EX-LIBRIS

I0836611

THE

GLOBE ENCYCLOPÆDIA

OF

Universal Information.

THE GLOBE ENCYCLOPÆDIA OF Universal Information.

EDITED BY

JOHN M. ROSS, LL.D.

FORMERLY ASSISTANT EDITOR OF "CHAMBERS'S ENCYCLOPÆDIA."

VOLUME III.

BOSTON:

ESTES & LAURIAT, 301 WASHINGTON STREET.

1877.

F, the sixth letter of the English alphabet, occupying the same position in the Phœnician alphabet as *vau*, from which it has been derived through the Latin; in Greek its place was originally occupied, both in form and sound, by the archaic digamma. Its proper phonetic value, which is that of a softened *v*, must be carefully distinguished from the sound of *ph*, the Greek φ, which is really an aspirated *p*. In transliteration from Oriental languages this confusion often arises. But though these two letters are etymologically distinct, few languages retain both, and either can be forced to serve the purpose. The Greek *ph* is often represented in primitive Latin words by F, as *phus*=*fui*, the same root as of Eng. 'be;' but in words directly borrowed, as *Philip*, it was retained, to be entirely discarded by modern Italian. The German pronunciation of *v* is hardly distinguished from our F. The interchanges of F are most numerous with the cognate labials and aspirates—Eng. 'father' is Ger. *vater* and Lat. *pater;* Lat. *fora* is Gr. *thura* and Eng. 'door;' Lat. *fero* is Eng. 'bear;' Eng. 'five' is Ger. *fünf*, Lat. *quinque*, and Gr. *pente*. As an abbreviation, FF. stands for *fragmenta*, used in referring to the Digest of Justinian. F. commonly stands for fellow, as F.R.S., Fellow of the Royal Society. F was also the letter formerly branded on felons in England who claimed the benefit of clergy.

F, in music, a note a perfect fourth above C. The vibration ratio F : C is equal to 4 : 3.

Faam', or **Fah'am** (*Angræcum fragrans*), a species of *Orchidaceæ* (q. v.) or orchids, found plentifully in the Mascarene Islands and the E. Indies. This plant is noted for the odour of its leaves, due to the presence of Coumarin (q. v.). The leaves are used in France for making an infusion popularly known as 'Isle of Bourbon tea,' greatly in vogue as a stomachic, and said to be also beneficial in consumption.

Faba'ceæ. See LEGUMINOSÆ.

Fa'ber, John, the name of two engravers in mezzotinto, of some repute in the 18th c., though of but little account now. The elder, who was born in Holland, and died at Bristol in 1721, besides engraving, drew portraits with the pen on vellum. His son, who died in London in 1756, was a superior artist. His best portraits are those of the beauties of Hampton Court, of the Kit-Cat Club, and of the Perceval family in the history of the House of Yvry.

Faber, Rev. George Stanley, an Anglican divine, was the eldest son of Rev. Thomas F., the descendant of a French Protestant refugee, and born 25th October 1773. After a successful career at Oxford, where he became fellow and tutor of Lincoln College, he was made Bampton Lecturer in 1801, and his discourses were published the same year under the title of *Horæ Mosaicæ* (2d ed. 1818). He married, and held various appointments, settling down finally in 1832 as master of Sherburn Hospital, near Durham, where he died, January 27, 1854. F. was a voluminous and popular writer on prophecy; among his works are *Dissertation on the Mysteries of the Cabiri* (1803); *The Origin of Pagan Idolatry* (1816); *Papal Infallibility* (1851); *The Revival of the French Emperorship Anticipated from the Necessity of Prophecy* (1853).—His nephew, **Francis William F.**, born June 28, 1815, is notable for having, while an Anglican clergyman and Rector of Elton, been converted to the Roman Catholic faith (1845), and joining Dr Newman's Oratory of St Philip Neri. F., who was an eloquent preacher and voluminous writer both of prose and of poetry, became superior of the Oratory at Brompton, and died September 26, 1863. Among his works, several of which have been translated into French, German, Dutch, &c., may be mentioned *Sir Lancelot, a Poem* (2d ed. 1858), *The Spirit and Genius of St Philip Neri* (1850), and *Spiritual Conferences* (1859). See Bowden's *Life of F. W. F.* (1869).

Fa'bius, the name of an old Roman patrician family, whose members were distinguished in war, literature, and the arts. From B.C. 485–479 a F. constantly appears in the list of consuls; but according to the family legend, which passes for history, having been alienated from their fellow-patricians, the clan retired to the river Cremera, where (B.C. 477) they were destroyed by the Veientes, one youth, left at Rome, alone having escaped.—**Quintus F. Rullianus**, or **Rullus**, who first of the Fabian gens bore the surname Maximus, was the most distinguished Roman general in the second Samnite war. His march through the Ciminian forest, though a rash and hazardous step, was followed by a decisive victory over the Etruscans at the Vadimonian lake, B.C. 310, and two years later he dispersed the Umbrians on the Upper Tiber.—**Quintus F. Maximus Verrucosus**, 'whose wise delay restored the Roman state,' was named *Cunctator*, or the 'Lingerer,' from the persistence with which, in the second Punic war, he avoided all direct encounter with Hannibal. Appointed dictator after the disaster at Lake Trasymene, his policy nearly achieved success when, following the invader on his retreat from Campania to Apulia, he closed the passes of the Apennines against him. Hannibal only escaped by a dexterous stratagem. The popular party at Rome misinterpreted the Fabian policy, and demanding more aggressive tactics, associated Minucius in command with the dictator; but the change of policy issued in the disgraceful rout at Cannæ. In his fifth consulship (B.C. 209) F. recaptured Tarentum. He died B.C. 203. Mommsen pictures him as a man 'zealous in his reverence for the good old times, for the political omnipotence of the senate, and for the command of the burgomasters—one who looked, next to sacrifices and prayer, to a methodical prosecution of the war as the main means of saving the state.'—**C. F. Pictor,** whose distinction as a painter acquired the name Pictor for a family of the Fabii. He lived about 300 B.C.—**Q. F. Pictor,** grandson of the preceding, flourished about 220 B.C. He was the earliest of the Roman annalists, and his work was of great value.

Fa'ble (Fr. *fable*, Lat. *fabula*, 'a narrative or story,' from *fari*, 'to speak'), a fictitious tale in prose or verse, in which animals or inanimate things are made to speak and act without regard to possibility, and which is intended to illustrate a moral truth or practical axiom, sometimes added to the story in the shape of a brief maxim called the *moral*. 'Jotham's F. of the trees (Judges ix.) is the oldest extant,' says Addison, 'and as beautiful as any made since.' Fables are especially popular in the East, and among the earliest known collections of them are Bidpai's (q. v.) or Pilpai's Indian and Lokman's Arabic fables. Some maintain the East to be the birthplace of F., and Max Müller traces La Fontaine's F. of the Milkmaid to a Sanskrit source. Among the most famous fabulists are the Greeks Æsop (q. v.) and Babrius (q. v.), the Latin Phædrus (q. v.) who recast the fables ascribed to Æsop, and added others of pure Roman origin, Aphthonius, a Greek prose writer, and Avianus, a Latin versifier of the 4th c., Planudes (q. v.), a Greek of the 14th c., Boner, and in modern times, La Fontaine (q. v.), who gave a novel piquancy to F. writing, Gay (q. v.), and the Spaniard Yriarte, who united the spirit of the Æsopian fables with the style of the Spanish romances. Fables were very popular in Germany in the 18th c., the best-known writers of them being Gellert (q. v.), Hagedorn (q. v.), Lichtwer, and Pfeffel. The greatest recent fabulist is the Russian Kriloff (q. v.), and many exquisite fables occur in Andersen's works. The most ambitious specimen of F. writing in England since Gay's time is the *Fables in Verse* of Lord Lytton ('Owen Meredith').

Fab'liau, pl. **Fabliaux** (formerly *fableau*, originally *fablel*, from Lat. *fabulellus*, a dim. of *fabula*, 'a story'), short metrical tales written by the early French poets, which, unlike the *sirventes* or songs of praise, the *tensons* or fantastic disquisitions on the 'art of love,' and the *lais* or miniature romances, were facetious and satirical, and mostly founded on proverbs and comic incidents. They are said to have originated at festive meetings, for which their brevity and piquancy were well adapted. While the *chansons de geste* deal with chivalrous adventure, the F. picture the humble and *bourgeois* life of the middle ages, and assail the vices and wrongs of the time, sparing neither king, baron, nor saint. Although stained with indecency, they evince fancy, pathos, and humour, bold satire, and greater narrative skill than the long rhyming romances. They belong principally to the 13th c., and are written generally in octosyllabic verse and in dialogue. Their sly banter and arch gaiety make them pleasanter reading than the prolix epics of the *trouvères*, or the lyrics embodying the amorous ritualism of the *troubadours*; and they were the delight and instruction of the people, until the the Church, dreading their anti-clerical influence, made them a medium for orthodox doctrine. This brought them into popular disrepute; they died away during the 15th c., and their place was taken by the *sotties* or farces. From the F. arose the French comedy. In *Maistre Pierre Pathelin*, the first French comedy, we see the very spirit of the F., the same love for ludicrous incident and merry cajolery. Molière's *Médecin Malgré Lui* and *Georges Dandin*, and Piron's comedy of *Le Fils Ingrat* were founded on old F. The subjects of the F. were drawn from very varied sources—from the Old and New Testament, the *Acta Sanctorum*, the *Gesta Romanorum*, Apuleius, Ovid, and especially from the East. Many were adapted from the *Romance of the Seven Sages*. But notwithstanding their frequent Eastern colouring, their character is distinctly French; their authors are the earliest representatives of that peculiar *esprit Gaulois* which sparkles in Villon, Marot, Voltaire, and La Fontaine, preserving the same character in Rutebeuf and in Béranger. This peculiarly French quality, which we first find in the F., consists of a laughing, poignant irony, a frolic piquancy, expressed with Attic lightness and clearness, distinct alike from the boisterous humour of Rabelais and the prim, chill graces of the classical school. The *fablieri* have supplied innumerable themes to succeeding writers. From them La Fontaine drew many of his raciest stories, and Boccaccio most of the plots for his *Decamerone*. Chaucer was indebted to them for his tales of the Reeve, Frankeleyn, and Schypman. Stories now known through Europe were first popularised by the F.; for example, the tale of Griselda was retold by Chaucer and Hans Sachs from Boccaccio, who took it from a *fableor*. After the Conquest Norman minstrels brought F. into England, where they were imitated in such poems as the *Owl and the Nightingale*, and the story of *Sir Cleges*. The *fablieri* were not mere sprightly, licentious humourists. They were bold satirists, whose writings were a check on the priests and nobles, and who anticipated Cervantes in ridiculing chivalry. Among the most noted of them were Bernier, Gautier de Coinsi, Henri d'Andeli, Hugues Piancelle, Jean de Boves, Jean le Chapelain, and, especially, Rutebeuf, a wandering minstrel of the 13th c., the representative *fablier*, author of *Charlot le Juif*, *Moine Sacristain*, &c. The *Vert-Vert* of Gresset is a perfect modern specimen of a F. See Demogeot's *Littérature Française* (Par. 1870), Besant's *French Humourists* (Lond. 1873), and Le Grand's *Fabliaux*, *Histoire de la Littérature Française*, by Charles Gidel (Par. 1875).

Fabrett'i, Raffaell'e, a famous Italian archæologist, born in 1618 at Urbino, repaired at an early age to Rome, and devoted himself to the study of its antiquities. His employments as papal treasurer, chancellor to the papal embassy at Madrid, and keeper of the papal archives in the castle of St Angelo gave him the best facilities for studying the classic works of the ancients. He is best known by his *De Aquæductibus Veteris Romæ* (Rome, 1680), his *De Columna Trajani* (Rome, 1683), and his *Inscriptionum Antiquarum, quæ in Ædibus Paternis asservantur, Explicatio* (Rome, 1699; 2d ed. 1702). He died in Rome, 7th January 1700. His valuable collections are preserved in the palace of Urbino.

Fabria'no, a city in the province of Macerata, Italy, 23 miles N.W. of the city of Macerata, has a cathedral and several churches containing numerous specimens of Italian sacred art. It has also been an important seat of paper manufacture for upwards of three centuries. Pop. 7500.

Fabriano, Gentile Da, an Italian painter, born at Fabriano about 1370, repaired at an early age to Florence to study under Fiesole. Among his first works were the fresco of the Madonna, preserved in the cathedral of Orvieto, which earned him the title of *magister magistrorum*, and an 'Adoration of the Kings,' now in the gallery of the Academy of Florence, a work dated 1423, and one of the finest works of the school of Giotto. He afterwards painted sacred subjects for the churches of Sienna, Perugia, Gubbio, Fabriano, &c., and eventually removed to Venice, where the senate gave him the pension of one ducat *per diem* and the privilege of wearing the toga of the patricians, in recognition of the merit of his great fresco—a sea-fight between the Venetian fleet and that of the Emperor Barbarossa—painted for the council hall of the Doge's palace. The work was destroyed by fire in 1574. F. was employed by Pope Martin V. to decorate the church of San Giovanni Laterano, in which he painted the history of St John, figures of several of the prophets, &c. He died in 1450. His works are bright and cheerful. Michael Angelo said of him, 'His genius is like his name—*gentile*.'

Fabri'cius or **Fabriz'io, ab Acquapenden'te, Geron'imo,** a famous Italian anatomist, was born at Acquapendente, near Orvietro, in 1537. He studied under Fallopius at Padua, where he was made professor of anatomy in 1565. F. soon became celebrated as a teacher, and his class-room was thronged by students from the various countries of Europe. After lecturing for fifty years he retired with a large fortune, and died at his country-seat on the Brenta, May 21, 1619. It was suspected that his heirs had poisoned him. Harvey, who attended F.'s lectures, states that his discovery of the circulation of the blood was suggested by F.'s remarks on the valves of the veins. F. wrote several Latin treatises on anatomy and surgery, showing careful, accurate investigation, and clear and vigorous in style. His complete works were published, with a memoir by Albinus, at Leyden in 1723, under the title *Opera Omnia Anatomica et Physiologica*. See Thuilius' *Memoria Hier. Fabricii* (Padua, 1619), and Salvadori's *Notitiæ Historico-Scientificæ de Fabricio* (Padua, 1837).

Fabricius, Johann Christian, a Danish entomologist, born at Tondern, Slesvig, 7th January 1743; studied medicine at Copenhagen, Edinburgh, and at Upsala under Linnæus; was chosen professor of natural history at Kiel in 1775; devoted himself to entomology; travelled over much of Europe, visiting Russia and England; and died at Kiel, 3d March 1808. His system of classification is by no means natural, yet entomology received from him a fresh impulse; and though later and better *savans* have pushed him into the background, he has a claim to be considered almost the founder of the science. His most important works are *Systema Entomologiæ* (Copen. 1775; revised and enlarged, 1792-94); *Supplementum Entomologiæ* (1797); and *Philosophica Entomologia* (Copen. 1778).

Fabricius Lusci'nus, Cajus, figures in Roman history as a model of antique simplicity, courage, and patriotism. When consul in B.C. 282, he delivered the city of Thurii, which was besieged by the Lucanians and Bruttii, and subsequently defeated the Samnites. When Pyrrhus came over from Greece to assist the Tarentines, F. was sent to confer with him, after the defeat at Heraclea (280), about a ransom of captives. The Greek monarch offered him gold if he would try to induce the senate to make peace, but F. was proof against both his bribes and his threats. Pyrrhus was so much impressed with his patriotic fidelity that he restored the prisoners without ransom. During F.'s second consulship, in 278, the physician of Pyrrhus secretly paid him a visit, and treacherously offered to poison his master for a reward. F. indignantly handed him over to the king, who again expressed his thanks by setting free all his Roman prisoners. While Pyrrhus was absent in Sicily, F. was victorious over the peoples of Lower Italy. He died poor, about 250, but the state charged itself with the upbringing of his only child.

Fabro'ni, An'gelo, an Italian biographer, born at Marradi in Tuscany, 25th September 1732, completed his studies at Rome. He wrote first in Latin, and afterwards in Italian; commenced at Pisa in 1771 his *Giornale de Letterati*, which at its close in 1796 formed 102 vols., and died at Pisa, 22d September 1803. Among his works are *Vitæ Italorum Doctrina Excellentium qui Sæculis XVII. et XVIII. floruerunt* (Pisa, 1778-1805, 20 vols.); *Laurentii Medicei Magnifici, Vita* (Pisa, 1784); *Magni Cosmi Medicei, Vita* (Pisa, 1789); *Elogi d' Illustri Italiani* (2 vols. Pisa, 1786-89).

Fa'byan, Robert, an English chronicler, born of a good Essex family in London, in the second half of the 15th c. He was a member of the Drapers' Company, and took an active part in civic affairs, becoming sheriff and alderman, and afterwards assessor of the London wards to Henry VII. He died February 28, 1512. He wrote a *Concordance of Histories* (first printed in 1516), compiled from monkish annalists, and marked by a strong ecclesiastical bias. It gives the history of Britain from Brut to 1504, in English prose, and has a prologue and seven episodes in verse.

Façade' (Fr.; from the Ital. *facciata*, Lat. *facies*), a term in architecture which at first signified the principal front of a building, but is now applied to any front or face of an edifice. It is chiefly used in speaking of important buildings.

Facciola'ti, Gia'como, an Italian scholar, was born at Torreglia, near Padua, January 4, 1682. He studied at the ecclesiastical seminary of Padua, of which he finally became the head. F. distinguished himself in criticism, grammar, antiquities, metaphysics, and theology, and wrote Ciceronian prose, but is remembered chiefly as a Latin lexicographer. He revised the lexicon of Schrevelius, and along with his pupil Forcellini produced a new edition of the *Calepine Lexicon*, or *Lexicon Septem Linguarum*. Finally, the same literary partners set to work to produce a new Latin dictionary, the basis of all subsequent dictionaries of the kind. F. did not live to see it completed (1771), as he died August 26, 1769.

Face. The F. is composed of fourteen bones, of which twelve are in pairs, viz., the superior maxillary, molar, nasal, lachrymal, inferior turbinated and palate bones; and two single, namely, the vomer and inferior maxilla. It contains the cavities of the orbits, of the nose, and of the mouth. These bones are covered by the muscles of expression and of mastication; and by the contour of the bones, the degree of development of these muscles, and the amount of fat beneath the skin, the countenance in life is formed. The forehead, eyelids, nose, mouth, lips, and cheeks have sets of muscles by the movements of which the various emotions may be expressed. (On the action of the facial muscles, as expressive of the emotions, see Sir Charles Bell's *Anatomy and Philosophy of Expression*.) By absorption of fat and atrophy of muscle the F. becomes much altered in disease, and the near approach of death is characterised by a peculiar expression of countenance—the *facies Hippocratica*, thus described by the ancient physician Hippocrates: 'nose pinched, eyes sunk, temples hollow, ears cold and retracted, the skin of the forehead tense and dry, the complexion livid, the lips pendant, relaxed, and cold.' The arteries of the F. come from the external carotid; its veins end in the jugular; its nerves originate in the brain.

Face-Ache. See TIC-DOULOUREUX.

Fa'cet (Fr. *facette*, 'a little face'), the name applied to the small faces of a crystal or cut gem. Steel jewellery and other metal ornaments are often *facetted*.

Fa'cial Angle. This is an angle formed by two lines, one of them descending from the most prominent part of the forehead to the incisor margin of the upper jaw, the other passing through the external auditory opening and the nasal spine. It was intended by Camper, the distinguished ethnologist, to indicate by the size of this angle the degree of projection of the face in different races of men, and the relative development of the face to the cranium. The following are several facial angles which have been measured:—(1) Faces in antique works of art, 90° or even more; (2) average European, 80°; (3) European below the average, 70°; (4) Negro, 70°; (5) young anthropoid apes, 56° to 60°; (6) old anthropoid apes, 30° to 47°. See SKULL.

Facil'ity, a term of Scotch law denoting the mental condition of a person unable in an ordinary degree to protect himself from imposition. On sufficient evidence of F. being given against any one by his heir or next-of-kin, the Court of Session will 'interdict' him. (See INTERDICTION.) Any one conscious of the infirmity may place himself under interdiction. There is no corresponding term in English law, nor any similar remedy. See IDIOTS and LUNATICS.

Fac'tor, in mathematics, is one of the numbers or symbols which go to make up a given product. Thus in the expression $3ab^2 (a^4 - b^4)$ the factors are 3, a, b^2, and $a^4 - b^4$; but of these the last two can be broken up into other factors, b, b, $a - b$, $a + b$, and $a^2 + b^2$. This process of breaking up an algebraic expression into its *elementary factors* is of great importance in analysis. The term *factorial* is given to those continued products of consecutive numbers, beginning with unity, which constantly occur in series and expansions. Thus 1.2.3.4.5 is called *factorial* five, and is usually written $\underline{|5}$.

Factor (Lat. 'doer'), in a general sense, is any one who does business for another. In English law, a F. is the agent of a merchant or trader constituted by letter of attorney. (See ATTORNEY, LETTER OF.) A F. is generally paid by commission. If he buy goods on account of his principal when he is accustomed to do so, the contract binds the principal. But if the goods have been bought or exchanged without order, the merchant may refuse to take them from the F. Formerly, the law was extremely hard on third parties in their transactions with factors. If an advance of money was made to one on the security of merchandise belonging to his principal, the principal was legally entitled to withdraw the security; and in the event of merchandise being bought from a F. not authorised to sell, the purchaser was liable, after paying the F., to have to pay the full value to the owner. To remove these hardships the Acts 4 and 6 Geo. IV. caps. 83-94 were passed, establishing the validity of contracts respecting merchandise intrusted to factors. Under 6 Geo. IV. the person in whose name goods are shipped is declared to be the owner unless the contrary can be proved.

In Scotland, the term F., besides its general legal meaning, which corresponds with the English, is especially applied to the manager for the proprietor of real (heritable) estates, for which the English equivalent is 'land-agent.' The great landowners have generally a F. resident on their estates, whose chief business it is to let the farms and draw the rents. The F. binds his principal to any engagement which he contracts within his powers. It has lately become to some extent customary to use the word *chamberlain* in Scotland as synonymous with F. in the above sense. Factors are also under certain circumstances appointed on estates in Scotland by the Court of Session. One so appointed is called a *Judicial F.* (q. v.).

Fac'tories and Mills, Law Regarding. Various Acts have been passed for the appointment of inspectors for the preservation of the health, and for regulating the education and hours of work, of children employed in M. and F. By 3 and 4 Will. IV. c. 103, children are required to attend a school chosen by parents or inspectors, to pay the expense of which one penny in each shilling is to be deducted from the child's earnings. It is rendered unlawful to employ children unless they produce weekly to the factory master the schoolmaster's ticket of attendance. Interior walls of mills and ceilings of rooms must be limewashed yearly.

Act 7 and 8 Vict. c. 15 empowers inspectors to enter factories by day and night, to examine the inmates, the register, and other documents kept in pursuance of the Act. Penalties are imposed on persons endeavouring to prevent the examination of any child by the inspector, or otherwise endeavouring to impede him in the execution of his duty. Inspectors are empowered within limits to fix the surgeon's fees and appoint the times of his visits. The Act makes stringent regulations for preventing injury to the health of the children and 'young persons'—those between thirteen and eighteen years old—and for prevention of accidents from the machinery. By 16 and 17 Vict. c. 104, no 'child'—that is, one under thirteen years old—shall be employed in any factory before six o'clock in the morning nor after six o'clock in the evening of any day, nor after two o'clock on Saturday. But between 30th September and 1st April children may be employed for one month on any day but Saturday from 7 A.M. to 7 P.M. There are various other Acts extending the operation of the Factory Acts, and making further regulations as to hours of employment and other matters concerning the health of the employed. Any manufactory in which fifty or more persons are employed is under the Acts a factory. See WORKSHOP REGULATION ACT.

Fac'ulty (Lat. *facultas*, a 'power,' 'means,' or 'opportunity'), in English law, is a privilege granted to do something generally prohibited by law. There is a court for the purpose under the Archbishop of Canterbury called the *Court of Faculties and Dispensations*, which has power to grant dispensations for marriages without publication of banns (see BANNS), for a deacon under age to be ordained, and for exceptional procedure in other matters connected with the Church. The bishop of the diocese may grant a F. for erection of a monument, or for other addition or alteration in a church. See PEW.

Faculty. See UNIVERSITY.

Faculty of Advocates (Scotland). See ADVOCATE.

Faculty, Dean of (Scotland). See DEAN OF FACULTY.

Fæ'ces (Lat. 'dregs,' 'impurities'). The undigested materials of the food, mixed with products excreted from the mucous membrane of the bowels, constitute the F. Microscopical examination shows usually disintegrated muscular fibre, cartilage cells, elastic fibres, free fatty matter, crystals of cholesterine, the chlorophyll of cells from plants, portions of broken-down vegetable matter, such as starch grains, spiral vessels, &c., bile salts, bile colouring matter, epithelium cells, mucous matter, corpuscles, saline matter, especially the crystals of the ammoniaco-magnesian or triple phosphate, &c., &c. Usually F. contain about 70 per cent. of water, and an estimation of the amount of nitrogen yielded by the F. was about 42 grains per day. The ash of F. consists of alkaline chlorides and sulphates, phosphate of soda, phosphates of lime and magnesia (in large amount), phosphate of iron, sulphate of lime and silica. About 8·55 of F. are evacuated daily. See DEFÆCATION.

Faed, John, a Scottish artist, son of a millwright, was born at Burley Mill, in the stewartry of Kirkcudbright, in 1820. He early showed a strong love of painting, and in 1841 went to Edinburgh, where in 1850 he exhibited several pictures, which soon made him widely known. In 1864 he removed to London. Among his works, which are mostly of humble Scottish life, are 'The Cottar's Saturday Night', 'The Wappenschaw,' 'Tam O'Shanter,' 'Auld Mare Maggie,' 'John Anderson my Jo,' &c.

—**Thomas F., R.A.,** brother of the above, was born at Burley Mill in 1826, joined the Edinburgh School of Design, where he received instruction from Sir W. Allan, and in 1849 was made an Associate of the Royal Scottish Academy. In 1852 he settled in London, and began to exhibit annually in the Royal Academy. His popularity continued to increase; he was made an A.R.A. in 1859, an R.A. in 1864, and an honorary member of the Vienna Royal Academy in 1875. Among his works are 'Scott and his Friends at Abbotsford,' 'The Mitherless Bairn,' 'The First Break in the Family,' 'From Dawn to Sunset,' 'Baith Faither and Mither,' &c. His paintings, which are rich in tint and free in execution, are mostly faithful transcripts of the pathetic and humorous aspects of Scottish rustic life.

Faen'za (the *Faventia* of the Romans), an episcopal town on the Lamone, in the province of Ravenna, N. Italy, on the railroad from Bologna to Ancona, and 20 miles S.W. of Ravenna. It is well built, four main streets branching off from the principal square, which is adorned with arcades and a fountain. The cathedral, courthouse, and theatre, are the chief public buildings. F. manufactures articles of Majolica, known from the name of the town as 'Faience' (q. v.) Pop. 17,486.

Fæ'sulæ. See FIESOLE.

Fagg'ing, the name given to a system peculiar to the great public schools of England, by which the upper boys are authorised to exact certain services from the lower boys. The system is explicitly recognised by the masters, and the services demanded are regulated only by the traditions of each particular school; some of them are of a menial character, while others are connected with the common school games. F. no doubt arose from the two circumstances, formerly almost universal in England—that all the boys were permanent boarders, and that the staff of masters was too limited to exercise supervision out of working hours. The first of these circumstances naturally engendered a private organisation among the boys, which the force of tradition has stereotyped; while the latter induced a semi-public sanction. Among day-boys the relation of master and servant could never have been instituted, and under ushers it would not have been allowed to take deep root. The advantages asserted of the system are that the fags are rendered handy, independent, and obedient, that an equality of condition is enforced upon all, and that unlicensed bullying is indirectly suppressed. The evils are that the smaller boys are harassed by perpetual forced employment, which is often capricious and degrading, and that the character of the bigger boys is not improved by the almost despotic exercise of indiscriminate power. Mr. Freeman, in his *Growth of the English Constitution*, asserts that F. is a remnant of the old Teutonic custom of *commendation*, by which a free man became the 'man,' or obedient follower of a chief. A somewhat similar system, under the name of 'the Garring Law,' grew up in Heriot's Hospital, Edinburgh, in the middle of the last century.

Fahr'enheit, Gabriel Daniel, a German physicist, born at Danzig, May 14, 1686, spent most of his life as a glass-blower in England, and later in Holland, where he died, 16th September 1736. About 1720 he improved the thermometer by substituting mercury for spirits of wine. (See THERMOMETER.) In the *Philosophical Transactions* for 1724 there are five papers by him, on the boiling and freezing of water, on specific gravity, and on a barometer of new construction.

Faid'herbe, Louis Léon César, a French general, born at Lille, June 3, 1818, served in Algeria, and as Governor of Senegal; commanded the *Armée du Nord* in the Franco-Prussian war, and was beaten, greatly through the want of artillery, at St Quentin, January 17, 1871. He joined Gambetta's party, and was elected by the central canton of Lille to the National Assembly in 1871, but retired into private life on the success of the Thiers Government. Besides proving himself an able soldier, F. has written valuable scientific articles, a *Notice sur la Colonie du Sénégal* (1859), and *Campagne de l'Armée du Nord* (1871).

Faïence', or **Fayence,** an old French term formerly applied to all kinds of glazed earthenware, now restricted to fine kinds of pottery, with a soft, opaque paste, and glazed.

Fai-Fo, a commercial town and seaport of Anam, about 70

miles S. by E. of Hué, has an extensive trade with China, to which it exports sugar and cinnamon. Pop. 15,000.

Faill'y, Pierre-Louis-Charles-Achille de, a French general, born at Rozoy-sur-Serre, Aisne, January 21, 1810. He served in Algeria, distinguished himself in the Crimean war, and in 1867 won unenviable notoriety as the conqueror of Mentana. He held a command in the Franco-Prussian war, and was captured at Sedan. F. was severely censured for incapacity by his countrymen, and has not been reinstalled in command.

Fai'néants Rois (Fr. 'do-nothing kings'), the name given to the Merwing kings, who nominally held the Frankish throne from the battle of Testry in 687 to the accession of the Karoling dynasty in 752. During this period the regal authority was wielded by the mayors of the palace. See FRANCE, HISTORY OF.

Fain'ting, or **Syn'cope** (Gr. *sun* and *koptō*, 'I fall down'), is a state in which the circulation of the blood is suddenly arrested or much diminished in force and volume, causing a deadly pallor and loss of consciousness and power. F. is thus a state of suspended animation, varying in duration, and sometimes ending in death. F. usually takes place in the upright position, but not always, and the first symptoms are sudden pallor and falling down in a swoon. There are no spasms, as in hysteria, epilepsy, and convulsive affections; and no pulsation or respiratory movements, as in catalepsy. F. most frequently occurs to those of a highly nervous temperament. Those of very delicate constitution, or who may have suffered from exhausting diseases or disease of the heart, are liable to attacks of F. from very slight exciting causes, such as the close atmosphere of a room or a start. The symptoms of F. and collapse, or shock, are similar, but the latter are much more serious, and are usually associated with accidents or surgical operations. *Treatment*:—The patient should be laid on the back, with the head and shoulders very slightly elevated; tight articles of dress should be loosened; and a current of cold air directed to the face and neck. Cold water dashed on the face, and ammonia or aromatic vinegar applied to the nostrils are highly useful in exciting the nervous system. The first symptoms of returning consciousness are twitchings of the muscles of the face, followed by a deep-drawn sigh. Artificial respiration, induced by compressing the ribs and allowing them to expand, as in natural breathing, rouses the respiratory movements. Friction over the region of the heart is also useful, and galvanism sometimes succeeds when all other means fail.

Fai'oum. See FAYUM.

Fair, a privileged market regularly convened at a particular place on certain periods of the year. The word is probably derived from the Lat. *feriæ*, holidays, or days exempt from labour, which, after the establishment of Christianity, included days set apart for religious festivals in honour of the saints. On such occasions large numbers of people assembled round the monasteries. These gatherings became the origin of fairs, which were held on feast-days and Sundays. The German word *messe* signifies F. as well as Mass, a further indication of the relation between the Church and fairs. Numerous fairs are held at stated periods in various towns of the United Kingdom, chiefly for the sale of horses, cattle, and agricultural produce. Railways, and improved means of inland communication generally, have rendered many unnecessary, and diverted most from their original purpose to mere gatherings for merrymaking. Some had, indeed, become such great public nuisances, scenes of riot and dissipation, that their abolition was secured by the Fairs Act, enacted in May 1871. Bartholomew F., in London, established in the 12th c., ceased to exist in 1855; for two centuries it was a gross carnival. Throughout Europe and Asia, however, many fairs are still devoted to legitimate trade. Those of Leipsic and Nijni-Novgorod are the principal. At Leipsic three annual fairs are now held—commencing on New Year's day, Easter, and Michaelmas—each extending over three weeks. Enormous trade is carried on, and the imports of the *Zollverein* and foreign manufactured goods steadily increase every year. Merchants from all parts of the world attend. The German book-trade, of which Leipsic is the great emporium, holds a half-yearly F. The annual F. of Nijni-Novgorod, sometimes called Macarieva, is the largest in the world. It begins early in July, and lasts over two months. Traders from all parts of Europe, Central Asia, and even China, frequent it. The F. of 1874 was visited by over one million persons; the value of its imports amounted to 180,000,000 roubles (three times the value of the imports of 1847), and eight-ninths of that sum were actually realised by sales. Other Russian and Siberian towns have periodical fairs, and at Frankfurt-on-the-Main, Brunswick, Frankfurt-on-the-Oder, Vienna, Cassel, Breslau, Lyon, St Germain, &c., considerable trade is similarly transacted.

Fair'bairn, Sir William, LL.D., F.R.S., an eminent engineer, was born at Kelso, Roxburghshire, Scotland, February 19, 1789. After receiving an elementary education at the parish school of Mallochy in Ross-shire, he became apprenticed to the trade of engine-wright at Percymain Colliery, North Shields. In 1817 F. was able to begin business for himself in Manchester as a machine-maker, and speedily won success and reputation. He is chiefly notable for being among the first to build iron ships, for substituting iron for wood in the shafting of cotton-mills, and for developing Stephenson's theory of tubular bridges, of which he successfully erected a large number. F. wrote various interesting papers, on such subjects as the tenacity of boiler plates, in the *Transactions* of the Royal Society and of the Philosophical Society of Manchester; and among his more important works are *Iron, its History and Manufactures* (1863), *Mills and Millwork* (1864–65), and *Iron Shipbuilding*. F., who during his later years had many honours bestowed upon him, such as the dignity of LL.D. of Glasgow, Fellow of the Royal Society, and corresponding Member of the Institute of France, held the office of president of the British Association for the Advancement of Science in 1861 and 1862, and in 1869 was made a baronet. He died August 18, 1874. See Smiles's *Lives of Engineers*.

Fair'fax, Edward, son of Sir Thomas F, of Denton, Yorkshire, was born in the reign of Elizabeth. He spent a studious tranquil life at Fuyistone, near Denton, and died about 1632. His translation of Tasso's *Gerusalemme Liberata*, first published in 1600, under the title of *Godfrey of Bulloigne*, preserves the octave rhyme and much of the music and voluptuous splendour of the original; and notwithstanding occasional obscurity and undue licence of fancy, remains an English classic and one of the best translations in our language. The 7th edition, published by Charles Knight in 1853, has a brief memoir of the translator. F. also wrote eclogues, &c., now lost, and a treatise on *Demonology*. See Leigh Hunt's *Essay on F.'s Tasso*.

Fairfax, Thomas Lord, an English general, son of Ferdinand Lord F., was born at Denton, Yorkshire, in January 1611. He served under Lord Vere in Holland, and when the civil war began in 1642, was made a general of cavalry in the army of the Parliament. In 1644 he defeated the Royalists under Bellasis, and commanded the right wing in the battle of Marston Moor. He succeeded Essex as leader of the Parliamentary forces, having Cromwell as his lieutenant-general, and commanded at the victory of Naseby in 1645. Henceforth, as Cromwell rose in power, F.'s influence lessened, though he was nominally commander-in-chief until 1650, when he resigned on being ordered to set out against the Scots, who had declared for the king. He then spent several years in retirement in Yorkshire, took part with Monk against Lambert in 1659, was elected member for Yorkshire in 1660, was one of the committee for promoting the Restoration, and died at Nun Appleton, Yorkshire, November 12, 1671. F. wrote *Short Memorials of Thomas Lord F.* (1699), and several works in prose and verse.

Fair Head (Scand. *farr*, 'a sheep'), otherwise **Benmore Head** (*i.e.*, 'great hill head'), a promontory on the coast of Antrim, Ireland, 3 miles S. by E. of the island of Rathlin, and rising perpendicularly from the sea 636 feet. Geologically it belongs to the coal-measures, but columnar greenstone forms its upper portion.

Fai'ries, or **Elves**. Several derivations of the word *fairy* are suggested, among others the Celtic *faer*, 'to charm;' Old Eng. *fere*, 'a companion,' from *faran*, 'to go;' and the Persian *peri*, pronounced in Arabic *feri*. The true root is probably the Lat. *fatum*, whence through the mediæval *fatare*, 'to enchant,' the Fr. *faer*, *feer*, from which came *faerie*, signifying first illusion, then the land of illusion, fairyland, and lastly an inhabitant of fairyland. Elf, on the other hand, is of Teutonic origin. It is the Old Eng. *ælf*, entering into the composition of many proper names, as Ælfred; the Ger. *elfe*, the Sw. *elf*, the

Norse *alf*, and is perhaps connected with the Lat. *alb*-us, 'white,' in allusion to their ghostly appearance. F. are imaginary beings of supernatural but limited power, and generally of tiny stature, a belief in whom has been common to almost all countries of Europe. They include beings of very different aspects and qualities. In particular the F. of romance differ from the F. of popular superstition. The former somewhat resemble the Greek nymphs, appear generally as damsels of angelic loveliness, and seduce knights into enchanted isles and palaces. The land of faerie was supposed to be sometimes underground, sometimes amid wildernesses, and sometimes in the ocean. It possessed brilliant but illusory splendours, and mortals were occasionally decoyed thither and detained for many years. Fairy mythology varies with different nations. The *peri* of the Persians, which correspond to the good *jinn* of the Arabs, resemble the *fays* of European romance, being of human stature and exquisite loveliness. They live mostly in the air, and wage war with the *deevs*, or evil spirits. The Scandinavian *alfar*, or elves, were supposed to be partly kind and beautiful, partly malicious, and 'blacker than pitch;' while the *duergar*, or dwarfs, were expert in metallurgy and in forging magical weapons. The English F. are more playful and innocent than those of Scotland and Germany, and appear as graceful, sportive pigmies, fond of dancing at night in the woods, and of sharing in household duties. The English sprite *Robin Goodfellow* corresponds to the German *Knecht Ruprecht*, the Scotch *Brownie*, and the French *Esprit Folet*, or *Gobelin* (goblin). He assumes various forms, misleads travellers, and is constantly playing tricks on mortals. He will sweep the house, and thresh corn at midnight, but if in return a bowl of cream be not set out for him, ill-luck will befall the negligent housekeepers. He is the same as Shakespeare's *Puck* (Old Eng. *pouke*, 'an evil spirit'), and probably as Jonson's *Puck Hairy*. The Cornish *pixies*—according to Keightley a diminutive from *Puck*—are supposed to be the souls of unbaptized children. They dwell in the mines, and, as Will-o'-the-wisps, mislead travellers, whence the term 'pixy-led.' The Scottish F. closely resemble the English. They were said to be small and handsome, to wear green dresses, to ride in splendid processions on Hallowe'en, and to indulge in moonlight revelry, marking the spots where they danced by circles of vivid green called *Fairy Rings* (q. v.). They were fickle and mischievous, kidnapping children to offer as yearly tribute to Satan, stealing the soul from the human body and replacing it by the soul of a fairy, and sometimes carrying away grown-up persons to fairyland. On this last belief are founded the ballad of *Tamlane* (see Scott's *Minstrelsy of the Border*), and Hogg's fine poem of *Kilmeny*. There is an element of sadness and fanciful weirdness in the Scottish tales of F. alien to the kindred English superstitions; thus, the *kelpie*, a wicked Scottish water-spirit, is unknown in the English rivers. The Gaelic F.—called *daoine shi* (dheenè shee), 'men of peace'—were said to inhabit turrets invisible by day but brilliantly illuminated at night. They enticed mortals into their abodes, and if these visitors partook of a fairy banquet, they forfeited the right to return to their fellowmen. According to tradition the Irish F. are the less wicked of the fallen angels, who were permitted to remain on earth. They have various names, apparently derived from *shia*, 'a spirit.' Among them are *pooka*, corresponding to the English *Puck*, who takes the form of a wild colt and indulges in evil frolics; *leprechaun*, a miserly spirit in the form of an old man; the *merrow*, or sea-maid, and the *banshee*, or guardian-spirit of a particular family. The F. of English poetry are different from the F. of popular superstition. Chaucer's F. are partly classic, partly Gothic, having Pluto and Proserpine for king and queen; Spenser's are idealised mortals; and the lovely diminutive spirits of Shakespeare's *Midsummer Night's Dream* are original creations, ruled by Oberon and Titania, who were unknown in the vulgar fairy superstitions. Oberon is *Le Petit Roy Oberon* who figures so conspicuously in mediæval fiction, and holds an intermediate place between the fays of romance and the elves of the north. He is the German Elberich, which the French softened into Oberon. Titania seems a derivative from Titan, since Diana, whom Ovid (*Metamorphoses*, iii. 173) styles Titania, was at one time regarded as a ruler of the F. The name of the tiny queen is thus derived from a word implying colossal stature and strength. Queen Mab, who in a certain degree has usurped the place of Titania, derives her name from the Welsh *mab*, 'a child.' There are frequent allusions to the F. in the Elizabethans, but, next to Shakespeare, Drayton, in *Nymphidia* and the *Poet's Elysium*, has been the most successful poet of fairyland. Fairy-tales became very popular in the last half of the 17th c. The *Contes de ma Mère l'Oye* (1697) of Perrault produced numerous imitations. Among recent authors of fairy-tales Hans Andersen stands unrivalled. See Keightley's *Fairy Mythology* (Bohn, Lond. 1860); Scott's *Essay on the F. of Popular Superstition*, in the *Minstrelsy of the Border*; Grimm's *Haus- und Kindermärchen*.

Fair Isle (Scand. *farr*, 'a sheep'), an island midway between the Orkney and Shetland groups, 29 miles S. by W. of Sumburgh Head, fully 3 miles long and nearly 2 broad, rising into three lofty promontories (one of which, 'Sheep Craig,' gives name to the isle), and accessible only at one point on the N.E. After the defeat of the Spanish Armada in 1588, its admiral, the Duke of Medina Sidonia, retreating northwards, was wrecked on F. I. The inhabitants live mainly by fishing. Pop. (1871) 226.

Fairy Rings, the name popularly given to green spots marked out in pasture lands, from the belief that they represented the meeting-place of fairies and elves. According to Roget, the occurrence of F. R. is explained by the exhaustion of the soil. The dark-green grass of the F. R. has been traced to the growth of fungi which have spread outwards. As the soil becomes deteriorated, the fungi spread themselves further and further outwards, in the form of successive and concentric circles. The succeeding grass crop which grows therein becomes necessarily more luxuriant than the surrounding grass, the soil having been enriched by the decay of the fungi. Way states that fungi which form F. R. (such as *Agaricus oreades* and *A. graveolens*) contain a large quantity of phosphoric acid and potash, which of course tend to enrich the soil.

Fairy Shrimp (*Chirocephalus diaphanus*), a genus of *Crustacea* (q. v.) belonging to a different order from that (*Decapoda*) in which the true shrimps are included—viz., to the order *Phyllopoda* (q. v.). They are so named from their delicate clear appearance. They occur in ponds, &c., in England and elsewhere. Their average length is about 1 inch, yet so clear are their bodies that they can scarcely be detected as they swim back-downwards. They have numerous feet, which are leaf-like in form.

Faith, in the widest sense of the word, is assent to the truth, or the persuasion of the mind that a thing is true. Thus the primary element of it is trust, as the primary idea of truth is that which is trustworthy; and it might be defined as a rational trust beyond the limits of knowledge, but founded upon it. It is often defined as if it were a special organ for the perception of a special kind of truth, but improperly so, although the complex state of mind involved in the act is, of course, different according to the nature of the object of F., and of the evidence on which it is founded. The ordinary definitions of F. may be divided into three classes:—Those founded (1) on its subjective nature; (2) on its object; (3) on its evidence. I. In the first class, F. has been defined as 'a persuasion of the truth stronger than opinion and weaker than knowledge;' otherwise, according to Locke, 'an assent of the mind to propositions which are probably, but not certainly, true;' or, according to Kant, 'the admission of a thing to be true on grounds sufficient subjectively, insufficient objectively.' Secondly, it is said to be a *voluntary* conviction or persuasion of the truth; which definition, however, admits of a number of meanings according to the sense attached to 'voluntary.' Thus it may mean that F. is not merely a speculative assent, but includes feeling; or, that F. does not depend on the nature of the object or the evidence, but on our choice to believe or disbelieve. II. Under the second class, F. is defined as the persuasion of the truth of things not seen. Here, again, 'sight' may be taken in three senses:—(1) Literally; we are said to know a thing which we have seen with our eyes, and to believe in the existence of things of whose existence we are certain without having seen them. (2) As mental perception; and we are said to believe on testimony what we might afterwards see or know by demonstration. (3) 'Things not seen' may mean all things not present to the mind; and we are said to know only the actual and the present, while what is mediately known, *e.g.*, by memory, is only believed to be. III. Under the third class, F. is defined to be (1) A conviction or persuasion of truth founded on feeling, not because of critical or philosophical research or of argument, but determined by inclination and inward necessity. (2) F. is a persuasion of the truth founded on testimony, and the F. of the Christian is the persuasion of the truth of the facts and doctrines recorded in the Scriptures on the testimony of God.

Having defined F., theologians further divide it into different kinds:—1. Speculative or dead F. is the F. of those who believe the Bible to be the Word of God, receive all it. teaches, and are perfectly orthodox, while yet they may be leading an immoral life. 2. Temporary F. is that temporary impression, more or less deep and lasting, produced by the gospel—*e.g.*, in the apprehension of death—and which is due to those influences of the Spirit of God common to all men. 3. Saving F. is that which makes us the sons of God, and secures eternal life, and is founded 'not on the external or the moral evidence of the truth, but on the testimony of the Spirit with and by the truth to the renewed soul.' See Hodge's *Systematic Theology* (Edinb. 1873).

Faith, Rule of, means a standard by which Christians are to be guided in what they believe in religious matters. The phrase originated with the early Christian fathers, but had a different meaning in the Greek and in the Latin Churches. In the latter, as, *e.g.*, in the writings of Irenæus, Tertullian, Novatian, and Jerome, R. of F. was, in fact, but a name for the Apostles' Creed, which was so called 'because it was the known standard of faith, by which orthodoxy and heresy were judged.' If a man adhered to this rule, he was considered orthodox; but if he deviated from it in any point, he was esteemed a heretic, one who had deserted the common faith and separated from the communion of the Church. In the Greek Church, on the other hand, as, *e.g.*, in the writings of Clement of Alexandria, the R. of F. meant an exegetical tradition or principle, by which the true meaning of Scripture was educed.

In modern times, all are agreed as to the meaning of R. of F. as regards its application, but there is a difference of opinion between Protestants and Roman Catholics as to what constitutes the standard. All Protestants hold that 'the Word of God, as contained in the Scriptures of the Old and New Testaments, is the only infallible rule of faith and practice.' According to Roman Catholics the R. of F. includes Tradition as well as the Scriptures, because 'some doctrines which all Christians are bound to believe are only imperfectly revealed in the Scriptures, others only obscurely intimated, and others not therein contained at all.' With regard to the Scriptures themselves, the Church of Rome differs from Protestants in admitting into the canon certain books which Protestants do not admit to be inspired, namely, the Apocrypha (q. v.). Further, while Protestants hold that the Bible is intelligible by all under the teaching of the Holy Spirit, and that therefore all are entitled and bound to search the Scriptures and judge for themselves what is the true meaning thereof, the Church of Rome teaches that the Bible cannot be properly understood by the people without a visible, present, and infallible interpreter, which interpreter exists in the Church, and the people are therefore bound to believe whatever the Church believes to be the true doctrine. With regard to Tradition, which the Church of Rome also holds to constitute a part of the R. of F., it teaches that many things were taught by Christ and his apostles which were not recorded in the New Testament, but which have been faithfully preserved and transmitted by the Church, and are now to be found, for the most part, in the works of the fathers, decisions of councils, ecclesiastical constitutions, and rescripts of popes. See Davidson's *Sacred Hermeneutics* (Edinb. 1843); Bingham's *Ecclesiast. Antiquities*; Hodge's *Systematic Theology* (Edinb. 1873).

Fai'thorne, Faithorn, or Faythorne, William, an English engraver, was born in London about 1625, took up arms for Charles I. in the civil war, was imprisoned, and afterwards went to France, where he seems to have come under the professional influence of Philippe de Champagne and of Nanteuil, and considerably modified his style as an artist. Returning to England in 1650, he entered upon a thriving business as a print-seller and engraver. Among his best portraits are those of Cromwell, Milton, Dryden, Hobbes, Prince Rupert, and Queen Anne (when Princess of Denmark). F., who wrote in 1662 an essay on *The Art of Graveing and Etching*, died May 1691.

Fakir', a name derived from the Arabic *faqutr*, 'poor,' and applied, especially in India, to Mohammedan mendicants who wander through the country, and are universally respected for their sanctity and self-mortification. It does not appear that their austerities have any necessary connection with the Mussulman faith; but they are rather to be derived from the singular spirit of devotion and indifference to pain which has characterised the religions of the East from the earliest times. They bear a close resemblance to the hermits of primitive Christianity, and also to the mendicant friars of later history. In India they are divided into ten classes, named either from their founders, or from a peculiarity of habit or doctrine. Some are jugglers, others dress like women, while others are accustomed to inflict the severest wounds upon themselves without apparent suffering. They travel from one end of the peninsula to another, and have been known to penetrate as far as Europe. In Persia and Turkey this class of holy men is represented by the dervishes. Their counterparts among the Hindus are termed Sanyasees and Byragees.

Falaise' (Fr. 'the cliff-town,' from Scand. *fell* or *felsen*, 'a rock'), a town in the department of Calvados, France, built on a natural terrace close by a rocky height, 23 miles S.E. of Caen. Remains of its ancient walls, and of the castle in which William the Conqueror was born, still exist. Its churches, and many of its houses, recall vividly the middle ages. The chief industry—the trade in leather and furs—which employs 4000 hands, has been carried on for centuries. Pop. (1872) 7634.

Fal'con, the name applied to various genera and species of Raptorial birds, included in the family *Falconidæ* (q. v.). In the typical genus *Falco*, the bill is strong and toothed at its tip. The cere is small, and the nostrils are round, having a central tubercle. The wings have their second and third quills longest, the first and second being notched near the tip. The feathers of the tarsi hang over the knee. The toes are long and powerful, and the talons strong. These birds are among the most typical of the *Raptores*. They exhibit the special structure of that group, and exemplify the bold, wary nature common to the eagles and other forms. The best-known falcons are the Jer or Gyr F. (*Falco gyrfalco*); the Peregrine F. (*F. peregrinus*); the Hobby (*Hypotriorchis subbuteo*); the Lanner (*Falco lannarius*); the Merlin (*Hypotriorchis æsalon*); the Kestrel (*Tinnunculus alaudarius*); the Notched F. (*Harpagus bidentatus*), &c. The name F. is given to various members of the kite subfamily (*Milvinæ*). Thus, the Crook-billed F. (*Cymindis uncinatus*) and Cayenne F. (*C. Cayanensis*) belong to this subfamily. The American Red-throated F. (*Ibycter Americanus*) belongs to the sub-family *Polyborinæ*, and the Rough-legged F. (*Archibuteo lagopus*) to the *Buteoninæ* or Buzzards.

The Falcon.

Falco'ne, Aniell'o, an Italian painter, was born at Naples in 1600, took part in Masaniello's insurrection, afterwards visited Paris, and died at Naples in 1665. Salvator Rosa was one of his pupils. His fame as a painter of battle-pieces was at one time so great as to earn him the title in Italy of 'Oracle of Battles.' His paintings are spirited and natural in design, and brilliant without being glaring in colour. See Lanzi's *Storia della Pittura*, vol. ii.

Fal'coner, William, an English poet, born at Edinburgh, 11th February 1732; entered the merchant service; and when eighteen became second mate of a vessel which was wrecked (1750) off Cape Colonna, F. and two others alone being saved. This disastrous voyage is the subject of F.'s *Shipwreck*. Through the influence of the Duke of York, to whom the *Shipwreck* (1762) was dedicated, F. joined the navy in 1763, and was lost at sea, when purser of the *Aurora* frigate, in 1769. The *Ship-*

wreck has passages of vigorous and pathetic description, but is essentially commonplace in structure and idea; while the contrast between F.'s frequent nautical technicalities and the names and conversation of his characters, who seem borrowed from a Queen Anne pastoral, jars upon the reader, and lessens the interest. F. wrote several verses of circumstance deservedly forgotten; *The Demagogue* (1765), an attack on Wilkes and Churchill; and a *Universal Marine Dictionary* (1769). The once popular song, *Cease, rude Boreas*, has also been attributed to him. See the Memoir by Stanier Clarke prefixed to his edition of the *Shipwreck* (1804), and that by Mitford in the Aldine edition of F.'s *Poetical Works* (Bell & Daldy, Lond. 1870).

Falcon'idæ, a large and well-known family of Raptorial birds, the members of which are distinguished by the fact that the bill has a partial cere, and is of compressed form, having the keel curved from the cere to the tip. The wings are long and pointed, and the tail broad. The tarsi are varied and of strong make, the claws being curved and sharp. The head and neck are feathered, and the eyes appear sunk and overarched by the brow. This family includes several well-marked sub-families. Chief of these are the *Aquilinæ* or Eagles (q. v.), the *Polyborinæ* (including the Caracaras and Brazilian kites), the *Buteoninæ* or buzzards, the *Milvinæ* or kites, the *Falconinæ* or falcons proper, and the *Accipitrinæ* or sparrow-hawks, &c. The F. are found in all parts of the world.

Fal'conry or **Hawk'ing**, the art of training Falcons (q. v.) and birds of Raptorial kind to pursue other birds in flight and capture them. The practice of F. dates from a remote period. It was probably derived from the East, and was most in vogue in England during the middle ages. The birds chiefly pursued as game were the heron, partridge, lark, pigeon, wild-duck, &c. The falcons used in the sport were the Peregrine (q. v.) and Gyr-Falcon (q. v.); but the Goshawk (q. v.) and Sparrow-Hawk (q. v.), birds of less powerful flight than the two former species, were also employed. The female birds, as a rule, were most valued by the falconer. They seemed to possess powers of endurance, agility, and cunning wanting in the males. The species which was most in favour was the peregrine falcon, which, when taken early from the nest and trained to the sport, excelled the other species in dexterity, and in the readiness with which it lent itself to the exercise. The course of training undergone by these birds was of a very complete and lengthy character. The falconer preferred to take the bird from the nest, but his art was, in lieu of nestlings, also practised on older birds. The young or nestling was named the *eyess*, and on being taken from the nest was carefully tended by the falconer, and was lodged in some outhouse, being fed on flesh of various kinds. Becoming thus familiarised with man, the *eyess* grew tamer. The food was generally attached to a *lure*—an apparatus consisting of a bunch of feathers, a cord, and tassel. The object of thus feeding the falcon was to accustom it to recognise the lure, and to associate it with its food; this association afterwards serving to recall and entice the bird to the falconer when its chase was unsuccessful. Another form of lure was that known as the *tabur stycke*, consisting of a short stick on which the semblance of a bird was borne; and a third form of lure was named the *drawer*. As the bird's powers of flight became developed, the lure was used to entice her back to hand after permitting her to fly abroad. The operation which was most important in the falcon's training is that known as *hooding*. This consisted in placing on the bird's head a close-fitting leather cap, made so as to cover the eyes, but to allow the protrusion of the beak. This procedure often repeated had the effect of making the bird tame and docile. The bird thus hooded was set on a 'block' of wood, and was secured thereto by an apparatus of *bells* and *jesses*; the former being two hollow metal globes attached by *bewits* or leather straps to the legs of the bird; whilst the jesses were leather bands 5 or 6 inches in length, and fixed to each leg below the bells. The jesses, in turn, were attached to another strap—the *leash*—by means of *varvels*, or two rings of silver, on which the owner's name was engraved. The apparatus thus described ultimately became permanent parts of the falcon's harness; and in addition to these structures, a long cord, named the *creance*, was tied to the leash, and served to afford further and wider scope to the movements of the bird in training. It was also trained to sit or perch itself steadily on the hand of its master or mistress. The falcon was further taught to circle and hover round the falconer, the lure being made use of to this end. The bird mostly pursued of old was the heron. The prey or *quarry* was attacked in its homeward flight against the wind. The falcons being unhooded, were cast off, and sought a greater elevation than the prey, on which they successively *stooped* or *swooped* down. If the first missed its aim, the second hawk *stooped* in like manner, the heron being soon seized. The falconer drew off the hawks from the prey after all three had descended, luring them by means of live pigeons and other birds. The heron was rarely killed outright, but was frequently liberated, being first marked with the name of the falcon's owner. It often proved a powerful adversary while on the ground, striking at the falcons with its powerful beak, and sometimes transfixing them. The Merlin (q. v.) is chiefly used for the capture of larks and other small birds, and the goshawk may be employed to secure pheasants, and even rabbits and hares. A special terminology, of which some examples have been given, characterised the sport. The most celebrated training-place for falconers was the village of Falconswaerd, near Bois-le-Duc, in Holland. Several old and a few modern treatises exist on F.; the best-known of the latter is Freeman and Salvin's *Falconry*, published in 1859.

Faler'ii, an Etruscan city, W. of the Tiber, and N. of Mount Soracte. It first appears in Roman history (B.C. 437) as the enemy of Rome, and after the fall of Veii it was besieged by the Romans under Camillus, whose treatment of the treacherous schoolmaster is a familiar fable. The friendly relations then established with Rome were broken on several occasions, and finally (B.C. 241) the inhabitants (called *Falisci*) were expelled from their old city and founded a new one, on whose site the 'Colonia Falisca' was subsequently established by the triumvirs. In the middle ages another city, named *Civita Castellana*, appeared on the site of the old F.

Faler'nian Wine occupied the second rank among the ancient wines of Italy. It was produced in a district of Campania, stretching from the Massican Hills to the river Vulturnus, and known as the *Falernus Ager*. The best variety was the *Faustianum*.

Falie'ri, an ancient Venetian family, several members of which held high offices in the state, and one of whom took part in the election of the first doge in 697. The most notable, however, was **Marino F.** He was born about 1284, and at the siege of Zara in 1346 defeated 80,000 Hungarians, at the same time checking the besieged. Appointed commander of the fleet, he took Capo d'Istria, and afterwards, while absent as ambassador at Rome, was chosen doge in 1354. In the following year, enraged because the Council of Forty passed what he thought too slight a sentence on a nobleman, Michele Steno, who had libelled the doge's young wife, F. conspired to overthrow the republic and win the sovereignty. The plot was betrayed, and the chief conspirators were executed. F. was beheaded, 17th April 1355, on the stone staircase where the doges took the oath after election. F. seems to have been brave, violent, and unforgiving. He was a personal friend of Petrarch, who mentions him in his letters. Among the pictures of the doges in the hall of the Grand Council is a space veiled and inscribed 'Hic est locus Marini Faletro, decapitati pro criminibus.' See Byron's *Marino F.* and its appendices, and Marino Sanuto's *Vite de' Duchi de Venezia*.

Fal'kirk (perhaps 'the kirk on the *Vallum*' or wall of Agricola; the Gaelic name is *Eglais-bhrac*, 'the speckled kirk'), a town of Stirlingshire, Scotland, 22 miles E.N.E of Glasgow, and 25 W. by N. of Edinburgh, and a station on the N. British Railway. It is in the immediate vicinity of extensive ironworks, of which the best known are the Carron, which have given name to a peculiar kind of ironmongery, and to a piece of ordnance known as a carronade, because both are made at Carron. Several firebrick, tile, and chemical works are in the neighbourhood. F. has also three famous trysts or cattle-fairs, known by its name. Two battles have occurred in the neighbourhood, the first in 1298 between the troops of Edward I. and the Scotch under Wallace, in which the latter was completely defeated; and the second between the royal forces and those of the Chevalier, Prince Charles Edward Stuart, in 1746, in which the former were repulsed. F. became a royal burgh in 1646. Along with

Airdrie, Hamilton, Lanark, and Linlithgow, it sends one member to Parliament. Pop. (1871) 11,762.

Falk'land, an ancient burgh of Scotland, Fifeshire, 10 miles S.W. of Cupar, its charter dating from 1458. (Pop. 1871) 1283, mostly hand-loom weavers. F. Palace, a famous royal residence, has given distinction to the place. It is mentioned by Sir David Lyndsay in his *Complaynt of the Papingo* as the 'forteress of Fyfe.'

Falkland Islands, otherwise the **Malouines'** or the **Malvi'nas**, an archipelago in the S. Atlantic belonging to Britain, and lying 230 miles E. of Magellan's Strait. They consist of two large islands, E. and W. F., and of about 200 smaller, with an area of 4741 sq. miles, and a pop. (1871) of 803. They were discovered in 1593 by Richard Hawkins, but it is only since 1833 that they have formed a British settlement, though they have been a British possession since 1771. Previously they had belonged in succession to France and Spain. These islands are principally valuable from their numerous commodious harbours. The pasturage is good and the surrounding seas teem with fish; seals also abound. Stanley, in E. F., is the seat of the government.

Falkland, Lucius Cary, Viscount, was born at Burford, Oxfordshire, in 1610. His father, Sir Henry Cary, filled for a time the post of deputy-lieutenant in Ireland, and F. was educated at Trinity College, Dublin, and St John's College, Cambridge. Inheriting from his grandfather an estate worth £2000 a year, he devoted himself to learned research, and was on terms of friendship with such men as Selden and Chillingworth. In 1640 he entered the House of Commons as member for Newport, in the Isle of Wight, and at first took an active part on the side of Hampden and Pym, and against the illegalities of the king and his tools. Ultimately, however, he separated from the popular party. After a vain attempt at mediation between king and Parliament, he espoused, though with sad forebodings, the side of the former in the civil war, fought gallantly at Edgehill, and fell in the first battle of Newbury, September 20, 1643. He was an author both in prose and verse, his best-known work being a *Discourse on the Infallibility of the Church of Rome*. Green, in his *Short History of the English People*, p. 525, finely describes him as 'the centre of a circle which embraced the most liberal thinkers of his day, a keen reasoner and able speaker, whose convictions still went with the Parliament, while his wavering and impulsive temper, his love of the Church, his passionate longings for peace, his sympathy for the fallen, led him to struggle for a king whom he distrusted, and to die in a cause that was not his own.' See Forster's *Historical and Biographical Essays* (1858).

Fall, The, is the name given by theologians to the sin committed by our first parents in disobeying the command of God and eating of the forbidden fruit in the garden of Eden, as described in the third chapter of Genesis. The details of that narrative, which are familiar to every one, have always been interpreted by theologians with a greater or less departure from the literal sense. Thus the ordinary interpretation is that the serpent was only a figurative designation of Satan, or actually Satan in disguise, or, at least, that the serpent, if real, was employed by Satan as his organ or instrument. According to this view, the effects of the disobedience recorded in the narrative were merely subordinate expressions of the divine displeasure, and consequences of that which was the real and primary effect, namely, spiritual death or absolute ruin analogous to that of the fallen angels; so that the F. is the very basis of the whole system of Christian theology, necessitating, as it does, the Atonement, which indeed is obscurely predicted in the words of God to the serpent:—'It (the seed of the woman) shall bruise thy head, and thou shalt bruise his heel.' Others, however, regard the serpent of the narrative as a real animal, but the narrative itself as a fable or allegory intended to explain philosophically the origin of evil, physical and moral, in which allegory the tree of Life represents spirituality, the tree of Knowledge sensuality, the serpent being the symbol of pleasure. According to this view, which has been held by some of the learned from the earliest times, *e.g.*, Philo, Clement of Alexandria, Origen, Eusebius, Augustine, &c., the allegory teaches 'that as soon as man's mind, through the weakness and treachery of his senses, became captivated and seduced by the allurements of lust and pleasure, he was driven by God out of Paradise, that is, lost and forfeited the happiness and prosperity which he had enjoyed in his innocence.' For the theological bearings of the F., see ORIGINAL SIN.

Traditions of a F. from a state of original innocence and happiness are to be found among every nation possessing a cosmogony and theogony. According to the Hindus, the first man was tempted by the Supreme Being, whose special symbol was the serpent, by means of a blossom dropped from heaven of the sacred Indian fig. Instigated by his wife, who had derived her being from him, the man determined to possess the blossom, with the expectation that it would make him immortal, and on gathering it actually believed himself to be so; but, on the appearance of the deity, the pair were banished from the Paradise in which they were. The Persian account, contained in the Zend-Avesta, is as follows:—'The first couple lived originally in purity and innocence. Perpetual happiness was promised to them by Ormuzd, the creator of every good gift, if they persevered in their virtue. But an evil demon was sent to them by Ahriman, the representative of everything noxious and sinful. He appeared unexpectedly in the form of a serpent, and gave them the fruit of a wonderful tree, Hom, which imparted immortality, and had the power of restoring the dead to life. Thus evil inclinations entered their hearts; all their moral excellences were destroyed. Ahriman himself appeared under the form of the same reptile, and completed the work of seduction. They acknowledged him instead of Ormuzd as the creator of everything good, and the consequence was that they forfeited for ever the eternal happiness for which they were destined.' A likeness has been remarked between the Greek myth of the garden of the Hesperides—in which was a tree with golden apples, guarded by a speaking dragon, the possession of which conferred immortality—and the story in Genesis; for which also some of the designs might stand as illustrations which appear on the ancient Greek gems and Etruscan pottery. To account for the similarity existing among all these traditions one school of divines supposes them all to have been derived from the Hebrew Scriptures, the oldest literature in existence; another school holds the theory that the Jews derived their literature on the early history of the human race from the Babylonians and Persians, during their captivity in Babylon. The latter view has lately received apparent confirmation from the discoveries of Chaldæan literature made by Mr. G. Smith. On the terra-cotta tablets dug from the ruins of Assyrian cities by himself and others, he has discovered accounts of the creation, F., deluge, &c., corresponding almost exactly, as far as the narrative on the tablets yet found goes, with those in Genesis, except that they are fuller. See Kalisch's *Commentary on Genesis*; C. Middleton's *Works* (2d ed. Lond. 1755); G. Smith's *Chaldæan Account of Genesis* (1876).

Fall'acy (Lat. *fallacia*) is the technical name given in logic to an error which arises not in observation by the senses, but in reasoning, or in the interpretation of what is directly seen. The line between fact and inference, between the original sense-impression and the form and colour which it receives from the mind, is no doubt hard to trace. A great many unapparent details are filled in unconsciously, and therefore the leading rule of all scientific inquiry is to remove, or minimise, or allow for your errors of observation. It is a F. to omit observation altogether, or to unduly limit its range; but every F. assumes a fact truly ascertained, which the mind then proceeds to distort. Fallacies might, therefore, be classified according to the particular kind of reasoning, inductive or deductive, in which they occur. In books on formal logic, where alone syllogistic reasoning is (at least, properly) treated, they are classified according to the canon of consistency violated. Elsewhere, as in Bentham's *Book of Fallacies*, or Bastiat's *Sophismes Économiques*, the leading errors on a particular subject are collected and analysed. But before we reach fallacies of inference or reasoning, there is (1) A class of natural prejudices, called by Mr. Mill 'fallacies of simple inspection,' which are held by the mind as self-evident, *i.e.*, without conscious reference to evidence. The strength of these prejudices often depends on the feelings as a remote predisposing cause, but the form of intellectual error is much the same in all cases, viz., that the course of nature must correspond to the current of human thought.

Under this class come most cases of omens, unlucky days or names, &c. Similar fallacies, however, may be found in philosophy and in cultivated opinion—*e.g.*, things we cannot think of apart must exist together, and things which we cannot think of together cannot coexist; every clear idea must correspond with an object—a principle at the root of the systems of Descartes, Spinoza, and Leibnitz; a thing can act only where it is; nature always works by the simplest means; the belief in the separate existence of abstract qualities or class names; the principle of sufficient reason, according to which nature does a certain thing because man can see no reason why she should not; the idea (held by Bacon) that there must be only *one* cause of the sensible qualities of objects; or that entertained by many metaphysicians, that the conditions of the phenomenon must, or probably will, *resemble* the phenomenon itself, exemplified in the medical doctrine of signatures, that the virtue of every substance is pointed out by some external character. (2) Another important class of fallacies is called by Mr. Mill 'fallacies of observation,' which consist in either *non-observation* or *mal-observation*. The mind is moved by the marvellous, and is also biassed by preconceived opinion or the desire to establish a particular conclusion. Hence comes a disposition not to observe, as in the famous Copernican dispute about the stone falling from the ship-mast. Or where a particular instance is examined, material circumstances may be overlooked, *e.g.*, the phlogistic theory, in which the gaseous products of combustion were overlooked. Mal-observation arises for the most part from the tendency above alluded to to confuse perception with inference, or sensation with judgment. (3) Fallacies of *generalisation*, in which inferences are drawn from the order of things in the known to that in the unknown universe, *e.g.*, the attempts made to analyse into one things generically distinct, as heat, light, and sensation into motion; the 'induction by enumeration,' or *per enum. simplicem*, of the ancients. A more special form is that called in formal logic *post hoc ergo propter hoc*, where a true cause is inferred from casual conjunction, as in the line of political reasoning which justifies existing institutions from the contemporaneous prosperity of the commonwealth. Common language is saturated with metaphor, especially with subtle exchanges of meaning between the bodily and the spiritual, and it is difficult to state a proposition on any complex subject without tacitly suggesting several very questionable trains of thought. (4) Fallacies of *ratiocination*, or what are generally given in works on formal logic. These include wrong conversion of universal affirmative and of hypothetical propositions. It is constantly supposed that, because the premisses cannot be true if the conclusion is false, therefore the premisses cannot be false if the conclusion is true. In the opposition of propositions, too, it is often forgotten that contrary propositions, though they cannot both be true, may both be false. The ordinary syllogistic fallacies all consist in having more than three terms, either expressly or by undistributed middle or *illicit process* of extremes. Frequently the premisses are changed in argument, as in the scholastic *a dicto secundum quid ad dictum simpliciter*, an absolute rule is substituted for one qualified. Examples of this are the mercantile theory in economics (which left out of view in its conclusion the purchasing power of money), and the argument that tithes fell on the landlord because, *under the tithe system*, the owner of tithed land received less than the owner of tithe-free land. (5) Fallacies of *confusion*, which include all those fallacies that consist not so much in mistaking the force of evidence, as in an indistinct notion of what the evidence is. The chief is the F. of an ambiguous middle, where the middle term of a syllogism is ambiguous, or one of the syllogistic terms is taken in one sense in the premisses, and in another sense in the conclusion. Etymology in this way becomes a prolific source of erroneous reasoning. In the F. of composition and division something is established separately concerning each *single* member of a certain class, and then the same is inferred of the whole *collectively*. The *petitio principii*, or reasoning in a circle, occurs where the premiss is the same as the conclusion, or can be proved from it alone. It is quite common, when discussion does not run to first principles, to prove A by B, though B really depends on A for proof. The conclusion, abstractly stated, often serves for a premiss, and the words nature and essence are very useful in this connection, and what Bentham calls 'question-begging appellatives,' *e.g.*, innovation. The *ignoratio elenchi* consists in the establishment of an irrelevant conclusion, a particular for a universal, or some proposition which excites the feelings. See the treatises on logic by Whately, Mill, De Morgan, and Sir William Hamilton.

Fall'en Angels. It appears from certain passages of Scripture that some of the angels 'kept not their first estate' (Jude 6), but 'sinned' and were 'cast down to hell' (2 Pet. ii. 4). The Apocalypse, with greater minuteness, tells that the archangel Michael and his angels made war against the dragon (Satan) and his angels, and prevailed, and the dragon was cast out, and his angels were cast out with him (xii. 7–9). These F. A. are thus the Demons (q. v.) who are so ready to obey the behests of their master the Devil in afflicting mankind, although St Jude and St Peter speak of their being bound in chains till the judgment day. It also appears from Eph. i. 21, vi. 12 (*cf.* iii. 10, Col. i. 16, 1 Pet. iii. 22), that the same grades existed among them as among those who had not fallen. As to the nature of the sin which led to their fall, various opinions have been held. Some have thought it was lust, founding on Gen. vi. 2; others, envy; but it is generally held to have been pride, from 1 Tim. iii. 6.

It is asserted by some, however, that all this doctrine of the Devil and his angels was derived by the Jews from the dualistic ideas of the Babylonians and Persians, during their Babylonian exile (see DEVIL), and that the allusions to the F. A. in the New Testament are derived from the Book of Enoch (q. v.), in which the following passage occurs:—'To Michael also the Lord said, Go, and announce his crime to Samyaza and to the others who are with him, who have been associated with women. . . . Bind them for seventy generations underneath the earth . . . until the judgment which will last for ever be completed. Then shall they be taken away into the lowest depths of the fire in torments, and in confinement shall they be shut up for ever' (x. 15, 16). Be that as it may, the Babylonians had fuller traditions than the Jews about the fall of the dragon and his angels, as appears from recently discovered Chaldæan literature. See G. Smith's *Chaldæan Account of Genesis* (Lond. 1876); *Book of Enoch.*

Fallmeray'er, Philipp Jakob, a German historian and traveller, was born of poor parents at Tschötsch, near Brixen, in Tyrol, December 10, 1791. He studied at the universities of Salzburg and Landshut, devoting himself chiefly to history and philology. After serving in the Bavarian forces against Napoleon, he was made a master in the gymnasium at Augsburg, and afterwards held the chair of philology at Landshut. From 1831 to 1834 he travelled in Egypt, Palestine, Syria, and Greece; and in 1840, and again in 1847, visited the East. He was elected to the Frankfurt Assembly, but shortly retired from public life. He died at Munich, April 26, 1860. Among his works are *Geschichte des Kaiserthums Trapezunt* (1831); *Geschichte der Halbinsel Morea im Mittelalter* (1830–36); *Fragmente aus dem Orient* (1845). His *Gesammelte Werke* were edited by Thomas in 3 vols. (Leips. 1861).

Falling Bodies. See PROJECTILES.

Falling Sickness. See EPILEPSY.

Fallo'pius, Gabrie'le, a famous anatomist, was born at Modena about 1523. He studied science in various universities throughout Europe, and in 1551 became professor of anatomy at Pisa. He died in 1562. F. was one of the earliest restorers of anatomy, but several discoveries claimed by him have been traced to Greek and Arabic physicians,—*e.g.*, the two tubes leading from the ovary to the Uterus (q. v.) were not discovered by him, though called the *Fallopian tubes*, having been accurately described by Herophilus and Rufus of Ephesus more than 300 years B.C. Among F.'s works are *Observationes Anatomicæ* (1561), *De Thermalibus Aquis* (1564), *De Morbo Gallico Tractatus* (1564), &c. See the collected edition of his works, entitled *Opera genuina omnia, tam practica quam theoretica* (Ven. 3 vols. 1584; Frankf. 4 vols. 1600).

Fallopius, Aqueduct of, a canal in the fibrous portion of the temporal, which transmits the facial nerve. It passes outwards and backwards over the labyrinth of the Ear (q. v.), and terminates at the stylo-mastoid foramen. On the anterior and upper surface of the bone there is a small foramen named the *hiatus Fallopii*, which transmits the large superficial petrosal nerve.

Fall'ow (Old Eng. *fealo*, a pale or reddish yellow; *cf.* Ger. *falb* and *fahl*, allied to Lat. *fulv*-us), a term in agriculture applied to land left bare of any crop for a season to free it from weeds, and to improve the mechanical condition of the soil. The practice of fallowing is one of very ancient origin, having been inculcated in the Mosaic law, which commanded that the ground should rest every seventh year. It was well known to the ancient Romans, by whom fallowing was introduced into England; but it was not till about the beginning of the 18th c. that the practice was begun in Scottish agriculture. Originally all kinds of land were fallowed indiscriminately; but the introduction of green crops, such as potatoes and turnips, had the effect of greatly limiting the area of land to which the system was applied. Now what is termed 'bare or summer F.' is only applied to very stiff retentive clay soils such as are found in the 'carse' land of Scotland, the fen clays of Huntingdon and Cambridgeshire, and the weald clay of Kent and Sussex in England. On the lighter soils, the periodical cultivation of green crops effects the same object, and is known as 'green-crop F.' Land under bare F. is ploughed up immediately on the removal of the crop, and so exposed to the rains, frosts, and atmospheric influences of the winter. In spring it is again ploughed across, and on very stiff soils it may receive as many as six or eight ploughings, besides scarifying and harrowing throughout the season. The soil so treated is thoroughly exposed to the oxidising influences of the atmosphere, and to the action of the carbonic acid contained in the air, as well as that dissolved in every shower of rain. While the land is thereby rendered more mellow and friable, the mineral substances which enter into the constitution of cultivated plants are fitted for assimilation, and injurious weeds are at the same time thoroughly eradicated.

Fallow Chat. See WHEATEAR.

Fallow Deer (*Dama vulgaris*), a species of *Cervidæ* or Deer (q. v.) nearly allied to the Stag (q. v.), but distinguished by its spotted coat, its smaller size, and the spreading palmated horns. The colour of the F. D. is a reddish brown spotted with white, and usually exhibiting a few whitish lines on the body. In winter it assumes a darker tint. The average height is about 3 feet at the shoulders. The food consists of grasses of various kinds. The original habitat of the F. D. is unknown. Tradition points to S. Europe or W. Asia as its probable home; but it is rarely if ever met with save in a domesticated state. F. D. are largely kept in parks and grounds. They are very docile, and readily tamed, the herd being governed by a 'master deer.' The flesh affords good venison, and from the skin leather is manufactured; while the shavings of the horns are used in making ammonia—hence popularly named 'hartshorn.' The females are hornless. The young are named *fawns*, the females *does*, and the males *bucks*.

Fallow Deer.

Fall River, a city of Massachusetts, U.S., at the mouth of a stream of the same name and of the Taunton River, 20 miles from the sea, and 48 S. of Boston by railway. It has two calico printworks, one woollen factory, thirty-eight cotton mills, having 1,269,788 spindles, large ironworks, and a bleaching business. It has also deep-water navigation, and is the terminus of steamboat communication with New York. It possesses a free library, a public park of 60 acres, two daily and three weekly newspapers, &c. Pop. (1870) 26,766. F. R., which was founded in 1659, was incorporated as a town in 1803, and as a city in 1854. —F. R., a small stream in Massachusetts, of great utility for its water-power. In its last half mile it descends about 130 feet, its banks being lined with extensive mills. It enters the eastern arm of the Narragansett Bay.

Fal'mouth, a town of Cornwall, England, at the mouth of the Fal, and formerly a station for the packet-boats to the S. of Europe and the W. Indies, 92 miles S.W. of Exeter and 266 W.S.W. of London. It is connected with Plymouth by the Cornwall Railway. The harbour, which is of unusual depth and capacity, is defended on the E. and W. respectively by St. Mawes and Pendennis Castles, built by Henry VIII. and strengthened by Elizabeth. The number of vessels that entered in 1875 was 1010; tonnage, 140,614; cleared, 589; tonnage, 49,167. The chief exports are tin, copper, granite, and fish (pilchards, oysters, &c.); the chief imports are timber, grain, flour, wine, hemp, fruit, and guano. Pop. (1871) of the municipal borough, 5294. F., with Penryn, returns two members to Parliament.

False Bay, a capacious inlet of the Southern Ocean in Cape Colony, S. Africa, the S.W. boundary of which is formed by the Cape of Good Hope It is about 22 miles long, and as many broad. Being protected from the N.W. monsoon, it has been chosen as the station of the British fleet in S. African waters.

False'hood, Le'gal, is defined to be a fraudulent imitation or suppression of truth to the injury of any one. *Forgery* and *swindling* are the main branches of the crime. See these articles; also FRAUD.

False Impris'onment consists in the unlawful detention of the person. All forcible confinement, even in a street, is by the law regarded as imprisonment. Legal restraint of the person must be by warrant of a court of law or legal officer, or by special power warranted by statute or common law, such as the obligation on every man who sees an act of felony committed to arrest the felon. (See APPREHEND.) F. I., however, may arise from executing a legal process at an illegal time, as by arresting in a civil process on Sunday. The imprisonment being committed under error is no excuse. The corresponding Scotch law term is Wrongous Imprisonment (q. v.). In England the safeguard of the subject is his power to require a court of law to issue in his favour a writ of Habeas Corpus (q. v.) *ad subjiciendum*.

False Point, a harbour at the mouth of the Mahanuddee river, in the district of Cuttack, province of Bengal, British India, 196 miles S. of Calcutta. In 1860 it was first formed into a port, though a lighthouse had been previously erected and buoys laid down; it now ranks as the third harbour of Bengal. Ships cannot proceed up the river, but native boats now bring down produce from the town of Cuttack through the Kendrapara Canal. In 1874-75 110 ships entered; tonnage, 118,375; value of the imports, £118,395; of the exports, chiefly rice, £170,047.

False Pretences, Obtaining Money by. To constitute this offence there must be a specific fraudulent misrepresentation of matter of fact by which property is obtained. If a man purchase goods, promising to pay for them next day or on some other specified day, should he fail to do so the failure is merely in an engagement. But if he obtain the goods in exchange for a cheque on a banker, stating falsely that he has funds in hands of the banker to meet the cheque, he commits the crime in question. But in a case in which a man induced a banker to pay his cheque by drawing a bill on one on whom he had no right to draw, the act was adjudged not to be a false pretence because he only obtained credit. It would have been otherwise had he obtained money on the bill. The distinction is a fine one, and obtaining credit by fraud is now punishable under the Bankrupt Act of 1869. The 24 and 25 Vict. c. 96 consolidates previous legislation on the subject. A minor obtaining money or goods by pretending to be of age may be punished as a common cheat. Under the Act, any one fraudulently inducing another to sign his name or to execute any document is guilty of felony; and liable to three years' penal servitude. Bills of exchange and all negotiable securities are included under this provision.

In Scotland the crime in question is punishable under common law. See FRAUD, SWINDLING.

False Return, Legal, renders the officer who makes it liable in damage.

False Swearing. See PERJURY, AFFIRMATION, DECLARATION. Under the English Bankruptcy Act, if the bankrupt make a false declaration, he is guilty of perjury. Under the Scotch Act, any one under oath is liable to prosecution at the instance of the Lord Advocate, or of the trustee in the sequestration, with concurrence of the Lord Advocate.

Falsett'o, a high register possessed by many male voices. It is seldom agreeable in itself, or used in serious concerted music.

False Verdict may arise from improper behaviour of the jury among themselves, or of the plaintiff towards them, by which their verdict is influenced, from misdirection of the judge, or from exorbitant award of damage. On these and similar grounds a new trial may be granted. But if two juries return the same or a similar verdict, a third trial is seldom conceded. Formerly, in England, a juror returning a F. V. might in certain circumstances incur heavy penalties under a writ of attaint, but the process was abolished by 6 Geo. IV. c. 50, and the universal rule now is that a juryman cannot on any ground be punished for his verdict.

False Weights and Measures. Possession of these for purpose of trade is in England punishable under common law. The penalty is imprisonment. In Scotland the users of false weights are by statute liable to confiscation of movables.

Fal'sifying Rec'ords. Any one injuring or obliterating any original document in legal process is liable to be punished with penal servitude. And any official whose business it is to furnish certified copies of documents, wilfully certifying a false copy is guilty of felony, and is liable to the punishment of penal servitude for life.

Fal'ster, a Danish island in the Baltic, 2½ miles S. of Seeland, and included in the amt of Maribo. Area, 181 sq. miles; pop. (1874) 32,413. It is flat, low, and rather unhealthy, but yields much corn and timber, and is celebrated for its fruits. Nykjöbing, the capital (pop. 3645), is on the Guldborgsund, and has a cathedral, castle, and some trade. F. became a royal domain in the 16th c., and was the chief residence of several Danish queens, of whom the last was Charlotte Amalie, 1700–14.

Fa'lun, or **Fah'lun** (otherwise *Gamla Kopparberget*, 'the old copper-mine'), the capital of the 'län' Ntora Kopparbergs, Dalarna, in Sweden, in a valley between lakes Warpan and Runn, 120 miles N.W. of Stockholm by railway. It has long been famous for its copper-mines, which are now, however, much less profitable than of yore. The mines were formerly the most extensive of the kind in Sweden, and indeed in the world. About the middle of the 17th c. the yield was 3000 tons; at present it is barely 700 tons. Since 1716 they have been in the hands of a joint-stock company, who own from sixty to seventy smelting furnaces. The smoke from these has given the town a dingy appearance. F. has also a mining-school and museum, cotton and flax mills, besides manufactures of cow-hair cloth, leather, tobacco, nails, &c. Pop. (1874) 6570.

Fa'ma (Lat.; Gr. *Phēmē*, or *Ossa*) was the personification of rumour or report. She is called by various ancient poets the messenger of Zeus, the daughter of Hope, and the daughter of Terra.

Fa'ma Clamo'sa in the ecclesiastical law of Scotland is a prevailing report imputing immoral conduct to a clergyman, probationer, or elder of the Church. No process is begun by the presbytery unless the F. C. be so clamant as to make it necessary to do so for their own vindication, or unless a complaint has been formally given in.

Famil'iar Spir'its is a name in which three different shades of meaning may be traced, or perhaps there have been three stages in the development of the idea expressed. 1. F. S. were originally the shades or ghosts of deceased persons brought up by magical arts from the abode of the dead, which, according to all ancient ideas, was in the bowels of the earth, in order that they might give information about future or doubtful things. This is necromancy pure and simple, and is well seen in the episode of the witch of Endor, to whom Saul said, 'Divine unto me by *a* familiar spirit, and bring me up whom I shall name unto thee' (1 Sam. xxviii. 8). The term familiar spirit has the same meaning in Isa. viii. 19, where the prophet asks, 'Why inquire at the dead concerning the living?' The shade of Samuel appears to have been seen by the witch; generally, however, the F. S. appeared to speak out of the ground: *cf.* Isa. xxix. 4, 'Thy voice shall be as of a familiar spirit out of the ground.' 2. Again F. S. were demons (in the original sense of disembodied spirits not necessarily evil) who took up their abode in the bodies of the magicians, who revealed matters communicated to them by the F. S. The persons so possessed were called by the Greeks *engastrimythoi* ('ventriloquists'), doubtless because designing men often imposed on people by means of the faculty of ventriloquism, and made sounds appear to come from their belly or breast, as well as from the ground. Isa. viii. 19 ('those that chirp and whisper') alludes to their imitating the chirping of bats. It is the name given in the LXX. to those having F. S., distinguishing them, as in Deut. xviii. 11, from necromancers, although, on the other hand, the term is also applied to the witch of Endor (1 Sam. xxviii. 7). They were also called *Pythones*, which is the term used Acts xvi. 16—'a spirit of Python.' 3. The third stage in the development of the idea was when demons came to be regarded by the Christian Church as altogether evil. Tertullian, in his *Apology for the Christians*, describes them as being 'everywhere in a single moment; the whole world is as one place to them; all that is done over the whole extent of it, it is as easy for them to know as to report. . . . The purposes of God, too, they took up of old from the lips of the prophets, even as they spoke them; and they gather them still from their works when they hear them read aloud. Thus getting, too, from this source some intimations of the future, they set themselves up as rivals of the true God, while they steal his divinations.' See DEMONS, NECROMANCY, and WITCHCRAFT.

Familiars. See INQUISITION.

Fam'ily. The word F. is derived from the Latin *familia*, and this from the Oscan *famal*, 'a servant,' or *faama*, 'a house.' This last corresponds to the Sanskrit *dhâman* (*cf.* Lat. *domus*), 'house,' from the radical *dhâ*, 'to place.' At Rome the primitive meaning of *familia* was the number of slaves or servants belonging to a person or a public office; then all those, whether masters or slaves, living under the same roof; lastly, all those connected by blood, whether living together or not. Its general meaning now is those persons connected by blood who live together, *i.e.*, father, mother, and children. But it has numerous other meanings. It is applied to the establishment of a cardinal, to the human race, to the children apart from the parents, to a political dynasty, to a religious order, to a group of organisms in botany or zoology, to a group of substances in chemistry, of allied words in philology, or of surfaces or curves in geometry having analytical or other properties in common. The legal conception of F., implying various reciprocal obligations and duties between parents and children, has been the subject of many theories. By one, the children became the property of the parents; by another, there was a tacit convention between parent and child; by a third, burdens were placed on the parents as a punishment for having sinned in bringing into existence creatures incapable of supporting themselves. Board, nourishment, education, are among the obvious positive obligations of parents; they, in turn, have a claim for support upon their children in case of old age and destitution. The limits and pecuniary amount of these obligations are of course varied by different municipal laws. The character of a nation, and the general laws which govern society, depend to a large extent on the kind of families of which society is composed. Originally, the domestic was a much more powerful and comprehensive form of association than it is now. In the primitive clan or tribe there are many features which suggest the F. relation. In Greece and Rome we find a close association of servants with the blood-relations. The inner life of the Roman F. deserves a few words. The powers of the head of a F. were three—*potestas*, *manus*, and *mancipium*. The first was either *potestas dominica* over slaves, or *potestas patria* over children; these two were different. *Manus* or marital power placed the wife on the footing of *filiafamilias*. The father had a legal power of selling (*mancipare*) his children into bondage; a *mancipium* was a *filiusfamilias* sold as a bondsman to another *paterfamilias*, to whom he stood in the position of a slave, though otherwise a free citizen, the exercise of political functions being probably suspended. The original power of the father was indeed that of life and death. But this disappeared long before Hadrian and Constantine (A.D. 319) included killing by a father under the crime of parricide. Trajan compelled a father to emancipate a son he had treated with inhumanity. The primitive option of a parent to nurture or to expose was also taken away, and is formally prohibited by a law of Valentinian (A.D. 374). In the same way a law of Diocletian and Maximian declares the sale, donation, and pledging of children to be unlawful. The surrender of a child to satisfy a claim of damages based on the child's wrong-doing lingered in the law, but even this was prohibited by Justinian. But in extreme poverty parents might sell children at birthtime (*sanguinolenti*). In polygamous countries a different set of conditions is presented, in which the influence of father and mother is entirely separate; while in Transylvania, Servia, and other Slavic countries in the S.E. of Europe, households of fifty and sixty are still found presided over by the house-father.

Family, a division of the animal and plant world used in classification. The F. is a group which embraces a number of more or less nearly-allied genera (see GENUS). Thus, the F. *Felidæ* (q. v.), forming one of the subdivisions of the great Carnivorous order of *Mammalia*, includes the principal genus *Felis* and allied genera, represented by such nearly-related animals as the lions, tigers, cats, lynxes, &c. The F. in turn forms one of the subdivisions of the higher 'order.' In some cases, where the animals to be classified are not numerous, the F. may be omitted altogether, the genera in such a case being directly included in the Order (q. v.).

Family of Love, a religious sect founded about the middle of the 16th c. by Henry Nicholas, a Münster Anabaptist, who, after making several converts in Holland, crossed to England, where his doctrines won considerable favour among the ignorant. He held himself to be greater than Moses or Christ, for while Moses preached hope, and Christ faith, he preached love. He made religion identical with love, independent of dogma; through love men could be absorbed in God, and even things forbidden were enjoyable by the pure. These teachings resulted in coarse license, and in 1580 Queen Elizabeth caused the sect to be scattered and their books burned. In 1604 they sought permission from James I. to answer the attacks made on them, and tried to ingratiate themselves with the king by slandering the Puritans, but their request was refused, and the sect gradually died out through the frequent exposure of their sensual practices. See Roger's *Displaying of an Horrible Secte of Grosse and Wicked Heretiques naming themselves the F. of L.* (Lond. 1579); Mosheim's *Ecclesiastical History*, ch. xvi.; and Collier's *Ecclesiastical History of England*.

Fan ('that which *blows*;' Old Eng. *fann*; *cf.* Ger. *wanne*, Fr. *van*, from Lat. *vannus*: the Fr. *éventail* is from *éventer*, 'to raise a wind'), an ornamental object used principally by ladies to cool their faces by agitating the air. The modern European F. usually consists of a decorated mount attached to a stick, composed of two master-pieces and slender radiating ribs, in such a manner that the fan may be folded or spread out at pleasure. The mount may be formed either of silk, paper, vellum, lace, or other thin and light material; and the stick, of ivory, bone, mother-of-pearl, wood, tortoiseshell, &c. The F. had its origin in the East, and among the civilised nations of antiquity it was regarded as an emblem of majesty and power. Rigid feather-plume fans with long handles were used by both sexes among the Greeks and Romans; and from the painted pottery preserved from remote ages we know that the opulent had servants to wave fans over them, as is customary in Oriental countries at the present time. The F. in one form or other is now common to all countries. Prior to the 15th c. the folding F. was unknown in Europe; but even then it had long been in use among the Japanese and Chinese, the latter people having adopted it from their more skilful and ingenious neighbours. From China it was brought to Europe by the Portuguese; and in the 16th c. it was common to Portugal, Spain, Italy, and France. In the time of Henry VIII. English ladies generally carried a feather F. suspended to the girdle, and till after the period of the Restoration folding fans were scarcely known in England. Some early English fans were provided with very long handles, so long, indeed, that ladies walked with them. They seem to have served to chastise the unruly and disobedient. In Beaumont and Fletcher's *Wit at Several Weapons*, occurs

> 'Wer't not better
> Your head were broken with the handle of a fan?'

and in 1 *Henry IV.* ii. 3, Hotspur says, 'I could brain him with his lady's fan.' One of the most exquisitely humorous of Addison's papers in the *Spectator* deals with the manipulation of the F. The Chinese fabricate cheap folding fans with palm-leaf or with painted silk or paper mounts for export. Fans of inferior quality are made at Vienna, London, and in parts of France and Belgium. In Spain a F. may be bought for a farthing; at a bull-fight exhibition every person buys one. Paris has no rival in the production of the highly artistic F. The *éventailliste*, or F.-maker, commands the services of eminent artists for designs, and only employs the most skilful workmen to carry them into effect. F.-making attained great excellence in the reign of Louis XIV., and many of the fans then produced were so costly that they were simply expanded for ostentation and not for utility. Fans belonging to the epoch of *le Grand Monarque* are much prized and eagerly sought after for private collections. The language of the F., in which most ladies of last century were deeply read, has now almost died out. In Spanish-speaking countries, however, the F. is still an instrument of diplomacy and intrigue, and by it a coquette can convey to her admirer her train of thought.

A special form of instrument for producing currents of air, used in certain industrial operations, is designated a F. See FANNERS.

Fanar'iots, a name given at first to the inhabitants of the Fanar or Greek quarter of Constantinople, so called from its beacon (Gr. *phanarion*). These Greeks, after the capture of Constantinople by the Turks, made themselves, by their adroitness and business talents, very useful as secretaries to Turkish ministers and dignitaries. Towards the close of the 17th c. all the dragomans were chosen solely from their ranks, and this greatly swelling their influence, they induced the Porte to choose the hospodars or governors of Wallachia and Moldavia from them exclusively. These hospodars were followed to their provinces by hosts of F., who held various offices, and wrung wealth from the provincials by the most unprincipled rapacity. The F. no longer exist as a distinct class. See Zallony's *Essai sur les F.* (Mars. 1824; 2d ed. 1830); and Finlay's *History of the Greek Revolution* (Edinb. 1861).

Fan'cy. See IMAGINATION.

Fandan'go, a lively Spanish national dance, in triple time, executed to the accompaniment of the guitar, the dancers beating time with castanets.

Fan'euil Hall, in Boston, Massachusetts, was built and given to the town by Peter Faneuil in 1742. It was frequently used for public assemblies during the War of Independence, and was hence known as 'the cradle of liberty.' It is still used as a public hall, and has several good paintings.

Fan'fare, a French term denoting a flourish of trumpets or other brass instruments. The music is of Moorish origin, and passed from Spain to France and other countries. A derivative from F. is *fanfaron*, meaning a braggart, probably from the noise he makes, while his braggadocia is called *fanfaronnade*.

Fanfish, or **Sailfish**, the name given to the *Histiophorus immaculatus*, a species of Teleostean fishes belonging to the family *Xiphiidæ* or swordfishes. The name is derived from the great height and size of the dorsal fin, which the fish appears to raise or depress at will. The ventral fins are very small, and the tail is deeply forked, its lobes being of equal size. The F. inhabits tropical seas, and is common round the coasts of Ceylon.

Fang (Old Eng. *fang*, 'that which *takes* or *seizes*,' from *fon*, a contraction of *fangan*, 'to seize;' *cf.* Ger. *fangen*, Dutch, *vangen*, Dan. *fange*). A thief captured while carrying stolen goods is, in Scottish legal phraseology, 'taken with the F.' As a noun it still survives in standard English, as in the 'fang' of a wild beast; while in Scotland people still speak of a well having lost its 'fang.' It was used as a verb by the Elizabethans; thus Webster says, 'He's in the law's clutches; you see he's *fanged*.'

Fann'ers, a deriv. from Fan (q. v.), a form of blowing apparatus used in agriculture for winnowing the chaff from the grain of corn. It consists essentially of a revolving fan with four or five arms or vanes, mounted within a box or case. The fan draws in air through openings at the side of the case, and throwing it forcibly forward against the mixed grain and chaff fed into the apparatus, drives the light chaff out at an opening at the opposite end of the case, the grain falling down and being delivered by spouts at the sides. The heavier and plumper grains fall nearest the fan, while lighter grains are carried further on, and may be delivered by a separate spout. It is thus possible to separate the grain fed into the hopper into three or four qualities, besides freeing it from the chaff. F. constitutes an essential part of a thrashing-machine, and farmers usually are supplied with a separate barn-F. The finishing F., or duster, is a simpler apparatus used for re-winnowing grain, or, as its name indicates, for dusting or cleaning grain which may have lain any time in the granary. The F. was invented by Andrew Cavers, a farmer in Roxburghshire, in the early part of the 18th c. The principle of the F. is adopted in many important metallurgical operations for creating a powerful blast of air.

Fa'no, an Italian watering-place in the province of Urbino e Pesaro, 30 miles N.W. of Ancona by railway. It stands a mile N. of the mouth of the Metauro, in a fertile plain, and is well built and girt with walls. It has a cathedral and thirteen churches, in which there are many fine paintings, frescoes, and marbles, among others Guido's 'Annunciation,' and several works by Guercino and Domenichino. The principal manufacture is of silk. The commerce has greatly declined, and the port has been largely silted up. Pop. 19,606. The chief classic relic is an arch of white marble raised in honour of Augustus. F. is the anc. *Fanum Fortunæ*, so called from the temple to Fortune built here by the Romans after the battle of the Metaurus.

Fan-Palm, a popular name (suggested by the form of the leaves or fronds) given to various species of Palms (q. v.) belonging to the genera *Mauritia*, *Hyphæna*, *Livistonia*, &c. The F.-P. of Europe (*Chamærops humilis*) and the palmetto of N. America are examples.

Fan'shawe, Sir Richard, a diplomatist and poet, was born at Warrenpark, Hertfortshire, in 1608. He studied at Cambridge, entered the Inner Temple, and was sent to Madrid by Charles I. in 1635 as secretary to the embassy. F. espoused the royal cause in the civil war, was taken prisoner at Worcester (1651), and on being freed, joined Charles II. at Breda. He was sent after the Restoration as ambassador to Madrid, where he died, 16th June 1666. F. translated Guarini's *Pastor Fido* (1647), Camoens' *Lusiad* (1655), Horace's *Odes*, and the fourth book of the *Æneid*. He wrote also original verse, *A Short Discourse on the Long Wars of Rome*, and a Latin version of Fletcher's *Faithful Shepherdess*. He was an elegant and spirited translator. His letters were published in 1701.

Fans, The, a race on the equatorial coast of W. Africa, chiefly on the Gaboon river, of a copper-brown colour and slight build. They have revolting cannibal practices, and are said to barter their dead with each other. They wear dresses of bark, stain themselves with red wood, and hold wild orgies at every full moon. Their traditions assert that they came from the N.E., and they seem to be the 'Yagas' of the old Portuguese writers. See Schweinfurth's *Heart of Africa* (Lond. 1873).

Fan'tail, the name given to several species of Insessorial birds belonging to the section *Dentirostres* of that order, and to the family of the *Muscicapidæ* or fly-catchers. Certain varieties of Pigeons (q. v.) are so called from the spreading nature of the tail-feathers. The *Rhipidura albiscapa* of Australia, popularly known as the white-shafted fantail, is a well-known species. The bill in this genus has long basal bristles, the nostrils being partly hidden by plumes; the first wing-quills are short, the fourth and fifth being longest. The tail is broad, and the tarsi are broadly scaled. The colour of the species just mentioned is a dusky olive-black on the upper parts, a white streak existing above and below the eye. The throat, edges of the wing-coverts, tips and shafts of the tail-feathers (excepting the two middle feathers) are white; and the tail-feathers when expanded form a fan-like structure. The average length of the bird is about five inches.

Fanta'sia, in music a composition in free form, like the Capriccio (q. v.). In modern music the F. is often an enlargment and embellishment of some popular air; or of melodies from an opera, arranged for performance as an instrumental solo.

Fan'ti or **Fantee**, a country of W. Africa, on the Guinea coast, lies between the rivers Sakuru on the E., and Kaku on the W., and is separated from Ashanti on the N. by dense forests. It is a rich strip of coast-land, yielding much gold-dust, and supporting a numerous people. The Fantis are closely allied in race to the Ashantis, who conquered them and greatly destroyed their country in 1807. See Captains Brackenbury and Wilson, *Fanti and Ashanti* (1874).

Fan-Tracery, a beautiful form of vaulting, invented by English architects in the 15th c. It is used in Late Perpen-

Fan-Vault of Chapel of Henry VII., Westminster.

dicular work, and is found only in England. The ribs which compose it spring from the capitals of the shafts with a uniform outward curve, and the spaces between these diverging ribs are filled by a rich tracery of foils and cusps. Fine examples of F.-T. are to be seen at Peterborough; King's College, Cambridge; Ely; St George's Chapel, Windsor; Henry VII.'s Chapel at Westminster; and in the cloisters at Gloucester. F.-T. was often used over tombs, in cloisters, chantry chapels, and other small buildings.

Far'aday, Michael, D.C.L., F.R.S., an illustrious English physicist, was born at Stoke-Newington, London, September 22, 1791. The son of poor parents, he received the most elementary education, and was apprenticed in 1805 to a bookbinder. Here he used well his opportunities for acquiring knowledge; and his reading, together with evening lectures by a Mr. Tatum, which he sometimes attended, gave his mind a strong bent towards physical and especially electrical subjects. While working as a journeyman bookbinder, he obtained the patronage of Sir Humphrey Davy, and became his assistant at the Royal Institution in 1813. He subsequently travelled with Davy on the Continent, and soon after his return in 1815, made his first published contribution to science, an analysis of some caustic lime from Tuscany. In 1820 his attention was directed to Œrsted's discovery of the action of a current upon a magnet, and his *History of the Progress of Electro-Magnetism* (1821) prepared him for his later celebrated researches in this and allied branches of physics. In 1823 he liquified chlorine, and in 1824 was elected a Fellow of the Royal Society. Of his chemical papers which appeared in the *Philosophical Transactions* about this time, that relating to the discovery of benzol deserves special notice. He succeeded Davy as lecturer at the Royal Institution in 1827, and was appointed Professor of Chemistry there in 1833. In 1831 he returned to his electrical researches, and made his great discovery of magneto-electric induction—the generation of electric currents in conductors moving relatively to a magnet or other current. This led to a series of investigations to establish the 'identity of electricities,' and later, in 1833, to the hitherto but little understood subject of electrolysis, his papers on which evince at once his high experimental skill and his profound mental acumen. From 1836 to 1838 frictional electricity engaged his attention, the outcome of his researches being the discovery of the specific inductive capacity of insulators or *dielectrics*, a discovery of the highest importance in submarine telegraphy. In 1841 he established the 'magnetisation of light,' or the rotation which a plane polarised ray of light undergoes in a magnetic field. Then followed his researches in diamagnetism, and his investigations on the magnetism of gases and atmospheric magnetism. In 1835, at the suggestion of Lord Melbourne, he received from Government a pension of £500, and in 1858 the Queen allotted him a residence in Hampton Court, where he died, August 25, 1867. F. was a man of simple and unaffected tastes, of open and unassuming character, and of deep personal piety. In physical science he is unquestionably the greatest experimentalist that England, perhaps the world, has ever seen. His principal works are *Experimental Researches on Electricity* (3 vols. 1839, 1844, 1855), *Lectures on Various Forces of Matter* (3d ed. 1862), and *Lectures on the Chemical History of a Candle* (2d ed. 1866). See *Life of F.* by Tyndall (1869), and by Bence Jones (2 vols. 1870).

Farai'zi, a name derived from the Arabic *farz*, 'a command,' and applied in India, and especially in Bengal, to the reformed sect of Mohammedans who are generally known as Wahabs. About the year 1827, a pilgrim from Mecca, on returning to his native village in the district of Furreedpore near Dacca, taught the new faith to his neighbours. It is supposed that the majority of the Mussulmans in Eastern Bengal, who there outnumber the Hindus, now belong to the F. sect. In 1831 the propagandism gave rise to serious riots, and again in 1870 the villagers of the Gangetic delta were found to be carrying on intrigues with the armed rebels on the frontier of the Punjaub; but at the present time there is no reason to doubt the loyalty of this portion of the Indian community.

Farce (from the Ital. *farsa*, Lat. *farcire*, 'to stuff,' or from the Provençal *farsum*, 'a ragout or mixture,' like the Lat. *satura*), a form of the drama which seeks to provoke mirth by dialogue and incident more ludicrous and less natural and refined than is admissible in comedy. The Greek *satyric plays* were essentially farces. *Saturæ*, or farces combining conversation with music and dancing, and *fabulæ Atellanæ*, or farces of Campanian origin, were the most popular of the Roman dramatic entertainments, and, even under the Cæsars, gave publicity to political feeling in their ribald, vigorous dialogue. In the middle ages, *jeux*, or profane dramatic performances, were common, and from these arose the farces of the *clercs de la Basoche*—a society founded in Paris in 1303. (See BASOCHES.) These early French farces were short, seldom exceeding 500 lines, mostly indecent, and without the stinging wit of the *fabliaux*. Coarse and frequently impromptu farces prevailed on the French stage until Molière founded genuine French comedy. In Italy the term *farsa* was applied to comic plays, which seem to have been modified from the ancient *fabulæ*, and which were greatly developed at the end of the 14th c. by Sannagarro. In mediæval Germany *farce* denoted a song chanted during divine service. In England farces appear distinct from comedy about the beginning of the 18th c. Perhaps the most notable name in English farcical literature is that of Samuel Foote (q. v.).

Far'cy, a disease of horses, closely associated with Glanders (q. v.), and distinguished by the inflammation and swelling of the lymphatic or absorbent vessels of either or both hind-limbs. The inflammatory process extends to the formation of ulcers, and of swellings known as 'F.-buds.' The treatment for the local affection is cauterisation with the hot iron; but constitutional remedies—such as the internal administration of copper and iodine—with good feeding and dry bedding, are also demanded. The poison producing these diseases is capable of being transmitted from the horse to the human subject, from one human being to another, and also to the horse and ass. It may be absorbed both by the cutaneous and mucous tissues, and thus infect the blood. The attention of the profession was first called to this disease in man by Mr. Muscroft in the *Edinburgh Medical and Surgical Journal* (1821).

Fardel-Bound, an old veterinary term for obstruction of the third stomach—the 'manyplies'—of cattle, generally caused by tough or indigestible food, such as leaves, moist clover, or grass, and the like. The results of this affection are inflammation of the stomach, together with paralysis from its distension. The bowels are constipated and the skin is hot, and feverish symptoms also prevail, whilst rumination is necessarily interfered with. The remedies to be adopted for the relief of this complaint consist in free purgation and injections; probably the latter are safest in the generality of cases. The food must be light, and consist chiefly of soft mashes. The stimulants needed in severe cases may consist of ale with ginger.

Fare'ham ('the dwelling at the ferry'), a market-town of Hampshire, England, on F. Creek, at the N.W. angle of Portsmouth Harbour, 5 miles N.N.W. of Spithead by railway, with manufactures of bricks, leather, and pottery. Vessels of good tonnage come close to F., which has an active trade. Pop. (1871) 7023.

Far'el, Guillaume, 'the pioneer of the Reformation in Switzerland and France,' was born at the hamlet of Farels, near Gap, Dauphiny, in 1489. His parents, who were Romanists, destined him for the army; but in 1500 he betook himself to Paris University, where he became a devoted disciple of Lefèvre d'Étaples, and gained a chair in the college of Cardinal de la Moine. Lefèvre's advanced views calling down the wrath of the Sorbonne, he and F. had to quit Paris for Meaux, then a stronghold of Lutheranism, where F. began to denounce the Catholic Church. In 1524 F. sustained at Basel thirteen theses on the chief points of controversy between the Catholics and Reformers, and about this time won the friendship of Haller and Zwingli. Thenceforth he gave himself up to the conversion of Switzerland, making the canton Bern the centre of his missionary labours, preaching with tireless and fervid zeal, and running great dangers from his rash and uncompromising iconoclasm. After the issuing of the Edict of the Reformation by the municipality of Geneva in 1535, F. laboured along with Calvin to organise there the new Protestant Church, a difficult task from the excesses of the *Libertins*, or Reformers who refused to obey any authorities in matters of religion. After allaying (1542) the disorders rife among the Protestants of Neufchâtel, and preaching at Metz, Montigny, and Gorge—where he was nearly killed in a skirmish—F. was sent in 1557 with Beza to seek the intervention of the German Reformed princes in behalf of the Vaudois, and after his return to Switzerland married a young girl, much to Calvin's displeasure. In 1561 he was imprisoned at Gap, but escaped by a basket lowered from the ramparts. Shortly after making a last visit to Calvin, who was then dying, F. ended his days at Neufchâtel, September 13, 1564. F. was not a systematic theologian, nor even a judicious ecclesiastic, but he was an admirable preacher, fluent, impressive, ardent, and as a missionary was the chief agent in the conversion of Switzerland. Among his numerous works, which, however, give no idea of his mastery of language, are *Themata Quædam Latine et Germanice Proposita* (1528), *De Oratione Dominica* (1524), and many epistles and treatises, many of which are inserted in Ruchat's *Hist. de la Réforme en Suisse*. See Kirchhofer's *Leben Wilhelm Farel's* (Zurich, 1831); Schmidt's *Études sur F.* (Strasb. 1834); Goguel's *Vie de F.* (1841); *F. und Viret* (Elberf. 1860); and MM. Haag's *La France Protestante* (Par. 1847-59).

Farewell, Cape, the southern extremity of Greenland, is dangerous to navigators from the masses of ice in its neighbourhood, which are constantly being forced by currents setting in from the N.E. round into Davis' Straits.

Fari'a Y Sousa, Manoel, a Portuguese critic, poet, and historian, was born 18th March 1590. His father's name was Amador Perez de Erro, but when, after a successful university career, he entered upon diplomatic life, he took the name of his mother. From 1631 till within a few years of his death, which took place June 3, 1649, he held the post of secretary to the Spanish embassy at Rome. F. is best known for his poems, consisting chiefly of eclogues, madrigals, and sonnets, written both in Portuguese and in Spanish; his treatises on poetry, which caused Lope de Vega to style him the first critic of the age, and of which his great commentary on the *Lusiad* (Mad. 1639) is the best; and his historical works, treating of Portugal and its dependencies. His *Imperio de China*, edited by Father Semmedo, and translated into French and Italian, is still recognised as one of the best of the elder authorities on the subject.—**Manoel Severim de F.**, a Portuguese historian and antiquary, born at Lisbon 1581, died at Evora, 16th September 1655. He wrote *Noticias de Portugal* (Evor. 1624; 3d ed. Lisb. 1791), and was reckoned one of the best numismatists of his age.

Fari'na, a name frequently applied to the flour or the starch of cereals or of other starchy plants, such as the cassava, arrowroot, &c. It is derived from the Latin *far*, meaning spelt wheat. In commercial circles the term F. is restricted to the starch obtained from potatoes, which is very extensively consumed as an adulterant of the more expensive starches, such as arrowroot, tapioca, &c., and of butter and other articles of food. It is also prepared as an article of food under the name of French sago, and it is largely employed as the basis of starch sugar, which, under the name of saccharine, is much used by brewers. Its chief consumption, however, is as a thickener in calico-printing, for which it is also prepared by torrefaction as dextrin or British gum. Fossil F. is an infusorial earth, the *berg-mehl* of the Swedes and Laplanders.

Farina Trit'ici, the grain of wheat, *Triticum vulgare*, ground and sifted, is used in medicine for the preparation of *Cataplasma fermenti*. When made into a paste with honey, it forms an excellent application for boils.

Fari'ni, Car'lo Lui'gi, an Italian politician and author, was born at Russi in the Romagna, October 22, 1812. He studied medicine at Bologna, and became known as a writer of scientific treatises, but being connected with the Liberal movement of 1841-43, had to quit the Papal territory, and resided successively at Marseille, Paris, Florence, and Turin. On Pius IX. granting an amnesty, F. established himself as a physician at Osimo, but shortly afterwards, entering on a political career, became under-secretary of state, and was sent in 1848 on a confidential mission to the camp of Carlo Alberto. He held aloof from the Roman Republic of 1849, and his services being rejected by the Church party after the French occupied Rome, he betook himself to Piedmont, where his moderate but liberal views secured him the royal favour. He was made minister of public education, knighted, elected to the Piedmontese National Assembly, and in 1859 named dictator of the duchy of Modena. He rendered important services in uniting central Italy to Piedmont, was appointed minister of state and royal secretary, refused in 1862 to join the Ratazzi ministry, became president of the cabinet, retired in 1863, and died at Gênes, August 1, 1866. He wrote *Storia dello Stato Romano dal Anno* 1814 *al* 1850, a valuable historic work, which has gone through several editions; *Storia d'Italia*, a continuation of Botta's history of Italy; and letters to Gladstone, &c. F. was one of the most sagacious of Italian statesmen, and Italy is greatly indebted to him for her present stable government.

Farm (Old. Eng. *feorm* and *feorme*, originally 'food;' next, the 'rent' (paid in kind) of land; finally, the 'rented land' itself), a portion of land or tract of country occupied as one undertaking for the cultivation of crops, or for the rearing and maintaining of cattle, sheep, and other creatures useful to man. Farming, viewed in its widest sense, is the greatest, as it is the primal and fundamental, industry of the human race. On its operations, to a great extent, depend not only the feeding, but the clothing of mankind, and most of the plants which are cultivated, and of the animals said to be domesticated, are so as a result of farming operations. Taking a narrower and technical view of farming, it embraces only those lands on which cereal, pasture, and green crops are cultivated, and sheep and cattle reared. Gardening and the cultivation of many products of human industry are embraced under other heads.

In Great Britain farms are classed under two heads—(1) arable farms, and (2) natural pasture and hill farms. Arable farms again are subdivided into (1) ordinary arable or grain-producing farms, (2) stock farms, and (3) dairy farms. These subdivisions are not sharply distinguished from each other, and they merely indicate the prevailing feature in the agricultural industry of any special locality or F., such features being generally controlled by circumstances of soil, situation, and climate. Thus on a F. in the great wheat-producing districts, a certain proportion of stock is fattened, and dairy produce is prepared, although its staple may be grain. The stock F. is principally devoted to the rearing and fattening of cattle for the fat market, and crops and field operations are all directed with a view to that chief object. In the case of a dairy F. the ultimate object of the farmer is the obtaining of milk for sale or for the manufacture of butter and cheese, and stock is selected and crops grown suitably for such objects. Natural pastures and uncultivated hill land are extensively laid out as sheep farms or sheep walks; and a F. of this description usually embraces a great area.

The size of farms is entirely regulated by convenience; but there is an increasing tendency to form farms of great extent. The scientific development of agricultural operations, and the introduction of expensive, yet economical, labour-saving appliances, render it necessary for a first-class F. to be one of considerable size, that it may yield a sufficient return for the capital sunk in appliances connected with its working. A great revolution in rural affairs has therefore taken place within recent times; the cottier and small farmer have disappeared, and small holdings have been combined to form large farms, which must be worked by persons having command of considerable capital. The modern farmer must also be possessed of a wide range of scientific and practical knowledge, of considerable mechanical skill, and much business aptitude. Concerning the laws which regulate the occupancy of land, see LAND LAWS, LANDLORD AND TENANT, and HYPOTHEC.

Farm Buildings. The various offices and structures required for the working of a farm are collectively known in England as the homestead, and in Scotland they are called the steading. The accommodation necessary varies in size and arrangement, according to the extent of the farm it serves, and the nature of the chief products cultivated. Thus on a dairy farm the cow byre and dairy offices are the chief feature, and on a stock farm prominence must be given to the feeding byres and arrangements for preparing food. As the health of his live-stock is an object of supreme importance to the farmer, F. B. ought to be placed in situations securing, as far as possible, abundant water supply, good drainage, freedom from damp, and a sheltered yet airy situation. The arrangement of F. B. is a matter of much practical importance, and the various parts should be so compacted that operations dependent on each other, or following in consecutive order, should be performed in immediate proximity; and the saving of all unnecessary labour, as well as the prompt and rapid execution of work, ought always to be kept prominently in view. The position of the thrashing mill and barn will generally be found to be the key to the arrangement of the whole range of F. B., as many of the most laborious duties of a farm, such as the feeding and littering of the live-stock are intimately connected with that department. It is usually found that F. B. of moderate extent come together most conveniently in the form of three sides of a square or parallelogram. The space lying between the projecting sides is either roofed over or left as an open court, and used as a yard for young cattle during the winter (if unroofed, with a covered shed attached), and as a repository for the manure from the stables and byres at its side. The ordinary F. B. comprise a thrashing-mill, granary and straw-barn, stables, stock and dairy byres, court and covered sheds for young cattle, calves' house, piggery, poultry house, sheds for storing turnips, boiler and food-preparing house, implement house, and cart-shed. The dairy is usually attached to the farmhouse, at once as a matter of convenience, and because that department must, as far as possible, be removed from all noxious smells. The farmer's house and labourers' cottages also form an essential part of F. B., but the arrangement and size of these are regulated by the principles of ordinary domestic architecture.

Farm Servants. The wages of F. S. is in Scotland a privileged debt. See WAGES.

Far'mer, Richard, D.D., an English scholar and archæologist, was born at Leicester, August 28, 1735. Educated at Emmanuel College, Cambridge, where he graduated in 1760, he was first appointed curate of Swavesey, near Cambridge, became Master of Emmanuel in 1775, and librarian to the university, and was successively canon of Lichfield, Canterbury, and St. Paul's. He died 8th September 1797. The following year his library, especially rich in works of Old English literature, was sold for £2210. F. collected copious materials for the history of Leicester, which he put into the hands of his friend Nichols. His sole work is his *Essay on the Learning of Shakespeare* (1776), reprinted by Steevens (1793), by Reed (1803), and by Harris (1812). In this he showed that Shakespeare's knowledge of the ancients was obtained from translations.

Farmers-General (Fr. *fermiers-généraux*) were persons who, under the *ancien régime* in France, obtained, for a fixed money payment, the right to collect one or more of the public taxes. This was the most expensive and least productive system of collection. Such rights, originally given to court favourites, were first exposed to public auction by Sully. After Colbert had detected the frauds of the individual collectors, a company or *ferme-générale* was formed in 1728, which, interrupted for a short time under the administration of Silhouette in 1759, continued in business till Necker's time, when it consisted of forty-four persons paying a rent of 186 millions of livres, and making an estimated profit of only two millions. The multiform and arbitrary nature of French taxation, and the quasi-official and yet practically irresponsible position of the F.-G. and their agents, led to great oppression. The French 'imposts' consisted in the first place in the '*taille roturière*,' at first a purely feudal contribution, but which the king, pressed by the expense of a standing army, gradually extended to the domains of his nobles. From 1,500,000 livres, in 1445, it rose under Henri IV. to fourteen millions, under Louis XIV. to thirty-five millions, under Louis XVI. to ninety-one millions. The *taillon* and the *crue* were additions to the *taille*. In 1710 Louis XIV. imposed a *dixième* on the revenues of the lands of nobles and churchmen, as well as of *roturiers*. Another *vingtième* was added for the war of American independence. In 1695 appeared the *capitation*, which affected the *roturier* class, the nobles, and public officers unequally, but from which the clergy were exempt. The *dîme*, estimated by Necker at 133 millions, went to the Church, but relieved the state of obligations towards the Church. Every five years the Church gave the king the *don gratuit*, about 3,600,000 livres. The *corvée* was a tax of eight days' labour, with cart and horse, on the public roads; its value was twenty millions. *Maîtrise* and *jurande* were taxes upon trade corporations and professions, which in 1788 produced 4,500,000 livres; and *vingtième d'industrie et de commerce* was a special tax on manufactured products and merchandise. The latter, along with all products whatever, were subject to the indirect tax or *aides*, which included *droits de sortie* or *traite foraine*; the tax on the extraction and sale of salt, which from 1345 was called *gabelle*; and certain dues on the sale of food, and the entry of wine into towns. As Charles VII. had dispensed with the consent of the States-General in imposing the *taille*, so François I. dispensed with their consent to the *aides* and *gabelle*. Certain of the *aides*, amounting in value to fifty-nine millions, were collected by the *régie générale des aides*, and were called *droits réunis*. The *ferme-générale* extended to the *gabelle*, which alone amounted to seventy-four millions, of which fifty-four reached the treasury; the monopoly introduced by Colbert for tobacco; the *droit d'entrée* on imported goods, originally one-thirtieth, imposed in 1581; the customs proper, internal and external. There was a third system of succession duties and feudal exactions, which were collected by the *régie des domaines*. The eighty *pays d'élection* formed twenty-four *généralités* for the purposes of collection, the gross amount being divided among the *généralités* by a *brevet-général*, but the further division among towns and parishes was at the pleasure of the *intendant*, and among different lands and persons by no fixed system of valuation. The *pays d'états* (such as Languedoc, Provence, Burgundy, Artois) had a much juster system, worked by *livres cadastrals*, or valued rent, and called *affouagement* (or 'hearth-tax'). In the *pays d'élection*, also, Necker's system of collection was to give three or five or six '*deniers pour livre*' to the various grades of officers, while the *pays d'état* put the collections up to auction in each province. The former were also called *pays de grande gabelle*, from the rate of salt-tax they paid; the latter, *petite gabelle*, or *franches* or *redimés*. The authorities on this important subject are Necker's *Administration des Finances*, Clamagéran's *Histoire de l'Impôt*, Laferrière's *Histoire du Droit Français*.

Farne or **Fern Isles**, or the **Stapes**, a group of small islands from 2 to 5 miles off the coast of Northumberland, and S.E. of Lindisfarne. Several are merely rocks hidden at high water. On one is a priory named after St. Cuthbert (q. v.), who spent the last two years of his life here. They render navigation very dangerous. There are two beacons 30 feet high on two of the islets. Here Grace Darling (q. v.) effected the heroic rescue of nine people from the wreck of the *Forfarshire* in 1838.

Farne'se, the name of a noble Roman family, dating from the 13th c., but first made important by **Alessandro F.**, who in 1534 became Pope Paul III.—His son, **Pietro Luigi**, who figures in the Life of Benvenuto Cellini, was about the worst man of his time. He got from his father the duchy of Castro as a fief of the Holy See, and Novara, an imperial fief, and the dukedom of Parma and Piacenza, subject to a payment of 8000 ducats to the pope. This division of papal property among popes' children was often practised. The new *gonfaloniere*, after a life of vice and tyranny, was murdered 10th September 1547 by Gonzaga, the governor of Milan, and others.—His son, **Ottavio** (born in 1520), recovered from Philip II. possession of Piacenza, which had been occupied by Milanese troops. His friendship for Henri II. of France was suspected by the emperor and the pope, and he owed much of his security to his wife Margaret, governor of the Low Countries, the natural daughter of Charles V. He died in 1587.—**Alessandro**, son of Ottavio, known as *the* Duke of Parma, became one of the great captains of the age. He was with Don John of Austria at Lepanto (1571), and in 1578 defeated the Flemish 'Beggars' at Gembloux. Wonderful stories are told of his *sang-froid*, or rather love of danger, at the sieges in the Low Countries—Oudenarde, Antwerp, &c. As governor of the Spanish Netherlands he fought long and bitterly with the Prince of Orange. Philip II. gave him the command of the force gathered at Dunkirk for the invasion of England in 1588, and in 1590 sent him to the relief of Paris, besieged by Henri of Navarre. Ill supported by the Catholic League, he was forced to yield to the superior force of the Huguenot prince, and died 3d December 1592, at Arras, of a wound received before Rouen.—His son, **Ranuzio I.** (born 1569, died 1622), lived on the worst terms with the other Italian princes, especially Gonzaga of Mantua. He built the beautiful theatre of Parma.—His son, **Odoardo** (born 28th April 1612, died 12th September 1646), having pledged the duchy of Castro in the *Mont de Piété*, formed an alliance with France in 1633, which protected him against Pope Urban VIII., wishing to forfeit Castro for the Barberini, his relatives. Muratori describes Odoardo as a brilliant and satirical talker, and of a splendid fashion of living.—**Ranuzio II.**, son of Odoardo, was born in 1630, and succeeded his father in 1646. He was ruled by a Provençal tutor and a Pavian tailor of a musical turn. In consequence, he lost the duchy of Castro to Innocent X. He died 11th December 1694, and was succeeded by his son **Francesco**, who was born 19th May 1678. During the reign of the latter occurred the Treaty of the Hague, by which it was agreed that Parma and Piacenza should become male fiefs of the empire; and that, when the succession opened, they should go to the eldest son of Elizabeth F., Queen of Spain, daughter of Odoardo, and his male issue, whom failing, to her other sons and their male issue. The undoubted legal claim of Innocent XIII. to the reversion of the duchies was coolly set aside. Francesco died 26th February 1727, and was succeeded by his brother **Antonio**. In him the hereditary corpulence of the family reached its utmost extent. He died 20th January 1731, and having no children, left the duchies by will to Don Carlos, the son of his aunt, Elizabeth of Spain. The name has been given to two palaces in Rome—one built by Pope Paul III., and adorned with some fine works of art; the other, known as the *Farnesina*, containing frescoes by Raphael—to a group of statuary representing 'Dirce Bound to the Horns of a Bull,' and to a Hercules copied by Glykon from an original by Lysippus.

Farn'ham ('the dwelling among the ferns'), a town in Surrey, England, on the Wey, 36 miles S.W. of London, with an interesting old castle, which has more than once been rebuilt or enlarged, and is a possession of the bishops of Winchester. The chief trade is in hops. William Cobbett was a native of F. Pop. (1871) 4461. At a distance of 6 miles lies the camp of Aldershot.

Farn'worth, a town of Lancashire, 12 miles S.E. of Liverpool, and a station on the Manchester and Bolton Railway. It has a chapel of the 15th c., a free grammar-school, and manufactures of watches, canvas, and iron tools. Pop. (1871) 9226.

Fa'ro (Gr. *pharos*, 'a lighthouse'), the chief town of the province of Algarve in the S. of Portugal, at the mouth of the Fermoso, 122 miles S.S.E. of Lisbon. It is a bishop's see, is well built, walled, and has a college, cathedral, and several hospitals. The harbour is small but safe, sheltered by islands, and defended by a fort. F. has a large fishery. The trade in fresh and dried fruit, wine, anchovies, sumach, and cork is carried on chiefly with England. Pop. 7900.

Faröe Isles (Dan. *Faareyjar*, 'sheep islands'), a group of twenty-two basaltic islands in the N. Atlantic, 185 miles N.W. of the Shetlands, in lat. 61° 20′–62° 20′ N., and long. 6°–8° W. Area, 504 sq. miles; pop. 9992. They are conical mountainous masses, some 2000 feet high, rising more or less abruptly from the sea, and are separated from each other by strong rapid currents. The precipitous shores, rendered dangerous by whirlpools, are broken by many deep inlets, which form secure havens. Stromö, the chief of the group, contains the capital,

Thorshavn (pop. 900), and is 8 miles broad and 27 long. Eight of the group are uninhabited islets. The shallow soil of all the islands affords rich pasture for the sheep and cattle, but there are no trees larger than a juniper or stunted willow. Although often visited by tempests, the climate of the F. I. is comparatively mild, allowing the cultivation of barley, rape, and potatoes. The snow only lies on the ground for about eight days in winter. There are 583 species of plants, of which 270 are flower-bearing. A seam of good Miocene coal was recently discovered on Syderö. The seas abound with fish, and the rocky coasts are haunted by myriads of seafowl, the capture of which is one of the perilous industries of the islanders. Among the exports, which are chiefly to Denmark, are salted mutton, skins, tallow, eider-down, goose-quills, and feathers. The F. I. were discovered and peopled by Norwegians in the 9th c., but have been Danish since 1380. A dialect of Old Norse is still spoken, but Danish is used in the churches, schools, courts, &c. The islands send a representative to the Danish *Rigsdag.* See R. Chambers's *Tracings of Iceland and the F. I.*

Far'quhar, George, son of a poor clergyman, was born at Londonderry in 1678. He studied at Trinity College, Dublin; at eighteen joined the stage, and shortly afterwards the Earl of Orrery's regiment in Ireland. Like Wycherley and Vanbrugh, he became a captain. His first comedy, *Love and a Bottle,* was brought out successfully at London in 1698. Duped into marrying a pretended heiress, he fell into poverty, and died in April 1707, 'leaving nothing,' he said, 'but two helpless girls.' His other plays are *The Constant Couple, Sir Harry Wildair, The Inconstant* (modelled on Fletcher's *Wild Goose Chase*), *The Stage-Coach, The Twin Rivals* (1705), *The Recruiting Officer* (1706), and his best piece *The Beaux Stratagem* (1707). F.'s plays are not imaginative and romantic. They are sprightly, natural transcripts of the life of his times. He will not rank with even the secondary Elizabethans, but his place is high among the Restoration dramatists. Inferior to Congreve in dazzling wit, he excels him in humour and invention. His plays are less gross, his characters more genial and lovable, than Wycherley's, Congreve's, or Vanbrugh's. The best edition of F. is Leigh Hunt's in Routledge's *Old Dramatists* (1875). See Hazlitt's *Comic Writers* and Ward's *English Dramatic Literature,* vol. ii.

Farr, William, M.D., F.R.S., D.C.L., was born at Kenley, Shropshire, in 1807, studied at the universities of Paris and London, practised medicine at London, and edited the *Medical Annual* and *British Annals of Medicine.* He was made compiler of abstracts in the Registrar-General's office in 1838, is now head of the statistical department in that office, and has been sent by Government to various international statistical congresses. He was made corresponding member of the French Institute in 1872. F. has written a number of articles for medical journals, and many statistical papers and reports.

Farr'agut, David Glasgow, a gallant and highly popular admiral of the American navy, was born near Knoxville, Tennessee, July 5, 1801. He entered the navy at the age of eleven, was lieutenant at twenty-one, and in 1833 commanded the *Natchez* on the Brazil station. In 1851 he was made assistant-inspector of ordnance, and in 1854 was appointed to construct a navy-yard in California. In January 1862 he commanded a naval expedition to the Gulf of Mexico, and on the 28th of April received the surrender of New Orleans. Ascending the Mississippi, he took Natchez, but failed before Vicksburg. Withdrawing to Pensacola, he was made Vice-Admiral of the Navy, and in March 1863 he sailed up the Mississippi, ran the Confederate batteries of Fort Hudson, and aided General Grant in his attack upon Vicksburg, which surrendered July 4, 1863. In August 1864, after a fierce conflict between his fleet and the Confederate forts and vessels of Mobile, he captured the forts and city. F. was raised to the rank of admiral in 1866. He died August 14, 1870.

Farr'ar, The Rev. Frederic William, M.D., F.R.S., son of a clergyman, was born at Bombay in 1831, and studied at Trinity College, Cambridge, of which he was made a Fellow in 1856. He was appointed assistant-master at Harrow in 1855, master of Marlborough School in 1869, and chaplain in ordinary to the Queen in 1873. F. has been a prolific author. Among his works are *Eric, or Little by Little,* and *Julian Home,* successful tales; *The Fall of Man* (1865); and *The Life of Christ* (1874). He edited *Essays on a Liberal Education* (1868).

Farr'ier (Old Fr. *ferrier,* from Lat. *ferrum,* 'iron'), a name given to the early representatives of the veterinary surgeon, who to their ordinary occupations as blacksmiths and horse-shoers added that of prescribing for the ailments of domestic animals. In many country districts the F. is still extant. It is needless to remark that his ideas on veterinary matters are marked by much prejudice and ignorance, not, however, unmingled with the rough and ready knowledge obtained by observation.

Farriers, Army, the name given to non-commissioned officers in cavalry regiments who assist the veterinary regimental surgeons, and act as horse-shoers. They rank with and receive the pay of sergeants, and have certain allowances arising out of their occupation.

Fars or **Fars'istan** ('Fars' is the native form of the classic *Pers*-ia), a province in the S. of Persia, bounded W. by Khuzistan, N. by Irak, E. by Kirman and Suristan, and S. by the Persian Gulf. Area, 55,000 sq. miles; pop. about 1,700,000. F. comprises the Dashtistan, a sandy, thinly-peopled plain fringing the Persian Gulf, and an upland district, formed by offshoots from the Yagros range, which rise in steep terraces, and are severed by long fertile plains abounding in rich pasture. Around Shiraz there are delightful woody valleys almost destitute of inhabitants, but the E. consists of arid sandy tracts. The chief rivers are the Band Amir or Araxes, the Nabon, and the upper waters of the Tab. F. contains the salt lakes of Bakhtigan and Dariacht. The chief products are fruit, opium, tobacco, sulphur, and lead; cutlery, arms, glasswork, cotton cloths, and wine are manufactured. The principal towns are Jahrum, Darabgird, Fasa, Firozabad, Kazinrum, and Shiraz. F. is famous for its antiquities, of which the most famous are the ruins of Persepolis, Pasargadæ, and Shapoor.

Farsan' Archipelago, a group of islands in the S.E. of the Red Sea. Only two are of any extent—F. Kebeer, 31 miles long, and F. Seggeer, 18 miles.

Far'thing (Old Eng. *feorthung* and *feorthling,* 'the fourth part of anything'), now denotes a copper coin, the fourth part of a penny. The term is sometimes applied to articles or circumstances of contemptible value, *e.g.,* a farthing rushlight.

Far'thingale (in 16th c. *verdingale;* from Fr. *verdugalle,* or *vertugade,* a corruption of *vertu-garde,* 'guard of modesty'), a large hooped petticoat worn in the 16th c. See CRINOLINE.

Fa'sa, a town in the province of Fars, Persia, 77 miles E.S.E. of Shiraz. It has manufactures of silk, wool, and cotton. The pop. has been estimated at 18,000. The *district* of F. is 45 miles long by 9 to 15 broad, and is generally known as the *Garm Sar,* or 'warm region.' It produces rice, Indian-corn, millet, cotton, and fine tobacco, and contains thirty-three villages.

Fasa'no, a town of S. Italy, in the province of Bari, on the highroad from Bari to Brindisi, near the coast, and 33 miles S.E. of Bari. It is famous for its olive plantations. Pop. 11,450. On the coast, near F., is the ruined *Egnazia.*

Fas'ces (from the same root as the English 'bind') were a bundle of birch (sometimes elm) rods, with an axe stuck in the midst, the iron of which projected from them. They were carried by officers called lictors before the superior magistrates of regal, republican, and imperial Rome, as a sign of their power of scourging and of capital punishment. When an inferior met a superior magistrate, he ordered his lictors to lower their F., as a mark of respect; and, in the same manner, the consuls at the public assemblies acknowledged the sovereignty of the people.

Fas'cia. These are strong membranes formed of connective tissue which cover the muscles, send septæ or partitions in between them so as to give them support, and in many cases give points of origin to muscular fibres. They are smooth, glistening, and opalescent in appearance to the naked eye. When a portion is teased out and examined under the microscope, they are found to be composed of delicate fibres of connective or white fibrous tissue firmly matted together.

Fascicula'ria, a well-known genus of *Polyzoa* (q. v.) (formerly known as *Meandropora*), and found in a fossil state in rocks of Tertiary age. This genus (of which *F. cerebriformis* of the Miocene rocks is a familiar species) presents a singular structure from the cœnœcium or connecting medium of the

Polyzoon being more or less spherical in form, and composed of vertical plates arranged not unlike the convolutions of the human brain.

Fascina'tion by Serpents. See SERPENTS, FASCINATION BY.

Fascines' (Lat. *fascis*, 'a bundle of twigs'), bundles of brushwood, generally about 9 inches in diameter, and from 6 to 12 feet long, used in war to fill up a ditch, &c. In civil engineering F. are used to protect the banks of rivers, &c.

Fasci'ola, the name of the genus of *Trematoda* (*Scolecida*) to which the Flukes (q. v.) belong. *F. hepaticum* is the scientific name for the common liver fluke, formerly known as *Distoma hepaticum*.

Fasciola'ria, a genus of Gasteropodous mollusca represented by the tulip whelk (*F. tulipa*) and allied species. These shells belong to the family of the *Muricidæ* or Whelks (q. v.).

Fash'ion (Fr. *façon*, 'a mode,' from the Lat. *facio*, 'I make'), literally a particular manner of making anything, is a term applied to a prevalent mode of dressing, speaking, and acting, and even to literary styles and to opinions current in society. F. may thus be an index of deep changes, a result of peculiar social conditions, or the passing reflection of the idlest whim. Thus the broad contrast between the flowing richly-coloured robes of the East and the dress of Europeans is due to differences of climate and manners of life, while the constant variations of dress in Europe arise mainly from caprice. F. in dress seems to have fluctuated far less in ancient than in modern times. In classic Greece there was comparatively slight variety in costume, and in the arrangement of the filleted or unfettered hair. Plautus, however, tells us that the Roman matrons often altered the materials and shape of their garments. In England there have been several broadly marked fashions of dress. The early English settlers in Britain wore ringed armour and square helmets in war, woollen tunics, short cloaks, and drawers in peace. Their hair was long, and they practised tattooing, though it was forbidden by an edict in 785 until the Norman conquest. The Normans introduced brighter and more costly dresses. Short mantles and long tunics, of brilliant silks and velvets, lined with furs, flowered with gold, and often stiff with jewels, were worn by the nobles, and peaked-toed shoes (*ocreæ rostratæ*) were common. The most minute and faithful picture of English mediæval fashions is to be found in Chaucer's Prologue to the *Canterbury Tales*. In the 16th c. French fashions spread into England, Germany, and Italy. In England during Elizabeth's reign the costume of the wealthy was remarkable for splendid colour and lavish and often fantastic ornament. Men wore slashed doublets of silk, velvet, or damask, jewelled and embroidered with gold and silver, trunk-hose of grotesque width, and cloaks, sometimes short, sometimes trailing on the ground, of red, white, violet, black, green, &c. The female apparel was specially marked by the high linen ruff, and huge Farthingale (q. v.). The reign of Charles I. is the age when English costume was most becoming and picturesque. Van Dyck's portraits have made us familiar with the cavalier dress—the crimson doublet or gold-worked buff coat, the broad plumed Flemish hat, the rich lace collar, the long fringed breeches, the cloak, baldric, and Spanish rapier. The female dress became very graceful, the ruff and farthingale being disused. In Charles II.'s time the King Charles costume was spoiled by extravagant additions, such as petticoat breeches and perukes. The dress of the ladies lost its tasteful simplicity, as is seen by comparing Lely's with Van Dyck's paintings. The 18th c. in England was the age of the Louis XIV. dress, the age of powdered wigs, blue or scarlet coats, embroidered waistcoats, knee-buckles, and high-heeled shoes. In this century it was at one time the F. to carry the hat under the arm instead of on the head, to place black patches on the face, and to stiffen the coat-skirts with wire. Fans, canes, and snuff-boxes were incessantly manipulated, a F. which evoked the raillery of Addison and Pope. After the French Revolution more sober costumes were adopted. F. in dress has at times gone to such excess as to call forth royal interference. Thus in England about the middle of the 16th c. there was such a mania for square-toed shoes, that an edict was passed forbidding any one to wear shoes above six inches broad at the toes. Queen Elizabeth, we are told, placed 'certain grave citizens' at the London gates to cut all ruffs above a 'nayle of a yeard' deep, and to break all rapiers above a yard long. Charles V. of France forbade the wearing of short and tight breeches, which had become a public scandal. There are fashions in literature as well as in dress and social etiquette. After the Renaissance it was the F. to write Ciceronian prose; Euphuism (q. v.) was a literary F. for a time prevalent in England; during one age the sonnet, during another the epic, has been the favourite form of poetry, each successful author inducing others to imitate his theme and manner by the example of his success and influence of his authority. Anagrams, *bouts-rimés*, and similar follies arose from a literary F. now happily decayed. See Planché's *British Costume*, La Bruyère (*Sur les Mœurs*), and Hazlitt's essay on F.

Fash'oda (formerly *Denab*), the most southerly Egyptian town and fort on the Upper Nile, lies in the Shilluk country, 380 miles S. of Khartum, in lat. 10° N. It is the seat of a mudir, and has a garrison of some 300 men. On account of the poll-tax all boats are compelled to stop at F. for several days. The town has arisen since 1869.

Fastern's, Fasten, or **Fasting Even**, an old Scotch and English name for Shrove Tuesday (q. v.).

Fasti (Lat. *fas*, 'divine law,' or *fari*, 'to speak;' hence *dies fasti* are *lawful days, i.e.*, on which business might lawfully be transacted before the prætor, or days on which judgment could be pronounced—court days) were arranged by the Romans in two divisions:—1. *Fasti sacri* or *kalendares*. These were tables closely resembling a modern almanac, and contained the lore with respect to the days of the year, &c., which for nearly four centuries and a half after the foundation of Rome was retained by the priests, but was then disclosed by Cn. Flavius, who had obtained access to the pontifical books. They contained the months and days of the year, with the nones, ides, market-days, lawful days, unlawful days, the different festivals, &c.; astronomical observations on the rising and setting of the fixed stars, and the commencement of the seasons; and notices of great victories, dedications of temples, &c. Specimens of these F. on stone and marble have been discovered from time to time, the most remarkable being that known as the *Kalendarium Prænestinum*, laid bare in 1770. The F. is the title of a well-known poem of Ovid, which treats of the festivals, &c., according to the order of the Julian Calendar. 2. *Fasti annales* or *historici*. From the resemblance in arrangement of the early historical records to the *F. Kalendares*, the name F. was extended to the registers of consuls, dictators, censors, &c., and generally to the chronicles of the events of each year. The *F. Capitolini*, excavated from the Forum in 1547, arranged by Cardinal Alessandro Farnese, and deposited in the Capitol, are regarded as a most important specimen of this class.

Fast'ing ('fast,' Old. Eng. *faest*, means lit. a 'keeping' away from food, and is the same word as the adj. fast = 'firm,' as in hold-*fast*, stead-*fast*) is a practice based upon the instincts of human nature, and common to all religions. As the effect of deep sorrow is to take away all desire for food, F. has always been regarded as a natural expression of sorrow for sin; and as a formal religious practice the object of it would be to afflict and humble the soul by withholding from the body its ordinary nourishment. 'Afflicting the soul' is the phrase used for it in the Bible (Lev. xvi. 29, 31), evidently as a familiar shortened expression for the fuller phrase of Ps. xxxv. 13, lxix. 10. Having, like asceticism generally, its original home in Asia, it was much practised by the ancient Hindus, Chinese, and Persians, and to a less extent by the Jews; it entered into the religious rites of the Egyptians, Greeks, and Romans, and descended to the Christian Church.

I. *Among the Jews*.—The only fast enjoined upon the Jews as a nation by the law of Moses was on the great day of atonement. Whosoever failed to keep that day with F. was to be cut off from among his people (Lev. xxiii. 29). But there are numerous instances recorded of individuals voluntarily imposing fasts upon themselves in seasons of penitential sorrow, as David (2 Sam. xii. 16), and Ahab (1 Kings xxi. 27); and the vow of Num. xxx. probably referred chiefly to F. A number of other individual cases recorded, as Hannah (1 Sam. i. 7), Jonathan (1 Sam. xx. 34), David (2 Sam. i. 12, iii. 35), had no special connection with religion, but were prompted by sheer grief. Even national fasts were imposed on special occasions, as when the Israelites were defeated by the rebel Benjamites (Judges xx.

26), at Mizpah on the restoration of the ark (1 Sam. vii. 6), under Ahab (1 Kings xxi. 12), and under Jehoshaphat (2 Chron. xx. 3). After the Temple was destroyed, and the people carried into captivity and prevented from worshipping God by means of sacrifices, they attempted to make up for this by an increased observance of fasts, as expressed in a prayer in the Talmud—'Lord of the universe! thou knowest that when the Temple existed, the man that sinned brought a sacrifice, and though only the fat and blood were offered, yet he was forgiven. Now that I fast, and my own fat and blood are consumed, let it please thee to accept this sacrifice . . . as if offered upon thine altar, and be merciful unto me.' The following fasts took their rise during the post-exilian period, and are observed by the Jews to the present day for the reasons assigned. 1. Annual national fasts: 1st, the fast held on the 17th of Tamuz, the fourth month, because on this day (1) the Golden Calf was made, (2) Moses broke the Tables of the Law (Exod. xxiv., *cf.* xxxii.), (3) the daily sacrifices ceased for want of cattle when the city was besieged, and (4) Jerusalem was stormed by Nebuchadnezzar (Zech. viii. 19; Jer. lii. 6). 2d, The fast held on the 9th of Ab, the fifth month, because on this day (1) God decreed that those who left Egypt should not enter Canaan (Num. xiv. 27–35), (2) the first Temple was destroyed by Nebuchadnezzar, and the second by Titus, (3) the city of Bethar was taken by Adrian, and 580,000 Jews massacred, and (4) the site of Jerusalem was ploughed up, as predicted by Micah (Jer. xxvi. 18; Zech. vii. 3, 5, viii. 19). 3d, The fast held on the 3d of Tishri, the seventh month, because on that day Gedaliah and other Jews were murdered at Mizpah (2 Kings xxv. 25; Jer. xli. 1–7; Zech. vii. 5, viii. 19). 4th, The fast held on the 10th of Tebeth, the tenth month, because on that day Nebuchadnezzar began the siege of Jerusalem (2 Kings xxv. 1; Zech. viii. 19). 5th, The fast of Esther, held on the 13th of Adar, the twelfth month (Esther iv. 16, 17, ix. 31). 6th, The first-born sons' fast, held on the day before the Passover (Exod. xii.). 2. Weekly fasts were kept every Monday and Thursday between the Feast of the Passover and that of Tabernacles, and between that which followed (Lev. xxiii. 36; Num. xxix. 35–37) and the Feast of the Dedication, because Moses went up to Mount Sinai to receive the second Tables of the Law on a Thursday and came down on a Monday, *cf.* Luke xviii. 12.

II. *In the Christian Church.*—Although our Lord condemned the Jewish manner of keeping their fasts (Matt. vi. 16), and did not impose F. regularly on his disciples (Matt. ix. 14), he yet speaks of it along with prayer as a source of spiritual strength (Matt. xvii. 21), indicates that it would be beneficial to his disciples after his removal from them (Matt. ix. 15), and even practised it himself on a memorable occasion (Matt. iv.). It was practised and recommended by the apostles (Acts xiii. 3, xiv. 23; 1 Cor. vii. 5). From a very early time F. was a part of the discipline of the catechumens, preparing them for baptism, and it soon came to be regarded as also necessary before partaking of the Eucharist. This could not be, so long as the latter was connected with the Agapæ (q. v.), but in the 4th c. Basil, Chrysostom, &c., insisted on the guilt of giving the Holy Communion to persons not F. The bi-weekly Jewish fasts described above were soon received into the Church, Monday and Thursday, however, being changed to Wednesday and Friday in commemoration of the betrayal and sufferings of Christ. These fasts, which were observed every week except between Easter and Pentecost, did not last all day, but only till three o'clock, and hence were called *stations*, as if watches of the soldiers of Christ, and *half-fasts*. By the 3d c. fasts came to be much practised as a safeguard against demons. But while the number of them increased, laxity in the observance of them also increased; for whereas at first F. meant entire abstinence from food, by the 4th c. many thought it sufficient to abstain from flesh and wine, which afterwards came to be the general understanding in the Western Church. The first four of the Jewish post-exilian fasts enumerated above were also introduced into the Church, according to tradition by Callistus, Bishop of Rome, about 223. To un-Judaise them they were connected with the four seasons (Lat. *jejunia quatuor temporum*, corrupted into Ember Fasts), being fixed by the Council of Mainz in the time of Karl the Great to the first week in March, the second week in June, the third week in September, and the week immediately preceding Christmas Day. More sacred than all the rest was the fast preceding Easter (see LENT), although up to the 4th c. it was left optional, and the exact length of it was not finally fixed till the 6th c., or, according to some, the 8th c. About the middle of the 5th c. a new fast was instituted in France and soon adopted elsewhere, under the name of the Litany or Rogation Days (q. v.), being the three days before Ascension Day. Besides these, and the Vigils (q. v.) or eves of holy-days, there were many other fasts having merely a local or partial observance. From the 6th c. F. began to be imposed as a mode of penance. In the *Penitentiary* of Theodore, Archbishop of Canterbury (668), three fasts of forty days each—before Easter, before the Nativity, and after Pentecost—are appointed to be held every year as special seasons of confession and penance. The fasts appointed to be observed by the Book of Common Prayer of the Anglican Church are Lent, the Ember days, the Rogation days, all Fridays except Christmas Day, and the vigils before certain festivals. See Blunt's *Dictionary of Doctrinal and Historical Theology* (1872); Smith's *Dictionary of Christian Antiquities* (1875); Bingham's *Ecclesiastical Antiquities.*

Fat is a tissue found in many parts of the body, and is composed of a meshwork of fine connective tissue, in which lie embedded cells called *F. cells.* These are round or oval if lying apart, but if they happen to be packed closely together, they may acquire an angular form. Their average size is from $\frac{1}{300}$ inch to $\frac{1}{800}$ inch in diameter. Each consists of a delicate transparent envelope of an albuminous substance, surrounding a single drop of fluid fatty matter. Young F. cells have a nucleus, but this becomes obscured, and may entirely disappear in old F. cells. Fatty tissue is sometimes termed adipose tissue. It is copiously supplied with blood-vessels.

Chemical Composition.—The F. of the human body is a mixture of margarin and olein, which are in turn formed of a base, glycerine, combined with the respective fatty acids, margaric and stearic acids. The F. of oxen and sheep contains, in addition, another substance called stearin. During life it is in the liquid state, but it solidifies after death.

Uses of Fat.—(1) It serves as a soft, elastic, and light packing for the various vacuities which are in the body. (2) It facilitates motion by diffusing pressure, and it also protects delicate organs from pressure. (3) It gives a smoothness to the contour of the body, specially observable in the graceful lines of the human female. (4) Being a bad conductor of heat, it prevents heat from escaping from the body, and thus assists in maintaining the equable temperature of the body. (5) Consisting largely of carbon and hydrogen, by its combustion in the lungs or in the tissues, it is a great source of animal heat, being converted, by union of its elements with oxygen, into carbonic acid and water. (6) It assists largely in the general nutrition of the body, almost every tissue containing more or less of this substance.

Source of Fat.—F. is derived in the body from three sources—(1) from F. introduced as such in the food; (2) from hydrocarbons, such as starch and sugar, which are converted into F.; and (3) from a special kind of retrograde metamorphosis, or splitting up of the albuminous tissues.

Fa'talism (from *fatum*, what is spoken and therefore irrevocable) is, according to Leibnitz, of three kinds. There is the F. of Mahomet, which supposes that if the effect were predetermined it happened without the cause—*Kismet*, 'it is fated;' 'ye cannot will, unless the Lord willeth.' Next comes the F. of the Stoics, which taught men to be quiescent, for they were powerless to resist the course of things. There is a third F. held by Christians, which admits a certain destiny of things regulated by the providence of God. 1. Pure F., based on the Greek idea *eimarmenē*, 'what is allotted,' or *moira*, 'the awarded lot' (which is perhaps seen in the Homeric *aisa, aei ousa*), or on the Chaldæan idea of astrological fate, undoubtedly means that our actions do not depend on our desires or volitions, and that a higher power bends us to its will, against which it is vain to struggle (*ineluctabile fatum*). The reasoning of the Turk under impending calamity is (or was)—'If this is fated to happen, I cannot prevent it; if not to happen, why should I exert myself.' 2. The description of Leibnitz is unfair to the Stoics. Chrysippus undoubtedly held that the human will is always determined by motives, but he did not even maintain the modified form of F. according to which our character is made *for* us, and not *by* us, so that we should in vain attempt to alter it, and are therefore not responsible for our actions. There is in this, of course, a portion of truth, viz., the law of heredity, which has frequently given a powerful interest to psychological romance, and which is occasionally illustrated in actual life. But the position of the Stoics was practically the reverse of this. They laid stress on a man's power to transform and discipline his own mind, controlling or suppressing some emotions, generating others, forming new intellectual associations. They recognised the unchangeable laws of life, and endeavoured to bring the character into harmony with the Kosmos. It was the man of ill-regulated life who came into conflict with the overruling force—*Ducunt volentem fata, nolentem trahunt.* 3. It is an interesting question whether Christians are fatalists to any extent. The verdict of psychology is simple enough; the normal healthy human character is amenable to moral discipline, and we can improve it if we desire. But apparently the volitions tending to improve character are theoretically as capable of prediction as others. This view is entirely consistent with the Christian doctrine of the foreknowledge of God, and with the predestination of the body of Christ. Nevertheless the Church has frequently condemned views of individual predestination. Many theologians contend that while free-will was lost by the fall, the bondage of the will to sin does not preclude absolute individual responsibility; although it is also maintained that nothing can be done without grace. But whatever may be said of Christian theology, it cannot be doubted that the preaching of the Christian religion has been one of the greatest anti-fatalistic influences in the world.

Fata Morga'na, the name of a sorceress in the Romance poetry of Italy, who showed her magic power by raising up visionary spectacles in the air; hence the name given in Italy to a mirage seen in the Strait of Messina—images of men, ships, houses, &c., showing themselves both in the air and the water.

Fates. See PARCÆ.

Fa'ther. See PARENT AND CHILD, FAMILY, and PATRIA POTESTAS.

Father Lasher (*Cottus bubalis*), a species of Teleostean fishes, belonging to the Gurnard family (*Triglidæ*), and to the sub-family *Cottinæ* or Bullheads (q. v.). In this genus the head is very broad and flat. No scales exist. The dorsal fins are of moderate size, and no palatine teeth are developed. The F. L. has its head armed with long sharp spines. It is common on our coasts, and is frequently found amongst rocks and tangle at low water. Its average length is 10 inches; its upper parts are brown coloured, and its under parts white. Both are marbled with darker colours, and the fins especially are so marked. The F. L. is also known by the names 'long-spined cottus' and 'lucky proach.'

Fathers, Christian, or **Fathers of the Church,** is a title given to the ancient Christian writers who belonged to the communion of the Church. The name of *Apostolic Fathers* (q. v.) is given to those of the 1st c. who, according to tradition, were disciples of the apostles. Various limits of time down to which the name ought to be applied have been adopted—any time from the 3d c. to the 7th c. A common division is to make the Patristic period end with the 6th c., and the Hierarchical begin with the 7th c. In its widest application the period extends to and includes St. Bernard in the 12th c., after which theologians receive the name of Scholastics. Not less various have been the estimates formed of the importance and value of their writings. As a rule, that estimate has been higher in the Roman Catholic Church than in the Protestant Churches. This is connected with the Roman Catholic doctrine regarding the Rule of Faith (q. v.), in which Tradition—at once the *interpreter* and the *supplement* of Scripture—plays so important a part. As the same authority is held to be due to the former as to the latter, it follows that the writings of the F., in which this tradition is chiefly contained, are inspired and infallible as well as Scripture. At the same time several Roman Catholic writers, when they started with the theory that doctrines were to be settled not by individuals, but by councils or the Church, have pointed out with remarkable candour the defects of the F. Protestants, who hold the Holy Scriptures to be the only infallible rule of faith and practice, in seeking to refute the Roman Catholic doctrine regarding tradition, went to the opposite extreme in their treatment of the F.: in seeking to drag to the light all the errors and faults of their writings, they naturally overlooked all that was valuable in them. Thus, although Daillé in his *De Vero Usu Patrum* (1631), the first thorough Protestant work that appeared on the subject, did not fail to point out their merits, the opinion generally adopted, at least by Calvinistic Protestants, was as one-sided as that of the Roman Catholics; and the prejudice against the F. which has been handed down among them, until quite recent times, as unreasonable as the adoration of the Church of Rome, for it was deemed right to despise, ridicule, and reject the whole body of their writings. It has been otherwise in the Church of England, which in her Church polity did not go so far as the Calvinistic Churches in opposition to Romanism, and in her doctrine did not so closely follow Augustine, who differed widely from the other F. She has always entertained great reverence for them, and the exaltation of them was a marked characteristic of the Tractarian revival.

Looked at without prejudice, the F. appear to be neither without great faults nor great excellences. Judged by the standards of the present day, they were very deficient. They were superstitious and credulous in a high degree. Only a few could be called learned, and as a body they were ill qualified to be interpreters of Scripture, being ignorant of the original languages, and too fond of allegorising. On the other hand, they were laborious and diligent, devotedly attached to the religion they professed, and zealous and courageous beyond all praise in its defence. To judge them fairly, they must be viewed in the light of their own time; and taken for neither more nor less than what they are, their writings are of incalculable value for tracing the development of doctrine and practice in the early Church. Among the more famous of the F. may be mentioned (1st c.) Clemens Romanus, Polycarp, Papias; (2d c.) Justin Martyr, Irenæus, Clemens Alexandrinus, Tertullian; (3d c.) Origen, Hippolytus, Cyprian; (4th c.) Eusebius Pamphili, Athanasius, Basil, Chrysostom, Gregory Nazianzen, Ephraem Syrus, Hilary, Lactantius, Ambrose, Jerome, Augustine; (5th c.) Cyril of Alexandria, Theodoret, Theodore of Mopsuestia, Pope Leo I., Orosius; (6th c.) Procopius, Gregory the Great, Gregory of Tours, Gildas, Isidore, all of whom receive separate treatment. See Donaldson's *Christian Literature and Doctrine* (Lond. 1864); Davidson's *Sacred Hermeneutics* (Edinb. 1843); Mosheim's *Church History* (Reid's ed.).

Fath'om (Old Eng. *faethm*; comp. Dutch *vadem*, Ger. *fadem*; perhaps connected with Lat. *spatium*, 'a space'), a measure of length in nautical surveying and in mining, 2 yards or 6 feet, *i.e.*, about the distance between the finger-tips of a man of average size when his arms are extended horizontally. It is also used metaphorically to express the reach of a man's capacity, 'I cannot fathom it' being equivalent to 'I cannot comprehend it.'

Fat'imides, or **Fat'imites,** a dynasty of califs who ruled Egypt and the N. of Africa from the 10th to the end of the 12th c. They were so called from their founder, Obeidallah Almahdi, declaring that he was descended from Fatima, daughter of Mohammed, and wife of Ali, an assertion which most Arab historians disbelieve. Obeidallah, with the help of the Berbers, dethroned the last of the Aglabites, who governed at Tunis, and made himself ruler of N. Africa from the Atlantic to the borders of Egypt. Moez, the fourth calif, subdued Egypt and founded Cairo. His fleets defeated the Spaniards, and his armies conquered Palestine and part of Syria. Hakem, the sixth calif, was a fanatic, who proclaimed himself a god, and is still worshipped by the Druses. He persecuted the Christians with fierce bigotry, and was assassinated in 1021. In the reign of Mostanser, the eighth of the F., the Turks were driven back from Egypt. Mostali, the ninth calif, was defeated by the Crusaders under Godfrey de Bouillon at Ascalon. During the reigns of his successors, the power of the F. dwindled away, until in 1169 the dynasty ended in Aladhed-Sidinallah, the fourteenth of the F., who was dethroned by Saladin, the founder of the Ayubite sultanate. See Mill's *History of Mohammedanism.*

Fats. The F. form an abundant group of compounds occurring both in the animal and vegetable kingdoms. In animals the secretion of fat takes place most abundantly immediately below the skin, and in the neighbourhood of the omentum and kidneys; in vegetables principally in the seed and fruit. All F. contain the elements carbon, hydrogen, and oxygen, united in various proportions. Together with many oils, they are characterised by the action which ensues when they are treated with superheated steam and caustic alkalies. By the first of these agents they are resolved into glycerine and a fatty acid; by the second, into glycerine and a salt of the fatty acid, or *soap.*

$$\underbrace{C_{57}H_{110}O_6}_{\text{Stearine.}} + \underbrace{3H_2O}_{\text{Water.}} = \underbrace{3C_{18}H_{36}O_2}_{\text{Stearic acid.}} + \underbrace{C_3H_8O_3}_{\text{Glycerine.}}$$

$$\underbrace{C_{57}H_{110}O_6}_{\text{Stearine.}} + \underbrace{3HNaO}_{\text{Caustic soda.}} = \underbrace{3C_{18}H_{35}NaO_2}_{\text{Stearate of soda (ordinary soap).}} + \underbrace{C_3H_8O_3}_{\text{Glycerine.}}$$

F. are indeed the ethers of glycerine, and may be formulated generally as $C_3H_5O_3(F)_3$, where F is the radical of the fatty acid. F. are lighter than water, in which liquid they are insoluble. They may be dissolved in ether, bisulphide of carbon, turpentine, &c. They melt when they are heated, their fusing point increasing with the proportion of carbon they contain. When strongly heated they are decomposed into acroleine, various hydrocarbons, &c. The most important of the animal F. is stearine, and of vegetable F. palmitine. They are employed in the manufacture of soap, glycerine, and candles, and in medicine in the preparation of ointments.

Fatt'y Acids. See OILS.

Fatty Degenera'tion is attended by a continually increasing accumulation of fat replacing the minute elements of tissue in different organs, and is essentially a sign of weakness or of death of the part, the elements of the tissues which perish being replaced by fat-granules. F. D. is quite distinct from accumulations of fat which do not replace other elements of tissue. Examples of F. D. may be seen in the minute elements of the muscular tissue, especially of the heart; in the acini of the liver, the blood-vessels, &c. Nearly all cell structures may undergo F. D., except, perhaps, red blood corpuscles, and the elements of nerve tissue. Yellow softening of the brain, however, is described as a form of F. D. *Arcus Senilis* (q. v.) is due to F. D. of the substance of the cornea, and is regarded as symptomatic of similar degeneration in other parts of the body. There is no kind of tissue, healthy or morbid, which may not undergo F. D., and it consequently gives rise to a great variety of local diseases. F. D. of the heart, or of the larger vessels, or of those passing through important organs, such as the brain, generally terminates in sudden death by rupture, followed by syncope.

Fatu'ity. See INSANITY.

Fat'uous, in law. A F. person, or an idiot, is legally incapable (see CAPACITY, LEGAL) of managing his affairs. See IDIOTS AND LUNATICS.

Fau'ces, the Latin name of the throat, or opening between the mouth and the pharynx.

Fau'cher, Léon, a French statesman, was born at Limoges, 8th September 1803, and first emerged into notice after the revolution of 1830, when he began to write for the Liberal opposition papers. He had already given his attention to economics, proposing a southern union to counterbalance the German *Zollverein*, and arguing for common work in prisons, and the separation of town and country convicts for different kinds of work. In 1845 he published his valuable *Études sur l'Angleterre* (chiefly of the industrial centres), which did much to spread free-trade principles in France. In 1846 he entered the Chamber of Deputies, and spoke on the currency and on the reform of the customs' tariff. In the revolution of 1848 he occupied an independent position, criticising the paper-money and other financial proposals of the Provisional Government, arguing against the limitation of the hours of labour, and suggesting that the masses in the national workshops, '*nourris par la patrie*,' being dangerous in Paris, should be sent to work on the railways. As Vice-President of the new Legislative Assembly he strongly opposed the tendency to sentimental, paternal government; he was always the unsparing critic of the Socialist budget. F., who believed in the possibility of a parliamentary government under the presidency of Napoleon, was for six months minister, but retired when the *plébiscite* by universal suffrage was proposed. He died at Marseille, 14th December 1854. See his *Mélanges d'Économie Politique et de Finance* (2 vols. Par. 1856), published by his friend Wolowski.

Fau'cit, Helen, an English actress, born in 1816, made a successful *début* as Julia in the *Hunchback*, at Covent Garden, London, in 1836. She soon rose to the summit of her profession, became a member of Macready's companies at Covent Garden and Drury Lane, and won wide repute for her refined, powerful rendering of Juliet, Beatrice, Imogen, Rosalind, Lady Macbeth, and other Shakespearian characters, and as the heroine in various pieces by Lytton, Browning, and Westland Marston. Her representation of Antigone was a remarkable success, and called forth an eloquent tribute from De Quincey. After her marriage with Theodore Martin, in 1851, this gifted actress continued to appear at intervals on the stage, from which she has now retired.

Fault, in geology, is a fracture, accompanied by a displacement, which breaks the continuity of the strata, altering the relative levels of contiguous portions.

Fault, in law. If the quality of a commodity sold prove inferior to what was represented, the buyer may reject it. Even if the buyer saw the goods, a *latent* F. may entitle him to reject them, and should they perish in consequence of it, he will be relieved from payment, or entitled to recover the price. But if the F. or deficiency of a commodity seen by the buyer is manifest, the rule is *Caveat emptor*, *i.e.*, the risk is the buyer's. Challenge on ground of F. must be without unnecessary delay. See ERROR IN ESSENTIALS.

Faun, or **Faun'us** ('the favourer,' from *faveo*, 'I favour'), in the mythic history of Italy was the third king of the Laurentes, and was noted for his devotion to hunting, cattle-breeding, and agriculture. He came to be worshipped both as a rural and as a prophetic divinity. His festival (the *Faunalia*) was celebrated on the 5th of December. F. was also the dream-god, hence he and his wife, Fauna, were known respectively as *Fatuus* and *Fatua*, the foretellers of destiny. His appearances under the images of fauns, half man, half goat, correspond with the satyrs of Greece; hence F. was identified with the Arcadian Pan after the myths of the Greeks had emigrated into Italy.

Faun'a, the name applied to indicate the entire *animal* population of any given continent, country, or region. The term is used in opposition to that of *flora*, applied to the *plant-life* of any district. The name F. is derived from the Roman fauns or satyrs, who were supposed to protect wild animals.

Fau'riel, Claude, a French scholar and critic, was born at St. Étienne, Loire, 21st October 1772. After acting as private secretary to Fouché from 1799 to 1802, he devoted himself to literature, and became one of the most profound and widely accomplished scholars of modern France. In 1830 he was appointed Professor of Foreign Languages at Paris; and there for fourteen years he delivered most ingenious and learned lectures on comparative philology, the sources of French and Italian, the Spanish drama, Servian poetry, &c. F. died at Paris, 15th July 1844. His great work is his *Histoire de la Gaule Méridionale sous la Domination des Conquérants Germains* (4 vols. Par. 1836). It is a masterpiece of learned research and brilliant art. Another admirable production is *Histoire de la Poésie Provençale* (3 vols. Par. 1846), in which he traces the origin of many of the chivalric ideas of honour, love, and gallantry in ancient poems of the Christians fighting with the Moors, or of the Aquitanians struggling against the Karoling kings. Another part forms a work on Dante and the Italian language (*Dante et les Origines de la Langue et de la Littérature Italiennes* (2 vols. 1854).

Fausse-Braye, a low rampart raised round a fortified place, now disused in fortification.

Fausse-Rivière ('false river'), a lake in Louisiana, U.S. of America, formerly a channel of the Mississippi; hence probably the origin of the name.

Faust. The F. legend, a favourite subject in European literature, arose during the struggles of Christianity with magic. Its main incident, the sale of a human soul to the devil, can be traced to the 6th c. tale of *Theophilus* by Eutychianus, which was translated by Germans and Scandinavians, occurs in Hroswitha and in the *Aurea Legenda*, and was popularised in the 13th c. by Rutebeuf's *Miracle de Théophile*. Hans Sachs has a similar story. In the 16th c. this legend of selling a soul was attached to the name of F. It has been said that the monks connected the tale with F. the printer in revenge for the injuries which his art caused their lucrative trade of book-copying; but the true protagonist of the modern version of the legend seems to have been a Georg or Johann F., perhaps the printer's son, *professor of magic* at Cracow

University early in the 16th c. He was a reputed necromancer, known to Melanchthon, 'who relates tales of his *diablerie*. The Polish legend of Twardowski, the printer of Cracow, who sold himself to Satan, seems to have grown from a confusion of F. of Cracow with F. the printer. The first version of the old legend, thus associated with the name F., was given in the *Volksbuch* of Spiess (1587), and on it Christopher Marlowe based his *Tragical History of Dr. Faustus*. In the narrative of Spiess and Widmann (1599), Helen of Greece is bestowed by Mephistopheles upon F. in place of a legitimate wife, but Margaret has not appeared. In Scheible's *Das Kloster* (1728) we meet with 'a beautiful but poor girl,' whom F. is prevented by supernatural interference from marrying, and who in succeeding versions gradually rises in importance, and finally becomes the Margaret of Goethe. Attempts have been made to find a common origin for the legend of F. and Don Juan (q. v.), and C. Grabbe, a German dramatist, wrote a play in which both F. and Don Juan appear. The story is still popular in Germany. The most notable poems upon it are Klinger's *F.'s Leben* and Goethe's masterpiece. Lessing wrote a drama on the F. legend, which, with the exception of a fragment, is unfortunately lost. Goethe's *F.*, having been turned into a libretto by Barbier and Carré, received an operatic form from Gounod. The plot of Calderon's *Magico Prodigioso* is similar to the F. legend, as is an old French play, *Mystère du Chevalier qui donna sa Femme au Diable* (1505), and, in a less degree, Byron's *Deformed Transformed*. See Düntzer's *Die Sage von Dr. Johann F.* (Stutt. 1846), and Peter's *Die Literatur der Faustsage* (Leips. 1857).—**Johann F.** or **Fust**, a goldsmith of Mainz, who, along with Gutenberg, Schöffer, and Coster, is accredited with the invention of printing by movable metal types. In 1450 he entered into partnership in the business of printing with Gutenberg (q. v.), whom he sued in 1455 for 2020 florins, which he had lent him—a loan which some maintain to be the only furtherance F. gave the new art. Decision being given against Gutenberg, F. acquired his printing apparatus, and, aided by Schöffer (q. v.), carried on the business prosperously until the sack of Mainz in 1462. F. died of the plague at Paris in 1466. See PRINTING and GUTENBERG.

Fausti'na, Annia Galeria, married Antoninus Pius several years before the death of Hadrian, and when he became emperor, A.D. 138, received the title of Augusta. She died A.D. 141.—**Annia F.**, daughter of the preceding, married Marcus Aurelius about A.D. 145, and died 175. Both mother and daughter are noted for their gross infidelity to their husbands, and for the honours which their husbands, faithful to the unfaithful, heaped upon them before and after their decease. Attempts have been recently made to construct a more favourable reading of the character of the wife of Marcus Aurelius.

Fausti'nus I., a negro emperor of Haiti, originally Faustinus Soulouque, was born at San Domingo, 1789, served in various humble capacities, rose to the rank of captain in the army, and was eventually elected president of the republic in 1847. He caused a frightful massacre of mulattoes at Port-au-Prince, 16th April 1848, and in the following year proclaimed himself emperor, continuing to reign till forced to abdicate by the revolution of 1859. He died 6th August 1867.

Fava'ra, a town of Sicily, 4 miles E. of Girgenti, and near the left bank of the Hypsas, a tributary of the Acragas. It has some trade in sulphur, olives, and other fruits. Pop. 12,829.

Fav'art, Charles Simon, born in Paris, November 13, 1710, may be called the author of the *opéra comique* of the 18th c. He aroused the jealousy of the French and Italian comedians, and for some time carried on his theatre in the Flemish camp of Marshal Saxe, who repaid him by seducing his wife, a lady who first had the courage to abandon the absurd *bergère de Watteau* dress on the stage, and to begin the reform of costume. The collected works of F. and his wife appeared as the *Théâtre de M. et Madame F.* (10 vols. Par. 1763-72). F., who composed about sixty comediettas of merit, died May 12, 1792. His son was an actor of some merit, and his grandson, **Antoine Pierre Charles F.** (born 1784), was also a dramatic author, a painter, and diplomatist, and with Dumolard issued the *Mémoires et Correspondence* of his grandfather (3 vols. 1809). An adopted daughter of Antoine, **Marie F.** (born in 1833), has become famous as an actress in comedy.

Fa'versham, a seaport of Kent, opposite Sheppey Island, on a stream flowing into the E. Swale, and 47 miles E.S.E. of London by the London, Chatham, and Dover Railway. It consists mainly of four streets, which form a cross, with the market-place in the centre. The trade is principally in coal, timber, corn, hops, and fruit. There are also breweries, brick-works, and large powder-mills. The oyster fisheries, however, are the chief industry. Pop. (1871) 7198. F. is the old English *Fifresham*, where King Æthelstan held a witenagemot in 930.

Favigna'na (anc. *Ægusa*), an island 6 miles off the N.W. coast of Sicily, forming one of the Trapani Islands, the ancient *Ægates*. It is 6 miles long by 2 broad, is well watered, has rich pastures, and produces wool and excellent wine. Its chief town, also called F., has a pop. of 3245.

Fav'osites (Lat. *favus*, 'a honeycomb'), a genus of Sclerodermic Corals (q. v.) found in a fossil state in the Silurian, Devonian, and Carboniferous rocks, but also represented by living species. They belong to the Tabulate division, and the family *Favositidæ* is recognised by having both septa and corallites distinct, with little or no connecting substance or cœnenchyma.

Favospon'gia, a well-known genus of fossil Sponges (q. v.) occurring in the Upper Silurian rocks. This genus belonged to the section *Calcarea*, or that of the calcareous or limy sponges.

Fa'vre, Jules Claude Gabriel, born at Lyon, March 21, 1809, of a mercantile family, came to the Paris bar about the time of the revolution of 1830, and soon made a reputation by his striking appearances in some of the great political trials. He was an extreme Radical, very independent in character, and a powerful and ready, though somewhat bitter, speaker. After the revolution of 1848 he held the office of home secretary, and drafted Ledru Rollin's election despatch to the local officials, which, though not unusual in French politics, was especially offensive in the case of a ministry pledged to the abstract rights of the people. On the President's election he passed into opposition, and spoke in favour of the freedom of the press and against the Roman expedition and the law of deportation. He refused to take the oath required by Napoleon after the *coup d'état*, and resumed his work at the bar. In 1858 he defended the political criminal Orsini, and subsequently entered the *Corps Législatif*, where he always spoke on the extreme Left, supporting the Austrian war of 1859 and condemning the Mexican expedition. At the Paris elections of 1869 he was run close by Rochefort, the editor of *La Lanterne*. In September 1870 F. became Minister of War, and attempted at Ferrières to negotiate an armistice, during which a Constituent Assembly might be elected, but the conditions required by Bismarck were too harsh. He afterwards held the portfolio of Foreign Affairs, but in 1871 withdrew again to the bar, of which he is *bâtonnier*. F. is a member of the French Academy, an honour merited by his classic eloquence. Besides a variety of speeches and pamphlets, F. has published *Rome et la République Française* (1871), and the *Gouvernement de la Défense Nationale* (1875), in which he narrates the events from the armistice to the taking of Paris, and recommends a moderate Conservative republic for France.

Fa'vus (Lat. 'a honeycomb') is a disease of the scalp, but in a few instances it has been observed on other parts of the body. F. is characterised by the presence of crusts of a bright yellow colour, situated under the epidermis, and scarcely rising above the level of the skin, sometimes exactly circular, but often with an outline representing numerous arcs of circles. The crusts are composed of the sporules and mycelia of a vegetable growth of the fungi order. The growth of the crust is eccentric, and spreads rapidly, and is unaccompanied by discharge of any kind. The hair bulbs are destroyed, and the hair falls out in patches, leaving permanently bald spots. F. is a disease of deranged nutrition, and generally occurs in childhood, and chiefly in families where no attention is paid to cleanliness. It is very common amongst the lower classes in France. Treatment:—Improved hygienic conditions, viz., fresh air, exercise, ablution, both local and general, and appropriate diet. The various preparations of iron are the most suitable medicines. The crusts may be removed by soaking the scalp thoroughly with oil in the evening, and washing it in the morning with soap and water.

Fawkes, Guy (properly **Guido**), an English gentleman, born of a Protestant family at York in 1570. At an early age he became a Roman Catholic, and on his return from the Low Countries, where he had served in the Spanish army, he became head of the Gunpowder Plot (q. v.), a conspiracy formed by several fanatical Catholics for blowing up James VI. and the members of the Commons and Lords, on November 5, 1605. F. was seized when about to fire the train, was put to torture, and executed in Palace Yard, Westminster, January 31, 1605-6. It was formerly the custom in English towns to burn his effigy every 5th November.

Fay, András, a Hungarian author, was born at Kohany in the county of Zemplén, May 30, 1786. Educated for the bar, he became an advocate and politician at Pesth, and in 1835 its deputy at the Diet. Feeble health, combined with the fact that although he was a Liberal, the tide of opinion was in advance of him, compelled him to retire from political life, and to devote himself to literature, social and educational improvements, &c. In 1820 appeared his prose Fables (*Mesek*), which from their charms of style and 'smack of the soil' are still very popular in Hungary. During his later years F. wrote two books on female education and the development of Hungary—*Nönevelés* (Pesth, 1840), and *Kelet népe nyn goton* (1841)—and a number of tragedies and comedies, while he contributed regularly to scientific and literary periodicals. A collected edition of his works, in 8 vols., was published at Pesth (1843-44). F. died 26th July 1864.

Fayal' (Port. *faya*, 'a beech-tree'), the chief island of the Azores (q. v.). It is extremely fruitful, abounds in myrtles and orange-trees, and exports largely fruit and wine. Pop. about 25,000. Its capital, Horta, has a pop. of 8549.

Fayette'ville, a town of N. Carolina, U.S., on Cape Fear River, 90 miles N.W. of Wilmington, with which it has regular communication by steamer. It lies in the centre of extensive pine forests, yielding much rosin, turpentine, and timber. It has four cotton-mills, a large general trade, an institute, a large school for coloured children, &c. Pop. (1870) 4660.

Fayûm' (from the Coptic *Pi-om*, rendered by Wilkinson 'the cultivated land,' and by Mariette 'the sea'), a division of Middle Egypt, on the W. side of the Nile, about 65 miles S.W. of Cairo, and 30 miles W. of Beni-Suef, on the Nile Valley Railway. It lies in a depression of the Libyan waste, and is only connected with the Nile valley by a single gorge. Area, 750 sq. miles, 100 of which are occupied by the Birket-el-Kerun ('the horned'), the Lake Mœris of the Greeks. In spite of an arid soil, F. is one of the richest parts of Egypt, yielding figs, dates, grapes, apricots, olives, and roses for the perfume factories. Medînet-el-F., the capital, stands on the E. shore of Lake Mœris, and on the site of the ancient Krokodilopolis.

Feal and Div'ot, a rural servitude in Scotland, in virtue of which the proprietor of a dominant tenement has a right to cut or remove turf to make fences or to thatch houses within the dominant lands. The kindred servitude of *fuel* gives a right to cut, winnow, and carry peats from the servient moss or peat-land. These servitudes may be constituted by express grants or by use or possession following on the usual clause of Parts and Pertinents (q. v.). There is an analogous right of common in England, called *common of estovers*. See ESTOVER.

Fealty (Old Fr. *féalté*, from the Lat. *fidelitas*), in English law, is the duty which the tenant of land owes to him from whom he holds it to perform the services of tenure. The word has not now any practical signification.

Feath'er, a beautiful river in a rich gold district of California, rises in the Sierra Nevada, and enters the Sacramento. Steamers ply on it to Yuba city, a distance of 100 miles from San Francisco.

Feather Grass (*Stipa*), a genus of grasses, so named from the great development of the awns, which in many species resemble a feather, as in the common F. G. (*S. pennata*). These grasses occur more abundantly on the Continent than in Britain, and are frequently used in room decorations, the long awns having an elegant and graceful appearance. They are often dyed. The awns are supposed to favour the dispersion of the seed, and its feration in the soil.

Feathers, the name given to the characteristic appendages of the skin of Birds (q. v.). They present the exoskeleton or outer skeleton of birds, just as scales represent that structure in fishes, reptiles, &c. They are formed in little *papillæ*, or rounded processes of the *dermis*, or true skin. The papilla which gives origin to a feather exhibits a deep middle groove on one side, this groove being broadest and deepest at its base, but shallower as it approaches the extremity of the papilla. Other grooves, which may be called *secondary* ones, are given off at right angles from the primary groove. These secondary grooves are closely set, and extend almost wholly round the papilla, but vanish at the side opposite to that on which the median primary groove is situated. Smaller grooves, which may be named *tertiary* grooves, are given off from the secondary ones, and these tertiary grooves lie in a manner parallel to the primary groove. A feather is formed on such a papilla much in the same manner as fluid metal is shaped in a mould. Horny matter secreted by the skin is pushed over the papilla, and naturally becomes thickest where the grooves are deepest. Thus, as the horny matter is pushed outwards, the material deposited in the central and primary groove becomes the *quill* or *shaft*; the matter deposited in the secondary grooves forms the *barbs*, which together compose the *web*; and the horny substance contained in the tertiary grooves forms the little *barbules*, or processes borne on the *barbs*, which bind the latter together to form the *vane* or *web*. These are the parts seen in any ordinary feather. The quill or barrel of the feather is its last-formed portion, and that by means of which it is inserted in the skin of the bird. The lower surface of the shaft exhibits a groove, the shaft itself consisting of a spongy white pith enclosed in a tough membrane. At the lower aspect of the shaft the barbs of the F. are disconnected, and form downy filaments; *down* itself, well seen in the under layer of F., especially in aquatic birds, consisting of a number of barbs, without any central shaft, united by a short quill. A small or miniature feather, often termed the *rachis*, *accessory plume*, or *plumule*, exists at the point where the quill and shaft unite. In some birds the rachis may be as large or larger than the feather itself, and in such birds as the ostriches, emus, and their allies, the barbs of the F. are not united to form a web, but are disconnected and free. It is this peculiarity of structure which gives to the ostrich F. their singular grace. In the cassowaries and other birds, the texture and appearance of the F. become singularly altered, and give to these birds the appearance of being clothed with long black hair.

The F. of birds receive various names, according to their situation. Those attached to the bones of the 'hand' are named *primaries*; the *secondaries* are attached to the fore-arm, and the *tertiaries* to the arm. The F. attached to the shoulder-blade are the *scapularies*. The *bastard wing* or *alula* is the name given to the collection of F. supported by the rudimentary *thumb*. The quills of the wings are covered at their bases by small F. forming the *wing-coverts*, the tail F. or *rectrices* being similarly protected by *tail-coverts*. F. once fully formed do not *grow*. They are mere appendages, and are therefore mostly renewed by new F. being developed, and by the moulting of the previously formed plumage. Changes of colour are also observed in F., due probably to chemical action.

F. are applied to many useful and ornamental purposes, especially those of the ostrich, the rhea or American ostrich, emu, birds of the heron kind, adjutant and Marabou stork, birds of paradise, argus pheasant, and many other common birds. The plumage of the male ostrich is most esteemed, that from the back and above the wings being preferred to that of the wings and tail. These F. adorn ladies' bonnets, and form military plumes, &c. Other ornamental F. are chiefly devoted to the preparation of ladies' head-dresses, artificial flowers, wreaths, fans, ornamental screens, &c. The soft F. and light elastic down procured from swans, geese, ducks, and fowls, are extensively used for stuffing beds, cushions, &c. Russia supplies Great Britain with large quantities of goose and duck produce, and smaller quantities are obtained from Ireland and Hudson's Bay. Goose F. are most appreciated for their softness and elasticity. The down of the eider-duck is much valued for quilts on account of its warmth and softness, but its matting character when lain upon keeps it from being much used for stuffing beds. Articles of clothing are made in different countries of birds' skins. Brazilian tribes make garments of the rich and varied plumage of native birds, and the Greenlanders wear the skins of waterfowl, turning the F. to the inside. Tippets, muffs, and many other articles used by ladies are likewise made of F. A new fabric, composed of an upper and lower layer of wool, and a thick intermediate one of down, the whole being carded together, is now manufactured in France for use as ladies' cloaks and other apparel. Spinning is performed by hand, and the wool-down is woven in the ordinary way with a warp of worsted.

Quill-pens are made from the hollow tubes of swan, goose, and crow feathers. In many parts of the world quills are employed for making ornamental baskets, cigar-cases, &c. Goose quills dyed various colours are made into ornamental articles by the Slave Indians of N. America, and in the East peacocks' quills are similarly used. The imports of F. into Great Britain during the year 1874 were as follows:—Ornamental, 273,705 lbs., valued at nearly £603,000; for beds, 2,419,984 lbs., worth about £128,000.

Feather Star (*Comatula* or *Antedon rosacea*), a species of *Crinoid* (q. v.) *Echinodermata* (q. v.), which in its earlier stages exists in a stalked condition, but in the adult state is met with as a free starfish form. The F. S. derives its name from its ten arms or rays being provided with numerous little *pinnæ* or processes, which give the arms a feathered appearance. The F. S. was formerly included in the order *Asteroidea* with ordinary starfishes, its early history being then unknown to naturalists. When first discovered in its young and attached state, it was thought to be a new form of *crinoid*, and as such was named *Pentacrinus Europæus*. But when this new crinoid was observed throughout its entire history, the star-like head was seen to detach itself from its stalk, and afterwards (as the F. S.) to live a free existence. The discovery of its early and attached condition at once showed that the F. S. was a true crinoid, and not an ordinary starfish, which is free and unattached throughout its entire existence. The arms are used by the F. S. as locomotive organs; and the internal organs are confined to the central body or *disc*, and do not, as in ordinary starfishes, send prolongations into the rays. The young or larva of the F. S. is an ovoid creature with four ciliated and transverse bands, and a small mouth and anus. The young F. S. is developed within this primitive embryo, or *pseudembryo* as it is called. The F. S. is widely distributed; it occurs in certain localities on the British coasts.

Febric'ula (Lat. 'a little fever') is a fever of short duration and mild character. The simplest form is Ephemera (q. v.), but the more severe, called *simple continued fever*, may last seventy-two or more hours. See FEVER.

Feb'rifuge (Lat. *febris*, 'a fever,' and *fugo*, 'I drive away'), a medicine having the property of curing a fever, such as mineral and vegetable acids, potassæ chloras, P. citras, P. nitras, &c.

Febro'nianism is a development or a phase of Jansenism (q. v.) which made its appearance in the Roman Catholic Church in Germany towards the end of last century. It was so called after Justinus Febronius, the *nom de plume* adopted by J. H. von Hontheim in his work *On the State of the Church and the Legitimate Authority of the Roman Pontiff* (1767).

Feb'ruary, the second month of the year, was, along with January, introduced into the Roman calendar by Numa Pompilius, who allotted twenty-nine days to it, except in leap years, when it had thirty. Augustus, however, transferred one day from F. to the month named in his honour, that it might be inferior to no other month of the year. The name F. is derived from *februare*, 'to purify,' because on the 15th of F. the *Februa* or *Lupercalia*, the Roman festivals of lustration and expiation, were held. Some consider (from the coincidence of the time of year) that the Christian festival of the Purification of the Virgin on Candlemas Day was engrafted upon the Roman rite.

Feb'ruus (Lat. *februa*, 'purifications,' a word of Sabine, or according to others of Etruscan origin), an ancient Italian divinity in whose honour lustrations were celebrated on the 15th of February, which thus took its name from him. As these were supposed to produce fertility among men and beasts, Juno likewise, as the goddess of marriage, was designated Februata. F. was sometimes identified with the god of the infernal world (*Hades*), because the festival for the dead (*Feralia*) was also celebrated in February.

Fécamp, earlier **Fescan** or **Fescamp** (Lat. *Fiscanium* or *Fiscarium*), a seaport of Seine Inférieure, France, on the English Channel, 38 miles N.N.E. of Le Havre by railway. The most interesting building is the church of Notre Dame, a fine specimen of 14th c. Gothic. F. has shipbuilding yards, forges, cotton, saw, oil, and bark mills, and breweries. Its sea-baths are famous. In 1874 there cleared the port 179 ships, of 23,200 tons; 60 boats were employed in the cod-fishery. Pop. (1872) 12,534.

Fech'ner's Psycho-Physical Law. This is as follows:—'Sensations increase proportionately to the logarithms of the strength of the stimulus.' See SENSORY IMPRESSIONS.

Fech'ter, Charles Albert, an actor of considerable originality and brilliance of style, was born in London, October 23, 1824. His father was a German, his mother an Englishwoman, while he himself by education is practically a Frenchman. He first appeared on the Paris stage, and afterwards joining a company, travelled through Italy, played in Berlin in 1846, and in Paris and London in 1847. Returning to Paris, he made the part of Duval in the *Dame aux Camélias*, and earned a reputation which has never since declined. In 1860 he appeared at the Princess's in *Ruy Blas*, and at once took a high position on the London stage. His Hamlet (20th March 1861) created great interest, and was the topic of much discussion. Originality of conception and rejection of stage traditions were the chief characteristics of F.'s Hamlet, and constitute it, perhaps, the first of what may be called the 'new light' interpretations of Shakespeare, of which we have had several since. In 1863 he became lessee of the Lyceum Theatre, in which he produced *The Duke's Motto*, *Bel Demonio*, &c. In America, to which he removed in 1870, he has achieved a brilliant success. After making the tour of the principal cities of the States, he was for some time lessee of the Globe Theatre, Boston.

Fecia'les, an order of priests among the Romans appointed to proclaim war and to negotiate peace. The *jus feciale* was the only principle recognised by the Romans corresponding to modern international law.

Fec'ula, or **Fæc'ula** (Lat. dim. of *fæx*, 'sediment,' Fr. *fécule*), organic matter obtained as a sediment after macerating the cellular tissue of plants with water. F. is frequently employed as a synonym for Starch (q. v.).

Fed'eral Gov'ernment, in the historical sense, has been said to exist wherever the bond of union between the members is closer than that of alliance, and the degree of independence possessed by the members is greater than that of municipal freedom. In the ideal federation each of the members ought to be wholly independent in those matters (*e.g.*, criminal and constitutional law) which concern itself; while the union itself is absolute sovereign on all matters affecting all the members, being chiefly external matters of international law, questions of peace and war, diplomatic intercourse, &c. There are four great examples—the Achaian League (B.C. 281–146); the Swiss cantons, converted in 1847 from a *Staaten-bund* into a *Bundestaat*; the Seven United Provinces of the Netherlands (A.D. 1579–1795); the United States of America (A.D. 1778). The minor confederations of ancient Greece, such as the Phokian, the Akarnanian, and the Epeirot Leagues in the N.; the Bœotian League; and in modern times the German Confederation (1815–66), followed by the North German Confederation, are much less developed specimens of union. Of the old leagues of the thirty cities of Latium, and of other cities in ancient Italy, history relates nothing certain. The league of the Hanse towns, though now of a special and restricted kind, is perhaps the oldest living form of political union; the youngest and least promising are among the republics of S. America. The change mentioned above in the Swiss constitution indicates the fundamental distinction between the 'system of confederated states,' and the 'composite state.' In the latter the federal government acts directly on all organic questions on the subjects of every state who are truly also its own subjects. In the former it must act by the intervention of the state governments. This was tried for the first few years of American independence, but emphatically repudiated by the great leaders, Hamilton, Jay, and Madison, who wrote the *Federalist* in support of the composite state. The older principle again appeared in the German *Bund*, which was not able even to maintain an alliance in peace and war. It had no executive power, and the arrangements as to currency and customs were really the work of Prussia. Mr. Mill has stated three conditions of useful federation—(1) A certain degree of mutual sympathy arising from common race, language, religion, political institutions; (2) that none of the members be sufficiently powerful to lose nothing by standing alone; (3) that there be no great inequality among the members. Even in the most successful federations it has been a delicate matter to preserve the balance of power between the federal government and the states. In the United States, questions on the constitution have frequently been decided in a peaceful way by the supreme court of justice; but the institution of slavery, being one naturally repugnant to civilised feeling, with its attendant questions of free soil, fugitive-slave law, &c., for a long time threatened, and at last nearly broke the Union. The American plan of a double chamber, one of which elected by a mass vote represents population, and the other elected by the legislatures of the states gives an equal representation to the states, seems wise and successful. It is always a question of circumstances whether federalism is better than an undivided government. The extent of territory, the commercial interests, the history of the inhabitants, must all be taken into account; and it must be remembered that much local autonomy, extending even to different systems of law and religion, may exist under a central monarchy. Generally, however, some great enthusiasm of race, the remembrance of a common history, devotion to a great family, or a political or religious principle, will be required to weld into unity the elements of difference. It has been suggested by Mr. Freeman that federalism combines to a certain extent the advantages of large states (viz., peace and the diminution of local prejudices and party strifes) with those of small states, of which the chief are a higher political intelligence and freedom from corruption.

Fee and Liferent (Scotch law). The first is the right of proprietorship, the second is the right to the use and profits of the subject during life. The rights may be held by one person, or they may coexist in different persons. It has been decided that a conveyance to a parent in liferent and to children unborn or unnamed in fee, imports a right of fee in the parent and a *Spes Successionis* (q.v.) only in the children. See FIAR.

Fee Fund, the name given in Scotland to the dues of court payable on the tabling of summonses, the extracting of decrees, &c. The clerks and other officers of the court are paid out of the fund.

Feel'ing. See EMOTION.

Fee-Simple. In England, a tenant in F.-S. is one who has unconditional and freehold possession of a property. He can dispose of his estate by will or deed. F.-S. is the largest interest that can be held in real property. To create it the conveyance must be to the grantee *and his heirs*, except in a will, in which equivalent expressions are admitted. The term is used in contradistinction to that of fee-tail, which is a limited tenure. See ENTAIL.

Fees in English Law Courts. All fees in courts of justice allowed by Act of Parliament are established fees, and the officers entitled to them may enforce their claim by law. Under the Supreme Court of Judicature (1875) Act, the Lord Chancellor, with the advice and consent of the judges of the supreme court, or any three of them, with concurrence of the Treasury, may fix the fees and percentages to be taken in the High Court of Justice or in the Court of Appeal, or in any court or office connected with these. The fees are to be taken in stamps, to counterfeit which is forgery, rendering the criminal liable to penal servitude.

Fees, Professional. In England it has been conclusively decided in the case of Kennedy *v.* Swinfen, that a barrister has no valid ground of action for his fees, which are given as a gratuity, not as hire; but a client cannot by law recover a fee paid to counsel, not even if he fail to attend the cause for which he has received the fee. It has been decided that it is in accordance with etiquette for a barrister to hold a brief in the county courts of England for a fee of one guinea. In Scotland it is considered that an advocate has no legal claim for a professional fee. By 21 and 22 Vict. c. 90, which applies to the United Kingdom, physicians, surgeons, and apothecaries are now entitled to recover reasonable charges, with costs of medicines and medical appliances, in any law-court. The general rule of law is that a member of any recognised profession has a legal claim for fees according to custom, if the custom be reasonable, for an unreasonable or unjust custom will not be upheld by law. In France the law with regard to legal enforcement of a barrister's claim for fees seems to be different from the English law, but from rule of the bar the result is practically the same. See RETAINER.

Fehérvár Székes (Ger. *Stuhlweissenburg*), a royal free town, and capital of the county of a same name, lies near the swamp Sár-Rét, 34 miles S.W. of Pesth by railway. Till 1527 it was the place of coronation and burial of the Hungarian kings. The seat of a bishop, F. has a cathedral, a bishop's palace, the beautiful Johanniskirche (1752), several higher schools, and a Hungarian theatre. Its manufactures are woollens, flannel, patent leather, soap, and cutlery. There are artesian wells. Pop. (1869) 22,683. F. occupies the site of the Roman *Floriana*. It suffered in the early wars with Austria, and fell in 1543, and again in 1602, into the hands of the Turks, who held it till 1688.

Feign'ed Iss'ue, in English law, is an action feigned to be brought with consent of parties to determine a question without pleading, so as to save time and costs.

Feign'ing of Disease' is of common occurrence in the army and navy, and amongst convicts and others desirous of escaping from discipline or avoiding compulsory service. In such cases it is technically called *malingering*. The diseases most commonly simulated are epilepsy, blindness, deafness, paralysis, insanity, neuralgia, and rheumatism causing lameness, &c. F. of D. is frequently practised by begging impostors, and in very many cases solely for the purpose of exciting sympathy and procuring notoriety. Detection, although difficult, is generally effected by very simple means. A little dry Scotch snuff, blown through a quill up the nostrils of a feigning epileptic, excites a fit of sneezing which may continue for an hour. When practised for a length of time, F. of D. often becomes a monomania, resulting in real mental disease, and cases are on record in which amputations have been submitted to for the removal of diseased parts, artificially produced. Feigning lunatics often become really insane.

Feint (Fr. *feindre*, 'to feign,' from the Lat. *fingere*), in warfare, is a seemingly offensive movement, usually made with the view of withdrawing the attention of the enemy from a position against which the real attack is to be made.

Feith, Rhijnvis, a Dutch poet, born February 7, 1753, at Zwoll, in Oberyssel. He studied at Leyden, became burgomaster of Zwoll, won considerable fame as a poet, was chosen member of the Institute of the Low Countries, and died in his birthplace, February 8, 1824. His chief productions are *Het Graf* ('The Grave,' Amst. 1792); a didactic poem, *De Ouderdom* ('Old Age,' Amst. 1802); *Odene n Gedichten* ('Odes and Miscellaneous Poems,' 1796–1810); *Thirza* (1791), and *Ines de Castro* (1793), tragedies; and *De Geuzen*, a patriotic lay on the water-beggars. A collection of his works appeared at Rotterdam (11 vols. 1824).

Feld'mann, Leopold, a German author of Jewish family and faith, was born at Munich, May 22, 1803. He first showed his poetical powers, according to common report, when a boy of thirteen and a cobbler's apprentice, by sending in a lady's pair of shoes which he had mended verses expressing his admiration of their owner. At the age of fourteen he produced a play, *Der Falsche Eid*. After spending a few years in trade, he was persuaded by Saphia, the poet, to throw himself into literature. His career as a man of letters has been eminently successful. The foundation of his fame was his comedy, *Der Sohn auf Reisen* (1841). In 1850 he was appointed histrionic teacher (*dramaturg*) at the National Theatre of Vienna. F.'s comedies, which are marked by spontaneity and sprightliness, have been published under the title *Deutsche Originallustspiele* (Vienna, 1844–52; 2d ed. 1855–57).

Felegyha'za, a market-town of Lesser Cumania, Hungary, on the railway between Pesth and Temesvar, 15 miles S.S.E. of Kecskemét, produces wine, fruit, and tobacco, and has cattle-markets. Pop. (1869) 21,313.

Feli'cians, the adherents of Felix, Bishop of Urgelles, in the Adoption Controversy (q. v.).

Fel'idæ or **Fe'line Animals**, a large family of Carnivorous mammalia, represented by the typical genus *Felis* and its varieties. It includes the lion, tiger, lynx, leopard, panther, cat, and other animals. The F. are *digitigrade Carnivora*, that is, they walk on the tips of their toes. The soles of the feet are hairy, and the metacarpus and heel are raised from the ground. The jaws are usually short, and the muscles of a great size and strength. The molar and præmolar teeth exist in fewer numbers than in any other *Carnivora*. They possess cutting edges, except the last upper molar, which is tuberculate, or provided with blunted points. The upper 'flesh' tooth (the last tooth but one in the upper jaw, and the last tooth in the lower jaw are named 'flesh teeth') in the F., has three lobes or divisions, and a blunt internal process. The lower flesh tooth has two cutting lobes. The typical arrangement of the teeth in F. is six incisors, and two canines in each jaw ; six præmolars in the upper, and four in the lower jaw ; and two molars in each jaw—making a total of thirty teeth. The legs are usually of equal size, and there are four toes on the hind, and five on the front feet. The toes are provided with retractile claws, which can be withdrawn at will within sheaths—an arrangement exemplified in the common cat. The tongue of the F. is rough, and its papillæ are horny ; this structure fitting it to serve as a rasp in scraping the flesh from the bones of the prey. The muscular system is well developed, the bones having prominent ridges for the attachment of muscles. The F. are very generally distributed throughout the world, but attain their greatest size in tropical regions. They approach their prey stealthily, and generally spring or bound upon it from a distance. It is doubtful if any other genus than the single genus *Felis* can with good reason be constructed in this family. Many varieties of its included forms exist, but these can hardly be regarded as distinct species.

Fe'lix, the Roman procurator of Judea in the reigns of Claudius and Nero, to whom St. Paul was consigned by the chief captain at Jerusalem when his life was in danger from the Jews (Acts xxiii.). Originally a slave, he was manumitted by Claudius Cæsar, from whom he took the prænomen Claudius. He had also the surname Antonius, after Antonia, the emperor's mother. He was loaded with military honours by the emperor, and finally made procurator of Judea, in which position he indulged in all kinds of cruelty and lust, relying on his influence at court to shield him from punishment for any crime he might commit. Superseded in 62 by Porcius Festus, he was accused by the Jews, and only escaped punishment through the influence of his brother Pallas with Nero.

Popes.—**Felix I.** (about 269-274) gained an adventitious importance owing to the following circumstance. Paul of Samosata (q. v.), Bishop of Antioch, after being deposed for heresy by the Council of Antioch (269), kept possession of the Church property. The Emperor Aurelius was appealed to by the orthodox party to compel Paul to resign his office. The emperor decided that he should be bishop who was recognised as such by F., the Bishop of Rome. F. is said to have perished in the persecution under Aurelius, about 274.—**Felix II.** was an archdeacon who acceded to the wishes of the Emperor Constantius when, in 356, he banished Bishop Liberius (q. v.) because he would not agree to the condemnation of Athanasius, and was elevated to the place of Liberius. After Liberius was restored, F. was banished, and is said to have spent the rest of his life in penance for his declension to Arianism.—**Felix III.** succeeded Simplicius in 483. The Emperor Zeno had (482) put forth a formula of concord, called *Henoticon*, intended to settle the dissensions caused by the Monophysite controversy. This Henoticon, for its concessions to the Monophysites (q. v.), was rejected by F., who also attacked Acacius, Bishop of Constantinople, by whose advice Zeno had acted, and got him deposed in a council of seventy bishops held at Rome (484). Acacius was supported by the emperor and the Eastern bishops, and thus arose the first schism between the Eastern and Western Churches, which lasted thirty-four years. F. died 492. —**Felix IV.** (526-530) was raised to the papacy by Theodoric, in opposition to the wishes of the senate and the people.—**Felix V.**, who became pope in 1439, was Amadeus VIII., Duke of Savoy, being elected by the fathers at Basel, who had deposed Eugenius IV. But as the majority of the Church adhered to Eugenius, there were two popes, and also two councils, the one sitting at Basel, the other at Constance. F. resigned his high dignity in 1449, leaving the undivided papacy to Nicolaus V., who had meantime succeeded to Eugenius.

Fell'ah (Arab. 'a peasant ;' plural *Fellahin*), the name of the agricultural labourer in Egypt, or of the peasant in contemptuous contradistinction to the inhabitant of the towns. They are the descendants of the ancient Egyptians, and form some three-fourths of the inhabitants. In the 7th c. they were forced to accept the religion and language of the Arabs, and the long period of their degrading toil and miserable subject condition has permanently influenced their character, habits, and appearance. They are from 5 to 6 feet in height, muscular and active, with an oval skull and a broad round face, a low retreating forehead, long deep-set eyes, large mouth, thick lips, and excellent teeth. The hands and feet, however, are of small size. A grinding system of taxation has lowered, if not broken, the spirit of the F., yet he is a brave, hardy soldier. Like the Egyptian of old, he is of grave, sustained temperament, and is distinguished equally for intelligence and immorality, sobriety and indolence. The women, who tattoo, marry often before eleven years of age. The Fellahin villages, which are scattered along the banks of the Nile and of the canals, are for the most part disorderly clusters of filthy huts, surrounding a mud-built mosque.

Fellata' (also called by the various tribes Fula, Fellani, Fulbe, &c.), the most intelligent of all the African races, now occupies a wide area in the W. of the Sudan, and includes many powerful states, as Flausse, Futa-Djalon, Senegal-Futa, Massina, &c. The F. advanced from Senegal in an easterly direction, and already in the 16th c. had spread beyond the Niger and comprised several large tribes. It was only, however, in the beginning of the 19th c. that they were stirred to conquest and to the spread of the Mohammedan religion by the Imam and reformer, Othman of Benue, on whose death (1816) the F. territory had increased to an area of 327,140 sq. miles. The people, who are of a reddish colour, and of great variety of type, are industrious and clever, but they are oppressed by a grasping aristocracy. The pop. is estimated at about 8,000,000.

Fell'enberg, Philip Emanuel von, a great improver of Swiss agriculture and education, was born of good family at Bern, 27th June 1771. After studying law at Tübingen, and travelling in different European countries, he finally devoted himself to a career of philanthropy. Purchasing the estate of Hofwyl, near his native city, he commenced a series of efforts to increase the productivity of the soil, and also to better the condition of the peasantry. He founded an asylum for forsaken children, a school of theoretical and practical agriculture, and in connection with it an institution for the education of the higher classes, which became quite famous and the model of similar institutions in other lands. F. died 21st November 1844. See Hamm, *F.'s Leben und Wirken* (Bern, 1845).

Fell'ows, Sir Charles, was born in August 1799, at Nottingham, where his father was a banker. From an early age F. took a delight in travelling, and had made himself familiar with Scotland, Switzerland, Italy, Greece, and Asia Minor, when, according to popular belief, the statement of Colonel Leake, that the valley of the Xanthus had never been explored, led him to make it the centre of archæological investigations, which he prosecuted with but slight intermissions to the end of his life. Lycia was explored by him in three different journeys in 1838, 1839, and 1841-42, the results of which were the discovery of the ruins of fifteen ancient cities, including Tlos and Xanthus, the original capital of Lycia, and the bringing home to England a great number of works of art from these cities, including twenty cases of marbles and casts, now in the Lycian Saloon of the British Museum. F., who was knighted in 1845, died November 8, 1860. For a description of his investigations see his published works, *The Xanthian Marbles* (1843); *An Account of the Ionic Trophy Monument excavated at Xanthus* (1848); *Travels and Researches in Asia Minor, particularly in the Province of Lycia* (1852), containing journals formerly published by him; and *Coins of Ancient Lycia before the Reign of Alexander* (1855).

Fell'owship, the name now applied, almost universally, to the holders of the larger endowed posts in the colleges of Oxford and Cambridge, being a translation of the 'socius' of the original statutes. The number varies in the different colleges, and there are several other minor differences, most of which have been created within the past few years. The following is an outline of the general system. Candidates must have qualified for the degree of B.A., and the selection is determined by an open examination. The post brings with it an equal vote in the government of the college, but involves no specific duties, and has no place in the life of the university proper. As a rule, it is tenable for life, subject only to the conditions of celibacy and the absence of a specified income from other permanent sources. The average value lies between £200 and £300 per annum, and the total sum thus annually appropriated at either university is about £90,000. About two-fifths of the fellowships at Oxford are still confined to clergymen of the Church of England, but otherwise there are now no religious disqualifications. Both universities are at present undergoing reform, in which the tenure of fellowships is the chief subject of discussion. The general tendency of modern changes is to divide fellowships into two classes, viz., mere prizes, and fellowships with teaching functions; to make all alike terminable; and to relax the restriction on marriage. It has also been proposed to attach to a proportion of these posts the obligation of literary study or scientific research.

Fe'lo de Se, a verdict in English law by which it is declared that one who has committed suicide has done so in sound mind, and has thereby become a felon. Formerly, the punishment was ignominious burial in the highway, with a stake driven through the body. As the ignominy, however, could only be felt by innocent survivors, the penalty was judiciously mitigated by 4 Geo. IV. c. 32. The funeral service is, however, still omitted at interment, which by law must be within twenty-four hours after the verdict, and between nine and twelve at night. Probably the same consideration which led to mitigation of penalty may ultimately lead to abolition of it.

Fel'ony (the word *fello*, 'a felon,' is found in the Capitularies of Karl the Bald, but its origin is unknown), a term of English law denoting the higher classes of offences. Though the punishment of death may legally be inflicted for various crimes, it is now practically restricted to that of murder. Burglary, arson, and various other crimes of magnitude are usually punished with from three years' penal servitude to penal servitude for life. The chief distinction between F. and *misdemeanour* used to be, that the former occasioned the forfeiture of lands or goods, or both, at common law. This distinction has been done away with by 33 and 34 Vict. c. 23, which abolishes forfeiture or Escheat (q. v.), except in so far as consequent upon 'Outlawry' (q. v.). But conviction for F. is a disqualification for certain offices.

Fel'spar (Ger. *feldspath*, 'field-spar'), a family of minerals, the most important of all in the structure of rocks. It is divided into two groups according to the crystallisation:—(1) *Orthoclase* (Gr. 'straight-cleavage') or monoclinic F.; (2) *Plagioclase* (Gr. 'oblique-cleavage') or triclinic F. The former group, comprehending the so-called *potash* felspars, comprises the varieties adularia, rhyacolite, sanidin, orthoclase, and loxoclase, which are composed of silica, alumina, potash, and soda, in varying proportions; are coloured white, grey, or flesh-red, with sometimes greenish and bluish tints; have a vitreous lustre, and are transparent to subtranslucent. F. is taken as one of the standards of the scale of hardness, being degree 6. *Moonstone* and *sunstone*, often set in jewellery, are opalescent varieties of adularia, the latter containing minute scales of mica. The members of the second group contain lime instead of potash, and are termed *soda* or *lime* felspars, according as soda or lime predominates. Of the soda felspars, albite and oligoclase are the chief varieties, having usually a white colour, a pearly or vitreous lustre, with physical and optical properties similar to the other felspars. The type of the lime felspars is labradorite, which varies in colour from dark grey to brown, frequently relieved by the play of rich delicate tints due to internal reflections. The felspars form the basis of all true igneous rocks, the *orthoclase* varieties occurring in granite, felstone, pitchstone, obsidian, syenite, orthoclase porphyry, trachyte, and phonolyte; and the *plagioclase* varieties in porphyrite, diorite, basalt, dolerite, andesite, diallage rock, and also granite. Plagioclase granite is distinguishable from orthoclase by its usually lighter colour. Grains of F. frequently occur in sandstones, which are named the *felspathic* sandstones, in distinction to the *micaceous*, *quartzose*, and *argillaceous* sandstones. *Kaolin* (q. v.) results from the decomposition of F.—the potash and part of the silica being removed and water added.

Fel'stone, the name given by Sedgwick to a class of igneous rocks, otherwise known as petrosilex, felsite, felsite porphyry, &c., is composed of orthoclase intimately mixed with quartz. It is smooth, compact, and flinty-like, varies in colour from dark-grey to white, and has a smooth fracture.

Felt (Ger. *filz*, 'woollen cloth,' allied to the Lat. *pileus*, 'a felt hat or cap') is a kind of cloth or texture made without any process of spinning and weaving, by matting together or interlacing fibrous substances. The property of felting which is possessed by certain fibres is due to the jagged or notched character of their surfaces, which enables them by the application of pressure, combined with a certain amount of moisture, to adhere firmly and closely together, so that if the moisture and pressure are applied to a lap, or evenly spread out layer, a uniform compact cloth may be produced. A certain amount of felting power must be possessed by all fibres in order that they may adhere sufficiently to enable them to be spun, but it is only wool and certain other animal fibres that are capable of being used for F. Examples of the felting property are found in the matting which takes place in mattresses and cushions filled with woollen flocks, and in the shrinking of flannels and woollen fabrics by washing. Woollen cloths in addition to the process of weaving receive a certain amount of felting in their finish. The property of felting is chiefly turned to account in the manufacture of F. hats (see HAT MANUFACTURE), for which, in addition to wool, the hair of the rabbit, hare, nutria, musquash, and various other mammals is employed. Felted cloth is very extensively employed for making tablecovers, crumbcloths, and cheap carpetings, which generally are ornamented with printed patterns, and sometimes in the case of tablecovers embossed. The Persians produce a felted carpet in which a pattern is produced by inlaying the various colours in the substance. A heavy coarse kind of F. is very extensively used by the Russian peasantry for their winter garments, and for boots and shoes, which are moulded in a single piece. F. prepared with artificial asphalt is employed for roofing buildings.

Fel'ton, Cornelius Conway, LL.D., a distinguished American scholar, was born at West Newbury, Massachusetts, U.S., November 6, 1807. He graduated at Harvard in 1827. In 1832 he became Professor of Greek in Harvard, and in 1860 President of the College. In 1853 he paid a visit to Europe, and published his *Familiar Letters from Europe* in 1865. He died February 26, 1862. F.'s chief works are—*Homer* with English notes (1833), a translation of Menzel's *Deutsche Literatur* (3 vols. 1840), *Panegyricus* of Isocrates (1849), *Birds* of Aristophanes (1852). Along with Sears and Edwards he published *Ancient Art and Literature* (1843).

Fel'tre (Ger. *Felters*), an old town in the province of Belluno, N. Italy, on a height overlooking the Piave, 50 miles N.N.W. of Venice. It has a cathedral, considerable manufactures of silk-twist, some trade in wine, oil, and grain, and extensive bleachfields. Pop. 6000.

Felucc'a (Ital., from Arab. *fulk*, 'a ship'), a small vessel used in the Mediterranean, rigged with lateen sails, but propelled also by oars when required.

Fe'male La'bour is illegal in mines and collieries under 5 and 6 Vict. c. 99. See COAL MINES REGULATIONS ACT, FACTORY ACTS, WORKSHOP REGULATION ACT.

Female Prostitu'tion. Under 34 Edw. III. c. 1, justices of the peace may hold all to bail that are not of good fame, and compel them to give surety for their good behaviour. This ancient statute has been revived in London for the purpose of bringing the keepers of notorious brothels under magisterial notice. Any female annoying a passenger may be apprehended by the police without warrant, and is liable to a penalty of 40s.

Female Whipp'ing was abolished as a penalty by 1 Geo. IV. c. 67, imprisonment or solitary confinement being substituted.

Feme Coverte' is the English law term for a married woman. Regarding a surviving husband's interest in his wife's real estate see COURTESY OR CURTESY. Regarding a widow's interest in her husband's estate see DOWER; see also DIVORCE, ADULTERY, MARRIAGE, DESERTION OF SPOUSE.

Fem'ern, or **Feh'marn** ('the place of cattle'), an island in the Baltic belonging formerly to Denmark but now to Prussia, separated from the N.E. point of Holstein by a narrow shallow channel, the Femersund. It is 16 miles long by 12 broad, is low and marshy, but fertile, producing much wheat and barley, which are largely exported. The fisheries are also valuable. The chief places are Burg and Petersdorf. Pop. 9600.

Feme Sole is the English law term for an unmarried woman. A married woman who by the *custom of London* trades on her own account without the husband being liable for her dealings is called a F. S. trader, because with respect to her trading her position is the same as that of a single woman. The *custom of London* is the general law of France, where any married woman can hold property irrespective of her husband and his creditors.

Fem'gerichte, or **Fæm'gerichte** (Old Ger. *fem*, 'punishment,' and *gericht*, 'a court of justice'), secret tribunals which arose during the middle ages in Westphalia, and took the place of the regular courts of justice. They seem to have grown out of the open-air meetings held by the German tribes in very early times, the notion that they took their origin from the courts held by the Missi Dominici, or imperial legates appointed by Karl the Great, being probably erroneous. Little is known of them before the end of the 12th c., when, on the deposition of the Emperor Heinrich the Lion (1180) and consequent removal of legal restraints, they were organised as a curb on feudal tyranny. They were centred in Westphalia, which was known among their members as the *Red Land*, but their influence was soon felt throughout Germany, and seems at first to have been a potent check on crime. They gradually, however, became a gigantic evil, wielding a terrible power, enhanced by the gloomy mystery which veiled them, and enforcing a system of irresponsible terrorism. Though at first the emperors made them occasional instruments of imperial designs, they grew strong enough to defy the civil government, and even on one occasion summoned the emperor to appear before them. The Pact of Westphalia in 1371 declared them lawful institutions, and during the 14th and 15th centuries their power rose to its height. In 1438 the Emperor Albrecht II. strove to abolish them; and in the second half of the 15th c. so flagrant were their evils, that in 1461 a league was formed against them by the Swiss commonwealth and several German cities and princes. In 1495 Maximilian I. made them accept a new code, which greatly weakened their authority; and on the *Landfriede* or general peace being established through Germany, and the administration of public justice secured, their influence rapidly waned, the last public F. being held at Celle, Hanover, in 1568. The secret meetings lingered on in Westphalia, though shorn of real power, until 1811, when they were suppressed by Jerome Bonaparte. The procedure at the secret meetings is somewhat obscure. The president of a court was called a *Freigraf* ('free-count'), while the members of the brotherhood who carried out his sentences were named *Freischöffen* ('free-justices') or *Scabini*. These *Freischöffen*, who at one time are said to have numbered 100,000, were also styled *Wissenden* ('wise' or 'initiated men'). At first none save a free Westphalian could be admitted into the brotherhood, but afterwards men from other districts were enrolled. They were sworn to secrecy by a terrible oath, and recognised each other by various signs, the chief of which was the mysterious S.S.G.G., whose meaning has never been revealed. The Freischöffen were bound to disclose any crime against 'the holy Fem,' or they were liable to the punishment due to the offence they had concealed. A man accused by one of the brotherhood was thrice summoned to appear by a citation secretly affixed to his door; and if he did not answer the command, was again called upon in a secret meeting named the *acht*, when, if he still disobeyed, the first Freischoff who met him was empowered to bind him to a tree, or, if he resisted, to slay him at once, in either case leaving the dagger borne by each of the members to show who had done the deed. The emperor was nominally head of the F., and the Archbishop of Köln was styled imperial lieutenant. Societies of like nature are said to have been organised in Italy. See Wigand's *Das Femgericht Westfalens* (Hamm. 1827), and Usener, *Die Frei- und heimlichen Gerichte Westfalens* (Frankf. 1832).

Fence (lit. 'that which defends' or 'guards'), a wall, hedge, or railing used for enclosing agricultural land, or for dividing it into fields. The F. most suitable for agricultural purposes consists of a rough stone dyke, but this form is only practicable in situations where stone is abundant and easily obtained. In many parts of Scotland most substantial and serviceable dykes are built from the boulders which have been removed from the fields they enclose. The lee side of a F. of this description affords excellent protection to cattle and sheep, while the F. occupies much less ground than hedges of any kind and needs no trimming. In England hedge fences are much more abundant than in Scotland, and their extent and abundance has occasioned great complaints of unnecessary waste of agricultural land. Hedges are most commonly formed of hawthorn, but the following trees and shrubs are also used:—Privet, beech, holly, crab-apple, barberry, furze, broom, maple, willow, yew, box, sweetbrier, and some others. To make and keep these living fences in an efficient condition, the plants require different methods of treatment according to their nature, and it is only in certain situations and conditions that some of them will succeed. Fences made of wooden rails and posts, or of shingles, are also very frequently employed in localities where wood is abundant and cheap, but in Great Britain it is now found to be much more economical to use fences of iron wire. These are made either entirely of iron, or the wire may be attached to wooden posts driven firmly into the ground. At certain intervals there are heavy straining posts, between which lighter posts sustain the various strands of wire in their proper relative positions. Where economy is not an object, strong fences of bar and rod iron built in short sections are employed.

Law regarding Fences.—Any one stealing any part of a live or dead F., or intentionally injuring it, is liable under statute for a first offence to a fine of £5, for a second offence to a year's imprisonment with hard labour. The Act does not apply to Scotland. In England a tenant is bound to keep fences in good repair, and with regard to them he must act according to rules of good husbandry. In Scotland a landlord is bound, without stipulation in the lease, to put fences on a farm in good repair on the entry of the tenant; but the tenant must maintain them and leave them in as good condition as when he received them. With regard to fences erected spontaneously by the tenant, it has been decided that if he is not entitled to remove them, he is not bound to repair them.

Fen'cible, a combatant or regiment of combatants levied to serve in defence of the country during a crisis, such as that of a threatened invasion. During the French war almost every country had its corps of 'Fencibles.' The name survives in the 'Royal Malta F. Artillery,' consisting in 1876–77 of 371 men of all ranks.

Fen'cing is the art of using the sword skilfully in attack or defence. It is one of the oldest of all modes of fighting, and was cultivated widely by the ancients. The Roman gladiators were well trained in handling the sword, but as they also defended themselves with armour and shields, their movements in fence were few and simple. As known in modern times, F. may be said first to have come into practice as the ponderous weapons and metal casings of feudalism were passing into disuse. During the religious wars of the Emperor Karl V., the prevailing sense of insecurity in Italy led to the general adoption of the small-sword as a safeguard by the civil classes. The Italians rapidly carried F. to great perfection, and subsequently introduced the art into Spain and France. A school was established for its prosecution in Paris, where fresh subtleties and improvements arose from day to day. The early Spanish and Italian schools generally drilled the fencer in the management of the dagger and the mantlet; to change position rapidly in avoiding attack was also regarded as necessary. But in more recent times all adjuncts were discarded in favour solely of the rapier, while the increased force and velocity of attack endangered the life of any one attempting to shift ground. As a ready and equable weapon, the rapier was long universally employed in Duelling (q. v.); and since the general abandonment of that practice, F. has continued to hold its ground firmly as an attractive, healthy pastime. In the modern exercise the Foil (q. v.) has supplanted the rapier, and the face of the fencer is defended by a strong wire mask. Space will only here permit of a description of the chief blows or thrusts and guards, together with a brief definition of the phrases in common use. The *guard* is the wary attitude which the swordsman most naturally assumes, advancing the right foot 24 inches in front of the left, slightly bending the knees, resting the weight of the body mainly on the left leg, and holding the foil extended at the height and in front of the breast. When on guard, it is essential, by supporting the foil over the right or left breast, to *cover* the side towards which the adversary's weapon points. The guard is a passive, the *parry* an active, defence. In F., the left arm, which is extended to the rear, is of great assistance in preserving the equilibrium. The *engagement* is the act of crossing foils. There are three engagements—(1) when the blades are brought in contact on the right side; (2) when on the left; and (3) when they cross obliquely from left to right, and the points are on a level with the groin. These may be changed rapidly, but from one or other of them all blows are made. The *blow* is the act of forcibly advancing the point towards one's antagonist either by simple thrust with the arm or by the heavier lunge, in which the right foot, and consequently the upper part of the body, is thrown quickly forward. There are three main points of attack. These are (1) the breast or, as it is called, the *inside;* (2) the face, on either side of the opponent's weapon, the *outside;* and (3) the body below the sword-arm, spoken of simply as *below.* Two of these points are always exposed, it only being possible to guard one at a time. To *parry,* which is done on the forte or part of the blade nearest the handle, is to divert the thrust of an antagonist's weapon. Ten guards are regarded as affording complete protection, and these are designated by the old French ordinal numbers—prime, seconde, tierce, quarte (carte), &c. Tierce, quarte, quinte, and six are called simple parries, only requiring the weapon to be slightly moved from guard. In prime, seconde, sept, and octave, which are called half-counters, the point describes a half-circle. The two remaining are known as counters, from the weapon having to sweep a complete circle in their execution. The counter has two advantages—(1) It cuts all the lines of attack in its ellipse, and (2) it throws the opponent's weapon to the side, leaving him exposed to a direct return blow. A *double counter* is a form of parry in which two rapid counters are made consecutively; it gives great command of the weapon, and should therefore enter regularly into practice. In assault, the *feint* is of great effect, being through all its modifications merely an attempt to throw one's adversary off his guard by illusive thrusts. The *riposte* is the name given to the blow with which one follows up a successful parry. A blow delivered at the flank of the antagonist when he menaces at the 'left' is called a *flanconade.* Fencers do not tierce, or carte, &c., at the same time, but A lunges while B guards. The motion of advancing and retreating is performed by rapidly withdrawing the left foot some 18 inches, and instantly following it with the other, and *vice versa.* One must retreat as the adversary advances, unless ready to offer him the sword-point. *Appels,* or beats with the right foot on the floor, and *glissades,* or glidings of one's weapon over the adversary's, are mainly intended to confuse and lay the enemy open to thrusts.

The cavalry sword exercise is only a modification of F. adapted to horseback, and the attack and defence with the foil is the basis for that of the sabre. Bayonet exercise, as another form of F., is cruder and clumsier, but extremely formidable. See A. & C. Black's *Army Book on F.*

Fén'élon, François de Salignac de la Mothe, a great French ecclesiastic, whose name is revered throughout Christendom, was born at Fénélon in Périgord, 6th August 1651. He was descended from the Marquis de la Mothe, a well-known diplomatist during the St. Bartholomew Massacre period. At the age of fifteen he passed from the college of Plessis to the seminary of St. Sulpice, where he took holy orders in 1675. He was then made superior of the 'New Catholics,' an institution patronised by Turenne for the edification of converts in the faith. Here he remained till 1691, composing his book *De l'Éducation des Filles* (1687), and joining in Bossuet's *promenades* and *conférences* at St. Germain. He also wrote a *Réfutation du Système de Malebranche sur la Nature et la Grâce,* revised by Bossuet, and a book against the *status* of Protestant ministers, which no doubt helped to pass the revocation of the Edict of Nantes. After that event he was sent with Fleury to convert in Poitou. In 1689 he was selected as tutor for the Duke of Burgundy, heir-presumptive to the crown, for whom he wrote his *Fables,* his *Dialogues des Morts,* and also the once famous *Les Aventures de Télémaque.* He was much in the good graces of Mme. de Maintenon, who consulted him about the rules of her new institution, St. Cyr. F. became successively abbé of St. Valery, near Amiens, and Archbishop of Cambray. Now begins his connection with Quietism. This was a form of spiritualism which aimed at producing a special kind of ecstatic existence in which all the daily duties of life would be performed, but everything with the immediate sense of God's presence. The tendency of this perpetual adoration was, however, to weaken the active powers. F. became acquainted with Mme. de Guyon and Father Lacombe, and did not share the dislike of Bossuet, Bourdaloue, and other eminent divines, for doctrines of 'pure love,' &c., which, whether within the compass of human nature or not, were hardly suited for a court of which De Maintenon was the head. On Mme. de Guyon's imprisonment, F. published his *Explication des Maximes des Saints* (1697), to show authority in the recognised Christian mystics for the gradual removal from the mind of the desire of reward and the fear of punishment. This Bossuet called 'fanaticism,' and the book was submitted to examination at Rome. After sixty-four congregations had met and discussed, the votes were discovered to be equal. In the meantime, the doctors of the French Sorbonne had condemned the book, and F. lost his pension and his post of royal teacher. While Bossuet damaged his cause by the offensive personalities contained in his *Account of Quietism,* the influence of the king easily procured from Innocent XII. a special verdict of the congregation of cardinals, setting forth twenty-three propositions in F.'s book as rash, scandalous, erroneous, &c. F. at once submitted but was never reconciled to the court, which soon after tried to suppress his *Télémaque.* This work had been stolen in MS. by a servant, and published without F.'s authority. Its success over a great part of Europe was immense. F.'s archiepiscopal life at Cambray was marked by strict performance of professional duty, and a simplicity of life and real sympathy with the poor very unusual in high dignitaries of the Church. One touching fact is that during the wars he was never molested, but equally revered by the hostile armies of English, German, and Dutch. F. was a man of great sweetness, piety, and dignity of character, and these fine qualities are always conspicuous in his writings. He was disinterested even to generosity in money matters, and zealous for the welfare of his Church. He desired that the rule forbidding the Scriptures to be read in the vernacular should be relaxed, at least in his diocese; and he defended the Jesuit missionaries from the charge of having adopted the superstitions of the Chinese. About 1702 the Jansenist war broke out again on the publication of the book called *Le Cas de Conscience.* F. took part in it on the side of the Church. He also wrote on political subjects, suggesting the revival of the States General (not as representative assemblies, but as royal councils, and denying the right of civil interference claimed for the Pope. F. died 7th January 1715. The most complete editions of F.'s *Œuvres* are those of Bausset (Par. 22 vols. 1821–24) and of Gosselin (10 vols. 1853). A favourite collection is that entitled *Œuvres Choisies de F.,* containing an *Éloge* by La Harpe and a biographical and critical sketch by Villemain (Par. 6 vols. 1825; new ed. 1829). The *Correspondance de F.,* from original documents, was published by Caron (Par. 11 vols. 1827–29). See Bausset's *Histoire de F.* (Par. 3 vols. 1808.)

Fenestell'a, a genus of *Polyzoa* (q. v.) including those forms familiarly known as 'lace corals,' from their close resemblance to delicate lace, although they have no relationship to the true Corals (q. v.). The species of F. are typically Palæozoic. They begin in the Lower Silurian rocks, and extend to the Permian series, but are most frequent in Carboniferous strata.

Fe'nian (so called from the mythical *Fionna Eirinn,* an Irish national militia, levied as early as 400 B.C., but which took its name from Finn or Fioun MacCumhail, the famous hero of Irish legend) is a national association, the main object of which, formerly kept secret, but now avowed, is to overthrow English rule in Ireland in favour of a native republic. This association, the origin of which is traced chiefly to the Irish famine of 1846–47, during which so many Irish were forced to emigrate, and to the insurrectionary movements of 1848, which increased the number of enforced exiles, was organised in America and Great Britain as a society for the restoration of Irish independence in 1859. The society was framed on the republican model. It consisted of social, district, and state 'circles,' each circle under the direction and control of a 'centre,' and the management of the whole organisation vested in a senate or 'congress.' F. congresses were held in Chicago in 1863, and in Cincinnati in 1865, and after the latter the order embraced 80,000 members in America. From this time the activity of the Fenians was unbounded, if for the most part ineffectual. In the United States several attempts were made in 1866 to invade Canada, which proved, however, ludicrous failures, and in 1867 an attempt, equally abortive, was made to create a revolution in Ireland. In September 1867 a number of daring leaders of the movement attacked a police van in Manchester, killed the officer in charge, and released the prisoners, who were under arrest for complicity in the late insurrection. The release of F. prisoners was the object of the attempt to break into Clerkenwell prison by blowing down its walls with gunpowder, an attempt attended with great destruction of life and property. At this period considerable excitement prevailed throughout England. A rising of the Irish was feared in London, and special constables were sworn in for the preservation of the peace. The number of suspected Fenians arrested from the 1st January 1867 to the 31st January 1868 was 265, of whom 95, including many most daring and influential offenders, had come from America, where having been engaged in the War of Secession, they refused to return to civil life. In May a party of 2000 invaded Canada from Vermont in the United States. They 'were ninety minutes on Canadian soil,' when they were driven back across the frontier with the loss of one man. At the close of the session of 1870 Mr. Gladstone granted an amnesty to the F. prisoners at Portland, on the condition that they should never return to the United Kingdom. In August 1871 a great meeting was held in Dublin to demand the release of the remaining F. prisoners, which resulted in a fight between the Fenians and the police, in which many persons received severe injuries. Subsequently several meetings took place for the same purpose, notably that of the 15th March 1874, when Mr. Disraeli was called to grant an amnesty to the forty prisoners then in gaol. Mr. Disraeli did not think it advisable to comply with the request; but since that date, by the natural expiry of the sentences, and by the escape early in 1876 of a number of prisoners from the convict settlement of Australia, the detention of prisoners for political offences has practically ceased to be an Irish grievance.

Fenn'ec (*Vulpes Zaarensis*), a species of Carnivorous Mammalia, belonging to the family *Canidæ* (q. v.) or Dogs (q. v.), and nearly allied to the foxes. It is also known by the name of 'Zerda,' and is found in Nubia and Egypt. Its average length is about 8 inches, and the colour is a pale fawn, the base and tip of the bushy tail being black. The F. is an active little animal, and appears to subsist, notwithstanding its carnivorous nature, almost entirely upon fruits. It inhabits burrows, which it excavates in sandy places. The fur is valued by the Arabs.

Fenn'el (*Fœniculum*), a genus of *Umbelliferous* plants belonging to the Harmless or Esculent section of the order. The common F. (*F. vulgare*) appears to have originally come from S. Europe. The fruit consists of a *cremocarp*, composed of two single-seeded portions or *achenes* united by their faces, and exhibiting a ribbed appearance. Common F. attains a height of 3 or 4 feet. It is a biennial plant, and its leaves are served with fish, either whole, or in the form of a sauce. Another species is sweet F. (*F. dulce*), also named Italian F. from being cultivated in S. Europe. It yields an aromatic, and *oil of F.* is obtained from it. Other species are Cape F. (*F. Capense*) of S. Africa, and the *F. panmorium* of India. The giant F. of S. Europe belongs to the genus *Ferula*.

Fennel.

Fenn'y (*Pheni*), a river of India which rises in the hill tracts of Chittagong, Bengal province, flows between Independent Tipperah and Noakolly district on the left bank and Chittagong district on the right bank, and falls into the N.E. corner of the Bay of Bengal. It brings down much hill produce, chiefly cotton, tobacco, and timber, which pays toll to the government. Near its mouth it divides into the Big and Little F.

Fens. See BEDFORD LEVEL.

Fen'ugreek (*Trigonella*), a genus of Exogenous plants included in the natural order *Leguminosæ* (q. v.), and in the *Papilionaceous* section of that group. The plant is distinguished by the appearance of the flowers, which have a small *carina* or keel, the *alæ vexillum*, together forming the most prominent parts of the flower. The leaves are obovate, and are stipulate. The common F. (*T. fœnum Græcum*) inhabits S. Europe, but is also largely cultivated in India. The name F., or 'Greek hay,' is derived from the fact that in Greece, as well as in India, it is used as fodder. The pods are cylindrical, and recently it has been stated that the seeds are exceedingly nutritious, and might with advantage be used as a dietary. *T. incisum* is a nearly-allied species also grown in India, and *T. esculenta* affords food in the latter country. *T. ornithopodioides* is a British species, which grows in sandy soil, generally near sea-coasts.

Fen'yes, Elek', a Hungarian geographer, was born at Csokaly, 7th July 1807, studied law at Debreczin and Presburg, and sat in the Presburg diet of 1830. He then devoted himself to geography and statistics, and settled at Pesth in 1836, where he became director of the Industrial Society, and editor of twc journals. During the Hungarian revolution he was appointed, in 1848, chief of the statistical department in the Ministry of the Interior. He was for some time president of the war tribunal at Pesth in 1849, and in the same year was imprisoned by the Austrians. He has since retired into private life. His works are comprehensive and accurate, and give the first reliable survey of Hungary. They were written in Magyar, but several of them have been translated into German. The chief are—*Magyarorszagnak's a hozzá kapcsolt Tartományoknak* ('State of Hungary and the Neighbouring Countries,' Pesth, 1839–40); *Magyar-ország Statistikaja* ('Statistics of Hungary,' Pesth, 1842–43); and *Közönségés Kezi's Iscolai Atlasz* ('General School Atlas,' Pesth, 1845).

Fe'odor (the Russian form of *Theodore*, Gr. 'Gift of God') is the name of three czars.—**Feodor I.**, son of Ivan the Terrible, was born 11th May 1557, succeeded to the throne in 1587, but left the government to his brother-in-law, Boris Godunov. He died 7th January 1598, the last of the race of Rurik.—**Feodor II.**, son of Boris Godunov, reigned only for a short time, being murdered 10th June 1605. To him succeeded the first of the 'false Dimitris.'—**Feodor III.**, the son of the Czar Alexei, was born in May 1661, and ruled from 1676 to his death, 26th April 1682. He warred with varying success against the Turks and Poles. In his reign the first learned academy was founded in Russia. F. was succeeded by his brother, the famous Peter the Great.

Feodo'sia. See KAFFA.

Feoff'ment, in English law, is a grant of lands to another in fee, to him and his heirs for ever, by the actual delivery of seisin. The granter is called the *Feoffer*, he that receives is the *Feoffee*. It is the oldest form of conveyance of real property. *Livery of Seisin* is the feudal investiture on delivery of the possession of the land or tenement to another, by giving him in the former case a piece of turf from it, or twig of a tree grown on it; in the latter case, by giving the latch or key, or by some similar act. The formality has been superseded by deed of grant under 8 and 9 Vict. c. 106.

Feoffment to Uses was an artifice of the clergy to avoid the prohibitions against Mortmain (q. v.). The feudal form was applied so as to give the possession to some one as a trustee for the Church or for an ecclesiastic. The evasion was regarded favourably by the judge of the Chancery Court, who in those days was usually a priest. See USE, USES AND TRUSTS. In Scotch law, see INFEFTMENT, SASINE.

Fer'æ Natu'ræ, a term applied in English law to all kinds of beasts and birds which do not become tame or domesticated. According to Roman law these became the property of any one catching them, though it was held that no one was entitled to enter the ground of another in the chase. But a trespasser who caught his game was held to be entitled to keep it, though liable in damage to the proprietor of the land on which he trespassed. In England if *game* be found in the possession of any one trespassing, he may, under statute, be required to deliver it to the person having the right, or to his servant or gamekeeper; and if delivery be refused, the game may be taken forcibly. But the statute does not apply to animals which are not game. (See GAME LAWS.) Curious questions of common law arise as to the right of property in animals F. N. For example, the question came before the supreme Scotch law court some years ago as to the right of property in a whale which, having been harpooned by one party, had broken the attached rope, and been subsequently secured by another whaling party. Eskimo witnesses were fully examined as to local custom, and decision was given, we believe, in favour of the actual captors. A swarm of bees, if it can be identified, belongs to the owner of the parent hive. See FORESTS, SALMON-FISHING, TROUT-FISHING.

Fer de Lance (*Craspedocephalus lanceolatus*), a well-known and most virulent species of Viperine snakes, included in the Rattlesnake (q. v.) family (*Crotalidæ*). It inhabits Brazil and some islands of the W. Indies, and is commonly found in sugar plantations. A large pit exists in each side of the head between the eye and nostril, as in other members of the family *Crotalidæ*. The usual length is 5 to 6 feet. The colour is olive above, with cross markings of darker hue, and whitish grey below, the head being of a brown colour. The tail has no 'rattle,' but is provided with a spinous process. The bite of the snake is fatal usually within a few hours; and even where recovery takes place, the effects of the poison may persist for long periods.

Fer'dinand, a name borne by the sovereigns of various European countries.

German Emperors.—**Ferdinand I.**, the second son of Philip the Handsome, Archduke of Austria and King of Castile, was born at Alcala, in Spain, in 1503. He married Anna, daughter of Ladislas VI.; and on the death of his brother-in-law, Ludwig II., at Mohacz, in 1526, he added the thrones of Bohemia and Hungary to the Austrian archduchy and the palatinate of Upper Alsace. His possession in right of his wife was, however, disputed by John Zapolya of Transylvania, seconded by Suleiman II. A long war was closed by the peace of Gross Waradein in 1538, but renewed by John Sigismund on his father's death. Named King of the Romans in 1531, F. became emperor in 1558 on the abdication of his brother Karl V. He was the last King of the Romans, or emperor elect, crowned at Aachen on the marble throne found in the tomb of Karl the Great. F., who had before oppressed the Calixtines and Lutherans in Bohemia, now urged the latter unsuccessfully to join the Council of Trent. He tried to get the double cup and priests' marriage from Pius IV., but failed. He died 25th July 1564. See Buchholz, *Gesch. der Regierung Kaiser F.'s I.* (10 vols. 1830–41).—His grandson, **Ferdinand II.**, born at Gratz, 9th July 1578, was the son of Archduke Karl of Carinthia and Styria, and Maria of Bavaria. He became King of Bohemia (1617) and Hungary (1618), and succeeded his cousin Matthias as emperor in 1619. His Ultramontane tendencies were well known, and there was a great revolt under Count Thorn in Bohemia, helped by Bethlen-Gabor and the Hungarians, Moravians, and Silesians. The siege of Vienna was raised, but with the approval of the Protestant Union the Bohemians elected as king Friedrich, the Elector Palatine. With the help of the Catholic League, especially of Johann Georg, Elector of Saxony, F.'s general Tilly crushed the Bohemians. The Charter of Rudolf II. was destroyed; the Reformed preachers sent out of the country, and with them thousands of the inhabitants. The alliance of Christian IV. of Denmark was, in spite of the bravery of Brunswick and Mansfield, overturned by Wallenstein, and the Peace of Lubeck (1629) was followed by the Edict of Restitution, directing the property of the Catholic clergy to be given back by the nobles, who had seized it so long ago as 1555, and excluding Protestants from the Peace of Religion. Now, however, Gustavus Adolphus was in the field, nor did the Catholic nobility relish the idea of restitution. Therefore, though Lutzen (1632) was soon followed by Nordlingen (1634), which left the Swedes almost alone in the cause of religious freedom, this edict was never properly carried out. F. died 15th February 1637. See Hurter, *Gesch. Kaisers F. II.* (11 vols. 1850–64).—**Ferdinand III.**, son of preceding, born at Gratz, 11th July 1608, succeeded his father on his imperial and royal thrones. He reluctantly continued the war against the Swedes, now backed by Richelieu, who wished to weaken the Hapsburg house. The preliminaries of Hamburg, ratified by the Congress of Münster and Osnabrück, at last led to the Peace of Westphalia (1648), just when the Swiss Wrangel had entered Prague. F. died 2d April 1657. A reform of the judicial arrangements in Germany took place during his reign. See Koch, *Gesch. des Deutsch. Reichs unter F. III.* (vol. i. 1865.)

'Emperors' of Austria.—**Ferdinand I.** (Karl Leopold Franz Marcellin), eldest son of the Emperor Franz I. and Maria Theresia of Naples, was born at Vienna, 19th April 1793. He was sickly in mind and body. In 1830 he was crowned *Rex Junior* of Hungary, and next year married Maria, daughter of Victor Emmanuel of Sardinia. Succeeding his father in 1835, he left foreign affairs in the hands of Metternich, but published an amnesty for political offences in Lombardy. The insurrection in Galicia was followed by the revolutionary movement of 1847–49. F. promised a constitution, dismissed Metternich, and then in 1848 abdicated in favour of his nephew, Franz Joseph. Roads and railways were largely constructed in Austria under F.'s influence. He died 29th June 1875.

Kings of Aragon or Castile. (1) *Aragon.*—**Ferdinand I.**, the Upright, King of Aragon and Sicily, the son of Juan I. of Castile, was born in 1373. His disinterested treatment of his nephew, Juan II. of Castile, and his successes against the Moors (especially in taking the city of Antequera), secured his election from a number of competitors to the throne of Aragon in 1412. His intervention in Sicily on behalf of Blanca, widow of Martin I., was marked by the same spirit of justice and courage; and in the Church he exerted himself on the side of peace, entreating Benedict XIII. to retire, and so end the schism. F. died in 1416, and was succeeded by his son, Alfonso V. the Wise. (2) *Castile.*—**Ferdinand I.**, the Great, was a son of Sancho III., King of Navarre, who first liberated Castile from the rule of Bermuda, or Veremund, III. of Leon. F. afterwards annexed Leon and Asturias to Castile. He confirmed the ancient *fueros* of the people, and collected the code of Visigothic law. A victory gained over his brother on the 'Field of Murder' confined the power of Navarre to a territory beyond the Ebro. F. then made a brilliant campaign against the Moors. He was the founder of Castile, and styled himself Emperor. This alarmed Heinrich the Swart, German Emperor, and the Pope was called in. The 'Cid' belonged to this reign. F. died in 1065.—**Ferdinand III.**, the Pious, was born in 1199, succeeded his mother as sovereign of Castile in 1217, and his father, Alfonzo IX., as King of Leon in 1230. He suppressed the revolt of the Lara family in Castile, and then attacking the Moors in Andalusia, captured Cordova in 1236. Twelve years later Seville fell, and the Emir of Granada was compelled to pay tribute. F. died in 1252. He burned the Albigenses who had fled to him for protection, but did much to check lawlessness, and founded the famous University of Salamanca. The Archbishop Rodrigo Ximenes of Toledo wrote his biography, *Cronica del Santo Rey Don F. III.*—**Ferdinand IV.**, the son of Sancho IV., the Brave, reigned over Castile from 1295 to 1312. A great war with Portugal and Aragon, each supporting a claimant to the crown, in which the heroic Perez de Guzman fought for F., was ended by double royal alliances. In his Moorish campaigns (1305–6) F. captured Gibraltar. He was on good terms with Pope Clement V., who gave him the right to levy a tithe on Church property, and to confiscate the property of the Templar order.

Kings of Spain.—**Ferdinand V.** of Aragon, known as F. the Catholic, born 10th March 1452, was the son of Juan II., King of Navarre and Aragon. In 1468 F. was declared by his father King of Sicily, and next year, in spite of the rivalry of Alfonso V. of Portugal and Louis XI. of France, he married Isabella, Princess of Asturias, daughter of Juan II. and sister of Enrique IV. of Castile. After some years skirmishing with the French, the death of Enrique (probably by poison) permitted F. and his wife to assume the royal power in Castile. A powerful party was formed against them by the Infanta Juana *Beltraneja*, or the Bastard, daughter of Enrique, who was affianced to

Alfonso V. F. soon routed the Portuguese army at Toro, and drove the French from Roussillon. The Pope having recalled the dispensation for the marriage of Juana and Alfonso, peace was made in 1479. Internal peace was also in great measure restored by the institution in towns and villages of the *Santa Hermandad* ('holy association'), half militia, half police, to suppress crime in each district. This incidentally weakened the powers of the feudal nobility. The consolidation of the Spanish monarchy was inaugurated in Castile by the abolition of franchises and the imposition of taxes. In 1481, with the approval of Pope Sixtus IV., F. started the Inquisition, nominally to punish those Jews and Moors in Andalusia who, having taken Christian baptism, were secretly practising their old religion, but quite as much that he might strike his political enemies in the dark. Owing to the divisions among the Moors, Muley Abul Hassan and Boabdil both claiming their allegiance, it was comparatively easy for Gonzalvo of Cordova to subdue Granada. After ten years' fighting, in 1492 the Spanish dominion was assured, the Moorish claims being renounced on condition that the Moorish inhabitants should be allowed the exercise of their religion. This agreement was afterwards broken. To the great hurt of Spanish commerce, the Jews, numbering, it is said, 800,000, were also expelled from Spain, except those who accepted baptism. The policy of F. was ably carried out by his minister, Cardinal Ximenes, and the glory of his reign enhanced by the expedition of Columbus. Queen Isabella by her will left Castile to Juana the Foolish, wife of Philip the Handsome, Archduke of Austria, F. to be regent. Philip, by an armed demonstration, forced F. to resign the regency, but soon after died, and F. reobtained the regency. Always zealous for the Church, F. now made two successful expeditions into Africa, where he was acknowledged by Tunis, Algiers, and Tripoli, and also lent assistance to Pope Julius II., who suffered a heavy defeat at Ravenna. The conquest of Navarre left him master of the whole of Spain. He died at Madrigalejo, January 23, 1516. See Prescott's *History of the Reign of F. and Isabella of Spain* (1838). —**Ferdinand VII.**, born 14th October 1784, was the son of Charles IV. of Spain and Maria Louisa of Parma. Weak in mind and body, he was entirely led by his tutor Escoiquiz, who gradually formed a party round the young prince hostile to the minister Godoy (q. v.) and the queen-mother, and therefore favourable to British influences. His young wife, Maria Antonietta of Naples, died in 1806; Escoiquiz was removed from court; and for some time F. lived in wretched solitude. He then began to correspond with Napoleon. This being discovered, he was tried in the famous case at the Escurial, and all his accomplices (whose names he confessed) were exiled. The French, however, entered Spain, the Spanish troops revolted at Aranjuez, Godoy fled, Charles IV. abdicated, and F. was proclaimed king under the auspices of Murat, stationed at Madrid. Still desiring French protection, F. foolishly met Napoleon at Bayonne in 1808, the result being that it was declared the Bourbons had ceased to rule in Spain; Joseph Bonaparte became king, and F. was sent to Talleyrand's house at Valençay, where he behaved in the most undignified manner. He had, in fact, sold his country's honour for a promise of Navarre and £32,000 a year. Although Joseph reintroduced the Cortes, he could not pacify the country; guerilla leaders appeared in almost every district, and after six years' fighting F. was at the end of 1813 sent back as king on condition that he would drive out the English. The Cortes made it a further condition that he should sign the moderately Liberal constitution which had been proclaimed at Cadiz in 1812. This F. repudiated by the Valentia Decree (4th May 1814). The document was applauded by the Absolute (*Netto*) or Servilest party, and a reign of terror and darkness began in Spain. The Inquisition was recalled, and education formally put in the hands of the Jesuits; and only by the intervention of Britain were the members of the late Cortes saved from death, many of them being sent to the galleys instead. At last, in 1820, the army revolted and proclaimed the Constitution of 1812, which F. swore to observe. This constitution did not guarantee religious liberty to any extent. The king did everything in his power to enfeeble the government, refusing his *veto* without reason, and dismissing ministers whenever the Cortes met. In 1823 Louis XVIII., acting on the principles of the Holy Alliance, sent 100,000 men to the help of F. The result was that the Cortes retreated to Cadiz and dissolved, and F. at once proceeded to declare null all the solemn acts of three years. Even the advice of ultra-royalist laymen was despised by this absolute king, and in 1826 there was an *auto-da-fé* at Valencia! In 1829 F. married his fourth wife, Maria Christina of Naples, on whose suggestion he issued the decree, which has cost Spain so much blood, that women may succeed to the throne. F. died 29th September 1833. See *Memoirs of F.*, translated by Quin (Lond. 1824).

Sovereigns in Italy.—(1) *Tuscany.*—**Ferdinand I.** of Medici, third Grand Duke of Tuscany, born in 1549, was a son of Cosmo the Great. He was made a cardinal by Pius IV., and succeeded his brother Francisco in 1587. F. energetically suppressed the Tuscan brigands under Piccolomini, and with the help of the Knights of St. Stephen he cleared the Italian coast of the Moslem pirates, whom he pursued to Cyprus and Africa. His policy was that of friendship to France, for he saw Spain threatening the liberties of Italy. He therefore lent large sums to Henri IV., and sowed discord between Pope Sixtus V. and Olivares, the ambassador of Philip II. F. also had friendly relations with the Protestant princes in Germany, and the Jews and other heretics expelled from Spain found a refuge in Leghorn. Dying in 1609, he left enormous wealth to his son Cosmo.—**Ferdinand III.**, born at Florence, 6th May 1769, was the son of the Grand Duke Pietro Leopold, who became German Emperor in 1791. F. was the first Italian sovereign who recognised the French republic in 1793. In spite of this, a provisional republican government was set up in Florence, which lasted till Suwarrow drove Moreau and Macdonald from Italy. After Marengo, when Tuscany was converted into the kingdom of Etruria, F. retired to Vienna, where, as Elector of Würzburg, he was admitted into the Confederation of the Rhine. In 1814 he returned, and spent his remaining years in carrying out a humane and liberal policy. He opened up communications and organised public schools, and Tuscany was not disgraced by those harsh and secret proceedings against *Carbonari* which were seen in other Italian states. He died 17th June 1824.

(2) *Naples.*—**Ferdinand I.**, born in 1423, was the natural son of Alfonso V. the Magnanimous, of Aragon, who bequeathed Naples to F., Sicily with Aragon going to Juan. Though Pope Nicholas V. had bound himself to recognise F., Calixtus III. refused the investiture on the ground that F. was born of adultery. By a bull he also forbade recognition by any other state. The next pope, Pius II., was, however, bribed to keep his predecessor's word by the gift of the town of Beneventum. The turbulent barons, the Count Piccinino, Jean d'Anjou, Duke of Calabria (whom Charles VII. of France had made Governor of Genoa), and the Prince of Tarentum, made war on F. in 1460, and gained a decisive victory near Nola in that year. This was compensated by the victory of Troja in 1462, for which F. was indebted to Scanderbeg of Albania. In 1480 F. retook the town of Otranto from Mohammed II. He died 25th January 1494. —**Ferdinand II.** was the son of Alfonso II., and the grandson of the preceding. When Charles VIII. marched into Italy, F., deserted by Trivulzio, was beaten at Faenza and San Germano (1495) by D'Aubigny and Armagnac, and compelled to retire to Sicily. Next year the influence of F. the Catholic in the Holy League caused the French evacuation of Naples, and the re-entry of F. He died 7th October 1496.—**Ferdinand IV.** (after 1817, First of the Kingdom of the Two Sicilies), born at Naples, 12th January 1751, was the son of Don Carlos, afterwards Charles III. of Spain. He was brought up to know nothing of public affairs, and the government was one long dispute between Tanucci, the minister, and the queen, Maria Caroline, Archduchess of Austria and a daughter of Maria Theresa. The vacillating policy of F. through the wars of the French republic met a proper end in the complete defeat of General Mack by the French in 1798, which caused the king to seek refuge on board Nelson's fleet. The population of Naples fought with desperate bravery against the disciplined troops of France, but the upper classes received them well, and tried to form a Parthenopean Republic. This exciting period has been described in Colletta's *History of Naples*, and in *Sketch of Popular Tumults* (Lond. 1837). Next year, Cardinal Ruffo and the Calabrian peasants besieged the republic in Naples, and finally F. re-entered his capital, having promised an amnesty which was at once violated by the most sweeping measures of political oppression, and unlicensed cruelty. In 1801 he arranged that a French army should again occupy part of his kingdom, and in 1805 he permitted a large army of British and Russians to land. This brought down Massena and 30,000 men, who drove out F.,

established Joseph Bonaparte, and subdued the country, except in Calabria, where opposition lingered for many years. (See Botta, *History*, book xx.) F. and the queen remained in Sicily, protected by the English fleet, till 1815, when F. resumed royal authority at Naples. In 1820 a revolt, inspired by the *Carbonari* societies, broke out. F. granted the same constitution as the Spanish Cortes had just obtained, but soon after went to a congress of the northern powers at Laybach, and returned with an Austrian army sent expressly to get rid of the troublesome constitution. He died 4th January 1825. His daughter Amelia married Louis Philippe.—**Ferdinand V.** (Second of the Two Sicilies), better known as 'Bomba,' born 12th January 1810, was the son of Francisco I., and grandson of the preceding. He began political life in 1830 by dismissing Viglia, Scaletta, and others from office, and carrying out a scheme of economy in the court and the public service. Unhappily his second marriage with Maria Theresa Isabella, daughter of the Archduke Karl, brought him more under Austrian influence. He introduced the Jesuits into Sicily, and suppressed the ancient constitution of the island. In 1840 he had a serious quarrel with Britain about the sulphur trade. The natural result of these arbitrary acts was repeated insurrection, which was cruelly punished. Ricciotti was the most popular of the leaders. The impulse of the election of Pius IX., 'the reforming pope,' at last gave to Sicily a constitution substantially the same as that of France in 1830. The example was followed on the mainland, and General Pepe marched northwards to assist the Lombards. But suddenly, on 15th May 1848, F. dissolved the Chambers, recalled everything, and by the battle of Custozza destroyed Sicily's last hope of independence. Then followed the state of things described in Mr. Gladstone's Letters—Mazza's Commission of Bastonnades, and every form of injustice. F. died 22d May 1859.

Ferenti'no, a town of Central Italy, 42 miles E.S.E. of Rome, on the Neapolitan Railway. F. is on the site of the ancient *Ferentinum*, and has a cathedral and remains of old Cyclopean walls and Roman buildings. Pop. 9096.

Fer'guson, Adam, a Scotch philosopher and author of eminence, was born at Logierait, Perthshire, 20th June 1723, and was educated for the Church at St. Andrews and Edinburgh Universities. After being for a short time chaplain to the 42d Regiment, during which he showed great gallantry at the battle of Fontenoy (1745), he settled in Edinburgh, where he became in succession Keeper of the Advocates' Library, Professor of Natural Philosophy, and (1764) Professor of Moral Philosophy. He wrote, besides other works, *Essay on the History of Civil Society* (1767), a reply to Dr. Price's work on the same subject, which resulted in his being sent out as secretary to the commission that attempted (1778-79) to bring to a peaceful close the quarrel between the American colonies and the mother country; *Institutes of Moral Philosophy* (1769); *History of the Progress and Termination of the Roman Republic* (1784), the most popular of his works, and translated almost immediately after its appearance into French and German; and *Principles of Moral and Political Science* (1792). F. died at St. Andrews, February 22, 1816.

Ferguson Bequest, The, was founded by John Ferguson of Cairnbrock, a native of Irvine, in Ayrshire, Scotland, where he died, January 8, 1856, aged sixty-nine. He left upwards of a million and a quarter sterling. Besides legacies for public purposes amounting to nearly £100,000, from one of which the Ferguson scholarships have been founded, he designed the residue of his estate, about £400,000, to form the permanent bequest fund. Its object is to aid in the erection of churches and schools, in supplementing the stipends of ministers and the salaries of missionaries and teachers of schools, and in maintaining public libraries. The benefits are confined to *quoad sacra* Established churches, Free, United Presbyterian, and Congregational churches. The annual income is upwards of £16,000. The fund is administered by trustees incorporated by Act of Parliament.

Ferguson, James, F.R.S., was born at Keith, Banffshire, 1710. Of poor parentage and little education, he early showed his mechanical talent in the construction of a wooden watch; and when engaged in tending his master's sheep spent his ample leisure time in contriving machines during the day, and in studying and mapping the stars at night. He thus attracted the attention of influential neighbours, who aided him in his mathematical studies and enabled him to go to Edinburgh, where he gained a livelihood by miniature-portrait drawing. In 1743 he removed to London, received a pension of £50 in 1760, became a Fellow of the Royal Society in 1763, and died November 16, 1776. His principal works are *Astronomy Explained on Sir Isaac Newton's Principles* (1756); *Lectures in Mechanics, Hydrostatics, Pneumatics, and Optics* (1760); *Select Mechanical Exercises* (1773); *The Art of Drawing in Perspective* (1775)—besides several papers in the *Philosophical Transactions*. Sir David Brewster re-edited several of his works. See F.'s Autobiography, prefixed to his *Select Mechanical Exercises*.

Ferguson or **Fergusson, Robert**, a poet, born at Edinburgh, September 5, 1751. He was educated at Dundee and at St. Andrews University, became clerk in an Edinburgh attorney's, and published several poems in the Scottish dialect which won considerable fame. Being thus led into society, he ruined his health by dissipation, and died insane, October 16, 1774. His poetry has a strain of pleasant fancy and humour, and is written in pure Lowland Scotch. Burns called F. his 'elder brother in the Muses,' and is said to have taken his idea of *The Cottar's Saturday Night* from *The Farmer's Ingle* of F. See F.'s works, with a biography by Dr. Irving (Glasg. 1813).

Fergusson, Sir William, Bart., F.R.S., a distinguished surgeon, was born at Prestonpans, East Lothian, March 20, 1808. Educated at Lochmaben grammar-school and at the High School and University of Edinburgh, he became assistant to Dr. Knox and Dr. Turner in the Edinburgh College of Surgeons, of which institution he was made a Licentiate in 1828 and a Fellow in 1829; began to lecture on surgery in 1831, was made Assistant-Surgeon in the Royal Infirmary in 1836, Fellow of the Royal Society, Edinburgh, in 1839, and Professor of Surgery in King's College, London, in 1840. F. was for five years Examiner in Surgery at London University, was made a baronet in 1865, and President of the Royal College of Surgeons of England in 1870. He is now Professor of Clinical Surgery at King's College, London, is a Fellow of the Royal Society of London, and consulting surgeon to various hospitals. F. has written several treatises on lithotomy, aneurism, &c., and an admirable *System of Practical Surgery*. He has also invented many surgical instruments.

Feriæ (probably for *fesiæ*, from *festus*) were days of rest, holidays in which all business (especially litigation) was suspended. F. were either private or public, according as their observance was limited to families and individuals or extended to the general community. Occasions for the former class of F. were found on birthdays. The public F. were of three kinds—*Stativæ*, observed regularly every year on a fixed day, such as the Lupercalia; the *conceptivæ*, observed regularly every year, but on days fixed from year to year by the priests or magistrates, such as the *F. Latinæ*; and *imperativæ*, days fixed by the magistrates for supplication or thanksgiving, in connection with some national event. On the F. the people generally visited the temples, and offered prayers and sacrifices, and were strictly prohibited from performing any kind of work. In Old Scotch, *ferial* (also *feryale* or *feriell* tymes) denoted the immunity from prosecution secured during *harvest*, as if every day of it had been devoted to religion.

Ferin'ghees, a name applied by Mohammedans to Christians generally, and derived from the 'Franks' or 'French.' In India it is appropriated to the descendants of the early Portuguese settlers, born of native women, who have retained the Roman Catholic faith, but have in all other respects, even in colour, sunk to the condition of the surrounding native population. They are especially numerous in the neighbourhood of Dacca and Chittagong, and are chiefly employed as cultivators and domestic servants.

Ferish'ta or **Firish'ta, Mohammed Kasim Hindu Shah**, a Persian historian, born at Astrabad about 1570. His father travelled to Ahmednuggur in the Dekkhan, and was there made tutor to Miran Hassein, the son of Murteza Nizam Shah. F. was patronised by Murteza and Miran, and on the latter's death repaired to Bijapur, where he was highly honoured by Ibrahim Adil Shah II., and where he devoted himself to his *Tarikhi*

Firishta, or history of the Mohammedans in India. He is supposed to have died about 1612. F.'s history consists of twelve books, is clear and impartial, but takes no notice of the institutions and social state of the people. It is very popular in India, where it has completely obscured the histories on which it was founded. The work was published at Bombay in 1831, edited by J. Briggs, who issued a translation of the whole (Lond. 1832).

Ferman'agh (Ir. Gael. 'the men of Monagh,' or from *Feor-magh-eanagh*, 'the country of the lakes'), a county in the W. of Ulster, Ireland, has an area of 715 sq. miles, and a pop. (1871) of 92,794, being a decrease of 12,974 since 1861, which is accounted for principally by emigration. F. is mostly covered with wild mountains (composed chiefly of limestones and sandstones of the Old Red Sandstone period) and a network of lakes and streams, but contains rich arable land and strips of fine wood and undulating pastures. In the central depression of the uplands lie the great Lakes Erne (q. v.). The chief summits are Dowbally, 2188 feet, and Slieve Baught, 1812 feet. The Erne and its tributaries are the principal rivers. In 1871 there were 106,530 acres under tillage, 243,251 in pasture, 5909 of plantation, and 55,248 of mountain, bog, and waste. Oats and dairy produce are the chief exports. Enniskillen is the chief town. The county proper returns two members to Parliament, and is traversed by the North-Western Railway.

Fer'mat, Pierre de, a French mathematician, was born at Beaumont-de-Lomagne, near Montauban, in August 1601, and spent the most of his life as an advocate at Toulouse, where he died in January 1665. He shares with Pascal the honour of having invented the calculus of probabilities, and in his method for finding maxima and minima anticipated the differential calculus; but his reputation rests chiefly upon his ingenious investigations into the properties of numbers. A collection of his works was published by his son Samuel in 1679, at Toulouse.

Ferma'ta, in music, the name of the pause, usually indicated by the sign 𝄐.

Fermenta'tion (from the Lat. *fermento*, and that from *fervere*, 'to boil') originally signified the boiling or bubbling up of a substance attended with disengagement of gas, and not produced by the action of heat; and in this sense it was employed by the alchemists and early chemists to denote such chemical changes as the solution of metals in acids, &c. The term now, however, has a different signification, and may be defined as the decomposition or change of an organic substance in a definite manner, produced by the action of another organic substance, which does not itself suffer any change, nor lose any of its own material during the process. The latter substance is termed a *ferment*. Fermentations may be divided into two kinds:—(1) Those in which the ferment possesses a definite organised structure, and is, in fact, a plant (or possibly in some cases an animal); (2) those in which the ferment is not organised, but consists of a small quantity of an azotised substance, very often occurring along with the fermentable material. In many instances mineral substance may be substituted for the ferment of the latter order, which is sometimes called a *false ferment*. As an example of the first or true F., the conversion of sugar into alcohol—the *vinous* F.—may be instanced. This is produced by adding to a dilute solution of sugar a small quantity of yeast, and maintaining the mixture at a temperature of from 21°–26° C. Shortly after the addition of the yeast, bubbles of gas begin to be disengaged, and the yeast rapidly increases in quantity, new cells being produced by a process of budding. This action continues until the whole of the sugar is decomposed. The chief products of this F. are alcohol and carbonic acid, the latter being the gaseous substance which causes the frothing, or, as it is technically called, the *working* of the mixture. The change which occurs in the sugar may be represented by a chemical equation thus—

$$\underbrace{C_6H_{12}O_6}_{\text{Grape sugar.}} = \underbrace{2CO_2}_{\text{Carbonic acid.}} + \underbrace{2C_2H_6O}_{\text{Alcohol.}}$$

It should be observed, however, that although alcohol and carbonic acid are undoubtedly the chief products of the decomposition of the sugar, yet small quantities of several other substances are formed, of which higher homologues of alcohol, glycerine, and succinic acid may be mentioned. Another familiar instance of F. is the souring of milk. This is due to the conversion of the sugar present in milk into lactic acid, and is also brought about by the action of a special organised ferment, differing, however, entirely from the yeast plant. Its spores are introduced into the milk either from the atmosphere, or by contact with vessels which are already contaminated with them. Milk undoubtedly grows sour more rapidly in a dairy than elsewhere, no doubt from the great number of the spores of the lactic ferment present. The change attending the conversion of sugar into lactic acid may be represented as follows:—

$$\underbrace{C_6H_{12}O_6}_{\text{Grape sugar.}} = \underbrace{2C_3H_6O_3}_{\text{Lactic acid.}}$$

Of the fermentations produced by the action of a non-organised ferment, the conversion of starch into dextrin, and eventually into dextrose, may be mentioned. The ferment in this case is Diastase (q. v.), a substance produced during the germination of grain. (See BEER.) Another very remarkable instance is the change brought about by the action of emulsine on Amygdaline (q. v.), both of which substances occur in the bitter almond.

Fermented and Distilled Drink, Consumption of. There are no means available of obtaining any reliable estimate of the quantity of alcoholic beverages made and consumed throughout the world; but as in one form or other such drinks are habitually consumed in all nations, the grand total must be prodigious. From customs and excise returns a fairly accurate statement of the consumption within Great Britain and Ireland can be framed. In the seventy years lapsed from 1801 to 1871 the population of the United Kingdom almost doubled itself; while in the same period the ostensible consumption of spirits of all kinds rose from 8,800,840 gallons to 29,151,000. The quantity of malt charged with duty in 1801 was 19,643,345 bushels, and in the year ending March 1871 it reached 52,929,000 bushels. These figures would appear to indicate a very serious increase in the drink consumed in Great Britain, but they must be regarded as quite untrustworthy, seeing to what a great extent smuggling prevailed during the early part of the century. The returns for the forty years from 1830 to 1870 afford a fairer basis of contrast, and show upon the whole a decline from 1·16 gallons to 0·95 gallons per head. In the case of Scotland the decrease is very marked, amounting to over 30 per cent., thus indicating a great change in national habits. The quantity of malt charged with duty in the United Kingdom in 1830 was 32,962,000 bushels, equal to 1·62 bushels per head; and in 1871 it had risen to 52,929,392, representing still only 1·68 bushels per head. The individual consumption of malt liquors has thus remained practically stationary over a period of forty-one years. On the other hand, the consumption of wine has increased enormously, and that increase has principally taken place since the rearrangement of the wine-duties in connection with the French Commercial Treaty of 1860. The home consumption of wine, which in 1851 was 6,280,653 gallons, and in 1859 was very little more, had by the year 1869 risen to 14,168,321 gallons, the greater part of the increase consisting of light non-alcoholic French wines. The total quantity of *all* kinds of wine retained for home consumption in 1874 amounted to 17,284,242 gallons. See *Journal of the London Statistical Society* (1872).

Fermented Liquors are alcoholic beverages prepared by the fermentation of infusions of starchy or saccharine substances. A few F. L. are enumerated under the head BEER, but that most extensively consumed throughout the world is wine, which is fermented from the juice of the grape. Cider and perry are fermented from the apple and pear respectively, toddy from the sap of various palm-trees, and Mexican pulque from the *Agave Americana*. There is, however, scarcely a juicy fruit or vegetable sap from which alcoholic beverages may not be prepared. All alcoholic drinks may be divided into (1) F. L.; (2) spirits distilled from fermented infusions or saps; and (3) *liqueurs*, which are sweetened and aromatised spirits, or spirits simply aromatised.

Fer'mo (anc. *Firmum*), a town of Central Italy, in the province of Ascoli-Piceno, 4 miles from the Adriatic, and 30 miles

S.E. of Ancona. It is circled by old walls, and has a cathedral and several churches and convents, is the seat of an archbishop, and has some trade in corn, wool, and silk, chiefly carried on by the small harbour, Porto F. Pop. 8011.

Fermoy' (Ir. Gael. *Feara-muighe*, 'men of the plains'), a town of Cork, in the rich and beautiful valley of the Blackwater, 18 miles N.E. of Cork. It lies on the highroad from Cork to Dublin, and is the E. terminus of the Great Southern and Western Railway. F. stands on both sides of the Blackwater, which is here spanned by a new stone bridge. It is an important military station. The chief buildings are the barracks, for 2700 troops, the Roman Catholic cathedral, the banks, and the parish church. There is some trade in agricultural produce. Pop. (1871) 7611.

Fern, Male, the old botanical name still retained to designate the *Lastræa filix-mas*, a species of ferns, the fronds or leaves of which are bipinnate in form, the pinnules or secondary fronds being oblong and serrated. This species is common enough in Britain, and obtains its importance from its root-stem or *rhizome* being used in medicine as an anthelmintic, or remedy for tapeworm. The rhizome may attain the length of a foot.

Fern, Sweet (*Comptonia asplenifolia*), a species of plants belonging not to the Fern order (*Filices*), but to the *Myricaceæ* or Gale order, the plants of which have generally aromatic, tonic, and astringent properties. S. F. is used in N. America as an antidote to diarrhœa. Its bark is aromatic and astringent, and its leaves possess a glandular structure.

Fernan'do de Nor'onha, a wooded island, about 8 miles long, in the S. Atlantic, 220 miles N.E. of Cape St. Roque. It belongs to the empire of Brazil, and is used as a convict establishment. In one place the surface attains an elevation of 1000 feet.

Fernando Po, properly **Fernan Po** (in Portuguese *Fernão Po*), an island in the Bight of Biafra, W. coast of Africa, 44 miles long by 20 broad. Area, 800 sq. miles; pop. with that of Annabon, 5590. F. P. is the chief of the Spanish Guinea Isles, the others being Carisco, Elobey, San Juan, and Annabon. F. P. is mountainous, rising in Clarence Peak to 10,714 feet; the soil is fertile, from the number of springs and streams. Discovered by the Portuguese in 1472, and originally named *Ilha Formosa* ('the beautiful isle'), it passed in 1778 into the possession of Spain. The capital is Clarence Cove, the seat of the palm-oil trade, and a station for English steam-vessels.

Ferns (*Filices*), an important order of Acotyledonous plants, which are sometimes also named Acrogens, or 'summit growers,' from their mode of growth. They are leafy plants; the leaves, or fronds, are rolled up within the bud after the fashion of a bishop's crosier—this being named *circinate vernation*. The stem exists either in the form of a rhizome or underground stem, or in that of a hollow erect stem. The fructification is borne on the veins of the lower surface of the fronds, or on the margins of the latter. The reproductive organs consist of *sporangia* or spore cases, which may be arranged either in round *sori* or clusters, or in an elongated manner, while sometimes they are covered by a layer of the Epidermis (q. v.) or skin, termed the *indusium*, or they may be entirely destitute of any covering. Occasionally (as in *Osmunda*, the royal fern) the fructification may appear in the form of a spike on the end of a frond. The sporangia or spore cases open or burst by the contraction of an *annulus* or ring, which may encircle the spore cases in various ways. Sometimes the ring may be wanting. The spores of F., when placed in suitable conditions, germinate, and give origin, not directly to F., but to soft cellular structures, each of which is known as a *prothallus* or *pro-embryo*. On the latter, peculiar reproductive cells, supposed to correspond to the ovules and pollen of higher plants, have been found; and by the contact of these latter elements a new embryo is produced which develops into the true fern. This process reminds us of the Alternation of Generations (q. v.) seen in some animals, such as zoophytes. F. grow best in moist places and climates. They flourish in greatest perfection in tropical islands, where they attain a great size and dimensions. In New Zealand they form the characteristic flora, and from 2000 to 3000 species are known. F. have been classified into the (1) *Polypodiaceæ*, with sori borne on the back of the fronds, and covered by an indusium—genera, *Polypodium*, *Adantium*, *Pteris*, &c.; (2) *Osmundaceæ*, or flowering F., represented by the genera *Osmunda*, *Todea*, &c., in which the spore cases are dorsal, or clustered on the sides of a modified frond; (3) *Ophioglossaceæ*, the adder's-tongue tribe, with spike-like sporangia; and (4) *Danæaceæ*, with spore cases forming dorsal masses, and represented by the genera *Danæa*, *Angiopteris*, &c.

Feroz' Canal, an irrigation work in the Punjaub, British India, N.W. of Delhi, first constructed by the Moghul emperor Feroz Shah (1351–88), to water his hunting-ground at Hissar. In 1568 the works were reopened by Akbar, and further developed in 1626 by the engineer Ali Murdan Khan, under orders from Shah Jehan, to bring water to Delhi. But by 1753 the canal had again become choked, and in 1823 it was restored by the British as part of the Western Jumna Canal (q. v.). The F. C. proper, which follows the old channel, leaves the main line near Kurnal, and passes to Hansi through the districts of Kurnal, Hissar, and Rohtuck. The water here is absolutely necessary, not only for agriculture, but even for the cattle.

Fero'zepore (Ferozpur), the chief town of the district of the same name in the Punjaub, British India, 3 miles from the left bank of the river Sutlej, and 1181 miles N.W. of Calcutta. Pop. (1855), including the cantonments, 36,231. It is an ancient town, with a strong fort, and was formerly very populous. For fifteen years it was the frontier station of the British power, and the scene of many military and diplomatic events. It contains a memorial church, inscribed with the names of those who fell in the Sikh campaigns. The present streets, shops, &c., were laid out, and the fort rebuilt, by Sir H. Lawrence. The river traffic is considerable; the exports being chiefly wheat, cotton, and wool; and the imports piece goods, iron, and spices. At the time of the Mutiny, in 1857, the three regiments of sepoys stationed here were partly disarmed and partly dispersed, and the immense magazine in the fort was thus saved.—F. *district* lies along the left bank of the Sutlej, S. of the territory of the Rajah of Cashmere; area, 2692 sq. miles; pop. (1868) 549,253. When acquired by the British in 1835, the country was desolate and covered with jungle; but it is now fairly populous and cultivated. It is well watered, and in some of the marshes rice can be grown; but wheat, barley, gram, and millet are the staple crops.

Fero'zeshah, a village in the district of Ferozepore, Punjaub, British India, 12 miles from the left bank of the Sutlej. It was the scene of the second battle of the first Sikh war, 21st December 1845, when the British, under Lord Gough and Lord Hardinge, stormed the Sikh entrenchments with great loss.

Feroz Shah, an Indian emperor of the Toghluk dynasty, reigned at Delhi from 1351 to 1388. In his reign the administration was improved and public works were lavishly undertaken. Of these last, the Feroz-Canal (q. v.) is the most celebrated; but F. is said to have constructed altogether 50 dams across rivers, 30 reservoirs, 100 caravanserais, as many hospitals and public baths, and 150 bridges. See the chronicle *Tarikh-i-Firoz Shahi* in Elliot's *History of India*, vol. iii. (Lond. 1871).

Ferr'alum, a mixture of the sulphates of iron and alumina, carbolic acid and terebine, has recently been introduced for crude deodorising purposes, where the coarser results of decomposition, such as sulphuretted hydrogen and ammonia, have to be neutralised, as in purifying drains, sewers, cesspools, urinals, stables, &c. See article by Dr. Bond, *On Some New Forms of Disinfectants* (*British Medical Journal*, February 20, 1875).

Ferra'ra (anc. *Forum-Alieni*, 'the market-place of the foreigners'), an Italian city in the province of F., on the Po di Volano, 4 miles S. of the main branch of the Po, and 26 miles N.N.E. of Bologna. It is a station on the railway from Florence to the Po. F. stands in a low unhealthy plain, is girt by walls, and consists mainly of wide and often grass-grown and deserted streets, with many crumbling palaces. In the centre of the city is a square castle of red brick, surrounded by a deep moat, the former residence of the Este family. The chief buildings are the cathedral of St. Paolo, which has a noble façade and massive campanile, and is rich in frescoes and statues; the churches of San Domenico, Campo Santo, Santa Maria del Vado, and San Benedetto, in which Ariosto was buried. These have many fine paintings, and the tombs of various artists of F. The house of Ariosto, and the cell of Sant' Anna, in which Tasso was imprisoned, are still shown. The university, now only a school of medicine and law, was founded in 1264, and possesses a valuable library of 80,000 vols. The town has some trade in corn, and caviare is made from the sturgeons caught in the Po. Pop. (1871) 28,509. F. began to rise in the 5th c., and was included in the exarchate of Ravenna. It was a great trading city in the middle ages, and at one time numbered 100,000 inhabitants. In 1240 it fell into the power of the Este family, under whom it became famous as a seat of literature and art, and of the most splendid court in Italy. It was seized by Clement VIII. in 1597, taken by the French in 1796, restored to the Pope in 1814, held by an Austrian garrison from 1849 to 1859, and in 1860 united to the kingdom of Italy.

Ferra'ri, Gauden'zio, one of the most famous painters of the Milanese school, was born at Valdugio in 1484, and executed some remarkable frescoes and highly-finished pictures when little more than twenty years of age. Afterwards he visited Rome, worked under Raffaelle, and modelled his style upon that of the great master. His numerous works—sacred subjects with a few portraits—are for the most part in Milan. His 'St. Paul in Meditation' at Paris, his 'Martyrdom of St. Catherine,' and his magnificent 'St. Jerome' at Milan are his *chefs-d'œuvres*. F. died at Milan in 1550. His composition is noble, his expression animated and true, his drawing correct, and his colour extremely gay, though somewhat deficient in harmony and tone.

Ferrei'ra, Antonio, 'the Portuguese Horace,' was born at Lisbon in 1528, studied law at Coimbra, where he became a professor, afterwards held an office at the court of João III., and was cut off by the plague in 1569. F. was a zealous student and imitator of the Greek and Latin poets, especially of Horace. His works, which include sonnets, odes, elegies, epistles, and dramas, are marked by depth of thought and graceful conciseness of diction, and belong to the Portuguese *classic* school. F. is particularly happy in his *Cartas* or epistles. His play *Inez de Castro* was the second tragedy written in Europe after the revival of letters, and his *Cioso* was the earliest comedy of character written in Portugal. F.'s *Poemas Lusitanas* were published at Lisbon in 1598; all his works appeared at Lisbon in 1771. See Sismondi's *La Littérature du Midi* (Par. 1813).

Ferr'et (*Mustela furo*), a species of Carnivorous Mammalia nearly allied to the polecats, weasels, &c., and included with these in the Digitigrade (q. v.) family *Mustelidæ*. The F. is employed chiefly in the extermination of rats and other vermin, and for hunting rabbits, its active lithe movements and its carnivorous propensities suiting it admirably for its work. The exact nature of the F. species or breed has been much disputed. Most naturalists agree in considering the F. to be an albino variety of the polecat, while a few have maintained its specific identity. The polecat and F. will breed together, but the latter appears to require a warmer climate than the former. The F. is said to have been originally brought from Africa. The common F. is the albino-like animal already alluded to, with a creamy-white body and pink eyes. The polecat-F. is larger and dark coloured. Both are very persistent and ferocious, especially if irritated. They breed twice annually, and produce from six to eight or nine young at a birth.

Ferricyan'ogen is the name given to a compound radical (or group of elements which can be transferred from one compound to another), having the composition expressed by the formula $Fe(CN)_6$.

The radical itself cannot be isolated, its compounds alone being known. Of these, the ferricyanide of potassium is the most important. This salt is prepared by the action of chlorine on ferricyanide of potassium, and differs from the latter only in that it contains an atomless metal.

$$\underbrace{K_4Fe(CN)_6}_{\text{Ferricyanide of potassium.}} + \underbrace{Cl}_{\text{Chlorine.}} = \underbrace{KCl}_{\text{Chloride of potassium.}} + \underbrace{K_3Fe(CN)_6}_{\text{Ferricyanide of potassium.}}$$

Ferricyanide of potassium crystallises in large prismatic bubbles, which are of a beautiful ruby-red colour. It is employed in the manufacture of *Turnbull's blue*. This compound is precipitated on mixing solutions of protosulphate of iron and ferricyanide of potassium, and when pure it has the composition expressed by the formula $Fe_3(Fe(CN)_6)_2$, and is the ferricyanide of iron or ferrous ferrocyanide. F. contains the element iron (Fe) and the group of elements called cyanogen (CN), but neither of these can be recognised in it by the ordinary test.

Ferr'ier, James Frederick, a subtle and strong metaphysician, was born at Edinburgh, November 1808. Educated at Oxford, where he took the degree of B.A. in 1832, he was called the following year to the Scotch bar, but did not practise. He became known in literature first as a contributor of articles, chiefly on metaphysical subjects, to *Blackwood's Magazine*, and his election to the chair of history in the University of Edinburgh in 1842 was followed in 1845 by his appointment to the professorship of moral philosophy in the University of St. Andrews. F.'s magazine 'studies' formed the basis of his *Institutes of Metaphysic, a Theory of Knowing and Being*, published in 1854 (3d ed. 1875), which, though cast in a mathematical form, has occasional bursts of radiant humour and paragraphs of the rarest literary beauty. It is on the whole the most keen and luminous exposition of Berkeleian idealism in the English tongue. In 1855 F., who had married a daughter of Professor John Wilson, published the collected works of his father-in-law. He died June 11, 1864. His *Lectures on Greek Philosophy*, and other philosophical remains (2 vols.), were published in 1864 (new ed. 1875), under the editorship of Sir Alexander Grant and Professor Lushington.—**Susan Edmonston F.**, aunt of the preceding, and sometimes called 'the Scottish Miss Edgeworth,' was born in Edinburgh in 1782, her father, James F., being, like Sir Walter Scott, one of the principal clerks of the Court of Session. Miss F. was herself on intimate terms of friendship with the great novelist. She first gained favour by her novel of *Marriage* (1818), which is rich in humour and in genuine portraits of Scottish character, although they occasionally verge on caricature. Her other works are *The Inheritance* (1824) and *Destiny* (1831), marked by the same enduring excellences as *Marriage*. Miss F. died 7th November 1854.

Ferr'o (Span. *Hierro*), the most westerly and the smallest inhabited island of the Canaries (q. v.). Area, 50 sq. miles. It attains a height of 3500 feet, is fruitful, but deficient in water. The chief place is the village of Valverde on the N.E. coast. All geographers at one time reckoned longitude from F., and maps are still constructed on this principle in Germany.

Ferrocyan'ogen is usually represented as having the same composition as ferricyanogen, $Fe(CN)_6$; but its salts differ from those of the latter compound, in that they contain more metal. Thus the ferrocyanide of potassium or yellow prussiate of potash has the composition expressed by the formula $K_4Fe(CN)_6$, whereas the corresponding ferricyanide is written $K_3Fe(CN)_6$. The most important compounds of F. are its potassium, iron, and copper salts. The first of these is obtained by heating animal refuse—horn, blood, clippings of hides, &c.—with carbonate of potash and scrap iron. The resulting mass is dissolved in water, filtered, and evaporated to crystallisation. Ferrocyanide of iron, or *Prussian blue*, $(Fe_2)_2(Fe(CN)6)_3$, is prepared by mixing solutions of a persalt of iron and ferrocyanide of potassium. Ferrocyanide of copper, $Cu_2Fe(CN)_6$, is called *Hatchett's brown*, and is also largely employed as a pigment; it is obtained by mixing solutions of sulphate of copper and ferrocyanide of potassium. Neither the iron nor cyanogen present in F. can be detected by the ordinary tests.

Ferr'ol (Span. *farol*, 'the beacon'), a fortified seaport in the province of Coruña, Spain, 12 miles N.E. of the town of Coruña, on a neck of land on the N. shore of the Bay or *Ria* of F., is the chief naval arsenal of Spain. The entrance to the harbour is so narrow that only a single ship of the line can pass at a time, and it is defended by the castles of San Felipe and Palma. The land side was fortified in 1769–74 with a wall on which 200 cannon can be mounted. Fifteen ships of the line could be built in F. at the same time. The arsenal is now much dilapidated, and the harbour has scarcely any mercantile importance. F. has manufactures of sailcloth, ropes, and leather. Pop. 16,640.

Ferr'otype, a photographic process published in 1844 by Mr. R. Hunt, whereby paper is sensitised by means of succinic acid, common salt, gum-arabic, and nitrate of silver; the image being developed by protosulphate of iron, and fixed by hyposulphite of soda. In the United States of America, cheap photographs on tin are called by the same name.

Ferru'ginous (from Lat. *ferrum*, 'iron'), a term in geology applied to rocks and soils which contain large quantities of red iron oxide. Its presence is easily recognised by the brownish-red colour which prevails.

Ferr'y (from Old Eng. *faran*, 'to move;' *cf.* Lat. *fero*), in law, is a right by prescription or by grant from the crown to keep a passage-boat on water, and to make a reasonable charge for the conveyance by it of passengers or goods. The right prevents another from setting up another F. in the same neighbourhood. It is not essential to a right of F. that the possessor should be the proprietor of the land on either side. By 8 and 9 Vict. c. 45, certain rules are laid down for the regulation of ferries.

Fertil'ity is the capability of producing progeny. This capability varies very much in the animal kingdom. It has been estimated by Leuckart that 'the yearly generative expenditure of the female organism is in the human female about one-fourteenth of the body weight, in the sow about one-half, in the mouse about three times the body weight, in the bee five times, and in the queen bee 110 times the body weight.' These facts indicate the tear and wear of the female body in these animals during reproduction. Another mode of estimating F. would be to note the number of real progeny resulting. This can rarely be done, but it may be stated generally that the number of the progeny stands in a certain relation to the mean duration of life of the species. The greater the mean duration of life the less will be the F., and *vice versâ*. The F. of the human being is affected by social influences and habits in a manner at present not understood.

Fescenn'ine Verses (from Lat. *fascinum*, 'a bewitching,' as they were supposed to be a protection against witchcraft) were the earliest attempt at versification made by the inhabitants of Italy. They were a rude kind of dramatic satire, in which the interlocutors ridiculed one another, and they were accompanied by music and dancing. In course of time they became malicious and libellous in character. At first they were confined to rustic gatherings, especially after harvest, but were subsequently introduced, probably in a more refined form, into the towns. It is a common error to suppose that the F. V. were of Etrurian origin, and that the name was derived from Fescennia, an Etrurian town.

Fesch, Joseph, Cardinal, an eminent ecclesiastic, who from the marriage of his father to the grandmother of the First Napoleon was considered uncle of the latter, was born at Ajaccio, January 3, 1763. He was educated for the Church of Rome, but entering into the spirit of the French Revolution, served in the army under General Montespan as storekeeper. When his nephew resolved to revive the Roman Catholic worship in France and to gain the favour of the Pope, he made use of F., who returned to his original profession, and proved himself an adroit and successful ecclesiastic. In 1802 he became Archbishop of Lyon; in 1803 he obtained a cardinal's hat; and in 1804, while ambassador at Rome, he induced the Pope to consecrate Napoleon as emperor. F., however, was too staunch a Churchman to approve of the policy which his nephew pursued towards the Pope; he declined to be made Archbishop of Paris; Eugène Beauharnais was preferred to him for the primacy of the Confederation of the Rhine, which he had been promised; and he retired with his half-sister Letitia to Rome. His later years were embittered by the persecutions of the Legitimist clergy, who compelled him to resign his charge. F. died May 13, 1839, leaving behind him one of the largest collections of paintings ever made by one person. See *Le Cardinal F., Fragments Biographiques* (Lyon, 1841), and *La Vérité sur le Cardinal F.* (Lyon, 1842). Napoleon's Correspondence with F. was published by Du Casse (2 vols. Par. 1855).

Fes'cue (*Festuca*), a genus of Grasses represented by various characteristic British species, and possessing spikelets with many flowers or florets, each floret having two lanceolate paleæ. The meadow F. (*F. pratensis*) attains a height of 2 or 3 feet, and is common in meadows and pastures in Europe, N. America, and N. Asia. The panicle in this species is of spreading form, and the spikelets are arranged in linear fashion. Spiked F. (*F. loliacea*) has the branches of the panicle represented by a single spikelet, and has a *raceme* arrangement of florets, or two-rowed spikes. It is otherwise nearly allied to the former species. *F. duriuscula*, or hard F., grows well on dry soils, and has a shortened panicle. Creeping or red F. (*F. rubra*) is allied to the preceding species, and is also of hardy nature. A smaller species is sheep F., or *F. ovina*, most common in hilly districts. Tall F. (*F. elatior*) may attain a height of 4 or 5 feet. It grows most profusely in moist soil, and near rivers and lakes. *F. heterophylla* is a native of the Continent, but has been cultivated with success in Britain; and *F. quadridentata* of Peru is used in that country for thatching roofs.

Fesse, in heraldry, one of the honourable ordinaries, is formed by two parallel lines drawn horizontally across the centre of the shield, so as to contain two-thirds, and is regarded as an emblem of the military girdle worn by mediæval knights. *Fess-point* is the centre of the shield; *F.-wise*, placed like a F.

Fess'enden, William Pitt, was born at Boscawen, New Hampshire, U.S., October 16, 1806. He graduated at Bowdoin College in 1823, established himself as a lawyer in Portland, Maine, in 1829, and soon acquired a high reputation in his profession. F. entered political life as a Whig, and was elected to the state legislature in 1832. In 1841 he was sent as representative to Congress; entered the United States Senate in 1854, and signalised himself by an able speech against the Nebraska bill. He became a leading Republican, and as chairman of the finance committee rendered invaluable service during the war. In 1864 he became Secretary of Treasury, but returned the following year to the Senate, where he voted for the acquittal of President Johnson. After suffering long from ill-health, he died September 8, 1869. F. was an eloquent debater, a skilful tactician, an able statesman, and a man of strict probity and honour.

Fes'tival Plays. See MYSTERIES, MORALITIES, AND MIRACLE PLAYS.

Festivals are, speaking generally, holy-days or 'solemn assemblies celebrated by cessation from labour, sacrifices, feasting, dancing, singing, or any other sign of joy.' They have been instituted chiefly from four causes:—First, in honour of the gods, for offering sacrifices and praises to them, out of gratitude for benefits received; secondly, in order to propitiate the gods, so as to obtain some particular blessings or deliverance from evils under which men were labouring; thirdly, in memory of deceased patriots or public benefactors; and fourthly, as times of rest and recreation to labourers. Perhaps the earliest of all F. were those connected with agriculture, as after harvest or vintage, when men rejoiced over the fruits they had gathered, eating and drinking plentifully. Astronomical phenomena would also be early observed, such as the moon's changes, the summer and winter solstices, &c., and F. celebrated in connection with them. Such celebrations have always had great attractions for primitive, half-civilised peoples, and have been of universal prevalence. The nation which was specially noted in ancient times for its attention to F. was the Egyptians, from whom probably the Greeks derived theirs to a great extent, the Romans again deriving theirs from the Greeks.

Greek and Roman Festivals.—The four great solemn F. of Greece were the Olympic, Pythian, Isthmian, and Nemean. The following, from their importance, also deserve notice:—The Adonia, in honour of Venus and Adonis; the Apaturia, of Bacchus; the Brauronia, of Diana Brauronia; the Dionysia, of Bacchus; the Eleusinia, of Ceres and Proserpine; the Thesmophoria, of Ceres the lawgiver; and the Panathenaia, of Minerva. F. to the same god were held in different localities, as the Apollonia at Sicyon, the Carneia at Sparta, the Daphnephoria at Thebes, the Delia at Delos—all in honour of Apollo. The Androgeonia and the Arateia (after Androgeus and Aratus) are examples of the numerous F. instituted in honour of heroes. The Romans freely enriched their mythology by foreign additions, but their F. were not at all so numerous as the Greek, never, indeed, having amounted to more than a hundred. The Epulum Jovis was held on the 13th November; the Matronalia, in honour of Juno, on the 1st March; the Quinquatrus, of Minerva, on the 19th March; and the other great gods were similarly honoured. Other notable sacred F. were the Cerealia, in honour of Ceres; the Consualia, of Consus, the god of secret deliberation; Matralia, of Mater Matula, or Aurora; Lupercalia, of Lupercus, the god of fertility, &c., &c. The Larentalia, in honour of Acca Larentia, nurse of Romulus and Remus, is an example of the F. that commemorated historical personages or events. Among the Romans, public games in the earlier ages were always regarded as religious rites. The chief athletic sports were the races, the mock fight (called the game of Troy), sham battles, sea-fights, and wild beast hunts.

The Hebrew F. may be divided into the Mosaic and post-exilian. 1. *Mosaic.*—The former are all connected with the sacred astronomical number *seven* (see WEEK), especially a series directly counted by sevens: (1) the Sabbath (q. v.) of Days; (2) the Sabbath of Weeks (see PENTECOST, FEAST OF); (3) the Sabbath of Months, kept on the first day of the 7th month (Tishri) as the beginning of the New Year, and called the Feast of Trumpets (Lev. xxiii. 23–25; Num. xxix. 1–6); (4) the Sabbath of Years, kept every seventh year as a year of remission (Exod. xxiii. 11; Lev. xxv. 1–7); (5) the Sabbath of Sabbath-years, kept every seven Sabbath-years, and called the year of Jubilee (q. v.). Besides these there were—(6) the Feast of the New Moon, kept at the beginning of every month, to connect the reckoning of weeks with the lunar month (Num. x. 10, xxviii. 11–15); (7) the Passover (q. v.), which had two real festival ('holy convocation') days—the first and seventh—and which was connected with the beginning of the harvest; (8) the Great Day of Atonement, on the 10th of the seventh month, which was a *fast* as well as a festival (Lev. xvi., xxiii. 26–32; Num. xxix. 7–11); (9) the Feast of Tabernacles (q. v.), or of the ingathering of the harvest; and (10) the feast which follows immediately on the Feast of Tabernacles, on the 23d Tishri (Num. xxix. 35–38). The annual F. also made up the sacred number seven, with their days of 'holy convocation' (*two* Passover, one Pentecost, Trumpets, Atonement, Tabernacles, and concluding festival), and of these seven the Great Day of Atonement was pre-eminent as the 'Sabbath of Sabbaths,' as the ordinary Sabbath was pre-eminent among the seven days of the week.

2. *The post-exilian* F. were all annual, and in their order in the year were as follows:—(1) The Feast of Acra, instituted by Simon Maccabæus, 141 B.C., and held on the 23d of the 2d month, in commemoration of the capture of Acra and the expulsion of the Hellenists from Jerusalem; (2) the Feast of Wood-carrying, kept on the 15th of the 5th month from the time of the return from Babylon (Neh. x. 35); (3) the Feast of Water-drawing, held on the 22d of the 7th month, the last day of the Feast of Tabernacles (*cf.* John vii. 37); (4) the Feast of Dedication (beginning on the 25th of the 8th month, and lasting eight days), instituted by Judas Maccabæus in commemoration of the purifying of the Temple (1 Macc. iv. 52–59; Jos. *Ant.* xii. 7, 7); (5) the Feast of Nicanor, instituted by Judas Maccabæus, and held on the 13th of the 12th month, in commemoration of the victory gained over Nicanor (1 Macc. vii. 49; Jos. *Ant.* xii. 10, 5); (6) the Feast of Purim, on the 14th of the 12th month, in commemoration of the deliverance of the Jews related in the Book of Esther (*cf.* iii. 7, ix. 20–28).

During the first few years of the existence of the Christian Church many of the Jewish F. were doubtless observed. As time went on the influence of Judaism diminished, and all Jewish F. were rejected except those which had been Christianised. At the end of the 2d c. there is no evidence of the existence of any other Christian F. than the Sabbath or Lord's Day, the Passover —observed as Good Friday (q. v.)—and Easter (q. v.), and Pentecost (q. v.). But gradually other F. were adopted, perhaps a good deal owing to the analogy of other religions. The earliest of these was Epiphany (q. v.), and then Christmas (q. v.) came to be observed as a separate festival. Ascension Day (q. v.) began to be observed in the 3d or 4th c., and the F. of the Presentation —Candlemas (q. v.)—and Annunciation in the 6th c. A very fruitful source of F. was the observance of the anniversaries of martyrs' deaths, reckoned as their birthdays (*i.e.*, their entrance into life), of which kind there was a widespread observance by the end of the 4th c. At first these saints'-days had only a local celebration, but in course of time those of the more eminent saints were celebrated by the whole Church. In the 7th c. a festival was instituted in honour of the Cross. At this time also (610), Pope Boniface IV., having got a gift of the Pantheon at Rome, which had been dedicated to Cybele and all the gods, dedicated it to the Virgin Mary and all the holy martyrs, and instituted the festival of All Saints (q. v.), which, however, had been observed in the Eastern Church from the 4th c. To this was added in the 10th c. the festival in memory of all departed souls.

The F. of the English Church are 149 in number (including Sundays):—sixty-three in honour of Christ, three of the Holy Ghost, one of the Trinity, one of the angels, five of the Virgin Mary, and seventy-six of saints. As the day on which Easter falls varies from year to year, those F. which depend upon Easter—Septuagesima, Rogation Sunday, Ascension Day, Whitsunday, Trinity Sunday, Ash-Wednesday—are also 'movable feasts.' See C. D. Ginsburg in Kitto's *Cyclo. of Bib. Lit.* (new ed. Edinb. 1863); Smith's *Dict. of Christ. Ants.* (Lond. 1875); Blunt's *Annotated Book of Com. Prayer* (6th ed. 1872); Bingham's *Ecclesiast. Antiquities.*

Festoon′, an architectural ornament, frequently occurring on the friezes of Roman and Renaissance buildings, and consisting usually of wreaths of flowers and fruit, alternating with heads of animals. In modern architecture the F. is much used as a decoration for cornices, panels, &c.

Fes′tus, Sex′tus Pompei′us, who is supposed to have lived in the 3d or 4th c. A.D., was the compiler of a valuable work in twenty books, entitled *De Verborum Significatione.* This work was a dictionary of notable Latin words, and consisted chiefly of an abstract of the *De Significatu Verborum* by Valerius Flaccus, an eminent grammarian of the time of Augustus. The epitome of F. was still further abridged by Paulus Diaconus, towards the close of the 8th c. Only one MS. of the work of F. has survived, the numerous blanks in which were filled up by Scaliger and Ursinus from Paulus, and from conjecture. The best edition is that of Müller (Leips. 1839).

Fesz′ler, Ignaz Aurelius, a Hungarian novelist and historian, born at Czorendorf in July 1756, joined the Capuchins, but afterwards became a Protestant, was reader to the Emperor Joseph in 1784, and from 1785–87 Professor of Oriental Languages at Lemberg. Being accused of atheism, he betook himself to Silesia, and finally to St. Petersburg, where he received the chair of Eastern languages in 1809, and died December 15, 1839. He wrote various novels, treatises, &c.; but his chief works, which are all in German, are *Marc-Aurel*, a romance (1790–92), *Mathias Corvinus* (1793), *Attila* (1794), and *Geschichte der Ungarn* (Leips. 1812–25). F. was a deep scholar and graceful writer. See his interesting autobiography, *Rückblicke auf meine 70 jährige Pilgerschaft* (Bresl. 1826).

Fetia′les. See FECIALES.

Fe′tichism, meaning the worship of fetiches (*fetich* is a corruption of the Portuguese *feitiço*, 'magic,' from the Lat. *ficticius*, 'what is feigned,' or perhaps from *fatidicus*, 'fate-telling'), is the first form of belief in the supernatural adopted by men altogether uncivilised. It is purely a worship of nature, the fetiches being natural objects, such as beasts, birds, reptiles, fishes, insects, trees, mountains, lakes, rivers, gems, metals, meteoric stones, the sun, moon, and stars, the earth, sea, and air, as well as artificial imitations of natural objects, which are credited with having a supernatural influence, and are appealed to by sacrifices and prayers against sickness, drought, &c., to cure insanity, barrenness, &c., to give rain, good crops, successful hunting, fishing, &c. The lowest form of F. is seen in what is also the first form of natural magic, when every man has his own amulet to protect him from all harm, and grant him all the success he desires in his occupations, being thus, at the same time, his own priest. Then family or household fetiches (teraphim, lares, &c.) are adopted, and the head of the house is the priest; or if wealthy, like Micah, 'the man of Mount Ephraim' (Judges xvii.), keeps a private chaplain. One step farther gives fetiches for the tribe, and a regular priesthood—medicine-men, rain-makers, jugglers, &c. The transition stage from F. to Polytheism is seen in the religion of the ancient Egyptians, with their unbounded use of amulets, and also their adoration of animals, or human forms with animals' heads, which were symbols of different attributes of deity. F. is systematised in the Shamanism (q. v.) of Tartary, and the Lamaism (q. v.) of Tibet and Mongolia. See MAGIC; also De Brosses's *Culte des Dieux fetiches* (1760); Pritchard's *Phys. Hist. of Mankind* (Lond. 1841); Catlin's *Letters, &c., on the N. American Indians* (New York, 1841); Theo. Parker's *Discourse of Religion* (*Works*, vol. i. Lond. 1866).

Fe′tid Lime′stone, called by the Germans *stinkstein*, is the name given to certain kinds of limestone, which, when struck with a hammer, emit a fetid odour, like that of sulphuretted hydrogen—a result probably of the decomposition of animal matter. In the carboniferous limestones of Ireland, such rocks are of frequent occurrence.

Fet'lock, or **Fett'erlock**, was at first probably an instrument fastened to a horse's leg to hinder his escape. In heraldry it is represented by a short rounded bar, to which a semicircular steel band or chain is fixed.

Feu (Low Lat. *feudum*, lit. 'land held on feudal tenure,' from the same root as *fee*, *i.e.*, Old Eng. *feoh*, 'cattle,' 'goods'), a term of Scotch law denoting a sale of land for a stipulated annual payment, called the *F.-duty*. The deed of conveyance is called a *F.-contract* or a *F.-charter*, there being some legal difference as to the mode of enforcing the two. The F.-contract, like other titles to land, has been simplified by the Titles to Land Act of 1858. A F.-duty is heritable, but an arrear is movable. It is a *Debitum Fundi* (q. v.), and in addition to his personal action, in the event of non-payment the superior may *poind* the ground. (See POINDING.) He has also a real right in the land, and consequently a preference over purchasers and creditors. He has also a *hypothec* (lien) over the crop for the last or current F.-duty. Sometimes the stipulation is for payment in grain, in which case the quantity agreed on is valued according to the *Fiar* (q. v.) prices of the year, and the payment is made in money accordingly. But most modern feus are payable in money. Proprietors of land in Scotland near towns, manufacturing villages, or places of summer resort, are generally glad to add to their income by feuing ground for building purposes. F.-duties, being usually a very safe investment, bring a high price in the market, usually from twenty-two to twenty-three years' purchase, thus yielding a return of about 4½ per cent. The system of building on F. tenure possesses considerable advantages over the English system of long leases. The tenure being perpetual, the holder is probably led to erect more substantial buildings than he would otherwise do, and Scotch houses are accordingly remarkable for durability and warmth. There is another kind of F.-duty called a *Ground Annual* (q. v.). For England see GROUND RENT.

Feud (Old Eng. *faehdth*, 'enmity,' 'deadly quarrel,' from *fian*, 'to hate;' *cf.* Frisic *faithe*, Dutch *veede*, Ger. *fehde*, Dan. *fejde*) was at first the war waged by the kindred of a murdered man to revenge his death, and then was applied to any strife between different clans or families, in the times before private disputes were settled by law. The word has no connection with 'feudal' or 'feudalism.'

Feu'dalism (for derivation see FEU), the principle of holding lands by military tenure which prevailed during the middle ages. The Roman republic granted land to be held by military service, the holder being subject to the state; and after the Goths seized the Roman empire this Roman custom was united with the Gothic custom of devotion to a personal chief, and men received lands from their kings and leaders on condition that they gave their services in war. Land thus granted by a Gothic king was called a *feudum* or *fief*, and was held by *feudal* tenure; while lands which were not held of any lord were said to be held by *allodial* tenure, *allodial* being either the Latinised form of the Teutonic *odal*, 'noble' (*cf.* Mod. Ger. *adel*), or a derivative from the Teutonic *loos*, 'a lot.' Besides feudal and allodial tenures, there was a feudal relation called *commendation*, which Hallam compares to the Roman relation of patron and client, and by which a vassal promised military service in return for the protection of a powerful lord. The great chiefs, who admitted only a very slight supremacy on the part of the king, bestowed parts of their lands as fiefs, also on condition of military service, and these fiefs or benefices were again divided in subinfeudations. Gradually all the land in several countries was held by feudal tenure, but there never was a definite organised *feudal system*. 'Every one,' says Mr. Freeman (*Essays*, 2d series), 'should be on his guard against believing that any such thing as a "feudal system" ever existed anywhere.' F., instead of being imposed as a uniform *system* upon the several European countries, grew up slowly and with great modifications in different lands, according to their previous history and the character of their inhabitants, and in no country was it largely developed before the 10th c. It was at first understood that the king could at will resume the great fiefs, but these were soon regarded as life-holdings; and after Karl the Bald, by the Diet of Chiersi in 877, gave his *leudes* or chief vassals hereditary possession of their benefices, allodial tenures lost their importance, and gradually changed into feudal fiefs, the protection of a strong over-lord being preferable to the perilous independence of an allodial landholder. Before the end of the 11th c. most allodial tenures were extinct, except in the S. of France. There was no clearly recognised hierarchy of landholders, but each feudal country may be said roughly to have been held by the king, the great vassals, and then the lords, barons, and lower vassals. The king was nominally lord of the whole country, but had a very lax control over his great feudatories, his real power being generally limited to his particular territories, which were granted to smaller holders in the same manner as were the fiefs of the great nobles. It was at one time held that the vassals of a feudal lord were not the 'men' of the king, but simply the 'men' of their over-lord, and that if an over-lord warred against the king, his vassals could support him without being guilty of treason. These doctrines were in great measure the cause of the temporary breaking up of the French monarchy, and of the prolonged disintegration of Germany. One man became the vassal of another by paying *homage* (Lat. *homo*, 'a man'), which consisted in his placing his hands in those of his lord and swearing to be his 'man,' and to aid him in war. The principal obligations of a vassal were *service in war*, each feudatory being bound to serve forty days, or if he were a *homo ligius*—*i.e.*, bound by a special arrangement—till the end of the war; *justitia*, the necessity of appearing to judge or be judged at his lord's court, a duty which, however, was generally discharged by proxy; *auxilia*, the obligation of paying sums when his lord had to be ransomed or went on a crusade, and when his lord's eldest or only son was knighted, or his daughter married. When the heir of a fief was a minor, the lord-superior was his guardian. If the ward was a female, the over-lord could propose a husband to her; and if she refused the suitor, she had to pay her feudal suzerein as much as any one would give him for the right of marrying her. The over-lord was also entitled to payments from his vassals on their inheriting lands, or on the alienating of a fief, but this seldom happened, as the right of alienation was a privilege opposed to the spirit of F. which was only slowly won by the humbler vassals. The relation of vassal and superior could be severed by the ending of the superior's line, or by the violation of the feudal oath taken when the vassal did *homage*. When women held fiefs, they had to find substitutes to perform military service. From the 4th to the 10th c. the clergy were looked on as a privileged class, and were free from any feudal burdens, but after the 10th c. they were made liable to military service for their estates, unless they purchased immunity, or held their lands by *frank almoigne*, *i.e.*, by saying masses for their superior's family. As the churchmen were often unable to guard their possessions, they generally obtained the protection of a noble, called their *advocate*, who was recompensed by lands or money. After the Church became feudalised, the clergy, as holders of fiefs, were considered to be the king's vassals; and as the Pope maintained that they were independent of the monarchy, struggles arose on this point between the regal and papal powers. Beneath the feudal landlords, lay or clerical, were the *villeins* and serfs, the original inhabitants of the countries conquered by the Gothic tribes. The *villeins* (Lat. *villanus*, 'one belonging to a *villa* or district') were small farmers bound to the soil (*ascripti glebæ*), who paid heavy rents, and could not leave the estates in which their farms lay. The serfs were miserable slaves, who had no common country, and almost no communication with each other, having no connections beyond their lord's territory. Towards these villeins and serfs a feudal chief stood in a different relation from that borne by the head of a clan towards his followers, the chief of a clan having a common lineage and common traditions with his dependants, while the feudal ruler and his inferior tenantry and serfs were quite alien from each other. F. varied greatly in different countries, some being far more thoroughly feudalised than others. Thus in France it was ruled that the eldest son should inherit all his father's lands, while in Germany fiefs were generally divided among all the last holder's male offspring. In France there were soon very few allodial tenures, while small freeholders were long numerous in Germany. The French fiefs early became hereditary, but it was not till the reign of Heinrich II. (1002–24) that the great German nobles were allowed to transmit their lands to their children. In Germany, partly from fear of invasion, considerable power was at first intrusted to the kings, who in the 9th and 10th centuries were actual rulers, while the contemporary French monarchs had only a nominal superiority. The German vassals were at first less independent than the French, but after the German monarchy became elective, the regal power sank in Germany, while it rose steadily in France. The decline of the kingly power and the continued existence of small fiefs made F. endure longer in Germany than in any other country. In the N. of France, where there was no regular law after the breaking up of the Roman empire, F. was early and fully developed, while in the S. of France it was greatly modified by Roman law and a riper and fairer civilisation. France N. of the Loire was called *Pays du droit coutoumier*, 'the land of customary law;' France S. of the Loire, in which F. was only firmly established in the beginning of the 13th c., after the Albigensian crusade, being styled *Pays du droit écrit*, 'the land of the written or Roman law.' In the 10th c. there were in France 70,000 separate fiefs, of which 300 gave titles to their holders, and many were almost independent states, their rulers levying taxes, legislating, and administering justice at their own will.

The beginnings of F. in England can be traced before the Conquest. The thegns held lands from the king by military service, and practised subinfeudation before the reign of William the Conqueror, who, however, greatly strengthened the custom of holding land by feudal tenure from the crown, while he checked the growth of F. as a system of government, and withstood its tendency to break up a kingdom. He prevented it from developing as it did in France by retaining the old English legislative, judicial, and administrative constitution; by preserving the courts of the shire and hundred, which were open to all freemen, but were subject to the decisions of the royal judicial assembly. In the 12th c. the royal power was far stronger in England than it was in France; and F. was also weakened in England by the national council, by the great mass of freemen, who neither ranked with the Norman nobles nor had lost their lands and sunk into villeinage, by the nobles' estates being smaller and more scattered than those in France, and by the fact that most of the English estates were granted as rewards to his followers by William, whereas in France the great nobles had held their lands before the accession of Hugo Capet. The English nobles never had the rights of private war and of coining, and being far feebler than the Continental lords, leagued with the people against the crown. F. in England came to an end after the Wars of the Roses, in which many of the old nobility perished. F. was brought into Italy in the time of the Karolings, but was unsuited to the genius of the people. F. in Italy was always an exotic, which faded with the rise of the commonwealths, and had greatly vanished before the close of the 12th c., though feudal rulers shone with a transient brilliancy in the N. and S. of the land. Feudal tenures were introduced into Spain at a very late date, and, except in Aragon, had no strong effect on Spain. Neither did F. leave any impress on Hungary or on the N. of Europe. Feudal principles did not prevail wherever the feudal form was found. The kingly power, the Church, and the cities, though they seemed to conform to F., were always its foes at heart, and clung to the monarchic, ecclesiastic, and democratic principles. As the kingly power gradually rose and leagued itself with the communes, as Roman law was restored, as the universities brought together men from different countries and broke down the old severance of nation from nation, F. gradually died away. It was greatly weakened in the 12th and 13th centuries by the battles of Mansourah, Courtrai, Crecy, and Poitiers, in all of which the French nobles were severely defeated. Money payments (*escuages*) began to be taken instead of military service; wider ideas were introduced by the crusades; the strength of the great feudatories was sapped by their mutual strifes; a new mode of warfare was necessitated by the use of gunpowder; the superiority of infantry to feudal cavalry was finally proved by the battles of Agincourt, Granson, and Morat; and before the end of the 15th c. F., as a system of government, had well-nigh disappeared. 'F.,' says Guizot, 'is perhaps the only tyranny which men have never been willing to endure. They have willingly yielded to monarchic and theocratic despotisms; to F., never.' F. seems to have been at first almost indispensable for restoring something of social order to Europe; but it established no legal bonds, no political rights; it isolated man from man, and nation from nation, fostered private strifes, and ruined national unity and patriotic feeling. It transferred the governing power in great measure from the towns to the country, being intensely opposed to the spirit of civic life, and substituting personal for political relations. It only admitted the right of individual resistance in the case of the nobles, and offered no recognised place of appeal to such as could not redress themselves by force. Though a kind of rude federative principle ran through F., it was impossible to carry it into effect, the seignorial courts being very seldom held and of very slight influence. In its infancy it served to check invasion, and restored a harsh iron order in the place of chaos; while from the feudal lord being almost cut off from society, it gave a new importance to family life, and consequently improved the social position of women. See Guizot's *Hist. de la Civilisation en l'Europe*, and Hallam's *Middle Ages*.

Feu-de-Joie (Fr. 'joy-fire') is strictly a fire lighted in the streets or public squares on occasions of general rejoicing—a bonfire. The English use of the term is to denote a 'running fire' of musketry, when troops in line fire rapidly in succession, beginning from the right-hand man of the line, so that the effect is an uninterrupted, rolling discharge. The F.-de-J. is fired in commemoration of victories, in honour of distinguished persons, &c.

Feu'erbach, Paul Johann Anselm von, born at Jena, 14th November 1775, devoted himself to the study of positive law, on which he lectured at Jena. In 1798 he published his *Anti-Hobbes* (on the limits of the civil power) and his *Untersuchungen über das Verbrechen des Hochverraths*. He soon became the head of the 'Rigorist' school, who maintain that in the administration of criminal law nothing should be left to the discretion of the judge. The importance of this position is very great, for nothing shakes the authority of law more than manifest inequality of punishment. Hence the attempts made in countries without codes to codify the penal law. On the other hand it is maintained that within certain limits the discretion of the judge may give effect to circumstances which the law cannot well define beforehand. The danger of the Rigorist principle is especially seen in the case of cumulative punishments for a series of offences. The chief work of F.'s life was the drafting of the Bavarian Penal Code of 1813, for which he had prepared himself by his *Revision der Grundsätze und Grundbegriffe des peinlichen Rechts* (Erf. 2 vols. 1799), and his *Lehrbuch des gemeinen in Deutschland geltenden peinlichen Rechts* (Giess. 1801; 14th ed. 1847). This code modified those of Saxony, Hanover, Würtemberg, and of four of the Swiss cantons. F. died at Frankfurt, 29th May 1833. His best-known book is the collection of *Merkwürdige Criminalfälle* (Giess. 2 vols. 1808–11), translated into English by Lady Duff Gordon, in which he explains and criticises the system of seclusion and mental torture by which the law endeavoured to extract a confession from prisoners, even after conviction on circumstantial evidence, for the purpose of justifying the infliction of capital punishment. F. had several sons, who became distinguished in archæology, law, Oriental science, and mathematics. See *Leben und Wirken Ans. von F.'s* (2 vols. Leips. 1852), edited by his son.—**Ludwig Andreas F.**, son of the preceding, was born at Landshut, 28th July 1804. Under the theological and philosophical influences of Paulus at Heidelberg and Hegel at Berlin, he soon went further than his masters from the orthodox schemes of thought. Schleiermacher had analysed emotional religion into a feeling of complete dependence on the universe of God. F., not content with demolishing the modes of thought which rest on sacrifice and prayer, attacks this feeling of dependence so far as it implies anything beyond the calculated result of human work, invention, culture. God is what man wishes to become. If he looks to God for what he wishes to get apart from his own striving, he loses the only true religion. The religion which consists in wishing, and trusting to an invisible power, is a perversion of human nature. Hence F. looks with disgust on the lamentations of Christians over their sins, on the privations of monastic life, on self-sacrifice for its own sake, and that wisdom of the cross which is opposed to the wisdom of the flesh. His chief work, *Das Wesen des Christenthums* (1841; Eng. trans. by George Eliot, 1871), is defiant and extravagant in its tone. Of his other works, the most notable are his *Theogonie* (2d ed. 1866), and his *Gott, Freiheit, und*

Unsterblichkeit (1866). A collection of his works in 9 vols. appeared at Leipsic, 1845–57.

Feuill'ans, the name of a reformed brotherhood of Cistercians founded in 1577 by Jean de la Barrière. The monastery of the order in the Rue St. Honoré, Paris, gave its name during the Revolution to a political club founded in 1790 by Lafayette, Sièyes, La Rochefoucauld, &c., who at first named their association the 'Society of 1789,' but afterwards, from the circumstance of their holding their meetings in the monastery of the F., were named F. The club advocated moderate and constitutional opinions in opposition to the Jacobins; but the latter rising in popular favour, the former came to be regarded with suspicion, and on the 28th March the club was violently suppressed by the populace.

Feuill'et, Octave, a French novelist, was born at St. Lô in Manche, 11th August 1812. He was educated at the college of Louis-le-Grand in Paris, and appeared for the first time as a writer in the columns of the *National* (1845). Since then he has sent forth an incredible number of tales, of which the best known are *Rédemption* (1849), *Bellah* (1850), *Le Cheveu Blanc* (1853), *La Petite Comtesse* (1856), *Le Roman d'un Jeune Homme Pauvre* (1858), *Histoire de Sibylle* (1862), *M. de Camors* (1867), and *Un Mariage dans le Monde* (1875). These are mainly distinguished by skilfully entangled plot, somewhat ambiguous morality, richly poetical descriptions, and lively satiric sketches of Paris society, not omitting its undercurrent of intrigue. F. is also the author of many successful comedies. In 1862 he was made a member of the Academy in place of Eugène Scribe, and in the following year officer of the Legion of Honour.

Feuille'ton (Fr. 'leaflet'), properly a portion of a political journal reserved for non-political matters, consisting generally of articles of criticism, light literature, art, belles-lettres, &c., usually printed in smaller characters at the bottom of the page, and separated from the matter above by a line. This system of publication was introduced by the *Journal des Débats*, and soon became highly popular. The *roman-F.*, a fiction published in this way, has extended from France to England, Germany, and America. The writer of such articles is a *feuilletoniste*.

Feve'da, an island of British Columbia, in the Gulf of Georgia, between Vancouver Island and the mainland. It is 32 miles long by 2 broad, and is valuable principally for its coal.

Fe'ver (Lat. *febris*, from *ferveo*, 'I grow warm,' or from *februo*, 'I cleanse') has been defined as a complex morbid state which accompanies many diseases as part of their phenomena, more or less constantly and regularly, but variously modified by the specific nature of the disease which it accompanies. The recognised characteristics of F. are those which relate either to the disintegration of the living substance of the body, or to the increase and diminished constancy of the bodily temperature. F. is both a state and a process, and has its beginning in the entrance into, or action on, the organism of some affecting or infecting cause. This event is followed by a period of latency, after which the first indications within the affected or infected organism begin to manifest themselves; but the F. process may vary indefinitely in its course, in its duration, and in the local inflammations which accompany it. In all cases, however, F. has its onset, accession, and declension, the onset being characterised by shivering, accompanied with rise of temperature of the internal parts of the body; the accession, by continued pyrexia and exhausting disorder of the bodily functions; the declension, epicrisis, or defervescence, by the restoration of these processes to their normal conditions and relations. Regarding the nature of F. and its relation to the febrile process, there are two possibilities, one being that F. originates in disorder of the nervous centres, and that by means of the influence of the nervous system on the systemic functions, the liberation of heat at the surface of the body is controlled or restrained, so that 'by retention' the temperature rises, and the increased temperature acts on the living substance of the body and disorders its nutrition; the other being that F. originates in the living tissues, and is, from first to last, a disorder of protoplasm, all the systemic disturbances being secondary. The most recent investigations have led to the conclusion 'that no disorder of the systemic functions, or of the nervous centres which preside over them, is capable of inducing a state which can be identified with febrile pyrexia; but that it is possible for such a state to originate and persist in the organism after the influence of the central nervous system has been withdrawn from the tissues by the severance of the spinal cord.' The tissue-origin of F. may, therefore, be adopted as the basis on which to construct an explanation of the F. process. This F. process is the prelude or accompaniment of a great variety of diseases, accidents, and surgical operations, but the term is most commonly applied to specific fevers, such as typhus and typhoid F., scarlet F., intermittent and remittent F., yellow F., puerperal F., and dengue. Small-pox and measles, although not usually called fevers, are so in reality. There being no single disease to which the term is applicable, no mode of treatment can be laid down suitable to every case of F. The treatment of F. will, therefore, be considered under the separate forms of the disease referred to. Dr. J. Burdon Sanderson has recently produced a compendious statement of the knowledge which at present exists as to the nature of the process of F. See *Reports of the Medical Officer of the Privy Council and Local Government Board*, new series, No. vi.

Fe'verfew (*Pyrethrum parthenium*), a genus of Composite plants, common in our gardens, and deriving its name from having long been employed as a popular remedy in ague and other fevers, and as an emmenagogue. It appears to possess stimulant and tonic properties. F. is a perennial plant, and may attain a height of 1 or 2 feet. Its leaves are flat and broad, its flowers small. It is nearly allied to Camomile (q. v.). The variety grown in gardens is generally of double nature. The Mayweed (*P. inodoratum*) has larger flowers with white ray and yellow disc florets. It is common in cornfields and hedgerows.

Fe'verwort (*Triosteum perfoliatum*), a genus of plants included in the natural order *Caprifoliaceæ*. They are found in N. America, where, under the name of Tinkar's Root (from Dr. Tinkar), they have been long employed as emetics and purgatives. The berries are also used as a substitute for coffee. The F. has an erect rounded stem, opposite leaves, axillary whorls of flowers, a tubular corolla, and three-seeded berries.

Fez, or properly **Fês** (Arab. 'the fertile'), the capital of Morocco, is picturesquely situated in the valley of the Sebu, 100 miles inland from its port, Mehedia. It is the Rome of the Western Arabs, and has, it is said, 360 mosques, of which the chief is the *El Karubin*—an inviolable sanctuary even for criminals of the deepest dye. There are several public schools, and a university, besides the sultan's palace, and numerous bazaars, caravanserais, baths, &c. The town walls are in great disrepair. F. is the centre of an active caravan trade reaching to Mecca in the E., and to Timbuctu in the S., and has manufactures of Beduin mantles, morocco leather, linen, fine tapestry, jewellery, carpets, silks, slippers, and F. caps. Pop. estimated at about 150,000, mostly Moors, Beduins, Berbers, Jews, and Negroes. F. was founded by Edris II. in 808 A.D., and was one of the largest and richest cities of the Mohammedan world in the middle ages.—The *province* of F., the most northerly in Morocco, was formerly an independent state. Area, 117,725 sq. miles; pop. 3,200,000.

Fezzan' (anc. *Phazania*), a great oasis of N. Africa, and the most southerly province of Tripoli, stretches from the springs of Meshru to the town of Bondshem, a distance of 350 miles. Area, 25,000 sq. miles; pop. 26,000, mostly Berbers and Beduins. It is traversed in the N.E. by two parallel ranges—the Black and White Mountains; and in the S. the fertility of its wadies, which yield wheat, maize, barley, &c., gives way to the burning sands of the Sahara. The climate is very unhealthy, the summer temperature frequently reaching 133° F. Journeys are performed on the camel or horse, and the plateaus are infested with the wild animals and birds of the great waste. Murzuk is the capital (pop. 4000), and there are many small towns and villages. The natives resemble negroes in colour, but are of Berber family, and speak a mixed Berber and Arabic language. See Barth's *Travels in Central Africa* (Lond. 1857).

Fi'ars (Fr. *feurs*, 'money for tillage,' or Icel. *fe*, *fiar*, 'money'), in Scotch law, are the prices of grain in the different counties fixed by their respective sheriffs, in February each year, with the assistance of juries. The form of striking the F. is prescribed by Acts of Sederunt of the Court of Session. They regulate the prices of all grain stipulated to be sold at fiar prices.

They also regulate the price in contracts concerning grain to be delivered, and in cases in which no price has been agreed to between parties. Results are arrived at by examining witnesses, whose testimony is digested by a skilled accountant. See *Historical Account of the Striking of the F. in Scotland*, by George Paterson, Esq., advocate (1852).

Fias'co, an Italian word (from Med. Lat. *flasco*, 'a flask,' but the reason for the derivation is unknown) applied to a failure generally, but originally an expression of frequenters of the theatre in Italy to mark a musical failure. The word has been introduced into France, Germany, and England.

Fi'at (Lat. 'let it be done'), a legal term for an order or warrant for the doing of an act. It was a term till lately of frequent use in the law of England under the Bankruptcy Act. But the term now in use under the Act of 1869 is Adjudication (q. v.).

Fi'ber. See BEAVER and MUSQUASH.

Fi'bres. By F. in histology is meant a microscopical solid filament. There are various kinds of F. found in the body, namely, white fibrous tissue, elastic tissue, involuntary muscular fibre, voluntary muscular fibre, and nerve fibre. These will be found described under their respective headings.

Fibres, Tex'tile, are all substances, mineral, animal, and vegetable, employed to form cordage or woven into webs. This definition includes all metallic wires from which cordage or wire cloth is formed, although such are not usually regarded as T. F. Besides these metallic substances, asbestos or amianthus is a fibrous material derived from the mineral kingdom, which has occasionally been woven into a kind of cloth, and in recent years has been much used for engine-packing, non-inflammable mill-board, and such purposes. The ordinary T. F. of commerce are, however, entirely derived from animal and vegetable sources, and all those of any economic importance will be noticed under their proper headings. We here simply enumerate the principal fibrous materials.

Animal Fibres.—The chief T. F. of animal origin are Silk (q. v.) and the Wool (q. v.) of sheep, closely allied to which is the pashm, or fine wool of the Cashmir goat, and Mohair (q. v.). Camels yield a woolly hair much used for weaving and felting in Russia and Western Asia. To this family belong the Guanaco, Vicuña, and Alpaca (q. v.). The hair of several other animals, including the rabbit, the hare, the nutria, &c., is used for felting purposes. Horsehair must also be included among T. F., being used for the seating of chairs, sofas, &c.; and as a simple curiosity among animal fibres, the byssus of a mollusc (*Pinna squamosa*) deserves mention, as being occasionally woven into small articles.

Vegetable Fibres.—Of all vegetable fibres the most important is Cotton (q. v.), and next to it is Flax (q. v.). Following these comes Jute (q. v.), and for cordage specially, but also for weaving purposes, Hemp (q. v.). Esparto (q. v.) grass is now of extensive use in making paper. China grass, the beautiful fibre yielded by *Bœhmeria nivea*, has not yet won the prominence it deserves, from the difficulties connected with its preparation. Phormium fibre or New Zealand flax, derived from *Phormium tenax*, is highly useful, as is also Coir (q. v.), obtained from the outer husk of the cocoa-nut, and Manilla hemp, the produce of *Musa textilis*. The following are also of some importance—Sunn hemp from various species of *Crotalaria*, bowstring hemp from species of *Sanseviera*, aloe fibres from species of *Agave*, plantain fibres from species of *Musa*, lime-tree bast from *Tilia Europæa*. The fronds of several palm-trees also yield fibrous materials of considerable value for weaving, plaiting, and basket-making, and wheat straw and the stalks of many other grasses are employed for hat and mat making.

Fi'brin, Fibrin'ogen, Fibrinoplas'tic Sub'stance. In the coagulation of the blood a substance is formed known as F. At one time it was supposed to exist as such in the blood, but now it is known that it is formed by the union of two other matters, namely, fibrinogen and fibrinoplastic substance. See BLOOD, COAGULATION OF.

Fi'bro-Se'rous a term used in anatomy to denote certain membranes, such as the pericardium, which are double, being composed of a layer of fibrous tissue lined by a layer of endothelial cells constituting a serous coat.

Fich'te, Johann Gottlieb, a German metaphysician, was born at Rammenau, Upper Lusatia, on 19th May 1762, and studied theology at Jena. During a visit to Switzerland he made the acquaintance of Lavater and of Johanna Rahn, the niece of Klopstock. He then taught Greek and philosophy privately at Leipsic, and in 1792 went to Königsberg to see Kant, to whom he presented his *Kritik aller Offenbarung*. Its publication rescued F. from starvation, and gave him a chair of philosophy at Jena. Here he lectured with such intensity of moral enthusiasm and such original power of speculation that he was accused of atheism and had to resign. In 1799 he retired to Erlangen, where he occupied the chair which he afterwards filled at Berlin. To Jena belong his *Wissenschaftslehre* (1795) and *System der Sittenlehre* (1798); to Berlin his *Ueber die Bestimmungen des Menschen* (1800), and his *Reden an die Deutschen* (1808), a series of heroic addresses to the German people after the disasters of Jena and Auerstadt; to Erlangen his *Ueber das Wesen des Gelehrten* (1805), *Grundzüge des gegenwärtigen Zeitalters* (1805), and *Anweisung zum seligen Leben oder die Religionslehre* (1806). The political tragedies of the time gave immense significance to his words. In 1810 he was employed to reconstruct Berlin University, of which, although there was a crowd of the most distinguished scholars in the chairs, he was made rector. When Germany rose against Bonaparte after his fatal campaign in Russia, F. enrolled himself as a volunteer in 1813, but died 28th January 1814, from a fever caught while nursing his wife, Johanna Rahn.

As regards F.'s philosophical position, we must recollect there were already many modifications of Kantianism. Reinhold added a representative faculty. Sigismund Beck pointed out that the assumption of a *ding an sich* or *noumenon* was not consistent with the spirit of the critical system. Jacobi had advocated an intellectual intuition as a source of spiritual truth. Bardili had already effected a monistic analysis—thought is the ground of all, for the concept of possibility precedes the apprehension of reality. Schultze and Maimon had arrived at pure scepticism. F.'s heresy from Kant consisted in referring the non-ego, the objective element in knowledge, to the pure activity of the ego. Substance is merely a mental synthesis of accidents. Without the ego, then, there is no non-ego, no object, no world; and unless the ego be regarded as a spontaneous activity (*thathandlung*), you get the contradiction of A and not-A each requiring the other as its condition. Mankind are quite correct in attributing a real existence to objects, but the object is not independent of the subject, they are identical. On any system of dualism you must be content with a knowledge of phenomena; but admit the unity of existence, and your knowledge becomes certain. F. is, however, compelled to assume an underlying force different from the ego (*anstoss*) which originates all the reflective power and self-limitation of the ego. Perhaps this force is what he calls the 'reine Form der Ichheit, welche noch nicht Individuum ist'—an impersonal reason, like the 'divine mind' of Berkeley. Morality, or the perfect freedom and development of the ego, consists in the gradual assimilation of the non-ego which at first appears in opposition to the ego. Thus human virtue creates the world, it is the incarnation of duty. God is the infinite moral order, and is the subject of faith, not inference. F.'s philosophy of history is contained in his *Grundzüge des gegenwärtigen Zeitalters*. There he deduces *a priori* the world-plan from the general conception of time, which again yields the conceptions of particular epochs. It is quite possible that empirical history, or the facts of experience, may not square with the world-plan: there are 'foreign elements' of which the philosopher is not bound to give an account. This seems an admission of dualism. In the *Wissenschaftslehre* he states the end of life to be the ordering of human relations with freedom according to reason, human life being assumed to be a necessary part or development of divine life. The five epochs are the state of innocence and instinct; the age of authority, external institutions, dogmatic creeds, and progressive sin; the age of indifference to truth, and the complete rejection of the authority of reason, conscious or unconscious; the age of science, in which the laws of reason are clearly seen, and truth is revered for its own sake; the age of art, in which humanity becomes beautiful by its cultivated and enlightened freedom. In the *Reden*, when Berlin was in the hands of the French, he contends that the *Mischvolk* (or mixed Romance nations, like the French) are now exhausted, while the *Urvolk* (primitive or German nations) have the world's future within them. F.'s *Sammtliche Werke* (8 vols. Berl. 1845–46) were edited by his son. See *F.'s Biography and Correspondence* (1830–31; 2d ed. 1862) by the same editor; Fischer's *Geschichte d. neuern Phil.* (vol. v. 1868); English translation of the *Wissenschaftslehre* by Kroeger, and of the *Popular Works* (with Memoir) by William Smith (1848).—**Immanuel Hermann F.**, son of the preceding, was born at Jena, July 18, 1797. He studied philology at Berlin, and was early devoted to history and philosophy. He spent his early life as a teacher, was made Professor of Philosophy at Bonn in 1836, and at Tübingen from 1842 to 1875. He died in 1876. His works, which are voluminous, include *Die speculative Theologie* (1846); *Grundzüge zur Entwickelung der künftigen deutschen Reichsverfassung; System der Ethik* (1850–53); *Anthropologie, neubegrundet auf naturwissenschaftlichem Wege* (1860); *Psychologie als Lehre vom bewussten Geiste des Menschen* (1864); *Fragen und Bedenken über die nächste Fortbildung deutscher Speculation* (vol. i. 1876). In philosophy F. was mainly a disciple of his father. He was strongly opposed to the Pantheistic doctrines of Hegel, against which he advocated what he called 'concrete theism,' maintaining the personality of God and the perfect dualism between God and the world. He held that the chief fact in the history of German philosophy was the contest between Theism and Pantheism; that the latter had been most ably developed by Hegel, who, however, had been refuted by Baader; that recent progressive German thought was represented by Krause, Weisse, and Lotze. Christianity, he believed, ought to become a great instrument of civil reform. He wrote several political pamphlets advocating moderate Liberalism and decrying revolution. His *Contributions to Mental Philosophy* have been translated by J. D. Morell (Lond. 1860).

Fici'no, Marsil'io, one of the leading scholars of the Renaissance, and one of the first who made Plato known to Western Europe, was born at Florence, October 19, 1433. His father was physician to Cosmo de Medici, who founded a Platonic school, of which he made F. the teacher. F. translated Plato and several of the Neo-Platonists, and lectured at Florence with shining success. His most distinguished pupils were Politiano and Lorenzo de Medici, the latter of whom gave him a canonry in Florence cathedral. He died at Careggi, October 1, 1499. Like his friend Mirandola, he sought to reconcile Platonic philosophy with Christianity, and developed a mystical theism enwoven with mediæval sentiment. Platonism, he held, was a foreshadowing and confirmation of Christianity, and he kept a lamp ever burning before the bust of Plato, as if it had been the image of a saint. He vastly aided the classical revival, while his fervent philosophy did much to counteract the immorality of the Church and the pagan licence favoured by many of the humanists. His works, of which the *Theologica Platonica* and the translation of Plato were issued at Venice in 1516, were published at Basel in 1491, 1576, and at Paris in 1641. See Corsi's *M. Ficini Vita*, written in 1506, but first published at Pisa by Bandini in 1772; and Symonds' *Renaissance in Italy* (Lond. 1875).

Fic'tion. See NOVELS.

Fiction of Law is a legal assumption that that is true which is either untrue or is as probably false as true. The law of England has adopted fictions more largely than that of any other country, but to some extent all nations have done so, dreading, according to Dr. Colquhoun (*Summary of the Roman Civil Law*) 'to adopt any abrupt measure which might disturb the practice and effect of former decisions.' By this he means that it is often considered desirable, in making a substantial change, to keep pace with social progress, to preserve an ancient form, and to force the change and the form into apparent harmony by means of a fiction. Thus while social progress has made it necessary that power which formerly belonged to the crown in England should be transferred to the House of Commons, the dignity of the crown—and consequently the social sentiment which has gathered round the institution from historical association—is preserved by important acts being still done in the name of the sovereign. No doubt the social weight of royalty is preserved by this fiction, and a practical end desired by the people of England is thus attained. But where there is no sentiment in question, it is difficult to see the use of legal fiction. A father in England can only get an award of damage for the seduction of his daughter on the fiction that she was his servant, and that he has suffered pecuniary loss from being deprived of her services. The award of damage must either be commensurate with the fictitious ground, or if in excess of it, the fiction is absolutely of no effect.

Fi'cus. See FIG.

Fid, a square bar of iron or wood which forms the support of topmasts. It is passed through a hole at the heel of the topmast, and its extremities rest on the tressel-trees. The *splicing-F.* is a pin tapering to a point at one end and made with an eye at the other, used by sailors in opening the strands of ropes preparatory to *splicing*.

Fid'dle. See VIOLIN.

Fid'eicommiss'um, a term of Roman law denoting the position of an estate bequeathed to an heir with the condition that he should bequeath it to a third person mentioned, that third person being sometimes directed to pass it to a fourth person, and so on. When the practice of so bequeathing property was first introduced in ancient Rome, it was not sanctioned by the laws; performance of the condition therefore depended on the good faith of the heir; but in the reign of Augustus that monarch instructed the prætor to enforce these trust obligations. The condition of F. might be either particular or universal. If the former, it only applied to part of the inheritance; if the latter, it applied to the whole of it. Estates *fideicommissa* are the earliest instance which we find of entails. (See ENTAIL.) The authority given to the prætors by Augustus was by Clodius extended to the consuls and governors of the provinces. In German civil law the *fideicommiss* is the regulation according to which the whole or part of a family property goes to a certain member of the family conditionally on his leaving it to the person indicated by the family arrangement. In Holland also the principle of F. has important application in regulating succession to land.

Fidic'ula, a small lyre-shaped musical instrument.

Fief. See FEUDALISM.

Field, in heraldry, the ground or whole area of the shield, said by old writers to be so named because the charges upon it originally represented the great deeds done upon the field of battle.

Field, Cyrus West, was born at Stockbridge, Massachusetts, November 30, 1819, and rose by energy and perseverance to be the head of a large mercantile business. He travelled in South America, and later became deeply interested in ocean telegraphy. In 1854 he took up the idea of an Atlantic cable, founded the two great transatlantic telegraphic companies, and toiled incessantly till he saw the realisation of his hopes in 1866. (See TELEGRAPH, SUBMARINE.) In the course of this work he crossed the Atlantic some fifty times. He received many medals and honours, and has since been engaged in helping to establish telegraphic communication between Europe, India, China, Australia, and S. America.

Field Allow'ance, a compensation allowed to British officers for service in the field, in consideration of the extra expense which such service entails. When in camp in the United Kingdom or in the colonies, *ordinary* F. A. is made; when engaged in active service, *i.e.*, during a campaign, *extra* F. A. is made. *Ordinary* F. A. for a general is £1, 10s. a day, *extra* £2, 10s.; for a subaltern, 1s. and 1s. 6d. respectively.

Field Bug (*Pentatoma*), a genus of Hemipterous insects belonging to the Heteropterous section of the order. These insects occur in fields and amongst grass, and possess mouths adapted for biting and suction.

Fieldfare (*Turdus pilaris*), a species of British thrushes included in the Dentirostral section of the order *Insessores* (q. v.). The F. arrives in Britain in winter, and departs in May or June for N. Europe to breed and build. The upper parts of the birds are ashen grey; the head is marked with dark-brown spots. The back, wings, and tail are dark brown; the chin and throat of a golden hue, spotted with black; the breast reddish brown, and the belly white. The average length of the

F. is 10 inches. Its nest is made of sticks, grasses, and clay. The eggs number three, four, or five, and are of light brown colour, spotted with dark brown.

Field-Glass is the lens interposed between the object-glass and eye-glass of a compound Microscope (q. v.), to receive the rays diverging from the focus of the former, and thus to render the image magnified by the eye-glass of more convenient dimensions and of greater distinctness than would otherwise be the case.

Field'ing, Copley Vandyke, the most distinguished member of an English family of painters, was born in 1787. A painter in water-colours and a teacher of art, he spent a singularly peaceful and prosperous life, was elected President of the Old Society of Painters in Water-colours, and held the office till his death, at Worthing in Sussex, March 3, 1855. He is one of the greatest of English landscape painters, though his manual dexterity and reputation led him latterly to produce many conventional pictures. The ideas which in these had become stereotyped he had originally taken from nature. His happiest efforts are vapoury perspectives in the Weald of Sussex, stormy sea-pieces off the chalky Kentish coast, and leafy dens in Hampshire.

Fielding, Henry, a famous English novelist, was born at Sharpham Park, near Glastonbury, Somersetshire, April 22, 1707. His father was Lieutenant-General Edmund F., a cadet of the Denbigh family, and thus connected with the imperial house of Hapsburg. After an education at Eton, where Fox and Lyttelton were among his friends, F. in his eighteenth year was removed to Leyden University. There he remained for two years, studying civil law, until his father's poverty compelled him to leave Germany for London. In his own words, he had to turn 'either hackney writer or hackney coachman,' and so, choosing the former alternative, he began to write comedies and farces. His first play, *Love in Several Masques*, was acted at Drury in 1728. From that time onwards he produced a constant succession of dramatic pieces, composing no fewer than six in the one year 1733. In 1736 F. married Miss Craddock of Salisbury, and about the same time fell heir to an estate in Dorsetshire of £200 a year. His improvidence, however, soon wasted this small fortune, and in 1739 he had to take refuge again in London. He resumed his legal studies with great diligence, and was called to the bar in 1740, but being prevented from practising by repeated attacks of gout, he had to fall back once more on the theatre and literature. In 1742 appeared his first novel, *Joseph Andrews*, originally intended as a parody on Richardson's *Pamela*. About this time his wife, to whom he was tenderly attached, died, and shortly after F. braved the conventional by marrying her maid. His next published works were the *Journey from this World to the Next*, and *Jonathan Wild* (1743); but in 1748 the interest of Lord Lyttelton made F. independent of authorship, by procuring for him the police-magistracy of Middlesex and Westminster, which office he filled with much conscientiousness and credit. In the same year *Tom Jones* was published, and two years later *Amelia*. For the former of these works F. received £600, and for the latter £1000. The great novelist's health was by this time entirely ruined, and in July 1754 he resolved, as a last resource under his complication of diseases, to seek the warmer climate of Portugal. This, however, was of little avail; he died at Lisbon, October 8, 1754. F. is in some respects the greatest of English novelists. His inspiration was received from Richardson, but he is, far more than Richardson, the creator of the English novel. His power lies greatly in his intense yet artistic realism; and this charm is enduring, for he was not more conversant with the manners and feelings of his own time than with those feelings of humanity which are the same at all times. Hence it is that Byron calls him 'the prose Homer of human nature.' He had seen both high and low life, and reproduced both, but especially the latter, with consummate art. Many of his best-known personages are drawn from living models. The immortal 'Parson Adams' had for prototype the Rev. William Young; 'Mr. and Mrs. Booth' were Fielding and his wife—the latter appears also as 'Sophia Western;' 'Parson Trulliber' was F.'s tutor; and 'Squire Allworthy,' 'Blifil,' and 'Lord Fellamar,' all had representatives in real life. F.'s skill in the construction of a plot is not great, and one can only regard Coleridge's dictum that the '*Œdipus Tyrannus*, the *Alchemist*, and *Tom Jones* are the three most perfect plots ever planned,' as a profound hallucination. Yet F.'s fertility of invention was not lawless or digressive. There is a certain unity of design in all his work, and he excites interest without violating probability. Some of the finest features of his genius reappear in Thackeray. The masterpiece of F. is *Tom Jones*, a work of fiction unsurpassed for wealth of character, artistic construction, and easy grace of style. Despite occasional coarseness, its morality is on the whole healthy. Gibbon has called *Tom Jones* 'the first of ancient or modern romances,' and La Harpe 'le premier roman du monde.' *Amelia* has been styled the Odyssey to F.'s Iliad; it is less varied and interesting than *Tom Jones*, but the heroine is exquisitely drawn. *Joseph Andrews*, begun as a caricature in the style of Cervantes, ended by becoming a serious fiction, and contains the inimitable character of 'Parson Adams.' *Jonathan Wild*, the least of his novels, is wonderful as a piece of sustained irony. F.'s collected works were published at London in 4 vols. 1762, again in 10 vols. 1764, in 14 vols. 1808, and again in 1821 and 1851. See Murphy's Life, Sir W. Scott's Life, Lawrence's Life, Lady M. Wortley Montagu's *Letters*, Thackeray's *English Humourists*, and Jesse's *Celebrated Etonians*, vol. i.

Field-Marshal, the highest military rank in Britain and some other countries. The title is the same as the *maréchal de camp* of the old French army, and the *feldmarschall* of the German service. The F.-M. is saluted with the standards of all the forces except the Household Troops, who would pay him that honour only in the case of his being their colonel. In peace his pay is the same as that of any other general, but in war he receives £16, 8s. 9d. a day, or nearly double the pay of his generals.

Field-Mouse, Wood-Mouse, or **Long-Tailed Field-Mouse,** the subject of at least one charming poem, is regarded as a nuisance and a pest wherever it occurs. Somewhat larger than a common mouse in tail, ears, and muzzle, it differs from it also in being lighter in the colour of the under parts of its body. It occurs throughout all the temperate regions of Europe, and the ravages it commits in the fields and gardens may be estimated from the immense stores of grain and other food found in its store-house among thick grass or in a hollow of the earth. Another species of F.-M. is the small harvest-mouse. See MOUSE.

Field-Officers are colonels, lieutenant-colonels, and majors, or such as may command battalions, and thus have charge of the field. They are always mounted in order to give ground for movements, circulate orders, &c.

Field of View is the space within which objects can be seen by a telescope or microscope which has been adjusted to its focus.

Field-Train is that department of the artillery intrusted with the charge and supply of stores and ammunition, and whose duty it is during an engagement to see that each gun is served with its full complement of men.

Field-Works are temporary fortifications, as trenches, ramparts, &c., constructed to cover an attacking, or protect an encamped force. See FORTIFICATION.

Fi'eri Fa'cias, a writ in English law for enforcing judgment against the goods of a debtor. If in execution the officer take the goods of a stranger, he is liable in damage. The writ cannot be enforced after a *Capias ad Satisfaciendum* (q. v.) has been issued. F. F. *de bonis ecclesiasticis* is a judicial writ directed to the bishop of a diocese, requiring him to attach the ecclesiastical goods of a clergyman within his diocese in satisfaction of judgment.

Fies'chi (sing. *Fiesco*), an ancient Italian family, Counts of Lavagna near Genoa, who are discernible in history as early as the 10th c. In the 12th c. we find them always quarrelling with the consuls and community of Genoa, of which, however, they finally became noble burgesses in 1198. The F. had possessions in Piedmont, Lombardy, Naples, Liguria, Umbria, and were owners of Massa and Cassara. The family produced two popes, Innocent IV. and Adrian V., thirty cardinals, more than 300 patriarchs, archbishops, and bishops, not to speak of soldiers and sailors. They were among the most zealous members of the Guelph faction. Few of them, however, possess much historical interest. We may note **Bartolomeo F.,** who flourished in the beginning of the 16th c. By an act of rudeness to a peasant he excited (1505) a revolution of the burgher and artisan class, who then desired a share with the nobles in the government of the republic of Genoa. The result was that French troops, sent by Louis XII., took possession of the town. —**Giovanni Luigi F.**, born in 1523, distinguished himself by a conspiracy against the ruling house of Doria, which was assisted by Duke Farnese, and approved of by François I. The plot miscarried through the accidental drowning of its chief, as he passed on board one of the admiral's ships, January 2, 1547. Schiller has dramatised this subject.

Fieschi, Joseph, born in Corsica, December 3, 1790, served in Murat's army, and afterwards led an obscure life in France till 1835, when, having lost his place by the Government suppressing it, he resolved, along with Pepin and Morey, to attempt the murder of Louis Philippe on the anniversary of the Revolution (28th July). They contrived the 'infernal machine,' of twenty small cannons, which was fired from a house in the Temple Boulevard, killing eighteen persons and hurting F., but not touching the king. The conspirators were guillotined, February 16, 1836.

Fie'sole, a small Italian town in Tuscany, crowning a hill above the Arno, about 3 miles from Florence. It is the seat of an archbishop, and possesses an old cathedral. The Franciscan church rises far above the rest of the town, and marks the site of the ancient *arx* or citadel. Pop. about 2500. F., the ancient *Fæsulæ*, has been an important military station from very early times. It was one of the oldest Etruscan towns, but was never a large place, and has sunk with the rise of Florence. There are parts of a Roman theatre, and remains of cyclopean walls, built with huge quadrangular stones, at F.; and various ancient relics have been found. See Freeman's *Historical and Architectural Sketches* (1876).

Fiesole, Giovanni da. See FRA ANGELICO.

Fife, a kind of octave or piccolo flute, used in military 'drum and F.' bands. Its tone is shrill and piercing—inspiring, but hardly pleasant. It has not keys like the piccolo used in the orchestra, and its musical capacities are thus extremely limited.

Fife-Ness, the eastmost point of land in Fifeshire, 2 miles E. by N. of Crail. From F.-N. a dangerous ridge of rocks, known as the Carr Rocks, projects a considerable way into the sea. On this a beacon, 35 feet high, has been erected.

Fifeshire, an almost peninsular county in the E. of Scotland, bounded N. by the Firth of Tay, E. by the North Sea, S. by the Firth of Forth. Its greatest length is 44 miles, and its greatest breadth 18 miles. Area, 328,427 acres; pop. (1871) 160,735. The coast is rocky in the N. and N.E., and along the Forth is steep, often luxuriantly wooded, and studded with many thriving towns. In the N. there are low offshoots from the Ochils, separated by the strath of the Eden, or Howe ('hollow') of F., from the central range of the Lomonds, which rise in W. Lomond to 1713 feet. Largo Law, in the S., is 1020 feet high. The chief rivers are the Eden and Leven. The climate is somewhat bleak and damp in the N., but dry and mild in the S. F. is well cultivated, the richest district being a belt of loam from 1 mile to 3 miles broad, which fringes the Firth of Forth. The county is well wooded, much grain is produced, but the N.W. is mostly heathy upland and barren moor. In 1873, of the 242,502 acres under cultivation, 91,102 were under corn crops, 48,770 under green crops, 47,732 under permanent grasses, and 53,367 under grasses. The formation is chiefly carboniferous, interspersed with trap. Limestone and freestone are much quarried, and there are valuable coal and iron mines. The principal manufacture is linen, and the most important exports are coal, lime, and fish. The chief places are Cupar, the county town, St. Andrews, Kirkcaldy, Kinghorn, Dunfermline, E. and W. Anstruther, Burntisland, Crail, and Dysart. F., which returns one member to Parliament, was anciently the most flourishing region in Scotland. Its thanes seem to have been the most powerful of Scottish nobles before the 11th c. It was styled the 'Kingdom of F.,' but does not figure greatly in Scottish history until the Reformation struggles.

Fifteenth', in music, an interval of two octaves.

Fifth Monarchy Men, a small fanatical sect which arose in England about 1654. They were sometimes called Millenarians, and believed that a fifth monarchy was to succeed the four monarchies of Daniel's vision—the monarchy of Christ on earth, which was to 'stand for ever,' or to remain for 1000 years. They anticipated the immediate advent of the Messiah on earth, and declared that whatever was opposed to the establishment of Christ's kingdom must be assailed by true believers. These tenets led to their conspiring to murder Cromwell in 1657, but their plot was disclosed and their leaders were flung into prison. Shortly after the Restoration they rebelled in London under one Venner, but were promptly suppressed, and Venner and others were executed. Others of the sect were executed in 1662 on a charge of having conspired to murder Charles II. The people seem to have confounded them with the early Münster Anabaptists, and their excesses drew odium on the Baptists, Quakers, and Independents, who had no connection with their risings.

Fig (*Ficus*), a genus of Exogenous plants, belonging to the *Urticaceæ* or nettle order, but also included by some botanists in the *Artocarpaceæ*, or bread-fruit and mulberry order, and in a special section (*Moreæ*) of the latter group. The *Moreæ* have flowers in heads, spikes, or catkins; the embryo being hooked, and the albumen fleshy. In the F. the fruit is named *polygynæcial* or *anthocarpous*, and consists of a hollow 'receptacle' of fleshy nature, within which numerous male and female flowers are contained. The *receptacle* is the extremity of the peduncle or flower-stalk, which becomes hollow and modified to contain the flowers. The seeds are single-seeded carpels, imbedded in the pulp of the fruit. The figs form numerous species, of which the most familiar is the common F. (*Ficus Carica*). This plant is a native of the East, but is cultivated with success in S. Europe, and in Britain in hothouses, although sometimes figs may ripen in this country as outside-growing plants. The F. is the *teenah* of Scripture, and is the first tree mentioned by name in the Bible. The figs imported into Britain come chiefly from Turkey. They are sent in 'drums,' or small boxes, from Smyrna. Figs are eaten simply as fruits, but are also used as mild purgatives or laxatives, and in the form of cataplasms are applied to painful boils, &c. The pulp contains about sixty per cent. of a saccharine substance named *sugar of F.* The common F. appears as a low shrub or tree, the leaves being palmate and deeply cleft. In the East two crops annually are yielded. Other species of figs are the *F. elastica*, which yields India-rubber, and which is frequently cultivated as a house-plant, on account of its green leaves and handsome appearance. The Banyan (q. v.) tree is a species of F.—*F. Indica;* and *F. Rumphii* and *F. religiosa* are objects of veneration to the Hindus. Many other species are familiar to botanists, the juice of certain forms (*F. toxicaria*) being acrid and poisonous.

Fig'aro, a celebrated character introduced by Beaumarchais about the end of last century into three of his comedies—*Barbier de Seville, Mariage de Figaro,* and *Mère Coupable*—and adopted from them by such operatic composers as Mozart and Rossini. F. is a barber, who by his dexterity, and what is better expressed in French than in English as an *esprit net et decidé*, succeeds in outwitting every one with whom he comes in contact. F. is also used to designate a collection of the writings of Spanish humourists, and as the name of satirical journals published in France and in England. The first French newspaper of the name was started on the restoration of the Bourbons, the second in 1854, by M. Villemessant, by whom it is still conducted.

Fi'geac, a town of France, in the department of Lot, 32 miles N.E. of Cahors, situated in a deep picturesque valley, amid rich woods and vineyards, and of a very antique aspect. Its chief buildings are the church of St. Sauveur, which dates from the 11th c., and the Château de la Baleine, an old feudal fortress now used as a courthouse. F. arose from a monastery founded here by Pippin the Short in 755. It has some trade in wine, manufacture of linen, and dyeworks. Pop. (1872) 5394.

Fight, Challenge to, by word or letter, is an indictable offence, punishable with fine or imprisonment. Any direct endeavour to provoke a challenge is a misdemeanour, though mere words which may tend to that issue—such as calling a man a liar or a rascal—are not necessarily criminal. See DUEL.

Fighting Fish (*Macropodus pugnax*), a small fish belonging to the family (*Anabasidæ*) of the Climbing Perches (q. v.), and found in rivers and lakes in Siam and other parts of S.E. Asia. It is exceedingly pugnacious, and when several of them are brought together in a confined space, they afford sport to the spectators by their combats, the exhibitions of which are said to be licensed by the state. Their anal and dorsal fins are elongated, and their colours, when they are excited, are very brilliant.

Figue'ras (Span. 'fig-trees'), a town in the province of Cataluña, Spain, 60 miles N.E. of Barcelona. It stands in a fertile plain near the confluence of the Muga and Manol, and is defended by the fortress of S. Fernando, which has been repeatedly taken by the French. F. has manufactures of paper and leather. Pop. 8350.

Fig'uline. See POTTER'S CLAY.

Fig'urantes, the name applied to the general body of dancers in a ballet—those that dance *en masse*, or are posed in the background—as distinct from the principal dancers.

Fig'urate Numbers are the numbers of a series formed from an arithmetical progression according to a certain definite rule. The *n*th number of the first series is equal to the *sum* of the first *n* numbers of the progression; and each term of the second series is formed in the same manner from the first series of F. N., and so on. *Polygonal* numbers are particular cases of F. N. Thus the series bearing the name of an *n*-sided figure is the first series of F. N. formed from the arithmetical progression whose first term is unity and whose common difference is $(n-2)$. The following are the first three series of polygonal numbers:—

Triangular	1	3	6	10	15	21	&c.
Quadrangular	1	4	9	16	25	36	&c.
Pentagonal	1	5	12	22	35	51	&c.

Pyramidal numbers are the F. N. formed from the polygonal numbers. These appellations, introduced as expressive of the properties of each class, very rarely appear in modern works. The operation is evidently the inverse of the fundamental operation in the calculus of finite differences, and is in itself of little practical importance.

Fig'ure, in geometry, is a finite space bounded by lines or surfaces. In arithmetic it is a name commonly given to the Arabian numerals.

Figure Stone. See SOAP-STONE.

Fig'worts (*Scrophulariaceæ*), the name given to a large natural order of Exogenous plants, represented by the calceolaria, veronica, foxglove (*Digitalis*), Eyebright (q. v.), Euphrasia (q. v.), and other genera. The plants of this order are herbs or small shrubs, with opposite, alternate, or whorled leaves. The calyx consists of four or five parts, and the corolla is irregular. Two or four stamens exist, five being rarely developed. The ovary is bilocular and the fruit, a capsule, or more rarely a berry. The seeds are albuminous. Many of the F. are showy plants; they are found in both cold and tropical regions.

Fiji', Feejee', or **Viti Islands,** an archipelago in the S. Pacific, lying between 15° 40' and 20° S. lat., and 177° E. long. and 178° W. long. The number of islands composing it is about 255, of which only 80 are inhabited, many being mere pinnacles of rock rising out of the sea. The total area of the group is about 8000 sq. miles, more than two-thirds of which are occupied by the two large islands of Viti Levu (4112 sq. miles) and Vanua Levu (2432 sq. miles). The areas of the islands of Taviuni and Kandavu, the next largest, are 217 and 124 sq. miles respectively. The archipelago was discovered by Tasman in 1643, and in 1776 was sighted by Captain Cook, though he did not touch there. In 1796 several missionaries proceeded to F., with the intention of starting a mission, but the threatening attitude of the natives caused them to abandon the enterprise without landing. In 1804 some convicts who had escaped from New South Wales in an open boat reached F., and became the advance guard of a chance white population of shipwrecked and runaway sailors. A Wesleyan mission was established in 1835, and in the same year commercial relations with New South Wales were set on foot. It was not until 1866, however, when an influx of European settlers from New Zealand began, that the trade of F. emerged from obscure insignificance. From that date settlers and capital poured into the group from the Australasian colonies, and at length, after repeated applications to that effect, both from the native king, Cakobau or Thakombau, and the European inhabitants, the islands were annexed to Britain as a crown colony. The annexation took place on 30th September 1874, but it was not until 1st September 1875 that the colony was formally proclaimed by its first governor, Sir Arthur Gordon.

The F. Islands are of volcanic origin, and consist almost entirely of steep mountains sloping abruptly to the sea, and girt by coral reefs. The climate being humid and the soil fertile, the vegetation is luxuriant. Cocoa-nut oil, yams, tortoiseshell, and *bêche de mer* were the staple articles of native commerce; but since European settlement fairly commenced, cotton, sugar, tobacco, coffee, and maize have been successfully cultivated. The chief obstacle in the way has been the scarcity of suitable labour, for the natives being indolent and inefficient, it has been found necessary to import labourers from neighbouring groups of islands. This traffic is now strictly regulated under Acts of the imperial legislature, and a number of armed cruisers are employed to see that the law is obeyed.

The aborigines of F. belong to the Melanesian race, and their colour varies from nearly black to a dark olive, which is the prevailing shade. They are a weak and cowardly race, and formerly indulged in cannibalism, which the missionaries succeeded in abolishing in 1854. In 1875 the islands were decimated by an epidemic of measles, introduced by H.M.S. *Dido*, by which it is estimated that 50,000 were carried off. The number left, according to an official calculation, is about 105,000, of whom 85,000 are professed Christians. The great majority of the latter are converts of the Wesleyan mission, which has 1000 native places of worship in the group. The Roman Catholic mission, established in 1846, has also a good many native members. The heathen natives, who are now confined to the more inaccessible mountain districts, are known by the name of 'devils.' They still give trouble occasionally to the Government.

The capital of F. is Levuka, situated on the small island of Ovalau. Its population at the census of 1876 was 1500, of whom half were whites. The imports of F. in 1875 amounted to £109,720, and the exports to £85,690. The island of Kandavu is the calling place of the mail steamers running between San Francisco, New Zealand, and New South Wales. The group is advantageously situated for becoming the entrepôt of a large portion of Melanesia and Polynesia; and now that a stable government exists, the islands may be expected to advance rapidly in prosperity. See J. H. de Ricci's *Fiji* (1875).

Fila'ria. See GUINEA-WORM and THREAD-WORM.

Fil'bert. See HAZEL.

File (Old Eng. *feol*, Ger. *feile*, allied to the Lat. *polio*, 'I polish'), a bar of cast steel, having one or more of its surfaces notched into teeth, which is used as a tool for making an approximately smooth surface upon metals or other hard substances. English-made files are known as Lancashire and Sheffield files, the two principal seats of their manufacture being Warrington and Sheffield. They are all made by hand, the attempts to manufacture them by machinery not having succeeded hitherto in this country. The process is as follows:—The *blank* is placed upon an anvil in front of the workman, and held in place by a foot-strap. The cutter then makes a series of nicks with a chisel in the surface of the blank, their direction making an angle of about 55° with the axis of the F. He is guided in fixing the position of each nick by bringing the chisel into contact with the burr thrown up at the last stroke; but the exact distance apart and depth of the cuts he regulates entirely by the inclination which he gives to the chisel and the weight of the hammer and force of the blow. So wonderful is the skill of some of the F.-cutters, that Mr. Holtzapffel, a great authority on all matters connected with tools, says he has known files with *nearly three hundred* cuts per inch. When the F. has been cut upon both sides in the way described, it may be at once straightened and hardened, and will be then ready for use. A F. thus made is called 'float-cut,' or 'single-cut.' In the majority of cases, however, another series of cuts is made on each side, crossing the first, and the ordinary 'double-cut' F. is produced. In files intended for use with softer materials, such as hard wood or bone, a pointed punch is used instead of the chisel, files made in this way being called 'rasps.' Each of the three classes of files—double-cut, single-cut, and rasp-cut—is made in about half-a-dozen degrees of fineness, the coarsest being called *rough*, the medium kinds *bastard* and *second-cut*, and the finest *dead-smooth* or *superfine*. All these varieties are made of many different lengths and cross sections, for different kinds of work. Unless otherwise mentioned, a F. is understood to have two flat parallel faces; a 'half-round' F. has one surface slightly convex, a 'three-square' F. is triangular in section. Square and round files, and other kinds, are also occasionally used.

File-Fish, the name given to various Teleostean fishes belonging to the order *Plectognathi*, and to the genus *Balistes*, *Diodon*, &c. Their bodies are covered with numerous spines, the presence of which has suggested their popular name. They are also known as 'trigger-fishes,' 'urchin-fishes,' and 'globe-fishes,' the latter name being given on account of their power of distending their bodies at will with air.

Filia'tion, in Scotch law, means the determination of a child's paternity. The presumption of law is that he is the father whom the marriage indicates (*Pater est quem nuptiæ demonstrant*), but this presumption may be overcome by showing that it cannot be fact. (See BIRTH, BASTARD AND BASTARDY.) Ten months is held by law to be the limit of gestation, but anterior intercourse is held to be an important article of proof. Actions of F. are usually brought in the Sheriff Court, but they may be brought in the Court of Session.

Filica'ja, Vincen'zo da, an Italian poet, born of a noble family at Florence, December 30, 1642. He was educated at the University of Pisa, and soon became distinguished as a jurist in his native town, where, in 1673, he was made a senator, and married one of the great house of Capponi. Six *canzoni* on Sobieski's raising the siege of Vienna by the Turks in 1683 made him known through Europe, and won him the congratulations of many sovereigns. A poem in praise of Christina of Sweden brought him liberal gifts from that queen, and in 1702 he was made one of the chief magistrates of Florence. He died September 24, 1707. F.'s odes, which are full of deep feeling, have now fallen into neglect, but his sonnets, partly devotional, partly breathing a sad scornful patriotism, and cast in vigorous and choice language, are still popular; the two finest, *La Providenza* and *L'Italia*, being known throughout the Continent. *L'Italia* is translated in Byron's *Childe Harold*, canto iv. His private character seems to have been almost without a blemish. His works were published shortly after his death; the best edition is that of Venice (1762). See his correspondence with Francesco Redi, Menzini, and Gori; Fabroni's *Vite Italiane*, and Tiraboschi's *Storia della Letteratura Italiana*.

Fil'ices. See FERNS.

Fil'igree (Fr. *filigrane*), fine gold and silver wire twisted into elegant forms, chiefly for use as personal ornaments. F. work was practised by the Etruscans, and their gold ornaments, combining fine wire (Lat. *filum*, 'a thread') with very minute beading (*granum*, 'a grain or bead'), cannot be equalled by modern goldsmiths. In Eastern countries great minuteness and delicacy are attained in F.-work with the rudest appliances. The Chinese are extremely adroit in silver F.; so also are the natives of Cuttack in India. Durable silver F. is largely manufactured in the S. of Europe.

Filio'que is a word which was subsequently added to the Nicene Creed, and formed a bone of contention between the Latin and Greek Churches. The Nicene Council (325), being chiefly concerned to establish the deity of the Son in opposition to the Arians, merely affirmed the existence of the Holy Spirit, without defining the nature and relations of the third person of the Trinity. Macedonius, Bishop of Constantinople (342), and many others, maintained the Holy Spirit to be a created being, as the Son was regarded by the Arians, and subordinate to the Son, as the Son was to the Father. By the Council of Constantinople (381) the simple phrase of the Nicene Creed, *and in the Holy Ghost*, was expanded into *and in the Holy Ghost, the Lord and giver of life, who proceedeth from the Father, who with the Father and the Son together is worshipped and glorified, who spake by the prophets*. But as this only affirmed that the Spirit proceeded from the Father, room was left for doubt whether the Council denied the procession from the Son. If it were meant that the Spirit did not proceed from the Son as well as the Father, this favoured the notion that the Son was subordinate to the Father; if the Spirit proceeded from both the Father and the Son, this seemed to be placing the Spirit in still greater dependence, namely, on two persons instead of one. Accordingly, the Greek fathers merely taught the procession of the Spirit from the Father, without denying the procession from the Son. The Latin fathers, on the contrary, taught the procession of the Spirit from both the Father and the Son, and at the third Council of Toledo (589)—or, according to Bingham, at Bracara (411)—inserted in the Creed of Constantinople the phrase *F.*, making it run :—'and (I believe) in the Holy Ghost, . . . who proceedeth from the Father *and the Son*,' &c. The Churches of the East refused to accept this as an addition to the faith of the Church, or to alter a single word of the Nicene Creed. This led to a schism between the two Churches, which was never thoroughly healed up, although a formal union was effected at Florence, 1439. See Blunt's *Dict. of Doctr. and Hist. Theology* (1872); *Pearson on the Creed*; Neale's *Hist. of the Holy Eastern Church*.

Fil'ipo d'Argi'ro, San, a town of Sicily, in the province of Catania, 27 miles W.N.W. of the town of Catania. It has a ruined Saracenic castle, and its church of St. Philip, whence it derived its name, was a great resort of pilgrims in the middle ages. Pop. about 7000. F. occupies the site of the ancient *Agyrium*, one of the oldest and wealthiest cities of Sicily.

Fill'an, St., more properly **Faolan**. There were two ecclesiastics of this name who flourished in the 7th and 8th centuries, and whose memories are still preserved both in Scotland and Ireland. The *first* is called Faelan the leper of Rath-eraan in Alba, and Cill-Fhaelain in Laighis, Leinster, Ireland. His day in the Irish calendar is June 20. Rath-erann is now known as Dundurn, in the parish of Comrie, Perthshire, and is near the E. end of Loch Erne (in Gaelic Loch Erinn), where there is also the village of St. Fillan's. There is a hill known as Dun-Fhaolain, at the foot of which is a well dedicated to the saint, and which in 1794, when the old *Statistical Account of Scotland* was published, was visited by scores of people who had faith in the healing virtues of its waters. The *second* Faolan is known as of Strath-Fillan, likewise in Perthshire, but quite on the edge of the old Drumalba, which separated Dalriada from the Pictish kingdom, or Argyleshire from Perthshire. His maternal grandfather is said to have been king of Leinster; his mother, St. Kentigerna of Inchcailleach, in Loch Lomond. In the Irish calendar he is styled of the church of Cluain Maoscna in Westmeath. Kilallan in Renfrew, written in old records Kilheylan, is named after him, and ought to be written *Cill Fhaolain*. In Strath-Fillan there are still some remains of a religious building consecrated to him. Some call it a priory, others a church. There is great sacredness attributed to this building, as well as to the river which flows beside it; and until a very late period frightful barbarity was practised in imparting their curative virtues to unhappy patients who needed them. Lunatics were brought by their friends and plunged in the river just at sunset, then bound hand and foot, and left all night in the ruins beside what is called (erroneously) St. Fillan's tomb. If in the morning they were found bound as they had been left, the case was given up as hopeless; but if the knots were untied, it was regarded as the merciful work of the saint, and the sufferers were for ever free of their malady. One very interesting relic of this second F. is still preserved, the silver head which belonged to his crosier, and known as the 'quigrich' (*coigreach*, 'stranger,' 'pilgrim'). In 1487 the right of keeping it was confirmed to Malise Doire or Dewar as its hereditary guardian. It remained in this family till 1877, when it was purchased from Mr. Alexander Dewar of Canada for the Antiquarian Museum, Edinburgh. (Dewar, originally *Deòraidh*, signifies first 'pilgrim.' It afterwards came to be applied to the bearer of the baculus or staff of a preacher; latterly it passed into a family name.) It is said by Hector Boece that Scotland owes much to another relic of St. F. At the battle of Bannockburn Bruce found himself and his companions greatly comforted and strengthened by St. F.'s crosier being carried in a silver shrine before them. After the victory he ordered the priory of the saint to be rebuilt.

Fill'et (Fr. *filet*, Lat. *filum*, 'thread'), a small flat face or band used both in Classic and Gothic architecture to separate mouldings.

Fillet, in heraldry, a diminutive of the Chief (q. v.), and containing one-fourth of it. The chief, unlike other honourable ordinaries, has only one diminutive (Boutell and Aveling).

Fillibust'ers. See BUCANEERS.

Fill'more, Millard, D.C.L., the thirteenth President of the United States, was born at Summer Hill, New York, January 7, 1800. He was apprenticed to a wool-carder, but afterwards studied law, and was admitted to the bar in 1823. He was elected to the New York Assembly in 1829, and was in Congress 1833–35, and 1837–41, where he supported J. Q. Adams on the slavery question. He was made in 1847 comptroller of New York state, in 1848 Vice-President, and in 1850 President of the United Sates. He retired from public life in 1856, and died March 8, 1874.

Filtra'tion is a mechanical process for removing substances suspended, or sometimes even dissolved, in water and other fluids. As the fluid passes through the fine pores of the filtering medium while suspended, matter is retained either on its surface or in the excessively fine meshes it presents. F. is of the greatest industrial importance, in many chemical manufactures, as, for example, in the refining of Sugar (q. v.). In the chemical laboratory, also, it is continually resorted to in order to separate precipitates which would only deposit slowly by mechanical subsidence. In laboratory practice, a cone of unsized paper is usually placed within a funnel, and the fluid to be filtered is allowed to percolate slowly through it.

On a great scale F. is generally required for the domestic water supply of any community. The water is first collected into reservoirs, where all heavy impurities subside, and from these it passes by gravitation through filtering beds, which are variously formed according to circumstances. Usually they consist of a substratum of gravel from 2 to 3 feet thick, covered with fine sharp sand to a depth of from 18 inches to 2 feet. A filter of this description removes by purely mechanical sifting all suspended matter, but it has little influence on dissolved organic impurities. Thick layers of sand, however, retain a good deal of dissolved mineral matter, such as common salt, and are said effectually to separate lead in solution. The sand in such F. beds gradually becomes encrusted with matter deposited from the water, and requires repeated cleaning or renewal.

In dealing with water on a smaller scale, it is possible to adopt many other expedients for F., and among the substances employed, nothing is equal in importance and efficacy to animal charcoal. The charcoal employed is freed by the action of acid from the phosphate and carbonate of lime, and it should be so compacted that the water is kept from percolating through it too quickly. By some manufacturers the charcoal is compressed into solid blocks. Wood and peat charcoal are also employed, and the charcoal obtained in Stanford's process for treating seaweed has also been shown to be an effective filtering agent. Combinations of iron and charcoal, powdered iron ores, manganese, mixed sand and carbon, sponge, flannel, and other woolly substances, have all been used in the fabrication of filters, and numerous patents have from time to time been secured for special forms or arrangements in domestic filters. A filter in extensive use in Paris consists of a series of diaphragms of wool prepared first with alum and cream of tartar, after which they are dyed in a solution of gall-nuts, and washed with sodium carbonate. Of the numerous forms of domestic filter, none is more effective than that shown in section in the accompanying figure, and which is manufactured by the Port Dundas Pottery Company, Glasgow. In this filter the water passes first through a piece of sponge, which is tightly plugged into an orifice in the upper reservoir. It then meets a stratum (1) of fine gravel A, and (2) of calcined sand B, of a pure white quality, after which it passes through a layer of animal charcoal C, well compacted, and again it percolates through another bed of fine sand D, and of gravel E. For the use of soldiers in campaign, or for travellers, a capital device is the pocket-filter, a small case or box containing animal charcoal, fitted at the top with an elastic tube, and pierced beneath with numerous small holes. The water to be drunk is drawn by suction through the charcoal and tube.

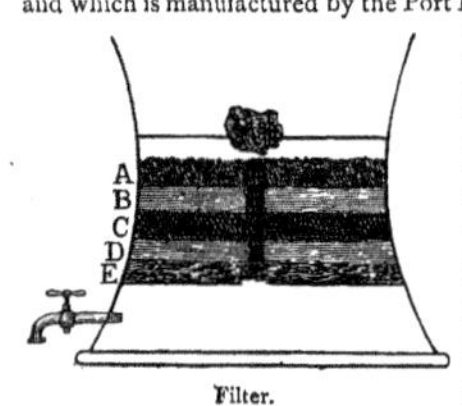

Filter.

Air Filter.—Charcoal has great power of absorbing noxious gases and vapours, a property taken advantage of for catching emanations from sewers, and for disinfecting the air passing out of fever wards in hospitals. Charcoal filters for placing on the mouth are useful in presence of very impure air, as in passing through smoke in a burning house. The filter chiefly recommended for such a purpose contains a layer of pure cotton wool, next the same saturated in glycerine, then powdered charcoal, followed by cotton saturated in glycerine, and dry cotton.

Fimbriated (Lat. *fimbria*, 'a border'), in heraldry, 'edged with a metal or tincture.'

Finale, in music, the last movement in a symphony or other instrumental composition, or the conclusion of the act of an opera. In the latter case its character is determined by the nature of the action; in the former it is always a quick movement.

Fi'nal Judg'ment, a term of Scotch law denoting in its widest sense a judgment which exhausts the merits of a cause, and is not subject to review. But the term is more frequently used in contradistinction to the term Interlocutory Judgment (q. v.). See also APPEAL.

Final Perseve'rance of the saints or of the elect is a tenet in the Calvinistic system of theology which flows necessarily from the doctrine of Election (q. v.). The logical chain of which F. P. is the last link is as follows:—From the mass of fallen men God elected a certain number to eternal life. For the salvation of those thus chosen God gave his own Son to become man, to obey and suffer for his people, thus making a full satisfaction for sin, and rendering the ultimate salvation of the elect absolutely certain. While the Holy Spirit in his common operations is present with every man, his certainly efficacious and saving power is exercised only in behalf of the elect. This efficacious grace is irresistible, not only at the time of conversion, but subsequently amid all the frailty and corruption of human nature, because it is the exertion of almighty power carrying out the divine purpose. With these premisses it is a moral impossibility that any of those for whom Christ died, and who subsequently become partakers of his grace, can fall from that grace, either totally—so as at any period of their lives to commit sins so heinous, and to persevere in them so obstinately, as to forfeit entirely the divine favour—or finally, so as not to be saved at last. See *Westminster Confession of Faith;* Hodge's *Systematic Theology* (Edinb. 1873).

Finance' means the management of revenue and expenditure, whether on a large or on a small scale, relatively to each other. See DEBT, NATIONAL; BALANCE OF TRADE; BULLION; BANK, BANKING; CAPITAL ACCOUNT; and DOMESTIC MANAGEMENT. The word *finances* denotes money itself.

Finch, a term applied indiscriminately to a large number of small song-birds, belonging to the order *Insessores* (q. v.). The family *Fringillidæ* is that which includes the great majority of the typical finches. (See CHAFFINCH, BULLFINCH, &c.) The *Fringillidæ* form a family of the *Conirostres* (q. v.).

Findhorn, a river of Scotland which rises in the Monadliadh Hills, Inverness-shire, flows through the counties of Inverness, Nairn, and Moray, and after a course of 90 miles enters the Moray Firth. The scenery along the F. is very fine. The river is broad and shallow, and often dangerous in flood. The village of F. (pop. 701), in the county of Moray, at the mouth of the river F., has large herring-fisheries.

Finding Goods, Law Regarding. It has been decided in England by the Court of Criminal Appeal (Reg. *v.* Wood, and Reg. *v.* Moore, 1861) that if the finder appropriates goods believing that the owner cannot be found, and believing the goods to be lost, the act is not theft; but that if he believe the owner can be found, the act is larceny. In the case the prisoner had found a bank-note, and had no means of knowing its owner. He was, however, told who the owner was. He then changed the note, and applied the money to his own use. He was held not guilty of larceny, because when he found the note he did not know that the owner could be found. The decision certainly seems strange, causing one to wonder what it would have been had the information as to the owner been received simultaneously with the finding, as suppose the money had been in a purse along with the owner's card having his name and address on it. However obscure the law of England may be on the subject, the moral obligation is clear enough.

Fine, in English law. This was an amicable composition by leave of the court, by which lands were declared to belong to one of the parties claiming them; and by it all the parties were barred who did not claim within a short period. But 3 and 4 Will. IV. c. 74 abolishes fines and recoveries, and substitutes more simple modes for assuring lands and barring estates tail. F. is also a sum of money paid for the grant of lands by lease, or on the admission to a copyhold interest. F. also signifies a pecuniary penalty imposed by a court of justice for an offence against the law.

Fin'gal, more properly **Fionn**, the great hero of Gaelic, as Arthur is of Cymric romance. It is impossible to determine whether he belonged to Ireland or to Scotland, or what was the exact period in which he lived, while some even maintain that he existed in name only. But if every national hero is a real person, however much his attributes be exaggerated by popular imagination, then perhaps the historical reality of F. may be conceded. In the *Book of Deer* (12th c.) we have mention of the *Féine*, *i.e.*, the followers of Fionn; he is represented as frequenting both the N. of Ireland and the N.W. of Scotland. There are many old heroic ballads, belonging alike to Ireland and to Scotland (see Mr. Campbell's *Book of the Féine*, 1872), in which F. is celebrated both as a great warrior and as a generous man; but in Ossian (Macpherson) the Gaelic muse has adorned him with every quality which can raise admiration or call forth affection. See OSSIAN.

Fingal's Cave. See STAFFA.

Finger-Board, in various stringed instruments, a piece of wood—generally ebony—lying underneath the strings, and upon which they can be pressed by the fingers so as to give the sounding part of them the required length.

Fingers. See HAND.

Fin'ial (Lat. *finis*, 'end'), the ornamental termination which in Gothic architecture usually surmounts and completes the design of spires, pinnacles, gables, the canopies of windows, porches, &c. By early writers the term was used to denote the pinnacle, canopy, or gable itself, as well as its ornamental termination. Finials proper first came into use in the 12th c.—although in the buildings of the ancients there are traces of foliated and other terminations surmounting the pediments—and during the 13th c. they were brought to perfection as an architectural ornament. During the 15th and 16th centuries it was customary to surmount finials with a gilded vane. Stone, wood, and metal were the materials in which these ornaments were carved; but the F. of modern times is usually a pyramidal termination in light metal-work, the designs being generally foliage and scrolls.

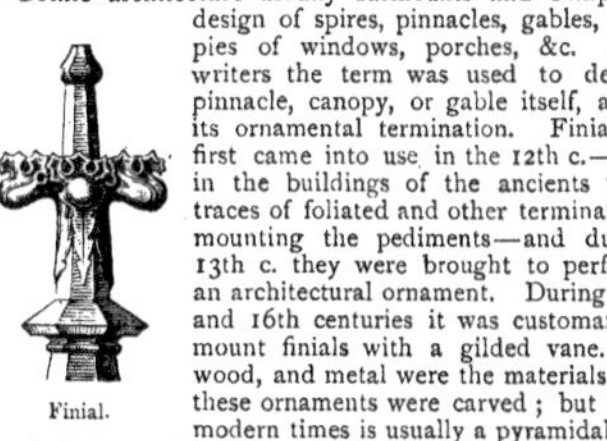
Finial.

Fi'ning. Some liquids holding impurities in suspension are cleared by straining through a porous body (see FILTRATION); others again, such as beer and wine, are clarified by adding substances which either precipitate or raise to the surface the impure matter; the latter process is termed F. The chief finings used are albumen, gelatine, blood, lime, acids, and alcohol. Beer and wines are clarified by dissolved isinglass, which combines with the tannic acid of the liquors, and subsides to the bottom, along with the impurities, in the form of a flocculent mass. In the case of wines containing little tannic acid, such as Burgundy, extract of nut-galls is added with the isinglass to the wine, to prevent decomposition by robbing the wine of one of its natural preservatives. White wines are cleared in Spain with powdered marble; gypsum and sand are elsewhere used. Lime or alum greatly assists the precipitation of impurities in beer or cider. The juices of plants may be clarified by heat, which calls into action the albumen present in them. Syrups are fined with white of egg, which coagulates with heat, and rises with the impurities, forming a scum on the surface.

Finistère' or **Finisterre** (Lat. *finis terræ*, 'land's end'), the most westerly department of France, once a portion of the province of Brittany, and lying between the English Channel and the Atlantic. Area, 2595 sq. miles; pop. (1872) 642,963. The climate is damp and dull. F. is a wild, hilly district. The coasts are deeply indented, and lined with rugged granite rocks; the interior is partly rich arable land, partly marshes and wide heaths. F. is watered by many small rivers, the chief being the Penzé and Aberbenoit, flowing into La Manche; the Odet, Arven, and Ellé, running S.; and the Aulne, Elorn, and Penfeld, flowing E. Barley, wheat, rye, flax, and hemp are largely cultivated, and much cider is made. There are valuable mines of silver and lead, iron and zinc are found, and much granite is quarried. The pilchard fisheries of the coast employ many of the inhabitants. The chief manufactures are of linen, canvas, ropes, leather, paper, pottery, sugar, soap, and tobacco; there is also some shipbuilding. F. comprises five arrondissements; the principal towns are Brest (the capital), Quimper, Landerneau, Morlaix, and Quimperlé.

Finisterre, Cape (Lat. *finis terræ*, 'land's end'), a cape on the N.W. of Spain, in the province of Galicia. F. was the Roman *Artabrium*, from the *Antabri* who dwelt there.

Fin'land, the most north-westerly province of Russia, is bounded W. by Sweden and the Gulf of Bothnia; N. by Norway; E. by the Russian governments of Archangel, Olonetz, and St. Petersburg; and S. by the Gulf of F. It is about 750 miles from N. to S., and on the average about 185 miles broad. Area, 140,000 sq. miles; pop. 1,857,035, whereof about 200,000 are Swedes, 40,000 Russians, 50,000 Lapps, 1000 Germans, and the rest Finns. The shores of F. are much indented, and enclosed with belts of islands; the interior is a plateau 500–700 feet high, precipitous towards the S., more level in the W., and sloping almost imperceptibly to the N. and E. In the N.W. part there are mountains of 2000 feet. F. consists in general of a mass of granite interspersed with trap, and yields some copper and lead, and many useful kinds of stone. Nitre, sulphur, arsenic, and iron are also found. The vast number of lakes and swamps, covering one-third of the entire surface, gave rise to the native name of F.—*Suomesimaa*, or 'fen-land.' The chief lakes are Ladoga, Saima (which drains two extensive chains of lakes, the largest among which are Kalla on the W. and Pieli), Näsi, Ulea, and Päjäne, with the Kymene as its outlet into the Gulf of F. The chief other rivers are the Tornea, which falls into the Gulf of Bothnia; the Tana, running into the Tanafjord in the Arctic Ocean; Kemi, Simo, Ijo, and Ulea, which fall into the Gulf of Bothnia. The climate of F. varies greatly, the mean temperature of Abo, under 60½° N. lat., being 40° F.; while that of Enontekis, under 68½° and 1370 feet above sea-level, is 27° F. The comparatively high summer temperature (that of Abo is 60° F.) has great influence on vegetation. F. is said to contain 1000 flowering plants. Corn is cultivated S. of the great lakes, but also to some extent in the fen-country, and even further N., and the oak thrives on the Kumo and about Björneborg. In the extensive woods covering most of F. are found bears, elk, wolves, and wildfowl, and the rivers and lakes abound in fish. Before the colonisation of F. by the Swedes, it was inhabited by petty tribes, the names of some of which survive in the names of the old provinces—*e.g.*, Oesterbotten, at the N. end of the Gulf of Bothnia, inhabited by the Kainu or Quains; F. proper, or Suomi, by the Suomians; Tavastland, by the Tavastians or Hæmians; Savolax and Karelia, by the Savolaxians and Karelians. F. is now divided into eight governments:—Nyland, Abo, Tavastehuus, Vasa, St. Michael, Viborg, Kuopio, and Uleaborg. The prevailing religion is the Lutheran, but about 40,000 Finns belong to the Greek Church.

In the 12th and 13th centuries F. was subdued by the Swedes, and gradually received Christianity and culture from its conquerors. While a Swedish province, it often suffered from the wars with Russia, of which it was the theatre. The Peace of Frederikshamn, in 1809, gave the country to Russia, and fixed the Tornea as the Swedish boundary. Under Russian rule the constitution is essentially unchanged. There are four social classes—nobles, clergy, burgesses, and farmers, the latter mostly freeholders. On the whole, F. has a perfectly independent internal government, with special customs-frontiers and financial arrangements proper to itself. The average revenue is about £429,000, and there is a public debt of £6,435,000, two-thirds of which was contracted by extensive construction of railways. Russian garrisons lie in the fortresses, but all public functionaries must be natives of F. The navy crews of F. are levied voluntarily. All Finnish affairs are laid before the 'Grand-Duke' (*i.e.*, the Czar) by a Secretary of State, who is the head of the Imperial F. Office. In F. itself the highest authority is the Imperial Senate for F., of which the Governor-general is Speaker, while a procurator watches over the administration of justice. There is a separate system of public instruction, and education is almost universal. The Finns are good seamen; their merchant shipping has a total burden of about 270,000 tons. The chief towns are Helsingfors (q. v.), Abo, Viborg, Björneborg, and Uleaborg; none of the rest reach 4000 inhabitants. See Stockfleth's *Bidrag til Kundskab om Finnerne* (*i.e.*, the Lapps) *og Dito om Qvænerne* (*i.e.*, the Finns) (1848); Milner's *The Baltic, its Gates, Shores, and Cities* (1854); Topelius' *F. fræmställdt i Teckning* (1860); Gerschau's *Versuch einer Gesch. F.'s* (1821); *Zeitschrift der Gesellschaft für Erdkunde* (vol. vi. 1871). See FINNS.

Finland, Gulf of, that part of the Baltic, 240 miles long, and from 10 to 70 miles wide, stretching from W. to E. between the coasts of Finland, St. Petersburg, and Esthonia. Its waters are only slightly salt. Along the Finnish coast it is studded with islands, rocks, and shoals, which render its navigation difficult. There are several excellent harbours, as Kronstadt and Revel, which, with Sveaborg, are also fortresses of the first rank.

Fin'lay, George, LL.D., one of the best of recent historians, was born in Scotland early in the present century, and in 1822 went out to Greece and fought in the cause of Greek independence. He then settled near Athens, and after an unsuccessful effort to better the state of agriculture in the country, devoted himself to writing the history of Greece from the time of Alexander, when he believed the history of the modern Greek nation began, down to the present day. An ardent Philhellene, he did not shrink from exposing the weaknesses of Greece in a series of shrewd, bold, and vigorous letters to the *Times*, which occasionally gave offence both in England and in Greece. His works were coldly received, but his studious zeal remained unchilled. He died January 26, 1875. F.'s chief writings are *Greece under the Romans* (1843, 2d ed. 1853); *History of the Byzantine Empire* (1852, 2d ed. 1856); *History of the Byzantine and Greek Empires* (1854); *History of Greece from its Conquest by the Crusaders to its Conquest by the Turks* (1851); *History of Greece under Othoman and Venetian Dominion* (1854); and *History of the Greek Revolution* (1861). These works have revolutionised our ideas of mediæval Eastern history, disclosing for the first time the true nature of the Eastern empire, and also shedding fresh light on the annals of modern Greece. They show deep, accurate learning, vivified by the author's strong practical intellect and generous love for the country, much of whose history he was the first to unfold to Western Europe.

Fin'mark, a province (*amt*) of Norway, and the most northerly part of Continental Europe. Area, 20,000 sq. miles; pop. (1871) 22,500. F. is a high barren tableland traversed by a range of snow-clad mountains, rising to a height of 4000 feet; its coasts are thickly studded by rugged islands and indented by wild narrow fiords. Barley and potatoes are grown near the sea, and the uplands support large herds of reindeer. The cod-fisheries occupy most of the inhabitants, and are very valuable, above 20,000 barrels of cod-liver oil being, on an average, annually produced. The inhabitants are partly Norwegians, but mostly Finns. The chief town is Hammerfest (q. v.).

Finn'er Whale, a name given to various kinds of whales belonging to the family *Balænidæ* or whalebone whales, and derived from their possessing a soft dorsal fin. Finner whales are of large size—the *Physalus Boops* or rorqual sometimes attaining a length of 90 or 100 feet. They are represented by the genera *Megaptera, Balænoptera*, in addition to *Physalus*. They are also named 'furrowed' whales, from the fact that the skin is plaited or folded. The whalebone plates are very small and commercially unimportant.

Finn'ish Language and Literature. Finnish, the most perfect of Ural-Altaic languages, is so rich in declensions and conjugations that Schwarze and Europæus class it among inflective rather than 'agglutinating' forms of speech. But its main characteristics discountenance the theory of its Aryan origin. The noun is without inflection, cases (fourteen in all), numbers, and genders being denoted by additional words. The prepositions (none of which are of pronominal origin) take the form of suffixes; and the verb, having only two tenses, a present and a past, expresses the future by adding some word or other which can indicate futurity. The syntax is comparatively rude and formless, and in all its wealth of cases there is scarcely a definite nominative or accusative; yet the language is so musical that Rask called it the 'most harmonious of tongues,' and, with the single exception of Magyar, it is the only branch of the Ugric (see FINNIC) stem in possession of a literature.

Swedish-speaking Finns fill the chief professional and mercantile positions in Finland. The people are as much Swedish in culture as the Irish are English, a large number of the Swedish-speaking Finns not even understanding Finnish. Yet the language has not wanted cultivation; it possesses translations of the best foreign works of a religious or popular character, and has a curious and ancient folk-poetry of its own. It was long known that there lived amongst the Finns a great number of lyrics known as *Runot* ('Runic songs'). These poems, some of which are late, others are witch-songs from heathen times, are collected under the title of *Kanteletar* (3 vols. Helsingf. 1840). It was also known that there were *improvisatori* among the Finns, as Paavno Korhoinen (1775-1840), whose poems have been collected from oral recitation into a volume. But in 1835 Lönnrot awoke general astonishment with the discovery that many of these *Runot* could be dovetailed into a true and noble epic, based on the old myths; it came out under the title *Kalevala;* but so many more fragments were afterwards found, that the edition of 1849 comprises thrice as many verses, divided into fifty songs. It was translated into Swedish by Castrén (1841), into French by Le Duc (1845), and into German by Schiefner (1852). In recent years the language has been much studied by the Finns themselves, and the Russian Government's careful encouragement of Finnish literature is well seconded by the eagerness of the peasantry for printed matter in their native tongue.

Finns, Finn'ic. The F. seem to be identical with the *Phinnoi* of Ptolemy and the *Finni* described by Tacitus as leading a miserable nomadic life in the N.E. of Europe, and together with the *Veneti* ('Venedi' in Pliny, the 'Wends') or Slavs (q. v.), bordering on the *Germani*. They are classed by philologists as one of the five sections of the Northern Turanian (q. v.) or Ural-Altaic family. The wide diffusion of F. races at the present day, as well as the allusions to them in Russian and Scandinavian writers, prove them to have been the oldest known inhabitants of Russia and Scandinavia. Yet, like other races composed of detached tribes, not recognising their own unity, they gave themselves no common name, *Finner* being the term applied to them by the Scandinavians and Germans, while the Russians knew them as *Tchud* (Chudians), in which some recognise the famous name of Scythians. Each branch of the F. stem formed a separate community, with its own name and customs. The people composing one of these, living in what is now called Finland (q. v.), named themselves *Suomalainen* (Suomians) or 'swamp-dwellers,' from the character of their country. Now, in the Germanic languages *fen* means swamp, and probably their German name is but a translation of their native name, which contains a word common to the F. tongues; for example, the Lapps, another F. race, call themselver *Samer* or *Sabmer*, and the same root appears in the name of the allied *Samoieds* or *Samoyedes* (q. v.). The ancient F. were in some respects superior to their more powerful neighbours, and though perhaps of shorter average stature, were strongly built and warlike. They were skilful in smelting and working metals, and especially renowned for their sorcery, a peculiar development of a mythology which influenced greatly that of the early Scandinavians, and was the origin of a rich popular poetry amongst themselves. *Fin* was a title of honour given to great Norwegians, and the leading families of Scandinavian kings and gods were traced to F. sources. But the patriarchal life of isolated tribes precluded political organisation, and they were never able effectually to join in resisting the attacks of neighbours who at first invaded their lands as robbers of their costly furs, and afterwards as zealous Christian proselytisers. From a remote period Norwegian chieftains levied *Finneskat* ('Finn-tax') in Finmark, a district extending from the White Sea to the banks of the Dvina, the abode of the Bjarmians. Erik the Saint of Sweden subdued Nyland or S. Finland in 1156, and in the 13th c. Swedish Christianity and culture took firm root. After this Russian conquest began. The princes and merchants of Novgorod penetrated into the country, and wisely developed its resources; it became, so to speak, Russianised, and missionaries gradually converted many of the inhabitants to the Greek faith. The F. were peaceful subjects, and Finland was the first and firmest foundation of the growth of Russia. The Esthonian and Livonian F. fared worse, for they fell into the hands of German nobles, who treated them as serfs. Of all the F. races, the Magyars alone attained autonomy, and that not in their native country of the Ural Hills, but in Hungary, which had a political existence before they conquered it. Generally speaking, all the other F. tribes have become scattered among greater peoples, but their dialects remain as oases of speech, though the races themselves are but fragments of what they once were. Their name has been applied with some confusion. By Norwegians it is often given to the 17,000 Lapps in Norway. Europe in general confers it only on the inhabitants of the Grand Duchy of Finland. Ethnologically, it is used of the whole class of which the F. and Lapps are members, but philologists would now denote this class by the Russian name *Chudic*, or the also Russian *Ugric*. The latter seems preferable, from its connection with the name *Ungarn* (Hungary), used in the middle ages to denote a great province in the N.E. of Europe and W. of Asia. The following list comprises the different peoples who speak these F. (Ugric, Chudic) tongues with their populations according to the latest authorities :—

			Inhab.
I.		Transuralian F. (in the valley of the Obi)—	
	1.	Woguls	6,500
	2.	Ostiaks	25,000
II.		Permic F. (Bjarmians), chiefly in the governments of Perm, Viatka, Vologda, Archangel, &c.—	
	3	Permians,	75,000
	4.	Siryanians	120,000
	5.	Wotiaks	214.000
III.		Volga F. (between Perm and Orenburg)—	
	6.	Cheremissians	200,000
	7.	Mordwins	780,000
IV.		Baltic F.—	
	8.	F. in Finland	1,600,000
		F. in St. Petersburg (government), Olonetz, &c., in Norway and Sweden	200,000
	9.	Esthonians and Livonians	635,000
V.	10.	Lapps in Norway, Sweden, and Russia	24,000
VI.	11.	Magyars in Hungary and Transylvania	4,820,000
		Total	8,699,500

Fins (allied to the Lat. *pinna* or *penna*, 'a feather'), the structures found typically in fishes, and which are adapted for locomotion in water. They are also found in certain mammals, as in whales and *Sirenia* (q. v.), the former having in some instances (see FINNER WHALE) a back or dorsal fin, and the latter a tail-fin. The pectoral or breast fins of fishes correspond to the fore-limbs, and the ventral fins to the hind-limbs, of other *Vertebrata*. The dorsal, anal, and caudal fins have no correspondence or homology with limbs, but are to be regarded as special developments of the skin in the middle line of the body. The swimming paddles of seals, walruses, &c., correspond to the pectoral fins of fishes, and represent the fore-limbs modified for locomotion in water.

Fins'bury ('fen town'), a parliamentary borough of Middlesex in the northern district of London (q. v.), returns two members. Pop. (1871) 452,484.

Fin'scale. See RED EYE.

Finsteraar'horn (Ger. 'the horn of the dark Aar'), so called because the dark Aar rises from it, the highest peak in the Bernese Alps, 14,000 feet high.

Fin'sterwalde (Ger. 'dark wood'), a town in the province of Brandenburg, Prussia, 40 miles N. of Dresden, with manufactures of linen, cotton, and flannel. Pop. (1871) 7289.

Fi'orin. See BENT GRASS.

Fir (Old Eng. *furh*, comp. Ger. *föhre* and Welsh *pyr*), a name given generally to many species of trees belonging to the natural order *Coniferæ* (q. v.). It may be botanically restricted to the species of the genus *Abies*, which also include the Spruce (q. v.); but many pines (*Pinus*) are also so denominated—the Scotch F. (*P. sylvestris*) being one of the most familiar examples. In the genus *Abies* the leaves are arranged singly, and are flat, whilst the scales of the cones are deciduous. Nearly allied to *Abies* is the genus *Picea*, or that represented by the silver firs, this latter genus having tetragonal leaves and persistent cone scales. Of the F. the Norway spruce or F. (*Abies excelsa*) is a good example. This tree attains a height of from 100 to 180 feet, and has an erect stem, whilst its branches are given off in the markedly symmetrical manner characteristic of these trees as a whole. It grows in Northern Europe, Asia, and even in the Arctic circle, and lives about 400 years. It yields *common frankincense* or *Thus*, and paper has been manufactured from its wood. Like most other species of F., it also yields resin, turpentine, tar, &c. The wood is very durable, and is known as *Danzig deal* and *white Christiania deal*. The soft sapwood is occasionally eaten in Sweden. Other species belonging to the genus *Abies* are the *A. balsamea* (the balm of Gilead fir) and *A. Canadensis*, from which 'Canada balsam' is obtained. The leaves of the latter, which is known as hemlock spruce, and also those of the *A. nigra*, yield the extract used in spruce beer. *A. pectinata*, the silver F., affords Strasburg turpentine. The white spruce (*A. alba*) is very common in N. America. *A. Douglasii*, the giant pine of California, thrives in Britain, and may attain a height of 245 feet with a circumference of 57½ feet at a height of 3 feet from the ground. To the genus *Pinus* belongs the typical Scotch F. (*P. sylvestris*), a tall tree with evergreen aciculate or needle-like leaves, naked flowers, and a cone or multiple fruit. The male flowers of the Scotch F. are arranged in short catkins composed of small overlapping scales, each scale having two anther lobes on its lower surface. The female flowers are in small dense catkins, each scale of which has at the base of its upper side two inverted seeds or ovules. The ovules are not enclosed in any seed vessel, and the F. and other Conifers are thus named Gymnospermous or naked-seeded plants. The Scotch F., the only pine now native in Britain, furnishes the wood known as yellow deal. Tar is distilled from it, and pitch is the residuum after the distillation of the liquid part of the tar. The inner bark of the Scotch F. yields the 'bark bread' of Norway. The firs, which are of Arctic type, flourish under conditions which would be fatal to the growth of other trees of their size. See PINE.

Fir Bholg, signifying 'men of the quiver,' a name given to one of the various tribes who invaded Ireland in prehistoric times. The S. of Ireland is sometimes called Bolga, and it is sought to identify the people with the Belgæ.

Firdu'si, Firdousi or **Firdewsi, Abou'l-Casim Mansur,** a great Persian poet, was born at Schadab, near Tus in Khorassan, in 940. He was called F. ('paradise') either from his father being in charge of an estate named F., or from the Sultan Mahmud saying that his poems were a true 'paradise.' F. early determined to frame an epic on the history of Persia; visited the court of the Sultan Mahmud at Ghuznee, then a famous seat of letters; and at Mahmud's request undertook to write an epic on the Persian kings from mythical times down to the 7th c., the sultan promising him a gold dirhem for each couplet. The work is said to have occupied F. for thirty years, and on its completion, Mahmud, prejudiced against F. by the poet's enemies, sent him 60,000 dirhems of silver, instead of the gold coins which he had promised. In return F. bitterly satirised Mahmud, whose resentment compelled him to wander from court to court, seeking protection which the various monarchs dared not bestow. F. seems to have died in his native place, about 1020. His life, and especially his latter years, are shrouded in legends, the stories regarding him being often very contradictory. F.'s great work, the *Shah-Nameh* ('Book of Kings'), is said to have at first contained 60,000 couplets, but no extant MS. comprises more than 56,685. The poem deals with mingled fable and history, and embraces 3600 years. It has no epical unity, being divided into separate tales, to each of which an introduction and epilogue are affixed. The chief theme is the war of Iran (Persia) with Turan (Turkestan). In the East it is regarded as of great historical value, but the only reliable portion seems to be that devoted to the Sassanids. It is one of the most interesting philological relics in Persian, is pure, though archaic, in style, with very few Arabic words. Sir William Jones says if it were understood in the original, it would 'contest the merit of invention with Homer himself.' It abounds in rich, daring, and often fantastic Oriental imagery, contains many fine passages of lofty and pathetic poetry, and its verse is softly musical. The *Shah-Nameh* was published at Calcutta in 1829, edited by Turner Macan, and at Paris in 1840, with a translation and commentary by Mohl. See Hammer's *Gesch. der schönen Redekunste Persiens*, and the biographies in Macan's and Mohl's editions.

Fire-Anni'hilator, a portable machine designed to extinguish fire by forcibly ejecting upon the burning mass a saturated solution of a gas or of other substances incapable of supporting combustion. The French call such a machine *l'extincteur*, a name which has been adopted by inventors in Great Britain. Mr. Phillips's F.-A. (1849), contrived to project steam, carbonic acid, and other gases, has not been much used. In 1873 Mr. W. B. Dick, of Glasgow, patented an extincteur, which consisted of a cylindrical vessel containing water saturated with bicarbonate of soda in the lower part, and in the upper of a bottle filled with sulphuric acid. The bottle may be readily broken by percussion applied to an external cap, and the ensuing chemical action of the acid on the bicarbonate produces carbonic acid, which by its own expansion is propelled through a stop and delivery hose as a super-saturated aqueous solution. Many public buildings, ships, &c., are provided with this extincteur. A novel and ingenious plan of extinguishing fires in buildings where steam power is used was patented in 1875 by Mr. Henry Lacy of Hebden Bridge, Yorkshire. His method is to connect a branch pipe, which may be carried to any part of the building with hose attached, to the water-supply pipe leading through an injector to the boiler of an engine. By means of stopcocks, the water is cut off from the boiler; and steam, being admitted into the injector, drives the water along the branch pipe with a force regulated by the pressure of steam. Provision is also made for mixing chemicals with the water in the branch pipe.

Fire'arms. The discovery of Gunpowder (q. v.) and its application to purposes of war led soon to the disuse of the old weapons of attack. The earliest form of goune (*canna*), or 'crake of war,' was probably an iron pot or 'mortar.' A specimen capable of throwing 160-lb. shot is preserved in the Rotunda at Woolwich. This gradually changed into a cylinder form, which may have been suggested by the practice of throwing 'feathered quarrels.' The early Cannon (q. v.) of the 14th c. were made of wrought-iron bars bound by iron girders, the shot used being generally stones. The larger cannon, Froissart's *grande artillerie*, subsequently called *bombardes*, of which Mons Meg at Edinburgh Castle is a specimen, projected granite balls. Some of these were breechloaders, and the largest could throw 200 lbs. It is said the Dulle Griette or Margot la Folle of Ghent, and Mahomet II.'s gun at Constantinople, now in the Woolwich Artillery Museum, threw each 600 lbs. In the 15th c. appear primitive *mitrailleuses*, called by the Germans 'death-organs,' and the lighter pieces for field-work with trunnions mounted on carriages with trails. At the end of the 15th c. hand-guns called culverins were used, two men for each; smaller petronels being supplied to the cavalry. Gustavus Adolphus (1630) first introduced small iron cannon for field purposes. In the middle of the 16th c. Henri II. of France had cannon of 34 lbs., culverins from 15 lbs. to 2 lbs., and falcons and falconets which threw small shot of 1 lb. and ½ lb. Grooved or rifled cannon (see RIFLED ARMS) occur in the 17th c., so that Benjamin Robins, who lived in the following century, was not the author of the idea. The long harquebus, and the longer and heavier muschite, or sparrow-hawk, which was fired from a rest, were both of Spanish origin. The old matchlock gradually gave place to the clumsy wheel-lock of Nürnberg and the snaphaunces, but not till about 1692 did the developed flintlock entirely supersede the matchlock. Casting guns was introduced to England by Sebastiani, under the patronage of Henry VIII.; many of the brass 'sakers' of that period still survive. The petard of this period was a kind of iron mortar, like a truncated cone, filled with gunpowder and yellow wax, or Greek fire. It was used for blowing up gates and bridges. There was a separate tube to carry the lighted match. Bombs were known in England in the 16th c. Ricochet-firing was first tried by Vauban at Philipsbourg in 1688. The bar-and-chain shot used in naval warfare were generally fired out of the guns called 'murtherers.' Many forms of hand-F. we have not yet mentioned. The iron hand-cannon, with a small pan under the right side to hold the powder, passed into the hand-gun proper cast in brass, the first step towards the gunlock. The *arquebus-à-croc*, or with a hook, was fired from a tripod, and therefore is not properly a hand-arm. The smaller haquebut, or hagbut, had a hooked or crooked stock, which gave greater facilities for aiming than the straight barrel. The demi-haque was merely a long pistol, with a semicircular butt. The musket (literally the male young of the sparrow-hawk), perhaps so called from mousquette, or muschetta, the iron part of the small arrows fired from guns, has been referred to a Russian as well as a Spanish origin. It was first largely used by Alva. The ramrod was called 'a scouring stick' or 'scorier;' and indeed wooden ramrods were used in the British army down to 1752. The so-called Vauban lock (really much older) was an attempt to combine the action of a flint and steel with that of a match-cord. The caliver was a short musket fired by a matchlock without rest. The name really refers to the calibre or bore—the height of the bullet—and marks the important change that all the men of a regiment must use the same ammunitions. The Fusil (q. v.) was a short musket (flintlock) used by the French army from 1700; it was fired not from the breast, but the shoulder. The Carbine (q. v.) was a wheel-locked arquebus of large calibre used by skirmishers in the French army (1576 to 1665) and by the English cavalry at the end of the 17th c. The currier was longer in barrel than the arquebus, but not of so wide a bore; it was used chiefly in sieges. The musquetoon was a smaller sort of musquet, not so long as the fusil, but differing from the carbine in having a firelock, and not a wheel-lock. The Pistol (q. v.) was an arquebus in miniature, and fired by the wheel-lock. It was much used by the German Reiters, and in one form with a snaphaunce lock in the Scotch Highlands. The dag was simply a pistol with a crooked stock. The petronel or petrinal (from *poitrine*, 'breast,' from which it was fired) was a sort of arquebus, shorter than the musquet, but of larger bore, in fact very like the modern carbine. The Blunderbuss (q. v.) was very short, with a wide bore, and was charged with several balls or slugs. The dragon (see DRAGOON) was a formidable small form of the blunderbuss; it was conveniently carried on horseback, and effectively used on foot. The hand-mortar was used for throwing shells or Grenades (q. v.). The patent of Forsyth for a percussion gun (1807) was followed in 1827 by Dreyse's invention of the needle-gun, which in 1836 was converted into a breechloader. In the Minie rifle the charge in exploding expands the end of the bullet, a result formerly obtained by the pressure of the ramrod, or more anciently in the rifled harquebus by a mallet. The chief forms of the needle-gun besides the Prussian are the Chassepot, the Snider, the Peabody (Swiss), the Werndl (Austrian), and the Remington (Danish). (See BREECHLOADING ARMS.) The recent improvements in large ordnance are noticed under CANNON. Among great collections of F. may be mentioned those of Dresden and the Musée d'Artillerie at Paris. Birmingham recently started one, which received help from the Government. The only large private collection in this country was that of Meyrich at Goodrich Court. See Louis Napoleon, *Études sur le Passé et l'Avenir de l'Artillerie*; Grose, *Military Antiquities*; Scott's *British Army*, vol. ii.

Firearms, Law Regarding. Before firearms are sold they must be tested in a public proof-house. The statute does not extend to Scotland or Ireland, and arms manufactured for the Queen are exempted. An Act granting a duty of excise in licenses to use guns was passed 9th August 1870.

Fire'balls, hollow projectiles filled with gunpowder, sulphur, naphtha, and similar combustibles, and discharged from cannon to illuminate or ignite an enemy's work. Rockets have greatly superseded their use.

Fire'bote, in English law, is the right of a tenant to cut wood for fuel on the ground held by him. See ESTOVER.

Fire'brick. See BRICK.

Fire-Brigade'. In London almost the whole of the fire-engines are under the control of the insurance companies. Up to 1825 each company had its own brigade; but in that year some of the principal associations joined together, and the advantages of conjoint action soon became so obvious that by 1833 nearly all the remaining companies had merged their establishments in the central one, and the present Metropolitan F.-B. was formed.

The skill and bravery of its men and excellency of its organisation have earned for it since its formation great popularity. In London each parish has under its own management a separate fire-engine. These machines are very small, and of little use in comparison with those of the brigade. In Edinburgh and most other cities the fire-engines belong to the municipal authorities, under whose control also the brigade is. On the Continent the fire establishment is generally under Government control; in America there are in most cities companies of volunteer firemen, who have certain immunities from taxation and militia service in lieu of pay.

Fire'clay is so named from its fire-resisting nature, which arises from the predominance of silica together with the small percentage of fluxes in its constitution. Pure F. is composed of silica, alumina, and water; but an alkali, lime, magnesia, or iron oxide is always present in variable proportions, tending to give fusibility to the clay. F. with over one per cent. of alkalies is unable to withstand very high temperatures for a prolonged period, but oxide of iron alone, to the extent of four per cent., is not detrimental. In Great Britain it is chiefly found in the coal measures, in beds of from 1 foot to 4 feet in thickness, forming the under clay of the coal seams. Valuable deposits occur at Stourbridge in Worcestershire, Garnkirk and other places in Lanarkshire, at Lilly Hill in Fifeshire, and at Blaydon on the Tyne. Stourbridge is the most celebrated of the British fireclays, and has the following percentage composition:—Silica, 63·30; alumina, 23·30; lime, 0·73; oxide of iron, 1·80; water, 10·30, with traces of titanic acid and carbonaceous matter. Gas retorts, glass-house pots, crucibles, furnace bricks, glazed drainage pipes, terra-cotta ornaments, and many other articles are made of F. When excavated, it is exposed to the disintegrating action of the weather; it is afterwards pulverised, mixed with water, kneaded in a pug-mill, then moulded by hand, and carefully dried and fired.

Fire'damp, an explosive mixture of Marsh Gas (q. v.) and air, is of frequent occurrence, and a source of great danger, in coal-mines. See SAFETY-LAMP.

Fire-Eating. Conjurors have at different times professed their ability to eat fire with impunity. Richardson, an Englishman, who travelled over Europe in the 17th c., chewed burning coals, poured melted lead upon his tongue, drank molten glass, and held red-hot iron in his mouth. Sir David Brewster (*Letters on Natural Magic*), commenting on these and similar performances, says, 'That these effects are produced partly by deception and partly by a previous preparation of the parts subjected to the heat, can scarcely admit of a doubt. The fusible metal—composed of mercury, bismuth, and tin, which melt at a low temperature—might easily have been substituted in place of lead, and fluids of easy ebullition may have been used in place of boiling water.' The skin becomes horny, and therefore insensible to intense heat, by continually compressing, singeing, or pricking it, or by frequently washing it with dilute sulphuric acid. Mediæval priests were acquainted with other protective preparations, which enabled them to pass 'the innocent' through the ordeal of fire with impunity.

Fire'-Engine, a pumping-machine for extinguishing fires. A double pump apparently for this purpose is described by Hero of Alexandria (B.C. 284–221), who calls it 'the syphons used at conflagrations.' There are now no means of saying how far such a machine (which was in principle identical with those employed at present) was used in the time of its inventor. We first hear of fire-engines definitely during the latter half of the 17th c., when they appear in very much the same form as that described by Hero. Up to this time huge squirts containing a few quarts of water were the principal means of extinguishing fires in this country. Two men held one of them, and a third pressed the piston upwards. The first F.-E. of which we have a trustworthy account was made at Nürnberg by Hautsch, and is described by Gaspar Schott in 1657. It carried its own water cistern, was worked by twenty-eight men, and seems to have had a kind of flexible discharge pipe. The general use of the leathern hose dates only from about 1670, when two brothers Van der Heide (fire-inspectors) introduced them at Amsterdam and obtained for them patent rights. Since then they have been universally employed, first of leather sewed, then riveted, and later of canvas and india-rubber, and of india-rubber alone. The first use of the *air vessel*, now an essential part of all fire-engines, is ascribed to a Frenchman, Perrault, in 1684. Subsequent improvements in the F.-E. down to 1830 were chiefly in details. In that year the first steam F.-E. was used by Mr Braithwaite, who shortly afterwards brought out a more powerful engine, and constructed also a *floating* steam F.-E. The use of steam did not make much progress at the time, and it was not until 1861 that Messrs. Shand & Mason made the first steam F.-E. used by the London Brigade. Since that time the steam F.-E. has become more and more important, there being few important towns without one or more. One of the largest kinds used weighs about 23 cwt., and can send a jet to a vertical height of 180 feet. These engines are specially constructed so that steam may be raised quickly—in the one just mentioned steam of 100 lbs. pressure per square inch can be obtained seven minutes after the fire is lit; of course this process may be going on as the engine is being driven to the fire, so that no time is lost. The modern F.-E. consists of one or more force-pumps (see PUMP), delivering water into an air chamber communicating with the discharge pipe and hose. By their action the air in the chamber is kept constantly compressed to any desired extent, and reacting by its elasticity upon the water, it forces it out in a continuous stream.

Fire-Escape', an apparatus for enabling persons in burning houses or buildings to escape. The name is strictly applied to a ladder 30 or 35 feet high, with a canvas trough behind it, and smaller sliding ladders attached to it, by which its length can be increased to 45 or 50 feet, and in some cases even more. The whole is supported in a nearly vertical position on two large wheels, so that it can readily be moved. In London there are about 120 fire-escapes, so placed that almost any house can be reached by one of them in five minutes. They belong to the 'Society for the Protection of Life from Fire,' an association founded in 1836, and supported by voluntary contributions. In our cities, where so many houses have only one narrow stair, communication by which sometimes becomes impossible at the very beginning of a fire, they have saved very many lives.

Fire-Fish, the name given to certain Teleostean fishes from their brilliant colouration. The best-known species is the red F.-F. (*Pteröis volitans*) of tropical seas, which belongs to the family *Triglidæ* or gurnards. The body is scaly, and has many spines and rays. The dorsal and pectoral fins are especially large, and their rays are prominent. The colour is a pinky brown with dark-brown markings. The average length is 8 or 9 inches. The flesh is eaten on the Ceylon coasts.

Firefly, a name sometimes applied generally to insects with phosphorescent or luminous properties, but restricted in a zoological sense to such forms as the Cucujo or F. of Brazil (*Pyrophorus luminosus*), the glow-worm (*Lampyris noctiluca*), and allied forms. The former insect belongs to the family *Elateridæ* of the *Coleoptera* or Beetle order of insects, and the latter is also a beetle belonging to the family *Lampyridæ*. The F. of Brazil is very luminous, the light proceeding from two spots at the base of the thorax, whilst two other shining patches exist beneath the wing-covers. These insects fly by night, and render the forests bright with their luminosity. Various other species are known. The glow-worm is familiar to all as a luminous insect or F. The females exhibit the utmost brilliance. The female glow-worm is wingless, the male being winged and of brown colour. Fireflies are most common in S. Europe and in tropical countries. How the luminosity is produced is still undetermined in an exact sense, but there appears to be little doubt that it is developed by the nerve-force acting through some special apparatus. See also LUMINOSITY and PHOSPHORESCENCE OF ANIMALS.

Fire Insu'rance, Law Regarding. When there has been damage by fire, notice should at once be given to the office, and an account given on oath or affirmation of the loss. Account-books and other vouchers should be shown in support of the account. It is well also to procure a certificate from the clergyman, and one or two others of position in the parish, not concerned in the loss, stating that they are well acquainted with the sufferer, and that they believe him to have sustained the damage alleged. To whatever amount persons insure, they can only recover the value of the loss sustained. A house being insured for £19,000 was totally destroyed by fire, but the company, though the premium on £19,000 had been paid for many years, refused to pay more than £12,000, alleging that this was ample value. If a policy be effected in several offices on the same subject, they are only liable proportionally to make good the loss. However small the damage to the subject insured, the office is liable; for example, under a policy on furniture, the office is liable for damage by a hot cinder. Most offices pay for damage caused by lightning or gas explosion, but the insurer should inquire as to this.

Firelock, the name given in the 16th c. to a musket or pistol with a wheel-lock, and afterwards to the musket with a flintlock, which in 1690 was introduced in place of the earlier matchlock. See FIREARMS.

Fire, Malicious Injuries by. See EXPLOSIVES.

Firenzuola, Agnolo, an Italian scholar and writer of fiction was born at Florence, September 28, 1493. He studied law at Siena and Perugia, but, while young, became a monk, and in 1525 was made abbot of a monastery at Spoleto. He was a friend of Aretin, is said to have led a profligate life, and died at Prato about 1545. His chief works are a free adaptation of the *Golden Ass* of Apuleius, *Apuleio, Dell' Asino d' Oro tradotto per Agnolo F.*, which excels the original in beauty of language; *Discorsi degli Animali*, partly imitations of Æsop; *Ragionamenti Amorosi*, *Novelli Otto*, licentious, sportive tales in the choicest Tuscan; *Dialogo delle Bellezze delle Donne;* two comedies, some satirical verses, &c. F. is one of the masters of Italian prose. His language is clear, flowing, and full of colour. See the Life in the edition of F.'s works published at Florence in 1848, and Maffei's *Storia della Letteratura Italiana* (Flor. 1853).

Fire-Proof Buildings. A building is fire-proof only when, in the event of a fire in one compartment, the fire burns itself out there without communicating with another compartment, or endangering the building. Considerable attention has been given to fire-proof construction, yet we have not made much progress in the art. Many buildings believed to be fire-proof, because in their construction brick, concrete, and iron are abundantly used, and wood very sparingly, when subjected to the fiery ordeal, assuredly succumb. The destruction of the London Pantechnicon in February 1874 is a case in point. Though constructed on the most approved principles, it was wholly consumed in a few hours. That conflagration proved the weakness of iron pillars as supports to brick arches, for they melted with the intense heat, or cracked when water was thrown upon them. Absolute fire-proof construction can only be attained at a great sacrifice of space. The compartments should be small, with thick firebrick walls supporting groined firebrick roofs. Where large floor areas are required, brick pillars should support the groined roofs. For valuable information on F.-P. B. see the *Transactions of the Society of Arts*.

Fire-Proofing, the art of diminishing the destructive effects of fire on inflammable materials. Textile fabrics are rendered non-inflammable by steeping them in any inorganic saline solution, whereby the fibres are coated with a protective crust that absorbs heat and excludes air. Fabrics so treated smoulder slowly when exposed to a high temperature, but do not burst into flame. For F.-P. light fabrics, phosphate of ammonium, alone or mixed with chloride of ammonium, sulphate of ammonium, or tungstate of sodium is recommended. The last named is most used for goods that require to be ironed. Little success has attended the efforts made to fix the protective agents in the fibre, by rendering the saline crust insoluble in water. Fire-proof clothing may be made with the fibrous mineral asbestos. The ancients were acquainted with the art of weaving it into garments. About the year 1828, Chevalier Aldini of Milan advocated its use for firemen's dress, in combination with cloth steeped in alum, and with wire-gauze. Wood is rendered incombustible, or nearly so, by painting it with silicate of soda, or by impregnating it with an aqueous solution of alum and sulphate of copper, or of common salt and alum. A new mode of F.-P. wood has recently been devised. Sulphate of zinc (2½ parts by weight), American potash (1 part), ammonium alum (2 parts), oxide of manganese (1 part), are mixed in a boiler, and water (2½ parts), at a temperature of 113° F., is run in. When the solution is effected, sulphuric acid (1 part), at 60°, is gradually introduced. The wood for F.-P. is submitted for three hours to the action of the solution, which is maintained in a state of ebullition during that time.

Fire-Proof Safes and other depositories. See SAFES.

Fire-Raising is in Scotch law the equivalent term to Arson (q. v.) in England. To constitute the crime there must have been actual burning, but it does not matter how small a portion of the subject has been consumed Ignition of furniture alone, when not a fixture (see FIXTURES) of a building, makes the culprit liable to a charge of an attempt at F.-R. Setting fire to one's own house, if so doing is not dangerous to the property of another, and if the act is not fraudulent, is not indictable. To set on fire growing crops, or to attempt to do so, is felony by statute. See EXPLOSIVE MIXTURES; GUNPOWDER, LAW REGARDING.

Fireship, a vessel laden with combustible matters, which in maritime warfare was sailed into an enemy's fleet, set on fire, and abandoned, in the hope that it might do damage or create confusion. The F. is of very early origin; we hear of its employment more than 2000 years ago. It is not used in modern warfare by civilised nations, although the Chinese employed fireships unsuccessfully against the British fleet before Canton in 1857.

Fireworks and Squibs. See PYROTECHNY, EXPLOSIVES.

Fire-Worshippers. See GUEBRES.

Fir'kin (Old Eng. *feower*, 'four'—Dan. *fire*—and dim. *kin*), the fourth part of a barrel, equal to seven and a half imperial gallons.

Fir'lot (Old Eng. *feower*, 'four'—Dan. *fire*—and Eng. *lot*, 'part or portion'), a dry measure Scots, equal to the fourth part of a Boll (q. v.).

Firm. See PARTNERSHIP.

Fir'mament is the Latin word (*firmamentum*) in the Vulgate for the Greek *stereōma* of the LXX. and the Hebrew *rakia* in Gen. i. 6, 7, &c. The literal meaning of the Hebrew word seems to be a thin solid plate which has been hammered out. Similar names for the sky, scientifically incorrect, but expressing its actual appearance, are found in other languages—Gr. *ouranos*, Eng. *heaven*, 'that which is elevated;' Gr. *koilon*, Lat. *cœlum*, 'the hollow place;' Ger. *heimeln*, 'a roof.' The Hebrew F., which was supported as if on pillars by mountains (2 Sam. xxii. 8; Job xxvi. 11), served a twofold purpose—first, of supporting a reservoir of water (Gen. i. 7; *cf.* Ps. civ. 3, cxlviii. 4), which descended as rain through windows (Gen. vii. 11, viii. 2; Mal. iii. 10) and doors (Ps. lxxviii. 23); secondly, of supporting the heavenly bodies—sun, moon, and stars (Gen. i. 15). According to the Christian fathers who commented on Genesis, as late at least as the Venerable Bede (8th c.), the earth was a flat plain skirted by mountains, on which the F. was supported like a dome, or stretched like a skin. In short, the fixity of the F. was necessarily combined with the flatness of the earth, a belief in which prevailed till the end of the 15th c., when the attempt of Columbus to prove its rotundity was condemned as irreligious by the Council of Salamanca. See Draper's *Conflict between Religion and Science* (International Science Series, 1875).

Fir'man (Pers. *ferman*, 'a command'), the official mandate of an Oriental sovereign, and especially of the Ottoman Porte. It also signifies the passport given to a traveller in the Turkish empire, and in India denotes a certificate giving permission to trade.

Firminy, a town in the department of Loire, France, 39 miles S.W. of Lyon by railway. It is surrounded by extensive coal-mines and stone-quarries. Pop. (1872) 8873.

Firola, a genus of Gasteropodous Molluscs belonging to the aberrant group *Heteropoda* or *Nudibranchiata*, in which the 'foot' of other *Gasteropoda* is modified to a flattened fin-like organ, used for swimming, the animals generally moving backdownwards through the water. The shell, at most rudimentary in the *Heteropoda*, is wanting in F. The genus gives the name to the family *Firolidæ*, in which a large body exists, and locomotion is performed by the modified foot, and by a tail-fin in addition. The body in F. is 4 or 5 inches long.

First'-Born. By the common instincts of human nature, which prompt parents to give their affection most fully to their F.-B., pre-eminent importance and privileges have always been granted to the eldest son in a family. According to the laws of most nations he succeeded to the official position and authority of his father, and for the same reason, as well as to enable him to sustain that dignity, received a larger share than his brothers of his father's wealth. According to the Mosaic law he inherited 'a double portion,' *i.e.*, twice as much as any of the other sons (Deut. xxi. 15-17). With the Hebrews, also, a special sanctity attached to the F.-B. both of man and beast, as devoted to the Lord in commemoration of the F.-B. of the Israelites being spared when those of the Egyptians were cut off. (See PASSOVER.) Of the animals, the clean (see Lev. xi.), if free from blemish, were offered in sacrifice (Deut. xv. 21); the unclean, not being fit for sacrifice, were to be put to death, to be sold, and the price given to the priest, or to be redeemed by the owner with a lamb or with six-fifths of its value (Exod. xiii. 13; Lev. xxvii. 11-13, 27). The F.-B. of man were all devoted to the Lord to be priests; but as they were superseded in this office by the Levites (q. v.), it was ordained that the F.-B. of the other tribes should be redeemed (Num. iii. 11-13, 40-46, xviii. 15).

First-Born, Law Regarding. See PRIMOGENITURE, HEIR, SUCCESSION.

First-Fruits. It was a common practice in ancient times to make an offering to the gods of the first of the fruits of the ground that were ripe, as an acknowledgment of their bounty in the past, and to procure from them good crops in the future. Such offerings were made by the Egyptians to Isis, by the Greeks to Demeter, Apollo, and Diana, and by the Romans to Ceres and Bacchus. Among the Hebrews, too, it was appointed by the Mosaic law not only that the first of all the produce of the ground should be offered to Jehovah, but also the first-born both of man and beast (Exod. xxii. 29, 30; Deut. xxvi. 2-11. (See FIRST-BORN.) Special occasions for the offering of F.-F. were—(1) At the Feast of the Passover, when the first sheaf of the harvest was brought to the priest, and by him waved before the Lord (Lev. xxiii. 5-12; (2) at the Feast of Pentecost, when a similar offering was made of two loaves of bread made from the new flour (Lev. xxiii. 15-17). Besides these public or national offerings, private offerings were to be made of the first-thrashed grain, of a cake of the first-ground meal (Num. xv. 17-21), of the best of the wine and the oil (Num. xviii. 12, 13), and in short, 'of all the fruit of the earth' (Deut. xxvi. 2). All these offerings fell to the priests, as part of their living (Deut. xviii. 3-5). The amount to be given as F.-F. was not fixed by the Levitical law; in the Mishna the minimum was fixed at one-sixtieth.

In the Christian Church the practice of dedicating F.-F. to God for the support of his servants was observed from an early period. At first the fathers represented the practice merely as becoming and expedient; but as the notion grew that the clergy had succeeded to the position and privileges of the Levites, the Levitical law on this matter was represented as binding on Christians, for which conclusive proof was found in Mal. iii. Full details on the subject are given in the *Apostolic Canons* and *Constitutions*. A species of F.-F. was latterly exacted from the clergy themselves by the popes. (See ANNATES.) See Spencer *De Legibus Hebræorum* (2d ed. Hag. 1686), and Smith's *Dict. of Christ. Antiquities* (1875).

Firth or **Frith** (Dan. and Norw. *fjord*, Sw. *fjärd*), an arm of the sea or the estuary of a river—a word in common use in Scotland, as the Moray F., the Firths of Clyde, Forth, Tay, &c.

Fischart', Johann, a German satirist, was born at Strasburg between 1545-50, studied law at Basel, visited England, lived as an advocate at Speier and as a bailiff at Forbach, where he died in 1589. F. was a man of considerable learning and great comic genius. He replied to the abusive attacks on Luther, which were common in his time, by fierce and telling satires and burlesques, full of rich, gross Aristophanic humour, and showing a marvellous command of language. Among his works are *Geschichtklitterung der Thaten der Helden Gargantua und Pantagruel* (1575), partly translated, partly imitated, from Rabelais; *Das Glückhafft-Schiff von Zürich* (1576); *Flöhatz Weibertratz* (1574); *Die zehn Alter der Wieber; Aller Praktik Grossmutter; Podagrammisch Trostbüchlein;* and *Psalmen und geistliche Lieder* (1576; new ed. Berl. 1849), which contain many fine sacred poems. A collected edition of F.'s poems was published by Kurz in 3 vols. (1866-68). See Wackernagel's *J. F.* (1870).

Fish, or **Fish-Plate,** a piece of wood or metal used in joining together the abutting ends of two members of a structure. The most familiar *fished joint* is that employed almost universally for connecting rails. Here the ends of the rails are made almost to touch, a F.-P. 15 to 18 inches long is placed upon each side of them, and the whole secured by two or three bolts through each rail. The importance of a sufficiently rigid rail-fastening is very great, not only on account of the increased comfort which it gives to travellers, owing to the smoothness of motion which it secures, but also because it greatly lessens the wear and tear of the rolling stock. Engineers have given much attention to the form and proportions of fish plates and joints with the view of finding out the best possible arrangement, and many patents have been taken out in connection with them. Fished joints are used also for timber ties and beams, for strengthening spring spars, and many other purposes.

Fish'er, John, Bishop of Rochester, was born at Beverley in Yorkshire about 1459, and after a distinguished college career at Cambridge, became Master of Michael House College in that university in 1495. As confessor to Margaret, Countess of Richmond, the mother of Henry VII., he induced her to found St. John's and Christ's Colleges. But for the Reformation F. would probably have had a peaceful and prosperous career. In 1501 he was chosen Chancellor of the University; in 1504 he became Bishop of Rochester. At first he was the favourite champion of Henry VIII., and wrote for him the pamphlet *Assertio Septem Sacramentorum*, for which that king obtained the title of 'Defender of the Faith.' But in 1527 he objected to the divorce of Queen Catherine, refused to acknowledge the legality of Henry's marriage with Anne Boleyn, and opposed Thomas Cromwell's scheme for the suppression of the monasteries. He was thrown into prison and released on paying a fine of £300; but in 1534, on refusing to acknowledge the king's supremacy in the Church, he was committed to the Tower, and his bishopric declared vacant. Pope Paul III. sent him a cardinal's hat as a consolation and mark of respect, but Henry brutally declared that F. would have to wear it on his shoulders, for he would not leave him a head. After a short trial for treason, the old man was beheaded, June 22, 1535. A biography of F., who was a writer of Scriptural commentaries, sermons, and controversial pamphlets, has been written by Lewis (2 vols. 1854).

Fish'eries. Under this term are generally included all the industries connected with procuring the creatures which inhabit either fresh or salt water, many of which have no connection with fish in their zoological relations. Thus the term includes the obtaining of such diverse animals and products as sponge, coral, pearl, shell-fish (including those valuable for their shells, as well as those sought for human food or as bait for other inhabitants of the sea), the crustaceans, as shrimps, crabs, and lobsters; and in the higher scale of animal life it is held to comprehend the capture of turtles, whales, seals, and their congeners. The only relation which these creatures bear to fish is the fact that they in common occupy the sea, and thus by F. are meant all animal products of the sea of whatever class. Here, however, will be noticed only the great industries for securing fish for human food from both salt and fresh water.

There is no way by which any approximately accurate estimate may be formed of the enormous value of the products annually drawn from the sea. Judging, however, by reliable statistics obtained for very limited areas, the wealth annually derived from the sea must be very great; and when the great extent of sea-board altogether neglected or only imperfectly fished is taken into account, there cannot be any doubt that F. are capable of indefinite expansion without crippling the productive resources of the sea. It is only in the case of a few minor creatures—noticeably the oyster, lobster, and crab on British coasts—that overfishing, or rather indiscriminate and wasteful habits of fishing, has resulted in any decline of productiveness, such as to call for legislative interference.

Fresh-Water Fisheries.—The one fresh-water fish of paramount economic importance is the salmon, the F. of which in many Scottish rivers, particularly the Tay, are of very great value to their proprietors. While salmon fishing is the most prominent fresh-water industry, it is also highly esteemed for sport. It is prosecuted with draw nets, or in certain positions with stake nets; and by sportsmen the fish is taken with fly-hooks. The rivers of Northern Europe and America abound in salmon, and the produce of the American rivers now appears largely in commerce as 'tinned' salmon. The trout and other species of the salmon kind come next to the salmon in importance as fresh-water fish. After these may be reckoned the eel, pike, and perch; and in Russia, various species of sturgeon, obtained from the Volga and other rivers, are sources of valuable food delicacies, as well as of isinglass.

Sea Fisheries are of much greater economic importance than fresh-water F. They are prosecuted in a variety of ways, the chief of which are:—(1) Trawling, (2) drift-net fishing, (3) line fishing, (4) sean fishing, (5) bag-net fishing, (6) kettle nets and weirs, and (7) trammel or set nets. (1) Trawling is performed with a triangular bag which has an arrangement for keeping its mouth open. The apparatus is called a trawl, and it is drawn along the bottom of the water. It is much employed by English fishers for catching haddocks, soles, turbots, plaice, and flat fish generally. (2) Drift nets are long nets having a definite size of mesh, and they are shot from boats and allowed to depend perpendicularly in the water, the upper side being kept at the surface by cork floats. They are used chiefly for the herring, pilchard, and mackerel fishing, the shoals of which, meeting these barriers in their course, attempt to push through them and so get entangled by their gills in the meshes of the nets. It is essential for the success of this style of fishing that it be conducted at night. (3) Line fishing is of two kinds—long-line fishing, in which many hooks are attached to a long central line, and baited for catching cod, ling, halibut, and haddocks; and short or hand line fishing, in which only a single hook is employed for the capture of cod. (4) The sean or sweep net is a long length of netting which is used for enclosing and sweeping a certain area of water in much the same way as in salmon fishing. It is employed for catching herrings, sprats, pilchard, mackerel, and various small fishes. (5) Bag nets are large open-mouthed bags like great trawls, used for sprat and whitebait catching, &c. (6) Kettle nets and weirs are structures placed along the coast between high and low water with the view of entrapping fish which may enter with the flowing tide, and which are secured when the water recedes. (7) Trammel nets are like drift nets in their action, but are fixed between stakes or other stays. The Cornish trammel consists of three nets set parallel to each other, the two outer having wide meshes, while that in the centre is fine in the mesh. The fish, passing through the outer net, pushes against the central net, forcing part of it through a mesh of the opposite outer net, thus forming a bag or pocket in which it is itself securely fastened.

Of all sea F. none equals in importance, extent, and value the herring fishery. It is most extensively cultivated along the N. and E. coasts of Scotland, the principal stations being Fraserburgh, Peterhead, Wick, and Stornoway. The quantity of herrings taken annually on the Scottish coasts alone is prodigious, and there is good reason to conclude that the number taken by fishermen is but a fraction of what is destroyed by cod, dog-fish, sea-birds, and other natural enemies of the herring. Notwithstanding all these causes, there is not the slightest appearance of any decrease in the productiveness of the herring fishery, but quite the opposite. From annual returns which have been made by the Fishery Board of Scotland since 1809, it appears that, with many violent fluctuations, there has been on the whole a steady increase in the quantity of herrings cured yearly down to the present time. The largest cure reported during that lapse of time occurred in 1874, when 1,000,561 barrels were cured, which, allowing 750 herrings to each barrel, would give a total of more than 750,000,000 separate fish. The cure of 1875 stands second on the list with 942,980 barrels, and the only other year in which 900,000 barrels were exceeded was in 1873, when 939,233¼ barrels were cured. These enormous numbers, it must be remembered, are exclusive of the incalculable quantity retailed throughout the country as fresh or as smoked herrings.

The Scottish Fishery Board also takes cognisance of the cod, ling, and hake fishing, which comes next in value to the herring industry. For these fishes the Shetland Islands are of more value than all the rest of Scotland together. The number returned as caught during 1875 was reported as 5,791,387 for the whole of Scotland, of which no less that 3,458,799 were taken on the Shetland stations. In 1875 there were cured dry 187,788½ cwt., and in pickle 8503½ cwt. were prepared. The fishing of 1875, judging by the weight of fish cured, was the most successful in the records of the Scottish Fishery Board. In 1873, 160,716¼ cwt. were reported as cured, and in no other year did the total weight cured reach so high as 150,000 cwt. The extent of Scottish sea F. may be computed by the fact that in 1875 there were employed in the industry 14,655 boats of a total tonnage of 105,506 tons, with 45,082 men and boys. The F. gave direct employment to 89,221 persons; and in boats, nets, and lines the capital invested was estimated to amount to £1,092,275.

The principal markets for cured herrings are found in Germany and Russia, and the system of branding barrels by Government authorities greatly facilitates the disposal of cargoes. Five grades of brand are adopted, according to quality. 'Full crown' indicates fish containing roe and milt. 'Crown maties' are fat fish of smaller size than fulls, and the remaining grades of brand are 'crown spent,' 'crown mixed,' and 'crown repacked.' A fee of 4d. per barrel is charged for branding, and from this source £8729, 16s. 6d. was obtained in 1875. Dried cod, ling, and hake are principally disposed of in Spain. The Dutch and Scandinavians also prosecuted sea fishing very extensively, and the inhabitants of Iceland and the Faröe Islands depend very largely for subsistence and commerce on the cod and ling F., with, in Iceland, shark fishing, from which a valuable liver-oil is obtained. On the American coast, Newfoundland is the seat of the most valuable F., and there, in addition to enormous quantities of cod, the salmon, capelin, Labrador herring, mackerel, halibut, and turbot are obtained in great quantities.

Fishery, Free, is in England an exclusive right of fishing in a public stream. It is a royal franchise, and must be at least as old as the reign of Henry II., to grant the right being expressly prohibited by Magna Charta.

Fish'es, the lowest group of Vertebrate animals, are adapted for locomotion in water by being provided with gills for breathing, during the whole of life; by the heart consisting of an auricle and a ventricle; by possessing cold blood, which is carried in an arterial condition from the gills to the body; by the body being usually covered with scales; by the limbs being developed in the form of fins; and by the embryo possessing neither an Amnion (q. v.) nor an Allantois (q. v.). The *form* of F. is that best adapted for easy locomotion in water. In the great majority of cases the body is pointed at each end, and flattened somewhat from side to side, whilst it is also rounded on the sides. In some F. it is apparently flattened above and below—as in the flounder, plaice, and other 'flat-F.' But in these cases, the body is greatly flattened *from side to side*, the two eyes being through a peculiarity in development brought round to one side of the head. The skates, rays, &c., are more truly *flat-F.* than the flounders, &c., since their dorsal or back surface really appears to be flattened, owing chiefly to the great enlargement of the pectoral or breast fins. The bodies of most F. are scaly. In some cases (such as the eels), where scales are either very small or altogether wanting, the body is generally covered with a *mucous* secretion, serving to protect it from the action of the water. The scales of F. may be *cycloid*, as in herrings, salmon, &c.; *placoid*, as in skates and sharks; *ctenoid*, as in perches, &c.; or *ganoid*, as in the sturgeons, bony pikes, &c. This last form of scale is most common in fossil F. Along the sides of most F. a line named the *lateral line* may be perceived. This line was formerly believed to be connected with the production of the mucous secretion which protected the body or scales, but it is now ascertained to be connected with the exercise of the sense of *touch*, since the terminations of nerves have been traced to a connection with this line; and the acts of many F. in rubbing the sides of their bodies against foreign objects seem to lend support to this latter belief. The *endoskeleton* of F. may be of very varied nature. Thus in the lowest fish of all, the *Amphioxus* or lancelet, there is no skeleton to speak of, this structure being represented by a soft cellular rod, the *Notochord* (q. v.), or *chorda dorsalis*, which represents the immature and imperfectly-developed spine. In other F., such as sharks, skates, rays, the skeleton is imperfectly ossified, and is composed of *cartilage;* whilst in the great majority, including the familiar food-F., it is of bony nature. The spine of F. (save in one instance, that of the bony pike or *Lepidosteus*) is composed of vertebræ, hollow at either end, and hence named *amphicælous*. When two vertebræ are opposed, a cavity is formed by the opposition of the vertebral bodies; and this cavity forms a kind of universal joint, permitting the freest possible motion and movement of the spine in swimming. In the bony pike the vertebræ are *opisthocælous*, that is, hollow behind and convex in front. The spine exhibits a division into two regions only—an *abdominal* and a *caudal* region, no distinct cervical, dorsal, or lumbar portions being recognisable. The vertebræ of the abdomen possess an upper or neural canal, neural spines, and two transverse processes, to which latter the ribs are attached. The caudal or tail vertebræ have an inferior or hæmal arch, but no distinct transverse processes. The ribs are not attached below to a sternum or breastbone, but simply imbedded in the muscles. The *interspinous bones* of F. are dagger-shaped bones which exist in the middle line of the body, and are attached below to the spines of the vertebræ; above they support the rays of the dorsal and anal fins. The *fins* of F. may be divided into two groups. The *pectoral* and *ventral* fins are paired, and represent the fore and hind limbs of other vertebrates respectively. The other fins are single or median, and are placed in the middle line of the body. Those on the back are the *dorsal* fins; the *anal* fin is placed near the *anus* or *vent* in the lower aspect of the body, and the *caudal* or *tail-fin* is the chief agent in locomotion. The fins are supported by bony rays or spines, and by soft rays. The *caudal* fin of F. is always set vertically, and works from side to side, the tail-fin of the whales and Sirenia amongst mammals being placed horizontally. The *digestive system* of F. comprehends a mouth, usually provided with numerous teeth, which are replaced when lost or injured, and which are not set in sockets, but attached by a ligament to the bones of the mouth. The stomach (*h*) is large, and provided at its hinder extremity with a number of blind sacs or appendages, varying from one to sixty or more in number, named *pyloric cæca*, which are supposed to represent a *pancreas* or sweetbread. The intestine (*e e*) is shut as a rule, and is often provided with a spiral coil, serving to increase its digestive area. The liver (*d*) is usually large and oily. The *kidneys* (*k*) are also large, and a true urinary bladder is doubtfully represented. The blood of F. is cold, and contains nucleated blood corpuscles. It is of red colour in all save the lancelet. The heart (*a*) is two-chambered, and consists of an *auricle*, which receives the venous blood from the body, and of a *ventricle* which propels it to the *gills* or *branchiæ* (*q*) for purification. In many F. a third chamber of the heart is formed by the dilatation of the great blood-vessels of the gills, this dilatation being named the *bulbus arteriosus*. In some F. (*e.g.*, sharks, &c.) this latter structure contracts in a rhythmical manner. The *gills* (*q q*) or breathing organs of F. consist of comb-like structures borne on branchial or gill arches, and composed of delicate filaments in which the blood is exposed to the aerating influences of the external water. In the sharks, rays, &c., the gills exist in the form of pouch-like cavities. The water for aeration is admitted by the mouth, and after passing over the gills and yielding up its oxygen, is ejected from the gill-chambers at the sides of the mouth, behind the *operculum* or gill-cover (*p*), or in the sharks, &c., by special apertures. The *air* or *swimming bladder* of F. (see AIR-BLADDER), or *sound*, as it is also called, is used for altering the specific gravity of these animals, and thus enabling them to rise or sink in the water. The *nervous system*, comprising a brain, spinal cord, and nerves, is distinct in all F. save the Lancelet (q. v.). The senses comprise large eyes, internal *ears*, touch (performed by the lateral line), and smell. The nostrils of all F., except the hag-F. (*Myxine*) and the *Lepidosirens* or mud-F., are simple closed or pocket-like sacs. F. are *oviparous* animals, producing eggs, from waries (*i i*), the young being afterwards hatched. But in some cases (skate, dog-F., &c.) the eggs may be enclosed in special cases or capsules, and in sharks there would appear to be an intimate connection between the parent and young, reminding one of the *placental* connection of *Mammalia*. As in all *Vertebrata*, the sexes are distinct. The *habits* of F. differ very widely. Migration is not uncommon with many, although the nature of the migratory movements is less susceptible of determination than in the case of land animals. An idea of the *classification of F.*, according to modern zoology, may be formed from the following table:—

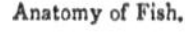
Anatomy of Fish.

Order.	Example.
1. *Pharyngobranchii* (pharynx-breathers).	The amphioxus or lancelet.
2. *Marsipobranchii* (pouch-gilled breathers).	Lampreys and hag-F.
3. *Teleostei* (F. with bony skeletons).	Cod, salmon, herrings, and all familiar F.
4. *Elasmobranchii* (plate-gilled breathers).	Sharks, rays, dog-F., &c.
5. *Ganoidei* (F. with ganoid scales).	Sturgeon, bony pike, &c., and many fossil F.
6. *Dipnoi* (F. breathing by gills and rudimentary lungs).	Lepidosirens or mud-F.

(By the majority of naturalists the *Dipnoi* are classified as a subdivision of the *Ganoidei*, this arrangement reducing the orders of F. to five in number.)

Fossil F.—The first traces of F. which appear in the rock formations occur in the Upper Silurian formations, these traces, consisting of the fin-spines and placoid scales, belonging to F. most nearly allied to the *Elasmobranchii*. In the Devonian or Old Red Sandstone rocks, fish remains are so plentiful that this epoch has been named the 'Age of F.' The Devonian fossil F. belong chiefly to the Ganoid order. The Teleostean or true bony F. do not make their appearance until the Cretaceous epoch at the close of the Mesozoic period; and three groups of F. (*Marsipobranchii*, *Pharnygobranchii*, and *Dipnoi*) have, as far as is yet known, left no traces of their existence in any rock formation.

Law Regarding F.—They become the property of him who catches them except royal fish. (See FISHES, ROYAL.) Though it requires a royal grant to entitle a man to fish for salmon, yet the salmon when taken by a man who has no grant belong to himself. 24 and 25 Vict. c. 96 imposes penalties on persons taking fish without permission from water which is private property. Persons found angling against the provisions of the Act, which does not extend to Scotland, may be required by the owner or his servant to deliver their fishing implements. On refusal they may be forcibly seized. But if the implements are taken, there is no further penalty or damage. To destroy the dam of any fishpond which is private property, with intent to destroy the fish, or to put lime or other noxious material into it with the same intent, renders the offender liable to penal servitude.

Fishes, Royal, are those which by common law belong to the crown, being the whale or the sturgeon when thrown ashore or caught near the coast. The law is a little obscure, however, and is modified or altered by local custom.

Fish-Hooks are made by a series of hand processes. The steel wire is first cut into lengths, and then slit with a lever knife near one end to form the barb. Each length, after being filed round the point and barb, is bent to the hook form by means of an instrument with a suitable core and pin. The end of the shank is then hammered flat to enable the hook to be secured to the line. The hook is next hardened, made stiff and elastic by tempering, and finished by blueing. F.-H. are sometimes swivelled at the head to prevent the twisting of the line. Redditch, in Worcestershire, is the great place for the manufacture of F.-H. In the United States they are made extensively by Crosby's automatic machine, which, it is said, is capable of turning out 6000 highly-finished F.-H. every hour.

Fish'ing-Tac'kle. See ANGLING.

Fish-Lice, or **Sea-Lice**, a name given to several genera and species of lower Crustaceans, from their parasitic habits. They attach themselves to the skin, gills, and other parts of fishes and other aquatic animals. One of the best-known forms is *Cymothöe œstrum*, which adheres to fishes by means of its hooked legs and suctorial mouth. Other genera are *Achtheres*, of which *A. percarum* of the perch is a good example; *Argulus*, of which *A. foliaceus*, common on fresh-water fishes, is a familiar species; and *Caligulus*, species of which are common on marine fishes. These fish-lice belong to the Crustacean orders *Rhizocephala* and *Ichthyophthira*. In their development they pass through a metamorphosis, appearing at first as lively free-swimming bodies, but eventually losing their limbs, &c., settle down to a parasitic life.

Fish'ponds. See PISCICULTURE.

Fish-Skin Disease, or **Ichthyo'sis Ve'ra**, is a disease of the epidermis characterised by a general dryness and roughness of the skin, modified in appearance in different regions of the body. The defective nutrition of the texture of the skin is most apparent in the limbs, particularly the arms, and there is a marked deficiency of subcutaneous adipose tissue. When the skin is hard, it may be moved about on the subcutaneous fascia as if there were no binding tissue between the under surface of the corium and the structures beneath; and it remains stiff like leather, apparently depending upon the lines of motion for its power of adaptation to the movements of the joints. The skin of the face may be perfectly normal, while that of the hands and arms may be dry and wrinkled, like the withered limbs of old age. Treatment:—General hygenic measures, nutritive diet with cod-liver oil; arseniate of soda, or Fowler's solution; Donovan's solution: locally, frictions and inunctions, bathing, &c. The disease is of a very obstinate nature, and its cure is difficult and seldom complete. See *Diseases of the Skin*, by Erasmus Wilson (Lond. 1857), T. Macall Anderson (Lond. 1874), and by Tilbury Fox (Lond. 1876).

Fissip'arous, a term used to describe reproduction by a process of division. It is well seen in the reproduction of many of the lower forms of animal and plant life, and it also probably takes place in the human body in the formation of colourless blood cells, pus corpuscles, modified epidermic cells, &c.

Fissiros'tres (Lat. 'split-beaked'), a sub-order of the order *Insessores* (q. v.) or Perching birds, distinguished by the so-called 'cleft' nature of the beak; the 'gape' or mouth-opening being very wide, prolonged far back on the head, and pointed with bristles, of service to these birds in the capture of insect prey. The beak itself is short. Typical examples are the swallows, &c. (*Hirundinidæ*), the swifts (*Cypselidæ*), and goat-suckers (*Caprimulgidæ*).

Fissurell'idæ, a family of Gasteropodous Molluscs including the forms popularly known as 'keyhole limpets.' The shells of these forms have an opening at the apex, which has suggested the popular name. The family belongs to the Holostomatous group of the Prosobranchiate Gasteropods. The shell is conical, and its aperture is subservient to the respiration or breathing of these forms. *Fissurella maxima* is a familiar species, and the family also includes the genera *Emarginula* and *Parmophorus*.

Fis'tula (Lat. 'a pipe'), or **Sin'us** (Lat. 'a winding'), a narrow passage, the walls of which are always indurated, consisting of a layer of imperfectly-formed granulations discharging ichorous pus. The passage, which is often long and winding, has an external orifice somewhat protuberant, situated under or in the midst of granulations. F. is, therefore, a chronic abscess without disposition to close. The causes of this non-closure may be—(1) the presence of some foreign body, such as a piece of dead bone; (2) the passage of irritating secretions, such as urine, fæces, saliva, &c.; and (3) the contraction of neighbouring muscles preventing the coalescence of the sides of the abscess, as when the abscess is situated in the neighbourhood of the sphincter ani. The treatment of F. must have reference to its cause, and the foreign body or irritating substance must be removed. In recent cases a cure may be effected by pressure; or a healthy inflammation may be excited by injecting the F. with tincture of iodine; by means of a seton; by actual cautery, or by galvanic cautery. The treatment of F. should always be intrusted to a skilful surgeon, and in such a case a complete cure may be effected in even the most distressing cases. That form of the disease called vesico-vaginal F., which renders life a burden to those who suffer from it, may now be cured by a simple and almost painless operation, for which the profession is indebted to the ingenuity of American surgeons, and especially to Dr. Marion Sims of New York.

Fistular'idæ, a group of Teleostean fishes, which from the prolongation of the jaws have been named 'pipe fishes,' 'tobacco-pipe fishes,' 'bellows fishes,' and the like. The genera *Centriscus*, *Fistularia*, are illustrative of this group, which is distinguished by the elongated body, by the tube-like jaws and small mouth, by the scaly body, and by the ventral fins being placed on the abdomen and possessing six spines. The true pipe-fishes or *Syngnathidæ* belong to a different group, that of the *Lophobranchii*.

Fistuli'na, a genus of fungi related to Boletus (q. v.), and represented by the British species *F. hepatica*, found growing on oaks, beeches, chestnuts, and walnut trees. The specific name *hepatica* is derived from the appearance of these fungi when old; the surface becoming brown, and not unlike the liver in outward aspect. The colour is red, and the fungus may attain a size of 5 feet in circumference, and a weight of 7 or 8 lbs. Berkeley gives an instance of one which weighed 30 lbs. The F. is an esculent, and is eaten on the Continent.

Fitch'y, or **Fitché**, in heraldry, pointed at the end; *e.g.*, *a cross fitchée* is a cross with one end sharply pointed.

Fits, a term popularly applied to any sudden seizure of disease, more particularly to those implying loss of consciousness or a change in the condition of the mind, such as apoplexy, convulsions, epilepsy, &c.

Fitz (Fr. *fils*, Old Fr. *fiz*, from Lat. *filius*, 'a son'), a prefix denoting at first merely descent, and afterwards applied to illegitimate sons of kings and princes of the blood—as *Fitzroy*, 'son of the king.'

Fitz'roy, a name of frequent occurrence in Australian topography, and derived from Sir Charles A. Fitzroy, who was governor of New South Wales from 1846 to 1855, and under whom the colony received the boon of responsible government. After him are named the following:—1. A town in Victoria, forming a suburb of Melbourne, but under distinct municipal government, and inhabited chiefly by the more well-to-do citizens. Pop. 16,500.—2. A county of New South Wales in the Clarence (N.E.) district.—3. A river in Queensland, which rises in the Peak Range, and after a tortuous course of 300 miles, falls into the S. Pacific at Port Curtis, in 23° 30′ S. lat., 151° 50′ E. long. The important town of Rockhampton (q. v.) is situated on the F., 35 miles from its mouth.

Fi'ume ('the river,' formerly *St. Veit am Flaum*, from the Lat. *Fanum St. Viti ad flumen*; Illyrian *Reka*), a town of Austro-Hungary, in the district of F., 40 miles S.E. of Trieste. It stands on the Adriatic, in a narrow and wild pass, where the Fiumara falls into the Adriatic. Rocky heights, on one of which is the old castle of Fersata, rise behind it, and before it the Bay of Quarnero is studded with green islands. The old town, straggling and gloomy, overhangs the new town, which has many handsome, spacious, and colonnaded streets. Among the finest buildings are the cathedral of St. Veit, the nunnery, gymnasium, and hospital. Near F. is a church much frequented by pilgrims. F. has manufactures of linen, wool, leather, paper, &c., and considerable shipbuilding. It was once the chief port of Hungary, but its trade has fallen greatly away. Pop. 13,314; of the district, 17,884.

Five Forks, a district in Dinwiddie county, Virginia, where the Federals, under General Sheridan, won a decisive victory over the Confederates, April 1, 1865.

Five Points is a name given to the five articles of doctrine which the Arminians presented to the States of Holland (1611), as embodying their views on predestination and grace, on which alone at that time they differed from Calvinists. See ARMINIUS.

Fives, a game played by striking a ball with the hand against a high wall, so named because the number of points, fifteen or twenty-five, necessary to score a win is a multiple of five. The 'bounds' of the game are marked by one chalk line on the wall, a yard from the ground, and a second on the ground, 10 feet from the wall. The players of each side engage the ball alternately, striking it either as it rebounds from the wall, or as it springs up from the ground. Missing the ball or striking it so that it falls within the 'bounds' counts one point for the opposing side. F. is an ancient game, and in England was formerly called 'hand tennis.' In 'bat-F.' the ball is struck with a bat in place of with the hand.

Fixed Air was the name given by Black, its discoverer, to carbonic acid gas. He so named it in consequence of the power possessed by certain substances (potash, lime, magnesia, &c.) of absorbing or *fixing* it.

Fixed Bodies are those which cannot be volatilised, nor which suffer change when they are exposed to a high temperature.

Fixed Oils are such as do not evaporate at ordinary temperatures; for example, the oils of olive, linseed, and rapeseed.

Fixed Stars. See STARS.

Fix'ing, the term applied in photography to the operation following development, and immediately preceding the exposure of the picture to diffused light. It consists in depriving the picture of the salts surrounding the image, which are still sensitive to light, by means of hyposulphite of soda or cyanide of potassium solution.

Fix'tures. Whatever is fixed to the soil or outhouse or farmyard wall so as to become a part of it, will at the expiration of a lease belong to the lessor, but a tenant may remove anything which he has placed for the convenience of his trade, such as engines, counters, &c., provided he does it during his term, and has not made an agreement to the contrary. Erections for the purpose of farming and agriculture do not come under the exceptions with respect to trade, and cannot be taken down again, but a nurseryman in England is allowed to remove his greenhouses and also his small trees and shrubs (Wyndham *v.* Way). Though on this special point a contrary decision has been come to in Scotland, the same considerations of public expediency will generally determine the law regarding F. in both countries. The general rule is, that things fixed with nails cannot be removed, but if fastened by a screw they may, provided the removal does not cause serious damage to the premises. All F. put in by the tenant must be removed during his term, otherwise on expiration of the term they become the landlord's. Mr. Commissioner Fonblanque lately came to the following conclusions in the case of a bankrupt :—That articles merely resting on the soil, however heavy, are goods and chattels (see CHATTELS); that if they are slightly connected with one another and with the freehold, but may be severed without material injury to the freehold, they are goods and chattels, as are also articles fixed to the freehold by bolts or screws; but that articles mainly sunk in the soil or built on it are real estate. In Dumergin *v.* Rumsey, it was held that tenant's F. are not chattels till severed, and it is competent to a landlord to make an agreement with his tenant which shall, notwithstanding an abandonment by the tenant of his property in the F. during the term, in the event of an execution against the tenant, enable the landlord to re-enter and retain the F. against the executing creditor. See FENCES.

Flacc'us, C. Valerius, a native of Padua, who is supposed to have died about 88 A.D., is now known only as the author of an unfinished epic poem in eight books on the Argonautic expedition. 'F. has attained to somewhat of the outward form, but to nothing of the inward spirit, of his great model the Æneid.' The *Argonautica* was translated into English verse by Nicholas Whyte (1565).

Flag (lit. 'that which flies or flutters,' from Old Eng. *fleogan*, 'to fly'), a light cloth worked in a specific shape or pattern, and displayed in the field or on board ship as an emblem or signal. Under this designation are included the royal standard, the colours of regiments, and all ensigns, banners, and the signals used in the army for marking off ground to be occupied by troops, and in the navy for the transmission of messages from ship to ship. The great flag of Britain is the royal standard, bearing the arms of the United Kingdom, and hoisted only in the presence of the sovereign or a member of the royal family; the next is that of the Lord High Admiral—an anchor on a red field; and the third in importance is the Union Jack (q. v.), the national flag of Great Britain. The British ensign is a red F. with the Union Jack borne as a *canton*, or occupying the upper corner next the flagstaff. In the British navy the centre squadron, commanded by the admiral, carry red ensigns at the *main*; the van-squadron, commanded by the vice-admiral, carry white ensigns at the *fore*; and the rear squadron, commanded by the rear-admiral, carry blue ensigns at the *mizen* or sternmost mast. The broad pennant is the special flag of an admiral, but every man-of-war carries a pennant, the colour of which defines the squadron to which the ship belongs. By means of flags of easily-distinguished shape and colour, each of them representing letters or numbers signifying words or sentences, and to which there is an official key, vessels can communicate with freedom, certainty, and rapidity. Nelson's famous message at Trafalgar was communicated by means of F. signals, and so rapidly, that, in recognition of it, all the ships of the fleet were manned simultaneously. In 1855 a new system of signalling for the merchant service was adopted by a specially-appointed committee, by means of which, using eighteen flags and three pennants, 78,642 signals can be made, each consisting of not more than four flags at a hoist.

Flag-Captain, the captain who sails in the flag-ship—*i.e.*, the admiral's ship in any squadron—and who relieves the admiral of many of the ordinary duties of command.

Fla'gellants (Lat. *flagellantes*, 'the scourgers'), the name given to those mediæval fanatics who believed in the possibility of expiating sin by self-inflicted castigation. This practice was not a very early one in the Christian Church, flagellation being used at first solely as a punishment. About the 11th c., however, it began to be employed as a substitute for pecuniary penance, a year of penance being commuted into the payment of 26 silver *solidi* (£4) or the infliction of 3000 lashes. It is told of one famous hermit, St. Dominic of the Iron Cuirass, that he inflicted on himself in six days so many stripes that he discharged a century of penance (Fleury's *Eccles. Hist.*, vol. xiii.). Numerous penitents of both sexes adopted this mode of self-torment, and it is said to have been a special favourite among ladies of quality (Chais's *Lettres sur les Indulgences*, vol. ii.). The practice continued down to the end of the 13th c. as one of the ordinary forms of penitential observance, but at that period there broke out in Italy an endemic of superstition, due to a belief in the approaching end of the world, which took the shape of flagellantism, and rapidly spread all over Europe. The F. became a regular society; they marched with naked shoulders through the streets of the towns, each one holding a scourge of leathern thongs, with which he lashed his back till the blood ran. Men, women, and even children of tender years joined in these processions, and all classes were represented. Sometimes the throng was led by a priest; banners, crucifixes, and at night lighted tapers, were borne before them. At times they would stretch themselves on the earth in the form of a cross, and in this attitude undergo the severest discipline at each other's hands. The chief 13th c. outbreak of this fanaticism began at Perugia in 1260, and though promptly suppressed in Italy, showed itself in various districts of France and Austria. The F. next became prominent in the middle of the 14th c., when the dreaded plague called the Black Death evoked a universal religious frenzy. This outbreak was both wider spread and more extravagant than the former. It reached as far as England, appearing in London. A band numbering 120 exhibited their self-imposed tortures in the streets of the city, but do not appear to have succeeded in making any converts (Lingard's *Hist. of Eng.*, vol. iii.). The Church, however, was at this period forced to interfere, flagellantism having been elevated by its votaries into the position of a sacrament, as a 'baptism of blood.' Clement VII. anathematised the F.; but they were not suppressed until their frequently impure excesses had overrun Germany, the Low Countries, Sweden, and Switzerland (Baluze's *Vitæ Pontif. Avenion.*, vol. i.). The third and final outbreak of the mania took place in 1414 in Thuringia and Lower

Saxony. Flagellantism here assumed its wildest phase, and became distinctly heretical, rejecting all practical religion, the sacraments, purgatory, prayer for the dead, &c. Salvation was to be secured by the scourge, and that alone. The leader of these fanatics was one Konrad Schmidt of Sangerhausen, who was burned in 1414 by Schönefeld the Inquisitor, along with many of his followers. Schmidt's 'Fifty Articles of the F.' were condemned by the Council of Constance (Von der Hardt's *Acta Concilii Constant.*, vol. i.), and the heresy was thus stamped out. Flagellantism, as an excess of religious revival, did not again appear; but the Romish Church to this day sanctions a discipline of self-castigation. See Schötgen's *Historia Flagellantium*, Boileau's *Histoire des Flagellans*, Delolme's *History of the F., or the Advantages of Discipline* (an English paraphrase of Boileau's work), Muratori's *Antiq. Ital. Medii Ævi* (vol. vii.), Baluze's *Miscellanea* (vol. i.), Forstemann's *Christliche Geisslergesellschaften*, Gerson's tract *Contra Sectam Flagellantium*, Wadding's *Annales Minorum Fratrum*, Mosheim's *Church History*, Hallam's *Middle Ages*, *Mysticism and the Mystics*, and Cooper's *Flagellation and the F.*

Flage'olet, an instrument with a mouthpiece like a whistle, and fingered like a flute. It is easy to play, and the quality of its tones is pleasant, but it does not possess sufficient individuality or richness to give it a place among orchestral instruments. The Harmonics (q. v.) of the violin and other stringed instruments have sometimes been called, very clumsily, F. tones.

Flag'-Lieutenant, the officer in a flag-ship who communicates the admiral's orders, either personally or by signal, to the ships in command, and performs generally such duties as an aide-de-camp is intrusted with in relation to a general.

Flag'-Officer, in the navy, is one who has the right to carry a flag at his mast-head denoting his rank—a privilege confined to admirals, vice-admirals, rear-admirals, and commodores, or captains in command.

Flag of the Prophet, the sacred flag (*Sanjak-Sherif*) of the Moslem, and the most highly-prized of the Mohammedan relics, is a black banner formed of the curtain that hung in front of the door of Ayesha, one of Mohammed's wives; was obtained by the followers of Omar at Damascus; and is preserved in a casket in the Seraglio, where it is guarded by emirs. It is never unfurled.

Flag'-Ship, the ship in which the admiral sails, and which carries his flag. From this ship, usually the largest in the squadron, orders are signalled to the other vessels.

Flag'stones are rocks of calcareous or argillaceous sandstones and limestones, which split easily into large flat slabs useful for paving. Those of Yorkshire and Caithness are well known for their hardness and durability.

Flahau'lt de la Billarderie, Auguste Charles Joseph, Comte de, a French soldier and diplomatist, was born at Paris, April 20, 1785, became aide-de-camp to Napoleon, distinguished himself in the Peninsular war and at Leipsic, was made a general and count, and fought at Waterloo. He afterwards married a Scottish heiress, Lady Keith, and in 1830 recovered his position in the French army. He was ambassador at Vienna from 1841 to 1848, and at London in 1860. He was made Grand Chancellor of the Legion of Honour in 1864, and died at Paris, 2d September 1870.

Flam'borough Head (Old Eng. *Fleamburh*, so named probably from its *flame* or beacon), a headland on the Yorkshire coast, on the N.E. boundary of Bridlington Bay. It is formed by a line of chalk cliffs, rising to 450 feet, and runs for 6 miles into the sea. It has a lighthouse 214 feet high, and is crossed by an old British work known as Danes' Dyke.

Flamboy'ant, the latest and feeblest style of Gothic architecture in France. It is named from the flame-like forms of its characteristic traceries—intricate reticulations of delicate gauzy texture, woven of thin, wavy lines into meshes of every diversity of size. There is good and bad F., the latter being that in which ornament is allowed to impair construction. Even good F. is Gothic without magnificence or serenity, and its restless caprice is only redeemed by endless variety and floral grace. Ruskin says, 'The F. leaf-mouldings are beautiful, because they nestle and run up the hollows, and fill the angles, and clasp the shafts' in the manner of natural leaves. A feature of the style is the twining of twigs and stalks into pillars. When mouldings meet, they are apparently interlaced or run through each other. While the windows and doors are generally large and richly carved, the wall surfaces are comparatively bare. A mark of the most debased F. is the figure of the *fleur-de-lis* in tracery bars. F., which prevailed in the 15th and 16th centuries, is well represented in the cathedral of Chartres, the pediment of the west front of Rouen, the lantern of St. Ouen (Rouen), the central tower of Bayeux, and the buttresses of St. Gervais at Falaise.

Flame (Lat. *flamma*) is the luminous appearance accompanying the gradual combustion of inflammable substances in the air. Combustion is really an evolution of heat produced by a transformation of the energy of chemical affinity existing between the combustible and oxygen; and if the heat produced be sufficiently intense, part of it will take the higher form of light. The luminosity of a F. is generally supposed to depend upon the presence of solid particles, probably carbon, which glow under the action of the intense heat; and this theory is supported by the continuous spectrum which luminous flames give. In the common gas F. the presence of such particles is little doubtful. This is readily shown by the deposition of soot upon a cold body held in the F. It is now known, however, that gases under pressure give out a continuous spectrum; and experiments of Dr. Frankland indicate that luminosity does not necessarily depend upon the presence of solid particles. Much of the luminosity of our ordinary flames is due to imperfect combustion; and if by any means a gas jet is diminished in light-giving power, it is increased in its heating capacity. This is well exemplified by Bunsen's burner—a simple contrivance of incalculable value in the laboratory. Its construction is such that the stream of gas issuing from the jet is first made to traverse a tube of comparatively wide bore, which is perforated at its lower extremity with holes for the admission of air. The gas is thus thoroughly mixed with air before it is lighted, and a continuous draught is produced, so that the combustion is rendered perfect. The Bunsen F. is of a transparent blue colour, and in its interior is a hollow cone containing a mixture of air and gas which is not sufficiently raised in temperature to permit of combustion. The hottest part of the F. is just above this cool cone. For combustion a certain temperature is necessary—the principle upon which Davy constructed his Safety-Lamp (q. v.), whose wire-gauze covering reduces the outside atmosphere to a temperature too low for the combustion.

Flam'en, a Roman priest, so named from the band (*filum, filamen, flamen*) of white wool which he wore round his head. These priests were fifteen in number, and their services were appropriated to a particular deity, from whom they derived a special name. The three principal flamens, known as the *Majores*, were the *F. Dialis*, *F. Martialis*, and *F. Quirinalis*—the priests respectively of Jupiter, Mars, and Quirinus—and were chosen always from the patricians, while the others—the *Minores*—might be plebeians. The special dress of the F. was the apex (a cap), the læna (a cloak), and a wreath of laurel. The *F. Dialis* was the most distinguished of the flamens, and enjoyed many privileges; as, for example, he had a right to a lictor, to the curule chair, and to a seat in the senate. His wife was called *Flaminica*, and on her death the *F. Dialis* was bound to resign.

Flamin'go (*Phœnicopterus*), a genus of birds usually included in the order *Grallatores* or Waders, to which it is allied by length of limb; but many ornithologists regard it as more appropriately ranked with Natatorial or Swimming birds, from the webbed feet. The three front toes are fully united by a web, and the bill is broad and lamellate, resembling that of the Lamellirostral *Natatores*. The bill is also of singular form, being bent abruptly downwards from the middle. The toes themselves are short, and the nostrils are placed in a groove and covered with membrane. The first and second quills are the longest of the wings. The tail is short. The typical example of the F. is the *Phœnicopterus ruber*, or common F. of S. Europe and other parts of the Old World. It inhabits the sea-coasts and marshes, and is gregarious in its habits. A sentinel bird watches over the safety of the flock. When at rest, the F. lies on the ground with its legs doubled under it, and its neck curiously bent. The nest is made of mud and earth so as to form a small hillock. The eggs are white, and number two or three. The colour is scarlet when in full plumage, the quill feathers being jetty black. The bill is orange-coloured at its base and black at the top. The average height of a full-grown F. is 6 feet. The common American species has received the name of *P. Americanus*.

Flamingo.

Flamin'ia Via, the famous highway leading N. from Rome, issued from the city by the Flaminian Gate at the northern angle of the Capitoline Hill. It proceeded to Narnia, in Umbria, and thence by Fulginia to Fanum Fortunæ on the Adriatic, from which it passed on to Ariminum, beyond which it extended under the name of the Æmilian Way through Cis-Alpine Gaul. One loop-line left the main road at Narnia, and passing through Interamna and Spoletium, rejoined it at Fulginia. Another, striking off at Nuceria, diverged to Ancona, and united with the main road at Fanum Fortunæ.

Flamini'nus, T. Quintius, the most distinguished representative of a family of the Quintian gens, was born about B.C. 230. He was elected consul B.C. 198, and obtained Macedonia as his province. He threw himself with great ardour into the war with Philip, and in the course of the struggle both achieved military successes and displayed great diplomatic skill. After the complete defeat of the Macedonians at Cynoscephalæ, B.C. 197, terms of peace were concluded, by which Philip relinquished all his Greek possessions in Europe and Asia; and during the Isthmian games of B.C. 196, F. proclaimed the freedom of Greece. He took leave of the Greeks B.C. 194, and on his return to Rome celebrated a splendid triumph of three days' duration. Peace was soon disturbed by the war in which the treacherous Nabis, tyrant of Sparta, was subdued. The most notable event in the subsequent career of F. was his connection with the death of Hannibal, who took poison, fearing lest he should be delivered up to the Romans by Prusias of Bithynia. F. died B.C. 174.

Flamin'ius, Caius, was tribune of the Roman people B.C. 230, and carried by popular support an agrarian law for the distribution of the recently-conquered territory of the Cis-Alpine Gauls. When consul (223), F. gained a great victory over the Insubians. His censorship (220) was distinguished by the two great works that bear his name, the *Circus F.* and the *Via Flaminia*. He was elected consul for a second time (217), and immediately marched against Hannibal, who was advancing southwards. F., with the greater part of his army, perished in the battle on the shores of Lake Trasimenus, B.C. 217.

Flam'steed, John, the first astronomer-royal of England, was born at Denby, near Derby, August 19, 1646, and at an early period showed so remarkable a power in the calculation of eclipses of the moon, that through Sir Jonas Moore, then Surveyor-General, he was appointed astronomer to the king in 1675. The same year he took holy orders, and nine years later was presented to the living of Burslow, in Surrey. Scientifically he is chiefly remarkable as the earliest of practical astronomers. He made the first valuable catalogue of the fixed stars, and was the first to introduce the method of simultaneously observing the right ascension of the sun and stars. F. died 31st December 1719. The partial publication of his leading work, *Historia Cœlestis Brittanica*, by Halley, against his wish, led (as was ascertained from the publication of some of his papers in 1835) to a quarrel between F. and Halley, in which Sir Isaac Newton was involved. This work, which was begun to be printed along with an *Atlas Cœlestis* in 1719, was not published till 1725. See Baily's *Account of F.* (Lond. 1835, Supp. 1837).

Flanch, The, in heraldry, is a segment of a circle drawn on each side of the shield, and is said to have had its origin in the dress of the 14th c. Guillin says that flanches are 'a proper reward for the services of a gentlewoman to her sovereign.'

Flan'ders (Flem. *Vlaendern*) is the name of a territory in the basins of the Scheldt and Lys which has often varied in extent, and which was formerly a powerful sovereign county. The ancient occupants of this country, whom Cæsar subdued, were the Celtic Morini, and various savage German tribes, as the Nervii and Menapii. The name F. was derived from the *Vlandergau* (*pagus Flandrensis*), but this was merely the district surrounding Sluis and Bruges. In the time of Karl the Great, F., then a region of wild morass and dense vegetation, was placed under a race of bold 'foresters,' who easily wrested the territory from his feeble descendants. By the Treaty of Verdun (843) F. and Artois were acquired by the Karolings of the newly-formed western Frankish kingdom. On the irruption of the Northmen the vassal rulers of the country were made wardens of the Frankish north-eastern coasts. In 864, Judith, daughter of Karl the Bald, and widow of Æthelwulf of England, was married to Baldwin (q. v.), surnamed *Bras-de-Fer*, who subsequently was created 'Count' of F., and who laid the foundation of the industrial greatness of his 'mark' or county. Among his more prominent successors was Baldwin IV., the Bearded (988–1036), who became a prince of the empire by receiving in fief from Heinrich II. the burgrafdom of Ghent, Walcheren, and the Seeland Islands. The son of Baldwin IV., the Pious, Baldwin V., gained a part of Lower Lothringen, between the Scheldt and Dender (the *Alosterland*), the episcopal supremacy of Cambray, and the county of Hainault (Hennegau), founding the Flemish-Hainault line in 1070. Of this line, the Flemish section died out with Baldwin VII. in 1120, whereupon some six claimants strove to gain the succession, which was finally secured by Dietrich of Elsass in 1128. Grown by this time into a flourishing state, F. had given crusading dynasties to Jerusalem and to the Latin empire of Constantinople. The Flemish weavers, rapidly becoming wealthy merchants, were beginning to receive a share of the political recognition foreshadowed by the first civic charter or *keur* granted to Middelburg in 1217. During the French and English wars of the 13th c., F. aided the latter power, although nominally a vassal of the former. In 1280 Margarethe II. died, leaving two sons by different marriages, John of Avennes and Guy Dampierre, who succeeded to Hainault and F. respectively. The revolt of Guy against Philippe le Bel (1297) led to the conquest of F. and its annexation to France; but the Flemings achieved their independence by the famous 'battle of spurs' at Courtrai in 1302. Under the oppressive rule of Count Louis I. of Dampierre, grandson of Guy, occurred the turbulent popular outbursts headed by the Arteveldes (q. v.). By the marriage of Philip I. of Burgundy the family of Valois-Burgundy replaced that of Dampierre in 1369, and F. was brought within the circle of the German empire. (See BURGUNDY.) Meanwhile F., along with Holland, was fast attaining its highest reach of material splendour; and its rich populous cities, Ghent, Bruges, Ypres, &c., were ready to resist any encroachment on their 'liberties.' After the death of Charles the Bold (1477), and the consequent disruption of the Burgundian possessions, F. went to his daughter Marie, who married Maximilian of Austria. The Treaty of Madrid (1526) formally abolished the vassalage of F. to France. On the abdication of Charles V. in 1556, F. came to the Spanish line of the House of Hapsburg with Philip II., but the territory was subsequently much diminished by the Peace of Westphalia (1648), which transferred a portion in the N. to the States-General, and by the conquests of Louis XIV. secured to France by the treaties of Aix-la-Chapelle, Nymwegen, and Utrecht. By the Congress of Rastadt (1714) the remainder of F. came again to the House of Hapsburg; but it was conquered by the French in 1794, and remained an integral part of the republic and empire till the Congress of Vienna (1814) conferred it on the kingdom of the Netherlands. It now forms the two Belgian provinces, East and West F. (q. v.). See Van Praet, *Histoire des Comtes des Flandres* (Bruss. 1828); Kervyn van Lettenhoven,

Histoire des Flandres (6 vols. Bruss. 1847–51); Le Glay, *Des Comtes de Flandres jusqu'à l'Avènement des Ducs de Bourgogne* (2 vols. Par. 1843); and Paul Fréderica, *Essai sur le Rôle Politique et Sociale des Ducs de Bourgogne dans le Pays-Bas* (Ghent, 1875).

Flanders, East (*Oost Vlanderen*), a province in the N.W. of Belgium, with an area of 1160 sq. miles, and a pop. (1873) of 854,366. It has a flat surface, and is watered by the Scheldt, and its tributaries the Dender and Lys. The sandy soil, which has undergone spade-culture, is very rich, yielding various grains, flax, hops, hemp, &c. Fine flax is produced in the *Land van Waes*, a region between Antwerp and Ghent, formerly a barren heath. E. F. is portioned into a great number of small farms, and is one of the most populous parts of Europe. There are large linen, cotton, woollen, lace, and silk industries, besides some 435 breweries and 170 distilleries. Ghent is the capital, and among the other towns are Alost, St. Renaix, Lokeren, and Eecloo.—**West F.**, the most westerly province of Belgium, is bounded N. by the North Sea, and W. and S. by France. Area, 1250 sq. miles; pop. (1873) 682,921. It is watered by the Lys and Iser, and is level and cultivated, except along the coast and in the N., where there are broad, low sand-dunes, in part covered with pine-trees. The chief towns are Bruges, Ostend, Courtrai, and Ypres.

Flange, in construction, a projecting rim placed round the edge of various parts of machines or apparatus. It serves commonly to afford the means of connecting (by bolts) the piece to which it belongs with other parts of the machine, but in some cases it has an entirely different purpose, as in the flanges of railway carriage wheels.

Flank (*i.e.*, 'the side') in a military sense means the extreme right and left of an army or encampment. To *flank* is to take up such a position as will strengthen the main body of an army or brigade, and at the same time have the men who perform the evolution well out of range of the enemy's fire. To *outflank* is to increase one's front so that by extending the line a general will be in a position to threaten or command the flanks of the opposing but less widely-extended line. *F. companies* is the name applied to the grenadiers and light infantry companies of regiments, as these generally occupy the right and left extremities when a battalion is in line. *Flanking parties* are bodies of cavalry and infantry employed to harass the flanks of an enemy. *Flanks of a frontier* are forts at the extremities of a frontier line, within which an attacking force will be careful not to enter, lest his retreat be cut off. For F. in fortification see FORTIFICATION.

Flann'el (Welsh *gwlanen*, Fr. *flanelle*), a woven woollen fabric of a loose texture, much used for underclothing, shirting, &c., on account of its softness and warmth. Wales still sustains the reputation it early earned for the excellence of its hand-made F. Many varieties of the fabric are produced at Rochdale, Halifax, Leeds, Bury, and Salisbury.

Flat, in music (denoted thus, ♭), a sign indicating the substitution of a note a semitone lower for the note on the staff before which it is placed. See NOTATION.

Flat-Fish, the common name for the flounder, plaice, sole, turbot, brill, halibut, and other Teleostean fishes belonging to the family *Pleuronectidæ* of the section *Anacanthini*. They can only be called *flat* in the sense that their *sides* are flattened to a much greater extent than is common in other fishes. Most people mistake the flat sides for the back and belly, but an examination will show that the paired breast-fins exist one on each flattened surface or side, whilst the dorsal and anal fins fringe the back and lower surface of the body respectively. These fishes swim on the light-coloured side; and both eyes, through a curious malformation of the bones of the skull, come to exist on one side of the body. The two sides of the mouth are of unequal size.

Flatt'ery, Cape, the name of two headlands—(1) One in the territory of Washington, U.S., on the S. side of the entrance to the Strait of Juan de Fuca. (2) One on the N.E. coast of Queensland, about 30 miles N. of Endeavour Bay.

Flat'ulence (from Lat. *flatus*, 'a breathing or blowing'), distension of the stomach or bowels by the formation of gases during digestion, depends more upon a disordered condition of the alimentary canal than upon the nature of the food partaken of. F. may be relieved by the use of aromatic medicines, such as anethi, carui, cinnamon, peppermint, cloves, ginger, cardamoms, &c.

Fla'vine is the name given to certain commercial colouring matters obtained from quercitron. The name is also given to a totally different substance, the diphenyl urea, $CON_2H_2(C_6H_5)_2$.

Flax (*Linum*), a genus of Exogenous plants belonging to the natural order *Linaceæ*. It has five imbricated sepals and five contorted petals. The ovary has five divisions, each of which is subdivided by a false septum or partition. The plants of this order are herbs with entire, sessile leaves. They are found in various quarters of the world, but most commonly in Europe and N. Africa. Common F. (*Linum usitatissimum*) is the best-known and most celebrated species. It grows as a smooth annual with a fibrous root, and attains a height of about two feet. The flowers are blue. At the present time F. is cultivated in Europe, Egypt, and India. F. is the Hebrew *pishtah* of Exod. ix. 31, the *linon* of Matt. xii. 20. The seeds are dark brown and of oblong shape, averaging about one line in length. A variety of the common F. named *L. humile* is grown to a large extent on the Continent. The F. plant becomes commercially of importance not only from the uses of the fibrous or woody tissue, obtained from the inner bark, in the manufacture of linen, but also from the drying oil expressed from the seeds, and known as 'linseed oil.' The crushed seeds form the 'oil-cake' so largely used in feeding cattle, and 'linseed meal' is obtained by grinding the crushed seeds after the oil has been expressed. Mixed with lime-water, linseed oil forms the 'carron oil' employed in the treatment of burns. 'Tow' is the product obtained in the process of 'heckling' the F. fibres. *F. cotton* is formed by steeping F. fibres, first in a solution of bicarbonate of soda, and then in a weak acid solution, so as to separate and break up the fibres to form a substance used in cotton manufacture. F. has been cultivated from the earliest times of which we have any authentic record. Thus F. linen was used to swathe the mummies of Egyptian tombs, and Herodotus refers to the extent of the Egyptian F. trade. In Ireland, F. is much more extensively grown than in England and Scotland, and in Belgium is cultivated to an extent probably unequalled elsewhere. *Brussels lace* is made from a fine F. grown in both W. and E. Flanders, and which sells at prices varying from £100 to £180 or more per ton. In 1849 Britain imported 1,806,786 cwts. of foreign-grown F., and in 1868, 1,816,669 cwts. of both dressed and undressed F. were imported from Russia, and other European countries, and from Egypt. In India F. appears to be grown chiefly for the seeds, which afford oil. When sown thickly, the F. plant yields the finest fibre, as also when the plants are pulled before the ripening of the seed. The name *purging F.* has been given to the *Linum catharticum* from its purgative properties. The latter is common enough in Britain, but is only used in popular and herbal systems of medical treatment.

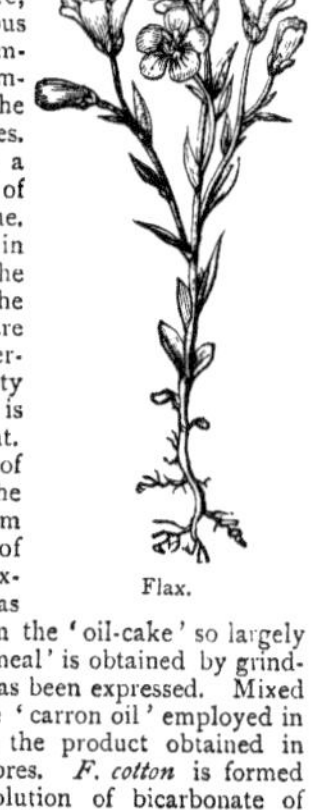
Flax.

Flax'-Dressing. The fibre of the flax plant is prepared for the spinners' use by the processes of seeding, steeping, rolling, drying, stacking, breaking, and scutching. Seeding is effected by quickly drawing the flax straw between two iron rollers, so fixed as to press out the seed without injuring it. An iron comb, called a ripple, with long and closely-set teeth, was formerly used for removing the seed-bolls. Steeping, or water-retting, is carried on by immersing the flax in a stream or pool of water. Fermentation ensues, and the glutinous matter which binds the fibre to its woody core is decomposed, facilitating the separation of the fibres. In Continental countries the flax is often sparsely spread on the ground, and exposed to the decomposing influence of dew and rain. This practice is distinguished as dew-retting. Improved methods of retting, by which a great saving of time is effected and the work more efficiently accomplished, are general. Schenck's plan was introduced into Ireland in 1847. The flax is placed in vats containing water, the temperature of which is raised to and maintained at 90° by means of steam-pipes placed under a perforated false bottom. The average duration of steeping by this method is sixty hours. On the removal of the flax from the vats it is passed between heavy cylinders on which a copious supply of water falls. By this rolling residual impurities are extracted and the fibres further loosened. Atmospheric drying follows, and then the straw is sheaved and stacked for two or three months to improve its quality and facilitate cleaning. Breaking and scutching, by which the fibres are cleaned of the woody part of the stem and separated from each other, are next proceeded with. On the successful performance of these operations chiefly depends the value of the flax. Breaking and scutching machines of varied construction are everywhere superseding manual labour. The woody part is crushed by passing the straw between fluted rollers, and then in the scutching machine the fibres are freed from the broken wood by beaters or brushes. The flax fibre is much injured in the last machine, which causes the production of an excessive quantity of tow. See LINEN MANUFACTURES and SPINNING.

Flax'man, John, a great English sculptor, born at York, July 6, 1755, was the son of a figure-moulder of the Strand, London, in whose studio he learned to draw and model, entered the Royal Academy, and exhibited a figure of Neptune in wax in his fifteenth year. He married in 1782, and in 1787 set out for Italy, where he executed his fine series of illustrations for the Iliad and the Odyssey, the beautiful marble group 'Cephalus,' 'Aurora,' &c. Returning to London in 1794, he was elected R.A. in 1800, and Professor of Sculpture in the Royal Academy in 1810. He died December 7, 1826. In his series of 109 illustrations of Dante he established his fame as a designer of noble conception and exhaustless invention. His numerous mural works, many of them in Westminster Abbey, and all inspired with noble simplicity and elevation of feeling, constitute F. one of the chief authors of the Renaissance of rilievo. Of his monuments, those in memory of Sir W. Jones (University College), Sir F. Baring's family (Micheldean church, Hants), Countess Spencer, and Mrs. Tighe, are among the most famous. A valuable collection of the models of many of his chief works may be seen in the Flaxman Museum, University College. See Flaxman's *Classical Compositions*, *Illustrations of Dante*, and *Acts of Mercy* (Bell & Sons, Lond. 1875).

Flax, New Zealand. See PHORMIUM.

Flea (*Pulex*), a genus of Insects belonging to the Holometabolic section of the class, and to the order *Aphaniptera* ('hidden winged'). They undergo a complete metamorphosis, but have no wings, these being represented by certain of the plates upon the thorax or chest-segments. The mouth is adapted for suction. The fleas, of which the common F. (*Pulex irritans*) is an example, are parasites. The larvæ first appear as footless grubs, which pass into a quiescent state within a cocoon in about twelve days. They emerge from the cocoon in about fourteen days. The F. bites sharply, and is exceedingly active in its movements, the legs being very long. The parts of the mouth are modified so as to provide the creature with a set of instruments admirably adapted for piercing the skin of the animals upon which it resides. Another and much more important species of F. is the Chigoe (q. v.) or *Pulex penetrans* of the W. Indies. Fleas have sometimes been trained to perform amazing feats, such as drawing miniature carriages to which they have been attached.

Flea'bane (*Pulicaria*), a genus of Dicotyledonous plants belonging to the natural order *Compositæ*, and so named from its strongly aromatic smell having been supposed to be serviceable in exterminating fleas and other insect pests. The *P. dysenterica*, a familiar species, commonly found in damp places, derives its specific name from having been used as a remedy for diarrhœa and dysentery.

Flèche, La (Fr. 'the spire'), a town of France in the department of Sarthe, on the right bank of the Loir, 24 miles S.S.W. of Le Mans. The church of St. Thomas, whose 'spire' gives name to the place, is a Romanesque structure of the 11th and 12th centuries. The College of Jesuits, founded by Henri IV. in 1603, is now the famous Prytanée, a military school, with accommodation for 800 pupils. In one of the squares of the town is a bronze statue of Henri IV. The principal manufactures are cloth, paper, hosiery, and glue; there are flour and bark mills, and quarries of tufa. There is a trade in cereals, wines, and fruits. Pop. (1872) 6542.

Fleck'noe, Richard, was a dramatist of the 17th c., who seems to have been originally a Roman Catholic priest, and to have come from Ireland to seek his fortune in London by his pen. F., who died about 1678, wrote a number of plays, including *Demoiselle à la Mode*, *Love's Dominion*, and *Marriage of Oceanus and Britannia*, all of which are now forgottten, and some fugitive verses which Southey has praised. F. is best known by Dryden's satire of *Mac Flecnoe.*

Fleet (Old Eng. *fliet*, 'what floats,' 'a ship'), now denotes a collection of vessels, but is generally applied to war-ships. The collective F. of a country is spoken of as its navy. The different divisions of this are known as 'fleets,' each being under the command of an admiral.

Fleet Prison, or **The Fleet**, for centuries a notorious London jail, stood on the E. side of Farringdon Street, on the banks of the Fleet stream, formerly a rapid affluent of the Thames, and now embraced within the system of the sewage of the city. It was king's prison and also debtors' prison from before the commencement of the 13th c. Here the religious martyrs of the reigns of Mary and Elizabeth were confined, and later the victims of the Star Chamber. The building was several times renewed. It was destroyed in the great fire of 1666, again burnt by the Gordon rioters in 1780, and finally abolished in 1845 as a public nuisance. It was the scene of much irregularity and brutality, arising mainly from the extortions of the keepers, and of the *Fleet Marriages*, which were contracted chiefly from the middle of the 17th to the middle of the 18th c. Prior to the passing of the Marriage Act of 1754, all that was required to render a marriage valid in England was the verbal and expressed consent of the parties; and as the Fleet at the time contained a number of dissolute ex-parsons, who were ready to celebrate a secret marriage for half-a-crown, or, according to Pennant, 'for a dram of gin or a pipe of tobacco,' persons wishing to marry, yet to keep their marriage secret, flocked to the Fleet. The Marriage Act of the 27th March 1754 put an end to the trade of the Fleet parsons.

Fleet'wood-on-Wyre ('the wood on the *fleet* or channel of the Wyre'), a seaport in Lancashire, at the mouth of the Wyre, 18 miles N.W. of Preston, and a terminus of a branch of the West Lancashire and Yorkshire Railway. It is a handsome modern town and a favourite watering-place. The chief buildings are the Whitworth Institute, the market-house, St. Peter's church, and the Roman Catholic church. F. has spacious barracks, and a fine harbour with extensive shipping. Pop. (1871) 4428.

Flem'ish Language and Literature. The name Flemish is now limited to the Germanic dialect of Belgium, though modern Dutch and Flemish, or *Vlaemish*, were at first the same tongue. The present Flemish speech differs from Dutch only in having fewer guttural sounds, and in having borrowed a number of French idioms; but while it has, until late years, received little cultivation, and been used almost solely for popular tales, songs, and farces, in Holland the old *Vlaemish* has long been a literary tongue under the distinct name of *Dutch*. By Flemish is now meant the language of Flanders, N. Brabant, and part of S. Brabant—the *Walloon*, a French dialect, prevailing in Walloon Brabant, Liége, Namur, and part of Limburg. Under FLEMISH LITERATURE, however, must be included the early writings in *Flemish*, whether produced in what is now Holland or in what is now Belgium, while the modern Dutch literature from the 16th c. onwards will be treated under LITERATURE OF THE NETHERLANDS. Among the earliest relics of Flemish are three works of the 12th c., *De Trojaensche Oorlog*, a poem of above 3000 lines on the siege of Troy, by Dieregodgaf; the *Reis van Sinte Brandaen*, a wild monkish tale of the wondrous adventures of St. Brandan, full of fantastic inventiveness; and *Reinaert de Vos*, a version of the famous satirical poem *Reynard the Fox*, written, according to Willems, most probably about 1170. To the 13th c. belong the poets Melis Stoke, Jan van Heelu, Heijnric van Holland,

Willem Utenhoven, and Jacob van Maerlent, 'the father of Dutch poetry.' The civil wars of the 14th c. checked the growth of literature, but chivalrous tales, borrowed largely from France, such as *The Holy Grail*, *Lancelot*, *Roland*, &c., became popular, and in 1394 the first of the *Kamern der Rederijkern*, or Chambers of Rhetoric, was founded. These *Rederijkern* were institutions corresponding to the guilds of the German *Meistersingers*, which offered prizes for poetic competitions, and gave public representations of farces and *Spelen van Sinne*, or moralities. They were founded in imitation of the French *Collèges de Rhétorique*, and had a baneful effect on the purity and correctness of the Flemish tongue. As their members were chiefly mechanics, though at first many of them were *sprekers*, or vagrant minstrels, they kept alive a taste for literature among the lower classes, but flooded the language with corrupt phrases, and rendered its grammar lax and uncertain. The lampoons and satiric dramas produced under their influence partly fulfilled the censorial functions of the modern press, and at times displayed an almost Aristophanic heartiness and extravagant vigour of ridicule and rebuke. Among the peculiar forms of poetry developed by the Rhetoricians were the *ketendichten*, 'chain-poems,' in which the last word of each line rhymed with the first word of the following; *dobbelsteert*, 'double tail,' in which each line ended with a double rhyme; and *scaekberd*, 'checker-board,' poems of sixty-eight rhyming lines, so arranged as to form in every direction a strophe of eight lines. From the 14th to the end of the 16th c. was the age of the Flemish ballads and popular songs, many of the latter being religious, and comprising Christmas carols, *Ave Marias*, Easter hymns, the ballads of Sister Bertha, &c. In the 16th c. Holland, after its struggle with Spain, continued to produce a national literature, whilst the Flemish literature died away in the Belgic provinces. In the 16th c. the Flemish language received a large French infusion, and after 1694, when the French invaded Belgium, French for a time superseded Flemish in the journals, and even in polite conversation. After the annexation of Belgium by Holland, the Dutch efforts to conciliate the Flemings by favouring the Flemish language were very coldly received, and tended on the whole to strengthen a reaction against the old dialect; until, after the separation of Belgium from Holland in 1830, a strong Flemish movement, headed by Willems, arose. Since then a Flemish literary school has developed, of which the chief representatives are Willems, Van Ryzwick, Van Deyse, Snellaert, Snieders, and Conscience, several of whose works have gained a European fame. The most elegant of Belgian periodicals, the *Nederduitsch Tijdschrift*, founded in 1862, is composed in Flemish. The chief Flemish authors have now agreed to write Flemish with the same orthography as the Dutch. See Vandenhoven, *La Langue Flamande, son Passé et son Avenir* (Brux. 1844).

Flemm'ing, Paul, a German poet, born at Hartenstein, Schönburg, October 15, 1609. He studied medicine at Leipsic, accompanied legations to Russia in 1633 and to Persia in 1635-39, and died at Hamburg, April 2, 1640. F. belonged to the first Silesian school founded by Opitz, and his works, *Geistliche und weltliche Poemata* (Jena, 1642; new ed. by Lappenberg, 1865), were unequalled by any German poet of the 17th c. They are vigorous and graceful in expression, lofty in thought, and full of interesting allusions to F.'s times. F.'s noble hymn *In allen meinen Thaten* is still sung in German churches. A selection of his poems was published by Schwab (Stutt. 1820), accompanied with a memoir of the poet's life. See also Varnhagen von Ense's *Biographische Denkmäler* (4 vols.) and Lappenberg's *Lexicon Hamburger Schriftsteller* (2 vols. Hamb. 1855).

Flens'borg, an old town in the province of Slesvig-Holstein, Prussia, on the F. Fjord, 20 miles N. of Slesvig by railway. It is the chief trading town in Slesvig, and has four steam and six wind mills, large breweries, and iron-smelting works, five brandy distilleries, a paper factory, and shipbuilding yards, besides manufactures of machinery, glass, soap, colours, tobacco, &c. In 1871 there cleared the harbour 1596 sailing and steam vessels of 471,660 tons, with cargoes. Pop (1872) 21,785, of whom 1635 were soldiers. F. is supposed to have been named from the knight Flenes, who is said to have founded it in the 12th c.

Flers, a town of France, department of Orne, on an affluent of the Noireau, 35 miles W.N.W. of Alençon, has cotton, linen, and other weaving manufactures, of the annual value of nearly £3,000,000 sterling. Pop. (1872) 7983.

Flesh, Chemical Composition of. F. or muscular fibre is composed mainly of fibrine in the coagulated condition, owing to the supply of blood constantly saturating the capillaries. Ordinary F. contains a certain quantity of that fluid, and therefore of its peculiar constituents, whilst in the juice which may be expressed from F., and which forms at least three-fourths of its weight, are found phosphoric, lactic, and butyric acids, partly in the free state, partly combined with potash and soda, lime and magnesia; chloride of sodium or common salt is also present. The juice of F. also contains a peculiar saccharine substance termed *Inosite* (q. v.), and an azotised body having feebly basic properties called *Creatine* (q. v.). The composition of muscle has been given as follows:—

Water	74·0	80·0
Solid constituents	26·0	20·0
	100·0	100·0
Albuminous substances insoluble in water	15·4	17·7
Gelatine	0·6	1·9
Albuminates of soda coagulating at 113° F.	2·2	3·0
Creatine	0·07	0·14
Fat	1·5	2·30
Lactic acid	1·5	2·30
Phosphoric acid	0·66	0.70
Potash	0·50	0·54
Soda	0·07	0·09
Chloride of sodium	0·04	0·09
Lime	0·02	0·03
Magnesia	0·04	0·05

Flesh-Fly (*Sarcophaga carnaria*), a species of *Diptera* or flies, so named from their depositing their eggs in decaying animal matter, and from their larvæ feeding on like substances. These larvæ thus become useful in removing putrefying material. Linnæus said that three flesh-flies could devour a horse in less time than a lion—meaning that the various broods of larvæ, produced in large numbers, would in turn attack and devour quantities of the putrescent matter. The eggs are hatched within the body of the parent F.-F., and the pupæ or chrysalides are contained within the larval skin.

Fletch'er, Andrew, of Saltoun, a Scottish patriot and political writer, was the son of Sir Robert F. of Saltoun, where he was born in 1653. After travelling on the Continent, F. entered the Scottish Parliament as member for East Lothian in 1681, but having borne part in the opposition to James Duke of York, then Royal Commissioner in Scotland, he was compelled to retire to England, and thence to Holland. Shortly afterwards he was outlawed, and his estate confiscated, whereupon he threw himself into the patriotic intrigues of the English refugees in the Netherlands. F. returned to England in 1683, and there became intimately associated with the leaders of the malcontent party—the famous Council of Six. The discovery of the Rye-House Plot (1683) scattered this party, and F. again fled to Holland. In 1685 he came back to England as volunteer in the Duke of Monmouth's invasion; but having killed the Mayor of Lyme in a private dispute, he was forced to quit the expedition at its very outset. F. then served in Hungary with distinction against the Turks. On the revolution of 1688 he came over from Holland with William of Orange, regained his lands, and again sat in the Scottish Parliament. The failure of the Darien scheme, in which F. had been a prime mover, embittered him towards King William's government, and in the Scottish Parliament he spoke violently against the projected union between England and Scotland. After the Union F. retired from public life. He died in London in 1716. F. was a passionate lover of freedom, but though a republican, was even more opposed to democracy than to monarchy. His views are set forth in several tracts—*Discourse of Government with Relation to Militias* (Edinb. 1698); *Two Discourses on the Affairs of Scotland* (1698); his *Speeches in Parliament* (1703); and *Conversation on Governments* (1704). These were reprinted at London in 1737 as *The Political Works of A. F.* There is an *Essay on the Life of F.* by the Earl of Buchan (1792). See also Macaulay's *History*.

Fletcher, Giles and **Phineas**, poets, sons of Dr. Giles F., uncle of F. the dramatist. Giles, born in 1588, was educated at Eton and Cambridge. In 1610 he published *Christ's Victory* *and Triumph in Heaven and Earth over and after Death*, a poem in an eight-line stanza. It is tedious and affected, but at times rises into lofty imaginative poetry. F. held the living of Alderton, Suffolk, where he died in 1623.—Phineas F. was born at Wanbrook, Kent, April 1582, was educated at Cambridge, obtained Hilgay Rectory in Norfolk, and died in 1650. His works include *The Locustes* (1627), a satire on the Jesuits; *Sicelides, a Piscatory;* and *The Purple Island*, a poem in ten cantos, in which the human body is allegorically described. It is written in a seven-lined stanza, and though grotesque and prolix, is smoothly versified, with rich descriptive and lofty moral passages. Like his brother, Phineas was an ardent disciple of Spenser. Quarles called him 'the Spenser of his age.' The poems of Giles and Phineas F. are contained in Anderson's *British Poets*, vol. iv.

Fletcher, John, one of the greatest of English dramatic poets, was born at Rye, Sussex, December 1579. He was the son of Richard F. who became Bishop of London, was sent to Bene't College, Cambridge, in 1591, and was left an orphan and in poverty on his father's death in 1596. Nothing is known of his life until 1607, when he produced commendatory lines on Jonson and the comedy of *The Woman-Hater*, in which he may have been assisted by Beaumont, with whom he formed the most famous of all literary partnerships. F. and Beaumont are said to have lived 'on the Banke side, not far from the Play-house,' and to have had even 'the same cloaths and cloake in common.' We know that F. was highly popular in the literary Bohemia of his times, with which he would be more closely connected than was his aristocratic associate. Beaumont died in 1616, and F. continued to write plays, alone or with other dramatists, until he was cut off by the plague in August 1625. Modern critics have sought to disentangle F.'s from Beaumont's writings; but while we know that a particular series of dramas was produced by F. after Beaumont's death, we must view with dubiety all attempts to separate the one poet's verses from the other's in the pieces of which it is certain that they were joint authors. Mr. Donne regards the problem of sifting Beaumont's writing from F.'s as insoluble. Professor Ward cannot trace any essential difference between the plays ascribed to both and those attributed to F. alone, while he can detect two styles in the plays written by F. along with another than Beaumont. The assertion that Beaumont merely pruned and chastened F.'s writings is contradicted by the verses of their contemporaries, and the plays (as *The Maid's Tragedy*) in which Beaumont unquestionably shared do not show calmer judgment than those written by F. alone. Dyce assigns the authorship thus:—By Beaumont and F.—*Four Plays in One, Wit at Several Weapons, Thierry and Theodoret, Maid's Tragedy, Philaster, King and No King, Knight of the Burning Pestle, Cupid's Revenge, Little French Lawyer, Scornful Lady, Coxcomb, Laws of Candy;* by Beaumont alone—*Masque;* by F. and Massinger—*False One, Very Woman;* by F. and Rowley—*Queen of Corinth, Maid of the Mill, Bloody Brother;* by F. and Shirley—*Noble Gentleman, Night Walker, Love's Pilgrimage;* by F. and Shakespeare—*The Two Noble Kinsmen;* and the remaining plays, except the *Nice Valour*, as to which he is uncertain, by F. alone. The plays of Beaumont and F. are marked by exuberant and fiery, joyous and wanton inventiveness, by unflagging dramatic interest, splendid rhetoric, and flowery poetic colour, and by a fascinating natural sportiveness which is found in no other Elizabethan writers. But they show little depth or subtlety of imaginative insight; they fail to portray intense passions; their characters are often weakened by the undue emphasis given to a leading quality; and their plots, though mostly woven with marvellous dexterity, are sometimes maimed and twisted to produce ingenious situations. So far as we can judge, Beaumont seems to have had the loftier tragic genius, F. the more active creativeness, the more sparkling wit, the nimbler and more versatile and graceful fancy. Beaumont's verse is more severe and simple than F.'s, which is distinguished by flowery volubility and liquid melody, by a sometimes too copious overflow of sweet and pellucid language. The comedies in which Beaumont seems to have especially shared display the parodistic vein and broad farce characteristic of Jonson, features absent from those pieces in which F.'s genius shines with the most brilliant and unborrowed lustre—his romantic comedies, plays which stand alone in our literature for a peculiar blending of varied qualities, for fluent grace of style, for tender sentiment brightened with dazzling wit, for delicate poetic beauties inwoven with humour and softly flushed with passion, for the captivating interest of the plot, and for the introduction of those pensive, aerial lyrics which are surpassed by Shakespeare's loveliest songs alone. See Dyce's edition of Beaumont and F. (13 vols. 1841–48); W. B. Donne's *Essays on the Drama* (1857); and Ward's *English Dramatic Literature* (2 vols. 1875).

Fleur-de-Lis (Fr. 'flower of the lily,' in Old English 'flower de luce'), the emblem of the French kings, whose royal banner, even in the time of the Merwings, seems to have been blue with gold lilies. Charles VI. is said to have reduced the number of lilies to three, as a symbol of the Trinity. There are many legends accounting for the adoption of the emblem; most probably it was at first meant to represent the head of a javelin, or it may owe its origin to the Frankish custom of placing a *reed* or *flag in blossom* instead of a sceptre in the hand of each newly-made king. In 1789 the F.-de-L. was displaced by the tricolour. During the middle ages the F.-de-L. was also the emblem of the Virgin, and was a favourite design on church decorations. See Rey's *Histoire du Drapeau, des Couleurs, et des Insignes de la Monarchie Française* (Par. 1837).

Fleuru's, a town in the province of Namur, Belgium, near the Sambre, 7 miles N. of Charleroi, and 2 N. of Ligny. Pop. (1873) 3823. An indecisive battle took place here between the troops of the Catholic League under Gonzalvo de Cordova, and those of the Protestant Union headed by the Dukes of Brunswick and Saxe-Weimar, 30th August 1622. F. was also the scene of the defeat of the Prince of Waldeck by the Duke of Luxembourg, 26th June 1794; and of a victory of Jourdan over the Allies, brought about by the bad strategy of the Prince of Saxe-Coburg, 26th June 1794.

Fleu'ry, André Hercule de, Cardinal, a French statesman and ecclesiastic, was born at Lodève, in Languedoc, June 22, 1653. He studied at the Jesuits' College, Paris, was made almoner to the queen of Louis XIV., and, in 1699, Bishop of Fréjus. He gave up his bishopric in 1715, became tutor to Louis XIV.'s grandson, afterwards Louis XV., and insinuated himself into that prince's favour. He was elected into the Academy in 1721, was admitted to the Council of State in 1723, and in 1726 became a cardinal and prime minister of France. His administration was tolerably successful. He strove to economise and lighten taxation, and at first sought to maintain peace at almost any cost, but sacrificed the freedom of the Gallican Church to Ultramontanism, and was nerveless and vacillating in his foreign policy. In 1733 the court party forced him into the war of the Polish succession, on behalf of Stanislaus Leczinsky, Louis XV.'s father-in-law. The struggle ended in 1736, and in 1741 F. was compelled by court influence to take part in the war of the Austrian succession. He died at Paris, January 29, 1743. F. was a well-meaning, benevolent, and peace-loving minister, but had not the energy needful in his position. He patronised learning, and added several valuable MSS. to the royal library. See St. Simon's *Mémoires*.

Fleury, Claude, Abbé, a French ecclesiastical historian, was born at Paris, 6th December 1640. He was educated at first for the law, and is said to have been one of the ablest advocates in the Parliament of Paris, but coming under the influence of Bossuet and Bourdaloue, took priest's orders, shortly after which he became tutor to the sons of the Prince of Conti. His legal knowledge was shown in 1674 in the publication of *L'Histoire du Droit Français*. Four years later appeared his translation in Latin of Bossuet's *Expositions de la Foi Catholique*, while between 1681 and 1683 he issued three little works, *Les Mœurs des Israélites, Les Mœurs des Chrétiens*, and *Le Grand Catéchisme Historique*. Through the influence of Fénelon F., who was a modest, amiable, and erudite man, was appointed first assistant tutor to the sons of the then dauphin, and subsequently confessor to the young king, Louis XV., as well as Prior of Argenteuil. The chief works written by F. during the latter part of his life are *Discours sur les Libertés de l'Église Gallicane*, published after his death, and his *Histoire Ecclésiastique* (1691–1720), published in twenty volumes. This work, in particular, has been much admired on account of its candour and impartiality, and F. himself, although a 'good Catholic,' was the reverse of a sectarian or a fanatic. He died

July 14, 1723. See Martin's *Œuvres de l'Abbé F.* (1837), to which there is prefixed an essay on his life and writings.

Fleu'ry, Flor'y, or **Fleurett'ée,** is applied in heraldry to an object of which the sides or ends terminate in *fleurs-de-lis.*

Flex'ure, in mathematics, is the bending or curving of a line or surface. A point of *contrary F.* or *inflexion* is the point at which a curve ceases to present convexity to a straight line without it, and begins to present concavity. Such a point cannot exist in curves lower than the third order. In engineering, F. denotes the bending of loaded beams, and is of great importance in the theory of construction. See STRENGTH OF MATERIALS.

Flied'ner, Rev. Theodor, D.D., a philanthropic clergyman, born at Eppstein, near Wiesbaden, January 21, 1800, studied at Göttingen, and in 1821 became pastor of a small Protestant community at Kaiserwerth, near Düsseldorf. F. is memorable as the founder of the Evangelical Deaconesses, who, though not a monastic body, correspond partly to the Catholic Sisters of Charity, visiting the sick and poor in their homes and in public institutions. F. laboured with great practical ability to organise these deaconesses, who have proved a boon to Germany, *e.g.,* in the Austro-Prussian war of 1866. Institutions modelled on F.'s establishment at Kaiserwerth have been founded at London, Paris, Berlin, Alexandria, &c. F. died at Kaiserwerth, October 4, 1864. See F.'s *Buch der Martyrer der evangel. Kirche* (1852), and Catherine Winkworth's *Life of F.* (Eng. trans. Lond. 1867).

Flies, Spanish. See CANTHARIS.

Flin'ders, Matthew, discoverer of great part of the coast of Australia, born at Donington in Lincolnshire in 1760, entered first the merchant service, and afterwards the royal navy. In 1798 F., in company with Surgeon George Bass, left Port Jackson, New South Wales, sailed S. along a coast previously unknown, and discovered and named Bass Strait between the continent and Tasmania. Subsequently in 1801–1803 he explored all the southern, eastern, and northern coast of Australia from Cape Leuwen near its S.W. angle round by Bass Strait, and along by the E. coast, Gulf of Carpentaria, &c., to the island of Timor. The voyage was one of romantic adventure as well as of great geographical achievement. On the return voyage F. was seized and retained prisoner in the Isle of France for six years. He reached England in 1810, and died there in 1815. His *Voyage to Terra Australia* (1814) is a work of high interest.

Flinder'sia, a genus of Exogenous trees belonging to the natural order *Cedrelaceæ,* or that including the mahogany trees. F. grows in Australia, and its hard wood is extensively used as a substitute for mahogany.

Flint is a variety of quartz, allied to chalcedony, from the purer specimens of which it differs in having usually a dark-grey or even black colour, and in being but feebly translucent. It is massive and compact, and breaks with sharp edges and a conchoidal fracture. It is found as concretionary nodules in the chalk formations, and is probably organic in its origin, Ehrenberg supposing it to consist for the most part of infusorial remains. *Hornstone* or *chert* is very similar, but is more brittle, and occurs in the limestones of older formations. The hardness and sharpness of F. ensured its early use as a material for the manufacture of knives, chisels, rasps, axes, &c.; and the facility with which it strikes fire upon steel is well known, though now of little practical importance since the invention of lucifer matches and percussion caps.

Flint, a town in Flintshire 14 miles S.W. of Chester by rail, on the W. bank of the Dee. Its chief buildings are a modern Gothic church, the town-hall, and the national school. It is a favourite watering-place, has chemical works, and exports coal and lead, which are obtained near it. The trade has of late increased. Vessels of 300 tons can discharge at its wharf. To the N.E. of the town are the ruins of a castle built by Henry II. F. seems to have been a Roman station from the number of Roman remains, such as coins, amulets, brooches, &c., found in its vicinity. Pop. (1871) 4269.

Flint, a river in Georgia, U.S., joins the Chattahoochee after a course of about 300 miles, 250 of which are navigable for steamboats.

Flint Arrow-Heads, the commonest of the weapons of the Stone Age, occur abundantly in every country of Europe. They have been found also in Asia Minor and Palestine, in China and Japan, and in N. and S. Africa. They are plentifully distributed over the whole of the New World, and are still in use among the uncivilised tribes both of N. and S. America. Though varying greatly in form, they may be classified in three groups,—the triangular, the leaf-shaped, and the lozenge-shaped. The triangular group presents varieties, with or without barbs, with or without a central stem or tang, and sometimes with the base hollowed or notched for the insertion of the shaft. The leaf and lozenge shaped forms, of which there are many varieties, were destitute of barbs and tang. They were inserted in the split end of the shaft, which was finely tapered off, so as to embrace the arrow-head almost up to its point. The grip of the split shaft on the flint was tightened by a lashing of sinew immediately behind the arrow-head, and seems in many cases to have been further strengthened by the use of gum or bitumen. Arrow-heads vary greatly in size, there being in fact no distinction between an arrow and a spear or lance head except that of size. The smaller arrow-heads are often not more than a quarter of an inch in length, and they vary from this size up to the largest that a bow would carry. Whatever their size, they are always fashioned of chipped flint, and never finished by grinding, like axes and other such implements of flint of greater size. They are, however, by far the most symmetrically-formed and exquisitely-finished specimens of the flint-worker's art. The smallest examples, though not much thicker than card-paper, will exhibit from thirty to forty facets, each of which represents a blow so skilfully delivered as to flake off a splinter from the surface without fracturing the flint or injuring the symmetry of the weapon. Although in all countries the general forms are much alike, there are special varieties which are characteristic of special areas. The triangular variety, with barbs and blunt-ended tang, is most abundant in N. Britain, while that with a notch in the base is most abundant in Scandinavia. In France, Italy, and N. Africa the form with a pointed tang is most common. In N. America the triangular form with side notches for the reception of the sinew by which they are lashed to the shaft is the prevailing variety. Only a very small proportion of the flint implements found in the drift or in the cave-dwellings of England, France, and Belgium, and the kitchen-middens of Denmark, can be regarded as arrow-heads, but in the lake-dwellings of Switzerland they are very numerous and well made. They are frequently found in the dolmens or cairns and sepulchral deposits both of the Stone and Bronze Ages, but they are chiefly found casually embedded in the soil. It may be assumed that as arrow-heads of bronze are extremely rare, flint was used for this purpose throughout the Bronze Age as being the more accessible and less costly material. Among the savage tribes by whom it is still used, arrow-making is a work of skill in which only few attain excellence. Longfellow's description of the 'ancient arrow-maker' in *Hiawatha* has made us familiar with a phase of the life of the Stone Age continued into our time, but which is now fast passing away. Not the least curious of the phenomena connected with this passing away of an ancient art is that which is exhibited, not by the barbarian, but by the cultured and civilised sections of humanity, in the translation of these once familiar objects from the region of common life into that of the supernatural. In most of the civilised countries of

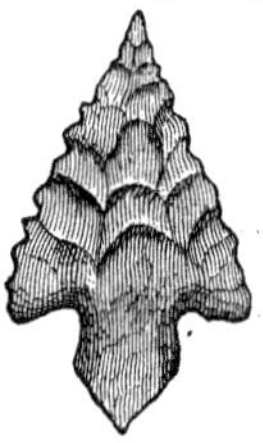

Serrated Flint Arrow-head.

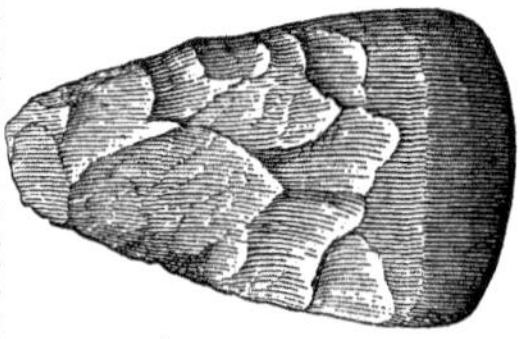

Flint Celt or Axe-head.

Europe F. A.-H. have been for many centuries associated with supernatural powers and regarded with superstitious veneration. Even among the Etruscans this feeling seems to have prevailed, for there is in the British Museum a beautiful gold necklace from an Etruscan tomb, the central pendant to which is a flint arrow-head.

Flint Glass. See GLASS.

Flint Im'plements, the tools of times when the use of metal was unknown, or when it was too rare and costly to be applied to the commoner purposes of the useful arts, are found in every country of the world whose antiquities have been made the subject of special investigation. Not only do they occur in regions that had not emerged from barbarism in prehistoric times, but on the sites of the most ancient civilisations of historic times their occurrence bears testimony to a previous condition of undeveloped civilisation of which history knows nothing. They underlie the relics of the most ancient civilisations of Europe, Africa, and Asia, in Greece and Italy, in Egypt, in Arabia, Palestine, Asia Minor, Assyria, Babylonia, India, China, and Japan. In all countries where flint is naturally accessible, it has been used by preference for the manufacture of implements and weapons on account of the facility with which it may be flaked and chipped into the desired form. The flint tools of primitive times were principally knives, saws, scrapers, awls, axes or adzes, chisels and gouges. In the manufacture of the smaller tools a peculiar process was employed. A suitable block of flint having been selected, it was first split, and then by a series of sharp blows delivered on the fractured face of the flint long splinters or flakes were separated from the block or core in such a manner that the ridge formed by the meeting edges of the two flakes previously struck off formed the midrib or back-bone of the third. Each flake was thus triangular in section, and broad or narrow in the base opposite to the midrib, according to the purpose for which it was wanted. Knives were usually made of a long thin flake, the natural edge of which is keener than any that can be produced by grinding, so keen, indeed, that flakes of obsidian were used to shave with by the Spaniards in Mexico when their European razors went out of order, and Mariette Bey records that he once saw an Arab having his head shaved with a flint flake at Abydos in Upper Egypt. This natural edge, however, is extremely brittle, and flint knives which were intended to retain their utility, and were not merely made for the temporary occasion, were worked to a more obtuse edge than is obtained by the natural fracture. In rare cases, and probably for special purposes, the edge was ground. Practically owing to the roughness of the edge all stone knives are saws, but the true saws were beautifully and often very finely notched or toothed with the utmost regularity. Both knives and saws were small, not usually exceeding 3 or 4 inches in length. Sometimes they were set in handles of wood or stag's-horn. Specimens thus handled are found in the Swiss lakes. The 'scraper,' so called because a similar tool mounted in a bone handle is used to this day by the Eskimos for scraping the fat off skins, was made from a flake by trimming one of its ends to a semicircular bevelled edge like that of a 'round-nosed turning chisel.' Judging by the large number of these tools of all sizes, from a quarter of an inch to 3 inches in length and width, that are found on every site of human occupancy during the Stone Age, it is probable that they were used for a great many purposes in which scraping or planing was required, including the manufacture of implements of bone or wood, as well as the preparation of skins for clothing. It is also probable that many of them were used as strike-lights with iron pyrites, nodules of this substance with the marks of use having been found in barrows in association with 'scrapers' of flint. Another form of 'scraper' with a semicircular hollow was used for planing arrow-shafts. Flint axes and adzes are sometimes merely chipped into shape, but more frequently they are ground sharp and smooth at the cutting edge, and occasionally smoothed or polished over the whole surface. They are extremely variable in size, ranging from 2 or 3 inches in length to as much as 14 or 16 inches in length. Axes or adzes were often made of other materials than flint, such as diorite, nephrite, greenstone, basalt, limestone, porphyry, serpentine, jasper, sandstone, and clayslate. Some of the modern savages, as those of New Guinea and the Barbadoes Islands, &c., make their axes of a large shell, extremely dense in texture. Chisels and gouges of flint are usually polished. They are well-made and effective tools, varying from 4 to 6 or 7 inches in length, and are most common in Scandinavia. Awls and borers are of various forms and sizes, but usually with a flattened shoulder or butt to be held between the finger and thumb. The most curious of these are the flint drills for piercing the 'eyes' of the bone needles found in the French caves. Besides the 'implements' properly so called, because their purpose is apparent from the form and finish that have been given to them, there is a class of 'F. I.' so called because they are artificially shaped, although they are so destitute of indications of destination or design, that it is impossible to suggest any special purpose of practical utility for which they could have been intended. They are usually found associated with remains of animals that are either totally or locally extinct, such as the mammoth, rhinoceros, lion, hyæna, reindeer, Irish elk, &c., and on this account, as well as from their rudeness of form and finish, an extremely high antiquity has been claimed for them. See Evans' *Ancient Stone Implements of Great Britain* (Lond. 1872); *Primitive Inhabitants of Scandinavia*, by Sven Nilsson, translated by Sir John Lubbock (Lond. 1868); Stevens' *Flint Chips, a Guide to Prehistoric Archæology*, &c. (Lond. 1870); *Catalogue of the National Museum of the Antiquaries of Scotland* (Edinb. 1876).

Flint'shire, a maritime county in N. Wales, bounded on the N. by the Irish Sea, on the E. by the Dee, and on the S. and W. by Denbighshire. Area, 288·9 sq. miles; pop. (1871) 76,312. F. chiefly consists of uplands, with hills of moderate height, the loftiest point being Moel-y-Famma, 1845 feet, in the S.W. The coast is low, and mostly sandy, but there are rich meadows on the estuary of the Dee. Many rivers, as the Elwy, Terrig, and Wheles, rise in F., but have their course chiefly in other counties. F. belongs mainly to the New Red Sandstone and Carboniferous formations, and has rich measures of coal, which are largely worked, and veins of iron, lead, and copper. Corn, barley, and green crops are grown in the plains and vales, and the uplands afford excellent pasture. The chief industries are mining, metal-working, and agriculture. There are also cotton manufactures. The principal towns are Mold (the county town), Flint, Holywell, and St. Asaph. F. returns two members to Parliament.

Flint'y Slate, a smooth, hard, brittle, splintery black rock, the result of the metamorphosis of slate or clay by contact with a mass of igneous rock. Rocks of this nature are found in the Lower Silurian of the S. of Scotland; and Lydian stone, used as a touchstone for testing precious metals, is probably of the same origin.

Float'ing Batt'ery, a name given to large vessels or hulks heavily armed and made as far shot-proof as possible. They were not built so as to attain high speed, or to be adapted for general service at sea, their principal use being in sieges, where rapidity of movement was not required. Wooden floating batteries were used against us by the French and Spaniards in the siege of Gibraltar (1779–80), and we employed iron ones—as did also the French—with success during the Russian war. Floating batteries are now superseded by armour-clad steamships, which unite a far greater degree of invulnerability than the others, with a speed such as the fastest cruisers scarcely ever attained.

Floating Docks. See DOCK.

Floating Islands may be formed either by nature or art, and consist mainly of masses of buoyant spongy soil, held together by the tenacious roots of plants. Portions of river banks are occasionally torn away by floods or swift currents, and carry with them to the ocean trees, reptiles, birds, and even large animals. Such 'straggling plots' are sometimes seen as far as 100 miles from the mouth of the Ganges, and were observed issuing from the Mississippi during the floods of 1874. F. I. have thus doubtless played an important part in the distribution of animal and vegetable life. Natural F. I. occur in great numbers in the marshy lakes bordering the Gulf of Venice. The lake of Gerdau, in Prussia, contains one of the largest in the world, while that in the lake of Kolk, in Osnabruck, is clad with elms. In Derwentwater, Cumberland, there is a small island which sinks below and rises to the surface of the water periodically like the fabled island of the Cutilian waters. This phenomenon is explained by the island rising only when the

Catgill, a stream which here enters the lake, is flooded by rains. The most celebrated artificial F. I. are the *chinampas* of the native Mexicans, and the aquatic gardens of Kashmir.

Float'stone, a light spongy-like variety of fibrous quartz, capable of floating on water, and occurring as flint incrustations in the limestones of the Paris chalk formations.

Flodd'en, Battle of, was fought on September 9, 1513, when James IV. of Scotland, who had sided with Louis XII. of France against Henry VIII. of England, was defeated by the Earl of Surrey, at F. Hill, one of the Cheviots, in Northumberland. There were about 30,000 on either side, and the Scots lost 10,000 men, among whom were James and the flower of his nobility. Miss Jean Elliot's exquisite ballad the *Flowers of the Forest* ('I've heard the lilting at our yowe-milking') is a lament for the calamity. The battle is described with more than Homeric fire and brilliancy in the 6th canto of Scott's *Marmion*. See Burton's *History of Scotland*, chap. xxx.

Flogg'ing, in the British army, is mentioned 'as strappadoe for drunkenness on guard' in the articles of war put forth by Charles I. in 1629, by advice of the council of war for the government of the troops in England. In every market there was to be a strappadoe as well as a gibbet. In the codes of 1639 and 1642 ordinary whipping by the provost is distinguished in the list of punishments. These codes also contained what was afterwards called by soldiers the 'devil's articles,' viz., for punishing indefinitely crimes for which no special order had been set down. In 1666 a jurisdiction in offences involving neither life nor limb was given to the then created regimental courts, which had also a power of 'arbitrary correction.' In 1672 'running the gantlet' was added. The Mutiny Act of 12 Anne confers on courts-martial a power to inflict corporal punishments 'for immorality, misbehaviour, or neglect of duty.' The disgraceful Act of 1715 declared every offence to be capital, with a discretion to the court-martial to award such other punishment as they should think proper. In 1812 both Houses of Parliament accepted the principle that for minor offences imprisonment might be inflicted as an alternative for corporal punishment, and the limitation of 300 lashes was introduced. A keen controversy raged down to 1868, when by 31 Vict. c. 14, sec. 22, the power to sentence any soldier to corporal punishment for any offence whatever during time of peace in her Majesty's dominions was abolished. But corporal punishment may be inflicted during active service or on board any ship not in commission for mutiny, insubordination, desertion, drunkenness on duty or on the line of march, disgraceful conduct (including embezzlement, theft, malingering, maiming, or tampering with the eyes), or any breach of the Articles of War, no punishment to exceed fifty lashes, or where punishment is also awarded, twenty-five lashes. This applies only to private and non-commissioned officers. In carrying out this sentence, the culprit is tied to a gun-wheel or a triangle of wood. For this purpose halberds were once used, hence the expression 'bringing a man to the halberds.' The drummers of infantry, and the trumpeters or shoeing smiths of cavalry, are selected for the work. The cat-o'-nine-tails consists of a drumstick with nine ends of whipcord, 16 inches long, and with three knots each. Steeping the cats in brine has been made the subject of a serious charge, and in the case of Governor Walls (28 *State Trials*), where a rope had been used, there was a conviction for murder. The barbarous practice of having right-hand and left-hand drummers is discontinued.

The law of F. in the navy during service is contained in the following passage of the Queen's Regulations :—'It being requisite for the maintenance of the efficiency, discipline, and even safety of H.M. ships of war, that the power of inflicting corporal punishment, when absolutely necessary, should be continued, such punishment is only to be inflicted under the responsibility and authority of the officers in command of the said ships, who are to exercise the power vested in them with the greatest discretion and forbearance.' No officer is subject to F., and petty or non-commissioned officers only in case of mutiny. Except also in case of mutiny, every soldier before sentence to F. is entitled to have an inquiry by one or more officers. But as regards marines during peace the prohibition of F. mentioned above in the case of the army is also inserted in every year's Marine Mutiny Act since 1868. The limit of punishment had previously been fixed at forty-eight lashes. In certain cases the possession of a good-conduct badge of the first or second class protected even common seamen against F. In all cases, of course, the man's health is looked to. Under the Juvenile Offenders Act, boys not older than fourteen may be sentenced to receive twelve strokes from the birch-rod.

Flood'ing is a term popularly applied to those copious hæmorrhagic discharges which occasionally occur after or during delivery. F. is caused by the non-closure of the uterine vessels, after the partial or complete separation of the placenta from the uterine surface, and the condition depends on the absence of contractile power in the uterus. F. very frequently follows abortion; and when such occurs during the early months of pregnancy, it is attended with great danger. Treatment :—procure delivery as early as possible, by exciting uterine action by means of friction and pressure, or by the administration of Ergot (q. v.).

Floor'cloth is generally formed of strong canvas oil-painted on both sides. (See LINOLEUM and KAMPTULICON.) The canvas is chiefly woven in Dundee in pieces of great length and width. The manufacture of F. is begun by stretching a piece of canvas containing about 210 or 220 sq. yards upon a vertical open wooden frame, a series of these frames being arranged parallel to each other at a distance of 30 inches with a tiered scaffolding between them, to enable the workmen to reach every part of the canvas. The cloth is washed on both sides with weak size, and then smoothed with pumice. This 'priming' solution preserves the pliability of the cloth by filling up the meshes to the exclusion of the oil-paint, which is next applied in the form of one 'trowel' and one 'brush' colour to the back, and afterwards of three coats of 'trowel' and one coat of 'brush' colour to the face. Each layer of paint, when dry, is rubbed down with pumice. The 'trowel' colour is so called because it is worked over the canvas with a trowel-shaped implement, the thick consistence of the paint not admitting of its being spread with a brush. When thoroughly dry, the painted cloth is transferred to the 'printing-room,' where it is passed over a long narrow table, and a pattern is hand-printed on the face by means of wooden blocks. Each colour has a separate block, the impressions of all producing an appropriate and harmonious design. From two to three months are occupied in the production of good floorcloths. The full-printed cloths are hung up in 'drying-rooms' to mature and season. This measure imparts strength to the cloth and brilliancy to the colours. F. is extensively made at Kirkcaldy in Fifeshire. There, one establishment alone can turn out 20,000 sq. yards per week, or an annual production of over 1,000,000 sq. yards. Painted baize and other light fabrics for covering furniture are produced in a manner similar to F.

Floors, in houses, the horizontal partitions between the stories. In the common or 'single-joisted' floor, a series of parallel wooden beams are laid across from wall to wall; these are not less than 8 or 9 inches deep, and 2 inches thick, and commonly more, and are called *joists*. To the top of these the flooring, which consists of narrow planks placed close together, is secured, and underneath them the laths for receiving the plaster of the ceiling are attached. 'Double-joisted' and 'framed' F. are more complex in construction, and are used where for any reason special strength is required, or where the length of the room is very great. The space between the flooring and the ceiling should be filled as far as possible with cement or other substance, as 'deafening.' In this country the flooring is of soft wood, and is most frequently planed tolerably smooth and left in that condition. In most parts of the Continent, where carpets are not so much used as with us, the F. are of hard wood, carefully jointed and kept always polished. The floor thus made looks better certainly than nine-tenths of the carpets used in this country. It is both clean, convenient, and economical to stain and varnish the edge of a soft-wood floor for a distance of about 2 feet 6 inches from the wall all round, and to put a border round the carpet, making it cover only as much of the floor as is unstained. This method can be used in any house floored in the ordinary way, by having the small spaces too often left between the planks stopped first with brown putty.

Flo'ra, the goddess of flowers and spring, was worshipped at Rome from the very earliest times. Her festival, the Floralia, lasted five days, from April 28 to May 1, and was celebrated with great licentiousness. The later Romans identified F. and

Chloris, the Greek goddess of flowers. In botany the word denotes the vegetable kingdom. See FAUNA.

Flor'ence (Lat. *Florentia*, 'the flourishing;' Ital. *Fiorenza*, now *Firenze*, surnamed *la bella*), one of the largest and fairest cities of Italy, capital of the province of the same name, is built on both sides of the Arno, but chiefly on the N. bank, 50 miles from the sea, and is connected by rail with Bologna and Rome. Its environs are singularly beautiful. It lies in the leafy valley of the Arno, in a gently undulating country, amid low hills covered with vineyards and terraced gardens, with white villas and old towers embosomed in groves of olives, cypresses, and mulberries, while to the N. the Apennines rise to a height of 3000 feet. The central and oldest part of F. is a maze of narrow, gloomy streets, where the massive castellated palaces of the nobles, used as fortresses during the middle ages, may still be seen. The Borghi, or outer quarters, which intervene between this central part and the old walls, are more spacious and regular; and beyond the walls lie the modern suburbs, consisting almost wholly of villas set among gardens. F. has lately been much changed. A new suburb has been built on the E. of the city, with handsome squares and boulevards, and the old quarters have been pierced by wide streets. The Arno, now confined to a channel 100 feet wide, is lined by broad quays known as the Lung Arno, which form a fine promenade, with a view of the sylvan Valdarno at one end, and of the Vallombrosan hills at the other. The river is spanned by six bridges, of which the Ponte alle Grazie is the oldest, having been built in 1235 (restored 1835). The Ponte Vecchio, still covered with quaint shops, dates from 1362. The walls are dismantled of the seventy or more towers which once crowned them, but the old gates are extant, the most interesting being the Porta Romana, Porta S. Miniata, Porta S. Gallo, and Porta alla Croce, built in 1284, the two last displaying frescoes by Ghirlandajo. F. has above twenty squares, of which the chief is the Piazza della Signoria, once the forum of the Florentine commonwealth, and still the great seat of trade. It contains a large fountain with bronze statues by Gian of Bologna. F. is rich in graceful and imposing buildings, in picturesque and historical piles. The Duomo, or cathedral, which stands near the centre of the city, was begun by Arnolfo di Lapo in 1294, was continued by Giotto, and was finished by Brunelleschi in 1436. The dome is 384 feet high, and the walls are cased with marble. By the side of the Duomo Giotto's campanile, or bell-tower, rises to a height of 292 feet. It is covered with delicately-tinted marbles and Gothic traceries, and according to Ruskin is the one building which unites in the highest degree the characteristics of beauty and power. The church of Santa Croce, 'the Westminster Abbey of Italy,' possesses eleven chapels and the tombs of Michael Angelo, Alfieri, and Macchiavelli, while the church of San Lorenzo contains the tomb of the Medici and the statues of Giuliano and Lorenzo de Medici by Michael Angelo. The Palazzo Vecchio or Palazzo della Signoria, built in 1285 by Arnolfo, is a square turreted pile, and was once the seat of the republic's magistrates. It has a lofty tower with the great bell which formerly called out the citizens. The Palazzo degli Uffizi possesses a library of 150,000 vols. and 12,000 MSS., and an unsurpassed collection of sculptures and paintings, amid which are the Venus de Medici and the famed group of Niobe and her children. The Palazzo Pitti, begun by Brunelleschi, and the residence of the King of Italy when he is at F., has a library of 70,000 vols. and a magnificent collection of paintings. Near the Pitti Palace, and on the summit of a hill S. of the Arno, are the Boboli Gardens, with statued avenues, terraced walks, fine fountains, and trees cut into formal shapes. The Bargello, built in 1255 as the abode of the Podestà, and known as the Palazzo di Giustizia, but for centuries used as the public prison, has been of late carefully restored and transformed into a museum for Tuscan antiquities. It has seven great halls and a richly-carved marble staircase. The church of Or San Michele is one of the finest Florentine relics. It is adorned with statues by Ghiberti, Donatello, and Gian of Bologna, which stand in niches of white marble carved into fanciful arabesques and inlaid with gold mosaic. There are many other palaces and churches and several theatres and hospitals. The commercial greatness of F. has departed; the silk, velvet, and woollen manufactures have declined, and trade is now mostly in mosaics, jewellery, porcelain, and works of art, though carpets and straw hats are still made. F. has two forts, but no regular defences. Pop. (1874) 123,463. F. has been compared to Athens for the turbulence, intellectual brightness, and keen political sympathies of its inhabitants, for its firm democratic leanings, and for its splendour as a home of literature and art. It was the centre of the Renaissance in Italy, and the focus of Italian culture; it gave birth to the modern literary dialect of the Italian language, produced the earliest school of political historians since the days of ancient Greece, and numbered among its sons several of the greatest names in the history of painting, sculpture, and architecture. See RENAISSANCE, ITALIAN LITERATURE, and ITALIAN ART.

F. was founded by the Romans in the 1st c. B.C., was pillaged in the dark ages by the barbarians, and was afterwards occupied by the Lombards. Karl the Great appointed a duke, afterwards called a count, over F., with officers under him chosen partly by the people, a government which seems to have been the germ of the Florentine commonwealth. The emperors, especially Otho the Great, favoured the city, which in the 10th c. had conquered several neighbouring places. F. was ruled by twelve *Angiani*, acting along with a foreign Podestà, and no distinction was made between plebeians and nobles, until, between 1282 and 1292, a mercantile commonwealth was established. It was decreed that no one could bear office who did not belong to the *Arti* or commercial guilds, and the nobles were forbidden to share in the government, which was administered by eight Priors and the Gonfalonier of Justice. These held office for two months. About 1300 party strife broke out between the Guelphs, known as the *Neri* ('blacks'), and the Ghibellines or *Bianchi* ('whites'), the latter, among whom was Dante, being in the end banished. In 1323 the constitution was changed, and Guelph citizens above 30 were alone declared eligible for the chief magistracies, and were chosen by lot. During the 14th c. a new aristocracy grew up and the Medici came into importance. In the beginning of the 15th c. the Medici dynasty was founded by Giovanni de Medici (died 1428), who was succeeded by Cosmo; and Cosmo's grandson Lorenzo in 1480 overthrew the old democratic constitution in place of a Council of Seventy, through which he controlled the state. In 1494 Pietro Medici was banished, and Savonarola founded a theocratic commonwealth, which ended in 1498; then the old republican government was restored under Soderini until 1512, when the Medici returned to power. A free commonwealth again existed from 1527 to 1530, when the Medici despotism was forced upon the city by the Emperor Karl V. Up to this time the Medici had ruled as commercial tyrants without princely titles, but in 1532 Alessandro de Medici was made hereditary president, and Cosmo, his successor, was declared Grand Duke of Tuscany in 1569. On the extinction of the Tuscan ducal line in 1737 F. became the appanage of the house of Lorraine, under whom, except during the episode of Napoleon's kingdom of Etruria, it remained until 1860, when Tuscany was united with the kingdom of Italy. In 1864 F. succeeded Turin as capital of Italy, but was superseded by Rome in 1870. In history F. is remarkable for her general adherence to the Guelphic party, for the instability of her government as contrasted with the permanence of the Venetian rule, for the bright, variable political activity of her citizens, and for surpassing every other Italian city in her interest in the welfare of all Italy. See Délécluze, *F. et ses Vicissitudes* (2 vols. Par. 1837); Reumont, *Tavole Cronologiche e Sincrone della Storia Fiorentina* (8 parts, Flor. 1841); Trollope, *History of the Republic of F.* (Lond. 1864); Symonds's *Renaissance in Italy* (Lond. 1875).

Florence of Worcester, a monkish chronicler, belonging to Worcester monastery, where he died 7th July 1118. He wrote a chronicle from the Creation to 1117, compiled chiefly from the *English Chronicle* and the work of Marianus Scotus, with additions from Bede, the so-called 'Asser,' and the Lives of the Saints. His chronicle deals mainly with English history, but also notices events abroad. It was brought down to 1141 by others of the brethren.

Flo'res (Port. 'flowers').—1. The most westerly island of the Azores, in lat. 39° 25′ N., and long. 31° 12′ W. It is very fertile, and has a pop. of 16,522. The chief town is Santa Cruz. —2. The largest island of the chain extending E. from Java to Timor, lies 200 miles S. of Celebes. It is 200 miles long and

35 broad, is in great part hilly, and has several lofty volcanic peaks on its S. side. The exports are sandal-wood, beeswax, and horses. There are Malay settlements on the coast, but the natives are of Nigritic race.—3. An islet of Uruguay, in the Plata, 20 miles below Monte Video.

Flor'iculture, or **Flower-Cultivation**, the art of cultivating flowers for the sake of their beauty, odour, and uses, has been practised from the most ancient times. In ancient history special reference is frequently made to floral decorations and to the selection of flowers for various purposes; while in modern times, not only has the art of gardening become very highly developed, but from a knowledge of the physiology of plant-life, florists are enabled to cultivate flowers under much more favourable auspices than formerly. The art of landscape-gardening has in fact become of late years highly specialised. In great towns and cities especially, flower-growing has been much facilitated by the invention of the *Wardian case*, a closely-glazed case invented by Mr. N. B. Ward. It consists of a strong box or trough to contain earth, which is placed over a substratum of gravel and broken bricks. The soil is well watered, and over the box a glass roof of tight-fitting nature is placed, this glass roof possessing a door or aperture permitting the removal of dead leaves, &c. By means of this principle of isolating, as it were, plant-life from the surrounding atmosphere, and supplying delicate or exotic forms with the necessary conditions for growth, many plants of rare nature can be successfully grown even in a very smoky atmosphere. The cultivation of flowers for commercial purposes may be said to form the practical application of the art of F. Thus the cultivation of Lavender (q. v.) assumes a high importance from the uses of that plant in the manufacture of perfumes. At Mitcham in Surrey vast quantities of lavender are grown. Otto or attar of roses, valued in some cases at five guineas per oz., also exemplifies the extent to which the successful results of F. may be carried. See Thomson's *Handy Book of the Flower-Garden* (1868), and Glenny's *Flower-Garden* (1871).

Flor'ida, the most southern of the United States of America, included chiefly in the bold peninsula projecting from the S.E. angle of the country, is bounded on the E. by the Atlantic, on the W. and S. by the Gulf of Mexico, and on the N. by the states of Georgia and Alabama. Area, 59,268 sq. miles, or somewhat larger than England and Wales. Pop. 188,248. The peninsular portion is 90 miles broad and 370 miles long. The coast-line is over 1150 miles in extent, and among its numerous harbours some of the chief are Pensacola, St. Marks, Cedar Keys, Tampa, Charlotte, Key West, St. Augustine, and Jacksonville. The capital is Tallahassee. From Cape F., near the southern extremity of the peninsula, a great series of reefs or keys sweep round to the S. and W., and end in a group of sandbanks and islets called *tortugas*. The chief of the keys are Key Largo and Key West, on the latter of which the important city and naval station of the same name is placed. The *surface* is level, the highest elevation being a ridge 180 feet above sea-level, extending from Fernandina on the E. to Cedar Keys on the W. coast, and traversed by railway. Streams, lagoons, and marshes abound all over the country. The chief rivers are the St. John's and the Suwannee. In southern F. the land seldom rises to more than 6 feet above the level of the tide. The soil is usually a light sandy loam, with a substratum of clay, and is of all qualities from the sandy pine barrens to the swamp lands of tropical productiveness. Nearly all the grains and fruits of temperate regions may be grown in the N., semi-tropical fruits are profitably cultivated in the eastern and central districts, tropical fruits in the S. Raising cotton and sugar-cane, for which the soil and climate of F. are especially suitable, are growing industries. The forests consist of yellow pine, live oak, hickory, magnolia, mahogany, satin-wood, &c. Though in the same latitude as the Sahara Desert and S. China, the climate of F., tempered by cool winds from the seas surrounding it, which blow from sunrise to sunset, is delightful during the greater part of the year, and in this connection F. is becoming to the northern states of America what southern France and Italy are to Europe—a national sanatorium, and a favourite place of resort for those suffering from pulmonary diseases. Of the entire area of about 38,000,000 acres, 2,000,000 are under cultivation. The cultivation and export of oranges, lemons, and citrons is the chief industry. Besides the numerous orange-groves in existence in 1870, 3,000,000 orange-trees planted since then were bearing in 1875. In 1872 the cotton production was 47,125 bales. The Indian corn crop in 1873 reached 2,320,000 bushels, of Irish potatoes 13,000 bushels, of sweet potatoes 1,037,000 bushels, of sugar 1300 hogsheads, of molasses 500,000 gallons, of tobacco 200,000 pounds. Hallock states that F. may at no distant date grow fruit for half the world, if she can only obtain a sufficiency of capital and labour. *History.*—Ponce de Leon, in search of an El Dorado that contained also the Fountain of Life, landed here in 1513, and gave the country its present name—the land of flowers. It was settled by the Spaniards in 1565, ceded to Britain in 1763, re-ceded to Spain in 1784, sold to the United States in 1819, and constituted a state of the Union in 1845. In 1861 F. joined the Southern Confederacy, and was the scene of many bloody conflicts until 1865. In 1868 the state was readmitted into the Union. See Townshend's *Wild Life in F.* (Lond. 1875); Charles Hallock's *Camp Life in F.* (1876); Lainer's *F., its Scenery, Climate, and History* (Lond. 1876).

Florida-Blan'ca, Don Josefo Moñino, Count of, a Spanish statesman, born at Murcia in 1728. He studied law, became ambassador at Rome, where he ably composed many differences between Spain and the Pope, and was a chief agent in the election of Pius VI. In 1777 Charles III. made him prime minister, in which office he promoted trade and science, improved the roads and beautified the cities of Spain, and allayed a dispute with Portugal. He united Spain with Russia and Prussia in an armed neutrality, of which the aim was to cripple England, but his foreign policy ended in failure. During his administration Algiers was bombarded, which checked piracy, many heavy dues were removed, and great judicial reforms were effected. F. created many powerful enemies, and in 1792 was imprisoned in the castle of Pampeluna. After several years' confinement, he was permitted to return to Murcia, where he lived in retirement until 1808, when he was called to preside over the central junta during the war with Napoleon. He died at Seville, 20th November 1809. F. wrote several treatises on jurisprudence.

Flor'idæ. See CERAMIACEÆ.

Florida Gulf, between the peninsula of Florida and the Bahamas, is practically the local name applied to that reach of the Gulf Stream which skirts the S.W. coast of Florida. See CURRENTS, OCEAN.

Florid'ia, a town of Sicily, province of Noto, near the Alfeo, 7 miles W. of Syracuse. It has some trade in grain, wine, and olives. Pop. 7030.

Flor'in, at first the name of a gold coin, so called either because it was made at Florence, or because on its reverse side there was a lily (Lat. *flos*, 'a flower'). The modern English coin so designated is of silver, and of the value of 2s.

Flor'ists' Flowers. These flowers are so named from having been made the subjects of special attention by the practisers of Floriculture (q. v.). The cultivation of roses, dahlias, tulips, fuchsias, hyacinths, and many other flowers, exemplifies the results of the florist's art. The liability of many flowers when cultivated to *sport*—*i.e.*, to produce varieties—and the knowledge that by fertilising together flowers of different species, varieties can be produced in some cases almost at will, form two facts of great importance to florists. The fertilisation of the seeds of one species by the pollen of a different species tends to produce a union, in the hybrid progeny, of the characters of the parent-species. And hence the colours of flowers and other characters can be manipulated often with great freedom. *Double flowers* result from the conversion of the stamens and pistil into whorls of flower leaves—this process resulting in the sterility of these flowers. The Dutch have long been famous for their cultivation of flowers, particularly Tulips (q. v.). In 1636–37 a 'tulipmania' seized Holland, and fabulous prices were given for rare varieties and bulbs. In S. Holland the cultivation of roses is also carried on with vigour, and in Britain, dahlias, hollyhocks, fuchsias, and other flowers are successfully grown.

Flo'rus, L. Annæ'us, or more probably **Julius**, the reputed author of a succinct but over-rhetorical history *Epitome Rerum Romanarum*, composed most probably in the reign of Augustus. It consists of two books, the first dealing with the foreign wars of Rome, the second with civil strifes, and ending at 20 A.D. The best editions are those of Otto Jahn (Leips. 1852), and of Halm (Leips. 1854). See Reber's *Das Geschichtswerk des F.*

(Freising, 1865), and C. Heyn's *De Floro Historico* (Bonn, 1865).

Flo'tant (Fr. 'floating'), an heraldic phrase applied to an unfurled flag.

Flo'tow, Friedrich von, a living German composer, born at Teutendorf, in Mecklenburg-Schwerin, 26th April 1812. He received his musical education in Paris, where also his first successful opera, *Le Naufrage de la Méduse*, was produced in 1839. His compositions are all operatic; they are pleasant and melodious, and in many ways more like the work of a musician than those of his Italian and French contemporaries. While extremely popular, however, both in Germany and France, they are not yet, with the exception of *Martha*, so much known in this country as they deserve to be. The principal are *Stradella, Die Grossfürstin, Rübezahl, Indra, Albin, Hilan, and L'Ombri.* Since 1863 F. has lived in Paris.

Flot'sam is a term of English law denoting goods floating in the sea, or goods which have been cast on shore by the sea. Where the owners are not known, F. goes to the crown or lord of the manor. When the owners are known, they have a year and a day to claim their goods. See DERELICT, JETSAM, and JETTISON.

Floun'der (*Platessa*), a species of *Pleuronectidæ* or flatfishes, common on the coasts of Britain, and esteemed as a food fish. It is distinguished by possessing a single row of teeth, the dorsal fin commencing over the eye, and the tail fin being distinct. The common F. (*P. flesus*) attains a length of 10 or more inches, and a maximum weight of 5 or 6 lbs. Smaller specimens, however, are more frequently met with. The eyes are on the right side of the body, this being the upper side of the animal, which swims and lies on the left side. Its colour is brown. The dab (*P. limanda*) is nearly allied to the F.

Flour, the grain of wheat or other cereals finely ground for human food. The term is also applied to many finely-powdered substances.

Flou'rens, Marie Jean Pierre, a French scientific writer, was born at Maureilhan, Hérault, April 15, 1794. He devoted himself from an early age to scientific study, at seventeen delivered a course of lectures on 'The Physiological Theory of Sensations,' and at nineteen obtained the degree of Doctor of Medicine, after which he went to Paris, where he made the acquaintance of St. Hilaire, Chaptal, the Cuviers, and other men of science. Admitted a member of the Académie des Sciences in 1828, he succeeded in 1832 to the professorship of natural history in the Jardin du Roi, and the following year became Perpetual Secretary of the Académie des Sciences. F. was a very voluminous writer, and from 1841 to 1851 published a number of books giving in a comprehensive form and in a singularly lucid style the 'history and philosophy' of several branches of science. Among his works are *Anatomie Générale de la Peau et des Membranes* (1843); *Théorie Expérimentale de la Formation des Os* (1847); and *De la Longévité Humaine et de la Quantité de Vie sur le Globe* (1854). F., who had been deputy to the French Chamber for Bériers, was made in 1840 a Peer of France, and in 1864 member of the Municipal Council of Paris. He died December 6, 1867.—**Gustave F.**, son of the above, and better known as a revolutionist than as a *savant*, was born August 4, 1838. In 1863 he filled his father's chair in the Collége de France, published (1865) *Science de l'Homme*, and aided in the preparation of a *Grand Dictionnaire du XIX. Siècle.* From 1866-68 he took part in the Cretan insurrection, about which he wrote a book. On his return he threw himself into conspiracies against the Second Empire, aided the celebrated Rochefort in editing the *Marseillaise*, was wounded in a duel with the Bonapartist M. Paul de Cassagnac, and on being sentenced in 1870 to three years' imprisonment, fled to England. After the fall of the Second Empire, he became commander of a regiment under the Commune, and was killed April 3, 1871.

Flour-Mite (*Acarus farinæ*), a species of *Acaridæ* or mites which belong to the spider class (*Arachnida*). They exist among flour, and resemble in form the cheese-mite or *A. domesticus.* The body is oval, has eight legs, and is covered with bristles. The female flour-mites are larger than the males.

Flour, St. (the ancient *Sanctus Florus*, surnamed *La Noire*), a town of France, department of Cantal, 34 miles E.N.E. of Aurillac. It stands on a basaltic highland, and is built almost entirely of volcanic *débris*. Its chief buildings are the cathedral (15th c.), the church of St. Vincent, and the corn-market. F. has manufactures of copper utensils, and trade in cattle and corn. Pop. (1872) 4046.

Flower (from Fr. *fleur*, Lat. *flos, floris*), the name given to the conspicuous series of organs found in higher plants, the ultimate function of which is *reproductive* in nature, and serves to mature and produce *seeds.* A perfect F. consists of four *whorls*, or concentric series of organs. Externally we find (1) the *calyx* (usually green, but sometimes coloured), composed of certain leaves named *sepals*; (2) within the calyx, the *corolla*, or showy part of the F., composed of leaves named *petals*, and coloured to attract insects to the F., for the purpose of fertilising the pistil by the conveyance of the pollen, or matter of the stamens; (3) the *stamens*, forming the third whorl, and existing each as a *filament*, bearing a head or *anther*, consisting of two lobes, within which the *pollen*, a yellow powder necessary for fertilising the seeds, is produced; (4) the *pistil*, which is the central whorl of the F., and is composed of one or more folded leaves named *carpels.* Each carpel consists of a lower portion (the *ovary*, containing the *ovules* or *seeds*), of a neck (the *style*), and of a little head surmounting the neck, and named the *stigma.* The stigma and style may be wanting. The stigma is borne directly on the ovary (as in the poppy) when the style is wanting. The calyx and corolla are collectively named the *floral envelopes*; while the stamens and pistil are together named the *essential organs*, because they are necessary for the production of seed. Every part of the F. is a leaf more or less modified. The leaf-type of the F. may be demonstrated in cases of abnormal flowering, as in *double flowers*, where the stamens and pistil are represented by floral leaves. Conspicuous flowers are only met with in higher plants, which are hence named *phanerogamous.* In ferns, mosses, and lower plants, the reproductive organs are not conspicuous, and such plants are hence named *cryptogamous.* The F. is usually borne on a *peduncle* or F.-stalk. Where no F.-stalk is developed, flowers are said to be *sessile.* Thus in a daisy numerous sessile flowers are borne on a common receptacle, and form a F.-head or *capitulum.* When all four whorls of the F. are present, the F. is *complete.* It is *incomplete* if one or more are absent. When (as in lilies, tulips, &c.) the calyx cannot be distinguished from the corolla, or when one whorl only is present, the floral envelopes receive the name of *perianth.* A F. with calyx and corolla is said to be *dichlamydeous*; with one envelope only, *monochlamydeous*; and with no true calyx or corolla, *achlamydeous.* Flowers are *irregular* when one part of the calyx or corolla exceeds in size the other parts—as in the corolla of dead-nettle; and *regular*, when all the parts are of equal size—as in the buttercup. A F. is *symmetrical* when its parts exist in similar numbers or in multiples of one another. When flowers depart from the ordinary type of floral structure or arrangement, their modifications are due—(1) to the *absence* or *suppression* of one or more whorls; (2) to the *form* of the whorls; (3) to the *separation* or *union* of parts of whorls; (4) to the *parts* of one whorl being united to the adjacent whorl on either side; and (5) to the *position* of each whorl on the floral receptacle. Flowers are *bisexual* when each has both stamens and pistil. They are *unisexual* when each F. has one series of essential organs (stamens or pistil) only. Flowers are called *monœcious* when staminate or stamen-bearing flowers are situated on the same *plant* with pistillate flowers; and *diœcious* when staminate flowers are situated on one plant and pistillate flowers on a distinct plant. The *arrangement* of flowers on the flowering-axis is named *inflorescence.* Inflorescence is determined by the manner in which flowers open. Thus when the centre F. opens first, and the external flowers open later, the inflorescence is said to be *centrifugal* or definite; such a mode of F.-expansion is seen in buttercup, chickweed, sweet-william, &c. In wallflower, foxglove, &c., the inflorescence is *centripetal* or *indefinite*, the flowers furthest from the axis opening first. The most common arrangements of inflorescence are—(1) the *spike*, as seen in plantain, where numerous sessile flowers are arranged on a common axis; (2) the *raceme* (as in red currant, foxglove, &c.), which is simply a spike with *stalked* flowers; (3) the *capitulum* or *head* (as in daisy, clover, &c.), where sessile flowers are arranged on a common receptacle; (4) *panicle* (as in oat, horse-chestnut, &c.), which is a compound raceme, each secondary F.-stalk or pedicel again dividing; (5) the *umbel* (as in cowslip, carrot, hemlock, &c.), where the pedicels or secondary F.-stalks spring from a common point, and bring the flowers to the same level; (6) the *corymb*, where the flowers reach the same level, but where the pedicels do not spring from the same point (as in elder and hawthorn). Flowers and F.-buds spring from modified leaves named *bracts*, those of the secondary F.-stalks being termed *bractlets*. Where a circle of bracts surrounds a F.-head (as in daisy), the circle is named an *involucre*. The coloration of flowers, their physiology as concerned with fertilisation of the seed and with plant reproduction generally, and many other points, will be found treated of in other articles relating to botanical subjects.

Flowers, Artifi'cial. The art of imitating the floral beauties of nature with varied materials is extensively practised in France and Italy. The chief seat of the art is Paris, and its productions are noted for great artistic beauty. Fine cambric is mostly used for petals, and taffeta for leaves; but velvet, gauze, silk, and crape are also in requisition. Stamens are represented with slender wire or stiffened silk threads, and stems are formed of stout copper wire. Veins, folds, and the peculiar markings of leaves are imitated by means of 'goffering' implements. Dyes for tinting are specially prepared. Most manufactories employ females, and produce only a component part of a flower, the parts being collected and grouped together by those who possess an intimate acquaintance with the natural objects. A. F. are much used for head-wreaths, dress-trimmings, bouquets, and table decorations. Great Britain carries on a large and annually-expanding import trade in A. F., chiefly with France. The value of the imports has more than quadrupled in twenty years; those of the year 1874 were valued at £447,050. Wax-flower making, which is almost exclusively practised in Great Britain, is quite a distinct art from the foregoing. (See WAX FLOWERS.) Other materials of the most diverse nature are employed in different countries for fabricating A. F. Feathers are widely used; the Austrians and Swiss use straw, the Brazilians gaudy insects' wings and fish-scales, and the natives of the Bahamas and Mauritius delicate sea-shells.

Flue. See CHIMNEY.

Flu'ids (from Lat. *fluo*, 'I flow') are bodies which yield without resistance to any given pressure, however small, unless they be supported by pressures in other directions. They thus embrace what are usually termed liquids and gases, and differ in this particular of non-resistance from solids, which comprehend all other known forms of matter. F., however, as we have them in nature, do not completely fulfil this condition. The *perfect* ideal fluid is not known; for in all viscosity, or what is termed fluid-friction, exists, in virtue of which work must be done to alter the relative positions of the component particles. As this viscosity gets greater and greater, the liquid fluid approaches more nearly the condition of a plastic solid, so that in certain instances it is impossible to say whether a given specimen of matter is a solid or a liquid. See GAS, LIQUID, SOLIDS.

Fluke, the name given to various species of parasitic animals belonging to the order *Trematoda* of the class *Scolecida* (q. v.). The *Trematoda* are nearly allied to the *Tæniada*, or the more familiar tapeworms. The flukes are sometimes called *suctorial worms*, from the fact that (as implied by the name *Trematoda*) they have one or more sucker-like pores whereby they adhere to the tissues of their hosts. The flukes are found as parasites and in a mature state in birds, fishes, and other *Vertebrata*. A very familiar form is the *Distoma* or *Fasciola hepaticum* or common liver F., which inhabits the liver and biliary ducts of the sheep, and when present in numbers produces the disease in that animal known to veterinarians as 'Rot' (q. v.). In the common F. the characters of the *Trematoda* may be conveniently studied. In all the flukes, with a single exception, a digestive system is present, although no true perivisceral or body cavity is developed. The digestive system is usually of branching shape, and opens externally by a single aperture only, which therefore serves both as mouth and anus. This opening is situated within the front or anterior sucker. The *sexes* in flukes are united in one and the same individual, and a *water-vascular system* is developed. The common F. attains an average length of an inch or more, and has a body of an oval and flattened conformation. The hinder sucker is not perforated, and between the two suckers the *generative pore*, or opening of the reproductive organs, is placed. The water-vascular system itself opens externally by a small aperture. The nervous system exists in the form of a ring of nerve-matter surrounding the gullet. The flukes pass through a complicated development. The young flukes appear to pass into water and gain access to the bodies of such forms as fresh-water snails. In this situation they develop into peculiar bodies called *Cercariæ* and *Cercaria-cysts*, each of which consists of a head-extremity and a tail. In some cases the *Cercariæ* appear to produce other *Cercariæ* like themselves. These latter, after some further changes, escape into the water, and gain access to the bodies of sheep along with water used for drinking. The flukes are not common parasites in man, although occasionally they are found in the human liver and its large veins. *D. lanceolatum* is another familiar species; and an Egyptian one, *D. hæmatobium*, occurs more frequently in man, and is dangerous to human life. An allied genus is *Diplostomum*, which occurs in numbers in the eyes of perches and other fresh-water fishes.

Fluores'cence, an optical phenomenon observed in certain substances (solution of sulphate of quinine, tincture of turmeric, uranium glass, &c.), which emit a diffused blue or green light when placed in the path of dark actinic rays of high refrangibility. Professor Stokes explains it as due to the degradation of the highly refrangible actinic rays into luminous rays of less refrangibility. It suggests a method for investigating the absorption lines of the ultra-violet rays of the spectrum, and is further a beautiful example of dissipation of Energy (q. v.) without the performance of useful work.

Flu'orine is classed amongst the elementary substances (see ELEMENTS, CHEMICAL), but up to the present time it has not been isolated. Its existence is surmised from the analogies existing between its compounds and those of chlorine, bromine, and iodine. It is, therefore, ranked with these substances, and they are called collectively the *haloids*, or salt-producers. F. occurs most abundantly combined with the metal calcium, as fluoride of calcium or fluor spar, and from this substance all compounds of F. are obtained. The only one of these of any practical importance is hydrofluoric acid, a compound of hydrogen and F., employed to etch glass. To prepare it, powdered fluor spar is heated with sulphuric acid in a leaden retort, when the gaseous hydrofluoric acid is disengaged, and may be used in this state, or conducted into water contained in leaden vessels, in which it is abundantly soluble. The reaction may be represented thus—

$$\underbrace{CaF_2}_{\text{Fluoride of calcium.}} + \underbrace{H_2SO_4}_{\text{Sulphuric acid.}} = \underbrace{2HF}_{\text{Hydrofluoric acid.}} + \underbrace{CaSO_4}_{\text{Sulphate of calcium.}}$$

Solution of hydrofluoric acid must be preserved in leaden or gutta-percha vessels, as it attacks all others. The atomic weight of F. is 17, and the symbol for its atom F.

Fluor'otype, a photographic process published in 1844 by Mr. R. Hunt. Paper is sensitised by means of a solution of bromide of potassium and fluoride of sodium, and afterwards with nitrate of silver. In developing, protosulphate of iron and weak hydrochloric acid are used; and in fixing, hyposulphite of soda is had recourse to.

Flu'or Spar, or **Derbyshire Spar**, a mineral of frequent occurrence in Derbyshire and Saxony, crystallises in the monometric system, and is usually found in veins, often as a gangue of galena and other ores, in granite, gneiss, mica-slate, clay-slate, limestone, &c. It is the fluoride of calcium (CaF_2), is commonly greenish, violet blue, or topaz-yellow in colour, though also found colourless, rose, crimson, or brown. It is transparent or translucent, is brittle, and of degree 4 in hardness. It is used as a flux for reducing metallic ores, and when heated with sulphuric acid yields hydrofluoric acid.

Flush, a nautical term applied to a ship's deck when it stretches from the bows to the stern in a uniform level, instead of curving upwards fore and aft.

Flush'ing (Dutch, *Vliessingen*, Fr. *Flessingue*, the town on the 'vliess' or 'channel' of the Scheldt), a fortified seaport of the Netherlands, province of Zealand, on the island of Walcheren, at the mouth of the Western Scheldt, 4 miles S. of Middelburg and 35 W. by S. of Bergen-op-Zoom by railway. It is one of the strongest maritime forts in the Netherlands, commanding the entrance to the Scheldt, and has two large harbours, a dry dock, good roads, dockyards, arsenals, magazines, &c. There is a considerable Indian trade, besides active fisheries, and numerous regular steam-lines. Opposite F. is the fort of Breskens. Pop. (1873) 8929. F. was the first town that declared against the Spaniards in 1572. It was pledged by the Prince of Orange to Queen Elizabeth in 1585, and remained with the English till 1616. At the beginning of the 19th c. it was taken by the French, and was stormed and captured by the English under Chatham in 1809.

Flus'træ, or **Sea-Mats**, a genus of *Polyzoa* (q. v.) or *Bryozoa* (q. v.). They are frequently cast ashore in great quantities on the English coasts, and present the appearance of masses of pale-brown seaweed. When microscopically examined, they are seen to consist of a colony of animal forms, each member of the colony or *polypide* being enclosed in a little cell. The cells exist on both sides of the structure, and their tough outer wall or *ectocyst* remains, after the delicate living parts of the organisms have disappeared. Each little member of the colony possesses a mouth, surrounded by retractile tentacles, a digestive system, and male and female generative organs. The colony springs from a single egg, and is produced by a process of continuous *gemmation* or *budding*. The tentacles of *Flustræ* are arranged in an *infundibulate* or funnel-shaped manner. Hence *Flustræ* are included among the Infundibulate *Polyzoa*, or *Gymnolæmata*.

Flute (Old Fr. *flaüte*, from *flaüter*, and that from Lat. *flatare*, 'to blow'), a wind instrument of ancient origin. It remained for a long time a very defective instrument, but recent improvements (especially those of Boehm) in the size and position of the holes, and in the fingering mechanism generally, have removed most of its imperfections. The natural scale of the concert F. is that of D major, and its compass is nearly three octaves. It is sometimes called a 'C' F. because its lowest note is C. The *piccolo*, or octave F., has nearly the same range as the concert F., but an octave higher. The sounds of the F. are produced by the vibration of the column of air in the tube, the length of that column being determined by the fingering. They are very nearly Simple Tones (q. v.), and therefore somewhat wanting in richness.

Flute, in classical architecture, is a vertical channel or hollow moulding on the shafts of columns. In a horizontal section of a fluted Doric column, the flutes, twenty in number, are segmental concaves, and sharply intersect each other. In Doric, also, the F. is not terminated before reaching the base and capital, as in the other orders. The Tuscan is the only column that is never fluted; the Ionic, Corinthian, and Composite have each twenty-four flutes. In Romanesque the F. was bent from the perpendicular into curved and twining forms. See CABLING.

Flute'work, a general name given to those stops in organs in which the sound is not produced or qualified by the vibrations of a metal tongue or *reed*.

Flux (Lat. *fluxus*, from *fluo*, 'I flow'), a substance easily fusible added to assist the fusion of refractory materials. Limestone, fluor spar, borax, nitre, sal-ammoniac, common salt, crude tartar, and glass are used as fluxes. *Black F.* is used in the reduction of metallic ores. It is formed of two parts of tartar to one of nitre, mixed in small quantities in a red-hot crucible. *White* or *refining F.* is composed of equal parts of the same ingredients.

Flux (Lat. *fluxus*, from *fluo*, 'I flow'), an extraordinary issue or evacuation, generally from a mucous membrane. Formerly the term was applied to a variety of diseases, such as diarrhœa, dysentery, cholera, bilious attacks, menorrhagia, &c., but it is now seldom used. Dysentery was long known as *bloody F.*

Flux'ions, the mathematical method invented by Newton which corresponds to our modern Calculus (q. v.). It is founded upon the kinematical considerations of the motion of a point, a manner of procedure fundamentally identical with that of *limits*, which is now generally recognised as the only true logical method of establishing the first principles of the differential and integral calculus. The *fluxion* of x was written $\dot{x}$, and corresponds to $\frac{dx}{dt}$, the differential coefficient of x with respect to time; $\ddot{x}$ corresponds to $\frac{d^2x}{dt^2}$, and so on. The notation, though now superseded in investigations in pure mathematics, is yet very convenient in many physical problems, where time is the only independent variable. $\dot{x}$ was the *fluxion* of x, and x was the *fluent* of $\dot{x}$; and the integral $\int z\,dx$ was written by Newton $\underline{\overline{z\,\dot{x}}|}$ and called the fluent of z.

Fly, a name given popularly to many insects, but zoologically restricted to members of the order *Diptera* (q. v.), or flies in which only two wings—the front pair—are developed, whilst the metamorphosis is perfect, and the mouth suctorial.

Fly'catcher, the name given to a large family (*Muscicapidæ*) of Insessorial birds belonging to the section *Dentirostres*, and also to various typical species of the family. The characters of the family are found in the bill being curved above and compressed at the tip. The tail and toes are long, and the tarsi short. The flycatchers are usually of small size, and their colours sober but pleasing. The familiar flycatchers of Britain are the pied F. (*Muscicapa atricapilla*) and the spotted F. (*M. grisola*). The former is found mostly in the N.W. of England, and appears to visit Norway and Sweden in summer. The colour of the female is a delicate brown above, and greyish beneath; the male being coloured dark brown above, the forehead having a white patch; while the tail is black, and the under parts white. The average length is 5 inches. The spotted F. arrives in England in May. It has been seen in S. Europe and S. Africa. Its general colour is a light brown above, the breast being white, and the sides yellowish brown. Its song is very feeble. The nest is ingeniously constructed of long hairs, grasses, mosses, &c.; and the eggs, numbering five, are bluish-white spotted with red. Exotic species are the paradise F. (*Tchitrea paradisea*) of India, and the fork-tailed F. (*Melvulus tyrannus*) of tropical America.

Fly'ing is the motion through the air of birds, insects, and bats. It does not include the leaping of fish, reptiles, and small quadrupeds, which is frequently assisted by membranes or fins acting as parachutes. As compared with walking and swimming, F. obviously is accompanied by the minimum of resistance from the atmosphere, and the maximum of displacement. The travelling surfaces or wings have therefore to be greatly increased; they act like twisted inclined planes. When the wing ascends and descends, it rotates within the *facettes* or depressions situated on the scapula and coracoid bones. The curves described by the wing and body in F. form waved lines intersecting at each beat of the wings. Professor Bell Pettigrew maintains that walking, swimming, and F. all take place in figure-of-8 curves; that wings (consisting of arm, forearm, and hand) are really screws, and reverse their planes at every stroke; and that they act not merely as elevators, but as buoys after the manner of kites. His experiments have been continued by Marey, Senecal, Ciotti, and others. The muscles being arranged in a certain cycle, the shortening of the flexor halves and the lengthening of the extensor halves diminish the angles formed by the lever bones, and by the opposite muscular actions these angles are increased, and this alternation makes F. The power of F. varies with the size of wing, the dragon-fly and the albatross being conspicuous examples. The weight of the bird is indispensable to flight, the body by its fall elevating the wings, which are opposed obliquely to the air. A good deal of exaggeration occurs in the descriptions of the air-sacs and hollow bones found in some flying animals. The fifteen air-sacs described by Sappey are more probably connected with respiration; they do not occur at all in the bat. The rapidity of vibration in wings has also been exaggerated; it has been said that the blow-fly vibrates its wings 300 times per second. The actual velocity of the wing is probably greater in the case of insects, as it arises from the thoracic muscle, while birds have muscles distributed upon the pinion. The *libellulæ* of the dragon-fly, however, enter the root of the wing. The buzzing, whirring, and whistling noises produced by wings have some relation to the rapidity of stroke. In the case of birds which skim, sail, or glide, the pinion is greatly elongated and ribbon-shaped, but generally there is a relation between the weight of the animal, the area of its wings, and the rate of oscillations.

Most flying animals seem to have much more wing than they absolutely require, as considerable portions have been detached without seriously affecting F. It is maintained by De Lacy that the larger the animal the smaller relatively are its flying surfaces. The pigeon weighs eight times less than the stork, and has twice as much surface. A singular mode of F. is that practised by the large-winged oceanic birds, who begin by beating the water with the tips of their wings so as to force the body up. An account of the manner in which the feathers are arranged to make the wing impervious to air in the down stroke, and to increase or diminish its area, is given in Pettigrew's *Animal Locomotion*, p. 180. By the flexing of the wing in flight, the *remiges* or 'rowing feathers' are opened up, and the air permitted to escape. The wing is elevated by the muscle *pectoralis minor*, and depressed by the *pectoralis major*. Professor Pettigrew is of opinion that the effective stroke is given downwards and forwards, but the weight of observation seems to be against this view. For an account of the attempts made at artificial flight by means of gas, see BALLOON. Attempts have also been made to fly, not by a machine specifically lighter than air, but by the use of rigid inclined planes driven forward in a straight line, or revolving planes (aërial screws), and also by the vertical flapping of wings. The *aërostat* of Henson and Stringfellow was invented in 1843. Its vanes or paddles were driven by a small steam-engine one-third of a horse power. It had huge fixed bamboo frames covered with canvas, and a rudder also made of canvas, but movable within limits. Its weight was 12 lbs. (including superimposed planes of canvas, or aëroplanes, added by Wenham in 1867), and its sustaining area 36 feet. This machine was started by being run rapidly down hill, the sails being set at a small angle to the ground. Sir George Cayley's *aërial screw* consisted of two corks, in which wing feathers were stuck. The corks were connected by a shaft, and a thread wound on to a bow of whalebone caused the corks to rotate in opposite directions. In 1842 Mr. Phillipps made a small metal steam-engine with fans (weighing 2 lbs.), which flew across several fields. In 1863 the Frenchmen Nadar and De la Landelle completed several clockwork models (*orthoptères*), but their chief success was in the *helicopteric*, in which the steam-driven screws were arranged in tiers upon two masts. As regards artificial wings, the earliest (not reckoning mere parachute falls) seem to be those constructed by Borelli (*De Motu Animalium*, Prop. 196, 1680). The wings consisted of a rigid rod in front, and flexible feathers behind. He conceived that the air's pressure drove the bird forward like a wedge in the direction of its base. It is generally admitted that the horizontal impulse depends on the yielding or *elevation* of the free extremities of the quills in the downward stroke. Marey further says that the converse takes place in the up stroke, the posterior margin of the wing in both cases making an angle of 30° with the horizon (*Méchanisme du Vol chez les Insectes*, 1869). The wings constructed by Marey and Straus-Durckheim do not seem to differ in principle from Borelli's. Pettigrew's wave wing, on the other hand, closely resembles the actual construction of a bird wing. It has no rigid margin, is twisted on itself, and tapers from the root to the tip. Elastic reeds or fine steel rods are covered with silk, india-rubber, linen, &c. The wing is valvular, so that during the up stroke the superimposed air passes through, and it is made to vibrate obliquely, not vertically. The experiments made seem to destroy Chalvier's theory that all the work of F. was done by the depressor muscles, the air forcing the wing upwards to its original position. See Bell-Pettigrew's *Animal Locomotion* (1873).

Flying Bridge, a ferryboat attached by a long chain or rope to a buoy anchored in the centre of a river. The position of the buoy depends upon the width of the river and the rapidity of the current, but when properly chosen, the action of the current combined with the resistance of the chain causes the boat to move across the river. By setting the boat obliquely to the current, by the help of the rudder, the action of the current is resolved into two forces—one tending to separate the boat from the chain, and the other to move it at right angles to the chain. The resistance of the chain to breaking counteracts the first of these, and the second only takes effect, the boat thus sweeping across the stream in an arc of a circle of which the buoy is the centre. Flying bridges are often used for military purposes.

Flying Drag'on or **Liz'ard** (*Draco volans*), a species of *Lacertilia*, or lizards, found in the E. Indies and Indian Archipelago, and so named from the possession of a *patagium* or wing-like membrane, enabling the animal to take flying leaps from tree to tree. The skin on each side of the body is extended and supported on six of the anterior ribs, which extend in a straight manner from the spine. This apparatus acts merely as a kind of parachute, and can in no sense be said to represent wings or organs of true *flight*. The colour of the F. D. is an olive brown, and the average length about 5 or 6 inches. An allied species is the fringed dragon, or *D. fimbriatus* of Sumatra. These lizards form the modern representatives of the great extinct reptiles known as *Pterodactyles* (q. v.).

Flying Dutch'man, The, like many other mediæval legends, is a growth by accretion rather than a single independent creation. It is traceable to the 16th c., and is typical of a time of rude religious feeling and of wild seafaring adventure. The germ of the story, in its varied forms, is akin to that of Odysseus and the Wandering Jew. For some great sin an accursed mariner is doomed to perpetual and aimless cruisings. In modern forms of the legend he is rescued from his fate by some holy interposition—a religious amulet or a faithful woman's love. According to a late version, the F. D. was an Amsterdam vessel, the master of which, Van der Decken, swore on a certain tempestuous night to make the Cape or to be 'eternally damned,' and 'though he should beat there till the day of judgment;' and there he is still to be seen, with crowded sail, tearing along in the wildest weather. Heine has made the legend the subject of a beautiful tale; Wagner weaves it into one of his finest operas, treating it as symbolical of the universal longing for rest from the storms of life.

Flying Fish, a name popularly given to all fishes which, from the large development of their pectoral fins, possess the power of leaping from the water and of supporting themselves for short distances in the air. The typical F. F. is the Teleostean species *Exocœtus volitans*, belonging to the family *Esocidæ*, or that of the pikes. In this fish, found in warm seas, the pectoral fins are elongated, as is also the lower lobe of the tail-fin. No teeth are borne on the palate. The swimming or Air Bladder (q. v.) is of very large size. The 'flight' of the F. F. is short and imperfect, and appears to result in greater part from the impetus which the fish gains in its primary rush through the water. Another species also known by the name F. F. is the Flying Gurnard (q. v.). The true F. F. swim in large shoals, and form the prey of other fishes. They are much esteemed on account of the delicacy of their flesh, and may be caught at night by exhibiting a torch or other light, this process seeming to attract them. The dolphin-fish, or *Coryphæna*, is the natural enemy of the F. F., and pursues them with great dexterity.

Flying Fox. See KALONG.

Flying Gur'nard (*Dactyloptera*), a species of *Triglidæ* or Gurnards (q. v.), so named from the large development of the pectoral or breast fins, by aid of which they are enabled to raise themselves from the water. The common F. G. is the *D. volitans* of naturalists, and is very common in the Mediterranean Sea. It attains a length of from 10 to 15 inches, and is of a brown colour above, variegated with bluish hues. The under parts are rose-coloured, and the fins are black and spotted with blue. An allied species is the *D. orientalis*, or Indian F. G. of the Indian Ocean, which is distinguished by the possession of two elongated filaments placed in front of the dorsal fin. Like the true flying fish, it is pursued by the dolphin-fish.

Flying Le'mur, or **Colu'go** (*Galeopithecus*), a peculiar genus of *Mammalia*, so named from the possession of an expansion of the skin along the sides of the body, uniting the fore and hind limbs, and also extending between the hind-limbs and tail. The possession of this membrane enables the animal to effect springing leaps from tree to tree, but does not confer upon it any power of true flight. The flying lemurs have been by some naturalists associated with the lemurs or lower *Quadrumana*, or monkeys, while other authorities have regarded them as forming a connecting link between the order *Insectivora* (moles, shrews, &c.) and that of the *Quadrumana*. The *G. volans* of the Eastern Archipelago is the most familiar species. The toes are free, and not united by or connected with the membrane. Each foot has five toes, but neither the great toes nor the thumbs can be opposed to the other digits, so as to convert the feet into hand-like organs, as in many monkeys. The teeth resemble in many respects those of *Insectivora*. There are four upper and six lower incisors, and two canines, four præmolars, and six molars in each jaw. The six lower incisors are divided into narrow strips or portions, like the teeth of a comb. The flying lemurs average in length about 1½ feet, are nocturnal in habits, and live chiefly on fruits, small birds, insects.

Flying Mouse. See FLYING PHALANGER.

Flying Phalan'ger or **Oposs'um** (*Petaurus*), a group of Marsupial (q. v.) mammals, allied to the kangaroos, &c., and included in the family *Phalangistidæ*, or that of the phalangers. The most familiar examples are the *P. sciureus*, or flying squirrel, the great F. P. or *P. Australis*, the Ariel P. or *P. Ariel*, and the *P. Taguanöides*, or Taguan. The opossum mouse, or flying mouse (*Acrobates pygmæus*), is also nearly allied. Like the Flying Lemur (q. v.), the F. P. has a fold of skin along each side of the body, uniting the fore and hind limbs. It is nocturnal in habits, and its *patagium* or fold of skin enables it to take flying leaps among the trees. The tail is not prehensile. The F. P. is confined in its distribution to Australia. The flying mouse attains a length of about 3½ inches, while the other species vary in length from 1½ to 2 feet. The prevailing colour is brown, and the fur is soft and glossy.

Flying Squid (*Ommastrephes*), a genus of *Cephalopoda* (q. v.), or cuttlefishes. These animals derive their popular name from their habit of leaping from the water, sometimes with force sufficient to land them on the deck of a ship. They belong to the Dibranchiate cuttles, and to the section *Decapoda* ('ten-armed'). They are included in the family *Teuthidæ*, or that of the Squids. The flying squids are most frequent in tropical seas, but are also found in temperate regions.

Flying Squirr'el, the name given to various genera of Rodent *Mammalia*, resembling the Flying Lemur (q. v.), and Flying Phalanger (q. v.), in that the body is provided with lateral expansions of the skin, forming a kind of parachute serving to sustain the animal in its flights from tree to tree. The flying squirrels occur in S. Asia, Polynesia, N.E. Europe, N. America, and Siberia. They belong to the genera *Pteromys* and *Sciuropterus*, and are included in the squirrel family (*Sciuridæ*). The Taguan F. S. (*Pteromys petaurista*) has no relationship with the phalangers. It inhabits India. The *Sciuropterus volucella*, or Assapan, is an example of the second genus, this form occurring in N. America, and attaining a length of 5 or 6 inches. The colour is brownish grey above, and white below. The fur is not of high value, but is frequently used along with that of other species of Squirrels (q. v.).

Fly-Pow'der is the name given to a compound of metallic arsenic and arsenious acid sold on the Continent for the purpose of killing flies. Such a dangerous compound should never be used for such a purpose. Flies and gnats are repelled by the odour of the oils of turpentine and rue, and quassia acts upon them as a poison.

Fly'trap. See DIONÆA.

Fly'wheel, in mechanism, a wheel fixed upon a revolving shaft and having a heavy rim, its use being to equalise the motion of the shaft, which without it would at some times rotate much faster than at others. Its theory can be most easily explained by reference to the F. of a steam-engine driving the machinery of a factory. Here, in ordinary cases, the resistance (due to the machinery) which has to be overcome by the engine changes continually throughout the day, but for any small interval of time (as that in which the engine makes one revolution) it is practically constant. The mean effort exerted by the engine in that period has been equal to the mean resistance to be overcome; but instead of being constant, it has varied continually, being at one instant smaller and at another greater than the resistance. *Of itself*, therefore, it could not drive the machinery continuously, but only by jerks. A heavy F. placed upon the shaft, however, entirely obviates this difficulty, and by its means any required degree of steadiness can be obtained. The engine expends energy, at starting, in accelerating the velocity of the mass forming the F., and this energy remains stored up in the wheel after it has attained the required velocity. When the resistance becomes greater than the effort, the deficiency is supplied from this storehouse of energy, the velocity being retarded in consequence; when the effort exceeds the resistance, the surplus is absorbed by the F. again with a corresponding acceleration. By making the F. heavy enough, the proportion borne by this surplus and deficiency to the whole energy stored up may be made as small as we please, and thus the fluctuations of speed may be made correspondingly small. In ordinary machinery the ratio borne by the difference between the maximum and minimum velocities to the mean velocity is about 30 : 1.

Any machine (as a punching machine, for instance) in which the resistance varies very greatly periodically should be fitted with a F. of its own besides the one on the engine. It may be mentioned that in certain cases flywheels, or their equivalent, are employed to store up energy in order that, by being brought suddenly to rest, they may be able to exert an enormous pressure through a very small distance, as in stamping a coin.

Foch'abers (Gael. *Faichaber*, 'the plain of the confluence;' anciently *Beul-ath*, 'the mouth of the ford'), a village of Elginshire, on the Spey, 9 miles E. of Elgin, and a station on the Inverness and Aberdeen Railway. F. is beautifully situated in a valley, and consists chiefly of a square and four main streets. The principal buildings are the Established, Free, and Episcopalian churches; and the Milne Free School, founded by A. Milne, a native of F., who died at New Orleans, U.S., and left 100,000 dollars for the purpose. Near F. is Gordon Castle, a seat of the Duke of Richmond. Pop. (1871) 1227.

Fo'cus (Lat. 'a fireplace'), in physics, is the point at which rays of light, heat, or sound meet after reflection or refraction. From certain important geometric properties of the conic sections with respect to certain points, the name was applied to these points, and has now undergone a much wider extension of signification in mathematics.

Fodd'er (Old Eng. *foder*, Dutch, *voeder*, Ger. *futter*), a name given to the food of cattle. The term is vaguely employed, but generally it is restricted to such plants and crops as are consumed in a green or fresh and succulent condition. F. is also an obsolete term for a weight of lead or other metal in England, the precise amount of which varied in different localities.

Law regarding F.—It is an implied obligation on a tenant of land that he shall cultivate it according to the rules of good husbandry, and these are commonly held to require the tenant to consume upon a farm the hay and straw produced by it. Local custom is, however, the rule of law in the matter; and it differs over England as regards a tenant's right to remove or sell hay and straw, the uniform rule, however, being that the manure afforded by the land must be returned to it. In Scotland the rule of good husbandry, and by consequence the law, is uniformly against the tenant having a right to sell or remove fodder. See LEASE.

Fœ'nus Naut'icum (Lat. 'interest on ships') is the rate of interest proportioned to the risk which a person lending money on a ship, on Bottomry Bond (q. v.), as it is called, is entitled to demand.

Fœ'tus (Lat. 'what is produced or bred,' from the obs. *feo*, 'I produce'), the term applied in medicine to the young of viviparous animals in the womb, and of oviparous animals in the egg, after its parts are distinctly formed, until its birth. Previous to the time of its complete formation it is called *embryo*. In the human subject the F. is developed at the end of about the fourth month of gestation; but there are certain points in which the F. at the full period differs anatomically from the child shortly after birth, and especially as regards the circulating apparatus. During pregnancy the *placenta* (popularly termed the after-birth) is developed on the inner wall of the uterus. This organ is chiefly composed of blood-vessels, and from it proceeds the umbilical cord, which conveys arterial blood to the F., and returns it to the placenta. The umbilical cord connects the placenta with the umbilicus or navel of the F., and is the channel by which the F. receives its nourishment from the maternal structures. The circulation of the blood in the F. differs from that in the child immediately after birth; for during fœtal life the circulation is carried on upon the mode of that of the higher reptiles, but afterwards, when certain changes have been accomplished, it becomes that of the complete warm-blooded animal. Up to the time of birth the partition between the auricles of the heart of the F. is incomplete, and the auricles communicate with each other by means of an aperture called the *foramen ovale*. There is also a direct communication between the pulmonary artery and the aorta by the *ductus arteriosus*, and another direct channel between the umbilical vein and the *vena cava*, by the *ductus venosus*. The blood brought from the placenta by the umbilical vein is partly conveyed at once to the *vena cava ascendens* by means of the ductus venosus, and it partly flows through two trunks that unite with the portal vein, returning the blood from the intestines into the liver, thence to be returned to the vena cava by the hepatic vein. The blood that enters the vena cava is purely arterial in its character, but it loses this character in some degree by the time that it reaches the heart, from its being mixed in the vessels with the venous blood returned from the trunk and the lower extremities. The arterial current, on entering the right auricle, is directed by the Eustachian valve into the *left* side of the heart through the *foramen ovale*, whilst the venous current that is being returned by the descending cava is directed into the right ventricle. When the ventricles contract, the arterial blood contained in the left ventricle is driven into the ascending aorta, and supplies the head and upper extremities before undergoing further admixture. The venous blood contained in the right ventricle is driven into the pulmonary artery, and thence through the *ductus arteriosus* into the descending aorta, supplying the trunk and lower extremities with a mixed fluid. The head and upper extremities are thus supplied with blood nearly as pure as that which returns from the placenta, but the rest of the body receives a mixed fluid, from part of it having previously circulated through the system. The changes which occur in the organs of circulation and respiration at birth are more immediately determined by the inflation of the lungs with air during the first inspiration, by the dilatation of the pulmonary blood-vessels with an increased quantity of blood, and by the interruption to the passage of the blood through the placental circulation. These changes are speedily followed by shrinking and obliteration of the *ductus arteriosus*, and of the umbilical arteries, from the hypogastric trunk to the place of their issue from the body by the umbilical cord—by the cessation of the passage of the blood through the *foramen ovale*—by the closure of the foramen, the obliteration of the umbilical vein as far as its entrance into the liver, and of the *ductus venosus* within that organ. Blood ceases at once to pass through the *foramen ovale* from the moment of birth, or as soon as the left auricle becomes filled with blood returning from the lungs; but the actual closure of the foramen may not take place for a considerable time, and it sometimes happens that the foramen remains open, constituting the malformation attending the *morbus cœruleus*.

The average length of time which elapses between conception and parturition in the human female is 280 days or forty weeks. Gestation, however, may be prolonged for two or even three weeks beyond that period; and it has been ascertained from observation among the lower animals, that the prolongation of the period may depend on some peculiarity in the embryo derived from the male parent. A case came under the observation of the writer in which a female, suffering from acute mania, admitted into an asylum, gave birth to a child 296 days after her admission. The shortest period at which gestation may terminate, consistently with the life of the child, has not been definitely fixed, owing to the difficulty of ascertaining the exact length of gestation. There are, however, satisfactory cases on record in which, from the degree of development of the F. at birth, it might be certainly known not to have attained twenty-six or twenty-seven weeks, or little more than six months, and in which the infant was reared in health and vigour.

Law Regarding F.—In medico-legal inquiries it is frequently of great importance to ascertain the age of the F., and to facilitate such conclusions, the main points regarding the physical characters of the F. during the stage of development have been carefully noted and described by physiologists. In the F. of nine months the length is from 17 to 21 inches, and the average weight about 6½ lbs. The length and weight of the male infant slightly exceeds that of the female. No period has been fixed by law beyond which a child born in wedlock may be pronounced illegitimate, nor has the shortest limit been fixed within which a child may be born capable of being mature. In consequence of this indefiniteness many important cases have appeared in the law courts. The question as to what constitutes live birth is of much importance, some maintaining that muscular movement is indicative of life, and others that where respiration has not taken place the child was still-born. The latter view is that more generally adopted in this country, and the question as to respiration having taken place can be easily determined, for the lungs previously to the act of inspiration are dense and solid in structure, and their specific gravity being greater than that of water, they sink when immersed in that fluid, whereas lungs or portions of lungs that have respired float in water. See Quain's *Elements of Anatomy*, edited by Professors W. Sharpey, Allen Thomson, and E. A. Schäfer (Lond. 1876).

The destruction of an unborn infant, though an indictable offence, is not murder. See ABORTION; GESTATION, LAW REGARDING; BIRTH, CONCEALMENT OF; PREGNANCY, CONCEALMENT OF.

Fog (of Danish origin), or **Mist** (Old Eng. *mist*, 'darkness'), is produced by the condensation due to cooling of the aqueous vapour in the air into the form of minute drops of water. The direct cause of its presence may therefore be either the indraught of a cold current into a warm mass of air, or of a warm current into a cold mass of air. The rapid cooling of the ground in contact with air is also frequently attended with the appearance of F., as in the case of the evening mists. Morning mists are often vaporised and dispelled as the day advances by the heat of the sun.

Fogarasy, János, a Hungarian scholar and lawyer, was born at Käsmárk in 1801. He gained considerable reputation from his works on jurisprudence, filled several public offices, and in 1848 was made a member of the financial council of Pesth. F. has zealously studied the Magyar tongue, and made important contributions to philology. Among his writings are *A' Magyar nyelo' metaphysicája* (1834), *A' Magyar nyelo szelleme* (1845), a Magyar-Latin dictionary (1835), and various legal and linguistic works. F. and another eminent Hungarian scholar, Czuczor, are the authors of the Dictionary of the Hungarian Academy.

Foggia, a town in the S. of Italy, in the province of the same name, 80 miles E.N.E. of Naples, on the river Cervara, and a station on the railway to Brindisi. It is the commercial centre of Apulia, and has great corn-stores, and a trade in cattle and wine. Pop. (1871) 34,181. F. is said to have been built from the remains of the old Arpi. The Emperor Friedrich II. held a parliament here in 1240. It was the scene of his wife's death in 1241, and of Manfred's victory over the Pope's troops in 1254. Towards the end of the 18th c. it was the seat of the court of Ferdinand I.

Fog-Signals, audible signals used on board ship, on the sea-coast, on railways, and elsewhere during fog or mist, when the ordinary visible signals cease to be of use. The signals commonly used at sea are the striking of a bell or gong, or the blowing of a horn or steam-whistle; the latter, where it can be used, being probably the most effective. Fog and mist very greatly interfere with the transmission of sound through the air, but further experiments are required in order that precise conclusions may be arrived at on this subject. Recent experiments (1874) by Dr. Tyndall have shown that an optically clear atmosphere is not always the best for transmitting sound, and that the report of a gun in certain circumstances is superior as a fog-signal to a horn or steam-whistle. Such signals as are mentioned above do no more than announce the presence, and approximately the position, of a vessel. In the navy a code of F.-S. is in use, by which the ships of a fleet can communicate in thick weather; there does not seem any reason to prevent the use in the merchant service of an alphabet 'of longs and shorts' (like the Morse alphabet), which would render communication, at present impossible, very easy. The F.-S. used on railways are small packets of detonating material, placed upon the rails and exploded by the wheels of the engine passing over them.

Föhr, an island belonging to Denmark, lies off the W. coast of Slesvig, in the North Sea. Area, 28 sq. miles; pop. 4500, mostly Frisians. It exports to Hamburg large quantities of oysters, cheese, and hosiery. Wyk, the chief town, is a bathing-place, and has had steamboat communication with Cuxhaven on the Elbe since 1833.

Foil, a sword-like weapon used in fencing, is a pliable, highly-tempered bar of steel, from 31 to 38 inches long. The blade is edgeless, and is protected at the point by a 'button.' The F. is only used for thrusting.

Foil (Fr. *feuille*, Lat. *folium*, 'a leaf'), in the arts, plates of metal beaten or rolled out to a state of great tenuity. Tin-F. not exceeding $\frac{1}{1000}$th of an inch in thickness is much used for lining boxes and packages in order to exclude moisture, or to preserve the flavour and aroma of their contents. When covered with mercury it is also employed for silvering looking-glasses. Till 1840, tin amalgam was exclusively employed for that purpose, but the pernicious effects its preparation had upon the health of the workmen, has chiefly led to the adoption of other methods of silvering. F. of copper and its alloys has long been manufactured at Nürnberg and Fürth in Bavaria; hence it is sometimes called *German F.* The manufacture of bronze powders is simultaneously carried on there in order to utilise the F. waste. Highly-polished thin sheets of silvered copper constitutes jeweller's F., which is coated with transparent-coloured varnishes, and placed under precious or factitious gems to enhance their brilliancy and colour.

Foix (Lat. *Fuxum*), a small French town in the department of Ariège, 467 miles S. of Paris. It stands on the Ariège, is very irregularly built, and is overlooked by three towers, part of the old château of the Counts of F. The chief building is the Gothic church of St. Volusien. F. has ironworks and some trade in pitch. Pop. (1872) 5429.

Foix, Comtes de, an old French family which arose in the 11th c. Among its chief members are **Roger**, who received from his uncle, Comte de Carcassonne, the lands of F., now the department of Ariège, whence he took the title Comte de F. He died in 1064. His nephew, **Roger II.**, joined the first crusade, and died in 1125. Roger II.'s grandson, **Roger-Bernard I.**, received large additions to his estates from Raymond V. of Toulouse, and in 1185 obtained the marquisate of Provence from Alfonso II. of Aragon. His son **Raymond-Roger** was the ally of Raymond VI. of Toulouse in the Albigensian crusade, and after a determined resistance to Simon de Montfort, in which he proved himself a brave and skilful soldier, died in 1223. He was a patron of the Troubadours, and wrote several poems. **Roger-Bernard II., the Great**, was the sole ally of Raymond VII. of Toulouse against the forces of Northern France. He was twice excommunicated, and died in 1241. His grandson, **Roger-Bernard III.**, one of the best French poets of the 13th c., fought against the house of Armagnac, a feud maintained after his death in 1302 by his son **Gaston I.**, and ended in the time of his grandson, **Gaston II.**, who contributed greatly to the victory of the Navarrese over the Castilians at Tudela in 1335, did good service against the English in France, and died in 1343. He was succeeded by **Gaston III.**, who was born in 1331, and surnamed *Phœbus* from his beauty. He was made king's lieutenant in Gascony and Languedoc, married a daughter of the King of Navarre, served against the Slavic heathens of Prussia, rescued the royal princesses when they were shut up in Meaux during the Jacquerie, and died in 1391. He was famous for his chivalrous courage and devotion to the chase. He is said to have kept 1600 dogs, and wrote a work *Phébus des deduitz de la Chasse des Bestes sauvaiges et des Oyseaulx de Proye*, which remained popular with the great nobles and gentry long after the middle ages had expired. Froissart, who spent a considerable time in Gaston III.'s residence of Orthes, where he picked up many of the most interesting tales in his Chronicle, has given a careful but over-flattering portrait of this prince. On his death the F. estates passed to another branch of the family. **Gaston IV.** ably opposed the English in Guienne, received the seignory of Carcassonne and the counties of Rouissillon and of Cerdagne from Louis XI., and died in 1472. His grandson, **Gaston de F., Duc de Nemours**, was the most famous of the family. He was the son of Jean de F., Vîcomte de Narbonne, and of Marie d'Orléans, sister of Louis XII.; was born in 1489; was made Duc de Nemours in 1505, and in 1511 commander of the French in Italy. He defeated the Swiss at Como and Milan by his brilliant strategy, routed the besiegers of Bologna, beat the Venetians near Brescia and took that city, and on April 11, 1512, gained the crowning victory of Ravenna over the Spaniards, but was killed through his rash daring, and his death rendered the success fruitless. He was surnamed the *Thunderbolt of Italy*, and is almost unsurpassed as an example of youthful military genius. On his death the estates of F. passed to the King of Navarre, and in the time of Henri IV. were united to the French crown.

Fok'shan, or **Fokchani**, a town of Rumania, on both banks of the Milkova, which partly separates Moldavia and Wallachia, 45 miles W.N.W. of Galacz. It is largest on the Moldavian side, and has a total pop. of 37,500. There is an active river trade, chiefly in corn, with Galacz, and in the vicinity is produced the best wine of Moldavia. The Turks, who were defeated at F. with great loss by the Greeks, 1st June 1821, set fire to the town in September 1822.

Folc'land, or **Folkland**, was the land belonging to the state, corresponding in the old English constitution to the Roman *ager publicus*, and opposed to *bocland* or hereditary estate. With the growth of the kingly power the people's land changed into the king's land, and, after the Norman conquest, the F. became the *terra regis*, the personal estate of the sovereign. When the hereditary nature of the English monarchy was established, any private estates which might belong to the several rulers were fused with the F., which from William I. to William III. was viewed as the king's personal property. Now, however, it is placed at the disposal of Parliament, to be used in the people's service in the same manner as the other state revenues. See Freeman's *Growth of the English Constitution*, chap. iii. (Lond. 1872)

Földvar (Magyar, 'land-fortress'), or **Földvar Duna**, a town of Hungary, on the right bank of the Danube, in the county of Tolna, 80 miles S. of Buda-Pesth. It is strongly and beautifully situated on a hill, is noted for its sturgeon-fishery, and has trade in wine, corn, and salt. Pop. 11,758.

Fo'ley, John Henry, R.A., a sculptor of rare force of genius and artistic accomplishment, born in Dublin, 24th May 1818, distinguished himself in the drawing and modelling schools of that city, and removing to London, entered the Royal Academy at the age of sixteen. He was elected Associate in 1849, and R.A. in 1855. He first exhibited in 1839, when his two models, 'Innocence' and 'Death of Abel,' attracted favourable notice. His 'Ino and Infant Bacchus' (1840), purchased by Lord Ellesmere, his 'Death of Lear' (1841), 'Lear and Cordelia' (1842), 'Venus rescuing Æneas' (1843), bear witness to the industry with which he followed up his first success. He afterwards produced 'Prospero and Miranda,' 'The Mourner,' 'Egeria,' &c. His fame, however, most securely rests on his fine marble statue of 'Hampden' in Westminster Palace, his 'Lord Hardinge,' now at Calcutta, and the magnificent equestrian statue of 'Sir James Outram'—a work inspired with vigour and heroic feeling, and the artist's masterpiece. Like the 'Hardinge,' the 'Outram' is now in Calcutta. F. died in London, 27th August 1874.

Folia'tion, in geology, is, according to Sedgwick, a 'separation into crystalline layers of different mineral composition,' differing thus from cleavage, which is merely a disposition to *split* without mineralogical changes. Darwin gives many fine examples in his *Geology of South America*, and suggests that F. and cleavage are really parts of the same process.

Folign'o, a town in the province of Perugia, Central Italy, on the Torpino, 15 miles S.E. of Perugia by railway. It has a fine cathedral, a Palazzo Communale, a theatre, promenades, &c. The 'Madonna di F.' by Raphael is now in the Vatican. The chief manufactures at F. are parchment, wax-candles, and playing-cards. Pop. 7890. F. is the Umbrian Fulginii and the Fulignum of the middle ages. It was partly destroyed by an earthquake in 1832.

Folkes, Martin, an English antiquary, was born in London, 29th October 1690, studied at Cambridge, was elected Fellow of the Royal Society in 1714, and in 1741 became its president. He was afterwards president of the Antiquarian Society, and a member of the Academy of Sciences at Paris. Oxford honoured him with the degree of D.C.L., and his own university with that of LL.D. He died 28th June 1754. F. contributed many dissertations to the *Transactions* of the Royal and Antiquarian Societies. One of these, *A Table of English*

Gold Coins, was reprinted in 1745 with additions, and a new edition appeared in 1763 under the title of *A Table of English Silver and Gold Coins, new reprinted with Explanation* (2 vols.).

Folkes'tone (Lat. *Lapis Populi*, 'the stone or fortress of the people'), a thriving seaport and bathing-place in the S.E. of Kent, lies in a hollow at the base of high cliffs, 5 miles W.S.W. of Dover, and 83 E.S.E. of London by railway. It has a good harbour and a pier, from which a view may be had of the French coast, and coastwise from Dover to Hastings. There is a considerable trade and regular steam communication with Boulogne, distant about 30 miles. In 1875 there entered the harbour 1166 vessels, of 183,103 tons, and cleared 844, of 141,953 tons. Pop. (1871) 12,698. F. returns one member to Parliament along with Hythe.

Folk'-Lore (Ger. *Volks-Lehre*), a term borrowed from the German to describe that floating mass of legendary narrative, song, and saying which takes its rise during the early life of a nation, and exists solely in the memory of the people, unless at a later date its remains be gathered up and preserved in literary form. F.-L. in its wide sense belongs to anthropology and antiquarianism as much as to literature, since religious myths, ethnic peculiarities, physical conditions, mental characteristics, and social customs all come within its scope. The term is, however, generally restricted to the literature originating in that period of national history which the Germans call *sagenzeit*, or tradition-time, a period through which all peoples pass. In regard to these early sagas, it must be noted that they are not, even in their most fantastic dress, deliberate fictions, but are believed by teller and hearers; and that they grow insensibly by a very natural process of accretion, until what has been a legend or a ballad may result in a complete cycle of connected traditions. There is a further tendency in many cases to group a set of tales and poems round the centre figure, such as Beowulf was to the Low German, Karl the Great to the Frank, Arthur to the Briton, Fingal to the Gael, the Cid to the Spaniard, or Hiawatha to the American Indian. F.-L. is seen at its perfection in Hesiod and Homer, in the poetical traditions of the Greeks, 'the abundance, the beauty, and the long continuance' of whose early literature Mr. Grote pronounces a 'phenomenon which has no parallel elsewhere.' The F.-L. of Rome, if less rich and splendid, is even more eminently national than that of Greece; her early history is but a collection of F.-L. recast by subsequent historians. Modern Italy has produced another legendary growth of a different character, exhibited in the collection of Mr. Busk (*Roman F.-L.*, Longmans, 1874). The literary history of Oriental nations is marked by a F.-L. equally abundant, of which the Arabian or Arabico-Egyptian *Thousand and One Nights*, the Persian *Sindibad Nameh*, the *Pantschatantra*, and the Hindu Vedistic and Brahmanical legends present distinctive phases, while the Slavic races have also their stock of popular traditions. (See Eichhoff's *History of Slavic Literature*, Paris, 1839; Ralston's *Russian F.-L.*, Lond. 1873). Among the Gothic peoples of early Europe, however, their F.-L., which flourished with great luxuriance, exercised an influence on the formation of national character not equalled in the case of any other people. Tacitus mentions the 'old songs' of the Germans, and Jacob Grimm (in his *Deutsche Mythologie*) has thoroughly investigated the growth of these ancient traditions, which comprise, among many others, the *Niebelungen Lied*, the *Volsunga Saga*, the *Eddas*, and the *Lay of Beowulf*. (See also Müller's *Saga Bibliothek*, Mallet's Introduction to the *History of Denmark*, Dahlmann's *Historische Forschungen*, Murray's *Manual of Mythology*, Baring-Gould's *Myths of the Middle Ages*.) The Welsh *Mabinogion* is a collection of Celtic F.-L. As specimens of French F.-L. may be mentioned the *Amadis de Gaul*, the *Chronique de St. Denis*, *Chronique de Turpin*, *Roman de Garin le Loherain*, and the *Chansons de Geste* (Fauriel's *Origine de l'Epopée Chevaleresque*, Paris's *Romans des Douze Paris de France*). In this country the antiquarian side of F.-L. has been treated of by such writers as Browne (*Antiquitates Vulgares*), Brand (*Observations on Popular Antiquities*), Hone in his *Every-Day Book*, Chambers in his *Book of Days*, and Swanson in his *Handbook of Weather F.-L.* English F.-L., in its purely literary aspect, is of great antiquity and interest. Geoffrey of Monmouth's *Chronicle* is apparently constructed of F.-L.; while *King Horn*, the *Romance of Alexander*, *Guy of Warwick*, *Bevis of Hampton*, *Havelok the Dane*, the *Proverbs of Hendying*, the *Robin Hood Ballads* (Wynken de Worde's collection), and *Chevy Chase*, are well-known instances of English popular traditions and ballads. See Percy's *Reliques*, Campbell's *Tales of the W. Highlands*, Warton's *History of English Poetry*, Scott's *Border Minstrelsy*, &c.

Folk'mot (Old Eng. *folc-gemot*, 'meeting of the folk or people'), the name given in early English times to the popular assembly of the shire, which was composed of representatives from hundreds and townships. The scirgerefa or sheriff presided over the F., by which he was at one period probably elected, though not within historical knowledge. The F., according to Edgar's law, was held twice in the year, but it assembled in arms on any occasion of emergency. It is incorrect to suppose, as Mr. Kemble does, that this was the origin of the Witenagemote, since the F. exercised no legislative authority, but only judicial functions, and the Witan was at no time a representative body. See Stubbs's *Constitutional History*, vol. i., Freeman's *Norman Conquest*, vol. i. (1870).

Folk'right, an old English law term denoting the rights of the people by common law.

Fomenta'tion (Lat. *fomentatio*, from *foveo*, 'I keep warm'), an application of warmth and moisture to a diseased or painful part. This may be done by means of a cloth moistened with water and covered with gutta-percha cloth, to prevent evaporation; or by cloths wrung out of hot water, and frequently renewed. The water may be medicated with vegetable infusions, and in this manner opium, belladonna, camomile, turpentine, &c., are used as topical applications.

Fonblanque', Albany William, a journalist of high ability and character, was born in London in 1793. His father was an equity barrister of Huguenot descent, and F. was for a time a pupil of Chitty, the special pleader; but before he was twenty years of age took to journalism. From 1820 to 1830 he wrote for the *Times* and *Morning Chronicle*, while he contributed to the *Examiner*, the *London Magazine*, and the *Westminster Review*. From 1830 to 1847 he edited the *Examiner*, and showed a humour and a trenchancy of style which have been compared to those of Swift. F. was a singularly conscientious and honourable as well as an able writer. In 1847 he retired from the *Examiner*, on being appointed by Lord John Russell to the post of statistical secretary to the Board of Trade, but continued to write at intervals for journals and magazines. He died October 13, 1872. In 1837 a number of his articles from the *Examiner* were reprinted under the title *England under Seven Administrations*. See *Life and Labours of F.* (1874), edited by his nephew.

Fon'di, a decayed town in the province of Caserta, S. Italy, 50 miles S.E. of Rome, near the miasmic *Lacus Fundanus*, and on the Appian Way, which is here in a very perfect state. It is enclosed in part by cyclopean walls, and has a fine cathedral, while the vicinity still produces richly the *vinum Cæcubum* of classic times. Pop. 6478.

Fond du Lac (Fr. 'bottom,' *i.e.*, 'inner end of the lake'), the capital of a county of the same name, Wisconsin, U.S., on Lake Winnebago, at the mouth of F. du L. River, 148 miles N.N.W. of Chicago. It is the junction of three railways, and has regular steam communication with the ports on the lake. There are over twenty churches, two free libraries, an opera-house, public gardens, and four newspapers. Water is supplied by about 1000 artesian wells, and is noted for its mineral properties. Among the principal works are twelve steam saw-mills, six planing-mills, four flour-mills, three foundries, ten waggon and carriage factories, two paper-mills, and six cigar factories, besides large blast-furnaces and tanneries. Pop. (1870) 12,764.

Fonse'ca, Bay of, or **Gulf of Concagua**, a Central American inlet of the Pacific, between San Salvador on the N.W., Honduras on the W., and Nicaragua on the S.E. It is 50 miles long from S.E. to N.W.

Font (Lat. *fons, fontis*, 'a spring or well') is the name given to the receptacle for the water used in Christian baptism. As this was performed in the early centuries by immersion, the F. was a large basin in the centre of the Baptistery (q. v.), generally about 6 feet across, and 3 or 4 deep, and below the level of the floor, like a tomb, with symbolical reference to the believer's being buried with Christ by baptism. The descent into it was generally by three steps, symbolical of the believer's renouncing the world, the flesh, and the devil; and the ascent by three, symbolical of his professing belief in the Trinity. The step on which the bishop stood celebrating the rite made up the sacred number, seven. When the innovation of baptism by aspersion was introduced in the Western Church, the F. took the form of a small vessel, such as is used at the present day. The *material* as a rule was stone, the basin marble. In *form* fonts were originally merely circular basins. In the 13th c., however, they were made octagonal, probably with reference to the eighth day of the child's life being the proper time for baptism, as it was for circumcision, between which and baptism the early Church held there was a strong analogy, the eighth being regarded as the first day of independent existence (*cf.* Gen. xvii. 12; Lev. xxii. 27). In the 14th c. and 15th c. they were richly sculptured. They were not at first raised on supports, but were afterwards supported on pillars, usually five, to represent our Lord and the four Evangelists. A F. at Hildesheim of the 13th c. rests on personifications of the rivers of Eden, for the four cardinal virtues; one at Salzburg, on four lions, and one at Liége, like the brazen sea of Solomon's temple, on twelve oxen. Latterly, too, the supports rested on a pedestal of three steps, for the same reason, as there were three steps in the old immersion F. As regards its *position*, as baptism is the rite of admission into the Church, the F. properly stood not far from the entrance of the church. Originally a F. was placed only in the bishop's church, which was therefore called 'the mother-church,' but latterly in all churches. See Walcott's *Sacred Archæology* (1868).

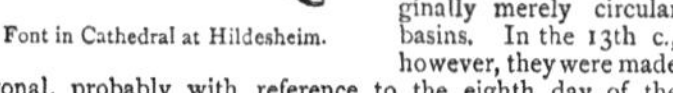

Font in Cathedral at Hildesheim.

Fon'tainebleau, a town and château in the department of Seine-et-Marne, France, 2 miles from the left bank of the Seine, and 35 miles S.S.E. of Paris. The town owes its origin to the château, which is one of the most magnificent buildings in France. As early as the time of Louis VII. it was a fine feudal structure, and it has been splendidly remodelled or extended by almost every succeeding king. It is a *mélange* of styles, and among its more interesting portions are the chapel of the Sainte Trinité, erected by François I., the gallery of frescoes of the 16th c., the gallery of Diana, restored by Napoleon I., the hall of council, decorated with pictures by Boucher, the ornate throne-room, and, grandest of all, the gallery of Henri II., containing a fine series of mythological pictures. The château, with its beautiful gardens, courts, and fountains, is surrounded by the grand old forest of F., which covers an area of 65 sq. miles. Of the historical events connected with the château, the more important are the execution of Monaldeschi in the Galerie des Cerfs by order of Christina of Sweden; the signing of the revocation of the Edict of Nantes by Louis XIV. in 1685; the celebration of Napoleon's marriage with Marie-Louise; and the imprisonment of Pope Pius VII. in 1816. The town has, among other good buildings, two large hospitals, one the gift of Madame de Montespan. There are large manufactures of porcelain and crockery, and an active trade in sandstone, grain, grapes (the famous *chasselas de F.*), and other fruits, horses and cattle. Pop. (1872) 10,941.

Fonta'na, the name of several Italian painters in the 16th and 17th centuries, of whom the most famous is **Domenico F.**, who was born at Mili, on Lake Lugano, in 1543. Trained to the profession of an architect at Rome, F. became the favourite of Cardinal Montalto; and when the latter succeeded to the popedom as Sixtus V., he was made papal architect, and as such completed the cupola of the basilica of St. Peter, placed on its piazza the obelisk which had been brought from Egypt in the reign of Caligula, designed the library of the Vatican, and restored the columns of Trajan and Antoninus. The successor of Sixtus V., Clement VIII., disgraced F., who took the post of architect to the King of Naples, and designed a royal palace and a harbour, which, however, he did not live to complete. F. died in 1607.—**Giovanni F.**, brother of the preceding (born 1540, died 1614), distinguished himself by his skill in hydraulic architecture.—**Carlo F.** (born 1634, died 1714) was also papal architect.

Fontanelles, membranous intervals or spaces found in the skulls of infants and of young animals, which the process of ossification has not reached. See SKULL.

Fontanes', Louis, Marquis de, known for his style of rhetoric and poetry as 'Racine's latest descendant,' belonged to an old Protestant family of Languedoc, and was born at Niort, 6th March 1757. He first became known in literature as the translator of Pope and Gray, and as the writer of two original poems, *Le Cri de mon Cœur* and *Le Verger*, both published in 1778. In politics F. was originally a royalist then a republican, although of a very moderate type, editing, during the Revolution, a journal entitled *Le Modérateur*. Compelled to take refuge in England after the 18th Fructidor, he there made the acquaintance of Chateaubriand. Returning to France after the 18th Brumaire, he became an ardent admirer of Napoleon, on whose fall he transferred his service to the Bourbons, and was raised to the peerage under Louis XVIII. His later years were devoted to an epic, *La Grèce délivrée*. His death took place 17th March 1821, in which year also a collection of his speeches was given to the public. A collection of his works both in prose and verse was edited by Sainte-Beuve in 1839.

Fon'tenay is the name of thirty-four places in France, of which the most important is **F.-le-Comte** (called during the Revolution *F.-le-Peuple*), a town in the department of Vendée, France, on the river Vendée, 25 miles S.E. of Napoléon Vendée. It has a fine Gothic church, with a crypt dating from the 11th c., a church of St. Jean, notable for the beauty of its spire, a Renaissance fountain, some manufactures of linen and coarse cloths, and a trade in timber, grain, hemp, wine, &c. Pop. (1873) 6129. F., which owes its origin to the château of the Comtes de Poitou, was ceded to the English, from whom it was taken by Du Guesclin after a heroic defence. It suffered ten sieges during the religious wars, and was dismantled under Louis XIII. The Vendéens gained one of their greatest victories here over the Republicans.

Fontenelle', Bernard Le Bovier de, a once famous French author, born at Rouen in 1657, was the son of a local procurator and of Martha, a sister of Pierre and Thomas Corneille. He began literary life at Paris under the auspices of his uncle. Here he made the friendship of St. Pierre, and soon joined in the great literary quarrel of Moderns *versus* Ancients, vehemently criticising the masterpieces of Greek art, held up as models by Racine and Boileau. Of Theocritus he said, 'Ses bergers sont trop bergers,' a phrase which has become classical. A few operas, his *Dialogues des Morts*, the *Entretiens sur la Pluralité des Mondes* (the speculative part of which is based on the Cartesian hypothesis of *vortices*), a translation of Van Dale's *History of Oracles*, in which and in his *Doutes sur le Système Physique des Causes Occasionelles* (of Malebranche) there is much covert scepticism, were the chief products of his pen down to 1688, when his *Poésies Pastorales* appeared. These were highly artificial in tone, and by no means justified his hard words against the great poets of antiquity. In 1697 he became secretary to the *Académie des Sciences*, of which he wrote a history; and during the next forty years he composed and pronounced those *Éloges des Académiciens,* which are the real monument of his literary fame. The range of knowledge required for the task may be inferred from the fact that the list includes Vauban, Malebranche, Leibnitz, Newton, Boerhaave, &c. His judgments, generally just, are always expressed with marvellous clearness and grace. He died in his hundredth year at Paris, 9th January 1757, a living connection between the 17th and 18th centuries of French literature. F.'s *Œuvres Complètes* have been frequently published, the best edition being that of Paris (1818). See Troublet's *Mémoires sur la Vie et les Ouvrages de F.*, Charma's *Biographie de F.* (1846), and Flourens' *F., ou de la Philosophie Moderne relativement aux Sciences Physiques* (Par. 1847).

Fon'tenoy, or **Fontenoy-en-Puisaye,** a village (pop. 872) in the department of Yonne, Burgundy, France, 18 miles S.W. of Auxerre, has, among several places of the same or similar name in that department, the best claim to be considered the old *Fontanetum* or *Fontanidus in pago Ætiodorensi,* where, on the 25th July 841, was fought the memorable battle between the sons of Hlodwig the Pious, which finally severed the connection between the Western and Eastern Franks, and from which we begin to date the separate existence of 'France' and 'Germany.'—F. is also the name of a village in the province of Hainault, Belgium, 4 miles S.E. of Tournay, where was fought 'the battle of F.,' a decisive contest in the war of Austrian succession, in which the French, under Marshal Saxe, defeated the English, Dutch, and Austrian allies, 11th May 1745. The forces were each some 60,000 strong, and the total loss amounted to about 7000 men.

Fonte'vrault (*Fons Ebraldi*), a small town in the department of Maine-et-Loire, France, 35 miles S.E. of Angers. It was formerly the seat of a celebrated abbey, the nucleus of the rich, influential order of F., founded by a Breton monk, Robert d'Arhissal, in 1099. The rule of the order was that of Benedict, but the monks were placed under abbesses, who were generally of illustrious family. In the 18th c. it had lost much of its wealth and power, but even at the time of the first French Revolution, when it was abolished, it held fifty-seven priories. The abbey is now occupied as a central prison. At F. are the tombs of the English Henry II., of his queen, Eleanor of Guienne, and of Richard I. Pop. (1874) 696.

Fontina'lis, a genus of *Musci* or mosses, distinguished by possessing the fructification within the leaves. The best-known species is the *F. antipyretica,* or greater water-moss, found growing on rocks and stones in the neighbourhood of water.

Food is whatever goes to the building up of the tissues and substance of a living being, and enables it to perform its necessary functions of life. All organisms, vegetable and animal, have their proper food which is essential to their existence. As a rule, vegetables build up, from the unorganised elements of the mineral kingdom, those compounds which serve for the nutrition of the animal kingdom. Animals, on the other hand, by feeding on the substances thus elaborated, decompose them, and return their constituents to the mineral kingdom; and thus the cycle of inter-dependent existence continues. Animals are classed according to their diet, as graminivorous or vegetable-eating, carnivorous or flesh-feeding, and omnivorous or eaters of both vegetable and animal F.; but primarily all animal F. is obtained from the vegetable world, carnivorous creatures only taking it at second-hand through the bodies of the animals on which they prey.

Human F. is frequently classified in a popular way under the two heads, F. and drink, which are regarded as functionally distinct, but such a subdivision is altogether fallacious, as there is no physiological or chemical ground to warrant the separation. Man is of all animals the most thoroughly omnivorous, drawing his F. from an endless variety of sources, and this he further varies indefinitely by cooking and compounding in every fashion that art can suggest. Notwithstanding this incalculable variety, the F. of man, as of every animal, is composed essentially of a limited number of alimentary principles. Analysis shows these principles to be—(1) Nitrogenous compounds, represented by casein in milk, and analogous substances found in cereals, peas, beans, &c., with a small proportion of albumen and other albuminates; (2) fat or butter; (3) a carbo-hydrate; (4) water; and (5) saline substances or ash, consisting of combinations of calcium, magnesium, sodium, &c., with chlorine, phosphoric acid, and other acid substances. Each of these five classes must be represented in every proper form of diet, and for the purpose of adequate nutrition they must be consumed in certain proportions, varying with conditions of climate and habits of life. The peculiar function of each has, however, not yet been definitely determined. The nitrogenous substances, the fats, and the carbo-hydrates become oxidised within the human body, and are thrown out as effete matter in the form of urea and carbonic acid. In becoming oxidised they give off within the human body the stores of energy which they contained, and that energy is manifested as vital heat, nerve and muscular action, &c. Water and saline substances, and the oxygen of the air inhaled by the lungs, are essential as oxidising agents. In addition to these principles there are, however, a variety of other substances taken into the human body, the functions of which obviously do not depend upon their being oxidised. They are various in their constitution, and are to be regarded as regulating the nutrition, or as having certain specific auxiliary or medicinal effects upon the essential ingredients of F. All kinds of F. thus come under one or other of the following heads, which are modified from a physiological and chemical classification of F. drawn up by Professors Huxley and Frankland:—Class I., Alimentary or necessary F., containing the five groups given above; and Class II., Medicinal or auxiliary F., subdivided into four groups, namely—(1) alcoholic substances, represented by beers, wines, and spirits; (2) spices and condiments, containing volatile oils, such as pepper, cinnamon, cloves, nutmegs, and mustard; (3) acid substances, such as apples, oranges, rhubarb, &c.; and (4) substances containing alkaloids or special active principles which act upon the nervous system as stimulants or sedatives, a most important group, embracing tea, coffee, and cocoa, with the various narcotics habitually indulged in by almost all races of mankind. See COOKERY, DIETETICS.

Fool. See COURT-FOOL.

Fools, Feast of (Lat. *Festum Stultorum, Festum Fatuorum*), was a festival instituted by the early Christian Church to take the place in the people's regards of the Roman Saturnalia (q. v.) or New Year festival. The great peculiarity of that festival, besides an unbounded extravagance of merriment, was that while it lasted all the ordinary conditions of society were reversed, slaves, *e.g.*, taking the place of their masters, arrayed in their clothes, and waited upon by them. And a similar inversion of the ordinary relations between the clergy and laity formed the principal feature in the F. of F. The festival extended from Christmas to the last Sunday of Epiphany, but the chief celebration was on Innocents' or New Year's Day. At first only the choristers took part in the ceremonies of the day, which consisted of the performance, with mock solemnity, of the ordinary religious rites, while the clergy formed the audience or part of it. But latterly all the servants of the Church, and even laymen, took part, and as time went on extraordinary license was introduced. A president being elected under the name of Pope of Fools, Archbishop of Dolts, Abbot of Unreason, Lord of Misrule, &c., the performers repaired to the church, where, dressed in the priests' vestments outside in, they read prayers from books turned upside down, with spectacles of orange-peel, and burned an old shoe or excrement in the censer; or, not sparing even the Church's most sacred rite of the Mass, ate sausages and puddings off the altar, or played at dice upon it. During and after the mock service, the church, which was thronged with a motley crowd of spectators, was a scene of the wildest riot and confusion, the maskers leaping and dancing like madmen, and singing obscene songs with obscene posturing, some of them being dressed up as dragons, hobby-horses, &c. Long before the Reformation the F. of F. had become such a scandal from the way in which everything sacred was turned to ridicule, that the clergy, who had themselves set the stone rolling, did everything in their power to put a stop to it; but all their attempts were unavailing, till the institution got its death-blow at the Reformation. See Du Tilliot's *Mémoire pour servir à l'Histoire de la Fête des Fous* (Laus. 1741, Par. 1751 and 1809).

Fool's Pars'ley (*Æthusa cynapium*), a species of poisonous *Umbelliferæ,* so named from its producing narcotic symptoms, and from its having been sometimes eaten in mistake for Parsley (q. v.). F. P. is a common British weed. It is distinguished from other and allied *Umbelliferæ* by its flowers having deflexed *involucres* or circles of *bracts*. Probably, as is the case with *Œnanthe crocata*, or 'dead-tongue,' a near ally of F. P., the poisonous properties of the plant depend greatly on the locality and mode of growth.

Foot. This important part of the body is formed of (1) the tarsus, (2) the metatarsus, and (3) the phalanges. The *tarsus* is composed of seven bones, namely, the os calcis (*d*), astragalus (*b*), cuboid (*h*), scaphoid (*a*), and the three cuneiform, internal (*e*), middle (*f*), and external (*g*). The astragalus articulates with the lower end of the tibia and fibula. The *metatarsus* is formed of five bones (I. to V.), which are shafted bones, like those forming the metacarpus, or palm of the hand. The *phalanges* are attached to the extremities of the metatarsal bones, and are usually numbered, first (1), second (2), and third (3), from behind forwards. It will be observed that the great toe has only two phalanges. Structurally the F. is an arch supported on three piers, two in front and one behind. The posterior pier ofthe arch is formed by the heel, and the anterior piers by the balls of the great and of the little toes. The weight of the body is transmitted to this arch from the tibia to the astragalus. The F. is also slightly arched transversely. These characteristics of the F. of man adapt it to the support of the body in the erect position, and to biped progression. It wants the prehensile power seen in the F. of the anthropomorphic apes. On the whole the human F. is, in proportion to the size of the whole body, larger, broader, and stronger than that of any other mammal save the kangaroo. The plane of the F. is at right angles to that of the leg, its sole is concave, its great toe is usually unopposable, and the upper surface of the astragalus looks almost vertically upwards. All of these peculiarities distinguish the F. of man from that of the ape. The great toe, though in man one of the largest digits, is rudimentary or entirely absent in many mammals. In climbing animals it is considerably developed, and has prehensile characteristics, as in the gorilla and orang.

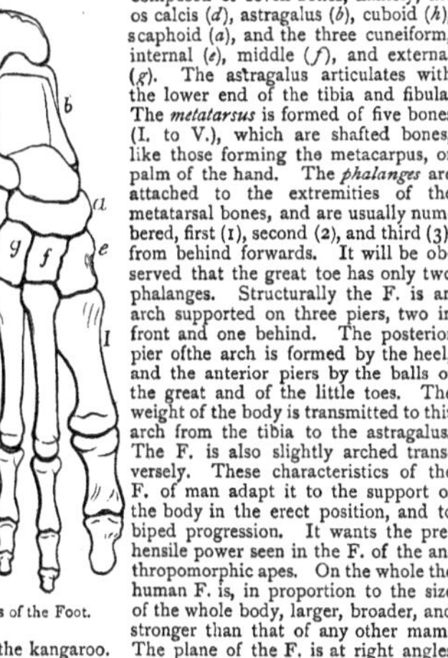

Bones of the Foot.

Foot, a measure of length, in almost universal use, and doubtless derived from the length of the human foot. Taking the English foot as unity, the lengths of the corresponding measure in other European countries and states are as follows:—Austria, ·964; Baden, 1·016; Bavaria, 1·044; France (Paris F.), ·938; Prussia and Denmark, ·971; Rhenish, 1·03; Russia, 1; Saxony, 1·076; Würtemberg, 1·064. It is usually divided according to the duodecimal scale. An English mile contains 5280 feet.

Foot, in organ-building, is sometimes used to qualify the word *tone*, as '4-foot tone,' '8-foot tone,' &c. It here indicates the length of an open organ-pipe which would produce the required sound. Thus middle C is 2-foot tone, &c. The expression '4-foot,' '8-foot,' &c., applied to an organ-stop indicates the length of the lowest C pipe in that stop.

Foot-and-Mouth Disease (synonyms, *Eczema contagiosa* or *E. epizootica*, *Epizootica Aphtha*, and *Murrain*), a contagious disease of a febrile nature, chiefly affecting cattle and sheep, and characterised by the presence of a vesicular eruption in the mouth, between the toes, and around the coronets. The mouth or feet alone may be affected. In cows, the eruption may extend to the mammary gland, and necessarily affects the milk. Pigs, poultry, dogs, and more rarely man, are subject to F.; but horned cattle are the chief sufferers. The temperature first increases, and a vesicular eruption appears after an incubatory period of from three to four days. The animal exhibits great restlessness and uneasiness; saliva runs from the mouth, and a watery discharge from the eyes. The disease is one of a specific type caused by the presence of a specific poison. Pasture lands receive the contagious material or virus, and the disease thus spreads. One attack is not a protection against a subsequent attack, but the animal is usually attacked only once in a season. Microscopic examination of the discharges has as yet failed to detect any specific form of fungus or other parasitic organism which might be credited with causing the disorder. The febrile symptoms may cease in a week; but if the weather be unfavourable or the animals be exposed, a rough tracheal cough with expectoration may persist for a long time. The treatment consists in giving the animals plenty of cold water to drink, in which nitrate of potash (one ounce to a bucketful) may be dissolved. Soft food—mashes, &c.—should be given, and the sores on the feet should be dressed with a mild astringent solution—*e.g.*, by one ounce of carbolic acid lotion (made by adding one part of pure carbolic acid to sixteen of hot water) added to twelve ounces of white lotion or a solution of acetate of lead. Stimulants may be demanded in extreme cases of prostration, but bleeding and purging are carefully to be avoided. Sheep, as a rule, suffer most violently in the feet, and require more careful watching and treatment than cattle. An affected flock should be made to walk or wade once or twice daily through a shallow trough containing the solution of acetate of lead and carbolic acid above mentioned.

Football, a popular national sport, played during the winter months at all higher-class public schools and colleges. There are two distinct types of game played, and nearly every public school in England has its own peculiar modifications. Both make use of a ball and two goals, each of which consists of two upright posts with a cross-bar or tape at the height of about ten feet. The goals are placed at the extremities of the course, which has fixed boundaries. If the ball is sent beyond these boundaries it is for the time out of game, and must be returned according to rule. In the *Association* or Harrow game, the ball is round, and must not on any account be touched with the hand, except by the goal-keeper of each side. One goal is scored when the ball is sent through the posts beneath the tape, each side working the ball towards the adversary's goal. In the *Rugby* game the ball is oval; and any player, if *on-side*, is entitled to catch or pick up the moving ball, and run with it towards the adversary's goal. If stopped, however, he has to relinquish the ball, and put it *down* to ground, when a *scrimmage* takes place, each side striving to drive it through towards the other's goal. A goal is won when the ball is kicked *over* the cross-bar between the goal-posts or the goal-posts produced. International matches, between chosen teams of English and Scotch, are yearly played according to both Association and Rugby rules, and excite great interest in F. circles. For full information regarding the rules of the games, the clubs, and matches, see Alcock's *F. Annual.*

Foote, Andrew Hull, rear-admiral in the American navy, was born at New Haven, Connecticut, May 4, 1808. He entered the navy December 4, 1822, became a commander in 1852, and a captain in 1861. In February 1862 he received the command of the western flotilla, took Fort Henry, attacked Fort Donelson, where he was wounded, and on April 7 took Island No. 10. He received the thanks of Congress, and was made rear-admiral, June 16, 1862. F. was appointed to relieve Admiral Dupont at Charleston, but died at New York, June 26, 1863. Admiral F. was not only a gallant, chivalrous naval officer, but a man of singularly strong moral character.

Foote, Samuel, a famous English wit and dramatist, was born at Truro, Cornwall, in 1719, and entered at the Temple, but finding the law uncongenial, went on the stage, and made his *début* as Othello in 1744. He was a comic writer as well as an actor, and led a brilliant and dissipated life, until in 1766 he lost his leg by falling from his horse. This misfortune did not extinguish his mercurial gaiety. He appeared in parts which turned the want of his limb to stage account, and remained to the last recklessly improvident and irresistibly vivacious. He died at Dover, October 21, 1777. F. was an admirable mimic, and the cleverest manufacturer of *bon-mots* of his day, but many of his witticisms are vulgarly broad and personal, and would no longer be tolerated in society. Among his pieces are some of the most amusing farces in the English language, but it is a sort of profanity to call him 'the modern Aristophanes.' A collection of his dramatic works appeared at London (4 vols. 1778; 2 vols. 1797). They were translated into German (4 vols. Berl. 1796–98). See Clarke's *Memoirs of Sam F.* (3 vols. Lond. 1805).

Foot-Guards. See GUARDS.

Foot-Pound is the work required to raise the weight of one pound through the distance of one foot at the surface of the earth; or it is the work which such a weight could perform in falling through the same distance in the same circumstances. The corresponding French unit of work is the *kilogrammètre*, which equals 7·233 foot-pounds.

Foot-Rot, a disease of sheep, characterised by the presence of cracks or fissures in the hoof, and by the subsequent appearance of ulcerated sores arising from the irritation consequent on the presence of dirt, sand, and other foreign particles. Occasionally the ulcerated action may proceed to a very great extent, the lesion being then termed 'foul-foot.' The milder forms of F.-R. appear to arise from unequal development or wearing of the hoof, consequent on the sheep being enclosed in soft meadow-lands where the hoof is subjected to the least amount of attrition. But in the more severe forms, F.-R. is probably connected with, and arises from, constitutional causes; and in the latter case, great attention to the general health is necessary, as well as the adoption of local treatment. The latter consists in the use of astringents and caustics where the ulceration is of any great extent. In mild cases, tar is a safe application, and butter of antimony, or a paste of flowers of sulphur and sulphate of copper in equal weight mixed with lard, is also to be recommended as useful in this complaint.

For'age (Low Lat. *foragium*, from the Goth. *fodur*, 'fodder'), the food of horses. In the army, field-officers, surgeons, and adjutants of infantry regiments receive an allowance in lieu of F. for every horse allowed by the regulations. The ration allowed for horses is 10 lbs. oats, 12 lbs. hay, and 8 lbs. straw in barracks; and 8 lbs. oats, 18 lbs. hay, and 6 lbs. straw in quarters. The troops in Great Britain and Ireland are supplied with F. under contract entered into by the commissariat department. The cost of F. and allowance in lieu of paillasse, according to the army estimates, was £612,000 for the year 1876–77.

Foraminif'era, an order of *Protozoa* (q. v.), or lowest animals, included in the class *Rhizopoda* (q. v.). The F. are distinguished by the possession of a shell or test of carbonate of lime, although the structure may occasionally be composed of sandy or *arenaceous* particles. Through holes or *foramina* in the shell the soft protoplasmic matter of their bodies can be protruded in the form of delicate interlacing filaments or *pseudopodia*. From the interlacing nature of these filaments, the name *Reticulosa* has been given to the F. by Dr. Carpenter, who describes the appearance of the pseudopodia as resembling 'an animated spider's web.' These filaments are used for grasping food-particles, and also subserve locomotion. In some cases (*e.g.*, *Miliola*) the pseudopodia are emitted, not through foramina, but by the mouth-opening or single aperture of the shell. The shells of F. have been divided into (*a*) the *porcellanous*, or those in which there are no foramina in the shell-wall; (*b*) the *arenaceous* shells, consisting of sandy particles; and (*c*) the *vitreous* or *hyaline* shells, which are glassy, transparent, and have their walls perforated. The shells of F. may be also divided into those consisting of a single chamber (*Monothalamia*), and those composed of many chambers (*Polythalamia*). The latter are originally single-chambered, and are produced by budding. If the budding of new segments proceeds in a straight line, a shell like that of *Nodosaria* is produced; whilst the spiral form of this process gives rise to a test like that of *Rotalina* or of *Discorbina*, &c. The shell-wall of F. appears to be perforated by a system of canals in addition to the foraminal apertures. The living matter of their bodies is of the simplest character, their protoplasm being destitute even of the nucleus and other structures found in most *Protozoa*. The F. are for the most part of microscopic size, and require the microscope for their investigation and recognition. Some extinct forms—notably the Nummulites (q. v.)—attained a larger size, the latter being found as large as a shilling, and frequently attaining even larger dimensions. The F. are found in the present day in waters of the sea, and in the bed of all our oceans, and most notably in those areas traversed by warm currents. Their shells form a thick layer of calcareous matter in the sea-bed. True chalk is a Foraminiferous deposit which was formed in this way in an ancient sea-bed. F. first appear as fossils in the Laurentian rocks where *Eozoon* (q. v.) is found. They occur in all the stratified formations up to the present day. Some species (*e.g.*, *Miliola* in Eocene rocks and *Nummulites* in the Middle Eocene) have attained a vast development in certain geological epochs.

Forbes', Duncan, of Culloden, one of the ablest and best men that Scotland has produced, was the second son of the proprietor of the estate of Culloden, and was born at Bunchrew—another estate belonging to the family—10th November 1685. His father, a stanch Presbyterian, had suffered much at the Restoration, and finally received a strange compensation in the privilege to distil whisky, under a merely nominal duty, on a third estate called Ferintosh, which privilege he used so extensively that to this day 'Ferintosh' in many parts of Scotland is synonymous with whisky. Duncan was sent to Edinburgh University when nineteen years of age, and lost his father the same year. Next year he was sent to Leyden, where he studied both law and Oriental languages. He returned home at the end of two years, passed as advocate in Edinburgh, was, through the influence of the Duke of Argyle (both a patron and a relation), appointed sheriff of Midlothian, and married Mary, a daughter of Mr. Rose of Kilravock. In 1715 he exerted himself to the utmost in suppressing the insurrection headed by the Earl of Mar; and when it was brought to a close, he showed the most active kindness in mitigating the fate of the unfortunate prisoners, who were treated with utmost rigour by the Government. He collected money for their defence, and publicly remonstrated with the Government on the cruelty they displayed. Some time after he proposed the plan, which Pitt sixty years later adopted with entire success, for the pacification of the Highlands, viz., restoring to the chiefs their forfeited estates, and employing the people in the service of the country. In 1716 F. was appointed depute to the Lord Advocate; in 1722 he was returned to Parliament for the Inverness burghs, and three years after was raised to the office of Lord Advocate. While in London, he was on intimate terms with Lords Mansfield, Lyttelton, and Hardwicke, as well as Sir R. Walpole, and was a valued member of the literary society in which Pope, Arbuthnot, and Swift held sway. In 1734, owing to the death of his elder brother, he succeeded to the family estate, and in 1737 was appointed President of the Court of Session. According to his best biographer, Dr. Hill Burton, he effected a thorough and most beneficial change in the proceedings of this court, having raised it to a state of efficiency which it has never surpassed. But it was in connection with the rebellion of the '45 that he rendered the most important services to the state. The members of the Government were singularly destitute of all resource, and for a length of time anything that was done in Scotland to save the country was mainly the work of Forbes. He kept the more reasonable of the Jacobites from rising, especially the great MacDonald and MacLeod clans in Skye and the islands, who themselves could have brought 8000 men into the field; and having restrained these, he may be said in a certain sense to have saved the Hanoverian throne. He gave not merely his great influence to this work, but he expended on it all the money he could raise, straining his credit to the utmost, yet the Government refused to repay him any portion of what he thus expended; and he died 10th December 1747, pressed by creditors whose claims he was unable to meet. Bishop Warburton calls him 'one of the greatest men that ever Scotland bred, as a judge, a patriot, and a Christian.' See Hill Burton's *Life of Duncan F.* (Edinb. 1848).

Forbes, Edward, a British naturalist, was born at Douglas, in the Isle of Man, February 12, 1815. At an early age he showed a bent towards the natural sciences, and when only seven had made a small collection of zoological and botanical specimens. In 1831 he entered Edinburgh University as a medical student. Here he studied till 1839, ultimately concentrating his whole attention on botany, zoology, and geology, to the exclusion of medicine, adding meanwhile to his stores of knowledge by excursions to Norway, the Alps, Austria, Algeria, and Southern Europe. In 1834 he became a member of the British Association, and in 1836 was one of the founders of the Edinburgh

Botanical Society, to both of which he contributed many valuable papers and reports. In 1841 he accompanied the *Beacon* in its surveying expedition to Asia Minor as naturalist, and from numerous dredging operations showed that the laws of geographical distribution in the depths of the sea were similar, and depended upon conditions similar, to those which held on land. On his return in 1842, he found that he had been elected Professor of Botany at King's College, London. In 1844 he became curator of the museum of the Geological Society, and palæontologist to the Ordnance Survey. In 1853 he was President of the Geological Society, and in May 1854 succeeded Professor Jamieson in the natural history chair at Edinburgh. This position he filled with great ability for only one short summer course, since his death occurred on 18th November of the same year. The peculiar merit of F. lay in his wide grasp of the whole range of the natural sciences, no one department being his peculiar study to the relative exclusion of the others. To a quick perceptive faculty of observation, and a retentive memory, he added a rare power of abstraction and generalisation, which is perhaps best displayed in his beautiful theory of the derivation of the present flora of the British Islands. His chief works are a *History of British Starfishes* (1841), *Travels in Lycia, Milyas, and Cibyratis* (1846), and, with Mr. Hanley, a *History of British Mollusca* (1850–53); but his great services to science can only be estimated from a consideration of his numerous memoirs on the classification of medusæ, mollusca, &c., on geographical distribution, and on subjects connected with every phase of natural science, all of which teem with novel and accurate information of varied description. He also drew up the valuable maps on distribution in Keith Johnstone's *Physical Atlas*. See *Memoir of Edward F.* (Camb. 1861) by G. Wilson and A. Geikie.

Forbes, James David, was born at Edinburgh, April 20, 1809, and passed most of his early life at his father's residence at Colinton, where he received private tuition along with his brother Charles. From 1825 to 1830, with the break of one year, he studied for law at Edinburgh University, devoting every spare moment, however, to astronomy, meteorology, and the physical sciences. In 1833 he threw up all legal pursuits, and was elected the successor of Sir John Leslie in the chair of natural philosophy at Edinburgh, a position which he resigned on account of failing health in April 1860, four months after he had become Principal of the United College in the University of St. Andrews. He died at Clifton, December 31, 1868. F. was a member of numerous scientific societies at home and abroad, and received the Royal and Rumford medals from the Royal Society of London, and two Keith medals from the Royal Society of Edinburgh for his contributions to science. The most important of these are the discovery in 1836 of the polarisation of heat by refraction and reflection, the subsequent investigations in its refrangibility and depolarisation, the observation in 1846 of the conditions of temperature at different depths in the soil, and experimental inquiry into the laws of thermal conduction in metal bars in 1861 and 1865, besides numerous valuable papers on climate, meteorology, and geology. His most famous work, however, is in connection with the motion of glaciers. The results of his investigations (see GLACIERS) are given in his *Travels through the Alps* (1843), *Norway and its Glaciers* (1853), *Tour of Mont Blanc and Monte Rosa* (1855), and *Occasional Papers on the Theory of Glaciers* (1859). These works display at once his high faculty as an observer of natural phenomena, his rare skill as an experimentalist, and his literary power as a graceful and lucid writer. His *Life and Letters*, the joint production of Principal Shairp of St. Andrews, of Professor Tait of Edinburgh, and of Mr. Adams-Reilly, the Alpine traveller, was published by Macmillan & Co., London, 1873.

Forbes, Sir John, a very able and successful physician, was born October 18, 1787, at Cuttlebrae, Banffshire. Educated at the universities of Aberdeen and Edinburgh, he was first a naval surgeon, but leaving the service in 1816, graduated at Edinburgh, and practised as a physician there, in Chichester, and finally in London, where he rose so much in favour with society that he was knighted and became Physician in Ordinary to the Queen in 1853. His death took place at Whitechurch, Oxfordshire, November 13, 1861. F., besides being a very successful practitioner of medicine, was a zealous man of science. He may be said to have introduced the stethoscope into this country, was one of the editors of the *Cyclopædia of Practical Medicine* (1835), translated the works of Auenbrugger and Laënnec on auscultation, helped to found the British Medical Association, and started the *British and Foreign Medical Review*, editing it for twelve years. Among the other works of F., who during his latter years was one of the most distinguished and popular members of his profession, may be mentioned his *Physician's Holiday* (1849), and *Nature and Art in the Cure of Diseases* (1857).

Forbes, Sir William, Bart., of Pitsligo, was born at Edinburgh, 5th April 1739, became a partner in the bank of Messrs. J. Coutts & Co. in 1761, and in 1773 rose to be head of the eminent firm of F. Hunter & Co., eventually converted into the Union Bank of Scotland in 1830. He purchased the estate of Pitsligo, forfeited by Lord Forbes during the rebellion of '45, and erected the village of New Pitsligo. Often in London, he was one of the earliest members of the Literary Club, along with Johnson, Burke, Reynolds, &c. He wrote a life of his friend Dr. Beattie, printed with a 4to edition of his works in 1805, and the *Memoirs of a Banking House*, published in 1860. His nobility and rectitude of character are happily delineated in one of the introductions to *Marmion*. He died 12th November 1806.

Forbes Macken'zie Act. This is the title of a very stringent 'Act for the better regulation of public-houses in Scotland.' It is so named after the author of the measure. It continues the classification of spirit-dealers, as under former statutes, into (1) inn or hotel keepers, (2) public-house keepers, and (3) grocers and provision dealers. The sale of spirits in the first class is only permitted between eight o'clock in the morning and eleven o'clock at night during week days, except to *bona fide* travellers and lodgers. On Sunday the sale is prohibited except to lodgers and *bona fide* travellers. The same regulations apply to the second class, without any exception in favour of lodgers or travellers. No certificate is allowed to be granted to any grocer or provision dealer for the sale of excisable liquors to be 'drunk on the premises,' if in these premises a sale is carried on of provisions to be consumed elsewhere. This latter class is also prohibited from keeping their premises open on Sunday, and from any sale of liquor between eleven at night and six in the morning. These are the leading provisions of this Act, which has given rise to so mnch vehement controversy N. of the Tweed. The supporters of the Act have cited voluminous statistics, which they contend prove that the Act has diminished drunkenness in Scotland. Its opponents, again, by a different manipulation of the figures, maintain that these statistics show a contrary result, and that even if they do show an apparent diminution in Sunday-drinking, the fact proves nothing; because to diminish public drinking on Sunday is only to increase drinking in private and in illicit houses. And public drinking, they maintain, is the smaller evil of the two; because it is better, they hold, that people should drink where the law can take cognisance of them than in places where it cannot. A bewildered public is thus almost led to acquiesce in Sydney Smith's celebrated dictum, that, except facts, there is nothing so misleading as figures. A Royal Commission was appointed in 1859 to inquire into the working of the Act. Its report, with two large volumes of conflicting evidence, has thrown little light on the vexed question. The *bona fide* traveller has also been a source of infinite perplexity to magistrates. It seems now that seven miles is the distance which requires to be travelled in order to constitute *bona fides* on the part of a traveller in Scotland. English law is more rational, as it holds that any exercise sufficient to make refreshments desirable constitutes a 'traveller' under the corresponding English Acts. See in English law, BEER ACTS, INNKEEPERS, HOTELS, LICENSED VICTUALLERS, LICENSING ACT.

Forbidd'en Fruit (*Citrus Paradisi*), a species of the genus *Citrus*, belonging to the *Aurantiaceæ* or orange order, also known by the name 'Adam's apple.' The Shaddock (q. v.) (*C. decumana*), another species of *Citrus*, is sold under the name of F. F. in the shops. *C. Paradisi* is common on the Continent, and appears to have been originally brought from China. The fruit is pear-shaped and has an irregular surface. The rind is thick, and constitutes the chief part of the fruit, the pulp being present in small quantity, and of an acid taste. The name F. F. has been occasionally given to the fruit of the *Tabernæmontana dichotoma* of Ceylon, a plant nearly allied to the *T. utilis* or cow-tree of Demerara, both species belonging to the Dogbane order (*Apocynaceæ*).

Force, according to Newton, is any cause which alters or tends to alter a body's state of rest or of uniform motions in a straight; and the change of motion is proportional to the impressed force, and takes place in the direction in which the F. acts. (See MOTION, LAWS OF.) This at once gives a method for measuring F., and implies that forces are to be composed and resolved in precisely the same manner as velocities, or indeed as any directed quantities. (See QUATERNIONS.) Now, change of motion is an evidence of a transformation of energy from a less to a more apparent form, and is the direct consequence of such a transformation, so that our definition leads us to regard F. as merely a convenient term for transformation of energy, and as having, therefore, no objective reality. When the effects of forces acting on a material system mutually balance, the result is equilibrium, and the study of this branch of dynamics is called Statics (q. v.). See ENERGY.

Force and Fear, if of sufficient degree, are grounds for the reduction of a contract. A threat of causing annoyance, as by bringing an action at law, is not sufficient to vitiate an agreement. But the requisite degree always depends on the circumstances and relative position of parties. It is generally held that a contract obtained by force or fear is not *ipso jure* void, but only voidable; from which it will follow that the wrong-doer can give a good title to a *bona fide* purchaser. See COMPULSION, CONSENT, EXTORTION.

Forcelli'ni, Egid'io, an eminent Italian lexicographer, was born near Padua, 26th August 1688. Although his education was so much neglected that he had almost reached manhood before he commenced regular study at the seminary of Padua, his industry and abilities soon attracted the attention, and secured him the lifelong favour, of Facciolati, its chief. The two cooperated in the production of a great Latin dictionary, entitled *Totius Latinitatis Lexicon Consilio et Cura Jac. Facciolati, Opera et Studio Æg. Forcellini Lucubratum* (4 vols. Pad. 1771). F. died at Padua, 4th April 1768, three years before the publication of their great work. Various editions of it have since appeared, the most complete being that of Furlanetto (Pad. 1828–31). It is the basis of all later lexicons of the Latin tongue, and is really a splendid treasury of scholarship and skill. Two new editions have recently appeared in Italy, that of Corradini (1859 *et seq.*), and De Vit (1860 *et seq.*).

For'ceps (Lat.), in surgery, are pincer-like instruments used for seizing, cutting, or removing substances that cannot be readily got at by the fingers. A complete set of F. are employed in tooth-drawing. Special kinds are required for securing a bleeding artery, extracting bullets, cleansing internal sores, assisting delivery in difficult midwifery cases, &c. Bones of great thickness can be cut by Liston's F.

For'cible En'try, in English law, is the public offence of violently taking or keeping possession of land or of a tenement without legal authority. The corresponding Scotch law terms are Ejection and Intrusion (q. v.).

For'cing, in horticulture, consists in stimulating the vegetation and growth of native or acclimatised plants at seasons other than their natural period of activity. It is practised by the application of artificial heat in hothouses and F. frames, and is resorted to in order to obtain fresh vegetable products in succession during periods when they cannot be procured by cultivation in the open air. In Great Britain F. is extensively prosecuted for obtaining early crops of culinary plants and vegetables, such as rhubarb, potatoes, and green peas.

Ford, John, an Elizabethan dramatist, was the second son of a Devonshire gentleman, and was born at Ilsington, N. Devon, in 1586. He entered at the Middle Temple in 1602, and in 1606 published *Fame's Memorial*, an elegy on the Earl of Devonshire. He was never called to the bar. As a dramatist he produced *The Lover's Melancholy* (1628), a beautiful romantic comedy; *'Tis Pity She's a Whore*, and *The Broken Heart* (1633), two tragedies of intense power, which are F.'s greatest works; *Love's Sacrifice*, a tragedy (1633); *The Chronicle Historie of Perkin Warbeck* (1634), an historical drama; *The Fancies Chaste and Noble*, and *The Lady's Trial*, comedies (1638). F. was a part author with Dekker, and probably with Rowley, in the domestic tragedy entitled *The Witch of Edinarton* (1623), and his masque *The Sun's Darling* (1624) was seemingly founded on Dekker's *Phaeton*. He appears to have retired to his birthplace before his death in 1640. The genius of F. is profound and sombre, but limited. He is wanting in variety, ease, and lightness; of humour and wit he has almost none, his comic scenes being the grossest and most tedious in the Elizabethan drama. As a tragic poet, however, he depicts passion with unerring subtlety and thrilling force. F.'s language is pure and vigorous; his verse has neither the effusive sweetness nor the charming felicities of Fletcher's; it is limpid and equably musical, though at times somewhat hard and unspontaneous. See *The Works of F.* by Gifford, new ed. by Dyce (3 vols. 1869), Swinburne's *Essays and Studies* (1875), Minto's *English Poets*, and Ward's *English Dramatic Literature* (2 vols. 1875).

Fords (from Old Eng. *faran*, 'to go,' hence 'to cross') are shallow parts of a river, which can be crossed simply by wading, without the aid of a bridge or a boat. They are of special importance in military operations; and in choosing a ford, great consideration must be given to its position, its depth in relation to the flow of water, the nature of its bottom, and the manner in which it may possibly be affected by changes of season, &c. For infantry the depth should not exceed 3 feet, and for cavalry 4 feet. Many of our towns, such as Oxford, Bedford, Bradford, Stratford, &c., indicate by their names their own origin, as well as the position of ancient and important F. now superseded by bridges.

For'dun, John of, a 14th c. chronicler, belonging (according to the slender authority of Camden) to Fordun, Kincardineshire, who is supposed to have died about 1385. He was probably a chantry priest of Aberdeen Cathedral. F. wrote what is now known as a *Scotichronicon*, or Chronicle of Scotland, tracing the history of the Scots from the times of Noah to 1153. He had collected additional materials before his death, which passed into the hands of Walter Bower, Abbot of Inchcolm, who carried the Chronicle of F. as far down as 1437, and whose work in 16 books, bearing the title of *Scotichronicon*, appeared between 1440 and 1447. A comparison of Bower's so-called 'Continuation' with the best MSS., especially with the Wolfenbüttel MS., has revealed the startling fact that Bower has so grossly tampered with the text of F. that the original is often unrecognisable and its character completely misrepresented. The best, indeed the only valuable, edition of F. is by Mr. Skene (Edinb. 1871) in the series of *The Historians of Scotland*. The researches of this profound and penetrating scholar must compel the re-writing of the early period of Scottish history.

Fore'castle (pron. *foks'le*), in a ship, strictly an elevated foredeck (see DECK) above the maindeck or the spardeck. Vessels are not frequently built with such a F. now, and the name is generally given to that portion of the fore part of the ship which constitutes the quarters for the crew.

For'eign Attach'ment. A defendant arrested abroad on an English judgment will in England be held to bail in action on the judgment. An English creditor may attach property in Scotland belonging to his debtor resident in England. With reference to Scotch law, see ARRESTMENT and ARRESTMENT FOR FOUNDING JURISDICTION.

Foreign Bill of Exchange. A bill is said to be foreign when drawn by a merchant abroad upon his correspondent in England, or the reverse; or when it is drawn and accepted abroad. Formerly, foreign bills were held by the law to be more important than inland ones, but now they are on nearly the same footing. Every bill drawn in this country must be stamped, and a bill drawn abroad must be stamped before it is presented for payment and before it is negotiated. In enforcing a bill drawn and accepted abroad, the courts of the United Kingdom will hold that whatever relates to the nature of the obligation—*ad valorem contractus*—is ruled by the law of the country where the contract is made, but that the mode of remedy is according to their own forms. See BILL OF EXCHANGE.

Foreign Debts, Recov'ery of. See DEBTS, RECOVERY OF; ENGLISH DEBT.

Foreign Enlist'ment Act. Under this statute of 1870, any British subject who, without the licence of Her Majesty, enlists in the service of any foreign state at war with any friendly state, or who induces another to do so, is guilty of an offence punishable by fine and imprisonment. The master or owner of any ship who takes illegally-enlisted persons on board, is guilty of an offence punishable in the same way. Penalties are also imposed on any one who, without Her Majesty's leave, builds, or agrees to build, any ship for the service of a foreign state at war with a friendly state. The Act gives special power to the Secretary of State for carrying out its provisions. It makes regulations with regard to foreigners enlisting in the Queen's service.

For'eigner. See ALIEN.

Foreign Law, Applica'tion of. It is provided by 22 and 23 Vict. c. 63, that if, in any action depending in any court of Her Majesty's dominions, the court shall think it expedient to ascertain the law in any part of the empire applicable to the case, a remit for the purpose may be made to the court having requisite jurisdiction. Her Majesty in Council, or the House of Lords on appeal, may adopt or reject the legal opinion so procured. By 24 Vict. c. 11, similar facilities are given for ascertaining, under similar circumstances, the law of any foreign country. No court in the United Kingdom will review the judgment of a foreign court, or allow a new suit to be opened on the matter affected by the judgment. In America the rule is the same. In England, and in most countries, foreigners may sue each other on the same terms as natives do. The French law courts, however, do not hold that they have jurisdiction in personal questions between undomiciled foreigners, except in commercial affairs. See DEBTS, RECOVERY OF ABROAD; ENGLISH DEBT; FOREIGN ATTACHMENT; FOREIGN BILL OF EXCHANGE; CONFLICT OF LAWS; JURISDICTION; DOMICILE; INTERNATIONAL LAW.

Fore'land, North (the *Cantium* of Ptolemy), is a chalky headland, 190 feet high, in the N.E. extremity of Kent, 2 miles E. of Margate. It has a fixed light visible at a distance of 24 miles.—**South F.**, a promontory, also of chalk, 16 miles S. of the N. F., and between Deal and Dover. It supports two fixed lights, at an elevation respectively of 380 and 275 feet above the sea. Between the two Forelands are the Downs and the Goodwin Sands.

Foreshort'ening, in painting and drawing, is the representation in correct perspective of an object presented obliquely to the eye, and the effect should be to give the object the appearance of projecting from the canvas. Cimon of Cleonæ was the first to apply the method to the human figure in any attitude, and in more recent times the art has been carried to perfection by Raphael, Angelo, Tintoretto, and Correggio.

For'est Fly (*Hippobosca*), the name given to flies belonging to the family *Hippoboscidæ* of the *Diptera* (q. v.). In this family the head is distinct, the legs short, and the fifth joint of the tarsi longest. The wings are large, and the nervures or supporting ribs do not extend to the tip. The *H. equina* is the most familiar species. It receives its popular name from its inhabiting forests, and its specific name of *equina* from its attacking horses by means of its suctorial mouth. The F. F. is about one-third of an inch in length, and is of brown colour, with yellow markings on the thorax. The eggs are retained within the body of the female until the larvæ are hatched, and ready to pass into the pupa stage.

Forest Mar'ble, a local deposit in the southern and midland counties of England, belonging to the Lower Oolites of the Jurassic period, and overlying the Great Oolite group. It consists of hard limestones, marls, shales, and fine oolitic freestone, and contains numerous lamellibranch shells characteristic of this period.

Forest Oak (*Casuarina torulosa*), a species of Australian trees, belonging to the *Casuarinaceæ* or beef-wood order. They are named beef-wood trees from the dark-red colour of their wood, which is hard and heavy, and used for ornamental upholstery.

Forests, Chas'es, Parks, and Warr'ens. By the common law of England, the possessor of land has the exclusive right to all the wild animals found upon it, and he may pursue and kill them. Besides the absolute right which the owner of land has over the soil, there may be a privilege of taking or killing wild animals to the exclusion of others, in virtue of a franchise to have a forest, chase, park, or warren. A forest is a royal domain for the preservation of the Queen's beasts and fowls of forest, and is subject to its own laws, courts, and officers. Before the *Charta de Foresta*, the sovereign could make a forest of any extent over the lands of his subjects. It is the highest franchise relating to game. There are sixty-nine forests in England, the four principal of which are New Forest on the Lea, Sherwood Forest on the Trent, Dean Forest on the Severn, and Windsor Forest on the Thames.

A *chase* is a franchise whose nature is between that of a *forest* and that of a park. It may be held by a subject, and is governed by the common, not by the forest, law. It is not enclosed. A man may have the right of chase over the ground of another, with privilege to keep royal game on it, protected even from the owner of the land. There are, we believe, thirteen chases in England.

To constitute a *legal* park there must be a royal grant; it must be enclosed by pale, wall, or hedge, and it must be stocked with deer; and if the deer are all killed, it is no longer a legal park, which is composed of *best venison* and *enclosure*, and failure in one is a total disparking. There are in England 780 parks.

The *warren* is a place privileged by prescription or royal grant for the keeping of beasts and fowls of the warren, which are hares and rabbits, partridges and pheasants. Some add quails, woodcocks, and waterfowl. Twenty years' undisturbed exercise of a claim of a warren or park will afford presumptive evidence of right in the party who has exercised it for the period. The owner of a warren may lawfully kill any dog found injuring the warren.

The rights of any forest, chase, or warren are not affected by the Game Laws (q. v.) The franchises mentioned above may be destroyed by reversion to the crown, or by surrender or forfeiture in consequence of a breach of the trust for which they were granted. In Scotland, lands granted by the crown with a right of forestry carried all the privileges of a royal forest, which were very oppressive to the country, and accordingly the right was reprobated in 1680 by the Court of Session. Nevertheless, the pretensions of royal foresters have survived to present times. In 1862 the Duke of Athole, in virtue of his supposed right of forestry, claimed the right to prevent his neighbour, the Laird of Lude, from killing deer on his own lands, and maintained that he, the Duke, and his servants were entitled to enter the lands of Lude and drive any deer found on them into the forest of Athole. Both points were decided against the Duke (1st March 1862).

For'far, the capital of Forfarshire, in the valley of Strathmore, near a small lake, 15 miles N.E. by N. of Dundee by railway. It has a large parish church, with a spire 150 feet high, a handsome townhall, and a considerable manufacture of brown linen and 'brogues.' Pop. (1871) 11,031. F., along with Montrose, Arbroath, Brechin, and Bervie, sends one member to Parliament. It is supposed to be the ancient *Orrea*, and received a royal charter in the reign of David I. There was formerly a royal castle here.

For'farshire, or **Ang'us**, a county on the E. coast of Scotland, bounded N. by Kincardine and Aberdeen, E. by the North Sea, S. by the Firth of Tay, and W. by Perthshire. Area, 890 sq. miles; pop. (1871) 237,567. It is entered in the N. by many spurs of the Grampians, known as the Braes of Angus, alternating with many romantic glens, as the Esk, Clova, Prosen, and Isla. The flat fertile belt of Strathmore bisects F. from S.W. to N.E., while to the S. the Sidlaw Hills run at a distance of 8 miles from, and in a direction parallel to, the Firth of Tay. The chief rivers are the Isla, an affluent of the Tay, and the N. and S. Esks. F. has a coast 45 miles long, part of which, from Arbroath to the promontory of Redhead, is a line of sandstone cliffs, worn into many deep caverns. Buddon Ness juts out at the entrance of the Tay Firth, and 13 miles to sea rises the Bell Rock Lighthouse. The soil of F. is partly fine alluvium, partly peat; and the chief formation is Old Red Sandstone. In 1873, 95,694 acres were under corn, 52,098 in green crops, 71,341 under various grasses, and 26,933 in permanent pasture. The chief manufactures are linen and jute, the former chiefly at Arbroath, the latter at Dundee. Among the towns are F. (the capital), Brechin, Montrose, and Kirriemuir. The county sends one member to Parliament, the burghs two. Angus, which was a possession of old Celtic Maarmors, is known as an earldom in the 12th c., and became subsequently a seat of the Umphravilles, the Stewarts, and Douglases. The antiquities are numerous, including several Roman camps, a vitrified fort at Finhaven, many sculptured stone pillars, the round tower and cathedral at Brechin, the ruins of Arbroath Abbey, Restennet Priory, the 'Bonnie House of Airlie,' and Edzell, a noble ruin overlooking the North Sea. The old baronial castle of Glammis is one of the finest in Scotland. The new residence of the Earl of Airlie, Cortachy Castle, is imposing, but does not occupy a commanding site.

For'feiture and Corrup'tion of Blood was formerly a penalty consequent on Attainder (q. v.) for treason or felony.

Forfeiture of Lands was in feudal law the penalty incurred by a tenant for an act of disloyalty to his over-lord.

Forfic'ula. See EARWIG.

Forge (Fr. *forge*, Prov. *faurga*, from Lat. *fabrica*, 'a workshop'), a place in which wrought-iron in the shape of bar or scrap is fashioned into the forms required in construction. Where only light work has to be done, the F. is generally called a *smithy*. In such a F. the furnaces for heating the iron are open hearths, air being supplied to each fire through a blast-pipe entering at the bottom of it. In the smithies of engineers a fan or Blowing Machine (q. v.) is employed to produce the blast, each hearth having a valve by which to regulate the quantity of air passing through it. Each hearth is attended to by at least two men, a smith and a striker, whose names sufficiently show their respective shares in the work. All the smaller forgings, which are hammered by hand, are made by these men. All smithies, except the smallest, are furnished with one or more Steam-Hammers (q. v.) to be used for larger work. In the F. proper, heavy forgings, such as crank shafts, armour plates (when not rolled), rudder posts, wrought-iron guns, &c., are made. Here large air-furnaces take the place of the open hearths, and all hammering is done by large steam-hammers instead of by hand. The 'portable F.' is a small iron hearth supported upon a movable framework (generally upon wheels), and fitted with a pair of bellows, or a small blowing machine worked by hand.

For'gery ('the art of fabricating') is the fraudulently making or uttering of a document to the injury of another, or the making or falsifying of a stamp to the loss of the revenue. To constitute F., it is not necessary that the whole instrument should be fictitious. Making a fraudulent insertion, alteration, or erasure in any material part of a true document, by which another may be defrauded, the fraudulent application of a false signature to a true instrument, or of a real signature to a false instrument, the alteration of the date of a bill after acceptance with fraudulent intention, are forgeries. A note being payable at a banker's who fails, to fix a piece of paper over the name of that banker, writing over it the name of another banker, is F. So is it also to put a fictitious signature to a bill of exchange. The essence of F. is an intent to defraud; therefore where the imitation of a signature or alteration of a writing can injure no one, the offence is not committed; but if the act can injure any one, there will be a presumption of fraudulent intention. If the counterfeited document be such as would be ineffectual if real, the crime may still be committed. Uttering (q. v.) is essential, and merely to show the forged instrument is not uttering. To have, without lawful excuse, the proof of which lies on the accused, forged-bank notes, or any appliances for making them, is punishable with penal servitude. (See BANK-NOTE.) Knowingly to make a false entry in any public register is F. Further provisions have been made against the crime by the F. Act (1870), which imposes severe penalties on the F. of stock certificates issued under the National Debts Act, and on the personation of owners of stock, and on engraving plates for stock certificates. The extreme penalty for F. is now penal servitude for life. Seven to fourteen years is commonly the term.

Forget'-me-not (*Myosotis palustris*), a well-known species of plants belonging to the *Boraginaceæ* or borage order. It is sometimes known also by the name of 'scorpion grass,' from its peculiar inflorescence. F. is a herb of annual or biennial nature. The calyx is five-cleft, and the corolla is *rotate* or *salver-shaped*. The flowers are blue, the leaves being alternate, and the stem of rounded form. An allied species is *M. sylvatica*, which has its calyx covered with stiff expanded hairs. *M. Azorica* occurs at the Azores, and *M. versicolor* is a common garden weed, the flowers of which are first coloured yellow, and then develop a blue colour. *M. Alpestris* is a mountain-growing species.

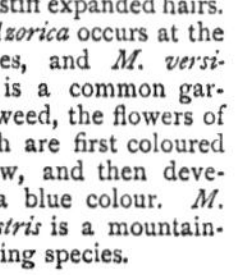

Forget-me-not (*Myosotis palustris*).

Forisfamilia'tion is a term of Scotch law denoting the separation of a child from the family of its father. Where a child has a separate estate from the father, the profits of which become his own, he is held to be forisfamiliated even though he remains in his father's family. F. takes place when a child is married or lives in a separate family with the consent of its father. The term is also used to signify either an onerous or gratuitous renunciation of *legitim* by a child. See LEGITIM, AGE.

Fork (Old Eng. *forc;* comp. Lat. *furca*), an instrument with two or more metal prongs, used, when small, at table for eating with, and, when large, in several farming and gardening operations. The nations of antiquity put their fingers to the use to which a table-F. is now applied; in England this custom universally prevailed till early in the 17th c., when the usefulness of the instrument, new from Italy, began to be appreciated. When and where table-forks were invented is not known. The wife of a Doge of Venice, according to Damiani, who died in 1073, used a golden F. to eat with. The name is occasionally met with in inventories of the 12th and later centuries, but the paucity of the references only goes to prove the extreme rarity of forks before the 15th c. In the following century they were in general use in Italy; the gastronomic art had then reached the greatest degree of magnificence and refinement in Venice, Florence, and Rome. A table instrument formed of a spoon and a two-pronged F. joined together was known in England long anterior to that time, even in the Pre-Norman epoch, but its use was for serving, not feeding. Coryate, the English traveller, visited Italy in 1608, and in his *Crudities* (1611) gives an interesting though quaint account of the use of the 'little F.' in that country. On his return to England he continued its use at meals, and was ridiculed for doing so. Slowly, thereafter, the F. became general at table, not however without opposition on the part of the clergy, who denounced the innovation as 'wicked,' and 'an abominable violation of primitive manners.' The washing of the hands before and after meals, which was rendered necessary by the primitive mode of eating, then fell into disuse. In Ben Jonson's comedy *The Devil is an Ass* an allusion is made to that circumstance—

> 'The laudable use of forks,
> Brought into custom here, as they are in Italy,
> To the sparing of napkins.'

The earliest forks were made of silver, and the introduction of others with steel prongs assisted in spreading the custom of using them among all classes. Asiatics do not use the F.; in China *chopsticks*, two slender rods of wood or ivory, take its place. An instance of the use of the F. among savages is reported of the Fijians, who twenty-five years ago were the most inveterate cannibals known; when eating human flesh, a large F., made of the hard wood of the *Casuarina*, was used, whereas at ordinary repasts the mode more befitting savages was followed.

For'li (the Roman *Forum Livii*), a walled town and capital of a province of the same name, N. Italy, between the rivers Ronco and Montone, at the base of the Appenines, 40 miles S.E. of Bologna by railway. It is the seat of a bishop, and has many splendid buildings, chief among which are the Palazzo

Guerini, designed by Michael Angelo, and the cathedral, containing pictures by Carlo Maratti, Guido, &c. There are some silk and salt industries, and a trade in hemp, corn, woad, and carthamus. Pop. (1872) 38,480. F. is supposed to derive its name from Marcus Livius Salinator, and to have been founded by him in 207 B.C. In the middle ages it formed a republic, and suffered greatly in the time of the Guelph and Ghibelline factions.

Forlorn' Hope, in warfare, is the name given to a body of picked troops or volunteers devoted to some desperate enterprise. The corresponding name in German is *Die verlornen posten*, in French *Les enfants perdus*.

For'ma Pau'peris, in the law of England and of Scotland, is the term denoting the mode in which an action may be maintained by one who is too poor to follow the usual way. In England it is provided by statute that any one having just cause of suit, who can take oath that, under deduction of his debts, his possessions are not worth £5, shall be entitled to sue without paying any fee to counsel, attorney, or clerks in court. The *just cause* must be certified by a barrister. If the case go against the person so suing, he may be imprisoned for the defendant's costs. The statute does not apply to defendants; but any one arrested on a *capias*, or information relating to the customs, may defend in F. P. In Scotland the privilege of so suing or defending is conferred by the court, on being satisfied that the applicant has *Probabilis Causa* (q. v.) (See also POOR'S ROLL.) While these arrangements for securing the administration of justice to the poor are perhaps on the whole commendable, their operation is frequently attended with considerable hardship to the opposing party. If the subject of dispute is inconsiderable, as it generally is, the opponent of the pauper knows that, however the case may be decided, he, the opponent, must be a loser, as he cannot get costs from the pauper. Thus, so far as money is concerned, it is better for him to abandon his case. Absolute paupers apart, when an unscrupulous agent has a client who can pay nothing if he looses, and the opponent can pay—or, in legal slang, is 'worth powder and shot'—the injustice that may be perpetrated in the position is evident; and it is perpetrated accordingly.

Forma'tion, in geology, is a somewhat vague term applied to a group or series of conformable strata, differing in lithological character and even in their fossil contents.

Formi'ca. See ANT.

For'mic A'cid derives its name from the fact that it is secreted by the ant (*formica*). When the insect is irritated it ejects the acid, which is at once recognised by its peculiar odour and by the stinging sensation it produces if it comes in contact with the skin. It also occurs in the free state in the nettle (*Urtica urens*), and is the cause of the disagreeable effect produced when the plant is touched. It may easily be obtained in a dilute state by distilling oxalic acid with its own weight of glycerine. The glycerine takes no apparent part in the decomposition of the oxalic acid, but simply exercises a catalytic action (see CATALYSIS) whereby the oxalic acid is split into formic and carbonic acids.

$$\underbrace{H_2C_2O_4}_{\text{Oxalic acid.}} = \underbrace{CO_2}_{\text{Carbonic acid.}} + \underbrace{H_2CO_2}_{\text{Formic acid.}}$$

In order to prepare it pure and anhydrous, dry sulphuretted hydrogen is passed over gently warmed formate of lead.

$$\underbrace{Pb(CO_2H)_2}_{\text{Formate of lead.}} + \underbrace{H_2S}_{\text{Sulphuretted hydrogen.}} = \underbrace{PbS}_{\text{Sulphide of lead.}} + \underbrace{2H_2CO_2}_{\text{Formic acid.}}$$

Pure F. A. is a pungent liquid, having a peculiar odour, and exercising a very corrosive action on the skin. It boils at 99° C., and crystallises when cooled to − 6° C. Its only compound of any practical importance is formic ether or artificial essence of rum, which is prepared by distilling a mixture of starch, alcohol, binoxide of manganese, and sulphuric acid.

Form'ing's Island, in the Pacific, to the N. of the Sandwich Islands, has a good harbour, on which account it was occupied by the English in 1860.

Formo'sa (Span.; Lat. *formosa*, 'beautiful;' Chinese, *Taiwan*, 'terrace;' Malay, *Pekan* and *Pakkando*), an island in the Chinese Sea, 90 miles off the province of Fu-kien, from which it is separated by the F. Channel. It is 237 miles long, with an average breadth of 70 miles, and is of great natural beauty. A central range, rising to about 12,000 feet, divides F. into a fertile western plain, and an eastern Alpine region. The mountains are of volcanic origin, fantastic in outline, and cleft by deep gorges running up from the sea, clothed with bright verdure and watered by many cascades. The western plain is cultivated like a garden by Chinese, who have settled there to the number of about 500,000; while the eastern high lands are held by wild tribes named Peppohoans, of Mongolian origin, whose numbers are not accurately known. Rich coal-mines have been opened in the N. of F. by the Chinese, who are encroaching on the E. coast. The mining is carried on very primitively, but much coal is exported to China, especially to Fu-chow. The interior has veins of sulphur and various metals. Besides coal, the chief exports are rice, for which F. is famous, tea, brimstone, timber, &c. The principal places are Tai-wan, the capital, opened to foreigners in 1858, and Ke-lung, a rising port in the N., and the centre of the coal trade. An atrocious massacre of some Japanese sailors who were wrecked on the E. coast of F. in December 1871 compelled the Japanese Government, who could obtain no redress from the Chinese authorities, to invade the island. General Saigo landed in May 1874 with a force of 3000 men, and inflicted severe punishment on the guilty tribes. The Chinese were greatly excited, and for some time war seemed imminent between the two empires, but peace was finally maintained, and on the 2d or 3d of December the Japanese troops withdrew. See *The Eastern Seas, being a Narrative of the Voyage of H.M.S. Dwarf*, by Captain B. W. Bax, R.N. (Lond. 1875).

Forms of Address are as various as the rank of those addressed, and a knowledge of the following may prove useful.

THE ROYAL FAMILY.

The Queen—Superscription, 'To the Queen's Most Excellent Majesty.' Commencement, 'Madam;' conclusion, 'I remain, with the profoundest veneration, Madam, Your Majesty's most faithful subject and dutiful servant.'

The Prince of Wales—Sup., 'To His Royal Highness the Prince of Wales.' Com., 'Sir;' conclusion, 'I remain, with the greatest respect, Sir, Your Royal Highness's most dutiful, most humble, and most obedient servant.'

Princes of the Blood Royal—Sup., 'To His Royal Highness the Prince ——.' Com., 'Sir;' conclusion, 'I remain, with the greatest respect, Your Royal Highness's most dutiful, and most obedient, humble servant.'

The Princess Royal—Sup., 'To Her Royal Highness the Princess Royal.' Com., 'Madam;' conclusion, 'I remain, with the greatest respect, Madam, Your Royal Highness's most obedient, devoted, and humble servant.'

Princesses of the Blood Royal—Sup., 'To Her Royal Highness the Princess ——.' Com., 'Madam;' conclusion, 'I remain, with the greatest respect, Madam, Your Royal Highness's most obedient, devoted, and humble servant;' refer, 'Your Royal Highness.'

Princes of the Blood, embracing the sovereign's nephews and cousins—Sup., 'To His Highness the Prince of ——.' Com., 'Sir;' conclusion, 'I have the honour to be, with great respect, Sir, Your Highness's most obedient, and very humble servant.'

Princesses of the Blood, embracing the Sovereign's nieces and cousins—Sup., 'To Her Highness the Princess —— of ——.' Com., 'Madam;' conclusion, as above, substituting *Madam* for *Sir*.

NOBILITY AND GENTRY.

Dukes—Superscription, 'To His Grace the Duke of ——.' Commencement, 'My Lord Duke.'

Duchesses—Sup., 'To Her Grace the Duchess of ——.' Com., 'Madam.'

Marquesses—Sup., 'To the Most Honourable the Marquess of ——.' Com., 'My Lord Marquess.'

Marchionesses—Sup., 'To the Most Honourable the Marchioness of ——.' Com., 'Madam.'

Earls, Viscounts, Barons—Sup., 'To the Right Honourable the Earl of ——.' 'To the Right Honourable the Lord

Viscount ——.' 'To the Right Honourable the Lord ——.' Com., 'My Lord.'

Countesses, Viscountesses, and Baronesses—Sup., 'To the Right Honourable the Countess of ——.' 'To the Right Honourable the Viscountess of ——.' 'To the Right Honourable the Lady ——.' Com., 'Madam.'

Baronets—Sup., 'To Sir William ——, Bart.' Com., 'Sir.'

Knights—Sup., 'To Sir John ——.' Com. as above.

The Wives of Baronets and Knights—Sup., 'To Lady ——.' Com., 'Madam.'

Sons of Peers—The younger sons of Dukes and Marquesses are also styled Lords, and addressed as such with the addition of their Christian names, as, 'To the Right Honourable Lord John ——.' The younger sons of Earls, and all the sons of Viscounts and Barons are styled Honourable, as, 'To the Honourable Mr. ——.' Com., 'Sir.'

Wives of the Sons of Peers—Sup., 'To the Right Honourable Lady William ——.' 'To the Honourable Mrs. ——.'

Daughters of Peers—Sup., 'To the Right Honourable Lady ——.' 'To the Honourable Miss ——.' Com., 'Madam.'

Privy Counsellors—Sup., 'To the Right Honourable ——.' Com., 'Sir.'

Army and Navy—Admirals when addressed officially have the rank of their flag added to their name and title, as, 'To the Right Honourable the Earl of ——, Admiral of the Red.' Commodores and captains take their rank and title after their designation on the *Naval List*. In the army all officers take their name and title after their rank in the *Army List*.

Governors of Colonies, &c.—Sup., 'To His Excellency Sir ——,' or, 'To His Excellency General ——, Governor of ——,' or, 'Governor and Commander-in-Chief.' Com., 'Sir.'

Archbishops—Sup., 'To His Grace the Lord Archbishop of Canterbury.' Com., 'My Lord Bishop.'

Bishops—Sup., 'To the Right Reverend The Lord Bishop of ——.' Com., 'My Lord Bishop.'

Deans—Sup., 'To the Very Reverend the Dean of ——.' Com., 'Mr. Dean,' or 'Reverend Sir.'

Archdeacons—Sup., 'To the Venerable the Archdeacon ——.' Com., 'Mr. Archdeacon,' or 'Reverend Sir.'

Lord Advocate (of Scotland)—Sup., 'Her Majesty's Advocate for Scotland,' but by courtesy, 'The Right Honourable the Lord Advocate.' Com., 'Sir,' but by courtesy, 'My Lord.'

Lord-Lieutenant of Ireland—Sup., 'His Excellency the Lord-Lieutenant.'

Lord Mayors are three in number, those of London, York, and Dublin—Sup., 'To the Right Honourable the Lord Mayor of ——.' Com., 'My Lord.'

Lady Mayoresses are addressed in the same style as their husbands.

Lord Provost of Edinburgh—Sup., 'The Honourable the Lord Provost.'

See the *Peerages* of Dod, Burke, Lodge, &c., also Kingdom's *Secretary's Assistant*.

Forms of Proced'ure. See PROCESS.

Fornica'tion (Lat. from *fornix*, 'an arch-vault,' because Roman brothels were underground), now usually regarded as an offence, has been at different periods, and in different countries, considered a crime meriting punishment of every degree of severity, including that of death. Among the Jews, F. was, under certain conditions, visited with capital punishment; and among certain religious communities, especially since the Reformation, the offence was prohibited under extreme penalties. By no class of religionists, probably, was F. more severely punished than by the English Puritans and the Puritan settlers in New England. During Cromwell's Protectorate, the Puritans made F. felony, including death without 'benefit of clergy.' Milder laws, however, with respect at least to moral offences, came in with the Restoration, and F., according to Blackstone, was treated with 'a great deal of tenderness and lenity.' In Scotland an Act was passed in 1567 providing that fornicators, whether male or female, shall for the first offence pay a fine of £40 Scots, and stand bareheaded at the market-place for two hours; for the second offence the fine was 100 merks; and for the third offence the fine was £100, and the culprit was also liable to be thrice ducked in the dirtiest pond in his parish, and then banished from it for ever. Scandalously-conducted houses of ill-fame are still punishable in Scotland by the civil authorities, but of 'simple' F. the law takes no cognisance.

Forr'es, an old royal burgh of Scotland, in Elginshire, on the Findhorn, 2 miles from the sea, and 10 miles W.S.W. of Elgin by railway. It stands on an old sea-terrace at the base of the Cleeny Hills, four gravelly elevations, on the highest of which—on the site of ancient fortifications—is the Nelson Tower (66 feet), erected in 1806. F. was formerly the seat of the Archdeacon of Moray, and there still remains a portion of the 'mantle wall' which once surrounded the college or cathedral kirk, and which contains the Paris Port, or bishop's entrance. To the W. are the ruins of a castle, to the E. a rudely-hewn pillar, 25 feet high, called Sueno's Stone, or the 'Stan'in' Stane.' The chief industries are distilling, brewing, and dyeing. F., along with Inverness, Nairn, and Fortrose, returns one member to Parliament. Pop. (1871) 3959.

Forr'est, Edwin, a celebrated American actor, born in Philadelphia, 9th March 1806, first appeared on the public stage at the age of fourteen as Douglas (November 27, 1820). After playing in the chief western cities during a long professional tour, he appeared at the Park Theatre, New York, as Othello, in 1826, and at once achieved reputation. He visited England in 1835, again in 1837, when he married Catherine Sinclair, and a third time in 1845. On the third visit to England the friendly relations that had previously subsisted between F. and Macready were severed; and on the occasion of the professional tour of the latter in America, F.'s partisans were the cause of a riot, 10th May 1849, from which the English tragedian barely escaped with his life. F. continued to play till 1871, after which he gave a few Shakespearian readings. He died at Philadelphia, December 12, 1872. F. added a fine presence to a distinct and even powerful histrionic genius. See Alger's *Life of E. F.* (Lond. and Philad. 1877).

For'ster, John, an eminent journalist and biographer, was born at Newcastle in 1812. Educated for the bar, he devoted himself to literature and journalism. He succeeded Charles Dickens as editor of the *Daily News*, but retired from the post in a year. A connection which F. formed with the *Examiner*, during the brilliant editorship of Albany Fonblanque, lasted for eighteen years, F. in the course of it becoming editor in 1846, and retiring from the office in 1856, on his having been appointed the year previous Secretary to the Lunacy Commission. Five years later he became Commissioner in Lunacy. He died 1st February 1876. F. will be chiefly memorable for his historical and biographical works. He devoted himself largely to the period immediately prior to the advent of Cromwell, and in discharge of his duty of 'righting wronged reputations,' as Fonblanque styled it, wrote *Statesmen of the Commonwealth of England* (1831–34), *Arrest of the Five Members*, and the *Grand Remonstrance* (1860), and *Sir John Eliot, a Biography* (1864). F. was the intimate friend of a number of the most eminent literary men of the day, such as Landor, Dickens, and Carlyle. He published a biography of Landor in 1868, and of Dickens in 1871–74. He also wrote a *Life of Oliver Goldsmith* (1848), and shortly before his death published the first volume of a *Life of Swift*.

Forster, Johann Reinhold, a celebrated naturalist and traveller, was born at Dirschau near Danzig, 22d October 1729. Educated for the Church, F. for some time after 1753 officiated as a pastor at Nassenhuben, but being devoted to philosophy, science, and mathematics, was employed by the Russian Government to investigate the condition of a colony at Saratov. He afterwards removed to England, and taught natural history and the French and German languages at Warrington, Lancashire. In 1772 he accompanied Captain Cook in his second voyage round the world as naturalist. On his return in 1775, the University of Oxford conferred on him the degree of LL.D., and three years later he published the results of his botanical observations, and *Observations made during a Voyage round the World*. Some disputes arising between F. and his English friends, he took the position of Professor of Natural History, &c., at Halle, in Saxony, and produced a number of works, of which *Geschichte der Entdeckungen und Schiff-fahrten im Norden* (Frankf. 1784) has been translated into English (1786). F. was a good scholar in classics and literature, and is said to have been able to speak and write seventeen different languages. He died at Halle,

December 9, 1798.—**Johann Georg Adam F.**, son of the preceding, was born at Nassenhuben, 26th November 1754. He was with his father in Russia and England, accompanied him in his voyage along with Captain Cook, and became Professor of Natural History first in Hesse Cassel (1778), and then in Wilna (1784). He settled in Mainz as a bookseller, and as librarian to the Elector. In 1790 he accompanied Alexander von Humboldt to Britain, France, and the Netherlands; finally he embraced republican opinions, and in 1793 was sent to Paris to solicit the incorporation of Mainz with the French Republic. When Mainz was taken by the Prussians, F. appears to have lost his books, MSS., &c., and was on the point of leaving for India and Turkistan, when he died in Paris, January 12, 1794. He was the author of a number of valuable works on ethnology, philosophy, politics, geography, and natural history. A collection of his letters was published by his widow, a daughter of Heyne (2 vols. Leips. 1828–29), and his complete works were edited by his daughter (9 vols. Leips. 1843–44). See König's *Clubisten in Mainz* (3 vols. 2d ed. Leips. 1857), and *F.'s Leben in Haus und Welt* (Leips. 2d ed. 1858), Moleschott's *F.* (2d ed. 1862), and Klein's *F. in Mainz* (Gotha, 1863).

Fort, Fort'ress (Lat. *fortis*, 'strong'), a place of strength, within the defences of which a small body of men may repulse a considerable force. The name *fort* is commonly applied to a star-shaped or a bastioned work of military engineering; the term *fortress* is of wider application, and may be used to designate a group or series of fortified works. See FORTIFICATION.

Fort, in British North America, is the name applied to the different posts or trading stations of the Hudson's Bay Company (q. v.) or other fur-trading corporations. These posts, usually log-built structures with sleeping, dining, and store rooms, are not in any sense strongholds.

Fort-Ad'jutant, an officer intrusted with the same duties in a fort as are discharged by a regimental adjutant on service. In 1876–77 the number of fort-adjutants was nine. The regimental pay of an adjutant is 17s. 6d. per diem, and fort-adjutants receive 4s. 9d. per diem as staff officers.

Fort Augus'tus (Gael. *Cilla-Chuimein*, 'the cell or church of Cumin,' probably the 'Cumineus albus' who was abbot of Iona 657–669), a small fort at the S. end of Loch Ness, 29 miles from Inverness, and in the very centre of the great glen of Scotland, built in 1718 with the view of bridling the N. Highlanders. It received its present name in 1746, in honour of the Duke of Cumberland. F. A. is a quadrangle with bastions, and was well fitted for about a hundred soldiers. It has been recently sold by Government to Lord Lovat, who has converted it into a Roman Catholic monastery.—F. A. is also the name of a small and very poor village in the immediate vicinity of the fort.

Fortè (Ital. 'strong or loud'), used in music as a mark of expression.

For'tescue, a noble English family said to have sprung from a certain Richard *le Fort* who accompanied William of Normandy to England, and at the battle of Hastings covered him with his shield, on account of which he received the name *Fort-escu* ('strong shield'). This pretty legend is embodied in the motto of the F. arms, *Forte scutum, salus ducum*. The most distinguished member of the family was **Sir John F.**, son of one of the bravest generals of Henry V. He was born about 1395, studied at Oxford, and in 1442 was Chief-Justice of the King's Bench. On the outbreak of the Wars of the Roses, he sided with the Lancastrians, and in 1461 fled with Queen Margaret to the Continent, where he wrote about 1463 for the young Prince Edward his famous treatise in dialogue, *De Laudibus Legum Angliæ* (best ed. Amos, Camb. 1825). In 1471 F. returned to England, submitted to the House of York, and died in 1485 at his estate of Ebrington in Gloucestershire. Another valuable work of F.'s is *The Difference between Absolute and Limited Monarchy* (Lond. 1714). In both of these F. proves himself a sound English Constitutionalist. **Sir Hugh F.**, a lineal descendant of Sir John, became Baron F. in 1746, but the first earl in the family was **Hugh F.** (born 1753, died 1841). **Hugh, second Earl of F.** (born 1783, died 1861), took an active part in the great debates on the first Reform Bill, and was Lord-Lieutenant of Ireland till the fall of the Whig Government in 1841. **Hugh, third Earl of F.**, born 4th April 1818, was educated at Harrow, entered Parliament in 1841 as Viscount Ebrington, was called to the Upper House on the death of his father, and has throughout his public career been an indefatigable sanitary reformer. He has written several pamphlets on social, political, and educational questions. The family of F. is noted for its fidelity to the Liberal party.

Fort George (Gael. *Aird-nan-saor*, 'height of the carpenters'), a fort in the county of Inverness, on a sand-spit in the Moray Firth, 9 miles N.E. of Inverness. It has barrack accommodation for 2000 men, and unlike the two smaller forts at one time connected with it, Fort Augustus and Fort William, is still kept in use. It mounts seventy guns, and is very scientifically defended, but would be of little avail against the artillery of the present day. It was built shortly after the Jacobite rising of the '45, at a cost of £160,000.

Forth, one of the most picturesque rivers of Scotland, rises in the N.W. of Stirlingshire, and has a direction mainly E. by S., forming part of the boundary between the shires of Perth and Stirling, and expanding into the Firth of F. near Alloa, after a very sinuous course of 70 miles. Its upper waters are the Duchray, 16 miles long, from the E. base of Ben Lomond, and the Avendhu, 12 miles, from the W. side of Ben Venue. The latter flows through Loch Chon, Dhu, and Ard, and the united stream leaves the romantic region of the Highlands at Aberfoyle. From the N. the F. receives the Teith, Allan, and Devon; the principal town it passes is Stirling, to which it is navigable for vessels of 100 tons. Below Alloa the estuary gradually widens, occasionally contracting, as at Queensferry (three-quarters of a mile), till it reaches its greatest breadth of 25 miles between Musselburgh and Largo Bay. The *Firth of F.* separates the counties of Stirling, Linlithgow, Edinburgh, and Haddington on the S. from Clackmannan, Perth, and Fife on the N.; and the chief towns on its shores are Leith, Portobello, North Berwick, Queensferry, Grangemouth, Culross, Burntisland, and Kirkcaldy. It receives from the S. the Carron, Avon, Almond, and Esk, from the N. the Leven, and its waters have a maximum depth of 30 fathoms. St. Margaret's Hope, above Queensferry, is one of the safest of British roadsteads. See *Guide to the Firth of F.*, by Messrs. Reid & Son (Leith, 1876).

Fortifica'tion, the art or science of strengthening a military position by means of defensive works, is resorted to equally by forces in attack and on defence. In warfare, the ultimate purpose of defensive works is to oblige the enemy to fight under the most disadvantageous circumstances, mainly by making use of natural or artificial cover as a protection against his fire, and as a shield from under which counter-fire may be delivered. Natural F. is the utilisation of natural objects—rivers, marshes, forests, ravines, &c.—to delay the assault of an enemy, and to render it more or less ineffectual when made. Artificial F. is constructive, and has been described as military architecture, or the art of strengthening natural obstacles to an enemy's advance, or, where such natural obstacles do not exist, of constructing works to serve the same purpose, by the skill of the engineer. The latter division of the subject falls to be considered under the two headings *Permanent* and *Field or Temporary F.* The purposes of both permanent and field works are identical, and in their construction the same principles are brought to bear. The principal features of both are a ditch to impede the enemy's assault, and a parapet on the side of the ditch occupied by the defence to afford the defenders protection against the enemy's fire, and at the same time enable them to deliver their own fire without exposing themselves to the enemy's marksmen. Field-works, thrown up for a temporary purpose, by unskilled labour, and with such materials as the locality affords, are often rude and slight; permanent fortifications, however, intended for the permanent protection of countries, capitals, arsenals, dockyards, &c., are deliberately built by the most skilful engineers, and with the best materials the age and the country can command, and are, so far, perfect as works of military engineering.

Permanent Fortification.—In the history of military science, the art of defence has gradually developed so as to meet the exigencies of a gradually-developing art of attack. In early days enclosing walls—the original *enceinte*—were considered sufficient to protect a city against a besieging force. Later the walls were strengthened by projecting towers at bowshot distance from each other, and from the loopholes of which an effective flank fire could be delivered along the face of the wall. After the invention of gunpowder and the introduction of artillery, the defensive wall and tower were lowered, so that guns mounted upon them might be fired at a level low enough to sweep the ground occupied by the enemy, and thus the tower became practically a *bastion*, and one of the chief features of modern F. was created. The bastioned system of F., due originally to the ingenuity of the Italian engineers of the early part of the 16th c., was developed by the genius of Vauban (q. v.), Cormontaigne, and other engineers, and all the French and many of the Continental fortresses of our own day are built on this system. The favourite type of permanent F. at present, however, the adoption of which has doubtless been due to the changed conditions of war consequent upon recent improvements in artillery, was advocated a century before Vauban's day by no less a person than Albrecht Durer, who in his work on F. in 1527 recommends what has always been known as the 'polygonal system.' This system was first adopted in Germany early in the present century, was subsequently employed (with modifications) by Belgium, and more recently by Great Britain in the construction of the defences of the great English dockyards. Of the polygonal system the chief characteristics are that the lines of parapet are traced with reference to the space they have to enclose and the direction from which it is probable an attack would be made, and not with reference to the reciprocal *flank defence of the ditches*. Still, in the polygonal system, the defence of the ditch is provided for, in the event of its being reached, by placing casemated buildings (masked batteries in fact) within the ditches, and in such positions as to sweep them to right and left, or otherwise, by reverse galleries in the counterscarps. The profile and arrangements of the works of the bastioned and polygonal systems of F. are similar though not identical. The accompanying figure will readily familiarise readers with the names, relative positions, &c., of the principal parts of the Enceinte (q. v.) of all regularly-fortified works.

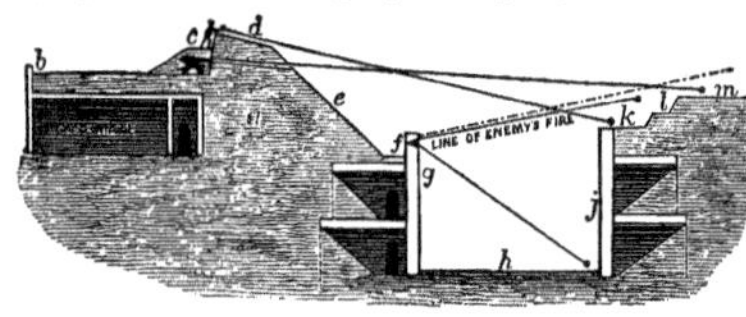

Fig. 1.—Section of Counter-Arched Revetments as adopted in England.

The *rampart* (*a*) is a mound of earth raised above the natural level of the country, and formed of the soil obtained by excavating the ditch, which extends in front of it all round the work. The *terreplein* (*b*) is the platform on which the guns are placed and worked. The *banquette* (*c*) is a tread or step of earth upon which the infantry stand to deliver their fire. The *parapet* (*d*) the highest part of the rampart, is a *breastwork* 30 feet thick and about 8 feet higher than the terreplein, the purpose of which is to protect the troops working the guns and the infantry on the banquette from the musketry and cannon of the enemy. The parapet is pierced with embrasures, usually about 18 feet apart, through which the guns are fired. The *crest* of the parapet (*c*) is usually about 22 feet above the natural level of the country. The *superior* or *upper slope* of the parapet is about 18 feet broad, and has a slope of 1 in 6. The *exterior* or *lower slope* (*e*), the remaining part of the parapet, has a slope of nearly 1 in 3. At the foot of the exterior slope in bastioned works is the *berm* (*f*), a narrow level space or path which affords a means of communication round the outside of the works. The same purpose is served in polygonal F. by the *chemin des rondes*. The *escarp* (*g*) is the inside wall of the ditch, lined with mason-work to retain the earth of the rampart in its place. (The strong structure of mason-work is called the *revetment*.) The *main ditch* (*h*) is usually about 12 feet deep, and is often from 100 to 180 feet wide, though usually its width is from 13 to 18 feet wide. The counterscarp (*j*) is the wall round the outside of the ditch. The covered way (*k*) is a space of about 30 feet extending round the counterscarp, enclosed or covered from fire by a parapet. The glacis (*m*), with a banquette (*l*), is the sloping space beyond the covered way. The slope of the glacis brings the troops of the enemy within direct fire of the cannon and musketry from the parapet. The enceinte, consisting of the ditch and rampart, with its subdivisions of parapet, banquette, and terreplein, runs completely round the fortress whatever be its shape, and presents the same profile of glacis, covered way, ditch, rampart, parapet, and terreplein on all sides of it. Where water can readily be procured the ditch is flooded, and its depth of 12 feet obliges the enemy to construct rafts to cross it, and thus delays the assault at the very moment when the defenders are delivering their most destructive fire. The defensive works of a fortress are not all on the interior side of the ditch. There are *outworks* placed outside the ditch but within the glacis. The chief outwork in either of the systems of F. above mentioned is the *ravelin*, a large *Redan* (q. v.), which is useful as affording an advanced position for artillery to flank the glacis and enfilade the enemy's trenches. It is defended by ditches, which in the bastioned system are flanked by the guns of the bastions, and in the polygonal system by low casemated batteries in flanks connected with the ravelins themselves. *Advanced works* are open works beyond the glacis, under the protection of the guns of the enceinte, and the use of which is to protect ground unprotected by the guns of the fortress. *Retrenchments* are works *within works*, so that when the outer lines are carried, the defence may still be maintained by the inner lines. In the bastioned system, retrenchments are of frequent occurrence, especially within the bastions of the enceinte and in the ravelins, portions of the faces of which are isolated by a small ditch and parapet called a *coupure*. *Casemates* are arched chambers, which are bombproof under all ordinary circumstances. Magazines are always casemated. In a gun casemate the embrasure is made in the end wall of the casemate. In the Spithead Forts, Portsmouth, these end walls of casemates are constructed of iron. *Caponieres*, in the polygonal system, are large casemated stone structures built within the ditch, the purpose of which is to defend the ditches of polygonal fortifications. In German enceintes, the caponieres are detached from the escarps, are built in two stories, and are situated in the middle of each long *face* or *side* of the angle. In England they are generally attached to the escarps, have only one floor, and are placed at the angles of the ditches, so as to command both faces of the work. Communication between the works and the caponieres is maintained by a tunnel, which, when it also communicates with the ditch and outworks, is called a *postern*. A novel feature in modern F. is the mortar casemate, a vaulted chamber, without a front wall, in which the mortar is secured against vertical fire, and from which its fire can be brought to bear on the enemy advancing over the glacis. Mortar casemates are placed behind the rampart of the enceinte. Unseen by the enemy, they are the means of a most destructive fire of large shells being thrown among his advancing troops. Having reached the covered way, there is nothing to obstruct an enemy's entrance into the works of a fortress except the escarp, for the counterscarp wall may readily be blown in by mining. Nor in these days does the escarp offer a very serious obstacle, for the accuracy of the curved fire of the present day, and the weight of the shells now used, enable the artillerist to strike and destroy the strongest escarp, unless the latter be well concealed below the crest of the glacis. To neutralise as far as possible the great improvements in the accuracy and range of large guns used in attack, the tendency in modern F. is to make the ditch narrower and deeper, so that the top of the escarp wall shall be 10 or 15 feet lower than the crest of the glacis. In the profile of the English forts (Fig. 1), in which a *chemin des rondes* (*f*), or path of communication, extends round the works, between the escarp and the exterior slope of the parapet, this plan has been adopted. It may here be stated, that in *counter-arched revetments* the pressure or lateral thrust of the earth of the rampart falls upon the arches, and not upon the actual wall of the revetment. The arches are arranged usually in two tiers, and the space they afford is sometimes converted into loopholed galleries for musketry-fire through the escarp. These galleries, known as escarp or counterscarp galleries, are utilised in English and German fortresses to flank the caponieres, and thus aid in defending the ditch. In the bastioned system, bastions are connected by a curtain, in front of which is an outwork called a *tenaille*, with a parapet for the musketry defence of the ditch. The tenaille also acts as a counter-guard, and to protect the postern and escarps of the curtain and flanks from being breached. The main differences between the bastioned and polygonal systems of F. having already been adverted to, it remains to describe Fig. 2, which exhibits the arrangement of works on a front of the German polygonal system, merely pre-

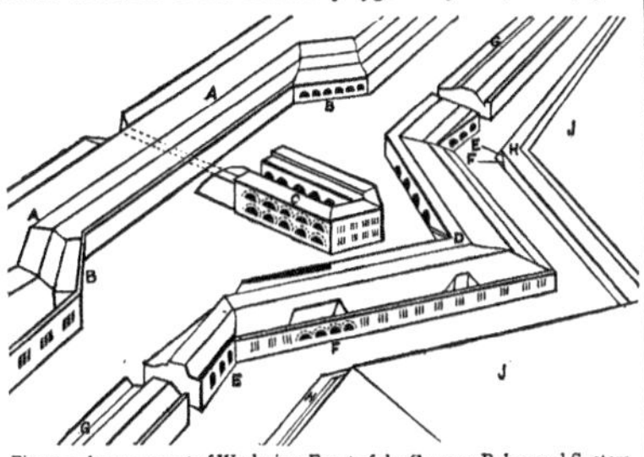

Fig. 2.—Arrangement of Works in a Front of the German Polygonal System.

mising that the great fortified works of England are constructed on similar, if not identical, principles. The figure given represents a portion of the enceinte which surrounds the work (if it be circular), and the profile of which is the same on all sides of the polygon. Beginning from the *interior* of the F., A A is the 'body of the place,' or the space enclosed by the enceinte; B B are casemated flanks in the *escarp of the rampart*, the purpose of which is to defend the ditch of the caponiere; C is a casemated caponiere, provided with two tiers of five guns, and built in the middle of the main ditch, which it commands to right and left; D is a ravelin with a ditch in front defended by the casemated flanks E E; F F are casemates in the ravelin to defend the ditch in front of the counter-guards G G; H H is the covered way, and J J the glacis.

The original works of Vauban were arranged, as to dimensions, &c., to be in harmony with the range, weight, &c., of the firearms of 1650, and are now obsolete. But apart from the matter of dimensions or relative proportion, the general arrangement of the fortified works of which he was the designer is still retained throughout France, and forms the basis of all the modern French systems, as exemplified in the fortifications of Paris, Metz, Lille, &c. One of the chief disadvantages of the Vauban or bastioned system, still prevalent in France, is the liability of the works to be swept by Enfilade (q. v.) or reverse fire. In the Franco-Prussian war, Forts Issy and Vanvers in Paris, and a number of the bastions of the Paris enceinte, were thus swept by the enemy's cannon, and the great number of *traverses* or covering parapets which the French found it necessary to erect along the lines of and at right angles to their covered ways and terrepleins, so as to afford protection against enfilade fire, is sufficient evidence to prove that, to this extent, they were forced to acknowledge the defect of their system. Perhaps the most complete and most interesting permanent works of modern Europe are the magnificent new fortifications of Antwerp constructed by General Brialmont. They consist of a most formidable and extensive enceinte, strengthened by a series of detached forts along the line at a distance from each other of about 2000 yards. A similar arrangement of defences—a continuous enceinte and a cordon of forts—may be seen at Paris, Metz, Lyon, Cologne, Coblentz, Mayence, &c., but Antwerp is *sui generis*, from the circumstance that in the construction and arrangement of its works the principles and details of the polygonal system have been applied and utilised with the greatest possible success.

Field Fortification.—The object of field as of permanent works is to enable a smaller to resist the attack of a larger body of men. When time is afforded for their careful construction, they are found to present a profile similar to that presented by permanent works, viz., a sheltering rampart, with parapet, ditch, and glacis. Field-works are of two kinds—open and closed. The simplest *open work* is a straight line, useful to close a gorge or defend an isthmus, but in ordinary ground liable to be destroyed by enfilade. The redan or *flèche* (Fr. 'arrow'), consisting of two straight lines or faces, forms what is called a *salient angle*. The line bisecting this angle is called a *capital*, and a line beween the open ends of the two lines or faces is called the *gorge*, which, being undefended, exposes the work to the liability of being taken in rear. A Russian redan was captured at Borodino by French cavalry riding in at the rear of the work by the gorge. Another defect of this field-work is that no provision is made for the defence of its ditch. Redans are commonly constructed for the defence of a bridge, defile, or any narrow passage. When flanks are added to redans at an angle of 100°, the work is vastly strengthened, as the flanks command the ditch as well as the ground in front of the salients. A *lunette* is a redan with two flanks running parallel to the *capital* or bisecting line of the two faces or lines forming the redan. A double redan is a work in which two redans are joined together, and provision thus made for the reciprocal defence of the inner ditches. *Enclosed field-works*, or such as are entirely surrounded by a parapet, are called *forts* when the ditches are flanked by the parapets; but where no flanking defence is afforded by the parapets, the work is called a *redoubt*. *Redoubts* may be of any shape, regular or irregular, provided the fire from any face of the rampart does not defend any line of ditch. Such works are readily constructed, and are defended by fewer men than forts. In redoubts, however, as in the polygonal system of F., the defence of the ditch is often provided for by placing caponieres so as to sweep it right and left, or by the construction of loopholed galleries in the counterscarp. Field-works comprise three kinds of forts—star, demi-bastioned, and bastioned forts. The bastioned fort is an elaborate work, constructed only in cases in which an important spot is to be fortified and an obstinate defence intended. Its ditch should be 12 feet deep, and its parapet 10 feet high and 16 feet thick, to resist a 16-lb. rifled gun. *Blockhouses*, usually formed of logs of wood, loopholed, and arranged vertically in the shape of a rectangle, polygon, or cross, are proof against rifle bullets, but offer no defence against artillery, and are only valuable in mountainous or thickly-wooded country, impracticable for field-guns. When built in the form of a cross, the blockhouse permits of a flank defence. In the Turko-Servian war (1876), field-works of this description were eminently serviceable. *Fortified lines* are either continued or interrupted by intervals. *Continued lines* are a connected line of field-works, the purpose of which is to enclose a front or connect isolated forts by a continuous parapet. They are now seldom used, from the circumstance that a parapet broken by salient and re-entering angles requires more men for its defence than are required for an ordinary line of battle, and that when once broken by the enemy, the lines may be regarded as lost. *Redan lines*, designed by Vauban, consist of a series of redans, the salients of which are 240 yards apart, and the inner faces connected by curtains. *Indented* or *crémaillère lines* consist of a series of alternate long and short faces, forming salient and re-entering angles of 90°. The defects of this trace are that the fire from the short faces is ineffective until the enemy arrives at the counterscarp of the line, and that they are exposed to enfilade fire. *Bastioned lines* consist of a series of connected bastions. The salients of the bastions are 360 yards apart, the perpendiculars are not more than 45 yards. In this trace the faces are much exposed to enfilade. *Lines with intervals* have, for almost all purposes, superseded continued lines, (1) because, as there is less extent of parapet to defend, they do not drain the garrison to an equal extent; (2) because, when one part of the line is forced, the whole does not fall; and (3) because the defending force can readily advance to the attack between the intervals. *Têtes-de-pont* or *bridge-heads* are bastioned works thrown up to cover the advance or retreat of an army across a river.

Obstacles.—In field F., the parapet is practically the only actual defensive work, and is usually constructed in haste, and often—in cases in which an earthen rampart cannot be thrown up—of materials which afford only insufficient cover. During the American civil war, a favourite form of parapet was constructed by cutting down trees and of these raising a rude breastwork. All such parapets, however, may be readily taken by assault, unless the approach to them (the glacis) is rendered difficult by what are termed obstacles. The purposes of obstacles are to impede the advance of the enemy at those points upon which the defenders can pour their most destructive fire. Obstacles may be of endless variety, dependent upon the ingenuity and resources of the commander; but 'good' obstacles must be placed well within the defenders' fire, must be sheltered from the artillery fire of the enemy, must afford no cover to the assailants, and must be so constructed as not to be easily removed or destroyed. The following are the obstacles most commonly used in field F:—The *trou-de-loup* ('wolf-hole'), a pit of the form of an inverted cone, from 6 to 10 feet deep, 6 feet diameter at the surface, and 1 foot wide at the bottom, into which a pointed stake is driven—a contrivance which, peculiarly successful in disabling cavalry, was used with effect at Bannockburn, and is still held in esteem; *pickets* or pointed stakes, one or two inches broad, and three feet long, driven firmly into the ground close together, also effective against cavalry, and when planted on the brow of a parapet (above the escarp), cause much trouble to escaladers; *crow's feet*, which fall so that they may always present an upward-pointing iron spike,—another contrivance *pour encourager* the enemy's cavalry; *Abattis* (q. v.); *entanglements*, young trees or brushwood picketed down to the ground; *Chevaux-de-frise* (q. v.); and fougasses, small mines filled with stones or shells, charged with gunpowder, and fired either by a hose or by electricity. See *Traité de Fortification Polygonale*, and kindred works, by General Brialmont, Belgian staff; *Fortification*, by Colonel O'Brian, Sandhurst; and *Field Fortification*, by Major W. W. Knollys, F.R.G.S. (Strahan, Lond. 1875).

Fortiguerr'a, Niccolo, an Italian churchman and poet, attached as chamberlain to the household of Pope Clement XI., was born at Pistoia, November 7th, 1674, and died at Rome, February 7, 1735. His fame rests chiefly on his light epic poem *Ricciardetto* (first published at Venice in 1738), abounding in comic incident and in satire on the morals of the clergy.

Fort'-Major, an officer acting under the governor of a fortress, and whose duty it chiefly is to inspect the defences and see that they are kept in repair. If under the rank of captain, the F.-M. takes rank as junior captain. Any field-officer appointed F.-M. must first resign his regimental appointment. The number of fort-majors in 1876–77 was five.

Fortrose', or **Fortross'**, a royal burgh and seaport in Ross-shire, on the W. side of the Moray Firth, 10 miles N.N.E. of Inverness, and opposite Fort George, with which it has communication by ferry. It was formerly a centre of culture in the N., and had a cathedral and bishop's palace, the stones of which were taken by Cromwell to build a fortress at Inverness. There is still some trade in grain, pork, eggs, &c. F., along with Inverness, Forres, and Nairn, sends one member to Parliament. (Pop. (1871) 911.

Fort Royal' (properly Fort-de-France), fortress, seaport, and capital of the island of Martinique (French) in the West Indies. Its bay of the same name is said to form the best port in the Antilles. There are grand promenades, some fine edifices, and 12,000 inhabitants.

Fort St. Da'vid, formerly a maritime fortress of India, in the province of Madras, 3 miles N. of Cuddalore. It was a strong position during the contests of the French and English, and was dismantled by the latter about 1760.

Fort St. George, the first fortified settlement of the British on the mainland of India, erected in 1639, and the nucleus of the present city of Madras (q. v.). It was captured by the French in 1744.

Fort Sumt'er, a celebrated stronghold of the Confederates during the War of Secession in S. Carolina, U.S., on the S. side of the entrance to Charleston inner harbour, and 3 miles from the city. It was built in 1829, and at the time of secession it mounted seventy-eight guns, and was held by a small body of troops under Major R. Anderson. Occupying a commanding position in the harbour of Charleston, it early became the centre of interest. The civil war was begun here by the Confederate batteries of General Beauregard on the 12th of April 1861, and the fort was surrendered on the following day. It was held undisturbedly for two years, repulsed a force of nine Northern iron-clads, August 17, 1863, was partly demolished by the land batteries, but was not evacuated till the final surrender of Charleston, February 18, 1865. It is now being rebuilt.

Fortu'na, among the Greeks **Tyche**, was the goddess of chance or luck. She was extensively worshipped in Greece and Italy, and was held in special honour at Rome. The Romans applied to her numerous epithets, such as *publica, privata, muliebris, conservatrix, regina*, indicative of the circumstances under which, and the persons to whom, she showed favour. F. was represented with a rudder, an emblem of her guiding power, and with a globe, to express her mutability.

For'tunate Is'lands. See CANARIES.

Fortuna'tus, the hero of an old popular story, who after undergoing great sufferings, obtains a wishing cap and exhaustless purse of gold, which eventually ruin F. and his sons. The story is of German origin, and has been recast in various forms in most of the languages of Europe. Its author is unknown, but F. seems at first to have been identical with Fortunio, another character in popular tales. The first printed edition of the story appeared at Augsburg in 1509. A Danish version was published at Copenhagen in 1664, a French at Rouen in 1670, an Italian at Naples in 1676, an Icelandic about 1690, and a Swedish in 1694, and a Dutch version at Amsterdam in 1796. The tale was dramatised in Hans Sachs' *Der F. mit dem Wunschseckel* (1553), and in Dekker's *Pleasant Comedie of Old F.* (1600). The tale is related poetically in Tieck's *Phantasus* (Berl. 1816), and the exhaustless purse reappears in Chamisso's story of *Peter Schlemil*, who sold his shadow for it. See Grässe's *Die Sagenkreise des Mittelalters* (Dresd. and Leips. 1842).

For'tune, Robert, a Scottish botanist, was born in Berwickshire, 1813, and was engaged at the Botanical Gardens of Edinburgh, and later at those of Chiswick. In 1842 he was sent by the Botanical Society of London to N. China, and the result of his visit appears in *Three Years' Wanderings in China* (1847). He spent other three years in China in the interest of the East India Company, and produced his *Two Visits to the Tea Countries of China* in 1851. This was followed by his *Residence among the Chinese Islands on the Coasts and at Sea, being the Third Visit*, 1853–56. In 1859 F. collected in China for the United States Government the seeds of the tea-shrub and other plants. His latest work, entitled *Yedo and Pekin* (1863), treats of the natural products and agriculture of Japan and China.

For'tune-Telling. Any one obtaining money or goods under pretext of foretelling is punishable, as so doing under pretence. Any one going about the country pretending to foretell is punishable as a 'rogue and vagabond' under the Vagrant Act. See BEGGARS, LAW OF ENGLAND RELATIVE TO.

Fortu'ny, Mariano, a modern Spanish painter, was born of poor parents at Reus, near Barcelona, 11th June 1839. His first experience in art was gained by assisting his grandfather, a showman, to paint wax figures. Later he studied at Madrid, and made two journeys through Morocco during the Spanish war, producing a vast number of oil and water-colour drawings. On his return he painted, on commission of the Spanish Government, his great picture, 'The Battle of Tetuan,' which procured for him a high reputation as a bold, original draughtsman, and a master of sunny, scintillating colour. He eventually settled at Rome, where he founded a school which sought inspiration from nature, and threw discredit on the 'Masters.' His splendid studio latterly became one of the public sights on account of its rare collection of enamels, ceramics, tapestries, &c. He died 21st November 1874. Among his best-known works are 'The Beach at Portici' (sold for £3952), 'The Siesta,' 'Academicians of Arcadia,' 'Marriage in the Cathedral of Madrid,' 'Snake-charmers,' and 'Madrid Procession Caught in the Rain.' He mainly held to Southern or Oriental *genre* painting. 'Le joli F.' was a perverted genius, cynical and frivolous, whose theatrical subjects lack the genuine feeling of humanity, and whose execution is always more or less feverish and flashy. He was influenced banefully by the artistic necromancy of his brother-in-law, Madrazo, and fell under the weird spell of Gérôme. The criticism of Théophile Gautier greatly helped to raise to a fabulous height the price of F.'s pictures. The unfinished works alone left at his death brought over £16,000. See *F., sa Vie, son Œuvre, sa Correspondance*, by Baron Davillier (Par. 1875).

Fort Wayne, a city of Indiana, U.S., situated at the point where the St. Joseph and St. Mary form the Maumee river, 94 miles S.W. of Lake Erie. It is a great railway centre, having the workshops of the Pittsburg, Fort Wayne, and Chicago Railways. The Wabash and Erie Canal passes through it. F. has manufactures of machinery, several newspapers, and numerous schools. The city derives its name from General Wayne, who built a fort here in 1794. Pop. (1870) 17,718.

Fort Will'iam (Gael. *Inbher Lochaidh*, 'the mouth of the dark river'), a burgh and fort in the county of Inverness, at the S. end of the Caledonian Canal, 63 miles from Inverness. The fort was first built by General Monk, rebuilt by General Mackay in 1689, and called Fort William in honour of King William. It is an irregular work, but withstood a siege by Prince Charlie's forces in 1745. It contained accommodation for 100 men. Like Fort Augustus, it has been sold by the Government, and is now occupied as private dwelling-houses. The burgh of F. W. (under the Lindsay Act), originally called Mary Burgh, afterwards Gordon's Burgh, contains a pop. of 1200, a public school, three banks, and four churches. Lying at the foot of Ben Nevis, it is very much frequented by summer tourists.

Fort William, the citadel of Calcutta (q. v.). The original fortification was erected in 1696, but was abandoned after the sack of the city by the Nawab Seraj-ud Dowlah; the present building dates from 1773.

Fo'rum (akin to *foris* and *foras*, hence 'that which is out of doors') meant originally a clear open space, and was applied specially to the central area in towns which in ancient times served as a market-place, and also as a place for the discussion of public affairs and the administration of justice. At Rome the F. was about 224 yards in length, and about 68 yards at its greatest breadth, stretching between the Capitoline and Palatine hills, and surrounded by spacious porticoes and the shops of bankers. It consisted of two parts, the Comitium, and the Lower F., occupying respectively one-fourth and three-fourths of the area. The Comitium was so named from having been the place of meeting of the Comitia Curiata, and contained the tribunal from which the prætor of the city administered justice, and the rostra, a platform from which public speakers addressed the people, and which was so called because it had been adorned with the *beaks* of ships won from the Antiates. In the Lower F. all general business was transacted, and the Comitia Tributa met. The famous Sacra Via was the boundary of the F. on the E. and N., entering near the temple of Vesta, and leaving at the Arch of Severus. Of the additional *fora judicialia*, erected by the emperors, the most important were the F. Julium and the F. Augustum, the works of Julius Cæsar and Augustus. There were numerous *fora venalia* in Rome, as the *F. boarium*, or cattle-market; the *F. olitorium*, or vegetable market; the *F. cupedinis*, or market for dainties, &c. F. was also the name of many market and assize towns, as F. Appii, F. Aurelium, &c.

Fosca'ri, Frances'co, a doge of Venice, familiar to English readers from Byron's tragedy. Born about 1372, he was doge from 1423 till 1457. Though during his long administration Venice was prosperous at home, and successful in the almost incessant wars undertaken by her energetic doge, the animosity of his enemies triumphed in compelling F. summarily and ignominiously to resign office in 1423. He had already lost three sons in battle, and had seen the fourth tortured and banished as a traitor. He was unable to survive the crowning calamity of 1423, and died immediately after his resignation.

Fos'colo, Niccolo Ugo, an Italian patriot, poet, and man of letters, born at Zante, 26th January 1777, was educated at Venice and the university of Padua. His first tragedy, *Tieste*, was performed with success at Venice in 1797. After Venice had become an Austrian town, F., still hoping great things for Italy from the soldiers of the republic, took service as an officer in the Lombard Legion at Milan, then capital of the Cisalpine Republic. He spent several years with the French army. F.'s first romance, *Ultime Lettere di Jacopo Ortis*, had appeared in 1802, and secured him a European reputation. The poem *I Sepolcri* was well received; and in 1808 F. was called to the chair of rhetoric at Pavia, which he occupied till the professorship was suppressed. The tragedies *Ajace* and *Ricciarda* were performed in 1811 and 1813. F. forsook Italy finally after the events of 1814, and soon settled in England, where he continued to be engaged in miscellaneous literary work, illustrative of Petrarch, Dante, and other great names of Italian literature. In spite of F.'s success as author and lecturer, the exile of this high-hearted but restless and impetuous Italian was embittered by pecuniary distress. He died at Turnham Green, 14th September 1827. In 1871 his ashes were brought to Florence, amid public solemnities. The best collective edition of F.'s works is that of Le Monnier (Flor. 11 vols.). See the Biographies of F. by Pecchio (Lugano, 1833) and Carrer (Ven. 1842).

Foss'a and Fur'ca. See PIT AND GALLOWS.

Fossa'no (Lat. *Fons Sanus*, 'the healing fount'), a walled town of N. Italy, province of Cuneo, on the Stura, an affluent of the Po, and 32 miles S. of Turin by railway. It is the seat of a bishop (since 1580), and has a cathedral of San Giovanni, a castle of the 14th c., an academy of science and art, a veterinary college, and a theatre. F. has paper, silk, and leather industries, and a trade in corn, hemp, and cattle. Pop. 7279. F. was an important fortress in the 13th and 14th centuries. It was stormed by the French in 1796, and was taken by the Austrians, 18th September 1799.

Foss Dyke. See CANAL.

Fosse, or **Foss** (Lat. *fossa*, from *fodio*, 'I dig'), is the dry or wet ditch immediately surrounding the rampart of a fortification.

Foss'il (Lat. *fossilis*, from *fodere*, 'to dig'), originally anything dug out of the earth, but now limited to the remains of plants and animals found imbedded in the rocks which form the earth's crust. These organic remains are found in all states of preservation, and are probably due to the replacement of the gradually-decaying organic matter by mineral products. Each stratum has its distinctive fossils or groups of fossils, which are consequently of the greatest value in fixing the age of the formations in which they occur. Without this aid, indeed, palæontology would have no existence, and geology would lose its most important component.

Fossil Ferns. The ferns or *Filices* are first certainly represented in a fossil state in the Devonian and Old Red Sandstone rocks. The Devonian F. F. present a close resemblance to the more luxuriant vegetation which prevailed in the succeeding Carboniferous epoch. The genera *Cyclopteris*, *Neuropteris*, and *Phenopteris* include smaller species, whilst trunks of tree-ferns are also found in Devonian strata, and are referred to the genera *Caulopteris*, *Protopteris*, &c. The former genus also occurs in Carboniferous strata, along with *Palæopteris* and other typical forms. The Coal period is very rich in smaller F. F. belonging to the genera already mentioned as occurring in the Devonian, and in addition to the genera *Pecopteris* (*Alethopteris*), *Odontopteris*, *Hymenophyllites*, &c. In the Permian rocks F. F. are abundant, but resemble those of the Coal period. Many Carboniferous genera also occur in the Trias, *Neuropteris elegans* being a characteristic Secondary form. In Tertiary strata F. F. are comparatively few in number, and are not represented in the profusion characteristic of the earlier formations.

Fossilif'erous Rocks, a comprehensive term in geology, embracing all formations which contain organic remains. It is nearly synonymous with *Aqueous Rocks* (q. v.), though not unfrequently fossils are found imbedded in volcanic tuff and similar fragmental rocks.

Fossombro'ne (the Roman *Forum Sempronii*), a town and bishop's see in Central Italy, province of Pesaro-Urbino, in the valley of the Metauro, and on the *Via Flaminia*, 16 miles W.S.W. of Pesaro. It has an old castle, and a cathedral, in which are many ancient inscriptions, besides the remains of a Roman theatre and bridge. The Metauro is here spanned by a modern bridge. F. produces the *Seta della Marca*, celebrated as the finest silk in Europe. Pop. 8464. Near F. Hasdrubal was defeated and slain by the Romans in 207 B.C.

Fos'ter, Birket, an English artist, was born at North Shields in 1812. He was educated at Hitchin, Herts, and after practising wood-engraving for some time with Landells, became a draughtsman, in which capacity he early showed an aptitude for the sympathetic treatment of rich pastoral and river landscape. His illustrations of the poetical works of Goldsmith and Scott, of Beattie's *Minstrel*, of *Evangeline*, &c., are artistic gems, crisp yet fluent in drawing, and in chiaroscuro singularly brilliant and true. Of late years F. has won a high reputation for water-colouring, but his lush bosky dells and bright sunny glades leave an impression more of airy daintiness than of great artistic strength or study. He was elected a member of the Water Colour Society in 1860.

Foster, John, an eminent English essayist, was born in Halifax, Yorkshire, September 17, 1770. For a brief period he was a weaver, but studied for the Baptist ministry at the Bristol College, and preached at Newcastle-upon-Tyne, Dublin, Downend, and Frome; but although his preaching was universally admitted to be able, it was not successful, and he gave himself up finally to literature. His great work is *Essays, in a Series of Letters*, published in 1805, when he was at Frome, and which have been much admired for their powerful if somewhat rugged thinking, and occasional imaginative outbursts. Marrying in 1808, he retired to lead a life devoted to literature and study at Bourton-on-the-Water, in Gloucestershire, preaching only at intervals. His chief work for eighteen years was writing papers for the *Eclectic Review*, his contributions to which, 'Biographical, Literary, and Philosophical,' were published in 1840. Among his other productions, the chief are *Essay on the Evils of Popular Ignorance* (1819), occasioned by his return to Downend in 1817, which first awoke the British nation to the perfect barbarism that prevailed in certain country districts; *Lectures delivered at Broadmead Chapel, Bristol* (1844 and 1847); and *Introductory Essay to Doddridge's Rise and Progress* (1825). F. died at Stapleton, near Bristol, October 15, 1843. *The Life and Correspondence of F.*, edited by J. E. Ryland, was published in 1846 (new ed. 1852).

Fou'cault, Jean Bernard Léon, a French savant, was born at Paris, September 18, 1819. Though educated as a physician, he devoted his life to experimental research in the physical sciences, and had charge of the scientific section of the *Journal des Débats* from 1845 till his death, which took place at Paris, February 13, 1868. He is widely known for the calculation of the velocity of light by means of a revolving mirror, and the establishing by direct comparison of the velocities of light in air and water the undulatory theory over the emission theory; for his invention of the Gyroscope (q. v.), and the application of it, as well as of the simple pendulum, to render the diurnal rotation of the earth evident to the bodily eye; and for his electric light apparatus, with the electro-magnetic regulator. F.'s memoirs are published in the *Comptes Rendus*, and some popular scientific treatises appear in the *Bibliothèque d'Instruction Populaire*.

Fou'ché, Joseph, born near Nantes in 1763, first appeared in public life in 1792 as member of the National Convention for Loire-Inférieure. Though a friend of Condorcet and Vergniaud, he showed much 'patriotic ferocity' in voting the king's death, in carrying out the 'Law of Suspects' in the W., and in suppressing with Chaumette the Catholic religion. At Lyon he and Collot d'Herbois perpetrated the judicial murders of which he afterwards ignobly tried to throw the blame on his enemy Robespierre. He was rewarded by the president's chair in the Jacobin Club. By lying and treachery, he survived the Reign of Terror, after which he curried favour with Director Barras by the betrayal of Babeuf's conspiracy. In the Ministry of Police, which he entered in 1799, he found the congenial task of suppressing the Jacobins, whom he had once led. The consuls being established, F. adopted milder measures, especially with regard to royalists, but his administration was disgraced by embezzlement on a grand scale. In 1802 F. was dismissed, the Ministry of Police being suppressed. The office and the man were restored under the Empire in 1804. Meantime F. resisted the murder of D'Enghien and saved the life of Moreau. To the former he applied the famous words—'It is worse than a crime; it is a blunder.' For several years F.'s administration of internal affairs was able, moderate, and popular. In 1809 he was made Duc d'Otrante; and was so popular that Napoleon became suspicious. In 1810 F. was replaced by Savary. He never recovered Napoleon's confidence, but was offered the Ministry of Police by Louis XVIII. in 1814. He resumed office during the Hundred Days, all the while maintaining friendly secret relations with leading royalists. In the Declaration of 1815 he unsuccessfully tried to obtain a recognition of the sovereignty of the people. After Waterloo F. was a member of the Provisional Government of Five, and arranged with De Vitrolles and Talleyrand the entry of the Bourbons. Once more Minister of Police, he exerted himself to reduce the list of proscriptions from 3000 to 57. Among these 57, however, were many of his old companions. This assumed moderation enraged the royalists, and F. was banished as a regicide. He died at Trieste, 25th December 1820. As regards his moral character, we may say with Robespierre—'He was a miserable impostor.' See *Mémoires de Fouché, Duc d'Otrante* (2 vols. Par. 1824), not authentic, but containing a good deal of credible matter; and *Vie de Fouché, depuis son Entrée à la Convention jusqu'à sa Mort* (Par. 1821).

Fougères', an old town in the department of Ille-et-Vilaine, France, at the confluence of the Nançon and Conesnon, 35 miles N.E. of Rennes by railway. It is overlooked by a ruined castle of the 12th c., has many quaint arcades, and is famous for its scarlet dye, the delicate tints of which are ascribed to the Nançon waters. Pop. 9805.

Fou'la, an outlying island of the Shetland group, 32 miles W. of Lerwick. It is an almost inaccessible sandstone and granitic mass, the haunt of myriads of sea-fowl, some 3 miles long, rising, in parts precipitously, 1285 feet above the sea. Pop. 250, chiefly engaged in fishing. F., which may be seen from Orkney, is supposed to be the ancient *Ultima Thule*. It is surrounded by dangerous rocks.

Fould, Achille, a French statesman, born at Paris, November 17, 1800. He was the son of a rich Jewish planter, and after travelling in Italy and the East, was returned to the Chamber of Deputies in 1842. He was a member of the Constituent Assembly in 1848, and of the Legislative Body in 1849. Under the presidency of Louis Napoleon he was four times Minister of Finances. In this post he showed great ability and disinterestedness, and though he repeatedly resigned from disapproval of Louis Napoleon's conduct, he was, after the *coup-d'état* of 1851, appointed a senator and minister of state. In 1852 he was made Commander of the Legion of Honour, and from 1861 to 1867 was again Minister of Finance. F. died at Tarbes, October 5, 1867.

Foul'is, Robert and Andrew, two celebrated Glasgow printers, born, the one April 20, 1707, the other, November 23, 1712. Robert was originally a barber with a good business, but under the advice of Dr. Francis Hutcheson, Professor of Moral Philosophy in Glasgow University, whose class he had attended, became a bookseller. The first work that brought him into reputation was an edition in Greek of *Demetrius Phalereus on Elocution* (1742). Next year he was appointed printer to the University, and soon after took into partnership his brother Andrew. During the next thirty years there followed a succession of classical reprints—Latin, Greek, English—among which may be mentioned Horace, Cicero, Homer, Herodotus, Milton, Pope, and Gray. Some of these were models of accuracy and elegance. Andrew died in 1775; Robert, in 1776. The sons of the latter maintained for some time the reputation of the firm.

Founda'tion (from the Lat. *fundus*, 'a bottom or basis'), a word applied both to the lowest part of any building or structure, and to the ground upon which it rests. The walls of a building are increased in thickness at the bottom—stepwise—in order to distribute the pressure due to the superincumbent masonry over a considerable area. Where the ground below is rock, no further preparation is needed than dressing its surface approximately level, or into a number of horizontal beds at different levels, if the surface slopes greatly. In ordinary cases, however, foundations have to be made upon material which is not only soft in itself, but which is liable to be rendered softer by the permeation of water. In these circumstances it is usual to provide a hard and impermeable base for the masonry or brickwork, and at the same time to extend the area over which the pressure acts, by putting down a layer of concrete of a thickness and breadth proportioned to the weight of the building, and the nature of the soil underneath. *Submerged* foundations, such as those for bridges, piers, &c., frequently present great difficulties to the engineer.

Foun'der, a name given to an inflammation of acute type of the laminar structures of the horse's foot, resulting usually from over-exertion. Occasionally the affection may appear as the result of derangement of the digestive system. The fore-feet are those most generally affected, but the disease is sometimes found in both fore and hind feet. The symptoms consist in heat and swelling of the feet, and in the inability of the horse to stand upon the affected feet. The treatment must first be directed to the removal of the inflammatory symptoms by antiphlogistic remedies. The shoes are to be removed and the hoof pared. Bleeding may be indicated, and the feet must be poulticed with bran-bags. The bowels must be freely evacuated, and if pus forms in the foot, it must have free vent given to it by incisions. Mild blisters may be afterwards required to reduce swelling.

Found'ling Hos'pitals are institutions for the nurture of children abandoned by their parents. It has been a much-mooted question whether or not the laws of political economy sanction the endowment of F. H.; the argument of the opponents of these institutions being that they promote sensual immorality, the parents being relieved of the charge of maintaining the child resulting from it. If it were the rule of the institution to receive no child unless deserted by its parents, this argument would have no more force against the maintenance of F. H. than it has against the present law of England, which obliges a *parish* to maintain a deserted child. It may be doubtful whether the law of political economy carried out in full rigour would sanction any general system for the keeping alive of deserted children; because there can be no doubt that the existence of such a system does promote sexual immorality for the reason above stated. But the laws of political economy apply only to the *wealth* of nations, and human benevolence and moral culture frequently require a mitigation of these. And they do require it regarding the matter in question. We could not see helpless children dying of hunger. We think, therefore, that under wise management F. H. are, at all events, harmless institutions. They simply relieve an individual, a parish, or a state of a pecuniary burden. The F. H. of London was established by Captain Coram in 1739 as 'an hospital for the exposed and deserted children.'

Foun'dry (from the verb 'to found,' Lat. *fundare*, 'to flow out'), a place where metal in the shape of 'pig' or ingot is cast into the forms required in construction or the arts. In the common iron F., the metal (pigs broken into pieces) is melted in a Cupola (q. v.) furnace with coke as fuel, and then run into large buckets or 'ladles,' which are slung from cranes, and so can be easily and quickly moved from the furnace to any part of the F. The sand or loam moulds into which it is then poured are made as follows:—A wooden pattern is prepared, having externally exactly the form of the required object, but having projections or 'prints' on it instead of holes wherever that object has openings. If the object be hollow, a box is then made, called a 'core-box,' having *internally* exactly the same shape as the interior of the required object, plus the 'prints' upon the pattern just alluded to. A mould is then made from the pattern in soft sand or loam (the *inside* of the mould having the same form as the *outside* of the object), and a 'core' is made of the same materials by means of the core-box (the *outside* of the core having the same form as the *inside* of the object); both mould and core are dried separately, and then the latter is placed inside the former, resting in it by means of the projections corresponding to the prints. The space between the core and the mould now corresponds exactly in form and thickness with the object to be cast. The whole is built up and strengthened as may be necessary (to prevent bursting); suitable air-holes and pipes are provided; and when all is ready, the molten metal is poured in. Sufficient metal is used not merely to fill the space left between the mould and the core, but also to form a 'head' above the casting, which can afterwards be cut or broken off, and which will contain impurities and sponginess that otherwise would spoil the casting itself. After the metal has had time to cool, the mould is broken up, and the casting cleaned by the removal of the sand still adhering to it, and of burrs or conspicuous roughnesses.

The process of casting other metals than iron does not essentially differ from that described above. For brass or gun-metal an air furnace takes the place of the cupola, and steel is most often melted in crucibles. With some geometrical forms, such as the cylinder, a complete pattern is not required, and in certain cases, when a number of copies of the same object are to be cast, the pattern is made of iron instead of wood.

Foun'tain (Fr. *fontaine*, Lat. *fons*), a jet of water springing up through a natural or artificial orifice in the surface of the earth in virtue of a hydrostatic law (see ARTESIAN WELLS); or a structure, usually decorated, from which water spouts forth, either by hydrostatic pressure, by the elasticity of compressed air, or by mechanical means. In Southern Europe, nearly all the water for domestic uses is drawn from public artificial fountains. Rome and Paris are noted for the number and beauty of their fountains, and the *Grandes Eaux* of Versailles are justly admired. London is exceptionally poor in fountains; the largest, in Trafalgar Square, is supplied from an artesian well. The Crystal Palace, at Sydenham, has one of its chief attractions in its fountains, and others of great beauty may be seen in the grounds of Chatsworth in Derbyshire. The Emperor F. at Chatsworth is the most remarkable *jet-d'eau* in the world; it rises to a perpendicular height of 267 feet.

Fountain, in heraldry, is one of the *roundels* formed of six alternate wavy lines, *argent* and *azure*, or more properly barry wavy of six. The F. is represented flat (Boutell and Aveling).

Fou'qué, Friedrich Heinrich Karl, Baron de la Motte, a German romance-writer and poet, was born at Brandenburg, February 12, 1777. He served in the campaigns of 1793, 1794, 1795, and, after living in rural retirement, in the war of 1813. He spent the rest of his life at his estate of Nennhausen, at Halle, Paris, and Berlin, where he died, January 23, 1843. F. was an ardent romanticist, and wrote many tales on mediæval and Scandinavian themes, full of wild fancy, and written in a poetic style, of which the best known are *Sigurd* (Berl. 1809); the exquisite fairy-story of *Undine* (Berl. 1811; 13th ed. 1864); *Der Zauberring* (1813; new ed. 1855); *Sängers Liebe* (Tüb. 1816); and *Die zwei Brüder* (1817). He likewise wrote many poems (*Gedichte*, 5 vols. Stuttg. 1816–27), dramas, &c. He has been blamed for the fantastic unreality of his conceptions, and the shadowiness of his characters. 'His heroes,' says Heine, 'are all iron and sentiment, without body or reason.' A selection of his works, edited by himself, was isued in 12 vols. (Halle, 1844–46). Carlyle has translated F.'s beautiful tale *Aslauga's Knight*. See Carlyle's notice of F. in *Miscellaneous Essays*.

Fou'quier-Tin'ville, Antoine Quentin, public accuser in the Reign of Terror, was born at the village of Hérouelles, department of Aisne, in 1747. He was educated for the bar, but led a dissipated life, and for misconduct lost a post he held as procurator at Châtelet. F. threw himself, however, with such vehemence into the Revolution, always giving his vote for death in the Assembly, that Robespierre made him public accuser. As such his name will be infamous for all time; he called the guillotine the coining machine of the Republic, and sent to it men of all opinions that came before him—Danton, Hébert, Camille Desmoulins, and even his master, Robespierre. Finally he himself was guillotined, 7th May 1795.

Four'chambault, a town in the department of Nièvre, France, near the right bank of the Loire, 5 miles N.W. of Nevers by railway. It has large iron-foundries, forges, and smelting furnaces, and an extensive manufacture of arms. The Loire is here crossed by a suspension bridge. Pop. (1872) 5835.

Four'croya, a genus of Exogenous plants, allied to the Agaves (q. v.), and belonging to the natural order *Amaryllidaceæ*. The stamens are shorter than the corolla. These plants grow in tropical climates.

Four Evan'gelists, the most easterly four of the group of twelve islands known as the Twelve Apostles, lying to the W. of Magellan's Strait.

Four'ier, François Marie Charles, born at Besançon, 7th April 1772, was the son of a wealthy merchant, lost his father's fortune during the Lyon insurrection of 1793, and served for a short time in the army. Returning to commerce, he received, it is said, his first inspiration of social reform from seeing a vessel of rice sunk at Marseille in order to raise the market price of the remainder. His article in a Lyon newspaper on the Continental triumvirate and the final struggle between France and Russia attracted some attention. In 1808 he published his *Théorie des Quatre Mouvements*, followed in 1822 by his *Traité d'Association*, republished by the disciples as *Théorie de l'Unité Universelle* (4 vols. 1841). His whole life was now given to the propagation of his doctrine, and in 1826 he fixed himself at Paris, where he died, 8th October 1837. In 1829 appeared *Le Nouveau Monde*, and in 1831 a violent attack on the 'charlatanism' of Saint Simon and Robert Owen, in which he offered to reorganise society in two months, with a profit of 300 per cent. In spite of the strange nomenclature (sometimes hieroglyphics were used) in which it was presented, F.'s theory became very popular, especially among women. The earth was for 80,000 years to pass through certain stages of development, the normal population being 30,000,000,000, all of whom should be seven feet high, and live for 144 years. The spirit, as well as the body, would become perfect. There would be 37,000,000 Homers, Newtons, Molières. Not less striking the industrial progress. One result of the universal *remboisement* would be restoration to equilibrium of the climate, and this would cause the ice at the N. Pole to melt. Each human soul lived through the 80,000 years until the golden age, but having alternately an existence within and without the material world. The unscrupulous selfishness of capitalists is constantly denounced, and F. looks forward to a time when the whole race, with one language, one coinage, and one system of weights and measures, would be employed harmoniously in one organisation of productive labour. His plan of reform was based on the transparent fallacy that psychological phenomena are amenable to the physical laws of motion. No institution—property, succession, marriage, the Church—was to be sacrificed. There are three forces, he says, in the individual—the desire for luxury, the tendency to separate in groups, the tendency to unity. On the combination of these depends the primitive group. By a gradual change of combinations the groups form a series, which finally compose the famous 'phalanx' of 1800 persons, chiefly pursuing different tasks of their own free will, on a piece of ground a square league in extent. There is what is pompously called an 'alternation of functions,' a protest against the mechanical effects of subdivided labour. The produce is partly profit on capital, partly wages for work, and partly given to talent. The scale of wages varies with the agreeable or disagreeable character of the work; but a minimum is first set aside for the subsistence of every person, whether capable of work or not. The capital may be owned in unequal shares. The phalanx would live in one building and have one store, so as to minimise the profits of distribution; but voluntary association in families would go on as before. The fundamental idea is that labour may and ought to be rendered attractive by the opportunity of free choice, and the prohibition of excess.

Fourier, Jean Baptiste Joseph, Baron, a French mathematician, was born at Auxerre, March 21, 1768, became Professor of Mathematics at the Central School of Public Works in 1794, was one of the *savans* who accompanied Napoleon to Egypt in 1798, was appointed prefect of Grenoble under the Empire, but after 1815 lived a retired life at Paris, where he died, May 16, 1830. His great work is his *Théorie de la Chaleur* (Par. 1822), a work which abounds in mathematical investigations of the highest originality, and which introduced a new epoch in the study of the laws of thermal conduction and absorption. Of his other works may be mentioned his *Discours Préliminaire*, or preface to the *Description d'Égypte*, his *Recherches Statistiques de la Ville de Paris*, and a posthumous work, *Analyse des Équations Déterminées*, published by Navier in 1831. See Arago's *Éloge de F.* (1833).

Four Lakes, a beautiful chain of lakes in a fertile part of Wisconsin, U.S. First Lake, the lowest and smallest, is 3 miles by 2, having its outlet in Catfish River. The largest, called Mendota, is 6 miles by 4. Between it and Third, or Monona, stands the state capital, Madison.

Foveaux' Strait separates the South or Middle Island of New Zealand from Stewart's Island. At its narrowest point it is 17 miles in width.

Fow'ey, or **Foy**, a seaport in the S. of Cornwall, near the mouth of the river of the same name, 28 miles W. of Plymouth, with which it is connected by railway. It carries on active pilchard-fisheries, has a good harbour, defended by three forts, and exports iron ore and 'china stone.' Pop. (1871) 7209. F. despatched 47 ships and 770 men to the siege of Calais in 1347, was partly burned by the French in 1457, and captured by Fairfax in 1646.

Fowl (Old Eng. *fugel* and *fugol;* Fris. *fugel;* Swed. *fogel;* Dut. and Ger. *vogel;* from a verb signifying 'to fly'), a name sometimes given to any bird of large size, but usually restricted to Gallinaceous or Rasorial birds domesticated by man, as the common barndoor fowls, turkeys, Guinea-fowls, &c. Such birds form a typical group of *Rasores* or 'scratchers,' are distinguished by their strong beak and claws, adapted for picking up seeds and for scratching in the ground respectively. The head is usually provided in the males with *wattles*, often brilliantly coloured and erectile. Fowls are polygamous, one male mating with several females. They form subjects of interest to the naturalist, from their susceptibility to variation under the hand of man. Their original habitat appears to have been E. Asia. The Bankiva jungle-F. (*Gallus Bankiva*) is credited with being the progenitor of all our domestic breeds. This F. is a native of Java. The male closely resembles the English gamecock. Its comb and wattles are bright red, the *hackles* or drooping feathers of the head and neck orange-red, and the upper part of the back a deep bluish black. The tail, which is long and drooping, is also bluish black glossed with green, and the breast and under parts are black. The chief breeds or varieties of fowls which may be more or less clearly traced to the Bankiva stock are:—The Cochin-China F., whose ungainly aspect is so well known. Fabulous prices were given for pure-bred Cochins on their first introduction into this country, but the breed has now somewhat deteriorated from its frequent mixture with other varieties. The game-fowls were formerly greatly cultivated for the sake of their pugilistic qualities. The Polish fowls are known by the great plume of feathers borne on the head. The Spanish breed is a particularly fine variety, possessing a large comb, and a patch of white skin destitute of feathers below the ear. The latter variety is of large size, and is in high repute amongst poultry fanciers, from the regularity with which the birds lay. The Dorking fowls are short-legged birds, and have frequently one or more supplementary toes. The bantams are fowls of small size, noted for their courageous bearing, but rarely bred save as fancy fowls. The name common F. or barndoor F. has now come to denote a large number of fowls belonging to no special breed, but representing the effects of interbreeding between the preceding well-marked varieties. The typical F. is the jungle-F. of India; but it has had less influence in the formation of the domesticated breeds than was formerly supposed. At any rate, its peculiarities are seldom, if ever, seen in domesticated fowls in the same proportion as those of the Bankiva F. The *Gallus Sonneratii* of India is a familiar example of a wild F. allied to the domestic breeds. It is of smaller size than our common F. The male is deep grey on the back and lower parts; the tail is long and arched, and coloured with purple and gold. The female wants the wattles of the male, and also his large and lustrous hackles. Other foreign species of F. are the silky F. (*G. lanatus*) of China and Japan, the frizzled F. (*G. crispus*), and the negro F. (*G. morio*). A large species is the *G. giganteus* or gigantic F. of Sumatra, and the fork-tailed F. (*G. Javanicus*) is abundant in the Javan forests.

Fowl'er's Solu'tion, or **Liq'uor Arsenica'lis**, a well-known preparation of arsenic and potassa introduced into medicine by Dr. Fowler, is used in various forms of skin-disease, and as an antiperiodic.

Fowl'ing, the name given to the killing of birds of various kinds, for the purpose of obtaining their feathers, flesh, or other products. This practice is carried on with much skill and daring, and in many different ways, in various parts of the world—*e.g.*, in the Faröe, Shetland, and Orkney Isles, Norway, Sweden, and other portions of N. Europe. The art of the fowler depended in former years much more on personal daring and prowess than in the present day. The introduction and general use of firearms have greatly aided and extended the capture of birds, although in some districts, from the nature of the birds to be caught, and from other considerations, the use of firearms is prohibited, and the pursuit of the birds is therefore attended with as much danger as before. Small birds are caught for the cage or for table by nets or snares of various kinds. But the exercise of the art of F. in its highest development can only be seen to advantage in rocky and inaccessible situations. In the northern islands, where such birds as gannets, guillemots, gulls, solan geese, and their allies are sought after and valued, not only for the sake of their feathers, but for their flesh and fat—the former serving as food, and the latter affording oil—F. is carried on by the hazardous proceeding of letting the fowler down the face of cliffs by means of a rope; and while thus slung in mid-air, he contrives to secure the eggs as well as the birds themselves. The ropes used are made of raw cowhide, and are very durable. A second rope is usually attached to the fowler for the purpose of giving signals to the persons on the top of the cliff, and for hoisting up the birds he secures. A simpler method of F. consists in securing birds by means of nets slung on the end of poles, but even in such a case the fowlers have to be let down the cliffs often for considerable distances.

Fowls of Warren. In the Duke of Devonshire *v.* Lodge (7 B. and C. 36) it was decided that grouse are not F. of W. See FORESTS, CHASES, WARRENS, and PARKS.

Fox (Old Eng. *fox*, Dut. *vos*, Ger. *fuchs;* perhaps allied to the Old Eng. *feax*, 'hair,' and so signifying 'the hairy animal') is the name given to *Canis vulpes* or *Vulpes vulgaris*, a genus of Carnivorous *Mammalia* closely allied to the dog and the wolf, but distinguished by the elongated pupil of the eye. The ears are pointed and triangular in shape, and the tail very bushy. The dental formula is similar to that of the dog, the teeth numbering forty-two, and consisting of six incisors, two canines, eight præmolars, and four molars in each jaw. Minor characteristics may be found in the peculiar scent or odour proceeding from the secretion of anal or tail glands, this scent often furnishing a clue to the whereabouts of the animal. The colour of the common F. is a reddish fawn, mixed with black and white hairs. The fur is coarse, and grows very thick in winter. The tail is tipped with white. The average length of the body is about 2½ feet, and the height about 12 inches. The F. lives in burrows, which he excavates in the ground, or forms by enlarging some natural opening. The burrow generally winds in a complicated manner, the entrance often being made in a circuitous fashion between the spreading roots of a large tree. The cunning and intelligence of the animal have become proverbial. When hunted, it will adopt ruses of the most extraordinary kind to throw its pursuers off the scent—*e.g.*, it will feign death when captured by man, taking advantage of a relaxed guard to escape quickly and noiselessly. A tame F., which was on friendly terms with the dogs of the household, cheated the cats of their milk by simply walking round the cats' dishes, well knowing that the cats, which exceedingly dislike the vulpine odour, would not taste the milk, which thus fell to reynard. The same animal was seen to rub himself against the dairymaid's pails so as to impregnate the milk with his odour, a due supply of the useless fluid naturally falling to his share. The female F. produces from four to six at a birth, and breeds but once annually. Varieties of the common F. are numerous. The cur F. is a small variety, and the greyhound F. has more slender limbs and a better-proportioned body than the common F. The genus *Vulpes* as now constituted includes several other well-marked species of F. The American F. (*V. fulvus*), sometimes named the red F. or cross F., varies much in colour, but is most generally of a pale yellow hue. Its name of cross F. is derived from the almost invariable presence of a blackish stripe across the shoulders. The Arctic F. (*V. lagopus*) is celebrated for the glossy nature of its white winter fur, the summer fur being grey or greyish brown. This F. occurs and is greatly hunted for its fur, in N. Europe and N. America. The soles of the feet are hairy, a peculiarity of structure which assists the animal to walk on the ice. The average length is about 3 feet. The asse or caama (*V. caama*) is a species of F. inhabiting S. Africa, the fur of which is highly valued. Other species are the *V. melanogaster* or black-bellied F. of S. Europe; the *V. Himalaicus* of the Himalaya slopes; the *V. Bengalensis* or Deccan F.; the black or coal F. (*V. alopex*) of Central Europe. The grey F. (*V. Virginianus*) of America is a commoner species than the *V. fulvus*, and exhibits all the characteristic traits of the British F.

Fox.

Law Regarding Foxes.—Foxes may be pursued and destroyed as vermin even on the property of another, the only liability being the damage done in pursuit. In England there is by common law a limited right of hunting foxes over the ground of another. In Scotland fox-hunting for sport without leave is punishable as a trespass.

Fox, Charles James, a Whig statesman and orator, born 24th January 1749, was third son of Right Honourable Henry Fox—created Lord Holland in 1763—and of Lady Georgiana Carolina, daughter of Charles Duke of Richmond, and was thus descended on one side from Charles II. He was educated at Eton and Oxford, had more Continental travel than most young men of his class, and before he had reached his majority was elected member for Midhurst, as a supporter of the Grafton Ministry. F.'s father, an old follower of Walpole, had left the Whig party, and F. began public life by supporting the absurd and unconstitutional defiance which the Commons, led by the Government, gave to the constituency of Middlesex, which had thrice returned Wilkes as member. Under Lord North's Ministry he was successively Lord of the Admiralty and Lord of the Treasury. A difference with the Premier on the Royal Marriage Bill was followed in 1774 by a serious quarrel relating to the censure of Woodfall, Horne Tooke's publisher. F. in consequence joined the Whig or Rockingham party, and came under the influence of Burke. This influence fixed and intensified his political principles, but though his reputation as an orator continued to grow, the scandal of his life (his father had recently paid £140,000 for the gaming debts of a single season) deprived him of moral leadership. He had, however, inherited the Walpole traditions of peace and civil liberty; and when in 1782 General Conway's motion for ending the American war was carried, and Rockingham, through the mediation of his rival Shelburne, constructed a cabinet, F. became Foreign Secretary. When Shelburne, the representative of Lord Chatham's policy, succeeded, F. with Keppel and Cavendish withdrew. By a junction of Lord North with the old Whig party a vote of censure was obtained (February 1783). The Portland or Coalition Ministry which followed was wrecked by the animosity of the king to F.'s East India Bill. From 1784 to 1792 F. was therefore reduced to the leadership of a powerful opposition to Pitt, and delivered great speeches on the Westminster Scrutiny, the Regency Bill, the Libel Bill, and the Russian Armament. He spoke with great effect against the abatement of impeachment by dissolution of Parliament, by which legal fiction it was attempted to defeat the trial of Warren Hastings, of which F. was a manager. In 1789 he moved the repeal of the Test and Corporation Acts, and supported Wilberforce in his holy crusade. The taking of the Bastille was hailed by him 'as the best event the world had seen.' The debate on the Quebec Government Bill (1791) severed the friendship that had so long existed between him and Burke. The Reign of Terror must have caused hesitation in the most sanguine minds; but F. from 1792 to 1797 vigorously pled the cause of peace with France. In 1795 he led the agitation against the Treason and Sedition Bills. He seconded the Grey motion for reform, called attention to the grievances of the Irish Catholics, and exposed the tyranny of crown and bench in the Scotch cases of Muir and Palmer. Though thoroughly persuaded of the advantages and necessity of party government, he retired into private life in 1797, saying that the House of Commons had ceased to discuss. His time until 1802 was occupied with literature and sport, and the beginning of his *History of James I.*, which he intended as an antidote to the brilliant misrepresentations of Hume's Charles I. After the death of Pitt in January 1806, F. again became Foreign Secretary under Granville. A further negotiation for peace, the passing of the Limited Service Bill, and a resolution to abolish the slave trade were the fruits of this short season of power. He died 13th September 1806. Opinions have varied much as to F.'s true character. Walpole describes him as first in Parliament, at Newmarket, and at the gaming-table. Pitt spoke of him as a magician. Mackintosh and Burke have confessed the splendid power of his passionate speech. Hazlitt and Bulwer Lytton accuse him of deserting Lord North through pique. He was doubtless the great champion of parliamentary freedom at a critical time, and Catherine II. did right to place his bust with those of Cicero and Demosthenes. He had the instinct of civil and religious liberty, and Villemain truly says he was the only English statesman who understood the French Revolution. His speeches were edited by Erskine (6 vols. Lond. 1815). See Lord John Russell's *Life and Times of F.* (2 vols. Lond. 1856–59), and *Memorials and Correspondence of F.* (4 vols. Lond. 1853–57).

Fox, George, the founder of the Society of Friends (q. v.), born at Drayton, in Leicestershire, in 1624, was first a shepherd and afterwards a shoemaker. About the age of nineteen he became deeply convinced that he had received a special call from

God, and began to wander through the country rapt in religious dreams. His garb was somewhat grotesque, consisting of a single garment of leather made by himself. About 1646 he resolved to give up attendance on Church ordinances, and content himself with the teaching of the 'Spirit.' Two years later he appeared as a preacher at Manchester, urging men to trust in the 'inner light,' and to cast aside as useless or pernicious the forms and ceremonies of worship. This was the burden of all his discourses. For upwards of forty years he may be said to have done nothing else than beseech men in a pathetic, wistful, and half-bewildered fashion to have faith in the 'inner light. The dogma-loving Puritans could not endure his wayward mysticism, and in spite of the fine moral simplicity and purity of his character, he and his 'people' suffered a good deal of persecution. In 1655 F. was brought to London, and had an interview with Cromwell, who recognised an honest soul under the 'leathern hull,' and dismissed him in a friendly way. In 1669 he married the widow of Judge Fell, one of his converts in Lancashire, after which he went to America, and on his return paid a visit to the N. of Germany. Before his death, 13th January 1690–91, the 'Society of Friends' had acquired considerable importance. F.'s writings, including his curious autobiographical *Journal*, were collected and published in 3 vols. 1694–1706. See also the Biographies of Marsh (Lond. 1847), Janney (Philadelphia, 1853), Watson (Lond. 1860), and Spurgeon (Lond. 1866).

Fox, sometimes **Foxe, John**, the martyrologist, was born at Boston, Lincolnshire, in 1517. Educated at Oxford, he was elected to a fellowship of Magdalen College, but having accepted the doctrines of the Reformation, was expelled from it, July 22, 1545. After some time he became a tutor, first in the family of Sir Thomas Lucy of Charlecote, and then in that of the Duchess of Richmond. In the reign of Edward VI., F. was ordained a deacon of the Reformed Church, but in that of Mary had to flee to the Continent, living for a time at Basel as a corrector of the press. Returning to England in the reign of Elizabeth, he held various offices in the Church, including a prebendal stall in the cathedral of Salisbury, and would have received further preferment, had he not been suspected of holding Nonconformist opinions, a belief strengthened by his refusal to subscribe to the Thirty-Nine Articles, and his interceding with the Queen for some Anabaptists who had been condemned to death. He died in 1587. F., who in early life had written some Latin 'Moralities,' one of which, *De Christo Triumphante*, was printed at London in 1557, and who was towards the end of his career a keen ecclesiastical controversialist, is remembered chiefly for his *History of the Acts and Monuments of the Church*, popularly styled *Foxe's Book of Martyrs* (first Latin ed. Stras. 1554; 2d Latin ed. enlarged, Basel, 1559, of which the English translation of 1563 was made), which has gone through innumerable editions, and is still looked upon as one of the manuals of Protestant literature. The first idea of the work was suggested to him by Lady Jane Grey. The truth of many of its statements has been questioned by Catholic critics, who have styled it *la légende dorée de F.*

Fox, William Johnston, an orator and preacher, the son of a small farmer, was born at Uggeshall, near Wrentham, Suffolk, March 1786. He was educated for the Independent ministry, but went over to the Unitarians, and finally took an independent position as a Rationalist, preaching for some time at the South Street Chapel, Finsbury. He was one of the earliest members of the Anti-Corn-Law League, the object of which he advocated with great ability, both as a speaker and a writer. He was returned to Parliament in 1847 for Oldham, which he represented with short intervals until his death, in London, June 3, 1864. F. was a Radical in politics, a 'Theist' in religion, a clear and vigorous writer, and a singularly effective orator. His chief works are *Letters of a Norwich Weaver-Boy*, *Letters addressed chiefly to the Working Classes*—telling political pamphlets—and *Religious Ideas*. F. was a frequent contributor to the *Westminster Review* and other periodicals. An edition of his selected works was published in 1868 (12 vols.).

Fox-Bats (*Pteropidæ*), the name applied to a family and section of *Cheiroptera* (q. v.) or bats. They are so named from the resemblance of the head to that of the fox. They are Frugivorous or fruit-eating, and possess a long pointed snout. The ears are of moderate size, and destitute of appendages. Incisors and cutting canine teeth are developed in both jaws. The F.-B. feed chiefly on vegetable matters, but they also subsist on small birds and mammals. The molar teeth have blunt tuberculate crowns. The tail is short or absent. Of the F.-B. the best-known species is the Kalong bat (*Pteropus edulis*) in the Eastern Archipelago, which attains an expanse of wing from 4 to 5 feet. The F.-B. are absent from the New World.

Fox'glove. See DIGITALIS.

Fox'hound. See FOX-HUNTING.

Fox'-Hunting, a thoroughly English sport, pursued by the middle and upper classes with courage and ardour, especially in the autumnal and winter months. It demands much organisation, not only as regards the breed and quality of the dogs employed, but in the training and appointment of the men connected with the pack and with the management of the dogs in the sport. The horses employed in hunting require also a certain degree of training and breeding; the qualities which render a horse a first-rate hunter being courage, agility, and a certain fondness or disposition for the work. The management and control of the pack of foxhounds is vested in a gentleman named the *master*, the appointment being generally given to some prominent country gentleman, who is elected by the subscribers to the pack, and who holds office either for a stated number of years, or for such time as may suit his tastes and convenience. Under the master are the *huntsman* and several *whippers-in* or *whips*. On the former devolves the duty of attending to the health of the dogs, and of seeing that they are properly housed and fed. He also directs their journey to the field, and exercises supreme control over their movements in the chase. The huntsman, in fact, is the active director of the sport, and is regarded as the leading character in the field, and as one whose directions all are expected to follow. The *whips* are so named from the fact that part of their duties consists in 'whipping' or bringing up lagging hounds to the front. But this duty—discharged in some instances by the second whipper-in—is a very subsidiary one in the office of *whip*, and this latter official may be said to be simply a qualified assistant to the huntsman himself. The dogs used in hunting the fox are named foxhounds, and 'Stonehenge' has justly remarked that 'the modern foxhound is one of the most wonderful animals in creation.' His acute scent, his wonderful sagacity in comprehending the difficulties of any position in the field, his efforts to circumvent the natural cunning of the fox, his speed and power of endurance, form traits which only require mention to be thoroughly appreciated. The breeding and training of foxhounds are tasks of no ordinary difficulty; the modern foxhound representing in itself a combination of a great variety of breeds. The average height of these dogs, in their thoroughbred state, is from 20 to 25 inches, and those forming a pack are usually selected of the same height. Their speed is sometimes very great. 'Bluecap,' a famous hound, ran over the Beacon course at Newmarket—a distance of 4 miles, 1 furlong, and 132 yards—in 8 minutes and a few seconds. The racehorse 'Flying Childers' ran the same distance in about 30 seconds less time. The country best adapted for F.-H. is that in which level and undulating ground, with a fair mixture of pasturage and plantation, are intermingled. The 'earths' or burrows of the foxes are duly 'stopped' by the *earth-stopper* or gamekeeper on the night preceding the hunt, after the foxes have left their dens on their nocturnal foraging expeditions. The foxes, shut out of their homes, usually seek refuge in thickets, and the localities of the 'stopped' earths being duly noted, the efforts of the huntsman are directed to these spots. The huntsmen and the hounds being assembled in the neighbourhood of the coverts, the dogs are 'thrown off,' and are encouraged to seek the fox in his temporary lair, the huntsman and whip following the pack. The master's duty chiefly consists in regulating the acts of the riders, in conformity with the huntsman's operations. Occasionally the riders may assist in searching the covert, and those outside watch eagerly for the first symptoms on the part of the hounds of having found or 'scented' a fox. Some old hound acts as leader, and betokens the presence of the fox or scent by a peculiar whimper. Sometimes a fox may be at once seized and *chopped* or torn to pieces, before he can escape; an incident which is of course a catastrophe so far as the sport is concerned. Sooner or later the fox leaves or *breaks cover*, and is allowed to gain a certain distance from the hounds. The person who notices his escape then gives the *View halloa!* as the warning cry is named. The *Tallyho!* of the huntsman is then heard, and the hounds are called together by the sound of the horn, while the whips collect the stragglers. Speedily the dogs *settle* to their work, and the pack, accompanied by the riders, are soon in *full cry* after the quarry. The sport thus begun continues to increase in excitement, the chase leading the huntsmen over mile after mile of country, swiftly or slowly as the scent is good or fails. In the latter case the dogs are said to be *at fault*, the sportsmen in such a case remaining at some distance, while the huntsman endeavours to set them once more on the scent. If the scent be recovered, the chase is resumed; but if it be lost, a fresh fox is drawn. The rider first *in* at the death of the fox lashes the hounds off, and secures the head, feet or *pads*, and tail or *brush* of the fox. The midland counties of England and Scotland are the chief localities in which the sport is carried on to any great extent. Large sums of money, amounting to thousands of pounds, may be annually spent on a pack of hounds and their maintenance.

Fox River, the name of two streams in the United States, both rising in Wisconsin, the more important of which, also known as the Neenah, is connected by canal with Wisconsin river, flows into Green Bay, after a course of 150 miles, is improved by means of a system of locks and jetties, and forms the connecting link between the great lakes and the Mississippi and its tributaries. The other flows S. and S.W. into the Illinois river, provides ample water-power, and has a course of 200 miles.

Fox-Shark (*Carcharias* or *Alopias vulpes*), a species of shark, also known as the 'thresher-shark,' from the excessive development of the upper lobe of the tail, which is thus more typically *heterocercal* or unequally lobed than in other sharks. This fish occurs in the Atlantic Ocean and Mediterranean Sea, and has been frequently found off the English coasts. It attains an average length of 12 or 13 feet. Its food consists of herrings and other fishes. The colour is slaty blue above, and the same hue mottled with white prevails on the under parts. The snout is shortened and conical, and the gill-openings are small, the hinder gill-slit being placed over the pectoral fins. The teeth are flat and three-sided. The tail is used as a defensive weapon. The other names applied to this fish are *sea-fox* and *sea-ape*.

Foxtail Grass (*Alopecurus*), a genus of *Gramineæ* or grasses having a *spiked panicle* of flowers with equal *glumes*. The meadow F.-G. (*A. pratensis*) is a familiar meadow-grass, and attains a height of from 1 to 2 feet. Another species is the jointed F.-G. (*A. geniculatus*), which has its culm bent at the joints. The slender F.-G. (*A. agrestis*) grows favourably on sandy and dry soils. *A. nigricans* is a European and N. Asiatic species, which thrive in Britain.

Foy, Maximilien Sébastien, a French general and orator, was born at Ham, in Picardy, February 3, 1775. He first served in 1792 under Dumouriez, and subsequently under Moreau, Massena, and finally Napoleon himself, gaining distinction by his daring bravery. Although opposed to the ambition of Napoleon, his ability was such that he was promoted to high and important commands. He successfully defended Constantinople in 1807 against Admiral Duckworth, became brigadier-general in Portugal in 1808, fought at Salamanca in 1812, was severely wounded at Orthez in 1814, and received his fifteenth wound at Waterloo. Retiring from military life, F. was elected in 1819 member of the Chamber of Deputies for the department of Aisne, and became very popular on account of his advocacy of constitutional liberty, his eloquence, and his political and economical knowledge. His health broke down, however, and he died at Paris, November 28, 1825. In 1826 appeared two volumes of his speeches, with a biography, and in 1827 his unfinished *Histoire de la Guerre de la Péninsule*, edited by Madame F. See Vidal's *Vie Militaire et Politique du Général F.* (1826).

Foy'ers, a mountain stream in Inverness-shire, rises in the Monadhliadh, flows N. through Strath Errick, and enters Loch Ness, 10 miles N.N.E. of Fort Augustus, after a course of 15 miles. It is famed on account of the two falls near its mouth, 90 and 30 feet high respectively, the former of which is a magnificent cascade, romantically hidden in a wild gorge.

Foyle, Lough, an extensive arm of the Atlantic in the N. of Ireland, separates Donegal from Derry, is of triangular shape, and has a length from N.E. to S.W. of 16 miles. It contracts at its mouth to 1 mile, is navigable to vessels of 200 tons along its W. side, but on the E. is very shallow. On the flat eastern beach was measured the base line of the Irish survey. The Irish North-Western Railway is continued from Londonderry completely round its E. shore.

Fra Angel'ico (often named *Giovanni da Fiesole*, but whose baptismal name appears to have been *Giovanni Guido Santi-Tosini*) was born at Mugello, a few miles N.E. of Florence, in 1387. In 1409 he entered the order of Predicants at the convent of Fiesole, and lived there eighteen years, during which he beautifully illuminated many of the books used in the choir, and painted a large number of frescoes and easel pictures in distemper. Invited to Florence in 1436, he there decorated the convent of San Marco and other public edifices with frescoes. About 1445 Pope Eugenius IV. called him to Rome to decorate a private chapel in the Vatican and the cathedral of Orvieto with frescoes. At the command of Niccolo V., the successor of Eugenius, and a liberal patron of the arts, F. A., leaving his works unfinished at Orvieto, repaired to Rome to decorate a chapel to be used as the Pope's private oratory. There he spent the remainder of his days, and died in 1455. He was offered the archbishopric of Florence by Niccolo, but declined it on the plea that to govern or to lead were equally incompatible with his nature. His art is distinguished by an ecstatic reverential sentiment, the truth and purity of which made his works the model for religious painters of his own and succeeding generations. Every work he began with prayer, and every original idea was welcomed as a divine inspiration. F. A. may be studied to most advantage in the convent of San Marco, Florence. Here are his 'Christ Appearing to St. Dominic,' 'The Image of St. Thomas Aquinas,' 'St. Peter the Martyr,' a 'Christ,' in which the expression of the features reaches the sublime. Here also is his greatest fresco, the 'Passion,' a work embracing twenty-three large figures, with Christ in the centre, and saints and founders of religious orders ranged below. Placed around are numerous figures and medallion portraits. All these works are in excellent preservation. Vasari has said that F. A.'s saints and angels 'must look the same in heaven.' The chapel of Niccolo V. is decorated on three sides with frescoes illustrating the lives of St. Stephen and St. Lawrence, works unrivalled in finish and in sweetness and harmony of colour, and evincing a command of light and shade which almost justifies the opinion that in chiaroscuro F. A. anticipated Correggio.

Fracasto'ro, Girola'mo, a physician and poet, distinguished for his miscellaneous learning, was born at Verona in 1483. At the age of nineteen he was Professor of Dialectic at Padua. His most famous work is a poem in three books, *Syphilis, sive de Morbo Gallico*, in excellent Latin verse, published at Verona in 1530, and frequently reprinted. Other works are *De Vini Temperatura* (Ven. 1534), *Homocentricorum* (Ven. 1535), *De Sympathia*, and *De Contagionibus* (Ven. 1546). F. died 8th August 1553. His *Opera Omnia* were published at Venice in 1555.

Frac'tion (Lat. *fractio*, 'a breaking into parts'), in arithmetic, is one or more aliquot parts or sub-multiples of unity. For instance, divide any magnitude into *eight* equal parts, and take *five* of these parts: this quantity is the F. *five-eighths*, and is written $\frac{5}{8}$, the lower number being termed the *denominator* and the upper the *numerator*. Such an expression as $\frac{11}{8}$ is termed an *improper* F., because it is greater than unity, being really *one* and $\frac{3}{8}$. It is immaterial whether we regard $\frac{5}{8}$ as being *five* of those parts *eight* of which make up unity, or as being the eighth part of five units. It is this latter conception which is chiefly present to the mind in algebra, in which a F. is simply a symbol of division, $\frac{a}{b}$ being equivalent to and treated as $a \div b$. From this definition the following rules for the four fundamental operations with respect to fractions follow naturally: $\frac{a}{b}+\frac{c}{d}=\frac{ad}{bd}+\frac{bc}{bd}=\frac{ad+bc}{bd}$; $\frac{a}{b}\times\frac{c}{d}=\frac{ac}{bd}$; $\frac{a}{b}\div\frac{c}{d}=\frac{a}{b}\times\frac{d}{c}=\frac{ad}{bc}$. For the usual rules for reduction and combination, reference must be made to an elementary treatise on algebra or arithmetic. When the denominator is a power of *ten*, the F. is called a *Decimal* F. (q. v.).

A *continued* F. is one which has in its denominator a F. which again in its denominator has a F., and so on. Such as

$$F = a + \cfrac{1}{b + \cfrac{1}{c + \cfrac{1}{d + \cfrac{1}{e + \&c.}}}}$$

or, more conveniently, $F = a + \frac{1}{b +}\, \frac{1}{c +}\, \frac{1}{d +}\, \frac{1}{e +}$ &c.

If the *quotients* a, b, c, &c., are finite in number, then we have a *terminating* continued F., and any ordinary F. may be expressed as such. Conversely, by breaking off at any quotient, the continued F. may be expressed as an ordinary F. If we write $a + \frac{1}{b} = B$, $a + \frac{1}{b +}\, \frac{1}{c} = C$, $a + \frac{1}{b +}\, \frac{1}{c +}\, \frac{1}{d} = D$, &c., B, C, D, &c. are termed *convergents* of the continued F., and these convergents are alternately greater and less in value than the F. Further, each convergent is nearer in value to the F. than the one immediately preceding it is, so that they may be said to oscillate from excess to defect with ever-decreasing amplitude. The theory of this branch of pure mathematics has been much studied by Wallis, Euler, Legendre, Sylvester, &c.

A *vanishing F.* is an algebraic F. which for a certain value of the variable takes the form $\frac{0}{0}$, or $\frac{\infty}{\infty}$. For instance, $\frac{x^2 - 1}{x - 1}$ and $\frac{\log. x}{x - 1}$ both become $\frac{0}{0}$, when $x = 1$. Now this shows that there is a common factor in numerator and denominator which becomes zero for the special case. In the first example this common factor is evidently $x - 1$, and the value of the F. becomes $x + 1 = 2$, when $x = 1$. The value of the second example may be found by putting $x - 1 = z$, when the expression becomes $\frac{\log. (1 + z)}{z} = \frac{1}{z}\left(z - \frac{z^2}{2} + \frac{z^3}{3} - \ldots\right) = 1$ when $z = 0$, that is when $x = 1$.

Frac'ture, in mineralogy, is the surface exhibited by a crystal when broken in a direction not coinciding with the planes of cleavage. The terms *conchoidal*, *even*, *uneven*, *hackly*, *splintery*, are used to distinguish the several kinds of fractures.

Fractures are almost invariably the result of direct or indirect external violence, the former being the more serious lesion, and generally complicated with considerable mischief to the soft parts. When caused by indirect violence, the bone is broken by being snapped between a resisting medium on one side, and the weight of the body on the other. F. are predisposed to by old age, cancerous and syphilitic diseases, scurvy, fragilitas ossium, frosty weather, &c. F. are called *simple* when the bone is broken across; *impacted* when one fragment is wedged into another; *comminuted* when the bone is broken into several fragments; *compound* when the soft parts covering the broken ends of bone are torn through so that the fracture communicates with the surface of the body; *complicated* when conjoined with other circumstances which may be of more importance than the fracture itself, as injury to some important internal organ, the laceration of a principal artery, or a dislocation. In general, F. are easily detected, the most obvious symptoms being increased mobility, displacement conjoined with crepitus, and a peculiar rough feeling caused by the broken extremities grating against each other. A fractured bone is ultimately united by the deposition of new bone around, within, and lastly between the broken fragments, the material for repair being termed *callus*. The callus deposited round the fracture is called *provisional*, as it merely serves as a wrapper and support, and is afterwards in great part reabsorbed, while that deposited between the broken ends is permanently left, and is called *definitive callus*. Treatment:—Wherever the fracture may be, the broken ends of the bone must be brought into as perfect apposition as possible; appropriate appliances must be adapted to prevent the recurrence of displacement; and the constitutional condition of the patient must be properly attended to. Various appliances are in use to prevent the recurrence of displacement. Splints are generally made of wood, pasteboard, gutta percha, or iron; and the bandage with which the limb is enveloped may be converted into a splint by means of starch or dextrine, or a shell may be formed for it by plaster of Paris. A simple fracture is pretty firmly united by the sixth or eighth week, but formerly three or four months elapsed before union of compound fractures took place. When compound fractures are treated by the antiseptic process, introduced by Professor Lister of Edinburgh, union takes place almost as speedily as in the case of simple F.

Fra Diav'olo, a name better known among musical connoisseurs than among students of history, was the *soubriquet* of one Michele Pezza, an Italian adventurer, born in Calabria about 1760, and who successively became a weaver, a soldier, a monk, and a brigand. His cruelty and rapacity were almost equalled by his ingenuity and resource. When pursued, he retired to the Calabrian mountains, amid which he frequently defeated the armed forces sent against him, though these were numerically superior to his own. Ardently loyal, he warmly espoused the cause of the royal house of Naples against the French in the beginning of the century. He was, however, taken prisoner, and executed in November 1806, for an attempt to raise a rebellion against the invaders. The name has been immortalised in Auber's famous opera, though his hero is a 'Devil' of much milder disposition than the Calabrian brigand.

Frame-Bridge, a name sometimes given to a timber bridge with trussed girders similar to those now used frequently in iron bridges. See BRACES, LATTICE GIRDER, TRUSS.

Fram'lingham (*i.e.*, 'strangers' town'), a market-town of Suffolk, on the Alde, 14 miles N.N.E. of Ipswich, and 90 N.E. of London by railway. It has extensive remains of an old castle, with thirteen towers, several of which are about 60 feet high, and a gateway carved with heraldic devices. To this the Princess Mary retired when Lady Jane Grey was proclaimed queen. The church of F. is built of flint, has a fine tower 100 feet high with a peal of eight bells, and contains many illustrious tombs and monuments, including those of the Howards, Fitzroys, &c. The Albert Memorial Middle Class College, for boys, was opened in 1865. F. has some trade in corn, and is the terminus of a branch line of the Great Eastern Railway. Pop. (1871) 2569.

Franc, the current silver coin of France, introduced in 1795 to supersede the *livre tournois*. Its value is very nearly $\frac{1}{25}$ of a pound sterling, or about 9¾d. The coin has also been adopted by Belgium and Switzerland, and by Italy under the name of *lira nuova*.

Francavill'a, a town in the province of Bari, S. Italy, 23 miles W. of Brindisi, is the seat of a college, and has cotton and woollen industries. The public buildings comprise three hospitals and many convents and churches. Pop. 17,600.

France (Lat. *Francia*, Ger. *Frankreich*), one of the largest and most important countries of Europe, extends from 42° 20′ to 51° 5′ N. lat., and from 8° 15′ to 4° 54′ W. long. It is bounded N. by the English Channel and the Strait of Dover; W. by the Bay of Biscay; S. by the Pyrenees and the Mediterranean Sea. The E. boundary begins in the S. with the Maritime Alps, the line running along the principal ridge from Colla Lunga to Mont Blanc. It then descends to the Lake of Geneva, and curving round the canton of Geneva follows the Jura mountains to the pass at Belfort, crossing which it keeps along the ridge of the Vosges. To the S. of the Dondon in the Lower Vosges it leaves the range, and ceasing to depend on natural features, becomes an arbitrary line, passing between Nancy and Metz, and holding a northwesterly direction, crosses the Meuse, Sambre, and Scheldt, and reaches the Straits of Dover 8 miles from Dunkirk. The country, which is of hexagonal shape, is extremely compact, its greatest extension from N. to S. being 600 miles, and from E. to W. 550, while in a diagonal direction from Finistère to Mentone it measures nearly 700 miles. The coast, which is flat and marshy in the S. along the Mediterranean, and bold and broken in the N.W., has an extreme length of 1500 miles, including Corsica. Among the promontories are the Gris-Nez, in Pas-de-Calais, the nearest point to England; Cap la Hague and Pointe de Barfleur in the N. of Manche; Pointes St. Matthieu and Raz in Finistère; and in the Mediterranean the Caps Cépet, Cicie, Couronne, &c. The coast is in part fringed with small islands, of which the chief are Corsica, now forming a department, Ushant and Belle Isle to the S. of Morbihan, Noirmoutier and Ile d'Yeu to the W. of Vendée, Ré and Oléron to the W. of Charente-Inférieure, the isles of Hyères and Lerins off the coast of Var. F. comprises

$\frac{1}{18}$th part of the area of Europe. The populations and areas of its divisions are as follows, according to the *Almanach de Gotha* for 1876 :—

Departments.	Pop. (1872).	Area in sq. miles.	Chief towns.
Ain	363,290	2258	Bourg.
Aisne	552,439	2830	Laon.
Allier	390,812	2830	Moulins.
Alpes, Basses	139,332	2680	Digne.
Alpes, Hautes	118,898	2136	Gap.
Alpes-Maritimes	199,037	2680	Nice.
Ardèche	380,277	1133	Privas.
Ardennes	320,217	2021	Mezières.
Ariège	246,298	2847	Foix.
Aube	255,687	1351	Troyes.
Aude	285,927	2438	Carcassonne.
Aveyron	402.474	2402	Rodez.
Belfort, Territoire de	56,781	3234	Belfort.
Bouches-du-Rhône	554,911	971	Marseille.
Calvados	454,012	1130	Caen.
Cantal	231,867	2216	Aurillac,
Charente	367,520	2200	Angoulême.
Charente-Inférieure	465,653	2740	La Rochelle.
Cher	335,392	2800	Bourges.
Corrèze	302,746	2265	Tulle.
Corse	258,507	2378	Ajaccio.
Côte-d'Or	374,510	3380	Dijon.
Côtes-du-Nord	622,295	3660	St. Brieuc.
Creuse	274,663	2153	Guéret.
Dordogne	480,141	2536	Périgueux.
Doubs	291,251	3018	Besançon.
Drôme	320,417	2519	Valence.
Eure	377,874	2300	Evreux.
Eure-et-Loire	282,622	2268	Chartres.
Finistère	642,963	2595	Quimper.
Gard	420,131	2252	Nîmes.
Garonne, Haute	479,362	2429	Toulouse.
Gers	284,717	2425	Auch.
Gironde	705,149	3761	Bordeaux.
Hérault	429,878	2393	Montpellier.
Ille-et-Vilaine	589,532	2597	Rennes.
Indre	277,693	2624	Châteauroux.
Indre-et-Loire	317,027	2360	Tours.
Isère	575,784	3200	Grenoble.
Jura	287,634	1924	Lons-le-Saunier.
Landes	300,528	3599	Mont-de-Marsan.
Loir-et-Cher	268,801	2452	Blois.
Loire	550,611	1838	St. Etienne,
Loire, Haute	308,732	1917	Le Puy.
Loire-Inférieure	602,206	2654	Nantes.
Loiret	353,021	2614	Orléans.
Lot	281,404	2012	Cahors.
Lot-et-Garonne	319,289	2067	Agen.
Lozère	135,190	1996	Mende.
Maine-et-Loire	518,471	2749	Angers.
Manche	544,776	2289	St. Lo.
Marne	386,157	3154	Châlon-sur-Marne.
Marne, Haute	251,196	2401	Chaumont.
Mayenne	350,637	1996	Laval.
Meurthe-et-Moselle	365,137	2025	Nancy.
Meuse	284.725	2405	Bar-le-Duc.
Morbihan	490,352	2623	Vannes.
Nièvre	339,917	2632	Nevers.
Nord	1,447,764	2193	Lille.
Oise	396,804	2260	Beauvais.
Orne	398,250	2354	Alençon.
Pas-de-Calais	761,158	2550	Arras.
Puy-de-Dôme	566,463	3108	Clermont.
Pyrénées, Basses	426,700	2943	Pau.
Pyrénées, Hautes	235,156	1749	Tarbes.
Pyrénées-Orientales	191,856	1592	Perpignan.
Rhône	670,247	1077	Lyon.
Saône, Haute	303,088	2062	Vesoul.
Saône-et-Loire	598,344	3302	Macon.
Sarthe	446,603	2396	Le Mans.
Savoie	267,958	2224	Chambéry.
Savoie, Haute	273,027	1667	Annecy.
Seine	2,220,060	184	Paris.
Seine-Inférieure	790,022	2329	Rouen.
Seine-et-Marne	341,490	2215	Melun.
Seine-et-Oise	580,180	2164	Versailles.
Sèvres, Deux	331,243	2316	Niort.
Somme	557,015	2379	Amiens.
Tarn	352,718	2217	Albi.
Tarn-et-Garonne	221,610	1436	Montauban.
Var	293,757	2349	Draguignan.
Vaucluse	263,451	1370	Avignon.
Vendée	401,446	2588	Napoléon Vendée.
Vienne	320,598	2691	Poitiers.
Vienne, Haute	322,447	2168	Limoges.
Vosges	392,988	2269	Epinal.
Yonne	363,608	2791	Auxerre.
	36,102,921	204,300	

Physical Aspect.—The surface of F. is on the whole a somewhat monotonous plain, inclining gently downwards from the Alps and the Pyrenees in a north-westerly direction to the Atlantic. It is rarely marked either by grandeur or variety. The mountain ranges may be divided into (1) an outer girdle, comprising the Pyrenees in the S., and the Vosges, Jura, and Alps in the E.; (2) the range of the Cevennes (q. v.), which stretch from the Pyrenees in a line parallel with the range of Lyon, and then N. along the western side of the Rhone basin, to be continued by the Côte-d'-Or and Plateau de Langres in a direction N.E. to the Vosges; (3) the mountains of Auvergne, separating the basins of the Dordogne and Lot in the S. from that of the Loire in the N., and sending off Mont Margeride towards the Cevennes in a south-easterly line, and several low ranges, as the Hauteurs de Gatine, in a direction N.W. and parallel with the Indre and other southern affluents of the Loire; and (4) the mountains of Bretagne, which run in sinuous masses E. and W., and extend into Lower Normandy, sending a spur N.N.E. into the peninsula of Cotentin. The Alps extend for about 280 miles along the frontier, and contain the highest summits in France, as Mont Blanc in Haute Savoie (15,781 feet), Grand Pelvoux (13,440), Mont Genèvre (11,782), and Mont Viso (12,586). Many ramifications trend E. towards the Rhone, forming a wild highland region, in which are the Alps of Vallais, Faucigny, Chablais, &c. The Jura range has a sharp rocky contour, and stretches N.N.E. for 450 miles. The Vosges, to the N. of the Jura, gradually lose the Alpine character, and are noted for their vast forests of beech, fir, &c. A considerable depression (Valdieu), known as the Pass of Belfort, divides the Jura mountains from the Vosges, and forms the great eastern gateway to F. Along the N.E. boundary the country rises to the wild, broken plateau of the Ardennes (q. v.). The Pyrenees (q. v.), though inferior in height to the Alps, are wilder and gloomier, consisting of sharp conical groups and ridges, crossed by difficult passes. The Cevennes have a length of 295 miles, and are precipitous mountains, rising in the S.E. in Mont Meyen to a height of 5794 feet, and sinking gradually in the N., where they give place to the Côte-d'Or, on the slopes of which are produced some of the finest wines of France. The mountains of Auvergne are volcanic, and include the Puy de Saucy (6187), Cantal (6093), Mont Dore (6188), and Puy de Dôme (4806). The chain of the Puys extending N. is a singular series of extinct volcanoes (*chéires*), now clad with verdure, but whose craters and lava-streams are easily distinguishable. To the S. of Auvergne stretches the vast expanse of the *Causses*, calcareous plateaux deeply cut by the Lot, Tarn, Aveyron, and other streams.

Hydrography.—The three great rivers of F. flowing W., the Seine, Loire, and Garonne, have their sources in the Cevennes. The Rhone, entering F. after issuing from the Lake of Geneva, flows S. on joining its great affluent, the Saône. The rivers to the N. of the Faucilles and Plateau de Langres, the Meuse, Moselle, and Scheldt, flow through Rhenish Prussia and Belgium to the Rhine or directly to the North Sea. F. has about 200 navigable streams, which are utilised to the extent of 5500 miles. Smaller rivers with basins of their own are the Somme and Orne, the Vilaine and Charente, and the Adour. Affluents of the Seine are the Aube, Oise, Yonne, and Marne; of the Loire, the Sarthe, Loiret, Allier, Maine; of the Garonne, the Dordogne, Lot, and Tarn; of the Rhone, besides the Saône, the Durance, Isère, Ain, and Ardèche. The extensive river system has been supplemented by 100 canals, with a total length of about 3000 miles. The rivers of F. flowing S. are liable to rapid inundations. Among the lakes of F., which are few, the largest are Bourget in Savoie, 12½ miles long and 2½ broad, and Grandlieu in the Vendée. There are numerous lagoons (*étangs*) along the coasts of Gascony, Roussillon, Languedoc, and especially about the mouth of the Rhone.

Climate.—Lying mainly between the annual isotherms 50°–60° F., F. enjoys a singularly fine climate. The climate of the N. generally corresponds to that of the S. of England, but in the S. the winters are much shorter and milder, and the sky is almost invariably clear. Along the Mediterranean the mean temperature is 57°. The regions towards the Alps and the Pyrenees are exposed to wild tempests and piercing winds. In the Rhone valley the temperature is subject to sudden change, owing to the alternations of the hot blast of the sirocco from the S., and the cold impetuous mistral from the N.W. The annual fall of rain on the W. coast is 24 inches, on the S. 23, on the N. 22. The number of rainy days on the W. coast is 152, in the interior 147, on the S. coast 66, at Paris 105.

Geology and Mineralogy.—The geology of F., like that of England, embraces almost all the stratified and non-stratified formations. The greatest area is covered by the Secondary strata, which prevail chiefly in the departments in the E. and N.E., stretching from the Mediterranean to the Moselle. In the W. also they extend from the Garonne to the mouth of the Seine, excluding Bretagne, which is mainly Silurian. The Tertiary series, next in extent to the Secondary, occurs between the Pyrenees and Garonne, and along the E. banks of the Rhone and Saône, and forms the extensive *Paris basin.* The Bretagne hills are chiefly of granitic rocks, and in Cantal and Puy-de-Dôme the rugged angular mountain masses are of volcanic origin. The coal deposits are most abundant in the central departments, in the Cevennes, and along the N.W. coast. French coal is unaccompanied by ironstone. Iron is widely distributed, and is wrought to the extent of half a million of tons yearly. Lead and silver are mined in Finistère, Isère, Puy-de-Dôme, &c.; copper in Haut-Rhin, the Rhone, and Basses-Pyrénées. In the E. the salt-mines are of great value. Besides marble and alabaster, there are also among the natural products some argentiferous galena, manganese, antimony, porcelain clay, lithographic stones, slates, &c. There are many mineral springs, of which the most frequented by invalids are in the Pyrenees at Vichy, Mont Dore, Plombières, and Bourbonne.

Botany and Agriculture.—In the number and variety of its indigenous plants F. surpasses all the other countries of Europe. Ruskin gives a verdict in favour of the trees of F. over those of all other countries for grace of stem and perfection of form in their transparent foliage, and for their beautiful modes of grouping and massing. The forest-trees occupy nearly one-eighth of the entire surface, and include the oak, beech, elm, ash, birch, &c. The largest forests are those of Compiègne, Chantilly, St. Germain, Fontainebleau, Orleans, and the Ardennes. Pines are plentiful in the Pyrenees and Landes, firs in the Jura and Vosges, larches in the Alps, cork-trees only in the basin of the Adour and in Provence. On the mountains of the S. and centre the chestnut abounds, and the walnut is found almost everywhere. The mulberry-tree, cultivated as support for the silkworm, is chiefly confined to the basin of the Rhone. Of the fruit-trees the principal is the vine, which grows in nearly all except the mountainous parts of F., yielding the best wines in Champagne, Burgundy, Franche-Comté, Dauphiné, Languedoc, and the Bordelais. Among the other fruits are the olive, apple, pear, cherry, plum, orange, citron, fig, pomegranate, lemon, and pistachio.

The country is essentially agricultural, and while the S. is rich in vines and fruits, the N. is equally productive in cereals. Everywhere, however, except between the Seine and the frontier of Belgium, husbandry is in a backward state. As a result of the equal division of land between the children of a proprietor, the area of F. is already held by some 5,550,000 owners, of whom 5,000,000 possess, on an average, not more than 6 acres each. One-half of the surface is under cultivation, one-seventh under forest and fruit trees, one-sixteenth is in permanent meadow, and one-seventh is unreclaimed waste. Three great agricultural belts traverse the country from S. to N. Thus the growth of the olive extends to a line stretching from the Corbières to the Alps of Dauphiné, the maize is cultivated to a boundary running from the island of Oléron to the middle of the Vosges, and the vine grows as far N. as the mouth of the Loire and the source of the Oise. More than a twentieth part of the surface is now covered with the vine, and the French have long borne the character of being the first of wine-makers. The production of wine greatly varies, and among the chief disturbing causes in recent years have been the fungus oïdium and the insect phylloxera. In 1869 the wine produced amounted to 1,364,000,000 gallons; and although of this quantity the great proportion is consumed in F., the value of the export to Great Britain alone, in 1874, was £2,616,355. The chief cereal in the W. is wheat, of which a considerable quantity is exported, and the average production of which is 275,000,000 bushels a year. In the S.W., as well as in the N., there is an extensive cultivation of flax and hemp, while the mulberry is a specialty in the vicinity of Lyon, the great centre of the silk manufacture. Among the other products are barley, oats, rye, buckwheat, hops, beans, peas, potatoes, and beetroot. There is also in the S. considerable production of rice, tobacco, madder, saffron, and other dye-stuffs.

Zoology and Live Stock.—The few wild animals yet remaining include the lynx, wolf, boar, chamois, and wild goat. Among the commoner animals are the roebuck, fox, marmot, ermine, hamster, squirrel, polecat, &c. Most kinds of game abound, but the red and fallow deer are scarce. Of birds the songsters resemble those of England; the more formidable birds of prey are the eagle, falcon, and buzzard. The flamingo haunts the Mediterranean shores. Several species of frogs, of vipers and harmless snakes, and of tortoises are the principal reptiles. Herring, mackerel, sardine, pilchard, turbot, sole, whiting, &c., are caught on the W. coast; tunny and anchovy in the Mediterranean, and salmon in the river estuaries. In the basin of the Arcachon, &c., there are large oyster and mussel beds. *Live stock.*—Of horses there are some 3,000,000; of asses, 413,000; of horned cattle, 10,000,000; of sheep, 35,000,000; and of swine, 5,000,000. The finest horses are reared in Normandy, while the Jura, the Vosges, and the basin of the Rhone are equally noted for their breeds of cattle. The yearly production of eggs is valued at £4,000,000, of which 28 per cent. is exported. There are £760,000 worth of honey and wax produced yearly in F. from 3,000,000 hives; the best honey is from Aude. Ardèche, Vaucluse, Drôme, and Gard are the great seats of the silk-culture, and previous to 1853, when disease broke out among the silkworms, the yield of cocoons amounted to 25,000 tons.

Industries.—F. has many and important industries, and of these perhaps the principal is the production of silks and velvets. Besides the raw silk produced at home, the amount yearly imported is over £4,000,000 worth. The weaving is done chiefly at Lyon, and in the department of the Rhone (120,000 looms), at St. Étienne and St. Chamond (ribbons and brocades), at Nîmes (light stuffs), and at Tours (silk furnishings). Silk lace is made at Alençon, Bayeux, Lille, Arras, &c. The northern towns (Rouen, St. Quentin, Amiens, &c.) are the most important seats of the cotton and woollen manufactures, while the linen industry is chiefly confined to Lille, Cambrai, &c. Since 1870 the making of printed calicoes has been limited to Paris and Rouen. Paris is noted for the variety and extent of its manufactures, including machinery, chemicals, porcelain, mirrors, clocks, watches, gloves, hosiery, *modes,* and above all jewellery. Another watchmaking centre is Besançon, where are mounted the pieces made in the Jura mountains. Over 200,000 tons of beet-sugar are produced (at Paris, Lille, Douai, &c.) from roots grown in F.; the total production is 325,000 tons. Raw sugar from abroad is refined at Marseille, Bordeaux, Havre, and Nantes. St. Étienne has great manufactures of firearms and hardware; Sèvres, of porcelain and glass wares; Rheims, of merinoes; Gobelins, of tapestry and cashmeres. Perfumery is extensively made in Paris and also in Provence.

Commerce.—In regard to commerce, F. ranks next to Britain among the countries of Europe. Its foreign trade nearly doubled in value from 1860 to 1874, rising from £167,000,000 to £304,000,000. In 1874 the total imports amounted to £148,720,440, and the exports to £155,110,120. The five chief articles of import were raw silk, corn and breadstuffs, wool, raw cotton, and coal. The exports were silk manufactures, woollens, wines, haberdashery and millinery, and refined sugar. The foreign commerce is mainly with Great Britain, Belgium, Germany, and Italy. The exports from Britain to F. in 1860 were £17,774,037; in 1870, £37,607,514; and in 1874, £46,518,571. The mercantile navy, exclusive of 'bateaux de la pêche côtière,' numbered in 1873 14,750 vessels of 1,064,379 tons, including 462 steamers of 141,520 tons and 57,510 horse-power. The chief ports are Bordeaux, Marseille, Havre, Nantes, Brest, Calais, Dunkirk, and Boulogne.

Railways, &c.—The growth of the modern railway system in F. dates from about 1840. The various railways, which are all subsidised by the state, are entirely in the hands of six great companies, viz., the Paris, Lyon, and Mediterranean, the Paris-Orleans, the Northern, the Southern, the Western, and the Eastern, having a total length (1874) of 12,822 miles, and a revenue of £31,894,612. At the end of 1874 there were 29,240 miles of telegraph lines, 78,174 of wires. The postal revenue from letters in 1873 was £3,560,550.

Finance.—The accounts of actual revenue and expenditure are seldom published by the Government of F. till the lapse of seven years. The last final account or *budget réglé* was for 1869, and in that year the real receipts were 1,798,187,538 francs, and the expenditure 1,740,213,970 francs, surplus 57,973,568 francs. In 1876 the budget gave the receipts at 2,575,028,582 francs, and the expenditure at 2,570,000,475 francs. The sources of the revenue are the direct and indirect taxes, arising from stamps, imposts, customs, *droits d'octroi*, produce of forests and telegraphs, &c. The enormous increase of expenditure of recent years has been met by the imposition of new indirect taxes on sugar, wines, salt, transports by railways, &c. In 1793 all the Government debts, annuities, &c., were consolidated in a perpetual five per cent. *rente*, entailing an annual charge of 174 millions of francs. At first the dividends were only paid in *assignats* or paper of fictitious value, but six years later the Government was forced to compound with its creditors, which it did out of the confiscated property of the Church and the nobles. Thus at the beginning of the 19th c. the annual charge of the national debt was reduced to £1,600,000, or less than one-tenth of that of Britain. By the date of the Restoration (1814) the interest of the debt had only increased to 63 millions of francs, but under Louis Philippe (1830–48) the indemnity to the *emigrés* and other heavy war-debts raised it to 244 millions. During the empire this sum was gradually augmented, and in 1870 it amounted to 358 millions, representing a capital of 11,500 millions of francs or £460,000,000. Having been more than doubled by the war of 1870–71, and by the indemnity to Germany of five milliards of francs, it amounted on 1st January 1875 to a nominal capital of £937,584,280, bearing an interest of £29,936,196. The number of fundholders (over four millions in 1875) has greatly increased of late years, and the debt seems to be steadily undergoing a process of complete subdivision among the freeholders in F. All the departments and many of the cities have their own budgets and debts. The nominal capital of the debt of Paris in 1875 was 78 millions sterling, including a loan of ten millions sterling issued in 1875.

Army.—The army has been reorganised on the basis of a law of 1872, which enacts universal liability to arms, and disallows substitution or exemption for money. The law of 1872 has been expanded and modified by two Acts of 1873 and 1875. All Frenchmen between the ages of twenty and forty, not legally exempted, are liable to serve for five years in the active army, for four in its reserve, for five in the territorial army, and for six in its reserve. Among the exempted are those physically unfit, men who are essential to the support of a family, the pupils of the École Polytechnique and the École Forestière, teachers in public schools, professors, ecclesiastics, and artists who have gained the Grand Prix of the Institute. Young men, by enlisting as self-supporting volunteers for a single year, may obtain exemption from service in the active army. Soldiers of the active army who have learnt their duties, and can read and write, may at the end of a year procure a furlough for an indefinite time. The total effective force of the French army in 1875 was 430,703, comprising 277,004 of infantry, 68,281 of cavalry, 65,096 of artillery, 10,930 engineers (*génie*), 9392 *équipages*. The expenditure for the army in 1869 was £15,359,192, in 1875 £19,751,052. The whole of F. is divided into eighteen military regions, each containing a mobilised *corp d'armée*. Included in the effective force are four regiments of Zouaves, three of Algerian *tirailleurs*, four of *chasseurs d'Afrique*, three of Spahis, and four battalions of the *Légion étrangère*. Since the German annexation of Metz and Strasbourg, the fortified *chefs-lieux* or headquarters have been Arras, Avignon, Bayonne, Besançon, Bourges, Brest, Cherbourg, Grenoble, Langres, La Rochelle, Havre, Lille, Lyon, Marseille, Montpellier, Nantes, Perpignan, Quiberon, Rouen, St. Omer, Toulon, and Toulouse.

Navy.—At the end of 1875 the navy was composed of 63 ironclads, of 700 guns and 29,250 horse-power; 264 unarmoured screw-steamers, of 1547 guns and 55,812 horse-power; 26 paddle-steamers, of 154 guns; and 113 sailing-vessels, of 672 guns. There are in active service 2 admirals, 15 vice-admirals, 31 rear-admirals, 100 captains of first-class men-of-war, 202 captains of frigates, 640 lieutenants, 505 ensigns, 1028 officers of marine, engineers, &c., and 28,431 men in the ironclads alone. The navy is manned partly by conscription, and there are constantly on the rolls some 150,000 names. In 1875 the National Assembly voted £1,200,000 for the construction of fifty vessels, to be applied within five years. The great Government docks are at Toulon, Brest, and Cherbourg.

Constitution and Government.—The present constitution, voted by the National Assembly of 1871, bears date of 25th February 1875, and vests the legislative power in an assembly of two Houses, a Chamber of Deputies of 532 members, and a Senate of 300 members, and the executive in a chief magistrate called President of the Republic. The Chamber of Deputies is elected by universal suffrage under the *Scrutin d'Arrondissement* of 11th November 1875. By this law every arrondissement elects one deputy, and if its population exceeds 100,000, an additional deputy for each 100,000, or portion thereof. Deputy and voter must each have the qualification of citizenship, while the former must be twenty-five, and the latter twenty-one, years of age. Of the 300 senators, 225 are elected by the departments and by the colonies, whilst 75 are nominated in the first instance by the National Assembly, and subsequently by the Chamber of Deputies. Those for the departments are elected for the term of nine years, the others for life. The only necessary qualifications of a senator are that he be a Frenchman and forty years of age. The two houses of legislature must remain in session for at least five months in the year. The President is bound to convoke an extraordinary meeting if it is demanded by one-half of the members of each chamber; he can also adjourn the Chambers, but the adjournment may not exceed the term of a month, nor occur in one session more than twice. The President, who is nominated for seven years, and is eligible for re-election, is elected by a majority of votes by the two Houses united in National Assembly. He has the control of the army, promulgates the laws when they are voted, and appoints to all civil and military posts. But every act of the President must be countersigned by a minister; and the ministers, of whom there are nine, are responsible to the Chambers for the general policy of the Government. The President is only responsible in case of high treason. His salary is fixed at £25,000, with an extra allowance for household expenses.

Administration of Justice.—A special Minister of State presides over the administration of justice. There are 357 *tribunaux de première instance* for the arrondissements, 2681 police courts, 216 tribunals of commerce, and 26 courts of appeal. A *cour de cassation*, of three chambers, pronounces on all the sentences of the police and assize courts; and a *haute cour de justice* gives final judgment on state offences. There are 387 department prisons, 21 central prisons, the two political prisons of Doullens and Belleisle, the *bagnes* of Toulon, and the penal settlements of Guiana and New Caledonia.

Education, &c.—Public education is entirely under the supervision of the Government, and to a great extent in the hands of the Roman Catholic clergy. An official report on the educational state of the nation was issued in 1872, and revealed the following results:—Nine-tenths of the children under six years of age, more than a fifth of the youth of both sexes under twenty, and over a third of the adult population of men and women are unable to read or write. Setting aside some four millions of children under six years of age, it is estimated that 30 per cent. of the French are entirely devoid of education. There is, however, a vast difference in the degree of education among the various departments, to the credit of those in the N. and N.E. With Alsace and Lorraine F. lost the most highly-educated portion of her inhabitants. Throughout F. there are 42,000 free and public schools for boys, and 14,000 communal schools for girls. The Roman Catholics of the lower classes, especially in the rural districts, rarely visit school after eleven or twelve, the age at which they receive their first communion, while Protestants usually attend school till their sixteenth year. The expense is borne partly by the departments, partly by the state. The higher education of F. is represented by the University of Paris, by eighteen colleges of instruction in special branches of knowledge, eighty-one academies, many Latin schools, three high military schools (St. Cyr, La Flèche, and Saumur), &c. Among the great literary and scientific institutions are the Institut de F. (q. v.), the Conservatoire de Musique, the École des Beaux-Arts, the Bibliothèque Nationale, &c. There are rich art and scientific collections, and many charitable institutions, receiving yearly from the state as much as nine millions of francs.

Religion.—In 1872 the population consisted of 35,387,703 Roman Catholics, 580,757 Protestants (Reformed and Lutheran),

49,439 Jews, and 85,022 of various minor creeds. All religions are allowed by law, but only the Roman Catholic, Protestant, and Jewish Churches receive state allowances. In the Roman Catholic Church there are 86 prelates, 17 archbishops, and 69 bishops, 192 vicars-general, 723 canons, 3531 *curés* or incumbents, and 31,569 *desservants* or curates. The Lutheran Protestants, 80,117 in number, are governed by a general consistory, while the Reformed Protestants or Calvinists (467,531) are under a council of administration, the seat of which is at Paris. Mohammedanism is recognised in Algeria.

Colonies.—The dependencies of F. have a total area of 463,827 sq. miles, and an aggregate pop. of over two and a half millions. They include Senegal, Île de Réunion and Ste. Marie, Nossi-Bé and Mayotte, East Indian possessions, Cochin-China, Martinique, Guadaloupe, Guiana, St. Pierre and Miquelon, Marquesas and Loyalty Islands, and New Caledonia. Algeria (q. v.) is an integral part of F. by constitution of 1852.

History.—The earliest historic inhabitants of F. were Celts, known as Gauls, who held all modern F. except the S.W., and who, a considerable time after they had settled in the land, were driven into the E. and S.E. by the Belgæ, a Celtic people with probably an infusion of Teutonic blood. The S.W. of the country belonged to the Aquitanians or Basques, a shorter and darker people akin to the Iberians, and probably a survival from pre-Aryan times. The Gauls and Belgæ were blue-eyed and yellow-haired, eminently brave and intelligent, the Belgæ being more thoughtful and patient than the Gauls, who were above all mobile and keen-witted, full of unstable heroism, and delighting in brilliant colours and barbaric display. Both peoples were ruled by Druids and chiefs, and were divided into clans. Long before Cæsar's invasion the strength of the Gauls had been sapped by the pleasures and splendours of Rome, which interfered in their tribal quarrels, and before 118 B.C. formed the Rhone valley from Geneva to the sea into a Roman province (*Provincia Romana*, hence Provence). Rome won no fresh land in Gaul until Cæsar's proconsulship, B.C. 58–51. In campaign after campaign he routed the Gauls, until the capture of Alesia laid the whole country at his feet (B.C. 51). From B.C. 50 to A.D. 476 Gaul was a province of the Roman state, and her inhabitants received that Roman impress to which France owes her language, her law, her religion, and even several features in the character of her people. From Rome the Gauls acquired the love for centralised city life, for severe logical theories of government, and for the conceptions of the equality of man and of universal empire which have played so large a part in the nation's career. Southern F. especially was so deeply Latinised as to become a different land from F. north of the Loire, and to retain, during the middle ages, part of the law and a faint reflex of the civic life of Rome. Before the 3d c. Gaul was studded with fair cities, centres of commerce and luxury, whose governments, modelled on the Roman *municipia*, were the germ of the French southern *communes*. But along with the civilisation came the corruption of the dying empire, and Christianity, introduced in its Greek form in 160 by Pothinus, made little progress until Roman missionaries entered the country in the 3d c. In 251, however, Dionysius founded the church of Paris, and the conversion of the Gauls quickly followed. In the first half of the 5th c. the barbarians, who were breaking up the empire, poured into Gaul, the Burgundians seizing the region between the Rhone and Jura, the Visigoths occupying the S.W., and the Franks making raids through the N. and establishing a fluctuating power along the Lower Rhine. These tribes did not seize Gaul by a united invasion, but broke up the unity of the country by intermittent incursions, and by settling in separate bodies through the land. Commerce and agriculture were thus arrested, the national life was palsied, and the towns were cut off from each other and gradually enfeebled. Guizot traces French civilisation to three sources—ancient Rome, the Germanic invasions, and the early Church. Rome, he says, gave F. the ideas of law and order; the Teutons brought the sentiment of individual independence and passionate love of freedom, while Christianity cleansed the land from the impurities of an effete paganism. The Teutons strove in their new settlements to conform to Roman institutions and ideas, while the cities of Southern F. preserved the relics of the Roman municipal government. The Franks consisted of two main branches, the Ripuarians, who dwelt near Köln, and the Salians, who held the districts at the mouths of the Rhine. They were ruled by princes called Merwings, one of whom, Hlodowig (Clovis), in 486 overthrew Syagrius, who governed in the Roman name at Soissons, then embraced the orthodox faith, crushed the Arian Burgundians and Visigoths, and before his death, in 511, established a Frankish monarchy embracing most of modern F. On the death of his son Hlotair (Clotaire) in 567, three clearly-defined kingdoms began to arise —that of N. Gaul or Neustria ('the W. kingdom'), between the Loire and Meuse; that of Austrasia ('the E. kingdom'), between the Maas (Meuse) and the Rhine; and that of Burgundy, including the Rhone valley and part of Switzerland. The Franks were comparatively numerous in the N., where Orleans, Paris, Soissons, and Metz became capitals of Frankish kingdoms, but they had few if any settlements in Aquitaine and Burgundy. Under Dagobert, king of Neustria, the power of the Merwings was at its highest, but on his death (638) the Merwing kingdom faded away, and after the battle of Testry (687), in which the Austrasians under Pippin of Heristal defeated the Neustrians, Pippin and his descendants ruled over Austrasia and Neustria as Mayors of the Palace, the *rois fainéants*, or Merwing kings, being allowed to retain the name of royalty until 752, when Pippin the Short, son of Karl the Hammer—the Mayor who drove back the Saracens in the fight of Tours (732)—was proclaimed king of the Franks. The reigns of the Karolings, the empire of Karl the Great, belong to the history of Germany. Under Karl the Great Gaul was simply a province of a great German empire, as it had formerly been of the empire of Rome. The Merwing monarchy was in a degree French, Neustria being mainly peopled by Gallo-Romans, but Austrasia was a purely German land, the Karolings were German in blood, speech, and customs, and their favourite abodes were Aachen (Aix-la-Chapelle) and Engelheim in the Rhine valley. The Merwing monarchy arose from the warrior kingship of the Franks, the Merwings being encircled with peculiar reverence, as the descendants of heroes and demigods; while the Karolings dazzled their subjects by claiming to wield the universal dominion of imperial Rome. From neither of these monarchies is modern F. descended. Modern F. dates from the rise of the Parisian monarchy of the Capets, which gradually absorbed most of the old province of Gaul. The treaty of Verdun (843) severed Neustria, now a distinctly Romance land, from Teutonic Austrasia; and, down to the 14th c., the kingdom of Paris, which grew into modern F., possessed neither Burgundy, Provence, Elsass, nor Lothringen, nor had it for 600 years any firm authority over Aquitaine. Celtic or Romance F., as distinguished from Teutonic F., first appears at the treaty of Verdun in 843; Parisian F. first appears in 888, when Karl the Fat, for a time ruler of Germany, Italy, and Neustria, was deposed, and the Karoling empire split into the W. kingdom or F., and the E. kingdom or Germany, Italy, and Burgundy. From the death of Karl the Great Paris had been steadily rising in power, and her noble defence against the Northmen in 885 decided her future as capital of F. north of the Loire. She was not, however, at once made the capital of an existing French kingdom, but, on the contrary, from being the chief place of the county of Paris, grew into the kingdom of F., a kingdom distinct alike from the Roman province of Gaul and the W. kingdom of the Karolings. In 888 the nobles of the N. of F. chose Odo, the chief defender of Paris against the Northmen, as king, but he had to declare himself a vassal of the king of the E. Franks, and a century of constant rivalry ensued between the Karolings, who held their court at Laon, near the German border, and the house of Capet, which ruled at Paris—between the slightly-Germanised Romance kingdom of the W., and the Teutonic kingdom of the E. About the close of the 9th c. the Northmen made permanent settlements in N. F., and at length in 911 Hrolf (Rollo) received the lordship of the region between the Epte and Brittany, where he founded the great dukedom of Normandy. The Karolings growing more incompetent as the 10th c. advanced, in 987 Hugues (Hugh) Capet abolished the monarchy of Laon, thus breaking the ties between F. and Germany, the native land of the Franks. The subsequent history of F. until the end of the 18th c. is mainly concerned with the slow fusion of various provinces into the monarchy of Paris, and the gradual change of the kingly office from a weak overlordship into a despotism. Hugues Capet was merely one of the great peers of F., having only a faint superiority, except in his own domain, a tract of land hemmed in by Normandy, Brittany, Burgundy, and Aquitaine. The Capetian was distinguished from the Karoling monarchy by making no claim to represent the Roman empire, and by its more essentially feudal nature. The fall of the Karolings had doubtless been hastened by the suspicions which the great barons, whose lands had been at first benefices granted in return for services at court, entertained towards the dynasty whose privileges they had usurped, and which had the right to reclaim the estates. A monarchy with less lofty pretensions was wished for, and was found in the purely feudal monarchy of the Capets. The new kings were more closely allied with the Church than were the earlier dynasties. A vague holiness began to be associated with the kingly office, and it is probably to ecclesiastical influence that we should ascribe the mildness and even feebleness of the early Capets, under whom the land was torn by feudal war, the nobles defying the kings, who could scarcely maintain the slight overlordship held by the first of their line. The Capetian kingdom was little more than a name until Louis VI. (1105–1137), with the aid of the Church, and by making common cause with the people, humbled the great feudatories of the crown. The king began to be looked on as the centre of justice, as the holder of a vague power which was dimly seen to be something apart from feudal overlordship, to represent the people and protect them from feudal oppression. Much of Louis VI.'s work was undone in the reign of his feeble son Louis VII., whose supremacy the nobles shook off, and who was overshadowed by Henry II. of England. That king made war in F., not as an English sovereign, but as a great French feudatory, and held more land in F. than belonged to all the other French nobles together, while his feudal superior, the king of F., was a comparatively unimportant ruler cooped up in a small central district. But the mysterious popular respect still clung to the kingly office, and Louis VII.'s successor, Philippe Auguste (1180–1223) changed an unstable superiority coloured by an indefinite moral influence into a vigorous though still a feudal monarchy. He added Normandy to his realm by the capture of Château Gaillard (1204), and in the victory of Bouvines (1214), where he crushed the feudal barons allied with Otho of Germany, secured the future of royalty in F. He was greatly aided in his struggle with feudalism by the *communes*, which he favoured, and by the lawyers, who were becoming important through the reviving interest in Roman law. During his reign the brilliant civilisation of Southern F. was almost extinguished in the crusade against the Albigenses. Up to this time the S. had held aloof from the N., the Loire flowing between two lands widely different in the customs and even the race of their inhabitants. The Frenchmen of the N. were a mixed people of Celts, Franks, and Norsemen; the Aquitanians were partly Basques, partly Visigoths; and the Provençals had a considerable infusion of Roman blood. The S. had preserved a fragmentary code of Roman law in preference to the northern feudal *custom-right*, and contained many rich free cities, full of refined and democratic citizens, with governments based on the Roman *municipia*. Hlodwig's invasions of the S. had kindled a bitter hatred among the southern Gallo-Romans and Visigoths for the N., the land of the Franks—a feeling which remained throughout the middle ages, the early dislike of Aquitaine and Provence for the Merwings and Karolings being transferred to the monarchy of Paris. While the N. was torn by feudal strife, in the S., where the power of the Church was almost extinct, poetry, art, and philosophical speculation were assiduously cultivated. Southern F., imbued with Arabic science and cherishing Roman municipal rights, was bringing on a sceptical, democratic movement, intensely hostile to feudalism and the Catholic Church. Therefore the Pope stirred up a crusade against the Albigenses (q. v.), or heretics of Languedoc, and from 1207 to 1215 the barons of the N. slew and ravaged in the S. country, which never recovered its old wealth, luxury, and culture, though it still is, in the speech, customs, and blood of its people, aloof from F. north of the Loire. Louis IX. (1226–44) added to the royal domains by treaties and purchases, and while scrupulously recognising certain feudal rights, determinedly strove to root out the feudal privileges of private war and judicial duels. He has been called the founder of the French absolute monarchy, and his virtues gave the kingly office a popularity which in a large measure enabled it to grow into the foul despotism of the 17th and 18th centuries. In his reign occurred the last of the crusades, expeditions which had indirectly strengthened the French monarchy. At first the royal power gained by the crusades carrying off hosts of turbulent barons to the East, many of whom never returned to F., while the kings prudently stayed at home; and, afterwards, when the kings became leaders of armies to Palestine, their influence was increased by the lofty position they thus held before all Europe. The cities also throve from the crusades, which quickened their trade, and enabled them to buy privileges from barons who needed money to travel to the Holy Land, while, as each man who became a crusader was thereby freed, a vast number of serfs thus won their liberty, and both the cities and the new freemen were warm supporters of the crown. Under Philippe le Bel (1285–1314) the old feudal monarchy began to change into a despotism. In his reign we see clearly the baneful tendency to concentrate all power in the king, which ended in a systematic depressing of national life, in a general political ignorance, that bore fearful fruits in the days of the Revolution. While in England the free Teutonic institutions always survived in theory, F. in the time of Philippe le Bel had lost all the old Frankish popular rights. Hence reform in F. has always required changes wrought by abstract theory, the country having been, unlike England, deprived of foundations on which to build. Under Philippe le Bel all laws and administration emanated from the crown, the nobles were only consulted when war was intended. The lawyers at this time did good service in lessening feudal and ecclesiastical influence, but lent themselves to foster despotism. Being raised to offices at the will of the king they became his instruments in special commissions, and the monarchy thus won vast judicial power. After Philippe's death the monarchy was severely shaken throughout the 14th c., being assailed both as to the nature of the succession and as to the nature of its power. During the reigns of the three sons of Philippe le Bel (1314–28), peasant rebellions, famine, and disease desolated F., and on the death of Charles IV., last son of Philippe le Bel, the succession to the throne was disputed between Philippe Comte de Valois, cousin of the last king, and Edward III. of England, who claimed the crown as the son of Isabella, Philippe le Bel's daughter. The nobles, along with the 'notables of Paris and the other good towns,' decided in favour of Philippe, who then provoked Edward to war with the hope of annexing Aquitaine, the last remnant of the Continental kingdom of Henry II. of England. In 1337 began the struggle known as the *Hundred Years' War*. Under Edward III. the English won the victories of Crécy (1346) and Poitiers (1356), and took Calais during the first period of the war, which ended at the peace of Bretigny (1360), Edward giving up his claim to the French crown, and being declared the independent ruler of Aquitaine, Calais, and several small districts. At this time the condition of F. was unspeakably wretched, agriculture and commerce were at a standstill, and in 1348 the land was ravaged by the Black Plague. At length the peasantry rose (1358), and slew and plundered until the nobles ruthlessly quelled the revolt. From the common nickname of the peasants—*Jacques Bonhomme*—the name *Jacquerie* was given to this and all succeeding rebellions of like nature. Now, too, the Parisians strove to establish a free commune, under Étienne Marcel the provost, and assumed for the first time a revolutionary cap of red and blue. This effort, like the Jacquerie, was suppressed by the barons. In the reign of Charles V. (1364–80) the French gradually drove back the English, who before Edward III.'s death lost nearly all Aquitaine except Bordeaux and Bayonne. From the death of Edward III. to the invasion of Henry V. there were occasional truces, but no definite peace. During the reign of Charles VI., F. was rent by party strife, and Henry V. of England entered the country, won the battle of Agincourt in 1415, and by the treaty of Troyes (1420) was acknowledged successor to Charles VI. on the French throne. Charles VI. and Henry died in 1422, and war continued between the English regent, the Duke of Bedford, and Charles VII., who, mainly through the patriotic ardour of Joan of Arc, was crowned at Rheims in 1429. After Bedford's death the English steadily lost ground, until in 1453 Bordeaux and Bayonne fell, and Calais alone remained of their Continental possessions. Thus ended the Hundred Years' War, which left F. in the darkest misery. The country was desolate; in many provinces there was scarcely a house outside of the walled towns; the roads were overgrown by thickets; the peasantry had fled to the cities, where many of them were sunk into beggary. But the strength of the lesser nobles was broken by the war, and the towns were thus enabled to wring new liberties from them. An upper class of traders arose, and the *bourgeoisie* carried their influence to the side of the crown. Louis XI. (1461-83) favoured the third estate, and jealously humbled the nobles. The 'third estate,' or the people, which now becomes somewhat important, sprang from the Roman municipal towns, which survived through the middle ages; from the *communes*, which won their independence by warring with the barons; and from the gatherings round a noble's dwelling of peasants and others, who, as they grew in numbers and practised trades, were enabled to win privileges from their over-lord. The royal officers and lawyers, being mostly of low birth, were also a powerful element in the third estate, which rose in influence throughout the 15th c., though the communal liberties were now disappearing. In 1494 Charles VIII. marched into Italy, and, though his conquest of the country was ephemeral, the results of his invasion were momentous, as they committed F. to a ruinous policy, and led to disastrous wars with Spain. The next French king, Louis XII., was likewise inflamed by the hope of Italian conquest, but wasted his strength in intrigues of which Austria reaped the benefit. François I., the successor of Louis, plunged into war with the Emperor Karl V., and was captured at Pavia, the struggle between F. and Spain going on until 1558, when the Spaniards having won the victories of St. Quentin and Gravelines, the peace of Cateau Cambresis was concluded. These wars cost F. a lavish waste of blood and treasure, and infected her with the luxury and seductive vices of the South, but they also brought the impressible French into contact with a refined people, imbued with the spirit of the Renaissance, which was now diffused by the French through other nations. From 1562 to 1595 French history is mainly occupied with the civil wars between the Catholics and Protestants. The last, who were Calvinists, were known as Huguenots. During the reigns of Henri III.'s three sons, François II. (1559–61), Charles IX. (1560–74), and Henri III. (1574–89), great authority rested with their mother Catherine of Medicis, a bigoted Catholic, who foully abused her power in persecuting the Huguenots. In 1572 the massacre of the Protestants known as the Massacre of St. Bartholomew was perpetrated at Paris, and the struggle continued with shifting fortune until 1589, when Henri III. died. Henri of Navarre, a descendant of Louis IX., was now the rightful heir to the throne, but Paris and most of F. would not obey him, until in 1593 he became a Catholic and was made sole ruler, changing the old title *King of the French* for the new title *King of F. and Navarre.* Henri IV. passed the Edict of Nantes (q. v.) in 1598, and, supported by Sully, reformed many financial abuses, chastised the nobles, and protected the people. His popularity and Sully's ability rendered it unnecessary to summon the States-General to confer supplies, and the centralisation of power was thus largely confirmed. On Henri's murder in 1610 the government was administered by the Queen until 1614, when Louis XIII. nominally began to reign. At this time the ecclesiastical power somewhat declined in F., the king confirming the Edict of Nantes and other measures in favour of the Protestants, and the Catholic statesmen abandoning their former intolerant policy. Richelieu, the minister who really governed France during the last eighteen years of Louis XIII.'s reign, broke away from the old religious alliances, checked ecclesiastical influence in the state, and enforced the principle that national interests and not religious differences must determine political relations. The kingly power was further strengthened by Richelieu's antagonism to the nobles. He cut down their privileges and political importance, though he could not lessen their social power, which retained its malign influence until the Revolution. Under his indulgent policy the Huguenot party lost its importance and many of its members passed over to Catholicism. The Calvinist clergy, however, stirred up a somewhat factious resistance to Richelieu, and a war broke out, which was ended in 1628 by the capture of Rochelle, the great stronghold of French Protestantism. On the death of Louis XIII. (1648), F. was ruled by Mazarin, whom the queen-mother had made prime minister. Mazarin's unpopularity and the exactions under which the people groaned led to the rebellion of the Fronde (q. v.), in which the nobles, the *bourgeoisie*, and the mob of Paris rose together against Anne of Austria's regency. Even princes of the blood shared in the insurrection, and the Parisian populace, inflamed by over-taxation, was led by one of the ablest of demagogues, the Cardinal de Retz. But the movement only proved the inherent strength of the monarchy. There was no sympathy between the aristocrats who headed the struggle and the people. The nobles were blind to popular interests and large political issues, while the people were too ignorant to produce leaders from their own ranks. Another century was needed to imbue the populace with clear political convictions, with revolutionary ideas as well as revolutionary fervour. In the 17th c. there was nothing to take the place of the monarchy in governing F., and after the Fronde collapsed the royal power shot up into unexampled splendour under Louis XIV. He came to the throne in 1661, and his reign is the culminating epoch of the French monarchy. Before Louis XIV. the kingly power was checked by other influences, and after Louis XIV. it passed into a rapid decay. Up to this reign there was a possibility of the crown and people uniting to remove abuses. But under Louis XIV. all political activity on the part of the nation was frozen, all co-operation ceased between the ruler and the people, on the latter of whom it was now impressed that the king must initiate and carry out everything. The country laboured under evils so vast as to render the warmest co-operation between the crown and its subjects indispensable for their correction; and when the reform could no longer be delayed, the monarchy, isolated from the people by its systematic repression of national spontaneity, was unable to cope with the task of reform. Louis's reign began with success, but closed in gloom. At the end of the Thirty Years' War F. was the chief power in Europe, and under Louis XIV. stepped into the place from which Spain had fallen. Louis's policy of aggrandisement was at first successful, but in the Spanish war of succession his ambitions were shivered. His armies were defeated, the revocation of the Edict of Nantes (1685) deprived F. of a large industrious population, the revenue was scandalously misapplied, and on Louis's death in 1715 the national debt amounted to £140,000,000 sterling. Under Louis XV. costly wars were carried on with England, Spain, and Austria, and by the treaty of Paris (1763) the larger part of the French colonial possessions was given up. So gross was the misgovernment that F. was brought to a state of seemingly incurable bankruptcy and misery. The country was dying under the weight of the monarchy, when, in the days of Louis XV.'s successor, Louis XVI., the changes began which led to the French Revolution. The monarchy had engrossed all power, feudal, legal, and clerical ideas having combined to swell its authority. The feudal theory of monarchy made F. the king's private estate; the lawyers' theory, based on Roman ideas, made him the sole representative of the nation; and the clerical theory made him the delegate of God. And the government, while narrowly concentrated and inquisitorially administered, was rude and ineffective, the king failing to perform the functions which his office had engrossed. The country was overrun by tax-collectors—about 250,000 in number—who veiled their extortions behind the royal name. The nobles, suspected by the king and hated by the people, remained in defenceless isolation, debarred from all share in the government, while they still kept their galling rights and immunities, and spent their lives in the costliest pleasures. Louis XV. made Versailles the scene of habitual revels, recalling the foul orgies of imperial Rome, and consumed one-fourth of the public revenue in keeping up his household. As the 18th c. advanced, the state of the people grew more and more wretched. They were the only class engaged in productive labour, their exertions were hampered by absurd restraints, and upon them rested the sole burden of supplying the public revenues, the nobles being free from taxation except a merely nominal class-duty. In 1715 a third of the poor classes perished from want; in 1725 St. Simon said the king was making F. a hospital of dying men and women; and in the middle of the 18th c. the majority of the rural population could not with the utmost efforts earn enough bread to keep themselves alive, and at the same time pay the subsidies. Wide tracts of land were deserted; the peasants, unable to maintain life in the country, became beggars in the towns; 'starvation,' says M. Taine, 'was an endemic disease.' The ancient regime by its monstrous waste of the public resources, its *lettres de cachet*, its secret system of police, its endless confiscation of individual possessions, its forced services, its grinding taxation, its inquisitorial interference with private rights, had broken F. into bitterly hostile sects, and was actually maintaining an anarchy worse than that of the worst days of the Revolution. Meanwhile the intellectual class was wholly at variance with the existing institutions. The literary men—who had been systematically persecuted by the monarchy, and debarred from all share in public life, while they had no practical knowledge of government, but were inspired by the old Gallic passion for equality, by an ardent belief in the perfectibility of man, and an intense hatred of existing social bonds, sentiments learned from Rousseau—were convinced that they could break with the nation's past, and mould society anew independent of its historic growth. As they were not mere speculative students, but lucid, fiery popular writers, they speedily imbued the people with their convictions; and to their wide influence, ignorance of practical politics, and passion for framing a government by theoretic doctrine, are due many of the wildest, emptiest follies of the Revolution. In 1789 Louis was forced by deficits to convoke the States-General, which had not met since 1614. On June 17 the third estate declared itself the National Assembly, and on June 23 proclaimed its members inviolable. The king then dissolved the ministry, and gathered a body of troops round Versailles, the result being that on July 12 insurrection flamed wildy out in Paris, and on the 14th the Bastile was taken by the mob. On August 4 the National Assembly—commonly known as the Constituent Assembly—abolished feudal rights; on October 6 the Parisian populace, their rage sharpened by accounts of the Versailles banquets, where royalists drank confusion to liberty, poured out, followed by the National Guard, to Versailles, and brought the king and queen back to Paris. This destroyed all the moral authority and mysterious inviolability which had till then clothed the French monarchy. In 1790 the king promised to conform to a new liberal constitution, while Austria, Prussia, England, Spain, and Saxony allied against his rebellious people. In 1791 the king and queen tried to escape from Paris, but were taken, and the Constituent Assembly gave place to the Legislative Assembly, which met October 1, 1791. At this time two great parties divided the revolutionists—the Girondins (q. v.) and the Jacobins (q. v.). The Austrians were now heard to be marching on F., and Paris broke out into mad fury. Henceforth until 1794 French history has to deal with two sets of events—with the repulse of the invaders, and with the violent struggles of factions in Paris. Each of 'the famous days of Paris' was prompted by the acts of the foreign enemies. On August 10 the Tuilleries were stormed in reply to the atrocious threats of the royalist Duke of Brunswick. The taking of Verdun and Longwy by the Prussians provoked the September massacres, F. being declared a republic September 25, 1792, and the loss of Cambrai led to the execution of Marie Antoinette. The king was guillotined on January 21, 1793, and the treachery of Dumouriez and rebellion of La Vendée called forth the rising of May 31, when supreme power passed over to the Jacobins, who won brilliant triumphs against the foreign enemy, and quelled insurrection at home, but, ignorant of ruling, and cruel through their fears and delusive hopes, plunged into the excesses of the Reign of Terror (q. v.), while the country yielded to them tamely, from its old habit of submitting to the crimes of the ancient regime. Reaction, however, swiftly set in. The leaders of the Jacobins fell, and the party broke up. (See DANTON, MARAT, HÉBERT, ROBESPIERRE, &c.) In 1795 the Convention made a new constitution, reposing the executive power with a Directory (q. v.) of five. Then followed the dazzling campaigns of Napoleon, who on November 9, 1799, overthrew the Directory and became Consul, and in 1804 Emperor of France. (See NAPOLEON). After Napoleon's final downfall in 1815, the Bourbon Charles X. was restored by the allies. Under him the dishonesty, incapacity, and priestly intolerance of the old regime were revived, until the revolution of 1830 placed Louis Philippe, Duc d'Orleans, on the throne. His stubborn enmity to reform caused his abdication in 1848, and the establishment of a republic. Louis Napoleon (q. v.) became president in 1848, and by the *coup-d'état* of 1851 Emperor of F. The Napoleonic absolutism endured until in 1870 the Emperor declared war against Prussia, and after sustaining a series of the most crushing defeats recorded in history, surrendered with 90,000 men at Sedan, September 2, 1870. He was then deposed, and a republic instituted at Paris, which city, after a resistance of four months, was entered by the Prussians, peace being made in March 1871. F. ceded Alsace and Lorraine, and paid an indemnity of £200,000,000. Since then a Conservative republic has been established, and now seems tolerably firm, having acted with wise patriotism, and shown itself free from the extravagance, intolerance, and imbecility of former republican rule. See the works of Michelet, Sismondi, De Tocqueville, and Taine on the *Ancien Régime*, Guizot's *Civilisation en F.*, and Kitchin's *History of F.*

France, Isle of. See MAURITIUS.

Franche Com'té ('free county') was a province of the kingdom of France comprising part of the Jura mountains and the lowlands to the westward. It is now represented by the departments of Doubs, Haute Saône, and Jura. Originally possessed by the Celtic Sequani, it was conquered by the Burgundians in the 5th c., and after many changes was finally handed over to France by the treaty of Nymwegen in 1678.

Fran'chise, or **Lib'erty,** in English law, is a privilege by a grant from the crown, or by prescription which supposes a grant. It may mean the privilege of corporation, exemption from special tribute, a right over land, as that of *forestry*, the right to vote for a member of Parliament, and so on.

Fran'cia, José Gaspar Rodriguez, popularly known as Dr. F., was born at Asuncion, Paraguay, about 1757. He was of French or Portuguese descent, studied for the Church, and took the degree of doctor of divinity at the University of Cordova de Tucuman. Subsequently he left divinity for law, and gained a high reputation for ability, uprightness of conduct, and industry as a legal practitioner. The revolution among the S. American republics which made Paraguay independent brought F. to the front. In 1813 he was appointed joint-consul along with General Fulgencio Yegros; next year he was made dictator; and in 1817, such was the confidence of the Paraguayans in him, that he was appointed dictator for life, his death, looked upon as a great calamity, occurring September 20, 1840. The most widely different accounts are given of this remarkable man. In a celebrated paper of Mr. Carlyle, reprinted in his *Miscellaneous Essays*, he is eulogised as a stern administrator of justice, while Mr. C. A. Washburn in his *History of Paraguay* (1871) paints him as an absolute tyrant. Unquestionably he did a great amount of good to Paraguay, promoted education, suppressed clerical abuses, encouraged agriculture, cattle-rearing, and every form of industry which he could naturalise in Paraguay, established defences against the Indians, and made injustice almost an impossibility. On the other hand, there can be little question that he was merciless toward those who plotted or were believed to have plotted against his life, and was bitterly opposed to the intermeddling or even the presence of foreigners—*e.g.*, Bonpland the naturalist, and the Swiss travellers Rengger and Longchamp, who published their experiences of him in an *Essai Historique*, &c. (1827). For a full and unfavourable account of F. see three vols. by J. P. and W. P. Robertson, two Scotchmen whom he expelled from Paraguay; *Letters on Paraguay* (2 vols. 1838); F.'s *Reign of Terror* (1839); and *Letters on S. America* (3 vols. 1843).

Fran'cis, St., of Assisi, the founder of the Franciscan order, and one of the most interesting and pure-spirited of Catholic devotees, was born at Assisi, near Naples, in 1182. He was the son of a rich merchant, Bernardone Mariconi, and was named *Il Francesco*, from his command of the Provençal speech. He was early noted for gaiety, kindness to the poor, and lavish splendour of living, the people of Assisi calling him 'the flower of youth.' Having been captured in a feud with Perugia, he was imprisoned for a year; and during this confinement and a subsequent illness at Spoleto, his ideas permanently changed; he resolved to devote himself to a life of worship and charity, abandoning in his twenty-fourth year all his worldly goods, becoming a hermit, and, in his own words, 'taking poverty as a bride.' He preached with loving fervour, wore the meanest dress, performed the lowliest offices to the poor and to the lepers in the hospital of Gubbio, and aided with his own hands in the building of St. Damian's church in Assisi. When as a preacher he visited the Umbrian villages, the people went joyfully to meet him with flags and green boughs and music. Gradually he was encircled by followers, whom in 1210 he formed into the Franciscan Order (q. v.), which was verbally approved of by Pope Innocent III. in the same year, though first confirmed by Honorius III. in 1223. The peculiarity of the order was its utter abnegation of personal property, the brethren disclaiming possession even of their robes and breviaries. The order increased rapidly, and in 1219 had 5000 members. F. likewise founded the orders of *Poor Ladies* and of *Tertiaries*. About 1220 he visited the East to convert the Sultan Meledin, whom he induced to promise kinder treatment of Christian prisoners, and to grant the Franciscans the privilege of being guardians of the Holy Sepulchre. On September 17, 1224, according to the Catholic legend, he received in a religious ecstasy on Monte Alverno the marks of the wounds of the Saviour. He died October 4, 1226, having caused himself immediately before expiring to be laid on the bare ground of the church. St. F. is the most beautiful character in the history of mediæval Christianity—simple, childlike, and glowing with the purest emotion. His burning ardour was tempered by meek sympathies and undimmed by bigotry. Dante, who tells the story of his life, speaks of him as a 'splendour of cherubic light.' No one since the rise of Christianity brought religion so powerfully home to the people; his mystical raptures never lessened his yearning love for the poor. He completely changed monachism, transformed lonely ascetics into missionaries, and founded the most popular of all the orders. His *Canticle of the Sun*, written in artless Tuscan and thrilling with strange fervour, marks the rise of the lofty religious poetry of the middle ages which culminated in Dante. See St. Bonaventura's *Life of St. F.*; the Bollandist *Acta Sanctorum*; Chalippe's *Vie de St. F.* (1728); Chavin's *Vie de St. F.* (1841); Milman's *Latin Christianity*, vol. iv.; Vogt's *Der Heilige F. von Assisi* (Tüb. 1840); Hase's *F. von Assisi* (Leips. 1856); and Stephen's *Ecclesiastical Biography*. Editions of F.'s works, which consist of letters, monastic treatises, parables, hymns, &c., are numerous. The most accurate is that of Père de la Haye (Par. 1641).

Francis, St., of Paula, born at Paula in the kingdom of Naples, 1416, was named after St. Francis d'Assisi, to whose intercession his parents believed they owed the birth of the child. Having manifested strong ascetic tendencies even as a child, he was sent at twelve years of age into the Franciscan monastery of St. Mark, in Calabria, where he surpassed all the friars in obedience to their *rule*. On the expiry of his year of probation, after making a pilgrimage with his parents to Rome and other holy places, he took up his abode in a cave on the sea-coast, and devoted himself to a life of extraordinary asceticism. The fame of his sanctity soon attracted to him a number of followers, who built for themselves a chapel and cell in the neighbourhood, and he gave to the new order he had thus founded the name of the Eremites of St. Francis. In 1436 the Archbishop of Cosenza sanctioned the building of a cloister and church, and monasteries of the new order soon sprang up in Spain, France, and Germany. In 1474 the *rule* was confirmed by Pope Sixtus IV., and Pope Alexander VI. changed the name of the order to Fratres Minimi. Louis XI. in his last illness summoned F. to France, where in a monastery at Plessis-le-Tours the saint died, 2d April 1507, He was canonised by Leo X., 1519.

Francis, St., of Sales, a bishop and prince of Geneva, was born at the château of Sales near Annecy, 21st August 1567. He studied rhetoric, theology, and Hebrew in the College of the Jesuits at Paris, and law at Padua, passed advocate at Chambery, and was strongly pressed by his father to become a jurist. But his heart was set on a sacred career, and in 1593 he entered the priesthood. The fame which he won by his first sermons pointed him out as a fit missionary for the district of Chablais, then filled with Protestants. In spite of great opposition, the brilliant young Catholic made numerous conversions, and inspired the Pope with the belief that he might perhaps succeed in winning over Beza (q. v.) himself, then the leader of French Calvinism. Three ineffectual conferences were held in 1597. In 1602 F. visited Paris, preached before Henri IV., who greatly admired him, and signalised himself by the miraculous conversion of courtiers. In the same year he succeeded to the bishopric of Geneva, and in 1607 founded the Florimontane Academy, and published his *Introduction à la Vie Dévote*, a work which excited a prodigious interest, was translated into several languages, and in less than half a century had gone through forty editions. Next year he again visited Paris, where his pious oratory once more brought the city to his feet. Every distinguished person sought his friendship or acquaintance. Cardinal Retz begged him to become his coadjutor and successor, but nothing could induce the modest bishop to abandon his Alpine diocese. Between 1610 and 1614 F. established the orders of the Visitation of the Barnabites at Annecy, and of the Carthusians at Ripaille. Two years later appeared his famous *Traité de l'Amour de Dieu*, which may be said to have evoked the admiration of Christendom. He now thought of resigning his episcopal functions, and passing the remainder of his days in some calm retreat, when the Duke of Savoy required his services at Avignon. On his return he fell ill, and died at Lyon, 28th November 1622. As a writer F. almost equals Montaigne in originality of style and the charm of diction. His *Œuvres Complètes* have been repeatedly published; the best edition is that of Blaise (16 vols. Par. 1835). F.'s letters in particular are exquisitely naïve and graceful. See Hamon's *Vie de Saint François de Sales* (2 vols. Par. 1854).

Francis'cans, Order of, named also 'Seraphic Brethren,' 'Minorites' (*Fratres Minores*) as a sign of humility, and 'Grey Friars' from the colour of their clothing, one of the great mendicant orders of the Romish Church, was founded by St. Francis in 1210, and confirmed by Honorius III. in 1223. The F. were vowed to chastity, poverty, and obedience, and their religious services were at first conducted with strict simplicity. They wore a grey cowl and robe, girded themselves with cords, and went bare-footed. The order grew with wonderful rapidity, and in the middle of the 13th c. had about 8000 convents and nearly 200,000 monks. 'Franciscanism,' says Milman, 'was the democracy of Christianity;' and at first, under the influence of Antony of Padua, one of their founder's disciples, the F. threatened to become bitter foes of the regular clergy; but they gradually forsook their early austerity, gathered riches, established a gorgeous ritual, and made their chief seat, Assisi, a centre of Christian art. During the 13th c. they were greatly favoured by the popes, who freed them from episcopal control, and allowed them to receive legacies, inter in churchyards, preach, and hear confession, independently of the regular clergy, by whom they were strongly opposed. From the frequency with which indulgences were granted them, the phrase *Portiuncula Indulgence* came into use, Portiuncula being the name of the church at Assisi where St. Francis had first collected his followers. The F. entered England in 1224, had a house first at Canterbury and afterwards at London, and in the beginning of the 14th c. the higher members of the order in England opposed Boniface because he refused to allow them to hold lands. There have been several offshoots from the F.—the Cæsarines separating in 1236, the Celestines in 1294, the Clarenines in 1302, and the Capuchins in 1525. Many who separated from the order were united in 1363 into the community of Soccolati, or sandal-wearers. The F. at first discarded learning, but afterwards included several of the greatest mediæval scholars, as Bonaventura, Roger Bacon, Hales, Occam, and especially Duns Scotus, who, with his followers, the *Scotists*, defended the doctrines of free-will and the immaculate conception of the Virgin against the Dominican Thomas Aquinas and his disciples the *Thomists*. To the F. also belonged the popes Nicholas IV., Alexander V., Sixtus IV., Sixtus V., and Clement XIV.; Thomas de Celano, author of the *Dies Iræ*, and Jacopone, author of the *Stabat Mater*. The order sank in the 15th and again in the 18th c. It now numbers about 100,000. The F. were once especially flourishing in S. America. The order of Tertiaries was founded by St. Francis in 1221 for such of both sexes as wished to observe some of the rules of the F., but were unwilling to take monastic vows. From the Tertiaries, who were in France called *Picpuses*, and who were very numerous in the 13th c., sprang the communities of the Fraticelli and Beghards. See Wadding's *Annales Minorum* (Rome, 1731–1744); Parkinson's *Collectanea Anglo-Minoritica*; and Milman's *Latin Christianity*.

Francis, Sir Philip, was born at Dublin, October 22, 1740. He entered public life on the Whig side in 1756, held a place in the Secretary of State's office, and from 1774 to 1781 was a member of the Council for Bengal, where he was wounded in a duel with Hastings. On returning to England he was elected to Parliament, and took part with eager enmity in the prosecution of Hastings. He left Parliament in 1807, and died in London, December 22, 1818. F. was an irritable but able man, and was influenced by sincere though splenetic patriotism. It is nearly certain that he was the author of the famous *Letters of Junius*. (See JUNIUS, LETTERS OF). See Merivale's and Parkes's *Memoirs of Sir P. F.* (Lond. 1867).

Francis'co, San. See SAN FRANCISCO.

Franck'e, August Hermann, a German educationalist, was born at Lubeck in 1663. Trained for the Church, he first became prominent through some lectures in Leipsic on biblical literature, which provoked persecution and made him leave that city in 1690 for Erfurt. Finally he obtained a professorship of theology in the University of Halle, and having also accepted the pastorate of the suburb of Glaucha, he conceived the idea of promoting the education of the children of the poor in his district. Successful class-work induced him in 1698 to lay the foundation of an orphan asylum. To this he afterwards united a missionary institution for the East Indies, a Latin seminary, and a boarding-school. He was warmly supported in his philanthropic efforts by his countrymen, and a chemist gave him a receipt for compounding certain medicines which was the means of bringing him a considerable income. The education given in these institutions was distinctly and elaborately religious, and is so yet, though not to the same extent. They have been extended, and certain industries are taught in connection with them, such as bookselling and printing. The pupils number about 2500. F. died June 8, 1727. See Guerike's *Aug. Herm. F.* (Halle, 1827); Kramer's *Beiträge zur Geschichte Aug. Herm. F.'s* (Halle, 1861), and *Die Stiftungen Aug. Herm. F.'s in Halle* (Halle, 1862).

François I., King of France, born at Cognac, 12th September 1494, was the son of Charles Comte d'Angoulême and Louise of Savoy. He succeeded to the French crown on the death of Louis XII. in 1515 without children. F. was educated in the traditions of romance and chivalry, but entirely without reference to his duties as a sovereign. His first project was to recover the duchy of Milan, which he claimed through his wife as descended from the Visconti. He crossed the Alps with 40,000 men, his mother Louise remaining as regent. The Swiss, who had combined with Spain and Pope Leo X. to defend the duchy, were completely defeated in a two days' battle at Marignano, which was followed by the surrender of Maximilian Sforza and the battle of Milan. F. made a very temperate use of his victory, entering into friendly relations with both the Swiss and the Pope. Next year Karl succeeding to Ferdinand V. of Spain and the Emperor Maximilian, entered into the treaty of Cambrai with F., who also obtained the alliance of Venice. The apparent security of his position carried the French throne a long way towards absolutism, but the death of Maximilian in 1519 brought F. and Karl into collision as rival claimants of the Roman Empire. Despite the festivities of the Field of the Cloth of Gold, Henry VIII. inclined to the side of Karl, who entered into a league with Leo X. to expel the French from Italy. F., after some feats of arms in the Netherlands, saw Milan occupied by Prosper Colonna, and the governor Lautrec with his Swiss and Venetian allies routed at Bicocca, 29th April 1522. Then the English invaded Picardy, Bourbon deserted to the empire, Venice joined the Papal League, Bonnivet was defeated, and Bayard killed on the Sesia, 1524; and at last, after expelling his enemies from Provence and retaking Milan, F. by his own ignorance of strategy was defeated at Pavia, 24th February 1525, and became the prisoner of Karl. After more than a year's captivity in Spain, he was freed on signing the treaty of Madrid, by which he gave up his claims on Milan, Genoa, Naples, Flanders, and Artois, and transferred Burgundy to the Emperor. By a secret protest of the same date F. declared the treaty null as signed under constraint. Then followed the Holy League (at Cognac, 22th May 1526) between Pope Clement VII., Venice, Florence, Milan, and F. against the Emperor. The result was another Italian war, in which, after Bourbon had taken Rome, Lautrec's army was destroyed in Naples, and the great Admiral Doria deserted to the imperialist side and liberated Genoa. After an exchange of cartels by the two monarchs, the Peace of the Ladies was negotiated at Cambrai by Louise of Savoy and Margaret of Austria, 5th August 1529. This confirmed F. in the possession of Burgundy, but stripped him of Flanders, Artois, and Italy. During the period of calm which followed, F. appears as the 'Father of Literature.' He patronised Budæus, Duchatel, Rabelais, and Robert Estienne, the great French printer of the Renaissance. But he never showed liberality to religious free thought, and his reign was marked by a series of *autos-da-fe.* The Edict of Toleration in 1535 was a mere political device to quiet the German Lutherans, whose neutrality he wished to gain, as well as the help of the Turks, in making another attempt on Italy. For this purpose also he had betrothed his son Henri to the Pope's niece, Catherine of Medici. Pope Paul III. at last reconciled Karl and F., who abandoned all his allies. In 1541, however, the murder in Milan of the French envoys on their way to Constantinople was made the occasion of another war. The Diet of Spires, indignant that F. should have brought the Turks to Nice, gave a large army to Karl, and Henry of England invaded Picardy. F., though victorious at Cerisolles (14th April 1544), was obliged to sign the peace of Crespy, which practically ratified those of Cambrai and Nice. Peace with England came two years later. The last years of his dishonourable reign were marked by an atrocious persecution of the Vaudois. He died at Rambouillet, 31st March 1547. F. founded the Royal College for three languages (Latin, Greek, Hebrew). See the *Mémoires* of Brantôme, Tavannes, Fleuranges, and De Montluc; also Gaillard's *Histoire de François I.* (7 vols. Par. 1760–69); Hermann's *Franz I.* (Leips. 1824); Röderer's *Louis XII. et François I.* (Par. 1825); and Kitchin's *History of France*, vol. ii. (1876).—**François II.**, born 19th January 1543, was the son of Henri II. and Catherine of Medici. He was married when Dauphin to Mary Stuart. He succeeded his father on the throne in 1559, but was entirely under the influence of the Guise family of Lorraine. St. André, Montmorency, the Bourbon princes, were driven from the court, and a wholesale persecution of Huguenots begun, which brought on the unsuccessful conspiracy of Amboise. Further troubles at Rouen and Grenoble suggested to the Chancellor L'Hôpital the Edict of Romorantur, which committed the crime of heresy to the clergy. This the Huguenots openly resisted; and the Assembly of Fontainebleau proving unequal to the occasion, the States-General were summoned to meet at Orleans, and in the midst of counterplot and treachery F. died, 5th December 1560. See Varillas' *Histoire de François II.*, and Kitchin's *History of France*, vol. ii. (1876).

Franc'olin (*Francolinus* or *Ithaginis*), a genus of Rasorial birds included in the *Tetraonidæ* or Grouse family, and nearly allied to the Quails (q. v.). They have short bills, the fourth, fifth, and sixth quills being the longest of the wings; the tarsi have one or two spurs, and the outer toe is longer than the inner. The hinder toe is elongated. These birds are natives of Europe, Asia, and Africa. The common F. (*F.* or *I. vulgaris*) is found in S. Europe, N. Africa, and in many parts of Asia. A very familiar species is the sanguine F. (*F.* or *I. cruentus*), inhabiting the Himalayas at an elevation, according to Hooker and Gould, of from 10,000 to 14,000 feet. The prevailing colour of the male is a slaty grey, with a black forehead and line round the eyes, a red chin and throat, a green breast and abdomen, and a tail tipped with white. The bill has a red base and black tip. The female is of a reddish-brown colour spotted with black on the upper parts. The average size is that of an ordinary fowl. The food consists of pine and juniper tops and berries.

Franco'nia, or **Eastern** or **Teuton'ic Fran'cia** (Ger. *Franken*), a name applied to the fatherland of the Franks to distinguish it from Latin *Francia* or *France*, was a region in the S.W. of modern Germany traversed by the Rhine, the Neckar, and the Main. It was the heart of the empire under the Karolings. On the death of the Emperor Heinrich II., he was succeeded (1024) by Konrad, Duke of F., and a descendant of Otto the Great. Konrad, the first of the Franconian emperors, united the kingdom of Burgundy to the empire on the death of its king, Rudolf, in 1032. His son, Heinrich III., 'one of the greatest of all the emperors,' greatly restored the imperial authority in Germany and Italy. The oppressive rule of Heinrich IV. drove the Saxons to revolt in 1073. Disputes with the popes chiefly occupied the reign of Heinrich V., on whose death in 1125 the dynasty came to an end, to be continued through female descent by that of Swabia (q. v.). The duchy of F. now sank in importance, and became split up from time to time into many small states, as Nassau, Katzenellenbogen, Hainau, Rhenish Palatinate, &c. The old circle of F. was re-established by Maximilian in 1512, and included Baireuth and Anspach, several counties and cities, and the sees of Bamberg, Eichstadt, and Würzburg. At the fall of the empire (1806) the greater part of F. passed to Bavaria (q. v.), where the name is preserved in that of the divisions Upper, Lower, and Middle F.; the rest was distributed between Würtemberg, Baden, Hessen, Hessen-Darmstadt, Prussia, and Saxony.

Fran'eker, an old town in the province of Friesland, Holland, on a canal, 10 miles W. of Leeuwarden by railway. It is notable as the seat of a university founded in 1585, and abolished by Napoleon in 1811, which boasted of many famous professors, as Heineccius, Vitringa, Schultens, Hemsterhuis, and Valckenaer. Pop. (1873) 4700.

Frangipa'ni, a noble Roman family which professed to trace its origin as far back as the 7th c., but which first becomes conspicuous in the 10th, when **Crescenzio F.** stands forward as the champion of the civil liberties of Rome against the encroachments of the popes. It played a prominent part in the long struggle between the popes and the German emperors. The F. uniformly took the imperial side; in particular, **Cencio F.** (12th c.) was the leader of the Ghibelline party in the time of the Emperor Heinrich V., but his career though turbulent has no abiding interest.

Frank'almoign ('free alms;' Lat. *libera eleemosyna*) is a kind of tenure in England by which a religious corporation held lands of the donor to them and to their successors for ever. The nature of the service under the tenure is not clearly defined, but the religious houses were bound by it to pray for the souls of the donor and of his heirs. Almost all the religious houses held their lands by F., and by it many ecclesiastical and charitable foundations hold them still, the nature of the service having at the Reformation been adapted to the doctrine of the Church of England.

Frank'enberg, a town in the kingdom of Saxony, on the Zschopau, 40 miles S.E. of Leipsic, with which it is connected by railway. It has large cotton and printing mills, besides manufactures of machinery, leather, Turkey-red dye, &c. Pop. (1871) 9710.

Frank'enhausen, a walled town in the principality of Schwarzburg-Rudolstadt, Germany, on the Wipper, 45 miles W.S.W. of Halle. It has a saltpetre refinery, and some trade in salt, corn, wool, and wine. Pop. (1871) 5221. On the neighbouring Schlachtberg ('Battle Mount') the Saxon, Brunswick, and Hessian troops quelled the peasant insurrection under Thomas Münzer, 15th May 1525.

Frank'enstein, an old town of Prussian Silesia, on the Pause, 45 miles S.S.E. of Breslau by railway. It has manufactures of linens, broadcloths, strawplait, and chemicals. Pop. (1871) 7171. About 7 miles to the S.W. is the strong rock-cut fortress of Silberberg, constructed by Friedrich the Great to command the road from Bohemia.

Frank'enthal, a town of Bavaria, in the Palatinate, on the Isenach, 3 miles W. of the Rhine, with which it is connected by a broad canal, and 9 miles S. of Worms by railway. It has large manufactures of woollen and cotton cloths, machinery, tobacco, &c. Pop. (1871) 7021.—There is another place of the same name in Upper Franconia, near the Thalrande, noted for its church (1743–72), which is visited on account of its 'miracles' by some 50,000 pilgrims yearly.

Frank'fort, the capital of Kentucky, U.S., picturesquely situated on the banks of the Kentucky River, is a station on the line of the Louisville and Lexington Railway. The State Capitol is a handsome building, and there are several important educational institutions. F. has two flour-mills, five saw-mills, a cotton-mill, and five distilleries. As the capital of Kentucky, it has been the centre of many stirring political events. Pop. (1870) 5396.

Frank'furt-on-the-Main, a city of Prussia, province of Hessen-Nassau, beautifully situated on the right bank of the Main, 20 miles above its confluence with the Rhine, and E.N.E. of Mainz. A place of great historical interest, it is now a great railway centre, and is entered by seven large gates, while its ramparts have given place (1804) to gardens and promenades. It has some twenty squares, of which the chief are the Rossmarkt ('horse-market'), with the monumental group of Fust, Gutenberg, and Schöffer, designed by Launitz; and the Goetheplatz, with the statue of Goethe (who was born in F.) by Schwanthaler. Among its sixteen churches is the cathedral of St. Bartholomew, begun in 1238 and finished in the 16th c., and in which the German emperors were crowned. It was restored in 1855, suffered from fire in 1867 and 1872, and been again restored (1876). The old stately townhouse, the Römer, still containing the Wahlzimmer ('election-room'), where the electors met, and the Kaisersaal, where the newly-elected emperor gave his first banquet, has of late years been enriched with portraits of all the emperors from Konrad I. to Franz II. Other public buildings are the Thurn-and-Taxis Palace, where the German Bund held its diets (1815–66), and the Saalhof, a modern imperial palace. There are also many educational and charitable institutions, literary and scientific societies, a medical institute (the Senckenberg), with a botanical garden and a large museum, a picture gallery, a public library of 100,000 vols., a theatre, &c. The chief street is the Zeil, 1215 feet long, in which are the large hotels. F. is visited annually by 120,000 persons, many of whom are attracted by the great fairs, which were already in their most flourishing state in the 16th c. The chief industries are printing, type-founding, and the making of jewellery, bijouterie, carpets, tobacco, sewing-machines; while as a place of trade, mainly in books, wine, timber, wool, silk, and leather, F. is one of the foremost centres in Europe. It is the banking-house of Germany, its exchange ruling the money market. The number of banks is over 100, while the aggregate capital is stated at twenty millions sterling, and the annual bills of exchange at twelve millions. The Rothschilds are the principal bankers; about one-third of the class are Jews. F. is connected with its suburb Sachsenhausen, on the opposite bank of the Main, by a stone bridge of fourteen arches (1340), by an iron suspension bridge, and by a railway bridge. The town is encircled by vineyards and orchards, which produce famous apple-wines. Pop. (1871) 91,040, of whom 25·8 per cent. are Roman Catholics, and 11 per cent. Jews, who once were restricted to a certain part of the city, the *Judengasse*. F. was the seat of a council convoked by Karl the Great in 794, and was the capital of the Eastern Frankish kingdom from 843 to 889. In 1248 it was made an imperial free city, and in 1356 the 'Golden Bull' of Karl IV. confirmed the custom of crowning the emperors here which had prevailed since the 12th c. Its geographical position early raised it to a high position as a place of trade. In 1806 Napoleon made it the capital of a grand duchy of the same name, and in 1815 it became the place of assembly of the Confederation Diet, at which it enjoyed an independent vote in the full council, and one in the united council conjointly with the other three free cities of Germany. F. sided with Austria in the war of 1866, and was annexed by Prussia, 18th October, after paying a fine of 31 million florins. The peace between France and Germany was concluded at F., the treaty being signed at the Swan Hotel by Bismarck and Jules Favre, 10th May 1871. See Böhmer's *Urkundenbuch der Reichstadt F.* (Frankf. 1836); Kirchner's *Geschichte der Stadt F.* (Frankf. 1807–10); Krug's *Historische topographische Beschreibung von F.* (Frankf. 1845); Battonn's *Oertliche Beschreibung der Stadt F.* (Frankf. 1863).

Frankfurt-on-the-Oder, a fortified town, and capital of a circle of the same name, in Brandenburg, Prussia, on the left bank of the Oder, 50 miles E.S.E. of Berlin by railway. It is connected by canals with the Elbe and Vistula, and has an extensive trade on the navigable Oder, which is here crossed by a bridge. F. was the seat of a university from 1506 till 1811, when the institution was incorporated with that of Breslau. It has a beautiful modern Marienkirche, several higher schools, manufactures of silk, leather, gloves, tobacco, mustard, &c., and large distilleries. There are three great annual fairs, attended largely by Poles, Silesians, &c. Pop. (1871) 43,214. F., an important Hanse town, was besieged by the Hussites in 1430, by the Poles in 1450, and by the Duke of Sagan in 1477, and suffered in the Thirty Years' War. Kunersdorf, 4½ miles from F., was the scene of a disastrous defeat of Friedrich the Great by the Russo-Austrian forces, 12th August 1759. See Sachse's *Geschichte der Stadt F.* (Frankf. 1830); and Spieker's *Geschichte der Stadt F.* (Frankf. 1853).

Frank'incense (Heb. *lebonah*, from *laban*, 'white,' Lat. *thus*) is a species of resin, of a white or pale-yellow colour, and agreeable odour when burned. There is much uncertainty as to the shrub or tree from which the resin exudes. According to Cant. iv. 6, 14, it was a native of Palestine, and according to Isa. lx. 6, and Jer. vi. 20, of Arabia, although these passages may merely refer to aromatic plants in general. At any rate, the F. now obtained in Arabia, of which it was said to be a native product by other ancient authorities besides the Bible, is of an inferior quality, and the best is brought from India, being the product of a tree called the *Boswellia serrata*, or *thurifera*. F. has always been much used in sacrificial worship, being burned on altars or in censers that its odour might rise up as 'a sweet savour' to heaven. In the Mosaic ritual it was used as an ingredient of Incense (q. v.), with which it is not to be confounded (as it is sometimes even in the Authorised Version), along with the meat-offering (Lev. ii. 1, 16, xxiv. 7; Num. v. 15). It is still used in the religious rites of various Churches.

Frankincense Plant.

Frank'ing Lett'ers, a privilege conferred on peers, members of the House of Commons, and some other officials, by 4 Geo. III. c. 24. It entitled those holding it to send ten letters per day, not over an ounce in weight, by the post free of charge, to any place in the United Kingdom, and to receive fifteen free. The person franking wrote his name or title on the corner of the letter. The privilege was much abused, and by statute of 1837 it was so trammelled as to be almost unavailable. It was abolished on the introduction of the uniform penny-postage system in 1840.

Frank'lin, Frank'leyn, or **Frank'eleyn**, was formerly the name of an English landholder whose estates were free (Fr. *franc*) of any feudal superior. Franklins, at first, seem to have been men of considerable property, belonging to the national as opposed to the feudal party in the 13th, 14th, and 15th centuries. The name is familiar to us from the F. who narrates one of the *Canterbury Tales*, and whom Chaucer describes in the Prologue as a rich country squire, with a sanguine complexion and white beard, a lover of good cheer, and free dispenser of it to others—

'Hit snewede in his hous of mete and drynke,
Of alle deyntees that men cowde thynke.'

He was likewise 'lord and sire' at sessions, and had been 'schirreve' and 'knight of the schire.' In John Russell's *Book of Nature* a F.'s feast is described, consisting of numerous rich and savoury dishes, the F. seeming to have been the type of plenteous hospitality. Spenser's F., Zele, the personification of Christian energy, is—

'Faire and free,
And entertaines with comely courteous glee'—(Bk. i. v. 10).

From such passages in Shakespeare as the clown's saying in *The Winter's Tale* (Act v. s. 2)—

'I am a gentleman,
Let boors and franklins say it, I'll swear it,'

and Imogen's request for a riding suit 'no costlier than would fit a franklin's housewife' (*Cymbeline*, Act iii. s. 2), the F. seems in Elizabeth's time to have sunk in the social scale, and was probably a small gentleman-farmer or wealthy yeoman. Sir Thomas Overbury describes a F. as an 'ancient yeoman of England,' and as a paragon of prudence and quiet virtue.

Frank'lin, Benjamin, an American philosopher, patriot, and philanthropist, was born at Boston, January 17, 1706. As an apprentice in his brother's printing-office, he eagerly devoted his leisure time to reading such books as he could get hold of. He was especially fascinated by the *Spectator*, whose simple and graceful style he strove to imitate. His first published literary efforts appeared in his brother's newspaper, the *New England Courant* (begun 1720); but the discovery of their authorship led to a quarrel between the brothers, which resulted in young F. breaking his indenture and running away to Philadelphia in 1723. Under the patronage of Governor Keith, he visited England in 1725-26, and after his return established in 1728 the *Pennsylvania Gazette*, which exerted a great influence in Philadelphia and the neighbouring provinces, and raised its owner rapidly to fame and fortune. In it, as well as in his *Poor Richard's Almanac* (1732-57), he developed his notions of morality, embodying his teachings in short pithy sentences, which have in not a few instances passed into proverbs. The precepts he enforced he practised himself; and in his *Art of Virtue* he enumerated thirteen virtues by which he proposed to reach perfection. He took an active interest in all reforms calculated to benefit society; founded the Philadelphia Library (1742), the Philosophical Society (1744), and the same year the first academy, now the university. He began his investigations on the nature of lightning in 1746, proving its identity with frictional Electricity (q. v.) in 1752; and for his papers on this subject he was elected F.R.S. in 1775, and received the Copley medal. In 1753, he became Postmaster-General for the Colonies, and four years later went to England to urge the claim of Penn's representatives for exemption from taxation. He visited Scotland in 1759, and returned home in 1762. On the passing of the Stamp Act (1764), F. was again sent to England to remonstrate; and his exertions procured its repeal in 1766. His efforts, however, could not prevent the War of Independence, and after the rupture in 1776 he was among the first to sign the 'Declaration.' The same year he was sent on a diplomatic mission to Paris, where he remained till 1785, and earned a lasting popularity by his natural, simple, and dignified bearing, and his practical wisdom. After his return he remained at Philadelphia till his death, April 17, 1790. F. combined in rare balance the inductive faculty of the true man of science, the native tact of the politician, and the shrewd common sense of the man of business. His improvements and inventions had all a practical turn; and the untiring energy of his mind is well shown in the curious calculations which he made in his moments of leisure and relaxation. He left an Autobiography going down to 1757, and a voluminous correspondence of later date, which were published by his grandson, W. T. Franklin, in 1817. A complete edition of his works was published by Jared Sparks (Boston, 10 vols.). Various biographies have been written—by Condorcet (1790), Chasus (1841), and Mignet, in French, by Bauer (1803-6), and Schmaltz (1840), in German, and by Parton (1864) and Theodore Parker in his *Historic Americans* (1870).

Franklin, Rear-Admiral Sir John, the greatest of the Arctic explorers, and the first discoverer of a North-West Passage, was born at Spilsby, Lincolnshire, 16th April 1786. He manifested a passion for the sea from early boyhood, and in 1800 was appointed midshipman on board the *Polyphemus*, which in the following year led the attack at the great battle of Copenhagen. Shortly afterwards F. was transferred to the *Investigator*, commanded by his relative Captain Flinders, who was commissioned to explore and survey the Australian coasts. In this expedition F. acquired a knowledge of practical seamanship and nautical surveying. In the *Porpoise*, which superseded the *Investigator*, he was wrecked, and left with ninety-four persons on a low sandbank for two months. Appointed to the *Bellerophon*, he acted as signal midshipman in that ship at the battle of Trafalgar. At the siege of New Orleans he signally distinguished himself in a gunboat action, in which he was wounded. Promoted lieutenant, he commanded the *Trent* in the Arctic expedition of 1818, sent out towards the Pole by the Spitzbergen route. He was intrusted with the command of the first overland expedition to the Polar Sea in 1819-22, and during these years performed perhaps the most extraordinary journey on record—traversing 5500 miles, and surveying the N. coast of America eastward from the Coppermine River to Coronation Gulf, amid unparalleled hardships and sufferings from want and extreme cold. In a second overland expedition (1825-27), he surveyed the Polar shores W. from the Mackenzie River halfway to Icy Cape. On his return he received the honour of knighthood. As Governor of Van Diemen's Land from 1838-44, he merited and won the affectionate esteem of the colonists. He was appointed to the command of the fatal Arctic expedition of 1845, consisting of the ships *Erebus* and *Terror*, which were last seen on the 26th July 1845, near the S. entrance to Melville Bay. After wintering off Beechey Island in 1845-46, he sailed up Wellington Channel for a considerable distance, then returning, he sought for a passage by a southern route. He died on board his ship, June 11, 1847, off the N. coast of King William's Island, after establishing the connection between Barrow Strait on the N. and the previously-explored arms of the Arctic Sea on the S., and thus demonstrating the existence of a North-West Passage (q. v.). F. is the author of the *Narratives* of his famous overland journeys.

LADY JANE F., second wife of Rear-Admiral Sir John F.,

and the daughter of John Griffen, Esq., born about 1805, was married in 1828. After the Arctic expedition commanded by her husband had been 'missing' for three years, she (in 1848) offered substantial rewards to any navigators who might rescue or afford relief to the *Erebus* and *Terror*, and from this date onward the one paramount object of her life was to succour the lost expedition. At the sacrifice of her whole fortune, she fitted out and despatched several vessels to prosecute the search —the *Prince Albert* in 1850 and again in 1851, the *Isabel* in 1852, and the *Fox* (Captain M'Clintock) in 1857. M'Clintock (q. v.) was successful in discovering the fate of F., the destruction of his ships, and the fact that he was the first to discover a North-West Passage. In recognition of her husband's discoveries, Lady F. was presented with the gold medal of the Royal Geographical Society in 1860. Lady F., whose devotion and self-sacrifice during so many years were warmly appreciated by her countrymen, died in London, 18th July 1875.

Frank-Marriage (Low Lat. *liberum maritagium*) arises where lands are given to a man along with a wife, the daughter or cousin of the donor, without further words. In these circumstances, or from the use of the words F.-M., the law inferred that the land was to be the property of the spouses, and after them of their lawful issue: it created a tenancy in special tail. F. has been superseded by modern conveyancing.

Frank'-Pledge, the Norman name of the old English **Frith'-borh** ('peace-pledge'), an association of ten men in common responsibility. It has often been confounded with the tithing, which though perhaps, like the hundred, originally a personal division of the host, certainly became in England a geographical division, the administrative unit for police and fiscal purposes. It was an English principle that every *landless* man should have a lord as his surety for judicial appearance; this was subsequently made universal. On the other hand, the tithing was bound to pursue a thief, and to do justice. But the laws of the Confessor direct men to combine in *frithborh*, or *ten-manne-tale* (in the N. of England), with a headman, or capital pledge, *borhs-ealdor*, or *frithborge-head*. These are mutual sureties: if a criminal escape, they must purge themselves of complicity, or answer for all damage done. The institution was, in cases of murder, extended by the Conqueror to the hundred. The 'view of F.-P.' consisted in keeping these associations in order by the infliction of fines. This was the duty of the local court, and the obligation of the *borhs-ealdor* to appear afterwards became useful as a machinery for representing the interests of towns. The duty passed as a manorial right to the court leet, where it still exists, at least in Yorkshire. For an account of the Irish system of F.-P., see O'Curry's *Manners and Customs of the Ancient Irish*, vol. i. pp. 196-205.

Franks, a great German nation, who first appear under that name on the Lower Rhine in the 3d c. A.D. They were probably formed by an amalgamation or confederacy of those tribes who dwelt in the same region in the 1st c.—the Sigambri, Chatti, Bructeri, &c.—and first became important when they overthrew Roman authority in Gaul. See FRANCE.

Franz I. (Stephen), German emperor, born at Nancy, 8th December 1708, was the son of Leopold Duke of Lothringen and the Princess of Orleans, niece of Louis XIV. In 1729 he succeeded to his father's duchies of Lothringen and Bar, but the preliminary treaty of Vienna (1735) provided that, on the impending extinction of the Medici family in the male line, the Duke of Lothringen should be made Grand Duke of Tuscany with right of succession in his family, and that the exiled King of Poland, Stanislas Leczinsky, should during his life have Lothringen and Bar, these duchies to revert to France. F., whom his Tuscan subjects disliked, and who had acted as commander-in-chief of the imperial army against the Turks, now became co-regent, and on the death of Karl VII. (1745) was elected emperor. By the peace of Dresden (1745) Prussia acknowledged F.'s imperial title. The history of the reign belongs rather to the life of Maria Theresa (q. v.). F. was a 'solid pacific gentleman,' engaged latterly in banking, farming the customs of Saxony, and for some time actually supplying the Prussian commissariat with meal. He was much opposed to the French alliance, and more interested in chemistry than in government. He died suddenly, 18th August 1765, at Innsbruck.—**Franz II. (Joseph Karl**, better known as Franz I., Emperor of Austria) was the eldest son of the Emperor Leopold I. and Maria Louisa, daughter of Charles III. of Spain. He was born at Florence, 12th February 1768, and on the death of his father in 1792 succeeded to the imperial title. He took part in the 'coalition of kings' against the French republic, but the brilliant campaigns of Napoleon in N. Italy forced on the peace of Campo Formio (1797), by which the Austrian Netherlands were ceded to France, and Venice was divided between the parties. The provisions of Campo Formio were substantially repeated at Luneville (1801), when the return of Napoleon from Egypt had destroyed the second coalition. In 1805, alarmed by Napoleon's assumption of the imperial title, F. called himself 'Erwählter Römischer Kaiser, Erbkaiser (hereditary emperor) von Oesterreich.' The third coalition was destroyed at Ulm and Austerlitz the same year, and by the treaty of Presburg F. gave up all his interest in Venice, recognised all the French institutions in Italy, and made large concessions of territory and privileges to Bavaria, Würtemberg, and Baden. On 6th August 1806 F. resigned the empire of the Romans. In 1809 he again declared war. The final result was the peace of Vienna and Schönbrunn. Salzburg and part of Upper Austria were given to Bavaria, the Illyrian Provinces to Napoleon as King of Italy, and parts of Galicia to Saxony and Russia. F. then gave his daughter Maria in marriage to Napoleon, and in 1812 agreed to assist him against Russia, England, and Sweden. After the tragedy of Moscow, he attempted to mediate, but failing, went over to the allies by the treaty of Töplitz, 9th September 1813. F. also succeeded in detaching Murat, now King of Naples, from his master's cause. The Congress of Vienna gave back to F. nearly all he had lost since Campo Formio except the Netherlands, and he retained his possessions in N. Italy. He also became the President of the new Germanic Confederation, which lasted till 1866. Austrian troops were in Lombardy and Naples in 1821, but otherwise the rest of F.'s reign was calm. He died 2d March 1835, and was succeeded by his eldest son, Ferdinand I. F.'s policy in the latter part of his reign was directed almost entirely by Metternich (q. v.).

Franz'ensbrunn, or **E'gerbad**, one of the most celebrated spas of Bohemia, 4 miles N.W. of Eger. It has four springs, mainly alkalo-saline, used in drinking and bathing. There are also mud and vapour baths. F. sends away yearly some 200,000 jars of mineral water. The springs were discovered in 1793.

Franz-Josef, Emperor of Austria, born 18th August 1830, was the son of Archduke Franz Karl and Sophia of Bavaria. The Italian revolution and that of the Hungarians made it necessary that F.'s uncle Ferdinand should abdicate, and his father having renounced his rights, F. succeeded (2d December 1848) with promise of a free constitution and equality of representation. This promise was broken, and the ancient rights of Hungary were destroyed. While Radezky drove the Sardinians out of Lombardy, F.'s generals, with the help of Russia, suppressed the rising of Kossuth. By the edicts of Schönbrunn, ministerial responsibility was declared at an end, and sheer absolutism expressly claimed. Government was centralised at Vienna, and several financial and commercial reforms were carried out. In 1855 F. arranged a Concordat with Rome, doing away with nearly all the reforms of Joseph II. The Franco-Italian war of 1859 and the Prusso-Italian war of 1866 stripped Austria of Lombardy and Venice, and excluded her from the Germanic Confederacy, and the emperor at last devoted himself to the adjustment of the Austro-Hungarian question. Meanwhile the constitution of the Reichsrath was enlarged, and in 1862 F. sanctioned the principle of ministerial responsibility. He increased his popularity by liberating the Polish patriot Langiewicz. In 1866 he chose Von Beust as his prime minister, who was succeeded in 1871 by Andrassy. Chiefly through the exertions of Déak and Beust, the Dual Constitution (giving a certain amount of autonomy to Hungary) was adopted in 1867. In that year F. was crowned King of Hungary at Pesth. The heir-apparent of the empire is the Archduke Rudolf, born 22d August 1858 of Elizabeth of Bavaria.

Franz-Josef's Land, a name given to the territory discovered by the Austro-Hungarian Polar expedition of 1873-74. It lies in lat. 80°-83° N., and long. 50°-70° W., 345 miles N. of Nova Zembla, and consists mainly of four promontories, named Vichy, Wilczek, König Oscar, and Petermann Lands, the connection between which was not completely traced, and which partly enclose a deep inlet of the sea, entered by 'Austria Sund.'

The shores of Wilczek Land rise in a rugged precipitous range of hills, which send down enormous glaciers. Great part of the explored surface is covered with ice. There are some thirty islands in and about the mouth of the Sund, five of which are of large size.

Frasca'ti, a town of Italy, on the slopes of the Sabine Hills, 10 miles E.S.E. of Rome by railway. It has a cathedral and many splendid villas, as the Mondragon and Traverna of the Borghese family. Pop. 6000. F. was named from the *frasche* or underwood with which, on the destruction of the neighbouring Tusculum by the Romans, A.D. 1191, the fugitive citizens here erected huts.

Fra'ser, Simon. See LOVAT, LORD.

Fra'sera, a genus of Dicotyledonous plants, belonging to the natural order *Gentianaceæ*. The flowers possess a four-cleft calyx and corolla, and four stamens. The fruit is a capsule. A familiar species is *F. Walteri*, which grows in Carolina and Virginia, and is known in commerce as *American Calumba*, its root being used in pharmacy.

Fra'serburgh, a seaport of Aberdeenshire, on a bay one side of which runs out into Kinnaird's Head, 46 miles N. of Aberdeen, and 19 N.N.W. of Peterhead by railway. It is the centre of large herring, cod, and ling fisheries, and has one of the best harbours on the E. coast, constructed at a cost of £50,000. A quadrangular building at the W. end of the town was intended for a college by Sir Alexander Fraser, who procured a crown charter in 1592, and had it renewed and enlarged in 1601. Pop. (1871) 4268. F. was formerly called Faithly, but its present name was conferred on it in honour of its proprietor, Sir Alexander Fraser, by James VI. (1592), who also made it a free port, free burgh of barony, and free regality.

Fraser River, the chief stream of British Columbia, rises in two branches, one of which is 250, and the other 200 miles in length. These, uniting at Fort George, flow S. and S.W. through the province, and enter the Pacific nearly opposite the southern extremity of Vancouver Island. The length of F. R. from Fort George is 800 miles. It is navigable by ocean ships for 75 miles (to New Westminster), and by steamers for 150 miles (to Fort Hope). Its main tributaries are the Stuart and Chilcotin on the right, and the Thompson on the left. The river, which flows for the most part in deep *cañons*, is rich in salmon and in the *oulachan*, or candle-fish, a nutritious, oil-yielding smelt. Its basin includes nearly the whole of the province, and its valley embraces valuable fur districts and pasture lands, while timber abounds, especially in the districts around its lower course. But the F. R. is best known for the rich gold-fields along its banks, the yield of which, since their discovery previously to 1857, has been such as to constitute them the rival of the best 'diggings' in Australia or California.

Frater'cula. See PUFFIN.

Fratricell'i (Lat. *fraterculi*, 'little brothers') was originally the Italian name of the whole Franciscan order. When that order adopted the milder interpretation of their *rule* given by Pope Gregory IX., the more ascetic members, who insisted on the rule being observed in its literal strictness, were called the Zealous, Spirituals, &c. In 1294 some of the Spirituals in Italy obtained permission from Pope Celestine V. to form themselves into a separate community, and to them was reserved the name of F. Being persecuted by the rest of the order, they fled (1307) into France, and joined themselves with a sect of Spirituals there, followers of Peter John Oliva, who had separated from the order for the same reason. Pope Clement V. attempted, at the Council of Vienne (1312–13), to put an end to the schism by a compromise. John XXII., on the other hand, ordered the extirpation of the F., along with the Beghards (from whom they differed only in being real monks), and immense numbers of both were put to death in Italy, France, and Spain. The only protection they found was in Germany, from the Emperor Ludwig of Bavaria, who sided with them against the Pope. After the death of John, Benedict XII. and Clement VI. tried to heal the schism by gentle measures, in consequence of which many returned to the order from which they had seceded. When, in 1368, the Franciscan order was divided into the two sections of the Conventual Brethren and the Brethren of the Observation, the latter, who were in fact the Spirituals inside the order, were joined by some of the Spirituals who had formerly left it; but the F. and the Beghards as a body still held out, and continued at open war with the popes. They were severely persecuted by Nicholas V. and succeeding popes, but were not extirpated before the Reformation, at which time those that were left became Protestants. Besides their controversy with the Franciscans regarding poverty, the F. were distinguished by certain peculiar tenets, which were chiefly those promulgated by the pseudo-Abbot Joachim. They inveighed against the corruptions of the Church, and predicted a reformation and the restoration of the true gospel of Jesus. They also held that the true and eternal gospel of God, which indeed was to supersede that of Christ, was manifested to mankind by St. Francis. Hence it was that his *rule* was more to them than any number of papal bulls. See Mosheim's *Church History* (Reid's ed. 1860), and Milman's *Latin Christianity*.

Fratt'a-Maggio're, a town in the province of Caserta, S. Italy, 6 miles N.E. of Naples by railway. It has, among other industries, extensive rope-making, silk-culture, and fruit-rearing. Pop. 10,687.

Fraud. When F. enters into a contract, it prevents consent, and the apparent contract is void *ab initio*. F. giving rise to an agreement may be a ground of reduction of a contract, but it will have no effect in a question with a *bona fide* assignee for consideration. When the F. is not that of the party contracting, but of a third party, compensation can only be required from that party. F. may be by false representation, concealment of material circumstance, underhand dealing, or by taking advantage of imbecility or intoxication. In mercantile dealings, ordinary artifices to enhance the value of goods is not F. Every one is supposed to understand these, and to be capable of protecting himself against them. Neither is concealment of fact necessarily F., though circumstances may make it so. A knows and B does not that there is a mine on B's estate. In negotiating a purchase of B's estate A is not obliged to tell B of the mine. But if one man be in confidential relationship to another, he must not in negotiating with that other conceal material knowledge arising from the relationship. In this case the law requires *uberrima fides*, perfect good faith. Thus in Maddeford *v.* Austwick (1 Sim. R. 89) a contract was reduced by which the partner of a firm purchased the share of a copartner, the grounds of reduction being that the purchaser kept the books of the firm, from which he must have known that the price was inadequate, and that he concealed the inadequacy. It was, however, proved in the case that the book-keeping was intricate, that the plaintiff was not conversant with accounts, and that the defendant kept a private book. A contract will not be set aside merely because an honourable man would not have entered into it. There must be circumstances falling within some legal definition of F.

Fraud'ulent Bank'ruptcy is the wilful cheating of creditors by a bankrupt. The offence is usually committed by the bankrupt concealing part of his property, by falsifying his books, by stating fictitious losses, by connivance with fictitious or exaggerated claims, or by concealing important information from his trustee. The Bankruptcy Acts give ample powers to trustees in cases of F. B.

Fraun'hofer, Joseph von, a German physicist and optician, was born at Straubing, in Bavaria, 6th March 1787. In 1818 he became Director of the Optical Institute in Benediktbeuren, and in 1823 professor and conservator of the physical cabinet at Munich, where he died, 7th June 1826. He is celebrated as one of the founders of Spectrum Analysis (q. v.), the dark absorption lines of the solar spectrum being commonly known as *Frauenhofer's lines*. Of optical instruments invented or improved by F., we may mention a heliometer, an achromatic microscope, an annular microscope, and the great Dorpat telescope called by Struve the *giant refractor*.

Frau'stadt (Polish *Wszowa*), a fortified town of Posen, Prussia, near the Silesian frontier, 25 miles N.E. of Glogau by railway. It lies in a sandy plain, in which one can count 100 windmills, and has manufactures of cloths, yarn, dyes, &c. Pop. (1871) 6595. F. was founded by Germans, and belonged to the Princes of Glogau till 1343.

Fraxinell'a. See DITTANY.

Frax'inus. See ASH.

Freck'les. See EPHELIS.

Fred'eric (German). See FRIEDRICH.

Fred'erik I., King of Denmark and Norway, born in 1471, succeeded his nephew Christian II. in 1523. His policy was reactionary. The laws in favour of the peasants and the newly-printed books were publicly burned, the poor-schools were closed, and the Lutheran preachers expelled from the country. Shortly before the Diet of Augsburg there was an utter change in F.'s religious policy. He died in 1533.—**Frederik II.**, born in 1534, the eldest son of Christian III., succeeded his father in 1559. He completely crushed the Ditmarshers at the battle of Hejde. His foolish claim to bear the three northern crowns on his arms provoked the Seven Years' War with Erik XIV. of Sweden, in which the Danes ravaged Vestgoland, Smaaland, and Ostgoland, while the Swedes wasted Blekingen. Peace was secured at Stettin in 1570, Denmark giving up all claim to Sweden, and getting confirmed her rights to Norway, Skaania, Halland, and Blekingen. The statesman Peder Oxe restored order to the finances, improved the condition of the serfs, and introduced to Denmark many agricultural novelties. F. was a Lutheran, and compelled subscription by all Danish residents of twenty-five articles drawn up by Jacob Andreæ of Tübingen. He died in 1588. His daughter Anne was married to James I. of England.—**Frederik III.**, the son of Christian IV. and Anna Katherina of Brandenburg, was born in 1609, and elected to the Danish throne on his father's death in 1648. In 1657 began a war with Karl X. of Sweden, the result of which was the cession to Sweden of Trondhjem and Aggerhus in Norway, the old Danish provinces of Skaania, Halland, and Bleking, with the islands of Lessö, Anholt, Femern, and Bornholm. In 1659 the crown of Denmark was suddenly declared hereditary, and the sovereign absolutely independent. The royal secretary, Peter Schumacher, introduced important administrative changes and reforms in the naval, military, financial, and university affairs. F. died 9th February 1670.—**Frederik IV.**, born 11th October 1671, succeeded his father, Christian V., in 1699, and fought with Sweden and her allies. The war was ended by the peace of Frederiksborg in 1720. In 1721 the frivolous 'type quarrel' between F. and Count Görtz, regent of the Gottorp territory, and formerly minister to Karl XII. of Sweden, again produced war, and the duchy of Holstein-Gottorp was reunited to the Danish crown lands. F. by economy was able greatly to reduce the national debt. He also showed great benevolence in dealing with the pestilence which in 1710 cut off 25,000 people in Copenhagen, the fire which in 1725 destroyed two-thirds of the city, the inundation which in 1717 made useless the Ditmarsh pastures. F. sent out Ziegenbalg to the Danish mission at Tranquebar, and assisted the Greenland missionary Hans Egede. He also started a Greenland trading company. At home he did much for the serfs, and opened a number of free schools.—**Frederik V.**, born 31st March 1723, was the son of Christian VI., and succeeded his father in 1746. He married Louisa, daughter of George II. of England. After his marriage with Juliana Maria of Brunswick he became dissipated, and incurred heavy debts. Public affairs, however, were ably administered by Counts Schimmelmann and Bernstorf, the latter of whom encouraged trade, manufactures, and science. From Catherine II. of Russia Bernstorf obtained the treaty renouncing the Russian claims to Gottorp in exchange for Oldenburg and Delmenhorst. F. died 14th January 1766.—**Frederik VI.**, son of Christian VII. and Caroline Matilda, sister of George III. of England, was born 28th January 1768, and began to rule for his half-witted father in 1784. In 1788 a law giving complete freedom to the peasants was passed, and in 1792 the slave-trade was declared illegal in the Danish W. Indian islands. After the formation of the Second Armed Neutrality in 1800, however, the Danish practice of sending armed convoys with their merchant vessels led to Nelson's famous attack on Copenhagen. In 1807, England, suspecting a treaty between Denmark and France, sent Gambier and Cathcart to the Baltic, who destroyed the Danish fleet. When F., therefore, succeeded his father as king in 1808, the country was in a miserable state. In 1809 he issued 142,000,000 paper notes, which afterwards were suddenly reduced to one-sixth of their nominal value. This saved the literal engagements of the state, but greatly aggravated private misfortune. Even after the battle of Leipsic F. remained true to Napoleon, but was finally forced by the peace of Kiel (1814) to yield Norway to Sweden, obtaining instead Swedish Pomerania and Rügen, which were at once ceded to Prussia in return for Lauenburg and 2,000,000 rixdollars. Heligoland was ceded to England, and at the Congress of Vienna F. had to submit to be admitted to the German Confederation as Duke of Holstein and Lauenburg. Denmark slowly recovered from its depression, F. contributing much to the process by the establishment of a National Bank, and by the voluntary concession of Provincial Chambers in 1831. He died 3d December 1839.—**Frederik VII.**, born 6th October 1808, was the son of Christian VIII. On his father's death in 1848 Russian intervention caused the evacuation of Jutland by Mangol, and after some help had arrived from Oscar of Sweden, the great powers arranged the seven months' truce of Malmo, the duchies being put under five joint-commissioners. The contention of the duchies and of Prussia at this time was that the former constituted one state, subject to a male line of succession and part of the German Confederation. The Vorparlement, therefore, had jurisdiction to interfere by military executions. After more fighting at Ulleruss and Frederits, another arrangement for joint rule was made. In 1850 the Prussian general Willisen and the insurgent army were completely defeated at Isted, and the old Danish frontier, the Dannevirke, reoccupied. The duchies were then put under a Danish, Prussian, and Austrian commission. In 1850 F. granted a liberal constitution, which Denmark at present enjoys. He died at Glücksburg, 15th November 1863.

Fred'erick City, a city of Maryland, U.S., on the Baltimore and Ohio Railway. It has twelve churches, a handsome new town-hall, two collegiate schools, three foundries, three planing-mills, four large tanneries, three newspapers, &c. Pop. (1871) 8526.

Fred'ericksburg, a city of Virginia, U.S., on the S. bank of the Rappahannock, 92 miles from its mouth, and 61 N. of Richmond by railway. It has several large flour-mills, which are supplied with water-power by a dam stretching across the river. There are also iron-foundries, woollen-mills, and paper factories. F. was in great part destroyed in a battle between the Federals under Burnside and the Confederates under Lee, when the former were forced back across the river, with a loss of 12,321 men, 13th December 1862. Pop. (1870) 4046.

Fred'ericton, the capital of New Brunswick, in the Dominion of Canada, on a beautiful plain stretching along the right bank of the St. John, 84 miles from its mouth, and 105 miles N.N.W. of St. John by railway. It is the seat of a bishop, and has a university, a cathedral church, Government-house, courts, public libraries, &c. The river is navigable up to F. for large steamers. A steam-ferry connects F. with St. Mary's on the opposite bank of the river. Pop. (1871) 6006.

Fred'erikshald, formerly **Hald'en**, a seaport in the S. of Norway, in the amt of Smaalenen, on the Tistedal-Elv, an inlet of the Swinesund, 60 miles S.S.E. of Christiania. It is a splendid rock-bound harbour, and has a large export trade in timber and lobsters. In 1869 there entered the port 419 ships of 54,600 tons. F. is connected with Christiania by a regular line of steamers. In the Tistedal are beautiful waterfalls. To the E. of the port is the rock fortress of Frederiksteen, 400 feet high, which can boast of never having been taken in spite of many assaults. In one of these Karl XII. of Sweden lost his life (1718), and a monument was raised on the spot where he was killed in 1814. Pop. (1871) 9200.

Free Bench, a custom of dower which prevailed in some parts of England, under which the widow had the whole or the half of the lands held by her husband in Socage (q. v.), *dum sola et casta vixerit.*

Free Church of Scotland is the name assumed by the party which in 1843 withdrew from the Established Church and formed themselves into a separate religious body. From the first establishment of the Church after the Reformation there had been a constant tendency on the part of some Churchmen to claim that the Church was independent of the State, notwithstanding—nay, as some affirmed, even in consequence of—her establishment. And although the Revolution settlement appeared to give less ground for this claim than did the statutes of King James I., the Westminster Confession contains the assertion that 'The Lord Jesus, as King and Head of his Church, hath therein appointed a government in the hand of church officers distinct from the civil magistrate.' It was a dispute regarding this claim that led to the Disruption of 1843, for the proper understanding of which it is necessary to go back to a point ten years previous to that event. The system of patronage, after being twice abolished by Parliament—in 1649 and 1690—was restored by the Act of Queen Anne, 1712. According to this statute a Presbytery was bound to ordain or induct to a vacant parish the qualified presentee of the patron, the call of the people being regarded as a mere form. The Evangelical party in the Church 'had always held it as a principle that the Church could not, without sin, act under any system of patronage which was subversive of the congregational call,' and that party, having now become the majority, passed in 1834 an Act called the Veto Act, according to which no minister was to be intruded on a parish contrary to the will of the people. In the autumn of that same year Mr. Young was presented by the patron to the parish of Auchterarder. But as a majority of the parishioners were opposed to his settlement, the non-intrusion party, as they were now called, in the Church declared the presentation to be null and void according to the Veto Act. Thereupon both the patron and the presentee appealed to the Court of Session, which decreed (1837) that the Presbytery proceed to ordain Mr. Young. The Court, in giving decree in this and all the subsequent cases, disclaimed any desire or any right to interfere with the Church, or to review or interfere with the decisions of her courts, when acting within her own recognised constitution; only it claimed, as representing the law, a third party, neither the Church nor the State, the right to decide, first, the *legal* point, that, in terms of the compact between the Church and the State, the former had no right to alter the constitution on the basis of which she was established, and therefore that passing the Veto Act was *ultra vires* of the Church; and, secondly, the *civil* case between parties within the Church, in which one party complained of being injuriously affected by the illegal proceedings of another.

As soon as this decision was given the non-intrusion party declared that the Church of Scotland was *the creature of the State,* or was Erastian in constitution, inasmuch as she recognised the right of the State to interfere, and of the civil courts to judge, in matters falling within the proper sphere and jurisdiction of the Church. And the same party declared in the General Assembly of 1838 (being a majority) that the supremacy and sole headship of the Lord Jesus Christ 'they would assert and at all hazards defend.' When the judgment had been confirmed on appeal by the House of Lords, May 1839, the General Assembly by a large majority passed a resolution pledging the Church implicitly to obey the civil courts in all matters of civil interest, but firmly refusing their control in things spiritual.

A case that had an important bearing on the controversy was the Stewarton case, which arose out of the Chapel Act, passed by the same Assembly which passed the Veto Act, and by the same party. According to that Act, districts in connection with 'chapels of ease' were to be erected into parishes *quoad sacra*, and their ministers to acquire the status of members of Presbytery. Such a parish was to be disjoined from the parish of Stewarton in 1840, when certain of the heritors applied for an interdict, which was granted, although the case was not decided by the Court of Session till January 1843. The non-intrusion party held the action of the civil courts in this case to be the most violent attack which had yet been made upon the Church, the foundation principle of which was Presbyterian—that all ministers are equal—and were prepared to accept an adverse decision as alone sufficient to drive them from the Church.

Meantime a number of other cases had been decided involving the same principle as the Auchterarder case. A second case arose out of the latter by the patron and presentee raising an action for damages against the Presbytery, which the Court of Session decided they were entitled to, a decision which was afterwards confirmed by the House of Lords. In the first case it had been decided by the Supreme Civil Court simply that the Presbytery had acted illegally in setting the presentee aside by the Veto Act; and from the injurious effects of this new interpretation (as the non-intrusion party considered it) of the law of patronage, the Church might have been protected by a change effected by the legislature in that law. When the negotiations for relief in that way failed, the party desiring it passed in the Assembly of 1842 their 'Claim, Declaration, and Protest,' which set forth the Church's constitutional principles concerning the headship of Christ, the various encroachments on her rights and liberties by the civil courts; the impossibility, consistently with her duty to Christ the Head, of submitting to the civil supremacy which had been assumed, and the necessity she would be under, if redress were denied, of withdrawing from her connection with the State. Matters were supposed to be made worse than ever by the decision of the House of Lords (August 1842), confirming on appeal that of the Court of Session in the second Auchterarder case. By this second decision it was declared that the obligation of the Presbytery to 'receive and admit' was a civil obligation, the violation of which was to be regarded and punished as a civil offence. The party held that the conditions produced by this new interpretation of the relation existing between the Church and the State (with which they always identified the civil courts, while the other party always regarded these as merely holding the legal balance between the Church and the State, and between different parties in the Church) were such that the Church could not fulfil them consistently with her principles. The crisis was produced by the decision in the Stewarton case (January 1843), and by the refusal of the Government (January) to take the Claim of Right into consideration, and the vote of the House of Commons (March) to the same effect. When the General Assembly met in May, the Moderator, Dr. Welsh, in his own name and that of 203 other members, read a protest, and the whole party withdrew and constituted themselves the Assembly of the F. C., with Dr. Chalmers as moderator. In the whole Church 474 ministers adhered to the Protest and resigned their livings. Since the Disruption, the F. C. has shared in the general prosperity of the nation. Its career has been marked (until recent years) by ecclesiastical vigour, well-defined policy, and able and energetic administration. As an evidence of the enthusiasm which marked its birth, it may be mentioned that the sum of £232,347 was contributed for its support during the sitting of its first Assembly. The maintenance of all the existing missions of the Establishment was boldly undertaken by the F. C., whose organisation was finally completed by the adoption of the Sustentation Fund (q. v.) and of an education scheme. In 1858 its doctrine of 'spiritual independence' brought it into something like collision with the State. The F. C. minister of Cardross was suspended for immorality. On the ground of irregularity in the ecclesiastical proceedings he appealed for redress to the civil courts. For this he was instantly deposed. The Court of Session, however, maintained its right to examine into the procedure of every 'voluntary association' for ecclesiastical purposes, not indeed to revise its ecclesiastical decisions, but to ascertain whether or not the compact between individual members and the society had been justly and equitably carried out. Negotiations with a view to the union of the Presbyterian Churches of Scotland were abandoned in 1873, mainly on account of the disinclination of the F. C. to modify its profession of the Establishment doctrine. The Reformed Presbyterian Church was received into the F. C. in May 1876. At the end of 1876 the F. C. had 984 ministerial charges, 34 'preaching stations,' and 39 foreign mission stations. Since the passing of the Education Act of 1872 most of the F. C. schools have passed into the hands of the School Boards. Colleges for the training of ministers and Normal Training Schools exist in Edinburgh, Glasgow, and Aberdeen. The aggregate sum raised by the F. C. of S. for all purposes from 1843 to March 31, 1876, was £11,782,978. See Innes's *Law of Creeds in Scotland* (Edinb. 1867); Buchanan's *Ten Years' Conflict* (Edinb. new ed. 1852); Brown's *Annals of the Disruption* (Edinb. 1876); Hanna's *Memoirs of Dr. Chalmers* (Edinb. 1854): on the other side, Bryce's *Ten Years of the Church of Scotland* (1850); *The Church of Scotland and the F. C., their Relation*, &c., by Veritas (Glasg. 1870); *Memoir of Dr. N. Macleod* (Lond. 1876).

Free Cities are in general those cities which became more or less independent during the middle ages, though the name is especially applied to the *free imperial cities* of Germany. These were at first closely connected with the emperors, and almost constantly at war with the nobles; but as the imperial power sank, they became practically independent, and formed leagues, such as the Rhenish League, which numbered seventy towns in the 13th c., and the great Hanseatic League, which, arising from a commercial treaty between Hamburg and Lübeck (1241), at one time included eighty towns, monopolised the Baltic trade, had fleets and armies of its own, and opposed successfully the Swedish and Danish kings. Its various towns were divided into four sections, presided over by Danzig, Köln, Brunswick, and Lübeck —where the Diet was held. The League was broken up in 1630, about which time the German free towns fell into the power of oligarchies or petty princes. In Italy free commonwealths shone more brightly during the middle ages than in any other country. (See ITALY, HISTORY OF.) The French *communes* or free cities were in the S. of France relics of the Roman *municipia*, but in the N. arose mostly after the 11th c., when a fierce struggle began between them and the nobles. Aided by the king, the *communes* became in the 12th c. in a great measure independent of the feudal seigniors, but they never approached the political power and brilliance of the Italian commonwealths. Though having extensive local liberties, they had no influence on the state in general, and showed slight political activity, being often much influenced by feudal ideas. Never forming leagues, and weakened by the jealousy between their wealthy citizens and their poor inhabitants, they speedily yielded to the centralising tendencies of the monarchy. F. C. also arose in Switzerland, where they were united into a federation, but where their power was modified by the rural democracies. In England F. C. were hindered from appearing by the strength of the central government, and by the early diffusion of political power. The cities of Aragon at one time held wide privileges. (See SPAIN, HISTORY OF.) See Gemeiner, *Ueber den Ursprung der Stadt Regensburg und aller alten Freistädte* (Munich, 1801); Guizot, *Civilisation en Europe* (Par. 6th ed. 1857).

Free'dom, Degrees of, in kinematics, are the number of independent variables in any displacement. For instance, a moving point has *three* D. of F., for the most general displacement it can take may be resolved into three parallel to three mutually independent directions, which are usually taken for convenience at right angles to each other. If the point be constrained to move on a surface, it has then two D. of F., for it cannot move along the normal, which may be chosen as one of three directions of resolution. If the point be constrained to remain on two intersecting surfaces, another degree of freedom is lost, the only possible motion being along the instantaneous tangent to the curve of intersection at the position occupied by the moving point. A free rigid system has evidently *six* D. of F., for besides having the three translations which the point has, it may have three independent rotations about three mutually rectangular axes. Fix one point, and the D. of F. are reduced to three—those, namely, of rotation. Fix another point, and the system has only *one* degree of freedom—a rotation round the straight line joining the two fixed points as axes. If a third point, not in line with the other two, be fixed, the system is fixed. If one point of the system be constrained to remain on a smooth surface, *five* D. of F. are left—two of translation and three of rotation; and each similar limitation to each of six points in succession removes one degree of freedom. A point constrained to move on a curve introduces two degrees of constraint, so the D. of F. are reduced to four. Other combinations will readily suggest themselves to the mind. See Thomson and Tait's *Natural Philosophy*, vol. i.

Free'hold Estate. The tenure of real estate in England is either freehold or copyhold. Freehold tenure owes no service to any one but to the sovereign.

Free Li'braries and Muse'ums. See LIBRARIES, FREE, and MUSEUMS, FREE.

Free'man, Edward Augustus, D.C.L., LL.D., one of the first of English historians, was born at Harborne, Staffordshire, in 1823. He is the son of John F. of Redmore Hall, Worcestershire, was elected scholar of Trinity College, Oxford, in 1841, and fellow in 1845. F. was examiner in the School of Law and Modern History in 1857–58 and 1863–64, and in the School of Modern History in 1873. He contested Mid-Somerset unsuccessfully in 1864; was made D.C.L. of Oxford in 1870, and LL.D. of Cambridge in 1874. He is a prolific author as well as a profound scholar. His works include *Church Restoration* (1846); *History of Architecture* (1849); *Architectural Antiquities of Gower* (1850); *Window Tracery in England* (1850); *Landaff Cathedral* (1860); *History of the Saracens* (1856; new ed. 1876); *History of Federal Government* (vol. i. 1863); *History of the Norman Conquest* (5 vols. 1867–76); *Old English History* (1869); *History of the Cathedral Church of Wells* (1870); *Growth of the English Constitution* (1872); *General Sketch of European History* (1872); *Historical Essays* (1st series, 1871); *Historical Essays* (2d series, 1873); *Comparative Politics and the Unity of History* (1873); *Disestablishment and Disendowment* (1874); *Historical and Architectural Sketches* (1876). Among the scholars who have devoted themselves to early English history, F. deserves the foremost place from his power of kindling interest in neglected epochs, and depth, freshness, and minute accuracy of learning, in which Gibbon alone is his peer among English historians. His *Norman Conquest* first disclosed the true nature of the Norman invasion, and in firm grasp of the subject, eloquence without exaggeration, and sound, far-reaching originality of judgment, is unequalled by any former English history. No book ever stated views so utterly subversive of all established opinion, which were yet so firmly based on historic fact. At times vividly pictorial, at times keenly critical and nobly reflective, the work is throughout steeped in learning, and bright with the enthusiasm of a patriot and a scholar. His *English Constitution* is a masterpiece of insight and brevity, and his *Essays* display his characteristic power of reconstructing without distorting history, of investing old-world contests with the interest of contemporary politics, and illuminating present questions from early annals.

Freeman's Roll. The Municipal Corporation Act directs that the town-clerks of nearly all the boroughs of England and Wales shall make out two lists of persons entitled to vote in the election of members of Parliament. One list is called the Burgess Roll (see BURGESS); the other is called the F. R. In it are the names of all who would have been entitled to vote before the passing of the Act.

Freema'sons are a fraternity consisting of persons of all ranks and professions, bound together by the ties of 'brotherly love, relief, and truth,' and founded in the 'practice of moral and social virtue.' In early times, prior to the invention of printing, freemasonry, or rather the masonic guild, was an institution of a more defined character, with an organisation springing immediately from the conditions under which building was carried on, with distinct purposes to subserve—with, in fact, a name to live. But the invention of printing has had an unfriendly influence upon it, mainly by abolishing the conditions in which the system naturally had its origin, and thus cutting away from it all justification for its continued existence. A minor evil which the printing-press has entailed upon freemasonry has been the facilities afforded for the ruinous support of injudicious literary 'brethren.' Masonic authors ascribe to the society an antiquity which varies more or less with the writer's credulity and ignorance. It is common, if not general, to date its origin from the period of the old Roman empire; but there are masonic writers who, unsatisfied with such a moderate degree of antiquity, trace the foundation of their system back to the days of the Pharaohs, to the building of Solomon's Temple, of the Tower of Babel, even to the days of the construction of the ark by Noah; while at least one author states that the founder of the brotherhood was Lamech, the sixth in direct descent from Adam, and that from his time the institution has been preserved inviolate and continuous down to the present day. That the institution of the thing now known as freemasonry is in any true sense ancient seems to be negatived on the ground that, were it so, an uninterrupted stream of architectural tradition, communicated to and understood by all the fraternity in every age, must have flowed onward through masonic societies down to the period when the invention of printing rendered tradition a superfluous method of transmitting information. But this was not the case, for we find that the technical secrets of the great builders of old died with them, and that even in comparatively modern times, after the age of ecclesiasticism had passed away, the Gothic architecture which in an earlier day it had called into being had vanished as a mode of architectural expression, and its principles, which by the theory of freemasonry should have been preserved and transmitted by tradition, were no longer known. The truth seems to be, that the masonic craft or guild, like the other crafts, sprang up after the Western nations had been taught to appreciate the luxuries of the East, and their growing wealth enabled them to gratify an improved taste. With the age of revival or *renaissance* crowds of artificers or craftsmen appeared, and guilds, crafts, or trade societies were formed everywhere. There were special reasons why masons should form themselves into one great society. They were under the necessity of travelling from place to place in search of employment, and as it was desirable that a master-mason should be recognised as such wherever he went without being under the necessity of giving a fresh proof of his skill by way of testimonial in every new locality to which the necessity of finding employment led him, it was found to be convenient to establish a set of signs, words, &c., which, as the knowledge of them was intrusted to master-masons exclusively, had only to be communicated to prove membership of the craft. English F. profess to trace the existence of their craft as far back as the convention of masons held at York in 926, but there is not a shadow of evidence for such antiquity. The full title of the craft is the 'United Grand Lodge of Ancient Free and Accepted Masons of England,' under the protection of which there are over a thousand lodges. The Scottish F. are content to trace their descent from the builders of the abbeys of Holyrood, Kelso, Melrose, Kilwinning, the cathedral of Glasgow, and other buildings of the 12th and 13th centuries; but the date of the institution of the first masonic lodge is really unknown. The Lodge of Edinburgh (Mary's Chapel), however, has minutes of its transactions dating back into the 16th c., and in this distinction it has an advantage over the most ancient lodges in England and Ireland. The records of the lodge are in six volumes, still in good preservation, and the first of which contains the earliest lodge MSS. extant. The first minute is that of a meeting in 1599. The Duke of Athole is the Grand Master of Scotland. Modern or 'speculative' freemasonry dates from 1646—the earliest date at which non-professional masons are known to have been admitted into an English lodge. It is an invention of Elias Ashmole and some antiquarian friends, and all its quaint symbols—sun, moon, compasses, square, triangle, &c.—owe their symbolic meaning to the same learned source. The initiation of Frederick Lewis, Prince of Wales (father of George III.), by Dr. Desaguliers, the learned brother who in 1721 instructed the Lodge of Edinburgh in the secret ceremonial of English masonry, is the first undoubted instance of the admission to lodge membership of a prince of the royal blood. The evidence of this is the diary of one of the persons so admitted. In Scotland, however, as early as the latter part of the 16th c. the membership of lodges was not exclusively *operative*. For much interesting information on this subject, see the admirably temperate and scholarly *History of Freemasonry*, by David Murray Lyon (Blackwood, Edinb. 1873).

Free Port, a port where ships may be unloaded and goods deposited without payment of customs. If goods so deposited are reshipped, a mere transit-due is exacted; if they pass inland for consumption, they must bear the full duty.

Free Spirit, Brethren and Sisters of the, derived their name from maintaining that they were the true sons of God, brought into the most perfect freedom from the law, according to the words of St. Paul in Rom. viii. 2, 14. The sect made its appearance first in Strasburg in 1212, under the name of *Ortlibenses*, from a leader *Ortlieb*. Their doctrines spread among the Waldenses and Beghards. In Germany they sometimes got the name of *Schwestriones* ('sisterers'), and in France of *Turlupins*. Their doctrines, founded on Pantheism, were probably a revival of the Averroism of Amalric of Bena, condemned by the University of Paris, 1204. Their fundamental tenets were, that 'the universe came by emanation from God, and would finally return to him by absorption; that the universe, considered as one great whole, is God; that rational souls are so many portions of the supreme deity; and that a man by withdrawing his attention from all sensible objects might be so identified with the great first cause as to attain to perfect freedom.' Consequently they made religion to consist entirely in internal worship. Some seem to have interpreted the freedom of spirit they claimed to be superiority to every form of sensuality; others, if their orthodox persecutors are to be believed, to be freedom from shame and all manner of restraint on sensuality.

Free'stone, any building-stone that admits of being *freely* tooled and dressed. In Scotland sandstones are invariably so called.

Free'thinkers, as an historical name, is an epithet applied in England to the Deists (q. v.) of the 17th and 18th centuries. Otherwise it might be used to designate the great school of Rationalists who are to be found among all classes of Christians, and whose attitude towards Christianity is to represent its spirit and ideal without its dogmatic system and supernatural narratives.

Free'town, or **St. George**, the capital of Sierra Leone, W. coast of Africa, on the left bank of the river Sierra Leone, 5 miles from its mouth. It is the seat of the administrative, and has a garrison and a pop. of some 16,000.

Free Trade. The term expresses the condition of commerce left to follow its natural course, without legislative interference with the view of improving or influencing it. It was long the belief of the majority in England that the unfettered exchange of articles of commerce between one country and another was contrary to the general interest. Thus it would have been held, if London could supply Edinburgh with hats better and cheaper than Edinburgh could supply itself with them, that it would have been wise on the part of Edinburgh to tax the admission of London hats into its markets so as to make them dearer than those of home produce. It is now understood that, in the supposed case, it would only have been the hat-makers of Edinburgh who would have suffered by the free import of London hats into that city, and that the rest of its hat-wearing public would have gained money or—which is the same thing—saved it. The capital, labour, and ingenuity so driven out of the hat manufactory in Edinburgh would have borne fruit in some other industrial branch in which circumstances enabled Edinburgh to excel. The general wealth of London and Edinburgh would thus be increased, and the law of political economy in F. T. which prevails between London and Edinburgh has equal force between London and New York or between any communities of the world, the fact that London and New York are under different governments making no difference in the operation of the law. If *protection* be good between London and New York, it is equally good between New York and Boston—between Leeds and Bradford, or between one district of a town and another. The great battle between F. T. and *protection* has been fought in England on the field of the Corn Laws (q. v.). Since the victory then won by the advocates of F. T., the country may almost be said to have unanimously pronounced in its favour, the practical result having convinced the most obstinate incredulity. The average British and Irish exports for the period 1841–50 were of the value of £57,412,494; for 1871 their value was £282,380,726, showing an increase for 1871 over the period 1841–50 of £224,968,232. To some extent duties continue to be levied on foreign goods imported into England, but this is owing to the necessity of raising the imperial revenue. See BALANCE OF TRADE.

Free-Will. All human action, all social institutions, all that is known about the human mind, suggest that mental states (including volitions) succeed to one another in an orderly manner, and with the same apparent uniformity as purely physical changes. The connection of the mind and body being admitted within certain limits, the hypothesis of disorder or want of uniformity in the mind would necessarily affect the uniformity of the physical world. In cases like politics and individual character, not only have laws been traced, but accurate prediction has been made; and what are called incalculable elements in human nature and society are only so because imperfectly ascertained. A different theory was held by Socrates, who, believing that man himself was the proper subject of scientific knowledge, confessed that physics and astronomy were entirely in the control of the gods, and therefore unknowable except through the ordinances of religion. The modern theory of particular providences, *e.g.*, in deciding the obscure issues of disease, or grace deciding the soul to seize salvation, is merely a refined version of the view that the world is not governed by fixed laws. With the stoics and Philo-Judæus the 'free' man was the virtuous man, not in the sense of being free from restraint (at least moral restraint), but as the more dignified and elevated character. On the other hand, the bondage of sin was described as slavery. The distinct conception of freedom, in the sense of self-determination, there being a margin of indifference after the influence of every possible motive has been allowed for, was quite unknown to Plato or Aristotle, and was introduced to explain theological difficulties, original sin, and the Augustinian theory of predestination. According to Augustine, Adam had F.-W., but none of his posterity. Evil was introduced by Adam's fall, and the human will is entirely governed by original sin on the one hand, and irresistible free grace on the other. Calvin went a step beyond this and rejected even Adam's F.-W. The opposite view of free choice (*liberum arbitrium*), as the foundation of the divine judgments and as limiting the divine foreknowledge, was upheld by Pelagius against Augustine, and in the 17th c. by Arminius against Gomar. Hobbes, in his tract on *Liberty and Necessity*, discusses the question without reference to theological interests. 'Doing or abstaining,' he says, 'necessarily follows the present thought a man hath of the good or evil consequence thereof to himself.' This occurs, however, only where the circumstances exclude deliberation, which is a succession of 'contrary appetites,' the last of them being the will. 'Liberty' he defines 'as the absence of all impediments to action that are not contained in the nature of the agent.' The will is the necessary cause of voluntary actions, and the will must have a cause else it would be eternal. Against this view Descartes appeals to consciousness: 'we are able to do or not to do the same thing,' however strong the motives on either side. It followed that the divine will was entirely indifferent, and this in a stricter sense than as regards the human will, because moral good and evil, the creatures of God's will, were not present to solicit it. Locke agrees with Hobbes and defines freedom as 'our being able to act or not to act according as we shall choose or will.' And he asks whether a man is free to will what he wills? Spinoza repudiates the notion of freedom in God, except in the sense of *unconditioned* existence and development, and of course human wills are not contingent, but are determined by the laws of the divine attributes. He points out that the favourite undetermined will of philosophers is a notion abstracted from all particular volitions, each of which has a cause. In his *Philosophical Inquiry concerning Liberty*, Anthony Collins adds a new argument to the controversy, viz., that except on the necessitarian view, punishment is inexcusable. Leibnitz applied to the problem his favourite principle of sufficient reason, which simply admits volition to be a case of universal causation, the agent being conscious. The pure-indifference notion was again stated by Samuel Clarke in the shape of a self-moving power which was equivalent to the spontaneity of the lower animals. This he defends by the whimsical objection that otherwise an abstract spiritual motive would be the cause of motion. The subject is nowhere better handled than in Jonathan Edwards' *Freedom of the Will*, which few books excel in clearness of language and vigour of thought. He examines in detail three meanings assigned to liberty:—(1) Self-determining power, the will causing its own volitions; (2) indifference or equilibrium; (3) contingency, or no fixed relations between motives and volitions. A thorough Calvinist, he supports his philosophical position by reference to the prescience of God. On the moral and practical side, Edwards truly says that what people love or hate is a good or a bad man, and not an ill-defined faculty of determination between two or more alternatives assumed to be perfectly neutral. A similar view was enforced by Priestley, who rashly declared that remorse was inconsistent with necessity. Reid reproduces at tedious length the opinions expressed much more clearly by Clarke and Price, and makes an impotent criticism of Leibnitz, saying that man is the cause of action. Hamilton, who said F.-W. was the only basis of morality and belief in God, considered the scheme of liberty, or of an absolute undetermined cause, and of necessity, or of an infinite retrogression of particular causes, as both inconceivable. Yet he rests his doctrine of liberty on the testimony of consciousness, or positive feeling, which is to be preferred to the causal judgment, because the latter depends on an infirmity of thought (the conditioned). Mr. J. S. Mill points out in his *Examination of Hamilton* that consciousness can only relate to what is or has been, and can therefore by no possibility disclose a power to do what is future. Mill also argues the point that it is just to punish a man for what he could not help, if that be the only way of enabling him or others to help it.

Free'zing and Fu'sing Points. One of the most important effects of heat is the alteration of the physical properties of bodies; the phenomena attending the transformation of solid into liquid or of liquid into solid will here be briefly noticed. When by the application of heat a solid *fuses* to a liquid, the temperature at which this change occurs is called the *fusing point*. When a liquid by cooling *freezes* to a solid, the temperature at which this change occurs is termed the *freezing point*. Thus when water, at ordinary pressure, is cooled to 0° C., it begins to freeze and become ice; and ice when heated to the same temperature begins to melt or fuse, and become water. Evidently, then, fusing point and freezing point, when used with reference to the same substance, represent one and the same temperature, though they imply reverse operations. When a solid fuses, it in general expands; and, according to the molecular theory, the molecules, formerly restrained to occupy the same mutually relative positions, now become free, through the diminution of the molecular forces of attraction, to shift about in the liquid. This has the obvious effect of giving to each molecule a motion of translation, that is, of increasing the internal energy of the substance, an effect which necessitates the disappearance of an equivalent amount of energy in some other form. Experiment shows that, as the solid is fusing, no rise or temperature is observed, though heat is being constantly applied. The thermal energy so absorbed is expended in changing the physical condition of the substance, and its equivalent is to be found in the probably increased internal energy. Precisely the reverse phenomenon is observed while a liquid is freezing or solidifying, the change of condition being accompanied with the evolution of heat. In all cases, however, while the change is taking place, there is no rise in temperature. That expansion is not essentially necessary for endowing the molecules with sufficient freedom of translatory motion is evidenced by the fact that some solids, notably ice, *contract* upon melting. Professor James Thomson deduced from the laws of thermo-dynamics that water, since it *expands* by freezing, should have its freezing point lowered by pressure, a theoretical result subsequently verified by the experiments of his brother, Sir William. The latter has extended the same law to embrace all similar phenomena, and has shown that solids which *expand* on fusing have their fusing points *raised* by pressure, and solids which *contract* on fusing have their fusing points *lowered* by pressure.

Freezing Mix'tures are combinations of two or more substances for the production of intense cold. One at least must be a solid, which is liquified when mixed with the other ingredients. This liquefaction requires the absorption of heat from surrounding objects, which is consequently lowered in temperature, and if liquid and near their freezing point, solidified. A quantity of pounded ice with half its weight of salt reduces a substance from + 10° C. to − 18° C.; while sulphate of sodium, nitrate of ammonium, and dilute nitric acid, in the proportions by weight of 6, 5, and 4, can reduce the temperature to − 26° C. Other mixtures may be employed, and by a skilful combination of the best, very much lower temperatures obtained; but the minimum temperature hitherto obtained is about − 90° C.

Fre'genal de la Sierr'a, a picturesque town in the province of Badajoz, Spain, in the wild valley of the Martiga, 30 miles S.E. of Badajoz. It has a quaint old castle, with a bullring, and industries in leather, linen, &c. Pop. 6948.

Frei'berg, a walled town of Saxony, on the Münzbach, a branch of the East Mulde, to the N. of the Erzgebirge, 20 miles S.W. of Dresden by railway. It is the administrative centre for the mines of Saxony, and the seat of a famous Mining Academy (since 1765), with thirteen professors and (1872) seventy-six students, Werner's celebrated mineral collection, and a library of 18,000 volumes. F. has a fine old townhouse (1410), and a cathedral with a 'golden gate' (1484–1512). Its manufactures are gold and silver wares, lace, woollens, chemicals, cutlery, and explosives: 150 mines of silver, copper, lead, cobalt, &c., are wrought in the vicinity. Pop. (1871) 21,673. The silver-mines of F. were discovered about 1190, but they have grown less productive of late years. See Benseler' *Geschichte F.'s* (1842).

Frei'burg ('the free or privileged city'), an old town in the Grand Duchy of Baden, lies on the Dreisam, at the W. base of the Black Forest, 45 miles S.S.E. of Strasburg by railway. It is the seat of an archbishop, and of a Roman Catholic university (since 1456). Its chief historical monuments are a beautiful Gothic minster in red sandstone (1152–1514), with a graceful tower 367 feet high, a quaint Kaufhaus (exhange) of the 16th c., and a grand ducal palace.

There are manufactures of leather, potash, starch, paper, &c., besides several dye-works, and a bell-foundry. Pop. (1871) 24,668.

Frei'burg, or the **Uecht'land** ('waste land,' so called because formerly a wild, uncultivated territory), is a western canton of Switzerland, lying between the lakes Neuchâtel and Geneva, and is bounded W. by Vaud and E. by Berne. Area, 563 sq. miles; pop. (1870) 110,832, of whom 93,051 are Roman Catholics, 16,819 Protestants, and 1400 Jews. F. is intersected in the S. by the Bernese Alps, which rise to the height in the Vanil Noir of 7346 feet, in Berra of 5307, in Dent de Brentlire of 7252, and in Follieran of 7215; it is watered by the Saane or Sarine, Broye, Seuse, &c. There is much fine wood and pasture. In 1870 the number of sheep was 23,206, of goats, 11,308, and of swine, 21,565. The chief industries besides husbandry are straw-plaiting, watchmaking, and the production of grass-tobacco, beet-sugar, and wine. Of the inhabitants 26 per cent. are German, 74 are French, the language of the latter prevailing, but in the form of a patois. The costumes are very picturesque. Since 1841 F. has been a member of the Swiss Confederation, and sends to the National Rath six representatives. The Jesuits were expelled in 1847.—**F.**, or **Fribourg**, capital of the above canton, is romantically situated in the deep valley of the Saane, and on its banks, which rise almost precipitously to a height of 918 feet. It is 17 miles S.W. of Berne by railway, is surrounded by old embattled walls, has twenty churches, five monasteries, four nunneries, one hundred inns, and many tanneries and dye-houses. The chief building is the beautiful Gothic church of St. Nicholas (1285–1500), which has a tower 280 feet high, a rare peal of bells, and a splendid organ of 67 stops and 7800 pipes. The river is crossed by four bridges, one of which has a single suspension span of 906 feet, a length exceeded by few bridges in the world. Pop. (1870) 10,904, mostly French Catholics. F. was founded by Berthold von Zähringen in 1175.

Freight (lit. 'that with which a ship is *fraught* or laded') is the price paid for the use of a ship to transport goods. It also denotes the goods transported. The terms of the F. are usually stated in the Charter-Party (q. v.), or in the Bill of Lading (q. v.). If a gross sum is stipulated to be paid for the whole ship or for any part of it, the money is payable though the freighter should not be liable to complete his lading. In payments by quantity, fractions of a ton, pipe, or pack, are not reckoned unless stipulated in the charter-party. F. is not due until the goods are delivered at the port of consignment; therefore if a ship be captured or lost, no F. can be claimed. But if advance-money has been paid, it cannot be recovered, nor can passage-money be paid in advance. If the agreement be for *landing* men or cattle, F. is due notwithstanding death, but if for transporting them, F. is not due for any dying during the voyage. No F. is due for an infant born at sea. If periodical payments are contracted for, and the ship be lost or captured, the owner is entitled to F. to the date of loss or capture. See AVERAGE, INSURANCE LAWS.

Frei'ligrath, Ferdinand, one of the most gifted of recent German poets, was born at Detmold, 17th June 1810, and was from 1825 till 1839 engaged in mercantile pursuits. Encouraged by the popularity of a collection of poems, he withdrew from commerce for a year or two, but political difficulties arising from the democratic spirit of his verses, led F. to return to business and settle in London in 1846. The commotions of 1848 brought him back to his fatherland, where he espoused the democratic side, and was prosecuted for his poem *Die Todten an die Lebenden*. Though acquitted now, F. had to retire to London again in 1851, where he was agent for a bank till its collapse in 1866. A national collection in Germany enabled him to spend his declining days in his native land. He published a few patriotic songs during the war of 1870, and died at Cannstadt, March 17, 1876. F.'s *Gedichte* reached a 27th edition in 1871, and collected editions of his works were published at New York (16 vols. 1858–59) and at Stuttgart (6 vols. 2d ed. 1871). F.'s translations have helped to make Burns and Longfellow known in Germany. His original poems are marked by wealth of imagery and glowing colour, with much true pathos, and a picturesque felicity of phrase more French than German; passion, however, often mars their beauty, especially in the numerous political and social pieces.

Frei'rina, a seaport of Chili, in the S. of Atacama, on the Huasco, with some export trade in copper. Pop. 10,000.

Frei'schütz is in German folklore the marksman who, by a paction with the devil, receives from him seven charmed bullets. Of these, six are sure to hit the mark, however distant; but over one of the seven the fiend has retained power to direct it as he wills. On this legend Weber's well-known opera is founded.

Frei'sing, an old town of Upper Bavaria, on the Isar, 20 miles N.E. of Munich by railway. It was the seat of a bishop from the 8th c. Its bishops were made episcopal princes by the Emperor Ferdinand (1619–37), but the see was secularised in 1803. The cathedral is a beautiful two-towered basilica of 1159. F. has manufactures of beer, spirits, tobacco, vinegar, &c. Pop. (1871) 7783.

Fre'jus, a town in the department of Var, France, on the Argens, 2 miles from the Mediterranean, and 45 N.E. of Toulon by railway. It is a bishop's see, and has many Roman remains, including an amphitheatre, part of an aqueduct, baths, &c. Pop. (1872) 2705. F. was founded by a colony from Marseille, and by the Romans was called *Forum Julii*, of which its modern name is a corruption. Its port, now silted up, was anciently of great importance. At St. Raphael, near F., Napoleon landed on returning from Egypt (1799).

Fremont', John Charles, a distinguished American explorer, of French extraction, was born in Savannah, Georgia, U.S., January 21, 1813, entered Charleston College in 1828, where he specially studied mathematics, engineering, and surveying, and where he graduated. In 1840 he was made lieutenant of engineers, and two years later explored the great South Pass in the Rocky Mountains, making valuable additions to our knowledge of the botany, geology, and geography of that region. During the next eleven years he made four expeditions westwards through territories then unknown, and in spite of terrible hardships and dangers, his dauntless courage and indomitable perseverance carried him successfully to the shores of the Pacific. His discoveries paved the way to the conquest of California, where he settled in 1849, and was chosen one of the United States' senators. The value of F.'s labours have been recognised in Europe. He is a member of the Geographical Society of Berlin, and has been awarded the founder's medal by the Royal Geographical Society of London. The new Republican party nominated him for president in 1856. His name elicited considerable enthusiasm, but he was defeated by Mr. Buchanan. He has since then devoted his time mainly to mining and to plans for trans-continental railways.

Fremont City, a town in Ohio, U.S., on the Sandusky river, and a station on the railway from Cleveland to Toledo, 30 miles E. of Toledo. It has three newspapers, good schools, a public park, and libraries, and carries on manufactures of cars, engines, boilers, and blinds. Pop. (1870) 5455.

French Beans. See KIDNEY BEANS.

French Berr'ies, or **Yell'ow Berries**, the fruit of the yellow buckthorn (*Rhamnus infectorius*), belonging to the *Rhamnaceæ* or buckthorn order. The name is also given to the fruit of the allied species *R. saxatilis* and *R. amygdalinus*. The berries afford a yellow dye when gathered in an unripe state. This dye, however, is not permanent, and has been superseded by mineral pigments. Y. B. are grown in the S. of France and in the Levant.

French Chalk, a variety of Steatite (q. v.) used for crayons.

French Hon'eysuckle (*Hedysarum coronarium*), a species of *Leguminosæ* included in the section *Papilionaceæ*, found in the S. of Europe, and having scarlet or white flowers. It grows to a height of 5 or 6 feet, and its pods, stem, and leaves are used as food for cattle. The stem is spreading, and the leaves are pinnate. F. H. is seen occasionally in gardens. *H. fruticosum* is a native of Siberia.

French Language and Literature. *French Language.*—The F. L. belongs to the Romance tongues which sprang from the Latin, and is at bottom a form, now vastly modified, of the *Lingua Romana Rustica*, or vulgar Latin spoken by the Roman provincials, as distinguished from the Latin of literature. This provincial Latin arose from the colloquial Latin of the Roman soldiers and populace, which differed widely in pronunciation and vocabulary from the Latin of the classic authors, as we see from fragments of the *Atellanæ* or popular farces; and while the literary Latin sank into a dead tongue, the *Lingua Romana Rustica*, a modification of the *sermo plebeius* of Rome, developed into the Romance languages of France, Italy, and Spain, the leading differences between these speeches being due to varieties of race and climate, and to the respective distances of certain places from Italy. Even the literary Latin showed a tendency, in the times of the Empire, to become less involved, and make more frequent use of prepositions; and this tendency to simplify speech advanced far more swiftly in the vulgar Latin, which was guided by no high literary models. The *Lingua Rustica*, however, after it became the universal speech of Gaul, did not sink into a mere lawless jargon, but preserved several grammatical rules and the nominative and accusative cases. The nominative singular ended in *s*, because many Latin words had that termination in the nominative alone of the singular cases; on the other hand, the accusative plural was distinguished from the nominative plural by having the *s* ending, because in Latin the accusative plural often ended in *s*, a letter never affixed in the plural to the Latin nominative. A few Celtic words crept into the *Lingua Rustica* on its adoption by the Gauls, as *alauda, cervisia, margula, leuca*, the modern *alouette, cervoise, marne, lieu;* but the Celtic element in French is so small that M. Brachet pronounces its influence insensible, though it had a certain effect on the pronunciation of the *Lingua Rustica*. As the Gothic barbarians settled in Gaul in small detached bands, and differed considerably among themselves in dialect, they were forced to adopt the general speech of the Gallo-Romans, the *Lingua Rustica*; but they aided immensely to relax its grammar, as they seized on the part of a word which was unaltered by inflection, and ignored the endings, whose changes bewildered them. They also gave to the speech of the Gallo-Romans a number of Teutonic words, probably about 500 in all, mostly applying to war and hunting, and afterwards to feudal relations, and these words, like the Celtic element, were softened down till they seemed to be of Latin origin. (See DIALECT.) On the other hand, the old Latin words were shortened of their unaccented syllables, *e.g.*, from *securus, fidelis, legalis, surdus, solus, corpus, nasum*, came *seur, feal, loyal, sourd, seul, corps, nez*. When two consonants came together in Latin, one was dropped out, as in *advocatus*, which became *avoué*, or one of them blended with and changed the sound of the other, as in *altar, autre;* and when a Latin word began with *s* followed by a consonant, an *e* was prefixed for the sake of euphony, *e.g.*, *species, spissus, stringere* are now represented by *espèce, épais* (through the old *espois*), *étreindre* (through the old *estreindre*). The Latin ending *-sionem* or *-tionem* became generally *-son*, *e.g.*, *mansionem*, modern *maison*, the French words being almost invariably formed from the Latin accusative; *iculus -a -um* became *-eil* or *-il*, *e.g.*, *periculum*, modern *peril*; *-ilia* became *-eille*, *e.g.*, *mirabilia*, *merveille*; *aculum* became *acle*; *arius, aire*; *aticus, age*, &c. In place of the adverbial suffixes in *ter* and *e*, which vanished, because they were unaccented, the Gallic *Lingua Rustica* added *mens*—which was meant to denote in the manner or spirit of, and which is seen in the French *l'egalement, hardiment*, &c. The old conjugations were broken down, the old tenses, moods, and voices were abandoned. In the 9th c. the F. L. began to define itself from the other Romance tongues. It became rapidly more different from the written Latin, and in 813 a Council of Tours directed the bishops to translate their homilies from the Latin into the popular Romance. Our earliest specimens of the latter idiom are the fragment of a glossary (*Glosses de Reichenau*, about 770), and the Oaths of Strasburg in 842. The latter show that the Romance was, in the middle of the 9th c., the speech of the whole French army—Karl taking the oath before the Germans in Frankish—Hludwig taking it before the Roman-Franks or Frenchmen in Romance. The change of the Latin, through the *Lingua Rustica*, into French now went on rapidly, and in the 10th c. there were in France two strongly marked dialects—the *Langue d'Oil*, spoken N. of the Loire, and so called from using *oil* (Latin *illud*) for yes, and the *Langue d'Oc* spoken S. of the Loire, which used *oc* (Lat. *hoc*) as an affirmative. The *Langue d'Oc*, which was softer, more melodious, and more closely akin to the ancient Latin than was the speech of the N., early received a high literary polish from the *Troubadours* (q. v.), but was reduced to a provincial dialect after the civilisation of the S. was almost trampled out in the Albigensian crusades. The *Langue d'Oil*, spoken in the N., the land of the Franks, besides being less euphonious and graceful than the *Langue d'Oc*, was, unlike the speech of the S., broken up into many dialects, of which the most broadly defined were those of Normandy, Picardy, Burgundy, and the Isle of France. The last, from its central position, and from the political greatness of Paris, rose into pre-eminence, and became the classic form of the F. L., which, from the 11th c. onwards, was increased by words lifted from the old Latin almost in their original form (*e.g.*, *innocent*) through the influence of the learned, instead of having been, like the main body of the language, gradually changed by popular use from their old Roman into their modern French form. In the 12th c. *Old French*, as distinct from the *Lingua Rustica*, was fully developed. It was less synthetic than the Latin, but more so than modern French, and for a time kept the nominative singular and accusative plural in *s*, *e.g.*, nom. sing. *amis*, acc. sing. *ami;* nom. plu. *ami*, acc. plu. *amis;* but after the 14th c. the nominative of both numbers was disused, and *s* became the French plural ending, *e.g. ami*, pl. *amis*, the F. L. thus receiving a somewhat deceptive likeness to English, which about the same time chose *s* as its plural termination from one of its various endings in the older stage of the language. During the 12th and 13th centuries many Oriental words were introduced by the Crusades, and a number of Greek medical and philosophical terms were adopted, while several old Latin words were lost. There is considerable difference in spelling between old and modern French; thus, wherever there is a circumflex in the present dialect there was formerly an *s*, *e.g.*, *feste, fête, karesme, carême*, &c. The modern *peu, appui, sus, si*, are represented by *poys, apuys, super, sic;* words now obsolete are found, *e.g.*, *antan*, from *ante annum*, *sade*, agreeable, *aie* for *aide*, *het* from *hilaritas*, *oy* for the modern *ai*, *tiengne* for *tienne*, *querra* for *cherchera*, &c. In the 15th c. the language becomes simpler and more analytic, and is henceforth spoken of as modern French. During the 16th c. the F. L. received a large Italian infusion from the French expeditions into Italy and from the union between the house of Valois and Medicis, and was likewise imbued with a considerable Spanish element from the invasions of the Spaniards into France. When the revival of letters began to act on France, novel and pedantic terms were freely borrowed from the Latin, but this movement, which was justly satirised by Rabelais, had not a lasting influence. In the 16th c. Ronsard and the other members of the Pleiad wrote with assiduous nicety, showing a peculiar daintiness of phrase, as in their fondness for diminutives—*ondelette, fondelette, doucelette*, &c.—and Malherbe, Amyot, and Montaigne composed with rare copiousness, liveliness, and fluency; but on the founding of the French Academy (1635), a movement to prune and chasten the language set in, and though writers such as Voiture, Balzac, and Boileau made French admirably elegant, pure, and correct, the result of the prolonged and finical refining was to reduce the speech in the 18th c. to a state of colourless tenuity. From the middle of the 17th to the middle of the 18th c. the men of letters and the members of the fashionable circles united to polish and enfeeble the language; from which learned and technical terms, homely, colloquial, and picturesque words and phrases were alike filtered away, as unfit for polite society. Classic French, or the French used by all the writers—except La Fontaine, La Bruyère, and Voltaire—who come between Montaigne on the one hand and Rousseau on the other, is distinguished by strict order, delightful clearness, and antithetic brilliance, by the preference of general to special terms, by the absence of the old *Gaulois* brusqueness and freedom, and by a vocabulary shrunk to about one-third of its early wealth. The French Revolution, however, again altered the complexion of the language, which became elastic, fiery, and affluent, and which has received in the 19th c. a development unexampled in its history. Writers such as Chateaubriand, Hugo, and Gautier have enriched its vocabulary and shaken off the bonds imposed by the 'classical' school, the Romanticists in particular having gone back to the ample, delicate, and long-forgotten stores of the early French poets, and shown that sonorous strength and flowing sweetness may be qualities as characteristic of French as its more familiar merits of ease, precision, and lucid vivacity.

French Literature. —The Latin literature which flourished luxuriantly in Southern Gaul under the Empire, and which was mainly a polished, shallow imitation of the ancient classics, perished during the barbaric invasions, and it was not until the 11th c. that two great schools of poets arose in Northern and in Southern France. S. of the Loire there sprang up the lyrical school of the *Troubadours* (q. v.), who brought a wholly new species of poetry into Europe. Among the chief *Troubadours* were Bernard de Ventadour, Giraud de Borneill, Pierre Vidal, Bertrand de Born, Marcabrus, Rambaud de Vaqueiras, Folquet, &c. Their lyrics were exquisitely varied in metre, full of sweet and delicate though at times overstrained sentiment, and blithe vernal imagery, often flushed with Oriental colour, and occasionally reflecting the mystical, rebellious spirit which prevailed in Southern France about the end of the 12th c. Their measures depended on accent, as in modern verse, and not, as in Latin verse, on quantity, and have descended to us through the Latin hymns of the middle ages. Alongside of the *Troubadour* love poetry, whose deep subjectivity and ideal intensity of passion made it a poetry for the refined few, there seems to have been a more simple, gay, and homely literature of ballads, songs, and prose tales, of which the only known specimen is the charming story of *Aucassin and Nicolette;* but the popular as well as the aristocratic Provençal literature withered rapidly after the Albigensian crusades, the Langue d'Oc giving way to the Langue d'Oïl as the classic French dialect, and the *Troubadour* school becoming extinct before the end of the 14th c. The *Trouvères* (q. v.), or narrative poets of Northern France, far more than the *Troubadours,* were the fathers of F. L. The *Troubadour* poetry, despite its subtle pensiveness and enchanting melody, was fated to early decay; a strange, faint sickliness clung to it even in the time of its brilliant ripeness; and the *Chansons de Geste* of the *Trouvères,* far below the Provençal lyrics in artistic charm, were much more truly a national poetry. They dealt with war and adventure, and were mainly Gothic in spirit, though tempered by Gallic clearness and grace of expression, and lightness of fancy. The earliest known example of this Northern epical poetry is the *Chanson de Roland,* a heroic lay of the 11th c., belonging to the Carolingian cycle of the *Chansons,* which treats of the mythical Charlemagne and his twelve peers. This cycle includes such poems as *Ogier le Danois, Le Roman des Loherains, Charlemagne,* and is strongly feudal, but not yet chivalrous in sentiment. Chivalrous ideas are the leading feature of the second or Arthurian cycle, which began about the end of the 12th c., was largely drawn from Breton sources (see ARTHURIAN ROMANCE), and was followed by the Classical cycle, which transforms the history of Alexander, the Greek legends of Ulysses, Helen, Hector, and others, into wild tales of magic and knight-errantry. Among the foremost *Trouvères* were Chrestien de Troyes, Marie de France, Renaud de Montauban, Jean de Flagy, &c. In the 13th c. most of the *Fabliaux* (q. v.) were written, and lyrical poetry began to be cultivated in the N. of France, its authors, of whom Thibaut of Champagne was the earliest of note, at first imitating the *Troubadour Chansons.* Mock-heroic poems burlesquing the long chivalrous poems became popular in the 13th c., especially the famous *Roman de Renart* (see REYNARD). The greatest of the northern *Chansonniers* was Rutebeuf (q. v.). The long chivalrous epics gradually fell into disrepute, and quaint and frigid allegorical poems became common, the passion for symbolism taking fullest shape in the *Roman de la Rose,* where two great streams of French medieval poetry—the allegorical and satirical—unite. (See MEUNG, JEAN DE, and LORRIS, GUILLAUME DE.) During the time of the Hundred Years' War, F. L. almost died out, Froissart (q. v.) being the only great French writer of the 14th c., and the poets Alain Chartier and Eustache Deschamps (q. v.) and the schoolman Gersen (q. v.) being almost the only notable authors in the first half of the 15th c. In 1402 the first dramatic company, *La Fraternité de la Passion,* was founded. (For the French drama, see DRAMA, BASSOCHE, MIRACLE PLAYS.) History—which arose with Villehardouin (q. v.), Joinville (q. v.), and Froissart—is further developed by Philippe de Comines (q. v.), who substitutes the shrewd insight of a diplomatist for the simple gossip of the old chroniclers. During the 15th c. poetry is mainly taken up with the now trite themes and fancies of the earlier *chansons,* the praises of the spring, the sun, the grass, and the warbling of birds being tediously repeated. There is little original thought or deep feeling except in Charles of Orleans (q. v.), Saint-Gelais, and François Villon (q. v.). The last is the greatest French poet before Corneille, and from his blending of sadness, rich fancy, and wild mockery, foreshadows a characteristic phase of later F. L. He was the chief of the *bourgeois* poets, who paint the lowly and vagrant life of the middle ages, while Charles of Orleans represents the knightly aristocratic writers. Clement Marot (q. v.), who lived in the first half of the 16th c., is the last great writer of the old school—the last French poet who reflects the middle ages. The Renaissance began to act strongly on France in the early years of the 16th c., but did not, as in England, completely alter the course and the complexion of the national literature. In France the Renaissance literature was not a sudden growth of dazzling novelty and beauty, but was to a large extent the last flowering of the medieval literature with a fresh artistic subtlety and chastened splendour brought from Italy, the home of the new learning. At the end of the 15th and beginning of the 16th c. the rough, boisterous Gothic element seemed, as in Rabelais, about to absorb the Gallic lightness and literary grace which had played furtively across the old *chansons de geste,* and which were saved when the Renaissance became a potent influence on French poetry and prose. In the middle of the 16th c. the Renaissance movement was at its height in France, and the Gothic spirit, which had mainly produced the Northern epics, was blended with a new delicacy of style, the leader of the movement to refine the literature being Ronsard (q. v.), who founded the Pleiad, a poetic school so called because it included seven important writers. Its members wrote French verse with unwonted nicety of diction and exquisite variety of lyrical form, delighting in fantastic imagery, quaint learning, and ingenious rhymes; but the charm of their work was somewhat ephemeral, and their insatiable thirst for fine turns of language and rhythm taking hold of other writers, rendered poetry for a time trite and flimsy, the imitators of the Pleiad pursuing mere verbal felicities, to the neglect of true feeling and original thought. Henceforth French lyrical poetry languished until the beginning of the 19th c.

The chief writers in the first half of the 16th c. are Amyot (q. v.), the translator of Plutarch; Brantôme (q. v.), one of the most entertaining of French memoir-writers; Montaigne (q. v.), the earliest essayist; Rabelais (q. v.), the greatest of French humourists, who seems to gather together the Gaulois mirthfulness which runs riot through French medieval literature; Ronsard (q. v.), who was called the 'prince of the French poets,' and his associates in the Pleiad—Jodelle (q. v.), the first writer of a tragedy modelled on the Greek drama, and Joachim du Bellay (q. v.), the earliest memorable French critic, and the author of at least one exquisite lyric. At the end of the 16th and beginning of the 17th c. F. L. became more trifling and affected, though more polished in manner. Except in the *Satyre Ménippée* (1593), a scathing attack on the League, and in the works of Théophile de Viaud (q. v.), a graceful and pathetic poet, and Regnier (q. v.), a satirist who imitated Horace, and in a measure anticipated Boileau, there was little passion or earnestness among the writers of verse. The fashionable poet Malherbe (q. v.) purified the language from the antique words which Ronsard and his followers had coined, but while he gave the tongue new lucidity and precision, stripped it of the mellow and autumnal richness which hangs around the writings of the Pleiad. (See FRENCH LANGUAGE.) From 1600 to about 1650 euphuism was at its height in France. Long and unspeakably tedious romances, embroidered with fantastic ornaments in the manner of Gongora, full of cold and insipid gallantries, and affecting a mawkish purity of sentiment and stilted dignity of language, were composed by Gomberville, La Calprènede, and Mdlle. de Scudéry (q. v.); there was an endless supply of madrigals and other verses of society, where unblushing indecency was conveyed in flowery periphrases; sparkling frivolous verses were produced by Voiture (q. v.); and Scarron (q. v.), a really original writer, introduced burlesque into France. To this period of Spanish literary influences, of dreary euphuism, and polished immodesties belong, however, three of France's chief writers—Corneille (q. v.), her first great dramatist, and Descartes (q. v.) and Pascal (q. v.), who rank among the deepest European thinkers. During the period from 1650 to 1700, which may be called the age of Louis XIV., F. L. flourished in unexampled luxuriance. Boileau and Molière destroyed the euphuistic school by the force of their ridicule, and a literature was developed rich in poetry, and marked by exquisite order, supreme good taste, and elegant rhetoric, but destitute of passion, depth, and spontaneous grace. The chief poets of the period were Molière (q. v.), Racine (q. v.), Boileau (q. v.), La Fontaine (q. v.); the leading prose writers were Malebranche (q. v.), Bossuet (q. v.), Fénélon (q. v.), Flechier, Bourdaloue, La Rochefoucauld (q. v.), La Bruyère (q. v.), and Madame de Sévigné (q. v.). In the 18th c. F. L. changes vastly in character; the formalism, equanimity, urbanity, and conservative indifference of the Louis XIV. period give place to bold sceptical discussion in politics and religion, and to a more free and varied literary manner. The old *esprit Gaulois* of Villon and Rabelais, which almost vanished under Louis XIV., reappears, while classical lucidity and order are in general preserved; literature, pervaded by a new philosophy born in England, no longer holds coldly aloof from everyday life; authors cease to re-set insipid generalities in graceful language, but grapple boldly and often rashly with practical questions. There is no longer the similarity between writers which prevailed during the latter half of the 17th c., the chief bond of union now being that the leading authors are mostly animated with identical philosophical tastes, and that all, save Buffon (q. v.), dabble in indecency. Saint Simon (q. v.), Fontenelle (q. v.), and Le Sage (q. v.) in a measure link the Louis XIV. school with the more characteristic authors of the 18th c., of whom the chief are Montesquieu (q. v.), Voltaire (q. v.), Diderot (q. v.), and Rousseau (q. v.). Montesquieu was the first to point out the true import and dignity of history; Voltaire, the incarnation of the century's scepticism, distilled the prevailing philosophy into tales, essays, histories, dramas, dictionaries, and burlesques, writing with unique piquancy and clearness; Diderot, a more vehement revolutionist, broke away wholly from the classic tradition, his powerful thoughts being mostly crudely though earnestly expressed; Rousseau is the earliest apostle of modern democracy, and from his passionate subjectivity, from the glowing liquid richness of his style, is the true parent of French Romanticism. The chief poet at the end of the 18th c. is Chenier (q. v.), and the chief dramatist is Beaumarchais (q. v.). Among the foremost writers during the early years of the 19th c. are Chateaubriand (q. v.), Du Staël (q. v.), Lamartine (q. v.), and Beranger (q. v.). In 1830 the French Romantic school was definitely recognised, and began a fierce struggle with the Classicists. Its leading members were Hugo (q. v.), De Musset (q. v.), Sainte Beuve (q. v.), Gautier (q. v.), De Vigny (q. v.), Dumas (q. v.), &c. (See ROMANTICISM.) Among the chief French authors of this century are Villemain (q. v.), Guizot (q. v.), Thierry (q. v.), Sismondi (q. v.), Michelet (q. v.), Thiers (q. v.), Louis Blanc (q. v.), in history; Hugo (q. v.), Nodier (q. v.), Balzac (q. v.), George Sand (q. v.), Mérimée (q. v.), Murger (q. v.), About (q. v.), Sandeau (q. v.), Dumas the Younger (q. v.), Gautier (q. v.), Janin (q. v.), Paul de Kock (q. v.), Alphonse Karr (q. v.), Madame Girardin (q. v.) Flaubert, Feuillet (q. v.), Sue (q. v.), &c., in fiction; Cousin (q. v.), Comte (q. v.), Courier (q. v.), Jouffroy (q. v.), Fourier (q. v.), St. Simon (q. v.), St. Marc Girardin (q. v.), Lamennais (q. v.), De Tocqueville (q. v.), Taine (q. v.), Ampère (q. v.), Littré (q. v.), Renan (q. v.), &c., in philosophy, politics, scholarship, and criticism; Hugo, Gautier, De Musset, Murger, Baudelaire, Banville, De Lisle, Deschamps, Dupont, Gérard de Nerval, Barbier, &c., in poetry. The Revolution inspired F. L. with novel audacity and wealth of thought, novel freedom and splendour of style. The French Romanticists, though they loved to select their subjects from the middle ages, did not, like the German Romanticists, become retrograde in politics from a false conception of medieval beliefs and manners of life. Their peculiar grace of style and bizarre fancifulness are still—as in Feuillet—visible in F. L.; but the most recent French fiction is largely characterised by feverish sensationalism and a coarse fondness for glaring colours, licentious plots, and morbid reflections. The French poetry of the 19th c. is rich in lyrical and dramatic masterpieces, is often full of deep passion and stormy ardour, and is generally characterised by a crystal lucidity combined with a sweetness of cadence formerly unknown to the language. See Villemain's *Tableau de la Littér. au Moyen Age* (1857), Fauriel's *Histoire de la Poésie Provençale* (Par. 1846), Littré's *Histoire de la Langue Française* (1867), Gerusez's *Histoire Littéraire de la France* (1865-73), Besant's *Early French Poetry* (1868), Gidel's *Histoire de la Littérature Française* (1875).

French Pol'ish is composed of shellac dissolved in wood-spirit or spirits of wine, and sometimes a little gum-elemi, copal, or mastic is added. The polish is applied to cabinet-work with a rubber, consisting of a woollen rag, gathered into a ball-form, and covered with linen. The rag is slightly soaked with the polish, and before commencing work, the surface of the linen is touched with raw linseed oil. The rubber is plied freely and lightly in short circular strokes till the whole surface has a smooth uniform coat of polish. The linseed oil is finally removed with a cloth moistened with spirits of wine, rubbed very lightly in the direction of the grain of the wood.

French Prot'estant Church. The first seeds of the Reformation in France were perhaps sown by Lefevre, a teacher in the Sorbonne, who, as early as 1512, turned from the study of the lives of the Saints to that of St. Paul's epistles. He it was who infected with his own love for the Bible his pupil Farel (q. v.), and perhaps also Olivetan (q. v.), the former of whom kindled the flame in Switzerland, after helping his master to do it in France, and the latter first translated the Scriptures into French-Swiss, and converted his nephew Calvin (q. v.) from the Romish doctrines. The Sorbonne raised the cry of 'Heresy' against Lefevre, and drove him from Paris; but the disciples of Luther had meanwhile arrived there, and multitudes 'assumed the liberty of interpreting the Bible for themselves.' Lefevre retired to Meaux, where, about 1521, he and Farel began openly to preach the new doctrines, and where, about 1523, he published a translation of the New Testament. The clergy were alarmed, and appealed to the Sorbonne, which succeeded in exciting the Parliament against 'the heretics of Meaux.' An interdict was issued against them in 1523, and the congregation there dispersed. Lefevre found an asylum with the Queen of Navarre; Farel fled to Basel; Pavanes was burnt in 1524, and Berguin in 1529. Calvin dedicated his *Institutes* to François (1529) in a preface imploring his protection for the Protestants, but the only effect of this was to increase the persecution. In 1534 Paris was thrown into excitement by placards which appeared all over the city, violently attacking the mass, the Pope, cardinals, bishops, and monks. Whether this was done by Protestants, or, as some say, by the clergy for a purpose, a rumour went that 'the Lutherans' had laid a plot to burn the city and massacre the Catholics, and soon the cry was raised of 'Death to the heretics.' The order was given to seize all heretics dead or alive, and the prisons were soon crowded. Six of the most prominent were burnt, and an ordinance published for the extermination of the sect. The Waldenses (q. v.) of Provence, who had declared the Protestants their brethren, were treated with indescribable barbarity. The same persecuting policy was pursued by Henri II., who succeeded his father in 1547; but all attempts to exterminate the Protestants were fruitless. In 1555 the first congregation was formed in Paris, and in 1559 a national synod met at the same place, when the F. P. C. was organised, with a Confession of Faith and an ecclesiastical polity essentially Calvinistic.

The same year Henri met his death, and was succeeded by François II., a youth of sixteen, and the husband of Mary Queen of Scots. The uncles of Mary, the Cardinal of Lorraine and the Duc de Guise, were appointed regents, and the Guise faction did their utmost to exterminate the Protestants. Under the leadership of the three brothers Coligny, D'Andelot, and Chatillon, nephews of the Constable Montmorency, they took up arms in desperation to relieve themselves from the tyranny of the Guises; but their plan failed, and many were slaughtered and imprisoned. About this time a third of the population of France were Protestants, and these the choice portion of the nation—the burgesses of the towns, three-fourths of the educated and learned, and half of the nobility, including the King of Navarre and the Prince of Condé. When François II. was succeeded in 1560 by his younger brother, Charles IX., through the influence of the queen-mother, Catherine de Medici, who was jealous of the power of the Guises, the Bourbon party were again received at court; and when the Guises entered into an alliance with Spain, to preserve the balance of power she sought the friendship of the Protestants, and showed them favour. In 1561 an edict of toleration was issued by Parliament to all the presidial courts; but the immediate consequence of this was an outbreak of intolerance, as the edict was rebelled against wherever the Catholics were more powerful than the Protestants. A second edict, to the effect that the Protestants might meet for worship outside the towns, was no better observed than the first, and a furious and cruel temper was displayed on both sides.

The massacre of a number of Protestants at Vassy by the followers of the Duc de Guise, which was followed by similar outrages elsewhere, was the signal for the outbreak of a civil war which raged, with intervals of peace, for forty years. On the assassination of the Duc de Guise in 1563 a peace was concluded, in terms of which the Protestant worship was to be tolerated in particular places. The war being renewed in 1567 by the Protestants under Condé and Coligny, they suffered a defeat in the battle of St. Denis; and after that the Protestant soldiers, who had hitherto submitted to strict discipline, were guilty of savage reprisals on the Catholics. After a peace of six months, in 1568 the fighting was resumed; the Protestants were again defeated, and Condé fell in the battle of Jarnac. The cause was all but lost, when Coligny suddenly defeated the royal army, and marched on Paris; and a peace on favourable terms was concluded in 1570. The lull was followed by the fearful tragedy of St. Bartholomew's Day (q. v.), which crushed the Church for twenty-six years, during which time only six national synods were held; but it revived after the publication (1598) of the celebrated Edict of Nantes (q. v.), the revocation of which in 1685 by Louis XIV. was fatal alike to France and Protestantism. The new edict enacted that all Protestant pastors should quit France within fifteen days; that the children of Protestants should be educated as Catholics; that Protestants found emigrating should be sent to the galleys for life if men, or imprisoned for life if women. Notwithstanding these penalties, a regular exodus took place. At least 300,000 found their way to other countries; thousands perished or were caught and imprisoned in the attempt; about 1,000,000 were left in the country.

Notwithstanding that there was now no longer a nobility to lead or a clergy to instruct them, and that persecution was unabated, the Protestant cause revived, for the heartless cruelty with which the Protestants were pursued had the effect of exciting much sympathy with them. So galling and atrocious was the persecution in the Cevennes, that in 1702 the inhabitants rose in rebellion. (See CAMISARDS.) They were able to hold their own so well that the Government was glad to come to terms with them, and there followed a period of comparative quiet. The fanaticism of the Camisards was held in check by Antoine Court, called 'the Restorer of Protestantism in France,' by whom the Church was now reorganised *in the wilderness*, and a theological seminary established at Lausanne, which supplied pastors to the Church till the time of Napoleon. Persecution again raged for a time when Louis XV. published (1724) a recapitulation of all the most severe measures passed during the reign of Louis XIV., but from 1730 to 1744 the Church enjoyed comparative quiet, and in the latter year a national synod was convened in Lower Languedoc. This, however, was the signal for the publication of enactments more tyrannical than ever, and a thousand acts of merciless oppression were perpetrated, so that a fresh emigration was the result. A sudden outburst of persecution in Languedoc in 1748 was followed by a period of comparative quietness. Two synods met in 1760, and the ordinary meetings for worship were unmolested. But this calm was interrupted by two wanton executions at Toulouse, which, however, had the opposite effect from that intended, for they excited a feeling of shame and indignation on the part even of many Catholics. Public opinion now gradually became so strong against persecution, that in 1787 the Edict of Toleration was passed by the Assembly of Notables, allowing Protestants to live in France unmolested for their religion, and to marry, baptize, and bury according to their own forms. In 1789 the Constituent Assembly declared 'all citizens equal in the eye of the law.' Under Napoleon as First Consul, the Catholic clergy and Protestant pastors were on an equal footing, with the one exception of state support, which the latter did not receive. But as this left the Protestant Church comparatively independent, along with supplementary support to the pastors, he gave it a new constitution, placing it entirely under the control of the state. On the restoration of the Bourbons in 1815, an attempt was made to renew the old persecution; indeed, 'another Bartholomew' was planned, and was near being executed. The second revolution in 1830 again placed all religions on an equal footing, and in spite of petty persecution by the Jesuits, Protestantism increased. In 1838 the Reformed (Calvinistic) Church had about 460 pastors; the Lutheran about 260. From 1659, when Louis XIV. intimated that such meetings would no longer be permitted, no synod had met with the sanction of the state till 1872. An attempt at one in 1848 was a comparative failure. The proposal to draw up a Confession of Faith was negatived, whereupon those who wished it seceded and formed themselves into the Union of the Evangelical Churches in France. Since no Confession was included in the constitution provided for the Church by Napoleon in 1802, and the old one was then obsolete, the Church had practically been without one from that time. Accordingly the conservative party in the synod of 1872 wished to endow the Church with a genuine Confession, and by a narrow majority succeeded in carrying their point; but its extremely general terms is an immense departure from the Predestinarian theology of the old one. Now that Alsace and a part of Lorraine, where a numerous Lutheran population had gathered, are severed from France, there do not remain in it above 800,000 Protestants, of whom 70,000 to 80,000 are Lutherans. See De Félice's *Hist. des Protestants de France* (Par. 1850), and MM. Haags' *La France Protestante* (Par. 1847–59).

French River, in the Dominion of Canada, province of Ontario, is an outlet of Lake Nipissing, and flows into Lake Huron after a course of 55 miles, part of which, through bare rock, looks like an artificial cutting. It is impeded by many rapids, but forms a channel for the fur trade of the Red River settlements.

Frere, John Hookham, was born in London in 1769, entered Parliament in 1796, and became Under Secretary of State for Foreign Affairs in 1799. He was one of the founders of the *Quarterly Review*, and the author of *Translations of Several Plays of Aristophanes* (1840), *Theognis Restitutus* (1842), and other writings, chiefly humorous. In 1808 he was appointed Minister to Spain, married the Countess of Erroll (1816), and removed to Malta, where he died at Pieta, 7th January 1846. His works were published with a memoir in 1872.—**Sir Bartle Edward F.**, nephew of the preceding, was born in 1815, educated at Haileybury College, and entered the Indian Civil Service in 1834. He was made British Resident in Scinde in 1856, and Chief Commissioner in 1860, and for his conduct during the Mutiny twice received the thanks of Parliament and was created a K.C.B. From 1862 to 1867 he was Governor of Bombay, and in the latter year was made a K.G.C.S.I., and returned to England, where he became Vice-President of the Royal Geographical Society. As special British commissioner he brought about the abolition of slavery by the Sultan of Zanzibar in 1873. He was sworn a member of the Privy Council on his return, and appointed Governor of Cape Colony in 1876. His writings include *Pandurang Hari, or Memoirs of a Hindoo* (new. ed. 1873), and *The Impending Famine in Bengal, and how to Prevent Future Famines in India* (1874).

Fre'ron, Élie-Catherine, a French critic and jealous champion of monarchy and the Christian faith against the tendencies of the time, was born in 1719 at Quimper. He is best known by his critical journal, which ultimately appeared under the name *L'Année Littéraire*, and which he conducted from 1746 till his death, 10th March 1776. F.'s fame is less due to his own talents than to his perpetual feud with Voltaire and the Encyclopedists, maintained on both sides with the intensest bitterness.

Fres'co (Ital. 'fresh'), a method of decorative painting executed upon wet or *fresh* plaster with raw pigments mixed with water or hydrate of lime. In drying, the colours are incorporated with the plaster, and are thereby rendered as durable as itself. The *intonaco* or F. ground is composed of two parts fine river sand and one part lime. It is floated on about one-eighth of an inch thick, and in quantities that the artist can overtake at one painting. A copy of the F. design on paper is laid on the wet plaster, and the outlines are indented through by means of a bone stylus. The colours, chiefly simple earths, are then applied with great breadth and freedom, brushes of hogs' and other hair being used. No colours of vegetable origin, and few compounded mineral pigments, withstand the chemical action of lime. To produce a successful F., considerable artistic and technical skill and experience are required. A design of masterly composition and careful drawing, the selection of permanent colours, and rapid work without retouching, are the chief essentials. A pure atmosphere is necessary for the permanence of a F., damp is fatal to it, and smoke and the products of the combustion of gas and coal are also very injurious. The failure of many of the experiments in F.-painting made in England of late years, in the Houses of Parliament and elsewhere, is traceable partly to climatic and other influences, and partly to the use of unsuitable pigments.

F.-painting is a most ancient art. Remains of it are still found in Egypt, and among the Romans it was extensively practised. Ancient examples of this mode of painting are to be seen in Pompeii, Rome, and other places. The art attained perfection on the revival of the arts in Italy. The highest pictorial efforts of Michael Angelo, Raphael, Giotto, Correggio, and others, are executed in F. in churches and palaces in Italy. After falling into disuse the art has been revived in Germany and in England.

Fresco Secco is distinguished from the foregoing, *buon* F., or true F., by the painting being executed on dry plaster, which is moistened with lime-water before the colours are applied. Many of the wall paintings of the ancients were executed by this method, and in Italy at the present time it is commonly practised.

Fresh'-Water Herr'ing. See COREGONUS.

Fresh'-Water Muss'el, a popular name applied to various kinds of Lamellibranchiate *Mollusca* inhabiting fresh-water streams and lakes. The genera *Unio* and *Anodonta* contain examples. This mussel is not to be confused with the true marine mussel, which belongs to an entirely different family—that of the *Mytilidæ*. The F.-W. M. has a shell generally equivalve, with a large external *ligament* used for opening the shell. The anterior hinge teeth are thick and striated, the posterior teeth being laminated in structure or wanting. The mantle-lobes are united between the (*siphonal*) apertures, and the foot, which is large and compressed, has the power in the embryonic state of secreting a *byssus* or 'beard,' such as is seen in the marine mussels. Of the genus *Unio* itself, the *U. littoralis* and *U. pictorum* are familiar species. The *U. margaritifera* produces pearls which, especially those found in Scotch rivers, are sometimes of large size and of considerable value. The swan or river mussel (*Anodonta cygnæa*), the *A. ensiformis*, and the *A. angulata* are examples of the second genus.

Fresh'-Water Stra'ta, in geology, are deposits which have been formed by lakes, rivers, or fresh water filtering into caverns. As a rule, they are of small extent compared with marine deposits, but they are important as indicating the presence of land, and frequently the nature of the fauna and flora of inland regions.

Fres'nel, Augustin Jean, a distinguished French mathematician and physicist, was born at Broglie (Eure), 10th May 1788. In his seventeenth year he entered the École Polytechnique, where he gained high distinction. He was afterwards appointed engineer to the department of Vendée, and later to that of Drôme, where he stayed till 1815. About the year 1814 he began the study of light, his researches in which in 1827 obtained the Rumford medal of the Royal Society of London. F. died at Paris, July 14, 1827. Though later in attacking the subject of light than the celebrated Young, his superior power of mathematical analysis enabled him to far outstrip that distinguished philosopher, and to establish still more the probability of the truth of the undulatory theory of light. The simplicity of his explanations of reflection, refraction, diffraction, and polarisation is itself a powerful argument in favour of his theory. He also greatly improved the apparatus for lighting lighthouses. His memoirs are published in the *Annals de Physique et de Chimie* and in the *Mémoires de l'Académie des Sciences*, which contain an *Éloge* on F. by Arago.

Fresnill'o, a town of Mexico, state of Zacatecas, on a branch of the Santiago, 30 miles N.W. of Zacatecas. It has a good mining school, and in the vicinity are rich copper and silver mines. Pop. 7015.

Fret, in heraldry, is a figure in which two lines, interlaced with a mascle, cross the shield transversely. The shield is said to be *fretty* ('broken,' from Lat. *fractus*) when it bears several such lines.

Freu'denstadt ('town of joy'), a town of Würtemberg, Germany, in the circle of the Black Forest, near the Murg, 40 miles S.W. of Stuttgart. It has some cotton-spinning, weaving, and smith-work, and a trade in wood, cattle, and fruit. Pop. (1872) 5145. F. was founded in 1559, and its first inhabitants were Lutheran refugees from Austria.

Frey'a, a Teutonic goddess, daughter of Niörd, and sister of Freyr, young and beautiful, was the wife of Odin, who deserted her, and the goddess of love but also of death. That she was originally the same as *Frigg*, another wife of Odin, is doubtful. The latter, however, was known to the Old English, Frisians, and other Low Germans as *Frea* and *Fria*, and her name is still preserved in *Friday*, originally *Frigdæg* (Old Ger. *Frîatac*).

Freyr, son of Niörd, a Teutonic god, worshipped in early times by the Swedes as the supreme deity. His temple was at Upsala and his festival at Yule. He was wise and peaceful, ruler of sea and air, and the giver of fertility to earth and to mankind.

Frey'stâdl (Hung. *Galgocz*), a town of Hungary, on the banks of the Waag, 84 miles N.W. of Pesth, and nearly opposite the fortified Leopoldstadt. It has a castle, a tower of supposed Turkish origin, some manufactures of wooden articles, and a trade in cattle. Pop. (1869) 6098.

Frey'tag, Gu'stav, called by his admirers 'the father of the modern German novel,' and known also as a poet and journalist, was born 13th July 1816, at Kreuzburg, in Silesia. After some years spent as a *docent* in the University of Breslau, he became, in 1848, editor of the journal *Die Grenzboten*, with which he was connected till 1870. He first acquired fame by his dramas *Valentine* (Leips. 1847) and *Graf Waldemar* (Leips. 1848). In 1855 appeared the successful comedy *Die Journalisten*, and in 1859 the antique drama *Die Fabier*. F.'s earlier novels are thoroughly modern in subject and spirit. *Soll und Haben* (1855), translated into English under the name *Debit and Credit* (1858), is a vigorous, truthful, and lively picture of the life in a German provincial town, and thoroughly deserves its great popularity (in 1871 the 16th edition appeared). Other works of F. are *Neue Bilder aus dem Leben des Deutschen Volkes* (Leips. 1862, Eng. trans. 4 vols. 1862–63), and *Die verlorene Handschrift* (1864, Eng. trans. 1865), which draws on university circles. In the novels *Bilder aus dem Deutschen Vergangenheit* (4 vols. 6th ed. 1871) F. has gone for his subjects to mediæval German history, and has treated them with patriotic spirit, deep insight, and artistic skill.

Fri'ar (Fr. *frère*, Lat. *frater*, 'brother') is a name common to members of all religious brotherhoods, but generally confined to the Mendicant Orders, which were reduced by Leo X. in the Council of Lyon (1272) to four—the Dominicans, Franciscans, Carmelites, and Augustinian Eremites. The Franciscans (q. v.), called by their founder *Fraterculi*, or *Fratres Minores* (Minor Friars), got the name in England of *Grey Friars*, from the colour of their habit. The Dominicans, first called *Preaching Friars*, were afterwards called *Major Friars*, in contradistinction to the Franciscans, and in England *Black Friars*. The Carmelites were the *White Friars*. In a more restricted sense still, F. is applied to the members of these orders who are not priests. Those in priest's orders are called Fathers.

Friar's Bal'sam (*Tinctura benzoini compositus*), sometimes called *traumatic B.*, is a compound of benzoin, 8 parts; prepared storax, 6; balsam of tolu, 2; socotrine aloes, 1½; and rectified spirit, 80; prepared by maceration and filtration. It is given internally for chronic cough, and is applied externally to languid ulcers, cuts, and wounds. See BENZOIN.

Fric'tion is the resistance to relative motion experienced at the surfaces of two portions of matter in contact. In the case of the sliding of solids, the laws of F. established by experiment are very simple, and require the mere statement for their comprehension. 1. F. is proportional to the pressure; 2. F. is independent, *ceteris paribus*, of the areas in contact; 3. F. is independent of the relative velocity. The same laws hold approximately for rolling bodies, except that in certain instances increase of velocity increases the F., an effect due no doubt to the *sliding* motion which must be present when the velocity is greatly increased. The resistance experienced by a solid moving through a fluid is due in great measure to *fluid F.*, which depends upon the viscosity of the fluid. On account of this viscosity, vortices or eddies are generated in the fluid when a solid moves through it, and this vortex motion necessitates the disappearance of a portion of the kinetic energy of the solid. It is thus apparent that the study of the phenomena arising from F. must hold an important place in many questions of practical moment. As examples, the gradual retardation of the earth's diurnal motion through the loss of energy by tidal F., and the diminution of the period of revolution of Encke's comet due to the presence of a resisting medium may be cited. In all cases, F. acts against the motion; and a definite quantity of energy must always be expended in overcoming it. The equivalent of this lost energy is to be found in the heat ultimately generated. Electrical effects also are known to accompany the rubbing of bodies together. Delicate experiments, however, have shown that contact of heterogeneous bodies and separation are sufficient without F. to generate electricity; and this suggests that F. may, partly at least, be due to attractive force which is called into action when separation is effected between the two oppositely-charged portions of matter originally in contact. The *coefficient of F.* for any two bodies is the ratio of the F. to the pressure, and is an important mathematical *constant* in the study of statics.

Frid'ericia, originally **Fred'eriks-Odde,** a fortified seaport of Denmark, on the E. coast of Jutland, occupies the peninsula of Skandse-Odde. It is the port where are collected the dues of the Little Belt, and it has twenty-two factories and an active manufacture of tobacco. Pop. (1873) 7186.

Fried'land, a small town of E. Prussia, on the Alle, 26 miles S.E. of Königsberg, notable as the scene of the victory of Napoleon I. over the Russians under Bennigsen, which led to the peace of Tilsit, 14th June 1807.—Another F., in Bohemia, on the Wittich, is the capital of a district, and gave the title Duke of F. to the great Wallenstein. Pop. (1869) 4260.

Friedland, Valentin, an eminent educationist, was born at Trotzendorf in Upper Lusatia, 14th February 1490, and from this place he derived his popular surname. After a course of study, chiefly memorable for the knowledge of Greek which he acquired, he embraced Lutheranism, formed at Wittenberg the acquaintance of Luther and Melancthon, and, according to report, placed himself in the service of a converted Jew for two years, on the understanding that as a salary he should obtain lessons in Hebrew. He is memorable for the success which attended his efforts as rector of the Gymnasium at Goldberg in Silesia, to which he was appointed in 1523. Pupils flocked to it not only from the surrounding district, but from neighbouring countries such as Poland, Austria, and Hungary. F. died at Liegnitz, April 26, 1556. See Pinzger's *Valentin F., genannt Trotzendorf* (Hirschberg, 1825; Breslau, 1856).

Fried'rich, a common name of German rulers. Some of the more famous are here noticed.

Romano-German Emperors.—**Friedrich I.**, surnamed *Barbarossa* ('red-beard'), the second of the Hohenstauffen line, was born in 1121, perhaps at Waiblingen. He was the son of Duke Friedrich of Swabia, and grandson of Emperor Heinrich IV. He succeeded his uncle Konrad III. in the imperial dignity in 1152, being crowned at Aachen by Arnold, Archbishop of Köln. Connected himself through his mother, Judith of Bavaria, with the Welf party, F. at once began a policy of conciliation. The quarrel of Knut V. about the Danish throne and the claims of Heinrich the Lion to Bavaria were settled; aid was promised to the Pope against Arnold of Brescia. It required some hard fighting to vindicate his authority in Milan, but in 1155 he opened the ancient *comitia* of the duchy at Roncaglia, and was crowned at Pavia. There was more fighting at Rome, where Arnold was burned alive. A difference now rose between F. and the Pope, Adrian IV., about the lands of the Countess Matilda of Tuscany, bequeathed to the Holy See, but claimed by F. as feudal suzerain. On his return to Germany, F. found ample employment in stopping the brigandage of the *burggrafen*, and in removing some of the heavier restrictions on commerce. He repaired the finances, controlled the dukes, exalted the central power by multiplying nobles of the second rank, afterwards the 'College of Princes,' and tried to supersede local and conflicting Teutonic customs by the Lombard feudal code, and the civil law which the new school of glossatores was now teaching in the great universities. To the great towns, *e.g.*, Köln, Trier, Mainz, Worms, Speyer, Nürnberg, &c., he gave municipal franchises and independent jurisdictions, which made them a counterweight to the local oligarchy. From 1158 to 1162 there was war in Italy, in which F., trying to impose an absolute government by Podestas of his own nomination on the towns which had democratic consular institutions, naturally roused them into fierce revolt. As an instance of the extent of the imperial power at the time, it may be mentioned that at the Diet of Besançon F. invested Waldemar with the royal dignities Denmark, Sweden, and Norway, and gave to Raymond of Provence a portion of the kingdom of Arles, and soon after compelled the Pope to canonise Karl the Great. The Lombard League of cities was now, however, gathering strength, and after several campaigns F. at last was defeated by the Milanese at Legnano, 29th May 1176, and by the good offices of Sebastian Ziani, the Doge of Venice, a meeting of peace was arranged between Pope Alexander and the Emperor, where the latter confessed the papal supremacy, the Antipope Calixtus III. retiring. In 1183 the more durable peace of Constance was entered into, which for some time was the guarantee of freedom in N. Italy. The news that Saladin had taken Jerusalem (1189) determined F. to lead a crusade to the Holy City. Crossing the Hellespont with 100,000 men, he obtained a great victory at Iconium (1190). Soon after he was accidentally drowned while bathing in the Cydnus. In the midst of his vast political and military activity F. found time to patronise the *Minnesingers*. It is an old German legend that F. still lives in a limestone cave in the Untersberg (Salzburg), whence he will issue with his crusaders and re-establish the golden age of Germany. When the German Empire was revived in 1871, men said the old legend had come true. See Prutz's *Kaiser Friedrich I.* (1871).—**Friedrich II.**, grandson of the preceding, was born at Jesi, in the March of Ancona, 26th December 1194. His father died in 1197, and his mother, Constance of Sicily, committed to Pope Innocent III. the education of her son. He became an accomplished scholar. The old description of him was—'Armorum strenuus, linguarum peritus, rigorosus, luxuriosus, epicurus, nihil curans vel credens nisi temporale: malleus Romanæ ecclesiæ.' In 1212 he married Constance of Aragon, and two years later was crowned King of the Romans at Aachen. The same year Innocent III., who had in 1201 published his celebrated brief to the effect that the empire really belonged to the Church, was succeeded by Honorius III., who at once insisted on F. performing his promise to make a crusade. The latter was, however, too much engaged with the rebellious Palatinate and the town of Brunswick to leave Europe, and by a series of ingenious excuses he delayed until 1220, when, after crowning his son Heinrich King of the Romans, he came to Rome, where he was himself crowned by the Pope, whose suspicions were allayed by the concessions of jurisdiction and exemption which F. had made to the ecclesiastical princes of the empire. For seven years F. governed the empire from Italy, or rather Sicily; he cultivated art and letters, founded the University of Naples, and his chancellor, Petrus de Vineis, published a code of laws. After his marriage with Jolante, daughter of Jean de Brienne, titular King of Jerusalem, F. was in 1227 driven by the new Pope, Gregory IX., to fulfil his promise of a crusade. By an injudicious attempt to curtail the freedom of the towns in N. Italy he resuscitated the old Lombard League, and by his reluctance to start for Palestine he drew down on himself the ban of excommunication. The angry letters which he now sent to Rome were the boldest which the world had yet seen. He calls the Pope an insatiable leech, who, unlike Christ, prefers war instead of peace, and amasses wealth by unjust means instead of remaining poor like Peter. He even entered Rome with a body of Arabian troops. The crusade consisted in a treaty or *mosapha* between F. and Kamel, the Sultan of Egypt, for a ten years' joint occupation of the Holy City by Christians and Mohammedans. Disputes with the Pope, the Lombards, and his son Heinrich fill up the period till 1235, when F. dethroned Heinrich, made his son Konrad King of Germany, and married Isabella of England, sister of Henry III. The victory of Corte Nuova on the Oglio (26th and 27th November 1237), in which Milan lost the *caroccio*, or standard-chariot, made the chief Lombard cities submit, and so alarmed Gregory that he again excommunicated the Emperor, alleging that he blasphemed, that he called Moses and Christ impostors, and denied the possibility of a birth from a virgin. In spite of F.'s services to Christendom in turning back the Mongol invader at Olmutz (1241), the new Pope, Innocent IV., continued the traditional hostility, and finally declared him to be deposed, and all his subjects freed from their allegiance. This encouraged Heinrich Raspe of Thuringia and Willem of Holland successively to declare themselves emperor. They were both defeated, but soon after F. died at Fiorentino, 12th December 1250. See Shirrmacher's *Kaiser F. II.* (Gött. 3 vols. 1859-64), and Winkelmann's *Geschichte Kaiser F.'s II. und seiner Reiche* (Berl. 1863).—**Friedrich III.**, the Pacific, twenty-ninth Romano-German emperor, the son of Duke Ernst of Styria, was born at Innsbruck, 21st September 1415. He succeeded to the imperial throne in 1440. He allowed Sforza to establish himself at Milan. The death of his ward Ladislaus brought him Lower Austria, but his expectations of Bohemia and Hungary were disappointed by Podiebrad and Corvinus. F. studied botany, alchemy, and the stars, while the Turks were advancing through Carniola to Salzburg. At last Bohemia and Hungary began war against him. He was obliged to renounce many of his possessions and claims, and retired from Vienna to the Netherlands, where his son Maximilian, by Eleanor of Portugal, had married Maria of Burgundy. The death of Corvinus in 1490 brought back Lower Austria, but Hungary fell to Podiebrad. After crowning Maximilian King of the Romans, F. died at Linz, 19th August 1493. The only good or vigorous work which he did in this stirring period of Hussite heresy, Turkish invasion, early renaissance, and the decay of feudal power, was the formation of a peace league among the Swabian cities. See Chmel's *Geschichte Kaiser F.'s IV.* (Hamb. 2 vols. 1840-43).

Electors of Brandenburg.—**Friedrich Wilhelm**, Elector of Brandenburg, known as the 'great Elector,' was born at Köln, on the Spree, February 6, 1620, and succeeded his father, Georg Wilhelm, as Elector of Brandenburg in 1640. In 1641 he entered into a treaty of neutrality with Sweden, and in 1644 reannexed Kleve and the county of Mark to his dominions by making an armistice with Hessen-Kassel. He devoted himself successfully to strengthening his army, by turns aided Poland and Sweden when war broke out in 1655, and entirely freed Prussia from the sway of Poland, on which it was till then dependent. In 1672 he formed an alliance with the Dutch Republic, but on the French invading the Netherlands, was crippled in his efforts to oppose them by the jealousy of the Austrians, and in 1673 made a treaty with France, breaking off his league with the Dutch. In 1675 he defeated the Swedes, who had invaded his territory, at Fehrbellin, but being unsupported by the other German rulers, was forced to yield to the French demands, and by the treaty of St. Germain, 1679, to restore the land which he had won from Sweden. He afterwards brought about an armistice between France and Germany, and sent 8000 men to aid Austria against the Turks. F. did much to consolidate and improve his possessions. On the revocation of the Edict of Nantes he afforded protection to 20,000 French refugees, who gave a great impulse to the industries of Prussia. He enlarged Berlin, and founded the University of Duisburg. He died at Potsdam, April 29, 1688. See Orlich's *Geschichte des Preuss. Staats im 17ten. Jahrh.* (3 vols. Berl. 1838-39); Förster's *Geschichte F. Wilhelm's des grossen Kurfürsten* (4 vols. Berl. 1855); Erdmannsdörffer's *Urkunden und Actenstücke zur Geschichte des Kurfürsten F. Wilhelm von Brandenburg* (Berl. 1864 *et seq.*); and Peter's *Der Krieg des grossen Kurfürsten gegen Frankreich* (1870).

Kings of Prussia.—**Friedrich I.**, King of Prussia, son of the Great Elector, was born at Königsberg, 22d July 1657. He succeeded his father in the Electorate of Brandenburg in 1688, and was a firm adherent of William of Orange and the other allies against Louis XIV. In 1700 he procured the title King of Prussia from the Emperor, whom, in return, he promised always to support in the Diet and in the field. In 1701 he placed the crown on his own head at Königsberg, and continued to oppose France until his death, February 25, 1713. He founded the order of the Black Eagle, the University of Halle, and the Royal Academy of Berlin, a city which he greatly beautified. Carlyle describes him as 'a perfect gentleman, and a courageous and high though thin-skinned man.'—**Friedrich Wilhelm I.**, King of Prussia, son of Friedrich I., was born August 2, 1688, married Sophia-Dorothea, daughter of the Elector of Hanover—afterwards George I. of England—in 1706, came to the throne in 1713, and devoted himself to improve the finances, and above all to strengthen the army of Prussia. He opposed Charles XII. of Sweden, interfered to protect the Protestants in adjoining states, and did much to develop the industries of his kingdom. He was ludicrously fond of tall soldiers, and spared no pains to procure them for his forces. He was a wise, vigorous monarch, but a man of coarse tastes and almost no culture. He died May 31, 1740, leaving Prussia with an army of 70,000 men, whom he had collected and drilled with unflagging assiduity. Probably Carlyle was the first to look wisely into his real character, and to detect the worth that lay beneath the transcendent rudeness and brutality of his manners.—**Friedrich II.**, the Great, the ablest ruler of the 18th c., son of the preceding, was born January 24, 1712. When 'one of the prettiest, sprightliest lads,' he quarrelled bitterly with his father, who thwarted his tastes for poetry and music, and forbade him to receive any other than a military training. The dissension increased, and F., taken when trying to fly to the court of his uncle the King of England, was kept in strict confinement, his father, it is said, having at one time been only deterred from sentencing him to death by the intercession of the Swedish and Polish kings. In 1733 he was brought back to court to marry the Princess Elizabeth-Christina, daughter of Ferdinand Albrecht, Duke of Brunswick-Bevern, and lived in retirement at Rheinsberg, where he wrote his *Anti-Machiavel* and other works, associated with *literati* and corresponded with scholars, especially with Voltaire, until on his father's death he became king in 1740. Taking advantage of the death of the Emperor Karl VI., he demanded from Maria Theresa the Silesian principalities of Jägerndorf, Liegnitz, Brieg, and Wohlau, to which the house of Brandenburg claimed a reversionary right. The demand being refused, F. entered Silesia and defeated the Austrians near Mollwitz, 10th April 1741. France and Bavaria now joined him, and after his victory at Czaslau (17th May 1742) the first Silesian war ended, Prussia obtaining Upper and Lower Silesia. After the second Silesian war, in which he defeated the Austrians and Saxons at Hohenfriedberg (4th June 1745) and Sorr (30th September), Hennersdorf (23d November) and Kesselsdorf (15th December), F. devoted himself during the eleven years of peace which followed to bettering the condition of Prussia, organising his army, and likewise to occasional literary labours, writing his *Mémoires de Brandenbourg*, and his poem *L'Art de la Guerre*. Hearing of an alliance between Austria, Russia, and Saxony, and dreading to lose Silesia, in 1756 F. entered Saxony, and the third Silesian or Seven Years' War (q. v.) began. Opposed by France, Austria, Russia, Saxony, with only England as an ally, F. triumphed signally over his enemies. Of the sixteen great battles which F. and his generals fought, he was victorious at Lowositz (1756), Prag, Rossbach, and Leuthen (1757), Krefeld and Zorndorf (1758), Liegnitz and Torgau (1760), and Freiberg (1762). When the war ended by the peace of Hubertsburg (1763), F. had shown a military genius previously unequalled in modern history, and had laid the foundation of a united Germany. Henceforth Prussia was recognised as a great force in European politics. F. now strove to lighten the taxation of his subjects, practised the strictest economy, founded various useful institutions, opened his magazines to aid the agricultural population, and established an excise on the French system. In 1772 he took part with Russia and Austria in the partition of Poland (q. v.), and by the treaty of Teschen (1779) brought about the union of Franconia with Prussia. In 1785 he formed the confederation of the German princes, and in August 17, 1786, died at Sans Souci, leaving Prussia in a flourishing financial condition, with a population raised from 2,240,000 to 6,000,000, an army of 200,000, and a greatly extended territory. F.'s moral character has many dark blemishes—he was dishonourable, vindictive, and callous, the somewhat fantastic sensibility of his youth hardening into icy cynicism, into an arch contempt for humanity which was embittered by his Voltairian creed. On the other hand, his intellectual breadth and keenness, his foresight and adroitness, his sagacious promptitude and marvellous firmness, his dazzling administrative and military genius are unexcelled in history. In all likelihood he was unaware of the mighty results of his policy, he probably looked merely to the founding of a strong, independent Prussia. In this he succeeded, but his career was pregnant with other consequences. He was a great leader of the movement which changed the old to the new Europe. His campaigns put an end to the dynastic and personal strifes which had racked Europe for a century before the Seven Years' War. He checked the Jesuits, who were strangling freedom; led the way in forwarding religious toleration; made international, not personal, relations the ground of war; and gave the first example to modern times of a new type of monarchy, which practised thrift, exercised a regal supervision over the kingdom, and favoured industry and the people's welfare, as opposed to the essentially mediæval despotisms of Austria and France. He strove to make Berlin an academic centre, and was a zealous admirer and student of French literature, though blind to the merits of the rising school of German authors. An edition of his works was issued by the Berlin Academy (1846–51). See Kolb's *Das Leben F.'s des Einzigen* (4 vols. Speyer and Leips. 1828); Förster's *Leben und Thaten F.'s des Grossen* (2d ed. Leips. 1842), and *F. der Grosse* (4 vols. Berl. 1860); Kugler's *Geschichte F.'s des Grossen* (Leips. 1860); and Carlyle's *History of F. II.* (4 vols. Lond. 1858–65).—**Friedrich Wilhelm II.**, nephew of the above, was born September 25, 1744. A coolness between him and the great Friedrich was dispelled by his courage at the battle of Neustädtel, in the war of the Bavarian succession (1778), and he came to the throne in 1786. He made various aimless and costly political interferences, declaring war with Holland and the French Republic, abandoned his uncle's wise neutrality in theological questions, squandered his revenues, indulged unworthy favourites, and shared in the second partition of Poland in 1793. He died November 17, 1797, leaving Prussia with additional territory, but with a debt of 22,000,000 thalers. See F. von Cölln's *Vertraute Briefe*, &c. (6 vols. 1801–9).—**Friedrich Wilhelm III.**, eldest son of the preceding, was born August 3, 1770, married the Princess Louise of Mecklenburg-Strelitz in 1793, and became king in 1797. He began his reign by retrenching the public expenditure, organising the finances, and abolishing monopolies. During the Napoleonic struggle he at first sought to remain neutral; then became an ally of France, receiving in reward Hildesheim, Paderborn, and Münster; and at length, after vacillating between Russia and Napoleon, who treated him with open contempt, declared war with France. The Prussians were defeated at Jena, Eylau, and Friedland, and by the treaty of Tilsit (1807) he was stripped of three-fourths of his dominions. He laboured vigorously, however, to improve the fraction of Prussia which remained to him, and passed several wise decrees, framing the constitution anew, removing the privileges of the nobles, and promoting free trade. To this period of political degradation also belongs the reorganisation of Prussia's educational system, which has raised her to the foremost place among civilised nations. After the French retreat from Moscow, F. again proclaimed war against Napoleon, who had continued to shower insults upon him while striving to restore his humbled kingdom. The Prussians were at first checked in the field, but afterwards had the largest share in the victory of Leipsic (1813). After the fall of Napoleon, F. recovered all his former and other additional territories. He divided Prussia into ten provinces, each ruled by an *ober-präsident*, enacted that every man must serve in the army, developed commerce by founding the *Zollverein*, and forwarded industry generally, but broke his promise to create a new constitution, and showed himself hostile to Liberal principles. He died June 7, 1840. See Eylert's *Characterzüge und historische Fragmente aus dem Leben des Königs von Preussen F. W.* (3 vols. Magdeb. 1842–46).—**Friedrich Wilhelm IV.**, eldest son of F. W. III., was born at Berlin, October 15, 1795. While a youth he was noted for his accomplishments, and served in the campaigns of 1813–14. After peace was made, he returned to artistic pursuits, and visited Paris and Italy. He began to reign in 1840, and at first raised bright hopes by promising reform and seeming to sympathise with Liberalism. But he soon discarded his Liberal counsellors, and pursued a retrograde and absolutist policy, until, in 1848, his guards being beaten in a street fight with the Berlin populace, he was forced to swear that he would grant a new constitution. This promise he never kept. He prosecuted the Liberals and favoured the Ultramontanes, besides being greatly under the influence of Russia. F. W. at last became partly insane, and in 1857 Prince Wilhelm of Prussia became regent, the king thenceforth living in retirement until his death at Sans-Souci, January 2, 1861. See Varnhagen's *Tagebücher* (14 vols. 1861–70), and his *Blätter aus der Preuss. Gesch.* (5 vols. 1868–69.) There were twice attempts to murder F. W.—in 1844 by Tschech, a burgomaster, and in 1850 by Sefeloge, a discharged soldier.

Friedrich, Karl Nikolaus, imperial prince of Germany, eldest son of Prince Karl, second brother of the emperor, was born March 20, 1828, commanded in the Danish war of 1864, led the first army through Saxony against Austria, and won the battle of Königgratz with the aid of the Crown Prince in 1866. In the Franco-Prussian war he commanded the second German army, defeated General Froissart at Speichern, and invested Metz until Bazaine capitulated. He then drove back the Army of the Loire, retook Orleans, and forced General Chanzy to retire. F. was made a field-marshal October 28, 1870.

Friedrich Wilhelm, Crown Prince of Prussia, and son of King Wilhelm I., was born 18th October 1831. He took part in the Slesvig-Holstein war (1864) under Wrangel, and in the war with Austria (1866) received the command of the second army, and fought at Nachod, Trautenau, Skalitz, Soor, Schweinschädel, Königinhof, and Königgratz. In the Franco-Prussian war of 1870 he was in command of the third army, and took part in the battles of Weissenburg, Wörth, and Sedan.

Friedrich Wilhelm, Duke of Brunswick, son of Karl Wilhelm Ferdinand, was born October 9, 1771, accompanied the Prussian army into France in 1792, was made commander of a regiment, and in 1806 was taken prisoner along with Blucher at Lübeck. His rights to the Duchy of Brunswick being set aside by Napoleon, he continued to fight in Bohemia until the Austrians were totally overthrown, when he executed a masterly retreat with 1500 men, defeating Reubel with 4000 troops at Aelper (1809), and sailed for England, where he was received with enthusiasm. Along with his men, the 'Black Brunswickers,' he joined the English service, fought in Spain, and fell bravely at Quatre Bras, June 16, 1815. His biography was written by Spohr (Brunsw. 1861).

Friend'ly or **Ton'ga Islands**, a group to the E. of the Fiji Islands, in the Pacific Ocean, between lat. 13°–25° S. and long. 172°–177° E. They are over 150 in number, the smaller ones being of coral formation, the larger ones of volcanic. Some 30 are inhabited, and the total population amounts to 25,000. They have few native animals, but are richly productive in yams, sweet potatoes, bread-fruits, cocoa-nuts, &c. The largest island is the Tongatabu or Sacred Tonga, with 8000 inhabitants. The group was discovered by Tasman in 1643, received its name from Cook, and was first visited by missionaries in 1797. A Wesleyan mission was founded here in 1827, and King George, the chief native ruler in the group, embraced Christianity.

Friendly Societies. See BENEVOLENT SOCIETIES.

Friends, Society of, is a sect of Christians better known by the name of Quakers. The name is derived from their practice of addressing each other as 'Friend,' rather than by any title. The history of the origin of the sect is simply a history of the life of George Fox (q. v.). At the outset his followers exposed themselves to imprisonments and other punishments by their rude and fanatical conduct. For the first few years they seem to have interrupted public worship in the parish church wherever they opened their missions—the example having been set by Fox himself—sometimes in a most annoying and indecent manner. They spoke in a most offensive way against what they called the abominations of all existing Churches. Some even desecrated the Lord's Day, as a legal ordinance which ought to be treated with contempt. But, on the other hand, their errors were magnified, and their indiscretions punished as outrageous crimes. In many cases the peculiar garb and mode of speech, proclaiming the simple fact of their being Quakers, were of themselves a sufficient condemnation. It is a sad proof of the intolerance of the age that they were treated worst of all under the Commonwealth by the Puritans, who themselves had just been relieved from the tender mercies of the Star Chamber and the Court of High Commission. Indeed, when some of them betook themselves to New England, expecting to receive at least indulgence from the Puritans who had fled thither on account of persecution for conscience' sake, they were persecuted with an intolerance which has no parallel but in the annals of the Inquisition. In 1658 a law was passed 'that for the first offence (*i.e.*, of being a Quaker), if the offender were a male, one of his ears should be cut off, and he be kept at work in the house of correction till he should be sent away on his own charge. For the second, the other ear, and be kept in the house of correction as aforesaid. If a woman, to be severely whipped and kept as aforesaid; and for the second offence, to be dealt withal as the first. And for the third, he or she should have their tongues bored through with a hot iron, and be kept in the house of correction close at work till they be sent away on their own charge.' This law, as a preventive measure, having proved an utter failure, another Act was passed the same year, which condemned Quakers to banishment, and inflicted the penalty of death if they revisited the colony. Under this Act many Quakers suffered exile, and some were put to death.

In England a paper was laid before Parliament in 1659, in which they recount their sufferings, from which document it appears that during the preceding six years about 2000 had suffered in their goods or persons. Some of their sufferings, it must be confessed, were the fruit of their own extravagance. After the Restoration in 1660, 700 Quakers were released from various prisons. The king was prepared even to grant them the free exercise of their religion, when Venner's insurrection happened. The Quakers were confounded with the Fifth Monarchy Men, and a general persecution began. An Act was passed in 1662 'for preventing mischiefs and dangers that may arise from certain persons called Quakers and others refusing to take lawful oaths.' Under this Act a Quaker thrice convicted of the offence might be sold into perpetual slavery at Tunis, Jamaica, Barbadoes, or Virginia; and the Act was rigidly enforced. Matters were only made worse by the Conventicle Act (q. v.) of 1670, under which William Penn (q. v.) was tried for preaching.

On the accession of James II. (1685) a petition was presented to the king and Parliament setting forth 'the suffering condition of the peaceable people called Quakers, only for tender conscience towards Almighty God.' During the previous reign above 5000 of their number had been imprisoned; about 1380, including 300 women, were still confined; of these, 300 were imprisoned only because they refused to take an oath. Since the Restoration above 320 had died in prison. In the gaol of Newgate they were crowded in such numbers that they died of suffocation and malignant fever. The tenderness of conscience for which they suffered implied, it is true, a refusal to pay tithes, and an obstinate perverseness in interrupting the public worship of other Christians; but the severity of the punishments inflicted, as described in this petition, was quite unjustifiable.

The persecution of the Friends came to an end when James II. set aside all penal laws against dissenters by his own 'dispensing power,' that is, by proclamation. The Toleration Act of 1689 permitted the Friends to hold their meetings in peace on condition of signing three documents, a declaration against transubstantiation, a promise of fidelity to the government, and a confession of Christian belief. Since that time there is little of importance to record in the history of the society. In America during the present century there have been some outbursts of latitudinarianism in the body—*e.g.*, the 'Hicksite' movement, which was begun in 1827 by Elias Hicks, and almost rent the sect in twain. The total number of members belonging to the society is about 120,000, of whom 90,000 are in the United States.

The following account of the doctrines, practice, and discipline of the S. of F. is taken from an authorised statement of their own published in 1800:—

1. *Doctrine and Practice.*—They agree with other professors of the Christian name in the belief in one eternal God, the creator and preserver of the universe, and in Jesus Christ, his Son, the Messiah and the Mediator of the new covenant. To Christ alone they give the title of the Word of God, and not to the Scriptures, although they highly esteem these sacred writings in subordination to the Spirit, from which they are given forth.

It is their belief that in order to enable mankind to put in practice the sacred precepts of Scripture, many of which are contradictory to the unregenerate will of man, every man coming into the world is endued with a measure of light, grace, or good spirit of Christ, by which, as it is attended to, he is enabled to distinguish good from evil, and to correct the disorderly passions and corrupt propensities of his nature. Being thus persuaded that man without the spirit of Christ inwardly revealed can do nothing to the glory of God or to effect his own salvation, they think this influence especially necessary to the performance of the highest act of which the human mind is capable, even the worship of the Father of lights and of spirits; therefore they consider as obstructions to pure worship all forms which divert the attention from the secret influence of this unction from the Holy One, and believe it to be their duty to wait in silence to have a true sight of their condition bestowed upon them. On the same principle it follows that the ministry they approve must have its origin from the same source. Hence arises their testimony against preaching for hire, in contradiction to Christ's positive command—'Freely ye have received, freely give;' and hence their conscientious refusal to support such ministry by tithes or other means.

As they cannot encourage any ministry but that which they believe to spring from the influence of the Holy Spirit, so they do not restrict this influence to the male sex alone, but allow such of the female sex as seem to be endued with a right qualification for the ministry to exercise their gifts.

The two sacraments in use among most Christians they regard as useless, holding, as regards baptism, that it belonged to an inferior dispensation, and as regards the Lord's Supper, that since communion between Christ and his Church is maintained only by a real participation of his divine nature through faith, it is unnecessary to attend to that which is merely the shadow of this reality.

Few of their tenets are better known than their testimony against oaths and against war. With respect to the former of these, they abide literally by Christ's command (Matt. v. 34), 'Swear not at all.' From the same authority (Matt. v. 39, 44, &c.), the example of Christ himself, and the convictions of his spirit in their hearts, they are led to believe that wars and fightings are utterly repugnant to the gospel. They inculcate submission to the laws in all cases where conscience is not violated. But they hold that as Christ's kingdom is not of this world, it is not the business of the civil magistrate to interfere in matters of religion at all.

They have always disused the ordinary names of the months and days because these were given in honour of heathen deities, and the custom of speaking to a single person in the plural number, because it arose from motives of adulation. They condemn all compliments, superfluity of apparel and furniture, outward shows of rejoicing and mourning, the observance of days and times, public diversions, and all other vain amusements.

2. *Discipline.*—The chief purposes which their discipline has in view are the relief of the poor, the maintenance of good order, and the recovery of such as are overtaken in faults. The principle on which their discipline is practised is that laid down by Christ himself (Matt. xviii. 15–17). For purposes of discipline quarterly meetings were at first appointed to be held. Afterwards subordinate monthly meetings were appointed for subdivisions of the districts which met quarterly, and in 1669 a yearly meeting was established to superintend the whole.

A monthly meeting is composed of several congregations. Its business is to provide for the subsistence of the poor, and for the education of their children; to judge of the fitness of persons desiring to be admitted as members; to excite due attention to the discharge of religious and moral duty, and to deal with disorderly members; to grant certificates of membership to members changing their residence; to allow marriages; and to appoint overseers to see that the rules of the discipline be put in practice. Several monthly meetings compose a quarterly meeting, at which are produced written answers from the monthly meetings to certain queries respecting the conduct of the members, which are sent, all digested into one set of answers to queries, to the yearly meeting. The yearly meeting has the general superintendence of the Society in the country, and therefore gives its advice and makes such regulations as circumstances seem to require. It also finally determines appeals from the quarterly meetings. As women are permitted to have a share in the support of their discipline, they also have their monthly, quarterly, and yearly meetings of their own sex. The yearly meeting of 1675 appointed a meeting to be held for the purpose of helping in cases of suffering for conscience' sake, which, as a standing committee of the yearly meeting, has continued to the present day under the name of the Meeting for Sufferings. See Fox's *Journal;* Sewel's *History of the Christian People called Quakers* (Lond. 1722); Bevan's *Refutation of some Modern Misrepresentations of the S. of F.* (Lond. 1800); Gurney's *Observations on the Peculiarities of the S. of F.* (Lond. 1824); *A Summary of the History, &c., of the S. of F.*, issued by the Meeting for Sufferings (1800); Neale's *History of the Puritans* (Toulmin's ed.).

Fries, Elias Magn., a Swedish botanist, born 15th August 1794, in the district of Femsjö in Smaland, studied at the University of Lund, and in 1824 became a titular professor there. In 1834 he left Lund for Upsala to hold the chair of Practical Economics, to which the professorship of Botany was united in 1851, but in 1859 he retired on a pension. F. was elected a member of the Swedish Academy in 1847. Most of his earlier works treat of fungi and lichens, *e.g.*, *Observationes Mycologicæ* (1815–18), *Scleromycetes Sueciæ Exsiccati* (1818), *Lichenes Sueciæ Exsiccati;* and it was as a mycologist and lichenologist that F. first took a place in science. His *Systema Mycologicum* (3 vols. 1820–32), with the supplementary *Elenchus Fungorum* (1828), *Epicrisis Systematis Mycologici* (1836–38), *Monographia Hymenomycetum Sueciæ* (2 vols. 1857–63), &c., made an epoch in this branch of botany. In *Lichenographia Europæa Reformata* (1831), a work which the Academy of Science rewarded with the Linnæan gold medal, he appears to mediate between old and new views, and especially he has struggled to preserve the often misunderstood Linnæan nomenclature in describing Scandinavian plants. Of his works in this direction, the chief are *Novitiæ Floræ Suecicæ* (2d ed. 1828), *Novitiæ Floræ Suecicæ Continuatio* (vols. i.–iii. 1832–42), *Flora Hollandica* (1817–18), *Flora Scanica* (1835), *Summa Vegetabilium Scandinaviæ* (1846–49). In the last-named works he unfolds a natural system, in many respects different from those of Jussieu and Decandolle, based on morphology and biology, the leading features of which he had already sketched in the incomplete *Systema Orbis Vegetabilis* (1st part, on fungi, algæ, and lichens, 1825). F. has also published some works of a practical kind, *e.g.*, *Sveriges ätliga och giftiga Svampar* (1860–66), &c., with many popular tracts on the history, physiology, and geography of plants. These last are mostly collected in the form of *Botaniska Utflygter* (3 vols. 1843–64).

Fries, Jakob Friedrich, a German philosopher, was born at Barby, in Prussian Saxony, 23d August 1773, studied at Leipsic and Jena, became a professor at Heidelberg in 1805, and died 10th August 1843. His standpoint is in the main that of Kant, with a supplementary doctrine of philosophical anthropology—an attempt to analyse the nature of the soul and the conditions under which it apprehends truth. The aim of his 'system' was to effect a reconciliation between the critical philosophy and faith. His chief works are *System der Philosophie als evidente Wissenschaft* (Leips. 1804); *Neue oder anthropologische Kritik der Vernunft* (3 vols. Heidelb. 1807); and *Die Lehren der Liebe, des Glaubens, und der Hoffnung* (Heidelb. 1823). See Henke's *Leben des F.* (1867).

Fries'land, or **Vries'land**.—1. W. F., or simply F., with the islands Ter Schelling, Ameland, and Schier Monnikoog, constituted by the Treaty of Utrecht in 1579 one of the Seven United Provinces, is a province of Holland, bounded by the North Sea, the Zuyder Zee, and the provinces Overyssel, Drenthe, and Gröningen. Area, 1253 sq. miles; pop. (1874) 311,246. It is a flat country, partly protected by dikes, the N. and W. being marsh, while in the S. and E. are found great heaths, and stretches of peat bog. Internal communication is easy, from the large number of canals, streams, and lakes. The soil is rich, and well suited for pasturage and tillage, especially where it is recovered fen-land. The chief productions are wheat and rye, but flax, hemp, chicory, colza, and clover are also largely cultivated. Butter and cheese are exported to England in great quantity. The chief towns are Leeuwarden, Harlingen, Francker, and Sneek. The inhabitants are well educated and prosperous, and are chiefly of the Calvinistic persuasion. All the dikes and canals are placed under a Board of Control, which levies a direct tax on landowners for their maintenance.

2. E. F., now known by the name Aurich, the smallest of the six high bailiwicks of Hanover, is bounded by the North Sea, Holland, Aremberg, and Oldenburg. Area, 1144 sq. miles; pop. (1871) 195,394. The natural features of the land and occupations of the people are the same as in W. F. Chief towns, Emden and Aurich.

Frieze (Fr. *frise*, Ital. *fregio*, 'a fringe of ornament'), in classical architecture, is the portion of an entablature between the cornice and architrave. The name was also applied to a broad band of relievo sculpture carried round the *cella* of a Greek temple, just under the ceiling of the portico. An ornamental F. is often added to the modern cornice.

Romanesque Frieze in Denkendorff.

Frig'ate (Fr. *frégate*, Ital. and Port. *fregata*, of doubtful origin, but probably meaning an 'undecked ship'), a name first given to a long, narrow, and swift vessel propelled by oars or sails, or both, used in the Mediterranean. During the last century and the first half of the present a F. was a ship of war built specially for speed, carrying not more than fifty guns, and belonging to a class below the larger, more powerful, but less handy, line-of-battle ship. With the alterations in the navy which have followed on the use of iron in construction, of steam propulsion, of armour plates and heavy guns, the name F. has lost its special meaning to a great extent, and is applied to such vessels as the *Warrior*, *Northumberland*, &c., which combine the highest speed and the greatest fighting power.

Frigate.

Frigate Bird (*Attagen* or *Tachypetes aquila*), a genus of Natatorial or Swimming birds, famous for their powers of flight. They are included in the Pelican family (*Pelecanidæ*), and are distinguished by the bill being longer than the head, rounded above, concave below, and hooked at its tip. The wings are very long and narrow, the first and second quills being longest. The tail is also elongated and deeply forked. The tarsi are short and partly feathered. The throat is naked, and appears capable of being dilated at will to form a kind of pouch, analogous to that structure in the Pelicans (q. v.). The colour is black glossed with green, but the throat 'pouch' is scarlet. The total length of the bird is 3 feet, and the expanse of wings from 6 to 8 feet. The F. B. inhabits the tropics, and is hence named the 'tropic bird.' It may be seen hovering for lengthened periods in mid air without a movement of the wings being perceptible.

Frigate Bird.

Frin'ges, in optics, are the coloured bands of light observed in Diffraction (q. v.) phenomena.

Fringe-Tree, a name given to a species of plants belonging to the *Oleaceæ* or olive order, and to the genus *Chionanthus*. The F.-T. or 'snow-flower,' as it is also named, is the *C. Virginica* of botanists, and grows in the United States of America, attaining a height of from 20 to 30 feet. The name is derived from the form of the corolla, which has the appearance of being divided into four elongated portions.

Fringill'idæ, a large family of Insessorial birds belonging to the Conirostral section of the order, and represented by the finches, sparrows, linnets, &c. A large number of sub-families are included in this group, in which the bill is conical with a sharp tip, the upper mandible not being toothed. The claw of the hinder toe is usually longer than that of the other digits. The neck is short, and the tarsi are of moderate size.

Frisch'es Haff (*i.e.*, 'fresh-water bay'), a lagoon of the Baltic, on the coast of Prussia, between Elbing and Königsberg, which receives the Fregel, Friesching, Passarge, and Vistula, is 60 miles long, from 4 to 12 broad, and has an area of 318 sq. miles. It was separated from the Baltic by a long narrow spit of land called the Frische Nehrung till 1510, when the waters of the Haff burst through the barrier and formed a *gatt* or channel of communication with the outer sea. The *gatt* is not more than 15 feet deep, and all large vessels, therefore, unload at Pillau at its mouth, whence the cargoes are conveyed to the lagoon ports by lighters.

Fris'ians (in their own language *Frisan;* the Lat. *Frisii*, later *Frisiones, Frisones*), a Low German people often referred to by Tacitus. The Romans first met with them in the N.W. corner of Germany and conquered them. They took part in Civilis' insurrection in 70 A.D. Including the kindred Chauci (between the Ems and Elbe), they peopled the coast of the North Sea from the islands of the Rhine and Scheldt as far N. as Slesvig. The Zuyder Zee divided them into Frisii Majores on the W. and Frisii Minores on the E. After their subjugation about the beginning of the 8th c. by Pippin of Heristal and Karl the Hammer, the name Frisian was restricted to the eastern section, whose lands were now divided into W. Friesland or simply Friesland, between the Zuyder Zee and the Lauwer Zee, and E. Friesland; while those on the peninsula of Jutland and the adjacent islands were called N. or Shore F. Among the descendants of the Frisii Minores (on the W. of the Zuyder Zee), the Old Frisian language, intermingling with Frankish and Lower Saxon, produced the 'Dutch' language. Among these there arose, from the 10th and 11th centuries, numerous hereditary lords and counts; but in the 13th c. the territory came under Holland. All these F. were distinguished for their free communal institutions, set forth in their old laws, which are recognised in the oldest English laws, for the F. were an essential element of the English conquerors of Britain. In 802 Karl the Great formulated their laws anew in the *Lex Frisionum*. In the 15th c. the F. were forced to become subjects of the German empire, and in 1523 they were joined to Burgundy by Karl V. Their subsequent history belongs to Holland and Hanover.

In free spirit and skilful seamanship the F. are very like their northern neighbours the Scandinavians, and Rask pointed out that Frisian is, much more than any other Low German dialect, a transition to Scandinavian. The resemblance of Frisian to English is still more striking. On this point see Davies *On the Races of Lancashire*, in the *Trans. of the Philol. Soc.* (1855), and *Archaic and Provincial English compared with Dutch and Friesic*, ibid. (1858), by M. de Haan Hettema, who gives 1000 words that are the same in those three languages. Several English poems, even some of Shakespeare's plays, have been put into Frisian almost word for word. The F. regarding, with some reason, Hengest as a Frisian exile, claim kinship with the English, as in their proverb :—

> 'Good butter and good cheese
> Is good English and good Freese.'

The likeness descends to inflexions, *e.g.*, the English sign of the infinitive *to* is found in Old Frisian, and in no other Germanic dialect.

The oldest form of the language is in the old law-books, the most interesting of which are *Emsiger Domen* (beginning of 14th c.), *Brokmerbrief* (after 1250), and *Asegabuch* (about 1200). Every district had its dialect. From the 15th c. onwards the Frisian language was pressed on all sides by Dutch, German, and Danish. New Frisian is the name given to country dialects spoken in the different Frisian districts. There are several minor poems written in this dialect by Hansen (the comedy *Di Gidtshals*, Sonderb. 1833) and Foocke Hoissen Müller (1857). Epkema published in 1820 the older poem *Friesche Rymlerye* of Gilbert Japicx, with a vocabulary. Noteworthy are the popular comedy *Waatze Gribbert's brilloft* (beginning of last century) and the popular book *It Libben fen Aagtje Ysbrandts*. Hettema, E. and J. G. Halbertsma, Salverda, and Veen are well-known philologists. *De Vrije Fries*, a Frisian periodical, has been published since 1850 by the Frisian Society, established at Franeker in 1829. Grimm has treated the language in his great German grammar. The best dictionaries are Richthofen's *Altfriesisches Wörterbuch* (1840) and Outzen's *Glossarium* (1837). Rask's highly useful *Frisisk Sproglaere* (Copenh. 1825) has been translated into Dutch by Hettema (Leeuw. 1832).

Frit, or **Fritt** (Fr. *fritte*, Lat. *frictus*, 'dried'), in glass-making, the calcined mixture of the constituents of glass before being melted.

Frit, a name given to the *Chlorops* or *Oscinis* F., a species of Dipterous insects or flies. The larvæ are exceedingly destructive to barley crops, especially in N. Europe. The adult fly is very small and of blackish colour.

Frith, William Powell, R.A., was born near Ripon in Yorkshire in 1819, entered the Royal Academy in 1838, and in 1839 exhibited his 'Malvolio before the Countess Olivia.' Since then he has produced an extraordinary number of bright and 'taking' works, always interesting in subject, graphic, gay in colour, and marked by a certain superficial finish. He has sought subjects chiefly in Shakespeare, Goldsmith, Molière, and Sterne; and among his principal pictures, most of which are well known from engravings, are his 'Duet Scene' from *Twelfth Night*, 'Falstaff and the Merry Wives of Windsor,' 'Sterne in the Grisette's Shop,' the 'Village Pastor' (which secured his election as Associate in 1845), and later his 'Coming of Age' (1849), one of his best works, and 'Life at the Seaside' (1854). F. was elected R.A. in 1853. His 'Derby Day' (1858) and 'Railway Station' (1862), his most popular works, were sold for immense sums—the latter, it is said, for about £10,000. In 1872 he was commissioned by the Queen to paint the 'Marriage of the Prince of Wales.'

Frit'illary, a name given to several distinct species of *Lepidoptera* or butterflies—the term being suggested by the resemblance presented by the wings of the insects to the coloration of the flower of the plant of the same name.

Fritillary (*Fritillaria*), a genus of Endogenous plants belonging to the natural order *Liliaceæ*, and represented by the 'crown imperial' (*F. imperialis*), so named from its depending flowers resembling the form of a crown. This beautiful plant is a native of Persia, and is grown in our gardens. Its bulb is said to be poisonous, and the leaves of its *perianth* or floral envelope (see FLOWER) have nectar glands or depressions at their bases. The common F. (*F. meleagris*) flowers in May or even earlier, and grows wild in the southern parts of England. Its flower is flesh-coloured.

Fritillaria imperialis.

Friu'li (Ger. *Friaul;* a corruption of the Lat. *Forum Julii*), a fertile stretch of coast-land in the N. of the Adriatic, which in the middle ages formed an independent duchy, but is now divided between the Italian province of Undine and the Austrian district of Görz-Gradiska. Area, 3905 sq. miles. The *Furlani* are mostly Italian, but speak a peculiar dialect.

Friv'olous and Vexa'tious, a legal term under the Act regulating the trial of election petitions. If a petition or opposition to a petition be reported to the House as F. and V. by its committee, the party in fault is liable in full costs.

Fröbel, Friedrich, a notable German educationist, was born at Oberweissbach, in Schwarzburg-Rudolstadt, 21st April 1782, studied at Jena, and in 1803 became a teacher in Frankfurt. His model was Pestalozzi, in whose Institute at Yverdun he worked as a private tutor during 1808–10. Thence he went to Göttingen and Berlin to complete his imperfect culture, took part in the campaigns of 1813–14 as a volunteer, and in 1817 established at Keilhau, near Rudolstadt, a school which soon became famous for its excellent teaching. Here he first gave to the world an outline of his pedagogic system in his *Die Menschenerziehung* (Keilhau, 1826), which consists in viewing the mind not as a series of independent faculties, which should be separately cultivated, but as a living organism in which all the parts should co-operate to produce an harmonious unity. The application of his 'idea' to the education of children of tender years was an undoubted benefit; and as the founder of the now famous *kindergärten* (1836–42) he is certain to be remembered in the annals of pedagogy. After spending some time in Switzerland, where he established some schools on his own system, he returned to Germany, and devoted himself exclusively to the education of children. He died at Marienthal, 21st June 1852. F.'s *Mutter- und Koselieder* (1843) is fairly described in its fuller title as 'poetry and pictures for the noble nurture of child-life,' with border-drawings, explanatory text, and accompanying songs. Its faults are superficial; its merits deep and enduring. The title-page also bears a characteristic summons: *Kommt, lasst uns unsern Kindern leben* ('Come, let us live for our children'). See Hanschmann's *Friedrich Fröbel* (Eisenach, 1875).—**Julius F.**, a nephew of the former, was born at Griesheim in 1805, held the mineralogy chair at Zürich University 1833–44, edited a Radical paper, removed to Germany (1846), and became a member of the Parliament at Frankfurt in 1848. Along with Blum (q. v.) he conveyed the congratulations of the 'Left' to the insurgents of Vienna, and was arrested on the recovery of the city. Escaping to Switzerland, he fled thence to the United States, where he was in turn editor, lecturer, merchant. In 1857 he returned to Germany, became editor of a journal first at Vienna (1862), then at Munich (1866), and was appointed German consul at Smyrna in 1873. His chief works are *System der Socialen Politik* (2 vols. 1847); *Theorie der Politik* (1861–64); *Aus Amerika* (2 vols. 1857–58; Eng. trans. 1859); and *Die Wirthschaft des Menschengeschlechtes* (1870).

Fro'bisher, Sir Martin, the first famous English navigator who devoted himself to the search for a N.W. passage from the Atlantic to the Pacific and to India, was born at Doncaster about the middle of the 16th c. Respecting the discovery of the passage, he considered that it 'was the only thing of the world that was left yet undone whereby a notable mind might be made famous and fortunate.' After vainly appealing to the London merchants for support, he obtained the patronage of Dudley, Earl of Warwick, and was enabled to fit out a squadron of three vessels, whose united burthen was under 70 tons, and set sail 8th June 1576. As the expedition passed Greenwich, Queen Elizabeth bade the mariners farewell 'by shaking her hand at them out of the window.' Passing the S. coast of Greenland, he crossed to Labrador, and discovered the inlet which still bears his name. Five of his sailors going ashore against orders were carried off by the natives and never heard of more. After collecting a quantity of mica, which was said to contain a large quantity of gold, F. set sail for England and arrived in October. A second voyage was undertaken in 1577, and a third in 1578, but without noteworthy results. F. died at Plymouth, 7th November 1594, of a wound received at an attack on Brest.

Frobisher Bay or **Inlet** (formerly misnamed a strait), extending W.N.W. from the S. of Davis Strait, on the N. side of the peninsula of Meta Incognita, which intervenes between it and Hudson Strait. The middle of its entrance is in lat. about 63° N. It is about 100 miles long and 20 broad.

Frog, the name given to various genera of Vertebrate animals included in the class *Amphibia* (q. v.), and in the order *Anoura* or *Batrachia*. Frogs are not *reptiles* in a zoological sense, since, like all Amphibians, they possess *gills* or branchiæ in early life, though afterwards they breathe solely by lungs. The order *Anoura* ('tailless'), to which the F. belongs, is characterised by the adult being destitute both of gills and tail, the larva possessing both. Two pairs of limbs are present, the hinder limbs exceeding the fore-limbs in length. In the F. the five hinder toes are webbed, the four toes of each anterior limb being free. The skin is soft and scaleless. The dorsal vertebræ are hollow in front and convex behind. There are no ribs, but the transverse processes of the dorsal vertebræ are very long. The F. breathes by *swallowing* air rather than by *inhaling* it. The radius and ulna of the fore-limb, and the tibia and fibula of the hind-limb are ossified together. The upper jaw carries small teeth; the lower jaw is edentulous. There are only ten vertebræ in the spine. The tongue is fleshy, and is attached in front to the jaw, but is free behind. Consequently, it is the hinder extremity of the tongue which is protruded. The tympanum of the ear is not covered externally. Like all other *Amphibia*, frogs undergo a series of changes in passing from the young to the mature form. These changes collectively constitute the *metamorphosis*. The *tadpole*, or larval F., is fish-like, and is provided soon after its birth with horny jaws, and with external gills springing from the sides of the neck. These give place to internal gills, connected with cartilaginous arches borne on the hyoid bone; the young F. thus breathing after the fashion of a fish. The hind-limbs first appear, and have the form of small protrusions, whilst the fore-limbs are found within the branchial or gill chamber of the embryo. The larval tail is retained up to this date, but now begins to decrease in size. Lungs are meanwhile being developed, and as the latter organs appear, the gills disappear; the F. ultimately leaving the water, and during its adult life breathing atmospheric air, like other terrestrial animals.

The oft-repeated stories of frogs being found enclosed in rocks reputed to have been of *solid* nature, are not to be credited. It is certainly true that these animals, on account of their cold-blooded nature and slow circulation, can maintain life on a limited supply of air, since the skin largely assists in the respiratory process. But the notions that they have been enclosed in solid rocks (often belonging to a geological period antecedent to that in which the earliest fossil traces of the F. are found), and that they could have lived thus for ages, only require mention to ensure their rejection as mere childish credulities. Dr. Buckland many years ago performed a series of experiments on frogs by enclosing them in cells cut in blocks of stone, with the view of testing whether or not any truth existed in such popular beliefs. He found that the duration of the existence of frogs and toads when enclosed in air-tight cavities was limited to a year or a little more. The common or grass F. (*Rana temporaria*) is too well known to need any description. The hind-limbs of the edible F. (*R. esculenta*) are, when properly cooked, esteemed delicate morsels by various nations on the continent of Europe, particularly the French. The latter species is somewhat larger than the grass F. The Bullfrog (q. v.) is another species common in America, and a second American species of the same name is the *R. clamitans* of naturalists. An African bullfrog is named *Tomopterna adspersa*, and to the genus *Rana* belong the pickerel F. (*R. palustris*) of N. America, and the shad F. (*R. halecina*) is also an American genus. The banded F. (*R. fasciata*) of S. Africa is a prettily-marked creature. Some more uncommon species of F. are the horned frogs (*Ceratophrys cornuta*) of S. America, which has horn-like points on the upper eyelids; and the nurse F. (*Alytes obstetricans*) of Europe, the males of which species have the curious habit of carrying the impregnated eggs in masses twisted round their legs, and of so supporting them during their development. The tree frogs or *Hylada* form a separate family.

Frog-Fish (*Batrachus*), a peculiar genus of Teleostean fishes belonging to the family *Batrachidæ*. The *B. grunniens* is a familiar example. It occurs in the Ganges and E. Indian seas, and is so named from the resemblance of the head to that of a toad or frog. The *Lophius piscatorius*, a great broad-headed fish frequently cast up on our shores, is also named F.-F., or more frequently 'fishing-frog.' See ANGLER-FISH.

Froissart, Jean, perhaps the most famous chronicler of the middle ages, was the son of a cabinet-painter, and was born at Valenciennes in 1337. At the age of twenty he undertook, at the request of Robert of Namur, to write the history of the wars of his time in France, England, Scotland, Spain, Brittany, Gascony, Flanders, &c., particularly those occurring after the battle of Poitiers. The first part of the Chronicle, which he laid at the feet of Queen Philippa at London in 1360, was founded on the Chronicle of Le Bel, the Canon of Liége. By Philippa's aid he travelled into Scotland, followed the Black Prince to Bordeaux, passed through Germany, and was present at the Visconti fêtes at Milan. In the employment as secretary of the Duke of Brabant, and then of the Comte de Blois, he continued to move about for the purpose of noting down what wars were being carried on, and to verify the narratives of past wars. In particular he visited the chivalrous court of Foix. Most of the Chronicle was written in 1390–94, after which F. visited England, and gave an illuminated and illustrated copy of the 'book in scarlet velvet, with ten large silver studs set in gold, and golden clasps with rosework, also in gold,' to Richard II. He died at Chiamy about 1410. F. is imbued with all the vices of the chivalric system. No word of sympathy for any class but the nobility escapes him. Courage, courtesy, and the patronage of letters are his three virtues; they are compatible with many unpleasant types of character. His moral tone is lower than that of Joinville and Villehardouin, the chroniclers of the crusades. It has not even the serious purpose of history, like the Chronicle of the Monk of St. Denis. It is written to amuse, and its quaint garrulity and vivid descriptions, its constantly repeated moral and religious commonplaces, are probably as amusing to this age as to the 14th c. The best editions of F. are those by Buchon (3 vols. 1835–36) in the *Panthéon Littéraire*, by Siméon-Luce for the *Société de l'Histoire de France* (4th vol. 1875), and by Baron Kervyn de Lettenhove (16th vol. Bruss. 1876). There are two English translations, one by Lord Berners (Lond. 1525), and another by Johnes (1803–5). The language used by F. is of varying inflection. He often uses the rustic Romance idiom of a final *s* in substantives, and also the dialect called *rouchi Français*, from the frequent occurrence of *ch*. F.'s *Poésies* have been collected and published by Buchon in his edition of the Chronicle.

Frome, or **Frome Selwood**, a picturesque old town in the E. of Somersetshire, on a small river of the same name, a branch of the Avon, 12 miles S.S.E. of Bath by railway. It is near the remaining portion of the famous forest of Selwood, and has a handsome principal church and a grammar-school founded under Edward VI. The river is here crossed by a bridge of five arches. F. is noted for its ale, and has manufactures of broadcloths, kerseymeres, &c. It returns one member to Parliament. Pop. (1871) 9753.

Frond (Lat. *frons, frondis*, 'foliage'), the name given to the so-called *leaves* of ferns and other cryptogamous plants. Fronds differ from the leaves in that they bear the *fructification* or fruit of Ferns (q. v.). The name *thallus* is frequently employed in a technical sense as synonymous with F.

Fronde (from Lat. *funda*, 'a sling'), a name which arose during the sittings of a committee appointed by the French Parliament in 1647 to consider the arbitrary rights of taxation claimed by Mazarin for the king. The Duc d'Orleans acted as a sort of mediator, and as the members of the committee spoke more boldly in his absence, one of them, Buchaumont, compared his colleagues to the schoolboys slinging under the city walls, who stopped as soon as they saw the police. Mdlle. Montpensier, however, says that the word was used in the debates for 'having a shy' at the Cardinal without naming him. The party was called *La Fronde*, and each member a *Frondeur*. This reforming committee had many public rights under discussion; but the subjects on which perhaps they felt most bitterly were the taxes on articles brought into Paris. The arrest, by the Queen, of Broussel was the signal for an insurrection in Paris, of which Gondi, the Coadjutor, and Madame Martineau were the leaders. Anne temporarily granted the constitutional demands, but immediately after withdrew them. At this there was an open rupture, and Conti, Longueville, and Beaufort, the King of the Markets, put themselves at the head of the popular party in Paris. After a few small victories had been gained by the troops of Condé, and many provincial parliaments had declared for the king, a temporary peace was arranged. Then Condé and D'Orleans joined the F., while Molé, Gondi, and ultimately Turenne, went over to the court. Turenne, not yet converted, marched into Picardy, demanding the liberation of Condé and the other princes whom Mazarin had thrown into prison. After a siege of Bordeaux, this stage of the contest was closed by the treaty of Bourg. Mazarin's position was strengthened by the defeat of Turenne in Champagne by the Marshal Duplessis Praslin; but immediately after he was compelled to free the princes, and the Parliament resolved to banish him and all his relatives. Mazarin retired to the Elector of Köln at Bruhl, Condé was made Governor of Guienne, and the young king fell into the power of Gaston of Orleans. The successful leaders soon quarrelled, and after a vast deal of plotting, the Coadjutor Gondi was selected by the queen-regent as minister in room of Mazarin, and was made Cardinal de Retz. Public favour now turned against Condé, who left Paris, and strove to rekindle civil war. In 1651 he assembled at Bordeaux a force of 5000. Against the rebels were Turenne and Harcourt, the ablest soldiers in France after Condé. A few defeats at Cognac and Rochelle were counterbalanced by the return of Mazarin, which caused a revulsion of feeling, the Parliament passing a sentence of outlawry. In 1652 the prince's friend De Rohan was defeated in Anjou by D'Hocquincourt, who then with Turenne invested Orleans, which was saved for the F. by the singular energy of Mdlle. de Montpensier. Condé now came to Orleans, and defeated the royal army at Blesneau. Then followed the march of the hostile armies to Paris, and the terrible fight of St. Antoine, where Condé and Turenne displayed equal skill and courage, and the brutal attack on the Town Council of Paris. Some months of anarchy followed, the Frondeurs being divided into factions. At last the Parliament withdrew to Pontoise, dismissed Mazarin, and proclaimed Condé guilty of high treason. The latter fled to the Champagne frontier, and the war was continued for some time in Guienne by Conti, Marsin, and Genet. See Sainte-Aulaire's *Histoire de la F.* (3 vols. Par. 1827), and *Mémoires* of De Retz, Montpensier, and Rochefoucault.

Fronti'nus, Sex'tus Jul'ius, a Roman writer of the 1st c. He was *prætor urbanus* in 70 A.D.; was in 75 A.D. made governor of Britain, where he conquered the Silures and extended the Roman power. He was afterwards appointed *curator aquarum* and augur, and from an epigram in Martial seems to have been twice consul. He died about 104 A.D. F.'s works comprise *Strategematicon* (ed. princ. Rome, 1487), which treats of military matters; *De Aquæductibus Romæ*; fragments on measuring land, &c. They throw considerable light on Roman architecture and land tenure. The best edition of the *Strategematicon* is by Oudendorp (Leyden, 1779); of the *De Aquæductibus*, by Dederich (Wesel, 1841).

Fron'tispiece (Fr. *frontispiece*; Lat. *frons*, 'front;' *specere*, 'to see,' 'look at') is sometimes, but seldom, used to denote the principal façade of a building. Commonly the name is applied to the title-page of a book when it is surrounded with ornamental work or enriched with a vignette, or to the engraving placed opposite the title-page, and the subject of which illustrates the subject or text of the work.

Front'let is the name in the Old Testament (Exod. xiii. 6; Deut. vi. 8, xi. 18) for the article worn by the Jews which in the New Testament is called Phylactery (q. v.).

Fron'to, Mar'cus Corne'lius, a famous rhetorician of the 2d c., born at Cirta, in Numidia, settled at Rome, and gained the favour of Hadrian and Antoninus Pius. He was made tutor to M. Aurelius and to Commodus, who both entertained a warm affection for him, was offered but declined the dignity of proconsul, amassed great riches, and died about 170. F.'s contemporaries declared him to be, as an orator, second to Cicero alone, and a body of rhetoricians arose who chose him as their model, and were styled *Frontoniani*. Except a treatise, *De Differentiis Vocabulorum*, no work of F.'s was known to be extant until 1819, when Mai discovered at Milan a number of letters by F., which he published in 1815. Mai afterwards unearthed, in the Vatican, additional correspondence between F. and M. Aurelius and Commodus. These letters mostly relate to trifles, and are very tamely written. F.'s works were published by Mai (Rome, 1823), and by Naber (Leips. 1867).

Frosch'dorf, or **Frohs'dorf**, a village and stately castle in Lower Austria, 30 miles S. of Vienna, on the Leitha, and at the foot of the great Kaiserwald. The castle belonged to the Crottendorf family in the 13th c., and after passing through many hands, became the residence of the Duchesse d'Angoulême in 1844. It was the refuge and rendezvous of the elder Bourbons. The Comte de Chambord, its present occupant, has greatly improved the castle.

Frosino'ne, an old town of S. Italy, province of Latium, built on heights overlooking the confluence of the Cossa and

Sacco, 48 miles S.S.E. of Rome by railway. It is identical with the Volscian *Frusino*, and has inconsiderable remains of an amphitheatre, walls, &c. The dresses of the inhabitants are very picturesque. Pop. 9234.

Frostbite is caused by cold of great severity, or applied for a long time to the surface of the body. It chiefly attacks those parts most distant from the centres of innervation and circulation, viz., the feet, hands, ears, nose, chin, cheeks, and the surface of the body generally. F. is characterised by insensibility or numbness, diminished or arrested circulation, and loss of motion or stiffness, and it may vary in severity from Chilblains (q. v.) to freezing and death of the part. In the one case there is suspension of vitality, and in the other complete death. When the stage of reaction occurs, the part not absolutely destroyed becomes red, swollen, and hot, and afterwards blue and livid, indicating a state of inflammation. This redness terminates in an abrupt line, called the *line of demarcation*, and the dead part remains contracted, and shrivelled, and finally becomes gangrenous, separating in a slough, or dropping off, if it be a part of a limb. Treatment:—Endeavour to bring about a return of sensibility and circulation *slowly* by placing the patient in a cold room, and applying friction with the hand. Snow or cold water may be rubbed on the part first, then friction by the hand alone, or with a little starch powder to prevent attrition. Afterwards some mild stimulating liniment may be used, and finally the part may be covered with cotton wool or flannel.

Froth-Fly, Frog-Fly, or **Froth-Hopper,** names applied to various species of Hemipterous insects, belonging to the family *Cercopidæ*, a group nearly allied to that of the *Cicadæ* or Cicadas. The common F.-F. or 'cuckoo spit,' as it is also named, is the *Aphrophora spumaria* of the entomologist. It produces while in the larval state a large quantity of a frothy exudation, formed from the juices of the plants to which these insects attach themselves. The larvæ and pupæ closely resemble the perfect insect, which, however, has wings. A Madagascar species (*A. Gondotii*) secretes a clear watery-like fluid without the frothy exudation. A second species common in England is the spotted hopper (*Cercopsis dorsivittata*).

Froude, James Anthony, an English historian, son of Archdeacon F., was born at Dartington, Devonshire, April 23, 1818, was educated at Westminster and at Oriel College, Oxford, and was made Fellow of Exeter College in 1842. He was at first a follower of the Rev. J. Newman. His *Shadows of the Clouds* (1847) and *Nemesis of Faith* (1849) were censured by the university authorities, who deprived F. of his fellowship. He wrote for *Fraser's Magazine* and the *Westminster Review* from 1850 to 1856, when he issued the first and second volumes of his *History of England from the Fall of Wolsey to the Defeat of the Spanish Armada*, the twelfth and last volume of which appeared in 1870. In 1867 his *Short Studies on Great Subjects* were published, and in 1869 he was elected Rector of St. Andrews University. F. was at one time editor of *Fraser's Magazine*, but gave up the position in 1871. In 1872 he lectured in the United States on the relations between England and Ireland, and his strictures on the Irish drew him into a lively controversy with Father Burke. In 1874 he was sent to the Cape of Good Hope by the Secretary of State for the Colonies to inquire into the Caffre insurrection. He returned to England in 1875. His latest work, *The English in Ireland in the Eighteenth Century* (3 vols. 1872–74), has been very severely criticised. F.'s history is, in a large degree, an elaborate defence of Henry VIII., and although the author is generally regarded as having failed in his special pleading, the work is of high value for the ample and fresh research which it displays, and for its glowing, polished, and animated English. F. has scarcely been surpassed as a master of language, but his authority has been greatly lessened by the animus which he has carried into history.

Fro'zen Strait, a passage leading N.W. along the N. coast of Southampton Island to Repulse Bay, is in lat. about 66° N., and is usually heavily encumbered with ice. It was navigated by Parry in 1821, but was found impenetrable in 1836–37 by Captain Back.

Fruc'ted, in heraldry, means fruited or bearing fruit, and the term is applied to a tree. The fruit is (heraldically) of a different colour from the tree.

Fruc'tidor ('fruit-month'), the name in the French republican calendar of 1792–1806 for the last month of the year, from August 18 to September 14. On September 4, 1797, Carnot's party in the Directory was overthrown, and sixty-five deputies were condemned to deportation on the charge of having conspired to restore monarchy.

Fruc'tose, or **Fruit-Sugar,** occurs, as its name implies, in ripe fruits. It is also present in molasses, the uncrystallisable syrup remaining after cane-sugar has been separated from the juice of the sugar-cane by concentration and crystallisation. F.-S. is uncrystallisable, and has the composition expressed by the formula $C_6H_{12}O_6$; but if it be boiled for some time with dilute sulphuric acid, it takes up a molecule of water, and becomes Glucose (q. v.), $C_6H_{12}O_6,H_2O$, a substance which may readily be obtained in the crystalline condition. The crystallisation of honey after it has been kept some time, and the formation of nodules of sugar in dried fruits—the raisin for example—are due to the same cause. The sugar of fruits is formed in all probability by the hydration of cellulose, brought about by the action of the acid of the unripe fruit. See CELLULOSE.

Frugo'ni, Carlo Innocenzo, an Italian poet, was born at Genoa, November 21, 1692. In his youth his family placed him against his will in a convent, from which he was freed by the influence of Cardinal Bentivoglio. He then filled the chairs of *belles lettres* at the universities of Brescia, Bologna, Modena, Genoa, and Rome, and was made poet-laureate, first to Antonio Farnese, Duke of Parma and afterwards (1749) to Philip of Spain, who had acquired Parma. F. died at Parma, December 20, 1768. He is an elegant prose writer, and his lyrics are pure in diction and smoothly versified. His *canzoni* are especially beautiful. His works were published at Parma in 1779; a more complete edition (15 vols.) at Lucca in the same year.

Fruit (Fr. *fruit*, from Lat. *fructus*), the name applied in botany to indicate the ripe *pistil;* but as popularly used, it denotes a great variety of structures. Botanically it should be confined to the result of the fertilisation and ripening of *one* pistil; but even in a scientific sense, it is given to collections of mature pistils which are aggregated together (as in the mulberry and pine cone) to form an apparently single fructification. The F. botanically may also include parts of the flower which, to a greater or less extent, have remained in contact with the pistil. Thus in the *acorn*, the fruit of the oak, the scale-like *bracts* or flower-leaves unite to form the 'cup' of the acorn; or in the strawberry, the bulk of the F. popularly so named is formed by the swollen fleshy *receptacle* (see FLOWER) covered with little yellow and ripe carpels or parts of the pistil. The study and determination of the F. involves several important considerations. (1) The due examination of the pistil itself is necessary for the determination of the nature and mode of formation of the F. (2) The result of certain parts or organs of the flower or pistil being *suppressed* in the F. has also to be allowed for. (3) The addition or formation of new parts or accessory organs which come in due time to form part of the F. Fruits have been very variously classified by botanists, but a proper classification founded on structural and physiological considerations is still a desideratum. A simple but hardly philosophical classification divides them into (1) *dehiscent* fruits, or those that open to allow of their contained seeds being scattered, and (2) *indehiscent*, or those fruits which simply rot on the ground, and allow the seeds to come in contact with the soil through their decay. Of dehiscent fruits, good examples are seen in the *pod* or *legume* of the pea, and in the *siliqua* or pod of the wallflower. Indehiscent fruits are exemplified by two sets—(1) those which are *dry*, such as *nuts* (acorn, &c.), and *achenes* (seen in buttercup, strawberry, &c.); and (2) those which are *fleshy* or *succulent*. The latter group of indehiscent fruits is exemplified by the apple, gooseberry, peach, &c. Such a mode of arranging fruits gives little or no information regarding their exact nature, and their relations to the flowers or plants of which they form part. A better classification may be founded on the homology of the pistil, and on its relations to the flower. Thus we may divide fruits (1) into *aggregate* or *multiple* fruits (such as are formed by *many* flowers), and (2) into *simple* fruits, formed by the pistil of *one* flower. Of the aggregate fruits the mulberry is a good example. It is formed of a 'head' of fruits, each derived from a single flower, and consisting of a little one-seeded indehiscent nut enclosed in four fleshy pieces representing the perianth or modified flower envelopes. The *fig* represents another example of this group, since the fig F. is formed by a hollowed *peduncle* or flower-stalk, contained within which are numerous fruits, each consisting of a little single-seeded *achene*, with withered floral envelopes. A *pine cone* is a third example of a truly multiple fruit, since each woody scale or modified bract has two seeds at its base. *Simple* fruits which are each formed by the pistil of *one* flower, may be divided into (1) *indehiscent*, fruits formed of *one carpel*, as in the plum, cherry, &c. The plum (or cherry) is a *drupe* or 'stone' F., its *pericarp* or seed-vessel possessing a fleshy outer and a stony inner coat, the 'stone' containing a single non-albuminous seed. In wheat we have an achene or single-seeded F. with a thin pericarp and an albuminous seed. In nettle we also find an achene, but with a non-albuminous seed. The fruits of thistle and dandelion may be classed in the present group, since each little floret gives rise to an achene, the persistent *calyx* being developed to form the superior woolly down or pappus by means of which the F. is wafted about by means of the winds. The second division of simple fruits is (2) that in which the F. is *dehiscent* and consists of *one* carpel. The pea or bean exemplifies this group, as also does the F. of the willow. A third division is formed by (3) *indehiscent* fruits of several *free* carpels. In the buttercup numerous free carpels form the pistil and F., each carpel becoming an achene, and containing a single albuminous seed. In the bramble and raspberry (liable to be confused with mulberry) we likewise find the product of a single flower consisting of many carpels, represented by fleshy drupes, placed on a dry elevated floral receptacle. In the strawberry, again, we have many separate carpels imbedded in a fleshy mass formed by the succulent receptacle. Here, as in the bramble and raspberry, the solitary seed of each achene is without albumen. In the rose we find few or many carpels (achenes) contained within the hollowed extremity of the peduncle or flower-stalk. The fourth division of simple fruits is constituted by (4) those *indehiscent* fruits which are each formed of several *united* carpels. In the ash, for example, the fruit is a dry-winged achene or 'key,' formed of two united carpels; in the maple it is almost identical in every respect; in mallow it is formed by a whorl or circle of single-seeded carpels (achenes) united by their faces. Dead-nettle has a F. formed of four dry achenes; holly has a drupe formed of four carpels; in olive the F. is also a drupe formed of two carpels; in the potato we find a berry consisting of two fleshy carpels; in the apple, pear, quince, &c., a fruit (named a *pome*) formed of five carpels enveloped in the succulent top of the peduncle; in the gooseberry and currant the F. exists as a berry composed of two carpels; in the carrot we find a similar number of carpels; and in the acorn three carpels exist, although only one of these is destined to ripen. A fifth division of simple fruits is that (5) in which *dehiscent* fruits, each composed of *several* united carpels, are included. Examples of this group are seen in the horse-chestnut, where a F. formed of three combined carpels is developed; and in the cowslip and primrose, where five carpels unite to form a pod. In the violet also three carpels combine to form a pod, and in wallflower two carpels unite to form the *siliqua* or pod, which opens or dehisces from below upwards. In the poppy many carpels form the F., the seeds escaping by pores under the stigma. The sixth group of simple fruits is that (6) in which *dehiscent* fruits are contained, each F. consisting of several *free* carpels. Of this group are the fruits of aconite, larkspur, &c., where three or more dry pods exist, and split in a longitudinal manner. Fruits present many interesting points in connection with their physiology. The dispersion of the seeds is secured by such contrivances as winged appendages (maple, ash), pappus (dandelion), hooked processes for attachment to the fur of animals, and means for forcible dehiscence (as in balsam, where the seeds are scattered by the valves of the F. acting after the fashion of miniature pop-guns). Of the facts connected with the physiology of F. the most important are, firstly, recognition of the fact that F. is not perfect, botanically speaking, unless it contains duly-fertilised seeds. Some *cultivated* fruits, however, such as certain varieties of oranges and grapes, contain no perfect seeds; and the banana and plantain fruits are most palatable when seedless. Old trees (*e.g.*, orange) often produce seedless F. Fruiting appears, and necessarily, to impoverish a plant. Annuals die after fructification. Fruits are often greatly improved by pruning operations, and by checking the growth of the roots, so that the energies of growth are detracted from the formation of wood to that of F. Cultivated fruits are greatly improved by allowing only a moderate quantity to ripen. The chemistry of fruits is a complicated subject, the composition of a F. varying greatly at various stages of its progress. Briefly stated, the changes which occur in the process of ripening consist chiefly in a diminution of the quantity of *water* and *woody matter*, and an increase in the quantity of *sugar*. The time which elapses between the expansion of the flower and the ripening of the F. varies considerably in different plants. Thus some oaks require eighteen months to produce F. after flowering; and cedars require twenty-seven months; strawberries ripen in two months; apples, walnuts, plums, &c., in from three to five; and lower plants (such as mosses) require usually a long period of twelve months or more. An increase of temperature accelerates *fruiting;* and different fruits ripen best in different climates. Apples and pears thrive best in temperate climates, while mangoes and breadfruit require a tropical heat. See FRUIT TRADE.

Law regarding Fruits.—Fruits, as part of the soil, belong to the proprietor of it; but when they are the produce of industry and yearly seed, they are in England and in Scotland held to be personal estate. Fruits gathered are the property of the *bona fide* possessor.

Fruit, Malicious Injury to. See GARDENS OR ORCHARDS, STEALING FROM.

Fruit-Crow, the name applied to several species of Conirostral *Insessores* belonging to the sub-family *Gymnoderinæ*. Of this group the *Gymnoderus fœtidus*, or bare-necked F.-C. of Brazil and Guiana, is a typical example. It attains a size averaging that of a common Jackdaw (q. v.), and derives its name from the naked state of the upper part of the head, neck, and throat. The bald F.-C. (*Gymnocephalus calvus*) is another example, and belongs to a different genus. It is common in Cayenne, Guiana, and other parts of S. America: the entire front of the body is destitute of feathers. This species is also named the 'capuchin baldhead.' The fruit-crows eat snails, worms, &c., in addition to their vegetable diet.

Fruit-Garden. The cultivation of fruits has been practised by man from the earliest times. Especially in the records of Eastern nations are evidences of the successful practice of fruit-culture even in very early times to be met with. Some facts relating to the cultivation of fruit have been detailed in a preceding article. The general law that the process of fruiting is one which detracts from the nutrition of the plant as a whole lies at the root and basis of the fruit-grower's operations. Thus, while due attention may be paid to the nourishment and growth of the plant prior to flowering, excessive attention to the general growth or flowering tends to lessen the fruit-producing qualities of the plant. Anything which deflects the nutritive powers fr m the fruit of necessity injures the latter; and hence we find that by checking the growth of the root, by 'ringing the bark' (that is, cutting out a ring of bark so as to accumulate sap above the wound and near the fruit), and by pruning, fruit-growers contrive to nourish the fruit at the expense of other parts and organs of the plant. The careful selection of a site for a F.-G. bears a most important relation to the successful growing of fruit; so does the construction of Hothouses (q. v.), &c. An acquaintance with the various methods of growing fruit-trees, and of providing for their nourishment, as also of the diseases to which they are liable, is necessary to the fruit-gardener. He must also be acquainted with such operations as Grafting (q. v.), Pruning (q. v.), and Transplanting (q. v.).

Fruit-Pigeon, the name given to a species of Pigeons (q. v.) belonging to the genus *Carpophaga*, in which a knob exists during the breeding season at the base of the upper mandible. The wings have the second to the fourth quills longest. The tail is long, and the outer toe longer than the inner. The Oceanic F.-P. (*C. Oceanica*) of the Pelew Islands is the best-known example. It attains a length of 14 inches, and is grey above glossed with green; the same colour, but of a lighter tint, also prevailing in the under parts. Fruit-pigeons aid in disseminating the nutmeg tree: they feed on the outer husk, swallowing the hard seed, which is voided along with the fæces, and is thus placed amid conditions favourable to its growth.

Fruit Trade, an industry of great and growing importance, extent, and variety. Two causes have of recent years conspired to give an enormous impetus to the trade—(1) the increased facility and rapidity of intercourse by steam communication, thus enabling fresh and tender fruits to be sent to distant markets; and (2) the development of the art of preserving fruits in many ways, such as by 'tinning,' by treatment with sugar, the manufacture of jams, jellies, &c. In the Board of Trade returns fruits are classified under various heads—as raw fruits, which apparently includes all fresh and succulent fruits excepting those of the orange tribe. Of these there were imported in 1874 2,622,914 bushels. Of oranges and lemons there were imported 2,405,054 bushels; fruits preserved in sugar and otherwise, 4,189,717 bushels; currants, 972,455 cwt.; and raisins, 505,361 cwt.; besides plums, prunes, and miscellaneous dried fruits. Among fruits are also reckoned almonds, of which there were imported 77,284 bushels; and nuts, which includes walnuts, hazel-nuts, and chestnuts, to the value of £550,463. These figures, of course, give only the faintest idea of the F. T., which in its proper signification includes the great vine culture, as well as the growth of apples for cider, cherries for Kirschwasser, and other fruits used for liqueurs.

Frumen'tius, St., the apostle of Ethiopia, was born at Tyre about the beginning of the 4th c. In his early life he sailed to Ethiopia, where all the ship's company were captured and slain, save himself and another youth named Edesius. These two were carried as slaves to the Ethiopian court, where F., soon winning the royal favour, was made secretary to the king, and, on the king's death, tutor to the young prince. The Queen placing wide authority in F.'s hands, he took advantage of his power to introduce Christianity, and founded the first Christian church built in Ethiopia. Aided by Edesius, who had likewise obtained considerable influence, he organised missions which made numerous converts, and on removing to Alexandria in 326, asked Athanasius, bishop of that city, to appoint a special bishop for Ethiopia. Athanasius made F. himself Bishop of Auxuma, whereupon he returned to Ethiopia and proselytised with great success. He died about 360. See Ludolf's *Historia Æthiopica* (Frankf. 1687).

Frus'tum, in solid geometry, is a portion of a solid, usually a pyramid or cone, bounded by two *plane* sections.

Fry, Elizabeth, an English philanthropist, was born at Bramerton, near Norwich, 21st May 1780. She was the daughter of John Gurney, a rich merchant and banker, and a member of the Society of Friends. After a gay visit to London, where she had met Peter Pindar (Dr. Wolcot), Mrs. Inchbald, and Amelia Opie, Elizabeth was greatly affected by the preaching of an American Quaker, William Savery. In 1800 she married a strict Quaker in Joseph Fry, and henceforth devoted herself to a life of pious charity. She visited Newgate (1813), and found some 300 women suffering, under the old prison system, the greatest privations and misery. Having supplied them with clothes, and otherwise relieved their condition, she further received permission to establish a school and factory in the prison (1817), and also organised a ladies' association for reforming prisoners. She subsequently carried improvements into most of the gaols, asylums, and hospitals of Britain, and made several journeys with a similar object into France and Central Europe. She died at Ramsgate, 12th October 1845. See *Memoirs of E. F.* (2 vols. Lond. 1847), by her daughters.

Fryxell', Anders, a Swedish historian, born 7th February 1795, at Hesselskog, in Dalsland, studied at Upsala, where he graduated in 1821, and in 1828 was made Rector of the Grammar-school of St. Mary in Stockholm. In 1834 he undertook a tour for historical inquiry in Denmark, Prussia, Poland, Austria, Belgium, and Holland, returning in 1835, when he was appointed parish minister of Sunne, in Vermland. He became a member of the Swedish Academy in 1840, doctor of theology in 1845, and a member of the Swedish Academy of Science in 1847. F.'s *Berättelser ur Svenska Historien* ('Narratives from Swedish History,' 40 vols. 1823–71) has made its author the most popular of all historians in Sweden. Other important works are *Handlingar rör. Sveriges Historia* (4 vols. 1836–43); *Om Aristokratfördömandet i Svenska Historien* (4 parts, 1845–50), a polemical work, directed against Geijer; and *Bidrag til Sveriges Literaturhistoria* (9 parts, 1860–62). Translations of the first volumes of the *Handlingar* have been published in English by Schoultz (2 vols. Lond. 1844), and in German by Homberg (2 vols. Stockh. 1843). The part relating to Gustav Adolf was translated into German by Homberg (2 vols. Leips. 1842–43), into French by Mademoiselle N. du Puget (Par. 1839), and into Dutch by Radijs (Utrecht, 1844), and the part treating of Gustav Vasa into German by Ekendahl (1831).

Fuad-Mehmed Pasha, a Turkish statesman and man of letters, was born in Constantinople about 1814. His father was a poet of eminence, but his property was confiscated by Sultan Mahmud, and F. had to study medicine. In 1834 he was appointed physician to the Admiralty, and as such accompanied an expedition to Tripoli. After this, however, he became a diplomatist, filling in succession the posts of attaché (1840) of the Turkish embassy in London, second dragoman of the Porte (1843), special commissioner during different years to Spain, Portugal, and Russia, first dragoman, grand referendary of the Divan, and commissioner-general in the Danubian Principalities, Minister of the Interior, and Minister of Foreign Affairs. He resigned this office in 1853, being opposed to the Russian policy of the time, but returned to it, and became in 1861 Grand Vizier. Throwing up his post in two years, he became Minister of War, returning however in 1867 to his old office of Minister of Foreign Affairs. He died at Nice, whither he had gone for the benefit of his health, February 11, 1869. F. was extremly popular on account of his knowledge of European languages and customs, his personal amiability, and his brilliant diplomatic powers. He published a *Turkish Grammar* in 1852, and was one of the earliest members of the Turkish Academy of Literature and Science. During the Eastern crisis he wrote a pamphlet, *La Vérité sur la Question des Saints Lieux* (1853), which irritated the Czar as much as it pleased his countrymen.

Fuca'ceæ, or **Melanosper'meæ**, a division of the great natural order *Algæ* or seaweeds. They include the brown-coloured seaweeds, or marine plants of an olive-green or brown colour composed of multicellular fronds. The fructification exists in the form of *conceptacles*, which contain moving cells. The typical genus is *Fucus*, and a large number of genera and species are included in the group. Most of the F. are provided with air-receptacles enabling them to float on the surface of the water. To the F. belong the tangles (*Laminaria*) and many other well-known Algæ—the genera *Sargassum* (Gulf weed), *Halidrys*, *Padina*, &c.

Fuca, San Juan de, Strait, between Washington Territory, U.S., and the S. shore of Vancouver's Island, leads from the Pacific to the Gulf of Georgia, is 60 miles long, and has a breadth of 10 miles. The possession of the largest of several islands in the strait, San Juan, was disputed by Great Britain and the United States, and was awarded to the latter on the arbitration of the Emperor of Germany in 1872. The strait was discovered by the navigator Juan de Fuca in 1592.

Fu-Chow-Fu ('happy city'), the capital of the province of Fu-Kien, China, on the river Min, 25 miles from its mouth. It has a good harbour, and is surrounded by old walls 30 feet high, 12 feet thick, 6 miles in circumference, and surmounted by many towers. The river, which is here crossed by a bridge of 40 or 50 arches 12 feet wide and 1200 feet long, presents a curious, lively appearance with its junks and floating houses. F. has a large arsenal on a European plan, which was founded in 1867, is superintended by a Frenchman, and employs fifty European engineers and teachers and some 1200 Chinese workmen. The city was opened to foreign commerce in 1842, and has a great tea trade. In 1872–73. 75,000,000 lbs. of tea were exported—50,000,000 to Great Britain, 17,000,000 to the colonies, and 8,000,000 to America. In 1874 the total value of imports from foreign ports, including Hong-Kong, was £1,332,388; of the exports, £4,397,321; while the number of British and other foreign vessels that cleared the port was 254 of 164,355 tons. The business of foreign houses is confined to ship brokerage, to the export of tea, and the import of opium, and lead for lining tea-chests. Native merchants import all the cotton and woollen goods from Hong-Kong. Some 500 vessels of 250,000 tons clear the port yearly. F. is noted for its lacquer-work, the making of which is the secret of a single family. Estimated pop. 600,000.

Fuchs'ia, a well-known genus of plants included in the natural order *Onagraceæ*, or that of the evening primroses. Many species and varieties of these beautiful and favourite plants are known, the process of cultivation causing them to exhibit many remarkable variations in colour. The fuchsias are remarkable for having a *coloured* and funnel-shaped calyx. The fruit is a four-celled *berry*. These plants are of moderate size. Their original habitat was S. America and the S. parts of N. America. The cultivation of fuchsias has largely increased, owing to the readiness with which they can be grafted and propagated by cuttings. The *F. gracilis*, *F. coccinea*, *F. globosa*, and *F. longiflora* are well-known species grown in hothouses.

Fuci'no, Lago di (the *Lacus Fucinus* of the ancients), a lake of S. Italy, in the Central Apennines, province of Aquila, 2181 feet above the sea. It has no natural outlet, and its sudden risings often proved disastrous to the ancient Marsi and to their descendants. In the reign of the Emperor Claudius, Monte Salviano was pierced with a tunnel (*emissarius*) 3½ miles long (1⅜ through solid rock) to let off the surplus waters. The completion of this work, in which some 30,000 men were employed for eleven years, and which is only inferior to the Mont Cenis Tunnel, was celebrated by a gladiatorial naval contest attended by vast numbers, A.D. 52. There were, however, serious defects in its construction, and despite the efforts of Trajan and Hadrian it gradually became choked up. Many vain attempts were made to reopen it, and the waters continued steadily to rise. In 1852 the Italian Government made a grant of the basin of the lake to a company on condition that they should drain it, a privilege subsequently sold to Prince Torlonia of Rome. Eventually the work of clearing and improving the old channel was completed in 1862, after an outlay of £1,200,000. Some 36,000 acres of good corn land have been reclaimed, but the work of further draining has been abandoned, partly on account of the valuable fisheries, chiefly because of the enormous expense of draining the deeper S. end of the lake. In 1861 its circumference was 37 miles and its depth 60 feet; these numbers were reduced to about one-third in 1871. The lake is occasionally frozen over, as in 1864. Its shores are dotted with charming antique villages. To the N. of the lake rises abruptly from the plain the double-peaked Monte Velino (8792 feet), visible from Rome.

Fu'cus. See FUCACEÆ.

Fu'el, a term applied to 'substances which may be burnt by means of air with sufficient rapidity to evolve heat capable of being applied to economical purposes' (Dr. Percy, *Metallurgy*, vol. i.). Numerous and different as these substances are, they all owe their special properties as F. to the presence of two elements only, carbon (C) and hydrogen (H). The chemical and physical properties of the various fuels will be found described under the headings COAL, COKE, PEAT, &c. We shall here consider their economical employment in relation to the theory of combustion.

In combustion the C or H combine with oxygen (O), and the combustion is said to be 'perfect' when combination takes place with the maximum amount of O with which the element can form a stable compound. The perfect combustion of C produces carbonic acid (CO_2); and of H, water (H_2O). The *calorific power* of a F. is the quantity of heat (in thermal units or in foot pounds) which can be developed by the *perfect* combustion of one unit of weight of it; it is independent of the *rate* of combustion. *Calorific intensity* (in degrees) is the thermometric effect of the same combustion, and is thus proportional in the same body to the rapidity with which the combustion takes place. Taking 1 lb. as the unit of weight, the calorific power of C is about 14,500 thermal units (*i.e.*, 1 lb. of it, in combining with 2⅔ lbs. of O to form CO_2, will develop sufficient heat to raise 14,500 lbs. of water 1° F.); and of H, about 62,000 thermal units. If 1 lb. of C undergo an *imperfect* combustion and be converted only into carbonic oxide (CO) instead of CO_2, only 4452 thermal units will be developed, *i.e.*, the calorific power will be reduced to less than one-third its former value. The importance of this will appear shortly. It may be noted here that the calorific power is *not* proportional to the quantity of O combining, as has often been stated.

If the required quantities of C and O were simply brought together and caused to combine, and the whole heat of combination were spent in raising the temperature of the CO_2 produced, the resulting calorific intensity would be 18,329° F. (supposing the pressure to be kept constant during the operation). The calorific intensity of the combustion of H, calculated in the same way, would be 12137°; and of C converted into CO, only 7697°. If the O were supplied in the form of air, the other conditions remaining the same, the temperature would be reduced, because of the quantity of nitrogen (N) which would have to be heated along with the other gases. The resulting calorific intensities would in this way be reduced to 4892°, 4831°, and 2674°.

The assumption here made that the whole heat generated by the combustion should be expended in raising the temperature of the gases produced is obviously not one of which the fulfilment would be desirable. The object of the combustion is generally to raise the temperature of some substance or object placed near or in contact with the F., and not that of the gases produced. We may examine the effect of this upon the available calorific power and intensity in the case of the furnace of an ordinary steam boiler. Here the escaping gases are required to be somewhat hotter than the air when it enters the furnace, in order to create a draught. This difference of temperature may be about 500° F. All the heat but what is required to create this rise of temperature should be absorbed by the water in the boiler, this absorption reducing the gases from the high temperature of the furnace to the required limit as they pass along the flues. By a simple calculation it can be shown that the heat available under these circumstances for heating the water will be—for each pound of C converted into CO_2, 13,000 thermal units; for each pound of H converted into H_2O, 47,000 thermal units; and for each pound of C converted into CO, 3600 thermal units. The usual standard of evaporative power is the number of pounds of water at 212° which one pound of the given F. will convert into steam of the same temperature. Each pound of steam so formed requires 966 thermal units for its formation, so that, dividing the quantities already given by 966, we obtain the following results:—

Combustion of	Number of pounds of water at 212° converted into steam of the same temperature by the combustion of one pound of F.	
	Total.	Available after raising gases 500°.
C into CO_2.	15·06	13·52.
C into CO.	4·61	3·75.
H into H_2O.	64·21	48·72.

The assumption is very commonly made that the calorific power of any F. containing known quantities of C and H can be found at once from data such as those just given. This involves the assumption that every pound of C or of H in the coal will behave in its combustion just as it would were it by itself. This assumption has not been verified by recent experiments, which have shown in many cases (*a*) that the calorific power of particular specimens of coal measured in the Calorimeter (q. v.) was considerably *greater* than that found by calculation from the percentage of C and H which they contained; and (*b*) that the calorific power of fuels having the same analysis often differs considerably. The cause of this may probably lie in the fact that as yet we are almost entirely ignorant of anything but the *ultimate* constitution of coal and other fuels; their *proximate* constitution, the way in which their constituents are combined among themselves, we know next to nothing of. In the absence of further experiment, it is at the same time often accurate enough for practical purposes to find the evaporative power of a unit of weight of any given F. by multiplying the quantities of C and H in it—expressed as fractions—by constants such as those given in the table above. It must be remembered that if there be any O in the F., only as much of its H must be considered available as F. as is *in excess* of the amount required to form water by combination with that O.

In practice no F. reaches such a high evaporative power as that given in the table above. The principal reasons for this are the following:—

(*a*) Radiation takes place from the boiler and the furnace; heat is wasted in heating the 'ash' or incombustible residue of the F., and is lost with the falling ash and cinder. These causes of loss cannot be entirely prevented, but by covering the boiler with non-conducting material and managing the fire carefully they can be kept within small limits.

(*b*) From 1½ to 2 times the net quantity of air required has to be passed through the furnace in order that sufficient O may come into contact with every portion of the F.; the whole of this air has to be raised to the temperature of the escaping gases. Considerable loss from this cause is unavoidable; it can in general only be reduced to a minimum by careful trials in each particular case.

(*c*) Some portion of the C passes away incompletely oxidised, *i.e.*, converted only into CO instead of CO_2. If the F. be in a tolerably thick layer, the CO_2 formed at the lower part of it will be converted into CO (by combination with another equivalent of C) as it passes upwards; and if there be a deficiency of air at the top of the F., it will pass away in this state.

(*d*) The compounds of H and C (hydrocarbons) which occur in many bituminous coals, and which are volatilised at an early stage of the combustion are decomposed if raised to a high temperature with any deficiency of air, and their C is deposited in the flues, &c., on cooling, as soot.

The last two causes of loss are both serious; they can only be obviated by a very careful adjustment both of the quantity of air admitted, the part of the furnace (above, below, at the side of, or behind the F.) at which it enters, and the time at which it is admitted. The hydrocarbons, for instance, require for their perfect combustion a considerable quantity of air entering above the F.; but they are all burnt within a short time after each supply of fresh F. is put on the grate; and after this such a quantity of air, if it were still to be supplied, would have no further result than to cause loss as mentioned at (*b*).

A F. of which the calculated calorific power is equivalent to the evaporation of about 15½ lbs. water from and at 212° may in exceptionally favourable circumstances evaporate as much as 12 lbs. in a very efficient boiler, but 10·5 lbs. would be considered very good work, and engineers are often contented with much less. With inferior fuels the evaporation is often as low as 5 or 6 lbs. of water per 1 lb. of coal.

Fuel, in law. See TURBARY, COMMON OF; FEAL AND DIVOT (Scotch law).

Fuen'te de Oveju'na (*i.e.*, 'the sheep's fountain,' so named from its springs), a walled town in the province of Cordova, Spain, on a hill between two tributaries of the Guadiata, 45 miles N.W. of Cordova. It has linen, woollen, and leather industries, and near it are several coal-mines. Pop. 5500.

Fuen'tes de Ono'ro (*i.e.*, 'the fountains of honour'), a Spanish village on the Portuguese frontier, and in the province of Salamanca, 14 miles W. of Ciudad Rodrigo, celebrated as the scene of a fiercely-contested battle between the English, commanded by Wellington, and superior numbers of the French under Massena, which terminated the French invasion of Portugal, 5th May 1811.

Fu'ero (from Lat. *forum*) is a Spanish word primarily meaning a place of justice, and then the customary law administered there. It is now confined to the rights and privileges of municipal constitutions of provinces and towns in the Basque provinces, including Navarre. The Visigothic code of Spain, collected by Egiza, 687–701, is called the *F. juzgo*. It is to some extent territorial in its character. It recognises slavery; a man may not marry a woman older than himself; the *arras* is the same as the Latin *dos* and German *morgengrab*; the *patria potestas* is asserted, and divorce is granted for adultery only; sexual crimes are severely punished. To this succeeds the period of many provincial and local customs, *e.g.*, *F. de Leon*, collected by Alfonso V. in 1020; *F. viejo de Castilla* (known also as *F. de hijos dalgo, libro de los jueces*), published by Pedro of Castile; *F. de Sobrarbe* of Aragon; and a crowd of *fueros municipales*—as of Salamanca, Toledo, Leon, Naxerd. Many singular institutions are contained in these fueros; they recognise, for instance, concubinage for life, settled by written contract, the concubine being entitled to bread, table, and knife (*a pan, mesa, e cuchello*). The F. of Plasencia goes so far as to say that the *barragania* who has been faithful has right to one-half the acquired property of her paramour. The amount of dowry on marriage is publicly regulated by many of the fueros. In Leon and Castile the rare custom of *gananciales* obtained, *i.e.*, all acquired property was divided equally between the spouses. There is also found a usage named *unidad*, by which the surviving spouse, *so long as not married*, has the possession of the whole estate. The bachelor suffers many penalties; he cannot give evidence nor acquire burghal rights. After this comes a period of consolidation, beginning with the *F. viejo*, known as the Statute of Burgos or Castile. Then comes the *F. real* of Alfonso the Wise, followed by the *partidas*; Isabella and Ferdinand published the eighty-four *Leyes de Toro* (7th March 1505). The final consolidation was by Philip II., in the famous *Recopilacion de las Leyes*. The *F. juzgo* and the *partidas* were also in force in Portugal. As already stated, however, greater interest attaches to the 'political' part of the fueros, especially in Biscaya and Navarre, in which districts their consolidation is traced to Count Juan in 1371 and King Theobald in 1236 respectively. In Biscaya there is a Junta General, meeting yearly; and the executive consists of a corregidor, with six regidores, together forming the regimiento. The King of Spain is entitled only to the name of Senor. In Navarre, again, there is a Great Council and a Contaduria, or Chamber of Finance. The Basque provinces claim exemption from military service, from direct land-taxes collected for the national treasury, and from the tobacco monopoly and other customs regulations. To such claims the Spanish Government has always been bitterly opposed; hence the support received by Don Carlos from the Basque people, who have besides a peculiar language and a territory separated from the rest of Spain. To the spirit of local management shown in the Basque *juntas forales*, and which has produced better charities, prisons, and roads than any other portion of Spain, the central Government has not recently been opposed. Spanish politics are in a state of continual fluctuation, but in the constitution of 1869 at least great prominence was given to the powers of *diputaciones provinciales* and *ayuntiamentos* (or municipalities).

Fuer'te de Andal'gala, a town in the province of Catamarca, Argentine Republic, near which are rich copper-mines. Pop. 5000.

Fuer'te Ventu'ra. See CANARIES.

Fugg'er, Family of, a race of merchant princes, were early admitted amongst the hereditary nobility of Germany. The founder of the family, Johann F., made a small fortune as a weaver at Graben near Augsburg. His eldest son, also named Johann, was a leading man amongst the weaver burgesses of Augsburg about 1370, and at his death in 1409 left 3000 florins. This sum was used to such purpose by his son Andreas that he was soon known as 'the rich F.;' for as a money-lender he had begun the business which was destined to establish the brilliant fortunes of the family. Andreas' three nephews, Ulrich (1441–1510), Georg (1453–1506), and Jakob (1459–1525), were ennobled by the Emperor, and were able on one occasion to lend Maximilian 170,000 ducats. But it was under Karl V. that the splendour of the family culminated. The brothers Anton (1493–1560) and Raimund (1489–1535), sons of Georg F., were made counts of the empire, and were permitted to coin gold and silver. Anton left a fortune of 6,000,000 crowns of gold. Both brothers were zealous Catholics. Their descendants were further favoured by Ferdinand II., under whom they held the highest offices of the state, while still continuing their commercial speculations. They were munificent patrons of art and science, and were zealous benefactors of the poor. Both of the branches which still boast the name of F. have long since given up commerce. The present representative of the line of Raimund is Count Raimund F., born 29th June 1810; and of Anton, Count Philipp F., born 9th November 1820. A collection of the portraits of the most important members of the family was published at Augsburg in 1593 (2d ed. enlarged, 1618; 3d ed. still further enlarged, at Ulm, 1754).

Fugita'tion, in Scotch law, is a sentence pronounced against one who does not obey a citation to answer a criminal charge. One of its consequences is Escheat (q. v.). The similar sentence in England is outlawry.

Fu'gleman (Ger. *flügelmann*, 'a file-leader,' from *flügel*, 'wing'), a soldier specially expert and well trained, who is placed in front of a rank on drill, as an example for time and movement in the ordinary exercises.

Fugue', in music (probably from the Lat. *fuga*, 'a running away or chase'), a composition in which a phrase is given out by one part alone, and afterwards taken up and repeated or imitated by the others, so that the different parts seem to fly from and pursue each other alternately. The earliest specimen of this imitative music which has come down to us is a canon composed by Guillaume Dufay, a Belgian, who was chapel-master and a tenor singer in the Papal Chapel at Rome from 1380 to 1432. After his time it developed—gradually at first and afterwards rapidly—until it became in the 18th c., the era of Bach and Handel, the principal form in which the greatest composers expressed in music their noblest thoughts. Before the time of Haydn, Mozart, and Beethoven, music was looked upon rather as a combination of melodies than as a succession of chords, and from that point of view the F. was the highest form which a composition could take. Composers have now better means—means more capable of varied expression, and less formal and rigid—of expressing their ideas, so that the F. has been displaced from its ancient superiority; but as the form in which so much of our finest music is written, it can never lose interest to us. Even now it is used in the choruses of oratorios and masses, where, probably through long familiarity, it not only does not seem antiquated, but appears most suitable and natural. The F. has many forms. A F. in four parts, with a single subject, is in its simplest form arranged somewhat as follows:—One of the parts commences with a melodic phrase called the *subject*, in the principal key, and is shortly answered by another part (the choice of parts is arbitrary) giving out the same subject in one of the two most nearly-related keys. This is called the answer, and is accompanied by a continuation in Counterpoint (q. v.) of the part which commenced. At a suitable point the key is changed back to the original one, and the third part enters with the subject in its first form, to be answered in its turn by the fourth in the same key as the second. Throughout the rest of the F. the subject and answer form the leading melodic ideas, appearing in different parts in different forms and in different keys, and accompanied by new counterpoint, as well as by the original counterpoint varied in an endless number of different ways.

The form we have described is only one of many which the F. takes, and for all of which the older musicians have laid down countless rules. In the *strict* F. the one subject and counterpoint are closely adhered to, and every rule rigidly observed; in the *free* F. episodes are introduced, and subsidiary themes only indirectly connected with the subject. There are also fugues with two subjects, double fugues, in which two subjects are treated simultaneously, and so on. The older composers were fond of showing their extreme ingenuity in manipulating the F. without transgressing rules; they inverted the subject, imitated it at all kinds of odd intervals, repeated it with its notes doubled in length or halved in length, and in many other ways twisted and turned it about so as to be almost unrecognisable. In the hands of ordinary musicians the result was merely the production of a mechanical curiosity; a F. came to be judged by its ingenuity, and not by its musical merit. Strangely enough, one of the most whimsical of oddities occurs in a sonata of Beethoven's (*Opus* 106, *finale*), where the subject, a very florid one, is absolutely *reversed*, that is, played backwards, note by note.

In the oratorios of Bach and Handel fugal writing reached its highest development; it has not been taken up, except to a very limited extent, by any of the great composers since their time. Bach has left also a collection of fugues for the pianoforte (*das wohltemperirte Clavier*), which will probably last as long as the instrument on which they are played, as fresh and interesting as if they had been written yesterday.

Füh'nen (Dan. *Fyen*), next to Seeland, the largest of the Danish islands, is separated from Jutland and Slesvig by the Little Belt, from Seeland by the Great Belt, and forms a province together with the small islands Langeland and Arröe, having a total area of 1148 sq. miles, and a pop. (1874) of 245,900. F. is 55 miles long and 45 broad, and has a rich level surface, rising in slight elevations to the S., while the coast is greatly indented by fjords. The longest river is the Odense-Aa (40 miles); of the lakes the Arreskov-See is specially rich in fish. F. exports barley, buckwheat, oats, flax, hemp, horses, cattle, honey, &c. Among the chief towns are Odense, Svendborg, Nyborg, and Assens (pop. 3461). The havens possess (1874) 315 vessels, of 31,366 tons. Langeland, formerly Lafvind, is 30 miles long and 5 broad, is well wooded in the N., and has a fruitful surface.

Fu'-Kien ('consummation of happiness'), one of the richest provinces of China, is bounded E. by the sea, N. by Chi-Kiang, W. by Kiang-si, and S. by Quang-tung, and has an area of 45,761 sq. miles, and a pop. of 22,799,556. It is bordered on the W. by the Tajü-ling range, has an undulating surface, and is mainly watered by Min river, yielding plentiful crops of tea, rice, and tobacco, besides the orange, li-chi, olive, plum, pomello, plantain, mulberry, &c. F. includes Formosa (q. v.). Its chief ports are Fu-Chow-Fu and Amoy.

Fu'lahs. See FELLATAHS.

Ful'crum is the fixed point round which a Lever (q. v.) acts.

Ful'da (anc. *Buchonia*, or *Buchgau*), a walled town in the Prussian province of Hessen-Nassau, on the F., a tributary of the Werra (90 miles long), 60 miles N.E. of Mainz by railway. It has a beautiful modern cathedral, the fourth church that has occupied the site, and within which is the shrine containing the body of St. Bonifacius, who was murdered by the Frisians in 754. There is also the palace of the former prince-bishops, the church of St. Michael (822), a Roman Catholic seminary, a public library, and an arsenal, besides manufactures of fine linen and woollen fabrics, leather, earthenware, tobacco, beer, vinegar, &c. F., the capital of the former grand duchy of F., was joined to that of Frankfurt by Napoleon in 1810, but in 1815 was ceded to Prussia and transferred to Hessen-Cassel, which in 1866 was annexed by Prussia. Pop. (1872) 9470.

Ful'gurites (Lat. *fulgur*, 'lightning') are vitrified tubes formed through the fusion of sand by the passage of lightning.

Fulham, (lit. 'the dirty place'), formerly an isolated village and parish of Middlesex, on the left bank of the Thames, and 4 miles S.W. from Hyde Park Corner, London, is now included in London without the walls, of which it forms a semi-suburban district.

Ful'ica. See COOT.

Fulig'ula. See POCHARD.

Full'er, Andrew, an able theologian, was born at Wicken, Cambridgeshire, England, February 6, 1754. He was of humble origin, and received only a limited education. When sixteen years of age he became a member of a Baptist church. Showing special gifts, he was ordained over the Baptist church in Soham, in 1775, on the small stipend of £21. He removed to the Baptist church in Kettering, Northamptonshire in 1782. In 1792 he assisted in the formation of the Baptist Missionary Society, and as its secretary rendered it signal services (without pay). In theology he was a moderate Calvinist, and his hand was often against both Socinians and hyper-Calvinists. The degree of D.D. was offered to him in 1793 by New Jersey College, U.S., and in 1805 by Yale College, U.S., but declined. He died May 7, 1815. He was noted for his sagacity and common sense, and has been called the 'Franklin of theology.' His chief works are *The Calvinistic and Socinian Systems* (Lond. 1794); *Socinianism Indefensible* (Lond. 1797); *Sandemanianism*; *Memoir of S. Pearce of Birmingham*; and *Expository Discourse on Genesis* (Lond. 1806). They have been frequently reprinted both in England and the United States. See the memoir of F. in the complete edition of his works by A. G. Fuller (Lond. 1846).

Fuller, Margaret, born in Cambridge Port, near Boston, Massachusetts, 23d May 1810, was the eldest daughter of a successful and highly-educated lawyer, who taught her himself. She read Latin at the age of six, and suffered the penalty of too much brain stimulation, becoming a somnambulist and a ghost-seer. After the classics, her father's library had chiefly the English writers of Queen Anne and the French writers of the Aufklärung, and so her mystic and imaginative nature was soon clad 'with that coarse but wearable stuff woven by the ages—common sense.' Her mother's flower-garden, and the view of distant hills, 'beyond which she placed her paradise,' were the chief sources of her finer experience, until one Sunday evening she wilfully disobeyed her father by reading Shakespeare, who was soon followed by Cervantes and Molière. 'The first angel of her life' was an English lady, a painter and musician, 'a *millefleur* beauty, the distilled product of ages of European culture,' who made up for much of the hard and superficial tone of New England village society. F. herself has described in *Mariana* her few years at the school of Dr. Parkes, Boston. In 1837, after her father's death, she became principal teacher in the Green Street School, Providence, Rhode Island, where she taught to boys and girls philosophy, rhetoric, history, poetry, and moral science. During 1839–44 she edited the Transcendentalist *Dial*, to which she contributed many striking articles. She loved gems, ciphers, talismans, omens, coincidences, drawing lots, anniversaries, dreams; she was the disciple of Swedenborg and Rosenkranz; she believed in fate, guardian genii, mesmerism. She wrote epistles to Beethoven as her patron saint. At the same time she was perfectly devoted to truth, and offended many by the plainness of her speech. In 1846 appeared her *Papers on Literature and Art.* During a tour in Europe she met at Rome the Marchese Ossoli, whom she married in December 1847. She spent the stirring times of the revolution at Rome. Her *Woman in the Nineteenth Century* (Lond. 1850) was one of the earliest vindications of the 'rights of women.' On 16th July 1850 the Marchesa, her husband, and their only child were drowned by shipwreck off the coast of Long Island. The magnetic flash of her grey eyes, and the marvellous and expressive grace of her head and neck, are still remembered by her friends. See *Memoirs of Margaret F., Marchesa Ossoli*, by Emerson and Channing (Lond. 1852).

Fuller, Thomas, D.D., an English divine and historian, born in 1608, was educated by his father, the rector of Aldwinkle, Northamptonshire, till he was twelve years of age. He was then sent to Cambridge, where he took orders in 1630. Shortly after he was presented to the living of St. Benet's, Cambridge, in which he gained great popularity as a preacher. The following year he obtained a prebendal stall in Salisbury Cathedral and a fellowship in Sidney Sussex College. He was next chosen rector of Broad Windsor, Dorset, and in 1640 lecturer at the Savoy Church, London. During the Civil War he shared the reverses of the Royalists, to whom he adhered; but in 1646 he was chosen lecturer at St. Clement's Lane, Lombard Street, and then at St. Bride's. About 1648 he was presented to the living of Waltham, Essex, and in 1658 to that of Cranford, Middlesex. Shortly before the Restoration he was reinstated in his Savoy lectureship and his stall at Salisbury; and soon after that event he was made one of the king's chaplains and D.D. He died 16th August 1661. His principal works were a *History of the Holy Warre* (1639); *The Holy and Profane State* (1642), one of the most characteristic of his writings; *A Pisgah Sight of Palestine* (1650); *The Church History of Britain* (1655); and *The Worthies of England* (1662), which is the best-known and most popular of all his productions. 'The quips and conceits of F.'s style represent the later Euphuism in its best form, for F. had religious feeling and high culture, good-humour, liberality, quick sense of character, and lively wit, which the taste of the day enabled him to pour out in an artificial form, with a complete freedom from affectation. Culture and natural wit make his quaintness individual and true' (Morley's *English Literature*). See Russell's *Memorials of Thomas F.* (1844), and J. E. Bailey's *Life* (Lond. 1874).

Fuller's Earth, a soft, greasy, detergent, earthy clay, formerly much used in the *fulling* or cleaning of woollen cloth from grease, hence its name. It is a hydrous silicate of alumina, having oxide of iron, lime, magnesia, and soda as impurities; in colour it is green, greenish yellow, or blue; it falls to powder in water, and with great heat it melts. F. E. is found in many localities in England, in the Oolitic and Cretaceous systems; and at Nutfield, near Reigate, Surrey, it is extensively worked.

Ful'mar, or **F. Petrel** (*Procellaria glacialis*), a species of Natatorial birds included in the family *Procellaridæ*, and found in large numbers at St. Kilda and other parts of the N. islands and coasts. It is also common in the Arctic regions, and feeds on the blubber of whales, on barnacles, shellfish, &c. The F. is coloured white on the head and belly, and pearl grey on the back. The hinder toe (as in all the *Procellaridæ*) is deficient and rudimentary; the first quill is the longest in the wings. The average length of the bird is 20 inches. The F. affords oil to the inhabitants of St. Kilda, who also value the eggs and down. A single egg of white colour is laid in a nest formed merely of a hollow in the turf.

Fulmin'ic Acid and the Ful'minates. The fulminates, as their name indicates, are explosive compounds. They are formed by the action of alcohol on the nitrate of a metal in presence of free nitric acid. Fulminate of mercury is largely employed as a detonating compound, principally in the manufacture of percussion caps. To prepare it mercury is dissolved in nitric acid and alcohol is added. A violent action takes place, and dense white fumes are evolved, the fulminate of mercury eventually subsiding as a white powder, which is purified by washing with cold water. Fulminate of silver is obtained in much the same manner, substituting silver for mercury: it is even more explosive than the mercury compound. Fulminate of mercury has the composition represented by the formula $HgC_2N_2O_2$, and fulminate of silver by the formula $Ag_2C_2N_2O_2$. F. A., which has never been obtained, and which is therefore hypothetical, would be represented by the formula $H_2C_2N_2O_2$. The fulminates are isomeric with the decyanates, and the salts of fulminaric acid ($H_3C_3N_3O_3$)—a derivative of F. A.—with the cyanurates. See ISOMERISM.

Ful'tah, or **Fal'da** (*Falta*), a village in the district of the Twenty-four Pergunnahs, Bengal, British India, 22 miles S. of Calcutta, near the mouth of the Hooghly, the site of an old Dutch factory, and known in history as the spot to which the English survivors retreated after the capture of Calcutta by Seraj-ûd-Dowlah in 1756.

Ful'ton, Robert, an American engineer and inventor, was born at Little Britain, Lancaster county, Pennsylvania, U.S., in 1765, although recently (1876) it has been contended that he was born at Beith, Ayrshire. Although at the age of three he lost his father, and received only a common school education, so earnestly did he give himself up to what he conceived to be his true vocation as artist and jeweller, that before he was twenty-one he was able to place his mother in a small farm. Going to London to study art, he was persuaded by the Duke of Bridgewater, whose patronage as well as that of Earl Stanhope he obtained, to become a civil engineer, and devoted himself in future entirely to mechanical invention. The early period of his career in England was marked by his invention of machines for spinning flax, making ropes, and sawing and polishing marble. Receiving a patent (1796) for canal improvements, he proceeded to Paris. His visit to France was rendered remarkable chiefly by his attempts to render perfect his scheme of steam navigation—on which he had been induced to enter chiefly by Lord Stanhope, if not by Watt—and his invention of a submarine boat called *Nautilus*. F.'s inventions, however, were not favourably received either in England or in France, and in 1806 he returned to his native country, where, after considerable difficulties, he succeeded in having the cost of his experiments with torpedoes defrayed by the Washington Government. Finally, with the help of Robert R. Livingston, U.S. minister at France, whose acquaintance he had made at Paris, into whose family he married, he was enabled to launch successfully a steamboat named the *Clermont* on the Hudson, in 1807. After this, although F. never made much money, his career was very successful, culminating (1814) in the construction of a new steamer, named first *Demologos* and afterwards *Fulton the First*, by which he may be said to have done for steam navigation what Watt did for the steam-engine. He died February 24, 1815. See Colden's *Life of R. F.* (1817).

Fu'mage (from Lat. *fumus*, 'smoke') is a tax mentioned in Domesday on every house having a chimney or fire-hearth. By 13 and 14 Car. II. c. 10, a tax of two shillings on each hearth paying to church and poor was granted to the king. The tax was abolished in the reign of William and Mary.

Fumaria'ceæ, a natural order of Exogenous plants, commonly named the Fumitory order, and represented by the common fumitory (*Fumaria officinalis*), and by a species of the genera *Diclytra*, *Corydalis*, &c. They have brittle stems and a watery juice; the leaves are alternate and exstipulate, and the flowers irregular and unsymmetrical. The sepals are two, and are deciduous; four cruciate irregular petals are developed. The stamens may number four when they are polyandrous, or six when united into two bundles (*diadelphous*). The fruit is a round indehiscent *nut*, or a pod composed of one cell and two valves. The fumeworts occur typically in temperate regions in the northern hemisphere. All have bitter and acrid properties. Some (such as *Diclytra spectabilis*) are showy, and are cultivated as hothouse plants. Common fumitory is a garden and field weed.

It was formerly held in esteem as a cure for scrofula, and as possessing tonic properties.

Fumar'ic Acid is obtained, along with its isomer malæic acid, by heating Malic Acid (q. v.). The change which occurs may be represented by the following equation :—

$$\underbrace{C_4H_6O_5}_{\text{Malic acid.}} = \underbrace{C_4H_4O_4}_{\text{Malæic and fumaric acid.}} + \underbrace{H_2O}_{\text{Water.}}$$

It has no practical importance.

Fu'migating Pas'tils are composed of various odoriferous ingredients, in combination with charcoal and nitrate of potash, which, while smouldering slowly, evolve agreeable odours. F. P. may be prepared thus :—Benzoin and dry balsam of Peru, of each 16 parts ; yellow sandalwood, 4 parts ; labdanum, 1 part ; charcoal of limetree wood, 96 parts ; nitrate of potash, 2 parts ; and mucilage of tragacanth, sufficient to form a pasty mass, which is then put into conical moulds and dried. The odoriferous materials may be varied indefinitely, but the relative proportions should be maintained. The 'ribbon of Bruges' is also employed for the same purpose, and is prepared as follows :—Dissolve two ounces of nitrate of potash in a pint of water, and steep in it undressed cotton tape; dry the tape and steep it in a strong aromatic tincture and dry. The aromatic tincture may be of any odour or of any combination of odours desired. When the fumigating pastil or the ribbon of Bruges is kindled, it burns slowly like match-paper ; and by regulating the quantity of nitrate of potash, combustion may be slow or quick as desired.

Fumiga'tion (Lat. *fumigatio*, from *fumus*, 'smoke'), the employment of fumes or vapours to purify articles of apparel and goods or apartments supposed to be imbued with some infectious or contagious poison. Formerly pastils were used for such purposes, but they merely disguise disagreeable smells without destroying the disease-germs. Since the recent discovery of the germ-origin of diseases of the zymotic type, or of those which are contagious and infectious, the value of F., or aerial disinfection, as it should be called, has been submitted to the test of rigid experiment, and valuable results have been obtained. Aerial disinfection, as commonly practised in the sick-room, is useless or positively objectionable, owing to the false sense of security which it gives ; for to make the air of a room smell strongly of carbolic acid or of chlorine is, so far as the destruction of specific contagion is concerned, an utterly futile proceeding. For purposes of sanitary F. the dioxide of sulphur, which is simply the fumes of ignited sulphur, is by far the most reliable and the most accessible. For an exhaustive examination of the subject, see Dr. Baxter's *Report of an Experimental Study of Certain Disinfectants*, in *Reports of the Medical Officer of the Privy Council and Local Government Board* (New Series, No. vi. 1875).

Funar'ia, a genus of Mosses (q. v.), and the type of a small natural order, characterised by its vesicular calyptra, which becomes sabulate above. *F. pygrometrica* is very common on charred and burned soils in this country, and occurs all over the world.

Funchal' (Port. 'a place abounding in *funcha*' or fennel), the sole town and port of the island of Madeira, and the capital of the Portuguese province composed of the islands of Madeira and Porto Santo, lies at the base of a picturesque mountain nearly 4000 feet high. It extends for a mile along the S. shore, and up the sides of the mountain in scattered villas for 2000 feet, ending in the double-towered church of 'Our Lady' (*Nossa-Senhora*). F. has a cathedral, many churches and convents, several forts, &c. Its appearance from the sea is magnificent, but the interior of the town in no way corresponds to the effect of the external view. The roadstead is exposed and the anchorage rocky. F. is a favourite residence for English people suffering from pulmonary complaints, and English modes of life and the English tongue may almost be said to prevail. F. is the coaling station for the West African and East Indian (Cape route) trade. Pop. 18,000.

Func'tion, a mathematical term of frequent occurrence, derived from Lat. *fungor*, 'I discharge.' One quantity is a F. of another when it depends for its value upon the value of the latter. Thus $y = ax + b$ is a F. of x, and is also of course a F. of a and b. The same is true of $y = ae^{bx}$, $y = a \sin x \cos b$, &c. The first is called an *algebraic* F., while the other two are distinguished as *transcendental* functions, which are easily recognised by the presence of exponental, logarithmic, or trigonometrical symbols. The fact that y is a function of x may be expressed by the notation $y = F(x)$. In the same way $F(y)$ would denote the quantity which involves y in exactly the same way that y involves x. $F(y)$ may obviously be written $F[F(x)]$, or more concisely $F^2(x)$. According to this symbolical notation, $F^m(x)$ signifies m successive operations of the same kind, each operation being performed upon the *result* of the preceding operation. The investigation of the *forms* of functions, without any regard to their values, has given rise to the *calculus of functions*—a branch of mathematics growing in importance. An idea of its nature may be gathered from the following example :—Required the *form* of F, so that the equation $F(x)F(y) = F(x+y)$. The F. is in this case $F(x) = a^x$, where a is any constant. For the general methods of investigation, see Babbage's *Treatise on the Calculus of Functions*, Lagrange's *Théorie des Fonctions Analytiques*, Cauchy's *Cours d'Analyse*, and Peacock's *Algebra*.

Functions, in physiology, the name given to those acts which are performed by animals and plants, and which together constitute the *life* of these beings. Every living organism performs the three great F. of *nutrition*, *reproduction*, and *innervation* ; and according as these are subserved by organs of high or low structure, the being is said to be of a superior or inferior type of organisation. *Physiology* is the 'science of F.,' or that which investigates the manner in which vital actions are performed.

Fund, Consolidated. See CONSOLIDATED FUND.

Fundamen'tal Note, in music, is the root of a chord. It is the lowest note if the chord be in its natural position, but is above some of the other notes in the inversions. See CHORD.

Fun'di, or **Fundun'gi**, a grain botanically known as *Paspalum exile*, grown in the W. parts of Africa, and allied in some degree to Millet (q. v.). It will be found described in the article *Paspalum* (q. v.). At Sierra Leone F. is largely used, either as an addition to stewed meat or in the form of porridge.

Funds. See DEBT, NATIONAL.

Fun'dy, Bay of (Fr. *Fond de la Baie*), on the E. coast of N. America, between Nova Scotia on the E. and New Brunswick and the state of Maine on the W., is 180 miles long from S.W. to N.E., and has an average breadth of 35 miles. It receives the St. John and St. Croix from the W., and at its head it forms the Minas Channel and Chignecto Bay, the latter of which is separated from Northumberland Strait in the Gulf of St. Lawrence by an isthmus only 13 miles in breadth, which it is proposed to cut through with a canal. The tides rise to the extraordinary height of some 70 feet, and render navigation dangerous.

Fu'neral Expen'ses. These, if reasonable, constitute a privileged debt in England and in Scotland, and are consequently payable before other debts. (See EXECUTOR, PRIVILEGED DEBT.) In England, if one dies in debt, the F. E. are usually limited to £10. In Scotland it has been decided (Buchanan *v.* Ferrier, February 1822) that mourning for the widow and children attending the funeral is included in F. E. The reverse has been decided in England (Johnson *v.* Baker, 2 C. and P. 207).

Fünf'haus, a town of Austria, 2 miles N. of Vienna by railway, with manufactures of silks, satins, woollens, red leather, &c., and a population (1869) of 27,065.

Fünf'kirchen (Ger. 'five churches ;' Slav. *Pécs*, 'fives'), one of the oldest towns of Hungary, county of Baranya, on the S. slope of the Mecseg mountains, between the Drave and Danube, 140 miles N.W. of Belgrade, and connected by railway with Agram and Pesth. It is a bishop's see, has the largest and finest cathedral in Hungary, and was formerly the seat of a university. Its manufactures are chiefly woollens, flannels, silks, leather, and ironwares, and it has an active trade in wine, gall-nuts, hogs, &c. There are coal-mines in the vicinity. Pop. (1869) 23,863. F. was held by the Turks from 1543 to 1686.

Fun'gi (Lat. ; a cognate of the Gr. *sphongos*, 'a sponge'), the name given to a large group of cryptogamous or cellular plants, which have neither leaves, roots, nor stems. They are nourished by means of whitish filaments named the *mycelium* or *spawn*, which form a kind of network by their union, and spread out amid the substances in which the F. grow. The mycelium gives origin to various structures which bear the *fructification*, and is itself composed of elongated colourless cells. F. are further distinguished by the fact that *spores* or seed-like bodies are produced, either enclosed within spore-cases or *thecæ*, or destitute of any such protection. Some of these spores named *antheridia* contain actively moving cells or spermatozoids, and seem to represent the *pollen* or male element of higher plants. Other cells, named *archegonia*, are analogous to the ovules or seeds produced by the pistil of flowering plants. The mycelium requires heat and moisture to produce its reproductive elements, and occasionally, as in the Puffballs (q. v.), when favourable conditions are supplied, the tissues of F. may grow with astonishing rapidity. In the spawn of the mushroom rapid growth may be observed to take place. F. grow in very various situations, and the difficulty experienced in following out the different stages of growth has rendered their classification a difficult task. Some are found growing beneath the soil, others on its surface. The Truffles (q. v.), for example, grow below ground, the Mushrooms (q. v.) above. Large numbers are parasites, feeding either upon or within the bodies of other animals and plants. In many animals serious diseases may be produced by the presence and growth of F. Thus the diseases in plants known as smut, mildew, ergot and dry rot, are caused by the growth of F., and the vine and potato diseases have also been traced to fungoid action, the *Peronospora infestans* having been recently traced through all its stages in the production of the potato disease. The Vinegar Plant (q. v.), Yeast Plant, (q. v.), and other familiar organisms exemplify F. developed in fluids, and which tend by their growth to assume putrefactive change. In animals, diseases are similarly induced by the development of F. The silkworms, as was proved by Pasteur in a series of beautiful researches, suffer from a minute fungus which grows and propagates at a rapid rate within the bodies of these larvæ, and is communicated by contact to surrounding animals. Many skin diseases in man and lower animals are traced to fungoid growths, and there can be little doubt that most, if not all, changes of a *putrefactive* nature are either caused or are in greater part induced by the growth of these lower forms of plant life. Many F. can be used for food, and are hence named *esculent F.*—*e.g.*, the mushroom (*Agaricus*). Poisonous F. may be recognised by being in general *highly coloured*, and by having the surface *spotted* or *scaly*. The flesh or substance is *tough* and contains much *water*. The poisonous species also grow in *clusters* or groups, and usually on wet marshy ground. *Edible F.*, on the other hand, are rarely coloured of bright or marked hues, but are either white or dull brown. They are soft and not particularly watery, and generally grow solitary in pasture and meadow lands. The F. which burn the fauces and are of bitter taste, or which yield a pungent juice, may be pronounced unsafe to eat, even if they be not actually poisonous. Dr. Badham perhaps goes to an extreme when he says that the great majority of F. are edible; but there can be little doubt that many now rejected as poisonous are so treated with little reason. Much may also depend on the nature of the ground and soil. These plants form exceptions to the general rule of plant life, in that they feed on *organic* substances, and probably inhale *oxygen gas* like animals. They have at any rate no power such as that possessed by plants with *chlorophyll* or green colouring matter, of decomposing carbonic acid gas and of emitting oxygen. The classification and arrangement of F. are points on which botanists, from the want of exact data, are not well agreed. One system divides the F. into—(1) *Basidiosporous* or *exosporous* F., or those in which the spores are developed on the outside of sacs named *basidia*; (2) *Thecasporous* F., in which the spores are developed within *thecæ* or spore-cases; and (3) *Myxosporous* F., or those in which the spores are produced in a gelatinous mass of tissue without being enclosed in any definite structure. See *F., their Nature, Influence, and Uses*, by Dr. M. C. Cooke, edited by Berkeley (International Scientific Series, H. S. King & Co., Lond. 1875).

Fun'gibles are in Roman law movable effects which may be estimated by weight, number, or measure, as grain or coin. Jewels and works of art are not F., there being no standard by which they may be valued.

Funn'el (Cymr. *ffynel*, 'an air-hole;' allied to the Lat. *infundibulum*, from *infundo*, 'I pour into'), in steamers, is the iron tube intended to remove the smoke and gaseous products from the furnace without inconveniencing those on the deck, and at the same time to secure a sufficient draught. In ships of war and other large vessels, the funnels are usually made telescopic, so that they can be easily altered in height. F. is also the name of the conical metallic glass or earthenware vessel ending in a tube which is used for filtering or for filling narrow-mouthed vessels.

Furid' Kote (*Farid Kot*), a tributary state of the Punjaub, in India, to the S.E. of Ferozepore district. Area, 600 sq. miles; pop. about 68,000; revenue, about £30,000. The military force is composed of 200 cavalry, 600 infantry and police, and three field-guns. The Rájá holds his territory by a grant dated 1863, by which his independence is considerably limited. The family are of Jat descent, and have uniformly adhered to the British cause.

Furid'pur (*Faridpur*), the chief town of the district of the same name, province of Bengal, British India, on an old channel of the Ganges, 115 miles N.E. of Calcutta. Pop. (1872) 8593. F. is merely a large village, with no important manufactures or commerce.—*F. district* (area, 1524 sq. miles; pop. (1872) 1,012,589) lies at the head of the Delta, just below the junction of the Ganges and the Brahmaputra. It is also intersected by numerous minor streams, which flood the entire country during the rainy season, leaving only the elevated sites of the villages above the water. The soil is extremely fertile. Rice is the staple crop, but pulses, jute, sugar-cane, date and betel-nut palms are grown. Sugar is largely manufactured, both from the cane and the date, and vine-grass mats form a specialty of the district. A considerable trade is carried on by water, and also by the Bengal Railway, whose terminus is at Goalunda.

Furios'ity, a term of Scotch law denoting the kind and degree of insanity which legally disqualifies a person from managing his own affairs. See CURATOR, BRIEVE, IDIOTS AND LUNATICS.

Fur'long (Old Eng. *furlang*, lit. 'a fur or furrow long'), an English measure of length, equal to 220 yards, or one-eighth of a mile.

Fur'lough (Dan. *forlov*, Dut. *verlof*, Ger. *verlaub*, 'leave of absence'), a military term signifying leave of absence. Non-commissioned officers or privates may apply to any officer not below the rank of a captain stationed in the district, or in the absence of such officer to a justice of the peace, for extension of F., which may be granted for a time not exceeding a month, on sufficient cause being shown. For a longer time the approval of the commanding officer of the district is requisite. A man on F. must have a pass, otherwise he may be treated as a deserter.

Fur'neaux Islands, a group of mountainous islets situated at the eastern entrance to Bass Strait, between Tasmania and Australia. Their total area is 513,000 acres, but the population numbers only 242, most of whom are half-castes, who live by sealing and bird-catching. The islands are named after the officer who was next in command to Captain Cook on his second voyage. They belong to Tasmania.

Furnes (Flem. *Veurne*), an old town of W. Flanders, Belgium, situated at the junction of four canals, 4 miles from the sea, and 27 S.S.W. of Bruges by railway. It has a quaint Gothic townhouse, remains of the old abbey of St. Willebrod, is the site of three great yearly fairs, and carries on a large trade in cattle, corn, cheese, linen, &c. Pop. (1870) 4500.

Fur'niture, Household, Law Regarding. Where furniture is lent on hire, as in a lodging-house, the hirer is not liable for damage done by accident, even though the accident be through himself. The tenant is, however, liable for damage arising from his own carelessness, or from his putting the furniture to an improper use. Should damage arise to the tenant from the furniture being insufficient for its proper use, the owner is probably liable in damage to the tenant. Usually all chattels found on the premises may, in England, be distrained for rent (see DISTRESS), the landlord having a right of lien over it. (See LIENS.) In Scotland the landlord has a similar right, called *Hypothec* (q. v.), under which even hired furniture may be seized; but furniture lent without rent cannot be taken. See LODGING-HOUSE, HIRE.

Furruck'ābād (*Farrakhabad*, 'the city of Farrakh Ser,' a Mogul emperor; *Farrakh* = happy), the chief town of the district of the same name, N.W. Province, British India, about 2 miles W. of the right bank of the Ganges, 660 miles N.W. of Calcutta, and 160 S.E. of Delhi. Pop. (1872) 79,204. F. was founded by the Mohammedans in the beginning of the 18th c., and soon acquired great commercial importance; its bankers were especially celebrated, and it retained the metropolitan privilege of a mint as late as 1824. The trade is still considerable, and the streets are wide, clean, and shaded with trees. The elevated mud fort, the palace of the Nawab, still exists, but the British cantonments are at Futtehgurh, about 3 miles E. of the town. F. was the scene of an engagement in 1804, when Holkar, at the head of his Mahratta cavalry, was entirely defeated by Lord Lake.—*F. district* forms the centre of the Doab, the triangle lying between the Ganges and Jumna rivers. Area, 1745 sq. miles; pop. (1872) 918,850. Near the Ganges the soil is naturally moist and fertile, and the sandy tract in the interior is now irrigated by a branch of the Ganges Canal (q. v.). The crops are wheat, barley, pulses, maize, sugar-cane, and indigo.

Furrucknugg'ur, a walled town in the district of Gurgaon, Punjaub, British India. Pop. (1868) 10,631. Along with the surrounding country, it formerly belonged to a chief who was hanged for rebellion in 1857. F. is the emporium of the important trade carried on in salt, manufactured in the district by evaporation from wells.

Furruck Shere (Farakh Siyyar), an emperor of Delhi of the Mogul dynasty, who succeeded to the throne by murdering his uncle, Jehander Shah, in 1713, and was himself assassinated in 1718. His reign is memorable for the privileges granted to the British East India Company at Calcutta through the court influence of an English surgeon.

Furs and Furr'iery (Span. *forro*, 'lining'). Fur is a name given to the skins of certain mammalian animals, generally characterised by short, close, and fine hair, prepared for use as human clothing, wrappers, or rugs. Though not generally classed among F., the fine, downy skins of certain birds, as the grebe and the swan, are used in the same way. Furriery is the art of preserving and preparing in various ways such skins for the uses to which they are applied. As F. are primarily valued on account of the protection they afford against cold, it is found that the skins of animals inhabiting Arctic regions, which themselves require protection from the extreme rigour of the climate, are most valuable for the purposes of the furrier. Accordingly the northern parts of Siberia, of European Russia, and of British N. America form the most valuable fur-hunting grounds. The Hudson's Bay Company, which for nearly two centuries possessed a monopoly of the fur trade in the vast tract known as Hudson's Bay Territory, is still the greatest fur-trading body in the world. As the demand for many F. is more regulated by the dictates of fashion than by absolute necessity, prices and values are subject to violent fluctuations. As a rule, the most valuable of all skins for fur is that of the Russian sable, next to which come the finer skins of the black or silver fox of N. America, which sometimes bring as much as £50 each. Of the greatest value, however, in respect of its total annual produce, is the trade in the skin of the northern fur-seal (*Callorhinus ursinus*), which is caught on the small islands off the coast of Alaska. About 130,000 skins are obtained from this source annually, while from various regions in the South Seas about 40,000 skins of the genus *Arctocephalus* are procured. These vary in value according to fashion from about 15s. to 30s. each. While nearly all haired animals may be more or less employed as sources of fur, the following list enumerates the principal varieties embraced in commerce:—Of the family *Canidæ* (dogs) there are the wolf, red fox, Arctic fox, silver fox, and cross fox; of the *Mustelidæ* or weasels, the ermine, the sable, Hudson's Bay sable, the kolinski, the various species of marten, and the sea-otter; of other carnivorous animals, the bears, black, grey, and white, and the various species of seal. Among rodents, the most valuable is the Beaver (q. v.), which, by an ingenious process of removing the long and coarse hairs and dyeing, is made to imitate and rival the fur-seal. There are also the musquash, the chinchilla of the Andes, the grey squirrel, and the rabbit. A vast number of black and grey lambskins, chiefly from Russia, are also used as F. under the trade name of 'Astracans.' The skins of several monkeys are also employed as F., such, for example, as the black monkey of W. Africa and the Abyssinian monkey. The skins of the larger *Carnivora*, the lion, tiger, leopard, &c., are also highly valued as carriage-rugs, &c.

Fürst, Julius, an illustrious Orientalist of Jewish descent, was born at Zerkovo in Posen, Prussia, 12th May 1805. He was educated for a rabbin, and even in his twelfth year showed a marvellously extensive acquaintance with Rabbinical literature. Studies at a German gymnasium and the University of Berlin led him, however, to devote himself to philological science, and he completed (1831) a regular course at Breslau and Halle. His lectures in Leipsic were recognised by the university in 1839, and in 1864 he became a professor. Before his death, 9th February 1873, F. had enriched Semitic learning by innumerable works, of which the best-known is his great concordance, *Concordantiæ Librorum Sacrorum Veteris Testamenti Hebraicæ et Chaldaicæ* (1837–40), and his Hebrew and Chaldee Lexicon (1857–61, 2d ed. 1863, Eng. trans. 1874). Others of great value are *Lehrgebäude der Aramäischen Idiome* (Leips. 1835); *Perlenschnüre Aramäischer Gnomen und Lieder* (Leips. 1836); *Die Israelitische Bibel* (Berl. 1838), translated from the original Hebrew into German; *Der Orient; Berichte, Studien, und Kritiken für Jüdische Geschichte und Literatur* (Leips. 1840); *Die Jüdischen Religionsphilosophen des Mittelalters* (Leips. 1845); *Geschichte der Juden in Asien* (Leips. 1849); *Bibliotheca Judaica* (1849–53); *Hebräisches und Chaldäisches Handwörterbuch* (Leips. 1857–61, 2d ed. 1863); *Geschichte des Karäerthums* (Leips. 1862–65); and a work on the canon of the Old Testament (the latter published in 1868).—**Livius F.**, son of the preceding, born at Leipsic, 27th May 1840, has acquired some reputation as a poet by his *Märchen von den Sieben Raben* (Leips. 1864), and *Dornröschen* (Leips. 1865).

Für'stenwalde, a walled town of Brandenburg, Prussia, on the Spree, 30 miles E.S.E. of Berlin by railway. Its chief building is a brick church of the 14th c. dedicated to the Virgin, and it has woollen and linen industries, and an active river trade. Pop. (1871) 8197.

Fürth ('the ford'), one of the most important towns of Middle Franconia, Bavaria, on the river Rednitz and the Ludwig's Canal, 5 miles N.W. of Nürnberg by railway. It has a Byzantine townhall with a tower 180 feet high, a large Roman Catholic church, and several synagogues, while its manufactures are chiefly mirrors, gold and bronze wares, machinery, optical and surgical instruments, paper, colours, &c. A fair, fourteen days in duration, is here held at Michaelmas. The railway between F. and Nürnberg, the first in Germany, was opened in 1865. Pop. (1871) 24,577, of whom 3116 are Jews. Karl the Great founded a chapel at F., and the place came subsequently into the hands of the Burggrafs of Nürnberg. In the Thirty Years' War (1634) the Croats burned F., and in 1680 it was almost completely destroyed by fire.

Fury and Hecla Strait, separating Cockburn Island on the N. from Melville Peninsula on the S., and connecting the Gulf of Boothia on the W. and Fox Channel on the E. It was discovered in 1823 by Parry, but is impracticable for ships. Its western entrance is in lat. 70° N.

Furze (*Ulex*), a genus of Leguminous plants belonging to the subdivision *Papilionaceæ*. The stamens are monadelphous, *i.e.*, united to form a single bundle; the branches spinous, and the leaves reduced to mere thorns in appearance. The calyx is bipartite. The common F. (*Ulex Europæus*) is a very familiar hardy shrub, sometimes growing in immense tracts on bare stony land. The flowers are numerous, solitary, and of yellow colour. F. appears to thrive best in temperate climates, and does not stand winter or severe frosts well. It is used for fodder. In Wales and in Flanders especially F. is highly esteemed for this purpose. Irish F. is the *U. strictus* of botanists, and has very dense branches. *U. nanus* is a very small species or variety.

Fusa'ro, Lago del (anc. *Acherusia Palus*), the supposed harbour of Cumæ (q. v.), in the province of Naples, on the peninsula of Baiæ, 11 miles W. of Naples. It is believed to be the crater of an extinct volcano, having emitted volumes of mephitic gas as late as 1838. In its centre is a pavilion erected by Ferdinand I. At the S. end an outlet of Roman construction

(*Foce de F.*) connects it with the sea, and in the vicinity is the vast ruined villa of Servilius Vatia, with many other relics of antiquity. The lake is still, as in ancient times, famous for its oysters.

Fuse (Fr. *fusée*, originally the *ball* of thread on a spindle, then a piece of artillery of that shape), in artillery, is a case of wood or metal fitted into a shell, and filled with slowly-burning combustible mixture. By a suitable arrangement the F. burns during the time of flight, and then communicates with the explosive mixture in the shell, which is thus calculated to burst as nearly as possible at the moment it touches the earth.

Fuse'li, Henry, a painter, designer, and art critic of great intellectual force but of limited artistic culture, was the son of a Swiss portrait-painter, and was born at Zürich in 1742. Educated for the Church, he entered holy orders in 1761, and soon after removed to London, where for some time he maintained himself by translating from and into the chief Continental languages. Among his works in this kind are a translation into German of Lady M. W. Montagu's Letters, and into English of Winckelmann's *Painting and Sculpture of the Ancients.* At Reynold's suggestion he devoted himself to painting, and removed to Italy in 1770. He returned in 1778, was elected R.A. in 1790, and in 1799 he was appointed Professor of Painting. He died 16th April 1825. F. studied Michael Angelo with great earnestness and much profit; and though his style is low in tone and bad in colour, he did much to emancipate English art from the prevailing mannerisms of the period by vindicating the superiority of design and expression to mere technical dexterity. His *Milton's Gallery*, a series of forty-seven designs from the poet's great epic, is a work of unquestioned genius. See the biographical memoir prefixed to Knowles's edition of his literary works (3 vols. Lond. 1831).

Fu'sel Oil is the name given to the less volatile products separated during the distillation of various alcoholic liquors. It consists chiefly of amyl alcohol ($C_5H_{11}OH$), but it also contains various other alcohols, the propylic, butylic, and hexylic, as well as the ethers of several fatty acids, chiefly those of capric or rutic acid. (See CAPRIC ACID.) Its constituents vary in amount and often in kind with the particular spirit manufactured. Most of the substances present in F. O. act very deleteriously on the system, and this is the reason why inferior spirits are so injurious in their effects, as they are imperfectly rectified. A small quantity of F. O. is present in most spirits, and frequently gives to them their characteristic taste. F. O. is employed officinally in the manufacture of nitrate of amyl. (See AMYL.)

Fusibil'ity, a property of certain kinds of matter, in virtue of which they change their solid for a liquid state under the influence of heat. All solids (except carbon) which do not decompose into their chemical constituents fuse if the temperature be sufficiently great, and the fusion of carbon will probably before long be effected, when our means of applying intense heat are improved. In most treatises on physics, tables are given showing the relative positions of fusible solids as regards their fusing-points. See FREEZING AND FUSING POINTS.

Fu'sible Metal. Many alloys melt at a comparatively low temperature, notably those containing bismuth, tin, lead, and cadmium. Such alloys are termed fusible metals. The following table shows the composition of a few of the more important of these with their fusing-points :—

	Bismuth.	Lead.	Tin.	Cadmium.	Fusing-Point.
Newton's Fusible Metal	8	5	3		94·5
Darcet's ,, ,,	2	1	1		93·0
Darcet's ,, ,,	5	3	2		91·0
Rose's ,, ,,	420	236	207		below 100·0
Wood's ,, ,,	7·8	2	2	1	66–71

Fu'sible Plug, a small plug made of an alloy which melts at a comparatively low temperature. It is placed upon the upper part of the firebox of a boiler, where, if it acts properly, it should melt if the temperature of the water becomes such as corresponds to a dangerous pressure of steam, or if the plate to which it is attached be left uncovered by water. In either case the result ought to be the blowing out of water or steam on to the fire, and the removal in this way in the one case of danger by bursting, and in the other of the risk of overheating the furnace plates. The F. P. is an excellent adjunct to a boiler, but cannot be depended on always to fulfil its intended purpose, so that or no account can it be allowed to supersede a Safety-Valve (q. v.).

Fu'sil (Old Fr. *fusel*, Mod. Fr. *fuseau*, 'a spindle or distaff'), in heraldry, a sub-ordinary, four-sided, presenting two angles perpendicularly and two horizontally. It is more elongated than the lozenge.

Fusil, Fusiliers' (Fr. *fusil*, Ital. *focile;* from Lat. *focus*, 'a fireplace,' in Low Lat. 'a fire'). The fusil was a firelock or light musket, formerly carried by certain British regiments, hence called Fusiliers. The Martini-Henry rifle has been selected for all British infantry regiments, but the name Fusilier is still retained by the following corps—Scots Fusilier Guards, Northumberland F., Royal F., Royal North British F., Royal Welsh F., Royal Irish F., Royal Bengal F., Royal Madras F., Royal Bombay F., and Bengal F.

Fu'sing-Point. See FREEZING AND FUSING POINTS.

Fus't.an (Fr. *futaigne*, formerly *fustaigne;* Ital. *fustagno;* from *Fostat*, a suburb of Cairo, where it was originally made; introduced through Italian commerce with the East), is a thick twilled cotton, of which varieties are velveteen and corduroy. From being an imitation of velvet, its name came to be applied to false, bombastic speech or writing.

Fus'tic. Two kinds of wood, both yielding yellow dyes, are known in commerce under this name, and they are distinguished as old F. and young or Zante F. respectively. The former is the wood of *Maclura tinctoria*, a large tree, native of the W. Indian Islands and S. America. The wood is of a pale-yellow colour, and was formerly much used in dyeing yellow, green, olive, and brown tints. The latter is the wood of a shrub, *Rhus cotinus*, belonging to the S. of Europe. The plant possesses a very peculiar feather-like inflorescence, and yields a fugitive yellow colour, which is only used in conjunction with other dyes to modify their effects.

Fu'sus, a genus of Gasteropodous *Mollusca*, the species of which are often popularly named 'spindle shells' from their shape, and in Scotland 'buckies.' They belong to the whelk family (*Muricidæ*), and have a short spire and a thin outer lip. The siphonal canal is very long. The best-known species is the *F. antiquus*, the 'roaring buckie' of the Scotch, so named from the curious sound resembling the roar of the sea which is heard on placing the shell to the ear. It attains a large size, and is used to form a rude lamp by the Shetlanders, the shell being filled with oil, and the wick drawn through the canal at the mouth. It is also extensively used for bait. *F. colossus*, the giant spindle, is a large species found in tropical seas. Fossil forms begin in the Oolite rocks, and are common in the Chalk, the Lower Greensand, and the Newer Pliocene rocks.

Futak' (Old and New), a village in the county of Bács, Hungary, on the left bank of the Danube, 9 miles W.S.W. of Neusatz. It has a fine castle, has a large trade in tobacco, vegetables, and corn, and a fair, visited by Turks, Armenians, Greeks, &c. Pop. (1869) 4642.

Futtehgunge' (*Fathiganj*, 'market of victory'), the name of two towns in Bareilly district, N.W. Province, British India, 23 miles distant from one another, known as Eastern and Western F. The former was founded by the Nawab of Oude, in commemoration of a victory gained by British troops which gave him Rohilcund, in 1774. The latter is also the site of a victory of the British over the Rohillas in 1796, and the spot is marked by an inscribed obelisk.

Futtehgurh' (*Fathigarh*, 'fort of victory'), a military cantonment on the left bank of the Ganges, 3 miles E. of Furruckabad Town (q. v.) in the N.W. Province. Pop. (1872) 10,335. It is a healthy and favourite station, and its importance has been increased by a branch of the Ganges Canal (q. v.), which here opens into the Ganges. At the mutiny of 1857, the Sepoys turned upon the English residents soon after the outbreak at Cawnpur, and the sufferings of those who escaped were only less dreadful than the fate of the prisoners at the latter place.

Futtehpur' (*Fathipur*, 'town of victory'), the chief town of the district of the same name in the N.W. Province, British India, is a station on the East Indian Railway, 571 miles N.W. of Calcutta, and 267 S.E. of Delhi. Pop. (1872) 20,478. F. has a spacious *sarai*, or lodging-house for travellers, and a small but elegant mosque. At the time of the mutiny of 1857 the English residents escaped with a single exception. The town was shortly afterwards sacked by Havelock, after he had won in the neighbourhood a victory over the troops of Nana Sahib.—*F. District* lies within the Doab, and is bordered both by the Ganges and Jumna. Area, 1586 sq. miles; pop. (1872) 663,877. The land is naturally fertile, and the upper portion is watered by the Ganges Canal (q. v.). The crops are wheat, barley, sugar-cane, indigo, cotton, poppy, and the exports are considerable.

Futtehpur' Sikri, a ruined town of the district of Agra, N.W. Province, British India, 23 miles W. of Agra city. It was the favourite residence of the Emperor Akbar (q. v.), and the ruins, still in a fair state of preservation, attest its former magnificence. The stone wall is 5 miles in circumference. The most striking object within is the mosque, 'which is hardly surpassed by any in India.' This building is 550 feet from E. to W., and 470 feet from N. to S., and contains two tombs of white marble, 'ornamented with pierced tracery of the most exquisite geometrical patterns.' The western gateway is the most celebrated feature, being of such elegant proportions as to be described by Fergusson as 'a romance in stone.' Its greatest height is 120 feet, and it is approached from below by a handsome flight of steps. In less good preservation is the Khas Mehal or palace, about 260 feet square. The Dewani Khas or throne-room contains a throne 'consisting of an enormous flower-like bracket supported on a richly-carved pillar.' Close by are three small pavilions, said to have been erected for three favourite sultanas. See Fergusson's *History of Indian Architecture* (Lond. 1876).

Futtuha' (*Fatwá* = a judicial sentence based on the Koran), a town in the district of Patna, Bengal, British India, at the junction of the Pûnpûn with the Ganges, and a station on the East Indian Railway, 390 miles N.W. of Calcutta, and 10 E. of Patna. Pop. (1872) 11,295. It is the seat of some trade, as well as the resort of multitudes of pilgrims, who flock hither at certain seasons to bathe in the Ganges.

Fu'ture Debt. In England, under common law, no procedure can under any circumstances be taken on a debt before the date on which it falls due. This legal doctrine formerly gave rise in bankruptcies to hardships and injustice, to obviate which various statutory provisions have been made. Under these, postponed or contingent debt can now be reduced to its immediate value, and procedure follow accordingly. In Scotland the doctrine of Roman law regarding F. D. has always been held—that in the event of the death or bankruptcy of the debtor, the creditor is entitled, by deducting a proper discount, to make his claim immediate. The Scotch law also gives to the future creditor the privilege of Arrestment (q. v.) in security. The contingent creditor in a Scotch sequestration may have his debt valued, and may vote and draw dividend accordingly.

Fyne, Loch, an inlet of the Firth of Clyde in the S. of Argyleshire, noted for its herring-fishing, is 43 miles long, 2 to 10 broad, and has a depth of from 40 to 70 fathoms. It begins in the N.E. of Cantire, has a N. and N.E. direction, separating first Cowal on the E. from Knapdale on the W., then Cowal from the Inverary and Loch Awe districts, and sends off to the W. Loch Gilp, which is linked by the Crinan Canal to the Sound of the Jura. The hilly shores are steep and bare, but round Inverary, near the top of the loch, there is finely-wooded scenery.

Fyzabad' (*Faizabad*, 'town of plenty'), the chief town of the district of the same name in the province of Oudh on the right bank of the Gogra, 89 miles E. of Lucknow. It is a station on the Oudh and Rohilcund Railway. Pop. (1869) 37,804. F. town, a modern suburb of the ruined city of Avadha or Oude, was founded about 1730 by the first Nawab of Oude; but the seat of government was removed to Lucknow in 1775, and since then the importance of F. has decreased. It was the residence of the Begums of Oude, whose title is known in connection with Warren Hastings. The Gogra is here navigable for large boats, which carry a considerable export trade in rice, wheats, and other cereals, oilseeds and sugar. The manufactures are native cloth, metal vessels, and firearms.—*F. district* contains an area of 2332 sq. miles; pop. (1869) 1,437,009.

G.

G the seventh letter in the English alphabet, occupying the same position in the Latin. In the Greek, as in the original Phœnician alphabet, it came third, and the names *gamma* and *gimel*, which it respectively bore in these tongues, show that in origin it was identical, both in sound and in shape, with its cognate *c*. In Latin the name Caius was long written as Gaius, and G always retained its proper phonetic value as a hard guttural, as it still does in German. The softened sound of G, which is closely analogous to the softened sound of *c*, came in when the Romance languages took shape, and was thence introduced into English. It is now always hard before *a*, *o*, and *u*, and usually soft before *e*, *i*, and *y*. In Italian, by means of the compound letter *gh*, the rules for pronunciation are more precise. In the same language before *l* it loses its own sound, and changes the sound of that letter to *ly*. It has a tendency to become altogether mute before *n* and *h*, and even to be dropped from the written tongue, as Latin *natus* *ognatus*. During the last century it was fashionable to insert *y* in the pronunciation of G when this letter commenced a word, as garden = *gyarden*. This shows the close affinity between these two letters, which may also be exemplified by the participial prefix *ge-* in Old English becoming in Transition English *y-*, as *y-clept*. G also interchanges with its cognates *c* and *k* and *ch*. Lat. *gnosco* is Eng. 'know;' Eng. 'eight' is Lat. *octo*, Greek *okto*, Ger. *acht*. As an abbreviation G. stands for Grand, as G.C.B. = (Knight) Grand Cross of the Bath.

G, in music, the tone which is a perfect fifth above or fourth below C. The particular G whose vibration number is 396 is represented by the second line of the treble stave.

Gaal, Jozsef, a Hungarian writer of considerable reputation, was born at Gross-Karoly in 1811. Educated at the University of Pesth, he has devoted himself chiefly to politics and literature, particularly humorous poetry, comedies, and sketches of Hungarian life. On the occasion of the rising of the Hungarians against Austria he was appointed Finance Minister to the Provisional Government. Among his works are *Szyrmay Ilona*, a novel in 2 vols. (Pesth, 1836); *Kirâlr Ludnom* (Pesth, 1837); *Peleskei Notarius* (Pesth, 1838), one of the best specimens of Hungarian comedy; and *Szerelem ès Champagnir* (Pesth, 1840).

Gabb'ion, or **Gab'ion** (Fr.; Span. *gavion*, Ital. *gabbione*, 'a large cage;' connected with Lat. *cavea*, 'a hollow'), a cylinder of wickerwork, or basket without lid or bottom, usually 3 feet in height. It is made by drawing a circle on the ground about 22 inches in diameter, driving from eight to twelve pickets, ⅝ths to ⅞ths of an inch in diameter, and pointed at both ends, into the earth at regular intervals on the circle described, and then constructing a web of basketwork upon the pickets with wattles or thin pliant rods. Gabbions filled with earth and ranged in one or more rows, form a useful and eminently manageable means of defence against musketry and even small field-guns. Disposed in alternate rows with fascines, they make a good revetment or lining of the escarp. Placed on the summit of the parapet, with narrow intervals between each for firing through, they afford valuable cover for the defenders of field fortifications. *Gabbionades* are lines of gabbions thrown up for cover.

Gabb'ro, the name given by Italian geologists to Diallage (q. v.).

Gabelentz', Hans Conon von der, a German philologist, born at Altenburg, October 13, 1807, and studied at Leipsic and Göttingen. He entered on a successful political career and in 1851 became President of the Altenburg Diet. He has throughout his life been devoted to philology, and has greatly advanced the study of various Turanian and other dialects. He was one of the founders of the *Zeitschrift für die Kunde des Morgenlandes* (1837, *et seq.*), in the second volume of which appeared his *Grammatik der Mordwinischen Sprache*. Other valuable works of G.'s are his *Grundzüge der Syrjänischen Grammatik* (Altenb. 1841); his critical edition of Ulfilas, with a Latin translation, glossary, and Gothic grammar (2 vols. Leips. 1843–46); *Beiträge zur Sprachenkunde* (Leips. 1852); *Ueber die Melanesischen Sprachen* (1860); *Ueber das Passivum* (1860); and (1864) Manchurian translations of the Chinese works *Se-Shu*, *Shu-King*, and *Shi-King*, with a glossary.

Gabelle', a French word denoting a tax on salt. In English law it may be applied to any other tax, or to rent, custom, or service. The word is of Teutonic origin. In Old Eng. it appears as *gafol*, 'tribute,' from the verb, *gifan*, 'to give.'

Ga'ble (Goth. *gibla*, 'a pinnacle') is the property of the party who builds it, even though partly resting on the ground of another, and the builder may prevent the owner of the other ground from using the G. until he has paid half the expense of building it.

Gaboon', a river of W. Africa, rises in the Crystal Mountains, and after a sinuous course of 120 miles, enters the Atlantic near the equator by a wide estuary. Much ivory is procured in the basin of the G., which is occupied by many native tribes. The climate is unhealthy. The French planted a colony at the mouth of the river in 1845, which was broken up in 1871, but has since been re-established.

Ga'briel (Heb. 'man of God,' a generic title of an angel), in the Jewish traditions was one of the seven Archangels (q. v.). In the Hebrew Scriptures, as with the ancient Persians, he appears as *the angel of revelations*. Thus he appeared to Daniel to make him understand his vision (viii. 16), and after his prayer to give him 'skill and understanding' (ix. 21–22). In the same character he appears to Zacharias and to Mary (Luke i. 19, 26–27). Hence Mohammed feigned that he received from G. the Koran (in which he is called the Holy Spirit and the Spirit of Truth) and instructions about a number of his actions. See Sale's *Koran*.

Gachard, Louis Prosper, an eminent archivist, born at Paris in 1801. He was at first a working printer, but devoted himself to history, and removed to Belgium, of which country he was made archivist in 1831. G. has thrown much fresh light on Belgian history, and especially the Spanish occupation of the Low Countries. Among his works are *Analectes Belgiques* (1830); *Documents Inédits* (1845); *Relations des Troubles de Gand sous Charles-Quint* (1846); *Correspondance de Guillaume le Taciturne* (5 vols. Bruss. 1847–65); *Correspondance de Philippe II. sur les Affaires des Pays-Bas* (3 vols. Bruss. 1848–59); *Don Carlos et Philippe II.* (Bruss. 1863); *Actes des États Généraux des Pays-Bas* 1576 *à* 1585 (1866), &c.

Gad was the seventh son of Jacob, by Zilpah, Leah's maid. The derivation of the name given in the A. V. (Gen. xxx. 11), which follows the Masoretic text, is very obscure. The best critics consider the original text would mean—'Leah said, *To my good fortune*' (*sc.* a son is born); 'and she called his name *Good Fortune*.' This would correspond with Isa. lxv. 11, where 'that troop' of the A. V. is understood by some to refer to the god or goddess of fortune under the form of the planet Jupiter or Venus respectively. The tribe of G., which numbered in the first census (Num. i.) 45,650 fighting men, in the second (xxvi.) 40,500, settled along with the tribe of Reuben and half tribe of Manasseh on the E. of Jordan (Num. xxxii.). See Delitzsch's *Commentary on the Pent.* (Clark's trans. 1867), and *Isaiah* (1869).

Gadames, or **Ghadames** (Lat. *Cydamus*), an oasis and town of Africa, in the S.W. of Tripoli, and on the border of the Sahara. It is a place of some traffic, lying on the routes between Tripoli, Tunis, Ghat, Tidikelt, &c. The tolls and land tributes amount to £1700 yearly. There are springs of 89° F., watering the gardens, which yield dates, wheat, millet, &c. The town has six mosques and seven schools, where the Koran is taught, along with a little Arabic writing. Pop. 5000.

Gadfly. See BOT and TABANUS.

Gadidæ, an important family of Teleostean fishes belonging to the section *Malacopterygii*, or 'soft-finned' fishes, and distinguished by having a long scaly body and a symmetrical head. The ventral fins are jugular in position, that is, are placed on the throat below the pectorals. To this family belong the cod, whiting, haddock, Dorse (q. v.), &c

Gad'wall (*Chaulelasmus strepera*), a species of *Anatidæ*, or Ducks (q. v.), common in N. America, in some parts of the continent of Europe and Asia, and occasionally found in the British Islands. It is imported from Holland in large quantities for the London market. The plumage is of sober colour, and the voice harsh and noisy. The nests are usually found in marshy ground, and from seven to nine eggs are generally laid.

Gadwall.

Gæ'a, or **Ge**, the Greek goddess of the earth, and, according to Hesiod, the first-born of Chaos and mother of Uranus. G. is one of the strange, gloomy Chthonian deities who seem to have belonged to an earlier, ruder religion than that of classic Greece. They are closely connected with the earth, and contrast strongly with the bright Olympian divinities who are native to the sky. G. corresponds to the Latin earth-goddess *Tellus*.

Gaelic Language and Literature. The Gaelic, as distinct from the Cymric family of the Celtic language, comprises three dialects, viz., Irish, Scottish, and Manx Gaelic, all of which show closer kinship with the Latin than with any other Aryan tongue.

The Book of the Dean of Lismore proves that 300 years ago Scotland possessed a native common, or Bardic, dialect widely differing from the foreign (Irish) and ecclesiastic. In the present day we find such differences still in existence—*e.g.*, the Irish use both the analytic and synthetic forms of the verb, the Scottish only the first. The Irish gives a present tense to the verb, the Scottish none. In Irish, nouns never take *n* in the plural, in Scottish they often do. In Irish what is called *eclipsis* is used to an extent altogether unknown in Scottish. In Irish the negative is *ni*, in Scottish *cha*; and in pronunciation, in idiom, and in vocables wide differences between the two are met with.

The lectures of Professor O'Curry on the 'MS. materials of Irish History' (Dublin, 1861) prove that many thousands of pages, written from the 10th to the 15th centuries, and embodying much written at an earlier period, are still to be found in public libraries and private collections throughout the kingdom, dealing with a great variety of subjects, and written often with great ability. Several volumes of the ancient laws and the historical annals of Ireland have been published at the national expense. The oldest Scottish Gaelic, strictly so called, which has been preserved is in the Dean of Lismore's Book, written from 1512 to 1540, a commonplace-book mainly filled with Gaelic heroic ballads, several of which are ascribed to the authorship of Ossian or his kindred. It proves that Ossianic heroic poetry was known and esteemed in the W. Highlands 300 years ago, and its peculiar orthography demonstrates, as already said, the existence of a separate Scottish Gaelic dialect. *Leabhar na Féinne* ('the Book of the Fingalians'), published by Mr. Campbell (Lond. 1872), contains the heroic ballads of the Dean's Book, placed side by side with all the other versions of them that have been gathered since, also a few not found in the Dean's collection, and is a work of immense labour. The poems of Ossian published by MacPherson (English translation 1762-63, Gaelic originals 1807) are undoubtedly Gaelic, whatever opinion be formed of their age or authorship, and in the opinion of scholars are unrivalled for sublimity and pathos by any other production of the Celtic muse. The fullest edition is that by Dr. Clerk (Edinb. 1870). 'The ancient poems,' *Sean Dàna*, published by Dr. Smith (1782), also deserve the highest praise. Of modern poets we may note a few of the best. Mary Macleod of Skye, born 1569, is an authoress full of Pindaric fire and freedom. John Lom or MacDonald, who was at the battle of Inverlochy (1645), is fully more of a politician than a poet, but he is a great favourite with his countrymen. Alasdair MacDonald of Ardnamurchan, 'the Tyrtæus of the '45,' was a classical scholar, and his *Birlinn* is probably the ablest modern poem in the language, but many of his pieces are disfigured by a pedantic display of learning, and an intolerable accumulation of synonymous epithets. Duncan Bàn MacIntyre, his contemporary, is beyond all question the 'Burns' of the Highlands. Rob Donn (q. v.) is a bard whose fame surpasses his merit. The names of John MacCodrum and William Ross are familiar to Gaelic ears. Buchanan and MacGregor have written religious poems of great merit, and there are crowds of lesser lyrists whose praise of love or war still kindles enthusiasm in Celtic breasts.

Mr. Campbell, already mentioned, published in 1866 a large collection of W. Highland tales in prose, but the only Gaelic prose worthy of the name was either edited or composed by the late Dr. Norman Macleod of St. Columba, Glasgow, in his periodicals. A collection of his own works—*Caraid nan Gäel*—edited by Dr. Clerk (Glasg. 1867) shows more of the flexibility and gracefulness of the language than any extant composition.

The first book ever printed in G. was a translation of Knox's Liturgy by Bishop Carsewell of Argyle in 1659. The Synod of Argyle in the same year published a translation of the first fifty Psalms and of the Shorter Catechism. The first Gaelic Bible was published in 1786. There are two good grammars of the language, Dr. Stewart's and Munro's; a good dictionary by Armstrong, a larger one by the Highland Society, and smaller ones by Dr. Macleod and Mr. Macalpine. Professor Blackie, who has successfully laboured to collect funds for the endowment of a Celtic Chair in Edinburgh, has written a very interesting and instructive work on the *Language and Literature of the Scottish Highlands* (1876), which may be recommended to English readers.

The Gaelic is rich in terms descriptive of *external* nature, and of the emotions of the mind, but entirely destitute of those relating to metaphysics and natural science. Notwithstanding the general impression of its ruggedness, it is in pronunciation soft and vocalic, like the French in its nasal tones, and also in loss of original vigour through the too frequent suppression of consonantal sounds both medial and terminal.

Gäeta (the ancient *Caieta*, perhaps from the Gr. *kaietas*, 'a hollow,' on account of its caves), an Italian town in the province of Caserta, 40 miles N.W. of Naples. It is situated on a high steep promontory, jutting into the beautiful Bay of G., is sheltered by wooded hills, and has some fisheries, and a coasting trade in wine, oil, fruits, &c. In its citadel, one of the strongest in Italy, is the tomb of Constable Bourbon, who sacked Rome in 1527. It possesses several ancient remains, of which the most interesting is the sepulchre of Munatius Plancus, a circular building, now known as the Torre di Orlando, which stands on the summit of the headland. G. was a busy port in the time of Cicero, and a favourite resort of the Roman nobility, who had many splendid villas along its shore. It was the first Italian town which became a commonwealth during the middle ages, and has sustained various sieges. After holding out bravely during three months for the King of Naples, it surrendered to Cialdini in 1861. Pop. 10,000.

Gætu'lia, the ancient name of a wild country in the N.W. of Libya, embracing the S. region of Morocco, and the W. part of the Great Desert. It extended from the Atlantic eastward to the region of the Garamantes, and was bounded on the S. by the river Niger. The Gætulians belonged to the great Berber (q. v.) stock. Those of the N. were of a yellowish-brown complexion, dark-haired and dark-eyed; while their southern neighbours, from mixing with the Negroes, were nearly black in colour, and were called *Melanogætuli* ('black Gætulians'). They were unsettled, warlike, savage, and implacable. They first appear in history as cavalry in the army of Jugurtha. In A.D. 6 they were defeated by Cornelius Cossus Lentulus, who, for his success, received the surname Gætulicus and the *ornamenta triumphalia*. The Berbers of Mount Atlas, and the Tuaricks of the desert, are thought to be the descendants of the ancient Gætulians.

Gaff (Dan. *gaffel*, Welsh *gafl*, 'a fork'), in a ship or sailing boat, is the spar to which the upper edge of a fore-and-aft sail is bent, the lower edge, except in a sprit-sail, being attached to a boom. The G. is probably so named from the fork-like appearance of the 'jaws,' with which it slides up or down the mast.

Gage. See GAUGE.

Gage, Thomas, governor of Massachusetts, was born in England in the early part of the 18th c. Having fought in the Seven Years' War, he was made governor of Montreal in 1760, obtained the chief command of the British forces in America in 1763, and finally arrived in Boston in May 1774 as governor of Massachusetts, when the dispute between the colonists and the mother country was assuming formidable dimensions. He excited odium by his policy and procedure, such as fortifying Boston, planning the expedition to Concord which ended in the battle of Lexington (April 19, 1775), and proclaiming martial law in Massachusetts. He was declared an enemy to America by the Congress then assembled. After the battle of Bunker's Hill, June 17, 1775, G., being superseded by General Howe, sailed for England. He died April 1787.

Gagea, a genus of Monocotyledonous plants belonging to the natural order *Liliaceæ*. It embraces numerous species found chiefly in Europe and the cooler parts of Asia and Africa. *G. lutea* is the only one indigenous to Britain.

Gag'ern, Hans Christoph Ernst, Freiherr von, a German writer and statesman, born at Klein-niederheim, near Worms, January 25, 1766, became Chief Minister to the House of Nassau in 1814, represented the Low Countries at the Vienna Congress, opposed the scheme of German federation, and died at Hornau, October 22, 1852. Among his works are *Die Fürsten* (Frankf. 1808); *Aristokratie* (Vienna, 1812); *Demokratie* (Frankf. 1816); *Politik* (Stuttg. 1818); *Die Nationalgeschichte der Deutschen* (2d ed. Frankf. 1825–26); his Memoirs, under the title *Mein Antheil an der Politik* (5 vols. Stuttg. and Leips. 1823–44); *Civilisation* (1847), &c.—**Friedrich Baldwin G.**, son of the above, born at Weilburg, October 24, 1794, joined the Austrian army, fought at Dresden, Kulm, Leipsic, &c., became a general, afterwards entered the Dutch service, and was killed at Kardern, April 20, 1848.—**Heinrich Wilhelm August, Freiherr von G.**, brother of the preceding, was born at Baireuth, August 20, 1799, entered the service of Nassau, and fought at Waterloo. He afterwards studied at Göttingen, Jena, and Heidelberg, and was one of the founders of the *Burschenschaft*. He then passed to the administrative service of the Duke of Hessen-Darmstadt, and became private secretary to the Minister of the Interior, a post which he had to give up on account of his Liberalism. In 1847 he was re-elected to the Darmstadt Diet, and in 1848 made Prime Minister. In 1852 he retired from public life. His favourite political project was to unite Germany into a confederacy of small free states, and to form a close alliance between them and Austria. His career has been marked by patriotism and moderation. From 1864 to 1870 G. was ambassador for Hessen-Darmstadt at the court of Vienna. He has written a life of his brother, *Das Leben des General Friedrich von G.* (3 vols. Heidelb. and Leips. 1856–57).

Gaill'ac, a town in the department of Tarn, France, on the river Tarn, 32 miles N.E. of Toulouse by railway. It lies in a rich wine district, and has some distilling, tanning, turnery, and dyeing. Its chief building is an abbey church of St. Michel of the 13th c. Pop. (1872) 5694. G. grew up about a Benedictine abbey founded by Raymond I., Comte de Toulouse, in the 10th c.

Gaill'ard, Gabriel Henri, a voluminous French author, was born at Ostel in 1726. He was educated for the bar, but chose a literary life, and cultivated history and rhetorical composition with much temporary success. He was during forty years the friend of Malesherbes. He finally retired to Saint-Firmir, near Chantilly, where he died, February 13, 1806. His works include *Histoire de la Rivalité de la France et de l'Angleterre* (1771–77); *Histoire de Charlemagne* (1782); *Histoire de la Rivalité de la France et de l'Espagne* (1801); *Essai de Rhétorique Française* (1745); *Éloge de René Descartes* (1765); *Epître aux Malheureux* (1766), &c.

Gai'mar, Geoffrey or **Geffrei**, a Norman-French *trouvère* who flourished in the middle of the 12th c. He lived in the household of Ralph Fitz-Gilbert, a baron of the N. of England, and translated Geoffrey of Monmouth's Latin chronicle into French verse, enlarging it with a series of tales of early English kings. His version known as *L'Estorie des Engles* was soon superseded by Wace's more popular rendering.

Gains'borough ('the town of the Ganii'), a seaport of England, in Lincolnshire, on the Trent, 20 miles above its mouth in the Humber, and 16 miles N.W. of Lincoln by railway. It consists chiefly of one long street parallel to the river, which is crossed by a stone bridge of three elliptical arches, erected in 1791. There is a curious old 'manor house,' partly tenanted by private families, which is said to have been the residence of the ancient lords of the manor. G. has also a grammar-school of date 1589, and an old church, rebuilt in 1736, with a tower of the 12th c. The harbour can be approached by vessels drawing 12 feet of water, has large manufactures of linseed oil, malt, and cordage, and does an active transit trade between the interior and the North Sea. Pop. (1871) 7564.

Gainsborough, Thomas, R.A., one of the greatest of English painters, was born at Sudbury, Suffolk, in 1727. His father was poor, and he received little education, passing his days mainly in sketching, until in his fifteenth year he went to London, where he studied painting for four years, and then resided for twelve years in Ipswich. In 1760 he settled in Bath, and worked there very successfully as a portrait-painter until 1774, when he returned to London, whither his fame had already spread. Henceforth his career was one of brilliant success. He was one of the thirty-six original members of the Royal Academy, and contributed regularly to its exhibitions. He died in London, August 2, 1781. Among G.'s best-known works are 'Hon. Mrs. Graham,' 'Shepherd Boy in the Shower,' 'The Seashore,' 'Cottage Girl with Dog and Pitcher,' 'Shepherd Boys with their Dogs Fighting,' and the 'Blue Boy,' painted to disprove the statement of Reynolds that blue should be excluded from masses of light. Uninfluenced by the foreign masters, G. developed a style 'pure in its English feeling, profound in its seriousness, graceful in its gaiety.' Ruskin says, 'G. is the greatest colourist since Rubens, and the last, I think, of the legitimate colourists.' His execution, however, is slightly mannered and always hasty, and his works are altogether lacking in 'affectionate details.' G. usually worked with cooler tints than Reynolds, and delighted in an enchanting play of blue and silver. In the treatment of a subject he combined audacity and finesse, and often produced most delicate effects by summary methods. His landscapes have idyllic feeling, and his portraits are marked by bewitching vivacity. See Fulcher's *Life of G.* (1856), and Wedmore's *Studies in English Art* (Lond. 1876).

Gai'us, a celebrated Roman jurist, flourished between 110 and 180 A.D. Of his personal history little is known. It is even uncertain whether his name should be written Gaius or Caius, and indeed whether it is a nomen or prænomen. By some he is considered a Greek, by others an Illyrian. Some learned civilians have erroneously thought him a Christian. G. is best known by his *Institutes*, which were compiled, or at all events completed, in the reign of M. Aurelius, and formed the basis of the more celebrated *Institutes* of Justinian. Before the reforms made by Justinian in the legal curriculum for students, this work and four other treatises by G. were honoured as text-books in the schools of law. The *Institutes* were lost till a palimpsest containing the MS. of the work of G. under that of the *Letters* of St. Jerome, was discovered at Verona by Niebuhr in 1816. The difficult task of deciphering the original MS. was successfully accomplished by two German scholars, Göschen and

Hollweg, and the result of their labours was published by the former in 1821. A second edition was issued in 1825, a third by Böcking in 1837, a fourth by Lachmann in 1842, and a fifth by Huschke in 1861. G. was the author of numerous other works. The chief are *Edictum Provinciale*, *Edictum Urbicum*, *Aureon*, *De Verborum Obligationibus*, *De Manumissionibus*, and *De Casibus*. In the *Digest* there are no fewer than 535 extracts from his works. See Huschke, *Zur Kritik und Interpretation von Gaius Institutionen*, in his *Studien des Römischen Rechts* (Breslau, 1830); Krüger, *Kritische Versuche im Gebiete des Römischen Rechts* (Berl. 1870); Teuffel, *Geschichte der Römischen Literatur*, sec. 357 (Leips. 1872).

Galac'tic Cir'cle (Gr. 'milky circle'), the name given by Sir John Herschel to the great circle in the heavens which most nearly corresponds to the position of the Milky Way (q. v.).

Galactoden'dron (Gr. 'milk-tree'), the generic name of the Cow-Tree (q. v.) of S. America.

Galactom'eter, or **Lactom'eter** (Gr. 'milk-measurer'), a form of apparatus for approximately testing the richness of milk by observing the amount of cream which rises from a given quantity. The apparatus is simply a graduated test-tube. The specific-gravity G. which is sometimes used is very delusive, seeing that milk deprived of cream is of higher gravity than pure new milk.

Galacz', the great river-port of Rumania, in Moldavia, between the left bank of the Danube and the Karamon or Bratych Lake, 15 miles above the confluence of the Danube and Pruth and N.E. of Bukarest by railway. It is one of the chief harbours on the Danube, has regular steam communication with Vienna, Constantinople, and Odessa, and is a free port for goods that are to be consumed in the town. The new portion of the town is built on an elevation, and includes most of the public buildings. G. has a good quarantine-hospital, large magazines and stores, extensive quays, &c. The trading people are chiefly Greeks, to whom belongs over half the home shipping. The Danube is frozen usually from the 16th December to the beginning of February. In 1874 there cleared the port 367 steamships of 218,603 tons, and 1072 sailing vessels of 146,922, 166 of the former being British, 466 of the latter belonging to Greece. The exports, chiefly wheat, barley, maize, flour, deal planks, oats, rye, colza, petroleum, and hides, amounted in value (1874) to £1,660,401; the imports, valued at £1,778,426, include cotton and woollen goods, building-stones, iron, coal, caviare, watches, jewellery, coffee, sugar, tea, tobacco, &c. G. is a station on the railway which, after traversing Moldavia, enters Austrian Galicia, and is merged in the systems of Central Europe. By a law (1874) of the Rumanian Government, G. will cease to be a free port on the 1st of January 1878. Pop. 80,000.

Gala'go, a genus of *Lemuridæ* or Lemurs (q. v.) having large naked ears and large eyes. The tarsus is elongated, and the tail long and thickly furred. The little G. (*G. minor*), and the Moholi G. (*G. Moholi*), are familiar species, inhabiting Madagascar and the adjoining African coast. The former, known as the 'Madagascar rat,' has a light-brown fur, and attains a length of about a foot; the latter is of grey colour, marked with darker tints, and attains a length of 16 inches. These animals are nocturnal in habits, and feed on insects, fruits, and small birds.

Galan'gal, or **Galan'gale**, the name applied to species of *Alpinia* belonging to the Ginger order. They are very aromatic, and are sometimes used in the East as ginger. From the rhizome of *A. Galanga*, a native of the Eastern Archipelago, an arrowroot is prepared. *A. alba* yields the fruits known as China cardamoms.

Galan'thus, the generic name of the Snowdrop (q. v.).

Galapa'gos (Span. *galapago*, 'a tortoise'), a group of six large and seven small islands in the Pacific, 200 miles off the Peruvian coast, near the equator, and in long. 89–92° W. They are volcanic in origin, and are almost solely tenanted by turtles and aquatic birds. The largest, Albemarle (60 miles long, 15 broad), reaches a height of 4000 feet.

Galashiels' ('the shielings or huts on the Gala'), a manufacturing town of Scotland, partly in Roxburgh, partly in Selkirk, on the Gala Water, just above its confluence with the Tweed, 4 miles N. of Melrose, and 33½ S. of Edinburgh. It is a railway junction, and the chief seat of the Scotch tweed manufacture, having (1876) 20 woollen factories, with 100 'sets' of carding-engines, using 220,000 stones of wool, and producing goods to the value of £750,000 yearly. There is here also a skinnery capable of preparing 35,000 skins weekly. The town, which is irregularly built in the confined valley of the Gala, was made a burgh of barony in 1630, and with Hawick and Selkirk sends one member to Parliament. Pop. (1871) 9678. Power was granted to extend the burgh and introduce a water supply by Act of 1875.

Gal'ata, a suburb of Constantinople, on the opposite side of the Golden Horn from the city proper, with which it is connected by two bridges. It is the business quarter, and is populous and filthy.

Gala'tia, or **Gallogræ'cia**, the ancient name of a beautiful and fertile country in the centre of Asia Minor. It was so called from the Gauls who migrated thither in the 3d c. B.C. These Gauls formed part of the immense hordes which under Brennus invaded Greece, and afterwards carried their arms across the Hellespont. In 239 B.C. they received a check from Attalus, King of Pergamus, and in 230 B.C. were constrained to settle down in a part of Phrygia, thenceforward called G. They adopted Greek customs, but for centuries retained their own language. They had a federal government, and were under their own chiefs till 36 B.C., when Amyntas, one of the tributary Asiatic kings set up by M. Antony in 39 B.C., received G., in the possession of which he was confirmed by Augustus, 31 B.C. G. became a Roman province in 25 B.C. Its chief towns were Pessinus, the seat of the worship of Cybele; Ancyra, the capital of the province under the Romans; and Gordium, where Alexander cut the Gordian Knot (q. v.).

Gala'tians, Epistle to the, was written by St. Paul not long after his journey through Galatia and Phrygia mentioned in Acts xviii. 23. This was his third missionary journey and his second visit to Galatia (about 55 A.D.). The word *strengthening*, or confirming, implies that the inhabitants had already been converted. The Galatian churches must therefore have been founded at a previous visit—that is, on the apostle's second missionary journey (Acts xvi.), or about 52. The question is how long after 55 the date is to be placed. Owing to the similarity between the epistle and those to the Corinthians and the Romans, the most likely position for it is considered to be after the former and before the latter; in other words, it was most probably written towards the close of his two to three years' sojourn at Ephesus (Acts xix. 55–57), or soon after he went to Corinth (57–58). The object of the epistle was to counteract the influence and refute the statements of certain Judaising teachers who had come after the apostle in Galatia, and who were seeking to undermine his teaching by contemning his apostolic authority (i. ii.), and by teaching directly that circumcision was necessary (iii.–v. 12). See Davidson's *Introd. to the New Test.* (new ed. 1868); Lightfoot's *Ep. to the G.* (2d ed. 1866).

Galati'na, a town in the S. of Italy, province of Lecce, 12 miles N.W. of Otranto. It has several fine churches, among others that of Santa Caterina, founded by a prince of Taranto, who is said also to have surrounded G. with walls in gratitude to its citizens for ransoming him from the Turks. Pop. 10,334.

Gala Water, a small Scottish river, which rises in the Moorfoot Hills, in Edinburghshire, flows through Selkirkshire, which it separates in part of its course from Roxburghshire, and after receiving the Heriot and other hill-streams, joins the Tweed near Abbotsford. It is 21 miles in length, and flows through romantic scenery famous in Scottish ballads. The G. is well known from one of Burns's songs.

Gal'axy, The (Gr. *gala*, *galaktos*, 'milk'), the name sometimes given to the Milky Way (q. v.).

Gal'ba, Ser'vius Sulpi'cius, Roman emperor from June 68 to 15th January 69 A.D., was the son of C. Sulpicius G. and Mummia Achaica. He was born 24th December 3 B.C. As a young man he evinced great ability, and attained the curule offices before the usual age. He received the province of Aquitania in 20 A.D., was consul in 33, and conducted the administration of Gaul in 39, and of Africa in 45 and 46 with equity, moderation, and diligence. In 61 Nero gave him the province of Hispania Tarraconensis, where he remained eight years. In 68, instigated by Julius Vindex, who had risen with the Gallic legions, and hearing that Nero plotted his death, he resolved to place himself on the throne. Meanwhile Nero was murdered, and G. assumed the title of Cæsar. Once emperor, he became the creature of his favourites. This, added to the character he bore for niggardliness and avarice, caused disaffection among the legions in Germany, and he was assassinated one day as he was being carried through the Forum in a litter.

Gal'banum, a gum resin obtained from an umbelliferous plant, is imported from India and the Levant in masses of greenish-yellow or reddish translucent tears. Its medicinal properties are similar to those of assafœtida, but less powerful. G. is used, *internally*, as a stimulating expectorant in chronic affections of the bronchial mucous membranes; and, *externally*, as a plaster to promote resolution or suppuration of indolent swellings. The preparations are *emplastrum galbani*, and *pilula galbani*, now known as *pilula assafœtidæ composita*. It is not definitely known from what plant the gum is derived.

Gale, Sweet Gale, or **Bog Myrtle**, popular names applied to the British shrub *Myrica G.*, the badge of the Clan Campbell. It is found most abundant in Scotland in bogs and moory ground, from the coast-line to about 1400 feet. Its leaves diffuse a very agreeable odour; they are bitter in taste, and have sometimes been used as hops. In the Western Highlands the inhabitants scent their clothes with the foliage, and in some parts of Scotland beds are made of the twigs. The Candleberry Myrtle (q. v.) of N. America is an allied species.

Ga'len, Christoph Bernhard von, a German prelate and general, was born at Bispink in Westphalia, October 15, 1600. After completing his studies he entered the military service of Ferdinand of Köln, on whose death he laid aside arms, took holy orders, and in 1650 became Bishop of Münster. The inhabitants, discontented with the rigid discipline which he enforced, applied to Holland in 1657 for aid against him; but G. quelled the insurrection by force of arms, and in 1661 built a citadel to keep the town in submission. As one of the directors of the *Rhein-Bund*, he proceeded with his own troops as far as Hungary to fight against the Turk, and materially assisted in the victory of St. Gothard. Engaged for a brief time in 1665 as England's ally against Holland, he united with France in 1672 against the same country, but having suffered great loss in 1674 through the flooding of his camp during the siege of Coevorden, concluded a treaty promising to restore his conquests. In the succeeding year he aided Christian V. of Denmark and the Elector of Brandenburg against Karl XI. of Sweden, and added the duchy of Bremen to his possessions. In 1678 he became involved in a war with Friesland, but died 19th September in the same year.

Gale'na, or native sulphide of lead, crystallises in the cubic system, is generally lead-grey in colour, with a shining metallic lustre. When pure it is composed of 86·55 lead and 13·45 sulphur, but frequently contains sulphide of silver and sometimes sulphide of zinc. It occurs in veins in granites, limestones, sandstones, gneiss, &c., often associated with zinc, silver and copper ores, and generally with quartz, heavy spar, sometimes fluor spar, as gangue. It occurs abundantly in the N. of England, in Saxony, Bohemia, and United States, and is widely wrought as the chief source of lead. Considerable quantities of silver are obtained from *argentiferous G.*

Gale'na, a city, Illinois, U.S., on the Fevre river, 5 miles from the E. bank of the Mississippi and 180 miles W.N.W. of Chicago. It is picturesquely built on bold bluffs, some of the streets being in terraces connected by flights of steps. G. derives its name and existence from the extensive lead-sulphide mines in the vicinity. It has also a trade in pork-packing, lumber, furniture, and pottery, with breweries, foundries, and flour-mills. Pop. (1870) 7019.

Gale'nus, Clau'dius, commonly called **Ga'len**, a famous physician, born at Pergamus, 130 A.D. His father, Nicon, was an architect and geometrician. After studying medicine in his native city, G. travelled extensively, prosecuting his studies under distinguished teachers at Smyrna, Corinth, and Alexandria. In 158 A.D. he returned to Pergamus, where he was appointed physician to a school of gladiators. In 163–164 he visited Rome, where he resided four years. His friends offered to recommend him to the Emperor, but this honour he declined. He returned to Pergamus in 167 or 168 A.D., whence he was summoned by M. Aurelius and L. Verus to Aquileia, where they were preparing for war with the hostile tribes. He reached Aquileia in 169 A.D. just on the eve of a pestilence which caused the Emperors to set out for Rome. L. Verus died of apoplexy on the way, and G. followed M. Aurelius to the capital, where he remained several years. Of the rest of his life little is known. He is generally supposed to have died in Sicily in 200 or 201 A.D., but several authorities place his decease ten years later. G.'s personal character, learning, and accomplishments entitle him to rank with the noblest patterns of antiquity. His works, which embraced a vast variety of medical, philosophical, and miscellaneous subjects, are said to have numbered about 500. They have certainly exercised a greater influence on medical science both in the East and West than those of any other writer ancient or modern. Most of his writings that have survived are in the original Greek; a few, however, are known to us only through Latin and Arabic translations. The works extant under his name consist of 83 treatises undoubtedly genuine, 19 doubtful, 45 spurious, 19 fragments, 15 commentaries on the works of Hippocrates, and over 50 pieces, many of them undoubtedly spurious, lying still unpublished in different European libraries. G.'s works were first published in a Latin translation, Venice, 1490, and they have appeared more than twenty times in that dress. The Greek text has been published four times—at Venice (Aldine), 1525, Basel, 1538, Paris, 1679, Leipsic (Kühn's edition), 1821–33. The last two are accompanied by a Latin version. See Smith's *Dictionary of Greek and Roman Biography*, art. 'Galenus;' Ackermann's *Historia Literaria*, prefixed to Kühn's edition; Choulant, *Handbuch der Bücherkunde für die ältere Medicin;* and the Histories of Medicine by Haller, Leclerc, and Sprengel.

Galeopith'ecus. See FLYING LEMUR.

Gal'erites, a genus of fossil sea-urchins or *Echini* belonging to the class *Echinodermata* and to the family *Echinoconidæ*. *G. albogalerus* from the White Chalk is a familiar species, and illustrates the character of the genus and family, which consists in the possession of a central mouth having 'teeth,' the spines of the shell being small, and the apical disc having five genital plates. The members of this family are confined to Mesozoic rocks.

Gale'rius Valerius Maximianus (known as Maximian II.), Roman emperor from 305 to 311 A.D., was the son of a Dacian shepherd. In early life he followed the calling of his father, but afterwards entered the Roman army, in which he rose rapidly. In 292 A.D. Diocletian raised him along with Constantius Chlorus to the dignity of a Cæsar, gave him his daughter in marriage, and assigned him the government of Illyria and Thrace. In 305 A.D., on the abdication of Diocletian and Maximian I., he and his colleague became joint-emperors. On the death of Chlorus at York in 306 A.D., the ambition of G., who aimed at the sole power, was frustrated by the troops declaring in favour of Constantine. This disappointment was followed by the usurpation of Maxentius, before whom he retired with the loss of Italy and Africa, A.D. 307. G. died in 311 A.D. of the *morbus pedicularis*, which the Christians believed to be a punishment for his pitiless persecution of them.

Galia'ceæ, a natural order of plants of which the genus *Galium* is the type. Some authors regard it as a sub-order of *Rubiaceæ* (q. v.). The Bedstraw (q. v.), the Woodruff (q. v.), and the Goose-Grass (q. v.) belong to the order.

Galia'ni, Fernan'do, an Italian wit, scholar, and political economist, was born at Chieti, 2d December 1728. Bred for the Church, he gained notoriety by a clever squib in 1746, and deserved serious attention for a very original economical treatise, *Della Moneta*, published anonymously in 1750. G. soon obtained a place in the Neapolitan Exchequer; and in 1760 he was sent as secretary of embassy to Paris, where he was a welcome and valued guest in the brilliant circle to which Grimm, Holbach, and Diderot belonged. Recalled in 1777, he held at home various influential posts in the service of the state till his death, 30th October 1787. His wit and originality he showed in his economical writings, so that even Voltaire pronounced his *Dialoghi* *sul Commercio del Grano* (French transl. 1770) to be as amusing as the best novels. G. wrote also *Della perfetta Conservatione del Grano* (1753), a treatise in 1779 on the eruption of Vesuvius, and in 1778 *Sur les Devoirs des Princes Neutres.* He maintained an extensive epistolary intercourse with European men of letters and statesmen, and at his death left a vast amount of interesting correspondence, part of which was published, 2 vols. Par. 1818–19, under the title *Correspondance inédite de G.*, 1765 *à* 1783, *Avec M. d'Epinay, le Baron d'Holbach, Grimm, Diderot,* with a biographical memoir by Guingené.

Gali'cia (Ger. *Galizien*), Latinised from the Polish *Halicz*, or *Galicz* (q. v.), the name of a crown-land in the N.E. of Austro-Hungary, and on the northern slope of the Carpathians, is bounded N. by Russia, W. by Silesia, S. by Hungary and Moldavia, and E. by Russia. Area, 30,308 sq. miles; pop. (1869) 5,444,689. It forms an extensive fertile plain in the N. and E., and is watered by the Dniester and its many tributaries in the E., and by the Vistula (which forms the border for 120 miles) and its branches the San, Donajec, and Bug in the W. and centre. Nearly a half of the surface is arable, rather more than a fourth wooded, and a tenth unproductive marsh and sandy waste. The chief crops are oats, barley, flax, tobacco, and beetroot, and there is much sheep and cattle breeding and horse-rearing. G. is rich in salt (Wieliczka and Bochnia), in coal and petroleum. The mass of the inhabitants are Slavs (4,544,000), Poles in the W. and Ruthenes in the E. There are 165,300 Germans and 575,918 Jews. The Poles are mostly Roman Catholic (two archiepiscopal sees, Lemberg and Cracow); the Ruthenes belong to the Greek Church. The trade, which is mainly transit, and is in the hands of the Jews and Armenians, has greatly increased since the construction of the railway from the Black Sea to Silesia. Lemberg is the capital, and Cracow the chief seat of industry. The old Ruthenes were already in the 9th c. subject to Poland. Their country belonged in the 11th c. to Hungary, but reverted to Poland in the 13th c., and on the partition of 1772 became Austrian. The present crown-land embraces, besides G., the kingdom of Lodomeria, the grand duchy of Cracow, and the duchies of Auschwitz and Zator. See Lipp's *Die Verkehrs- und Handelsverhältnisse G.'s* (1870).

Galicia (anc. *Gallæcia*, 'the land of the *Gallæci* or *Callæci*,' perhaps a Gallic people), a former province in the N.W. of Spain, bounded S. by Portugal, and N. and W. by the Atlantic. Area, 11,195 sq. miles; pop. (1870) 1,989,281. It is intersected from E. to W. by several irregular ranges of the well-wooded Cantabrian mountains, reaching the sea in lofty rugged promontaries, as in Capes Ortegal and Finisterre. Alternating with these are many fertile valleys, yielding corn, fruits, &c. The coast is much indented. The estuaries of the rivers, the chief of which is the Minho, with its affluents the Sil and Avia, afford several of the safest harbours in Europe (*e.g.*, Ferrol and Coruña). The chief town is Santiago. The 'Gallegos' are industrious and enterprising. In 1833 G. was divided into the provinces Coruña, Lugo, Orense, and Pontevedra.

Galicz', or properly **Halicz**, a town of Austrian Galicia, on the Dniester, 14 miles N. of Stanislawow by railway. It dates from the 12th c., and was the capital of the former principality of H. Pop. (1869) 2813.

Galigna'ni, Jean-Antoine and Guillaume, celebrated French publishers, were born in London, the former 13th October 1796, the latter 10th March 1798. Their father, who was a native of Brescia, and a skilled linguist, opened an English library at Paris in 1800, and established a *Monthly Repertory of English Literature, Arts, and Science* (1808), and the well-known *G.'s Messenger* in 1814. On his death (1821) the *Messenger* was greatly improved and enlarged by the brothers, who subsequently raised it to a highly-honoured position, adopting as its chief object the advocacy of a cordial political relationship between England and France. They each received the cross of the Legion of Honour from Louis Philippe, and were presented with a splendid silver épergne by the English Government (1866) through Lord Cowley in recognition of their efforts to promote the well-being of British subjects, and more especially for having erected the G. Hospital for distressed Englishmen, near Paris. The brothers also built the large hospital of Corbeil at their own expense. Jean-Antoine died December 1873.

Galilee (Heb. *Galil*, a 'circle' or 'circuit'), the name originally given to part of the land belonging to the tribe of Naphtali, but at the beginning of the Christian era used to denote the northernmost of the three provinces into which Palestine was divided. In this latter application it embraced an area about 50 miles long by 25 broad, corresponding nearly to the former tribal territories of Asher, Naphtali, Issachar, and Zebulon. 'Upper G.,' the northern portion, was hilly but well wooded, 'Lower G.' level and luxuriantly fertile. Late in being colonised by the Hebrews, great part of this territory remained 'G. of the nations' in Isaiah's time. The Book of the Maccabees represents G. as almost wholly peopled by heathens, and in Josephus's days the Jews of G. lived among Phœnician, Syrian, Arab, and Greek neighbours. This was especially the case in the larger towns of Tiberias, Tarichæa, and Sepphoris. The dialect of the Galileans sounded strange in the ears of a Judæan; and, doubtless owing to their intercourse with non-Jewish races, the Galileans were much less strict in their observance of the law than their southern kinsfolk. Hence 'Galilean' was a term of reproach at Jerusalem; yet after the destruction of the capital, G. became, and for four centuries continued to be, the home of Jewish learning.

The *Sea of G.*, also called the *Lake of Gennesaret* and the *Sea of Chinnereth*, bordering G. on the E., was about 12½ geographical miles long by 6 wide, and is 640 feet or more below sea-level.

Galile'i, Galile'o, the celebrated astronomer and experimental philosopher, was born at Pisa, on the 15th or 18th of February 1564. In 1581 he entered the university of his native town, with the view of studying medicine and philosophy, but these he soon forsook for the more congenial studies of mechanics and mathematics. His power of rare observation was shown, when he was scarcely nineteen years old, in connection with the swinging lamp in the cathedral of Pisa, which resulted in the discovery of the law of motion of a pendulum. Under Ostilio Ricci he made such rapid progress in mathematical studies, that in 1589 he was chosen Professor of Mathematics at Pisa. His opposition to the Aristotelian philosophy, however, so roused the hatred of the schoolmen, that he was forced, in 1592, to remove to Padua. Here his fame as a teacher attracted students from all countries; and his habit of lecturing in Italian necessitated many idiomatic modifications to suit the requirements of science. His attention had been early directed to the fall of bodies, and his demonstration at Pisa that all bodies fall from the same height in precisely the same time, was supplemented in 1602 by the discovery that the spaces described by a falling mass in successive equal intervals of time increase like the odd numbers 1, 3, 5, 7, &c., so that the whole space described from the beginning of the motion is proportional to the square of the time. The rumour of the invention in Holland of an optical instrument for observing distant objects led him, in 1610, to the construction of his telescope, which consists of a plano-convex object-glass and a plano-concave eyeglass. This he at once directed to the moon, whose surface he thus demonstrated to be uneven and rugged, and covered with mountains often far exceeding in height those on the earth. He proved its axial rotation, and discovered, but did not satisfactorily explain, its librations. With the same instrument he next examined and resolved certain nebulæ, discovered Jupiter's satellites in January 7, 1610, observed what he called the *three-bodied* character of Saturn—his telescope being too imperfect to sufficiently distinguish the ring—proved the sun's rotation, and the inclination of its axis to the ecliptic, by observing the motion of the spots, and finally demonstrated that Venus, Mercury, and Mars exhibited phases like the moon, thus dealing the death-blow to the Ptolemaic system of the universe. The history of these discoveries is narrated in his *Nuncius Sidereus* (1610). In 1611 he visited Rome, and was received with great honour; but his controversies with the Aristotelians—*i.e.*, the clergy—continued with greater virulence than ever, and resulted, in 1616, in a papal admonition through Cardinal Bellarmine not to teach publicly the Copernican system. This might have had the effect of turning him from the study of astronomy, if the appearance of three comets in 1618 had not strongly attracted his attention. In 1623 he published *Il Saggiatore*, an eloquent and masterly reply to the Jesuit Grassi, whose direct antagonism was aroused by a work written by Marco

Guiducci, G.'s pupil, but supposed by Grassi to have been written by G. himself. This could not but tend to embitter the mutual animosity, and more fuel was added to the fire by the publication in 1632 of G.'s great work, *Dialogo di Galileo G. sopra i due massimi Systemi del Mondo Tolemaico e Copernicano*, in which the Ptolemaic partisan came off decidedly the worse in the argument. This publication not only increased the enmity of the clergy, but roused the hatred of Pope Urban VIII., who had hitherto been G.'s personal friend, and accordingly in the spring of 1633 he was summoned to Rome. On the 22d of June he was brought before the Inquisitors, and forced, under fear of threatened torture, to abjure upon his knees his belief in the doctrine of Copernicus. The remainder of his life he passed chiefly at Arcetri, near Florence. In 1636 he became quite blind, just as he was completing his treatise on motion (published 1638), and deafness, sleeplessness, and other infirmities of old age severely tried him till his death on January 8, 1642. He wrote many works on subjects of natural philosophy for the use of his students, and collective editions have been published in 1718 at Florence (3 vols.), in 1744 at Padua (4 vols.), in 1808 at Milan (13 vols.), and in 1842-56 at Florence (16 vols.). His biography has been written by Viviani, his disciple, in the annals of the Florentine Academy, by Nelli (Lausanne, 1793), Brewster (Lond. 1841), Caspar (Stuttgart, 1854), Chasles (Par. 1862), and by Drinkwater in the *Library of Useful Knowledge*. See also Madden, *G. and the Inquisition* (Lond. 1863); Vosen, *G. und die Röm. Verurtheilung des Kopernikanischen Systems* (Frankf. 1865); and Gebler, *G. G. und die Römische Curie* (Stuttg. 1876). A Vatican MS. published by Signor Bert! (Rome, 1876) proves that G. escaped torture only through the interposition of an influential friend.

Gal'ingale, a name sometimes applied to *Cyperus longus*, a rare plant found in England, whose tuberous roots contain a bitter principle. Hence they have been used as a tonic. See CYPERUS.

Galipea, a genus of plants belonging to the Rue family, found in tropical America. They are chiefly shrubs. The bark of several species is highly aromatic and tonic. See ANGOSTURA BARK.

Gal'ium, the typical genus of the order *Galiaceæ* (q. v.), and the generic name for the Bedstraw (q. v.).

Galiz'yn (spelt also **Galitzin** and **Golizyn**) is the name of one of the most distinguished princely families of Russia. From the time that the Princes Dmitrij and Michael commanded Russian armies in 1514 down to the present day, members of this house have at all times been prominent in Russian diplomacy or in Russian campaigns.—**Wassilij**, 'the Great G.,' born 1633, was the favourite of Sophia, Peter the Great's sister, and strove, not without success, to import Western civilisation into Russia. For aspiring to marry Sophia, he was banished to a prison on the shores of the Arctic Ocean, where he died of poison. His cousin Dmitrij headed the party which wished to restrict the authority of the Czar, and died in the dungeons of Schüsselburg.—**Dmitrij Alexejevitch G.** (born 1735, died 1803), was the ambassador of Catherine II. at Paris and the Hague, a friend of Voltaire and the Encyclopédists. His wife, **Amalie, Princess G.**, born 21st March 1748, was the daughter of a Prussian general, Graf von Schmettau, who gathered round her at Münster a circle of brilliant authors, including Jacobi, Hamann, and Hemsterhuis, the last of whom addressed to her his *Lettres sur l'Athéisme* (1785). She was not less distinguished for accomplishments than for intense devoutness. Her own influence and that of the circle in which she moved was mainly influential in producing the extravagant religious sentimentality which for a time characterised large sections of cultured German society. She died 24th August 1806. A son of the Princess, **Dmitrij**, born in 1770, died as a Catholic missionary in N. America, 6th May 1840.

Gall. See BILE.

Gall, St., a canton in the N.E. of Switzerland, bounded N. by Thurgau and Lake Constance, E. by Vorarlberg and Lichtenstein, S. by the Grisons and Glarus, and W. by Zürich and Schwyz. Area, 747 square miles; pop. (1870) 191,015. It is very mountainous in the S., where the greatest heights are Schirbe (9000 feet) and Galanda (8800). In the N. the rich valleys and plateaux yield maize, corn, grapes, cherries, apples, &c. Partly included in G. are the Lakes Constance, Zürich, and Wallenstadt, while it is further watered by the Secz, Thur, and Tamina. It surrounds Appenell, is intersected by various lines of railway, and produces iron (at Gunzenberg), linens, muslins, cottons, embroidery, lace, glass, leather, &c. The inhabitants, who speak a Swabian dialect, comprise 38 per cent. of Protestants, 60·8 per cent. of Roman Catholics, and 1·92 Jews. The canton was formed out of the territory of the old abbey of St. Gall and various minor districts in 1805. It sends ten members to the National Council, and has a military contingent of 12,474 men and a debt of 9,000,000 francs. The local constitution (1861) is extremely democratic, the citizens exercising a veto on the transactions of the two elective chambers.

Gall, St., the capital of the Swiss canton of the same name, lies on the Steinach, 20 miles S.W. of Lake Constance and 45 E.N.E. of Zürich by railway. It is 2081 feet above the level of the sea; has important manufactures of cottons, linens, muslins, embroidery, &c.; receives the cotton goods of the W. of Switzerland; and does a large export trade with the various countries of Europe. The seat of a bishop, its chief buildings are the cathedral, rebuilt in 1756, with two towers 266 feet high; the famous abbey, founded 612, secularised 1805, still a Catholic seminary, and containing the great library of 1506 codices dating from the 3d c.; and the large cantonal school (1855), in which are a museum and a town library. The deep valley of the Seinach is spanned by a stone bridge and by a new iron railway-bridge. Pop. (1870) 16,616, of whom one-fourth are Roman Catholics.

THE ABBEY OF G. (Ger. *St. Gallen*) was raised by Pippin of Heristal in memory of St. Gallus, an Irish missionary who came with St. Columban to France, and about 612 founded a monastery here. It was largely rebuilt between 820 and 830 by the Abbot Gospertius, and during many years great wealth and architectural skill were devoted to its embellishment. In the 17th c. Mabillon found a plan of a monastery at St. G., which he conjectures to have been prepared by Eginhard for Gospertius; but from the many architectural changes which St. G. has undergone we cannot tell whether or not it was rebuilt according to this drawing, which, however, throws interesting light on the arrangement of a Benedictine monastery in the 9th c. From the 8th c. onwards St. G. was a celebrated school, and to the labours of its monks as copyists we are indebted for the preservation of several of the classics. It was specially famed for cultivating music. Though its abbots were for some time subject to the Bishop of Constance, they afterwards became independent suzerains of a large part of Switzerland, and at one time ranked as princes of the Empire. The abbey was secularised at the French Revolution, but a bishopric of St. G. was created in 1847.

Gall, Franz Joseph, the eminent phrenologist, was born at Tiefenbrunn, near Pforzheim, in Suabia, March 9, 1758. He studied medicine at Vienna, practised as a physician, and was led to make a close examination of the structure and functions of the brain. After a series of observations conducted in lunatic asylums, prisons, courts of justice, &c., he first gave to the public his celebrated theory of mind and brain (see PHRENOLOGY) in a series of lectures at Vienna in 1796. Considerable opposition arose. G.'s views were declared to be subversive of religion and morality, and in 1802 he was prohibited from re-delivering them by the Austrian Government. Two years before, G. had made a valuable disciple in Spurzheim, who was a better anatomist and psychologist, and a more popular expositor of science than himself. M. Villers, the translator of Kant, wrote a letter to Cuvier on G.'s theory, and phrenology soon had many disciples. During a term of partnership which lasted till 1813, when they quarrelled, G. and Spurzheim made a lecturing tour in Germany, Switzerland, and Sweden, and in 1809 presented to the Institute of France, in answer to an unfavourable report by Cuvier and others, *Recherches sur le Système Nerveux en général, et sur celui du Cerveau en particulier*. This led the way to their famous work, the first edition of which appeared at Paris in 1810 under the title of *Anatomie et Physiologie du Système Nerveux*. After the quarrel with Spurzheim, who went to England, G. settled in Paris as physician, remodelled the work, and published the bulk of it as *Fonctions du Cerveau* (6 vols. Par. 1825). Fragmentary translations of this have appeared in various languages, including one in six volumes by D. Winslow Lewis, jun. (Boston, U.S. 1835). G. died at

Montrouge, near Paris, 22d August 1828; and the facts disclosed at the post-mortem examination of his body, that his skull was twice the usual thickness, and that there was a tumour in the cerebellum, caused considerable remark. Whatever may be the fate of G.'s theory, there can be no doubt about his conscientiousness as an investigator, or about his valuable discoveries in anatomy. See the works of Combe and Laycock, and for G.'s influence on philosophy, Mr. G. H. Lewes's *History of Philosophy* (3d ed. vol. ii. pp. 394-435).

Galland, Antoine, a French Orientalist, was born at Rollot in Picardy, in 1646. He travelled in the East, first in the suite of the French ambassador, and afterwards independently; was made Arabic professor in the Collége de France in 1709, and died 17th February 1715. He was a voluminous writer on numismatics, but his claim to be remembered rests on his *Mille et Une Nuits, Contes Arabes* (12 vols. Par. 1704-14), the first translation of the *Arabian Nights' Entertainments* (q. v.) into any European tongue.

Gall'a Ox, or **San'ga**, a species or variety of ox found in Abyssinia, and distinguished by the size of the horns, which form a lyre-shaped figure by their curve. The shoulder is humped, and the horns sometimes attain a length of nearly four feet.

Gallara'te, an old walled town in the province of Milan, N. Italy, 24 miles N.W. of Milan by railway. It lies at the S.E. base of the Somma Hills, and on the margin of a vast plain reaching to Milan, and yielding maize, mulberries, and vines. G. has large steam cotton-mills. Pop. 5200.

Gall'as (*i.e.*, 'invaders'), or **Oroma** (*orma*, 'men'), a large native race of E. Africa, chiefly occupying the romantic highlands in the S. and E. of Abyssinia and a tract of country S. of the river Jub. They appeared first in the 16th c. as invaders, pressing their conquests from the interior in the direction of the Red Sea, and are supposed to be only partially of negro origin, being active, intelligent, and warlike. Their colour is brown, and they have frizzled hair. Many of the G. pursue pastoral occupations in the deep valleys of Godsham and Amhara; others live by hunting and slave-trading. The majority are heathens; while there is a sprinkling of Mohammedans, and a few have accepted Coptic Christianity. See Beke *On the Origin of the G.* (Lond. 1848); Dr. James Christie, *Cholera Epidemics in E. Africa* (1876).

Gall'atin, Albert, L.L.D., an American statesman, was born of good family in Geneva, Switzerland, January 29, 1761. Inspired with enthusiasm for the American cause, he emigrated to the New World in 1780. Entering the army, he was for a while in command at Fort Passamaquoddy. In 1783 he became Professor of French in Harvard College, but in 1786 settled in Pennsylvania. In 1790 he was elected to the State Legislature, and entered Congress in 1795. He soon became a leader of the Republican party of that period, was the author of many brilliant financial measures, and also signalised himself as an ardent advocate of free trade. In 1801 President Jefferson made him Secretary of the Treasury, a position which he held for twelve years. He was opposed to the war with England in 1812, and he assisted in negotiating the treaty of peace at Ghent in 1814. G. was minister at the court of France (1815–23), and envoy extraordinary to Great Britain in 1826. Returning to the United States in 1827, he withdrew from political life and settled at New York. His later years were devoted to history and ethnology, and he published many papers on these subjects, and on currency, banks, and trade. He died at Astoria, Long Island, August 12, 1849. G. was a brilliant and versatile genius, and his honourable career reflected a lustre at once on his native state and on the land of his adoption.

Gall-Bladder. This is a receptacle or reservoir for the bile placed on the under surface of the right lobe of the liver. It is a pear-shaped organ, the broad end of which projects beyond the anterior border of the liver, while the narrow end terminates in a duct, called the cystic duct, which joining with the duct coming from the liver forms the common bile duct. The capacity of the G.-B. is about ten fluid drachms. It is covered by a layer of the peritoneum, or lining of the abdominal cavity, and its wall consists of a strong fibrous coat composed of connective tissue and involuntary muscular fibre, which is lined by a mucous coat. The function of the G.-B. appears to be for the purpose of storing up the bile, and of mixing it with mucous; but it would seem not to be an essential organ, as it is absent in many animals, such as the horse. See LIVER.

Galle'go, an affluent of the Ebro, rises in the Pyrenees, near the Pic du Midi d'Osan, receives the Guarga from the E., and after a course of ninety miles joins the Ebro near Zaragoza.

Gall'eon (Span. *galeon*, 'a great galley'), the name of a class of large ships formerly used by the Spaniards in war and commerce. They were tall clumsy vessels, occasionally with four gun-decks. Their towering poops were encrusted with gilding, and their bulwarks were about four feet thick. They were employed to convey treasure from S. America to Spain.

Galleon.

Gall'ery (Fr. *galerie*), in architecture, a long narrow room used as a passage, or for containing paintings. The name is also applied to a raised floor commonly found in old English halls, and often known as a loft. Raised wooden galleries are frequently seen in churches, and are named *rood-lofts* from having carried a large cross or *rood*. A G., *in fortification*, is a covered passage through earthwork or masonry, sometimes loopholed for firing. A G., *in mining*, is a passage from one part of the mine to another.

Gall'ey (Old Fr. *galie*, Prov. *galea*, Old Span. *galea*, Low Lat. *galea*; *cf.* Lat. *galea*, 'a helmet,' dim. *galeola*, 'a hollow vessel'), a long, low, one-decked vessel, propelled by sails or oars, and still used in the Mediterranean. The G. was the sole form of war-vessel among the ancients. (See TRIREME and NAVY.) During the middle ages galleys were the commonest class of vessels in the Mediterranean, and were only disused in naval war at the end of the 17th c. They were generally rowed by slaves chained to the oars, and it was long customary to sentence criminals in France, Spain, and other Mediterranean countries to row in them—a punishment which came into disuse in France after the reign of Louis XIV. G. is likewise applied to the general cooking-place aboard ship, and to a light swift boat belonging to a man-of-war.

Galley, or *Lymphad*, in heraldry, an ancient one-masted ship, with oars, flying colours, and furled sails. It is the emblem of the Lord of Lorne.

Galley-Slave. See BAGNES.

Gall-Fly (*Cynips*), a genus of Hymenopterous insects belonging to the family *Cynipidæ*, in which the antennæ are straight and the ovipositor internal. The abdomen in *Cynips* is egg-shaped, and the antennæ of the male are fifteen-jointed, those of the female possessing a joint less. The wings are large. *C. rosæ* is the *Bedeguar* of the rose, and *C. insana* forms the 'Dead Sea apples.' *C. quercus-folii* is the G.-F. of the oak-leaf, and *C. gallæ-tinctoriæ* produces the 'galls' which are so largely used in commerce in the manufacture of ink. The insects puncture the leaves and bark of trees with their ovipositors in order to deposit their eggs; the puncture of the vegetable substance is probably accompanied by the injection of some irritating fluid which has the effect of exciting an abnormal growth in the vegetable tissues; this growth finally appears as an excrescence known as a 'gall.' Within the gall the young larva undergoes development, ultimately eating its way out after attaining its mature state. The oak is frequently attacked. The best galls are gathered before the insect makes its escape, and the astringent juice is thus preserved. See GALLS.

Gall-Fly.

Gall'iard (Fr. *gaillard*, from *gai*), a sprightly dance-tune, popular 300 years ago, perhaps of Italian origin, and preceding the *minuet*, which it resembles. Many specimens of the G. survive. Scott mentions it in his ballad of *Lochinvar*.

Gallia'te, a town in the province of Novaro, N. Italy, 4 miles E.N.E. of Novaro by railway. It has an old castle, silk and cotton mills, &c. Pop. 6700.

Gall'ic Acid is a crystalline substance contained in small quantities in gall-nuts, in the seeds of the mango, in the leaves of the arbutus, in sumach, &c. It is obtained either by allowing an aqueous solution of Tannin (q. v.) (or powdered gall-nuts moistened with water) to remain for some weeks exposed to the air, or by boiling a solution of tannin with dilute sulphuric acid. The chemical change is the same in both these processes, viz., that the tannin absorbs water and splits into G. A. and grape-sugar—

$$\underbrace{C_{27}H_{22}O_{17}}_{\text{Tannin.}} + \underbrace{4H_2O}_{\text{Water.}} = \underbrace{3(C_7H_6O_5)}_{\text{Gallic acid.}} + \underbrace{C_6H_{12}O_6}_{\text{Grape-sugar.}}$$

The crude G. A. thus obtained is purified by crystallisation from boiling water. G. A. crystallises from a hot aqueous solution in white needles, which have the composition expressed by the formula $C_7H_6O_5H_2O$. When these are heated to 100° C., they lose the molecule of water of crystallisation and become $C_7H_6O_5$. At 200° C. G. A. melts and then decomposes into carbonic acid gas and a new substance, the pyrogallic acid or pyrogallol—

$$\underbrace{C_7H_6O_5}_{\text{Gallic acid.}} = \underbrace{CO_2}_{\text{Carbonic acid.}} + \underbrace{C_6H_6O_3}_{\text{Pyrogallic acid.}}$$

G. A. is only slightly soluble in cold water, though readily soluble in boiling water. It is also easily dissolved by alcohol and ether. Its aqueous solution reduces gold and silver from their salts, and gives with perchloride of iron a bluish-black precipitate. When G. A. is cautiously heated with concentrated sulphuric acid to a temperature of 140° C., and the solution thus obtained is poured into water, a new acid separates, called rufigallic acid, which differs from crystallised G. A. in containing no water of crystallisation. When rufigallic acid is heated to 120° C. it loses a molecule of water, and then has the composition represented by the formula $C_7H_4O_4$; at a higher temperature the acid sublimes in red crystals. Rufigallic acid dyes cloth of a fine red colour if it be mordanted with alumina. Another acid called ellagic acid separates occasionally as a yellow powder from an aqueous extract of gall-nuts which has long been exposed to the air. This acid can also be prepared by oxidising G. A. by means of arsenic acid, and is interesting as forming certain intestinal calculi called *bezoars*, which occur in the antelopes of Central Asia.

Gall'ican Church is the Roman Catholic Church in France, which has always maintained a peculiar position in relation to the Papal supremacy. The foundation of the rights which the French clergy claimed from the earliest times was an exemption in particular cases from that general control in ecclesiastical matters which was assumed by the Roman see. During the vacancy of the Papal chair after the death of Clement IV., Louis IX. of France published (1268-69) an edict against the encroachments of the popes, who had lately claimed the right of electing prelates and taxing benefices. This edict or Pragmatic Sanction (q. v.) consisted of six articles, the sixth of which preserves all privileges and immunities formerly granted, showing that there had been former edicts of a similar kind, and that the liberties then guaranteed had before been granted to the Church, but through the usurpations of the popes had in great measure been lost.

After this the anti-Papal spirit grew still stronger, fostered by the desire of the bishops to recover their authority, which had long been overridden by the popes; by the intolerable extortions and disgraceful conduct of the popes, whose authority was further greatly weakened by their dependence on the French kings during the seventy years' residence at Avignon; and by the influence of the University of Paris, at which an independent and liberal spirit was developed. At the Council of Constance, assembled 1414 to extinguish the schism between the rival popes, the principle was established which has since been regarded as the leading dogma of Gallicanism, namely, that the Pope is subject to a general council. In 1438 the Council of Basel passed several canons restricting the power of the popes. The Pope, Eugenius IV., transferred the council to Florence and rejected the canons, but the anti-Papal party continued to sit at Basel, and sought the protection of Charles VII. of France. The latter summoned the estates of his kingdom to a council at Bourges (1438), which has been called the Pragmatic Council, and which embodied in a pragmatic sanction the enactments of the councils of Constance and Basel, limiting the Papal authority in the exercise of patronage in the G. C.

This edict was the great bulwark of the liberties of the G. C., and remained in force (although Louis XI. attempted to repeal it) till 1516, when Pope Leo X. persuaded François I. to substitute for it the Concordat by which annates and some other privileges were restored to the popes, and the nomination to bishoprics and higher benefices secured to the kings. In 1682 an assembly of the clergy, called by Louis XIV. to settle a dispute between himself and certain of the bishops who opposed his claim of *régale*, or right to administer the revenues and present to vacant sees, published four propositions commonly called the 'Gallican Liberties,' and founded on the Pragmatic Sanction of 1438 :—1. Neither St. Peter nor his successors received from God any power to interfere, directly or indirectly, in what concerns the temporal interests of states; kings cannot be deposed by them, nor their subjects freed from allegiance. 2. In the popes the full power over spiritual things is in such sort vested as that the Decrees of Constance concerning the authority of general councils are at the same time in full force and remain unshaken. 3. The exercise of the apostolic power is to be regulated by the canons of general councils, and the usages of the G. C. are to remain unshaken. 4. Although in questions of faith the chief place belongs to the Pope, and his decrees extend to all particular churches, yet his judgment is not unalterable, unless it have the concurrence of the Church universal.

After the Revolution the G. C. was established by a Concordat (carried into effect 1802) between Pope Pius VII. and Bonaparte, according to which bishops were to be presented to the sees by the First Consul, and the presentation confirmed by the Pope. At the same time it was enacted by the Government that no bull or missive should be received without the authority of the Government. In 1810 a decree was issued by Bonaparte confirming the Declaration of 1682. On the restoration of the Bourbons the Concordat of 1802 was annulled, and that of 1516 re-established. Since the revolution of 1848 Ultramontane principles have made rapid progress, and the once boasted liberties of the G. C. are now contended for only by a small minority in the Church. See *Report of Com. of House of Commons on the Regulations of Roman Catholic Subjects in Foreign Countries* (1816); Burnet's *Hist. of the Reformation of the Church of England* (1681-1714); *The Power of the Popes*, translated from the French (Lond. 1838); and Blunt's *Dict. of Doct. and Hist. Theology* (1872).

Gallie'nus, Publius Licinius Valerianus Egnatius, son of the Emperor Valerian, was born 218 A.D. He was associated on the throne with his father from 253 to 260 A.D., after which he became sole emperor. G. was not wanting in bravery and warlike qualities, but his victories while co-regent appear to have been a series of pompous frauds. On becoming sole ruler, he devoted himself to the most shocking debauchery. During his reign a number of usurpers, known as the *Thirty Tyrants*, scorning the feeble emperor, aspired to the purple, while foreign invaders on every side threatened the empire, the safety of which was maintained only by the energetic conduct of Claudius, Aurelian, and Probus. G., fairly roused by the gathering dangers, redeemed for a brief season his contemptible character by a singular display of valour and military skill, defeated his opponent Aureolus, and shut him up in Milan; but while pressing the siege of that city, he was murdered by his own soldiers in March 268 A. D.

Gallina'ceous Birds, or **Raso'res** (Lat. 'scrapers'), the name given to an order of *Aves* or Birds (q. v.), represented by the fowls, pheasants, partridges, pigeons, and their allies. The group is distinguished by the toes being of very strong construction and provided with blunt nails adapted for *scraping* in the ground for food. The upper mandible is vaulted and convex, and the nostrils open at its base in a membranous space, and are covered with a cartilaginous scale. The legs are stout, and feathered to the tibial and tarso-metatarsal joint. Four toes exist, the hinder one being short, and placed at a higher level than the front toes, except in the pigeons, in which it is placed on the same level as the front ones. The food consists of seeds and grain, and a powerful *gizzard* is developed for the trituration of the food. The nests are built chiefly on the ground, and never evince any great constructive powers. The G. B. are mostly *polygamous*—*i.e.*, one male mates with several females; and the former are generally provided with brilliantly-coloured *wattles* and other appendages. The wings, save in the pigeons, are never very powerful. The G. B. are divided into the *Gallinacei*, represented by the fowls, partridges, &c., and the *Columbacei*, represented by the pigeons. The latter have sometimes been elevated to the rank of a distinct order. Their powers of flight are better developed than those of the *Gallinacei*, but they are less adapted for running and for a ground life than the latter. The pigeons are also *monogamous*, and pair usually for life. The young of the *Gallinacei* are *autophagous*, that is, can run about immediately after being hatched, whilst those of the pigeons are *heterophagous*, and are dependent for a longer or shorter period upon the care of the parent.

Gall'inule (*Gallinula*), a genus of Grallatorial or Wading birds, belonging to the family *Rallidæ* or Rails, and to the sub-family *Gallinulinæ*. The typical genus *Gallinula* is represented by the Waterhen (*G. chloropus*), or moorhen, whilst the other genera are *Fulica*, including the coots, and *Porphyrio*, represented by *P. veterum*, or the Hyacinthine G. of Africa, Asia, and some parts of Europe. The bill in the G. is curved at the tip; the nostrils are placed in a groove near the middle of the bill; and the second to the fourth quills are the longest of the wings. The waterhen inhabits moors and marshes. It attains a length of about 12 inches, and is coloured dark olive above, the head, neck, and under parts being of a dark grey hue. The bill is green at the tip and red at the base, and the legs and toes are green. The bird dives and swims with great ease, and is much sought after for the delicacy of its flesh.

Gallinule.

Gall'iot (Fr. *galiote*, 'a half-galley'), a small two-masted Dutch vessel, flat-bottomed, bluff-bowed, and carrying a large boom mainsail. A G. has its shorter mast aft.

Gallip'oli (Gr. *Callipolis*, 'the fair city'), a fortified seaport of S. Italy, province of Lecce, on a rocky island in the Gulf of Taranto, connected with the mainland by a bridge of twelve arches. It is a bishop's see, has a castle and a cathedral (1629), and is celebrated for its olive-oil. The oil is stored for a long time in vast cisterns cut in the solid limestone, whence it is drawn for exportation in a thoroughly clarified state. G. is supplied with water by an old aqueduct, which ends in a splendid fountain bearing many fine bas-reliefs and Latin inscriptions. It is a chief station for the steam-navigation between Ancona, Messina, and Naples. The date-palm is often seen in the gardens of the beautiful villas in the vicinity. Pop. 9951. G. is the *Urbs Graia Callipolis* of the geographer Mela, and the *Anxa* of Pliny. In the middle ages it sustained many severe sieges. In 1429 it was surprised by Turkish corsairs, and many of the inhabitants were carried off.

Gallipoli (Gr. *Callipolis*, Turk. *Gelibolu*), a seaport of European Turkey, vilayet of Adrianople, on the peninsula of G., 90 miles S. of Adrianople. It is the most important town on the Dardanelles, the chief station of the Turkish fleet, is the see of a Greek bishop, and has two good harbours, an old castle, extensive bazaars, many mosques, fountains, &c. Its trade, which is in a flourishing state, is chiefly in corn, barley, cotton, oil, and wine. A magazine and cellars built by Justinian are among the antiquities in the vicinity. In 1872 the exports amounted to £128,290, the imports to £97,766. Pop. 20,000, composed of Turks, Greeks, Armenians, and Jews. G. was taken by the Turks in 1357, and formed their first European conquest.—**Peninsula of G.**, separating the Ægean Sea from the Gulf of Saros, is 55 miles long, and from 4 to 13 broad.

Gall'ipot (Dutch *gleye*, 'potter's clay,' and 'pot'), a small painted and glazed earthenware pot or jar used by apothecaries for holding medicine.

Gall'on, the standard measure of capacity for liquids and dry goods used throughout the British Islands. According to the Act of Parliament of 1826, the G. contains 10 lbs. avoirdupois of distilled water, weighed in air at a temperature of 62° F., and a barometric pressure of 30 inches. It is thus equivalent to 277·274 cubic inches. In 1825, just before the passing of the Act, there were three different gallons in common use—the dry measure, of 269; the wine measure, of 231; and the beer measure, of 282 cubic inches.

Galloon' (Fr. *galon*), a close kind of lace made of silk, or of gold or silver, in narrow width suitable for binding, trimming, &c.

Gallotann'ic Acid. See TANNIN.

Gall'oway, a district in the S.W. of Scotland, now including the counties of Wigton and Kirkcudbright. There is considerable uncertainty as to the history of G., and varying extent of the territory to which the name has been given. G. seems to have been at first inhabited by the body of Picts whom Bede styles the Niduari, probably from the frontier river Nid (Nith), and who remained half independent until the 12th c. Mr. Skene contends that they were Gaelic, as they did not merge with the Cymric people around them, and long clung to a distinct dialect. The district formed for several centuries a province of the Anglian kingdom of Northumbria, and received the name *Galwydel* in Welsh, *Gallaidel* in Irish (whence the modern G.), most probably from its people being thus ruled by foreigners, from *gall*, 'a stranger,' and *Gaidhel*, the name of the Gaelic race. At one time G. seems to have been applied to the land between the Firths of Clyde and Solway. G. appears to have been practically severed from Northumbria in the 9th c., and was known as the land of the Picts till the 12th c. It was in a large degree independent of the Scottish crown until the 13th c. See Skene's *Celtic Scotland* (Edinb. 1876).

Galloway, Mull of, the most southern point of Scotland, in Wigtonshire. It forms the extremity of the Rinns of Galloway, and is a precipitous headland, supporting a lighthouse 325 feet above the sea, with a light visible for 24 miles.

Gall'ows-Bitts, a nautical term for a frame in which spare spars are held.

Galls are of great variety of form and composition, according to the plants on which they are formed and the insects producing them. Several varieties possess great economic value on account of the large proportion of tannic and gallic acid which they contain, which in some amounts to from 60 to 70 per cent. of the whole weight. These G. are very largely employed in dyeing and tanning, and for the manufacture of black ink; in addition to which, the principles they contain are valuable as astringents in medicine. The most important are known as Aleppo G. They are divided into blue, black, or grey G., which embrace such as are of a dark greenish-grey colour, and are heavy and unpunctured; and white or false G., which are light, and punctured with a channel through which the insect has escaped. The unperforated or blue G. are much more valuable than those punctured by the gall-insect. Recognised commercial varieties of these are obtained from Greece, Italy, France, and Algeria. Knoppern, or Hungarian G., constitute a peculiar variety, formed on the acorn-cups of the common oak. They are obtained in Hungary, Rumania, Styria, Piedmont, and the neighbouring countries. The Chio turpentine-tree (*Pistacia terebinthus*) bears a gall which is used for tanning and dyeing, a variety of morocco leather being tanned with it. In the East several species of *Rhus* produce G. which yield large proportions of tannic and gallic acid. A very peculiar horn-like gall is obtained in India from *Rhus kakrasinghee*; and in China hollow spherical G. are yielded by *Rhus semialata*, while a closely-allied species produces Japanese G. Tamarisk G., formed abundantly in Arabia on a species of *Tamarix*, form a sweet manna-like substance, which is regarded by the Bedouins as a great luxury; and in Australia a similar manna-gall is formed on the *Eucalyptus dumosa*.

Gall-Stone. See CALCULUS.

Galop, a quick dance-tune in double time.

Galt, a town in the province of Ontario, Dominion of Canada, on both banks of the Grand River, 14 miles S.W. of Guelph, on a branch of the Great Western Railway. It has good water-power, which is utilised by many flour and other mills. Pop. (1871) 3827, mostly Scotch.

Galt, John, a famous Scottish novelist, the son of a sea-captain, was born at Irvine, Ayrshire, May 2, 1779. After being a clerk in the Greenock customhouse, he went to London in 1804, with an epic on the battle of Largs, part of which appeared in the *Scots Magazine*. Failing in business, he began to study law, but his health being feeble, he was forced to travel for three years in S. Europe, where he was for a time a companion of Byron and Hobhouse. After his return G. worked on the staff of his father-in-law Dr. Tulloch's paper, the *Star*, and published *Letters from the Levant* and other works, but it was not until 1820 that his characteristic power was displayed in the *Ayrshire Legatees*, which appeared in *Blackwood*, and was cordially received. The *Annals of the Parish* (1821), his best work, established his fame, and was followed by *Sir Andrew Wylie*, *The Entail*, *The Gathering of the West*, *The Steamboat*, and the less successful historical romances of *Ringan Gilhaize*, *The Spaewife*, *Rothelan*, and *The Omen*. In 1826 G. went out to Canada as secretary to the Canada Company, but becoming at variance with the directors, returned to England in 1829 and lost his appointment. He again devoted himself to authorship, produced *Lawrie Todd*, a tale of a Scotch settler, which became very popular, *Southennan*, a romance of Queen Mary's times, and a *Life of Lord Byron*. In 1834 he came back to Scotland poverty-stricken and broken in health, and after suffering repeated shocks of paralysis, died at Greenock, April 11, 1839. G.'s poems, dramas, biographies, and essays are now deservedly forgotten, and his ambitious historical romances, though often vigorous and impressive, are wanting in animation and freshness. The modern tales, however, in which he depicts the quaint, sleepy life of Scottish provincial towns, are rich in homely humour, shrewd knowledge of character, and simple pathos, and while they have had many imitators, still possess a unique Doric flavour and a lasting popularity. See G.'s *Autobiography*, his *Literary Life and Miscellanies*, and *Memoirs* by Delta.—**Sir Alexander Tulloch G.**, son of the preceding, was born at Chelsea, September 6, 1817, and was from 1833-56 in the service of the American Land Company, becoming in 1844 manager of all their estates. In 1849 he entered the Canadian Parliament, and was finance minister 1858-62 and 1864-66. He was knighted in 1869, was one of the chief founders of the Canadian railway system, and is held to be the ablest financier in Canada.

Galva'ni, Lui'gi, an Italian physiologist, was born September 9, 1737, at Bologna, where he studied first theology, then anatomy and physiology, and became Professor of Anatomy in 1762. As a lecturer he was very popular, but his writings are few, the chief being two treatises on the urinary organs (*De Renibus atque Ureteribus Volatilium*) and on the organs of hearing of birds (*De Aure Volatilium*), and his *De Viribus Electricitatis in Motu Musculari Commentarius* (Modena, 1792). This last work treats of the results of his great discovery in 1780 of the convulsive motions of the limb of a frog in connection with an electric machine—a discovery which, in the hands of Volta (q. v.), led to the foundation of the science of current electricity. G. died at Bologna, December 4, 1798. A collection of his writings was published at Bologna in 1841.

Gal'vanised Iron is the name given to iron which has been covered by a thin coating of zinc to guard against the oxidising action of air and water. It is widely used for sheeting purposes, and is formed into telegraph wires and bolts for ships; but care must be taken that it is not placed where steam is of frequent occurrence, otherwise a rapid decomposition is the consequence. See ZINC.

Gal'vanism. See ELECTRICITY.

Gal'veston, the chief city of Texas, U.S., on G. Island, at the mouth of a bay of the same name. Its harbour, one of the best in the Gulf of Mexico, has at its entrance 12 feet of water at low tide. G. is a great centre of the cotton trade. In 1872 its exports amounted to 333,502 bales. It has also a trade in wool, hides, beeves, pecan-nuts, and beeswax. In 1874 the total exports were valued at $35,334,747. The city has street railways, and is lighted with gas. Railways connect it with the interior, and steam-ships ply between it and New Orleans and New York. G. is the see of a Roman Catholic bishop, has a Roman Catholic college, and a good medical school, two daily and four weekly newspapers. Pop. (1870) 13,818.—*G. Island*, 28 miles long, is only from 3 to 4 feet above the sea.

Gal'way, a county in the W. of Ireland, province of Connaught, is bounded E. by the Shannon and its tributary the Suck, N. by counties Mayo and Roscommon, W. by the Atlantic, and S. by county Clare and Lake Derg. Area, 2383 sq. miles; pop. (1871) 235,072. It is nearly divided into two portions by the beautiful Loughs Corrib (20 by 12 miles) and Mask, which extends into Mayo. The western portion, known as Connemara (Ir. Gael. *Conmaicne-mara*, 'the seaside tract of the children of Conmac,' a son of Fergus, King of Ulster), is a wild region of hill, glen, and morass, with a precipitous coast-line, containing many deep indentations, as Kilkieren, Birterbury, Mannin, Ballynakill, and Killary Bays. In the E. the surface is in part arable, and is watered by the Suck (a feeder of the Shannon) and its affluents. The Slieve-Baughta Mountains enter G. in the S., while in the N. of Connemara, known as 'Joyce's Country,' is the group of the celebrated Twelve Pins, some 2200 feet high. Oats and potatoes are extensively grown, and much attention is given to the rearing of a fine breed of cattle. In 1871, 230,902 acres were under tillage, 794,710 in pasture, 23,910 of plantation, and 426,600 waste, bog, mountain, &c. The lough and coast fisheries are of considerable value, while there are also manufactures of woollens, linens, friezes, &c. G. contains iron, copper, lead, marble, and limestone. It is traversed from E. to W. by the Irish Midland Railway. The chief towns are G. (the capital), Tuam, Loughrea, Athenry, and Ballinasloe. The county sends two members to Parliament. Among its many antiquities are seven round towers, various raths, cromlechs, &c.

G., BAY OF, the inlet separating the counties of G. and Clare, extends from E. to W., is 30 miles long, and has an average breadth of 10 miles. It is a splendid natural harbour, the Isles of Aran dividing its entrance into the N. and S. Sounds.

Galway, the capital of the county of the same name, Ireland, at the mouth and on both banks of the Corrib, and on the N. shore of G. Bay, 50 miles N.N.W. of Limerick and 130 W.S.W. of Dublin by railway. It is the chief town in the W. of Ireland, is the see of a bishop, and has a parish church of St. Nicholas (1320) in the Decorated English style, a Queen's College (opened 1849), Erasmus Smith's endowed collegiate school, many Roman Catholic churches, three monasteries, five nunneries, a handsome courthouse, barracks, &c. G. is a bonding port, with a floating-dock of five acres, capable of admitting vessels of 14 feet draught. The harbour light on Mutton Island is visible for 28 miles, and there are other two lights on the Arans. In 1875 there cleared the port 104 vessels, of 14,982 tons; entered 178, of 36,511 tons. The chief exports are fine marbles, corn, flour, fish, bacon, and kelp. G. has large breweries, distilleries, tanneries, foundries, flour and paper mills, &c. The extensive herring and salmon fisheries are the sole industries of the inhabitants of Claddagh (Ir. Gael. 'the muddy seashore'), a suburb forming an isolated community, where strangers are excluded, and Irish alone is spoken. The river is crossed by three bridges. Pop. (1871) of parliamentary borough, 19,843. G. returns two members to Parliament. It is doubtless an ancient place, but it first emerges clearly into history when it was seized by Richard de Burgo in 1232. In 1396 it obtained a grant of incorporation, and subsequently under Henry IV. a license to coin money. In the 16th c. a prosperous trade sprang up with Spain, which has left its trace in many old Spanish-like houses, with arms carved over their gateways. During the rebellion of 1641 the Earl of Clanricarde held G. against the Catholic insurgents, but was eventually obliged to yield to Captain Willoughby. The pestilence broke out among the terror-stricken thousands who had here sought refuge, and carried off some 3700. In 1652 G. surrendered, after a lengthened blockade, to Sir Charles Coote for the King. It was garrisoned by James II. (1690), and taken by William III.'s troops under General de Ginkell in 1691. The mails to America were despatched from G. from 1858 to 1861, and again from 1862 to 1864, in which latter year the steamer *Anglia* having struck on the Black Rocks, the line was abandoned.

Galyz'in. See GALIZYN.

Ga'ma, Dom Vasco da, discoverer of the sea route to India by the Cape of Good Hope, was born of an old family at Sines, in the Portuguese province of Alemtejo, in 1469, and was early distinguished as an enterprising sailor. The success of the expedition under Bartolommeo Diaz, who had fairly doubled the Cape (1487), encouraged King João II. to pursue the scheme of reaching India by this route. Early in the reign of João's successor Manoel, a small expedition of four ships under the command of G. sailed for India from Lisbon, 8th July 1497, and on the 20th November rounded the Cape. At Christmas they were off Natal, hence named; and thence by way of Mozambique, Mombassa in Zanguebar, and Melinda, where they secured the services of a Gujerati pilot, they reached Calicut on the Malabar coast, 20th May 1498. Through the hostility of the Moorish traders, who here, as on the African coast, recognised their hereditary enemies under the Portuguese flag, G. made no very favourable impression on the Zamori (*Samudri-Rajah*, 'the Prince of the Coast'), but satisfied with the attained results of his enterprise, sailed for home in August. He anchored in Lisbon harbour 14th July 1499, and was received with distinctions and well-merited rewards. A second expedition under G. as Admiral of the Seas of India, set out in 1502, and already in 1503 he was able to return with his thirteen ships all richly laden. G. now spent a term of years in peace at home. Meanwhile Portuguese affairs in India were far from prosperous, and in 1524 G. sailed once more for India, this time with the commission of viceroy. He had but fairly begun by his vigorous administration to re-establish order and restore the fallen Portuguese credit, when he became ill and died at Cochin, 24th December 1524. His remains were brought to Portugal, and there reinterred with all honour in 1538. G.'s character was marked not merely by the resoluteness and presence of mind necessary to every great explorer, but by a degree of good faith, uprightness, and piety unusual amongst the navigators of the 16th and 17th centuries. G.'s great achievement is the theme of the national epic of Portugal—the *Lusiad* of Camoens (q. v.). It appears that Castanheda, who even earlier than Barros wrote the history of G.'s discoveries, founded his account on the *Roteiro da Viagem que em Descolerimento da India selo Cabo de Boa Esperança fez Dom Vasco da Gama em* 1497, drawn up by Alvaro Velho, one of G.'s fellow-voyagers. The MS. of this invaluable document was discovered at Oporto by MM. Kopfe and Paiva, who published it in 1838; a French translation was made by Ferdinand Denis in 1855.

Gama Grass, a name applied to *Tripsacum dactyloides*, a grass of the Southern States of America, where it is also called buffalo grass. It is considered excellent forage, for which it is cultivated in America and Southern Europe, but it is too tender a plant for the climate of Britain.

Gama'liel (the Gr. form of the Heb. *gamliel*, 'gift,' or 'benefit of God'), the teacher of the Apostle Paul, is generally identified with the celebrated Jewish doctor, son of Rabbi Simeon, and grandson of Hillel, who was called the 'glory of the law,' who was the first to receive the title of Rabban, 'our master,' and with whose death, according to the Mishna, 'the reverence for the law ceased, and purity and abstinence died away.' He became president of the Sanhedrim, A.D. 30, and is said to have died eighteen years before the destruction of Jerusalem, or about 50. As far as the personal opinions of G. can be separated from the conclusions of the school of Hillel (q. v.), they show that he 'was endowed with great intellectual powers, a fondness for study and for definitely settling every point of difficulty, refined taste, and good judgment; that he was humane, anxious to ameliorate the condition of the helpless, a strict Pharisee, yet liberal-minded, and averse to persecute those who differ from him.' The liberality of his opinions and tastes is shown by his study of Greek literature, a taste which he seems to have communicated to his disciples (*cf.* Acts xvii. 28; 1 Cor. xv. 33; Titus i. 12); by the law he passed regarding the observance of the Sabbath, 'that all persons called to assist either at hostile invasions, or inundations, or fires, or at the falling down of houses, or even at childbirth, might walk 2000 paces in any direction;' by his humane laws that the heathen poor should have the same right as poor Jews to gather the gleanings after harvest, that Jews on meeting heathen should greet them 'Peace be with you,' and for the relief of wives and widows from the abuses to which they were exposed from unprincipled husbands and children; as also by his tolerance of the Christians (Acts v. 34-40).—**G.**, grandson of the former, who was born about 50, succeeded to the presidency about 80, and died about 116, was the teacher of Aquila, the Greek translator of the O. T., and of Onkelos, the Chaldee translator of the Pentateuch. It was he, and not the former, who sanctioned the famous prayer against all heretics, and to whom Onkelos raised a royal funeral pile. It was he, too, who put an end to the extravagant Jewish practice, so hard on the poor, of burying their dead in costly apparel, and introduced the practice, ever since followed, of burying in a simple white shroud. See Ginsburg in Kitto's *Bib. Cyclo.* (new ed. 1865), Frankel's *Hodegetica in Mischnam* (Leips. 1859).

Gamb (Fr. *jambe*, 'the leg'), in heraldry, the whole fore-leg of an animal.

Gam'ba. See VIOL DA GAMBA.

Gambett'a, Léon, a brilliant French statesman of Genoese descent, was born at Cahors, October 30, 1838. He entered at the Parisian bar in 1859, and soon became known as a fervid and trenchant orator, especially in political cases, and won great popularity from his advanced republican tenets. In 1869, on the prosecution of the *Emancipation* newspaper, he was enthusiastically received through the S. of France, and in the same year was returned to the Chamber for Paris and Marseille. In September 1870, after the fall of Napoleon III., he was made Minister of the Interior in the Government of the National Defence, and evinced conspicuous administrative energy. In October 1870 he crossed the Prussian lines round Paris in a balloon, and became head of the Delegate Government which sat at Tours. He was thenceforth for some months practically the ruler of all France unoccupied by the Germans, against whom he organised a fruitless resistance; but the Paris Government annulling his decree that former officials of the Empire should be stripped of the privileges of electors, he resigned his office and retired for a few months to Spain. He was afterwards returned to the Assembly, where he became leader of the extreme republicans. Of late (1875-76) his opinions seem to have modified, his sympathies with the Reds have cooled, and he has done much to strengthen French Liberalism by his political sagacity and moderation.

Gam'bia, a British settlement in W. Africa, consisting of Bathurst; Fort James; Fort George (M'Carthy's Island), 180 miles inland; a strip of land, 40 miles by 1, stretching along the N. bank of the river; and a triangular patch of 12 sq. miles on the S. bank, known as Cape St. Mary. Area, 21 sq. miles; pop. (1871) 14,190, of whom 80 are whites. It is a fertile country, and has a fair climate for W. Africa, the temperature ranging from 58° F. to 72° at Bathurst (where the Trades blow for some eight months); and at other parts never exceeding 96° in the shade. There is considerable commerce not only with Britain, but with France and the United States. G. imports much rice, and exports ground-nuts, wax, hides, some twisted gold rings, ivory, &c. Fort James is on an island near the mouth of the river, and Bathurst, the capital, is on St. Mary's Island, 7 miles from Cape St. Mary. G. is now subject to Sierra Leone.—G., the *river*, rises in the Tenda range, near the source of the Senegal, and flows N.W. and W. till it enters the Atlantic after a course of about 500 miles. Its mouth is 10 miles broad, and is free from bars and rollers. The G. is navigable for large vessels to Bathurst, and for vessels drawing 9 feet of water to Yabatenda, a distance inland of 300 miles.

Gam'bier, James, Lord, a British admiral, born in the Bahamas, October 13, 1756. He entered the navy when very young, became a post-captain in 1778, was engaged in the repulse of the French at Jersey in 1781, and was the first to break the French line with his ship the *Defence* in the action off Brest, June 1, 1793. He was made rear-admiral in 1795, vice-admiral in 1799, and Governor of Newfoundland in 1801. In 1807 he bombarded Copenhagen, and captured the Danish fleet of nineteen ships of the line, and many smaller vessels. He was then made a baron, and was offered, but declined, a pension. In 1808 he received command of the Channel Fleet, and in 1809 successfully attacked a French squadron off Aix, but a dispute which arose on this occasion with his subordinate, Lord Cochrane, led him to demand a court-martial, by which he was honourably acquitted. He was made Admiral of the Fleet on William IV.'s accession, and died at Iver, near Uxbridge, April 19, 1833.

Gam'bier Islands, a group of some ten coral islets in the S. Pacific, important as a station for good water, in lat. 23° 8′ S., long. 134° 55′ W. They are under a French protectorate.

Gam'bling. See GAMING, &c.

Gamboge', an acrid, purgative yellow gum-resin, the product of various species of the *Guttiferæ* or *Clusiaceæ* order. G. occurs in commerce in three forms:—(1) in *rolls*, (2) in *pipes*, and (3) in *cakes*, the two first being the purest. The best G. comes in the form of *pipes* from Siam, the produce of *Garcinia morella*. That which occurs in *cakes*, called Ceylon G., has been said to be derived from *Gambogia gutta*, but this is doubtful, as the tears of *G. gutta* are altogether distinct from true G. G., in combination with elaterium, bitartrate of potash, or jalap, is employed in the treatment of dropsy attended with torpidity of the bowels; in cases of obstinate constipation, and in the expulsion of tapeworm. As it occasions nausea and griping, it is best given in small doses in pill or emulsion, or dissolved in an alkaline solution, until it operates. Dose of the gum-resin:—One to five grains; of the pharmaceutical preparation *Pilula gambogiæ composita*, five to ten grains. Test:—An emulsion made with boiling water and cooled does not become green on addition of solution of iodine, indicating absence of flower or starch.

Game Laws. Hares, pheasants, partridges, grouse, heath or moor game, black game, and bustards constitute game in a legal sense of the word. Snipes, woodcocks, quails, landrails, rabbits, &c., though not game, are by the Certificate Act protected at certain seasons of the year. The Act 1 and 2 Will. IV. c. 32, made important alterations in the G. L., bringing them more into harmony with the spirit of the age than formerly. No qualification from rank or property is now required in England to entitle a man to kill game. An annual license entitles the holder to sell it. Two justices are required to try an offender, except for trespass, which may be tried by one. Appeal is allowed to the Quarter Sessions. Any one killing game on Sunday or on Christmas Day is liable to a penalty of £5, with costs. The Act imposes penalties for killing or taking a partridge between 1st February and 1st September, or pheasant from 1st February to 1st October, or black game or grouse between 10th December and 12th August (or 1st September in the counties of Somerset and Devon, and in the New Forest), or bustard between 1st March and 1st September. Hares may be killed and sold at any season. The price of a license to shoot is from £2 to £3, according to circumstances; to deal in game it is £2; the gun-license 10s. Under a lease granted subsequent to 1 and 2 Will. IV. c. 32, where there is no provision to the contrary, the tenant has the exclusive right to kill the game. When the landlord has reserved the right to himself, he may authorise others to exercise it. Justices may hold a special session as often as they think fit for the purpose of granting annual licenses to deal in game. Every licensed person must put outside his shop or stall a board with his Christian name and surname, having the words 'licensed to deal in game' upon it. Servants of licensed dealers may sell game on the premises of their employer, and one licensed dealer may sell on account of another. The provisions of the Act as regards licenses to deal in game apply to the United Kingdom. There are, however, material differences in the G. L. of England and those of Scotland. In the latter country, under a lease where there is no provision to the contrary, the game belongs to the landlord, the tenant having, however, a legal right to recompense for excessive preserving if material injury be thereby done to his crops. This right does not exist in England nor in Ireland. In Scotland possession of a Ploughgate (q. v.) of land, or leave from one having it, is required to give a title to take or kill game. Pheasants taken in lawful time, and kept in a mew or breeding-place, may be killed at any time. The Act 11 and 12 Vict. c. 30, empowers all persons having a right to kill hares in Scotland to do so, and to authorise others to do so, without a game certificate. As regards POACHING and TRESPASS IN SPORTING, see those articles. On the G. L. generally, see Irvine's *G. L.*, Paterson's *G. L.*, Levinge's *G. L.* For Scotland specially see *Stair*, B. ii. tit. 3, 68–76; *Bell's Princ.*, 948.

Laws Regarding Gamekeepers.—A corporation may appoint a gamekeeper. So may the devisee of a Manor (q. v.) in trust, and the owner of a free warren (see FORESTS, CHASES, PARKS, AND WARRENS), but the lord of a Hundred (q. v.) or Wapentake (q. v.) cannot do so. All appointments of G. must be registered with the clerk of the peace, and their powers cease on revocation of the appointment. A gamekeeper may seize guns used by persons not certified, but he cannot seize hounds or game. A park-keeper or warrener may destroy dogs pursuing deer or rabbits; but being merely owner of the land on which a dog is trespassing, though in pursuit of game, does not entitle the owner to shoot the dog. A gamekeeper is not entitled to carry or use firearms for the capture of poachers, nor can any proprietor do so.

Ga'ming, Bett'ing, Lott'eries, Laws Regarding. By 8 and 9 Vict. c. 109, keeping 'a common gaming-house' is an offence punishable by a fine of £100 or by six months' imprisonment. Gaming implements found in any suspected place are held to be proof of its being 'a common gaming-house,' and persons found in the place are held to be guilty of gaming, unless the contrary can be proved in either case. Playing for money in a public-house is not, however, necessarily an offence under the Act. To be illegal there must be an inequality of chance of winning among the players; thus if any one keeps a *bank*, with chance in his favour, the offence of gaming is committed. Games otherwise lawful, such as billiards, bagatelle, &c., are prohibited in licensed houses between one and eight o'clock A.M. and on Sundays in England and Scotland, and in England on Christmas Day and Good Friday. Any one cheating at cards, dice, or in wagering on the event of any game, sport, or pastime, and winning money by so doing, is guilty of having obtained it under *false pretence*, and punishable accordingly. All contracts, either by parole or writing, for gaming and wagering are null. The keeper of a common gaming-house is liable to a penalty of £500 or twelve months' imprisonment with hard labour. State lotteries were abolished by 4 Geo. IV. c. 60; and by 9 and 10 Will. III. c. 17, any one keeping a place for a lottery is liable to a penalty of £500. It is also an offence punishable by fine to advertise for sale any ticket or share in a foreign lottery, unless authorised by Parliament. Raffles and other devices equivalent to lotteries are also prohibited. Any one gaming or betting in any 'open or public place' may be treated as a vagrant. See BEGGARS, LAW OF ENGLAND RELATIVE TO.

Gamm'arus, a genus of *Crustacea* (q. v.) belonging to the order *Amphipoda* (q. v.), and represented by the *G. pulex* or fresh-water shrimp, common in our ponds and brooks. They swim on their side, and have slender upper antennæ.

Gam'ut, or **Gamm'ut**, the scale or series of musical sounds. For the historical meaning of the word, see NOTATION, MUSICAL.

Gan'dia, an old walled town in the Spanish province of Valencia, about 2 miles from the mouth of the river Alcoy, and 25 miles N.E. of the city of that name. Besides numerous churches, it contains an elaborately ornate palace. G. has some trade, and manufactures of linen, woollen, and silk fabrics. Pop. 7000.

Gan'do, a native African state in the Sudan, to the N.W. of Sokoto. It is traversed by the Niger, and is luxuriantly fertile, producing abundance of yams, dates, bananas, &c. The inhabitants are Fulahs, of Mohammedan faith, and are dispersed throughout various semi-independent provinces. G. is also the name of the capital, which is delightfully situated on a shallow stream, and has successful cotton-weaving industries.

Gandolf'o. See CASTEL-GANDOLFO.

Gan'ga, or **Sand-Grouse** (*Pterocles*), a genus of Rasorial birds, represented by the *P. bicinctus* of the sandy deserts of Europe, Asia, and Africa, and by the *P. setarius*, the pin-tailed S.-G. of Persia. These birds belong to the sub-family *Tetraonidæ*, or that of the true grouse, and are distinguished by the small size of the bill, the nostrils being partly hidden by membrane. The first and second quills are the longest; the tarsi are feathered. The toes are short, and united at the base by membrane.

Gan'ges (*Borra Ganga*, 'the great river'), the first river in India both in sanctity and historical associations, in agricultural and commercial utility, but in actual length surpassed by the Indus, and probably by the Brahmaputra. In some parts of its course it is called the Bhagirutti (*Bhagirathi*), a name which always marks the more holy channel; and at the head of the delta, after the departure of the Bhagirutti southwards, the main stream is known as the Podda (*Padma*). The Bhagirutti rises in the Himalayas, in the native state of Gurhwal, issuing from under a glacier cave, the cow's mouth of Hindu legend. This spot is 13,800 feet above the sea, and the surrounding mountains tower 7000 feet higher. The stream first flows N.W. past Gangotri (q. v.) till it is joined by the Jahnuvi, which both in volume and length of course may claim to be the original river. The united stream now pursues a sinuous course, which is on the whole S.W. for 150 miles, and dashes upon the plain of Hindustan at Hurdwar (q. v.), 1024 feet above the sea, having fallen about 60 feet per mile. It has already received many tributary torrents, of which the Aluknunda is said to be at least one-half bigger than the G. itself, which takes its well-known name only after this junction. From Hurdwar it flows S. for 130 miles, and then S.E. for 350 miles to Allahabad, where it is joined on the right bank by the Jumna, its largest tributary. In the latter reach it has also received the Ramgunga, passed the town of Cawnpore, and been twice crossed by bridges of the Oude and Rohilkund Railway. In this part of its course are many shoals and rapids, and it is fordable in several places during the hot weather. Boat traffic, however, is extremely brisk at Cawnpore, 150 miles above Allahabad; large boats can go 260 miles higher, and the river is reckoned navigable as high as Hurdwar, 488 miles above Allahabad, and 1334 miles from the sea. From Allahabad it proceeds almost due E. for about 500 miles, as far as the hills of Rajmehal. This is the grandest portion of its course, in which it passes by the holy city of Benares and the great mart of Patna, and is augmented by the Gumti, Gogra, Gunduck, Bagmutti, and Cusi from the N., and by the Sone and other minor streams on the right bank. At Rajmehal it turns sharp S.E., but the deserted channel, still called the Bhagirutti, which passes under the ruins of Gaur, still marks the former course further to the E. The first offshoot that contributes to form the delta branches off from the right bank at the town of Suti, about 60 miles below Rajmehal, and 280 miles from the sea. This offshoot, which is not now easily navigable except during the rains, is also called the Bhagirutti, and preserves the sanctity which the main stream henceforth loses. Its course is almost due S. past Murshedabad, and the high bluffs of clay on the right bank indicate the western limit of the delta. After being joined by the Jellinghi, the second offshoot of the G., it presently takes the name of the Hooghly, and passing Chandernagore and Calcutta, opens into the Bay of Bengal at Saugor Island, the most S.W. mouth of the G., and the only one navigable for large ships, which can come up as high as Chandernagore, 115 miles from the sea. The total length of the river, according to the course described above, is about 1500 miles. The main stream, the Podda, after throwing off the Bhagirutti, receives the Mahanunda and other minor streams from the N., and loses several offshoots to the S. at Goalundo (q. v.), is the confluence of the Jumuna, as the Brahmaputra is here called, whose volume is far larger than that of the G. The united stream flows S.E., and after throwing off innumerable branches towards the S., is joined by the Meghna, and finally under that name enters the Bay of Bengal, amid a network of islands and marshes, at the extreme N.E. of the delta. The entire length of the G., measuring from the source of the Jahnuvi to the mouth of the Meghna, is 1570 miles. The influence of the tide is felt about 200 miles inland; and lower down the phenomenon of the 'bore' is frequently to be observed, and is occasionally productive of disastrous consequences. To understand the general character of the G., all notions derived from English or even European rivers must be laid aside. We must attempt to realise a river which receives several tributaries as large as itself, but whose average volume is not thereby augmented; which wanders over a sandy bed at least two miles broad, and changes its main channel year by year, throwing up sandbanks and habitable islands several square miles in area, and again washing them away; which rises about 30 feet, more than double its average depth, between June and October, when swollen by the annual rains, at which time it is estimated to bring down 1,350,000 cubic feet of water per second; which disperses itself in fertilising flood over thousands of square miles in the lower part of its course, and loses in backwaters and swamps the greater portion of its volume before ever it reaches the sea. The delta extends in a triangular shape, Suti being at the apex, 180 miles from the sea, and the base reaching from the Hooghly to the Meghna, more than 200 miles. The upper portion of this delta forms the most fertile portion of Bengal, where the rice crop never fails; but a wide strip along the sea, the Sunderbuns (q. v.), where the process of land-making goes on day by day, is an unsurveyed wilderness of jungle, marshes, and creeks, inhabited only by tigers and other wild animals. The total quantity of solid matter annually brought down has been estimated at 6,368,000,000 cubic feet; the area of the drainage basin at 391,000 sq. miles.

As far as the head of the delta, the services of the river to agriculture are limited to within a few miles from its banks, except where they have been artificially extended by the G. Canal (q. v.); but below that point the whole country is annually inundated, and it has been found unprofitable to attempt to interfere with this natural irrigation by means of confining embankments. In an ordinary year the floods bring down a top-dressing of silt, which renders all manure unnecessary, and even ploughing a mere form, and sometimes allows three crops to be taken off the same field in a single year. The villages are placed on high lands, artificially raised; and the peasants become boatmen during the rainy season. Occasionally, indeed, the inundation is excessive, and villages, cattle, and crops are all swept away; but such a misfortune is rare, and almost compensated by the extra fertility caused to the soil.

The utility of the G. as a means of water traffic cannot be over-estimated. The great towns on its banks, especially Cawnpore and Patna, owe their greatness to this cause; but the opening of the East Indian Railway has somewhat interfered with the native boats, especially in the upper part, and has driven steamers off the river. The total traffic registered at Sahibgunge, just above Rajmehal, in 1873 amounted to about 220,000 tons coming down stream, and about 200,000 tons going up. The exports down stream are chiefly oilseeds, pulses, wheat, sugar, saltpetre, timber, and tobacco; the imports up stream are almost confined to rice; next come salt and pulses. The down-stream traffic is most brisk during the floods; and the boats return up stream from December to April, being towed from the bank the greater part of the way. At Cawnpore, Patna, and Sahibgunge the local boat-traffic is transferred to and from the railway. From the head of the delta there are two alternate routes to Calcutta, the one straight down the Bhagirutti, which is only open during the rainy season; and the second round through the Sunderbuns, along recognised natural and artificial channels. By this latter route also comes the produce of Eastern Bengal and Assam.

The sanctity of the G. dates from the Puranic period, the second classical era of Sanskrit literature. The most popular legend is that contained in the *Ramayana*, which explains the associations which still cling to the names Ganga, Bhagirutti, Jahnuvi, and Saugor. The river is there described as being brought down from heaven to atone for unparalleled sacrilege. The most frequented spots of pilgrimage on its banks are Gangotri, Hurdwar, Allahabad, Benares, Nuddea, and Saugor Island, but ghauts or bathing places abound everywhere throughout its course. 'The offences of any man who bathes in this river are immediately expiated; and those who, even at the distance of a hundred leagues, say *Ganga, ganga*, atone for the sins committed during three previous lives.'

Ganges Canal, described in an official document as 'the greatest work of irrigation ever constructed,' is designed to irrigate the Doab, the dry tract between the Ganges and Jumna rivers, extending roughly from Delhi to Cawnpore. Its services to navigation are of secondary importance. The head of the G. C. is 2½ miles N. of Hurdwar, where the Ganges debouches from the mountains. At first it has to encounter many cross torrents, some of which are suffered to cross it on a level, others are conducted over it by bridges, and over others it passes by aqueducts. The Solani Aqueduct is 920 feet long, in 15 arches of 50 span each. The canal proceeds along the centre of the country between the two rivers, throwing off branches at intervals, of which the two largest fall into the Jumna near Etawah and into the Ganges at Cawnpore. The work, which is entirely of British origin, was commenced in 1848, and opened by Lord Dalhousie in 1854. The total length, including branches, is 614 miles, and the distributaries are an additional 3111 miles. Irrigation commences 22 miles below the headworks, and is diffused over an area 320 miles long by 50 broad. In 1872–73, there were irrigated 685,170 acres; the net profits were £70,764, or 2·74 per cent. on the capital; and the navigation returns were £3237.

A Lower G. C. was commenced in 1872, with a capacity equal to the above canal, to water the remainder of the Doab from Futtehgurh to Allahabad, at an estimated cost of £1,825,000. The water will be diverted from the Ganges by a weir at Rajghat. An Eastern G. C. has also been determined upon to irrigate 3000 sq. miles in Western Rohilkund, between the Ganges and the Ramgunga. It will pass through several miles of deep cutting.

Gan'gi, an old town of Sicily, province of Palermo, in a hilly region, 12 miles W. by N. of Nicosia. It is near the remains of the Sikelian *Enguium*, originally a Phœnician colony, where in Cicero's time was a famous temple of *Magna Mater* (or Aschera), despoiled by Verres. This older G. was destroyed by Friedrich II. in 1299. Guiseppe Salerno, a famous painter of the 17th c., was born at G., and was called *Lo Zoppo* ('the lame') *di G.* His 'Last Judgment' is in one of the churches. Pop. 10,535.

Gang'lia. These are little knots or swellings found in connection with nerves. They vary in form and size, from being almost microscopic to about half an inch in length. Each ganglion has a strong, tough, fibrous coat, composed of connective tissue, which sends partitions into its interior, dividing it into a meshwork. In this meshwork numerous large round or oval nerve-cells are found. These nerve-cells are undoubtedly in connection with nerve-fibres, of which there are usually several bundles entering into or issuing from G. G. are found on the posterior roots of each of the spinal nerves, on one of the roots of the fifth cranial nerve, in connection with the seventh pair of nerves, the glosso-pharyngeal and pneumo-gastric nerves, on the branches of certain cerebro-spinal nerves, and in connection with the sympathetic nerve. The functions of G. are not well understood, but they are generally believed either to act as reflex centres or to have an important relation to the nutrition of the nerves with which they are associated. See NERVES.

Ganglion, in surgery, is of two distinct kinds, *simple* and *compound*, the former being situated on the sheaths of tendons, and the latter consisting in a dilatation of the sheath itself. Simple ganglia consist of cysts, varying in size, containing a transparent yellowish fluid, thin and serous, or gelatinous and semi-coagulated. They are smooth, globular, and elastic, and are usually situated on the back of the wrist or dorsum of the foot. They are considered to be cystic transformations of the fringe-like processes of the synovial membrane lining the sheaths of the tendons; and they give rise to painful sensations from pressure on neighbouring parts. Compound ganglia chiefly occur in the palm of the hand and the dorsum, sole, and inner side of the foot. They often attain a large size, owing to several tendons being implicated, the sheaths of which are vascular and lined by a red fringed membrane, the fluid contents being dark and bloody, containing masses of fibrine, or granular bodies similar to those met with in certain forms of enlarged bursæ. This form of disease is extremely chronic, and may occupy a very extensive surface, frequently assuming an almost malignant appearance. Treatment:—When small and simple, they may be got rid of by being ruptured by forcible pressure, by puncturing them by means of a valvular opening, or they may be dissected out. The injection of a small quantity of the tincture of iodine, or the introduction of a seton, often effects a cure.

Gangot'ri, a place of pilgrimage high up in the Himalayas, in the state of Gurwhal. Here is a temple about 8 miles below the actual source of the Bhagirutti or Ganges, 10,319 feet above the sea, whither devout Hindus come to bathe, pay fees to the guardian Brahmins, and carry away to the plains flasks of the holy water, which is supposed to possess peculiar efficacy. Higher than this temple the pilgrims do not go.

Gangpur', one of the tributary states of Chota Nagpore, a division of the province of Bengal, British India. Area, 2484 sq. miles; pop. (1872) 73,637; estimated revenue, £2000; tribute to the British, £50. The state, which was ceded to the British in 1803, is very hilly, and overgrown with jungle. The river valleys produce rice, oilseeds, and tobacco. Diamonds and gold are found in the rivers, and coal has been ascertained to exist. The chief town is Suadi, on the Ib river, a tributary of the Mahanaddi.

Gan'grene, or **Mortifica'tion**, the local death of a part of the body, external or internal, the result of disease or injury. There are certain local phenomena common to all forms of G., such as complete loss of motion and sensation, depression of temperature, an odour of putrescence, emphysematous crackling from development of gas in the tissues, and a dark, purplish, or greenish-black colour, more or less mottled with red. In the dry form the skin shrivels, becomes dry, wrinkled, and semi-transparent, the colour of the skin being pale, tallowy white with a mottled appearance. When G. is strictly local, and the parts affected are unimportant, the constitutional symptoms are slight; but if important parts are affected, as the intestines or lungs, the symptoms are severe, comprising, first, the symptoms of inflammation, followed by great depression of the vital powers, anxietas, feeble, quick, and compressible pulse, cessation of pain, hiccup, vomiting, and death, with delirium, twitchings, and coma. Treatment:—When G. occurs in any part of the body, the part affected must be separated from the living tissues by a *natural process* or by a surgical operation. Surgical interference is applicable only when external surfaces or portions of limbs are involved, and even in such cases the necessity for operation must depend upon the nature and cause of the disease. G. invariably involves the destruction of the part affected, and if that part is essential to life, death is the necessary sequence.

Gangue is the mineral product which accompanies the ores in metalliferous veins.

Gang'way (Old Eng. *gang*, 'a going,' and *weg*, 'a way'), a narrow roped or railed platform running along a vessel's side, or from the forecastle to the quarterdeck, especially in deep-waisted ships. G. is also the name of a plank or planking for entering a ship from the shore, and of the part of a ship's side to which steps are nailed for climbing aboard.

Gan-Hwuy. See NGAN-HOI.

Ganjam', a town in the district of the same name, province of Madras, British India, 536 miles N.E. of Madras, and 315 S.W. of Calcutta. It was formerly the chief town of the district, with military cantonments and other fine buildings; but in 1815 it was desolated by a fever, and the headquarters were removed to Chicacole. It still retains some trade. Exports in 1872-73, £32,602; pop. about 5000.—*G. district* is the most northerly portion of the Madras Presidency, being bordered on the N.W., the N., and N.E. by the Bengal province of Orissa. Area, 8313 sq. miles; pop. (1871) 1,520,088. It is sharply divided into hill country, and alluvial plains. The former, which is inhabited by the aboriginal Kondhs, supplies valuable jungle products; the latter yield abundant crops of rice, maize, sugar-cane, cotton, pulses, and oilseed. Refined sugar is now largely manufactured under European supervision. The chief towns are Berhampur and the ports of Chicacole, Gopaulpur, and G. town. The seaboard has no proper harbours, but a considerable coasting trade is carried on. Exports in 1872-73, £303,097; imports, £79,521.

Gann'at, a town in the department of Allier, France, on the Andelot, a branch of the Allier, in a richly-wooded hilly district, 12 miles W. by S. of La Palisse by railway. It has tanneries, breweries, and some trade in wine, corn, cattle, &c. Pop. (1872) 5202.

Gann'et (*Sula Bassana*), a species of Natatorial birds included in the family *Pelecanidæ*, and also known by the name Solan goose. The bill is straight, and slightly curved towards the tip. The first and second quills are the longest. The tail is of graduated conformation, and the tarsi have a posterior keel. The claw of the middle toe is notched or indented, the hinder toe possessing only a rudimentary nail. A space destitute of feathers exists on the breast. The average length of the bird is about 32 inches. Its colour is buff on the head and neck, the primary wing feathers being black, and the rest of the plumage white. The nest is constructed out of grass and seaweed, and one egg of a pale blue colour is laid. The G. feeds on fishes, and is especially active

Gannet.

in its movements during the winter and spring months when the sprat-fishing is carried on. The great home of these birds in Britain is the Bass Rock in the Firth of Forth, where they exist in large numbers, but are sometimes subjected to a wanton and indiscriminate slaughter. They are also found at Lundy Island, Ailsa Craig, St. Kilda, on the S. coast of England, Labrador, &c. The feathers are made use of, but the flesh is coarse and oily. The Booby (q. v.) (*S. fusca*) is a species nearly allied to the G.

Gan'oid Fishes, or **Ganoi'dei**, an order of Fishes represented by very many fossil forms (*Pterichthys, Cephalaspis, Dipterus Pteraspis, Coccosteus, Diplacanthus*, &c.), mostly found in the Devonian or Old Red Sandstone rocks, and by a few families and genera of living fishes, chief among which are the sturgeons (*Sturionidæ*), amia (*Amiadæ*), bony pikes (*Lepidosteidæ*), *Polypterus*, &c. By many naturalists the genera *Ceratodus* (the 'Barramunda' (q. v.) of Australian rivers) and *Lepidosiren* (the 'mud-fishes' of Africa and S. America) are included among the G. F., being removed from the order *Dipnoi* (q. v.). (See also FISHES.) The G. F. forming the order *Ganoidei* are distinguished by the presence of the peculiar *ganoid* (Gr. *ganos*, 'splendour') scales, which consist of hard plates of bone, coated with a kind of enamel known as *ganoine*. These scales are placed edge to edge, and are generally articulated together by means of processes, so as to envelop the fishes in a kind of armour. Ganoid scales, it may be noted, are found in one or two groups (*Lophobranchii* and *Plectognathi*) of the Teleostean order of fishes. The endoskeleton of G. F. is usually imperfect, the spine and skull frequently remaining cartilaginous throughout life. Both sets of paired fins—*pectorals* and *ventrals*—are present, the latter being abdominal in position. The tail fin is *heterocercal*. The swimming-bladder is provided with a duct, and the intestine has a spiral coil. The heart has an auricle and ventricle, and a contractile arterial bulb, which is provided with several rows of valves.

Gant'let, or **Gaunt'let** (Fr. *gantelet*, from *gant*, 'a glove'), an armed glove worn by knights in armour. Prior to its introduction in the reign of Edward I. the hand was protected by a bag or mitten of mail attached to the sleeve of the hauberk. The first G. had separate fingers, and was formed of leather covered with scales or overlapping plates of iron. The G. was thrown down in token of challenge; 'to take up the G.' was to accept the challenge. 'To run the G.' means to pass quickly between two rows of soldiers or sailors, and be scourged by each. G. in this connection is a corruption of the Swed. *gattlopp*, from *gata*, 'a street or lane,' and *lopp*, 'a leaping.'

Gan'tung Pass, between the feudatory state of Bussahir, in the Punjab, and Tibet, crosses the Western Himalayas at a height of 18,295 feet, and is covered with perpetual snow. It is overhung by a peak 3000 feet higher than itself, and presents a wild and savage appearance.

Ganyme'des, in Greek mythology, a beautiful youth, son of Tros and Callirhoë, carried to Olympus by Zeus, where he was made cup-bearer to the immortals. According to Homer, G. was transported to heaven by the gods in general, while other myths make Zeus bear him to Olympus, either in his own shape, or in the form of an eagle, or by means of the eagle. G. is also said to have been beloved by Zeus, and to have been carried off from Mount Ida. The story was the subject of innumerable sculptures, paintings, and cameos. G. is usually represented as a youth of exquisite loveliness, with a Phrygian cap, and with the eagle standing beside him, or bearing him through the sky. Horace describes him as yellow-haired (*Ganymede flavo*).

Gaol. See PRISON.

Gaol Deliv'ery, Commiss'ion of, is one of the five commissions under which judges of assize in England discharge their duties when on circuit. It commands two or more of the judges and other law officers of the crown on circuit to try prisoners or those on bail at the date of the commission. The court has power to suppress publication of procedure before it till the end of the trial, and to punish infraction of its order as contempt of court.

Gaol'ers and Offi'cers. To oppose an officer in the execution of his duty in a criminal case makes the opposer an accomplice in the crime (see for Scotch law, DEFORCEMENT); and if he kill the officer, he is guilty of murder. If the officer kill the opposer, it is justifiable homicide. Gaolers permitting the sale of spirituous or fermented liquors in prison are liable to a penalty of £20. They have power to punish certain breaches of discipline by keeping the offender on bread and water for a period not exceeding three days. They are required to attend the Quarter Sessions, to report the state of prisons, and to keep regular books, which are to be examined periodically; and lists of prisoners tried for felony are to be transmitted to the Home Secretary of State; omission so to do entails a penalty of £20. Under the Act persons introducing or attempting to introduce letters or other articles not allowed by the rules of the prison may be fined; and any officer of the prison so doing forfeits his office.

Gap, chief town of the French department of Hautes Alpes, on the Luye, 50 miles S.E. of Grenoble. It is ill built, and in spite of its manufactures of linen, silk, cotton, leather, and agricultural implements, has a far from thriving appearance. The cathedral is handsome. G. is the ancient *Vapinicium*. It was destroyed successively by Goths, Lombards, and Saracens. Between the plague of 1630 and the Revocation of the Edict of Nantes G. was nearly depopulated, and in 1690 it was sacked and burned. The pop. in 1872 was 6938.

Ga'per Shell, the popular name of a well-known genus of Lamellibranchiate (q. v.) *Mollusca*, scientifically known as the *Mya arenaria*. The shell is common on many parts of the British coasts, the animal burrowing in sand and mud, and possessing long siphons or breathing-tubes for the purpose of conveying water to the gills. It is much sought after for bait, and is also eaten in many districts. The family *Myacidæ* is distinguished by the thick shell with 'gapes' behind, and by the foot being of small size. The genus *Mya* itself possesses an oblong shell, a straight 'foot,' a siphon fringed at its extremity, while the gills do not project into the siphon.

Gapes, a disease of fowls and other Rasorial birds depending upon the presence in the trachea or windpipe of small parasitic worms, allied to the Flukes (q. v.), and named *Fasciola trachealis*. These worms attain a length of three-quarters of an inch. The disease is named 'G.' from the worms causing the bird to frequently open its mouth as if anxious to get rid of its troublesome guests. An oiled feather introduced into the bird's windpipe dislodges them.

Gar'ancin, a dyeing substance prepared from Madder Root (q. v.) by the action of sulphuric acid. To prepare G., madder is first treated for a few hours with water which has been acidulated, and afterwards it is acted on with strong sulphuric acid, which is added to it to the extent of 30 per cent. of the weight of madder under treatment. The mixture of madder and acid is kept boiling in a covered tank by means of steam for about four hours, after which it is repeatedly washed with pure water in a tank having a perforated false bottom. The washed product when drained, dried, pressed into a cake, and ground to a fine powder constitutes the G. of commerce. One hundred parts of madder yield from 34 to 37 parts of G., but the tinctorial effect of the product is much greater than that of the original dyestuff. The acid is supposed to disintegrate a certain proportion of the woody fibre of the roots, and to bring the tinctorial principle into a more readily soluble condition. G. is more easily and expeditiously applied in calico-printing than madder, but it does not possess the solidity and permanence of that dye. The introduction of artificial alizarine has greatly decreased its importance.

Gar'anceux, a dye prepared from spent madder in the same way that garancin is made from the unexhausted roots. See GARANCIN.

Garay, János, a Hungarian poet and journalist, was born at Zsekzard, in Tolna county, Hungary, 10th October 1812, studied at Fünfkirchen and Pesth, and spent his life in editing various native papers. He died at Pesth, 5th November 1853. G. wrote dramas, tales, and poems, mostly of a historical character. They were published in a collected form by Franz Ney at Pesth in the year of the author's death (German selection and translation by Kertbeny, 2d ed. Vienna, 1857). The most notable are *Csab* (1835) and *Arbocz* (1837), tragedies; *Orszâgh Ilona* (1837) and *Bâtory Erzsebet* (1840), historical dramas; and his *Arpadok* (1847), a splendid cycle of historic ballads. Some of G.'s pieces are reckoned among the pearls of Hungarian literature.

Garb, or **Garbe** (Old Fr. *garbe*, Mod. Fr. *gerbe*, from Old High Ger. *garba*, 'a sheaf'), in heraldry, a sheaf of wheat; or, if it is not blazoned, a G. simply of any other grain.

Garba'les Dec'imæ mean in the law of Scotland the tithes of corn. They were also termed *decimæ rectoriæ*, or parsonage tithes. (See TEINDS.) The word G. is from the Old High Ger. *garba*, 'a sheaf.'

Gar'cia, Manuel, was born at Seville, Spain, in 1775, and was first a chorister in Seville Cathedral. After gaining distinction as an operatic tenor at Cadiz, Madrid, Paris, and Naples, he sang in London and Paris from 1818 to 1824. In 1825 he took a select operatic company to the United States and Mexico, but was not fortunate. In his latter years he taught singing at Paris, where he died, 9th June 1832. His eldest daughter, **Maria Felicita**, was the famous Madame Malibran (q. v.); his second daughter is **Pauline Viardot-G.** (q. v.). His son **Manuel**, born at Madrid in 1805, became a teacher of singing at the Paris Conservatoire in 1835, and afterwards in London. His *École de G.* (Par. 1841; 4th ed. 1856) has won him an honourable name in musical literature.

Garcilass'o (abbreviated for **Garcias Lasso**) **de la Vega**, known as the *Inca*, was the son of a Spanish *conquistador* and governor of Peru, and was born at Cuzco about 1540. Descended on the mother's side from the old royal Peruvian stock, he was well fitted both by his sympathies and his acquaintance with the native language for his life-work, the investigation of Peruvian history. Though always zealous to be a good Spaniard and Catholic, G.'s popularity with the aborigines excited suspicion at home. He was finally ordered to return to Spain, and was interned at Valladolid. He died there in 1620. G.'s history of the Incas (*Los Comentarios reales que tratan del Origen de los Incas*) was published at Lisbon (2 vols. 1609–17), and repeatedly translated into French. A continuation of this work, *Historia general del Peru*, appeared in 1616, and was often republished before 1730. There is an English translation by Sir Paul Rycaut (Lond. 1688). G.'s work is the great source of our knowledge of the ancient Peruvians.

Garcilasso (a contraction of **Garcias Lasso**) **de la Vega**, a Spanish poet, was born of a noble family at Toledo in 1500 or 1503. His father received the name Vega from King Ferdinand in recognition of his bravery in combat on the Vega, or plain of Grenada. G. went when young to the Spanish court, and in 1529 was one of a Spanish corps which distinguished itself against the Turks in Austria. At this time he became entangled in an intrigue between a court lady and one of his relatives, incurred the Emperor's dislike, and was imprisoned on an island in the Danube, where he composed several melancholy poems. Regaining the imperial favour, he accompanied Karl V. in his expedition against Tunis in 1535, and during the following year was given an important command; but on the Emperor invading Provence, was mortally wounded near Frejus, at a fortified tower, of which he was the first to mount the breach. G. died shortly afterwards at Nice, November 1536. His poems (first published in 1543) include eclogues, sonnets, epistles, and cançiones. He imitated Petrarch, Ariosto, and Sannazarro, and, following the example of his contemporary Boscan, introduced the Italian poetic style and hendecasyllabic measure into Spain. His first eclogue is one of the most precious treasures of the national literature. His active military life finds no reflex in his verse, which is pervaded by tender, and at times even effeminate, pensiveness, expressed in language occasionally diffuse and affected, but singularly copious and graceful, and full of rich languid melody. The best edition of G.'s poems is that of Azara (Mad. 1765). There is an English translation by Wiffen (Lond. 1823). See Sismondi's *Literature of the South of Europe* (1846), and Ticknor's *History of Spanish Literature* (New York, 1849).

Garcin'ia, a genus of plants of the natural order *Guttiferæ* (q. v.), to which the Mangosteen (q. v.) and Gamboge (q. v.) belong.

Gard, a department of France, lies between the Cevennes and the Rhone, and is bounded S. by the Mediterranean, and N. by Ardèche. Area, 2252 sq. miles; pop. (1872) 420,131. It is hilly in the N. and W., slopes gradually towards the Rhone and the sea, and has a marshy coast-line of 10 miles. Rich tracts along the Rhone, G., Herault, Vidorra, and Ceze produce wine (26,000,000 gallons yearly), olives, and mulberry. G. is noted for its silk-culture, its cattle, and a fine breed of white horses. Its minerals include coal, iron, lead, sulphur, zinc, and salt, while it has large exports of dyeing and medicinal plants. The chief manufactures are silks, woollens, cottons, ribbons, and gloves. G. is traversed by a branch line of the Tarascon à Cette railway. Nîmes is the chief town; others are Alais, Uzès, and Vigan. The *Pont du G.*, 15 miles N.E. of Nîmes, is one of the grandest Roman relics in France. It is an aqueduct, and is supposed to have been built by Agrippa to convey water to Nîmes.

Gar'da, Lago di (Lat. *Lacus Benacus*), the largest lake of Italy, lies between the territory of Trent, in the Italian Tyrol, and the provinces of Verona, Brescia, and Mantua. On both sides rugged Alpine masses, opening here and there in smiling valleys, are mirrored in its singularly clear waters. Beautiful villas are dotted along its shores, and on the Sermione (Lat. *Sirmio*), a tiny peninsula, are the remains of the country seat of Catullus. The lake is 32 miles long, from 2 to 10 broad, and its greatest ascertained depth is 1900 feet. It contains the islands Trimelone, Olivé, and St. Pietro, and receives the Sarca and many minor streams, while its only outlet is the Mincio, a tributary of the Po. The name is derived from the village of G. (pop. 3000) on the E. shore.

Gardai'a, or **Gharda'ja**, a walled town in the S. of Algeria, on the N. border of the Sahara, 315 miles S.S.E. of Algiers. It is girt with orchards, watered from many deep wells, has six mosques, and carries on a large caravan trade, chiefly in oil, gold-dust, ivory, woollens, cottons, indigo, and dates. Pop. 13,000.

Gar'dant, or **Guardant**, an heraldic term, applied to beasts of prey when they are looking toward the spectator.

Gardele'gen, earlier **Gardeleben** and **Garleben**, a town of Prussian Saxony, on the Milde, 28 miles N.N.W. of Magdeburg. It has a well-endowed hospital founded in 1285, some tanneries, distilleries, and mills, and five yearly fairs. The town was once noted for its beer. Pop. (1871) 6266.

Garde Nationale, of France, was a guard of armed citizens instituted in Paris to protect liberty and preserve order, July 13, 1789. Similar bodies had previously been maintained in other French towns. The colours of the G. N. were red and blue, to which white was afterwards added, whence arose the famous tricolor. It numbered at first 48,000 men, but being organised throughout the country, speedily comprised 300,000. The G. N. offered no check to the excesses of the revolutionists until 1795, when it helped to disarm the mob of Paris. It was maintained in efficiency by Napoleon, and its members took a large part in the revolution of 1830, though it had been nominally abolished but not disarmed by Charles X. Under Louis Philippe it grew in power and republican tendencies, and in 1848 supported the revolutionists, but it was generally opposed to the Socialist party. Its privileges were largely curtailed in 1852, when it was placed beneath strict Government control, and in 1871 it was dissolved by a decree of the National Assembly.

Gar'dener's Gar'ters, the popular name given to the variegated variety of *Phalaris arundinacea*, a grass frequently cultivated in cottage gardens.

Garde'nia, a genus of trees and shrubs belonging to the natural order *Cinchonaceæ* (q. v.), found in Asia and in Africa. Several species are cultivated in hothouses for their beautiful and fragrant blossoms, such as *G. florida*, the Cape jasmine, which has double flowers, and *G. Stanleyana*. A fragrant resin is obtained from *G. gummifera*, in India, where also the fruit of *G. campanulata* is said to be used as a cathartic, and to take stains out of silk.

Gar'dening. See HORTICULTURE.

Gar'dens or Orchards, Stealing from. By 24 and 25 Vict. c. 96, to steal or injure with intent to steal any plant or fruit growing in a garden, orchard, nursery ground, hothouse, greenhouse, or conservatory, makes the offender liable to six month's imprisonment with or without hard labour, or to pay £20 above the value of the article stolen, or of the injury done. A second conviction renders the offender liable to penal servitude for three years.

Garden Spider. See EPEIRA.

Gardes Suisses, a famous corps in the French army formed in 1616. They numbered about 2000, and at the French Revolution made a desperate defence of the Louvre against the Parisians, August 10, 1792, when they were massacred almost to a man. The corps was re-organised in 1815, and disbanded in 1830.

Garde-Visure', in heraldry, the visor, or front part of the helmet.

Gar'diner, a town of Kennebec county, Maine, U.S., on the right bank of the Kennebec, and on the Maine Central Railway. The Cobossec, with a fall of 133 feet in a mile, affording valuable water-power, here enters the Kennebec. The industries of G. include saw and paper mills, woollen goods, furniture, tanning, and ice. Pop. (1870) 4497.

Gardiner, Colonel James, a soldier noted for his bravery and piety, was the son of Captain Philip G., and was born at Carriden, Linlithgowshire, January 11, 1688. He entered the Dutch service at an early age, but exchanged it for the English under Marlborough, and was wounded at Ramilies in 1706. G., who became aide-de-camp to the Earl of Stair, had a reputation at once for great courage and profligacy. According to Doddridge, who says that he had his information from G. himself, he was converted to Christianity in an almost supernatural manner in the year 1719. The accuracy of Doddridge's narrative is denied by Dr. Alexander Carlyle in his *Autobiography* (Edinb. 1860). The fact, however, unquestionably is, that after this period G. certainly became a pronounced Christian. In 1743 he was appointed colonel of a new regiment of dragoons, but was killed in an attempt to beat back the onset of Prince Charles Edward and the Highlanders at the battle of Prestonpans, September 21, 1745. See Doddridge's *Life of Col. Gardiner* (1747).

Gardiner, Stephen, Bishop of Winchester, born at Bury St. Edmunds in 1483, was the illegitimate son of Lionel Woodville, brother-in-law of Edward IV. He studied at Trinity College, Cambridge, and entered political life as secretary to Cardinal Wolsey. Gaining the favour of Henry VIII. by his efforts to secure that monarch's divorce from Catharine of Aragon, G. received rapid promotion as politician and churchman, being made Secretary of State, special ambassador to France and Germany, and (1531) Bishop of Winchester. For a time it seemed likely that he would fall before Thomas Cromwell on account of his objections to a genuine reformation, which are all the more remarkable that he wrote a work, *De Vera Obedientia*, in favour of the doctrine of the king's supremacy in the Church; yet he not only survived that statesman, but aided in his overthrow. He fell into disgrace, however, through his opposition to Catharine Parr, and during the reign of Edward VI. was imprisoned and deprived of his bishopric. The accession of Mary, on the other hand, made him the first subject in England; he was restored to the bishopric, was made Lord Chancellor and Prime Minister, and officiated at the marriage of Mary and Philip of Spain. The infamy of the persecutions of this reign is often assigned to him, but according to Lingard 'more from conjecture and prejudice than from real information.' He died 12th November 1555. Among G.'s other works are *The Necessary Doctrine of a Christian Man* (1543), the authorship of a portion of which is ascribed to Cranmer; and *Confutatio Cavillationis* (1552). See Maitland's *Essays on the Reformation*, and Froude's *History of England.*

Garess'io, an old town of N. Italy, province of Coni, on the Tanaro, at the N. base of the Maritime Alps, 45 miles W. by S. of Genoa. It has many Roman remains, and in the vicinity are quarries of fine marble (*Persigliano*). Pop. 6500.

Gar-Fish (*Belone vulgaris*), a name given to a species of Teleostean fishes, belonging to the family Esocidæ (q. v.), or pikes, and distinguished by its long and slender body, and by the length of its jaws. The G.-F. is also known by the names 'sea-pike,' 'long-bill,' 'sea-needle,' 'green-bone' (from the colour of the bones after boiling), and by other terms. Its average length is 2 feet; its colour a dark or bluish-green above, and silvery white below. It obtains the name of 'mackerel guide,' from the fact that it invariably appears before the mackerel: a circumstance probably due to the proximity of the spawning seasons.

Gar'ganey, Gargany, or **Summer Teal** (*Pterveyanea circia*), a species of *Anatinæ* or Ducks, closely allied to the Teals (q. v.), rarely found in Britain, but common in S. Europe, in India, in Africa, and distributed pretty generally over the Old World. The G. is somewhat larger than the teal. Its colour is a dark brown, variegated with white, the eye being marked above by a conspicuous white streak running backwards into the neck. The flesh of the bird is palatable and nutritious.

Garga'no, a mass of mountains in the province of Foggia, Italy, running for 20 miles into the Adriatic, and also stretching for some distance inland, but severed from the Apeninnes by a wide plain. It is wild and sterile on the S., but on the N. is richly wooded, and contains many picturesque gorges and ravines. Its highest point is 5120 feet above the sea. G. consists mostly of limestone, and has large alabaster quarries. It is the ancient *Garganus* which Horace speaks of as covered with oaks, and praises for its fine honey, an article for which G. is still famed. Horace's name *Matinus* still clings to the village Mattinasa S. of G.

Gar'garus. See IDA.

Gar'gle, or **Gar'garism,** a liquid preparation for washing the mouth and throat. Gargles are used for cleansing the parts, and also as topical applications in diseases of the mouth and throat, as in relaxed sore throat, inflammation, ulceration, &c. For such purposes alum, borax, capsicum, myrrh, chlorate of potass, and permanganate of potass, and Condy's fluid are used. A useful G. may be prepared thus:—Borax, 1 dr.; honey, 2 drs.; water, 4 oz.

Gar'goyle, or **Gur'goyle** (Fr. *garguille*, 'a waterspout;' *garguillu*; Ital. *gargagliare*; compare with *gurgle*, 'to murmur'), in Gothic architecture is a projecting spout to discharge the water from the gutter of the roof. It was generally carved into a grotesque figure of a man, animal, or monster, from whose mouth the water was often made to gush. Gargoyles were sometimes caricatures of real persons. They seem to have been first used in the Early English style. They are generally longer on old French and Flemish than on English buildings.

Garibal'di, Giusepp'e, was born at Nice, July 22, 1807. Under his father, a poor man who owned a little coasting vessel, G. took to the sea, and made numerous voyages to Odessa, Genoa, Rome, and other ports. In 1830 he was himself in command of a trading vessel, *Notre Dame de Grace.* About this time his deep and fervid nature became impressed with patriotic sentiments. In 1833 he made the acquaintance of Mazzini, and entered heartily into the Liberal movements of the time for the regeneration of Italy. Sharing in a revolutionary movement at Genoa (1834), he had to flee, first to France, then to Africa, where he offered his services to the Bey of Tunis, and finally to S. America, where he fought in the interest of republican freedom for Rio Grande against Brazil, and for Paraguay against Rosas, the dictator of Buenos Ayres. This period in his history gave G. considerable military experience. In 1848 revolutionary movements in Italy brought him back to his native country. He commanded the forces of the Provisional Government in Rome, fought with heroic but unavailing courage against the French army, and only left the city when Oudinot began to enter it. His retreat in a N.E. direction to the Adriatic, through a country overrun with Austrian soldiery, can still be followed with breathless interest. His beloved wife Anita, the companion of all his perils, succumbed to the hardships of the march, but G. himself finally reached Genoa in safety. Thence he went to Tunis, but was forced to leave through the intrigues of the French consul. He was sent to the Isle of Maddalena, where he lived as a kind of state-prisoner till 1851, and during some hunting and fishing tours made his first acquaintance with Caprera, his future home. Thence he went to America, made some money in trade, came back to Italy in 1854, and bought the northern part of Caprera. Here he occupied himself quietly in farming for some years. The Franco-Sardinian war with Austria in 1859 induced G. to offer his sword to King Victor Emanuel; and as a leader of volunteers he gained many small victories over the Austrians. The next year he attained the height of his military success in the brilliant Sicilian campaign. Leaving Genoa with about 1000 volunteers, he landed at Marsala, 11th May; four days later won a decisive victory over the Royalist troops at Catalfimi, and took Palermo. The battle of Melazzo, July 20, placed

Messina and the whole of Sicily in his possession. Next month he crossed to Calabria. Volunteers in thousands joined his standard; he entered Naples without striking a blow, and was proclaimed Dictator. A desperate attack on the part of the Royalists on the Garibaldian army stationed on the Volturno failed; King Victor Emanuel at the head of his army marched to the scene of action; G. saluted him as 'King of Italy,' Gaeta capitulated, and the hero withdrew to Caprera. In 1862 he made a second descent on Sicily, with the view of driving the French out of Rome and securing the city for the Italian people. The situation was embarrassing to the Government, who could not afford to break with France. At last an Italian force was sent against the rash patriot, who was wounded and captured on the 29th of August at Aspromonte in Calabria. Pardoned by the Italian Government for his indiscretion (as he always has been), he returned to Caprera. In 1864 he visited England, and was received with unprecedented enthusiasm, but suddenly and not very intelligibly returned to Italy in the Duke of Sutherland's yacht. In 1866 the war with Austria brought him to the front as a leader of irregulars in the Tyrol, but he was unable to accomplish much. Next year all attempts to prevent him making an invasion of Pontifical territory failed. At the head of a band of volunteers he beat the Pontifical troops at Monte Astundo (October 26th), but these being reinforced by French, he was defeated at Mentana (November 4th). Once more arrested and set at liberty, he did not appear much in public until the collapse of the Third Empire during the Franco-German war made him offer his services to the new republic, and even then, although appointed commander of the army of the Vosges, he could do little beyond showing his personal gallantry. In 1871 he resigned the post to which he had been elected as representative to the National Assembly at Bordeaux, but took his seat as a member of the Italian Parliament at Rome, June 25, 1875. He has frequently owned and disowned his king, but has lately been reconciled to him with a view to getting the assistance for the scheme, now abandoned, of draining the Campagna, giving another course to the Tiber, and a new port to Rome. G. has come before the world both as poet and novelist, but none of his efforts have added to his fame. The biographies of G. are innumerable; that of Cuneo (Turin, 1865) is probably the best. G. has two sons, **Menotti** and **Ricciotti G.**, both of whom have appeared by the side of their father on the field of battle. Menotti took part in the disastrous campaign of 1862, and also in the Franco-Prussian war on the side of the Republic.

Gar'iep. See ORANGE RIVER.

Gariglia'no (perhaps from Arabic *garil*, 'a marsh'), a river which rises W. of Lake Tricino, in the Central Apennines, flows through Campania in a slow stream, and enters the Bay of Gaeta at Cangliano. Its chief affluent is the Sacco. In its lower course it traverses marshy unhealthy districts. It was anciently named the *Liris*, and more anciently the *Clanis* or *Glanis*. It separated Latium from Campania. Horace notices its gentle current (Carm. I. xxxi. 7, 8.).

Gar'lic, the common name for *Allium sativum*, a bulbous plant belonging to the Lily family, and a native of Southern Europe. The bulb, which is composed of several small bulblets called cloves, is the part which is used. G. is extensively employed in Spain, Italy, and other parts of Europe for flavouring dishes. Among the Greeks and Romans it formed a favourite viand even of the common people. Several species of *Allium* (q. v.) are popularly known as G.

Broad-Leaved Garlic (*Allium ursinum*).

Garlic, Oil of. When the bulbs of the garlic (*Allium sativum*) are distilled with water, an oily liquid passes over and condenses in the receiver along with the water, from which it may be separated by decantation. This is the crude O. of G., which may, however, be purified by rectification. From 50 kilogrammes of garlic not more than from 100 to 120 grammes of the crude oil can be obtained. O. of G. is also contained in the different parts of several species of the *Cruciferæ* and asphodels. It is present in onions, together with oil of mustard in the leaves and grains of *Thlaspi arvense* and of *Iberis amara*, in the leaves of *Alliaria officinalis*, &c. O. of G. does not always exist ready formed in the different plants from which it may be obtained, but appears to be produced by a species of fermentation similar to that which gives rise to oil of mustard from the myronate of potash contained in mustard seed. O. of G. when pure is the sulphide of allyl, and has the composition represented by the formula $(C_3H_5)_2S$. The crude oil contains small quantities of oxide of allyl $(C_3H_5)_2O$, and of bisulphide of allyl $(C_3H_5)_2S_2$. Pure O. of G. is colourless, transparent, slightly soluble in water, readily soluble in alcohol and ether. It has the peculiar and characteristic odour of the garlic. It boils at 140° C. O. of G. has been prepared artificially from oil of mustard, which is the sulphocyanate of allyl (C_3H_5CNS), by heating it with sulphide of potassium—

$$\underbrace{2(C_3H_5CNS)}_{\text{Oil of mustard.}} + \underbrace{K_2S}_{\text{Sulphide of potassium.}} = \underbrace{2KCNS}_{\text{Sulphocyanate of potassium.}} + \underbrace{(C_3H_5)_2S}_{\text{Oil of garlic.}}$$

It has also been obtained from the iodide of allyl (C_3H_5I), prepared from glycerine $(C_3H_5(OH)_3)$ by mixing it with an alcoholic solution of sulphide of potassium—

$$\underbrace{2C_3H_5I}_{\text{Iodide of allyl.}} + \underbrace{K_2S}_{\text{Sulphide of potassium.}} = \underbrace{2KI}_{\text{Iodide of potassium.}} + \underbrace{(C_3H_5)_2S}_{\text{Oil of garlic.}}$$

For compounds of allyl see OIL OF MUSTARD.

Gar'net, a mineral group belonging to the monometric system of crystallisation, the most common form being the dodecahedron. It is of various colours, has a vitreous lustre, is brittle, and from 6·5 to 7·5 in the scale of hardness. It occurs abundantly in mica slate, hornblende slate, and gneiss, and is also found in granite, granular limestone, serpentine, and lava. G. is a compound of four silicates (alumina, lime, iron, manganese), which in varying proportions give rise to the different varieties. *Precious G.* or *almandine*, the best specimens of which are from Pegu, Ceylon, and Greenland, is of a clear deep-red colour, sometimes almost black; *cinnamon stone*, from Ceylon and Sweden, is light yellow in colour with a high lustre; *melanite* or *black G.* occurs in the lavas of Vesuvius; *grossularite*, a green variety, is got from Siberia and Norway; *ouvarovite*, of a rich emerald shade, from Bissersk in Russia; and *aplome*, deep brown or orange in colour, from Siberia and Saxony. *Common G.* is brownish red, imperfectly translucent or opaque, and is easily recognised by its dodecahedral crystals.

Gar'netberry, a common name given to the fruit of the red currant (*Ribes rubrum*). See CURRANT.

Gar'nett, Rev. Richard, a distinguished philologist, born at Otley, Wharfedale, July 25, 1789. His literary and scholarly bias led him to quit a business life and join the Church. In 1815 he became a curate at Blackburn, in 1821 priest-vicar in Lichfield Cathedral, in 1836 vicar of Chebsey near Stafford, and in 1838 assistant-keeper of printed books in the British Museum. He contributed frequently to periodicals, and died at London, September 27, 1850. G. united vast learning, a keen scientific faculty, and a singular gift of luminous expression. His *Philological Essays* (Edinb. 1859), a selection from his contributions to journals, are a treasury of fresh research, lucid statement, and penetrating speculation. His essay on the Celtic tongues is an especially valuable contribution to the science of language. In the mellow humour and racy anecdotage with which he occasionally flavours his erudition he somewhat recalls the great scholars of the 16th c. See the memoir by his son prefixed to his *Philological Essays* (Lond. 1859).

Gar'nish (Fr. *garnir*, 'to furnish') was formerly a kind of tax which gaolers levied on their prisoners. It is now prohibited by statute.

Gar'nished, in heraldry, is applied to an ornament set on a charge.

Garonne′ (Gael. *garbh* and Cymr. *garw*, 'rough,' seen in *Garry*, *Yarrow*, &c., 'the rough stream,' Lat. *Garumna*), a river of the S. of France, which rises in the Val d'Aran in the Spanish Pyrenees, flows N.E. as far as Toulouse, and afterwards N.W. through Gascony and Guyenne, passes by Bordeaux across sandy and marshy tracts, and widens into the estuary of the Gironde (q. v.), which opens on the Bay of Biscay. Its total length is 350 miles, and it is navigable for about 250 miles. It is enlarged in its course by thirty-two affluents, eight of which are navigable. From the Pyrenees it receives the Salat, Ariege, Gers; from the highlands of the Cevennes and of the Auvergne region, the Tarn, Lot, and Dordogne, the last of which is its largest tributary. The G. waters a beautiful valley, rich in corn and wine. The Canal du Midi connects it with the Mediterranean. It may be called the boundary between the Celtic and the Basque population of France.

Garonne, Haute, a department in the S. of France, on the borders of Spain. Area, 2429 sq. miles; pop. (1872) 479,362. The S., covered by spurs of the Pyrenees, is a picturesque region of snowy peaks, lakes, and beautiful valleys, containing fine pastures and dense forests, and watered by wild torrents. The N. consists of low hills and plains rich in corn, fruit, and maize, and, especially around Toulouse, famous for their vines. The chief river is the G. (q. v.). Lead, copper, iron, zinc are found, and white and finely-variegated marble is quarried. The leading manufactures are cottons, woollens, and pottery. The exports consist mostly of grain, wine, wood, horses, and cattle. G. is traversed by the Boulogne-à-Cette Railway, and by the Canal du Midi. The chief town is Toulouse. G. belongs to the old Euskarian land; its inhabitants are mostly Basque (Iberian), a non-Gallic, probably a non-Aryan race.

Garr′ick, David, was the son of a half-pay captain in the army, and born at Hereford, 20th February 1716. In 1735 he was for some months a pupil of Samuel Johnson at Edial, near Lichfield, and accompanied his master to London. After trying various professions, including law, he chose the stage, and in 1741, under the assumed name of Lyddal, he appeared at Ipswich as 'Aboan' in *Oroonoko*. From the provinces he proceeded to London, and at Goodman's Fields, October 19, 1741, as 'Richard III.' achieved so pronounced a success, that after that day his career was one long triumph. He was as popular in comedy as in tragedy. As a playwright he produced a number of pieces which are now forgotten, but which 'took' at the time, and his managerial career culminated (1773) in his becoming sole director of Drury Lane Theatre. In 1749 he married the celebrated dancer Mdlle. Violette, who brought him £6000, proved a good wife, and survived till 1822. His extraordinary versatility has recently been doubted, and it is questioned whether as a Shakespearian actor he was not surpassed by Edmund Kean; but his fame certainly surpasses that of any other English actor. In 1769 he conducted the Shakespeare Jubilee at Stratford-upon-Avon. He died 20th January 1779, leaving a large fortune, estimated at about £150,000. G. had many good qualities in private life, but was vain, jealous, and morbidly sensitive to ridicule. See P. Fitzgerald's *Life of G.* (1868), and for a clever sketch of his character, Goldsmith's *Retaliation*.

Garr′ison (Fr. *garnison*, from *garnir*, derived from a Teutonic source: comp. Old Eng. *warnian*, 'to take care,' 'to defend'), a body of men placed in a fortress or fortified town, to defend it against the enemy or to keep the inhabitants in subjection. The name is also given to a place where troops are placed in barracks.

Garrison, William Lloyd, the leader of the American abolitionists, was born in Newburyport, Massachusetts, U.S., December 12, 1804. From being a compositor, he became editor of the *Free Press* in his native town, and in 1828 went to Bennington, Vermont, to conduct a paper in which he espoused temperance and emancipation. In 1829 he united with B. Lundy in editing the *Genius of Universal Emancipation*, in Baltimore. In this paper he advocated *immediate* emancipation 'in the name of God and humanity.' He opposed colonisation, and for an article on the domestic slave trade was convicted for libel and imprisoned until his fine was paid by a friend. In January 1831 his real life-work began in the founding of the *Liberator* in Boston. He made this paper an organ for temperance, women's suffrage, and the abolition of capital punishment. In January 1832 he organised the New England, and in 1833 the American, Anti-Slavery Society. From 1843 till 1865 he was president of the latter. Great agitation both N. and S. attended his movements. In October 1835 he was assailed by a mob led on by men of property and standing in Boston. He was led through the streets by a rope around his body, and was with difficulty rescued and lodged in gaol for safety. G. denounced the Union as a 'covenant with death and an agreement with hell.' In the darkest time his 'clarion voice' was oft and long heard in behalf of freedom; and his fiery invectives against Church and State in league with slavery kindled a passionate enthusiasm in generous breasts, not only in America, but even in England. His cause being finally crowned with success, he closed the agitation in 1865, the *Liberator* expiring at the end of that year. G. visited England in 1832, 1840, 1846, and in 1867, on the last occasion receiving much honour. His works consist of *Thoughts on African Colonisation* (1832); *Sonnets and other Poems* (1843); *Selections from his Writings and Speeches* (1852).

Garr′ot (*Clangula*), a genus of *Anatidæ* or Ducks (q. v.), in which the bill is somewhat shorter than the head. To it belong the golden-eyed duck or G. (*C. glaucion*), the harlequin duck (*C. histrionica*), and the spirit or buffel-headed duck (*C. albeola*). The first-mentioned species visits Britain in winter, and appears to breed in the Arctic regions. The nests are commonly constructed in holes—a fact of which the Laplanders are said to take advantage by inducing the birds to lay their eggs in boxes, and thus securing them. The harlequin duck derives its name from its curiously-marked and mottled plumage; the buffel-head is a familiar N. American species of G.

Garrott′ing (Span. *garrote*, 'a stick' or 'cudgel'). By 24 and 25 Vict. c. 96, any one using personal violence to another in an attempt to rob him is liable to penal servitude for life, and by c. 100 an attempt to choke is made an aggravation, rendering the offender liable to being whipped in addition to the other punishment.

Garr′ow (Garo) Hills, a district of Assam, British India, S. of the Brahmaputra, bounded N. by Kamrup, S. by Mymensing. Area, 3390 sq. miles; pop. (1872) about 80,000. This tract was first brought under direct British management in 1866, and in 1872 the intervention of an armed force was required. The hills produce valuable timber and cotton. Elephants are numerous. The headquarters of the Deputy Commissioner are at Tura. The G. people, of whom there are about 13,000 in Bengal proper, and 14,000 in the rest of Assam, are a very primitive race. They are divided into villages, with headmen and priests, and into clans; descent and inheritance of property is traced through the female line. Human sacrifice was formerly practised. Slaves are numerous (Dalton's *Ethnology of Bengal*, Calcutta, 1872).

Gar′ter, Order of the, a military order of knighthood founded by Edward III. in 1344. It consisted at first of twenty-six members, of whom the king was head, but in 1786 the number was raised to thirty-two. The chief sign of the order is a garter of blue velvet, edged with gold, and inscribed *Honi soit qui mal y pense* ('Evil be to him who evil thinks'). The mantle is of blue velvet lined with white. The order is also known as the Order of St. George, that saint being regarded as its principal patron. *Garter king-at-arms*, next to the Earl-marshal the chief officer of the Heralds' College, is herald to the O. of the G., and principal king-at-arms in England. His office was instituted by Henry V. in 1420. In 1874 there were forty-nine knights, none below an earl in rank. The Bishop of Winchester is prelate, and the Bishop of Oxford is the dean of the order. See Ashmole's *History of the O. of the G.* (1672).

Order of the Garter

Garth, Sir Samuel, a distinguished physician and wit, was born of a good family at Bolam, Yorkshire, in the latter half of the 17th c. He studied at Cambridge, and settled in 1692 in London, where he gained a very wide practice, and was famed as a conversationalist among the brilliant Whig society of the time. In 1700 he procured interment for the body of Dryden in Westminster Abbey, and delivered the poet's funeral oration. As chosen poet of the Kitcat Club, he produced numerous verses, praising Whig beauties and decrying the Tories, and in reward for his political constancy and fervour was knighted by George I. in 1714, and appointed physician in ordinary to the king. He died at London, January 18, 1718. Pope, who was always grateful to G. for having 'inflamed him with early praise,' and who very often alludes to him, said that 'if there ever was a good Christian without knowing himself to be so, it was Dr. G.' The chief work of G. is his *Dispensary* (1699), a mock-heroic attack on the physicians and apothecaries who were opposed to supplying medicine gratis to the poor. It was at first very popular, but its personalities are now without interest, and its satire somewhat blunted. He also wrote a poem on the house of Clare (1715), and took part in a translation of Ovid's *Metamorphoses*, to which Gay, Congreve, and Pope contributed. See Johnson's *Lives of the Poets*, and Spence's *Anecdotes*.

Gärt'ner, Friedrich von, a German architect, born at Koblenz in 1792. He is chiefly notable for his efforts to revive mediæval architecture. Among the positions held by G., were those of Professor of Architecture (since 1820), director of the Academy of Arts, and head Government surveyor in Munich. He died 21st April 1847. G. is best known by his *Ansichten der am meisten erhaltenen Monumente Siciliens* (1819), an account of the chief monuments preserved in Italy; but specimens of his work as an architect are found in Munich and other cities of Germany. The Romanesque style appears in all his buildings.

Gartsherr'ie, a village of Lanarkshire, and a station on the Caledonian Railway, 6¼ miles E. by N. of Glasgow. It has extensive ironworks and collieries, which formed the original lease of the Baird (q. v.) family. Pop. (1871) 1915.

Gas Anal'ysis. The analysis of a gaseous mixture is a problem of frequent occurrence to the chemist, and it is therefore of importance that he should possess accurate methods for its accomplishment. The existence of substances similar to air in physical properties, but altogether different from it in chemical composition, was scarcely considered before the discovery of hydrogen by Cavendish and of oxygen by Priestley; and consequently previous to these discoveries G. A. was not needed. The first method of G. A. was suggested and employed by Priestley. He had discovered that nitric oxide unites with oxygen, and that after the mixture of the two gases had been made, a contraction in volume took place.. Priestley showed that from this contraction an estimate might be made of the quantity of oxygen present in air. The apparatus for observing this contraction, and, therefore, for judging of the purity of the air, or the amount of oxygen it contained, was called a *eudiometer* (*eudios*, 'fine,' and *metron*, 'a measure'). Priestley's method, however, was inaccurate, as were others subsequently introduced. The analysis of a gas was first made an accurate and simple operation by Bunsen of Heidelberg more than thirty years ago. The apparatus employed in the analysis of gases has since been modified by Williamson and Russell, Regnault and Reiset, Frankland and Ward; but Bunsen's method still remains in practice. The limits of this article prevent us from entering into a discussion of the various apparatus; we can only point out the principle of the method now in use in the analysis of gases. Gases may be divided (for the consideration of their analysis) into two groups:—(1) Those which can be absorbed, and therefore removed from a gaseous mixture by the action of solid or liquid substances; (2) those which cannot be so absorbed. In analysing a mixture containing gases of the first group, a certain quantity is first introduced into the eudiometer tube. (This consists of a glass tube graduated from above downwards, and having platinum wires sealed to its upper part, which nearly touch one another and permit an electric spark to pass between them.) In introducing the gaseous mixture under examination into this tube, it is first filled with mercury and inverted in a vessel of mercury. A sufficient quantity of gas is then made to bubble up into it, and thus to displace the mercury. Careful observations are then made (1) of the volume of the gas; (2) of its temperature (or, what comes to the same thing, if the gas has remained long enough in the tube, of the temperature of the room); (3) of the height of the column of mercury in the tube above the level of the mercury in the outer vessel; (4) of the height of the barometer. The difference between the fourth and third observation gives the pressure of the gas. A knowledge of the pressure and the temperature is of the greatest importance, because the volume of a gas alters considerably if either of these change. A certain volume, then, of the gas having been introduced into the tube, and its temperature and pressure noted, the absorbent is introduced either in the solid or liquid condition, as the case may be; and when no further contraction is observed, the volume of the residual gas is measured and its temperature and pressure observed as before. In ascertaining the results of the analysis, it is necessary to compare the volumes before and after absorption under the same conditions of temperature and pressure. The temperature and pressure at which gases are compared with one another are 0° C. and 760 millimetres. A calculation is therefore necessary to arrive at the volume which the gases *would* occupy if measured under these conditions. This is accomplished by means of the formula

Eudiometer Tube.

$$V' = V \times \frac{B}{760} \times \frac{273}{273 + t}$$

In which

V' = The volume at 0° C. and 760.
V = The observed volume.
B = The height of the barometer in millimetres.
t = The observed temperature.

The volume which a gas occupies at 0° C. and 760 millimetres is called its normal volume. To arrive at the normal volume of the absorbed gas, the normal volume of the gas after absorption is subtracted from the normal volume of the mixture before absorption. The gases which can be determined by absorption are as follows:—

(1) Hydrochloric acid, hydrobromic acid, hydriodic acid. These are absorbed in sulphate of sodium.

(2) Hydrosulphuric acid (sulphuretted hydrogen), sulphurous acid, carbonic acid. These are absorbed by caustic potash, but not by sulphate of sodium.

(3) Oxygen, nitric oxide, carbonic oxide, olefiant gas. These are absorbed neither by sulphate of sodium nor by caustic potash. Oxygen is absorbed by a solution of pyrogallic acid and caustic potash. Nitric oxide is determined by the addition of a small quantity of oxygen to convert it into nitrous acid, and then the latter is absorbed by caustic potash. Carbonic oxide is absorbed by a solution of cuprous chloride, olefiant gas by fuming sulphuric acid.

The gases of the second group (*i.e.*, those which cannot be determined by absorption) are estimated indirectly. They consist of nitrogen, hydrogen, and gaseous hydrocarbons (marsh gas, ethane, &c.). Nitrogen is determined by removing all the other gases and measuring the residual volume; hydrogen, by adding to the mixture excess of oxygen, closing the tube with the thumb, and exploding by means of an electric spark. Two-thirds of the contraction which occurs represents the volume of hydrogen. The gaseous hydrocarbons are estimated in much the same manner, but after the contraction which follows the explosion has been observed, the carbonic acid is absorbed by caustic potash, and the contraction again observed. Two-thirds of the first contraction represents the volume of the hydrogen, the whole of the second that of the carbonic acid which has been formed by the oxidation of the carbon. The weight of carbon and hydrogen is easily ascertained from a knowledge of the facts that 22·33 cubic centimetres of the latter at 0° C. and 760 millimetres weigh 0·002 grammes, and that the same volume of the former contains 0·012 grammes of carbon.

Gas, Lighting by. Gas, the popular name of coal-gas, was first turned to useful account for purposes of illumination in 1792 by Mr. W. Murdoch, who lighted his premises at Redruth, in Cornwall, with it. Twelve years later he applied it to the illumination of Messrs. Boulton & Watt's factory at Soho, Birmingham, and other works were soon thereafter similarly lighted. In 1810 the London and Westminster Gaslight Company was incorporated by Act of Parliament, and in 1813 gas superseded the use of oil in certain London thoroughfares. From remote times gas had been observed as a natural product issuing from rents in the earth's crust, and for some years before Mr. Murdoch's success its production from coal formed a common laboratory experiment. Whenever the utility of gas for artificial lighting was demonstrated, it ceased to be regarded as a scientific curiosity, and its manufacture soon developed into an important branch of industry. Since that period the use of gas has gradually spread throughout the civilised world, lightening labour, stimulating research, creating new branches of industry, and otherwise conferring inestimable benefits on mankind. It has been calculated, on trustworthy data, that in 1874 not less than 7,300,000 tons of coal were used in the United Kingdom in gasmaking.

When coal is subjected to destructive distillation in retorts or close vessels, various volatile products are expelled, and coke remains as residue. The products evolved are permanent gaseous compounds of hydrogen, carbon, oxygen, nitrogen, and sulphur mixed with vapours condensable into liquids and solids. Part of the permanent gases consists of impurities, and these, together with the condensable products, are removed as far as practicable in the subsequent processes of manufacture. The purified gas contains marsh gas, hydrogen, carbonic oxide, olefiant gas, various hydrocarbons, and nitrogen, with traces of other impurities. In the course of manufacture, tar and volatile oils, ammonia compounds, sulphuretted hydrogen, carbonic acid, and bisulphide of carbon are eliminated. The illuminating power of gas is chiefly due to olefiant gas and other heavy hydrocarbons, which all burn with a bright flame. Marsh gas, hydrogen, and carbonic oxide compose the great bulk of gas, and have more value as heat-producers than light-givers; nitrogen is incombustible and useless, and is regarded as an impurity. The relative proportions of the whole volatilised products are governed by the temperature and duration of the destructive distillation. A low temperature favours the production of a large proportion of condensable hydrocarbon vapours, while a high heat decomposes the luminous gases, and evolves many of little practical value. It is a matter, therefore, of the utmost importance to employ a temperature that will yield the highest proportion of the more valuable and less injurious heavy hydrocarbons.

Highly bituminous coal is best adapted for gasmaking. Cannel and Scotch parrot coal yield good gas with little coke, and English caking coals much gas of an inferior quality with superior coke. A ton of the latter yields on an average 10,000 cubic feet of gas, and the cannel coal of Wigan and Lesmahago, yield respectively 9500 and 11,300 cubic feet per ton. The richest coal for gasmaking yet discovered in the United Kingdom is the cannel of Boghead near Bathgate. It yields 15,000 cubic feet of gas per ton, of an illuminating power equivalent to from 35 to 40 standard candles.

The apparatus used in the manufacture of gas consists essentially of a series of retorts which communicate with a hydraulic main, in which part of the tar is deposited; the cooling apparatus, where the condensation of the liquids is completed; various purifiers for removing gaseous impurities; and a gas-holder for storing the purified gas.

The *retorts* are usually D-shaped or oval tubes of fireclay, 7 to 10 feet long, 12 inches high, and 18 inches wide. They are placed horizontally in groups of five or six in a furnace. The open end of each retort has a mouthpiece of cast iron, with a lid which can be tightly screwed down and luted after the charge of coal (about 1½ cwt.) is introduced. From the neck a cast-iron stand-pipe rises up perpendicularly, and with a curve dips down into the large horizontal cylinder of cast iron called the *hydraulic main.* The main is kept half filled with tar, into which the ends of the *dip-pipes* enter, the return of the gas to the retorts when opened for recharging being thus effectually prevented. The gas, charged with impurities, escapes from the retorts by the stand-pipes and dip-pipes to the hydraulic main, and under the reduced temperature a considerable portion of its vapours is condensed. Large quantities of the tar and ammoniacal products liquefy in the main, whence they pass by an overflow pipe into the tar well, to be subsequently withdrawn. The hot gas then passes into the *condenser*, to be freed of all the residual vaporous liquids. The condensed vapours flow into a cistern, and the gas leaves the condenser greatly reduced in temperature. The noxious gases sulphuretted hydrogen, ammonia, and carbonic acid still remain, and their elimination must be effected as thoroughly as possible. A portion of them is got rid of by the use of the *lime purifier*, between which and the condenser an *exhauster* or pumping engine is commonly placed, which relieves the retorts from internal pressure, and causes a continuous flow of the gas from the hydraulic main through the whole apparatus to the gas-holder. Slaked lime, either in the form of a powder or milk of lime is the most effective agent in removing the impurities still in the gas. The *dry*-lime purifier is composed of a rectangular iron vessel containing sieves or perforated shelves spread over with fresh-slaked lime. The gas is led in at the bottom of the purifier, and in passing through the layers of lime it leaves behind the sulphuretted hydrogen and carbonic acid and part of the ammonia. Three such purifiers are used in succession. The quantity of lime required depends upon the amount of impurities in the gas. One thousand cubic feet of gas, with 5 per cent. of impurities, requires 15 lbs. of lime.

In the *wet*-lime purifier the gas is brought into contact with milk of lime agitated by a stirrer. Spent gas lime, which possesses a most fetid odour, is, after drying, partly used for luting the retorts and partly sold for manure. A mixture of hydrated oxide of iron and sawdust has been found to be a very efficient substitute for lime, but it does not remove the carbonic acid, and consequently entails the subsequent use of lime. The remaining ammonia is removed by leading the gas from the dry-lime purifier to the bottom of an apparatus called a *scrubber*, which is filled with small coke, furze, or other material. Water percolates through it, and dissolves out the ammonia as the gas ascends. The thoroughness of the purifying processes may be tested as follows:—If sulphuretted hydrogen be present, it will blacken a test paper dipped in acetate of lead; ammonia will impart a brown colour to a turmeric test paper slightly moistened; and a turbidity in lime-water will ensue if the gas passed through it contain carbonic acid. The purified gas then passes to the *station-meter*, which measures and registers the quantity and rate of production, and thence it makes its exit to the *gas-holder* to be stored for use. A gas-holder consists of a large cylindrical tank of wrought iron, inverted into a tank of masonry or brick-work containing water. The inverted tank is confined in its position by cast-iron columns, provided with guiding rods, up and down which the tank moves freely. Sometimes it is suspended from the columns by chains with heavy counterbalancing weights; but the use of an exhauster renders this unnecessary, as the pressure of gas flowing in is always sufficient to raise the tank, and occasionally it has to be weighted to drive the gas through the street mains. The outlet and inlet pipes for the gas rise above the level of the water. Evaporation is to a great extent retarded by a layer of coal oil, which soon collects. Telescopic gas-holders—two or three tanks sliding into each other—are in use in some large works. The amount of gas to be consumed within a certain time regulates the size of the tank.

The gas is distributed for consumption through large cast-iron conduit-pipes or *mains*, with smaller ramifications, called *service pipes*, leading to and connected with the *gas-fittings* of the dwelling-house or place where the gas is to be consumed. The gas-fittings—small tubes of tin or pipe-metal—serve to convey the gas to the burner. Between the gas-holder and the mains a *governor*, resembling a small gas-holder, is placed to regulate the flow of the gas and maintain a uniform pressure. It is so contrived that the orifice of the inlet pipe is contracted if the pressure of gas in the gas-holder exceed that in the mains, and *vice versa.* Governors are also introduced into mains to correct variations arising from different levels. *Regulators*, acting on the same principle, are placed near meters or on burners to control the delivery pressure to $\frac{6}{10}$ths of a inch column of water, representing $\frac{1}{50}$th of a lb. per square inch. Gas practically increases in pressure $\frac{1}{10}$th of an inch of water for every 10 feet of altitude on account of atmospheric pressure diminishing.

Gas meters are self-acting machines for measuring the quantity of gas burned by a consumer. In the early days of gas-lighting meters were unknown, and the consumer was charged according to the number and size of his burners, and the duration of lighting. The first gas meter was made about 1815 by Mr. Samuel Clegg, a name inseparably associated with the early improvements in gas machinery. Two kind of meters are now used, *wet* and *dry*. The wet meter consists of an iron cylindrical case, more than half filled with water, enclosing a smaller cylinder or drum closed at the ends and rotating on a horizontal axis. The drum is divided by four curved radii into five chambers, four around a central one. Each of the four outer chambers communicates by one small aperture with the space between the two cylinders leading to the outlet pipe, and by another with the axial chamber into which the gas is led by a pipe bent above the level of the water. These apertures are opened and closed in succession as the drum revolves through the water. The gas on passing into the central chamber escapes into one of the compartments, and by expansive action on the upper side and on the water causes the drum to rotate. Each of the chambers is in turn subjected to this process, the rotation being thereby maintained; and while the gas is passing into one chamber, it is escaping from another and making its way to the burners. The drum has a known capacity, and the number of cubic feet passed through it in one revolution is indicated on separate dials marking from 1 to 10,000 cubic feet by means of an arrangement of toothed wheels driven by the axle of the drum. The wet meter has several defects. The flow of gas is apt to cease if the water be not maintained at its proper level; aqueous vapour may condense in the gas-pipes, and either choke them or cause unsteadiness in the flame; and an exposed meter is liable to derangement from frost. To remedy these and other defects the dry meter has been invented. In it there are two or more measuring chambers from which the gas is displaced by the piston-like action of metal discs. By each backward and forward motion, controlled by nicely-contrived valves, a certain constant quantity of gas is discharged, and its registration is effected by suitable clockwork connected by levers with the discs. The dry meter is not so durable as the wet meter, and faulty working is not so easily detected. Various forms of it are gradually being introduced by English gas companies and on the Continent, and in the United States they are extensively adopted.

The Sale of Gas Act (1859) regulates the construction of meters, and provides for their public inspection, and sealing if found correct. The adoption of the Act, however, is optional. The economical consumption of gas is in a great measure promoted by the use of proper *gas-burners*. Those chiefly used are the union jet or fishtail, bat's-wing, Argand, and its various modifications. The nipple of the former is pierced obliquely with two holes meeting at the top and producing a flat flame; the bat's-wing has a fine slit and gives a flame of the form implied. These two are best suited for burning cannel gas issuing at a pressure of five to six tenths of an inch of water. In the Argand burner the gas issues from a number of minute holes on the upper surface of a hollow ring, and burns with a circular flame. The Bude burner is a concentric series of Argand rings. Glass chimneys are used with the Argand burners in order to effect the complete combustion of the gas, which to be burned to best advantage should not exceed 18 to 19 candle power.

As the value of gas depends upon its illuminating power, it is of the utmost importance to estimate it. This is effected, among other methods, by the use of a Photometer (q. v.). By it a comparison is made between the light of a gas flame consuming at the rate of 5 cubic feet per hour, and a sperm candle, one-sixth of 1 lb. weight, burning 120 grains per hour, called a *standard candle*. The comparative cost of different lighting materials giving the same amount of light has been shown by experiment to be as follows:—Spermaceti candles, 6s. 8d., paraffin candle, 3s. 10d.; tallow candles, 2s. 8d.; sperm oil, 1s. 10d.; and gas, 4½d.

In regard to wholesomeness gas contrasts favourably with other artificial lights, as well as in its safety. Unlike candles and lamps, it is not carried about, it emits no sparks, and dispenses with 'snuffing' or trimming. Its peculiar smell quickly permeates the air and leads to the detection of leakage. Gas is explosive only when mixed with air in the proportions of from 3 to 9 of air to 1 of gas. Gas of a highly illuminating quality may be obtained from substances other than coal, as peat, wood, resin, oil, and petroleum. None of these, however, have as yet entered into serious commercial competition with coal for the manufacture of gas.

Gascoigne′, George, an Elizabethan poet, son of Sir John G. of Cardigan, Bedfordshire, was born about 1525. He was educated at Trinity College, Cambridge, studied law at Gray's Inn, was imprisoned in 1548 on a charge of dicing, and after a course of dissipation, served as a soldier in Holland under William of Orange. He returned to England in 1573, and in 1575 recited verses before Queen Elizabeth at Kenilworth. Henceforth he lived by his pen, producing numerous pieces, mostly of a satirical cast, until his death at Stamford in 1577. G. was a prolific and versatile writer. His play *The Supposes*, translated from Ariosto, is the earliest English prose comedy; his *Dan Bartholemew* is the first English imitation of the Italian mock-heroic poetry; his *Jeronini* is the forerunner of the euphuistic prose tales of Greene and Lyly; and his *Steel Glas* (1576), one of the earliest long English satires. G. possessed uncommon literary energy. His verse is remarkably clear and abounds in rough mirthful vigour and pathetic personal retrospects. Minto compares G. to Byron in his life and the style of his writing. A complete edition of his works by W. C. Hazlitt has been issued in the 'Roxburghe Library.' See Minto's *English Poets* and Skeat's *Specimens of English Literature*.

Gascoigne, Sir William, an English judge, who has obtained a place in history, was born at Gawthorp, Yorkshire, about 1350. On the accession of Henry IV. he was made a Justice of Common Pleas, and in 1401 Chief Justice of the King's Bench. His courageous vindication of law as something higher than royal mandate was exemplified in his refusal to pass sentence of death upon Archbishop Scroop as a traitor. Still more famous is the incident immortalised by Shakespeare when he ordered Prince Henry to be committed to prison for striking him on the bench. G. died 17th December 1413.

Gasconade′, a river rising in Missouri, U.S., and flowing N.E. to the Missouri, which it joins 36 miles below Jefferson city, after a course of 250 miles. It gives name to a village, and to a county rich in yellow pine and other timber.

Gasconnade, in French, is a boastful or extravagant statement, the Gascons having been proverbial for braggadocio. The word *Gascon* is also used as synonymous with boaster, and a verb *gasconner*, to boast, has been formed.

Gas′cony (Fr. *Gascogne*, Lat. *Vasconia*, 'the land of the *Basques*,' *Vascons* or *Gascons*), an old province of the S. of France, which lay between the Atlantic, Pyrenees, and Garonne. It included the present departments of Hautes Pyrénées, Landes, and Gers, and parts of Haute-Garonne, Tarn-et-Garonne, and Lot-et-Garonne. It was united with Aquitaine, passed to Henry II. of England in 1152 on his marriage with Eleanor, the divorced wife of Louis VII., and was not joined to the French monarchy until 1453.

Gas′-Engine is an engine of the same general structure as the ordinary steam-engine, but differs in obtaining its motive power from the explosion of a mixture of inflammable gas and air. As early as 1799 Lebon, a French artisan, had constructed and patented such a machine. The inflammable mixture, introduced alternately on each side of the piston, was fired by an electric spark. It was found to work well and effectively, but coal gas not having been at that time introduced for illuminating purposes, the expense of preparing the mixture rendered the scheme a practical failure. Lenoir's engine, patented in 1860, was very much a reproduction of Lebon's; while the chief points of difference in Hugon's machine, constructed about the same time, consisted in firing the mixture by a gas jet and in introducing a little water, which, converted into steam by the great heat, lessened the violence of the action. Very different in action, and much more economical in the consumption of its fuel than any of its predecessors, is the invention of Otto and Langen of Köln, exhibited at Paris in 1867. The gaseous mixture, introduced beneath and fired by a permanent gas jet, shoots up the heavy piston to the top of the vertical cylinder. A partial vacuum ensues and the piston descends, urged down by its own weight and the atmospheric pressure. A heavy fly-wheel equalises the motion as far as possible, and maintains the action during the moments when the piston is ineffective.

Gas′es are fluids which ultimately fill the vessel in which they are contained. This power of indefinite expansion distinguishes them at once from liquids, and renders it impossible for them to be contained in open vessels. When a gas is kept in a closed vessel, it exerts upon the walls of the vessel an outward pressure, an explanation of which is readily found upon the hypothesis, first advanced by Daniel Bernoulli, and now universally accepted, that a gas consists of a crowd of minute particles, shooting about in all directions with generally great velocities. The pressure, then, obviously depends upon the number of impacts which take place over unit surface in unit time. Hence, if the number of particles in the given enclosed space be increased—in other words, if the density be made greater—the pressure must also increase; and experiment proves that this increase of pressure follows the very simple numerical law that *at constant temperature the pressure is proportional to the density.* This law was first enunciated by Robert Boyle in 1668 under the form: the volume of a portion of a gas varies inversely as the pressure. Another and very suggestive statement proposed by Rankine is, that any portion of gaseous matter exerts the same pressure against the sides of a vessel as if the other portions had not been there; and this, as shown by Dalton, whether these portions be of the same gas or not.

It is known from experiment that matter, whether it be solid, liquid, or gaseous, is raised in temperature when heat is applied, provided that during the operation there is no change in condition; and further, that this rise of temperature is *generally* accompanied by an increase of volume. In the case of G., a very simple numerical law, discovered by Charles in 1787, holds. It is, that under constant pressure, and for a given rise of temperature, the volume of a gas expands by a fraction of itself, which is the same for all G. Thus, a gas at 0° C. expands by $\frac{1}{273}$ of its volume for a rise of 1°; and a gas at 1° C. expands by $\frac{1}{274}$ of its volume for a further rise of 1°, and so on. Or, if we take a gas of 273 cubic inches at 0° C., and under a given pressure, its volume at 1° C. will be 274; at 2°, 275; at 10°, 283; at 100°, 373, &c. This hints at an absolute zero of temperature 273° below zero Centigrade, a result fully corroborated by other thermo-dynamic relations, and permits us to enunciate Charles's law in the much simpler form, that *at constant pressure the volume of a gas is proportional to its absolute temperature.* Boyle's and Charles's laws may now be combined in the formula $pv = Ct$, where p is the pressure, v the volume, t the absolute temperature, and C a constant depending upon the particular gas used. No gas accurately fulfils this law; and when the gas is near its point of liquefaction, the deviations from it are considerable. The non-condensable G.—hydrogen, oxygen, nitrogen, carbonic oxide, nitric oxide, and marsh gas—however, very nearly fulfil it, and more nearly the higher the temperature and greater the volume. When a gas is permitted to expand of itself, its temperature falls, since part of its thermal energy is transformed into mechanical work to effect the expansion; and when a gas is suddenly condensed, an evolution of heat is the consequence, which of course ultimately tends to raise the temperature of the gas. According to the Kinetic Theory given above, which regards a gas as a crowd of molecules moving in all directions with various velocities, the absolute temperature of a gas is proportional to the arithmetic mean of the squares of the individual velocities. The square root of this mean is called the velocity of mean square, and by it we compare different gaseous systems. Calling the velocity V, the equation $pv = Ct$ may be written $p = a\rho V^2$, where ρ is the density, and a a constant equal to one-third for the ideal perfect gas. This equation may be put in the form $p = amnV^2$, where m is the mass of an individual molecule, and n the number of molecules in unit volume. For another given gas, $p' = a\,m'\,n'\,V'^2$; hence, if the pressure is the same for both, $mnV^2 = m'\,n'\,V'^2$. If their temperatures are equal, evidently $m\,V^2 = m'\,V'^2$; and hence (dividing the one equation by the other) follows Avogadro's law, that *two G. at the same temperature and pressure have the same number of molecules in unit volume.* A direct consequence of this is $\rho : \rho' :: m : m'$, or the densities of two G. at the same temperature and pressure are proportional to the masses of their individual molecules—a relation first given by Gay-Lussac in the form that the densities of G. are proportional to their atomic weights.

The majority of G. can be condensed to the liquid form, and in general there is a distinct transition stage from the one form to the other. Dr. Andrews of Belfast has shown, however, in the case of carbonic acid, and probably of all G., that if the condensation be effected by pressure while the gas is kept at a temperature above a certain critical value, it is impossible to fix the moment of transition or to tell when the substance ceases to be gas and begins to be liquid. Under EVAPORATION, the chief phenomena attending the transformation of liquids into G. are noticed. In certain circumstances G. may condense at once into the solid state, as exemplified by the sublimation of sulphur and the formation of hoar-frost. The resistance which G. present to solids passing through them is of great importance in the practice of Gunnery (q. v.). It increases with the velocity; but except for moderate velocities, when it may be taken as proportional to the *square*, the resistance is related to the velocity according to a complex and only approximately determinable law. In the phenomenon of Winds (q. v.), we have the relative motion of large portions of the same gaseous material, a motion which also experiences resistance. In this case, however, the resistance is probably due chiefly to the mutual diffusion of contiguous portions. Under the headings HEAT, LIGHT, SOUND, &c., other properties of G. will be noticed. See also MOLECULAR THEORY. In Clerk Maxwell's *Theory of Heat* and Balfour Stewart's *Treatise on Heat*, the Kinetic Theory is discussed with fulness and lucidity.

Gas'kell, Elizabeth Cleghorn, an English novelist, born in 1822. She became the wife of the Rev. William G., a Unitarian minister at Manchester, and died November 12, 1865. Her leading works are *Mary Barton* (1848), a touching tale of factory life in Manchester, *The Moorland Cottage* (1850), *Ruth* (1853), *North and South* (1855), *Lizzie Leigh, Cranford, Sylvia's Lovers* (1863), *Cousin Phyllis*, and a *Life of Charlotte Brontë* (1857). Her novels give faithful and graphic pictures of artisan life and forcible delineations of character, besides showing tender human sympathy, quiet humour, and fine descriptive power.

Gas-Lighting in Railway Trains. Gas has been applied to the lighting of railway carriages, but to a very limited extent. Several plans have been suggested, but the fact that gas-light in trains has not been generally adopted is evidence that no method yet devised meets the exigencies of the case. These are, that little room be occupied by the apparatus, that each carriage be lighted independently of the others, and that the light be as brilliant, as cheap, and as certain under all circumstances as oil on long journeys. Gas, under the ordinary pressure, has been used for many years on the Metropolitan Underground Railway. The gas-holder is replenished at the end of a double journey. This plan, it is obvious, is quite impracticable in journeys of some hours' duration. The difficulty to be overcome, before the general adoption of gas-lighting, is to reduce gas, stored under a pressure of 10 or 15 atmospheres, to a pressure of $\frac{6}{8}$ths of an inch column of water, and to maintain it thereat under all circumstances during consumption.

Gasom'eter. See GAS, LIGHTING BY.

Gaspé Basin, a prosperous village in the province of Quebec, on the beautiful Bay of Gaspé, which stretches about 20 miles inland from the Gulf of St. Lawrence. It is the chief port of entry under the free port system, has new wharves and stores, and bids fair to become the capital of the fertile district of Gaspé. There are valuable whale and cod fisheries, and petroleum is obtained in the neighbourhood. Pop. 700.

Gassen'di, Pierre, a French philosopher and astronomer, was born at Champtercier (Basses Alpes), January 22, 1592. He studied at Aix, where in 1616 he was chosen Professor of Philosophy and Theology. Relinquishing this post in 1623, he obtained a benefice at Digne, where he wrote his *Exercitationes Paradoxicæ adversus Aristotelem* (Grenoble, 1624), a work in which he asserted his utter disbelief in the prevailing dogma that the Church and the scholastic philosophy were inseparable. After a visit to Paris in 1624, and to Holland in 1628, he became Professor of Mathematics in the Collége-Royal de France at Paris, where he died, 24th October 1655. He adopted the philosophy of Epicurus; and though his views were in direct antagonism to those of Descartes, he had for that philosopher a deep admiration, and even a warm friendship, which, however, ceased for a time after the publication of his *Disquisitio Metaphysica adversus Cartesium* (Par. 1642). His greatest work is his *De Vita, Moribus et Placitis Epicuri* (Lyon, 1649), of which his *Syntagma Epicuri* forms a part. As an astronomer and mathematician G. did not display much original talent, but he strongly favoured the study of physical science. He was the first to observe the transit of Mercury predicted by Kepler, and wrote biographies of Tycho Brahé, Copernicus, Puerbach, and Regiomontanus (which form together a history of the early progress of astronomy), a treatise on *Parhelia* (Par. 1630), and a descriptive catalogue of astronomical observations taken between 1618 and 1655. G. was a steady and courageous friend of men like Kepler, Galileo, and Hobbes. His collected works were published by Montmort and Sorbière at Lyon in 1658, and by Averrani at Florence in 1728. See Bugerel's *Vie de G.* (Par. 1737).

Gasse'rian Gang'lion is a swelling on one of the roots of the fifth cranial nerve, situated on the upper part of the petrous portion of the temporal bone. It gives off three branches—(1) the ophthalmic, which enters the orbit; (2) the superior maxillary, for the upper jaw; and (3) the inferior maxillary, for the external ear, the tongue, the lower teeth, and the muscles of mastication. The G. G. is on the sensory root of the nerve. Its special functions are unknown.

Gass'ner, Johann Joseph, an 'exorcist' of the last century, was born at Bratz, in the Tyrol, August 28, 1727. Entering the Catholic Church, he became priest at Klösherbe, in the diocese of Coire, and in a short time acquired a reputation for curing with a mere prayer or command persons in fits or otherwise 'possessed of devils.' For a time he had crowds of believers, and although some prelates opposed, others, including the Bishop of Ratisbon, supported him; and even yet, in spite of efforts made to convict him of imposture, there are many who consider him to have possessed some equivalent to the 'mesmerism' or 'psychic force' of the present day. He died Dean of Berndorf, 4th April 1779.

Gas-Tar. See TAR.

Gasteromycetes, one of the six orders into which the *Fungi* (q. v.) are divided, of which the Puffball (q. v.) is an example.

Gasterop'oda (Gr. 'belly-footed'), a large class of Higher or Cephalous *Mollusca*, distinguished generally by having a *shell*, commonly *univalve* or composed of one piece (as seen in the whelks), or which exists in one family (that of the *Chitonidæ*) as a *multivalve* structure, *i.e.*, composed of more than two pieces. In no case is the shell of G. *bivalve*, or composed of two pieces, as in *Lamellibranchiata* (q. v.). A shell may be wanting, however, in many G., as in the slugs, sea-lemons (*Doris*), sea-hares (*Aplysia*), &c. The locomotion of the G. is performed, as seen in the snail or whelk, by a broad ventral 'foot,' from which the class derives its name. Occasionally, as in the *Heteropoda*, this 'foot' may be modified from the more typical form to a flattened fin-like organ. The foot is generally divisible into a *propodium*, *mesopodium*, and *metapodium*, these divisions being the front, middle, and posterior portions of the organ; and the metapodium frequently develops a horny or limy plate, the *operculum*, which is used to close the shell when the animal has withdrawn into its abode. The head of the G. has *tentacles* and eyes, and the mouth contains a *tongue* or *odontophore*. Organs of hearing are also developed in the form of *otoliths* or ear-sacs. The digestive system comprehends a *stomach, intestine, liver*, and *salivary glands*. The *heart* consists of an auricle and ventricle, and is purely *systemic*, in that it serves only to propel pure blood throughout the system. Breathing is carried on by gills or pulmonary sacs, or simply by the walls of the *mantle cavity*; the *pallium* or mantle being the general investment or skin of the body, which, as in other *Mollusca*, secretes and enlarges the *shell*. This structure in the G. exists essentially in the shape of a spiral cone, seen in its simplest form in the limpets, and from it the spiral shell of the whelks and other G. is formed by the shell being rolled upon itself. The G. shell may be *discoid* (as in *Planorbis*, where the whorls of the body lie in one plane), or it may be *turreted, trochoid*, or more commonly *turbinated*. A central axis or *columella* is seen in G. shells, this axis having the embryonic or first-formed shell at its apex, so as to constitute a kind of *nucleus*. The mouth aperture may be unindented (*holostomatous shells, e.g.*, snail), or indented by a groove for the passage of a breathing-siphon (*e.g.*, whelk), when the shell is said to be *siphonostomatous*. The *nervous system* consists of three chief ganglia, one in the head (*cephalic* or *cerebral*), a second in the foot (*pedal*), and a third in the neighbourhood of the heart and gills (*branchial* or *parieto-splanchnic*). The sexes may be distinct or united in the same individual, and the young Gasteropod (whether possessing a shell or not when adult) is invariably provided with a small shell. The G. are *classified* in two chief divisions, the *Branchio-G.*, or those breathing by means of gills, and the *Pulmo-G.*, or those breathing by lung-sacs. The chief families of the first division are the *Muricidæ* and *Buccinidæ* (whelks), *Cypræidæ* (cowries), *Conidæ* (cone-shells), *Littorinidæ* (periwinkles), *Patellidæ* (limpets), *Chitonidæ* (chitons), *Aplysidæ* (sea-hares), *Doridæ* (sea-lemons), &c. In the Pulmo-G. the snails (*Helicidæ*), slugs (*Limacidæ*), and other families are included.

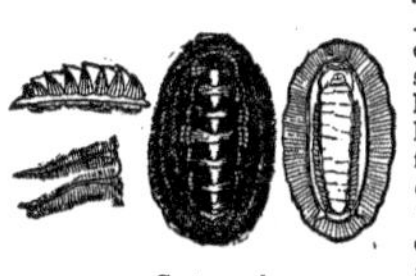

Gasteropod.

Fossil G.—These *Mollusca* appear to be first represented as fossils in the Upper Cambrian rocks, and they hold a place in all the stratified formations down to the present day, when they attain perhaps the maximum of their development.

Gasteros'teus. See STICKLEBACK.

Gastral'gia, or **Stomach Colic,** is a severe pain in the stomach frequently arising from slight causes. In some cases it is invariably produced by certain articles of diet, such as an egg; in others by irregularities in diet; and in others again every sort of diet produces it, so that each meal is followed by severe pain. Women are more subject to G. than men, but cases occur of this disease among men otherwise robust and healthy. The seizure is sudden, and the pain is most severe round or above the umbilicus. G. may continue from a few moments to a few hours, and it subsides almost as rapidly as it appears, leaving, however, a soreness. G. is generally accompanied by sickness, vomiting, flatulence, and diarrhœa. In G. the pulse is natural; there is no fever; and the pain is relieved by pressure, features which distinguish it from Enteritis (q. v.). Treatment:—Hot fomentations, mustard poultices, and friction. When the bowels are confined, an aperient should be given, followed by opiates or diffusible stimulants, as ether, chlorodyne, &c.

Gas'tric Juice. This is the juice secreted by various small glands in the mucous membrane of the Stomach (q. v.). When obtained without mixture with saliva, it is a clear, colourless, slightly viscid, acid fluid, which under the microscope shows only a few cells derived from the glands. As obtained from man, it has the following chemical composition in 1000 parts:—Water, 994·4, solids, 5·60—the solids consisting of (*a*) *organic matter*, a peculiar ferment termed *Pepsin* (q. v.), 3·19, and (*b*) *inorganic matter*, consisting of chloride of sodium, 1·46, chloride of potassium, 0·55, chloride of calcium, 0·06, phosphates of magnesia, lime, and iron, 0·12, and a slight trace of free acid, which some chemists have determined to be hydrochloric, while others assert it is lactic acid. The active principle of the G. J. is pepsin, which has the property of acting upon the albuminous materials in food, converting these into Peptones (q. v.). The juice is secreted during digestion, the stimulus apparently being the contact of any solid or fluid matter with the inner surface of the stomach. See DIGESTION.

Gastri'tis, and **Gastro-Enteritis.** See ENTERITIS.

Gastrochæ'na, a genus of Lamellibranchiate *Mollusca* forming the type of a family (*Gastrochænidæ*). The shell is wedge-shaped, and closed behind, but open in front. The foot is grooved, and the siphons are united nearly to their tips. *G. modiolina*, the typical British species, has a habit of burrowing into sand, rocks, or amongst oyster-shells, and of lining its burrow with a limy structure. It is also common on the Mediterranean coasts. The watering-pot shell or *Aspergillum* (q. v.) belongs to this family.

Gastrocne'mius (Gr. 'the calf of the leg') is the most external of three superficial muscles which form the calf of the leg, and which end in the strong tendon above the heel called the *tendo*

Achilles. The other two muscles of the group are the *soleus* and *plantaris.* See LEG.

Gastrolo'bium, a genus of Leguminous plants embracing many species peculiar to Australia. They are chiefly shrubs with yellow flowers, and are very poisonous to cattle, large numbers of which die yearly by eating the foliage. The most fatal species are *G. bilobum* and *G. spinosum.* Several species are grown in British greenhouses.

Gastros'tomy (Gr. *gastēr,* 'the belly or stomach,' and *stoma,* 'the mouth'), an operation which has been performed to relieve the patient from starvation by making an incision through the abdomen into the stomach for the purpose of introducing food directly into the stomach. By such means life may be prolonged for a short time, and the patient may be sustained until the obstruction is removed, as in cases of stricture of the gullet.

Gastrot'omy (Gr. *gastēr,* 'the belly,' and *tomē,* 'an incision'), an incision into the cavity of the Abdomen (q. v.) for the purpose of removing some foreign body, diseased tissue, or the fœtus *in utero,* in which latter case the operation is called Cæsarean Operation (q. v.). G. is very frequently had recourse to in modern surgery for the purpose of removing diseased ovaries, and such operations are designated Ovariotomy (q. v.).

Gates, Horatio, a general of the American revolution, born in England in 1728. He entered the British army, served with General Braddock in 1755, and was wounded at Fort Duquesne, now Pittsburg. At the close of the war he settled in Virginia. On the breaking out of the War of Independence in 1775, he was made adjutant-general, and accompanied Washington to Cambridge (Massachusetts). He received command of the troops N. of Albany, and in October 1777 compelled General Burgoyne and his whole army to surrender at Saratoga. Defeated at Camden, 16th August 1780, by Lord Cornwallis, he was then superseded by General Greene, but was restored in 1782. In 1790 he freed all his slaves, and retired to New York, where he died, April 10, 1806.

Gates, Stealing or Injuring. Under 24 and 25 Vict. c. 97, persons maliciously damaging any fence, wall, stile, or gate are punishable by a fine of £5 above the amount of the injury done. A second offence is punishable by imprisonment with hard labour. See MALICIOUS INJURIES TO PROPERTY; FENCES, LAW REGARDING.

Gates'head, a town of England in the county of Durham, on the steep southern bank of the Tyne, opposite Newcastle, of which it practically forms a part, and with which it is connected by three bridges. It has a large parish church with a lofty tower, besides some fifty other established and dissenting churches; a handsome townhall (1869); a charitable hospital (St. Edmund's), restored by James I., and since known by his name; the Albert Memorial Reformatory; a mechanics' institute; and an ably-conducted dispensary, since an outbreak of cholera in 1831–32. The houses are mainly brick-built, and in the older parts of the town are squalid and rickety. There are extensive ironworks, foundries, brickfields, and special manufactures of anchors, chain-cables, iron-wire, chemicals, soap, glass, and tiles. The quarries for the world-famed 'Newcastle grindstones' are at G. Fell. Pop. (1871) 48,627. G., which sends one member to Parliament, became a municipal borough in 1826, having been previously (since 1317) governed by a bailiff and patentee officer under the bishops-palatine of the county. Roman relics (coins, &c.) found here have given rise to the supposition that G. was an outwork of the station at Newcastle. The town was partly destroyed by a great explosion and fire in 1854.

Gate'way. The gateways of the Greek and Roman cities were generally imposing buildings, and in the middle ages large gateways were raised at the entrances to castles, religious houses, colleges, &c. In fortified buildings the G. was most commonly an arch flanked by towers crowned by battlements, and loop-holed in the ceiling. Modern gateways are often large arches for carriages with smaller arches for foot-passengers, but there is now much variety in their construction. Fine examples of old gateways may be seen at Canterbury, Oxford, Cambridge, Bristol, &c. In Russia each city had formerly a sacred G., the best known being the sacred gate of the Kremlin, Moscow, which is one of the most important of Russian antiquities.

Gath (Heb. 'a wine-press') was one of the five royal cities of the Philistines (Josh. xiii. 3). It was captured by David when he came to the throne, but does not seem to have remained long in the hands of the Israelites (1 Chr. xviii. 1; *cf.* 1 Kings ii. 39). It was captured by Hazael, King of Syria, in the reign of Jehoash of Israel, 856 B.C. (2 Kings xii. 17), and by Uzziah, King of Judah, who dismantled it (2 Chr. xxvi. 6). In the time of Amos it was in ruins (vi. 2), and after that is no more heard of, except in a proverb (Mic. i. 10).

Gat'ineau, the name of a river and lake of Canada, in the province of Quebec. The lake lies about 150 miles W. of Grand Lake, in lat. 48° N., and is one of a series out of which rises the river, which flows S.S.W. and then S., expands into lakelets at various points, receives the Jean de Terre, and enters the Ottawa opposite the city of Ottawa, after a course of nearly 300 miles.

Gat'ling, Richard Jordan, an American inventor, was born in N. Carolina, U.S., 12th September 1818. At an early age he was anticipated by Ericsson in the discovery of screw propulsion, but his ingenuity was successfully shown in devising a machine for sowing wheat in drills. G. studied medicine at Ohio and Cincinnati, 1847–49, and subsequently engaged in railway and real estate speculations. In 1850 he invented a double-acting hemp-breaker, and in 1861–62 elaborated his masterpiece, a mitrailleuse, or repeating machine gun. At the first trial of the 'G. gun,' in 1862, it fired 200 shots per minute. It has since been adopted in the United States, as well as by several European Governments, for use with troops, and for the flank defence of fortifications.

Gatschi'na, a town of Russia, on Lake Ishora, 30 miles S.S.W. of St. Petersburg. It is the seat of a beautiful royal palace (1770), the favourite residence of Paul I., which has 600 rooms, and is encircled by splendid gardens. G. has porcelain industries, and includes among its buildings a horticultural school, and a school for foundlings. Pop. 8890.

Gau, a German word meaning generally a district, as in *gau-graf,* 'count of a district,' and more specially an old political division of Germany, which embraced several villages, and was governed by several grafs. The division was abolished in the 12th c., but the name survives in *Thurgau, Aargau, Rheingau,* &c.

Gauge, a word of various applications, signifying usually an instrument for measuring dimensions, capacity, pressure, &c. Thus we have the *button G.* for finding the dimensions of buttons; the *rain G.* for measuring the rainfall; the *steam G.* for registering the pressure of steam in a boiler; the *tide G.* for determining the height of the tide; the *wind G.* for indicating the velocity of the wind (see ANEMOMETER), &c. The railway G. is the distance between the rails of a railway; hence the *narrow G.* (4 feet 8½ inches) and the *broad G.* (7 feet).

Gauge of Railways, Law Regarding. The Act 9 and 10 Vict. c. 57 renders it unlawful to make a railway for the conveyance of passengers on any other gauge than one of 4 feet 8½ inches in Great Britain, unless the whole railway is S. of the Great Western; but railways already made on a different gauge may be so maintained: 5 feet 3 inches is the Irish gauge under the Act. The penalty for making a railway contrary to the Act is £10 per mile for every day the railway is in use.

Gau'ger (Old Fr. *gauger,* 'to measure,' probably through *galger,* from Lat. *qualificare,* 'to ascertain qualities of a thing'), an excise officer who *gauges* or measures casks of excisable liquor. A G. may not, under a penalty of forfeiting his office, traffic in excisable goods, and if he accept a bribe, is liable to a penalty of £500, and is rendered incapable of holding any Government post.

Gau'ging, in mensuration, is the measurement of the capacity of a vessel of any kind, and is of great importance in the collection of the revenue. In most instances the determination is only approximate, the vessel being taken as some simple surface of revolution, such as a spheroid or paraboloid or simply a cylinder, to which it may bear some approximate resemblance.

Gaul. See FRANCE.

Gault, the lowest member of the Upper Cretaceous formations, intermediate in position between the Lower and Upper

Greensands. It consists of a stiff compact blue clay, often used for brickmaking, and contains fossils (chiefly *Lamellibranchiata* and *Gasteropoda*) in a beautiful state of preservation. G. is developed principally at Folkestone and in Cambridgeshire. Contemporaneous rocks are found in the compact sandstones of the Blackdown Hills of Devon, in the *Lower* Pläner of N. Germany, in the schistose beds near the Swiss canton of Glarus, and in the corresponding formations of France.

Gaulthe'ria, a genus of shrubby plants belonging to the order *Ericaceæ* (q. v.). The species, which are numerous, are found in various parts of the globe, but are most abundant in America. *G. procumbens*, commonly called 'winter-green' in the United States, contains a peculiar aromatic volatile oil, which separates by distillation, and is used in medicine and perfumery under the name of 'winter-green oil.' Its leaves are astringent, and have been used as a substitute for tea; hence it has also been called 'mountain tea.' Its berries supply food during early winter to many animals, hence the plant has received the names partridge-berry, deer-berry, box-berry, &c. *G. Shallon* is a shrubby plant about 2 feet high, found in the N.W. of America. It has been introduced into Britain for a considerable time, where it flourishes in pleasure-grounds and open woods, and yearly bears abundance of berries much relished by game. The fruit makes excellent tarts. *G. hispida* of New Zealand produces white berries which are eaten.

Gaunt, John of, Duke of Lancaster, third son of Edward III., was born at Ghent—whence his name—in 1339, and married his cousin Blanche, daughter of the Duke of Lancaster, in 1359, succeeding to his father-in-law's estates in 1362. After fighting in Spain, he led an English army into France in 1372, but met no resistance, and retreated to Bordeaux with only a remnant of his troops. During Edward III.'s latter years he took a large share in the government, and rendered himself very unpopular by his overbearing insolence towards the commons, and by striving as the leader of the barons against the national party to undo the reforms of the Good Parliament. Being anxious to sieze the wealth of the great churchmen, he for a time supported Wiclif, but afterwards withdrew his favour from the reformer. The peasant revolt of 1381 forced him to fly to Scotland, whence he shortly returned to England. Claiming the throne of Castile through his marriage with a daughter of Pedro the Cruel, he invaded Spain, and in 1388 married his daughter to the Prince of the Asturias. He afterwards tried fruitlessly to rule Guienne. G. died in 1399. He was the patron of Chaucer, and is the knight of *The Boke of the Duchesse.* He is the 'time-honoured G.' of Shakespeare's *Richard II.*, where he delivers the famous panegyric on England. See Green's *Short History of the English People* (Lond. 1875).

Gaunt'lett, Dr. H. J. G., musician, was born at Wellington, Salop, in 1805, and practised as a lawyer in London. He became organist of St. Olave's, Southwark, in 1827, was made Doctor in Music in 1842, and died in 1876. He was a vigorous writer, a good organist, a prolific composer of hymn-tunes and anthems, and a strenuous promoter of congregational psalmody.

Gaur, or **Gour,** the ancient Hindu capital of Bengal, of which only ruins now remain, situated in Maldah district, on the left bank of the Ganges, about 180 miles N. of Calcutta. The original Sanskrit name was Lakshmanawati or Lucknouti. Its history has been traced back to the 7th c. A.D. In 1202 it was taken by the Mohammedans, and remained the seat of government under the Afghan dynasty until the triumph of the Mogul Akbar in 1574. About this latter date the main stream of the Ganges deserted its old bed, and the city was depopulated by a pestilence. The area now covered by ruins was estimated by Rennell to extend over 30 sq. miles, and the population could hardly have been less than one million souls. The whole has relapsed into jungle, the most renowned shooting-ground for tigers in Bengal. A few mosques and gateways still stand, in an indifferent state of repair, but the majority of the buildings have been pulled down, and the materials used in the towns for fifty miles round. The most celebrated monument is a circular minar or tower, 81 feet high and 21 feet in diameter, which is described in Fergusson's *Indian Architecture.* There are several large tanks, with masonry banks, containing good drinking water, one of which is nearly one mile long and half a mile wide.

Gaur, or **Gour** (*Bibos gaurus*), a variety of oxen (*Bovidæ*) found in small herds in S. Bahar, and other parts of Hindustan. The horns are depressed at the base; the shoulders high and prominent; the spinous processes of the dorsal vertebræ very largely developed. The general colour is a deep brown, the females being of lighter hue than the males. The average height is about 6 feet at the shoulders. A distinctive mark of the G. consists in the fore-legs being white from the knees downwards. Attempts to domesticate the G. have not been very successful. The flesh is tender and palatable, and the hides furnish strong leather.

Gauss, Karl Friedrich, a mathematician of the highest order, was born at Brunswick, 30th April 1777. In 1795 he went to the University of Göttingen, where in 1807 he became professor and director of the Observatory. Before this date he had earned a wide reputation by his *Disquisitiones Arithmeticæ* (Leips. 1801), and by his elaborate calculations of the elements of Ceres and Pallas. His *Theoria Motus Corporum Cœlestium* (Hamburg, 1809; Ger. by Haase, 1865) displays, like all his works, a marvellous combination of the greatest power of theoretical generalisation with the utmost possible practical application. In this work appears his discussion of the methods of Least Squares (q. v.), introduced by D'Alembert, and now of immense practical importance. In 1811 he calculated with singular accuracy and detail the parabolic course of the famous comet of that year. For a considerable time after this geodetic measurements engaged his attention; and during 1821-24, at the instance of the Hanoverian Government, he measured the meridian arc between Göttingen and Altona, introducing into his system of triangulation many highly original and important improvements. His principles are explained in his *Theoria Combinationis Observationum Erroribus Minimis Obnoxiæ* (Gött. 1821-23), with *Supplementum* (1826). The arrival of Weber at Göttingen in 1831 directed him to the study of the magnetism of the earth. He invented most refined and delicate instruments for recording magnetic variations and declinations; and his energy was rewarded by the formation of observatories in different localities for determining these magnetic elements. The results were published at Göttingen (6 vols. 1837-43). In 1840 his *Atlas des Erdmagnetismus* (3 vols. Leips.) was given to the world, containing the whole theory, which has undergone little extension since then. In it he introduces the function now known as the *Potential* (q. v.), proving by its means, notwithstanding, the great generality and complicacy which necessarily existed in such a subject, many important theorems, such as the impossibility of there being more than *two* magnetic poles on the earth's surface. Dioptrics, equations, series, the rotation of the earth, and other subjects in pure and mixed mathematics successively engaged his attention. His last great work was *Untersuchungen über Gegenstände der höhern Geodäsie* (Gött. 1845-47). G. died at Göttingen, February 23, 1855. Until his numerous papers, which are scattered through the various scientific and mathematical publications of the day, are collected, it will be impossible to fully realise how much he has done to science, and how much he has influenced its progress. His correspondence with Schumacher has been published by Peters (4 vols. Altona, 1860-62), that with A. von Humboldt, by Bruhns (Leips. 1877), and *Ein Umriss seines Lebens und Wirkens* by Winnecke (Bruns. 1877).

Gau'tier, Théophile, one of the finest French poets and prose writers, was born at Tarbes in Gascony, August 31, 1808. He was educated at the Colléges Louis-le-Grand and Charlemagne, and was in early life an eager student of Villon, Rabelais, and the old French authors. In 1830 he published his first volume of poems. G. was one of the most ardent of Hugo's disciples during the strife between the Romantic and Classical schools, which he has described in his *Romanticism.* In 1833 he issued *Albertus*, a poem, and in 1835 *Mademoiselle de Maupin*, a tale, which has been called the most perfect book of modern times, and which attracted the attention of Balzac, who placed G. on the staff of the *Chronique de Paris.* From 1838 onwards he wrote tales and criticisms for the leading French journals. He visited Spain in 1840, Algeria in 1845, Italy in 1850, Constantinople in 1852, and Russia in 1858. He became very popular as a prose writer, but his fame is not equal to his merit as a poet. G. died in Paris, October 23, 1872. His works include *Premières Poésies*, *Les Jeunes Francs*, *Mademoiselle de Maupin*, *Le Roman de la Momie* (a fascinating tale of ancient Egypt), *Voyage en Russie*, *Voyage en Espagne* (1843), *Théâtre* (comedies and brief humorous pieces), *Les Grotesques* (1844), notices of Villon, St. Amant, and other old French poets, *Nouvelles* (1845), *Romans et Contes*, *Émaux et Camées* (1852), *Constantinople* (1854), *La Capitaine Fracassé* (1863), *La Belle Jenny* (1865), *Peau de Tigre* (1865), *Spirite* (1866), *Tableau de Siège* (1872), &c. As a poet G. is only surpassed in French literature by one or two names, and for beauty of prose style is unexcelled by any of his countrymen. In his poetry, which has been well described as 'the faultless expression of a worship for things formally beautiful,' the French language appears endowed with new flexibility, richness, and metrical variety. See the autobiographic sketch in G.'s *Portraits Contemporains*, his *Romantisme*, and C. Baudelaire's *L'Art Romantique*.

Gauze, a thin delicate texture woven of very fine hard-spun fibre. It was originally made of silk alone, and previous to the development of the cotton trade its manufacture constituted an important industry in the W. of Scotland, of which some traces still survive. Silk G. is much used by millers in flour sifting. The name is said to be derived from *Gaza* in Palestine, where G. was first manufactured.

Gavar'ni, the well-known pseudonym of Sulpice Guillaume Paul Chevalier, a French caricaturist, who was born in Paris in 1801. Beginning life as a mechanical draughtsman, he early discovered a genius for burlesque pencilling. He first published sketches of the valley of Gavarni in the Pyrenees; hence his *nom de plume*. About 1835 he began to contribute regularly to *Charivari* and other comic journals the wonderful series of ever-varying social and character sketches, instinct with artful originality and scathing cynicism, which earned for him the name of the 'arch-fiend of caricature.' Among his best-known works are *Les Enfants Terribles*, *Les Parents Terribles*, *Les Rêves*, *Comme l'on dîne à Paris*, *Les Fourberies de Femmes*, and *Impressions de Ménage*. He successfully illustrated many popular works, as Eugene Sue's *Wandering Jew* and Balzac's *Diable à Paris*. G. died at Auteuil, 23d November 1866. A selection from his sketches was published in Paris, 1845, in 4 vols. 8vo, with notes by Théophile Gautier, and 2 vols. subsequently under the title of *Perles et Parures* (1850).

Gavazz'i, Alessandro, a celebrated anti-Papal agitator, was born at Bologna in 1809. Admitted in 1825 into the order of Barnabites, he showed great natural powers of eloquence, and became Professor of Rhetoric in Naples. In 1846 he threw himself heartily into the liberal policy of the 'reforming Pope,' Pius IX., and was appointed chaplain-general of the Roman patriotic legion sent to the aid of the Milanese. The Pope, however, becoming reactionary, withdrew the legion, whereupon G. abandoned his allegiance, and joined in the agitation which ended in the flight of the Pope and the establishment of a republic. After the failure of the struggle with France, G. left Italy for England, and since 1851 has figured chiefly as a lecturer against the Papacy. His addresses in various countries have been received with much enthusiasm, although in some places, *e.g.*, Canada, they have led to riots. G. has frequently revisited Italy, and was with Garibaldi during his campaign in the Two Sicilies. In 1876 he was again active in Britain speaking against 'Papalism.' His Protestantism is simple, broad, and humane, evangelical in sentiment, but not rigid in creed.

Gav'elkind, Tenure in. In some of the counties of England lands and tenements are by immemorial custom held in gavelkind, all the sons having an equal share in the real estate of a deceased father. The custom is ancient, but whether Celtic or English in origin is still in dispute.

Gav'ial (*Gavialis*), a genus of *Crocodilia* or crocodiles, often named the Gangetic crocodile and the 'nakoo.' Its distinctive features are the remarkable prolongation of the jawbones to form a prominent snout. The teeth, numbering about 120, are nearly of equal size, and similar in form in both jaws. The nostrils open at the extremity of the snout. The gavials, which are confined to the large rivers of India, are typically represented by the *G. Gangeticus*, a large reptile attaining a length of 25 feet, but, in spite of its size, less carnivorous and dreaded than the crocodiles and alligators. The colour is dark olive-brown spotted with black. The feet are webbed, and the tail has a well-marked spiny ridge. The bony plates covering the back are united with those covering the neck, and form one set. The food consists chiefly of fishes. Fossil G. occur in Eocene rocks in the S.W. of England and elsewhere.

Gavina'na, a village of N. Italy, province of Lucca, in the romantic valley of the Lima, 35 miles N.W. of Florence, is notable as the scene of the final overthrow of the army of republican Florence under the chivalric Ferruccio, at the hands of the imperialist Philibert, Prince of Orange, in 1530.

Gavot, Gavotte', a dance-tune somewhat resembling the country-dance, which was in fashion principally from 1670 to 1760. On it was founded an instrumental piece or movement much employed in the 'suites' of Bach and Handel. It was originally a dance of the *Gavotes*, *i.e.*, the people of Gap in France.

Gay, John, an English poet, was born near Barnstaple in 1688. He was sent to London as a silk-weaver, but in 1712 became secretary to the Duchess of Monmouth, having the year before published *Rural Sports*, a poem dedicated to Pope, with whom he formed a warm friendship, and at whose suggestion he wrote *The Shepherd's Week* (1714), a burlesque on the eclogues of Philips. It contains, however, some of the most natural pastoral poetry in the language, and resembles Spenser's *Shepherd's Calendar* in its English colour. Through the influence of the Tories G. accompanied the Earl of Clarendon as secretary to Hanover, whence he returned in two months to England. In 1715 his burlesque *What d'ye Call It* was well received, but his next piece, the farce *Three Weeks after Marriage*, entirely failed. In 1726 his *Fables* appeared, and in 1727 his *Beggar's Opera*, the idea of which was suggested by Swift, was received with enthusiasm, and ran for sixty-three nights. Its chief characters, 'Macheath,' 'Polly,' and 'Lucy,' were a delightful change from conventional heroes and heroines, and its humorous mimicry of the Italian opera, then a fashionable novelty in England, its sparkling wit, touching simplicity, charming songs, and delightful music, combined to ensure it a brilliant popularity, the memory of which is not yet forgotten. G. died December 4, 1732, and was buried in Westminster Abbey. He was a natural and graceful poet. In his *Beggar's Opera*, 'he extracted,' says Hazlitt, 'an essence of refinement from the dregs of human life.' His *Fables* (best ed. Owen, Lond. 1856), though somewhat tedious, are easy and fluent; his *Trivia, or the Art of Walking the Streets of London*, gives interesting glimpses into the life of his times; but his fame rests on his lyrics, which have a flowing melody and pathetic sweetness peculiar to G. An edition of his poetical works in 3 vols. appeared at London in 1797, and another in 2 vols. 1806.

Gay, Marie-Françoise-Sophie, a French authoress, whose maiden name was Nichault de Lavalette, born at Paris, July 1, 1776, married M. Gay, and wrote many romances and several dramatic pieces. Her salon was a famous resort of authors and artists. She died at Paris, March 5, 1852. Among her works are *Laure d'Estelle* (1802), *Anatole* (1815), *Le Moqueur Amoureux* (1830), *Scènes de Jeune Age* (1833), *La Duchesse de Châteauroux* (1834), *Les Salons Célèbres* (1837), *Le Mari Confident* (1849). See Gautier's *Notices Contemporaines*.—**Delphine G.**, afterwards **Madame de Girardin**, a French poetess and novelist, daughter of the above, was born at Aix-la-Chapelle, January 26, 1804. When only seventeen she wrote a prize poem, which, though unsuccessful, was read publicly before the French Academy. Shortly afterwards she produced several poems, for which a pension was bestowed on her mother, whom she then accompanied to Rome. There she was enthusiastically received and crowned in the Capitol. On her return to Paris she became the ornament of a literary circle which included Lamartine, Balzac, Hugo, and Gautier, the last of whom describes her as a dazzling beauty. In 1831 she married the journalist Émile de Girardin, and afterwards issued several novels, which were well received. From 1836 to 1848 she contributed to her husband's paper *La Presse* her well-known *Lettres Parisiennes*—letters on literature, art, and current topics, written with charming airiness and vivacity. She died at Paris, June 29, 1855. Sainte-Beuve, Gautier, and Jules Janin have extolled her beauty, wit, and literary genius. Among her numerous works are *Essais Poétiques* (1824), *Nouveaux Essais Poétiques* (1825), *Contes d'une Vielle Fille à ses Neveux* (1832), *La Canne de M. de Balzac* (1836), *Lettres Parisiennes* (1836–39), *Nouvelles* (1853), *Marguerite* (1853). See Sainte-Beuve's *Causeries du Lundi*.

Gay'a, or **Gyah** (the name of a god), the chief town of a district of the same name, province of Bengal, British India, on the Phalgu river, about 265 miles N.W. of Calcutta, and 55 miles S. of Patna. The old town is inhabited by the priests and their followers, and the new town (called Sahibgunge) contains the official and trading population. G. is one of the most celebrated centres of pilgrimage in India, and was known even in the Buddhist period. At present it is frequented by Hindus, who come to worship the infernal deity Gaya, for the sake of the souls of their ancestors. It is estimated that 100,000 pilgrims come to G. every year; and a single Mahratta prince has been known to pay £10,000. The old town is unusually picturesque; the houses are mostly of brick and stone, with ornamented verandahs. Pop. (1872) 66,843.—The *district* of G. contains 4718 sq. miles and (1872) 1,949,750 souls. The soil is fertile, but the density of the population is excessive. The old manufactures of weaving and paper-making are dying out. In the E. and N. of G. district are situated the most ancient stone memorials of Buddhism in all India.

Ga'yal (*Bos Gavæus*), a variety of oxen found in a wild state in Central Asia and N. India, and in a domesticated state in Bengal. The form of the body resembles that of the buffalo; and although the body is not humped, the front portion of the back is very prominent. The head is broad and flat, the muzzle prominent, and the horns of small size, and directed outwards and slightly upwards. The colour is a dark brown. The gayals are domesticated for the sake of the flesh and hides, and the milk is said to be very rich and plentiful.

Gay-Lussac', Joseph Louis, a French chemist and physicist, was born December 6, 1778, at St. Leonard (Haute-Vienne). In 1794 he went to Paris, and in 1797 entered the École Polytechnique, where he became Professor of Chemistry in 1809. In 1804 he performed his celebrated balloon ascents, the first with Biot, and the second alone. Most of his early investigations in specific gravities, specific heats, gaseous laws, the decomposing action of the voltaic pile, &c., appear in his *Recherches Physico-chimiques* (2 vols. Par. 1811). In 1816 he began the *Annales de Chimie et de Physique* with Arago; and in this and the *Comptes Rendus* many of his numerous memoirs are published. He is specially famous in connection with iodine, cyanogen (which he discovered), bleaching chlorides, alcohols, ethers, alkalies, the manufacture of sulphuric acid, &c. In 1832 he obtained the chair of general chemistry at the Jardin des Plantes, in 1839 was made a peer of France, and died at Paris May 9, 1850. G.'s chief works, besides those already mentioned, are his *Cours de Physique* (edited by Grosselin, Par. 1827), and his *Leçons de Chimie* (collected by Marmet, 2 vols. Par. 1828). See the *Éloge de Gay-Lussac* by Arago, read at the *Académie des Sciences*, 20th December 1852.

Ga'za (Gr., Heb. *Azzah*, Deut. ii. 23) was one of the most ancient towns in Palestine and the capital of the Philistines, by whom it was taken from the *Avim*, the earliest inhabitants of whom there is any notice (Deut. ii. 23; Josh. xiii. 2, 3). G. formed the limit on the S.W. of the territories of the ancient Canaanites (Gen. x. 19) and of Joshua's conquests (Josh. x. 41). It fell to the lot of the men of Judah, who indeed took it, but were unable to keep it (Judges i. 18, 19). Alexander the Great besieged G. after taking Tyre, and only took it after a five years' siege. Captured and razed to the ground (about B.C. 96) by Alexander Jannæus, it was rebuilt by Gabinius, governor of Syria (Jos. *Ants.* xiii. 13, 3, and xiv. 5, 3). It was again destroyed by the Jews about A.D. 65 (*Bell. Jud.* ii. 18, 1), but soon recovered. The secret of its importance and prosperity was its situation; it lay in the line of communication between Egypt and the whole region of Syria. In Christian times G. remained a stronghold of idolatry. It was taken by the Mohammedans in 634, and since that time has gradually declined. The modern town (*Ghuzzeh*) has about 15,000 inhabitants.

Gaza, Theodorus, one of the Renaissance scholars, was born about 1405 at Thessalonica, whence, after its capture by the Turks in 1430, he removed to Italy. He became Professor of Greek at Ferrara, was patronised by Pope Nicholas V., Cardinal Bessarion, and King Alfonso of Naples, and finally obtained a benefice in S. Italy, where he died in 1478. He translated Aristotle's *History of Animals*, the *History of Plants* by Theophrastus, and other Greek works into Latin; wrote a treatise *De Mensibus Atticis*, a Greek grammar, *Introductivæ Grammatices* in 4 books, and various literary epistles. Scaliger said he envied only three scholars—G., Poliziano, and Mirandola.

Gaze. In heraldry, a beast of the chase is *at gaze* when it looks towards the spectator.

Gazelle (Arab. *gazal*, 'a wild goat'), the name of a well-known genus of Antelopes (q. v.), more especially applied to the *Gazella Dorcas* of Arabia and N. Africa—a small animal of a light-fawn colour on the back, which deepens into a darker tint on the sides, and passes into pure white on the abdomen. The face is marked with a dark-brown stripe passing from each eye to the angle of the mouth, and by a white streak extending between the horns and the muzzle. The hinder quarters have also white markings. The horns are lyre-shaped and of moderate size, and taper to a point. The females are hornless, and the *crumen* or tear-bag is distinctly developed below the eyes. The eyes of these graceful creatures are large and lustrous, and have long been celebrated in Eastern poetry. The gazelles are found in large herds, and sometimes act against their enemies the *Carnivora* with much courage and boldness. An allied species, regarded by some naturalists as a mere variety, is the Ariel G. (*G. Ariel* or *Arabica*) of Syria and Arabia, which differs from the preceding species chiefly in the darker tints of its hair. Its average height is 21 inches at the shoulder. In Asia several characteristic species are found.

Gazelle.

Gazette'. This name is especially applied in England and in Scotland to the official newspaper of each country in which government and legal notices are given to the public. The *London G.* is published on Tuesdays and Fridays, and the *Edinburgh G.* on the same days. It seems to be held that publication in the G. of notice of dissolution of partnership is not alone sufficient to free the partners from liability for debt afterwards contracted in the name of the company with any one formerly in the habit of dealing with it. With regard to parties dealing with the company for the first time, there is a difference between English and Scotch law. By the former it is doubtful whether notice in the G. is always sufficient even in a question with a stranger. By the latter it is held that persons dealing for the first time with a company ought to make previous inquiry into its circumstances, and that notice even in a provincial newspaper is effectual. But all reasonable means ought to be taken to publish the dissolution. Under the Bankruptcy Acts and some other statutes, certain notices are directed to be given in the Gazettes. The word G. is derived from the Ital. *gazzetta*, a Venetian coin about ¾d. in value, the sum charged for permission to read the first Venetian newspaper, which appeared in the 15th c. See NEWSPAPER.

Gaz'ogene. See AERATED WATERS.

Gazons (Fr. *gazon*, 'turf'), sods used to line the faces of earthworks.

Gean, the English name for the wild cherry (*Prunus avium*), the origin of the cultivated garden cherry. See CHERRY.

Gear'ing, or **Geer'ing**, in machinery, sometimes means those parts which are used to transmit motion from one machine to another (most frequently from a prime mover to a direct actor), sometimes a combination which forms part of one machine, and is employed for transmitting motion between two different portions of it having generally different velocities. G. consists in some cases of leather belts, ropes, &c., with pulleys and shafts, in other cases of toothed wheels. The word is more commonly used for the latter, and spur G., bevil G., screw G., &c., is spoken of, according to the arrangement of the wheels employed.

Gebang' Palm, the name given in Java to *Corypha Gebanga*, one of the fan-palms. A kind of sago is obtained from the interior of the stem, and a strong fibre from the leaf-stalks, which is used for making ropes, cloth, &c.

Ge'ber, the name under which **Abu Musa Jafar al-Sofi**, the earliest of the great Arabian chemists or alchemists, was regarded as an oracle by the chemists of the middle ages, and is said to have written 500 works on his art. Of these, the most noted is the *Summa Perfectionis Magisterii*, published at Rome between 1490 and 1520, at Danzig in 1682. A fundamental belief of G.'s was that metals are convertible, and are all composed of sulphur, mercury, and arsenic. G.'s date is uncertain, but he lived about the end of the 8th or beginning of the 9th c. There is an English edition (Lond. 1678). A minute and complete analysis of G.'s works will be found in Höfer's *Histoire de la Chimie* (Par. 1842).

Gecko' (*Gecko*), a name given to various kinds of lizards (*Lacertilia*), included in a large family, that of the *Geckotidæ*, in the typical genus of which the toes are dilated, and furnished on their lower surfaces with expansions of the skin, enabling these animals to hold on firmly to any smooth or perpendicular surface. The tongue is flat, wide, and scarcely protrusible. The eyes are large, the eyelids short, and the pupil of linear shape, but occasionally of circular conformation. The teeth are small, compressed, and set on the inner side of the jaw; hence the creatures are *Pleurodonts*. The nails are hooked, and can be retracted at will, and the tail possesses a ridge. The G. are widely distributed in the warm parts of both hemispheres. They feed on insects, and inhabit houses, running up and down walls with great ease. The common G. (*G. verus*) is found in N. Africa, and may be known by having the back studded with large tubercles. Its colour is reddish grey, spotted with white. The house G., named 'fan-foot' from the expanded nature of the toes (*Ptyodactylus G.*), likewise occurs in the same region. Another species of G. is the fringed-tree G. (*Ptychozoon homalocephala*) of Java, known as the smooth-headed G. It is brown in colour above, with a yellowish spine-marking, and variations of darker brown wavy lines. The top of the head is similarly marked, and the under parts are a dirty white.

Gedd'es, Alexander, LL.D., a Scottish scholar of considerable note, was born at Pathhead, Enzie, Banffshire, in 1737. At the age of fourteen he was sent to the Roman Catholic Seminary of Scalan, from which he passed in 1758 to the Scots College at Paris. Returning to Scotland in priest's orders (1764), he was appointed chaplain at Traquair, where with a good library he had the best opportunity of pursuing his favourite study of Biblical Criticism. From this post he was removed (1768) and sent back to Paris by the vicar-apostolic (Bishop G. Hay), for the indiscretion of falling in love with a female relative of the Earl of Traquair. He returned to Scotland next year, and was appointed to the mission at Auchenhalrig. There he employed his leisure translating the select odes of Horace into English blank verse, in which, as well as in a number of fugitive pieces in English, Scotch, Latin, and French, he showed considerable poetical powers. His too free expression of liberal opinions, and particularly his attending service in the parish church of Cullen, brought upon him censure and harsh treatment from Bishop Hay, who finally (1779) suspended him in his diocese. In 1780 he got the degree of LL.D. from the University of Aberdeen, and the same year went to London, where by the liberality of Lord Petre, who settled an annuity upon him, he was enabled to carry out what had been the aim and ambition of his life, namely, to make a translation of the Bible for English Roman Catholics. The first volume of this work appeared in 1792, the second (and last published) next year. In 1800 appeared the first volume (and all that was published) of *Critical Remarks on the Hebrew Scriptures, corresponding with a New Translation of the Bible*, in which a very pronounced Rationalism was freely expressed. G. died in 1802. See Good's *Memoirs of G.* (1803), Irving's *Lives of the Scottish Poets* (Edinb. 1804), Gordon's *Catholic Church in Scotland* (1869).

Geefs, Guillaume, a Belgian sculptor, born at Antwerp, September 10, 1806. He studied in Paris, and settled in Brussels in 1830, when he exhibited his work 'A Young Herdsman strewing Flowers on a Tomb.' This composition established his reputation, which was increased by his 'Victims of the Revolution,' a colossal work in the Place des Martyrs, at Brussels. He was made premier sculptor to the king, Chevalier of the Legion of Honour, and member of various fine art academies. He died May 10, 1860. G. executed statues of historic characters, busts of contemporaries, and many purely imaginative compositions. His style is soft, delicate, and picturesque, rather than severe and classical.—**Joseph G.**, brother of the preceding, born at Antwerp in 1808, was also a sculptor of reputation. Among his works are 'Godfrey of Bouillon,' 'Thierry Maertens,' 'Baldwin of Constantinople,' &c. He died at Brussels, May, 1860.—**Aloys G.**, youngest brother of Guillaume G., was a sculptor of promise, but died prematurely in 1841.

Geel, Jakob, an eminent Dutch Hellenist, was born at Amsterdam in 1789. He received a good classical education, and in 1833 was appointed head librarian at Leyden, where he died, 11th November 1862. G. is well known for his translations from German and English into Dutch, contributions to library literature, his treatises on æsthetics, such as *Gesprek op dem Drachenfels* (Leips. 1836); and above all his editions of *Theocritus* (1820), Dio Chrysostom's *Olympicus* (1840), *Excerpta Vaticana* of Polybius (1829), *Historia Critica Sophistarum* (1823), and the *Phœnissæ* (1846). His *Catalogus Codicum Manuscriptorum qui inde ab Anno* 1741 *Bibliothecæ Lugduni Batavorum accesserunt* (Leyd. 1852) is a learned and useful work.

Gee'long, a town in Victoria, situated on Corio Bay, a western arm of Port Philip, 45 miles S.W. of Melbourne. The trade of G., which has a good harbour, has been swallowed up by Melbourne since the establishment of railway communication between the two places; but various industries, the chief of which are woollen manufactures, meat-preserving, and tanning, are now causing the town to revive. Pop. within the municipal boundary, 12,000; but including the new borough of Geelong W., and that of Newtown and Chilwell, 23,000.

Gef'le (pron. *yävle*), the capital of the *län* of Gefleborg, Sweden, on an island at the mouth of the broad and rapid Gefle-A, 50 miles W. of Falun by railway. It is the third trading town in Sweden, has a beautiful town-house, and is overlooked by an old castle, and girt with fine gardens. There is a good harbour, and the exports include iron, timber, flax, linen, and tar, while among the manufactures are sailcloth, linen, leather, tobacco, sugar, &c. Pop. (1874) 16,787. G. is one of the oldest towns of the Swedish Norrlands, and formerly enjoyed a monopoly of trade.

Gehenn'a (Gr. from Heb. *ge-hinnom*, or *ge-ben*, or *bne*, *hinnom*, valley of the son or sons of Hinnom, of whom nothing further is known) was a glen which, descending from the level of the plateau on the W. of Jerusalem, and gradually deepening, ran along the W. and S. sides of the city, joining the Valley of Jehoshaphat at the S.E. corner. It was the deep, narrow gorge on the S. side which was Hinnom proper, and was also called Topheth (q. v.). The place became notorious as the scene of the rites (human sacrifices, &c.) paid to Chemosh (q. v.) and Molech (q. v.), first introduced by Solomon (1 Kings xi. 7), and restored by Ahaz and Manasseh (2 Chron. xxviii. 3, and xxxiii. 6). On the reformation by Josiah, it was polluted or rendered ceremonially unclean (2 Kings xxiii. 10), and afterwards became the lay-stall of the city, where the larvæ of insects fattened on the corruption, and fires were continually kept up to consume some of the offal. G. thus came to be used as a figure of the eternal torment of the wicked in the world to come (Isa. lxvi. 24, *cf.* Mark ix. 47, 48).

Gei'bel, Emanuel, a German poet, son of an Evangelical Reformed pastor, was born at Lübeck, October 18, 1815, studied at Bonn, and in 1838 visited Athens as tutor to a Russian prince. In 1852 he was made Professor of Æsthetics at Munich. His works include *Classische Studien* (Bonn, 1840); *Gedichte* (Berl. 1840; 58th ed. 1865); *Juniuslieder* (Stuttg. 1848; 16th ed. 1866); *Neue Gedichte* (Stuttg. 1856; 8th ed. 1865); *Brunhild* (Stuttg. 1857; 2d ed. 1861); *Sophonisbe* (2d ed. 1870), &c. G. has won an extraordinary popularity, due to his love of freedom, simplicity, tender melancholy, religious vein, and exquisite music, rather than to originality or imaginative power.

Gei'ger, Abraham, a Jewish rabbi and well-known Orientalist, born at Frankfurt-on-the-Main, May 24, 1810, studied at Heidelberg and Bonn, in 1832 went as rabbi to Wiesbaden, in 1835 took part in editing the *Zeitschrift für Jüdische Theologie*, and in 1838 became assessor to the rabbis at Breslau. G. has been a deep student of Judaism, and has been led into fierce controversies from his endeavour to break down the exclusiveness of the Jewish religion. His works—among which are *Lehr- und Lesebuch zur Sprache der Mischna* (Bresl. 1845); *Urschrift und*

Uebersetzungen der Bibel in ihrer Abhängigkeit von der inneren Entwickelung des Judenthums (Bresl. 1857); and various sermons and pamphlets, &c.—show a wide and thorough knowledge of history and of Eastern languages.

Gei'jer, Erik Gustaf, a great Swedish historian and poet, born 12th January 1783, at Ransätter in Vermland. At sixteen he left the Carlstad Gymnasium for Upsala University, and at twenty wrote a celebrated prize essay on Sten Sture the elder. He graduated in 1806, and in 1810, after a year's stay in England, was appointed 'docent' in history at Upsala, but soon left for a post in the public record office in Stockholm. Together with some friends he instituted the *Götiska Forbund*, to whose journal *Iduna* he contributed many prose tracts and a few remarkable poems, some of which have been set by himself to fine music, which has greatly contributed to their popularity in Sweden. In 1812 G. published *Försök till Psalmer*, but in 1815 he laid aside poetry and devoted himself to public lectures in history, the chair of which at Upsala became his in 1817. To regain strength exhausted in the preparation of *Svea Rikes Häfder*, of which work, however, only a single part appeared (1825), he went on a tour (1835) through Denmark and part of Germany, giving his impressions in *Minnen* (1834). In 1832 and 1836 appeared *Svenska Folkets Historia*, breaking off at the end of Christina's reign, and followed by *Sveriges Tilstand fran* 1718 *till* 1771 (1838), *Gustav III.'s efterlemnade Papper* (1843). His lectures greatly influenced his students, who showed their warm attachment during the unsuccessful indictment for heresies in *Thorild* (1820). Failing health forced G.'s retirement in 1846; and going to Stockholm to complete his *History of the Swedish People*, he died 23d April 1847. The collected edition of his writings (13 vols. 1849–55) comprises also many papers written for periodicals and articles for *Literaturbladet*, a newspaper edited by him and expounding democratic views opposed to those he held in 1828, when, as again in 1840, he represented his university in the Swedish Parliament.

Geik'ie, Archibald, F.R.S., LL.D., a distinguished geologist, was born at Edinburgh, December 28, 1835, and educated at the High School and University of that city. In 1855 he was appointed to the geological survey of Scotland, of which he became the director in 1867, and in 1870 obtained the Murchison chair of mineralogy and geology at Edinburgh University. Besides various geological memoirs in the journals of the Geological Society and elsewhere, which entitle him to a foremost place among geologists, he has published several works bearing more or less on his special department. The principal of these are *The Story of a Boulder* (1858); *The Life of Professor Edward Forbes*, in conjunction with Professor George Wilson (1861); *The Phenomena of Glacial Drift of Scotland* (1863); *The Scenery of Scotland viewed in Connection with its Physical Geography* (1865); Jukes and G.'s *Manual of Geology* (3d ed. 1872); and *Memoir of Sir Roderick J. Murchison*, &c. (2 vols. 1872).—**James G.**, the brother of the preceding, was born at Edinburgh August 23, 1839, and was appointed to the geological survey in 1861. He is the author of *The Great Ice Age* (2d ed. 1876).

Gei'ler von Kaisersberg, Johann, an able but somewhat eccentric German preacher, was born at Schaffhausen, March 16, 1455, studied at Freiburg and Basel, became rector of Freiburg University, and in 1478 settled as a cathedral preacher in Strasburg, where he gained wide popularity, and where he died, March 10, 1510. He was a bold opponent of clerical abuses, and an earnest, vigorous preacher, using keen and homely illustrations. He did much to found useful institutions in Strasburg, and his death was regretted through Germany. His writings are now very rare. See Ammon's *G. von K.'s Leben, Lehren, und Predigten* (Erl. 1826), and Meick's *Joh. G. von K.* (3 vols. Frankf. 1829).

Ge'la, an ancient city on the river G., in the S. of Sicily, was founded by a Rhodian and Cretan colony 690 B.C. It grew rapidly, and in 582 B.C. the Geloans founded Agrigentum, which soon eclipsed G., and was for a time the most powerful state in the island. The form of government at G. was at first an oligarchy, which was subverted by the 'tyrant' Cleander, under whom (505–498 B.C.) and his brother Hippocrates (498–491 B.C.) G. flourished greatly. Gelon (q. v.), who succeeded Hippocrates by the conquest of Syracuse in 485 B.C., made G. the first city in Sicily. This position it might have kept, had not Gelon shown a preference for Syracuse, and compelled great numbers of the inhabitants to migrate thither. Under his brother Hiero G. continued to decline, but after the expulsion of Thrasybulus it again experienced a period of great prosperity (466–406 B.C.). During the Punic wars it suffered terribly. It was finally laid in ruins by Phintias, tyrant of Agrigentum, who transferred its inhabitants to a city founded by himself near the mouth of the Himera in 280 B.C., and called by his name. G. was the scene of the death and burial of the poet Æschylus, and possessed among other monuments a colossal statue of Apollo, which was carried off by the Carthaginians in 405 B.C. and sent to Tyre, where it remained till the taking of that city by Alexander the Great. *Terra Nova* occupies the site of the ancient G.

Gel'atine (from the Lat. *gelo*, 'I freeze or congeal') is a product obtained from various animal tissues, and employed in the arts and as human food according to the sources whence it is obtained and the care exercised in its preparation. When the preparation is pure and transparent in colour, yielding a solution free from smell, it is commercially known as G. and chiefly employed as food; but when brown in colour and impure in its constitution, it is called glue. Both, however, insensibly merge into each other, and excepting difference of purity they have no other distinction. The following may be regarded as the sources of the varieties of commercial G., using the term in its wide sense:—(1) The fine, clean, and fresh cuttings of sheep and ox skins, tendons, &c., from which G. for cooking and calf's-foot jelly are prepared; (2) hide-cuttings, ears, tails, &c., from tanneries, and animal refuse generally, which yield common glue; (3) bones, from which bone glue is made; and (4) swimming bladders of fish, which constitute isinglass. As the methods of preparing common G. and glue differ only in the care with which the materials are selected and the cleanliness of manipulation in the case of the former, it is to be understood that the manufacturing processes here indicated are those adopted for both. The raw materials are first treated with lime in tanks or lime-post for the purpose of cleansing them from fragments of flesh, blood, &c., the lime at the same time saponifying adherent fatty matter, and preventing putrefactive decay. Lime-water is added from day to day, and after two or three weeks the materials are removed from the tank, thoroughly washed free from lime and dried. The materials so prepared are next boiled, by which they yield up a gelatinising compound. Different degrees of temperature are required for extracting the gelatinous substance from different materials, and the operation of boiling is conducted in three separate ways:—(1) By acting on the tissues by high-pressure steam, whereby a highly concentrated solution is obtained with great rapidity—a process very generally adopted in Great Britain; (2) by fractional boiling, that is, in treating a change of material with a small proportion of water which is periodically run off, and renewed so long as a gelatinising solution continues to be obtained; (3) by boiling the glue-yielding mass in a caldron with a sufficiency of water to exhaust it. The last of these ways is the least satisfactory, as the first portion of G. formed by being kept at a high temperature for a prolonged period loses its power of gelatinising when cooled. The G. solution, by whatever process obtained, is poured into flat shallow moulds, and after being hardened sufficiently, it is cut up into cakes of the size and form required. The drying operation to which it is next subjected is one of the greatest difficulty and delicacy. The cakes are placed on twine nets stretched between frames in a drying chamber, and when practicable the drying is conducted by exposure to the heat of the sun. In the application of artificial heat great care must be exercised to keep the temperature at a uniform pitch, so that the G. does not become fluid by too high heat, or crack and bend by irregular and unequal temperature. The cakes are then polished and finished by immersion in hot water, brushing, and drying. In preparing bone glue, the bones are first freed from grease by boiling, after which they are treated with hydrochloric acid till they become soft and transparent. When freed from acid by neutralising with lime and repeated washing with fresh water, the gelatinous matter is separated by the action of steam in a closed boiler, and the solution treated as in the case of ordinary glue. A non-gelatinising glue yielded by cartilaginous matter, and known chemically as chondrin, is prepared and used as size. Ordinary glue, if dissolved in water to which nitric or acetic acid is added, remains liquid, while it retains its adhesive properties unimpaired.

The ordinary varieties of glue have multitudinous applications for cementing or 'glueing' in joinery, &c., and as 'size' in papermaking, painting, and numerous other arts. The more pure varieties of G. are almost exclusively used in food and cookery. G. of a transparent quality is very frequently artificially coloured, and run into excessively thin plates for use as ornamental wrappings for confectionery and other fanciful purposes. Nauseous medicines are also much administered in capsules of G.

Isinglass, although the source of fish glue, being more used in its native condition than as a source of G., will be treated of under its own heading. Several substitutes for glue, as an adhesive and sizing agent, have been introduced, the most important of which are albumen glue and casein glue. The first of these is made from the gluten obtained as a bye-product of the manufacture of wheaten starch, and is largely used like ordinary glue, besides being available as a substitute for egg albumen in calico-printing and for clarifying liquids. Casein glue is obtained by dissolving the casein of milk in a strong solution of borax, and it forms a very useful glueing material for joiners and bookbinders.

Gelat'inous Tiss'ues and Gelatine, the name given to various tissues found in the bodies of man and higher animals, and from which a jelly-like substance named G. is obtained by boiling. The characteristics of these tissues and of the products they afford consist in their being (1) sparingly soluble in cold water; (2) readily soluble in hot water; and (3) their free precipitation by tannic acid and chlorine-water, whilst ferrocyanide of potassium has no action upon them, this fact distinguishing them from *albuminous* compounds. The comparative chemical composition of the two forms of gelatinous compounds—*chondrin* and *gelatine*—may be seen by an inspection of the following table :—

	Gelatine.		Chondrin.	
	Mulder's analysis.	Scherer's analysis.	Mulder.	Scherer.
Carbon	50·4	50·8	50·0	50·7
Hydrogen	6·7	7·1	6·6	6·9
Nitrogen	18·3	18·3	14·4	14·7
Oxygen } Sulphur }	24·6	23·8	29·0	27·7
	100·0	100·0	100·0	100·0

Gel'derland, a province in the E. of Holland, is bounded N. by Overyssel, S. by N. Brabant, E. by Westphalia, and W. by Utrecht and the Zuider Zee. Area, 1964 sq. miles; pop. (1873) 441,088. The centre is occupied by the sandy plateau of the Veluwe (formerly *Felua*), while the S. and E. (Veluwezoom), the dryest part of Holland despite its many springs, is an undulating region covered with rich copsewood and dotted with beautiful country-seats. A tract of arid sand-dunes stretches along the Zuider Zee. The Rhine, Waal, Yssel, and Maas traverse G., and between the first two lies the fertile lowland of Betuwe (hence Roman *Batavia*), 'good meadow land,' divided into E. and W. portions by the Nieuwe Dijk. In the extreme S., between the Waal and Maas, rises the Hunenberg, clad with the Nederrijks Forest. The river valleys are highly cultivated, yielding much wheat, rye, buckwheat, hops, tobacco, &c. G. has a large trade in butter and eels. Arnhem is the capital, and other towns are Nymwegen, Zutphen, Tiel, and Harderwijk.

Gelid'ium, a genus of rose-spored seaweeds including several species, one of which is said to form the gelatinous substance of which the Chinese edible birds'-nests are made. (See NESTS.) *G. corneum* is a very common but variable species on the British coast.

Gell, Sir William, an English archæologist, was born in 1777 at Hopton, Derbyshire, and studied at Cambridge, where he graduated in 1804. In 1814 he travelled abroad with the Princess of Wales as one of her chamberlains, and appeared as a witness at her trial (1820). He subsequently settled in Italy, living chiefly in Rome and Naples, in the latter of which he died, February 4, 1836. G. is best known by writings on classical antiquities, several of which are still authorities. The chief are *Topography of Troy* (1804); *Itinerary of Greece* (1810); *Attica* (1817); *Pompeiiana, or Observations upon the Topography, Edifices, and Ornaments of Pompeii* (with J. P. Gandy, 1817–32; 3d ed. of first series, 1832); and *The Topography of Rome,* and *Rome and its Environs* (1834).

Gell'ert, Christian Fürchtegott, a German poet, was born at Haynichen, Saxony, July 4, 1715, and studied at Leipsic University, where, after labouring as a tutor, he became professor in 1751. He was a very successful lecturer on philosophy and rhetoric, and his writings were popular throughout Germany. G. died at Leipsic, 13th December 1769. G. was peculiarly shy and gentle, and Friedrich the Great called him 'the most rational of German professors.' His works, consisting of fables, hymns, and a few other pieces, display a pure though somewhat thin vein of poetry, glimpses of quiet humour, and deep and tender piety. They were published at Leipsic in 1769–74 (10 vols.) and in 1840–41 (6 vols). See Döring's *G.'s Leben* (Leips. 1833).

Gell'ius, Au'lus, a Latin grammarian of good family, flourished 117–180 A.D. The dates of his birth and death are unknown. He studied rhetoric at Rome and philosophy at Athens. On his return to Rome he devoted himself to the legal profession, in which he seems to have been busily occupied during the remainder of his life. His work *Noctes Atticæ,* so called because it was begun and in great part written during the long winter nights in a country-house near Athens, contains dissertations and discussions on an endless variety of subjects, including history, philology, antiquities, and philosophy, and abounds in quotations, many of them from Greek and Latin authors whose works have perished. It originally consisted of 20 books, all of which have come down to us except the 8th, the index of which only has been preserved. The style of G. is marred by the constant occurrence of obsolete words and phrases; but his work is thoroughly readable, and eminently valuable for the light it throws on many points that would have otherwise remained obscure. The *editio princeps* was printed at Rome (fol. 1469). The best critical edition is that of J. Fr. and Jak. Gronovius (Leyd. 1706); the latest is that of Hertz (2 vols. Leips. 1853).

Ge'lon, son of Deinomenes, sprung from one of the most ancient and illustrious families of Gela in Sicily. On the death of Hippocrates in 491 B.C. he became 'tyrant' of Gela, and in 485 B.C. of Syracuse, which he made his capital, and to which he transferred the majority of the inhabitants of Gela and Camarina. By this means he soon raised Syracuse to unexampled power. When the Greeks sought his aid against Xerxes, G. offered to assist them with 200 triremes and a land force of 28,000 men if they would make him commander-in-chief, but to this condition they would not accede. Soon after he assisted Theron of Agrigentum against Terillus of Himera, who was aided by the Carthaginians, and on the day of the battle of Salamis (according to Herodotus), or of Thermopylæ (according to Diodorus), gained the decisive battle of Himera, in which Hamilcar was slain (480 B.C.). Thereupon G. concluded a treaty with the Carthaginians by which they paid the expenses of the war. This sum he devoted to the erection of temples and to offerings at Delphi and other shrines. He died 478 B.C. The Syracusans built a splendid tomb to his memory and decreed him heroic honours.

Gema'ra. See TALMUD.

Gemblou'x (Flem. *Gemblours,* pron. *Changblu*), a quaint old town of Belgium, province of Namur, 25 miles S.E. of Brussels by railway. It has a famous Benedictine abbey, the origin of which is assigned to the 9th c., and from which proceeded the very useful *Chronik des Siegebert von G.* Since 1860 the abbey buildings have been used as a Royal Agricultural Institute. Don John of Austria gained a victory here over the Netherlanders, 31st January 1578. Pop. 3018.

Gem'ini (Lat. 'The Twins'), a constellation of the northern hemisphere, easily recognised in the winter months by its two conspicuous stars Castor and Pollux, the latter of which is of the first magnitude, and in the line joining Procyon and the Pole Star. G. is also the name of the third sign of the zodiac.

Gemis'tus Ple'tho, Geor'gius, one of those learned Greeks who so powerfully contributed to the revival of letters in Italy during the 15th c. Born in Constantinople, after the middle of the 14th c. he came to attend the council at Ferrara in 1438, and was persuaded to reside at the court of Cosmo de Medici. He wrote scholia to Thucydides and a history of Greece; but his fame rests on the success of his efforts to revive the Platonic and Neo-Platonic philosophy, and on his zeal as an opponent of the Aristotelians. In this cause he wrote on the differences between Plato and Aristotle (Venice, 1532). His enthusiasm for the pagan philosophy chilled, if it did not entirely destroy, his belief in Christianity. His treatise on Fate was edited at Leyden in 1722; that on the Four Cardinal Virtues appeared at Basel in 1552. G. died about 1441 in the Peloponnesus.

Gemma'tion. See BUDD'ING.

Gemot' (Old Eng. 'a meeting,' from *metan*, 'to meet'), the old English name for a council, as the *Scir-G.*, or assembly of the shire, the *Burh-G.*, *Hundred-G.*, and the *Micel-G.*, or assembly of the whole nation, also known as the Witenagemot (q. v.).

Gems, Ancient. The term gem, though often used to indicate precious stones used for ornamental purposes, properly belongs only to such hard and precious stones (the *pierres fines* of the French) as have engraved upon them devices, figures, portraits, pictorial groups, &c. Minute engravings were in ancient times executed on nearly all the hard precious stones now known, except the diamond, which on account of its hardness presents insuperable difficulties to the engraver's tools. But the stones most suitable for gem engraving were the various forms of coloured and banded quartz and colourless rock crystal. The banded quartzes—the onyx, sardonyx, nicolo, and agate, which only differ from each other in the colours and arrangement of their various strata—were the favourite media for engraving in relief (cameo engraving), the different layers giving great boldness and clearness of outline to their work. For intaglio, or sunk engraving, on the other hand, carnelian quartz, and its fine variety known as sard, chalcedony, and jasper, were very frequently employed. Of much less frequent use were such precious stones as beryls, emeralds, sapphires, rubies, garnets, jacinths, &c.; but many examples of antique engraving on these, as well as on lapis-lazuli, tourmaline, aventurine, obsidian, &c., are still found in collections of A. G. Next to the quartzes, the material most frequently employed was 'paste' or glass imitations of precious stones, in the preparation of which the Romans were highly skilled. Such pastes were evidently in great demand in early times, as imitation jewellery is in the present day.

The implements which the early gem-engravers used were probably only two—the drill and the 'diamond' point. The drill was used for producing the deeper portions of any engraving by making a succession of small holes or depressions in the material. Its cutting effect was produced by feeding its point with fine emery powder mixed with oil. The diamond point, which effected its working by a succession of scratches, was composed of minute splinters of corundum (the *adamantis crustæ* of remote times). These splinters, Pliny remarks, 'gem-engravers greatly value, and mount them in an iron tool, there being nothing so hard that they will not hollow out with facility.' The 'wheel,' an instrument much used by Renaissance and modern artists, was not known to the engravers of the classical period. It consists of a minute disc of copper fixed on the point of a spindle, which is caused to revolve with great rapidity. The edge of the disc, charged with emery or diamond dust mixed with oil, is applied to the surface to be cut away, and it bites its way into the hardest materials with great rapidity. It is evident that under any circumstances the work of gem engraving is of a nature requiring the greatest patience, as well as skilful and delicate manipulation, and considering that ancient engravers worked entirely without magnifiers, the artistic feeling and individuality of their works are marvellous.

The art of gem engraving was developed from the very ancient practice of engraving signets for securing property by their impressions, and for various official purposes. Numerous remains of such signets in Assyrian and Egyptian workmanship still exist, containing rude representations of human and other figures, having no traces of hieroglyphic or alphabetic characters, and therefore presumably more ancient than the invention of arbitrary modes of representing ideas. These primitive engravings are succeeded by another series upon which inscribed characters appear. In the case of the Assyrian they were chiefly executed upon serpentine, and took the form of cylinders engraved around their whole surface. The Egyptian work was cut in the form of *scarabei* or beetles, the material used being soapstone or glazed terra-cotta. Real gem engraving can be traced to Assyrian work dating about the 7th c. B.C., although it is maintained that at least one engraved jasper of Egyptian origin belonging to the 15th c. B.C. exists. It is, however, most probable, as maintained by King (*Handbook of Engraved Gems*), that the Egyptians were long preceded by the Assyrians in the cultivation of the art, and that the former people continued to use soft materials and gold for their signets down to the times of the Ptolemies. From the Assyrians the art passed in succession to the Phœnicians and the Greeks, by the latter of whom gems were for the first time secured in gold settings and worn as finger rings. Gem engraving was a well-recognised art in Greece 600 years B.C., and about that date the famous ring of Polycrates was made by a Samian artist. About the same period the art was cultivated by the Etruscans, who, however, obviously derived their inspiration from Asia and Egypt, and using the scarabeus form, engraved first representations of the lower animals, only rising to the drawing of human figures under the influence of the Greeks. An archaic intaglio of Etruscan workmanship, 'The Five Heroes before Thebes,' is pronounced by Winckelmann to be 'not only the most ancient monument of the art of the Etruscans, but also of art in general.' From the Etruscans the art passed to the Romans, under whom it reached its zenith of perfection and variety.

Down to about 150 B.C. gem engraving was confined to works in intaglio, but then an altogether new branch, cameo engraving, was introduced, which gave an enormous impetus to the development of the art. The primary purpose for which intaglio engravings were executed had always been for use as signets, whereas cameos were introduced purely from artistic motives; and although many magnificent works of art were achieved in intaglio, they cannot compare in artistic and historical value with some of the cameos which are preserved to our own times. Although any engraving on a hard or precious stone executed in relief may be regarded as a cameo gem, yet true cameo engraving requires for its perfection such stones as enable the artist to throw his work into distinct relief by two or more coloured strata. Gem portraits, which began to appear in the era of Alexander the Great, soon came to be executed in great abundance in cameos, and the authentic portraits we possess of many of the most prominent persons in ancient history are derived from these. The most valuable cameo still extant is the 'Tiberius,' or great cameo of the Sainte Chapelle, preserved in the Bibliothèque Nationale, Paris. It is a work containing twenty-four figures and accessories representing the triumph of Germanicus, executed on a sardonyx of five layers. This magnificent gem was sold to St. Louis of France by Baldwin II. (q. v.), the last of the Latin Emperors of the East, along with various relics of our Saviour, for £20,000. Though less in size, the Vienna cameo, 'The Coronation of Augustus,' is even of greater artistic excellence. The Carpegna cameo in the Vatican collection is by far the largest gem in existence, measuring 16 inches long by 12 deep, its subject being Bacchus and Ceres.

Gem engraving in all its departments, including the fabrication of pastes, reached its highest perfection during the period of Augustus, and for two or three centuries thereafter the art was maintained in its fullest vigour and development. But after the reign of Severus it rapidly declined, and in the 5th c. Roman gem-cutting may be said to have become extinct, dying away in fantastic and ill-executed works which were employed and valued as amulets and charms. It was not till the Renaissance period, about the beginning of the 16th c., that it was again revived on the very soil where it had flourished so vigorously more than a thousand years before; and attained even greater perfection than in classic times. In the last century many instances occurred of the fabrication of spurious antiques and the falsification of genuine ancient gems by inserting inscriptions purporting to be the names of their original engraver. The Poniatowsky collection was the most remarkable example of such, containing as it did about 3000 works all signed ostensibly by the greatest artists of ancient times. The prevalence of these forgeries did infinite harm to the art, introducing doubt and confusion into the minds even of the most experienced amateurs; and to the disgraceful practice was doubtless due in large measure the extinction of the art. Gem engraving is now only practised as a handicraft for producing seals or small works altogether devoid of artistic significance. Cameo cutting is confined to works in shell and other soft material, which do not bring it within the province of gem engraving. See CAMEO.

In addition to the artistic value which A. G. possess, they preserve to modern times the most faithful representations of the dress, habits, and usages of the remote periods whence they have come down. On many historical events they throw much light, and they help to interpret innumerable obscure allusions and remarks in classical writers. No less valuable are they for preserving a faithful representation of the features of the great rulers, statesmen, poets, and philosophers of antiquity, and thus knitting in closer ties the thought and life of widely-removed epochs. See Marriette's *Pierres Gravées* (1750); Raspe's *Catalogue der Impreintes der Pierres Gravées; Tassie Gems* (1791); King's *Antique Gems* (2d ed. 1866); *Handbook of Engraved Gems* (1866); *Antique Gems and Rings* (1872).

Gems, Artificial. The artificial production of precious stones is a subject that has of recent years engaged the attention of some chemists, among others Ebelmen, Sainte-Claire Deville, Caron, Becquerel, and Wöhler. In 1858 Deville and Caron communicated to the *Académie des Sciences* of Paris the fact that they had produced small gems of the corundum class—as the ruby and sapphire—by exposing to a white heat the fluoride of aluminum mixed with a little charcoal and boracic acid in a crucible. Their process is detailed in *Comptes Rendus, Annales de Chimie*. In 1870 M. Gaudin, and in 1873 M. Ch. Feil, gave to the same learned Society the results of their researches in this field. In fusing the materials they employed the flame of the oxyhydrogen blow-pipe. Gaudin's A. G. were deficient in hardness, but possessed the other qualities and composition of the natural stones. Feil has produced a rose-coloured stone, composed of almost pure alumina fused with the aid of borax, that emits the phosphorescent light of the ruby.

Gems, Imitation, or **Pastes,** are composed of a dense transparent glass of great purity and lustre. The Romans produced, among other mock gems, admirable imitations of the emerald and lapis-lazuli. Early in last century Strass, a German chemist, fabricated a vitreous base, which now bears his name, and employed it for I. G. Its percentage composition is thus given by Dumas:—Silica, 38·5, potash, 7·5, alumina, 1·0, oxide of lead, 53. The diamond is imitated with white strass; for coloured gems a little of the metallic oxides used by enamellers is added to the base. Large quantities of cheap I. G. are made at Septmoncal in the Jura. The Parisians take the lead in this art. They employ, besides strass, a paste called *diamant de bore*, of which borax is believed to be the main ingredient. The paste possesses great hardness, with the brilliancy and refractive power of the diamond; and when skilfully cut, polished, and set, it is difficult to distinguish it from true brilliants. In the manufacture of I. G. great care is taken. The ingredients are selected of great purity, and well pulverised and sifted; the fitness of the crucibles to resist intense heat and chemical action is tested; and the fusion and cooling of the paste are slowly conducted.

Gems-Boc, or **Gems-Bok** (*Oryx gazella*), a species of Antelope (q. v.), also known as the *kookaamis*, a typical inhabitant of S. Africa, and distinguished by its grey colour, which is varied by a deep black spinal marking, the latter hue also being found on the hinder quarters, flanks, and face. A short mane is developed. The tail is long and black, and the horns are straight and slope backwards, while they are annulated at their bases only. No *crumen* or 'tear-bag' exists. The G. inhabits arid plains and barren wastes, and appears to feed largely upon succulent plants, the juices of which serve in lieu of water. It will resist the attack of the lion, and defend itself with great courage and skill by means of its sharp horns. The flesh is very highly esteemed.

Gen'darmes, or **Gens d'Armes** (Fr. 'men-at-arms'), the name given first to the heavy French cavalry during the 14th and 15th centuries, then to a cavalry corps which formed a royal body-guard to the Bourbons, and now applied to the French military police, which contains both cavalry and infantry.

Gen'der (Fr. *genre*, formed from the ablative of the Lat. *genus*), in grammar, is the distinction of nouns according to sex. In English all names applied to males are said to be of the *masculine* G., those applied to females of the *feminine* G.; all others are said to be of the *neuter*, *i.e.*, of *neither* G. Properly speaking, as there are only two sexes, there are only two genders; but the term neuter G. is sanctioned by universal usage, and under this head all names of inanimate objects ought to fall. Owing, however, to the process of personification, such objects are often spoken of as animate, conscious, or sentient beings, and as such are invested with sex according to the analogy suggested. Thus the sun, considered as a god, is masculine; the moon, as a goddess, is feminine. So also in figurative language *time* is masculine, while such nouns as *earth, ship, country, town, virtue*, &c., are feminine. In Latin Greek, Sanskrit, &c., many nouns of inanimate objects have from this cause become masculine, others feminine; their G. must accordingly be ascertained from their terminations, which are in all probability the remnant of suffixes indicative of the sex originally assigned to the object spoken of. For example, the terminations *us, a, um* in Latin, *os, ē* or *a, on* in Greek, in many instances represent the masculine, feminine, and neuter genders respectively, both in nouns and adjectives. In English the G. of the noun affects the form of the third personal pronoun (*he, she, it*) alone; whereas in all the highly-inflected languages adjectives (including articles and participles) have different forms for the different genders. Hebrew, Italian, French, Spanish, and Portuguese have no neuter G.; German, like the classic languages, distributes inanimate objects over the three genders. In the matter of G., English, strictly following the order of nature, is the most rational of all tongues. Indeed, nothing can be more absurd than that the name of any one thing should be both masculine and feminine, or masculine and neuter, in the same language, or masculine in one language and feminine or neuter in another. In English there are three methods of distinguishing the G.—(1) by different words, as *bachelor, maid*; (2) by a difference of termination, as *actor, actress*; (3) by prefixing a noun, pronoun, or adjective to the substantive, as *man-servant, maid-servant; he-goat, she-goat; male-child, female-child.*

Geneal'ogy (Gr. *genealogia*, from *genos*, 'race,' and *logos*, 'a discourse') is the science of family origin and descent. It embraces the history of the succession of families from remote ancestors, of the various families which have a common origin, and of the different lines which centre in each individual. In the earliest historical ages we find that genealogy was carefully attended to. No nation has excelled the Jews in this respect. Some of the princely families of India and of other Eastern nations can show pedigrees that almost make *parvenus* of the oldest European families. G. was of supreme importance in feudal times, and it is still of great value in a legal point of view from the inheritance of land and the succession to hereditary titles. It also possesses a deep interest from a scientific and historical point of view. It has an intimate connection with physiology and psychology, and by exhibiting the growth, transmission, and combination of hereditary qualities it may yet throw much light upon many mysteries in character and conduct. G. has become within the present generation a very important study in the United States, having an extensive literature of its own. See for England, Collins's *Peerage of England* (new ed. 9 vols. 1812); Henry Drummond's *Histories of British Families* (2 vols. Lond. 1846): for Scotland, Douglas' *Peerage of Scotland* (2 vols. Edinb. 1813), and his *Baronage* (Edinb. 1796); Crawford's *Peerage* and other works; Anderson's *Scottish Nation* (3 vols. Edinb. 1863); *Retours*, or *Inquisitionum ad Capellam Domini Regis Retornatarum, Scotiæ*, &c. (3 vols. 1811–16): for the United States, Savage's *Genealogical Dictionary of the First Settlers of New England* (4 vols. Bost. 1860–62); *The New England Hist. and Genealogical Register* (periodical). For Europe generally

Hübner's *Genealogische Tabellen* (4 vols. Leips. 1725–33, new ed. 1737–66); Gatterer's *Abriss der Genealogie* (Gött. 1788); Koch's *Tables Généalogiques des Maisons Souveraines d'Europe* (Ger. Berl. 1808); Voigtel's *Geneal. Tabellen* (1810); also Vehse's *Geschichte*. On royal families, Lavoisne's *Atlas* (Phil. 1820; new ed. Lond. 1841) is very useful. For the literature of the subject consult Moule's *Bibliotheca Heraldica* (Lond. 1822).

Gen'eral, used of monastic institutions, is the term for the supreme head of a religious order, who is responsible to the Pope alone. He is elected, usually for three years, by the general chapter of the order, over which he then presides. The general chapter consists of the provincials, each of whom is head of all the communities belonging to an order throughout a province. The *admonitor* appointed by the order as adviser to its G. has no control over his decision.

General Assembly. See ASSEMBLY, GENERAL.

Generalisa'tion, as defined by Whately, is the act of comprehending under a common name several objects agreeing in some point which we abstract from each of them, and which that common term serves to indicate. This may, at least, be taken as a definition of the G. of *notions*. Thus from the consideration of the earth as a body moving round the sun, we arrive at a conception of the generalised notion implied by the word planet. The grouping of individuals in families, species, genera, orders, &c., is a succession of generalisations, each of which is wider than its predecessor. It is therefore apparent that G. leads up to classification, depending itself upon the process of abstraction. To generalise we must first abstract; though it is conceivable, as pointed out by Herbert Spencer, that abstraction may be possible without G.

A higher species of G. is what may be termed the G. of *propositions* or inductive G. (See INDUCTION.) For instance, consider the proposition that the earth moves round the sun in an ellipse. Inasmuch as the earth moves round the sun, it is, as we saw above, a planet; and when we extend this other attribute of the earth's motion, ellipticity, to such bodies, we form a generalised proposition which may or may not be true, viz., Planets move round the sun in ellipses. To generalise thus is necessarily hazardous, but the process has always played a most important part in the progress of science. When Werner, towards the close of last century, from careful observation of the succession of strata in his own neighbourhood, concluded that all formations in all parts of the world were laid down in the same order, and must have been deposited by the same agency—a universal ocean—his generalisations were hasty and false. On the other hand, the enunciation by Newton of the universal law of gravitation, which was the result of the demonstration by calculation that the moon was held in its path by the same force which made a stone fall to the ground, is a most perfect example of a true G. Of all generalisations the grandest is the modern theory of the Conservation of Energy—a true induction from our only source of accurate knowledge, experience.

General Officer. In the middle ages a commander who had captains under him was styled a captain-general, and the adjective *general* has from this use become a substantive signifying an officer with independent command. G. O. is applied to any officer higher than a colonel. At the head of all is the commander-in-chief or field-marshal, beneath whom come generals, lieutenant-generals, major-generals, and brigadier-generals. In England the office captain-general is merely nominal, and is held by the sovereign.

General Quarter Sessions, Court of. This court is held in England by two or more justices of the peace in every county and division of a county once every quarter of a year, for the trial of misdemeanours and other breaches of the peace. Under 1 Will. IV. c. 70, these sessions must be held in the first week after 31st March, 24th June, 11th October, and 28th December. Justices may, however, direct the April quarter sessions to be held any time between 7th March and 22d April, so as not to interfere with the spring assizes. For Scotland, see QUARTER SESSIONS, JUSTICES OF THE PEACE.

General Ship. A trading ship is so called which has been advertised to carry goods from a particular port at a stated time, and which is under no special contract. If the destination be stated, and an alteration subsequently made, the owners must give notice of the change; and should they omit to do so, they are liable for the consequences. Contracts should be made with the master, not with the owner, of the vessel. Usually there is no other evidence of contract except the advertisement and the bill of lading. These may be supplemented by parole evidence.

General Verdicts. In criminal cases the usual verdict is 'guilty' or 'not guilty,' or in Scotland 'not proven;' in civil cases it is a verdict for the plaintiff or for the defender. These are called G. V. in contradistinction to Special Verdicts (q. v.).

Genera'tion, the function of living bodies whereby the losses which death is continually making upon the species of animals and plants are repaired and made good. Reproduction of the *species* stands in a manner antagonistic to the *nutrition* of the individual, since the reproductive energies act antagonistically to the nutrition of the form, by demanding the exercise of powers which weaken and destroy it. G. in the animal world is accomplished in various ways. The various modes of reproduction may thus be tabulated:—

REPRODUCTION may be effected	(A.) ASEXUALLY, without the operation of the elements of *sex*, as by	(*a.*) *Fission*, or simple division of the body.
		(*b.*) *Gemmation* or budding, which may be (1) *continuous* or (2) *discontinuous*.
	(B.) SEXUALLY, by the operation of the *male* and *female* elements, and may be performed by individuals which are	(*a.*) *Diœcious, i.e.*, having the sexes in distinct and separate individuals.
		(*b.*) *Monœcious* or *Hermaphrodite, i.e.*, having both sexes in one and the same individual.

In the plant creation, similarly, G. may be performed by monœcious or diœcious individuals. Some plants are sexually *perfect, i.e.*, have *stamens and pistil* (corresponding to male and female organs respectively) in the *same flower*; or *monœcious, i.e.*, have stamens in one flower and pistils in other flowers of the *same plant*; or *diœcious, i.e.*, have staminate flowers in one plant, and pistillate flowers in another and *distinct plant*. Asexual modes of G. in animals are exemplified in many *Invertebrata*. Thus the *Vorticellæ* or 'bell animalcules' among the *Infusoria*, and other members of the latter class, illustrate the process of fission, the bell-shaped heads of these animalcules dividing into two separate beings. The *Amœbæ* and other *Rhizopoda*, among the lower *Protozoa* do the same. The process of *gemmation* or *budding* is well seen in the fresh-water polypes, or *Hydræ* (q. v.), in which a young form buds out from the side of the parent, but sooner or later detaches itself. This is termed *discontinuous* gemmation. In the zoophytes and corals the buds may grow into forms resembling the parent organism, and may remain permanently attached thereto, thus constituting a *compound* animal. In the latter case, the budding is said to be *continuous*. A *compound* animal consists of separate organisms, each of which is termed a *zoöid*; and as the *individual* animal in zoology is regarded *as the total result of the development of a single ovum or egg*, the entire organism of a compound form forms the individual, since it may be proved to have originally sprung by continuous budding from a single egg. In *sexual reproduction*, as already defined, the elements of the *male* and *female* sexes take part. These elements consist in the production by the female of an *ovum* or egg, and by the male of the *seminal fluid* or *semen*, the characteristic parts of which fluid consist of certain minute animalcular and living bodies named *spermatozoöids*, or *spermatozoa*. The performance of the sexual mode of reproduction consists essentially in the *fertilisation* or *impregnation* of the egg of the female by contact with the spermatozoöids of the male. Thereby a certain series of changes is induced, which results in the formation of a new being. What the exact nature of the contact is, which takes place between the male and female elements, physiology cannot as yet tell. But it appears highly probable that this contact is not only effected by the spermatozooids actually penetrating the covering of the egg, but that the influence of the male may in some cases extend or be transmitted thus to many subsequent generations of progeny. Occasionally certain cases may occur in the animal series, as among the plant-lice or *Aphides* (see APHIS) (*Hemiptera*), in which virgin or unimpregnated females appear to be capable of producing progeny without contact with a male. This peculiarity has received the name of *Parthenogenesis* (q. v.). The explanation of this anomaly appears to be that the bodies which give rise to the young of such females are not true *ova* or eggs, which would require fertilisation before developing new beings, but are simply *pseudova* or false eggs, resembling *internal* buds or *gemmæ*, and produced by an *asexual* process of G.

The presence of sexuality in plants has already been referred to —the *stamens* constituting the male organs and the *pistil* the female organs of vegetables. In early times the Egyptians knew that dates were produced by bringing the two kinds of flowers into contact. Theophrastus mentions the *sexes* of plants, and Pliny speaks of *male* and *female* palms. Grey in 1676 first definitely determined the sexuality of plants, in a paper read before the Royal Society; and this botanist appears to have had pretty clear notions that the *pollen* from the stamens was the matter which fertilised the seeds contained in the *pistil*. Ray and Camerarius—the latter of Tübingen—advocated the views of Grey, and in due time Linnæus (1736) definitely expressed his belief in the sexuality of plants. Linnæus, however, was not aware that in the lower (cryptogamic or flowerless) plants truly-defined sexual organs also existed. This subject was finally investigated by Treviranus (1815), Amici, and Robert Brown, whilst the researches of Hofmeister, Suminski, and others on cryptogams have enabled us to clearly comprehend the reproductive processes of the lower groups of plants.

Generation, Eternal. See TRINITY.

Generation, Sponta'neous, the name given to indicate a belief in the origin of living beings, and especially of the lower forms of animal and plant life, from inorganic matter. When living beings are said to come *spontaneously* into existence, they are believed to originate without the *pre-existence* of a parent organism or organisms. The ancients, with imperfect knowledge of the development and general physiology of living beings, were firm believers in S. G., or *abiogenesis* as it is more commonly termed in modern biology. That putrefaction and the decay of animal and vegetable matters should give origin to living beings appeared to be a fact which the daily experience of life seemed in every way to corroborate, and it was only about the middle of the 17th c. that Francesco Redi, a physician of Florence, first refuted the common belief by showing that the maggots which appeared in decaying meat sprang from eggs deposited in the meat by the parent flies. Redi's experiment consisted in placing gauze over the meat to exclude the flesh-flies, when the process of decomposition went on as before, without the production of maggots or larval flies. Redi adopted as his motto the expression *Omne vivum ex vivo.*

After Redi's day and generation the microscope began to be perfected; and although the idea of animals of such high organisation as insects being spontaneously generated was given up, the discovery of many forms of animalcular life renewed the theory of S. G., as explanatory of the origin of the lowest animals and plants. Needham and Buffon in the middle of the 18th c. experimented upon the production of animalcules in infusions, and came to the conclusion that these animalcules were produced by S. G.; inasmuch as, notwithstanding their precautions of boiling and carefully sealing their infusions, they continually found animalcules developed in them. They therefore supported the doctrine of abiogenesis, against that of *biogenesis;* according to which all living things originate from pre-existing forms of life. The Abbé Spallanzani repeated Needham's experiments, and by the exercise of greater care showed that it was possible to keep sealed infusions without developing any animalcules; and in 1836-37 Schulze and Schwann, filtering the air admitted to infusions through sulphuric acid and through red-hot tubes, found that no animalcular life was developed. In 1854-59 Schröder and Dutsch used cotton-wool to filter the air and so to protect their infusions, with the same result. Quite recently the experiments of Tyndall have proved that the air contains multitudes of germs, and that the atmosphere therefore acts as the medium for the conveyance of these germs to situations (as among decaying matters) in which they may spring up into their mature and adult forms. The 'germ theory' of disease, which accounts for the spread of infectious diseases on the assumption that these germs are conveyed by the atmosphere, rests on the facts just stated, and receives much support from the experiments and surgical practice of Professor Lister of Edinburgh, who prevents suppuration and putrefaction in wounds by protecting raw surfaces with gauze and dressings rendered antiseptic or germ-destroying by being steeped in carbolic acid. The doctrine of *biogenesis* is thus accepted in the present day by almost all naturalists. Some few authorities (amongst whom Dr. H. C. Bastian of London stands pre-eminent), however, still declare their adherence to the doctrine of S. G., and believe that the lower forms of life may be developed from inorganic matters and without the pre-existence of parent organisms. The reader will find in Dr. Bastian's work entitled *The Beginnings of Life* a full *résumé* of the subject, and of experiments conducted in support of his views.

In the present day the following statements may be held to briefly summarise this great controversy:—(1) Whether or not S. G. be ever proved to be a possibility or to actually occur, there can be no doubt whatever that many lower organisms are propagated in decaying matters through their *germs*, borne by the atmosphere, finding an appropriate resting-place in such matter, and there springing up into adult forms of life. (2) It has been abundantly proved that the atmosphere contains a large quantity of *germinal* or *organic* matter amongst the floating *débris* and dust it carries mechanically suspended in it. (3) Experiments which seem to favour the idea that S. G. may occur are liable to fallacy and error, since it has not been proved that germs are destroyed by even intense heat. The belief that cases of living beings appearing in infusions carefully protected from the atmosphere, are explicable on the ground that the germs may have previously been contained in the fluids of the infusion, and have not been destroyed by heat, is thoroughly warranted and feasible. (4) The advocate of S. G. has the disadvantage of having to maintain that the ordinary laws of nature and of reproduction must be continually set aside. And lastly, when cases of Dormant Vitality (q. v.) occur among such highly organised creatures as the *Rotifera* (q. v.), or 'wheel animalcules,' it may be reasonably assumed that living matter may simulate states of seeming death, and yet be capable of easy and quick revival.

Generations, Alternation of. See ALTERNATION OF GENERATIONS.

Genera'tor, in mathematics, is a point, line, or surface by whose motion a curve or surface may be described or *generated.* Thus a point moving round a fixed point at a constant distance from it describes a circle, and a straight line rotating round a fixed line not in the same plane generates an hyberboloid.

Genesee', an American river which rises in Pennsylvania, flows through New York, and, after a course of 120 miles, through a fertile and romantic district, enters Lake Ontario, 7 miles N. of Rochester. It is navigable for 5 miles, and has remarkable falls at Portageville and in the neighbourhood of Rochester.

Gen'esis, the first book of the Hebrew Scriptures, received its name (in full Gr. *genesis kosmou*, 'creation or origin of the universe') from the subject of its contents. The plan of the book, as it now stands, is easy to be seen. It is, in a word, to trace the history of Israel as the chosen people of God from the creation of the world. The history, which embraces a period of 2390 years (from Adam to the Flood, 1656, v., vii. 11; till Abram left Haran, 368, xi., xii. 4; to the death of Joseph, 286, xxi. 5, xxv. 26, xlvii. 9, add 71 of Joseph's life, l. 26, *cf.* xli. 46, and add 7 years of plenty and 2 of famine), is divided naturally into two eras by the Flood. The history of the creation of the world, and of the fall of man from a state of primeval innocence (i.-iii.), is followed by the history of Adam's descendants to the death of Noah (iv.-ix.). From the nature of the case the history so far is entirely general, and is therefore a mere introduction to what follows. But from the Flood the history traces step by step how the children of Israel were chosen out of all the families of the earth to be the people of God. After the descendants of Noah are enumerated, by whom the earth was peopled (x.-xi. 9), two of the three sons are dropped, and only the generations of Shem traced, down to Abraham (xi. 10-32). Of Abraham's children, Ishmael and those by Keturah are summarily dismissed (xxi. 9-21, xxv. 1-6, 12-18), because the history is chiefly concerned with the history of Isaac (xii.-xxiv.). In his sons the final election takes place; Jacob obtains the birthright, his father's blessing, and also the title of 'Israel' (xxv.-xxxv.), while the descendants of Esau are dismissed with a genealogy (xxxvi.). After that the history of Jacob's sons is carried on to the death of Joseph (xxxvii.–l.). Otherwise, the contents are divided into ten sections besides the first chapter, beginning each with the heading *These are the generations*:—1. Of the heavens and earth (ii. 4–iv. 26); 2. of Adam (*This is the book of the generations*, v. 1–vi. 8); 3. of Noah (vi. 9–ix. 29); 4. of the sons of Noah (x. 1–xi. 9); 5. of Shem (xi. 10–26); 6. of Terah (xi. 27–xxv. 11); 7. of Ishmael (xxv. 12–18); 8. of Isaac (xxv. 19–xxxv. 29); 9. of Esau (xxxvi.); 10. of Jacob (xxxvii. 2–l.). Such is the design and plan of the book as it now stands.

Authorship.—The general or common belief is that G. was written by Moses when he wrote the rest of the Pentateuch, its facts having been communicated to him by supernatural revelation. But from various indications in the book itself the opinion was broached as early as the 17th c. (*e.g.*, by Simon and Le Clerc) that he derived his information from previously-existing documents. The view that G. is founded on older documents has been adopted still more strongly by those critics who place the composition of the Pentateuch at a later time than that of Moses altogether. The warrant for the assumption is found (1) in certain supposed indications of a later date, (2) in the introductory clauses by which certain portions are separated from what goes before, (3) in the repetitions of the same or very similar events, and (4) in the difference in style and language which is evident when various parts are compared, and particularly in *the naming of the deity*. For example—(1) The mention of *Dan* (xiv. 14), a name which the town did not receive till long after Moses (Josh. xix. 47; *cf.* xiv. 2, 3, 7, 17, xxiii. 2, xxxv. 19, 27); ch. xxxvi. 31, which seems to imply that one or more kings had reigned over the children of Israel; ch. xii. 6 and ch. xiii. 7, which seem to imply that when they were written the Canaanite was no longer in the land; ch. l. 11, which would seem to imply a writer who lived in the land of Canaan, &c. (2) The headings of the ten sections mentioned above. (3) The adventure which happened to Abraham and Sarah, and to Isaac and Rebecca, in both cases with Abimelech, King of Gerar (xx. xxvi.); the twofold account of the creation (i.–ii. 3, and ii. 3 to end), of the entering into the ark (vi. 9–22, vii. 9–16, and vii. 1–8), of Esau's wives (xxvi. 34 and xxviii. 9, and xxxvi. 2, 3), and of the origin of the names Bethel (xxviii. 19 and xxxv. 9–15), Israel (xxxii. 28 and xxxv. 10), and Beersheba (xxi. 22–32 and xxvi. 17–33). (4) Varieties of style and language, the most conspicuous of which is the use of the two chief names of the Deity—Elohim (A. V. God) and Jehovah (Lord). Sometimes the one name is used throughout a passage, sometimes the other—a peculiarity which is rendered the more striking by the fact that the difference is observed just in those passages which there appear to be *other grounds* for believing to be composed by different writers, *e.g.*, in the two accounts of the creation, the entering into the ark, and the origin of Beersheba above.

The first who laid particular stress on the names of the Deity, of which so much has been made by modern critics, was Astruc, a French physician, in his *Conjectures sur les Mémoires Originaux, dont il parait que Moyse s'est servi pour composer le Livre de Genèse* (Bruss. 1753). He assumed the existence of two chief sources which pervaded the whole of G., an Elohim document and a Jehovah document, and other ten minor ones. Eichhorn held (*Einleitung ins A. T.*, 1823) that G. was founded on two pre-Mosaic documents, Elohistic and Jehovistic. De Wette (*Einleitung*, 1806) supposed that the chief source of G. is a continuous Elohistic writing, extending down to Exodus vi., with which the author of the existing book interwove matter out of one or more Jehovistic documents. He was followed in essential points by Von Bohlen, Bleek, Tuch, Knobel, Delitzsch, and Bishop Colenso. The theory of the last is that the Book of G. grew to its present shape by degrees, different writers (whom he distinguishes as the second Elohist, first, second, and third Jehovist, and the Deuteronomist) introducing from time to time into the original narrative such matter, generally supplementary, as they considered important. He professes to be able to pick our from the whole book the Elohistic narrative, in a series of passages which may be read continuously—i.–ii. 3, v., vi. 9–22, vii. 6–24, viii. 1–19, ix. 1–17, 28, 29, xi. 10–32, xii. 4*b*, 5, xiii. 6, 12, xvi. 1, 3, 15, 16, xvii., xix. 29, xxi. 2–5, xxiii., xxv. 7–26, xxvi. 34, 35, xxviii. 1–9, hiatus, xxix. 24, 29, 32–35, xxx. 1–24, xxxi. 18, xxxv. 9–29, xxxvi. 1–19, 31–43, xxxvii. 1, 2, 28*a*, 36, xlvi. 6–27, xlvii. 7–11, 27, 28, xlviii. 3–7, xlix. 1*a*, 29–33, l. 13.

On the other hand, many eminent scholars have all along opposed these opinions. Ewald, *e.g.*, in his first work (*Die Composition d. G.*, 1823), sought to weaken the argument from the different names used for God by showing that the use of them in G. is always fixed by rules grounded on the usages of the Hebrew language. In the opinion that no written documents were made use of by Moses in the composition of G., an opinion which he afterwards abandoned, he has been followed by Sack, Hengstenberg, Havernick, Ranke, Drechsler, M. Baumgarten, Wette, J. H. Kurtz, Keil, and Smith's *Chaldæan Account of Genesis* (1875). Since the publication of this last work, the question as to the authorship of G. has entered on an entirely new phase. See PENTATEUCH.

Genette' (*Genetta*), a genus of Carnivorous *Mammalia*, very nearly allied to the *Viverridæ* or Civets (q. v.). The genettes have a musk pouch, although in a less perfectly developed state than that of the civets. They are nocturnal in their habits. The common or blotched G. (*G. tigrina*) inhabits S. Africa, but also occurs in S. Europe. Its colour is greyish yellow, with bands and patches of black. The claws are semi-retractile. The pale or Senegal G. (*G. Senegalensis*) is a second species, which, like the common G., is susceptible of domestication. The Amer G. (*G. Amer*), a native of Abyssinia, has a fur spotted with dark markings.

Gene'va (F. *Genève*, Ger. *Genf*, Ital. *Ginevra*), the most westerly canton of Switzerland, lies at the S.W. end of the lake of the same name, and is encircled on the E., S., and W. by the French department of Haute Savoie. Area, 109 sq. miles; pop. (1870) 93,239. It has an undulating surface, rising to a height of 1620 feet above the sea-level, and is traversed by the winding Rhone, which receives the Arve 2 miles S. of the lake. Industry has triumphed over an unpromising soil, and of the surface 40 per cent. is under the vine. G. has 3000 horses, 7950 horned cattle, 1900 swine, 920 sheep, and 1165 goats. The chief mechanical industry is the making of watches (100,000 are yearly exported), musical boxes, scientific instruments, and bijouterie. The people, who almost entirely speak French, belong in nearly equal proportion to the Roman Catholic and Reformed Calvinistic Churches. G. is a representative democracy, there being a member of the Grand Conseil for every 666 inhabitants. The members must be over twenty-five years of age, the voters over twenty-one. A council of state of seven members, elected for two years, holds the executive. All forms of worship are allowed. The chief towns are G. and Carouge.—**Lake of G.** (the *Lacus Lemanus* of the Romans), lies mainly between the French department of Haute Savoie in the S. and the Swiss canton of Vaud in the N., is of crescent shape, and touches in the W. and E. the cantons G. and Valais respectively. It is 55 miles in length along the N. bank, 48½ along the S. bank, and has an extreme width of 9 miles, and a depth of 1014 feet near Meillerie. The E. horn has been silted up for 9 miles by the alluvium brought down by the Rhone, which flows through the lake. The wild rocky southern shore contrasts with that of the N., where the gentle slopes are clad with the walnut, the sweet and wild chestnut, the magnolia, the cedar of Lebanon, and the vine. The deep-blue colour of the lake distinguishes it from the other Swiss lakes, the waters of which are of a greenish hue. It occasionally rises several feet without any apparent cause, currents (*ardyres*) are very strong, and waterspouts now and then occur. The lake, which is never entirely frozen over, has but slight navigation. Of fish there are twenty-one different kinds, the chief being the *ferraz*. The L. of G. is inferior in grandeur to the Lake of Lucerne, while in charm of picturesqueness it is far surpassed by Lake Zürich. Mont Blanc is visible only from the W. bank; from the S. Jura may be seen. Among those who have written, however, with enthusiasm on the scenery of the lake are Voltaire, Rousseau, Goethe; it is also the theme of some exquisite stanzas in the third canto of *Childe Harold*.

Geneva, the capital of the canton of G., and the largest and wealthiest town of Switzerland, lies on both sides of the Rhone where, with the swiftness of an arrow, it leaves the Lake of G., and is 70 miles N.E. of Lyon, with which it is connected by railway. It consists of the city proper, the G. of history, on the left bank of the river, the industrial portion of St. Gervais on the opposite bank, and between these the small Quartier de l'Isle, 831 by 139 feet. The river, which is 600 feet broad, is crossed by six bridges, and of these the handsomest, the Pont du Mont Blanc, nearest to the lake, was completed in 1862. A second little island called Rousseau's, from its having a bronze statue of Jean Jacques (by Pardier, 1834), is planted with trees, and is reached by a small chain suspension bridge from the middle of the Pont des Berques. G. was formerly fortified, but only in the S.E. are there portions of the walls remaining, where they have been converted into promenades. The best and broadest streets are La Corraterie, part of the ancient fosse; the Rues Basses, a series of streets intersecting G. from E. to W.; the Rue de Rhone, running parallel to the river; and the Boulevard Helvétique. Great improvements have been made, especially in St. Gervais, since the construction of the railway. Fine quays extend along both banks of the Rhone, and two jetties projecting on either side into the lake form the new harbour. From the Quai de Mont Blanc, on the left, a magnificent view is obtained of the Mont Blanc group. The Jardin Anglais stretches along the Grand Quai du Lac, and at the city end rises the National Monument, a bronze group of Helvetia and G. on a lofty pedestal, by Dover, in memory of the union of G. with the Confederation in 1814. Among the chief buildings are the cathedral of St. Pierre, completed in 1024 by the Emperor Konrad II., in pure Romanesque, but much altered in the 12th and 13th centuries, and finally disfigured by the addition of a Corinthian portico in the 18th c.; the Hotel de Ville, in the Florentine style, has in the interior planes instead of staircases; the Academy, with lecture-rooms, laboratories, and collections, erected 1867-71 by the city and canton at a cost of £50,000; the Bibliothèque Publique, founded by Bonnivard, the prisoner of Chillon, in 1551, and containing 80,000 vols. and 500 MSS. G. has also a university dating as far back as 1368, but reorganised by Calvin in 1538; an arsenal; a botanic garden laid out by De Candolle in 1816; a fine art athenæum; a museum of pictures, casts, &c., founded by the Russian General Rath; another, with fine Etruscan collections, originated by M. W. Fol; a natural history museum, containing the famous collections of Delesseret, Pictet, De Saussure, Melly, Reviliod, &c.; a Russian church with glittering domes, a synagogue, a conservatoire de musique, and a theatre (1782). The environs of G. are very beautiful, both banks of the lake being studded with fine villas. Chief among the industries is the making of watches, of which 200,000 are produced yearly. The annual value of the bijouterie is about £480,000. Other manufactures are mountain shoes, carved wooden articles, musical boxes, &c. Pop. (1870) 46,783, of whom more than half are Calvinists. French is the prevailing language.

G., which is first mentioned by Cæsar, early belonged to the Allobroges, with whom it passed under Roman rule. On the decay of the empire it fell under the power of the Burgundians, who had settled in Eastern Gaul. In 536 it passed to the Franks, and in 879 to the new kingdom of Burgundy. Konrad II., after subduing Burgundy, was proclaimed king here for the second time in 1034. The bishopric of G., which had existed from the 5th c., became an object of fierce dissension between the Counts of Savoy and those of G., and in the midst of their struggles the citizens joined the Swiss Confederation by concluding an alliance with Freiburg (1518) and Bern (1526). Two parties were thus formed in G., the Confederates (Ger. *Eidgenossen*, by the Fr. pron. *Higuenos*, whence probably the term Huguenots) and the 'Mamelukes,' partisans of the House of Savoy. After the outbreak of the Reformation the bishop transferred his seat to Gex in 1535, and the Reformed religion was legally established, and vigorously preached by Farel (q. v.). In 1541 Calvin (q. v.) settled here to enter on his rigorous career of religious dictator, and henceforth G. became a centre of Protestant education and intense mental life. Opening its gates to evangelical refugees, it received also many philosophers and free-thinkers. The last effort of the Dukes of Savoy to recover G. in 1602 was abortive. In the 18th c. G. was torn by intestine strife, which was eventually settled in behalf of the aristocratic party. The government, however, was overthrown in 1794, and replaced by a national convention. The French annexed G. in 1798, making it capital of the department *Du Léman*, but it was liberated, and admitted into the Swiss confederation in 1814. The attempt to introduce Jesuits led to a violent change of the aristocratic for a republican government in 1848. G. was the seat of a violent peace congress in 1867 and of the Alabama Commission in 1871-72. Monseigneur Mermillod was nominated Bishop of G., but expelled in the latter year. See, besides the older histories of G. by Spon, Picot and Berenger, Pictet de Sergy's *Genève, Origine et Développement de cette République* (Gen. 1845); Thourel's *Histoire de Genève* (3 vols. Gen. 1833); Galiffe's *Quelques Pages d'Histoire* (Gen. 1863); Roget's *Histoire du Peuple du Genève* (3 vols. 1876).

Geneva, the name of twelve towns and villages of the United States, the chief of which is in New York State, at the N.W. end of Seneca Lake, half-way between Rochester and Syracuse, and 50 miles distant from either. It is a great railway terminus, and owes its prosperity to the nurseries, which cover 10,000 acres, and export over one million dollars worth of stock to the various states and to Canada. G. is the seat of Hobart College (1824), and has ten churches, two fine parks, &c. Pop. (1870) 5521.

Généviève (Celtic, 'white wand'), a saint of the Roman Catholic Church, is said to have been born at Nanterre, near Paris, in 422. According to the poetical story of her life, she was first a shepherd-maid of spotless purity and holiness; afterwards removed to Paris, and joined a sisterhood of Christian virgins. When Attila was marching on Paris (451), G.'s prayers were believed to have at least contributed to turn him aside, and when that city was taken by the Franks, she moved the heathen kings Hlodwig and Frederik to treat the Parisians with clemency and to set free many of their captives. G. died in 512, when she was made the chief patron saint of Paris. Her name is a favourite with the Parisiennes. A society of priests, bearing her name, was founded in the 12th c. and lasted till the Revolution. The 'Sisters of St. G.,' an order created in 1636, took no monastic vow, but devoted themselves to teaching young girls, and to the care of the sick.

Gen'ghis Khan, also spelt **Zen'ghis Khan**, but properly **Chingiz Káan** ('greatest of khans'), a famous Mongol conqueror, whose original name was Temudjin, 'best steel,' was born at Deylun Yeldak, on the Upper Hoangho, January 25, 1155. His father, chief of the tribe Neyrun, dwellers N. of the wall of China, dying when G. K. was thirteen, civil war broke out, and the young prince had to fly to Toghrul Ungh, Khan of the Keraites, whose armies he led so successfully that at length Toghrul, from jealousy, planned his assassination. G. K., however, escaped to his native country, raised an army, and made himself master of Toghrul's dominions. In 1204 he defeated the tribe of the Naimans, and in 1205 received the title G. K. or Chingiz Khan, as the acknowledged chief ruler in Mongolia. He had already projected the invasion of China, with which design he published his great code, and enforced strict discipline through his troops. After five years of war with rebellious Mongol chiefs, he fell upon N. China, and though his career of conquest was stayed for a time by a treaty, and by his marriage with the Emperor of China's daughter, in 1215 he seized Pekin and annexed the N. provinces of China. Having now united the Mongols under his single sway and subdued E. Asia, he attacked Mohammed Kothbeddin, who held a sultanate stretching from the Indus to the Black Sea. Mohammed was defeated near the Jaxartes (Scidaria) in 1218, and his realms devastated by G. K.'s followers, who now, under various generals, conquered Persia, advanced into the plains of India, and swept over Europe as far W. as the Dneiper. In 1224 G. K., who had ravaged the fairest regions of Central Asia, spilt the blood of 5,000,000 of men, and formed an empire stretching from the Black Sea to the Sea of Okhotsk, returned to his capital of Kara-Korum in the N. of Mongolia, from which he had been absent seven years. But his thirst for conquest was still unslaked. In 1225, though he was above sixty years of age, he led a horde of fierce nomads across the desert of Gobi, in the depth of winter, and overthrew the King of Tangut. He then descended on S. China, but after taking Nankin and other cities, died in the full flush of victory, August 24, 1227. His aim was to conquer the whole world, and the design was never, says Sir Rutherford Alcock, nearer its accomplishment than in his lifetime. He was reckless of bloodshed, cruel and merciless to his foes, but to his subjects he was a considerate as well as a strict ruler. His path was marked by desolation, but he gave a kind of national organisation to the previously scattered and lawless tribes of Central Asia, and enforced obedience to the civil authority throughout his vast dominions. He made rigid edicts against crime, and established a great postal system. He was a firm monotheist, but tolerated all beliefs. His empire was afterwards divided among his four sons. See Erdmann's *Temudschin* (1862), and Howorth's *History of the Mongols* (Lond. 2 vols. 1876).

Ge'nii, a name given to the Arabic *Jinn* ('the invisible'), from a mistaken belief that the word was cognate with the Latin *genii*, or tutelary spirits. (See GENIUS.) The *Jinn*, belief in whom is enjoined by the Koran, are supposed to have dwelt in the world before the creation of man, but having rebelled against Allah, were expelled to the realm of *Jinnistan*. Though inferior to men in dignity, they are more powerful, and cause much misery and happiness to mortals, visiting the earth in storms and taking whatever form they please, which is generally that of a monster. Many are said to have been converted by Mahommed. The good ones are known as *Peri*. The *Jinn* play a large part in Arabian and Persian fiction, and appear very frequently in the *Thousand and One Nights*.

Genis'ta, a genus of Leguminous plants containing over a hundred species. *G. tinctoria*, found throughout Europe, and common in some parts of England, was formerly extensively used as a yellow dye, and called Greenweed (q. v.) or woodwaxen. *G. Anglica* is another shrubby species found in Britain, commonly called petty whin and needle greenweed. The Plantagenet kings took their name from wearing a sprig of the *Planta genista* as a badge.

Gen'itive, properly **Gen'etive**, one of the cases in grammar. According to the common explanation the G. (Lat. *genitus* from *gigno*) denotes descent from something, as *regis filius*, 'the king's son.' The words *regis* and *king's* are here said to be in the G. case as denoting the son's origin. That this explanation is erroneous will be seen at once by a glance at such expressions as *pueri pater*, 'the boy's father,' *regis domus*, 'the king's house.' A much more rational theory, and more in keeping with the nature of the case, is that offered by Professor Max Müller in his *Science of Language*, and now universally adopted by grammarians. According to his view the G. (Lat. *genus, generis*), that is, the *generic* case, defines the class or genus to which anything belongs. Thus in the phrase *regis filius* the G. *regis* distinguishes the *filius* from the *filii* of other parents, and limits him to a particular class, viz., *king's sons*. The G. may stand to the governing substantive in a variety of relations. The relation may be possessive, as *regis domus*, 'the king's house;' attributive, as *regis domus* = *regia domus*, 'the royal house;' or appositional, as *vox gloriæ*, 'the term glory.' Sometimes the G. may represent either the subject or the object. It is then termed the *subjective* or *objective* G. as the case may be. Thus *amor Dei* may either mean 'the love of God to man,' *i.e.*, God's love to man (subjective), or 'the love of God by man,' *i.e.*, man's love of God (objective); *injuria militum*, 'the injury done by' (subjective) or 'to the soldiers' (objective). The relations of the G. case are expressed in English by *'s*, the form being termed the *possessive* case from the frequency with which it indicates possession; by a preposition (generally *of*); or by an Adjective (q. v.). The old theory that the *'s* in English is the pronominal adjective *his* is absurd. For although it may seem to explain such a phrase as 'the king's son,' *i.e.*, the king his son, it really does not remove the difficulty one whit, *his* (*i.e.*, *he's*) being itself the possessive form of *he*. While in such forms as 'the queen's crown,' 'the book's cover,' 'the men's horses,' it utterly fails. It is simply the relic of *es*, the prevalent inflection for the G. singular in Old English, and which in Transition English absorbed all the others.

Ge'nius (Lat. *genius*, from *gigno, genitum*), properly the superior or spiritual nature that is innate in everything, was the name applied by the Romans, as *daimōn* was by the Greeks, to the protecting spirit that was supposed to accompany every created thing from its origin to its end. Hesiod estimates the number of the *daimones* at 30,000, and considers them to be the souls of just men who lived in the golden age. On this idea the Greek philosophers framed their elaborate theory of demons. In Pindar the *genethlios daimōn* is the G. who watches over man from his cradle to his grave. The G. was looked on as an emanation from the divinity; and that he must have been in some way connected with Jupiter we infer from the fact that the G. of a woman was called a *Juno*. The genii were frequently confounded with the *Manes, Lares*, and *Penates*, to whom they were closely allied in one important feature, viz., the protection of mortals, but from whom they were wholly distinct. A G. was represented as black or white, according as the future of the person of whom he was the guardian angel was dark or fair (Hor. *Epist.* ii. 2, 187-189). The bridal bed (*lectus genialis*) was sacred to the G., who was worshipped on birthdays with incense, flowers, and libations of wine. Not only individuals but places had their G. The image of the national G. of Rome may be seen on coins of Hadrian and Trajan. The G. of a male was represented as a beautiful boy, naked with the exception of a *chlamys* on his shoulders, and furnished with the wings of a bird. A *Juno* (guardian spirit of a female) was represented as a young girl with the wings of a bat or moth, and entirely draped. The G. of a place was portrayed as a serpent eating fruit. See Schömann's *De Diis Manibus, Laribus, et Geniis* (Greifswald, 1840); Ukert's *Ueber Dämonen, Heroen, und Genien* (Leips. 1850). With the Christian writers the G. (*kakodaimōn*) is an evil spirit condemned to endless punishment for his pride and insubordination. See DEMONS.

Gen'lis, Stéphanie Felicité Ducrest de St. Aubin, Comtesse de, a French authoress of good family, was born near Autun, 25th January 1746. At an early age she married the Comte de G., and in 1782 was intrusted with the education of the children of the Duc de Chartres, afterwards Duc d'Orléans. At this time she published several works on education, &c., which attracted a good deal of attention. In 1793 she withdrew with her young wards to Switzerland, where she heard that her husband had perished by the guillotine. In 1800 she returned to France, won the favour of Napoleon, who when he became emperor gave her a pension, which ceased on the Bourbon restoration. She continued her literary labours until her death, December 31, 1830. Among her writings are *Théâtre d'Éducation; Adèle et Théodore; Madame de la Vallière; Henri le Grand*, a biography; *Les Chevaliers du Cyne*, an indefensible political work; *Dîners du Baron Holbach*, an attack on the French philosophers of the 18th c.; *Mademoiselle de Clermont*, a tale, perhaps her most popular work; and her *Mémoires*, written when she was above eighty years of age. Madame G.'s character was by no means estimable. She was a voluminous and popular writer, but her works show slight traces of genius. See her *Mémoires* (10 vols. Par. 1825), and Sainte-Beuve's *Causeries du Lundi*.

Gen'oa (Ital. *Genŏva*, Fr. *Gênes*), surnamed *La Superba*, the chief commercial city in Italy, stands at the foot of the Apennines, on the Gulf of G., in the province of the same name, 79 miles S.E. of Turin, with which it is joined by rail. Pop. (1872) 130,269. From the sea G. has a magnificent appearance, its houses rising in tiers up the steep slope of hills, whose barren summits are crowned with turreted forts. The upper city consists of streets of palaces—noble piles with vast halls and marble staircases and terraces, but mostly disfigured by stucco. Many are crumbling away, others are changed into warehouses, but some are still the dwellings of the rich. Among the chief buildings are the cathedral of S. Lorenzo, built in 1100, but which has been greatly altered, and is now partly Romanesque, partly Renaissance, and partly French Gothic; S. Ambrogio, which has many splendid chapels founded by noble Genoese families, and is lavishly adorned with gilding, mosaics, and paintings; S. Annunziata, with fluted columns of red marble and rich vaultings; the Palazzo dei Principi Doria, whose garden has a large *loggia*; the Palazzo Balbi, which possesses an excellent picture gallery, and affords delightful glimpses of foliage through its colonnades; the Palazzo Ducale, which is all of white marble, and was once the abode of the Doges, but is now used as the townhall; and the Palazzo dell' Universitat, formerly the seat of a Jesuit college, but transformed in 1812 into a university, with a library, museum, botanical garden, and the finest court and staircase in G. The finest streets are the spacious Via Balbi and the Via Nuova, which is lined with palaces, many having marble fronts. The Carlo Felice is the chief theatre, and the Acqua Sola, a high park at the N.E. of the city, is the favourite promenade. In the Piazza Acquaverole is a statue of Columbus (q. v.). It was raised in 1862, is all of white marble, and is placed on a pedestal ornamented with ships' prows. The lower part of G. is a maze of narrow, winding, and very steep and filthy lanes and streets, which are partly separated from the harbour by a high wall with arcades and marble platforms. The harbour is semicircular and sheltered by two long piers, the

Molo Vecchio and Molo Nuovo. It is too small for the growing trade, and can with difficulty be enlarged from the very great depth of the water. The manufactures are considerable and various, consisting chiefly of silk, velvets, lace, cotton, candles, soap, and oil. The making of household furniture and filigree work in coral and silver employs a good number of the Genoese, and shipbuilding is an important industry. The imports, of which about one-third is from England and the rest mainly from France and N. America, are valued at 300 million francs annually, and the exports at 120 millions.

G. (the ancient *Genua*) was early famous as a harbour, and in the Roman times had great trade in the products of the Ligurian coasts. It was a Roman *municipium*, and after the breaking up of Karl the Great's empire constituted itself a republic, presided over by Doges. During the middle ages it was commonly known as *Janua*. It carried on a large Levantine trade even before Venice—with which city as well as with Pisa it had fierce and frequent strife (see VENICE)—and rose to its zenith of power and wealth in the middle of the 13th c. The Genoese shared largely in the crusades, and at one time monopolised the traffic with the Black Sea, had a lucrative trade with India, and held many rich possessions in the East. G. was long convulsed by party struggles, begun by the Doria and Spinola families, who were Ghibellines, and the Grimaldi and Fieschi families, who were Guelphs. At last Andrea Doria (q. v.) established an oligarchical government, against which the Fieschi (q. v.) conspired unsuccessfully in 1547. Gradually the city lost its foreign possessions, the Turks seizing its eastern conquests. Corsica, which remained last of all its foreign territories, was annexed in 1797 by the French, who in 1802 captured G. itself. In 1815 the city was added to the kingdom of Sardinia, and now belongs to the kingdom of Italy. See Serra's *Storia della Liguria* (4 vols. Tur. 1834); Canale's *Storia Civile, Commerciale, e Litteraria dei Genovesi* (9 vols. Gen. 1844–54), and *Nuova Storia della Repubblica di Genova* (Flor. 1862–64).—**Gulf of G.**, a bay rather than a gulf, on the coast of Italy, between Spezia and Oneglia. It is sheltered on the N. by the Apennines, which approach the sea very closely here.

Genouillère, in fortification, the part of the parapet between the ground and the *sill* of the embrasure. It derives its name from being about the height of a man's knee (Fr. *genou*).

Genre Painting (Fr. *genre*, Lat. *genus*, 'kind, variety'), the name of a department of art distinct on the one hand from historical (*genre historique*), and on the other from landscape (*genre du paysage*) painting, but nevertheless given to works in which both historical figures (when they are represented under conditions common in everyday life) and natural scenery (when it assists the composition, but does not preponderate) may be introduced. As this style of painting does not concern itself with strictly historical incidents or historical personages *as such*, it is not regarded as what has been loosely termed 'high art.' On the other hand, although it has been carried perhaps to its highest perfection by the painters of the Dutch school (Ostade, Teniers, and the tavern school generally), it is by no means limited in its range to subjects arising out of 'low life.' The Dutch genre picture, which has familiarised us with the pleasures and pastimes of the Netherlands in a past age, is well known. In the modern English school the name is applied to all compositions with figures, whether interiors or works having a landscape background, all dramatic compositions, and all pictures in which humour is the quality most fully expressed.

Gens (root *gen*, from Lat. *geno, gigno*, 'I beget or bring forth') primarily signifies *kin* or lineage. Among the Romans it denoted sometimes a nation or community like *natio* and *populus*, but specially a clan embracing several families united by a common name and by common religious rites. In the Roman constitution and in Roman law the term G. is always used in the latter signification, and the words G. and *gentiles* had thus a special and definite meaning. At first the G. was purely patrician, but after the passing of the *Lex Canuleia* (445 B.C.), which granted *connubium* between patricians and plebeians, plebeian also. Before this, however, some of the *gentes* contained plebeian *familiæ*, though it is by no means clear how they are to be accounted for. According to the Pontifex Scævola (see Cic. Top. 6), those alone were *gentiles* who (1) bore the same name, (2) were born of freemen (*ingenui*), (3) had no slave among their ancestors, (4) had suffered no *diminutio capitis* or reduction to an inferior condition. Of the *diminutio capitis* there were three grades, which it may be convenient to note briefly here. The first (*maxima*) consisted in the loss of personal freedom (*libertas*), and of course the loss of the *civitas*; the second (*minor*), the loss of *civitas*, or of full *civitas* without loss of personal freedom; and the third (*minima*) had reference neither to *civitas* nor *libertas*, but resulted from a change of family. For example, a man who was his own master (*sui juris*), by adoption (*adrogatio*) into another family, became subject to parental control (*patria potestas*). Each G. was composed of a number of *familiæ* or branches, all supposed to be sprung from a common ancestor; each *familia* was made up of individual members. The *gentes* and *familiæ* were thus the social divisions of the original Roman tribes, which were divided politically into *curiæ* and *decuriæ*. Niebuhr argues that the *decuriæ*, or decades, and *gentes* were the same, in which case the G. would be the smallest political division without reference to kindred; but it seems much more reasonable to suppose that the *familiæ* of each G., as well as the individual members of each *familia*, referred their origin, as in the case of the Celtic clans, to which the Roman *gentes* bear a marked resemblance, to a common ancestor, and that all who were *gentiles* were regarded as connected by blood, however remotely. See Niebuhr's *Roman History*; Malden's *History of Rome*; Göttling's *Geschichte der Römischen Staatsverfassung*; Becker's *Handbuch der Römischen Alterthümer*; Wachsmuth's *Die ältere Geschichte des Römischen Staates*.

Gen'seric, or **Gai'serich** ('spear-prince'), king of the Vandals, one of the barbarian leaders who destroyed the Roman empire, was the son of Godigiselus, who founded a Vandal kingdom in Spain. In 429 G. invaded and ravaged N. Africa, taking Hippo in 431 and Carthage in 439. Invited by Eudoxia, wife of the Roman Emperor Maximus, to be her champion against her husband, as Attila had been the champion of Honoria, he fell upon Italy with a motley host of Vandals, Moors, Ausurians, and Mediterranean pirates, sacked Rome in 455, and carried off the chief art treasures of the city in his ships. The Western emperor Majorian sent an expedition against G., which was destroyed in the Bay of Carthagena in 457, and the fleet despatched against him by the Eastern emperor Leo was burned off Bona in 468. G. died at a great age in 477. He was a man of ruthless cruelty, and being an Arian, persecuted the Catholics of N. Africa with terrible severity. See Gibbon's *Decline and Fall of the Roman Empire*, ch. xxxiii.-xxxvi.

Gentia'na, the typical genus of the Corollifloral order *Gentianaceæ* (q. v.). It contains many herbaceous species, with very showy—generally blue—flowers, natives of temperate countries. Almost all the species possess a more or less bitter principle, employed as a tonic. *G. acaulis* is cultivated in British gardens under the name *Gentianella* (q. v.). *G. nivalis*, an annual, is only found in Scotland, where it is confined to the mountains of Perthshire and Forfarshire.

Gentiana lutea.

Medicinal Properties and Preparations of Gentiana.—The active principles of G. are obtained from the dried root of *G. lutea*, a plant collected in the Alps, Apennines, and other mountainous districts of Europe. G. being a tonic bitter, without astringency, is used in cases of pure debility of the digestive organs, or when a general tonic is required. It is administered in *powder*, in doses of from 10 to 40 grains; in *extract*, 10 to 15 grains; in *infusion*, 1 to 2 oz; in *mixture*, ½ oz. to 1 oz.; and in *tincture*, 1 to 2 drachms. Incompatibles—Sulphate of iron, nitrate of silver, and lead salts.

Gentiana'ceæ, a natural order of Dicotyledonous plants, embracing about 70 genera and 500 species. The plants of the order are chiefly herbaceous, very few being shrubby, and are generally distributed both in cold and warm countries, but are rare in the Arctic and Antarctic islands. The principal property of the order is bitterness. The Buckbean (q. v.) (*Menyanthes trifoliata*), a common British marsh plant, and the Centaury *Erythræa*, belong to the order.

Gentianell'a, the common name generally given to *Gentiana acaulis*, the large blue-flowered gentian cultivated in gardens for edgings, &c.

Gentill'y, a village to the S. of Paris and just beyond the fortifications, in the valley of the Bièvre. It has several charitable institutions, a lunatic asylum (*Bicêtre*), extensive manufactures of wax-candles, buttons, ices, and a trade in timber, charcoal, and forage. Pop. (1872) 8871.

Gen'tleman (Fr. *gentilhomme*, from the Lat. *gens* and *homo*) is a man who belongs to a known family, a meaning which the name partly retains. But it has also a wider signification, for, according to Blackstone, a G. is a student of law or in the university, or one who professes the liberal sciences, or can live idly without manual labour and bear the charge and countenance of a G. In the case of an apportionment of a charitable allowance, a court of equity directed the master to include in the definition of G., 'magistrates, esquires, members of the three learned professions, graduates of the universities, attorneys, surgeons, apothecaries, and *the like*' (*Law Mag.* xii. 202).

Gentlemen-at-Arms (formerly the Band of Gentlemen Pensioners), a corps founded in 1509 as the royal body-guard by Henry VIII. In 1834 William IV. ordered it to be called His Majesty's corps of G.-at-A., and it now consists of a captain, lieutenant, clerk of the cheque, and forty members. The G.-at-A. are only called out on a few state occasions.

Gentoo' (Port. *gentio;* Lat. *gentilis*, 'gentile or foreigner') was the name originally given by the Portuguese, and afterwards by the English, to the inhabitants of Hindustan. The word has now fallen out of use, but has a place in history.

Gentz, Friedrich von, a distinguished German political writer and statesman. Born in 1764 at Breslau, he entered the Prussian public service in 1786. On the outbreak of the French Revolution, he was for a time its enthusiastic defender, but ere long became the most fanatical opponent of all attempts to establish free institutions. Both before and after G. passed from the Prussian to the Austrian service in 1802, he was zealous and influential in stirring up war against Napoleon; it was he who drew up the Berlin manifestoes of 1806 and the Austrian manifestoes of 1809 and 1813, and he was present at the Congress of Paris as first secretary. Soon he was known to Europe merely as the tool of Metternich, and to the policy of reaction he wholly devoted his versatile and brilliant talents. He died suddenly, 9th June 1832. His political writings have been twice published in 5 vols. (by Weick in 1836–38 and by Schlesier in 1838–40), his letters in 1841, and his diaries (*Tagebücher*) in 1861. See also the valuable *Dépêches inédites du Chevalier de Gentz aux Hospodars de Valachie*, by Count Prokesch-Osten (Par. 1876).

Genuflex'ion (Lat. *genu*, 'knee,' and *flectio*, 'bending'). The common posture in prayer among the Jews was standing (Matt. vi. 5), although they also knelt (Dan. vi. 10), and prostrated themselves (1 Kings xviii. 39). The early Christians used five different postures—standing upright, standing bending forward, kneeling on one knee, and on both knees, and lying prostrate. No distinction was made in language, however, between kneeling and prostration, as in kneeling they supported themselves with their hands on the ground. Kneeling, being always regarded as a token of penitence and sorrow, was more practised by Christians than Jews, as if, from a better knowledge of God, they had a deeper sense of their own unworthiness. This principle ruled the occasions on which they knelt. Kneeling was probably the general posture except on Sundays, and between Easter and Whitsuntide, at which times the standing posture was adopted as a sign of the Resurrection.

Gen'us, a division of animals and plants comprising Species (q. v.) which are nearly related to each other by some strongly marked characteristics. Thus the G. *Mus* includes the species of rats and the species of mice, these animals being closely allied in all points of their structure, and the G. *Aquila* includes the various species of true Eagles (q. v.). In botany, the G. *Rosa* includes the various species of roses, and the G. *Rubus* the raspberry, bramble, and their allies. In naming animals and plants scientifically, after the *binomial* system, first used by Linnæus, we give to each organism two names. The first of these indicates the G. to which the animal or plant belongs, and is hence termed the *generic* name; the second is the name of the species to which the animal or plant belongs, and is known as the *specific* name. The common mouse is thus named *Mus domesticus*, and the rat *Mus rattus;* the golden eagle is the *Aquila chrysaëtos*, and the jerfalcon *Falco gyrfalco*.

Geocen'tric (Gr. *gē*, 'earth,' and *kentron*, 'centre'), an expression in astronomy used in the case of a celestial body when its position and motion are considered in relation to a celestial sphere whose centre coincides with the earth's centre, and whose fixed plane of reference is the ecliptic.

Ge'odes (Gr. 'earthy') are hollow nodules, frequently lined in the interior with quartz, calspar, and other crystals. In Somerset and neighbouring counties they go by the name of *potato stones*.

Geod'esy (Gr. *gē* and *daiō*, 'I divide') is the science of determining by measurement and calculation the size and figure of the earth or of any portion of it. Upon it, therefore, depends the construction of maps and charts, the fixing of artificial boundaries of countries, the determination of the lengths of rivers, mountain chains, &c. The chief difficulties encountered arise from meteorological changes affecting the instruments in use, the unevenness of the ground, the practically spherical form of the surface for smaller, and its recognisable ellipticity for larger, areas. The measurement of the base line and angles (see TRIANGULATION) is of course attended with error; but the great number of triangles, and the probability of the error happening on the one side being as great as its probability in happening on the other, probably render the ultimate error arising from the angular measurements very small.

Geoff'rey de Vin'sauf, an English didactic poet of the reign of Richard I., also known as Galfridus Anglicus. He studied at Oxford and in France and Italy, and was in Rome at the end of the 12th c. His metrical treatise *De Nova Poetria*—the earliest attempt at literary criticism made by an Englishman—was very popular in the middle ages. In it G. advocates a return to the style and measures of classic Latin poetry, and protests against the mediæval rhyming Latin verse. A lively *Itinerary of King Richard* has been ascribed, but probably wrongly, to G.

Geoffrey of Monmouth, also named **Jeffrey ap Arthur**, one of the most famous of English mediæval writers, was born about the beginning of the 12th c. at Monmouth, and educated at the Benedictine monastery of that town. He was made Bishop of St. Asaph in 1152, and died about 1154. G.'s Latin *Historia Britonum* has been one of the most important additions ever made to our literature. It deals with the 'history' of Britain from the times of the Trojan Brut to the death of Cadwallo, relating the wildest fictions with an air of perfect gravity, and, as the author remarks, without tiring the reader by rhetorical ornament; blending mediæval legends with Welsh fancies of past greatness and future victory over the English. The work for the first time introduced into England the tales of Arthur and the Round Table, with which English literature has become so deeply imbued, which so many writers have retold, from Walter Mapes to Tennyson. (See ARTHURIAN ROMANCE.) G.'s pre-Arthurian legends, though much less popular and fascinating than his Arthurian stories, have given many themes to our poets, *e.g.*, the tales of Brut, Ferrex and Porrex, Locrine, and Lear, adapted by Sackville, Warner, Spenser, Milton, and Shakespeare. Alhough G.'s statement that he translated the book from one Walter Calenius—who has been wrongly confounded with Walter Mapes—was most likely a mere jest, the fabulous chronicle is undoubtedly based on old Cymric legends which had passed into Wales from the Celts of Brittany. The book became at once widely popular, was abridged by Henry of Huntingdon, and recast by Wace and Gaimar. It was first printed at Paris in 1508. There is an English translation by Aaron Thompson (Lond. 1718), which is reprinted in Bohn's *Antiquarian Library*.

Geoff'rin, Marie Thérèse, *née* **Rodet**, a celebrated French patroness of letters, was born at Paris, June 2, 1699. Her station was originally humble, since she was the daughter of a valet; but having at the age of fourteen married a rich tradesman, she was left on his death with such a colossal fortune as secured her an entrance to the highest circles of Parisian society. Madame G., though without education, was a woman of much natural cleverness, and she succeeded in forming a *salon* of literary and philosophic celebrities without any rival at that day. Diderot, D'Alembert, Marmontel, and Thomas were members of her circle; Horace Walpole, Hume, and Gibbon among her foreign guests; and she so befriended Stanislas Poniatowsky, before he became King of Poland, that he was ever after accustomed to call himself her son. Madame G. contributed largely to the publication of the *Encyclopédie;* and her munificent liberality procured her a wide reputation, not in Paris alone, but all over the Continent. She died in October 1777, and *éloges* upon her were written by D'Alembert, Morellet, and Thomas. Her *Mémoires* were published by Marmontel; her *Correspondance* was edited by Grimm and Diderot; and her *Treatise on Conversation* by Morellet.

Geoffroya, a genus of trees occurring in S. America, belonging to the *Leguminosæ*, but differing from most of that order in having succulent fruits. The principal species is *G. superba*, a magnificently branched tree with beautiful green foliage and bright yellow flowers. Its wood is hard; and its fruit when boiled is said to be largely used by the inhabitants of the Ilha de St. Pedro.

Geoffroy St. Hilaire, Étienne, a French naturalist, was born at Étampes (Seine-et-Oise), April 15, 1772. He first studied for the Church at the Collége de Navarre, after which he went to Paris, where his taste for natural science strengthened under the fostering of Haüy and Daubenton. Through the influence of these he was nominated, at the age of twenty-one, Professor of Zoology in the Jardin des Plantes. In 1798 G. accompanied Napoleon to Egypt, returning in 1801 with valuable collections of natural history specimens. His labours secured his admission to the Académie des Sciences in 1807; and after his return from Portugal, whither he had been sent in 1808 on a scientific mission, he was elected Professor of Zoology in the medical faculty at Paris. As a theorist he maintained a great unity of plan throughout the organic kingdom, a principle which was keenly opposed by Cuvier. His constant endeavour was to establish this theory, which is developed and discussed in all his chief works—*Philosophie Anatomique* (Par. 1818–20), *Sur le Principe de l'Unité de Composition Organique* (Par. 1828), and *Principes de la Philosophie Principe* (Par. 1830). G. died at Paris, June 19, 1844. He wrote numerous and valuable treatises and memoirs, the number of which alone indicates the extraordinary energy of his nature. See *Vie, Travaux, et Doctrine Scientifique d'É. Geoffroy St. Hilaire* (Par. 1847) by his son,—**Isidore G. St. H.**, son of the preceding, was born December 16, 1805. He first assisted his father, and in 1841 became Professor in the Museum, and in 1845 General Inspector of Studies. In 1850 he succeeded Blainville in the chair of Zoology in the Faculty of Science, and died November 10, 1861. He early took up the subject of monstrosities, publishing his *Histoire Générale et Particulière des Anomalies de l'Organisation chez l'Homme et les Animaux* (3 vols. Par. 1832–37). Among his other works are *Essai de Zoologie Générale* (Par. 1840); *Histoire Naturelle des Insectes et des Mollusques* (2 vols. Par. 1841); and *Histoire Naturelle Générale des Règnes Organiques* (2 vols. Par. 1854–59).

Geog'nosy (Gr. *gē*, 'the earth,' and *gnōsis*, 'knowledge'), a term much used by German geologists, but rarely met with in English treatises. It designates that branch of Geology (q. v.) which treats merely of observation, or the practical part of the science without any regard to theory.

Geograph'ical Distribu'tion of An'imals. The fact that each country or region of the earth's surface has a fauna or collection of animals more or less peculiar to itself is well known. The investigation of the causes to which the distribution of the various species of animals is due has only recently received the attention which it deserves. The recent work of Mr. Alfred Russel Wallace on *The Geographical Distribution of Animals* (Lond. 1876) is the first philosophical contribution of any importance which has been made to the literature of the subject; while the distribution of the mammalia is the only part of the subject which has been investigated with due precision. The G. D. of A. was formerly explained—by Professor Edward Forbes, among other naturalists—on the *special creation* hypothesis, by supposing that each species of animal was created in a special district or region—named its *specific centre*—and that the form extended its range of distribution to a greater or less extent, according as physical conditions (such as the presence of mountains, lakes, seas, &c., the presence or absence of a due food-supply, &c.) were more or less favourable. It is obvious that this explanation admits of no further elaboration—it is a statement of belief, susceptible of no direct or indirect proof or corroboration. The other mode of explaining the facts of the G. D. of A. rests on the recognition of the truth and feasibility of the Darwinian and other evolutionary hypotheses. The chief facts which the consideration of the subject brings under notice are—(1) That the more remote and distant countries are, the more dissimilar will their animals be, and *vice versa;* (2) that where the animals of two countries are similar or alike, these two countries must at present be, or must in the recent past have been, in geographical connection; (3) that each species has its definite area, as also has each genus and family; and that locality or distribution is thus as much a characteristic of animal life as the possession of a special structure or other marks of individuality. The near resemblance, for example, seen between the animals of Britain and those of the adjacent parts of the continent of Europe is explicable on the supposition of the recent continuity of the two regions. Similarly, the peculiarities of its fauna which separate Trinidad from the other W. India Islands, and the resemblance of its fauna to that of Venezuela and the adjoining part of the S. American continent, strongly suggest the probability that Trinidad was recently in connection with the S. American region. The faunas of Sumatra and Borneo are alike; that of Java is mostly different from either. Java is nearer to Sumatra than Borneo, and, therefore, the dissimilarity of the Javan fauna is explained by assuming that Sumatra and Borneo have been in connection more recently than Sumatra and Java. On the Darwinian hypothesis, which is founded on the natural tendency of animals to vary, the likeness between the fauna of two near regions is explained on the ground that they have not had time to vary or to spread themselves, and thereby acquire differences. The differences, on the other hand, between the animals of the widely-separated regions are attributed to the great length of time which has elapsed since the regions were in continuity, and which has, therefore, permitted variations and differences to become developed. The fact of the individuals of each species being confined to a certain defined locality is explained by assuming them to be the descendants of ancestors or pre-existing species which inhabited the same area.

Mr. Sclater's zoographical provinces appear to be those which hold good for the entire animal creation, although, as has been remarked, they have as yet been applied to indicate the distribution of only a few groups of the animal world. These provinces are as follows, the characteristic mammals of each region being indicated:—I. PALÆARCTIC REGION, including the world N. of a line drawn S. of the Atlas, and passing E. through the S. of Palestine and Persia, and along the Himalayas through Central Asia and China to the Pacific. This region has no monkeys, lemurs, or fruit-eating bats; Carnivora (wolves, foxes, gluttons, bears, lynxes, &c.) abound; and Rodents and Ungulata (sheep, deer, &c.) also occur. Neither the elephant nor the hyrax, however, exists. II. ETHIOPIAN REGION, including Africa S. of Atlas and Arabia up to the Persian Gulf and Madagascar. The characteristic mammals are the highest apes, the African elephant, hyrax, rhinoceros, hippopotamus, wart-hog, antelope, giraffe, and manis, but no bears. Madagascar and the Mascarene Islands are sometimes regarded as forming the (II. *a*) LEMURIAN SUB-REGION, and are distinguished by the prevalence of lemurs and the absence of Felidæ and Ruminants. III. INDIAN REGION, including Asia S. of the Palæarctic Region and the E. Archipelago, down to Wallace's line—a line running between the islands of Bali and Lombok to the S., and Borneo and Celebes to the northward. Here are found the orang and other monkeys, flying lemurs, tigers, leopards, &c., the Indian elephant, Malayan tapir, rhinoceros, and the manis. IV. NEARCTIC REGION, including America down to the Isthmus of Tehuantepec. This region contains mammals resembling those of the first region, and which have probably come from the W.; *e.g.*, bears, beavers, sheep, and deer are found, but the prong buck, musquash, and pouched mice are peculiar. The racoon and opossum probably originated here. V. NEOTROPICAL REGION, comprising America S. of Tehuantepec. The monkeys are those of the families *Cebidæ* and *Hapalidæ* (spider monkeys, &c., and marmosets);

vampire bats exist, but no fruit-eating bats; porcupines are plentiful; the opossum, sloth, armadillo, ant-eater, Insectivora, civets, and tapirs occur; but there are no elephants. The (V. *a*) ANTILLEAN SUB-REGION has a few mammals, but these are peculiar (*Solenodon*, *Capromys*, &c.). VI. AUSTRALIAN REGION, including Australia, New Guinea, and the Moluccas up to Wallace's line. No higher mammals are here found native, except a few rodents and bats, the Australian territory being the home of the Didelphia and Ornithodelphia—kangaroos, Ornithorhynchus, Echidna, &c.

Geographical Distribution of Disease, also called **Medical Geography** and **Noso-Geography,** is that branch of medical science which treats of the manner and conditions under which diseases are distributed over the globe or confined to certain districts. The science is thus intimately connected with physical geography and vital statistics. The geographical limits of particular diseases and their regulated distribution frequently depend upon atmospheric influences, such as temperature, moisture, density, and electricity, and upon telluric influences, such as geological formation, topographical situation, elevation of the soil, vegetation, drainage, and cultivation. Such diseases depend in great measure, both in origin and propagation, on the manners and customs of the inhabitants, their position in civilisation, and their attention to personal and general hygiene. There are certain diseases peculiar to localities which are not found elsewhere, and certain miasmatic diseases of an infectious type, as yellow fever, plague, enteric fever, typhus fever, and cholera, which have particular climates or zones where each predominates, and beyond which they rarely pass, and they may thus be arranged systematically in zones of distribution N. and S. of the equator, bounded in great measure by isothermal lines, approaching to but not identical with the degrees of latitude. (See ISOTHERMS.) In countries under the line of the equator of greatest heat, where the mean temperature is 82° F., malarial fevers, yellow fever, cholera, dysentery, diarrhœa, and hepatic affections attain their maximum intensity; but each of these diseases has its peculiar habitat, within this circumscribed area, depending upon local causes. Cholera is endemic in certain parts of British India, yellow fever on the shores of the Gulf of Mexico and the Antilles, and malarial fevers in flat low-lying countries, the vicinity of marshes, lakes, and rivers, more especially where there is a damp argillaceous or ferruginous sub-soil. A certain amount of heat and moisture is necessary for the development of certain maladies in intertropical regions; and the period of disease follows the course of the sun, the unhealthy season occurring at opposite times on the N. and S. of the equator. Cholera and yellow fever frequently move out of their endemic areas as virulent epidemics, but the range of the latter is more circumscribed than that of the former, for with a temperature under 55° F. its persistent existence and propagation become impossible.

Within the temperate isothermic zone the varied forms of continued febrile disease take the place of the malarial fevers of the tropics; but as we approach the tropics the continued form merges into the intermittent type. This zone is the most healthy in the world, the prevailing causes of ill-health being mainly due to condensation of population, vicious modes of life, and inattention to personal and general hygiene; but within it nearly every type of disease is represented as it embraces the extremes of temperature of the torrid and frigid zones. The diseases which furnish the greatest mortality are the zymotic and constitutional. Typhus and enteric fevers are endemic, more especially between 30° and 40° N. lat.; measles, scarlatina, whooping-cough, diseases of the respiratory organs, and rheumatism prevail everywhere; intermittent and remittent fevers occur in Sweden and Italy; pellagra in Italy, France, and Spain; plica polonica in Poland and Tartary; leprosy and elephantiasis are met with in Scandinavia.

The prevalent diseases of the polar isothermic zone are asthmatic and catarrhal affections, influenza, scurvy, erysipelas, diseases of the skin and digestive organs. The majority of the natives of Greenland, Labrador, and Iceland die from asthmatic and catarrhal affections before the age of fifty.

There is a distinct connection between the geological nature of the soil and certain pathological conditions of man by means of which diseases existing in one place may be predicated as existing in another. Goitre and cretinism are endemic in the Alps and Pyrenees, and it was predicated that the same diseases would be met with in the Himalayas and Cordilleras. Experience verified the prediction. Probably many of the diseases peculiar to particular localities depend more upon deleterious ingredients contained in the water supply than upon any direct telluric influence.

The first important communication on the G. D. of D. was made by Alexander Keith Johnston, F.R.S.E., see *Trans. Epidem. Society* (Lond. 1856). The most important works are Mühry's *Outlines of Noso-Geography* and Boudin's *Traité de Géographie et de Statistique Médicales Endémiques* (Par. 1857). See also Sir Ranald Martin's work on the *Influence of Tropical Climate;* Inspector-General Lawson's *Observations on the Influence of Pandemic Waves in the Production of Fevers and Cholera*, and article on PANDEMIC WAVE THEORY OF DISEASE.

Geographical Distribution of Fossil Animals. See PALÆONTOLOGY.

Geographical Distribution of Plants. The causes which determine the distribution of plant life throughout the globe are numerous and varied. The influences exercised by climate, the geological changes and configuration of a continent, and the fitness of the plants themselves to carry on the struggle for existence, are the great factors. Schouw enumerates twenty-five phyto-geographical regions.

1. Alpine Arctic Flora. Here are met with the most northern limits of vegetation in the form of mosses and lichens, grasses, sedges, willows, saxifrages, gentians; and caryophyllaceous plants, remarkable for their neat style of growth and the size and beauty of the flowers as compared with the low habit of the plants that bear them, are seen. Forests of birch and fir also occur. There are no cultivated plants in this region, which embraces all the land within the Arctic circle, together with some tracts which lie external to it, and the summits of the loftier mountain ranges of Europe.

2. The region of umbelliferæ and cruciferæ is characterised by the abundance of the above-named orders, together with the cichoraceæ and cynarocephalæ. Ranunculaceæ, amentiferæ, coniferæ, carices, and fungi are plentiful. The various cereals are cultivated, as also are the potato, buckwheat, leguminosæ, fruit-trees, and vegetables common to the remainder of Northern Europe not included in the first region.

3. The region of labiatæ and caryophyllaceæ, comprehending S. Europe, N.W. Africa, the Azores, and Canaries. Here we meet with salvias and scabiosæ, sempervivums and euphorbiaceæ, evergreen trees, and some more tropical plants—as the date-palm. The castor-oil, oleander, and aloe are seen; rice, millet, figs, olive, cotton, and oranges are cultivated.

4. The region of asters and solidagos includes the eastern part of N. America. Oaks, firs, and vacciniaceæ are abundant; cruciferæ, umbelliferæ, cichoraceæ, and cynarocephalæ are scarce. The genus *erica* is absent. In the northern part there is no cultivation; in the southern agriculture is similar to that in the second region, but maize prevails to a greater extent.

5. The region of magnolias, the southern parts of N. America. Many tropical forms—anonaceæ, sapindaceæ, melastomaceæ, acaciaceæ, zingiberaceæ, cassias, and laurus. Plants cultivated as in the third region. In the Californian and Oregon districts many showy annuals are found, and interesting coniferæ.

6. The region of ternstrœmiaceæ and celastraceæ comprises Japan, N. China, and Chinese Tartary. Peculiar coniferæ abound. Bananas, palms, cycads, camellias, the Indian fig, and the tallow-tree (stillingia sebifera) are seen. Tea, melons, oranges, shaddocks, loquats, peaches, apples, rice, and the cereals are grown.

7. The region of zingiberaceæ, or India generally and Ceylon. Coco-nut, cotton, indigo, opium, turmeric, clove, and pepper occur and are cultivated, along with coffee, bananas, guava, and sugar-cane. The region of Cochin China and Southern China presents many peculiar features. Here we meet with the rice-paper plant, the lorgan and litchi, bamboos, orchids, and caoutchouc-yielding trees.

8. The region of tree rhododendrons, the Alpine district S. of the Himalaya. In the lower parts tropical forms appear; as we ascend, coniferæ, rhododendrons, oaks, &c., are met with. Some European grains and fruit are cultivated.

9. The region of the Asiatic islands, Polynesia. In Sumatra the curious rafflesia is met with; orchids and Australian forms

are seen. Breadfruit, casava, nutmeg, camphor, and the cultivated plants are similar to those of the Indian region.

10. The region of Upper Java and the islands, which rise from 5000 to 12,000 feet above the sea-level, have a flora somewhat similar to that of the mountains of India (8). The tea order, oaks, and thibaudias are seen.

11. The Polynesian or Oceanic region, which includes the tropical islands of the Pacific, has a flora allied to the Asiatic and Australian. Arums, dioscoreas, ferns, boehmerias, gourds, and species of morus are met with. The breadfruit-tree, coconut, double coco-nut (lodoicea), yams, plantain, kava, and cabbage-palm are cultivated.

12. The region of amyridaceæ. Here we meet with gum-yielding leguminosæ and shrubs producing aromatic resins—as boswellias. This district corresponds to the floras of Arabia and Persia. Stone-fruits, coco-nut and date-palms, maize, millet, rice, coffee, cotton, ginger, and indigo are cultivated.

13. The desert region of Africa and N. Arabia. Cultivation is confined to the valley of the Nile and oases, where we find the date and doom palms, wheat, barley, and the S. European and Indian grains.

14. The region of tropical Africa, from between the parallel 15° and the tropic of Capricorn, excepting Abyssinia. Members of the sterculiaceæ, as the baobab and kola are found in Senegal. We also meet with species of elais yielding palm-oil, the Calabar bean, and welwitschia. Towards the E. coast there is a more peculiar flora, which perhaps is most specialised in Madagascar. Here are found the sanglimia or ordeal bean, the lattice-leaf plant (*Ouvirandra*), and traveller's tree (*Urania*). Maize, rice, Guinea corn, millet, yams, cassava, banana, mango, pine-apple, coffee, sugar, cotton, ginger, cardamoms, earth-nut, and oil-palms are grown.

15. The region of cactaceæ and piperaceæ. These are specially abundant in Mexico, New Grenada, Guiana, and Peru. The ivory-palm and Victoria regia grow here, as also do leguminosæ, melastomaceæ, cinchonaceæ, orchids, and ferns. The cultivated plants are maize, Guinea corn, cassava, yams, batatas, arracacha, arrowroot, custard-apple, guava, tamarind, chocolate, vanilla, coffee, sugar, cerennial cactus, capsicum, cotton, earth-nut.

16. The region of the highlands of Mexico, that is, districts more than 5000 feet above sea-level, is remarkable for its coniferæ and species of mirabilis, zinnia, and dahlia.

17. The region of cinchonas, which are peculiar to this region. On the Andes we also find the wax-palm (*Ceroxylon*). On the more elevated parts the potato and quinoa are grown, and in the lower coffee and maize. This district extends from 5000 to 9000 feet above the sea-level in the mountainous parts of the Andes.

18. The region of escallonias and calceolarias, including that part of the Andes over 9000 feet above sea-level. Alpine plants occur here, as saxifrages, gentians, carices, grapes, and compositæ.

19. The W. Indian region comprehends the Antilles. Tropical fruits are abundant, and cultivated as in the Mexican region (15).

20. The region of palms and melastomads is that part lying E. of the Andes between the equator and tropic of Capricorn. Vellozias and lychnophoras are seen. The forest vegetation is extremely luxuriant; tillandsias, gesneras, bignonias, cover the trees, as also do wondrous epiphytical orchids; and fuchsias, compositæ, gigantic leguminosæ, ficus, and laurus are prevalent. The cultivated plants are the same as those in the 15th region.

21. The region of arborescent or shrubby compositæ corresponds to the lower basin of La Plata and the plains W. of Buenos Ayres towards Chili. The habit of the compositæ and the natural order calyceraceæ characterise this region. The Chilian flora itself resembles that of New Zealand, Australia, and the Cape, in its proteas, araucarias, and goodenias. Calceolarias, escallonias, and buddleias abound. There are also curious coniferæ. European plants are cultivated here.

22. The Antarctic region includes the countries near the Straits of Magellan. Here are met with Polar plants corresponding to those seen in the Arctic region. Saxifrages, gentians, and primroses, veronicas, pernettias, and empetrum rubrum are found. There are a few British plants. The fuschia, the tussac grass and bolax glebaria or misery-ball are seen. Species of beech and drimys winteri are found. There is no cultivation.

23. The region of mesembryanthemums and stapelias, a S. African flora, extends from the Tropic of Capricorn to the Cape Coast. Ericaceæ are very abundant. Geraniaceæ, Cape bulbs, as ixias, &c., proteaceæ, iridaceæ, acacias, aloes, euphorbias, and leguminosæ occur. Various plants introduced by the colonists are cultivated, as also are yams, plantains, guava, and shaddocks.

24. The region of epacridaceæ and eucalyptia, a flora of Australia and Tasmania. The eucalypti or gum-trees give a peculiar aspect to the country from their vertically-placed leaves. There are many remarkable coniferæ, as the various species of calitris, dacrydium, and araucaria. Proteaceæ, casuarineæ, acacias, compositæ, leguminosæ, stackhousiaceæ, and tremandraceæ abound. Some of the trees rival the wellingtonias of California. The various European plants and grains are cultivated, and in many cases are establishing themselves and taking the place of the original vegetation.

25. The region of New Zealand contains many peculiar coniferæ species of podocarpus and dacrydium. Epacridaceæ, umbelliferæ, and scrophulariaceæ are found, together with a great number of ferns and tree-ferns. The native phormium or New Zealand flax and many introduced European plants are cultivated.

These twenty-five regions may again be further subdivided into smaller districts. In this way we find that various valleys, mountains, and tablelands have special floras. Some plants are only to be found in one particular spot, while others follow the footsteps of man and are almost cosmopolitan. The destruction of forests has affected the prosperity of countries materially by rendering the climate less humid until so little rain fell that vegetation generally became impaired, as in the Mauritius and Azores; and again, the growth of trees, as in Australia, by increasing the rainfall has altered what was almost a desert into a fertile plain.

Geog'raphy (Gr. *gē*, 'the earth,' and *graphō*, 'I write'), a name literally meaning a description of the earth. In its highest sense G. is the science that deals (1) with the earth as a planet, or member of the solar system; (2) with the cosmical distribution of its surface into areas of land and water; (3) with its natural phenomena and their dependence upon physical laws; and (4) with the political and arbitrary division of its surface. A comprehensive view of G. entitles it to be defined as the science of the organic and inorganic life of the earth and of the reciprocal relations of the constituent parts of that life. When geodesy, geology, zoology, and ethnography have done their special work, it then remains for G. to gather and group the results together, and from their conjunction to explain more completely the action of each of the natural sciences that it thus embraces. And as it is an indisputable fact that the character of a nation is developed or modified by conditions of locality, climate, and the structure of a country, so G. comes to have an historico-philosophical side and to hold a definite relation to the history of civilisation.

The science is commonly divided into the three departments of astronomical, physical, and political G. The first of these, dealing with the figure, magnitude, and density of the earth, is treated at length in the articles EARTH, and LATITUDE AND LONGITUDE. The aspects of physical G. are dealt with in such articles as ATMOSPHERE, CLOUDS, CURRENTS, EARTHQUAKES, GEOLOGY, GLACIERS, RIVERS, SEAS, SEASONS, VOLCANOES, WINDS, &c. Political G., mainly relating to the arbitrary allotment of countries among various Governments, is fully illustrated in articles on the different states, kingdoms, and empires.

The *history* of geographical discovery will serve to outline the growth and scope of the modern science. Among the earliest records incidentally tinged with G. are the Pentateuch and Book of Joshua, which contain frequent and singularly correct reference to contemporary Egypt and Arabia. Homer represents the earth as the shield of Achilles surrounded by the sea, and describes for the first time 'the isles of Greece.' In 568 B.C. Anaximander of Miletus is supposed to have invented geographical maps. Herodotus (born 484 B.C.) may fairly be regarded as the father not only of history but of G., his work describing minutely the various countries he had visited in his wide travels. The world of Herodotus extends from the Red Sea or Indian Ocean to the amber-lands of the Baltic, and from the Atlantic to the W. boundary of Persia. In the 4th c. B.C. the victories of Alexander the Great opened up the path to Northern and Eastern Asia, about the same time that Pytheas of Massilia (modern Marseille) was sailing along the E. coast of Britain into the Northern Ocean as far as Thule (supposed to be Iceland), and returning by the Baltic, where he heard of Goths and Teutons. Eratosthenes (born 276 B.C.) tried to base the construction of maps on mathematical principles, and invented the parallels of latitude and longitude. His work on G. is lost, but from Strabo we learn that he regarded the world as a sphere 'revolving with its surrounding atmosphere on one and the same axis, and having one centre.' Many large works on G. which are lost were written during the 200 years that elapse till we come to Strabo (born 66 B.C.), whose great work, giving an account of his travels in Egypt, Palestine, Syria, &c., is singularly accurate and interesting. G. made vast strides under the Romans, who carefully took account of the material resources of every conquered territory. A survey of the empire, begun by Julius Cæsar and completed by Augustus, gave descriptions and measurements of each province by the greatest living geometricians. The *Historia Naturalis* of Pliny, containing a digest of the works of Sallust, Cæsar, Tacitus, &c., together with results of his own travels in Spain, Gaul, Germany, and Africa, shows the great increase of geographical knowledge that had taken place. Here there is mention of the Scandinavian lands and of Arctic regions, of settlements in various parts of Africa, of the course of the Niger, of the *island* of Ceylon, &c. The *G.* of Ptolemy embodied the latest contributions to the study of G. in ancient times, and remained the acknowledged canon during the middle ages. In the 8th c. the Arabs eagerly seized upon the study of G., and towards the end of the middle ages a great accession of knowledge resulted from the travels of the Venetians, Genoese, and Portuguese. The works of Carpini (q. v.), Marco Polo (q. v.), and Sir John Mandeville (q. v.) first gave information regarding Central and Eastern Asia. Then followed the discovery of America (q. v.) in 1492, and the doubling of the Cape of Good Hope by Vasco da Gama in 1497. In the 16th c. took place the remarkable Arctic expeditions of Willoughby, Frobisher, and Davis, while one of the earliest works on G. appeared in Sebastian Franck's *Weltbuoch* (1534). Other geographers of the period were Sebastian Münster, Ortelius, Cluver, and Merian. The discoveries by Tasman (q. v.) and Van Diemen (q. v.) in Australasia were greatly extended by those of Cook in the 18th c. Meantime the sciences had been enlisted in the service of the study, and physical G. had been founded by Bergmann (died 1787). 'Comparative G.' itself was raised to the dignity of a science by the labours of Karl Ritter (q. v.). The 19th c. has witnessed the discovery of the Antarctic continent in 1840, the opening up of the African interior by the explorations of Barth, Burton, Speke, Vogel, Livingstone, Stanley, Schweinfurth, and Cameron; the investigation of Central Australia (q. v.); the survey of Central Asia by the Russian Government; the appearance of such works as those of Burnes, Vansberg, Schuyler, &c.; and the Arctic expeditions of various Governments. (See ARCTIC OCEAN and POLAR VOYAGES.) Geographical Societies were established at Paris in 1821, at Berlin in 1828, at London (the most important) in 1830, at Frankfurt in 1836, at St. Petersburg in 1845, at Darmstadt in 1845, at New York in 1852, at Vienna in 1856, at Geneva in 1858, at Leipsic in 1861, at Dresden in 1863, at Kiel in 1867, at Florence in 1867, &c. In 1876 a geographical conference was held at Brussels, at which a scheme was projected for the national endowment of exploration in Africa.

For the history of G. see the works of Malte Brun, Humboldt, Ritter, Peschel, and Löwenberg. Among the best bodies of G. are the *Handbuch* by Gaspari, Hassel, Gutsmuths, and Ukert (23 vols. 1819–31) and the works of Stein (new ed. by Wappäus, 11 parts 1850–71), Ritter, Berghaus, Roon, Klöden, *Erdkunde*, new ed. 1874–77), Daniel, Ungewitter, Cannabich, &c. Cartography has been carried to great perfection in the atlases of Stieler, Johnston, Kiepert, Ravenstein, Berghaus, and Spruner. Of many admirable journals are those of Behm and Wagner, Petermann's *Mittheilungen*, and the *Geographical Magazine*.

Geology (Gr. *gē*, 'the earth,' and *logos*, 'doctrine') is, in its modern signification, the science which treats of the structure, surface configuration, and composition of the earth, of the causes which influence these, and which have brought them to be as they are, and of the structure and history of the once living beings whose remains are left imbedded in its crust. In the early cosmogonies of the Hindus, Chinese, and Egyptians some of the more evident geological operations, such as the alternate submersion and emersion of dry land, earthquakes, volcanoes, &c., are recognised, but only for the purpose of explaining the origin of the earth. According to Herodotus, the Egyptian priests regarded Lower Egypt as the gift of the sea. The Greeks probably borrowed much of their knowledge from Egypt and the East. Anaximander (born 610 B.C.), a pupil of Thales, is said to have been the first to write a philosophical treatise on G., of which there is now no trace. According to Plutarch and Eusebius, he taught that man was not originally created in an adult state, and must therefore have depended for nourishment in the first instance upon some lower animal—foreshadowing in a vague way the modern theory of evolution. Pythagoras (about 580 B.C.), if we may judge from the doctrines ascribed to him by Ovid, seems to have established a system far more philosophical than any before his day. He taught that the total quantity of matter in the world was constant, that sea became land and land sea, and that valleys were formed by the wearing action of running water. The same ideas of continual change and fluctuation are found in Aristotle's *Meteorologica*, and the same philosopher in his discussion of respiration distinctly mentions fossil fishes. The last of these ancient geologists is Strabo, who flourished under Augustus in the beginning of the Christian era. In the second book of his geography he discusses the explanations which had been given of the occurrence of sea-shells high up on dry land. Xanthus the Lydian had ascribed the emersion of land to long-continued droughts; and Strato to the emptying of an inland sea, gradually raised in level through the deposition of mud brought down by rivers upon its bottom, till in the end it forced an outlet into an adjacent body of water. Dissatisfied with these, Strabo enunciated his own theory, that the land, not the sea, was subject to changes of level. He also studied the nature of volcanoes, regarded them as safety valves, and recognised in Vesuvius an extinct crater, although in his day there was neither record nor tradition of an eruption. For fifteen centuries after the time of Strabo, science was practically unknown in Europe; and among the Arabs G. was not cultivated with any great success. In the 10th c. Avicenna, a physician, wrote a treatise *On the Formation and Classification of Minerals*, and Omar El Aalem ('the learned') was persecuted and forced into voluntary exile for having represented the sea as receding and leaving the land dry, a theory which was held to be contradictory to the Koran. Early in the 16th c. G. revived in Europe. In Italy a sharp controversy sprang up regarding the nature and origin of the Apennine fossil shells. The celebrated Leonardo da Vinci maintained that these remains, and the gravel of rounded pebbles found at various heights, conclusively proved the presence and action of water at those localities. In 1517 Fracastoro clearly showed the absurdity of attributing the shells to some 'plastic force' or to the Mosaic deluge, which he argued was far too transient, and could not have buried them at great depths in the heart of mountains. His cogent arguments were unconvincing in an age of superstition, which rather accepted such fantastic theories as those of Mattioli and Fallopio, who imagined the remains to be the result of fermentation. Cardan (1552), Palissy (1580), Colonna (1592), Majoli (1597), and others, supported the sounder views of Fracastoro, mixing, however, much error with truth. For a century the controversy raged, and the organic origin of fossils was generally allowed only after the publication of the works of Steno (1669) and Scilla (1670). The former, a Dane, but long resident in N. Italy, showed the specific identity of the Tuscan fossils with living Mediterranean forms, and declared that he had proof that the country had been twice submerged. Theologians now entered the field, and roused a controversy which lasted a century and a half. Fracastoro had long before shown the physical impossibility of the diluvial theory of the origin of the Apennine shells, and yet to the Deluge were the fossils attributed by the Church generally, and indeed were regarded as proving the truth of the Mosaic narrative. To reject this dogma was equivalent to disbelieving the whole Scriptures. The anxiety of naturalists to reconcile their theories with the sacred writings led to hopeless error and confusion. Woodward (1695) referred the origin of all strata to deposition from the chaos of matter produced at the Flood, the fossils settling down into their places according to their specific gravities. Ray, who protested against the diluvial hypothesis, accused Woodward of inventing facts to harmonise with his theory, since the order of fossils in no way depended on their weights. Another of these early English cosmogonists was Burnett (1690), who gave a picture of the earth before the Deluge, explaining how it enjoyed a perpetual spring before the Flood, which burst through the crust cracked by the sun's rays. The works of Hooke and Ray, on the other hand, exhibit a more philosophical spirit. The latter especially enlarged on surface denudation and the encroachment of the sea. Italian geologists, however, were still the pioneers of progress. Vallisneri (1721) demonstrated by observation that Italy had been wholly submerged for a lengthened period, and that the water had gradually subsided. Spada of Grezzana (1737), Mattani, and others powerfully resisted the diluvianists, and prepared the way for Lazzaro Moro (1740), who recognised in earthquakes and volcanic eruptions a grand agent in the formation of continents. His doctrine he supported by solid arguments, such as the existence of faults and dislocations. He was, however, much hampered by the accepted age of the world, and he fell into evident error in attributing *all* strata to volcanic ejection. Buffon (1749) developed the theory of Leibnitz (1680), that the earth was originally of volcanic origin, and that Stratified rocks were formed subsequently by the deposition of the waste produced on the nucleus by the denuding action of a universal ocean. G. now began to occupy a prominent place in Germany. Lehman (1756), a mineralogist, divided mountains into three classes—those formed originally with the globe, those produced by a general revolution, and those produced by local revolutions. Two years later, Gesner of Zürich published a treatise on petrifactions. He discussed the filling up of lakes and seas by sediment, the effects of earthquakes, the retreat of the sea, and calculated from observed data that it would require 80,000 years to raise the Apennines to their present height. In 1760 John Michell, Professor of Mineralogy at Cambridge, anticipated many of the theories in stratigraphical G. established forty years later by William Smith. His papers were not published at the time, otherwise they would have certainly formed an era in the history of the science. Turning again to Germany, we find Raspe (1763) discussing with a philosophical fairness the doctrines of Hooke, Ray, Moro, and others, and indicating many of the obscurer problems in G., such as the former tropical climate of Europe and the changes in the typical species. Fuchsel (1762-73) recognised the differences in character and age of several groups of strata, referring their derangement from the horizontal to oscillations of the ground subsequent to their deposition. In 1775 Werner, Professor of Mineralogy at Freyberg in Saxony, by pointing out the great importance of G. in the art of mining, gave a grand impulse to the study of the science. His lectures on the subject roused to enthusiasm his hearers, who soon spread the fame of Werner's school far and wide. He carefully examined the rocks in his own vicinity, tabulated them according to their mineralogical character, propounded a theory for their origin, and generalised this theory to apply to *all* strata throughout the world. He regarded all formations as having been deposited on the bed of a universal ocean, which had now subsided. His disciples accepted his hypothesis *in toto*, and wherever they went strove to reconcile observed facts with it. They received the name of Neptunists or Wernerians. Their doctrines were powerfully combated by the French geologists Desmarest and Dolomieu. The former executed an admirable geological map of the volcanic district of Auvergne, and the latter maintained the volcanic origin of the rocks of Southern France. The controversy thus provoked between the Neptunists and Vulcanists was carried on with an almost unprecedented bitterness, and extended even as far as Scotland, where Hutton was laying the first foundations of his theory. Meanwhile Pallas and De Saussure were prosecuting their philosophic travels—the former in the dreary *steppes* of Northern Russia and among the recent strata bordering on the Caspian Sea, the latter studying the glaciers and highly-contorted formations of the Alps and Jura. Hutton's *Theory of the Earth* was published in 1795, and it forms a marked epoch in the progress of G. The most striking points advanced by Hutton were the constant denudation of the earth's surface and the consequent formation of valleys by running water, the deposition of this waste on the bed of the ocean, the subsequent upheaval of the bed by volcanic action, and the igneous origin of whinstone and granite. In 1797 Playfair published his *Illustrations of Hutton's Theory*, and in the succeeding year Sir James Hall proved by laboratory experiments one of Hutton's positions, that molten rock may give rise to lava or to basalt according to the pressure under which the cooling takes place. While the Wernerians and Huttonians were engaged in their fierce controversy, William Smith, an English surveyor, was establishing the bases of stratigraphical G. His *Tabular View of the British Strata* was published in 1790, and was followed in 1815 by his geological map of England—a work which well earned for its persevering author the title of the 'father of British G.' He classified all the strata now known as the Secondary formations, grouping them according to their fossil contents. The Tertiary formations were similarly treated by the French naturalists Cuvier and Brongniart, whose joint work *On the Mineral Geography and Organic Remains of the Neighbourhood of Paris* (1808) may be regarded as having laid the foundation of Palæontology (q. v.), a growingly important branch of G. By this time a new school of G. was rising, whose votaries preferred to simply amass facts rather than excite controversy by advancing theories. The Geological Society of London, established in 1807, did much to foster this reform, encouraging pure observation, and affording a means by which geologists could become easily acquainted with the labours of others. The example set by London was followed by Paris in 1830, by Dublin in 1832, and by Edinburgh in 1834. The Huttonian and Wernerian struggle gradually died out, but was succeeded by the milder controversy between the Convulsionists and Uniformitarians. The former maintained that the configuration of the surface of the earth, the rugged peaks and gorges, the distorted strata, &c., were produced by sudden throes or convulsions; while the latter, of whose views Lyell was the great exponent, argued that contortion did not necessitate suddenness, and that a gradual but continued movement was quite able to produce the most irregularly-contorted appearances if only sufficient time be granted. The position taken at present by the majority of geologists is intermediate to these, inclining rather to the Uniformitarian side. It is impossible to do more than touch upon the great advances during the last half century. Since William Smith's time the whole series of primary formations has been opened up by men whose names are still fresh in the memories of the present generation. We have had Hugh Miller revealing the treasures of the Old Red Sandstone, Murchison unravelling the mysteries of the Silurian, and more recently Logan attacking the wide unknown deposits of the still more ancient Laurentian in N. America. Sedgwick, Von Buch, Elie de Beaumont, De la Beche, Delauny, Daubeny, Humboldt, Agassiz, Buckland, Lonsdale, among others, are names well known to the student of G. The services which Sir Charles Lyell has rendered to the science are inestimable. The theory of evolution, which received such an impulse from the publication of Darwin's *Origin of Species*, was accepted by the majority of naturalists as affording a philosophical explanation of the succession of life exhibited in the fossils imbedded in the earth's crust. The Uniformitarians, headed by Darwin, Huxley, and Lyell, urged that the agents at work now were the same as had been at work countless ages back, and as will be at work for countless ages to come; that the evolution of species, genera, orders, and kingdoms from the primordial germ must have proceeded by the gradual accumulation of countless variations through a practically infinite time, and that three hundred millions of years would cover a comparatively short geological period. This doctrine received its deathblow at the hands of Sir William Thomson, who, upon physical grounds, demonstrated that one hundred millions of years ago the earth, if it existed at all, would have been a globe of molten red-hot liquid, utterly incompatible with the existence of life. The geologists calculated their time from the thickness of geological strata, assuming the rate of deposition in past time to be equal to the present rate—an unwarrantable assumption. Sir William Thomson based his calculations on two distinct and undisputed facts, namely, the tidal retardation of the earth, and the fact that the earth is a cooling solid. There is a growing disposition to accept Thomson's theory, and this has shown itself in a recent endeavour to rearrange the order of formations, taking account of the possible contemporaneity of unlike strata. Thus the lacustrine Cambrian may be contemporaneous with the marine Silurian, the Permian with the Jurassic, the Miocene with the Cretaceous, &c., the different characters of these conjoined groups being referable to the varying conditions under which they were deposited. G., in its several divisions, is continually touching upon other branches of science. Mineralogy (q. v.) is allied to chemistry and mathematics, palæontology to botany and zoology, physical geography to meteorology and the wide subject of natural philosophy. The principal works on G. are Lyell's *Principles* and *Elementary Geology*; Ansted's *Geology*; Philip's *Guide to Geology*; De la Beche's *How to Observe in Geology*; Jukes and Geikie's *Manual*; Page's text-books; Geikie's *Life of Murchison*, giving an account of the modern progress of G.; Dana's *Mineralogy*; Nicolson's *Palæontology*; besides the writings of Darwin, Murchison, Mantell, Ramsay, Woodward, and others, on special parts of the subject. See the sub-references of PALÆOZOIC or PRIMARY, MESOZOIC or SECONDARY, KAINOZOIC or TERTIARY.

Ge′omancy (Gr. *gē*, 'the earth,' and *manteia*, 'divination') is an ancient mode of divination by points, marks, or circles drawn on the earth, or by casting pebbles on the ground. G. was practised, as a more recondite science, by the Arabian astrologers, who from earthquakes, rents in the ground, and all manner of rumblings and movements beneath the earth's surface pretended to forecast the future and interpret the divine will. Like other modes of divination, it has long been relegated to the domain of the unscrupulous fortune-teller.

Geomet′rical Progres′sion, in algebra, is a series each term of which bears to the one preceding it a constant ratio. Thus, 1, 2, 4, 8, &c., is a G. P. whose common ratio is 2; and 1, $\frac{1}{2}$, $\frac{1}{4}$, $\frac{1}{8}$, &c. is one whose common ratio is $\frac{1}{2}$. The general series may be represented by a, ar, ar^2, ar^3, &c., where a, the first term, is any algebraic quantity, integral or fractional, positive or negative, and r, the common ratio, any other algebraic quantity. To sum such a series, *i.e.*, to find

$$S = a + ar + ar^2 + ar^3 \ldots \text{ to } n \text{ terms,}$$

observe that the last term must be ar^{n-1}, from which it is easily deducible that

$$S = a\,\frac{1 - r^n}{1 - r}.$$

If r is a fraction and n infinite, S assumes the simple form $S = \frac{a}{1 - r}$. Hence, $1 + \frac{1}{2} + \frac{1}{4} + \frac{1}{8} + \ldots$ to infinity $= \frac{1}{1 - \frac{1}{2}} = 2$; which is equivalent to saying that the value of the series can be made to differ from 2 by less than any assignable quantity, by simply continuing the series far enough. *Geometrical mean* of any two quantities is the square root of their product, and is evidently the middle term of a G. P. of three terms, the first and last terms of which are the given quantities.

Geom′etry (Gr. *geometria*, 'earth-measurement'), as defined by Sir W. R. Hamilton of Dublin, is the science of pure space, while algebra, which takes no direct cognisance of space, is in contradistinction the science of pure time. Kinematics (q. v.) or the *G. of motion*, combines these two fundamental motions; and, by the introduction of the unit of mass, merges into dynamics. The early origin of G. is wrapped in obscurity; and the ancient tradition that the Egyptians were led by necessity to the invention of the science in order to furnish them with a means of recovering their old landmarks obliterated yearly by the Nile inundations, has no foundation in fact, though backed by the authority of Herodotus. The Greeks undoubtedly obtained much of their knowledge from Egypt; but the Egyptians, in this as in other sciences, probably borrowed largely from the Hindus. The Hindu records are very uncertain as regards date; but Bhascari in the 12th c. A.D. gives a much nearer approximation (3·1416) to the ratio between the circumference and diameter of a circle than was known in Europe at that time. The Hindus also possessed the method of calculating the area of a triangle when the sides are given, and this would of itself necessitate a considerable amount of mathematical knowledge. The Chinese do not seem to have made much progress in the investigation of the properties of space, being barely acquainted with the property of the right-angled triangle; so that it is to India that we must look for the source of G. as well as of the decimal arithmetic and algebra. Thales (600 B.C.) commonly gets the credit of having transported G. from Egypt and founded the first Greek school; but Pythagoras (540 B.C.), according to Proclus, was the first to give it in the form of a science. After him come Anaxagoras, who wrote on the quadrature of the circle, Hippocrates, who invented the quadrature of the lunules, Theodorus of Cyrene, and Plato (400 B.C.), who powerfully influenced the progress of the science, and gave a simple and elegant solution of the duplication of the cube. Contemporary with Plato were Leodamas of Thasos, Archytas of Tarentum, and Theætetus of Athens; and a few years later appeared Leo, Eudoxus, Theudius of Athens, Hermotimus, who wrote on *Loci*, Philippus, and Euclid (q. v.). G. had now been extended beyond the straight line and circle, and many of the properties of cones, cylinders, spheres, and conic sections, and even higher curves, were known. Archytas, indeed, is said to have imagined and applied a curve of double curvature. Euclid's great merit lies in his having collected and arranged consecutively all the more important theorems and problems of pure G., although the best evidences of his high mathematical originality are found in the little-known book upon the classification of incommensurable quantities (Book x. of the *Elements*). Several of his works are lost, notably that on *Porisms* (q. v.). After Euclid appeared Archimedes (240 B.C.), who applied mathematics to hydrostatics and other branches of physical science; Apollonius, famous as the discoverer of the subcontrary sections of the cone, and Eratosthenes; and about a century later flourished Nicomedes, the inventor of the conchoid, Hipparchus, who seems to have made some progress in spherical trigonometry, and Hypsicles. After the Christian era, the Alexandrine school continued to prosper under Menelaus (80 A.D.), Ptolemy (125), Pappus (390), and Proclus (440). Diophantus, the introducer of methods more algebraic in character, probably lived about a century later than the last named. The first Latin edition of Euclid's *Elements* was that of Adelard, about 1150 A.D.; but two or three centuries elapsed before G. began to be studied to any extent in Europe. Vieta (1540–1603), by introducing algebraic symbols, prepared the way for Descartes (see GEOMETRY, ANALYTICAL), and for the subsequent development by Newton, Leibnitz, and the Bernoullis of the ancient method of Exhaustions, and Cavalieri's Method of Indivisibles, into the powerful *Calculus*, handled so effectively in physical investigations by Lagrange and Laplace. The rapid growth of this new *Analysis* was accompanied with an evident retrogression in the study of pure G., a result to be deplored, since, in any investigation by the former method, the meaning of the symbols is generally completely lost sight of, and little scope is offered for the cultivation of true mathematical originality. Men like Desargues, Halley, and Maclaurin, however, show in their writings a decided predilection for G. proper; and from these, through the labours of Carnot, Monge, Poncelet, Chasles, and Hamilton, has sprung the ever-growing, and growingly-important modern G. Monge's *Descriptive G.* established the whole theory of *projections*, so important in perspective, in the planning of roads and canals, in naval constructions, in mining, and in fortification, on a firm basis; and Carnot's *Theory of Transversals*, dimly foreshadowed in the works of Pappus, developed, in the hands of Poncelet, into the beautiful and prolific theory of reciprocal Polars (q. v.). Sir W. R. Hamilton's *Quaternions*, the most potent mathematical method at present known, is a still higher stage in the progress of G., for, though it is symbolic in the extreme, the geometrical meaning of the symbols can never for an instant be lost sight of, so that mathematical science is further than ever from sinking into a mere succession of symbolic operations which in themselves mean nothing.

Geometry, Analytical or **Algebraic**, is a branch of pure mathematics, first formed into a systematic method by Descartes. It is more than a mere expression of geometrical relations by algebraic symbols; its great peculiarity rather lies in regarding + and − as no longer simply the symbols of multiplication and division, but as expressing *direction* according to certain conventional rules. Thus if we speak of north as positive, then south will be negative; or if east be positive, west will be negative, and so on. Now a point in space is fixed if we know its Co-ordinates (q. v.) with respect to three given non-coplanar axes meeting at a point; and if this point lie on a certain continuous curve or surface, a relation will hold for its co-ordinates which is true for the co-ordinates of every point on the same curve or surface. The mathematical expression of this relation may be put in the form of an equation, which is known as the equation of the curve in question. The cultivation of this branch of mathematics is of great importance, especially when viewed in connection with dynamics. The best English works on the subject are Salmon's

Conic Sections, *Higher Plane Curves*, and *A. G. of Three Dimensions*.

Georg (*Der Bärtige*, 'the bearded'), Duke of Sachsen, was born August 27, 1471, and became Duke of Sachsen in 1500. He at first favoured the Reformation, but afterwards became, along with the Duke of Bavaria, its chief opponent in Germany, and forbade Luther's translation of the Bible to be circulated in his dominions. The loss during his latter years of his wife and eight children, and the knowledge that he would be succeeded by his Protestant brother Henrich of Freiberg, cast him into deep melancholy. He led an ascetic life, and let his beard grow to his waist—whence his surname of *Der Bärtige*—for some time before his death, April 17, 1539.

Georg I. (**Christian William Ferdinand Adolf Georg**), King of Greece, second son of Christian IV. of Denmark and younger brother of the Princess of Wales, was born 24th December 1845. He was educated at Copenhagen, entered the navy, and was chosen King of Greece in 1863. G. married the Princess Olga, daughter of the Grand Duke Constantine and niece of the Czar of Russia, in 1867. See GREECE.

George, a district of the W. Province, Cape Colony, is bounded N. by the Zwarte Berge, S. by the G., W. by the district of Zwellendam, E. by Uitenhage. Area, 4032 sq. miles; pop. 20,000. It is well wooded, is watered chiefly by the Gauritz, and has a good wheat-growing soil of loam and clay mixed with gravel and decomposed granite. Georgetown is the capital, and Mossel Bay indents the coast-line.

George (Lake), or **Horicon**, a beautiful lake in New York State, 36 miles long, from 1 to 3 broad, and in parts 400 feet deep. It is studded by about 300 islands, and has an outlet to Lake Champlain.

George, St., a saint in the Latin and Greek Churches, and the national saint of England. One legend makes him a soldier martyred under Diocletian, but according to Gibbon the St. G. of the Catholics is identical with the Arian persecutor George of Cappadocia. This man, who was born about the beginning of the 4th c. at Epiphania, Cilicia, after acquiring wealth by the most flagrant dishonesty, was chosen by the Arians to succeed Athanasius as Archbishop of Alexandria in 356, and ruled there as a cruel, insolent tyrant, persecuting alike Catholics and pagans, until on Julian's accession he was cast into prison, and shortly afterwards was killed by the people, who flung his body into the sea (361). He was viewed as a saint by the Arians, and, says Gibbon, their seeming conversion introduced his worship into the Catholic Church. 'The odious stranger assumed the mask of a martyr, a saint, and a Christian hero; and the infamous George of Cappadocia has been transformed into the renowned St. G. of England, the patron of arms, of chivalry, and of the Garter.' On the other hand, it is contended that the Catholics would never have admitted their bitter persecutor into their hierarchy of saints. St. G., however, though revered in Palestine and Armenia in the 6th c., was not generally known in Europe until the crusades, which first made him famous in England. In 1330 Edward III. made St. G. patron of the Order of the Garter. See Gibbon, ch. xviii., and Heylin's *History of St. G.* (Lond. 2d ed. 1633).

George, St., one of the Bermudas (q. v.).

George, St., Banner of, a white banner with a red cross. In the 14th c. all English soldiers in the royal service wore the red cross of St. George, the patron saint of England, over their armour, and the St. George banner was the national flag until transformed into the Union Jack (q. v.) by being combined with the crosses of St. Andrew and St. Patrick.

George, The, the badge of the Order of the Garter. It represents St. George mounted and piercing the dragon.

George Lewis, known as **George I.**, King of Great Britain and Ireland, was the son of Ernst August, Elector of Hanover and Duke of Brunswick-Lüneburg, and Sophia, grand-daughter of James I. He was born May 28, 1660. On the death of Queen Anne he became, by the Revolution Settlement, which secured the Protestant succession, King of Great Britain; and although he allowed six weeks to elapse before he came from Hanover to take his throne, and although he was seen by his subjects when he landed at Greenwich to be a little awkward man of fifty-four, who could not speak a word of English, he was heartily welcomed for the cause he represented; and Oxford and Bolingbroke, if they ever contemplated enthroning the Pretender, made no demonstration in his favour. Personally the 'foreign tyrant,' the 'wee, wee, German lairdie,' as G. was dubbed, was never liked, and did not deserve to be. He was honest, and Mr. Carlyle admires him for possessing the gift of silence, probably because he had nothing to say; but his 'temper was that of a gentleman usher,' his manners and morals were coarse and his tastes low; and a French critic has lately not inaccurately summed up his private history by saying that he 'kept his wife in prison thirty-two years, and got drunk every night with his two plain mistresses.' His wife was Sophia Dorothea of Zelle, by whom he had two children, George, who succeeded him, and Sophia, the mother of Friedrich the Great. Believing her to have been unfaithful with Count Philipp von Koningsmark, he shut her up in the castle of Ahlden, where she died, after an incarceration of thirty-two years, at the age of sixty, and only a few months before her husband. But whether from imbecility or not, G. understood the duties of a constitutional sovereign, and threw himself into the hands of the Whig party, which then fortunately had for its leader Sir Robert Walpole, the first of that brilliant series of peace and finance ministers who have made this country a 'nation of shopkeepers.' The chief events of G.'s reign are the Jacobite rising of 1715, which ended in failure; the mad South Sea scheme (1720); a war with Spain, chiefly noted for an unsuccessful attempt on the part of that country to recover Gibraltar; and the passing of the Septennial Act, which is still in force. G. died in his carriage, of apoplexy, June 11, 1727, when proceeding to the palace of his brother the Bishop of Osnabrück.—**G. II.** was born at Hanover, 30th October 1683, and was in his forty-fifth year when he ascended the British throne. Although he could speak English, he was thoroughly German at heart, and preferred his electorate to his kingdom. He has been described as a 'drill-sergeant who believed himself master of his realm, while he repeated the lessons he had learned from his wife, and which his wife had learned from the minister.' This wife was the handsome and accomplished Carolina Wilhelmina, daughter of the Markgraf of Anspach. By her he had two sons, both of whom died before him, and three daughters. She died in 1737 to the great grief of her husband, although the tone of his morals may be judged from his declaration to her that he would never marry again, but only keep mistresses. G.'s reign is one of the most eventful in British history. It witnessed the fall of Walpole and the rise of Pitt; the last attempt of the Jacobites, which ended in the battle of Culloden (q. v.); wars with Spain and France, chequered by the victory of Dettingen (1743) and the defeat of Fontenoy (1748), and ending in the peace of Aix-la-Chapelle (1748); the capture of French Canada, closing with the victory and death of Wolfe (1759); the foundation of the English empire in India by Clive, who won the great battle of Plassey in 1756; and the victory of Minden (1759), all part of the Seven Years' War; the rise of Methodism, of which the chief promoters were John Wesley and George Whitfield; the adoption (1752) of the Gregorian reform in the calendar; a great development of literature and art, showing itself especially in fiction and caricature; and the doubling—chiefly owing to the Seven Years' War—of the National Debt. G. died suddenly of heart-disease at Kensington, October 25, 1760.—**G. III.**, eldest son of Frederick Louis, Prince of Wales, was born June 4, 1738, and succeeded his grandfather, G. II., on the throne in 1760. On 8th September of next year he married the Princess Charlotte Sophia of Mecklenburg-Strelitz, a lady of exemplary and even pious character, by whom he had fifteen children. G.'s mind was naturally narrow, and he was trained carefully in the matter of morals, wretchedly as regards the development of the intellect. The dullest and most respectable of kings, he did more public mischief than all the other Georges put together; the British public condoned in the 'good old king' and 'Farmer G.' what they would have resented and resisted in another. Although his general education was so defective that he spoke impatiently of Shakespeare as 'such stuff,' his mother had taught him to assert himself as a monarch; and his efforts—honest no doubt—to do this, finding a tool in Lord North, 'the most amiable of men, the worst of ministers,' were the means of bringing about the separation between the country and her American colonies. G.'s personal life is chiefly notable for his attacks of insanity in 1764, 1788, 1801, 1804, and 1811—the last continuing to the end of his reign; his troubles with his family, particularly with his eldest son, afterwards George IV.; and his Royal Marriage Bill (12 Geo. III. c. 11), forbidding (1772) the members of the royal family to marry without the consent of the monarch if under twenty-five years of age, and the consent of Parliament if above that age. The reign of G. III. is one of the most eventful in the history of Britain and of mankind. Here we need only make an enumeration of the leading events. The two most important were the American War of Independence and the French Revolution. The former, caused by the attempt of the government of the day to tax the colonists against their will, began in the battle of Lexington (19th April 1775), and ended in the capitulation (1781) of Earl Cornwallis at York Town to French and American troops, followed by the recognition (1783) of the United States. During this period Spain, France, and Holland joined in war against Britain; and the remarkable point in connection with the war is the ability which Britain showed to contend against the world in arms. During this war British gallantry and seamanship were evidenced in Rodney's great victory (1782) over the Comte de Grasse, and Elliot's defence of Gibraltar against the forces of France and Spain for three years and seven months. Elsewhere we record the wars occasioned by or subsequent to the French Revolution, which were marked by the great naval victories of Howe, Duncan, Jervis, and Nelson, and the subsidising of Continental coalition upon coalition against Napoleon Bonaparte by Pitt, and which ended in the battle of Waterloo, June 18, 1815. Among the other events of the reign are the consummation of the Union with Ireland, 1st January 1801, which, however, did not put a stop to Irish troubles and grievances; the Wilkes and Lord George Gordon Riots; the consolidation of our Indian empire under Warren Hastings and Earl Cornwallis; and a second war with the United States, ending in 1815; the reform of prison management promoted by Howard; and the passing in 1807—mainly through the exertions of Clarkson and Wilberforce—of an Act abolishing the slave trade. In this reign the chief statesmen were the elder and the younger Pitt, Fox, Burke, Shelburne, Liverpool, and Castlereagh. The 'strike system' commenced with the outbreaks of the 'Luddites;' scientific invention began under the auspices of the James Watt steam-engine to revolutionise the world; trade and commerce flourished in spite of the war; vaccination and gas became necessities; Captain Cook and others found new fields for emigration in Australia and New Zealand; the punishment of death for minor offences was removed from the statute book; and literature and thought of all kinds, especially poetical, found fresh vents and vigorous expression, as the names of Walpole, Johnson, Burke, Sheridan, Burns, Cowper, Crabbe, Wordsworth, Coleridge, Scott, Byron, Shelley, and Keats are sufficient to show. G. died at Windsor Castle, 29th January 1820, leaving six sons and five daughters.—**G. IV.** was born 12th August 1762, and succeeded to the throne on the death of his father. He was a man of considerable amiability and of fascinating manners, which in the eyes of many covered the multitude of his sins, but his private life was almost as great a scandal to the British monarchy as that of Charles II. It has indeed been said that he was 'a sort of coachman, gamester, scandalous roysterer, unprincipled betting-man, whose proceedings all but got him expelled from the Jockey Club.' On August 8, 1794, when Prince of Wales and deeply in debt, he married his cousin Caroline Amelia Elizabeth, Princess of Brunswick-Wolfenbüttel. There was little affection between G. and his wife, who seems to have been a person of somewhat coarse manners, and altogether indiscreet in her conduct. The only issue of the marriage was the Princess Charlotte Augusta (born 7th January 1796), who married Prince Leopold of Belgium, and died 6th November 1817. One of the most famous events of the reign of G. was his attempt to procure a divorce from Queen Caroline on the ground of immorality. It broke down, but Caroline, who was very popular with the nation, was much chagrined by being prevented from being present at G.'s coronation in Westminster Abbey, and died August 7, 1821. The other leading events of the reign were the break-up of the alliance of the European powers, followed by the formation of a league between Great Britain, France, and Russia, on behalf of Greece, which ended in the battle of Navarino (October 20, 1827), the passing of the Catholic Emancipation Act (13th April 1829), a Burmese war (1824–26), a financial panic (1825), the placing (1829) of the metropolitan police force upon a proper footing, and the death of Canning followed by the rise of Peel. G., who had led a secluded life for some time, died at Windsor Castle, January 26, 1830.

For details of the private and official history of the four Georges, see, among other works, Coxe's *Life of Sir Robert Walpole*; Horace Walpole's *Memoirs of the Reign of George II.*, *Letters to Sir Horace Mann*, and *Memoirs of Early Reign of George III.*; Hervey's *Memoirs from the Accession of George II. to the Death of Queen Caroline*; Stanhope's *History of England from the Peace of Utrecht*; Bancroft's *History of the United States*; Massey's *History of England from the Accession of George II.*; May's *Constitutional History*; Napier's *History of the Peninsular War*; F. Thackeray's *Life of Chatham*; W. M. Thackeray's *Lectures on the Four Georges*; Southey's and Tyerman's biographies of Wesley; *The Rockingham Memoirs*; *The Greville Papers*; Earl Russell's *Life and Correspondence of C. J. Fox*; *The Correspondence of George III. with Lord North*; *Greville's Diary*, edited by W. Reeve; Fitzmaurice's *Life of Lord Shelburne* (3 vols. 1876); and Leslie Stephen's *History of English Thought in the Eighteenth Century* (1876).

George's Channel, St., lies between Wales and the coast of Ireland from Dublin to Wexford, and communicates in the S. with the Atlantic, in the N. with the Irish Sea. It varies in width from 75 to 60 miles, and is about 100 miles long.

George'town, a town of Maryland, on the Potomac, 2 miles W.N.W. of Washington, and a terminus of the Chesapeake and Ohio Canal. It stands on a series of heights, and has many fine buildings, a college under Catholic management, and several schools. Its trade has somewhat declined, but its flour manufactures are very large, and there are paper, leather, iron works, &c. Pop. (1870) 11,384.

Georgetown, the capital of British Guiana, at the mouth of the Demerara. It is the see of an Anglican bishop, is regularly built but unhealthy, and the streets, which are traversed by many canals, are shaded by rows of cabbage-palms, cocoa-nut, and orange trees. The chief buildings are a handsome town-hall with beautiful marble pavements, an episcopal cathedral, a colonial hospital, a mariners' hospital, barracks, and a theatre. G. exports mainly sugar and coffee. A line of rail is being carried hence to New Amsterdam, a distance eastward of 60 miles. Pop. 26,000, of whom 6000 are whites.

Geor'gia (Pers. *Gurjestan*, Russ. *Grusia*, native *Iberia*), a district in the Russian lieutenancy of the Caucasus (q. v.), formerly an independent state, so named either from St. George or from the many Georges who ruled over the country. It now includes the governments of Tiflis and Kutais, and has an area of 38,250 sq. miles, and a pop. of 1,100,000. The country, which is watered by the Kur and its many tributaries, is very fertile, and has a mild, healthy climate. The Georgians, who are of Iranic race, and mostly belong to the Greek Christian Church, are famed for their strength and beauty. Of the four branches into which they are divided, the Karthuli speak the purest Georgian. The history of G. emerges from fable in the time of Alexander the Great, who brought the land under subjection. Freed from the Macedonian yoke by Pharnawas on the death of Alexander in 324 B.C., G. remained, with interruptions, for upwards of 2000 years under its own kings or *mephé*. In the 4th c. it received Christianity, and subsequently suffered much from the raids of the Sassanides and the Arabs, till eventually it was made a province of the Califate in the 8th c. After a brief gleam of liberty, G. again passed into the power of Mohammedan rulers of Persia in the 9th c. Towards the end of the 10th c. it once more struggled into independence under Bagrat III., to enter on a period of wise internal rule and of flourishing trade. The reign of Bagrat VI. (1360–96) was disturbed by the irruption of Timur, who forced the faith of Mohammed on the inhabitants. Georg VII. (1396–1407) restored Christianity. His successor, Alexander I., divided the kingdom between his three sons. Subdivision once begun was carried on till G. had twenty-six princes. The eastern states Karthuli and Kachetien early came under the dominion of the Persian Shahs, and the Georgian princes sought by aid of the Czar (since 1579) to obtain freedom. In 1783 Heraclius II. formally declared himself a Russian vassal, and George XI. resigned in favour of the Emperor Paul in 1799. The western states Imerethi, Mingrelia, and Guria suffered greatly from civil conflict, were overrun by Caucasian mountain tribes, and finally were brought under allegiance to the Turks in 1536. One by one the states have been transferred to Russia (1803–38). See Brosset, *Histoire Ancienne et Moderne de la Georgie* (5 vols. St. Petersb. 1849–57); Bodenstedt, *Die Völker des Kaukasus* (2 vols. Frankf. 1855); Haxthausen, *Transkaukasia* (Leips. 1856). The Georgian speech, rude in sound, but strong and regular, agglutinative in character, is descended from old Colchian, Albanian, and Iberian, and together with Suanen and Lasen forms a special branch of language, which has an alphabet of its own, and which assumed a written form in the 10th c. A literature sprang up under the influence of the Byzantine empire, and includes chiefly translations of the Bible, of the fathers, of Plato, Aristotle, &c. In the 12th c. appeared a few heroic poems; in the 17th c. many songs and chronicles attest the influence of Armenia and Persia. Under the Russians G. has made great advances in education and culture. The national archives were removed to St. Petersburg in 1807. See Brosset, *Éléments de la Langue Georgienne* (Par. 1837), and *Rapport sur un Voyage Archéologique dans la Georgie* (St. Petersb. 1850–51).

Georgia, one of the original states of the American Union, is bounded N. by N. Carolina and Tennessee, W. by Alabama, S. by Florida, E. by the Atlantic and S. Carolina. Area, 58,000 sq. miles; pop. (1871) 1,184,109, of whom 545,142 are coloured, and 40 Indians. The surface for 20 miles from the coast is low and swampy, and is partly under rice crops and partly covered by saw-palmettoes, cypress, cedar, live-oak, magnolias, gum-trees, canes, and other semitropical trees. Two terraces, of 20 and 100 miles' breadth respectively, extend to the centre of G., where a height is attained of 575 feet. The N.W. portion of the state is intersected from S.W. to N.E. by the parallel ranges of the Appalachians and Blue Mountains, which rise to an extreme height of 4000 feet, and between which extends a wild romantic region of narrow gorge, winding valley, and foaming cascade. The Chatta and Etowah rivers flow S.W. between the two hill-ranges; the Savannah forms the N.E., and the Chattahoochee part of the W. boundary; while other rivers flowing S. are the Alatamaha, Flint, Alapahaw, &c. The coast-line is indented by many river estuaries, and fringed with small islands (the largest Cumberland), which yield fine cotton. The staples of G. are Indian-corn (in 1873 23,500,000 bushels), and cotton, the produce of which amounted in 1873 to 614,039 bales. Other crops are rice (in 1870, 22,277,380 lbs.), wheat, oats, rye, sweet potatoes, tobacco, ground-nuts, sugar-cane, &c. In the centre of G. are large forests of black walnut, chestnut, tulip-tree, hickory, poplar, sycamore, beech, maple, &c.; while in the S.E. flourish the orange, lemon, banana, olive, and vine. A vast deposit of fine bituminous coal enters in the N.E., while the hill region is rich in iron ore, gold, copper, silver, lead, zinc, talc, marble, and petroleum, chalybeate, and sulphur springs. Gold-mining was discontinued in 1861, but is being renewed by means of the hydraulic process on a large scale. The climate in the lower valleys and levels is unhealthy. Among the wild animals are the black bear, panther, wild cat, opossum, and racoon; the tick, sandfly, and mosquito are the chief insect pests. Atlanta (q. v.) is the capital, and other cities are Augusta, Macon, and Columbus. G. sends nine representatives to Congress. It derived its name from George II., and received its first colony in 1733. The Creeks and Cherokees were frequently troublesome, but the former finally ceded their territory in 1802, and the latter removed to the Indian territory W. of Arkansas in 1838. As a slave-holding state G. suffered greatly in the late war, Sherman's devastating 'march to the sea' ending with the capture of Savannah.

Georgia, Gulf of, is, strictly speaking, a channel and a northerly extension of Puget's Sound, separating Vancouver's Island from the mainland of British Columbia. It terminates in the N. in Queen Charlotte's Sound, in the S. in the Strait of Fuca (q. v.), receives the Fraser river, and is 20 miles broad on an average, and 100 miles long.

Geoteu'this, a genus of fossil Dibranchiate or two-gilled Cuttlefishes (q. v.), belonging to the family *Teuthidæ*, but referred by some palæontologists to that of the Belemnites (q. v.). Species occur in the Oolitic rocks.

Gephyr'ea, the name given to a class of lower *Annulosa* (q. v.), represented by such forms as the *Sipunculi* or 'spoon-worms,' found in the sand of the English coasts. They are nearly allied to the *Annelida* (q. v.) or true worms, but differ from them in some important particulars. Thus, while the body is usually annulated or segmented, it may be perfectly smooth. In the majority of cases it wants appendages, and the ventral nervous cord is not provided with ganglia or nervous enlargements. The sexes are distinct and the young appear to undergo a metamorphosis in the course of their development. *Sipunculus Bernhardus*, found burrowing in the sand of the coasts, is a familiar species. The anterior extremity is provided with a retractile trunk or proboscis, and the digestive system is convoluted. *Syrinx* is a second genus of G., and *Echiurus*, which occurs in the N. Sea, has posterior bristles.

Gepi'dæ, or **Gepi'di**, one of the chief Gothic tribes, are first mentioned about 280 A.D. as dwelling near the mouth of the Vistula. They gradually moved S. into Pannonia, and settled between the E. and W. Goths. Their power was destroyed by Alboin (q. v.) the Longobard in 566.

Ge'ra, a German town in Reuss-Schleiz, the principality of the younger branch of the Reuss family. It stands on the White Elster 35 miles S.S.W. of Leipsic, and is connected by railway with the Thuringian line of Central Germany. G. is a thriving place, has broad streets and several fine buildings, a castle, townhall, and gymnasium. The chief manufacture is woollen stuffs, but cotton, harmoniums and pianos, soap, and leather are also made. There is a large brewery, and much gardening is carried on. Pop. (1871) 17,957.

Gera'ce, an old town of S. Italy, in the province of Reggio di Calabre, on a hill 4 miles from the sea, and 3 miles N.E. of Reggio. It is a bishop's see, and has a trade in silk and wine. Near it are lead, zinc, and iron mines. Pop. 7200. On the destruction of the ancient Locri (q. v.) by the Saracens in the 12th c., its inhabitants built a new town *Santa Ciriace*—corrupted into G.—about 4 miles from Locri, the ruins of which lie in the plain between G. and the sea. G. was greatly injured by an earthquake in 1783.

Gerania'ceæ, a natural order of Thalamifloral Dicotyledonous plants, including about seven genera and 700 species. They are found in various parts of the world. The species of *Pelargonium* (q. v.), which have very showy flowers, and of which numerous hybrids are now cultivated in greenhouses, abound at the Cape of Good Hope. The genus *Pelargonium* is distinguished from that of *Geranium* (q. v.) by having the flowers irregular and spurred. The plants of the order are aromatic and astringent.

Gera'nium, the genus of plants from which the Dicotyledonous natural order *Geraniaceæ* (q. v.) takes its name. There are thirteen species found growing wild in Britain, which are called crane-bills, from the long beak of their fruit. The tuberous roots of *G. parviflorum* of Tasmania and those of *G. tuberosum* of the S. of Europe are used as food. The rhizome of *G. maculatum* of N. America is called Alum Root (q. v.).

Gér'ard, Étienne Maurice, Comte, a distinguished French soldier, was born at Damvilliers in Lorraine, April 4, 1773. He figures first in Dumouriez' celebrated campaign of 1792–93, then attached himself especially to Bernadotte, to whom in 1805 he became aide-de-camp, while he contributed greatly to some of the greatest victories of the Emperor—such as Austerlitz, Jena, and Wagram. Made a count of the empire, G., who had fought both in the Peninsular and in the Russian war, yet received various appointments and honours after the Bourbon restoration. After his former master's return from Elba, G. joined him, and gave Grouchy the bold advice (which was not taken) on the day of Waterloo to march to the assistance of the Emperor. In 1822 he returned to public life as a member of the Chamber of Deputies, put down revolutionary movements in Paris in 1830, became a marshal of France in 1831, took Antwerp, December 23, 1832, was made the same year a peer of France, in 1835 was appointed Grand Chancellor of the Legion of Honour, and in 1838 general of the National Guards of the Seine. Under the Third Empire G. became (1853) a senator. His death took place 17th April 1855.

Gérard, François Pascal Simon, Baron, a distinguished painter, was born of a French father and Italian mother at Rome, 11th March 1770. He studied painting under David in Paris, became known through his 'Blind Belisarius' in 1795, and rose to be the first of contemporary French portrait-painters. He was made a baron by Louis XVIII. for his 'Entry of Henri IV. into Paris,' his masterpiece, and died at Paris, January 11, 1837. Among his works, which comprise many historical pictures as well as portraits, are 'Cupid and Psyche,' 'Battle of Austerlitz,' 'Coronation of Charles X.,' 'Thetis bearing the Armour of Achilles,' 'Ossian's Dream,' 'Daphne and Chloe,' 'Philip V.,' 'Homer,' &c. In his early paintings G. imitated the antique statuesque style of David, but several of his later works are spirited in design, glowing, varied, and harmonious in colour, and scrupulously accurate in costume. His portraits represent a number of the celebrities of his time.

Ger'asa, one of the ten cities of Decapolis (q. v.), and one of the finest cities of Palestine under the Antonines (130–180 A.D.), lay among the mountains of Gilead, 20 miles E. of Jordan. Its ruins are the most magnificent in the Trans-Jordanic country, surpassing even those of Palmyra. See Porter's *Handbook for Travellers in Syria and Palestine* (new ed. Lond 1868); Buckingham's *Travels in Palestine*, &c. (Lond. 1821).

Ger'ba, or **Jer'ba**, an island of Tunis, in the Gulf of Cabes, 130 miles N.W. of Tripoli, is 12 miles broad and 20 long. It is noted for its manufactures of coloured shawls, fine silks and woollens, blankets, &c.

Ger'hard, Johann, born at Quedlinburg, 17th October 1582, died Professor of Theology at Jena, 17th August 1637. He is generally ranked next to Luther and Chemnitz amongst the great Lutheran divines. His *Loci Theologici* are the foundation of the more developed systematic form of orthodox Lutheranism, and were first published in 1610 in 10 vols. An enlarged edition (22 vols.) appeared 1622–89, of which a reprint was begun by Ed. Preuss in 1863. The *Confessio Catholica* is polemic, while the *Meditationes Sacræ* are an outcome of the warmest personal piety.

Ger'hardt, Charles Frédéric, a French chemist, was born at Strasburg, August 21, 1816. After studying for two years at Karlsruhe, he proceeded to Leipsic in 1833, and under Erdmann developed his taste for chemistry. In 1835 he was working in Liebig's laboratory at Giessen, and in 1838 at Paris, where he was soon engaged with Cahours experimenting on the essential oils. From 1844 to 1848 he was Professor of the Sciences at Montpellier, a position which he resigned in order to establish a chemical laboratory in Paris. Here he worked upon *homologous series*, the *theory of types*, *anhydrous acids*, &c., till 1855, when he was appointed Professor of Chemistry at the École Supérieure of Strasburg. He was shortly after elected corresponding member of the Académie des Sciences. G. died August 19, 1856. His theories and discoveries, which have greatly influenced modern chemistry, are sketched and developed in his two principal works, *Précis de Chimie Organique* (1844–45), and *Traité de Chimie Organique* (4 vols. 1853–56).

Gerhardt, Paul, one of the foremost of German hymn-writers, was born 12th March 1607, at Gräfenhainichen, in Saxony. After he came to Berlin as pastor in 1657, he was known as the leader of the extreme Lutheran party in the embittered theological strife of that period. As such he was deposed by the Government in 1666, though soon reponed. He died an archdeacon at Lübben, 7th June 1676. G.'s hymns (*Geistl. Andachten*), first published in 1666, are very popular; they have been frequently reprinted, the latest edition being that of Bachmann in 1866. Biographies of G. have been written by Langbecker (Berl. 1841) and Bachmann (Berl. 1863).

Ger'izim and E'bal, according to the almost unanimous opinion of travellers, are the mountains which form the sides of the valley in which lies Nablus, the ancient Shechem—E. on the N. and G. on the S. In this valley the Israelites assembled soon after their arrival in Canaan, in obedience to the instructions of Moses. The law, with the blessings and cursings attached to it, was read by Joshua surrounded by the Levites, and stationed apparently in the middle valley. Six of the tribes on the slopes of E. gave back the response 'Amen' when the curses were read, and the other six on G., when the blessings were read (Deut. xi. 29, xxvii.; Josh. viii. 30–35). This is the only mention of E. in the Old Testament history, and the only other mention of G. is in connection with the parable of Jotham (Judges ix. 7). It was on E. that Joshua built the altar to Jehovah (viii. 30); according to the Samaritan Pentateuch it was on G. There are two Samaritan traditions regarding G.—the one that it was the spot where Melchizedek met Abram (Gen. xiv. 18–24), the other, which Stanley thinks much more likely to be true, that it was the place where Abraham was to offer up Isaac (Gen. xxii.). Sanballat, the Persian satrap, built a temple on G., about B.C. 420, for his son-in-law, a son of the high-priest's, who had been excommunicated for the foreign alliance (Neh. xiii. 28; Jos. *Ant.* xi. 8, 2–4). This temple was destroyed by John Hyrcanus about 129 B.C., and does not appear to have been rebuilt, but G. continued to be a holy place to the Samaritans for centuries. For their attacks on the Christians they were driven from G. about 487 A.D., and a Christian church built on it. The ruins which now crown its summit are probably those of the fortifications built by Justinian for the defence of the church. The Samaritans annually celebrate the Passover on G. to this day. See Porter's *Handbook for Travellers in Syria and Palestine* (new ed. Lond. 1868); Robinson's *Bib. Researches* (3d ed. Lond. 1867); Stanley's *Sinai and Palestine* (new ed. 1871).

Ger'ki, a walled town of Africa, in the Sudan, near the E. frontier of Sokoto, and on the border of Bornu, 11 miles N.E. of Kano. The inhabitants, who are Fellatas, and are of noted predatory habits, number some 15,000.

Ger'lache, Étienne Constantine, Baron de, a Belgian politician, was born at Biourge, in Luxemburg, December 26, 1785. He entered the second chamber of the États-Généraux as deputy from Liége in 1824; became President of Congress in 1831, receiving as such the oath of allegiance to King Leopold; and was nominated first president of the Cour de Cassation in October 1833, after which he retired from active legislation, still, however, occupying a prominent position as one of the chief leaders of the Catholic party. He has written several historical works, such as *La Révolution de Liége sous Louis de Bourbon* (1831); *L'Histoire du Royaume des Pays-Bas* (2d ed. 3 vols. 1842); *L'Histoire de Liége* (1843); *Essais sur les Grandes Époques de notre Histoire Nationale* (1852); and *Observations Critiques sur l'Histoire de Jules César par Napoléon III.* (1865).

Ger'man (Lat. *germanus*, 'derived from the same *germen*,' 'germ') is a term applied to those born or descended from the same father or mother, and thus related in full blood.

German, Cousins, or **First Cousins**, are all those not being brothers and sisters who have had the same grandfather.

German (San), a town in the S.W. of Puerto Rico, in the W. Indies, on a small river, 10 miles from its mouth. It has some trade in cotton, coffee, cattle, &c. Pop. 9125.

German Barm. See YEAST.

Ger'man Cath'olics (*Deutschkatholiken*) is the usual name for a sect formed about 1844 by secession from the Catholic Church in Germany. The immediate occasion of the secession was the solemn exhibition of the Holy Coat at Treves in 1844, accompanied by an episcopal promise of remission of sins as reward for a pilgrimage to this sacred relic. Johann Ronge, a Silesian priest, became spokesman of the widespread feeling of contempt for this mummery; and he soon found a helpmeet in Czerski, a priest who had already seceded from the Catholic Church. Their united labours produced a powerful effect in many parts of Germany, and separatist congregations soon began to form themselves. The earliest, organised at Schneidemühl in Posen, under the pastorate of Czerski, published its confession of faith in 1844—a formula which departs but little either from the doctrine or ritual of the Catholic Church, while rejecting the use of Latin in the service. The confession drawn up by Ronge for his congregation at Breslau went much further in its dissent from Rome, and the spirit of Ronge's manifesto was that which triumphed in the first council of the G. C., held at Leipsic in 1845. Scripture interpreted by the unfettered reason was declared the only rule of faith; belief in God as Creator and in Christ as Saviour was retained; the celibacy of the clergy was abolished; and congregations were declared to have the right to elect their pastors and officers. By the end of 1845 there were as many as 298 congregations of G. C. A few Protestants joined them, and leading men of all parties regarded the movement as full of significance for the future of German ecclesiastical life. The highly repressive measures of almost all the German Governments was less a check to the development of the body than the diversity of aim and of belief that speedily showed itself between Ronge and Czerski and the parties headed by them. Ronge moved steadily in the direction of free-thinking, and he and his adherents began to show their zeal less in matters religious and ecclesiastical than in the field of politics. The democratic and socialistic views of Ronge's party shocked all who retained anything of conservatism in religion or in politics, and not merely led to open secession and the disruption of numerous congregations, but drew on the whole body in a still higher degree the suspicion and hostility of the German Governments. The reactionary policy that predominated after 1848 told heavily on the German Catholic associations, even when they were not, as was frequently the case, formally prohibited from assembling. Ronge retired to London; the whole organisation began to fall to pieces. Such German Catholic congregations as still remained saw their way in 1850 to join the association of the 'Free Churches' (*Freie Gemeinden*). These Churches were the result of the continued struggle between the rationalistic and the orthodox sections within the Protestant Church. The desire for entire theological freedom led numerous congregations to secede from the national churches, the first being formed in 1841. These separatists have been always much more fully agreed in what they are to disbelieve than in any positive articles of faith, and are generally regarded as wholly without the pale of Christianity. About the time of their union with the G. C., the free-thinking congregations numbered 104. The united body has not thriven, the council held in 1865 at Gotha was attended by only fifty-six members.

German'der, a common name for the species of *Teucrium*, a genus named from Teucer, Prince of Troy, who is said to have first used G. medicinally. *T. chamædrys* is the common G. or wall G., which has been introduced into Britain, and was formerly used in cases of gout and rheumatism. *T. scorodonia*, the wood G., is frequent in Britain. It is extremely bitter, and has been used in place of hops. *T. scordium* is the water G., and *T. marum* is called cat thyme, which causes sneezing. The plants belong to the natural order *Labiatæ* (q. v.).

Germa'nia, called *G. Magna, Transrhenana*, or *Barbara* in contradistinction to *G. Prima* and *G. Secunda* (the N. and N.E. of *Gallia Belgica*), was bounded on the N. by the *Mare Germanicum* (German Ocean) and the *Mare Suevicum* (Baltic), on the E. by the Vistula, on the S. by the Danube, and on the W. by the Rhine and the German Ocean. The name G. is supposed to be derived from the Celtic *gaire, gairm, gairmean* ('a cry'), the habit of the Germans being to utter the war-shout as they rushed to battle. Tacitus divides the Germans into three great groups—the *Ingævones* in the N.W., the *Hermiones* in the centre, and the *Istævones* in the E. and S. The Teutones are the first German tribe known to history. They were defeated by the Consul Papirius 113 B.C., and were completely crushed by Marius 102–101 B.C. From 72 to 55 B.C. some German tribes under Ariovistus, chief of the Marcomanni, overran the greater part of Eastern Gaul. In the latter year this prince was defeated by Cæsar in the territory of the Sequani, and forced to recross the Rhine. In 55 and 54 B.C. Cæsar twice entered German territory, but was compelled to retire. In 12 B.C., Drusus, stepson of Augustus, led an expedition against the Germans, advanced as far as the *Albis* (Elbe), subdued the Frisii, Batavi, and Chauci, and inflicted a severe blow on the Catti. Being killed by a fall from his horse 9 B.C., he was succeeded in the command by his brother Tiberius, who conquered the tribes between the Rhine and the Weser. In A.D. 9, under Arminius, chief of the Cherusci, they again rose and defeated the Romans in the Teutoburg Forest, and freed themselves from foreign sway. Violent commotions now broke out among the Germans, and the Romans gradually established themselves in the S.W. of G. From A.D. 16–68, the *agri decumates*, or tithe-lands, were formed on the E. of the Upper Rhine, and on the N. of the Upper Danube. In A.D. 70–71 the Batavi revolted. This was followed by a series of struggles which culminated in the sanguinary Marcomannian war, when the Germans invaded Italy and besieged Aquileia (166 A.D.). In 180 A.D. the Emperor Commodus purchased peace and surrendered the forts on the Danube. After this the Roman power in G. rapidly waned; the Germans began to harass their old neighbours, and at last, pouring forth in countless hordes, swept like a hurricane the countries of Gaul, Italy, and Spain, and planted their victorious standards in Britain and Africa. By the end of the 5th c. nearly the whole of Western Europe was subject to German sway.

G. is described as a country of swamps and forests. Its chief rivers are the Rhenus, Danubius, Amisia (*Ems*), Visurgis (*Weser*), Albis (*Elbe*), Viadrus (*Oder*), and Vistula. The people were a branch of the Aryan race. They are described by Cæsar and Tacitus as tall, strong, fair-complexioned, yellow-haired, and animated by an intense love of liberty. Their women were distinguished for their chastity. Their dwellings were rude huts, generally separate, and, though villages were not uncommon, towns were regarded by them with great aversion, and hardly existed except on the banks of the Rhine. The territory was divided for political purposes into districts (*pagi*), each of which had its own magistrate. The people were divided into four classes—nobles, freemen, freedmen, and slaves. The chiefs, and probably the magistrates, were elected from the nobles. Of the religion of the Germans little is known. They worshipped the sun, moon, and stars, Tuisco, the ancestor of their race, and his son Mannus, and a number of greater gods. Their sacred rites were celebrated in groves and forests or on the lone hillsides. They practised divination, cherished a belief in a future state, and peopled air and earth and water with numberless inferior deities, such as elves, nixes, dwarfs, and giants. See Müller, *Geschichte und System der altdeutsch. Religion* (1844); and Kuhn, *Zur ältesten Gesch. der Indogerman. Völker* (Berl. 1850).

German'ic Folk-Laws. After the migrations of the Germanic races had subsided, their old laws were gradually embodied in Latin, generally by private effort. They are chiefly of a penal character, and are distinguished from the Roman law and the capitularies of the Frankish kings as *Leges Barbarorum:*—(1) *Lex Salica* and *Lex Ripuariorum*, the laws respectively of the Salic and Rhenish Franks; (2) *L. Burgundiorum* (before 501), or *L. Gundobaldi*, or *Loi Gombette* (from King Gundobald), a formal code, with traces of the influence of the Roman law; (3) *L. Visigothorum*, recorded by King Enrik at the end of the 5th c., but, after the West Goths were driven back to Spain, so grafted on Roman law as to become a distinct growth, the main stem of the modern law of Spain, and which, incorporated into a law-book (the *Forum Judicum*) about the middle of the 7th c., was in the 13th c. translated into Spanish under the name *Fuero Juzgo*; (4) *L. Longobardorum* (the oldest part, 'Edictum Lotharis,' dating from 643), extended by successive Longobardic, Frankish, and German kings and emperors, and recognised as a system of law for all Italy, the whole being collected (beginning of 12th c.) under the title *Lombarda*, or *Liber Legis Longobardicæ*, and enriched with the glosses of the University of Bologna; (5) *L. Alamannorum* (the modern Swabians), coeval with the Ripuaric or Rhenish; (6) *L. Baiuvariorum* (or Bavarians), recorded between 622 and 638, and very like the preceding; (7) *L. Saxonum*, from the same time; and (8) *L. Angliorum et Werinorum, i.e., Thuringorum*, also from the beginning of the 9th c.

German'icus Cæ'sar, son of Nero Claudius Drusus and Antonia, daughter of M. Antony and niece of Augustus, was born 15 B.C. In A.D. 4 he was adopted by his uncle Tiberius. In A.D. 7 he was quæstor, and in the same year accompanied Tiberius against the Pannonians and Dalmatians. He returned in A.D. 10 to announce the successful issue of the war, and was honoured with triumphal insignia and the rank of prætor. In A.D. 12 he was elected consul. On the death of Augustus, 14 A.D., the legions in Germany and Illyricum, dissatisfied with their pay, the long period of service, and the severity of the military tasks, rose in revolt. G. whose frank and open manners made him the idol of the army hastened from Gaul to establish order in the camp. He was offered the imperial power by the troops, but declared that he would rather die than turn traitor. Having satisfied the demands of the soldiery, he continued the German war in A.D. 15, and in the following year defeated Arminius, whereupon Tiberius jealous of his glory recalled him to Rome. On his return he was received with great enthusiasm, and on the 26th May A.D. 17 he celebrated a triumph over the conquered tribes, Thusnelda, wife of Arminius, following in the procession of captives. The eastern provinces were now assigned to G., but his influence was thwarted by Cn. Piso, whom Tiberius had appointed governor of Syria. In 18 A.D. G. entered on his second consulship at Nicopolis, after which he visited Egypt. On his return he was seized with a serious illness, and died at Epidaphne, 9th October A.D. 19, in the thirty-fourth year of his age. His ashes were carried to Italy by his heroic wife, Agrippina (q. v.), and deposited in the mausoleum of Augustus. G. was learned, benevolent, and generous. He wrote a verse translation of the *Phænomena* of Aratus; a physical poem, entitled *Diosemeia* or *Prognostica*, compiled from Greek sources; and a number of epigrams, one of which, on a Thracian boy, has been much admired. G.'s remains were first printed at Bologna (fol. 1474). The latest edition is that of A. Breysig (Ber. 1867).

German Ocean. See NORTH SEA.

Germa'no, San, or **Casi'no,** a town in the province of Caserta, S. Italy, 50 miles N.N.W. of Naples. It stands picturesquely on the small river Rapido, is overlooked by an old castle of very great antiquity, and occupies the site of the Volscian *Casinum*, which was made a Roman colony in 312 B.C., and from the ruins of which G. arose in the middle ages. An alliance was formed here by Gregory IX. and Friedrich II. in 1230. Near G. is the famous monastery of Monte Casino (q. v.).

German Paste, the name of a preparation for feeding cage singing-birds, made with peameal (1 lb.), blanched sweet almonds (½ lb.), lard (2 oz.), raw sugar (3 oz.), and hay saffron (7 grains). The addition of an egg is an improvement. Beat these materials into a paste with water, strain, and dry or use.

German Silver, a hard, silvery-white compound of copper, zinc, and nickel in variable proportions, used extensively in the arts. Two kinds for *casting* have the following percentage composition:—First quality, copper 50, zinc 25, nickel 25; second quality, copper 62·5, zinc 25, nickel 12·5. The alloy for *rolling* contains 100 parts—57·1 of copper, 19 of zinc, and 23·9 of nickel. This has entirely superseded copper as the foundation of electro-plated goods. In the rolling mill it is reduced to sheets of the required thicknesses, which are by the process of 'raising,' 'beating up,' 'spinning,' or stamping, formed into forks, spoons, bodies and other parts of table-dishes, vases, &c. Hard solder, composed of 5 parts of G. S. and 4 parts zinc, is used to unite the parts before the article is submitted to the electro-depositing bath. In melting the ingredients of the alloy, care has to be taken to prevent the volatilisation of the zinc.

Germans, St., a market-town of Cornwall, on the Fal, 9½ miles W.N.W. of Plymouth by the Cornwall Railway. It has a grand old church, with a Norman west front and towers, and in the vicinity is Port Eliot, the seat of the Earl of St. G. There is an export of coal and some fisheries. Pop. (1871) 2678.

German Tinder. See AMADOU.

Ger'mantown. See PHILADELPHIA.

Ger'many (Lat. *Germania*, Ger. *Deutschland*, Fr. *Allemagne*), in the wide ethnographic sense, is that portion of Central Europe which is occupied by the Germanic race and where the German language is spoken, extending from the Slavic E. to the Romanic W., and from the Alps to the North Sea and the Baltic. In the ordinary political sense—that with which we have now to deal—it comprises the greater part of this area as the German Empire, and is bounded E. by Russia and Austria; W. by France, Belgium, and the Netherlands; N. by the North Sea, Jutland, and the Baltic; and S. by Switzerland and Austria, in lat. 49° 7′–55° 50′ N. and long. 6°–22° 40′ E. It embraces one-eighteenth of the area of Europe, and is of irregular cuboid shape. Its extreme length from S.W. (about Aachen) to N.E. (Tilsit) is 740 miles, and from N. to S. 580 miles, while it has 1008 miles of a coast-line. The chief indentations in the N.W. are the estuaries of the Ems, Weser, and Elbe; in the Baltic, the Gulf of Lübeck, the Haff of the Oder, the Gulf of Danzig, and the Kurische Haff. The N. Frisian group off the W. coast of Slesvig, and Fehmern and Rügen in the Baltic, are the principal islands. G. consists of twenty-five states, the areas and populations of which are as follows according to the census of 1st December 1875:—

States.	Area in sq. miles.	Pop. (1875).	Chief towns.
KINGDOMS—			
Preussen (Prussia, with Lauenburg)	134,431	25,772,562	Berlin.
Bayern (Bavaria)	29,138	5,022,904	Munich.
Würtemberg	7,527	1,881,505	Stuttgart.
Sachsen (Saxony)	5,785	2,760,342	Dresden.
GRAND-DUCHIES—			
Baden	5,910	1,506,531	Karlsruhe.
Mecklenburg-Schwerin	5,135	553,734	Schwerin.
Hessen-Darmstadt	2,963	882,349	Darmstadt.
Oldenburg	2,469	319,314	Oldenburg.
Sachsen-Weimar-Eisenach	1,403	292,933	Weimar.
Mecklenburg-Strelitz	1,131	95,673	New Strelitz.
DUCHIES—			
Braunschweig (Brunswick)	1,420	327,493	Brunswick.
Sachsen-Meiningen	953	194,494	Meiningen.
Anhalt	880	213,689	Dessau.
Sachsen-Koburg-Gotha	759	182,599	Koburg & Gotha
Sachsen-Altenburg	516	145,844	Altenburg.
PRINCIPALITIES—			
Waldeck	438	54,711	Arolsen.
Lippe	438	112,442	Detmold.
Schwarzburg-Rudolstadt	364	76,676	Rudolstadt.
Do. Sondershausen	333	67,480	Sondershausen.
Reuss-Gera	122	92,375	Gera.
Schaumburg-Lippe	171	33,133	Bückeburg.
Reuss-Greiz	320	46,985	Greiz.
REICHSLAND—			
Elsass-Lothringen	5,603	1,529,408	Strassburg.
FREE TOWNS—			
Hamburg	157	388,618	
Lübeck	109	56,912	
Bremen	100	141,848	
Total	208,575	42,752,554	

Physical Aspect.—The surface of G. is naturally divided into three well-defined portions:—(1) The Alpine region in the S. with the Bavario-Suabian plateau stretching northwards; (2) the district of the German Mittelgebirge; and (3) the great sandy plain in the N. of G., which stretches E. and W. from Russia to the Netherlands, includes Slesvig-Holstein, and covers an area of 124,000 sq. miles. A branch of the Rhætian and Noric Alps forms the S. boundary of Bavaria and Würtemberg, sending northwards occasional offsets, but nowhere attaining the limit of perpetual snow, which is 8900 feet in the Alps. Of the ranges forming the Mittelgebirge, and converging more or less directly in the N. of Bavaria, are the Böhmer Wald (4800 feet), trending N.W. along the E. Bavarian frontier; the continuous chain of the Sudetic Mountains, Riesengebirge, and Erzgebirge (with the beautiful 'Saxon Switzerland'), forming the southern boundary of Silesia and Saxony; the Teutoburger Wald, Solling, Fichtelgebirge, and Thuringer Wald, extending S.E. in a somewhat broken line from the N. of Westphalia; the Rhöngebirge and Vogelsgebirge, from Hessen and Bavaria; and the Spessart and Odenwald, stretching N.N.E. from Baden, and connecting with the central chain the Schwarzwald (see BLACK FOREST) and the Suabian Alps. Several low ranges run at right angles to the Rhine in its lower course, chief of which are the Hunsrück, Gifel, Ardennes, Taunus, Westerwald, Siebengebirge, and Sauerländgebirge. The Rhine is enclosed on the side of Elsass by the Vosges (q. v.). The Harz Mountains (q. v.) are an isolated group (3470 feet), partly in Brunswick, Hanover, and Prussian Saxony. As the common affix *wald* implies, the mountains of G. are generally clad with forests, which give richness to the scenery and tone down the austerity of wild peaks and ridges. The great northern plain has an average elevation of 350 feet, while parts of the Slesvig-Holstein coast are below the level of the sea, protected by dykes.

Hydrography.—The rivers of G. are numerous, and have for the most part a northerly course. Of those entering the North Sea the principal are the Rhine, Ems, Weser and Elbe; the Oder, Vistula, Niemen flow into the Baltic. The great river of the S. is the Danube (q. v.), which rises in the Schwarzwald, some 40 miles N.E. of Lake Constance. The Etsch (Ital. Adige) connects G. with the Adriatic. The Rhine is the longest river in G., the Weser the longest purely German river. There are many canals, of which the chief are the Elbing-Oderländisch, the Bromberger, Müllroser, Finow, Eider, Plauen, and Main-Donau or Ludwig's Canal. The lakes in the N. of G. are very numerous, but of no great size. The Spirding See and Mauer See, in Prussia Proper, are drained by the Pregel and Vistula respectively; the Plau, Malchow, Flesen, Kölpin, and Müritz, in Mecklenburg, by the Elbe and the Dümer. In E. Prussia the surface covered by lakes and marshes is 553½ sq. miles; in Mecklenburg, 255; in the Mark, 223; in Pomerania, 255. Besides Lake Constance, there are in the S. the Ammer, Würm, and Chiem Lakes, drained by affluents of the Isar and Inn.

Climate.—The climate throughout the empire is characterised by great uniformity, and is on the whole temperate and healthy. The S. Tyrol and the Rhine valley are the warmest parts, but the greater general altitude of S. than of N. G. counteracts the effects of a lower latitude. In the S., however, there is less rain and a clearer sky. Advancing N. the decrease of temperature is 1° F. in 52 miles; from W. to E. it is 1° F. in 72 miles. The mean annual temperature is at Hamburg 47° F., at Berlin 46·5°, at Hanover 48°, at Frankfurt-on-the-Main 48·5°, at Dresden 48°, and at Königsberg 43°. The mean temperature at Berlin in summer is 66° F., in winter 27°, or 3½ degrees lower than at London. Exposed to the cold winds of the N., the great northern plain is visited by severe winters, during which the ground is under deep snow for several months, and the water surfaces are covered with ice of great thickness. G. has a mean annual rainfall of 20 inches. There are eighty-five meteorological stations in the empire, mostly in Prussia.

Geology and Mineralogy.—The chief formations in the great northern plain are Tertiary, covered with mud and sand of a recent date, while the district stretching from Hanover to the Danube consists of Secondary strata. Primary beds, containing true coal, occur in Rhenish Prussia. The Trias rocks, of which the best types are bunter-sandstein, muschel-kalk, and keuper, are rich in fossils, marine shells, labyrinthodont saurians, &c. In the more recent Tertiary of the Lower Rhine basin have been found the bones of the mammoth, rhinoceros, &c. Westphalia and Central Germany are covered with Oolitic formations, confusedly erupted in many places by igneous rocks, and embracing much valuable coal and ironstone. Among the rocks of the Mittelgebirge are basalt, trachyte, granite, &c. The *minerals* of G. are numerous and valuable. In the Erzgebirge and Harz Mountains are rich mines of gold, silver, iron, copper, lead, salt, coal, alum, and sulphur. Coal and iron abound in Silesia, Rhenish Prussia, Elsass-Lothringen, Bavaria, Würtemberg, Hessen-Darmstadt, &c. Other minerals exported are cobalt, arsenic, gypsum, bismuth, quicksilver, pumice-stone, kaolin, and emery. Immense deposits of pure rock-salt have been discovered near Stettin, in Pomerania. Along the Baltic coast valuable amber is obtained from beds of lignite in large quantities. Of the vast number of mineral springs in G. some of the most noted are those of Aachen, Wiesbaden, Ems, Selters Homburg, Kissingen, Rosenheim, Brückenau, and Baden-Baden.

Botany and Agriculture.—There are 50,000 sq. miles of wooded land in the whole empire. The large forests, which chiefly occur in the central mountain region and in the W. portion of the great plain, consist of elms, poplars, beeches, oaks, birches, pines, Scotch and silver firs, &c. The Black Forest is famed for its wealth of sombre foliage, and many of its trees are of gigantic size, some attaining a height of 180 feet. Of indigenous plants G. reckons some 7000 species, of which 2566 are flowering. Fruit-trees are extensively cultivated, and comprise the apple, pear, chestnut, plum, almond, walnut, apricot, &c. The vine is grown chiefly in Rhenish-Prussia, Nassau, and the Bavarian Palatinate; the best Rhenish wine is produced on the slopes of a ridge which extends in Nassau and along the right bank of the Rhine for 25 miles. Of German wines perhaps the best known is *hock*, which is distinguished by its delicate flavour and extraordinary durability. But other fine kinds are Asmannshaüser and Rüdesheimer. Among the cereals are rye, wheat, oats, and buckwheat; in the S. spelt, potatoes, maize. Elsass-Lothringen and Prussian Saxony yield much beetroot; the Rhine valley produces tobacco; while flax and hemp are most largely obtained from Baden, Hessen-Nassau, and Hanover. Other crops are saffron, madder, hops, rapeseed, poppy, anise seed, coriander and liquorice. The soil is for the most part fertile, and agriculture, for which there are various colleges, is in a thriving state. There are 102,115 sq. miles of surface under cultivation, 37,227 of meadows and pasture, and 17,944 of waste land; the most thoroughly developed parts being Prussian Saxony, Thuringia, Slesvig-Holstein, Posen, and Hessen. Husbandry engages some three-fourths of the inhabitants. There is abundance of excellent pasture.

Zoology and Live-Stock.—The forests of G. are still haunted by many wild animals, as the wolf, deer, hog, fox, lynx, martin, weasel, &c. In the Alpine S. are seen the eagle and vulture, while the northern plain (Pomerania) abounds in storks, wild-geese, ducks, &c. Bavaria is noted for pheasants and other kinds of game. Among domestic animals the chief are the horse in the N.; horned cattle (15,776,702) in the centre; sheep (3,352,231) mainly in Saxony, Silesia, Bohemia, and Thuringia; and swine (7,124,088) in Westphalia and Mecklenburg. Asses, mules (13,315), and goats (2,320,002) are also bred in large numbers; in the S. the silkworm is reared extensively, and the bee in the northern meadows. The rivers and lakes are rich in fish, of which the chief are the salmon, carp, trout, pike, perch, and eels. Crayfish, pearl-bearing mussels, and leeches are found in the rivers.

Industries.—The manufacturing industries of G., which have fluctuated greatly of late years, are mainly centred in Rhenish Prussia, Brandenburg, Westphalia, Prussian Saxony, and Silesia. The woollen industry employs some 250,000 persons, and causes an import of raw material amounting in 1873 to 1,088,700 cwt. To provide the cloth-factories with yarn, there are spinning factories with 1,750,000 spindles. Aachen is noted for its doeskins and other cloths, of which America takes 5,000,000 marks' worth yearly. In Greiz and Zeulenroda, the 'German Tibet,' the annual value of woollen stuffs produced is 20,000,000 marks. Apolda is noted for hosiery, Berlin for carpets and shawls, Schmiedeberg in Silesia for Turkey carpets. In the whole empire there are some 60 flax-spinning mills, with 280,000 spindles, and about 458,000 looms for the manufacture of linen, of which 250,000 are in the E. provinces of Prussia. The cotton industry, which is chiefly carried on in Elsass-Lothringen and Saxony, has greatly increased of late years, and in 1872 there were 430 mills, with 225,000 mills and 5,000,000 spindles. Silks and velvets, chiefly made in Crefeld, Elberfeld, Barmen, and Viersen, are exported in great quantity to Great Britain. The lighter velvets and half-silk goods are superior to those of France. Other branches of weaving industry are lace-making and embroidery in Saxony, galloons and fringes in Barmen and Berlin, and corset stuffs in Würtemberg. The valley of the Wupper is famed for its calico-printing and Turkey-red dyeing. Leather is an important manufacture in the S. and W., and among the exports are fine boots and gloves. Paper is made (chiefly near Aachen) in 950 mills, employing 25,000 persons. There are 3600 tobacco and cigar factories, in which 70,000 persons are engaged. Bavaria is famed for beer, while the N. German states alone have 10,220 breweries. G. has also 25,000 brandy-distilleries, 1600 vinegar-factories, 7000 oil-mills and refineries, 650 chemical works, 180 perfume-factories, 300 glass-works, 110 porcelain-factories, 18,000 brick-kilns, 10,000 saw-mills, and 5200 lime-kilns. In 1874 there were 336 beetroot-sugar factories, producing 5,640,700 cwt. of raw sugar. Berlin, Mühlhausen, and Chemnitz are the great seats of the machine manufacture (locomotives and sewing-machines), which is now conducted in 750 works, employing 90,000 hands. The iron and steel industries are chiefly confined to Prussia. The shipbuilding ports are Hamburg, Bremerhaven, and, for war vessels, Kiel, Danzig, and Wilhelmshaven on the Jade. Large ironclads are, however, procured from other countries. A specialty in G. is the manufacture of musical instruments—organs (at Dresden), harmoniums (at Gera), violins, pianofortes, &c. In the Black Forest watch-making employs 10,300 persons: other industrial products are musical boxes and straw goods. Typical manufactures of G. are also carved goods in bone, wood, meerschaum, mother-of-pearl, brass, bronze, and silver wares, and articles in vulcanite.

Commerce.—The trade and commerce of all G., except Hamburg and Bremen, are under the administration of the Zollverein or Customs' League, which is represented by a parliament, merged in the imperial Reichstag in 1871, and by a council of three permanent committees dealing separately with finance, taxes and customs, and trade. All receipts of the Zollverein, arising mainly from custom dues on imports and taxes on spirits, wines, beetroot-sugar, and tobacco, are paid into a common exchequer, and are distributed equally among the various states *pro rata* of inhabitants. The total value of imports in 1874 was £188,655,000; of exports, £121,640,000. The direct imports from and exports to Great Britain in the same year amounted to £24,799,846 and £19,947,195 respectively. Among the exports are wheat, barley, flour, oxen, sheep, flax, timber, sugar, wool, and textiles. In 1875 the mercantile navy numbered 4495 vessels of 1,033,725 tons, 253 being steamers of 167,633 tons. There are some twelve trading ports.

Railways, &c.—In the beginning of 1876 the railways of G. open for traffic had a total length of 17,386 miles, of which 7463 belonged to the state. In 1875 there were 28,132 miles of telegraph lines, 101,422 miles of wires, and 5434 stations. The telegraph receipts amounted in the year ending March 1875 to £588,368, and the expenditure to £870,839. The imperial post-office in 1875 transmitted 576,013,557 letters, 64,662,503 post-cards, 9,302,611 patterns, and 92,956,908 stamped wrappers.

Finance.—The common imperial expenditure is defrayed from the revenues arising from customs, excise dues, and profits of the posts and telegraphs, and failing these, from an assessment on the various states in proportion to their populations. In 1876 the revenue was £23,712,849, and the expenditure £20,162,253. The £200,000,000 received as war indemnity from France was not entered in the budget, but was converted into a separate account by itself along with £6,000,000 indemnity from the city of Paris, and £14,000,000 from various French departments. Of this sum nearly one-half was portioned out among the states of the empire. The other half was disposed of in the following sums:—To France for the railways of Elsass-Lothringen, £13,000,000; to persons and corporations in Elsass and parts of G. for damage and expense sustained during the war, £5,505,000; similar compensation to shipowners, £840,000; for rolling-stock, &c., to the Elsass-Lothringen railways, £2,761,800; for the fortress of the empire, £6,000,000; to the Invalid Fund, £4,050,000; for extra expenditure incurred by the occupation, £4,350,000; and for the armament and disarmament of fortresses, the purchase of fresh siege material, and naval re-equipments, £4,200,000. Further a sum of £3,000,000 was repaid to the customs department, £1,650,000 went to liquidate treasury bonds, £525,000 were handed over to Bavaria and Würtemberg, whose military administration is not under the empire, £515,000 went to the imperial railway fund, £600,000 to generals as allowances, £6,000,000 was set aside as a war reserve fund, while the remainder was chiefly applied to the working capital of the imperial exchequer, and to several special branches of the military service.

Army.—By the constitution of April 16, 1871, the Prussian system of conscription was extended to the whole empire. Thus every German capable of bearing arms (*wehrfähig*) must pass three years in the line, three in the army of reserve, and five in the *Landwehr*—the support of the standing army. Substitution is not allowed, but teachers from the primary schools have only to go through infantry exercise for six weeks. Self-supporting volunteers, who pass certain examinations, only require to serve one year. The strength of the army on a peace footing was fixed, in the Army Bill of 1874, at 401,659 men, for a term of seven years beginning January 1, 1875. On a war footing the force can be raised to 1,273,346 men, with 31,195 officers, 281,546 horses, and 2700 guns. In 1875 the army consisted of 401,659 men, 18,079 officers, with 97,379 horses, and 1200 guns, in 148 infantry regiments, 26 battalions of Jäger, 93 regiments of cavalry, 36 of field artillery, 26 battalions of fort artillery, 19 of engineers, 18 of train, 274 depôts of Landwehr, and a staff division. By a law of 1874, the military strength was greatly augmented by the organisation of the *Landsturm*, which only becomes an active force in the event of invasion. It is divided into two classes, the first including all able-bodied men up to the age of forty-two who are not already in the army, the second embracing all fit subjects above that age. The first class is organised into 293 battalions, and adds 175,000 men to the army, so that, without the second class of the Landsturm, which, is not to be formed for the present, the German forces will be raised to some 1,800,000 men. The whole land forces 'form a united army in war and peace under the orders of the emperor,' and 'all German troops are bound to obey unconditionally the orders of the emperor,' who has the right of erecting fortresses, and of declaring a turbulent district in a state of siege.

Navy.—In November 1875 the navy consisted of 62 steamers of 80,580 tons, 70,340 horse-power, and 4268 guns. It comprises 3 turret-ships and 8 ironclad frigates, two of which, the *Kaiser* and *Deutschland*, launched in 1874, have ten-inch armour plate, and were built on the Thames. In 1875 the navy was manned by 5500 seamen, and officered by 1 admiral, 1 vice-admiral, 1 rear-admiral, 28 captains, and 224 lieutenants. There are also 9 companies of marines, 6 of infantry, and 3 of artillery, consisting of 1500 men. The crews are raised by conscription among the seafaring class. Wilhelmshaven, Kiel, and Danzig are the three war ports.

Constitution and Government.—The imperial constitution of April 16, 1871, binding together all the states of G., enacts an 'eternal union for the protection of the realm, and the care of the welfare of the German people.' The supreme control of affairs, military and political, is vested in the King of Prussia, who, as emperor, can declare war, if defensive, make peace, enter into treaties, and appoint and receive ambassadors. The legislature consists of the Bundesrath, or Federal Council of the individual states, and the Reichstag, representing the German nation. The former body numbers fifty-nine members, appointed for each session by the Governments of the different states; the latter 397 members, elected by universal suffrage and ballot for three years. The Bundesrath is presided over by the chancellor of the empire; the president of the Reichstag is elected by the deputies. All imperial laws before they take effect must receive an absolute majority of votes of both houses, and be assented to by the emperor and countersigned by the chancellor. The Bundesrath, under the direction of the chancellor, also exercises supreme administrative and consultative functions.

Education.—The educational system of G. is singularly comprehensive and complete, and since 1872 much has been done to counteract the effects of the obstructive policy adopted by the Ultramontanes. Ecclesiastics have been removed from the direction of schools in Prussia, Elsass-Lothringen, and several other states. Primary schools, of which there are 60,000, with 75,000 teachers, are maintained in all towns and villages out of local rates, and the attendance of children for four or five years is compulsory. A means of transition from the primary schools to the higher is furnished by middle schools of various names and organisations. The higher schools, over 500, are divided into *realschulen* and *gymnasia*. At the realschulen, modern languages, mathematics, Latin, and physical science, especially in its industrial applications, are taught; the gymnasia prepare for the higher government offices and the universities. In 1875 G. had twenty-one universities, with 1729 professors and 16,359 students. Of the universities fourteen are Protestant, *i.e.*, in the theological faculty teach only Protestant theology, while four are Roman Catholic. The remaining three are of a mixed character. There are many special schools for technology, agriculture, commerce, military science, music, design, &c. G. is rich in museums (over 150), art and science academies, picture-galleries, botanical gardens, &c. The press is free (since 1848), and from 8000 to 10,000 works issue from it annually. There are also some 3000 newspapers and journals, several of which have a high reputation beyond the empire.

Religion and Race.—While Protestantism prevails in the N., Roman Catholicism predominates in the S., but no state can be said to belong exclusively to either faith. The constitution of the Protestant Church varies in the different states. At the end of 1871 there were altogether 25,580,615 Protestants, 14,868,608 Roman Catholics, 49,351 (1876) Old Catholics, 512,158 Jews, some 82,155 Herrnhutters, Mennonites, &c. The Protestant Church has 16,000 clergy; while of the Roman Catholics there are 5 archbishops, 20 bishoprics, 3 vicariates-apostolic, 20,000 priests, and 800 monasteries. The Jesuits were excluded from the territory of the empire July 4, 1872.

In 1871 the population of the empire, exclusive of 80,000 foreign residents, comprised 37,820,000 Germans, 2,450,000 Poles, 140,000 Wends, 50,000 Czechs, 150,000 Lithuanians and Kurlanders, 150,000 Danes, and 220,000 French and Walloons.

History.—On the breaking up of the Roman empire, the Germanic tribe of the Franks (q. v.) founded a kingdom partly in N. Gaul and partly in what is now G., which was ruled by the Merwing princes. The Franks who remained by the Rhine, however, became severed from the

Frankish settlers among the Gallo-Romans, and in the middle of the 8th c. the purely Germanic kingdom of Austrasia held sway under the Karolings (q. v.) over the rival Gallicised kingdom of Neustria (see FRANCE, HISTORY OF). When Karl the Great was made Emperor of the Romans, the Karoling power was at its highest, Karl ruling over the lands from the Eider to the Tiber, and from Hungary to the Pyrenees. But this great Teutonic empire was dismembered by the treaty of Verdun (843), when the kingdom of the W. Franks or France was separated from the kingdom of the E. Franks or G. These realms were reunited under Karl the Fat, and permanently severed on his death in 887. The House of Capet now became kings of N. France, while the Karolings ruled E. Franconia, which corresponds loosely to modern G., until 911, when the line became extinct. The most lasting work of Karl the Great was to give something of unity to G., but the land still preserved old tribal distinctions in the great dukedoms of Saxony, Franconia, Suabia, Lotharingia, and Bavaria. Konrad, Duke of Franconia, was chosen king by the great nobles, who now seized the right of electing the monarch, and on Konrad's death in 918, Heinrich the Fowler, Duke of Saxony, was appointed his successor. Heinrich, the founder of the Saxon dynasty, warred victoriously against the Magyars, and strengthened the royal power against feudalism. His son, Otto the Great, again united the offices King of G. and Emperor of Rome. Up to this time the imperial throne had not been specially connected with any kingdom, having been in theory open to all Christian freemen, and having been filled by rulers of various countries. Now, however, it was acknowledged that the King of G. had a right to be crowned King of Italy at Milan and Emperor at Rome. Under Otto's successors the Popes shook off their old dependence on the Empire, and the royal power sank, while the feudal and ecclesiastical power increased, but Konrad I. of the Franconian line (1024–1039) revived the kingly authority, enforced order, and checked the Papal pretensions. Heinrich III. (1039–1056) continued to increase the extent of the royal power, but under his successor, Heinrich IV., strife and confusion ensued, Pope Hildebrand opposing Heinrich with unflinching determination, and stirring up the feudal barons to revolt. In 1137 the first of the Hohenstaufens, Konrad III., became king, and in the reign of his son, Friedrich Barbarossa (1152–92), Italian politics began greatly to influence German history. The Guelphs and Ghibellines (q. v.) had now arisen, and the emperors were called on for help by the small Guelphic commonwealths. The evil effects of the imperial dignity on G. now became manifold. It led the emperors to interfere in Italian politics, to waste their strength on fruitless Italian expeditions, and neglect their own and their people's interest; it drew them into strife with the Popes, who inflamed the German barons against them at home. After the death of the great Friedrich II. (1212–50), whose reign was mainly occupied in warring with the Pope, the imperial power sank, succeeding emperors having almost no direct influence beyond G., where their power was steadily shrinking. Meanwhile numerous Free Cities (q. v.) had arisen; the commerce of G. had greatly increased; and, especially under the Hohenstaufens, many serfs had won liberty by the Crusades and by flying to the towns. Unfortunately there was little advance in national unity and constitutional freedom. The Diet, a faint shadow of the old Teutonic assemblies, was an aristocratic, not a national, body. While in France feudalism destroyed the old Teutonic institutions, and so cleared away all constitutional checks on monarchy, in G. feudalism changed the old institutions into oligarchical tools for breaking up the country and lessening the royal power. In the 12th c. the right of choosing the king was confined to the seven chief princes called the Electors (q. v.). On the death of Friedrich II.'s son, Konrad IV., in 1254, the line of Hohenstaufen emperors ended. Up to this time the Empire had been partly elective, partly hereditary. Henceforth a time follows in which birth is almost ignored, until the middle of the 15th c., when Austrian princes began to be regularly chosen. From 1254 G. had no actual king until 1273, this period, one of terrible suffering and anarchy, being known as the *Great Interregnum*. In 1273 Rudolf, Count of Hapsburg in Suabia, was made king. He was a brave, well-meaning, and able ruler, and, aided by the Church and people, curbed the robber-barons and vindicated the civil power. Rudolf's son, Albrecht, becoming Duke of Austria, the electors, jealous of Austria, made Heinrich, Count of Lützelburg or Luxembourg, king. He was the first German monarch crowned emperor since Friedrich II. After Heinrich's death civil war raged between Ludwig of Bavaria and Friedrich Duke of Austria, the towns mostly supporting the former, and the nobles the latter. Ludwig finally became king, and was succeeded in 1347 by Karl IV., who in 1356 published the *Golden Bull* (q. v.). The reign of his son Wenceslaus (1378–1410) was marked by the beginning of the Hussite movement, and by the fierce struggles between the towns and the nobles, both parties uniting in leagues or confederations. The Femgerichte (q. v.) now grew vastly in power, and the Hansa League was very thriving. In 1410 Siegmund, King of Hungary, was made king, and in 1433 emperor, his reign being the beginning of the particular connection between the empire and Hungary which afterwards had a grave influence on German history. Siegmund strove to reform the Church, and died in 1437. The emperor's office had now become an almost empty honour, and it was necessary to elect a prince to it who held power independent of his imperial position. The emperor was no longer recognised as the overlord of Europe; and the Empire was held from the time of Albrecht II., Duke of Austria (1437–38), to 1806 by princes of the House of Austria. The last emperor crowned at Rome was Friedrich III. (1440–93). His son, Maximilian, did something to further justice by dividing G. into circles, and appointing the special court known as the *Imperial Chamber*. Meanwhile feudalism and the system of chivalry were vanishing, the princes and great nobles having after the introduction of gunpowder begun to carry on war with mercenaries (*Landsknechte*), instead of exacting military service from their vassals. During Maximilian's reign the Reformation began to agitate G., and in the time of Maximilian's successor, Karl V. (1519–56), spread rapidly through the land. (See REFORMATION.) On the death of Karl V. his empire, which included G., Austro-Hungary, Spain, Holland, Belgium, and parts of Italy, was broken up, and G. went to Karl's brother, Ferdinand I. (1556–64). The religious differences finally resulted in the Thirty Years' War (q. v.), which lasted from 1618 to 1648. It was carried on between the Protestant princes of G. and the Emperor Ferdinand II. The emperor at first seemed about to crush the German Protestants, but the victories of Gustavus Adolphus restored the fortunes of the former; and the subsequent espousal of their cause by France changed a religious into a political struggle, which was ended by the peace of Westphalia in 1648. G. was terribly enfeebled by the long strife. Half, if not more, of her people had perished in the intestine fighting. The land was almost untilled, and many of the towns were in ruins. All national feeling seemed dead, the differences of creed which arose at the Reformation tending strongly to split up the country. Henceforth, until recently, G. was merely a loose cluster of petty states ruled by despots or oligarchs over whom the emperor had no control, while the Diet of the Confederation which sat permanently after 1654, and nominally held the rights formerly belonging to the emperor, of making war and peace, passing laws, &c., was never powerful, and became notorious for its formal trifling. After the war G. continued to sink into degradation. The Diets of the various states were mostly abolished; the Free Cities, no longer united in leagues, lost their old political influence, while many of them fell into the hands of the small princes, who pursued a purely unnational policy, and aped the luxury and sensuality of the French court. Louis XIV. of France, taking advantage of the weakness of G., in a time of peace, in 1687, seized the free city of Strassburg, and in 1689 ravaged the Palatinate. The German princes, instead of uniting together, partly sided with Louis, who had more power in G. than belonged to the emperor. Towards the end of the 17th c. Prussia began to rise under the Electors of Brandenburg, and in 1701 was declared a kingdom independent of Poland. Friedrich Wilhelm I. and Friedrich the Great built up the power of Prussia by able government, thrift, and thorough military organisation, while the other German princes wasted the strength of their territories in shameful prodigality and selfish jealousies. After the Seven Years' War (1756–63) (see SEVEN YEARS' WAR and FRIEDRICH II.), Prussia and Austria remained rivals for the mastery over the various German states. In 1777 the Emperor Joseph II. sought to annex Bavaria, but was hindered by Friedrich the Great. Joseph was succeeded by his brother Leopold, who was followed by Franz II., the last of the Austro-Germanic emperors. Austria and Prussia united against France at the time of the French Revolution, and were both humbled in the wars of Napoleon. By the peace of Luneville (1801) all G. left of the Rhine was joined to France; and after Prussia and Saxony were crushed at Jena (1806), the states of Southern G. were united into the Confederation of the Rhine (q. v.), under Napoleon's protectorate. A kingdom of Westphalia was set up under Jerome Bonaparte, and finally North-Western G., with the free cities Lübeck, Bremen, and Hamburg, was added to France. In 1813 came the great rising of G. against Napoleon, and after the battle of Leipsic the Congress of Vienna (1814–15) made a new settlement of German affairs. The boundaries of the states were all shifted; many of the smaller states were absorbed; the kingdoms of Würtemberg, Saxony, and Bavaria, which Bonaparte had created, were suffered to remain; but much of Saxony was added to Prussia. No strong federal principle allied the petty states, for the supremacy over which Prussia and Austria soon reappeared as rivals. The princes broke their promises to form constitutional governments, and until 1848 Metternich, the Austrian Minister, held the chief authority throughout G. There had arisen, however, a fervent national sentiment, an eager wish for union and progress, which was strengthened by Prussia establishing the commercial union of the *Zollverein* in 1833. The members of this union, of which Prussia was the centre, and which was joined by most of the German states, agreed not to levy duties on merchandise passing from one state to the other, an arrangement which did much to prepare the country for political unity. After the revolutions of 1848 in Prussia, Austria, and other states, a fruitless effort was made to form a German empire and a great German parliament. G. seemed about to relapse into her old condition, when, in 1863, Bismarck, the Prussian Minister, inaugurated a new policy, by wrenching Slesvig and Holstein from Denmark. In 1866 war broke out between Prussia and Austria, and the Austrians, utterly beaten at Sadowa (1866), were forced by the peace of Prague to withdraw altogether from the German confederation. The North German states were then formed into the North German Confederation under the presidency of Prussia. Still the union of G. seemed doubtful, until it was unexpectedly brought about by the Franco-Prussian war, which was provoked by Napoleon III.'s jealousy of Prussia and hope of redeeming his lost popularity. The French emperor also expected that the S. of G. would aid him or remain neutral, but all G. supported Prussia. On August 4, 1870, the first battle was fought at Weissenburg, where the French were driven back. Then the Germans, after winning the victories of Wörth and Saarbrücken (August 6), advanced with about a million of men to the Moselle, and defeated the French at Vionville and Gravelotte. Bazaine, who had taken chief command of the French, was now hemmed in at Metz, and Macmahon, while marching to relieve him, was beaten at Beaumont, after which the French were driven from different sides into Sedan, where Napoleon III. surrendered with 90,000 men, September 4, 1870. On September 5 the Germans began the siege of Paris, the French vainly striving to break their lines. The army of the Loire was now formed, and Faidherbe raised a force in the N. But Bazaine surrendered with 180,000 men on October 17, and the army of the Loire was driven back from Paris, and divided into two divisions under Generals Chanzy and Bourbaki. Chanzy's force was soon dispersed, but Bourbaki marched towards Southern G., which he seriously endangered, until he was checked at Hericault, and finally forced across the Swiss frontier on February 1. On January 18, 1871, King Wilhelm was proclaimed, at Versailles, German Emperor, the North German Confederation having been changed into the German Confederation. Faidherbe, who had struggled with great ability, was beaten at St. Quentin on January 19, and on January 28 Paris surrendered. The preliminaries of peace were signed on February 26, and on May 16, the peace of Frankfurt was concluded, by which France ceded Alsace and Lorraine, and agreed to pay 5,000,000,000 francs. The present German empire includes twenty-five states, which retain considerable local privileges. The executive power rests with the emperor, the legislative with the Diet and Federal Council. The present empire is not a revival of the Holy Roman Empire. That was a medieval restoration of the Roman Empire, while the new imperial office partly represents the old dignity of 'King of the Germans.'

See Menzel's *Geschichte der Deutschen* (8 vols. 1815–22), and *Neuere Geschichte der Deutschen* (12 vols. 1826–48); Luden's *Geschichte des Deutschen Volks* (12 vols. 1825–39); Wenzel's *Geschichte der Deutschen* (5 vols. 1855); Mayer's *Deutsche Geschichte* (2 vols. 1858); and Giesebrecht's *Geschichte der Deutschen Kaiserzeit* (1862–68).

German Language and Literature. *Language.*—The G. L. is a branch of the Teutonic family of Aryan speech, as is illustrated by the Germans still calling it *Deut-sch*, the name *German* having probably been given by some Continental Celts. Greek and Latin authors supply incidentally the only specimens of Germanic speech preserved from heathen times; but after the diffusion of Christianity several of its dialects gradually began to be moulded through popular translations by the clergy of prayers and ecclesiastical formularies. At least 300 years earlier than any of these MSS. is the unique translation of the Bible into Gothic by Bishop Ulfilas (318–388), highly interesting as affording the groundwork of the history of the language. Already in the 7th c. we find the Germanic dialects divided into two main sections, the Upper or High German, and the Lower or Plain (*Platt*) German, separated then as (generally speaking) now by a line roughly drawn from the mouths of the Ruhr and Sieg to the Harz, the High German being subdivided into the pure Upper German (or South German) and the Middle German (to which belong the Upper Saxon and Franconian dialects); and the Plain or Low German (spoken in the western part of the N. German lowland, *i.e.*, N. of a line drawn through Aachen, Bonn, Cassel, Nordhausen, and Wittenberg) into the Lower Saxon (in Holstein, Mecklenburg, and part of Brandenburg and Pomerania) and the Westphalian.

High German eventually prevailed over Low German, and in the form known as *Old High German* flourished for six centuries, from the foundation of the Frankish dominion (about 500 A.D.) to the beginning of the Crusades (1096), a period in which, Latin being the recognised medium of the court, the clergy, and the learned and cultured classes generally, the native language was confined to popular religious literature and some popular songs. The influence of the Crusades, of the spirit of chivalry, and of the new relation to Italy, &c., resulted in greater breadth and freshness of ideas, and created a new era in the national mind, which found fitting expression in a great chivalrous court poetry in *Middle High German*, a form at first used by the nobles and princes, but gradually by the people as well. As this poetry soon diffused itself throughout Germany, it speedily lost all provincial peculiarities, till at last the Swabian dialect, used not only at court, but by the best and most poets, predominated over the rest, and was employed by writers of Low German or even wholly alien origin. But as literature and art sank with the fall of the House of Hohenstaufen, so also the language received much injury. The dialects again gained the mastery; alike in speech and writing arose a bewildering confusion, until at length the Upper Saxon dialect rose above the rest, and won a greater than common diffusion. This Luther employed in his translation of the Bible and in his other writings, and through him the *New High German* form by degrees extended its dominion over all German literature; being destined, despite foreign corruption (against which Opitz, &c., fought persistently) and the well-nigh ruinous influence of the Thirty Years' War, to become the final exponent of all writers and men of culture. Gottsched laid the foundation for a coherent treatment of the grammar, and the G. L. came constantly nearer to its highest development and polish in the hands of Klopstock, Lessing, Wieland, Herder, Goethe, Schiller, Winckelmann, Kant, &c. The influence of translations, in which Voss was the first master, as well as of the study of the writings transmitted from antiquity and the middle ages, was very marked. Benecke was the founder of such philological study, but it received its greatest impetus from the labours of the brothers Grimm in early Germanic language and history, and the philological criticism of *Old High German* by Lachmann, the discoverer of its metrical laws. The most noteworthy followers of these have been Gabelenz, Schulz, Diefenbach, Graff, Schmeller, and Wackernagel. The grammar has also been treated philosophically by Becker (K. F.), Herling, &c. See Wackernagel's *Deutsches Lesebuch;* Pischon's *Denkmäler der Deutschen Sprache* (1838–51); *Germaniens Völkerstimmen* (1843, *et seq.*), by Firmenich; Bernhardi's *Sprachkarte von Deutschland* (2d ed. 1849); Grimm's *Geschichte der Deutschen Sprache*, and *Deutsche Grammatik* (Göttingen, 1819–40); Bopp's *Comparative Grammar;* Bessel, *Ueber das Leben des Ulfila;* Max Müller's *Science of Language* (1861–64); Helfenstein's *Comparative Grammar of the Teutonic Languages* (Lond. 1870); Schleicher's *Compendium der vergleichenden Grammatik der Indo-germanischen Sprachen* (Weimar, 1866); Whitney *On Language* (3d ed. 1870).

Literature.—I. *From the Earliest Times to* 1200.—Unlike English and French literature, G. L. has had no continuous growth, and its chief works belong to very recent times. The wild pagan war-songs and mythic tales died out after the time of Karl the Great under the influence of Christianity, and the brood of Latin hymns, prayers, and paraphrases which took their place had no literary vitality. Of the pieces on Christian subjects, the best was *Heliand*, written in Low German in the 9th c. by an Old-Saxon poet. Except Eginhard (q. v.), the biographer of Karl the Great, there was scarcely a German author of European reputation before the 13th c., the period of the *Minnesänger* ('love-singers'). II. 1200–1300.—The *Minnesänger* poetry was awakened partly by the *Troubadour* and *Trouvère* songs and epics, partly by the influence of the Crusades, and centred in the brilliant Suabian court. Among its chief writers were Walther von der Vogelweide (q. v.), Wolfram von Eschenbach (q. v.), Gottfried von Strassburg (q. v.), Konrad von Würzburg (q. v.), Hartmann von Aue, Heinrich von Ofterdingen, Hugo von Trimberg, &c. They wrote lyrics, generally musical and joyous, though somewhat monotonous in their praise of love, chivalry, and the spring-time, and long ballads resembling the *Chansons de Geste*, celebrating the deeds of Arthur, Roland, and Charlemagne. Meanwhile the old heathen and heroic poetry lingered in popular ballads sung by wandering minstrels; and in this period a number of these old lays were gathered together into the *Heldenbuch* ('Book of Heroes') and the great national epic of the *Nibelungenlied* (q. v.). Besides the gay, sentimental, knightly poetry, there arose a comic, mocking literature, best represented by *Reinaert de Vos*, the famous satirical allegory translated from Flemish into German in the 12th c. III. 1300–1600.—The *Minnesänger* poetry declined on the fall of the Hohenstaufen dynasty, which had fostered it with genial patronage, and died out in the 14th c. Meanwhile the burgher class had been rising in power, and a new literature of stories, fables, and satires, sometimes blunt and clumsy, sometimes coarsely pungent, and essentially *bourgeois* in style and sentiment, was created. The comic drama began to develop from the medieval theatre (see MIRACLE PLAYS and DRAMA), and in the 15th c. the great schools of the *Meistersänger* were formed. The *Meistersänger* were wholly popular, as the *Minnesänger* were purely aristocratic poets. They were mostly artisans who sang the praises of their various crafts, and united into Guilds (q. v.) to compose and recite verses. The most famous of the *Meistersänger* was Hans Sachs (q. v.), and the most famous guilds were in Ulm, Mainz, and Nürnberg. In the 15th c. the Renaissance learning entered Germany, and the Greek and Latin classics began to be studied. A new freedom of thought followed on the studies of the humanists, and spread down to the people, who delighted in satirical and facetious tales, such as *Eulenspiegel* (q. v.), and the *Narrenschiff* of Brandt (q. v.). The chief writers of the early Reformation times were Luther (q. v.), Ulrich von Hutten (q. v.), and Fischart (q. v.). Other authors of the 16th c. are Schede, Knaust, Ringwaldt, Belitz, Metzger, Hager, and Denaisius. IV. 1600–1700.—The 17th c. was the darkest period in G. L. Poetry withered amid the dull dogmatic strifes that followed the Reformation, and is found almost solely in the religious hymns. At length literature was for a time almost extinguished by the Thirty Years' War. Martin Opitz (q. v.) established a new theory of German verse, and founded the First Silesian school, which included Flemming (q. v.), Gryphius, Van Zesen, and Gerhardt (q. v.), and aided to polish and purify the speech, but which by its slavish imitation of the French *classical* writers sank into empty affectation. A reaction against this Gallicising tendency began with the Second Silesian school, which, led by Hofmann von Hofmannswaldau and Kaspar von Löwenstein, substituted frantic bombast and exciting plots for the insipidities of Opitz's followers. V. 1700–1770.—During the first half of the 18th c. the language became more copious and nervous, and English began to displace French authors as literary models. Gottsched (q. v.) assailed the sterile mimicry of the Second Silesian school; and with Klopstock (q. v.), Lessing (q. v.), and Wieland (q. v.) a national imaginative literature arose, not yet, however, fully emancipated from the 18th c. classical style. Among other writers of this period were Haller (q. v.), Bodmer (q. v.), Breitinger, Gessner (q. v.), Gellert (q. v.), Lichtwer, Gärtner, Giseke, Kreuz, Weisse, Hagedorn (q. v.), Kramer, Gleim, Ramler, &c. Lessing inaugurated a national drama; Klopstock taught the Germans to sing the praises of the 'Fatherland;' Wieland introduced a fresh and natural gaiety and lightness of thought and style; and Winckelmann (q. v.) began a new era in the history of æsthetic criticism, and disclosed the true nature of Greek art and culture. VI. 1770 *to the Present Time.*—This is by far the richest period of G. L. alike for the number, beauty, and originality of the works which belong to it. Henceforth German writers, instead of wrangling over the respective merits of French or English writers, and feebly aping French polish and clearness, began to give voice to their nation's sentiments, to create an impassioned, unimitative literature. This last period may be subdivided. From 1770 to 1794 is the *Sturm-und-Drang Periode* ('Storm-and-Pressure Period'). A wildly violent reaction arose against the old 'classical' schools, and poems full of strained rhapsodies and furious passion, but foreshadowing a more free and varied literature, were written by Stolberg (q. v.), Heinse, Müller (q. v.), Klinger (q. v.), Lenz (q. v.), Bürger (q. v.), and Goethe (q. v.). But this period, with its pathos and weirdness, its stormy novelties and grotesque rant, passed swiftly away; G. L., guided to new and lofty issues by Goethe and Schiller (q. v.), became purified from the *Sturm-und-Drang* excesses, and along with vivid energy and passion revealed an unlooked-for beauty of execution. About this time the German Romantic school arose, a school comprising poets, critics, and historians, and of which the leading features were a somewhat exaggerated love for nature, an intense fondness for medieval themes, an enthusiastic worship of Shakespeare, a sentimental and mistaken admiration of the middle ages, and a general tendency to a glowing, dreamy, and fantastic style. To the earlier Romantic school belonged the brothers Schlegel (q. v.), Wackenroder, Tieck (q. v.), and Novalis (q. v.). After 1813 the War of Liberation called forth a number of patriotic poets, as Körner (q. v.), Rückert (q. v.), and Schenkendorf (q. v.); but the Romantic school, swayed by medieval predilections, began to show reactionary tendencies in politics. The later Romantic school was devoted mainly to weird, fanciful, and florid prose romances, and included Fouqué (q. v.), Arnim (q. v.), Brentano (q. v.), Eichendorff, and Hoffmann (q. v.). The first half of the 9th c. is the golden age of G. L. The masterpieces of Goethe and Schiller moulded the national taste anew, and a magnificent poetry was created, wonderfully many-sided, profound, and passionate, expressing with almost unequalled subtlety and power the philosophical questions and political aspirations characteristic of modern times, and especially remarkable for the number and beauty of its lyrics. These have not in general the sunny blitheness of the old *Minnelieder;* they are mostly steeped in pathos, and clouded by mystical suggestions, and have an endless charm in the melodious flow and haunting melancholy of their rhythm. Goethe united the variety, glowing colour, and deep subjectivity of the Romantic with the breadth, repose, and transparency of the Classical spirit, but, notwithstanding his vast influence, both the Romantic and Classical tendencies have recently given place to a strong realistic movement, which in a measure discards the Classical polish as well as the whimsical Romantic fervours. Alongside of the magnificent poetry of the 19th c. a great prose literature grew up, represented in history by Müller (q. v.), Schlosser (q. v.), Ranke (q. v.), Niebuhr (q. v.), Menzel (q. v.), Dahlmann (q. v.), Droysen (q. v.), Gervinus (q. v.), Mommsen (q. v.), &c.; in philological criticism, by Bopp (q. v.), the brothers Grimm (q. v.), Adelung (q. v.), the Humboldts (q. v.), Wolf (q. v.), Hermann (q. v.), Heeren (q. v.), Heyse (q. v.), Steinthal (q. v.); in theology, by Schleiermacher (q. v.), Neander (q. v.), Bunsen (q. v.); in philosophy, by Kant (q. v.), Fichte (q. v.), Jacobi (q. v.), Hegel (q. v.), Schopenhauer (q. v.), Feuerbach (q. v.), Stahl (q. v.), &c. In fiction the chief names are Richter (q. v.), Börne, Hoffmann (q. v.), Mundt, Sternberg, Freytag (q. v.), Gerstäcker (q. v.), Heyse (q. v.), Grimm (q. v.), Auerbach (q. v.), &c. The foremost poets, not yet mentioned, from 1813 to the present time are, in lyrical poetry, Heine (q. v.), next to Goethe perhaps the greater German lyrist, Platen (q. v.), Spitta, Uhland (q. v.), Herwegh, Geibel (q. v.), Grün, Lenau, Schneckenburger, Kinkel, Hartmann, and Gottschall; in the drama, Halm, Hebbel (q. v.), Freytag, Gutzkow, Ludwig. An important element in G. L. is the innumerable number of *Volkslieder*, or popular songs by unknown authors, which are mostly instinct with the tenderest melody and a strange old-world charm, couched in exquisitely simple language, and, like the early *Minnelieder*, bright with fresh vivid descriptive touches. See Gervinus' *Geschichte der Deutschen Dichtung* (5th ed. 1871); Koberstein's *Grundriss der Deutschen National-Lit.* (1845); Vilmar's *Vorlesungen über die Gesch. der Deutschen National-Lit.* (4th ed. 1851); Gruppe's *Leben und Werke Deutscher Dichter* (1861-68); Schmidt's *Gesch. der Deutschen Lit.* (5th ed. 1865-67); Gottschall's *Die Deutsche National-Lit.* (3d ed. 1871).

Ger'men, or **O'vary,** the name for the lower portion of the Pistil (q. v.), or central part of a flower, which ultimately becomes the Fruit (q. v.). It contains the young seeds or Ovules (q. v.). The G. is said to be *superior* when the other parts of the flower are placed below it, as in the lily; and *inferior* when the parts are placed above, as in the gooseberry.

Ger'mersheim, a town of Rhenish Bavaria, at the confluence of the Queich and the Rhine, 8 miles S.S.W. of Speyer. It has some trade in corn, hemp, flax, &c. Pop. 10,180. G. was originally a Roman fortress and station. A 'burg' was built here by Konrad II., but the place first emerges as a town in the time of Rudolf of Hapsburg, who died at G. in 1291.

Germina'tion, the term applied to the sprouting or beginning of growth of the young plant in the seed. Certain conditions are essential to G., such as moisture, heat, and air. Darkness is also favourable. Internal changes take place in seeds during G. Starch is converted into dextrine or sugar by oxidation, and diastase is developed. During these changes considerable heat is evolved, and substances which were before insoluble become soluble. The seed becomes swollen; the embryo enlarges, ruptures the integument, and protrudes; and the growth of a new plant commences.

Germ Theory of Disease. Various theories have been adduced regarding the mode by which diseases of the contagious and infectious type gain entrance to the body and produce their pathological effects. Two centuries ago the celebrated Robert Boyle said 'that he that thoroughly understands the nature of ferments and fermentations shall probably be much better able than he that ignores them to give a fair account of divers phenomena of several diseases (as well fevers as others), which will perhaps be never properly understood without an insight into the doctrine of fermentation.' The prediction of Boyle has been verified; for the recent exhaustive observations, by aid of the microscope, of the process of Fermentation (q. v.) have been the foundation of the G. T. of D. The air contains numberless germs that act as ferments when brought into contact with a medium suitable for their development, some of them producing alcohol, some acid, and others putrefaction. When pure meat is exposed to the air, it becomes, after cooling, either sour or putrid, and on microscopic examination, that which is sour is found to be swarming with organisms called *vibrio*, and that which is putrid with *bactria*. Reasoning from such data, Professor Lister of Edinburgh inferred that the putrefaction of wounds might be arrested by the destruction of the *bactria*, and to effect this, he introduced the antiseptic system of treating wounds, the most important advance ever made in surgery. The most striking analogy between a *contagium* and a ferment consists in the power of self-multiplication possessed and exercised by both; for a particle of *contagium* may spread through the body and be so multiplied as to decimate whole populations. In 1850 MM. Davainne and Rayer made observations on the blood of animals which died of splenic fever, and discovered small microscopic organisms resembling transparent rods. Some time afterwards a German physician, Koch, studied the habits of these organisms, and his observations were confirmed by the celebrated naturalist Cohn of Breslau. The rod-like organisms, when placed in a drop of the aqueous humour of the eye, began to lengthen, and in a few hours they formed filaments a hundred times the length of the original rods. Within the filaments little dots appeared, gradually becoming more and more numerous and distinct until the whole organism was studded with them, being converted into a long row of seeds or spores. Koch proved, by actual experiment, that the spores as distinguished from the rods constituted the *contagium* of splenic fever. According to the G. T. of D. many diseases, but particularly those of the contagious and infectious class, depend for their development on similar principles, and each specific disease has its peculiar germ or seed. The nature of the morbid action depending on the enormous multiplication of the germs within the body is merely in process of investigation; but as regards specific fevers it is probable that the characteristic features of the febrile state are due to the growth of the germs or contagious particles, and that the disturbance to which they give rise results from the appropriation by them of the essential constituents of the blood, rather than from any special action as poisons which they may possess. See *The Germ Theory applied to the Explanation of the Phenomena of Disease: The Specific Fevers*, by T. Maclagan, M.D. (Lond. 1876, Macmillan & Co.).

Gerôme, Jean-Léon, a great French painter, was born 11th May 1824, at Vésoul, Haute-Saône, went to Paris and became a pupil of Paul Delaroche and a student at the Fine Arts School in 1841. He travelled in Italy with Delaroche in 1844, and studied and sketched in Turkey and Egypt from 1853 to 1856. Since 1847 G. has produced an immense number of pictures, some of which, as the 'Gladiators before Cæsar—*Ave, Cæsar Imperator, morituri te salutant*,' and the 'Death of the Vanquished Gladiator—*Pollice Verso*,' are almost too absorbing and painful in the character of the interest they excite. Other great works are 'Bacchus et l'Amour' (1848); 'Le Siècle d'Auguste et la Naissance de Jésus Christ' (1855); 'La Sortie du Bal Masqué,' and 'Memnon et Sesostris' (1857); portrait of Rachel, and 'Phryne devant le Tribunal' (1861); 'Louis XIV. et Molière,' 'Cleopatra et Cæsar (1866); 'La Mort de Cæsar (1867); 'Promenade de Harem' (1869); and the wall painting 'La Peste à Marseille' in one of the chapels of Sainte-Séverin. G. is well known through photography. His works, often sombre and even sinister, are always highly imaginative and instinct with a sensuous dramatic life. He strikingly combines the leading traits of the Romantic and Classical schools.

Gero'na, a city in the N.E. of Spain, capital of the province of the same name, 60 miles N.N.E. of Barcelona, with which it is connected by rail. It stands on the Ter, near the foot of the Gavarras Mountains. Its streets are narrow and picturesque; it has a large collegiate church; and its Gothic cathedral, begun in 1316, is one of the finest and most original of medieval buildings. G. is enclosed by massive walls, and defended by four forts. There is some trade in soap, leather, cotton, and wool. Pop. 14,615. G., the *Gerunda* of the Romans, was made the see of a bishop in 786, was the residence of the Aragonese kings, and is said to have sustained twenty-eight sieges, the most famous being that of 1809, when it held out for above seven months against the French.

Gers, a department in the S.W. of France, is named from the river G., which traverses it from N. to S., and is bounded N. by Lot-et-Garonne; S. by the Hautes and Basses Pyrénées; E. by Haute-Garonne and Tarn-et-Garonne; and W. by Landes. Area, 2425 sq. miles; pop. (1872) 284,717. It is entered in the S. by six parallel offshoots of the Pyrenees, but extends in a flat fertile plain in the N., watered by the G., Adour, L'Osse, Baise, Arratz, Gimone, and Save. There are several forests. Wine is produced to the extent of 20,000,000 francs, but is mainly used for making Armagnac brandy, which is exported largely to N. America. At the last census G. had 298,000 sheep, 145,000 cattle, 56,000 pigs, and 6000 mules, reared mainly for the Spanish markets. Auch is the capital, and the terminus of the Agen-à-Auch Railway. The patois of G. is a mixture of Gascon and the Langue d'Oc.

Ger'son, Jean Charlier de, a great medieval theologian, was born at Gerson in the diocese of Rheims, December 14, 1363, and studied at Paris University, of which, in 1395, he became chancellor. He earned a wide fame as a scholar and the surname 'Most Christian Doctor,' and laboured sedulously to end the Great Schism, urging that the two (and afterwards the three) rival Popes should resign. In 1414 he figured in the Council of Constance, and sullied his character by advocating the burning of John Huss. A warm champion of the Orleanist or national party in France, G. denounced the Duke of Burgundy for the murder of the Duke of Orleans, and the resentment of the great noble forced him to quit France and wander as a pilgrim over Germany. He was kindly welcomed by the Duke of Austria, and spent some time at Vienna, returning to France after Burgundy's death, in 1419. G. spent his last years within the Celestine monastery at Lyon, where he died, July 12, 1429. He was a Nominalist and strictly orthodox theologian, but denounced the worldliness and license of the Popes. Among his works are *De Consolatione Theologiæ*, partly in verse, and imitated from the *De Consolatione Philosophiæ* of Boethius; *De Unitate Ecclesiæ; Contra Sectam Flagellatorum; De Probatione Spirituum*. The *De Imitatione Christi* has been ascribed to G., but is the work of Thomas à Kempis. See Schmidt's *Essai sur G.* (Strasb. 1839), and Thomassy's *Jean G.* (Par. 1843).

Ger'stäcker, Friedrich, a German author, born at Hamburg, May 16, 1816. He emigrated to America in 1837, and after a chequered life as a sailor, hunter, trapper, and woodcutter, returned to Germany in 1843, and published an account of his wanderings in 1844. He went round the world in 1849-52; travelled across S. America in 1860-61; journeyed in Africa with Duke Ernst of Gotha in 1862; visited Central America in 1863; and died at Vienna, May 31, 1872. Among his works are *Die Flusspiraten des Mississippi* (3 vols. Leips. 1848); *Amerik. Wald- und Strombilder* (2 vols. Leips. 1849); *Reisen* (5 vols. Stutt. 1853-54); *Nach Amerika* (1855); *Neue Reisen* (1868); &c. His writings have won great popularity, and several of them have been translated into French and English. G.'s travels give entertaining accounts of his varied roving career, and graphic pictures of Transatlantic life and scenery. His fictions are fresh, exciting, and realistic.

Ger'und (Lat. *gero*, 'I carry on') is a part of the Latin verb which expresses a *state* or *action* in a general way. It is a verbal noun possessing the power of governing the same case as its verb. It is used only in the oblique cases, the nominative being supplied by the infinitive, thus—nom. *amare*, 'loving;' gen. *amandi*, 'of loving;' dat. *amando*, 'to loving;' acc. *amandum*, 'loving;' abl. *amando*, 'with loving.' It has no plural.—The **Gerundive**, on the other hand, is a passive participle, denoting that something is *to be done*, and generally implying possibility, expediency, or necessity, as *amandus, a, um*, 'to be loved, deserving or requiring to be loved.'

Ger'vas, or **Gervao**, a Brazilian name for *Stachytarpha et Jamaicensis*, a shrubby aromatic plant belonging to the natural order *Verbenaceæ*. Its leaves have been extensively used for adulterating tea.

Ger'vase of Til'bury, an English chronicler of the 13th c., was born at Tilbury in Essex, studied in France and Germany, and won the favour of the Emperor Otho IV., who made him marshal of the kingdom of Arles, and to whom he dedicated his *Otia Imperialia*. G. died about 1218. He is said to have been a nephew of Henry II. of England. His chief work, *Otia Imperialia*, deals with the history of the world from the creation to the rule of the Norman kings in England. It is, according to Morley (*English Literature*, p. 71), 'full of learning borrowed without acknowledgment from Petrus Comestor;' but is interesting as a storehouse of popular legends belonging to England and the country round Arles. G. also wrote *Illustrationes Galfridi Monemuthensis*, and *De Origine Burgundiorum*. See Wright's *Biographia Brit. Liter.*, vol. ii.

Gervi'nus, Georg Gottfried, a very eminent German historian and literary critic, born at Darmstadt, 20th May 1805. Though designed for a mercantile life, the influence of Schlosser on him while a student at Heidelberg attached G. to the science of history. The merit of historical sketches published by G. in 1833 secured him a call to the University of Göttingen. He was one of the seven professors who were, in 1837, deposed and banished for their protest against the change in the Hanoverian constitution. In 1844 he was called to Heidelberg, and in 1847 founded the *Deutsche Zeitung* in the interests of constitutional freedom. He was a member of the Frankfurt National Assembly, but soon withdrew from all political activity in disgust at the course of events. He died at Heidelberg, 18th March 1871. G.'s most important writings are the great work known since its fourth edition as *Geschichte der Deutschen Dichtung* (1st ed. 1835-42; 5th ed. 1870); the *Grundzüge der Historik* (1837); *Shakespeare* (4 vols. 1849-52; 3d ed. 2 vols. 1862), the *Geschichte des 19ten Jahrhunderts* (8 vols. 1855-66). His *Hinterlassene Schriften* appeared in 1871. G. treated history not as a mere series of events, but as an organic growth; and in poetry he saw an outcome of the social and political conditions of the period which gave it birth. See the Lives of G. by Gosche (Leips. 1871) and by Lehmann (1871).

Gese'nius, Friedrich Heinrich Wilhelm, an Orientalist and an exegete whose labours form an era in the history of Semitic philology, was born at Nordhausen, 3d February 1785. In 1811 he became a professor at Halle, where he taught till his death, 23d October 1842. G.'s linguistic-critical method of interpreting the Old Testament produced in his hands rationalistic results, which excited much opposition from the orthodox party. Of his works, the best are the universally-known lexicon, the *Hebr. und Chaldäisches Handwörterbuch* (1810-12, 6th ed. 1863; Latin translation, 1846; English translation by Robinson and by Tregelles); *Hebr. Elementarbuch*, consisting of a grammar (1813; 18th ed. by Rödiger, 1857; also familiar to all English students as translated by Davies), and a reading-book; a more elaborate grammar in 1817; and the *Thesaurus Philologico-Criticus Linguæ Hebr. et Chald.* (completed by Rödiger, 1829-58); besides a commentary on Isaiah, a history of the Hebrew languages, and treatises on Samaritan theology and Phœnician inscriptions.

Ges'ner, Johann Matthias, a celebrated German humanist, born at Roth, near Nürnberg, 9th April 1691. After completing his studies at Jena, he became in 1715 con-rector and librarian at Weimar, in 1728 rector of the gymnasium at Ansbach, in 1730 rector of St. Thomas School, Leipsic, in 1734 Professor of Rhetoric, and in 1735 librarian in the University of Göttingen. He died 3d August 1761. G. laboured with intelligence and zeal for the improvement of classical studies, and formed a wider and higher idea of culture than was customary among pedagogues. His chief works are his editions of the *Scriptores de Re Rustica*, of Quintilian, Claudian, Pliny the Younger, and Horace; his *Primæ Liniæ Isagoges in Eruditionem Universam* (new ed. Leips. 1784); *Novus Linguæ et Eruditionis Romanæ Thesaurus* (4 vols. Leips. 1749); *Opuscula Varii Argumenti* (8 vols. Bresl. 1743-45); and *Thesaurus Epistolarum Gesneri* (Halle, 1768).

Gesnera'ceæ, a natural order of Corollifloral plants embracing about 80 genera and 300 species. They are principally herbs, rarely shrubs, found in various quarters of the globe, but chiefly in the warmer regions of America. Several species of *Gloxinia, Achimenes*, and *Gesneria* are cultivated in hothouses for their showy flowers and foliage.

Gess'ler, Albrecht, in the tradition of Tell (q. v.), figures as the governor set over the Forest Cantons of Schwyz, Unterwalden, and Uri by Albrecht I. of Austria in 1300. He is painted as a cruel oppressor who was shot by the Swiss hero in a defile near the castle of Küssnacht in 1307. But there is no governor of that name mentioned in the still extant charters of the 14th c. relating to Küssnacht, and the story is therefore either not historical at all, or has lost its strict historical outline during its oral preservation as a legend. See *Tell und G. in Sage und Geschichte*, by E. L. Rochholz (Lond. 1876).

Gess'ner (Lat. *Gesnerius*), **Konrad**, a Swiss polyhistor and naturalist, was born at Zürich, March 26, 1516. After studying at Strasburg and Paris, he became schoolmaster in his native town. Resolving to study medicine, he resigned his post, went to Basel, and later to Lausanne, where he was appointed Professor of Greek. After three years G. proceeded to Montpellier to complete his medical studies, returning ultimately to Basel, where he received his doctor's degree in 1541. He then began practice at Zürich, where he was soon elected Professor of Philosophy, a post which he occupied till his death, December 13, 1565. G. was a most prolific writer on medical, zoological, historical, and philological subjects. His greatest works are *Bibliotheca Universalis* (1545-49), and *Historia Animalium* (5 vols. 1551-87), which was planned in six volumes but never completed, the fifth volume being published posthumously. See Hanhart, *Biographie G.'s* (Winterth. 1824).

Gessner, Salomon, a Swiss painter and poet, was born at Zürich, April 1, 1730. After an imperfect education, he was apprenticed by his father to a bookseller at Berlin, but soon deserted trade, and sought to gain a subsistence as a landscape painter. At Hamburg he formed a friendship with Hagedorn, and returning from that town to his native place, devoted himself to the cultivation of poetry. In 1754 he produced a work in verse called *Daphnis*, and some time after, *Inkle and Yarico*, *Idylls*, and the *Death of Abel*. This last is a kind of prose epic, which gained a celebrity beyond its deserts. In 1762 G. published four volumes of *Poems*, and after that period gave much attention to engraving. In 1772 he published a collected edition of his works, and on March 2, 1788, died at Zürich. G.'s Life has been written by Hottinger (Zür. 1796).—His son, **Konrad G.** (born 1764, died 1826), distinguished himself as a landscape-painter.

Ges'ta Romano'rum (Lat. 'the deeds of the Romans'), a collection of stories, mostly intended to convey moral lessons, highly popular in the middle ages, the authors of which in their mediæval form are unknown. Warton wrongly ascribes them to Petrus Berchorius, a Benedictine prior who lived at Paris in the 14th c.; their real compiler seems to have been an English or German monk named Elinandus. They are partly tales of Greece and Rome, especially of the Roman Empire, partly Eastern apologues, and partly chivalrous and saintly legends of the middle ages; but all these varying times and themes are harmonised by a naïve, charming anachronism—Romans and Greeks being represented as chivalrous knights, and placed amid Gothic surroundings. A moral is added to each tale, and the whole work is marked by a strange, delightful, and almost infantile simplicity of manner and incident. Ovid, Valerius Maximus, Aulus Gellius, Pliny, Seneca, Boethius, are referred to for several of the classical tales, and many of the Oriental fictions are taken from the Arabian stories in the *De Clericali Disciplina* of Petrus Alphonsus and the romance of *Baarlam and Josaphat* (q. v.). English poets have been largely indebted to the G. R. Chaucer and Gower each borrowed two of their stories from them; they contain the plot of Shakespeare's *Pericles*, and the stories of the caskets, the bond of the pound of flesh, and Portia's judgment, which reappear in the *Merchant of Venice*. We also find in the G. R. the basis of the spectral episode in *Marmion*, the magic mirror which occurs in the *Faerie Queene* and in the pseudo-legend of Surrey and Geraldine, the story of Parnell's *Hermit*, and an early version of the *Three Black Crows*. The G. R. have likewise supplied many themes to the Italian poets and novelists, *e.g.*, the story of the nobleman who made his wife drink nightly from the skull of her slain adulterer, which occurs in various Italian poems, in a tragedy by Rucellai, in the thirty-second tale of the Queen of Navarre, and in a ballad by Stolberg. It was perhaps from the G. R. that the Italian writers caught their love for tales of magic and enchantment. The German fabulists also borrowed freely from the G. R. These tales were known in England before the end of the 13th c., and were widely popular till the 16th c.—their fame waning at the Reformation. The first edition of the original Latin work was issued at Köln in 1472, the first Dutch translation appeared in 1481, and the first German at Augsburg in 1498. See the Rev. C. Swan's *G. R. translated from the Latin* (Lond. 1824, new ed. revised by Wynnard Hooper, 1877).

Gesta'tion (Lat. *gestatio*, from *gesto*, 'I carry on'), the term applied collectively to the series of actions and processes involved in the development and nutrition of the embryo or young animal within the *uterus* or *womb*. The name is also used to indicate the *period* of intra-uterine development. G. follows the *impregnation* of the ovum. In cases of *abnormal* G., this process may take place *without* the uterus, when the process is known as that of *extra-uterine* G. The embryo may thus be developed within the *Fallopian tube* or *oviduct*, such instances being named cases of *tubal pregnancy*; or sometimes the process may be more or less intimately related to the abdominal cavity itself. The period of human G. is usually estimated at forty weeks—nine months or 280 days; but these limits may in many instances be exceeded, and cases of G. lasting for a less period may frequently be met with. Occasionally grave points of law have had to be settled by the determination of the length of the period of G. in particular cases. As a general rule, where many young are produced at a birth, the period of G. is short. Its duration varies greatly in different animals. The elephant goes with young for twenty or twenty-one months, producing but a single young one at a birth. The period of G. in the giraffe is about fourteen months, of the camel twelve months, of the horse eleven months; that of the cow is nine months, and that of most of the deer eight months. The sheep carries her young for five, and the pig for four months. The lion appears to go with young for about three or three and a half months, and the bear for about six months, whilst the dog's period of G. is sixty-three days, and that of the cat fifty-five or fifty-six days. See also FŒTUS, PARTURITION, &c.

Ge'tæ. See DACIA.

Gethsem'ane (Aram. 'oil-press') was a place between the Brook Kedron and the Mount of Olives, about half a mile from the E. wall of Jerusalem, where was a garden to which our Lord retired on the night of his betrayal, where his agony took place, and where he was apprehended by the emissaries of the Jews, led by Judas (Matt. xxvi. 30–56; Mark xiv. 26–50; Luke xxii. 39–54; John xviii. 1–12). See Stanley's *Sinai and Palestine* (new ed. Lond. 1871).

Gett'ysburg, a town on the S. border of Pennsylvania, U.S., 28 miles W. by S. of York by railway. It is the seat of the state college, and has some carriage-making and granite quarrying. Pop. (1870) 3074. In and around the town was fought the fierce battle of G., between the army of the Union under General Meade and the Confederates under General Lee, which lasted for three days, ending in favour of the former on 3d July 1863. Although it had an important bearing on the course of the war, it was but a desperate 'soldiers' battle.' The killed and wounded on the side of the victors were 16,500; on the side of the South 18,000. See Bates' *Battle of G.* (Phil. 1875).

Ge'um, a genus of perennial plants belonging to the natural order *Rosaceæ* (q. v.). There are a number of species found in the temperate parts of the northern hemisphere. Only two are indigenous to Britain, viz., *G. urbanum*, the common or wood avens, and *G. rivale*, the water avens. The root of the former is aromatic, and possesses astringent properties. The root of *G. Canadense*, called chocolate or blood root in America, has been used as a tonic. *G. coccineum* is cultivated in gardens for its handsome scarlet flowers.

Gey'sers are a class of hot springs characterised by periodic eruptions. The name is of Icelandic origin (*geysa*, 'to be forced out with violence'), and is strikingly descriptive of these springs, which are very numerous in the volcanic regions in the S.W. of Iceland. The most remarkable in that island are the Great Geyser and Strokkr (Eng. 'churn'), about 70 miles E. of Reikiavik. The former consists of a cylindrical tube, about 12 feet wide and 80 feet deep, which opens into a bowl-shaped trough, 6 or 7 feet deep, with an average diameter of 60 feet, and situated on the summit of a circular mound from 26 to 32 feet high and 210 feet in diameter. The cylinder and bowl are always filled with water (except immediately after an eruption), the temperature of which varies on the upper surface from 76° to 89° C., but attains in the tube at a depth of 60 or 70 feet a point as much as 20° above the boiling-point. Bunsen in 1846 observed a temperature of 127° C. (261° F.) a few minutes before an eruption. The possibility of water remaining water at such a high temperature is due no doubt to the increased pressure at those depths, and also to the comparative freedom of the water from air. Every few hours the Great Geyser becomes tumultuous, a condition which is accompanied by underground rumblings; but it is only at intervals of a day or so that this tumult becomes so intensified as to produce the characteristic feature of geyser action, the forcible ejection of volumes of steaming liquid to a height of 60 or 80 feet. After some fifteen minutes' activity the eruption ceases; and the tube and basin, left almost empty, gradually fill with clear sea-green water, which then trickles slowly over the margin and down the slope, where, through evaporation, it deposits the silica which is the main constituent in the formation of the mound and the smooth sides of the basin. The Strokkr, which lies 100 paces from the Great Geyser, presents a curious funnel-shaped tube, and its eruptions take place every two or three days. These natural wonders, long supposed to be peculiar to Iceland, have more recently been discovered in New Zealand and the United States. The region to the N. of Lake Taupo in the province of Auckland abounds in hot springs, fumaroles, solfataras, &c. In many places the country is beautifully terraced by siliceous deposits, and whole lakes—Rotamahana for example—are maintained at an average temperature of from 70° to 80° C. At the N.E. end of this lake is the Tetarata spring, which presents usually the appearance of an immense cauldron, 80 feet long and 60 wide, and filled with clear, ever-boiling water, and which is probably a geyser with long intervals of quiet. In the vicinity of Lake Rotorna are seven or eight periodic G., the principal one being the Waikite near the native settlement of Whakarewarewa. It sometimes spouts to a height of 30 or 40 feet. See Hochstetter's *New Zealand* (1867). The Yellowstone National Park in the N.W. of Wyoming Territory, U.S., abounds in G., hot springs, and sulphur springs of every description. One of the most remarkable of the G. is Old Faithful, which spouts on an average once an hour, each eruption lasting not quite five minutes, and the column of water attaining a height of 120 or 130 feet. The Bee-Hive is surmounted by a dome-shaped chimney through which the water and steam forcibly escape, rising to a great height in the form of a fine spray and ultimately evaporating in the air. The Grand Geyser has magnificent eruptions, the column sometimes attaining a height of over 200 feet. The Grotto, the Giant, and the Giantess are also first-rate spouters, quite throwing into the shade their Icelandic brethren. For full information regarding the G. and hot springs of this curious region see Hayden's *Sixth Annual Report of the United States Geological Survey* (1873), and Jones' *Report upon the Reconnaissance of North-Western Wyoming, including Yellowstone National Park* (1875).

The first theory of geyser action was stated by Sir George Mackenzie, who visited Iceland in 1810. He explained the ejection of water as produced by the expansion of steam which had accumulated under constantly increasing pressure in an underground cavern connected by a duct with the geyser tube. Bunsen in 1846 showed that a simple tube was quite sufficient to account for any eruption; and a veritable geyser may be exhibited on a small scale by heating a tube filled with water in two places—at the bottom and about half-way up. In the geyser tube, by lateral heating, the body of water at a certain depth is raised to its boiling-point, expands, and pushes the superincumbent column of water up. This necessitates an overflow of water at the margins of the basin, therefore a diminished pressure and a consequent lowering of the boiling-point of the water in the tube. Any portion of the column which was formerly at its boiling-point will be now suddenly converted into steam, whose expansive energy will be evidenced in the sudden ejection of the superimposed water. Such is a brief outline of Bunsen's theory, which does not, however, in itself give a full explanation of several curious points recently brought to light in the Yellowstone region regarding a physical connection between contiguous G. The study of these sympathetic fountains will no doubt throw much light on the nature of their workings. Besides the works already cited, see Mackenzie's *Travels in Iceland* (1810), Klöden's *Erdkunde* (1873), and Lyell's *Principles of Geology* (10th ed. 1868).

Gfrö'rer, August Friedrich, a German historian, was born at Calw in the Black Forest, 5th March 1803, and was educated for the Protestant ministry. In 1830 he forsook theology for literature. Even his earlier works, *Philo* (Stuttg. 1831), *Geschichte des Urchristenthums* (3 vols. Stuttg. 1838), and *Gustav Adolf* (2 vols. Stuttg. 1835–37, 4th ed. 1863), showed a leaning to Catholicism, and in his *Allgemeine Kirchengeschichte* (4 vols. Stuttg. 1841–46) he professed himself a Catholic. In 1846 he became professor in the Catholic University of Freiburg, and was active as a keen Ultramontane till his death, 10th July 1861. The chief of his later works are *Untersuchung über die Decretalen des falschen Isidorus* (Freib. 1848), *Geschichte der Ost- und Westfränk. Karolinger* (2 vols. Freib. 1858), *Papst Gregor VII.* (7 vols. Schaff. 1859–64), *Gesch. des 18ten Jahrhunderts* (3 vols. Schaff. 1862–63).

Gha'ra, the name given to the Sutlej river in N.W. India, for a distance of about 300 miles between the confluence of the Beas and its final junction with the Chenab.

Ghas'el, or **Ghazel** (Arab. 'love-poem'), a form of lyrical poetry among the Turks and Persians which has been compared to the Western sonnet. It consists of not less than fifteen, and not more than seventeen strophes of two lines each, and the last strophe invariably contains the real or assumed name (*tachallus*) of the author. The finest specimens are by Hafiz (q. v.), many of whose ghasels are mystical and philosophical under a bacchanalian guise.

Ghaut (*ghat*), the Indian name for a passage or gateway, usually applied to the structures erected on the sides of rivers, tanks, or lakes, to facilitate the access of bathers. These consist of wide masonry steps, sometimes protected above with walls and porticoes. They are most numerous and most highly ornamented on the Ganges, especially at Benares and other sacred spots. See Fergusson's *Hist. of Ind. Architect.* (Lond. 1876).

Ghauts, Western and Eastern. The name given by Europeans to the two parallel hill-ranges which fringe either coast of the Indian peninsula. The W. G., which alone can be called mountains, start from the central plateau, and first stretch W. along the left bank of the Tapti, where they are sometimes called the N. G.; presently they turn due S. and run down almost continuously to Cape Comorin, at a distance from the Indian Ocean which nowhere exceeds 70 miles. The total length may be 1000 miles, the average height about 4000 feet, the highest point about 7000 feet. They form an absolute watershed, being pierced by no rivers, and sending all their water to the E. They cut off the clouds from the Indian Ocean, and their W. slope has an annual rainfall of more than 100 inches. They are twice crossed by the Great Indian Peninsula Railway, near Nasik and near Poonah; and also by the Madras Railway, at the gap of Palghaut, which is 16 miles broad, and practically divides the W. G. into two distinct portions. The E. G. are altogether less important. They commence in Orissa, S. of the Mahanadi river, and run S.W. at a considerable distance from the Bay of Bengal, and in a very broken chain, till they cross the point of the peninsula and join the W. G. N. of the gap of Palghaut. Their average height is not more than 1500 feet, and they are penetrated by the valleys of the Godavari and Kistna. The Neilgherries form the junction between the two ranges, and contain Dodabetta Mountain (8640 feet), but not even here has snow been known to fall.

Ghazi, an Arabic word signifying 'champion or hero,' especially assumed by those Mohammedans who have slain infidels in battle, in the form of *ghazi-ūd-din*, 'champion of the faith.'

Ghazipore' (*Ghazipur*), the chief town of the district of the same name in the N.W. Province, British India, on the left bank of the Ganges, 431 miles N.W. of Calcutta and 46 N.E. of Benares. Pop. (1871) 38,853. It has a ruined palace, now a custom-house, said to have been built by Mîr Cossim, Nawab of Bengal, and a stone obelisk in memory of Lord Cornwallis, who died here in 1805. The military cantonments lie to the S.W. G. is celebrated for its rose-water, and also for its horse races.—G. *district* is intersected by the Ganges and many minor streams, and bordered by the Gogra. Area, 2168 sq. miles; pop. (1872) 1,345,570. The spring crops are maize, rice, pulses, and oil-seeds; the summer crops, wheat, barley, opium, and sugar-cane, which last is of especially fine quality. The exports towards Bengal are sugar, saltpetre, cereals, and oil-seeds, from the river marts of G., Balia G., and Moniar; the imports are rice and piece goods. The latter come by the East Indian Railway, which traverses the S. of the district.

Ghazzali-al-Abou-Ibn-Hamid-Mohammed, an Arabian philosopher, born at Tus, Persia, in 1058, son of a merchant in cotton (*ghazal*), whence his surname G. After studying at Djorshan and Nishapur, he was made Professor of Theology at Bagdad, and after holding various offices as a teacher, died at Tus in 1111. G. is one of the foremost Arabian authors, and has been surnamed *Zain Eddin* ('glory of the law'), though he does not always adhere to strict orthodoxy. His chief work is the *Ihjá Olúm ad-Din* ('Restoration of Religious Sciences'), of which it has been said 'If all the books of Islam were lost and we had only this one left, we should not miss the others.' Among his other writings are *Kitabunnahali-Filásafa* ('On the Opinions of Philosophers'), *Tahâfat Al-Filásafa*) ('The Destruction of Philosophers'), &c., and various moral and philosophical treatises. Most of his works are lost. See Schmolders's *Essai sur les Écoles Philosophiques chez les Arabes, et notamment sur la Doctrine d'Al-Gazzan* (Par. 1842).

Ghee (*ghî*), the name given to the boiled butter which is in universal use among the natives of India in cooking and for sweetmeats. The best is prepared from the milk of the buffalo, and where those animals are kept G. forms an important article of manufacture and of local trade.

Gheel, or **Geel**, a town in the province of Antwerp, Belgium, in the Campine, 25 miles W. of Antwerp. It has a shrine of St. Dymphnea, to which the insane have resorted for cure since the 7th c. This class has settled in large numbers at G., partly in the hope of miraculous cure, partly because of the kind treatment they receive from the citizens and the neighbouring farmers. In recent years a medical staff has been organised, and cottage asylums have been established under the control of Government. Pop. 11,614. See Duval's *G., ou une Colonie d'Aliénés vivant en Famille et en Liberté* (Par. 1860).

Ghent (Flem. *Gend*, Ger. *Gent*, Fr. *Gand*), the capital of East Flanders, Belgium, at the confluence of the Lys, Scheldt, Lieve, and Moère, 35 miles W.N.W. of Brussels by railway. It is a quaint old town, rising here and there in ornate dusky brick piles, and enclosed by walls eight miles in circuit, girt with pleasant gardens and promenades. Separated into some twenty-six islands by various canals and branches of the rivers, it is bound together by means of about 300 bridges, of which forty-two are of stone. The Great Canal, connected with the Scheldt, enables vessels drawing 18 feet of water to enter the docks of G., which can accommodate some 400 vessels. G. has a cathedral of St. Bavo, with a grand interior, a crypt of date 941, a beautiful choir and chapel of 1228, and many fine pictures, including four of the original thirteen famous *Agnus* studies by the brothers Eyck. Other notable buildings are the Gothic church of St. Michael of 1480; the church of St. Peter, rebuilt in 1720, and containing rare pictures; part of an old abbey, converted into barracks for 4000 men; a new (1830) citadel on the Blandinus Mount, the sole height in the district; a university with 450 students since 1816; the Beguin establishment, with 130 houses, 18 convents, 2 chapels, and 700 nuns; the townhouse (begun 1200), with a richly-carved façade; a palace of justice (1844), designed by Roelandt; an art academy; the best botanical garden in Belgium; a library of 100,000 volumes and 700 MSS.; a fine theatre (1848); and a large casino (1836) for concerts. From the centre of G. rises the old Belfroot or Beffroi (1183–1339), a square watch-tower 387 feet high, with an iron peak (renewed in 1854), a peal of forty-four bells, and a gilt dragon-vane, brought by Baldwin IX. from Constantinople in 1204. In the historic and picturesque Vrydag Markt a statue of Jakob van Artevelde was raised in 1863. G. has 29 cotton factories, with 480,000 spindles and 4800 hands, several large flax-spinning factories, extensive cotton-print and dye works, sugar refineries, &c., and a large floricultural trade. Sluices 15 miles to the N. can lay the whole district under water. Pop. (1873) 116,693. G. is first mentioned in the 7th c. A fortress was built here in 868 by Baldwin Bras-de-Fer as a defence against the Norsemen; in the 13th c. it became the chief seat of the Counts of Flanders, and rose in the 15th to be the richest and most populous city in Europe. Under Jakob van Artevelde (q. v.) G., with an army of 50,000 men, resisted Louis of Flanders. It struggled long against the Dukes of Burgundy, but at last was obliged to yield. Under Karl V. its splendour began to fade. By the *Pacification of G.*, Holland, Zeeland, and the S. provinces of the Netherlands joined against Spain in 1576, and took an active part in the War of Independence, until it succumbed under the cruelties of the Duke of Parma. When the Netherlands was overrun by the French in 1792 G. became capital of the department of the Scheldt, and so remained till the overthrow of Napoleon. By the *Treaty of G.* peace was concluded between England and the United States, December 24, 1814.

Gherardes'ca, a Tuscan family which played a large part during the middle ages in the history of Pisa, and supported the Ghibelline cause. The most notable of the house was Count Ugolino, whose story is immortalised in the 33d canto of Dante's *Inferno*. Banished for plotting to make himself tyrant of Pisa, he was restored by the aid of Florence and Pisa, and in 1284 betrayed the Pisan forces to the Genoese in the battle of La Meloria. Through intrigues with the Guelphic enemies of the republic, he maintained a despotism over the Pisans, governing with the darkest treachery and cruelty, until in 1288 a revolt broke out, led by Archbishop Ruggieri, and G. was seized and cast, along with his two sons and two grandsons, into the dungeon of a tower, where they perished of hunger. The tower was afterwards known as the Tower of Hunger (*Torre della Fame*). Dante places G. in the icy lake in hell. The family again rose to power in the first half of the 14th c. See Sismondi's *Histoire des Républiques Italiennes*, vol. iv.

Gher'iah, the name of two places celebrated in Indian military history. One of these, also called Viziadrug, 170 miles S. of Bombay on the sea-coast, was captured from the Mahrattas in 1755 by a British fleet and army under Admiral Watson and Colonel Clive. At another G., near Mûrshedabad, on the Ganges, 140 miles N. of Calcutta, Major Adams, after a hard-fought battle, defeated the Nawab Mîr Cossim in 1763, and finally established the pre-eminence of the East India Company in Bengal.

Ghib'ellines. See GUELPHS AND GHIBELLINES.

Ghiber'ti, Loren'zo, sculptor and designer, was born at Florence in 1378, and in 1401 joined in a competition to which all sculptors were invited by the guild of merchants of Florence, and the object of which was to produce a design in basso-relievo for a gate to the baptistery of San Giovanni. G.'s design was allowed to be the best even by the other competitors, among whom were Brunelleschi and Donatello. In carrying out his design—the 'Sacrifice of Isaac'—G. was occupied twenty years, after which his townsmen commissioned him to design and carve a companion gate for the same building. The subject of this splendid work was also biblical. These two works contain the best sculpture of the 15th c., and to this day they remain unrivalled for the highest qualities of art. Michael Angelo said they were worthy to adorn the gateway to paradise. He died at Florence in 1455. Twelve beautiful etchings of these gates were published by Feodor Ivanovitch in 1798. See Hagen's *Chronik seiner Vaterstadt vom Florentiner Lorenz G.* (Leips. 2 vols. 1833; 2d ed. 1861).

Ghi'ka Family, a noble house of Albanian origin, many of whose members have been hospodars of Moldavia and Wallachia.—**Gregor G.**, an Albanian peasant, founded the house in the 17th c. He entered the service of the Governor of Moldavia, went to Constantinople, and by intriguing obtained the hospodarship of Wallachia in 1657. He was succeeded by his son **Gregor II.**, who was poisoned at Constantinople about 1680. The most famous of the later members of the family are—**Alexander G.**, born in 1795, and hospodar of Wallachia from 1822 to 1825, and from 1834 to 1842. He did much to better the condition of his subjects, and pursued a liberal and wise policy until the Sultan stripped him of his power. He then lived at Dresden and Vienna until 1853, when he returned to Wallachia, of which he was made *caimacum* in 1856. He died at Torre-del-Monte, near Naples, in 1862.—**Gregor X.**, born in 1803, was made hospodar of Moldavia in 1849. His government was marked by anti-Russian leanings, and by zealous efforts to improve education, establish order, remove abuses, and forward the union of the Danubian principalities. He freed the serfs, removed the censorship of the press, and carried many liberal measures. On retiring from office in 1856, G. removed to France. He died in July 1857. For Helena G., see DORA D'ISTRIA.

Ghilan' (Arab. *ghil*, 'mud'), a province in the N.W. of Persia, bounded N. by the Caspian, E. by Mazandaran, S. by Khamseh, and W. by Azer'bijan. Area, 4673 sq. miles; estimated pop. 100,000. It is low-lying and jungle-clad towards the Caspian, but to the S. is traversed by the lofty Bagra Koh or Talish Mountains and the Elbruz range, both densely wooded and covered with snow in winter. The wild animals include the tiger, panther, boar, jackal, vaspen, and deer, while the marshy coast and reedy islands are swarming with wild-fowl. The climate is damp and malarious, especially from June to September; much rheumatism, small-pox, and cutaneous disease prevails. The natives, who are handsome though often sickly, are chiefly engaged in the cultivation of silk (£75,000 worth yearly), oranges, lemons, and limes, and in rearing ponies, humped cattle, and fat-tailed sheep. They speak a rapid dialect (*Ghilaik*) of Persian, and are bigoted Mohammedans. Resht and Lahijan are the only considerable towns. G. was ceded to Peter the Great in 1724 for aid granted to drive out the Afghans. The Russians, however, were forced to retire by Nadir Shah in 1736, and since then have always claimed the territory.

Ghirlanda'jo, properly **Domenico Corradi**, one of the greatest painters of his time, was born at Florence in 1451, and was instructed in goldsmith's work by his father, who, as the designer of a garland (Ital. *ghirlanda*) or head-dress much esteemed by the Florentine ladies, was named Il Ghirlandajo. He afterwards devoted himself to painting, and acquired the highest fame as a painter and designer in mosaic. He died in 1495. To his school in Florence many of the greatest Italian painters owe their training. His chief work, the 'Massacre of the Innocents,' together with other great frescoes, is in the choir of Santa Maria Novella, Florence. He painted portraits, wonderful in their fidelity and freshness, of Lorenzo de Medici and other famous Florentines. His brothers Benedetto and Davidde, and his son Rodolfo G. (born 1485, died 1560), were also celebrated painters. G. is supposed to have discovered the laws of aerial perspective.

Ghiz'eh, or **Gizeh** (Copt. *Tpersioi*), the capital of a province of the same name in Lower Egypt, on the left bank of the Nile, opposite ancient Cairo. It was formerly a flourishing fortified place of the Mamlukes, but is now a miserable village. There are still here ovens for egg-hatching, and in the vicinity are three of the largest Pyramids (q. v.) and the great Sphinx.

Ghiz'ni. See GHUZNI.

Ghost-Moth (*Hepialus humuli*), so called from the silvery-white colour on the upper parts of the male, and from the suddenness with which it disappears from sight. The under parts are brown in both sexes. The male insects have the habit of hovering over the female at twilight as the latter lie concealed in the grass. The rapid and spectral-like disappearance of the moth when alarmed is due to the insect's fluttering to the ground, and there concealing itself from view by turning the lower and brown side of its body uppermost. The larvæ commit ravages in hop-fields, and also live on nettles, &c.

Ghümuldji'na, or **Komuldsi'na**, a town in the vilayet of Adrianople, European Turkey, on the Karaji, near the S. base of the Karlyk Bagh, 80 miles S.W. of Adrianople and N.E. of Lagos Bay. It has a citadel and a trade in silks, opium, and perfumes. Pop. 9000.

Ghur, a small town in Afghanistan, has given its name to the Ghurian dynasty, which succeeded the Ghiznevides in Hindustan in 1186 A.D., but only maintained itself for a few generations. It fixed the Mohammedan power in India more permanently than its predecessor, but was itself overwhelmed by Genghis Khan.

Ghuz'ni, or **Ghizni** (*Ghazni*), an ancient town and fortress of Afghanistan, 7726 feet above the sea, 85 miles S.W. of Cabul. A still older G., first heard of in the 10th c., was the capital of the great conqueror Mahmud of G., and was taken and destroyed by Allah-ud-dîn of Ghur in 1151. The only old building remaining is the tomb of Mahmud, before which used to stand the supposed sandal-wood gates of Somnauth. The existing G., 3 miles to the S.W., on the G. river, is still strongly fortified, and there is some trade. In 1839 it was stormed by the British under Sir J. Keane, and in 1842 evacuated and again retaken by General Nott. On this last occasion the Somnauth gates, as they were called, were carried off to Agra. Pop. 8000. G. has given name to the *Ghiznevide dynasty*, which dominated over Central Asia from 961 to 1186. The founder was Abastakîn, an adventurer from Bokhara; his grandson Mahmud (q. v.) ravaged Hindustan five times, and extended his empire from the Tigris to the Ganges. The last king, Khusrû Melek, was killed at Lahore by the King of Ghur, who had previously expelled the dynasty from G.

Gianibell'i, Federigo, an architect and military engineer, was born about 1530 at Mantua. After failing to obtain the patronage of Philip II. of Spain, he removed to England, and offered his services to Queen Elizabeth, by whom he was sent in 1585 to relieve Antwerp, then closely besieged by the Duke of Parma, Spain's generalissimo. After a little he succeeded in inventing an infernal machine which annihilated the huge bridge built by the Spaniards across the Scheldt, and which completely barred the entrance to the city. But the internal discord of the citizens hindered them from reaping any benefit from his ingenuity, and G. returned to England. The fire-ships which wrought such confusion in the fleet of the Armada were also the fruits of his inventive genius. After this no more is heard of him, but he presumably died in London.

Gianno'ne, Pietro, an Italian historian and jurist, was born at Ischitella in Naples, 7th May 1676. After a distinguished career at the Neapolitan bar, he withdrew from the practice of his profession, and assiduously devoted himself to historical literature. The fruits of his studies appeared in 1723, when he published his great work, *Storia Civile del Regno di Napoli*, in 4 vols. (new ed. Milan, 5 vols. 1845–47). It is characterised by wide and various learning, critical insight, and a philosophic spirit. In a thoroughly modern fashion G. illustrates the political, social, and religious influence of the successive civilisations that established themselves in Southern Italy. His ecclesiastical opinions excited the hostility of the clergy, and G. was forced to abandon his country and seek a refuge in Vienna. After some years he went to Venice, and thence to Modena, Milan, Turin, and Geneva, where he wrote a fierce diatribe against the Papacy, entitled *Il Triregno, Ossia de Regno, del Cielo, della Terra e del Papa*, and seems to have even adopted the doctrines of Calvin. Induced by false representations to re-enter Sardinia, he was arrested and imprisoned at Turin, where he died, 7th March 1748. Other works of G. were posthumously published. There is some evidence to support the opinion that, in spite of his high qualities, G. was proud, dictatorial, and intolerant in the expression of his sentiments, and had a way of making enemies rather than friends. See Panzini's *Vita di P. G.*

Gi'ants and Dwarfs. A giant (Gr. *gigas*, 'a giant,' Fr. *géant*, from *gēgenēs*, 'earth-born; '*gē*, 'the earth,' and *gignomai*, 'I am born'), is a man greatly exceeding the average of his species in height and bulk, while a dwarf (Goth. *dvairg*, which Grimm thinks may be identified with the Gr. *theurgos*, 'a divine worker') is an individual of diminutive stature. The belief, almost universal until the beginning of the 19th c., that giants of colossal size had formerly existed is now exploded, the huge bones which were thought to have belonged to enormous men having been proved to be the remains of mammoths and other great quadrupeds. Two races of giants are mentioned in Scripture—the Nephilim, who lived before the Flood, and the Rephaim, who dwelt in Palestine in the days of Joshua. Some, however, are of opinion that Nephilim merely signifies bearded, or cruel, or violent men. Individual giants, such as Og, King of Bashan, and Goliath, are also spoken of in Scripture. There are several dubious references to giants in ancient Greek and Latin authors. Thus Arrian tells us that Porus, King of India, was 5 cubits high, and Pliny speaks of an Arab of 9 feet 9 inches high who lived in the reign of Claudius. Men have been known to attain a height of between 8 and 9 feet, and even this stature may have been exceeded. In the museum of Trinity College, Dublin, there is a skeleton, that of O'Brien, 8 feet 6 inches high, and the museum of the College of Surgeons, England, contains a skeleton of 8 feet 2 inches. Bishop Berkeley is said to have tried to rear a giant on hygienic principles. The orphan named Magrath whom he selected for the experiment died at the age of twenty when he was 7 feet 8 inches high. Dwarfs were common among the Romans who called them *nani* and *nanæ*, and occasionally sought to check the growth of the children of slaves by means of bandages. The most famous dwarf of ancient times was Philetas of Cos, who was one of the best poets of his time, and tutor to Ptolemy Philadelphus, and of whom the story runs that he had to carry weights to escape being blown away. In the middle ages dwarfs were generally kept at the courts of princes and nobles, a custom which did not become extinct until the end of the 18th c. Among the smallest dwarfs of whom we have thoroughly reliable information are Bebè, the dwarf of Stanislaus, King of Poland, who was under 3 feet when he died, at the age of twenty-three, and Count Joseph Borowlaski, who was 2 feet 4 inches high at the age of twenty, and 3 feet 3 inches high at the age of thirty. He died aged ninety-eight, and had a brother 3 feet 6 inches high. As compared with dwarfs, giants are for the most part much shorter lived, dwarfs often attaining a very old age; and much feebler in mind, dwarfs being generally lively and keen witted; giants are also often malformed or badly proportioned, while dwarfs have often great symmetry of shape. The belief that races of dwarfs lived in certain parts of the world was once widely diffused, and is now seen to have a certain basis of truth. The Greeks, and among others Herodotus and Aristotle, held that a race of pygmies lived on the Upper Nile, and the Portuguese writers of the 17th c. speak of a dwarfish race in the interior of Africa named Bakka-Bakka. These beliefs seem to have been founded on facts. Dr. Schweinfurth (*Heart of Africa*, 1873), when travelling on the Upper Nile, saw several specimens of a dwarfish people named Akka, who inhabit an unknown district between lat. 2° and 1° N. Their average height, he says, was 4 feet 10 inches, and they were distinguished by a redder or brighter complexion from the other native races. His description substantially agrees with Du Chaillu's account of the Obongo, a wandering race whom he met in the Ashango territory, and whose average height he estimates at 4 feet 7 inches. Natives of stunted growth are reported to inhabit parts of E. Tropical Africa, as the Doko, who dwell on the Upper Juba, and who are said to be about the height of boys ten years old. Schweinfurth considers it almost certain that these people of small stature, who may have given rise to the Greek tales of pygmies, are the 'scattered remains of an aboriginal population now becoming extinct.' There are very conflicting accounts as to a race of dwarfs said to inhabit Madagascar; it seems probable that an under-sized people dwells in the interior of the island. Another people considerably shorter than the average are the Esquimaux (q. v.). Until recently it was credited that the Patagonians were of gigantic stature, but it is now proved that, though generally tall, they are by no means giants.

Giants and Dwarfs in Mythology.—There are various legends of the *Gigantes* or giants in Greek mythology. Homer describes them as a race of wild huge men who dwelt in the far west, in the island of Thrinacia, but does not speak of their strife with the gods. Eurymedon, he says, slew them for their insolence to the immortals. According to Hesiod the Gigantes were the offspring of Ge, 'the earth,' and Tartarus, while later writers confound them with the Titans (q. v.), and make them, like the Titans, war with the Olympians. The legends of Hercules and Theseus represent these hordes as slayers of giants. The Gigantes are mostly placed in volcanic regions, as Cos and Sicily, and the legends relating to them seem connected with volcanic phenomena. Giants are much more important in Norse than in Greek mythology. This is in all likelihood due to the Northern nations being brought into close contact with gloomy and terrible natural phenomena comparatively unknown in the bright, warm climate of Greece. In the Northern mythology the giants (*Joetter, Jötuns*, and *Rimthurser*) were the incarnation of evil. They dwelt in a dark land of wild, snow-clad mountains, known as Jötunheim ('giant land'), on the shores of the great ocean, separated from the gods by the 'unfreezing river' Ising. They were the offspring of darkness and cold, were hideous and deformed, and had often several heads. The giantesses, however, were sometimes fair, *e.g.*, Gerde, whose beauty woke the love of Freyr, and are represented as stirring up discord among the gods. The Northern mythology represents the giant Ymir, who was produced from heat and ice, as the earliest of created beings. He was slain by the gods Odin, Vili, and Ve, who made the sea from his blood, and heaven and earth from his body. All the other frost-giants were slain save Bergelmir, who, escaping with his wife, became the father of the Jötuns, against whom the gods reared a wall made from the eyebrows of Ymir. Dwarfs are likewise important actors in Northern mythology and folk-lore. According to the younger Edda, the dwarfs were produced as maggots on the dead Ymir, and afterwards received human form and reason from the Aesir or gods. They were afraid of light, and lived in caves and in the bowels of the earth. They were very skilful in metallurgy, and especially in forging magic arms and armour. Thus the dwarfs Darin and Daalin forged the wonderful sword Tyrsing. The dwarfs occasionally aid men and are hostile to the giants. The north, south, east, and west are sometimes spoken of as dwarfs who uphold the four corners of heaven. It has been suggested that many of the tales of the Northern dwarf have arisen from the migration of a race of Lapps into Scandinavia. Both G. and D. appear constantly in medieval romance, whence they have passed into nursery tales. In the mythical English history of Brut and his descendants giants are mentioned as dwelling in Albion; and Cornish and Welsh giants are often met with in English folk-lore. See Geoffroy Saint Hilaire's *Histoire des Anomalies de l'Organisation*; Mallet's *Northern Antiquities*; Thorpe's *Northern Mythology*; Grundtvig's *Nordens Mythologie*; Grimm's *Deutsche Mythologie*.

Giant's Causeway, a singular promontory of most perfect columnar basalt in the N. of Ireland, running into the North Channel from the coast of Antrim, midway between the mouth of the Bann and Bally Castle. It consists of the lowest of three beds of highly crystalline basalt, and appears at Bengore Head, where the cliffs are from 400 to 500 feet high, forming a great mole or paved way 30 feet wide and 300 yards long, which dips towards the sea. The perpendicular columns are closely packed together, and are mainly hexagonal; but there are also columns with nine, eight, seven, five, and even three sides. There is great beauty in the transition of colour from the snow-white chalk which overlies to the almost black basalt, and in the lively tints of intervening beds of ochre and of green and red sandstones. Two similar promontories of minor size are known as the Middle and Little Causeways. The Irish name of the G. C. is *Clochan-na-bh Fomharaigh*, pron. *Cloghan-avowry*, *i.e.*, 'the stepping-stones or causeway of the Fomorians,' a race of pirates, who in semi-mythical times infested the Irish coasts, but were transformed by later legend into giants who wished to make a road to Scotland.

Giaour (the Turkish form of the Pers. *geber*, which in turn is borrowed from the Arabic *kafir*, 'infidel'), the name given by the Turks to those who do not hold the Mohammedan faith. It is generally, but not necessarily, used as a term of reproach.

Giarr'e, a large town in the province of Catania, Sicily, near the sea, and 42 miles S.S.W. of Messina. The vicinity is famous for its wine, and about 5 miles above the town, on the side of Mount Etna, are several trees of remarkable size and age, and the remains of the famous *Castagno di Cento Cavalli*, held to have been formerly the largest chestnut-tree in the world. Pop. 17,197.—**G. Riposto**, about a mile distant to the E. of G., of which it is the port, is a station on the railway from Giardini to Catania. Pop. 6530.

Giave'no, a walled town in the province of Turin, N. Italy, on the Sangone, 17 miles W.S.W. of Turin. It has a castle of date 1369, and some manufactures of silks, linens, leather, and ironwares. Pop. 9683.

Gibbet. See HANGING.

Gibb'on (*Hylobates*), a genus of Catarhine or higher apes found in the E. Indies and E. Archipelago. They are distinguished by the great length of the anterior limbs, the hands reaching the ground when the animal is in the erect posture. The tail is abortive, but *callosities* or hard parts exist on the nates. The fur is thick and woolly. The common G. (*Hylobates lar*) is one of the best-known species. It is sometimes known as the white-handed G., and occurs in Malacca and Siam. The colour is black; the face bordered with a grey colour. The agile G. (*H. agilis*) and the silvery G. (*H. leuciscus*) are well-known forms, as is also the Siamang (*H. Siamang* or *syndactylus*) of Sumatra. The latter is an exceedingly man-like ape, and is the largest of the gibbons. The index and middle toes of the hind-feet (as indicated by the specific name *syndactylus*) are united by the skin as far as the nail-joint.

Gibbon, Edward, the greatest of English historians, was the son of a rich proprietor in Surrey and Hampshire, and was born at Putney, 27th April 1737. Being a weak child, he was allowed largely to educate himself, and from his early years read widely, especially in history. In his fifteenth year, at which age he proposed to write a history of the times of Sesostris, he was sent to Magdalen College, Oxford, where he remained only fourteen months, being converted to Roman Catholicism from reading two works by Bossuet, and consequently being forced to quit the university, to which he afterwards averred he owed no obligation. He was then placed at Lausanne under the care of a clergyman, who induced him to reaccept Protestantism. In 1758 he returned to Hampshire, entering no profession, but devoting himself to study. In 1761 he issued an essay in French *Sur l'Étude de la Littérature*, which was well received abroad. About this time he became a captain in the Hampshire Militia, and gained an experience of military movements which was, he says, useful to him when composing his history. He visited Paris and Lausanne in 1763, and while at Rome in 1764 formed the idea of writing his great work, as he sat 'musing amidst the ruins of the Capitol, while the barefooted friars were singing vespers in the Temple of Jupiter.' In 1770 his father's death made him master of a large fortune, whereupon he devoted himself to writing the history of the *Decline and Fall of the Roman Empire*. The first volume appeared in 1776, and the whole edition was sold off in a few days. The book was completed at Lausanne in 1787 and published in 1788. G.'s attempt in his great work (chap. xv., xvi.) to explain the rise of Christianity by 'secondary causes' exposed him to much, and, on the whole, unmerited obloquy. He does not deny 'the ruling providence of the great Author' of Christianity, but thinks 'we may still be permitted, though with becoming submission, to ask, not indeed what were the first, but what were the secondary causes of the rapid growth of the Christian Church.' He returned to England in 1793, and died in his fifty-seventh year, January 16, 1794. G.'s was a cold, placid nature, almost untouched by passion or enthusiasm. Indifferent rather than cynical, he has been well called the perfect type of the conservative sceptic. When we turn, however, from the man to the author, it is impossible to refuse him an unbounded admiration. He is the loftiest example of historical genius in English literature. His theme was the grandest that ever fell to the lot of an historian, and no writer ever possessed learning more expansive and minutely accurate, or turned his studies to more splendid account. 'The work of G.,' says Mr. Freeman, 'as the grandest of historical designs carried out with wonderful power and accuracy, must ever keep its place; whatever else is read G. must be read too.' Carlyle has called G.'s work the splendid bridge between the old world and the new; and its special value lies in the parts which describe the transition from Roman to modern Europe, but nowhere is the scope of G.'s learning more manifest than in the picturesque episodes—such as the famous chapter on Mohammed—which enliven the march of the narrative. Unfortunately G. cannot always rise to the epical grandeur of his subject. He cannot, from the want of imaginative sympathy, breathe life into the great figures of the past nor reveal the natures of heroic characters. A skilful analyst of a dead civilisation, he cannot set forth the development of a living society. His style is at times obscured by allusive brevity, and is overburdened throughout by Latin derivatives; but it is nobly majestic, copious, and vivid, full of ornate picturesqueness, and rich in a kind of sombre, stately, and ironical epigram, expressed with a rhythmic elegance peculiar to its author. His *Autobiography* is deeply interesting as a frank revelation of character, and is marked by a delightful felicity of manner. The best editions of G. are those by Milman (12 vols. 1838–39), which contains a valuable Memoir, and Smith (5 vols. 1854–55). See also Minto's *English Prose Writers* (1872); and Stephen's *History of English Thought in the 18th c.* (Lond. 1876).

Gibb'ons, Grin'ling, the greatest of all English wood-carvers, supposed to be of Dutch extraction, was born in London in 1648. He received an appointment in the Board of Works from Charles II., and was employed to do much of the ornamental carved work for the chapel of Windsor. The stalls of St. Paul's choir are rich with foliage and festoon work from his hand, but the highest products of his genius are the beautifully executed fantasies of flower, fruit, and birds which adorn the panels, staircases, and pillars of the famous English mansions of the 17th c.—Chatsworth, Petworth, Burleigh, Southwick, &c. His delicacy and truth to nature evince high genius; his executive *finesse* is still unrivalled. He carved a point-lace cravat in wood for the Duke of Devonshire, and he could represent a feather in the same material with all the lightness of nature. G. died August 3, 1721.

Gibb'ons, Orlan'do, 'one of the rarest musicians of his time' (Anthony Wood), was born in Cambridge in 1583. At the age of twenty-one he was appointed organist of the Chapel-Royal, and in 1622 was made Doctor of Music by Oxford University. In 1625 he died of smallpox, caught on the occasion of King Charles's marriage, for which ceremony he had composed the music. He was buried in Canterbury Cathedral. Though he wrote other music besides, he owes his fame to his anthems, of which eighty have come down to us. They are simple, grand, and harmonious compositions. His brothers Edward and Ellis were also fine musicians, and his son Dr. Christopher G. was one of the best organists in the second half of the 17th c.

Gibbos'ity (Lat. *gibbus*, Gr. *kūbos*, *kuphos*, 'humpbacked'), the name given to a protuberance of part of the body, generally of the spinal column. This malformation depends on caries of the bodies of the vertebræ, with disintegration of the intervertebræ fibro-cartilage, and occurs most commonly in young children. It is almost always a strumous affection. See STRUMA.

Gibb'ous (Lat. *gibbosus*, from *gibba*, 'a hump'), in astronomy, is the term used to describe the moon's figure when it is within a week of the full. Mars is the only planet which presents marked G. phases.

Gib'eah (Heb. 'a hill') was the name applied to several towns and places in Palestine—a city of Judah (Josh. xv. 57), and of Benjamin (xviii. 28); the place where the Ark remained for a time (1 Sam. vii. 1; 2 Sam. vi. 3); G. of Benjamin, the scene of the outrage on the Levite's concubine (Judges xix., xx.), mentioned during the wars of Saul (1 Sam. xiii., xiv.), in 2 Sam. xxiii. 29, and by Hosea (v. 8, &c.), which is most probably the same as G. of Saul (1 Sam. xi. 4), and as the modern *Tuleil-el-Ful.*

Gi'bel (*Cyprinus gibelio*), the name given to a species of the Carp (q. v.). It has, however, no *barbules* or mouth filaments, and has a hooked tail. The G. is found in many British ponds and rivers, but appears to be somewhat local in its distribution. It is more common on the Continent, and may attain a weight of 1½ or 2 lbs. Its common English designation is the 'Prussian carp.'

Gibelli'na, a small town of Sicily, in the province of Trapani, 34 miles S.E. of the town of Trapani. It stands among mountains, and near it is a hill named *Le Fenestrelle*, from being cut into a number of curious cells, supposed to have been troglodyte dwelling-places. Pop. about 5000.

Gib'eon (Heb. 'belonging to a hill') was the city—one of the four of the Hivites—whose inhabitants by a stratagem induced Joshua to make a league with them (Josh. ix. 3–15, 17), which was in the territory of Benjamin (most probably the modern *El-Jib*), and afterwards became a Levitical city (xxi. 17). G. was the scene of the encounter between the men of David and of Ishbosheth, under Joab and Abner (2 Sam. ii. 12–32), and there Amasa was afterwards slain by Joab (2 Sam. xx. 8–12). On the high-place at G. the tabernacle was placed for some time (1 Chron. xvi. 39, xxi. 29), where it was one of the first acts of Solomon, after coming to the throne, to visit it (1 Kings iii. 4). See Stanley's *Sin. and Pal.* (new ed. Lond. 1871).

Gibral'tar (a corruption of the Arab. *Gebel el Tarik*, *i.e.*, 'Tarik's hill'), one of the most southerly points of Spain, 60 miles S.W. of Cadiz, and an almost isolated promontory of towering rock, only connected with the mainland of Andalusia by the 'neutral ground,' a low sandy isthmus about half a mile broad and 1½ miles long. To the W. a deep crescent-shaped inlet between G. and Algeciras, known as G. or Algeciras Bay, has an extreme width of 5½ miles, a depth of 218 fathoms, is marked by five lights, and affords good anchorage. The 'Rock' extends N. and S. for some 3 miles, has an extreme breadth of three-quarters of a mile, and rises to a height of 1439 feet. It is a mass of grey primary marble, of a reddish colour towards the base, and presenting almost perpendicular cliffs to the N., E., and S., but sloping accessibly though abruptly on the W. side to the plateau or *pied à terre* on which the town is built, and which is protected by strong batteries and works of defence. Some points along the ridge, beginning at the N., are Rock-gun Fort (1337 feet), Middle Hill (1010), Signal Station (1255), Mount Misery (1300), O'Hara Tower (1408), and the highest peak, known as the Sugar Loaf. The headland to the S., Point Europa (in lat. 36° 2′ 30″ N., and long. 5° 15′ 12″ W.), supports the lighthouse of G. The rock is perforated by many large caves, the principal being the *Cueva de San Miguel*, which has an entrance 1000 feet above the sea, and which has been descended for 500 feet through a series of narrow passages and vast chambers hung with stalactites. The limited vegetation comprises asparagus, capers, palmitas, aloes, cacti, and various mosses; while among the animals are cattle, sheep, goats, rabbits, partridges, pigeons, woodcocks, and Barbary apes (the N. African *Simia ecaudatus*). Although G. has the warmest climate in Europe, it is now one of the healthiest places in the world. From July to November is the hottest season, and the 'G. fever' only appears once in about twelve years. The home supply of water is limited to one rich spring, but there are eight bomb-proof cisterns for rain-water capable of holding 40,000 tons. G., which may be regarded as the key to the Mediterranean, constantly maintains a garrison of some 5000 infantry and 1000 artillery. While to the N. it is honeycombed by strongly appointed galleries, towards the S. magazines, rock-hewn batteries, and steep escarps stretch out to Point Europa.

It is placed under a governor, who decides in civil cases, subject in those of importance to an appeal to the British Privy Council. In 1871 the revenue derived from customs, port and quarantine dues, land revenues, stamps, and licences, amounted to £38,156, the expenditure to £42,015. Next to Malta G. is the most expensive of the British possessions, the cost of maintenance being £306,433 in 1872–73. All religions are tolerated, and G. is the seat of a Protestant and of a Roman Catholic bishop. The *town* of G. consists of a lower and upper portion, with a difference of 100 feet of altitude. It is irregularly built, and the houses, many of which are in the English style, are generally painted in a dark colour. The chief buildings are those of the Government (formerly a Franciscan monastery), the Roman Catholic cathedral, the Protestant church, the hospital, three synagogues, a mosque, and, in the upper part of the town, part of a Moorish castle of the 8th c., now used as a military prison. In front of G. is the beautiful Almaden Garden decked with exotic plants. G. is a free port, and has an active transit trade with Spain, Portugal, Morocco, France, and Italy. It is a source of much Spanish smuggling. Pop. (1871) 18,695, of whom the majority are Roman Catholics, and 1800 Jews.

History.—The classical G., named *Calpe*, a corruption of the Phœnician *Alube*, formed part of Hispania Bætica, and was one of the Pillars of Hercules, Abyla (mod. *Ceuta*) on the African coast being the other. In 711, as the Arabs poured into Spain, a castle was erected on the rock by Tarik Ibn-Zeyad, a general of the Calif Al Walid, from which circumstance it was called *Gebel el Tarik*. G. remained a Moorish stronghold till 1309, when it was recovered by the Christians under Antonio de Guzman. Ferdinand IV. then strengthened the defence, and erected a dockyard at the Old Mole. In 1333 G. yielded to the Moorish King of Fez, and was only regained by treachery in 1462. During the Spanish war of succession a Dutch and English naval force, under the Prince of Hessen-Darmstadt and Sir George Rooke, bombarded G. and forced the governor to capitulate, 4th August 1704. It was vigorously but vainly besieged by the Spanish in 1704–5, was formally ceded to Great Britain in 1713, and again attacked by a force of 20,000 men under the Count de las Torres in 1727. When England was engaged in the struggle with her colonies and was at war with France, the Spanish made their grand and final attempt to overwhelm the garrison of G., and were met by one of the most obstinate and brilliant defences in history. It began on the 21st June 1779, and ended on the 6th February 1783, having lasted three years, seven months, and twelve days. The blockade began unexpectedly, but Admiral Rodney was able to force the lines, convey provisions, add 1000 men to the garrison (making it 6382), and remove civilians. The defence devolved on General Elliot (q. v.), the governor, and General Ross. Matters began to assume a serious aspect when the Spanish seized the African ports opposite in 1780; but in April of the following year G. was relieved for a time by Admiral Darby, who led 100 merchant vessels into the bay. All this time an active bombardment was going on by land and sea; for weeks together 6000 shells were daily thrown into the town. With a combined Spanish and French fleet of 47 sail of the line, 10 floating batteries, and 15 gun and mortar boats, 1000 pieces of heavy ordnance, and covered boats to land 40,000 men, a crowning onset under the Duc de Crillon was made on the 8th September 1782, and lasted till the 13th, when it was only repulsed by the use of red-hot balls and incendiary shells. The munitions used by the enemy in one night were estimated at £2,000,000. A peace was declared on the 2d February 1783; the thanks of Parliament were conveyed to the garrison, and General Elliot (q. v.) was made a Knight of the Bath and afterwards Lord Heathfield. An engagement took place here between the French and English fleets, 6th July 1801.

Gibraltar, Strait of (Sp. *El Estrecho de G.*, the *Fretum Herculeum* of the Romans), is the channel between the coasts of Morocco and Andalusia, and connecting the Mediterranean and the Atlantic. It is 36 miles long from E. to W., 900 fathoms deep, and has a breadth between Capes Trafalgar and Spartel of 25 miles, and between G. and Ceuta of 14 miles. There is a constant current eastwards.

Gib'son, John, an English sculptor, was the son of a landscape gardener, was born at Conway, N. Wales, in 1791, removed with his family to Liverpool in the beginning of the century, and there, at the age of sixteen (having previously manifested taste and power in drawing), was invited to enter the marble works of Messrs. Francis, under whom he soon became highly esteemed for his skill in designing, modelling, and carving. The friendship of Mr. Roscoe (the biographer of Lorenzo de Medici) enabled G. in 1817 to repair to Rome, where he was an apt and favoured student under Canova and Thorwaldsen successively. He made Rome his home, and though elected A.R.A. in 1833, and R.A. in 1836, he did not revisit England till 1845, and then only to return immediately to Italy. He died January 27, 1866. In his works the perfect form and spirit of the antique are revived. His first commissions were his group 'Mars and Cupid,' executed in marble for the Duke of Devonshire, and his 'Psyche borne by Zephyrs,' for Sir George Beaumont. Among other famous works are 'Sleeping Shepherd Boy,' 'Aurora,' and the 'Wounded Amazon.' His 'Helens,' 'Sapphos,' 'Proserpines,' &c., are numerous; and while these are classic in form and ideal, they are also informed with a character and personality directly the outcome of G.'s own genius. But the constant effort to bring sculptural art back to the conventions of Greek design led to the waste of his skill in the creation of beautiful anachronisms. His 'tinted' Venus, Hebe, &c., slightly coloured and gilt, were defended by himself as having precedents in Greek art; but the experiment has had no effect upon recent sculpture. G. also executed a number of noteworthy portraits, statues, and busts. He left a representative collection of his works to the Royal Academy, where the 'G. Gallery' was opened in November 1876. See Eastlake's *Life* (1870).

Gibson, Thomas Milner, an English politician, born at Trinidad in 1807, was the son of Major T. M. G. After an education at the Charterhouse and at Trinity College, Cambridge, where he became a wrangler, he entered Parliament (1837) as Conservative member for Ipswich. He soon, however, became a 'philosophical Radical and free-trader,' and lost his seat in 1839, but was returned as one of the representatives of Manchester in 1841. After this G. became a prominent member of the Anti-Corn-Law League, and an eloquent exponent of the principles of the Manchester school. In 1857 he and Mr. John Bright were ousted from Manchester on account of the views they held on the subject of the Crimean war, but the same year he found a seat for Ashton-under-Lyne. The most successful thing as a parliamentary tactician he ever did was to overthrow the Palmerston Administration (February 19, 1858) by a majority of 234 to 215 through an amendment to the celebrated Conspiracy to Murder Bill. In the next Government of Lord Palmerston, G., who had once under Earl (then Lord John) Russell been Vice-President of the Board of Trade, became its President, and held the office till the Russell-Gladstone Ministry broke down on the question of Reform in 1866. G. is best known for his efforts in repealing the newspaper stamp, the advertisement duty, and the tax on paper—known as 'taxes on knowledge.' He retired from public life and Parliament at the general election of 1868.

Gidd'iness. See Vertigo.

Gid'eon (Heb. 'hewer' or 'destroyer') was the fifth of the Judges of Israel. Roving bands of Midianites had for seven years periodically carried off the crops and cattle of the Israelites, when 'an angel of Jehovah' appeared to G. and commissioned him to deliver the people from this oppression, which the narrative implies was inflicted as a punishment for indulging in the worship of Baal (Judges vi. 1, 25). G. accordingly inaugurated his mission by casting down the altar of Baal in Ophrah. The Midianites having encamped in great force in the Valley of Jezreel, he called together the men of the neighbouring tribes. With a band of 300 chosen from these, he gained an easy victory over the enemy, having first produced a panic in their camp by a stratagem (Judges vi., vii.). Pursuing the fugitives over the upper fords of the Jordan, he defeated them a second time, and took their two kings Zeba and Zalmunna, whom he afterwards slew. Meantime the Ephraimites had seized the lower fords, and took and slew, doubtless with many others, two chiefs, Oreb and Zeeb. G. declined the honour which was now offered to him of becoming king, but lapsed into idolatry so far as to set up an Ephod (q. v.) (Judges viii.). Having thus shattered the power of the Midianites, he secured for his country safety from such depredations till his death, forty years afterwards.

Gien, a French town in the department of Loiret, on the right bank of the Loire, 38 miles E.S.E. of Orleans. It has a castle dating from the 15th c., and several very old buildings; the chief industries are printing and the making of crockery and whiting; and there is trade in corn, bay salt, saffron, wool, serges, coal, &c. G., the *Genabum* of Cæsar, was at one time a separate county. Pop. (1872) 7068.

Gies'eler, Johann Karl Ludwig, an ecclesiastical historian, was born at Petershagen, near Minden, 3d March 1792. He was educated at the University of Halle, and had entered upon a career as a teacher, but it was interrupted by his becoming a volunteer in the patriotic war against France. In 1815 he resumed his profession, and became in succession *con-rector* of the gymnasium at Minden, director of the gymnasium at Kleve, ordinary professor of theology at Bonn, and professor at Göttingen. His death took place July 8, 1854. G. was a philanthropist, a writer in magazines and of books on various subjects. See his *Narratio de Bogomilis* of Euthymius Zygabenus (Gött. 1842), and Siculus' *Historia Manicheorum seu Paulicianorum* (Gött. 1846); but he has attained his chief eminence by his *Lehrbuch der Kirchengeschichte*, of which three vols. were published in his life, two posthumous ones appearing under the editorship of his pupil, E. R. Redepenning, who has also given a notice of his life. It is particularly valuable for its apt and instructive quotations. There is a good English translation by Professor Henry B. Smith (4 vols. New York, 1856–59).

Giess'en, the capital of the province of Upper Hessen, in the grand-duchy of Hessen-Darmstadt, at the confluence of the Wieseck and Lahn, 35 miles N. of Frankfurt by railway. It has a Protestant university (*Ludoviciana*), founded by Prince Ludwig V. in 1607, which has extensive scientific collections, a celebrated laboratory, a botanical garden, and a staff (1875) of 55 professors and 340 students. In the time of Liebig there were 700 students. G. has several quaint old public buildings, and its streets are crooked and narrow. The chief industries are in tobacco and liqueurs; and in the vicinity are iron and manganese mines. Pop. (1872) 12,225. G. arose in the 12th c., and was fortified in 1530. See Nebel's *Geschichte der Universität G.* (Marb. 1828), and Duller's *G. und Umgebungen* (2d ed. Gies. 1851).

Giff'ord, William, critic and satirist, was born at Ashburton, Devonshire, April 1756, and served in a coaster and as a shoemaker's apprentice, until several poems which he wrote won the notice of William Cookesley, a surgeon, who enabled him to study at Exeter College, Oxford. In 1794 he produced the *Baviad*, and in 1795 the *Mæviad*, two crushing satires against the Della-Cruscans (q. v.). He was made editor of the *Anti-Jacobin* in 1797, issued a translation of Juvenal in 1802, an edition of Massinger in 1805 and of Ben Jonson in 1816, and edited the *Quarterly Review* from 1808 to 1824. G. died in London, December 31, 1826. His editions of Ford and Shirley appeared after his death. G.'s editions of the old English dramatists have still some value, but his criticisms are now well-nigh forgotten, and his satires are as dead as the verses which they annihilated. He had a vigorous, but coarse and narrow mind; his criticism was wholly swayed by political prejudice; and his strictures were for the most part bluntly abusive, with occasional touches of malignant pungency and sour wit. See G.'s Autobiography prefixed to his *Juvenal*.

Gift means in English law a gratuitous transfer of property, real or personal. In the former case the transfer can only be made by deed. In the latter it may be made by deed or by delivery of the property with words of G. A gratuitous promise to give is not binding in law. A G. by a person insolvent at the date of it, though effectual against himself, is void against his creditors; and if any one give heritage to another and then sell the same, the gratuitous deed is void against a *bona fide* purchaser. No personal property can pass by G. of which absolute possession is not given by the donor; thus delivery of a stock receipt will not give the stock—there must be a transfer; but delivery of a bank-note transfers the property. In Scotch law G. is usually called a Donation (q. v.). In Scotland, as in England, a G. by an insolvent person is ineffectual against his creditor.

Gigue. See JIG.

Gijon', a Spanish town in the province of Oviedo, on the Bay of Biscay, 20 miles N.N.E. of the town of Oviedo. It is well built, is partly encircled by old walls, has an ancient castle, batteries, and an educational institution, *Instituto Asturiano*, with several professorships. The harbour is dangerous of access, but is safe and commodious within. There are large cigar manufactures and trade in coal and fruit. G. is the chief seaport and trading town in Asturias. Pop. 10,378.

Gi'la, a river of the United States, rises in the state of New Mexico, flows W. through Arizona, and joins the Colorado 70 miles from its mouth in the Gulf of California, after a course of 450 miles, 180 of which are navigable for flat boats. It is partly hemmed in by precipitous cliffs nearly 1000 feet high, and along its banks are found traces of a vanished civilisation.

Gil'bert, Sir Humphrey, a famous Devonshire gentleman of the Elizabethan era, born at Dartmouth in 1539, educated at Eton and Oxford, adopted the profession of arms, and rendered distinguished service in the Irish wars (for which the Queen conferred upon him the honour of knighthood) and in the Low Countries. He sat in the Parliament of 1571. In 1576 he wrote a treatise on the N.W. Passage to India, and two years after succeeded in obtaining from Elizabeth a patent authorising him to 'discover and take possession of any remote heathen and barbarous lands not being actually possessed by any Christian prince or people.' Aided by his half-brother, Sir Walter Raleigh (G.'s mother was twice married, the second time to Walter Raleigh of Fardel, Devonshire), he fitted out a naval squadron for discovery and conquest in 1579; but his ships, damaged by tempest and beaten in an engagement with the Spaniards, were driven back to England. In 1583 he organised another expedition of five vessels and 260 men, which was still more disastrous. With four out of his five vessels G. reached Newfoundland, and in terms of his patent took possession of it in the Queen's name. Sailing southward G. lost the largest of his three remaining ships, with nearly all on board, off Cape Breton. On the 9th September in the midst of a storm, G., 'sitting abaft with a book in his hand,' more than once exclaimed 'We are as near to heaven by sea as by land.' On the evening of the same day the frigate in which he sailed went down with all on board. Besides being a conspicuously brilliant, chivalrous figure in an age renowned for brilliance and chivalry, G. is to be remembered as taking a prominent part in laying the foundations of English colonisation in America.

Gilbert, William, an English physician and natural philosopher, was born at Colchester in 1540. He graduated at St. John's College, Cambridge, as M.A. in 1564, and M.D. in 1569, after which he travelled abroad for a time. On his return he settled in London in 1573, entered the Royal College of Physicians, and ultimately became physician to Queen Elizabeth. His pension enabled him to carry on the researches in magnetism for which his name is famous. In his work *De Magnete Magneticisque Corporibus, et de Magno Magnete, Tellure, Physiologia Nova* (1600), he establishes the polar property of the magnet, shows the earth to be magnetic, and calls those poles by the same name which repel each other, so that it is the S. pole of a magnetic needle which points to the N. He further gives a list of substances which, like amber, become electrified by friction, and lays down the fundamental laws of electricity. He was continued in his position as royal physician by King James, but died at Colchester, November 30, 1603, soon after. His other work, *De Mundo nostro Sublunari Philosophia Nova* (Amst. 1651), was printed from a MS. in the library of Sir William Boston.

Gilbert Islands, or **Kingsmill Group**, the name given to sixteen inhabited coral islands of Mulgrave Archipelago, in the Pacific, lat. 1° S.–2° 30′ N., long. 172°–174° 30′ E. They are low-lying, and are covered with a thin layer of rich soil, in which grow coco-nut, taro, and pandanus trees. The two largest, Drummond's Isle and Knox's Isle, are 30 and 20 miles long respectively. The inhabitants, 60,000 in number, are like the Malays in feature, and have been known to practise cannibalism. Missions are maintained here by the Hawaiian and American Congregationalists.

Gilbo'a (Heb. 'bubbling fountain'), a mountain range in the E. of the plain of Esdraelon, which is only mentioned in the Bible in connection with the defeat and death of Saul and Jonathan by the Philistines (1 Sam. xxxi. 1; 2 Sam. i. 6, &c.).

Gil'das, a writer who probably flourished in the 6th c., but whose life has come down to us only in two legends, neither of which is credible. According to one of his editors, Mr. Stevenson, 'we are unable to speak with certainty as to his parentage, his country, or even his name, the period when he lived, or the works of which he was the author.' Mr. Skene, a better authority, in his *Four Ancient Books of Wales* (vol. i. pp. 33–37), expresses himself more moderately. He says—'The treatise [of G.] is evidently the work of one man, and there is evidence in the work itself of his date. The writer states that he was born in the year in which the battle of Badon was fought, and that he wrote forty-four years after. According to the oldest Welsh annals, the battle of Badon was fought in the year 516, which would place the composition of the treatise in the year 560, and the Irish annals record the death of G. in 570, ten years later.' The work of G. is in Latin, and is sometimes called the *De Excidio Britanniæ*. It consists (1) of a 'Preface,' in which he explains why he undertook his task; (2) a brief 'History of Britain during the confusions before and after the withdrawal of the Romans;' (3) an 'Epistle,' containing chiefly denunciations of the British 'kings' for their wickedness, out of which with difficulty some fragments of fact can be extracted, and ending with a long string of warnings from the Old Testament. Three MSS. of G. once existed; there are now only two, both in the public library at Cambridge, the one belonging to the 13th, the other to the close of the 14th c. The best editions are those of Stevenson, published by the 'English Historical Society' in 1838, and Petrie in the *Monumenta Historica Britannica* (Lond. 1848). There is an English translation by Habington (1638), which has been reproduced with certain 'modernisations' by Dr. Giles in Bohn's *Antiquarian Library*. See Skene's *Four Ancient Books of Wales* (2 vols. Edinb. 1868).

Gil'ding, the art of applying a superficial coating of gold to wood, metal, and other bodies. This is accomplished by several distinct methods.

With wood two kinds of G. are practised, called burnish G. and oil G. *Burnish* G. as applied to picture-frames consists principally of the following processes:—(1) Priming with *thin white*, a composition of whiting and pure size, and closing pores and irregularities with fine putty made without oil. (2) Coating four or five times with a whiting and size mixture, termed *thick white*, each coat being allowed to dry, the moulding being kept open and sharp by means of suitable tools, and the edges and surface smoothed with pumice and glass-paper. (3) Gold-sizing, or preparing the ground on which the gold leaf is to be laid. The burnish gold size is a soft mixture of pipeclay, Armenian bole, black lead, suet, and bullock's blood. A portion of it is melted in hot clear size, and from four to eight coats of the warm creamy mixture are laid on the moulding. Care is taken to make each coat equally thick, and to give it time to dry before another is applied. The whole is then smoothed, especially the parts to be produced in *matt* or dull gold, and the parts to be burnished are recoated with gold size. (4) G., in which the workman cuts the gold-leaf into narrow strips corresponding to the width of the depressions or prominences of the moulding. He then moistens with water a few inches of the surface, lays down a strip of gold with the aid of a *tip* brush, and presses out the superfluous water with a dry brush. The whole moulding is thus covered, and dried, and then burnished with agate. (5) Deadening the unburnished parts with weak size. (6) Faulting or covering little holes, previously wetted, with leaf, and strengthening the dull parts with another coat of size.

Oil G. differs slightly from the foregoing. A thin coat of white lead in oil is first applied, then red or yellow oil paint, next oil gold size, a mixture of boiled linseed oil and ochre. When the gold size is partially dry and sticky the gold leaf is laid on. Varnish may afterwards be brushed over it. Oil G. cannot be burnished, and alone can be washed.

Leather is gilded by applying *glaire* or egg albumen, and pressing down the gold leaf upon it with heated implements. Agate is used for burnishing.

Metal G. is accomplished by chemical means. *Wash G.*, formerly much practised, is still employed to some extent on account of its durability. Amalgam of gold of a pasty consistence is applied to the surface of the article to be gilded, and the mercury is dissipated by heat, leaving a thin film of gold, which is burnished with bloodstone.

G. by Immersion.—Copper articles may be coated by immersing them in a boiling-hot solution of perchloride of gold and bicarbonate of potash.

Electro G.—In this process, for details of which see ELECTRO-METALLURGY, the metal article is dipped into a bath containing a hot solution of auro-cyanide of potassium. Wood or any substance that can be coated with blacklead may be electro-gilded.

Porcelain or *glass* is gilded by painting it with powdered gold mixed with oxide of bismuth, borax, and gum-water. Heat in a muffle fixes the gold, which has to be burnished to enhance its lustre.

Gil'ead (Heb. 'a hard rocky region'), a mountainous region E. of the Jordan, first mentioned in connection with Jacob's flight from Laban (Gen. xxxi. 21), was taken possession of by the tribes of Reuben and Gad and half-tribe of Manasseh on the arrival of the Israelites at Canaan (Num. xxxii. 1, 29; Josh. xii. 1–6). Under the Romans G. prospered greatly, and several splendid towns were built. Under Turkish rule its population consists of a few wandering tribes.

Gilfill'an, Rev. George, was born at Comrie, Perthshire, in 1813. He was educated at Glasgow University, and in 1836 became minister of the School Wynd U.P. Church, Dundee, a charge which he still holds. He has won considerable popularity as an author and lecturer. Among his works are *A Gallery of Literary Portraits* (1845); *The Bards of the Bible* (1850); *The Martyrs, Heroes, and Bards of the Scottish Covenant* (1852); *History of Man* (1856); *Christianity and our Era* (1857); *Alpha and Omega* (1860); *Night*, a poem (1867); *Modern Christian Heroes* (1869); *Life of Sir Walter Scott* (1870). His writings are overcharged with metaphors, vehement and rhapsodical, but display some insight into the nature of poetry, and are not without flashes of genius and accidental felicities of erratic criticism.

Gill (Old Fr. *gaille* or *jale*, from Low Lat. *gillo* or *gello*, 'a flask') is a measure of capacity, the fourth part of a pint, and $\frac{1}{32}$ of a gallon.

Gill (Lat. *gula*, 'the throat'), or **Bran'chia**, the name given to the typical form of breathing organ in aquatic animals. In the typical fishes, for example, the gills consist of a number of filaments borne on the *branchial* or gill arches, each filament being composed of a network of minute blood-vessels, in which the air is exposed to the action of the oxygen of the surrounding water. In other fishes (as in the lampreys, sharks, rays, &c.) the gills exist as closed pouches or sacs, the lining-membrane of which consists of a network of capillary vessels. In fishes the gills are usually covered by an *operculum* or G.-cover, and water taken in by the mouth for the purpose of breathing is ejected, after passing over the G., behind the *operculum*. In some forms, such as proteus and axolotl amongst the *Amphibia* (q. v.), external gills exist, and in the tadpole stage of the frogs and toads both external and internal gills are temporarily developed. Among lower or invertebrate types gills of various kinds are found. Thus among Molluscs they form the breathing organs of cuttlefishes, Lamellibranchiates (q. v.) (mussels, oysters, &c.), of many Gasteropods (q. v.) (whelks, &c.), and of *Pteropoda* (q. v.). Lobsters, crabs, and other crustaceans breathe by gills, which exist as vascular processes adapted for bringing venous blood in contact with the oxygen of the surrounding water.

Gilles, St., an old French town in the department of Gard, 12 miles S.S.E. of Nîmes. It has a beautiful Romanesque church of the 11th c., and is noted for its fine wines. Pop. (1872) 6211.

Gilles'pie, George, a notable Scotch divine, born at Kirkcaldy in 1612. He was ordained minister of Wemyss in 1638, translated to Edinburgh in 1642, and in the following year was appointed commissioner from the Church of Scotland to the famous Westminster Assembly. The ability which he showed in theological discussion excited the admiration even of his Erastian opponents. In 1648 G. was elected moderator, but died prematurely in the same year. His *Dispute against the English Popish Ceremonies*, *Aaron's Rod Blossoming*, and *Miscellany Questions*, are meritorious works, but his historic eminence is greater than his literary fame.

Gill'ies, John, LL.D., a Scottish historian and classical scholar, was born at Brechin, Forfarshire, January 18, 1747.

Educated in Glasgow, he tried his fortune in London as a man of letters, was for some time travelling tutor to the sons of the second Earl of Hopetoun, and in 1793 succeeded Robertson as historiographer-royal for Scotland. He produced a number of histories and translations—*History of Ancient Greece* (1786), translations of the *Orations of Isocrates and those of Lysias* (1778), *Aristotle's Ethics and Politics* (1804), *Aristotle's Rhetoric* (1823), and *View of the Reign of Frederick II. of Prussia* (1789)—all of which are nearly quite forgotten. G. died February 5, 1836, at Clapham, London.

Gill'ray, James, an English caricaturist of Scotch parentage, was born at Chelsea in 1757. He was apprenticed to a letter-engraver, but it was not until, throwing aside his graver, he spent some time with a troop of strolling players, that he seems to have discovered that caricature was his true vocation. After studying at the Royal Academy, he allied himself with a publisher named Humphreys, with whom he continued to live till his death, and who printed and sold his drawings, which amounted in all to over 1200 in number. His caricatures, political and social, are often marred by the coarseness that characterised his time, but are always humorous and patriotic, and often savage in their moral intensity. He died June 1, 1815. G. has been restored to his rightful place in the history of intellectual life in England by the splendid edition of his *Works, with a History of his Life and Times*, by Thomas Wright, F.R.S. (Lond. 1873).

Gill'yflower (frequently written *gilloflower*, and corrupted into *July-flower*, from the French *giroflée*). G. is generally applied to varieties of the garden stock, the origin of which is *Matthiola incana*, a Cruciferous plant indigenous to Britain, and *M. annua*. Clove G. is applied to *Dianthus caryophyllus*, the clove-pink of gardens, and marsh G., sometimes to *Lychnis floscuculi* or Ragged Robin.

Gilo'lo (*Halmahera*), the chief island of a group of the same name in the Moluccas, in long. 128° E., and on the equator. It is separated from Celebes by the Molucca Passage, from New Guinea by G. Channel, and from Ceram by Pitt's Passage. Area, 6500 sq. miles. It is of volcanic origin, is mountainous and luxuriantly wooded, and exports spices, fruits, sago, cattle, horses, gold-dust, pearls, edible bird's-nests, &c. G. belongs in part to the Dutch. Its chief town is of the same name.

Gil Polo, Gaspar, a poet of Spain, born at Valencia about the beginning of the 16th c., held various honorary posts under Philip II. of Spain, and died at Barcelona in 1591. He is chiefly notable as a lyric poet, and as continuator of Montemayor's *Diana*, under the title *Primera Parte de Diana enamorada Cinco Libros, que prosique los Sieta de Jorge Montemayor* (1564; Cerda's ed. with G.'s *Canto de Turia*, 1802). His works were much admired when they appeared, and still give the impression of strength and lucidity.

Gilt'head, a name applied to at least two distinct species of Teleostean fishes. One of these (*Chrysophrys aurata*), found in the Mediterranean, belongs to the family of the *Sparidæ*, which includes the sea-bream, and in its turn forms a division of the *Acanthopterygii*. The Mullets (q. v.) are nearly allied to the *Sparidæ*. The *C. aurata* possesses a crescentic golden spot over the eye, and a violet patch over the gill-cover. The back is blue, and the sides marked with golden bands. The fins are bluish, and the bases of the dorsal and anal fins are bordered by very prominent scales. The teeth are large and powerful, and are used for bruising and crushing the shell-fish on which the fish feeds. The G. was a favourite in the *aquaria* of classic times. The name is also applied to the *Pagellus centrodontus*, or common sea-bream, from the silvery hues of its head. The eye is very large and yellow; the body colour, a grey tinted with red; while a dark patch occurs at the base of the pectoral fins, which with the tail-fin are coloured red. This fish is very common on the S. coasts of Britain.

Gilt Toys, a technical name for cheap jewellery, comprising lockets, brooches, and all kinds of personal ornaments, largely manufactured at Birmingham. By the aid of the stamp and screw-press the requisite form is given to the metal, which is then electro-plated with a very thin film of gold. Sometimes imitation gems, shell cameos, jet, and other materials are used in combination with the gilt metal. In this way the finest jewellery is imitated, and may be obtained at an astonishingly low price.

Gil Vicen'te, 'the Plautus of Portugal,' was born about 1470, his birthplace being still a matter of dispute. After studying law at Lisbon University, he devoted himself to producing dramas for the courts of Emmanuele and of Joao III., the latter king even taking a part in one of his comedies. He seems to have been an actor as well as an author, but little is known of his life. He died at Evora in 1557. G. is the founder of the Portuguese, and, in some degree, of the Spanish drama. His works consist of *autos*, or religious pieces, comedies, tragi-comedies, and farces. The mythological machinery of G.'s plays is often grotesquely absurd, and their plots are loose and careless, but they show rich invention and humour, and, especially in the farces, which are really comedies, much insight into character and lively natural dialogue. The verse is flowing and harmonious. G.'s complete works were edited by Feio and Monteiro (Hamb. 1832). See Bouterwek's *Geschichte der neueren Poesie und Beredsamkeit* (1801–19).

Gim'bals (Lat. *gemelli*, 'twins') are two concentric metallic rings, the inner of which is movable about a diameter of the outer as axis, while the outer is movable round a horizontal axis perpendicular to the former. By such an arrangement, an object attached to the inner ring will preserve its originally horizontal position for *any* motion. The principle is applied in the mounting of ships' compasses, portable barometers, &c.

Gim'blet (Fr. *gibelet*, probably connected with *wimble*, 'to twist'), a tool for boring holes in wood. Its conical point combines the principles of the wedge and screw, and is followed by a groove for clearing, which may be either straight or spiral.

Gimigna'no, San, an old Italian town in the province of Siena, 22 miles S.S.W. of Florence. It has a medieval appearance, and its tall towers, whence it was called *San G. delle belle torri*, are still standing. Of its churches the most interesting are *La Collegiata*, built in the 11th c., and *S. Agostino*, begun in 1280. G. was a thriving place in the 13th c. Pop. 7425.

Gimp, or **Gymp**, a kind of silk, cotton, or woollen braid, with a wire or coarse thread twisted through it, used as edging by upholsterers.

Gin (contr. from 'engine;' Lat. *ingenium*, 'a contrivance' or 'invention') is a word that was at one time often used by engineers and millwrights for certain descriptions of windlass employed to raise weights, drive piles, &c., either by hand or by animal power. It now generally denotes a machine for cleaning and preparing cotton or wool.

Gin, a spirit for drinking, prepared either from malt or from raw grain, and flavoured properly with juniper berries, whence the name, which is an abbreviation of Geneva, itself a corruption of the French *genièvre*, 'juniper.' The manufacture of G. is peculiarly a Dutch industry, centring at Schiedam, whence the spirit is very frequently known as Hollands or Schiedam. From that country it is largely exported to most quarters of the globe, but Great Britain and the United States of America are the principal customers. Hollands G. is usually imported in peculiar quadrangular bottles. The spirit when pure and genuine has a powerful diuretic influence, owing to the essential oil of juniper it contains, which renders it medicinally of considerable value, but more than any other intoxicating beverage it is subject to adulterations of a most pernicious character. It is the favourite drink of the lower orders in London, and to meet their tastes for a potent and pungent stimulant, a harsh, ill-rectified spirit is compounded with oil of turpentine, common salt, and many deleterious essential oils, which communicate a factitious strength to the spirit. The imports of Hollands G. into Great Britain during 1874 amounted to 324,260 proof gallons, valued at £59,535.

Gin'gal, or **Gingall**, a Chinese piece of ordnance of great antiquity, and still employed as a wall-gun. It is said that breech-loading gingals which have been in use for centuries may be seen in Northern China.

Gin'ger (formerly *gingiber*, Fr. *gingembre*, Lat. *zinziberum*, from Sansk. *Gringa-bera*, 'horn-shaped'), the name applied to the root-stock or rhizome of *Zingiber officinale*, a plant belonging to the Monocotyledonous order *Zingiberaceæ*, and a native of the E. Indies, where it is also extensively cultivated, as well as in the W. Indies, Africa, and China. G. is either preserved green in syrup or dried. There are several white and black varieties. Upwards of 550 tons are annually imported into Britain. It is an aromatic stimulant, and is largely used as a condiment for flavouring.

Ginger-Beer', a pleasant, refreshing, non-alcoholic beverage, frequently prepared on a small scale for domestic use. The following recipe produces an excellent quality:—To each gallon of water used add one pound of refined sugar and about one-third of an ounce of ground ginger. Boil this for an hour, then add the white of two eggs, and remove the scum. Strain the liquor into a vessel to cool, then cask it up with the juice and peel, fine cut, of a lemon. To this add a very small quantity of brewer's yeast, and bung tightly up for a fortnight, then bottle, and a fortnight thereafter the G.-B. will be fit for use.

Gin'gerbread, an ancient and (especially with children) a favourite sweet cake. There are two kinds, one baked thick and soft; the other, thin and crimp when baked. Of the numerous ways of making soft G., the following is an example:—Half a pound of butter, a quart of treacle, eight eggs, four table-spoonfuls of ginger, two tea-spoonfuls of carbonate of ammonia, kneaded thoroughly up with flour into a very stiff dough. Lemon peel and almonds are frequently added, and the whole baked in an oven. Hard G. requires no 'raising,' and it is rolled out thin and baked in flat pans in a moderately hot oven.

Ginger-Wine', or **British Wine**, is a popular and cheap liqueur manufactured on a considerable scale in Great Britain. To every fourteen gallons of water are added six pounds of fine pounded sugar, four ounces of ground ginger, and the white of two eggs. The mixture after boiling a quarter of an hour is skimmed and decanted into an earthenware vessel to cool, when the juice and peel of four lemons and half a pint of brewer's yeast are added. After fermenting for a day the liquor is racked off into a cask, and kept closely bunged up for two weeks. Before bottling, a little alcohol is generally added to improve its keeping qualities.

Gingh'am (Fr. *guingan*), a cotton fabric originally manufactured in India, and thence introduced into Europe. It differs from calico in this respect—that the colours are produced by dyeing the yarn, and not by printing the cloth. Britain has now largely taken the Eastern trade out of the hands of the native manufacturers. The chief kinds of G. are Earlston ginghams, power-loom seersuckers and checks, muslin grounds, coloured diapers, derries, Hungarians, umbrella ginghams. Glasgow is a great seat of the G. trade.

Gink'go, or **Gin'go**, the Japanese name for *Salisburia adiantifolia*, or maidenhair tree, a large tree belonging to the natural order *Taxaceæ*. It is grown in China and Japan, and also in Britain as an ornamental object. Its fruit is astringent and resinous, and an oil is extracted from the seed. Its wood is yellowish white and takes on a fine polish.

Gin'seng, the name given to the roots of the species of *Panax*, a genus belonging to the natural order *Araliaceæ*. G. is greatly esteemed by the Chinese, who believe that it can remove fatigue and completely restore exhausted animal power. The word G. is said to mean the 'wonder of the world.' The root is aromatic and mucilaginous.

Giober'ti, Vincen'zo, an Italian philosopher and political writer, was born at Turin, 5th April 1801. He was educated for the Church, in 1825 was made Professor of Theology in his native city, and in 1833 court chaplain. Suspected of sympathy with Young Italy, and accused of complicity in a republican plot, G. was sent into exile; and till 1847 he lived abroad, chiefly in Brussels, busied with literature. The works published during this period are mostly on philosophical subjects, and comprise an *Introduzione allo Studio della Filosofia* (1839) and a treatise *Dello Bello*. But the political ideal advocated in *Il Primato civile e morale degli Italiani* (1843) immediately left an abiding mark on the history of Italian political thought; and when G. returned to Italy in 1847, he was received with popular enthusiasm, immediately obtained political appointment, and soon stood at the head of a short-lived democratic Ministry. The new premier sent G. to Paris in 1849, where he died, 26th October 1852, ever faithful to the central thought of the *Primato*, that the new birth of Italy was to be found in a confederation of the Italian states under the primacy of the Pope, with the Piedmontese King as military protector. G. was buried with public honours at Turin. G. was a zealous but enlightened Catholic. His *Il Gesuita moderno* appeared in 1847, *Il Rinuovamento civile dell' Italia* in 1851. G.'s philosophy has of late attracted notice. A collected edition of his works was published in 9 vols. (1843-45), and his posthumous writings appeared in 1859. See Spaventa, *La Filosofia di G.* (2 vols. Nap. 1864).

Gio'ja, Melchiore, an Italian political economist, was born at Piacenza, 20th September 1767. He was educated at the College Alberoni, and first attracted notice by a prize essay in favour of the Republican form of government. In 1797 he was appointed state historiographer at Milan, and in 1809 was employed to draw up a statistical report of Italy. He was a keen satirist (as his *Il Povero Diabolo* shows), and a sharp critic, especially of those who criticised him; but at the same time he did very substantial work as a statistician. G. died at Milan, January 2, 1828. His best works are *Dell' ingiuria, dei danni, del soddisfaci mento e relative basi di stima* (Milan, 1802); *Nuovo prospetto delle scienze economiche ossia somma totale delle idea teoriche e pratiche in ogni ramo d'amministrazione privata e pubblica* (1815-19); and *Filosofia della Statistica* (1826).

Gioja del Colle, a town in the province of Bari, S. Italy, 26 miles S. of Bari by railway. It was founded in the 6th c., and in the vicinity, at Monte Sannace and Santa Sophia, have been found valuable ancient vases and Greco-Roman coins. Pop. 13,094. G. is also the name of three small towns in S. Italy.

Giojo'sa, a town in the S. of Italy, province of Catanzaro, on a fertile slope of the Apennines, and near the railway from Taranto to Reggio. Its inhabitants are noted for their beauty. G. stands near the site of *Locri Epizephyrii*, and seems to have arisen after the destruction of that place in the 12th c. Pop. 6889.

Giorda'no, Luca (surnamed *Luca, fa presto*, from the rapidity with which he worked), a dexterous painter, born at Naples in 1632, studied under Spagnoletto, and at the age of sixteen entered the studio of Pietro da Cortona at Rome. The art of his later years shows the distinct influence of Paolo Veronese. G. is said to have painted the large altar-piece of the Jesuits at Naples in less than thirty-six hours. He was fertile in invention, a master of perspective, his colour was tender and harmonious and his touch free and vigorous; but he was wanting in individuality, and in all his pictures the same types of character are reproduced. In 1679, on the invitation of Charles II. of Spain, he visited that country, and was employed in the decoration of the Escorial, in which he painted a vast number of immense pictures—'Death of the Virgin,' 'Last Judgment,' 'Passage of the Red Sea,' 'Triumph of the Church Militant,' &c. He died about 1704. G.'s works are everywhere. His frescoes may be best studied at Naples, Rome, and at the Escorial; his easel pictures in the Louvre and the museum of Madrid. See Sir William Stirling-Maxwell's *Annals of the Artists in Spain* (1848).

Giorgio'ne, properly **Gior'gio Barbarell'i**, one of the greatest of the Venetian colourists, was born at Castelfranco in the N.E. of Italy, in 1478, and studied, together with Titian, under Giovanni Bellini. He decorated a number of the buildings of Venice with noble frescoes. His portraits are among the most beautiful of the Italian school. His compositions, mostly scriptural and pastoral scenes, are fresh and original, and his colour royally rich. No one before his day wielded the pencil with his decision and firmness of touch, and no one carried the art of producing effect at a certain distance higher than he. G. died prematurely at Venice in 1533. A 'Holy Family' and 'Concert' are in the Louvre; numerous portraits and a 'Virgin and Child' in Venice; a 'Nymph and Satyr,' 'Moses Rescued,' and 'Concert' at Florence; and many other examples in Madrid, Vienna, Dresden, and Munich. See Vasari, *Vite de' più eccellenti Pittori* (Flor. 1550); and Rigollot, *Essai sur le Giorgione* (Amiens, 1852).

Giott'o, properly **Angiolott'o** or **Ambrogiott'o Bordo'ne,** one of the greatest of the old Italian masters, distinguished as painter, sculptor, architect, and poet, was born about 1276 at Colle, about 33 miles S. of Florence. In boyhood, while engaged tending sheep, it was his custom to amuse himself drawing on slates and rocks. One of his sketches came under the notice of Cimabue, who took the boy into his studio and instructed him in art. The pupil eventually excelled the master, chiefly by abandoning the traditions of the Byzantine school and devoting himself to nature and truth. His series of thirty-two pictures at Assisi, representing the life of St. Francis, may be said to be the earliest example of allegorical painting. His mosaic of the 'Navicella' or boat of St. Peter, in the great church at Rome, is considered his greatest work. It has been much injured by successive restorations. 'The Last Supper' in the refectory, and 'The Coronation of the Virgin' in the church of Santa Croce, Florence; 'St. Francis,' now in the Louvre; his six great frescoes representing 'The History of Job' for the convent of Campo Santo, Pisa, are also fine specimens of his genius. The beautiful campanile of the cathedral, Florence, was built after G.'s design, and the *bassi-rilievi* of that building were executed by him. His portraits of Dante, Donati, and other famous contemporaries are not more remarkable as works of art than valuable for fidelity and individuality. He went to France on the invitation of Pope Clement V., and painted many frescoes there. He was the author of a poem, *Giotti, pintor di Florentia, sopra la poverta.* G. died 8th January 1336 at Florence, and was buried in the church of Santa-Maria-del-Fiore, which he himself had designed. See Vasari, *Vite de' più eccellenti Pittori* (Flor. 1550).

Giovann'i (San) a Teduccio, a small straggling town, 3 miles E. of Naples, on the highroad to Pompeii. It stands in a fertile, densely-peopled district, and its name is said to be a corruption of Theodosius, that emperor's name having been found on a column near G. It is a place of great antiquity. Pop. 7298.—**San Giovanni in Fiore,** a town in the S. of Italy, province of Cosenza, 20 miles N.W. of Cotrone. It stands on the Neto, in the beautiful hilly region of La Silva, amid rich woods and pastures. Pop. 9239.—**San Giovanni Rotondo,** a small town of S. Italy in the province of Foggia, near the Adriatic, 7 miles N.W. of Manfredonia. It stands in a hilly district, and has linen and woollen manufactures. Pop. 6865.

Giovinazz'o, a seaport in the province of Bari, S. Italy, 15 miles N.W. of Bari by railway. It has an active trade in oil, wine, and fruits, and is richly girt with olive and almond groves. Among its public institutions are an asylum for the poor and a large reformatory. Pop. 9108. G., supposed to be the Roman Natiolum, has remains of ancient walls towards the sea. It was taken by the Greeks in the 11th c., and subsequently passed to the Gonzaga family.

Gip'sies. See GYPSIES.

Gipsy-Moth (*Hypogymna dispar*), a species of Moths (q. v.) belonging to the family *Arctiidæ*, in which the antennæ of the males are deeply notched, the wings being bent downwards in repose, and the proboscis small or wanting. The genus *Hypogymna* has no proboscis, and the wings are opaque. The feelers are comb-like in both sexes, and the male abdomen has a tuft at its tip. The male G.-M. is of dark-brown colour; the female, greyish white. The front wings are marked with four transverse and wavy brown bands, and a V-shaped mark exists at the middle of their anterior margin. The G.-M. is common on the Continent.

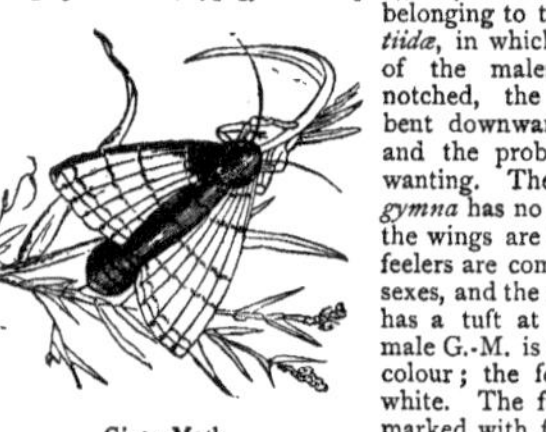

Gipsy-Moth.

Giraffe' (*Camelopardalis giraffa*), a remarkable genus of *Mammalia* belonging to the *Ruminant* section of the *Ungulate* or hoofed order. It is the only living species of its genus, and occurs in Africa. The horns are covered with a hairy skin, and tufted at their tips; the neck is exceedingly long, but consists of only seven vertebræ, the ordinary number among mammalia; the lips are hairy and not grooved; the tongue is extensile; and the tail, which is of moderate length, has a tuft of hair at the tip. The height of the full-grown G. is about 18 to 20 feet. The back slopes in a very marked manner, but the legs are of nearly equal length. The tongue is well adapted for seizing the foliage of trees, which the animal is enabled to reach by the length of its neck. The general colour of the body is a very light brown, marked by definitely rounded patches scattered over the entire surface. The food of the G. consists of grasses in addition to the leaves of trees. The G. is of a gentle disposition, but when enraged, manages to defend itself most effectually by kicking with its strong hoofs. It is easily tracked by its *spoor* or footprints, and runs awkwardly owing to the great weight and size of its fore-parts. It lives gregariously in small herds of from five or six to fourteen or more in number, one large male being the leader of his herd. The flesh is palatable, and the hide is made into strong leather.

Giraffe.

Giral'dus Cambren'sis ('Gerald the Welshman,' the name usually given to Gerald de Barri), the son of William de Barri, a Norman noble, and Angharad, the daughter of a Welsh princess, is one of the liveliest and most interesting of English mediæval authors. He was born in the castle of Manorbeer, Pembrokeshire, about 1146, and was educated by his uncle, the Bishop of St. David's. He distinguished himself at Paris University, returned to England in 1172, and obtained church preferment; but the king refusing to sanction his election to St. David's bishopric, he resumed his scholar's life at Paris until 1180, when he came back to England, and was made administrator of St. David's see. In 1185 he travelled with Prince John through Ireland, and in 1187 accompanied the Archbishop of Canterbury on a tour through Wales—these journeys forming the subjects of his *Topographiæ Hiberniæ* and *Itinerarium Cambriæ.* G. visited France with Henry II. in 1189, and after being again elected to St. David's bishopric, and set aside by the Archbishop of Canterbury's influence, spent his last years in studious retirement, and died at St. David's in 1223. G. was both a fine scholar and a keen-witted man of the world. His works give the vivid impressions of a traveller through Ireland and Wales in the middle ages, and afford a valuable and entertaining picture of his times. They are full of quaint gossip and bright witty sallies, their credulity and frank egotism are pleasing rather than otherwise, and their Latin is delightfully clear and vivacious. G. was the earliest English pamphleteer, and has been called the 'father of our popular literature.' He made fearless attacks on the civil government, and poured forth fierce invectives against the Angevin kings. Besides the accounts of his Welsh and Irish tours, G. wrote *Expugnatio Hiberniæ, Descriptio Cambriæ; De Vita Galfridi Archiepiscopi Eboracensis; Speculum Ecclesiæ,* an attack on the monkish orders, &c. See the edition by Brewer and Dimock, of which 6 vols. had appeared in 1875. There is an English version of G. in Bohn's *Antiquarian Library.*

Girar'din, Émile de, a French journalist noted for his sparkling style and his political fickleness, was the illegitimate son of General Alexandre de G., and was born in Switzerland about 1802. After working in a stockbroker's office, he became connected with various periodicals, married Mdlle. Delphine Gay (q. v.) in 1831, and in 1836 produced *La Presse,* the earliest penny paper, which met with vast popularity. G. has shifted incessantly in his political opinions, writing with equal ability and with seemingly equal ardour in favour of conservatism, republicanism, constitutionalism, and socialism, and justly earning the sobriquet of *La Girandole* ('the weathercock'). He sold his share in *La Presse* for £32,000 in 1856, again became editor of the paper in 1862, but soon retired from it to edit *La Liberté,* and in 1867 was fined 5000 francs for assailing the Napoleonic administration in his new journal. He ceased to edit *La Liberté* in 1870. He has written several dramatic pieces and a number of pamphlets. A collection of his articles was issued in 1858, entitled *Questions de mon Temps*, 1836 *à* 1856.

Girardin, St. Marc, a French professor and author, born at Paris, February 19, 1801. He studied at the Collége Henri IV., and in 1827 was made professor in the Collége Louis le Grand, and received a prize from the Academy for an *éloge* on Bossuet. In 1830 he visited Germany, where he became intimate with Hegel, and on returning to France, was chosen to succeed Guizot as Professor of History in the Faculty of Letters. He received the chair of Poetry in 1834, and being already known by his political articles in the *Débats*, was elected to the Chamber of Deputies in the same year. He was made an Academician in 1844, and Minister of Public Instruction in 1848. He continued to work as a professor and as a journalist until 1863, when he gave up his chair in the Sorbonne. In 1869 he succeeded St. Beuve as editor of the *Journal des Savants*. Among his works are *Tableau de la Marche et des Progrès de la Littérature Française au XVIème Siècle* (1828); *Rapport sur l'Instruction Intermédiaire en Allemagne* (1835–38); *Cours de Littérature Dramatique*, his chief work (1843–68); *Tableau de la Littérature Française* (1861); *Souvenirs et Voyages* (1861); *Essai de Littérature et de Morale* (2d ed. 1863); *La Fontaine et les Fabulistes* (1867), &c. He is a moderate Liberal in politics, and is very clear-sighted, impartial, and catholic in his critical verdicts.

Gir'asol (Lat. *gyrus*, 'a circuit,' and *sol*, 'the sun'), a variety of Opal (q. v.), bluish white, translucent with reddish reflections when turned to the sun or any bright light; also applied to the asteriated sapphire (Pliny's *asteria*), which exhibits a pale star-like opalescence.

Gir'der, a structure supported at the ends, and used for carrying a load placed between the points of support. It is thus the same as *beam*, the latter word being commonly used in theoretical works, while G. is more distinctly technical. A G. is commonly made either of cast or wrought iron or steel. The first-named material is used frequently for such girders as occur in buildings, on account of its comparative cheapness in these cases. In Bridges (q. v.), on the other hand, cast iron is seldom used, wrought iron being employed in the great majority of cases. A 'continuous' G. is one supported vertically at one or more places besides the ends. Such girders have many advantages over simple girders in economy of material, but their theory is much more complex. They are now largely used by engineers. A G. bridge differs from a suspension bridge or an arch in being complete in itself, requiring only vertical support, and not being dependent on the pull of anchor chains or the thrust of abutments for its stability.

Gir'dle of Ve'nus (*Cestum Veneris*), a peculiar animal organism belonging to the *Cœlenterata* (q. v.), and to the order *Ctenophora* (q. v.) of the class *Actinozoa*. It is met with off the British coasts and in warm seas, and is a long ribbon or band-like structure, which may attain a length of 3 or 4 feet and a breadth of 3 or 4 inches. It is allied in its nature and structure to the more familiar *Beröe* or *Cydippe*. Two tentacles extend away from the mouth. The G. of V. is markedly phosphorescent, and resembles at night, as it swims through the sea, a long waving band of flame. See also PHOSPHORESCENCE, ANIMAL.

Gir'geh (from *Girgis* or George, the patron saint of the Coptic Church), a town of Upper Egypt, of which it was formerly the capital, on the left bank of the Nile, 108 miles W.N.W. of Thebes. It is beautifully embowered among palms, above which rise its eight minarets. Its Roman Catholic convent is the oldest in Egypt, and it has a fine bazaar and some cotton industry. G., however, is suffering much from the encroachment of the Nile. Pop. 10,000.

Girgen'ti. See AGRIGENTUM.

Girnar, a mountain in the peninsula of Kattywar, India, rising abruptly about 3000 feet. It is a frequented place of pilgrimage, and the summit is studded with Jain temples. At the foot is a rock with Pali inscriptions, which date back to the 3d c. B.C.

Gironde', the largest department of France, is formed out of part of Guienne, and is bounded N. by Charente-Inférieure, E. by Dordogne and Lot-et-Garonne, S. by Landes, and W. by the Bay of Biscay. Area, 3761 sq. miles; pop. (1872) 705,149. The surface is for the most part flat or undulating. In the W. stretch the Landes de la G., a sterile waste of heath and shifting sand, broken only by occasional forests of pine; while in the E., and especially along the beautiful banks of the Garonne, most of the soil is under the vine. G. is watered by the Garonne and its tributaries. It produces much wheat, maize, hemp, garden fruit, and famous wines (Lafitte, Latour, Château-Margaux, Sauterne, and Vin de Grave) to the extent of 44,000,000 gallons annually. Other industries are the rearing of sheep and cattle, fishing, sugar-refining, shipbuilding, and iron-smelting. The coast, 90 miles long, is lined with lagoons (as the Bassin d'Arcachon and Étang de Carcan), which yield much salt. Turpentine, pitch, and charcoal are got from the pine forests. Bordeaux is the capital, and other towns are Lesparre, Blaye, Bazas, and Libourne. G. is traversed by the Paris-à-Bordeaux and Bordeaux-à-Bayonne Railways.

Giron'dists, or **Giron'dins**, the name given to the moderate party which sat in the French Legislative Assembly from 1791 to 1793, because several of its chief members came from the Gironde. At first the G., who were ardent patriots and men of greater culture than most of their associates in the Assembly, opposed the court and proposed stringent edicts against the priests and nobles. The king chose four of them for his ministers in 1792, but shortly dismissed them, the consequence being a rising in Paris which led to their recall, August 11, 1792. They then showed utter incapacity to meet the difficulties of the time, threatened the Jacobins with the guillotine, and before the middle of 1793 had brought France to the brink of ruin. Marat, whom they had sought to impeach, in turn demanded their arrest, and in 1793 the Parisian rabble drove them from the Convention. Several of the G. fled into the provinces and strove to gather an army at Caen, but their supporters were easily crushed by the energy of the Jacobins. A number of their leaders—among others Brissot, Vergniaud, Sillery, Lacaze, Ducos, Fauchet, Lasource—were sent to the guillotine, October 31, 1793, singing the *Marseillaise* on their way to execution. During 1794 many others of the G. perished. The G. were well-intentioned and true lovers of freedom, who wished to establish a moderate republic, but they had not the energy, determination, and zeal of the Jacobins. See Lamartine's *Histoire des G.* (Par. 1847).

Gironné ('girdled;' from Lat. *giro*, 'the lower part of the tunic, a skirt;' a word, however, of Teutonic origin), in heraldry, a field divided into several parts or gyrons. A gyron is an ordinary composed of two lines issuing from the dexter chief point, and meeting in an acute angle at the fesse point.

Gir'van, a seaport of Ayrshire, Scotland, at the mouth of a small river of the same name (Celt. 'the short stream'), opposite Ailsa Craig, and 21 miles S.W. of Ayr by the Glasgow and South-Western Railway. It has a good harbour and a brisk export trade in coal, chiefly to Belfast, distant 65 miles. Its fine beach and beautiful environs attract many summer visitors. Pop. (1871) 4776.

Gi'sors, a town of France, department of Eure, on the Epte, 30 miles N.W. of Paris, with which it is joined by railway. It has an old castle and a church which dates from the 13th c., some trade in grain, wool, cattle, and copper and zinc works. Pop. (1872) 3834. Here Richard I. defeated the French, October 10, 1198.

Gitsch'in (*Jičin*), a town of Bohemia, capital of a circle of the same name, on the Cydlina, 50 miles N.E. of Prague, with which it is connected by railway. It was formerly the capital of the duchy of Friedland; became the residence of Wallenstein, whose bones were placed in a neighbouring Carthusian monastery in 1636; and has a beautiful church after a Spanish model, a Jesuits' college turned into barracks, and an active corn trade. Pop. (1869) 5715. A victory was gained by the Prussians over the Austrians at G. on the night of June 29, 1866.

Giuli'ni, Giorgio, an Italian historian, born at Milan in 1794. He studied at Padua, and, after a life of learned research, died in 1780. Of his works, which are marked by deep erudition and incisive criticism, the chief are *Memorie spettanti alla Storia, al Governo, ed alla Descrizione della Città e della Campagna di Milano ne' Secoli bassi* (1760–75), which throws much light on the mediæval history of Milan; *Continuazione delle Memorie spettanti*, &c., which carries the Milanese history down to 1447; *Di Giulia Drusilla* (1756); *Sopra l' Anfiteatro di Milano* (1757). G. likewise wrote dissertations on Latin poetry, antique gems and inscriptions, &c. See Fabroni's *Vitæ Italorum* (Pisa, 1778–1805).

Giu'lio Roma'no, properly **Pippi**, the favourite pupil, the heir, and the artistic successor of Raffaelle, and a painter, architect, and engineer of high original genius, was born at Rome in 1492. Raffaelle, who had availed himself of G.'s assistance in carrying out some of his greatest designs, as 'The Battle of Constantine' and the frescoes in the Vatican, left directions at his death (1520) that his unfinished pictures should also be completed by G. One of these works, so completed, was the famous 'Transfiguration.' Of the great works independently executed by G., and which still show the influence of Raffaelle, are the embellishments of the villas Madama and Lante, both of which he had himself built, and which are distinguished for nobleness, variety, and elegance in design. Among his frescoes of the earlier period is 'The Martyrdom,' in the church of St. Stephen, Genoa, which for splendour of colour recals 'The Transfiguration.' A well-known and favourite picture of the same period is 'The Holy Family' (Dresden), in which the mother is preparing to wash the child. The child stands in a basin, and the young St. John sportively sprinkles him with water. G. was docile and tractable under the master-spirit of Raffaelle, and seemed at times to breathe the same air. After the death of his preceptor, however, he abandoned himself to an inferior class of compositions. He painted classical and mythological subjects—many of the latter being treated with reprehensible license. Invited to Mantua by Duke Frederico Gonzaga, he resided there many years, during which he built and decorated the famous Palazzo del Te. The Hall of Giants, in which he represents the defeat of the Titans, shows astonishing power, and proves G. to have been in some respects equal to Buonarotti. At Mantua he built the severely fine cathedral and a number of palaces and churches. He also drained the Mantuan marshes, which had previously suffered from the overflowing of the Po and Mincio. G. died at Rome, 1st November 1546.

Giurge'vo ('St. George's town'), the chief town of the district of Vlachka, and the river-port of Bucharest, in Wallachia, on the left bank of the Danube, opposite Rustchuk, and 40 miles S. of Bucharest by railway. It has a thriving trade, the exports chiefly consisting of grain, maize, and salt. In 1873 the imports amounted in value to £750,000, and 1237 steamers cleared, of which number 669 belonged to the Austrian Danube Co. The town is connected by a bridge with the fortified island of Slobodse. G. was originally the Genoese settlement of St. George, and later a fortress of the Turks, who were defeated here by the Russians in 1854. Pop. 15,000.

Gius'ti, Giusepp'e, a great Italian poet, was born at Monsuannano, near Pescia in Tuscany, in 1809. He studied law at Pisa, but the subject was distasteful to him, and he early withdrew into a retired life, mingling only with a few such friends as Manzoni, D'Azeglio, and Capponi, and issued patriotic and satiric lyrics, which became universally popular, and did much to stir up his countrymen against Austria. He was elected to the Tuscan Chamber in 1848, and after the fall of Capponi's Ministry was attacked as a reactionary. G. died at Florence in 1850. He was an ardent patriot, and a moderate Liberal in politics. His writings are full of satiric wrath relieved by playful and incisive wit. Among his works are *Stivale*, an exquisitely humorous and sarcastic allegory, in which Italy is represented as a *boot* that has undergone no end of misfits, repairs, bad usage, &c.; *Gingillino*; and *Re Travicello*. A complete edition of his writings was published at Florence in 1852. See Horner, *The Tuscan Poet Giuseppe Giusti and his Times* (Lond. 1864).

Gi'vet, a fortified French town in the department of Ardennes, on the Meuse, 145 miles N.E. of Paris. It consists of three parts, *Le Grand G.*, *Le Petit G.*, and the *Citadelle-de-Charlemont*. It is well built, was fortified by Vauban, and is still a place of strength. It has manufactures of leather, glue, lead pencils, and clay pipes. It belonged to Luxembourg until 1699. Pop. (1872) 5104.

Givors, a town of France, department of the Rhone, at the confluence of the Rhone and Gier, 14 miles S. of Lyon. It has considerable trade, the chief manufactures being silk, leather, and glass. There are also foundries and brickworks. Pop. (1872) 9886.

Gla'ciers (Lat. *glacies*, 'ice') are fields of ice which rest on the flanks or fill the lower valleys and ravines of snow-capped mountain ranges. They are the result of the gradual descent of the accumulated snow below the line of perpetual winter. The continual formation of snow on the heights, and the melting of the glacier ice and abstraction of the water to form rivers, lakes, and seas, while the glacier itself does not sensibly recede or diminish in size, prove conclusively that G. move down the valleys. This motion, however produced, must exert a powerful influence in wearing away the rocks over which the ice-mass passes; and the resulting waste is shown in the existence of the *moraines*, which are differently named according to their position. The *lateral moraines* are lines of débris, composed of blocks of varying sizes, which form along the margins of the glacier. When two G. unite, the moraines along their contiguous margins combine to form one; and the single glacier thus produced has three longitudinal moraines, two *lateral* and one *medial*. In this way, by the union of several of these ice-streams, a glacier may ultimately present on its surface a number of medial moraines. The heat of the sun is constantly melting the surface of the glacier; and by this means a block originally imbedded in the ice seems to rise towards the surface, while one on the surface, by the protection it affords to the ice on which it rests, is gradually raised upon a pillar of ice as the surrounding surface melts away. This pillar of course ultimately gives way; but the block, precipitated on the surface, again rears for itself a pillar. A glacier is thus a powerful agent in the transportation of more or less huge blocks of stone; and these, deposited at the termination of the glacier, form the *terminal moraine*. The curved form of this moraine, with its convexity presented *down* the valley, has an important bearing upon the theory of glacier motion, which will be considered afterwards. Another striking feature is the crevassed appearance of the mass. These crevasses are due to the splitting of the ice, and run, as a rule, from the margin towards the centre, generally directed obliquely *up* the glacier. Such are the general characteristics of a glacier. Its effects are seen in the worn surface of the rocks, in the scooping out of valleys, and in the deposition of boulders far from their parent rock. These peculiar appearances, especially the *roches moutonnées*, the striated rocks, and the terminal moraines stretching across the mouths of valleys, are visible in many regions where G. do not now exist, and indicate to the geologist a time when a more rigorous climate rendered their existence a possibility, and even a necessity.

To account for the motion of G., two theories were early put forward—the *gravitation* theory of De Saussure, which regarded the glacier as merely sliding down an inclined plane by its own weight, aided by the fusion of the ice in contact with the warmer earth; and the *dilatation* theory of De Charpentier, which explained the motion as due to the expansion of the water in the innumerable fissures as it became ice, thus forcing the mass in the direction of least resistance, *i.e.*, down the valley. The former cannot explain of itself the motion of a glacier through a *sinuous* channel, while the latter is in direct contradiction to physical law. For water at 0° C. cannot be frozen through contact with ice at the same temperature, and the presence of water as well as ice in a glacier renders it impossible for the ice to be of a lower temperature. Besides, if the dilatation theory were true, the lower portions would be pushed forwards further, on account of the accumulation of displacements, than the higher portions, and the distance between any two points on the glacier would be constantly increasing. To test these theories all that was necessary was a series of accurate observations; but no great step was taken in this direction until the late Principal Forbes took the subject in hand. The estimates of the rate of motion of G. were especially varied and conflicting. According to Ebel, the G. of Chamouni advance 14 feet every year, and those of Grindelwald 25 feet, while De la Beche gives 200 yards a year as the motion of the Mer de Glace. Hugi was perhaps the first to point out the correct method to measure the advance of a glacier, and he determined the motion of the glacier of the Aar at about 240 feet a year, an estimate which is now known to be very correct. The complete confusion that existed regarding this most important point is brought out by Rendu, Bishop of Annecy, in his most ingenious paper on G. 400 feet and 40 feet a year are both given as the rate of motion of the Mer de Glace. This discrepancy Rendu attributes to the different velocities of the centres and sides. The same author compares a glacier to a river, and forestalls in some measure Forbes' viscous theory. He, however, felt the lack of observations, and was unable to decide which of his various speculations was the true one. For several years previous to 1840 Agassiz had been at work among the G. of the Alps, testing the various theories which had been given. He adopted a modification of De Charpentier's theory, and regarded the sides of a glacier as moving faster than the centre, being more rapidly melted by the heat reflected from the rocks, and this theory he deemed supported by the generally upwardly-directed *crevasses*. In company with him, in the autumn of 1841, Forbes visited the glacier of the Aar. It was at this time that Forbes observed the veined structure of glacier ice—perhaps his greatest discovery in the subject—which has such an important bearing on the theory of stresses in general, and of glacier motion in particular. He at once saw the necessity of making accurate scientific measurements; and the succeeding year saw him on the Mer de Glace with his theodolite, prepared for a thorough investigation, and quite unbiassed by a belief in any theory. Later observations in the Alps and in Norway fully bore out the theory to which he was led, and which, in his own words, is as follows:—'A glacier is an imperfect fluid, or a viscous body, which is urged down the slopes of a certain inclination by the mutual pressure of its parts.' The facts established by Forbes are—the greater velocity of the centre and surface than of the sides and the bottom, the deep-seated character of the longitudinal ribboned structure produced by stress parallel to its direction; and his theory furnishes complete explanation of many minuter points, such as the concavity of the dirt-bands, and the convexity of the crevasses, to the source of the glacier; for, as demonstrated by Sir W. Thomson, a viscous mass under action of a stress splits in a direction perpendicular to the line of greatest tension. Hopkins took objection to Forbes' theory on the ground that ice was rigid; but it must be remembered that viscosity or plasticity (Forbes used the terms indiscriminately) merely expresses the capability of a body to continuously alter its form under the action of a continuous stress. This capability glacier ice evidently possesses; but the *property* of ice upon which this capability depends is quite a different question. The next conspicuous Alpine traveller is Professor Tyndall, who fell foul of Forbes' theory on the same grounds as Hopkins, arguing that, though ice may act as a viscous body under pressure, the existence of crevasses proves that under tension it splits like a brittle substance. He advances a theory, which, he professes, accounts for the plasticity possessed by ice under pressure, viz., that the 'brittle' ice by its descent is crushed and broken in small fragments, which, however, freeze together in accordance with the phenomenon known as *regelation*. This phenomenon, which might be better termed 'congelation,' was first observed by Dollfuss-Ausset, who compressed into one mass fragments of ice under a Bramah press, and later and independently by Faraday. This alternate fracturing and freezing may and probably does occur along the surfaces of contact of the ice and rock; but of its existence in the body of the glacier, where the ice is strained by a shearing stress, there is no evidence. And does not this regelation require explanation as much as glacier motion? The discovery by Professor James Thomson of the lowering of the freezing-point of water has thrown a flood of light upon the whole question. This property of water, which is merely a particular case of the conservation of energy, affords an explanation of the physical phenomenon exhibited in the making of a snow-ball, and of the curious laboratory experiment in which a thin wire hung over a block of ice, and stretched by suspended weights, passes through the block without permanently cutting it. Under pressure ice melts, cools, contracts. The contraction relieves the pressure, and the water freezes, warms, expands. Thus by compression, with the necessary alternation of melting and freezing, the descending snow becomes ice, and the ice moulds itself to the configuration of the valley in which it accumulates, flowing down as a glacier under the action of gravitation. The ice of G. differs considerably from the ice produced by the freezing of water. The latter possesses a stratified construction, which is not present in the former, and glacier ice has besides a peculiar deep blue colour.

The G. of the Alps, which are undoubtedly the best known throughout the world, occupy a superficial area of nearly 1500 sq. miles. The largest is the Aletsch Glacier, which is 15 miles long, while the famous Mer de Glace above Chamouni is only 9 miles. G. of unknown extent abound in the fjords of Scandinavia, in Spitzbergen, Novaya Zemlya, Greenland, Patagonia, and the inaccessible shores of the Antarctic. Among the Himalayas huge ice-rivers exist, one in Tibet measuring, upon the authority of Captain Austin of the Indian Survey, 36 miles in length. The Southern Alps of New Zealand vie with the Alps of Switzerland in the grandeur of their glacier system—the largest one, the Tasman Glacier, being about 18 miles long. The G. of Europe formerly extended to much lower altitudes, as evidenced by the ice-markings on the rocks. This, however, does not imply that they were much larger, because the snow-line itself was also probably lower. To account for this Glacial Period several theories have been advanced, the most plausible of which is the coincidence in some past time of the maximum eccentricity of the earth's orbit with the earth's aphelion falling in our winter. See Rendu's *Théorie des Glaciers de la Savoie* (1841; edited and translated by Prof. G. Forbes, 1875); Agassiz's *Études sur les Glaciers* (1841), and *Nouvelles Études sur les Glaciers* (1847); Forbes' *Travels through the Alps* (1843), *Norway and its Glaciers* (1853), and *Occasional Papers on the Theory of Glaciers* (1859); Tyndall's *The Glaciers of the Alps* (1860), and *The Forms of Water* (1872); Croll's *Climate and Time* (1875); and James Geikie's *Great Ice Age* (2d ed. 1876).

Gla'cis (Fr.; from Lat. *glacies*, 'ice;' hence 'what slides or is slippery like ice'), in fortification, a smoothly sloping mass of earth serving as the parapet or breastwork of the covered way, also to mask or protect the general works of the enceinte; but chiefly to bring assailants within the direct sweeping fire of the fortified works.

Glad'bach (*Mönchen-G.*), the chief industrial town in Rhenish Prussia, on the Niers, 16 miles W. of Düsseldorf by railway. It has active manufactures of linens, cottons, silks, ribbons, druggets, velvets, tobacco, machinery, &c., besides large bleach-fields and dye-works. Pop. (1875) 31,962. G. was founded in the end of the 8th c.—**G.** (*Bergisch-G.*), a town of Rhenish Prussia, 8 miles E.N.E. of Köln by railway. It has manufactures of paper, nets, and percussion-caps, and was included in the former Duchy of Berg. Pop. (1871) 6195.

Glad'iator (Lat. *gladius*, 'a sword'), a general name applied to men trained to fight with deadly weapons for the amusement of the Romans at public funerals, in the circus, and in the amphitheatre. The practice originated in the ancient belief that the spirits of the dead took pleasure in human blood. Gladiatorial exhibitions were imported from Etruria to Rome in 264 B.C., when M. and D. Brutus matched three pairs of gladiators in the Forum Boarium at the funeral rites of their father. In the Ludi Funebres 216 B.C. twenty-two pairs fought, the same number in 200 B.C., and sixty pairs in 183 B.C. These combats rapidly grew in popularity. On one occasion Julius Cæsar presented 320 pairs of gladiators to the people. Under the Empire this brutal taste rose to a frenzy. Titus regaled the Romans with an exhibition for 100 days. When Trajan triumphed over the Dacians, 10,000 men were matched together or with wild beasts during a period of 123 days. Cicero, Augustus, Tiberius, and others tried to limit these contests; but no attempt to interdict them was made till the time of Constantine (325 A.D.). They were revived by succeeding emperors, and finally suppressed by Honorius. Gladiators were instructed in schools (*ludi gladiatorii*) by a trainer (*lanista*), at first with heavy wooden swords (*rudes*), then with steel. They consisted at first of captives, malefactors, and slaves; but under the more worthless emperors, knights, priests, senators, and even high-born ladies entered the arena. Gladiators were classed according to their equipments. In all cases they were sworn to fight to the death. The shows were announced by bills, containing a description of the numbers, names, and exploits of the combatants. The contest began on a signal given by the president (*editor*). When a G. was wounded his antagonist cried *Hoc habet* ('it is a hit'), whereupon the president, if the injury were such as to disable the sufferer, replied *Habet.* The wounded G. then held up his finger in token of submission, and his life or death depended on the president, who generally allowed the spectators to decide. If they raised their thumbs, he was spared; if they depressed them, he was slain by the victor. In the latter event the corpse was dragged away by a hook, and the arena was sprinkled with fresh sand for fresh combatants.

Gladi'olus (Lat. 'a little sword'), a large and very beautiful genus of Iridaceous plants, found principally in Eastern Europe and Africa. Many fine hybrid forms with very showy flowers are cultivated in gardens under the name of sword-lilies. They have starchy underground corms or stems, which are eaten by the Hottentots.

Gladiolus communis.

Glado'va, or **Klado'vo** (Turk. *Fet-ül-Islam*, 'rock of Islam'), a village of Servia, on the Danube, immediately below the 'Iron Gate' (*Dolni-Demir-Kapu*), and 2½ miles above the remains of Trajan's Bridge. The goods of the Danube Navigation Co. are conveyed to G. overland from Orsova, a distance of 13 miles, to avoid the rapids. Pop. 1125.

Glad'stone, The Right Hon. William Ewart, an illustrious English statesman and author, was born at Liverpool, December 29, 1809. He was the fourth son of the late Sir John G., Bart., of Fasque, in Kincardineshire, a Liverpool merchant who originally belonged to Leith. Educated at Eton and at Oxford, where he graduated with a double first class in 1831, he was returned to Parliament in the Conservative interest in 1832, and soon won the notice of Sir Robert Peel, who made him a junior Lord of the Treasury in 1834, and in 1835 Under Secretary for Colonial Affairs. In 1838 he published *The State in its Relations with the Church,* which called forth a vigorously hostile review from Macaulay, the critic, however, praising G.'s 'desire to penetrate beneath the surface of questions.' He was appointed Vice-President of the Board of Trade in 1841, and President of the Board in 1843. In 1846 he succeeded Lord Stanley, the late Earl of Derby, as Colonial Secretary, and during the Corn-Law struggle supported Peel with great ardour and eloquence. His labours to repeal the Corn-Laws lost him his seat for Newark (a pocket borough of the Duke of Newcastle), but after being a short time out of Parliament, he was returned for Oxford University in 1847. In 1850–51 he visited Naples and published *Two Letters to the Earl of Aberdeen on the State Prosecutions of the Neapolitan Government*, exposing the loathsome cruelties to which the Bourbons of Naples subjected their political opponents. These letters had a vast circulation, and made a deep impression throughout Europe. G., who had become gradually alienated from the Tories, despite his High-Church sympathies, during the discussions on University Reform and the removal of the Jewish disabilities (1847–51), finally withdrew from his old party in 1851. When Lord Aberdeen's 'Coalition' Ministry was formed in 1852, G. was made Chancellor of the Exchequer, and on the fall of that Ministry before Mr. Roebuck's motion to inquire into the state of the army at Sebastopol, became a member of the Palmerston Government, but resigned in a few weeks. G. was then partly in opposition to Lord Palmerston, to whose defeat on the China question in 1857 he greatly contributed by a powerful speech. He declined to take office under Lord Derby, but went as a special commissioner to the Ionian Islands in 1858–59, and in 1859 became again Chancellor of the Exchequer under Lord Palmerston. In the same year he was chosen Rector of Edinburgh University. His bill to repeal the paper-duty, after being passed in the Commons, was flung out by the Lords in 1860, but was carried in 1861. He lost his seat for Oxford in 1865, but was returned in the same year for South Lancashire. On the death of Lord Palmerston in 1865 he became leader of the House of Commons and Chancellor of the Exchequer in Lord Russell's Ministry, which resigned in 1866 on the rejection of Lord Russell's Reform Bill. G. then vigorously attacked and successfully amended Mr. Disraeli's curious Reform Bill, and brought forward in 1868 resolutions to disestablish the Irish Church, which were carried through the Commons, but were rejected in the Lords. In 1868 G. lost his seat for South Lancashire, but the Greenwich electors, anticipating his defeat, had a few days before returned him for their town, which he has since represented. In the same year, on the resignation of the Disraeli Government, he became First Lord of the Treasury; and the Liberal party being at this time firmly united and having a majority in the Commons of about a hundred members, G. was enabled to carry a series of important measures. The Irish Church Disestablishment Act was passed in 1869, the Irish Land Act and the Elementary Education Act in 1870, and religious tests for admission to university degrees and offices were abolished in 1871, and in the same year purchase in the army was removed by the exercise of the royal prerogative; the Ballot Act was passed in 1872, and the Judicature Act in 1873. The University Education Bill was, however, flung out in 1873, through the union of the Catholic with the Conservative members, whereupon G. resigned; but Mr. Disraeli refusing to take office, G. was forced to rearrange the Cabinet, himself taking the offices of First Lord of the Treasury and Chancellor of the Exchequer. In 1874 he suddenly dissolved Parliament, and in the ensuing election a Conservative majority of nearly seventy members being returned, G. resigned, and for a time was seldom seen in the House, withdrawing in 1875 from the Liberal leadership. He has of late, however, again taken part in political questions, and has repeatedly engaged in the Eastern discussion with characteristic earnestness and fervour. G. is a scholar as well as a brilliant statesman, but his *Homer and the Heroic Age* (1858); *Juventus Mundi, Gods and Men of the Heroic Age* (1869); *Homeric Synchronism* (1876), though replete with evidence of the most thorough scholarship and even clear intelligence, do not indicate a very sagacious or penetrating critical faculty. Among G.'s numerous pamphlets and articles are *Ritualism*, which appeared in the *Contemporary Review* for 1874; *The Vatican Decrees in their Bearing on Civil Allegiance,* a pamphlet against the Roman Catholic Church (1874); *Vaticanism, an Answer to Replies and Reproofs* (1875); and *The Turk in Europe* (1876), a fierce denunciation of the Bulgarian atrocities and the Turkish rule. G. as a statesman is remarkably honest in intention, bold in design, and, when supported by popular sentiment, resolute of purpose. His sagacity, however, is not equal to his genius, he lacks the instinct of patriotism, and his earnestness is unaccompanied by sufficient tact and pliancy, so that his character somehow wants the charm that clings to his more amiable though perhaps less admirable rival Disraeli. As a speaker he has been excelled by no contemporary; his oratory is distinguished by swift and fiery energy of utterance and by a marvellously rapid and copious rush of glowing and emphatic language.

Glagolitz'a, or **Glag'ola** (*i.e.*, 'word,' 'letter'), the name given to the Old Slavic, in contrast to the Cyrillic, alphabet. Concerning its origin, antiquity, and extension much uncertainty prevails. Undoubtedly it was devised for the old Slovenian language, and passed from the Slovenians in Pannonia to those in Bulgaria. Amongst the Croats its use was maintained till modern times; and profane as well as ecclesiastical works continued to be printed in it at Venice and at Rome up till the end of the 18th c. In Russia, Servia, and Bohemia it was also known. The oldest document in this character is the *Glagolita Clozianus*, dating from the 11th c., and published at Vienna in 1836. Tradition assigned the invention of the G. to St. Jerome.

Glamor'ganshire (Cymr. *Glann Morgant*, 'the valley by the sea-shore'), the most important county of Wales, lies between the rivers Burry and Rumney, and is bounded S. by the Bristol Channel, W. by Caermarthen, N. by Brecknock, and E. by Monmouth. Area, 547,070 acres; pop. (1871) 397,859. The surface in the N. is hilly, reaching an elevation of 1859 feet in the Llangeinor; the broad woody expanse of the S. is known as 'the Vale of Glamorgan.' Among the rivers, all of which flow S. to the Bristol Channel, are the Taff, Neath, Llwchwr, and Tawe;

The chief features of the coast-line (90 miles long) are the peninsula of Gower and Swansea Bay. The climate is mild and healthy. A rich soil, chiefly of reddish clay, yields good crops of wheat, barley, oats, and potatoes; dairy-farming and cattle-rearing are extensively pursued in the beautiful upland pastures and valleys of the N. The formation of G. is almost entirely Carboniferous, and includes one of the largest coal-beds in Great Britain, consisting of true coal, anthracite, and coking coal. Ironstone, lead, and limestone are also found, while the iron-works (chiefly Merthyr-Tydvil and Dowlais) are among the largest in the world; and there are extensive copper, tin, and lead-smelting works at Swansea, Neath, &c. The county, which has an excellent railway and canal system, returns two members to Parliament. Its pop. has increased with great rapidity during the present century—in 1801, 70,879; in 1851, 231,849; in 1861, 317,752; and in 1871, 397,859. The finest architectural remains are Oystermouth, Caerphilly, Cardiff, Coch, and Coity castles, and Morgan Abbey.

Glan'ders is defined as a contagious malignant disorder, chiefly seen in horses, and arising from the introduction within the system of a poison which, besides its effects generally upon the system, specially affects the Schneiderian or mucous membrane of the nose, the lungs, and the lymphatic system. A variety of G. named Farcy (q. v.), together with G. itself, appears to originate spontaneously in the horse, ass, and mule. From these animals the disease is capable of being transmitted in all its virulence to man, and from man it may in turn affect these animals. Aristotle and other ancient writers noted it. The disease occurs in temperate climates, and is rarely seen in hot or cold regions. It exhibits four varieties, known as *acute G.*, *acute farcy*, *chronic G.*, and *chronic farcy*. Its cause appears to consist in some special poison generated under such influences as old age, insufficient or bad food, exhausting diseases, overcrowding, and bad ventilation. Horses crowded on board ship, for example, are very liable to G. The disease is preceded usually by a form of *diabetes* (*D. insipidus* or *polyuria*), in which large quantities of urine, indicating an increased tissue-waste, are passed. The *latent period* of G. is short; on the second or third day after inoculation the glands swell, and at periods varying from the third to the sixth day a discharge from the nostrils appears. The general *symptoms* of G. in the acute form, which is always and very rapidly fatal, are found in the presence of high *fever*, inflammation and ulceration of the pituitary membrane and of the lymphatic glands, while from the eyes and nostrils a foul and irritating discharge flows. In bad cases the nasal bones may become necrosed. The lungs evince symptoms and conditions analogous to those seen in cases of tubercular disintegration, and many authorities hence argue for the near relationship of G. and *tubercle*. Modes of treatment are only available for chronic G. The Contagious Diseases (Animals) Act provides for the destruction of horses affected with G. The general treatment includes attention to diet, good food, tonics, such as copper and iron and arsenite of strychnia (5 gr. doses of arsenious acid with 1 drachm of nux vomica); whilst the local applications include the treatment of swellings by blistering and by the application of the biniodide of mercury ointment. Ulcerated surfaces are to be treated by the application of nitrate of silver, and carbolic acid lotion must be freely used both as a curative and as an antiseptic measure. The *preventive* treatment consists in cleaning and disinfecting the stables, and in giving horses liable to be affected, 2 oz. of the hyposulphite of soda or 2 drachms of chlorate of potash with every meal for two or three weeks.

Glandford Brigg, or simply **Brigg**, a market-town in Lincolnshire, on the Ancholme, 18 miles W. of Great Grimsby by railway. It has a corn exchange, a horticultural society, railway works, malthouses, breweries, cornmills, and a large river trade in corn, coal, and timber. The river is navigable for sloops from the Humber. Pop. (1871) 2646.

Glands. These are special organs distributed throughout the body for the purpose of secreting or separating certain materials from the blood. Although differing amongst themselves very much in structure, they are all essentially formed on the same general type. A secreting apparatus essentially consists of a simple membrane named the *basement membrane*, on one side of which we find a layer of secreting cells, and on the other numerous blood-vessels. By modifications of this simple structure, all the various G. are formed. There appear to be four types of gland structure, viz.:—(1) *Simple glands*, including a straight tube as found in the gastric G. of the stomach, a sack or pouch, and a coiled tube, as seen in the sweat G. of the skin; (2) *multilocular crypts*, which may be either of a tubular or of a saccular form, as exemplified in the wax G. of the ear; (3) *racemose glands*, which contain a number of little saccules clustered round the extremities of a branch duct; and (4) *compound tubular glands*, consisting of numerous tubes opening into each other, as seen in the structure of the kidney. Racemose G. are so termed on account of their resemblance to such an object as a bunch of grapes, in which the stalks represent the various ducts of the gland. As examples of this kind of gland may be mentioned the pancreas, the salivary, lachrymal, and mammary G., the G. of Brunner in the small intestine, and numerous small G. in the mouth, throat, and windpipe. The various parts of G. are intimately bound together by connective tissue and blood-vessels, and recently it has been shown that they are richly supplied with nerves, some filaments of which actually terminate in the cells of the gland. For details as to the functions of G. see SECRETION.

Glands, Diseases of.—The lymphatic glands are subject to enlargement from acute inflammation, as in Adenitis (q. v.), frequently resulting from inflammation of the lymphatics connected with them. There may be also chronic hypertrophy, without inflammation, depending upon strumous disease or chronic irritation, which may be permanent or may terminate in suppuration. The glands principally affected in such cases are the submaxillary, the glandulæ concatenatæ, the axillary and inguinal; and they frequently have the appearance of large, indurated, and nodulated tumours. D. of G. are dependent upon various causes, and no line of treatment applicable to all cases can be indicated.

Glan'vill, Ranulf de, the author of the earliest work on English law, was sheriff of Yorkshire in 1174, when he captured William the Lion of Scotland near Alnwick, and in 1180 was chief justiciar of England. He was imprisoned by Richard I., who extorted a large fine from him, and whom he accompanied to Palestine. G. died at Acre in 1190. His *Tractatus de Legibus et Consuetudinibus Regni Angliæ* is very valuable for the light which it throws on the early English constitution, and for preserving a number of old and interesting customs.

Gla'rus, a Swiss canton of triangular shape, is bounded N.E. by St. Gall, S.E. by the Grisons, and W. by Schwytz and Uri, and in the W. and N. touches the lakes Lucerne, Zuger, Zürich, and Wallenstadt. Area, 267 sq. miles; pop. (1870) 35,150. It is almost entirely covered by the Sand Alps, which reach their greatest height of 11,887 feet in Tödiberg or Piz Rusein, and are intersected by the beautiful valleys of the Linth, Sernf, and various minor streams. The Linth rises at the base of the Tödi, and flows N. to the Wallenstadt lake, which is now connected with Lake Zürich by the Linth Canal, constructed (1807–22) at a cost of £60,000. G. has a severe climate, and is rich in rare plants, crystals, minerals, springs, glaciers, petrifactions, &c. The chief occupations are cattle-breeding and the manufacture of cottons (250,000 spindles), woollens, silks, paper, &c. 'Schabziger,' or 'scraping cheese,' the famous aromatic green cheese of G., is coloured by an infusion of meliot or blue pansy, and its odour is perceptible in most of the villages. The chief towns, all in the Linth valley, are G., Nettstall, Mollis, and Näfels. G. is a pure democracy, under constitution of 22d May 1842. G. achieved its independence of the Hapsburgs by the victories of Näfels, and joined the Swiss confederation in 1388.—**G.** (Lat. *Glarona*), the chief town, on the Linth, and at the base of the Vorder-Glärnisch and Schilt, has some weaving industries, and a pop., with Klönthal (1870), of 5517. It was in great part destroyed by a fire in 1861; and the site of the old church where Zwingli preached from 1506 to 1516 is now occupied by the courts of justice. The new Romanesque church is used for both Protestants and Catholics.

Glas'gow, a city and a royal and parliamentary burgh in the lower ward of the county of Lanark, Scotland, is situated on both banks of the Clyde, the larger part lying on the N. side of the river. For the importance of its commerce and manufactures, G. hardly yields precedence to any city in the United Kingdom except London. It occupies an area of nearly 5 miles E. and W., by 2½ from N. to S., and is distant by rail from London 405¼ miles, and 47 from Edinburgh. The principal streets run E. and W., parallel to the river, and the houses are substantially built. The handsome crescents and terraces on the rising ground to the W. of the city are the homes of the wealthier citizens. The oldest part of the city, lying between the Cathedral and the river, has long been notorious for the squalid misery of a great part of its inhabitants, though, under the City Improvement Act of 1866, the Town Council has been diligent in replacing streets of noisome dens, never free from pestilence, by airy and wholesome habitations. The Royal Exchange, the new Stock Exchange, the City Hall, capable of holding 4000 persons, a still larger new Public Hall, and the Post-Office, now (1877) being entirely rebuilt, are prominent public buildings; and many of the banks and other commercial houses possess handsome offices. The venerable Old College has made way for a railway station; but the magnificent new University buildings, on a very advantageous site at Gilmorehill, westwards from the city, is the most imposing of the public structures. G. is proud of its old cathedral church, an admirable specimen of the Early English style, founded in 1176. Among its public and charitable institutions are the Infirmary, the Fever Hospital, the Blind Asylum, and Gartnavel Lunatic Asylum. Besides the ancient University, the institution known as the 'Andersonian University' provides a varied educational course; the municipality has established a museum in Kelvingrove Park, and it possesses a collection of pictures in the Corporation Galleries; there are normal seminaries for the training of teachers; the Free Church has here a theological college; and numerous schools provide for primary and secondary education. Statues of John Knox, Sir Walter Scott, Sir John Moore, Watt, Peel, Nelson, the Queen and Prince Albert, are found in the streets or public places of G.; and there are four large public parks.

A chief source of the wealth of G. is the river. The Clyde, now spanned by five bridges, was once a narrow and shallow stream navigable only by flat-bottomed boats. Some attempt was made to deepen its channel as early as 1566; in 1775 it was so effectively deepened as to admit vessels of 7 feet draught to the Broomielaw. Now there are upwards of 2 miles of quays, and ships of nearly 2000 tons are able to lie in the river. The influx of sewage and of refuse from manufactories has reduced the water to a very filthy condition, and called forth numerous schemes for its purification, none of which has yet been adopted. The Highland scenery of the Firth, however, provides in some measure for the health and recreation of the citizens; and a perfect fleet of passenger steamers plies perpetually between G. and the innumerable watering-places on the Clyde. Coal and iron are abundantly found in the W. of Scotland, and contribute largely to the prosperity of the trade of G. Iron is extensively manufactured as well as exported. G. shipbuilding, both in iron and timber, is one of the greatest industries in the kingdom. Clyde-built vessels are known all over the world, and sail under every flag. G. has long been a centre of the cotton trade in Scotland; and linen, woollen, silk, and mixed fabrics are woven in large quantities. Carpet-weaving, cotton printing, bleaching, and dyeing, are carried on on a large scale. The chemical industries of G. are the most varied in the world, and include, on a large scale, the soda and bleaching-powder manufacture, the preparation of alum, bichromate of potash, dynamite, gunpowder, iodine and other products of seaweed, soap, matches, tin, salts, acids, india-rubber, prussiates of potash, &c., copper, zinc, and lead. Two great chemical manufactories have chimneys, the one 435, the other 454 feet high. Pottery is largely made, and there are great distilleries and breweries. An abundant supply of the best water is drawn from Loch Katrine, 34 miles distant. The works required for the undertaking were completed in 1859 at a cost of £918,000. G. has established public wash-houses and bathing institutions. G. is a terminus of the Caledonian, the North British, and the Glasgow and South-Western Railways; and in September 1876 a new central station in the heart of the city was partially opened for traffic. In 1875 there entered the harbour 5131 vessels of 1,410,324 tons, and cleared 6195 of 1,774,170 tons.

The extent of the leading industries of G. may be estimated from the following figures:—In 1874 there were in Scotland 163 blast-furnaces, nearly the whole of which belonged to the G. district. Their output of pig-iron was 807,677 tons. In the nineteen malleable-iron works which centre in G. there are 342 puddling furnaces, and 49 rolling mills in operation, while a very extensive steel-work on the Siemens-Martin principle turns out about 30,000 tons of steel rails, &c., annually. The following table represents the Clyde shipbuilding of the six years 1871–76:—

	Vessels.	Tonnage.		Vessels.	Tonnage.
1871 ...	231	196,200	1874 ...	225	266,800
1872 ...	227	224,000	1875 ...	276	228,200
1873 ...	194	261,500	1876 ...	260	200,000

In 1875 the cotton factories of G. numbered 84, and contained 1,500,000 spindles and 27,500 power-looms, giving employment in all to 33,276 persons. At St. Rollox Chemical Works alone 1200 people are employed; 80,000 tons of raw material are annually transformed into soda, bleaching-powder, and sulphuric acid, the coal consumed in the various processes weighing 110,000 tons.

Besides several evening and weekly journals, G. has three daily papers, the *Glasgow Herald*, the *North British Daily Mail*, and the *Glasgow News*.

The city sprang up around the abode of St. Kentigern, now commonly known as *Mungo*, 'the beloved,' who is said to have settled here in 580. The etymology of the Celtic name of the city is variously given; either from *glas gow*, 'white smith;' from *clais ghu*, 'dark ravine;' or from *eaglais dhu*, 'black church.' The Cathedral was founded by Joceline, Abbot of Melrose, in 1176 on the site of a still more ancient church. In 1180 G. became a burgh of barony by royal charter, with the right of holding an annual fair. The first stone bridge over the Clyde was built by Bishop Rae in 1345. The see was made archiepiscopal in the time of Blacader, who died in 1550; the University having been founded in virtue of a bull from Pope Nicholas V. in 1450. The Cathedral was defended by the craftsmen of the city from the demolition decreed against it in 1578. The population of G. was in the 14th c. between 2000 and 3000, in the 16th about 5000, and at the end of the 17th c. had reached about 12,000, G. becoming now the second city of Scotland. The subsequent rapid growth of G. in size and prosperity began with the opening of the West Indian trade, especially the tobacco trade, to Scotland. Soon after the Union G. began to trade with Virginia, Maryland, and Barbadoes, but the first G. vessel that ever crossed the Atlantic left G. in 1718—the pioneer of that fleet of merchant ships now found in every quarter of the globe. A new and powerful impulse was given to the enterprise and wealth of G. by the application of steam-power to navigation, carried out on the Clyde in 1812 by Henry Bell. Since the beginning of the century, the population has been very rapidly increasing. In 1801 the pop. was 77,058 (less than that of Edinburgh and Leith); in 1871 it was 477,156. The city returns three members to Parliament.

Glasgow, University of, was founded in 1450 by a bull of Pope Nicholas V., obtained through the exertions of Bishop Turnbull. In 1460 a college was established by James Lord Hamilton on the site in High Street, where, with various additions, it remained for 410 years. The new foundation was declared to have the same powers of creating masters and doctors as any other *studium generale* in Christendom, and consisted of a chancellor and rector, of various masters and doctors in the faculties of theology, canon law, and the arts, and of the incorporated students. The Reformation caused great confusion in the University; and in 1577 James VI., besides granting additional endowments, modified the constitution of the University by a new charter, drawn up according to the suggestions of the then principal, the famous scholar Andrew Melville. This *nova erectio* made provision for the support of a principal and three regents. The principal was to teach theology and the Hebrew and Syriac languages. Of the regents, the first taught Greek and rhetoric; the second, dialectics, morals and politics, arithmetic and geometry; while the third had assigned to him the provinces of physiology and geography, chronology and astronomy. Contrary to the former arrangement, the regents were to abide from year to year by the same subjects. Hitherto each regent carried the same students through their whole curriculum. At the Restoration the University suffered much, and remained in a depressed condition till the Revolution. Since then it has steadily increased in prosperity. Twelve of the professorships have been founded in the present century. As early as 1846 there had been negotiations for the transfer of the University buildings to a better site; but it was not till 1864 that the

Old College was sold to the City of Glasgow Union Railway. An admirable site was obtained on Gilmore Hill, an eminence near the West End Park; and the present handsome edifice, built from designs by Sir G. Gilbert Scott at an estimated cost of £350,000 (since considerably exceeded), was formally opened in 1870. Besides £100,000 obtained for the Old College and a grant of £120,000 from Government, nearly £160,000 has been raised by voluntary subscription. Some of the Glasgow citizens showed a princely munificence in their gifts. The University Library—now extensive and valuable—is nearly coeval with the University, and enjoys, besides occasional donations, an annual grant of £707 from the Treasury. There is a separate Divinity Hall Library. One of the most valuable possessions of the University is the Hunterian Museum, bequeathed by the eminent physician William Hunter, and consisting of books, manuscripts, coins, paintings, anatomical preparations, zoological and mineral specimens, and archæological relics. Amongst the famous names on the roll of the University are those of John Major, Andrew Melville, James Melville, Boyd of Trochrig, Robert Baillie, Zachary Boyd, John Spottiswoode, Robert Simson, Francis Hutcheson, Adam Smith, Thomas Reid, William Cullen, and Joseph Black.

The University is a corporate body, consisting of a chancellor, rector, dean of faculties, principal, professors, and students. Its governing bodies are the University Court, the Senatus, and the General Council of Graduates, which last has, along with the Council of Aberdeen University, the privilege of sending a member to Parliament. The chancellor is elected for life by the General Council, over which he presides. The rector is chosen every third year by the matriculated students, divided for the purpose into four 'nations,' according to birthplace (*Natio Glottiana*, consisting of students born in Lanarkshire; *N. Transforthiana*, of those born N. of the Forth; *N. Rotheseiana*, of students from the counties of Bute, Renfrew, and Ayr; *N. Loudoniana*, of all students not included in the other nations). Another ancient system of nomenclature divided the students into four classes according to their year of study—the first year's class being designated *Bajan*; the second year's, *Semi*; the third, *Baccalour*; the fourth, *Magistrand*. The dean of faculties is elected yearly by the Senatus, and the principal is appointed for life by the crown. There are twenty-eight professors—nine in the faculty of arts, four in theology, two in law, and thirteen in medicine. The number of matriculated students in session 1875–76 was 1601, viz., in the faculty of arts, 942; in theology, 74; in medicine, 415; and in law, 170. Students of humanity, Greek, logic, ethics, and natural philosophy are *Togati*, wearing a red cloak or gown during the University session. The University has the power of conferring the following degrees—D.D., LL.D. (both honorary), M.A., B.D., LL.B., B.L., M.B., C.M., M.D., and B.Sc. It has in its gift over 230 bursaries, university prizes, and scholarships, of which the most considerable are fourteen Snell exhibitions of £110 each, which enable Glasgow students to proceed to Oxford, and four Clark scholarships, each worth £200 a year and tenable for four years.

Glass (Lat. *glacies*, 'ice') is an amorphous compound consisting essentially of silicates of sodium or potassium and calcium, and of other basic substances, which vary according to the nature and purposes for which the G. may be intended. G. is usually transparent, but by the admixture of various substances it may be prepared of an opaque white or any other desired colour. Its manufacture dates from a very remote antiquity, the earliest traces of it being found in Egypt. In the British Museum there is an amulet of G. bearing the name of Nuantef IV., a monarch of the eleventh dynasty, who, according to Lepsius, reigned between B.C. 2423 and 2380; and Sir J. Gardner Wilkinson states that representations of G. bottles containing red wine occur on monuments of the fourth dynasty, besides contemporary paintings illustrating all the processes of the manufacture. The British Museum also contains a G. vase from Nineveh, inscribed with the name of a king who reigned about B.C. 700. From Egypt the Phœnicians probably obtained the secret of the manufacture, and to them are attributed the numerous small vases of brilliantly coloured G. which are found in tombs on the shores of the Mediterranean. Both by the Egyptians and the Phœnicians beads of G. were very extensively fabricated, and used as a medium of barter with the barbarous races in the interior of Africa, and with the tribes of Western Europe. Among the later examples of Phœnician workmanship are numerous specimens in the form of fruit, heads, &c., which obviously have been prepared in moulds.

From these ancient centres a knowledge of G.-making travelled with the progress of civilisation into the various countries which border on the Mediterranean; and in Rome especially the art reached a high degree of excellence. The Romans applied the material to a great variety of purposes, including the glazing of windows. The splendid iridescence displayed by most of the ancient Roman G. is the result of a partial decomposition induced by its great age. The Romans moulded, engraved, and stained G., and combined opaque coloured G. into mosaics of great beauty, which were much used for lining walls and forming the floors of rooms. Engraving is found on G. vessels, cameos and intaglios in imitation of gems. The famous Portland or Barberini Vase in the British Museum is the most magnificent ancient example of cameo engraving, and shows the perfection of technique as well as artistic treatment to which the Romans attained. The estimation in which fine works in G. was held in Rome may be judged from the fact that the Emperor Nero paid 6000 sestertia for two small vases.

With the fall of the Roman Empire the glory of G.-making, as well as of many other important arts, passed away for centuries, although G. continued to be made at Constantinople. In mediæval times some highly prized vessels of G. manufactured at Damascus, gilt and enamelled, found their way into Western Europe, a few of which are still preserved. But it was not till towards the end of the 13th c. that the art again revived in Europe, and then at Venice it quickly attained an artistic perfection unequalled in classical times, and which cannot be rivalled by the knowledge, skill, and resources of the present age. It is probable that the fall of Constantinople in 1204 drove many workers in G. from that capital to settle in Venice, and thus gave the first impulse to the craft in that famous centre. In the earlier years the manufacture was chiefly confined to the fabrication of beads and imitations of precious stones and gems, and no authentic Venetian G. vessel of a date earlier than the middle of the 15th c. is known to exist. Ancient Venetian G. is generally very thin and light, being blown with marvellous skill into infinite varieties of graceful shapes. It is found to be very often ornamented in gold and enamel colours after the fashion of the Oriental G., which doubtless served as patterns for the early workers. The stems of the vessels were frequently worked in an elaborate manner in knots, wings, and various graceful and fantastic forms. The varieties of early Venetian G. have been thus classified by Mr. A. W. Franks:—1st, Vessels of transparent or of single-coloured G., the beauty of which depended on the skill of the blower. 2d, Gilt and enamelled G., which was necessarily made heavy to bear the heat of the enamelling kiln without losing its form. 3d, Cracked G., the rough surface of which was produced by sudden cooling when the object was half-blown, then reheating and expanding the cracked surface to its full size. 4th, Schmelz G., an opaque variety of mixed colours, imitating agates, jasper, chalcedony, and other stones. 5th, Millefiori or mosaic glass, made by combining numerous small rods of many colours of opaque G. into one cane, from which beads were made; or it was sometimes worked into vases and other forms. 6th, Reticulated or lace G. had fine threads of opaque, generally white, but sometimes coloured G., running through it. It was in making this variety that the greatest triumphs of the mediæval Venetian artists were attained.

The manufacture of decorative or artistic G. is known to have been prosecuted in France and Germany about the middle of the 16th c. The German works consist most frequently of large cylindrical cups of greenish G. ornamented in enamel colours with arms, heraldic devices, and figures. Vessels made in imitation of characteristic Venetian forms are wanting in the lightness and elegance which belong to the work of their Southern rivals. The beautiful ruby G. of Germany is said to have been first made in 1679 by Kunckel, the director of the G.-works at Potsdam, and one of the early specimens bears the cypher of Friedrich the Great.

Evidence exists that G. was manufactured in England as early as 1447, as in that year it was stipulated that for the windows of Beauchamp Chapel at Warwick there was to be used 'no glasse of England.' Stow the historian states that 'the first making of Venice glasses in England began in London about the beginning of the reign of Queen Elizabeth by one Jacob Vessalina, an Italian.' In 1670 under the patronage of the Duke of Buckingham, a G.-work was established at Lambeth by Venetian workmen, and there bevelled mirrors in imitation of Venetian and coach G. were manufactured.

Manufacture of Glass.—G.-making, as conducted at the present day, embraces many distinct industries; the material has very numerous applications, and a large number of distinct styles of ornamentation are applied to it. The different varieties of G. may be classified as follows, the classification being based partly on composition, and partly also on method of manufacture and application:—1. Window G., including (*a*) sheet or rolled G., (*b*) crown G., (*c*) patent or blown plate G., (*d*) cast plate G. 2. Bottle G., including ordinary dark-green or 'black bottle' G., and the greenish-tinted G. used for aerated waters, acid carboys, &c. 3. Flint G., under which are included (*a*) crystal or cut table G., (*b*) pressed or moulded table G., (*c*) optical G., (*d*) Strass or paste G. 4. Enamel or opaque G. The raw materials and processes employed in the manufacture of these different varieties of G. will be briefly noticed under their respective heads. In the preparation of the molten material, or 'metal,' as it is termed, the following details and operations are common to all kinds of G.

The raw materials are melted in *pots*, which are placed in *furnaces* in the *G.-house*. The G.-house is usually a conical erection open at the top, and in the centre of the area is placed the furnace. As this construction is subject to an enormous heat, the bricks and fireclay of which it is built must be of the most refractory and infusible description. The arrangement of the furnace is modified in several particulars for the different kinds of G., but the accompanying plans of an ordinary window-G. furnace will serve to indicate the general features of the structure. The ground plan and perpendicular section of such a furnace are represented in the accompanying illustrations. It consists essentially of an arched space *A*, in the middle of which is the fire-grate *B*, above the *cave* or ash-pit *C*. On each side of the fire space are two raised banks or *sieges D*, on which are placed the pots *e*. Opposite each pot is a small

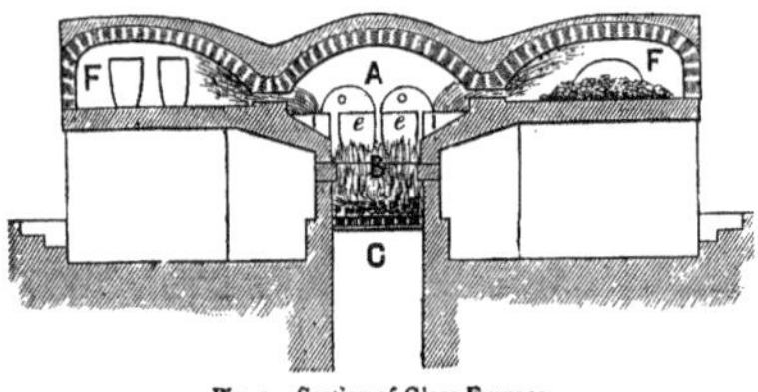

Fig. 1.—Section of Glass Furnace.

opening—the *work-hole*—through which the pots are charged and emptied. Between each work-hole there is a short dividing wall. The flame, after being reverberated from the arched roof on the surface of the G. pots, partly passes into two lateral

Fig. 2.—Ground Plan of Glass Furnace.

ovens *F*, called *arches*, in which new pots are prepared for being placed in the furnace, and the mixed ingredients for charging the pots are calcined and fritted. Two principal forms of pot or vessel in which the raw materials are melted are employed. The pot for bottle or ordinary window G. is an open vessel (*a*, Fig. 3) of the form of a truncated cone, the narrow end of which forms the bottom; but for melting flint G. a closed or covered pot (*b*, Fig. 3) is used, with a mouth or opening in its upper side towards the work-hole. The material of which melting-pots are made in this country is exclusively a kind of fire-clay obtained at Stourbridge, and their preparation is a work of the greatest labour and patience. The clay is ground up with a proportion of fragments of old pots to a fine dust, mixed with water, and left for some time in wooden bins to temper or sour, during which time it is periodically turned over and kneaded under the naked feet of the workmen. The pots are built up very gradually of small pieces firmly kneaded together, not more than from three or four inches in height being added to any pot in a day. After finishing they are allowed to dry very gradually in a loft, and subsequently the drying is completed in a heated chamber. They are then stored for a considerable time. Before being placed in position, they are taken to the annealing furnace or arch, in which they are slowly raised to a red heat, in which state they are moved as rapidly as possible into the furnace. The setting of a pot is not only a very critical but also a most laborious and difficult task, requiring severe exertion in the presence of a temperature which the workmen cannot endure more than a few moments at a time.

a b

Fig. 3.

The various ingredients of G. are intimately mixed, and usually calcined or fritted in the arches—an operation in which carbonic acid and water are driven off, and a partial agglomeration effected. It is then in a succession of charges introduced into the pots, and all openings being closed up, the heat is forced as much as possible. From time to time test samples are withdrawn to determine the progress of vitrification. When the whole mass is reduced to a fluid condition, a scum consisting of the uncombined alkaline substances forms on the surface. This scum, which is termed G. gall or sandiver, is skimmed off. The molten mass is kept as highly fluid as is practicable for some time, to clear it and to expel all air-bubbles, after which the temperature is lowered to a point which renders the metal sufficiently viscous to be worked.

After G. has been fashioned into the form it is intended to retain by the processes hereafter indicated, it undergoes the operation of Annealing (q. v.). G. which is very suddenly cooled from the heat of fusion assumes the peculiar condition exemplified in the well-known Rupert's drops. These consist of drops of G. allowed to fall into water, when they assume a pear-like form. The G. is externally excessively hard, but if the smallest fraction is broken from the thin end, the whole mass crumbles into fine dust with explosive violence. This result is owing to the unequal tension of the molecules of the G., caused by rapid external cooling and setting, while the interior is yet hot and dilated. In the annealing furnace the material is first exposed to a high temperature, which by various expedients is so gradually lowered that all parts of the G. are throughout the process kept at a uniform and gradually-decreasing temperature. A method of annealing by which a hardened (improperly called a toughened) G. is prepared has been introduced and patented within very recent times by M. de la Bastie. Bastie's process consists in plunging the article to be annealed at a red heat into an oleaginous bath of high temperature, which, however, varies for different qualities and thicknesses of G. The effect produced is analogous to case hardening, a thin external skin of excessively hard G. being produced, by which the breaking strain of the material is very greatly increased. When, however, such hardened G. does fracture, it resolves itself into innumerable fragments like Rupert's drops, to which it is, indeed, analogous. Bastie's process can only be applied to G. made in one piece, and is consequently inapplicable to stalked vessels like wine-glasses, &c. It cannot be cut with the diamond.

Sheet Glass.—This, as well as *Crown G.*, noticed below, is a compound of silicates of sodium and calcium, the materials used for both being composed of 100 parts of sand, 35 to 40 of chalk, 30 to 35 of soda ash, and 100 to 150 of cullet, or fragments of broken G. All these materials, excepting the cullet, are mixed and fritted, as before mentioned, previous to their introduction into the melting-pot. When the metal is in a state fit for working, the blower gathers on the end of a long iron tube, in successive layers, a ball of G. sufficient for the sheet to be made. The ball, by manipulation on an iron table, assumes a pear form (*a*, Fig. 4), and the workman first moulds this mass by combined

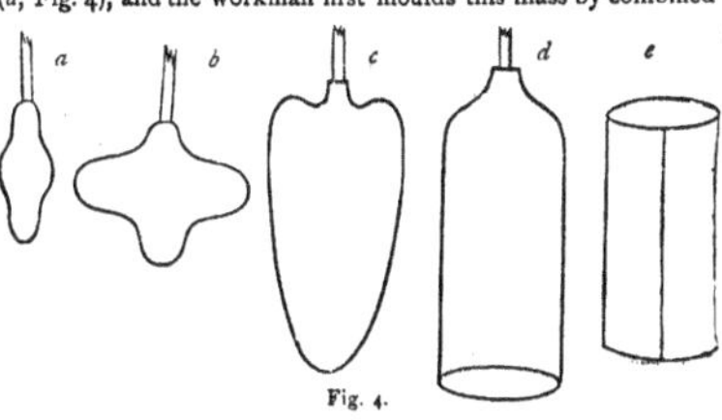

Fig. 4.

rotation and blowing into the form shown in *b*, and by degrees the cylinder is expanded till it assumes the form shown at *c*. Thereafter it is burst at the lower end, which is then opened out to the form shown at *d*. The neck is next detached from the blowing tube, and to obtain a cylinder open at both ends it is only necessary then to detach the shoulder or upper bent portion. This and the longitudinal slitting of the cylinder are accomplished by passing a red-hot iron around the neck and then along the surface of *e*. The opening of the cylinders is a subsequent operation, performed in a flattening or annealing furnace, which is divided into two compartments. In the first of these, the cylinders are gradually raised to a heat which allows of their being opened out flat on a smooth table in the lower part of the furnace, and when so flattened they are piled up in the next chamber for annealing.

Crown Glass is a much older form of window G. than the above, but sheets of only limited dimensions can be obtained from it. A globular gathering of metal is obtained on the end of the blowing tube, and this the blower distends till it forms a very flat spheroid. When so dilated, a solid rod tipped with a small piece of glass is attached to the nipple or prominence in the centre of the lower part of the spheroid, and the blowing tube is detached. The opening thus made is gradually enlarged, and the operative, holding the G. in front of a circular opening in the furnace, by a rapid twirling motion gradually still further spreads out the opened sides till it is ultimately flashed into a disc or flat circular table. By holding this disc in front of the furnace fire, and continuing the rapid rotation, centrifugal force expands the disc to a diameter of 5 to 6 feet, the sheet thus formed being remarkably smooth and of uniform thickness, except at the centre, where the 'bull's eye' or thick portion remains, on account of the slow motion of rotation at that point. Crown G. containing potassium is used for optical purposes.

Patent Plate or *Polished Sheet Glass* consists of sheets of selected sheet G., which are smoothed by rubbing two together with emery powder placed between them, and subsequent polishing with very fine emery and rouge.

Plate Glass is generally of similar composition to crown and sheet, but it sometimes contains a small proportion of potash. The materials for this kind must be selected with great care, in order to produce a pure bright metal, as otherwise, owing to its thickness, any colour would be readily perceptible. The ingredients are usually 300 parts of pure white sand, 100 of carbonate of soda, 43 of slaked lime, to which about 300 parts of cullet are added. When the materials are thoroughly melted, the pots are taken from the furnace to the casting-table, on which the metal is poured out in front of a heavy iron roller. The roller is moved from end to end of the table, and spreads out the metal in a plate of uniform thickness, which thickness is regulated by strips of iron at the sides on which the roller moves. After solidifying sufficiently to bear removal, it is conveyed to the annealing furnace, and after annealing, the G. is in the condition of rough plate, frequently used for glazing roofs and other places where perfect transparency is not required. In this state the G. has a very wavy irregular surface, to remove which it has to undergo a tedious process of polishing. For this purpose one side of the plate is embedded in plaster of Paris, and the opposite surface is first ground to a uniform plane with sand and water. It is then polished by the aid of machinery with seven different qualities of emery powder, increasing in fineness, and the polishing is finished by means of fine rouge in a liquid state, and rubbing with the hand. Plates are made up to about 17 feet long by 10 wide, and in the rough state they vary from $\frac{3}{8}$ to $\frac{3}{4}$ of an inch in thickness. The polishing of plate G. makes the material necessarily much more expensive than ordinary kinds, but the mechanical improvements introduced in recent years have both greatly reduced its price, and rendered the production of sheets of great size practicable.

Bottle Glass, which varies in colour from the opaque dark green of the ordinary black bottle to the slightly tinged variety seen in acid carboys, soda-water bottles, &c., is a compound, of greater or less impurity, of numerous silicates. The materials for ordinary bottle G. are about 100 parts of ferruginous sand, 80 parts of soap-maker's waste, 5 of common clay, and 3 of rock salt. The G., therefore, consists of silicates of aluminum, calcium, iron, magnesium, and sodium. The olive-green tint of the clearer varieties of bottle G. made with more carefully selected materials is due to the presence of magnetic oxide of iron. The making of G. bottles is a very extensive industry, and although the bottles are partly fashioned in moulds, the processes involved are numerous, and demand great dexterity on the part of the workmen. Messrs. Chance of Birmingham at one time made a G. similar in appearance to black bottle G. from a kind of basalt called Rowley rag, and recently a patent has been obtained for utilising blast-furnace slag for the manufacture of bottles and similar articles.

Flint Glass is the type of those varieties which contain lead instead of the calcium or lime, and potash in place of soda is used. It is the glass generally used for table and decorative purposes, being remarkably brilliant and highly refractive. When it is massive and cut, it usually receives the name crystal or crystal G. It is very dense, and much more fusible than the other varieties of G., but it is comparatively soft, and scratches readily. In addition to being used as table G., it is much employed for optical purposes. According to the purpose for which it is designed, the proportion of lead used varies, but the following may be taken as the average quantities of the various ingredients:—300 parts of fine white sand, such as is obtained at Lynn in Norfolk, or from Fontainebleau in France; 200 of minium (red oxide of lead); 100 of pearl ash, or its equivalent in potash or other potassium salt; and about 30 of nitre. From a half to a third of cullet or broken glass is added to these materials. Flint G., as before mentioned, is always made in pots with covered or enclosed tops; and the materials, being thus screened from the direct action of the heat, are longer in melting than the charges in open pots, although the mixture is really much more fusible. Flint G. is fashioned into an innumerable variety of forms by the blowers, and within recent years moulded or pressed G. has attained a perfection which in sharpness of outline almost rivals the numerous articles made of cut flint G. *Strass* or *Paste* only differs from ordinary flint G. in having an excessively high proportion, never less than 53 per cent., of lead in its composition. On account of its high refractive power, it is employed to imitate the diamond, and, when properly coloured, other precious stones. See GEMS, IMITATION.

Enamel Glass consists of coloured or white G. rendered opaque by the addition of oxide of tin. It is prepared by first calcining at a low red heat a mixture of 1 part of tin with from 1 to 6 parts of lead, the ash so prepared being added to the other ordinary ingredients of G. Various other substances communicate opacity to G., among which may be mentioned phosphate of lime, which yields the opalescent shade used for thermometer scales, gas globes, &c.

Coloured Glass.—Many metallic oxides communicate various shades of colour to G. without destroying its transparency, but some colours so produced are so intense that only a thin coating of the coloured material can be flashed over a body of ordinary pure G. Thus we have two varieties of coloured G.—(1) Whole-coloured or pot-metal, and (2) flashed G. The flashing is accomplished by the workman first gathering a proportion of uncoloured metal on his blowing tube, which he then inserts into a pot of coloured G. He has thus a nucleus of uncoloured covered with a skin of coloured G.; and in blowing, both expand together, a stratum of coloured G. always remaining on the surface, thick in proportion to the quantities originally gathered. Red colours are obtained by means of chloride of gold, protoxide of copper, and iron oxide; yellows are yielded by antimoniate of potassium (G. of antimony), and various silver salts. Oxide of wianium yields a greenish yellow; blue is produced by oxide of cobalt, and sometimes oxide of copper; green results from chrome oxide, oxide of copper, and protoxide of iron; violet is yielded by black oxide of manganese; and from a mixture of oxides of iron, copper manganese, and cobalt, black is obtained.

Decoration of Glass.—G., in addition to the decorative forms it assumes under the hands of the skilled workman, is ornamented in several ways by operations not connected with the art of the G.-blower. In addition to painting in enamel colours and gilding, it is ornamented by cutting, engraving, and etching. Cutting is done on wheels with materials of varying degrees of fineness, and besides its decorative application, it is much resorted to in preparing G. for optical purposes. The G. is first ground with sand and water, and the rough surface so left is gradually smoothed and polished with increasingly fine emery powder, putty powder (oxide of tin), and rouge. G. engraving is done on small copper wheels, and in this art everything depends on the taste and artistic ability of the workman. G. etching or hyalography results from exposing certain surfaces of G. to the attacks of hydrofluoric acid, which combines with the silica. The sheet or article to be etched is covered with a protecting coat of wax; the pattern is then traced out, and the wax removed from the portions to be acted upon.

Water Glass or *Soluble Glass* consists of silicates of sodium or of potassium; but this material has neither the properties nor applications of ordinary G. It is soluble in water, and is used as a *dung substitute* in calico-printing; for rendering wood, linen, cotton, &c., uninflammable; as a cement; for preparing artificial stone; and as a basis for external paint-work, &c. See Neri, *De Arte Vitraria* (Amst. 1669); Vinnkel, *Vollständige Glasmacherkunst* (Nürn. 1785); Sanzay, *Marvels of Glassmaking in all Ages* (1870); and Apsley Pellat's *Curiosities of Glassmaking.*

Glass-Painting, the art of painting on transparent white or stained glass with vitrescent pigments. The colours employed are oxides or other combinations of metals, and nearly all of them are mixed or fused with fluxes and applied to the glass in a finely-powdered state in a vehicle of thickened oil of turpentine. G.-P. is practised by two methods, distinguished as the *mosaic* and the *enamel* methods. In the mosaic method several pieces of stained glass, either *pot metal* with the colour throughout, or *flashed*, that is, with only a coating of colour on one side, are joined together with ribs of lead, which add to the general effect by marking the outlines of the parts of the figure. A working drawing shows the disposition of the leads and pieces of coloured glass. The pieces of glass, first 'matted' or brushed over with tracing colour, are arranged on a sheet of plain glass over the cartoon, and shading and outlining details not expressed by leads are painted on, and graded lights are formed by removing the mat and clearing the glass. The colours are then burned into the glass in a kiln at red heat, after which the glass is allowed to cool slowly. The glazier next adjusts and solders the pieces in the leaden ribs. White glass stippled and hatched with colour is employed for flesh-tints in stained glass-work. In enamel G.-P. a large sheet of pure white glass is employed, and on it the outlines of the design are traced in a dark colour, and the enamel pigments are applied in varying thicknesses according to the depth of colour required. By red-heat firing the colours are fused on the surface of the glass, and are usually intensified by retouching and refiring.

Glass Painting in the Marienburg Church, Helmstadt.

The use of coloured glass in windows can be traced back to the 5th c. of our era. The earliest existing painted windows are believed to be those of the Abbey of Tegernsee in Bavaria, belonging to the 10th c. Early windows were formed by the mosaic method, and a striking feature in them is the intensity of the colours, among which ruby and blue predominate. The art of G.-P. was carried to great perfection in the 13th c., and it continued to flourish till the 16th c., when the use of semi-opaque enamel colours began. These furnished a greater variety of tints, but were inferior in beauty and brilliant transparency. The art declined in the 17th c. The 19th c., however, has witnessed a great revival of G.-P. in England, Germany, and France; and stained or painted glass is becoming a popular feature not only of ecclesiastical but of domestic decoration. See GLASS.

Glass'ites are a sect of Christians who derive their name from John Glass, who was born 1695, ordained minister of the Established Church at Tealing, Forfarshire, 1719, and died in 1773. For uttering views differing from those of the Church regarding the kingdom of Christ, Glass was deposed in 1730. A small body of his parishioners adhered to him, and the first Glassite congregation was formed. He maintained that all national establishments of religion 'were unlawful and utterly inconsistent with the true nature of the Church of Christ,' with other opinions which have since received the name of Voluntaryism. In regard to church government, he maintained 'that a congregation with its presbytery or eldership is in its discipline subject to no jurisdiction under heaven, but to Christ alone.' His followers were hence called Independents, but had no connection with the English Congregationalists, from whom indeed they differed on several points. The distinctive teaching of the sect was before long affected by the views of Robert Sandeman, Glass's son-in-law, from whom the sect received in England and America the name of Sandemanians. The chief tenets peculiar to the G., besides the above, are:—A plurality of pastors in each congregation, for which office no special education or separation from secular employment is required; a weekly observance of the Lord's Supper, with a love-feast between morning and evening services; the washing of each other's feet; and the kiss of charity to new members. They hold it unlawful to eat or drink with excommunicated members, to join in prayer with one not a brother or sister in Christ, to lay up treasure on earth, and to eat blood or things strangled. See Glass's *Testimony of the King of Martyrs* (1728), and *Acts of the Gen. Assembly.*

Glass-Snake (*Ophisaurus ventralis*), a species of *Lacertilia* or Lizards found in N. America, and so named from its snake-like aspect, the limbs being wanting. It is included in the family *Chalcidæ*, to which also belong several peculiar lizards, such as the *Chirotes* of Mexico, in which only the front limbs are developed; and the African *Bipes*, in which only the hind limbs are represented. The palate in the G.-S. is toothed, and two deep grooves extend along the sides of the body, which is marked with lines of black, yellow, and green, the belly being bright yellow, and the head mottled on its upper surface. The upper parts are occasionally black, and the under grey; but great variations of colour are observable. The name 'G.-S.' is derived from the brittle nature of the animal's body, the sudden contraction of the tail-muscles causing the body to break in two when the animal is incautiously handled. The common blindworm (*Anguis fragilis*) exhibits the same peculiarity. The G.-S. is very common in plantations, and is often dug up in autumn along with the sweet potato (*Convolvulus batatas*). It feeds on insects, smaller reptiles, &c.

Glass'wort, a common name for species of *Salicornia*, a genus of Chenopodiaceous marine plants. Several species grow abundantly on the coast in S. Europe and N. Africa, and yield a large quantity of soda, which is used in the manufacture of soda and glass, hence the popular name G. *S. herbacea*, not uncommon in salt marshes, is the only species indigenous to Britain. The *Salsola kali* (saltwort or prickly G.) and *Suæda maritima* (the white G. or sea-blite) are both British plants.

Glas'tonbury ('the town of the Glaestings'), a town in Somersetshire, 25 miles S.W. of Bath, and 158 from London by rail, stands on the river Brue, on a height almost surrounded by marshes. It has several interesting buildings, among which are the Church of St. John the Baptist, with a tower 140 feet high, the Church of St. Benedict, and the ruins of the old abbey. The best-preserved part of the abbey is St. Joseph's Chapel, a very fine example of Transition architecture. Near the town is the Tor Hill, on which formerly stood the monastery of St. Michael, of which only a tower remains. The chief industry is the making of gloves, and leather, tiles, bricks, and pottery are also manufactured. The monastery was founded by Ine, King of Wessex, about the beginning of the 8th c., and probably took its name from the English family of the *Glaestings*, who had settled here. G. was a famous seat of learning in pre-Norman times, the story that a second St. Patrick had rested here making it the resort of many Irish scholars. Dunstan was born at G., and was for a time abbot of its monastery. It was long believed that King Arthur and Queen Guinevere were buried in the abbey, and their supposed tomb was visited by Henry II. In 1539 the monastery was seized, its abbot hanged, and its wealth confiscated by Henry VIII. Pop. (1871) 3670.

Glatz (Bohem. *Kladsko*), a fortified town of Silesia, Prussia, on the left bank of the Neisse, between the mouths of the Biela and Steina, 50 miles S.S.W. of Breslau by railway. It has an old castle 1070 feet above the sea, forts on the surrounding heights and on the opposite bank of the river, an old church with tombs of the Silesian dukes, three nunneries, large barracks, and manufactures of linens, damasks, plush, rose garlands, wooden wares, brandy, &c. The valley of the Neisse can be laid under water. Pop. (1871) 11,821 (including a garrison of 2000), most of whom are Roman Catholics. G. suffered in the Thirty Years' War, and capitulated to the Prussians in 1742.

Glau'ber's Salt. See SODA.

Glauch'au, the second manufacturing town in the kingdom of Saxony, on the Mulde, 15 miles W. of Chemnitz by railway. It has two castles, and its manufactures are chiefly cottons, woollens, mixed textiles, iron, and machinery. Pop. (1875) 21,743.

Glau'cium, a small genus of Herbaceous plants, belonging to the Poppy family, found generally on the sea-coasts of Europe and America. There are two British species, viz., *G. luteum*, the yellow horned poppy, and *G. phœniceum*, the scarlet horned poppy. Several species are cultivated for their showy flowers. Most of them have an acrid poisonous juice.

Glauco'ma (Gr. *glaukos*, 'sea-green'), a disease of the eye, the distinctive character of which is a green or greenish colour of the pupil. It occurs in cases of arthritic iritis, and in acute and chronic choroiditis, the eye presenting a green reflection behind the pupil. G. is generally a disease of the crystalline lens alone, but it is sometimes accompanied with Amaurosis (q. v.) from the very commencement.

Glau'cus (*Glaucus*), a beautiful genus of Gasteropodous *Mollusca*, belonging to the Nudibranchiate or 'naked-gilled' section of that class, and to the family *Æolidæ*, of which the nearly allied *Eolis* (q. v.) is the type. The G., of which *G. Pacificus* is a familiar example, is also named the 'sea-lizard.' Its colour is dark blue, streaked with white above, and pearly white on the under parts. The head is white with a median line of blue. The G. is very commonly met with floating in the Atlantic Ocean, and, according to Mr. F. D. Bennett, subsists on the jellyfishes, *Velellæ*, &c., which exist in immense numbers in the track of the ocean currents. The gills are supported on three stalks or lobes on each side of the body.

Glaux, the generic name of a pretty little Herbaceous plant of the Primrose family. It grows abundantly in salt marshes in Britain, hence its Latin name *G. maritima*, and its popular names sea-milkwort and black saltwort. G. has been used as a pickle.

Glaze. See POTTERY.

Glean'ing. It used to be thought that by the law of England the poor might glean on another's ground after harvest. It has now, however, been decided otherwise, the practice having been held to be productive of vagrancy and other evil consequences. But in spite of the legal authority, G. is generally allowed to the poor by the proprietors and farmers of England. At a meeting of farmers in Hertfordshire, August 11, 1845, certain hours of the day were fixed during which G. would be permitted, and a resolution was passed depriving able-bodied labourers between eighteen and sixty years old of the liberty. In Scotland it has been repeatedly decided that the poor have no legal right to glean.

Glebe (Lat. *gleba*, 'a clod or lump of earth') is the land belonging to a parish church in England, or of which the rector or vicar is seised in right of the church. By 5 and 6 Vict. c. 54, the Commissioners for the Commutation of Tithes (q. v.) are empowered, with consent of the ordinary and of the patron, to exchange the G. lands for others, if conveniently situated. The executor of an incumbent who has manured the G. lands and sown them with corn is entitled to the profits of the crop; but if the successor be inducted before severance of the crop from the ground, he is entitled to the tithe. In Scotland, as in England, the parish minister is generally entitled to a G. in addition to his stipend, but ministers in royal burghs proper cannot claim a G., unless there be a landward district annexed. The G. must be taken as near the manse and as convenient for the minister as possible, a provision intended for the benefit of the proprietors as well as of the incumbent, so that the latter is not entitled to choose remote lands on account of the superiority of the soil. The incumbent cannot alienate any part of the G., and in Scotland it is doubtful if he can make a feu contract (see FEU) regarding it. The court has refused to sanction this, even when the feu-duty offered was four times the agricultural rent, the reason being that the value of land continually increases, while that of money does the reverse. Trees in the G. are thought to belong to the incumbent.

Glee (Old Eng. *glig*), a vocal composition for three or more parts, each part being in a manner an independent melody. The great G. period was 1760–1830, and among G. writers may be named Callcott, Stevens, and Bishop.

Gleim, Johann Wilhelm Ludwig, a German poet, was born near Halberstadt, 2d April 1719. Till 1747, when he settled finally in Halberstadt as cathedral secretary, he had been engaged as tutor and secretary in families of distinction. G.'s indefatigable efforts to encourage poetical and literary promise, and his zeal in promoting German unity and national feeling, have, quite as much as his own writings, secured for him the affectionate title of *Father Gleim*, by which he is generally called. He died 18th February 1803. Of his own poems, his *Kriegslieder* (Berl. 1778) are by far the best. *Halladat*, a didactic poem, had appeared in 1774; and *Fabeln und Erzählungen* were posthumously published in 1810. G.'s *Sämmtliche Werke* were edited in 7 vols. (Halb. 1811–13; new ed. 8 vols. 1841) by by Körte, who also wrote his life (Halb. 1811).

Glei'witz, a garrison town in the S.E. of Prussian Silesia, on the Klodnitz, a branch of the Oder, 115 miles S.E. of Breslau by railway. It is the central point of trade in Upper Silesia, and has large coal and iron mining and smelting industries. Pop. (1871) 13,018, of whom many are Polish-speaking Jews.

Glencoe (Gael. *Glencōin*, 'the narrow pass,' not 'the vale of weeping'), a wild, solitary glen in the N. of Argyleshire, is traversed by the Cona of Ossian, which rises in a dreary tarn, and enters Loch Leven on the E. side at Invercol, the residence of Macdonald of G. The glen is enclosed by two lofty porphyritic ranges, and its mouth, fringed with beech, pine, and ash trees, looks out on Loch Leven to the island burial-place. *The Massacre of G.*—To break the power of the disaffected Highlanders in William's reign a plan was devised by the Earl of Breadalbane, and assented to by the Master of Stair, then Secretary of State, the former receiving £20,000 to gain the allegiance of the chiefs, while a proclamation was issued by the Privy Council declaring all to be traitors who did not take the oath by the 1st January 1692. Old Mac-Ian Macdonald of G. offered to do this at Fort-William only on the 1st January. He found that the sheriff was at Inverary, and this occasioned a further delay of a few days. The roll was then returned with a certificate explaining the delay. The certificate was suppressed, and G.'s oath deleted from the roll, for which more than suspicion attaches to Stair, who immediately procured the signature of William to an order 'to extirpate that set of thieves.' Some 120 soldiers, mostly Campbells, the sworn foes of the doomed clan, were quartered at G., and were received with unsuspecting hospitality. At four o'clock on the morning of the 12th February they massacred thirty-eight men and women, about 150 escaping to the hills. The tale of perfidy and blood excited widespread indignation. A parliamentary inquiry was only averted by the nomination of a royal commission, which found (1695) 'that William's instructions afforded no warrant for the measure.' Stair was severely censured, but was left to be dealt with by the king. William was addressed to prosecute Glenlyon, Major Duncanson, Captain Drummond, &c., then in Flanders. And so the matter ended. See the histories of Macaulay and Burton; *Report of the Commission; Papers Illustrative of the Condition of the Highlands*, issued by the Maitland Club; and Paget's *Examen*.

Glendower', or **Glendwr, Owen**, or **Owen of Glendowerdy**, a Welsh leader who, in the reign of Henry IV., declared himself the descendant of the old Welsh princes, and stirred up a rebellion against the English, being provoked by Lord Grey de Ruthyn's seizure of part of his lands. 'The whole country rose at his call' (Green). G. strove with varied success until 1402, when he decoyed Lord Grey into an ambush and captured him, receiving 10,000 marks for his ransom. Along with Earl Percy (Hotspur) and his Scotch prisoner, Earl Douglas, he formed a conspiracy against Henry IV., but arrived too late to save his confederates from defeat at Shrewsbury in 1403. G. next entered into an alliance with Charles VI. of France against England in 1404, but this gave him no substantial aid, and after several years of perilous guerilla warfare, in which his fortunes alternately darkened and brightened, he was driven back when invading Shropshire and forced to fly to the mountains of Snowdon. He died in his daughter's house in 1415. So far as we can judge, G. seems to have been a brave, patriotic, and able, though rash and ambitious, leader. His character is portrayed in Shakespeare's *Henry IV.*

Glenliv'et, a valley in Banffshire, about 20 miles W.S.W. of Huntly, watered by the Livet, which joins the Avon, an affluent of the Spey. The whisky made in the district is deservedly famous.

Glenroy' is a narrow precipitous glen in the county of Inverness, Scotland, through which the Roy, a small tributary of the Spean, flows. It lies in the Lochaber district, a few miles N. of Ben Nevis. Its great interest arises from the three distinctly-marked terraces, known as the *Parallel Roads of G.*, which can be traced almost continuously on both sides of the valley. Each forms a gently sloping shelf from 3 to 30 feet in width, and the most striking characteristic of all is their absolutely constant level. The highest (1144 to 1155 feet) can be traced from the col, 1151 feet in height, at the head of G.—which forms the lowest part of the watershed between the Roy and the Spey—to Bohuntine Hill, near the mouth of the glen. The second shelf (1062 to 1077 feet) runs parallel to the first, but can be traced round Glen Glaster, which opens into G. just below where the first road terminates. This second road corresponds in height to the col (1075 feet) at the S.E. end of Glen Glaster, which is part of the watershed between the Glaster and the Feitheil, a small tributary of the Spean. The third and lowest shelf (850 to 862 feet) can be traced right round Glen Roy, Glen Glaster, and Bohuntine Hill, and away eastward along Glen Spean to a little below Loch Laggan. It corresponds in height to the col (848 feet) at Muckall above Loch Laggan, which forms part of the watershed between the Spean and Maskie, a tributary of the Spey. In Glen Gloy, to the W. of G., is another similar road at a height of from 1156 to 1175 feet. The col at the head of this glen, which looks over to G., is 1172 feet above the sea-level.

The constant level at which each of these roads remains suggests at once that they have been the shores of former lakes or seas. The marine theory advanced by Darwin, who regarded the glens as former arms of the sea, is not now generally believed. The hypothesis which ascribes them to fresh-water lakes was first brought forward by Macculloch, and taken up by Sir T. Dick Lauder. They were forced to assume the former existence of gigantic barriers of *débris*, which were gradually washed away by the water, kept for more lengthened periods at the heights of the various shelves. The difficulties of this theory are, first, where did the *débris* come from; and second, where did it disappear to, without leaving even the slightest trace of its existence. Such difficulties do not exist in the bold speculation of Agassiz, who finds the necessary barrier in a huge glacier which slid down from Ben Nevis. This theory is supported by the numerous evidences of former glaciers in the district. Suppose a glacier to fill all the lower portion of G. up to where the highest road terminates above Glen Glaster. The water collected in the glen could escape only at the col at the head of G. Let the glacier now recede till it reaches the points where the second road terminates on Bohuntine Hill. Glen Glaster will now be open, and the waters will be discharged over the lower col at the head of that glen. Let the glacier now recede quite out of G. and stretch across Glen Spean below Roy Bridge. The water will then fall to the level of the lowest possible outlet, which is the col at Muckall above Loch Laggan. See Tyndall's Lecture in the *Pop. Science Rev.* (1876).

Glidd'on, George Robins, antiquarian and ethnologist, was born in Devonshire, England, in 1809. His father was United States' consul in Egypt, where he himself lived for twenty-three years, and filled for some time the post of vice-consul at Cairo. In 1840 he visited London, Paris, and the United States, where he lectured in all the principal cities on Egyptian antiquities. In 1857 he became agent of the Honduras Inter-Oceanic Railway, and died the same year, November 16, at Panama. His works are *Ancient Egypt, her Monuments, Hieroglyphics, History, and Archæology, &c.* (1850); *Discourses on Egyptian Archæology* (1841); *Memoir on the Cotton of Egypt* (1841); *Appeal to the Antiquaries on the Destruction of the Monuments of Egypt* (1841); *Otia Ægyptica* (1849); and, together with Dr. J. C. Nott of Mobile, Alabama, *Types of Mankind* (1854), and *Indigenous Races of the Earth* (1857). G.'s knowledge was great in certain directions, and his industry was unflagging; but his writings, especially the *Types of Mankind*, are so marred by bitter prejudice, rash speculation, and bad reasoning, that they have not been received even with the modified respect to which they are entitled.

Gli'res (pl. of Lat. *glis*, 'a dormouse'), a name formerly given by zoologists to an order of *Mammalia* (q. v.) now better known as *Rodentia* (q. v.) or gnawing quadrupeds. It is represented by the rats, mice, squirrels, porcupines, beavers, dormice, &c.

Globe (Lat. *globus*) is a round spherical body, and is frequently used as a synonym for the earth. *Artificial globes*, constructed of pasteboard, wood, metal, &c., are intended to give a clear notion of the arrangement of the stars and constellations in the heavens, or of the form of the earth, and of the true surface configuration of land and water. These are termed respectively *celestial* and *terrestrial* globes. In the celestial G. the constellations are not represented as they appear to an observer on the earth; they are drawn as viewed from the *outside*, and are therefore reversed. The Armillary Sphere (q. v.) is a particular form of G. in which all but certain important circles are cut away.

Globe-Fishes, the popular name applied collectively to various genera (*Diodon, Balistes, Tetraodon*, &c.) of Teleostean fishes, belonging to the division *Plectognathi* of that order, from the peculiar appearance of their bodies, produced by their inflating themselves with air. See DIODON, FILE-FISHES, &c.

Globe-Flower, the popular name given to *Trollius Europæus*, a Herbaceous perennial plant belonging to the natural order *Ranunculaceæ* (q. v.). It is not uncommon in mountainous pastures and open woods in sub-alpine districts throughout Britain; it is also abundant on the Swiss Alps. The G.-F. is frequently grown in gardens for its large globose, pale-yellow flowers. In Scotland it is called the 'lucken gowan.'

Globe-Flower (*Trollius Europæus*).

Globigeri'na, a very common genus of *Foraminifera* (q. v.) found in great abundance in existing oceans, and also in the true chalk formations. The latter are, in fact, made up in very considerable part of the minute shells of these Foraminifera. *G. bulloides* is the familiar species, and the G. of the chalk appear to be indistinguishable from their existing representatives. It would appear from recent researches that the shells of G. in their perfect state have an outer coating of delicate spines, which become detached, when the shells fall to the bottom of the ocean, where they aid in forming the ever-accumulating mass of chalky ooze, which only requires elevation and consolidation to convert it into a true chalk deposit. The shell of the G. consists of a number of minute rounded spheres or chambers of limy matter, aggregated in an irregular fashion; the walls of the chambers being perforated for the emission of the *pseudopodia*, or extensions of the soft protoplasm of the body.

Glo'bus Hyster'icus, or **Ball in the Throat**, a term applied to one of the more marked symptoms of Hysteria (q. v.).

Glock'ner, Gross, the chief peak in the Noric Alps, 12,431 feet high, and on the border of Tyrol, Carinthia, and Salzburg in Upper Austria.

Glog'au, Gross, a fortified town in Prussian Silesia, on the Oder, 35 miles N.N.W. of Liegnitz by railway. It has a cathedral of 1120, beautifully situated on a river island; also a castle, two gymnasia, and manufactures of woollens, printed calicoes, tobacco, paper, sugar, &c. Pop., including the garrison (1871), 22,265. In Slavic, *glog* means 'the whitethorn,' and Glogau is therefore 'the town of the whitethorn.'

Glogg'nitz (Slav. 'the town of the whitethorn'), a market-town of Lower Austria, on the Schwarza, at the N. base of the Semmering Alps, 45 miles S.S.W. of Vienna by railway. It has a castle, and manufactures of machinery, white-lead, &c. G. is the station at the beginning of the ascent of the railway from Vienna to Trieste, which goes over the Semmering. Pop. (1869) 3777.

Glomm'en, the greatest river of Norway, rises in Lake Aursund, 2419 feet above the sea, flows first S.W., then S.E., and again S.W. into Skager Rack at Fredrikstad after a course of 400 miles. After being joined by the Vormen, it is called the *Stor-Elv* or 'great river.' Its course is much impeded by falls, of which the chief is Sarp-fos, 60 feet in descent, and 10 miles from the sea.

Glo'ria in Excel'sis (Angelic Hymn or Greater Doxology) originally consisted of its opening sentence, taken from Luke ii. 14. Variously ascribed to Telesphorus, Bishop of Rome (128–138), and to Hilary of Poictiers (350–367), it was probably adopted as a Eucharistic hymn in its present form in the 6th c. —**Gloria Patri**, or Little Doxology, which originally consisted of its first clause, taken from Matt. xxviii. 19, 20, in its present form is the result of the Arian controversy.

Glorio'sa (**Methon'ica** of some authors), a genus of Liliaceous climbing herbaceous plants, natives of India and Africa. All the species have remarkably handsome flowers, several of which are grown in hothouses. They are said to be extremely poisonous.

Glo'rious Vir'gin, or **St. Mary the Glorious**, an ecclesiastico-military order of knighthood in Venice, the organisation of which was sanctioned in 1260 by Pope Urban IV. The protection of widows and orphans, and the furtherance of the interests of Italy, were the objects of the society.

Gloss, in its first departure from the classical usage of Gr. *glôssa* 'tongue, speech,' meant a word requiring explanation, a book containing all such words with their explanations being a *glossary*. G. next came to mean the explanation itself, and thus to have its modern meaning of a note to any word or phrase, for the purpose of interpretation or illustration. Scripture glosses are of two kinds—(1) Explanations drawn from the Greek glossarists on words occurring in the Scriptures; (2) marginal notes, which in the Hebrew gave rise to some of the K'ri readings, and in the LXX. and the New Testament to a number of the various readings. There is still another meaning of G. in the history of exegesis. When the *catenæ* of comments, which were so common in the 6th c., became too copious, abridgments were compiled from them, which were called glosses. Such was the *Glossa Ordinaria* of Walafried Strabo (9th c.), a *marginal* G. The first *interlineary* G. was made by Anselm in the 12th c.

Glossi'tis (Gr. *glôssa*, 'the tongue'), inflammation of the tongue, is a rare affection, more particularly when occurring idiopathically; but it may result from acrid substances taken into the mouth, from the specific action of mercury, or from such zymotic diseases as scarlet-fever or small-pox. The tongue in such cases is greatly infiltrated with serum and blood, becomes much enlarged, causing inability to swallow or to speak, and even threatening suffocation. G. is frequently accompanied with profuse salivation. Treatment:—A long and free incision along the dorsum of the tongue, on either side of the medial line, should be made; but if the patient can swallow, saline purgatives should be administered first.

Gloss'op, a town of Derbyshire, England, on high ground to the N. of the Peak, and overlooking the Dinting Vale, 11 miles E.S.E. of Manchester by railway. It is the chief seat of the cotton industry in Derby, and has, besides, woollen and paper mills, iron-foundries, dyeworks, bleachfields, &c. Pop. (1871) 17,046.

Glott'is. This is the chink or opening forming the superior aperture of the Larynx (q. v.).

Gloucester, the titular name of several English historic families, of which the following are the most prominent members: —1. **Robert, Earl of G.**, a natural son of Henry I. He took the part of his sister Maud in the long civil war between her and Stephen, in obedience to the oath he had sworn to their common father; defeated and captured Stephen at Lincoln in 1141, but was himself made prisoner in the same year. He and Stephen were exchanged for each other. G. subsequently went to France to persuade Matilda's husband, the Comte d'Anjou, to come to her help. He did not succeed, but he brought back with him the young Prince Henry (afterwards Henry II.), and by his persistent efforts not only made it impossible for Stephen to securely maintain himself on the throne, but prepared the way for the succession of Matilda's son. He died 31st October 1147. G. was the Mæcenas of his age, and a man of great talent, sagacity, and accomplishment. To him William of Malmesbury dedicated his *History of the Kings of England*, and Geoffrey of Monmouth his *Historia Britonum*. The former closes his work with an eloquent tribute to the virtues and munificence of the Earl, while the latter pronounces him 'an accomplished scholar and philosopher, as well as a brave soldier and expert commander.'—2. **Gilbert de Clare, Earl of G. and Hertford**, fought at the battle of Lewes on the side of Simon de Montfort, Earl of Leicester. Afterwards he quarrelled with his leader, who justly suspected the sincerity of his alliance, and on the escape of Edward from captivity, put himself at the head of his forces and joined the Prince. He had a share in the victory of Evesham in 1265, where De Montfort was slain. A later revolt in which he was concerned cost him by way of penalty 20,000 marks. During the absence of Prince Edward in the East he was appointed chancellor of the kingdom by Henry III., and died in 1295. Like his father, a turbulent and fickle member of the baronage, G. lacked insight, conviction, and patriotism. His only son, **Gilbert, Earl of G.**, by his marriage with Johanna, daughter of Edward I., fell at Bannockburn in 1314—

> 'The Erl of Glousister ded was thar,
> That men callit Schir Gilbert of Clar.'
>
> —*Brus.* cvii. l. 27, 28.

3. **Thomas of Woodstock, Duke of G.**, youngest son of Edward III., was born 7th January 1355, and married Eleanor Bohun, eldest daughter of Humphrey, Earl of Hereford, Essex, and Northampton—a union which brought him great wealth and the dignity of Grand Constable of England. In 1377 he was made Earl of Buckingham, and in 1385 Duke of G. He was the head of the party among the nobles who wished to carry on the war with France, crushed the peace party, and by a bill of impeachment hurried its leader, the Earl of Suffolk, into exile and death. Popular resentment was aroused against him, and the young king, Richard II., threw off his guardianship. G. was seized and carried off to Calais, where he was murdered in September 1397.—4. **Humphrey, Duke of G.**, youngest son of Henry IV. by his marriage with the second daughter of Humphrey Bohun, became after the death of his brother, Henry V., guardian of the infant king, Henry VI., along with the Duke of Bedford (q. v.). While the latter carried on the war in France, G. governed the realm at home. On the death of Bedford in 1435, he became sole guardian of the king. He married Jacqueline of Brabant in 1425, divorced her in 1430, quarrelled with Burgundy, and after the marriage of Henry VI. with Margaret of Anjou, fell into disgrace through the intrigues of

the Bishop of Rochester, the Earl of Suffolk, and the Queen. Accused of high treason in 1446 and thrown into prison, he was one morning found dead in his bed. He was the leader of the war party among the English nobles, and as long as his great brother the Duke of Bedford was alive to be the terror of France, G.'s position was secure. But the disasters that followed Bedford's death made peace necessary, and enabled his enemies to accomplish his overthrow, and encouraged them to complete it with a crime.—5. **Richard, Duke of G.**, son of Richard, Duke of York, ascended the throne of England in 1483 as Richard III. (q. v.).—6. **William Henry, Duke of G.**, born 25th November 1743, was the third son of Frederick, Prince of Wales, a brother of George III., and was proclaimed Duke of G. in 1764. Two years later he was privately married to the widowed Countess of Waldegrave. This morganatic union was the cause of animated discussions in Parliament. His career was otherwise insignificant, and he died in dignified obscurity, 25th August 1805. His son, **William Frederick, Duke of G.**, born at Rome, 15th January 1776, distinguished himself in the campaign of 1799 in Holland, and married in 1816 the Princess Mary, a daughter of George III. He nevertheless ranged himself on the side of the Whig opposition, especially in the trial of Queen Caroline, but latterly went over to the Tories, and died childless at Bagshot Park, 30th November 1834.

Gloucester, Robert of, a monk of Gloucester Abbey who lived in the latter half of the 13th c., and wrote a chronicle of England from the siege of Troy to 1272. This work, which must have been composed after 1297, as the author alludes to the canonisation of St. Louis in that year, is largely based on Geoffrey of Monmouth's *Historia Britonum*, and is written in rhyming English verse, the lines being very long and somewhat irregular. It is cast in the Southern dialect, and is very free from Romance words. R. of G. is also held to have written metrical *Lives and Legends of the English Saints.* The only complete edition of his chronicle is that by Hearne (Oxford, 1724). Several of the *Lives of the Saints* appear in Furnivall's *Early English Poems* (1862). See Morris and Skeat's *Specimens of Early English* (Oxford, 1872).

Gloucester, the chief place in the county of G., stands in a fertile district on the left bank of the Severn, 114 miles W.N.W. of London by rail. It is a very handsome town, with several fine public buildings. The cathedral, begun in 1058 (and restored 1875), a beautiful building in various styles, is 427 feet long, 154 feet in extreme breadth, and has a fine tower 223 feet high, topped by four singularly graceful pinnacles. The choir is scarcely surpassed as an example of Perpendicular architecture, and its roof is covered with exquisite fan-tracery. There are twelve churches, several other places of worship, a theatre, assembly rooms, gaol, and lunatic asylum. The two channels of the Severn are spanned by two fine stone bridges, and the G. and Berkeley Canal enables large vessels to enter the docks. G. has considerable coasting and foreign trade. In 1875, 2785 vessels of 301,623 tons entered, and 3500 of 165,045 cleared. The chief imports are timber, corn, wine, and spirits; the chief exports, iron, coal, bricks, salt, malt, and pottery. There are brass and iron foundries, flour and saw mills, chemical, soap, marble, and slate works, tanneries, &c., and ship-building is also carried on. The city returns two members to Parliament. Pop. (1871) 18,341. G. was the British *Caer-Glow* ('the bright fortress'), the Roman '*colonia*' *Glevum*, and the *Gleaw-Ceaster* of the West Saxons, who occupied it about 580. It afterwards belonged to Mercia, and suffered greatly from the Danish invaders. It was a favourite abode of William I., was almost destroyed in 1087 during the struggle between William II. and his brother Robert, and supported Maud firmly against Stephen in 1141. Edward I., Richard II., and Henry IV. held parliaments at G., which stubbornly and successfully resisted the Royalists in the great civil war. The see of G. was united with that of Bristol in 1842. Many Roman remains have been found here.

Gloucester, a seaport of Massachusetts, U.S., 28 miles N.E. of Boston, with which it is connected by railway. It has a fine harbour, is much resorted to for summer bathing, and carries on a large fishing trade. In 1873 the produce of the fisheries amounted to $4,000,000. Pop. (1870) 15,389. G. was settled in 1623, incorporated a town in 1642, and became a city in 1874.

Gloucestershire, an inland county in the S.W. of England, bounded N. by Warwickshire and Worcestershire, E. by Oxfordshire, S. by Somersetshire and Wiltshire, and W. by Herefordshire and Monmouthshire. Area, 1258 sq. miles; pop. (1871) 534,640. The surface of G. is very varied. In the W. of the county is the picturesque sylvan district known as the Forest of Dean; along the river lies the rich grassy Vale of the Severn, and in the E. the Coteswold Hills (q. v.) separate the basins of the Severn and Thames. The formations are mainly oolite and lias, with new red and carboniferous limestone in the W. The chief rivers are the Severn, Wye, Upper and Lower Avon, the Churn, and the Thames or Isis, which drains the district E. of the Coteswolds. The climate is mild; the Vale of the Severn produces large crops of wheat, barley, and rye, and abounds in fruit, which ripens very early, while the Coteswolds afford excellent pasture. The chief products of G. are butter and cheese, and the G. cows and Coteswold sheep are famous breeds. Much cider is made in the Forest of Dean. The chief manufactures are woollens, cotton, and iron, brass, &c., at Bristol. The chief places are Gloucester, Bristol, Stroud, Cheltenham, Cirencester, Berkeley, and Tewkesbury. There are many Roman relics and remains of British, Old English, and Danish works. The county returns four members to Parliament.

Glove, a word of uncertain origin, but probably meaning a covering for the hand, and perhaps connected with the Scotch *loof.* Gloves appear to have been worn in England early in the 11th, but were not common till the 13th c. White silk gloves beautifully embroidered and jewelled were worn by the clergy. In the 16th c. New Year's gifts took the form of gloves, and when money was given it was called 'G.-money.' Leather is the chief material of which gloves are now made—silk, cotton, and worsted, however, being also used. The manufacture of gloves in England is conducted at the following places:—Worcester, Yeovil, Ludlow, and London for leather; Derby and Nottingham for cotton and silk; and Leicester for mixed woollen gloves. Large quantities of leather gloves are made in France, Belgium, Denmark, and Italy. Britain imported in 1874 from Continental countries, especially France, 1,126,078 dozen pairs of leather gloves, valued at £1,546,716. The finest leather G. is made of the skin of the sucking kid. Cheap 'kid' gloves are invariably made of fine thin lambskin, and 'dogskin' gloves of ordinary sheepskin. Cheveril, the skin of the young goat, buckskin, doeskin, and shamoyed leather are also used for G.-making. Kid is cured and rendered soft and pliable by 'tawing' in a paste consisting of wheaten flour, egg yolk, alum, common salt, and water. Spotted kid is unsuitable for white or delicately-dyed gloves, it is therefore dyed of a dark colour. In 'cutting out' care is taken to have as little waste as possible, and in this the French excel. Kid gloves may be cleaned by stretching them on a wooden stock and rubbing them over with benzine, spirits of turpentine, or with an inodorous composition of one part of soap shavings dissolved in two parts of distilled water, to which a small quantity of ammonia is added.

Glov'er, Richard, an English poet, born at London in 1712, became a merchant in his native city, entered Parliament as member for Weymouth in 1760, and died in 1785. His chief poem, *Leonidas*, published in his twenty-fifth year, is a serious epic, was popular for a generation, and passed through several editions, but has now dropped out of human remembrance. A continuation entitled the *Atheniad*, which appeared two years after G.'s death, is equally forgotten; but his ballad of *Hosier's Ghost* (1739), intended to rouse the national feeling against Spain, has still some faint vitality, though not enough to awaken interest. G. also wrote two tragedies, *Boadicea* and *Medea.*

Glow-Worm (*Lampyris noctiluca*), a genus of insects belonging to the *Coleoptera* or Beetle order, and to the family *Lampyridæ*, in which the body is long and flat, the head small, the chest or thorax extending over the head, and the antennæ toothed. In the genus *Lampyris* itself, no rostrum or beak exists, and the females are wingless. Both males and females are luminous, although the males do not emit such brilliant phosphorescence as their mates. The females are grub or larva-like, and their appearance has suggested the popular name, 'glow-*worm*.' The light appears to be emitted from the extremity of the abdomen, and its function is supposed to be that of guiding the males to their mates. The female G.-W. attains a length of about half an inch, and is of a blackish colour, the legs being red. The eyes of the male are very prominent. The larva feeds on snails, slugs, and other insects, and has a kind of brush-like appendage attached to the abdomen. The G.-W. is common in the S. of England, and is but rarely found in Scotland. See also FIRE-FLY and PHOSPHORESCENCE, ANIMAL.

Gloxin'ia, a genus of tropical American plants belonging to the order *Gesneraceæ* (q. v.), several species of which are grown in British hothouses for their richly-coloured foliage and graceful flowers.

Gluchov', a town in the S. of Russia, on an affluent of the Seim, 112 miles E. of Tchernigov. It stands in a fertile district, is girt by an earth-wall, and has cloth manufactures and a trade in corn and brandy made from a fine kind of cherry. Fine porcelain clay is found in the vicinity. Pop. about 9000.

Gluci'na. See GLUCINUM.

Gluci'num, or **Beryll'ium**, is a comparatively rare metal contained in certain precious stones and minerals. The emerald is a double silicate of aluminum and G., coloured green by a small quantity of chromium. Beryl has much the same composition, but is paler in colour than the emerald. Chrysoberyl is a compound of the oxides of aluminum and G. G. is also contained in euclase, gadolinite, leucophane, phenacite, helvine, &c. G., or rather its oxide glucina, was discovered in the year 1797 by Vauquelin in the emerald. Metallic G. was obtained by Wöhler in 1827 by the action of potassium on its fused chloride. It is a white, very light metal (sp. gr. 2·1), and may be hammered into leaves and rolled at ordinary temperatures. It does not decompose water even at a red heat. Its atomic weight is 9·25, and the symbol for its atom Gl or Be. In its chemical properties it resembles on the one hand magnesium, on the other aluminum. The first observers, indeed, mistook its oxide (glucina) for the oxide of aluminum (alumina). Glucina (GlO) is obtained from beryl by fusing that mineral with carbonate of soda. The fused mass is then dissolved in water acidulated with hydrochloric acid, and evaporated to dryness, to render the silica insoluble. It is again dissolved in water, the solution filtered from the silica, and carbonate of ammonia is added in excess; this precipitates alumina, but dissolves the glucina. On cooling the solution, carbonate of glucina ($GlCO_3$) separates as a white precipitate, and this when heated gives up carbonic acid, and glucina (GlO) remains. The salts of G. are characterised by their sweet taste—whence the name of the element.

Gluck, Christoph Willibald, Ritter von, a famous musical composer, was born at Weidenwang, near Neumarkt, in the Upper Palatinate, Germany, 2d July 1714. When only three years old, his father removed to Bohemia, where G. received his education. At the age of twenty-two he went to Vienna, where Prince Melzi of Lombardy having heard him sing and play, brought him to Italy and put him under the training of Sammartini of Milan, then a very celebrated teacher. Here he brought out his first opera, *Artaserse* (1741). It was followed by seven others in the received Italian style. Meanwhile, he had gone to London, where his fame had preceded him, but in 1746 returned to the Continent. His great triumphs were achieved in Vienna and Paris. He conceived the design of reforming the abuses of the existing opera, and began to compose works after a nobler and fuller plan. Genius, industry, and a quick impetuous mind fitted him for this task. He studied literature, and especially poetry, with earnestness, and was much furthered in his projects by the poet who wrote his librettos. His great operas, which give him the right to be called the founder of 'a new era in dramatic music,' are *Orpheus and Eurydice; Alcestis* (1762); *Iphigenia in Aulis* (1774); *Armide* (1777); and *Iphigenia in Tauris* (1779). G. died at Vienna, 15th November 1787. See Schmid's *Christoph Willibad, Ritter von G.* (Leips. 1854).

Glück'stadt, a port of Slesvig-Holstein, Prussia, on the Elbe, near the Kremper Marsh, 30 miles N.W. of Hamburg. It has harbour room for 200 vessels, is intersected by canals, and sends out ships to the whale-fishing. Pop. (1871) 5073. G., which was formerly the chief town in the duchy of Holstein, was founded in 1620, and had fortifications till 1815.

Glu'cosides. The G. form a large group of substances derived from animal or vegetable products. They possess the common property of yielding Glucose (q. v.) and other products when they are boiled with dilute acids, or are acted on by certain ferments. They may be regarded as ethers of glucose. Most of them occur in the vegetable kingdom, comparatively few are of animal origin. The majority contain the elements carbon, hydrogen, and oxygen only; others contain nitrogen and a few other elements. None of the G. have been prepared artificially. The following are among the most interesting:—

Amygdaline, a crystalline body occurring in bitter almonds. When gently warmed in aqueous solution with *emulsine* (the ferment which occurs along with it in the almond), amygdaline is resolved into oil of bitter almonds, hydrocyanic acid, and glucose—

$$\underbrace{C_{20}H_{27}NO_{11}}_{\text{Amygdaline.}} + \underbrace{2H_2O}_{\text{Water.}} = \underbrace{C_7H_6O}_{\text{Oil of bitter almonds.}} + \underbrace{HCN}_{\text{Hydrocyanic acid.}} + \underbrace{2C_6H_{12}O_6}_{\text{Glucose.}}$$

Chitine (q. v.), the substance forming the solid parts of insects. When boiled with dilute acids, it takes up water and is resolved into lactamide and glucose—

$$\underbrace{C_9H_{15}NO_6}_{\text{Chitine.}} + \underbrace{2H_2O}_{\text{Water.}} = \underbrace{C_6H_{12}O_6}_{\text{Glucose.}} + \underbrace{C_3H_7NO_2}_{\text{Lactamide.}}$$

Gallotannic Acid or Tannin (q. v.) is contained in gall-nuts. When boiled with dilute acids, it takes up water and yields glucose and Gallic Acid (q. v.)—

$$\underbrace{C_{27}H_{22}O_{17}}_{\text{Tannin.}} + \underbrace{4H_2O}_{\text{Water.}} = \underbrace{C_6H_{12}O_6}_{\text{Glucose.}} + \underbrace{3C_7H_6O_5}_{\text{Gallic acid.}}$$

Myronate of Potash is contained in the seeds of the black mustard, and is resolved by the action of *myrosine* (a ferment which occurs along with it in the mustard-seed) into sulphocyanate of allyl (oil of mustard), acid sulphate of potash, and glucose—

$$\underbrace{C_{10}H_{18}KNS_2O_{10}}_{\text{Myronate of potash.}} = \underbrace{C_3H_5CNS}_{\text{Oil of mustard.}} + \underbrace{KHSO_4}_{\text{Acid sulphate of potash.}} + \underbrace{C_6H_{12}O_6}_{\text{Glucose.}}$$

Indican, a colourless substance occurring in woad (*Isatis tinctoria*). Boiled with dilute acids, it takes up water and yields indigo blue and indiglucine—

$$\underbrace{C_{26}H_{31}NO_{17}}_{\text{Indican.}} + \underbrace{2H_2O}_{\text{Water.}} = \underbrace{C_8H_5NO}_{\text{Indigo blue.}} + \underbrace{3C_6H_{10}O_6}_{\text{Indiglucine.}}$$

Salicine, a crystalline substance occurring in the leaves and young bark of the poplar. When boiled with emulsine (the ferment contained in bitter almonds), it takes up water and is resolved into glucose and saligenine—

$$\underbrace{C_{13}H_{18}O_7}_{\text{Salicine.}} + \underbrace{H_2O}_{\text{Water.}} = \underbrace{C_6H_{12}O_6}_{\text{Glucose.}} + \underbrace{C_7H_8O_2}_{\text{Saligenine.}}$$

Coniferine, the crystalline principle contained in the different species of the pine-tree. When treated with emulsine, it takes up water and yields glucose and another substance—

$$\underbrace{C_{16}H_{22}O_8}_{\text{Coniferine.}} + \underbrace{H_2O}_{\text{Water.}} = \underbrace{C_6H_{12}O_6}_{\text{Glucose.}} + \underbrace{C_{10}H_{12}O_3}$$

The substance thus obtained along with glucose when oxidised with a mixture of bichromate of potash and sulphuric acid is converted into *vanilline* ($C_8H_8O_3$), the aromatic principle of vanilla.

Glu'cose. Under this title are included several distinct substances having the common formula $C_6H_{12}O_6$. They more or less closely resemble one another in their properties, and are either directly or indirectly prepared from animal or vegetable products. The most important members of the family of glucoses are the following:—

Ordinary G., Dextrose, or Grape-Sugar.—This occurs in considerable quantity in the juice of ripe fruits, especially in that of the grape; associated with lævulose in unripe fruits and in honey; and in considerable quantity in the urine of patients suffering from diabetes. It may be obtained by boiling starch, Dextrine (q. v.), Cellulose (q. v.), and cane-sugar with dilute acids, but in the case of cane-sugar lævulose is also produced. It may be prepared from the *Glucosides* (q. v.) by a similar treatment. Dextrose may be extracted from honey which has become crystalline, by treating it with cold alcohol to dissolve lævulose, and then boiling the residue with alcohol. The solution on cooling deposits dextrose in crystals. To prepare dextrose from starch, 1 part of that substance, 4 parts of water, and from $\frac{1}{100}$th to $\frac{1}{10}$th part of sulphuric acid are boiled together for from six to thirty-six hours. The liquid is then neutralised with chalk, filtered, decolorised with animal charcoal, and evaporated to a syrup. From this syrup dextrose very slowly separates in the crystalline state. The conversion of starch into dextrose is also accomplished during the germination of seeds, and is brought about by the action of a peculiar ferment called *Diastase* (q. v.).

Dextrose crystallises from its aqueous solution in warty masses. These crystals contain a molecule of water of crystallisation, and therefore have the formula $C_6H_{12}O_6H_2O$. The water of crystallisation is driven off by exposing the dextrose to a temperature of 60° C. in dry air. Dextrose is characterised by the property possessed by its solution of rotating the plane of a ray of polarised light to the right (whence its name). It is less sweet and less soluble than cane-sugar. Heated to 170° C. it loses a molecule of water and becomes *glucosan* ($C_6H_{10}O_5$). At a higher temperature it loses more water and is converted into caramel and other products. It forms crystalline compounds with lime, baryta, oxide of lead, &c., and with certain salts—chloride of sodium or common salt, for instance. Boiled with a solution of caustic potash and sulphate of copper (or any other cupric compound), dextrose is rapidly oxidised, and the copper salt is reduced to red cuprous oxide (Cu_2O). Upon this reaction is based the ordinary qualitative and quantitative test for dextrose. Cane-sugar does not reduce the alkaline copper solution. A dilute solution of dextrose mixed with yeast, and maintained at a temperature of from 21–26° C., ferments, and is resolved into alcohol and carbonic acid—

$$\underbrace{C_6H_{12}O_6}_{\text{Dextrose.}} = \underbrace{2CO_2}_{\text{Carbonic acid.}} + \underbrace{2C_2H_6O}_{\text{Alcohol.}}$$

Lævulose generally occurs with dextrose. It is present along with that body in honey and in the juice of fruits. It is obtained in equal quantities with dextrose when cane-sugar is boiled with dilute acids. The mixture of the two sugars thus prepared is called *inverted* sugar. The dilute acid simply causes the cane-sugar to take up water, and to split into equal parts of dextrose and lævulose—

$$\underbrace{C_{12}H_{22}O_{11}}_{\text{Cane-sugar.}} + \underbrace{H_2O}_{\text{Water.}} = \underbrace{C_6H_{12}O_6}_{\text{Dextrose.}} + \underbrace{C_6H_{12}O_6}_{\text{Lævulose.}}$$

Lævulose may be separated from dextrose by taking advantage of the property it possesses of forming an insoluble compound with lime. The inverted sugar obtained from 10 grammes of cane-sugar is mixed with 6 grammes of slaked lime and 100 grammes of water. A solution at first results, but after a time the whole of the lævulose separates, in combination with the lime, as a white precipitate. This is separated from the soluble lime compound of the dextrose by pressure, and is decomposed by an equivalent quantity of oxalic acid dissolved in water. Lævulose remains in solution, and by evaporating off the water may be obtained as an uncrystallisable syrup. In most of its properties lævulose resembles dextrose. It is distinguished from dextrose, however, by its action on polarised light, its solution rotating the polarised ray to the left; also by its forming the insoluble lime compound before alluded to, and by its fermenting less rapidly than dextrose.

Galactose, produced by boiling sugar of milk (see LACTOSE) with dilute acids, is more readily crystallisable than dextrose, ferments with greater rapidity, and has a greater dextro-rotatory power on the polarised ray. Unlike dextrose and lævulose, it does not yield saccharic acid when oxidised with nitric acid, but an isomeric substance called mucic acid.

Maltose, a variety of dextrose, produced by the action of diastase on starch, differs from dextrose only in its greater dextro-rotatory power. It is converted into dextrose by boiling with dilute acids. The other glucoses are unimportant.

Mannitose is produced by the slow oxidation of Mannite (q. v.) by platinum black.

Inosite occurs in the muscles of the heart and other organs, also in green kidney-beans and in the unripe fruit of several plants. It does not ferment with yeast.

Sorbin occurs in the juice of ripe berries of the mountain-ash. It does not ferment with yeast.

Eucalyn, an uncrystallisable and unfermentable glucose, separates during the fermentation of melitose—a variety of saccharose occurring in the Tasmanian eucalyptus. It is dextro-rotatory.

Glucosu'ria. See DIABETES.

Glue, Marine. In shipbuilding and other arts glue is required that will resist the solvent action of water. M. G., having no gelatine in its composition, meets this requirement. It is prepared by dissolving caoutchouc in naphtha, and adding shell-lac to the solution.

Glume, the term applied to the outer scales of the flowers of Grasses (q. v.) and sedges. (See CAREX.) Hence these plants have been placed in the Monocotyledonous sub-class *Glumiferæ*.

Glutæ'us (Gr. *gloutos*, 'the buttock') is a term applied to various muscles which form that region. In man they are three in number, viz., the G. maximus, the G. medius, and the G. minimus—of which the first is the chief extensor of the hip-joint, while the two latter remove the thigh from the median plane of the body (that is, they are *abductors*), and they assist in supporting the body on one limb during the act of walking.

Glu'ten (Lat.) is readily obtained from white fibrous tissue and from the animal part of bone. It forms a thick jelly from a solution 1 part to 100 of water; and tannic acid forms a cheesy precipitate with it, even when added to a solution of the strength of 1 part of G. to 5000 of water. Creosote gives with G. a 'milky turbidity.' By boiling G. in caustic potash it is decomposed, and along with the escape of ammonia, glycine and leucine are produced. Chondrin is obtained from cartilage alone, and most acids which have no effect on G. will precipitate chondrin. Gelatine cannot be detected in the blood or in the healthy tissues of the body. Probably gelatinous compounds are formed from the protean or albuminous ones, when the latter are converted into fibrous tissue. Modern physiologists incline to the belief that gelatinous compounds never serve as a formative basis for any of the structures of the body, but are to be simply regarded as presenting material for vital combustion. Again, the gelatinous tissues are never associated in the living body with other than purely mechanical uses, exemplified by their forming ligaments for the union of bones, whereas vital and actively functional organs are of albuminous composition.

Glutt'on (*Gulo luscus*), a genus of Carnivorous *Mammalia*, belonging to the family *Mustelidæ* (q. v.), or that of the Weasels (q. v.), and also known by the name of wolverene. The popular name of the animal originated from the tales of its ferocity, which are now well ascertained to be without foundation. It was said to pounce upon animals from the branches of trees, and to exceed larger carnivora in its rapacity. The G. inhabits N. America, Siberia, and N. Europe. It is of bear-like aspect, and attains a length of about 2½ feet. Its fur is a brownish-black, the muzzle and paws black, the large claws white and lustrous, and highly esteemed as ornaments by savages. A lightish-brown band runs across the head from ear to ear. The paws are large when compared with the size of the body. The tail is short and somewhat bushy, and a rudimentary anal gland exists. The ears are short and rounded. The teeth number six incisors, two canines, and eight premolars in each jaw; while two upper and four lower molars are developed. The food of the G. consists of small quadrupeds; and the flesh of the beaver in particular is said to be a favourite, while it causes much annoyance to the fur-trappers by stealing their bait, and taking the captured animals out of the traps. The G. itself is caught in traps, and its fur is highly valued. The young, numbering two at each birth, are born in May.

Glutton.

Glyce'ria, a genus of Grasses (q. v.). See MANNA GRASS.

Glycerine was first obtained in the year 1779 by Scheele by boiling fats with oxide of lead and water, and was called by him *the sweet principle of oils*. All the oils and fats occurring in nature which can be *saponified—i.e.*, which yield soap when boiled with an alkali—are ethers of G. These compounds are all formed on the same type or plan, and may be represented by the formula $C_3H_5O_3F_3$, where F. denotes the radical of a fatty acid. When these bodies are boiled with an alkali (caustic soda, for example) they are resolved into three molecules of the alkaline salt of the fatty acid (*soap*), and one molecule of G.—

$$\underbrace{C_3H_5O_3F_3}_{\text{Oil or fat.}} + \underbrace{3NaHO}_{\text{Caustic soda.}} = \underbrace{3NaOF}_{\text{Soap.}} + \underbrace{C_3H_5(OH)_3}_{\text{Glycerine.}}$$

The old process for preparing G. consisted in heating olive oil with litharge (oxide of lead) and water. The oxide of lead gradually decomposed the oil, and united with its fatty acid (oleic acid) to form insoluble oleate of lead (lead plaster), whilst the G. remained in solution, and was purified by removing traces of lead by a current of sulphuretted hydrogen, and concentrating to remove water.

This process, however, is now entirely superseded by a method indicated by Guy-Lussac and Chevreul in 1825, but first carried out on the manufacturing scale by Wilson and Payne in 1854. This method consists in heating fats in copper or iron stills, and passing a current of superheated steam through them, at such a temperature that a thermometer placed in the still stands at from 288–315° C. Under these conditions the fats absorb water, and are resolved into fatty acid and G.—a reaction precisely similar to the saponification of a fat by an alkali. Thus with stearine (the most common animal fat)—

$$\underbrace{C_3H_5O_3(C_{18}H_{35}O)_3}_{\text{Stearine.}} + \underbrace{3HOH}_{\text{Water.}} = \underbrace{3HOC_{18}H_{35}O}_{\text{Stearic acid.}} + \underbrace{C_3H_5(OH)_3}_{\text{Glycerine.}}$$

$$\underbrace{C_3H_5O_3(C_{18}H_{35}O)_3}_{\text{Stearine.}} + \underbrace{3NaOH}_{\text{Caustic soda.}} = \underbrace{3NaOC_{18}H_{35}O}_{\text{Hard soap (stearate of soda).}} + \underbrace{C_3H_5(OH)_3}_{\text{Glycerine.}}$$

Both the fatty acid and G. are carried over with the steam, and are found in the condenser. The fatty acids, being specifically lighter than the solution of G., rise to the surface, and are removed by decantation. The solution of G. is concentrated by evaporation.

Pure G. is a colourless syruppy liquid of sp. gr. 1·260 at 15° C. Occasionally crystals of G. separate from cold liquid G., but the exact conditions necessary for the formation of this crystalline G. are not understood. G. rapidly attracts moisture from the air, and for this reason is often employed as an application in cases of chapped hands, cracked lips, &c., in order that the skin may be kept moist. It has also been employed in the manufacture of moist water-colours, which retain their consistency in a dry atmosphere.

When heated, a certain quantity of G. volatilises unchanged; but the greater part is decomposed into acrolein and other products. G. cannot therefore be distilled under ordinary conditions, but in vacuo it passes over unchanged.

G. is a triatomic alcohol (see ALCOHOLS), and contains a radical called glyceryl (C_3H_5'''), which under certain conditions becomes monatomic, and is then called allyl. Iodide of allyl (C_3H_5) is prepared by acting on G. with phosphorus and iodine, or with concentrated hydriodic acid—

$$\underbrace{2C_3H_5'''(OH)_3}_{\text{Glycerine.}} + \underbrace{P_2I_4}_{\text{Iodide of phosphorus.}} = \underbrace{2C_3H_5I}_{\text{Iodide of allyl.}} + \underbrace{2P(OH)_3}_{\text{Phosphorus acid.}} + \underbrace{I_2}_{\text{Iodine.}}$$

From the iodide of allyl thus prepared Oil of Mustard (q. v.) and Oil of Garlic (see GARLIC, OIL OF) have been obtained.

Ethers of G. are obtained by heating it with the corresponding acids, and in this manner Berthollet succeeded in preparing fats artificially.

The following are among the most interesting derivations of glyceryl and allyl:—Glycerine $C_3H_5(OH)_3$; monochloryhydrine $C_3H_5(OH)_2Cl$; dichlorhydrine $C_3H_5(OH)Cl_2$; trichlorhydrine $C_3H_5Cl_3$; acrolein C_3H_4O; acrylic acid $C_3H_4O_2$; glyceric acid $C_3H_6O_4$; allyl alcohol C_3H_5OH; iodide of allyl C_3H_5I; oil of garlic (sulphide of allyl) $(C_3H_5)_2S$; oil of mustard (sulphocyanate of allyl) C_3H_5CNS.

Glyc'ogen, a substance identical in chemical composition with starch, found in the liver, placenta, tissues of the embryo, and in many of the tissues of the adult. Its formula is $C_6H_{10}O_5$, and when separated from the liver is a white mealy powder. It is insoluble in alcohol, and is turned brownish-red by the action of iodine. Regarding its important physiological relations, see LIVER. Bernard, its discoverer, believes that G. is converted into sugar either by a ferment present in the liver or in the blood. G. is isomeric with starch, both having the composition represented by the formula $C_6H_{10}O_5$. It may be obtained from the liver by washing it with water, straining and filtering the aqueous extract and precipitation with alcohol. The G., separating in white flocks, is purified by boiling it with potash; dissolving in acetic acid, re-precipitating with alcohol, and subsequent treatment with ether, give a white amorphous substance closely resembling starch in appearance and properties. It is, however, coloured brownish red by iodine, and not blue, as is the case with starch. Boiled with dilute acids, it yields dextrine (or a substance closely resembling it), and later dextrose.

Glyc'ol. This substance was discovered in the year 1856 by Würz, and was the first diatomic alcohol obtained. (See ALCOHOLS.) To prepare it, bromide or iodide of ethylene is heated for some days with acetate of silver and acetic acid, when bromide or iodide of silver and acetate of ethylene results—

$$\underbrace{C_2H_4Br_2}_{\text{Bromide of ethylene.}} + \underbrace{2AgC_2H_3O_2}_{\text{Acetate of silver.}} = \underbrace{2AgBr}_{\text{Bromide of silver.}} + \underbrace{C_2H_4(C_2H_3O_2)_2}_{\text{Acetate of ethylene.}}$$

The acetate of ethylene thus prepared, when boiled with baryta or potash, yields G. and acetate of barium or potassium—

$$\underbrace{C_2H_4(C_2H_3O_2)_2}_{\text{Acetate of ethylene.}} + \underbrace{2KHO}_{\text{Caustic potash.}} = \underbrace{C_2H_4(OH)_2}_{\text{Glycol.}} + \underbrace{2KC_2H_3O_2}_{\text{Acetate of potassium.}}$$

G. is a colourless, inodorous, slightly viscid liquid, having a sweet taste. It is rather heavier than water (sp. gr. 1·125), and boils at 197·5° C. It is soluble in all proportions in alcohol and water, but is insoluble in ether. Like other alcohols, G. yields ethers when heated with acids. A whole series of diatomic alcohols, similar in properties to G., and having the general formula $C_nH_{2n}(OH)_2$ (when *n* represents the number of carbon atoms), have since been obtained. These diatomic alcohols are called as a class the Glycols.

Glyc'ocoll, Gly'cine, Glyc'ocine, Ami'do-Acet'ic Acid, or **Sugar of Gelatine**, a crystalline nitrogenous substance, first obtained by Bracconu by acting on gelatine with sulphuric acid. It may also be prepared from bile, from uric acid, and from various animal products. Its synthesis was accomplished by Perkins by heating bromacetic acid with ammonia—

$$\underbrace{\begin{array}{c}CH_2Br\\ |\\ CO_2H\end{array}}_{\text{Bromacetic acid.}} + \underbrace{2NH_3}_{\text{Ammonia.}} = \underbrace{NH_4Br}_{\text{Bromide of ammonium.}} + \underbrace{\begin{array}{c}CH_2NH_2\\ |\\ CO_2H\end{array}}_{\text{Glycocoll.}}$$

Gerhardt obtained it by acting on formic aldehyde with hydrocyanic acid and water—

$$\underbrace{CHOH}_{\text{Formic aldehyde.}} + \underbrace{HCN}_{\text{Hydrocyanic acid.}} + \underbrace{H_2O}_{\text{Water.}} = \underbrace{C_2H_5NO_2}_{\text{Glycocoll.}}$$

G. is a crystalline substance. It has a sweet taste, and its solution reddens litmus paper. It unites with acids, bases, and salts.

Glycos'mis, a genus of Asiatic trees and shrubs belonging to the orange order. *G. citrifolia*, is the best-known species, from its deliciously flavoured fruit.

Glycyrrhiz'æ Radix, or **Liquorice Root**, the root or underground stem of the *G. glabra*, fresh and dried, cultivated in Great Britain. G. is used in medicine, in catarrhal affections, irritation of the mucous membrane of the bowels and urinary passages, and as an adjunct to bitter and irritating vegetable substances. It is prescribed in the form of extracts and powders.

Glyp'todon, an extinct genus of Edentate quadrupeds most nearly allied to the existing Armadilloes (q. v.). The fossil remains of the G. occur in the Recent or Post-tertiary deposits of S. America—that is, in the region where existing armadilloes are found. This coincidence exemplifies Owen's 'organic succession of animal forms.' A well-known specimen is the *G. clavipes*, 9 feet long. The G. had no divisions of its armour-plating, which, as in the armadilloes, consists of bony pieces of hexagonal shape, firmly united by suture, thus rendering all movement of the casing impossible. The head and tail had each a cuirass of plates. The vertebræ of the spine were fused into a solid mass. The feet were large, and the last joints of the toes short and massive. No canine or incisor teeth were developed, but there were eight molars on each side of each jaw. The crowns of the latter teeth were fluted and divided into lobes.

Gme'lin, the name of a German family continuously distinguished in science for nearly two centuries. The first was **Johann Georg G.** (1674–1728), in his time a famous chemist. His son (1709–55), who bore the same name, was one of the first botanists of his age, and his *Flora Sibirica* (4 vols. St. Petersb. 1749–70) is still remembered. **Johann Friedrich G.** (1748–1804), nephew of the preceding, was Professor of Medicine and Chemistry in Göttingen. His edition (the 13th) of the Linnæan *Systema Plantarum* was a work absolutely indispensable to his contemporaries. But probably the most distinguished member of the family was **Leopold G.**, son of Johann Friedrich, who was born August 2, 1788, at Göttingen. After completing his studies at Tübingen and Vienna, and travelling for a year in Italy, he settled in 1813 at Heidelberg, where he was appointed Professor of Chemistry in 1817, and where he died, April 13, 1853. His principal work is his *Handbuch der theoretischen Chemie* (4 vols., completed by Schossberger and List, Heidel. 1841–55), which is a masterpiece of clearness, fulness, and method.

Gmünd (*Schwäbisch-G.*), a town of Würtemberg, on the Rems, 30 miles E. of Stuttgart by railway. It was formerly a free city of the empire, was added to Würtemberg in 1803, and has considerable manufactures of hardware, hosiery, bijouterie, &c., and a large trade in hops. Pop. (1871) 10,739.

Gmun'den, a town of Upper Austria, at the outflow of the Traun from the Traun or G. Lake, 36 miles S.W. of Linz by railway. It is the seat of an imperial 'direction' for salt-mines and forests, and has considerable fisheries and an active river trade. The fine castle of Ebenzweirer stands out in the lake. Pop. (1869) 5623.

Gnapha'lium, a genus of Composite plants. See CUDWEED.

Gnat (*Culex*), a genus of *Diptera* or Flies, forming the type of the family *Culicidæ*, which is distinguished by a very long rostrum or beak composed of seven pieces. The head is small, and the antennæ of the males are plume-like. In the genus *Culex* itself, the palpi of the males are larger than the thorax, while those of the female are small. The common G. (*C. pipiens*) is noted for its power of inflicting irritating wounds. The female gnats are most voracious, and have a proboscis of sharp-pointed bristles, adapted for puncturing the skin of animals, and for sucking up blood. Gnats' eggs are deposited in water, and appear to be glued together in masses for security. The larvæ, active, large-headed creatures, breathe by means of air-tubes in the terminal joints of the tail, which is exposed above the surface of the water. The pupæ are also aquatic, and the perfect insect emerges from the pupal skin. Swarms of these insects may be seen rising from the water on a summer day, exercising their newly-found powers of flight. The Mosquito (q. v.) is closely allied to the G.

Gneis'enau, August, Graf Neidhardt von, one of the most distinguished Prussian commanders in the wars of 1813–15, was the son of a lieutenant of artillery, and was born at Schilda, in Prussian Saxony, 27th October 1760. He served amongst the German auxiliaries during the American revolution, and entered the army of Friedrich the Great in 1786. Here he rose steadily, and as lieutenant-colonel gained distinction by his defence of Tilsit in 1807. He retired from service during the peace, but joined the army at the rising in 1813, and took a very distinguished part in the war of liberation. After the peace of Paris he was raised to the rank of Graf, and was presented by the King with an estate. In 1815 G. was the chief of Blücher's general staff, and had his full share in the glories of Waterloo, especially in leading the Prussian pursuit. In 1825 G. became general field-marshal, and died at Posen, 24th August 1831. See his Biography by Pertz (1864–69).

Gneiss is a Metamorphic rock with the same mineral ingredients as granite, from which it differs in having a more or less stratified structure. This arrangement in layers is sometimes so evident that it closely resembles the fissile mica-schist, and at other times is so hidden that it becomes very difficult to distinguish the rock, especially hand specimens, from granite. It has been sometimes termed schistose granite; but this is somewhat misleading, since G. is not really a granitic or igneous rock, but has been formed from an originally laminated sandstone.

Gne'sen (Pol. *Gniezno*), a town of Prussia, province of Posen, 30 miles E.N.E. of the town of Posen. It lies on the Wrzesnia among hills and lakes, has a fine old cathedral, and is the residence of the Archbishop of Gnesen-Posen. Here the Polish kings were crowned up to 1320. There are some slight manufactures of linen cloth, and two horse and cattle fairs are held here. Pop. (1871) 9050.

Gneta'ceæ, a natural order of small Monochlamydeous trees. See SEA-GRAPE.

Gnome (Gr. *gnōmōn*, 'wise'), in the Cabalistic and Rosicrucian mythology, a spirit who dwelt underground and guarded hidden treasures. They were male and female, the former being hideous dwarfs. A G., Umbriel, plays an important part in Pope's *Rape of the Lock*. See ELEMENTAL SPIRITS and ROSICRUCIANS.

Gno'mon, in geometry, is the six-sided figure made up of any three of the four parts into which a parallelogram is divided by two lines intersecting at a point in its interior, and drawn parallel to the sides.

Gnos'tic, a name afterwards appropriated to heretics, was originally applied, although not in the New Testament, to Christians possessed of the so-called *gnosis* (Gr. 'knowledge'), or true spiritual knowledge. *Gnosis*, as used in the New Testament, means a more profound spiritual perception of the truths revealed for the salvation of man, in this sense, that it is regarded as a gift of God not less than faith, which is the basis of it, and to which *gnosis* is sometimes opposed as an additional and pre-eminent quality (*cf.* 1 Cor. xii. 8, 9, xiii. 2). It is also to be accompanied by a development of holiness, and, in short, is to be a comprehension of 'the breadth, and length, and depth, and height of the love of Christ,' so that those who have it may 'be filled with the fulness of God' (Eph. iii. 18, 19). In the First Epistle to Timothy (vi. 30) there is mention of a *gnosis* which was unaccompanied by this progressive holiness, but was rather associated with speculations about the oppositions of good and evil, and which is declared to be a *gnosis* 'falsely so called.' In the tendency here referred to is apparent the germ of what was known as Gnosticism. Clement of Alexandria, however, applies the epithet G. to orthodox Christians who cultivated the true *gnosis*. According to the Alexandrian theology the *gnosis* consists of absolute knowledge, such as agrees with the reality of existing objects. It presupposes faith as the basis on which it rests, the Scriptures forming the objective source of both, so that the G. Christian is described as one who has grown grey in the study of the Scriptures. An essential part of this *gnosis* is allegorical interpretation, by which it is able to explain all Scripture in its harmony with reason and with itself. It is thus the spiritual interpretation taught by Christ to his disciples (Matt. xiii. 11), and became the possession of the Gnostics by education (being transmitted from the apostles through those who succeeded them in presiding over churches), faith, and reason, through the inworking of God's Holy Spirit. From this it appears that whilst the G. Christian professed to adhere to apostolic tradition alone, the ultimate principle by which he determined the meaning of the Scriptures was speculation. Further progress in the same direction produced the heresy of Gnosticism.

Among the Alexandrian Jews, under the influence of Platonism, a philosophical system of religion had been formed which exalted itself above the popular faith. The presence of a similar tendency in Christianity almost from the first is apparent from the use of *gnosis* as indicated above, which denoted the religion of absolute knowledge as contrasted with the faith of the multitude. The genuine Pauline conception of faith, which implied an accompanying elevation of mind, had been lost sight of, and instead 'faith was regarded as a kind of trust on outward authority, which by itself alone could not obtain the reward of eternal life.' Such a faith might reasonably be regarded as a subordinate phase of the Christian life, and furnished Gnosticism with a pretext for depreciating it. The first principle of Gnosticism was that the beginning of perfection is the knowledge of man, and absolute perfection the knowledge of God. Again, Christianity had furnished a simple, practical solution of every problem that had occupied thinking minds, in the shape of a faith in great historical facts on which the religious convictions of men were to depend; whereas Gnosticism wished to make religion depend on a speculative solution of these questions.

Gnosticism was produced, then, speaking generally, by the craving for a philosophy of religion to which the old faiths of the world, as well as Christianity, should each contribute their share. Accordingly in all the G. systems there are to be traced in various proportions elements of Greek philosophy, especially Platonism, Jewish theology, and Oriental theosophy. The so-called founders of the different systems properly only gave expression to different phases of the spirit of inquiry which pervaded the intelligent part of the Christian world, and which, according to the local colouring, produced a mythological, cabbalistic, or Zoroastrian G. Claiming to be philosophical Christians, and also the possessors of a secret tradition on which their system was founded, as that of the common herd of Christians was on certain external historical facts, the Gnostics desired to found schools of Christian *mysteries*, to which should be admitted only the select few who possessed the higher spiritual faculty withheld from the commonalty.

Different classifications of Gnostics have been made on various principles. Mosheim treats Gnosticism as produced exclusively by the combination of Oriental philosophy with Christianity. Neander classifies them according to their affinity with or opposition to Judaism; Gieseler, according to countries and the preponderance of dualism or emanation, as Syrian and Egyptian; Matter, as Syrian, Roman, Egyptian, and of Asia Minor; Hase, as Hellenistic, Syrian, and Christian. Baur's classification is :—(1) The Valentinian, which admits the claims of Paganism, together with Judaism and Christianity; (2) the Marcionite, which refers especially to Christianity; and (3) the Pseudo-Clementine, which espouses the cause of Judaism in particular. Referring for details to the several articles BARDESANES, BASILIDES, CARPOCRATES, CERINTHUS, MARCION, OPHITES, SATURNINUS, SIMONIANS, VALENTINUS, it must suffice here to indicate the general character of Gnosticism. The problems to be solved were these :—'How the transition from the infinite to the finite, and the beginning of creation, are to be explained?—how it is possible to conceive of God as the author of a material world so alien to his own nature?—whence, if God is perfect, are the imperfections of this world?—whence the destructive powers in nature?—whence is moral evil, if a holy God is man's creator?—whence the great diversity of characters among men themselves, from the truly godlike to those which appear to be utterly abandoned to blind passions, without a vestige of a rational and moral nature?' The theory which in its fundamental principles was held by Gnostics in general, with many variations in detail, and in which a solution of these questions was found, was as follows :—One supreme, infinite, and self-existent Being has existed from all eternity, and is the original source of all beings, having within his own intelligence the Pleroma (Gr. 'fulness, sum') of Æons (Gr. 'ages'). By the impulsive principle of love 'the only-begotten Son,' the Nous, is evolved from the Supreme, and from him a series of emanations (see EMANATION), coming each from the preceding in successive evolution. But with each successive emanation in the series the divine life diminishes, and the connection with the Supreme becomes feebler, till the boundary of the Pleroma is reached. At this point there arises a defective or abortive emanation, which, being unable to retain its connection with the divine life, sinks into the dead, the unsubstantial, the darkness, the void, the chaos, the sluggish stagnant water which limits from without this evolution of life. The hitherto dead and inert mass receives vitality from this drop of the divine life, and there arises an active opposition to the divine on the part of this nature—power or matter—direct products of which are evil spirits and wicked men. Otherwise, the abortive emanation referred to above produced the Demiurge, whose mission it was to give life and a plastic energy to matter. Under his hand evil spirits of every grade took their being from the unmixed principle of evil in matter. But good and evil are variously combined in human souls, which were classed as Spiritual, or those who seek to return into the Pleroma; Psychical, or those who are subject to the Demiurge; and Carnal, or those entirely under the power of matter. The only essential variation from the above, which is the Alexandrian theory, and which regards the Demiurge as a remote emanation from the Supreme, and as fashioning matter according to the ideas of the Supreme, is to be noted in the Oriental Gnosticism, according to which matter was eternally the residence of evil, or the Demiurge or creator of the world was a being directly opposed to the Supreme, who sought continually to check and suppress the divine life by confining it in a prison of matter.

All systems of Gnosticism alike had a scheme of redemption, the effect of which was to be the final separation of good from evil, or the liberation of the divine life from its degrading confinement in matter. In the Saviour Jesus Christ were united, without amalgamation, a human form—real according to Alexandrian Gnosticism, a mere vision according to the Oriental—and one of the divine Æons. The passion of Christ was brought about by the Demiurge, in a vain attempt to defeat the plans of the Supreme, and retain the souls of men under his control. See Burton's *Bampton Lectures* (1829); Neander's *Geschichte d. Christl. Rel. u. Kirche* (Hamb. 1852, Eng. trans. 1858); *Pflanz. u. Leit. d. Christl. Kirche* (Hamb. 1833; Eng. trans. 1859); Baur's *Die Christl. Gnosis* (Tüb. 1835); Irenæus' *Adv. Hæreses* (Camb. ed.); Hippolytus' *Philosophoumena* (ed. Miller); Mansell's *Gnostic Heresies of the First and Second Centuries* (Lond. 1875).

Gnu, or **Gnoo** (*Connochetes* or *Catoblepas*), a peculiar genus of *Antilopidæ* or Antelopes (q. v.) inhabiting S. Africa, and known under the name of 'wildebeest' by the Dutch settlers. The horns are broad at the base, are curved outwards and downwards on the sides of the head, and recurved at the tip. The tail is long and hairy throughout. The head is very large; and the massive, shaggy chest and neck contrast with the slender hind quarters and limbs. These animals live in large herds, and appear to be active, watchful, and timorous. When alarmed, they paw the ground and pursue each other in circles. Attempts to domesticate the G. have not been successful. The common G. (*C. Gnu*) is brownish-black, and has a black chest-mane. The brindled G. has no mane, and is brown striped with grey. The average length is 6½ feet, and the height about 3½ feet.

Gnu.

Go'a (*Crocodilus palustris*), a species of Crocodiles (q. v.) belonging to Asia and Australia, known also as the 'marsh crocodile,' and 'mugger.' A large specimen may attain a length of 33 feet. The G. travels overland for considerable distances during the dry season in search of water.

Goa, the capital of the Portuguese dominions in India, on the western coast, about 250 miles S. of Bombay. It was conquered from the Mohammedans by the great Albuquerque in 1503. Three cities have successively borne the name; the present G. is the nearest to the sea on a river mouth that is gradually silting up; pop. estimated at 10,000. The second G. is still the headquarters of the Catholic mission; it contains a fine church with the bones of St. Xavier and many relics. Area of the territory, 1451 sq. miles; pop. about 537,517, mostly Roman Catholics; revenue estimated at £80,000.

Goalpa'ra, the chief town of the district of the same name, province of Assam, British India, on the left bank of the Brahmaputra. Pop. about 6000.—The *district* of G. was originally part of Bengal, and G. town was long the N.E. frontier town of the empire. The district was transferred to Assam in 1874, having previously been augmented by the Eastern Dwars, which were annexed from Bhotan after the war of 1863-64. Area, 4433 sq. miles; pop. (1872) 444,761.

Goalun'do, a town in the district of Furidpur, province of

Bengal, British India, at the junction of the main streams of the Ganges and Brahmaputra, 152 miles N. of Calcutta by rail. It is the terminus of the E. Bengal Railway, from whence the Assam steamers start, and the registration depôt of the coolies for the tea plantations. The railway station and protective works against the river currents, erected at a total cost of £100,000, were swept away in the floods of October 1874, and are now abandoned. There is a trade in dried and salted fish. During the first six months of 1876 the traffic in boats was valued at £700,000; by railway at £600,000.

Goat (Old Eng. *gât*, 'the goer or leaper:' comp. Gr. *aix*, from *aïssō*, 'I leap or spring'), a genus of Ruminant (*Ungulata*) *Mammalia* belonging to the family *Ovidæ*. There are horns in both sexes, and the lachrymal glands are undeveloped. The throat has a 'beard,' which may be present in both sexes, or in the males alone. The horns are erect and compressed, are curved backwards and outwards, and have a prominent ridge in front. All goats emit a strong and peculiar odour, which is wanting in sheep. The common G. (*Hircus ægagrus*, or *Capra hircus*) is known by the horns being compressed in front and rounded behind, the anterior ridge being rugged or irregular. These animals in their wild state live in herds. They inhabit mountainous districts, and are fleet and agile, climbing the most inaccessible places. Their food is mainly grass and herbage. The milk of the G. has a somewhat disagreeable flavour, but is highly esteemed for its nutritious qualities. The G. generally produces two young at a birth. The G. and sheep have been bred together; and though the hybrids have been sparingly fertile, the experiment seems to prove the specific identity of these animals. Two of the best-known varieties are the Cashmere G. (q. v.) and the Angora G. (q. v.). The Jemla G. (*C. Jemlaica* or *Hemitragus Jemlaica*) and the Berbera or Ram Sagul of India are also well known. The former inhabits the loftiest mountain ranges of India, and is distinguished by the hairy mane which depends on each side of the head and neck. The colour is a pale greyish fawn, with a black spine-mark and a brown mark on the forehead. The Berbera G. has no beard, but a very large 'dewlap.' The Syrian G. has long pendant ears, and the Spanish G. is hornless. See also BOQUETIN and IBEX.

Goat, Rocky Mountain, is generally included in the Antelope family, under the designation of the *Antilocapra furcifera*. It is sometimes known as the Prongbuck or Cabrit, and appears to combine the characters of the antelopes and the goats. Its horns, which are oval, rise straight from the forehead, and then curve inwards and backwards. A short prong is given off in front of each horn. This animal is found in the central prairies of N. America, and between the Rocky Mountains and Pacific.

Rocky Mountain Goat.

Goat-Moth (*Cossus ligniperda*), a species of nocturnal *Lepidoptera* (q. v.), or Moths (q. v.), belonging to the family *Hepialidæ*, in which group the antennæ are short and the proboscis rudimentary or wanting. In the genus *Cossus* the antennæ are as long as the thorax, and are serrated quite to the tip in both the male and female. The G.-M. is one of the largest British moths. The wings are large and downy, and like the body are of a sombre grey and brown colour, banded with dark markings. The larva is large, and has a smooth reddish body, with an oval patch of chestnut on the upper surface of each joint. The head is triangular. The larval condition lasts for three years. The larvæ exude a strong-smelling fetid substance; they enclose themselves, in their pupa or chrysalis stage, in holes which they excavate in the trunks of trees.

Goat-Moth.

Goat's-Beard, the common name for the species of *Tragopogon*, a genus of plants belonging to the natural order *Compositæ* (q. v.). There are three indigenous to Britain, one of which is *T. porrifolius*, the purple G.-B., or Salsafy (q. v.).

Goat's-Rue, the popular name for *Galega officinalis*, a Leguminous plant indigenous to the S. of Europe. It is grown for forage, and is said to increase the milk of cows that feed upon it. Formerly it was medicinally used in cases of fevers.

Goat'sucker, a very large family of Fissirostral *Insessores* (q. v.), or perching birds, so named from an absurd notion, formerly current, that they sucked the teats of goats and sheep. They form the family *Caprimulgidæ*, in which the bill is short, flat, and broad, and the tarsi short; the toes are long and powerful, and the hinder toe is united at its base to the inner digit. Like all *Fissirostres* (q. v.) the G. has a wide 'gape' fringed with bristles, to assist them in securing their insect prey. The colours of these birds are, as a rule, sombre—black, grey, and brown being the prevailing tints. The genera *Steatornis*, *Podargus*, *Ægotheles*, *Caprimulgus*, *Scotornis*, *Macrodiptex*, and *Chordeiles* include various species of this interesting group. The genus *Caprimulgus* includes the typical species, and is distinguished by the second quill being the longest, and by the tail being long and broad and occasionally forked. The middle toe is longest, and has a singular comblike development of its claw, the function of which appears to be that of clearing the bristles of the gape. The European G., or nightjar, is found throughout Europe, and arrives in Britain in May or June. The plumage is a pleasing variety of shades of black, grey, white, and brown; the male birds having white spots of oval shape on the inner side of the first three quill-feathers of the wings. The average length is 10 inches. These birds are useful to man from their devouring large numbers of cockchafers. The European G. is also known by the names of 'churn-owl' and 'jar-owl.' The Carolina G. (*C. Carolinensis*) is an allied American species, and the *C. vexillarius*, or long-winged G. of W. Africa, an exotic species.

Gobb'o, a name given to the pods of a species of Abelmoschus (q. v.) or Hibiscus (q. v.).

Go'belins, The, a celebrated manufactory of tapestry at Paris, deriving its name from Jean Gobelin, who in the reign of François I. erected a dye-factory on the banks of the stream Bièvre. Rabelais ridiculed the idea, and dubbed the concern *Folie-G.* Gobelin's successors carried on the manufacture of tapestry with great success. Subsequently Louis XIV. acquired the building for the nation, styled it the *Hôtel Royal des G.*, and devoted it to the production of the choicest works in Tapestry (q. v.).

Go'bi, or **Ko'bi**, the Mongolian name of the great wilderness of Central Asia, known to the Chinese as **Sha'mo** ('sand-sea'), between about lat. 40° and 50° N. and long. 90° and 120° E., 1800 miles long, with an average width of from 300 to 400 miles. Though not absolutely barren, no part of it is fertile, its sterility being partly due to its great elevation (on an average 3500 feet) above the sea. It forms a tableland between the Altai and the Kuen-Lun, with only slight varieties of level, except in the eastern portion, which is cleft by a great rugged valley. In the W. the surface is mainly sand, which is sometimes drifted before the wind in great waves; in the E. it is rocky and gravelly, and sprinkled with many salt lakes and strips of pasture and wood.

Gob'lins and Bo'gles, spirits of popular superstition, generally held to be sinister in nature and grotesque in appearance. Goblin (Fr. *gobelin*, Armorican *gobilin*, 'a will-o'-the-wisp;' comp. Ger. *kobold*) perhaps comes through the Low Lat. *gobelinus* from the Gr. *kobalos*, 'a knave,' or is perhaps derived from the Fr. *gober*, 'to swallow.' The conjecture that *elf* and *goblin* are corruptions of Guelph and Ghibelline is an ignorant absurdity, as the former word occurs in *Beowulf* (v. 112), a poem written ages before the imperial-papal strife began, or the families had risen into notice who gave it name. Goblin sometimes signifies merely a spirit, *e.g.*, Shakespeare: 'Be thou a spirit of health or goblin damned;' Milton: 'To whom the goblin full of wrath replied.' *Hobgoblin* may come from *Hop-goblin*, but is more likely a corruption from Robin, the spirit Robin Goodfellow or Puck being specially known as Goblin or Hobgoblin. Bogle, or Bogey, may be from the Welsh *brogwly*, 'to frighten;' Gael. *bwgwl*, 'fear;' N. Eng. *bogle*, 'to frighten.' The word *bogey* is used in Scotland for a bugbear.

Go'bony. See COMPONÉ.

Go'by (*Gobius*), a genus of Teleostean fishes belonging to the *Acanthopterygii* and to the family *Gobiidæ*. The body is long, the teeth small, the spinous and front part of the dorsal fin flexible, and less perfectly developed than the soft posterior part. The anal fin is soft, and the ventral fins are spinous. The latter are sucker-like, but are not adherent to the abdomen; and dorsal fins are developed. The rock-fish or black G. (*G. niger*) is a familiar example of the group, and is found in rock pools adhering to fixed objects by its sucker-like ventral fins. The body, like that of the Eels (q. v.), is covered by a mucous secretion. The polewig or spotted G. (*G. minutus*), another familiar species, is coloured grey, with black spots on the back and darkish patches on the sides, and a black spot on the dorsal fin. The two-spotted G. (*G. Ruthen-sparii*) has two brown spots on each side of the pectoral fin and tail. The Lumpsuckers (q. v.) or *Cyclopteri* are nearly allied to the G., and the Dragonets (q. v.) are also included in the G. family.

God (Ger. *Gott*, Goth. *Guth*; of uncertain derivation, but *not* connected with the adj. 'good') is the English name for the Supreme Being who is worshipped by most civilised nations. But belief in G., conceived as the primordial, self-sufficing being, the author and upholder of the universe, belongs to man in an advanced state of civilisation. It is a philosophical idea. The case of the Jews is an exception. It is difficult, if not impossible, to understand the first chapter of Genesis—assuming it to be the work of Moses—on any other hypothesis than that of a 'revelation.' But at any rate, no such view of G. is met with among savage tribes. It has been asserted that there is no tribe of men so degraded as to have no idea of a G., but this is contradicted at the present day by the best authorities (*e.g.*, Lubbock, *The Origin of Civilisation* and *Prehistoric Man*). The truth is, that the adoption of any religious ideas whatever marks an era in human development. The first G. that a savage worships is whatever he fears, whatever seems to have the power of doing him injury (see FETICHISM). And as his conceptions of G. are simply reflections of his own ideas, the gods of savages are invariably cruel and malignant. The next step, taken when the phenomena of nature are considered, is to Dualism (q. v.) and Polytheism (q. v.). Nature appears rent into two realms—a kingdom of light, virtue, and happiness, and one of darkness, sin, and misery—and a G., good or bad, is given to every newly-observed phenomenon, according as it is beneficial or hurtful. The highest phase, Monotheism (q. v.), passes of necessity through an inferior stage of anthropomorphism. The earliest Jewish conceptions of G. are from a philosophical point of view anthropomorphic in some respects; but the absolute creative power and self-sufficing being are not altogether absent; and as the nation grew, the conception of 'Jehovah' expanded and became profoundly spiritual. The point on which the East and the West were prevalently divided was—the relation of G. to nature or matter. The ancient Persian religion, while acknowledging one supreme being, was practically dualistic. The Greek philosophers agreed with the Hebrew prophets as to the harmony of nature with G., who was the cause of all movement, all production, all mental action. The Hindu religion, in the earliest Vedantic period, the later Brahmanic development, and as Buddhism, is fundamentally a system of Pantheism (q. v.). The G. of Christianity is a profounder expression of the Hebrew Jehovah. The paternal and providential features become clearer, but the divine nature is enveloped in a new mystery by the doctrine of the Trinity (q. v.).

Godav'ery (*Godavari*), a large river of India, rises near Nassick, a station on the E. Indian Railway, on the E. slope of the Western Ghauts, only 50 miles from the Arabian Sea, and flows through the S. of the Deccan, mostly in the dominions of the Nizam and the Central Provinces, until it breaks through the Eastern Ghauts in the province of Madras by a narrow pass at the village of Polaveram. It then passes Rajahmundry, and divides into two main branches, each about 55 miles long, flowing E. into the Bay of Bengal, the one at Point Gordeware, the other to the S. at Narsipur. The total length is 898 miles, and it drains an area of 112,200 sq. miles.—The *district* of G. lies in the N.E. of the Madras Presidency, at the mouth of the G. river. Area, 6224 sq. miles; pop. (1871) 1,592,939. The products are rice, maize, cotton, and sugar. The towns are Rajahmundry, Ellore, and Coconada, of which the last conducts a considerable coasting trade. The exports by sea were valued at £643,980 in 1872–73; and the imports at £138,321.—The *district of the Upper G.* is the name lately given to the S.E. tract of the Central Provinces. Area, 1971 sq. miles; pop. (1872) 52,120. The population is very sparse, consisting of hill tribes who cultivate by burning down the jungle; but the district has lately been opened out by the extension of navigation on the G. river.

Godavery Irrigation Works, commenced in 1844 to save the delta of the G. river from the vicissitudes of drought and flood, and also to assist navigation, extend over 840 miles of main channels, and command 780,000 acres. The water is taken off at Dhaleswaram, at the head of the delta, 22 feet above high water, by a masonry dam or anicut, 2½ miles long, 12 feet high, and 130 feet broad at the base. Branches are diverted along both banks, one of which is carried over an offshoot of the river by the Gunnarum brick aqueduct, 2248 feet long, on 49 arches. In 1864 an extension was sanctioned to connect with the Kistna Works (q. v.). In 1872–73 the total area irrigated was 264,717 acres, and traffic was conducted by 51,957 boats and rafts. The navigation project, on which three-quarters of a million had been expended, was finally abandoned in 1871.

Godd'ard, Arabella, an English pianist, was born in Brittany, January 1836. In 1848 she was placed under Mrs. Anderson, the Queen's pianist, and afterwards became the pupil of Kalkbrenner and Thalberg. Her first public appearance was in 1850. In 1854–56 she visited the Continent, and in 1873–76 America and Australia. She is again (1877) in London. G. excels in the performance of both classical and modern music.

Go'desberg, a village in the circle of Köln, Rhenish Prussia, on the left bank of the Rhine, 4 miles S. of Bonn. It has mineral springs and the beautiful ruins of a castle, commanding a splendid view of the Rhine valley and the Siebengebirge. Pop. (1871) 1775. The castle of G., built by Dietrich, Archbishop of Köln (1208–13), afforded temporary refuge to the deposed Archbishop Gebhard in 1582, suffered severely in the Thirty Years' War, and later was nearly destroyed by the French.

God'father and **God'mother** are the names given to Sponsors (q. v.), from the spiritual parental relationship which they are supposed to contract with those for whom they stand surety in baptism, and who, on the same principle, are called their godchildren. By a law of Justinian a man was forbidden to marry a woman for whom he had been godfather, 'because nothing does induce a more paternal affection or juster prohibition of marriage than this tie, by which their souls were in a divine manner united together.' The Council of Trullo (691) further decreed that it was unlawful for the godfather to marry the mother of the child; and the Council of Trent still further forbade marriage between the sponsors themselves. No such restrictions exist in the Anglican Church. The rubric of the English Prayer-Book appoints that 'there shall be for every male child to be baptized two godfathers and one godmother,' and for every female one godfather and two godmothers.'

Godfrey of Bouillon. See BOUILLON, GODFREY DE.

Godi'va, Lady, the wife of Leofric, Earl of the Mercians, according to a beautiful old legend (first recorded by Matthew of Westminster 200 years after the event), besought her husband to free the people of Coventry from a tax. He agreed to do so if she would ride naked through the streets, whereupon she ordered all the people to go indoors and shut their windows, and rode naked through the town, freed the people from the tax, 'and made herself an everlasting name.' Only one man, named Peeping Tom, looked out, and he was struck blind. The story forms the subject of an exquisite poem by Tennyson, and of another by Leigh Hunt. The worst thing about the legend is that it distorts and perverts the character of the great Mercian Earl of the 11th c., who was a genuine Englishman. The true name of the wife of Leofric was *Godgifu*, who founded a number of churches, and lived to a very old age. Mr. Freeman points out that 'Peeping Tom must have been one of King Eadward's Frenchmen,' for Englishmen did not use Scripture names at the time when Lady G. is said to have ridden through Coventry (q.v.)

Gödöll'ö, a small town of Hungary, 16 miles N.E. of Pesth by rail. It has a stately château, formerly the residence of the

Grassalkovich princes. On the neighbouring hills Gorgei gained two bloody victories over the Austrians, under Prince Windisch-grätz and the Ban Jellachich, April 14, 1849. Pop. 3361.

Godol'phin, Sydney, Earl of G., an English statesman, belonging to an old Cornish family, originally known as Godolcan, was born about 1635. He was made Secretary of State in 1664, was sent to Holland to forward an alliance between that country and England against France in 1678, became one of the Lords of the Treasury in 1679, and, along with Viscount Hyde and the Earl of Sunderland, had the chief direction of public affairs. He ingratiated himself into the favour of Charles II., whom he aided in the scandalous negotiations with Louis XIV., and who placed him at the head of the Treasury in 1684. Under James II. he held a post in the Treasury, and was Lord Chamberlain to the Queen. On the landing of William of Orange, G. was sent to treat with him, a task which he executed adroitly. William III. soon recognised his abilities, and he was one of the council which governed the country during the King's absence in 1695. Detected in carrying on a treasonable correspondence with James II. in 1697, he was deprived of office till 1700. After Anne's accession G. acted in concert with Marlborough, was made Lord High Treasurer in 1702, became Earl of G. in 1706, and about this time left the Tories for the Whigs. In the struggle which then began between him and Harley, G. was finally defeated, being ejected from office in 1710. G. died at St. Albans, September 13, 1712. He was cold, astute, and taciturn; and as a financier was unequalled by any contemporary.

Godoy'. See ALCUDIA, MANUEL DE GODOY, DUKE OF.

God Save the King, a formula appended to British state proclamations, and the refrain and title of the national anthem. The anthem, which bears some resemblance in language to the Roman Catholic *Domine Salvum*, was first sung at a dinner of the London Mercers' Company on George II.'s birthday, 1740, and appears in the *Harmonia Anglicana* of 1742 and *Gentleman's Magazine* of 1745. Both words and music are now generally assigned to Henry Cary, who was born in London about 1696, and died 1743. They were long ascribed to Dr. John Bull (died 1622) on account of his *God save Great James, our King*. See Chappell's *Popular Music of the Olden Time*.

God's Truce (Lat. *Treuga Dei*), the name given in the middle ages to the period of the year during which all private feuds were suspended by command of the Church. In a council held at Limoges in the 10th c. the nobles vowed to cease from private strifes and to protect the weak. In 1027 a synod held in Roussillon decreed that no one should assail another from Saturday to Monday. The G. T. being constantly broken, an attempt was made by a council which assembled in Aquitaine in 1041 to render it more stringent, by limiting it to the days between the Wednesday and Monday of the Passion Week. Eadward the Confessor introduced the G. T. into England. The institution was confirmed by various councils, but gradually fell into disuse. See Milman's *Latin Christianity*, book viii.

God'unov, Boris Feodorovitch, a Russian noble of Tartar descent, was born in 1552. After he had long been the virtual ruler under the weak Feodor I., and had by the final conquest of Siberia done much to strengthen and extend the empire, he was in 1598 called by the Bojars to the throne. Although he inaugurated serfdom (1595), his reign greatly advanced civilisation in Russia by many wise measures for the promotion of trade, education, and the strict administration of justice. He poisoned himself, 13th April 1605. His son Feodor G. (born 1589) succeeded his father as Czar, but was murdered in June of the same year by Demetrius, brother of Feodor I., who returned at the head of a Polish army. See DEMETRIUS.

God'win, Mary Wollstonecroft, an English authoress, born at Beverley, Yorkshire, April 27, 1759. In her youth she left her father's house and maintained herself as a schoolmistress and governess until 1787, when she entered on a literary life in London. Several tales which she issued won some notice, and in 1791 her *Vindication of the Rights of Women* made her generally known. She then visited Paris, where she became intimate with the leading Girondins, and formed a *liaison* with an American named Imlay, who left her in great distress. In 1797 she married William G., whose Radicalism she shared, and died in London, September 10 of the same year, in giving birth to Mary G., afterwards the wife of Shelley and authoress of *Frankenstein*. See William G.'s remarkably candid *Memoirs of Mary Wollstonecroft G.* (1798).

Godwin, William, an English political writer and novelist, the son of a Presbyterian minister, was born at Wisbeach, Cambridgeshire, March 3, 1756. He was a dissenting clergyman at Stowmarket 1778–83, but a study of the French 18th c. writers leading him into unbelief, he gave up the Church for literature. G. published *Sketches of History* in 1784, and nine years later his once famous *Political Justice*. *Caleb Williams* appeared in 1794, and was followed by other inferior novels, of which the best is *St. Leon*. In 1798 he married Mary Wollstonecroft, who died shortly after, and G. took another wife in 1801. Though for a time a celebrity, and even in a way a power, G. was never in easy circumstances, and during his later years, when the excitement caused by his early works was almost forgotten, was forced to write for his bread. Among his other works are *Life of Chaucer* (1801), *Lives of Edward and John Phillips, Nephews and Pupils of Milton* (1815), *Treatise on Population* (1820), *History of the Commonwealth of England* (1824–1828), *Thoughts on Man* (1833), *Lives of the Necromancers*, &c. Finally, the intractable revolutionist was made yeoman-usher of the Exchequer. He died in London, April 7, 1836. Though G. has lately come into notice from the publication of his *Autobiography* and *Letters*, he will perhaps be chiefly remembered as the father-in-law of Shelley. His *Political Justice* is lofty and generous in sentiment, and often ingeniously and closely reasoned. Its doctrines were borrowed from Rousseau, G., though he rejected the *a priori* theory of the rights of man, arguing for the abolition of all existing political institutions. G. has been called the 'father of English philosophic Radicalism,' but the title is far more applicable to Bentham. *Caleb Williams*, which was written to enforce G.'s political views, is an almost unique novel. Hazlitt said it could never be begun without being finished, and despite occasional clumsiness and a want of reality in the characters, it exerts an irresistible and sombre fascination over the reader. *St. Leon*, the only other novel of G.'s which is still read, is much less interesting, being in great measure an attack on the Inquisition. See C. K. Paul's *G., his Friends and Contemporaries* (2 vols. Lond. 1876), containing G.'s letters and a portion of an autobiography; also L. Stephen's *History of English Thought in the Eighteenth Century* (Lond. 1876).

Godwi'ne, Earl of Wessex, the first English noble who was distinguished as a statesman, was born about the close of the 10th c. He is said to have been at first a cowherd, and to have been raised by the favour of King Cnut's brother-in-law, whose daughter he married. He proved himself a bold and skilful leader in Cnut's Scandinavian wars, and after Cnut's death supported the Danish cause until after Harthacnut's reign, when a strong feeling arising in favour of the English dynasty of Wessex, he became the chief agent in bringing Eadward to the throne. Eadward's incapacity flung the chief power into G.'s hands, and for some time he governed wisely and successfully, until his love of self-aggrandisement and the unjust favour which he extended to his unruly son Swegen lessened his influence so greatly, that when he stood forward as the champion of the English against the king's Norman favourites, he was unsupported by the people, and Eadward was enabled to banish him and confiscate his estates in 1051. G. then withdrew to Flanders, but his old popularity among the English quickly revived, and when, after about a year, his fleet entered the Thames, the people forced Eadward to restore him to his estates and to expel a number of the Norman strangers. G. died shortly after this, in 1054, and was succeeded in his estates by his son Harold, afterwards King of England. G. was full of bold and subtle ambition, but he followed a truly national policy, and showed high administrative genius, being at once adroit, prudent, and courageous. See Freeman's *Norman Conquest*, vol. i., and Green's *History of the English People* (Lond. 1875).

God'wit (*Limosa*), a genus of Grallatorial or wading birds included in the family *Scolopacidæ* or Snipes (q. v.), and in the sub-family *Limosinæ*. The godwits are distinguished by the bill being curved and inclined towards the tip. The first quill is the longest, and the outer toe is united to the middle one up to the first joint. Two species occur in England—the common G. (*L. rufa*), the tail of which is marked by brown and grey bars, and the black-tailed G. (*L. ægocephala*). The birds haunt marshy districts, and their nests are built on the ground, the eggs numbering four, and being of a light brown tinted with green. The general colour of the body in both species is brown above and grey below. The average length is sixteen inches, the females being larger than the males. The voice is harsh and shrill.

Godwit.

Goe'deke, Karl, a critic and historian of German literature, was born in 1814 at Celle, in Hanover, taught privately for many years at Göttingen, and was subsequently appointed a professor in the university there. G.'s principal work is a history of German poetry, ***Grundriss zur Geschichte der Deutschen Dichtung***(3 vols. 1856–70). He has also published ***Elf Bücher Deutscher Dichtung*** (2 vols. 1849), ***Deutsche Dichtung im Mittelalter*** (1852), and has edited Lessing, Schiller, and Goethe, with notes and biographical introductions. His biography of Goethe has been published as a separate work.

Goes, or **Tergoes,** a fortified port of Holland, in the province of Zeeland, and in the N. of the island of S. Beveland, 10 miles E.N.E. of Flushing by railway. It has some shipbuilding, and a trade in hops, grain, salt, &c. Its harbour is linked by a canal to the E. Scheldt. Pop. (1873) 5205.

Goe'the, Johann Wolfgang von, one of the greatest poets of all ages, and the most brilliant and many-sided genius of modern times. He was born at Frankfurt-am-Main on the 28th August 1749. His father, the grandson of a Thuringian blacksmith, stood high in the esteem of his fellow-citizens, was a Doctor of Laws, and held the dignity of Imperial Councillor. To his mother, Elizabeth Textor, G. always traced his own universal receptivity, that poetic sympathy with all human and natural interests which distinguished him while yet a mere boy. The theatre maintained by the French army of occupation during the Seven Years' War, and the otherwise unwelcome presence of a French officer in his father's house, gave G. an early opportunity of mastering the French language. G.'s father destined him for the profession of law, and to this end he was in 1765 sent to the University of Leipsic. Here he took more delight in the lectures of Ernesti and Gellert than in the study of legal technicalities; and as the influence of Gottsched was still dominant, the poetical efforts made by G. at this time (*Die Laune des Verliebten, Die Mitschuldigen*) are marked rather by French taste than by the sympathy G. confessedly felt for Klopstock. In Leipsic, already boasting to be a 'little Paris,' G. mixed freely both in academic and in general society, and one of his many love affairs quickened his experience of life. A visit to Dresden was not without effect on his artistic tastes. At the old University of Strassburg in 1770 G. studied the *corpus juris* less than anatomy and chemistry, but took his degree in law after a session or two. Under the shadow of the fairy minster, G. fully felt the charm of medieval art; and the influence of Herder, whose acquaintance G. made here, combined with his enthusiastic study of Shakespeare, Rousseau, and Hans Sachs to remove G. still further from the formal spirit of French art, and awakened that contempt for the conventional which made G. the apostle of the 'Storm and Stress' revolution in German literature. At Wetzlar, then the seat of the high courts of the empire, G. was supposed in 1772 to complete his law studies, and here he passed through the experience that afterwards thrilled Europe in *Werther*. G.'s first great work, *Götz von Berlichingen* (1773), which took the heart of Germany by storm, was pronounced by Friedrich the Great, as mouthpiece of the old school, an *imitation détestable des mauvaises pièces Anglaises*. In 1775 happened an event that coloured all G.'s after-life. The Duke of Sachsen-Weimar invited G. to his court, and gave him a seat in the Privy Council. In the Duke's capital G. made henceforward his home, and save during a journey to Switzerland, a residence of two years in Italy, and a short sojourn with the army in Champagne during the invasion of France in 1792, he was seldom far from Weimar. Here he was the brightest ornament of the brilliant court circle which made the Thuringian court the heart and eye of Germany. Besides directing the theatre, which was a school for the whole nation, G. held important state offices. In 1779 he became a Privy Councillor, in 1782 President of the Chamber, in 1815 First Minister. He had been ennobled in 1782. After the death of his friend and patron in 1828, G. withdrew from all state affairs, but continued to busy with the delights of art and with the vigilant surveyal of all that was new in literature the last years of a serene and cheerful old age, active to the last, and till his death, on the 22d March 1832, revered by the world of letters as its archpriest and king. In 1806 G. was formally married to Christiane Vulpius, with whom he had lived in terms of closest intimacy since 1788. Their only son, **Johann August Walther von G.**, was born on the 25th December of that year, and after having held several offices in the service of the Duke, died in Italy in 1830, leaving three children, of whom two sons are still alive.

G.'s entry on court service at Weimar coincides with a marked change in the style of his poetic workmanship. In his first period of power he was substantially a popular poet, a poet of and for the people; and the novelty of matter, or the keenness and freshness of feeling and of thought, is much more remarkable than ingenuity of construction or polish of style. *Götz von Berlichingen* sets before us with vigour and almost naïve simplicity a true 16th c. knight at feud with his surroundings. In *Werther's Leiden* (1774) we have the experiences and the fate of a hero who succumbs to the agony of unrequited love. By writing *Werther* G. succeeded in shaking himself free of the morbid sentimentality of that period; but too many of his readers saw in the romance a justification of passionate self-indulgence in the luxury of sorrow, and even an apology for suicide. *Clavigo* (1778) and *Stella* (1776) are poor in comparison with their prototypes *Götz* and *Werther*, and the *Grosskophta* (1789) is but a minor work. But the lyrics, many of which belong to this period, are inimitable and unexcelled, possessing warmth of feeling and all the indefinable charms of true songs. For years after G. came to Weimar he published nothing of importance, but was at work on more than one of his second series of great works, though none was finished till the Italian tour. These are all marked by singular melody of language and beauty of form. As G.'s first period has been called *sentimental*, the second is frequently characterised as *ideal*. In *Iphigenia* (1786) G. has endeavoured with success to solve a problem he consciously set before him, that of clothing the wealth of modern thought with the grace and elegance of the ancient classics. As in *Iphigenia*, so in *Tasso* (1789) there is a striking want of outward action. In the latter especially the struggle of feelings takes the place of deeds, though for most readers they fail to inspire the same interest. *Egmont* (1785), with much of excellence in detail, is tame as an historical drama, and is irregular in the style of its execution. *Wilhelm Meister's Lehrjahre* (1796) illustrates more than any other work save *Faust* the marvellous universality of their author's genius; it is the first classical attempt to promote as well as depict social culture by means of romance, and, like all G.'s prose works, has done unspeakable service in smoothing and polishing the prose style of Germany. *Hermann und Dorothea* (1796), in hexameters, is unique amongst G.'s poems as glorifying, under forms of idyllic simplicity, strength, and beauty, the homely virtues of everyday life. *Faust*, the first part of which was published as a fragment in 1790, is a work unparalleled in ancient or modern literature. It is essentially a psychological drama, though the hero plunges into the vortex of life, and illustrates his inmost thoughts and passions in action on the human stage. The subject of *Faust* is man—man in the fulness of his unsatisfied cravings for superhuman wisdom, power, delight; and at least one of the deep lessons of the poem is the inability of human power to solve the problems which life sets us. *Faust* is intensely German, but being also intensely human, it has become a portion of universal literature. The *Xenien* (1796), full of humour, the translations from Voltaire, and *Die Wahlverwandtschaften* (1808) may all be reckoned to the second period. The latter work is unquestionably, in respect of composition, a very perfect romance, whatever may be thought of its ethical teaching, and it shows that G.'s original productive power was still vigorous. *Dichtung und Wahrheit* (1811), a beautiful though not entirely accurate retrospect of his life as it appeared to the patriarch of literature, may be regarded as the transition to G.'s third period, in which the *didactic* and scientific tendencies predominate over the creative impulse. Under this head comes the *West-östlicher Divan* (1813). *Wilhelm Meister's Wanderjahre* (1821) is unequal and often tedious. The second part of *Faust*, completed the evening before the poet's last birthday (1831), is strangely unlike the first part; it is rich in beauties of detail, but full of mystical allegories. In these years G. worked with zeal at studies in the realm of natural science, and the published results comprise articles and treatises on subjects too numerous and various to be mentioned. Though many of G.'s views, especially that on which his theory of colours (*Farbenlehre*) is based, are at variance with scientific certainties, yet they almost all abound in fruitful thought, and in his *Morphologie* G. positively anticipated modern science.

The vast influence exerted by G. on the world ever since *Götz* and *Werther* were published is, of course, mainly due to the unfathomable power of the true poet; but it also partly depends on the fact that G. appeared after a period barren of poetic inspiration in all European countries. Besides his originality and force, some outstanding features of G. deserve to be noted. It was his maxim that all his poetry should be the outcome of his own experience, yet so faithfully did he strive to regulate and mould his inward impulses by the realities of nature, of life, of the world, that he is to be reckoned amongst objective, realistic poets. The harmony of form and matter in G.'s works is not more remarkable than is the harmony of development between the many sides in the nature of the poet, of the apostle of culture. The universality of G.'s interests is appreciated only by those who study his multifarious writings. Even within the realm of poetry the versatility of his powers is remarkable. He is equally at home in the merriest lyric trifle and in the lofty ode, in warm love strains or eerie ballads. But in G.'s very various dramatic efforts the limit of his genius is most plainly revealed. He had no enthusiasm for great historical movements, little sympathy or understanding for keenly national efforts and designs; so that, although one of the most German of men, although his works contributed powerfully to the national regeneration of Germany, he was too consciously cosmopolitan to be much moved by the outburst of the new national life in the War of Liberation; and it is also noteworthy that he failed to find a personal interest in that other great factor in the intellectual revival of Germany, the Kantian and post-Kantian philosophy. Hardly ever has any poet in his lifetime become so truly the hero of his country. Probably none has ever been so entirely idolised by his worshippers, or had the minutest details of his life so indefatigably sought out and chronicled.

Among biographies, that most accessible to Englishmen is practically as yet the best, *The Life and Works of G.*, by George Henry Lewes (1855, 2d ed. 1864, 8th ed. of German trans. 1872). Briefer is that by Goedeke (1st ed. 1859). Viehoff's work had reached a 5th ed. in 1872. The biographer had rich material in *Eckermann's Gespräche mit G.* (3d ed. 1869, trans. by Winkworth), and in G.'s copious correspondence with his friends, especially with Schiller. See also Bernay's *Der Junge Goethe* (Leips. 1875.) Criticisms and even commentaries on his several works are very numerous. As early as 1799 Scott translated *Götz*. *Werther* has been translated into French and English by many different hands (the first French being in 1776; first English trans. in 1779). There are numerous English versions of *Faust*, the best being that by Bayard Taylor. *Wilhelm Meister* has been well rendered by Carlyle. The last edition of his own works, revised by G., was published in 1827-32, in 40 vols., to which a supplement of 20 vols. was afterwards added.

Gog and Magog, two warriors mentioned in the Scriptures, and the names of two figures 14 feet high, which stand on pedestals in the Guildhall, London. According to legend, G. and M. were giants whom the Trojans under Brut led captive to London, where they were kept as porters chained to the gate. G. and M. have been associated with London from very early times. Their effigies, which were carried in the Lord Mayor's procession, were burned in the great fire of 1666. The present statues were raised in 1708.

Gog'ari, a river of India, which rises among the hills of Nepaul, under the name of the Kamla, flows first S.W. and then S.E. through the British districts of Tirhut, Monghyr, Bhagulpore, and Purniah, and finally falls into the Coosy, a tributary of the Ganges, after a course of about 230 miles.

Go'go, a seaport in the district of Ahmedabad, Province of Bombay, British India, on the W. coast of the Gulf of Cambay, 190 miles N. of Bombay. Pop. (1872) 9571. The port is a safe anchorage, with a muddy bottom, and the inhabitants make excellent lascars.

Go'gol-Ivanov'ski, Nikola'i Vassilje'vitz, one of the most celebrated novelists of Russia, born at Vassiljevka, in the government of Poltava in 1808. He came to St. Petersburg in the beginning of 1829, and sought to be admitted to the theatre, but his *début* was unsuccessful. After some time he obtained a Government appointment, and in 1831 was appointed Professor of History at the Patriotic Institute. In 1843 he was made Professor of General History in the University of St.Petersburg, but held the post barely a year and a half. He afterwards lived abroad, principally at Rome, but returned to Russia, a victim of religious *melancholia*, and died at Moscow, 4th March 1852. G.'s great strength as a novelist lay in representing popularly and humorously the essential characteristic qualities of his countrymen. His chief works are *Vechera na Khutorie*, 'Evenings at a Farmhouse' (St. Petersb. 1832), which manifests vigorous talents, and is valuable as an accurate representation of peasant life in Little Russia; *Mirgorod* (1834), a volume of similar tales, permeated, however, by rare poetic feeling, and equally remarkable for powerful development of plot and dramatic and consistent management of character; *Revisor*, a comedy, in which the corruption of official life in the Russian provinces is ably satirised, and which won the commendation of the Emperor Nicolas; and the *Dead Souls* (1842), a satirical work written with the view of laughing serfdom out of existence. The collected works of G. appeared in 6 vols. (Moscow, 1856-57), and in 4 vols. (Moscow, 1862).

Gog'ra or **Ghog'ra** (*Ghagra*), a large river of India, which, in its upper part, is also called the Kali, Sarda, and Sarju. It rises, under the name of Kali, at an elevation of 18,000 feet, among the Himalayas, on the frontier of the district of Kumaon. It first flows S.W., receiving many hill torrents on either side, and forming the boundary with Nepaul, till it reaches the plain of Hindustan at Burmdeo, after a course of 148 miles. It then becomes navigable, and continues in the same direction through the districts of Oudh and the N.W. Province. After bordering the Bengal district of Sarun, it finally falls into the Ganges a little above Patna, after a total course of 600 miles. Its largest tributary is the Rapti on the left bank. The large traffic which it brings down, chiefly oilseeds, rice, wheat, and sugar, is now registered at Durowli in Sarun district; much of it is transhipped into larger boats at Revelgunge, or forwarded by rail from Patna.

Goil, Loch, a beautiful western arm of Loch Long, in Argyleshire, 6 miles long, and from 1 to 2 broad, is fringed on the E. with hazel woods, and overshadowed by lofty rugged hills. On a low sea-girt rock on the W. side stands Carrick Castle, a fortress of the Dunmore family. At the head of the inlet lies the village of Loch Goil-Head, which in summer has daily communication by steamer with Glasgow, and is a favourite summer residence.

Go'ito, a town of N. Italy, province of Mantua, on the Mincio, 15 miles N.W. of Mantua. It was taken by the Imperialists in 1630, by the allies and Imperialists successively in the Spanish Succession wars in 1701, and by the French in 1796. G. was also the scene of a battle between the Austrians and Italians in 1814, and of two encounters in the war of independence in 1848. Pop. 5274.

Goi'tre (Lat. *guttur*, 'the throat'), or **Bron'chocele**, a specific affection of the thyroid gland generally ascribed to the persistent use of water which has percolated through magnesian limestone rocks or strata, and containing in solution salts of lime. G. is a very widespread affection, having no connection with climate, for it is met with in certain districts having a similar geological formation, both in the tropics and the polar regions. It prevails in places where *pump-water* rather than *surface-water* is used, and more especially where water is obtained by tapping a magnesian limestone rock. There are some goitrous districts in Switzerland, where the use of water issuing from the hollows of certain rocks and trickling along crevices in the mountains will produce G., or aggravate the disease in the course of a few days, while those who avoid such water are free from it. Captain Franklin, in his expedition to the polar sea, found G. to be very prevalent at Edmonton, but confined to those only who drank from the water of the river Saskatchewan; those who used *snow-water* only, or that derived from the rivulets which flow through the plains in summer, being exempt from it. G. is common in Derbyshire, where it is called *Derbyshire neck*; in Switzerland, where it is often associated with *Cretinism* or *Cagot* (q. v.); and in Oude and Nepaul, where it affects the inferior animals as well as man. G. may be simply hypertrophy of the thyroid gland, or it may be associated with *cystic tumours* in the gland, and in either case it may attain an immense size. The usual treatment consists in removing the exciting cause and the administration of iodide of iron internally and of iodine externally. In some cases a cure has been effected by the ligature of the thyroid artery, and occasionally by excision of the tumour. See Nièpce, *Traité du G.* (Par. 1851).

Go'lab Singh, the founder of the present dynasty of Cashmere, feudatory to the British Government of India. By descent a Dogra Rajput, he entered the service of Runjit Singh, the Sikh Rajah of the Punjaub, in 1820. Though he himself never joined the Sikh sect, he became the most favoured minister of Runjit, who conferred upon him the fief of Jummu, which lies at the mouth of the Cashmere valley. He used the Sikh soldiery to conquer for himself the additional province of Ladakh; and after the first Sikh war, in 1845–46, he received from the British the state of Cashmere, in consideration of paying £750,000 in a lump sum and an annual tribute of a few goats and shawls. Though often suspected, he continued loyal to the treaty then made, and on his death in 1857 his son succeeded to the state on the same terms. See CASHMERE, and Cunningham's *History of the Sikhs* (Lond. 1853).

Golcon'da, a fortress and ruined city in the Nizam's dominions, India, 7 miles W. of Hyderabad. It was the former capital of the Deccan, and contains many handsome tombs of granite with stucco ornaments. It is still the treasury and state prison of the Nizam. The far-famed diamonds of G. really came from a considerable distance, and were only cut and polished here.

Gold (Old Eng. and Low Ger. *gold*, Dut. and Low. Sc. *goud*, Dan. and Sw. *guld*, from the adj. *gelew* or *gealew*, 'yellow, bright') has been known from the earliest ages, and is frequently mentioned in the Bible. In the second chapter of Genesis it is spoken of as occurring before the Flood. Its brilliancy and unalterability, together with the ease with which it may be hammered and fashioned into various shapes, must have early attracted the attention of man—the more so as G. almost always occurs in the native or uncombined condition, and therefore requires no preliminary treatment to obtain it pure. The alchemists regarded G. as the most perfect, and therefore as the king of metals. They compared it with the sun, no doubt on account of its colour and brilliancy, and frequently called it 'sol' in their writings; indeed, the metal is always represented by them symbolically by the sun. The great effort of the alchemists was to convert the baser or less perfect metals into the perfect metal G., and to extract medicines from it. The physical properties of G. were described by Pliny, and according to him the metal was discovered by Cadmus, the Phœnician, on Mount Pangæus. Its discovery was also attributed to Thoas or Eactis, or to Sol, the son of Oceanus. Some of the chemical properties of G.—its solubility in a mixture of nitric and hydrochloric acids (aqua regia), for instance—were known to the alchemists; so also were a few preparations of the metal—fulminating G. amongst others.

G. is a brilliant yellow metal, capable of taking and retaining a high polish. In the pure state it is scarcely harder than lead, and therefore is unsuitable for the purposes of coinage, &c. To increase its hardness it is alloyed with small quantities of other metals. G. coin in this country contains 1 part of copper and 11 parts of G.; and G. jewellery, varying quantities of silver and copper. The addition of a small quantity of alloy produces very considerable changes in the colour of the G.

G. is remarkable for its ductility and malleability. An ounce of it may be hammered into 100 square feet of leaf; 15 grains may be drawn into a wire more than 2000 yards in length. In the manufacture of G. thread for embroidery, a cylinder of silver is coated with G. and passed through the draw-plates. In this manner 200 miles of thread may be obtained from 6 oz. of G. The metal is also remarkable for its high specific gravity (19·3); with the exception of platinum, it is the heaviest in general use. It melts at a higher temperature than either copper or silver, and crystallises in beautiful fernlike forms in cooling. It does not combine directly with oxygen, and for this reason it does not become tarnished by exposure to the air; neither is it acted upon by sulphuric, hydrochloric, or nitric acid. A mixture of the two latter, however, dissolves it, and on that account was called by the alchemists *Aqua Regia* (q. v.). G. is readily precipitated from its solutions as a purple powder by the action of reducing agents, such as sulphate of iron, oxalic acid, &c. The atomic weight of G. is 197, and the chemical symbol for its atom Au (from Lat. *aurum*, 'gold'). Among the more important compounds of G. are the following:—

Terchloride of G. (*Auric Chloride*), $AuCl_3$, obtained by dissolving G. in aqua regia, and evaporating in a water bath to a small bulk. On cooling, a compound of the chloride of G. and hydrochloric acid separates in yellow needles. From this the hydrochloric acid may be removed by exposure to a gentle heat. Heated to 150° C., the chloride loses two atoms of chlorine, and sub-chloride of G. (aurous chloride), AuCl, remains.

Peroxide of G. or *Auric Acid*, Au_2O_3, and the protoxide, or aurous oxide, Au_2O, are obtained by the action of caustic potash on the corresponding chlorine compounds.

Fulminating G. is obtained by adding ammonia to a solution of the terchloride. It explodes violently when heated.

Sel d'Or, used by the photographer, is a double hyposulphite of G. and sodium ($Au_2S_2O_3$, $3Na_2S_2O_3$, $4H_2O$), obtained in white needles by precipitating a mixture of the terchloride of G. and hyposulphite of soda with alcohol.

Purple of Cassius (q. v.) is obtained by mixing terchloride of G. with protochloride of tin.

Salts of G. are employed in glass and porcelain painting and staining to produce a rose colour.

Law Regarding G.—In England the standard for G. and silver coin is 22 parts pure and 2 of copper or brass; and 11 oz. 2 dwts. of fine silver and 18 dwts. of copper melted together are held the standard for silver coin, and are called sterling silver. By 7 and 8 Vict. c. 22, all G. wares of the standard fineness of 22 carats of fine G. in every pound troy, made since October 1, 1844, must be marked with a crown and the number 22, instead of the lion passant. By 17 and 18 Vict. c. 96, the Queen in Council is empowered to allow any standard for gold wares not less than one-third part in the whole of fine gold, and to appoint a stamp setting forth in figures the actual fineness according to the standard so declared. Any assayer or other officer marking gold ware with the mark of a higher standard than is due to its quality, incurs a penalty of £20 and dismission from his office; and all wares so stamped improperly are liable to seizure. By 18 and 19 Vict. c. 60, gold wedding-rings must be assayed and marked. See ASSAY, or ASSAYING. For Scotch law, see SILVER AND GOLD PLATE.

Gol'dau, a former village of Switzerland, canton of Schwyz, in a valley between the Rossberg and Mount Rigi, 5 miles N.W. of Schwyz. It had some 400 inhabitants, and, together with four minor villages, was overwhelmed by a sudden landslip from the side of Mount Rigi on the 2d of September 1806. One-third of Lake Lauwerz was choked up by the dislodged mass of rock and earth, and further devastation was wrought by the expulsion of its waters.

Gold-Beating, the art of reducing gold to infinitesimally thin leaves by hammering. The gold, pure or alloyed with silver or copper in variable proportions according to the colour required, is cast into a thin ingot, ¾ of an inch wide, 1½ inches long, and weighing about 2 oz. The ingot is then reduced between steel rollers to a long narrow ribbon, about $\frac{1}{800}$ of an inch in thickness, which, after being softened, is carefully divided into square inch pieces. Squares to the number of 150, with as many pieces of vellum 4 inches square, are next alternately piled up and enclosed in a parchment case called a *kutch*. This packet is beaten until the 1 inch squares of gold are expanded to nearly the size of the vellum. The leaf is then quartered, and the pieces, placed between gold-beater's skin, are again beaten. Another quartering and beating follows, by which the leaf is reduced to about $\frac{1}{300000}$ of an inch in thickness. The finished leaves are next trimmed to an equal size of 3¼ inches, twenty-five of which are placed in a book, the leaves of which are rubbed over with red chalk. The book is sold for 15d.

Gold-Beater's Skin, the peritoneal or outer membrane of the cæcum of neat cattle, used by gold-beaters for placing between leaves of gold. It is prepared by immersion in a weak potash solution, is scraped with a knife, then beaten, soaked in water, and stretched on a frame, where it is treated with alum water, isinglass, and egg-albumen. When dry, it is pressed and cut up into squares of 4½ inches, ready for use. Nine hundred squares of this membrane constitute a gold-beater's *mould*, and it takes 500 oxen to furnish this quantity.

Gold'berg ('gold mount'), a walled town of Prussian Silesia, on the Katzbach, 50 miles W. of Breslau. It was formerly noted for its gold-mines, which are said to have yielded 150 lbs. of pure gold weekly in the 12th c. There are now manufactures of broadcloth, hosiery, gloves, &c., and an active fruit trade. Pop. (1871) 6716. G. was seized by the Mongols in 1241, suffered in the Thirty Years' War, and was the scene of a Franco-Russian and a Franco-Prussian battle in 1813.

Gold Coast, a purely geographical name given to the maritime portion of Guinea lying between the Ivory and Slave Coasts, and including the seaboard of Ashanti (q. v.), Cape Coast Castle (q. v.), and Fanti (q. v.). The name is derived from the local gold-dust trade. See GUINEA.

Golden Age, the name given in classic mythology to that period in the infancy of the human race when men, untainted by degrading passions and vices, lived like the gods in happy security and plenty till death like a gentle slumber carried them away from their herds and harvests. The kindly earth then produced spontaneously all things necessary for the welfare of man, and war and bloodshed were unknown. Hesiod, Virgil, Tibullus, and Ovid have dedicated some of their finest verses to this charming theme, the last portraying with singular power and beauty not only the G. A. but the Silver, Brass, and Iron Ages which followed, each fraught with increasing wickedness and woe.

Golden Beetle, a general name given to various genera and species of beetles or *Coleoptera* (q. v.), but more especially to the genera of the family *Chrysomelidæ*, in which the body is rounded and the colours usually most brilliant, golden tints prevailing. These beetles belong to the *Tetramerous* group of the order, and have the antennæ widely separated, and the mandibles or larger jaws notched at their tips.

Golden Bull (Lat. *Bulla Aurea ;* Ger. *Goldene Bulle*), a decree of Karl IV., King of the Germans and Emperor of the Holy Roman Empire, issued in 1356, which regulated everything in regard to the election of the King of the Germans. The number of Electors (q. v.) was fixed at seven ; a majority of their votes was to decide every question ; the election was always to be at Frankfurt ; and the coronation at Aachen ; the King of Bohemia was to be the first secular elector, and the Archbishop of Mainz the convener of the Electoral College. The G. B. added to the power of the electors, declaring their persons sacred, and making them independent princes within their own possessions. A G. B. of Andreas II. of Hungary fixed the privileges of the nobility in 1222.

Golden-Crested Wren (*Regulus cristatus*), a common British species of *Dentirostral* (*Insessores*) birds belonging to the family *Sylviadæ*, and to the sub-family of the nightingales (*Luscininæ*). In the genus *Regulus* itself the bill is short and broad at the base, and the nostrils are crescent-shaped and covered by a scale. The first quills of the wings are very short, and the fourth and fifth feathers are longest. The tail is slightly forked, and the tarsi are covered in front with one long scale. The G.-C. W. is common in hedgerows and copses, and is distinguished by the crest of golden feathers, which the bird can raise or depress. The average length is 3½ inches, and the colour is brown and green above, white on the wing-coverts, and yellowish grey on the throat. The crest is yellow tipped with orange.

Golden-Eye Fly (*Hemerobius perla*), a species of *Neuropterous* insects, so named from their large lustrous eyes. They are also called 'lace-winged flies,' from the delicate texture of their wings. They attain a length of about 1½ inches. The eggs are attached in moss-like clusters to plants, each egg being fixed on a stalk of a hardened glutinous secretion.

Golden Fleece. See ARGONAUTS.

Golden Fleece, Order of the, an order of knighthood founded by Philippe III., Duke of Burgundy, in 1429. It chose the fleece as its emblem, probably from wool being the chief manufacture of the Netherlands. Its grand-mastership was hereditary in the Dukes of Burgundy, until the order, along with their dominions, passed to Austria. Since Karl V.'s death the order has been held by the Spanish monarchs, though their claim has been disputed by the Austrian sovereigns. The order is at present the highest bestowed at the Spanish and Austrian courts.

Golden Legend (Lat. *Legenda Aurea*), a medieval collection of saintly legends and other tales written by Jacobus de Voragine, a Genoese Dominican of the 13th c. He based his work partly on a similar book in Greek by Simon Metaphrastus, and was indebted to the *Gesta Longobardorum* for many of the beautiful tales which he interspersed amid the stories of the saints, whence the G. L. was at one time known as the *Historia Lombardica*. Voragine's book was translated into French by Jean de Vignai, and was one of the sources from which Caxton's G. L. was compiled. The lives of the well-known saints were afterwards extracted from the G. L. The work contains several familiar tales, as the stories of the 'Seven Sleepers' and 'St. George and the Dragon.' It reflects the simple, credulous medieval devotion, as distinct from the logical casuistic theology of the schoolmen and the lofty mystical religion of men like Dante and St. Francis.

Golden Number. See EPACTS, METONIC CYCLE.

Golden Rod, the common name given to species of *Solidago*, a genus of Composite plants mostly natives of N. America. *S. Virgaurea* is the only British species, and at one time was largely used as a vulnerary. The fragrant leaves of *S. odora* have also been used in medicine. Several species are cultivated in gardens for their large spikes of yellow flowers.

Golden Rose was an ornament in use from about the end of the 11th c., of gold, musk, and balsam, typical of the divinity, body, and soul of Christ, of joy, spring, and Easter, by its sweetness, beauty, and pleasant taste. It was anointed with chrism and sprinkled with perfumed dust, and, after benediction and lying on the altar during mass, was sent or even carried by the Pope to some distinguished personage or eminent church. See Walcott's *Sacred Archæology* (1868).

Goldfields and Gold-Diggings. Gold is a widely-diffused metal, but nowhere has it ever been found in large quantities. It occurs only in the metallic condition, and generally, when found in veins, it is as minute specks or spread out in thin plates, which occasionally show an arborescent crystalline structure. The auriferous veins, which are found traversing rocks of various ages and different composition, are composed chiefly of quartz, with sometimes calc-spar and baryta. In these veins the gold is most frequently associated with iron pyrites and other metallic sulphides. By far the larger proportion of gold is, however, obtained from alluvial diggings in which the metal has been deposited by the denudation of auriferous veins. In these diggings the metal is found mostly distributed in loose specks, having been separated from the rock by the disintegrating action of the atmosphere and water. Occasionally, but not often, pellets and masses of considerable size are found in alluvial diggings, and these, when of the size of a hazel-nut and upwards, are known as nuggets. The largest mass known to have been found was the 'Welcome Stranger' nugget, which weighed 2280 oz., obtained in 1869 near Dunolly, Victoria, and numerous single pieces weighing from 100 to 400 or 500 oz. troy are recorded. There are few countries in which gold does not exist, but generally it is so sparsely disseminated that its extraction cannot be profitably undertaken. It is usually only on the first discovery of a goldfield that the alluvial diggings yield, without skilled labour or expensive appliances, exceptionally profitable results, and taking all circumstances and conditions into account, there is no reason to believe that gold-mining is more lucrative than other industrial pursuits. A small quantity of gold is obtained as a by-product of certain metallurgical industries. Thus Spanish coppery pyrites contain very minute traces of both gold and silver; and in the treatment of that ore by the wet method for the extraction of copper, it is possible to extract both precious metals with profitable results.

Gold has been worked at various periods on a commercial scale in the United Kingdom, but at no time has the produce been sufficient to sensibly affect the total yield of the gold-producing countries of the world. In England, between the years 1860 and 1866, 12,800 oz. of gold were obtained in N. Wales, chiefly in the Vigra and Clogau mines in Merionethshire. In Scotland, during the reign of James VI., a considerable quantity of gold was obtained in the Leadhills, and in the winter of 1869–70 a good deal of agitation arose in connection with the discovery of auriferous deposits at Kildonan in Sutherlandshire. For a few months the so-called field was diligently worked, and although some amount of gold was obtained, the labour was not sufficiently remunerative to encourage its prosecution, and the undertaking was quickly abandoned. In Ireland, about the close of last century, a good deal of gold in the form of nuggets was obtained in Wicklow. One nugget weighing 22 oz. was obtained, and specimens are yet occasionally picked up.

The two most remarkable discoveries of gold in modern times have occurred in California and in the colony of Victoria, Australia. The produce of these localities had, and still exercises, a powerful influence on the commerce of the world, as, taken together, the regions they may be regarded as embracing produce more than one-half of the gold annually brought into the market. The discovery of gold took place in California about the beginning of March 1848, and the announcement of the fact produced a sensation throughout the world which is almost without parallel. Emigrants flocked thither from every quarter, and within a few months a teeming population filled the river valley in which the first discovery was made. Within four years—in 1852—the annual output of gold from the diggings exceeded £12,000,000, and in 1854 the produce reached £14,100,000. Since that period, although the auriferous region has been found to be widespread throughout the Pacific states, the yearly return has decreased; but it is estimated that California and its neighbouring states have already added £200,000,000 to the available bullion of the world. The G. of Victoria were practically opened up in 1851, and the discovery produced an effect scarcely less marked than in the case of California. In 1852 not less than £15,900,000 in value of gold was produced in the colony; but from that maximum the yield has declined, and in 1875 the output was only valued at £4,332,300. Victoria is estimated to have added upwards of £150,000,000 to the gold of the world since 1851. The other Australian colonies, and especially New S. Wales, S. Australia, and Queensland, as well as New Zealand, have all either developed important G. or otherwise demonstrated their wealth in the precious metal. The remaining gold-yielding regions of the world are indicated in the accompanying statement of their comparative yield in 1869, taking the produce of the Californian region as the standard at 100:—

Australian colonies (with New Zealand) .	127
California and Pacific States	100
British North America	45
Mexico	35
Russia	31
Brazil, &c.	20
Asia and Africa	14
Europe	10
American localities not enumerated . .	9

The yield of the whole world for that year has been estimated at £60,000,000, but there is reason to believe that the total amount fell very much short of that amount. A more reliable calculation for 1874 puts the total produce of all G. at about £23,000,000.

In dealing with alluvial deposits gold-mining is a very simple process, as the gold can be readily washed out of the clay, sand, and gravel in which it rests by virtue of the superior gravity of its particles. To effect this washing a variety of devices are employed, the object in view in all cases being to remove by a current of water the light clayey particles of the 'pay dirt' or 'wash dirt,' as the auriferous soil is termed, and leave the gold either in the bottom of the vessel employed, or in the 'ripples' or cross bars of the sluice or shoot through which the current is sent. In some cases the gold, instead of being permitted simply to subside, is caught in and amalgamated with mercury, from which it is subsequently separated by distillation. In vein-mining, the auriferous quartz or other rock is obtained by blasting, and reduced to a fine powder in a stamping mill, after which the material is in a condition to be treated by washing and amalgamation in the same manner as wash dirt.

Native gold invariably contains some proportion of silver, and frequently it has traces of iron and several of the rare metals, such as platinum, iridium, and palladium. The following represents the analysis of the native gold of the principal auriferous regions:—

	Hungary.	Russia.	California.	Australia.
Gold	64·77	86·50	89·60	95·7
Silver	35·23	13·20	10·06	3 9
Iron and other metals .	..	0·30	0·34	0·2

Gold'finch (*Fringilla carduelis*), a typical British species of Finches (q. v.) or *Fringillidæ*, distinguished by the greyish-brown tint of the upper parts, by the crimson band encircling the bill, and by the top of the head being black. The sides of the head are white, and the wing-coverts and the outer edge of the primary feathers of the wing yellow. The tail is black, and the under parts greyish white. The average length is 5 inches. The nest is made of grasses, wool, and hair; the eggs, numbering four or five, are white, with purple-brown markings. The G. is very readily domesticated, and can be taught to perform tricks requiring considerable dexterity. The food consists of thistledown and seeds of various kinds. The bird is found throughout Europe and in Asia. It is nearly allied to the Siskin (q. v.) or aberdevine and to the chaffinch (*F. cœlebs*).

Gold'fish (*Cyprinus auratus*), a species of the Carp (q. v.) genus (*Cyprinus*), distinguished by the golden colour of the scales. The familiar G. varies in colour; occasionally the golden is replaced by a silvery tint and dark markings. The G. was first domesticated by the Chinese, and was brought from China to Europe by the Dutch. It may be fed on bread-crumbs, flies, worms, &c. It appears to be acclimatised to the cold of our climate, and thrives in open-air ponds and lakes.

Goldfish.

Gold-Lace, a gold-thread tissue, the thread of which is formed by twining round a filament of yellow silk flattened narrow strips of gold, or more commonly of gilded silver, so closely that the edges meet and conceal the silk. The gilded silver is made by applying gold-leaf to a rod of silver, and drawing the rod out to a very fine wire, which is afterwards flattened between rollers. The ductility of the gold is so great that the wire is perfectly coated with gold surpassing gold-leaf in thinness. During the middle ages the G.-L. of Cyprus and Venice was much esteemed. In very early gold tissues, flattened gold wire was inserted with the needle, and the Chinese and natives of India still practise this primitive method.

Goldo'ni, Carlo, the chief comic dramatist of Italy, was born at Venice in 1707. He at first studied medicine at Rimini, and afterwards law at Pavia University, from which he was expelled for composing a satire against the citizens. On his father's death he settled as an advocate in Venice, but shortly abandoned the law, and led a wandering life with strolling players until 1736, when he married and returned to his birthplace. He now devoted himself to writing comedies of character modelled on Molière, but the fondness of the public for the improvised buffooneries of the *Commedie dell' Arte* debarred his plays from winning popularity. From 1741 to 1746 he journeyed to various Italian cities composing pieces for different theatrical companies, and for a time renewing his legal practice. On returning to Venice his comedies gained wide popularity, and began to displace the extemporised burlesques; but a piece of his bitter opponent Gozzi for a time depriving his dramas of favour, G. repaired in 1761 to Paris, where several of his plays were acted with success, and where he was made Italian master to Louis XV.'s daughters. Shortly afterwards he was accorded a yearly pension of 3600 francs, which was suppressed at the Revolution, and restored to him on the day of his death, January 7, 1793. G.'s plays quickly regained possession of the Italian stage, and have been the model for all the chief modern writers of Italian comedy. He has been called the Italian Molière, and he thoroughly reformed the Italian comic drama. His plays are admirably fluent and sprightly, picturing the surface of society with entertaining fidelity, but the rapidity with which he was forced to write—he produced on an average one play a month—hindered him from giving due proportion to his work. Among the numerous editions of G.'s works, that published at Venice (44 vols. 1788–94) is the most complete; that of Florence (53 vols. 1827) the most elegant. See the *Mémoires de G.* (Par. 1787); the Biographies of Carrer (3 vols. Ven. 1824), Calvi (Mil. 1826), and Meneghezzi (Mil. 1827); and Copping's *Alfieri and G.* (Lond. 1857).

Gold'schmidt, Madame (*née* **Jenny Lind**), a great Swedish singer, was the daughter of a poor teacher, and born at Stockholm, October 6, 1821. She appeared in children's parts at the age of ten, but her upper notes failing somewhat in her twelfth year, she was withdrawn from the stage for four years. At the age of sixteen she appeared with success at Stockholm as Agatha in *Der Freischütz*. In 1841 she removed to Paris, where she was a pupil of Garcia, but failed at the Grand Opera—a failure which, it is said, made her determine never to sing again in France. On returning to Sweden she was welcomed with enthusiasm, and in 1847 appeared with triumphant success in London. In 1850 she visited the United States, receiving 302,000 dollars for her tour there, and in 1851 married M. Otto G., the pianist who accompanied her on her tour. Since her marriage, Madame G. has seldom sung in public. She has expended large sums on charities, and has laid out £40,000 in endowing schools in Sweden. Her voice is a peculiarly sweet and powerful contralto.

Gold'sinny, or **Gold'finny**, a popular name of certain *Teleostean* fishes allied to the Wrasse (q. v.) (*Labridæ*), and found on the N. European coasts. Their colour is a bright yellow, and the dorsal fin is very long. The G. is included in the genus *Crenilabrus*.

Goldsmith, Oliver, was born at Pallas, County Longford, Ireland, November 10, 1728. His father, the Rev. Charles G., removed in 1730 from Pallas to Lissoy, where Oliver was taught in the village school kept by an old quartermaster. At the age of eight he was deeply marked by the small-pox, and was sent after recovering to various schools, where he was generally viewed as 'impenetrably stupid.' In 1745 he went as a sizar to Trinity College, Dublin, where he studied little, and where his great delight was to hear his ballads sung on the streets. After a brief truanting from college, the first of his long wanderings, he took the degree of B.A. in 1749, and set out to study law in London, but having lost at a Dublin gaming-table the £50 given him for his outfit, came home and resolved to be a doctor. After staying eighteen months in Edinburgh without taking his degree, and spending some time at Leyden, he roamed on foot across Flanders, France, Switzerland, and part of Italy, maintaining himself by playing on his flute. He came back to England in 1756, and for some years was in deep distress, failing completely as a physician, and with difficulty supporting himself by writing for the *Monthly Review*. He now wholly abandoned medicine for literature. His *Inquiry into the Present State of Polite Learning in Europe* (1759) had considerable success, and his *Chinese Letters*—afterwards issued as *The Citizen of the World*—which began in the *Public Ledger* for 1760, made him well known in London. In 1761 he was introduced to Dr. Johnson, and thenceforth mingled with the chief authors of the town. The *Traveller* (1764) established his reputation, which was increased by the appearance of the *Vicar of Wakefield* in 1766. His comedy of the *Good-Natured Man* was produced in 1767, his *Deserted Village* was published in 1770, and *She Stoops to Conquer*, the best English comedy of the 18th c., was acted successfully in 1773, and has ever since kept possession of the stage. During his last years he earned about £400 annually, equal, says Macaulay, to £800 at present, but his constant charities, his fondness for gambling, fine clothes, and fine living, plunged him in embarrassment, and at his death, of a nervous fever, April 4, 1774, he was £2000 in debt. Among his other works are histories of England, Rome, and Greece, *Life of Beau Nash*, *History of Animated Nature*, *Retaliation*, a poem, &c. Thackeray calls G. 'the most beloved of English writers;' and there is an irresistible fascination in his gentleness, simplicity, and generosity, even in his half pathetic, half comic failings, as well as in the romantic story of his life, and in his exquisite and versatile literary powers. The *Vicar of Wakefield* has an undying charm from its graceful idyllicism and natural pathos; the *Citizen of the World* is full of piquant, naïve satire; *She Stoops to Conquer* abounds in the purest and most frolicsome humour; the *Traveller* and *Deserted Village* are suffused with a tender glow of descriptive beauty and reflective sentiment, and display in their polished verse a peculiarly rich music and pensive monotony of cadence; while *Retaliation* sparkles with playful, apt, and incisive epigram. G.'s prose style has been seldom rivalled in elegance, sweetness, and captivating ease. His *Miscellaneous Works*, in 4 vols., were published by Washington Irving in 1825, who also wrote a charming biography (Lond. 1849). But the standard work on G. is Forster's *Life of G.* (3d ed. 1862).

Golf, formerly **Goff** and **Gouf** (Dutch, *kolf*, Ger. *kolbe*, 'a club'), an outdoor game in Scotland, and a pastime that of late years has found many votaries S. of the Tweed. The game consists in driving a small gutta-percha ball round a course, and into a series of 'holes' (distant from each other not more than 500 yards), in the fewest number of strokes. It is played with clubs of various forms, of which the chief are known as the play-club, putter, spoon, sand-iron, cleek, and niblick or track-iron. These consist of two distinct parts—(1) the shaft, in all cases of hickory or lance wood; and (2) the head, which in the three clubs last mentioned is of iron, in the others of well-seasoned apple-tree or thorn, weighted with lead, and faced with a rim of horn. The different kinds of clubs are adapted to the 'hazards' or diversities of surface in the 'links' or downs where G. is played. The most suitable links are broken with deep furrows, sand-pits, pebbly reaches, furzy knolls, &c. The rival players are usually in pairs, but two may play against two, the partners striking the ball alternately. The game is reckoned either by the aggregate strokes in a 'round' or by scoring the holes won. Strength is required for driving 'long-balls,' skill in avoiding hazards, and a sure eye and steady hand for 'putting' or holing. Among the finest links in Scotland are those at St. Andrews, Prestwick, Leven, Musselburgh, Edinburgh, N. Berwick, Gullane, Aberdeen, Carnoustie, and Montrose; in England those at Hoylake, Westward Ho, Wimbledon, and Crookham on the Berkshire Downs. Chief of the many organised golfing clubs in Scotland is the Royal and Ancient Union of St. Andrews; in England the Blackheath Club, dating from the reign of James I. G. was popular in Scotland as early as the 15th c., when many of the statutes refer discouragingly to 'golfe and uther sic unprofitabill sportis.' Among the royal players of G. are James IV. of Scotland, James I., Charles I., James II., and William III. See *G., a Royal and Ancient Game* (Edinb. R. & R. Clark, 1875).

Gol'fo Dul'ce ('sweet gulf'), a lagoon in Costa Rica, Central America, 25 miles long and 10 broad, communicating with the Gulf of Honduras by a small stream known as the Rio Dulce. The lagoon is 8 fathoms deep, but the mouth of the river is impeded by sand bars.

Gol'gotha is a Hebrew word meaning 'skull,' and the name of the place where our Lord was crucified. See CALVARY.

Goli'ath (Heb. 'an exile,' or perhaps from an Arabic word meaning 'stout'), a famous Philistine giant, belonging to Gath, who was slain by David in single combat (1 Sam. xvii.). His height was six cubits and a span, that is, about 10½ feet, or, according to the LXX. and Josephus, four cubits and a span, that is, about 7 feet. His conspicuous position in Scripture has made his name a personified symbol of huge size.

Goliath Beetle (*Goliathus*), a genus of *Coleoptera* or Beetles belonging to the *Pentamerous* group of the order, and so named from the large size of several species. These insects are found in tropical regions, especially in Africa.

Göll'nitz, or **Gölnicz** (a corruption of *Jelenze*, 'stag-town'), a town of Hungary on the river G., 130 miles N.E. of Pesth.

It has hardware industries, and in the vicinity are extensive copper and iron mines. Pop. (1869) 5205.

Goll'now, a walled town of Prussia, in Pomerania, on the Ihna, 15 miles N.E. of Stettin, has manufactures of woollens, silks, paper, tobacco, &c. Pop. (1871) 7444.

Golomyn'ka (*Comephorus Baikalensis*), a Teleostean fish found in Lake Baikal, and nearly allied to the gobies. (See GOBY.) It attains a length of 12 inches, and has no scales. Its flesh is oily, and its outer surface is protected by a mucous secretion, seen in other members of the goby family.

Golosh', or **Galosh** (Fr. *galoche*, 'a clog;' from Med. Lat. *calopedia*, 'a wooden shoe,' 'a patten or wooden shoe fastened to the foot with latchets'), an overshoe, generally made of vulcanised india-rubber, worn to protect the foot from damp, and made to clasp the boot firmly without fastenings. The sole and upper are cut from sheet rubber to the size of a metal pattern. The pieces are then arranged round an iron last, and the edges are cemented together with india-rubber solution. A glossy coating is next imparted to the shoe, which is afterwards submitted to the vulcanising process, which destroys the adhesive properties of the rubber, and renders it unaffected by heat or cold, while it preserves its elasticity.

Golun'da (*G. Barbara*), a genus of *Muridæ*, or Mice (q. v.), familiarly known as the Barbary mouse, from its occurring in that country. This elegant animal has a rich brown fur, striped longitudinally with yellow, while the under parts are white. It is about the size of the common mouse. The G. becomes very tame in captivity.

Go'marists were the Supralapsarian Calvinistic party in the Reformed Church at the time of the Synod of Dort. They derived their name from Francis Gomar, a colleague of Arminius in the University of Leyden, who took a leading part against the Arminians both at the Hague in 1610, and at Dort in 1618.

Gombrûn' (pron. *Gamrun*), or **Ban'dar Abb'as**, a seaport of Persia, at the mouth of the Persian Gulf, on the Strait of Ormuz, 198 miles S.E. of Shiraz. In the 17th c. it was the emporium of Persia, and still has a considerable trade, exporting carpets, tobacco, dried fruits, fish, and sulphur, and importing piece-goods, Indian cloths, China ware, &c. The port, destitute of any pier, in S. and S.E. winds is lashed by heavy surf. In the hot summer all but the very poorest desert G. for Minab, a town 14 miles inland, on the slope of lofty hills. Pop. 8000 or 9000. G. was founded in 1622 by Shah Abbas, after ousting the Portuguese from Ormuz, in which he was aided by the English. The English, Dutch, and French had factories at G., but internal commotions soon drove the trade to other ports. G. is farmed to the Sultan of Muscat.

Gome'ra, one of the Canary Islands (q. v.) to the S.W. of Teneriffe, is 12 miles long, 9 broad, and has a pop. of 11,742. Its two towns are St. Sebastian and Villa Hermosa.

Gomorr'ah. See SODOM.

Gomu'to, Gommu'ti, or **Ejoo**, names given to the bristly horsehair-like fibre obtained from *Arenga* (*Saguerus* of some authors) *saccharifer*, or areng, a frequent palm in the Indian islands. The fibre is largely used for cordage and strong cables. Sago is also obtained from the arenga stem, and palm-wine or toddy from its flowering spike.

Gonaives', Les, a town on the coast of Hayti, on a bay of the same name, has a good harbour and trade. Pop. 4000.

Gon'da, the chief town of the district of the same name in the province of Oudh, British India, about 120 miles N. of Allahabad. Pop. (1869) 11,966.—G. *district*, which lies under the Himalaya, is watered by the Bapti and Gogra rivers, by which it exports to Bengal rice, other cereals, and oilseeds, and receives salt and iron. Area, 2629 sq. miles; pop. (1869) 1,167,816.

Gon'dar, or properly **Guendar**, the nominal capital of Abyssinia, on a ridge of the Wogra Mountains, 7000 feet above the sea, and 30 miles N. of Lake Dembea. It consists in great part of thatched huts, and is embowered in trees, above which rise the pinnacles and towers of its royal palace (the *Gemp*), and the high conical roofs of its forty-four churches. There are Mohammedan and Jewish quarters, and a considerable trade is carried on, chiefly in firearms, musk, wax, ivory, coffee, pottery, &c. The mean temperature is about 69° F., while much rain falls. The dirty, crooked streets are badly paved with basalt, and are often invaded by hyænas, foxes, &c. In the 17th c. G. is said to have had a pop. of 50,000, now decreased to 7000.

Gondhwa'na, a geographical name given to the large hilly and jungly tract of Central India, which is inhabited to a great extent by the Gondhs, a wild race akin to the Kandhs of Orissa, and believed to be of Dravidian (q. v.) origin. Their number amounts to upwards of a million, and before the incursions of the Mahrattas they were ruled by a powerful native dynasty. They are very backward in civilisation, devotees to demon-worship, and are known to have made a practice of human sacrifice up to a late period.

Gondok'oro, a trading place in the Bari country, on the steep left bank of the White Nile, 200 miles N. of Albert N'yanza Lake. It has been from antiquity a centre of the ivory and slave trade. A Roman Catholic mission was founded here by Dr. Knoblecher in 1849, and from that time to 1857, when the position was abandoned, sixteen out of twenty-four priests succumbed to the climate. G. was the headquarters of Baker during the Anti-Slave-Trade Expedition of 1871.

Gon'dola (Ital. diminutive of *gonda*), a boat from 25 to 30 feet long and 4 or 5 feet broad, much used on the canals and lagoons of Venice. Its two sharp ends rise high out of the water, the stem and stern are decked over, and amidships a cabin is placed for passengers. The hull is painted black, and the drapery of the cabin is of the same colour, giving the whole a funereal aspect; hence Byron (*Beppo*) describes the G. 'just like a coffin clapped in a canoe.' The rowers are called *gondolieri*.

Gondola.

Gon'falon (Ital. *gonfalone*), a flag the bearer of which, or *gonfalonier*, was the chief magistrate in many Italian republics of the middle ages, and notably in Florence.

Gong (Javanese), an Eastern instrument of percussion, usually made of bronze, 78 parts copper and 22 tin, and used for signalling in peace, and as a martial instrument in war.

Gon'gora, Luis y Argote, a Spanish poet, born 11th June 1561, at Cordova, studied law at the University of Salamanca, and after vainly courting fortune for many years, was appointed almoner to Philip III. He died at Cordova, 24th May 1627. G.'s early works, mainly songs, lyrics, and satires, are national in their spirit, and are among the best productions, in that kind, of Spanish genius. Desirous, however, of surpassing all his predecessors and creating a new and distinct school of poetry, he abandoned the old national feeling and form of expression, and adopted the *estilo culto*, or cultivated style, of which affectation, pedantry, obscurity, and confusion were the chief characteristics. His chief works in this style, besides numerous sonnets, *octavas*, *tercetos*, &c., were the long poems *Las Soledades*, *El Poliphemo*, *Pyramo y Thisbe*, published after his death. His followers were named *Gongoristas* or *Cultoristas*, and his poems gave rise in Spain to the school of the *cultismo*, which was vigorously attacked by Lope de Vega, who, however, did not always avoid its vices. The earliest edition of G.'s works is that of Lopez de Vicuña (Madr. 1627); the most complete, that of Gonzalo de Florez y Cordoba (Madr. 1633). There is a good *Coleccion* by Ramon Fernandez (Madr. 1789).

Gonias'ter, a genus of Starfishes (*Echinodermata*), including those familiarly named 'cushion stars.' The body is pentagonal, and flat on either side; the rays inconspicuous, and only to be seen distinctly on the under surface. The 'knotty cushion star'

(*G. equestris*) occurs abundantly round the British coasts. The genus is first represented in a fossil state in the Jurassic rocks.

Goniati'tes, a fossil genus of *Cephalopoda* (q. v.) belonging to the family *Ammonitidæ* or Ammonites (q. v.). The shells of G. occur first in the Upper Silurian rocks, attain the maximum of their development in the Carboniferous system, and die out in the Trias. They are discoidal in shape, and the 'sutures' (or external markings of the *septa* or partitions of the shell) are lobed or angulated, the *sipuncle* being dorsal in position. *G. Jossæ*, from the Carboniferous formations, is a well-known specimen. *Bactrites* (q. v.) is very nearly allied to G., as is also the genus *Ceratite* (q. v.).

Gonid'ia, a name given to the bright-green globular cells which form a layer under the cortical covering of the thallus of Lichens (q. v.). They partake of the character of both vegetative and reproductive cells.

Goniom'eter (Gr. *gōnia*, 'angle,' *metron*, 'measure'), an instrument for measuring angles formed by the sides of a crystal. That in common use is Wollaston's reflecting G., which by bringing two contiguous sides into the same position relatively to an outside object, and its reflected image viewed by the operator, is capable of measuring angles accurately to an error not exceeding one minute. The crystal is rotated with a graduated circle, and the angle through which it is rotated during the operation is the supplement of the angle of the crystal.

Gonorrhœ'a (Gr. *gonos*, 'progeny' or 'seed,' and *reō*, 'I flow') is a specific disease affecting the urethra, the mucous membranes of the genital organs in the male, and the vulva and vagina in the female. It is accompanied by inflammation and an abundant muco-purulent discharge of a highly contagious nature. In the early stages G. is a strictly local affection; but in many cases it is followed by a particular train of characteristic symptoms, apparently the result of constitutional infection, such as affections of the fibrous tissues, giving rise to rheumatism and inflammation of the testicles and the sclerotica, affections of the mucous membrane of the throat and eyes, and certain eruptions of the skin assuming a specific type. The first or incubative stage usually appears from the third to the fifth day after exposure, the symptoms being heat, itching, and general irritation of the parts. The second or inflammatory stage is characterised by a copious and thick muco-purulent discharge, great pain during micturition, and a diminished stream of urine. These symptoms usually continue for about a fortnight, when the sub-acute stage commences, which under proper treatment may subside in two or three weeks, but which may last for months or years and degenerate into a *gleet*. Though the inflammatory symptoms subside, the specific and contagious character of the discharge does not disappear, and the infective power may continue so long as the discharge keeps up. G. may be followed by *Stricture* (q. v.) after an interval of many years, resulting in the most serious consequences, or even in death, from retention of urine.

Gon'ville and Ca'ius College. See CAIUS COLLEGE.

Gonza'ga, a town of Northern Italy, in the province and 15 miles S. of the city of Mantua by railway. It stands amid fertile plains, was doubtless formerly of great strength, and is said erroneously to have been the cradle of the Gonzaga (q. v.) family. Pop. 17,526.

Gonzaga, House of, an old princely family of Italy, owes its origin to the Emperor Lothar. Ludovico G. brought the long-continued contention with the Bonacossi family respecting the supremacy of Mantua to a close by the murder (14th August 1328) of Passerino de Bonacossi and the expulsion of his dependants. Ludovico, now captain-general of Mantua, was appointed imperial vicar of the district by Kaiser Ludwig the Bavarian, and after his death the supremacy remained vested in his descendants with the title of Counts (from 1432 to 1530) and Dukes (1530 to 1707) of Mantua. Through the three sons of Ludovico III. the H. of G. came to be divided into three lines. From Federico, the eldest, sprang the Counts of Mantua, who were created dukes under Karl V. in 1530, and died out in 1726. From the younger sons, Giovanni Francesco and Ridolfo, sprang respectively the Dukes of Sabioneta and Castiglione, whose dukedoms were confiscated by the Emperor in 1692. The Guastalla branch of the G. family, founded by Ferrante G., governor of the dukedom of Milan for Karl V., became extinct in 1746. Petrino, younger son of Ludovico I., founded the family of the Counts of Novellara, extinct in 1728. Among the more notable members of the H. of G. are Ludovico III. (1444–78), named the 'Turk' on account of his successful campaigns as general of the Florentines and Venetians against the Infidel; Francesco II. (1484–1519), commander-in-chief of the united armies in Italy in the battle of Fornovo against Charles VIII. of France; Vincenzio I. (1587–1611), who fortified Mantua, and distinguished himself fighting on the side of the Hungarians against the Turks. His three sons were Francesco IV., Fernando IV., and Vicenzio II., the last of whom died in 1627. The nearest heirs should have been the Duc de Nevers, but Ferdinand II. of Guastalla laid claim to the whole inheritance and Carlo Emanuele of Savoy to Montferrat. In the Mantuan war of succession which followed, France, Venice, and the Pope supported the Duc de Nevers, Spain and Austria the Duke of Savoy. Peace was concluded in 1631, by which the Duc de Nevers was enfeoffed in Mantua and Montferrat. Charles I. (of Nevers) was succeeded by his uncle and afterwards by Carlo II., one of whose sisters (Maria) was first married to Vladislav IV. and afterwards to John Kasimir, King of Poland, while the other (Anna) became the wife of the Count Palatine of the Rhine, who, after playing a distinguished part at the French court, died at Paris in 1684, leaving behind him very attractive Memoirs (Lond. and Par. 1686). Carlo IV., who died in 1708 without issue, admitted a French garrison into Mantua, and joined the side of France in the Spanish war of succession. For this the Emperor Joseph I. placed him under the ban of the empire, whereupon Savoy took possession of Montferrat, and Austria of the dukedom of Mantua.

Gonzal'vo di Cordova (properly **G. Hernandez y Aguilar**), surnamed *El Gran Capitan*, 'the great general,' was born in 1453 at Montilla near Cordova, in Andalusia. When only fifteen he fought under his father, Don Diego G., against the Moors in Granada. In this war he displayed so much gallantry, especially at the capture of Tejara, Illora, and Monte-Frio, and he conducted the negotiations with King Boabdil for the surrender of Granada with so much ability, that the Spanish rulers conferred upon him a pension and an estate. His splendid successes against the French in Naples earned him the surname of *Gran Capitan*, and freed Italy from the invaders. He returned to Spain in August 1498, after having received from the King of Naples an estate in the Abruzzi and the title of Duke of San-Angelo. At the close of the 15th c. Louis XII. of France renewed the attack upon Naples, and G. was again sent to Naples to protect the Spanish interests there. Having previously captured Zante and Cephalonia, and restored them to the Turks, he landed at Sicily and took possession of Naples and Calabria. Dissensions naturally arose on the partition of Naples between the Spaniards and French, and again G.'s arms proved invincible against the latter, who were finally driven out of the peninsula. About this time King Ferdinand of Spain, moved by jealousy of the splendid success of his great general, and of the affection with which he was regarded by the people, withdrew his favour from G. Troubles again arising in Naples, the king commanded G. in April 1512 to organise another expedition to Italy. The force was no sooner assembled than Ferdinand ordered its disbandment in a slighting, capricious, insulting manner. The old warrior never regained the favour of his king, and, crushed by neglect and chagrin, he died at Granada, 2d December 1515. See Le Père du Poncet's *Histoire de Gonzalve de Cordoue*; Paul Jove's *Vita magni Consalvi*; and Quintana's *Vidas de Españoles celebres* (Madr. 1807).

Good, John Mason, M.D., was the son of an Independent minister at Epping, where he was born, 25th May 1764. He studied at Guy's Hospital, and practised medicine for a few years, but is chiefly known as an author. He died 2d January 1827. G. wrote dissertations *On the Diseases of Prisons and Poorhouses* (1795) and *On Medical Technology* (1808), *A History of Medicine* (1795), *A Physiological System of Nosology* (1817), *The Study of Medicine* (1822), and *The Book of Nature* (1826). He published besides translations of the Song of Solomon (1803), Job (1812), and of Proverbs (1821), and an English version of Lucretius in blank verse (1805). See the Memoir of G. by Dr. Olinthus Gregory, published in 1828.

Good'all, Frederick, R.A., an English painter, was born in London, September 17, 1822. He gained the Isis medal of the Society of Arts at the age of fourteen, and in 1839 exhibited his first picture at the Academy, 'French Soldiers Drinking in a Cabaret.' His 'Return from Christening' gained a prize of £50 from the British Institution, and in 1847 his 'Village Festival' won wide admiration. He was made an Associate of the Royal Academy in 1852, and a Royal Academician in 1863. His earlier pictures were largely representations of Breton life, G. having travelled in Brittany; but of late years he has essayed more ambitious subjects. Among his works are 'The Soldier's Dream,' 'Raising the Maypole,' 'The Swing,' 'The Return of the Pilgrims from Mecca,' 'Hagar and Ishmael,' 'Mater Dolorosa,' &c.

Good-Con'duct Pay, an increase of pay awarded in the army and navy for continued good conduct.

Goodenia'ceæ, a Dicotyledonous order of plants embracing twenty-three genera and about 200 species, chiefly natives of Australia and the South Sea Islands. *Scævola Taccada* of India and Ceylon, which belongs to the order, yields a fine pith, which has been used as rice-paper. Its young leaves are eaten as a pot-herb.

Good Friday is the Friday before Easter Sunday, and the anniversary of our Saviour's crucifixion, called in early times the Pasch of the Cross, Paraskeue ('Preparation') (*cf.* Mark xv. 42), &c., and in Germany, Still Friday. Observed from very early times as a solemn fast, it came afterwards to be distinguished by a peculiar ritual and customs: the bells were silent from midnight of Wednesday; the kiss of peace was prohibited; the altar was stripped of its ornaments and covering; the processions were without chanting; the lamps and candles were gradually extinguished during matins; a long series of intercessory collects were used; a cross was erected in front of the altar, blessed, and adored; there was no consecration of the Lord's Supper or celebration of the Mass, although until the 10th c. the faithful were permitted to partake in silence of what was reserved from the previous day. At the present day in the Roman Catholic Church no one partakes of the Eucharist but the celebrant.

Good Hope, Cape of, next to Cape Agulhas (q. v.) the most southerly point of Africa, and the turning-point from S. to E. in the voyage from Europe to India, in lat. 34° 22′ S. and long. 18° 29′ E. It is 25 miles S. of Cape Town, and is a bold promontory rising 800 feet above the sea, and forming the termination of the Table Mountain. Diaz, a Portuguese, who doubled it for the first time in 1486, named it *Cabo Tormentoso*, on account of the storms that he encountered; but the King of Portugal changed this forbidding appellation into that which it now bears, *Cabo de Bona Esperanza*. See CAPE COLONY.

Goods, Purchase and Sale of. By the Statute of Frauds (see FRAUDS, STATUTE OF), no contract for the sale of goods to the value of £10 or upwards is valid unless the buyer receive part of the goods, or give an Earnest (q. v.) to bind the bargain or towards payment, or unless there be written proof of the contract. With regard to goods under the value of £10, no contract is binding unless the goods are to be delivered within a year, or unless the contract be in writing. Delivery of a penny or of a glove is sufficient *earnest*. Acceptance of the key of the warehouse in which goods are deposited, or the payment of warehouse rent, is affirmative of the bargain. When no act remains to be done by the vendor, such as counting, weighing, or measuring, the moment the bargain is struck the property of the goods vests in the vendee, and the risk is his if they remain with the vendor. So if a horse die in the interval between sale and delivery, the conditions of the statute having been complied with, the vendor is entitled to his money. The general rule of law is that sale in open market not only binds the parties to it, but also binds any one having a right of property in the article sold. Open market in the country is only held in certain towns in a particular spot and on special days by charter or prescription, but in London every day except Sunday is market-day, and every shop in which goods are publicly exposed to sale is open market for such goods as the owner professes to trade in. Pawnbrokers in London or within two miles of London are excluded from this protection, and any goods wrongfully taken to them may be claimed by the owner. No writ of attachment against the goods of a debtor will affect the title to them acquired by a *bona fide* purchaser before execution, provided he has not had notice of the writ having been delivered to the sheriff. See SALE OR RETURN; WARRANTY OF GOODS; BILL OF SALE, under BILL. For Scotch law, see SALE and MARKET OVERT.

Goods and Chattels, a legal phrase signifying personal property. In Scotch law the corresponding phrase is goods and gear. The terms are seldom used except in wills.

Goods in Commun'ion are in Scotch law the movable effects belonging in common to a husband and wife. They comprehend all the movable property of both, except that which has been settled on the wife exclusive of the *Jus Mariti* (q. v.), and of the wife's *Paraphernalia* (q. v.). By the Act 18 and 19 Vict. c. 23, the representatives of a wife who predeceases her husband have not now, as they had previous to the Act, a share of the G. in C., and no bequest by the wife can affect them. When marriage is dissolved by predecease of the husband, and there is no child, the G. in C. are divided into two equal parts; one of which, the *Jus Relictæ* (q. v.), goes to the wife, the other, the Dead's Part (q. v.), going to the legatees or executors of the husband. When there is a child or children, the division is into three equal parts; one of which goes to the widow, another, the *Legitim* (q. v.), to the child or children, who are also entitled to the third part, unless otherwise disposed of by the father's will. The same division takes place in England by statute, if there is no will. (See DISTRIBUTIONS, STATUTE OF.) In Scotland the destination, which is by common law, prevails notwithstanding a will to the contrary; hence in Scotland, as regards movable property, a man cannot disinherit his wife and children; in England he can. In both countries the rights of a wife and children may be altered or set aside by antenuptial contract. See CONTRACT OF MARRIAGE, MARRIAGE, CONFIRMATION, EXECUTOR.

Good'sir, John, anatomist, was born at Anstruther in Fife. March 20, 1814. He was originally intended for the practice of dentistry, but after a short trial relinquished it for the medical profession. In 1835 he obtained the diploma of L.R.C.S.E., and shortly afterwards settled in Anstruther as a general practitioner. It was here that he made his first great contribution to anatomy, an essay *On the Origin and Development of the Pulps and Sacs of the Human Teeth*. This paper was so replete with originality and research, that it brought him at once into notice as one of the most gifted young anatomists of the period. Several important contributions to natural history rapidly followed. In 1840 G. removed from Anstruther to Edinburgh, which at that period was adorned by a wealth of young scientific talent. In 1841 he was elected curator of the Museum of the Royal College of Surgeons. In 1844 he was appointed demonstrator of anatomy to the third Monro, and on his death in 1846 G. was elected his successor in the anatomical chair. Notwithstanding the great amount of work which his professorial duties entailed, G. was constantly engaged in important and laborious original researches. His contributions to the literature of his department were numerous and important. His doctrine of nutritive centres, which paved the way for Virchow's cellular pathology, his researches on the inflammation of cartilage, his views on the motion and construction of joints, his lectures upon the structural dignity of man, &c., possess the highest merit. But it was not as a writer that G. was most distinguished, although he wrote clearly and forcibly. He excelled most as a teacher. Brimful of learning, not only relating to anatomy, but to physics, mathematics, history, and theology, he was able to bring the truths of every science to bear upon the elucidation of the subject in hand, as occasion required. G. prosecuted the study and advancement of anatomical science with such unremitting ardour that his health broke down in 1853. He passed the following winter abroad, but returned next summer to Edinburgh, and continued, in spite of increasing suffering, to deliver his lectures till within a few months of his death, which took place at South Cottage, Wardie, March 6, 1867. Such records of his labours and researches as could be collected are included in the two volumes of memorials, edited by Professor Turner and Dr. Lonsdale (Edinb. 1868). On account of his natural genius, his originality, his scientific enthusiasm, his Herculean energy and industry, and his numerous anatomical discoveries, G. deserves to be remembered better than many who bulk much more largely in the annals of the medical profession.

Goodwin, Thomas, D.D., an English divine, born at Rollesley, Norfolk, 1600, studied at Cambridge, where he was made vicar of Trinity Church in 1632. Shortly afterwards he left the English Church, and withdrew to Holland, where he became pastor of the English church at Arnheim. He returned to England about 1640. In 1649 the Parliament made him President of Magdalen College, Oxford. After the Restoration he led a studious life in London until his death, February 23, 1679. Anthony Wood speaks of him as 'one of the Atlasses and patriots of Independency.' His works, which are theological, were published (Lond. 5 vols.) 1681-1704.

Goodwin Sands, a dangerous shoal off the E. coast of Kent, distant 5½ miles from the mainland, with which it runs parallel from N.E. to S.W. for 13 miles. The G. S. are 2½ miles broad, are visible at low tide, and are marked at various points by lightships. The sunken, shifting sands are extremely fatal to navigation, but they form a breakwater to secure the anchorage in the Downs (q. v.), which lie to the W., and between the N. and S. Foreland. Terrible shipwrecks occur on the treacherous sands almost every winter, although the lightships are provided with every means of signalling. A class of idle but intrepid boatmen along the coast, known as 'hovellers,' live by appropriating portions of wrecks, and often effect daring rescues. An account is given of the origin of the shoal, but is supported by slight evidence. The sands, it is said, consisted formerly of some 4000 acres of low land belonging to Earl Godwine, which were seized by William the Conqueror and bestowed on St. Augustine's Abbey at Canterbury. The abbot subsequently neglected the protecting dykes, and the sea bursting through, submerged the whole in 1100. A lighthouse, on fixed iron piles, was erected here in 1846, but was overwhelmed in the following year.

Good'year, Charles, born at New Haven, Connecticut, December 29, 1800, became an iron manufacturer in Philadelphia, and in 1830 began to experiment on the uses of india-rubber. In 1836 he invented a nitric acid process for fitting it to be worn as waterproof shoes, &c., and in 1839 he perfected a method of vulcanising india-rubber by sulphur. G. received many marks of distinction, but, owing to infringements of his patents, gained slight pecuniary reward for his important inventions. He died at New York, July 1, 1860.

Goole, a river port and market-town in the West Riding of Yorkshire, 25 miles S.W. of Hull, on the river Ouse, at its confluence with the Don. G. is the terminus of a branch of the Lancashire and Yorkshire Railway, and, though recently but an inconsiderable village, it has now large docks and a thriving Continental and coasting trade. The chief exports are coal, woollen manufactures, and machinery; amongst the imports are fruit, butter, wool, and timber. G. has also alum and sugar works, iron foundries, and corn mills, and makes agricultural implements. In 1875, 1727 vessels of 27,835 tons cleared the port. Pop. (1871) 7680.

Gooroo', or **Guru** (derived from a Sanskrit word signifying 'heavy'), 'a person of weight or respectability,' a word used throughout India in two special senses—(1) for the village schoolmaster in the indigenous *pathsala;* and (2) the religious teacher or guide who communicates to his disciple the peculiar prayer which initiates him into any particular sect. In this latter sense it was commonly applied to the ten Sikh Gurus, from Nanuk to Govind Singh, whose succession has now ceased. To this day the watchword of the Sikhs is *Wah gooroo* = 'Hail G.,' and Gurumuki is the name of the peculiar modification of the Sanskrit alphabet adopted by that sect. See Cunningham's *History of the Sikhs* (Lond. 1853).

Goose, the name given to various genera of Natatorial or swimming birds belonging to the sub-family *Anserinæ*, in which the bill is not longer than the head, while its ridge or keel is elevated at the base, and slopes to the tip of the bill, which is hard and horny. The knee is bare, and the hinder toe, short and furnished with a rudimentary lobe. The name G. is given to birds belonging to different sub-families; 'Solan G.,' for example, being given to the *Gannet* (q. v.), which belongs to the genus *Sula*, and to the sub-family *Pelecaninæ;* while the spur-winged G. (*Plectrophanes Gambensis*) belongs to a special sub-family, although it is nearly allied to the true G. Beginning with the genus *Anser* itself, we find the grey lag or wild G. (*A. ferus*) and the bean G. (*A. segetum*) exemplifying two familiar forms, from which the domestic G. and its varieties are believed to be descended. The former is common throughout the Old World, and has a pink bill tipped by a whitish 'nail.' The head and upper parts are ashy brown, the hinder part of the back bluish grey. The lower parts are white, and the neck and breast grey. The full-grown male attains a length of 3 feet. The bean G. arrives in Britain from its Arctic habitat about October. Its beak is more slender and pointed than that of the wild G., and is coloured black with an orange centre. The upper surface is brownish grey, the tail-coverts and belly white, and the breast grey. The average length is about 2¾ feet. The domestic G. is of a white colour, although the darker grey of its progenitors is often noticeable. The flavour of the flesh of the wild G. is rather fishy and disagreeable, and to remove it sportsmen are accustomed to bury the bird for an hour or two in the ground. The curious genus *Cereopsis* includes the *C. Novæ Hollandiæ* or Cape Barron G., found in Bass's Straits. Its technical name is derived from the presence of a large *Cere* (q. v.), which forms a prominent object on the beak. The bill is short, the nostrils large and rounded, and covered by the cere. The first quill of the wing is short, and the hinder toe is not lobed. The colour of this bird is brownish grey marked with black on the wing-coverts; the head a light grey tint, while the bill is black, and the cere greenish yellow. The legs are pink. The bird breeds freely in England, but is less decidedly aquatic in its habits than the other species of G. The flesh is palatable. The spur-winged G., already mentioned, inhabits Gambia and Senegal, and is so named from having 'spurs' or horny appendages on the wings. The head bears a red crest, springing from the base of the bill, and forming an intimate part of the skull. The plumage is mostly a deep black, but the breast and belly are white. The tail is short and round, and the second, third, and fourth quills are the longest. Other species of G., more or less closely related to the genera and species just described, are represented by the Egyptian G. (*Chenalopex Ægyptiaca*), the Brent G. (*Bernicla Brenta*), and the red-breasted G. (*B. ruficollis*). The Canada G. (*B. Canadensis*) is very common in N. America, but lives and breeds freely in Britain. It is somewhat swan-like in appearance and proportions. Its colour is black with a semi-lunar patch of white on the throat. The pink-footed G. (*A. brachyrhynchus*) is noted for the shortness of its bill; this species is rare in Britain, but common in the Hebrides. The white-fronted G. (*A. erythropus*), sometimes named the laughing G., is found both in the Old and New World, chiefly in the Arctic regions. The average length is 26 or 27 inches, and the colour, grey with a white head. The Chinese G. (*A. Cygnoides*), has a protuberance on its mandible, from which it is also named the 'knobbed G.' Its native country is supposed to be Guinea, but it is domesticated in Britain. Geese are typically inhabitants of the northern regions, and usually fly southwards in winter in immense flocks, which appear to be led by regularly appointed leaders; each flock flying in the form of the letter V—the apex of the letter pointed forwards. They breed once a year as a rule, and pair during the breeding season. The varieties of the common G. most famous are the Emden and Toulouse G.; the latter including birds of large size. Lincolnshire with its fenny districts affords the chief supply of these birds to the London market.

Goose.

Goose'berry (a corruption of the Ger. *krausel-beere*, 'hairy berry:' 'krausel' was Latinised in the medieval ages into *grosella*, whence the Fr. *groseille*, and the Low. Scotch *grozet* or *groset*), the common name for the fruit of *Ribes grossularia*, a prickly shrub belonging to the natural order Grossulariaceæ, and indigenous to Britain, many parts of Europe, and to Nepaul. There are now many varieties of G. cultivated in gardens. The ripe fruit, which is very wholesome, and varies much in flavour, is either red, yellow, or green, and hairy or smooth on the surface. It is extensively used as a preserve, and in the unripe state for tarts. A champagne is also manufactured from it. The Peruvian G. is a species of *Physalis* (q. v.), a plant belonging to a different natural order.

Gooseberry Caterpillar, the name given to the larva of a moth (*Abraxas grossulariata*), striped with white and black, and moving by bending its body into 'loops.' It is very destructive to the leaves of gooseberry and currant bushes. The moth itself is a dirty white, marked with black and yellow. The larvæ of various other species of moths (*e.g.*, *Halias Vanaria*) also feed on the leaves of these plants, and are also known by this name.

Gooseberry Fly (*Nematus grossulariæ*), a species of *Neuropterous* insects allied to the well-known Sand-Flies (q. v.), and included in the family *Tenthredinidæ*. The antennæ are simple in the genus Nematus, and the tarsi are jointed. The G. F. is noteworthy from the ravages of its larvæ on the gooseberry trees and fruit.

Goose'bill Shell. See LINGULA.

Goose Grass, or **Cleavers**, the popular names given to *Galium aparine*, a common hedge plant. See BED STRAW.

Goph'er or **Mungofa Tortoise** (*Testudo gopher*), a species of *Testudinidæ* or tortoises found in America, of a brownish-yellow colour, mottled with dark brown. It attains a length of 13 or 14 inches, and the female is larger than the male. The back is greatly arched. The food of the G. T. consists of vegetable matter, and it is specially fond of the sweet potato. The eggs are larger than those of pigeons, and are highly esteemed as food.

Gopher Wood, the wood of which the ark was constructed (Gen. vi. 14), is supposed to be the produce of a species of Cypress (q. v.), or some other tree belonging to the same order.

Göpp'ingen, an industrious and thriving town of Würtemberg, on the river Fils, about half-way by rail between Stuttgart and Ulm. Its acidulous mineral waters are in high repute. The manufactures comprise linen, cotton, and woollen fabrics. Pop. (1871) 8649.

Go'ral (*Antilope Goral*), a species of *Antilopiodæ* or Antelopes (q. v.) found in the mountainous districts of Nepal, and somewhat resembling the Chamois (q. v.) in habits. The colour is a light brown marked with black, and the horns are short, pointed, and curved inwards.

Gora'my (*Osphromenus olfax*), a peculiar species of Teleostean fishes, included in the family *Anabasidæ* of which the *Anabas* (q. v.) *Scandens* or Climbing Perch (q. v.) of India is a familiar example. The G. appears to be a native of rivers in China and the Malay Archipelago, and has been acclimatised in the W. Indies. The body is broad, the tail prominent, and the head small. The dorsal and anal fins are spinous, and the ventral fins are peculiar, as the first ray of each is prolonged, and forms a long and slender filament. This fish was introduced into the Mauritius in the 18th c., and is now found native in the streams; while in Java the Dutch have long kept the G. in tanks. The nest is formed of plants, both male and female watching the eggs during their development.

Gor'dian Knot. The tradition regarding this celebrated knot may be briefly stated. When Gordius, a poor Phrygian peasant, was ploughing, an eagle settled on his yoke of oxen, and remained till night. Curious to know the meaning of the prodigy, he went to Telmissus to consult the soothsayers. On his way he met a prophetic girl who told him to offer sacrifice to Zeus Basileus. She directed the rites, and the grateful Gordius married her, and became by her the father of Midas. After a time dissensions arose in Phrygia which an oracle declared would be quelled by a king who should come riding in a car. Gordius arrived in this fashion, was chosen king, and dedicated his car and yoke of oxen to Zeus, at the same time tying the yoke to the pole in such a cunning manner that the ends of the thong could not be detected. An oracle, or at least a rumour, promised the sovereignty of Asia to him who should untie the knot. When Alexander the Great came to Gordium (the city of King Gordius) he cut the G. K. with his sword, and declared the oracle fulfilled. The term G. K. is commonly applied to any apparently inextricable difficulty.

Gordia'nus, the name of three Roman Emperors, father, son, and grandson :—1. **M. Antonius G.**, surnamed **Africanus**, Emperor 238 A.D., descended on his father's side from the Gracchi, and on his mother's from Trajan. He spent his life in study and in the practice of virtue. When quæstor he was famed for his liberality, and when ædile he exhibited the games with unusual splendour. He was twice consul, first in 213 A.D., and afterwards with Alexander Severus. Soon after he was nominated Proconsul of Africa. In his eightieth year, during the tyrannical reign of Maximinus, he was compelled much against his will to accept the purple. His election was ratified by the senate, and G. and his son were proclaimed Augusti. Meanwhile Capelliannus, governor of Numidia, refused to acknowledge G.'s authority; advanced towards Carthage, and defeated and slew the younger G., who had taken the field against him. On hearing of this disaster the elder G. slew himself in despair, after a reign of less than two months.—2. **M. Antonius G.**, son of and joint-emperor with (1), was born 192 A.D., and died as stated above, in his forty-sixth year. G., who was a man of considerable culture and literary taste, was chiefly remarkable for the largeness of his library (60,000 volumes, left him by his tutor), and the number of his mistresses.—3. **M. Antonius G.**, grandson of (1), was raised when very young to the rank of Cæsar, and associated with Balbinus and Pupienus Maximus, who were elected emperors in opposition to Maximinus on the death of the two elder Gordians. In a few months all three were slain, and G. was declared emperor. In 241 A.D. he married Sabinia Tranquillina, daughter of the learned and virtuous Misitheus. Next year he undertook the war against Sapor, King of Persia, whom, chiefly owing to the ability of Misitheus, he defeated, and compelled to evacuate Mesopotamia. Misitheus soon died, and Philip, his successor, having created disaffection in the army, G. was assassinated 244 A.D.

Gor'dius, a genius of *Scolecida* (q. v.), popularly known from their slender form under the name of 'hair-worms,' and erroneously included in some works in the class *Annelida* (q. v.), or that of the true worms. The genus G. forms the type of an order (*Gordiacea*) of Nematoid or 'round' worms (*Nematelmia*). It occurs parasitically in the earlier stages of its existence within the bodies of grasshoppers and beetles, and may be found of a length far exceeding that of the insect in which it is located. When sexually perfect, it escapes from the body of its host, and subsequently breeds; the sexes being situated in distinct individuals. The eggs are deposited in long strings in water, and although the G. parasite has a mouth and digestive system, the alimentary canal of the sexually mature G. becomes obliterated. The young G. appears to have hooklets and a retractile proboscis, and at first leads a free existence in water, but soon enters the body of some insect. *G. Aquaticus* is the familiar species.

Gor'don is the surname of one of the most ancient and illustrious Scottish families. The origin of the name and family is unknown, but the fictions of a certain Duke of G. who was Constable of Charlemagne, and of a family who took their name from Gordunia in Macedonia, and flourished as early as the time of Julius Cæsar, are more than usually absurd; nor are accounts of Gourdons in Normandy or of Gordons in Scotland in the time of Malcolm Canmore much more worthy of belief. There seems, however, no doubt that the family was settled in its original seat of G. in the Merse sometime in the 12th c. The first G. of any note was an Adam de G., who joined the crusade of Louis IX., and died during the expedition in 1270. His grandson, Sir Adam, Lord of G., was one of the most notable men of his time. At first in the service of Edward I., he joined Bruce after the death of John Baliol in 1313. For various services he was rewarded with a grant of the lands of Strathbogie in Aberdeenshire, whither in 1333 he transferred the family seat. His second son, William, was ancestor of the Gordons of Kenmure. A descendant of this Adam, another Sir Adam, fell at Homildon in 1402, leaving an only daughter, who married Alexander Seton of Seton. The latter came in consequence to be styled Lord of G. and Huntly, and is the ancestor of the main branch of the family.

GORDONS OF HUNTLY AND GORDON.—Alexander, son of the last-mentioned lord, was created Earl of Huntly in 1449.

The succeeding Earls were noted for their loyalty to the Stuart family and the Roman Catholic Church. George, fourth Earl, was head of the Scots Catholics at the time of the Reformation, and his son, the fifth Earl, was one of Queen Mary's most determined adherents. The sixth Earl, created Marquis of Huntly in 1599, was at first a zealous Catholic, but conformed to the Established Church in 1610; and George, second Marquis and Earl of Enzie, was beheaded in 1649 for his unyielding fidelity to Charles I. George, fourth Marquis, was created Duke of G. in 1684; but the title became extinct on the death of George, fifth Duke, in 1836, being confined to heirs male of the body of the first Duke. It was, however, revived in 1876, and conferred on the Duke of Richmond and Lennox, who, as sister's son of the last Duke, had inherited most of the G. estates, while the second title—Marquis of Huntly—devolved on George, fifth Earl of Aboyne. The Duke of G., as head of the great Clan G., was wont to be called 'Cock of the North,' but the most ancient appellation was 'gudeman of the Bog,' from the Bog of Gight, the site of Gordon Castle.

THE GORDONS OF KENMURE AND LOCHINVAR were descended from William de G., second son of that Sir Adam who was killed at Halidon Hill in 1333. In 1633 Sir John G. of Lochinvar was created Viscount Kenmure and Lord Lochinvar. Alexander, fifth Viscount, the hero of 'Kenmure's on and awa', Willie,' was executed in 1716 for his part in the Rebellion of the previous year, and the title and estates were forfeited. The honours of the family were restored by Act of Parliament in 1784; but since the death in 1847 of Adam, eleventh Viscount in succession, but eighth in possession owing to the attainder, the title has been dormant.

GORDONS OF ABOYNE.—Lord Charles G., fourth son of the second Marquess of Huntly, was in 1660, for his great services to the Royalist cause, raised to the dignity of Earl of Aboyne and Lord of Strathaven and Glenlivet by Charles II. The fifth Earl, George, became Marquis of Huntly, as above mentioned, on the death of the fifth Duke of G. in 1836, and died in 1853 in his ninety-second year. The present Marquess of Huntly is the premier marquess of Scotland. He was born in 1847, and succeeded his father in 1863.

The GORDONS OF METHLIC AND HADDO are said to be descended from Sir William G. of Cowdenknowes in Berwickshire, son of that Sir Adam who took part in the last crusade. The groundless tradition that they, with the other Gordons, are sprung from Bertrand de Gourdon, who killed Richard Cœur de Lion, is an event commemorated by the family arms. The family was ennobled in the person of Sir George G., Lord Chancellor of Scotland (3d baronet, 1642), under the title of Earl of Aberdeen, &c. (Viscount Formantine, and Lord Haddo, Methlic, Tarves, and Killie). George, fourth Earl (q. v.), was Premier from 1852 till 1855, and his second son, Lieutenant-General Sir Alexander Hamilton G., was elected M.P. for E. Aberdeenshire in 1875.

GORDONS OF SUTHERLAND.—In 1512, Adam, Lord of Aboyne, second son of the second Earl of Huntly, married Elizabeth, Countess of Sutherland, and became in her right Earl of Sutherland. Their descendants long retained the name of G. There are many other families of the name throughout Scotland, all more or less directly sprung from the same stock, among whom may be mentioned the Gordons of Gight, of whom Lord Byron, through his mother, was the last descendant.

Besides two unprinted compilations of the history of the G. family—one by an Italian monk, written at Kinloss in 1545, and the other by Robert G. of Straloch, an eminent antiquary who died in 1661—there have been published *A History of the Ancient, Noble, and Illustrious Family of G.*, by William G. (2 vols. 8vo, Edinb. 1726); *A Concise History of the Ancient and Illustrious House of G.*, by C. A. G. (1 vol. 12mo, Aberd. 1754), both of which are rare; and a *Genealogical History of the Earldom of Sutherland, from its Origin to the year* 1630, by Sir Robert G. of Gordonston, with a continuation to the year 1687, by Gilbert G. of Salloch, published at Edinburgh in 1813.

Gordon, General Patrick, a distinguished general in the Russian service, was born at Easter Auchleuchries, in Aberdeenshire, Scotland, 31st March 1635. He left his native country at an early age, and after spending some time in N. Germany, went to Russia in 1661, where he shortly afterwards entered the army. His talent soon gained him promotion, and he at last became General-in-Chief of the Russian army, and the great favourite of Czar Peter. He subdued the Cossacks of the Ukraine (1670 *et seq.*), repelled the assaults of Turks and Tartars (1677), and crushed the revolt of the Strelitzes (1698). The unwillingness of Peter to part with him, obliged G. to decline several highly-flattering offers of command in the service of his own sovereign. To the great grief of the Czar, G. died at Moscow on the 9th December 1699. For many years before his death, G. had kept a diary (in English), of which the MS., in 4 vols. 4to, is preserved in Moscow. Besides some fragments of it to be found in Müller (*Samml. Russ. Geschichte*) two abridgments have been published—*Tagebuch des General Patrick G.*, edited by Dr. Posselt (Mosc. and St. Petersb. 1849–53); and *Passages from the Diary of General Patrick G.*, printed for the Spalding Club. (1 vol. 4to, 1859).

Gordon, Lord George, whose name is best known from the part he took in the Protestant riots of 1780, was the third son of Cosmo George, third Duke of G., and was born in December 1750. After spending some time in the navy, in which he rose to the rank of lieutenant, he entered Parliament in 1774, and so distinguished himself by his attacks on all parties, that it was usual to say 'that there were three parties in Parliament—the Ministry, the Opposition, and Lord George G.' Having been elected President of the Protestant Association in 1779, he headed a procession of about 100,000 excited citizens to the House of Commons on the 2d June 1780, to present a petition against the Catholic Emancipation Act of 1778. The result was a riot which lasted several days, during which many Catholic chapels and private houses, including the house of Lord Mansfield, were sacked, Newgate destroyed, and many of the prisons burst open and set in flames. Lord George was arrested on a charge of high treason, but was acquitted for lack of evidence. In 1787 he was convicted of libel on Marie Antoinette, and of reflecting on the administration of law and justice in his own country in a petition drawn up and presented by him. He fled to Holland, but in 1788 was committed to Newgate, where he spent the remainder of his life in study. Some time before his apprehension he embraced the Jewish religion, of which he continued to be a firm adherent till his death, which occurred at Newgate, 1st November 1793.

Gordon, Sir John Watson, R.A., an eminent Scottish painter, was born in Edinburgh about 1790, studied at the Art Academy of that city, and devoted himself at first to historical subjects, but afterwards to portrait painting, in which he became highly successful. In 1850 he was elected president of the Royal Scottish Academy, and was shortly afterwards knighted. He died June 1, 1864. G. painted many of the chief members of the Edinburgh society of his time, Scott, De Quincey, Wilson, Chalmers, Principal Lee, Cockburn, &c. But his *chef-d'œuvre* is the 'Provost of Peterhead.' His portraits are very realistic and solidly painted.

Gordon, Lucy, Lady Duff, daughter of Mrs. Austin, was born in 1821, married Sir A. G. in 1840, and became known as an excellent translator of French and German works. She died at Cairo, July 14, 1869. Among her translations are Ranke's *History of Prussia*, Niebuhr's *Greek Legends*, *The Amber Witch*, *The Village Doctor*, &c. Her original works, marked no less by an exquisite feminine lightness and grace than by an almost perplexing freedom of religious sentiment, are *Letters from the Cape* (1864) and *Letters from Egypt* (1865), and *Last Letters from Egypt* (1875), with a *Memoir* by her daughter, Mrs. Ross.

Gore, in heraldry, a charge consisting of a third of the shield marked off by a line from the foot of the escutcheon, and a line from the dexter or sinister chief.

Gore, Mrs. Catherine Frances, an English novelist and dramatist, born at East Retford, Nottinghamshire, in 1799. She married Captain G. in 1823, spent several years on the Continent, and died at Lynwood, Hampshire, October 19, 1861. She wrote about seventy novels, among which are *The Cabinet Minister*; *Preferment*; *Cecil, or the Adventures of a Coxcomb*; *Greville, or a Season in Paris*; *The Banker's Wife*, &c. They consist mostly of shallow, lively pictures of fashionable English life, with almost no feeling, but a good deal of caustic cleverness. Mrs. G. also wrote *The School for Coquettes*, a prize comedy; *Lord*

Dacre of the South, a tragedy, and numerous short tales, sketches, verses, &c.

Gorée', an islet off the W. coast of Africa, 2 miles S.E. of Cape Verd, and 3 miles in circumference. It has a good harbour, and some trade in gold-dust, ivory, wax, &c. Two-thirds of its surface are occupied by a fortified town (pop. 3042) of the same name. Pop. 7000.

Go'rey, a town in the county of Wexford, Ireland, 3 miles from the sea and 11 W.S.W. of Arklow by railway. It consists mainly of a long straggling street, and has a modern Roman Catholic church, which includes a nunnery, and is built in the Pointed style. The trade is in wheat, oats, barley, cattle, pigs, &c. Pop. (1871) 3620. G. received its municipal charter from James I.

Gorge. See FORTIFICATION.

Gorged, in heraldry, having a collar round the neck.

Gor'gei, Arthur, a Hungarian general, descended from a noble Protestant family, was born at Toporcz, in the county of Zips, 5th February 1818, and educated for the army. He forsook the military profession in 1845 for the study of chemistry, and was writing chemical dissertations when the Revolution of 1848 called him back to the army again. After Moga's defeat at Schwechat G. was made commander, and his energy and military talent were signally displayed in his defence of the retreat to the hilly country. Though often defeated by superior forces, he was always able to keep in the field. The suspicion of the Hungarian Government, excited by G.'s famous declaration of loyalty to the constitution promised by Ferdinand V., removed G. from the command; but after Dembinski's failure, G. was replaced at the head of one of the armies, and on April 7th, 1849, began at Godöllo that brilliant series of victories which ended on the 28th in Welden's retreat on Pressburg. The Austrians now retained only a few fortresses and a mere strip of Hungarian territory. But the tedious siege of Buda proved fatal. A Russian army was now co-operating with the Austrians; and, despairing of success against their combined forces, G. determined, in spite of his orders, to operate immediately against the Austrians, and sustained repeated repulses. He ventured on a last effort at Komorn, 11th July 1849, and was defeated. On 11th August Kossuth resigned in G.'s favour: G. became dictator, and having certain information of the total defeat of Dembinski's army, he submitted unconditionally to the Russians at Világos on the 13th August. The fact that G. had then under his command 20,000 infantry and 2000 cavalry, and the leniency with which he was personally treated, have provoked charges of treachery. At first interned at Klaqenfurt, in Carinthia, G. was permitted in 1866 to return to Hungary. In 1851 G. published an account of his campaigns, *Mein Leben und Wirken in Ungarn in* 1848 *und* 1849.

Gor'get (Fr. *gorge*, 'a throat'), a piece of armour which covered the throat. It was retained in the 17th c. after other body armour was disused.

Gor'gias, a celebrated Greek rhetorician, was born at Leontini, in Sicily, about 480 B.C., and lived to the advanced age of 105 or 109. Of his early life little is known. In 427 B.C. he was sent by his fellow-citizens to Athens to solicit aid against the Syracusans. After his return to Leontini his stay was but short; and he seems to have spent the remainder of his long life for the most part at Athens, and Larissa, in Thessaly. G. was the expounder of an art which he deemed superior to all others, and his aim was to enable his pupils to convince by the spell of eloquence alone. He did not profess to impart virtue; and he is said to have preferred the name of rhetorician to that of sophist. Two works ascribed to him are extant, *The Apology of Palamedes* and the *Encomium on Helena*. Their genuineness is admitted by Reiske and Schönborn, but doubted by Foss and others. G. owes much of his reputation to Plato's dialogue, which bears his name.

Gor'go, or **Gor'gon**, according to Homer, one of the frightful shapes in Hades. Hesiod mentions three Gorgons—Stheno, Euryale, and Medusa, daughters of Phorcys and Ceto (hence called *Phorcides*), and assigns them a dwelling-place in the western ocean, in the vicinity of Night and the Hesperides. Later writers place their haunt near Lake Triton in Libya. They are described as winged forms, having hair entwined with serpents, brazen claws, and enormous teeth. Medusa, to whom the name G. is most frequently applied, was the only one of the three who was mortal. According to Ovid and later mythologists, she was originally a very beautiful maiden with luxuriant hair; and had received her terrific visage and serpent locks from Athena as a punishment for having gratified the passion of Poseidon in one of her temples. So frightful was her aspect, that every one who looked on her was turned into stone. She was at last slain by Perseus (q. v.). Athena placed her head in the centre of her shield.

Gorgo'nia, Sea-Shrub, or **Sea-Fan**, a genus of *Cœlenterate* (q. v.) animals belonging to the class *Actinozoa* (q. v.), and to the order *Alcyonaria*. The G. is closely allied to the red coral of commerce, which is, in fact, included in the family *Gorgonidæ*. In this group the cœnosarc (or connecting medium which unites the various and different animals of these compound organisms) is of branched tree-like form, and is permanently rooted to the sea-bed. Each little polyp has a mouth surrounded by eight pinnate tentacles. The spreading coral substance of G. is of a horny and flexible texture, while the living polyps are spread over the extended branches of the flattened organism. *G. flabellum* is a familiar species, and occurs in the W. Indian Seas. The coral substance is usually blackish in hue, but occasionally exhibits various tints.

Gor'ham Controversy was a remarkable episode in the history of the Tractarian revival in the Church of England. Mr. Gorham being presented (1847) to a living in the diocese of Exeter, the bishop refused to institute him until he should submit to an examination on the subject of Baptism. On receiving Mr. Gorham's answers to the forty-nine questions proposed to him 'on the single subject of baptismal efficacy,' the bishop persisted in his refusal to institute, on the ground of unsoundness in doctrine; the whole question at issue between them being whether the efficacy of baptism, in the case of infants, be conditional or unconditional, the bishop holding that it is unconditional, and Mr. Gorham that it is conditional. The Court of Arches, when appealed to by Mr. Gorham, confirmed the bishop's decision, when the judge said:—'The Church has declared that the thing signified is given at the moment. There is no hindrance in the way when infants are baptized, therefore they receive the benefit, whatever it may be, and it is spiritual regeneration according to the formularies of the Church.' The Judicial Committee of the Privy Council, however, being appealed to by Mr. Gorham, reversed the decision of the Court of Arches, and gave a final decision (1850) in favour of the 'Evangelical' view. At least, it declared that the view that the child in baptism is regenerated only if it be one of the elect, or if it be presented in faith, is not inadmissible.

Gorill'a (*Troglodytes gorilla*), one of the highest of the Catarhine, Old World, or anthropoid ('man-like') apes, inhabiting Lower Guinea and Equatorial Africa, and distinguished, among other characteristics, by its large size, the G. attaining a height of between 5 and 6 feet. The genus *Troglodytes* also includes the Chimpanzee (q. v.) (*T. niger*), to which the G. is most nearly related. The distinctive characteristics of this ape are that the arm is longer than the fore-arm, the foot longer than the hand, and both feet and hands broader than in any other ape. The heel is well developed, and the erect posture can therefore be assumed with comparative ease by the G. The thumbs and great toes have well-developed nails; and the first or basal joints of the three middle toes are united by the integument. The points in which the G. approaches most nearly of all the apes to the human type of structure, are the proportions of the leg to the body, the proportions of the hand to the foot, the size of the heel, and the curves of the spine, together with the form of the pelvis. The 'absolute capacity of the cranium' is also closely related to that of the human subject. As measured from a typical skeleton, the spine of the G. measures 27 inches along its front face; the arm 31½ inches without the hand; the leg without the foot 26½ inches. The foot is 11¼ inches, and the hand 9¾ inches long. Certain peculiarities in the skeleton of the G. may be briefly noticed. It has thirteen pairs of ribs, the first lumbar vertebra bearing a pair of ribs—a development occasionally seen in man, who has nominally only twelve pairs of ribs, borne by the twelve dorsal vertebræ. The last lumbar vertebra of the G. frequently becomes ossified with the *sacrum*—an abnormal feature also seen in man. The frontal sinuses of the G.'s skull are large, and the brow ridges well marked. The jaws are largest in proportion to the size of the brain-case in the G. and in the orang. The nasal bones are convex, and rise above the facial level. In the wrist of the G. eight bones are found, as in man, and the thumb is at least one-third the length of the hand. The female G. has a shorter pelvis than the male. The brain of the G. has recently (December 1876) been fully described by Dr. Pansch of Germany, who dissected along with Dr. Bolau a specimen which lived for some time in the Berlin Zoological Gardens (see *Nature*, No. 372, vol. xv. p. 142). In the G. the brain has a capacity of about 35 cubic inches, that of man being over 60 cubic inches. In external appearance, the G. presents a brute-like aspect. The body is covered with very dark brown hair, which has in some cases been described as of black colour. The hairs from the shoulder to the elbow point downwards, those from the elbow to the fingers are directed upwards, and meet the hairs of the upper arm in a tuft at the elbow. The G. has small ears, the tail is abortive, and a large laryngeal sac giving great resonance to the voice is developed. One male appears to mate with several females. The existence of the animal appears to have been first discovered by Dr. Savage of the United States of America, who in 1847 procured the skull of an ape hitherto unknown to zoologists, and which he named the 'G.' In 1861 M. Paul Du Chaillu published his *Explorations in Africa*, and gave a series of descriptions of the G., the truth and correctness of which have been greatly disputed. Making allowance for some exaggeration, Du Chaillu's accounts present no features which render their acceptance a matter of hesitation. It is curious to note that Hanno, the Carthaginian voyager, dating from about 350 B.C., makes mention of an ape-like animal which he named the 'gorilla,' but which may possibly have been the chimpanzee. Of the immense strength and natural ferocity of the G. no doubt can be entertained. The voice is loud and powerful, and the food consists of fruits and leaves. It is an expert climber, and appears to construct 'nests' amid the boughs of trees or in shady places.

Gor'kum, or **Gorinchem**, a strongly fortified town in the province of S. Holland, Netherlands, on the river Merwede, at the point where it is joined by the Linge, and 12 miles E. of Dort. Except the church and the townhouse, the chief buildings are military. G. has a brisk trade in agricultural produce and fish. Its system of relief for the poor is remarkable. Pop. (1875) 8725.

Gör'litz, an old town in Prussian Silesia, on the left bank of the Neisse, and 90 miles W. of Breslau by railway. Its chief ecclesiastical structures are the church of St. Peter and Paul (1423–97), with a splendid organ, and a bell of 12½ tons; the Frauenkirche (1450–90), with a magnificent choir and doorway; and a kreuz-kapelle built on the model of the holy sepulchre. Other notable buildings are the gymnasium (Gothic style), containing a large library; and a town theatre built in 1851. The Neisse is spanned by a bridge 115 feet high and 1500 long. G. is the seat of extensive cotton factories, employing some 2000 men; and among its other manufactures are linens, leather, and tobacco. Pop. (1875) 45,348. G. was strongly fortified till the end of the 12th c.

Gör'res, Jakob Joseph von, a German scholar, journalist, and politician, was born at Coblenz, 25th January 1776. Both by his speeches, and by a journal which he edited, G. directed for years the republican zeal of his native district; but after Napoleon became supreme in France, G. retired from politics in disgust. As a lecturer at Coblenz and at Heidelberg, he discoursed and published on subjects as various as physiology, medieval poetry, and Asiatic mythology. The great national German movement of 1814 reawakened his political energies and patriotic hopefulness, and G. edited the vigorous *Rheinischer Mercur*. The work *Deutschland und die Revolution* (1820) exposed G. to the risk of imprisonment; he fled to France, and busied himself with literature. In 1827 he was invited to occupy the chair of literature in the new university of Munich, and was afterwards known as a zealous Catholic, and defender of Catholic measures. He died 29th January 1848. Among G.'s principal works may be mentioned *Athanasius* (1837); *Die Christliche Mystik* (1836–42); and *Die Japhetiden* (1844). G.'s collected works, 8 vols., appeared in 1854–60. His son, **Guido G.** (born 1805, died 1852), distinguished himself as a poet and as a writer for the young.

Gort'schakoff, a princely Russian family, which claims descent from Rurik, and of which the chief members are:—**Peter**, who held Smolensk against Sigismund of Poland from 1609 to 1611.—**Dmitri**, great grandson of the above, was a popular lyrical poet, who wrote odes, satires, epistles, &c., and died in 1824.—**Alexander**, brother of Dmitri, born in 1764, served against the Turks under Suwarroff, his uncle, became a general in 1798, defeated Marshal Laures at Fleilsberg, was made War Minister in 1811, and died in 1825.—**Peter**, son of Dmitri, born about 1790, fought against the French in the campaigns of 1812 and 1813, was made commander of a division in 1826, and in 1829 governor-general of Western Siberia—the condition of which he greatly bettered. He held commands at the battle of the Alma and at Inkermann.—**Michael**, brother of the above, born in 1795, joined the army, commanded at the sieges of Schumla and Silistria in 1829, and distinguished himself at the battle of Ostrolenka and capture of Warsaw in the Polish campaign of 1831. He was made governor of Warsaw in 1846, took part in the Hungarian war of 1849, led the Russian troops in the Danubian Principalities in 1853, and in 1855 took command of the army in the Crimea. His defence of Sebastopol against the French and English was a triumph of military skill, and he conducted his retreat from the fortress with consummate ability. He was made lieutenant-general of Poland on the close of the war, and died May 30, 1861.—**Alexander Michaelovich**, cousin of the above, was born in 1798, became secretary to the Russian embassy in London in 1824, *chargé d'affairés* at Florence in 1830, and a member of the legation to Vienna in 1832. In 1841 he arranged the marriage of the Grand Duchess Olga of Russia with the Prince Royal of Würtemberg. He represented Russia in the Vienna Conference of 1854, and in 1856 became Minister for Foreign Affairs. In 1870 he announced that Russia would no longer submit to the restrictions on her rights in the Black Sea imposed by the treaty of 1856, and gained his demands at the London Conference of 1871. He is still (1877) Russian Foreign Minister.

Goruckpore' (*Gorakhpur*), the chief town of the District of the same name in the N.W. Province, British India, on the left bank of the Rapti, 430 miles N.W. of Calcutta. Pop. (1872) 51,117. It has an old ruined fort with two mosques, and a Hindu temple with a tank much frequented by pilgrims. The military cantonment lies to the E.—The *district* of G., bounded N. by Nepaul, has an area of 4579 sq. miles, and a pop. (1872) of 2,019,361. It is flat, studded with marshy lakes, and watered by the Gogra, Rapti, Gunduck, and their tributaries. Rice is the staple crop, but wheat, barley, opium, and sugar-cane are also grown. A large trade is conducted with Bengal, by means of the rivers, the chief marts being Burhej, Gopalpore, and G. During the first half of 1876, they were valued at £290,000.

Go'ry-Dew, a common name for *Palmella cruenta*, a cellular plant belonging to the order *Palmelleæ* (q. v.), or green-spored Algæ (q. v.). It occurs on damp walls in the form of gelatinous spots resembling blood, hence its name. It is nearly allied to the Red-snow (q. v.) plant.

Görz, or **Göricz** (Slav. 'the town on the hill'), the capital of a district of the same name, in the Kustenland of Austria, on the Isonzo, 25 miles N.N.W. of Trieste by railway. It lies between the Karste and Tarnovane forests, and has a cathedral and an old castle of the former Counts of G. There are large sugar-refineries, and silk, linen, cotton, and leather industries. Pop. (1869) 15,300.—**G.** or **Gorica Velica**, a town of Austria in Croatia, in the valley of the Save, 10 miles S.S.E. of Agram by railway. Pop. (1869) 8000.

Gosain', or **Goswa'mi** (Sansk. lit. 'one who is master of his passions'), is the term used throughout India for a special class of professed religious mendicants. In S. India, they are chiefly the reputed descendants of the religious reformer, Sankara Acharya; they are gathered into *maths* or convents, and profess celibacy. In N. India, they are generally members of the Vaishnav sect, who may marry and follow secular pursuits; but the name is loosely applied to all sorts of disreputable vagrants.

Gos'hawk (*Astur palumbarius*), a species of *Raptorial* birds belonging to the sub-family *Acciptrinæ*, or that of the sparrow-hawks. In the genus *Astur*, to which the G. belongs, the bill is broad at the base, and compressed at the tip; the nostrils are large and oval, and placed in the middle of a *Cere* (q. v.). The wings are very long, and have their third, fourth, and fifth quills longest. The tarsi are long, and are scaled in front and behind. The G. is found in Europe, Asia, and N. Africa. Its length is about 18 inches. The colour is a grey-brown above; white, beneath; the body, and particularly the under part, being marked with black bars. The legs and toes are yellow. The female G. is a more powerful bird than the male, but neither is able to take long flights. When trained, the G. becomes an adept in the capture of hares and rabbits. The nests are placed on the highest branches of trees, and the eggs, numbering three or four, are of a bluish-white. An allied species is the *Astur Novæ Hollandiæ*, or white eagle of New Holland.

Goshawk.

Go'shen (Heb.) was the part of Egypt where the children of Israel dwelt during the period of their residence in that country (Gen. xlv. 10). According to the best authorities it lies between the desert of Arabia and Palestine on the E., the Pelusiac arm of the Nile on the W., and the Mediterranean on the N., corresponding nearly with the modern *Wadi-t-Tumeylat*.

Gos'lar, ('the town or site on the Gose'), an old town of Prussia, in the S.E. of the province of Hanover, at the foot of the Rammelsberg, on the Gose, 25 miles W. of Halberstadt by railway. It has remains of fortifications, and of a cathedral of 1040, part of an old imperial palace, now used as a corn-magazine, and a Gothic church of 1521. There were formerly (from 986) gold, silver, copper, lead, and zinc mines in the vicinity. Pop. (1875) 9823. G., founded by Heinrich I. about 920, and often an imperial residence, was the seat of splendid diets (in 1009 and 1015), and remained a free city till 1801. It was incorporated with Hanover in 1814. See Crusius, *Geschichte von G.* (1814), and *G. am Harz, sonst und jetzt* (1863).

Gos'pels (Old Eng. *god-spell*, 'good news') are the four memoirs of the life of Christ in the New Testament under the names of Matthew, Mark, Luke, and John.

I. *Their Mutual Relation.*—1. *John v. the Synoptics.*—Even the most careless reader of these books cannot fail to be struck with two circumstances: the marked agreement that exists among the first three, and their common difference from the fourth. In the first place, prior to the arrival of Jesus at Bethany six days before the Passover, John relates only two incidents in common with the other three—the feeding of the 5000 people, and the storm on the Sea of Galilee. But this is not the whole of the difference, neither is the difference a mere diversity of style or plan. It affects the fundamental distribution of the events of Christ's public ministry, if not even the whole conception of his person and teaching. The first three describe Jesus as baptized by John, like many of his countrymen, and not beginning his public ministry till that of John was finished (Matt. iv. 12, 17); confining his labours exclusively to Galilee and the N.; appealing to the Messianic expectations of the time, and teaching the common people, and performing countless miracles as he journeyed from place to place; gradually unfolding to a select few his claims and destiny, while warning them not to reveal the same to the common people (Matt. xvi. 20); and only at the very close of his ministry coming to Jerusalem, where he came into collision with the sacerdotal and rabbinical party, who accomplished his death. Further, his teaching, as set forth in the three, is remarkable for its casual and aphoristic nature, and, with the exception of the Sermon on the Mount, for never expanding into any lengthened argumentation. His public ministry is divided into two distinctly-marked periods—that which was passed in Galilee, and that in Jerusalem; the one introduced by the descent of the Holy Ghost upon him at his baptism; the other, by the Transfiguration. Finally, the Last Supper was an ordinary Jewish Passover. In all these particulars the fourth Gospel stands out in decided contrast to the first three, but is in no sense contradictory of them. It differs, but does not disagree. Thus it omits the baptism altogether, and presents the Messiahship of Jesus as a thing distinctly comprehended from the first (ch. i. 29-34, 41, 45), indeed, openly proclaimed by himself (ch. i., ii., iii.). In keeping with this is the position given to the incident of the expulsion of the traders from the temple, namely, at the very beginning of his ministry, instead of the end, as in the three. Instead of the daily miracle-working of the three, the fourth gives what is evidently a selection of (seven) miracles. The time of Christ is also divided almost equally between Galilee and Jerusalem from the first, and he attends two, if not three, Passovers in the Holy City. But in nothing is the difference more marked than in the discourses delivered by Christ. The parables and short aphoristic sayings of the three give place in the fourth to long argumentative discourses. Instead of a varied 'miscellany of history and doctrine, of miracle and parable, there is an almost uninterrupted flow of exhortation and disputation.' Finally, according to this Gospel, Christ was crucified on the day of the Jewish Passover. Regarding the explanation of the difference here briefly sketched, critics are greatly divided. Some maintain that the explanation first broached by Eusebius (*H. E.*, iii. 4), namely, 'that John, writing last, at the close of the 1st c., had seen the other G., and purposely abstained from writing anew what they had sufficiently recorded,' is quite satisfactory. Others maintain that it is impossible to harmonise the two forms of the narrative; and that the theory of Clement of Alexandria (*apud* Eus. *H. E.*, vi. 4), properly understood, is nearer the truth, namely, 'that whereas the three earlier G. contained the *corporeal* side of the history, John . . . produced a *spiritual* Gospel.

2. *The Synoptics, per se.*—Not less remarkable than the variation of the fourth Gospel from the first three is their general harmony among themselves; from which harmony they have received the name of the Synoptics. 'If the synoptic text be divided into 124 sections, 47 are common to the 3; 12 are in Matthew and Mark, 2 in Matthew and Luke, 6 in Mark and Luke; while 17 are in Matthew alone, 2 in Mark, and 38 in Luke alone.' The examples in which all the three verbally coincide are not numerous, and contain generally only from one to three sentences. The examples of verbal agreement between Matthew and Mark are very numerous; between Mark and Luke they are but slight. These verbal coincidences are more numerous in reporting the words of Jesus, or the words of others spoken in connection with his language, than in the narrative parts; being in the proportion in Matthew of about one to two, in Mark of one to four, and in Luke of one to ten. But, notwithstanding this similarity of matter, there is great diversity among them in its arrangement. Exact chronological sequence is not found in any of them. Matthew comes nearest to it. In arrangement Mark agrees more nearly with Luke than Matthew.

II. *Origin of the G.*—In view of the above peculiarities, a great number of theories have been propounded to account for the origin of the G. (1.) The first that may be mentioned is, that the Evangelists made use of each other's work. On this theory many critics (*e.g.*, Grotius, Mill, Wetstein, Griesbach, &c.) have tried to determine which of the three was the first written, which was copied from the first, and which from the other two; it being always understood that the fourth came last of all. Of the six possible combinations, each has found advocates. The difficulty of this theory, whatever the order adopted, is the omission by the second and third of matter inserted by the first, which indicates an arbitrary selection, for which there are no apparent grounds. (2.) The theory of Eichhorn (*Einleitung ins N. T.*), which was followed by Marsh (Edn. of Michaelis) with certain modifications, was that the G. were derived from a common written source or sources: the portions common to the three, from a certain document from which they all drew; that the sections common to Matthew and Mark, but not to Luke, were additions made in the copies used by Matthew and Mark, but not in the copy used by Luke; and that the portions common to Mark and Luke, but not to Matthew, were additions made in the copies used only by Mark and Luke. (3.) Both of the above theories are now to a great extent abandoned; a third, adopted by Gieseler (*Historisch-krit. Versuch*, 1818), is that they were derived from oral tradition, after it had assumed a fixed form. The objection to this theory is, that while accounting for many resemblances and discordances in the G., 'it fails to explain their numerous verbal coincidences.' This objection the Archbishop of York, in his exposition of the theory (Smith's *Dict. of the Bible*), endeavours to meet as follows :—The preaching of the apostles must have been in great part historical, 'of such a kind as to be to the hearers what the reading of lessons from the G. is to us ;' their preaching would probably begin to take one settled form during the first years of their ministry ; the guidance of the Holy Spirit, 'which consisted not in whispering to them facts which they had not witnessed, but rather in reviving the fading remembrance, and throwing out into their true importance events and sayings that had been esteemed too lightly at the time they took place,' would supply for a time such aid as made a written Gospel unnecessary ; 'there is nothing unnatural in the supposition that the apostles intentionally uttered their witness in the same order, and even, for the most part, in the same form of words ;' the vernacular language was the Syro-Chaldæan, which was a poor and scanty language, and the Greek, as used by the Jews, partook of the poverty of the speech which it replaced ; and while modern taste abhors a repetition of the same phrases as monotonous, the simplicity of the Evangelists, and their language and education, would all keep them from having any such feeling. It is necessary for the completeness and success of this theory to assume that the G. were written by the apostles, or during their lifetime. (4.) A fourth theory, held by more 'advanced' critics, is that earlier G. were used in the composition of the later ones ; otherwise, the writers used earlier G., 'with other written documents now lost, some of them preserved only in fragments, others entirely unknown except in name,' not excluding oral tradition, although 'it formed a small element in the composition of each, because it had been incorporated into written collections of the evangelical history when the canonical G. appeared.'

III. *Language.*—The earliest MSS. of the G. we have cannot be dated earlier than the 4th c., but these are understood to be copies of the originals as they first appeared, with the exception, perhaps, of Matthew (q. v.). Consequently as these MSS. are all in Greek, it is assumed that that language was understood by the people of Palestine to whom Jesus and the apostles preached, and for whose instruction the G. were written. Thus Dean Alford says (*Com. Acts* vii. 1) that 'Greek was almost universally understood at Jerusalem ;' and Dr. Roberts (*Discussions on the G.*, Lond. 1862) maintains 'that Greek was, in several important respects, the then prevailing language of Palestine, that it was, in particular, the language of literature and commerce, the language generally employed in public intercourse, the language which a religious teacher would have no hesitation in selecting and making use of, for the most part, as the vehicle for conveying his instructions, whether orally or in writing, and the language accordingly which was thus employed both by our Lord and his apostles.' As this is a question which has an important bearing on the origin of the G., it may be well to inquire briefly into the actual facts of the case. If Greek were understood at Jerusalem in the time of Jesus, it must have been still more familiar in the time of Josephus, a generation later. Yet Josephus himself says in the last chapter of his *Antiquities*, 'I am so bold as to say, now I have so completely performed the work I proposed to myself to do, that no other person, whether he were a Jew or a foreigner, had he ever so great an inclination for it, could so accurately deliver these accounts to the Greeks as is done in these books. For . . . I have also taken a great deal of pains to obtain the learning of the Greeks, and understand the elements of the Greek language, although I have so long accustomed myself to speak our own tongue that I cannot pronounce Greek with sufficient exactness. For our nation does not encourage those that learn the languages of many nations.' In his treatise *Contra Apion*, he tells us (i. 9), 'I sold them (the books of the *Wars of the Jews*) also to many of our own men who understood Greek, among whom were Julius Africanus, Herod (of Chalcis), and King Agrippa;' and in the preface to the *Wars of the Jews*, that he had translated those books into Greek which he had formerly composed in the language of his own country. Again, when at the siege of Jerusalem with Titus, he was several times employed as an interpreter. He was the only man who understood the deserters, and was sent several times to parley with the besieged in their native tongue (*Contra Apion*) ; and in the *Book of the Wars* (bk. vi.) he gives in Greek a long address which he delivered to them, by command of Cæsar, in the Hebrew language. The above information furnished by Josephus, who was the only Jew born in Judea in those times whose testimony we have before us independently of the G., seems to afford evidence that Greek was not generally understood at Jerusalem, even by the higher classes of the people. And although the question of the original language of Matthew has been keenly discussed, this evidence, as an element in the problem of the origin of the G. generally, has not received the attention which it deserves. See MATTHEW, MARK, LUKE, JOHN, GOSPEL OF ; Smith's *Dict. of the Bible* (1863) ; Norton's *Int. Evid. of the Genuineness of the G.* (Bost. 1855) ; Westcott's *Introd. to the study of the G.* (Camb. 1860) ; Marsh's Michaelis' *Introd. to N. T.* (1803) ; Tischendorf's *Wann wurden unsere Evangelien verfasset?* (1867, Eng. trans. 1869.)

Gospel Side of the Altar is the N., on which side the G. was read in the time of St. Augustine, in allusion to Jer. iii. 12. At Rome the deacon turned to the S., because the men sat there (1 Cor. xiv. 35), or rather as defying Satan (Isa. xiv. 13). In some parts of England the G. S. of the A. was the S. side as late as the 15th c.

Gos'port ('God's port'), a fortified seaport of Hampshire, on the W. side of Portsmouth harbour, opposite Portsmouth, and 14 miles S.E. of Southampton, with which it is connected by railway. A steam ferry and floating bridge give it communication with Portsmouth ; and the chief public works are the Royal Clarence Victualling Yard, comprising large granaries, a brewery, a steam-bakery capable of making 10 tons of biscuit in an hour, and the Haslar shipyard for the repair of gunboats. The Haslar Hospital (1762), one mile to the S., can accommodate 2000 invalid sailors. G. has some shipbuilding, and manufactures of iron anchors, chain cables, &c. Pop. (1871) 7366.

Goss, Sir John, an eminent composer, was born at Fareham in Hants in 1800. In 1811 he became one of the 'young gentlemen' of St. James' Chapel Royal, and in 1856 was made composer to the Chapels-Royal. He was organist of St. Paul's Cathedral from 1838 to 1872, and till recently Professor of Harmony at the Royal Academy. G. has published an *Introduction to Harmony and Thorough Bass* (1833), a collection of voluntaries (1864), and numerous glees and anthems. He composed the music for the funeral ceremony of the Duke of Wellington in 1852, and for the thanksgiving service for the Prince of Wales' recovery from fever in 1872 ; on the latter occasion he was knighted.

Goss'amer, the name given to the light and almost invisible filaments which sometimes exist in great quantities in the air, and which are secreted by certain species of Spiders (q. v.). Various explanations were formerly given of the formation of G. threads, which, when loaded with dewdrops and extended from plant to plant, present an appearance which has frequently been alluded to in poetical works as symbolical of an airy, graceful, and ethereal substance. The exact relation of G. threads to the silky secretion of spiders is not well determined. The theory has been advanced that G. represents the secretion of young spiders, but this explanation is not a probable one, as the G.-producing spiders do not appear to be capable of producing any other kind of thread ; and insects are not frequently detained by these slight threads. The idea has also been thrown out that possibly the water or dewdrops attracted by the G. threads may be acceptable to the spiders. Altogether the subject is one which requires further elucidation—at any rate, as to the exact functions of the G. threads ; while the more exact determination of the species of spiders which secrete this substance will materially aid our understanding of the uses subserved by G.

Gossan'der (*Mergus*), the name of a well-known genus of Natatorial birds, belonging to the family *Anatidæ* or ducks, and to the special sub-family *Merginæ*. It is distinguished by the straight, compressed bill, which has its edges prominently toothed, by the short and rounded tail, and by the front toes being webbed, while the hinder toe has only an edging of membrane. The G. (*Mergus merganser*) arrives in Britain in November, and migrates northwards in March. A few specimens may be found remaining throughout the year in Britain. The northern coasts are the habitat of these birds, which subsist on fishes, and secure their prey by means of the sharp-toothed projections of the bill. These projections are merely prominences of the horny lining of the bill, and are in no sense to be regarded as physiologically corresponding to teeth. The average length of the G. is 2 feet. Its colour is a deep metallic green on the neck and upper part of the back, the latter region being black, and the tail dark grey. The wing-coverts are white, and the breast and belly of a ruddy buff hue. The bill and legs are scarlet. The female has a reddish-brown head and neck, and a grey back. The nest is constructed in the neighbourhood of water, and the eggs, which number six or seven, are of a pale buff colour.

Gosse'lies, a town of Belgium, province of Hainault, 4 miles N.W. of Charleroi. There are coal-mines in the neighbourhood, and G. has manufactures of woollen cloth, hats, &c., tanneries and bleachfields. Pop. (1870) 7000.

Gossyp'ium, the generic name of the cotton plant. See COTTON.

Go'tha, the capital of the duchy of Sachsen-Koburg-Gotha, is situated on the Leine Canal, and about 15 miles W. of Erfurt by rail. It lies just on the northern border of the Thuringian Forest, and besides being the most beautiful town in this region, is also the most prosperous. It is surrounded by pretty avenues, and is handsomely built. The ducal palace Friedenstein was erected in 1643, and contains a fine picture gallery, and other collections of valuables and curiosities, with a library of 200,000 volumes and 3000 MSS. The park is admirably laid out. The five churches and other public buildings are not very remarkable; the observatory has been newly refitted. G. is the seat of Perthes' geographical publishing house, and has considerable manufactures of porcelain, tobacco, sugar, paper, leather, shoes, sausages, and musical instruments. Pop. (1875) 22,928.

Gotha, Almanach de (Ger. *Gothaischer Almanach*), is a universal political and statistical compend, published annually at Gotha since 1764 by the firm of Perthes. It gives the pedigree and dignities of all royal and princely families, the members of the various governments, the diplomatic and other public officials, and a multitude of tables illustrating the constitutional features, the area, population, army, navy, the national finance, and the commerce of all nations. The almanack gives further a chronicle of the chief political events of the past year, and an annual necrology; and within its 1000 small pages, it contains probably more information than any other work of the same size. Originally appearing in German, the A. de G. was issued in French alone from the time of Napoleon I. down to the restoration of the German Empire; now it is published in both languages.

Gö'thaland, or **Gö'taland** (also called **Göta Rike**, 'the Gothic kingdom'), southmost of the three provinces of Sweden, embracing eight läns or districts with the islands Gotland and Oland. Area, 28,126 sq. miles; pop. (1874) 1,991,021. The surface, though in general mountainous, is well watered and wooded, and presents many fertile tracts. The chief river is the Götha or Göta, once unnavigable from cataracts (Trolhättan, &c.), but now so fitted with canals and locks that vessels can reach Lake Venern, from whence the Göta Canal affords free passage to the Baltic. The chief towns are Göteborg, Malmö, Norrköping, Carlskrona, Jönköping, Lund, and Calmar. To Englishmen it possesses a special interest as the native land of the hero Beówulf (q. v.) whose adventures have been celebrated in one of the oldest and greatest of English poems. See SWEDEN.

Go'thard, St., the name of a group of the Helvetian Alps, having an extreme height in Tritthorn of 9852 feet, and of a mountain pass and carriage way 6867 feet, from Altdorf on Lake Lucerne to the Valentino (*Vallis Lepontina*), or valley of the Ticino and the Lago Maggiore. The road was made in 1820–32, and suffered greatly from two terrible storms of 1834 and 1839. The Sasso di San Gottardo (8235 feet) rises above the summit of the pass. There are several hotels on the road, and near the summit is a hospice, erected by the canton of Ticino, with fifteen beds, receiving yearly some 10,000 visitors.

Gö'theborg, or **Gö'teborg** (Ger. and Eng. *Gothenburg*), the chief town of a län of the same name, and the second port in Sweden after Stockholm, from which it is distant 145 miles W.S.W. by railway, stands near the mouth of Göta river. In the last half of the 18th c. it grew rapidly through its great herring fishery, on the decline of which it profited greatly by the 'Continental system,' as it became a depôt for English colonial goods. G. has been steadily increasing, especially since the completion of the Göta Canal and the western railway; and its fine harbour has now an extensive foreign traffic. In 1874 there belonged to the port 240 vessels of 25,000 tons. The town is regularly built, and in the part within the moats intersected with canals crossed by twenty-four iron bridges. Pop. (1874) 63,748. The chief industries are shipbuilding, linen and cotton weaving, and brewing. G. is well provided with educational and benevolent institutions, and its peculiar public-house system has of late years excited attention in England.

Goth'ic Ar'chitecture. The Gothic style of architecture is directly descended from the Romanesque, an adaptation of the classical Roman form to the requirements of Christian worship, and which continued to be the prevailing style of the early churches down to the 6th and 7th centuries. After the destruction of the Roman Empire by successive tribes of barbarians, and during the period of confusion among the Western nations of Europe that followed that event, the practice of the arts was suspended, and the traditions of Romanesque architecture appear to have been partly lost or abandoned. When the practice of elaborating their places of worship by the nations of Western Europe was resumed, the prevailing system of architecture was found to embody what were believed to be 'Barbarian' ideas, and the name 'Gothic' was consequently applied to it by the Italians. G. A., the architecture of the pointed arch and vault, first appeared in the Isle de France (Paris) and its neighbourhood during 1170–1200, and in the 13th c. extended all over the N.W. and some parts of the S. of Europe. It is by no means to be inferred here that the European medieval architects were the discoverers of the arch and vault. Stone arches, perfect in construction, have been discovered in the porches of the pyramids, and belonging to an age between the era of Solomon and that of Cambyses, and Layard discovered both circular and pointed arches forming underground vaults at Nimroud of the 8th or 9th c. before our era. The arch was also thoroughly understood by the Pelasgian Greeks, by the Romans, and, indeed, by all the great building nations of antiquity. The true Gothic Pointed style, however, was invented in the N. of France toward the close of the 12th c. From the N. of France the new architectural method was carried into Normandy and across to England with astonishing rapidity. G. A. was only invented thirty years before the close of the 12th c., yet the choir of Canterbury Cathedral was rebuilt in this style in 1174–85.

The Christian architects of the 12th c. had recourse to the employment of groined vaults, pointed arches, and flying buttresses, which enabled them to dispense with the massive walls of the Norman builders. The introduction of high-pointed arches, in which the weight of superincumbent wall rested upon a single point (the *crown* of the arch), and thus diminished the powerful outward thrust of the round or heavily-loaded arch to the utmost possible extent, gave quite a new character to the architecture of the time. The walls were now light and *lofty*, and the supporting piers were made correspondingly light, there being no longer any necessity for constructing them of the vast Norman proportions. The result was the Gothic cathedral with its spacious nave and choir, its airy spire, its infinite variety of graceful and fanciful decoration.

The name given by the French to the style of architecture under consideration, and which arose in France, is *Ogival*. (See OGEE.) Its essential characteristics are that the arches are always pointed; the pillars are attenuated to a point at which all resemblance to the classic column ends, and they are frequently combined and grouped together into a *sheaf* of columns; the mouldings, cornices, and the capitals are entirely different from those of the Romanesque style; and the rectangular surfaces, the pilasters, and entablature of classic architecture no longer exist. The elements of the design in G. A., or Ogival architecture, are much more slender than in the ancient styles; and instead of the flat surfaces and strongly-marked features of classic construction, there is a constant repetition and multiplication, all but confusion, of details. It may be said that the openings, the doors and windows, are the characteristics of G. A., instead of the solidly-constructed portions—columns, entablatures, &c., of the ancient art. Vertical lines predominate in the later, as horizontal lines do in the early style. The outline of the pillars is carried up to the vault, which is divided by the prolonged stems into numerous regular compartments; and between these compartments and the windows of the clerestory, the form of the triforium, and the decoration of the nave, a subtle harmony is preserved. Finally, the buttresses have a considerable outward slope, and variety and interest are given to the lines of the roof by the pinnacles and towers which pass through or rise above them. During the three centuries in which G. A. prevailed in France—from the close of the 12th c. to the classic revival of the commencement of the 16th c.—the style underwent continuous development. There are, therefore, several phases in which, at different times, the art manifests itself. Owing to the length of time employed in building a cathedral, it often happens that several of these phases of development may be observable in the same structure. In France, the style named *Ogival Primaire*, or *Gothique à Lancettes*, prevailed from the close of the 12th c. to the end of the 13th c. It owes the latter name to the high-pointed style of its windows, arcades, &c. In this style the doorways, which are deeply recessed into the wall, are often divided into two bays by a central pillar. The arch which surrounds the entrances is enriched with numerous mouldings, and the sides (jambs) are decorated with pillars standing free from the wall. Similar pillars enrich the windows, niches, &c. The windows are usually long and narrow, and they often occur in groups of two, three, and sometimes five together. Above such a group a pointed arch frequently rises, and the space between the apex of the arch and the window-heads is often pierced with a circular, trefoil, or quatrefoil opening. The *Second Ogival style*, or *Style Gothique Rayonnant*, is regarded as the completely developed form, and existed in perfection during the 14th c. Without losing severity and sublimity of form, it shows all the lightness and elegance compatible with the inspiring religious idea of which the churches and cathedrals of the period named were the symbols. The churches of the Rayonnant or Second Ogival do not differ in any essential particulars from those of the Primary Ogival style. They show, however, considerable difference in details. The windows and doorways are much larger, and the mullions that divide them are more slender and more numerous. The tracery of the window becomes more complicated, the forms, which are remarkably varied, being for the most part geometrical. The great circular *rose-windows* of this period were on an immense scale. Strassburg Cathedral is the best example of this perfect style of French Gothic. The *Third Ogival style* inaugurated the period of decline. During the 14th c. immense progress had been made in the *technique* of the art. Stone had become, so to speak, as ductile as wax in the hands of the builders, who had surmounted every difficulty of construction. There was now a constant temptation to attempt *tours de force*, with the view of doing better than, or at least of doing differently from, their predecessors. The consequence was that the architecture of the 15th c. became more remarkable for audacity and fantastic invention than for purity of taste. Feats of construction were attempted in stone that could only suitably be executed in metal, and church architecture now began to lose the gravity of religious art. This period of decadence set in at the same time in France, in Germany, and in England. In France the debased form of the art was known as Flamboyant (q. v.), while in England it became known as Perpendicular (q. v.).

The new era in architecture had already been inaugurated in England in the middle of the 11th c. During the Heptarchy, when the dominant race was Saxon or Danish, the building enterprise of king and noble was inconsiderable. After the Norman conquest in 1066, when a brilliant inventive nobility and a cultivated and wealthy clergy took possession of the country, the rude Saxon churches were superseded by edifices designed by foreign architects in the Norman or late Romanesque style, the distinctive feature of which was its massiveness. But though heavy from the clumsiness of its enormous piers and round arches, it must be stated that the Norman nave in some instances remains to this day unsurpassed for impressiveness. The vivifying influence of Norman culture continued to animate the architectural art of England for about four centuries. From the date of the building of Canterbury Cathedral (q. v.) the national architectural style of the country has been Gothic. Originally foreign, the style soon became naturalised on English soil. From the earliest times the extreme length of the English churches and cathedrals in proportion to their breadth has given to these structures a peculiar and original character. It was customary on the Continent during the middle ages to give to churches the proportion of about 4 in length to 1 in breadth. Canterbury and Winchester Cathedrals, which were built under French supervision, were originally less than 5 in length to 1 in breadth; but the early English architects were so convinced that greater length in proportion to breadth would give greatly increased artistic effect, that they increased the proportions of these great cathedrals to 7 to 1. Again, the English plans, even of the churches of the Norman period, were further peculiar for the great height of the nave, and consequently they vastly excel the Continental cathedrals for pictorial effect. York Minster, mainly of the 13th and 14th centuries, is one of the noblest

York Minster.

cathedrals in the world. Originality of plan and of constructive details was cultivated with great success in Yorkshire, in which there was great activity in church-building during the 12th c., but which, from its remote distance from the S. coast, remained practically unaffected by the influence of foreign architects. Thus it happened that when Lincoln was rebuilt (1200), the English style was distinct from the Norman or French. (See EARLY ENGLISH.) In Salisbury Cathedral (1220–58) the plan and general arrangements are not only thoroughly original, but remarkably beautiful, and in its design the English nation, for the first time, asserted that national scorn and independence of foreign interference, 'which,' says Fergusson, 'eventually led to the reformation,' and he might have added, to the decay, of ecclesiastical art in Britain. But perhaps the most original and the boldest of the great distinctive conceptions of English architects was the vaulted octagon at the intersection of Ely Cathedral, built by Alan of Walsingham in 1322. It is 'the only true Gothic dome in existence,' and is 'surpassingly beautiful' (Fergusson). After the death of Edward III. (see DECORATED STYLE), few really great architectural works were commenced in England. The Decorated style existed from 1272 to 1377, after which the finest age of G. A. in England is at an end. Still, though English middle-age architects appear, after the close of the 14th c., to lose something in wealth of spontaneous invention, and become somewhat formal in their treatment of exteriors (see PERPENDICULAR), the feeling for beauty of ornamental work was not yet to decay till at least the royal chapels of Windsor, Westminster, and Cambridge, and other fascinating fan-roofed buildings, were finished, with which the true G. A. of England went out 'in a blaze of glory' under the Tudors. See FAN TRACERY.

Domestic Architecture.—It is a curious circumstance, that of *lay* buildings, as distinct from cathedrals and churches, England cannot show a single *municipal* building in Gothic, while in *Castles* (q. v.) or Gothic military structures she is richer than any country in Europe. The mansions, also, manor-houses, granges, &c., of the latest Gothic period, the Tudor, usually called the Elizabethan (see ELIZABETHAN ARCHITECTURE)—the domestic establishments of nobles and gentry after the period of the

Restoration—which, with their spacious halls, heavily mullioned windows rich in stained glass, and their appearance of peaceful, sunny comfort, are specially beautiful examples of Domestic Gothic in England. The universities, colleges, and the Eton, Winchester, and other schools, are noble examples of semi-ecclesiastical foundations in late Perpendicular. Although, with the construction of the churches and cathedrals of the 13th and 14th centuries, the vitality of Gothic as a pure style of construction came to an end, yet many great schools, &c., in which a futile attempt to reproduce the style was made, continued to be built down to the death of Queen Elizabeth (1602). But by this time the great object for which Gothic had been invented—the suitable celebration of a gorgeous religious ceremonial by which an unlettered nation might be instructed, impressed, and governed—had ceased to exist,and after the Reformation, as soon as other means for the instruction of the people were provided, the Gothic cathedral was employed for other purposes, the Gothic style of architecture died out, and even its traditions, its constructive principles and processes were forgotten by English architects. Little wonder, then, that when Horace Walpole attempted to reproduce the glories of Westminster Abbey in a suburban villa near Twickenham, he performed an act which has immortalised him more surely than his cleverest letter or his best story—in the ridicule of posterity. Still the attempt awakened an ignorant interest in Gothic, and since 1750 there has been a sort of Gothic revival throughout the land, until, at the present day, a large class of persons advocate Gothic indiscriminately for churches, cottages, villas, assembly-rooms, law-courts, and houses of parliament.

Gothic Architecture in Scotland.—Among the old churches of Scotland, one of the most characteristic and beautiful is that of Leuchars or Dalmeny, in which the details are at once rich, bold, and elegant, and the ornament most skilfully distributed. The churches of Jedburgh and Kelso are of the end of the 12th or the beginning of the 13th centuries. Much of the decoration is of the Early English period. Kirkwall Cathedral was founded in 1137. The arch of the tower and the vaulting are in the Gothic of the 14th c. Glasgow Cathedral, the best preserved, is also the best Gothic work in the country. Its crypt is unrivalled in Britain, perhaps in Europe, for peculiarity of solid construction, rich vaulting, and variety of perspective. The cathedral of Elgin, in the Decorated or Edwardian style, was probably the most beautiful building in Scotland. Next to it was Melrose, a great Cistercian abbey, originally founded by David I. in 1136. The building erected by the 'sair saunt for the croun' disappeared in the Wars of the Succession, and the present ruins are the remains of a new monastery begun in the reign of Robert Bruce, and not finished for nearly 250 years. It is a specimen of the Perpendicular or Lancastrian style. The tracery and carvings are of unsurpassable excellence. Scott thus speaks of them—

> 'The moon on the east oriel shone,
> Through slender shafts of shapely stone,
> By foliaged tracery combined:
> Thou would'st have thought some fairy's hand
> 'Twixt poplars straight the osier wand
> In many a freakish knot had twined;
> Then framed a spell when the work was done,
> And changed the willow wreaths to stone.'

Roslyn Chapel (1446) is believed to owe its structure and ornament to a Spanish source. Holyrood Chapel was originally founded in 1128, but its remains are of the Decorated style of the 13th c. Much of its ornamentation has a rich but foreign look. St. Andrew's Cathedral was probably not inferior to Elgin and Melrose in beauty of ornamentation. Doorways in St. Giles', Edinburgh, and Pluscarden Abbey are beautiful examples of the round arch beautifully enriched. The fine remains on Iona are of Continental design.

Gothic Architecture in France.—The principal French works of the first epoch (corresponding with that of Early English) are the cathedrals of Sens, Amiens, Reims, St. Denis, Fontenay Abbey, La Chapelle (Paris), the churches of Pontigny and St. Germen. Of the second epoch (corresponding with our Decorated), are the churches of St. Ouen, Rouen, and parts of the cathedrals of Rouen, Tours, Amiens, Paris, Bayeux, Poictiers, Nevers, Narbonne. Of the third epoch, the Flamboyant (q. v.), are the churches of St. Nisier at Lyon, Pont l'Evêque, Caudebec, Louvois, St. Brieux cathedral.

Gothic Architecture in Germany.—The chief examples of German Gothic are—First epoch, the nave at St. Gereon at Köln, the Madonna church at Treves, St. Elizabeth at Marburg, the choirs of the cathedrals at Magdeburg, Meissen, and Köln, the naves of the minsters at Strassburg and Freiburg, and the cathedrals at Halberstadt and Minden; Second epoch, the nave and aisles of Meissen cathedral, choir of St. Stephen's at Vienna, the church of Lamberti and that of Our Lady at Munster; Third epoch, the church of Our Lady at Esseingen, St. Lorenz, and St. Sebald at Nuremburg, St. Peter and St. Paul at Gorlitz, and Church in the Fields at Soest. See Lubke's *Ecclesiastical Art in Germany*, Fergusson's *History of Architecture*, Ruskin's *Seven Lamps of Architecture*, works of Violet-le-Duc, &c.

Goths. Though the term Gothic is sometimes used as synonymous with Teutonic, the G. were only the chief of the Teutonic tribes who broke up the Roman Empire. According to one derivation, Goth or Yuth signifies 'war;' while Dr. Latham asserts that G. was not the aboriginal name of the race, but was given to them after they came to the mouths of the Danube, the land of the Getal, 'as the Kentings of England took their name from the Celtic Kent.' The Lithuanians, he says, were first called *Gothini* or *Gothones* by the Sclavonic peoples. The G. in all likelihood come originally from Scandinavia, whence Gotha-land, and in the earliest historic times seem to have held the Prussian coast from the Vistula to Braunsberg. In Pliny and Tacitus G. are mentioned as dwelling near the Baltic, and Ptolemy speaks of the Guthones, a tribe living E. of the Vistula. In the 3d c. the G. had spread over the S. of Russia and along the Danube into Hungary. In the reign of Philip (244–249) they seized Dacia, and in 250, being assailed by Decius, almost wholly destroyed a Roman army near Philippopolis. In 251 they routed Decius with terrible carnage near Forum Trebonii, and from about 250 to about 270 made piratical expeditions in the Euxine, and ravaged the Greek and Illyrian coasts. Though they were severely beaten by Claudius in 269, the Romans were forced in 272 to yield them Dacia, where they remained for the next fifty years at peace with the empire. In 332 they crossed the Danube under an Alaric, but were repulsed, and did not again attack the Romans until the latter half of the 4th c., when their dominion stretched from the Black to the Baltic Sea. At that time they were split into two great divisions, the Ostro-G. ('East G.') or Grutungs, who lay between the Volga and the Dniester, the Visi-G. ('West G.') or Thervings or Thüringer, who lay mainly between the Dniester and the Theiss. They were beginning to become Arian Christians, chiefly through the teachings of Bishop Wulfila or Ulfilas, when in 376 the Huns, guided, says the Gothic legend, across the steppes by a magic hind, fell upon them, defeated their great king Ermanaric ('powerful warrior'), and forced most of the Visi-G. to cross the Danube, and with the Roman permission to settle in Mœsia. Being ill-treated by the Romans, who established a slave trade in the Gothic children, they rose against the empire, routed the Roman general Lupicinus, and in 378 overthrew and killed Valens at Adrianople—a crushing disaster from which the Roman power never recovered. Recruited by great bands from the N., the G. now became so powerful that the Romans sought to avert destruction by hiring them as mercenaries, and conferring imperial offices on their leaders, a policy which was partly successful, until, after the death of Theodosius (395), the great chief Alaric (q. v.) led the West G. into Greece and then into Italy, from which, however, he was forced to retire. But in 410 he sacked Rome, and his successor, King Athaulf ('helping father'), having married Placidia, sister of the Emperor Honorius, passed into Spain and here founded a Visi-Gothic kingdom which lasted until the 8th c. (See HISTORY OF SPAIN.) It seemed at this time that the G. might raise a great western empire, but they wasted their strength by dividing into small bands, and their Arian creed was a barrier to their union with the inhabitants of Gaul and Italy. Athaulf was succeeded by Wallia (415–418), who aided the Romans against the Vandals and Alans, and was followed by Theodoric I. (418–451), son of Alaric. When the Huns (q. v.) under Attila swept down on the empire, the Visi-G., under Theodoric, united against them with the Romans and drove them back in the great battle of Chalons—the *Hunnenschlacht*—in 451, a victory which saved European civilisation. The history of the Visi-Gothic kingdom in the West belongs to the history of Spain, on which, notwithstanding its destruction by the Mohammedans in the 8th c., it exerted a great influence. The Visi-G., who were at first severed from the original Spaniards by their heresy, afterwards appeared as the deliverers of the country from the Moors, and regained their old position as its rulers. The early Visi-Gothic customs helped greatly to mould the Castilian institutions, and were not displaced by the Justinian law until the 14th c. Another kingdom, more brilliant, but much shorter lived than the Visi-Gothic in Spain, was founded by the Ostro-G. At the end of the 4th c. many of the latter yielded to the Huns, and the Romans refusing to allow them to settle within the imperial boundaries, they again and again ravaged the frontier, but sustained a severe check in 386 when seeking to cross the Danube. They afterwards settled in Asia Minor, and on Attila's invading Southern Europe, joined the Huns in large numbers, and fell fighting against the Visi-G. and Romans at Chalons. Afterwards the majority of them settled in Pannonia, and the Emperor Leo agreed to pay them 300 pounds of gold yearly if they would leave the Eastern Empire in peace. Theodoric (q. v.), who became King of the Ostro-G. in 475, after fighting for and against the Byzantine Emperor Zeno, gathered together his people along with other Teutons, fought his way into Italy, where he overthrew Odoacer at Verona in 488, and established a great Gothic kingdom with a Roman organisation. He ruled with admirable justice and firmness, and restored Italy to peace and prosperity; but after his death in 526, civil war broke out among the G., and Queen Amalasuentha invited Justinian to seize Italy. The Ostro-G. maintained a lingering struggle with Belisarius, but that general's successor, Narses, defeated their king Totila in 542 at Tagina, and after a desperate battle at Vesuvius, where Teia, the last of the Ostro-Gothic kings was slain, the remnant of his people withdrew from Italy, and henceforth disappear as a nation, being absorbed in other Teutonic peoples. Their kingdom fell mainly through their intestine strifes, the enervating effects of a southern climate, and because, holding aloof from the conquered races, they could not, when cut off from their northern kinsmen, sufficiently recruit their numbers in the war with Rome.

The Gothic invasions are often compared to a deluge, as if the G. had swept into the empire by vast united movements, whereas they really destroyed it by endless incursions and battles, by ravaging it in small bands, by breaking off fragments from the imperial dominion. Most of these leaders seem to have been awed by the Roman greatness, and many of them seem to have dreamed of themselves filling the emperor's throne. The G. who seized on Italy, Spain, and part of Gaul were not mere destroyers, but allowed the Romans to keep their own laws and customs, and even portions of the land. As they were, however, smaller in number than the Romanised peoples, they gradually lost their distinct language and manners. (See ROMANCE LANGUAGES.) When they began to stream into the empire, the G. were believers in Wodenism (see NORTHERN MYTHOLOGY), and were ruled by two races of kings, both held to be descended from Woden—the Amalungs ('heavenly race'), and the Balthungs ('bold race'). They were a tall, fair-haired people, said to be the noblest and least cruel of all the Teutons, and were considerably removed from savagery when they first came down to the lower Danube. Their foremost warriors prided themselves on the skill with which they could forge armour and weapons, and the war Geats or Geátas who appear in *Beówulf*, and who were a section of the Gothic race, are described as equipped with chain-mail, helmets with plumes and devices, with dress of linen and hide, and gold and silver ornaments. Their lands were chiefly tilled by slaves, most of whom were probably Sclavs, and according to Dr. Latham, they numbered among their fighting men a large Germanised Sclavic element. They were closely akin to the Low German tribes who conquered Britain, and their language was certainly a Low German speech. The only specimen of it is the translation of the Scriptures executed in the 4th c. by Bishop Ulfilas (q. v.). See Jornandes, *De Getarum Origine et Rebus Gestis*; Procopius, *De Bello Gothico*; and Gibbon, *Decline and Fall of the Roman Empire.*

Gott'fried von Strassburg, one of the leading *minnesingers*, belonged to the second half of the 12th c., and probably was born or lived at Strassburg. His chief work, *Tristan*, written about 1207–1210, surpasses all the productions of his contemporaries in grace and ease of style. He tells the story, moreover, with considerable power, and at times displays an almost Chaucerian vein of bantering pleasantry. G. likewise wrote lyrics, several of which are extant. His works were edited by F. van der Hagen (Bres. 1823), and Bechstein (1869), and modern German translations of *Tristan* have been published by Kurtz (Stuttg. 1844), and Simrock (Leips. 1855).

Göttingen, an ancient town in the province of Hanover, Prussia, pleasantly situated in the fertile valley of the Leine, about 50 miles S. of Hanover. G., once a Hanse town, thrives under Prussian rule; the rapidly-multiplying villas that have recently sprung up outside the old city fortifications (now a promenade with beautiful lime-tree avenues) give G. a more lively appearance than of old. G. has some industries, but its well-being depends mainly on its famous university, to which the only important buildings of G. save the churches belong. The university was founded in 1734 under George II. of England as Elector, and under the fostering care of the minister Münchhausen speedily became one of the foremost in Germany. Its professors long enjoyed a then unparalleled freedom of research and speech, and had amongst them men such as Heyne, the Eichhorns, Blumenbach, and O. Müller. In 1823 the university had 1547 students, but political troubles, culminating in the expulsion of the well-known seven professors (Dahlmann, Albrecht, Ewald, Gervinus, the brothers Grimm, and Weber), sadly reduced the number of students. But better times soon restored prosperity. In 1874 the university had 81 professors, besides *privatdocenten*, and 1018 students. Its library contains 360,000 volumes and 5000 MSS. Pop. (1875) 17,038.

Gott'sched, Johann Christoph, for a great part of his life the literary dictator of Germany, was born 2d February 1700, at Judithenkirch, near Königsberg, at which latter place he studied. In 1724 he came to Leipsic, and in 1730 was called to a chair in the university, a post he retained till his death, 12th December 1766. G.'s merits were great as well as his defects. He asserted the rights of the German tongue, and did much to purify it from foreign admixture. He brought utter discredit on the turgidity of style then prevalent, and, seeking his models in France, strove in numerous works and in magazines to prove that accuracy of form is the cardinal virtue of poetry. As a necessary result, poetry became in his hands formal to a degree, cold, stiff, and soulless. G.'s fierce controversy with the Swiss school, with Bodmer at its head, prepared the ground for the glorious age of German literature, and meanwhile effectually sapped G.'s influence. His principal works are *Die Deutsche Schaubühne* (6 vols. 1741–45, 2d ed. 1746–50); *Versuch einer kritischen Dichtkunst* (1730, 4th ed. 1751). G.'s example did little to commend his precepts; his *Gedichte* (1736) and his *Der sterbende Cato* (though the latter, imitated from Addison, went through ten editions) are of small interest. See Danzel, *G. und seine Zeit* (Leips. 1848).

Gou'da, or **Ter Gouw**, a Dutch town in the province of S. Holland, on the right bank of the Yssel, at its confluence with the Gouw, 11 miles N.E. of Rotterdam by railway. The chief building is the church of St. John, with its forty-four famous stained windows (two 60 feet high), contributed, after the burning of the old church in 1552, by various European sovereigns and cities, and executed by the brothers Dirk and Walter Crabeth (1560–1603). In the market-place, which is one of the finest and largest in Europe, stands the townhall, with painted roof and pinnacled façade. There is a weekly market for the sale of cattle and of the well-known G. cheese made of new milk. G. has extensive potteries, brickfields, clay-pipe factories, cotton mills, &c. Pop. (1873) 15,174.

Gough, Hugh, Lord, a distinguished English general, born at Woodstown in the county of Limerick, Ireland, 3d November 1779, entered the army in 1794, served at the Cape of Good Hope and in the W. Indies, and was present at most of the battles of the Peninsular war, in which he was more than once severely wounded. He was sent to India in 1837, and to China in 1840, in command of the land forces; for his services in the latter country he was made G.C.B. and a baronet. From 1843 to 1850 he was commander-in-chief in India, and commanded in person throughout the two bloody Sikh campaigns of 1845–46 and 1848–49. On his return to England he was created baron and viscount, and received a pension for three generations; subsequently also he obtained a field marshal's staff. He died 3d March 1869. Personally he was regardless of danger, and he was not sparing of the lives of his soldiers, preferring an immediate bayonet-charge to the proper use of artillery.

Gough, Richard, an antiquary, born in London in 1735, studied at Cambridge University, and, after a life of research, died at Enfield in 1809. His works include *Anecdotes of British Topography, The Sepulchral Monuments of Great Britain, The History of Pleshy in Essex, Plates of the Coins of the Seleucidæ, Account of the Missal presented to Henry VI. by the Duchess of Bedford.* G. left all his MSS. to Oxford University.

Goul'burn, a town in New South Wales, 128 miles S.W. of Sydney, with which it is connected by railway. It is the centre of an important agricultural district; while gold is found in the vicinity, though not in rich quantities. Copper is also beginning to be worked. G. is a see of the Anglican and Roman Catholic Churches. Pop. of the town (in 1875), 4453; of the district, 13,756.

Gou'nod, Charles-François, a brilliant operatic composer, was born at Paris, June 17, 1818. As a pupil in the Conservatoire he learned composition under Halévy. In 1839 he gained the first prize at the 'Institut,' and, receiving a Government pension, went to Rome to study further. There he was appointed honorary *maestro di capella* for life. He next held in Paris the posts of chapel-master to the church of foreign missions and director of the Orphéonists, an important musical organisation. He resigned the latter in 1860. He wrote operas from 1851, obtaining little favour till 1859, when he produced *Faust.* Of later date are *Mireille* (1864) and *Romeo and Juliet* (1867). In 1866 he was made a member of the French Institute. G.'s recent compositions are principally songs. G.'s music shows 'great depth of sentiment and decided originality of thought,' though in sustained power he falls below his great model, Gluck.

Gou'ra (*Goura Coronata*), a species of *Columbidæ* or Pigeons (q. v.), found in Saya, New Guinea, and the Moluccas, and distinguished by having an expanded crest of light silky feathers. The colour is a slate-blue with dark tints on the wings and tail, and a patch of red and white on each wing. The nostrils exist in a groove in the middle of the bill, and the fourth, fifth, and sixth quills are the longest. The cry of the G. is sonorous and loud.

Gourd, a name commonly given to many species and varieties of *Cucurbita* and other genera belonging to the natural order Cucurbitaceæ (q. v.). They are principally found in Asia, N. America, and Europe. The fruit of some is poisonous, that of others is largely used as a culinary vegetable. The species chiefly grown in British gardens are the white G. or G. pumpkin (*Cucurbita pepo*), the red G. (*C. maxima*), and especially the succade G. or vegetable marrow (*C. ovifera saccada*). Many species of G. are exceedingly ornamental. The orange G. (*C. aurantia*) is sometimes grown in gardens for its beautiful orange-like fruit, but as colocynth is frequently developed, it is unsafe for use. The snake G. of India (*Trichosanthes anguina*) is eaten, and the shell of the fruit of *Lagenaria vulgaris* serves as a vessel to hold fluid, hence it is called 'bottle G.' The name 'sour G.' is given to a tree of a different natural order. (See ADANSONIA). The squash (*C. melopepo*) is largely cultivated in America, and produces an acceptable food for men, cattle, and swine. The bitter G. or colocynth is furnished by *Citrullus colocynthis*, and the round fruits from which the drug is prepared are principally the produce of countries bordering the Mediterranean. The gooseberry G. is the fruit of *Momordica echinata.* The white G. of India is *Benincasa cerifera*, and in its unripe state is universally employed by the natives in their curries. What are known as 'club G.' or 'trumpet G.' are different forms of the 'bottle G.' above mentioned, the fruit of which is at first long and cylindrical, like a cucumber, but swelling as it ripens, ultimately assumes a shape like a Venetian bottle. After being gathered the neck end is cut off, the internal pulp with the seeds carefully removed through the orifice, and the interior repeatedly washed to remove the bitter principle which constitutes the poison. G. are sometimes grown to weigh as much as 200 lbs. each.

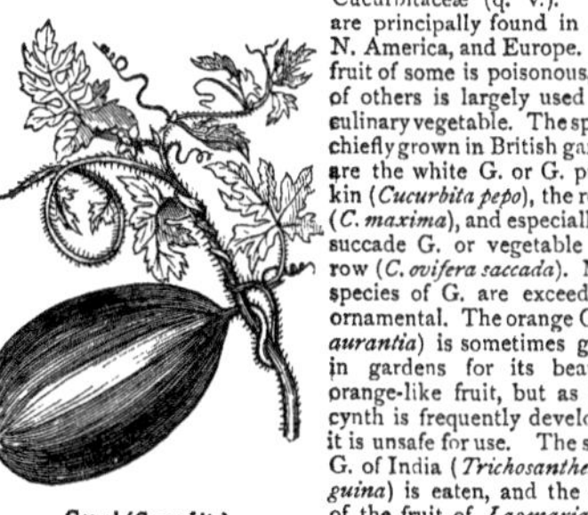

Gourd (*Cucurbita*).

Gout (Lat. *gutta*, 'a drop'), or **Pod'agra**, a disease attended with febrile excitement, and a specific form of inflammation, usually associated with disorder of the digestive and other internal organs, and especially with an affection of the joints, as the first joint of the great toe. G. is predisposed to by congenital or hereditary constitution, and generally occurs in paroxysms or 'fits of the G.' at indefinite intervals, and is characterised by nocturnal exacerbations and morning remissions. It has been proved experimentally that the blood, in cases of acute G., contains *lithic acid* in the form of *lithate of soda*, and that, in cases of chronic G., with chalky deposits round the joints, *lithic acid* is *always* present in the blood and deficient in the urine, both absolutely and relatively to the other organic matters. Uric acid is also found to exist in the blood-serum, the fluid effused by blisters, and in the abdominal and pericardial fluids. The gouty inflammations are distinguished from the rheumatic by a tendency of the former to the deposition of urate of soda, a discovery made by the late Dr. Wollaston. The urate of soda is deposited first as a white fluid, and after a time the fluid portion is absorbed, leaving concretions of crystals of urate of soda, which eventually harden and form what have been termed *chalk-stones.* Sometimes these concretions are accompanied with deposits of phosphate and carbonate of lime. A paroxysm of G. is simply an effort of nature to eliminate from the system ingredients which act as blood-poisons. G. is equally common among the plebeian and aristocratic, the degraded and the highly cultivated. It may be acute or chronic, and when the viscera are affected it is termed irregular, retrocedent, or misplaced G. This metastasis may be to the stomach and intestines, or to other parts, as to the testicles, bladder, rectum, or the head, causing death, in the latter case, from apoplexy. The intervals between paroxysms of G. vary, but in general they are shorter the younger the patient. The most common is the biennial or triennial attack for the space of eight or ten years, and then the attacks become more frequent, the tendency of the disease being to acquire a chronic form, terminating in complete lameness, helplessness, and debility, or in death by metastasis to the heart or brain. The treatment of G. is complicated, but as the disease is clearly of constitutional origin, the indications are the administration of remedies to control or subdue the constitutional tendency, and to modify the severity of the paroxysms. This must be done cautiously, as the paroxysm is the means by which nature seeks to relieve itself of the *materies morbi.* Iodide of potassium and alkaline remedies, as the bicarbonate, the citrate, or the acetate of potash, have been recommended, and benefit has been derived from the continuous administration of small doses of salines, in a very dilute form, taken two or three times a day on an empty stomach, shortly before food. See Dr. Adams' *Treatise on Rheumatic Gout* (Lond. 1873).

Gout-Weed, Bishop-Weed, or Herb-Gerard, popular names given to *Ægopodium Podagraria*, a common umbelliferous plant.

Gov'an, a borough of Lanarkshire, Scotland, on the left bank of the Clyde, 3 miles W. of Glasgow, of which it is virtually a suburb. It has extensive shipbuilding yards, silk, cotton, and paper mills, blast furnaces, cotton-printing and dye works, &c. Pop. (1871) 19,200. G. was known before the 17th c. as 'meikle Govane.'

Gov'ernment. See CONSTITUTION, PRIVY COUNCIL, MINISTRY.

Government Purchase of Annuities. See ANNUITY, in English law.

Govind', or **Gobind' Singh'**, the tenth and last *guru* of the Sikhs, flourished 1660-1708. It was he who developed what had previously been a mere religious sect into a nationality of disciplined warriors. He gave the name of *khalsa* = 'select or liberated;' and a great part of the *Grunth* or Holy Book is composed of the elaborate ceremonies and rules of conduct which he imposed on his followers. See Cunningham's *History of the Sikhs* (Lond. 1853).

Gow'die, a name given to the Gemmeous Dragonet (q. v.), a Teleostean fish allied to the Goby (q. v.), and known scientifically as the *Callionymus lyra*. The term 'G.' refers to the golden lustre of the body.

Gower, John, an English poet, born about 1320. He was an esquire of Kent, and held the living of Great Braxted, Essex. Little is known of his life, which was that of a recluse. He died in 1408. G. was probably the greatest English scholar of his day, and his voluminous works are brimful of learning. His *Speculum Meditantis*, a didactic poem in French, is lost, but several French *Balades* are extant. In *Vox Clamantis*, a Latin political poem, he defends Richard II., and satirises the social evils of the time. His chief English work is the *Confessio Amantis*, a dialogue in verse between a penitent and his confessor, a priest of Venus. It contains tales of love, magic, astrology, &c. The work is overburdened with learning, but seldom rises to poetry, and is generally so wearisome as to justify Professor Lowell's remark, that G. has 'positively raised tediousness to the precision of a science.' G.'s English is wanting in the ease and grace of Chaucer, and has a larger Norman element. The best edition of G. is that by Dr. Reinhold Pauli (3 vols. 1857). See Minto's *English Poets* (1874), and Morley's *English Writers* (1864-67).

Gowhat'i (*Gauhati*), the chief town in the district of the Kamrup, province of Assam, British India, on the left bank of the Brahmaputra. Pop. (1872) 11,492. It was the capital of Assam under the early Hindu dynasty, and the fortifications can still be traced for miles on both sides of the river. All buildings have now entirely disappeared, but the soil is mainly composed of decaying brick and mortar, and sculptured stones are continually turned up by the plough. It is by far the most populous town in the province, indeed the only town, and is the seat of a considerable river trade; but owing to its unhealthiness, the headquarters of the Chief Commissioner have been removed to Debrugurh.

Gowrie, Carse of, a fertile reach of land on the N. side of the Tay in Perthshire. It formerly belonged to the Ruthvens, who hence derived their title of Earls of G.

Gowrie Conspiracy, an attempt made by John Ruthven, Earl of Gowrie, his brother Alexander Ruthven, and others to murder, or more likely to seize the person of, James VI., whom they decoyed into Gowrie's house in Perth on August 5, 1584. The King, however, was rescued by his followers, and both the Ruthvens were killed. The conspiracy is still involved in mystery. Gowrie may have been actuated by revenge, his father having been executed in 1584; but the object of the plot seems to have been by keeping the King a prisoner to govern in his name in favour of Presbyterianism. See Burton's *History of Scotland* (vol. v. ed. 1867).

Goyann'a, a city in the province of Pernambuco, Brazil, on a river of the same name, 30 miles S. of Parahyba. It has some trade in hides, rum, dyewoods, &c. Pop. 12,000.

Goy'a y Lucientes, Francisco, a Spanish painter, was born at Fuente de Todos, Aragon, March 31, 1746. Studying at Rome, he returned to Spain, where he soon became famous, and was made court painter by Charles IV. He led a gay, dissipated life, and in his 78th year removed to Paris for his health. G. died at Bordeaux, April 16, 1828. He was a most fertile and original artist, painting numerous portraits, historical pictures, and scenes from everyday Spanish life. He delighted in Rembrandtesque shades and fantastic colour, his style is peculiarly bold and vivid, and he sometimes displays a subtle, lurking satiric purpose. See Théophile Gautier in *Le Cabinet de l'Artiste et de l'Amateur* for 1842.

Goyaz', chief town of an inland province of the same name, Brazil, on the Vermelho, a tributary of the Araguaya. Pop. 8000.—The *province* lies near the centre of the empire, between the Tocatins and Araguaya, two affluents of the Amazon, and is a fertile but neglected region with no exports. It had formerly rich gold-mines; there is now only some insufficient husbandry and cattle-rearing. Area, 263,335 sq. miles; pop. 160,395, most of whom are Indians.

Gozz'i, Count Carlo, an Italian dramatist, born at Venice in 1722. When a youth he joined the army in Dalmatia, and after spending three years there returned to Venice, where he began to write fanciful fairy dramas, one of which, *L'Amore delle tre Melarance*, brought out in 1761, had such a complete success that G. for a time quite eclipsed his rival Goldoni. He produced many other wild romantic pieces, full of spectacle and bustle, and not without humour and pathos amid their lively trivialities. G. died April 6, 1806. His pieces were speedily displaced by Goldoni's. An edition of his works in 10 vols. was published in 1792. See his autobiography, called *Memorie inutili di Carlo G.* (Venice, 1797).

Gozz'o, an island in the Mediterranean, 4 miles N.W. of Malta, belongs to England. Area, 36 sq. miles; pop. 17,000. It has many rare plants, abounds in game, and yields heavy crops of cotton and grain, &c. There is here a fine breed of large asses. G. has two harbours, and the governor resides at Castel del G. In the centre of G. is the chief town, Rabato. The 'Giant's Tower' is an interesting relic of remote antiquity. G. was known to the Romans under the name *Gaulos*.

Gozz'oli, Benozz'o, an Italian fresco painter, born at Florence about 1408. He was a favourite pupil of Fra Angelico, who greatly influenced his style and choice of subject. He painted at Florence, Rome, Volterra, and Pisa, and died in the last city in 1478. His masterpiece is the series of scriptural frescoes in the Campo Santo of Pisa. G.'s colour is rich, and his drawing accurate, though sometimes over formal. He was less sentimental in style than Angelico, and worked in the accessories to his figures with lavish care.

Graaf, Regnier de, a Dutch physician, born at Schoonhaven, 30th July 1641. His fame rests on his investigations on the use of the pancreatic juice, and on the physiology of human generation. The results of these were published in the treatises *De Natura et Usu Succi Pancreatici* (Leyden, 1663), *De Mulierum Organis Generationi Inservientibus* (1672), and other brief works. G. died at Delft, 17th August 1673. His *Opera Omnia* appeared in 1667, and were republished in 1608 and 1705.

Graaff-Rey'net, the chief town of a county of the same name, Cape Colony, on the Zondag, to the S. of the Schnee Berge, and 130 miles N.N.W. of Port Elizabeth. It has some trade in pastoral produce, and a pop. of 9000. The province is intersected from W. to E. by the Koudveld and Schnee Berge, which in Compass Peak attain a height of 8500 feet.

Graaf'ian Ves'icles, are structures found in the ovary, developed for the special purpose of expelling the ovum, and named after Regnier de Graaf (q. v.).

Graal, or **Gréal** (probably from the Old Fr. *gréal*, Prov. *grazal*, Med. Lat. *gradalis*, 'a dish'), a sacred and miraculous cup, which forms the centre of various medieval legends and poems, and which was generally spoken of as the *san graal* ('sacred dish'). The stories of the G. probably arose from the Breton tradition of a marvellous golden chalice studded with diamonds, and concealed in a magic lake or grotto, which endowed its possessor with vast knowledge and the gift of prophecy. In the Christian legend the G. was a chalice, brought by angels to earth, from which Christ drank at the Last Supper. Joseph of Arimathea caught in it the last drops of the blood of Christ, and carried it to Brittany, and afterwards to England, where he left it to his descendants. The G. wrought strange miracles if its possessor were devout and stainless, and became the symbol of holiness and purity. Some time after Joseph of Arimathea died the G. was lost, and Uther Pendragon founded the order of the Round Table to recover it. In Arthur's time many knights set out in search of it, and the quest was achieved by Galahad, according to Walter Mapes (q. v.), who added the legend of the G. to the English Arthurian cycle. According to some French *trouvères* the G. was found by Parcival le Gallois, whose story was begun by Chrétien of Troyes, continued by Gerbert and Gauthier de Denet, and ended by Manessier at the close of the 12th c. Wolfram von Eschenbach (q. v.) introduced the story of the G. into German literature. The legends of the G. were at one time very popular throughout Western Europe, and interest in them has been lately awakened by Tennyson's *Holy Grail* in the *Idylls of the King*.

Grac'chus, the name of a Roman family of the Sempronian gens, which gave to the state many citizens eminent for bravery, magnanimity, and patriotism. **Tiberius Sempronius G.**, the first known to history, was consul 238 B.C., and carried on war in Sardinia and Corsica after the rising of the Carthaginian mercenaries. The next was **T. Sempronius G.**, who achieved renown in the Second Punic War. He was ædile 216 B.C., consul 215 B.C., defeated Hanno 214 B.C. with great loss near Beneventum, was consul a second time 213 B.C., and in 212 B.C., while bravely resisting the Carthaginian arms in Lucania, was slain in the struggle with Mago, or fell into his hands by treachery. Mago sent his body to Hannibal, who gave it distinguished burial. His son, of the same name, augur 203 B.C., died augur 174 B.C. **T. Sempronius G.**, who waged war with the Gauls 196 B.C., and **P. Sempronius G.**, tribune 189 B.C., also deserve mention. But the three most illustrious members of the family are—1. **Tiberius Sempronius G.**, a man whose life was adorned by public and private virtues of the highest order. He was born 210 B.C., was tribune 187 B.C., ædile 182 B.C., prætor 181 B.C., consul 177 B.C., censor 169 B.C., and again consul 163 B.C. His military career in Spain (181–178 B.C.) was a brilliant one; and in the latter year he celebrated a splendid triumph over the Celtiberians and their allies. He afterwards subdued the Sardinians, for which he was again honoured with a triumph, 175 B.C. About 186 B.C. he married Cornelia, youngest daughter of Scipio Africanus, by whom he had twelve children, nine of whom died young. The survivors were Cornelia, wife of Scipio Africanus the younger, and the two famous tribunes T. and C. Sempronius G., known in history as the 'Gracchi.'—2. **Tiberius Sempronius G.**, the elder of the 'Gracchi,' was born, according to Plutarch's statement, about 164 B.C., but probably four years earlier. While still young he lost his father. The education of G. and of his brother, however, was carefully superintended by their mother, and under the best Greek teachers they received a training that enabled them to outstrip all the youths of the time. When G. arrived at manhood, he was elected augur. In 149 B.C. he accompanied his brother-in-law, Scipio Africanus the younger, into Africa, and was present at the siege of Carthage, the walls of which, it is said, he was the first to scale. In 137 B.C. he was appointed quæstor to the army under the consul C. Hostilius Mancinus in Hither Spain. Here he gained the esteem of the soldiery and the confidence of the enemy. Forty years before this the Spaniards had experienced the upright dealing of his father, and now, in their turn victorious, they declined to treat with any other than the son. G. was thus enabled to save the lives of 20,000 men who were entirely at the mercy of the Numantines, and to conclude an equitable peace. The terms, however, were deemed disgraceful at Rome, and Mancinus was sent back to the Numantines naked, with hands bound, that the treaty might be set aside (136 B.C.). Meanwhile G.'s popularity increased. But he was daily becoming more and more impressed with the desert look of the fields of Italy, and the terrible destitution of the poorer classes. These evils he resolved to remedy by checking the avarice of the aristocracy, and by creating an industrious middle class of husbandmen. To this end he stood for and gained the tribuneship, 133 B.C. He then brought in a bill for the renewal of the Agrarian Law (q. v.) of Licinius Stolo, which with certain modifications he carried amid violent opposition. The triumvirs appointed to carry out the law were G., his father-in-law Appius Claudius, and his brother Caius, then with Scipio at Numantia. Though G, still continued the idol of the people, the death of one of his intimate friends by poison warned him of danger. He therefore ceased to appear alone in public. Meanwhile Attalus died leaving his kingdom and wealth to the Roman people. G. wished the money thus left to be divided among the poor, and further entertained the idea of extending the franchise; but fortune turned against him. Rumours were circulated that he aimed at being King of Rome. At every turn his life was in danger, and his heart became filled with fears and misgivings. The people deserted their champion, and at next election for the tribuneship he was slain in a scuffle at the entrance to the temple of Fides. Upwards of 300 men were killed in the tumult by sticks and stones, but none by the sword. G. was a man of amiable nature, noble bearing, and simple yet dignified demeanour. As a speaker he was temperate, graceful, and persuasive; but in talent, energy, and intensity he was inferior to his younger brother.—3. **Caius Sempronius G.** was, according to Plutarch's account, nine years younger than Tiberius. At his brother's death G. was in Spain, and the aristocracy, jealous of his abilities, were nowise anxious for his return. He came back, however, in the following year, but kept aloof from public affairs. In 126 B.C. he was sent as quæstor to Sardinia under the consul L. Aurelius Orestes, a mission which removed him from the jealous eyes of his enemies for a time. Like his brother, he soon became popular in the camp. After an absence of two years, urged by his brother's shade, which appeared to him in a dream, he returned to Rome. In 123 B.C. he was elected tribune. As such, his first acts were directed against his brother's murderers. He then proceeded to carry out his brother's Agrarian Law, which was being thwarted by the nobles on all hands, and to pursue a policy for the improvement of the poor, the regeneration of his country, and the development of its resources. A law was enacted that corn should be sold every month to the poor at a low and fixed price. He next directed his weapons against the senate, and carried a law by which the *judicia publica* were transferred to a court of 300 equites. G. was re-elected tribune for the following year, when one of his colleagues, M. Livius Drusus, bribed by the nobles, succeeded in outbidding him in the proposal of popular measures. The result was that G. failed next year to obtain the tribuneship, and the consul Opimius began to repeal his laws. In the tumult which followed G. fled to the temple of Diana, and thence to the grove of the Furies, where he was slain at his own request by his slave Philocrates. More than 3000 are said to have perished with him. All his friends who fell into the hands of their enemies were thrown into prison and strangled. After this fearful scene of bloodshed, the senate, in blasphemous mockery, dedicated a temple to Concord! Many specimens and fragments of the oratory of G. may be found in Meyer's *Fragment. Orat. Rom.*, pp. 227–249, 2d ed.

Grace (Gr. *charis*) means a favourable or kind feeling, especially towards an unworthy object. In the New Testament it is represented as the crowning attribute of the divine nature, the manifestation of which was the grand end of the whole scheme of redemption (Eph. i. 3–6, ii. 6, 7). In theology various kinds of G. are distinguished. Common G. is 'that influence of the Holy Spirit which, in a greater or less measure, is granted to all who hear the truth.' Sufficient G. means 'such kind and degree of the Spirit's influence as is sufficient to lead men to repentance, faith, and a holy life.' Effectual G. is 'such an influence of the Spirit as is certainly effectual in producing regeneration and conversion.' Preventing G. 'means that operation of the Spirit on the mind which precedes and excites its efforts to return to God.' Co-operating G. is 'that influence of the Spirit which aids the people of God in all the exercises of the divine life.' Habitual G. is that permanent state of mind which is due to the abiding presence and power of the Holy Spirit. See Hodge's *Systematic Theology* (Edinb. 1872).

Grace, Days of. See BILL OF EXCHANGE, under BILL.

Gra'ces (Lat. *Gratiæ*; Gr. *Charites*), the goddesses of grace, beauty, refinement, and loveliness. Homer in the Iliad (xviii. 382) describes the Grace Charis as the wife of Hephæstus. In the same poem (xiv. 269) he speaks of the G. as an indefinite number, and calls one of them the destined wife of Sleep. In the Homeric poems the G. are elsewhere spoken of in the plural. According to the Odyssey, Aphrodite is the goddess of love and beauty, and the G. are her attendants. Hesiod mentions three G.—Thalia, Aglaia, and Euphrosyne. The G. are generally represented as the daughters of Zeus by Hera, Eurynome, Eurydomene, Eunomia, Harmonia, or Lethe; of Apollo by Ægle or Euanthe; or of Dionysus by Aphrodite. The Spartans and Athenians worshipped only *two* G., though under different names. The worship of the G. was introduced into Bœotia by Eteocles. They are represented as the companions of many divinities besides Aphrodite, *e.g.*, of Hera, Hermes, Eros, Dionysus, and the Muses. They are generally portrayed as slightly draped or nude, and as carrying musical instruments, myrtles, roses, or dice. Among later Roman writers the G. appear as symbols of gratitude and benevolence—a phase unknown to Greek mythology, and springing from the radical meaning of the term *gratia* in the Roman tongue. Apropos of this later meaning of the term may be noted the Feast of the Charities (*Charistia*), an annual family banquet for the adjustment of differences—'the Feast of the Reconciliation'—celebrated on the 19th or 20th of February, and called from its character the 'Kinsmen's Day'—*Lux Propinquorum*. See Mart., *Epigr.* ix. 56.

Gracio'sa, one of the Azores (q. v.).

Gra'dient (Lat. *gradus*, 'a step'), in heraldry, signifies 'walking,' and is applied to the tortoise.

Gradient, of a railway, road, or canal, is its inclination to the horizontal, and is measured as a rise of 1 foot in so many measured horizontally. The *barometric G.* of any two localities is the geographical distance of the two places in nautical miles, divided by the difference of barometric pressure in inches.

Gradisk', a town in the S. of Russia, province of Poltava, near the left bank of the Dnieper, 65 miles S.W. of Poltava. It has four churches, a monastery, and some grain and cattle trade. Pop. (1870) 7107.

Grad'ual (from Lat. *gradus*, 'a step') was—(1) An anthem or response, originally an entire psalm, varying with the day, sung in the Western Church, between the reading of the Epistle and the Gospel, from the same step of the ambo as the Epistle was read from; hence probably the name G. Strictly the G. was only the first verse of the anthem; the rest, when sung to the end by the chanter alone, was called the Tract; when he was interrupted by the choir, it was called the Verse or Responsory. (2) The book containing the anthems, although the name was also applied to the Antiphonary, containing everything sung antiphonally at the Eucharist.

Gradual Psalms is the liturgical name for the fifteen psalms entitled 'Songs of Degrees,' cxx. to cxxxiv. The term 'degrees' has been variously explained. Some make the psalms to have been songs of the pilgrims returning from Babylom (*cf.* Ezra vii. 9); others refer them to the journeys to Jerusalem at the great feasts. Later Jewish expositors say they got their name from fifteen steps in the Temple. Most probably they got it from the step-like progress of the thoughts and the rhythm (*cf.* cxxi. 1, 2, '. . . from whence cometh my help. My help cometh,' &c.)

Gradua'tion is the art of dividing a given length into a required number of equal parts. The geometry of the straight line and circle supplies a method by which any straight line may be so subdivided, but in practice this method is neither convenient nor accurate. The principle was made use of in constructing the Diagonal Scale (q. v.), which has been, however, in our modern instruments for astronomical, geodesic, and other purposes, wholly superseded by the Vernier (q. v.). The growing necessity for accurate measurements has developed the art into one of great delicacy. Most instruments are graduated by the aid of a *dividing engine*, which has been constructed with the greatest possible care. This of course requires a scale graduated originally with the aid of such a simple form of machine as the beam compasses, and the difficulties of original G. are such as to have rendered the few who have attained to excellence in it as famous as the illustrious investigators who have used their instruments—such men for instance are Graham, Ramsden, Troughton, Simms, and others. The most practically accurate method for original G. is that of successive bisections until the different intervals are so small as to be easily divided, by the process of *stepping*, into the required number. Stepping is accomplished by setting the compass points as near as may be to the needed interval, and then, by stepping over the whole distance to be divided, discovering by how much this interval repeated so many times exceeds or falls short of the true interval taken the same number of times, and adjusting the compass points accordingly. A dividing engine consists essentially of an endless screw, on which a nut works backwards and forwards. If this screw be provided with a graduated circle, by which the number of turns may be fairly estimated, we have a machine by which any given distance not exceeding the screw in length may be divided into any number of equal parts, with a greater or less degree of accuracy depending on the operator. For example, if it is required to divide a length into n equal parts, first count how many turns and fractions of a turn are necessary to make the nut travel the given distance, then work the nut backwards, marking the positions which correspond to $\frac{1}{n}$, $\frac{2}{n}$, $\frac{3}{n}$, &c., of the whole distance, found by calculating the number of turns necessary to make the nut move through each subdivision.

Graduation, the ceremony of conferring an academic degree. See DEGREE, UNIVERSITY.

Græ'cia Mag'na. See MAGNA GRÆCIA.

Graf is the German form of the Old Eng. *geréfa*, perhaps a variant of *gefera*, 'a companion or associate' (Mod. Eng. *reeve*, 'a bailiff;' Low. Sc. *grieve*, 'a farm-steward'), and if so, the equivalent in meaning of the Lat. *comes*, and the Fr. *comte*. The name first occurs among the Franks in the *Lex Salica* under the Latinised form of *grafio*, and there it denotes an officer appointed by the king to govern a 'gau' or district. The office grew in importance and dignity with the growth of the kingly power, and various kinds of 'grafs' gradually appear. The chief of these, however, is the district-G., who superseded the older *thunginus* or *centenarius* chosen by the people themselves. His duties were to preside in the justiciary court, to protect the Church and all who deserved help, to proclaim the royal summons to arms, to lift the royal revenues, and to inspect the royal demesnes. His management of Church property ultimately gave rise to abuses, such as the appointment of laymen to the office of abbots, hence the word *comites* or *grafen* sometimes stands for *abbates*. Among the more notable of the other grafs who figure in Frankish history are the *stall-G.* (Lat. *comes stabuli*, Fr. *connétable*, Eng. *constable*) or *marschalk* (Lat. *marescalcus*, Fr. *maréchal*, Eng. *marshal*), who had charge of the horses in the king's stable; the *pfalz-G.* (Lat. *comes palatii*), who assisted the king in his personal administration of justice; the *send-G.*, who was sent as an extraordinary delegate of the king to control or report upon the district-G.; the *mark-G.* ('border earl'), a creation of Karl the Great's, made necessary by his extensive conquests. As early as the 9th c. we see a tendency in these offices to become hereditary, and it gradually increased with the development of feudalism until the family succession to lands and offices was formally recognised and invested with the authority of feudal law. Towards the close of the middle ages many *herren* ('lords') who had never held any office under the Emperor took the title of G.; and in modern times the fundamental changes in the mode of governing a country, exemplified in the separation of the judicial office from territorial possessions, have transformed the G. in Germany, like his counterparts elsewhere in Europe, into a mere titled noble. See COMES, COUNT, EARL.

Gräf'enberg, a village in Austrian Silesia, on the slopes of the Grafenberge, overlooking the Biele, 1250 feet above the sea, and 65 miles S.W. of Oppeln. It has the first hydropathic establishments in Europe, founded by Vincenz Priessnitz in 1828. G. receives annually from 500 to 1000 visitors.

Graffi'ti (from Ital. *graffiare*, 'to scratch') is the name applied to a class of ancient inscriptions rudely scratched by a style or other hard-pointed instrument on walls, door-posts, and the like. They have been found in some of the most famous Roman palaces and in the Catacombs, but chiefly in Pompeii. Though their literary merit is of no account, their value to scholars is nevertheless great; and when we have more knowledge of them than we possess, even after the labours of Wordsworth, Garrucci, and others, we may be in a better position to appreciate the 'slang' and 'street-life' of Rome, and to account for many obscure allusions in the writers of the pre-Augustan and Augustan periods. G. are found written in Greek in a few instances; in Oscan, at a time, moreover, when that language is generally supposed to have passed away; but more frequently in Latin. The subjects, scribbled on door-posts, walls, and pillars, include jokes, caricatures, witty or wicked epigrammatic touches, and simple statements of passing events; those in the Catacombs, again, are symbolical of Christian life and hope. For collections of Pompeian G. see Wordsworth's *Ancient Writings on Walls of Pompeii* (8vo, Lond. 1837); and Garrucci's compilation, a still better one (Par. 1856); while, for an exhaustive essay on the whole subject, the reader may consult the *Edinburgh Review* (vol. cx. pp. 411–437).

Graft'ing. In its broad sense, G. is the operation by which a bud portion of one plant is implanted upon the nourishment-yielding portion of another, and there made to grow. The numerous methods of G. are conveniently divided into three groups—namely, Budding (q. v.), Inarching (q. v.), and G. proper. The part transferred is termed the *graft* or *scion* (*bud* in the case of budding), and that to which transferred, its future support, the *stock*. Most of our valuable fruit-trees have been produced by long cultivation and selection from comparatively worthless originals, *e.g.*, all the kinds of apple are an accumulated succession of improvements upon the wild austere crab. When patient labour is rewarded with a desirable variety, that variety could not with any certainty be reproduced from its own seed, there being always a tendency to revert to the parent state; moreover, self-fertilisation is not the rule in nature, and cross-fertilisation might quite alter the characteristics of the offspring. The object of the horticulturist is therefore to obtain a method of propagation by division of the special individual he has secured, and one great means to accomplish this is G. In addition to this, G. also accelerates the production of fruit and flowers, and induces fertility. Consequently it is evident that G. is an art of the highest importance in horticulture. The whole system of artificial G. is founded upon the capacity inherent in plants of uniting together under certain circumstances and in a given mode. As to circumstances, it is absolutely necessary that stock and graft bear a near natural affinity to each other; in other words, that G. may be successful, the sap of the stock must contain all that the engrafted bud or shoot requires in every stage of its growth. As to mode, it is essential that those parts of graft and stock which have the power of generating new tissues be brought into juxtaposition. This growing element of the plant is termed its *cambium*, and is the layer of delicate cells between the last formation of new wood and the inner bark. When graft and stock are properly placed, the new tissue produced by their respective cambium meets together, coalesces, and thus institutes a vital connection between the buds of the scion and the roots of the stock. No real union ever takes place between the adjacent surfaces of the *existing* wood. G. is most simple when both stock and scion are equally the same size: in such a case a smooth sloping cut is made in an upward direction on the former, while a corresponding downward cut is made in the latter, the two surfaces are then brought together, secured by matting, and covered with clay or other adhesive material to exclude air, &c. But the multitudinous conditions of plant-life practically render G. so varied in plan of operation that the inquirer must consult special treatises on the subject. In all the methods of procedure the chief point to remember is that the closer the contact between the respective cambium layers the greater the prospect of success. The period of operation is entirely guided by the state of the ascent of the sap: the spring, therefore, is the proper season for the hardy trees in our climate. The vine is best grafted when in leaf. The following are the principal current names in connection with G.—namely, splice-G., whip or tongue G., saddle-G., cleft-G., crown-G., peg-G., shoulder-G., root-G., inarching, and budding. The art of G. is so ancient that anything connected with its origin is lost in the obscurity of ages. Accounts, such as Pliny's, of a tree so grafted as to bear apples, pears, plums, almonds, olives, figs, and grapes, are based simply on ingenious deceptions.

Gragna'no, a town of Italy, province of Naples, 2 miles S.E. of Castellamare di Stabia, on the slope of Mount Gaurano. It is a bishop's see, and is noted for its wines. Pop. 12,278.

Graham, Grahame, or Graeme, the variously-spelled name of an ancient Scottish family, is probably derived from a Celtic root, *grym*, signifying strength (Gael. *grumach*, 'stern'), from which we have also *Grime's*, popularly called *Graham's* Dyke. The first member of the family known in Scotland was Sir William de Graham (so spelled in a charter witnessed by him at Holyrood), who came from England in the reign of David I. The elder line of his descendants having terminated with Sir John de G. in the 14th c., the younger branch, derived from John, second son of Sir William, became the representative of the family. David, son of this Sir John, obtained from William the Lion a grant of land near Montrose, from which the present ducal title is derived. His elder son (?), Sir Patrick, fell at Dunbar in 1296, while his younger son was the famous Sir John the G., the friend and comrade of Wallace. In 1451 Sir Patrick G. of Kincardine, a cousin of Patrick G., Archbishop of St. Andrews, was created a peer of Parliament by the title of Lord G. William, third Lord G., who fell at Flodden in 1513, was created Earl of Montrose in 1503. Third in descent from him was James, first Marquess of Montrose (q. v.), born 1612. The ducal title was granted in 1707 to James, fourth Marquess. The Grahams of Claverhouse (q. v.) were a branch of the house of Montrose; and the Grahams of Balgowan, of whom General Thomas G., Lord Lynedoch (q. v.), was a representative, were sprung from the same noble family.

Graham, John, of Claverhouse, Viscount Dundee, celebrated as a zealous Royalist and a relentless opponent of the Scottish Covenanters. He was the eldest son of Sir William G. of Claverhouse, near Dundee, a descendant of the noble house of Montrose, and Lady Jane Carnegie, fourth daughter of the first Earl of Northesk. G. was born in 1643; and after completing his education at the University of St. Andrews, entered the French service as a volunteer, but left it in 1672 for that of the Prince of Orange. He received a captain's commission in the Dutch army in 1674, having, it is said, saved the life of the Prince at the battle of Seneff in August of that year. Returning to Scotland in 1677, he was appointed to the command of one of the independent bodies of cavalry raised to suppress the Covenanters, and soon distinguished himself by his merciless ardour in hunting out and persecuting these unhappy people, earning for himself the title by which he is still generally spoken of in the W. of Scotland—'The Bloody Claver'se.' The only regular engagements in which he took part against the Covenanters were those of Drumclog and Bothwell Brig, both in June 1679, in the former of which he was surprised and beaten. In 1682 G. became Sheriff of Wigton. His discipline of his own soldiers was almost as severe as his treatment of the 'hill people,' death being the only punishment he inflicted. For his services he was in 1684 appointed captain of horse, and received as a gift the Castle of Dudhope and the constabulary of Dundee. Under James II. he rose to be major-general, and in 1688 was created Viscount Dundee and Lord G. of Claverhouse. After the Revolution he raised an army in the Highlands in support of King James, and marched to Killiecrankie, where he was met on July 27, 1689, by General Mackay with nearly 4000 men. Dundee's troops amounted to only about 2500; but Mackay could not withstand the furious onset of the Highlanders, and retreated with a loss of over 2000 men. The victory was, however, dearly purchased with the loss of Dundee, who was mortally wounded by a musket-ball. He died shortly after the battle, and was buried in the church of Blair Athole. With him died the hopes of King James' cause in Scotland. See Napier's *Memorials and Letters illustrative of the Life and Times of Dundee* (Edinb. 1859).

Graham, Sir James Robert George, of Netherby, Bart., an English statesman, was the eldest son of Sir James, first baronet, and Lady Catherine Stewart, eldest daughter of the seventh Earl of Galloway. He was born June 1, 1792, and was educated at Westminster and Christ-Church College, Oxford. He afterwards spent two years in foreign travels, during part of which time he acted as private secretary to Lord Montgomery in Sicily; and owing to the illness of his superior, G. had entire charge of the negotiations by which Murat, King of Naples, was detached from his alliance with Napoleon. Returning to England in 1815, he began to take an eager interest in politics, and having declared himself a Whig, was in 1818 elected member for Hull. In 1824 he succeeded to the baronetcy, and in 1830 became First Lord of the Admiralty in Earl Grey's Ministry, and was soon a Privy Councillor. He helped to pass the Reform Bill of 1832, but in 1834, differing from his colleagues, he resigned along with Lord Stanley and the Earl of Ripon. In 1835 his political doctrines underwent a considerable change, in consequence of which he lost his seat for Cumberland in 1837; but he was returned as a Conservative for Pembroke, and in 1841 accepted office as Home Secretary in the Government of Sir Robert Peel. While at the head of the Home Department he incurred much unpopularity from the unyielding attitude by which he precipitated the Disruption of the Scottish Kirk, from opening the letters of Mazzini, and, in Ireland, from the proceedings against O'Connell. The Ministry fell in 1846, and G. remained out of office till 1852, when he again became First Lord of the Admiralty in the Coalition Ministry of Lord Aberdeen, a post which he retained till a few days after Lord Palmerston became Premier in 1855. Having latterly embraced Liberal views, G. generally supported Palmerston during the rest of his parliamentary career till his death, which occurred 25th October 1861; but he refused to take office in his Government. G.'s Life, by Mr. M'Cullagh Torrens, was published in 1863 (2 vols. Lond.).

Graham, Thomas, a celebrated chemist, was born December 20, 1805, in Glasgow, where he studied till 1826, when he removed to Edinburgh. In 1830 he was elected Professor of Chemistry in the Andersonian University, and in 1837 succeeded Dr. Turner in the chemical chair of University College, London. In 1855 he was made Master of the Mint, a post which he held till his death, September 16, 1869. G. was a skilful experimenter, and is especially famous for his researches on the Diffusion (q. v.) of gases and liquids, and his contributions to the atomic theory of matter. His valuable memoirs on this and other physical and chemical subjects are printed in the *Transactions* of the Royal Society of Edinburgh, and in the *Philosophical Transactions*. His *Elements of Chemistry* has gone through several editions. His papers have been collected and printed for private circulation by Mr. James Young and Dr. Angus Smith, under the title of *Chemical and Physical Researches* (1876).

Grahame, Rev. James, a Scottish poet, born at Glasgow, 22d April 1765. After studying law and practising for some years at the bar, he took orders in the English Church, and became curate of Shipton, Gloucestershire, and of Sedgefield, Durham. Ill-health forced him to return to Scotland, and he died at his brother's house near Glasgow, September 14, 1811. G.'s writings include *Mary Queen of Scotland*, a dramatic poem; *The Sabbath*, his best work; *Sabbath Walks*, &c. His verse is tame and monotonous, and his sentiment is mostly a reproduction of Cowper's, somewhat dulled by the lack of genius, yet not without a certain sweet and tender piety. He shows strong sympathy with Scottish life, and his descriptions have an unmistakable Scottish impress.

Grahams, The, of the Border, are descendants from Sir John G. of Kilbride, second son of Malice 'with the bright sword,' first Earl of Strathern, and afterwards Earl of Menteith. The principal families are those of Plomp, Esk, and Netherby.

Graham's Town, the capital of the eastern county of Albany, Cape Colony, South Africa, 25 miles from the sea. It is the see of a Protestant and Roman Catholic bishop, and has a cathedral, hospital, barracks, public library, botanic garden, &c. Its harbour is Port Alfred, next in importance to Port Elizabeth, with £50,000 yearly of custom dues. Pop. 9000.

Grain (Lat. *granum*, probably allied to *gramen*, 'grass,' anything that can be eaten), the name generally applied in botany to the caryopsis or fruit of the cereal grasses.

Grain, the origin of all weights in England, was a G. of dried wheat from the middle of the ear. Thirty-two grains made one pennyweight, twenty pennyweights one ounce, and twelve ounces one pound. Now twenty-four grains make one pennyweight. The G. is the smallest weight in common use.

Grain Coast, also known as **Pepper Coast**, is the name given to the seaboard of Liberia, W. Africa, on account of the Malaguetta pepper, or 'grains of paradise,' formerly exported in large quantity. See GUINEA.

Grain'ing (*Leuciscus Lancastriensis*), a species of *Teleostean* fishes belonging to the family *Cyprinidæ*, or that of the Carps (q. v.), and nearly allied to the Dace (q. v.). It is found on the Continent, but also inhabits a few English rivers. The G. has a single prominent dorsal fin, the tail is forked, and the head short and compressed.

Grains of Paradise and Malaguetta Pepper, the names given to the seeds of two species of *Amomum*—viz., *A. grana-paradisi* and *A. Meleguetta*—belonging to the ginger order. A few tons of the seeds are annually imported into Britain from the Guinea coast, where the plants are indigenous. They are sometimes illegally used to give a fictitious strength to spirits, and a hot, strong flavour to gin. In Africa they are largely used as a spice, and in some parts of Europe as a veterinary medicine. The name Guinea Pepper (q. v.) has also been applied to the seeds.

Grak'le (*Gracula*), a name popularly applied to many Insessorial birds allied to the Starlings (q. v.), but specially limited by zoologists to members of the genus *Gracula* included in the sub-family *Graculinæ* of the *Conirostres*. In this group the bill is broad at the base and compressed, but is also curved above. The nostrils are exposed, and the wings are long, the first quill being short, and the third and fourth longest. The tail and tarsi are short, and the toes long. The genus G. itself has a long bill, with a strong hinder toe, parts of the head being unfeathered. The grakles inhabit India and New Guinea. The crowned G. (*G. coronata*) is of a very dark-green colour, glossed with blue and black. The head and nape of the neck are yellow, and the skin around the eye pink. The tail is short and square-shaped. The Mina bird (*G. musica*), found in India and the E. Archipelago, is of a deep-black colour, with a white mark at the base of the wing-quills. The head bears two prominent yellow wattles. The average size of the G. is about that of the common thrush. This bird, which is a rare visitant in England, seems to possess talking powers, and imitates various sounds in a very perfect manner.

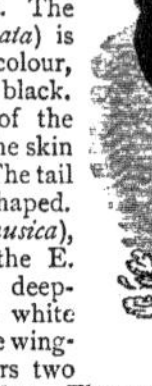

Grakle.

Grallato'res, Grall'æ, or **Waders**, an important order of Birds (q. v.) represented by the cranes, herons, ibises, storks, coots, waterhens, rails, woodcocks, plovers, bustards, &c. In this group the legs are for the most part very long, as is also the bill. The legs are destitute of feathers from the lower end of the tibia or shinbone downwards. The toes are long and straight, and a short hinder toe or *hallux* may be developed, but is frequently absent. The wings are long, but the tail is short, and in flight the G. (as is well seen in the herons) fly with the legs extended behind them, the legs supplying the place of the tail in guiding their flight. The neck is long. The food consists of worms, slugs, mollusca, fishes, and small mammalia. The G. inhabit shallow pools and lakes and the estuaries of rivers or the sea-coasts. They are either monogamous or polygamous, and the young run about as soon as they are hatched.

Gram, the Indian name for the Chick-Pea (q. v.).

Gramin'eæ, the natural order of Grasses (q. v.).

Gramm'ar (from Gr. *gramma*, 'a letter'), in its common and restricted sense, is the art of writing and speaking a language with accuracy and elegance. Its object is to investigate, systematise, and apply the component 'parts of speech,' as exhibited in the best writers and speakers of any particular tongue. The four main divisions of the subject are—(1) Orthography, (2) Etymology, (3) Syntax, (4) Prosody. The first treats of the forms and sounds of letters, and the formation of syllables from letters, and of words from syllables; the second, of the derivation, composition, inflection, and classification of words; the third, of their collocation or order in a sentence; and the fourth, of their correct accentuation and pronunciation with special reference to the metrical value of the syllables. G. is not one of the early births of language. To Homer, as an art, it was unknown. In the days of Plato it was still in its infancy. G., in the sense in which we are using the term, was a nursling of the Alexandrine writers; and the analysis and classification of words and other phenomena of language, as exemplified in the early poets, philosophers, and historians, furnished it with nourishment. The earliest Greek G., systematically compiled, for the use of Roman students, was not published till about 80 B.C. This work, the production of one Dionysius Thrax, a pupil of the Alexandrine school, formed the basis of European grammars. Within the present century, in all the countries of Europe, immense advances have been made in the treatment and study of the subject; and now, under the names of comparative G., comparative philology, and science of language, G. possesses an elaborate nomenclature, and takes a foremost place among the sciences. In the essentials all languages agree. Setting out with this dictum, comparative G. undertakes not only the investigation, arrangement, and comparison of the different parts of human speech, but also the classification of the different varieties of language into families and groups according to their affinities and differences. It even seeks to account for the origin, growth, and manifold phenomena of language. For the different terms in G., see under their special heads.

Grammar Schools. This was the name given to schools before the grammar of our language was written or taught, and when all grammatical knowledge was obtained through the study of the ancient languages. Latin, the language of the Church and of the learned, was the chief subject of instruction in the early G. S. The learning of Latin, of course, involved the translation of it into some living language. In England this tongue was French till 1350, when John Cornwall, a schoolmaster, introduced the practice of making his pupils translate Latin into English. In the 16th c. Hebrew, Greek, Latin, French, and Gaelic were allowed to be spoken in the Grammar School of Aberdeen, but not English. In course of time 'Lecture' schools were added, and subsequently schools for arithmetic and writing. In connection with the G. S. in Scotland, the 'Sang' schools deserve mention. These, as their name implies, were originally for music. G. S. have now in great measure lost their distinctive character as colleges for classics alone, and aim at giving a liberal and general education. In most of them mathematics and other sciences are now on an equal footing with the classic tongues. German and French are becoming indispensable; while a critical study of the English language—a powerful instrument of culture far too long neglected or but inadequately recognised—and the historic sequence of English literature, history, geography, &c., are rapidly attaining their rightful place.

Law Regarding Grammar Schools.—Act 3 and 4 Vict. c. 77, was passed for improving and enlarging the sphere of G. S., defined as all endowed schools founded or maintained for the teaching of Latin or Greek. The Act empowers the Court of Chancery, on being properly petitioned, to make decrees extending the system of education in any school, and regulating the system of admission and the application of its revenues. The intention of the founders is to be considered. The teaching of Greek and Latin may be given up if the revenues are insufficient. The Act 23 Vict. c. 11, provides for the secular instruction of children whose parents do not hold the religious doctrine taught under the endowment, unless the deed specially appoints the teaching of the formularies of a specified Church or religious sect.

Gramme (Gr. *gramma*), the standard unit of weight in France, was originally fixed as the weight of a cubic centimètre of distilled water at 0° C., and is equal to 15·43234874 grains Troy. The method of nomenclature of the multiple and submultiple weights is considered under METRIC SYSTEM.

Gram'mont, or **Gramont,** the name of an old French family belonging to the S.W. of France. In the 15th c. it split into two branches, the younger of which found a second home in Dauphiné, while the elder became extinct in the male line in the 16th c. But a daughter, **Claire de G.**, carried on the succession, and on her marriage in 1525 with Menaud d'Aure, Vicomte d'Astre, the latter took the name and arms of G. His great-grandson was the famous courtier, **Philibert, Comte de G.**, born about 1621. He distinguished himself in his youth under Condé and Turenne, but eclipsed his early fame as a soldier by his accomplishments as a courtier. Banished from France for seeking to win the affections of one of the royal mistresses, he betook himself to the court of Charles II. of England, where he became a great favourite from his wit and gallantry. He afterwards returned to France, and died in 1707. His brother-in-law, Anthony Count Hamilton, published memoirs of G., which sparkle with wit, and give a lively and seemingly faithful picture of the licentious Restoration society. See *Memoir of the Comte de G.*, edited by Sir Walter Scott (1811), and reprinted in Bohn's 'extra volumes.' His brother Antoine (born 1604), distinguished as a diplomatist and soldier, was made **Duc de G.** in 1663. He also left *Mémoires* (published by his son in 1716). To this family belongs the present **Antoine Alfred Agenor, Duc de G.**, born at Paris, 14th August 1819. He was educated at the École Polytechnique, entered the army in 1840, allied himself with Louis Napoleon after the Restoration of 1848, was appointed French ambassador at the court of Würtemberg in 1852, at Sardinia in 1853, at Rome in 1857, and Vienna in 1861. In May 1870 he was appointed Foreign Minister, became the leader of the war party, and after the fall of the Napoleonic dynasty fled to England, where he wrote *La France et la Prusse avant la Guerre* (1872).

Gram'mont, an industrial town of Belgium, province of E. Flanders, on the Dender, 25 miles W.S.W. of Brussels by railway. Its chief manufactures are linens, lace, damasks, woollens, leather, tobacco, &c. Pop. (1873) 9362.

Gram'pians, the great mountain system of Scotland, stretching as a principal chain in a W. and S.W. direction from Kincardineshire to near the southern end of the Caledonian Canal. The Cairngorm range is an offset to the N. into Banffshire and Aberdeenshire; and the Southern G. of Argyle and Perthshire, exending as far S. as Loch Lomond, form the southern limit of the system. The strata, which are violently contorted and upturned, belong to the Silurian age, and rest upon granitic rocks. On the S. they touch unconformably upon the Old Red Sandstone of Forfarshire and Perthshire. The chief heights are, in the principal chain, Ben Nevis (4406 feet), Lochnagar (3786); in the Cairngorm range, Ben Macdhui (4296), Cairntoul (4245), Cairngorm (4090), Ben-na-Buird (3860); and in the Southern G., Ben Cruachan (3668), Ben Lawers (3935), Schiehallion (3564), and Ben Lomond (3192).—G. is also the name of a mountain group extending N. and S. in the S.W. of Victoria, Australia. It forms two parallel chains, the Victoria and Serra ranges, in the latter of which is Mount William, 3825 feet high. The name is taken from the *Mons Grampius*, or rather *Graupius*, of Tacitus.

Gram'pus (*Phocæna*), a genus of *Cetacea* (q. v.) or Whales belonging to the family *Delphinidæ* or Dolphins. The characters of the genus are the presence of teeth of compressed form in both jaws, and a triangular dorsal fin, placed near the middle of the back. The common G. (*P. orca*, or *Delphinus G.*) attains a length of from eighteen to thirty feet, and a girth of from ten to twelve feet. The teeth number forty-four. The colour is black on the upper parts, and white on the belly, and there is a patch of white over each eye. The tail is broad and deeply forked, and the body tapers towards the posterior extremity. The food consists of salmon, herrings, and other fishes, and the grampuses are frequently taken in rivers or shallow waters, into which they have pursued their prey. The habitat of the G. is the northern seas, but it often appears in warmer latitudes. The name G. is derived from the French *grand poisson* ('great fish').

Grampus.

Gran (Hung. *Esztergom*), the chief town of a comität of the same name in Hungary, at the mouth of the river G., on the right bank of the Danube, 25 miles N.W. of Pesth, and opposite Párkány, a station on the Vienna and Pesth Railway. It is the seat of the archbishop and primate of Hungary, and has a beautiful cathedral (1821–56) and other fine buildings. Its wine trade is considerable. Pop. (1869) 11,215. G. was the birthplace of St. Stephen, the first King of Hungary.

Grana'da (Span. *Granata*, Arab. *Garnathah*, perhaps a corruption of *Karnathah*, the name of the old Phœnician fortress which stood here, or perhaps from *granatum*, 'a pomegranate,' as the city bore a resemblance to that fruit half opened, and as a pomegranate was part of its arms), once called by the Arabs 'the Damascus of Spain,' the former capital of the kingdom of G., and now the chief place in the province of G., in the S. of Spain, is situated 2445 feet above the sea, and 140 miles E.S.E. of Seville. It overlooks the wide and fertile plain known as the Vega of G., and lies in a deep valley between two hills, one of which is crowned by the Alhambra (q. v.), and the other by the suburb of Albaycin. G. is belted by high ruined walls, once studded with 1030 towers, outside of which are villas embosomed in groves. It lies partly between the Xenil, which flows through it, and the Darro, which joins the Xenil about a mile below G. The city has a picturesque aspect from its neighbouring mountains and Saracenic piles, its white walls, airy minarets, gilded cupolas, and intervening masses of verdure. The streets are crooked and narrow, and the houses mostly flat-roofed, with balconies. G. is enlivened by many fountains, and has several fine squares, of which the chief are La Plaza Mayor,

La Bivirambla, and El Campo. The cathedral is a splendid but irregular building. There are some silk and woollen manufactures. Pop. (1870) 67,326. G. was founded by the Arabs in the 10th c., when it belonged to the caliphate of Cordova. In 1236 it became capital of the Kingdom of G. (q. v.), and became a famous seat of Moorish power, wealth, and luxury. It is said to have had 200,000 inhabitants at the beginning of the 14th c., and in later times to have been able to send out an army of 50,000. After a long resistance it was taken by the Spaniards in 1492.

Granada, a former province in the S. of Spain, bounded N.W. by Andalusia, E. by Murcia, and S. and S.E. by the Mediterranean. Area, 11,063 sq. miles; pop. (1870) 1,351,909. It is a fruitful and picturesque region, traversed by the rugged, snow-capped range of the Sierra Nevada, by the Sierra de Ronda, and the Alpujarras, and watered by the Guadalhorce, Almeria, and Almanzora, which flow into the Mediterranean, and by the Xenil, and other affluents of the Guadalquiver. Its mountains shelter deep and fertile valleys, and descend to the lowland by beautiful, richly cultivated terraces. The plains abound in corn and vines, and there are valuable mines of iron, lead, silver, and copper. G., now subdivided into the provinces of G., Malaga, and Almeria, formed the ancient kingdom of G., which in 1235 was made an independent Moorish dominion, and became a famous seat of culture and wealth, exercising considerable influence on Western Europe by the refinement, chivalrous courtesy, and artistic, literary, and scientific activity of its inhabitants. In 1492 it was seized by Ferdinand and Isabella, and in 1510 the Moors were driven from Spain.

Granada, a town of Nicaragua, Central America, on the N.W. shore of Lake Nicaragua. It was founded by Spaniards in 1522, and was once very prosperous, but has not recovered from its siege in 1854–56 during a civil war. Pop. about 8000.

Granadill'a, the name usually given to the edible fruit of several species of *Passiflora* or Passion-Flower (q. v.). *P. quadrangularis* produces the large G., a well-known W. Indian fruit. The roots of the plant are narcotic. Several species are grown in hothouses in Britain.

Gran'ary Weevil. See CORN WEEVIL.

Grana'ti Rad'icis Cor'tex, or **Pomegranate Root Bark**, the dried bark of the root *Punica granatum*, chiefly imported from the S. of Europe, is used in medicine as an astringent and anthelmintic, and, in the latter case, it is more effective than turpentine in expelling tapeworm. For this purpose two ounces of the bruised bark are macerated in twenty-four ounces of boiling water for twenty-four hours, and then boiled down to eighteen ounces. A dose of castor-oil should be administered on the morning of the day previous to taking the medicine, and solid food should be abstained from during the day. A third part of the decoction should be taken early in the morning, another third in half an hour after, and the remainder in another half-hour. The worm is generally expelled entire within about two hours after.

Gran'by, John Manners, Marquis of, son of the third Duke of Rutland, born 2d January 1721. He had already sat for several Parliaments in the House of Commons, when in 1745 he raised the regiment which he commanded at Culloden. Choosing the military career, he served in Germany under Prince Ferdinand of Brunswick, and gained the battle of Minden by disobeying the orders of his superior officer, Lord George Sackville. He further distinguished himself in the other battles of the campaign, but at the peace in 1763 returned to Parliament. He was soon called to a place in the Cabinet, and was in this capacity one of the most bitterly assailed in the *Letters of Junius*. G. died at Scarborough, 19th October 1770. In his lifetime he was much admired by his countrymen.

Gran Chaco, El (*i.e.*, 'the great hunting-ground'), also called **Chaco Gualamba**, is a wide expanse of llanos in S. America, comprising the N.E. of the Argentine Republic and the S.E. of Bolivia. Area and population uncertain. The surface is very level, in the S. waste, in the N. covered with luxuriant vegetation. It is watered by the Rio Salado, Vermego, Pilcomayo, &c. Little is known of the interior, which is occupied by scattered tribes of nomadic Indians.

Grandchildren. See GRANDFATHER.

Grand Combe, La, a town of France, department of Gard, 9 miles N.N.W. of Alais by railway, has important manufactures of iron, and one of the richest coal-pits in France, yielding annually 15,000 tons of fuel. Pop. (1872) 9367.

Grand Days, in English law, were days solemnly kept in the Inns of Court and Chancery during the terms, and on which the famous revels of the Inns were held. They were Ascension Day, St. John the Baptist's Day, All Saints' Day, All Souls' Day, and Candlemas Day. The benchers now decide what days shall be observed as G. D. See Pearce's *Inns of Court and Chancery*.

Grandees' (Span. *grandes*) was as early as the 13th c. the term for a special class of nobles in the kingdom of Castile. The G. included amongst their number, besides the members of the blood royal, all the most distinguished members of the higher nobility of Spain, and enjoyed many peculiar privileges, both formal and real. Ferdinand and Isabella broke their power, and G. became at last merely a court title. Even this dignity was abolished at the Revolution, though subsequently restored.

Grand'father. By the common law of England a G. is not obliged to maintain his grandchildren, but by 43 Eliz. c. 2, he may, if able, be called on by the parish to help to do so. In Scotland, when the father fails, the G. is bound to support his indigent grandchildren, the burden falling first on the paternal G., failing whom it falls on the maternal. The liability is by common law.

Grand Haven, a town of Michigan, U.S., on Lake Michigan. It is the terminus of the Detroit and Milwaukee Railway, has a public bank, eight churches, and a trade in timber, leather, flour, fish, &c. G. is a favourite summer resort. Pop. (1870) 3147.

Grand Jury. After committal of a prisoner, or after acceptance of Bail (q. v.), the next step is to present an Indictment (q. v.) against him to the G. J. This is summoned by the sheriff, and consists of not fewer than twelve, nor more than twenty-three, of the principal men of the county. Before trial they are instructed by the bench as to the subject of it. They only hear evidence for the prosecution. For expediting the proceedings of the G. J., by 19 and 20 Vict. c. 54, persons attending to give evidence before them may be sworn in the presence of the jurors and examined on oath. After evidence has been led, the jury, if they think the accusation groundless, write on the back of the bill of indictment 'Not a true bill,' or 'Not found.' The prisoner is then discharged. But a new bill may be preferred to a subsequent G. J. If the accusation be held to have good ground, the indorsation is 'A true bill.' The indictment is then said to be *found*. But to effect this at least twelve of the jury must concur. As to convict requires the unanimous verdict of the petty jury of twelve men, it follows that no prisoner can be found guilty except by the votes of twenty-four of his countrymen. (See JURIES; JURY, TRIAL BY.) In Scotland, the duties of the G. J. are discharged by a public prosecutor. See ADVOCATE, LORD; CRIMINAL PROCEDURE; PRECOGNITION; PROCURATOR-FISCAL.

Grand Master (Lat. *magnus magister*, Ger. *hochmeister*), the head of the Templars (q. v.), Hospitallers (q. v.), Teutonic Knights (q. v.), and Dominicans.

Grand Pen'sionary, in the Dutch Republic, was State Secretary for the province of Holland, for which he was also Advocate-General until the time of Olden Barneveldt. Afterwards the G. P. was practically Foreign Minister. The office, which was held for five years, was abolished in 1795.

Grand Rapids, a city of Michigan, U.S., on the Grand River, 30 miles E. of Lake Michigan. It is an important railway centre, stands in a thriving agricultural district, and has a large trade in pine and other wood, and manufactures of furniture, agricultural implements, &c. Grand River is here 900 feet wide, and, falling seventeen feet in two miles, supplies excellent water-power to numerous mills. Pop. of G. (1870) 16,507.

Grand River, a river of Michigan, U.S., enters Lake Michigan, after a course of 270 miles, at Grand Haven. It is navigable for 40 miles, to Grand Rapids.

Grandville, Jean Ignace Isidore Gérard, a French artist, born at Nancy, 3d September 1803, removed to Paris in 1823, where in 1828 he published his *Metamorphoses du Jour*, and at once found himself famous. This series of designs represents persons with the heads of animals, and in the selection of the heads and their treatment as expressive of the assumed character of the person represented, G. was wonderfully successful. He afterwards designed series of illustrations for the works of Beranger, for *Gulliver's Travels*, La Fontaine, *Robinson Crusoe*, *Don Quixote*. A posthumous work, *Les Étoiles*, was published in Paris in 1856-57. His *Magasin Pittoresque* embraced many curious designs, as the *Scènes de la Vie Privée des Animaux*, and many others of equal humour and peculiarity. The illustrated periodicals for which he produced the majority of his political and other fugitive sketches were *La Caricature*, *Figaro*, and *L'Illustration*. G. died in Paris, 17th March 1847.

Gra'ne, or **Qua'de**, a seaport of Arabia, in the N.W. angle of the Persian Gulf. It has some trade in carpets, fruits, &c. Pop. 8000.

Grani'cus, the ancient name of a river in Mysia, rising in Mount Cotylus, a branch of Ida, and flowing through the Adrastian plain into the Propontis. It is small, and, like the rest of the rivers in the Troad, unnavigable; but, like them also, it is famous in poetry. It is, moreover, celebrated in history for two great victories gained on its banks—one in B.C. 334 by Alexander the Great with 30,000 men over Darius with 600,000 Persians, when 100,000 of the latter were left dead on the field; the other by the Roman general Lucullus over the great Mithridates in 73, 71, or 69 B.C. (The chronology of the events in the Mithridatic war is very confused and perplexing.) Famous as this small stream has been, there is considerable difficulty in identifying it with any modern river. Some travellers consider it to be the *Kodsha-su*, others the *Dimotico*.

Gran'ier de Cassagnac (Adolphe de), born at Aveyron-Bergelle (Gers.) in 1808, reached Paris in 1832, and, introduced by Victor Hugo, became a contributor to the *Journal des Debats* and the *Revue de Paris*. The acerbity of his style gained him a position on the staff of the *Press*. He visited the Antilles in 1840, was elected *délégué* for Guadaloupe, and having married a creole, Madle. de Beauvallon, returned to France. He became editor of the *Pouvoir* in 1850, afterwards joined the staff of the *Constitutionnel*. He eagerly espoused the Government inaugurated by the *coup d'état*, and was elected deputy to the Corps Legislative. He was re-elected deputy in 1857, in 1863, and 1869. In conjunction with others he founded the *Réveil*, later he undertook the editorship of the *Pays*, in which, after 1866, he was assisted by his son, Paul de Cassagnac. He was promoted 'officier' of the Legion of Honour in 1857, and 'commandeur,' 1865. Throughout his career he has signalised himself as a violent partisan of successive conservative Governments, and has used every weapon, fair and unfair, against his adversaries. He has been engaged in many duels, some of them, it is said, not of a strictly honourable character, and has been implicated in numerous affairs which have necessitated his visiting the Palais de Justice. His principal substantive works are *Histoire des Causes de la Revolution Française* (1850), *Histoire de la Chute de Louis-Philippe* (1857), and *Les Girondins et les Massacres de Septembre* (1860)—productions marked by imperfect research and unwarranted conclusions.—**Paul de G. de C.**, son of the preceding, notorious as a literary and political writer and otherwise, was born about 1841. He commenced his career as a journalist in 1866 on the *Pays*, of which he afterwards became *rédacteur en chef*. Early in his career he fought a duel with M. A. Scholl, a satirical journalist; he fought M. Vermorel in 1867, Lieutenant Luiller in 1868, and M. Gustave Flourens (see FLOURENS) in 1869. This last fight, in which G.'s antagonist received many wounds, one of which endangered his life, lasted for twenty-five minutes, and is one of the most determined duels of recent times. G., who has spilt about as much blood as ink, has steadily supported the cause of the Imperialists, and at present (1877) is one of the most audacious and scornful Bonapartists in the National Assembly.

Gran'ite (Ital. *granito*, 'grained,' from Lat. *granum*), a well-known and easily recognised igneous rock, composed of the three minerals felspar, mica, and quartz in varying proportions. The felspar is always an essential ingredient, forming rarely less than a half of the mass, but the mica and quartz may exist in minute almost unrecognisable quantity. The texture of G. also varies greatly, and its colour is red, grey, or white, with intermediate tints depending upon the proportion and colour of the constituent minerals. The felspar is usually orthoclase. Oligoclase, however, is also found, being recognisable by its finely striated surfaces; and, more rarely, albite. The quartz but seldom forms perfect crystals, an interesting and remarkable fact when it is observed that both the felspathic and micaceous ingredients not unfrequently are most distinctly crystallised. This may probably be due to the physical phenomena attending the production of granitic rocks, which are now generally believed to have solidified by cooling. Differences between the fusing-points of the various minerals easily account for the more perfect crystallisation of the felspar and mica, which may have solidified while the quartz was still viscous. As proved by Hutton towards the close of last century, G. is, in certain circumstances, an igneous rock. It forms the heart of all the great primitive mountain chains, and is regarded as the original source of all the felspathic or highly silicated traps and lavas. It is also conceivable that it may have given rise to the more basic traps, if the circumstances in which it was fused admitted of the admixture of some fusible bases. In many cases, however, undoubted metamorphic rocks have been observed undistinguishable in character from a true igneous G. It is, in such instances, the ultimate metamorphosis of gneiss, mica-schist, or other schistose rock, losing in the process all trace of stratified structure. Syenite may be regarded as a variety of G. in which hornblende replaces the mica. *Graphic G.* is distinguished by the peculiar regularity of the crystallisation of the quartz in the felspar, presenting on a cross section an appearance somewhat resembling Hebrew writing. *Protogine* has the felspar replaced by talc, and occurs in the metamorphic rocks of the Alps. G. is important from an industrial point of view, since in it are found ores of tin, copper, zinc, iron, antimony, nickel, cobalt, bismuth, silver, &c., and also the emerald, topaz, fluorspar, garnet, tourmaline, and other precious and useful minerals. As a building material G. is very valuable, especially the finer in texture and more quartzose varieties, which, if free from pyrites or other iron ore, are very durable.

Gran Sass'o d' Ital'ia ('great rock of Italy'), or **Monte Corno** ('horn mountain'), the highest peak of the Apennines, in Abruzzo, province of Teramo. It is a towering, snow-capped mass of calcareous rock, nearly 10,000 feet high, rising in a sublime series of wild mural slopes and vast overhanging cliffs.

Grant, in English law, formerly signified a conveyance of incorporeal things, as reversions, tithes, &c. But by 8 and 9 Vict. c. 106, it is enacted that incorporeal as well as corporeal estate may pass by G.

Grant, a name of several distinguished Scotchmen and Scotchwomen of different families, of whom the following are the most notable:—1. **Mrs. Anne G.**, a Scottish authoress, born at Glasgow, February 21, 1755. In 1779 she married the Rev. Mr. G. of Laggan, on whose death in 1801 she was forced to support herself and family by literature, and produced, among other works, *The Highlanders* (1803), a volume of verse, which was well received; *Letters from the Mountains* (1806), a collection of her own letters; *Memoirs of an American Lady* (1808); *On the Superstitions of the Highlanders* (1811); *Eighteen Hundred and Thirteen* (1814), a poem of very little worth. She received a pension in 1825, and died at Edinburgh, November 7, 1838. See her Life by her son, J. G. (1844).—2. **Mrs. G. of Carron** (born 1745, died 1814), authoress of *Roy's Wife of Aldivalloch*, a song of exquisite humour and vivacity.—3. **Charles G., Lord Glenelg**, born of a Highland family at Kidderpore, Bengal, in 1799. He studied at Cambridge University, was called to the bar in 1807, and in 1811 was elected M.P. for the Inverness burghs. After being for five years a Lord of the Treasury, he was in 1819 made Secretary for Ireland, and in this office showed great impartiality, and strove to carry out a policy of conciliation. He was made Vice-President of the Board of Trade in 1823, President of the Board of Control in 1830, and Secretary of State to the Colonies in 1834. After 1839 he took little part in politics. G. died at Cannes in 1866. He was a Liberal in politics, an eloquent speaker, and a pure-spirited statesman.—4. **Sir Robert G.**, brother of the preceding, born in 1788, studied at Cambridge, was called to the bar in 1807, sat for several years in Parliament, was knighted and made Governor of Bombay in 1834. He died at Dapoorie in 1838. G. wrote two treatises on Indian affairs, and some hymns inspired by an evangelical devotion, which were collected and published by his brother in 1839.—5. **Sir Francis G., P.R.A.**, fourth son of Francis G. of Kilgraston, Perthshire, was born at Edinburgh in 1803. He was intended for the bar, but abandoned law for painting; was elected an Associate in 1842, a R.A. in 1851, and President of the Royal Academy in 1866, shortly after which he was knighted. He was made D.C.L. of Oxford in 1870. Among his portraits are those of Macaulay, Landseer, Sir J. H. Grant, Disraeli, Lords Palmerston, and Russell.—6. **Sir James Hope G., G.C.B.**, brother of the preceding, was born in 1808, distinguished himself as brigade-major in China; was commander in the battles of Chillianwallah and Gujerat; was made brevet-colonel in 1854; showed great ability at the siege of Delhi and relief of Lucknow; and was appointed major-general and K.C.B. in 1858; led the army which took Pekin in 1860; was made lieutenant-general in 1861, and general in 1872. He died March 7, 1875. He wrote *Incidents of the Chinese War of* 1860 (Lond. 1874).—7. **Sir William G.**, born at Elchies, Morayshire, in 1754. He went out in 1775 to Canada, where he was made attorney-general, and in 1787 he was called to the English bar. In 1790 he was returned to Parliament, and in 1793 was made a judge by Pitt, of whom he had been a firm supporter. In 1801 he became Master of the Rolls, retired from Parliament in 1812, and died in 1832. He was a strict Conservative in politics, an admirable debater, and a learned and sagacious lawyer.

Grant, Ulysses Simpson, late President of the United States, was the son of a leather merchant of Scottish descent, and was born at Point Pleasant, Ohio, April 27, 1822. He entered the Military Academy at West Point in 1839, received a commission as second lieutenant in 1842, took part in all the battles, save Buena Vista, of the Mexican war, and in 1848 married the daughter of a St. Louis merchant. In 1854 he was made captain, when he resigned his commission, and after engaging in farming near St. Louis, went into business with his father. Until the civil war G. was quite unknown; but shortly after its outbreak he was made brigadier-general of volunteers, and after the battle of Belmont and the capture of Fort Donelson became commander of W. Tennessee. He drove back Beauregard at Shiloh (April 7, 1862), repulsed the Confederates at Corinth (October 4, 1862), took Vicksburg (July 4, 1863), and (November 23, 24, 25) defeated General Bragg at Chattanooga, a victory which opened up Georgia to the Federals. In February 1864 G. was made lieutenant-general, and on 17th March took command of all the Northern forces. He now set out against the army of N. Virginia under Lee, which he drove back after several desperate battles, while Sherman fought his way through Georgia. G. then held Lee shut up at Richmond, the siege of which he pushed on with unflinching energy, notwithstanding the impatient murmurs of the Northern States, while Sherman, Schofield, and Sheridan routed the other Confederate leaders. After he was joined by Sheridan, G. captured Richmond, April 3, 1865, and on April 9 surrounded Lee at Appomatox, where the Confederate general surrendered with 27,000 men, G. granting him very generous terms. This ended the civil war, and immediately after Abraham Lincoln was assassinated and Andrew Johnson became President. G., who was hailed throughout the North with boundless enthusiasm, and loaded with honours, was now placed in opposition to Johnson, interposing in behalf of the South, and averting the prosecution of Lee. Johnson afterwards in a measure severed himself from the Federals, and in 1868 G. was elected President. During his administration the enmities engendered by the war were greatly allayed, the national debt largely reduced, and the Alabama question settled. In 1872 G. was re-elected President over Horace Greeley (q. v.), the candidate of the Democrats and 'Liberal Republicans.' His second presidentship was marked by financial difficulties and troubles in the South, which culminated (1876–77) in the contest regarding his successor. G. is the greatest general that America has produced, and may even rank among the foremost generals in modern times. Without undervaluing the brilliant military genius of Sherman and Sheridan on the one side, or of Stonewall Jackson and Lee on the other, a comparison of the work done by the host of able soldiers that the civil war brought to the front distinctly shows G. to be the man who most thoroughly grasped the whole situation, and who saw most clearly how the end could be attained.

Gran'tham, a town of Lincolnshire, England, on the Witham, 26 miles S. of Lincoln by railway. It has a beautiful parish church (St. Wolfran's) of the 13th c. (restored by Sir G. G. Scott, 1865–68), with pointed windows and a spire 273 feet high; a free grammar-school (with an endowment of £800 yearly), where Sir Isaac Newton received part of his early training; two large corn-exchanges, a new townhall, and a philosophical institute. G. is connected with the Trent by a canal, and carries on a trade in malt, coal, corn, &c. Here are Messrs. Hornsby's agricultural implement factory and ironfoundry. It returns two members to Parliament. Pop. (1871) 5028.

Gran'ton, a port of Midlothian, on the S. shore of the Firth of Forth, opposite Burntisland, and 3 miles N.W. of Edinburgh by railway. It has a good harbour of 130 acres, a pier 1700 feet long and 200 broad, an eastern breakwater 3170 feet long, and a western breakwater 3100 feet, the greater part of which is converted into wharfage, with steam-cranes and special appliances for shipping coal (in 1876, 230,000 tons). The trade is in grain, timber, iron, oil, tobacco, &c. G. is the ferry port of the North British Railway, and has regular steam traffic with London, Aberdeen, Shetland, Norway, and Sweden, &c. In 1876 there entered and cleared the port 1924 vessels of 670,956 tons. The customs revenue (1876) was £73,762. G. has one of the finest tobacco bonding warehouses in the country, with an area of 14,000 feet; also large sawmills, foundries, engineering, ink, and chemical works. Pop. (1871) 976. The docks are the property of the Duke of Buccleuch.

Granula'tion is one of the modes by which a wound or sore, or part previously acutely inflamed, heals. G. is always a reparative process, which may occur with or without suppuration, and is associated with an exudation of inflammatory lymph, into which old vessels extend, and in which new ones are formed. See INFLAMMATION, ULCER, WOUND.

Granvell'a, Antoine Perrenot, Cardinal de, the accomplished but unscrupulous Minister of the Emperor Karl V. and of Philip II., was born at Ornans, in Burgundy, 20th August 1517. In 1540 he became Bishop of Arras, and soon entered the diplomatic service of Karl V., under whom G.'s father had kept the great seal. G.'s sagacity and linguistic attainments—so great that he had perfect command of seven languages—soon raised him to high favour, and his influence over the great political negotiations of his time renders him one of the most prominent men of the 16th c. G. was present at the Diets of Worms and Ratisbon, and at the Council of Trent. He negotiated the marriage of Philip II. with Mary of England, and, as Minister of Margaret of Parma, he conducted the affairs of the Netherlands from 1559 till his unpopularity compelled him to retire in 1564. In 1570 he concluded the alliance of Spain and the Pope against the Turks, was for a time vice-king of Naples, and died at Madrid, 21st September 1586. For his services to Church and State, G. was successively rewarded with the archbishoprics of Mechlin and Besançon, and in 1561 he was raised to the cardinalate. The papers left by G. illustrate all the negotiations in which he was engaged, and extend to eighty folio volumes of MS. In 1842 the publication of them was begun. See Gerlache's *Philippe II. et G.* (Bruss. 1843).

Gran'ville, a fortified seaport in the department of La Manche, France, on a rocky peninsula 60 miles S.W. of Caen, and 12 N.W. of Avranches. It has a Flamboyant church of grey granite, and a new pier and floating-dock. The harbour is dry at ebb tide. Many English people resort hither for sea-bathing, and there are shipbuilding industries and oyster fisheries. Pop. (1872) 14,747. G. was burned by the English in 1695, and was besieged by the Vendeans in 1793.

Grape-Shot is a combination of a number of small balls to be fired from a cannon, and contained in a strong canvas bag firmly bound with a network of cord, the whole being attached to a circular iron plate, the diameter of which is adapted to the gun. This species of shot is very destructive.

Graph'ic Representa'tion is the practical application of the principles of co-ordinate geometry to the construction of curves, which show readily to the eye the relations existing between a series of numbers which refer to some one physical phenomenon. The construction of maps by means of meridians and parallels is a very perfect example of the nature of the methods commonly employed, except that in this particular case the co-ordinates are not referred to *rectangular* axes. In the elucidation of the laws by which a continually and regularly varying phenomenon is governed, the method of G. R. is of singular power. As an example, take the variation of barometric pressure throughout the day. Measure along a horizontal line twenty-four equal spaces to represent hours, and at each point raise a perpendicular representing by its length the height of the mercury at the corresponding hour. The result will be a series of points, the curve through which will indicate on mere inspection the general variation of barometric pressure from hour to hour. In our best observations the barometer is made to record its variation in this way for every instant. A strong electric or lime light is thrown through the barometer tube upon a strip of sensitive photographic paper, which is moved slowly and equally along by clockwork. The column of mercury of course shuts off the light from the lower part of the paper, which is therefore not acted upon, and by this means a sharp line of demarcation is obtained upon the paper, which gives at once the law of variation. When there are three variables involved in the progression of any phenomenon, G. R. on a plane surface becomes more difficult. For instance, in mapping a country, we must take account of vertical elevation, as well as of latitude and longitude. The usual method of representing mountains on maps is not only inaccurate, but, as a rule, misleading. The true scientific method is by *contour lines*. A glance at an Ordnance Survey map will show at once the nature of this representation, which consists in drawing through points at the same elevation a line, which must be ultimately a closed curve. The principle is the same as in the drawing of Isotherms (q. v.) or equipotential lines (see POTENTIAL). The closer two different contour lines are, the steeper is the slope at that place; and if they touch, they indicate a perpendicular precipice.

In all branches of science graphical methods are coming into greater favour, and in practical science the Continental engineers have developed a kind of applied geometry which they call graphical statics. By its methods the engineer can solve numerous statical problems by simple construction more easily and with as much accuracy as by calculations founded on analytical investigations. The leading treatise on this subject is the *Graphische Statik* of Professor Culman of Zürich (2d ed. 1875). See also Professor Dubois' *Elements of Graphical Statics* (New York, 1875).

Graph'is, a genus of Lichens (q. v.) which have their fructification resembling Oriental writing, hence they have been called 'scripture worts.' There are several species in Britain which grow on the bark of trees.

Graph'ite. See BLACKLEAD and CARBON.

Graph'otype, a cheap and rapid process of engraving, which, it was expected, would before this have supplanted wood-engraving. But while it is well adapted for the rougher work of maps and diagrams, it would prove a poor substitute for highly finished wood-engravings. In 1860 Mr. De Witt C. Hitchcock, a draughtsman on wood, had occasion to remove the white enamel from a visiting card, and discovered that the printed portion resisted the action of his brush, and stood out in relief. This circumstance suggested to him the idea of the G., and after a series of experiments the following process was perfected:—A metallic plate is coated under hydraulic pressure with French chalk, finely pulverised and sifted. The surface is then sized, and a drawing made upon it with ink composed of lamp-black and glue. The chalk not drawn upon is next brushed off with silk velvet, and the drawing left in relief is hardened by soaking the block in water-glass. Finally a stereotype cast is taken, which is used for printing the impressions.

Grap'nel, Grap'line, or **Grapp'ling Iron**, an anchor-shaped iron instrument with four or six bent and pointed claws springing from a stem, at the end of which is a ring to which a rope is attached. Made on a small scale, it is used as an anchor for boats or small craft. Formerly grapnels of a large size were frequently used in naval engagements, to draw ships closer, and facilitate the attack of boarders.

Grapp'le-Plant, the common name for *Uncaria* (Harpagophytum) *procumbens*, an African plant belonging to the order Pedaliaceæ. It has received the name G.-P. from its fruits being furnished with very strong, sharp, branching hooks, which lay hold of animals and travellers' garments, and with difficulty can be removed.

Grap'tolites, an important fossil genus of *Cœlenterata*, allied to the existing *Sertularidæ*, or 'sea-firs,' which belong to the class *Hydrozoa*, or that including the zoophytes, jellyfishes, &c. The G. occur as fossils in a very distinct and limited series of rocks—the Upper Cambrian and Silurian, attaining the maximum of their development in the former. The best-known genera of G. are *Graptolites*, *Rastrites*, *Didymograpsus*, *Dichograpsus*, *Diplograpsus*, &c. These fossils were probably not rooted and attached like our existing zoophytes, but were free-floating bodies; at least no disc or attaching part has yet been discovered in any specimen. The outer portion of the organism was protected by a horny covering, and the polypites or distinct animals of each graptolite were enclosed in horny cups or *cellules*, a conformation also seen in living 'sea-firs,' in which the cups are named *hydrothecæ*. Further, the interior of each graptolite was strengthened by a central solid rod or axis, this latter structure being unrepresented in living zoophytes. Certain bodies supposed to represent the *ovarian bodies* or *egg-capsules* of the G. have also been discovered in a fossil state. The G. are divided into the *Monoprionidia* and *Diprionidia*, the former (*e.g.*, *G. priodon*) having only a single row of cellules, and the latter (*e.g.*, *Diplograpsus*) a row of cellules on each side of the axis. About sixteen genera of G. are known.

Gras'litz, an industrial town of Bohemia, on the Zwoda, 88 miles N.W. of Prague. The manufactures are cottons, paper, machinery, scientific instruments, &c. Pop. (1869) 5786.

Gras'mere ('the lake of swine'), one of the smallest, but also one of the finest, of the Westmoreland lakes, a mile long and half a mile broad, and situated about three miles N.W. of Ambleside. The vale, lake, and mountain girdle of G. exhibit a rare harmony of natural forms, and their beauty, once seen, can never be forgotten. Wordsworth, who for many years lived on a rising ground overlooking the lake, and whose plain grave, worn by the feet of pilgrims, is in the village churchyard, has sung the praises of every striking feature of the scene.

Grass, Law Regarding. Growing grass belongs to the owner of the soil, and is real estate. In Scotland, the landlord's Hypothec (q. v.) extends over the grass-mail of fields let for pasture.

Grass Cloth, a popular name for a fine soft fabric made from the fibre of *Bœhmeria nivea*, extensively and carefully cultivated in China and other Eastern countries. As the plant belongs to the nettleworts, G. C. is a misnomer.

Grasse', a town of France, department of Alpes-Maritimes, on steep southern slopes 20 miles W. of Nice. It is embowered amid rich flower gardens and citron groves, looks out over the sea to the blue hills of Corsica, and has an old cathedral and hospital with many good pictures. There are extensive manufactures of perfumes (exports 11,000,000 francs' worth yearly), soap, silks, &c. Pop. (1872) 8382. G. was founded by Sardinian Jews in the 6th c.

Grass'es (Old Eng. *gærs* and *graes*, 'that which grows;' comp. Lat. *cresco*, 'I grow,' Gr. *graō*, 'I gnaw,' and Sansk. *gras*, 'to devour') belong to the class Monocotyledons (q. v.), sub-class Glumiferæ, and natural order Gramineæ. They constitute a well-marked order, which is characterised by round, generally hollow, jointed stems. Their leaves are furnished with a projecting membrane called a ligule. The flowers, usually produced in spikelets with outer scales called glumes, have two styles and three stamens. The plants of the order are generally low, tufted herbs, but some species, such as the sugar-cane and bamboo, attain a considerable height. They have all slender stems strengthened by a deposit of silica in the epidermis. G. are one of the most useful and widely distributed families of plants known. As furnishing the chief article of food, they are cultivated in all parts of the civilised world, man and beast being alike dependent on them. Among the more useful G. may be enumerated the various cereals. Barley (*Hordeum vulgare*) and oats (*Avena sativa*) extend to the northern parts of Scandinavia and Siberia. Rye (*Secale cereale*) is grown along the shores of the Baltic, Russia, and N. Germany. Wheat (*Triticum vulgare*) is cultivated in Great Britain, the middle of Europe, Hungary, and in the southern parts of the Russian empire. In Southern Europe, America, and in the tropics, as

Central Africa, maize (*Zea mais*) appears. Rice (*Oryza sativa*), the staple article of food for the greater part of mankind, is met with throughout all the warmer parts of Asia and the Old World, as well as in the Southern States of N. America. The seeds of *Sorghum vulgare* and *Panicum miliaceum* are known as Guinea corn and millet. All these grains have been cultivated from time immemorial, and no trace of their origin remains. Sugar-cane is chiefly grown in the E. and W. Indies, in Hong-Kong, Java, Jamaica, and Demerara. The bamboos rival the palms in usefulness. Various G. are grown as fodder, as the rye-grass (Lolium); others (*Andropogon*) yield aromatic oils; while many G. fulfil a most important purpose by binding together loose sand shores with their long creeping roots, and thus form a natural bulwark against the inroads of the sea. There are no poisonous plants in this order.

Grass'hopper, a name given to the various genera of insects belonging to the order *Orthoptera* (q. v.), and nearly allied to the locusts, crickets, &c. The genus *Acrida*, represented by the *A. viridissima*, or great green G., is one of the best-known groups. The wings are long, the wing-covers (formed by the front wings) form a slanting roof, and the ovipositor is flat and sword-shaped. The abdomen bears four straight spines. This G. attains a length of from two to two and a half inches. Its colour is a delicate green. The ovipositor is used to bore holes in the earth, for the purpose of burying the eggs. The young are like the adult, and the pupa does not pass through any quiescent stage (as in butterflies); the *Metamorphosis* (q. v.) is therefore said to be *incomplete* or *hemimetabolic*. The characteristic 'chirp' of the G. is produced, as in the crickets, by a peculiar arrangement of the anterior wings or *elytra*. The tarsi are four-jointed, and the ocelli or simple eyes are usually wanting. The food consists of leaves and the soft parts of plants.

Grass of Parnass'us, the common name for *Parnassia palustris*, a beautiful bog plant, placed by some authors in the natural order *Hypericaceæ*; by others, in *Saxifragaceæ*. It is not uncommon in Northern Britain and other parts of Europe, and has been named from Mount Parnassus, to which, however, it is not peculiar. Dioscorides called it *Agrostis en to Parnasso*; in France it is the *fleur du Parnassus*, and in Germany the *Einblatt*.

Grass Tree, the common name for the species of *Xanthorrhœa*, a remarkable genus of Australian Liliaceous plants resembling small palms. Two kinds of fragrant resin, one yellow and the other red, are obtained from them, and their foliage affords fodder for cattle. *X. arborea* and *X. hastilis* are the most conspicuous.

Grass'um, in Scotch law, is an immediate payment in consideration of a lease for a term of years. When the title of an heir in possession prohibits alienation, the general rule seems to be that he must administer the estate *secundum bonum et æquum*, taking no more of the profits than he leaves to his successor. The equivalent terms of English law are *premium* and *fine*. A freeholder may let his land at any rent and for any premium or fine which he can get.

Grass Wrack, or **Sea Wrack**, the popular name for *Zostera marina*, a salt-water plant belonging to the natural order *Zosteraceæ*. It has a wide distribution, and is common on the shores of Britain. It is largely used for packing glass and earthenware. In Russia it has been found in old tombs among pottery. In the N. of Europe beds are frequently stuffed with it, and it is sold in this country for similar purposes under the name of *Alva* (*Ulva* or *Alga*) *marina*.

Grate (Ital. *grata*, 'a lattice;' from Lat. *crates*, 'a hurdle'), a contrivance consisting essentially of an iron sparred basket for burning fuel placed in an open fireplace. The sides and back are commonly lined with firebrick to conserve and radiate the heat. By placing a thin metal plate in the bottom in place of bars, which cause an excessive draught, a great saving of fuel is effected. As five-sixths of the heat produced in an open fireplace passes up the chimney, it should be contracted at the throat. 'Register grates' are provided with movable plates for this purpose. Many kinds of 'smokeless grates' have been designed on Franklin's idea of a reversible box-G., in which the coal is ignited at the top and burns downwards. When the charge is nearly exhausted but still red hot, the G. is replenished, then closed with a lid, and turned upside down. In Dr. Arnott's smokeless G. a large box for holding a large supply of coal is placed beneath the fire-bars, at the level of which the burning coal is maintained by raising a false bottom in the box. In this way the coal beneath is subjected to a crude process of distillation, and the carbon vapours emitted are consumed as they pass through the burning layer.

Grate, in mining, signifies a perforated metal plate used for riddling disintegrated ores.

Gra'tian, or **Grazia'no**, the collector of a great body of ecclesiastical acts and decrees, commonly called the 'Decretum Gratiani,' was born at Chiusi in Tuscany in the beginning of the 12th c. Nothing is known of the personal history of this celebrated canonist except that he passed a considerable portion of his life in the monastery of St. Felice at Bologna. The 'Decretum' was probably compiled between the years 1130 and 1151. How far it is the work of G. himself cannot now be ascertained. Historical criticism has shown much of it—for instance, the so-called 'Isodorian Decretals'—to be apocryphal. In addition to decrees of councils and popes, the Decretum contains numerous quotations from the Scriptures, the fathers, and the Roman law. The first part of the work treats of the hierarchical constitution of the Church, with special reference to doctrine and morals; the second is occupied with external jurisdiction; and the third and last with the Church's inner life, ritual, and ordinances. G. died at Bologna, but the date of his death is unknown.

Gratia'nus, Augustus, son of Valentinian I. by his first wife Severa, was born at Sirmium in Pannonia, 19th April A.D. 359. In A.D. 366 he was made consul, and on 24th August 367 he was raised to the rank of Augustus. In 368 A.D. he accompanied his father against the Alemanni, more that he might learn the art of war than experience its hardships. The poet Ausonius was his tutor, and it is to the credit of G. that he afterwards raised him to the consulship in token of his gratitude (379 A.D.). On the death of Valentinian at Bregenz A.D. 375, the troops declared G.'s half-brother, Valentinian II., a child of four years, his partner in the empire. As the eastern provinces were subject to Valens, brother and colleague of Valentinian I., the western provinces fell to be divided between the young emperors. The part allotted to G. included Gaul, Spain, and Britain. G. fixed his residence at Treviri (*Trèves*). In the early part of his reign Illyricum and the Danubian provinces were the scenes of ceaseless strife, and G. was on the eve of starting for Thrace to assist his uncle, when the Lentienses, a German tribe, to the number of 40,000, invaded his dominions. They were cut to pieces by the imperial army in May 378 A.D. G. now pressed towards the eastern portion of the empire, where he heard of the defeat and death of Valens near Adrianople, August 378 A.D. The eastern empire now fell to G.; but feeling himself unequal to the task of the undivided sovereignty, he recalled Theodosius from Spain, and assumed him as his colleague, 19th January 379. After this we hear but little of G.'s warlike or other transactions. He seems to have persecuted with great severity both the pagans and heretic Christians, and thereby to have alienated the affections of many of his subjects. The frivolous amusements and low company with which he occupied his time increased his unpopularity with the army. At this crisis Maximus, being chosen by the legions in Britain, crossed into Gaul and defeated G. near Paris. Deserted by his troops, he was pursued and slain by Andragathius, 25th August 383 A.D.

Grati'ola, a genus of herbaceous plants of the natural order *Scrophulariaceæ*, found in Europe, N. and S. America, and Australia. *G. officinalis* is the hedge hyssop of Europe, which was formerly held in great esteem as a medicine. It is very bitter, and acts as a purgative and an emetic. Cattle have been poisoned by it in Switzerland.

Gratt'an, The Right Honourable Henry, a great Irish statesman and orator, was born in Dublin, July 3, 1746. After studying at Trinity College, Dublin, he entered at the Temple, London, and in 1772 was called to the Irish bar. He won no success as a lawyer, soon devoted himself wholly to politics, and in 1775 was returned to the Irish Parliament by the borough of Charlemont. He now vindicated the constitutional rights of Ireland with such effective fervour of eloquence that in 1782 the Irish House won the privilege of conducting its business without the control of the English Parliament or Privy Council. For this service the Irish Parliament proposed to make him a grant of £100,000, which was at his request reduced to £50,000. G.'s popularity now greatly waned, and he was ably opposed by Henry Flood (q. v.); but his successful resistance in 1785 to the unjust restrictions which it was sought to lay on Irish commerce made him again the idol of his countrymen. In 1790 he was returned for Dublin, and in 1805, after the Union—of which he had been a determined foe—was elected to the Imperial Parliament for the English borough of Malton. In 1806 he was again elected by Dublin, which he thenceforth represented until 1820. He continued to labour in the interests of his country until his death, June 4, 1820, in London, whither he had gone, against the advice of his physicians, to contend for Catholic emancipation. He was buried in Westminster Abbey. G.'s character seems to have been unimpeachable, and his fiery patriotism was unstained by revolutionary sentiment. His oratory was admirably varied; his speeches abound in pathos and sarcasm, in stormy invective, close reasoning, felicitous epigram, and terse antithesis. G.'s *Speeches* (4 vols. Dub. 1821) were collected by his son, who also wrote *Life and Times of Henry G.* (5 vols. Lond. 1839-45). See also Lecky's *Leaders of Public Opinion in Ireland* (1871-72).

Gratu'itous Deed, in Scotch law, means a deed granted without value given for it. A person cannot dispose of his property to the injury of his creditors, or of those to whom he is under legal obligation. The granter of a G. D. with a future obligation in favour of children or grandchildren who falls into poverty before the date of fulfilment may draw back so far as to provide for his own subsistence. The rule does not, as in Roman law, extend to a Donation (q. v.) to a stranger. In England a G. D. is usually called a Gift (q. v.).

Gratz, formerly **Grätz** (Slav. 'the fortified place'), the capital of Styria, Austro-Hungary, on the Mur, 1047 feet above the sea, and 140 miles S.S.W. of Vienna by the Vienna and Trieste Railway. The old part of the city, on the left bank, is girt with walls and shady promenades, and has a cathedral of St. Ægidi of 1462, the church of St. Leonhard of 1283, the old 'burg' of the Styrian dukes, the arsenal, many fine palaces, a university (founded 1585, and rebuilt in 1863) with a library of 55,000 volumes, a museum, picture gallery, &c. The river is crossed by two chain and two wooden bridges. G. has manufactures of steel and iron wares, saltpetre, cottons, woollens, paper, &c. It is a bishop's see. Pop. (1869) 81,119, of whom many are Italians and Jews.

Grau'denz (Slav. 'the fortified place'), a fortified town of W. Prussia, on the Vistula, 20 miles S.S.W. of Marienwerder. It has a Catholic seminary (formerly a Jesuit college), a convent of 1635, a Protestant seminary for female teachers, extensive barracks, woollen and cotton industries, and a trade in cattle, corn, tobacco, &c. The Vistula is here crossed by a bridge of boats. One mile to the N. is the bombproof fort of G., built by Friedrich II. in 1770-76, and bravely defended by Courbière against the French in 1807. Pop. (1871) 14,844.

Grauw'acke, or Grey'wacke, a name given to certain metamorphosed sandstones, consisting of rounded or angular grains of quartz, felspar, mica, or slate, cemented together by an altered arenaceous or argillaceous base. Its colour is usually grey, but may be brown, red, or blue. The name is of German origin, and was applied by Werner and his disciples to what was deemed a highly important unfossiliferous rock, which was supposed to occupy a certain geological position. G., however, belongs to all periods, and in most cases contains fossils.

Grav'el. See CALCULUS.

Gravel, in geology, is any accumulation of rounded pebbles and sand. Beds of G. occur of all ages, but the most extensive belong to the Tertiary formations. The Glacial Period is especially rich in such deposits, and along the slopes of the valleys through which certain rivers—notably the Somme in France—flow, terraces of G. are found indicating the much greater extension in former times of the river's channel. All gravels have been deposited by running streams or water currents, or through the wearing action of the sea along the coast-line; and the more ancient accumulations have almost always consolidated, by the infiltration of some cementing material, into conglomerate or pudding-stone.

Grave'lines (Flem. *Gravelinghe*, 'count's ditch,' so named because Count Theoderic of Flanders here constructed a canal), a fortified seaport of France, in the department Du Nord, at the mouth of the Aa, 10 miles S.W. of Dunkirk. It is defended by Fort Philippe, and has a church of the 16th c., a fine market-place, a trade in timber from the Baltic, and in butter, eggs, cheese, &c., to London, several salt-refineries and linen-factories, &c. The harbour is left dry at ebb tide. Pop. (1872) 7723. G. was founded by Count Theoderic in 1066, taken by the English under the Bishop of Norwich in 1383, and ravaged by the Duke of Burgundy in 1405. The Spanish, under Count Egmont, gained here a famous victory over the French, under Marshal Tromes, 13th July 1558. By the peace of the Pyrenees, G. was finally ceded to Louis XIV.

Grave'lotte, a village in the German province of Elsass-Lothringen, 7 miles W. of Metz and 35 E. of Verdun, was the scene of one of the fiercest battles in the late Franco-German war. Prevented by the first and second armies of Germany under King Wilhelm from marching W. to Verdun, the French army under Bazaine was placed in a strong defensive position on the elevation marked by St. Privat, Amanvillers, Rozerieulles, and Verneville. At 10 o'clock on the morning of August 18, 1870, the French centre was vigorously attacked, the 9th German corps by noon gaining the height of Verneville, and pouring a terrific fire into the batteries of Ste. Marie, St. Privat, and Amanvillers. By seven o'clock St. Privat was taken, but it was quite dark when the contest was finally decided by the failure of an attempt to break through the German lines at G. The French had then to fall back on Metz. The Germans, numbering 211,000, lost 904 officers and 19,658 men; the French, 140,000 in number, lost 609 officers and 11,605 men. St. Privat and Rezonville have also given name to the battle.

Graves, Robbing. It appears to be the doctrine of the common law of England that a human body, living or dead, is not the subject of theft. (See LARCENY or THEFT. See, however, ABDUCTION.) Thus stealing a dead body is not felony, unless some of the grave-clothes be taken. But it is an offence not to bury a dead body; and in Rex *v.* Young the master of a workhouse and a surgeon were convicted of a conspiracy to prevent the burial of a person who died in a workhouse; and in Rex *v.* Cundick the defendant was found guilty of a misdemeanour for not having buried the body of an executed felon intrusted to him by the gaoler for that purpose (Surrey Spring Assizes, 1822). See ANATOMY, IN LAW; CHURCHYARDS.

Graves'end ('the town at the end of the *graef* or moat'), a parliamentary and municipal borough in the county of Kent, England, and a thriving port on the Thames, opposite Tilbury Fort, and 24 miles E. of London by rail. Its townhall is a handsome classical edifice, and there are a number of interesting churches, old and new. From Windmill Hill a fine view may be obtained of the river and the constantly passing craft, the flat banks of the Thames, and the wooded hills inland. G. is the outport of London, at which emigrant and other outward-bound ships stop to take passengers on board, and inward-bound ships are inspected by revenue officers. G. is the headquarters of the Royal Thames Yacht Club, and of various other boating clubs. It is customary for royal and other distinguished visitors from foreign shores to land here and proceed to London by rail or road; and G. has consequently been the scene of many splendid pageants and welcomes conducted with festive ceremonial, among the last of which was the reception given to the Duchess of Edinburgh on her arrival in England in March 1874. Coal and timber are imported, and the shrimp and turbot fisheries are important. Rosherville Gardens, on the outskirts, is one of the principal resorts of Londoners for 'a happy day.' Steamers ply regularly from Rosherville and G. pier on the S. to Tilbury pier, in connection with Tilbury Railway, on the N. bank of the Thames. Asparagus and rhubarb are raised in great quantity for the London market. G. returns one member to Parliament. Pop. (1871) 21,265. G., the Gravesham of Doomsday Book, was sacked, and many of its inhabitants carried off, by French galleys, in the reign of Richard II. Its early history is meagre. It was fortified by Henry VIII., and in 1861-66 £148,000 were spent upon its defensive works.

Gravestones. In England, the ordinary, who is usually the bishop, has the power of granting or refusing permission to erect G. or monuments in the church or churchyard. In Scotland, this power belongs to the *heritors*, *i.e.*, the proprietors of the lands in the parish. As to the admissibility of G. as evidence in questions of pedigree, see *Dickson on Evidence*, 591, 592.

Gravi'na, an Italian town in the province of Terra di' Bari, 37 miles S.W. of Bari. It stands in a district famed for its pastures, on a hill above the river G., an affluent of the Bradano, is girt by a wall with towers, and has a cathedral and several churches. It is a bishop's see, and has a yearly cattle fair. Pop. 10,849.

Gravita'tion is the great law which regulates all the motions of the planets, satellites, and comets of our system. It was discovered by Newton, who was led to its enunciation by a brilliant train of inductive reasoning perhaps never equalled in the history of science. Assuming the truth of Kepler's Laws (q. v.), he showed that the planets would so move under the action of an attraction force directed to the centre of the sun and varying inversely as the square of the distance from it. The motion of the moon round the earth strongly resembled in its general characters the motion of the earth round the sun, and therefore was presumably due to a similar force. The possibility of this force being the same which made a body fall at the surface of the earth soon suggested itself to Newton's mind; and to test this he compared the distance through which the moon falls *towards* the earth in a given time with the space traversed by a falling body at the earth's surface in the same time. The calculations brought out that the force which drew the moon towards the earth was less than that which made a body fall in the ratio of 3600 : 1 or of 60^2 : 1. Now the moon's distance from the earth's centre is about sixty times the earth's radius, and consequently the earth's attraction, or force of gravity, as it is termed, varies inversely as the square of the distance from the earth's centre—the same relation which Kepler's laws necessarily involve. This governing principle, viewed in the light of his own laws of motion (see MOTION, LAWS OF), was generalised by Newton into the law of universal G., which is that 'every particle in the universe attracts every other particle with a force which acts in the straight line joining them, and is proportional to the square of the distance inversely and to the product of the masses directly.' This law proves that Kepler's laws, to a first approximation, are true, but when applied in all its strictness to such a system as our own solar system, it shows that the path described by any planet deviates from the exact ellipse, and that the area swept out by its radius vector in a given time is not constant, on account of the perturbing effects due to the attraction of the other planets, and also that the planet does not move round the sun, but that both move round the common centre of gravity. Almost all the lunar inequalities are due to the secondary effects of this principle, which seems to rule throughout the whole visible universe.

To regard G. as merely an action at a distance is unscientific in the extreme. In mathematics it may be treated as such, but in physics we are bound in the light of analogy to inquire into the direct cause of the attraction, for *force* in itself has no existence. It must be due to a transmission of energy, and for transmission a medium is necessary. The only plausible theory which has ever been advanced is that of Le Sage, who supposes this medium to consist of an infinite number of particles, minuter far than even the ultimate particles of matter, darting about in all directions with great velocities. One material particle, placed in the heart of such a conflicting crowd, would be equally battered all round, and would remain stationary. Two particles, however, would, so to speak, shield each other, and the better the nearer they were, and accordingly they would approach each other with ever-increasing velocity. The exact law of the inverse square also would hold; but when large masses are considered, a difficulty is encountered as regards the effect of density—a difficulty which is overcome only by supposing the molecules of matter to be separated by a distance large in comparison to their diameter, or by supposing the molecules or atoms themselves to be cage-like in their construction. Sir William Thomson's vortex atoms are essentially such, and his theory has of late years brought Le Sage's hypothesis much into notice. See VORTEX.

Gravity is the force of attraction which the earth exerts upon a mass of its substance, and is measured by the acceleration it produces on a falling body in unit time. It varies from point to point of the earth's surface, thus indicating that our world is not a true sphere. Its maximum value is at the poles, and its minimum at the equator, while in any given locality it diminishes as the height above the sea-level increases. At Greenwich the acceleration due to gravity is 32·1912 feet per second; at Edinburgh, 32·2; at Paris, 32·1819; at Stockholm, 32·2122; at Spitzbergen, 32·2528; at New York, 32·1594; at Rawak, 32·088; and at Ascension, 32·0956. The most accurate method for finding the force of gravity at any locality is by pendulum experiments. See PENDULUM.

Gravity, Specific. See SPECIFIC GRAVITY.

Gray, a town of France in the department of Haute-Saône, on the left bank of the Saône, 26 miles W.N.W. of Besançon. It has a townhouse with a fine façade, a church built in the Renaissance style, and other interesting buildings. It is a thriving place, with manufactures of haircloth, starch, &c., boatbuilding, ironworks, and trade in corn, wine, timber, &c. Pop. (1872) 6965.

Gray, Asa, a distinguished savant, born at Paris, New York, U.S., November 18, 1810, studied medicine, was made in 1842 Professor of Natural History in Harvard University, and has become widely known as a botanist. Among his many works are *Elements of Botany* (1836), *Manual of Botany* (1848), *Botany of the U.S. Pacific Exploring Expedition* (1844), &c. He is a part author with Dr. Torrey of the *Flora of N. America*, a book begun in 1838.

Gray, David, was born at Merkland, Dumbartonshire, 29th January 1838, studied at Glasgow University, and in May 1860 removed to London, where symptoms of consumption showed themselves. Sent by his friends (chief among them, Lord Houghton) to Italy, he derived no benefit from the change of climate, and returning to his father's house at Merkland, January 1861, died there, 3d December of the same year. His work, *The Luggie and Other Poems*, abounds in delicate and subtle descriptions of natural scenery, and in melodious and suggestive lines. Had he lived he might have won fame. See *Life and Works of D. G.* (Lond. 1862), and *Poems of D. G.*, edited by Henry Glassford Bell (Glasg. 1874).

Gray, John Edward, naturalist, was born at Walsall in 1800, studied medicine, was made assistant in the natural history department of the British Museum in 1824, and in 1840 keeper of the zoological collections. G. wrote many works on zoology, among which are *Illustrations of Indian Zoology*, *The Knowsley Menagerie*, *Spicilegia Zoologica*, &c. He died 7th March 1875.

Gray, Thomas, a familiar English poet, was born at London, December 26, 1716. He was the son of a money-scrivener, and was educated at Eton and at Cambridge. After travelling through France and Italy with Horace Walpole, he fixed his abode at Cambridge, where he led a secluded, scholarly life, acquiring great stores of learning, slowly polishing and maturing his verses, and corresponding with accomplished friends. He published his *Ode to Eton College* in 1747, his *Elegy Written in a Country Churchyard*—which became at once popular—in 1751, and his *Pindaric Odes* in 1757. He was offered but declined the situation of poet-laureate, and was in 1768 made Professor of Modern History at Cambridge, with a yearly income of £400. G. died at Cambridge, July 30, 1771. His poems, of which the best-known is the *Elegy*, are elaborated with infinite painstaking, and each of them may, as a whole, be considered an original work, though their diction is in a large degree a mosaic of the 'curious felicities' of other poets. They are sometimes overloaded by personification, and are not free from a false glitter and an obvious artificiality, but they glow with splendid epithets and images, and their verse has a peculiar richness and stateliness of rhythm. G.'s letters are among the finest in English literature, models of scholarly grace, refined humour, and exquisite description. See Mason's memoir in his edition of G.'s works (4th ed. 2 vols. 1807), and Mitford's, prefixed to the Aldine edition of G.'s poems.

Gray'ling (*Thymallus vulgaris*), a genus of Teleostean fishes belonging to the family of the salmons (*Salmonidæ*). The mouth and teeth are small, but the dorsal fin is of great length. The scales are also large. The G. is very local in its distribution, but occurs in many English and some Scotch rivers. It lives in clear water and seems to prefer a gravelly bottom. It attains a weight of 4 to 5 lbs., and its general colour is a silvery grey, the body being distinctly marked by longitudinal streaks of dark colour. The dorsal fin is marked by transverse rows of dark spots, and the abdominal or lateral line is straight. The flesh is very palatable, and is finest in the autumn. The breeding season is in April or May. The G. is caught with trout bait, and rises readily to the fly. An allied species is *T. signifer* of N. American streams.

Grayling.

Gray's Inn is one of the four Inns of Court (q. v.).

Grazale'ma, a town of Spain in the province and 60 miles E.N.E. of the city of Cadiz, and 50 miles N. of Gibraltar. It lies to the E. of the Cerro de S. Cristobal at a height of 3130 feet, and is only approached by a narrow ledge. It has considerable smuggling trade. Pop. 6000. G. has withstood severe sieges.

Grazio'so (Ital.), a term in music meaning 'with graceful expression.'

Grease (Fr. *graisse* from *gras*, 'fat;' Lat. *crassus*, 'gross,' 'fat'), any soft thick unctuous matter of a refuse kind, more especially animal fats which are variable in consistence. G. is extensively used as a lubricant, and in certain processes, as currying leather, is in great demand. Curriers' G. is composed of tallow and cod oil. Cart-wheel G. is a mixture of equal parts of tallow or train oil and common tar. Railway-axle G. is a compound of tallow, palm oil, common soda, and water, the ingredients are mixed by heat and agitated while cooling. The proportions of tallow and palm oil vary in summer and in winter. G. is also the name of a disease which attacks badly cared-for horses in the heels and surrounding parts. See Dick's *Manual of Vet. Science.*

Great Bear Lake. See BEAR LAKE, GREAT.

Great Britain and Ireland, United Kingdom of, the official name given to the British Isles, of which the principal members are Great Britain (comprising England, Wales, and Scotland) and Ireland, and also including 1127 smaller islands. They lie within lat. 49° 13′–60° 49′ N., and long. 1° 45′ E. and 10° 32′ W., are separated from the Continent by the North Sea, the Strait of Dover, and the English Channel, and are bounded N. and W. by the Atlantic. The extreme length of Great Britain, from Dunnet Head to Lizard Point, is 610 miles; of Ireland, from Fair Head to Crow in Kerry, 306 miles; while the entire coast-line has a length of 4300 miles. The archipelago occupies 11⅓° of lat. and 12¼° of long., and the trapezium formed by the meridians and parallels that pass through its extreme points is 800 miles long and 490 broad, enclosing an area of about 392,000 sq. miles, of which, however, over two-thirds are covered with water. The actual area of the land (exclusive of 2662 sq. miles of lakes and rivers) is 118,946 sq. miles, or rather more than one-thirtieth of the area of Continental Europe. Of the 1127 islands along the coasts, only 224 are inhabited. The chief groups are the Orkneys (320 sq. miles), the Shetlands (615), the Hebrides (3141), Isle of Man (227), Anglesey (192), Scilly Islands (6), the Isle of Wight (156), and the Channel Islands (112). According to the census of April 3, 1871, the populations and areas of the British Isles are as follows:—

	Area in sq. miles.	Pop. (1871).
England and Wales . .	58,311	22,712,266
Scotland (including islands) .	30,463	3,360,018
Ireland (do.) . .	32,531	5,411,416
The Isle of Man and the Channel Isles . .	303	144,638
	121,608	31,628,338

The details of areas and populations, of physical geography, climate, geology and mineralogy, botany and agriculture, zoology, and industries of the British Isles are given in separate articles on England and Wales, Scotland, Ireland, Isle of Man, Jersey, Guernsey, &c. The present article confines itself to a sketch of the physical geography, to statistical details for the United Kingdom, and to the history of England and Scotland from the Union in 1707, and of Ireland from the Union in 1801.

Physical Aspect.—The British Isles are based on a submarine plateau issuing from the coasts of Denmark, Germany, the Netherlands, and France. A fall of the sea-level of 180 feet would convert almost the entire southern half of the German Ocean into dry land, while a fall of 240 feet would unite Ireland to Britain. From 20 to 50 miles N. and W. of Ireland, the Shetland Islands, and Hebrides, the depth of the sea increases rapidly. In Great Britain no point is distant more than 75 miles from the sea, in Ireland no point more than 50 miles. The E. coast of Great Britain is only indented by the sand-choked Wash, the Moray Firth, and by the estuaries of a few rivers, as the Thames, Humber, Forth, and Tay. The great inlets in the W. are the Firth of Clyde, the Irish Sea, and Bristol Channel, while Wales and the Scottish Highlands present bold and broken coast-lines. Ireland, almost unindented in the E., has also a wild, rugged western coast, in which the chief openings are the Donegal, Sligo, Clew, Galway, Dingle, and Bantry Bays, and the estuaries of the Shannon and Kenmare. The British Isles, with a mean height of little more than 700 feet, have a great variety of surface. England and Ireland are comparatively flat, the former, however, rising in the Pennine chain and in the Cumbrian and Cambrian groups into veritable mountain heights. Scotland is far more mountainous than either, having a mean height of 800 feet. The Grampians (q. v.) form its chief range, and in the W. culminate in Ben Nevis, the highest point in Britain, with an altitude of 4406 feet. The chief rivers of Great Britain are the Thames (201 miles long), Severn (186), Humber (185), Shannon (160), Ouse (143), Suir (114), Tay (103), and Tweed (96). The rivers of Great Britain, though small compared with those of the Continent, are all abundantly supplied with water throughout the year, and are of great industrial and commercial importance.

Commerce.—Great Britain holds the first rank among the commercial nations of the world for both home and foreign trade. It possesses some 57 per cent. of all steam-vessels, 37 per cent. of all sailing vessels, and not only carries out the exchange of its own immense industrial products for the raw material of other countries, but acts extensively as foreign agent and carrier for the Continental markets. An analysis of the imports shows them to consist of over 40 per cent. of breadstuffs, condiments, and stimulants, about an equal amount of raw material for industrial purposes, and only 9 per cent. of manufactured goods. Of the exports, on the other hand, manufactured goods constitute 82 per cent. of the whole. The following returns are exclusive of the movement of bullion and specie, and also of the merchandise trans-shipped in British ports (amounting in 1875 to £12,137,064):—

	Imports.	Exports.
1854	£152,389,053	£115,821,092
1860	210,530,873	164,521,351
1865	271,072,285	165,835,725
1870	303,257,493	199,586,822
1873	371,287,372	255,164,603
1874	370,082,701	239 558,121
1875	373,939,577	223,465,963

The imports are, in order of importance, mainly from the United States, France, India, Russia, Germany, Egypt, Australasia, Belgium, Holland, the Dominion of Canada, Sweden, and Norway, China, and Spain; the exports of home produce are chiefly to the United States, Germany, India, Australasia, France, and the Netherlands. In 1874 the value of several of the principal imports was as follows:—Raw cotton, £50,696,496; corn and flour, £51,070,202; sugar (raw and refined), £20,009,730; wool, £21,116,184; timber, £21,968,138; tea, £11,532,896; coffee, £7,103,000; silk, £15,713,000; metal ores, £11,109,000; spirits, £2,612,000; wines, £6,868,000. The exports (1874) comprise—Cotton manufactures and yarn, £74,247,615; woollens and worsted goods, £28,359,512; linens, £8,832,533; silks, £3,130,000; haberdashery and millinery wares, £9,328,000; earthenware and glass, £3,152,000; iron and steel, £31,190,256; coals, £11,954; hardware, £4,413,000; machinery, £9,790,914; leather and leather wares, £3,547,000; beer and ale, £2,451,000; soda, £2,602,000; books and stationery, £1,587,000, &c. The declared value of gold bullion and specie imported, mainly from Australia, Mexico, S. America, the W. Indies, and the United States, in 1875, was £23,140,834; of silver, £10,123,955; of gold exported, £18,648,296; of silver, £8,979,746. There are neither export nor protective duties; customs levied on imports from abroad are balanced by articles manufactured within the kingdom being made to bear corresponding excise or stamp duties. The tariff, which is exceedingly simple, includes (since the expiry of the sugar-duties in 1874) but four great articles of customs' produce, namely, spirits, tea, wine, and tobacco. In 1874 the gross receipts of customs amounted in England and Wales to £15,475,043, in Scotland to £1,666,215, and in Ireland to £1,752,736.

The British *mercantile marine* in the home and foreign trade in 1800 comprised 15,724 vessels, of 1,698,515 tons; in 1845, 23,472 vessels, of 3,004,398 tons; in 1860, 27,663 vessels, of 5,758,687 tons; and in 1876, 25,461 vessels, of 6,152,000 tons. There has been a decrease in the number of sailing vessels, and no great increase in the tonnage since 1860, but the number of steamers has risen from 997 to 2970; while their tonnage has advanced from 441,184 to 1,847,188. In 1876 the equipment extended to 199,667 men. The total tonnage of the vessels in the foreign trade that entered British ports was, in 1875, 22,693,163, of which 7,502,172 was foreign; cleared, 23,583,675, of which 7,829,922 was foreign. The coast trade is represented by 22,944,265 tons, all but 138,541 tons being in British ships. Adding to the registered fleet of Great Britain its colonial marine (in 1876, 11,675 vessels, of 1,592,000 tons), there is under the British flag a total of over 37,136 vessels, of 7,744,000 tons. In 1875 there were 923 vessels of 420,551 tons (357 steamers of 178,905 tons) built in the United Kingdom. The British Isles are encircled by a ring of 360 shore-lights and 50 lightships, under the direction of the Trinity Board, and of Scottish and Irish boards. There are also 250 lifeboat stations supported by public charity and managed by a private association.

Railways, &c.—From 1825, the date of the opening of the first railway, to 1850, Great Britain constructed 6621 miles of line; at the end of 1860 there were 10,433 miles open for traffic; in 1876, 16,664. The railways are entirely the property of private companies. In 1875 the total amount of paid-up capital was £630,226,942; of traffic receipts, £58,977,518; and the number of passengers 507,532,187. The amount invested (1874) in railway stock in England and Wales was £508,720,097; in Scotland, £71,327,140; and in Ireland, £29,902,682; while of traffic receipts (1875), England and Wales contributed £49,766,684; Scotland, £6,577,731; and Ireland, £2,633,103. The railway lines in the British colonies have a total length (1875) of 12,158 miles. In 1870 the telegraph lines were taken over by the State, and in 1874 the total length of wires was 107,000 miles, of which 5487 were rented by private persons. The revenue has increased from £697,933 in 1871 to £1,120,000 in 1875; the expenditure was £1,083,275 in the latter year. The post-office in 1875 transmitted 1,009,000,000 letters, 280,000,000 newspapers and book-packets, and 16,485,661 money orders to the aggregate value of £26,493,090. The savings' banks of the post-office, with a capital of £25,187,345, received £9,355,436, of an average deposit of £2, 14s. 10d. The life insurance and annuity department granted 278 insurance policies, amounting to £21,622; 1,814 immediate annuities of £12,259 value, and 53 deferred annuities of £992. The gross revenue of the post-office (1874) was £5,751,600, and the expenditure £3,009,588. Since the introduction of penny postage in 1840 the revenue has quintupled, while there is more than a tenfold increase of the correspondence.

Finance.—The actual revenue of Great Britain for the year ending 31st March 1876 was £77,131,693, and the expenditure £76,621,773. The yearly returns have varied little for upwards of twenty years. In 1876 the sources of revenue were—Customs £20,196,691, excise £27,569,323, stamps £11,023,374, land-tax and house duty £2,440,000, property and income tax £4,306,000, post-office £5,670,000, telegraph service £1,120,000, &c. The items of expenditure were—Interest on and 'management' of national debt £27,094,479, civil list and civil charges £1,583,589, army £14,519,433, army purchase commission £579,114, navy £10,680,404, civil service £11,974,127, customs and inland revenue £2,694,908, post-office £2,911,917, telegraph service £1,193,065, packet service £972,000, localisation of the military forces £200,000, purchase of Suez Canal shares £76,566. The annual value of property and profits on which the income-tax is assessed amounts (1874) to £543,025,761. At 31st March 1876 the national debt (see DEBT, NATIONAL) was £776,970,544, of which £713,657,517 was consolidated, and £10,701,800 unconsolidated, and £51,911,227 of terminable annuities. The balance in the Exchequer (1875) was £6,265,322. By an Act of 1875 the national debt is to be reduced by a new permanent Sinking Fund (q. v.) maintained by annual votes of the Legislature. The charge of the sinking fund, to be entered under the consolidated fund, was fixed for 1875-76 at £27,400,000, for 1876-77 at £27,700,000, and for every subsequent year at £28,000,000. In 1875 there was coined at the Royal Mint £243,264 of gold, £594,000 of silver, £69,813 of copper. See BANKING.

Army and Navy.—See BRITISH ARMY and BRITISH NAVY.

Constitution and Government.—The government of Great Britain is a constitutional monarchy, in which the sovereign alone represents the supreme executive, and the sovereign jointly with Parliament (q. v.) the supreme legislative power. There are three estates of the realm—the Lords Temporal, the Lords Spiritual, and the Commons. The Act of Settlement secures the succession in either male or female line of the family of Brunswick. Since the time of Edward I. the heir-apparent has borne the title of Prince of Wales. The civil list granted to the Queen amounts to £363,760 a year, in addition to the revenue of the Duchy of Lancaster (£37,000); the various members of the royal family receive separate revenues and annuities. Parliament comprises the sovereign, the House of Lords, and the House of Commons. An Act, to obtain the force of law, requires to be passed by all three. The customary session of Parliament extends over six months of the year. (See CONSTITUTION, PRIVY COUNCIL, CABINET MINISTRY.) The sovereign nominates to the orders of chivalry, chief of which are those of the Garter, Thistle, St. Patrick, Star of India, the Bath, St. Michael, and St. George (the Maltese cross). Valorous conduct in the field is rewarded by the Victoria cross.

Administration of Justice.—The judicial system of Britain comprises Courts of Common Law (q. v.) and Courts of Equity (q. v.). The former include the Courts of Queen's Bench, of Common Pleas, of Exchequer, of Probate and Divorce and Matrimonial Causes; the latter those of the Lord Chancellor, of the Lords Justices of Appeal, of the Master of the Rolls, of the three Vice-Chancellors, and of Appeal in Chancery of the County Palatine of Lancaster. The new Court of Judicature (q. v.) of 1873-75 combines these in a 'High Court of Justice,' from which an appeal lies to the newly constituted 'Court of Appeal.' The House of Lords and Judicial Committee of the Privy Council retain their appellate jurisdiction in Scotch, Irish, colonial, ecclesiastical, and admiralty cases. There are also Courts of Bankruptcy, three Ecclesiastical Courts, the Lord Mayor's Court, the Sheriffs' Courts, and sixty County Courts. Inferior jurisdiction is in the hands of justices of the peace in petty and quarter sessions, and of stipendiary magistrates in larger towns. Together with the Lord Chancellor and Lord Chief-Justice there are forty-six superior judges in England. In Great Britain the number of salaried judges is 450, and their joint salaries £550,000. (See JUDGES.) In Scotland the Court of Session (q. v.) is supreme in civil cases, the Court of Justiciary in criminal cases. In Ireland the system resembles that of England, with the special feature of a Landed Estates Court. The sessions of justices of peace are presided over by a salaried barrister. In 1874 the number of offenders convicted in England and Wales was 10,954, in Scotland 2143, in Ireland 2484. The police (in England and Wales 28,550, Scotland 3200, Ireland 12,000) are maintained by local rates. But in the metropolis the police (except those of the city) depend on the Home Secretary.

Education.—Great Britain possesses a national system of primary education. By the Public Elementary Education Act of 1870 the various 'educational districts' of England are provided with schools supported by local rates, fees, and parliamentary grants, and are placed under the control of popularly elected 'school boards,' invested with the power of compelling the attendance of all children between the age of five and thirteen. Children may be admitted free, and the schools are open to

Government inspection at all times. In England and Wales the number of day-schools inspected (1874) was 12,167; of pupils in average attendance, 1,678,759; of teachers, 51,216. The Government grants amounted to £1,050,259, In Scotland the number of day-schools inspected (1875) was 2329; of pupils in average attendance, 233,130; of teachers, 7606. The Government grants amounted to £134,053. In Ireland the primary schools have been under the management of the Commissioners of National Education since 1833, and are professedly based on the principle of the separation of religious from secular instruction. In 1871 the number of schools was 6914, and of pupils 1,021,700, while the grant amounted to £408,388. According to the returns of 1871, 15·7 of the whole population attend school, namely, 16·3 in England, 17·1 in Scotland, and 12·1 in Ireland. In England the most famous schools for higher-class education are Eton, Rugby, Westminster, Harrow, Charterhouse, Winchester, Cheltenham, Marlborough, and Clifton; in Scotland, the High School of Edinburgh, the Edinburgh Academy, and the Aberdeen Grammar-School. The great universities are those of Oxford (q. v.) and Cambridge (q. v.) for England; Edinburgh (q. v.), Glasgow (q. v.), Aberdeen (q. v.), and St. Andrews for Scotland; and the Trinity College or Dublin University (q. v.) and Queen's University for Ireland. The last of these, like the London University, is strictly a mere examining board, and has three affiliated colleges—Belfast, Cork, and Galway. There are many medical schools in connection with the leading hospitals. Besides the great national institutions above mentioned, the Nonconformist communions have important colleges of their own. There are colleges of physical science, as Owen's College, Manchester (to which, however, a literary faculty is attached), and Bristol College (1876); military schools, as Sandhurst, Woolwich, &c.; various Dissenting Church colleges; schools of art and design. Other of the higher educational institutions are the Royal Society, Royal Geographical Society, the Royal Academy, the British Museum (q. v.), South Kensington Museum, the National Art Gallery, the Royal Academy of Music, the recently established National School of Music, &c.

Religion.—The Established Church of England and Wales is Episcopal, of Scotland Presbyterian; that of Ireland was a branch of the English Episcopal Church till its disestablishment in 1871. It is impossible to obtain trustworthy statistics regarding the numbers belonging to the different ecclesiastical communions. The *Almanach de Gotha* (1877), from calculations based on those of Ravenstein (*Denominational Statistics of England and Wales*, Lond. 1870), arrives at the following result; but as regards the Church of England it seems a gross exaggeration, 13,000,000 being probably nearer the mark, leaving 4,780,000 more to be distributed among the other Nonconformist communions:—

England.	
Church of England	17,781,000
Protestant Dissenters	3,971,000
Roman Catholics	1,058,000
Jews	39,000
Scotland.	
Church of Scotland	1,473,000
Presbyterian Dissenters (Free, U.P., &c.)	1,486,000
Anglicans	73,200
Roman Catholics	320,000
Jews	6,400
Ireland (Census 1871).	
Roman Catholics	4,150,867
Anglicans	667,079
Presbyterians	497,648
Methodists	43,441

The Established Churches of England and Scotland are in possession of valuable endowments; the others, several of which have accumulated large funds, depend on voluntary contributions. According to the census of 1871, the number of Protestant ministers in England and Wales was 29,958, in Scotland 4105, in Ireland 3243; of missionaries, scripture readers, &c., in England and Wales 3261, in Scotland 252, in Ireland 24; of Roman Catholic priests and monks in England 1620, in Scotland 224, in Ireland 3505; of nuns in England and Wales 2474, in Scotland 243, in Ireland 3719.

Colonies.—The colonies and dependencies of Great Britain embrace nearly a seventh of the land surface of the earth, and fully a seventh of its inhabitants. In 1875 the various colonial possessions were grouped into thirty-nine administrative divisions, of which several embraced formerly separate colonies. The following table gives the colonies and possessions with areas and populations, according to the *Almanach de Gotha* for 1877:—

	Area in sq. miles.	Pop. 1869–76.
British India	905,046	190,840,848
Ceylon	24,454	2,418,741
Straits Settlement	1,206	308,097
Keeling Islands, Aden, Perim, Labuan, Hong-Kong	96	156,996
Australia	2,967,500	1,117,929
Tasmania	26,215	104,176
New Zealand	104,272	211,246
Chatham and Norfolk Islands	630	661
Fiji Islands	8,033	142,150
Dominion of Canada	3,483,952	3,602,321
Newfoundland	40,200	161,386
Bermuda	40	15,309
W. India Islands	13,754	1,063,886
Honduras	13,500	24,710
British Guiana	85,425	215,200
Falkland Islands	4,741	933
Cape Colony (including Kaffraria since June 1876)	214,914	746,461
Bassuto Land	8,450	75,000
Griqua Land (West)	16,632	25,477
Natal	18,750	307,241
West African Settlements	17,115	633,417
Mauritius (and dependencies)	1,088	352,762
St. Helena	47	6,241
Ascension	34	27
Tristan da Cunha	45	85
Gibraltar	2	25,143
Malta	142	145,604
Nicobar Islands	725	5,000
Andaman Islands	2,551	13,500
Laccadives	744	6,800
Kuria Muria Islands	21	
Kamaran	64	500
Auckland Isle	196	
Lord Howe Isle	3	37
Fanning Malden, Starbuck and Caroline	46	150
New Amsterdam	25	
	7,960,658	202,727,934

The cost of the colonies, which has long been gradually declining, scarcely now amounts to two millions sterling, of which more than one half goes to maintain nine of the possessions, classed as general military and naval stations—Gibraltar, Malta, Cape Colony, Mauritius, Bermuda, St. Helena, Heligoland, Falkland Islands, and Hong-Kong. In 1875 the total effective strength of the British army in the colonies, exclusive of India (q. v.), was 23,063 rank and file.

History.—After the union of the English and Scottish Parliaments was effected, May 1, 1707, the two nations were together designated the United Kingdom of Great Britain. Discontent with the Act of Union lingered for some time in Scotland, but the measure, fruitful as it has been in good results, did not lead to an immediate change in the home or foreign policy. During the latter part of Anne's reign Bolingbroke and Harley, the leaders of the Tories, who were then in power, schemed incessantly to secure the succession for the Pretender, but these intrigues were ruined by the Queen's sudden death in 1714, when the Elector George of Hanover, a descendant through his mother of Elizabeth, daughter of James I., became king as George I. (1714–17). The two chief consequences of the Guelphic accession were, first, that the power of the crown was reduced in the reigns of George I. and George II. to sheer insignificance, the country being then ruled by a Whig oligarchy, who advocated constitutional principles, and jealously narrowed the royal power, now divorced from its old allies the Tories; second, that the Tories through their Jacobite leanings became alienated from the mass of the nation, hostile to the new dynasty, and identified with rebelliousness and disorder. The most notable events of George I.'s reign were the overthrow of a Jacobite revolt in 1715, the forming of the Quadruple Alliance in 1718, the collapse of the South Sea scheme in 1720, and the beginning of Walpole's Ministry in 1721. During the reign of George II. (1727–60) the government was prudently administered by Walpole, who controlled Parliament by a system of general bribery, and skilfully fostered commerce and averted war until 1739, when he was forced into an inglorious struggle with Spain. In 1742 Walpole was ousted from office because he opposed

England's engaging in the Austrian War of Succession (q. v.). In that struggle the English won the battle of Dettingen (1743), but were beaten at Fontenoy (1745), and at the close of the contest in 1748 Great Britain and France remained on the same political footing as before the war. The revolt of the Highland clans to restore Prince Charles Edward Stuart, which broke out in 1745, was completely crushed at Culloden in 1746. During the Seven Years' War (q. v.) Great Britain took part with Prussia, and though the British arms were unsuccessful on the Continent, the Duke of Cumberland surrendering in Hanover with 40,000 men, in the progress of the struggle Wolfe added Canada to the British Empire, and Clive swept the French almost out of India. The war was still going on at the accession of George III. (1760–1820). A great change now affected British politics. The Whigs, after their triumphant defence of the Revolution settlement against Jacobites at home and Louis XIV. abroad, had lost their old patriotism and unity, and were mainly occupied in scuffling for places; the Tories, formerly the opponents of the Guelphs, now flung aside their Jacobitism and allied themselves against the Whigs with the King, who was obstinately bent on winning a despotic control over the nation. Instead of politics being a mere strife of factions and aristocratic cabals, weighty differences began to distinguish the rival parties, and the questions whether the King or Parliament should be the chief seat of government, whether the popular or despotic theory of the constitution should prevail, whether the Ministry should be a united body, plastic to the nation's will and pursuing a harmonious line of policy, or whether each Minister should be merely a royal official responsible only to the King, were first seen in this reign to underlie the chronic faction fights, combinations, and squabbles of the country's rulers. Outside of politics and foreign wars, the reign of George III. was marked by a great Christian revival—notably by the Wesleyan movement—by great scientific and speculative progress, by great industrial inventions and improvements, Brindley beginning the Grand Trunk Canal, Wedgewood establishing his potteries, Hargreaves inventing the spinning-jenny, Watt the steam-engine, and Crompton the 'mule' between 1761 and 1776. George III., in his efforts after fresh monarchical power, placed himself in serious opposition to the country. Bute, his first Minister, by shameless bribery and 'borough-jobbing,' made Parliament for a time the tool of the royal will, but was forced by popular indignation to resign in 1763. His successor, Grenville, kindled a violent excitement by his arbitrary prosecution of Wilkes (q. v.); and the Ministry of Lord North, by seeking to impose unjust duties on the American colonies, stirred up the war of American Independence (1774–83), which led to the formation of the United States. On the break-up of the Coalition Ministry—which was formed by a union of Fox's with North's followers—Pitt became Prime Minister in 1783. Supported by a great Tory majority, and backed by the royal favour, Pitt at first devoted himself to economical and financial measures, but in 1793 he declared a groundless war against the French Republic, which plunged his country in debt and disaster. Napoleon was at first universally victorious by land, and Great Britain was left without an ally to face a powerful European coalition, with her trade crippled by the exclusion of her merchandise from Continental ports, though she remained irresistible by sea. At length fortune changed, Napoleon (q. v.) failed in his Russian expedition; various states began to join against him, and he was finally crushed at Waterloo (1815). These long wars were a terrible source of suffering to the English poor, and at the end of the struggle the popular discontent was embittered by a series of bad harvests and the stagnation of trade, while the corn laws kept the price of corn up to the war rates. The democratic movement that arose at the end of the War of Independence, that gained new force at the beginning of the French outbreak against feudalism, and that was almost extinguished in England through the reaction caused by the excesses of the French revolutionaries, burst forth irresistibly shortly after 1815. In France the reaction against democracy was aided by the association of French democracy with atheism; while in England the democratic cause was strengthened by the great Evangelical movement, which was mainly confined to the Dissenters, who were mostly Radicals in politics. In the reign of George IV. (1820–30) reform slowly began. Canning and Huskisson introduced excellent commercial measures, trade revived, and in 1829 Catholic Emancipation was passed. Under William IV. (1830–37) the Whigs were restored to office, from which they had been excluded for above fifty years. They carried the Reform Bill in 1832 (see REFORM), enacted the abolition of slavery in 1833, improved the state of the poor-laws, and in 1834 founded a system of national education in Ireland. Queen Victoria ascended the throne in 1837, and the Whigs were displaced by the Ministry of Sir Robert Peel in 1841. But the principles of free trade advocated by numerous speakers throughout the country, and especially by Cobden and Bright, produced such excitement that in 1846 the corn laws were repealed. Numbers of the working classes about this time banded together as Chartists (q. v.), but the Chartist agitation, which brought Great Britain to the brink of revolution, was suppressed in 1848. In 1852 the Tories regained office but had to retire within a year, and the next Ministry, Lord Aberdeen's, gave way to Lord Palmerston's in 1855. In 1854 Great Britain entered into an alliance with France in defence of Turkey against Russia, and the Crimean war, which began in the same year, was ended by the taking of Sebastopol in 1855. The Indian Mutiny which burst forth in 1857 was stringently and heroically suppressed, and in 1858 the government of India was transferred from the East India Company to the Queen, who in 1876 took the title of Empress of India. Except for a short interval in 1858 when Lord Derby was Prime Minister, Lord Palmerston held office from 1855 to 1865, pursuing a policy of inaction at home and non-intervention abroad. His successor, Lord Russell, resigned office in 1866 on his Reform Bill being flung out, but the Tory Government which followed with Lord Derby as Prime Minister passed a more sweeping measure. The new constituencies returning a Liberal majority of over 100, the Tories retired and Mr. Gladstone became head of the Government. A succession of measures, some great, and all drastic, followed—the disestablishment and disendowment of the Protestant Church of Ireland in 1869, and the legalising of tenant-right in Ireland by the Land Bill of 1870, the abolition of compulsory church rates in 1868, and of religious tests for admission to offices and degrees in the English universities in 1871. A bill for securing national education was also passed in 1870. Purchase was abolished in the army and the Ballot Bill was passed in 1871. But incessant changes finally created a deep feeling of alarm and distrust; and in 1874, when Mr. Gladstone dissolved Parliament, a Tory majority of nearly seventy was returned, and Mr. Disraeli again became Prime Minister. Since 1874 the question of most moment has been the relations of Great Britain, Turkey, and Russia in regard to the complicated 'Eastern Question.' See Stanhope's *History of England from the Peace of Utrecht to the Peace of Versailles*, Macaulay's *Essays*, Massey's *History of England from the Accession of George III.*, Sir Erskine May's *Constitutional History*, Bancroft's *History of America*, Alison's *History of Europe*, Napier's *History of the Peninsular War*, Kinglake's *History of the Invasion of the Crimea*, Molesworth's *History of England to the Resignation of the Gladstone Ministry*, &c.

Great Britain, Royal Arms of. The royal heraldry of England dates from about the middle of the 12th c.; the arms ascribed to kings of an earlier date, whether English or Norman, are not authentic. The shields of the Plantagenets (1154–1340)

bore gules, three lions passant gardant, in pale, or. In 1340 the royal arms of the French kings were introduced into the English shield by Edward III. Henry VI., Edward IV., Richard III., and the Tudor sovereigns Henry VII., Henry VIII., Edward VI., Mary, and Elizabeth all bore the same arms, viz., quarterly 1 and 4 *France, modern* (*i.e.*, bearing three fleurs-de-lis only);

2 and 3 *England*. Elizabeth, however, sometimes bore *Ireland*. James I. incorporated the arms of Scotland (*or, a lion rampant gu.*), and those of Ireland (*azure*, a harp *or*, stringed *argent*). William III. introduced in pretence his paternal arms of Nassau; Mary his queen bore the Stuart shield with the royal arms impaled. After the accession of George I., the royal shield was blazoned—quarterly—1 England impaling Scotland, 2 France, 3 Ireland, 4 Hanover. The French fleur-de-lis were removed from the arms of England 1st January 1801. The kingdom of Hanover passed from the sovereign of Great Britain on the accession of her Majesty Queen Victoria, when the Hanoverian escutcheon was removed from the royal shield, which now bears only the insignia of the realms of the United Kingdom—England 1 and 4, Scotland 2, and Ireland 3.

Great Circle Sailing. The shortest distance between any two points on a sphere lies along the great circle which passes through these points, *i.e.*, the circle whose centre coincides with the centre of the sphere. In the art of navigation, therefore, it becomes a question of practical value to be able to sail along a great circle in passing from one position to another. The difficulty in doing this will be evident when it is considered that any great circle (excluding the equator and the meridians) cuts successive parallels and meridians at varying angles, so that a vessel in pursuing the theoretically shortest course must be continually altering its direction of motion. In practice G. C. S. can only be effected by approximation. The great circle connecting the two stations is first laid down on the chart; and along this line convenient points are chosen, sufficiently near so as to render the straight line joining any successive two nowhere much deviating from the corresponding portion of the great circle. The vessel then makes for each point in succession, following the direction represented on the map. See NAVIGATION.

Great Fish River, an unnavigable stream in British America, has a course of about 500 miles, and flows into Cockburn Bay, an inlet of the Arctic Ocean, its mouth being in lat. 67° 8′ N., long. 94° 40′ W.—**G. F. R.** is also the name of a river of Cape Colony, which rises in the Snowy Mountains, and enters the Indian Ocean after a course of 231 miles.

Great Kanawha River, a river of W. Virginia, U.S., formed by the confluence of the Gauley and the New rivers, which, after a course of 100 miles through a picturesque and fertile region, joins the Ohio at Point Pleasant. It is a narrow rapid stream, navigable for small vessels for 98 miles to the Falls, which are of about 50 feet.

Great Marlow (orig. *Merelow*, 'the hill by the marsh'), a market-town of Buckinghamshire, England, 29 miles N.W. of London by rail. It stands in a hollow near the Thames, which is here crossed by a suspension bridge of 225 feet span. G. has paper, copper, rope, and wire works, and a considerable trade in corn, timber, and hops. It returns one member to Parliament. Pop. (1871) 6627.

Great Salt Lake, a sheet of water in the N. of Utah, U.S., 70 miles long, 45 broad, 4250 feet above the sea, with an average depth of 12 and a maximum of 66 feet. Its coasts are wild and rugged, and it is studded with many rocky islands, of which Antelope Island, 15 miles long, is the largest. It receives the Blue River, Weber, Jordan, and other streams, but has no outlet. It contains 20·196 per cent. of common salt, and a slight percentage of other salts. Its specific gravity, 1·170, is almost that of the Dead Sea. Steamers ply upon it between Corinne and Black Rock. The G. S. L. was first explored by Colonel Fremont in 1843, and first thoroughly surveyed by Captain Stansbury, U.S. Navy, in 1849-50.

Great Seal. The office of Lord Chancellor is conferred by the sovereign delivering the G. S. to him who is to hold the office, the sovereign addressing him by the title which he is to bear. The G. S. is held to be the emblem of sovereignty—the *clavis regni*—the only instrument by which, on solemn occasions, the will of the sovereign can be expressed. Faith is universally given to every document purporting to be under the G. S., as having been duly sealed with it by the authority of the sovereign. When in a new reign, or on a change of the royal arms or style, an order is made by the sovereign in council for using a new G. S., the old one is publicly broken. The ceremony of publicly breaking the seal consists in the sovereign giving it a gentle blow with a hammer, after which it is supposed to be broken, when, according to Lord Campbell (*Lives of the Lord Chancellors*, vol. i. p. 261), it has lost its virtue, and becomes the perquisite of the Lord Chancellor for the time being. At the union of England and Scotland a G. S. for the United Kingdom became necessary for public Acts and instruments. But this G. S. not being appropriate for those private grants which had formerly passed the G. S. of Scotland, by article 24 of the Treaty of Union a G. S. for sealing private grants in Scotland was ordered to be made, and declared to have the same effect with the ancient G. S. of Scotland.

Great Slave Lake, one of the largest of that chain of lakes which extend in a N.W. direction through the Dominion of Canada from the United States frontier almost to the shores of the Arctic Ocean. It is, next to the Great Bear Lake, the most northernly of the chain; lies in lat. 60° 40′-63° N., long. 109° 30′-117° 30′ W.; is irregular in shape, about 300 miles in length, with a breadth, at its greatest, of 50 miles. It has numerous islands, some of which are covered with wood; its northern shores are steep, and it is frozen for half the year. G. S. L. receives the waters of Lake Athabasca by the Great Slave River, and discharges its own by the Mackenzie.

Great Wall of China. See CHINESE EMPIRE.

Greaves (Old Fr. *grèves*, Span. and Port. *grevas*, from Lat. *gravis*, 'heavy;' Low Lat. name *bainbergæ*, from Ger. *beinbergen*, 'leg-coverers'), armour for the legs, made of metal in classical times. Homer's Greeks are always 'well-greaved,' and examples of G. found at Pompeii are in metal richly ornamented. In the middle ages they were frequently made of leather.

Grebe (*Podiceps*), a genus of Natatorial or swimming birds, having the toes provided with very broad flaps or lobes of skin, the hinder toe being rudimentary. The nostrils are in a short groove, the tail is very short, and the first quill is the longest. The feet are not webbed; the lobed appearance is produced by the web being divided into a portion for each toe. In swimming, and during the forward or ineffective stroke of the foot, the lobes allow the water to pass freely between them, but during the backward stroke they expand and oppose a firm surface to the water. When at rest, the G. sits in an erect position like the penguins and puffins, the legs being extremely short. The great crested G. (*P. cristatus*) is a familiar example of the genus. It occurs in the fen districts of England, and swims and dives with great ease. Its food consists of fish. The head is brown, and the cheeks, which are provided with expanded feathers, are of reddish-chestnut colour. The neck and upper parts are dark brown, and the under surface is white, glossed with a peculiar satin-like lustre. The average length is 22 inches. The eared G. (*P. auritus*) possesses tufts of golden feathers behind each eye, and attains a length of 12 inches. The head and neck are black, the back dark brown, and the under parts white. The horned G. (*P. cornutus*) has a tuft of dark-brown feathers, and is noted for its habit of diving when alarmed, with the young borne on its back. The dabchick or little G. (*P. minor*) is the most common British species, and measures about 9 inches in length. Its colour is dark brown above, and greyish white below. The nest is made of water-plants, and is scarcely raised above the surface of the ground. The eggs are white, and number six. The skin of the G. is much used for making muffs, and for bordering cloaks and fur garments.

Crested Grebe.

Grecian Architecture, universally recognised as the highest, most complete form of structural invention and expression as yet developed, was itself, in a measure, a development out of the earlier architectural systems of Egypt and Assyria. It is now generally acknowledged that nearly every idea and every architectural feature of the renowned works that crowned the Acropolis were derived from already ancient structures in Asia Minor and on the banks of the Nile. Yet the Greek temple was as distinctively a *creation* as is a Shakespearian play, and owed no more to the Egyptian temples or Assyrian palaces than did *Romeo and Juliet* to the old Italian tales. Wherever the original types of the various architectural elements of the Parthenon were gathered, that work, as one complete and perfect whole—a distinctive conception faultlessly realised—was essentially the creation of native Hellenic genius. The earliest architectural remains of Greece are ascribed to the 'Pelasgians'—a name that expresses nothing beyond vague tradition or pure ignorance. Among these are the Treasury or tomb of Atreus at Mycenæ, a city of Homeric times. The tomb is an immense horizontal pointed arch, enclosing a chamber 48 feet 6 inches in diameter. At the doorway of the tomb were the fragments of two pillars richly covered with sculptured ornamentation, purely *Asiatic*, or rather Persepolitan in character. Other so-called 'Pelasgic' remains are a pointed arched gateway at Thoricus in Attica, an exact counterpart of which exists at Assos in Asia Minor; an arched roof at Delos formed by placing two large stones together at a certain angle; a wall in the Peloponnesus, the lower courses of which are in excellent *ashlar* work, while above the masonry is irregular or 'Cyclopean;' and the Gate of Lions, the principal gate of the Acropolis of Mycenæ, which has been said to stand to the art of Greece somewhat in the same relation as the *Iliad* to her literature. These remains, the antiquity of which ranges beyond the historic into the heroic age, clearly attest the intimate connection which subsisted between Greece and Asia long before the age of Homer.

But though so ancient, these extraordinary ruins, especially the tomb and gateway of Mycenæ, show wonderful knowledge and constructional skill, and like all Asiatic art are remarkable for elegance of form and rich ornamentation. But a new influence which had long been at work in the ancient country, and which was now to become paramount, completely altered the character of the primitive architecture of Greece. When the supremacy of the pre-Hellenic tribes came to a close, and the Hellenes began to appear as the dominant element in Greece late in the 8th c. B.C., then the ingenious and ornate Asiatic art gave way before the graver genius of the Hellenic nation. The earliest known example of this new G. A. is the Doric temple of Corinth, of about the middle of the 7th c. B.C., in the construction of which anterior tradition seems to have been abandoned, and the Hellenes sought their model in the massive temples of Egypt. It is asserted by Falkener (*Museum of Classical Antiquities*) that already twenty-seven proto-Doric columns are enumerated as still existing in eight different buildings, ranging from the Third Cataract to Lower Egypt. It is hardly questioned now, however, that the Greeks borrowed their idea of the Doric order from the rock-cut temple of Beni-Hassan (Lower Egypt), which is known to have been in existence a thousand years before the erection of the temple at Corinth. The 'Proto-Doric pillar of Beni-Hassan,' as it has been called, was a very short, massive, fluted column. Those of the Doric temple at Corinth were equally primitive and massive. Their diameter was 5 feet 10 inches, and their height was less than four diameters, or under 23 feet. The architrave—the only part of the superstructure still existing—was proportionately heavy. The next known and notable work of G. A. was the small temple of Ægina (94 feet by 45), supposed to have been erected in the middle of the 6th c. B.C. Other contemporary temples, of which, however, little is known, are supposed to have existed in all the considerable cities of Greece. These were all destroyed during or immediately after the Persian war, and in the exultation of the Greeks after the famous victories of Salamis and Platæa, new temples were erected to the gods that had fought with them against the Persian. The consequence was that a great building era set in in Greece, so that within forty or fifty years after the defeat of Xerxes and the destruction of his thousand ships, nearly all the great temples now found in Greece were built, including the Parthenon, the most beautiful building of its class in the world.

The character of G. A., however subtle in its refinements and minute and complex from the technical point of view, is simple in itself. Its essential element is the pillar and beam—the column and entablature. (See COLUMN, ENTABLATURE, ARCHITRAVE, CORNICE, FRIEZE, CAPITAL, PEDIMENT, &c.) The column and entablature taken together form what is called the order of an architectural style. There are three styles in G. A., the Doric, Ionic, and Corinthian, the difference of the orders of which consists in the different proportional relations between the column and the superincumbent entablature. Before noting the special features of the three orders, a few words may be said about the character and the forms of temples. In the earliest ages of Greece trees were often selected by devotees as the dwelling-places of their gods, and mountains, as Parnassus, Olympus, &c., were regarded as their favourite seats. The simplest Grecian temples were small square *cells*, in which the image was placed. The name cell remained, for however large and splendid the temple might become, the interior enclosure in which stood the image of the divinity was still called the cell or cella. Afterwards the square apartment was divided into two—the cell and the porch or doorway. The fronts of these small temples were *distyle in antis*, that is, they consisted of two pillars between *antæ* or square piers, which terminated the flat side-walls. As the temple was enlarged, the number of the pillars of the front increased, and the step from the picturesque hexastyle (six-pillar) front to a peristyle temple (one surrounded by pillars on all its four sides) was an easy and natural one. As the Greek temple was usually twice as long as it was wide, the number of pillars extending along each side of a hexastyle structure was usually either thirteen or fifteen. In such a temple an inner range of pillars usually surrounded the *cella*, which was thus a temple in itself, and which, curiously enough, occupied a position near the back of the temple similar to that occupied by the altar in Christian churches. The plan of the Parthenon was somewhat peculiar. Its porticoes were octostyle (eight-pillared), with seventeen pillars in all down each side, but there was an inner hexastyle portico at each end of the cell. These temples were lighted from the roof by an ingenious contrivance which, while admitting light, excluded rain.

The Doric order is readily recognised by the short, massive, fluted column, without base, and with a plain capital composed merely of the echinus and Abacus (q. v.), and by the simple ornamentation of the frieze, in which the joints of the primitive wooden structure which preceded the classic temple are represented by tablets carved with two vertical grooves or glyphs in the centre and two half grooves at the sides. These tablets are called *triglyphs*. The plain spaces between them are named *metopes*. The distinguishing mark of the Ionic order is a longer and more slender column, the capital of which is ornamented with volutes or scrolls. The Corinthian order is remarkable for its very slender column, with capital richly carved in acanthus and honeysuckle foliage and blossom.

The Greek temple being rectilinear, all its horizontal and perpendicular lines are nominally straight. But were they perfectly straight, they would not appear so; for by a law of perspective all perfectly straight lines projected far above the spectator appear to have a slight inclination upwards, while those extending on either side of him appear to be also slightly deflected. The Greeks discovered this law, and by giving every straight line a very slight curve they counteracted the optical illusion and made every line appear to the eye to be mathematically straight. There are no really straight lines in any temple of the best age of G. A., though all appear so, and hence the perfect satisfaction with which the eye rests upon these marvellous structures. The steps of their temples have a convex curve of 3 inches in 100 feet. Even the pillars have a scarcely perceptible convex curve near the middle, the swelling which causes the curve being named *entasis* ('a stretching or distension'). In all the orders sculpture and painting, and in some cases gilding, were employed. The Doric order, the first, severest, but grandest and most beautiful, may be understood as expressive of power, the Ionic of decoration, the Corinthian of luxury and incipient decline. The main characteristics of the three orders are given under COLUMN. Compare also ACROPOLIS, AMPHITHEATRE, BATHS, CARYATIDES, &c. See Sharpe's *History of Egypt*; Guhl and Koner's *Life of the Greeks and Romans* (Lond. 1875), and Fergusson's *History of Architecture* (2d ed. 1874).

Greece, or the modern **Kingdom of the Hellenes**, is the southern portion of the most eastern of the three European peninsulas that project into the Mediterranean Sea, lat. 37° 30′–39° N., long. 21° 10′–24° 5′ E. The name G. (*Græcia*) was first given to the country by the Romans, who probably derived it from the *Graikoi*, a tribe in Epirus near Dodona, with whom, from proximity, they must early have come into contact. *Hellas*, however, was the name by which the ancient Greeks themselves knew their own land; and in a separate article under this heading the ancient geography, history, and culture of G. are treated. Modern G. is bounded N. by Turkish Albania and Thessaly, W. by the Ionian Sea, S. by the Cretan Sea, and

E. by the Ægean Sea. It excludes not only Epirus and Macedonia, but Hellenic Thessaly and part of Acarnania, while of the islands of ancient G. it embraces the Ionian Islands (q. v.)—Corfu, Cephallenia, Zante, Santa Maura, Ithaki, Cerigo, &c.—Eubœa (q. v.), Salamis (q. v.), and the Cyclades (see ARCHIPELAGO)—Delos, Naxos, Tinos, Andros, Thermia, Serpho, Syra, Paros, Milos, Scyro, Sciatho, Scopelo, &c. The mainland has an extreme length from N. to S. of some 200 miles, and a breadth of 180 miles. G. is now divided into thirteen nomarchies, which correspond in name, and often in extent, with the old Hellenic states. The nomarchies are subdivided into fifty-nine eparchies. The areas, populations, and chief towns of the nomarchies are as follows:—

Nomarchies.	Area in sq. miles.	Pop. 1870.	Chief towns.
Attica and Bœotia	2,481	136,804	Athens.
Evripo (*Eubœa*)	1,574	82,541	Chalcis.
Phthiotis and Phocis	2,053	108,421	Lamia.
Acarnania and Ætolia	3,025	121,693	Missolonghi.
Achaia and Elis	1,908	149,561	Patras.
Arcadia	2,028	131,740	Tripolitza.
Laconia	1,678	105,851	Sparta.
Messenia	1,226	130,417	Kalamæ.
Argolis and Corinthia	1,448	127,820	Nauplia.
Cyclades	926	123,299	Syra.
Corfu (*Corcyra*)	427	96,940	Corfu.
Cephallenia (*Cephalonia*)	302	77,382	Argostoli.
Zante (*Zacynthos*)	278	44,557	Zante.
	19,354	1,437,026	
Soldiers and sailors		20,868	
		1,457,894	

Physical Aspect.—G. has a singularly diversified surface, and a very irregular coast-line. It is almost encircled by the sea, and is somewhat triangular in shape, having a northerly base. Near the middle it is all but intersected by the Gulf of Corinth (*Lepanto*) on the W., and the Saronic Gulf on the E., which approach each other to within 3½ miles. Thus G. is generally regarded as consisting of three great divisions—(1) The northern portion (7500 sq. miles) between the Gulf of Corinth in the S., and the range of Mount Othrys in the N., indented in the N.W. angle by the Gulf of Arta (q. v.), and running out in the promontory of Attica in the S.E. parallel to Eubœa, from which it is separated by the narrow channels of Evripo, Talanti, and Orei; (2) the Morea (anc. *Peloponnesus*), or southerly portion (8500 sq. miles), connected with N. Greece by the Isthmus of Corinth, and sending out to the S. three promontories, which enclose the Gulfs of Koron (*Messene*) and Marathonisi (*Laconia*); and (3) insular G., including the Cyclades and the Northern Sporades in the Ægean, having a total area of 3300 sq. miles. G. is distinguished among European countries, as Europe is among continents, for the great extent of its coast-line. Little larger than Portugal, its coast-line is longer than that of 'the whole Pyrenean peninsula,' having a length of 2700 miles. The Morea is indented on the W. by the Gulf of Arcadia, on the E. by the Gulf of Nauplia (*Argolis*), and on the N.E. by Megara Bay. No point in G. is further than 46 miles from the sea. *Mountains.*—The mountain-ranges of G. are irregular, extensive, and often boldly precipitous, but are of no great altitude. The lofty Pindus chain, which separates Thessaly from Epirus, enters G. in the N.E. of Ætolia, at 39° N. lat., and sends off to the E. the Mount Othrys range (highest point Geracovuni, 6110 feet), which forms the N. boundary of G. to the Gulf of Volo, and to the S.E. the Mount Katavothra (*Œta*) range, which, again, in the N.W. of Phocis, separates into several diverging ranges. Of these, the most easterly (in Mount Saromata, 5780 feet) runs close to Gulf of Zituni, contains the famous pass of Thermopylæ (q. v.), and after separating Phocis from Locris, enters Bœotia. From Mount Katavothra (6310), in a westerly direction, trend several minor ranges, while the great irregular central chain, comprising Liakura (*Parnassus*) (8068), Palæovúni (*Helicon*) (4963), Elaté (*Cithæron*) (4630), and Telo-Vuni (*Hymettus*) (5366), extends S.E. as far as Cape Sunium or Colonna in Attica. The great system of the N. is connected with that of the Morea by the Geranean Mountains, which stretch over the Isthmus of Corinth. Covered with a maze of lesser mountain ranges, the Morea is traversed in a southerly direction from Mounts Zyria (*Cyllene*) (7778 feet) and Olonos (*Erymanthus*) (7297) in Arcadia, by the chains Pentedactylon (*Taÿgetus*) (7902) and Malevó (*Parnon*) (6355), which terminate in Capes Matapan and Malia. The islands, almost without exception, are mountainous and irregular in shape. The mountains of G. are all below the line of perpetual snow. They enclose innumerable narrow valleys, and are parted here and there along the coast by fertile plains. Most notable are the plains of Bœotia, Marathon, Argos, and Messenia. *Rivers, &c.*—Few of the rivers of G. are perennial, and none are navigable. The most important is the Aspropotamo (*Achelous*), which rises in Mount Pindus, flows in a southerly direction through Epirus, Ætolia, and Acarnania, and enters the Ionian Sea near the Gulf of Corinth, after a course of 130 miles. On the E. side of the Pindus range rises the Ellada (*Spercheus*) (60 miles long), which flows E. through a wide vale between the Othrys and Œta ranges to the Malic Gulf. Liakura sends forth the Mavronero (*Cephissus*) (55 miles) over the Bœotian plain to Lake Topolias (*Copais*). The Evenus (70 miles) waters the E. of Ætolia, and flows into the Gulf of Corinth. Several meagre streams in Bœotia, Attica, and Phocis appear in the rainy seasons. Almost the only notable rivers in the Morea are the Vasilipotamo (*Eurotas*) in Laconia, and the Alpheus (*Rufēa*) in Arcadia and Elis. The Rufēa (*Alpheus*, q. v.) is consecrated by the memory of the great Olympic games. The largest of the permanent lakes are Topolias in Bœotia, Phonia (*Stymphalus*) in Arcadia, and Arta (*Ambracia*) in Acarnania. Many lakelets are formed in the valleys during spring-time, but in summer these evaporate and give place to malarious swamps.

Climate.—G. has every diversity of climate, from the winter severity of Arcadia and of the northern highlands, where snow lies for many months in the year, to the sultry heat of the marshy plains. Attica is pre-eminent for its pure atmosphere and clear blue sky. Bœotia is proverbially notable as the land of fogs. The lively Athenians supposed that their neighbours over the hills had got fog on the brain. The chill winds of the N. and N.W. prevail even in summer, while the temperature of the S. is often raised by the sudden visits of the parching sirocco. The rains of spring and autumn come with the mild S.E. winds. The climate of G. is said to be affected to a greater extent than in ancient times by malaria, and this is ascribed to the diminution of tillage and the destruction of forests. The mean temperature in the N. is 59° F., in the S. 64° F.; at Athens it is 60°–41° in winter, 77° in summer.

Agriculture and Botany.—One-half of the land consists of mountain and marsh, and only a fifth of the remainder is under cultivation, although nearly half of the male inhabitants are employed in agriculture. The soil is rich but thin, the implements and resources are exceedingly primitive; oxen for ploughing are scarce, and the country people are for the most part lodged in miserable huts. Upwards of three-fourths of the land belongs to the State. The *metayer* or tenant is in many cases supplied by the proprietor with oxen and seed, holds his farm by the year, and pays rent in kind to the extent of one-third of the net produce. Wheat, barley, and maize are the chief crops, but grain has to be imported, chiefly from the S. of Russia, for the subsistence of the population. The currant (Ital. *papolina*) or small Corinthian grape is successfully cultivated along the shore of the Gulf of Corinth, between Corinth and Patras, and on the islands of Cephalonia and Zante. The marshy regions and plains (especially those of Argos and Marathon) produce rice, cotton, madder, and tobacco. Among the fruits are the vine, olive, almond, orange, lemon, and fig. The island of Santorin exports (mainly to Russia) in considerable quantity a fine wine to which it gives name. Many of the mountains have been stripped of their forests, but the ancient Taÿgetus, Parnassus, Helicon, &c., are still richly clad with foliage. The pine is the common tree; others are the beech, chestnut, oak, and cypress.

Zoology.—The principal wild animals still left in the mountains are the bear, wolf, boar, lynx, jackal, deer, and wild-cat. Game abounds in great variety, and of typical birds there are eagles, vultures, hawks, and owls. G. is more a pastoral than an agricultural country, and its great sources of wealth are its flocks of sheep and herds of goats. Arcadia is still, as of old, the land of shepherds.

Geology and Mineralogy.—G. has no volcanoes, but is marked by volcanic action in its wild, contorted mountains, mineral springs (as those of Thermopylæ and Delphi), deep caverns, &c.

The prevailing rock is hard, grey limestone, often assuming the form of finest marble. Other rocks of G. are granite, mica schist, and serpentine. Among the minerals are gold, silver, copper, iron, lead, sulphur, salt, cobalt, manganese, and antimony. The quarries of Mount Mendeli (*Pentelicus*) produce beautiful white marble, those of the Morea and the islands, rare green and red marbles. At Laurium in Attica are the once valuable silver mines. There are many quarries of gypsum and porphyry.

Industries and Commerce.—G. is of little industrial importance. The chief manufactures are cottons, woollens, silks, gauze stuffs, cutlery, carpets (in Andros), gold and silver embroidery, straw-hats (at Epakto), earthenware, &c. Shipbuilding, dyeing, and marble-cutting are special occupations. In 1874 the exports amounted to £2,678,000, the imports to £4,763,000. The principal exports are currants (£1,319,000), lead, skins, olive-oil, figs, wine, silk, and tobacco. The imports include grain from Russia, and manufactured goods from Great Britain and France. G. trades chiefly with Great Britain, Turkey, Austria, France, and Russia. In 1874 the total number of vessels that entered and cleared the ports was 142,503, of 7,945,000 tons. The trading ports are Syra, Piræus, Patras, and Nauplia; and the mercantile marine numbers (1874) 5202 vessels, with an equipment of 25,838 men. Greek vessels are much engaged in the carrying trade of the Mediterranean and Black Seas. In the almost total absence of carriage roads, internal communication is wretchedly defective. The only line of railway is that from Athens to Piræus (7 miles). In 1875 there were 1156 miles of telegraph wires, while the post, with 136 offices, transmitted 2,573,481 letters, 1,300,019 papers and journals, and 670,914 official despatches.

Government.—The constitution of G., of date 1863–64, vests the whole legislative power in a chamber of representatives, the Boulé, of not less than 150 members, which is balloted for by universal suffrage, for a term of four years. The constitution guarantees religious liberty, the establishment of the Greek Church, inviolate personal liberty, the non-existence of slavery and of titles of nobility, trial by jury, the freedom of the press, &c. The Boulé meets for not less than three nor more than six months in the year; a sitting is only valid when one-half of the members are present, and no measure can become law without the vote of an absolute majority. A council of state examines all bills, and may propose amendments. The assembly has no power to alter the constitution. Executive power is vested in a hereditary king, and in Ministers of the interior, of finance, of justice, of education, of ecclesiastical affairs, of war, of marine, and of foreign affairs. The king must belong to the Greek Church. Since 1863 ministerial changes have occurred on an average three times a year.

Army and Navy.—In 1867 military service for three years in the 'active army' and nine in the reserve was made obligatory. G. has a national guard for home defence. In 1876 the effective comprised 12,188 men (754 officers) and 636 horses. In time of war the army can be raised to a force of 29,584 men, besides volunteers. In 1875 the fleet consisted of 1 ironclad, 6 screw steamers, 4 schooners, 2 cutters, and a royal yacht. In 1876 it had 76 officers and 581 men. The cost of the army was (1875) £279,600; of the navy £64,298.

Finance.—In 1875 the revenue was £1,415,857, and the expenditure £1,421,125. The public debt, foreign and internal, amounted in 1875 to £15,360,000, on only a small portion of which is the interest paid. Starting on a borrowed capital, G. has had few financial terms without a deficit. The constant excess of expenditure is in great part due to the employment of so many public officials (18,860 or one-twelfth of the population) at salaries amounting to about one-half of the total revenue. G. has, in addition to her funded debt, a floating one estimated at about £6,000,000 sterling. The unit of the monetary system is the *drachma* = 8½d.; of weight, the *oke* = 2 lbs. 11 oz. avoirdupois; of lineal measure, the *pique* = 27 inches. A *stremma* is about one-third of an English acre.

Justice.—G. is divided into four judicial districts each having a royal court of appeal. The supreme court is the Areopagus. There are 13 courts of appeal and 120 of justices of the peace. The laws are mainly based on the Code Napoleon; the judges, appointed by the King, are reputed for integrity. Cases of brigandage and murder are common, but there are not many of drunkenness and immorality. Besides passing a special examination, advocates must hold the degree of LL.D. from the University of Athens or from some other university of Europe.

Education and Religion.—In 1834 education was made compulsory and free, but according to the census of 1870 only 33 per cent. of men and but 17 of women were able to read or write. There are 370 communal schools, 180 schools where ancient Greek is taught, some fifty gymnasia, four medical schools, one theological, one military, one agricultural, one school of arts, and universities at Athens and Corfu. The professors and teachers number about 500, and the pupils 64,061; the state estimate of grants for education and religion was (1875) £75,825. Nearly all the inhabitants belong to the Greek Church (q. v.). Only 12,555 are members of other Christian churches, and 2582 are Jews. The monks are numerous, ignorant, and degraded. The press is free, and there are 120 political, literary, and religious newspapers. In the Neo-Hellenic literature that is slowly developing, perhaps the most illustrious names are those of the historians Tricoupis (q. v.) and Perrævos; of the dramatists, Soustos, Neroulos, Rangavis, and Charmouzis. Barnvas, Gennadios, and Byzantino are authors of works on the language.

Nationality.—In 1870 there were in G., besides the Greek-speaking inhabitants, 37,598 Albanians, 1217 Macedo-Wallachians, and 29,216 others. The number of resident Turks was 15,051, of English 2099, of Italians 1539, of Germans 526, of French 415, of Russians 141.

History.—After the fall of the Comnenian dynasty (see BYZANTINE EMPIRE) in 1203, a dukedom of Athens was one of the divisions into which the empire was split. The dukedom remained in the hands of various families till after the final siege of Constantinople in 1453, when G. passed under the Moslem yoke. On the signal defeat of the Turks at Vienna (1684), the Venetians invaded and took possession of Athens and the Peloponnesus, but were forced to withdraw in 1718. G. had to endure for a century longer the cruel despotism of Turkey. At last, in 1821, broke forth the rebellion in which Greek nationality worked out its independence, aided by the allied fleets of England, France, and Russia. The chief events of the war of independence were the Turkish massacre in Scio (q. v.); the brilliant midnight attack of Marcos Bozzaris (q. v.) on the Turkish camp at Carpenesia (1823); the capture of Missolonghi (1825), and of Athens (1826), by the Turks; the rejection by the Porte of all diplomatic interference; and the destruction of Ibrahim Pasha's fleet in the harbour of Navarino (1827). The Count Capo d'Istria, who had assumed the presidency of G. in 1828, was assassinated in 1831. Otho, second son of Ludwig of Bavaria, was chosen king, and began to reign in February 1833. G. compelled Otho to grant a constitution in 1843, and eventually banished him in 1863. The crown was then almost unanimously offered to Prince Alfred of England, but its acceptance was prevented by standing conditions between the protecting powers. Prince Georg, son of Christian IX. of Denmark, and brother of the Princess of Wales, was crowned as Georgios I. (see GEORG) in October 1863. He married the Princess Olga, niece of the Emperor of Russia (1867), and had several sons. See Bernardaki, *Le Présent et l'Avenir de la G.* (Par. 1870); Brockhaus, *Griechenland, geographisch, geschichtlich und kultur-historisch von den ältesten Zeiten bis auf die Gegenwart dargestellt* (Leips. 1870); Edward Strickland, *G., its Condition and Resources* (Lond. 1863); Tuckerman, *The Greeks of To-day* (Lond. 1873); and Dr. R. Nicolai, *Geschichte der neu-griechischen Literatur* (Leips. 1876).

Greece, Ancient. See HELLAS.

Greek Church, which assumes to itself the name of 'Orthodox,' and might most properly be called the Eastern Church, comprises in its wider sense three main groups of churches. 1. Those fragments of the Christian Church in Asia and Africa, all of which, with the exception of the last, rendered themselves heretical by protesting against the innovations of the see of Constantinople. (1) The Chaldean Christians of Kurdistan, who trace their origin to the mission of Thaddæus to Abgarus, King of Edessa, their sacred city. They only recognise the first two general councils of the Church, rejecting the third (of Ephesus), which condemned Nestorius, and receive the epithet of Nestorians. (2) The Armenians (q. v.), inhabiting the mountainous tract around Ararat, converted by Gregory the Illuminator in the 4th c., who have been called the 'Quakers' of the East, the 'Jews' of the Oriental Church; their sacred city and seat of the patriarch is Etschmiadzin (q. v.). (3) The Church of Syria, with its capital Antioch, which is the oldest of the Gentile churches, and to whose chief pastor 'alone in the world by right belongs the title of patriarch.' It comprises two different communities—(*a*) The Jacobite or Monophysite (q. v.) Church, with its patriarch at Diarbekr (q. v.); and (*b*) the Maronites of Mount Lebanon, founded by Maro in the 5th c., the only relic of the Monothelite (q. v.) heretics. (4) The Coptic Church (q. v.) of Egypt, with its patriarch formerly at Alexandria, now at Cairo, which, like the Syrian, is Monophysite, rejects all but the first three general councils, and protests against the heterodoxy not only of the whole West, but of the whole East beside themselves. A daughter of the last is the Church of Abyssinia, founded by the Church of Alexandria in the 4th c. In the usages of this Church 'whatever there is of Jewish or of old Egyptian ritual in the Coptic Church, whatever of extravagant ritualism, of excessive dogmatism, of the fatal division between religion and morality, that disfigures to so large an extent the rest of Oriental Christianity, is carried to excess.' (5) The Church of Georgia. The king of this country was converted nearly at the same time as Constantine (312). The allegiance of the Church, which at first belonged to Antioch, was afterwards transferred to Constantinople. 2. The G. C. proper, the Orthodox Imperial Church, or 'the great Church,' which includes the whole Greek-speaking race, has its centre in Greece and Constantinople, and the sanctuary of which is the 'Holy Mountain' of Athos. The main characteristic of this Church is its lineal descent from the first Christian empire (the Byzantine), and of that Church at new Rome which was for a period more truly the centre of Christendom than that at old Rome. 3. The barbarian tribes of the North who were converted by the Byzantine Church—(1) The tribes on the Lower Danube. Bulgaria was first converted to Christianity by Cyril (q. v.) and Methodius in the 9th c., and communicated the new religion to Servia, Moldavia, and Wallachia. There is besides a colony of Greek Christians, called 'Raitzen,' who occupy large districts in Hungary. (2) The Church of Russia, which is the present representative of the Imperial Church of Constantine, the Czar being the personal head of the whole G. C.

II. The history of the G. C. has been divided into three periods. 1. The first period is that of the first seven general councils, which were as peculiarly councils of the Eastern Church as those of Constance and Trent were of the Western. Of these, the Council of Nice (325), the confession of which has been received by the whole of Christendom as the earliest, the most solemn, and the most universal expression of Christian theology, may be considered both as the most significant and also as the most enduring monument of the Oriental Church. 2. The second epoch is the birth and growth of Mohammedanism, which is essentially interwoven with the G. C. There are points which Mohammedanism owes to its Oriental origin in common with the G. C.; in other points it is a reaction against that Church. The history of the Slavonic races has been continually affected by their conflict with Arabs, Tartars, and Turks. 3. The third epoch is the establishment of the Russian Church, and through it of the Russian Empire.

III. The characteristics which are common more or less to all parts of the G. C., and which distinguish it from the Western Church. The final external separation between the Eastern and the Western Church, which took place in the 12th c., was directly due to a multitude of concurrent external causes: (1) Political—the jealousy between the two rival capitals of Rome and Constantinople, specially represented by their bishops; the rival claims of the Eastern and the Western Crusaders, &c. (2) Religious—as the doctrine regarding the procession of the Holy Spirit (see FILIOQUE); the use of leavened or unleavened bread, &c. But the real elements of discord between these two great divisions of the Christian Church were more deep-seated than any of the above-mentioned pretexts. 1. Perhaps the most prominent distinction between the two is that of the speculative tendency of the G. C. and the practical tendency of the Western which is manifested in the theology of the two. 'The East,' it has been said, 'enacted creeds, the West discipline;' the truth of which is seen from the fact that the first decree of an Eastern council was to settle the relations of the Godhead, the first decree of the Pope of Rome was to interdict the marriage of the clergy. 'Latin Christianity contemplated with almost equal indifference Nestorianism and all its prolific race, Eutychianism, Monophysitism, Monothelitism. While in this great contest the two great patriarchates of the East, Constantinople and Alexandria, strove to establish their right to ascendancy, . . . in the West there was not a Nestorian or Eutychian sect.' 2. This contrast 'appears not only in the theology but in the ecclesiastical, and especially in the monastic, system of the East.' Monasticism was not only born in the East, but has thriven there with an unrivalled intensity. The active life generally exhibited by Western monachism—*e.g.*, by the Benedictines and the Sisters of Mercy—is regarded in the East as an abuse of the system. So, too, fasting, which in the West is chiefly confined to the special season of Lent, is liable to wide dispensations, and amounts for the most part only to abstinence from particular kinds of food, in the East extends over long periods of the year, and means abstinence from all food. 3. Another important difference is that the G. C., like the East generally, has remained stationary and unchanged, while the Western has been progressive. This conservatism in the G. C. is exhibited, *e.g.*, (1) in the rite of baptism, in which the original, primitive practice of immersion is kept up, and in the following practices also descending from primitive times:—(2) the laying on of hands immediately after baptism, in the case of infants as well as adults, that they might receive 'the gifts of the Spirit,' which in the Western Church has been made into a separate rite of Confirmation; (3) the administration of the Eucharist to infants; and (4) calling in the elders of the Church (James v. 14) *for the recovery of the sick*, a rite which in the Western Church has developed into extreme unction for those not expected to recover. Minor points in which the same spirit is exhibited are, keeping up the primitive posture of standing at public prayer, excluding musical instruments of every kind from public worship, and refusing to adopt the 'new style' of reckoning time. 4. Another point of difference is that in general the G. C. has never shown either a missionary or a persecuting spirit; the conversion of the Russian nation, what would appear to be a great missionary effort, was effected, not by the preaching of the Byzantine clergy, but by the marriage of a Byzantine princess. 5. Another difference, which is a marked indication of the stagnant spirit of the G. C., is that its theology has not been systematically developed, as in the Western Church. Its doctrines remain very much in the rigid, undefined state in which they were in the beginning of the 4th c. 6. The organisation of the hierarchy of the G. C. shows a marked contrast to that of the Western Church. (1) The ordination of a priest in the G. C. is not indelible. (2) The monastic orders in the East are to a great extent lay institutions. (3) The centralisation displayed in the Papacy is unknown in the G. C. Its place is taken by the Patriarchate, so that the constitution of the one Church is monarchic; of the other, aristocratic. (4) The whole body of the parochial clergy of the G. C. must always be married before they enter on their office, except the bishops, who, being selected from the monasteries, are single. In the Western Church the enforcement of celibacy was one of the first steps for the organisation of the clergy. See Stanley's *Lectures on the Eastern Church* (4th ed. Lond. 1869); Neale's *Hist. of the Holy Eastern Church* (2 vols. 1850); Palmer's *Diss. on the Eastern Communion* (1853); Gibbon's *Decline and Fall of the Rom. Empire.*

Greek Fire, an inflammable compound very extensively employed in warfare for causing conflagrations during the middle ages. It was well known in the East in the 7th c., and its invention has been ascribed to the Arabs. The definite composition of G. F. is not known; its ingredients are supposed to have been naphtha, bitumen, sulphur, resins, and numerous fatty substances. The fire was thrown in fragile pots or other vessels from catapults or other warlike engines. Through the Crusaders it came to be known in Western Europe, and it was one of the many incendiary compositions in use at the time gunpowder was discovered. A modern instance of the employment of a kind of G. F. occurred in the siege of Charleston, U.S., by the Federals in 1863.

Greek Music is a very obscure subject. The Greek name for music was *harmonikē*, and the Greek instrument was the lyre. The Greeks understood the nature of *intervals*, and Pythagoras is said to have discovered the law on which the construction of stringed instruments depends. Terpander (flourished probably about 670 B.C.) added three to the four strings of the lyre, and successive additions were made to the number corresponding to successive extensions of the scale. The centre of the Greek system is the *tetrachord* (four notes—*e.g.*, B, C, D, E), and by adding and 'fitting' together tetrachords, they reached a 'system' of two octaves, which they called 'perfect.' Two tetrachords were 'fitted' together when they had a note in common, and this was usually, but not always, the case. The above 'system,' corresponding to our minor scale with minor seventh, was called the 'diatonic genus;' besides, the Greeks had the chromatic and the enharmonic genera, in which the notes proceeded by different degrees. G. M. was used almost exclusively to accompany poetry.

Gree'ley, Horace, an important American writer and politician, was born at Amherst, New Hampshire, February 3, 1811. He was the son of a poor farmer, and spent his youth in rural labours until he was apprenticed to a printer. In 1831 he went to seek his fortune in New York, and worked there as a journalist on various papers, one of which, the *Log Cabin*, rose to a circulation of 80,000, and in 1841 was merged in the *New York Tribune*, of which G. was the founder, and with which he was henceforth always associated. He was elected to Congress in 1848, visited Europe in 1851, and was chairman of one of the juries in the Great Exhibition. He travelled again to Europe in 1855, and to California in 1859. On the close of the civil war he earnestly advocated a universal amnesty, and in 1867 was a member of the New York State Constitutional Convention. In 1872 he was brought forward against General Grant (q. v.) as a candidate for the presidentship, but was defeated, and shortly afterwards died near Chappaqua, November 29, 1872. G. was not only a singularly able writer and speaker, but a man of so unique a character that he may be said to have approached the confines of genius. Impetuous yet generous, broadly tolerant yet keenly opinionative, he was perhaps one of the best representatives of American vigour and enthusiasm, and was held in honour both in England and on the Continent of Europe. Among his works are *Hints towards Reforms* (1850), *Glances at Europe* (1851), *History of the Struggle for Slavery Extension* (1856), *Overland Journey to San Francisco* (1860), *The American Conflict* (1864), *Recollections of a Busy Life* (1869). See G.'s *Life* by J. Parton (new ed. Bost. 1868).

Green is one of the constituent colours of white light, and occupies a position in the solar spectrum intermediate between yellow and blue. It is regarded by Clerk Maxwell as one of the three primary colour sensations, deep red and violet being the others; and this theory is supported by the now well-known fact that from a pure yellow and a pure blue (such as are present in the spectrum) it is impossible by mixture to form a G. The reason why yellow and blue pigments, when mixed, produce G. is simply because they do not severally produce upon the retina the same simple sensations which the pure spectrum colours do, and the consequence is a blurred resultant sensation, which, though apparently the same as the pure spectrum G., is as different as a mixed sound from a pure note. The production of a G. by the combination of blue and yellow is very common both in oil and water-colour painting and in dyeing. There are, however, certain greens which are formed directly by a chemical process, such as *Scheele's G.*, *Brunswick G.*, *Emerald G.*, *Schweinfurth G.*, *Mineral G.*, which are all salts of copper, and *Sap G.*, formed from the fermented juice of buckthorn berries. An allied species gives also *Chinese G. Indigo*, which is used for dyeing silk. The copper greens are all highly poisonous. *G. Vitriol* is the sulphate of Iron (q. v.), having the composition $FeSO_47H_2O$. It crystallises in rhombic prisms, is soluble in water, and is employed in dyeing and in the manufacture of ink and Prussian blue.

Green'backs, the popular name for the paper money of the United States, first issued by the Government in 1862.

Green Earth, a mineral consisting of the silicate of ferric oxide with potash, alumina, magnesia, water, and other ingredients, usually found occupying cavities in amygdaloid. In the arts it is used as a pigment under the name of *mountain green*.

Green Eb'ony, the wood of the *Jacaranda ovalifolia* (see JACARANDA), a tree of S. America belonging to the natural order Bignoniaceæ (q. v.). It is imported into Britain as a dyewood.

Greene, Nathan'iel, an American general, born of Quaker parents at Powtowhommet, Rhode Island, May 27, 1742. He became a member of Rhode Island Assembly in 1770, and in 1774 enlisted in the American army. He was made brigadier-general in 1775, and major-general in 1776; and after distinguishing himself in the battles of Trenton and Princeton, by a rapid march saved the American army at Brandywine. In 1780 he presided at the trial of Major André, and was made commander of the army of the S., which he found in great want and disorganisation. Having restored his troops to efficiency, he was attacked by Cornwallis, who, though he defeated G. at Guildford, was shortly forced to retreat before him. In 1781 he gained the battle of Eutaw Springs, one of the most fiercely contested in the whole war, for which a medal was struck in his honour by Congress, while Georgia and N. and S. Carolina gave him large grants of land. At the end of the war he returned to Rhode Island, and in 1785 retired to his estate of Savannah, Georgia, where he died, June 19, 1786. G. is one of the foremost heroes of the War of Independence, and in the eyes of his countrymen ranks second only to Washington himself. No more energetic, skilful, or intrepid leader figured in the strife.

Greene, Robert, an Elizabethan dramatist, lyrist, and writer of fiction, was born at Norwich about 1560, became B.A. of Cambridge in 1578, travelled in Spain and Italy, and, after hesitating whether to be a clergyman or a physician, 'became an author of plays and a penner of love pamphlets.' His first work, *Mamilia*, a prose tale (1583), was followed by other euphuistic stories which became at once popular. Henceforth his career was one of incessant literary work and reckless debauchery until his death, September 3, 1592. His *Repentance of Robert G.*, published after his death, gives a frank, touching account of his wild life. Only six of his plays are preserved, *Orlando Furioso*, *Looking-Glass for London and England*, *Friar Bacon and Friar Bungay*, *James the Fourth*, *Alphonsus*, and *George-a-Greene*. These show slender dramatic art, but are often graceful, natural, and pathetic. *Friar Bacon* and *George-a-Greene* are delightfully English in descriptive colouring, and combine a sweet and simple pastoralism with a vein of rich classical allusion peculiarly characteristic of the Renaissance spirit. Many of G.'s lyrics are exquisitely musical, and full of a glowing voluptuousness of imagery. See Dyce's *Works of G. and Peele* (new ed. 1874).

Green'finch (*Fringilla chloris*), a well-known species of *Fringillidæ* of Finches (q. v.), and one of the commonest hedge-birds of Britain. The colour is yellow on the upper parts in the adult male, the yellow being tinted with green, and the wings edged with yellow. The quill feathers are greyish black, and the under parts yellowish fading into grey. The female is similarly coloured, but the tints are less bright than in the male. The average length is 6 inches. The song is sweet, but not powerful. The nest is not completed till May, and the eggs, which number from three to five, are a bluish white spotted with grey and brown. In winter the G. frequents farmyards and barns.

Greengage', the common name given to a cultivated variety of *Prunus domestica* or common plum, from the green appearance of its round fruit. It is regarded from its delicate flavour when ripe as one of the best dessert plums. In France it is called *Reine Claude*.

Green'heart, Bibiri, or **Bebeeru**, names given to *Nectandra Rodiæi*, a valuable timber tree of British Guiana belonging to the natural order *Lauraceæ* (q. v.). The wood is hard and durable, and so heavy as to sink in water. It is employed in ship-building, and for a variety of purposes where strength and durability are requisite. Its bark is valued in medicine as a tonic and febrifuge. It owes its properties to an alkaloid called Bebeerine (q. v.).

Green'house, in horticulture, a structure glazed on the sides and roof, for rearing tender plants, such as *Pelargonium*, *Fuchsia*, *Camellia*, *Azalea*, *Calceolaria*, *Cineraria*, &c., and for protecting during winter hardier kinds that in summer are grown out of doors. In cold weather heat is maintained by artificial means, and in order to admit air the sashes of the roof are made movable. The plants are placed in pots—a G. differing only in this respect from a Conservatory (q. v.), and are arranged on benches or shelves so as to reap the full benefit of the sun's rays. A G. is usually in direct communication with the dwelling-house, for convenience of being resorted to in inclement weather.

Green'land, a polar region belonging to Denmark, being a large island or cluster of islands of unknown size N.E. of the N. American continent, bounded on the N. by the Arctic Ocean,

E. and S. by the Arctic and Atlantic Oceans, and W. by Davis Strait, Baffin's Bay, Smith Sound, Kennedy Channel, &c. The E. coast is quite desolate and almost inaccessible, being beset by immense icefields, from which great floes constantly pass round Cape Farewell to the W. coast, the only part of G. hitherto at all explored. For about 1000 miles this W. part presents first an outer seaboard strip from 15 to 150 miles broad, cut with bays 45 to 90 miles deep, and skirted with large and small islands. Its area, about 35,000 sq. miles in extent, is in general rocky, having a lower formation of gneiss and granite covered with sandstone and coal-layers, and in the N. with an extensive trap formation. Its shores are steep, with many cliffs of from 3000 to 5000 feet, some even from 5000 to 6000 feet, and plateaux from 2000 to 3000 feet high, with edges scarped to the sea. Seen from Davis Strait and Baffin's Bay, it offers the same features from S. to N.—high, naked, black mountains towering above a white sheet of ice and snow, which on closer approach proves to be the ice-clad highland of the coast, hiding an 'underland' less bleak, yet well-nigh barren of plant-life, owing to the fog and sea-wind from Baffin's Bay. Farther inland the vegetation becomes less stinted, though still restricted to the valleys and lower slopes. Beyond this the interior of G. is a monotonous wilderness of ice, about 2000 feet high at its western part, but slowly rising to nearly 4000 feet, whence the eye sees to a great distance eastward one level unvarying desert, destitute of every sign of life. This inland ice has a constant tendency to compensate its yearly increase by pushing its edge westward over the outer borderland into the sea. The descent of the 'ice-streams' is very gradual, but river-like; they slide down into the fjords, and their edges, often 1000 feet thick, are lifted up by the sea, and form icebergs. There are thirty-two such 'ice-fjords' on the W. coast of G. In some places where the inland ice extends to the cliffs of the shore itself, it falls down into the fjords in smaller pieces, called 'calf-ice.' The presence of these masses, as well as the neighbourhood of the Arctic Ocean, renders the cold in G. exceptionally severe. In North G. the ground is always frozen to a depth of 8-12 inches. The average temperature is 3·22° F. South G., having a moister and more uncertain though generally warmer climate than North G., and therefore a more uneven surface, is less favourable for communication by dog-sledges. At Godhavn the sun is six, at Upernavik eleven and a half weeks below the horizon; but there always remain two or three hours clear enough for reading the smallest print. The dry atmosphere of G. keeps wood long sound and food long fresh. The islands only produce lichens and carices, but on the mainland are found grass and shrubby plants yielding 'ling-fuel,' chiefly willows and dwarf-birches, and also whortleberries, bilberries, and crake-berries, which are universally used as food. Further inland grow the birch, willow, alder, and juniper, but nowhere higher than 5 feet from the ground. Corn cannot be ripened. For fuel, turf, drift-timber, and train-oil are chiefly used. Of animals, the natives have only the dog. The hunting of reindeer, once very extensive, has now nearly ceased, and is succeeded by that of hares, foxes, bears, and sea-birds. But it is the capture of seals (90,000 to 100,000 are taken yearly) that supports the life of the Greenlanders, and makes G. of any importance. The few minerals are chiefly graphite, alum, lime, vitriol, cryolite (of which 9147 tons, valued at £21,660, were exported to Philadelphia in 1869), and coal. The chief imports are wheat, coffee, sugar, brandy, tobacco, and firewood. The pop. (10,000) is composed of native Eskimos (q. v.), and some Danes. Taxes are unknown. Judicially, the country is divided into two 'inspectorates' subdivided into thirteen districts. G., discovered by an Icelander named Gunbjörn, at the beginning of the 10th c., was first colonised by Erik the Red about 982. Gradually two settlements arose, called the 'East Parish' and the 'West Parish.' While the 'Black Death' raged in Norway (from 1349), all communication with that country, from which the Scandinavians in G. had drawn their supplies, was cut off, and the distressed settlers gradually dwindled away under the attacks of the 'Skrællinger' (*lit.* 'parings,' *i.e.*, 'puny wretches'), as they were wont to call the Eskimos. In 1721 Hans Egede (q. v.) went to G. to Christianise the natives. In 1874 the first native pastor was ordained. Some attempts had been made in the 17th c. by the Danes to found a trade with G., but these were unsuccessful till 1774, when they instituted the Government monopoly that is still kept up to the great advantage of G. See Richardson's *Polar Regions* (Edinb. 1861), and Rink's *Tales and Traditions of the Eskimo* (Edinb. 1875).

Green Mountains. See APPALACHIANS and VERMONT.

Green'ock (Gael. 'the sunny knoll'), a thriving seaport of Scotland, in Renfrewshire, on the left shore of the Firth of Clyde, opposite Helensburgh (q. v.), the Gare Loch, and peninsula of Roseneath, 4 miles N.W. of Port Glasgow, and 21 W.N.W. of Glasgow by railway. Stretching along the shore for about 5 miles, and climbing the slopes of a range of hills 800 feet high, it looks N. to the rugged peaks of the Highlands, across the Clyde, which has here a breadth of 2⅞ miles. It is a bonding port, and its fine custom-house was erected in 1818 at a cost of £30,000. Other public buildings are the courthouse, townhall, Wood's Mariners' Asylum (1851), the sugar exchange, the academy, a mechanics' institute, a hospital, temperance institute, Watt Institute (with bust of Watt by Chantrey), museum, and library of 100,000 vols. G. has been supplied with water from large reservoirs behind the neighbouring hills since 1825, at a total cost till the present time of over £300,000. On the line of falls in the water system there have been erected fifteen sugar refineries, woollen, flour, and saw mills, yielding a revenue for water supply of £10,000 yearly. The harbours stretch about 3 miles, cost over £1,000,000 sterling, and include four tidal docks, three graving docks, a large wet dock in course of construction (1877), and the Princess Pier, opened in 1870. The Gavel Park graving dock is one of the finest in Britain; the harbour cranes (two of which are 70 and 50 tons respectively) are worked by hydraulics. The harbour revenue in 1876 was £69,212; in the foreign trade 667 vessels of 307,957 tons entered, and 516 of 299,015 tons cleared, while there was an active coasting trade. The trade is chiefly in sugar, timber, coal, and iron. The sugar imported in 1876 amounted to 237,799 tons; the timber to 98,740 loads; the coal exported to 36,713 tons; the iron to 8950 tons. The chief industries are shipbuilding, engineering, spinning, distilling, and sugar refining. In 1876 the fifteen sugar refineries sent out 239,410 tons, being 31 to every 100 tons refined in the British Isles (772,700 tons) in the same year. The valuation of the burgh in 1876 was £337,085, while 429 vessels of 200,374 tons belonged to the port. The corporation revenue was £119,197 in 1876. G. is the great starting-point for tourists to the W. Highlands, and as many as fifty steamers call at its quays in a day. It returns one member to Parliament. Pop. (1871) 57,821; estimated in 1876, 68,000. Prior to the Union (1707) G. was a mere fishing village, though a burgh of barony from 1635.

Green River, a river of Kentucky, U.S., which, after a course of over 300 miles, joins the Ohio 6 miles above Evansville, Indiana. It is navigable for small vessels for about 20 miles. The river in the Mammoth Cave is a subterranean offshoot from the G. R.

Greens, a familiar name for all the open-hearted varieties of cabbage, but more especially applied to the curled leaves of German G. or kale. *Brassica oleracea*, a cruciferous plant, is the origin of G. See CABBAGE.

Green'sand, the name given to two formations belonging to the Cretaceous Period (q. v.). They are known as the *Upper* and *Lower G.*, and are separated by the Gault (q. v.). The former is of comparatively little importance, and is probably a shore deposit formed while the Chalk (q. v.) was being laid down in deeper water. By a subsidence of the land, it was removed to a greater depth, and there became covered with the chalk. It attains a maximum thickness of 100 feet in the Isle of Wight. The *Lower G.* is the upper member of the Lower Cretaceous, overlying the Wealden Beds, and corresponding in position to the Neocomian of the Continental geologists, which is specially developed at Neuchâtel in Switzerland. It is a marine formation, abounding in Lamellibranch fossils and other molluscs and invertebrata. Reptiles characteristic of the Wealden formations are also found, indicating the proximity of land, and suggesting that these formations were formed after a depression of the fresh-water Wealden, which brought it under the waters of a sea. The name G. arises in both cases from the frequent presence of dark-green specks of silicate of iron in the sand, but this is not a constant character, and the name must be taken, as in every other similar case, to refer merely to a certain period of geological time.

Green'stone, an old and generic name for a numerous class of trappean rocks (see TRAP), which consist essentially of oligoclase felspar with hornblende or augite. They are highly crystalline, and sometimes become porphyritic. Their colour is generally greenish, and on the weathered surfaces dark brown. Diorite, diallage rock, hypersthene rock, &c., are well-known species belonging to the G. group.

Green'weed, the common name generally applied to *Genista tinctoria*, a British plant at one time largely used as a yellow dye for wool. See GENISTA.

Greenwich, a borough of Kent, on the Thames, and 5 miles S.E. of London by rail. The old town, which was low and irregular, has all but disappeared, and new and pleasant garden-bordered streets, with handsome lines of villas erected, give to the town a cheerful, holiday appearance. Quite a feature of G. are its taverns, which occupy a whole street leading from the river to the Royal Observatory, and which are daily patronised during the season by thousands of Londoners. From the Observatory (see OBSERVATORIES), a grassy hill in the middle of the fine Park, a noble view is obtained of the winding reaches of the Thames, studded with sails, and the rich low country on its banks. Engineering, steamboat-building, and the industries that feed these, are the chief employments. The manufactures comprise electric telegraph cables, ship-rockets, wire ropes, india-rubber, soap, and artificial stone. Pop. (1871) 40,412. G., together with Deptford, returns two members to Parliament.

Greenwich Hospital, a former home for disabled sailors, on the right bank of the Thames at Greenwich, was founded by William and Mary in 1694. The grand building, originally a palace, in which were born Henry VIII. and his daughters Mary and Elizabeth, was extended and adapted to hospital service by Wren (1694–1705), and in the latter year received 100 sailors. By 1708 the royal grant had been increased by bequests and contributions exacted from sailors to a sum of £12,000 a year. In 1735, under George II., the estates of the attainted Earl of Derwentwater (beheaded in 1716) were bestowed on the hospital, amounting yearly to £6000. An annual grant of £20,000 from the Consolidated Fund was substituted (1797) for the sailors' compulsory contributions. The hospital had reached the highest point of its prosperity in 1853, when it was lodging 2710 seamen, and drawing a revenue of £150,000. The staff comprised a governor (salary £1500), a lieutenant-governor (£800), four captains, four commanders, eight lieutenants, two masters, two chaplains, and a large body of medical officers and nurses. After much public discussion on the merits of the splendid charity and its administration, an Act of Parliament (28 and 29 Vict. c. 89) of 1865 converted the hospital into an infirmary, and dismissed 900 seamen with addition to their pensions. By 1869 all but thirty-one bedridden inmates had left the place, and the patients of the *Dreadnought* hospital were removed hither in the following year. The G. H. out-pensions or 'naval pension,' regulated by Acts of 1869–72, provide for a far greater number than the hospital could ever accommodate. These pensions, varying from £3 to £57 a year, are distributed by district staff-officers of military pensions. The hospital buildings have been occupied by a royal naval college and a free school for 800 sailors' sons since 1873.

Greg, William Rathbone, was born at Manchester in 1809, was made a Commissioner of Customs in 1856, and Controller of the Stationery Office in 1864. He has become well known as the author of *Essays on Political and Social Science*, *Enigmas of Life* (1872, 5th ed. 1873), *Literary and Social Judgments*, *Political Problems*, *The Creed of Christendom* (3d ed. 1873), *Rocks Ahead, or the Warnings of Cassandra* (1874). He is a singularly lucid and graceful writer, and a clear and original thinker, but his teachings are somewhat narrow, cold, and dogmatic. In his fidelity to fact, in his earnest attachment to what truth he knows, no less than in his rigid attitude of hostility to convictions which he does not share, we can recognise both the good and the evil of his Puritan training.

Gregari'na, a genus of lower *Protozoa* (q.v.), forming the type of the class *Gregarinida*. The gregarinæ exemplify some of the lowest animal forms known to the naturalist. They are defined as Protozoa destitute of a mouth, and not having the power of emitting *pseudopodia*, or processes of the body substance. All gregarinæ are parasitic in habits, and exist chiefly in the digestive system of *Annulose* animals, such as worms, insects, lobsters, &c. A very common form is *G. lumbricis*, found in the alimentary canal of the earthworm, whilst *G. gigantea* inhabits the digestive system of the lobster. The latter attains a length of one-third of an inch, but the other species are of microscopic size. The G. of the earthworm, which may be selected as a typical form, consists of a little speck of protoplasm of granular nature. When magnified, it is seen to be long and oval in shape, and to have a *nucleus* and *nucleolus*. Living in the digestive canal of its host, the G. absorbs nourishment by imbibition, and thus, like a true parasite, lives at the expense of its host. No distinct body-wall exists, but in some cases (as in *G. gigantea*) one extremity of the body may be provided with hooked processes for attachment to the tissues of its host. Occasionally the interior of the body has been described as divided into two or more portions, but this appearance has probably some connection with the process of reproduction and development. The latter begins by two gregarinæ uniting, although changes may be observed in single gregarinæ; and the interior or central protoplasm of the body next divides into small portions, the outer part of the body having become thickened to form a cyst-like wall, whilst the body itself assumes a globular form. The cyst-like body sooner or later ruptures, and the small contained particles (*pseudonavicellæ*) escape as young gregarinæ. Some of the particles may exhibit *amœboid* movements, or those observed in the nearly allied *Amœba* (q. v.); hence some naturalists have maintained that gregarinæ are simply Amœba degraded by parasitism. The process of development in G. and the internal division of the body bear a strong analogy to the segmentation of the yolk seen in the eggs of higher animals. (See DEVELOPMENT OF THE EMBRYO.) Certain little bodies known as *Psorospermiæ* (q. v.) found as parasites on fishes are regarded as peculiar forms of G.

Gré'goire, Henri, a French priest and revolutionist, was the son of humble parents, and was born in the village of Vého near Lunéville, 4th December 1750. Educated by the Jesuits, he taught for a time in their seminary at Pont-à-Mousson, and was subsequently for years the zealous pastor of Embermésnil in Lorraine. In 1789 he gained a prize for an essay on the regeneration of the Jews. That same year G. was sent as a deputy to the States-General, and was soon known as a thorough-going democrat. He had no hesitation in accepting the new constitution of the clergy, decreed by the National Assembly in 1790, and under that constitution G. was next year elected Bishop of Mans. He sat also in the National Convention, yet never forgot the bishop in the statesman; and when it was demanded of him by the Convention that he should abjure Christianity, he rejected the notion with horror, and remained then and to the end faithful to his Christian profession in spite of scorn, hatred, and solitariness. In the Council of the Five Hundred G. used his influence indefatigably for the restoration of the Christian faith; and he presided over two national assemblies of the clergy held for that end. But as G. favoured Gallicanism, and in theology approached Jansenism, he was never in favour at Rome, and was compelled to demit his bishopric in 1801, and Bonaparte, though he made him a senator, preferred the friendship of the Pope to a reformed French Church. The Restoration regarded G. with the utmost disfavour. He devoted himself to study, declined to withdraw his oath to the revolutionary constitution, and, in spite of the hierarchy, had the last rites of the Church administered to him on his death-bed, 28th May 1831. G. wrote a *Histoire des Sectes Religieuses* (1810, 2d ed. 5 vols. 1828); *Essai Historique sur les Libertés de l'Église Gallicane* (1818, 2d ed. 1826); *De l'Influence du Christianisme sur la Condition des Femmes* (1821). See Carnot, *Mémoires de G.* (1837); Krüger, *Heinrich G.* (1838).

Gregorian Chant or **Tones**, the choral melodies introduced into the Roman Catholic liturgy by Gregory the Great (q. v.), and still used by the Roman, and, to some extent, by the Protestant Church. Gregory was the author of a musical system, as well as the organiser and composer of actual church song. He carried on the work of St. Ambrose (q. v.), Bishop of Milan in the 4th c., inventor of the 'Ambrosian chant.' The latter was founded on what was thought to be the Greek system of scales, and that again is thought by some to be identical with 'the tonality of the Hebrew music.' G. retained from the Ambrosian system four scales, called the Dorian, Phrygian, Lydian, and Mixolydian, under the name of 'authentic modes,' and added to each of these another called 'plagal.' (See diagram.)

It should be noticed that each authentic mode has the same keynote or 'final' (F) as its 'plagal' companion, and that they have a perfect fifth in common; also that every scale is made up of a perfect fifth added to a perfect fourth, and has a note called the 'dominant' (D), which was next in importance to the 'final' in the liturgical recitation. The notes are all 'naturals;' to speak more strictly, they are all *in one key, in the modern sense of that word.* The semitones thus occur in a different place in each scale.

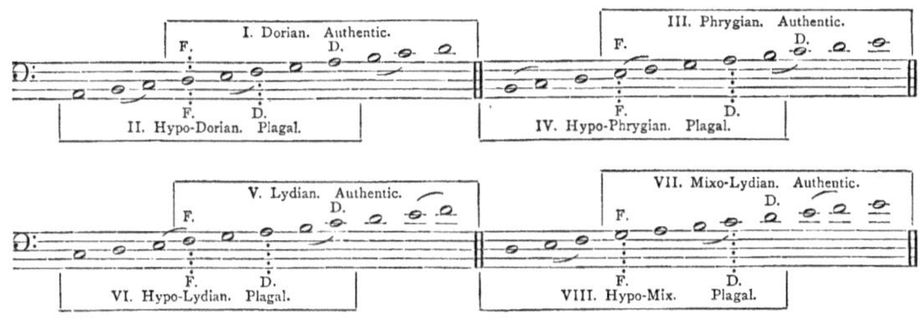

Three more couples are required to give us seven 'finals,' an octave of finals. One (couple) was rejected for reasons of harmony, and the other two were the subject of dispute on the ground of alleged 'superfluity.' A decree of Karl the Great said, 'Octo toni sufficere videntur' (*tonus* = scale). The rhythm of Gregorian music follows the irregular accentuation of spoken language. See Coussemaker's *Histoire de l'Harmonie au Moyen Age*, and Stainer's *Dictionary of Musical Terms.*

Greg'ory I., surnamed **The Great**, the son of a Roman senator, and the grandson of Pope Felix, was born in Rome about 540. He was very carefully educated, and early held offices under the Roman Government. In 574 the Emperor Justin the Younger appointed him Prefect of Rome, but in 576 he resigned the post and entered a monastery on the Cælian Hill, and lived with the strictest austerity. Benedict I. made him a deacon, and in 579 Pelagius II. sent him as Nuncio to seek aid at Constantinople against the Lombards. He discharged his mission with great firmness and dexterity, resumed the rule of his monastery in 584, and in 590 was chosen as Pope. He devoted himself to the double task of spreading Christianity, and of reforming the monks and clergy. He aided Queen Theodolinda in converting the Lombards, sent missionaries to Sardinia, checked Nestorianism, repressed simony, and is linked to English history by his efforts to win over our forefathers from paganism. According to a beautiful story in Bede, G., when a young deacon, noticed several fair-haired slaves in the Roman market, and asked from what land they came. Being told they were Angles, he answered they would be, not Angles, but Angels if they were Christians, and thenceforth resolved to labour for the conversion of that people. Accordingly, in 597, he sent Augustine (q. v.) to Kent, and Christianity was planted in England. G. died at Rome in 604. He was zealous, mild, and strongly averse to persecution. He did more, it has been said, than any other Pope to extend the ecclesiastical power of Rome. Besides bringing about the conversion of the English, he won over Spain to orthodoxy, spread his influence throughout the West, and even into Greece, successfully withstanding the Patriarch of Constantinople, who claimed the title 'Universal Bishop.' He reorganised the Church funds, regulated the calendar, and instituted a new and solemn ritual. Unfortunately he had an illiberal dislike of classical literature and art, and, more than any other pontiff, fostered that excessive veneration of saints, martyrs, and relics, which afterwards sapped the strength of the Church. Among his works are letters, dialogues, homilies, and a treatise on the duties of bishops. The best edition of G.'s works is that published by the Benedictines of St. Maur (4 vols. Par. 1705), which contains the lives of G. written by Paulus Diaconus and Joannes Diaconus. See Gibbon's *Decline and Fall of the Rom. Empire;* Milman's *History of Lat. Christianity;* Lau's *Gregor I. nach Leben und Lehre* (Leips. 1845); Pfahler's *Gregor der Gr. und seine Zeit.* (Frankf. 1853).—**G. II.**, afterwards **Saint**, was born at Rome, and bred a Benedictine. He held the see of Rome from 715 till 731, at a time when Italy was distracted by the advance of the Lombards, and when the unity of the Church in the East and West was seriously threatened by the controversy about image-worship. Both circumstances served to loosen the hold of the Eastern Emperors on Italy, and to compel the Popes to independent negotiations with the Franks, so that the pontificate of G. is justly regarded as having greatly promoted the independence and the supremacy of the see of Rome.—**G. III.**, a Syrian by birth, was consecrated Bishop of Rome in 731, and, so long as he guided the Church of the West, carried out in all respects the policy of his predecessor, G. II. The latter had defended image-worship, and had treated the Emperor Leo the Isaurian like a disobedient child; G. III. formally sanctioned, at a council, the Western usage, and excommunicated the Emperor along with all enemies of the images. G. II. had given his support to the mission of Boniface, the English apostle of Germany; G. III. made Boniface archbishop. And, like his predecessor, G. III. invoked the help of the Franks against the Lombards. He is said to have written a work in favour of the use of images, and died 28th November 741.—**G. VII.**, the type of papalism in its loftiest aims as well as in its proudest spirit, was Pope from 1073 to 1085, but his influence on the affairs of the Roman Church had been decisive for nearly twenty years before he assumed the tiara. His own name was Hildebrand, and he was born about 1020, of humble parentage. Whether or not he was a native of Rome, he spent there most of his childhood, and was chaplain to Pope G. VI. For a time a monk at Cluny, he returned to Rome under Leo IX. and was raised to the cardinalate. Hildebrand's first great work for the reformation of the Church, begun in 1058, was to destroy the influence of the Roman nobility on the papal elections. This he accomplished, not without violence and bloodshed, by the help of the Norman dukes of S. Italy, who were content to become vassals to the successor of St. Peter. A still more arduous and ambitious venture was the attempt to make the papal election itself entirely independent of the Emperor. But circumstances favoured Hildebrand. Pope Nicolas was deposed in 1061; without waiting for the advice or initiative of the German court, Hildebrand and the other cardinals elected Alexander II. The mother of Heinrich IV., the young King of the Germans, had nominated another Pope, but soon after died; and the new regent saw it to be for his advantage to recognise the cardinals' choice. But that which completed Hildebrand's triumph in this matter, was when, on the very day of Alexander's death, he was chosen his successor by clergy and people, and took the name of G. VII. A rebellion of the Saxon princes constrained the king (afterwards emperor), Heinrich IV., to sanction the election, and even to submit to a penance imposed by the new Pope for having held intercourse with counsellors who had been excommunicated by Pope Alexander. The third of the great aims promoted by G. was finally and completely to impose celibacy on all clergy. Since the time of Leo IX. several synods had forbidden the married state to priests, but ineffectually. Taking advantage of the prejudices of the populace of Milan, G. in 1074 forbade the laity to receive the sacrament at the hand of a married priest, and commanded them to compel all such to separate from their wives. The sufferings of the parochial clergy in consequence of this were indescribable, and lower clergy and bishops were alike bitterly incensed against a Pope who conferred such powers on the rabble. G.'s fourth and greatest undertaking was that of securing the freedom of the Church in the matter of the investiture of bishops and abbots. He regarded it as profanation and invasion of the Church's rights that bishops, selected by the Emperor for the most part arbitrarily, should receive purely spiritual appointments from the temporal power, and in the 'abominable usage' that had hitherto permitted this G. saw an open door for simony. His contention was that people and clergy should freely select the bishop, solely with regard to his fitness for office. So the monks, their abbot; and the thus elected bishop should receive investiture from his archbishop, the abbot from the bishop of the diocese. But G. was content that bishop and abbot should do homage to the king in respect of the temporalities of their offices. G.'s famous decree was first drawn up in 1075, though formally published only in 1078, and was to the effect that henceforth no clergyman should receive any spiritual office from the hand of a laic, and that no prince or other temporal potentate should hereafter confer any appointment in the Church. G.'s great contest with Heinrich IV. began in 1076. In 1073 the King had appointed a new Archbishop of Milan. The common people, enthusiastic for the Pope, chose another. Neither obtained general recognition, and in 1075 the nobility and higher citizens, determined to put an end to the perpetual tumults, petitioned the King to name a new and worthy archbishop. So that, when Heinrich had nominated Tedald, there were three archbishops of Milan, of whom two had been appointed by the King. G. was enraged, and when, in the course of the same year, an embassy came requesting him to crown Heinrich Emperor of the Romans, G.'s reply was substantially a threat to deprive Heinrich of his kingdom now and of salvation hereafter. On receipt of this, in January 1076, Heinrich was imprudent enough to decree the deposition of the Pope. G. replied by excommunication. The unlucky ruler's enemies at home insisted on his submission to the Pope, and compelled him to consent that G. should be invited to take part in a diet of the empire. G., delighted at the prospect of sitting as mediator between the King of the Germans and his princes, immediately hastened north. But when he reached the Po he learned to his dismay that Heinrich was in Italy. G. fled to Canossa, whither he was followed by Heinrich. And here the Pope was persuaded to absolve Heinrich, who did penance for three days. The German princes, enraged that the Pope had in so far yielded, chose in 1077 an anti-king, but in 1080 the rebels were crushed. The Pope, disappointed in his hope of securing power over the King, put him a second time under excommunication, while Heinrich again appointed an anti-pope, Clemens III. In spring 1081 the indefatigable soldier was marching southward through Italy against Rome; but his army was small, and twice he had encamped before the city ere in 1083 he took a part of it, and established his anti-pope in the Lateran. But on the approach of Robert Guiscard, who at last listened to G.'s entreaties for help, Heinrich retired; and Robert, entering the city, carried G. off with him to Salerno, where, after eleven months, G. died, 25th May 1085. He did not live to see the issue of his work, and many of his schemes—such as those for making the several European states fiefs of the apostolic see, and his design of a crusade—were entirely absorbed in the struggle with the imperial power. But he lived long enough to set a movement going which turned the course of European history into new channels, and of which we still feel the effects. G. was a great man, and was inspired by an ambition that was at least as noble as it was perilous to liberty. Nothing mean or selfish urged him to advance his portentous claims. If he desired to be the Vicar of Christ on earth, it was to do the work of Christ, to confront and overcome evil-doers, and to lift up the down-trodden and the oppressed. See Milman's *History of Lat. Christianity;* Voigt's *Hildibrandt als Papst Gregor VII.* (2d ed. 1846); Floto's *Kaiser Heinrich IV.* (1855-57); Gfrörer's *Gregor der Siebente* (7 vols. 1859-64).—**G. XIII.** was born at Bologna, January 7, 1502, and educated in his native city. He had for eight years taught canon law with success at Bologna, when the learning and activity displayed by him at the Council of Trent recommended him to the dignity of cardinal. He was chosen Pope chiefly at the instance of Cardinal Granvella. Though formerly far from an ascetic in his life, he entered with zeal and self-devotion into the great work of Catholic restoration, and was indefatigable in the struggle against Protestantism. He celebrated the massacre of St. Bartholomew by processions and medals, and did his best to suppress the Gallican liberties, as well as the Huguenots. No less than twenty-two Jesuit colleges owe to him their origin. He was zealous in the cause of foreign missions. The new edition of the *Corpus Juris* was due to G., and he has the credit of having succeeded in carrying out the reform of the Julian calendar. But his many undertakings involved the papal treasury deep in debt. He died in 1585. See Ranke's *History of the Popes* (Eng. trans. Lond. 1843 and 1847).—**G. XVI.** was born at Belluno, 18th September 1765. He entered the order of the Camaldulites, and became a profound student of theology and the Oriental languages. Called to Rome as general of his order in 1814, he held the offices of Consultor of the Inquisition, of the Propaganda College, Examiner of Bishops, &c., was made a cardinal in 1826, and at the same time Prefect of the Propaganda. In 1831 he was elected Pope. Alarmed by the outbreaks which in Italy followed the French revolution of July 1832, he made liberal promises, which on the suppression of the insurrections he failed to keep, and for some years after 1836 his rule was marked in an unseemly way by proscriptions and punishments of the severest kind. The shameful treatment of the Roman Catholics of Poland by the Russian Czar did not evoke from G. the stern denunciations that became his exalted office. He died 1st June 1846. See La Farina's *Storia d'Italia dal* 1815 *al* 1850.

Gregory Thaumatur'gus ('the wonder-worker') belonged to a wealthy heathen family at New Cæsarea in Pontus. Even after his conversion to Christianity at the age of fourteen, he was resolved to devote himself to the study of law. But circumstances having in A.D. 231 led him to Cæsarea, he there came under the powerful influence of Origen, whose conception of Christianity G. was ever after zealous in defending and disseminating. Leaving Origen at Alexandria in 239, he went homewards with the design of leading a hermit's life, but was induced to become bishop of his native city, where, it is said, there were then only seventeen Christians, while at G.'s death in 270 there were only seventeen heathens. G. was strong in word and in deed; and to his miracles, especially in casting out devils, he owes his name. He escaped the Decian persecution by flight, and survived to ward off a fearful pestilence from all good Christians or converts. G. was zealous against heretics, but was himself accused of a leaning towards Sabellianism. His extant works, including the Panegyric on Origen, were published by Vossius at Mainz in 1604 (Par. 1622); his life, at least the miraculous part of it, was descanted on by Gregory of Nyssa.—**G.**, surnamed **the Illuminator,** because he enlightened his country with a knowledge of the gospel, was born at Vagarchabad in 257, escaped from a massacre of his family at the court of Armenia, and was carried to Cæsarea by his nurse, who brought him up in the Christian faith. Returning to Armenia in the train of Tiridates II., he was soon thrown into prison for his attachment to his religion; but having cured the king of a deadly malady, he was not only liberated from his dungeon, but converted his royal patient. Christianity rapidly spread. To persuasion G. added violence. The idols were shattered, the pagan temples destroyed, and churches erected in their stead. G. was now consecrated Bishop of Armenia, and in his turn made numerous priests. He founded monasteries, hospitals, schools, and libraries, and fixed his episcopal residence at Vagarchabad, the ruins of which may still be seen in the neighbourhood of the monastery of Etschmiadzin (q. v.). He was invited to attend the Council of Nice in 325, but sent a deputy instead. After discharging the duty of patriarch for many years, G. withdrew from all human society to a cave in Mount Sebu, where his lifeless frame was afterwards discovered, about 332. His relics are now scattered over Western Asia and Europe. The homilies, orisons, and prayers ascribed to G. are collected in the work entitled *Le Celèbre Omelie e Preci del Nostro S. Padre Gregorio Illuminatore* (Ven. 1838). The legend of G.'s life, given in the *Acta Sanctorum* of the Bollandists, is taken from the Greek text of Agathangelos.—**G. of Nazian'zus,** one of the famous 'three Cappadocians,' combined the highest culture of Greek theology and sacred eloquence with Nicene orthodoxy, and was in his time one of the most influential apostles of Trinitarianism. Born about 330 in or near Nazianus, in the S.W. of Cappadocia he was early dedicated to the clerical life by his father, who was afterwards Bishop of Nazianzus. The young theologian visited Cæsarea and Alexandria, and at Athens devoted years to the study of grammar, mathematics, rhetoric, and philosophy, in the company of his countryman Basil. At the age of thirty he returned home, and in 361 was ordained a presbyter in his native city, but withdrew into retirement. The bishopric of Sosima was forced on him, but he soon fled from its responsibilities, and in 374 became the vicar of his aged father. His life passed between official activity and monkish seclusion till he was called to a charge in the Eastern capital, where the orthodox party was still in a depressed minority. G.'s success as apologist and pulpit orator was marked; and in 381 he was compelled to accept the metropolitan bishopric, which, however, he soon abdicated. He returned to Cappadocia, and till his death in 389 or 390 devoted himself to private studies. Neither so powerful a churchman as Basil, nor so original a thinker as his own namesake and friend of Nyssa, G. was distinguished by rhetorical power, versatility, and general culture. His intensity of feeling often passed into bitterness, and his repeated resignations of influential position are not to be wholly attributed to commendable humility. Some of G.'s hymns are good, but his most important works are his discourses on various subjects, especially the five dedicated to the exposition and defence of the Nicene doctrine, which earned for him the title of 'the theologian.' The best edition of G.'s works is the Benedictine (not finished till 1840); and the most valuable memoir is the monograph of Ullmann, *Gregorius von Nazianz der Theologe* (1825).—**G. of Nyss'a**, the brother of Basil the Great, was born about 331 of a family distinguished in Cappadocia both for piety and social standing, but he does not seem to have enjoyed the very unusual opportunities of study, both at home and in Greece, that were permitted to his brother. After he had held for a time the ecclesiastical function of lector, he, to the great grief of his friends, forsook the Church for the profession of orator. But he was soon persuaded to return to pastoral office, and in 371 or 372 was, against his will, and in spite of his being a married man, consecrated Bishop of Nyssa by his brother Basil. It was probably less his energy of character that commended him to the post than his power of oratory and his dogmatic subtlety—gifts of great value while Antitrinitarian heresy was still in the ascendant. In 375 G. was condemned and banished by a court of synod; and he remained in exile, and subject to persecution, till the death of the Emperor Valens permitted him to return to Nyssa with enthusiastic welcome. In 381 G. was present at the second Œcumenical Council, and it is doubtful whether or not the additions then made to the Nicene Creed are from G.'s pen. He visited Jerusalem, made various public appearances in Constantinople, and is last heard of at a council held there in 394. G.'s importance depended on his zeal and ability in defence of the mystery of the Trinity. On this head he is one of the great pillars of orthodoxy, though here and there he shows traces of Origen's theology. His sermons, orations, homilies, and letters first appeared in 2 vols. at Paris in 1615. There are several good monographs on G., especially that of Möller (1854).—**G. of Tours**, born about 540 at Clermont in Auvergne, belonged to one of the most distinguished Roman families in Gaul, and was originally named Florentius. Coming on a pilgrimage to the grave of St. Martin at Tours, he secured the favour of King Siegbert and the goodwill of the clergy, and in 573 was made Bishop of Tours. With self-denying zeal, resolution, and prudence, he watched in troublous times over both the spiritual well-being of his diocese and the temporal interests of the city. G. died 17th November 594. His earlier works on the miracles of St. Martin, and on the lives of other saints and confessors, are of small importance, but his ten books on the history of the Franks remain a valuable treasury of the contemporary history of the 6th c. First printed in 1511-12, and critically edited in 1699, G.'s chronicle has been repeatedly translated. See Löbell's *Gregorius von Tours und seine Zeit* (1839). The best edition is that given by Pertz in the *Monumenta Germaniæ Historica*.

Gregory, a Scottish family, many members of which have been eminent in science, and of which sixteen members have held professorships in England and Scotland.—**James G.**, son of David G., a landed proprietor, was born at Aberdeen in 1638, studied at Aberdeen University, devoted himself to science, and in 1674 was made Professor of Mathematics in Edinburgh University. In October 1675, while showing his pupils Jupiter's satellites through a telescope, he was struck blind, and died in a few days. G. wrote *Optica Promota* (1663), which describes his great invention of the 'Gregorian' reflecting telescope; *Vera Circuli et Hyperbolæ Quadratura* (1667); *Geometriæ Pars Universalis* (1668); *Exercitationes Geometricæ* (1668); *The Great and New Art of Weighing Vanity*, an attack on a Glasgow professor.—His son, **James G.**, born in 1674, founded the School of Medicine in Aberdeen, where he was Professor of Medicine.—**John G.**, son of the last, born at Aberdeen, June 3, 1724, studied at Aberdeen and Leyden, held chairs of medicine at Aberdeen and Edinburgh, becoming in the latter place highly famous as a teacher and as a member of the brilliant literary society of the time. G. died February 9, 1773. Among his works are *Elements of the Practice of Physic* (1772); *A Comparative View of the State and Faculties of Man with those of the Animal World* (1765); *A Father's Legacy to his Daughters* (1793).—**James G.**, son of the above, born at Aberdeen in 1753, became in 1776 Professor of Medicine in Edinburgh, and died April 2, 1820. He was a fine classical scholar, as well as a thorough scientist. His chief works are *Conspectus Medicinæ Theoreticæ* (1778), and *Literary and Philosophical Essays* (1792).—His son, **William G.**, born in Edinburgh, December 25, 1803, held the chair of chemistry in Aberdeen and in Edinburgh, and died April 24, 1858. He made several important contributions to chemistry, and was one of the first exponents of Liebig's theory. He translated Liebig's *Principles of Agricultural Chemistry* (1855), and edited part of Turner's *Elements of Chemistry*.—Another branch of the G. family descended from **David G. of Kinardie**, who was a brother of James G. the inventor of the 'Gregorian' telescope, and whose son, **David G.**, born at Aberdeen in 1661, was mathematical professor in Edinburgh, and in 1691 was made Professor of Astronomy in Oxford, chiefly through the influence of Newton, whose *Principia* he had introduced into Edinburgh University. He died at Maidenhead, Berkshire, in 1710. Among his works are *Exercitatio Geometrica de Dimensione Figurarum* (1684), *Catoptricæ et Dioptricæ Sphæricæ Elementa* (1695), *Astronomiæ Physicæ et Geometricæ Elementa* (1782).—**James G.**, brother of the above, succeeded him as Professor of Mathematics in Edinburgh University; and his brother, **Charles G.**, was Professor of Mathematics in St. Andrews University from 1707 to 1739, when he was succeeded by his son, **David G.**

Greif'enberg, a walled town of Pommern, Prussia, on the Rega, 20 miles from its mouth and 40 N.E. of Stettin. It has a garrison, and is noted for its linens. Pop. (1871) 5619. G. is also the name of a small town (pop. 1485) in the Ukermark, province of Brandenburg, and of another (pop. 2496) in Prussian Silesia.

Greif'enhagen, a town of Pommern, Prussia, on the Reglitz, 12 miles S. of Stettin, has cloth factories and distilleries. Pop. (1871) 6611.

Greifs'wald, a town of Pommern, Prussia, on the Rick, about 3 miles from its mouth, and 22 miles S.E. of Stralsund by railway. G. has a saltwork, manufactures some paper and tobacco, does a little weaving, and carries on a coasting trade (G. had fifty-five ships in 1872). The University of G., founded in 1456, has forty-six professors besides ten *privat-docents*, and over 460 students. The Agricultural Science Academy at Eldena, about 2 miles off, is associated with the university. Pop. (1871) 17,238.

Greiz, capital of the principality of Reuss-G., Germany, on the White Elster, and 50 miles S.S.W. of Leipsic, with which it is connected by rail. G. is prettily situated, and has three palaces. It has some manufactures, especially of woollen, half-woollen, and cotton stuffs; a little silk is also wrought. Pop. (1871) 11,582.

Grena'da, one of the most beautiful of the Windward Islands, in the British W. Indies, lies in lat. 11° 58'-12° 30' N., and long. 61° 20'-61° 35 W. Area, 133 sq. miles; pop. (1871) 37,684, of whom 1344 were Asiatic coolies, and 1135 Africans. G. is of volcanic origin, is traversed by a mountain range attaining, in Mount St. Catherine, a height of 3000 feet, and exports sugar, cotton, rum, tobacco, and cocoa. The capital is St. George, and other towns with good harbours are St. Mark,

Charlotte-Town, St. Patrick, and St. Andrew. G. was discovered by Columbus in 1498, occupied by the French in the 17th c., and taken by the English in 1783.

Grenade' (Prov. *granada*, from Lat. *granata*, 'pomegranate'). The hand-G., so called from its resemblance in shape to a pomegranate, is a hollow ball of iron or glass 2½ inches in diameter, charged with powder, and having a tube and fuse attached. When the fuse burns sufficiently low, the powder is fired and explosion takes place. These missiles, which are no longer used in ordinary warfare, were invented in 1594, and were long found useful in field and siege operations. The Bomb (q. v.) is practically a G. fired from a mortar or howitzer.

Gren'adier Guards, the first of the three regiments of foot guards in the British army, numbering, in 1876–77, 2543 officers and men. The Scots Greys form a regiment of horse-grenadiers. In both of these regiments the men wear high bearskin caps. See *The Grenadier Guards, their Origin and History*, by Lieut.-General Sir F. W. Hamilton, K.C.B. (Lond. 1875).

Gren'adiers were first employed (1667) in the French army to throw grenades into the covered way of a fortress, remove the obstacles to the advance of the troops, lead in the assault, &c. The G., who, as they were exposed to special dangers, enjoyed special privileges, were the select men of their corps. In the armies of the present day, the tallest and stoutest men of every regiment of infantry are selected to form a company of G. This company usually leads in the attack, and occupies the place of honour (the right) when the regiment is in line. They are clothed and accoutred like the men of the other companies, with the exception of slight peculiarities in the ornaments of the coat and hat.

Gren'adines, or **Gren'adilles,** a southerly group of the Windward Islands, in the West Indies, belonging to Great Britain, and stretching between St. Vincent and Grenada. They number 23 islets, have a total area of 7000 acres, and a pop. of 3000. The largest are Carriacon and Begnia.

Gren'oble, the chief town in the department of Isère, France, on both banks of the Isère, at the foot of Mont-Rachais, 58 miles S.E. of Lyon. It has many fine streets and boulevards with numerous fountains. The river is lined with spacious quays and spanned by two handsome bridges. Among the chief buildings are the church of Notre-Dame, partly Gothic, partly Romanesque, and said to have been founded by Karl the Great; St. Laurent, belonging to the 11th c., and St. André, which contains Bayard's tomb, and the Palais de Justice, built in the styles of the 15th and 16th centuries. G. has several literary and scientific societies, and a library of 80,000 volumes. The town is very strongly fortified, has large manufactures of gloves, and some trade in wine, liqueurs, wood, grain, &c. Pop. (1872) 42,660. G., originally a town of the Allobroges, when it was called Eularo, was walled anew by the Romans in 288, and in 379 enlarged by the Emperor Gratian, who gave it the name of *Gratianopolis*, of which G. is a corruption. It was the see of a bishop as early as the 4th c.

Gren'ville, an important English family connected with the county of Buckingham since the reign of Henry I., became conspicuous in the 18th c., when **Richard G.**, by his marriage with Hester, daughter of Sir Richard Temple, afterwards the Countess Temple, acquired great wealth and influence. Their son, **Richard G.**, succeeded through his mother to the title and estates of the Temple family. In 1757 he was made Keeper of the Great Seal, and in the political strifes of the time was first the friend and afterwards the foe of Chatham, who had married his sister Hester. It is a compliment to his powers that some have attributed to him the authorship of the *Letters of Junius*. He died childless, 11th September 1779. His brother, **George G.**, was born October 14, 1712. He studied at Oxford, entered Parliament in 1741, was made Lord of the Treasury in 1747, and Treasurer of the Navy in 1754. He became Secretary of State in 1761, and in 1763 succeeded Bute, of whom he was a supporter, as Prime Minister. While holding this office, in which he was merely a tool of Bute, he urged on the prosecution of Wilkes (q. v.), and introduced the Stamp Act (q. v.), which led to the war with the American colonies. His Ministry was thrown out by the Regency Bill in 1765, and G. died 13th November 1770.—**William Wyndham, Lord G.**, third son of the preceding, was born 25th October 1759. He entered Parliament in 1782, and in 1789 was made Speaker of the House of Commons despite the opposition of Fox and Burke. Shortly afterwards he was chosen Secretary of State for Home Affairs, was Pitt's chief supporter, and in 1790 was raised to the peerage as Baron G. He became Foreign Secretary in 1791, quitted office in 1801, and shortly joined Fox in opposition to the Addington Administration. He was Premier in 1806–7, and acted in unison with Lord Grey until 1815, when G. advocated the prosecution of war with Napoleon. He afterwards supported Canning, being a zealous advocate for the removal of the Catholic disabilities. G. died at Dropmore, Buckingham, January 12, 1834. See the *Grenville Papers* (4 vols. Lond. 1852–53), a collection of G.'s family documents.

Gresh'am, Sir Thomas, son of Sir Richard G., was born in 1519, studied at Cambridge University, became a member of the Mercers' Company in 1543, and in 1552 was sent as 'king's agent' to Antwerp, where he skilfully negotiated for loans with the Flemish merchants. From this post he was dismissed by Queen Mary, but was soon reinstated through his successor's incapacity, and in 1559 was knighted by Elizabeth, and sent as ambassador to Antwerp. In 1564 he gave a large sum to raise an Exchange for the London merchants, the building being opened in 1570 by Elizabeth, who named it the Royal Exchange. In 1569 he persuaded the crown to borrow from the London instead of from the foreign merchants, a change which produced much financial good. G. died November 21, 1579, having by his will set aside large sums for charitable institutions, and arranged that his house in Bishopsgate Street should be converted into a college. This building was pulled down in 1768, but 'Gresham College' still exists, the lectures being given in a hall in Gresham Street.

Gret'na Green Marriages. Prior to the passing of the Marriage Act (England) of the 27th March 1754, persons in England desirous of marrying secretly could effect their purpose by repairing to the Fleet Prison (q. v.). After the passing of that Act, which provided that every marriage celebrated in England should be public or in presence of witnesses, English persons wishing to marry secretly required to get away out of England, to which alone the Act referred. Thus the practice arose of posting to the Border and crossing into Scotland, where every facility was afforded for the consummation of the act. The nearest and most convenient spot across the Border was Gretna Green. In Scotland the law was that mutual declaration of acceptance as husband and wife before witnesses constituted a legal marriage; and as the rule is that marriage contracted according to the law extending to the spot in which the contract is made shall be legal all the world over, the G. G. M. were indisputable. Such marriages are still legal, under the condition of the residence of one of the parties in Scotland for twenty-one days; but as the English law now recognises marriages before the superintendent registrar as legal, there is little or no occasion now to have recourse to the once-famous 'blacksmith.'

Gré'try, André Erneste Modeste, a musical composer, was born at Liége, Belgium, February 11, 1741, became a choir boy in the Collegiate Church at the age of six, and in 1759 went to Rome to study counterpoint under Casali. He studied little, but he brought out an 'Intermezzo' in 1765 at a Roman theatre. In 1767 he went to Paris. Between this and 1803 he wrote fifty—chiefly comic—operas, *e.g.*, *Le Huron* (1768), *Le Tableau Parlant* (1769), *L'Amant Jaloux* (1778), *Richard Cœur de Lion* (1785), *Guillaume Tell* (1791), *Delphis et Mopsa* (1803). G. acquired great renown, had a street named after him, was made member of many learned bodies, and received substantial benefits from Napoleon to compensate him for the loss of his wealth during the Revolution. He died at Montmorency, near Paris, 24th September 1813. G.'s works suffered neglect at the time that Méhul and Cherubini began to compose, but they were afterwards revived with new honours. He lived among a circle of admirers, and is said to have disdained all music but his own. Strong in graceful and original melody and dramatic expression, he was extremely ignorant of the principles of his art, as his works abundantly show.

Greuze, Jean Baptiste, a famous French genre painter, was born at Tournus, Burgundy, in 1726. He studied at Lyon, Paris, and Rome, and for a time misdirected his powers through ambition to be an historical painter, but afterwards limited his efforts to genre and portraits, and achieved a remarkable success. He was long an Associate of the French Academy of Painting, and died at Paris, March 21, 1805. Among his chief works are 'La Petite Fille au Chien,' perhaps his masterpiece, 'La Bonne Mère,' 'Le Gâteau des Rois,' 'La Fille Confuse,' 'Une Jeune Fille tenant une Colombe,' &c. G.'s treatment is sometimes meretricious, and his modelling defective. He was especially successful in subjects from common life, and above all in roguish or languorous female faces, which he executed with peculiar softness and grace, with combined delicacy and richness of colour.

Grew'ia, a genus of small trees and shrubs belonging to the order Tiliaceæ found in warm regions, but absent from America. The wood of *G. elastica* and *G. occidentalis* is used for making bows and carriage shafts. The inner bark of many of the species yields a strong fibre.

Grey, Charles, first Earl, belonged to the old Northumberland house of G., of which the Barons G. of Werk and the Earls of Tankerville were branches. He was born in 1728, was at first Sir Charles G. of Howick, commanded in the wars with the American colonies and the French Republic, was made for his services Baron G. de Howick in 1804, and Earl G. in 1806. He died 14th November 1807.—**Charles G., K.G.**, second Earl, son of the above, was born at Fallowden, Northumberland, March 13, 1764. He was educated at Eton and King's College, Cambridge, and in 1786 entered Parliament as a Whig, and soon became so distinguished for forcible and graceful oratory, that he was chosen at the age of twenty-four, along with Burke, Fox, Sheridan, and Windham, to conduct the impeachment of Warren Hastings. During the times of the Revolution he adhered to Fox, and always strove to end the war between France and England. He early stood forth as the advocate of parliamentary reform, exposing the abuses of the Government, and resisting its arbitrary measures. In 1797 his proposal to extend the suffrage was thrown out; in 1799 he opposed the union with Ireland; and in 1806, when the Grenville Ministry was formed, became, as Lord Howick, First Lord of the Admiralty; shortly after succeeded Fox as Foreign Secretary and leader of the Commons, and carried a bill to abolish the slave trade. In 1807, after the dissolution of the Grenville Ministry, he became Earl G., and thenceforth for several years led the Opposition in the Lords, though his adhesion to the Government was repeatedly sought for. He defended Queen Caroline with remarkable power; attacked Canning with deadly point in 1827; and at length, in 1830, when the stubborn resistance to reform had brought the country to the brink of revolution, became Premier of a Whig Administration. A Reform Bill was introduced, and, after its rejection by the Lords had almost kindled a rebellion, was carried, June 4, 1832. The first reformed Parliament carried several weighty measures, freeing the slaves in the colonies, destroying the monopoly of the East India Company, passing the bill for National Education in Ireland, the Irish Church Temporalities Bill, &c. The Irish Coercion Bill breaking up the Ministry in 1834, G. resigned the office of Premier, and retired with an unsullied character and with general admiration and respect. He died at Howick House, Northumberland, July 17, 1845. See *Life and Opinions of the Second Earl G.* (Lond. 1861), edited by his son.—**Henry George G.**, third Earl, was born 28th December 1802, studied at Cambridge, entered Parliament as Lord Howick in 1829 for Winchelsea, was Under Secretary for the Colonies in his father's Administration (1830–33). When the Whigs re-entered office in 1835 he became War Secretary with a seat in the Cabinet, but resigned in 1839. In 1842 he supported the motion of Villiers for the repeal of the corn laws. Called to the House of Lords by the death of his father, he was appointed Secretary for the Colonies in the Ministry of Russell. In this position he displayed great powers both as a debater and orator, but overweening pride and egotism made him intensely unpopular. Since the fall of the Russell Ministry (1852) he has occupied an isolated position, with a disposition to criticise in a hostile spirit the policy of his former associates. He is the author of *Colonial Policy of Lord J. Russell's Administration* (2 vols. Lond. 1853), and *Parliamentary Government considered in Reference to Reform* (new ed. 1864).

Grey, Lady Jane, famous for her accomplishments and misfortunes, was born at Broadgate, Leicestershire, in 1537. She was the eldest daughter of Henry Grey, Duke of Suffolk, and Lady Frances Brandon, niece of Henry VIII., was educated with the utmost care, and early displayed a singular scholarly aptitude, becoming thoroughly versed in Greek, Latin, French, and Italian, and even dipping into Hebrew and Arabic. A well-known passage in Ascham tells how he found her reading Plato's *Phædon* in the original, while the family were out hunting. In 1553 the Duke of Northumberland (q. v.), bent on altering the succession, dictated a 'plan' to Edward VI. (q. v.), by which that king set aside his sisters Mary and Elizabeth, and named as his successor Lady Jane G., whom Northumberland had married to his son Guildford Dudley. On Edward's death (1553), Lady Jane G. was, against her will, proclaimed queen, but the people, especially in the eastern counties, supported Mary. Northumberland was defeated and beheaded, and Lady Jane imprisoned in the Tower after being queen for ten days. On February 8, Mary pronounced sentence of death against her hapless rival, who was executed on February 12, 1553. Lady Jane G. has left in her letters to Bullinger, says Mr. Froude, a portrait of herself drawn by her own hand—a portrait of piety, purity, and free noble innocence, uncoloured even to a fault with the emotional weaknesses of humanity. See Harris Nicholas' *Memoirs and Remains of Lady Jane G.* (new ed. Lond. 1832), and Froude's *History of England* (vols. v. and vi.).

Grey, Sir George, K.C.B., an explorer and colonial governor, born in Ireland, after the death of his father, who fell at the storming of Badajos, 7th April 1812, entered the army in 1829, and in 1837–39 led a number of expeditions into the interior of Western Australia, displaying great courage and skill. He was governor of South Australia from 1841 to 1846, when he was made governor of New Zealand, and in that office showed rare administrative powers. He was made a K.C.B. in 1848, governor of the Cape of Good Hope in 1854, and in 1861 was replaced in the governorship of New Zealand, where the Maories and English were at war. Through his address and firmness, and the ability of General Cameron, the strife was satisfactorily ended, and in 1867 G. returned to England. He is the author of *Journals of Two Expeditions in N.W. and W. Australia* (1841); *Polynesian Mythology* (1855); and *Proverbial Sayings of the Ancestors of the New Zealand Race* (1858).

Grey'hound, a variety of Dogs (q. v.) distinguished by the lithe, slender body, the shapely and delicate limbs, the length of the muzzle, and the thin, long tail. The chest is deep, allowing free play for the lungs in an extended chase, whilst the hinder quarters are somewhat sloped and narrow. The G. is used for hunting hares, or in 'coursing,' as the sport is named, and a great deal of attention is paid to its breeding and training. In order to give to the breed the powers of endurance necessary for the chase, breeders have been accustomed to unite the bulldog with the G.—the coarser features of the former being toned down after the lapse of time, and by the effects of interbreeding. In the chase of the hare, the latter evades the G. by 'doubling,' or suddenly turning in a direction opposite to that in which it was running, the G. being carried far past its prey before it can recover itself, and start on the fresh line of pursuit. The original habitat of the G. is difficult to trace. The best-known varieties are the *Irish G.*, noted for its strong build, its somewhat coarse hair, and pale fawn colour. The average length is 62 inches. The *Scotch G.* has also a rough coat, and is nearly related to the Deerhound (q. v.). The latter is smaller than the Irish G. The *Russian G.* is thick, and rough at the extremities of the body, while the tail is tolerably bushy. The *Persian* variety, used for hunting the antelope and wild ass, is of light colour. The *Italian G.* is a small breed, kept as a mere pet, and noted for the general delicacy of its frame, the weight of a highly-bred specimen being about 8 lbs., and the height 14¼ inches. The Italian G. is singularly liable in Britain to affections of the lungs. See *Stonehenge on the G.* (new ed. Lond. 1875).

Grey'ness of the Hair, or **Canit'ies**, may be congenital, accidental, or senile. Congenital greyness is usually partial, occurring in the form of round patches; but cases have been met with in which the hair on one side of the head was brilliantly white, while on the other side it was jetty black. Accidental and senile greyness present varieties in extent. When white hair falls off it is not reproduced. Blanching of the hair commences at the root, and the coloured part is gradually carried onwards, further and further from the integument. Black and brown hair is most liable to greyness, but blonde and auburn hair is more liable to fall off. When the hair is 'snowy,' of an opaque white, and of the thickness of ordinary hair, it contains abundance of calcareous salts; but when it is clear and transparent, assuming a yellowish tint on exposure to the atmosphere, it contains little or no calcareous salts. Senile greyness depends on diminished powers of the nervous system, resulting in the alteration of pigmentary deposits in the formative cells of the hair. In most cases the effects are gradual; but there are numerous instances on record in which the change took place within a few hours, owing to violent mental emotions. The hair of Marie Antoinette, the wife of Louis XVI., became grey in a short period, from grief. So also with Mary Queen of Scots, Sir Thomas More, and others. Rayer mentions a case in which several of the cilia became blanched within a short time in consequence of mental agitation, and the writer had at one time under his care a young lady suffering from acute mania, whose eyelashes became white within ten hours, the hair of the scalp not being affected.

Grey'wacke. See GRAUWACKE.

Gries'bach, Johann Jakob, an illustrious biblical critic, was born at Butzbach in Hessen, 4th January 1745, and early in life resolved to devote himself entirely to the critical study of the New Testament text. After studying at Tübingen, Halle (where he came under the influence of Semler), and Leipsic (where he formed a friendship with Ernesti), he visited the great scholastic libraries of Germany, Holland, France, and England. In 1771 he attached himself to the University of Halle, and in 1776 was called to Jena, where he laboured for more than thirty years, dying 24th March 1812. G.'s edition is generally regarded as the earliest really critical edition of the New Testament Scriptures. It appeared in 1775–77 in two volumes, a third edition being begun in 1827 under the superintendence of D. Schulz. The *Populäre Dogmatik* was issued in 1719 (4th ed. 1789), the *Symbolæ Criticæ* in 1785–93, and the *Commentarius Criticus in Textum N. T.* in 1798–1811. G.'s name is associated with a threefold classification of the New Testament MSS. into—(1) the Alexandrine recensions, (2) the Latin or Western recensions, (3) the Byzantine recensions. Although this classification varies in some respects from that of other scholars, it is in the main a sound division. See *Outlines of Textual Criticism applied to the New Testament* (Oxf. Clar. Pr. 1872). G.'s life has been written by Köthe (1812), Augusti (1812), and Eichstädt (1815).

Griff'ard (*Spizaëtus bellicosus*), a species of Eagle (q. v.) sometimes known as the martial eagle, occurring in S. Africa. The colour is dark brown, the feathers bordered by paler brown, and the quill feathers black. The tarsi are long and slender, the inner toe exceeding the outer in length. The nostrils are large and oblique. The bird is powerful and rapacious, and its cry is shrill and disagreeable.

Griff'in (Gr. *gryps*, 'the hook-beaked'), a fabulous animal in Greek mythology, with the body of a lion and head and wings of an eagle. It seems to have been the offspring of Eastern, not of Hellenic fancy. The earliest Greek writer who mentions the G. is Hesiod, and Philostratus includes it among the creatures which were set over the gold of India. The figure of the G. was sometimes included in Greek works of art. It is, however, more often met with in romantic than in classical fiction, and in the medieval romance is the most common custodier of treasures and captive princesses. Its existence was believed in even during the 16th c. The G. is a prominent bearing in heraldry.

Griffin, Gerald, an Irish poet and novelist, was born at Limerick, December 12, 1803. After several years of literary work in London, he joined the monastic order of the Christian Brothers of Cork, and died there, June 12, 1840. Several of his lyrics are tender and musical. Of his novels, the best is the *Collegians* (1828), a powerful tragic story, which won considerable popularity, and which is the groundwork of Boucicault's *Colleen Bawn.*

Griffin, or **Griffon Vulture,** a name given to the Fulvous Vulture (*Gyps fulvus*), a bird distributed very generally throughout the Old World. Its colour is a dirty yellowish brown above, the wings and tail are black, and the head and neck covered with white down. The average length is 4 feet. The G. is remarkable for its keen scent and sight, which enable it to ascertain the presence of carrion and prey at a considerable distance.

Grigoriop'ol, a fortified town of Russia, government of Kherson, on the left bank of the Dniester, 78 miles N.W. of Odessa. Founded by Armenian settlers in 1793, it was named after the national saint, Gregory the Illuminator (q. v.). It has some manufactures of silks and cottons. Pop. 6477.

Grill'parzer, Franz, an Austrian dramatist, was born at Vienna, 15th January 1790. After studying law, he entered the Austrian public service, in which he attained the rank of Reichsrath. He died 21st January 1872. G. first attracted public notice by his 'fate-tragedy,' *Die Ahnfrau* (1816, 6th ed. 1844), in which the fatalistic element was carried to an extreme. His later works are characterised by melodious language and sentimentality. G. wrote, besides minor pieces, *Das Goldene Vlies* (1822); *König Ottokar's Glück und Ende* (1825), generally thought his best piece; *Melusine*, an opera (1833); *Der Traum, ein Leben* (1834); *Weh dem, der lügt* (1840); and *Esther* (1863). An edition of G.'s *Sämmtliche Werke* began to be published in 1872. See the sketch of G. by K. von Wurzbach (1871), and Carlyle's *Essay on German Playwrights.*

Grilse. See SALMON.

Grimm, Friedrich Melchior, a distinguished French critic of German birth, was born at Regensberg, 25th December 1723. While still a mere youth, he accompanied a young nobleman to Paris as his tutor, and there settled permanently. He made Rousseau's acquaintance about 1749, and was by him introduced to Diderot, Holbach, and others of that brilliant circle in which he was himself to shine; and as secretary to the nephew of Marshal Saxe, G. early found his way into the most select society of Paris. In 1776 he was made a baron, and was appointed Minister at the French capital of the Duke of Gotha. Long ere this G. had begun with several German princes that extensive literary correspondence which he preserved to our day—a complete review of all that is noteworthy in French literature from 1753 to 1790. At the Revolution G. retired to Gotha; was made Russian Minister at Hamburg by the Empress Catherine in 1795; and died at Gotha, 19th December 1807. The 16 volumes of his *Correspondance Littéraire, Philosophique et Critique*, were published in 1812 at Paris; a new and complete edition appeared in 1829–31 (15 vols.).

Grimm, Jacob Ludwig, one of the greatest of philologists, may be said to have given the scientific foundation to all subsequent investigations as to the origin, history, character, and relations of the Germanic language. He was born at Hanau in Hessen, studied law at Marburg, and while holding the office of War Secretary, found time to explain the literature of the middle ages. He held various offices of responsibility under the Elector, and from 1816 till 1829 was librarian at Kassel. In 1830 he accepted a call to a chair in Göttingen, and lectured on the German language and literature and on legal antiquities. G. was one of the seven professors who, in 1837, formally protested against the suspension by the King of the national constitution, and was therefore deposed and banished. He was called to Berlin in 1841, where he died, 20th September 1863. G.'s powerful mind and deep poetic insight were mainly devoted to the successful task of tracing the growth and character of the spirit of the German race, as displayed in its language and its poetry, its religion, laws, and customs. The chief monuments of his labours are the well-known *Deutsche Grammatik* (1819–37, new ed. 1869), *Deutsche Rechts-Alterthümer* (1835, 3d ed. 1854), *Geschichte der Deutschen Sprache* (1848, 3d ed. 1868). Along with his brother he edited *Kinder- und Hausmärchen* (1812–1813, 9th ed. 1870), and began the great unfinished dictionary, *Deutsches Wörterbuch* (1854, continued from vol. iv. by Hildebrand, Heyne, and Weigand).—**Wilhelm Karl G.,** brother of the preceding, and closely associated with him all his life, was born 24th February 1786 at Hanau, and went to Marburg University to study law. In 1814 he was librarian at Kassel; in 1830 went with his brother to Göttingen, where, in 1835, he became professor. Like his elder brother, he protested in 1837 against the abolition of the constitution, and was deposed for the same cause. To him also a chair in Berlin was offered in 1841;

and there on the 16th December 1859 he died. Besides work done by the brothers in conjunction, G. edited numerous ancient German poems, *e.g.*, *Grave Ruodolf* (Gött. 1828, 2d. ed. 1844), *Hildebrandslied* (Gött. 1830), *Freidank* (Gött. 1834, 2d ed. 1860), *Rosengarten* (Gött. 1836), *Rolandslied* (Gött. 1838), *Wernher vom Nieder-Rhein* (Gött. 1839), the *Silvester* of Konrad of Würzburg (Gott. 1841), *Alt-Deutsche Gespräche* (Berl. 1851), &c. His great work is *Die Deutsche Heldensage* (Gött. 1829), a collection made with a fine critical taste, and accompanied with a treatise on the origin and development of the sagas. See Denhard's *Die Gebrüder G.* (1860).

Grimm'a, a town in the kingdom of Saxony, on the Mulde, 18 miles S.E. of Leipsic by railway. It was a flourishing place of trade in the middle ages, and has still some cotton and woollen manufactures. G. is the seat of a famous classical school. Pop. (1871) 6476.

Grimm'ia, a genus of Mosses (q. v.) found on walls and rocks, growing in cushion-like tufts, throughout the world. In Britain there are over a dozen species, found in Alpine and sub-Alpine districts. *G. pulvinata* is the commonest. G. is named in honour of Grimm, a German botanist.

Grimm's Law, the principle, discovered by Jakob Ludwig Grimm, which regulates the interchange of mute consonants in the Aryan tongues. Thus *p*, *b*, and *f* in Latin, Greek, and Sanskrit become respectively *f*, *p*, and *b* in Gothic, and *b*, *f*, and *p* in Old High German, as in the Sansk. *purna*, 'full,' Lat. *plenus*, which becomes in Goth. *fulls*; and in Sansk. *upari*, 'over,' Lat. *super*, which becomes in Goth. *ufar*, and in O. H. Ger. *ubar* (Ger. *über*). The Sansk. *bh* becomes the Gr. *ph*, the Lat. *f*, the Goth. *b*, and O. H. Ger. *p*, *e.g.*, Sansk. *bhrati*, Gr. *phratēr*, Lat. *frater*, Goth. *brôthar*, O. H. Ger. *pruoder* (Ger. *bruder*), Eng. *brother*; the Sansk. *dh* becomes the Gr. *th*, Lat. *f*, Goth. *d*, O. H. Ger. *t*, *e.g.*, Sansk. *dvâra*, Gr. *thura*, Lat. *fores*, Goth. *daur*, O. H. Ger. *tor*, Eng. *door*; the Sansk. *gh* becomes the Gr. *h*, Lat. *h*, Goth. *g*, O. H. Ger. *k*; *b* in Sansk., Gr., and Lat. becomes *p* in Goth. and *f* in O. H. Ger.; *d* in Sansk, Gr., and Lat. becomes *t* in Goth. and *z* in O. H. Ger.; *h* in Sansk., Gr., and Lat. becomes *f* in Goth. and O. H. Ger., *e.g.*, Sansk. *panchan* becomes Goth. *fimf*, Eng. *five*; *t* in Sansk., Gr., and Lat. becomes Goth. *th* and *d*, *e.g.*, Sansk. *tvam*, Gr. and Lat. *tu* becomes in Goth. *thu*, in O. H. Ger. *du*, Eng. *thou*; *k* in Sansk., Gr., and Lat. becomes Goth. *h* (*g*), O. H. Ger. *h* (*g*), *e.g.*, Lat. *caput*, Goth. *haubith*, O. H. Ger. *houpit*, Eng. *head*; Sansk. *j* (*g*), Lat. *g*, becomes in Goth. *k*, O. H. Ger. *ch*, *e.g.*, Sansk. *jnâ*, Gr. *gnômi*, Lat. *gnosco*, Goth. *kunnan*, Eng. *ken*, *con*, *know*. There are, however, numerous exceptions to G. L.

Grims'by, Great, a seaport of Lincolnshire, England, on the right shore of the Humber, opposite Spurn Head, 7 miles from the sea, and 15 N. of Louth by railway. It is an old shipping town, and has docks covering an area of 150 acres, capable of accommodating ships of war. Its chief buildings are a fine old church, St. James', with a tower and peal of bells, a new townhall, custom-house, mechanics' institute, free grammar school, &c. The industries include fishing, shipbuilding, iron and brass founding, tanning, and timber-sawing. In 1875 there entered the port 2543 vessels of 438,520 tons, and cleared 2071 of 508,898. Pop. (1871) 20,244.

Grim'sel, a mountain pass in the Bernese Alps, Switzerland, 7103 feet high. It connects the valleys of the Aar and Rhone, which have just emerged from their respective glaciers, and on its ridge lies the Todtensee ('lake of death'), where the Austrians and French buried their dead in the summer campaign of 1799. At the N. entrance of the pass is the G. Hospice (6148 feet above the sea-level), a few miles W. of which the Aar glacier terminates.

Grin'delwald, a beautiful Swiss valley in the S.E. of the canton of Bern, 7 miles S.S.E. of Thun Lake. It is 15 miles long, 2 broad, and 3852 feet above the sea. It is hemmed in to the S. by the giants of the Bernese Alps, the Eiger (13,041 feet), Mettenberg (10,197), forming the base of the Schreckhorn, and the Wetterhorn (12,165). On its S. side it is entered by two fine glaciers, which rise in a splendid *eismeer* ('ice-sea'), and form the course of the Black Lütschine. The village of G. or Gydisdorf consists of wooden houses scattered over the valley, and has a pop. of 3135.

Grind'ing, in the industrial arts, is the operation by which form is given to a body by abrasion with hard substances. For example, cutlery and edge-tools are shaped by pressing them against grindstones revolving towards the article to be ground; in this way the particles rubbed off are more easily carried away, and the progress of the work better seen. In producing a cutting edge with a stone revolving in the opposite direction, it is not easy to tell when the edge is fully ground in consequence of the formation of a 'feather-edge.' Plate-glass, stones, and metals are ground by rubbing them with hard, coarse powders, such as emery. The term G. is also applied to the act of disintegrating or pulverising ores, &c., between two stones or metal rollers, with their peripheries nearly touching, and again to the reduction of pigments to an impalpable powder with a *muller*, a conoid stone with a perfectly flat base, and a *slab* of close-grained porphyry.

Grind'stones are cylindrical pieces of sandstone or gritstone used for shaping and sharpening cutlery, tools, &c. They are secured to an axle which is turned round by means of a winch handle, or an endless belt moved by steam power. They vary in diameter and thickness, in solidity and granular texture. The famed Newcastle G. are obtained from the coal measures abounding in that district. Bilston in Staffordshire, and Wickersley and Haderley near Sheffield, also furnish good G. Artificial G., formed by binding together grains of sand with silicate of lime (Rawsome's method), are now largely superseding natural G.

Grip'ing, or **Gripes**. See Colic.

Gri'qua Land, West, better known as the S. African Diamond Field, the western portion of the land formerly occupied solely by the Griquas (*i.e.*, 'bastards'), a mixed Dutch and Hottentot race, lies to the N.E. of Cape Colony, and to the W. of the Transvaal Republic and the Orange River Free State. It is a pastoral country, confined on the S. and E. by the Orange and Vaal rivers, and intersected from N.E. to S.W. by low ranges, as the Asbesto, Mosib, Lange, and Schurve hills. Area, 16,632 sq. miles; pop. (1873) 25,477. In the W. the surface descends in terraces towards a wide region of sandy plains. The diamond 'rush' took place between 1868 and 1870, when the country was in the possession of a 'Captain' Waterboer and his people. Unable to hold his own, Waterboer offered his territory to Britain; it was accepted by proclamation of October 27, 1871, and subsequently a lieutenant-governor and a Government staff were appointed, the territory being vested by commission in the Governor of Cape Colony. This led to considerable dispute between the English and Dutch colonies. In 1875 the revenue was £70,000. The 'farm' on which has sprung up the town of Kimberley, was recently purchased by the local government for £100,000, a sum already far more than realised by mines and building sites. The Government has raised a large sum by selling farms, and retaining the mineral rights. Till the beginning of 1876 the total value of the diamonds found was £12,000,000. The stones are mostly small and of inferior colour, but the famous 'Star of S. Africa,' found in 1869, weighed 83½ carats, and was valued at £20,000. Another of 147 carats was found in 1873, and a valuable blue one in 1876.—*East* Griqua Land is now included in Kaffraria.

Gri'si, Giu'lia, or **Guliett'a**, 'the most distinguished singer of our time,' was born at Milan, 28th July 1812. She was educated in a convent at Girizia, and afterwards took singing-lessons at Bologna. In 1828 and 1829 she sang in the opera at Bologna and Milan. Then becoming the pupil of Marliani, she followed him to Paris in 1832, and became, by Rossini's influence, Prima Donna at the Italian Opera there. From 1834 to 1861 she sang continuously in London, missing only one opera season. G. died at Berlin, November 28, 1869. Her principal parts were in *Norma*, *I Puritani* (written for her), and *Don Pasquale*. See Fétis, *Biographie des Musiciens* (Par. 1862).

Gris-Nez ('grey nose or ness'), a cape on the W. coast of France, department of Pas-de-Calais, 10 miles N. of Boulogne. It supports a lighthouse, and is the point nearest to England, being distant from Dover only 21 miles.

Gri'sons (Ger. *Graubünden*, 'the grey league'), a canton in the S.E. of Switzerland, is bounded N. by Glarus, St. Gall, and the Vorarlberg, S. by Lombardy, W. by Uri and Ticino, and E. by Tyrol. Area, 2774 sq. miles; pop. (1870) 91,782. It lies among the Rhætian Alps, which here reach a height of 11,208 feet in Piz Linard, and of 13,294 in Piz Bernina, and is intersected by the valleys of the Lower Rhine and the Inn. (See ENGADINE.) Several tributaries flow S. to the Adda and Ticino. The climate varies; the productions are rye, barley, maize, the vine, almond, and fig. There is much cattle-breeding, and a large transit trade. G. has a constitution of 1853. The people are three-fifths Protestant and one-third German. Two Romanic dialects are spoken, *Ladin* in the Engadine, Albula, and Münster valleys, and Romanic in the valleys of Disentis, Ilanz, &c. In the latter there is a slight literature, chiefly of religious and educational works. (See grammars and dictionaries by Conrad, Carisch, and Palioppi.) Coire (anc. *Curia*) is the capital, with a pop. (1870) of 7552. G., the country of the ancient Rhætii, was conquered by the Romans in the 4th c., passed to the German empire in the 9th c., and remained under the Suabian dukes till 1268. It then became an independent province of the empire, and the residence of many nobles, against whom the people were subsequently driven to form leagues. The 'Grey League' dates from 1424. The heroism shown by the confederates in the Suabian war in 1499 gave them great celebrity. The Reformation found an entrance into the canton in 1521, but it was not till quite recently (1803) that G. joined the Swiss Confederation.

Gris'wold, Rufus Wilmot, born at Boston, U.S., February 15, 1815, travelled in Europe and America, became a printer, a Baptist preacher, and finally a journalist, edited *Graham's Magazine* (1842-43), the *New York International Magazine* (1850–54), and died in New York, August 27, 1857. He was the author of *Poets and Poetry of America, Washington and the Generals of the Revolution, Curiosities of American Literature, Prose Writers of America, The Republican Court*, &c. His attack on Edgar Poe has called forth very severe strictures.

Grit, a term vaguely given to coarse-grained silicious sandstones. See SANDSTONE.

Grivegn'ée, a town of Belgium, province of Liége, on the Ourthe, near the height of Espérance, 2 miles S.E. of Liége. It has large machine-works, fulling-mills, and coal-mines. Pop. (1873) 6234.

Groat (Dutch *groot*, from the same root as the French *gros* and the English *great*), originally used as a qualifying word to distinguish the thick from the thin coins, but long current in England since the time of Henry III. (1351) as a definite silver coin valued at 4d. In 1835 the coin was revived when the mint issued *fourpenny-pieces.*

Groats, or **Grits** (Old Eng. *greót*, Dutch *grut*, Ger. *grutze*, 'husked and bruised grain'), oats shelled, or deprived of their husks; when ground they constitute *Embden G.*

Gro'cyn, William, one of the great scholars who brought the Renaissance learning into England, was born at Bristol in 1442. He was educated at Winchester and New College, Oxford, became divinity reader in Magdalen College, and in 1479 rector of Newton Longville in Buckinghamshire, and afterwards prebendary of Lincoln. From 1488 to 1491 he studied Greek under Chalcondylas in Italy. On returning to England, he taught the new language in Exeter College, Oxford, where its introduction, and especially G.'s new mode of pronunciation, were strongly opposed—the University being divided into two factions of Greeks and Trojans. G.'s lectures, however, were highly successful, and Oxford became a centre of Hellenic culture. Erasmus, who studied under G., spoke with admiration of his wide knowledge. In 1506 G. was made Master of Allhallows College, at Maidstone, Kent, where he died in 1519. A Latin epistle to Aldus Manutius is his only extant work.

Grod'no, a government of W. Russia, formerly a part of Lithuania, lies along the N.W. boundary of Poland. Area, 14,700 sq. miles; pop. 958,852. It is a flat sylvan country, thickly wooded with beech and pine in the N., where it is watered by the Niemen, and covered in the S. with 500 sq. miles of morass, in which rise the head waters of the Pripet, a tributary of the Dnieper. There is extensive cultivation of rye, barley, flax, and hops, much cattle-rearing, timber-hewing, and iron-smelting. The forests are still a refuge of the bear, wolf, lynx, and buffalo. Of the inhabitants, 225,000 are Poles and 95,000 Jews.—**G.**, the capital of the government of G., lies on the right bank of the Niemen, 160 miles N.E. of Warsaw by railway. It has several decayed Lithuanian palaces, a grand modern palace erected by Augustus III., a medical academy, botanic garden, considerable scientific collections, and a large library. There are manufactures of silks, woollens, and weapons. Pop. 31,000, of whom some three-fourths are Jews. The name is Slavonic, and denotes 'a fortified town.'

Grog is a mixture of rum and cold water, allowances of which were first regularly served in the navy about the middle of the 18th c. under Admiral Vernon. It is said to have been christened from a nickname—'Old G.'—given by the sailors to Vernon on account of his wearing a *grogram* (Fr. *gros-grain*) cloak on deck in foul weather.

Groined Vaulting. See VAULTING and GOTHIC ARCHITECTURE.

Gron'ingen, or **Grön'ingen.** 1. A province of the kingdom of Holland, surrounded by the North Sea, Hanover, and the provinces Drenthe and Friesland. Area, 915 sq. miles; pop. (1875) 238,662. The northern part is marshy, but fruitful, intersected with canals, and fenced with dykes; in the E. there are extensive moors yielding abundance of turf; and the S. has several wide stretches of heath. The streams, though small, are, with the help of canals, skilfully made available for communication, and the largest river, the Hunse, is navigable inland as far as the town of G. The main occupation of the people is the rearing of cattle, sheep, and horses; butter, cheese, and wool, as well as live-stock, being the chief exports. Chief towns, G. and Winschoten. G. in early times was under bailiffs of the Holy Roman Empire, who assumed the title of Burgh Counts (Burcgravii, Præfectii, Comites Urbis or Civitatis) in the 11th c. Afterwards the Bishop of Lüttich (Liège) exercised a sort of supremacy over the country. After much contention it yielded to the Emperor Karl V. in 1536, and in 1580 became one of the Seven United Provinces, with William of Orange as stadtholder. —2. A well-built and fortified town in the province of G., on the river Hunse, 94 miles N.E. of Amsterdam. Pop. (1875) 40,165. It has a beautifully built university (founded in 1614), an imposing townhall, a church of St. Martin with a lofty tower and magnificent organ, a picture gallery, a botanic garden, shipbuilding yards, extensive quays, tobacco and linen factories, gold and silver workshops, and a large trade in cattle, wool, cheese, butter, and corn. G. belonged to the Hanse League. In 1874 there entered the port 190 vessels of 16,157 tons; cleared, 179, of 17,002 tons.

Groo'te Ey'landt (Dut. 'great island'), the largest island in the Gulf of Carpentaria, on the N. coast of Australia. Its shape is very irregular, but the maximum length and breadth of the island are about 40 miles each. The shores are sandy and barren, but the interior, which is still unexplored, appears to be mountainous and well wooded.

Gros, Antoine Jean, Baron, a French painter, the son of an excellent miniaturist, was born in Paris, 16th March 1771. A pupil of David, he gained the patronage of Napoleon by a picture of the 'Victor of Arcola,' and subsequently painted, by commission of the Government, the chief events of Bonaparte's career—the battles of Aboukir, of the Pyramids, of Wagram, and of Eylau, &c. The 'Peste de Jaffa' (1804) was received with immense enthusiasm, and was publicly crowned in the Louvre. G.'s historical pictures exhibit great dramatic power and rapid vigour of execution. His miniature portraits are full of rich refined beauty. The celebrated cupola of St. Geneviève, in Paris, a work of great decorative skill, procured him (1824) the rank of baron. Later his fame was diminished and his life embittered by the attacks of the rising Romantic school. G. was drowned in the Seine, whence, near Meudon, his body was taken, 26th June 1835, and interred in Père-la-Chaise. See Rougct's *Notes*, and J. B. Delestre's *G. et ses Ouvrages* (Par. 1845).

Gros'beak, or **Haw'finch**, the popular name of a group of *Conirostral Insessores* (q. v.) or perching birds belonging to the sub-family *Coccothraustinæ*, in which the bill is large and somewhat clumsy, broad at the base and curved towards the tip.

The tail is short, the wings long and pointed. The common G. or H. (*Coccothraustes vulgaris*) is a familiar British bird. Its bill has angular or sharp edges at the base; the nostrils are oval, and hidden by feathers. The second and third quills are longest, and the tail is short and forked. The G. is found in large flocks, especially at the middle of April, this being the breeding season; the young are hatched about the end of May. In the male the head and neck are fawn-coloured, the back being brown, and the chin and throat black. The wing coverts are white, black, and fawn; the tail black and white; and the under parts of a lighter brown than the back. The average length of the bird is 7 inches. Its food consists chiefly of berries and seeds. The black and yellow G. (*C. melanoxanthus*) of India, is an exotic species, coloured black above and yellow below, the female being mottled with yellow alone. The cardinal G. (*Cardinalis Virginianus*) or scarlet G. is a well-known American species, also termed the 'Virginian nightingale' from its pleasing song. The colour is a dusky red above, and the other parts are a brilliant scarlet, with the exception of the feathers of the chin and forehead, which are black. The bill is also scarlet. The female is of a brownish olive on the upper parts. The eggs, numbering five, are greyish white marked with brown.

Grosbeak.

Gross'enhain (Ger. 'thick grove'), a town in the kingdom of Saxony, on the Röder, 20 miles N.N.W. of Dresden by railway. It has a fine church of date 1748, and is the seat of important woollen and cotton industries. Pop. (1875) 10,686. G. was already a town in the 10th c., and belonged successively to Bohemia, Meissen, and Brandenburg. It suffered severely in the Thirty Years' War and Seven Years' War.

Grosseteste, Robert, one of the great ecclesiastical statesmen of England during the middle ages, was born at Stradbrook, Suffolk, about 1180, studied at the Universities of Oxford and Paris, was made lecturer in the Franciscan school at Oxford, and in 1235 Bishop of Lincoln. He immediately entered on an earnest career as a clerical reformer and champion of political freedom, striving to check the worldliness of the churchmen, and consistently opposing at once the royal tyranny and the papal ambition and venality. In 1244 he took a leading part among the prelates and nobles who demanded that Henry III. should rule through a ministry, and in 1253 he boldly and eloquently combated Innocent III., who had appointed his nephew, a young Italian, to the first canonry vacant in Lincoln cathedral. Throughout his life he resisted the papal efforts to intrude foreigners on English benefices, was several times the leader of the constitutional party in Parliament, and was the intimate friend of Simon de Montfort. G. died October 9, 1253. Mr. Stubbs calls him 'the most learned, the most acute, and the most holy man of his time,' and adds that he represented 'a school, part of whose teaching descended through the Franciscans to Ockham and the Nominalists, and through them to Wycliffe.' See Sward's *Roberti G. Episcopi Quandam Lincolensis Epistolæ* (1862), and Stubbs's *Constitutional History of England*, vol. ii. (1876).

Grosse'to, the fortified capital of a province of the same name, Central Italy, on the Ombrone, 8 miles from the sea, and 65 S. of Florence by railway. The seat of a bishop, it has a beautiful cathedral, a *Compagnia di Misericordia*, several sugar refineries, a trade in coals, chemicals, wine-casks, &c. Pop. (1871) 4151. The huge ruins of the Etruscan *Rusellæ* lie 5 miles N.E., where are also the Bagni di Roselle (*Aquæ Rusellarum*), copious springs with a temperature of 28° 5′ R., rich in various salts.

Grossularia'ceæ, or **Ribesia'ceæ,** a natural order of Calycifloral dicotyledonous shrubs found in Europe, Asia, and America. The order includes three or four genera, and about sixty species—many of which yield edible fruits. The different kinds of Gooseberry (q. v.) (*Ribes grossularia*) and Currant (q. v.) (*R. rubrum* and *R. nigrum*) belong to this order.

Grosswar'dein (Magyar *Nagy-Várad*), a town of Hungary, capital of the comitát of Bihar, on the Sebes ('rapid') Körös, 38 miles S.S.E. of Debreczin, and 135 of Pesth by railway. It is the seat of a Roman Catholic and of a Greek Catholic bishop, has a beautiful cathedral, is enclosed by walls and girt by eight suburbs. There is an active wine and cattle trade. Pop. (1869) 22,443. G. was occupied by the Turks from 1660 to 1692.

Grote, George, one of the greatest of English historians, was the son of a London banker, and was born at Clay Hill, Beckenham, Kent, November 17, 1794. He entered his father's bank when sixteen years old, and early devoted his leisure to study. A friend of James Mill, and a 'philosophical Radical,' he had resolved as far back as 1823 to write a history of Greece vindicating Greek democracy. He took part keenly in the Reform struggle, publishing a pamphlet, *Essentials of Reform*, in 1831, and in 1832 was chosen at the top of the poll as member for the city of London. He annually brought forward a motion for the ballot, and repeatedly advocated his Radical views with great force and ingenuity. He retired into private life in 1843, and issued the first volume of his *History of Greece* in 1846, the twelfth and last appearing in 1856. In 1865 he produced a work on Plato, and was largely occupied during his last years on a book on Aristotle, which, however, he left unfinished. He became President of University College, London, in 1869, and died in London, June 18, 1871. His *Aristotle* (3 vols.) was published in 1872, and his *Minor Works, Essays, and Reviews*, in 1873. G.'s *History of Greece* is the standard history of that country. It is marked by solid research, strong and penetrative criticism, the keen insight of a practical politician, and especially by an ardent, original, and masterly championship of the Athenian democracy, most of the charges against which G. has in the opinion of many successfully rebutted. The book overthrew the conventional ideas of Greek history, shed a fresh light on very many questions previously misunderstood, and inspired the subject with a novel, varied, and living interest. G.'s style is full, clear, and vigorous, though sometimes wordy, heavy, and tediously parenthetical. See Mrs. G.'s *Memoirs of G. G.* (Lond. 1873), and *Character and Writings of G. G.*, prefixed to G.'s *Minor Works*.

Grotesque', a term applied from the 13th c. onwards to a fanciful and picturesquely unnatural style of ornament, because the first specimens of it were found in old Roman subterranean chambers, called in Italian *grottos*. In G. decorations, which became popular at the end of the middle ages, animals, leaves, flowers, fruits, &c., are fantastically but often gracefully mingled. At the Renaissance, however, the G. style sank into uncouth and unmeaning capriciousness.

Gro'tius, Hugo, the Latinised form of the Dutch **De Groot,** a great jurist and theologian, was born April 10, 1583, at Delft, where his father was burgomaster. He studied at Leyden University under Joseph Scaliger, and in 1598 accompanied the Dutch embassy to Paris, where he won the favour of Henri IV. by his talents and manners. He returned to Holland in 1599, published editions of *Martianus Capella*, and the *Phænomena* of Aratus, three original Latin tragedies, &c., and practised with success as an advocate. In 1613 he was chosen councilpensionary of Rotterdam, but becoming involved in the controversy between the Dutch Calvinists and Arminians, he was, on the triumph of the former, sentenced to lifelong imprisonment. In 1621 he escaped from Lowenstein castle in a book-chest, while his wife remained in his stead, and fled to France, where Louis XIII. pensioned him, and where he wrote his chief work *De Jure Belli et Pacis*. Richelieu's displeasure causing him to quit France, he betook himself to Sweden, and was appointed by Queen Christina, in 1635, ambassador to the French court, an office which he filled with rare ability for ten years. When travelling to Sweden in 1645 he met with a most flattering ovation at Amsterdam, and afterwards received an equally honourable welcome at Stockholm. Disliking the Swedish court and climate, however, he resigned his post, and left Sweden for Holland. Stress of weather drove the ship in which he sailed to the Pomeranian coast, and G. while journeying by road fell ill and died at Rostock, August 28, 1645. His character is untarnished, and he was, notwithstanding his active forensic and diplomatic life, perhaps the widest scholar of his age. His fame is highest as a writer on law, his masterly treatise *De Jure Belli* (1625) being the origin of the modern system of international law, and generally remarkable for its solid learning and its humane and philosophic spirit. Of his other works the chief are *Mare Liberum* (1609), *Florum Sparsio ad Jus Justinianeum* (1642), *De Imperio Summarum Potestatum circa sacra* (1646), &c., which discuss legal questions; *Defensio Fidei Catholicæ* (1617), *De Veritate Religionis Christianæ* (1627), *Via ad Pacem Ecclesiasticam*, *Annotationes in Vetus et Novum Testamentum* (1641–51), &c., which treat of theology; and various historical and miscellaneous writings, as *De Antiquitate Reipublicæ Bataviæ* (1610), *De Origine Gentium Americanarum* (1642), *Annales et Historiæ Belgicæ* (1657); poems in Dutch, Greek, and Latin, &c. As a theologian G. is distinguished by moderation and clear, sound judgment, and displays both a wealth of philological learning remarkable for his times, and a singularly apt command of illustrations from the ancient classics. His editions of Lucan and Tacitus, and his translations from the Greek poets into choice Latin verse, show him to have been an elegant as well as a profound scholar, and his Latin prose style was admirably terse and vigorous. See Butler's *Life of G.* (Lond. 1826); Creuzer's *Luther und Hugo G.* (Heidel. 1846).

Grott'a del Ca'ne (Ital. 'dog's grotto'), a well-known mephitic cave, 2 miles W. of Naples, near the Lago d' Agnano, is 10 feet by 4, and 9 feet high. The carbonic acid gas which it exhales is known to extinguish lights and even to kill dogs. It is described by Pliny (*Hist. Nat.* ii. 93).

Grottagl'ie, a town in the province of Lecce, S. Italy, 12 miles N.E. of Taranto. It lies at the base of a hill, from the caves (*grotte*) in which it takes its name, and has several cotton factories. G. was founded in the 10th c. by the refugees from neighbouring villages ravaged by the Saracens. Pop. (1871) 8747.

Grou'chy, Emmanuel, Marquis de, a noted French marshal, belonged to an ancient family of Normandy, was born at Paris, 23d October 1766. He entered the army at the age of fourteen, was a sub-lieutenant in the king's bodyguard in 1789, but eagerly embraced the cause of the Revolution. In 1792 he was made a brigadier-general, received the command of the cavalry in the army of the Alps, and took part in the conquest of Savoy. In 1793 he was engaged in the suppression of the Vendean revolt. The decree of the National Convention ordering the expulsion from the army of all aristocrats induced him to throw aside his title and re-enter the ranks as a private. In 1795 he was reappointed a general of division, served under Hoche in the army of the West, under Joubert in the army of Italy (1798), when he induced the Sardinian king to abdicate and deliver up his fortresses to France. He was with Moreau in his memorable Piedmontese campaign against the Austrians, commanded a division of the army of the Rhine, contributed to the success of Hohenlinden, and was made inspector-general of cavalry. In 1805 he commanded one of the divisions of the camp at Brest, distinguished himself (1806–7) in the war against Prussia, his corps being the first to enter Berlin after Jena. His brilliant cavalry charges at Eylau helped to decide the day. For his services at Friedland (1807) he obtained the grand cordon of the Legion of Honour; at Wagram (1809) the title of colonel-general of chasseurs and commander of the Iron Crown, which made him a grand officer of the empire. In the Russian campaign of 1812 he fought at Wilna, Krasnoï, Smolensk, Moskow, and commanded the *escadron sacré* which guarded Napoleon on the retreat. A quarrel with the Emperor prevented him from taking part in the Leipsic campaign, but he fought against the allies when they invaded France. On the return of Napoleon from Elba, G. received the command of four divisions, forced the Duc d'Angoulême to surrender at Lyon, was made marshal, cleared the royalists out of the south, defeated Blucher at Ligny, 16th June 1815, but was unable to give the Emperor any help on the decisive day of Waterloo, owing to a rigid adherence to the orders he had received. Exiled after the second restoration of the Bourbons, G. went to live in America, but was permitted to return in 1821. The revolution of 1830 restored him his military honours, and two years later he was called to the House of Peers. He died at St. Étienne, 29th May 1847. G.'s conduct at Waterloo has been severely censured, and a whole library of acrimonious literature has been written on the subject, but no one now believes the base insinuation of his opponents that he betrayed his master or his country. See Thiers' *Histoire du Consulat et de l'Empire.*

Ground, the term used in painting to denote the whole of the surface unoccupied by the figures, &c., and which is of level uniform colour. The richness and harmony of the design depend to a great extent upon the degree of tonic sympathy which exists between the G. and the colours of the objects of the design. In Indian and Japanese designs the grounds are always in the truest tonic accord with the figured work.

Ground Ann'ual, a term of Scotch law denoting the perpetual annuity which is sometimes given as the price of land instead of an immediate sum. When a sub-feu (see FEU) is prohibited, those who speculate in building-ground with the intention of disposing of it in small portions to builders attain their end by the creation of a G. A. The disposition is granted to be held public (see PUBLIC RIGHT) in compliance with the condition of the feu-charter, but the subject is charged with an annual payment to the disponer and his heirs and assignees; and either a burden or annuity is reserved, which is declared a real burden, or a bond and disposition in security of the annuity is granted by the purchaser, on which Infeftment (q. v.) is taken. The similar term in the law of England is Ground Rent (q. v.).

Ground Dove or **Pigeon**, a name given to various species of *Columbidæ* or pigeons, belonging to the family *Gouridæ*, of which the genus *Goura* (q. v.) is the type. The bill is of moderate size, and arched at its apex. The G. D. seems to approach most nearly of all the pigeons to the ordinary Rasorial birds (such as the fowl, grouse, &c.), which are thoroughly terrestrial in their habits. The G. D. does not, as a rule, perch upon trees, and the food consists of seeds, &c., which it picks up on the ground. Besides the genus *Goura*, the genus *Calænas*, represented by the *C. Nicobarica*, or Nicobar pigeon (a native of India), may be selected as a good example of the G. D.

Ground Ivy, the popular name of *Glechoma hederacea*, a pretty little trailing herbaceous plant common in open woods and on hedge banks throughout Britain. It was formerly used medicinally, and for flavouring ale; hence it was called ale-hoof. Country herbalists still use it in England. It belongs to the natural order *Labiatæ* (q. v.).

Groundling (*Botia tænia*), a small Teleostean fish belonging to the Carp family (*Cyprinidæ*), and attaining a length of 3 or 4 inches. It inhabits the bottom of rivers, and hence its name. It resembles the Loach (q. v.), and has a spinous process below each eye. The G. is found here and there in English rivers.

Ground Nut, a name generally applied to the pods of *Arachis hypogæa*. See ARACHIS.

Ground Rent, in the law of England, is the rent which the person who builds on a piece of ground pays to the landlord. In letting the house the builder includes in the rent the G. R., or a proportionate part of it. The landlord, if the G. R. is in arrear, is entitled to distrain all goods and chattels on the premises, even though the tenant has paid the whole rent to his immediate landlord; but in this case he may deduct the twice-paid G. R. from the payment at next term. The usual duration of a building lease in England is ninety-nine years. On its expiry the building becomes the property of the landlord.

Ground'sel, the popular name for *Senecio vulgaris*, a very common weed throughout Europe.

Ground Squirrel (*Tamias*), a genus of Squirrels (*Sciuridæ*) represented in Europe, Asia, and America, and allied in some respects to the Marmot (q. v.) or prairie dog. They have cheek-pouches, but their feet are shorter than those of the true squirrels, and the tail is shorter than the body. The most familiar example of the G. S. is the *Tamias Lysteri*, the Hackee or chipping squirrel of N. America. Its colour is a brownish grey above, passing into orange brown on the head and the quarters. The sides and back are marked by longitudinal stripes of black and yellowish white, giving the animal a somewhat piebald appearance. The under parts are white. Its food consists of wheat, buckwheat, and corn. The G. S. inhabits burrows, which it excavates for a considerable distance below ground. Its average length is 11 inches, the tail measuring 4 inches. From four to five young are produced in May, and a second brood appears in August.

Grouse (*Tetrao*), a genus of *Rasorial* or Gallinaceous birds, forming the type of a large family (*Tetraonidæ*), which includes a number of sub-families, such as those of the partridges, quails, &c. The sub-family *Tetraoninæ* includes the genus *Tetrao* itself, and is distinguished by the feathered nostrils and the short, broad bill, the wings being rounded, the tarsi feathered, and the toes long. The third and fourth quills are the longest; the eyebrows are bare, and covered with a reddish warty skin. To the genus *Tetrao* belong the Capercailzie (q. v.) (*T. urogallus*), the Cock of the Plains (q. v.) (*T. urophasianus*), and the Blackcock (q. v.) (*T.*) or Black G. (*T. tetrix*). The pinnated G. (*T. cupido*) is a N. American form, attaining a length of 19 inches, and distinguished by the males having two wing-like appendages to the neck, composed each of about eighteen feathers, and a slight crest on the head. The neck is provided with brilliantly-coloured *wattles*. The colour is brown, marked with white and black, the brown being lightest below. The ruffed G. (*Tetrao umbellus*) derives its name from the curious tufts of feathers on the shoulders. These are of a velvet-black colour, and have a bare patch of skin under each. The colour is a rich chestnut brown above, marked with darker brown and grey, and the tail is grey marked with blackish bars. The average length is 18 inches. The genus *Lagopus* is nearly allied to the genus *Tetrao*, but is distinguished by the tarsi and toes being fully feathered—the latter even to their tips. The common or red G. (*Lagopus Scoticus*) is the best-known member of the G. sub-family. It appears to be peculiar to the northern parts of Britain, and inhabits moors, feeding on the tips of heather. The colour is a reddish brown speckled and marked with black, although lighter-tinted varieties are not uncommon. The average length is from 12 to 14 inches. This bird is subject to various grave forms of disease (see G. DISEASE), and in particular seasons large numbers die off. The Ptarmigan (q. v.) (*L. vulgaris*) is an allied species of the G. The sand-G. of the East is represented by the *Pterocles bicinctus*, and inhabits the sandy tracts of Africa, Asia, and S. Europe. The tarsi have their front and inner sides feathered. The bill is small, and the nostrils are partly hidden by membrane. The toes are short, and united at their bases by membrane, the hinder toe being especially small. In colour it approaches very nearly to that of the sandy tracts amid which it dwells.

Grouse.

Grouse Disease, the name given to a peculiar epidemic disorder affecting Grouse (q. v.) in certain seasons, and causing a great mortality in the moors. The disorder has received various explanations, some authorities, *e.g.*, Dr. Cobbold of London, ascribing the disease to the presence of parasites of various kinds, while others, *e.g.*, Dr. Farquharson of London and Dr. Andrew Wilson of Edinburgh, favour the theory of an infectious disorder of an epidemic and febrile type. That the latter view is correct is supported by the fact that even so-called healthy grouse are almost invariably infested with parasites (such as the *Tænia calva* and a species of *Strongylus*), whilst mere parasitism will not explain the sudden spread and extension of the disorder. Dr. Wilson, from his researches (see *Edinburgh Medical Journal*, April 1875), inclines to the belief that the respiratory mucous membrane is specially affected, and that the disease, in some cases at any rate, assumes the form of an acute inflammatory affection. A paper by Dr. Farquharson of London on the G. D. will also be found in the vol. of the *Edinburgh Medical Journal* for 1875, and Dr. Cobbold's contributions to this subject are contained chiefly in the British Association Reports.

Growing Corn, on land let to a tenant, is in England subject to Distress (q. v.) for rent in arrear. In Scotland G. C. is subject to Poinding (q. v.), but procedure is not competent till the corn is cut down and measured. The landlord in virtue of his Hypothec (q. v.) has a claim preferable to that of a poinding creditor. A symbolical delivery of G. C. has in Scotland been held to exclude creditors.

Growl'er (*Grystes salmoides*), a Teleostean fish belonging to the *Percidæ* or Perch family, and found in N. American rivers, an allied species occurring in Australian streams. It attains a length of 2 feet, and has small scales and teeth of minute kind. The flesh is very palatable. The name G. is given to the fish from the grunting sound it emits.

Growth. During early life the tissues of the body increase in size by taking up materials from the blood which they convert into substances similar to themselves. For example, muscle grows by matters obtained from the blood, which are assimilated by the substance of the muscle. This increase in size constitutes G., as regards the individual tissues. Up to a certain period of life the body generally increases in size and weight. It may then remain nearly stationary in these respects for many years, in consequence of the amount of waste of tissue being nearly equal to the amount of repair. During this middle period of life, in one sense the body may have ceased growing, but still G. may be taking place in one or more of the tissues, as, for instance, in muscular tissue in consequence of being habitually exercised, or in fatty tissue. In the later years of life, the waste is in excess of the repair, and consequently the body decreases in size and weight. The general conditions regulating G. may be briefly stated as follows:—(1) A healthy quality of the blood; (2) a proper quantity of blood; (3) a proper influence of the nervous system; and (4) a healthy state of the various tissues of the body. See NUTRITION.

Grub (lit. 'the digger,' because of its picking its way into plants), a general term applied to the larval or caterpillar stage of most insects. It is spoken of frequently by agriculturists in connection with injury done to crops, the larvæ of the Beetle (q. v.) being specially pernicious.

Grubb'er (lit. 'the digger'), an agricultural implement for tearing up and loosening the soil without turning it over like the plough, and for cleaning land of roots of plants, &c. It consists of a handled and wheeled iron frame with cross bars, from which depend iron tines with cutting edges capable of being closed or widened. The most approved forms of the G. have three wheels, one in front and two behind, and have an arrangement for regulating the depth of penetration of the soil, and for withdrawing the tines when requisite. In Scotland, Kirkwood's and Scoular's three-wheeled implements, and Tennant's and Scoular's one-wheeled are principally used. In England, Coleman's and Johnston's cultivators, Biddell's scarifiers, and other machines all designed on the principle of the G., are much esteemed.

Gru'gru, the name given by negroes to the Grub (q. v.) or larva of a W. Indian insect (*Calandra palmarum*) belonging to the *Coleoptera* or beetles, and popularly known as the palm weevil. The weevil itself attains a length of 2 inches, and the larva is even larger. It burrows in the canes and cabbage palms (*Euterpe oleracea*), and is esteemed as a luxury in diet by the negroes, who eat the G. after roasting it.

Grün'berg ('green mount'), a town of Prussian Silesia, on the Golden Lunse, amid vine-clad hills, 54 miles S.E. of Frankfurt-on-the-Oder by railway. The old town is surrounded by a wall with three gates. G. produces 667,000 gallons of sparkling wine yearly, and has manufactures of woollens, silks, tobacco, &c. Pop. (1875) 12,248.

Grundt'vig, Nikolai Frederik Severin, a distinguished Danish theologian, born 8th September 1783 near Vordingborg in Zealand, was educated at Aarhus 'Latin school,' and Copenhagen University, and early chose as his favourite studies religion and mythology. In 1805, after a period of strong spiritual excitement, he caught an enthusiasm for Scandinavian antiquity from the poetry of Oehlenschläger, and for a poetic Christianity from the study of Schelling and Steffens. G.'s remarkable literary activity for the popular enforcement of his gradually developed views dates from 1807. A course of sermons delivered at Copenhagen in 1810 awoke great interest, and led to his rebuke by the University 'Consistorium.' In 1811 he became curate of his father's parish, and the next year published the first of a number of able and characteristic works on the history of the world, quickly followed by the first struggles of the many-sided literary warfare that stimulated most years of G.'s long life, whether he opposed Molbech, Oersted, Heiberg,

Clausen, Rudelbach, or Martensen. After living at Copenhagen from 1813, in 1821 he became minister of Prœstö, and the year after curate of St. Saviour's at Christianshavn, but resigned in 1825 under a censure, which was only removed in 1838. In 1839 he was appointed chaplain of Vartou Hospital, and in 1861 was made a bishop. He died in 1872. G.'s chief writings are *Nordens Mythologi* (1808), *Nordens Kæmpeliv* (1810), *Nytaarsnat* (1811), *Bibelske Prædikener* (1816), *Bjovulfs Drapa* (1820), *Nytaarsmorgen* (1824), *Nordens Mythologi og Sindbilledsprog* (1832), *Verdenshistorien* (1833–36), *Christenhedens Syvstjerne* (1860).

Grunth (Sansk. *grantha*, 'a book'), the holy book of the Sikhs, divided into the *adi* or first G., which contains chiefly the sayings of Nanuk, the founder of the sect; and the tenth G., compiled by Govind Singh, the tenth and last *guru*. Both are in verse, and the language used is Hindi rather than Punjaubi; but the written character is that known as Punjaubi or Gurumukhi, from its having been adopted by the Sikh *gurus*. The earliest writer is Arjun, the fifth *guru* (1581–1606). The contents are chiefly prayers addressed to the One Great God, with some mythological stories. See Cunningham's *History of the Sikhs* (Lond. 1853).

Gruyères (Ger. *Greierz*), a Swiss town in the canton and 16 miles S.S.W. of Freiburg. It has an old castle, and a trade in the famous G. cheese made in the district. Pop. (1870) 973.

Gryll'us, a genus of *Orthopterous* insects, represented by the grasshoppers, crickets, &c., but occasionally subdivided into other genera. See GRASSHOPPER, LOCUST, &c.

Grys'boc (*Calotragus melanotis*), a species of antelopes inhabiting S. Africa, and attaining an average height at the shoulder of from 19 to 20 inches. The colour is a deep or reddish chestnut interspersed with white, the greyish tint thus produced giving origin to the Dutch name of G. or 'grey buck.' The ears are prominent, and have black tips; the tail is short; and the horns (which only the males possess) are erect and tapering.

Gua'charo, or **Trinidad Goat-Sucker** (*Steatornis Caripensis*), also known as the 'fat bird,' a genus of *Insessorial* birds belonging to the *Fissirostral* section of the order, and to the family *Caprimulgidæ* or goat-suckers. The bill has a hooked tip, and its base is provided with feathers and bristles. The wings are long and pointed, the tail broad and graduated, and the outer toe longer than the inner. The G. is found in Guadeloupe, Trinidad, and Colombia, and inhabits caves. The fat of the young is melted down by the Indians in clay pots, and yields a soft limpid oil, which keeps for a long period without becoming rancid. The colour of the G. is a reddish fawn mottled with brown, the plumage being varied by the presence of square white marks.

Gua'chos, or **Gau'chos**, a kind of Mestizo (Fr. *mestis*, from Lat. *mixtus*) descending from the early Spanish colonists and native Indians, and inhabiting, as nomad hunters and cattle-rearers, the Pampas of S. America, especially those of the Argentine Republic.

Guadalajara, the capital of the state of Jalisco, Mexico, near the Rio Grande de Santiago, in the fruitful valley of Atemaxac, 150 miles from the Pacific. It is a bishop's see since 1863, has fourteen public squares, a poorly endowed university with 750 students, an art academy, the great hospital Belén or San-Miguel, a fine cathedral, the appearance of which was impaired by the destruction of its cupolas by the earthquake of 1818. Its *alameda* (promenade) is beautiful, and there are twelve large fountains supplied with water from the Cerro del Col by an aqueduct 3 miles long. The manufactures are gold and silver wares, leather, shawls, earthenware, &c. Pop. (1873) 70,947. G. was founded in 1543. In the vicinity are many silver-mines.

Guadalaviar', or **Tu'ria**, a Spanish river, 130 miles long, rises in the S.W. of Aragon, near the source of the Tagus, flows S.S.E. to the Mediterranean at Grao, 1½ miles E. of Valencia. It is employed in irrigating the fine gardens along its banks, but its mouth is silting.

Guadalja'ra, the capital of the Spanish province of the same name, on the left bank of the Henares, 35 miles N.E. of Madrid by railway. It lies in the fine pastoral district of Alcaria; has ten churches, seven nunneries, and six monasteries, a royal cloth factory, an academy of military engineering, the great palace of the Dukes of Infantado, the Panteon, containing the tombs of the dukes, and erected on the model of the Escorial (1696–1728), at a cost of £225,000. The Henares is here crossed by a new stone bridge, and its valley is malarious. Pop. 6500. G. is the ancient *Arriaca*, and was taken from the Visigoths in 714 by the Arabs, who called it *Wadi-l-Hadjarra*, and eventually lost it to Alfonso I. of Castile in 1081.

Guadalquivir' (Arab. *Wad-al-Kebir*, 'the great river'), the chief river in the S. of Spain, rises in the Sierra de Cazorla, flows S.W. through Andalusia, passing Andujar, Montoro, Cordova, and Sevilla, receiving on the right the Guadalimar and Guadiato, on the left the Xenil and Guadajos, and entering the Atlantic at San Lucar de Barrameda, 20 miles N.W. of Cadiz, after a course of 260 miles. It is navigable to Sevilla (80 miles), below which it encloses the Isla Menor ('lesser isle') and Isla Mayor ('larger isle'). The stream is loaded with alluvium, while its lower course lies in a luxuriant but malarious half-deserted country. G. is the ancient *Bætis*.

Guadalupe', the name (1) of a long spur of the Rocky Mountains between the Rio Grande and the Pecos; (2) of a beautiful grain-growing and sylvan county in the S.W. of Texas, U.S.; and (3) of a river rising in the S. of Texas, which flows S.E. through a fair, fertile region, and, after a course of 200 miles, joins the San Antonio, 13 miles from its mouth, in Esperitu Santo Bay.

Guadalupe-y-Calvo, a town of Mexico, state of Chihuahua, in a hilly region, has a pop. of 10,000, and several rich silver-mines worked by an English company.

Guadeloupe', the chief W. Indian possession of France among the Windward Islands, in lat. 16° N. and long. 61°. Area, along with the islet dependencies La Désirade, Marie Galante, and Les Saintes, 534 sq. miles; pop. (1872) 163,657, including 15,210 coolies. It consists of two islands, G. proper on the W. and Grand Terre on the E., separated by a strait 40 yards wide, called the Rivière Salée ('salt river'). G. proper is traversed by a mountain chain, rising in the volcanic La Souffrière ('sulphur-mine') to a height of 5018 feet; Grand Terre, which is of coral formation, is for the most part low and fertile. The hot climate is tempered by the regular sea breeze, but there are frequent hurricanes, high tides, and earthquakes. Basse-Terre, the capital, is on the W. island, and Pointe-à-Pitre, the only other port, is on the E. The exports (amounting yearly to some 18,000,000 francs) are sugar, rum, coffee, dye-stuffs, cabinet-woods, and tobacco. In 1874, 138 vessels of 37,300 tons entered and cleared the ports from France. G., discovered by Columbus in 1493, was colonised by the French in 1635, passed several times into the hands of the English, and was finally ceded to France in 1816.

Guadia'na (anc. *Anas*), a river of Spain, rises in the Sierra Alcarez, Murcia, 8 miles N.W. of Alcaraz. After 30 miles of its course, it flows for a similar distance underground, throwing up lakelets (*ojos*, 'eyes') here and there. It emerges at Daymiel, and continues W. through Lamancha and Estremadura, passes Badajoz, and then turns S. to form for 35 miles the E. boundary of Spain. It makes an incursion into Portuguese Alemtejo, again becomes the boundary for 30 miles, and finally enters the Atlantic after a course of 420 miles, only 35 of which are navigable. The chief affluent on the right is the Javalon; on the left, the Ardila. The G., though one of the longest rivers of Spain, has a comparatively small volume of water.

Guaia'cum, a genus of S. American and W. Indian trees belonging to the natural order *Zygophyllaceæ*. *G. officinalis* is a beautiful tree with hard wood, called lignum-vitæ, which sinks in water. It yields a resinous substance known as resin of guaiac, or gum-guaiac. Both the wood and the resin are used medicinally, on account of their stimulating diaphoretic properties. *G. sanctum* also yields G. resin, while its leaves are used in the W. Indies for soap.

Guan' (*Penelope*), a genus of Rasorial or Gallinaceous birds belonging to the family *Cracidæ*, or Curassows (q. v.). The crested G. (*P. cristata*), inhabiting the forests of tropical America, attains a length of 30 inches. The throat of the G. is naked, and has a dilatable skin. The bird is solitary in its habits, and appears to feed on fruits. Its flesh is highly esteemed. It can be domesticated with difficulty.

Guana'co, a variety or sub-species of Llama (q. v.) inhabiting Patagonia, and distinguished by its long neck and its ruddy brown colour. The height at the shoulder is about 3½ feet. The G. lives in herds of from ten to thirty or forty in number, and is kept for the sake of its wool, skin, flesh, and milk. It is wonderfully sure-footed, and in its native state is quiet and timid, but when domesticated shows fight on being irritated, and discharges saliva over its assailant.

Guanaha'ni, or **Cat Island**, a small island of the Bahamas, W. Indies, has a pop. of 2378. Till recently it was supposed to be the island first discovered by Columbus, and called by him San Salvador. Watling's Island is, however, now regarded as the island in question, and has therefore received the official name San Salvador.

Guanajuato, Sante Fé de, the capital of an inland state of the same name, Mexico, lies at an elevation of 6017 feet above the sea, and on steep, broken slopes. It has a cathedral, eight monasteries, a college, a theatre, and manufactures of soap, linen, tobacco, &c. The vicinity is rich in silver-mines. Pop. (1873) 63,000.—The *state* of G. is partly a plateau 6000 feet above the sea, traversed by mountains 11,000 feet high. It is very rich in silver, and yields maize, red pepper, wine, and olives.

Guana're, a city of Venezuela, S. America, in Barinas, near the river from which it takes its name, 220 miles S.W. of Caracas. It exports hides, coffee, cocoa, &c. Pop. 12,000. The river G. is the upper water of the Apure.

Guanine is a basic nitrogenous substance, first obtained from guano, but it also occurs in the pancreatic juice of the mammalia and in the excrement of certain insects. It may be prepared from guano by boiling with slaked lime and water till the solution is only slightly coloured, filtering, and precipitating with acetic acid. The G. is precipitated in a somewhat impure condition, but may be purified by solution in hydrochloric acid, and precipitation by ammonia. G. is a colourless crystalline powder, insoluble in ether, alcohol, and water, but soluble in acids and solution of potash. Its composition is represented by the formula $C_5H_5N_5O$. It unites with acids to form salts.

Guano (Per. *huano*, 'dung') consists of the excrement deposits of animals, chiefly of sea-birds, which, owing to peculiar conditions, has been allowed to accumulate in extraordinary masses in various regions of the earth. It is used as manure, and is by far the most important and valuable of all imported manures in any agricultural country. The preservation of G. deposits is dependent on the freedom of the locality in which the fæcal matter is dropped from rain or other forms of moisture which would wash away the important fertilising constituents for which it is valued. As observed by Professor Johnston, 'a single day of English rain would dissolve out and carry into the sea a considerable portion of one of the largest accumulations; a single year of English weather would cause many of them entirely to disappear.' It is on this account found that the most valuable deposits of G. occur in hot, arid regions on or near sea-coasts, where little or no rain falls, and these conditions prevail chiefly on certain parts of the Peruvian and Bolivian coasts of S. America, and on islands lying off these coasts. According to the amount of rain or dew which may have operated upon G. deposits, they are roughly separated into three classes as follows:—(1) Nitrogenous G., consisting of droppings which have been little affected by moisture, and which consequently retain the greater part of the soluble constituents of bird-dung, as urea, uric acid with other ammoniacal salts, and soluble phosphates. These guanos contain from 16 to 21 per cent. of ammonia. (2) G. which has lost a large proportion of its nitrogenous matter through the solvent action of rain, but in which from 2 to 4 per cent. of ammonia is still present. (3) Phosphatic G., from which all the soluble nitrogenous compounds are washed away, and which are valuable almost entirely on account of the earthy phosphates remaining in them. These varieties contain also some organic compounds which have resisted the action of water with sulphates and carbonates of lime, and they are frequently mixed with a considerable proportion of sand. The phosphatic varieties are generally treated with sulphuric acid to render the phosphates they contain more soluble, or they are used similarly to bones, coprolites, &c., as a source of 'superphosphates.' Although it is convenient thus to classify the varieties of G., there is no distinct line of demarcation between the three classes, and some kinds may be considered as much phosphatic as nitrogenous. The freshest, most recent, and least altered G. imported into Great Britain consists of Angamos G., obtained from a rocky promontory in Bolivia. It is obtained only in small qnantities, and though the most valuable of all, it is practically interesting only as the extreme type of nitrogenous G. Next to it comes the ordinary Peruvian G., of which the now exhausted deposits of Chincha Island were the most characteristic and valuablě, containing from 16 to 17 per cent. of ammonia. The Falkland Islands on the Patagonian coast, Ichaboe, Saldanha Bay, certain parts of Bolivia, and Upper Peru, Chili, and California are the sources of the varieties generally containing less than 5 per cent. of ammonia. The phosphatic guanos are obtained from S. America, S. Africa, certain of the W. Indian Islands, and some uninhabited islands in the S. Pacific. The chief commercial varieties are Mejillones, Patagonian, Californian, Curaçoa, Birds' Island, Malden Island, and Starbuck Island. The following analyses by Dr. Voelcker of two extreme varieties indicate the effect of weather on the deposits and their variation in fertilising influence:—

	Angamos Guano.
Moisture	7·24
Organic matter and ammoniacal salts	69·01
Phosphates of lime and magnesia (bone phosphates)	12·06
Alkaline salts (potash and soda salts)	9·02
Insoluble siliceous matter	2·67
	100·00

	Starbuck Island Crust Guano.
Moisture and organic matter	8·75
Phosphoric acid	45·57
Lime	40·94
Magnesia	·64
Sulphuric acid	3·56
Alkaline matter and silica	·54
	100·00

Nitrogenous guanos have a brownish-yellow appearance, and so very pungent an ammoniacal odour that they produce watering of the eyes. Frequent masses of comparatively pure carbonate of ammonia are obtained from them, and they also sometimes enclose remains of birds, &c. They exercise a powerful stimulating and forcing influence on the crops on lands to which they are applied; and containing a large proportion of soluble matter, their valuable principles are communicated to the soil with great rapidity. Phosphatic guanos have a yellow or chocolate colour, and a fine powdery texture, with much less odour than the nitrogenous kinds. They produce a very beneficial effect on root crops when applied in their native condition; but as already stated, they should be washed with sulphuric acid to render their phosphates readily soluble.

The earliest known mention of G. is in the *Commentaries of the Incas* by Garcilaso de la Vega in 1568. Attention was called to its fertilising qualities by Humboldt, who sent samples analysed by Fourcroy and Vauquelin to France in 1805. Regular importations began about 1842 and rapidly rose in amount to 500,000 tons a year, at the rate of £20 a ton. In 1875, 114,454 tons were imported into Great Britain, the value being £1,293,436. The import of France (1870) was 100,186 tons; of Belgium, 68,837; of Germany, 36,412; of Spain, 34,366; of the United States, 30,798.

Guapey', a tributary of the Mamore, a branch of the Amazon, rises in Bolivia, and has a length of 550 miles.

Guapo're, a head water of the Amazon, flows through the Mamore and Madera in Brazil, and has a course of 400 miles.

Guara'na, a native Brazilian name for a valuable food preparation of the seeds of *Paullinia sorbilis* (natural order *Sapin-*

daceæ), a low, wide-spreading tree abounding along the banks of the Amazon and its tributaries. The fruit, about the size of a walnut, contains five or six seeds. These are roasted, powdered, mixed with water, and shaped into rolls which are dried in the sun. For use a quantity is grated off a roll and boiled with water. The decoction acts as a stimulant and nervous restorative, owing to the alkaloid theine which is present, to the extent of 5·07 per cent., more than twice the quantity contained in good black tea.

Guar'antee, or **Guar'anty**, in law, is a contract by which one person binds himself to do some act, in the event of the person primarily liable failing to do it, or some other specified act. G. is either continuous or limited. It is continuous when one pledges himself for another to a certain amount in any dealing. It is limited when restricted to a particular transaction, person, or time. The Statute of Frauds provides that no person shall be liable on any special promise to answer for the debts or default of another, unless the G. can be proved by writing, and that the surety shall not be bound beyond the express words of the engagement. 19 and 20 Vict. c. 60 enacts that the G. to or for a firm shall cease on a change in its members, unless it appears to have been otherwise meant by the parties to the contract. By the same Act every surety who discharges his liability to a creditor is entitled to any security held by that creditor. If a creditor discharges or gives indulgence to his debtor, the surety is released. A letter of recommendation, though spontaneously given, is not held to be a G. unless it refers to a particular transaction, and contains assurances of its being a safe one.

Guardafui', Cape, or **Ras Asser**, the most easterly point of Africa, in the Somali territory, and running E.N.E. between the Indian Ocean and the Gulf of Aden. It was the *Aromatum Promontorium* of the ancients.

Guar'dian, in English law, is the legal custodier and representative of a boy or girl who is under Age (q. v.). If an estate be left to an infant, the father is by common law the G. and must account to his child for the profits. A father may by deed or will appoint a G. of his child till the twenty-first anniversary of its birthday. A G. so appointed is called *G. by statute*, or *testamentary G.* The reciprocal duties of G. and ward are the same as those of Parent and Child (q. v.), but that on the ward coming of age, the G. must account to him for all transactions on his behalf, and the G. is answerable for loss by his wilful default or negligence. To marry a ward of Chancery without consent of that division, is a contempt for which the offender may be committed or indicted, though he was ignorant of the wardship. A proper settlement made on the ward is sometimes, but not always, held to counteract the contempt.

Guardian ad Litem is a person, usually the father, appointed by the Chancery division to carry on a suit for an infant.

Guardian of the Poor.—This is, by 4 and 5 Will. IV. c. 76, any qualified person elected to the office by the ratepayers and owners in the parish or union. The qualification is not to exceed a rental of £40 a year. County magistrates are guardians *ex officio*.

For *Guardian* in Scotch law, see CURATOR, MINOR, TUTOR, JUDICIAL FACTOR.

Guards, in the British army, are during peace the garrison of London, and guard of the monarch at Windsor. The G. include, in cavalry, the 1st and 2d, and the Royal Horse G. (Blue); in infantry, the Grenadier G., Coldstream G., and Scots Fusilier G. Formerly an ensign in the Foot G. ranked with a lieutenant in another regiment, and a lieutenant with a captain; but this distinction between the G. and other troops vanished on the abolition of purchase in 1871.

Guardship, a war-ship placed to guard a port, and generally used to receive seamen before they are appointed to other vessels.

Guar'ea, a genus of trees belonging to the natural order *Meliaceæ*, having purgative and emetic properties, found in N. America. The wood of *G. trichilioides* and other species has been used as a perfume owing to its strong musk odour.

Guari'ni of Verona, generally called **Guari'no** (Latinised *Varinus*), one of the first scholars of the 15th c., was born at Verona in 1370. He went to Constantinople in 1390 to study Greek under Chrysoloras, and returning to Italy after five years, became Professor of Greek successively at Florence, Venice, Verona, and Ferrara, where he died in 1460. G. did much to revive learning in the West. His principal works are Latin translations of Plutarch and Strabo, and several grammatical treatises, of which the most important are *Grammaticæ Institutiones* (Verona, 1487), and *Chrysoloræ Erotemata Linguæ Græcæ*. See Rosmini's *Vita e Disciplina di G.* (Brescia, 1805).

Guari'ni, Giovanni Battista, an Italian poet, was born at Ferrara, 10th December 1537. After studying at Pisa and Padua, he entered the service of the Duke of Ferrara, who sent him as ambassador to Venice, Rome, Germany, &c. After quitting and returning to the Ferrarese court and engaging in diplomatic labours for various Italian rulers, he died at Venice, 4th October 1612. G.'s brilliant gifts were greatly neutralised by his vanity, irritability, and puerile craving for court favour. His chief work, the *Pastor Fido*, a tragi-comic pastoral written in imitation of Tasso's *Aminta*, was once immensely popular, and is musically versified, pure in diction, and full of colour, but its characters are artificial, and its language often affected and licentious. An edition of G.'s works was issued at Ferrara (4 vols. 1737).

Guatema'la, a republic of Central America, bounded N. by Yucatan, W. by Mexico, S. by the Pacific, and E. by St. Salvador, Honduras, and the Caribbean Sea. Area, 41,830 sq. miles; pop. 1,190,800, of whom about 90,000 are Indians, 20,000 whites, and the rest mestizoes. The country is traversed by mountains which may be regarded as a continuation of the Andes. From these, spurs branch off, with deep valleys between, to the Caribbean Sea. There are several active volcanoes, the highest being Sapoetlan (13,050 feet) and Atitlan (12,500 feet), and the country is subject to earthquakes. The soil is fertile, and wheat, rice, maize, sugar, cotton, vanilla, indigo, tobacco, and cochineal are grown. The revenue for 1874 amounted to £520,200, and the expenditure to £508,520. The national debt in 1875 was £872,645. The value of the imports for 1874 was £610,801, and of the exports for the same year £657,744. The trade, which is chiefly with Great Britain and the United States, is mostly in cochineal, indigo, and coffee. G. was from 1804 to 1839 included in the confederation of Central America. In 1839 it was formed into a separate republic, and was ruled by an oligarchy of dissolute priests and nobles until 1871, when the priestly party was stripped of power. The executive is vested in the president, who is chosen for four years. General Rufino Barrios now (1877) holds the office. —**New G.**, or **Santiago de G.**, capital of the republic of G., stands on a wide fertile plateau 4961 feet above the sea. It is spacious and well built, the houses being generally, for fear of earthquakes, only one story high. It is an archbishop's see, and has manufactures of muslin, cotton yarn, silver-ware, &c., and a brisk trade in agricultural produce. Pop. (1874) 45,000, about a tenth of whom are of European descent.—**Old G.**, or **La Antigua G.**, former capital of G., is beautifully situated at the foot of Volcan d'Agua, 30 miles W. of New G. It was founded in 1524 by the Spaniards, was destroyed in 1541 by an eruption, and in 1773 by an earthquake. Pop. (1874) 20,000.

Gua'va, the common name given to the species of a genus (Psidium) of tropical American and W. Indian trees and shrubs, belonging to the natural order Myrtaceæ (q. v.). Their fruits are edible. The common G., sometimes called white G., is the *P. guaiava*, a well-known tropical fruit. The red G. (*P. pomiferum*) is an agreeable but more acid fruit than the common G. The China or purple G. (*P. Cattleianum*) is cultivated in British hothouses, where it fruits freely. Large quantities of G. jelly and G. cheese are imported annually into Britain from the W. Indies.

Guayaquil', the name of a department, city, and river of Ecuador, S. America. The *department* of G. is a belt of fertile lowland between the Pacific and the Andes. Area, 14,401; pop. 92,696.—The *city* of G., capital of the above department, stands at the mouth of the river G., and has the best port on the W. coast of S. America. It is, however, very unhealthy, lying amid swamps, and is mostly built of wood. It has a considerable trade, the chief exports being cocoa, timber, india-rubber, and tobacco; the chief imports, cotton, wine, and hardware. Pop. 20,000.—The *river* G., the only navigable stream on the W. coast of S. America, rises in the Andes, receives the Daule and Babo, and flows through a marshy plain into the Gulf of G. Vessels of considerable size can ascend it for about 100 miles.

Guay'ra, La, a town of Venezuela, S. America, 6 miles from Caraccas, of which it is the port, stands on a narrow strip of plain between the sea and the mountains, which here rise with an almost sheer ascent of 3000 feet. The climate is very hot and unhealthy, and earthquakes are frequent. G. is the chief port of Venezuela, but has no harbour, and the roadstead is very exposed. Coffee, cocoa, sugar, cotton, indigo, and hides are largely exported. In 1875 its exports amounted to £814,886, and its imports to £1,022,975. Pop. 8000.

Gubb'io (anc. *Eugubium* or *Iguvium*), a town in the province of Perugia, Central Italy, 27 miles S. of the town of Urbino, lies in a valley circled by mountains. It has a quaint medieval aspect, and among its chief buildings are the Palazzo del Comune, begun in 1332, the ducal palace, and the cathedral. Outside G. are the ruins of a theatre, supposed to belong to the age of the Roman republic, and of the temple of Jupiter Apenninus. The Eugubine Tables (q. v.) were found here in 1444. Pop. (1871) 5343. G. was the *Iguvium* mentioned by Cicero, was destroyed by the Goths, afterwards rebuilt, and became an independent state at the end of the 12th c.

Gu'ben, a thriving town of Prussia, province of Brandenburg, at the confluence of the Lubst and Neisse, 28 miles S.S.E. of Frankfurt-on-the-Oder. It has an active river trade, woollen and tobacco industries, and produces much excellent red wine. The gymnasium is its chief building. Pop. (1875) 23,738.

Gud'geon (*Gobio*), a genus of fresh-water Teleostean fishes included in the carp family (*Cyprinidæ*), and distinguished by large scales, small dorsal and anal fins, a forked tail, and a mouth pointed with *barbules*, or tentacular filaments. The G. (*G. fluviatilis*) is a common fresh-water fish in most English ponds and rivers. The average length is 8 inches, and the colour an olive brown with black spots; the under parts are white. The G. appears to be gregarious in habits. Its food consists of worms, &c., and it is readily caught with this bait by juvenile anglers whose only equipment is a piece of string and a bent pin. The flesh is very palatable and delicate.

Gueb'res, a small sect in the E. of Persia, nearly confined to the two cities of Yezd and Kirman and the villages in their neighbourhood, and in 1858 numbering about 7000, are the only known representatives, besides the Parsees of India, of the Zoroastrian religion. When the Sassanian dynasty fell before the advance of the Arabs, and Zoroastrianism had to give place to Mohammedanism, a persecuted remnant fled to the mountainous district of Khorassan; part of whom found their way to India, and became the ancestors of the Parsees there, the G. being the descendants of those who remained behind. The great majority of the latter are in extreme poverty, owing to the harsh persecution to which they have all along been subjected. Their condition, however, is so far ameliorated by the kind assistance of their co-religionists in India, who, for one thing, have established schools for the gratuitous education of their children. They have been able, on the other hand, to repay the kindness of the Parsees with copies of their sacred books. The copies originally brought to India were no longer in existence in the 14th c., the originals of the present Indian MSS. being brought from Yezd between the 14th c. and 18th c. See PARSEES, SUN-WORSHIP, and ZOROASTER.

Guebwill'er, a German town in the province of Elsass-Lothringen, on the Lauch, 15 miles S.S.W. of Kolmar. Its church of Saint Leger is a very interesting edifice of the 12th c., and it has also a Dominican church of the 14th c. There is considerable trade in white wine; and ribbons, cottons and woollens, &c., are made. Pop. (1871) 11,338.

Guelderland. See GELDERLAND.

Guelder Rose, or more properly **Gueldres Rose**, a common name given to the cultivated form of *Viburnum opulus*, a shrub native in Britain. It is also sometimes called snow-ball tree, from the round form of its clusters of flowers. It belongs to the natural order Caprifoliaceæ (q. v.).

Guelphs, Order of, often incorrectly styled the **Guelphic Order**, a military and civil order of knights founded in 1815 by George IV. of England for his Hanoverian subjects, but into which many Englishmen have been admitted. The badge is a gold cross, with a lion passant in its divisions, surmounted by the Hanoverian crown. The Prussian Government does not recognise the order, and its members are not considered as knights in Great Britain.

Guelphs and Ghib'ellines, the names of the two great rival parties in the political history of medieval Italy, the Guelphs being the advocates of the Papal, the Ghibellines of the Imperial power. The names are Italianised forms of the German *Welf* and *Waiblingen*, the *Welfs* being a Saxon house hostile to the Hohenstaufens or *Waiblingen*. According to the most probable tradition of the rise of the names, when Konrad III.'s forces were besieging the revolted town of Weinsberg, in 1140, the rebels used *Welf*, the name of their leader, the brother of the Duke of Saxony, as a war-cry, while the King's troops in reply shouted *Waiblingen*, the name of their commander Friedrich of Suabia's native village, and these war-cries were adopted as distinctive titles by the two hostile German parties. Afterwards, it is said, the foes of the Hohenstaufens in Italy took the name of that family's German rivals. At the beginning of the struggle between the emperors and popes, however, the Italian Guelphic party had not arisen, and it was not until the reign of Friedrich Barbarossa that the true Guelphic faction appeared, when the Pope allied with the republics of Northern Italy against the Emperor. Friedrich then invaded Italy, but not as a mere foreign aggressor. The Ghibellines viewed him as the assertor of strictly legal claims, as the lawful successor to the dominion of the Roman emperors, nor did even the republican Guelphs deny his supremacy over Italy—they merely questioned its nature and extent. His predecessors, Otto and Heinrich III., had been invited into Italy by the Italians to repress papal wrong-doing and feudal anarchy, but after Heinrich's time the imperial rights had fallen into disuse, and free commonwealths had arisen in Lombardy and Tuscany, jealous of a foreign ruler's supremacy. The quarrels of the Italian cities favoured the imperial pretensions. Milan refused to pay tribute to Friedrich, and strove to subdue Como, Lodi, and other cities which sought help from the Emperor. Friedrich then entered Italy, while the Northern Guelphic cities united against him in the Lombard League (q. v.), and finally defeated him at Legnano, after which the Emperor was left only a titular supremacy. This was the greatest struggle between the two parties, and during it both may be said to have been truly warring for principles. Afterwards the names were merely used to give colour to aggression and kindle discord. In 1334 Pope Benedict XII. forbade their use, and at the end of the 14th c. they ceased to have any true meaning. The rivalry of the two great parties, even when their followers were the earnest advocates of two antagonistic theories of government, and when there was true nobility of purpose on either side, was most baneful to Italy. They carried discord into every section of Italian society, and led to ceaseless revolutions in the cities, each of which, whether it were Guelph or Ghibelline, included among its citizens many of the opposite party, the nobles being in general Ghibellines. Our sympathy, says Mr. Bryce, must go with the Guelphic cities, 'in whose victory we recognise the triumph of freedom and civilisation' (Bryce's *Holy Roman Empire*). But the Guelphs never fancied they were fighting for Italy against Germany, and had no stronger national feeling than the Italian Ghibellines who were by no means traitors, though supporters of the less noble cause. In the S. of Italy the names Guelph and Ghibelline never represented rival principles, but were merely used in a contest between the house of Hohenstaufen and the house of Anjou, which grew into a struggle between France and Spain. The Guelphic badge was an eagle tearing a dragon crowned with a lily, that flower as well as a red rose being the symbol of the Ghibellines. See Freeman's essays on the *Holy Roman Empire*, and on *Frederick I., King of Italy* (*Essays*, 1st series), and Bryce's *Holy Roman Empire* (5th ed. 1875).

Guerci'no ('the squint-eyed'), the name given to Gian Francesco Barbieri, a famous painter, born at Cento, between Bologna and Ferrara, February 2, 1590. He early showed strong artistic genius, became a follower first of the Caracci, and afterwards of Guido, won great fame at Rome, where he was patronised by Gregory XV., and settled in 1642 at Bologna, where he acquired large wealth. He died at Bologna, December 22, 1666. Among his works are 'Æneas carrying his Father,' 'Endymion Asleep,' 'St. Antony of Padua,' 'St. Paul,' 'St. Francis,' 'Circe,' 'St. John in the Desert,' 'Persian Sibyl,' 'St. Petronilla,' and 'Aurora,' the three last being probably his masterpieces. His style was nobly facile and vigorous, and at first characterised by the preponderance of sombre shadows, but afterwards, as he came under the influence of Guido, became much more refined and delicate. He was far more successful in colour than in design.

Guer'icke, Otto von, a celebrated natural philosopher, was born at Magdeburg in Prussian Saxony, November 20, 1602. After studying at Leipsic, Helmstedt, Jena, and Leyden, and travelling for some time in France and England, he settled in his native town, where he became a member of the senate in 1627, and burgomaster in 1646. Here he made his famous discoveries in science, inventing the air-pump in 1650. By it he emptied spherical vessels, and proved that air had weight, and exhibited the great pressure exerted by the atmosphere by means of the well-known *Magdeburg hemispheres.* He was the constructor of the first frictional electrical machine, and was the earliest to hint at the periodicity of comets. His most important researches are found in his *Experimenta Nova, ut vocant, Magdeburgica de Vacuo Spatio* (Amsterdam, 1672). In 1681 G. followed his son to Hamburg, where he died, May 11, 1686.

Guerill'a (Sp. 'petty war,' derived from Sp. *guérra*, 'war'), the name given to the war carried on in Spain by irregular bands of peasants, &c., during the French invasion of 1810–14. These bands, of which the most famous was Mina's, that afterwards did good service under Wellington, were at first called *partidas*, but were afterwards spoken of as guerillas, a name now applied to irregular troops carrying on a desultory struggle.

Guér'in, Pierre Narcisse, Baron, a French painter, born at Paris, May 13, 1774. He served in his youth in the army, and first became known in 1796 by his 'Corps de Brutus rapporté à Rome.' He gained great popularity, was successful as a teacher, was made a baron in 1829, and died at Rome, July 16, 1833. Among his chief works are 'Phèdre et Hippolyte' (1802), 'Orphée au Tombeau d'Eurydice' (1802), 'Andromaque' (1810), 'Didon et Énée' (1817), 'Clytemnestre' (1817). G. belonged to the French Classical school. His style was cold and often theatrical, but his colour is pure and harmonious, and his designs are marked by great taste in the details and skill in the grouping.

Guern'sey, the most westerly, and, next to Jersey, the largest of the Channel Islands (q. v.), is 69 miles S.E. of Start Point, in Devonshire, and 46 S.W. of Cherbourg. Area, 25 sq. miles; pop. (1871) 30,667. It is 9 miles long and 6 broad, and is difficult of approach for rocks and currents. The surface is flat and fertile in the N., but rises in the S. to rocky eminences overhanging the sea. Though subject to Britain, G. has its own legislature. Its climate is singularly fine, and its inhabitants, who speak a Norman-French dialect, are intelligent and thrifty. St. Peter's, the only town, is in the S.E.

Guerra'ra, El, or **Gerra'ra,** a town S. of Algeria, on the river Zegerin, in the oasis of Wady-Nizab, 40 miles N.E. of Ghardaia. It is encircled with walls, and has a large trade in gold-dust, ivory, cotton, ostrich feathers, horses, cattle, &c. Pop. 14,000.

Guerrazz'i, Francesco Domenico, an Italian statesman and lawyer, was born at Leghorn in 1805. He studied law at Pisa, but early engaged in literature, and produced a number of patriotic tales bearing on Italian politics. After suffering imprisonment for his republican opinions, he was elected deputy in 1848, and on the flight of the Grand Duke of Tuscany was appointed triumvir with Montanelli and Mazoni. Soon after he was proclaimed dictator, but on the restoration of the ducal power was, in spite of his masterly defence, *Apologia della Vita Politica di G.* (1851), imprisoned for three years, and condemned to banishment for life. He then betook himself to Corsica, but was enabled by the results of the Franco-Sardinian war with Austria to renew his political career, and after the establishment of the Italian kingdom was repeatedly elected to Parliament. G. died September 25, 1873. Among his works are *Battaglio di Benevento, L'Assedio di Firenze, Isabella Orsini, Veronica Cybo, Nuovi Tartufi, Beatrice Cenci, Torre di Nonza, Fides, Il Bucaniel Muro,* and *Il Secolo che Muove.* His works are full of noble imagination, ardour, and eloquence, often shot through with satire and humour in a manner that greatly resembles Byron.

Gues'clin, Bertrand du, Comte de Longueville, and Constable of France, a famous French soldier, was the son of a poor Breton gentleman, and born at Rennes about 1320. He was distinguished in his youth for skill in the tilt-yard, and early became known as a fearless and able captain of free-lances. He supported Charles Comte de Blois against Jean de Montfort in a struggle for the dukedom of Brittany, but in 1364 was beaten and captured at Auray by an inferior English force under Sir John Chandos. Ransomed by Charles V., he drove Pedro the Cruel from Aragon, but was utterly routed and captured by the Black Prince at Najara in 1367. Again ransomed, he defeated Pedro in 1369, and raised Henry of Trastamare to the throne, being in return made Duke of Molina and Constable of Castile. In 1369 he was appointed Constable of France, and began to clear the country of the English, whom he never beat in a great battle, but whom he adroitly harassed and out-manœuvred until their strength was utterly broken. G. died while besieging Château-Neuf de Randor in Languedoc, July 3, 1380. He was one of the chief instruments in building up France, but his character has been generally misrepresented. He was not a high-souled chivalrous warrior; on the contrary, more than any other man he helped to destroy chivalry in France, and make war a mercenary pursuit. He was rude and ignorant, insolent to the nobles, but kind and generous to the poor and to his free-lances; a marvel of strength and ferocious courage, and a singularly wily and dexterous tactician. See Cuvelier's *La Vie du vaillant Bertrand du G.*, a metrical chronicle published by M. Charrière (Par. 1839); De Berville's *Histoire de G.* (2 vols. Par. 1767); and Kitchin's *History of France* (1873).

Gueux ('beggars'), the name given in scorn to the confederate nobles of the Low Countries on the occasion (5th April 1566) of their presenting a remonstrance to the Regent Margaret, Duchess of Parma, against the despotic policy of their sovereign, Philip II. of Spain, and particularly against the proposed introduction of the Inquisition into the country. A great gathering was held three nights after, under the presidency of Henry Count Brederode. 'They call us beggars,' said the Count; 'let us accept the name. We will contend with the Inquisition, but remain loyal to the King, even till compelled to wear the beggar's sack.' This was enthusiastically agreed to, and an appropriate costume was fixed on, the G. soon appearing in the streets with common felt hats on their heads, and beggars' pouches and bowls at their sides. After a long and strenuous opposition to the policy of Philip, they were finally crushed and destroyed by the overpowering force of Alva. See Motley's *Rise of the Dutch Republic* (Lond. 1856).

Gugliel'mi, Pietro, an Italian composer, was born at Massa-Carrara in May 1727. Instructed first by his father, and then by Durante of Naples, he wrote operas from 1755, making a successful beginning in the Italian towns. After spending some time in Vienna, Dresden, &c., he went in 1767 to London, where he remained till 1772. Five years later he returned to Naples. From 1793 to his death, 19th November 1804, he was maestro-di-capella of St. Peter's at Rome. Fétis (*Biographical Dictionary of Musicians*) enumerates seventy-eight operas, sacred and secular, written by G.

Guian'a (Fr. *Guyane*, Span. *Guayana*, Port. *Guianna*), the name of an extensive tract of country in the N.E. of S. America, extending along the coast of the Atlantic from the mouth of the Amazon to that of the Orinoco, in lat. 8° 40′ N.–3° 30′ S., and long. 50°–68° W. It is divided politically between Brazil, Venezuela, Great Britain, France, and the Netherlands. Brazil and Venezuela have incorporated their portions in provinces. Its extreme length is 1090 miles, its breadth 710, and its distribution between the three European Powers is as follows:—

	Area in sq. miles.	Population.	Chief towns.
Great Britain, 1874 . .	85,425	215,200	Georgetown.
Netherlands, 1875 . .	46,049	69,834	Paramaribo.
France, 1872 . . .	46,856	24,171	Cayenne.
	178,330	309,205	

There is little geographical diversity between the various divisions. Along the seaboard stretches a belt of low land, from 10 to 40 miles in width, with a soil of bluish clay enriched by vegetable matter and impregnated by marine salts. When drained this soil sinks for nearly a foot, and requires to be protected against the inroads of the sea by dykes. Much alluvium is brought down by the numerous rivers, of which the most important are Essequibo (q. v.), Demerara (q. v.), Berbice (q. v.), Corentyn (q. v.), the boundary between British and Dutch G., the Maroni, that between French and Dutch G., and the Gyapok, forming a boundary of Fronch G. on the E. The rivers are greatly impeded by rapids and cataracts; the Kaiateur waterfall, first described by Barrington Brown, has a drop of 822 feet and a width of 269, and is splendidly set off by all the leafy wealth of the tropics. Advancing inland, the alluvial coast flats give place to sandy uplands, stretching away in the S.W. to the little-known mountain ranges of the Sierra Pacaraima and Sierra Parime. The chief rocks of this rugged region are granite, gneiss, and white quartz. The abundant presence of mica in the quartz gives to the hills in sunshine a glittering appearance, and to this peculiarity has been ascribed the belief in the mythical El Dorado (q. v.), or 'golden land,' that was here sought by Francisco Orellana and the ill-fated Raleigh. According to the report of Schomburgk, published in Leipsic in 1848, the region is somewhat barren of minerals. In British G. is the unique rock plateau of Roraima, which is inaccessible, resembles a vast fortification surrounded by glacis, and is crowned by forests and drained by cataracts. The sculptured rocks in the interior of G. are supposed to relate to the history of an ancient people. G. has a hot, moist climate, the mean temperature being 81° F. The two rainy seasons cover the months of June, July, and August, and December, January, and February. The climatic changes are sudden, and are generally accompanied by violent hurricanes and thunderstorms. G. is only cultivated along the coast flats and for a short distance up several of the rivers. The chief products are sugar, timber, cacao, rum, gums, balsams, drugs, cloves, pepper, rice, and maize; cotton and coffee, formerly grown to a considerable extent, have been abandoned for sugar since the introduction of improved machinery. In French and Dutch G. gold is found in some quantity, and of late years its pursuit has been taking the place of agriculture. The various kinds of woods exported are among the most valuable in commerce; the timber of the gigantic mira tree, which attains a height of 150 feet, is said to be as durable as teak. Among the fruits of G. are the banana, pine-apple, guava, &c. Chief of its gorgeous flowers is the *Victoria regia*, one of the largest of water-lilies. The most notable of the animals are the 'Warra caba' tiger, tapir, ant-eaters, and various turtles, besides anacondas, alligators, iguanas, and several poisonous snakes. There is a great variety of excellent fish, and birds of splendid plumage abound, including the parrots, humming-birds, flamingoes.

It is not known whether Columbus ever landed on the shores of G., but the Spaniards had certainly settled in the region as early as the 16th c., for they opposed the entrance of the Dutch in 1580. The Dutch, however, effected a settlement on the Essequibo in 1602, and the French near the Gyapok in 1633. After much internal disturbance, and frequent raids of the French, part of the Dutch possessions, at the desire of the colonists, was transferred to Britain in 1796. At the peace of Amiens (1802) the colonies were handed over to the Batavian Republic, only to be restored to Britain in 1803.

British Guiana, the most westerly of the three colonies, lies between Venezuela on the W. and Dutch G. on the E. It is divided into the counties Essequibo, Demerara, and Berbice, and its chief towns are Georgetown (q. v.) and New Amsterdam (q. v.). Of its inhabitants (1871), 113,570 were born in British G.; 13,385 in the West India Islands; 7925 in Madeira, Azores, &c.; 1444 in Europe; 7541 are immigrant coolies from Africa; 2535 from Madras; 40,146 from Calcutta; and 6295 from China. The aboriginal Indians, who are not included in the census returns, are variously estimated at from 7000 to 20,000. The colony, which has been making steady progress under British sovereignty, in 1871 had a revenue of £379,647, an expenditure of £338,053, and a public debt, in process of reduction, of £512,865. In 1875 the value of the exports to Great Britain alone amounted to £1,911,981, and of the imports from Great Britain to £852,977. The value of (unrefined) sugar exported was £1,430,861 (1,210,193 cwt.); of rum, £394,044 (3,624,294 proof gallons); of woods, £55,024. Of the imports, the value of cotton was £106,993; of iron, £52,695; of machinery, £63,964, and of manure, £57,477. The total exports (1871) amounted to £2,748,720, the imports to £1,897,184. A submarine cable is (1877) being laid down between Pará in Brazil and Demerara, with stations at Cayenne and Paramaribo, thus connecting the colonies by telegraph with Europe. The political constitution of the colony is little altered since the time of the Dutch. The governor presides over the legislative body, and over the 'combined court,' which meets annually to pass the tax ordinance, and which includes the 'college of financial representatives.' The latter body, comprising six members, is popularly elected; of the legislative body, five members are nominated by the crown, and five by the 'college of electors,' which again is returned by electoral franchise. The judicial system is still partially based on the Roman code, but English criminal law was introduced in 1846. The churches maintained by public funds are Presbyterian, Episcopalian, Roman Catholic, and Wesleyan; there are also voluntary missions. See *Reisen der Brüder Schomburgk in Britisch. G.* (Frankf. 1852), and *Canoe and Camp Life in British G.* by C. Barrington Brown, late Government surveyor (Lond. 1876).

Dutch Guiana or *Surinam*, lies between British and French G., is bounded by the rivers Corentyn and Maroni. It is called by the Dutch Surinam, from its principal river. The population comprised in 1875, 706 Europeans, 3779 immigrants, and 45,363 natives, exclusive of the aborigines and of the Maroons, descendants of runaway slaves, who live in the interior. In 1875 the value of the exports was £200,778; of imports, £260,451. The trade is chiefly with Great Britain, Holland, and the United States. The sugar trade has greatly fallen off since the emancipation of the slaves in 1863; the field-labourers, who are greatly deficient in number, now mainly come from China, the W. Indies, and India. Gold diggings and washings have become so general as to bring to the treasury a considerable revenue for the granting of 'prospects' at 2d. a hectare, but the result till 1876 had only covered the preliminary outlay and daily expenses. The colony is under a governor-general and council of native freeholders. There is full religious toleration; the labouring classes mostly belong to the Moravian and Roman Catholic Churches. In 1875 the revenue was £70,938, the expenditure £101,085, and the subsidy from the mother country £30,147. The chief towns are Paramaribo (the capital), Batavia, Groningen, and Nassau. See Palgrave's *Dutch G.* (Lond. 1876).

French Guiana, or *Cayenne*, the most easterly of the colonies, is bounded by the navigable rivers Maroni and Oyapok. The low alluvial lands are in part covered with forests of mango-trees and palms, and with swamps formed by the overflowing of the rivers. The climate is less oppressive here on account of the trade winds. G. has a rich soil, well adapted for cultivation; but agriculture has of late years been almost abandoned for gold-digging. In 1874 the exports amounted to £191,411, of which gold formed £163,268, and cabinet woods £15,237; the imports to £274,738. In 1874, 1808 coolies were brought from Calcutta, Pondicherry, and Carical to work at the mines. Almost the whole of the settled part of the colony from N. to S. is taken up for gold-seeking; the richest and most populous field is Sinnamary. In 1874 the declared export of gold was 81,156 oz., but much more was smuggled out of the colony. The revenue of G. in 1874 was £40,434; the expenditure, £37,026. The receipts for concessions of land for gold-exploring alone was £7821. G. includes several islands, of which the chief are Cayenne, Le Grand Connétable, and Le Petit Connétable. Cayenne (q. v.), the capital, is on the island of the same name. The colony is under a privy council and a governor.

Guicciardi'ni, Francesco, one of the greatest Italian historians, was born at Florence, 6th March 1482. He early distinguished himself as a law-student and eloquent advocate, and in 1512 was sent by the Signoria on an embassy to Ferdinand of Aragon, and in 1515 was chosen to confer with Leo X., who took him into his favour, and made him governor of Reggio, Modena, and Parma. Clement VII. appointed him viceroy of Romagna in 1523, and lieutenant-general of the Papal troops in 1526. In 1531 he was appointed governor of Bologna, and in 1534 he returned to Florence as an adherent of the Medici. Mainly through his influence Cosmo de Medici became ruler of

Florence, and as Cosmo immediately afterwards discarded him, G. retired from public affairs and devoted himself to writing history. He died, aged fifty-eight, 22d May 1540. G. is a frigid, astute cynic, but ranks among the best of historians. His *Istoria d' Italia* (1561–64) is prolix and cumbrous in style, G. lamely following the manner of Livy; but the *Istoria Fiorentine* is far more succinct and thoughtful, and gives a peculiarly valuable analysis of Italian politics, and a peculiarly vivid picture of Italian society in the writer's times. It deals with Florentine history from 1378 to 1509, and is pregnant with calm and ripe reflection. The *Reggimento di Firenze* is a masterly treatise on the best form of government for Florence, G. declaring in favour of an oligarchy. His *Ricordi Politici e Civili* are a collection of occasional remarks, many of which have a truly proverbial terseness and point. An edition of G.'s works was published by Rosini (10 vols. Pisa, 1819). See Rosini's *Saggio sulle Azioni e sulle Opere di F. G.* (Pisa, 1822), and Symonds' *Renaissance in Italy* (Lond. 1875).

Gui'cowar (*gaekwar*, 'a cowherd'), the hereditary title of one of the great Mahratta families, who rule at Baroda (q. v.) in E. India, so called from the caste, of the founder, Pilaji G., who rose to eminence by the Mahratta characteristics of valour and treachery, and first occupied Baroda in 1730. In 1755 his grandson wrested the province of Guzerat from the Mohammedans, as the nominal feudatory of the Peishwa (q. v.). In 1805 the G. accepted a treaty with the British, by which he bound himself to support a subsidiary force, and to enter into a regular alliance. See BARODA, and Grant Duff's *History of the Mahrattas* (Lond. 1826).

Gui'do, Carlo Alessandro, an Italian poet born at Pavia in 1650, won the favour of the Duke of Pavia, and afterwards of Christina, Queen of Sweden, who met him at Rome, worked with him on a pastoral drama, and received him into her literary academy. He died at Rome, June 10, 1712. G. was a sweet lyrical poet, writing with Horatian finish, and helped to check the euphuism introduced by Marini. Among his works are *Poesie Liriche* (1681); *Amalsunta in Italia* (1681); *Endimione*, a pastoral (1692); *La Dafne* (1692); *Lei Omelie di N. S. Clemente spigeate in versi* (1712). A complete edition of his works was issued at Padua in 1818.

Guido of Arez'zo, a Benedictine monk devoted to music, flourished about A.D. 1020. Scarcely anything else is known about him than that he was a native of Arezzo in Tuscany, and that he settled at Pomposa in Ferrara. For many centuries a host of musical inventions were loosely and fancifully attributed to him. G. certainly wrought a needed reform by discovering a *method* of teaching church-singing. He made use of a simple instrument called the *monochord*, and of the mnemonic syllables *ut, re, mi, fa, sol, la*, already associated with a certain melody, for teaching correct intonation. He wrote the *Micrologus*, the *Antiphonary*, and other theoretical works, which still exist in MS. See Burney's *History of Music*, vol. ii., and Fétis' *Biographie des Musiciens* (Par. 1862).

Guido Reni, one of the chief Bolognese painters, was the son of a musician, and was born at Bologna in 1575. When a youth he was trained by Denis Calvaert, a Dutch artist then in Bologna, in whose school he is said to have studied the works of Dürer. He afterwards joined the school of the Caracci, and on visiting Rome imitated Caravaggio. At Rome G. soon became famous, and was employed by several popes in decorating chapels, painting portraits, &c., but having quarrelled with the treasurer of Urban VIII. respecting the price of a picture, he returned to his native city, whence he was soon recalled to the capital. After a brief residence in Naples he taught a large school in Bologna, but became involved in debt through his passion for gambling. G. died at Bologna in 1642. Among his works are the famous 'Aurora' of the Rospigliosi Palace—his masterpiece—the 'Portrait of Beatrice Cenci,' 'Rape of Helen,' 'Fortune,' 'Michael Vanquishing Satan,' 'Crucifixion of St. Peter,' &c. He excelled in religious and pathetic subjects. His early productions show the influence of Caravaggio in their violent contrasts of light and shade; but his later works, though wanting in vigour and expression, are marked by exquisite sweetness, harmony, and grace. G.'s numerous paintings are scattered through the great European collections, and there are several in the National Gallery, London.

Guienne' (a corruption of Aquitaine), one of the thirty-two old French provinces, lay on the Lower Garonne, and comprised the modern departments of Gironde, Lot, Dordogne, Aveyron, with portions of Tarn-et-Garonne and Lot-et-Garonne. It was part of Aquitaine, and was of great importance as 'the English doorway into France' during the Hundred Years' War, when its nobles clung to England from dread of French aggrandisement, and its merchants because they were chiefly engaged in English trade. G. belonged to England from 1154 to 1451. See Kitchin's *History of France* (1873).

Guignes, Joseph de, a celebrated French Orientalist, was born at Pontoise, 19th October 1721. He studied Oriental languages, especially Chinese, under Étienne Fourmont, with such success that on the death of the latter he was, at the age of twenty, appointed to the vacant post of secretary and interpreter for Oriental languages to the King of France. In 1757 he became Professor of Syriac in the Collége Royale de France. His great work, the *Histoire Générale des Huns, Turcs, Mogols et autres Tartares Occidentaux* (published at Paris 1756–58, in 5 vols. 4to), is a monument of profound and accurate learning. He published also a life of Fourmont (1747), and contributed many articles to the journals. He also edited *L'Éloge de Moukden* (1770) and *Chou-King*, one of the Chinese sacred books. He was reduced to great distress by the French Revolution, and died at Paris, March 22, 1800. His son, **Chr. Louis Joseph de G.** (born 1759, died 1845), was also an eminent Orientalist, his chief work being his *Dictionnaire Chinois-Français et Latin* (Par. 1813).

Guilandi'na, a genus of Leguminous shrubs, embracing few species, found in warm countries. *G. Bonduc* and *G. Bonducella* are the best known. The seeds of the former, which are yellow, and of the latter lead-coloured, are very hard and used as beads; they are popularly known as nicker-nuts; they are tonic, and yield an oil which is used medicinally in India.

Guild'ford, the county town of Surrey, England, on the Wey, in a hollow of the N. Downs, 30 miles S.W. of London by railway. It is a quaint old town, ranging in long narrow streets along the E. side of the Wey, which is here crossed by a bridge of five arches. Besides the fine ruins of a Norman castle, G. has a charitable hospital (Archbishop Abbot's), an old church of St. Mary (restored in 1863), and another of the Holy Trinity dating from the 18th c., a royal free grammar-school founded by Edward VI., a townhall, a cornmarket, a county hall and assize court (1862), and a county hospital (1866). It is noted for its trade in 'Surrey wheats,' and has corn, paper, and powder mills, iron-foundries, breweries, &c., cattle, lamb, and pig markets, horse and sheep fairs, and sends one member to Parliament. Six newspapers are published weekly. Pop. (1871) 9801. G., formerly *Guldford* or *Gyldeford*, was bequeathed by Ælfred to his nephew Æthelwald, and under the Confessor it ranked among the royal demesnes. An occasional residence of the English kings, it was bestowed by Charles I. on the Earls of Annandale, and eventually passed to the Onslow family.

Guildhall, the townhall or hôtel-de-ville of the city of London, at the foot of King Street, Cheapside, was originally built 1411–31, was almost totally destroyed by the great fire of London, 1666, was rebuilt in a debased style by Dance in 1789, and restored in better taste in 1865–68. The fine open timber roof of the Great Hall was constructed in 1867 at the cost of £3000. Several police and other courts are held here, and here the Lord Mayor and Sheriffs of the city are elected. The famous Lord Mayor's dinner is held in the Great Hall annually on the 9th November. The Hall is 153 feet long by 48 feet wide, and 55 feet high. The E. and W. windows are filled with fine stained glass, and the great, hollow, wooden figures of Gog and Magog flank the W. window. In this chief apartment, as well as in the numerous rooms around, are many interesting works in painting and sculpture. The very handsome Free Library, Reading-Room, and Museum, form a suite of noble halls, built 1871–72, and presented by the Corporation to the City of London.

Guilds, or **Gilds** (Old Eng. *gild*, 'a money payment'), were voluntary associations to maintain order and bestow mutual aid and defence, formed in many European towns during the middle ages. They closely resemble the *collegia opificum*—corporations of artisans who united for mutual aid under the later

Roman empire—but the attempt to trace the English G. to a Roman source is quite fallacious. G. arose in England partly as a protection against feudalism, partly because society had grown too complex to rest on the old Teutonic family union, about the end of the 9th and beginning of the 10th c. The earliest of these fraternities in England were formed for religious purposes, each member contributing to keep up the regular guild feasts, to defray the burial of a guild brother, and to have masses sung for his soul. From the religious G. sprung the more complex *frith G.* or peace G., which made regulations to protect the members against theft and violence. London had a strong *frith gild* in the time of Æthelstan, organised into parties of ten, each under a leader. A third form of G. was the *ceapmanne gilde*, or merchant G., which came into existence at least as early as the Conquest. These at first only regulated the trade of the town, but gradually engrossed various municipal rights, first superintending public works as a supplementary body to the municipal government, and finally holding the position of the modern town-council. Membership in a *ceapmanne gilde* became indispensable to one seeking full burghership or right to trade in a town. They won valuable commercial privileges from the king and nobles, and separated themselves from the poor artisans, who united into the latest and most democratic G., the crafts G., which laid down strict rules as to the quality of work, the rate of wages, and strove to check competition among workmen. These crafts G. grew in influence from the 11th c. onwards, and became powerful rivals to the merchant G. The royal sanction was necessary to give them corporate legal rights, and from the number of fines which the kings imposed on them, they seem to have been viewed with great jealousy. The work of the *gegildan*, or guild-brothers, was inspected by a committee of artisans, disobedience to whose orders was punished by fine or expulsion, the last penalty taking away a man's right to trade. A villein who gained admission into a guild, if he were unclaimed by his lord for a year and a day, became free, his guild-membership giving him a social standing much above other freedmen. Though the different G. were long hindered from uniting by the varying social position of their members, they gradually began to coalesce, and thus forced the towns into compact, well-organised communities. The English G., some of which corresponded to the modern club, others to the modern town-council, and others to the modern trade union, were distinguished from the French *communes* by the social element which characterised them all, their members holding a festive meeting generally every month in the *hans-hus* or guild-hall. They helped to forward the political influence of the towns, but they engrossed, says Mr. Stubbs, many of the old rights of the people. They became very wealthy, and the property of many of them was confiscated by Henry VIII. The law by which no one could trade in a town unless he were a member of a guild was only formally abolished in 1835. The name guild is still kept up in some places in Scotland, and the dean of guild is the second municipal magistrate in a Scottish burgh. G. were formed in the German towns during the 10th c., and at first had no political influence, but afterwards struggled against the nobles. In this strife the G. were mainly successful, winning a share in the government of most towns, and even establishing a purely democratic rule in some places. During the 15th c. the German artisans joined themselves in literary G., which met to compose, sing, and recite verses. (See MEISTERSÄNGER.) At Florence, in the middle ages, all the trades were associated into twenty-one *arti* or G., each of which had a mansion where the brethren met to elect officers, settle accounts, &c. These *arti* originated in 1282, when the people overthrew the nobles, and no one could be a burgher of Florence unless he or one of his ancestors had entered a Florentine guild, whether or not he practised its particular trade. G. were peculiarly numerous and thriving during the middle ages in Catalonia, where trade, which the Castilians looked upon as degrading, was considered highly honourable, and where the various craftsmen were banded into companies, probably in imitation of the Italian *arti*, Catalonia having then close commercial intercourse with Italy. See Brentano, *On the History of G.* (1870), and Stubbs, *Constitutional History of England* (1875–76).

Guiliel'ma, a small genus of palms found in S. America. *G. speciosa* is the peach palm, largely grown on the banks of the Amazon by the Indians for food. The fruit, about the size of a fowl's egg, contains a quantity of starchy matter, and is either roasted or boiled. A beverage is also made from the fruit by fermentation.

Guille'mot (*Uria*), the name given to various species of Natatorial birds belonging to the genus *Uria*, which is included in the family of the *Alcidæ* or auks, and in the special subfamily of the *Urinæ*, in which the bill is of moderate length, the tip scooped, and the nostrils contained in a groove. The hinder toe is wanting. The wings are pointed, and the first quill is the longest. The tail is short and rounded. The tarsi have small scales. The common G. (*U. Troile*) is the best-known species. It occurs very plentifully on the northern coasts of Britain, and is of a dull black colour above, the secondary wing feathers being tipped with white. The under parts are white, the bill black, and the legs and toes brown. The average length is 18 inches. The G. lays a single egg, the colour of which varies, but the prevailing tint is a bluish green with reddish-brown markings. The bird swims and dives well, and is said to carry its young into the water on its back. The black G. (*U. grylli*) is of smaller size than the common G., and of a black colour, with a white mark on each wing. The under parts are white in winter. This species is common in the Arctic regions, and occurs very plentifully, like the common G., in N. America. The eggs number three, and are deposited on bare rocks, &c., without the protection of a nest. The eggs of the G. are gathered in great quantities in Newfoundland and Labrador. In summer the G. appears to migrate to the Arctic regions.

Guilloche (Fr. *guillochis*), in classical architecture, is an ornament formed by bands or fillets which intertwine regularly.

Guill'otine, a machine used for decapitation during the French Revolution, and so called from Dr. Joseph Ignace Guillotin, who, from humane motives, counselled its adoption. It consisted of two posts, joined by a cross-beam, and with grooves in which a heavy blade with an oblique edge fell on the neck of the condemned. A similar machine, known as the *Mannaia* in Italy, as the *Maiden* in Scotland, and as the *Demoiselle* in France, had been used to decapitate criminals throughout various parts of Europe several centuries before the adoption of the G. during the Terror.

Guilt'y. This is the verdict of the jury in England when a crime charged has been found proved. If the crime is found to be not proved, the verdict is *Not Guilty*. In Scotland there is a third verdict—*Not Proven*. This may be given when the jury think that strong ground of suspicion has been shown against the person charged, but not sufficient to convict him. Its effect is to leave a stigma on his character.

Guimar'ães, one of the oldest towns of Portugal, in the province of Entre Douro e Minho, beautifully situated in a fertile vale, girt by woody hills, 37 miles N.E. of Oporto. It has a cathedral of 1385, a Flamboyant castle of the 12th c., and an old Dominican convent with ornate cloisters. The walls, mounted by pointed parapets, now enclose only the older part of the town, with its narrow streets, picturesque Moorish buildings, and quaint red verandahs and balconies. In the vicinity are sulphureous springs, ranging from 91° to 120° in temperature. G. has leather and paper industries, and an export trade in dried plums, figs, &c. Pop. 8000. G. was the residence of Count Henriquez, and the birthplace of his son, the first King of Portugal, Alfonso Henriquez (q. v.), in 1110.

Guin'ea, the general name given to a tract of country which stretches along the west coast of Africa from Cape Verga on the southern boundary of Senegambia to Cape Negro, S. of Benguela. It is divided into two portions—Upper G., lying to the N., and Lower G., to the S., of the equator. The coast-line is upwards of 2000 miles in length. The shores, especially of Upper G., are low and barren, and round the mouths of the Niger, Congo, and other rivers, extremely unhealthy; but towards the interior the country rises into fertile plateaux, luxuriant in vegetation, and yielding maize, rice, yams, tobacco, sugar, coffee, palm-oil, manive, banana, and other tropical products. Minerals are abundant, but are at present beyond the reach of the European powers that have established colonies along the coast. Lower G. comprises the territories of Loango (q. v.), Congo (q. v.), Angola (q. v.), and Benguela (q. v.), all but the first of which are nominally under the rule of Portugal. Upper G. includes Sierra Leone (q. v.) (English), the republic of Liberia (q. v.), the Ivory Coast, the Gold Coast (q. v.) (English), the kingdom of Ashanti (q. v.), in the interior, the Slave Coast (q. v.), with English ports, and the kingdom of Dahomey (q. v.); to the N. the coasts of Benin and Biafra; and to the S. the French settlement at the mouth of the Gaboon (q. v.).

The Gulf of Guinea is a great inlet of the Southern Atlantic, washing part of the shores of the foregoing territory. The outlying delta of the Niger forms two secondary gulfs, the Bight of Benin (q. v.) and the Bight of Biafra (q. v.). The chief islands in the Gulf of G. are Fernando Po, Princes Island, and St. Thomas.

Guinea, an English gold coin, first issued in 1662, of gold brought from G. (whence the name), and originally bearing the impression of an elephant. It weighed 129½ grains, and contained 118·7 grains of pure gold. It was superseded in 1817 by the sovereign, but the name is still used as a synonym for twenty-one shillings.

Guinea-Corn, a common name for species of *Sorghum*, cultivated as cereal grasses in the S. of Europe, Africa, and India, where they are called Durra (q. v.). See also MILLET.

Guinea-Fowl, or **Pintado** (*Numida meleagris*), a genus of Rasorial or Gallinaceous birds, domesticated in England, and originally inhabiting Africa. The genus is included in the *Meleagrinæ* or turkey sub-family. The bill is strong, and the nostrils large, oval, and partly covered by membrane. The fifth quill is the longest, and the tarsi are covered with broad scales. The outer toe is longer than the inner. The G.-F. is common in most poultry yards, and bears a close resemblance to the turkey in form and habits. It seems to prefer marshy lands, and its powers of flight are by no means great. The eggs number from ten to twenty or more, and are yellowish red spotted with dark-brown spots of small size. They have a very tough shell. The colour of the G.-F. is a kind of slaty blue, variegated with small white spots. The head is ornamented with a hard protuberance or 'casque,' and the wattles are very prominent, being purplish red in the males and red in the females. A white or pale-brown variety of the G.-F. is common; and a second species, the crested G.-F. (*N. cristata*), having a blue-black plumage, is also known.

Guinea-Grass, a species of *Panicum* cultivated in warm countries as a forage grass. See MILLET.

Guinea-Pepper, an old commercial name for Grains of Paradise (q. v.), otherwise called in Western Africa *melegueta* (*melegette, mallaguetta, maniguette*) pepper. Formerly the name was sometimes applied to the pods of Capsicum (q. v.).

Guinea-Pig. See CAVY.

Guinea-Worm (*Dracunculus* or *Filaria Medinensis*), a genus of *Scolecida* (q. v.), not allied to the true worms, and included in the section *Nematelina* or round worms. The genus *Dracunculus* belongs to the order *Nematoda*, in which a distinct mouth, alimentary canal, and anus are present. The sexes are distinct, and the males, curiously enough, are not only smaller than the females, but are very seldom met with. Thus in the case of the G.-W. the curious fact is recorded that no male worm has ever been observed, all the specimens which have been examined being found to be impregnated females, within which the young were contained in great numbers. The habits of the G.-W. are very peculiar. It inhabits the *cellular tissue* of the human body, and most frequently selects for its residence the cellular tissue of the feet and legs. In this situation it grows to a length of several feet, its presence being attended by severe symptoms of pain, swelling, and inflammation, while emaciation is not an uncommon result. After a period, in some cases of over a year, but in other cases of a few weeks, the G.-W. appears to attain its maturity, and the head-extremity of the animal projects from a little sore which forms. The negroes are skilful in removing the worm, the method practised consisting in winding the body of the animal slowly and gradually round a reel or similar object, the great care of the operator being to avoid breaking the worm. The G.-W. comes to the surface of the skin for the purpose of getting rid of its young. The body is thread-like in conformation, and of white colour. No external aperture of the reproductive organs can be discovered, and the manner in which the young are produced within the body of the parent has led to the supposition that it is by a process of internal *Gemmation* (q. v.), or budding. The G.-W. occurs in India, Persia, Egypt, Abyssinia, &c., and appears to be most frequently observed after the prevalence of rains and floods, by means of which it may be presumed the ova or eggs are widely distributed. The development of the G.-W. has yet to be fully determined, and the elucidation of this subject would undoubtedly lead to the determination of its exact reproductive history. The young G.-W. has a thread-like tail, and most probably exists as a 'tank worm'—a form very common in water-cisterns and tanks in India. Dr. Bastian of London thinks that the G.-W. is merely an accidental parasite, and that formerly it was a free or non-parasitic Nematoid. By many authorities, ancient and modern, it is believed to represent the 'fiery serpents' of Scripture.

Guingamp, a town of France, department of the Côtes-du-Nord, on the Trieux, 21 miles N.W. of St. Brieux. It has a college, two old churches, and several tanneries and water-mills. The chief trade is in linen. Pop. (1872) 7045. G. was formerly the capital of the duchy of Penthièvre.

Guine'gate, Battle of, was fought August 16, 1513, at G. near Tournai, Hainault, between the English under Henry VIII. and the French, who were defeated and fled so hastily that the engagement was styled the *Battle of the Spurs.*

Guis'borough, a town in the North Riding of Yorkshire, England, at the foot of the Cleveland Hills, 5 miles from the mouth of the Tees. It is a station on a branch line of the North-Eastern Railway. G. has roperies, tanneries, and brickworks; and ironstone mining is carried on in the neighbourhood. Pop. (1871) 5202. Some ruins are still extant of a famous monastery built in 1119 by Robert de Brus.

Guis'card, Robert, a famous Norman adventurer, was the sixth of the twelve sons of a Norman baron, Tancred of Hauteville in Lower Normandy, and was born in 1015. About 1053 he followed his brothers to Southern Italy, where he distinguished himself as a military leader, and succeeded his brother Humphrey as Count of Apulia in 1057. Pope Nicholas II. made him gonfalonier of the Church, and gave him permission to conquer the parts of Italy held by the Saracens and Greeks. After adding Calabria to his possessions, he invaded Sicily, and, aided by his brother Roger, defeated the Saracens at Enna in 1061, and founded the kingdom of Sicily, which lasted till 1860. In 1081 he entered Epirus, and overthrew the Byzantine forces at Durazzo in the following year; but was recalled when marching on Constantinople by the tidings that Heinrich IV. had invaded Italy. Returning to Italy, G. drove back the Emperor, and freed Hildebrand, who was shut up in the castle of St. Angelo. In 1084 he won a naval victory over the Byzantines and Venetians off Corfu, and died at Cephalonia, while again advancing on Constantinople, July 17, 1085. G. was the beau-ideal of Norman knighthood, combining the highest chivalrous daring with admirable military skill. His career had grave historic results, notably from his establishment of a Sicilian kingdom, and opportune vindication of the papal against the imperial power in the chief crisis of the struggle. See Galfridus a Mala Terra's *De Gestis Roberti Guiscardi*, and Gualtier d'Arc's *Histoire des Conquêtes des Normands en Italie, en Sicile, et en Grèce* (Par. 1830).

Guise, a town in the department of Aisne, France, on the left bank of the Oise, 13 miles W.N.W. of Veroins. It was formerly strongly fortified, and has a castle built in 1649. Shawls, wool, and cotton are manufactured, and there are iron and copper foundries. Pop. (1872) 5659. G. has been repeatedly besieged in medieval and modern times. In 1443 it was handed over to Charles of Anjou; it afterwards passed to a branch of the house of Lorraine, who took from it their title of Duc de G.

Guise, the name of a famous French family which greatly influenced the history of France in the 16th c., its members rising to power not so much by the extension of their lands as by their important services to the crown, their ability, courage, and unscrupulous advocacy of the Roman Church. The chief representatives of the house were:—**Claude**, 1st **Duc de G.**, fifth son of René II., Duc de Lorraine, born in 1496. He served with distinction in the Italian campaigns of François I., married

Antoinette de Bourbon in 1513, and drove back the German Imperialists who invaded Champagne in 1523. He became Comte de G., an estate which the house of Lorraine held in Picardy, in 1520, and was in 1527 made Duc de G. He fought in Flanders in 1542, treated the Protestants of Elsass with great cruelty, and died at Joinville, April 14, 1550. His daughter, **Marie**, became the wife of James V., King of Scotland, and the mother of Mary Queen of Scots. This alliance greatly strengthened the power of the Guises.—**François**, 2d **Duc de G.**, son of the above, was born February 17, 1519. He soon became famous as a general—the Spaniards called him 'the great captain'—and in 1552–53 held Metz for two months against Karl V., who was forced to raise the siege. This successful defence gave him a European renown. He drove back an army of Spaniards and Flemings which had entered France, and in 1558 seized Calais, the last of the English continental possessions. The accession to the French throne of François I., the husband of Mary Queen of Scots, greatly advanced the influence of the Guises, and François was looked on as the head of the Romish party in France. Along with his brother Charles the cardinal, G. became guardian of the weak king, banished his rival Montmorency, dismissed Diana of Poictiers, persecuted the Huguenots with vindictive zeal, and sought to establish the Inquisition in France. He defeated the French Protestants at Dreux in 1559, but on the death of François I., Catherine de Medicis claimed the guardianship of the young Charles IX., and deprived G. of his almost absolute power. At the siege of Orleans, February 1563, G. was assassinated by a Calvinist named Polbrot.—**Charles, Cardinal of Lorraine**, the ablest of the G. family, was born at Joinville, February 17, 1524, became Archbishop of Rheims in 1538, Cardinal of Lorraine in 1547, and went to the Council of Trent in 1562. During the reigns of Henri II. and François II. he was, along with his brother, the chief ruler of France. He was ambitious of becoming Pope, and making his brother François, Duc de G., King of France. He prompted despotic measures and persecuted the Protestants, through united bigotry and statecraft, but on the death of François II., when his niece, Mary Queen of Scots became no longer Queen of France, his power began to decline. He founded the University of Rheims, and died at Avignon, December 26, 1574. He was able and learned, but heartless, deceitful, and licentious. —**Henri**, 3d **Duc de G.**, surnamed *Balafré* ('scarred'), eldest son of François, Duc de G., was born in 1550, became Duc in 1563, fought in Hungary against the Turks in 1566, and at Jarnac and Moncontour in 1569, forcing Coligny in the same year to raise the siege of Poictiers. He was one of the chief agents in the massacre of St. Bartholomew (August 21, 1572), and took command of the chief party of assassins. He defeated the Huguenots in 1575 near Chateau-Thierry, and there received the wound in the face from which he was surnamed *Balafré*. He was afterwards the real head of the League, which determined to make him King of France in place of the feeble Henri III., though the next heir to the throne was Henri of Navarre. This led to the 'War of the Three Henris,' which was followed by a brief and hollow reconciliation. The King, however, was bent on his rival's death, and had him assassinated at Blois, December 23, 1588. His brother Louis, Cardinal of G., was murdered on the following day.—**Charles**, 4th **Duc de G.**, the son of the above, was born in 1571, and after his father's murder was imprisoned in the castle of Tours until 1591, when he escaped, and joined the garrison which held Paris against Henri IV. Along with the Duc de Mayence he became the chief commander of the League, and after Henri IV. became king was pardoned, and made governor of Provence. He was banished by Richelieu in 1631, and died near Sienna in 1640. His son **Henri, 5th Duc de G.**, was born April 4, 1614. He was educated for the Church, and was made Archbishop of Rheims at the age of fifteen, but on the death of his elder brother, abandoned a clerical life, and became Duc de G. Having conspired against Richelieu, he was condemned to death, but fled to Germany, and on the death of Louis XIII. returned to France. In 1647 he set out, in hopes of winning a kingdom, to aid the Neapolitans who had revolted against Spain. He was enthusiastically welcomed by the people of Naples, but was betrayed to the Spaniards, and was kept a prisoner in Spain from 1648 to 1652. On gaining his liberty he joined first the Fronde, and then the court party, and finally became grand chamberlain to Louis XIV. He died at Paris in 1664. He was famed for his capricious gallantry and chivalrous courage, and his character, notwithstanding his fickleness and knight-errantry, is a pleasant contrast to the callous, sombre nature of the other leading members of the family. He was succeeded by his nephew, Louis, who died in 1664, and left an infant son, at whose decease, in 1675, the line of the Guises became extinct. See Sismondi's *Histoire des Français*, Da Trousset de Valincourt's *Vie de François de Lorraine, Duc de G.* (Par. 1681), Brantôme's *Vies des Grands Capitaines*.

Guitar (Span. *guitarra*, Ital. *chitarra*, from Lat. *cithara*, Gr. *kithara*, 'a lute'), a musical instrument with six strings used in France, Spain, and Italy to accompany the voice or dancing. The right hand of the performer *plucks* the strings, while the left hand *presses* them, and so forms the notes.

Gui'zot, François-Pierre-Guillaume, a French statesman and historian, was born at Nîmes, 4th October 1787. His father, a Protestant advocate, died on the scaffold, 8th April 1794; and Madame Guizot fled to Geneva, where her son received his education, having at the age of twelve mastered the learned languages, besides English, German, and Italian. Coming to Paris in 1805 to study law, G. was at first obliged to eke out his means by teaching, but adopting the profession of letters, he had by 1811 published three original works and a translation of Gibbon's *Decline and Fall*. He had also written for a magazine, *Le Publiciste*, edited by Mdlle. de Meulan, and this lady, though fourteen years his senior, he married in 1812, in the same year becoming Professor of Modern History in the Sorbonne. On the fall of the Empire, G., whose wife had great influence with the royalist party, received the Secretaryship of the Interior, which he vacated during the Hundred Days, but on the second restoration he again took office as Secretary of Justice and Director of the Indemnity Administration. A constitutional royalist, and with Royer-Collard a founder of the *Doctrinaire* (q. v.) school, he went out with the Decazes Ministry in 1820, and for ten years resumed the labours of author and professor, in his twelve works on history and politics belonging to that period maintaining so firm an opposition to the illegal measures of the Villèle Government as evoked a three years' interdict (1825) on his lectures at the Sorbonne. The July revolution of 1830 brought G. once more to the front. He was named in quick succession Minister of Instruction and of the Interior, and for eighteen years held a portfolio under every administration, except during a short residence in London as French ambassador (1840). But he failed as a politician. His adhesion to the 'peace at any price' policy, his action in the Tahiti question, and again in the Spanish marriages, had estranged his former partisans, and the part he took in the prohibition of the Reform Banquet (February 22, 1848) led not only to his fall, but to three years of exile in England. He returned to France shortly after the *coup-d'état*, and stood for Calvados in 1852, but being defeated, retired to his country seat of Val Richer in Normandy, whence he only issued to attend the sittings of the French Academy (of which he was director in 1861) or of the Protestant Conference, and where he died, September 12, 1874. It is by his historical writings that G. will be best remembered. His literary activity extended over upwards of sixty years, and in that time he produced between thirty and forty works, most of which have been translated into English. Manly and thoughtful, pure alike in style and sentiment, they are marred by an exaltation of theory over fact, and by that excessive dogmatism which won for their author among his co-religionists the title of 'Pope G.' The following are the most important:—*Histoire de la Révolution d'Angleterre* (2 vols. 1826); *Histoire de la Civilisation en France* (5 vols. 1828–30); *Histoire de la Civilisation en Europe* (1830); *Vie de Washington* (2 vols. 1839–40); *Mémoires pour servir à la Histoire de mon Temps* (9 vols. 1858–68); and an unfinished *Histoire de France, racontée à mes Petits-Enfants* (4 vols. 1875).—**Élizabeth-Charlotte-Pauline G.** (*née* **De Meulan**), wife of the preceding, was born at Paris, November 2, 1773. The death of her father in 1790, and the ruin in which the Revolution had involved her family, leading her to seek a livelihood by her pen, she produced a novelette, *Les Contradictions*, in 1800, which won a considerable reputation. It was followed by other romances, tales for children, and reviews, which appeared in a collected form as *Essais de Littérature et de Morale* (Par. 1802). She assumed the joint editorship of Suard's *Publiciste* in 1807, married G. in 1812, and died 1st August 1827. Her best work, *Lettres sur l'Éducation*, was crowned by the Academy.

Gu'jerat, the chief town of the district of the same name, Punjaub, British India, 8 miles from the right bank of the Chenaub. It is a walled town, of some strategic importance, and the scene of the concluding battle of the second Sikh war, in which Lord Gough completely defeated 60,000 Sikhs.—The *district* of G. has an area of 1900 sq. miles; pop. (1868) 616,347.

Gujranwall'a, the chief town of the district of the same name, Punjaub, British India, N. E. of Lahore. It possesses a large square mud fort, the original residence of the family of Runjit Sing.—The *district* of G. has an area of 2657 sq. miles; pop. (1868) 550,576. It is bounded N. by the Chenaub river; the crops are wheat, rice, other cereals, and sugar-cane; the exports are wheat, wool, and ghee.

Gulan'cha, or **Galun'cha**, the name in India for an extract prepared from *Tinospora cordifolia* and *T. crispa*, two plants belonging to the order *Menispermaceæ*. G. is used as a tonic and diuretic, and also as a specific for the poisonous bites of insects.

Gul'den is the German name for a coin, originally of gold, and first made at Florence in 1252. It was called in Latin *florenus* (see FLORIN), and *Fl.* is still the usual written designation of the G. The golden G. disappeared in the 17th c., and the silver G., varying much in value according to time and place of coinage, took its place in Germany. In Southern Germany, where, till 1875, the G. was the standard, it was worth 1s. 8d.; the Dutch G. (*guilder*) has the same value; and the Austrian G. is valued at about 2s.

Gules (Fr. *gueule*, Lat. *gula*, 'the mouth and throat,' hence, from the colour of the throat, 'red'), in heraldry, red, the most honourable colour, denoting magnanimity or courage, and ranking next to *or* and *argent*.

Gulf Stream. See CURRENTS, OCEAN.

Gulf Weed, the common name for *Sargassum bacciferum*, a dark-coloured seaweed (Algæ, q. v.), which occurs in immense quantities in some parts of the Atlantic, forming what is known as the Sargasso or Sargazo sea. It is not native on the British coast, although it is occasionally brought thither by the Gulf Stream (q. v.).

Gull (of uncertain derivation), the name given to a large number of Natatorial or Swimming birds, the typical G. belonging to the family *Laridæ*, in which the wings are long and pointed and the bill straight. The hinder toe is usually short and the tail long. In the *Larinæ* or true G. the bill is long, straight at the base, and curved at the tip. The common G. or seamew (*Larus canus*) is one of the most familiar of British coast birds; and has a white head and neck a grey upper surface; the tail, tail-coverts, and under parts pure white, while the wing feathers are variously marked with black. The average length is 18 inches. The G. often follows in the wake of ships for many miles for the purpose of picking up morsels of food. It is readily domesticated, and destroys large quantities of slugs and worms in gardens. It has the habit of dancing or tapping with its feet on the ground, especially after rain, in order to attract the worms to the surface. The black-backed G. (*Larus maximus*) is less common than the preceding species, and is found on the British coasts at the mouth of the Thames, on the Swedish and Norwegian coasts, &c. The colour is a dark leaden grey above and white beneath; the head and neck are white. The average length is 30 inches. The little G. (*Larus minutus*) has a jet-black head and neck, and attains a length of 10 inches. The laughing G. (*Larus atricilla*) is so named from its hoarse cry. The herring G. (*Larus argentatus*) is a beautiful species, also known as the silvery G., and is white on the head and neck, the back being a silvery grey. The ivory G. (*Pagophila eburnea*) is so named from its white plumage. The genus *Rissa*, distinguished by the bill being longer than the head, is represented by the kittiwake G. (*R. tridactyla*), in which the hind toe is quite rudimentary. The name is derived from the bird's cry. The length of the kittiwake G. is about 16 inches; the head and neck are white; the upper parts a light grey; and the wings black and white. The genus *Stercorarius* is represented by several typical species of G., among which the best known is the skua G. (*S. catarrhactes*). This is a bird of large size, and of predatory habits. It robs other gulls of the fishes they have caught, and attacks smaller birds. It is also said to devour eggs. Its general colour is brown. In the genus *Stercorarius* the bill is curved at its base by the *Cere* (q. v.); and the nostrils are narrow, and lodged in the front portion of the cere.

Herring Gull.

Ivory Gull.

Gull'et. See ŒSOPHAGUS.

Gum is an exudation obtained from numerous plants, the name being applied to several classes of substances chemically and physically distinct from each other, and having different applications in the arts. True gums, of which G. Arabic may be taken as the type, are wholly soluble in water, making in their dissolved condition a strongly adhesive viscous mucilage, upon which property their value as a commercial commodity almost wholly depends. The entirely soluble chemical principle contained in a true G. is known as *Arabin*. A second class of G., of which tragacanth G. is an example, does not wholly dissolve in water, but partly swells up and softens and partly is dissolved. The insoluble portion in such gums is known as *Bassorin*. A third class is wholly insoluble in water, the material only swelling up and forming a kind of pasty or gelatinous mass. Such gums, of which there are numerous varieties produced in India, possess no adhesive properties, and though they may be useful as thickeners, they have little economic value. Various astringent vegetable extracts are also commercially recognised as gums, but they are really valuable only as tanning and dyeing materials or for medicinal purposes, and ought strictly to be classed with vegetable extracts like catechu, &c. G. resins again embrace a class of substances which, as their name indicates, possess in part the characters of both gums and resins. British G. or dextrine is an artificial preparation, obtained by roasting common starch, and it possesses the soluble and adhesive properties of a true G. The name G. is also very often improperly applied to a variety of the commoner true resins, as, for example, G. copal, G. asafœtida, &c. Of the true or soluble gums, the most important is G. arabic, the produce of *Acacia vera*, which is chiefly obtained from Turkish and other Mediterranean ports. Numerous closely allied commercial varieties, also the produce of various species of *Acacia*, exist, of which the most prominent are known as East Indian G., Barbary or Morocco G., G. Senegal, G. Gedda, and Australian G. Several acacia gums also occur in South America, some of which, however, are only partly soluble. True gums should not only be perfectly soluble, and yield a smooth uniform mucilage, but should be transparent, or as little coloured as possible. The commercial variety which most perfectly fulfils this condition is 'elect' or picked Turkey Arabic. Of the partly soluble gums, tragacanth, which is obtained from two or three species of *astragalus* in the South of Europe, is the only important commercial variety, and it is of more value in its medicinal relations than for industrial purposes. The common cherry-tree yields a G. having similar properties to tragacanth, for which it may be used as a substitute. Of the so-called astringent gums, the most important is kino.

Gumbinn'en, a town of E. Prussia, on the Pissa, an affluent of the Pregel, 68 miles E.S.E. of Königsberg. It has weaving, dyeing, brewing, and distilling industries, two hospitals, a public library, a gymnasium (1813), &c. Pop. (1875) 9116. G. was founded in 1724, and received many Protestant refugees, chiefly from Salzburg.

Gummi Rubrum, an exudation from the bark of the *Eucalyptus rostrata*, imported from Australia, and introduced into

European practice by the late Sir Ranald Martin in cases of diarrhœa and dysentery. G. R. adheres with great tenacity to mucous surfaces, and is much used, in the form of lozenges, for the relaxed throat of public speakers; and, in combination with Cayenne, in cases of relaxed uvula. It is also administered in decoction, extract, syrup, and tincture.

Gum'ri, now **Alexandropol**, a fortified town in the government of Erivan, Russian Armenia, on the Arpa-Chai river, 85 miles S.W. of Tiflis. It stands 5860 feet above the sea, is the key to Armenia, and its fort can hold 10,000 men. Pop. 17,300.

Gums, Diseases of. Abscess of the gums is of very frequent occurrence from the inflammation of decayed teeth. A free and early incision should be made to give exit to the pus. Spongy and sloughing ulceration of the gums frequently occurs as the result of malaria, scurvy, syphilis, and from the use of mercury. Treatment:—*Internally*, tonics, with the chlorate of potass and mineral acids; *externally*, solution of nitrate of silver, with chlorinated or tannin washes, or escharotics, as muriatic acid, creosote, or permanganate of potass. Epulis is a fibrous tumour springing from the periosteum and edge of the Alveolus (q. v.), which grows up between and loosens the neighbouring teeth. It is most frequently met with in the lower jaw and about the molar teeth. Treatment—Removal of the whole mass, and of that portion of the alveolus from which it springs. The gums are also subject to cancerous ulcers and fungous growths from the alveolar processes. Treatment—as in epulis.

Gumsur', a town in the district of Ganjam, province of Madras, British India, notorious for the human sacrifices practised by the Konds, which required to be suppressed by armed force in 1845.

Gum'ti ('winding'), a river in India, which rises in the district of Shah-jehanpore, and flows through the province of Oude, with a very sinuous course, past Lucknow, where navigation begins. It falls into the Ganges below Benares. Total length, about 480 miles.

Gun. This general name may be said to include every species of firearm, be the calibre large or small, from the barrel of which there is forcibly discharged either ball, shell, or small shot by means of gunpowder or any of its modern substitutes. As guns of large calibre, however, have been or will be treated of under the headings ARTILLERY, CANNON, ORDNANCE, &c., this article will be confined to smooth-bore guns used for sporting purposes; to what, as a rule, sportsmen call 'a G.' or fowling-piece. This will of necessity exclude rifled small-arms, but these will be described under the heading RIFLE.

From the time of Nimrod till now, the killing of wild animals for food or sport has afforded employment or pastime to large numbers of the human race, and the invention or improvement of weapons intended to facilitate their capture has exercised the ingenuity of men during the same period of time. In the early ages (and, indeed, among savage races to the present day) the bow and arrow was the favourite weapon employed to secure the coveted prize, and it was a considerable time after the discovery of gunpowder that firearms for sporting purposes began to be used. The first of these portable firearms were merely clumsy and unwieldy iron tubes fixed on a straight wooden stock, and fired by a lighted piece of tow applied by hand to a small orifice at the breech end; but from this rude weapon has been developed the light, handy, and serviceable G. of the present day.

According to the most authentic accounts, portable firearms were first introduced into England in the reign of Henry IV. Shortly after an improvement was made in the means of ignition by the introduction of the match-lock, which was superseded in the time of Henry VIII. by the Italian wheel-lock. This latter method of ignition lasted till the reign of Charles I., when the flint-lock (a Dutch invention) took its place. Only forty years ago (in 1837), the Rev. Alexander John Forsyth, an Aberdeenshire clergyman, called attention to the advantages of igniting the charge by means of a fulminating substance, and patented his percussion lock, which was shortly afterwards followed by the invention of the percussion cap and nipple gun, the predecessors of the present central-fire cartridges and breech-loading guns. So far as regards the means of igniting the charge. The next important change was reducing the weight of the G. by the decrease of the metal in the barrels, and at the same time improving its quality, so as to supply the sportsman with a weapon that would not unduly fatigue him, and which, at the same time, would be safe, and capable of killing game at long distances.

Sporting guns are, as a rule, double-barrelled, *i.e.*, with two barrels placed side by side, the charge in each being fired by means of separate locks on each side of the stock. Till within a comparatively recent period muzzle-loading guns only were used. About twenty-five years ago breechloaders, now in general use, began to be talked of among sportsmen, owing to the invention of M. Lefaucheux, a Frenchman, the main features of which are preserved in the most modern breechloading guns of the present day. The principle of the Lefaucheux G. consists in an iron body fastened to the wooden stock, which, as a rule, is made of walnut, and of which it may be said to form a part. The barrels are attached by a hinge joint a short distance in front of the breech, and are allowed to turn down at an angle from breech to muzzle, so as to raise the breech end far enough above the top of the action to allow of the insertion of the cartridge. When closed, the breech end of the barrels fits accurately against the face of the action, and are secured in that position by a lever engaging with recesses in the 'lump,' which is brazed or dove-tailed between the barrels. During the last fourteen or fifteen years breech actions have been the subject of the most fertile invention. Most of them, however, are based on the Lefaucheux system, so far at least as the falling barrels are concerned, the chief improvement being an increase in the ease and rapidity with which the G. can be loaded and fired.

The accompanying woodcut represents one of the best-known of the numerous systems of snap actions for guns, showing the

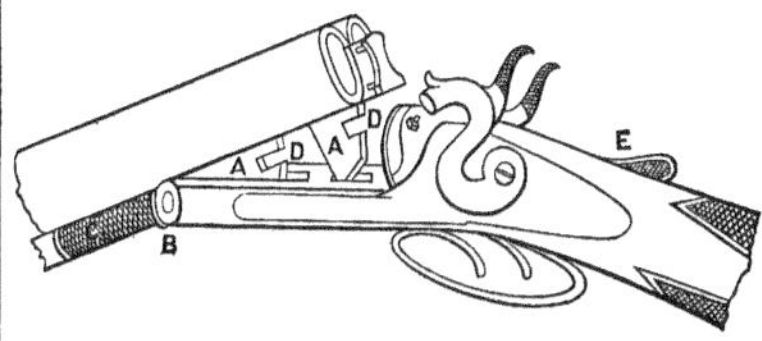

barrels opened and ready for loading. AA is a solid steel lump brazed between the breech end of the barrels, the forward part of which hooks on to the axle B, and with the fore-end C makes a hinge joint forming the centre of motion for the barrels. A sliding bolt, with catches corresponding to the recesses DD in the lump, works in a horizontal slot in the body of the G. When the barrels are being shut down, a bevelled face on the lump pushes back the bolt, and the latter, on the complete closing of the barrels, is forced by a spring into the recesses in the lump. In opening the G., the bolt is actuated by the lever E, which has a vertical axis between the hammers, the bottom being provided with an eccentric fitting into a notch in the back end of the bolt. On pushing aside the lever E, a partial rotation is given to the axis, and the eccentric motion of the projection at the bottom draws the bolt out of the recesses DD, and allows the barrels to drop into the position for loading.

Among recent inventions for facilitating the rapidity of loading is the rebounding lock, which, by means of a compensating mainspring, raises the hammer to half cock after driving it against the cap, the special action of raising the hammer to half-cock position by hand being thus avoided. Further improvements have recently been attempted in the way of making the locks self-cocking, but as yet these have not met with much favour. The most recent attempted improvement, only brought prominently forward within the last two years, has been in the direction of increasing the range, penetration, and pattern of the G., by making the barrels 'choke bore,' *i.e.*, contracting the bore at the muzzle, and there can be no doubt that the object aimed at has been to a certain extent obtained, though a great controversy is still maintained as to its practical advantages. Many gunmakers have adopted the system, or a modification of it, while many others are using a plan which at first sight would seem entirely opposite, but which produces as good, or, it is said by some, better, because more uniform results, viz., making a slight recess in the barrels near the muzzle, so as to form a small chamber, which concentrates the shot just before leaving the barrel, and makes it carry closer and further than when propelled from the ordinary bored G. Sporting guns vary in calibre from twenty to eight bore (see BORE), the gauge most used, however, being twelve, with barrels 30 inches long, and the complete G. weighing about 7 lbs. For the charge for breech-loading guns and means of ignition, see CARTRIDGE.

Gunboat. See NAVY.

Gun-Carriage, the carriages upon which cannon are mounted, the particular form depending upon the nature of the service for which the gun is required. The earliest gun-carriages of which there is record were *carts of war*, for conveying light artillery, mentioned in a Scotch Act of Parliament of 1456. A field-piece is mounted on a two-wheeled carriage, to which is attached a single shaft, known as the 'trail,' under the breech end of the G. In transport the end of the trail is attached to the 'limber,' which may be described as a small two-wheeled cart with shafts, to which the horses are harnessed, and carrying the ammunition boxes for the service of the gun. When in action, the trail is detached from the limber, and its end rests on the ground. Cannon for naval or garrison service are mounted on strong frames with four low wheels. Siege guns are mounted much in the same way as field-pieces, the carriages being, of course, much stronger, to bear the greater weight of the gun, and the limber carrying no ammunition. A number of inventions for the improvement of the different kinds of gun-carriages have been brought forward within recent years, notably by Sir Joseph Whitworth, Sir William Armstrong, and Major Moncrieff. The latter gentleman is the inventor of the well-known 'protected barbette G-C.,' which is said to combine the security of a protecting parapet without embrasures. To obtain this the force of the recoil is utilised to lower the gun behind the protecting parapet (or below the level of the pit in which it may be mounted), in which position it is retained by a catch working on a toothed wheel till it is loaded, the gunners being all the time under shelter. A counterweight is suspended below the gun, which, on the removal of the catch, elevates it to the firing position.

Gun-Cott'on, an explosive substance of great power possessing weight for weight about six times the destructive force of ordinary gunpowder. It was discovered in 1846 by Professor Schönbein, of Basel, who in that year exhibited it at a meeting of the British Association at Southampton, under the name 'explosive cotton.' He kept the method of preparation secret, and proposed selling his invention to the German Government as a substitute for gunpowder. Pelouse, a French chemist, had previously prepared a somewhat similar explosive by the action of nitric acid on wood, and in consequence claimed the priority of discovery. In December of the same year (1846) in which Schönbein announced that he had converted cotton into an explosive, Professor Ellet of South Carolina College, U.S., communicated to the Legislature of that State a method of manufacturing G.-C.

The new explosive gained immediate favour, and its manufacture was eagerly proceeded with, both in this and other countries, the impression being that it was to supersede gunpowder for all purposes for which the latter was used, and from its great destructive power effect a revolution in modern warfare. A number of terribly disastrous explosions, however, occurring during manufacture or storage, it was almost entirely given up for some years. The subject of manufacturing and storing G.-C. with safety was from time to time revived, and in 1863 a committee was appointed by the Government to investigate the whole matter, and Professor Abel, chemist to the War Department, effected many improvements in the mode of manufacture; so much so, that it was thought the means of making and storing the material with perfect safety had been arrived at. A disastrous and fatal explosion at Stowmarket factory in 1871 dissipated this idea, and in 1872 the Government appointed a special committee to inquire into the subject. This committee recommended that G.-C. should be stored wet, and dried in small quantities as required—a mode of procedure that would have had many inconveniences; but in the course of subsequent experiments it was discovered that wet G.-C. could be exploded if only a small portion in immediate contact with the detonator employed to set off the charge be dry, thus allowing of the great bulk of the cotton being stored wet, and reducing to a minimum the danger of accidents.

The component parts of G.-C. are common cotton and sulphuric and nitric acids. The cotton fibre is finely carded, thoroughly cleaned and dried, and dipped into a mixture of three parts of sulphuric to one of nitric acid. After being drained over the tank, it is put into jars, which stand in water for some hours. It is then placed in a revolving drum, where it discharges most of the spare acids, is next thoroughly washed till all trace of acid has vanished, then pulped and dried, and finally pressed into cartridges of such size and shape as will suit the purposes for which they are intended. G.-C. is ignited at a temperature of about 400°, and when not confined, and fired by simple ignition, burns with a flash without smoke or report, but when fired by concussion its destructive force is immense. G.-C. has not proved so effective for artillery purposes as was anticipated, but it is largely used for mining purposes and the charging of torpedoes. The Government has a large establishment for its manufacture at Waltham Abbey.

Gundamuk', an Afghan village, 28 miles W. of Jellalabad, where, during the retreat from Cabul (q. v.) in 1843, the remaining British force of 100 soldiers and 300 camp-followers was massacred, only one man escaping.

Gunduk' (*Gandaki*), the name of several rivers in the N. of Behar, India. The G. proper, a large river, is formed by the junction of the Narayani or Salagrami, which is supposed to have its source to the N. of Mount Dhawalagiri in the Himalayas, with the Trisulgunga, which also rises in Nepaul. These two streams meet near Bhelaunji, where they first touch British territory and also become navigable. The G. then flows through Chumparun, Goruckpore, Sarun, and Tirhut, usually forming a district boundary, and falls into the Ganges at Hajipore, directly opposite to Patna, after an estimated course of 450 miles. It is confined within strong embankments throughout the lower part of its course, where, like other rivers in alluvial plains, its channel is considerably above the level of the surrounding country. It carries a considerable amount of traffic, especially with Nepaul. The Bara or Old G. flows to the W. of the former river, and after a course of 170 miles falls into the Gogra in Sarun district. The Chota or Little G. flows to the E. and joins the Baghmutti, after about 190 miles, in Tirhut district.

Gun Factories, the name given to establishments for the manufacture of cannon. The principal factories in Great Britain, excluding the Royal Factory, are those of Sir William Armstrong & Co. and Sir Joseph Whitworth & Co. At the former establishment there was turned out last year (1876) for the Italian Government the largest gun ever manufactured in this country, its weight being 100 tons. Artillery for the use of the British navy and army are for the most part made at the Royal Factory at Woolwich, first started in 1855. There machinery of the most powerful and elaborate kind has been erected for the production of cannon of all kinds and sizes. The greatest effort as yet made in the Royal Factory has been in the production of the 80 ton gun, but a gun to weigh 200 tons is about (1877) to be commenced, the resources of the establishment in steam-hammer power, boring machines, &c., being said to be fully equal to this gigantic undertaking.

Gunge (*ganj*), a word of Persian derivation, used throughout India (commonly in compounds, as Sahibgunge) for a village with a market-place containing grain and other necessaries of life.

Gun'ja (*ganja*), a narcotic drug akin to bhang and haschisch, prepared from the leaves and flowers of the hemp plant (*Cannabis sativa* or *Indica*), which is extensively smoked throughout India. The cultivation is almost entirely confined to a small tract in the district of Rajshahye, Bengal, where about 1,000,000 lbs. are annually produced. It is the policy of the Government to check the consumption by a gradual enhancement of the excise duty, which has hitherto been effected without any diminution in the revenue. In 1874-75 the duty on G. in Bengal alone amounted to £105,817.

Gun'making includes the manufacture of all kinds of sporting weapons and military small arms. The mode of manufacture, however, of the two classes named differs so very considerably that they must be treated of separately.

Sporting Weapons.—The manufacture of sporting weapons is divided into a number of different branches, such as barrel making (already noticed under BARREL), action filing, lock making, stocking, &c. The chief seat of the barrel-making trade in this country is Birmingham, and the lock trade is extensively carried on in London, Wolverhampton, and Birmingham. The stocks of sporting guns and rifles are made almost exclusively of walnut wood, which is tough, durable, often finely figured, and takes on a beautiful polish. Space does not permit of details being given of the manufacture of the component parts of a rifle or fowling-piece, the processes being so varied and intricate, but a sketch may be given of the mode of making up a gun. Suppose a pair of barrels welded, bored, ground, and filed, the next process is to braze the steel lump, for attaching them to the action, between the breech ends, and fit and solder 'ribs,' both on the top and bottom sides; plugs are then screwed into the breech ends, and they are sent for provisional proof. Next they are handed to the action filer, who makes the action and fits the barrels to it, when the whole goes for definite proof. The action and barrels with the locks and mountings are then handed to the stocker, who stocks the gun in the rough, and passes it on to have the hammers fitted. At this stage the gun or rifle is usually shot and the barrels adjusted. The stocker then makes off, *i.e.*, trims up and buffs and chequers the stock, and 'strips' the gun. The ironwork is handed to the polisher, by him passed to the engraver, and by the latter to the hardener, who case-hardens the action lock-plates, &c., and 'blues' some of the other parts. The barrels, meantime, have been finely polished and browned, and the whole work now goes back to the stocker, who puts the parts carefully together, and the gun is complete. There are few finer or more beautiful pieces of mechanism than a well-made and highly-finished shot gun or rifle.

Military Small Arms.—These at the present day may be said to be entirely made by machinery, barrels, action, locks, and stocks being all machined, so that it only remains to put the parts together by hand labour. For the introduction of machinery we are mainly indebted to the Americans, who, some years previous to 1853, had a Government small-arm manufactory at Springfield fitted up with most ingenious machinery. A commission from this country to the New York Exhibition in 1853 was allowed to visit this manufactory, and their report induced our Government to establish a similar factory at Enfield in Middlesex. From being at first on a small scale, this manufactory has been developed and extended, till it is now capable of turning out over 1000 complete Martini-Henry rifles weekly. Large manufactories belonging to public or private companies also exist in London and Birmingham. In the Government factory and most of those large establishments the arms are made on the interchangeable system, *i.e.*, each particular part of a gun is made so exactly the same, that if any number of guns are taken to pieces and the parts mixed together, any series of parts can be assembled and put together as a perfect gun. The manufacture of arms, both sporting and military, is in this country a very important industry, Birmingham alone employing over 10,000 men in the trade.

Gunn'el, or Butt'erfish (*Centronotus*), a genus of Teleostean fishes belonging to the family *Blenniidæ*, or that of the Blennies (q. v.). The ventral fins are either small or wanting, and the scales are also small. The gill membranes are united below the throat, and no lateral line exists. The common or spotted G. (*C. gunellus*) is well known on the British coasts, and is an eel-like fish, about 6 inches in length, coloured brown, with black spots along the base of the dorsal fin. The head is small, and the muzzle blunt. The G. derives its name of 'butterfish' from the quantity of mucous secretion which, like the eel, it is capable of emitting from its skin. It is commonly found in rock pools after the tide has receded.

Gunn'er, in the British army, is a private artillery soldier, who is paid at the rate of 1s. 2½d. daily. Master gunners are pensioned artillery sergeants, who receive from 3s. to 5s. a day. G. in the navy is the highest warrant officer, and has charge of the great guns and the powder-magazine, and exercises the men in gun practice. His pay varies from 5s. 6d. to 9s. a day.

Gunn'era, a genus belonging to the natural order *Haloragaceæ* (q. v.), but some authors place it in *Araliaceæ* (q. v.). There are about a dozen species of G. known, chiefly natives of New Zealand, Java, and S. America. *G. scabra* or '*panke*' is grown in British gardens and pleasure-grounds as an ornamental plant. When growing in sheltered damp places, its leaves, which are very rough, attain a large size, and it produces a conical fleshy spike of minute flowers. Its roots are astringent, and are employed for tanning, and its leaf stalks eaten as rhubarb.

Gunnera scabra.

Gunn'ery, as a science, treats of the theory of Projectiles (q. v.), particularly in its military bearings; and, as an art, is concerned with the management of ordnance and the application of the theoretical principles to practice. In the 15th c. Leonardo da Vinci displayed a knowledge of the fundamental laws far in advance of his contemporaries. Tartaglia, in his *Nuova Scienza* (1537), was the first to endeavour to enunciate the principles of G. He explained the motion of a projectile, taking into account the resistance of the air, showed that the maximum range was obtained with an elevation of 45°, and proved that no part of the *trajectory* or line of flight was a straight line. Galileo followed this up in his *Dialogues on Motion* (1646) by demonstrating the parabolic form of the trajectory, leaving out of account the resistance of the air. Newton found that by reason of this resistance the path deviated much from the true parabola, and that, therefore, in the practice of G. this resistance must not be neglected—a principle which Galileo also urged. Not till the time of Benjamin Robins, however, did these suggestions receive the attention they deserved. His *New Principles of G.* (1742) formed unquestionably the foundation on which the science has been built. His Ballistic Pendulum (q. v.) provided a means of determining the velocities of cannon-balls at any point of their range; and from experiments with it Dr. Hutton of Woolwich, towards the end of the century, deduced formulæ which have been successfully used in the approximate determination of some of the most difficult problems in G. This instrument has only lately been superseded by the much more accurate and refined apparatus of Navez, Noble, Bashforth, and others, whose electric chronographs can record with perfect accuracy to tenths, and even much smaller fractions, of a second.

The forces which act upon a projectile during its flight are the explosive force of the gunpowder, which gives it its initial velocity; the force of gravity, which continually drags it down; and the resistance of the air, which acts against its motion, so as to diminish its velocity. While the bullet is in the bore of the gun, it experiences further resistance to its progress from the friction between the shot and the bore, and in rifled cannon this resistance is increased by the necessity of giving to the projectile rotatory motion. The advantages of rifling were early pointed out by Robins, but it is only within the last thirty or forty years that they have been generally recognised Under RIFLE the details of rifling will be noticed. Here it is sufficient to mention the general advantages accruing from its use. In the first place, by making possible the introduction of elongated in place of spherical projectiles, it greatly increases the range; while the rotatory motion given to the shot as it leaves the gun tends better to preserve it in its initial plane of projection, thus rendering the art of aiming a greater certainty. Experiment shows that the shot, while travelling the bore, gradually increases in velocity, so that it is going fastest just when it leaves the muzzle. The resistance of the air is an exceedingly important element, and depends chiefly upon the velocity of the projectile. For slow motions, this resistance varies as the square of the velocity; but for the high velocities attainable in modern artillery, other considerations come into play. Hutton made numerous experiments on this subject, and showed that the formula $r = mv^2 + nv$ (where m, n are experimentally determined constants, r the resistance, and v the velocity) gave results very approximately concordant with observation. All his results were obtained with spherical projectiles. Other investigators have used other formulæ. General Didion, for instance, made the second term proportional to the cube of the velocity, and St. Robert of the Sardinian artillery to the fourth power. Bashforth from 1866–68 made a series of experiments to test the cubic law of resistance ($r = mv^3$); and this law, by making use of a *varying* coefficient, is found to be approximately accurate and very convenient for practical purposes. Experiments indicate that the *form* of projectile has a marked influence on the resistance of the air, the elongated being preferable to the spherical, and the ogival-headed (like a pointed arch in longitudinal section) to the conical, rounded, or square. See Owen's *Modern Artillery* (1871) and Bashforth's *Motion of Projectiles* (1874).

Gunn'y, a name of uncertain derivation given in India to the fabric of indigenous manufacture woven from the fibre of the well-known jute plant (*Corchorus*). G. bags are made in village households all over Eastern Bengal, and now also in mills worked by European capital. They are largely exported to serve for packing the wheat of Australia, California, and Egypt, and the rice of Burmah and the Straits Settlements. In 1875–76 the exports from Calcutta to foreign ports were valued at £431,000, having more than doubled in two years. The exports to British Indian ports, principally Bombay and Burmah, were valued at £587,000. G. cloth was also exported to the value of £44,000.

Gun'powder, an explosive agent, is a mechanical mixture of nitre, charcoal, and sulphur, in determinate proportions. It is employed in propelling projectiles from firearms, in blasting, and in pyrotechny. When first used for firearms in Europe, towards the close of the 13th or early in the 14th c., a thorough revolution was effected in the art of war. The place and time of the invention of G. are involved in obscurity. Its discovery about 1320 has long been popularly ascribed to Schwarz, a monk of Cologne, but Roger Bacon, who died in 1292, gives, in one of his treatises, the composition of G., and describes its properties, and in no way indicates that it was then new. No European writer prior to Bacon refers to G., except Marcus Græcus, who names its ingredients with their proportions. Some aver that he wrote in the 9th, and not in the 13th c., as others, with more probability, maintain. In early Arabic MSS., however, there are unmistakable allusions to it, and it is now generally accepted that G. was known and used for purposes of deflagration in the East centuries before it was known in Europe. India, where the soil is rich in nitre, is probably the country that gave it birth in some remote age.

The explosive force of G. on combustion arises from the rapid conversion of the nitre, charcoal, and sulphur, into an enormous volume of very expansible gases at a high temperature. The bulk of the gases chiefly consists of carbonic anhydride, and nitrogen. They are produced by the dissociation of the elements of the nitre, the nitrogen for the most part remaining free, and part of the oxygen uniting with part of the carbon of the charcoal. Sulphur is not essential to the formation of G., the other two ingredients alone forming an explosive mixture. Its action, however, is comparatively slow, and the addition of sulphur, which ignites at a lower temperature than the other ingredients, accelerates the decomposition of the nitre, while it unites with the potassium to form various compounds. The oxygen is also more speedily liberated for union with the carbon. The combustion of the sulphur also augments the temperature of the gases and thereby expands them. The products of the combustion of G. are very complex. The proportions of the ingredients of G. vary very little in different countries, and it is remarkable, considering that they are empirical, how closely they approximate to the theoretical proportions—two molecules of nitre, three atoms of carbon, and one atom of sulphur—which in 100 parts yield 74·9 of nitre, 13·3 of carbon, and 11·8 of sulphur. The proportions employed in different powders are as follows :—

	Nitre.	Charcoal.	Sulphur.
English and Austrian (war)	75 parts	15 parts	10 parts
„ (sporting)	77 „	14 „	9 „
French and United States (war)	75 „	12·5 „	12·5 „
„ (sporting)	76·9 „	13·5 „	9·6 „
Prussian (war)	75 „	13·5 „	11·5 „
Russian „	73·8 „	13·6 „	12·6 „
Chinese	75·7 „	9·9 „	14·4 „

Blasting powder is made with a less proportion of nitre and more charcoal; the mixture is cheaper than ordinary G., but less rapid in action.

The manufacture of G. for the English Government is conducted at the Waltham Abbey Mills by the following processes. The first essential is to obtain the ingredients in a state of purity. The nitre, as imported from India, contains several impurities, chiefly the deliquescent salts (cubical nitre) and chloride of sodium, which unfit it for making G. until purified by lixiviation and crystallisation. From the crude sulphur of commerce fine yellow crystals are obtained by a process of distillation. The charcoal is prepared by the carbonisation of light woods yielding little ash imported from Holland and Germany. Three kinds of wood are employed—dogwood for fine rifle powder, and alder and willow for more common varieties. The nitre, sulphur, and charcoal are separately ground to a fine powder and sifted. The definite proportions for a charge of 50 lbs. are then weighed out and mixed in a 'churn,' or revolving drum, with internal projecting arms. The mixture, or 'green charge,' is now conveyed to an incorporating mill, water is added to make a stiff paste, and the whole is thoroughly ground and blended under iron runners. The incorporated product, called 'mill-cake,' is then broken up into 'meal,' and placed between gun-metal plates in a hydraulic press by which it is compressed into hard and dense cakes of different thickness, according as rifle or heavy G. is required. The thin 'press-cake' for rifle powder is broken up and granulated by toothed cylinders, and the grains in falling are received by the uppermost of a series of three tiered screens or sieves, placed in an inclined position, and designed to sift the powder into large and fine grains and dust. The sifted grains are then rounded and polished in rotating 'glazing barrels,' by friction of particle against particle. This operation renders the powder less liable to absorb moisture, and better adapts it for transport. The powder is afterwards dried by heated currents of air. It is then freed from dust, and passed again through the glazing barrels, and finally it is put up in barrels holding 100 lbs. 'Pebble powder,' for heavy rifled guns, is made by cutting thick 'press cake' into cubes, which vary in size with the projectile. One and a half inch cubes are employed for the 81-ton gun. After being dried, the cubes or pebbles are passed through the glazing barrels, a small quantity of blacklead being placed in them to impart a high gloss. Pebble powder is denser than small-grained powder, bulk for bulk, and this quality, as well as the degree of glaze, retards ignition.

The characteristic qualities of good G. are uniformity of texture, absence of light specks or glittering points, resistance to pressure between the fingers, crispness and cleanliness, paper not being soiled by contact, and rapid combustion with little residue. The specific gravity should not be less than 1·755. G. explodes at a temperature of about 600° F., or a little above the heat necessary to ignite sulphur. The size, form, and density of the grains modify their rapidity of combustion, hence the employment and value of pebble powder for charging heavy rifled guns. Small grains are unsuitable for this purpose, because of their instantaneous conversion into gas, whereby an excessive strain would be put upon the sides of the gun tending to rupture it. With pebble powder, however, the ignition and combustion proceeds comparatively slow, and the gases being gradually evolved, exert their greatest propelling force just as the projectile reaches the mouth of the gun. The exports of G. from Great Britain in 1874 amounted to 14,930,995 lbs., valued at £415,716.

Laws Regarding G.—Former Acts on the keeping and carriage of G. are superseded by 23 and 24 Vict. c. 139. It enacts that no charcoal be kept within 20 yards of any mill or engine for making G. No dealer in it may keep more than 200 lbs. in his premises. 300 lbs. is the most allowed to be kept in store for blasting. Not more than 30 barrels may be sent at one time by land, nor more than 2500 lbs. by water. Any one smoking on board of a ship carrying G. is liable to a fine of £5. The Act transfers the power of granting licences from justices in Quarter Sessions to justices in Petty Sessions. Special regulations are made for the security of the shipping in the Thames. See EXPLOSIVE MIXTURES.

Gunpowder Plot, the conspiracy of a number of English Catholics to destroy King James I. and his Parliament by blowing up the Parliament House on the 5th of November 1605. The king's children were then to be seized and an open revolt carried out. The G. P. was originally formed by a small band of desperate men headed by Robert Catesby; later a few Catholics of fortune were made privy to the design. One of the latter, Tresham, betrayed the plot to a relative (Lord Mounteagle) endangered by it; Guido Fawkes was found in charge of the arrangements in the cellar beneath the Parliament House; and most of the conspirators were brought to the block. The horror of the Protestants at the G. P. and their delight at its frustration were long celebrated on every anniversary of the day.

Gunroom, a cabin on a man-of-war's lower gundeck situated aft, and used as a messroom by certain of the officers.

Güns (Magyar *Köszeg*), a town of Hungary, in the county of Eisenburg, on the river G., 57 miles S.S.E. of Vienna. It successfully resisted the Turks under Solyman for twenty-eight days in 1532, thus affording the Emperor Karl V. time to gather his forces. G. is inhabited by the descendants of Bavarian colonists, who speak a dialect of German peculiar to themselves. Pop. (1869) 6915.

Gun'shot Wounds constitute a species of contused and lacerated wounds varying in severity from a simple bruise to the tearing away of a whole limb or the destruction of the body, differing according to the nature of the projectile, its size, form, and momentum, as also the distance from which it has been projected, and its angle of incidence. G. W. may cause serious injury by concussion only, as of the heart; or by the powder charge only, as when driven into the mouth or abdomen. Wadding and soft material, as pieces of clothing, may inflict severe wounds according to the momentum; and such accidents frequently take place at reviews, fairs, and on the stage. Small shot often inflict serious injuries if the person wounded be within a few feet of the muzzle of the gun, and if at a greater distance, the scattered shot may injure an important or vital part, as the eye, the heart, or the femoral vein. Similar injuries are inflicted by splinters of metal, wood, or stone in blasting and mining operations, and in naval practice. Bullets, slugs, and grapeshot occasion more serious wounds, and give rise to every possible variety of injury. G. W. from bullets may have one aperture only, that of entrance, the bullet remaining in the part, dropping out of it, or injuring by concussion, as in the case of a spent ball; or they may have two or more openings, one being of entrance and the other of exit. A ball may split against the sharp edge of a bone and have two apertures of exit, or it may pass through two parts of the body, as the thighs. The direction of these openings is often of great importance in a medico-legal as well as a surgical point of view. In a case of murder Sir Astley Cooper ascertained that the fatal shot must have been fired by a left-handed man, and thus led to the detection of the criminal. By careful attention to this point the relative positions of the criminal and his victim, the distance between the two, and other points of importance may be ascertained. G. W. may be so situated as to render it impossible for them to have been self-inflicted, and they may be so situated as to render it in the highest degree improbable that they should have been inflicted by another, such as when a bullet has passed through the roof of the mouth. The entrance aperture of a gunshot wound is small, depressed, and circular, while the exit aperture is relatively large, everted, and irregular. There are differences in the apertures of round and conical bullets, and there are also differences depending on the momentum of the ball and on the resistance it meets with. If it strikes when at the maximum of its velocity, it makes a small round hole, smaller than the bullet itself, owing to the elasticity of the skin; and if it passes through soft parts, the point of exit is much like that of entrance; but if it meets with resistance, the point of exit is torn, large, and rugged. On the second day after infliction the aperture of entrance may appear to be larger than that of exit, owing to the protrusion of an eschar. Bullets are frequently deflected in their course, owing to the elasticity of the skin, the angle of incidence, or by their striking against a bone at a low momentum: thus the apertures may be so situated as to lead to the impression that the bullet had passed through the body or the skull, whereas it had passed along a rib or round the cranium. A case occurred in the experience of the writer in which a bullet passed through the body of one man, causing instant death, and was afterwards deflected on the body of the soldier next to him, the relative positions of the wounds in both cases being almost identical. See Taylor's *Medical Jurisprudence* (Lond. 1873).

Gun'ter, Edmund, an English mathematician, was born in Hertfordshire in 1581, studied at Christ Church, Oxford, where he took the degree of B.D. in 1615, and became Professor of Astronomy in Gresham College in 1619. He died December 10, 1626. G.'s *Canon Triangulorum* (1620) was the first table of logarithmic sines, tangents, &c., and in it are introduced for the first time, cosine, co-tangent, &c. He observed also the variations of magnetic declination, but is best known for his improvement of the Sector (q. v.), and for the invention of Gunter's Scale (see GUNTER'S LINE), which are described in his treatise *Of the Sector, Cross Staff, and Other Instruments* (1624). The fifth edition of his works was published by Leybourn in 1673.

Gunter's Chain. See CHAIN.

Gunter's Line is a scale on which are marked off lengths corresponding to the logarithms of the natural number, so that by the aid of a pair of compasses, simple questions in multiplication, division, involution, and evolution may be worked. Logarithmic sines and tangents of angles may be laid down in the same way; and if the limbs of a Sector (q. v.) are engraved with these lines (marked *N*, *S*, *T* respectively), the instrument goes by the name of *Gunter's Line* or *Scale*. It is used for solving simple problems in navigation, the results so obtained being sufficiently accurate for practical purposes.

Guntur' (*Gantur*), a town in the district of Kistna, province of Madras, British India, 225 miles N. of Madras and 47 W. of Masulipatam. Pop. (1871) 18,033, of whom many are Christians. G. was formerly the chief town of a district of the same name. The neighbourhood yields abundant rice and cotton; the breed of cattle is famous; and there is some manufacture of cotton cloth.

Gun'wale, or **Gunn'el**, the upper part of a boat's side, also the topmost bend of a ship's bulwarks.

Gur, the Indian name for unrefined sugar, made from the date-palm. It is extensively manufactured in the districts of Jessore and Nuddea, in the delta of Bengal, and it enters largely into native sweetmeats.

Gur'ges, in heraldry, is a charge representing a whirlpool. It is azure and argent, and occupies the whole field.

Gurgoon', the chief town, but by no means the most populous, in the district of the same name, province of the Punjaub, British India, 918 miles N.W. of Calcutta. Pop. (1868) 3539. It was formerly a military cantonment, and is now a station on the Rajputana State Railway.—The *district* of G. occupies the southernmost corner of the Punjaub, and is bordered on the E. by the Jumna river; area, 2016 sq. miles; pop. (1868) 696,646. The territory has been acquired at different periods since 1803, a considerable portion by forfeiture after the Mutiny of 1857. The soil is undulating, with numerous marshes, and is irrigated by wells. The staple crops are barley, millet, wheat, and cotton. Salt is made by evaporation from wells near the Mujufgarh marsh, and at Noh, to the amount of about 30,000 tons annually. The chief towns are Rewaree, Pulwul, Furrucknuggur, Ferozepur, and Sonah. The exports are salt, cotton, wool, and food grains.

Gurh (*garh*), a word of Sanskrit derivation, used throughout India (especially in composition) for a fort, particularly when the walls are of mud.

Gurhwal', the name of a district in the North-West Province, British India, and also of an adjoining native state. The British *district*, which has been formed out of Kumaon, has an area of 5500 sq. miles; pop. (1872) 310,288. It lies on the southern slope of the Himalayas, and contains the sacred source of the Ganges. There are copper-mines, and some trade in timber, wool, and fibrous hemp. In all respects it resembles the neighbouring more important district of Kumaon (q. v.). The native state, distinguished by the name of Tehri-G., which lies on the W. of the Aluknunda river, is still more entirely mountainous. Area, 4180 sq. miles; pop. about 150,000; revenue, £8000. The dynasty is very old, but owes its present security to the protection of the British after the Gurkha war of 1815.

Gur'jun Bal'sam, or **Wood Oil** (*Balsamum dipterocarpi*), an oleo-resinous substance, imported from India, resembles copaiba in appearance, and possesses similar properties. G. B. is procured from the *dipterocarpeæ*, gigantic trees found in the districts E. of Bengal, by the double process of incision, and heat by fire, to promote exudation, each tree yielding as much as forty gallons in a single season. G. B. was introduced into English medicine in 1838 as a substitute for copaiba, and it has recently been extensively employed by Dr. Dougall in India as a specific in the tubercular thickenings and cachectic ulcerations of leprosy. It has also been employed in this country by Erasmus Wilson and others in cases of chronic eczema, lupus, and lepra with favourable results. It is stated to have afforded great relief at the Sultanpore dispensary in Oude, twelve lepers there having expressed the decided benefit they had received from its use. See *Lectures on Dermatology*, by Erasmus Wilson (Lond. 1875), and *Report on Sanitary Measures in India in* 1874-75 (Lond. 1876).

Gur'kha, a town in the state of Nepaul, India, 53 miles N.W. of Katmandu. It was the former capital of the present dynasty. The war between England and Nepaul in 1814 is known as the G. war. There are at present five battalions of Gurkhas in the Indian army, who have done good service both during the Mutiny of 1858 and in all subsequent border campaigns. They were sent to the Malay peninsula on the occasion of the disturbances at Perak in 1875. Accurately speaking the Gurkhas, who are an aboriginal tribe, ought to be distinguished from the Gurkhalis, who are the ruling race, are of mixed Hindustani origin, and claim to be Rajputs.

Gurmuktesar' (*Garhmuktisar*), a town in the district of Meerut, North-West Province, British India, on the right bank of the Ganges, 887 miles N.W. of Calcutta, and 31 S.E. of Meerut. Pop. (1872) 7962. The river is always navigable to this point; and G., besides being the site of an important ferry and bridge of boats to Moradabad, carries on a thriving trade as the port of Meerut. There are four temples here dedicated to the goddess of the Ganges; and a fair is said to be annually attended by 200,000 persons.

Gur'nard (*Trigla*), a genus of Teleostean fishes belonging to the *Acanthopterygious* section of the order and to the family *Triglidæ*, in which the scales and ventral fins are of small size. The head is large, and the opercular bones spinous. The pectoral fins attain a large size, and the dorsal and anal fins are also well developed, the former being frequently separated into two portions. The G. inhabits deep water, and is a fish of ungainly appearance. The sapphirine G. (*T. hirundo*) derives its name from the deep-blue colour of the inner surface of the pectoral fins. The flesh of this species is highly palatable. The scales are small, and the head is armed with spines. The red or 'cuckoo' G. (*T. pini*) is another common species; the colour of its body is a light red above, and silvery white beneath. The grey G. (*T. gurnardus*) has short pectoral fins, and a body of greenish-brown colour, spotted with white. It is the kind most frequently captured on the English coasts. The long-finned G. (*T. obscura*) has a very long second spine in the dorsal fin. The colour is red above and white below. The fins are red, with the exception of the pectorals, which are blue. The Oriental G. (*Peristethus Orientalis*) and the mailed G. (*P. cataphractum*) belong to a different genus from the preceding. See also BULLHEADS and FLYING GURNARD.

Gur'ney, Joseph John, a Quaker writer and philanthropist, and a younger brother of Elizabeth Fry (q. v.), was born near Norwich in 1788. He was educated at Oxford, became a Quaker minister in 1818, and died in 1847. G. devoted himself earnestly to benevolent labours, contributing largely to charities, &c., inspecting prisons and hospitals, and composing many religious works. Among his writings are *Notes on Prison Discipline* (1819), *Essays on Christianity*, *Biblical Notes*, *A Winter in the West Indies* (1840), &c.

Guss'et, in heraldry, part of the side of the shield. A G. was an *abatement* or sign of disgrace, indicating cowardice, adultery, or drunkenness.

Gustaf, the name of four Swedish kings.—**G. I.** ('Gustaf Vasa'), son of Councillor Erik Johansson (*Vasa*), and born at Lindholm in Upland, probably 12th May 1496. He was educated at an Upsala school, and in 1514 received at the court of his kinsman the regent Sten Sture. His first exploit against the Danes was in the campaign of 1517, and in 1518 he was chief standard-bearer at Brännkyrka. The ensuing negotiations placed G. in the custody of a distant relation, Erik Eriksön Banner of Kalö on the E. coast of Jutland; but hearing of Christiern II.'s preparations against Sweden, he fled to Lübeck, yet could not reach Calmar before the following year (1520). Having vainly tried to move the populace of Smaaland and Oestergotland, and being alarmed at the news of the massacre at Stockholm, he fled to 'The Dales' (Dalarne). Here, in hiding, he worked at daily toil for bread, protected by the fidelity of 'The Dalesmen' (Dalkarlarne). The new taxes imposed by Christiern at length led to an insurrection, of which G. became leader. Successful in the first action (at Vesteraas), he seized that town and Upsala. The revolution now became general. Seventy nobles and many representatives of the other classes held a diet at Badstena (24th August 1521), where G., refusing the crown, received their allegiance as regent. Though within a year Bleking, Bohuslän, and all the fortresses in the interior were his, the stinted aid of the merchants of Lübeck, who had undertaken to supply war-ships, &c., prevented him from becoming master of Stockholm and Calmar, as well as of Finland, before the latter half of 1523. Before the taking of Stockholm, a diet at Strengnäs (7th June 1523) had chosen G. king. Gotland was still Danish; an expedition against it in 1524 failed, and the 'Malmö Reces,' concluded at the mediation of Lübeck, gave it and Bleking to Denmark. The internal affairs of Sweden were almost desperate. The war of liberation had created a large debt to Lübeck, which had bargained for the exclusive trade of Sweden till its payment; the wars of a whole century had impoverished the people. One-third of the land was in the hands of the Church, and the revenue only covered one-third of the expenditure. G. now set himself to better the internal condition of Sweden, and diffuse Protestantism, to which he had been converted through Laurentius Andreæ. The bitter opposition of the bishops led him to offer to abdicate, but he accepted the compromise called 'Vesteraas Recess och Ordinantia' (1527), which gave him the appointment of all ecclesiastics, as well as the general direction of the Church. The Diet of Orebro (1529) did away with a large number of the Church rites. The plots, however, of the Church party gave G. much trouble; he had even twice to curb the unruliness of the Dalesmen. Christiern II. again attempted to win back his lost dominions, and Lübeck sought to check in the 'Count's War' the effort to be rid of its monopoly, but had to be content with the peace of 1537. Two years afterwards came the 'Dacke War,' the most dangerous outbreak of G.'s reign. In 1540 a diet at Orebro settled the succession on G.'s descendants (a resolution confirmed by 'Arveforeningen' at Vesteraas in 1544). The only other war of this reign was with Russia (1554-57), chiefly confined to mutual plundering on the Finnish border. Two years afterwards (1559) G. assembled the estates of the kingdom to hear his testament, and died the next year, at Stockholm, 29th September 1560. He was thrice married. G. was a stern and wise ruler. He promoted trade by fair legislation and treaties of commerce with England, France, Russia, and Holland; taxation, education, and the marine were brought into an excellent condition. His private character was spotless, and his piety sincere and fervent without being puritanical. See Fryxell's *Biography of G.* (Ger. trans. 1831).—**G. II., Adolf**, born at Stockholm 9th December 1594, was the son of Karl IX. (youngest son of Gustaf Vasa) and Christine of Holstein. His great natural faculties received an excellent education. From his tenth year he was present at cabinet councils, and when sixteen he held his first military command. Though yet a minor at his father's death in 1611, he received the crown on the resignation of the provisional government appointed by his father. Sweden was then engaged in a general war with all her neighbours, which closed in 1613 with the peace of Knœröd, leaving G. free to turn against the Russians, whom the peace of Stolbova (27th February 1617) deprived of Karelia and Ingermanland, and thereby excluded from the Baltic for a century. G. availed himself of the comparative quiet that followed for the internal improvement of Sweden. The army, the administration, and the courts of law were placed on a better footing, and just laws were enacted to regulate education and commerce. The war with Poland, however, continued till the six years' truce of 1629, and the next year G. landed in Germany (23d June 1630) with 15,000 men. He broke the power of the League at Breitenfeld, near Leipsic, 7th September 1631, delivered the hard-pressed Protestants of Mainz and the Rhine districts, and had already penetrated Bavaria, when Wallenstein's incursion into Saxony forced his return for its defence, and he fell victorious at Lützen, 6th November 1632. (See THIRTY YEARS' WAR.) G.'s life-object was to realise his father's idea of placing Sweden at the head of a great Protestant power in Europe, and to oppose Ferdinand II.'s encroachments on freedom of belief, as well as his schemes against the balance of power, and the political independence of the north. His full programme he had not time to carry out, but through him Sweden learnt her own power, and Germany won freedom of opinion. Though an ardent Protestant, he checked all unwarrantable retaliation against the Catholics, and his martinet discipline never lessened the deep love felt for him by his own army. See the important biographies of Gfrörer (4th ed. 1863) and Droysen (1870), and E. de Parieu's *Histoire de Gustave-Adolphe* (Par. 1875).—**G. III.**, eldest son of King Adolf Frederik and Louise Ulrike, sister of Friedrich II. of Prussia, was born at Stockholm, 24th January 1746. At his accession the people were in a state of discontent with the conduct of the nobles, and readily supported G. in the bloodless *coup d'état* of 19th August 1772, which, under pretence of suppressing a counterfeit rebellion, established a new form of government, assigning the executive, except the right of declaring war, to the king alone, and legislation to the king and the estates of the realm in common. G.'s moderation won the confidence of the Swedes; he abolished torture, gave freedom to the press, regulated the money system, established numerous trading companies, &c., for their welfare; but his love of display and imitation of French extravagance gradually alienated the affection of his people. In 1788 he entered on a war with Russia, but the greater number of his officers by common agreement ('Anjalaforbundet') refused to serve, on the ground that the king had not the right to initiate an offensive war. The Danes, in alliance with Russia, invaded Sweden, and their action roused the Swedes to support their king. The menaces of England erelong induced Denmark to withdraw, and G. took the opportunity to establish a new form of government under an act of security ('Säkerhetsakt'). The war lasted one and a half years longer, and was closed by the peace of Werelä (24th August 1790). Friendship for the house of Bourbon, and dread of revolutionary ideas, now tempted him to join the coalition against France. A diet was held at Gefle to deal with the national debt; but the nobles were displeased with the king's proposals, and conspired against him. At a masked ball, one of the conspirators named Anckarström wounded him with a pistol-shot, of which he died thirteen days after (29th March 1792). Judgments the most diverse have been formed of G. III., yet all must admit his great services in promoting the national taste and learning. He was the greatest orator of his time in Sweden. His speeches (chiefly political), dramas, letters, &c., were printed after his death under the title *Kon. G. III.'s Skrifter* (6 vols. 1806-12), having been published in French (by Dechaux) and German the year previous. Certain additional papers, forbid by G. to be published till fifty years after his death, appeared as *G. III.'s Efterlemnade Papper* (1843-44), but were found to be unimportant. See Beskow's *Biography of G.* (1868).—**G. IV., Adolf**, born November 1, 1778, at Stockholm, was still a minor at G. III.'s death, wherefore the government was intrusted till 1796 to his uncle, Duke Karl (afterwards Karl XIII.). G.'s reign began well, but his conduct gradually degenerated from firmness, justice, and the love of order to unfeeling self-will, with a trifling regard for forms. Some of his nobles saw fit to resign their titles, and the people became thoroughly disaffected through his attempts to curtail freedom of speech and of the press. To rescue trade from the English supremacy at sea, he formed an alliance in 1800 with Denmark, Russia, and Prussia, a step which also led to closer relations with France. In 1803 he undertook a journey to Baden, and during his stay there the imprisonment and death of the Duc d'Enghien occurred, to the great disgust of G., who refused to recognise Napoleon as emperor, and joined the Anglo-Russian coalition in 1805. With unparalleled obstinacy he rejected all offers of peace after the treaties of Tilsit, and would not sanction even an armistice concluded by the Swedish general in Pommern, in consequence of which that province was seized by the French, and Sweden became involved in war with Russia and Denmark. In this war the Swedes lost Finland. At last, when G. refused to assemble the estates, or hear any proposals of peace, and either his fall or that of Sweden seemed fated, he was seized and imprisoned by Adlercreutz on March 13, 1809. Seeking to abdicate in favour of his son, he, with his heirs, was declared in May to have for ever lost the crown of Sweden. The diet voted him and his family a yearly pension of 100,000 rigsdaler, which was some time afterwards discharged at a single payment. At the end of 1809 he went abroad, to live, at first as 'Count of Gottorp,' a rambling life in Germany apart from his family, then as 'Colonel Gustafsson' to become a citizen of Basel, though still continuing to travel in Germany and Switzerland till February 7, 1837, when he died at St. Gall. G. has given his own history in *Mémorial du Colonel Gustafsson* (1829; German trans. 1839), and *La Journée du 13 Mars 1809* (1835).

Güs'trow, the chief town in the Wendish circle, Mecklenburg-Schwerin, on the Nebel, 45 miles N.E. of Schwerin by rail. It was the fortified capital of the former duchy of G., and has a Gothic cathedral. It has distilleries, breweries, and a pop. (1875) of 10,923.

Gu'tenberg, Johannes, or **Henne**, also called **Gensfleisch**, who seems to have the best right to be regarded as inventor of the art of printing with movable types, was born at Mainz between 1395 and 1400, and was sprung from an old patrician family, taking the names of G. and of Gensfleisch from two estates in its possession. Of G.'s early life but little is known. Political troubles drove him about 1420 to Eltville and then to Strassburg, where he was certainly living in 1434. In 1438 he made a contract with Andreas Dryzehn and others for the prosecution in common of certain secret arts. From the records of a lawsuit in which G. had soon, unsuccessfully, to engage with Dryzehn's brother, it would appear that these secret arts included the rudiments of typography. In 1443 G. returned to his native city; and in 1450 we find him in company with Johann Faust (q. v.) or Fust, a wealthy goldsmith, who apparently provided the funds necessary for their common enterprise of printing. But ere long a quarrel separated the partners, and G. was compelled by the law courts to repay Faust for his advances. Faust also retained the printing apparatus, which he improved and wrought in partnership with Peter Schöffer (q. v.). G., on the other hand, obtained pecuniary backing from Hummer, one of the councillors of the city; and it seems that it was from G.'s new press that the *Catholicon* of 1460 came, as well as the Bible with 36 lines in the page, and the Letters of Indulgence of 1454 and 1455, &c. About 1465 G. was ennobled and attached to the court of Adolf of Nassau; he died 24th February 1468. The debt which the civilised world owes to G. for the art of printing has been very copiously discussed, and the most divergent opinions have been maintained concerning the relations of G., of Coster (q. v.), of Faust (q. v.), and of Schöffer (q. v.) to the development of the art. As the early printers practised their craft as a secret art, it is not singular that the controversy about the origin of an invention so recent and important should not have secured results clear and conclusive on every point. But against the view that G. stole the idea of using movable types from Coster (maintained most energetically by Koning in his *Verhandeling over het Oorsprong, &c. der Boekdrukkunst*, Haarlem, 1816), those who maintain G.'s sole right to be regarded as the inventor can allege the direct contemporary testimony of Ulrich Zell, who introduced printing into Köln, of the Alsatian scholar Wimpfeling, of Trithemus (who died in 1516), and of Johann, son of Peter Schöffer, and son-in-law of Faust. These all attribute the invention to G.; whereas the earliest positive testimony for Coster's claims is only the allegation of Junius in his work *Batavia* (Leyden, 1588). Schaab (in *Die Geschichte der Erfindung der Buchdruckerkunst*, Mainz, 1830-33) asserts that the printed works attributed to Coster are late and from types modelled on those of G. But a middle view, represented by Sotzmann (*G. und seine Mitbewerber*, 1841), grants that G. was excited to the discovery by specimens of Dutch xylography, but that to him belongs the grand idea of superseding copying in all its branches by printing; while the later xylographs and earliest type-printed works of Holland form a continuous series independent of foreign influence, though the superior German methods soon suppressed the Dutch art. See PRINTING.

Guth'rie, James, son of the laird of Guthrie, was a zealous minister of the Kirk of Scotland, and one of the first to suffer for his opinions after the Restoration. He was born before 1617, and was educated at St. Andrews, where he afterwards became professor of philosophy. In 1638 he was ordained at Lauder, and in 1649 was translated to Stirling, where he remained till his death. G. was the leader of the Protesters or extreme Presbyterian party in Church politics, and in 1650 publicly excommunicated the Earl of Middleton for his hostility to the covenant. In 1651 G. was deposed for disowning the king's authority in spiritual matters, and in 1661 he was brought to trial for the same offence, for writing two pamphlets *The Western Remonstrance* and *The Causes of the Lord's Wrath.* He defended himself with great eloquence, but was found guilty of treason, and condemned to death. The sentence was executed 1st June 1661. G. was also the author of an attack on Cromwell (*Considerations, &c., concerning Dangers which threaten Religion*, 1660; reprinted 1738), of sermons, and a treatise on ruling elders and deacons.—**William G.**, cousin of the preceding, was also an eminent Scottish churchman and divine. He was born 1620, and studied at St. Andrews. On receiving licence to preach, he resigned his family estate of Pitforthy to one of his brothers, and was ordained minister of Fenwick, near Kilmarnock, in 1644. He soon became a popular preacher, and was appointed chaplain to the Scots army, in which capacity he was present at the battle of Dunbar. Like his cousin, G. was a leader of the party of the Protesters. As a parish minister, he was much addicted to rural sports, especially fishing and fowling, and was popular even with those who did not adopt his views. Shortly after the Restoration in 1664, he was suspended from his charge by Archbishop Burnet, and never preached again. He died 10th October 1665. G. was author of the well-known work *The Christian's Great Interest*, which was translated into Dutch, German, and French. See Muir's *Memoirs and Letters of G.* (Edinb. 1827).

Guthrie, Thomas, D.D., an eminent preacher and philanthropist, sprung from the same family as the preceding, was born at Brechin in Forfarshire, 12th July 1803. Having entered the University of Edinburgh, he completed in 1824 the course in arts and theology necessary for the ministry of the Church of Scotland, but remained two years longer at the university, attending classes in anatomy, chemistry, and natural history. He was licensed in 1825, and after spending six months at Paris in the study of the natural sciences, managed a bank at Brechin till 1830, when he was presented to the parish of Arbirlot in his native county. In 1837 he became collegiate minister of Old Greyfriars, Edinburgh. To this congregation and its mission charge, St. John's, he was attached till the Disruption of the Scottish Church in 1843, when he left the Establishment and removed to Free St. John's. Of this congregation he continued to be nominally minister till his death at St. Leonard's-on-the-Sea, 24th February 1873, though failing health had compelled him to cease regular work several years before. His rhetorical powers, chief elements of which were freshness of style, effective delivery, and force and copiousness of illustration, rendered G. one of the most popular speakers of his time, and till the end drew crowds of all classes to his church. While at Arbirlot he attracted notice by the ability of his defence of the Established Church during what is known as the Voluntary controversy; in the 'Ten Years' Conflict' he was a zealous non-intrusionist, and in 1848 he devoted himself with singular zeal and success to the raising of a fund to provide manses for the country ministers of the Free Church. The cause, however, in connection with which his name is best and most widely known is that of the 'Ragged Schools,' of which, at least in their present form, he may be said to be the originator. In 1849 he received the honorary degree of D.D. from the University of Edinburgh, and in 1862 he was chosen Moderator of the Free Church Assembly. G. contributed to religious journals, edited for years the *Sunday Magazine*, and published volumes of sermons. Of his many popular works the best known are *Pleas for Ragged Schools, The Gospel in Ezekiel, Christ and the Inheritance of the Saints*, and *Speaking to the Heart.* An autobiography and memoir by his sons was published in 1875.

Guthrie, William, a compiler of histories, was the son of an episcopal minister, and was born at Brechin in 1701 or 1708. He graduated at King's College, Aberdeen, and about 1730 came to London. Here he was at first employed on the *Gentleman's Magazine.* In some of the very numerous works that bear his name, it appears that he was only one of several authors employed. Besides numerous translations of Cicero and Quintilian, G. compiled, wholly or partly, *A General History of England* (1744), *A Complete History of the English Peerage* (1763), *A General History of the World* (1764), *A New System of Modern Geography* (1770), *A General History of Scotland* (1746). G. had a pension from the Pelham Ministry, and died March 9, 1770.

Guth'rum the Dane, or **Guthrum of East Anglia**, a Danish leader who long opposed King Ælfred. He was beaten by Alfred in a great battle at Edington in 878, and forced to surrender after standing a siege of fourteen days in his camp. He was then baptized as a Christian, and the peace of Wedmore was concluded.

Gut Manufacture. This art is concerned with the preparation of Catgut (q. v.), Gold-Beater's Skin (q. v.), bags for preserved meats, coverings for jars, &c., from the intestines of oxen, sheep, pigs, and other animals. Lathe cords are made chiefly from the muscular coat of horses' intestines, which, after being cured and dried, is cut into strips and twisted. The gut bags used by sausage-makers are prepared by scouring and washing in water, and by scraping off with a peculiar knife the mucous and peritoneal membranes, incipient putrefaction being induced to facilitate their separation. The middle or muscular membrane is thereafter freely treated with water until no taint is perceptible, after which one end is tied with a ligature, and the whole insufflated, closed, and dried. The ligature is then cut, and the air expelled, and the gut is finally bleached and protected from insect ravages by fumigation with sulphur.

Guts Muths, Johann Christoph Friedrich, a German educationist, was born at Quedlinburg in Prussian Saxony, 9th August 1759. In the practical work of a teacher, he was led to realise the value of systematic physical training. This he developed in the educational institute at Schnepfenthal, while his *Gymnastik für die Jugend* (1793, 3d ed. 1845) taught all Germany the importance of this branch of education, and was long the basis of all similar works. Besides writing other treatises on gymnastics, G. M. was editor of the *Bibliothek für Pädagogik, Schulwesen und die gesammte pädagogische Literatur Deutschlands* (1800–20), and composed a *Handbuch der Geographie* (1810, several times reprinted). He died 21st May 1839.

Guttæ (Lat. *gutta*, 'drop;' Fr. *gouttes*), small drop-shaped ornaments worked on the cornice of classical buildings, on the under side of the mutules, and below the triglyphs in the Doric order of Grecian architecture.

Gutt'a Opa'ca, an old name for Cataract (q. v.).

Gutta-Per'cha (Malay for Sumatra gum), or **Gum Tu'ban**, is the inspissated juice of *Isonandra gutta*, a tree growing in Sumatra, Borneo, and various other islands of the East Indian archipelago. The juice, which has a dirty milky colour, is obtained by making deep incisions in the trunk of the tree; but in the early years of its collection the trees were cut down entirely and the bark stripped off, a procedure which would soon have resulted in the complete extermination of the species. The juice quickly solidifies and hardens on exposure to the air, when the G.-P. assumes its well-known brown leathery aspect and texture. The deep reddish-brown tint it usually presents is, however, due to the presence of accidental impurities, as pure G.-P. has a dirty greyish-white appearance. At ordinary temperatures G.-P. is hard, tough, and only slightly elastic; at from 110° to 120° F. it becomes soft and doughy; heated in boiling water it becomes very soft, and two surfaces pressed together then unite and thoroughly amalgamate; above 230° it boils and distils, yielding an oil analogous to the oil of caoutchouc. G.-P. consists of a mixture of three chemical principles, from 75 to 80 per cent. being the pure *gutta* upon which the properties of the article chiefly depend, 14 to 16 per cent. being a white crystalline resin called *albin*, and from 4 to 6 per cent. consisting of an amorphous yellow resin termed *fluavil.* G.-P. is not acted on by water, alcohol, or dilute acids or alkalies, but chloroform and bisulphide of carbon dissolve it completely. It is an excellent insulator of electricity.

G.-P. was not known in Europe till 1843, when the first specimen was sent to the Society of Arts, London, and Dr. Montgomerie, by observing the uses made of it by the Malays, brought its properties prominently into public notice. On its first introduction it was applied to a great variety of uses, many of which were abandoned, but the consumption of the raw material has nevertheless steadily increased. For manufacturing purposes it is purified and kneaded with powerful machinery with the aid of hot water and bleaching powder. It is then rolled out into thick sheets or plates ready for use. On account of its insulating properties G.-P. is much used for covering telegraph wires and as insulators. Its plasticity when heated is taken advantage of for obtaining the impression of seals, medals, coins, and also for preparing moulds of larger sculptured objects in the making of plaster casts. It is moulded into tubes in the same manner as lead and block tubes are prepared, and it is prepared in thin sheets for surgical purposes, and for wrapping up substances securely from air and moisture. It is extensively utilised as a cheap substitute for leather in the soles of boots and shoes, and it is moulded into many useful and decorative articles. Dissolved in bisulphide of carbon it forms a most tenacious cement, much used by shoemakers in patching, and combined with two parts of caoutchouc the advantages of both substances are obtained in the compound. Balata Gum (q. v.) is the produce of a South American tree *Sapota mullieri* having properties and composition the same as G.-P.

Gutta Sere'na, an old name for Amaurosis (q. v.).

Gutt'ée, Gutt'y, or **Goutt'ée** (Lat. *gutta*, 'a drop'), in heraldry, is applied to a field sprinkled with drops, which may be of various tinctures and convey various meanings.

Guttif'eræ, an important natural order of trees and shrubs. See CLUSIACEÆ.

Gutz'kow, Karl Ferdinand, one of the most prominent among recent German poets, essayists, and novelists, was born 17th March 1811 at Berlin. His early efforts were miscellaneous, and chiefly connected with journalism. Denounced in 1835 as a leader of the 'Young Germany' (*Junges Deutschland*) party, he was imprisoned, and for many years afterwards suspected by the German Government. After 1839 G. has chiefly been known as a dramatist, and as the author of novels bearing on the social questions of the time. His works are very numerous. Of his tragedies *Richard Savage* (1839) and *Uriel Acosta* (1847) are the most important, and of his comedies *Zopf und Schwert* (1844). His novels *Die Ritter vom Geiste* (in 9 vols. 1850, 4th ed. 1865) and *Der Zauberer von Rom* (also in 9 vols. 1859, 3d ed. 1863), at once made their mark, are rich in character and incident, and display a great power of grasping and delineating the different aspects of Roman Catholic and Protestant life. His *Gesammelte Werke* in 13 vols. appeared 1845–52; his *Dramatische Werke* in 20 vols. 1862–63, 3d ed. 1871.

Gutz'laff, Karl, a missionary to China, was born 8th July 1803, at Pyritz in Pommern, Prussia, and learnt the trade of saddler, but to his great joy was in 1821 admitted to a missionary college in Berlin. In 1826 he was sent as agent of a Dutch missionary society to Sumatra, but owing to a war then raging was detained at Batavia. Here he was thrown much into contact with Chinese settlers, acquired their language, and resolved to devote himself to evangelising China. After a short residence at Siam, G. came to Macao, and did his utmost to carry Christianity into the heart of the empire. Besides preaching and distributing tracts, G., along with Mr. Medhurst, began a new translation of the Bible into Chinese; with Morrison founded a society for widening the intellectual horizon of the Celestials; and edited a monthly Chinese magazine. He visited various parts of the empire (see his *Journal of Three Voyages along the Coast of China in* 1831, 1832, and 1833, Lond. 1834; Ger. trans. Basel, 1835). In 1835 he was appointed chief interpreter to the British representatives in China, and when all his missionary efforts were systematically thwarted by the Chinese authorities, G. made himself most useful to Britain during the Chinese war, and in the negotiations of 1842. In 1842 he founded a society for the employment of native Chinese as missionary agents. He visited Europe in 1849, and shortly after his return to China died at Hong-Kong, 9th August 1851. His most important works are *China Opened* (2 vols. Lond. 1838); *Geschichte des Chinesischen Reichs* (Stuttg. 1847); *The Life of Tao-Kuang* (Lond. 1851; Ger. trans. Leips. 1852).

Guy, Thomas, a philanthropist and the founder of Guy's Hospital, was born in Horsleydown, Southwark, London, in 1645. He started in trade as a bookseller, and obtained the privilege of printing Bibles for the University of Oxford. Among his public acts of benevolence were large benefactions to Stationers' Company and Christ's Hospital, the founding and endowing of almshouses and a free library at Tamworth, the building and endowing of three wards in St. Thomas's Hospital (1707). By lucky investments in the South Sea stock (1720) G. amassed his fortune of near half a million. In 1722 he built the hospital in Southwark which bears his name, and bequeathed nearly £220,000 towards its maintenance. He sat in Parliament from 1695 to 1702, and died 27th December 1724.

Guy's Hospital, in Southwark, was built by Thomas Guy (q. v.), who just lived to see it completed in 1724. It cost £18,793 to build and furnish. In addition to the £219,499 left by its founder, it received from Mr. Hunt in 1829 £180,000, and it has since been enlarged (the last addition in 1871) and enriched by several other bequests to the extent of £10,000. The hospital, managed by a body of sixty self-elected governors, has now (1877) accommodation for 700 patients, and an annual income of £40,000. The celebrated school of medicine and surgery attached to G. H. dates from 1769, and comprises some thirty lecturers. The school buildings include extensive museums and theatres, a library, and an improved chemical laboratory built in 1872.

Guy'on, Jeanne Marie Bouvier de la Motte, a famous French mystic, was born at Montargis, April 13, 1648. She married M. Guyon in 1664, and being left a widow at the age of twenty-five, settled her property on her children, and engaged almost wholly in a life of religious contemplation. When residing at Gex she fell under the influence of Père La Combe, a Barnabite, who imbued her with an extravagant mysticism. Her peculiar tenets exposed her to repeated persecutions, and after wandering to various French and Italian cities, and gaining many converts to La Combe's doctrine of Quietism (q. v.), she was imprisoned in 1688 in the convent of St. Marie, Paris. Liberated at the instance of Mde. de Maintenon, she mingled with the highest Parisian society, amid which her mysticism spread so rapidly that her numerous works were handed over for examination to Bossuet, who, infuriated by her grotesque language and unintelligible teachings, assailed Mde. G. with indignant zeal, while her cause was espoused by Fénélon, who strove to show that her doctrines were those of St. Francis de Sales, St. Theresa, and other mystics unimpugned by the Church. Bossuet, however, prevailed, and Mde. G. was imprisoned for heresy at Vincennes, Vangirard, and finally in the Bastille, where she remained for four years, being released in 1702. She then retired to Blois, where she died, 9th June 1717. Mde. G. was a woman of pure and lofty piety, but her mysticism was irrational and enervating, and often incoherently and fantastically expressed. Among her works are *Torrens Spirituels* (Köln, 1704); *Poésies Spirituelles* (Amst. 1689); *Cantiques Spirituels, Lettres Chrétiennes* (Köln, 1716); *L'Ame amante de son Dieu* (Köln, 1716); *Opuscules Spirituels* (Köln, 1704), &c. See the articles FÉNÉLON and QUIETISM, and *Vie de Madame G., écrite par elle-même* (Köln, 1720), a work which seems to have been written by Poiret, who obtained several of her papers.

Guyon, Richard Debaufre, a distinguished officer in the Hungarian war of independence, was the son of a commander in the English navy, and was born at Walcot, near Bristol, 31st March 1813. He took service in the Austrian army in 1831, married a daughter of an Austrian field-marshal in 1838, and shortly after quitted the army to live on his wife's estates. In 1848 G. received a command in the Pesth volunteers, and headed his battalion at Sukoro and Schwechet, commanded the advanced guard during Görgei's retreat, and distinguished himself by his valour in several of the most important battles of the war. After Temesvar, G. fled to Turkey, and soon obtained, without renouncing Christianity, an appointment in the Turkish service. In the Crimean war G. became chief of the staff in Asia Minor, and showed great energy and skill in organising the army, and in the defence of Kars. He died of cholera at Constantinople, October 13, 1856. See Kinglake's *History of the Invasion of the Crimea*.

Gu'zerat, or **Gujrat** (so called from the Gujar caste), a geographical division of India, lying N. and N.W. of Bombay, which includes the dominions of the Gaekwar of Baroda, the Kattywar peninsula, and the British districts of Ahmedabad, Broach, and Surat. G. had a place in history, but has no longer any political importance. It has given its name to famous breeds of cattle and horses, and to the Guzerati dialect, which is a vernacular derivative from the Sanskrit stock, and is the official language for a population of about 3,000,000. See Durnall's *Chronological and Historical Chart of India* (Lond. 1877).

Gwal'ior, a native state of Central India, covers a great part of the ancient province of Malwa. Area, 33,119 sq. miles; pop. 2,500,000; revenue, including tribute from feudatories, £1,200,000. G. is chiefly watered by the Chumbul, and is very fertile; produces the well-known Malwa opium, cotton, tobacco, iron, &c.; and has manufactures of iron, brassware, cotton and silk cloth. The ruler, Scindia, is one of the three great Mahratta chiefs. The first of the name was slipper-bearer to the Peishwa; the second founded the kingdom, and dominated over the Mogul Emperor; the third came into collision with the British and was defeated at Assaye and Laswari. Anarchy then prevailed for some time, but the present Maharajah, who succeeded in 1843, is a most enlightened ruler, with the military instincts of his family. He was loyal during the Mutiny of 1857, together with his minister, Dinkur Rao, but his army revolted. The present force consists of 48 guns, 6000 horse and 5000 foot, and is most efficient. Railways have been constructed at the cost of a million and a half sterling.

Gwalior, the capital of the preceding state, is 65 miles S. of Agra. Its most notable feature is the fort, which consists of a sandstone rock, 342 feet high, made precipitous by nature and art, and capable of containing a garrison of 15,000 men. It has been famous throughout Indian history, and was captured by the British in 1779; it is still occupied by the G. contingent, officered by Englishmen. A fine palace on the plain is now being built in the Italian style. The town lies W., and the Lashkar or military camps S. of the fort. In 1875 a person falsely supposed to be the Nana Sahib was arrested here by Scindia. The Prince of Wales was magnificently entertained at G. in the spring of 1876. On the 1st of January 1877 the Maharajah was made G.C.B., and honorary general in the British army.

Gwyn'iad (*Coregonus pennanti*), a species of Teleostean fishes belonging to the genus *Coregonus* (q. v.), found in the Welsh and Cumberland lakes, and known under the popular name of 'fresh-water herring.' The Powan (q. v.) of Loch Lomond is an allied species. The average length of the G. is 10 or 12 inches. It has a prominent first dorsal fin, but the mouth is small. The tail is forked.

Gwynne, Nell, a fascinating actress and a mistress of Charles II., born in London, February 2, 1650. At the Portugal Street Theatre and at Drury Lane she won the hearts of the town, especially by personating youthful gallants. Pepys calls her 'a mighty pretty soul!' She was a generous, witty, and very beautiful madcap, with a laughing face and curling golden-brown hair. It is said she received £60,000 in four years from Charles II., who intended to make her Countess of Greenwich, and whose last words were, 'Do not let poor Nelly starve.' She was pensioned by James II., and died in her thirty-eighth year, November 1687.

Gy'ges. 1. A Lydian who dethroned Candaules, married his queen and ascended the throne of Lydia about 716 B.C. According to Herodotus, Candaules, vain of the beauty of his queen, Nyssia, exhibited her naked charms to G. his favourite officer. Writhing under the affront, and bent on vengeance, she summoned G. and ordered him either to prepare for death, or to slay her husband and accept his kingdom together with her hand. G. chose the latter alternative, and became the founder of the dynasty of the Mermnadæ. The Lydians were at first unwilling to submit to his rule, but eventually accepted it in consequence of an oracle from Delphi. In gratitude G. sent splendid gifts to the shrine. He carried on war with several Asiatic cities, and his wealth passed into a proverb. He reigned thirty-eight years. Plato's well-known fable of the 'ring of G.,' reproduced by Cicero (*De Offic.* iii. 9), and frequently alluded to by medieval writers, is a moral allegory founded on the story of the Lydian king.—2, **Gyges**, called also **Gyas** or **Gyes**, a son of Cœlus and Terra, had fifty heads and a hundred hands. With the rest of the giants he made war against the gods, and was doomed to endless punishment in Tartarus for his impious and rebellious conduct.

Gymna'sium and Gymnas'tics. The gymnasium (from Gr. *gymnos*, 'naked') was the public building in which a Greek youth received his education. This education included grammar, music, and gymnastics. The last subject was deemed by the Greeks the most important; and while training in the others was left off after a certain period, gymnastic exercises were continued even to an advanced age by persons of culture, these exercises in the case of elderly persons being necessarily of a lighter and less fatiguing character. The practice arose from the conviction that bodily health was conducive to mental vigour. As the word denotes, gymnastic exercises were undergone by persons either quite nude or but lightly clad. The benefit of such public training, not only to the general health, but also to the arts of sculpture and painting, can hardly be over-estimated. On the other hand, at a later period of Greek history, it must be confessed that the effects of the public exhibition were most pernicious. Nearly every town in Greece had a gymnasium. Athens possessed three—the Lyceum, Cynosarges, and the Academia—all splendid structures, and containing covered and open apartments, colonnades, walks, baths, &c. The earliest regulations for the gymnasia are contained in the laws of Solon. From these we learn that they were open from sunrise to sunset; that adults were excluded while the boys were taking their exercises; and that slaves were not admitted to training. In Athens and in the Ionian States women were excluded from the gymnasium. In Sparta and other Doric States maidens took part in the exercises. The instructions were given by *gymnastæ* and *paidotribæ*. Among games may be mentioned those of ball and top, and a variety of amusements with the rope. Of the exercises, the most important were running, leaping, wrestling, boxing, dancing, and throwing the discus or quoit. Many gymnasia were erected by the Romans, but they never became popular, the thermæ and amphitheatres possessing for the Italian races a superior charm. In course of time gymnastics fell out of repute; indeed the science was not revived in Europe till the beginning of the present century. Prussia led the way in this revival, and also in the institution of gymnastic exercises as a branch of military training. In 1806 gymnasia were opened by Basedow (q. v.) and Salzmann; that of the latter at Schnepfenthal being under the direction of Guts Muths. (q. v.). Sweden followed, then France in 1844, and last of all Britain about twenty years ago set about establishing gymnastics at Aldershott and elsewhere. The system of instruction consists of two parts: the first—elementary gymnastics—embracing special movements for the purpose of developing the muscles, and giving the performer confidence and self-command; the second—applied gymnastics—comprising such exercises as leaping, climbing, vaulting, suspension, &c. Swimming (q. v.), Boating (q. v.), Golf (q. v.), Cricket (q. v.), Football (q. v.) are among the best of gymnastic exercises. The treatises on gymnastics—English and Continental—form a considerable library.

The term gymnasium is applied in Germany to a higher school—corresponding to the public school, high school, or grammar school in this country—in which boys are trained for the universities. The gymnasia differ, however, essentially from such public schools as Eton, Harrow, and Rugby, in respect that all the pupils are day scholars, and do not reside in the buildings.

Gymne'ma, the genus to which the Cow Plant (q. v.) of Ceylon belongs.

Gymne'trus, a genus of Teleostean fishes, including those popularly named 'Ribbon-Fishes' (q. v.) and 'tape-fishes,' from the great length and narrow conformation of their bodies. The familiar species is the *G.* (or *Regalecus*) *Banksii*, which is frequently captured off our coasts, and may attain a length of 11 or 12 feet. One specimen is mentioned as having measured over 60 feet, and the appearance of such a fish, seen at a distance swimming through the sea, may possibly have given rise to many of the tales of the Sea Serpent (q. v.).

Gymnoc'ladus, a genus in the order *Leguminosæ*, having only one species, *G. Canadensis*, a large N. American tree, popularly called Kentucky coffee-tree and chicot. Its fruit is preserved like tamarind, its seeds are used as coffee, and its wood, which is hard, is valued by cabinetmakers.

Gym'nogens, or **Gym'nosperms**, a section under the sub-class *Monochlamydeæ* in the natural system of classification of plants. G. include the natural orders *Coniferæ* (q. v.) and *Cycadaceæ* (q. v.).

Gymnoso'mata (Gr. 'naked-bodied'), one of the two groups into which the class *Pteropoda* (q. v.) of the Molluscan (q. v.) sub-kingdom is divided. This division includes the pteropods, such as *Clio* (q. v.), &c., in which no shell is developed.

Gymnos'ophists (Gr. 'naked sages'), a class of philosophical or religious ascetics in India, who denied themselves the luxury of raiment or other bodily pleasures.

Gymno'tus, a genus of Teleostean fishes, represented by the *G. electricus*, an electrical eel of S. American marshes, and included in the division *Malacopteri*, of the order *Teleosti*, and in the section *Apoda*, in which the ventral fins are entirely wanting. The G. derives its zoological fame from having organs adapted for converting nerve-force into electricity. (See ELECTRICITY, ANIMAL.) Its length is from 4 to 5 feet. The skin is soft, and is destitute of scales. The G. is caught by the Indians, who drive horses and mules into the water, and thus cause the eel to exhaust the full force of its electrical apparatus upon these animals. When the fish is exhausted it seeks the shore, and can then be captured without danger.

Gym'pie, a town in Queensland, Australia, 116 miles N. of Brisbane. It is entirely dependent upon the yield of the auriferous quartz reefs which surround it, and to the discovery of which, in 1867, it owes its existence. The value of the gold produced at G. since that date is about £1,500,000. Pop. (1875) 5793.

Gyne'rium, the generic name of the Pampas Grass (q. v.) (*G. argenteum*) of S. America. It is a splendid grass, and is frequently grown in British gardens as an ornamental plant.

Gynerium argenteum.

Gyo'ma, a town of Hungary, on the Körös, 89 miles S.E. of Pesth by railway. It is celebrated for its wine. Pop. (1869) 8587.

Gyöngyös, a town in the centre of Hungary on a stream of the same name, at the S. base of the Matra mountains, 55 miles N.E. of Pesth by railway. It has a large trade in a celebrated red wine, and in grain, fruit, horses, and cattle. Pop. (1869) 15,830.

Gypae'tos. See LAMMERGEYER.

Gyps, a genus of vultures, represented by the Griffon (q. v.), or fulvous vulture, and by other species.

Gyp'sies (Early Eng. *Gyptians*, corrupted from Egyptians), a singular wandering race, formerly believed to have come from Egypt, but now understood to be originally an Indian tribe or group of tribes, made their first appearance in Asia Minor and in the Greek-speaking countries in the S.E. of Europe early in the Middle Ages—the exact date is unknown. The earliest mention of them is in 1322. The only existing record of their history is to be sought for in their language, and this line of investigation into the early annals of the race was first followed with success by Rüdiger in his *Neuester Zuwachs der Sprachkunde* (Halle, 1782–93), and has since been successfully prosecuted by recent scholars in Germany, England, America, &c. In 1417 considerable numbers of G. (followed in a few years by still larger hordes) appeared in the north of Germany, whence they gradually spread themselves over every country in Europe—to Britain on the W. and Spain on the S. They were led by a 'duke' and 'count,' and they carried with them commendatory letters from kings and princes, including one (probably a forgery) from the Emperor Sigismund. From the earliest times their character as a race has remained unchanged—they were vagabonds, tricksters, thieves on their first appearance in Europe, and such the *tent-G.* remain to the present day; though those who have become 'house-dwellers' conform more or less to the usages of the people among whom they are domiciled. With their own ever-varying accounts of their origin as a people, and of the reasons which caused them to migrate from the East into Europe, it is needless to concern ourselves, as such accounts were invented and coloured as occasion and necessity required. Certain swarms described themselves as having come from 'Little Egypt,' hence the name they bear in England. The immigrants of 1417, however, were named *Secani*, and they are now almost universally spoken of as *Cingari* or *Chingani*. In Italy the name is *Zingari*, in Spain *Zincali*, in Germany *Zigeuner*, &c. They never, however, speak of themselves by any of these names, but always as *Rommany*. Among other Indian tribes who tell fortunes by chiromancy, and are addicted to legerdemain, cheating and thieving, are the *Nats*; and the later immigrations of G. into Europe are supposed to have belonged to that race. To the investigations into the language of the G. by Pott of Halle and Miklosich of Vienna we owe a number of facts bearing upon the early history and successive migrations of this singular people. Their language was originally spoken by a border tribe of Northern India. During the continuous wanderings of swarms cast off from this tribe the original language became much modified, until in modern times it appears as Rommany. Many of the original words were lost and many new words were adopted from every country through which the vagrants passed. An analysis of the language as it at present exists, and a calculation of the number of foreign and corrupted words which have been engrafted upon it, prove that the G. entered and remained long in Persia, that they thence passed to a Greek-speaking country (many of the Rommany words, numbers, &c., are still Greek), and that they thence passed through Hungary into Central Europe. They paused in immense numbers in Bohemia before penetrating further west, and to the French they are still 'Bohemians.' We learn from Lieut.-Col. MacGregor's *Central Asia* that in Ghilan (Persia) G. are still very numerous. 'There they preserve the characteristics of their race, as in other parts of the world. Fortune-telling is the occupation of the women. They live in little camps formed of miserable tents, in which they migrate from the hot to the cold country according to the season. The donkey is their companion, and his master is the professional vendor of pots and pans. In features and habits they differ but little from their brethren in the W.' It is curious that among the English G. Leland has collected an immense number of Indian and Persian words, which have not yet been collected among the different Rommany tribes on the Continent, and thus this writer is led to believe that the English branch is a separate migration. The G. in England are described by those who have lived with them, and who have devoted years to the study of their language, habits, and character, as a robust and extremely handsome race. Writing in 1846, Borrow states that in no country do the G.—everywhere a strikingly handsome people—reach such perfection of form and complexion as in England. 'The women while young are of a very high type of beauty, but after the prime is past they become unusually ugly. The men are taller than the English peasantry, and far more active.' They first appeared in the S. of England in considerable numbers in 1512, and immediately began to develop their vagabond and thieving propensities with great industry and success. Native thieves joined them, and the old thieves' slang of the country, as well as a considerable portion of the more modern slang, is based upon Rommany. The authorities began to frown upon them in 1522, and regarded them as exercising 'no craft but palmistry and robbery.' Though 'wanted' by the authorities, in terms of an Act for the apprehension of vagabonds, G., conspirators, prophesiers, players, and such like, their numbers continued to increase, and it is said that there were 10,000 of them in England in 1563. The circumstance that Acts for their suppression were unavailing led to the enactment of unduly severe laws against them. A few years prior to the Restoration, thirteen G. were executed simply because they belonged to the vagabond class. They still furnish the majority of our hawkers and tinkers, chair-menders, mat and basket sellers, &c., and according to Leland, there is not a theatre or music-hall, either in England or America, that does not include one or more persons of gypsy descent, near or remote. At present (1877) the full-blooded or *tent-G.* in England are only a few thousands in number, while the *Kairengroes* or house-dwellers, those who keep their gypsy blood a secret, and half-breeds, all of whom speak Rommany more or less perfectly, number perhaps as many as 20,000. In Scotland the wanderers first appeared in 1460, *i.e.*, if Simson's conjecture that they are referred to under the name 'Saracens' be correct, which is, however, very doubtful. In 1506 they were favoured so far by James IV. as to receive a grant of special privileges. During the 16th c. they multiplied and increased amazingly, and married well among the natives, their thieving habits, as Simson remarks, being no bar to matrimonial alliances among a people so accustomed to thieving as the Scotch. Early in the 17th c., however, several oppressive edicts were issued against them, and to be a gypsy was declared to be a capital crime. Nevertheless, the G. in Scotland were always in favour with the people; for though they were generally robbers and villains of the worst description, yet they were invested with a certain air at once of gallantry and 'uncannyness' which had their due effect among the peasantry. The consequence was that in Scotland the G. flourished so long as they were persecuted, but began to decline and decay as soon as persecution was withdrawn. At one time the small town of Yetholm in Roxburghshire was inhabited by them exclusively, but now few are found in the neighbourhood. The majority of the Scottish G. have emigrated to America. In the New World these wanderers have generally become 'house-dwellers,' and have become lost to view as a distinctive race. In Europe the number of G., who are massed principally in the basin of the lower Drave and in Hungary and Wallachia, is about 500,000. There are, it is computed, between two and three hundred works on the G. The following are probably the best:—Dr. R. Bright, *Travels from Vienna through Hungary* (Edinb. 1818); Dr. A. F. Pott, *Die Zigeuner in Europa und Asien* (Halle, 1844); Dr. A. G. Paspati, *Études sur les Tchinghianés* (Constan. 1870)—a most important work; Dr. F. Miklosich, *Ueber die Mundarten und die Wanderungen der Zigeuner Europa's*, published in the *Denkschriften der Wiener Akademie der Wissenschaften* (Vienna, 1872–76); C. G. Leland, *The English G. and their Language* (1874), *Egyptian Sketch-Book* (1873), and *English Gypsy Songs in Rommany* (1875); G. Borrow, *Romano Lavo-lil* (Lond. 1874); Dr. B. C. Smart and H. T. Crofton, *The Dialect of the English G.* (Lond. 1875). This last is by far the best work on the English G. For everything relating to the history of the G., apart from the language, the best works are those of P. Bataillard, *De l'Apparition et de la Dispersion des Bohémiens en Europe* (Par. 1849), &c.

Gyp'sum, a widely-distributed mineral, composed essentially of sulphate of lime and water. It crystallises in the monoclinic system, and is between degrees 1·5 and 2 in the scale of hardness. Pure and crystallised specimens are clear and transparent, with a pearly lustre; but varieties are obtained of all shades of grey, red, brown, and black. Before the blowpipe it becomes white and opaque, crumbling readily in the fingers to loose powder. It is frequently met with forming twin crystals, and it occurs also in laminar, fibrous, stellated, granular, and compact masses. *Selenite* includes all the transparent crystallised varieties, which generally cleave easily into thin flexible laminæ. Of uncrystallised variety, *alabaster* is the finest. It is fine-grained, compact, white, and semi-transparent, and easily workable into vases and small articles of ornament. Its slight solubility in water ultimately renders its surface rough and opaque. *Satin-spar* is a white, delicately fibrous variety, characterised by a fine play of colours. Though employed for ornamental purposes, its softness and liability to being scratched prevent its very extensive use. G., rendered anhydrous by burning, reduces easily to a powder, which is known as *plaster of Paris*. This powder, when mixed with its own bulk of water, sets almost at once into a firm white solid. G. is also ground down and used as a manure.

Gypsy-Wort, the English name for *Lycopus Europæus*, a labiate plant found by ditches and river-banks in Britain and throughout Europe. It yields a black dye, which is used by gypsies to render their skins darker, hence the name G.-W.

Gyr'falcon (*Falco gyrfalco*), a species of Falcons (q. v.) found in N. Europe, Iceland, and N. and S. America. The average length is about 2 feet, or rather less. The colour is nearly white, only the upper parts being marked by light-brown bars. The toes are yellow and the claws black. The G. is trained in Falconry (q. v.) to pursue other birds, and is capable of a high degree of training. It is sometimes named the Iceland falcon and Greenland falcon.

Gyri'nus, or **Whirl'igig Bee'tles**, a genus of *Coleoptera* (q. v.) or beetles common in ponds and rivers, and so named from their peculiar movements on the surface of the water. The *G. natator* is a familiar example. These insects are nearly allied to the species of the genus *Dytiscus* (q. v.). They dive and swim well, and are of small size. Their eggs are deposited on aquatic plants.

Gy'romancy (Gr. *gyros*, 'a circle,' and *manteia*, 'prophecy'), a mode of divination practised by means of a circle with letters or symbols placed or inscribed thereon. Round this circle the gyromancist walked repeating a formula of incantation and stopping at intervals. At each stoppage the letters or symbols were carefully noted, and at the conclusion of his rounds all these were collected, disposed into words or sentences, and interpreted. The result thus obtained was supposed to be the intimation of the will of Heaven. See DIVINATION.

Gyroph'ora, the generic name of the lichens called *Tripe de Roche* (q. v.).

Gy'roscope and Gy'rostat are instruments which show to the eye many curious dynamical effects of rotational motion. When any symmetrical body is set rotating round a principal axis, it will continue to so rotate, and, unless an external force act upon it, the axis will retain its original direction. It is this persistency in the direction of the earth's axis that gives rise to the succession of the seasons, and to the same principle we owe the greater efficiency of rifled arms, which project the bullet with a rotatory motion, as compared with that of smooth-bored weapons. The gyroscope consists of a heavy rimmed disc, whose axis of rotation is fitted in Gimbals (q. v.), like the box of a mariner's compass. If an effort be made to change the direction of this axis, while the disc is rotating, a powerful resistance will be experienced. A very curious effect is produced if a downward-acting force, such as a suspended weight, act at the one extremity of the axis of rotation. The extremity is, of course, depressed a certain distance, but there results a precessional rotation of the axis—a motion precisely analogous to that presented by a common spinning-top whose axis is off the perpendicular. When this instrument was first made is not known, but to Foucault (q. v.) is due the credit of bringing it into general notice. He used it to prove by ocular demonstration the diurnal rotation of the earth. More recently Professor Piazzi Smyth, Astronomer-Royal for Scotland, has employed it with considerable success to the steadying of a telescope at sea. The gyrostat of Sir William Thomson is simply a gyroscope enclosed in a rigid case, which is flat and wheel-like in shape. Such an instrument can stand upon its rim in any set position while the internal disc is rotating; and if it be made the bob of a pendulum under certain conditions, the plane of oscillation revolves in accordance with the laws of the composition of rotations. The same physicist has recently constructed a liquid gyrostat, which consists of a spheroidal metallic case filled with liquid. The equatorial axis is greater than the polar axis by one-tenth of either, and with this ellipticity the gyrostat when set in rapid rotation behaves in the same way as those of common construction—though the action of fluid friction introduces curious theoretical considerations. See *Nature*, vol. xv., February 1, 1877.

Gyu'la, a town of Hungary, in the circle of Békés, 30 miles N. of Arad by railway. It is divided by the White Körös into Hungarian and German quarters, and has a trade in cattle, oil, angel-fish, &c. Pop. (1869) 18,495.

H.

H the eighth letter in the English alphabet, occupying the same position as in the Latin and the original Phœnician. In the last-mentioned alphabet, its form was *cheth*, a hard guttural, which the Greeks, who used no proper H, took to represent their long *e* or *eta;* but in Latin the same ideograph was recovered as the sign of the aspirate, but pronounced soft as in English. Though etymologically it is very valuable, as representing its cognates *c, k,* and *ch,* its pronunciation is very irregular. In modern Italian its very existence has been lost; the best French pronunciation of the present day omits it altogether; in English its use is apparently on the increase; while in the lisping Spanish and guttural German it occupies a prominent place. Its superfluous insertion in the spoken language, which is so prominent a mark of vulgar provincialism, was also reprobated at Rome by Cicero and Catullus. But, on the other hand, its disappearance from many English words which had it in their primary or Old English form has been injurious to philology. H is sometimes mute in the middle of a word, as in 'right;' and it has a peculiar sound in 'which,' &c., as preceding and not following the *w.* Examples of its interchanges are—Eng. 'horn' = Lat. *cornu* = Gr. *keras;* Span. *hembra* = Lat. *femina;* Span. *hermano* = Lat. *germanus.*

As an abbreviation H.R.H. stands for his royal highness; H.M.S. for her Majesty's ship; H.P. for half-pay.

Haar'lem ('the clayey mound'), the chief town of the province of N. Holland, in the Netherlands, on both banks of the Spaarne, 4 miles from the sea and 12 W. of Amsterdam by railway. One of the finest and healthiest towns in the Netherlands, it was formerly the residence of the Counts of Holland, is the see of a Catholic and of a Jansenist bishop, and has many fine buildings, of which the chief are the church of De Groote or St. Bavo's Kerk, dating from the 15th c., with its tower 138 feet high, and its world-famous organ (1735–38) 34 feet high, of register 68, and 8000 pipes; the old townhall, richly ornamented with carving; the well-endowed, half charitable, half scientific Teyler Institution, with its fine collections of physical instruments, large library, and astronomical observatory; the Royal Academy of Science, founded in 1752; and the royal palace of Welgeleque in the beautiful H. Hout (Ger. *Holz*) or Bosch. There is a famous royal school for teachers, another of clinical surgery, and many charitable refuges (*hofjes*). In the market-place a marble statue was erected to Laurens Coster (q. v.) in 1856. H. is intersected by the river, here crossed by five bridges, and by various canals. It is the centre of the great Dutch trade in flowers, bulbs, and seeds, and has considerable manufactures of velvet, silk, linen, gold and silver stuffs, the cotton and linen mixtures called *H. boutjes*, carpets, lace, &c. Pop. (1875) 34,132. H. was a place of importance as early as the middle of the 12th c., and took an active part in the wars against the W. Frisians. In 1492 it sided with the peasant or 'cheese-and-bread' insurgents, and was partly destroyed and deprived of its privileges. In the war of independence of the 16th c. it took the part of the allies, and heroically withstood a seven months' siege by the Spaniards, only surrendering eventually on fair conditions, which were violated with foulest treachery.

Haarlem Lake, a former lagoon in the vicinity of the above city, from which it took its name, and connected with the Zuider Zee. By the beginning of the 19th c. it had been increased by the advance of the sea to an area of 45,000 acres. Much damage was done to Amsterdam and Leyden by an overflow in 1836. At last a company of English engineers commissioned by the Government succeeded in draining the lake by cutting deep canals and using gigantic pumps. The work, which is one of the engineering triumphs of modern times, occupied from 1839 to 1852. See Gevers d'Eude-Geest, *Du Dessèchement du Lac de H.* (1853) and *Journal des Ponts et Chaussées* (1842–63).

Haar'lingen (Fries. *Harns*), the fourth seaport in Holland, and the great trade centre in the province of Friesland, on the coast near the mouth of the Zuider Zee, 12 miles W. of Leeuwarden by railway. It is intersected by canals, has old fortifications, and is protected from the sea by immense dykes 40 feet high. As the headquarters of the Friesian Steam Shipping Company it has regular communication with Amsterdam, the Nieuwe Diep, Hull, and the Thames. The exports are chiefly butter, cheese, and cattle. In 1874 there entered the port 705 vessels of 196,110 tons, and cleared 689 of 192,197 tons. H. has a Latin school, a drawing academy, and school of navigation. Pop. (1875) 9968. A town that formerly stood here was submerged in 1134.

Habakk'uk (Heb. 'the embracing'), **The Book of,** one of the Hebrew prophets, is divided into two parts—chaps. i. and ii., entitled 'The burden which Habakkuk the prophet did see,' and chap. iii. 'A prayer of Habakkuk the prophet.' Both parts refer to the judgment which Jehovah either threatens or executes on his people by means of a foreign nation, the Chaldæans (i. 6). Very various opinions have been entertained as to the age to which Habakkuk belonged, and the date of the composition of his book. All that can be gathered from the contents, which is the only source of information on the subject, is (1) that the Chaldæans had already extended their march to the west, and (2) that this march had only very recently begun, so that they had not yet arrived at Jerusalem, and were little known there (i. 6–11). These circumstances seem to render it most probable that the prophet wrote in the reign of Jehoiakim. The book, especially chap. iii., is one of the most beautiful and sublime remains of Hebrew literature.

Ha'beas Cor'pus Act is in England one of the main guarantees of the Rights of the People (q. v.). Under the Act 31 Car. II. c. 10, if any one be imprisoned he may have a writ of Habeas Corpus to bring him before the Queen's Bench or Common Pleas division, who shall determine whether the cause of his committal be just. This Act embraces only criminal committals, but 53 Geo. III. c. 100 extends the remedy to all cases, and the power of issuing the writ to all judges. By 25 and 26 Vict. c. 20, no writ of Habeas Corpus can issue out of England into any colony or foreign dominion of the crown, in which there is a law court having power to issue and execute the writ. In times of great political excitement, if treasonable conspiracies are suspected, the H. C. A. has sometimes been suspended. It was so in Ireland in 1866. But suspension does not entitle any authority to imprison a man without cause. It only prevents persons committed (see COMMITTAL) from being bailed, tried, or discharged during the suspension, leaving to the committing magistrate all the responsibility of illegal imprisonment. It is not uncommon therefore to pass subsequent to suspension an Act of Indemnity (q. v.) for the protection of those who either could not defend themselves in an action for false imprisonment without making an inexpedient disclosure, or who have acted illegally believing the illegal act to be for the public good. There are various sorts of Habeas Corpus. That which secures the liberty of the subject is the writ of Habeas Corpus *ad subjiciendum*, directed to the person detaining another, and commanding him to produce the body of the prisoner, with a specification of the day and cause of the caption and detention, and commanding the captor to obey the decree of the judge or court issuing the writ. The Scotch Act corresponding to the English Habeas Corpus is the Act of 1701, c. 6. See WRONGOUS IMPRISONMENT.

Haben'dum, in English law, is, in a deed of grant, the name of the clause descriptive of the estate granted, and of the length of time for which it is to be held.

Haber'geon (a French diminutive from Old Eng. *heals beorga*, 'a protection for the neck') was a short jacket of chain-mail reaching from the neck to the middle. Readers of Chaucer will remember the garb of the 'verray perfight gentil knight,'

> 'Of fustyan he werede a gepoun
> Al bysmotered with his *habergeon*.'

Hab'it may be defined as the specialised effect of repetition on the human mind. There are, in the first place, certain purely mechanical acquirements which depend on the endowments of the active organs concerned, the delicacy of the particular senses concerned, and any special interest which the mind may have in the process under consideration. Sets of muscles vary very much, not only in their contractile force, but in their spontaneity and their sensibility to degrees of expenditure. This last is most important, as no amount of flexibility or compass will enable us to rise above the discrimination of the effect produced. Effective training depends on the freshness of the system. Hence military drill takes place in early morning, after breakfast, and after dinner. Among the more strictly intellectual habits are language, the scientific faculty, and acquisitions in the fine arts. Language of course depends on the opportunities of hearing and speaking, but it is in most cases greatly modified by special interests. Hence the peculiar styles of great writers and speakers. There are, however, singular instances of pure verbal memory coinciding with total ignorance of the connection of names and things. The science of mnemonics addresses itself to this form of mental H. But the moral habits, or the acquirements relating to feelings and volitions, are the more generally interesting. Conscious control by self or others is more frequently directed to moral than to purely intellectual ends. The general conditions of moral acquirement are mental concentration and natural retentiveness. It is very important to avoid defeat. A simple case is the H. of morning bathing in cold water in all weathers. Here, ideal conceptions of ultimate good gradually weaken the repulsion of the physical shock. Another case is where the mind becomes indifferent to and is able to work amid noise and bustle originally of the most distracting kind. Habitual sympathy, stimulation, and encouragement have a great effect in developing a generally emotional character, often to the great detriment, sometimes to the complete starvation, of the intellect and will. Then, as regards special emotions, anger, terror, or some tender feeling, they are all capable of culture and of being put more or less under control. Apart from these, however, and from the command of trains of ideas which long practice gives, there is a distinct cultivation of the will which issues in the most valuable of all human qualities—endurance and persistence.

Habit (*Physiology*).—It is apparently a law in the organism of animals that after any function has been frequently performed, there is a tendency to a repetition of the function. This constitutes H. Thus all excito-motor and sensori-motor actions are repeatedly performed without any effort on the part of the individual, or even without his consciousness. It is also observed that actions which were at first acquired with painstaking care become after a time easily performed, thus also exemplifying the force of H.

Habit and Repute', a phrase of Scotch law denoting a force of public belief so strong as legally to prove the matter believed in. The most common application of the phrase is to marriage, which in Scotland may be constituted by the mere fact of a man and woman living together as husband and wife. That is, the law presumes that there has been consent on the part of each to the contract of marriage, and the presumption thus afforded is so strong that no evidence to the contrary will be listened to. H. and R. is also a phrase of the criminal law of Scotland applied to one who is notoriously a thief. The convict must have borne the character for at least six months to merit the severer sentence generally passed on the thief by H. and R.

Habita'tion, in Roman law, denoted a rule under which a dwelling-house could only be used as such. In England and Scotland the restriction can only be under contract.

Offences against Habitations are by law Arson (q. v.), Burglary (q. v.), Housebreaking (q. v.), and Stealing. See LARCENY OR THEFT.

Habit'ual Crim'inals Act. This Act was passed in 1869 to make further provision for the suppression of crime committed by convicts under Ticket of Leave (q. v.), but this statute was repealed, and 34 and 35 Vict. c. 112 put in place of it. Under this Act, any constable, if so authorised by the chief officer of police of his district, may take into custody any convict holding a licence, if there are reasonable grounds for believing that he is getting his livelihood dishonestly, and on proof before a court of summary jurisdiction, his licence is to be forfeited. A convict holding a licence must notify his residence to the chief officer of police of the district, and also any change of his residence. Criminals are to be registered and photographed. Persons twice convicted on indictment may be specially punished and subjected to police supervision. New penalties are imposed on harbouring thieves, and powers are given to search for stolen property, and to seize and secure property believed to be stolen.

Hack'berry, the common name for the fruit of certain species of *Celtis*, a genus of plants belonging to the natural order *Ulmaceæ*. See NETTLE-TREE.

Hack'länder, Friedrich Wilhelm, a German novelist and dramatist, was born 1st November 1816, at Burtschien near Aachen, was at first engaged in commerce, then in the state service of Würtemberg, and has since 1864 retired into private life. H. is a keen humorist, and has been called 'the German Dickens.' His works are very numerous, but of the tales the *Bilder aus dem Soldatenleben* (Stutt. 1847, 7th ed. 1862), *Humorist. Erzählungen* (3d. ed. 1862), have been most popular; of his novels, *Eugen Stillfried* (1852), *Tag und Nacht* (2d ed. 1861), *Fürst und Kavalier* (1865), may be mentioned. His dramas *Der geheime Agent* (1850), and *Der verlorene Sohn* (1865), are the best known. Later works are *Die Marionetten* (1868) and *Der letze Bombardier* (1870). Several of H.'s tales have been translated into English.

Hack'ney, a suburban borough of London, in the county of Middlesex, lies to the N. of Victoria Park, 3 miles N.N.E. of St. Paul's. It is traversed from E. to W. by the North London Railway. The division of Tower Hamlets by the Reform Act of 1867 erected H. into a borough, including the parishes of H., Bethnal Green, and Shoreditch, and having an area of 4696 acres, and a pop. (1871) of 124,951. The inhabitants are of the poorer classes. There are many large establishments for the manufacture of chemicals, india-rubber, drugs, varnish, soap, tar, &c. G. returns two members to Parliament.

Hackney Coach (Fr. *coche-à-haquenée*, 'a coach let out for hire;' *haquenée* is from the Old Fr. *haque*, 'a pony,' or any small horse not required for military service). In London a H. C. is by statute declared to be every carriage except a stage carriage driven by animal power, and plying for hire at any place within ten miles of the General Post-Office. Drivers may ply on Sunday. Any one refusing to pay the driver, or to compensate him for loss of time in summoning for the fare, or to pay him properly for damage done by the hirer to his vehicle, may be imprisoned for one calendar month. Drivers refusing to go, or not going reasonably fast, or exacting more than their legal fare, are liable to a penalty of 40s.

Hadd'ington, the chief town in the county of H., Scotland, stands in an undulating district, sheltered by the Garleton Hills, on the Tyne, 16 miles E. of Edinburgh by rail. Among the chief buildings are the corn exchange and the parish church, an old Gothic building with a tower 90 feet high. H. is one of the most important grain markets in Scotland; it has also cattle sales, and brewing, distilling, tanning, iron-working, &c., are carried on. Here John Knox was born in 1505. H., North Berwick, Dunbar, Jedburgh, and Lauder unite to send a member to Parliament. Pop. (1871) 4004.

Hadd'ingtonshire, or **East Lo'thian**, a maritime county in the S.E. of Scotland, bound S.W. by Edinburghshire, S. and S.E. by Berwickshire, W. and N.E. by the German Ocean, and N. and N.W. by the Firth of Forth. Area, 280 sq. miles; pop. (1871) 37,771. Part of H. is traversed by spurs of the Lammermuir Hills, of which the highest points are Berwick Law (800 feet) and Traprain Law (700 feet). The centre and N. are level. The coast is steep and rocky in the N. and N.E.

the cliffs at Tantallon being 100 feet high. The chief stream is the Tyne, which after a course of twenty miles enters the sea near Dunbar. Geologically, H. is trap in the N., Devonian in the centre, carboniferous in the W., and Silurian in the S. The soil is mostly a clayey loam, and is very fertile. In agriculture H. is reckoned the foremost county in Scotland. Wheat, beans, and turnips are largely produced, and cattle are now largely bred. Recent disclosures, however (*Scotsman*, February 6, 1877), seem to prove that the high farming of this county has not rewarded the farmer in proportion to his outlay of money and skill. The fault is not in the farming, but in the rack-renting of the farms, and that must in time cure itself. H. is rich in coal and limestone, and also affords a supply of iron, fireclay, shale, and potter's clay. The leading manufactures are salt, pottery, and distilling; and fishing is extensively carried on at Prestonpans and Dunbar. In 1674 the land rental was £14,072; in 1874-75 it amounted to £311,526. The chief towns are Haddington, North Berwick, Prestonpans, and Dunbar. H. contains many interesting antiquities, notably the old castles of Tantallon, Dunbar, Innerwick, Dunglass, Winton, and Dirleton. There are various encampments and tumuli, and Roman, British, and Danish works. H. returns one member to Parliament.

Hadd'ock (*Morrhua æglefinus*), a species of Teleostean fishes belonging to the sub-order Anacanthini, and to the *Gadidæ* (q. v.) or cod family. It attains an average length of a foot. In general conformation the H. resembles the Cod (q. v.). The lower jaw is provided with a small *barbule* or filament; the dorsal fins are three in number, two anal fins being developed. The lateral line is very prominent, and the colour is a brown on the upper parts and silvery white beneath. A black spot, not at all unlike the impress of a thumb, exists behind the pectoral fin on each side; and a peculiarly grotesque popular fancy has ascribed its origin to the apostle Peter's thumb, the H. being assumed to be the fish which was taken out of the fresh-water lake of Gennesaret to obtain the tribute money! The H. is most plentiful on the N.E. coasts of Britain, but it also occurs round other portions of the coast, and is common on some parts of the Irish coast. It is caught chiefly with the line, and is greatly relished as an article of diet both in its fresh state and also when dried and smoked. In the latter form it is known as *Finnan H.*

Had'ersleben (Dan. *Haderslev*, in the middle ages *Hatharslöf*, 'the property of Hada'), a town of Prussia in the N. of Slesvig-Holstein, on a fjord of the Little Belt, 45 miles N.N.E. of Flensborg by railway. It has some glove-making and fishing, and its harbour admits small vessels. Pop. (1875) 8362. H. was formerly an imperial free city, and the seat of a bishop till the Reformation. Its castle, which stood without the walls, suffered many sieges. Christoph of Oldenburg, the founder of the present Danish dynasty, was born here in 1448. H. was taken by the Prussians in 1864.

Ha'dēs (Gr. *Aidēs* or *Hadēs*, probably 'the concealer'), popularly called Pluto (Gr. *Ploutōn*, 'the wealth-giver'), the Roman Dis, Orcus, or Tartarus, was worshipped in ancient Greece and Italy as the god of the lower world. He was brother of Zeus and Poseidon, and husband of Persephone, and was believed to be a stern and relentless deity. In the extant representations of H. he wears a gloomy aspect, is attended by the dog Cerberus, and bears the key of his shade-peopled realm, which was also called H. by the Greeks after Homer's time.

Had'ji Khal'fah, the title given to Mustafa Ben Abdallah, a Turkish historian and biographer, was born at Constantinople towards the close of the 16th c. After taking an active part in several campaigns, and performing a pilgrimage to Mecca, he returned to Constantinople in 1635, and there devoted himself to literary work until his death in 1658. His *Fedzlikeh* or *Tarikh-Kebir*, a universal history from the days of Adam down to 1655, is a work of vast information, containing notices of 150 Eastern dynasties. H.'s *magnum opus*, however, is his *Asam Kotoul ve alfonoum* ('Names of Books and Sciences'). It is, in fact, a comprehensive history of science, with a catalogue of books containing 25,000 names, and also notices of their authors. Flügel has translated it under the title *Lexicon Bibliographicum et Encyclopædicum* (7 vols. Leips. 1835-58), and it forms the basis of D'Herbelot's *Bibliotheca Orientalis* and Von Hammer's *Encyclopædia of Universal Knowledge*.

Had'ley, John, an English mathematician, was born about 1670. In 1717 he became a member of the Royal Society, before which he read his description of the quadrant or Sextant (q. v.) in 1731. In 1742, however, it transpired that Sir Isaac Newton in 1727 had described the instrument in a private letter to Halley (q. v.), who for some unaccountable reason suppressed it. This gave rise to a lengthened dispute as to priority, Newton's partisans going the length of accusing H. of plagiarism; but there seems little doubt that the two invented the instrument quite independently of each other, and that H. was the first who constructed it. H. died February 15, 1744.

Had'ramaut, the *Adramitæ* of Strabo, is the part of Arabia to the S. and S.E. of the great central waste. The name is more strictly applied to the smaller coast district to the N.W. of Aden, of which the chief town is Makulla. In the interior it is confined by the angle of the mountains Wadi Masilah and Wadi Doân, while a series of hills are dotted along the coast. The people, mostly in towns and villages, are of many tribes, and trade in camels, fine horses, dates, gums, &c. The country is rich in coal and copper. See Wrede's *Reise in H.* (1870).

Hadria'nus, P. Ælius, the fourteenth of the Roman emperors, was born at Rome, 24th January 76 A.D. His father, Ælius Hadrianus Afer, was married to Trajan's aunt. At fifteen H. went to Spain in a military capacity, was soon recalled, and became military tribune in 95, when he served in Lower Mœsia. In 98 he bore to Trajan the intelligence of Nerva's death. In 101 he attained the office of quæstor; in 105 he was tribune, and two years after prætor. In Trajan's expedition against the Dacians he greatly distinguished himself, and in 108 was sent as prætorian legate against the Lower Pannonians, in 109 he was consul suffectus, in 114 legate in the war against the Parthians, and in 117 consul-elect for the following year. Trajan, accompanied by H., now carried on war against the Parthians. In this campaign he was taken seriously ill, and having placed the command in the hands of H., set out for Rome, but died on the way at Selinus in Cilicia. H., then at Antioch, was proclaimed emperor, 11th August 117. The state of affairs in the empire was now perilous in the extreme; the eastern provinces were invaded; others were in a state of revolt. H.'s policy was peace. He made great but necessary sacrifices, settled the affairs of the empire, and returned to Rome 118, only to receive news of the invasion of Mœsia by the Sarmatæ and Roxolani. The Sarmatian war lasted, according to the Eusebian Chronicle, to 120. In 119 H. made his memorable 'progress.' First he went to Gaul, then to Germany, thence to Britain—everywhere introducing improvements and strengthening the empire. At this time was constructed the celebrated wall from the Solway to the mouth of the Tyne, of which many traces still remain. See *Lapidarium Septentrionale* (Soc. of Antiq., Newcastle-on-Tyne, 1875). H. returned through Gaul, went to Spain 121-122, and in the latter year visited Africa, from which he crossed to Asia. Western Asia was now (123) the scene of his travels, after which he visited the islands of the Ægean, Achaia, and Athens. At the last place he stayed three years. Thence he returned to Rome in 126 or 127. There he was saluted *Pater Patriæ*, and his wife *Augusta*. For some years, with the single exception of a visit to Africa, he remained at Rome, introducing Greek rites and culture. In 129 he made his second journey to the East. In 131 he returned to Rome, and in 132 built the temple of Venus and Roma, and promulgated the *Edictum Perpetuum*. Then followed the Jewish war, which H. successfully terminated, and thereafter the outbreak of the Albanians and Iberians, which he also quelled. In the autumn of 132 he went to Athens, and in 134 to Egypt. He returned by Syria, superintended the settlement of a colony in Jerusalem, and fixed its constitution. H. died at Baiæ, whither he had gone in search of health, 10th July 138, at the age of sixty-three, and after a reign of twenty years. The senate, indignant at the cruelties which marked the latter part of his reign, wished to deny him the title of *Divus*, but Antoninus prevailed on them to be lenient towards his memory on account of the mental darkness that clouded his later years. The character of H. may be briefly sketched:—His reign was one of peace; his policy not cowardly, as some have said, but mild and wise; his liberality great; his military system well devised; his patronage of literature and art liberal and enlightened. He erected many splendid edifices, among which may be mentioned the

Moles Hadriani and the Ælian Bridge leading thereto. He founded several cities, the most famous of which was Adrianopolis, which still exists to perpetuate his name. Not less honourable to him than any of these was the *Athenæum*, a scientific institution which was founded and fostered by him at Rome, and which long retained its vitality. In the Latin Anthology are six epigrams by H.; in the Greek Anthology six; but not one is touched by the finger of genius.

Hæmatem'esis (Gr. *haima*, 'blood,' and *emesis*, 'vomiting'), vomiting of blood, may depend on some morbid change in the mucous membrane of the stomach, or on the rupture of some of its vessels. Treatment:—Small pieces of ice should be swallowed, and the horizontal position maintained. Astringents, such as oil of turpentine, acetate of lead and opium, alum and tannic acid, should be administered. The oil of turpentine should be given in doses varying from 10 to 20 minims in cold water, and repeated more or less frequently according to the urgency of the symptoms. See STOMACH, DISEASES OF.

Hæ'matine, a substance obtained from the colouring matter of the blood, having the chemical formula of $C_{34}H_{34}N_4FeO_5$. It is a reddish-brown amorphous powder, insoluble in water, alcohol, and chloroform, but soluble in alkaline solutions. With hydrochloric acid it forms crystals of the hydrochloride of H., of a rhomboidal form, the appearance of which constitutes one of the most important tests for blood stains. These crystals may be seen by adding to a drop of blood on a piece of glass a few crystals of common salt, and a drop or two of glacial acetic acid. This is placed in a warm atmosphere or before a fire for a few hours, at the expiry of which the microscope will show the characteristic crystals. This test is of considerable importance in cases where it is necessary to determine whether or not certain stains are due to blood.

Hæ'matite, one of the principal ores of iron, so named on account of the blood-red colour of its principal variety, *red H.*, which is a sesquioxide of iron, Fe_2O_3, occurring in large kidney-shaped masses in Great Britain, at the Garleton Hills, Haddington, Cumberland, and Cornwall. *Brown H.* is a hydrated sesquioxide, $F_2O_3, 3H_2O$, frequently found in small pellets, whence it is called pea iron ore. It is of great importance in France. H. has risen much in value since the introduction of the Bessemer process for steel manufacture.

Hæmat'ocele (Gr. *haima*, 'blood,' and *kēlē*, 'tumour'), a tumour containing blood, but specially an accumulation of blood in the tunica vaginalis, distending the sac and compressing the testis.

Hæmatox'yline is the colouring principle of Logwood (q. v.) (*Hæmatoxylon campechianum*). It is probable that the H. does not exist ready formed in the living wood, but in the form of a *Glucoside* (q. v.), as the colour of the wood does not develop till after it has been cut down, and exposed to the action of air and moisture. H. may be obtained in yellowish white crystals from a dried aqueous decoction of logwood by extraction with hot alcohol. Its composition is represented by the formula $C_{16}H_{14}O_6 3H_2O$. When heated to 100° C. it loses two of the three molecules of water, and the monohydrated compound $C_{16}H_{14}O_6H_2O$ remains. When an alkaline solution of H. is exposed to the air, exudation takes place, and a new substance called hæmateine is formed.

$$\underbrace{C_{16}H_{14}O_6}_{\text{Hæmatoxyline.}} + \underbrace{O}_{\text{Oxygen.}} = \underbrace{C_{16}H_{12}O_6}_{\text{Hæmateine.}} + \underbrace{H_2O}_{\text{Water.}}$$

It is hæmateine and not H. that is employed by the dyer and calico-printer for producing shades of purple and black. Shades of violet and purple are produced by mordanting the fabrics with oxide of tin previous to passing them through the logwood decoction; black with a mordant of iron and bichromate of potash.

Hæmatozo'a, the name given to such parasitic animals as inhabit the blood-vessels of man and higher animals. The most common form is the *Bilharzia hæmatobia* (once known under the names *Distoma hæmatobium* and *Schistæoma hæmatobium*), which occurs chiefly in the *portal veins* of man—or those veins which carry venous blood to the liver for the manufacture of bile. Dr. Bilharz of Cairo was the discoverer of this parasite, the generic designation being derived from his name. Another form, at first supposed to be a new species (*B. magna*), was found by Dr. Cobbold in the portal vein of a Sooty monkey (*Cercopithecus fuliginosus*) which died in the London Zoological Gardens in 1857. This species, however, is now believed to be identical with the human parasite. *Bilharzia* is very common in Egypt. It was found in 117 cases out of 363 cases of death in which post-mortem examinations were made. The male is a cylindrical worm, attaining a length of about half an inch; the female being longer and narrower than the male. As in other Flukes (q. v.), suckers exist, and by one of these organs the animal attaches itself to the tissues of its host. Its effect in man appears to consist chiefly in dropsical and allied symptoms, along with hæmaturia and anæmia. Another species of H. is *Hexastorna* or *Hexathyridium venarum*, which also occurs in the human veins. In India Dr. Lewis has recently described a new hæmatozoon under the name of *Filaria sanguinis hominis*, which is said to induce *chyluria* and *elephantiasis*.

Hæmatu'ria (Gr. *haima*, 'blood,' and *ouron*, 'urine'), or **Bloody Urine**, may depend upon congestion of the kidneys, ulceration or malignant disease of the bladder or Prostate Gland (q. v.), or upon irritation caused by calculi in the Uretere (q. v.) or bladder. Lesions in the bladder, resulting in H. are also effected by the existence of a Distoma (*Bilharzia hæmatobia*) in the bladder. H. depending upon the existence of these parasites is endemic in Africa at the Cape of Good Hope, Uitenhage, Port Elizabeth, the Zambezi regions, and in certain parts of the Zanzibar territories, and especially at Tula. In ordinary cases H. may be checked by the administration of gallic acid or the sesquichloride of iron.

Hæmidro'sis (Gr. *haima*, 'blood,' and *idroō*, 'I perspire'), or **Bloody Sweat**, is a morbid condition which has been frequently observed and described by medical men. The greater number of cases of H. occur in young women, and are referable to vicarious menstruation. Cases have been described in which H. affected the greater part of the body, and others in which it flowed from the axilla during a paroxysm of fever. Mr. Erasmus Wilson describes several cases of H. referable to vicarious menstruation. In one case H. took place every fortnight from four circular spots, each about the size of a half-crown, and situated symmetrically on the face, one being on each cheek, one on the forehead, and one on the chin. In another case a young woman suffered a loss of blood from her ears, a little after at the points of her fingers, and then at her toes; presently after, at the umbilicus and corner of the eye; several times by sweat; and at length it burst out from the middle of her breast; afterwards on the foot, where the saphena is pricked in bleeding; then at both palms and backs of her hands. Two days after it flowed from her chin, and all this in a fortnight's time. Whenever it flowed from her breast or other parts like sweat, there was no vestige of an orifice to be seen. This curious affection seems to be identical with those extraordinary cases of religious neuropathia which are manifested by hæmorrhage from the hands and feet and from the left hypochondriác region—the so-called *stigmata* of the crucifixion of our Lord. Mr. Erasmus Wilson describes this disease as *neurotic excoriations*. A striking example of this affection, associated with hysterical and ecstatic phenomena, recently occurred in Belgium in the person of Anne Louise Lateau, born at Bois d'Haine, Belgium, in 1850. Her father died of malignant small-pox when she was only ten weeks old. Twelve days after the father's death the infant was seized with the same disease, and narrowly escaped with her life. At the age of eight she had to commence work for her own support, and continued to do so till she was seventeen, when she became ill with the ordinary phenomena of chlorosis. She had also a severe attack of pharyngites, with neuralgia, eczema, and axillary abscess. At eighteen, menstruation occurred for the first time, and during the period she evinced certain mental phenomena supposed to be a visitation of divine light. Shortly after, the bleeding stigma appeared for the first time on her left breast; the week after, it appeared on the breast and back of the feet, and the following week on the breast, feet, and hands. Five months later it appeared on the forehead, and ten months after, she became the subject of trance. Instances of H. are noted as having taken place during vehement terror, and not unfrequently during the agony of hanging or the torture. One memorable instance of this kind occurred in the experience of the founder of Christianity. See Buchner's *Repertorium*, 2d series, vol. v.; Stark's *General Pathology; Medical Essays*, abridged from the *Philosophical Transactions*, vol. i.; Essay by Dr. F. Lefebure, Professor of General Pathology and Therapeutics; Louvain on *Louise Lateau, de Bois d'Haine, sa Vie, ses Ecstases, ses Stigmates* (1870); *Lectures on Dermatology*, by Erasmus Wilson (Lond. 1875); Bartholinus, *Epistola*, i. p. 718.

Hæmodora'ceæ, a natural order of Monocotyledonous plants, embracing thirteen genera and about fifty species. The plants receive the name of blood-root from the red colour of the roots of many of the species which are used for dyeing. They are distributed in N. and S. America, Africa, and Australia. The vellozias or tree-lilies belong to the order, and give a striking feature to the mountain vegetation in Brazil.

Hæmoglo'bin, the colouring matter of the blood, is sometimes termed Hæmoglobulin or Hæmato-crystalline. It is the most complex substance known to chemists, as shown by its formula—$C_{600}H_{960}N_{154}FeS_3O_{179}$. This formula of course is quite empirical, but as it represents in the simplest numbers the ratios of the different elements in the percentage composition of the substance, it will at once be seen that it is extremely complex in chemical structure. It may be separated from the blood by various methods, and it is remarkable that it is more easily separated from the blood of certain animals than from that of others. It may be obtained readily from the blood of the guinea-pig or of the horse by simply diluting the fluid with water, and keeping it for several hours at freezing-point. In these circumstances, the coloured blood corpuscles apparently break down, and their colouring matter crystallises out as H. The crystalline form of H. varies in different animals. Usually it appears as elongated rhombodedra, but in some, as in the guinea-pig, it assumes the form of *texa* or octahedra. It is soluble in water, the solution having the red colour of blood; heat, in the presence of alkalies, augments the degree of its solubility; it may be split up into (1) *globin* or *globuline*, a coagulable albuminous substance, and (2) *hæmin* or *hæmatine*, a matter containing all the iron (Fe) of the blood. H. is of importance physiologically, inasmuch as it is the substance which combines with oxygen in the lungs, becoming a compound called *oxyhæmoglobin*, which is carried by the blood corpuscles to the tissues of the body. In the ultimate capillaries the *oxyhæmoglobin* gives up its oxygen to the tissues, and is reduced to H., which again goes to the lungs to receive a new burden of oxygen. Spectrum analysis distinguishes readily between the two conditions in which H. may exist. Thus a solution of *oxyhæmoglobin* gives two absorption bands in the spectrum between D. and E., while under the action of reducing agents (or those which take away its oxygen), such as sulphide of ammonium, these two bands disappear, and are replaced by a *single* band, which occupies the interval between the two preceding. H. forms compounds with other substances than oxygen, as, for example, with carbonic oxide. H., acted on by this gas, gives with the spectroscope two bands like those of *oxyhæmoglobin*, but these bands are not affected by reducing agents. Thus it would appear that carbonic oxide gas acts as a poison, because it prevents H. from carrying oxygen to the tissues.

Hæmop'tysis (Gr. *haima*, 'blood,' and *ptysis*, 'spitting'), expectoration of blood, is always indicative of organic disease of the lungs, such as engorgement of the pulmonary vessels, disorganisation of pulmonary tissue, as in tuberculosis, pneumonia, or cancer of the lungs, disease of the heart or thoracic aneurism. H. may occur from sudden changes of atmospheric pressure, as in ascending mountains, or descending in diving bells, or from violent straining or plethora. H. is always a serious symptom of disease, but the gravity of the symptoms depends upon the disease with which it is associated. In tubercular disease H. is frequently a fatal symptom. Treatment:—Bitartrate of potash in drachm doses, and the mineral acids in doses of from three to five drops, combined with opium or morphia, every four or six hours. Cupping, and the application of ice upon the spine, are useful in many cases, but afford only temporary relief, H. being a symptom of several diseases.

Hæ'morrhage (Gr. *haima*, 'blood,' and *hrēgnumi*, 'I burst forth'), a flow of blood from injured arteries, veins, or capillaries. The characters of the H. differ according to the nature of the vessel from which the blood escapes. If from a *vein*, the blood is of a dark colour, and flows in a uniform stream; and if there be any pressure applied between the wound and the heart, the force of the flow of blood will be increased. To arrest H., in such cases, pressure must be applied between the wound and the extremities. When an *artery* is wounded, the blood is of a bright scarlet colour, and flows by jets, synchronous with the contraction of the left ventricle, and between each jet the stream is continuous. To arrest arterial H. a ligature, or pressure, or other means must be applied to the cardiac end of the injured vessel. When there is H. from a wounded vessel into the cellular tissue of a part, the substance of organs, or internal cavities, it is termed Extravasation (q. v.). When H. is produced intentionally by surgeons it is called Blood-Letting (q. v.) and Cupping (q. v.). Treatment:—After the flow of blood has been arrested it may be necessary to adopt means to prevent fatal syncope. The patient should be placed in the recumbent posture, with the head low, and pressure should be applied to the abdominal aorta, and the main arteries of the limbs, to confine the blood as much as possible to the nervous and circulatory centres. When death appears imminent from the effects of H., as sometimes happens in cases of Flooding (q. v.), Transfusion of Blood (q. v.) may be had recourse to.

Hæ'morrhoids, or **Piles**. See ANUS, DISEASES OF.

Hæmus, Mount. See BALKAN.

Hæred'itas Ja'cens, a term of Scotch law denoting an estate to which the heir has not made up a title after the death of his predecessor.

Hæret'ico Comburen'do was a writ against a heretic who, having been convicted of heresy by the bishop, was delivered to the secular power to be burnt. It was abolished by 21 Car. II. It was put in execution upon two Anabaptists in the seventeenth year of the reign of Elizabeth, and upon two Arians in the 9th of James I.

Haff, a disused Danish word meaning 'the sea.' It occurs in the proper name of inlets of the Baltic—the Frisches H. (q. v.), Stettiner H. (q. v.), and Kurisches H. (q. v.).

Há'fiz (*Schems-ed-dîn-Mohammed*), the representative poet of Persia, whose name is inseparably associated with the city of Shiraz, where he lived and died, and whose lyrics throughout the East fill the position occupied by the poems of Homer among the Greeks. Of his life little is known, except that it extended throughout the greater part of the 14th c. He was undoubtedly at one time a dervish, professing the mystical system of doctrines known as Sufiism, which colours all his writings. He chiefly wrote in praise of love, wine, and every form of pleasure; and his felicity of language, readiness of wit, and flow of metre have won for him the name of the Eastern Anacreon. It is still a disputed question among commentators whether his erotic appeals are not to be understood in a semi-theological sense, as with the Song of Solomon. His magnificent tomb at Shiraz, which had become a place of pilgrimage, was overthrown by the destructive earthquake of 1853. The collection of the poems of H. called *The Divan* is used for purposes of divination, after the manner of the *sortes Virgilianæ*. It has been several times printed in the original—at Calcutta (1791); Cairo (1834); Constantinople (1840); Leipsic (1854-61); the best and most complete English version is that of Herman Bicknell, illustrated by J. Herbert, R.A. (Lond. 1875), in which the Persian metres are preserved.

Ha'gar (Heb. 'flight') was an Egyptian slave belonging to Sarah, Abraham's wife, whom Sarah gave to her husband for a concubine when she had no children of her own (Gen. xvi.). The story, true to human nature, describes how, when H. 'saw that she had conceived, her mistress was despised in her eyes.' 'And when Sarah dealt hardly with her, she fled from her face.' Having taken the way to her native land, she was found in the wilderness, 'in the way to Shur,' by an angel of Jehovah, who sent her back, and she gave birth to Ishmael (q. v.). At the feast on the occasion of the weaning of Isaac, Ishmael, being then seventeen years of age, was observed 'mocking' by Sarah, who was mortally offended, and prevailed on her husband to send away H. and her son. They went and dwelt in the wilderness of Paran, and H. took for her son 'a wife out of the land of Egypt,' probably one of her own kindred (Gen. xxi.). She is held in honour by the Mohammedans as the mother of the Ismaelite Arabs, and her 'grave' at Mecca is much visited by devout pilgrims.

Hag'berry, a name applied to the Bird-Cherry (q. v.), and as an equivalent of Hackberry (q. v.).

Ha'gedorn, Friedrich von, a German poet, was born at Hamburg, 23d April 1708. He studied law at Jena, published a collection of poems in 1729, and shortly thereafter went to London. In 1733 he was appointed secretary to an English company at Hamburg, and there, having had abundant leisure to cultivate his muse and enjoy the delights of social intercourse, he died, 28th October 1754. Though lacking original power, H. was very successful in fables, short tales, and such poetic trifles as had hitherto been disfigured by the clumsiness of an imperfectly polished tongue. In purity of style and eloquence of versification, H. stands far above most of his contemporaries. An edition of his *Poetische Werke*, accompanied by a memoir, was published by Eschenburg at Hamburg in 1800 in 5 vols.

Ha'gen, a manufacturing town in the province of Westphalia, Prussia, 14 miles E.N.E. of Elberfield by rail, at the confluence of the Empe and the Volme rivers. A good deal of cloth is woven here. The town has dye and print works, also manufactures of wire, of iron and steel, and of tin and copper. Pop. (1875) 24,218.

Hagen, Friedrich Heinrich von der, a scholar who did much to awaken interest in the study of ancient German poetry, was born February 19th, at Schmiedeberg, in the N. of Brandenburg, entered into the public service at Berlin in 1803, and was in 1810 appointed Professor of the German Language and Literature at the newly-founded university, where he for the first time made the old German tongue a branch of university study. He died at Berlin, June 11, 1856. Besides editing the *Nibelungenlied* four times (viz., 1810, 1816, 1820, and 1822), the works of the *Minnesänger* (1838), and other ancient German poems, H. wrote a *Grundriss der Geschichte der Deutschen Poesie* (Berl. 1812).

Ha'genau (Fr. *Haguenau*, 'the enclosed meadow'), a town of Elsass-Lothringen, Germany, on the Moder, and in the great Hagenauer Forst, 20 miles N. of Strassburg by railway. It is girt with old towering walls and broad moats, and has manufactures of leather, oil, soaps, madder, and other dyes. Pop. (1875) 11,726. H. was founded by Friedrich Barbarossa in 1164, suffered in the Thirty Years' War, and passed to France in 1648. The French gained two bloody victories over the Austrians here in 1793. In the Franco-German war G. was taken the day after the battle of Wörth by Badenese troops under General La Roche, August 7, 1870.

Ha'genbach, Karl Rudolf, a German divine, was born March 4, 1801, at Basel, Switzerland, and became Professor in the university of his native city in 1828. H. is a representative of the 'Mediation School' (*Vermittelungs-Schule*) of modern German theology—the school, created mainly by the reviving influence of Schleiermacher, latitudinarian in all matters of confessional detail, free in its attitude towards critical questions, but earnest and hearty in support of the cardinal points of evangelical truth. H.'s sympathies are rather with the Reformed than with the Lutheran theology. His numerous works comprise a complete history of the Christian Church, published between 1834 and 1860 (new ed. in 7 vols. 1868–72, *Vorlesungen über Kirchengeschichte*), a valuable *Lehrbuch der Dogmengeschichte* (Leips. 1840–41, 5th ed. 1867), the well-known *Theologische Encyclopädie* (a manual of reference to the principal works in all departments of theology; 7th ed. 1864), and the *Grundlinien der Homiletik* (1863).

Ha'gerstown, a city of Maryland, U.S., 6 miles E. of the Potomac river, and 30 S.W. of Gettysburg by railway. It is a meeting point of three railways, and has some manufactures of machinery. Pop. (1870) 5779.

Hag'fish, or **Bo'rer** (*Myxine glutinosa*), a peculiar species of fish belonging to the order *Marsipobranchii*, which includes but another genus, the well-known Lamprey (q. v.). It is of slender, eel-like form, and has a circular mouth, furnished with eight *cirrhi* or filaments. The palate bears a single large tooth or fang, which is, in its turn, serrated or toothed on each side. By means of this great fang the H. bores its way into the bodies of other fishes. The cod is frequently assailed. A peculiar feature of the H. is the power it has of secreting a large quantity of *mucus* from the surface of the skin. The gills exist in the form of closed sacs or pouches which open into a common tube, the outer aperture of which is found on the lower body-surface. No paired fins or lower jaw are developed; and the skull is cartilaginous; while the spine is represented by the soft structure known as the notochord.

Hagg'adah (Heb. 'legend,' 'saga'; pl. *Haggadoth*), a certain element in the Jewish Talmud, so called in contradistinction to Halacah (q. v.), because it consisted of mere sayings without authority, of allegories, parables, or tales, the sole value of which was to point a moral or illustrate a subject. From its popular nature, however, the people clung to it, and in course of time gave to it alone the name of Midrash (q. v.) It has an exegesis, a system, and a method of its own, and transforms Scripture into a thousand themes for its variations. Everything being bound up in the Bible, there must be an answer in it to all questions; all the riddles in it are solved if only the key be found. 'The persons of the Bible—what they did and suffered, their happiness and their doom, their words and their lives—became, apart from their historical reality, a symbol and an allegory.' Besides, the H. supplied much that the narrative had omitted, filling up the gaps, explaining the motives, and finding connections between the remotest countries, ages, and persons; drawing sublime morals from the most commonplace facts. See E. Deutsch on *The Talmud* in his *Lit. Remains* (Lond. 1874).

Hagg'ai (Heb. 'the festal one'), was one of the twelve 'minor' Jewish prophets, and the first of the three who prophesied after the return from Babylon. Regarding his personal history there is nothing but unreliable tradition. In all probability he was one of the exiles who returned with Zerubbabel and Joshua. His four prophetic utterances, delivered between the sixth and the ninth month of the second year of the reign of Darius Hystaspis (B.C. 520), all relate to the rebuilding of the Temple. In the first he reproves the people for their selfishness and indifference in dwelling in their 'ceiled houses' while the house of the Lord was lying waste, and warns them that Jehovah will punish them therefor by unfruitfulness in the land (i. 1–11). The effect of this admonition is such that the building of the Temple is at once resumed (i. 12–15). The second message is intended to reconcile the people to the diminished splendour of the new Temple as compared with the old one (ii. 1–9). Two months after the prophet has again to rebuke the people for their sluggishness in carrying on the work of the Lord, but repeats the promise of the blessing of Jehovah (ii. 10–19); and in his last prophecy, delivered to Zerubbabel the same day, foreshadows the establishment of the Messiah's kingdom (ii. 20–23).

Haghe, Louis, a Belgian artist, was born at Tournay in 1802. He first acquired a name as a lithographer, but is best known as a member of the New Watercolour Society, and an illustrator of Flemish interiors. His picture 'L'Hôtel de Ville de Courtray' gained him a great reputation, and for fidelity as a historical painter he has few superiors. His eminence as a lithographer gained him a second-class medal in the Paris Exhibition of 1855.

Hagiog'rapha (Gr. 'holy writings') is a name which has been used by some writers as synonymous with Holy Scriptures; in the middle ages it was frequently used as synonymous with Apocrypha (q. v.). In its special and most limited sense it means the third division of the Jewish canon (see BIBLE), including Job, Psalms, Proverbs, Song, Ruth, Lamentations, Ecclesiastes, Esther, Daniel, Ezra, Nehemiah, Chronicles.

Hague, The (Dut. *S'Gravenhage*, lit. 'the graf's hedge' or enclosure; Ger. *Der Haag;* Fr. *La Haye*), politically the chief city of the Netherlands, the residence of the king, and seat of the States-General, in the province of S. Holland, 3 miles from the coast, and 15 N.W. of Rotterdam by railway. A handsome, fashionable, healthy city, with many fine streets and squares (Weiher, Buitenhof, and Binnenhof), and stately buildings, it is intersected by numerous canals fringed with rows of linden trees, and spanned by elegant bridges. The finest parts of the H. are Het Vorhout, the Vyverberg, and the former Willemspark; and towards the centre, on the *Vyver*, or 'pond,' is the *hof* of the Counts of Holland, and later of the Stadtholders. Other notable buildings are the irregular pile of the States-General; the Buitenhof, where Oldenbarnevelt was confined and executed; the Gevangenpoort, a prison of historic interest over the entrance of the Buitenhof; the royal palace, with splendid interior (1815); the so-called Mauritz Huis; and the national museum, containing valuable collections of Dutch paintings; the church of St. James of 1309, with its hexagonal tower and chime of thirty-eight bells; and the townhouse, with a beautiful façade of 1525. In the archives of Het Plein are rare documents relating to the history of Europe for the last four centuries. The H. has a royal library of 100,000 vols., with rich collections of MSS., coins, medals, and gems; a Latin school, a technical school, and a royal academy of music. Its manufactures are chiefly gold and silver wares, furniture, brushes, soaps, perfumery, and carriages, but its prosperity greatly depends on the number of foreign residents. French, English, and German are widely spoken languages. The sea-bathing at Schevingen attracts crowds of summer visitors. Near the H., and in the heart of a beautiful wood is the Huis in 't Bosch, a royal summer palace, the walls and ceiling of which bear frescoes by Rubens. Also in the vicinity is Ryswick (q. v.), where was signed the treaty of peace in 1697. Pop. (1875) 100,254. A hunting castle built here by the Counts of Holland gave place to a palace erected by Willem, Duke of Holland and King of the Germans in 1250. In the 16th c. it became the residence of the States-General, and during the 17th c. was the centre of European diplomacy. It was the birthplace of William III. of England, and of other members of the House of Orange.

Hahn'emann, Samuel Christian Friedrich, born at Meissen in Saxony, 10th April 1755, was the founder of homœopathy. His father was a poor painter on porcelain. Going to study medicine at Leipsic, he supported himself by translating scientific works from French and English. It is said that at this time he slept only on alternate nights. After acting as physician and librarian to the governor of Transylvania at Hermannstadt, and taking his doctor's degree at Erlangen (1779), H., much to the disgust of his wife, left a good practice at Dresden, to return to study and translation at Leipsic. The chemistry of drugs engaged him chiefly; for, as appears in his letters to Hufeland, the great Berlin physician, he did not like the notion of prescribing unknown substances to be applied to unknown morbid states. Convinced that Providence must have supplied a simple remedy not far off from the disease, he was led to his fancied discovery that 'like cures like.' This he attempted to put in practice at Brunswick in 1794, but the ignorant trades-unionism of the allopaths drove him from town to town, and he retired to Leipsic, where he prescribed and taught publicly from 1811 to 1829. It was a matter of conscience with him to prepare his drugs; hence his enemies founded on the custom that no physician should deal in drugs. Until 1815 he remained at Anhalt Koethen, consulted from all parts of Europe, but persecuted shamelessly, the mob being instigated more than once to attack his house. His second wife took him to Paris, where he continued to practise down to his death (2d July 1843), strong in mind and healthy in body to the last. H.'s principal work is his *Organon der rationellen Heilkunde* (Dresd. 1810, 5th ed. 1833). The principle that a morbid physiological state may be abated or cured by the application of a substance which produces a similar morbid state in the healthy organism is apparently confirmed by a large number of incontestable empirical facts. The idea is expressed by Hippocrates, Stahl, and others, and implied in many unscientific customs. The really characteristic parts of H.'s doctrine are his explanation of chronic diseases (which he regards as inherited forms of psoriasis) and his theory of *infinitesimal attenuation.* The latter was parodied in the prescription 'Put in a grain of the specific above Schaffhausen, and take out a glass from the Rhine below Bingen.'

Hahn-Hahn, Ida, Countess, a German poetess and novelist, was born at Tressow, in Mecklenburg-Schwerin, June 22, 1805. The extravagance of her father, Count von Hahn, had impaired his large fortune; and in 1826 she was married to her cousin Friedrich Count Hahn, the owner of the finest baronial estate in North Germany. This union proving very unhappy, was terminated in three years by a separation, after which the countess gave herself up to foreign travel and authorship. Her first published works were poetical; but she is best known for her novels, which are clever and showy, though marred by much false sentiment and absurd prejudices of rank. In 1850 Countess H. suddenly became a convert to Romanism, entered a convent at Angers, and subsequently published an account of her conversion under the title *From Babylon to Jerusalem.* Her later writings have been on ecclesiastical topics.

Hai'ducks (Magyar, 'drivers'), originally cowherds, was in the 16th c. a name for a class of mercenary soldiers, who in 1605 had a district of country allotted to them on the E. side of the Theiss with several peculiar privileges. This territory has over 60,000 inhabitants, chiefly Magyars, and is still directly under the supreme Government. In the 18th c. the word came to be used for the servants of Hungarian officials and magnates.

Hail (Old Eng. *hagal* and *hagol*, Ger. *hagel*, Lat. *grando*, from an Aryan root meaning 'to rattle') is the name given to those discrete particles of ice which descend as a shower, usually before a heavy rain. The conditions under which H. is formed are not well understood, but they must be of a transient nature, since hailstorms last but a brief period, rarely so long as fifteen minutes. Immediately before the shower begins, a peculiar rustling sound is heard, like that produced by the shaking of peas or small pebbles in a bag, and at the same time the atmospheric electricity is greatly disturbed. The constant presence of electrical phenomena during a hailstorm early suggested an electrical origin; but it is quite as likely, so far as we at present know, that the electricity is an effect, not a cause, of H. There is no doubt, however, that to produce the material necessary for the formation of H. the cooling of a mass of moisture-laden air below the freezing-point is required. This cooling may result either from the indraught of a cold current of air, or from the sudden expansion of the mass of air itself. In the latter case a diminution of pressure must ensue, and in the former the condensation of the moisture may produce a like result. Thus an area of low pressure would be formed, and the inrushing air, on all sides, would gradually raise the temperature, and destroy the conditions necessary for the formation of H. The hailstones, which vary in size from that of a small pea to not unfrequently several inches in diameter, seem to grow by accretion in much the same manner as rain-drops grow. The larger and more rapidly falling stones overtake, and come into collision with the smaller ones, and the pressure at the moment of concussion melts the surfaces in contact which then freeze together again, and form thus one stone. Professor Osborne Reynolds has lately investigated the shapes which on this supposition hailstorms would assume, and finds the theory supported by observation.

Haimu'ra (*Erythrinus macrodon*), a Teleostean fish, found in the rivers of Guiana, and most nearly allied to the *Salmonidæ* and to the *Clupeidæ* or herrings. It may attain a length of 3 or 4 feet, and derives its specific name (*macrodon*) from the size of its teeth. The flesh is palatable.

Hainan', an island of China, in the province of Canton, lies partly in the Gulf of Tonquin, 300 miles S.S.W. of Canton, in lat. 18°-20° N., and long. 108°-111° E. Area, 12,000 sq. miles; pop. 1,500,000. It is 180 miles long, and 100 broad, and is separated from the Lui Chu peninsula on the N. by a channel 5 miles in breadth, navigable only for junks. The climate is unhealthy; in summer typhoons are frequent along the coasts. In the interior it is mountainous and woody, and is occupied in part by wild tribes. The W. coast is low and fertile, yielding rice, sugar, indigo, &c., but is girt with shoals and sandbanks. The coast in the S., though rocky, has several good harbours, among them the chief town of H., Kiang Chu (q. v.), with a pop. of 200,000, open to foreign commerce since 1858.

Hainault, French, a district in the N.E. of France, annexed from the Belgian province of H. in 1678, and now included in the department of Nord.

Hainau't, formerly **Hainault** (Flem. *Henegouwen*), a province of Belgium, bounded N. and N.E. by Brabant and E. and W. Flanders, E. by Namur, W. by W. Flanders and France, and S. by France. Area, 1424 sq. miles; pop. (1874) 949,346. The surface is mainly level and very fertile. The forest of

Ardennes in the S. and S.E. is partly hilly. The chief rivers are the Scheldt, Sambre, Dendre, and Haine, from which the province takes its name. H. contains the richest coal-seams in Belgium, and also affords supplies of lead, slate, marble, and lime. Wheat, rye, barley, and flax, are largely grown; and cattle, horses, and sheep are numerous. The chief towns are Mons, Tournay, and Charleroi.

Hain'ichen, a town in the kingdom of Saxony, Germany, 10 miles N.E. of Chemnitz by railway. It spins and weaves woollens, has cotton manufactures, and extensive bleaching and dye works. Pop. (1875) 8468.

Hair (Old Eng. *hær;* Ger. *haar;* comp. Lat. *hirtus*, 'hairy') is a growth of the epidermis. Each particular hair consists of a root embedded in the skin, of a shaft or stem, and of a point. The root expands at its lower end into a swelling or knob, called the *hair bulb*, and it grows from a recess or pouch in the skin called the *hair follicle*. This pouch receives near its mouth the openings of one or more sebaceous or oil glands. The shaft of the H. is usually round, but occasionally it may be somewhat flattened. The surface presents the edges of fine scales which are placed over each other like slates on a roof. In some specimens these project so far as to present sharp edges which interlock with those of adjoining hairs and thus form a felt. Each hair usually tapers to a point, and after reaching maturity tends to split up. When placed under the microscope with a magnifying power of about 300 diameters, it is seen to consist of a fibrous cortical portion, and of a cellular medulla or pith, and frequently the cells of the pith are filled with air, and occasionally with pigment. Sometimes hairs are met with having no pith, but composed entirely of fibrous structure, made up of highly compressed epidermic cells. Hairs vary in appearance in different animals. They may be classified as follows:—(1) *Fibrous* hairs, having no pith, and usually strong and coarse; (2) *cellular* hairs, consisting entirely of cells, which often contain air, an example of which we have in the H. of the roe-deer; (3) *fibrocellular* hairs, composed of a cortical and medullary portion, the most common form of H.; and (4) *irregular* hairs, which are characterised by their edges being serrated, as in the hairs of bats, or by being of irregular form, neither flattened nor cylindrical, as in ordinary hairs, but having expansions near their extremity, as may be seen in the H. of the *Ornithorhynchus paradoxus*, or Duck-Bill Platypus (q. v.). Many hairs have slender muscles attached to the follicles, by the contraction of which hairs may be erected, as seen after sudden fright or exposure to cold. The first hairs of the human being are a soft down called the *lanugo*, which disappear soon after birth, giving place to other hairs which are developed from a minute papilla at the bottom of the follicle. Each H. has a certain average duration of life, at the end of which it drops out and is succeeded by another. If the papilla be destroyed, or if it undergo atrophy, no H. will be developed. This is the probable cause of *baldness*. The animal matter of H. contains fat and a substance yielding gelatin on prolonged boiling. The mineral substances in H. consist of peroxide of iron, traces of manganese, silica, chlorides of sodium and potassium, sulphates of lime and magnesia, and phosphate of lime. H. is preserved long after the decomposition of the body, and consequently is frequently found in tombs and sarcophagi after all other remains of their occupants have disappeared.

Diseases of Hair.—The hair and hair follicles are liable to a variety of morbid conditions resulting from altered nutrition, or from inflammation of the formative structure of the hair, or of the hair-follicles. There may be augmentation of the hair cells, giving rise to simple increase in quantity or length, in situations naturally occupied by hair, or there may be increase of quantity or length in abnormal situations. The hair may also be diminished in quantity from arrested formation, resulting in simple thinning of the hair, and finally in complete alopecia or baldness. It is likewise subject to alteration of colour from disorder of the chromatogenous function of the formative organ, and is generally associated with an alteration of the *rete mucosum* of the skin. The most common change which takes place is blanching or Greyness (q. v.). There are several diseases closely associated with the hair, such as *ringworm, plica polonica, favus, sycosis*, &c.

Hair-Dressing. The natural covering for the head has ever been regarded as an ornament, and as such special care has been devoted to its arrangement. In most countries great diversity of style has shown itself at different periods. Most extravagant styles of dressing the hair are met with among uncivilised races, especially in Africa and the islands of the Pacific. The ancient Egyptians shaved the head and face, and wore wigs and false beards; ladies dressed their hair in innumerable plaits, which hung down the back and covered the sides of the face. The Assyrians wore their hair in luxuriant curls and plaited their beards. The Greeks, in ancient times, after reaching manhood wore the hair long; so did the Romans till about 300 B.C., when barbers were introduced, and short hair came into vogue. The coiffures of Greek and early Roman ladies were characterised by great simplicity and taste, but in the decline of the Roman empire, ladies overdressed their hair in costly and extravagant modes. Dyeing the hair, too, was then practised. The Teutonic tribes were distinguished for their long hair. The Britons, like the Gauls, allowed the hair to grow long and bushy. In England, since the Norman conquest, fashion in H.-D. has fluctuated violently. Previous to that event men cropped their hair and shaved their beards, but in the reign of Henry I., William of Malmesbury states that barons and gallants 'vied with women in the length of their locks,' and false tresses were even worn. At this period ladies wore long plaits reaching to the knees; sometimes they were looped up at the back of the head under the couvre-chef. A century later they appear to have adopted an Oriental mode of confining the hair in a caul or net of gold-thread or silk. In the 13th c. men wore thick wavy locks curled up at the ends, and short hair across the forehead. The fantastic caps of the ladies of the 15th c. entirely concealed their hair. Short hair was fashionable with men in the reign of Henry VIII. In Elizabeth's time ladies' hair was most elaborately dressed, and pins and wires were used to prop the 'curled, frizzled, and crisped' hair into many *outré* forms. Charles I.'s reign is noted for the introduction by the Cavaliers of the French 'love-lock,' a ringlet worn on the left side, and occasionally reaching to the elbow. The otherwise full flowing locks of this period contrasted greatly with the closely-cropped heads of the Puritans. Towards the end of the 17th c. the Sevigné style—curls on the forehead and ringlets at the side of the face—was followed by ladies, and gentlemen wore perukes of various forms, which remained in fashion till about 1760. Much of the extravagance of Elizabeth's reign was revived by the ladies of the 18th c., whose hair and head-dresses swelled upwards to inordinate dimensions. Hair-powder was then largely patronised. After the French Revolution short hair, *à la Titus*, became common among males. It is not possible, and, if it were, it is not necessary, to note the ever-changing female fashions of the present day.

Hair Dyes. The agents commonly employed to dye the hair are solutions of nitrate of silver or various preparations of lead with sulphur, pyrogallic acid, the juice of green walnut shells, and various other vegetable astringents. These substances are chiefly used to darken grey hairs, and it is affirmed that the use of leaden combs also tends to produce the same effect. The Arabs produce a yellow colour in their hair by the use of *Henna* (q. v.). When in recent years golden locks were fashionable, a poor bleached substitute for the warm yellow tint was artificially produced by the use of a preparation called *Auricome* or golden-hair water which consisted essentially of peroxide of hydrogen.

Hair Grass, the common name for species of Aira, a genus of grasses with narrow wiry leaves. There are about thirty known species, of which six are natives of Britain. They are of little or no agricultural value. *A. cæspitosa* is the tufted H. G., which is so useful in walking through bogs.

Hair Manufactures. The hair of different animals is applied industrially to a considerable variety of purposes according to its length, toughness, and other qualities. Human hair itself forms an article of commercial value for the purposes of wig-making, and for supplementary tresses and plaits for ladies. It is also frequently worked up into watchguards, bracelets, necklets, and other articles of ornament. The short hair of oxen and some other animals is of value in plastering for mixing with the mortar to bind it together on walls and roofs, &c. The short hair of other animals, again, principally the rabbit, hare, and vicuña, is extensively employed in felting (see FELT). Camels' hair, mohair, &c., are treated like sheep's wool for spinning and weaving into dress fabrics; and in recent years a fabric like Irish frieze has been woven entirely of cows' hair with the view of passing it into the American market free of the duty levied on woollen articles. The stout thick hairs, called bristles, of the wild hog are used in Brushmaking (q. v.); and for certain kinds of soft brushes, the hair of the badger, polecat, marten, &c., and camels' hair are found serviceable. Artists' pencils or brushes are made from sable and camels' hair. The long and strong hair obtained from the tails of horses forms an important article for weaving into haircloth used for covering the seats of chairs, sofas, and other articles of furniture. It is very largely imported from South America. All dark-coloured hair is dyed a uniform glossy black with logwood and copperas, the pure white hair being either employed in its natural state or dyed in bright colours for damasked and fancy haircloth. This peculiar fabric is generally composed of worsted, cotton, or linen warp, and as the weft is composed of single separate hairs a peculiar hooked shuttle or long rod is used by the weaver for shooting them through the web as they are supplied one by one by an attendant who takes them from a box in which they are kept moist with water. Tail hair is also woven both as warp and weft for sieve cloth used for sieves and strainers in dairy and cooking operations. It is besides employed for twisting into salmon and trout fishing lines, and white hair plaited or woven under the name of crinoline is occasionally a fashionable material for ladies' hats and bonnets. The stiff petticoats which at one period distended ladies' dresses were originally made of horsehair, whence the name Crinoline (q. v.). The shorter hair of manes and cows' tails is twisted into ropy pieces and boiled, after which it is dried in an oven, and when uncoiled it preserves its curly structure, thus forming a very elastic material for stuffing seats, cushions, and mattresses, &c. The comparatively limited supply of hair for these varied purposes has led to the introduction of many substitutes, especially for brushmaking and stuffing-hair; but no article possesses the strength, elasticity, cleanliness, and freedom from felting which characterises hair, and from which its peculiar value arises.

Hair-Powder, composed of perfumed ground wheaten starch, was introduced into England from France about the end of the 16th c., and notwithstanding the inconvenience attending its application, was extensively patronised for two centuries. Taylor, the water poet, thus alludes (*Superbiæ Flagellum*) to its use in his time—

> 'Some every day do powder so their hair
> That they like ghosts or millers do appear.'

H.-P. was lavishly used by the beaux and belles of the 18th c. to impart a softness to the features. In 1795 a tax was imposed on the use of H.-P., which thereafter was gradually laid aside. The impost was repealed by 32 and 33 Vict. c. 14.

Hairs, in botany, are conical projections from individual epidermal cells. Leaves which have no H. are said to be glabrous. In the cells of the H. of *Tradescantia* or Virginian spiderwort, movements of protoplasm are easily seen under the microscope. The loasa or Chili nettle and the common nettle (*Urtica*) have stinging H. Cotton (q. v.) consists of the H. which surround the seeds of *Gossypium herbaceum*. On the leaves of different species of sundew there are numerous glandular H.

Hair-Tail, the name given to various Teleostean fishes included in the special family *Trichiuridæ*. They are so named from the presence of the filaments which are attached to the tail, which is itself of attenuated form. The body is very long and much compressed. The dorsal fin is long, and both ventrals and pectorals are of small size. The silvery H.-T. (*Trichiurus lepturus*) has no tail-fin, the tail simply tapering to a hair-like point. This species occurs in the Atlantic, and off the W. Indian Islands. An allied species is the Savala (*T. savala*) of the E. Indian seas.

Hajipur' ('town of the pilgrim') is the name of several towns in India. The best known is at the confluence of the Gunduck with the Ganges, in the district of Mozufferpur, province of Bengal, just opposite Patna city. Pop. (1872) 22,306. In the neighbourhood is held the great cattle fair of Sonepur in November, and H. itself has a large trade, valued at £600,000 a year: exports, indigo and saltpetre; imports, piece goods, indigo seed, and grain. It was a place of some importance under the Mohammedans.

Hake (*Merlucius vulgaris*), a genus of Teleostean fishes belonging to the *Gadidæ* or cod family. It is common round the British coasts, and is also found in the Mediterranean Sea. Its colour is grey above and white below, and its length varies from 3 to 4 feet. The head is flat, and the fore part of the body is somewhat deeper than the hinder portion. The first dorsal fin is short, the second long, as is also the anal fin. No barbules or mouth-filaments exist. The flesh is coarse, but the fish is captured in great quantities for the purpose of being dried and salted like ling and cod.

Hak'im, Ben All'ah, or **Ben Hash'em,** surnamed **Mokann'a** ('the Veiled,' or 'the One-Eyed'), was the chief of an Arabic sect which took its rise in the second half of the 8th c. He first appears in A.D. 774 at Meru, the capital of Khorassan, as a private soldier in the service of the Abassidian Calif Mahadi. He seems from the first to have exercised a powerful influence over the minds of his fellows, and, rising to be captain in the army of the calif, subsequently obtained command of a troop of his own. He is next found simulating himself to be God in human form, feigning to have been previously incarnate by the transmigration of souls in Adam, Noah, and other famous personages, down to Abu Muslem, a prince of Khorassan. One of his eyes having been pierced in battle by an arrow, he constantly wore a veil over his face in order to conceal the defect, and hence was called the 'veiled prophet.' So formidable did his party speedily become, that the calif had in 780 to march against him in person; and after standing a long siege in his fortress, the prophet was finally reduced to the last extremities. The end of H. was consistent with his extraordinary life; for, after poisoning his partisans with wine at a feast, he threw himself into a vessel filled with some powerful acid, so that his body might be completely dissolved, and his followers believe in an apotheosis. The sect founded by H. sunk into insignificance after the death of its leader. The story of H. forms the subject of Moore's first tale in *Lalla Rookh*—the *Veiled Prophet of Khorassan*. See D'Herbelot's *Bibliotheca Orientalis*.

Hak'luyt, or **Hack'luyt, Richard,** an Elizabethan author, was born in 1553, studied at Westminster School and at Christ Church, Oxford, becoming lecturer on cosmography in his university. He accompanied the English embassy to Paris in 1584 as chaplain, on returning to England began to collect accounts of English maritime discovery—a work in which he was aided by Raleigh; published *The Principal Navigations, Voyages, Traffiques, and Discoveries of the English Nation* in 1598–1600; received a prebend in Westminster Abbey and a living in Suffolk, and died in 1616. H. seems also to have been the chief compiler of *A Selection of Curious, Rare, and Early Voyages, &c.* His works are full of invaluable details regarding our early navigators, and are written with pleasing simplicity and quaintness. Mr. Froude calls them 'the prose epic of the modern English nation,' adding that 'their plain, broad narratives rival legend in interest and grandeur.' *H.'s Voyages* have been issued by the Hakluyt Society, founded in 1846, with the aim of publishing records of early voyages and travels, but no good edition has yet appeared.

Hakod'ate, or **Hakoda'de,** the most northerly of the open ports of Japan, on the S. coast of the island of Yesso, at the base of a lofty promontory, on the Strait of Tzagar, with a background of wild hill scenery, 440 miles N. of Yeddo. It has a splendid harbour, somewhat difficult of access, and was connected by telegraph cable with Yeddo in 1875. The chief industry is fishing, and a foreign trade, which has developed since the opening of the port in 1859. The climate is severe in winter—the temperature has been known to reach 18° below zero. Snow lies till April, and is followed by heavy rains brought from the Pacific by S.E. winds. In 1875 there entered and cleared the port 77 vessels of 24,179 tons, of which 44 vessels of 16,290 tons were British. The exports, chiefly seaweed, irico, cuttlefish, awabi, dried fish, deer horns, and sharks' fins, amounted in value to £89,078; the imports, coals, kerosine oil, and manufactured goods, to £15,103. Customs and shipping dues amounted (1875) to £3754. Of the resident firms thirteen are British, six American, three Russian, two French, two German, and two Danish. Pop. (1872) 14,633.

Hal'acah (Heb. 'rule,' 'guide;' pl. *Halacoth*), an element in the Jewish Talmud, consisted of traditionary legal dicta and decisions bearing on the Jewish law after the captivity, and intended to harmonise the precepts of the law with the altered circumstances of the people. They were of the highest authority as precedents, Moses himself being said to have promulgated some H. in explanation of certain precepts of the law; in which respect they differed specially from the Haggadah (q. v.). Of the greater part of the H. Hillel (q. v.) was the reputed author. He probably collected what were in existence in his time, and added others. They are classified by Maimonides as follows:—(1) Mosaic and scriptural; (2) Mosaic and traditional; (3) generally received though questionable; (4) decisions of the wise as 'hedges of the law;' (5) counsels of prudence, well to follow, but not having the force of law. See E. Deutsch on the *Talmud* in his *Literary Remains* (Lond. 1874).

Halas', a town of Hungary, in Lesser Cumania, on Lake Halastó, 80 miles S.S.W. of Pesth. It has a large wine trade. Pop. (1869) 13,339.

Hal'berd, or **Halbert** (Fr. *hallebarde*, Ger. *hellebarde*, Old Ger. *helmbarte*, 'a pole-axe'), a weapon consisting of a long pole, on which was mounted a steel head, comprising a spike for thrusting, an axe face for hacking, with a hook behind. Formerly used by companies of halberdiers in foot regiments; it is now borne only for ornamental purposes on civic occasions.

Hal'berstadt, an old town in Prussian Saxony, on the Holzemme, a branch of the Saale, 30 miles S.W. of Magdeburg by railway. It has many quaint, picturesque houses, ornamented with curious wood carvings, and its cathedral of the 13th c. is in the purest Gothic style. The church of Our Lady (1005–1284) is a fine Byzantine structure. H. has rich collections of pictures, antiquities, &c., a 'Poetical Society' founded by the poet Gleim, and two large libraries. The manufactures are woollens, cottons, leather, soap, gloves, oil, cigars, &c. Pop. (1875) 27,800.

Hal'cyon Days (Gr. *alkyonides hēmerai*; Lat. *alcedonia*), fourteen days, seven before and as many after the winter solstice, during which the halcyon (Gr. *alkyōn*; Lat. *alcedo*) or kingfisher was fabled by the Greeks to brood, the sea meanwhile remaining profoundly calm. The term H. D. is often used as a synonym for quiet and peaceful times, *e.g.*, De Quincey, 'Deep, *halcyon* repose.'

Halcyon'idæ. See KINGFISHER.

Hale, Sir Matthew, a notable English lawyer, was born at Alderly, Gloucester, 1st November 1609, and studied at Oxford. Bred to equity under Sergeant Glanvil at Lincoln's Inn, he was called to the bar shortly before the Civil War, during which, by his affected indifference, he managed to secure the custom and confidence of both parties. H. signed the Solemn League and Covenant, and sat in the Westminster Assembly. Cromwell made him a commissioner for reforming the law, and a Judge of the Common Bench (1653). In 1660 he became Chief Baron of Exchequer, in 1671 Chief Justice of the King's Bench. He died on Christmas day 1676. It is interesting that H., although a judge, was elected a member of the House of Commons for the Three Kingdoms, there being then no House of Lords. He also sat in the Convention Parliament of 1660, where he moved that the Restoration should be agreed to only on constitutional conditions resembling those in the Treaty of Newfort. No one has disputed H.'s eminence as a Common Law judge; his impartiality was perfect, and indeed sometimes carried to absurdity, *e.g.*, when he refused a circuit-dinner as a bribe. It is a reproach more to his age than to himself that at Bury St. Edmunds he sentenced to death two women accused of witchcraft, but against whom no substantial evidence had been brought. H. wrote two important works, *History of the Pleas of the Crown* and *History of the Common Law of England*; and he left many valuable MSS., including his Commonplace Book, to the library at Lincoln's Inn. Richard Baxter called him 'the pattern of honest plainness and humility.' See Williams' *Memoirs of the Life, Character, and Writings of Sir Matthew Hale* (Lond. 1835).

Hales, Stephen, an English naturalist, was born at Beckesbourn, in Kent, September 17, 1677. He studied at Benet (now Corpus Christi) College, Cambridge, where he took his degree of Bachelor of Divinity in 1711. About the same time he was presented to the living of Teddington, and there devoted himself to his favourite studies, botany, anatomy, and physics. As a fellow of the Royal Society he communicated many papers of scientific interest, especially on methods of ventilation; and was the author of several works, the most important of which are *Vegetable Staticks* (1727); *Hæmastaticks* (1733); and *Philosophical Experiments on Sea Water, Corn, Flesh, and other Substances* (1739). H. died at Teddington, January 4, 1761.

Hal'évy, Jacques Fromental, a distinguished musical composer and teacher, was born at Paris, May 27, 1799. He entered the Conservatoire in 1809, became a teacher of 'solfeggio' there in 1816, of harmony in 1827, and of counterpoint and fugue in 1833. He studied five years under Cherubini and two at Rome. Among his operas represented at Paris, *La Juive* (1835), *La Reine de Chypre* (1841), and *Les Mousquetaires* (1846) deserve mention. He died at Nice, 17th March 1862. See Léon Halévy's memoir, *F. Halévy, sa Vie et ses Œuvres* (Paris, 1862).

Half Blood. The term in law, and generally, denotes the relationship of those who have had only one common ancestor. When that is a male, the relationship is called *consanguinean*; when a female, it is called *uterine*. By the succession law of England the H.-B. relation by the father's side succeeds to real estate (see ESTATE IN LAW) after the full-blood relation. As regards personal estate, the H.-B. relations on both sides share equally with the full blood. In Scotland, in collateral succession the H.-B. consanguinean succeeds after the full blood; thus, if a man die leaving a son and daughter by his first marriage and a son by his second marriage, and if the son of the first marriage takes the succession and dies without issue, being survived by his full sister and half brother consanguinean, his sister by the full blood will succeed as *her brother's* heir-at-law. But if the eldest son of the first marriage had predeceased his father, the son of the second marriage would have succeeded as *his father's* heir-at-law to the exclusion of the daughter of the first marriage.

Half-Pay. Under the Consolidated Royal Warrant of 1870, the following are the *daily* rates fixed for combatant officers:—

Rank.	Cavalry.	Infantry.	Artillery and Engineers.
	£ s. d.	£ s. d.	£ s. d.
Col.-Commandant	...	...	1 15 4
Colonel	0 15 6	0 14 6	0 16 9
Lieut.-Colonel	0 12 6	0 11 0	0 11 8
Major	0 10 0	0 9 6	...
Captain	0 7 6	0 7 0	0 7 4
Lieutenant	...	0 4 6	0 4 8
Cornet	0 3 6	...	...
Ensign	...	0 2 6	...

Officers who have enjoyed 'Distinguished Service Pay' obtain slightly increased rates when they retire on a reduction, or on account of wounds, or of illness contracted during service. On the other hand, those exchanging for their own convenience to H.-P. before seven years' service receive reduced rates. After twenty-five years' full-pay service, every officer of the household troops, or cavalry, or infantry of the line, has an unqualified right to retire on H.-P. If twelve years have been spent in the W. Indies, or sixteen on the W. coast of Africa, the period is reduced to twenty-one and sixteen years respectively. The Secretary of State may suspend H.-P. The period of service entitling quartermasters, adjutants, and ridingmasters is generally thirty years, the rate of daily pay being 10s. After the same period a chaplain gets 17s. 6d. a day; a controller, £1, 10s.; a commissary, 16s. 8d.; a paymaster, 12s. 6d.; an inspector-general, £1, 17s. 6d.; an apothecary, 9s. For fifteen years' service a surgeon is entitled to 13s. 6d. a day. Originally H.-P. was just a *retainer* for future services. The Commons always jealously watched the payments to 'Reformado' officers, as they were called. In 1718 and 1811 movements were made towards the principle of recognising the *past* services of officers. See the history of the subject, as well as of pensions and unattached pay in Clode's *British Army*, vol. i. App. G.

Halibur'ton, Thomas Chandler, an Anglo-American humourist and historian, was the son of a Nova Scotia judge, and was born at Windsor, in that province, in 1796. After leaving college he joined the bar, and made rapid progress in his profession, finally becoming Judge of the Supreme Court of Nova Scotia in 1840. In 1829 he published a *Historical and Statistical Account of Nova Scotia*, in 2 vols., and in 1837 appeared his famous *Clockmaker*. Allowing for some exaggerated touches, Sam Slick has been accepted as a type of the 'cute,' inventive, ready-witted, and inextinguishable Yankee, and his *naïve* and ingenious 'sayings and doings' have since produced a host of imitations. A visit to England in 1840 resulted in the publication of *The Attaché, or Sam Slick in England* (4 vols. Lond. 1843–44). In 1850, resigning his judgeship, H. settled in England, where he published *Sam Slick's Traits of American Humour*, and *Rule and Misrule of the English in America* (1852), and *Nature and Human Nature* (1855). He entered Parliament in the Conservative interest as member for Launceston in 1859. H. died August 27, 1865, when engaged on a new edition of his works, which includes, beside those enumerated, *Bubbles from Canada; The Letter-Bag of the Great Western; The Old Judge, or Life in a Colony*, &c.

Hal'ibut, or **Hol'ibut** (*Hippoglossus vulgaris*), a genus of Flat-fishes (q. v.), or *Pleuronectidæ*, attaining a length of 4 or 5 feet, and common off the British coasts. The H. has been known to measure over 7 feet, and to weigh more than 300 lbs. The colour of the upper side is brown, the surface being smooth. The body is longer, in proportion to its width, than is usually the case with the flat-fishes. The scales are of small size, of oval shape, and of soft consistence. The flesh is firm, but somewhat dry. The Greenlanders capture the H. in great numbers, and store the flesh up in a dried state for winter food; while oil is obtained in considerable quantity from the liver and other parts.

Halicarnass'us (originally *Zephyra*, now *Budrum*), a Dorian city on a S.W. promontory of Caria in Asia Minor, facing the island Cos, and nearly opposite Cnidus on the other side of the Ceramic Gulf. It was the birthplace of the historian Herodotus and the rhetorician Dionysius, but was chiefly famous for the magnificent sepulchre of Mausolus, erected by his queen, Artemisia, the name of which has become generic for a costly tomb. Sculptures from this building may be found in the British Museum. H. was early isolated from the Dorian Hexapolis, fell in time under the power of the Persians, during whose rule it was held by the dynasty of Lygdamis, sided with Athens in the Peloponnesian war, and (before B.C. 380) was included in an independent Carian kingdom governed by the dynasty of Hecatomnus. On its capture by Alexander the Great in 334 B.C., the city was burned to the ground, and it never regained importance. After the conquest of Antiochus the Great by the Romans, H. was made a part of the government of Rhodes, and later of the province of Asia.

Halicore. See DUGONG.

Halicz'. See GALICZ.

Hal'idon Hill, a strong military position about a mile from the town of Berwick, and between the Tweed and the Whiteadder, was the scene of a battle in the Scottish war of independence, 19th July 1333, between Edward III. of England and Douglas, Regent of Scotland acting for David Bruce. The Scotch, abandoning the defensive tactics of Bannockburn, rushed, after a long march, right up H. H. to storm the English position, and were thoroughly routed by the showers of arrows from the ranks of their opponents. The defeat, in which Douglas and the flower of the Scotch nobility fell, gave a temporary lease of power to Edward Baliol, and occasioned a renewal of English attempts upon Scotch independence; but its chief result was the final surrender of Berwick to England.

Hal'ifax ('holy face,' said to be named from an image of St. John once kept here), a town of England in the W. Riding of Yorkshire, on the right bank of the Ribble, 7 miles S.W. of Bradford, 16 W.S.W. of Leeds, 25 N.E. of Manchester, 203 N.N.W. of London by railway. It is pleasantly encircled by hills, and has a natural position of great industrial importance. Its principal buildings are the townhall, designed by Sir C. Barry, and opened by the Prince of Wales in 1863; the Piece Hall, covering 10,000 sq. yards, built in 1779 as a market for piece-goods, and now used as a wholesale market for fish and vegetables; the parish church of St. John, in Late Perpendicular style, with a length of 180 feet; the church of All Souls, one of the chief works of Sir G. G. Scott (1861), a structure in the Early Decorated style, rich in ornamental granite, serpentine, marbles, in mural paintings, stained glass, and elaborate sculpture, and built at the sole cost of Edward Akroyd, Esq.; and St. Mary's church, built by the late M. Stocks, Esq., from designs by Mr. W. S. Barber, also in the Early Decorated style. H. possesses three parks, viz., Savile Park of 50 acres; the People's Park of 12½ acres, given by the late Sir Francis Crossley; and the Shroggs Park of 25 acres, laid out in 1877. H. has many charities, including the great Crossley Orphanage for 300 children. The free grammar-school at Heath was founded under royal charter in the reign of Elizabeth. A new school, at a cost of nearly £10,000, is to be built shortly. H. has also a mechanics' institute (1856) with a public hall and library, an extensive infirmary (1864), a museum, assembly and concert rooms, and a theatre. The great manufactures are carpets, woollens, worsted, damasks, camlets, cottons, cotton cards, rugs, silks, serges, shalloons, tammies, kerseys, and calimancoes. Many of the inhabitants are employed in the neighbouring coal-mines, ironworks, stone quarries, chemical works, dyeworks, &c. Pop. (1871) 65,510. The old 'H. gibbet law' applied to all offenders within a certain area accused of theft to the value of 13½d., who were tried by the frith-burgers of the liberty, and if convicted were executed by a kind of guillotine on the first market-day following. The axe is preserved by the lord of the manor at Wakefield. H. sends two members to Parliament.

Halifax, the capital of Nova Scotia, is the military head-quarters of the Dominion of Canada, and the chief naval station for British N. America and the W. Indies. It is situated near the head of Chebucto Bay. Its harbour, regarded as one of the best in the world, runs over 15 miles inland. The city and harbour are defended by the citadel on a hill behind, by six forts, and by masked batteries and martello towers. H. is well built, with spacious streets, and has an area of about two miles in length by three-quarters of a mile in breadth. The chief public buildings are Province Building, the Post-Office, Government House, Admiralty House, Dalhousie College (with sixteen professors), Insane Asylum, the barracks, hospital, and jail. Several of the twenty-three churches and of the seven banks are handsome structures. The commerce of H. is considerable; the exports amounting in 1869 to £660,320, and the imports to £1,500,520. The city, called Chedabucto or Chebucto till 1749, received its present name from the Earl of H., a zealous promoter of enterprise in Nova Scotia. H. is 189 miles from St. John, N.B., and 786 from Ottawa. Its pop. was 1400 in 1749, 11,516 in 1818, and about 30,000 in 1870.

Halifax, Charles Montagu, Earl of, statesman and poet, grandson of the first Earl of Manchester, was born at Horton, Northamptonshire, 16th April 1661, and educated at Westminster and Cambridge. A poem on the death of Charles II. procured for him the patronage of Lord Dorset, under whose auspices he entered Parliament. He voted for the dethronement of James II., and became a staunch adherent of William III., from whom he received, partly as a reward for a poem on the battle of the Boyne, a pension of £500. He was appointed in 1692 a Commissioner of the Treasury, in 1694 Chancellor of the Exchequer, in 1697 Premier, and on his resignation in 1700 was created Baron Halifax. While in office H. displayed great financial ability. In 1692, in order to raise a million of money for war purposes when the exchequer was severely strained, he conceived the idea of a national debt; in 1694 he adopted William Paterson's scheme for the formation of the Bank of England with great success; and in 1694 he carried out a recoinage with the assistance of Sir Isaac Newton. Although out of office during the whole of the reign of Queen Anne, H. rendered effective aid toward the Union of 1707. He warmly supported the Hanoverian succession, and on George I.'s accession became Prime Minister with the rank of earl. He died 19th May 1715. H.s poems and speeches were collected and published with a biography, for which he supplied the materials, in the year of his death.

Halio'tis, or **Ear-Shell**, a genus of Gasteropodous molluscs, forming the type of the family *Haliotidæ*, in which the shell is ear-shaped, with a very large, expanded lip and aperture, and very small whorls. No operculum exists, and the outer lip is perforated for the passage of a respiratory siphon. The siphon is periodically shifted in position as the shell increases in size, so that old shells possess a row of apertures along the outer side. The H. is very common in the Channel Islands, the *H. tuberculatus* being known as the Guernsey sea-ear or 'ormer.' The ass's ear (*H. asinus*) is another species. These shells are highly valued for the beautiful hues and lustre of their lining, which is largely used in the manufacture and decoration of *papier maché* ornaments.

Hall is the name of several German towns, and, like Halle and Hallein, signifies that the places so named possess salt springs or saltworks. The root is probably Celtic, and connected with the Gr. *hals*, 'the salt sea.'—1. **H.**, called commonly, to distinguish it, **Schwäbisch-H.**, is an old, irregularly-built town of Würtemberg, situated on the Kocher, and is 40 miles N.E. of Stuttgart, with which it is connected by rail. The salt-mine at Wilhelms Glück (nearly 3 miles distant) produces annually from 90,000 to 100,000 cwt. of salt, mostly used for baths. A little cotton-spinning is done at H., which was once an imperial city. Pop. (1871) 7793.—2. **H.**, in Tyrol, Austria, is 6 miles E. of Innsbruck on the main line of railway, and lies on the river Inn. Its industry depends mainly on the salt, which is brought in a state of solution to the saltworks in pipes from the mines, 10 miles further N. amongst the mountains. The annual produce is close on 14,500 tons of salt. The pop. of H. is (1869) 5010.

Hall, Mrs. Anna Maria, an English novelist, was born in Dublin in 1802. The name of her father was Fielding, and her mother was of Swiss and French descent. In 1824, after a nine years' residence in London, she married Mr. Spencer Carter Hall, whom she has assisted in many works, such as *Ireland* (1841-43), and in literary efforts in the interests of temperance. Her own writings as a novelist, dramatist, and author of books for children are very numerous, but her most successful works are those which deal with her native country, such as *Sketches of Irish Character*, *The Groves of Blarney* (acted 1838), *Stories of the Irish Peasantry*, and *The Whiteboy* (1845). Mrs. Hall's style is graphic and touching. The 'golden wedding' of Mr. and Mrs. H. was celebrated in 1874.

Hall, Basil, Captain, R.N., a popular English writer, son of Sir James Hall of Dunglass, was born at Edinburgh in 1788. He joined the navy at fourteen, and served in the junior grades of the service in American and East Indian waters. In 1813 he accompanied Admiral Sir Samuel Hood in a journey through Java, and three years later had the command of a sloop, forming part of Lord Amherst's expedition to China. His experiences during the latter cruise were published in 1818, under the title *An Account of a Voyage of Discovery to the Western Coast of Corea and the Great Loo Choo Island.* As post-captain of the *Conway*, he was stationed on the S. American coast at the time of the disputes between Spain and her colonies from 1820-22, *Extracts from a Journal* then kept by him appearing in 2 vols. in 1824. Five years later appeared his *Travels in North America.* Between 1831-40 he published 9 vols. of *Fragments of Voyages and Travels. The Castle of Hainfield*, published in 1836, and *Patchwork*, a fascinating collection of reminiscences of travel in the form of tales (3 vols. 1842), complete the list of his larger works. H.'s industry brought on an attack of mental aberration in 1842, and he died in the Royal Hospital at Haslar on 11th September 1844.

Hall, Joseph, distinguished as a churchman and author, was born July 1, 1574, at Bristow Park, near Ashby-de-la-Zouch; and after an education at the public school of that town, entered Emanuel College, Cambridge. When twenty-three years of age, he published six books of satires, under the title *Virgidemiarum, or a Gathering of Rods*, which assail with some wit the follies and abuses of the time, and were burned by command of the Archbishop of Canterbury. H. eventually took holy orders, and after filling the incumbencies of Halstead and Waltham, became in 1617 Dean of Worcester. He attended the Synod of Dort in the next year as one of the English delegates, and was decreed a gold medal by the Synod as a token of respect. In 1627 he accepted the bishopric of Exeter, and was translated to the see of Norwich in 1641; but at this period his zeal and honesty had begun to expose him to the suspicion of Puritanism. His numerous pamphlets in favour of the divine right of episcopacy, however, might have secured him from any such aspersion; and in November 1641, having united with the bishops who protested against all measures passed during their enforced absence from Parliament, H. was sent to the Tower. In June of the next year he was released on bail for £5000; but in 1643 his estates were sequestrated by the Parliament. He then retired to Higham near Norwich, where he died, 8th September 1656. The chief works of Bishop H. are his *Contemplations* (on historical passages of the Bible), his *Sermons*, his *Characters of Virtues and Vices*, his *Occasional Meditations*, and his *Three Centuries of Meditations and Vows*, all of which, but especially the last two, are full of subtle beauties of illustration, exquisitely cogent reasoning, and a devout and tender sentiment. The only contemporary churchman who surpassed him in genius was the 'modern Chrysostom,' Jeremy Taylor. His collected works were published in 12 vols. at Oxford (1837-39).

Hall, Robert, a learned and eloquent Baptist divine, was born 2d May 1764 at Arnsby in Leicestershire, England, where his father was a pastor. He early showed signs of a powerful intellect and a taste for study, and in 1781 was sent to the University of Aberdeen, where he took the degree of M.A. He thereafter became a minister in the Baptist connection, and held a charge successively at Bristol, Cambridge, Leicester, and again at Bristol, where he died, 21st February 1831. In consequence of his intense devotion to his studies he was thrice afflicted with mental derangement, from which, however, he completely recovered. H. was one of the foremost and most powerful pulpit orators of his time, and his works are still ranked amongst English classics. Among the more notable are *Christianity Consistent with a Love of Freedom* (1791), *Apology for the Freedom of the Press* (1793), *Modern Infidelity* (1799), *Reflections on War* (1802), *The Sentiments Proper to the Present Crisis* (1803), and a *Funeral Sermon on the Princess Charlotte* (1817). A collected edition of his writings, with a *Life of H.* by Dr. Olinthus Gregory, was published in 6 vols. (1831-33).

Hall'a, a town in Scinde, British India, near the left bank of the Indus, 36 miles N. of Hydrabad. Pop. (1872) 4096. It is famed for the manufacture of glazed pottery, and conducts a trade in agricultural produce valued at £11,000 a year. In the neighbourhood are some old Mohammedan tombs.

Hall'am, Henry, a great English historian, son of the Dean of Bristol, was born at Windsor in 1777, and educated at Eton and Oxford. After leaving the university H. joined the Whig party in London, and wrote for the *Edinburgh Review.* His profound linguistic acquirements are alluded to by Byron in *English Bards and Scotch Reviewers*—'the classic H., much renowned for Greek.' In 1818 appeared his *View of the State of Europe in the Middle Ages*, which gives valuable sketches of the growth of ecclesiastical power, of civil organisation, of feudalism and chivalry; in 1827 his *Constitutional History of England from the Accession of Henry VII. to the Death of George II.* In 1837-39 he produced his *Introduction to the Literature of Europe in the 15th, 16th, and 17th Centuries*, a full account of the revival of letters, and of the development of a literature in each of the great vernacular languages of Europe. H. died at Penshurst, 21st January 1859. As Macaulay has said, H. is a critical and argumentative historian, of great industry, acuteness, and impartiality, with a massive style which sometimes rises into a grave and sober eloquence. He has been called an anatomist, and compared to Macchiavelli; but his appreciation of the inner currents of political feeling indicates some spiritual insight, and his somewhat unimpassioned conclusions generally are based on the best-authenticated facts. The value of his critical judgments, however, is impaired by the fact that in his survey of European literature he is necessarily forced to rely in great measure on the knowledge and criticism of foreign historians.—**Arthur Henry H.**, eldest son of the preceding, was born in London on 18th February 1811. Morally and intellectually he was precocious. Educated at Eton and Cambridge, he probably owed the decisive tone of his mind to spiritual poetry and art to a long stay which he made in Italy in 1827-28. He did not attempt any university honours except the English Declamation Prize of 1831. But his metaphysical acumen, his imaginative power, and his literary taste made him in fact one of the most distinguished men of his time. In 1832 he began to study law at the Inner Temple, but found time to reply to Rossetti's work on the *Antipapal Spirit* in the great Italian poets, and to write memoirs of Petrarch, Voltaire, and Burke for the *Gallery of Portraits.* He died suddenly at Pesth, 15th September 1833. His character has been immortalised in Tennyson's *In Memoriam.* His poetical remains, with a preface by his father, were published in 1863 (Murray, Lond.).—**Henry Fitzmaurice H.**, younger brother of the preceding, was born on 31st August 1824, and was educated at Eton and Cambridge. He was a very distinguished scholar, and before leaving for the bar founded the Historical Debating Society. His quiet, sincere, strongly intellectual, and deeply religious nature was very like his father's. He died suddenly in 1851. See *Memoir* by Sir H. S. Maine and F. Lushington (Lond. 1863), prefixed to an edition of his brother's *Remains*.

Hall'e, an important city and railway centre in the province of Saxony, Prussia, on the river Saale, 20 miles N.W. of Leipsic, on the Leipsic-Magdeburg Railway. It is ancient and irregularly built, the streets being narrow and very crooked. Of its six churches one dates from the 12th, another from the 14th, a third from the 16th c. It has manufactures of starch, beetroot-sugar, chemicals, carpets, machinery, and beer. The saltworks of H. are famous, and produce over 10,000 tons annually. The brine comes from springs within the town, and is worked partly by a private company, partly by Government. The workmen connected with the salt manufacture form a special class in the community. They are called *Halloren*, and are distinguished from the other natives of the district by features, dialect, and costume, though they now intermarry with their neighbours. The *Halloren* are presumed to be of Wendish, or more probably of Celtic origin, and still enjoy some special privileges.—The *University* of H., founded in 1694, had the still older one of Wittenberg incorporated with it in 1817. The university nearly expired in Napoleon's time, but is now one of the most influential in Germany, having in 1875 95 professors and teachers and 989 students. The important educational institution founded by and named after Francke (q. v.) consists of an orphanage, an elementary school, a gymnasium or classical academy, a commercial school, a school for the poor, a workshop, a printing-work, and a book warehouse. H. first appears in 806 as a German border-fortress of Karl the Great's on Slavic soil. In 965 the Emperor Otto I. gave it to the Archbishops of Magdeburg. In 981 Otto II. made it a town. In the beginning of the 12th c. it began to be a thriving place of trade, and was a member of the Hansa in the 13th and 14th centuries. At the Reformation it finally threw off the authority of its ecclesiastical princes. Pop. (1871) of H., with its suburbs Glaucha and Neustadt, 52,615 (including 526 soldiers).

Hall'e, Charles, pianist, was born April 11, 1819, at Hagen, in Westphalia. Early in life he went to Paris, where he became a professor. But in February 1848, in consequence of the Revolution, he came to England, and attracted notice as a pianist at the matinées of Mr. Ella, director of the Musical Union in London. Soon afterwards he settled in Manchester as director of the Musical Institution. He appears every season in London and Edinburgh. Although H. has published few compositions, he has done very much to elevate musical taste in England, and to introduce the best orchestral works. His own playing is exquisitely classical.

Hall'eck, Henry Wager, an American general, was born at Waterville, New York, U.S., 16th January 1815, graduated at West Point in 1839, and entered the army as an engineer. He served in Mexico and California, but resigned his commission in 1854 to establish himself at San Francisco as a lawyer. Soon after the outbreak of the civil war he became general of the Western Federal Army at St. Louis, and afterwards held the command-in-chief of all the United States' armies from July 1862 till March 1864, when he was made chief of the staff. During a few months in 1865 he was commander at Richmond, whence he was transferred to the division of the Pacific, and in March 1869 to Louisville, where he died, 9th January 1872. He is the author of *Elements of Military Art and Science* (1846, 2d ed. with critical notes on the Mexican and Crimean wars, 1858); the *Mining Laws of Spain and Mexico* (1859); a treatise on *International Law* (1861); a translation of Jomini's *Life of Napoleon I.* (1864), &c.

Halleck, Fitzgreene, an American poet, was born at Guildford, Connecticut, U.S., 8th July 1790. Most of his life, from 1811 to 1849, was spent in a New York bank, and he also acted as secretary to J. J. Astor, the millionaire, but his practical and commercial surroundings did not prevent his wooing the Muses with fair success. *Twilight*, which appeared in a New York paper in 1818, was his first printed poetical effort; and in the following year, in conjunction with J. R. Drake, whose early death he touchingly commemorates, he contributed the *Croaker Papers* to the *Evening Post*. *Fanny*, a biting satire in verse on the follies and fashions of the day, was anonymously published by him in 1819, and achieving great popularity, passed through several editions. In 1827 he issued a volume containing *Burns*, *Alnwick Castle*, *Marco Bozzaris*, and other poems, principally suggested by a visit to Europe in 1822. Enlarged editions of his works appeared in 1836, 1842, 1849, and 1858; a poem, *Young America*, in 1864; and a complete edition of his works after his death, which took place at Guildford on 19th November 1867. An obelisk at Guildford and a statue at New York testify to the affectionate regard in which he is held by his fellow-countrymen.

Hall'el ('Heb. 'praise') is a hymn of praise which was used by the Jews at certain of their festivals. The Egyptian H., consisting of Psalms cxiii.–cxviii., was chanted in the temple at the festivals of the Passover, Pentecost, Tabernacles, and Dedication, and in private families at the celebration of the Passover. From the 2d c. A.D. it was also recited by the Jews at Babylon at every festival of the new moon. The Great H., Ps. cxviii. (according to some authorities cxx., or even cxxxv. 4)–cxxxvi., was recited at the Passover Supper by those who wished to have a fifth cup. At the present day the Jews recite the Egyptian H. on all the festivals of the year except the New Year and the Day of Atonement.

Hallelu'jah (Heb. 'sing ye praises to Jehovah;' Gr. Alleluia) occurs in Psalm cxvii., and in the headings of several other Psalms, *e.g.*, cxiii., cxviii. (see HALLEL), and was used by the Jews as a general formulary of praise; from whom it passed into the Christian Church. Being deemed fitting, however, only for joyful occasions, its use was in many churches limited to the season between Easter and Whitsunday, but afterwards its use was forbidden in the West only between Septuagesima and Easter. In the early days of the Church 'the people sang it together in divine service, monks assembled to its sound, and it was chanted at funerals, by labourers in the field, and seamen on shipboard.'

Hall'er, Albrecht von, a Swiss anatomist, physiologer, and botanist, who was also distinguished as a poet, was born at Bern, 8th October 1708, and educated at the gymnasium there. He studied medicine at Tübingen and Leyden, and afterwards visited England and France. In 1728 he devoted himself to the study of the higher mathematics at Basel, but was compelled by failing health to make a tour among the Alps. Here his love for botany was awakened, and here he wrote his great didactic poem, *Die Alpen*. In 1729 he settled in Bern as a medical practitioner; in 1736 he accepted a call to a professorship in Göttingen, where he laboured for seventeen years, and published eighty-six works on medical and scientific subjects. The most important are *Enumeratio Methodica Stirpium Helveticarum* (1742), *Icones Anatomicæ* (1743), *Primæ Lineæ Physiologiæ* (1745), *Elementa Physiologiæ Corporis Humani*, and Boerhaave's *Methodus Studii Medicinæ* (1751). To the *Götting'sche Gelehrte Anzeigen* H. contributed, it is said, upwards of 12,000 reviews and articles. His fame was in all countries, and honours from all quarters were showered on him. In 1753 he returned to his native town, and devoted himself to the promotion of education, of industrial and agricultural science in Switzerland, but found time to write three political romances (*Usong*, *Alfred*, *Fabius und Cato*), and to maintain, in five languages, a correspondence with the leaders of European thought. He died 12th December 1777. His services to natural science and medicine are imperishable; amongst them his observations on irritability in organic life, the processes of generation, and the development of life in the fertilised egg. His poetry is didactic, like that of his English models, but is distinguished by richness of thought, depth, and earnestness. The first collection of his *Schweizerische Gedichte* appeared 1732; the twelfth in 1828, accompanied by a memoir by Wyss. See his own *Tagebuch* (Bern, 1787), his *Leben* by Zimmermann (Zur. 1755), and Baggesen's *H. als Christ* (Bern. 1865).

Hall'ey, Edmund, an English astronomer, was born at Haggerston, near London, October 29, 1656. While studying at Queen's College, Oxford, he published, in 1676, the calculation of the time of the sun's axial rotation from observations of the motion of a spot. In the same year he went to St. Helena, where for two years he worked at the preparation of a catalogue of the southern stars (published 1679). On his return he became a Fellow of the Royal Society; and in 1680, took a year's tour through Europe, during which he made observations of the comet which goes by his name. In 1684, he made the acquaintance of Newton, who intrusted him with the publication of the *Principia*. In 1698, he was sent as commander of a vessel to the Western ocean to test the truth of his theory of magnetic variation. The mutiny of the crew obliged him to return, but the next year he set sail again, and got as far S. as the Antarctic ice would allow. The results of this voyage he published in a general chart, and soon after his return home was employed in making a chart to represent the correct course of the Channel tides. In 1703 he succeeded Dr. Wallis as Savilian Professor of Geometry at Oxford, and in 1710 published a new edition of the works of Apollonius of Perga. On the death of Flamsteed in 1719, he was appointed Astronomer-Royal. The remainder of his life was spent in astronomical observations and calculations, and especially in studying the motions of the moon. One of his last services was pointing out, for the benefit of his successors, the great importance of accurately observing the approaching transit of Venus across the sun's disc. H. died at Greenwich, 14th January 1742. His *Tabulæ Astronomicæ* were published in 1749.

Halley's Comet. See COMETS.

Hall'iwell, James Orchard, F.R.S., was born at Chelsea, June 21, 1820, and studied at Cambridge University. He has devoted himself to Shakespearian criticism, and among his many works are *Shakespeariana* (1841), *A History of Freemasonry* (1842), *Dictionary of Provincial and Archaic Words* (1844-45), *Life of Shakespeare* (1845), *Popular Rhymes and Nursery Tales* (1849), *An Account of the New Place, Stratford-on-Avon* (1864), an edition of *Shakespeare*—his greatest labour (1865), and *Illustrations of the Life of Shakespeare* (Part I. 1874). He has published large numbers of forgotten pamphlets, plays, &c., of the Elizabethan age, and has enriched his edition of *Shakespeare* with many archæological notes. A peculiarity of H.'s *Shakespeare* is its containing the novels and tales which supplied the plots of the dramas.

Hall'ow Even, or **Halloween**, the night of October 31, being the eve before All Saints' or All Hallows' Day, which falls on November 1. During the middle ages it was believed that every invisible spirit walked about on this night, and hence it was long customary in the rural parts of England and Scotland to celebrate H. with half-sportive, half-superstitious customs, which are humorously and minutely described in Burns's *Halloween*. There seems to be a connection between H. and the German Walpurgis Nacht.

Hallu'cinations (Lat. *hallucinatio*, 'a blunder') are morbid conditions of the mind, resulting in perceptions where no impression has been made upon the brain or the external organs of the special senses. These organs may be morbidly affected, causing sensations, not dependent upon any external object, but upon the morbid conditions of the organs themselves. Such phenomena are termed Illusions (q. v.), and sometimes H. There may be also incipient disease or morbid excitation of the brain, giving rise to sensations or trains of thought not adequately referable to any external cause, and such phenomena are strictly H. H. may be transient, recurrent, or permanent. They often occur in those of a highly excitable nervous temperament, and also after great mental concentration and exhaustion. Sir Walter Scott was subject to them; the late Earl Grey was haunted by a gory head; Luther seems to have been affected in a similar manner; and Swedenborg imagined that he saw members of the heavenly hierarchy seated among the ministers at the council board when he was at the head of the government. H. are of very frequent occurrence amongst the insane; those of vision and of hearing are the most numerous; those of taste, smell, and touch, less frequent. Esquirol held that of 100 lunatics four-fifths at least would be affected with H., and M. Baudry found that of 145 insane people at Bicêtre 56 presented H. When the organ of hearing is affected, or that part of the brain through which the sensation is transmitted, the insane persons may be dangerously suicidal or homicidal, for in such cases the voices and commands are frequently ascribed to God, and implicit obedience is given. See Brière de Boismont *Des Hallucinations* (Par. 1845); Aubanel and Thore, *Recherches Statistiques faites à l'Hospice de Bicêtre;* Michéa, *Du Délire des Sensations* (Par. 1848); *Psychological Journal* (Lond.); Bucknill and Tuke, *Manual of Psychological Medicine* (Lond. 1874).

Hall'uin, a town in France, department of Nord, 10 miles N.N.E. of Lille. It carries on weaving, cotton-spinning, bleaching linen, and calico printing. Pop. (1872) 12,946.

Hal'malille, a name given to *Berrya Ammonilla*, a large Ceylon tree belonging to the lime-tree order. It yields a valuable light timber much used for building purposes and making oil casks. In Madras, to which the wood is exported, it is called *trincomali wood*.

Hal'ogens. The H. consist of a group of the four elements *chlorine*, *bromine*, *iodine*, and *fluorine*, all of which possess many properties in common, and are, in fact, closely related to one another chemically. They derive their name of H., or 'salt-producers' (Gr. *hals*, 'sea,' and *gennaō*, 'I produce'), from the readiness with which they combine with metals to form salts—common salt, indeed, being itself a compound of a haloid (chlorine) and a metal (sodium). Of the H., fluorine has never been isolated, at least in quantities sufficient to admit of an examination of its properties; but there can be no question that, could it be obtained in the pure condition, its properties would resemble those of the other haloids. In its compounds at least, this analogy is well marked. In comparing, then, the properties of the H. in the free state there remain but three, viz., chlorine, bromine, and iodine. The first is a gas, the second a liquid, and the third a solid at ordinary temperatures. The colour of chlorine is pale green (Gr. *chlōros*, 'pale green'), that of bromine dark red, and of iodine black or dark grey, except in the condition of vapour, when it is of a beautiful violet (Gr. *iōdēs*, 'violet'). This gradation in physical properties is also apparent in the specific gravities of the three haloids, which are as follows:—

Liquified chlorine.	Bromine.	Iodine.
1·38	3·19	4·95

It will be observed that the specific gravity of bromine is very nearly the mean of the specific gravities of iodine and chlorine. Similar differences are observed in the atomic weights of the haloids, which are as under:—

Fluorine.	Chlorine.	Bromine.	Iodine.
19	35·5	80	127

Thus the atomic weights gradually increase from fluorine to iodine. The haloids are remarkable for the compounds which they form with hydrogen, each of them forming a single compound, containing an atom of haloid and an atom of hydrogen. These compounds form the important group of acids known as the hydracids. Their names and formulæ are as follows:—

HF	Hydrofluoric acid.
HCl	Hydrochloric acid.
HBr	Hydrobromic acid.
HI	Hydriodic acid.

The hydracids are gaseous. They have a powerful affinity for water, actually condensing it from the atmosphere as a cloud. They readily act on many metals (both in solution and in the gaseous state), yielding the haloid salt of the metal and free hydrogen; on oxides, yielding water and haloid salt; and on peroxides, forming water, a haloid salt, and free haloid. It is upon this last reaction that the ordinary method of preparing the haloids depends. The affinity of the haloids for hydrogen varies, being so powerful in the case of fluorine, that when once the compound is set at liberty, its hydrogen cannot be removed by oxidation. With chlorine it is also powerful, a mixture of the two gases exploding when brought into sunlight. With bromine the affinity is much slighter, the two bodies only combining directly when strongly heated; and with iodine so weak that no compound can be obtained by direct synthesis. The haloids may be arranged in the order of their affinity for hydrogen as follows:—

Fluorine,
Chlorine,
Bromine,
Iodine.

It should be observed that this is also the order of their affinity for the metals. As a consequence of this difference of affinity, the haloids may be made to replace one another in their compounds. Thus a metallic bromide or hydrobromic acid when treated with chlorine is decomposed, with formation of the chlorind of the metal or hydrochloric and free bromine. An iodide when treated either with bromine or chlorine yields the bromide or chloride and free iodine. These facts are turned to account in the manufacture of bromine and iodine.

The affinity of the haloids for oxygen is in the reverse order, that of iodine being the most powerful, and of fluorine so slight that no compound of the two can be obtained. It follows that the haloids replace one another in their oxygen compounds in exactly the reverse order of that just described for the hydrogen and metallic compounds, iodine decomposing a compound of bromine and oxygen, and both bromine and iodine one of chlorine and oxygen.

The oxides of chlorine are numerous but unstable; the stability, however, increases with the amount of oxygen they contain. Owing to this instability they are powerful oxidising agents. No simple compounds of bromine and oxygen exist, but acids containing bromine, hydrogen, and oxygen. Iodine yields two oxides and the corresponding acids. They are comparatively stable bodies.

With the exception of fluorine the haloids occur in sea water, chlorine in the largest proportion. Iodine and bromine are abstracted from the water by marine plants, and it is from the burnt seaweeds (kelp) that most of the iodine is obtained. Fluorine occurs in tolerable abundance in fluor spar or fluoride of calcium.

Hal'oid Salts are compounds of the halogens with metals. Common salt is the most familiar substance of a haloid salt. It consists of a compound of an atom of chlorine and one of the metal sodium (NaCL). The existence of H. S. could not be accounted for on the old hypothesis that a salt was a compound of an acid and a base, and that an acid contained oxygen. After the discovery of the hydracids, however, and when acids were defined as compounds of hydrogen with *salt radicals—i.e.*, elements or groups of elements which can combine with a metal to form a salt—the existence of H. S. was satisfactorily explained, and their relations to the hydracids and oxyacids, as well as to the oxysalts, at once made clear. Thus

Hydrochloric acid,	H(CL)	Nitric acid,	$H(NO_3)$
Chloride of sodium,	Na(CL)	Nitrate of sodium,	$Na(NO_3)$.

Haloragea'ceæ, an order of calycifloral dicotyledons, embracing nine genera and about eighty species, many of which are aquatic plants found in various parts of the world. They have no properties of importance. In Britain the order is represented by the mare's-tail (*Hippuris vulgaris*), and three species of *Myriophyllum* or water-milfoils. The genus *Gunnera* belongs to the order, the species of which are found in various countries and have large coarse leaves. *G. scabra* and *G. manicata* are cultivated in gardens for ornament. See GUNNERA.

Halorageaceæ.

Ha'los (Lat. *halos*, Gr. *halōs*, 'a threshing-floor,' which among the ancients was *circular*) are coloured concentric rings which, under certain conditions, are observed round the sun and moon. There are many distinct phenomena included under this general term, which receive particular names, and which are due to different causes. For instance, *coronæ* are coloured rings of a few degrees in diameter, which may be almost always seen round the sun or moon when either is shining through a mist or cloud (which is not a cirrus). This appearance is due to Diffraction (q. v.), occasioned by the presence of small spheres of water floating in the air through which the rays of light are passing. To the same cause are referred the *glories* or *Anthelia* (q. v.) which surround the shadow of the spectator's head when cast by the sun on a fog bank. Rainbows (q. v.), which present the same alternation of colours, though not included under this head, are due simply to combined reflection and refraction through spherical drops of water, which are too large to produce any diffraction phenomena.

The most interesting of all H., however, are those great concentric rings which, though rarely seen in our latitudes, surround the sun in Polar regions with dazzling brilliancy. They depend upon the presence of innumerable minute *crystals* of ice, which float as a cirrus cloud in the higher strata of the atmosphere; and are often accompanied by *parhelia* or mock suns. Huyghens was the first to attempt the explanation of these; but he was ignorant of the crystalline form which ice takes, and also of its refractive index, so that his theory was necessarily far from complete. Marriotte, with fuller knowledge, explained many of the curious attendant phenomena; and Young and Kaemtz may be regarded as having finally perfected the theory. Bravais' memoir, published in the *Journal de l'École Polytechnique*, gives a systematic treatment of the whole question, and is indeed the great authority upon the subject.

The characteristic features of a solar halo, with its accompanying phenomena, are as follows:—(1) *The halo of 22° radius.* This is due to the refraction of the sunlight through those prisms with refracting angles of 60°, which are in the position of *minimum deviation* (see SPECTRUM ANALYSIS), with respect to the sun and the observer. Since the different coloured lights are differently refracted, it follows that the halo is variously coloured like the rainbow, passing from red on the inside through yellow and green to purple on the outside. Again, the ice-crystals are slowly falling through the air, and they consequently take up certain positions depending on their form. Long and thin crystals probably fall with their axes vertical, while flat hexagonal plates most likely descend edgewise. If the majority have their axes placed vertically, the laws of optics indicate that besides the halo there ought to be bright-coloured images of the sun, at the same altitude as that body, and distant from it, one on each side, by an angular distance which depends upon the angle of incidence made by the refracted ray. If the sun be on the horizon, these so-called *mock-suns* or *parhelia* lie on the halo of 22°; if otherwise, they are external to it. Observation in this instance corroborates the results of theory. The light *reflected* from the vertical prisms gives rise, in accordance with optical laws, to a white horizontal line passing through the sun and parhelia—a phenomenon often observed. (2) *Tangent arcs to the halo of* 22°. These are the result of the overlapping of innumerable parhelia, formed each by refraction through short hexagonal plate-like crystals with their horizontal axes all pointing in the same direction. The more acute the angle which the parallel axes make with the line joining the sun and the observer, the further removed from the medial line is the parhelion corresponding to that position; and, as there are crystals in all conceivable positions, the result is two curved lines of coloured light touching the circular halo at its highest and lowest points, and extending outwards on both sides. For certain altitudes these tangent arcs curve downwards and meet, forming a closed elliptical curve. (3) *The halo of* 46° *radius.* This is formed by refraction through the *right angle* which the sides of the hexagonal prisms make with the terminal plane. Its explanation is the same as that given for the small halo of 22° radius, the only difference being in the greater angle of refraction and the consequently greater size of the halo. It also has its parhelia and tangent arcs, which, when present, surpass in magnificence of colouring the attendants on the smaller halo. The parhelia may themselves give rise to *secondary* H., which, though necessarily fainter than the *primary* appearances, have been observed under favourable circumstances. There are other phenomena resulting from the various combinations of planes which are possible in a prism terminated by a six-sided pyramid; but their explanation is scarcely possible without the use of mathematics. The fullest details are found in Bravais' memoir above mentioned.

Hal'stead, a market-town of Essex, England, on the Colne, 43 miles N.N.E. of London. It has a very fine parish church, a grammar-school (Lady Mary Ramsay's), and carries on manufactures of silk, crape, velvet, &c. Pop. (1871) 5783.

Hal'yards (from *haul* and *yard*), ropes aboard ship for hoisting sails and yards.

Hal'yburton, Thomas, a Scottish theologian, born at Dupplin, near Perth, in December 1674, became minister of Ceres, in Fife, in 1700, and in 1710 Professor of Divinity in St. Leonard's College, St. Andrews. He died at the age of thirty-eight, on September 1712. H.'s best-known writings are directed against the Deists. The chief are *Natural Religion Insufficient, and Revealed Necessary to Man's Happiness* (Edinb. 1714); *Memoirs of his Life* (1715); *The Great Concern of Salvation* (1718); *Ten Sermons* (1722). The memoirs of H.'s life appeared in 1715; a complete edition of his works at Glasgow in 1836.

Ham, a name most frequently applied to the hind-legs of pigs, cured and preserved for use in a variety of ways, but also given to the preserved flesh of other animals, more especially mutton and beef. Bacon or pork H. is cured, among numerous other ways, by thoroughly rubbing over the fresh meat with a mixture of equal parts, say 1 lb. of salt and sugar, with 4 oz. of saltpetre, and keeping it for four or five weeks in the brine from this mixture, occasionally turning over the meat. Thereafter it is removed from the brine, drained, and hung up to dry in a cool place, and finally sewed up in canvas. The flavour of the H. is, however, improved by *smoking* after its removal from the brine. This is done by hanging the H. over a fire of any non-resinous wood. Beef is corned or made into H. by treating it with salt and a little saltpetre to preserve its red colour, and spices are sometimes added in the curing process. Mutton H. is prepared in the same way as pork H., but requires less time to cure it. What is termed goose H. is extensively prepared in Pomerania, where geese in vast numbers are cured, being salted, and so hard dried in smoking that they require no further dressing. The best hams are Westphalian and Belfast, and curing is an important industry at Cincinnati, &c., in America.

Ham, an old town in the department of Somme, France, on the river Somme, 70 miles N.N.E. of Paris. As early as the 9th c. coins were struck at H., the seigniory of which, successively held by the families of Courcy, Orleans, Luxembourg, and Vendome, was raised to a duchy in 1407. The massive fortress or castle of H. built in 1470, has in recent time, as a state prison, received many distinguished visitors. Louis Napoleon, the late Emperor of the French, was confined here 1840–46. Pop. (1872) 2836.

Ham (Heb. 'sun-burnt') was one of Noah's three sons (Gen. v. 32), apparently the youngest (*cf.* ix. 24, and Jos. *Ant.* i. 6, 3), and according to the Biblical narrative, the ancestor of all the Southern nations of the earth (x. 6–20). His sons are: (1) Cush, whose descendants are made to people the whole region from Ethiopia across the South of Arabia to Babylonia; (2) Mizraim (Egypt); (3) Phut [the Libyans (called in Old Egypt. *Phet*, in Coptic *Phaiat*), or North Africans]; and (4) Canaan, whose descendants peopled the region from the boundaries of Syria in the north to Gaza.

Hamadan', the ancient *Ecbatana* (q. v.), a town of Persia, in the province of Irak-Ajemi, at the N. base of Mount Elwund, 180 miles W.S.W. of Teheran, at a converging point of several important caravan routes. It is embowered in gardens and orchards, and has a fine climate, except for four winter months of extreme cold. There are many mosques, baths, and bazaars, and manufactures of leather, carpets, coarse woollens and cottons, &c. At H. are the reputed tombs of Mordecai and Esther, much visited by Jews, and that of Avicenna (q. v.), which attracts crowds of pilgrims. Estimated pop. 40,000.

Hamadry'ads. See NYMPHS.

Ham'ah (Gr. *Epiphania*, the Biblical *Hamath*), a town of Syria, Asiatic Turkey, on the river Orontes, 120 miles N. of Damascus. The chief buildings are the residence of the governor, the mosques, bazaars, baths, and aqueducts. It has manufactures of silk, cotton, and woollen goods. Pop. 30,000. H. is one of the oldest cities in the world. It was the capital of a kingdom as early as the exodus of the Israelites from Egypt.

Hamamelid'eæ. See WITCH HAZEL.

Ham'ann, Johann Georg, a German philosopher, known as 'the Magus of the North,' was born at Königsberg, East Prussia, August 27, 1730. He studied philology and law, and after a wandering life, during which he acted as tutor, clerk, and commercial traveller, settled at Königsberg in 1777 as superintendent of a bonded warehouse. He died at Münster, June 21, 1788. Faith is the central thought of H.'s philosophy. He was consequently a keen opponent of rationalism in philosophy and religion. He took delight in the mysteries of the Christian faith, and in spite of his intense religious fervour, and the admiration for him expressed by Herder, Jean Paul, and Goethe, he was almost wholly neglected by his contemporaries. His thought is unsystematic, his style very abstruse, and his writings chiefly in the pamphlet form; but his *Schriften* were at last collected and edited by Roth in 1821–25. See Gildemeister, *H.'s Leben und Schriften* (5 vols. Gotha, 1857–68).

Hamba'to, a town of Ecuador, S. America, at the N.E. base of Chimborazo, and 8860 feet above the sea, has a trade in wheat and other grains, cochineal, and sugar. Pop. 10,000. H. was destroyed by an eruption of Cotopaxi, which is 25 miles distant, in 1698, and again by an earthquake in 1796.

Ham'burg ('harbour town'), the largest of the three Hanse towns of the German empire, the greatest port of the Continent, and, next to London, Liverpool, and Glasgow, the most important commercial place in Europe, is situated on the N. bank of the Elbe, 75 miles W.S.W. of its mouth, 67 N.E. of Bremen, and 170 N.W. of Berlin by railway. It is a gay, bustling city, with a quaint Altstadt of picturesque houses, tortuous streets, and sluggish canals, and a fair, stately Neustadt, enclosing a beautiful lakelet, the Binnen-Alster, upwards of a mile in circumference, and girt on three sides by quays (the Alte and Neue Jungfernstieg, and the Alsterdamm) planted with trees, and flanked by lines of splendid mansions, hotels, and shops. The Alster (q. v.), a small stream from the N., forms a basin, the Aussen-Alster, 2 miles long and 1100 feet broad, on the outskirt of the city, the Binnen-Alster within it, and is then discharged by locks and canals (*fleths*) into the many branches of the Elbe that intersect the mercantile quarter. Among the principal buildings are the church of St. Nicolai (1842) on the Hopfenmarkt, designed by Sir G. G. Scott, and erected at a cost of over £200,000, in the rich Gothic style of the 13th c., with one of the highest (483 feet) spires in Europe; the Grosse Michaeliskirche, of 1750–65, in Renaissance style, with a spire 450 feet high; the exchange (1842), where some 5000 merchants and brokers congregate daily, and which has a commercial library of 40,000 vols.; the Johanneum or grammar-school, a large Italian edifice founded in 1529; the gymnasium, established in 1611; the H. *real schule*; the town library of 250,000 vols., 5000 MSS., &c.; the Kunsthalle (1863–69), containing fine specimens of Flemish, Italian, and modern German art; the new Zollvereins Niederlage, covering 13 acres, &c.; and the Thalia theatre (1842). H. has also large hospitals, an asylum, extensive botanical and zoological gardens, and innumerable music halls and other places of amusement. The old fortifications have been transformed into gardens and walks, which encircle the city proper, and beyond which are the suburbs of St. Georg in the N.E., Dammsthor in the N., and St. Pauli or Hamburger Berg in the W. Altona (q. v.) is now connected with H. by St. Pauli. The environs, thickly dotted with the villas of merchants, are singularly beautiful, especially along the steep, woody N. bank of the Elbe in the direction of Blankenese (q. v.). A fine view is commanded from the Elbhöhe or Stintfang of the low-lying city, of the harbour with its forest of masts, and of the many branches and islands of the Elbe to the S. The quays, which now stretch along the river for three miles, can accommodate 400 sea-going vessels, and as many river craft and barges, and are provided with steam cranes and rails in connection with the main lines. Besides the outer quays, and the great Nieder Hafen for the protection of vessels in the season of floating ice, there are extensive inner harbours, as the Sandthor Hafen ('Sandgate Harbour'), 1100 yards long and 100–140 wide, the Grasbrook Hafen, 1000 yards long, the Holz Hafen ('timber harbour'), with an area of 400 acres, and the Binnen Hafen, receiving many of the canals, which are navigated by *schuten* or flat-bottomed boats for the conveyance of wares to the storehouses. Opposite H., on the large islands Steinwärder and Kleine Grasbrook, to which steam ferryboats cross, there are wharves, dry docks, and shipbuilding-yards. In 1875 there entered the port 5260 vessels, 2739 steamers, of 2,117,822 tons, with crews of 61,305; while 6000 barges and 100 rafts arrived from the Upper Elbe. The imports (including bullion, £12,000,000), amounted in value to £96,151,421, of which

£57,078,182 were by sea, and £39,073,239 by land and river; while the exports were estimated at £12,000,000. H. is a packet port, and trades extensively with Great Britain (imports, 1875, £24,692,483), the United States, W. Indies, Brazil, France, Holland, Venezuela, Chili, Peru, and China. The imports are cotton yarn and twist, raw cotton, wool, sugar, dyes, coffee, drugs, pig-iron, coals and coke, &c.; and the exports by sea are grain, refined sugar, machinery, cigars, musical instruments, and fancy goods. The value of ships and cargoes insured here in 1875 was £87,686,000. H. is the great emigrant port for N. Europe. Next to London it has also the largest money exchange business in Europe. Its chief industries are shipbuilding, sugar-refining, and the manufacture of steam-engines, tobacco, cigars, &c. Pop. (1875) 239,107, of whom 14,000 are Jews and 7800 Roman Catholics. A 'burg' was founded here by Karl the Great in 811, and H. became the seat of a bishop in 831, and of an archbishop in 834, though then but a fishing village. In 1215 it was made a free city by Otto IV., but was seized by the Danish Knut IV. in 1223. The citizens recovered it for 1500 marks silver, and by its covenant with Lübeck was founded the Hanseatic League (q. v.) in 1241. H. adopted the Reformed faith in 1529, and remained completely unaffected by the Thirty Years' War. Its commerce increased immensely during the American war of independence; but in 1806 it was seized by the French, and held almost continuously till 1814, during which period the loss sustained is estimated at £13,000,000 sterling. The citizens were treated by Davout with merciless severity. The only great subsequent disaster in the annals of H. is the fire that raged from 5th to 8th May 1842, destroying nearly a quarter of the city. H. became a member of the German empire in 1871.

The small republic of H. has an area of 158 sq. miles, and a pop. (1875) of 338,974. According to its constitution of 1860, the legislative power is vested in a senate of eighteen members, and a municipal council of 192; the executive in the senate alone. In 1876 the estimated expenditure was £1,263,230, the revenue £1,263,230, and the public debt £7,040,000. H. is outside of the German Zollverein, to which it pays for exemption £156,860. It only levies slight dues on a few articles for local consumption. H. sends three members to the Imperial Parliament, and with Bremen and Lübeck furnishes as its military contingent the 75th and 76th regiments of infantry. See Lappenberg, *Hamburg. Urkundenbuch* (Hamb. 1842), and *Hamburgische Chroniken* (1860), and Gallois, *Geschichte der Stadt H.* (1867).

Ham'eln, a town in the province of Hannover, Prussia, 26 miles S.W. by rail of the town of Hannover, where the Hamel joins the Weser. Formerly a fortified city, it still preserves its walls and towers. H. was the scene of the exploits of a sorcerer who in 1284 undertook for a handsome sum to free the town from a plague of rats, and by means of a strain on his pipe compelled them all into the river. When the town-council refused the promised reward, the piper again tuned his lay, and led the children of the town into a chasm of the Kuppelberg, which yawned to receive them. The children were believed to have come to light again in Transylvania. Robert Browning, in his *Pied Piper of Hamelin City*, has made Englishmen familiar with the quaint miracle. H. has some trade, and makes beer, paper, cement, cloth, and carpets. Pop. (1871) 8530.

Hame'sucken, in Scotch law, is the offence of feloniously beating or assaulting a person in his own house. A shop is not held to be a house as regards H. Premeditated design is essential to the crime. Punishment is usually arbitrary, but when serious injury is done, the offence is capital. For English law see BEATING AND WOUNDING, BATTERY.

Hamil'car, a name borne by many illustrious Carthaginians, of whom the following are the most notable:—1. The commander of the Carthaginian expedition to Sicily, defeated and slain by Gelon at Himera, 480 B.C. 2. A commander in the Carthaginian army, defeated by Timoleon at the passage of the Crimissus, 339 B.C. 3. A Carthaginian general in the first Punic War, who gained several important victories over the Romans in Sicily, but was defeated in the naval engagement off Ecnomus, on the southern coast of the island, 256 B.C., after which he was recalled to Carthage, now menaced by the Romans. 4. H., surnamed *Barca* (an epithet supposed to be akin to Heb. *Barak*, and to mean 'lightning'). In 247 B.C., while still a youth, he received the command of the Carthaginian forces in Sicily. The Romans then possessed the whole island except the strongholds of Drepanum and Lilybœum. H., after ravaging the shores of Bruttium, landed on the N. coast of Sicily and established his army on Mount Hercte (*Pellegrino*), a position which he held for nearly three years. In 244 B.C. he suddenly removed to the foot of Mount Eryx and converted the town of that name into a fortified camp. Here, notwithstanding that the Romans held the fort on the summit of the hill, and that one of their armies lay entrenched at its base, H. for two years defied all their efforts to dislodge him. The Romans, in despair, now endeavoured to regain their supremacy by sea; and the total defeat of Hanno, the Carthaginian admiral, off the Ægates in 241 B.C., compelled H. to resign his command and leave the island. After suppressing the revolt of the mercenaries (239–238) he was appointed generalissimo of the Carthaginian army, and entered on his Spanish campaign about 237 B.C. In Spain he saw the possibility of founding a new empire which should more than compensate for the loss of Sicily and Sardinia, and afford, at the same time, a basis of operation against Rome. Setting out from Carthage, he marched westward, crossed at the Strait of Gibraltar, penetrated the country, and subdued many tribes. The wealth he acquired both by pillage and from the silver mines was enormous. Altogether he spent nine years in Spain, but of his history during this long period we know next to nothing. He was slain in battle with the Vettones, 229 B.C. Of H.'s private character we know little. He seems to have been liberal, generous, and lenient where leniency was possible, impatient of control, a man of undoubted patriotism, and by the unanimous testimony of antiquity a military genius second only to his son Hannibal.

Ham'ilton, a town of Scotland, in Lanarkshire, on the left bank of the Clyde, above its junction with the Avon, 11 miles S.E. of Glasgow by railway. It has a townhall, county buildings, large cavalry and infantry barracks, a fine railway station, mechanics' library, several charities, Hamilton Academy (higher-class school), St. John's (middle-class school), Gilbertfield House (a high-class boarding and day school), &c. The Clyde is spanned by a five-arched bridge, and there is a railway bridge over the Avon. Hand-loom weaving and tambouring have given place to industries in the coal and ironstone with which the district abounds. Near H. is H. Palace, the seat of the Dukes of H. and Brandon, in the midst of a finely wooded park of 1600 acres, and containing the finest private art collection in Scotland. The famous Cadzow Castle and oak forest are also in the neighbourhood. At Cadzow a herd of the original white cattle or *Urus* is still preserved. Pop. (1871) 11,299.

Hamilton, a flourishing port of entry in the Dominion of Canada, province of Ontario, on Burlington Bay, at the W. extremity of Lake Ontario, 40 miles S.W. of Toronto by the Great Western Railway. It has excellent water and gas works, and is connected by the Desjardins Canal, a deepened channel, with Dundas (q. v.). The manufactures are machinery, iron wires, sewing-machines, paper, glass, gunpowder, soap, carriages, &c. H. is the see of a Roman Catholic bishop, and among its institutions are a technical college, a public library, six benevolent associations, a hospital, a deaf and dumb asylum, &c. It is known locally as the 'ambitious city.' Pop. in 1841, 3500; in 1850, 10,312; and in 1871, 26,716.

Hamilton, the surname of a noble Scottish race, the members of which have played a leading part in court and camp at many an eventful epoch of Scottish story. In 1542 the head of the house of H. was declared by the estates of Scotland the second person of the realm, and a popular delusion continued to regard this noble line as, after the royal family, next heirs to the Scottish crown, even long after the Union and the accession of the Brunswick family. The name is derived from the manor of Hambledon in Leicestershire. A William de H. is found in Yorkshire in 1274; but the first H. who is positively known to have been established N. of the Border is Walter de H., also called Fitz-Gilbert, who figures in the Paisley chartulary in 1294. This Walter adhered to the English interest during Bruce's wars, and was made Governor of Berwick by Edward II. But he soon made his peace with Robert Bruce, from whom he received in gift the barony of Cadyow in Lanark and other domains. His son, Sir David de H., Dominus de Cadzow (Cadyow), was, like his father, a faithful and valued servant of

David Bruce. Sir David's grandson and great-grandson were repeatedly sent on important political missions to the English court, and James, great-grandson of the latter, was in 1445 created a lord of Parliament under the title of Lord H. of Cadyow. James joined the confederacy headed by Douglas in 1452, and, after taking the field with the murdered Douglas' successor, became reconciled to the King, and filled several high official posts. He died in 1479. The second Lord H., James' son, was one of the commissioners who negotiated the marriage of James IV. with the Princess Margaret of England, and at the marriage received from his grateful sovereign a gift of the island of Arran, being at the same time created earl thereof. During the expedition which ended at Flodden, Earl James was ambassador in France. On his return he became one of the principal personages that stand prominent throughout the stormy period of James V.'s minority, aiming steadfastly at the regency, and venturing repeatedly to measure his strength with Albany and Angus. Dying in 1529, he was succeeded by his son James, who, on the death of James V., was declared regent of the kingdom. At first, in treaty with England, the regent did much to promote the Reformation movement in Scotland; but, becoming reconciled to Cardinal Beaton, he was persuaded to form a new league with France, and in 1544 had to face the English army on the fatal day of Pinkie. Still faithful to the French alliance, he was, in 1548, created by the French king Duke of Chatelherault in Poitou—a title still claimed by the Dukes of H., and by the Marquises of Abercorn. He afterwards joined the Lords of the Congregation, and was induced to agree to Moray's regency after the battle of Langside, though the Hamiltons were mostly 'queen's men.' He died at H. Palace, in 1575. His son James, third earl, succeeded as Earl of Arran, the dukedom of Chatelherault being resumed by the crown of France. He was a suitor for the hand of Queen Mary, but died childless and insane in 1609 (Captain James Stewart, the notorious favourite of James VI., was titular Earl of Arran, and held possession of the H. estates from 1581 till 1585). Meanwhile, Lord John H., the second son of the regent, Duke of Chatelherault, and Lord Claud, fourth son, had been amongst the most zealous of Queen Mary's supporters, and now returned from banishment in 1585. Both were kindly received by the King: John was received into special favour, and was created Marquis of H. in 1599. He died in 1604, and was followed by his second son, James, the second Marquis of H., who, on the death of his uncle James, third earl, in 1609, came into the possession of the H. estates and dignities as fourth earl. He was further created a peer of England as Earl of Cambridge in 1519, and died in 1625. James, third marquis and son of the second, was first a courtier, then served under Gustavus Adolphus, was commissioner to the famous General Assembly of 1638, and in 1639 led an English army against the Covenanters. In 1646 he was made hereditary keeper of the Palace of Holyrood, headed the forces raised in 1648 by the Scots Parliament for the defence of the King, was defeated at Preston, and was beheaded in Palace Yard, Westminster, on March 9, 1649. William, second duke, was, like his brother the first duke, a zealous adherent of Charles I., accompanied Charles II. from Holland into Scotland, and in 1651 entered England with the Scotch army. He died September 12, 1651, of wounds received in the battle of Worcester. The estates and the title of Duchess of H. now devolved on Anne, eldest surviving daughter of the first duke, while the representation of the house of H. in the male line fell to James, second Earl of Abercorn (see below).

Anne, Duchess of H., married Lord William Douglas, eldest son of William, first Marquis of Douglas. Lord William obtained the title of Earl of Selkirk, and at the Restoration was, in consideration of his marriage, made Duke of H. for life, since which time the title of Duke of H. has been held by a branch of the Douglas family, but bearing the H. name. The new duke honourably distinguished himself by his opposition to the arbitrary and barbarous administration of Lauderdale, and at the Revolution was president of the meeting of the Convention of the Scottish Estates which declared the crown vacant, and offered it to William and Mary. James, eldest son of the preceding, adhered to King James, but in 1698, when his mother (who survived her husband) resigned her title, became fourth duke. He was zealous in the effort to secure for Scotland commercial privileges equal to those of England, and in 1707 was a determined opponent of the Union. In 1711 he was, nevertheless, created Duke of Brandon in the peerage of Great Britain. He fell in a duel with Lord Mohun, November 15, 1712. James George, seventh Duke of H., great-grandson of the fourth, became in 1761 male representative of the ancient house of Douglas, as Marquis of Douglas and Earl of Angus, and in the famous 'Douglas cause' asserted the right to the estates also, but unsuccessfully. The present Duke of H. (with the family name of Douglas-H.) is twelfth Duke of H. and ninth Duke of Brandon in regular succession.

The male line of H. is represented by the Abercorn family. James, first Earl of Abercorn, was eldest son of Lord Claud H. mentioned above, who was fourth son of the first Duke of Chatelherault. He was a lord in high favour with James VI., and was raised to the dignity of earl in 1606. James, eighth earl (born 1712), was a man of great ability; he was one of the first to powerfully promote systematic agriculture in Scotland, and to him in great measure the town of Paisley is indebted for its commercial advancement.

The title of Earl of Haddington was in 1627 conferred on Sir Thomas H., son of Sir Thomas H. of Priestfield, who was descended from a branch of the original stock of the Hamiltons of Cadyow. Sir Thomas, honoured by King James' friendship under the name of 'Tam o' the Cowgate,' became eminent in the legal profession, and in 1616 attained to the dignity of Lord President of the Court of Session. He was one of the King's Commissioners to the notorious General Assembly of Perth (where the 'Six Articles' were passed), and had been created Lord Binning and Byres and Earl of Melrose before the earldom of Haddington was conferred. On the death of the ninth earl, the succession passed to a member of the Baillie family, who as tenth Earl of Haddington, assumed the surname of H. The present earl is the eleventh in succession.

Lord Charles H., third son of the Duchess Anne, became Earl of Selkirk in 1688. But his successors never returned to the ancient name of Douglas, which is now borne by the sixth Earl of Selkirk. The fifth son of the Duchess Anne was in 1696 created Earl of Orkney. The present earl is his descendant, but is of the family of Fitzmaurice.

Sir James H., descended from Thomas, brother of James first Lord H. of Cadyow (1445), was created Lord Belhaven and Stenton in 1647. On the death of the eighth Lord the title was for some time dormant, but in August 1875 the House of Lords declared James H., born 1822, to be the nearest heir. On members of the same great family the titles Viscount Boyne in the peerage of Ireland, and that of Viscount Clanboy and Earl of Clanbrassil were conferred. But the most ancient cadet branch of the Hamiltons is the family of H. of Preston and Fingalton, on which a Nova Scotia baronetcy was conferred in 1673. The second baronet was the Sir Robert who commanded the Covenanters at Drumclog and at Bothwell Brig. To his family belongs the illustrious metaphysician Sir William Hamilton (q. v.).

Of the numerous families of position priding themselves on their descent from the original H. stock, the most noted are the Hamiltons of Airdrie, sprung from John, second son of the seventh representative of the house of Preston; the Hamiltons of Silvertonhill, possessing a Nova Scotia baronetcy, and descended from Alexander de H., second son of Sir James H., dominus de Cadyow; and the Hamiltons of Kincavil, descended from Sir Patrick H., natural son of James, first Lord H., and brother of the first Earl of Arran. For the history of the Hamiltons, see *Historical and Genealogical Memoirs of the House of H.* by Anderson (Edinb. 1825). A MS. *Account of the Family of H.* by Dr. James Baillie (first half of 17th c.) is preserved in the Advocates' Library at Edinburgh.

Hamilton, Alexander, a celebrated American statesman of Scotch extraction, was born in the Island of St. Kitts, 11th January 1757, and studied at Columbia College, New York. In 1774 he made a speech at a great revolutionary meeting, and ever afterwards wrote, spoke, and acted for his country's freedom. When the war broke out, he became Washington's favourite aide-de-camp. In 1782 he was chosen to represent New York in the Congress which adjusted the Constitution. Distrusting the abstract principle of self-government, he supported with great eloquence and political insight the doctrine of Federalism, afterwards expounded in a series of letters to the *Daily Advertiser*, which were collected and republished in *The Federalist.* As the first Secretary to the Treasury, H. had to face all the financial problems presented by a large and hastily incurred national debt. In spite of the clamour of the Democratic party, he put all the common war expenses to one joint account, instead of letting each state pay its own war debts, imposed taxation sufficient to meet the current charges, and to provide for gradual writing off, and founded the national bank. He supported the proclamation of neutrality when the French wars began, and the sending of Jay to England. In 1795 he withdrew from the cabinet to legal practice. When in 1798 the Army of Defence was organised, Washington insisted that H. should be first major-general of his command. With his usual sagacity and patriotism, H. strongly opposed the election of the adventurer Burr as against Jefferson, although the former was the Federalist candidate. The second disappointment of Burr, when Jefferson was re-elected president in 1804, so infuriated him that he found means to entrap H. into a duel, and shot him dead, 12th July 1804. His premature death caused profound and widespread sorrow. See the memoir of H. by his son, who has published his father's writings in 7 vols.

Hamilton, Anthony, Comte de, born in Ireland in 1646, was descended from the Scottish Dukes of H. He entered the army of Louis XIV., afterwards joined the Irish service, was made governor of Limerick, and on the dethronement of James II., accompanied that king to St. Germain, where he died in 1720. He was famed as a wit and author. Among his works are *Contes de Féerie*, a French translation of Pope's *Art of Criticism*, and the lively and interesting *Mémoires du Chevalier de Grammont* (Lond. 1772). H.'s works were issued at Paris in 1805 (3 vols), and in 1812 (4 vols.).

Hamilton, Patrick, the protomartyr of the Scottish Reformation, was born in 1503 or 1504 in or near Glasgow. He was of noble descent, his father being a natural brother of the first Earl of Arran, and his mother daughter of the Duke of Albany, second son of King James II. Having taken his master's degree at Paris in 1520, he was for a time at Louvain and at Basel, and in 1523 became a member of the University of St. Andrews. H. had already attached himself to the views of Erasmus, but he was regarded with much greater suspicion by the ecclesiastical authorities when he adopted and defended the heresies of Luther. He fled to Germany in 1527, and at Marburg, and, perhaps, at Wittenberg also, became confirmed in his sympathies with the German Reformation. When he returned to Scotland in the same year, the zeal with which he preached the new doctrines, his learning, courtesy, blameless character, and noble birth, gave great weight to his teaching, and made him specially obnoxious to the clergy. He was apprehended, and, on March 1, 1528, brought to trial before Cardinal Beaton. After examination he was condemned as an obstinate heretic, delivered over to the secular arm, and on the afternoon of the same day he was burnt at the stake in front of St. Salvator's College. H. left a brief statement of his views in a work called *Patrick's Places or Commonplaces*, originally in Latin, but translated into English by John Frith, and republished in 1807 as a *Treatise on the Law and Gospel*. See Dr. Lorimer's *Life of Patrick H.* (1857).

Hamilton, Sir William, the most learned and potent metaphysician that Scotland has yet produced, was the son of Dr. Thomas Hamilton, Professor of Anatomy and Natural History in Glasgow College, and was born there, March 8, 1791. He studied at Glasgow (1803-7), went up as Snell exhibitioner to Oxford, and when going in for his degree astonished his examiners by the number of works in philosophy in which he offered himself for examination. In 1812 he settled as an advocate in Edinburgh, and married, but did not obtain practice. In 1820 he was defeated by John Wilson in a competition for the Chair of Moral Philosophy, but in 1821 succeeded Mr. Fraser Tytler in the Chair of History, which he held till 1836. During this period, after a sharp criticism of the popular phrenology, he produced his famous *Edinburgh Review* articles on the Philosophy of the Conditioned (in which he annihilated M. Cousin's Semi-Hegelian Intuition of the Absolute), on Perception (in which he criticises Brown's view of the irresistible suggestion of the non-ego, and tries to develop his own doctrine of natural realism out of the common-sense of Dr. Reid), and on Logic (in which, using his extensive knowledge of Aristotle and his commentators, he tries to make the formal syllogism cover the facts of inductive reasoning). This last subject he afterwards elaborated into his theory of the Quantification of the Predicate, which is described in the *New Analytic of Logical Forms*, by Professor Spencer Baynes. In 1836 he succeeded Mr. Ritchie in the Chair of Logic and Metaphysics, defeating Isaac Taylor and Mr. George Combe, and began those original and learned lectures which were posthumously edited by Dean Mansel and Professor Veitch (4 vols. 1859-61). He had a large and enthusiastic class, and whatever may be the ultimate fate of his philosophy, his influence in stimulating speculation in Great Britain was great and beneficial. Besides the lectures and the discussions on philosophy (1852), which include papers on Oxford University reform, and against the utility of mathematical education, he wrote valuable notes and dissertations to his collected edition of Reid's works. He died May 6, 1856. H.'s fundamental position is that on the one hand consciousness is to be trusted, and on the other hand that it relates only to the conditioned. Hence a vein of contradiction which runs through all his writings. He accepts the doctrine of relativity of human knowledge, insists upon cognitive limitations, and admits the apparent universality of causation. But, by a resort to faith, or a consciousness which is indistinct and inconsistent with itself, he asserts a direct knowledge of external material objects and their primary qualities, the analysis of which he declines to enter on; a consciousness or belief in the absolute, infinite, and the conditioned, and also a belief in the freedom of the will as the foundation of human responsibility. He imperfectly realised the operation of the laws of inseparable association, obliviscence, and necessary dissociation. His views on these subjects, and his teaching on logic as the science of the fundamental and applied laws of pure mental consistency, have been criticised by Mr. J. S. Mill in his examination of H.'s philosophy (1865). See also Stirling's *Philosophy of Perception*, and Bolton's *Inquisitio Philosophica*. Professor Veitch has written a memoir of H.

Hamilton, Sir William, born in Scotland 1730, was English ambassador at Naples from 1764 to 1800, and took an active part in the excavations at Pompeii and Herculaneum. He spent his time in preparing his *Campi Phlegræi*, a series of scientifically arranged coloured plates, showing the local volcanic phenomena, and his *Etruscan, Greek, and Roman Antiquities*, published in 1766. He acquired the Porcinari collection of vases, &c., and some of his marbles are still in the Townley Gallery. H. died in London, 6th April 1803.

Hamilton, Sir William Rowan, the most original of the mathematicians of this century, was born in Dublin, August 4, 1805. At the age of ten he began the study of mathematics, and when only thirteen had a fair knowledge of thirteen languages. In 1822 he presented to Dr. Brinkley, Astronomer-Royal for Ireland, his first original paper on *Contacts between Algebraic Curves and Surfaces.* He entered Trinity College in 1823, and his course was marked by most unprecedented success. While still an undergraduate, he succeeded Dr. Brinkley in 1827 as Astronomer-Royal and Professor of Astronomy in the university. He entered ardently upon his new duties, and his lectures were characterised by an eloquence which is rare in exact science. Meanwhile he had applied algebraic geometry to problems in optics, and his first paper before the Royal Irish Academy, entitled *Theory of Systems of Rays*, is a most elaborate development of his earlier investigations on contact of curves. He continued the subject in several subsequent papers, and in 1833 predicted, as a mathematical consequence of the undulatory theory of light, the existence of two kinds of conical refraction. This was experimentally verified by Lloyd. In 1834 his *General Method in Dynamics* appeared in the *Philosophical Transactions* —a paper which attracted more attention in the mathematical world than probably any other single paper has ever done. These researches all turn upon the differentiation of *one* function with respect to different variables. All H.'s memoirs are characterised by a grasp of the fundamental conceptions of mathematics, and by a power of generalisation, which have perhaps never been equalled; and that for which his name is most famous, the invention of Quaternions (q. v.), is no mere development of older methods, but has for its very basis notions of the properties of space which, though known to previous mathematicians, were not recognised in their full importance.

H. was knighted in 1835, was president of the Irish Academy in 1837, and died at Dublin, September 2, 1865. His great works are *Lectures on Quaternions* (1853), and *Elements of Quaternions* (1866).

Hamm, a town in the province of Westphalia, Prussia, at the confluence of the Lippe and Ahse, 17 miles S.S.E. of Münster by railway. It has a castle, a gymnasium, linen and iron industries, and is girt by old walls now converted into promenades. Pop. (1875) 18,904. H. was a member of the Hanse League. It figures as a strong fortress in the Thirty Years' War, and was bombarded by the French in 1761 and 1762.

Hamm'er. An immense number of varieties of this well-known tool exist, each adapted for some particular work or for some particular material. All possess the same general features, each consisting of a long wooden handle to which is attached a metal head, the size and form of which is the principal characteristic of the tool. In general the head is of iron or steel, or of iron faced with steel, but for some special purposes lead, copper, and even tin heads are employed. The heaviest class of hand hammers is that used for forging by the 'strikers' in smithies, and called a 'sledge H.' The head of a sledge H. sometimes weighs 25 or 30 pounds.

At a very early stage of manufacturing art it became necessary to have a more powerful forging tool than the hand-worked H., and this want was met by the tilt H. or 'helve,' which for an immense period was the only power H. in existence. It was simply a large hand H. with the end of the handle fixed to a rocking shaft. The H. was raised at intervals by projecting teeth, called wipers or tappets, attached to a continuously revolving disc, set in motion at first by a water-wheel, and in later times by a steam-engine. As soon as each wiper had done its work and lifted the H. to its full height, the latter was released, and the head fell by its own weight, the piece to be forged being placed, of course, on an anvil underneath it. This tool was a very rough one in all ways, and no means existed of regulating the force of the blow, which obviously had the smallest force when the piece of iron on the anvil was largest, that is just when the heaviest blow was required.

It has been found with the H., as with the sewing-machine and in so many other cases, that the very natural attempt to imitate manual methods in machinery is a mistake. A machine may do the same work as the hand, but in almost all cases it does it best in a very different manner. Both James Watt (1784) and a Mr. Deverell (1806) patented a power H. in which the head should be attached directly to the piston rod of a steam-engine, but in neither case does the matter seem to have been carried further than the patent specification. It is only within the last forty years that this direct-acting H., now familiar everywhere, has come into use. In 1838 some difficulty arose as to the forging of a paddle-wheel shaft of unprecedented size, which no forge in the country would undertake to make. Mr. Nasmyth, of Patricroft (the firm being then Nasmyth & Gaskell) was applied to about the matter, and at once gave its solution in what proved to be the germ of the present 'steam H.' This consists of an anvil resting on the ground, a framing carrying a vertical steam cylinder directly over the anvil, and a block of iron for giving the blow attached to the rod of a piston working in the cylinder. This block is so guided that it can move up and down only; it is lifted by admitting steam under the piston, and then allowed to fall by its own weight. Owing to various circumstances the first H. made in this country (in the meantime a Nasmyth H. had been set to work by M. Schneider, at Creusôt) was not constructed until the beginning of 1843. Although a great improvement on the helve, it was yet by no means altogether satisfactory, its principal drawbacks being the considerable manual labour required to work the valves, and the want of adjustability in the force of the blow. The self-acting valve gear which remedied these defects, and without which the Nasmyth H. would have had little general value, was invented by Mr. Robert Wilson (who has now for many years been managing partner at the Patricroft works) in 1843, and it was to this gear that the early steam-hammers owed the extraordinary delicacy and adaptability to all kinds of work which brought the new tool so rapidly into general use. For many years Wilson's valve gear formed an essential part of direct-acting hammers, but latterly this has been superseded by other arrangements scarcely more perfect in their action, but much simpler, invented both by Mr. Wilson himself and by others. Into these we cannot here enter. We need only mention that in many hammers now used steam is admitted above the piston to aid the blow, and in this way the power of the H. is enormously increased. In armour plate, gun factories, and other large works, hammers are now used of which the weight of the falling mass is from 25 tons to 40 tons, and in a few cases even more.

Hamm'erfest (Scand. 'the rock fortress'), the most northerly town in Europe, and port of the amt of Finmark, in Norway, on the bare island of Kvalö ('the whale'), in Soro Sund, lat. 70° 40′ N., and long. 23° 30′ E. It lies at the base of a rocky ledge, is sheltered by the island of Soro and the Fuglenäs peninsula, and has a temperature never below 3° F. Its exports, valued in 1873 at £119,280, are chiefly stock-fish, train-oil, reindeer hides and horns, walrus skins and tusks, and the skins of the seal, fox, and otter. The copperworks at Kaafiord were taken over by an English company in 1847. In 1873 there entered the port 152 vessels of 17,125 tons, of which 97 were Russian and 30 German. For two months in summer the sun never sets, and fishing is carried on during the whole year. H. has regular steam communication with Trondhjem. Pop. (1876) 2125.

Hamm'erhead, or **H. Shark** (*Zygæna* or *Sphyrinas*), the name given to various species of *Squalidæ* or Sharks (q. v.), distinguished by having the head produced at each side into two prominent processes or lobes, on the extremities of which the eyes are borne. The common species (*Z. malleus*) attains a length of 7 or 8 feet, and is most common in warm seas. Occasionally it is found in British waters. It produces living young, the eggs being retained within the parent-body until the young are hatched. One specimen captured at Tenby in 1839 measured 10 feet in length, and contained thirty-nine young. Other species are the *S.* or *Z. laticeps*, the *Z. tiburo*, and the *Z. tudes* of the Mediterranean Sea.

Hamm'er-Purg'stall, Joseph, Freiherr Von, a celebrated Orientalist, was born at Gratz, in Styria, June 9, 1774, and educated at Vienna. After a long and varied official career, he died in the Austrian capital, November 23, 1856. H.-P. was a most voluminous author, and his writings are valuable. Though deficient in critical insight, and not adequately equipped in philology, he has immensely enlarged our knowledge of Eastern tongues and of Eastern history and literature. Among his more important works are *Des Osmanischen Reichs Staatsverfassung und Staatsverwaltung* (2 vols. Tüb. 1816); *Geschichte des Osmanischen Reichs* (10 vols. Pesth, 1827–34), still the standard authority on Turkish history; *Geschichte der Assassinen* (Stutt. and Tüb. 1819); *Gemäldesaal Moslemischer Herrscher* (6 vols. Darmst. 1837–39); *Geschichte der Khane der Krim* (Vienna, 1856); *Geschichte der schönen Redekünste Persiens* (Tüb. 1818); *Geschichte der Osman. Dichtkunst* (4 vols. Pesth, 1836-38); *Geschichte der Arab. Literatur* (7 vols. Vienna, 1850–57), besides editions of numerous Eastern authors—Turkish, Persian, and Arabic. See Schlottmann's *Joseph von H.* (1857).

Hamm'ersmith, a parish of Middlesex, and member of the parliamentary borough of Chelsea, on the Thames, 3½ miles W. by S. of Hyde Park Corner by the Metropolitan and N. London Railway. It is united to London by continuous lines of streets, and its once famous market-gardens are now mostly covered with buildings. Its parish church dates from 1631, and was consecrated by Bishop Laud; other public buildings are the church of St. John the Evangelist (1860), a Roman Catholic chapel (1866) and training college, three convents, the W. London hospital, and William Godolphin's school, re-erected in 1862. Here are the extensive works of the W. Middlesex water company. The Thames at H. is spanned by a bridge completed in 1827 at a cost of £80,000. Pop. of parish (1871) 42,691.

Hamme-sur-Durme, a fortified town of Belgium, province of W. Flanders, 3 miles N. of Bruges. It lies at the intersecting point of two important canals, and has considerable trade and some industry in linens and lace. Pop. (1874) 10,518.

Hamm'ock, the strong piece of hempen cloth, about 6 feet long, which forms the framework of the sailor's bed, and is swung from hooks in the deck overhead. The name is derived from a W. Indian word *hamaca*, meaning a network used as bed.

Hamm'ond, Henry, D.D., an Anglican divine, born at Chertsey, Surrey, August 18, 1605, and educated at Eton and Oxford. He was appointed Fellow of Magdalen College in 1625, rector of Penshurst in 1633, archdeacon of Chichester in 1643, and subsequently canon of Christ Church. A keen Royalist, he acted as chaplain to Charles I. during the king's captivity until 1647, when he was chosen sub-dean of Christ Church. Stripped of his offices by the Parliament in March 1648, he devoted the remainder of his life to literature and charitable schemes at Westwood, Worcestershire. At the Restoration he was selected for the bishopric of Rochester, but died before consecration, 25th April 1660. His works, which are learned and mainly controversial, were collected in 4 vols. folio, 1674–84. His celebrated *Paraphrase and Annotations on the New Testament* was published in 1653, and in an improved edition in 1702.

Hamoon'. See SEISTAN LAKE.

Hamp'den, John, an English statesman and patriot, born in London in 1594, was the son of a Buckinghamshire squire, whose family was historical as early as the 13th c. He was educated at Oxford, and studied for the bar. In the stormy Parliaments of the reign of Charles I., he represented successively the boroughs of Grampound and Wendover, and the county of Buckingham. He at once joined the party of Pym, Selden, and others, who were resolved to assert popular liberties against the encroachment of the prerogative. His refusal to contribute to the compulsory loan or benevolence of the second Parliament was followed by the great ship-money case of 1637, which was decided against him by the servility of all the judges but two. It had been clearly shown that the tax had formerly been levied only in cases of sudden emergency, and only on the coast and in the port towns. Matters were now becoming serious, many were leaving England to escape tyranny, and it was chiefly the noble stand made by H. and others in the Long Parliament that precipitated the civil war. Once war was declared, the hero of the constitution displayed (chiefly in Berkshire, Oxford, &c.) the highest military skill. As a member of the Committee of Public Safety, he condemned the Fabian policy of Essex, and received his death-wound at Chalgrove Field, 18th June 1643, dying six days after. The pathos and dignity of his dying prayer are well known. He has been described as a 'man of consummate ability, unequalled power of persuasion, keen intelligence, ripe learning, and a character singularly pure and lovable.' See Nugent's *Memorials of H.* (2 vols. Lond. 1831; new ed. 1854), and Clarendon's *History of the Rebellion*.

Hamp'shire, Southamp'tonshire, or **Hants**, a maritime county in the S. of England, bounded N. by Berkshire, E. by Surrey and Sussex, S. by the English Channel, and W. by Wiltshire and Dorsetshire. Including the Isle of Wight, its area is 1,070,216 acres; pop. (1871) 544,684. The coast is often deeply indented, generally low in the E., but high and steep W. of Hurst Castle. The surface is undulating and irregular, the county being traversed by the N. Downs, S. Downs, and Alton Hills. The chief rivers are the Anton or Test, the Itchen, and Hamble, which flow into Southampton Water, and the Avon, which drains the W. of the county. H. is richly and beautifully wooded, including the New Forest in the W., which covers 63,000 acres, and belongs to the crown, Bere Forest in the S.E., of 11,000 acres, and the smaller forests of Woolmer, Harewood, Alice Holt, and Waltham Chase. Geologically H. is chalky in the N. and tertiary in the S. The climate is peculiarly mild, and the soil is fertile in the N., but sandy and gravelly W. of the lower Avon. Large crops of wheat, barley, oats, rye, peas, and trefoil are raised; fruit and hops are also grown, and sheep are extensively reared on the chalk downs. Apart from the naval yards at Portsmouth and Gosport, the manufactures are not important, but brewing, tanning, and the making of paper, bricks, pottery, &c., are carried on. The chief towns are Winchester, Portsmouth, Southampton, Andover, Alton, Bishop's Waltham, Basingstoke, Fareham, Fordinbridge, Romsey, Havant, Kingsclere, &c. Excluding the Isle of Wight, H. returns four members to Parliament. H. was the heart of the old kingdom of Wessex, and the scene of many important events in early English history. It suffered greatly from the Danish invasions, and from William the Conqueror's arbitrary extension of the New Forest, in which two of his sons and his grandson met their deaths. H. abounds in Roman remains.

Hamp'stead (Old Eng. *Hamstede*, 'homestead'), a suburban district of London, on the S. slope of a hill, the summit of which forms H. Heath, covering 260 acres, and commanding a fine view of London. H. was once famed for its mineral springs, and is still much frequented on holidays. The chief streets are High Street and Heath Street, and there are many fine villas in the neighbourhood. H. is rich in literary associations, having been a favourite resort of Pope, Gay, Arbuthnot, Akenside, Johnson, Coleridge, Keats, Leigh Hunt, Hazlitt, and Moore. A private house on the heath was formerly the Upper Flask Inn, where the Kit-Kat Club (q. v.), of which Addison, Steele, Richardson, Marlborough, and Walpole were members, used to assemble. Pop. (1871) 32,281.

Hamp'ton, a village in the county of Middlesex, England, on the left bank of the Thames, 12 miles S.W. of London. It is a station on the South-Western Railway. Pop. (1871) 2207. A mile below the village stands **Hampton Court Palace**, a splendid building, formerly a royal residence. It was founded by Wolsey, who lived here in great splendour, and was afterwards enlarged by Henry VIII. and William III., the more modern portions, including the Fountain Court and grand front, having been added by Sir Christopher Wren. It has been partly restored during the present reign, and comprises three quadrangles and several smaller courts, and is surrounded by gardens laid out in the Dutch style. Its picture gallery contains above 1000 paintings, among which are seven cartoons by Raphael, various specimens of the old masters, Lely's 'Beauties of the Court of Charles II.,' and works by Holbein, Kneller, West, &c.

Hampton, a village on Chesapeake Bay, Virginia, U.S., which gives name to Hampton Roads, the wide deep channel by which the James, Nansemond, and Elizabeth rivers flow into Chesapeake Bay. These roads are defended by Fort Monroe and Fort Wool. On March 8 and 9, 1862, the U.S. frigates *Congress* and *Cumberland* were sunk here, and the first engagement between ironclads—the *Monitor* and *Virginia*—took place.

Hampton Court Conference was held 12th–18th January 1604 in presence of King James I., to settle the dispute between the High Church party and the Puritans. The questions discussed were not doctrinal, for the doctrine of both parties was Calvinistic. The objections of the Puritans 'lay entirely against matters of form and ceremony, or against expressions in the Prayer-book capable of misapprehension.' Some slight concessions were made to them: private baptism by women was forbidden, the Church Catechism was enlarged by the addition of the explanations of the sacraments, and it was on the suggestion of Dr. Reynolds that the authorised version of the Bible was undertaken; but their request that the sign of the cross should be omitted in baptism was treated with contempt; and the Puritans retired browbeaten and dismayed.

Ham'ster (*Cricetus frumentarius*), a species of *Rodents* belonging to the *Muridæ*, or rat and mouse family, and inhabiting N. Europe. It is a short, thick-set animal, attaining a length of 15 inches. The tail is about 3 inches. The H. is provided with cheek-pouches, in which food, consisting of grain, peas, beans, &c., can be temporarily stored. The colour is grey tinted with brown on the back; the under parts are black; the cheeks, sides, and shoulders are marked with yellowish tints. The skin is of considerable value. The H. lives in burrows. From six to eight young are produced at a birth, and several broods appear annually. The H. is exceedingly destructive to grain-crops and stores; upwards of 60 lbs. of corn having been found in the burrow of one specimen.

Han'au, a town in the province of Hessen-Nassau, Prussia, on the Kinzig, near its junction with the Main, and 11 miles E. of Frankfurt, on a main line of railway. For its thriving industries in silks and woollen wares, in jewellery, and in gold and silver work, H. is indebted to Flemish and Walloon refugees who settled here in the 17th c. It has also carpet factories and coachworks, and manufactures buttons, tobacco, &c. Pop. (1871) 20,294. Here, on 30th and 31st October 1813, Napoleon fought the disastrous battle of H., the last he fought in Germany. See *Die Schlacht bei H.* (Han. 1864).

Hand. This part of the body, by its peculiar construction and mechanism fitting it for grasping minute objects and for executing delicate movements, constitutes one of the special bodily characteristics of man. Existing in a more or less rudimentary form in the lower vertebrates, and used as an instrument of prehension only in the highest, it attains its greatest degree of complexity in man, and serves as the most important instrument he possesses in carrying out the commands of his high cerebral organisation. Anatomically it consists of three parts, which may be specially studied in the skeleton.

These three parts are (1) the *carpus*, or bones of the wrist; (2) the *metacarpus*, or palm; and (3) the *phalanges*, or fingers.

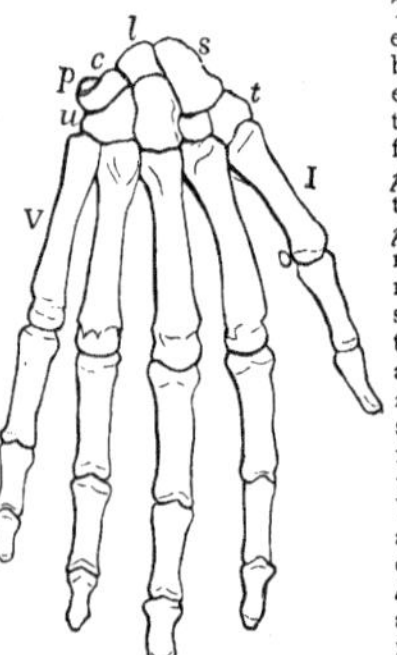

The carpus is composed of eight short irregularly-shaped bones, in two rows, four in each row. Enumerated from the side next the thumb, the first row consists of the *scaphoid* (*s*), the *semilunar* (*l*), the *cuneiform* (*c*), and the *pisiform* (*p*); and the second row, or that next to the metacarpus, contains, in the same order, the *trapezium* (*t*), the *trapezoid*, the *os magnum*, and the *unciform* (*u*). The *metacarpus* consists of five shafted bones, of which the first is that of the thumb while the others are numbered successively 2, 3, 4, and 5, the latter being that of the little finger. The *phalanges*, or bones of the fingers, are fourteen in number, three for each finger, except the thumb, which has only two. See *The Hand, its Mechanism and Endowments*, by Sir Charles Bell, late Professor of Surgery, University of Edinburgh (Lond. 1852).

These various bones are more or less connected together by ligaments, and have joints between them which admit of a certain amount of movement. These movements are effected by the action of numerous muscles, part of which originate in the forearm, while the others belong to the hand itself. Without going into anatomical details, it may be briefly stated that these muscles consist of (1) *flexors*, for bending the fingers, which arise from the inner aspect of the limb; (2) of *extensors*, for extending the fingers, arising from the outer or posterior aspect of the limb; (3) of special extensors for the thumb and index or fore finger, which permit accurate movements to be effected; (4) of the *muscles of the thumb*, which form the prominence or ball of the thumb, consisting of four muscles—an abductor, an opponens, a short flexor, and an adductor; (5) of the *muscles of the little finger*, forming the fleshy mass at the inner border of the hand, consisting of three muscles, viz., an abductor, a short flexor, and an opponens; and (6) of seven *interosseous* muscles which occupy the intervals between the metacarpal bones. These muscles are supplied by vessels and nerves, are firmly bound together by fascia, and are covered over by skin, in which the sense of touch is largely developed.

Comparative Anatomy of the Hand.—The number of carpal bones is increased to ten in chelonians, and it is reduced to two in birds. In the number of metacarpal bones man agrees with many vertebrates, but in some the number is much reduced. Thus there may be only a single metacarpal (the third) with the rudiments of two others, as in the horse, or there may be a single bone formed of the third and fourth fused together, as in the sheep. In the birds we have the second and third metacarpals, along with a rudiment of the first, fused together to form a single bone. The number of fingers which may be developed varies. Thus there may be only one, as in the horse; two, as in the ox; three, as in the rhinoceros; or four, as in the pig or dog. There are never more than five. When one is wanting, it is usually the thumb; but it may be the fifth, or the fourth and fifth, as in birds. The thumb may be opposable, as in most monkeys; or two fingers may be opposed to three, as in the chameleon. The fingers may be remarkably short, as in the tortoise; or of extreme length, as in the hand of a bat, commonly called the wing. There are many variations in the arrangement of the muscles, which in no animal are so specialised as in man. The thumb of the human hand can be brought into contact with the tips of all the fingers, whereas in the higher monkeys the fingers are so long and the thumb is so short as to make this almost impossible. The hand of a monkey is specially suitable for grasping a cylindrical object, such as a branch; but the hand of man, from its concave form, as produced by the great development of the eminences of the thumb and little finger, is adapted for grasping a sphere. In addition, from the great multiplicity of its muscular arrangements, the amount of movement possible in its various joints, and its elaborate nervous arrangements, the hand of man is capable of doing work requiring most delicate adjustment and manipulation.

Hän'del, Georg Friedrich, one of the greatest composers that ever lived, was born at Halle, in Prussian Saxony, February 23, 1685. His father, a surgeon, though at first not wishing the boy to give himself wholly to music, was persuaded to place him, at the age of seven, under Zachau, organist of Halle Cathedral, who sent him to Berlin in 1696, confessing he had no more to teach him. Under Zachau H. studied harmony and composition, and learned the organ, harpsichord, violin, and oboe. He was again in Halle from 1697 to 1703, when he went to Hamburg, being thrown on his own resources by his father's death in the former year. At Hamburg he wrote a *Passion Music*, his first recorded work, and *Almira*, his first opera. From 1706 to 1709 he was in Italy, remaining in turn at Florence, Venice, Rome, and Naples, exciting the highest admiration by his readily-written operas and oratorios (the Venice theatre resounded with 'Viva il caro Sassone' when *Agrippina* was played), and meeting with splendid hospitality from the Marchese de Ruspoli and others. As he found no settled employment, however, in Italy, he accepted the post of chapel-master to the Elector of Brunswick, afterwards George I. of England. Twice, viz., in 1710 and 1712, he visited London. After the latter date it became his home, and only on four occasions did he return to the Continent—in 1716 to Hanover with the King, in 1729 to Italy to prepare for opening a London opera season, and to Germany to see his mother, in 1736 to Aix-la-Chapelle to recover his health, and in 1750 to Germany just after making his will. H. received pensions from Queen Anne and George I. and accumulated much money besides; but he twice lost large fortunes (in 1737 and 1745), the first time through the expense and failure of theatre management. Yet he accumulated a third fortune, which again enabled him to exercise his large generosity, especially to poor musicians. In 1752 he became blind. He died at London, 13th April 1759. It is unnecessary to name the many Italian operas which H. composed from 1712 to 1741; his fame rests on his sublime oratorios, of which it is not too much to say that they are the noblest tribute ever offered by music to religion—*Esther* (1720), *Deborah* (1733), *Saul* and *Israel in Egypt* (1739), *The Messiah* (1742), *Samson* (1743), *Belshazzar* (1745), *Joshua* and *Judas Maccabæus* (1747), *Solomon* and *Theodora* (1749), *Jephtha* (1751). Other notable compositions of H.'s are the *Te Deum and Jubilate* for peace of Utrecht (1713), *Coronation Anthems* (1727), *Acis and Galatea* (1721), *Alexander's Feast* (1736), *Ode to St. Cecilia's Day* (1739), and instrumental music, including organ *Concertos* and harpsichord *Suites*. See Schoelcher's *Life of H.* (Lond. 1857) and Chrysander's *Georg Friedrich H.* (2 vols. Leips. 1858–60).

Hand'icapping, is the term given in horse-racing and other sports to the placing of competitors upon an equal footing by artificial means. Thus a superior horse is made to carry certain weights—the adjustment of which is left to a chosen handicapper. See HORSE-RACING.

Hands, Imposition of, as a symbol of blessing and consecration, was in use from the most primitive times (Gen. xlviii. 14–20; Num. xxvii. 18–20). 'It was as though the superior desired to let his whole spirit stream over through the glowing nerves of his hands on to him whom he honoured with his blessing and highest commissions.' Virtually the same thing was done when the priest, in greeting and blessing a multitude of people, stretched his hands over the crowd (Lev. ix. 22). So when the priest or the offerer laid his hands on the head of the victim to be offered, it indicated that he desired to transfer his own feelings to the creature which was, as it were, to appear in the presence of God for him (Exod. xxix. 10, 15, 19; Lev. i. 4,

&c.). The practice kept its hold down to Christian times, when it came to life again with new vigour, and the I. of H. was regarded as the symbol, the means, and the commencement of the communication of a divine influence of salvation, and especially of the Holy Spirit (Mark vii. 32; Acts viii. 18; 1 Tim. iv. 14; Heb. vi. 2).

Hand'sale. Anciently among Northern nations shaking of hands was held essential to complete a bargain. A sale thus made was called a H. In time the word came to mean the Earnest (q. v.) money given after the shaking of hands, or instead of it. In Scotland it is pronounced *hansel*, and means a small pecuniary gift, or *tip*. In that country the practice is not yet discontinued of making a present on or about the first Monday in the year (hence called *Hansel Monday*) to postmen, lamplighters, message-boys, &c.

Hand'writing. The strongest direct proof of any one having executed a writing is his own avowal, when he is a competent witness. The next best is the evidence of any one who saw the writing executed. The best indirect evidence is that of one acquainted with the H. of the individual; but this is insufficient in a criminal case. Writings in question are sometimes submitted along with the admittedly genuine writing of the individual to engravers and other skilled persons; but this latter mode of proof is considered somewhat inconclusive and unsatisfactory. In England, a jury is now allowed to form its own opinion by comparison of the disputed H. with that admitted to be genuine. In Scotland a Holograph (q. v.) will is held genuine without attestation, but it is not so held in England or Ireland.

Hang-Chow-Fu, the finest city in China, and the capital of the province of Chi-Kiang, on the Tsien-Tang, 20 miles from its mouth, in the Bay of H.-C.-F., and 150 miles S.E. of Nankin. It lies at the S. terminus of the Grand Canal, the various branches of which are spanned by innumerable bridges. A lofty wall, 20 miles in circumference, with ten monumental gateways, encloses but a portion of the city, which spreads over an immense area, most of the houses being of only one story. The 'Tartar city' (the name given to the Mantchu military colony or garrison) is hemmed off in the N.E. by a low wall. The streets, comparatively wide, are well paved, and there are many splendid temples and other stately buildings. Of these, the most remarkable are the palace of Kien-lung, containing the imperial library, a temple with 500 life-sized richly-gilded images of the Buddhist saints (*Jo-han*), and the ruined tower 'of the thundering winds.' There are several colleges and literary institutions, and in the vicinity many vast rock-cut images of a religious and mythological character, to which pilgrims resort in crowds. The neighbourhood is enriched by the arbor vitæ, and by camphor and tallow trees, and every available spot within the city is devoted to the cultivation of the mulberry. H.-C.-F. is widely celebrated for its silks, and especially for its embroidery. Its port is Chapu, on the N. shore of the bay, distant 50 miles. The great equinoctial *eagre* or bore, rising to a height of 30 feet, though guarded against by dykes and other works costing yearly some 130,000 dollars, is often very destructive. Estimated pop. 800,000. H.-C.-F. was the imperial capital under the Mongols, and was visited by Marco Polo in the 14th c.

Hang'ing is the mode of executing Capital Punishment (q. v.) most common in the countries of Western Europe. It was adopted in England as early as 1241, in the case of William Marise, a man of rank, who was hanged for piracy. Hanging murderers in chains near the scene of their crime, and dissecting the body after execution, were long prescribed in brutal cases by statute, but were abolished by 6 and 7 Will. IV. c. 30. Between the passing of sentence and the infliction of death there may elapse not less than fifteen, nor more than twenty-seven days. Public executions ceased in England in 1868. Reprieves are granted on certain legal and other grounds, and on account of mental alienation or pregnancy. Death in H. is produced by Strangulation (q. v.). The windpipe is compressed, the flow of the blood is stopped, and in some cases the jerk of the cord fractures the vertebræ. In France the substitute for H. is the guillotine, and in Spain the garotte.

Hanging Gardens, The, of Babylon, were regarded as one of the Seven Wonders of the world, and were said to have been the work of Semiramis or Nebuchadnezzar. The H. G. were a mass of terraces supported by pillars and elaborate masonry, forming an artificial hill of pyramidal shape in the vast plain of the Euphrates. They had an area of four acres, and were covered with luxuriant vegetation of all kinds, irrigated from a reservoir at the summit of the whole. The evidence for the existence of the H. G. has been questioned both in ancient and modern times.

Hankow' (*i.e.*, 'Han-port'), a great trading city in the heart of China, in the province of Hu-pé, at the confluence of the Han-kiang and Yang-tse-kiang, 600 miles from the mouth of the latter river. It is strictly a suburb of Wu-chang-fu, on the opposite side of the Yang-tse-kiang, and faces another suburb, Han-yang-fu, on the W. side of the Han-kiang. The river is navigable as far as H. for large steamers, and the cost and delay of transhipment has been abolished by securer lighting and pilotage. In the vicinity of H. are several large sheets of water; the surrounding country and great part of the settlement is submerged by the periodical floodings of the river. H. is fast becoming the chief market for the Hunan and Hu-pé teas and the depôt for the supply of the minor ports. The choicest teas are bought for Russia, and there are here a number of Russian firms and three factories, with steam apparatus for making brick-tea. Coal is found in considerable quantity in the vicinity. H. is a centre of various Chinese manufactures, notably ribbons, felt, and velvets. Regular steam lines are established with England and Odessa. In 1875 there entered the port 383 vessels of 284,944 tons; and cleared, 483 of 294,288 tons. Of these, 352 were British, 285 American, 203 Chinese, 22 German, and 4 Russian. In 1875 the value of the exports was £5,652,094; of the imports, foreign, £2,677,717; native, £2,176,091. The value of black tea exported was £3,067,903, of brick tea £197,290, of green tea £30,365, of raw silk £83,718, of tobacco (a new staple) £356,217, of fungus £136,920, of hemp £146,200, drugs £192,335, wood oil £444,364, and coal £24,851. The chief imports are cotton and woollen goods, opium, sugar, pepper, and fish from Japan and the Straits, and metals. The tobacco, which is of good quality, and of which 13,548,431 lbs. were exported in 1875, is sent *viâ* America to the European markets as genuine Havana. Estimated pop. of H., together with Wu-chang-fu and Han-yang-fu, 1,000,000. H. was opened to foreign commerce in 1858, and partly destroyed in the Tae-ping rebellion in 1861.

Han'ley, a market-town of Staffordshire, ranking since 1857 as a municipal borough, is 1½ miles from Stoke-upon-Trent, and is a terminus of a branch of the N. Staffordshire Railway. H., a comparatively modern town, is one of the most prosperous in the region of the Potteries. Its staple manufactures are those of earthenware, porcelain, and encaustic tiles, and has coal and iron pits in the neighbourhood. Of public buildings the town-hall, the mechanics' institute, the school of design, the North Staffordshire museum, the theatre, and three large covered markets. For parliamentary purposes H. is part of the borough of Stoke-upon-Trent; the township of Skelton is included in the municipality of H. Pop. (1871) 39,976.

Hann'ibal, a city of Missouri, U.S., on the W. bank of the Mississippi, 150 miles above St. Louis by river, and 130 W. of Springfield by railway. It has a large lumber, grain, and tobacco trade, railway engineering works, and iron foundries. The river is here spanned by the splendid iron bridge of the Toledo, Wabash, and Western Railways, erected in 1872. Pop. (1870) 10,125.

Hannibal ('the grace or favour of Baal'). Many persons of this name occur in the history of Carthage, but by far the most celebrated was H. 'Barca,' born 247 B.C. When nine years old he accompanied his father Hamilcar to Spain after taking the memorable vow of everlasting enmity to Rome. He received his early training under the eye of his father, at whose death in battle he was present 229 B.C. Though only eighteen years of age at the time, he was intrusted by Hasdrubal (the son-in-law and successor of Hamilcar) with many important military enterprises, and on the assassination of the latter 221 B.C., was appointed commander-in-chief of the Carthaginian army. H., now twenty-six years of age, steadily followed in the footsteps of his father, and already contemplated the conquest of Italy. His first act was to complete the subjugation of Spain. In the spring of 219 B.C. he attacked Saguntum, a city in alliance with the Romans, and took it after a siege of eight months. Embassy after embassy was sent by the Romans vainly demanding the surrender of H. War was therefore declared, 218 B.C., and thus began the tremendous struggle known as the second Punic War. Starting from New Carthage in the spring of 218 B.C. with 90,000 foot and 12,000 horse—a force that was considerably diminished by the assignment of 11,000 men to Hanno to keep the conquered province, by repeated encounters with the tribes between the Iberus and the Pyrenees, and by desertion—he pushed on towards Italy. From the foot of the Pyrenees he marched to the Rhone unopposed, crossed the river, though Scipio was at Marseille only four days' journey distant, continued his march along the left bank of the river to its confluence with the Isère, and by a timely interposition in his favour secured the efficient assistance of one of the chiefs of the Allobroges. He then crossed the Alps in fifteen days—one of the most memorable achievements on record, encountering almost insurmountable difficulties. Whether H. crossed the Cottian Alps by the pass of Mount Cenis, or the Graian Alps by the Little St. Bernard, will probably never be settled. Both theories have found eminent advocates; but, as Dr. Liddell observes, 'the controversy will probably last for ever; the data seem insufficient to enable us to form a positive judgment.' In five months H. had reached the plains of Italy. He now rested, and recruited his army, then marched against the Taurini, whom he soon subdued. Meanwhile Scipio, who had sent his own army into Spain, hastened to the N. of Italy, undertook the command there, and met H. on the plains to the W. of the Ticinus. H.'s Numidian horse were irresistible. Scipio, himself severely wounded, was defeated and recrossed the Po. At the Trebia the Romans fared no better. After the winter was over H. pushed southward through Liguria and the fens of the Arno with great loss (217 B.C.). Here he lost the sight of one eye by an attack of ophthalmia. He next reached Fesulæ, where he gave his troops a brief repose. He then defeated the consul Flaminius near Lake Thrasymenus with terrible disaster, crossed the Apennines to Picenum and Apulia, recrossed the Apennines, and descended into the rich Campanian plains, which he laid waste far and wide. He endeavoured to draw into battle the consul Fabius (q. v.)—surnamed, from his policy, *Cunctator*—who had been sent against him, but in this he was unsuccessful. H., however, managed to get out of the net which the wary Roman had spread for him, established himself in Apulia, and laid in provisions. He wintered at Geronium, and late in the spring of next year surprised the Romans at Cannæ, where he fixed his headquarters. About the middle of June, on the banks of the Aufidus, quite near to Cannæ, he attacked and nearly annihilated the Roman army of 90,000 men under Terentius Varro and Æmilius Paulus. About 50,000 Romans were left on the field of battle, among whom were the consul Paulus, both the consuls of the past year, above eighty senators, and a host of knights and men of mark. Had H. now marched direct to Rome, he might have taken it without difficulty, and another civilisation might have influenced the destinies of Western Europe. But the blunder was irreparable. H. now tried to make himself master of Naples, but without success. Capua, however, opened its gates to receive him, and there he wintered (216-215 B.C.). The luxury of this city, is said to have demoralised his troops. Be this as it may, the star of H. now began to wane. He tried to turn the Italian nations against Rome, and to crush her by her own allies. In this he failed. In 211 B.C. he marched to Rome, and received a check. Still he traversed Italy, gained many signal victories, took many towns; but he was no nearer Rome than ever. The defeat and death of Hasdrubal, and the total loss of his army on the Metaurus 207 B.C., effectually turned the scale against H. For four years more (207-203 B.C.) he held his own in Bruttium, and at last, after fifteen years in Italy, during which the Romans estimated their loss in the field at not less than 300,000 men, he was recalled to Carthage, now in turn threatened by Scipio. The two generals met near Zama, and H., notwithstanding the heroic conduct of his veterans, was defeated with the loss of 20,000 men (202 B.C.). This blow was fatal to Carthage, and a peace was concluded in the following year. H., thwarted in his cherished scheme, now set about reforms at home; but his enemies accused him to the Romans of setting Antiochus III., King of Syria, against them, and he was compelled to leave Carthage. He fled to the court of Antiochus at Ephesus, where he was received with great honour. H. advised Antiochus, now (193 B.C.) on the eve of a war with Rome, to carry his arms into Italy, but without effect. On the conclusion of the war, one of the conditions was the surrender of H., who sought an asylum at the court of Prusias, King of Bithynia. But Rome could not rest while her arch-enemy lived, and T. Quintius Flamininus was sent to demand his immediate surrender. To avoid falling into the hands of his enemies he poisoned himself about 183 B.C. As a man H. was humane and magnanimous; as a general he was unrivalled. Among ancient authorities, Polybius, Dion Cassius, Plutarch, and Nepos may be consulted. See also the histories of Rome by Niebuhr, Arnold, Mommsen, &c., and, for the noblest tribute yet paid to the genius of the great Carthaginian, Professor Nichol's *H., a Historical Drama* (Glasg. 1873).

Hann'o, a more common name at Carthage than even Hamilcar or Hannibal. The most distinguished men who bore it were (1) H., the navigator and author of the *Periplus* (see next art.); (2) H., commander of the Carthaginians in Sicily in one of their wars with Dionysius, afterwards crucified by his countrymen for exciting a rebellion, 356-346 B.C.; (3) H., commander of the Carthaginian garrison at Messana, 264 B.C. For surrendering the citadel to the Romans he was condemned to be crucified on his return to Carthage; (4) H., son of Hamilcar, one of the three ambassadors sent to Regulus to sue for peace after the defeat near Adis; (5) H., commander of the Carthaginian fleet, defeated by Catulus off the Ægates, 241 B.C.; (6) H., surnamed the *Great*, on account of his successes in Africa, was long the leader of the aristocratic party at Carthage. While still young he held a command in Africa in the first Punic War. So great was his fame that he was regarded as the rival of Hamilcar Barca. When the mercenaries who had been employed in Sicily under Hamilcar returned to Africa, H. was sent to treat with them regarding the abatement of a part of their promised pay. Being unsuccessful, he was superseded by Hamilcar (q. v.). After his displacement H. refused to act with Hamilcar, but in time a formal reconciliation was effected. The two completed the subjection of Africa by the reduction of Utica and Hippo. After this H. was powerful in the councils of his country, uniformly opposed the Barcidæ, and thwarted to the utmost of his power the measures of that ambitious family.

Hanno, a celebrated navigator, whose work, the *Periplus*, written in the Punic language, still survives in a Greek translation. All that we know of his period is that he lived when Carthage was in the zenith of its power ('Punicis rebus florentissimis, Carthaginis potentia florente'). He was sent with sixty ships and 30,000 souls—an incredible number—to found colonies beyond the Pillars of Hercules. How far S. along the W. coast of Africa the fleet sailed is still matter of dispute. The *Periplus* of H. was first published at Basel, 1534; again at Strassburg, 1661; at Leyden, 1674; and with an English translation by Thomas Falconer at London, 1797, 8vo.

Hanno'ver (Eng. **Han'over**), a province of Prussia in the N.W. of Germany, has an area of 14,855 sq. miles, and a pop. (1875) of 2,018,868. The country belongs for the most part to the great N. German plain, only about a fourth of its area being hilly, chiefly in the region of the Harz. H. is watered by the Elbe, the Weser, and the Ems, with their numerous tributaries. The soil is generally poor, the great moor of Lüneburg and the marshy region and peat mosses of the N.W. comprising much ground wholly unfit even for pasture. All available ground is, however, diligently cultivated, and agriculture and cattle-breeding are the main occupations of the inhabitants. Manufactures are progressing, especially metal-working and the linen manufactures. The forests of the Harz, as well as its mineral treasures, are a source of wealth. Along the flat coast of E. Friesland shipbuilding and the fisheries are of importance. The people mainly belong to the Old Saxon stock. In most of the rural districts *Platt-Deutsch* (Low German) is the prevailing language, cognate to the Dutch and Frisian extensively spoken in the N.W.

History.—H. forms part of the land occupied by the Old Saxons, who furnished a large proportion of the Low German invaders and conquerors of Britain in the 5th c., and who three centuries later, under their leader Wittikind, offered a stubborn and protracted, though in the end unavailing resistance to the arms of Karl the Great. For a notice of the earlier history of the country, see BRUNSWICK and SAXONY. The Brunswick-Lüneburg family, of which the dispossessed King of H. is the representative, was founded by Wilhelm the Younger, who in 1569 divided the territories of the Brunswick family with his brother Heinrich, the founder of the reigning ducal house of Brunswick. Wilhelm's descendant Friedrich left at his death in 1648 several sons, of whom Christian Ludwig and Georg Wilhelm founded the houses of Celle and H. respectively. But dying without male issue, they were succeeded in 1679 by a younger brother, Ernst August, who was in 1692 raised to the dignity of *Kurfürst* ('Elector'). By his marriage with the Princess Sophia, daughter of the unfortunate Friedrich, King of Bohemia, and Elizabeth, daughter of James I. of England, Ernst August secured to the house of H. the succession to the English throne, and in 1714 his son Georg Ludwig became George I. of England, as the nearest Protestant kinsman of Queen Anne. His new dignity did not alienate the affections of the English sovereign from his ancestral Hanoverian possessions, which in many ways benefited by their connection with England, the ports of H. becoming the main inlet and outlet of all German commerce with England and her colonies. During the great French war, especially between 1801 and 1806, H. was alternately in the possession of Prussia and of France. In 1807 a great part of it was transferred to the new kingdom of Westphalia, and in 1810 the remainder followed, with the exception of a strip along the coast, which was retained by the French Empire. In 1813 the British rights in H. were restored, the ancient feudal institutions being re-established, and next year H. was made a kingdom. A considerable addition of territory was secured in 1815. The next great event in the history of H. was in 1833, when a new constitution, based on liberal principles, was introduced. In 1837, on the accession of Victoria to the British throne, the crown of H. fell to the Duke of Cumberland, women being excluded from the succession in H. The new king Ernst August signalised the beginning of his reign by the abolition of the liberal institutions of 1833 by royal patent, and a return to the old constitution of 1819. Protest was unavailing, and the seven professors of Göttingen who declined the oath of allegiance under the new conditions were summarily deposed. In 1848 it was found necessary for the Government to sanction reforms much more advanced than those withdrawn by Ernst August, and it was not till 1855 that a thoroughly reactionary Ministry came into power. This Government ventured to modify the constitution in its own spirit, and showed itself distinctly hostile to German aspirations towards national unity. Alliance with the enemies of Prussia at the outbreak of the Austro-Prussian war in 1866 was fatal to H. The issue was the occupation of Hannoverian territory by Prussian troops on the 17th June, three days after the declaration of H.'s policy, the hopeless and fruitless battle at Langensalza on the 27th June, and the final incorporation of H. with Prussia on the 17th August. The new Prussian province retained but one or two distinctive privileges; amongst others, the state church in H. is still the Lutheran, and not, as in the old Prussian provinces, the United (Lutheran and Reformed).

The history of H. has been written by Spittler (1798), Havemann (1853-57), Schaumann (1864), and Oppermann (1860).

Hannover, capital of the province, is an important railway centre, and is situated on the navigable river Seine. It consists of an old town irregularly built, and a handsome new town which has come into existence since 1837, the line of the ancient fortifications being now occupied by wide avenues of trees. The palace in H. was restored in 1817. The magnificent townhouse dates from 1439, and the Marktkische was built in 1349. There is a large museum and a polytechnic school; and the town possesses one of the handsomest theatres in Germany. The industry of H. is considerable, and includes iron founding and iron manufacturing, sugar refining, flax spinning, and cotton weaving. Machinery, chemicals, cement, linseed oil, and varnish are largely made. Near the town are the castles of Welfenschloss and Herrenhausen. Pop. of H., including the suburbs of Glocksee and Linden (1871), 104,248.

Han'sard, the name of a family and firm which has long been identified with the printing of British parliamentary documents, and especially of the semi-official reports of the debates. The founder, Luke H., was born at Norwich, 5th July 1752, succeeded Hughes as sole printer to the House of Commons in 1800, and died in London, 29th October 1828. His career, based on high intelligence, zeal, and probity, is ably sketched in the *Gentleman's Magazine* for December 1828. Although parliamentary printing is now no longer confined to one firm, the Messrs. H. produce, besides the debates, the bills before Parliament, the reports of committees, &c. The report of the debates, or *H.*, as it is specifically called, is compiled from the London newspapers. Each speech, however, is generally revised by the individual speaker, and to this is due the character of authenticity that attaches to the reports. Copies are procurable by purchase.

Hanseat'ic League, or **Hansa** (Ger. *hanse;* Goth. *hansa*, 'a league'), the most powerful of all the German confederations of cities, arose from a union made in 1241, between Hamburg and Lübeck, to protect their commerce, Brunswick entering into the alliance in 1247. The league was soon joined by other towns on the Baltic and in the neighbouring states, and in 1261 the first diet was held at Lübeck, the head city. There were at one time eighty-five towns in the confederacy, which sent representatives to the triennial diet, and which were divided into four circles:—(1) The Wendien, of which the chief city was Lübeck; (2) the Western, presided over by Köln; (3) the Saxon, of which the capital was Brunswick; and (4) the Eastern or Russian and Livonian, at the head of which was Danzig. The four chief foreign depots were at London, Bruges, Novgorod, and Bergen. The Hansa soon became very wealthy and powerful, maintained large fleets, defended Eric and Hakon of Norway, and Waldemar III. of Denmark, deposed Magnus of Sweden in 1348, and forced the rulers of England and France to form alliances favourable to the league. In the 14th c. much of the English export trade was in the hands of Hanseatic merchants, who were spoken of as *Easterlings*, whence the modern *sterling*. Had the union between the cities been closely cemented, and had they continued to act on broad commercial principles, they might have become rulers of all Northern Germany. But after their commercial monopoly was confirmed by the treaty of Colmar in 1285, they showed a narrow and jealous mercantile spirit, pursuing a ruinous, exclusive policy, and denying foreign merchants the privileges accorded to Hanseatic traders in other countries. The H. L. came to the height of its power in the 15th c., but the discovery of America turned trade into new channels. The strength of the League was sapped in constant embroilments, and after an unsuccessful struggle in the first half of the 16th c. with the Scandinavian kingdoms, whose union under Christiern II. the League had sought to break up, and against the German aristocratic party, the H. L. were decisively defeated at Assens, a blow from which they never recovered. In 1598 the blind adherence of the H. L. to their old prerogatives provoked Queen Elizabeth to expel their traders from London, while Drake seized sixty-one of their ships. The League, which was never formally recognised by the Empire, was practically dissolved in 1630, on the plea that most of the towns were no longer able to pay the expenses necessary to keep it up. Lübeck, Hamburg, Bremen, and Danzig, however, maintained their old alliance until 1810, when they were united to the French Empire. In 1813 they joined Frankfurt to form the league of free Hanseatic cities. In 1866 Frankfurt was added to Prussia; but Lübeck, Hamburg, and Bremen are still nominally free Hanse towns. The H. L. was at first formed to check feudal and kingly aggression, suppress piracy, and regulate and foster commerce. In these aims it was at first highly successful, and at one time exerted a most beneficial influence, stimulating enterprise, strengthening a love of freedom, and inculcating the general principles on which modern mercantile law is based, besides vastly increasing the wealth of the cities, and favouring agriculture, mining, and fisheries, as well as manufactures and trade. See Sartorius, *Geschichte des Hanseatischen Bundes* (3 vols. Gött. 1802-8); Lappenberg, *Urkundliche Geschichte des Ursprungs der Deutschen H.* (2 vols. Hamb. 1830); Barthold, *Geschichte der Deutschen H.* (3 vols. Leips. 1854); Falke, *Die H., als Deutsche See- und Handelsmacht* (Berl. 1862).

Han'sen, Peter Andreas, a German astronomer, was born at Tondern, in Schleswig, December 8, 1795. In 1825 he became director of the Lieberg Observatory in Gotha, a position which he still holds. He is the author of several astronomical works, as *Untersuchungen über die gegenseitigen Störungen des Jupiter und Saturn* (1838); *Theorie des Aequatoreals* (1854); *Geodätische Untersuchungen* (1865); and *Anwendung der Methode der kleinsten Quadrate auf Geodäsie* (1868). His great reputation, however, rests upon his *Sonnentafeln* (1854) and *Mondtafeln* (1857). In the preparation of the latter he was led to call in question the then universally accepted value for the sun's parallax, which had been deduced from the transit observations of 1761 and 1769. He found that, for the concordance of theory and observation, the parallax would require to be increased (*i.e.*, the sun's distance diminished) by 1-30th. Leverrier was somewhat later led to the same conclusion, and their deductions have been fully verified by subsequent and more accurate determinations.

Han'si, an old town in the district of Hissar, Punjaub, British India, on the canal of Feroz Shah, 89 miles N.W. of Delhi. Pop. (1868) 13,563. It was fortified by the adventurer George Thomas at the end of the last century, and was the former capital of Hureeanah. Since the Mutiny, when the sepoys stationed here murdered the Europeans, the cantonment has been removed.

Han'steen, Christoffer, a Norwegian astronomer and physicist, was born at Christiania, September 26, 1784. In 1814 he was chosen Professor of Mathematics in the University of Christiania, and in 1819 published his great work on terrestrial magnetism, which attracted wide notice, and brought into general use his methods of observing magnetic phenomena. Two years later he discovered the regular daily variation of the horizontal intensity; and in following up his investigation travelled to various places, remaining in Siberia from 1828 to 1830. On his return to Norway, his exertions procured the erection, in 1833, of an observatory at Government expense, especially intended for magnetic observations. In 1837 he undertook the direction of the trigonometrical survey of Norway. He wrote treatises on geometry (1835) and mechanics (2 vols. 1836–38), and numerous memoirs in the *Magazin für Naturvidenskaberne*. More recently he published *Observations on Magnetic Inclination from* 1855 *to* 1864 (1865), and *On the Secular Variations of Magnetism* (1865). H. died 11th April 1873.

Han-Yang-Fu, a suburb of Wu-chang-fu, China, on the Yang-tse-kiang, at the point where it is joined by the Han-kiang, and on the opposite side of the latter river from Han-kow (q. v.). It has manufactures of silks, velvets, ribbons, felts, &c., but most of the inhabitants are engaged in the tea trade. Estimated pop. 300,000.

Haps'burg, or Habs'burg, House of, the family to which the present royal family of Austria belongs, received its name from the castle of Habsburg or Habichtsburg ('hawk castle') in Aargau, Switzerland, which was founded in 1020 by Bishop Werner of Strassburg, first Count of H., through whose brother Kanzeline it passed to Werner, second Count of H. The great-grandson of the last Albrecht III. ruled over Aargau, Elsass, and part of Suabia, and on the death of his son Rudolf I. in 1232 the possessions of the house were shared between Albrecht IV. and Rudolf II. The latter founded the Hapsburg-Lauenburg line, which became extinct in the male branch in 1408, though represented by the Denbigh family in England, and in 1415 the possessions of Rudolf II.'s descendants reverted to the Hapsburg-Hapsburgs, descendants of Albrecht IV., whose son Rudolf III. had been made King of the Germans in 1273, and had added the duchy of Austria, Styria, and Carinthia to his dominions, after defeating Ottocar of Bohemia in 1278. Rudolf's descendants held the office of Holy Roman Emperor from 1438 to 1806, and besides governing Austria have ruled in Spain, Burgundy, Tuscany, and Modena. See Coxe's *House of Austria*. Lieknowski's *Geschichte des Hauses Habsburg* (2 vols. Vienna, 1836–37).

Har'ald I., Haar'fager ('fair-haired'), the founder of the kingdom of Norway, was the son of Halfdan Svarte ('swarthy'), a great jarl (earl) in the S. of Norway, and a descendant of the Ynglinga family, the earliest Swedish dynasty. His father was accidentally drowned when H. was only ten, probably in 860, and the chieftains whom he had subdued and confirmed as his subjects by the 'Eidsiva Law' (*Heidsævis lög, Sefs lög*), sought to dismember the young king's inheritance, but were gradually reduced under the military skill of Hertug (Duke) Gutorm. Success awaking higher ambition, H. did not rest for ten or twelve years, till, as king of all Norway, he had won the Lady Gyda's hand, which the legend tells could only be gained at this price. A feudal system of government was then established, the udal-right ('Odel') of the common people was taken away, and the petty kings replaced by 'jarler,' and (under them) 'herser' (bailiffs)—the chief of all these being his stout helper Hakon Griotgardsön. H.'s good fortune in this was largely due to the desire of many prominent men, and especially Ragnvald, afterwards Mörejarl, to check the bloody feuds of the *smaa-konger* ('sma' kings') by placing the whole land under one head. At last, in the decisive battle of Hafrsfjord, near Stavanger, in 872, he defeated the combined fleet of the southern chieftains, after which many of them fled over seas, as 'Vikinger,' to escape from his stern rule. Iceland, the Faröes, Shetland, and the Orkneys were colonised by these exiles, and Normandy seized by Rolf, a powerful young viking from Möre. H. extended his dominion to the Hebrides. His rule was wise, and he greatly discountenanced the general piracy of his time, but his last years were embittered by the perpetual bickering and misconduct of his many sons, among whom at first he divided his kingdom. To restore unity, in 930 he made over the crown to his son Erik (Blodöxe), and died three years after, aged eighty-three.—**Harald III., Haardraade** ('hard-ruling'), son of Harald Haarfager's descendant, Sigurd Syr, 'jarl' of the uplands of Ringerike in Norway, fought at the battle of Stiklesbad (1030), along with his half-brother Olaf the Saint, when only fifteen. After this defeat he had to leave Norway, and passed through Russia to Constantinople, where he took service among the Emperor's mercenaries, the Varangians, still, however, keeping up connection with the Russian grand-dukes. After twelve years' eventful warfare had brought him great riches, he came to Norway at the end of his nephew Magnus the Good's reign. Joining Magnus's enemy, the Danish king Svend Estridsön, he forced his nephew to give him a share in the government, an arrangement which led to many quarrels, Magnus's death in 1047 alone preventing a civil war. Though on his death-bed he had resigned to Svend his claims to the Danish crown, H. continued the war, now mainly confined to forays. The warlike, unquiet H. knew not how to conquer. He wanted one essential quality of a military ruler—the power of gaining the love of his own army and his own land. His avarice and severity often caused disobedience and the desertion of his own supporters, and his assassination of the brave Einar Tambeskjœlver roused popular hatred against him. At last he was persuaded by Tostig, the brother of Harold Godwineson, to join an expedition against this, the last of the pre-Norman kings of England, but suffered a defeat at Stamfordbridge, near York, in which he fell (1066).

Har'bour (Old Eng. *hereberga*, lit. 'a station or resting-place for the army' on its march, but afterwards applied to a station for ships) is a port or haven which by its natural configuration or artificial construction affords a safe refuge and anchorage to vessels. The essentials of a good H. are protection from the violence of the waves and easy accessibility; and if to these is added sufficient depth of water at all tides, its value as a H. is greatly enhanced. The great majority of harbours are, however, *tidal*, so that, though they may be useful as harbours of refuge, they are very inconvenient for purposes of lading and unlading. Accordingly, when such a H. is of any commercial importance, it is provided with an enclosed dock, into which ships enter at time of high water. (See DOCK.) Permanent harbours, which have always a sufficient depth of water, may dispense with the dock; but the same inconvenience in shipping and unshipping cargo is present on account of the rising and falling of the tide. In the Mediterranean, Caspian, and other inland seas and lakes, where the tides are hardly perceptible, this disadvantage does not exist. These permanent harbours are employed either for military or civil purposes. To the former class belong the extensive harbours of Plymouth, Portsmouth, Cherbourg, Brest, &c.; and to the latter the smaller harbours of Southampton, Liverpool, Glasgow, London, Bordeaux, Havre, &c.

The construction of harbours necessarily accompanies the rise of commerce, and the remains of the great H. works at Tyre attest the genius and energy of the early Phœnician engineers. The coast of Greece was so well provided with natural harbours that this art of naval construction did not develop to more than the erection of simple moles, breakwaters, or other minor works. The Romans, however, were forced through circumstances to resort to the formation of artificial ports; and perhaps their most perfect undertaking was the H. of Ostia, at the mouth of the Tiber. The revival of commerce in the middle ages resulted in the construction of the ports at Genoa and Venice. France soon followed the example of Italy; but not till the latter half of last century was England impressed with the importance of having ports and havens for the protection of its commerce and the safety of its shipping.

In constructing a H. the engineer must take into account many local characteristics, such as the geological features of the coast, the direction of prevailing winds and currents, the line of greatest reach of open sea in front, the maximum height of the waves and the character of the breakers, the effects of tidal influence, and other minor details. The protecting walls must be of the form best suited to resist the force of the waves; but engineers are not decided upon which really is the best, some arguing in favour of a perpendicular front, others maintaining the superiority of a gradual slope. Another important consideration is the relation which the width of the entrance bears to the area of H.; for upon this depends the tranquillity or reductive power of the H. Mr. Thomas Stevenson, the author of a work upon harbours, gives the following formula for the reductive power:—$x = \frac{H}{\sqrt{B}} \left\{ \sqrt{b} - \frac{1}{50} (\sqrt{B} + \sqrt{b}\sqrt[4]{D}) \right\}$ where x = height of wave at place of observation; H = height of wave at entrance; B = breadth of H. at place of observation; b = breadth of entrance; D = distance from mouth of H. to place of observation. $x \div H$ is the reductive power. The material employed for constructing the walls of harbours may be wood, metal, or stone. Wood, however, is not suitable for positions of great exposure; and all three are gradually wasted away by mechanical or chemical action. The great improvement of late years has been the introduction of Portland cement, which can be formed into blocks of any size, and which, when hardened, is nearly as durable as sandstone. Besides Stevenson's work above mentioned, see Sir J. Rennie's *Harbours* and the *Minutes of Proceedings of the Institute of Civil Engineers.*

Laws Regarding Harbours or Ports.—Ports are *inter regalia;* the right to erect or hold them being vested in the crown, except when the right is given by royal or parliamentary grant to a subject. Any one obtaining a grant of a harbour is bound to keep it in proper repair, and is entitled to levy harbour dues for the purpose, the rate of dues being regulated by custom. The granter is not bound to repair or improve the harbour at his own expense; but he is not entitled, without the authority of Parliament, to exact additional dues to indemnify himself for any extraordinary expenditure or improvement. The Act 10 Vict. c. 27 applies to the United Kingdom. It regulates the procedure of all bodies having charge of piers, docks, and harbours. It also defines their duties as regards the levying.

Har'burg, a town of Hanover, Prussia, on the southern branch of the Elbe, 6 miles S. of Hamburg, with which it is connected by railway. H. has foundries and machine works, manufactures of india-rubber, waxcloth, and sailcloth, and has a thriving trade. In 1871 1227 sea-going ships of 43,220 tons entered the port. Pop. (1875) 17,131.

Har'denberg, Friedrich, Freiherr von, better known by his asssumed name *Novalis*, was born on the family estate near Mansfeld, in Prussian Saxony, May 2, 1772, studied philosophy and law at Jena, Leipsic, and Wittenberg, but in 1795 accepted a post in connection with the saltworks at Weissenfels. His early death, March 25, 1801, prevented the fulfilment of the rich promise of his youth; yet the originality and poetic power of his unfinished novel, *Heinrich von Ofterdingen*, entitle H. to rank as one of the best representatives of the 'Romantic school.' His religious poems are among the most beautiful that exist in the German tongue. H. regarded his *Hymnen an die Nacht* as his most perfect work. He is often fantastic, more frequently obscure; but the mystical form never conceals the wealth of pure and tender feeling that everywhere lurks under it. His friends Tieck and F. Schlegel superintended an edition of H.'s *Sämmtliche Schriften* in 1804 (5th ed. Berl. 1837–46). See Carlyle's *Miscellaneous Essays.*

Hardenberg, Karl August, Fürst von, born 31st May 1750 at Essenroda, in Hanover, of a noble family, early devoted himself to the political service of his native state. The seduction of his wife by the 'first gentleman of Europe,' the Prince of Wales of the period, was the occasion of his accepting a public post from the Duke of Brunswick, whom in 1791 he left for the service of Friedrich Wilhelm II. of Prussia. Under Friedrich Wilhelm III., H. in 1804 succeeded Haugwitz as Prime Minister, the French policy of the latter having ended in the military occupation of Hanover. H. endeavoured to maintain neutrality, and also to cultivate English interests. After the disaster of Jena he undertook for a short time the *portfolio* of foreign affairs. When Stein came into power in 1810 he was made chancellor, and began that brilliant series of internal reforms which are associated with his name, and to which Prussia owes her present position. He swept away ecclesiastical and aristocratic exemptions and corporation abuses. He created the class of free peasants, permitting them to redeem feudal burdens by the surrender of a portion of their lands. His labours, both diplomatic and legislative, were rewarded in 1814 by the title of prince. He next revised the political constitution and the municipal organisation of his country. He equalised custom duties, improved the system of public records, and was favourable to the introduction of a representative system. Having gone to Rome to sign a concordat, he fell ill, and died at Genoa, 26th November 1822. See Klose's *Leben Karl August's, Fürsten von H.* (Halle, 1851). His autobiography and papers were issued by L. von Ranke as *Denkwürdigkeiten des Staats Kanzlers Fürsten von H.* (4 vols. Leips. 1877).

Har'derwijk, a seaport of Holland, province of Gelderland, on the E. shore of the Zuider Zee, 20 miles S.W. of Zwolle by railway. It has extensive fisheries and an export trade in grain, butter, eels, herrings, &c. Pop. (1873) 5067. H. is an old Hanse town, and has frequently suffered the misfortunes of war.

Har'dicanute. See HARTHACNUT.

Har'dinge, Henry, Viscount, an English general and statesman, was the son of a Durhamshire rector, and was born 30th March 1785, entered the army in 1800, and served through the Peninsular and Waterloo campaigns; at the battle of Ligny he lost a hand. He afterwards became Secretary of State for War, Secretary for Ireland, and finally Commander-in-Chief of the British army on the death of the Duke of Wellington in 1852. But he is best known as Governor-General of India from 1844 to 1848, a period which included the first Sikh war, in which Lord H. took a personal share by the side of Lord Gough, the commander-in-chief, and was made a Viscount for his services. He died 24th September 1856. His pension of £3000 a year is continued to his two next successors in the peerage.

Hard'ness is a property of matter possessed only by solids. In mineralogy, the H. of a body is measured by its power of scratching other substances. Thus the garnet scratches felspar, but is scratched by topaz, and accordingly it is intermediate in hardness to these. For comparison, a *scale of H.* has been constructed of ten well-known minerals, which increase gradually in H. from *talc* to diamond. This scale is as follows—(1) *talc;* (2) *rock salt;* (3) *calc spar*, transparent variety; (4) *fluor spar*, crystallised variety; (5) *apatite*, transparent crystal; (6) *felspar*, cleavable variety; (7) *quartz*, transparent variety; (8) *topaz*, transparent crystal; (9) *sapphire*, cleavable variety; (10) *diamond.* The first six can be scratched with a knife, so that by one simple trial the position of any substance in the scale can be approximately determined.

Har'douin, Jean, commonly called **Père H.,** a French scholar, born of humble parents at Quimper, Brittany, in 1627. He early became a Jesuit, devoted himself to ancient literature and numismatology, and sought to establish the wild theory that most of the Greek and Latin classics, except Plautus, Virgil's *Georgics*, Pliny's *Natural History*, Horace's *Satires* and *Epistles*, Homer's *Iliad*, and Herodotus, were monastic forgeries of the 13th c. He declared that Virgil's *Æneid* was an allegorical account of St. Peter's journey to Rome, and that the New Testament was originally written in Latin. H. was made librarian of the Collège Louis-le-Grand in 1683, and died September 3, 1729. Among his works are an edition of Pliny's *Natural History* (1685); *Chronologia ex nummis antiquis restituta* (1697); *Conciliorum Collectio* (1715); *Apologie d'Homère* (1716); *Opera Varia* (1733); and *Prolegomena ad Censuram Veterum Scripto-*

rum (1766), in which his strange opinions on ancient literature are set forth.

Hard'ware, a trade term signifying all kinds of articles manufactured from the base metals, as iron, steel, copper, brass, &c. Birmingham, Wolverhampton, and Sheffield are important seats of the industry.

Hard Wood, applied to the *duramen* or heart wood of exogenous trees. Hard-wooded trees are those in which the timber is hard and heavy, such as oak, elm, beech, ash, &c.; while soft-wooded trees are those in which the timber is soft and light such as poplars, willows, &c.

Hare (*Lepus timidus*), a species of *Rodentia* belonging to the family *Leporidæ*, of which group it and the Rabbit (q. v.) are the typical examples. The family is distinguished by the presence of four incisor teeth in the upper jaw, but the H. has two additional incisors of small size. The molars are rootless. The fore-feet have five, and the hind-feet four toes. The tail is rudimentary. The ears in the H. are larger than in the rabbit; the hind limbs also attain a greater relative length. No canine teeth are found. There are six premolars in the upper and four in the lower jaw, while the molars number six in each jaw. The fur of the H. is redder than that of the rabbit. The average weight of the animal is from 8 to 13 or 14 lbs., the length about 2 feet. The under parts are white, as also the breast. The H. is usually accounted of a timid disposition, but instances are on record of its turning upon its oppressor with considerable fury. That it possesses no small amount of instinct is evident from the skilful way in which it contrives to double, and to take every advantage of inequalities in the ground when pursued by the Greyhound (q. v.) and other dogs. Many of the popular notions regarding its timidity have probably arisen from the fact that its habits have seldom been carefully studied, and that we oftenest associate the H. with its pursuit by a pack of hounds. Other varieties are the Irish H. (*Lepus Hibernicus*), which is generally believed to represent a distinct species. It has shorter limbs and ears, and a head of more rounded conformation than the common H.; the Alpine or blue H. (*Lepus variabilis*), noted for its change of coat in winter, hence called 'the changing' H.; the Arctic H. (*L. glacialis*), which also assumes a white colour in winter, its summer fur being of a brownish-grey hue. Various other species occur in India, N. America, N. and S. Africa, &c.

Law Regarding Hares.—It is a misdemeanour in England punishable by fine or imprisonment to take or kill a hare in any warren or ground used for keeping them between the first hour after sunset and the beginning of the last hour before sunrise. The same offence in the daytime is punishable by a fine not exceeding £5. The owner of enclosed land may kill hares without a license; so may the tenant if his lease entitle him to kill them. Nor is a license required to hunt them with greyhounds or beagles. The Act 11 and 12 Vict. c. 31 enables all persons having a right to kill hares in Scotland to do so, or to authorise others to do so, without a game certificate. See GAME LAWS.

Hare'bell, the popular name for *Campanula rotundifolia*, called also bluebell, and witches' thimbles in Scotland. *Hyacinthus nonscriptus* (*Scilla nutans*), a plant belonging to the lily order, is the bluebell of England.

Hare's-Ear, applied to species of *Bupleurum*, a genus of plants belonging to the natural order Umbelliferæ (q. v.), and natives of temperate regions. They have no economic value, although early medical authors ascribe certain virtues to them. *B. rotundifolia* is one of the four British species, and is called thorow-wax from the stem 'waxing' or growing through the leaf. Several species are cultivated in gardens for the curious inflorescence.

Har'fleur (anc. *Arefluctus*; medieval, *Hare-flot*), a village in the department of Seine-Inférieure, France, near the mouth of the Lézarde, on the right bank of the Seine, about 4 miles E. of Havre. It stands in a marshy district, and has a castle in the Renaissance style, and a fine Gothic church built by the English to commemorate Agincourt. In the middle ages H. was a place of commercial importance, and had a strong fortress, taken, after a brave resistance, by Henry V. of England in 1415. H. was again taken by the French in 1433, by the English in 1448, and by Charles VII. of France in 1450. Pop. 1800.

Har'greaves, James, inventor of the spinning-jenny, was born at Stanhill, near Blackburn. He was an uneducated weaver and spinner, and in 1760 invented the carding-machine. After unsuccessfully trying to spin several cotton threads at once, having noticed on one occasion when his child upset the spinning-wheel that the spindle revolved vertically, while the wheel revolved horizontally, the idea flashed on him of placing several vertical spindles side by side, and from this idea he developed his invention of the Spinning-Jenny (q. v.) in 1764. The invention was at first kept a secret, but his neighbours, noticing how much cotton he and his family spun, entered his house and broke his machine, whereupon, in 1768, he established a spinning-mill at Nottingham. Having unfortunately sold machines before they were patented, he lost the claim to the patent on his invention, and died a poor man in April 1788.

Hari-Kari, a Chinese expression signifying a 'happy despatch,' and used of suicide effected by the infliction of two cross gashes in the abdomen—a form of self-destruction much practised in Japan. Officials guilty of a grave offence are invited by the authorities to perform H.-K., and are thus enabled to escape formal degradation and disgrace. H.-K. is also had recourse to by private persons who have received any intolerable affront.

Här'ing, Wilhelm, a German novelist, known by the pseudonym of Wilibald Alexis, was born at Breslau, 23d June 1797. He studied law, but soon devoted himself wholly to literature, and attained great celebrity in the field of 'historical romance.' His first successful work, *Walladmor*, which appeared as a translation from Sir Walter Scott (3d ed. Berl. 1823–24); *Schloss Avalon* (1827); *Cabanis* (1832); *Der Roland von Berlin* (1842); *Der falsche Waldemar* (1842); and *Dorothea* are H.'s best-known works. He also published tales of travel, and edited a collection of criminal trials. His *Gesammelte Werke* in 18 vols. appeared at Berlin in 1861–66. H. died at Arnstadt in Thuringia, 16th December 1871.

Hari'ri, Abu Mohammed al Kassim Ben Ali, an Arabic philosopher and poet, was born at Bassorah about A.D. 1054. The name H. means 'the silk-worker,' and refers to the occupation of his parents, who were wealthy. In spite of the troubles caused by the invasion of Malek Shah, the Turk, H. probably received a good education. He became *Sahib-al-Khabar*, or political intelligence agent, about the time when Baldwin of Flanders led the crusade to Edessa and some of these events are alluded to in his work the *Makamas* (1101), a collection of fifty short dramas, partly verse, partly prose, which was modelled on the work of Hamadani, and is probably after the Koran the greatest of Arabic classics. The leading characters are the wise and decorous Haret, and the clever vagabond, Abu-Seid. Some of these dramas H. read in public at the mosque. They contain many proverbs and literary and grammatical observations, and some verses which became popular songs. Assonance, or the incomplete rhyme which consists in the repetition of vowel sounds, is much used. During his life H. was accused of being a mere *mushi* or compiler, and also of treating frivolous subjects in opposition to the text of the Koran. H. died in September 1122. While H.'s works are much more artificial than the early poems such as the *Moallakat* of the 6th c. or the *Hamasa* of Abu Temman (A.D. 830), they represent a reaction in favour of natural simplicity of taste against the extravagant conceits of Motanabbi and Abul-Ola. The *Makamas* have been largely imitated, and commented on in Hebrew and Syriac as well as Arabic; a similar work, called *The Meeting of the Two Seas*, was produced by a Maronite writer as lately as 1857. The same author (Nasif-al-Jazidji) published, in 1848, a criticism of Silvestre de Sacy's edition of the *Makamas*, now superseded by that of Reinaud and Derenbourg (1847–53). The *Makamas* have been translated into German by the poet Rückert (1826), and into English by Preston (1850), who translates *Makamat* as 'rhetorical anecdote.' H. also wrote the *Molhat-al-Irab*, or 'The Delights of Grammatical Analysis,' and the *Dorrat-al-Gaouas*, 'The Pearl of the Diver,' a work on subtle errors of speech. See Chenery's translation of the 'Assemblies' (Lond. 1867).

Harlaw', Battle of, took place in the year 1411. It was caused by a conflict over the earldom of Ross between the great Highland chieftain of the times, Donald, Lord of the Isles, and the Regent of Scotland, the Duke of Albany. Donald, being promised the support of an English fleet, invaded the Eastern

Lowlands at the head of 10,000 men, ravaged the country as far as Aberdeenshire, when he was confronted at Harlaw, on the Ury, 18 miles from Aberdeen, by a force of Gordons, Buchans, and others, under the Earl of Mar, on the 20th July 1411. Although Mar was confronted by an army outnumbering his by ten to one, a desperate struggle ensued, in which the Lowlanders stood their ground, but with a fearful loss of gentry and men-at-arms. The provost and chief magistrates of Aberdeen were also killed. The retreat of the 'hieland kern' next day gave the fruits of the victory to the Earl of Mar, and ultimately the Duke of Albany was able to force from the Lord of the Isles the earldom of Ross, and vassalage to the Scottish crown. Of the ballads commemorating the fight Scott's fragment in the *Antiquary* is by far the finest. See Fullarton's *Scottish Highlands* (new ed.), and Burton (*History of Scotland*, vol. iv.), who says that the defeat of Donald of the Isles 'was felt as a more memorable deliverance even than that of Bannockburn.'

Harlequin, Clown, Pantalcon, and Columbine, the chief characters in the harlequinade of the modern pantomime. The harlequin is the *arlechino* (Fr. *arlequin*) of the Italian *Commedia dell' Arte*, and was transferred to the Italian stage from the Roman *Fabulæ Atellanæ*. (See PANTOMIME.) In the modern pantomime he is supposed to be the hero of the 'burlesque opening' transformed into a magician, who is the lover of the columbine, and the stroke of whose wand produces sudden changes of scenery. In Italy the harlequin was at first the same as the mime, or actor who mimicked everyday life; he afterwards sank into a stupid glutton, the butt of his companion who was named *Brighella*. Goldoni changed him into a wit, in which capacity he was transported to the French theatre. The character of harlequin is said to have been introduced to the English stage by Rich in the 18th c. The clown, who is descended from the *sannio* or jester of the Roman *Fabulæ Atellanæ* through the Italian *zanni*, is perpetually engaged in knavery and comic, and is assisted in his mischief-making by the pantaloon, represented as a weak old man. The last character, as well as the columbine, are of later origin than the harlequin and clown. The pantaloon arose from the Spanish *capitan* or captain, who was at first represented as a hectoring bravo, and who, after kicking a Spanish *capitan*, was caned by the harlequin. But when the Spanish power in Italy waned, the Spanish *capitan* was turned into an abject coward, who still wore the Spanish dress, and who is the pantaloon of the modern English pantomime. The columbine is the heroine of the burlesque introduction to the pantomime, whose function now lies merely in dancing. The H., C., P., and C. all appeared in the old *Commedia dell' Arte* of the Italians.

Harlequin Duck (*Clangula histrionica*), a species of duck belonging to the genus *Clangula*, distinguished by the peculiar mottling and variegation of its plumage, which is marked with hues of black, white, and grey. It is an inhabitant of northern regions. The average length is 16 inches.

Har'ley, Robert, Earl of Oxford, an English politician, belonging to a Herefordshire family at one time prominent among the Presbyterians, but afterwards devoted to the Restoration, was born at London in 1661. Soon after entering Parliament H. became a Tory, and was elected Speaker when Rochester and Godolphin came into office in 1701. When, in spite of the Occasional Conformity and Queen Anne's Bounty Bills, Lord Nottingham quarrelled with Marlborough in 1704, H. and St. John entered the Cabinet as Secretary of State and Secretary for War respectively. H.'s interest was promoted by his cousin, Abigail Hill, soon to become Mrs. Masham. The introduction of Cowper and Sunderland to the Ministry rendered his position insecure, and the conviction of his clerk Gregg for treasonable correspondence with France decided his dismissal in 1708. When the peace party triumphed over Marlborough in 1710, H. became Chancellor of the Exchequer. The absurd incident of the Guiscard assault made him very popular, and he became Lord High Treasurer, and was created Earl of Oxford and Mortimer. He and Bolingbroke negotiated the Peace of Utrecht (1713), and passed the Schism Act, and began to intrigue with St. Germains. On the Queen's death they both were impeached by the House of Commons. After two years' imprisonment, H. was discharged without trial. He died May 21, 1724. H. bequeathed to the British Museum the Harleian MSS., which include the two golden Latin Gospels, the oldest *Odyssey*, and a great number of topographical and historical papers, abbey registers, parliamentary regal records, antiphonars, &c. See Defoe's *Eleven Opinions of Mr. H.* (1711), and *The Secret History of Arlus and Adolphus* (H. and Godolphin), *Minister to the Empress of Grandinsula* (Lond. 1710).

Har'lingen. See HAARLINGEN.

Har'maline and **Har'mine** are two Alkaloids (q. v.) which occur in the husk of the seeds of the Syrian rue (*Peganum harmala*), a plant which is cultivated in the steppes of Southern Russia, and is employed in dyeing silk shades of red. Harmaline is a white crystalline substance, having a bitter astringent taste, and colours the saliva yellow. It is but slightly soluble in water and ether, but is readily dissolved by hot alcohol. It forms yellow salts with acids. Its composition is represented by the formula $C_{13}H_{14}N_2O$. By limited oxidation harmaline may be made to lose two atoms of hydrogen, and to become transformed into harmine, $C_{13}H_{12}N_2O$—a substance which, as just stated, is also found in the Syrian rue. Harmine is crystalline, only slightly soluble in alcohol and ether, and nearly insoluble in water. It is a powerful bane, actually expelling ammonia from its salts when boiled with their solutions, and uniting with the acids they contain. It forms colourless salts with acids, the solutions of which are bluish in colour when dilute, yellow when concentrated. When harmaline is submitted to the prolonged action of oxidising agents it yields a red substance, the salts of which form the red colouring matter known as *Harmaline Red*.

Harmatt'an, a dry and withering hot wind that blows from the interior of Africa along the coast of Guinea. Its influence, injurious alike to the human frame and to vegetation, is felt chiefly in the months of January, February, and March. The H. has the same origin as the Sirocco (q. v.) of the Mediterranean.

Harmo'dius and **Aristogei'ton,** two Athenian youths who, to revenge a private insult, conspired to destroy the Pisistratidæ. During the Panathenaic festival, B.C. 514, they attacked and slew Hipparchus, but H. was cut down by the guards, and A. was seized and executed by Hippias. Though the Pisistratidæ were not expelled till 510, the two friends were regarded by posterity as the true restorers of freedom. Their descendants had admission to the free table in the Prytaneum, statues were erected to their honour, and their glory sung by the poets, especially in the *Scholia* or 'table-songs.'

Harmon'ica, the name given to several different musical instruments. In all, the tones are produced by the friction of the finger or the striking of a hammer on *glass*. The harmonica invented by Dr. Franklin consisted of bell-shaped glasses, tuned in semitones, which revolved round a spindle and were touched by the moistened fingers.

Harmon'ic Mo'tion, in kinematics, is any motion which recurs periodically. *Simple H. M.*, which plays such an important part in many physical phenomena, is rigidly defined as the orthogonal projection upon a straight line of uniform circular motion. Now, this motion is approximately that of a pendulum, or of the simplest vibrations of a tuning-fork, and of the media through which sound, light, heat, &c., are propagated. Considering the motion of a long pendulum, it is observed that the bob has a certain range on each side of the position it would occupy when at rest. The greatest range from the mean position is called the *amplitude*; and the smaller the amplitude in comparison to the length of the pendulum the more approximately is the motion a simple H. M. The *period* is the time which elapses from any instant till the bob again moves through the same point in the same direction. The *epoch* is the time which elapses from the era of reckoning (an arbitrarily chosen element) till the bob first comes to its greatest distance from the middle position measured in the positive direction. Simple H. M. is intimately related to all wave motions. This will be at once evident when it is observed that a water wave, for instance, travels along the surface of the water in virtue of the up and down motion imparted to each particle. For a detailed discussion, see Thomson and Tait's *Natural Philosophy*, vol. i.

Harmonic Progress'ion is a series whose successive terms are the reciprocals of the terms of an arithmetical progression, such as $1, \frac{1}{4}, \frac{1}{7}, \frac{1}{10}$, &c. $\frac{1}{a-b}, \frac{1}{a}, \frac{1}{a+b}$ is an H. P. of three terms; and $\frac{1}{a}$ is the harmonic mean between $\frac{1}{a-b}$ and $\frac{1}{a+b}$. In geometry, a straight line is said to be divided in *harmonic ratio* when the ratio of the parts into which it is divided by an internal section is equal to the ratio of its parts by an external section. The base of a triangle, intersected by the lines which bisect the interior and exterior vertical angles, is divided in harmonic ratio.

Harmon'ics, the sounds which go to make up what to the ordinary ear is itself *one sound*. As the vibrations of a whole string, or a whole column of air, produce a tone of a certain pitch, so the vibrations of its aliquot parts, which proceed along with those of the whole, produce higher, weaker, but not inaudible tones, which play their part in the total effect of the 'note' in question. The experiments which prove this cannot be described here; the reader may consult Sedley Taylor's *Sound and Music* (Macmillan, Lond. 1873). The H. are produced by vibrations whose numbers per second are respectively 2, 3, 4, &c., times as great as those of the fundamental tone of the string (if we use the 'string' as the most convenient example), in other words, by the vibrations of $\frac{1}{2}$, $\frac{1}{3}$, $\frac{1}{4}$, &c., of the length of the whole string. We give the H. of a low 'C,' or at least 10 of them—9 'overtones' and the 'fundamental.'

&c.

A sound need not contain the full number of H., but 'in no case can a tone intermediate in pitch between any two consecutive members of the series make its appearance.' A tuning-fork, again, furnishes an example of a simple, indivisible sound.

Harmo'nium. A musical instrument, with keyboard, whose sounds are produced by the passage of air through vibrating 'reeds.' A reed, in this sense, is a slip of metal of rectangular shape, free to move except at one end; it forms part of a larger piece, and moves up and down in a slit just its own size. The bellows are moved by means of footboards, and, as the air is sent into a wind-chest, a continuous stream presses against the reeds. The stops draw away wooden slides, and so open the particular sets of reeds—according to the number of stops, there may be one reed or several to each note—to the influence of the wind. The 'expression' stop brings the action of the wind on the reeds under the more direct and rapid control of the player. The instrument has a range of five octaves, from C to C, but sometimes there are stops which add an octave above and below, each note giving a sound an octave higher or lower than its normal one. The harmoniums used in this country are principally of French manufacture. Debain (the inventor), and Alexandre (at Paris), Schiedmayer (at Stuttgard), and Kaufmann (at Dresden) are the chief makers.

Har'mony. In a musical sense this word means the simultaneous sounding of different tones. In the vibrations of *one* string or column of air there are heard various tones, but the physical facts underlying the 'consonance' or agreement of tones must not be confounded with that consonance itself. The first answer to the question, 'What tones sound well together?' is 'Any tone along with its major or minor third and its fifth.' (See INTERVAL.) Such a combination is called a 'common chord' or 'triad.' Of the triads in the major scale, that on the seventh tone—with imperfect fifth——and that on the third tone are the least common. Of course it is sufficient to consider one key—if the minor be only a 'mode' of the major—in order to get a complete view of the chords of all keys. The tones G, B, D make up *different chords* in keys G and C respectively. At intervals within the octave, we find, next, 'chords of the seventh,' in which a fourth tone is used—

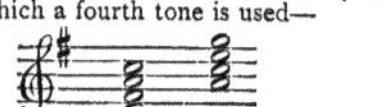

The seventh is discordant with the 'root' (D, A, are the roots in diagram), and is employed under certain limitations. Even ninths, elevenths, and thirteenths to any given tone sometimes bring into existence distinct and original chords, though as intervals they are only compound forms of smaller intervals (the octave being merely a reduplication). Any single chord may stand in various positions, thus—

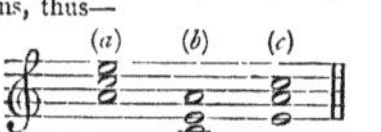

Moreover, the parts may stand at different distances from one another, and may be more or fewer in number, and wider or narrower in extent, thus—

H. involves also the *progression* of chords, and many other essential matters that cannot even be named here. See Banister's *Music* (Bell & Sons, Lond.); Curwen's *How to Observe H.*; and Macfarren's *Lectures on H.* (new ed. Lond. 1877).

Harmony, although in its more extended sense it means a book in which the Scriptures, either of the Old or the New Testament, are arranged in chronological order, in its original and more limited sense deals only with the Gospels, which are four narratives of the life of Christ requiring to be harmonised on account of their real or apparent discrepancies. (See GOSPELS.) The first work of the kind was that of Tatian (q. v.), in the 2d c., which, however, was not a H. proper, but a *diatessaron*, that is, a single continuous narrative extracted from the four Gospels. The first H. proper, in which the four Gospels were arranged in two, three, or four parallel columns, according as a narrative of the same particular occurs in two, three, or four of them, was compiled in the 3d c. by Ammonius of Alexandria, who, taking Matthew as his standard, arranged in parallel columns the corresponding passages of the other three. On this work was founded the more elaborate *Ten Indexes* of Eusebius. Since the Reformation at least two hundred attempts have been made to compile a H., showing both the interest taken in the subject and the difficulty of the undertaking. Four of the latest and best are those by Stroud (1853), Anger (1851), Tischendorf (1851), Robinson (1845), Greswell (1830).

Harmony of the Spheres, the music made, according to an ancient fancy, by the orderly motions of the stars and planets. See Shakespeare's *Merchant of Venice*, act v. scene 1, and Milton's *Hymn on the Nativity*.

Harms, Klaus, a revered leader of Lutheran orthodoxy, was born at Fahrstedt, in S. Ditmarsch, Holstein, May 25, 1778, and till his nineteenth year assisted his father in the management of a cornmill and attached farm. But his zealous desire to study theology triumphed. He became pastor in 1806, archdeacon at Kiel in 1816, and died there as *oberconsistorialrath*, 1st February 1855. H. was a powerful preacher, and was throughout his life an earnest and energetic enemy of Rationalism in all its forms. In 1817, in remembrance of Luther's theses just 300 years earlier, he nailed ninety-five theses against the religion of nature to the door of the University Church in Kiel, and published in 1819 a large work to the same effect. His sermons, *Winter- und Sommer-Postille* (published 1808–15), reached a sixth edition in 1846. His *Pastoral Theologie* appeared in 1830. See H.'s Autobiography (Kiel, 1851).

Har'old I., surnamed **Harefoot**, King of England, was the son of Cnut, whom he succeeded in 1035. It was not until 1037, however, that he had any real control over Wessex. His reign was marked by lawlessness and bloodshed. Little is known of his character. He is said to have received his surname from his swiftness. To this time belongs the great Mercian earl, Leofric, the husband of Lady Godiva (q. v.).—**H. II.**, known also as **H. Godwineson**, the second son of Earl Godwine of Kent, and of Gytha, a Danish lady. During the latter part of Eadward the Confessor's reign, the chief administrative power rested with H., who followed out his father's wise and peaceful national policy, preserving strict justice and order, and developing the kingdom's resources. He invaded Wales successfully in 1063, drove his brother Tostig—who was plotting to succeed Eadward—to Flanders, and on Edward's death was chosen king, January 10, 1066. Shortly before he had been shipwrecked on the coast of Normandy, where William, duke of the country, had forced him to swear on the bones of Norman saints to aid the duke in his claim to the English throne, a claim which William prepared to enforce on H.'s accession. Tostig now invaded Yorkshire with a great host under Harald Hardrada, King of Norway. H. routed them decisively at Stamford Bridge, September 25, 1066, shortly before William of Normandy landed on the southern coast. When that event took place, H. at once marched against the new enemy without having time to muster his kingdom's strength, and was slain by an arrow which pierced his right eye in the battle of Senlac, or Hastings, October 14, 1066. H. was a skilful and fearless soldier, and a clear-headed, strong-willed, prudent, and just ruler. As the last of the dynasty of purely English kings, and the antagonist of the Normans, he has been raised into a kind of national hero, and painted in somewhat deceptive romantic colours. See Freeman's *Norman Conquest*, vol. i.

Harp (Old Eng. *hearpa*, Ger. *harfe*, Fr. *harpe*, probably named from the way of sounding it by 'snatching' at the strings; if so, comp. Gr. *harpazō* and Lat. *carpo* and *rapio*), a musical stringed instrument that was in some forms known to the Hebrews, the Egyptians, the Assyrians, and the old Celtic and Teutonic nations. With the Greeks the *lyre* was commoner, and the Roman 'cithara' is indifferently translated 'H., lyre, lute, guitar,' &c. Harps and harpists were highly honoured by our forefathers, as the stories about King Ælfred, Caedmon the poet, and many others testify. The H. is still in use in Wales, and occasionally appears in a modern orchestra. A revival of its popularity took place about 1820, but of this few traces are left. Of the several kinds of H. now in use the most important is Erard's, which has given the modern impetus to H.-playing. The compass of this instrument is from

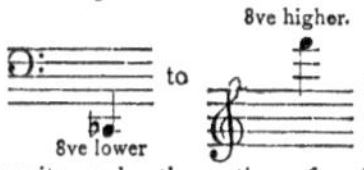

8ve lower — to — 8ve higher. Each string can be altered two semitones by the action of pedals, so that it represents three notes in all.

Harpe, Jean François de la, a French author whose reputation has faded, was born at Paris, 20th November 1739. He lost his parents when young, received a good education by charity, and began a literary life at twenty with a volume of heroic verses, which was followed by the tragedy of *Warwick*, called by Grimm 'the first effort of a young man of sixty.' In spite of its want of force and originality, the play was a success. His other dramas were failures, and after a residence of three years at Ferney in the intimate friendship of Voltaire, he began the more congenial career of a critic in the *Mercure*. *Mélanie or the Nun*, written against forced vows, gained him admission to the French Academy. But his greatest hit was his *Cours de Littérature* at the Lyceum, opened in 1786. He did not know or understand much of classical literature, or of the historical beginnings of French literature. But the authors of the 17th and 18th centuries, and especially the French tragedy as understood by Racine and Voltaire, he expounded with perfect knowledge and considerable force. Of this he printed twelve volumes during his life. The last edition, with additions, contains 18 vols. (1825–26). When the Revolution came, H., who had adopted the philosophical standpoint of Voltaire, welcomed it with enthusiasm. This did not save him from being thrown into prison in April 1794. There he seems to have suffered conversion to Catholicism, and when he came out he was an ardent Royalist. He died at Paris, 11th February 1803. See Petitot's *Memoirs of H.*, and a notice by Daunon.

Har'per's Ferr'y, a village of Virginia, U.S., at the confluence of the Potomac and Shenandoah, 70 miles W. of Baltimore by railway. It is a railway junction, and the seat of a Government arsenal and armoury. Pop. (1870) 2500. H. F. was held for a few hours by John Brown and the Abolitionists in 1859. In April 1861 it was occupied by the Confederates, who, on being forced to retire, destroyed the bridge over the Potomac, the arsenal, and armoury. During Lee's invasion of Maryland, in September 1862, the Confederates compelled it to surrender, and received 12,000 prisoners, 73 guns, 13,000 small arms, besides a large quantity of stores.

Har'pies (Gr. *harpyiai*, 'the snatchers') are in Greek mythology the symbols of the rushing storm-wind. In Homer, who gives the name of one, Podarge, they are swift goddesses, the ravishers of all that disappear without trace. Hesiod mentions Aello and Okypete, the winged and fair-locked daughters of Thaumas and Electra; but afterwards their number grew, and they were represented as winged monsters, half maidens, half birds. In the legend of the Argonauts, they are the tormentors of the blind seer Phineus, who seize and soil his food, until driven away and slain by Zetes and Calais, the winged sons of Boreas; or, as others say, pursued to the Strophades, and there compelled to pledge their oath to leave Phineus in peace. It is there that they are met with in Virgil. In the story of the Argo, however, the H. are personifications, not of the storm-wind, but of foul, omnivorous hunger.

Harpoc'rates (the *Har-pe-chret*, 'the child Horus' of the hieroglyphics), youngest son of Osiris and Isis, was regarded by the Greeks as the god of silence. Among the Egyptians H. was properly only a surname of the young Horus, considered as the rising sun. He was represented as a child, naked, and in a sitting posture, with his finger on his mouth.

Harpoon' (Fr. *harpon*, from *harper*, 'to seize with the nails;' of Teutonic origin), a kind of spear with flattened barbs used for striking whales and other large fish. The H., attached to a long line, is generally thrown from the hand, though gun harpoons, projected from a small swivel cannon fixed in the whaling boat, are also employed.

Harp-Shell (*Harpa*), the popular name given to various species of Gasteropodous mollusca belonging to the family of the whelks (*Buccinidæ*). Of the H.-S. the best-known species are the imperial H.-S. (*H. imperialis*) and the little H.-S. (*H. minor*). They are found in tropical seas, and are distinguished by the regular ridges developed on the outer surface of the shell. The colour of the former is chestnut and white with yellow tints; the latter is darker, and about 1½ inches in length.

Harp'sichord (Ital. *cembalo*, Fr. *clavecin*, Ger. *flügel*), a keyed musical instrument, in shape like a grand pianoforte, whose strings were twanged by pieces of crowquill or hard leather. The date of its invention is uncertain, but it was in use in the 16th c., was introduced into England early in the 17th c., and was manufactured here in the 18th c. principally by Kirkman, Broadwood, and Schudi. Important music was written for it, *e.g.*, by Händel. In its most improved form it could give forth differences of tone, but was deficient in the *shading* of loud and soft into each other. See PIANOFORTE.

Harpy Eagle (*Thrasætus harpyia*), also known as the crested eagle, inhabits S. America, and attains a size even exceeding that of the Golden Eagle (q. v.). The feathers of the head and neck form a ruff or crest, which under excitement is capable of being raised or erected, and entirely changes the aspect of the bird. The general colour is a very dark slate grey, the under parts being white, and the tail barred with black and grey. The crest itself is grey, the feathers having black tips. The H. E. is very rapacious, killing and carrying off young deer, sheep, and smaller animals. The wings have their fourth, fifth, and sixth quills longest, and the talons are especially powerful.

Har'quebus. See ARQUEBUS.

Harr'ier, a collective name applied to various species of Raptorial birds nearly allied to the sparrow-hawks, but included in a special sub-family—that of the *Circinæ*. Their characters are found in the wavy form of the bill-margins, and in the large oval nostrils hidden by feathers. The third and fourth quills are the longest. The tail is long and rounded. The outer toe is longer than the inner, and the claws are long and slender. These birds are distributed throughout the world. The common or hen H. (*Circus cyaneus*) is found in Britain, and is the enemy of small field animals, of lizards, snakes, frogs, &c. The general colour is an ashen grey; the hinder parts are white; the toes, beak, and cere yellow. The average length is 18 inches, but the females are somewhat larger, and of darker colour. The marsh H. or moor buzzard (*C. æruginosus*) is a second species. Its plumage is grey, and it attains a length of 2 feet. Jardine's H. (*C. Jardinii*), inhabiting Australia, has the under surface spotted with white on a chestnut ground.

Hen Harrier.

Harrier, a variety of dog, so named from its being generally used in the pursuit of the hare. It is very closely allied to the foxhound, many authorities regarding it as simply a foxhound of small size. The average height is 17 or 18 inches, and the colours are generally of the boldly-marked nature seen in the foxhound. The scent of the H. is keen.

Harr'ington, James, an English political author, the son of Sir Sapcotes H., was born in Rutlandshire in January 1611. Educated at Oxford under Chillingworth, he visited several of the European courts, and became the intimate friend of Elizabeth of Bohemia and the Prince of Orange. After the execution of Charles I. he withdrew into private life to think out a political system for England, and in 1656 published his rigorously republican romance, *The Commonwealth of Oceana*, which he dedicated to Cromwell. H.'s leading idea is that political power is necessarily founded on property in land. Hence the whole people should practically be the landlords. Olphaus Megaletos (Cromwell) appears as Lord Archon of Oceana, 'the sea-girt isle.' The whole people is divided into freemen and servants, and government carried on by a council of fifty, deliberating by ballot, which is also used in the election of clergy, local judges and officers, deputies, &c. The *Oceana*, abridged into the *Art of Lawgiving* (1659), was the subject of discussion at the Rota Club, formed by H., of which Cyriac Skinner, Milton's friend, was a member. In 1661 he was thrown into the Tower, and in spite of *Habeas Corpus* detained prisoner at St. Nicholas Island, Plymouth, on a charge of treasonable practices, but was afterwards released. He died 11th September 1667. Montesquieu has reproached H. with building air-castles instead of studying the noble constitution of his country. The best edition of H.'s works is that of Hollis (1771). See the *Life of H.* (1700) by Toland.—**Sir John H.**, an English poet, born in 1561, died in 1612, is known as the translator of the *Orlando Furioso* (1591), and the author of the *Metamorphosis of Ajax* (Lond. 1596, new ed. 1814), and of the *Epigrams* (Lond. 1615).

Harr'is, a parish of Scotland, comprising the S. portion of Lewis (q. v.), and the islets Taransay, Scarpa, Pabbay, &c.

Harris, James, an English philologist, was born at Salisbury, 20th July 1709. His mother was Lady Elizabeth Cooper, sister of Lord Shaftesbury. After studying at Oxford, he devoted most of his leisure to the classics, entered Parliament in 1761 for Christchurch, held some Government posts, became Comptroller to the Queen, and died 22d December 1780. His chief work is the now almost forgotten *Hermes, or a Philosophical Inquiry concerning Language and Universal Grammar* (1751). Sentences he divides into forms of assertion and forms of command. Words are significant either by themselves or by relation. These give him nouns and verbs on the one hand, and articles and conjunctions on the other. Along with verbs, he takes adjectives and participles, and translates a good deal of unintelligible matter from Aristotle about the 'latent parts' and the 'supposed affections' of verbs. Conjunctions, he says, are void of meaning, and language itself he puts on the basis of an 'original compact.' It is obvious that this book is without scientific value. *Hermes* was preceded by *Essays on the Fine Arts and Happiness*, and followed by *Philosophical Arrangements*, the first part of a work on Aristotle's logic, and by *Philological Inquiries*. His Life, by his son, Lord Malmesbury, is prefixed to the edition of his works in 1801.

Harr'isburg, capital of Pennsylvania, U.S., lies on the E. bank of the Susquehanna, 60 miles from its mouth, and 106 W.N.W. of Philadelphia by railway. It is the junction of five railways, the terminus of the Pennsylvania Canal, and a great depôt for lumber *viâ* the Susquehanna, which is here spanned by three railway bridges and a carriage one, each over a mile long. Besides handsome state buildings in the midst of a fine park, H. has thirty-eight churches, a state library of 40,000 volumes, an opera-house, a lunatic asylum, three daily and six weekly newspapers, &c. It is the seat of a Roman Catholic bishop. The chief industrial establishments are Bessemer steel-works, blast-furnaces, ironworks, cotton, flour, and saw mills, and broom factories. Pop. (1870) 23,104. H. was settled by John Harris in 1733.

Harr'ison, John, an English mechanician, was born at Faulby, Yorkshire, in 1693. He made many improvements in watchmaking, and is specially celebrated as the inventor of the *compensation curb* and the *gridiron pendulum*, which modify and lessen the effects of varying temperature upon the rate at which the timepiece goes. His *going fusee* and *remontoir escapement* were also important improvements in horology. H. was the first who constructed a chronometer for determining longitude, which, after two successful voyages to Jamaica (1761–64), obtained for him the Government award of £20,000. He died in London, March 24, 1776.

Harrison, William Henry, ninth President of the United States, was the third son of Governor Benjamin Harrison, and was born at Berkeley, Virginia, 9th February 1773. When nineteen years of age he entered the army, and distinguished himself in the frontier wars with the Indians, resigning his commission in 1797. From 1801 to 1812 he acted as Governor of Indiana, when he was appointed brigadier, and subsequently major-general in command of the north-western frontier. He became a senator in 1824, and was the unsuccessful Whig candidate for the Presidency in 1836. In 1840 he was elected President by 234 votes against 60 for Mr. Van Buren, but only lived to reign at the White House for one month. He died on 4th April 1841 from illness brought on by excitement and fatigue.

Harr'ogate, a town in Yorkshire, England, beautifully situated in Knaresborough Forest, near the river Nidd, 3 miles S.W. of Knaresborough, and 15½ N. of Leeds by railway. It is a fashionable spa, with many sulphurous, saline, and chalybeate springs, pleasure grounds, baths, hotels, &c. The visitors are said to number 40,000 annually. The springs, discovered in 1571, were minutely reported on by Professor Hoffmann in 1854. The former villages, Low and High H., the latter 596 feet above the sea and commanding a splendid view, are united by what is now called Central H., consisting of lines of modern houses. Pop. (1871) 6843.

Harr'ow (Old Eng. *hyrwe*, 'anything that *tears up*'), an agricultural implement consisting of a series of long iron teeth or tines set in a strong wooden or iron framework, and so arranged that, when dragged over the ground, each tine makes a separate groove or rut. The H. is used principally for covering over seed after it has been sown in ploughed land, and being dragged across the ploughed ridges it at once smooths the ground and disposes the seed roughly in lines corresponding to the depressions between the ridges. A drill-H. is a two-handed implement with strong curved tines for pulverising and cleaning between the furrows of green crops. A grubber is an implement of a similar nature to the drill-H., employed for pulverising ploughed or fallow land previous to depositing seed therein.

Harr'ow-on-the-Hill, a town of Middlesex, England, on an elevation commanding a view over thirteen counties, is 11 miles N.W. of London by railway. Its church of St. Mary has a square embattled tower visible for many miles, and contains the tombs of Sir Samuel Garth, John Lyon, the founder of H.-on-the-H. school, &c. It is gas-lit and has a good water supply. Pop. (1871) 4997. H.-on-the-H. is chiefly notable on account of the famous grammar-school founded here and endowed by John Lyon, a wealthy yeoman, in 1571, for the education of poor boys of the parish, but which has developed into one of the most famous higher-class schools in the kingdom. The many modern additions have been kept strictly in harmony with the original brick Elizabethan building. An elegant school chapel was built from designs by Sir G. G. Scott in 1859. In 1877 the school had twenty classical masters, including the head-master, the Rev. Dr. Montagu Butler, and over 500 pupils. There are ten scholarships at Oxford and Cambridge, the annual value of which is £625. Among illustrious Harrovians are Dr. Parr, Sir William Jones, Richard Sheridan, Lord Byron, Sir Robert Peel, and George Canning.

Harry, Blind, or **Henry the Minstrel,** a Scottish author of the 15th c., who about 1470 wrote *The Adventures of Sir William Wallace*, which he pretended was based on a Latin life of Wallace by his chaplain Arnold Blair. Almost our only knowledge of B. H. is derived from a passage in Joannes Major's Latin *History of Scotland.* He is mentioned in the Treasury accounts of the King as an occasional recipient of the royal bounty, the last of these notices occurring in January 1492. It is therefore improbable that he survived the close of the 15th c. The oldest existing transcript of the poem bears the date 1488, and curiously enough neither it nor the first printed editions (1520 and 1570) say who was the author. It was repeatedly reissued in the 17th c., and was immensely popular. In the 18th c. Hamilton of Gilbertfield executed a modernised version (1722), which kept alive the national enthusiasm. Burns says, 'The story of Wallace poured a Scottish prejudice into my veins, which will boil along there till the floodgates of life shut in eternal rest.' The work, generally rough and bold in style, is in no sense whatever historical. Its animosities are those of the 15th, and not of the 13th c. Admitting that the poem abounds with evidence of topographical knowledge, and that the wandering minstrel had gathered from every nook and corner of the land the romantic traditions of a heroic life, it must still be pronounced in its great outlines a tissue of wild fiction, told with a somewhat blatant energy of patriotism, and marked by a coarse and even ludicrous zest for bloodshed and revenge.

Hart. See STAG.

Hart, Solomon Alexander, R.A., an English artist, born at Plymouth in 1806, became a student in the Royal Academy in 1823, worked first as a miniature painter, but afterwards devoted himself to oil-painting, and soon gained a wide reputation. He was made A.R.A. in 1835, R.A. in 1840, Professor of Painting in the Royal Academy in 1857, and librarian to the Royal Academy in 1868. Among his works are 'The Elevation of the Law' (1830); 'Wolsey and Buckingham' (1834); 'Cœur-de-Lion and the Soldan Saladin' (1835); 'Milton Visiting Galileo in Prison' (1847); 'The Three Inventors of Printing' (1852); 'Lady Jane Grey in the Tower' (1860).

Harte, Francis Bret, an American novelist and poet, born in Albany, New York, on 25th August 1839. In 1854, while the gold fever was raging, he went to California, and, mining, teaching, and travelling, there gleaned that ripe experience of life which characterises his works. After three years' wanderings, he settled down as a compositor in the office of the *Golden Era*, San Francisco; and some happy original sketches put into type by himself attracting the attention of the proprietor, he was transferred to the literary department of that journal. From 1864 to 1870 he acted as Secretary to the United States Mint in San Francisco, and during this time *John Burns of Gettysburg, The Society upon the Stanislaws*, &c., appeared in Californian newspapers. In July 1868 H. started the *Overland Mail*, in which his best works appeared. Of these, the best known are *The Luck of Roaring Camp, The Outcasts of Poker Flat, Tennessee's Partner*, and *Plain Language from Truthful James, or The Heathen Chinee.* A volume of clever parodies, *Condensed Novels*, was published in New York in 1867, republished in Boston in 1871, and it has since been followed by four new volumes of the same kind. In 1870 H. was appointed Professor of Modern Literature in the University of California, but he resigned his appointment with the editorship of the *Overland* in 1871, when he removed to New York. *East and West Poems* appeared in 1871, *Poetical Works Illustrated* in the same year, *Select Poems* in 1874, *Gabriel Conroy*, a novel, and in 1876 *Thankful Blossom*, a tale. His style is terse, but often abrupt, and his tales abound in graphic descriptions. His colours are dashed on with a bold and powerful brush, and with a few skilful strokes he produces grand effects. The characters of his stories are rough and rugged as the land in which they move, but they stand out in fresh, true realism—outcasts, vagabonds, adventurers—their human weaknesses not blinked, but their human virtues tenderly revealed. Unknown a few years ago, he is now widely read in French and German, and M. Deutzon, in the *Revue des Deux Mondes*, has given an elaborate analysis of his powers.

Har'tebeest, a Dutch name given to several kinds of antelopes, of which the most typical example is the H. (*Alcephalus Caäma*) of S. and Central Africa. The genus to which it belongs is distinguished by horns of a lyrate shape, which are thick at the base and bent acutely backwards at their tips. The muzzle is broad, and the 'muffle' small. The colour is a greyish brown, and the animal may be readily known by a large white patch on the haunches, and a black mark on the cheek. The average height is about 5 feet. The bastard H. (*Damalis lunatus*) is of reddish-brown colour, and has simple lyre-shaped horns, widely separated at the tips. It inhabits districts near the tropic of Capricorn.

Hart'ford, the capital of Connecticut, U.S., on the W. bank of the Connecticut river, and 60 miles from its mouth, 111 N.E. of New York by railway. It is a great railway centre, has daily steamboat communication with New York, and freight lines to Philadelphia, Baltimore, and Albany, besides some 200 sailing craft in the coasting trade. In 1873, after years of controversy, and after sharing the honour with New Haven, it was made sole capital of the state, and a grand state legislative building of white marble was erected at a cost of 2,500,000 dollars. H. is the seat of Trinity College (Episcopal), founded in 1823, and of a Roman Catholic bishopric, and has, among many other churches, the first Congregational Church in New England (1638), a library of reference of 25,000 volumes, a free library of 25,000, an athenæum, an arsenal, a lunatic and a deaf and dumb asylum, a picture gallery, three daily newspapers, &c. The leading business is insurance, the gross assets of its ten companies being 14,420,411 dollars. Two offices have granite buildings that cost 750,000 dollars each; the cost to the companies of H. by the fires of Chicago and Boston alone (1871–72) was 12,000,000 dollars. Among the chief manufactures are firearms, silks, tobacco, cottons, carriages, machinery, boilers, &c. The Colt's firearms works (capital, 1,000,000 dollars) are confined within a dyke 1½ miles long, 32½ feet high, and 50 feet wide at its base, reclaiming 123 acres from the overflow of the river. Pop. (1870) 37,743. H. was settled in 1635, and named after Hertford in England, the birthplace of Rev. Samuel Stone, a Congregationalist. It had the first written constitution in America, of date 1639; and the first code of laws was drawn up here, reducing the criminal offences (160 in England) to fifteen, in 1650. In 1662 Charles II. granted the colony a charter, secreted for safety (1687–89) in the hollow of an oak, which hence came to be called 'the charter oak,' and gave to H. the name of 'charter oak city.'

Hartford Convention was an assembly at H. (15th December 1814 to 5th January 1815) of several leading citizens of Federal politics nominated by the Legislatures of Massachusetts, Connecticut, and Rhode Island, and opposed to the war with Great Britain of 1812–15, for the purpose of proposing the amendment of defects in the constitution disclosed by the condition of things in New England during the war. They were held to be treasonably contemplating a dissolution of the Union, and subsequently incurred much unmerited obloquy. Theodore Dwight, secretary of the Convention, published its journal with a sketch of the time in 1833.

Harth'acnut, later **Hardicanute,** King of England, was the son of King Cnut and Emma of Normandy, widow of Æthelred II. Being absent in Denmark on Cnut's death, H. became King of Denmark, and in 1040 he succeeded his brother Harold as King of England. During his short reign he indulged in brutal murder and sensuality, dug up his brother's body and cast it into a marsh, and provoked a revolt at Winchester by burning the town. He died in 1042, 'as he stood at his drink in the house of Osgod Clofa at Lambeth.' With him the Danish dynasty in England came to an end.

Hart'lepool, a seaport of England, in the county of Durham, on the N. side of a small headland forming the Bay of H., opposite W. H., 4 miles N. of the Tees estuary, 20 E.S.E. of Durham, and 10 N.E. of Middlesborough by railway. It has a good harbour, extensive docks, iron-shipbuilding yards, ironworks, puddling furnaces, brass and iron foundries, mast and block lofts, sawing and planing mills, &c. It is supplied with hard water for domestic use by tapping the springs in the magnesian limestone upon which the town is built, and with soft for industrial purposes by the rain stored in reservoirs at Hart, 3 miles distant, capable of holding 25,000,000 gallons, and now being enlarged. Besides several churches, one a fine specimen of Norman architecture, recently restored, H. has a townhouse of brick and stone in the Italian style, built in 1866, and covering a market 300 feet square. Its trade is chiefly in the export of coal and coke, cottons, woollens, machinery, &c., and in the import of timber, grain, flax, cattle, cheese, spirits, &c. In 1875 there entered the ports of the two Hartlepools 2208 vessels of 525,637 tons, and cleared 5170 of 964,528 tons. Pop. (1871) 13,166. H. is said to derive its name from the pool or slake of Hart (Nor.-Fr. *Hart-le-pol*), into which flows a rivulet or beck, called by Bede 'Hart's Water.' Its first charter was granted by King John. The Bruces of that period were largely interested in H. Robert Bruce, who was claimant with Baliol to the Scottish throne, enclosed the town and built a wall round the haven.—**West H.** lies on the S. side of the bay, 1 mile distant from H., with which it is united by railway. The docks extend between the two towns, and are the property of the North-Eastern Railway Company, who are now constructing extensions. The area of the present docks (1877) is 32¼ acres, and the new docks 34 acres, making 66¼ in all, besides timber ponds covering 132¼ acres. W. H. was founded by Ralph Ward Jackson, a railway speculator, in 1847, rapidly grew, and now has a similar and more extensive trade than old H., as well as greater industries. The official trade-returns of the two ports are given jointly under H. The two Hartlepools, with the adjacent Throston, Stranton, and Seaton Carew, send one member to Parliament. Pop. (1871) 26,804.

Hart'mann, Von der Aue, or **Von Aue**, one of the German Minnesänger, was born in Suabia about 1170, joined Friedrich Barbarossa's crusade in 1189, and died between 1210 and 1220. Among his works are *Erek* (ed. by Haupt., Leips. 1839; trans. by Fistes, 1851); *Iwein* (ed. by Benecke and Lachmann, Berl. 1827; trans. by Baudissin, 1844); *Gregor auf dem Steine* (ed. by Lachmann, Berl. 1838; trans. by Fistes, 1851); *Der arme Heinrich* (ed. by W. Müller, Gött. 1842; trans. by Simrock, 1830), which tells the same story as Longfellow's *Golden Legend; Lieder und Büchlein* (ed. by Haupt., Leips. 1842). His poems are mostly adaptations of Breton legends; they are pathetic, simple, and melodious. An edition of his writings was issued by Bech in 1869.

Hart'ley, David, an English philosopher, the son of a Yorkshire clergyman, was born August 30, 1705. He studied at Cambridge for the Church, but not being able to sign the Articles, became a physician, and practised successively at Newark, Bury St. Edmunds, London, and Bath, where he died, August 25, 1757. His uneventful life was marked by piety and benevolence. In 1748 H. published his *Observations on Man—his Frame, his Duty, and his Expectations* (2 vols.), the theory of which he had suggested in *Conjecturæ quædam de Sensu, Motu, et Idearum Generatione*. The possibility of deducing the intellectual pleasures and pains from associations had been first maintained by Gay in a dissertation prefixed to Law's translation of King *On the Origin of Evil*. Newton, at the end of the *Principia*, and in the questions annexed to his *Optics*, had hinted that vibrations of an ether might be a cause of sensation. Premising that the *white* medullary substance of the brain, spinal marrow, and nerves are the instruments of sensation and motion (physiology now regards the *grey* matter as the immediate organ), H. argues that external objects cause continuing vibrations of the infinitesimal medullary particles of nerve and brain, which are propagated by an ether penetrating the pores of the nervous substance. He even supposed there might be an infinitesimal elementary body intermediate between the soul and the gross body. All this remained, like the 'vibrations' of Descartes, and the 'transformed sensations' of Condillac, the rudest hypothesis. H. knew nothing of the length or duration of the objective vibrations, on which the sensations of light, sound, and heat have now been ascertained to depend, and he did not even imagine a law of nervous vibration, according to which the simplest mental operation might physiologically be explained. Accordingly the theory is omitted from the abstract of the observations by Dr. Priestley. The real psychological value of the work lies in the application to some of the lower processes, called automatic and secondarily automatic, of the principles of association already enunciated by Hobbes and Locke. This is done with a simplicity and vigour of style which has fascinated many, notably Coleridge, who used to sleep with the book under his pillow.

Hart'mann, Edward von, a retired officer of Prussian cavalry, and author of the most paradoxical and popular of recent metaphysical systems. H. was born in Berlin, 23d February 1842, was disabled by an accident from entering on active military service, and devoted himself to philosophy in 1864. The *Philosophie des Unbewussten* ('Philosophy of the Unconscious'), to which H. owes his fame, appeared in 1869, and in 1874 had reached a sixth edition. H.'s system is strictly monistic, the basis, principle, or cause of the universe being regarded as unconscious spirit, with the attributes of will and ideation. Both attributes attain to consciousness only in the animal world. With Schopenhauer H. is convinced that the universe contains upon the whole much more evil than good, and that it were much better that the universe did not exist. In so far H. is thoroughly pessimistic; but he declines to affirm that ours is the worst of possible worlds. On the contrary, the teleological perfection which an unconscious providence has brought about goes far to prove that this is the best of *possible* worlds. Still, man's chief end is to hope for, and to strive, according to prescribed methods, towards the extinction of existence, towards the blessedness of *Nirvana*. Like Schopenhauer, with whose system H.'s has the nearest affinity, H. has the deepest contempt for 'professor-philosophy,' and the professors are in return agreed that H.'s system is but dillettanti philosophising. H. has also, though an adherent of the development theory, written against the mechanical aspect of Darwinism; and as an advocate of a return to a purified Brahmanical faith, published a work on the *Selbstzersetzung des Christenthums* ('Self-Dissolution of Christianity,' 2d ed. 1875). His *Gesammelte Studien und Aufsätze-gemeinverständlichen Inhalts* began to appear in Berlin in 1876.

Harto'gia, a genus of Dicotyledons belonging to the natural order *Celestraceæ*, represented by one species (*H. Capensis*) found in S. Africa. It is a small shrubby tree, the wood of which is often used for veneers at the Cape of Good Hope. The genus is named in honour of Hartog, a celebrated Dutch traveller.

Harts'horn, or **Spirits of Hartshorn**, is still employed to designate a solution of Ammonia (q. v.). The name is derived from the solution having been formerly prepared by distilling shavings of horn.

Hart's-Tongue, a species of *Scolopendrium*, a genus of Ferns (q. v.) characterised by their simple tufted fronds. They are highly ornamental plants. There are about a dozen known species—one, *S. vulgare*, is British—of which there are innumerable varieties cultivated.

Hart's-Tongue (*Scolopendrium*).

Hartz'enbusch, Juan Eugenio, a dramatic author of German descent, born at Madrid, Spain, September 6, 1806. He was educated by the Jesuits, but gave up the Church for literature, working also as a carpenter until 1835, when he was placed as a reporter on the staff of the *Madrid Gazette*. He afterwards held a post in the royal library, Madrid, and was made president of the theatrical council in 1852. He has produced many dramas, of which the chief are *Doña Mencia* (1838); *La Redoma Encantada* (1839); *La Visionaria* (1846); *Alfonso el Casto* (1841); *Primero Yo* (1842); *La Coja y el Encogido* (1843); *La Madre de Pelayo* (1846); *La Archiduquesáta* (1854); *Vida por Honra* (1854); *El mal Apostol y el buen Ladron* (1860). His plays are original, imaginative, and vigorous in language, imitating the ancient dramatists without being frigid or affected. H. has also produced excellent editions of Molina (12 vols. 1839–42); Calderon (1849–51); Alarcon (1852); and Lope de

Vega (4 vols. 1853). More recently he has published *Cuentos y Fabulas* (2 vols. 1861); *Obras de Encargo* (1864); and *Obras Escogidas* (1865).

Hârun' al Rash'îd ('Aaron the Just'), the most famous of the Abbasides, and the second son of the Calif Mohammed Mehdi, was born at Rei, Persia, in 765. He was trained to arms from his youth, and while still in his minority took part in several military expeditions. In 781, when only sixteen, he attacked the Byzantine empire, and forced the Empress Irene to pay a yearly tribute of 70,000 gold dinars. On the death of his elder brother Hadi in 786, he succeeded to the califate, and thenceforth intrusted the control of his dominions, which spread from Khorassan to Egypt, to the Barmecides Yahya and Giaffar, who ruled with great energy and wisdom, maintaining H.'s empire in prosperity and order. H. is specially famous for his patronage of literature, science, and art. He fostered commerce and industry, bestowed great attention to the teaching and practice of medicine, founded a university at his capital, Bagdad, and made that city a brilliant centre of learning and poetry. He forced the Emperor Michael III. to pay a yearly tribute of Greek books, and it is said that during his reign camels laden with volumes entered Bagdad daily. He kept up a political relation by means of Jewish ambassadors with Karl the Great, to whom, according to a rather dubious story, he sent the keys of the Holy Sepulchre, along with an elephant and a wonderful clock. During his later years he became capriciously jealous of the Barmecides, whom he caused to be massacred in 803, not sparing even his favourite, Giaffar. On the deaths of these wise administrators his affairs were plunged into confusion, revolts broke out, and H., while marching against the rebels of Khorassan, died of apoplexy at Tus in 809. The glory which encircles his name is partly fictitious. His character was blemished by avarice, cruelty, and indolence, and much of his fame is due to the *Arabian Nights*, which represents him as a generous, good-humoured sovereign, pursuing romantic nocturnal adventures in the streets of Bagdad. See D'Herbelot's *Bibliothèque Orientale*, and Gibbon's *Decline and Fall of the Roman Empire.*

Harus'pices (sing. *haruspex*, containing the root *spec*, 'behold,' in the second part, the first being akin to Lat. *hira*, Sansk. *hirâ*, Old Norse, *gar-nir*, all meaning 'the entrails,' and also to Lat. *harviga*, 'a sacrificial ram'), or **Extispices**, those who practised *haruspicina* or divination from signs in victims' entrails (*exta*), an art originally derived from Etruria. The H. also took cognisance of uncommon natural phenomena (*portenta*), as thunder and lightning. Though inferior to the Augurs (see AUGURIES and AUSPICES) in estimation and importance, they were recognised by the state. During the Empire they kept in vogue the Chaldean astrology. Claudius particularly favoured them, forming their class into a regular *collegium*. They were, however, in 419 abolished by a law of Honorius directed against all soothsayers (*Mathematici*).

Har'vard University, the oldest and most important educational institution in the United States, is situated at Cambridge (q. v.), in Massachusetts, 3 miles W. of Boston. As early as 1636 the general court of the colony of Massachusetts Bay voted £400 for the purpose of founding a college. In 1639, John Harvard, an English Nonconformist clergyman, bequeathed upwards of £800 and his library of 300 volumes; and in the following year was opened *Harvard College*. The college was incorporated by charter of 1650. In 1873 the vested funds of the university amounted to 2,750,000 dollars, besides its grounds, libraries, buildings, &c. It is under a board consisting of the president, treasurer, and thirty others elected by the graduates for a term of six years; has forty-six professors, twenty-five assistant professors, twenty-three tutors and instructors, and some 1200 students; is unsectarian and (since 1865) independent of the state. Voluntary courses of study are allowed after the first year. The buildings comprise nine dormitories, with 400 rooms, various class-rooms, laboratories, a general library (150,000 volumes, 100,000 pamphlets), a chapel, and a memorial hall erected by subscription in 1874. The medical school (founded 1782) is connected with Boston hospitals. Other professional schools are those of theology (founded in 1812), with a special library of 16,000 volumes; of law (1817), with a library of 15,000 volumes; and of science (1847), the gift of Abbot Lawrence of Boston, with which has been connected a school of mining and practical geology since 1865. The Agassiz zoological museum (1859) has a library of 12,000 volumes. There is also a botanic garden and herbarium, an astronomical observatory (1846), a department of agriculture (the 'Bussey Institution'), and a Peabody archæological museum.

Har'vest (Old Eng. *hærfæst* and *harfest*, Low. Sc. *hairst*, Ger. *herbst*, 'autumn;' probably connected with Gr. *harp*—Lat. *carp*—'to snatch, gather'), the season of gathering in, or reaping corn and grain, or any crop. H. is also applied to the corn gathered in, and that which is reaped.

Harvest Bug (*Leptus autumnalis*) a little mite belonging to the *Acarina* or mite order of the class *Arachnida* (q. v.), common in fields, especially in autumn, and of a dark red colour. It infests plants, rabbits, dogs, &c., and is able to bite so severely that small pustules are formed. The treatment consists in bathing the bitten parts with a weak solution of ammonia, and afterwards using simple oil, or other emollient applications.

Harvest Moon, an astronomical phenomenon observed in our latitudes at the autumnal equinox, when the full moon rises nearly at the same time for several successive evenings. It follows from the fact that the moon's retardation is for all northern latitudes then at its minimum, and at its maximum for all southern latitudes. In March, again, there is minimum retardation in the S. latitudes.

Harvest Spider (*Phalangium longipes*), a genus of Spiders (q. v.) common in fields and gardens in autumn, and distinguished by the great length of the legs, the feet being pointed with a single claw, and the tarsi consisting of from 10 to 15 joints. The cephalothorax or front portion of the body is closely united to the abdomen, the latter region being plaited or folded in a transverse manner. These animals have the singular habit of throwing off one or more of their legs when irritated.

Har'vey, Sir George, a Scottish painter, was born at St. Ninians, near Stirling, in 1805. At an early age he showed a keen taste for drawing; and, studying at the Trustees' Academy, Edinburgh, made great progress in his art. He took much interest in the origin of the Royal Scottish Academy; became an Associate in 1826, and an Academician in 1829, and showed the interest he took in the institution by publishing (1870) *Notes of the Early History of the Royal Scottish Academy.* His subjects were chiefly religious and pastoral. H. was, perhaps, too exclusively national to be adequately admired beyond the Tweed, but no painter has more tenderly expressed the poetry of nature in her grassy solitudes, none has with subtler magic of art revealed the soft mystery of mountain scenery, and imbued his canvas with 'the sleep that is among the lonely hills.' Among his best known works are 'Covenanters' Preaching' (1830); 'Curlers' (1835); 'Battle of Drumclog' (1836); 'John Bunyan in Gaol' (1838); 'Quitting the Manse' (1840); 'Dawn Revealing the New World to Columbus;' 'A Highland Funeral' (1844); and 'The Penny Bank' (1864). He succeeded (1864) Sir John Watson Gordon as president of the Royal Scottish Academy, and was knighted in 1867. He died at Edinburgh, 22d January 1876.

Harvey, William, an illustrious English physician, born at Folkestone, in Kent, 1st April 1578, was educated at Cambridge and Padua, where Casserius and Aquapendente were his teachers, became physician to Bartholomew's Hospital about 1610, and in the Lumleian Lectures for 1615 first suggested his hypothesis of the circulation of the blood. Before this it was thought that the veins distributed blood to the body, that the arteries distributed vital spirits (formed from air and blood), the vapours or *fuligines* being returned to the lungs by the left ventricle. How the blood came to the left side of the heart was the subject of mere guesswork. According to Boyle in his *Treatise on Final Causes*, the idea of circulation was suggested to H. by the form of the valves of the veins. This he followed up by extensive dissections and vivisections, which proved the correspondence between the systole or contraction of the heart and the supply of blood through the pulmonary arteries and the aorta. After describing the return of fœtal blood by the *foramen ovale*, he explained the course of the blood in the adult through the lungs to the left ventricle, thus developing the conception of Galen, and by the simple experiment of ligature demonstrated its return to the heart. These views remained very unpopular till near the end of H.'s life, Parisanus, Riolanus, and other learned men combating them. Besides his *Exercitatio Anatomica de Motu Cordis et Sanguinis* (1628), he published a work on *Generation*, in which he minutely examines the formation of the common fowl's egg, which he took as the universal type of reproduction. H. was appointed physician-extraordinary to James I., and in 1632 physician to Charles I. He attended the latter monarch in the early part of the Civil War, and was made Master of Merton College, Oxford, in 1645. When Oxford surrendered in the following year, many of his MSS. were lost in the disgraceful burning of his house by the Parliamentary troops, and H. withdrew to London. In 1654 he was elected President of the College of Physicians. He died 3d June 1657, and was buried at Hampstead, Essex. A life by Lawrence is prefixed to the 4th edition of H.'s works, 1766. See also Flourens' *History of the Discovery of the Circulation of the Blood.* The best edition is that of Willis, published by the Sydenham Society in 1847.

Har'wich, a seaport and fashionable watering-place of England, in the county of Essex, on a headland, at the point where the estuaries of the Stour and the Orwell unite, 5 miles N. of the Naze, and 65 N.E. of London by railway. It has a good harbour, that is only entered by a narrow channel, marked out by lights and buoys. The coast here is bold and cliffy, and the beach well adapted for bathing. H. has some ship-building, considerable fisheries, and manufactures of Roman cement, artificial manure, sails and tackle, &c. A few years ago the harbour was in danger of being choked by the increase of shingle on the Suffolk coast, but this was avoided by the construction of two groins or jetties, respectively 1350 and 1000 feet long. In 1875 there entered the port 878 vessels of 239,738 tons, and cleared 897 of 223,021 tons. H. is defended by a redoubt with heavy guns and by three martello towers. Its suburb of Dovercourt has a fine promenade and a chalybeate spring, over which stands the Spa House, containing a museum and library. Pop. (1871) 6079. The town seems to have got its name from being the 'wick' or 'vik' where the Danish 'army' had a depot.

Harz Mountains ('the forest mountains'), a congeries of mountain ranges in North Germany, 23 miles wide, 70 miles in length from N.W. to S.E., and occupying an area of about 880 sq. miles, of which 450 belong to Prussia (province of Hanover), the remainder mostly to Brunswick, but partly also to Anhalt. They form the watershed between the rivers Leine and Saale. The most northerly portion, the *Oberharz*, is for the most part wild and dreary, but has valuable mineral treasures. The highest summit, the Brocken, rich in tales of diablerie, is the scene of the Walpurgisnacht in *Faust.* The *Unterharz*, more varied in picturesque beauty, is richly wooded. Both are much frequented by tourists. The minerals include silver, iron, lead, copper, zinc, and arsenic.

Has'drubal ('helped by Baal'), a name of common occurrence in Carthaginian history. The most prominent of the name are—1. The son of Mago, one of the chief founders of the military power of Carthage. He had three sons, Hannibal, Hasdrubal, and Sappho, who, with their three more celebrated cousins, sons of Hamilcar (q. v.), had much to do with Carthaginian affairs. 2. A famous general in the first Punic War, called by Polybius a son of Hanno. He took the field against Regulus 256 B.C., mismanaged the affairs of his country, was virtually superseded by Xanthippus, but never actually deposed. He was totally defeated by the Roman consul L. Caecilius Metellus at Panormus, 250 B.C. 3. The son-in-law of Hamilcar Barca, whom he accompanied into Spain 238 B.C., where he distinguished himself at first by his astute policy and conciliatory manners. He founded Nova Carthago, and did much to consolidate the Carthaginian empire in Spain. After holding the command in Spain for eight or nine years, he was murdered by a slave, 221 B.C. 4. The son of the great Hamilcar Barca, and brother of Hannibal. He was present at the battle in which his father was slain, bore a distinguished part in the second Punic War, opposed the Scipios, conquered Cn. Scipio in Spain 212 B.C., afterwards commanded the Carthaginian army in Italy, and was defeated and slain by the consuls C. Nero and M. Livius at the battle of the Metaurus, 207 B.C. Nothing of the character of H. is known to us. He seems, however, to have possessed all the qualities of generalship for which his family was so distinguished. 5. The son of Gisco, general in Spain in the second Punic War, is first mentioned in 214 B.C. as an auxiliary of Hannibal and Mago. He was defeated along with Syphax by Scipio in Africa 204 B.C., was condemned to death for his ill success, had his sentence reversed on Hannibal's return from Italy, but, finding his enemies implacable, poisoned himself. His head was struck off by the populace and paraded through Carthage in triumph.

Ha'se, Karl August, one of the most venerable of living German theological professors, was born at Steinbach, in Saxony, 25th August 1800, and studied theology at Leipzig, Erlangen, and Tübingen. The share he took in the political movement of the German students in 1822 cost him eleven months' imprisonment in the state prison of Hohenasperg. Since 1830 H. has been attached to the theological faculty of Jena, where his jubilee as professor was celebrated in 1870. H. belongs to the theological school technically termed Æsthetic-Rationalists, but, save in the freedom of thought which he demands, has little in common with the 'vulgar rationalists,' of whom he has always been an opponent. On his theology the influence of Fichte, Schelling, and Schleiermacher is apparent; Christ as the ideal man is the centre of his teaching. Amongst his many works may be mentioned *Lehrbuch der Evangelisch. Dogmatik* (Stutt. 1825, 6th ed. 1870); *Gnosis* (Leips. 1826); *Leben Jesu* (1829, 5th ed. 1865); *Hutterus Redivivus* (Leips. 1828, 11th ed. 1868); *Kirchengeschichte* (Leips. 1834, 9th ed. 1867), and many valuable and delightfully-written monographs, such as *Franz von Assisi* (Leips. 1854); *Geistliche Schauspiele* (Leips. 1858); *Caterina von Siena* (Leips. 1862).

Hashish', is the Oriental name for the flowering tops of the female plant of the *Cannabis Sativa,* from which the resin has not been removed. H. is the *majoon* of Calcutta, the *mapouchari* of Cairo, and the *dawames* or *dawamese* of the Arabs. Dr. Moreau of Tours (*Du Hachisch et de l'Aliénation Mentale,* 1845) describes in highly coloured terms the *real happiness* produced by H., but the use of the drug more frequently produces violent homicidal mania. The writer of this article has seen many cases in which those intoxicated with H. have suddenly rushed out into the streets and market-places with drawn dagger or sword, stabbing and cutting every one whom they met.

Has'lingden, a town of Lancashire, England, on an eminence 20 miles N.N.E. of Manchester by railway. It lies on the border of the Forest of Rossendale, and has a church of St. James, rebuilt in 1780, a handsome townhall, a literary institute of 1861, large cotton-mills, iron-foundries, fulling and sheeting mills, size-works, &c. Near H. are many collieries and stone and slate quarries. Pop. (1871) 7698.

Hasp and Sta'ple, in Scotch law, is the term denoting the old form of entering an heir under Burgage Tenure (q. v.). The heir took hold of the H. and S. of the house door, then entered and bolted himself in.

Hass'an, the chief town of the district of the same name, in the state of Mysore, India, 114 miles W. of Bangalore; pop. (1871) 6305. The *district* of H., which is mountainous, has an area of 3291 sq. miles; pop. (1871) 668,417. The crops are *ragee* (largely exported), rice, tobacco, chillies, and areca nuts. Coffee, introduced in 1843, is now grown on 50,000 acres; every native has a few coffee-trees. There is a fine breed of cattle, used for draught. Brassware of excellent quality is manufactured.

Hass'elt, the capital of the province of Limbourg, Belgium, on the left bank of the Demer, 47 miles E.N.E. of Brussels by railway. It is walled, and has twenty-nine distilleries, large salt-refineries, lace and linen industries, and a trade in madder, tobacco, cattle, &c. Pop. (1874) 11,379.

Has'tings (Old Eng. *Hæstingas, Hæstingaceaster*), a watering-place of England, in the county of Sussex, midway between Beachy Head and Dungeness, and 75 miles S.E. of London by railway. It is situated at the base of high cliffs, which shelter it from the N. and E. winds. The chief industry is fishing, but the boats (some 160) have to be beached for want of a harbour. St. Leonard's-on-Sea, the fashionable western suburb, has sprung into existence since 1828. A splendid 'parade' skirts the beach, and on the summit of the West Cliff, 400 feet above the sea, are the ruins of a castle of unknown antiquity. From Fairlight, 600 feet above the sea, is obtained a view of the Dover cliffs and the coast of France. Pop. (1871) 29,291. In his *Saxons in England*, Mr. Kemble suggests that H. was the fortress of the tribe called *Hæstingas*. A mint was established here by Æthelstan in 924. H. was the landing-place of William the Conqueror in 1066, and there are traces of a supposed Norman camp in the vicinity. The 'battle of H.' was fought on a heath between H. and Battle (q. v.) on the 14th October 1066. In the time of the Confessor, H. was made a Cinque Port, but the harbour was destroyed by a storm in the reign of Elizabeth. It has returned two members to Parliament since Edward III.'s time.

Hastings, a famous viking or sea-rover of the 9th c., born most probably in Denmark, who ravaged the shores of France, Spain, Portugal, and Italy, sailed up the Seine, Garonne, Loire, Tagus, and Guadalquiver, and sacked Rouen, Lisbon, Seville, Spezzia, and many other cities. H. invaded England in Ælfred's reign, but after an unsuccessful struggle of a year in Wessex, was defeated at Benfleet by the Mercian leader Æthelred. He afterwards renewed his plunderings in France. The manner of his death is unknown. Many wild legends were told of him, and it has been held that the exploits of other rovers of the same name have been wrongly attributed to him.

Hastings, Warren, first Governor-General of India, was born 6th December 1732. He belonged to a cadet branch of the ancient family of H. of Daylesford in Worcestershire, which was ruined by the Civil War. Losing both parents at an early age, he was sent by an uncle to Westminster School, where among his schoolfellows were Cowper the poet, Churchill, Colmar, and Cumberland. In 1750 he obtained a writership in the service of the E. India Company, and spent the next few years at Fort William and Cossimbazar (the river port of Moorshedabad), doing purely mercantile work. His political services during the war with Surajah Dowlah brought him under the notice of Clive, who appointed him agent at the court of Meeraffier. From 1761 to 1764 he served at Calcutta as member of council, taking no part in the systematic plunder of the natives which the feeble rule of Vansittart permitted to English servants. On one occasion he was openly insulted on this account, and struck in the face in council. In the latter year he returned to England, where he lived for the next five years. In 1769 he accepted the post of member of council at Madras, and on his way out fell in love with the Baroness Imhoff, whose husband he paid to procure a divorce. Appointed president of the Supreme Council of Bengal in 1772, he found in the fall of the Mussulman minister Mohammed Reza an opportunity of establishing a system of internal administration by English servants. He sold Allahabad and Corah to the ruling family of Oude, and cut down the pension of the Nabob of Bengal. The assistance he gave for a large sum of money to the conquest of the Rohillas was sharply condemned by Clavering, Francis, and Monson, the majority of the new council which, from 1773, acted with H. as Governor-General over all the presidencies. Then began the disgraceful controversy in which Nuncomar and other worthless natives were encouraged to bring charges of corruption against H., while the latter, on the other hand, by his influence with Impey, the Chief Justice, obtained the execution of Nuncomar on a charge of forgery. This event brought back to H. his power and patronage. His London agent, fearing an impeachment, now sent in a formal resignation by his principal. H. denied the authority, obtained from Impey a judgment on his position under the Regulating Act, and, in spite of the opposition of Clavering, continued to act as Governor-General. This was acquiesced in at home, where American troubles had now led to war. When France took up arms, H. lost no time in fortifying the settlements, seizing the French factories, and countermining French influence in the W. and centre by taking a side in a great feud among the Mahratta chiefs. A bribe to Impey ended the claims of jurisdiction asserted over the natives by the supreme court; and H. was able to send Sir Eyre Coote **to Madras** in time to check the victorious advance of Hyder Ali of Mysore. The war expenses he provided for by an arbitrary tribute from Chayte Sing of Benares, whose territory he soon after took by force of arms. The Princesses or Begums of Oude were next robbed of the treasure lying in the 'Beautiful Dwelling' at Fyzabad. Impey was concerned in this, and was soon recalled by Parliament. H., however, retained the confidence of the Company till 1785. In fact he voluntarily resigned, and found on his return to England that both the Company, the Government, and the court were friendly. Burke, however, undertook an impeachment. He was assisted by Fox, Sheridan, Windham, and Grey, in speeches which have become classical. After eight years' trial H. was acquitted of all the charges; but his fortune was ruined by the expenses. Accepting a handsome annuity from the Company, he retired to Daylesford, where he died, 22d August 1818. See Gleig's *Memoirs of the Life of W. H.* (Lond. 3 vols. 1841), and Lord Macaulay's Essay.

Hat, the prevailing head covering of both sexes among civilised races, includes articles of the most diverse material, shape, and construction. As an article of male attire, the principal form is the silk or so-called dress hat, a tall cylindrical structure, which, from an obvious resemblance, is also known as the chimney-pot. Hats of felt and straw are also common head-coverings of the male sex. Ladies' hats run such riot in form and material, that it is impossible to define them. The chief material consists of straw, after which come felt, silk, and fancy materials. The silk hat is the modern substitute for the beaver hat, which, introduced in the reign of Queen Elizabeth, is now entirely superseded. The manufacture is divided into two departments, body-making and finishing. The body or shell is composed of stout calico, prepared with a hard varnish which at once stiffens and renders it waterproof. Pieces of the prepared calico, after it has been dried on a stretching frame, are cut to size and folded round a hat-block of the size and shape of the hat to be made. It is brought into shape by hot-ironing. The finisher cuts out three pieces of plush for the crown, the side, and the upper brim, and the body being coated with varnish, these are neatly fitted on and made to adhere without showing any joints. The whole is then polished and smoothed by hot ironing and 'lureing,' the under brim is covered with merino, the rim is bound and turned over, the interior lined, a silk band put round the body at the junction with the brim, and the hat is ready for use. Innumerable patents for easy-fitting, ventilating, and grease-proofing hats have been taken out, but these are valuable only for advertising purposes. Felt hats are made chiefly of sheep's wool, rabbit and hare fur, and occasionally of the hair of other animals. Mechanical processes are now adopted for felting operations, the details of which vary according as wool or short fur is used for felting. For a simple felt hat, a loose triangular cone of wool or fur, technically termed the 'bat,' has first to be formed. The bat is slightly hardened so as to admit of free handling, by moistening it with steam and pressing it under a piece of leather till it attains some degree of consolidation. It is then 'planked' or felted at the 'battery,' a leaden vessel containing hot water acidulated with sulphuric acid, into which the material is occasionally dipped, while it is rolled and hard pressed on a wooden board till the fibres interlace into a firm texture. The body so formed is stiffened, if hard felt is desired, by dipping in a shellac varnish; it is next dyed, then blocked and drawn into shape. It is now ready for finishing by smoothing with sandpaper, trimming, and lining. The French excel in the manufacture of felts of fine quality. See also STRAW MANUFACTURE.

Hatch, Hatchway. A hatch is the covering of the hatchway or opening in a ship's deck leading to the hold or to a deck below. In a large ship there are the fore hatchway, close abaft the foremast, the main hatchway close before the mainmast, and the after hatchway between the mainmast and the mizen. Hatchways are generally covered with gratings, but in rough weather they are securely battened down to hinder the water from entering between decks.

Hatch'ment (a corrupted form of *Achievement*, a word generally used in the same sense), is a lozen-shaped frame displaying the armorial bearings of a deceased person, which is placed in front of the house, in the church, or on the hearse at the funeral. The H. varies according as the deceased was husband, wife, widower, bachelor, &c.

Hat'field, or **Bishop's Hatfield**, an old town of England, in the county of Herts, on the slope of a ridge between the valleys of the Lea and Colne, 7 miles S.W. of Hertford, and 20 of London by railway. It has a parish church of St. Ethelreda of the 13th c., some silk and paper industries, and militia barracks. In the vicinity is H. House, a fine Elizabethan structure (1605–11), the seat of the Marquis of Salisbury. Pop. (1871) 3998. The palace of the bishops of Ely stood near H. House, and was appropriated with the manor of H. by Henry VIII. It was the temporary residence of Edward VI., of Elizabeth, and of Charles I., and was destroyed by fire in 1835.

Hat Money, or **Primage**, is the small sum besides the freight paid to the master of a ship for his care of the cargo. The amount is regulated by the custom of the port.

Hatras', a town in the district of Allygurh, N.W. Province, British India, 97 miles S.S.E. of Delhi, and 33 miles N. of Agra; pop. (1872) 23,589. It was formerly fortified with a strong citadel, which was bombarded and dismantled by the British in 1817. During the Mutiny of 1857, it was loyally held by the Hindu Rajah, and was a refuge for the Europeans. A light provincial railway is now in course of construction to this town from the main line, 5½ miles distant. H. is the commercial centre for all the neighbourhood, the exports being grain, oil-seeds, cotton, sugar, and ghee. The sugar alone amounts to 6000 tons a year. The imports are iron, piece-goods, and all articles of native consumption.

Hatt'eras, Cape, the E. point of a low angular island, separated from N. Carolina, U.S., by Pamlico Sound, in lat. 35° 15′ N. and long. 75° 30′ W. Shoals extend here far out to sea, and two miles N. of the cape rises a lighthouse, 190 feet high, with a flashing dioptric light.

Hatt'i Sherif' (*i.e.*, 'exalted writing'), the Turkish name for the Sultan's edicts or rescripts, which are irrevocable, are written in Divani, the Arabian court-hand, and are marked by the Tugra or Rishani Sherif, an intricate flourish in black, red, or gold, as a sign of authority. The celebrated H. S. of Gulhane, guaranteeing the life and property of all subjects of the empire, was promulgated by Abdul Medjid in 1839, and renewed in 1856, but has been practically a dead letter. Recent events (1876–77) have not inspired Europeans with increased faith in the value of such documents.

Hatt'o, the second Archbishop of Mainz bearing that name, was consecrated in 968. He is famous in connection with the legend recorded by the Centuriators of Magdeburg, and commemorated by Southey in his ballad, *God's Judgment on a Wicked Bishop.* During a famine H. is said to have shut up a large number of starving poor in a barn, and to have burnt them alive. When their despairing cries were heard, H. is reported to have asked the horrified bystanders whether they heard the mice squeaking. As a punishment, the cruel archbishop was so unmercifully beset with swarms of mice, that to escape them he built the so-called 'mouse-tower' (*Mäusethurm*, perhaps for *Mauth-thurm*, 'toll-tower') near Bingen (q. v.). But even here his persistent enemies found him, and ate him piecemeal.

Hau'berk, was a shirt or tunic of chain-mail, or rather of interwoven steel rings. It had a hood of one piece with it, the sleeves varied in length. See HABERGEON.

Hauch, Johannes Carsten, a great Danish poet, born at Frederikshald, in Norway, 12th May 1790. Coming to Denmark with his father in 1802, H. became a student at Copenhagen University in 1809, and graduated the year following. He became deeply impressed with the poetry of Oehlenschläger, which led to a careful reading of Shakespeare, Goethe, Tieck, Novalis, and Jean Paul, and resulted in the dramas *Contrasterne* and *Rosaura* (1816–17). In the literary war with Baggesen he was a prominent partisan of Oehlenschläger. After 1821 he travelled for six years in France, Germany, and Italy, where he wrote *Hamadryaden* and the tragedy *Bajazet*, and the dramas *Tiberius* and *Gregorius VII.* On his return to Denmark, he was erelong again at war with the poetic successor of Baggesen, J. L. Heiberg. In 1846 he became Professor of Northern Languages and Literature at Kiel; but coming to the capital during the troubles of 1848, he was appointed professor there in 1851. He died at Rome, 4th March 1872. H. is most famous for his novels *Wilhelm Zahern*, *Guldmageren*, *En polsk Familie*, *Slottet ved Rhinen Robert Fulton*, and *Charles de la Bussière*, which appeared from 1834 to 1859. He also wrote several other tragedies of great merit, *Carl V.'s Död* (1831), *Maastrichts Beleiring* (1832), *Svend Grathe* (1841), &c., and his *Lyriske Digte* (1842) is one of the choicest of Danish books. H.'s writings are everywhere tinged with the mysticism of Novalis, and marked throughout by high and pure feeling.

Hauff, Wilhelm, a popular German novelist, whose works very plainly show the influence of Sir Walter Scott, was born at Stuttgart, November 29, 1802, where he died, 18th December 1827. His principal historical romance is *Lichtenstein* (1826); his *Märchen* reached a 9th edition in 1861. H. also wrote *Phantasien im Bremer Rathskeller*, *Memoiren des Satan*, and *Der Mann im Monde* (all in 1827), together with many short tales.

Haupt, Moritz, a philologist, highly esteemed for his labours as an editor of classical texts and of the works of the early German authors. He was born 27th July 1808, at Zittau, in Saxony, studied at Leipsic, and became professor there in 1838. H.'s sympathy with the revolutionary movements in 1848 and 1849 led to his being expelled from his post; but in 1853 he was appointed to the chair in the University of Berlin, vacated by the death of Lachmann, and is a secretary of the Berlin *Akademie.* In the department of classics H. has given editions of Ovid, Horace, Catullus, Tibullus, Propertius, and Virgil. In the native field H.'s most important publications are his critical editions of *Erec* (1839), of *Armer Heinrich* (1842), and of *Guter Gerhard* (1840); he has also superintended new issues of Lachmann's text of the *Nibelungen*, of Wolfram, and of Walther von der Vogelweide. He died in 1874. The first two volumes of his philological *Opuscula* appeared at Leipsic in 1876.

Hau'riant, a term applied in heraldry to the figure of a fish when represented in an upright position, as if rising to the surface to draw breath.

Hau'ser, Kaspar, a remarkable foundling, observed in the streets of Nürnberg in the afternoon of the 26th May 1828. He was then apparently sixteen or seventeen years of age, about five feet in height, and well-proportioned, had a tender skin and delicately fair complexion; he walked with difficulty, and could speak but a few words in the Bavarian dialect. He was taken in charge by the authorities and carefully educated. His intense curiosity and desire to learn, the abnormal acuteness of his sense-perceptions, and his unusual strength of memory decayed in proportion as his knowledge extended. So far as could be learned from H., he had from his infancy been reared in perfect solitude in a dark cave, whence he was never allowed to go out till the day he came to Nürnberg, and had bread and water put within his reach while he was asleep. A mysterious stranger attacked and wounded H. severely in October 1829, but he recovered. He was adopted by Lord Stanhope, and sent to Anspach to continue his education. He was here again attacked and severely wounded in the park, and died three days afterwards, 17th December 1833. By whom or wherefore H. was murdered remains as much a mystery as his parentage. See the works on K. H. by Feuerbach (1832) and Broch (1859).

Hauss'mann, Baron Georges Eugène, the rebuilder of Paris, was born in that city, March 27, 1809. He was educated at the Conservatoire de Musique, and subsequently received a legal training; but his marked administrative capacities brought him under the notice of Louis Napoleon, who in 1853 appointed him Préfet of the Seine. In this office H. displayed the utmost energy and resource; and the works which he undertook by way of developing the natural and architectural beauties of Paris completely changed the aspect of the capital. Public gardens, squares, markets, official buildings, bridges, hospitals, and asylums were all formed under his direction; and among his more important schemes may be mentioned the improvement of the Bois de Boulogne, the prolongation of the Rue de Rivoli, the construction of the Boulevard de Sebastopol, and the formation of about a score of additional boulevards in various quarters in the city. The success of his projects made H. for a time exceedingly popular; and he also stood high in favour at court, being promoted to the rank of Grand Officer of the Legion of Honour in 1856, and Grand Cross in 1862. In 1858 he was created a senator; and he became also a member of the Academy of Fine Arts, and of the Imperial Council of Public Instruction. His magnificent notions, however, could only be realised by an enormous expenditure of money; and as one loan succeeded another, public discontent began to be manifested. After several loans had been exhausted, the Municipality of Paris, by special powers, raised a further sum of 250,000,000 francs in 1865, and another of 260,000,000 four years later. On the formation of the constitutional Ministry under Ollivier (1870), H. was requested to resign his ædileship; and on refusing to do so, was dismissed by an imperial decree. After the fall of the Empire, he left France for a time; but ultimately returned, and became in 1871 Director of the Crédit Mobilier.

Hautbois. See OBOE.

Haüy, René Just, a celebrated French mineralogist, was born at St. Just in Picardie, February 28, 1743. He studied for the Church, in which he took orders, but his life was devoted to science. About 1780–81, a lecture of Daubenton's on mineralogy, which he chanced to hear, turned his attention to crystallography; and from this time till his death he published close upon a hundred memoirs bearing upon this and allied subjects. In 1802 he became Professor of Mineralogy in the Museum of Natural History, and died at Paris, June 3, 1822. H.'s chief works are *Traité de Mineralogie* (4 vols. 1801, 2d ed. 1822–23); *Traité Élémentaire de Physique* (2 vols. 1804, 3d ed. 1821); *Traité de Crystallographie* (2 vols. 1822); besides his memoirs in the *Journal de Physique*, *Annales de Physiques et de Chimie*, *Journal des Mines*, and other scientific periodicals. See Cuvier's *Eloge* before the Académie des Sciences, June 2, 1823.

Havan'a (Span. *La Habana*, 'the haven'), the principal city in the W. Indies, and the capital of Cuba, situated on the N. shore of the island. It is the see of a Roman Catholic bishop, and has a splendid harbour, entered by a strongly fortified channel three-eighths of a mile long, and opening into a basin lined with wharves, and capable of accommodating a thousand of the largest vessels. The massive houses, like those in the S. of Spain, are of only one or two stories, with flat roofs and large windows, shaded by iron shutters or wooden blinds. H. is unsurpassed by any city in the world for its beautiful public parks, shady drives, and promenades, and numerous fountains. An excellent water supply is brought by an aqueduct from Chorrera, distant 7 miles. H. has a university, a cathedral of 1724, the palace of the governor-general, a large opera-house, spacious botanical gardens, various scientific and benevolent institutions, &c. The average temperature in summer is 87° F., in winter 85° F. There are large tobacco industries. In 1873 there entered the port 2194 vessels of 921,632 tons. The exports were chiefly sugar (796,179 tons), molasses (242,308 tons), tobacco leaf (17,442,600 lbs.), and cigars (224,765,000). The imports are codfish, flour, rice, wine, coals, oil, and timber shooks. H. is a railway centre, and communicates by weekly lines of steamers with Spain, France, England, and the United States, and by telegraph with Key West, Kingston, Aspinwall, &c. Pop. 205,676, of whom 138,895 are white, 66,781 are coloured, 29,013 being slaves. H. was founded by the Spaniards in 1511, was taken by the English in 1762, but restored to Spain in the following year.

Hav'el, The, an important tributary of the Lower Elbe, rises about 6 miles E. of Neu-Strelitz in Mecklenburg, and after a circuitous course of 180 miles, joins the Elbe on its right bank a little below Havelberg. The H. is navigable as far as Fürstenberg, and is throughout a great part of its course a chain of lakes. Its importance for the transit trade of a large district is increased by the fact that by means of the Finow Canal, the H. is connected with the Oder. The H. flows past the towns of Spandau, Potsdam, and Brandenburg, and it receives as tributaries the Rhin, the Dosse, and the Spree.

Have'lock, Sir Henry, K.C.B., a hero of the Indian Mutiny, was the son of a merchant, and was born at Bishopwearmouth, in Durham, 5th April 1795. He entered the army in 1815, and served through the Burmese, Afghan, and Sikh wars. After forty years' regimental service and slow promotion, despite his military zeal, he first received an independent command in 1857, when the tidings of the Mutiny brought him from Persia to Calcutta. He was placed by Lord Canning at the head of a movable column, and marched from Allahabad to relieve Cawnpore. He defeated the mutineers, headed by the Nana Sahib in person, in several battles, but arrived at Cawnpore too late to prevent the massacre. He then moved towards Lucknow, which was also besieged, but after eight more engagements was compelled to retire, until reinforced by his old friend and general, Sir J. Outram, whose chivalrous spirit would not allow him to take over the command. H. again advanced and fought his way into Lucknow, only to be himself surrounded until finally delivered by Sir Colin Campbell (Lord Clyde). He died of dysentery, 24th November 1857, at Lucknow, within a few days after the final relief. A pension of £1000 a year was given to his widow, and a baronetcy and a similar annuity to his eldest son, Sir H. Marshman H., who had acted as his father's aide-de-camp, and is now M.P. for Sunderland. A statue was erected by public subscription in Trafalgar Square. His campaign showed great military genius. But what has perhaps most highly exalted him in the eyes of his countryman, is his pure, severe, religious faith. See Marshman's *Memoirs of Sir Henry H.* (Lond. 1860, new ed. 1874). H. himself published histories of the Afghan and Burmese wars.

Ha'ver, a term of Scotch law denoting the holder of a writing who is called on judicially to produce it. The form of process for compelling the holder to produce the writing is by letters of incident diligence. There is no corresponding form in English law, the end being only attainable by summoning the holder as a witness, and telling him in the subpœna that he must bring the writing with him.

Hav'erfordwest, the chief town of Pembrokeshire, and a county of itself, in S. Wales, on the West Cleddau river, in a beautiful hilly district, 8 miles N.E. of Milford, and 275 W.N.W. of London. The river is navigable at spring tides for vessels of 150 tons, but the only manufacture of the town is paper. Its fine church of St. Mary was restored in 1862, and is widely noted for its richly carved timber roof and stalls. The grammar-school has two exhibitions to Oxford. H., with Fishguard and Narbeth, returns one member to Parliament. Pop. (1871) 6622.

Ha'verhill, a city of Massachusetts, U.S., on the N. bank of the Merrimac, 18 miles from its mouth, and 32 N. of Boston by railway. It has boot and shoe manufactures to the value of ten million dollars annually, and also produces hats and woollen goods. On the opposite bank of the river are the thriving towns of Bradford and Groveland, which communicate with H. by two bridges. Pop. (1870) 13,092. H. was settled in 1640, incorporated as a town in 1645, and as a city in 1870.

Ha'versack, the canvas bag in which a soldier on the march carries his rations. It is also used for a case in which the gunner carries cartridges from the ammunition chest to the gun.

Hav're, Le, or **Le Havre de Grâce**, the port of Paris, and next to Marseilles the most important trading place of France in the department of Seine-Inférieure, at the mouth and on the N. side of the Seine's estuary, which has here a breadth of 9 miles. It is 54 miles W.N.W. of Rouen, and 135 N.W. of Paris by rail, and lies at the base of a slight range of chalky hills commanding beautiful views of the sea, the slopes of which are clad with foliage and dotted with elegant villas. A project was announced in 1875 to construct a boulevard along the seashore (1919 mètres) from the pier to the picturesque suburb of St. Adresse. The town is regularly built, has several squares, fountains, and tree-shaded streets, and now extends far beyond the old walls. Among the principal buildings are the sombre church of Notre Dame, dating from the 15th c., the church of St. François, begun under Henri II., the modern Hôtel de Ville, the arsenal, the museum and library (34,000 vols. in 1876), the Palais de Justice, a theatre, new law courts (1875), and an English episcopal church of the Holy Trinity, opened in 1876. Other institutions are schools of navigation and of applied geometry, a chamber of commerce, a lyceum, an observatory, and an English institute and reading-room. The harbour is very accessible, and consists of an *avant-port* of 52 acres, the entrance to which has a depth of 31 feet at spring tides and of 26 at neap tides, and is protected by two long jetties. It has seven wet docks, with a total area (1876) of 126 acres, and 8320 mètres of quays. In 1871 a dry dock, 515 feet long and 112 broad, was opened for the repairing of large steamers. The basin of L'Eure covers 53 acres. In 1876 the works in progress, besides the Eure and Vauban docks, were the large half-tide basin, and the substitution of pivot-bridges for the old-fashioned draw-bridges between the various docks, at an estimate cost of £560,000. In 1875 there entered the port 2728 vessels of 1,408,780 tons; of these, 1211 were British vessels of 565,919 tons. In 1876 there entered 1343 British vessels of 635,291 tons, and the customs receipts were £1,068,455. The imports, chiefly coal, pig-iron, cement, woollens and cottons, machinery, colonial produce, and metal wares, amount in value to £25,000,000; the exports, mainly Paris and Lyon manufactures, wines, spirits, flour, oil, seeds, fruits, chalk, and flints, to £27,000,000 H. transacts one-fifth of the foreign commerce of France, and has direct lines of steam-navigation with New York, Havana, Brazil, La Plata, and all the chief ports of Europe. It has a large Government tobacco factory, much shipbuilding (in 1875 seven steamers of 3284 tons), sugar-refining, papermaking, cotton-weaving, and engineering. Many visitors are attracted in summer by the sea-bathing. Pop. in 1872, 81,785, and in 1876, 92,068. H. was a fishing village in 1509, when Louis XII. began to convert it into a harbour of refuge for the navy. The subsequent silting up of Harfleur determined its importance. It was bombarded by the English in 1694, 1759, and 1794-95, and under Louis XIV. was made the entrepôt for the E. India, Senegal, and Guinea companies. An International Maritime Exhibition was held here in 1868.

Hav'restraw, a town of New York, U.S., on the W. bank of the Hudson River, 38 miles N. of New York by railway. It has extensive brickmaking, large printworks and papermills, and a rolling-mill for copper. Pop. (1870) 6412.

Hawai'i (formerly spelled *Owhyhee*), the largest and most southerly of the Sandwich Islands (q. v.), to which group it gives an alternative name. It lies in the N. Pacific Ocean, and has a length of 800 miles, an area of 4500 sq. miles, and a pop. of 21,480. It is generally mountainous, and attains in Manna Kea an altitude of 13,953 feet, in Manna Loa of 13,760 feet. The sides of the mountains are densely clad with forests, and send down numerous streams to water the rich arable plains. There are two active volcanoes, Kilanea (3970 feet) and Manna Loa, the latter of which erupted destructively in 1868. The centre of the island is occupied by a lava plain, but the coast is encircled by many towns and harbours. The chief town and port is Hilo.

Ha'wash, a river of Abyssinia, rises in the S.W. of Shoa, of which it forms part of the boundary. It has a general north-easterly direction, and enters Lake Aussa, after a course of 350 miles. Habesh, the Arab name of Abyssinia, is probably derived from that of the river.

Haw'finch (*Coccothraustes vulgaris*), a species of Insessorial birds, belonging to the group of grosbeaks. The H. inhabits Britain, and is gregarious. The average length is about 7 inches. The back and upper parts are of a chestnut-brown colour, the wing coverts and tail variegated with black and white, the under parts and breast a light brown, the head of a fawn colour, the chin and throat black. The food consists of berries of all kinds, and the nest is constructed of twigs and mosses. The eggs number from four to six, and are of an olive-green hue, spotted with black. The H. also occurs on the Continent, and on the European borders of Asia.

Haw'ick, a town of Scotland, in Roxburghshire, at the confluence of the Teviot and the Slitrig, 10 miles S.W. of Jedburgh, and 52½ S. of Edinburgh by railway. It is a thriving town, with many fine mansions and villas, and has a handsome exchange built in 1865, several other good buildings, a parish church of 1767 (now St. Mary's), fourteen other churches, part of an old fortress of the barons of Drumlanrig, now built into the Tower Inn, and a moat or mound, supposed to have been the judicial rendezvous of the neighbouring chiefs. H. is one of the great centres for the manufacture in Scotland of tweeds, yarns, hosiery, and plaids. It has (1877) over 650 power looms, 180 hand looms, 88 carding engines, and 900 stocking frames, of which 86 are power frames. The water supply is brought from the Allan, distant 5 miles. Pop. (1871) 11,355. H. is one of the three Border burghs that together send one member to Parliament. Near it rise the towers of Goldielands and Branxholm, the former a unique old Border castle, the latter the ancient ducal seat of the Buccleuchs. On the opposite side of the Teviot lies the manufacturing village of Wilton, which is practically part of H.

Hawi'za, a town in a fertile district of Khuzistan, Persia, 60 miles N. of Bassora, is the principal place under the sway of the Vali of Arabistan. The river Kerkah used to pass through H., but has been diverted thence by a canal; so that H., once a populous town, has decayed till it contains only about 500 houses, occupied chiefly by Arabs.

Hawk, a very general term applied indiscriminately to many members of the family *Falconidæ* or Falcons (q. v.), and to other kinds of raptorial birds. The various species and chief genera of H. are described in special articles, such as GOSHAWK (q. v.), SPARROW-HAWK (q. v.), &c.

Hawk.

Hawk'ers and Ped'lars. Hawkers are itinerant traders. A pedlar is a hawker who deals in trifling commodities. The Pedlars' Act, 1870, now regulates the trade. No one is allowed to act as a pedlar without a certificate, nor is any one to act in any district in which his certificate does not authorise him to act, under a penalty of 10s. for the first offence, and £1 for every subsequent offence. A certificate is to be granted by the chief officer of police of the district to any applicant of good character residing in the district. The certificate is not to cost more than sixpence, and is to be in force for a year. Its authority may be extended by endorsement by other chief officers of police to their respective districts, at a charge of not more than sixpence for each endorsement. An appeal against refusal of certificate can be made to a Justice of the Peace. The license of a H. who uses beasts of burden is valid over the kingdom. The cost is £4 a year for each beast used. He may sell tea and coffee, but not spirits. He must not sell by auction without an auctioneer's license, nor may he sell plated goods without special license. Commercial travellers, sellers in fairs or markets, and book agents, require neither license or certificate.

Hawkes'bury, a river of New South Wales, formed by the junction of the Grose and Nepean rivers. After a very tortuous course of 330 miles it falls into the S. Pacific, 14 miles N. of Port Jackson (q. v.). The H. is liable to tremendous floods, and has been known to rise 97 feet above its usual level. It is navigable by vessels of 100 tons for 140 miles.

Haw'kins, Sir John, one of the 'sea lions' of the Elizabethan period, was born at Plymouth about 1520. The relative of Drake, he was frequently associated with him in naval enterprises, particularly against the Spaniards in 1555; while he fought so well against the Armada that he was knighted in 1558. Magnanimous and generous in many things, as in founding a hospital at Chatham for the relief of poor and disabled seamen, he made a blunder in maintaining, if not initiating, the slave trade. His death took place November 21, 1595.

Hawk'weed, the name given to species of *Hieracium*, a genus of plants belonging to the natural order *Compositæ*. They are perennial hairy herbs with yellow heads of flowers, and are natives of temperate and Arctic regions. Much doubt prevails as to the number of true species, owing to the difficulty of distinguishing them from one another. For the most part they are mere weeds. *H. pilosella* is the common mouse-ear H., and *H. aurantiacum* with orange flowers is called *Grim-the-collier* in England. Formerly birds of prey were imagined to employ H. to strengthen their powers of vision, hence the name.

Hawse (Old Eng. *hals*, 'the neck'), the space directly ahead of a ship, between her anchors and her bow. A ship has a *clear H.* when she is riding with two anchors out and their cables are not crossing; when the cables cross, a ship is said to have a *cross in her H.* To *freshen H.* is to veer out fresh rope at the H.-holes—apertures at the bows through which the cables run.

Haw'thorn (Old Eng. *hagathorn*, 'hedgethorn;' comp. Ger. *hagedorn*), or **White'thorn**, is the *Cratægus oxyacantha*, belonging to the natural order *Rosaceæ* (q. v.). It is a small branching tree or hedge-shrub. The plant is covered in early summer with numerous corymbs of white scented flowers. The fruit, which is usually produced in abundance, consists of small red drupes called 'haws.' It is common in Britain, where it is used principally for Hedges (q. v.). It is found throughout Europe, in Northern Africa, Siberia, Western Asia, and India, and has been introduced into N. America, where there are several other species. H. is the badge of the Clan Ogilvie.

Hawthorne, Nathaniel, the most subtle and original of American writers of fiction, was born at Salem, Massachusetts, July 4, 1804. He graduated at Bowdoin College in 1825, and then resided at Salem, writing tales and articles for magazines, until 1836, when he became editor of the *American Magazine* in Boston. The first series of his *Twice-Told Tales* appeared in 1827, the second series in 1842 and in 1843. He married, and settled in an old parsonage at Concord, Massachusetts, in 1843, where he associated with Emerson, Channing, Ellery, and Thoreau. From 1846 to 1850 he was surveyor of Salem port, and from 1853 to 1857 United States consul at Liverpool. He then travelled in Italy, returned to Concord in 1860, and died at Plymouth, New Hampshire, May 19, 1864. His works include *Twice-Told Tales* (1837 and 1842), *Mosses from an Old Manse* (1846), *The Scarlet Letter* (1850), *House of the Seven Gables* (1850), *True Stories from History* (1851), *The Wonderbook* (1851), *The Blithedale Romance* (1852), *Life of Franklin Pierce* (1852), *The Snow Image* (1852), *Tanglewood Tales* (1853), *Transformation* (1860), *Our Old Home* (1863), *Notebooks* (1868–72), *Septimius Felton* (1872). His tales are marvels of daring, fantastic, and subtle imagination, abounding in wild and occasionally ghastly incidents, wrought out with the most vivid realism and keen analysis of character—H. being unexcelled for the skill with which he blends the supernatural and the commonplace—while the thrilling gloom of the narrative is relieved by the poetic beauty of the descriptive setting. He shares with Washington Irving the praise of being the most exquisite of American prose-writers, his style having scarcely been surpassed for purity, sweetness of cadence, and delicate touches of colour.—**Julian H.**, son of the above, was born in Boston, June 22, 1846, studied at Harvard College and at Dresden, and was an engineer in New York during 1870–72. He has written novels for periodicals, and published *Bressant* (1873), *Idolatry* (1874), both novels, and *Saxon Studies* (1876), bright caustic sketches of German life.

Hay (Old Eng. *heg*, Fr. *hea*, Pl. Deut. *heu, hau*, Dut. *hooi*, Dan. *höe*, Swed. *hö*, Icel. *hey*—perhaps from the same root as the verb to 'hew' or cut down), an important fodder for horses and cattle, consisting of dried grasses frequently mixed with clover or other allied plants. Two kinds of H. may be distinguished in the agriculture of Great Britain: natural or meadow-grass H. and artificial-grass H. In England and Ireland the first of these is the most important, but in Scotland the second is far more common. In the preparation of meadow-grass H., the points to be attended to are the cutting of the grass at the particular stage in its growth when it contains the largest proportion of nutritive matter in a soluble condition, and the drying of it so as to retain and preserve for use the nutritive principles it contains. It is found that the nutritive value of native grasses generally is much greater at the period of flowering than when the seed has ripened and the culm become hard and woody; and in several of the most important species the difference in value is as much as 3 to 1. It is therefore of great importance that the condition of the grasses in this respect should be understood, and that the mowing should take place when the grass is at its richest stage. The weather has a most important bearing upon the drying of H. in fine condition, and it is only with bright sunshine that it can be properly made. In dry sunny weather the H. is tedded or turned in the swathe, then gathered into windrows (in Scotland into small mounds called 'coles' or 'cocks'), and when it is so thoroughly dry that there is no fear of it fermenting or heating when pressed together in bulk, it is ready for forming the haystack or 'sow.' The artificial-grass H. made in Scotland consists generally of Italian ryegrass (*Lolium Italicum*), or perennial ryegrass (*L. perenne*), combined with clover or sanifoin, which latter plants yield an abundant 'aftermath,' generally consumed in the green state. The ryegrass is allowed almost or altogether to ripen its seed before the H. is cut, and, indeed, many farmers thrash out a certain proportion of their H. for the sake of seed for sowing. H., of recent years, has become a very valuable article, and a large quantity, in compressed bundles, is now annually imported from the Continent, especially from the meadow lands of Holland. According to Dr. Lyon Playfair, 100 lbs. of ordinary H. contain 76½ lbs. of dry organic matter or real food, 16 lbs. of water, and 7½ lbs. of ash. New H. contains a much larger proportion of water than old H.

Hay'bote, in English law, is the right which a tenant of land has to take wood 'from it to repair the hedges, gates, and fences upon it.' It also denotes the wood which may be taken to make implements for gathering the hay.

Hay'dn, Franz Joseph, a great German composer, was born at Rohrau, in the duchy of Austria, of poor parents, March 31, 1732. At the age of eight he entered the choir of St. Stephen's Cathedral, Vienna, where he remained till his sixteenth year, when his voice broke, and he lost his situation. He now began to give lessons in music, and in his leisure hours mastered theoretical works by Fux and Mattheson. After a nine years' struggle with poverty, Prince Esterhazy made H. his private chapel-master in 1760. Meanwhile H. had made the acquaintance of the singer Porpora, Wagenseil, and the poet Metastasio. He now lived with the Prince, partly in the country and partly at Vienna, diligently composing for orchestra, opera, and chapel. After Esterhazy's death in 1790, H. visited London twice, viz., in 1791 and 1794, where his genius received an enthusiastic recognition. He died at Gumpendorf, a suburb of Vienna, 31st May 1809. H. wrote 83 string quartets, 118 (published) symphonies, of which 12 were composed for Salomon's concerts in London, 24 concertos for various instruments, 24 trios, 44 sonatas, 163 pieces for the 'baryton' (a sort of violoncello), 19 operas, 15 masses; *Tobia*, an oratorio (1775); *The Creation* (1797–98); *The Seasons* (1801); and various other compositions, sacred and secular, such as the *Seven Last Words of Christ* (1785), and the English canzonets. His greatness appears chiefly in his quartets and symphonies, and in *The Creation* and *The Seasons*. A brilliant joyousness and a happy humour marked both his character and his music. See the *Life of H.* (Lond. 1818), abridged from Carpani's work (Padua, 1812–23), and Griesinger's *Biographische Notizen*.

Hay'don, Benjamin Robert, an English historical painter, was the son of a bookseller, and was born at Plymouth, January 23, 1786. Much against his father's will he resolved to be a painter, and in 1805 entered as a student the Royal Academy, where he was taught by Fuseli and became intimate with Wilkie. In 1807 his 'Joseph and Mary Reposing' was exhibited and sold for a high price, and in 1809 the Academy awarded a first prize to his 'Dentatus,' but H.'s idea that the picture was unfairly hung led to his lifelong rupture with the Academy. He afterwards opened independent exhibitions, began a school of painting—in which Landseer and Eastlake studied—in 1815, and was largely instrumental in inducing the English Government to buy the Elgin Marbles in 1816. He became involved in pecuniary difficulties, and his life was embittered by his excessive ambition, vanity, irritability, and sensitiveness. In 1840 he delivered lectures on painting, which were published in 1844–46. The failure of an exhibition of two of his pictures in 1846 wounded him so poignantly, that, added to his other troubles, it led to his suicide, June 22, 1846. His difficulties were mainly due to himself, as many of his pictures were sold for large sums. Among his works are 'Curtius Leaping the Gulf,' 'Uriel and Satan,' 'Nero Watching the Burning of Rome,' 'The Judgment of Solomon,' 'The Maid of Saragossa,' 'Alexander and Bucephalus.' His works are generally disproportioned and exaggerated, but impressive in design, and warm though somewhat coarse in colour. See *Life of H.* by Tom Taylor (2d ed. 1853), and *B. H., Correspondence and Table-Talk* (1876), edited by his son.

Hayes, Augustus Allen, M.D., an American chemist, was born at Windsor, Vermont, February 28, 1806. H. studied chemistry under Dr. Dana, devoted himself absolutely to that science, and filled various important posts. Among his discoveries is that of the organic alkaloid sanguinaria, which produces most brilliant salts. He has also investigated the properties of chromium, and written on chemical differences in varieties of guano, and the action of sea-water below the surface.

Hayes, Rutherford Birchard, President of the United States, is a descendant of New England Puritans, was educated at Harvard, became a successful lawyer and a vigorous Abolitionist. He served with distinction in the Civil War, rising to the rank of brigadier-general, and was subsequently thrice made governor of Ohio, and twice returned by the state to Congress. A prominent Bepublican, he strongly favours national education, the friendly pacification of the South, civil service reform, and the resumption of specie payments. After nearly four months' delay in attesting the votes, which was finally done by a joint convention of the two legislative Houses, H. was held to be duly elected President, 2d March 1877. See Howell's *Life and Character of H.* (1876).

Hay-Fever, or **Hay-Asthma** (*Catarrhus æstivus*), consists in excessive irritation of the eyes, nose, and the whole of the air-passages, causing paroxysms of sneezing, with a copious defluxion from the nostrils; pricking sensations in the throat; cough and difficulty of breathing, with or without mucous expectoration. H.-F. attacks certain persons only, and always at the same period of the year (and only then), when the grass comes into blossom or when hay-making is going on. If such persons avoid meadows and hayfields, and the neighbourhood of haystacks they escape the malady. It is supposed that the irritation is due to parasites of animal or vegetable origin. The powder of ipecacuanha and the odour of cats produce, in some persons, similar bronchial irritation. The only remedy consists in removal from the exciting cause, by going to those parts of the coast that are barren of grass, or by remaining within doors, and shutting out as much as possible the external air during the hay crop. Excessive symptoms may be relieved by *Belladonna*, *Camphor*, *Indian hemp*, *Lobelia inflata*, and *Stramonium* (q. v.).

Hay'nau, Julius Jakob, Freiherr von, an Austrian general, was a son of the Elector of Hessen, and was born at Kassel, 14th October 1786, entered the Austrian service in 1801, served in the campaigns of 1805 and 1809, but was not conspicuous till 1848, when he held a command in Italy, and crushed the revolt in Brescia (1849) with bloody severity. In May of that year he commanded the artillery of the army in Hungary, stormed Raab, besieged Szegedin, and had a share in the concluding battle of Temesvar. But the wholesale executions ordered by him in Pesth and Arad excited such horror, even in Austria, that he was removed from his command in 1850, and on a visit to London in 1851 he was severely handled by a London mob. He died at Vienna, 16th March 1853. See Schönhals' *Biography of H.* (1853).

Hay'ti (Carib. 'mountainous'), **Hispaniola**, or **Santo Domingo**, next to Cuba the largest of the W. Indian islands, in the Greater Antilles, lies to the S. of the Bahamas, in lat. 17° 36'-19° 59' N., and long. 68° 20'-74° 38' W. Area, 28,000 sq. miles; pop. 850,000, comprising whites, creoles, mestizos, and creole negroes. The Mona Passage, 58 miles broad, separates it on the E. from Puerto Rico, and the Windward Channel on the W. from Cuba and Jamaica, distant 43 and 107 miles respectively. It is 405 miles long from Cape Engaño in the E. to Cape Tiburon in the W., and 165 miles broad from Cape Isabella in the N. to Cape Mongon in the S. Its shape, though irregular, is that of an acute angle with its base in the W., where it is indented by an immense bay, enclosing the island of Gonaive. Other inlets are Samana Bay in the N.E., of great importance to shipping, and the bays of Neyva and Ocoa in the E. The island has a coast-line of 1500 miles, and is traversed by the Cibao mountains, which reach a height of 9000 feet in the peak of Yaque, and with their lateral spurs cover great part of the surface. The mountains, which are clad with virgin forest, descend abruptly on the N., but have a gentle southern slope. Among the characteristic trees are the oak, mahogany, cedar, walnut, ebony, satin-wood, fustic, and wax palm. Everywhere the forests are richly festooned with the twining vanilla, and with a wild vine that yields a muscadel wine. Along the coast and in the valleys are many rich tracts, watered by voluminous streams, as the Yuna, Great Yaque, Artibonite, Ozoma, and Neyva. The rivers are generally swift flowing, turbid, and alive with caymans. Enriquillo, near Neyva Bay, is one of several salt lakes, and has a length of 25 miles. The season of rain and tempests extends from May to July, and in August the heat increases in the daytime to 104° F. in the plains, and to 77° in the mountains. Changes from the dry to the wet season are sudden, accompanied sometimes by hurricanes and earthquakes, and the rivers often overflow, causing great destruction in the cultivated parts. The products are coffee, sugar, cacao, maize, rice, cotton, tobacco, indigo, cochineal, figs, &c. There is no mining enterprise, but H. is rich in minerals, including coal, copper, iron, gold, silver, mercury, salt, tin, jasper, marble, &c.

The island is divided into the republics of H. in the W., and of Santo Domingo in the E. (see DOMINICAN REPUBLIC), the former of which has an area of 1024 sq. miles, and a pop. of about 572,000, of whom three-fourths are negroes and the rest mulattoes, with the exception of 600 Europeans. The constitution of H., dating from 1867, vests the legislative power in a national assembly of two houses, and the executive in a president, to be elected for a term of four years by the people. The language is French, and the state religion is Roman Catholicism. Port-au-Prince (q. v.) is the capital. The finances are sadly entangled by previous misgovernment, and there is besides large foreign loans a vast floating debt, chiefly in depreciated paper money. In late years the estimated revenue has been £1,100,000, and the expenditure £1,700,000. The custom receipts amounted to £893,353 in 1874, and in 1875 the value of the exports, chiefly coffee, raw cotton, mahogany, and logwood, was £1,820,000, and of the imports, mainly manufactured goods from Britain and the United States, £1,250,000.

The island of H. was the second place in the New World visited by Columbus, and received a Spanish colony, which took the name of Isabella, in 1492. To the whole island was given the name Hispaniola, and the new colony of San Domingo, founded in 1496, became a bishopric in 1511. The colonies prospered immensely, but at the reckless sacrifice of the natives, who were made to toil like beasts in the mines, and who only rebelled to incur a swifter death. Although at their entrance the Spaniards had found some 2,000,000 natives, negro slaves had to be introduced as early as 1522; by 1711 there were only 21,000 natives. French buccaneers began to appear on the N. coast of the island in 1630, and formed an independent settlement in 1714. By the treaty of Ryswick (1697) Spain ceded the W. part of H. to the French, under whom it prospered rapidly, having a population in 1792 of 780,000, comprising 40,000 whites, 40,000 half-breeds, and 700,000 slaves. But the conflicting diversity of race, and monopoly of political power by the whites, led to a rupture on the outbreak of revolution in the mother-country. After fierce revolts of the mulattoes and negroes, and inroads of the English and Spanish, all the inhabitants of the colony were declared free and equal in 1793, and the command of the army was given to Toussaint l'Ouverture, who expelled the hostile intruders, and once more restored peace. In 1795, by the treaty of Basel, the Spanish territory was ceded to France. Napoleon I. attempted unsuccessfully to reinstitute slavery in 1801, and San Domingo declared itself an independent republic, 30th November 1803. Dessalines (q. v.), who was chosen governor for life, assumed the fantastic title of Emperor of H., and consequently brought about a long, wasting civil war, ending in almost complete anarchy. On his assassination in 1806 the E. part of the island returned to Spanish rule, while the W. part remained divided between various rival chiefs till Boyer (q. v.) succeeded in bringing the whole island under his government in 1822. France in 1825 acknowledged the independence of the republic. But in 1842 the negroes rose in insurrection, and the E. portion formed itself into the republic of Santo Domingo, while H. was again split into petty rival states. Soulouque (see FAUSTINUS I.) assumed the imperial title in 1849, but was deposed in 1858. Of its later presidents, Geffard fled in 1867, and Salnave was expelled in 1870. General Boisrond-Canal was elected for four years in 1876. See Jordan's *Geschichte der Insel H.* (Leips. 1846); Madion, *Histoire d'H.* (Port-au-Prince, 1855); Ardonin, *Etudes sur l'Histoire de H.* (10 vols. Par. 1853-61); Bonneau, *H., ses Progrès, &c.* (Par. 1862); and Hazard, *Santo Domingo, with a Glance at H.* (Lond. 1873).

Hay'ward (lit. 'Hedgeward'), the keeper of the herd of cattle belonging to a town or manor, who prevents them from injuring the hedges. H. is also an officer who impounds strayed cattle.

Hazard (Fr.; Sp. *azar;* Ital. *zara*), a game of chance played with the Dice (q. v.) for money. The thrower of the dice is called the *castor*, his opponent the *setter*, and the throw itself a *main.*

Hazaribagh' ('thousand gardens'), the chief town of the district of the same name, Province of Bengal, British India, 239 miles N.W. of Calcutta, 1750 feet above the sea; pop. (1872) 11,050. It has a military cantonment, but the European troops were removed in 1874 on account of an outbreak of typhoid fever; a few are left to guard the European penitentiary, which contains about forty prisoners. The town has frequently been chosen as the residence of dethroned native chiefs. The *district* of H. has an area of 7021 sq. miles; pop. (1872) 771,875, chiefly Sonthals and other aborigines. It is very hilly and covered with jungle; but the heads of the valleys are dammed up, wherever possible, for rice cultivation. There are many coalfields, of which the Kurhurbari mine, the best in India, is profitably worked by the railway company. The output in 1874 was 105,000 tons, and the consignments are despatched as far as Madras and Scinde. There are also copper and mica mines, and four tea-gardens, which yielded an outturn in 1874 of more than 100,000 lbs.

Haze'brouck, a town in the department of Nord, France, on the H. canal, 25 miles W.N.W. of Lille, at the junction of the Dunkirque and Calais Railways. Its church of St. Eloi dates from the 15th c. Linen is manufactured, and there are several breweries, limekilns, soapworks, and dyeworks. Pop. (1872) 9435.

Ha'zel (Pl. Deut. Dan. and Sw. *hassel;* Ger. *hazel;* Dut. *hazelaar*), the English name for *Coylus avellana*, a small tree or coppice-shrub frequent throughout Britain and the Continent. The small flowers, which are produced before the foliage, are in long pendulous catkins. The fruit consists of the well-known nut surrounded by a large spreading husk. Filberts and cobnuts are cultivated forms of the H. Besides this one British species, there are five others found within the temperate region of the northern hemisphere. The long flexible tough shoots of H. are used for making crates and fishing-rods.

Haz'litt, William, a great English critic and essayist, of Irish descent, was born at Maidstone, Kent, April 10, 1778. His father was a Unitarian minister at Wem, Shropshire, and H. was trained for the same profession at the Unitarian College, Hackney. At the age of seventeen he abandoned theology and devoted himself to painting. Disappointed with his artistic efforts, he went to London in 1803, published his *Principles of Human Action* in 1805, and thenceforth lived by literature, publishing an abridgment of Tucker's *Light of Nature* in 1807, the *Eloquence of the British Senate*, a collection of parliamentary speeches, in 1808; *English Poets* in 1818; *English Comic Writers* in 1819; *Dramatic Literature of the Age of Elizabeth* and *Characters of Shakespeare's Plays* in 1821; *Table-Talk* in 1821–22; *Spirit of the Age* in 1825; *Plain Speaker* in 1826; *Life of Napoleon* in 1828–30. He contributed to the *London Magazine, Edinburgh Review, New Monthly*, and various political, literary, and theatrical journals. H. died September 18, 1830. His *Literary Remains* (Lond. 2 vols. 1836) were published by his son. The genius of H. never found full expression in his works. He was a man of intense feelings, warm-hearted, excitable, aggressive, and capricious. His criticism is generally passionate and eloquent, often acute and nobly sympathetic, often wayward, intemperate, and paradoxical. His style is fluent, rich, and graceful, sparkling with epigrammatic terseness, but sometimes overstrained and flowery beyond the limits of good taste. The best edition of his works is that edited by his grandson, W. C. Hazlitt, published by Bell & Daldy, London. See Bulwer Lytton's *Quarterley Essays* (1875) and L. Stephen's *Hours in a Library*, 2d series (1876).

Head. See CRANIUM, BRAIN, and ENCEPHELON.

Head, Sir Edmund Walker, son of the Rev. Sir John H., Bart., was born near Maidstone, Kent, in 1805, stood first in classics at Oriel College, Oxford, in 1827, succeeded to the baronetcy in 1838, and was successively appointed poor-law commissioner in 1841, lieutenant-governor of New Brunswick in 1847, and governor-general of Canada in 1854. He is author of *Painting* in the *Penny Cyclopædia*, of a *Handbook of the Spanish and French Schools of Painting* (a sequel to Kugler's *Handbook*), &c. He returned to England in 1861, and died in London, 28th January 1868.—**Sir George H.**, born in 1782, served as an officer of commissariat in Spain and Canada, and was knighted in 1831. His *Forest Scenes and Incidents in N. America* appeared in 1829, and he translated Cardinal Pacca's *Memoirs* (1850), and the *Metamorphosis of Apuleius* (1851). He died 2d May 1855. —**Sir Francis Bond H.**, brother of the preceding, was born near Rochester in 1793, entered the Royal Engineers, undertook in 1825 to work a gold and silver mine in Rio de la Plata, and described a ride of 6000 miles in *Rough Notes of Rapid Journeys Across the Pampas* (1826). He was appointed lieutenant-governor of Upper Canada in 1835, and suppressed an insurrection, for which he was created a baronet in 1838. Among his many works are *Bubbbes from the Brünnen of Nassau* (1833), a *Life of Bruce the Traveller* (1844), *The Emigrant* (1847), *The Defenceless State of Great Britain* (1850), *Descriptive Essays* (1856), *The Horse and his Rider* (1860), *The Royal Engineer* (1860). He died 23d July 1875.

Head'ache, or **Cephalal'gia**, a pain referred to the head, or to the front, side, or back thereof, varying in intensity according to its cause. H. very frequently depends upon or is connected with deranged digestion. During attacks of *Indigestion* (q. v.) there are, together with a violent H., frequently nausea and vomiting, the complaint being popularly known as *sick H.* or *bilious H. Hemicrania* (q. v.) is simply headache confined to one side, and occupying generally the brow and forehead, but sometimes affecting very exactly half of the head. *Tic Douloureux* (q. v.), another neuralgic disease, is frequently situated in the facial branches of the fifth pair of nerves, nerves of sensation. Neuralgic H. has a tendency to recur at regular intervals. H. is a frequent, and, in many cases, an unvarying symptom of disease processes within the cranium, and also in other parts of the body. Violent attacks of H. may thus be caused by disease of the bony structure, as necrosis and exostosis; by abnormal growths, as fungous tumours of the dura mater; by inflammatory action in the membranes of the brain, as Meningitis (q. v.), or in the brain substance itself, as Cerebritis or Encephalitis (q. v.), and by increase or diminution of the contents of the serous cavities, H. is also a frequent accompaniment of such diseases as Chorea, Hysteria, Catalepsy, Epilepsy, Apoplexy, and Sunstroke (q. v.); and of exanthematous and malarial fevers, as Small-pox and Ague (q. v.). H. is also frequently caused by congestion of the vessels of the brain, depending on relaxation of the coats of the vessels themselves, or on an abnormal quantity of blood being present owing to obstruction of the circulation in other parts of the body. In such cases, depletion, gentle purgatives, and restriction in diet afford relief, and may obviate, in some cases, an attack of apoplexy.

Headborough was anciently the head of the Frankpledge (q. v.) in boroughs. The word now denotes a kind of constable or peace-officer.

Healds, or **Heddles**, in weaving, the name given to that part of the *harness* of a loom which alternately raises and depresses the warp threads for the passage of the weft, and which consists of vertical lines of plaited yarn or wire with loops or eyes in the centre through which the warp threads pass. H. were formerly made by hand-knitting, but both yarn and metallic kinds are now made by machinery, by which uniformity and durability—points of great importance—are attained.

Health (Old Eng. *hælth*, from *hælan*, 'to heal;' connected with 'whole'), is that state of an animal or living body in which all the parts are sound, well organised, and developed, performing freely their natural functions without pain. Every deviation from this condition of the system constitutes Disease (q. v.). Absolute bodily H., although possible, must be one of the rarest endowments. Life may be divided into three periods, viz., growth or development, maturity and decay, terminating in Death (q. v.). In absolute bodily H. the form of death is euthanasia, the final result of gradual decay. The absolute and extreme duration of human life is uncertain, but the physiological limit is certainly much greater than that attained by the longest livers within historical times. There is probably no individual born in a state of perfect H., without any hereditary predisposition or taint; and no one passes through the stages of development, maturity, and decay without having suffered from derangement of H., necessarily shortening life. Hereditary taint varies in degree, and so also diseases depending on an almost infinite variety of causes. In point of fact, no community of human beings can be said to fulfil all the conditions of a healthy existence, and it is notoriously the case that the laws of H. are flagrantly violated by nearly all. That department of medical science which embraces a consideration of the means of preventing disease, or, in other words, of preserving H., is called Hygiene (q. v.). The means of preserving H. are in a great measure, but not altogether, at the command of each individual of the community. In every condition in which human beings may be placed there are agencies at work which operate injuriously on their H., and which can be removed or guarded against by the joint action of the community only. Such agencies are numerous and varied, some depending upon atmospheric and telluric influences, capable, nevertheless, of being removed or guarded against; while others may originate in the various modes of life of other members of the community who violate the laws of H. From the remotest antiquity, and in all civilised countries, laws have been made with the intention of removing conditions which injure the H. of the people. The growth of the population in town and country necessitates a code of sanitary regulations for the preservation of the public H., and such regulations, based upon sound hygienic principles, constitute Sanitary Science (q. v.). The necessity for such regulations is obvious from a view of the phenomena of the death-rate as affecting the calculation of premature mortality; for even where adults are more than commonly long-lived, and while there is no reason why a healthy child, the offspring of healthy parents, should not survive to a good old age, there is always a considerable mortality at very early ages, more especially under the age of five, which tends to reduce the *Vital Statistics* (q. v.) of the whole community. These departments of science, *hygiene*, *sanitary science*, and *vital statistics*, have assumed great importance of late years, and constitute the object of the 'public H.' movement in this country, a movement which has accomplished many valuable practical results. See DISEASE, ACTS RESPECTING.

Health, Bill of. See BILL.

Health, General Board of. The G. B. of H. has ceased to exist, its powers having been transferred by 21 and 22 Vict. c. 77, s. 1 to the Local Government Board (q. v.). See also SUPERVISION, BOARD OF.

Health, Medical Officer of. After the invasion of Great Britain by cholera in 1831, attention was directed to the existence of certain duties in reference to health, the observance of which, in the public interest, required to be enforced; and from time to time, by various statutes, these were consigned to certain authorities. Just as in questions of law and procedure the need of legal advisers soon appeared, so in reference to health and medicine the necessity for public medical advisers became apparent. In the Towns' Improvement Clauses Act, 1847, power was first given to appoint medical officers of health. Under the Metropolitan Management Act, 1855, every vestry might make such an appointment—an extension to the metropolis of the provisions of the Public Health Act of 1848. Although in all the important cities and towns, either under this or local Acts, medical officers were appointed, no appointments were made, in the country generally, until after the passing of the Public Health Act, 1872, by which such appointments were made *compulsory* upon all authorities, urban and rural. In Scotland, under the Nuisance Removal Act (1846 and 1848), the sanitary authority, such as it was, was vested in parochial authorities, and, consequently, poor-law officers performed such duties in connection with public health as received attention, chiefly in matters referring to epidemic diseases and the like. Under the Burgh Police Act, 1862, the commissioners were empowered to appoint 'a person of competent skill and experience who shall be styled the "Officer of Health."' In the same year, under a local Act, the city of Glasgow obtained similar power. The Public Health Act, 1867, was the first general Act applicable to Scotland constituting local authorities for health purposes in every locality who have power to appoint medical officers of health. This power is *not* compulsory, as it is in England. The difference between the duties of the officer in the two countries is well stated by Sheriff Spens as follows:—'Under the English system the M. O. of H. discharges the duties of Sanitary Inspector (q. v.) and medical officer of the Scotch local boards *minus* those of the inspector of nuisances.' This is well shown by comparing the byelaws recommended by the Board of Supervision for regulating the duties of medical officers with those of the local government board. They agree with the omission of rules 5, 8, 10, 14, and 16, under section iv. It is noteworthy that the M. O. of H. in England can be removed from office by the central board only, whereas in Scotland he is not so protected. In Ireland, the public health has always been conjoined with the poor-law service. In 1844 the hospital treatment of all persons suffering from contagious diseases, whether paupers or not, devolved on the unions. By the Medical Charities Act of 1851 the country was divided into above seven hundred dispensary districts, with dispensaries numbering above one thousand, and medical officers in proportion. These were parochial officials, and, although not so designated, performed the duties of medical officers of health, in so far as such were performed. The first statutory recognition of this fact was made by the Public Health Act (Ireland) of 1874, by which every dispensary doctor was appointed a M. O. of H. for his district. In 1875 the Irish Local Government Board reports as follows:—'We are now in a position to state, that the whole surface of Ireland is, for sanitary purposes, divided into districts, as nearly as practicable uniform in regard to population and area, each district being served by one or more sanitary officers—in other words, dispensary officers with both medical and surgical diplomas—whose annual official emoluments amount to an average of £147, 16s. per annum each.' The official designation is not M. O. of H., but 'sanitary officer,' the person corresponding to the sanitary inspector of Scotland and England being the 'sanitary sub-officer.' Their respective duties are similar, but are apportioned more after the English than the Scotch practice. There are three classes of medical officers of health:—(1) Those in cities and combined districts, whose whole time is devoted to the office; (2) those who are also in general practice, their salary not being sufficiently remunerative; and (3) union and parochial medical officers, who receive a paltry annual fee for the nominal performance of nominal duties. See *Dictionary of Hygiène and Public Health*, by Alexander Wynter Blyth (Lond. 1876); *Sanitary System of Scotland*, by Sheriff Spens (Edinb. 1876).

Hear'ing. See EAR.

Hearing of a Cause is the phrase used in English law to denote the argument on the merits of a case before the chancery division or before a magistrate. 'The trial' is the corresponding term at common law in a jury case in England and in Scotland. In the latter country, before a judge, it is called 'the debate.'

Hearing in Presence, in Scotch law, means the debating of a case before all the judges of the Court of Session (q. v.). It is only resorted to in difficult and important cases.

Hearne, Thomas, an English antiquary, born at White Waltham, Berkshire, in 1678, studied at Edmund Hall, Oxford, became assistant librarian in the Bodleian in 1701, and lived in Edmund Hall till his death, June 10, 1735. His chief works are editions of Justin, Eutropius, Livy, Spelman's *Life of Alfred; Leland's Itinerary; Lelandi de Rebus Britannicis Collectanea;* Langtoft's *Chronicle; Aluredi Beverlacencis Annales*, &c. He also wrote *Ductor Historicus*, and *The History and Antiquities of Glastonbury.*

Hear'say Ev'idence is the name given by lawyers to evidence in which the witness tells what he has heard said by another. H. E. is usually inadmissible, but there are exceptions to the general rule. For the most important one see DECLARATION, DYING. When a witness depones to a conversation, he must give the exact words if he can, and an opposing counsel will probably ask him to repeat them on cross-examination. If the exact words cannot be given, the substance must, as a witness is not allowed to give his impression of a result apart from words or substance. See EVIDENCE.

Hearse, or Herse (Fr. *herse*, Old. Fr. *herce*, Ital. *erpice*, from Lat. *hirpex* or *irpex*, 'a harrow'), a pyramidal candlestick, or a triangular iron frame resembling a harrow, set with spikes for holding candles tier above tier; a decorated carriage for conveying the dead to the grave. The transition of meaning is curious, and is thus traced: The candlestick called *hercia* in the 12th c., being part of the furniture of a church, was used at funeral solemnities. In course of time, the light wooden frame for supporting the pall over the bier during the service for the dead was called H., from the arrangement of H. lights around it. Later, the name was applied to a lofty structure or canopy, draped with black hangings, and decorated with waxen figures, tapers, and banners, which was erected temporarily in a church for holding the bier. At times such herses were allowed to remain for months in honour of the dead. From meaning a funeral canopy the transition was easy to a decorated car mounted on wheels, which was introduced in the 16th c. for carrying the dead to burial. See Wedgwood's *Dictionary of English Etymology*.

Heart. See CIRCULATION OF THE BLOOD.

Heart, Disease of the. Like all other organs of complex structure, and formed of different tissues, the heart is subject to a variety of diseases of more or less serious import; for the office of the heart is as essential to life and health as is that of the brain or of the lungs. It seldom happens that the whole heart is affected; the component tissues and different portions of the organ being more frequently separately diseased. The left side is more liable to disease than the right, and when both sides are affected, the morbid changes are more conspicuous in the left than the right chambers. The inflammations of the heart embrace *pericarditis*, an inflammation of the *Pericardium* (q. v.),—the fibro-serous membrane containing the heart, and investing it on its external aspect; *endocarditis*, a similar affection of the *Endocardium* (q. v.) covering the valves and lining the chambers of the heart; and *carditis* or *myocarditis*, an inflammation of the muscular structure of the heart, occasionally terminating in suppuration, ulceration, rupture, ramollissement, and induration. The pathological conditions and changes dependent upon inflammations of the heart are identical with the morbid appearances induced by the inflammatory process affecting similar structures in other parts of the body, so that the gravity of the symptoms depend more upon the important nature of the organ affected than upon the gravity of the disease *per se*. All serous membranes are liable to Inflammations (q. v.), acute or chronic, which may terminate by resolution, or in an increased effusion of serous fluid, which may become purulent, or may coagulate upon the opposed surfaces, become vascular and glue them together. Lymph, which is generally formed in much greater quantity from the serous membrane of the heart than from any other serous membranes, may render the serum turbid, or may float in it in flakes; but it is more frequently disposed as a membrane, measuring from two to several lines in thickness. When the result of inflammation is a purulent exudation, the pus is generally of a healthy character. It occasionally happens that blood, as well as serum, is effused within the cavity from the highly congested vessels, or from the new formed vessels, which, being tender, give way. In chronic forms of the disease the effused lymph is commonly found organised, forming adhesions, and frequently it becomes converted into cartilaginous and even osseous patches. D. of the H. is diagnosed by constitutional and local symptoms, the latter being chiefly elicited by auscultation and percussion. Although the disease processes in Pericarditis and Endocarditis (q. v.) are precisely the same, the symptoms are markedly dissimilar; but in the early stages there may be some difficulty in diagnosis. In acute pericarditis there is pain in the præcordial region, radiating over the sternum, often extending to the brachial plexus and the left arm; disturbance of the heart's action; a sensation of constriction over the chest; pain on inspiration, during coughing, and on pressure; inability to lie on the left side; dulness on percussion, and generally an exocardial friction sound. In endocarditis the impulse of the heart is more extensive, forcible, and abrupt than is natural. There is much discomfort and uneasiness at the heart, but no special sensation of dyspnœa unless there be valvular disease. The greatest ease is obtained by lying on the back, and there is frequently an inclination to toss about the arms. As the disease advances endocardial sounds are apparent. The exocardial friction murmur, soft and bellows-like, accompanies both the diastole and the systole; it is limited to the region of the heart, varies over different parts of the heart, and is not constant; it precedes and follows the impulse of the heart, but does not correspond with its rhythm. Pressure over the region of the heart intensifies the murmur, and converts the sound into a rustle or rub. In all these respects the exocardial are distinguished from the endocardial or valve murmurs, which may depend upon aortic or mitral obstruction and regurgitation, or upon both combined. Both diseases may coexist in the same subject, so that the friction sound, pathognomic of pericarditis, must be looked for in the heart's region, and the endocardial murmurs beyond the region of the heart. Chronic endocarditis almost invariably results in valvular lesions, which tend to thicken the walls and enlarge the cavities of the heart, owing to the great increase of the heart's action necessary to propel the blood through the valves. Aortic regurgitation induces dilatation of the left ventricle, enlargement of the left auricle and the right ventricle and auricle. Disease of the pulmonic valves causes dilatation of the right cavities, and mitral disease leads to enlargement of the left auricle, dilatation of the pulmonary veins, congestion of the lungs, enlargement of the right ventricle and auricle, and of the *venæ cavæ*, engorgement of the liver, and enlargement of the left ventricle itself. So long as the muscular tissue of the heart is sound, valvular disease has but little influence on health, but the persistence of the disease implies (1) *an enlarged heart, or simple hypertrophy*; (2) *hypertrophy with dilatation of one or more of the cavities*; and (3) *simple dilatation with or without attenuation of the walls of the cavities*. Atrophy is an abnormal wasting and loss of the muscular substance of the heart, and may be general or partial, and is generally associated with enlargement of the cavities; but the whole heart may be atrophied and reduced in size, as is often seen in phthisis. Carditis (q. v.), or inflammation of the heart, is extremely rare as an idiopathic disease, and has been seldom met with unless complicated with pericarditis. The arteries supplying the heart itself are also liable to disease, and diseases of the aorta and thoracic aneurism are intimately associated with D. of the H. Hydatids or 'echinococcus' cysts have been found between the walls of the heart, beneath the inner membrane, and such parasitic cysts abound in sheep and oxen. The heart is also subject to degeneration of its minute tissues, the muscular fibres being replaced by fatty or fibrinous molecular particles, as in Fatty Degeneration (q. v.), tending to sudden death from syncope or rupture of the heart. *Breast-pang*, or *Angina Pectoris* (q. v.), ought to be regarded rather as a symptom of organic D. of the H. than as a distinct form of disease. *Cyanosis* (q. v.) is symptomatic of various malformations of the heart and great vessels, so that only a small portion of the blood is aërated in the lungs. Cyanosis may depend upon obstructions in the pulmonary artery and systemic venous circulation, a patulous condition of the ductus arteriosus, an open foramen ovale, a deficiency in the septum of the ventricles, or a heart formed of one ventricle and one auricle only, depending upon arrestment of development during fœtal life.

There are also various functional derangements of the heart, unconnected with organic mischief, but which simulate organic disease, such as palpitation, and fainting (q. v.), spasms, and metastatic gout (q. v.), but all such derangements are apt to terminate in organic D. of the H.

The causes of D. of the H. are various and numerous. Pericarditis and endocarditis are frequently associated with rheumatic affections, pleurisy, and inflammation of the lungs. Endocarditis is frequently caused by abnormal conditions of the blood, as in exanthematous or zymotic diseases, or when the blood is habitually impregnated with alcohol. Functional derangement is frequently associated with hysteria and dyspepsia, and is traceable to excessive mental exertion, sedentary occupations, strong mental emotions, and nervous exhaustion from various causes. The medical literature of D. of the H. is peculiarly rich. See the works of Corvisart, Lænnec, Stokes, Graves, Walshe, Sibson, Latham, Fuller, and *Clinical Lectures on Diseases of the Heart and Aorta*, by Dr. G. W. Balfour (Lond. 1876).

Heart-Urchin, the name given to certain genera of *Echini*, or 'Sea-urchins,' from their heart-like or cordate shape. These 'urchins' are called 'irregular,' on account of their difference in form from the Common Echinus (q. v.), which is spherical. The purple H.-E. is the *Spatangus purpureus* of the naturalist; the common species, the *Amphidotus cordatus*. A curious form is the 'Fiddle H.-E.' (*Brissus lyrifer*), so named from a mark of that shape on the shell or 'test.'

Heat. The familiar terms *hot* and *cold* are used to express certain well-known sensations, which are experienced on touching certain objects. They are understood also as descriptive of a certain state in which the object is—any given body containing more or less H. according as it is hotter or colder. This agent, H., if it has an existence at all, must be either matter or energy, for excepting the inevitable *time* and *space*, these are the only elementary notions which are recognised in the physical universe. Till far on in the present century the *material* hypothesis was generally adopted; but the discoveries of Rumford (1798), Davy (1799), and Joule (1843) have for ever overthrown it, and established on the most unequivocal evidence that H. is *energy*—energy of motion. The history and development of this branch of science bears intimately upon the *theory* of H., or Thermodynamics, and to that article accordingly we refer the reader, purposing here only to enter upon what might be termed the truly experimental portion.

It is of the greatest importance to have a clear conception of the true scientific meaning of the word *temperature* as distinguished from *heat*. When two bodies at the same temperature are placed in contact, neither parts with H. to the other. This is the first great principle upon which the science of thermometry is based. The second principle is, that when two bodies at different temperatures are placed in contact, the one which is at the higher temperature parts with H. to the other, until both are reduced to the same temperature. In other words, the hotter body cools, and the colder becomes warm. The temperature of a body is then simply its thermal state considered with reference to its power of communicating heat to other bodies, and bears exactly the same relation to H. which pressure bears to fluid in hydrodynamics. Practical methods for measuring temperature depend in all cases upon other *effects* of H. which occur simultaneously with the changes which temperature undergoes; and to the consideration of these effects we will now turn.

As a general rule, when a substance, whether solid, liquid, or gaseous, is raised in temperature, it expands in volume. The expansion of a solid under the action of H. is measured in two ways, according as it is the *linear* or *cubical* expansion which is considered. In the former case the *co-efficient* of linear dilatation for any substance is measured by the ratio which the increase in length, due to the rise of temperature by one unit, of a long narrow rod formed of that substance bears to the original length. For instance, if the original length of the rod be L, and its length after having its temperature raised by one unit $L + l$, the co-efficient of linear dilatation is $l : L$. If the substance, instead of being in the form of a thin rod, is cubical in shape, then it is the cubical dilatation that is considered; and for all solid substances, which increase equally in all directions, the co-efficient of cubical dilatation is practically three times the co-efficient of linear dilatation. Certain crystalline solids, however, do not expand equally in all directions; and Mitscherlich has shown that this peculiarity is closely connected with the optical properties of the crystals. Thus simple regular crystals which do not cause double refraction (see LIGHT) dilate uniformly in all directions; uniaxal crystals have two co-efficients of dilatation, one along the principal axis, and the other along each of the three secondaries; and biaxal crystals have a different co-efficient for each of the three axes. The heating of a solid is then accompanied by a rise of temperature, and in general an increase of volume. But at a certain stage the solid begins to alter its physical state, in other words, to melt; and as long as this change of state is taking place, little if any alteration is produced in the temperature. As soon as the solid is wholly transformed into liquid, the temperature again begins to rise as the heating is continued, the liquid at the same time dilating. This dilatation of liquids when heated is the phenomenon upon which the common practical method for measuring temperature depends. (See THERMOMETER.) The mercuric thermometer is that which is used for all common purposes; and the temperature is indicated by the height at which a column of mercury stands in a narrow glass tube, which has been made as perfect a vacuum as possible. Mercury is especially convenient, because for usual temperatures it expands very uniformly, and having a low specific H., does not lower the temperature of the body with which it is in contact by an appreciable amount. Throughout this article the thermometer scale chosen is the *centigrade*, which has for its zero the freezing-point of water, and for its hundredth degree the boiling-point. We have seen how a substance may exist in both the solid and liquid state at the same temperature and pressure, the only difference being that the liquid contains more H. The H. which disappears while the substance is changing from solid to liquid is called the *latent H. of liquefaction*. It has really, of course, no existence, but is the thermal equivalent of the mechanical work required to be done to effect the physical change. The latent H. of water is in thermal units 79·25, where a thermal unit is the amount of H. required to raise the temperature of 1 lb. of water 1° C.,—*i.e.*, it requires 79·25 units of H. to be expended in order to transform one pound of ice at 0° C. into one pound of water at the same temperature and pressure. Now, exactly as H. disappears, when the solid is melting, without an accompanying rise of temperature, so H. disappears in converting the liquid into gas. All liquids which do not chemically decompose under the operation are convertible into the gaseous form if sufficiently heated, and the temperature at which this occurs is called the boiling-point of the liquid. The quantity of H. which disappears during the conversion of unit mass of the liquid into gas is called the *latent H. of vaporisation*, and is measured in the same way as the latent H. of liquefaction. Thus the latent H. of steam is 537 units of H. Regnault, Andrews, and others, have made numerous experiments on this subject, and their results indicate that of all vapours, steam has the greatest latent H., and of all liquids, water. The effects of H. upon gaseous substances are simply stated in the laws of Boyle and Charles. (See GASES.) These are—(1) That at constant temperature the density of a gas is directly proportional to the pressure; and (2) that under constant pressure, and for a given rise of temperature, the volume of a gas expands by a fraction of itself, which is the same for all gases. All gases tend to expand when heated, but amongst liquids and solids there are some which contract when heated. Thus water at 0° C. contracts when heated till it reaches a temperature of 4° C., when it begins to expand. India-rubber, again, when heated under tension, contracts—a phenomenon which has an important bearing upon the theory of Energy (q. v.).

If there is no change of physical condition, heating is accompanied by rise of temperature; and the number of thermal units necessary to raise the temperature of unit mass of a given substance by one degree is called the *specific H.* of the substance. The specific H. of a substance in its liquid state is greater than the specific heats in its solid or gaseous states; thus water has twice as great a specific H. as ice, and more than twice as great as steam. Experiments show that for solids and liquids, the specific H. is greater for a higher temperature. Of all known substances, water has the greatest specific H., and it is this phenomenon upon which depends the important climatic effects of water. The specific heat of gases may be measured in two ways; or, rather, every gas has two specific heats—the specific H. at constant pressure, and the specific H. at constant volume. Their determination is one of excessive difficulty, but Regnault has made a successful series of experiments, and deduced the curious relation, that for the non-condensable gases (air, hydrogen, oxygen, &c.) the ratio of the specific H. at constant volume to that at constant pressure is about 1·408 : 1. This result is closely concordant with theory. There are other effects of H., which can be merely indicated here. Of these, we may cite the electric polarity acquired by Tourmaline (q. v.), the whole subject of Thermo-Electricity (q. v.), the demagnetising effect upon a magnet, and the chemical effects as evidenced in dissociation.

The *transference* of H. from one substance to another may be effected in three different ways: by radiation, convection, or conduction. *Radiation* consists in the transmission of H. from one body to another by propagation through the intervening medium. Radiant H. is of precisely the same nature as Light (q. v.). Both are wave motions due to transverse vibrations; both travel in straight lines and with the same velocity; both are reflected and refracted according to the same laws; and both can be polarised. Radiant H. differs from light only in its wave length, which is too long to affect our retinas. The difference is therefore only one of degree, and is precisely the same as the difference between a low musical note and a high musical note. Now, let a number of bodies, all at the same temperature, be placed in a chamber the walls of which are maintained at that temperature and are besides impervious to H. In such a state of affairs no change of temperature will occur, and the whole system will be in thermal equilibrium. But if a colder body be introduced into the chamber, all the other bodies as well as the enclosing walls will begin to part with H. to the colder body. Now, it is quite out of the question to suppose that the mere introduction of the colder body should suddenly cause the surrounding bodies to begin to emit radiations; and accordingly we conclude that a body is always radiating H., but that, if there be no colder body in the vicinity, it receives from radiation by the surrounding bodies exactly what it radiates towards them, so that its temperature remains constant. If two bodies are at the same temperature, the H. radiated by the first and absorbed by the second is equal to the H. radiated by the second and absorbed by the first. Further, the higher the temperature of a body the greater the radiation, so that if the bodies be at different temperatures, the hotter will radiate more than the colder, and the colder will absorb more than the hotter; and, consequently, H. will be lost by the hotter and gained by the colder, till both are at the same temperature. This is Prevost's famous *Theory of Exchanges;* and it has been extended and fully verified by the researches of Stokes, Balfour Stewart, Kirchhoff, and De la Provostaye. (See SPECTRUM ANALYSIS.) If a part of a fluid be heated so as to expand or contract, the hydrostatic equilibrium will be destroyed; and the heated fluid, if acted on by gravity, will ascend or descend, giving rise to a current. Such currents are called *convection* currents, and they are seen on a large scale in the operation of winds and ocean currents. If a liquid, which expands when heated, is heated from below, the lower strata, becoming lighter than the upper, must ascend and give place to the heavier (because colder) liquid. By this means H. is conveyed from one portion to another; and considering the great mobility of gases, it is evident that convection currents must play in them a most important part. If the liquid were heated from above, of course there would be no convection currents; but the H. would be transmitted solely by *conduction*. This means of transmitting H. is easiest studied in solids, which are quite free from the effects of convection. All substances conduct H. more or less easily; and according to their power of conduction they are relatively termed good and bad conductors. The metals are the best conductors—silver, copper, gold, brass, tin, and iron, ranking the highest; woollen materials, india-rubber, &c., are bad conductors. See CONDUCTIVITY.

The production of H. is an action which is constantly going on in the universe. Wherever there is a transformation of Energy (q. v.), or whenever *work* is done, H. is necessarily evolved—and all forms of energy tend ultimately to take the form of H. This part of the subject, which treats more especially of the nature of H. and of its economical uses, is best studied under Thermodynamics.

The best works on the subject are Tyndall's *H. Considered as a Mode of Motion* (1863); Balfour Stewart's *Elementary Treatise on H.* (1866, 2d ed. 1876); Tait's *Thermodynamics* (1868, 2d ed. 1877); and Clerk Maxwell's *Theory of H.* (1871). All these are written on totally different plans. Tyndall's is specially intended for the non-scientific public; Stewart's enters more fully into the methods of experimentally determining the various thermal constants and co-efficients; Tait's is chiefly an historical sketch of the subject, with an accompanying account of the development of the modern theory of energy; while Clerk Maxwell's touches only upon those portions which bear intimately upon the theory. See also Rankine's *Steam-Engine and other Prime Movers* (1859).

Heat, Animal. See ANIMAL HEAT.

Heath (so called from where it grows), the common name for the species of *Erica*, a genus of plants belonging to the natural order *Ericaceæ*. They are wiry, much-branched shrubs, with rigid narrow leaves. About 400 species are distributed throughout Europe, N. Asia, and the Cape of Good Hope. The chief British species is the ling, *E.* (*Calluna*) *vulgaris*, so common on the moors. It is also found sparingly in N. America. On the Scottish mountains it is met with from their base to 3300 feet above the sea; it forms the food and shelter of the grouse and other birds. 'Heather honey,' which is much sought after, has received its name from the bees having been fed from the flowers of this plant. In the Highlands, H. is much used for thatching cottages, making besoms, and for tanning; it also yields a yellow dye. *E. tetralix* and *E. cinerea*, although less frequent than the ling, are still abundant, and are occasionally found with white flowers. The former is the badge of the Clan Macdonald, and the latter that of the Clan M'Alister. The numerous species of Cape H. are well-known ornamental greenhouse plants.

The Law Regarding H.—In England the malicious burning of H. is felony by statute. For Scotch law, see MUIRBURN.

Heaven (Old Eng. *heofon* and *heofen*, 'what is lifted up,' from pp. of *hebban* 'to lift up,') means originally the sky, which was popularly conceived as a solid expanse raised above the earth. The Hebrew terms used to express the idea of H., in its various shades of meaning, are—1. *Shamaim* (*lit.* 'height,' 'elevation'), Gen. i. 8, &c. 2. *Marom*, 'heights,' 'high place' or 'places,' Ps. lxviii. 18 (*on high*), xciii. 4, cii. 19. 3. *Galgal* (*lit.* 'a wheel'), Ps. lxxvii. 18. 4. *Shchakim* (*lit.* 'something beaten out'), 'the sky' or 'skies,' Deut. xxxiii. 26, 2 Sam. xxii. 12, and 'clouds,' Job. xxxv. 5. 5. *Rakia*, 'firmament,' Gen. i. Three regions are distinguished in the Hebrew Scriptures under the name of H.:—1. The region of the clouds or the air, Gen. vii. 3, 23; 2. the region of the stars, Gen. xxvi. 4; and 3. the region inhabited by the angels and God himself, which last is variously expressed as (1) 'the heaven of heaven' (Deut. x. 14); (2) 'the third heaven' (2 Cor. xii. 2); (3) 'the high and holy' [place] (Isa. lvii. 15); (4) 'the highest' (Matt. xxi. 9). This threefold distinction was adopted by Latin theologians, who spoke of Cœlum Aqueum, C. Sidereum, and C. Empyreum. A twofold division is also referred to in the Bible—into 'the heaven,' and 'the heaven of heavens' (Deut. x. 14, 1 Kings viii. 27, Ps. cxv. 16). The Rabbinical writers divided H. into *seven* regions, in the highest of which was the throne of the Eternal, and of which the throne of King Solomon, with the six steps leading up to it, was regarded as a symbol (1 Kings x. 18–20). This classification was followed by some of the Fathers and in the Koran.

Besides the meanings of H. in the Old Testament enumerated above, in the New Testament it sometimes means (1) a state answering to 'the kingdom of H.' (Eph. ii. 6, where 'heavenly places' stands for H.; *cf.* Phil. iii. 20). (2) It means also the place where God dwells (Matt. vi. 9), where the angels and the spirits of the just are congregated, whence Christ came, and to which he has returned (John xiv. 2).

Hebb'el, Friedrich, a dramatic poet of great originality, but with a tendency towards the unnatural and monstrous. He was born at Wesselburen in Ditmarsh, 18th March 1813, and died at Vienna, where since 1842 he had been resident, on the 13th December 1863. Of his tragedies, *Judith* (1841), *Genoveva* (1843), *Maria Magdalena* (1844), *Herodes und Mariamne* (1850), *Die Nibelungen* (1862), deserve mention; of his comedies, *Der Diamant* (1847) and *Der Rubin* (1851). His *Gedichte* went through a second edition in 1848, and his *Werke* were published 1866–68 in 12 vols. See Emil Kuh's *Life of F. H.* (1876).

He'be, in Greek mythology, the goddess of youth, daughter of Zeus and Hera, and sister of Ares. She was the cup-bearer of the gods, and the wife of Heraclês. She was worshipped at Rome under the name Juventas.

He'ber, Reg'inald, Bishop of Calcutta, was born at Malpas in Cheshire, England, 21st April 1783. He distinguished himself greatly at Oxford, gaining at the age of nineteen the university prize poem on the subject of *Palestine*. In 1808 he graduated as M.A., and next year was presented to the family living of Hodnet. In 1810 appeared his *Hymns*, some of which are exquisitely musical, tinged with Oriental hues, and inspired with the sweetest devotion. In 1822 he published his *Life of Jeremy Taylor*, accompanying an edition of his works, and was elected preacher to Lincoln's Inn. Shortly afterwards he was appointed Bishop of Calcutta, and landed there 10th October 1823. But his arduous labours and the Indian climate soon proved too much for a constitution never strong, and H. died at Trichinopoly, 2d April 1826, in the forty-third year of his age. Besides the works already mentioned, H. was author of sermons published at various dates, and of an Indian *Journal*, published after his death in 1828. His Life, by his widow, appeared in 1830 in 2 vols. 4to.—**H., Richard**, brother of the above, born at Westminster, January 5, 1773, studied at Oxford, became a well-known collector of rare and curious books, and died at Pimlico, October 24, 1833. He was the 'dear H.' whom Scott addresses in the Introduction to the sixth canto of *Marmion*.

Hébert, Jacques René, nicknamed the **Père Duchesne**, was born at Alençon in 1755. Almost without education, he came to Paris in early youth, lost two situations through embezzlement, and lived in misery till the Revolution, when he published some savage and outrageously expressed pamphlets, and also became known as a blatant speaker at various clubs (chiefly the Cordéliers). He now started a radical newspaper called the *Père Duchesne*, in opposition to Lemaire's Royalist journal of the same name. Thiers says it was even more violent and vile than Marat's *Ami du Peuple*. H. constantly preached the sacred right of insurrection, and advised death on all occasions. He thus became a considerable person in the municipality, and was deputy-procureur under Chaumette. He was arrested for a while by the moderate Commission of Twelve. This provoked an insurrection, and H. was presented with a civic crown (an oak garland), which he placed on the bust of Rousseau. It was he who suggested the summary process which led to the conviction of the twenty-two Girondins, who denounced the Revolutionary tribunal for hesitating about the execution of Custine, who brought the disgusting accusation of incest against the queen, and who along with Chaumette and Clootz invented the worship of Reason. He was, in fact, the black soul of the ultra-revolutionary party. On the withering denunciation of St. Just, he was finally brought to trial with eighteen others (including Clootz, Vincent, Mamdro, Kock, &c.), and executed 24th March 1794. He showed great cowardice at the end, and no man was more hooted at the scaffold. While pretending in public to purity of republican principle, he lived privately in ill-gotten luxury. His widow, Jacqueline, the ex-nun of the Convent of the Conception, was executed along with Lucile Desmoulins.

He'brew is an appellation first applied to Abram (Gen xiv. 13), and afterwards to his descendants (Gen. xl. 15; Exod. ii. 6). It is derived either from Eber, the great-grandson of Shem (Gen. x. 21, 25), which indeed seems to be applied in the narrative, or from Heb. *abar*, 'to pass over or through,' so that 'Abram the H.' would mean either, 'he who had come across' (the Euphrates), or 'he who was passing through,' or merely a sojourner in the country (*cf.* Heb. xi. 13). See JEWS, JEWISH LANGUAGE AND LITERATURE.

Hebrews, The Epistle to the, has been assigned to many authors: to Clement of Rome; to Barnabas, the friend of Paul; to Luke; to Silas; to Apollos; and, according to the received opinion, to Paul. For the Pauline authorship the external evidence is divided and conflicting. In the Western Church the Epistle was not considered canonical till the 4th c., when it was assigned to Paul; in the Eastern Church tradition was from an early period (in Syria not till the 3d c.) almost uniformly in favour of the Pauline authorship. The weight of internal evidence is now considered to be against it: *e.g.*, 1. The absence of a title and the name of the writer is contrary to Paul's practice. 2. The writer appears to know the Old Testament only in the LXX., and to betray an imperfect acquaintance with the Temple. 3. The statement in chap. ii. 3 seems inconsistent with Paul's claim to apostleship in the Epistle to the Galatians. 4. The doctrine of the Epistle seems to differ from that of Paul, *e.g.*, in (1) the relation of Judaism to Christianity, (2) the Christology, (3) the atonement, and (4) the relation of *faith* to *law*, &c. 5. The language and style are unlike Paul's. The opinion which seems to find most support from good critics in recent times is that the author was Apollos. The 'Hebrews,' to whom it appears the Epistle was written, were the Jewish Christians either at Jerusalem or at Alexandria. All that can be known as to the time when it was written is that it was probably before the destruction of Jerusalem (70 A.D.), otherwise the writer would not have failed to refer to that event in connection with his argument. The object of the Epistle was to warn those to whom it was addressed against relapsing into Judaism. It is shown that the Jewish economy was preparatory and typical of the Christian, and that the shadow has given place to the substance.

Heb'rides, or **Western Islands,** the name of the great island group stretching along the W. coast of Scotland, and belonging to the counties of Ross, Inverness, and Argyle, and comprising some 490 islands, of which only about 90 are inhabited. Estimated area, 3000 sq. miles; pop. 150,000. They are divided by Tiree Passage, Little Minch, and N. Minch into the Outer H., chief of which are Lewis, Harris, N. and S. Uist, Benbecula, Barra, Coll, Tiree, and the isle of St. Kilda, 'placed far amid the melancholy main;' and the Inner H., of which the most notable are Skye, Rum, Eigg, Mull, Iona, Staffa, Ulva, Lismore, Kerrera, Easdale, Scarba, Colonsay, Jura, and Islay. It is inaccurate to reckon the islands in the Firth of Clyde (Arran, Bute, &c.), as part of the H. The H. are generally wild, rocky, and picturesque, rising in jagged peaks, or extending in bleak moors studded with gloomy tarns. A mild, moist climate, due to the presence of the Gulf Stream, clothes the valleys and hillsides with finest verdure. The industries are chiefly the rearing of cattle and sheep, fishing and fowling. Among the principal towns are Stornoway in Lewis, Portree in Skye, and Tobermory in Mull. The H. are much visited by tourists, and have regular communication with Glasgow by several steam lines. They are the *Hebudes* of Pliny, their present names being a corruption, some say a misprint. The Norwegians, who fled hither from the tyranny of Harald Haarfager and to a great extent supplanted the Celtic inhabitants, called them the *Sudreyjar*, or 'S. isles,' as distinguished from the *Orkneyjar* or 'N. isles.' The H. were brought under the rule of Norway about 870, but were transferred to Scotland in 1266. In 1346 they fell under the sway of the chief of the Macdonalds, who took the title of the 'Lord of the Isles.' They were finally annexed to the Scottish crown by James V. in 1540. See, besides the works of Martin, Sir Joseph Banks, Pennant, and Dr. Johnson, Macculloch's *Geological Account of the H.* (2 vols. 1819); Professor Munch's *Chronica Regum Manniæ et Insularum* (Christiania, 1860); Hugh Miller's *Cruise of the Betsey* (new ed. 1875); and W. A. Smith's *Lewisiana, or Life in the Outer H.* (Lond. 1875).

Hebrides, New. See NEW HEBRIDES.

He'bron, a town of Palestine, 18 miles S. of Jerusalem, is one of the oldest cities of the world (*cf.* Gen. xii. 18; Num. xiii. 22). Its original name was Kirjath-Arba ('city of Arba:' Gen. xxiii. 2; Josh. xiv. 15, xv. 13), but it was also called Mamre (Gen. xxiii. 19). H. was the headquarters of Abraham, Isaac, and Jacob, while they lived, and here they were buried, in the cave of Machpelah. On the return of the Israelites from Egypt, it was taken by Joshua and given to Caleb (Josh. x, 36, 37, xiv. 13, 14), and was afterwards made one of the cities of refuge (Josh. xx. 7). During David's reign of seven and a half years over Judah, H. was the royal residence. It was rebuilt after the Babylonish captivity (Neh. xi. 25), but soon fell into the hands of the Edomites, from whom it was rescued by Judas Maccabæus (1 Macc. v. 65; Josh. *Ant.* xii. 8, 6). The modern city, *El-Khulil* [Arab. 'the friend' (of God), *i.e.*, Abraham], contains about 5000 inhabitants.

Hecatæ'us (Gr. *Hekataios*), one of the early Greek historians and geographers, was born of a noble and rich family at Miletus, about 550 B.C. He visited Greece, Thrace, the Euxine coasts, and perhaps Spain and Libya; opposed Aristagoras, who prompted the Ionians to rise against Persia, and, after the insurrection was quelled, won more lenient terms for his countrymen from the satrap Artaphernes. He seems to have died about 476 B.C. His works include *Periodos Gēs* ('Tour of the World'), which consists of two books, one relating to Europe, the other to parts of Asia, Egypt, and Libya; and four books of *Histories*, containing a number of the old Hellenic legends. The extant fragments of his works are collected in Klauser's *Hecatæi Fragmenta* (Berl. 1831). See Mure's *History of Greek Literature.*

Hec'ate (Gr. *Hekatē*), a mystic goddess in Greek mythology, mentioned by Hesiod as the daughter of the Titan Perses and Asteria, the bringer of good and averter of evil fortune. Later, she appears in connection with Persephone as a dreadful infernal deity, in possession of the magic forces of heaven, earth, and sea. In the Eleusinian and Cabiric mysteries of Samothrace and Lemnos she played a prominent part, and her worship was generally diffused throughout Hellas; offerings to her were placed in front of the houses, in public meeting-places, at cross-roads, &c. As an infernal goddess she is represented in a terrific form, with snakes in her hair, torches and a sword in her hand, snake-footed, and accompanied by a long-haired dog. Afterwards, when a magic influence was more and more commonly attributed to the moon, H. became identified with it. From her many-sided character, the myths of H. are very different, and artistic representations of her display a corresponding variety.

Hec'atomb (Gr. *hekaton*, 'a hundred,' and *bous*, 'an ox'), literally, the sacrifice of a hundred oxen, signified among the Greeks any sacrifice of numerous victims. In a H. the whole of each victim was sometimes burned, but more often the thighs, legs, and hides were alone consumed, while the flesh was eaten by the worshippers.

Heck'er, Friedrich Karl Franz, born 28th September 1811, at Eichtersheim in Baden, became in 1838 public prosecutor at Mannheim. In 1842 he sat as a member of the opposition in the Lower Chamber of Baden, and was soon one of the leaders of the republican movement. He organised a rising on the Swiss frontier, but had to flee in September 1848 to the United States. Here he settled as a farmer in Illinois; and in the civil war commanded a regiment.

Heck'les, or **Hack'les** (Dut. *hekel*, Fin. *hakylar*, 'a comb'), are instruments with sharp-pointed steel teeth from one to two inches in length, through which flax, hemp, or jute fibre is drawn, in order to split it up into parallel filaments and separate the tow. The fibre is drawn repeatedly through H. of increasing degrees of fineness till the required quality is obtained. Heckling-machines with various arrangements of combing apparatus have now almost entirely displaced hand-H.

Heck'mondwike, a town of Yorkshire, England, 2 miles N.W. of Dewsbury, and 10 S.W. of Leeds by railway. It is a centre of the blanket trade, and has carpet factories, breweries, &c. In the vicinity are many collieries. Pop. (1871) 8300.

Hec'la, or **Hek'la,** a famous volcano in Iceland, 60 miles E. of Reykiavik, is an irregular cone about 20 miles in circumference, rising from a mountain mass 420 sq. miles in extent. Its height, which has hitherto been over-estimated, is 5282 feet. Of its five craters, the largest is over a mile in diameter, and from 200 to 300 feet deep. Since the year 1104 there have been eighteen eruptions, of which the most violent continued from September 1845 to April 1846. On this occasion, at a distance of 2 miles, the lava torrent was from 40 to 50 feet deep, and the dust of the eruption was carried as far as the Orkney Isles.

Hectare'. See ARE.

Hectic Fever (Gr. *heptikos*, 'habitual'), a peculiar type of Fever (q. v.), frequently depending upon inflammation or suppuration of an internal organ, as the lungs; or associated with some analogous wasting of the bodily substance, as in prolonged lactation. H. F. is distinguished from inflammatory and typhoid forms of fever by its periodical intermissions, &c., and excessive waste of the tissues. The symptoms of H. F. are heat of skin during the paroxysm, quick and short respiration, *hectic flush* of the cheek, limited to a spot in the centre, gradual wasting and loss of strength, terminating often in mild delirium and death. See PHTHISIS.

Hec'tor (Gr. *Hektōr*), the bravest hero in the Trojan army, was the son of King Priam and Hecabe, and husband of Andromache, by whom he had the son Astyanax, and, according to others, also Laodamas and Amphinous. When in battle with the Greeks, he had killed Achilles' friend Patroclus. Achilles became reconciled to Agamemnon, again entered the war, and avenged his friend's death by the slaughter of H. H. is one of the noblest characters of the Iliad, and his leave-taking of Andromache is one of the finest episodes in that poem.

Hec'uba (Gr. *Hekabē*), the Trojan king Priam's wife, mother of Hector and Paris, was, after the capture of Troy, carried off as a slave by the Greeks. For blinding Polymestor, who had killed her youngest son Polydorus, she was changed to a dog, and cast herself into the sea. Euripides paints her in the tragedy bearing her name as the unfortunate victim of destiny, but a noble princess, a good wife, and an affectionate mother.

Hed'era, the generic name of the Ivy (q. v.).

Hedge (Old Eng. *hege*, *haeg*, Ger. *hage*, Dan. *hekke*, Sw. *hage*) is something planted either to make fences round enclosures or to part off and divide the several parts of an enclosure. When designed as outside fences, hawthorn or quick is most frequently used, but blackthorn (sloe), crab, elm, beech, holly, and briars are often employed, singly or in combination. Inner hedges of gardens are made of various sorts of plants that will bear clipping, according to the fancy of the owner, as privet, yew, holly, hornbeam, &c. Before forming the H., it is proper to consider what sort of plants will thrive best in the soil, whether it be clay, gravel, sand, &c. The extent to which hedges are used for the division of land into fields and to bound roads, differs very much in various countries, and in different parts of the same country; the local surroundings and local prejudices generally establishing the custom. Nowhere do they form such a factor of the scenery as in England, yet there are large districts where all the required divisions are effected by stone walls or water-courses, and not a H. to be seen. Planting trees in hedgerows is commonly adopted, the result being a wooded appearance of the country. Modern farming has much reduced the wild hedgerows of the old farmers, and the H. is becoming more and more supplanted by the iron fence. Hedges are stated to have been introduced into Scotland and Ireland during the Commonwealth.

Hedge'bote, in English law, is the same as *Haybote* (q. v.).

Hedge'hog (*Erinaceus*), a well-known genus of *Insectivorous* mammalia, has the hairy covering of the upper part of the body modified to form spiny-fluted hairs. The feet are not adapted for burrowing. The common H. (*E. Europæus*) has five toes on each foot, the entire sole being applied to the ground (*plantigrade*). The nose is prolonged to form a flexible snout; the eyes and rounded ears are small. The vertebræ of the back number fifteen, those of the loins six; and fifteen pairs of ribs exist, eight being attached to the breastbone. The teeth number thirty-six; no canines are developed; six incisors and six molars occur in each jaw; also six premolars in the upper and four in the lower jaw. The milk-teeth number twenty-four, and fall out seven weeks after birth (*Rousseau*). The power possessed by these animals of rolling themselves up into a ball-like form as a means of defence is effected through the action of a special muscle, the *orbicularis panniculi*, which literally surrounds or encircles the body. The muscle acts in bringing the head and tail together only when the tail and head are first flexed; while, when the head and tail are extended, the action of the muscle erects the spines. The brain of the H. is almost entirely smooth, or destitute of convolutions, like that of other insectivora. The testes of the male are abdominal, and do not leave the cavity of the abdomen; and the *cornua* or horns of the uterus are long. The food consists of slugs, earthworms, and insects. The average length is 10 inches. The long-eared H. (*E. auritius*) occurs in N. Asia and N. Africa, and is of smaller size than the common H. The Tenrec (q. v.) (*Centetes*) is sometimes named the 'Madagascar H.'

Hedgehog Plant is applied to species of *Medicago* (more particularly *M. intertexta*) on account of the prickly legume being spirally twisted into a sort of ball. In like manner *Caucalis daucoides*, belonging to the *Umbelliferæ*, is called *Hedgehog Parsley* from its spiny fruit.

Hedge Mustard, a common name for species of *Sisymbrium*, a genus of cruciferous plants. The common H. M. (*S. officinale*) occurs abundantly as a weed in waste places. *S. Irio* is called *London wild rocket*, on account of its having sprung up in great profusion immediately after the great fire in London in 1666. There are about eighty species of S. distributed in the northern hemisphere. They are of no economic importance.

Hedge Sparrow, or **Accen'tor** (*Accentor modularius*), a common species of Insessorial birds, belonging to the *Dentirostres*, has narrow nostrils, the first quill short, and the fourth and fifth longest. The tarsi have broad scales in front, and the claw of the hind-toe is long and compressed. The bird derives its name from its habit of frequenting hedges. Its colour is a bluish or slaty grey variegated with brown; the back and wings are brown, the under parts grey and white. The average length is 5 or 6 inches. The nest is built near the ground, and the eggs, five in number, are of a bluish-green. The Alpine accentor (*A. Alpinus*) is an allied species, attaining a length of 6½ inches, and found in France, Italy, and Germany.

Hedjas', a maritime district of the W. coast of Arabia, was ceded to the Ottoman Empire in 1867, since which time it has formed a vilayet or general government, of which the seaport Jidda is the capital. Its soil is unproductive, and besides the seat of government, the only port is Yambo. It contains the cities of Mecca and Medina, the birthplace of Mohammed and his place of sepulture. It is therefore the Holy Land of the Mohammedan world, and attracts crowds of pious Moslems annually.

Hedj'rah, or **Hegira** (a contraction from the Arabic *Hedjrat-al-Nebi*, 'the prophet's departure'), the era fixed by the Calif Omar, and since adhered to among Mohammedans, for the computation of time. The first day of the era was July 16, 622, on which date Mohammed fled to Medina from Mecca, where the Koreish sought his life.

Heem, Jan David de, the greatest of the Dutch fruit and flower painters, was born at Utrecht in 1600. His life was uneventful, honourable, and exceedingly prosperous. His pictures of flower-filled vases in gold, silver, or crystal standing on tables strewn with fruit are marvels of freshness, truth, and strength of colour. During his lifetime they commanded almost unheard-of prices, and since his death, which took place at Antwerp in 1674, they are only to be seen in the more celebrated galleries. See Descamps' *La Vie des Peintres Hollandais*.

Hee'ren, Arnold Herman Ludwig, a noted German historian, was born at Arbergen near Bremen, 25th October 1760, studied at Göttingen, and became lecturer in classics there in 1785. He attracted notice by editing the texts of some less-known classical authors; was made, after a sojourn in Italy, Professor of Philosophy at Göttingen in 1787, and Professor of History in 1801. He died 7th March 1842. His best-known works are *Ideen über Politik, den Verkehr und den Handel der Alten* (Gott. 1793-96, 4to ed. 1824); *Geschichte des Studiums der Classichen Literatur* (1797-1802); *Geschichte der Staaten des Alterthums* (1799, 5th ed. 1826); *Geschichte des Europäischen Staatensystems und seiner Colonien* (1809, 4th ed. 1822). His *Historische Werke* (15 vols. 1821-26) are mainly a reprint of these and other smaller publications.

Hef'ele, Karl Joseph von, an ecclesiastical historian, was born 15th March 1809 at Unterkochen, in the E. of Würtemberg, became in 1840 professor in the Catholic theological faculty of the university at Tübingen, and in 1870 Bishop of Rottenburg. He was known before and at the Vatican Council as a zealous opponent of the dogma of infallibility, but has since tacitly accepted it. H. published an edition of the *Patres Apostolici* (1839, 4th ed. 1855); *Der Cardinal Ximenes* (1844, Eng. trans. 1860); but is best known by his great work the *Konciliengeschichte* (vols i.-vii. 1855 to 1874), of which an English translation is at present (1877) appearing.

He'gel, George Friedrich Wilhelm, one of the greatest of German metaphysicians, was born at Stuttgart, August 27, 1770. When eighteen he went to the University of Tübingen, where he was a fellow-student of Schelling. After having been a private tutor for some years, he qualified as privat-docent at Jena in 1801. Here he joined Schelling for a time in editing *Das Kritische Journal für Philosophie*, but shortly after the battle of Jena went first to Bamberg, where he edited a political journal, and then to Nürnberg, where he became rector of the academy. In 1816 H. was made Professor of Philosophy at Heidelberg, and in 1818 accepted a call to Berlin, where, for a dozen years, he reigned supreme in philosophical, and exercised a very great influence in political, circles. He died of cholera in 1831, not long after his election to the rectorship of the university. A collected edition of H.'s works was published at Berlin in 1832-41. See Rosenkranz, *Hegel's Leben* (Berl. 1844).

In H.'s system are to be found elements drawn from all quarters. Plato, Aristotle, and the Neoplatonists, Jacob Böhm and Spinoza in more modern times, and Kant, Fichte, and Schelling among his immediate predecessors, seem to have influenced him more than any others. In the main, however, he may be directly affiliated to Kant, provided we bear in mind the immense aid he derived from the systems of Fichte and Schelling. Kant maintained that there was a system of absolute acts of thought, constitutive of not merely all experience or nature (by ordering the vague chaos of given sensations in definite relations in the forms of time and space), but also, by means of nature, of all individual minds, which are thus so far absolutely identical, being but the one absolute reason, which is realised in a plurality of self-conscious individuals. H. followed out this conception. He showed that the supposed necessary causes of sensations, things in themselves, were meaningless fictions, and that space and time, which Kant supposed to belong to a faculty different from the categories, were in reality intelligible relations logically derived from them, and constituted by thought. Sensations he showed also to derive their whole existence from the categories, to be as it were *potential* thought. H. was accordingly left with pure thought or reason as creative (not *in time*, for time belongs to that very sphere of nature which thought constitutes, but *logically*), and the problem was how to discover the intelligible system of reason which manifests itself in the categories. These Kant had deduced from the empirical classification of formal judgments afforded by ordinary logic; but H., seeing that this inductive procedure, which involved the conception of experience as given to instead of built up by thought, was futile, invented a presuppositionless dialectical method for the discovery of their mutual relations. To illustrate this we may take the simplest and emptiest of all abstractions, the category of being. But this has no meaning save as the correlative of the category of non-being, and the two are only realised by their union in the notion becoming, of which they are the logical constituents. This category is in its turn only real as the correlative to fixed determinate being, the two notions mutually involving each other. By following out this dialectical process, passing through on our path the categories of substantiality, causality, and many others, we reach a point where the region of pure thought terminates, and the logically implied sphere of nature is entered, where reason finds its correlative in irrationality or contingency. The antithesis of reason and nature is finally reconciled in the higher notion of self-consciousness, which includes all personal and individual relations, psychological, ethical, and religious. It must be borne in mind that this dialectical development of reason is not evolution in time, but pure logical explication of notions implicated in one another, in which each higher category presupposes and is yet presupposed by two lower correlatives, itself forming one of a higher pair of correlatives. Accordingly, the crowning notion of the Hegelian system, self-consciousness, is that which is logically last, since it is also logically first, as being that in which all the lower ones attain reality. This point was foreshadowed in the doctrines of the active reason of Aristotle and the Arabian Averroes. Self-conscious knowledge is thus the one fact in which all else finds its meaning and existence (*cf.* Berkeley's *New Question*, leading to the result that *esse* means *percipe*), and the categories with their derivative nature, while constituting, only become real in the plurality of individual *egos*. Shortly after the death of H. there appeared divisions among his disciples, at first principally in connection with the doctrines of the personality of the absolute, the immortality of the individual consciousness, and the person of Christ, but afterwards to a great extent in the region of politics also. The so-called 'Hegelians of the Left' may be said, speaking generally, to have denied the empirical reality of the three first-mentioned conceptions, and to have maintained Radicalism in politics. Of this school, Michelet, Ruge, and Strauss may be taken as representatives. Those of the 'Right' (Erdmann, Göschel, &c.) maintained for these conceptions empirical reality, in addition to their admitted position in the dialectical development of the notion. There was also a school (represented by Rosenkranz) which sought to adopt a position midway between the two extremes.

The Hegelian metaphysic, once the almost unanimous creed of philosophical Germany, has, since the great movement of 1848, almost died out in that country, where the tendency is at present towards materialism in so far as it is reconcilable with Kant's theory of perception. Hegelianism has of late, however, taken root in England, its psychological side, as dealing with the problem of the origin of knowledge, receiving the chief share of attention. This tendency first assumed adequate shape in Dr. Stirling's *Secret of H.*, and has reappeared in Mr. Green's *Introduction to the Works of Hume*, two books which, combined with a thorough study of Kant, form, perhaps, the best introduction to Hegelianism for the English student of philosophy.

Hegesipp'us (Gr. *Hēgēsippos*), a Christian writer of Asia Minor, who about the middle of the 2d c. composed a collection of historical traditions drawn from the apostolic period, of which a few fragments are now all that remain. See Grabe, *Spicilegium*, tom. ii., Fabricius, *Bibl. Græca*, vii. 156.

Hegi'ra. See HEDJRAH.

Hei'de, a market-town in the province of Slesvig-Holstein, Prussia, 25 miles W.S.W. of Rendsburg. It lies in the Ditmarsh district, and has some trade in agricultural produce. Pop. (1875) 6772.

Hei'delberg, a town in the grand duchy of Baden, Germany, magnificently situated at the mouth of the Neckar valley, where the river forsakes the richly wooded hill country for the great plain of the Rhine. H. is 45 miles distant by rail from Frankfurt. The glorious ruin of the castle, for 500 years the seat of the electors palatine, stands on the hill behind the town. The castle was begun in the 13th c., was partially blown up by the French in 1689, and wholly destroyed by fire in 1769; but its cellars still preserve the enormous H. wine-cask. The University of H. is one of the oldest in Germany, having been founded in 1356. In 1875 it had 99 teachers in its staff, and 534 students. The library contains about 175,000 vols. and 2000 MSS. Pop. (1871) 19,983.

Heights, Measurement of, may be effected in four different ways, viz., by levelling, by trigonometrical survey, by the temperature of the boiling-point, and by barometrical observations. The last two methods depend upon the same phenomenon, the rarefaction of the atmosphere, and consequent diminution of pressure, as the distance from the earth's surface is increased. By both methods the difference of pressure at the sea-level and at the height can be calculated, and from this, by means of a formula, the height can be obtained. On account of the non-homogeneous nature of our atmosphere, this formula is complicated, and, as given by Clerk Maxwell, is as follows, where h is the height in feet, P the pressure at the bottom, p that at the top, and t the temperature in Fahrenheit degrees :—

$$h = \log. \frac{P}{p} \times \left\{ 60360 + (t - 32^\circ) \times 122{\cdot}68 \right\}$$

Roughly, the difference of the logarithms of the heights of the barometer multiplied by 10,000 gives the difference of the heights in fathoms. The other methods will be considered under the articles LEVEL and TRIGONOMETRY.

Heijn, or **Heyn, Peter Petersen**, a famous Dutch naval commander, was born in 1577 at Delftshaven, and by his own bravery and skill rose from a cabin-boy to be admiral of Holland. In the services of the Dutch West India Company he, in 1626, defeated a Spanish fleet, and captured forty-five vessels at one stroke; and in 1628 made a prize of a flotilla of Spanish galleons, carrying silver and jewels to the value of 12,000,000 of Dutch gulden. Made Admiral of Holland in 1629, he fell in an action with two Dunkirk vessels that same year.

Heilbronn (originally *Heligbronn*, 'holy well'), a town of Würtemberg, on the Neckar, 23 miles N. of Stuttgart by rail, was once a free imperial city, and still possesses monuments of its former grandeur. Its Gothic church of St. Kilian dates from the 11th c. It is now the most important commercial and industrial town in the kingdom, manufacturing beet-sugar, tobacco, paper, woollens, machinery, iron goods, silver wares, and chemicals. Pop. (1871) 18,995.

Heil'igenstadt ('holy town'), a town of Prussian Saxony, on the Leine, 60 miles N.W. of Erfurt by railway. It has manufactures of woollen and paper, and some dyeing, a former Jesuits' college, and a pop (1875) of 5201.

Heils'berg, a town of E. Prussia, on the Alle, 43 miles S. of Königsberg, has manufactures of cloth, yarn, thread, beer, &c. Its castle was the residence of the former Bishops of Ermeland, in Poland. Pop. (1875) 5770.

Heils'bronn, or **Klos'ter Heils'bronn**, a market-town of Bavaria, in Middle Franconia (pop. 996), formerly the seat of a Cistercian abbey (suppressed in 1555), still a church, containing the tombs of the Hohenzollern Burggrafs of Nürnberg and of the Markgrafs of Ansbach, restored by Friedrich Wilhelm IV. of Prussia. See Hocker's *Heilsbronnisches Antiquitätenschatz* (2 vols. 1731-40).

Hei'ne, Hein'rich, one of the greatest lyrical poets of any country, was born of Jewish parents, at Düsseldorf, in Rhenish Prussia, December 12, 1799. In his youth he was sent to Hamburg to learn business, but, disliking a commercial life, began to study law in 1819 at Bonn, and afterwards proceeded to Göttingen and Berlin. He produced a volume of poems in 1822, which was almost unnoticed, and his two tragedies *Almanzor* and *Radcliff*, issued in 1823, were even more signally unsuccessful. In 1825 he was baptized a Christian. After residing at Munich and visiting Italy, he published *Reisebilder* (1826-31), a description of his travels, which was at once favourably received, and in which his characteristic vivacity of ridicule and lucid elegance of style were first clearly visible. In 1827 appeared his *Buch der Lieder*, a volume of lyrics which captivated the German public by their wondrous melody, thrilling sadness, and faultless simplicity. He resided partly at Munich, where he edited the *Politische Annalen*, and at Berlin until 1831, when he removed to Paris. There he spent an erratic life among a congenially brilliant, gay, and careless society until 1848, when he became paralysed in the spine, and thenceforth seldom left his couch until his death, February 17, 1856. He forbade that his remains should be carried to Germany, and was buried in Montmartre cemetery at Paris. His character showed a strange mingling of fickleness, sensuality, and reckless scepticism, with intense susceptibility, wayward playfulness, and ideal intensity of passion. His poems are French in their sprightliness and lucidity, German in their rhythmical sweetness and deep simple feeling; and while they move to old ballad forms, and their cadences seem to have floated up from bygone times, they are intensely modern in spirit, and are especially marked by a pathos which again and again effervesces into mockery. His prose works are beautifully written, and abound in fantastic and scathing wit, in sunny, sportive, and mellow humour. 'On H.,' says Matthew Arnold, 'of all German authors who survived Goethe, incomparably the largest portion of Goethe's mantle fell.' The best edition of H. is his *Sämmtliche Werke* (18 vols. 1867–68). See Strodtmann's *Biographie* (2 vols. 1869); Stigand's *Life, Work, and Opinions of H.* (1875).

Heinec'cius, Johann Gottlieb, a learned German jurist, was born at Eisenberg in Sachsen-Altenburg, studied theology and law, became Professor of Philosophy at Halle in 1713, and was afterwards Professor of Law there, at Franeker, and at Halle again, where he died, 31st August 1741. H.'s special departments were those of German and Roman law; and his text-books (*Elementa Juris Civilis Secundum Ordinem Institutionum*, 1725; *Elementa Juris Civilis Secundum Ordinem Pandectarum*, 1728; *Historia Juris Romani et Germanici*, 1733), were long classical works, not merely in virtue of their completeness, but by reason of their logical method and excellent Latin. The *Opera Omnia* of H. were published by his son at Geneva, in 9 vols. (1771).

Hein'rich I., 'the fowler,' King of the Germans, was born in 876, succeeded his father, Otto I., as Duke of Saxony in 912, and was chosen king in 919. He repelled the Magyars and Wends, won back Lotharingia, and by his energetic but conciliatory policy greatly strengthened German monarchy. Until his reign there was no civic life in Germany, but he founded numerous towns both as fortresses against the Hungarians and as centres of industry. H. died at Mansleben, July 2, 936. He was never made Holy Roman Emperor, and only bore the imperial title because his soldiers hailed him as *Imperator*.—**H. II.**, Saint, was born May 6, 972, became Duke of Bavaria in 995, King of the Germans in 1002, and Holy Roman Emperor in 1014. He warred with the Poles, and with France and Italy, and died July 14, 1024. He was canonised in 1154 from his favours to the Church.—**H. III.**, surnamed the Black and the Pious, succeeded Konrad II. in 1026, and was elected Emperor in 1046. Under him the imperial power came to its zenith. He suppressed intestine feuds, and placed the great duchies, the constant rivals of the kingly power, in the hands of his relatives. He forced Hungary to pay tribute, and no emperor ever wielded such authority over Rome. He compelled the Roman priesthood to receive German pontiffs, and gained the right of always appointing the Pope. But when, owing to his sudden death in 1056, a child, **H. IV.**, inherited his dominions, the great fabric of imperial power which he had reared broke down. H. IV. was born November 11, 1050, was elected King in 1054, and succeeded H. III. in 1056. During his youth Germany was rent by feudal discord, and in 1074 he appealed to Pope Gregory VII. (q. v.) to decide between him and his unruly vassals, whereupon Gregory forbade H. to sell and grant benefices until the quarrel was ended, a command which H. ignored after defeating the insurgents at Hohenburg. A long struggle ensued between the Pope and Emperor, the details of which are given in the article GREGORY VII. The central incident was the humiliation of H. at Canossa in 1077, when the Emperor remained three days and nights barefooted on the snow until Gregory deigned to absolve him, and 'Christendom saw her greatest and most venerable institution dishonoured and helpless' (Bryce's *Holy Roman Empire*). After protracted wars with Saxon vassals stirred up by the Pope, H. entered Italy and besieged Gregory in the castle of St. Angelo, but was recalled to Germany by the news that Heinrich of Luxenburg had been elected King. Having crushed the rebellion, he again carried on a successful war in Italy from 1090 to 1096, when he heard that his son Konrad had joined the revolt against him at home. Returning to Germany, he ruled with great popularity until 1105, when his son, H. V., deposed him and flung him into prison, whence, however, he escaped. H. died at Liége, when preparing to oppose his son, August 7, 1106.—**H. V.**, son of the above, was born in 1081, elected King in 1099, and dethroned his father in 1106. He was a firm foe of the Papacy. At his coronation as Emperor at Rome in 1106, he flung Pope Paschal II.—who resented his claim to all the rights over the Church which any emperor had held—into prison, and only freed him on the pontiff accepting his terms. A long strife with the Pope immediately began, and when it ended at the Concordat of Worms in 1122, the imperial power was greatly shaken, and H. retained only half of his former rights of investiture. Besides civil dissensions, H. had wars with Flanders, Poland, and Hungary. He married Matilda, daughter of Henry V. of England, died at Utrecht, May 23, 1125.—**H. VI.**, the Cruel, son of Friedrich Barbarossa, was born in 1165, and began to reign in 1190. His marriage with Constance, the heiress of the Norman rulers, by making him master of Sicily and Naples, gave him a strong influence over the Pope, as these countries had formerly been held by the chief papal adherents. His efforts to build up a centralised system of government were cut short by his death, which some attribute to his wife's poisoning him, at Messina, September 28, 1197.—**H. VII.**, son of Heinrich, Count of Luxembourg, was born in 1262, was made King of the Romans in 1308, and Emperor in 1312. Although the struggle between the Empire and the Papacy had now ceased, H. interfered between the Italian factions, which still bore the names of Guelphs and Ghibellines, invaded Italy, and died on his march against Naples, at Buonconvento, August 24, 1313. Some say he was poisoned by a Dominican while taking the eucharist.

Heinrich the Lion, Duke of Saxony, a famous German prince, son of Heinrich the Proud, was born in 1129, and began to rule in 1146. When Konrad III. set out on the second crusade, H. carried on war against the Wends, and on Konrad's enterprise ending in gloom, claimed all Bavaria as his own. Konrad shortly returned, and H. was reduced to submission, but Bavaria was given up to him by the next Emperor, Friedrich Barbarossa. In 1154 he accompanied Friedrich into Italy, and courageously saved the Emperor's life in a tumult at Rome. H. now strove to swell his dominions by cruel wars against the Slavs, and in 1171, to avoid aiding Friedrich in his Italian campaigns, made a pilgrimage to Jerusalem. On his return he set up a lion as a symbol of his power in the market-place of Brunswick, whence arose the legend of his being accompanied on his pilgrimage by a lion. In 1154 he entered Lombardy with the Emperor, whom he deserted before the battle of Legnano. On Friedrich's return from Italy, H. was assailed by the Emperor and all the German nobles save those of Saxony. He resisted bravely, and won a great victory in 1180, but was finally forced to yield, and stripped of all his dominions except Brunswick. He died at Brunswick in 1198. He was a bold, ambitious, and able prince, and at one time ruled dominions spreading from Lombardy to the Black Sea. He gave great privileges to his towns, which clung firmly to him in his struggle with the Emperor. He was twice married, his second wife being Matilda, daughter of Henry II. of England.

Heinrich von Veldeke, one of the chief of the Minnesänger, and founder of the medieval German court poetry, flourished during the 12th c., resided at the court of Hermann, Landgraf of Thuringia, and took part in the wars of Wartburg. His works include *Eneid*, a love story, partly based on Virgil's *Æneid*, but drawing its inspiration mainly from French sources; *Herzog Ernst von Baiern*, and various love songs. A legend of St. Gervais is also ascribed to him. Gervinus says he was the first who gave German verse cadence and melody, and subjected it to fixed laws. See Ettmüller's *H. von V.* (Leips. 1854).

Heir, in English law. The person next in the line of succession to the holder of real estate is called the H. *apparent* or the H. *presumptive*. The former is one whose right of inheritance is certain, if he outlives his predecessor; the latter is one who would succeed to his predecessor under existing circumstances, but whose right may be defeated by birth of a child. The only H. apparent is an eldest son, or one holding his right. Any relative may be an H. presumptive. In English law, see INTESTACY. In Scotch law, SUCCESSION, HEIR, and HEIRS-PORTIONERS. In both, see HEIR AND EXECUTOR, HEIRESS, HEIRLOOMS.

Heir, in Scotch law. The word denotes the H. at law, and the H. *by destination*, that is, the person named in the deed of conveyance, failing the person to whom the estate is conveyed. A series of heirs is sometimes named in general terms, as to *A. B.*, and the heirs male of his body. The word is also sometimes loosely applied to the person who succeeds to the movable (English, personal) estate. To displace the legal H. to any subject or estate, the testator must convey the estate or subject to the person whom he wishes to succeed to it, and he may call to the succession a series of strangers.

After an H. has completed his title every right possessed by his predecessor is vested in him. Heirs are liable for the debts of their ancestor in a certain order. The H. at law—sometimes called the heir of line—is primarily liable; next is the H. of conquest (see CONQUEST); then follows the H. male, the H. by destination, and lastly the H. under a marriage contract. This is the order in which those heirs must be discussed. See DISCUSSION.

Heir and Exec'utor, a phrase denoting the legal distinction between two kinds of property which may be left by one deceased, *i.e.*, *real* and *personal*, in Scotland *heritable* and *movable*. Real property goes to the heir, personal property to the executors or administrators. Some property is heritable in Scotland which in England is personal. See EXECUTOR, EXECUTOR IN SCOTLAND, EXECUTRY, HEIRLOOMS.

Heir'ess. Sisters having a joint right of inheritance are called *coparceners* in England (see COPARCENERY), in Scotland, *Heirs-Portioners* (q. v.).

Heir'ess, in heraldry, a lady whose brothers leave no issue is an H. Alliance with an H. is expressed by quartered arms; if her husband bear her arms upon a shield of pretence upon his own shield, their descendants would quarter her quartered shield. See MARSHALLING.

Heir'looms are certain chattels (see CHATTELS) which by custom go to the heir at law, such as family pictures, plate, jewels, &c. The extent of the right is very vague. In Scotch law, *heirship movables* is a similar but much more comprehensive term. They consist of the best of certain kinds of movable (personal) goods belonging to the predecessor. The right to inherit them only arises under peculiar circumstances.

Heirs-Por'tioners a term of Scotch law. Failing male issue and their issue, succession to heritage opens in favour of the female issue. Females, or their representatives in the same degree of relationship to the deceased, inherit equally and *pro indiviso* with H.-P. The eldest heir-portioner has a right to the mansion-house of a country estate, without compensation to her sisters. She is also entitled to any peerage or dignity not otherwise destined.

Hel, in the Scandinavian mythology, the daughter of Loki and the giantess Angerbodi. Alfader cast her down to Niflheim, and gave her power over nine worlds as a place of maintenance for those sent to her, that is, those who died of age or sickness. There she had great mansions within courts of excessive height, fenced with massive gratings. Her threshold was a devouring abyss, her hangings threatening sorrow, her dish famine, her knife hunger, her bed a sick-bed, and her slaves sluggish. She was half of a bluish-black and half of human complexion, and had a head bent down, presenting a fierce aspect.

Hel'denbuch (Ger. *Book of Heroes*), a famous collection of old German heroic poems dealing with events which happened in the time of the barbaric invasions of the Empire. It includes the tales of Dietrich of Bern (q. v.), of the famous rose-garden of Worms, of the dwarf Elberich, and the emperor Otnit, &c. These were written at various times, but mostly in the 13th c., and among their authors were Heinrich von Ofterdingen and Wolfram von Eschenbach. The first printed edition of the H. appeared in 1491 (new ed. by A. Von Keller, 1867). A modernised edition was issued by Von der Hagen (Berl. 1811), and again by Simrock (6 vols. 2d ed. 1851); the original was published by Von der Hagen and Prunissier (Berl. 2 vols. 1820–24).

Hel'der, a fortified seaport of the Netherlands, in the province of N. Holland, on the Texelgat or Marsdiep, 4 miles broad, separating the island of Texel from the mainland, and uniting the German Ocean with the Zuider Zee. Lying at the N. end of the peninsula of N. Holland, where the sand dunes are most enfeebled, the H. is protected by massive works, including a dyke of Norwegian granite and Belgian limestone 6 miles long. It was made a naval station by Napoleon I., and since the N. Holland Canal was constructed to avoid the difficult passage of the Zuider Zee (1820) has been the out-port for the larger vessels with cargo for Amsterdam. In 1874 there entered the port 463 vessels of 243,038 tons, and cleared 473 of 264,684 tons. Pop. (1875) 21,328.

Hel'en (Gr. *Helena*), daughter of Zeus and Leda, and sister of Castor and Pollux, was the fairest of all women, and the cause of the siege of Troy. At the age of ten she was carried off by Theseus and Pirithous, but was rescued by her brothers. She was sought in marriage by noble suitors from all Greece, who by the advice of Odysseus bound themselves to support the husband whom she might choose, should any strive to carry her off. She chose Menelaus, King of Sparta, and when Paris bore her away to Troy, the Greek princes set out to recover her, which led to the great war of Troy. Legend varies as to her fate after the taking of Troy. She returned with Menelaus to Sparta, bore him a daughter Hermione, and lived in wealth and happiness until his death, when, according to one story, she was driven from Sparta and slain by the queen of Rhodes. Another legend says that both Menelaus and H. were sacrificed by Iphigenia in Tauris to Artemis. H. figures very largely in ancient poetry, and is depicted by Greek artists as the perfection of female loveliness, while modern poets, *e.g.*, Marlowe, Goethe, Landor, and Rossetti, have recurred again and again to the story of her surpassing beauty.

Hel'ena, the name of various Christian saints, of whom the most famous is the Empress Helena Flavia Julia, mother of Constantine the Great. She was of lowly origin, and was born most probably in Bithynia in 247, though some assert that she was a native of Gloucester in Britain. She was married to Constantine Chlorus, who, when he was made Cæsar by Diocletian in 292, was forced to divorce her in place of the step-daughter of Maximinius. After Constantine became Emperor in 306, H., who was treated with great honour, and had received the title of *Augusta*, embraced Christianity, and, according to the Christian legend, made a pilgrimage to Jerusalem, where she discovered the holy sepulchre and the wood of the true cross. H. died at an advanced age in 328.

Hele'na, St., a solitary island in the Atlantic, belonging to Great Britain, 863 miles S.E. of Ascension Island, and 1140 W. of the African, and 1800 E. of the American shore, in lat. 15° 55′ S., and long. 5° 49′ W. Area, 47 sq. miles; pop. (1871) 6241. It is 10½ miles long, 7 broad, and presents to the sea a line of cliffs from 600 to 1200 feet high, broken only by an occasional fortified gorge. The only good harbour is James's Bay, on which is situated James's Town, a port regularly visited by vessels bound for the Cape. St. H. is of volcanic origin, and rises in Diana's Peak to a height of 2700 feet. It has a delightful climate, and some agriculture and goat-breeding, but provisions have to be imported. The island was discovered by Juan de Nova Castella on St. H.'s Day, 22d May 1502. It was subsequently occupied by the Dutch, who ceded it to the English East India Company in the 17th c. It was the islet-prison of Napoleon from 1815 till his death in 1821. See *St. H., a Physical, Historical, and Topographical Description*, by J. C. Melliss (Lond. 1875).

Hel'ensburgh, a pretty watering-place in Dumbartonshire, Scotland, on the right side of the Firth of Clyde at the entrance to Gair Loch, opposite Greenock, and 23 miles W.N.W. of Glasgow by rail. It has a promenade, a landing stage, and some weaving and fishing. In the vicinity are many fine mansions. Pop. (1871) 5975.

Heli'acal (*hēliakos*, 'belonging to the sun'), an expression in astronomy, formerly used with reference to the rising of a star which rose just a sufficient time before the sun to be visible in the early dawn.

He'liand (Gr. *heiland*, 'saviour'), a Low German poem of the 9th c., which narrates the life of Christ in alliterative verse, in a style derived from the old heathen ballads. It contains some interesting traits of the times when it was composed, and is said to have been written by command of the Frankish King Hhlodwig, or Ludwig the Pious (the *Louis le Débonnaire* of French historians). There are two manuscripts of the H., one in the British Museum, London, and one at Munich. It was published by A. Schmeller, Munich (1830–40).

Helian'thus, a genus of herbaceous composite plants, chiefly natives of North America. *H. tuberosus*, the Jerusalem Artichoke (q. v.) and *H. annuus*, the Sunflower (q. v.), belong to the genus.

Helianthus annuus.

Heli'cidæ, (from Gr. *helix*, 'a spiral,' the family of *Gasteropodous* Mollusca, including the snails. The shell is external, and contains the whole animal when it is withdrawn. No *Operculum* (q. v.) exists for the closure of the shell aperture. See SNAIL.

Hel'icon, a mountain of Bœotia, Greece, between Lake Copais and the Gulf of Corinth. It may be considered a continuation of the range of Parnassus, and its topmost summit (now *Paleovuni*) is about 5000 feet high. Its western slopes are bare and rugged, but its eastern are fertile and woody. It was famed as the chosen abode of the Muses, who had a sacred grove here, near which were the sacred wells of Hippocrene and Aganippe, which inspired all who drank of them. The village of Ascra, at the foot of H., was the seat of the early Hesiodic school of poets.

Helig'oland, or **Hel'goland** (*i.e.*, 'holy land'), the smallest of the British possessions, and an islet in the North Sea, about 30 miles from the mouths of the Elbe, Weser, and Eider. Area, one-fifth of a sq. mile; pop. 1913. It is formed of hard red clay and marl, and on three sides rises nearly perpendicularly from the sea to a height of 150 feet. On the S.E. side there is a low, flat bank of sand called the Unterland, on which stands the principal group of houses, restaurants, a theatre, &c., and from which a flight of 190 wooden steps leads to the Oberland, or plateau, where, on the margin of the cliff, is the village of Falm. The pastures of the Oberland support goats and some 300 sheep, and there is some cultivation of potatoes. Opposite the Unterland, and separated from it by a strait half a mile wide, is the *Düne* or *Sandinsel*, appropriated to the bathers who flock hither in the holiday season from Bremen and Hamburg. The inhabitants, who are mostly Frisians, are occupied as pilots and lobster-fishers, and have peculiarities of dialect and costume. The maintenance of batteries and a lighthouse costs the Government £1000 yearly. H. has been greatly diminished by the action of the sea. It was anciently the residence of the chief of the Sicambri, and the seat of the worship of the Saxon goddess Hertha. Its old name of Fosetisland gave place to that of H. when it received Christianity in the 7th c. from St. Williberond. It belonged to Slesvig till the English seized it in 1807. During the blockade of 1812 it was a great resort of smugglers, and more recently of gamblers.

Heliocen'tric, an astronomical term, used with reference to the positions or motions of a planet or other body, which is supposed to be viewed from the sun. See GEOCENTRIC.

Heliodo'rus, the author of the earliest Greek romance, was born at Emesa, Syria, and flourished about the end of the 4th c., becoming Bishop of Trikka, Thessaly. His tale, named *Æthiopica*, which describes the loves of Theagenes, a youth of Thessaly, and Charicleia, daughter of an Æthiopian king, is full of romantic interest, and is told with delightful art in a sweet, simple, and poetical style. The *Æthiopica* was imitated by Tatius and other Greek writers of fiction, and had a great influence on the heroic romances and poems of Italy and France, Tasso in particular confessing himself much indebted to H. It has been translated into most modern languages. The best editions are in the *Scriptorum Græcorum Bibliotheca* of Didot; the *Scriptores Græci Erotici* of Mitscherlich (Strass. 1798); and that by Coraes (2 vols. Par. 1805).

Heliogab'alus. See ELAGABALUS.

Heliom'eter was originally a small telescope with a divided object-glass, used for determining the diameter of the sun; but the name now denotes any instrument which has its object-glass constructed on the same peculiar principle, and which measures with great accuracy small angular distances, such as the distance between the individual members of a multiple star system. Frauenhofer was the first to construct a H. of any size; and his instrument was productive of most valuable results in the hands of Bessel. Merz and Repsold have successfully followed up Frauenhofer's example; and the fine instrument at Oxford observatory is the work of the latter. The principle is explained in Herschel's *Outlines of Astronomy*. See also Bessel's memoir on the *Königsberg Observations*, and Professor Johnston's paper in the *Radcliffe Observations* (Oxford).

Hēlios, the Greek name for the sun and the sun-god. H., the god, was the son of Hyperion and Theia, and the brother of Selēnē, the moon, and Eōs, the dawn. Homer describes him as rising in the morning from a marsh formed by the ocean stream, and as sinking in the ocean at evening. The later poets represent him as sailing nightly under the earth, back to the E., in a golden boat, or while slumbering in a golden bed, and as dwelling in a gorgeous palace in the E. and W. The eastern palace is splendidly described in Ovid's story of Phaethon (Met. ii.). H. was partly identified with Phœbus Apollo, and was widely worshipped, Rhodes being his chief seat. The cock was peculiarly sacred to H., and white rams, boars, lambs, and especially white horses were sacrificed to him. The myth of H. is certainly of Hindu origin. See Cox's *Manual of Mythology* (Lond. 1867).

He'liostat, an instrument for keeping a celestial object constantly in the field of view of the telescope. It effects this by throwing a reflected image of the object into the tube of the telescope from a plane mirror, which is kept in the necessary position by clockwork.

He'liotrope, a name given to species of *Heliotropium*, a large genus of herbs or under-shrubs belonging to the natural order *Boraginaceæ* (q. v.). They occur chiefly in warm countries, only a few being met with in Central and Southern Europe. *H. Peruvianum* is cultivated in gardens for its sweet-scented flowers. Some authors place H. in the natural order *Ehretiaceæ*.

Heliotrope, or **Bloodstone**, a deep green uncrystallised variety of quartz, faintly translucent, with bright red spots, as if intermixed with carnelion. The red colour is due to iron. H. is pretty widely distributed, but the most valuable specimens are obtained in the S. of Asia.

Hell, in modern language, means the place of torture which is the abode of the wicked after death. The word itself is Teutonic, and primarily in its heathen usage denoted the realm of Hel (q. v.), the Scandinavian goddess of the dead or the under world. Even in the rude Northern myth we can discern some faint perception of H. as not merely an abode of misery but a place of punishment, but the word did not acquire its dread import till the perfervid ethics of Christianity had obtained dominion over the Teutonic mind. Then, from denoting 'thrilling regions of thick-ribbed ice,' it passed to signify a realm of scorching flame such as appalled the fancy of Oriental nations. In the Old Testament the word occurs thirty-one times as the equivalent of the Heb. *sheol*. In the New Testament it occurs twenty-three times, twelve times standing for Gehenna (q. v.), and eleven times for Hades (q. v.). The meaning to be attached to H., therefore, depends on the meanings of these three words. 1. *Sheol* (1) in many passages means simply the *grave*, in the general sense in which it is co-extensive with death, and in fact it is so translated thirty-one times, or as often as by H. It is also thrice translated *pit*, in much the same sense. (2) Even when the idea of retribution is connected with it, as when it is translated H., the reference is more to the danger of a sudden and terrible death, than to a place of infernal anguish (Ps. ix. 17; Prov. v. 5, ix. 18, xv. 24), for until a late period of their national existence the Jews had no vivid apprehension of a future life at all (*cf.* Isa. xxxviii. 9–20; Ps. vi. 5; Eccles. ix. 10). 2. *Hades* in the New Testament means also the abode in the region of the dead of good and bad, or of happy and miserable alike. The separate condition of the happy is indicated by Paradise (q. v.), which has a threefold meaning—the Garden of Eden, 'the Hades of departed saints, and the heaven of their glorious rest,' or by the peculiar phrase, 'Abraham's bosom.' 3. *Gehenna* denotes both Tartarus (2 Pet. ii. 4), and the final condition of the lost (Matt. xxiii. 33).

Helladothe'rium, a remarkable extinct genus of *Ungulate* (q. v.) or 'hoofed' quadrupeds, allied to the existing Giraffe (q. v.). The H. fossils occur in the Upper Miocene (Tertiary) rocks of Attica. No horns were developed in these singular beings, and as regards their dentition they appear to have resembled the antelopes. Fossil giraffes occur in the tertiary deposits in the Siwalik Hills of India.

Hell'as is an ethnological rather than a geographical term, signifying the abode of the Hellenes or ancient Greeks, and thus varying in application with the changing distribution of the Hellenes throughout parts of Europe and Asia. In the time of Homer H. was applied to a small region in the S. of Thessaly, while in the time of Herodotus it included not only the greater portion of modern Greece, but also Hellenic colonies in Italy, Sicily, Africa, and Asia Minor. H. was, however, sometimes restricted to the district bounded by the Peneus and the Corinthian and Ambracian gulfs, while after the Roman conquest the name was extended to Macedonia, Illyria, and Epirus. The Romans gave the name of Græcia to the Peloponnesus (q. v.), and the districts immediately N. of it, which are now comprised in modern Greece and the S. of Turkey, the name being probably derived from the Græci, a tribe of Epirus. From the earliest times the centre of H. was the peninsula now known as Greece, where the whole population was Hellenic, the Hellenes, one of the first Aryan peoples who entered Europe, having settled there probably about the 14th c. B.C. The situation of Greece was peculiarly favourable for colonising and maritime adventure when the Levant was the chief commercial highway, as it had a very wide seaboard, was separated from Italy by a channel in parts only 38 miles wide, lay opposite a fertile part of Africa, and was connected with Asia Minor by clusters of islands. The Hellenes early took to seafaring, placed most of their great cities near the coast, and began to found colonies in Italy and Asia Minor. (See IONIA and MAGNA GRÆCIA.) During the heroic age, reflected in the poems of Homer, they seem to have been a warlike, adventurous, and even piratical race, of considerable artistic skill, and possessing the institutions common to the Aryans. When they first appear in semi-historic times, they are divided into cities, each of which is ruled by a king. The royal office is generally hereditary, but its power is limited by the *Boulē*, or council of chiefs, and the *Agŏra*, or assembly of the people. The *Heroic Age* is the period when the mythical heroes, of whom the chief were Heraklês or Hercules, Theseus, and Jason, are supposed to have performed their exploits, which probably symbolise the gradual triumph among the Hellenes of order over lawlessness. The chief legends of the heroic age gather round the siege of Troy (q. v.), the Homeric account of which is in all likelihood a poetic rearrangement of some historic fact, it being certain that the early Hellenes had wars on the Asiatic shores of the Hellespont, and that Mycene, of which Homer makes Agamemnon the king, was the great city of the Achæans, the leading Hellenic people before the 12th c. B.C. In that century the Dorians passed from Thessaly to the Peloponnesus, and overcame the Achæans, and ruled in their cities of Sparta, Argos, and Corinth. In the heroic age the Ionians also settled in Attica and along the Corinthian gulf, while the Æolians occupied the W. of the Peloponnesus. In the 8th c. B.C. myth begins to disappear before history, and the Hellenes are seen clearly subdivided into numerous small states, which never, even up to the time of their final subdual, united into a compact federation. The intense passion of the Hellenes for town-autonomy was favoured by the configuration of Greece, which is broken up into plains isolated from one another by rugged mountains, and frequently open only to the sea. Thus Attica was cut off from the neighbouring states by high ridges, and the Peloponnesus was divided into several states separated by the lofty ranges branching out from the central 'mountain-vase' of Arcadia. Moreover, even the cities in a district such as Phocis or Bœotia were generally independent of each other, and while the half-barbarous regions of Macedonia, Molossis, and Ætolia preserved kingly government and a rude federation of towns, the cities of the true H. clung to their cardinal principle of the independence of every city. The result of this ineradicable passion for town-autonomy was to produce an intensely keen and brilliant life, both intellectual and political, which was doomed to swift disappearance from the want of national unity. There was, however, an enduring Pan-Hellenic feeling among the Hellenes, who applied the word *Barbarians* to all non-Hellenic peoples; who had language, religion, and many political and intellectual tendencies in common; and who were loosely bound together by the Pan-Hellenic institutions of the Olympic, Pythian, Isthmian, and Nemean games—open to all Hellenes, and to none but Hellenes—the central oracle of Delphi (q. v.), and the Amphictyonic Council (q. v.). The last consisted of deputies from the various states, who met twice a year to check dissensions and protect the Delphic oracle; but during the palmy age of Hellenic history the council wielded no real power, and the fact that the votes were counted by tribes, not by cities, proves it to have been mainly an empty survival from a past age. In the 7th c. we find bits of genuine history in the poetry of the time, *e.g.*, the war-songs of Tyrtæus, relating to a struggle in which Sparta crushed Messene. After this triumph Sparta defeated the Arcadians and Argives, and became the leading power in H., Athens being as yet insignificant. Before the 7th c., monarchy, the Hellenic form of government during the heroic age, had been superseded by various aristocracies, which in their turn gave way to government by *tyrants*, the name applied by the Hellenes to those who had illegally won royal power, whether they ruled well or ill. From about 650 to 600 is the age of the tyrants, after which democratic and aristocratic governments prevail, till the rise of a new brood of despots in the age immediately before H. yielded to Rome. The tyrants had mostly vanished before 500 B.C., and in the 5th c. B.C. began the most glorious war in all history—the struggle between H. and Persia—a contest of epical grandeur, from the splendid heroism of the Hellenes, the overwhelming disproportion of strength between the antagonists, and the mighty issues involved. In the 6th c. Cyrus raised Persia into a vast empire which absorbed the Hellenic colonies in Asia Minor. These rebelled against the Persian king Darius, and were aided by the Athenians, whose forces burned Sardis (500 B.C.). The Athenians, refusing to take back their expelled tyrant at the demand of the Persian king, Darius sent a force of 110,000 men against them, but this vast host was routed at Marathon (q. v.) in 490 by an army of 10,000 Athenians. After this victory—the greatest of all the 'decisive battles of the world'—Athens rose rapidly to the head of Hellenic affairs. A successful war with Ægina laid the foundation of her maritime power, and under the wise administration of Themistoclês she became mistress of the most powerful fleet in H. In 480 the Persian wars were renewed, Xerxes, son of Darius, setting out against the Hellenes with a motley army of, it is said, about 3,000,000. Thebes and other Hellenic cities sided with Xerxes, while others succumbed to him; but Sparta and Athens, though almost deserted by the rest of H., resolved to withstand the barbarians. The first battle was at Thermopylæ (q. v.), where King Leonidas and the three hundred Spartans fell. Xerxes then burnt Athens, which had been deserted by its citizens. But his fleet, after being severely handled off Artemisium, was defeated with terrible carnage at Salamis (480 B.C.), whereupon he fled to Asia, leaving Mardonius with 350,000 men to continue the war. Mardonius was decisively beaten at Platæa (q. v.) on the same day that the Hellenes won the sea-fight of Mycalê (q. v.), on the coast of Asia Minor. The glory of Salamis rests mainly with the Athenians under Themistocles, the glory of Platæa with the Spartans under Pausanias. Athens now rose swiftly to the zenith of her power. Her naval superiority over Sparta made her the fitting head of the confederacy of Delos, a Hellenic league against Persia; and she received contributions in ships and afterwards in money from the other states, whom she protected against the common foe. From 490 B.C. to 431 B.C. is the most brilliant epoch in Hellenic history—the time of the Athenian supremacy in literature, art, and war—Athens becoming under the rule of Pericles the most flourishing of Hellenic cities. (See PERICLES.) But jealousy and discontent were excited by her somewhat arbitrary application of the common fund raised by the Hellenic confederacy, and by her haughty and aggrandising policy; and in 431 the Peloponnesian War (q. v.), which lasted about twenty-seven years, broke out. It was waged between Athens and Sparta, the latter having for allies most of the Peloponnesian cities. It was a war of races and principles, between Ionians, represented by Athens, and Dorians, represented by the Peloponnesians; between democracy, represented by Athens, and aristocracy, represented by Sparta, neither party being entitled wholly to engross our sympathies. After the first ten years of the struggle neither had gained a decisive advantage, the Spartans being stronger by land, the Athenians by sea. But in 415 the Athenians sent an expedition against the Dorian colony of Syracuse, and besieged that city for two years. The Spartans took the part of their kinsmen, and the Athenians were signally beaten—a blow from which they never recovered. Their allies began to revolt, while the friends of Sparta clung to her firmly; and finally, in 405, Lysander the Spartan defeated their fleet at Ægospotamus in the Hellespont, and took Athens in 404. But the oligarchy of the Thirty Tyrants, by which the Spartans supplanted the Athenian democracy, was driven out in 403, and Athens won back freedom. The Spartans were now supreme in H. Numbers of them went to support Cyrus the Younger against Artaxerxes, and in 401 began the famous march known as the Retreat of the Ten Thousand. (See XENOPHON.) In 396 the great Spartan Agesilaus overthrew the Persian armies in Asia, and the Spartan power continued to increase until it suddenly paled before Thebes, which, under the control of Epaminondas (q. v.) and Pelopidas, now began to play the leading part in Hellenic politics, the Thebans defeating the Spartans, who had never before lost a pitched battle, at Leuctra in 371. Athens, siding first with Thebes and then with Sparta, regained much of her old influence, and after the death of Epaminondas, who fell at Mantinea, fighting against the Spartans and Athenians, the Theban power swiftly collapsed, and Macedonia emerged as the dominant state. Philip, the Macedonian king, engaged in the Sacred War, beat the allied Athenians and Thebans at Chæronea (338), and had himself elected captain-general to lead the Hellenes against Persia—the Spartans alone holding sullenly aloof. Alexander, son of Philip, in 334 led the Hellenes into Asia, and advanced in a line of dazzling conquest to the Indus. Although, after his death in 323, his vast empire crumbled away, the effects of his expedition remained. Hellenic culture was diffused through the east, Hellenic colonies were planted in Egypt, Persia, and Bactria, and Alexander's generals became rulers of half-Hellenised kingdoms whose history cannot strictly be included under that of H. (See PTOLEMY and SELEUCIDÆ.) The career of Alexander gave a vast outlet to Hellenic influence, through which there arose peoples of naturalised Hellenes, the history of the modern Greek nation beginning, according to Mr. Finlay, with Alexander's conquests. The Macedonians, who now ruled H., though not pure Hellenes, were closely akin in blood and language, besides having a capacity for receiving a Hellenic impress wanting to the other semi-Hellenic peoples who bordered on H. proper. They never sought to absorb H. in Macedonia, but to make Macedonia the leading Hellenic state. The history of the Macedonian period will be treated under MACEDONIA. It is a time of bloody, chaotic, and selfish strife. The power of the Macedonians over the Hellenes fluctuates greatly; Epirus springs into sudden power under Pyrrhus; and Ætolia and Achæa become rivals of Macedonia and Sparta. During the 3d c. tyrants began to snatch power, and leagues were formed—the most famous being the Ætolian and Achæan, which embraced all H. except Sparta, now flourishing vigorously and freed from its old oligarchy. But the Achæans, instead of uniting with Sparta, which might have enabled them to repel Macedonian and even delay Roman aggression, treacherously supported the Macedonians, against whom Rome began war on behalf of Athens in 200 B.C. After subduing Macedonia, the Romans crushed the Achæans in 146, when Mummius destroyed

Corinth, and the independence of Greece passed away, though Athens and several other cities continued to be nominally free. Until the time of the Roman empire, however, the republics of Byzantium, Rhodes, and the Lycian federation, though they held no external dominions, were internally free, and Cherson, on the Black Sea, the 'last of the Greek republics,' remained until the 9th c. practically independent, and to the end partly Hellenic. See the histories of Herodotus, Thucydides, Polybius, Thirlwall, Grote, Curtius, Cox, and Finlay; Donaldson's *Dorians*, Freeman's *Essays* (1st series), and *History of Federal Government*.

Hell'ebore, applied properly to species of *Helleborus*, a genus of plants belonging to the natural order *Ranunculaceæ* (q. v.). Nearly all the species have long been noted for their irritant qualities. Many of them act as drastic purgatives, hence their use in ancient times in cases of mania. They are natives chiefly of Southern Europe and Asia. Several species are grown in gardens, such as *H. niger* or Christmas-rose, which blooms in mid-winter, and *H. officinalis* or black H., which was used by the Greeks as a medicine. *H. fœtidus* or stinking H., and *H. viridis* or green H., are natives of Britain. H. has also been applied to species of *Veratrum*, a genus of plants belonging to *Melanthaceæ* (q. v.).

Helleborus niger.

Hellen'ic Literature. In Hellas, as has been the case in all nations, poetry was the earliest birth of literature. Indeed, if we were to judge solely from the poems of Homer and Hesiod—the most ancient works which remain to us—we should be tempted to believe that it burst forth at once, as did Minerva from the brain of Jupiter in the highest perfection. Long, however, before Homer's time, the wandering rhapsodist sang the stories of gods and heroes, the tender tale of love, and the 'pomp and circumstance of war;' and long ere the art of writing was practised, the records of the past were imprinted on the tablets of memory by aid of the rhythmic flow and recurrent chime of verse. Of the earliest lays of the Hellenic bards nothing has come down to us. Linus, 1280 B.C., the father of mythic hymnology, the minstrel Orpheus, 1260 B.C., and Musæus, the founder of the religious epic, 1180 B.C., are to us names only—names, however, which their followers in the realm of song ever delighted to honour. The earliest extant Hellenic poems, and certainly the greatest, are the *Iliad* of Homer (962-927 B.C.), an epic which has for its subject the siege of Troy and the contests of the gods and heroes that took part in the struggle; and the *Odyssey*, which contains a charming account of the wandering of Odysseus (Ulysses). This period, which also includes the Homeric hymns and the writings of the Cyclic bards, closes with the name of Hesiod (flor. 850 B.C.), author of the *Theogony*, a genealogy of the gods; the *Works and Days*, an agricultural poem; and an epyllion entitled the *Shield of Hercules*. The century 950–850 B.C. may be said to have witnessed the dawn, the noon, and the sunset of epic poetry in Hellas. Next in order came the lyric, elegiac, and iambic poets (800–530 B.C.), chief of whom were Archilochus, celebrated for his keen iambics (708 B.C.), and Simonides of Amorgus (693–662 B.C.), who disputes with Archilochus the invention of iambic verse; Tyrtæus (685 B.C.), and Callinus (678 B.C.), writers of martial elegy; Alcman of Sparta (670 B.C.), inventor of love elegy; Mimnermus of Smyrna (629 B.C.), writer of mournful elegy; Arion, dithyrambic poet (625–610 B.C.), Stesichorus of Himera (612 B.C.), esteemed by Quintilian the equal of Pindar in sublimity, harmony, and beauty of language; Sappho (610 B.C.), and Alcæus (604 B.C.), with whom the Æolian Melic attained its highest perfection; Anacreon of Teos (560 B.C.), the gay, luxurious, and festive lyric bard; Theognis of Megara (541 B.C.), gnomic poet; and Ibycus (540 B.C.), lyric poet.

In the tragedians Æschylus (524–456 B.C.), Sophocles (495–405 B.C.), and Euripides (480–406 B.C.), Hellenic literature reached the highest pitch of excellence; while in Simonides of Ceos (flor. 490 B.C.), and Pindar the Theban (522–442 B.C.)—the latter incomparably the greatest of all the lyric poets of Hellas—lyric poetry attained the greatest perfection. About this period we have the dawn of history in the Ionic logographers Hecatæus of Miletus, Charon of Lampsacus, Pherecydes of Scyros, Xanthus the Lydian, and Hellanicus of Mitylene. These were followed by the historians, whose claim to the title is paramount, and who in their respective styles are unequalled—Herodotus, called the 'Father of History' (484–408 B.C.), the concise, vigorous, and energetic Thucydides (471–402 B.C.), and the smooth and graceful Xenophon (444–362 B.C.). Between 450 B.C. and 380 B.C. flourished Magnes, Cratinus, Eupolis, and Aristophanes—all famous in the old Attic comedy. To this period—the golden age of Attic prose—belong the celebrated orators, Pericles (499–429 B.C.), Antiphon (480–411 B.C.), Lysias (459–380 B.C.), Andocides (440–390 B.C.), Isocrates (436–338 B.C.), Isæus (420–350 B.C.), Æschines (389–314 B.C.), Demosthenes (382–322 B.C.), and Hyperides (flor. 346 B.C.). The years 400–336 B.C.—the age of Spartan and Theban supremacy and of Philip of Macedon—produced the middle comedy, which numbered a long list of writers whose works have perished. After 336 B.C. the new comedy flourished. The two most important names connected therewith are those of Menander and Philemon, of whose works only fragments remain. Aratus of Soli (or Tarsus), poet and epistolary writer (flor. about 270 B.C.); the bucolic poets Theocritus (280 B.C.), Bion and Moschus (270 B.C.); the elegiac poet Callimachus and the epic poet Apollonius Rhodius (238–188 B.C.), with a number of what are known as the learned poets of the Alexandrine school, adorn the period immediately preceding the Roman age. Nor must we omit the epigrammatists who flourished greatly at this time; the historians Polybius (207–122 B.C.) and Zeno (160 B.C.); the grammarians Aristarchus (flor. 156 B.C.) and Apollodorus (146 B.C.), and the geographers Strabo (66 B.C. to 22 A.D.) and Pausanias (174 A.D.). The Hellenic prose of Polybius and the Alexandrine prose of Philo were succeeded by the revived Atticism of Lucian, satirist and sceptical wit (120–200 A.D.); Plutarch (40–120 A.D.), whose biographies of eminent men possess an enduring charm; the historians Dionysius of Halicarnassus, Appian, Arrian, and Dion Cassius, with the Erotic (q. v.) writers complete the list of later names worthy of notice.

Hellenic Mythology. The H. M. or religion was from various historical causes, as well as from the geographical isolation of the people, essentially unique. It was, moreover, at once poetical and humane. Though made up of apparently heterogeneous elements, it was not therefore inharmonious, as a brief survey of it will show. From the instinct of the Hellenes to explain everything through the medium of their emotional nature, their divinities were only human beings in a more exalted and refined condition. They invested their deities with the passions, desires, and feelings of humanity, and the worship which they accorded to them was regulated accordingly. Moreover, the creed of every individual district was framed to suit the natural dispositions and religious instincts of the people, and to accord with their aims and aspirations. This is the prime point in the creeds of all the nations of antiquity. The Hebrew Jehovah was worshipped at Jerusalem, Zeus at Olympia, Aphroditē had her shrine at Cyprus, so had Astarte in Phœnicia.

By Hesiod, the earliest genealogist of the divinities, and by the epic poets of his time, the theogony was framed, and a hierarchy of gods, similar in every respect to a conclave of human potentates, received the adoration of man. Through the medium of poesy various genealogies were promulgated, but all of these were based on *human character*, and all of the deities were clothed in *human shape*. These features pervade the H. M. Another characteristic trait is its purely *national* character. Special cultus there might be, but the religion as a whole was *national*. The gods were classed as celestial, earthly, maritime, and infernal. Each deity was held supreme in his own domain. To such an extent did the idea of local godship pervade the Hellenic mind.

The H. M. presents at least three dynasties of gods. Their periods are, however, ill defined, and at times they seem to merge in such a way that only one—the third—remains as the genuine product of the mythographers. The earlier dynasties may have been merely commentaries by an ancient priesthood actuated by heroic sympathies or national pride. In those times the profession of a genealogist, if not a lucrative one, must have been a favourite occupation of bards and seers. The earliest Hellenic account of the creation which we possess is by Hesiod. It runs thus:—(1) Chaos, from which were fashioned Gæa (*earth*), and Eros (*love*); (2) Erebos (*darkness*), and Nux (*night*). By virtue of love Erebos and Nux produced Aithēr (*clear sky*), and Hemera (*day*). Then Gæa of herself produced Ouranos (*heaven*), Pontos (*sea*), &c.; and again from her union with Ouranos she brought forth the giants, Cyclops, and Titans. Ouranos was then god supreme. He was dethroned by Kronos, who in turn was dethroned by Zeus.

Of the third dynasty of Olympian gods, twelve or more (the number is indefinite) were esteemed in power and privileges superior to the others. The chief were (1) Zeus, father of gods and men, dethroner of Kronos and the Titans (earlier dynasty); (2) Hēra, sister and wife of Zeus, worshipped especially at Samos and Argos; (3) Apollōn, worshipped with great pomp at Delos and at Delphi in Phocis, and esteemed by the Dorians the greatest of all the Hellenic gods; (4) Poseidōn, brother of Zeus, god of the sea; (5) Athēnē, proctectress of Athens; (6) Arēs, the god of war; (7) Aphroditē, the goddess of love and beauty; (8) Eros, the personification of desire; (9) Artemis, the goddess of the chase, twin sister of Apollōn, and, like him, specially worshipped at Delos; (10) Dēmētēr, the goddess of the soil, worshipped at Eleusis with mysterious rites along with her daughter; (11) Cora (*Persephonē*); (12) Ploutōn, brother of Zeus and husband of Persephonē, king of the nether world; (13) Hermēs, the messenger of the gods and conductor of the dead. It remains to mention (14) Hestia, the goddess of the domestic hearth; (15) Hephaistos, the god of fire; (16) Dionusos, the god of wine—a purely national god—whose marriage with Ariadnē is immortal, and the festive rejoicings in honour of which were celebrated when fruits were ripe. Hēraklēs, Hēbē, and Ganymede, translated to Olympus, almost complete the catalogue of the *Dii Majores*, or Olympian gods.

The marine deities, Amphitritē, the personification of the sea in all its phases, called also wife of Poseidōn; Nereus, father of the ocean-nymphs, and Tritōn, the horn-blower of the sea-god; and the earthly deities, including Pan, the Oreads, dryads, &c., were all duly honoured in their sphere.

The catalogue of Chthōnian or infernal deities, under which terms are comprised Ploutōn, Persephonē, and Hermēs, already mentioned among the Olympiads, comprehended the heroes and the ancestors of those who had altars assigned to them. These were the *Dii Manes* of Roman mythology.

Apart from the deities above mentioned, an infinite variety of divine beings claim notice. Such are the personifications (1) of the fertility of nature:—Pan, the Satyrs, Mænads, Silvanus, Priapus, &c.; (2) of the visible beauty of nature:—The Charites, Hōrai, and Hesperides; (3) of the vocal beauty of nature:—The muses and nymphs; (4) of the ætherial spirits:—Winds, &c.; (5) of the veiled mysteries:—Thanatos, Hypnos, &c. In addition to all these and many other divinities, the Greeks recognised in an eminent degree Themis, the goddess of justice; Nemesis, the avenger of wrong; the Furies (Erinues), and the Fates (Moirai). The last, who were beyond the control of even Zeus, are, according to Plato (*Rep.* 317), seated on thrones, white-robed and chapleted—Lachesis singing the past, Clōthō the present, and Atropos the future, touching and turning the spindle of necessity.

Hellenic Philosophy. Hellas, so famous for her poets, historians, orators, and statesmen, was no less distinguished for her schools of philosophy. Thales of Miletus (644–548 B.C.), one of the 'seven sages,' is justly considered as the father of Hellenic speculation, and his name marks an epoch in H. P. The distinctive characteristic of his system and that of his followers—known as the Ionian School—was an inquiry into the origin and constitution of the universe. He taught that water was the beginning of things. Anaximander of Miletus (611–547 B.C.), the first to use the term *arche* for the fundamental principle, asserted that the infinite (*to apeiron*) was the origin of things, and that water, air, earth, and fire were generated thereby, and thereinto again resolved—the parts of the whole constantly changing while the whole was unchangeable. Anaximenes, by Ritter and Lewes placed next to Thales, mainly on the ground that the doctrines of the former are a development of those of the latter, declared that air was the first principle. Pythagoras (flor. 531 B.C.), one of the great founders of mathematics, whose life is enshrouded in myth and legend, taught that number was the cause of the material existence of all things; in other words, that while individual things change, the numerical attribute—the One—is indestructible. The infinite, therefore, must be one. This involved the belief that numbers were real, not merely symbolical. A notable feature in the teaching of Pythagoras was the doctrine of the transmigration of souls (*metempsychōsis*). Xenophanes of Colophon (538 B.C.) was distinguished as an opponent of the polytheism of the time, and as an asserter of the unity and perfection of the Godhead. The one, the infinite, philosophy taught him could not be infinite, nor yet finite; could not be moved, nor unmoved. Though neither a clear nor an exact thinker, Xenophanes nevertheless greatly influenced the progress of H. P. He was followed by Parmenides of Elea (flor. 505 B.C.), a man of great logical acumen. He evolved the theory of the duality of human thought and asserted the doctrine of the one—the *ens* (Gr. *on*), self-existent—to satisfy the reason, and of the many to accord with the testimony of sense. He admitted, however, the uncertainty of knowledge, but maintained the certainty of reason. Contemporary with him was Heracleitus of Ephesus, 'the weeping philosopher,' who took his stand on the principle of flux or ceaseless change, as exemplified in fire—ever self-kindled, ever self-extinguished. 'All,' said he, 'is and is not'—an enigmatical expression of his theory that nothing *is* but is always *becoming*. About this time Leucippus originated his famous Atomic (q. v.) theory. Anaxagoras (500–428 B.C.) treated the universe as composed of an indefinite number of elements (Gr. *homaiomeriai*); but at the same time held to the Pythagorean and Eleatic principle of the one. While he saw that things were many, he saw also the necessity for the one. He thus admitted both sense and reason. Diogenes of Apollonia (flor. 468 B.C.) adopted in a modified form the tenet of Anaximenes that all things have their origin in air; but gave to it a broader and deeper signification. In air he saw that there was not only life but intelligence, and that intelligence must have been the first of things. Next in point of time came Zeno of Elea (flor. 464 B.C.), one of the most distinguished of the ancient philosophers. He was the inventor of that system of logic called *Dialectics*—a method which produced the Sophists and Sceptics, and which became an instrument of terrible power in the hands of Socrates and Plato. Democritus of Abdera (flor. 460 B.C.), 'the laughing philosopher,' whose system was an expansion of the atomic theory of Leucippus, received the universe as a congeries of atoms, and attributed the formation of all things to destiny (or necessity); but whether by that term an intelligent cause is to be understood or not, it is impossible to say. Empedocles of Agrigentum (flor. 444 B.C.) in his philosophy has something in common with all the schools before his time; but the cardinal point in his system is his assuming the four elements as the primary principles from which all things proceed by the action thereon of love, the mingler or creator, and hate or discord, the destroyer. Meanwhile the uncertainties incident to all yet promulgated philosophical theories, and the proved insufficiency of all attempts towards a solution of the great problems of existence and human knowledge, produced an intellectual crisis; and a class arose under the name of Sophists, who by objections and counter-arguments sought to overthrow the systems of the past. From the nature of the case it will be evident that the Sophists formed not so much a philosophical sect as a school of rhetoricians. Their avowed object was 'to make the worse appear the better reason.' For their instructions they exacted enormous fees, which were ungrudgingly paid by the rich. But hereby they incurred the odium of the poor and the contempt of the philosophers. By many authors they are said to have corrupted the public morality. One eminent modern historian, Mr. Grote, takes, we think with good reason, an opposite view. At all events, they were the natural outgrowth of the age. Their scepticism, however, in the main was shallow—the shadow without the substance; and with Socrates (468–399 B.C.) H. P. again asserted her rightful reign. With this second dawn Hellenic speculation assumed a new phase. The great problems affecting the end of life, human happiness, social duty, &c., were to be solved with regard to new and deeper considerations. Virtue and vice were no longer to be looked at from a utilitarian point of view, but to be determined by fresh canons and reconciled with man's religious convictions. Socrates proclaimed his ethical creed. Virtue was enthroned by him as the supreme guide of life; justice was declared the sole passport to happiness. Ethical terms, such as justice, injustice; piety, impiety; nobility, baseness; temperance, intemperance; citizenship, government; and the like, were rigidly defined. And for this grand and noble work, for which every succeeding age has done him honour, the saintly sage suffered martyrdom. But the seeds he had sown were to blossom in his pupils Xenophon and Plato—the former of whom in his *Memorabilia* of the sage has left us a tender and graceful tribute to his memory, the latter a splendid exposition of his philosophy. The conflicting sects represented by Euclid of Megara (flor. 400 B.C.), Antisthenes the Cynic (426–371 B.C.), with his more famous pupil Diogenes (419–324 B.C.), both 'imposing blasphemers,' according to Mr. Lewes, and Aristippus of Cyrene (400–362 B.C.), whose abstract conception of the good was reduced to the concrete pleasure, were more or less influenced and moulded by Socrates, and partially adopted his method. In Plato (q. v.) (429–347 B.C.), as we have indicated, we have a complete and clear adoption and application of the Socratic method. But Plato was more than a mere exponent of the Socratic philosophy. He was the inheritor of all the wisdom of the past, and added largely to it. The Socratic school was succeeded by that of Aristotle (q. v.) (384–322 B.C.), the founder of the Peripatetics, for twenty years pupil of Socrates, but no servile follower of his philosophy. To the region of speculation he restored physics and metaphysics, in great measure neglected during the reign of ethics inaugurated by Socrates—a restoration that was succeeded by a second crisis in H. P. In 350 B.C. flourished Pyrrho the Sceptic; in 366–264 B.C., Zeno the Stoic; in 341–270 B.C., Epicurus; in 300–241 B.C., Arcesilaus of Pitane; and in 213–129 B.C., Carneades of Cyrene. Pyrrho was the natural successor of the Sophists; Zeno and Epicurus were but modifications of the leaders of the Cynic and Cyrenaic schools respectively; Arcesilaus and Carneades evolved a form of scepticism totally different from that of Pyrrho. With these names H. P., properly so called, ends; for the genius of philosophy no longer dwelt in Hellas. Speculation, however, again appeared at Alexandria under the name of Neo-Platonism, in the companionship of faith; and after a protracted struggle for life, the old philosophy expired with Proclus, 485 A.D.

Hell'enists (Gr. *Hellenistai*), a general name for those learned in matters of Greek antiquity, especially the language and literature. More particularly the name is applied to the great numbers of Jews who immigrated into Egypt, and there became nationalised, adopting the Greek language and philosophy, and gradually establishing a new epoch of Græco-Jewish culture, which from its more prominent element received the name Hellenistic. The chief of these Jewish-Hellenistic philosophers was Philo (q. v.). An important memorial of the literary diligence of these Alexandrian Jews is the Greek translation of the Old Testament (Septuaginta). The name H. was often given to the Jews who lived among the Greeks, and Hellenistic to the Greek spoken by them, always more or less betraying the influence of the Hebrew idiom.

Hell'espont. See DARDANELLES.

Hellevœt'sluis, a strongly fortified seaport of the Netherlands, in the province of S. Holland, on the island of Voorne, and on the Haring Vliet, 17 miles S.W. of Rotterdam. It is an important naval station, with an artillery magazine, an arsenal, an hospital, a vast sluice, &c. Through the Voorne Canal, which here enters the Haring Vliet, comes much of the Rotterdam trade. Pop. (1873) 4284. William of Orange sailed hence to England, with 50 vessels and 14,000 men, on 11th November 1666. H. was taken by the French in 1795 and besieged by the English in 1813.

Hell Gate (originally Dutch, *Helle Gat*), a narrow part of the East River, United States, between New York city (nearly opposite Croton Reservoir, beyond Central Park), Ward's Island and Hallet's Point on Long Island, and within the corporate limits of New York and neighbouring cities. It receives strong tides from Long Island Sound in the E. and Sandy Hook in the W., and is rendered dangerous by its violent currents and its formidable reefs of thinly stratified gneiss. Since 1851 works have been carried on for the removal of the rocks by means of engine-drilling, tunnelling, and blasting by electricity. It is surmised that by opening up the channel the eastern trade of Sandy Hook will be diverted hence, while New York will have the advantage for defence of an additional outlet to the sea. But the Sound, though 12 miles shorter, is foggy, tortuous, and shoaly. Many of the reefs, including Pot Rock, Frying Pan, Shelldrake, Bald-headed Billy, have been removed at a cost, at the end of 1875, of over 14,000,000 dollars. The last explosion was that off Hallet's Point, on the 24th October 1876, when were used in charges 28,901 lbs. of dynamite, 9061½ lbs. of 'rendrock,' and 14,244 lbs. of 'vulcan' powder, an aggregate of 52,206½ lbs. of preparations of nitro-glycerine. The cartridges were disposed in 4462 cavities, inter-connected by 100,000 feet of telegraph wire, and placed in communication with the batteries by 120,000 feet more. Nearly three acres were undermined by 7600 feet of tunnels, so as to give a uniform depth of 30 feet, and the explosion dislodged 43,000 cubic feet of gneiss rock, weighing 90,000 tons, and supporting the pressure of 143,000 cubic yards of water. The work of opening H. G. is, however, not more than one-third done.

Hellin' (the ancient *Illunum*), a town in the province of Albacete, Spain, on the Menedo, 52 miles N.W. of Murcia. It has a fine old church, several Roman remains, and is well built and paved. Near it are rich sulphur mines, and sulphurous springs used for bathing. Pop. 10,200.

Helm (Icel. *hialmun*, perhaps from its being the *helve* or handle which guides the ship), is the steering mechanism of a ship, consisting of the wheel, tiller, and rudder. In boats and small vessels the wheel, which is used to give greater leverage to the steersman, is dispensed with. To *put the H. up* is to put the tiller to the weather side and allow the vessel to fall off before the wind; to *put the H. down* is to put the tiller to the leeside and so throw the ship's head into the wind. See STEERING and RUDDER.

Hel'met (Goth. *hilms*, Old Norse, *hialmr*, Ger. *helm*, Fr. *heaume*), the metal or leather covering for the head worn by soldiers. The Greek and Roman helmets carried plumes, but left the face exposed. In the middle ages the helmets, which were formed of steel, and often richly inlaid, covered the face by a part called the *visor* or *vizor*, which lifted up by a pivot over each ear. The introduction of gunpowder has led to the general disuse of helmets, though they are still worn, chiefly as ornament, by heavy cavalry.—**H.**, in heraldry. The form of H. came to vary with the rank of the wearer, and, consequently, in heraldry, representations of helmets were placed above the chief part of the shield, to carry the crest and to indicate its bearer's rank. There are four forms of H. in heraldry—(1) The sovereign's, of gold, full-faced, and six-barred; (2) the noble's, of steel, in profile, and five-barred; (3) the knight's and baron's, of steel, garnished with silver, full-faced, with the visor raised and without bars; (4) the esquire's, of steel, in profile, and with the visor closed.

Helm'holtz, Hermann Ludwig Ferdinand, the German physicist and physiologist, was born August 31, 1821, at Potsdam in Brandenburg. He began his career in 1842 as an army surgeon, and in 1849 became Professor of Physiology at Königsberg. In 1855 he removed to Bonn, and in 1858 to Heidelberg. In 1870 he gave up his physiology chair for that of physics at Berlin, a position which he now (1877) occupies. As a physiologist he has specially directed his attention to the organs of sense, and the results of his researches are embodied in his *Beschreibung des Augenspiegels* (1851), *Uber das Sehen* (1855), and *Handbuch der Physiologischen Optik* (1867), the last a most exhaustive treatise. In pure physical and mathematical science he is widely known through his valuable paper on the conservation of energy (*Die Erhaltung der Kraft*, 1849), his *Populäre Vorträge* (1865 and 1870), and his splendid mathematical memoirs in Crelle's *Journal* on *Vortex Motion in Liquids and Air-Vibrations in Open Pipes*. Under his direction also was the German edition of Thomson and Tait's *Natural Philosophy* published. His most original work has been in connection with the physiology and physics of musical sounds; and his masterly treatise on the sensations of tone, *Lehre von den Sonempfindungen* (1862, 3d ed. 1870, Eng. trans. 1875), has thrown a flood of light upon the whole science of acoustics.

Hel'mont, Jan Baptista van, the great chemist, was born of a good family at Brussels in 1577. Educated at Louvain, he became a mystic, had visions of God, and felt called on to resign his property to his sister. He now began the study of medicine that he might serve Christ in ministering to the poor. Appointed a professor of surgery, he soon found out the absurdity of the old-world system then in vogue in medicine, a stupid commentary on the crude notions of Hippocrates and Galen. Like Paracelsus, he resolved to travel, and spent ten years in Italy and Germany. A voice in a dream bade him take up the science of chemistry. He experimented on fossils, on animal and vegetable substances, thought he had confounded the 'humorist' school by the discovery of a panacea, adopted the title *medicus per ignem*, and attended the sick gratuitously. His opinions were attacked by the orthodox philosophy and medicine of the day, and also by the Church. He, however, enjoyed the favour of Rudolf II. and of the Elector of Köln. He died at Vilvorde, December 30, 1644. In spite of an overheated imagination, H. made some steps on the road of true science. He introduced the word 'gas,' applying it to the 'woody spirit,' the product of the combustion of wood, fermentation, putrefaction, &c. The different kinds of gas he classified as inflammable and non-inflammable. Hydrochloric acid he called 'gas of salt.' Coal-gas he considered to be water, which he held to be the real food of plants and vegetables, 'the blood of the earth.' All his theories and speculations are, however, tainted by the uncertainty which then prevailed with regard to the question of ultimate chemical elements. Sometimes he leans to the alchemistic view of 'salt, sulphur, and mercury,' at another time to the ancient 'water, air, and earth.' In his measurements of heat, he used melting ice and boiling water as fixed points. He introduced the word 'saturation' to express the combination of an acid with its base, which it had previously been said to destroy. Several diseases he traced to the excess of a specific acid, the gastric juice. His system of *archai*, or spiritual forces presiding over the kingdom of nature, was taken from Paracelsus. The *archē* of the animal kingdom was the *aura vitalis*, called *janitor stomachi*, because its seat was the cardiac orifice. The *spiritus vitalis*, a gas produced in the left heart, originates respiration, circulation, muscular contractility, and nervous force. The soul resided in the stomach. The centre of the earth he regarded as full of hot water, and the interstellar spaces as full of an ether which penetrated the atmosphere of the earth. H.'s chief work is the *Ortus Medicinæ* (Amst. 1648). See the sketches of Elmotte, Crasso, and Frænkel, and Hœfer's *History of Chemistry*.

Helm'stedt, a town in the duchy of Brunswick, 20 miles E. of the town of Brunswick by rail. It is known mainly as the seat of a former university, founded in 1575 and suppressed in 1809. A little iron and coal is found in the neighbourhood of H., and pottery is manufactured. Pop. (1875) 7783.

Hel'mund, a considerable river of Afghanistan, which rises in the mountains of Paghman, and after a S.W. course of over 700 miles, falls into the lake of Seistan. It is never without a plentiful supply of water, which is used for irrigation, though not to such an extent as in former times. Navigation is not practised anywhere.

Heloise'. See ABELARD.

He'lots (*i.e.*, either 'captives,' from Gr. *helein*, 'to capture,' or 'inhabitants of Helos,' a town of Laconia), the lowest of the four classes into which the population of Sparta was anciently divided, appear to have been the original inhabitants of Laconia, who were reduced to serfdom on the Dorian invasion of the Peloponnesus. They were treated with great cruelty and indignity by the Spartans, who made them serve in war, till the soil, wait at meals, and massacred them when their numbers seemed to grow dangerously great—companies known as *Crypteiai* being formed to secretly slay them. The H. were occasionally rendered drunk as a warning to the Spartan youth, and the name Helot has become synonymous with a degraded slave.

Helps, Arthur, an English essayist and historian, was born about 1817, and educated at Trinity College, Cambridge, where he graduated in 1838. He became private secretary to Lord Monteagle, Chancellor of the Exchequer; commissioner of French, Danish, and Spanish claims; and in 1859 clerk of the Privy Council. H. died in London, March 7, 1875. His works include *Thoughts in the Cloister and the Crowd* (1835); *Essays Written in the Intervals of Business* (1841); *Henry II.; Catherine Douglas; The Claims of Labour* (1845); *Friends in Council* (1st series, 1841; 2d series, 1859); *Companions of my Solitude* (1851); *Conquerors of the New World* (1852); *The Spanish Conquest of America* (1855-61); *Life of Pizarro* (1869); *Brevia* (1870); *Casimir Maremma* (1870); *Life of Cortes* (1871); *Thoughts upon Government* (1871); *Ivan de Biron* (1874); *Social Pressure* (1874). His essays, which are mainly in the form of dialogue, are full of ripe sober reflection, occasionally lightened with mellow humour; and as a historian he excels both in thorough mastery of his subject and in lucid picturesque narration. His style is admirably pure and graceful, abounding in quiet beauties of diction. He composed several plays, but was almost wholly lacking in dramatic variety and fire.

Hels'ingborg, a bathing-place and port of Sweden, in the län of Malmöhus, on the Sound, opposite Elsinore. It has frequent steam communication with Copenhagen, and carries on a trade in iron wares and pottery. Pop. (1874) 8103.

Hels'ingfors (Fin. *Helsinki*), the strongly fortified capital of Finland, in the government of Nyland, on the peninsula Estnäs ('east nose'), in the Gulf of Finland, 190 miles West of St. Petersburg. It is the finest town in Finland. It originally rose around the old palace *Helsingfors* (*fors* meaning a waterfall or 'force'), and has now extensive foreign commerce. It is the seat of the governor-general of Finland, has a university (fifty-two professors, 500 students, and a library of 100,000 vols.), transferred hither from Aabo in 1828, a church of St. Nicholas (1830–52), a hospital, and a large theatre in a beautiful park. Visitors come in great numbers from St. Petersburg in summer for bathing. In 1874 the imports amounted in value to £2,054,338. The trade is chiefly with England, Germany, Russia, America, and Scandinavia. About half of the imports were cotton and yarn; the staple export is timber. In 1874 there entered 880 vessels (559 Finnish) of 85,332 lasts. To the S. of H. lie the seven fortified islets of Sveaborg (Viapori), called the northern Gibraltar; pop. (1867) 32,130. H. was made the capital of Finland in 1812. Sveaborg was bombarded in vain by a French and English naval force in August 1855.

Helst, Bartholomaus van der, one of the greatest portrait painters of the Dutch school, was born at Haarlem in 1613, and afterwards removed to Amsterdam, where he died in 1678. His 'Feast of the Town Guard of Amsterdam,' is a portrait composition, astonishing for its freedom, truth, and beauty of colour, and vividly recalling the masterpieces of Van Dyck. His draperies are masterly, his figures firmly modelled, and even in minor details he follows nature with unswerving fidelity and invariable success.

Hel'stone, a market-town of England, county of Cornwall, in the beautiful valley of the river Cobre, 12 miles E. of Penzance. It has a corn trade, but greatly depends on the many mines and quarries in the vicinity. The mouth of the Cobre, 3 miles distant, is obstructed by a sandbank that forms the Loe Pool. May-games are still celebrated here. Pop. (1871) 8760. H. was made a borough in 1201, and returns one member to Parliament.

Helvell'a, a genus of *Fungi* (q. v.), allied to the morels. Six species are found in woods in Britain, several of which are esculent, such as *H. crispa*, *H. lacunosa*, on *H. esculenta*. The last of these is now referred to the genus *Gyromitra*.

Helvell'yn, a mountain of Cumberland, England, towering 3055 feet over Ulleswater, on the road between Keswick and Ambleside. It is associated with the poetry both of Wordsworth and Scott.

Helvet'ic Confess'ion is the name given to two distinct documents: the first presented to the assembled divines at Wittenberg (1536) by Martin Bucer (q. v.) in his attempt to settle the controversy between the Lutherans and Zwinglians. The second was drawn up by Bullinger (q. v.) at the desire of Friedrich III., Elector of the Palatinate, published 1566, and adopted in Switzerland, the Palatinate, Poland, Hungary, France, and Scotland.

Helvet'ii, a Celtic people who, in Cæsar's time, held the lands between the Rhône and the Lake of Geneva on the S., the Rhine on the E. and N., and the Jura on the W., a district corresponding loosely to modern Switzerland. In B.C. 58 they sought to migrate to the S. of Gaul, but were turned back at Geneva by Cæsar, who, when they endeavoured to follow another route, fell upon them at Bibracte, the modern Autun (?), Burgundy, and routed them with dreadful slaughter, only 110,000 returning of the 368,000 who had quitted Switzerland. The H. suffered another severe defeat in 70 A.D. from Vitellius.

Helve'tius, Claude Adrien, a French writer of Swiss extraction, was born at Paris in 1715. He was sent to business at Caree, but occupied himself wholly with literary criticism. In philosophy he became a disciple of Locke. The Queen, Maria Leczinska, knowing his father, gave him the post of fermier-général, worth 100,000 dollars per annum. Out of his large income he managed to pension several less fortunate literary men. In 1751 he resigned his post, and married Mlle. de Ligneville, with whom he retired for eight months of the year to his estate of Voré, spending the other four in Paris. His country life was one of unwearying benevolence, sometimes carried to the point of absurdity. In 1758 he published his chief work, *De l'Esprit Humain,* in which he tries to prove that men praise actions just as they tend to their own advantage, a position which he illustrates by tracing the variations in private, municipal, national, and international equity. Character was an affair of education, and religion was a dangerous perturbing force, which should be repressed in the interests of society. This brilliant and beautifully-written book was inspired by a love of reputation rather than of science. It, however, contained some bold thoughts on the basis of political authority and the need of social reform. This roused the fears of the court, while the Church denounced the sceptical tendencies of the work. The license for publication was withdrawn; Pope Clement XIII. and the Sorbonne, the Jesuits and the Jansenists, combined against H., and he was forced to publish a miserable retractation. It is curious to compare the tone of depreciation with which H.'s French contemporaries spoke of his book, with the praise of Hume, Robertson, and other foreigners. The truth is, that H., while throwing out many valuable suggestions and some paradoxes, had not a really scientific mind. 'The well-fed farmer-general enlivening his Sybaritic life with metaphysic paradox.'—*Carlyle.* In 1764-65 H. was the guest of George III. and Friedrich the Great. After writing a frigid poem called *Le Bonheur,* and a development of his philosophy called *De l'Homme, de ses Facultés, et de son Éducation* (2 vols. 1772), H. died, September 17, 1775. See St. Lambert's *Essai sur la Vie et les Ouvrages d'Helvetius.*

He'mans, Felicia Dorothea, *née* **Browne,** a popular English poetess, was born at Liverpool, September 25, 1793. Her first volume of poems was published in 1808, when she was only fourteen years of age. It was followed by another, entitled *The Domestic Affections,* in 1812, and in the same year the authoress married Captain Hemans of the 4th Regiment. This marriage did not prove a very happy one, and when the failing health of her husband induced him in 1818 to take up his residence at Rome, Mrs. H. remained in England. After this she lived for the most part at her brother's seat, Bronwylfa, near St. Asaph, Flintshire, occupied in literary work and the education of her children, of whom she had five, all sons. *Lays of Many Lands,* a volume of translations, was published in 1818, followed by *Tales and Historic Scenes,* and in 1820 by the poem of *The Sceptic; The Vespers of Palermo,* produced at Covent Garden Theatre under Mr. Kemble's management in 1823, *The Siege of Valencia* (1823), *The Last Constantine, Belshazzar's Feast, The Forest Sanctuary* (1826), and the *Songs of the Affections* (1830). In 1831 Mrs. H. went to reside in Dublin, where she died, May 16, 1835. A memorial has been erected to her memory in the Cathedral of St. Asaph. Her poetic genius was pure, tender, and delicate. A womanly sweetness everywhere breathes through her verse. Some of her lyrics are permanently enshrined in the memory of the English nation, as *The Graves of a Household, The Voice of Spring, The Homes of England, The Treasures of the Deep,* and *The Palm-Tree.* The most complete edition of her writings is that published by the Messrs. Blackwood, Edinburgh (6 vols. 1840, new ed. 1859), accompanied by a *Memoir of the Life and Writings of Mrs. H.,* by her sister. —Her son, **Charles H.,** author of a *History of Medieval Christianity and Sacred Art in Italy, Historic and Monumental Rome,* &c., died at Rome, 26th October 1876.

Hemicra'nia (Gr. *hēmi,* 'one-half,' and *kranion,* 'the skull'), sometimes called *megrims* (Fr. *migraine,* a corruption of H.), a variety of Headache (q. v.), affecting only one side of the head at a time, and generally intermittent. H. is often connected with a hysterical diathesis, with pregnancy, or occurs during the debility brought on by suckling. Treatment—Quinine, arsenical solution, sarsaparilla, and bromide of potassium.

Hemides'mus, a genus of plants belonging to the natural order *Asclepiadaceæ* (q. v.). The fragrant roots of *H. Indicus* are what are known as Indian sarsaparilla in Madras, where they are also called country sarza, nannári or ananto-múl.

Hemio'pia (Gr. *hēmi,* 'one-half,' and *ōps,* 'the eye'), a peculiar variety of Amaurosis (q. v.) signifying a partial blindness obscuring about half of the field of vision. See Dr. Wollaston's paper *On Semi-Decussation of the Optic Nerves, Philosophical Transactions* for 1824.

Hemiple'gia (Gr. *hēmi,* 'one-half,' and *plēssō,* 'I strike'), a form of Paralysis (q. v.), limited to one side of the face and body, depending upon disease of the brain, or Embolism (q. v.), opposed in signification to Paraplegia (q. v.).

Hem'ipode (*Hemipodius*), a genus of *Grallatorial* or wading birds, in which the hinder toe is wanting. They are allied to the Quails (q. v.), and are all of small size. The common species is the *H. tachydromus,* occurring in Spain, Italy, and other parts of the Continent, and also in the N. of Africa. Its average length is 5 or 6 inches.

Hemip'tera, an order of insects, in which the mouth is suctorial, and consists of a *rostrum* or *beak,* formed by the modified *labium* or under-lip, which exists as a protective sheath for the mandibles and maxillæ. These are adapted for piercing the skins of animals, and for sucking blood from the wounds thus made. The eyes are of the compound variety, but simple eyes or *ocelli* are developed in addition. The wings may be absent altogether (as in the plant-lice and cochineal insects), but two pairs of these organs are more usually developed. The order derives its name from the fact that the first pair of wings in one section at least possess horny bases, the remainder being membranous. The H. are divisible into (1) *Homoptera,* in which the wings are wholly membranous; the parts of the mouth turned backwards, and the wings folded over each other when at rest; (2) *Heteroptera,* in which the bases of the wings are horny, the beak springing from the front of the head.

Hem'isphere. See SPHERE.

Hem'lock (Old Eng. *hemleac—leac* means a plant), is the name used in connection with two genera of the order *Umbelliferæ,* respectively represented in Britain by common H. (*Conium maculatum*) and water-H. (*Cicuta virosa*). Both are highly poisonous, though not unfrequently deaths have been attributed by non-botanical medical men to H. which have arisen from persons eating the root of Water-Dropwort (q. v.) in mistake for the wild parsnip. Common H. is a widely-distributed plant through Britain, generally growing in waste places and about hedgebanks. Without entering minutely into its botanical characteristics, yet, on account of its poisonous qualities and its common occurrence around the outskirts of towns, &c., the following points may be prudently mentioned:—Height, 2 to 5 feet; stem quite smooth, and more or less sprinkled (as with a brush) with purple spots; leaves finely divided into numerous deep-green segments, which when bruised emit a peculiarly nauseous odour. The partial umbels or umbellules (q. v.) have only a half circuit of bracts at their base; and each half of the somewhat globular fruits bears five wavy crenate ridges. There is no other plant of the order that combines these different points of structure. The active principle of H. is conia, which pervades the whole plant, but, as is usually the case, exists especially in the fruit. (See CONIINE.) It acts as an irritant poison, subsequently causing muscular paralysis, convulsions, and death; and there is a general impression that it was employed to carry into effect the sentence of death decreed against Socrates by the Athenian law courts. The water-H. is most frequently found along the margin of lochs, ponds, &c., but is much rarer than common H. Instances are on record of its occasioning human death; there can, however, be little temptation for any one to gather it except the botanist. Its poisoning attributes have not unfrequently been exemplified upon cattle, hence its more generally recognised name of Cowbane. These losses having usually been noted to take place in the early part of the year, it is suggested that in spring, when cattle enter their pasturage, they in eagerness make a raid upon all before them without that appreciation of quality which is afterwards developed. Consequently it behoves farmers to see that the water-H. is not within the limits of their pasture grounds.

Medicinal Properties of H.—The active ingredients are contained in the leaves of the *conium maculatum*, collected when the fruit begins to form, and thereafter dried. H., a powerful narcotic, is anodyne, antispasmodic and deobstruent, and is chiefly used in chronic enlargements of the liver, rheumatism, syphilis, neuralgic affections, and to allay irritation in bronchial affections, pertussis, and phthisis. H. acts as a *direct sedative*, especially on the spinal cord, and in very large doses causes paralysis or stupor, coma, and slight convulsions. Antidote in cases of poisoning: According to Pereira, an infusion of galls may be serviceable.

Hemp (Old Eng. *hænep*, Ger. *hanf*, Lat. *cannabis*, Sansk. *kana*). As commonly employed, H. designates various fibres used for manufacturing purposes, as also the plants that supply them. Strictly speaking, its limit is *Cannabis sativa*, the only species of the genus that is the type of the natural order Cannabaceæ (q. v.). The plant is valued for two widely separate reasons. In India, where it is indigenous, and in other hot countries, the yield from it held highest in estimation is a peculiar resin. This resin is used to produce intoxication, and gives rise to native synonyms for H.—such as 'increase of pleasure,' 'leaf of delusion,' 'cementer of friendship,' &c. The resin itself is termed *churrus*, whilst the drink of which it is the stimulant is known as *bhang*, and a preparation for use with tobacco is sold in the bazaars under the name *gunjah*. (See HASHISH.) But it is a far different product that renders H. appreciated with us, and has caused its wide-spread cultivation through the temperate regions of the northern hemisphere. The thin bark of the plant yields a fibre that has been of high recognised merit from the earliest historic times to the present day, when its import value into Great Britain is yearly more than a million sterling. The chief supplies are drawn from the Russian empire, but Italy produces the finest quality. For successful cultivation the soil must be rich, and the seed should be sown close, so as to produce straight stems without branches. Harvesting, in the generality of cases, takes place at two periods, the male individuals being pulled as soon as the pollen is shed, and the female when the seeds are ripe. After the leaves are removed, the stems tied in bundles are subjected to the 'retting' process as with flax, and are then spread out to dry and bleach. The fibre is removed either by hand labour or machinery. The fruit, for which the female plant is allowed to remain to maturity, is commonly known as 'hemp seed,' and is largely sold for pet birds, &c.; by pressure an oil is also obtained from it.

Hemp.

The principal other fibre-yielding plants to which the name H. is loosely applied are Manilla H. (*Musa textilis*) (see ABACA), Canadian H. (*Apocynum Cannabinum*), Ambaree H. (*Hibiscus Cannabinus*), Sunn H. (*Crotalaria juncea*), Bowstring H. (*Sanseviera guineensis*, &c.). The Indian H. (*Cannabis Indica*) is simply a climatological variety of common H. (*C. sativa*).

Hemlock Spruce, the common name for *Abies Canadensis*, N. American fir-tree. See FIR.

Hemp Palm, a species of Chamœrops (q. v.) from the fibre of which a coarse cordage is made in China, &c.

Hems, the *Emesa* of the Romans, a city of Syria, Asiatic Turkey, near the right bank of the Orontes, 65 miles N.E. of Baalbec, and 48 N. of Damascus. It was formerly celebrated for its splendid temple of the sun, and the elevation of its priest Bassianus or Elagabalus (Syr. *Elagabal*, 'high-priest') at the age of fourteen to the imperial dignity. Here the Emperor Aurelian repulsed Zenobia in 273 A.D. The Arabs, who seized the city in 636, revived the old Semitic name that it has since borne. It is still a busy trading place, with a pop. of 23,000, of whom 6500 are Greek Christians.

Hem'sterhuis, Tiberius, one of the chief philologers of the 18th c., was born at Groningen, 9th January 1685, and educated at Leyden University. After filling for some years the mathematical professorship of Amsterdam, H. became in 1740 Professor of Greek at Leyden, where he died, April 7, 1766. H. was, perhaps, next to Bentley, the most distinguished Grecian of his day. Ruhnken and Valkenaer are his most famous pupils. His chief works are the completion of Lederlin's edition of the *Onomasticon* of Pollux (Amst. 1706); the *Dialogues of Lucian and Timon* (1708); the *Plutus* of Aristophanes (1744); *Observations on the Homilies of Chrysostom* (1784); and various Latin *Orations*, published by Valkenaer in 1784. See Ruhnken's *Elogium Hemsterhusii* (Leyd. 1768). His son, **Franz H.** (born 1722, died 1790), acquired distinction as a writer on philosophy and art. His collected works were published in 1792.

Hen'bane, the name in common use for a genus of *Solanaceæ* (q. v.), of which the most important species is *Hyoscyamus niger*, or common H., a plant found growing spontaneously in Great Britain in the vicinity of old ruins, on rubbish heaps, and not unfrequently on sandy ground near the coast. Covered with a woven felt of sticky hairs, and rendered further unpleasant by its heavy-smelling exudation, and bearing dingy yellow flowers veined with purple—in the very plucking of a specimen the narcotic poisonous qualities of the plant are suggested. Medicinally, the alkaloid extracted from it is used where the administration of opium is undesirable. To some extent common H. is cultivated in Southern England, but the crop is an uncertain one, and the price of the leaf varies considerably in consequence. Other species of the genus possess more or less the same qualities as the above. The name H. expresses an early knowledge of the baneful effects of the seed upon poultry. See Matthioli, b. iv. c. 64.

Hen'derson, Thomas, a Scottish astronomer, was born at Dundee, December 28, 1798. In 1831 he was appointed director of the royal observatory at the Cape of Good Hope. Here he made those observations which resulted in the calculation of the parallax of a *Centauri*—the nearest fixed star to our system, and the first whose distance was calculated. In 1833 his health compelled him to return to England, and the succeeding year he was appointed Astronomer-Royal for Scotland, and Professor of Astronomy in the University of Edinburgh. H. died November 23, 1842.

Hen'gest and Hor'sa. See ANGLO-SAXONS.

Heng'stenberg, Ernst Wilhelm, the foremost representative of recent German orthodoxy, born at Fröndenberg in Westphalia, 20th October 1802, studied at Bonn, and, after a short residence at Basel, settled at Berlin in 1824 as a privat-docent, where he soon became known as the leader of a band of youthful champions of orthodoxy. In 1826 he was appointed a Professor of Theology in the Berlin University, an office he held till his death, 28th May 1869. Though bred in the Reformed Church, H. adopted Lutheranism; and since the union of the two creeds in Prussia, he was the chief advocate of Lutheran Confessionalism within the national Prussian Church. As editor of the *Evangelische Kirchenzeitung*, H. was unwearied in lifting up a vehement testimony against all innovations or defections, and in treating all views differing from his own as anti-evangelical. He has the credit of having done much to re-awaken zeal for a pious and profound study of the Old Testament, and showed much acuteness in defending almost all the portions of the Old Testament of which the genuineness or authenticity had been disputed. His principal works are *Christologie des A. T.* 1829, 2d ed. 1854); *Beiträge zur Einleitung ins A. T.* (1831–39); *Die Bücher Mosis und Aegypten* (1841); *Geschichte Bileams* (1842); *Die Opfer der Heiligen Schrift* (1852); *Geschichte des Reiches Gottes unter dem Alten Bund* (1869–70); and commentaries on the Psalms, the Apocalypse, the Canticles, Ecclesiastes, Ezekiel, and the Gospel of John.

Hen'ley-on-Thames, a picturesque town of England, in Oxfordshire, on the left bank of the Thames, under shelter of the Chiltern hills, 23 miles S.E. of Oxford, and 35 W. of London by railway. It is a favourite summer resort, and has an inn of high repute. Its trade is in flour, malt, beech-wood, grain, &c. The river, which here abounds with pike, perch, and eels, is crossed at H. by a bridge of five arches. Pop. (1871) 4523. H. was incorporated in the reign of Elizabeth as *Hemley-gang* or *Hanneburg*.

Henn'a (Arab. *Al-hinna*, 'the cypress,' hence the Span. *Alcaña*), a pigment made from catechu and the powdered leaves of the *Lawsonia inermis* or *L. spinosa*, shrubs of the order *Lytheraceæ*. It is much used in Eastern countries, especially in Egypt and Persia, for staining the nails and finger-tips of an orange colour. In dyeing the hair with H., the dye is converted into a deep black by a subsequent application of indigo. The leaves are used in Europe for dyeing leather, and are obtained chiefly from moist places in the N. of Africa, Arabia, Persia, and the E. Indies.

Henri, the name of four French kings.—**H. I.** of France, son of King Robert and Constance of Provence, came to the throne in 1031. His reign was at first disturbed by civil wars with his brother Robert, who was supported by the Counts of Champagne and Flanders, and afterwards he had actual control only over a comparatively small part of central France. H. died in 1060.—**H. II.** was born in 1518, and succeeded his father, François I., in 1547. In 1552 he sided with the Elector of Saxony against Karl V., and armed Metz, Toul, and Verden, under the pretence of assisting the German Protestants. But the troops were defeated at St. Quentin in 1557 and checked by Alva in Italy, and peace was made by the treaty of Cateau-Cambresis in 1559, when Philip II. of Spain married H.'s daughter. At a tournament held amid other rejoicings to celebrate the union, H. was accidentally wounded in the ribs by the broken spear-shaft of the Comte de Montgomery, and shortly afterwards died, July 10, 1559.—**H. III.**, last of the Valois line, was the third son of H. II., and was born at Fontainebleau, September 19, 1551. He served against the Huguenots from 1569 to 1573, taking part in the battles of Jarnac and Moncontour; was made King of Poland in 1573, and in 1574 succeeded his brother Charles IX. on the French throne. During his reign France was convulsed by the wars of the three Henris. H. was a miserable sensualist, who spent his life in a round of costly orgies, while the Spanish Catholic party of the League, headed by the Duc de Guise, who aimed at the succession to the throne, sapped the royal influence and inflamed the Parisians at once against the imbecile sovereign and the Huguenot Henri of Navarre. H. was surrounded by a host of licentious parasites known as the 'Mignons,' who frivolously squandered the revenues and violated the liberty of the people. Guise at length becoming virtual king of France, H. had him assassinated at Blois in 1588, and was forced by the rage of the Catholics into a reconcilement with Henri of Navarre. The two Henris then marched on Paris, which they would probably have seized, when H. was stabbed by a Dominican, Jacques Clément, and died August 2, 1589. See Adrien de Valois, *De Vita Henrici Valesii* (Par. 1677); Sauvigny, *Histoire de H. III.*; and the histories of Mézeray, Sismondi, Martin, Michelet, and Kitchin (Lond. 1877).—**H. IV.**, surnamed 'the Great' and 'the Good,' and known as H. of Navarre, was the third son of Antoine de Bourbon and Jeanne d'Albret, daughter of Henri, King of Navarre and Béarn. H. was born at Pau, December 14, 1553, was brought up as a Protestant, and was trained in hardy exercises among the mountains of Béarn. In his youth he took a prominent part in the wars of the Huguenots, and after the peace of St. Germain was drawn into marriage with Marguerite of Valois, sister of Charles IX. To avoid being murdered he now proclaimed himself a Catholic, and was kept a prisoner at court until 1576, acquiring consummate diplomatic skill amid the Medicean schemes and conspiracies. Escaping to the Huguenots, he renounced Catholicism, and the death of the Duc d'Anjou made him legitimate heir to the French crown. After the murder of H. III. (1589), the Catholic party, abetted by Philip II. of Spain, forced him to retire to the fastnesses of the S., and his position was for a time full of peril. But his cause was strengthened by the dissensions in the League, and in 1590 he won a great victory over Mayenne at Ivry, a fierce cavalry fight, where H. showed the most splendid chivalry and alert generalship. He then besieged Paris, and reduced its citizens, who held out with misguided heroism, to dreadful straits, when the Duke of Parma advanced to relieve the siege and out-generalled H. Unable to end the protracted conflict in 1593, he embraced the Catholic creed, whereupon Paris and the other great cities surrendered, and H. became King of France. In 1598 peace was made between France and Spain, and H. signed the Edict of Nantes (q. v.). He now ruled with admirable wisdom and patriotism, rooted out the confusion engendered by the long wars, practised strict economy, developed the resources of his kingdom, and showed an anxiety for order, justice, and the welfare of his subjects which endeared him to his people—Catholics and Protestants alike. The finance reforms of his reign were carried out by his able minister Sully (q. v.), and France was raised to a state of unexampled prosperity. On May 14, 1610, the great king was assassinated by one Ravaillac, a tool of the Jesuits, and the whole country mourned his death, his old foes the Parisians in particular becoming frenzied with rage and grief. H. is by far the most fascinating character in the roll of French kings. He possessed a dazzling courage, the most sanguine confidence, the most winning amiability, careless mirthfulness, and flashing wit, allied to keen Gascon shrewdness, far-seeing statesmanship, and iron tenacity of purpose. He seems to have had the good of France seriously at heart, but to have regarded religion mainly as a diplomatic instrument. The great stain on his temperament was his licentiousness; he was all his life the slave of one mistress or another. He is said to have been present in seven distinct wars, a hundred pitched battles, and two hundred sieges. See Reboul, *Les Fortunes et Vertus de Henry, Roy de France et de Navarre* (Par. 1604); Matthieu, *Histoire de France durant sept Années de Paix du Règne d'H. IV.* (Par. 1605); Peleus, *Histoire de la Vie et Faits de H. le Grand*; Poirson, *Histoire du Règne d'H. IV.* (Par. 1857); MM. Haag, *La France Protestante* (1847-59); the histories of Michelet, Martin, Ranke, and Kitchin (Lond. 1877).—**H. V.** is the title assumed by the Comte de Chambord (q. v.).

Henry. For French kings of this name, see HENRI; for German kings, see HEINRICH.

Henry I., King of England, the youngest son of William the Conqueror and Matilda of Flanders, was born at Selby, Yorkshire, 1068. On the 2d August 1100, his brother William II. having been pierced with an arrow while hunting in the New Forest, H. speedily took possession of the royal treasures, and was crowned at Westminster, thereby forestalling Robert, Duke of Normandy, his elder brother, who was returning from a crusade. To conciliate the baronage, he granted a charter of liberties, exchanging the exactions under which they laboured for customary fees, and thus removing the old system of plundering the Church. He recalled Archbishop Anselm, who had been driven from court during the previous reign, and took the strongest step towards popularity by marrying Matilda, daughter of King Malcolm of Scotland and of Margaret, the sister of Eadgar Ætheling. The nobles remained unfriendly, and at their invitation Robert landed with his followers at Pevensey (July 19, 1101). Through the influence of Anselm the dispute was at that time made up, but it broke out again, and in 1106, at Tenchebray, H. gained a decisive victory over his brother on Norman soil, captured and kept him a prisoner until his death (in 1134), and added the dukedom to his own possessions. The king having sternly suppressed his rebellious baronage, gave grants of their estates to new men, whilst charters and the foundation of trade-guilds were allowed to create in the towns a counterbalancing force to feudalism. The whole system of justice and finance was reorganised. A great grief overtook the king (1129) when his son William was drowned in the Channel. He, however, settled the crown upon his daughter Matilda, widow of the Emperor Heinrich V., and married her to Geoffrey, eldest son of the Comte d'Anjou, making the nobles and priests on these occasions swear allegiance to her and her son. H. died in Normandy, December 1, 1135, owing, it is said, to a surfeit of eels. The central aim of his policy was to depress the nobles through an alliance with the people, to whom, though he treated them as slaves, he was always sternly just. See Stubbs's *Select Charters and other Illustrations of English Constitutional History* (1870), Freeman's *History of the Norman Conquest*, and Green's *Short History of the English People* (1875).—**H. II.**, son of Geoffrey Comte d'Anjou and Matilda, was born at Le Mans, Normandy,

1133. He was recognised by H. I. as his successor directly after his birth, but Stephen of Blois, Comte de Boulogne, disregarding his oath to Matilda, seized the crown for himself. H. was brought to England when eight years of age, and trained to the use of arms. In 1151 he succeeded to Normandy, Anjou, and Maine, and a year later he married the Duchess Eleanor of Aquitaine, who had been divorced from Louis VII. By this connection he gained the county of Poitou and the Duchy of Aquitaine. H. landed in England (January 1153) in order to recover the kingdom, for which his mother had long fought with varying degrees of success; and many friends gathering round him, he began negotiations at Wallingford which were concluded at Westminster (in November) with the result that Stephen recognised him as his heir. On the 19th December 1154, H. was crowned, and Thomas à Becket (q. v.) became his chancellor. H. at once began to demolish the castles, which had become the strongholds of feudal lawlessness. The administration of justice was restored upon a stronger footing, and he set himself to the study of law, holding numerous councils. He altered the conditions of scutage, under which every freeman was bound to serve in arms for the defence of his country, taking money instead of service from the whole of his dominions. Circuits were made by itinerant judges, and the supreme court was rearranged so as to secure easy justice to all. H. got his chancellor elected to the Archbishopric of Canterbury in June 1162, and Becket in this capacity immediately began to oppose him. In January 1164 the Council of Clarendon was held, and the clergy were brought under the criminal jurisdiction of the ordinary courts, but Becket refused to set his seal to the acceptance. At Northampton he was tried, and went into voluntary exile for six years. Through fear of the Pope, H. recalled him (1170), but his first acts were so irritating that a hasty speech of the king's incited some private enemies of the archbishop to seek him at Canterbury, where they slew him in the cathedral, December 29, 1170. With Ireland, Wales, Scotland, and France, H. at different periods engaged in hostilities. The Earl of Pembroke, Robert Fitzstephen, and Maurice Fitzgerald, having obtained royal permission to join Dermot of Leinster with an army (1169), carried everything before them; and in 1171 H. crossed to Ireland, and received a general acknowledgment of supremacy. In 1163 the Welsh princes did homage to him at Woodstock. His relations with the King of France were extremely complicated, not only through the geographical extent of his dominions, but owing to the difficulties of the feudal relationship between them. The last years of H. were embittered by the revolts of his sons, who were stirred up against him by their mother. His eldest son, Henry, joined (1173) a confederation of the French lords and English barons, who were aided by Louis of France, Philippe of Flanders, the Comte de Champagne, and the King of Scots, William the Lion. An incident of this revolt was the capture of King William, whom (1175) H. compelled to do homage and to acknowledge the supremacy of the English crown and Church over the Scottish. His sons were again at war (1183), and, after the death of Henry and Geoffrey, Richard, who had received Aquitaine, intrigued with Philippe, King of France, and their allied forces drove H. to Chinon, where he died (July 6, 1189). H. was strong in the sterling qualities of kinghood. He was a great soldier, mingling caution and prudence with rapidity and determination in his movements. Though restless and passionate in disposition, he was a consummate man of business, both in law and finance. As a politician, his aims were ambitious but definite. All that he possessed through marriage and inheritance he determined to keep, while he intended his family by similar means to add to his territory, and to form an imperial federation under himself. He understood that the well-being of his people was the strongest basis upon which to build his own power, and in all his relations with them he was firm, politic, just, aiming at subjugation through order. His constitutional ideal was a strong personal government unembarrassed by church or baronage. See *Life of Henry II.* by Lord Lyttleton; Stubbs's *Constitutional History of England* (1875); Freeman's *Essays* (1st series, 1871); *Select Charters* and *Early Plantagenets* (1877), and Green's *Short History of the English People* (1875).—**H. III.**, son of John by his second wife, Isabel of Angoulême, was born at Winchester in 1207. In the ninth year of his age he was crowned at Gloucester, and for fifty-six years he reigned over England. At the time of his accession Prince Louis of France was in England, at the head of the English baronage, prosecuting a claim to the crown, but when John was removed a disruption of the party took place. After the battle of Lincoln (1217), and the dispersion of his fleet at Thanet, Louis withdrew, and Alexander, King of Scots, and Llywelyn, Prince of N. Wales, both acknowledged H. Until 1219 William Marshal, Earl of Pembroke, was the king's guardian; he was succeeded by Peter des Roches, while Hubert de Burgh acted as Prime Minister. In 1220 a second coronation took place, and in 1228 the great charter was confirmed for the third time. H. came of age in 1227, and, according to Professor Stubbs, 'the history of the thirty-one years (1227 to 1258) which form the period of his personal administration is one long series of impolitic and unprincipled acts. They may be divided,' continues the same writer, 'into the three heads of internal misgovernment, a mischievous foreign policy formed under the guidance of the Popes, and the unfortunate line adopted with regard to the French provinces on which the king still retained his hold.' In 1236 H. married Eleanor of Provence, and two years later he gave his sister Eleanor in marriage to Simon de Montfort. Meanwhile a struggle about taxation was kept up in the assembly of barons and bishops until, in 1244, the lay and clerical estates acted together, and chose twelve representatives to demand confirmation of the charters. From the time of his marriage H. was surrounded by foreigners, upon whom he lavished estates, and to whom a sixth of the royal revenue passed in pensions. The administration of justice became debased, forced loans were exacted, and (1255) H. brought matters to a climax by accepting a papal offer of the kingdom of Sicily for his son Edmund, which occasioned immense expense. At the Parliament of Oxford, held 11th June 1258, where his son was presented as King of Sicily, H. had to consent to certain conditions known as the Provisions of Oxford, by which it was stipulated that there should be a permanent council of fifteen, three annual parliaments, and the representation of the community of the realm through twelve representative barons. But the members of this government quarrelled among themselves, and Louis IX., having been called to arbitrate, annulled the Provisions (1264). The result was the Barons' War, in which Simon de Montfort (q. v.) led the nobility. The battle of Lewes, fought May 14, 1264, threw the King into their power. A new constitution, entitled the Mise of Lewes, was formed, and on January 20, 1265, the first Parliament, in which representatives of the borough towns sat, was called. Dissensions again sprung up among the nobles, and at the battle of Evesham, Simon de Montfort, who led the King in his train, fell, and his fall restored peace. H. died November 16, 1272, England being then at peace. Though not wanting in personal bravery, H. was in every important respect a weak king. He lacked firmness and fibre. His actions were the outcome of no abiding purpose, and his tastes were satisfied by empty ostentation. As a husband and father he shows improvement upon his predecessors, but his falseness of character was unrelieved by any touch of the greater qualities exhibited by them as warriors. His vanity was excessive, and the hatred of his people towards him cordial and sincere. See Matthew Paris's *Chronicle*, Stubbs's *Constitutional History of England*, and *Early Plantagenets*, Freeman's *English Constitution*, Green's *Short History of the English People*, Pearson's *History of England*, and Hallam's *Middle Ages*.—**H. IV.**, eldest son of John of Gaunt and Blanche, daughter of Henry, Duke of Lancaster, was born at Bolingbroke, Lincolnshire, 1366. In 1387 H. acted with the party which exiled the favourites of Richard II. He was banished the kingdom in 1398, but during Richard's absence in Ireland he returned, and was joined by Archbishop Arundel and the Percy family. Richard, who was betrayed into his hands, resigned the crown, and on September 30, 1399, H. claimed it as being a descendant of H. III. A conspiracy was detected (January 4, 1400), which resulted in the beheading of the Earls of Kent, Huntingdon, Salisbury, and Lord Spenser. Next month Richard II. was either starved or assassinated in prison, and his body was exposed in London. In the same year H. invaded Scotland, but famine compelled him to withdraw from Edinburgh. Troublesome rumours that Richard was still alive began to be disseminated, and intrigue entered the very palace. Wales, which had ceased to give trouble since the time of Edward I., rose in rebellion (1402) under Owen Glendower (q. v.). At the same time the Scots invaded Northumberland, but were defeated at Homildon Hill, and their leader, Earl Douglas, taken prisoner by the Earl of

Northumberland and his son Henry Percy. Owing to the refusal of H. to allow Sir Edmund Mortimer to be ransomed from Glendower, the Percys revolted, but at Shrewsbury (July 21, 1403), they were intercepted by the King, Hotspur slain, and his father ordered into confinement. Yet the Welsh maintained their independence of England during the whole reign. An incident occurred in 1405 which laid H.'s mind to rest concerning Scotland. Prince James of Scotland (q. v.) was taken prisoner on his road to France, and detained in England. A new confederacy sprung up (1405), in which the liberated Earl of Northumberland, Mowbray, the Earl Marshal, the Lord Bardolf, and Richard Scroop, united to advance the pretensions of the Earl of March, who was descended from Lionel, Duke of Clarence, elder brother of John of Gaunt. By the year 1408 the chief actors in this revolt had all disappeared. H. died 20th March 1413. See Lord Brougham's *England under the House of Lancaster*, James Gairdner's *Lancaster and York*, and Green's *Short History of the English People.*—**H. V.**, son of the preceding and Mary de Bohun, was born at Monmouth, 1388. H. was distinguished in youth for his excess of animal spirits and his dislike to the restraints of court-life, and his love of frolic and practical joking are immortalised in Shakespeare's *Henry IV.* At the battle of Shrewsbury, by the exercise of courage and prowess he showed himself possessed of sterner stuff, and when he came to the throne he dismissed the companions of his pleasures and took into confidence the councillors of his father. At the outset his reign was troubled by the importunity of the Lollards, who were encouraged by Sir John Oldcastle. Proceedings were taken against Oldcastle, though he was a favourite, and belonged to the royal household, and a conspiracy of the Lollards was put down promptly (January 27, 1414) at St. Giles's Fields. H. revived the claims of Edward III. to the French crown, and followed up his unreasonable demand (1415) by crossing from Southampton to Harfleur. Though dysentery broke out in his army and reduced it from 30,000 to 9000 men, he fought a great battle at Agincourt (October 25, 1415) against overwhelming odds, routed the French, and slew the flower of their nobility. In 1417 he again invaded France; and at the beginning of 1419, Rouen having capitulated, he became master of Normandy, Maine, and Isle of France. H. married (June 2, 1420) Princess Catherine, daughter of the French king, and (1421) entered Paris in triumph. A third invasion of France had to be made after the battle of Beaugé, in which H.'s brother, the Duke of Clarence, was defeated. King James of Scotland, still a prisoner, accompanied H. on this campaign. The N. of France was brought under subjection (by 1422), but H. was struck down with dysentery, and died at Vincennes (August 1422). He was one of the most popular of English kings, and possessed a very high genius for war and diplomacy. His splendid military achievements dazzled the nation, and his death at so early an age contributed to the estimate of his greatness. His policy in reference to France though not to be justified, is easily explicable. His title to the throne being but indifferent, he was compelled to divert public attention from his own descent, and to create a right by virtue of his own deeds. See Lord Brougham's *England under the House of Lancaster*, James Gairdner's *Lancaster and York*, and Green's *Short History of the English People* (1875).—**H. VI.**, son of the preceding and of Catherine of France, was born at Windsor, December 6, 1421, and two months after his father's death, when yet an infant, was declared King of France. John, Duke of Bedford, was appointed Regent of France for his nephew, and Humphrey, Duke of Gloucester, received the title of Protector, with the care of defending the kingdom of England. For the first twenty years of H.'s reign all interest centres in the struggle to preserve the French kingdom against the claims of the Dauphin, who reigned at Bourges as Charles VII. For some years the Duke of Bedford succeeded in maintaining the English conquests; but in February 1429, Jeanne D'Arc (q. v.) appeared to Charles at Chinon, and declared she was sent from Heaven to conduct him to Rheims for his coronation. Under her leadership the English were compelled to raise the siege of Orleans. At Patay she defeated Lord Talbot and took him prisoner, but on May 25, 1430, she was captured by the Burgundians at Compiègne, and handed over to the English, who had her burnt as a witch at Rouen. The Duke of Bedford died in 1435, and bit by bit the inheritance of Henry II. and the conquests of his successors in France were lost beyond recovery. Cherbourg, the last English stronghold, was surrendered (1450), and though the people of Bordeaux revolted (1452) against Charles, and sought to return to the English Government, they were forced to yield. From this event dates the end of the Hundred Years' War between the two countries. During these years in England a great struggle for power had been going on between Humphrey, Duke of Gloucester, and Henry Beaufort, Bishop of Winchester, who became Cardinal. On the rise of William de la Pole, Earl of Suffolk, to power, he recommended to H. the policy of a match with Marguerite, daughter of René, Duc d'Anjou, titular king of Naples and Jerusalem. H. married her (1445), but Suffolk was disliked by the people as negotiator of the match, and blamed for the military losses in France. Suffolk was, therefore, impeached, banished, and murdered on his passage to Calais (1450). Complaints at this time arose concerning the extortions of the king's officers who collected the revenue, and culminated in Jack Cade's rebellion (1450), which was rapidly quelled. Cade was an Irishman, and professed to be cousin of the Duke of York. Two rival factions now began to show among the nobility, headed by the Dukes of York and Somerset. York was made Protector (1454), the king having lost his faculties. When H. recovered, Somerset, the representative of an illegitimate branch of the House of Lancaster, and a favourite of the King, was recalled to power. York raised an army, and met his rival, whom he slew at the Battle of St. Albans (1455). In 1459, the struggle became the Wars of the Roses, so called from the family emblem of a white rose affected by the Lancastrians, and a red rose by the Yorkists. With varying fortune battles were fought (see Edward IV.) between the families and their adherents—at Northampton, where H. was captured and compelled to recognise York as his successor; at Wakefield, where York was slain; at Mortimer's Cross, where York's son avenged his death; at St. Alban's, where the queen and her friends defeated the Earl of Warwick. In March 9, 1461, H.'s reign came to an end by the assembly of peers, prelates, and citizens, declaring Edward, Duke of York, king. H. was liberated from the Tower (1470) and reinstated in his kingdom by the Earl of Warwick, but on the 21st he died, or was murdered in prison (May 21, 1471), on the triumphant entry of Edward into London. H. was a weak and harmless king, who throughout his life was made the tool of more powerful men. He had no positive vices, was amiable in disposition, inclined to peace and the ordinances of religion. See Lord Brougham's *England under the House of Lancaster*, James Gairdner's *Lancaster and York*, and Green's *Short History of the English People* (1875).—**H. VII.**, son of Edmund Tudor, Earl of Richmond, and Margaret Beaufort, was born at Pembroke Castle, 21st January 1456. During the civil wars he was an exile in Brittany, from which he crossed August 19, 1485. Landing at Milford Haven, he met Richard III. at Market Bosworth, overpowered him, and gained the crown. H. married Elizabeth of York, January 18, 1486, and thereby united the contending houses. In 1487, a youth calling himself Earl of Warwick, having secured the support of Margaret, widow of the Duke of Burgundy, was crowned king in Ireland. This pretender, named Lambert Simnel, who was the son of a joiner, was defeated and captured at the battle of Stoke (June 16, 1487). A second claimant, Perkin Warbeck by name, professing to be the Duke of York, whom Richard III. had caused to be murdered in the Tower, appeared in 1496. He was supported by the Duchess of Burgundy and the kings of France and Scotland, but was taken prisoner (1497), and beheaded (1499). H., in his foreign policy, aimed at peace and alliance with Spain, and to this end he married (1501) Prince Arthur to Catharine of Aragon, Princess of Spain. H.'s besetting sin was avarice, and towards the end of his reign he became unpopular from the number of his exactions, which were chiefly put into effect by Richard Empson and Edmund Dudley, who revived and applied forgotten statutes, and filled the royal coffers with fines. H., who sent out Sebastian Cabot to America, was the founder of the colonial empire of England. He died April 21, 1509. H. was a hard and commonplace man, but his severe economy was not without purpose. His aim was to accumulate a treasure which would render him independent of the House of Commons, and in this he succeeded so well that at his death he left nearly two millions. See Seebohm's *Era of the Protestant Revolution*; James Gairdner's *Letters and Papers of Richard III. and H. VII.*; Lord Bacon's *H. VII.*; Hallam's *Constitutional History* (vol. i.); Green's *Short History of the English People* (1875).—**H. VIII.**, the son of Henry VII. and of Elizabeth of York, was born at Greenwich, 1491. Catharine of Aragon, widow of his brother Arthur, was betrothed to him in 1501. H. married her in 1509 on arriving at the throne. The opening years of his reign were full of promise, and in the midst of revelry part of his life was given up to study. H. soon found a pretext for renewing the ancient struggle with France. Allied with the Emperor-elect Maximilian, he in 1513 won the Battle of the Spurs at Guinegate (q. v.). In the same year, at the Battle of Flodden, the Scots were disastrously defeated by the Earl of Surrey, and their king slain. The King of France tried to retain H.'s friendship by an interview at the Field of the Cloth of Gold near Guisnes, but Karl V., who had become Emperor on the death of Ferdinand, tempted him to a war policy. But though France lost the Milanese and was defeated at Pavia, it was the Emperor who profited and not H. Peace was therefore made (1525), and at the end of the war H. found he could no longer rely on Karl V. and the Pope. Thomas Wolsey (q. v.), Chancellor and Cardinal, who aided a renewal of the French alliance, saw a chance of widening the breach between England and Spain. Catharine had only one child alive, her daughter Mary. The succession to the throne was uncertain, and superstitious doubts as to the validity of the marriage rose in H.'s mind. At the same time he contracted a passion for Anne Boleyn (q. v.), a young lady of his court. A divorce was asked from Pope Clement VII., who wished to gratify H., but was afraid of the Emperor. Cardinals Wolsey and Campeggio were appointed as a commission to inquire into the fact, but they delayed. In 1529 Wolsey fell from power, and in the year following he died. Cranmer (q. v.) was now Archbishop of Canterbury, and after consultation with the chief European universities, he pronounced the marriage with Catharine null and void. H. married Anne Boleyn in January 1532. Thus H., who in 1521 had received from the Pope the title of 'Defender of the Faith' for writing a Latin treatise against Luther, completely broke with Rome. Sir Thomas More (q. v.) resigned his post of Lord Chancellor, because he continued to believe that the Pope was head of the Church by divine authority, and his convictions on this point afterwards brought him to the scaffold. During the next ten years the new monarchy reached the height of its absolute power, and the revolt from the ecclesiastical empire was completed. H. became 'Protector and Supreme Head of the Church and Clergy of England' in 1531. A purified Catholicism became the religion of the country, but the Lutherans and Protestants were persecuted as heretics. Thomas Cromwell, created Earl of Essex, who had been in Wolsey's service, now aided H. in the policy of reducing the Church to a department of state. Being appointed vicegerent of the King in ecclesiastical affairs, he selected royal commissioners to make a general visitation of the religious houses, and the whole of them with an income of less than £200 a year were suppressed. In 1536 agrarian discontent and reaction in favour of the old religion stirred up a revolt in Lincolnshire, which being crushed, reappeared in Yorkshire. This insurrection, styled the 'Pilgrimage of Grace,' was put down with ruthless severity (1537). A papal bull of deposition was, at the instigation of Cardinal Pole, levelled at H. (1538), but was answered by the execution of his mother, the Countess of Salisbury, and his brother, Lord Montague. Under Cranmer and Cromwell, who were really carrying on the work set agoing by the Oxford Reformers, an English translation of the Bible was placed in all the churches. But the zeal of the Protestants and their attack on the mass roused H.'s indignation, and the law of the Six Articles was passed (1539) to check them. Meanwhile Anne Boleyn was beheaded (1536) on a charge of unfaithfulness, and H. married Jane Seymour, who died at the birth of Edward. In 1540 H.'s marriage with Anne of Cleves, which was brought about by Thomas Cromwell, was the occasion of that minister's fall and execution. After the annulment of Anne's marriage H. took Catherine Howard to wife, who being beheaded for misconduct (1542), was succeeded in 1543 by Catherine Parr, who survived him. The Earl of Norfolk filled the place of Cromwell, and carried on his policy. A Scotch army was defeated (1542) at Solway Moss, and (1544) H. carried war into France. During his reign Wales was incorporated with England, and Ireland was raised from a lordship to a kingdom. H. died June 28, 1547. His character has been variously estimated, according to the reading of the events of the period given by different historians, but under any view, he was a man of vigorous intellect, strong passions, and immense force of will. See Froude's *History of England* (vols. i.-v.); Hallam's *Constitutional History* (vol. i.); Green's *Short History of the English People*; Seebohm's *Era of the Protestant Revolution*; and *Letters and Papers, Foreign and Domestic, of the Reign of Henry VIII., arranged and catalogued by J. S. Brewer*, of which four vols. had appeared in 1876.

Henry, surnamed 'The Navigator,' was the third son of John I. of Portugal and Philippina of Lancaster, sister of Henry IV. of England. He was born at Oporto in 1394, and showed great courage in the Portuguese conquest of Ceuta in 1417. He was from boyhood devoted to geography, and after his father's death took up his abode at Sagres on the coast of Algarve, where he constructed docks, arsenals, and an observatory, and gathered round him voyagers and men of science. Under his auspices many expeditions were sent out, which explored the W. coast of Africa, established a trading company at Lagos in 1442, and discovered the Azores in 1448. H. caused various plants and animals to be introduced into the newly discovered lands, and bore the expense of the expeditions until his nation awakened to the importance of prosecuting the W. African trade. H. died at Sagres, November, 13, 1460. He left a few works which are extant in MS. There is no prince to whom geographical discovery is so deeply indebted as to H. See *Vida do Infante Di Henrique* (Lisbon, 1758).

Henry, Matthew, an English commentator on Scripture, was born at Broadoak, near Whitchurch in Shropshire, in 1662. He at first studied law at Gray's Inn, but afterwards became a Nonconformist clergyman. H. was pastor of a congregation of dissenters at Chester from 1687 to 1712, when he removed to Hackney. He died at Nantwich, June 22, 1714. His works include *A Discourse on Schism*; *Life of Mr. Philip H.*, his father; *A Scripture Catechism*; *Family Hymns*; *A Method of Prayer*; *Exposition of the Old and New Testament*, his chief work (1710), and still highly valued in Dissenting circles. See Yong's *Life of M. H.* (1716), and Williams's *Life, Character, and Writings of the Rev. M. H.* (1828).

Henry of Huntingdon, an English chronicler of the 12th c., who became canon of Lincoln and archdeacon of Huntingdon, and wrote a Latin history of England to the death of Stephen in 1154; a treatise, *De Mundi Contemptu*, which contains many interesting anecdotes of his contemporaries; several Latin verses, partly in the manner of Martial, &c. The date of his death is not known. H.'s history is, in the early part, based chiefly on Bede—whose style he imitates—and on Geoffrey of Monmouth, but in the later books has an independent value. An edition of it was published by Sir H. Saville among the *Scriptores Post Bedam* (Lond. 1596), and there is an English version in Bohn's *Antiquarian Library*.

Henry, Patrick, a famous American politician and orator, was born at Studley, Virginia, U.S., May 29, 1736, his father being a nephew of Robertson the historian. At the age of twenty-four he was admitted to the American bar, but had no practice until, in 1765, by boldly and ably introducing in the house of burgesses resolutions against the Stamp Act, he became known as a gifted orator and ardent patriot, and shortly rose to affluence by his forensic powers. In 1774 he was the first Speaker of the General Congress at Philadelphia; and in 1775 the resolve of the Convention to resist George III. was largely due to his eloquence. After the declaration of independence he was made commander of the Virginian forces, and he was governor of Virginia during 1776-79 and 1781-86. Washington and Adams afterwards offered him several high posts, which he declined. H. opposed the formation of a Federal constitution in 1788, quitted public life in 1794, and died at Red Hill, Virginia, June 6, 1799. He was an ardent democrat and a zealous patriot, and his thrilling oratory had a most momentous influence on several critical occasions in his country's history.

Henry, Robert, D.D., a Scottish historian, born at St. Ninians, Stirlingshire, February 18, 1718. He studied at Edinburgh University, became a schoolmaster at Annan, was a minister in Carlisle and Berwick, and latterly in Edinburgh. He died in November 1790. H. wrote a *History of Great Britain on a New Plan* (6 vols. 1771-93), which goes down to the reign of Henry VIII. It is a dreary, inaccurate work, but was novel in so far as it gave pictures of the country's varying social state.

Henry, William, an English chemist and physician, was born at Manchester, December 12, 1775. He studied successively at Manchester, York, and Edinburgh, where he graduated M.D. in 1807. He then settled as a practitioner in his native town, but subsequently became the superintendent of the chemical establishment founded by his father. His papers in the *Philosophical Transactions*, and in the *Memoirs* of the Philosophical Society of Manchester, bearing for the most part upon the chemistry of gases, attest the extent of his knowledge and his admirable skill as an experimental philosopher. H. was elected a Fellow of the Royal Society in 1808, and obtained the Copley prize in 1809. His *Elements of Experimental Philosophy* (1799, 11th ed. 1829) was long the standard treatise on the science. H. died September 2, 1836, at Pendlebury, near Manchester.

Hen'ryson, Robert, one of the best of the old Scottish poets, flourished during the 15th c., but of his birth and early years nothing is known. In 1462 he was made a member of Glasgow University, and is there referred to as the 'venerable.' He spent the most of his life at Dunfermline, where he was schoolmaster, and the date of his death is uncertain, but it must have been shortly before the close of the 15th c., about which time the plague ravaged Scotland. Dunbar, in his *Lament for the Death of the Makaris*, published in 1508, says of Death that—

> 'In Dunfermline he has done roun
> Gud Maister Robert Henrysoun.'

H., as a poet, shows deep, simple feeling, rich humour, varied descriptive power, and a full command of melodious verse. His chief work is *The Testament of Cresseid*, which continues Chaucer's *Troilus and Creseide*, and tells with exquisite pathos and quaint felicity of language how Cressida was punished by leprosy for her faithlessness. His other writings comprise *Orpheus and Eurydice*, mainly interesting as a reflection of the classical learning of the time; *The Bludy Serk*, an allegorical ballad; *The Moral Fables of Æsop in Scottish Metre*, abounding in naïve vivacity and quiet humour; and *Robene and Makyne*, a delightfully natural, animated, and musical Scottish pastoral, in the form of a dialogue between a youth and a girl. See *The Poems of R. H.* edited with a memoir by Laing (Edinb. 1865).

Hep'ar Sulphuris, the term used in the U.S. Pharmacopœia for Potassa Sulphurata (q. v.).

Hepati'tis (Gr. *hepar*, 'the liver'), or inflammation of the liver, may have its seat in the fibrous covering of the liver, the sheath of the vessels in Glisson's capsule, or in the glandular paunchyma, the portal or hepatic veins, or the bile ducts, and may terminate in simple or granular induration, or in softening and acute atrophy, associated with Jaundice (q. v.) and severe febrile symptoms. In tropical climates H. has a tendency to result in suppuration, and is called *suppurative H.* Symptoms:—Deranged stomach, loaded tongue, heartburn, nausea, vomiting, flatulence, constipation, distension and tenderness of the epigastrium, pain in the right shoulder, and a yellowish colour. See LIVER, DISEASE OF.

Hepat'icæ, a section of Cryptogams (q. v.) known popularly under the name Liverworts, differ from Mosses (q. v.), to which they are closely allied, in their capsule never having a distinct lid, and consequently no trace of a peristome. Considerable difficulty has been experienced in dividing H. into satisfactory groups. Hooker, in his beautiful work (1816) devoted to these plants, placed the whole under the one genus *Jungermannia*; Gray, in his *Arrangement of British Plants* (1821), instituted numerous genera, some of which are now resuscitated; and the Belgian botanist Du Mortier, who has been a writer on H. for more than fifty years, has been continually altering his arrangement. Dr. Lindberg, as the latest reformer, adopts three sections —(1) Marchantiaceæ, for those with stem and leaves confluent in a frond; (2) Jungermanniaceæ, with stem and leaves distinct; (3) Anthocerotaceæ, consisting of species with solitary capsule, filiform, bivalved, stalked, with a free central placentation. These he again groups into sub-sections, according to whether the valves of the capsule split into pieces when ripe (*Schizocarpæ*) or remain whole (*Cleistocarpæ*). H. are world-wide in distribution, occurring under much the same condition as mosses, with which they agree in the development of the fruit and the manner of impregnation. They are also extensively propagated by gemmæ. See Hofmeister's *Higher Cryptogams* (Ray Society), and for a description of British species Dr. B. Carrington's *British H.* (1877).

Hephæs'tus (Gr. *Hēphaistos*), the Greek god of fire, was the son of Zeus and Hera, or of Hera alone. In disgust at his being born lame, Hera threw him from Olympus, but the Nereids, Thetis and Eurynome, received him in the bosom of the sea, and kept him for nine years, after which he was restored to Olympus, and became the artist of the gods. His mother's harshness he repaid with tenderness; but one morning his interference on her behalf in a quarrel between her and Zeus so enraged the latter that he threw him down from heaven. About evening he alighted on Lemnos, where he was kindly welcomed by the Sinties. After his fall, to which later writers ascribe his lameness, he was again restored to Olympus. He had there a glorious palace of his own, which contained his tools, and where, aided by the Cyclops, he made an endless variety of wondrous works. Other workshops of H. were Hiera, Imbros, Lipara, and Sicily. Charis, Aglaia, and Aphrodite are variously given as his wife. The story of Aphrodite's intrigue with Ares, for which H. made the god of war a laughing-stock to the other Olympians, is often alluded to. In common with Athena, H. patronised artists of every kind, and most of the epithets by which the poets characterise him either refer to this or to his lameness. In artistic representations H. appears as a strong bearded man, with a hammer, an oval cap, or a chiton as attributes. For the Italian deity, with which the Romans identified H., see VULCANUS.

Hep'tagon, a plane figure enclosed by *seven* sides. It has, therefore, seven angles; and when these are all equal, the figure is called a *regular* H.

Hep'tarchy (Gr. *hepta*, 'seven,' and *archo*, 'I govern'), the name given to the seven kingdoms founded by the Teutonic settlers in Britain before the Norman conquest. At no period did these seven kingdoms exist side by side, but one was constantly gaining supremacy over the other, the kingdoms of Northumbria, Mercia, and Wessex being successively pre-eminent. The seven kingdoms consisted of—(1) Kent; (2) Sussex; (3) Essex, which corresponded roughly to the present counties of Kent, Sussex, Essex, and Middlesex; (4) East Anglia, which included Norfolk and Suffolk; (5) Northumbria, which stretched from the Humber to the Forth, being bounded on the west by the Celtic district of Strathclyde; (6) Mercia, which included the Midlands from the Thames to the Humber; (7) Wessex, which comprised at first England W. of Sussex and S. of the Thames and E. as far as Devonshire, but which afterwards embraced part of Cornwall, and finally, under Eagberht, brought the rest of England beneath its sway about 830. With this date the H. is by some said to have ended, but the old kingdoms were not thoroughly welded together until the Norman conquest. See ANGLO-SAXONS, Freeman's *Early English History and Norman Conquest*, and Green's *Short History of the English People*.

He'ra (Gr. *Hēra* or *Hērē*, 'mistress') was, in Greek mythology, the eldest daughter of Kronus and Rhea, and sister and wife of Zeus, by whom she was the mother of Ares, Hebe, and Hephæstus. Many places in Hellas claimed to be her birthplace, but particularly Samos and Argos, where were also her two finest temples. Homer says that she was brought up by Oceanus and Tethys, but the Argives believed it was by the three daughters of the river-god Asterion, near Mycenæ. Her 'sacred marriage' (*Hieros gamos*) was said to have been at Cnossus or on Mount Thornax, or in Samos or in Eubæa. On its occasion she received gifts from all the Olympians, and Ge gave her the famous tree of the Hesperides (q. v.), which bore golden fruit. As the only goddess that could be considered married, she was the patroness of marriage and child-bearing, from which she was surnamed Gamelia, Zygia, Teleia, Ilithyia, &c. In the legend of the Argonauts she is kind to Jason, but in the Trojan war her spite against Paris makes her the enemy of Troy. She is a relentless persecutor of Hercules, Dionysus, and all children of Zeus by other mothers. Though honoured with the chief confidence of her lord, and treated by the rest of the gods as on a level with him, H. is only so by courtesy, and must obey her lord implicitly, suffering chastisement if disobedient. Yet her stubborn and imperious temper breeds many quarrels, and often taxes severely the patience of Zeus. In later mythology, however, she is raised to the dignity of queen of heaven. Though some of the ancients connected H. with the atmosphere, or the stars, or the moon, it is most probable that the conception of her character originally sprang from her being the great goddess of nature, universally worshipped in the earliest times. The Romans identified H. with their Juno (q. v.). She is represented as a fully-developed woman of superhuman size, with handsome features, and an aspect of majesty. Her head, draped in a bridal veil, is crowned with a diadem. She also bears a sceptre, and is attended by a peacock.

Heracle'a (Gr. *Hērakleia*, 'Herakles's town,' now *Erekli*), a name common to more than twenty ancient Greek cities. Of greatest political importance was H. in Bithynia, on the Black Sea, hence called *Pontica*, of which ruins still remain. Founded by Megarensian colonists about 550 B.C., it stood long under an aristocratic government, then, from 364, was held by 'tyrants,' but was finally reduced under Roman dominion by Aurelius Cotta during the Mithridatic war.—**H.**, in Lucania, on the river Siris, founded in 432 B.C. by Thurian and Tarentine colonists. It became an important city, and the meeting-place of the congress of the Italiot Greeks, until this was transferred to Thurii by Alexander of Epirus. It was the scene of Pyrrhus's victory in 280 B.C., and from 278 it had a very favourable treaty of alliance with Rome. During the Social War it suffered greatly. This H. is supposed to have been the birthplace of the painter Zeuxis. Near a farm named Policoro, on the site of the ancient city, many coins and other relics have been found, but especially interesting are two bronze tables, known as the *Tabulæ Heraclienses*, presenting a copy of the Lex Julia Municipalis of 45 B.C. The inscriptions have been published by Mazocchi (2 vols. Naples, 1754–55) and by Muratori (*Inscriptionum*, vol. ii. p. 582, 1739–43). There are also valuable commentaries by Dirksen (Berl. 1820) and Savigny (*Vermischte Schriften*, vol. iii. Berl. 1850).

Herac'leum, a genus of umbelliferous plants found in Europe, America, and India. *H. giganteum*, a native of Siberia, which is cultivated in gardens as an ornamental plant, grows from 12 to 14 feet high. *H. sphondylium*, a common British species, popularly known as cow-parsnip, is used for feeding pigs. In the Caucasus, the young shoots of *H. pubescens*, which are aromatic, are used as food.

Heracleum pubescens.

Heracli'dæ (Gr. *Hērakleidai*), the general name of the sons and later descendants of Hercules generally, but particularly applied to those of them who (according to the Greek legend), with the help of the Dorians, pressed their hereditary claim on the Peloponnesus, and possessed themselves of the provinces Argos, Laconia, and Messenia, which had been seized by the Dorians. Of their five expeditions, the last, which was eighty years after the destruction of Troy, was the greatest. The first four had passed over the Corinthian isthmus, but in this Oxylus, son of Andræmon, led them over the strait from Naupactus in Ætolia to Rhium, and after they had conquered in a great battle Tisamenes, son of Orestes, they seized the whole peninsula, and divided it among their number. Argos fell to Temenos, Lacedæmon to the twin sons of Aristodemus, Procles and Eurysthenes; Cresphontes obtained Messenia by stratagem, and Oxylus was rewarded with Elis.

Heracli'tus (Gr. *Hērakleitos*), a Greek philosopher, born at Ephesus about 500 B.C. He is said to have been a great traveller, and from his sorrowful scorn of mankind was spoken of as the 'weeping philosopher,' while Democritus was surnamed the 'laughing philosopher.' He held that the world was evolved from fire 'not made by God or man,' and wrote a work *On Nature*, fragments of which are collected in Wolf and Buttmann's *Museum der Alterthums-Wissenschaften* (Berl. 1805).

Herac'lius, a famous Byzantine emperor, was the son of Heraclius, exarch of Africa, and was born about 575 A.D. Little is known of his early life, but in 610 he sailed with a fleet from Carthage, and took an important part in dethroning the Emperor Phocas, in whose stead he ascended the imperial throne. The empire was at this time torn by internal strife and barbaric invasions. Chosroes of Persia ravaged the Asiatic provinces and the Avars advanced on Constantinople. H. narrowly escaped being captured by the latter enemy, but bought them off by 200,000 gold pieces, and prepared to assail the Persians, who in 616 took Chalcedon, opposite Constantinople. After carefully disciplining his army, H. invaded Cilicia in 622, routed a Persian army near Issus, and leaving his army to winter in Pontus, returned to Constantinople, whence he sailed with a select force to Trebizonde in 623. He then marched through Armenia and along the Caspian, making an advantageous alliance with the Khasars, who lay N. of the Caucasus. After thoroughly defeating Chosroes, he re-entered Cilicia and inflicted a crushing defeat on Sarbar, the general of Chosroes, on the Sihun, displaying remarkable courage as well as generalship. He now advanced into Persia, while the Avars swept down on Constantinople, and Sarbar lay with a new army on the Asiatic shore of the Bosphorus. H., instead of flying to succour his capital, struck at the heart of the Persian empire, again beat the Persians near the confluence of the Little Zab and Tigris in 627, and seized Artemita, a royal residence near Ctesiphon, where his soldiers acquired a vast booty. Chosroes now fled to the interior of his empire, the Persians were forced to conclude peace, and H. returned in a triumphal progress to Constantinople. The fame of his wonderful victories spread over Europe, and ambassadors from Europe and Asia, from India and from the Merwing Dagobert sought Constantinople to congratulate him on his restoring the old military renown of the Roman Empire. The latter years of his reign are in striking contrast to the earlier. While the Arabs, who were recently converted to Mohammedanism overthrew his generals and occupied Syria, Palestine, Mesopotamia, and Egypt, H. remained in Constantinople, seemingly given up to lassitude and empty theological disputes until his death in 641. Some ascribe this remarkable change in H.'s character to mental derangement, others to bodily pain arising from the many wounds and hardships which he suffered while pursuing his heroic career of conquest. 'Since the days of Scipio and Hannibal,' says Gibbon, 'no bolder enterprise has been attempted than that which H. achieved for the deliverance of the empire.'

Her'ald, during the middle ages, was an officer who bore messages from one king or noble to another, laid out the lists for tournaments, looked on at combats, counted the dead after a battle, and superintended matters relating to ceremonies and the bearing of coat-armour. Heralds gradually became mainly associated with the interpretation of coats-of-arms and with blazoning devices; in modern times they have merely to perform ceremonial duties on important public occasions, and to keep records of crests and arms. There are now fourteen heralds in England, four kings-at-arms—Garter, Clarencieux, Norroy, and Bath—six heralds, and four pursuivants.

Her'aldry (lit. 'the art of a herald,' from Old Fr. *herald*, Ger. *herold*, from *haren*, 'to shout') is the science of interpreting and arranging the various devices borne on shields, banners, &c., and the art of conducting public solemnities. The present article will deal only with H. as a science. In very ancient times, though H. did not exist, distinctive badges were carried on shields and helmets. The children of Israel in Numbers (i. 52 and ii. 2) are commanded to pitch their tents 'each by his own standard,' and 'with the ensign of their father's house.' In Æschylus's drama of *The Seven against Thebes*, the shields of the leaders are described as being blazoned with distinguishing emblems. The kings of Media are said by Xenophon to have carried the representation of a golden eagle on their shields, and though the Romans did not adopt the custom of distinguishing every leader by his carrying hereditary symbols on his armour, traces of such a custom occasionally appear in Roman history. Thus Suetonius tells us that Domitian carried the representation of a golden beard as a coat of arms. Nations, moreover, as opposed to individuals, adopted various distinctive emblems in very ancient periods of history. The Athenians, for example, chose an owl as their national standard, while the Romans bore an eagle. The first Teutonic invaders of England had a horse on their standard, and the Norse pirates adopted the raven as the device for their banner. But it was not until the middle ages that separate personal devices began to be so generally borne, that the knowledge of their various significations gradually developed into a kind of science. The date when H. originated cannot, of course, be definitely fixed, but in the latter half of the 12th c. it was beginning to develop into a system, and in the 13th c. it emerges as a distinct branch of knowledge, though the devices which it had then to interpret were very simple, generally symbolising some heroic act of the bearer or of his immediate ancestor, and being free from the complicated hereditary significance which they afterwards assumed. The use of these devices was largely due to the tournaments, in which it would have been difficult, without some such distinguishing marks, to have known one warrior from another, encased as they all were in very similar coats of mail. When a new knight appeared at a tournament, he carried the visor of his helmet shut, and the herald had to proclaim the import of the coat of arms which he bore on his shield. From this custom, the so-called science of explaining armorial bearings came to be known as H. In a tournament it was also the custom for each knight to hang up his helmet, with his shield below it, in the lists; and from this practice arose the peculiar pictorial representations used in H., and which are still to be seen on the panels of noblemen's carriages, &c. These representations consist of a shield surmounted by a helmet, the latter being generally encircled by a wreath. The distinctive colours of these shields, known in H. as *tinctures*, are said to have originated in the old German custom, mentioned by Tacitus, of marking each warrior's shield with brilliant tints. In the middle ages these colours borne on the shields were regarded as symbolising particular meanings. Afterwards it became usual to divide the shield into sections, it being the practice of any knight who had proclaimed himself the champion of more than one lady to carry all their respective colours on his armour. In the 11th c., when the crusades drew the nobles of Europe to the Holy Land, H. received a rapid development, it being absolutely necessary, in the mingling of so many warriors, that each should select bearings by which he could be recognised. Before the 11th c. we can find no tomb which is engraved with armorial bearings, the oldest tomb which carries an escutcheon being, so far as is known, that of Vormond, Count of Wasserburg, at Ratisbon. H. was mainly systematised by the French and Normans, and all the terms that are at present used in English H. are derived from the French, though it is asserted that the *ordinaries* and *metals*, as well as the *tinctures*, are of Teutonic origin, while it is said that many of the devices were brought from the East during the times of the crusades. The chief duties of the herald were (1) *Blazoning*—probably from Ger. *blasen*, to blow a horn, from the practice of blowing a trumpet when a new knight appeared at a tournament—which consisted in giving a description of a bearing; (2) *marshalling*, *i.e.*, preparing a new escutcheon; and (3) *historifying*, *i.e.*, explaining the origin of a coat of arms, and the successive modifications which it has undergone. In H., arms have many various names, according to the causes of their adoption. Thus there are *arms of dominion*, *i.e.*, arms borne by sovereigns, and appertaining to different countries—*e.g.*, the arms of England; *arms of patronage*, *i.e.*, arms borne by lords of manors, governors of provinces, &c.; *arms of pretension*, *i.e.*, arms borne by a ruler who has a claim on a territory which belongs to another, and who adds the arms of the territory so claimed to his own arms; *arms of community*, borne by cities, bishops, &c.; *arms of family*, borne by individuals, apart from their position as rulers of any territory or city; *arms of succession*, borne *quartered* on their original arms by those who inherited other than their original estates; *arms of alliance*, borne to indicate the union of families; *arms of assumption*, which are arms assumed by persons who have no legal title to them, or arms assumed with the approval of the king of arms. The shield and helmet were the parts of the armour on which these arms were borne. The shields of the knights were distinguished by various *tinctures*, *ordinaries*, and *charges*, from which all H. has developed. Tinctures are divided into metals, colours, and furs. There are two metals, gold, called in H. *or*, and silver, called in H. *argent*. The heraldic colours are blue, denoting charity; red, courage; green, youth; purple and black, called respectively *azure*, *gules*, *vert*, *purpure*, and *sable*, grief and prudence. Some writers add to these orange or tawny, *jaune*, and dark-red or blood colour, *sanguine*. These they call *stainard* colours, or colours denoting abatements of honour, which, of course, no one would ever carry on his shield. The furs are *ermine*, *ermines*, *erminois* or *contre-ermine*; *pean* and *vair*, with its derivative *counter-vair* and *vair-en-point*; *potent* and *potent-counter-potent*. *Ermine* is represented by a field *argent* sprinkled with *sable* spots and triangles; *ermines* by a field *sable* sprinkled with *argent* spots and triangles; *erminois* by a field *or* powdered with *sable*; *pean* by a field *sable*, powdered *or*. *Potent* is a field covered with figures of *potents* (*i.e.*, crutches, Fr. *potence*); while *potent-counter-potent* is distinguished from *potent* by having the *potents* of the same tincture base to base and point to point. *Vair* is distinguished by alternate shield-shaped figures of argent and azure, the figures of the same tincture being placed base to base, while in *vair-en-point* the point of one figure is placed opposite the base of another. To these furs some add *ermynites*, which is the same as *ermine* with the exception of a red mark on each side of the sable spots. The surface of the *escutcheon* (Old Fr. *escusson*, Lat. *scutum*, 'a shield') or shield is called the *field*, because it was covered with honourable emblems formerly won in the field of battle. The upper part of the escutcheon is called the *chief*; immediately below the *chief* is the *collar* or *honour-point*; the centre is variously known as the *cœur* or heart, the *centre*, and the *fesse-point*. Beneath the *centre* is the *nombril* or *navel-point*, while the lowest part of the escutcheon is termed the *base*. The side of the shield which would be the right side to its bearer is called the *dexter* side, the other side being designated the sinister; thus there is a *dexter chief* and *sinister chief*, a dexter base and sinister base. The divisions of the escutcheon, *chief*, *base*, &c., are styled the *points of the escutcheon*, and are used to distinguish coats-of-arms which, though charged with the same figures, have these figures differently placed on the shield. The escutcheon is divided into parts by lines, which are known either as *crooked* lines, which distinguish bearings, and *partition* lines, which divide the shield into two or more parts. Crooked lines are divided into *wavy*, an undulating line; *indented*, toothed like a saw; *dancette*, similar to indented, but deeper in the indentations; *crenellé*, representing a castle's battlements; *nebulé*, intended to resemble a cloud; *raguelv*, representing a tree-trunk; *dove-tail*, imitating dove-tail joints; *invecked*, a line of semicircles, with the points downwards; and *engrailed*, a line of semicircles with the points upwards. The shield may be divided by partition lines, as *party per pale*, when the partition line is perpendicular; *party per fesse*, when the shield is crossed in the middle by a horizontal line; *party per bend*, when a diagonal line runs from the dexter chief to the sinister base; *party per chevron*, when a diagonal line rising from the dexter base meets at the collar point with a diagonal line running from the sinister base; *party per cross*, when the field is divided by a horizontal and by a vertical line; and *party per saltire*, when the diagonal lines running from corners of the escutcheon meet in the centre.

Figures in H. consist of *ordinaries*, *charges*, and *differences*. The ordinaries consist of the bar, bend, bend-sinister, chevron, chief, cross, pale and saltire, which are known as the *honourable ordinaries*; and the *sub-ordinaries*, which include the billet, bordure, canton, flanche, frette, fusil, gusse, gyron, inescutcheon, lozenge, mascle, quarter, rounde, rustre, and tressure. The honourable ordinaries are so called because they were added to bearings as marks of honour by emperors and kings. (For the meanings of the various classes of ordinaries see the separate article on each.) Ordinaries are figures of squares, circles, &c., while *charges* represent natural things, *e.g.*, animals, birds, fishes, trees, fruits, &c. These animals are *blazoned* (*i.e.*, described) by a peculiar and rich heraldic vocabulary. Thus animals are *blazoned* as couchant, courant, rampant, passant, sejant, gardant, saliant, dormant, &c., and again as rampant regardant, counter-saliant, counter-passant, &c. Trees are *fructed*, *raguled*, *trunked*, *eradicated*, *blasted*, &c.; birds are *displayed*, *close*, *indorsed*, *erect*, &c.; a man is *in armour*, *in robes*, *naked*, *habited*, *rustre*; a castle is *towered*, a weapon *imbrued*, a key *endorsed*, a horse *furnished*. (For the meanings of these terms see the article on each.) Beside the shield a heraldic bearing includes the Helmet (q. v.), the mantling crest, or mantle, derived from the mantle with which it was customary to cover the helmet; the crest, which represents the distinguishing crest formerly carried on the helmet in battle; the motto, the word or words adopted as a characteristic phrase to be carried on armorial bearings; or to the *supporters*, so called because they seem to support the shield; crowns can only be borne by sovereign princes, while coronets, which are smaller and simpler, are borne by nobles.

Differences are devices which are carried on the escutcheon to indicate the branch of a family to which the bearer belongs, and his particular position in that branch. This is shown by means of small charges named *brisures*, *marks of filiation*, and *cadency*. Thus, during the father's lifetime, the eldest son was distinguished from his brothers by bearing a *label*, *i.e.*, a figure of three points; while a second son bore a crescent; a third son, a *mullet* or *mollet*, *i.e.*, a figure of five points; a fourth son, a *martlet*, *i.e.*, a representation of a swallow with long wings and without legs; a fifth son, an *amulet* or small ring; a sixth, a *fleur-de-lys*, or conventional lily; a seventh, a rose; an eighth, a *crossmoline;* a ninth, a *double quatrefoil*, *i.e.*, a double four-leaved grass. In the family of a second son these differences are repeated, added to the paternal marks of filiation. Females could not carry differences, unless they were daughters of the royal family, or unless the differences had become permanent parts of the shield, *i.e.*, that were not dropped on their bearer's position in the family changing, but became integral parts of the arms. All the marks by which members of a family are distinguished from each other are generally spoken of as marks of *cadency*, while *differencing* is applied to the distinguishing of the arms of families and individuals, who are not connected by blood, but by dependency or feudal alliance. H. also appears on certain modern flags. In the middle ages the three varieties of flags, the pennon, banner, and standard, all carried armorial bearings. The national flags of England, Scotland, and Ireland, carry respectively the crosses of St. George, St. Andrew, and St. Patrick; the Union Jack is a combination of the flag of James I., in which the English and Scotch flags were combined with the flag of St. Patrick. Heraldic devices are also seen on seals and coins. During the middle ages even the lower classes were familiar with the signification of heraldic devices. Armorial insignia were displayed not only on shields and banners, but on the sails of ships, the dresses of servants, the windows of mansions. Men were exceedingly jealous of their particular devices, and to appropriate another's heraldic insignia was regarded in much the same light as a theft of another's property is at present.

H. was, long after the fall of chivalry as an institution, a favourite study among the nobility. Gradually, however, it fell into disrepute from the stupid fancifulness and exaggerated pretensions of its upholders. Latterly it has somewhat risen in repute, as it has been recognised that it may at times shed some light upon history. See Clark's *Grammar of H.* (1776), of which fourteen editions have appeared; Parker's *Glossary of H.* (1847); Fairbairn's *Crests of Great Britain and Ireland* (2 vols., Edinb., T. C. Jack, 1876); Knight and Rumley's *Heraldic Illustrations* (2 vols., Edinb., T. C. Jack, 1876); *H. Ancient and Modern*, by Boutell and Aveling (Lond. 1873); and the works of Lowen, Planché, Porny, Berry, Lodge, and of John and Sir Bernard Burke.

Heralds' College, or **College of Arms,** a corporation founded 1483 by charter of Richard III., with a house assigned to its officers called Colde Arbor in All-Hallows-the-Less, London. Philip and Mary granted them Derby House, which being destroyed in the Great Fire (1666), the present building was erected by Sir Christopher Wren. The H. C. consists of three kings-of-arms, six heralds, and four pursuivants, all nominated by the president, the Duke of Norfolk. To it belongs the right of granting new arms and sanctioning their reassumption after disuse. The officers are salaried, but rely for their income mainly on fees for arms, pedigrees, &c. The Scottish H. C. is known as the Lyon Court (q. v.).

Herat', a city of Afghanistan, the chief town of a province of the same name, on the right bank of the Harri Rood, 369 miles N.W. of Candahar and 700 E. of Teheran. It lies in a fertile valley, and the bread, water, and grapes, are proverbial for their excellence. The inhabitants are mostly of Persian origin, and belong to the Shiah sect of Mohammedans. The town is strongly fortified, and contains some handsome mosques, palaces, and reservoirs. It is the great emporium of trade between Afghanistan, India, and Persia. The chief manufacture is that of carpets. Iron and lead are found in the vicinity. The climate is salubrious. H. has the reputation of having stood more assaults than any other city in Central Asia. In 1232 it was destroyed by Genghis Khan. Thirteen more assaults are counted up to 1837, when the Persians were repulsed after a ten months' siege, chiefly by the exertions of Eldred Pottinger, an Indian artillery officer, who happened to be within the walls. H. has since been the apple of discord between Afghanistan and Persia, and also between the rival members of the Afghan royal family. Some regard this town as the key of India, and the objective mark of all Russian intrigue.

Hérault, a department of France, lies between the Lower Cevennes and the Gulf of Lyon. Area, 2393 sq. miles; pop. (1872) 429,878. The chief river is the H., which rises in L'Aigonal, and has a length of 102 miles. The coast, 66 miles long, is marshy and malarious; elsewhere the climate is fine. H. is in great part covered with forest and pasture, but yields annually 4,297,000 hectolitres of excellent wine, of the value of 27,000,000 francs. There are mines of iron, lignite, zinc, coal, &c., and quarries of marble and granite. H. also yields much salt, manufactures woollens, cottons, and silks, and is traversed by three railway lines. The chief town is Montpellier.

Herba'ceous Plants or **Herbs** are those having a permanent woody underground stem or 'crown,' which sends up annual shoots to bear the leaves and flowers.

Her'bal, a book-title that in the early days of botany meant a descriptive account of all known plants, with a statement of their places of growth, medicinal uses, &c. Thus Gerard's well-known folio published in 1597 is entitled *Herbal, or General History of Plants.* The word has now passed into the hands of quacks and herb-doctors as a title for their worse than worthless publications. In like manner *herbalist* or *herbarist* has been degraded.

Herba'rium, a collection of plants dried for scientific purposes, and scientifically arranged, thus bearing the same relation to botany that a museum does to zoology. Preserved specimens have one great advantage over living ones—that they can be collected in infinitely greater numbers, maintained in juxtaposition and compared, however distant the time and places at which found. They are often the only materials from which the botanist can obtain a knowledge of his subject of study. The necessity of having herbaria was soon evident to those who raised botany into a science, and the collections of several of these 'fathers' still exist. The oldest in England are preserved in the Sloane Collection at the British Museum and the Sherardian Collection at Oxford. Of a later date, the most notable is that of Linnæus, now the property of the Linnean Society. During the past eighty to ninety years the exploration of the globe has led to the rapid increase of herbaria and of their contents. That at Kew is now supreme, and one of the most available for study; it contains upwards of 110,000 species of flowering plants and ferns. There are also herbaria of considerable extent at Edinburgh (Botanic Garden), Oxford and Cambridge Universities, and at Trinity College, Dublin. On the Continent there is a rich H. at the Jardin des Plantes, Paris; the valuable herbaria of De Candolle, Boissier, and Delessert at Geneva; the Imperial H. at Vienna; the Royal H. at Berlin; the Von Martius H. at Brussels; that of Webb at Florence; and a good national H. at St. Petersburg, Stockholm, Upsala, Copenhagen, and Leyden. In the United States the H. of Asa Gray belongs to Harvard University. At Melbourne is a large one founded by Mueller; and another, pretty extensive, at Calcutta Botanic Garden. For useful instruction regarding the arrangements of a H. see Dr. Greville's 'Directions' published in the *Third Annual Report of the Edinburgh Botanical Society* (1840), and *Notes on Collecting and Preserving Natural History Objects*, by various authors (Hardwicke, 1876).

Her'bart, Johann Friedrich, a German philosopher, was born at Oldenburg, 4th May 1776, studied philosophy under Fichte at Jena, became professor at Königsberg in 1809, and accepted a call to Göttingen in 1833, where he died, 14th August 1841. H. was a consistent opponent of Fichte and the main line of post-Kantian idealism, in opposition to which he called his own system *realism.* The main thought of his metaphysic is that real beings are simple qualities, and that the notion of a thing with many qualities and the notion of change contain contradictions. H.'s chief peculiarity lies in his psychology, which he endeavoured to render an exact science by the application to it of an elaborate mathematical calculus. In ethics he is determinist, attaching much weight to the development of character through experience; and his works on pædagogic are valued by those who do not accept his philosophy as a whole. H's chief works are *Psychologie als Wissenschaft* (1824–25); *Allegemeine Metaphysik* (1828–29). His works in 12 vols. were published (1850–52) by Hartenstein. See Ziller on H. (1871).

Herbert, the name of a noble English family of great antiquity. The first who belongs to English history is **H., Comte de Vermandois,** who followed William the Conqueror to England, was chamberlain to William II., received a gift of lands, and married the Conqueror's granddaughter. Since that time the Herberts have often taken a prominent part in the public life of England. The family has very numerous untitled branches in Ireland as well as in England. The Earls of Powis (a race still surviving, though not in the male line) were of the same noble family as the Lords H. of Cherbury. The race is still represented by the Earl of Pembroke and by the Earl of Carnarvon (q. v.), though the direct representation of the main line seems to be the head of the house Muckross, in county Kerry, Ireland. Among the more illustrious or memorable persons bearing the name are—1. **Edward, Lord H. of Cherbury,** 'the father of deism,' a brave soldier and an original thinker, who was born at Montgomery Castle in 1581, and educated at Oxford. He married early, was knighted by James I., and in 1608 went to reside in France, becoming distinguished for a keen sense of honour and great intrepidity in maintaining it. In 1610 he served under the Prince of Orange, and showed extreme valour in the field. He travelled in Italy, was appointed ambassador extraordinary to the court of France in 1616, recalled, and again sent as permanent ambassador to Paris, where he lived on intimate terms alike with the most distinguished courtiers and the foremost scholars and wits. Created baron of Castle-Island in Ireland in 1625, he was in 1631 made a baron of England as Lord H. of Cherbury. In the civil war he at first sided with the Parliament, but afterwards sympathised with the King. He died 20th August 1648. H.'s treatise, *De Veritate,* published at Paris in 1624, though it does not wholly break with the whole philosophy, is remarkable as one of the first modern attempts to solve on independent grounds the fundamental problem of Locke and of Kant as to the nature and limits of human knowledge. H. abided by the belief that there are *Notitiæ Communes* rooted in the reason of all men. The most important of these trace for H. fair fundamentals of religious belief, which, in *De Religione Gentilium* (1645), H. asserted to lie at the basis of all the heathen religions. Regarding these truths of natural religion as the only necessary doctrines, H. is entitled to be taken as the earliest of the deists, though he makes no direct attack on the revealed doctrines of Christianity. H. also wrote a history of Henry VIII.; and his interesting *Autobiography* was published in 1764. —2. **George H.,** poet and divine, a brother of Lord H. of Cherbury, was born at the family seat, Montgomery Castle, April 3, 1593. He studied at Trinity College, Cambridge, in 1615 became major-fellow of his college, and was elected public master in 1619. The scholarship he displayed in this office so pleased James I. and Lord Bacon, that H. began to entertain high hopes of court preferment. All that he received, however, being a sinecure worth £150 a year, H., after the death of the king, carried out a design he had long secretly entertained, and in 1625 took holy orders. He was made prebend of Layton Ecclesia in Huntingdonshire; married in 1630; and three months after became rector of Bremerton. There he laboured with as much zeal as his feeble health permitted, and there he died in 1632. *The Temple: Sacred Poems, and Private Ejaculations* (1631) is the title of H.'s chief work in verse. It is unsurpassably quaint and fantastic, but abounds in subtle poetic conceits, and everywhere breathes that spirit of 'holiness' which was attributed to its author as a distinguishing characteristic. *The Country Parson* (1632) is a work in prose, describing the life of the ideal parish priest; it is written in a natural and unconstrained manner. H. has found in Izaak Walton an appreciative biographer.—3. **Sidney H.** (**Lord H. of Lea**), a distinguished politician and statesman, son of the eleventh Earl of Pembroke by his second wife, the daughter of the Russian Count Woronzow, was born at Richmond, September 16, 1810. He was educated at Harrow, and Oriel College, Oxford, where he took a fourth in classics. Having chosen politics as a career, H. entered the House of Commons in 1832, representing South Wilts in the Conservative interest. After holding a subordinate office in Sir Robert Peel's first Ministry, he was appointed Secretary to the Admiralty in 1841, and Secretary at War in 1845; but retired for a time from public life after the defeat of his political chief on the Corn-Laws Repeal question in 1846. In that year, H. married Elizabeth, daughter of General Ashe A'Court. In 1852, H. again became Secretary at War in Lord Aberdeen's Coalition Ministry, in which arduous post he had to face much of the hostile criticism excited by the mismanagement of the Crimean war. On the resignation of Lord Aberdeen, and the formation of the Palmerston Ministry, H. became Colonial Secretary; but resigned this office immediately on the Premier accepting the Committee of Inquiry into the state of the Army before Sebastopol. When Lord Palmerston formed his second Administration, however, H. was once more appointed to the War Office; and in this department effected many important reforms—among others, the reorganisation of the militia, the organisation of the volunteer forces, the fortification of dockyards, the amalgamation of the Indian with the royal army, and the reconstitution of Sandhurst College. His health finally became impaired by these unremitting labours; he was forced to resign his seat; and in January of 1861 was called to the House of Peers by the title of Baron H. of Lea. This period of repose, however, came too late, for he died in August 2d of the same year. Lord H. was heir-presumptive to the earldom of Pembroke, and to this his eldest son succeeded in 1867.

Hercula'neum was, in ancient times, one of the most important cities of Campania; it lay on the coast between Naples and Pompeii, was founded by Oscans, but afterwards chiefly inhabited by Greeks. During the reign of Titus H. was, with the neighbouring towns Pompeii and Stabiæ, overwhelmed by an eruption of Vesuvius (79 A.D.), and so deeply buried in ashes (68–100 feet) that afterwards its site was not recognised, and the villages Portici and Resina were built where it stood. Earlier excavations (*e.g.*, in 1689) were as good as forgotten, when in 1720 three statues were discovered in digging a well. Excavations were renewed in 1738, and Pompeii and Stabiæ found in 1750. More systematic exertions were made from 1806 to 1815, and, after ceasing awhile, were again begun in 1828. Besides the remains of buildings, which are not so important at H. as at Pompeii, there have been found many fine frescoes, numerous statues, and a large number of papyrus rolls. Reference may be made to *Delle Antichità d'Ercolano del Museo Borbonico;* Roux Ainé et M. L. Barré, *H. et Pompeii;* Finati, *Manuale per Ercolano, Pompeii e Stabia;* Selvatico, *Le Arti del Disegno in Italia* (Milan, 1874); Beulé, *Le Drame du Vesuve* (Paris, 1872). See POMPEII.

Hercula'no de Carval'ho, Alesandro, a well-known Portuguese novelist and historian, was born in 1796 at Guimaraes, and received his education at Paris. Having there imbibed liberal ideas in politics, H. took part in those revolutionary measures which aimed at securing a constitutional government for Portugal, and which in 1820 effected this result. The earliest writings of H. were poetical, but he published in 1828 a volume of poetry called *A Voz do Propheta* ('The Voice of the Prophet'), in which he predicted a most unhappy future for his country, then distracted by civil war. This work produced a great sensation, and was followed in 1832 by *A Harpo do Crente* ('The Harp of the Believer'), a volume of romantic verse. H.'s next literary production was a novel, *Eurich, Priest of the Goths,* which proved less successful than his poetry, and from this time the author gave himself up to historical writing, his chief work, *Historia de Portugal,* appearing between 1845 and 1853. It shows great industry and erudition, is written in a pure and attractive style, and is marked by general fairness and moderation. Another important work of H.'s is *Da Origem e Estabelecimento da Inquisição em Portugal* (1854).

Her'cules (Gr. *Hēraklēs*), surnamed **Alci'des,** from his grandfather Alcæus, was the son of Zeus and Alcmene. He was renowned for his immense strength, and was the ideal hero of the heroic age. Never had Hera been so jealous of her husband as then; even before his birth H. was persecuted by her, and as Zeus had sworn that the child to be born that day should rule the whole race of Perseus, she, by delaying the birth of H., and hastening the labour of the wife of Sthenelus, son of Perseus, secured the supremacy to her son Eurystheus. We are told by Homer and Hesiod that he grew so strong and confident as to challenge the gods themselves, and, but for the favour of Zeus and Athena, would have felt the wrath of Hera, whom, with Ares, he had wounded. Later writers tell of his strangling in his cradle two serpents sent against him by Hera, of his being instructed in every manly exercise by the first masters, of his killing Linus with a lyre, and being sent away by Amphitryon for safety's sake to feed cattle. He was thus occupied till his eighteenth year. During his shepherd life he slew for Amphitryon and Thespius of Thespiæ the huge lion of Mount Cithæron, which had devoured part of their flocks, and afterwards wore its skin as a covering. Returning to Thebes, he fell in with the messengers sent by Erginus, king of Orchomenus, to claim the yearly tribute of 100 oxen extorted from the Thebans. He sent them back mutilated to Erginus, who then took the field against Thebes, but was slain by H., who imposed on Orchomenus a tribute twice as great as that paid before by Thebes. According to the legend, Amphitryon fell in the battle, though in the tragedians he appears still alive after the campaign. As the reward, H. received from Creon, king of Thebes, his daughter Megara in marriage; from Hephæstus, a golden cuirass; from Apollo, a bow and arrows; from Athena, a peplus; and from Hermes, a sword and brazen club. Another account makes the club of wood be cut by H. in Nemea. Being after this struck mad by Hera, he killed his own children by Megara, as well as two of his half-brother Iphicles, but remorse drove him into exile, where he was purified by Thespius. The Delphic oracle, calling him for the first time 'Herakles,' bade him live twelve years at Tiryns subject to Eurystheus, for that thereby he should become immortal. Neither in Homer nor Hesiod do we find any account of twelve labours as specially imposed on him by Eurystheus. Homer mentions the descent to Hades in quest of Cerberus, his adventure with a sea-monster, his expedition to Troy to revenge himself on Laomedon, and his war against the Pylians; but the following works are commonly called 'The Twelve Labours of H.':—(1) He strangled with his hands the great lion of Nemea, and took its skin (which, and not that of the Cithæron lion, another account makes him wear); (2) killed the Lernæan hydra; (3) caught the swift-footed stag of Artemis; and (4) the wild boar that ravaged the district about Mount Erymanthus; (5) cleansed in one day the stables of Augeas, king of Elis, in which 3000 oxen had stood for thirty years, by leading through them the rivers Alpheus and Peneus; (6) killed the birds of Lake Stymphalus, which devoured human flesh; (7) captured the Cretan bull, famous for its strength and beauty; (8) brought to Eurystheus the man-eating horses of the Thracian king Diomedes; and (9) to his daughter Admete the girdle of Hippolyte, queen of the Amazons; (10) captured the oxen of the giant Geryones; (11) fetched the golden apples from the garden of the Hesperides; and (12) brought up Cerberus from Hades. While roving through the world engaged in these works, he did many other exploits ('Parerga'), such as joining in the war with the Centaurs, and in the Argonautic expedition, erecting the 'Pillars of H.,' freeing Prometheus, and bringing up Theseus from Hades. To expiate the killing of Iphitus, he followed the command of the oracle by becoming for three years slave to the Lydian queen Omphale ('H. at the spinning-wheel'), after which he did many great feats, and finally married Dejanira, daughter of Œneus. She became the innocent cause of his death, for, fearing his infidelity, she sent him a robe that the Centaur Nessus had given her, and which he had said would preserve her husband's love to her. No sooner was it put on by H. than he suffered fearful agony, amid which he ordered a funeral pile to be placed on Mount Œta, and placed himself in its flames. A cloud carried him to Olympus, where, being reconciled to Hera, he married Hebe. His worship, though general throughout Hellas, was most prevalent amongst the Dorians, and the usual victims offered to him were lambs, rams, bulls, and boars. At the feasts held in his honour he was celebrated in songs as a hero, and thus arose a class of longer poems, the so-called *Heraclea*, the subject of which was his life and exploits. The dramatic poets set off his life with many comic additions. Representations of H. at every stage of life abound, all characterised by energy. The most famous is the 'Farnese' H. of Glycon. Roman traditions make H. on his expedition against Geryones visit Italy, where, abolishing the Sabine custom of sacrificing human beings, and establishing fire-worship, he destroyed a monster named Cacus, who had plundered some of the oxen taken from Geryones by H. Evander paid him especial honour, and H. gave two great families, the Pinarii and Potitii, the task of seeing to his worship. There were two temples of H. at Rome. Those who wish to see what becomes of a Greek myth in the hands of a solar mythologist may consult Max Müller's *Comparative Mythology* in the *Oxford Essays* of 1856. Several other heroes of this name are mentioned by ancient writers:—(1) the **Cretan H.**, one of the Dactyli of Mount Ida, who founded the temple of Zeus at Olympia, and was believed to be a magician; (2) the **Phœnician H.**, worshipped at Carthage, Gades, and all the other Phœnician colonies till the 4th c.; (3) the **Egyptian H.**, a son of Nilus or Amon, and otherwise called Dsom, Chon, and Maceris; (4) the **Indian H.**, or Dorsanes, believed by the Greeks to be their own H., and the founder of the Indian royal race; and (5) the **Celtic and Germanic H.**, founder of Alesia and Nemausus.

Hercules Beetle (*Dynastes Hercules*), a genus of Lamellicorn beetles, attaining a length of 5 inches, and distinguished by large mandibles, the upper being very large and projecting. This beetle occurs chiefly in S. America.

Hercules, Pillars of, the ancient name of the two opposing promontories, Calpe (Gibraltar) and Abyla (Ceuta), at the entrance to the Mediterranean Sea. They were fabled variously to have been rent asunder or forced together to serve as a bridge by Hercules. In the Spanish arms they are supporters; the national motto, *Ne plus ultra*, refers to the ancient belief that the pillars marked the end of the earth. The pillars appear on Spanish coins, and it is conjectured that with a fillet for the motto they form the sign $ for dollars.

Hercyn'ian Forest (Lat. *Hercynia Silva*; the root appears in Harz and Erz), a common name by which the Romans in the time of Cæsar denoted the several mountain masses ranging from the Rhine to the eastern Carpathians, and which are generally called the Mid-German Mountains. Later writers, such as Tacitus and Pliny, use the name specially for that range between the Carpathians on the E. and the Thüringerwald on the W.

Her'der, Johann Gottfried von, one of the most original, many-sided, and influential thinkers of Germany, at once poet, philosopher, and theologian, was born 24th August 1744, at Mohrungen, in E. Prussia, and at an early age showed rare gifts, in spite of the narrow-minded limitation of his studies by his father. He studied philosophy and theology in Königsberg, coming more under the influence of Hamann than of Kant, but read with avidity in all realms of literature. In 1764 H. became, with marked success, a teacher and preacher in Riga, but in 1767 went on a lengthened tour. In 1771 he was called to be court preacher at Bückeburg, and in 1776 accepted an invitation to fill a like post at Weimar, where he lived, increasing in honour and in power to mould the minds of his contemporaries, till his death, 18th December 1803. A sacred enthusiasm for all that is truly and nobly human, for what he himself called *humanität*, breathes through his numerous works. As poet and critic he purified taste and inspired life into the hearts of his time, seeking out especially all that is characteristic of peoples and periods in the literature of the world, and finding materials in popular legends, in Homer, Ossian, Shakespeare, and the national poetry of the South, as well as in old German poetry. But though of enormous importance in the æsthetic development of Germany, H. cannot rank as a great creative poet. H.'s spirit is seen in his *Geist der Hebräischen Poesie*, where a thoroughly sympathetic attempt is made to appreciate the Hebrew Scriptures as a monument of human genius apart from their inspiration or theological significance. H.'s conception of God and the divine shows in the main a leaning towards an unsystematic pantheism. In *Metakritik* he maintains a vigorous but bitter polemic against the sharply defined and radical dualism of the Kantian philosophy. Throughout, H. contends for the close communion and sympathy of nature and man, of matter and spirit; and his greatest work, the unfinished *Ideen zur Geschichte der Menschheit*, the earliest consistent scheme of a philosophy of history, regards all history as a continuous and connected development towards a great end.

H.'s *Schriften*, in 45 vols., were published at Stuttgart in 1806–20; the *Gedichte*, the *Volkslieder*, and the *Cid* being given in a separate form. See *Erinnerungen aus H.'s Leben* (1820), by his widow; *H.'s Lebensbild* (1841), by his son; and several collections of his letters.

Heredit'ament, a term of English law denoting all property which goes to the heir-at-law. Hereditaments are divided into *corporeal* or *incorporeal*. Houses and lands are of the former class; rents and annuities of the latter.

Hered'itary Right means, in law, the right of the heir-at-law to succeed on the death of his predecessor. See BIRTHRIGHT, PRIMOGENITURE, INTESTACY, BROTHERS, LAW OF SUCCESSION AMONG, HEIR, and articles referred to under these.

Hereditary Transmiss'ion. By this term is understood the transmission of peculiarities from parents to offspring. Thus children are like their parents, and any special peculiarity in the parent may be transmitted to the child. Sometimes the peculiarity may be transmitted by the father and sometimes by the mother. Many strange examples of transmission have been in recent years carefully observed, and it has been ascertained that if the individuals possessing the hereditary peculiarity are permitted to inter-breed, the peculiarity may become constant. The laws regulating H. T. are quite unknown. For details see Huxley (*Westminster Review*, 1860) on Darwin's *Origin of Species*, Huxley *On our Knowledge of the Causes of the Phenomena of Organic Nature, Six Lectures to Working Men*, 1863, pp. 95–97; *Philosophical Transactions*, vol. xiv., No. 160, 1730, and vol. xlix., part 1 for 1755; Galton's *Hereditary Genius* (Lond. 1869); Ribot's *Heredity* (Eng. trans. Lond. 1875); and *The History of Creation* by Hæckel (Lond. 1876).

Her'eford ('the ford of the army,' or a mistranslation of the original Celtic name *Caer-ffawydd*, 'the town of the beech-trees'), capital of the county of the same name, on a gentle eminence rising from the N. bank of the Wye, 144 miles W.N.W. of London by railway. It is the see of a bishop, and has a beautiful cathedral, with a tower 160 feet high, partly built about 1115 on the site of an older building, and restored by Sir G. G. Scott in 1863. There is also a fine church of St. James (1868), slight industries in gloves, hats, and flannels, and important cattle and cheese fairs. H. returns two members to Parliament. Pop. (1871) 18,347. The city received its charter from Richard I. in 1189. It was among the last places that surrendered to the Parliamentary forces (1643), in token of which it was granted a new charter, with the motto *Invictæ Fidelitatis Præmium*, from Charles II. H. is the birthplace of Nell Gwynne and David Garrick.

Her'efordshire, a western county of England, lying between Worcester and Gloucester on the E., and S. Wales on the W., and bordered by the Black Mountains and the Malvern Hills. Area, 833 sq. miles; pop. (1871) 125,370. It contains some of the most richly diversified scenery in England, is watered by the Wye, Lugg, Arrow, Teme, &c., all finding their way to the Severn. Its soil is a red well-cultivated loam, yielding wheat, barley, oats, beans, peas, rye, &c. In 1875 there were 111,965 acres under corn crops, 37,647 under green crops, 231,569 in permanent pasture, exclusive of mountain and heath. Other products are oak-bark, apples, and excellent cider (20,000 hogsheads yearly). H., almost entirely of Devonian formation, has a good climate, and celebrated breeds of sheep and cattle. H. was conquered by the Romans about 73 A.D., for a time was included in Mercia, and later formed part of the Welsh borderland or 'marches.' It sends three members to Parliament.

Heren'cia, a town in the Spanish province of Ciudad Real, is situated on the river Gigucla, a tributary of the Guadiana, and is about 42 miles N.E. of the capital of the province. Pop. 7317.

Her'esy (Gr. *hairesis*, 'choice'), in the New Testament means a sect or party distinguished by holding certain opinions, as the sect of the Pharisees (Acts xv. 5; Gr. *hairesis; cf.* Jos. *Ant.* xiii. 5, 9). Hence it was applied to the Christians themselves (Acts xxiv. 5, 'Nazarenes'), and then, within the Church, to dissension produced by party spirit (1 Cor. xi. 19). It also has the meaning of the opinion which one chooses to hold (2 Peter ii. 1), and in the early Christian writers indicates those opinions which deviated in any particular from the true Christian faith, or even systems which adopted any Christian element whatever. According to the canonical definition, which has regulated the practice of the Church, H. consists (1) in a departure, not from the implied belief of Christianity, but from that which the Church through her creeds and canons has declared to be a matter of faith; (2) the error must be persistent and wilful, and after admonition; and (3) it must not only be suspected, but detected and adjudicated upon.

The position of heretics as regards the Church was the same as that of Jews or pagans; they were not regarded as Christians at all. The penalties, both ecclesiastical and civil, to which they were liable were very severe. (1) By ecclesiastical law they were excommunicated, prevented from being present at public worship, at least, during the more sacred ceremonies, and their evidence against a Catholic refused in the ecclesiastical courts, and social intercourse with them was prohibited. (2) Of the civil penalties (comprised in the Theodosian code, *De Hæreticis*), eleven distinct kinds have been enumerated, besides the laws against their teachers, aiders and abettors, and meetings. They were styled generally infamous persons, and special names of reproach were attached to particular sects; all commerce was forbidden to be held with them; they were deprived of all offices of profit or dignity in the state; they could neither receive nor bequeath property, nor give or receive donations; no contract with them was binding; they were fined, banished, subjected to corporal punishment, and even sentenced to death. In this country many persons were imprisoned and burned for H. at the time of the Reformation. Nowadays all civil penalties have fallen into desuetude, although there are yet unrepealed laws to inflict them. The worst that is now inflicted on a heretic is the penalty of excommunication, and social ostracism.

Her'ford, a manufacturing town in the province of Westphalia, Prussia, is situated on the Werre, and on the railway from Köln to Minden, 15 miles from the latter town. It has manufactures of cotton, flax, and carpets. H. was formerly a free city, and possessed a great nunnery, secularised in 1803. Pop. (1871) 10,974.

Her'iot, in English law, signified originally a tribute to the lord of the manor on his preparing for war. It now denotes a fine payable to the lord on the death of a copyholder. It is usually the best beast which he dies possessed of. The right can be enforced by action, or the subject may be forcibly taken. The corresponding Scotch law term is *Herizeld*, but the exaction has long been obsolete in Scotland, though what is called Relief (q. v.) may still become due from the vassal's heir to the superior on the vassal's death.

Her'iot, George, a descendant of the Heriots of Trabroun, and son of a wealthy goldsmith, was born in Edinburgh, June 1563. He was bred to his father's occupation, entered the Edinburgh incorporation of goldsmiths in 1588, became jeweller to James VI. of Scotland about 1597, and removed to London as banker and court-jeweller when James succeeded to the English throne in 1603. He was twice married; first to burgess Marjoribanks's daughter, Christian (1586), and then to Alison, daughter of James Primrose, ancestor of the Earls of Roseberry, but died without issue, February 12, 1624. H. amassed a fortune, and was a great favourite with the king, who familiarly nicknamed him 'Gingling Geordie.' The bulk of his riches he bequeathed to the town-council and ministers of Edinburgh, that they might found an hospital for the maintenance and education of sons of poor or deceased burgesses. The building, a grand Gothic quadrangle, is said to have been designed by Inigo Jones in 1628, but was not completed till 1659. So immensely have the funds increased, that in addition to Heriot's Hospital, with 300 boys and twelve teachers, they support eighteen day-schools and ten evening-schools also in Edinburgh, for the gratuitous education of poor children, attended by upwards of 4000 boys and girls. In connection with the hospital there are (1876–77) thirty-nine university bursaries. See *Heriot's Hospital, with a Memoir of the Founder*, by Dr. W. Steven (3d ed. revised and enlarged by Dr. Bedford, Edinb. 1874).

Her'istal, or **Herstal,** a town of Belgium, in the province of Liège, on the Meuse. It has large coal-mines, and steel and iron works, and is now almost a suburb of Liège. It was the birthplace of Pippin, the founder of the Karoling dynasty. Pop. 9326.

Her'itable and Mov'able are Scotch law words denoting the classes of property which respectively fall to the heir-at-law and to the executor or administrator. *Real* and *Personal* are the corresponding words of English law, and the distinction is similar to that indicated by the phrase 'Heir and Executor' (q. v.) in England.

Heritable Bond. See BOND, in law.

Heritable Jurisdic'tions were, in Scotland, grants from the crown of criminal jurisdictions to great families. They were abolished after the Rebellion of 1745 by statute. The abolition was followed by the appointment of sheriffs on a proper footing.

Heritable Secu'rity, in the law of Scotland, corresponds to Mortgage (q. v.) in English law. See also for English law, EQUITY OF REDEMPTION. The bond must be recorded in the Register of Sasines. (See SASINES.) It is assignable.

Her'itor, the Scotch law term for a landowner in connection with parochial law.

Hermandad', The, (Span. 'brotherhood'), a confederation of the chief cities of Aragon and Castile to maintain order and defend their liberties. The first H. was founded in Aragon about the middle of the 13th c., and the H. of 1315 embraced 100 Castilian and Aragonese cities. The cities united in a H. were bound together by 'a *solemn* covenant,' to remit the aggression of the nobles, to revenge any injury to any of their members, and to kill any one trying, even by the king's orders, to collect an unlawful tax, the decisions of their councils being carried out by armed forces. In 1496 their power was greatly increased, and they did good service in suppressing brigandage until 1498, when they were lowered to the condition of a police force. They were generally known as the *Santa Hermandad,* or Holy Brotherhood, and were occasionally spoken of as 'Cortes Extraordinary.' See *Quaderno de las Leyes nuevas de la H.* (Burgos, 1527), and Prescott's *History of Ferdinand and Isabella.*

Her'mann, or **Herman,** the German name erroneously conferred on the warrior called by Latin authors Arminius, who, in the days of Augustus and Tiberius, asserted the freedom of Germany against Rome. The tribes of the N.W. had for the most part accommodated themselves to the Roman supremacy, when H., son of a prince of the Cherusci, and born in 16 B.C., commanded a battalion of his fellow-countrymen in the Roman service, and learned the arts of war from Roman generals. But when Quintilius Varus replaced the forbearance of former governors by the insolence of a conqueror, the Latin yoke galled German shoulders. Seeing the hopelessness of open rebellion against a force of 50,000 veterans, H. secured the co-operation of numerous allied tribes, contrived that the Roman forces should be scattered, and then, in the autumn of 9 A.D., attacking the reduced main body in the Teutoburger forest, after three days' fighting wholly annihilated it. Germanicus, appointed commander in the Lower Rhine in 14 A.D., had to use all his skill in coping with H., and was assisted by the hostility of H.'s father-in-law, who delivered Thusnelda, his wife, into the hands of Germanicus. A great battle was fought near Hameln in 16 A.D., when the Germans were defeated with the loss of a third of their number, but even after again joining battle unsuccessfully, remained unbroken in spirit. Germanicus was withdrawn by his jealous uncle ere the supremacy of Rome could be secured. H. was subsequently victorious in war with Marbod, a prince of the Marcomanni, but fell in an intestine struggle in 21 A.D. Thusnelda had in 17 been made to grace the triumph accorded to Germanicus. See Wietersheim, *Der Feldzug des Germanicus* (1850); Massmann, *Arminius* (1839); Reinking, *Die Kriege der Römer in Germania* (1863). On the 16th of August 1875 a monumental statue, 40 feet high, in honour of H., by Ernst von Bandell (q. v.), was unveiled near Detmold by the German Emperor in presence of the princes of the empire, senates of the Hanse towns, and an audience of 40,000 persons.

Hermann, Johann Gottfried Jakob, a scholar who gave a great impulse to classical learning in Germany, was born at Leipsic, 28th November 1772. He became a lecturer at the university there in 1794, was made Professor of Philosophy in 1798, and of Eloquence in 1803, with which the chair of Poetry was conjoined in 1809. In this congenial work he spent the rest of his days, dying 31st December 1848. H.'s lectures were powerfully attractive by their vivacity, clearness, and completeness. His efforts as an academical teacher to awaken independent thought in his pupils were indefatigable; and to all his work H. brought the support of a vigorous and truth-loving character. He first signalised himself by works on the metres of the classics, as *De Metris Græcorum et Romanorum Poetarum* (Leips. 1796); *Epitome Doctrinæ Metricæ* (1818); *De Metris Pindari* (1817). By his *De emendanda Ratione Græcæ Grammaticæ* (1801) and *De Græcæ Dictionis Idiotismis* (1802) he sought to reform the treatment of the Greek grammar. The acuteness and accuracy of his scholarship are further displayed in his editions of Sophocles, Euripides, *The Clouds,* the Homeric hymns, the *Trinummus* of Plautus, Aristotle's *De Arte Poetica,* &c.; and by those of Bion and Moschus, and of Æschylus, published after his death. The seven vols. of his *Opuscula* (1827–30) contain numerous essays and short treatises, with poems, in excellent Latin. See Jahn, *Gottfried H. eine Gedächtnissrede* (Leips. 1849).

Her'mannstadt (Magyar, *Nagy-Szeben;* Ruman, *Sibenin*), the capital of Transylvania, Austro-Hungaria, on a hill overlooking the Zibin, 60 miles S.S.E. of Klausenburg by railway. It consists of a walled upper and lower town and three suburbs, is the seat of a Greek archbishop, and of the governor of Transylvania; has a Gothic Lutheran church with a high tower, a townhouse containing Saxon archives, and national museum, a theatre, &c. The manufactures are woollens, linens, leather, tobacco, and pottery. Pop. (1869) 19,000, mostly German Protestants, but also including many Rumanians, Magyars, and Gypsies. H. is said to have been founded in the 12th c. by a German colony from Nürnberg, led by a citizen named Hermann.

Hermaph'rodite, the name given to such animals as possess, in each individual of their species, distinct male and female generative organs. The term *monœcious* (Gr. *monos,* 'single,' *oikos,* 'house') is also employed synonymously with H. Very many lower animals are H. Thus the snails exemplify familiar examples of this condition; but it is also a curious fact that the mutual sexual congress of *two H. individuals* is necessary to ensure the fertilisation of the eggs. In the tapeworm, again, H. are met with; each segment or joint of the tapeworm being provided with a complete set of male and female reproductive organs. The vertebrata or highest animals never—save abnormally—exhibit hermaphroditism; this condition being occasionally met with in the human subject.

Hermaphrodite (in botany). When a flower contains sexual organs of both kinds it is called H. or bisexual; if it contains only male or only female sexual organs, and is, therefore, unisexual, it is termed *diclinous;* when flowers of both sexes occur on the same individual plant, the species is *monœcious;* when on different individuals, it is *diœcious.*

Her'mas, one of the Christians at Rome to whom St. Paul sent a greeting in his epistle (Rom. xvi. 14), is the reputed author of a work entitled *The Shepherd* or *Pastor of Hermas* (although, according to the Fragment of Muratori, H., the author, was the brother of Pius I., Bishop of Rome, in the 2d c.), which many Christians from the 2d to the 4th c. placed, along with the epistle of Barnabas, side by side with the inspired writings of the New Testament. It was included in the MS. of the New Testament discovered (1859) by Tischendorf in the convent of Mount Sinai. The contents have been divided into three books: the first, containing four visions, the second twelve commands, and the third ten similitudes. The name is derived from the author asserting that he wrote the 2d and 3d books to the dictation of the angel Repentance in the guise of a *shepherd.* The work is accessible to English readers in Clark's *Ante-Nicene Fathers* (vol. containing the 'Apostolic Fathers').

Hermeneu'tics (Gr. *hermeneutikē,* (sc. *technē,* 'art'), from *hermeneuō,* 'I interpret') stands to exegesis in the relation of theory or principles to practice. Strictly to distinguish between the two is purely arbitrary. See EXEGESIS.

Her'mes (Gr. *Hermēs, Hermeias*), identified by the Romans with their Mercurius (q. v.), was a son of Zeus and Maia, daughter of Atlas, and born on Mount Cyllene in Arcadia. In the *Iliad* and *Odyssey* he is described as thievish, and in a 'Homeric' hymn it is said that, escaping from his cradle, four hours after his birth, he stole from Pieria some of the oxen of

Apollo's herd, which he drove to Pylos, and concealed in a cave there, after slaughtering two of them, his feet being covered with sandals during the journey that his footsteps might not be traced. Thereafter returning to Cyllene, he found a tortoise, whose shell he took and formed into a lyre by placing strings across it. Apollo then went to Cyllene to demand his oxen, but Maia showed him H. in his cradle, whereupon Apollo seized and carried him before Zeus, who bade him restore them. H., persistently denying the theft, was disbelieved, and compelled to accompany Apollo to Pylos, where he so charmed the god with the sound of the *chelys* that he was allowed to keep the cattle. His next invention of the *syrinx* or pipe further cemented their good relations, which Apollo confirmed by teaching him how to divine with dice, and by presenting him with his own shepherd's staff of gold. He became the herald of Zeus and of the gods of Hades. Though H. seems originally to have been an Arcadian god of nature, whose special function was to make the soil fruitful and bless the efforts of husbandmen, it is mainly as herald of the Olympians that he appears in the legends and in the poets. Hence he was considered the god of eloquence, and the tongues of victims were held sacred to him. He was also the god of shrewdness in affairs, as well as of deceit and theft, always, however, set off with a foil of gracefulness, through which the 'vice itself lost half its evil, by losing all its grossness.' He was further credited with the invention of the alphabet, music, numbers, and astronomy, with the introduction of weights and measures, olive culture, &c., and with imparting skill in these to his favourites. Of his many missions, chiefly undertaken at the command of Zeus, the abduction of Io, with the slaying of the hundred-headed Argus (q. v.), is oftenest alluded to, and from this feat he had the surname *Argeiphontes.* With most versatile activity H. appears also as the charioteer and cupbearer of Zeus, the bringer of dreams and sleep, of wealth, luck, and sudden gain, the promoter of trade and social courtesy, the preserver of peace and protector of wayfarers, and the conductor of the shades of the dead from earth to Hades. The Athenian generals sacrificed to H. before starting on any expedition, and shepherds paid him special reverence, as he was thought to promote the fertility of their flocks. His first temple was believed to have been built by Lycaon, king of Arcadia, from whence his worship spread to Athens, where he was first invoked as the patron of athletic exercises. Festivals called *Hermæa* were celebrated there, and in various other parts of Hellas. It is probable that the first statues of any god that presented the likeness of a head above the more primitive square block of stone were those of H., whence the name *Hermæ* grew to be applied to the whole class of tetragonal torsos, of which one stood before every door in Athens, and the mutilation of which caused consternation there just before the Sicilian Expedition. (See ALCIBIADES.) The usual sacrifices to H. were lambs, pigs, goats, honey, cakes, and incense, and the number four, the palm-tree, the tortoise, and some kinds of fish were sacred to him. He is usually represented as a youth with finely formed limbs, bearing a herald's staff (*skēptron*), and wearing a broad-brimmed hat (*petasos*), and beautiful golden sandals (*pedila*), winged at the ankles.

Her'mes, Trismegis'tus (Gr. *Hermēs Trismegistos*, or 'thrice-great,' *cf.* Milton's *Il Penseroso*), the name applied by the Greeks to the Egyptian Thoth as early as the 4th c. B.C. He was believed to be the origin of everything formed and produced by the human mind, and was therefore the inventor of all arts and sciences; hieroglyphics, astronomy, arithmetic, geometry, music, agriculture, law, medicine, worship, &c., being instituted by him. The sacred books of the Egyptians were attributed to him, and were called by the Greeks after him the *Hermetic Books.* They were inaccessible to all but the priests, and were shown to the common people only from a distance on great festivals. The Neo-Platonists regarded H. as the embodied Logos, and it was in their age, when theosophy, alchemy, and magic developed themselves, that he received the surname 'Trismegistus.' All secret knowledge was believed to be propagated by a series of wise men called the 'Hermetic chain.' Of the writings attributed to H., the chief now extant are *Pœmander sive de Potestate ac Sapientia Divina* (Lat. trans., ed. princ. Treviso, 1471; Gr. original by Hadr. Turnebus, Par. 1554; Germ. trans. by Tiedemann, Berl. 1781); *Æsculapii Definitiones, Iatromathematica, Horoscopica* (collected in Patricius, *Nova de Universis Philosophia,* Venice, 1593). Later, H. and his reputed writings were held in great esteem by all kinds of enthusiasts, who called themselves from him 'Hermetici.' Thus originated the 'hermetic medicine' of Paracelsus, 'hermetic freemasonry,' and the expression 'hermetically sealed,' applied to whatever is so securely closed as to prevent the entrance of air, as the magic seal of H. was thought to have the power of making anything whatever inaccessible.

Her'mit. See EREMITES.

Hermit Crab, a name applied to several genera of Crustacea (q. v.) belonging to the *Decapoda* (q. v.)—the order including the lobsters, crabs, &c.—and to the section *Anomura* of that order. This section is distinguished by the soft and comparatively rudimentary nature of the abdomen. The best-known H. C. is the common species—the *Pagurus Bernhardus*—commonly found round the British coasts, inhabiting the cast-off shells of whelks and other molluscs. In this genus the abdomen is perfectly soft, and destitute of appendages, but has terminal suckers, and a few rudimentary feet, adapted for enabling the animal to retain a hold of the whorls of the shell. The carapace or shell covering the body is membranous, and has little calcareous or limy matter in its composition; one of the great *chelæ* or pincer-like claws is much more developed than the other, and is used by the animal for closing the entrance to the shell when it has withdrawn into its abode. These crabs are also named 'soldier crabs,' from their pugnacious habits. A curious instance of that form of animal association named *commensalism* occurs in the invariable association of a species of sea-anemone (*Adamsia palliata*) with the H. C., the anemone adhering persistently to the exterior of the shell in which the crab dwells. The crafty H. C. (*P. calidus*) is found in the Mediterranean Sea, and is of larger size than the common species. The Diogenes H. C. (*Cenobita Diogenes*) of Brazil and the W. Indies is a well-known tropical species, and appears, like the land crab, to inhabit damp places inland.

Her'mitage, the cell of a hermit, or several cells close together.

Hermosill'o, a town of Mexico, in the state of Sonora, 90 miles N. of Guaymas, a port on the Gulf of California. It is an entrepôt for the produce of the interior, and carries on a large trade in wine and brandy. Pop. 14,000.

Her'nia, in its widest sense, means the protrusion of any organ from its natural cavity through an abnormal or accidental opening in its walls. There may be thus H. of the brain, of the cornea, of the iris, of the lungs, &c.; but the term chiefly designates protrusions that occur in the abdomen. H. most frequently occurs at parts where the muscular and tendinous structures are weakened by natural passages, as the spermatic cord in the male, the round ligament in the female, and the large vessels to the lower extremity, constituting crenal and inquinal H. The umbilicus, the thyroid pramen, the sciatic notch, the vagina, the perineum, the muscular parietes of the abdomen, the diaphragm, &c., may be the seat of H., which is invariably composed of a *sac* and its *contents*, the sac being the prolongation of the Peritoneum (q. v.), which overlies the aperture through which the H. protrudes, and the contents being, most frequently, a portion of the small intestine, more particularly of the ileum, constituting the form of H. called *enterocele.* When intestum and Omentum (q. v.) are found in a H. it is called *entero-epiplocele*, but when omentum alone, *epiplocele.* Intestinal H. is smooth, gurgling on pressure, and conveys a well-marked impulse on coughing. Omental H. is soft, doughy, irregular in outline, and conveys no impulse on coughing. H. may be congenital, and in Africa, where no artificial support by bandage is afforded, umbilical H. is almost universal. H. generally appears in consequence of some forcible effort, and men are more liable to the disease than women. When a H. may be readily pushed back into the abdomen it is called *reducible?* otherwise it is *irreducible*, and may be *strangulated.* A reducible H. is best treated by the application of a truss to retain the protrusion within the abdomen, and various means have been adopted for the radical cure of H. Irreducibility of H. may depend on its shape, on the existence of adhesions, or on the nature of its contents. Strangulation is probably, in all cases, the result of congestion of the protruded parts, induced by the constriction to which they have been subjected, which, unless speedily removed, may terminate in gangrene. Irreducibility is a serious affection; but strangulation is of the gravest import, and frequently necessitates a surgical operation. In such cases purgatives should never be administered by the mouth, but enemata often afford relief, and so also the hot bath, inhalation of chloroform, and, in certain cases, blood-letting to the verge of faintness.

He'ro, according to the famous Greek story, was a priestess of Aphroditê in Sestos, on the coast of Thrace, and was beloved by Leander, a youth of Abydos. As his union with H. was forbidden by her parents, he nightly swam the Hellespont to visit her, guided by a torch which H. held on the top of a tower. One stormy night the light was extinguished, and Leander was drowned. Next morning, when his body was washed ashore, H. saw it, and in despair threw herself from her tower into the sea. The legend has been told by Musæus, Statius, Virgil, and Ovid, but the most beautiful version of the tale is that in Marlowe's *H. and Leander*. Schiller has a fine ballad on the same subject.

Hero, or **Heron**, of Alexandria, a Greek mathematician, was a pupil of Ctesibius, and flourished from 284 to 221 B.C. He displayed a remarkably inventive genius, and constructed several philosophical toys. The most interesting were his *fountain*, in which a jet of water was projected upwards by the action of air, itself compressed under water; and his *eolipyle* or steam-engine, which consisted of a spherical vessel filled with boiling water, and perforated in such a way that the escaping steam forced it to rotate exactly like a Barker's Mill (q. v.). His most valuable extant work is his *Pneumatica*, which describes the above and other inventions; but besides that, there have come down to us fragments upon the construction of darts, military instruments, and automata. H.'s works are published in the *Mathematici Veteres* (Par. 1693).

Her'od the Great, the second son of Antipater, an Arabian, was made Governor of Galilee at the age of fifteen (B.C. 47), and soon after of Cœle-Syria. In B.C. 41, H. and his brother Phasael were appointed by Antony tetrarchs of Judæa. But next year, on the invasion of the Parthians, he had to flee to Rome, where he was appointed by the Senate King of Judæa, a dignity in which he was established by Octavian (B.C. 31) after the conclusion of the civil war. His reign was on the one hand distinguished by great magnificence, and on the other disgraced by innumerable acts of horrid cruelty. He built a temple at Samaria, and a number of new towns altogether, and adorned Jerusalem with many fine buildings. His great work, the restoration of the temple there, which was begun B.C. 20, although the mere temple was finished in a year and a half, was not completed at his death B.C. 4. All this munificence was but a poor offset to his bloodthirsty jealousy, through which a vast number of the people—high and low, young and old—lost their lives. His own relations even—*e.g.*, his wife Mariamne, her grandfather and two sons, and his own son Antipater—were not spared. The Evangelist Matthew gives an instance of his cruelty not recorded by Josephus, of the slaughter of the boys in Bethlehem under two years of age (Matt. ii. 16).—**H. Antipas**, son of the above, succeeded on his father's death to the tetrarchy of Galilee and Peræa. He married first a daughter of Aretas, King of Arabia Petræa, but afterwards Herodias, the wife of his half-brother, Herod Philip. In A.D. 38 he went to Rome to try to get for himself the title of king, but instead he was condemned to perpetual banishment at Lugdunum (Lyon), and died in Spain. See also AGRIPPA HEROD.

Herod'otus, the most ancient Greek historian, properly so called, hence styled the 'Father of History,' was born at Halicarnassus in Caria, 484 B.C. According to Suidas he was the son of Lyxes and Dryo. Regarding his youth and upbringing we have no certain information; but it seems that he early formed the idea of travelling and of writing history. Unable to bear the tyranny of Lygdamis, ruler of Halicarnassus, he is said to have emigrated to Samos, where he acquired the Ionic dialect. After a time he returned to his native place, and assisted in delivering it from the rule of the tyrant. H. afterwards withdrew to Thurii in Italy, where he finally settled. This fact is one of the best attested in the life of H., but the date of it is uncertain. Where H. composed his great work is also a disputed point. According to Lucian—an untrustworthy authority—he wrote it at Halicarnassus; according to Suidas, in Samos; according to Pliny, at Thurii. Lucian says that H. read his history during the Olympic games, and that it was received with unbounded applause. He adds that Thucydides—then a mere boy—was present, and was moved to tears by the recital. This would fix the time at about 456 B.C. H. would then be about twenty-eight years of age. Now, it is simply incredible that H. could have finished his travels and his history at that early age. Moreover, the historian alludes to events of much later date than the year referred to. Lucian's account, as has been ably shown by Dahlmann, must, therefore, be treated as a mere invention. Plutarch, moreover, would not have ignored the fact. The statement of Dio Chrysostom that H. read his history to the Corinthians is probably equally groundless. The averment of Suidas rests on no better foundation. The only reasonable theory is that the work was written, as Pliny says, at Thurii, during the old age of H. The abrupt termination of the work, moreover, goes to prove that it was the production of the writer's later years, and that death alone prevented its completion. The preparations which H. made in order to write his great work were enormous. He visited Greece proper and the coasts of Asia Minor. Samos, Athens, Corinth, and Thebes were surveyed by him with special attention. The great battlefields of Greece were visited and studied, and the route of Xerxes and his army from the Hellespont to Athens closely followed and mastered. He visited the isles of Greece—in the Ionian and Ægean alike—sailed through the Hellespont, Propontis, and the Euxine, and visited Thrace and Scythia. He traversed Lydia, Phœnicia, and Egypt. Indeed, his contributions to the history of the last-mentioned country are beyond anything done in ancient times, and even now they rank with the achievements of modern explorers. From Egypt he made excursions to Arabia and Libya. Whether or not he went to Carthage is not clear. He visited Palestine, saw the Euphrates and the Tigris, and the city of Babylon, and pushed northward to Ecbatana. Susa was perhaps the limit of his travels in this direction. The Greek settlements in Italy and Sicily seem to have been pretty well known to him, but, on the whole, his knowledge of Western Europe was meagre. But not from his travels alone did H. draw his inspiration. He knew Homer and Hesiod by heart. He was acquainted also, though perhaps in a less degree, with Alcaeus, Sappho, Æschylus, Pindar, and others. From these he drew his literary culture; the sources of his knowledge and actual humanity were his own observations and experiences. The object of the great work of H. was to relate the struggle between the Greeks and Persians. Had this been the sole ground covered by his writings, the achievement would have been great indeed; but the value of his work is immeasurably enhanced by the interesting digressions and episodes which he has interwoven into his narrative. For these the reader must go to the history—the nine books of which bear the names of the nine Muses. The dialect in which H. wrote is Ionic intermixed with Epic, Doric, and Attic forms. The simplicity, vigour, and charming style of his narrative have never failed to delight his readers, while his reverent spirit has ever secured their admiration and respect. As an observer he was quick and shrewd; as a historian, thoroughly honest and faithful; and many of his statements that have been scouted as absurd have been shown, by the light of modern travel and discovery, to be strictly accurate and true. According to Suidas, H. died and was buried at Thurii, 408 B.C. The first edition of his history appeared in a Latin translation by Laurentius Valla at Venice (1474). The first Greek edition is that of Aldus Manutius (fol. Venice, 1502). The editions of Schweighäuser (6 vols. Stras. and Par. 1806), of Garsford (4 vols. Oxf. 1824), of Bähr (Leips. 1830–34), and of Müller (Par. 1844) may be mentioned; but the best English edition, with copious notes, is the conjoint work of Canon Rawlinson, Sir H. Rawlinson, and Sir G. Wilkinson (4 vols. Lond. 1858–60).

Hero'ic Verse is a name given by the ancients to their Hexameter (q. v.) verse, because it was used to celebrate the deeds of heroes, as in the *Iliad* of Homer and the *Æneid* of Virgil. The phrase has been transplanted into English, where it denotes decasyllabic or Iambic pentameter verse, in which most of the great English poetry, dramatic and non-dramatic, has been written.

Her'on' (*Ardea*), a genus of *Grallatorial* or Wading birds included in the sub-family *Ardeinæ*, the members of which have a long, sharp bill, the gape extending to beneath the eyes, and the nostrils, guarded by a membranous scale, existing in a lateral groove. The tail is short, and the legs extend behind in flight to compensate for the want of the tail, and thus act as an aerial rudder. The second and third quills are the longest, and the outer toe is longer than the inner. The common H. (*Ardea cinerea*), also named the grey H., is now scarcer than it used to be. It inhabits swampy places, and feeds on slugs, snails, frogs, and lizards. Its colour is a slaty grey on the upper parts, the primary quill-feathers being black. The breast and under parts are of a lighter tint, the throat and neck white, while the long plume of feathers extending behind the head is grey. The average length is 3 feet. The egret or white H. (*A. egretta*) is found in the New World. It attains a length of 4 feet, and is pure white in colour, the tail being of a yellowish tint. The long feathers are much in request for the manufacture of plumes. The purple H. (*A. purpurea*) is a rare species. The night herons belong to the genus *Nycticorax*, the familiar species being the *N. Gardeni;* others are the *N. Europæus*, and the Australian or Nankeen night H. (*N. Caledonicus*). The latter is of a cinnamon-brown hue.

Heroph'ilus, a Greek physician, was a native of Chalcedon in Bithynia, and settled at Alexandria under the first Ptolemy (q. v.). Physiology and anatomy were his favourite pursuits, and the latter he prosecuted with such ardour as even, it is said, to dissect criminals alive. Of the works of H., who was one of the chief founders of medical science in Alexandria, only a few fragments remain, which have been published by Marx, *De Herophili Vita*, &c. (Gött. 1840).

Heros'tratus, an Ephesian who, through desire to make his name immortal, set fire to the renowned temple of Artemis (Diana) at Ephesus in 356 B.C. He was put to death; but one of the Ionian cities, decreeing that he should be consigned to perpetual oblivion, thereby only gave rise to the proverb 'Herostratic celebrity.' On the night of the deed Alexander the Great was born, and the ancients believed that Artemis had been unable to defend her temple only because her presence as Lucina was necessary at Alexander's birth.

Her'pes is an affection of the skin, characterised by an eruption of clusters of vesicles on an inflamed base, rarely lasting more than two or three weeks, and generally unaccompanied by constitutional disturbance. Each vesicle runs a course of about ten days, and terminates in desquamation. The varieties of H. depend on the form and arrangement of the clusters, or on their locality; thus the *phlyctenoid* group is irregular in the form and distribution of its clusters, while the *circinate* group has its clusters disposed in a circular form. The itching, pricking, smarting, and intense burning heat is relieved by emollient ointments, as the benzoated oxide of zinc, glycerine, or a weak lotion of acetate of lead, and by the internal use of ferri arsenias. According to Dr. Tilbury Fox, *H. circinatus* is a parasitic disease, the fungus being the *Trichophyton tonsurans*. See *Parasitic Skin Diseases* (Lond. 1863).

Herre'ra, Antonio, a Spanish historian, was born at Cuellar in 1549, passed his youth as secretary to Gonzalo, viceroy of Navarre, was appointed by Philip II. 'historiographer of the Indies and Castile,' and died at Madrid, 29th March 1625. The historical writings of H. are numerous and important; and his fairness, accuracy, and industry render him a valuable authority on a most interesting period of Spanish history. Chief among his works is the *Historia General de los Hechos de los Castellanos en las Islas y Tierra Firme del Mar Oceano* (Mad. 1601-15). The first two volumes contain the famous *Descripcion de las Indias*. Besides these may be mentioned his *Historia del Mundo en el Reynado del Rey D. Felipe II.* (3 vols. Mad. 1601-12), and also the *Historia de Portugal* (Mad. 1591).—**Ferando de H.**, a Spanish poet, was born at Seville in 1534, and died in 1597. He was in orders, but that did not prevent him from writing much poetry of a decidedly amorous character. His countrymen conferred on him the title of 'Divine,' and his odes, founded on the Pindaric model, display undoubted genius; that on the *Battle of Lepanto* and the *Ode to Sleep* being particularly fine. His *Obras en Verso* were published at Seville in 1582, and republished in the *Coleccion* of Fernandez (Mad. 1786, new ed. 1808). H. was also the author of a historical work, the *Relacion de la Guerra de Chipre* (Seville, 1572).—**Francesco H., El Viejo** ('the elder'), the most distinguished painter, with the exception of Pacheco, of the school of Seville, was born in that city in 1576. He speedily became noted both for frescoes and easel pictures, excelled also as a graver in bronze, and probably from this circumstance was accused of having coined false money. In 1650 he left Seville for Madrid, and lived there in high repute till his death in 1656. Among his great works, of which there are many specimens both at Seville, Madrid, and in the Louvre, may be named the gigantic 'Last Judgment' in the church of San Bernardo, Seville; the 'Descent from the Cross,' 'Effusion of the Holy Spirit,' and 'Holy Family,' in the church of Santa Inez, Seville; and his decoration of the convent of La Merced. His style is marked by boldness of execution, freedom in colouring, and a thorough mastery of technique.—**Francesco H., El Mozo** ('the younger'), son of the preceding, was born at Seville in 1622, studied under his father, and worked as an architect and fresco-painter at Rome. After the death of his father H. returned to Seville, and followed his art till his death at Madrid in 1685. His chief paintings are at Seville, Madrid, and the Escorial. Among them are the 'St. Francis' in the Seville cathedral, and the 'Ascension of the Virgin' at Atocha.

Herr'ick, Robert, an English poet of good family, was born in Cheapside, London, in August 1591, and educated at St. John's College, Cambridge. After spending a wild youth in his native city, he took orders in 1629 at the mature age of thirty-eight, and was presented to the living of Dean Prior in Devonshire, from which he was ousted by the Puritans in 1648, but replaced at the Restoration. He died 15th October 1674. The work which will keep green the memory of H. is the *Hesperides*, so called because it was composed in the *West* of England. It is a medley of love-lyrics, epigrams, pictures of rural scenery, pastimes, &c. There is a vast deal of rubbish in the collection, and at times a low sensuality defiles the verse, but some of the songs for dainty tenderness of sentiment, artless beauty of language, and joyous music with an undertone of sadness, have no peers in the English tongue. The pieces entitled *Noble Numbers* show that H. was not unvisited by higher emotions than those that spring from love or wine. See *The Complete Works of Robert H.*, by the Rev. Alex. B. Grosart (Lond. 1876).

Herr'ing (*Clupæa harengus*), a well-known species of *Teleostean* fishes, forming the type of the family *Clupæidæ*, which is included in the *Malacopterous* ('soft-finned') sub-order of the class. In this genus the ventral fins are abdominal in position, the body being covered with very large and distinct scales. One dorsal fin only exists, and the abdomen is sharply ridged or 'keeled.' The body is much compressed and of elegant shape, and the teeth are of very small size. The H. is one of the most valuable of fishes, and affords employment to large numbers of men and boats in its fishery. It appears to inhabit deep water during the greater part of the year, but in autumn and winter approaches the shore to spawn. Vast shoals visit the British coasts at the spawning season, and are caught with nets. The H. cannot live out of the water; it dies almost immediately on being taken from its native element. It has, however, been kept in confinement in the Brighton and other aquaria. The flesh is inferior to that of no other fish in delicacy, but the herrings of different localities undoubtedly vary greatly in their quality. Those of Loch Fyne on the W. coast of Scotland have perhaps the finest delicacy and flavour, and certainly the highest reputation. The H. is a somewhat uncertain fish in its movements; occasionally shoals appear round the British coasts in such numbers that the beach has been strewed with them; in other years, again, the H. almost vanishes from British shores. Probably the cause of the plenty or scarcity of the H. depends very greatly upon the prevailing *temperature*. The facilities for railway transport have largely extended the sale of the H., and herrings caught in the N. of Scotland now reach the London market twelve or fourteen hours later.

The name H. is given to fresh-water fishes such as *Coregonus* (q. v.); and an allied species, the *C. Leachii*, is common in winter round the coasts of Britain.

Herring Fishery is by far the most important maritime industry, yielding a much greater addition to human food than any other, and probably not much less than the whole produce of the other sea-fisheries. Although the herring does not appear to have been known to the Greeks and Romans, there is evidence that the fishery was prosecuted in the 10th c. At particular seasons in the year the herring approaches in vast shoals certain coasts of the N. Atlantic, over which it is found widespread. Thus the H. F. is prosecuted off the Newfoundland and Nova Scotian coasts of America, off the coasts of Norway, in the North Sea, and around the shores of the British Islands In Norway the H. F. has been regarded as an important source of national wealth for many centuries, and among the Dutch, who prosecute the fishery in the North Sea, it is distinguished as the 'great fishery,' while whaling is spoken of as the 'little fishery.' In the early part of this century the Dutch fishery was most injuriously affected by the Revolutionary wars, and at that period the H. F. sprung into great importance as a British industry. In Scotland especially it has continued to grow in importance with great steadiness and rapidity, till it now annually yields an inconceivably great amount of human food. The whole quantity cured in Great Britain in the year 1811 was 91,827 barrels; in 1875, around the Scottish coasts alone, there were cured 942,980 barrels, while in the preceding year the barrels cured slightly exceeded 1,000,000. Allowing a low average of 750 fish to each barrel, there were thus cured in Scotland alone, in 1874, more than 750,000,000 herrings, but that number probably does not represent half the total catch, as immense quantities were sold and consumed fresh, or otherwise disposed of.

H. F. is carried on during the night by means of drift nets, which are 'shot' out from the boats, in situations where the shoals are supposed to be. The nets depend from the surface downwards, like long meshed walls, being kept afloat by cork floats attached to the upper edge. The legal size of mesh for herring nets is one inch from knot to knot, but beyond the three mile coastline a smaller mesh may be used. The herrings in their progress through the water push their heads through the meshes, but are unable further to squeeze through, and the twine catching in their gill-covers prevents them from drawing back. Trawling, or the use of the seine net, is common in the sea lochs of the W. coast, and is the occasion of much controversy. The fish taken, according to their condition, are classified as 'maties,' or herring with milt and roe not fully developed, 'full' fish, and 'spents.' The H. F. is open all the year round, but the great Scottish harvest begins about Stornoway in June, and gradually it comes round and southward on the N.E. coast from the early part of July. It does not reach Yarmouth till October, and on the S.W. English coast it begins in December. As the fishery thus occurs at different dates at the various stations, the boats and various classes of persons employed follow it from station to station, and thus secure more than one herring harvest. The great Scottish centres of the industry are Stornoway, Wick, Fraserburgh, Peterhead, and Aberdeen, at which 1200, 730, 900, 730, and 300 boats respectively are employed during the season. Further statistical and other information will be found under FISHERIES.

Herrings, King of the. See CHIMÆRA.

Herr'ison (Fr. *hérisson*), in heraldry, the hedgehog borne as a charge by the families of Herres, De Heriz, or Harris, and Speechly.

Herrn'hut, the cradle and the headquarters of the *Herrnhuter* or Moravian Brethren, founded by them in 1722, is a village of nearly 1000 inhabitants in Saxony, about 35 miles E. of Dresden. The cleanliness and orderliness of the place are remarkable. Noteworthy among the larger buildings are the two meeting-houses and the four institutions in which widowers, widows, unmarried brethren and sisters are respectively lodged. The articles made by the brethren are sent far and near, being chiefly cloth, leather-work, paper, and candles. See MORAVIANS.

Her'schel, Sir William, D.C.L., F.R.S., &c., a famous astronomer, was born in the town of Hanover, Germany, November 15, 1738. His father was a musician, and he and his four brothers were trained to the same profession. Towards the close of 1757 he came to England as an oboe-player in the band of the Hanoverian Foot-guards, which he soon left for more lucrative appointments. In 1766 he became organist at Halifax, and later in the Octagon Chapel at Bath. From his early years his mind had a philosophical turn, and astronomy was ever a favourite study. About 1770, not having the means to purchase a telescope of sufficient power, he set to work to construct one. In 1776 he completed a Newtonian telescope five feet in focal length, with which he observed Saturn's rings and Jupiter's belts and satellites. In 1781 he discovered the planet Uranus (q. v.), which he at first mistook for a comet. This discovery carried his fame far and wide, and obtained for him a Government salary of £400 per aunum. Thereafter he devoted himself wholly to astronomical research, settling for the remainder of his life at Slough, near Windsor. He catalogued double, triple, and multiple stars, nebulæ and clusters, and investigated the motion of our system among the fixed stars and its position with respect to the Milky Way. On January 11, 1787, he discovered the second and fourth satellites of Uranus, and sighted the rest of the six between 1790 and 1800. His great 40-foot telescope was begun in 1785, and completed August 27, 1789, on which evening H. by its aid discovered the *sixth* satellite of Saturn, and the discovery of the *seventh* followed in a few weeks. It is impossible here to give even a catalogue of his researches and discoveries, which were published in the *Philosophical Transactions*, and in the *Transactions of the Astronomical Society*, of which he was elected the first president in 1822. Perhaps his most remarkable labours are his *star-gauging*, his investigations into the motions of binary stellar systems, his researches among nebulæ, his observation of the revolution of Saturn's ring and of Jupiter's satellites, and his discovery of spots in the polar regions of Mars. He was a member of numerous scientific societies both at home and abroad, was knighted in 1816, and died at Slough, August 25, 1822.—**Caroline Lucretia H.**, sister of the preceding, was born at Hanover, March 16, 1750. In 1772 she came to England, followed for the first ten years the profession of a singer and player at concerts, and proved throughout a most valuable assistant to her brother in his life-labours. At his death, in 1822, she returned to Hanover, where she died, January 9, 1848. She drew up a *Catalogue of Stars* (1798), discovered eight comets, and wrote several memoirs, which appear in the *Proceedings of the Royal Society* of London. She received a pension from George III., and was elected an honorary member of the Royal Society—an honour which has been conferred on only one other lady, Mrs. Somerville. The *Memoirs and Correspondence of Caroline H.*, edited by Mrs. John H. (Lond. 1876), give an almost complete biography of Sir William himself.—**Sir John Frederick William H., Bart., F.R.S.,** the only son of the eminent astronomer, and himself one of the foremost of European scientists, was born at Slough, March 7, 1792. He graduated at Cambridge in 1813, coming out as Senior Wrangler and first Smith's Prizeman. During the years 1821–23, he worked with Sir James South in making observations of the positions and distances of stars, and published his results in the *Philosophical Transactions* for 1824. For the next eight years he followed in the footsteps of his father, and drew up a catalogue of 2300 nebulæ, 525 of which he had himself discovered. In 1834, he established, at his own expense, an observatory at the Cape of Good Hope, and began a regular course of 'sweeping' the heavens, which he continued till 1838. His valuable results were published in a separate form in 1847. On his return to England he was received with every possible honour, was created a baronet at the Queen's coronation, made a D.C.L. of Oxford in 1839, and elected an honorary and corresponding member of almost every scientific association on the Continent. In 1848 he became President of the Royal Astronomical Society, and two years later he was appointed Master of the Mint, a post which he resigned on account of failing health in 1855. He died at Collingwood, near Hawkhurst, Kent, May 11, 1871. As an author he ranks high among men of science. He wrote the articles *Isoperimetrical Problems* and *Mathematics* in the *Edinburgh Encyclopædia*, *Meteorology* and *Physical Geography* in the *Encyclopædia Britannica* (8th ed.), and *Sound* in the *Encyclopædia Metropolitana*. The last three have been published separately. Of his larger works, we have a *Treatise on Light* (1831); *Preliminary Discourse on the Study of Natural Philosophy* (*Lardner's Cyclopædia*, 1835); and for the same series, a *Treatise on Astronomy* (1836), which grew into the larger and more complete *Outlines of Astronomy* (1849); *Instructions for Making and Registering Meteorological Observations at Various Stations in Southern Africa* (1844); and *A Manual of Scientific Inquiry, prepared for the Use of Her Majesty's Navy, and adapted for Travellers in General* (1849).

Hers'feld, a town in the province of Hessen-Nassau, Prussia, on the Fulda, in a hilly region, 40 miles S.S.E. of Kassel by railway. It has manufactures of woollen stuffs, serge, &c. Its cathedral of the 12th c. was partly destroyed by the French in 1761. Pop. (1875) 6537.

Hert'ford ('the hart's ford'), the chief town of the county of the same name, England, on the Lea, 26 miles N. of London by railway. In its castle, now a residence of the Marquis of Salisbury, Queen Elizabeth several times held her court, but only a small part of the original building exists. H. has a branch of Christ's Hospital, a large county-hall, a corn-exchange, an infirmary, besides iron-foundries, malt-houses, breweries, flour and linseed mills, &c. In the vicinity are brickfields, limekilns, rose-gardens, and nursery grounds. Pop. (1871) 7896. A national synod was held here as early as 673. The town sends two members to Parliament.

Haileybury College, a large classical structure 3 miles from H., was formerly a training college of the East India Company, but is now converted into a public school with about 500 pupils.

Hert'fordshire, or **Herts**, a county of England, lying between Middlesex and Cambridge. Area, 611 sq. miles; pop. (1871) 192,725. It has an undulating, well-wooded surface, and is sheltered in the N. by low offsets of the Chiltern Hills. The Lea and Colne, its chief waters, are branches of the Thames. Its formation is mainly Cretaceous, except in the S., where it is Tertiary. The climate is mild, and the soil a fertile loam mixed with flints. In 1875 there were 152,011 acres under corn crops, 44,337 under green crops, and 93,568 in pasture; 13,625 horses used solely in agriculture, 32,442 head of cattle, 188,040 sheep, and 30,650 pigs. The chief products are wheat, barley, turnips, hay, straw, apples, pears, and cherries. H. sends fruit, flowers, and vegetables to the London market, and its roses are seldom surpassed in the great horticultural shows. Among its industries are malting, strawplaiting, and papermaking. It returns three members to Parliament.

Herto'genbosch ('the duke's forest'), or simply **Den Bosch**, the Dutch name of Bois-le-Duc (q. v.).

Hertz, Henrik, born of Jewish parents, 25th August 1798, at Copenhagen, one of the greatest of recent Danish poets, who from his earliest years showed a love for poetry. Becoming a student at Copenhagen in 1817, he greatly distinguished himself in æsthetics and law, and graduated in the latter in 1825. In 1827 appeared his first work, *Hr. Burckhardt og hans Familie*, a comedy, followed by *Kjærlighed og Politi*, *Flyttedagen* (1828), *Arvingerne* (1829), *Amors Genistreger* (1830). In 1830 he also wrote *Gjengangerbrevene*, whose ripe and tasteful criticism decided the controversy between Heiberg in 'Soranerne,' in favour of the former. In 1832 he cast off anonymity for the first time, and the year after travelled at the public cost in Germany, Italy, Switzerland, and France. From 1836 to his death, 25th February 1870, H. wrote with great activity a large number of character-comedies, which have essentially contributed to form Danish taste and strengthen a love for the stage. *Kong Renés Datter* (Ger. trans. by Leo, 10th ed. 1869), *Scheik Hassan* (Ger. trans. by Baudissin, 1861), *Sparekassen* (1836), the great romantic tragedy *Svend Dyrings Huus*, *Svanehammen*, *Indqvarteringen*, *Ninon*, *Tonietta*, *De Deporterede*, *Den Yngste*, and *Besöget i Kjöbenhavn* are best known. In poetry H. is a master of the erotic lyric. His narrative poems, and his larger novelistic pictures in verse, *Stemninger og Tilstande*, *De Frifarvede*, *Eventyr og Fortællinger*, *Johannes Johnsen*, have been very popular. In 1850 he collected his *Digte fra forskjellige Perioder*, and in 1853 his *Dramatiske Værker*.

Her'uli, or **Er'uli**, a Teutonic people, who seem originally to have dwelt in Scandinavia, and who, along with the Goths, invaded the Roman empire in 262 A.D. Numbers of them afterwards joined Attila's host, and they formed the greater part of the armies with which Odoacer founded a kingdom in Italy in 476 A.D. Others of the H. formed a kingdom along the Theiss and Danube, which was conquered by the Langobardi.

Herz, Henri, a distinguished pianist, born at Vienna, January 6, 1806, settled at Paris in 1816, and won considerable reputation by his *Air Tyrolien* and *Rondo alla Cosacco*. His execution as a pianist is marked by exquisite lightness and elegance, and his compositions for the piano have had a remarkable popularity. His fantasies on *Othello*, *Norma*, *Euryante*, &c., are very widely known.

Herzegovi'na, a sanjak in the S.W. of the villayet of Bosnia (q. v.), European Turkey. Area, 6420 sq. miles; pop. 71,954. It is bounded W. by Austrian Dalmatia and at two points by the Adriatic, N. and E. by Bosnia, S. by Montenegro, and contains the three divisions of Mostar, Trebinje, Plevlje. The surface is broken by the ramifications of the Dinaric Alps. In the E. the Dormitor rises to a height of 8000 feet. Along the W. there are stretches of waste and swamp, but the climate is warm, and Southern fruits flourish; while in the E. the woods and Alpine meadows resemble those of Bosnia. The chief river is the Narenta and its affluents. Among the products are grain, tobacco, honey, wine, and figs. The pop., mostly of Slavic origin, comprised at the last census 29,472 Mohammedans, 23,492 Greek Catholics, 18,289 Roman Catholics, 459 Jews, and 677 Gypsies. The capital is Mostar, and other towns are Trebinje, Fotsha, Stolatz, and Kolashin. H. first appears in the 9th c. as a Servian dependency, the principality of Zachlum. It passed to the Ban of Bosnia in 1154, to Andreas of Hungary in 1197, and again to Bosnia in 1326. In 1440 the Emperor Friedrich conferred on Prince Stephen (*Kosaca*) the title of duke, and henceforth the territory was known as H. (or 'Duke's Land'), also as H. Sancta Saba, in recognition of its patron, St. Sebastian. H. was conquered by the Sultan Mohammed II. in 1466, was long the battlefield of Moslem and Christian, and was finally ceded to Turkey by the treaty of Carlovicz in 1699. After being united to Bosnia since 1483, H. was made a separate division of Turkey in 1832. It revolted against the Porte unsuccessfully in 1737, 1851, and 1861, and was the original seat of the insurrection of 1875, which has led to the reopening of the Eastern Question. See articles BOSNIA, TURKEY; Forsyth's *Slavonic Provinces S. of the Danube* (Lond. 1876); and Evans's *Through Bosnia and the H. on Foot* (Lond. 1877).

Herz'en, Alexander, a Russian novelist and journalist, was born at Moscow, 25th May 1812. Hostility to the Imperial Government was the motive power of H.'s life; it brought about his exile to Siberia in 1854 while yet a student, and though suffered five years later to return to St. Petersburg, he did not renounce his Socialistic opinions. In order to remove him from the capital, H. was created member of the Council at Novgorod; but becoming possessed of considerable fortune in 1846, on the death of his father, he requested permission to travel. Obtaining this in the next year, he visited Italy, France, Switzerland, and England, and returned no more to his native country. At Geneva he established a free Russian press, from which issued translations into his native tongue of the writings of the chief European democrats, such as Mazzini and Louis Blanc, and also a newspaper advocating similar political views. H. died at Paris, January 21, 1870. Among his chief works are *Dilettantism in Science* (1842), *Whose is the Fault?* (1847), and *From the Other Side* (1850), *On the Development of Revolutionary Ideas in Russia* (1854), and *My Exile* (Lond. 1855).

He'siod, one of the earliest Greek poets, supposed to have flourished about the middle of the 8th c. He tells us in his *Erga kai Hemerai* ('Works and Days') that he was born at Ascra in Bœotia, and that his father was an emigrant from the Æolian Cyme, in Asia Minor. From a passage in his *Theogonia* he seems to have been a shepherd on Helicon, and to have won a first prize in a poetic competition at Chalcis. On his father's death he removed to Orchomenus, and there probably ended his days. The *Works and Days* is the earliest instance of Greek didactic verse, and marks the transition from heroic to ethical poetry in Greek literature. It resembles Homer's works in dialect, is homely in style, and paints the life of the *thetes* or common people. It abounds in doleful and even fretful lamentations, but contains several rural pictures touched with quiet soothing beauty. The *Theogonia* gives a genealogy of gods and heroes, and is much less interesting than the *Erga kai Hemerai*. Its genuineness as a work of H.'s was questioned by the Greeks. In all likelihood H. has been accredited with parts of the compositions of a school of poets who lived near Mount Helicon, and the works attributed to him consist partly of his own writings, partly of alterations from earlier and of interpolations from later writers. The *Katalogoi Gynaikōn* ('Catalogues of Women'), now lost, is ascribed to H., but the extant fragment, the *Aspis Hēraklēos* ('Shield of Hēraklēs'), was probably part of it. The best edition of H. is by Göttling (Gotha and Erfurt, 1843).

Hesper'ides, the daughters of Night, or of Zeus and Themis, who inhabited, according to Hesiod, an island of the ocean on the western edge of the world. Their number is variously given as three (Ægle, Erytheis, Hesperia), four, and seven. They were gifted with the faculty of song, and, along with the hundred-headed dragon Ladon, watched over the golden apples that Hera had as a wedding-present from Ge. The apples were brought by Hercules to Eurystheus, who gave them back to him, whereupon Hercules presented them to Athena, by whom they were restored to the *Garden of the H.*

Hess, the name of several distinguished painters.—1. **Karl Adolf Heinrich H.**, known chiefly for his success in painting horses, left many proofs of his skill in military subjects. He was born at Dresden in 1769, and died near Vienna, 3d July 1849.—2. **Peter von H.**, a painter of battle scenes, born at Düsseldorf, 29th July 1792, was the son of a famous engraver. He died 5th April 1871.—3. His brother, **Heinrich von H.**, devoted himself chiefly to historical subjects in his art. He was born 19th April 1798, became Professor in the Academy at Munich in 1827, and died 29th March 1863.

Hess'en, the name of an old German stock, in ancient times called the Catti or Chatti, which now peoples Ober-H. and Nieder-H., the land between the Neckar, Rhine, Main, Lahn, and Fulda, as far as the Grabfield in the S. and Thuringia in the E. Germanicus, the first who speaks of the Catti, destroyed their chief settlement of Mattium, near the present Gudensberg, in 15 A.D. In the following century the tribe lost its separate identity among the Franks, and after the general emigration to Belgium and Gaul, the Saxons, from Thuringia, pushed into part of the country subsequently called Sächs-Hessengau. In Frankish Hessengau and Oberlahngau several abbeys were established by St. Boniface (q. v.), and these portions were governed by grafs till the extinction of the direct Karling line, when Konrad, Graf of Franconia and H., and nephew of the Emperor Arnulf, was elected King of the Germans in 911. Through marriage, H. and Thuringia were subsequently united, but the death of Heinrich Raspe (1247) was followed by a succession-war that led to the separation of the two principalities in 1263. Sophia, wife of Heinrich of Brabant, obtained H., and her son Heinrich I., surnamed the Child, became landgraf, with his residence at Kassel, and founded the Hessian dynasty. One of his descendants, Philipp I., the Magnanimous, introduced the reformed faith, applied the convent revenues to the establishment of Marburg University, and divided H. among his four sons at his death in 1567. Two of the sons died leaving the whole territory, divided as H.-Kassel (q. v.) and H.-Darmstadt (q. v.), to Wilhelm IV. and Georg I. See Landau, *Beschreibung des Hessengaues* (Kass. 1856; Teuthorn, *Ausführliche Geschichte der H.*, 11 vols. Frankf 1777–80); and Rommel, *Geschichte von H.* (10 vols. Gotha, 1820–58).

Hess'en-Darm'stadt, a grand duchy of Germany, consisting of two large and eighteen small parts detached from each other, and lying between Prussia, Bavaria, and Baden, and partly within the Prussian frontier. Area, 2963 sq. miles; pop. (1875) 882,349. H. is divided into three provinces, Starkenburg, Ober-Hessen, and Rhein-Hessen. It is rough and hilly in the N., where it is traversed by the Vogelsberg, and offsets of the Westerfeld and Taunus. In the S. the fertile valleys open on extensive plains, stretching away in the E. to the base of the Odenwald mountains. The principal rivers are the Rhine, Neckar, Main, Nahe, Lahn, Nidda, Edder, and Wetter. The soil is rich and well cultivated, yielding heavy crops of maize, wheat, flax, hemp, tobacco, and poppies, as well as the vine, figs, almonds, chestnuts, &c. H. produces about 120,000 hogsheads of wine yearly, of which the chief kinds are grown near Mainz, and Worms, and Bingen. Among the mineral products are iron, salt, coal (£138,300 yearly). Mainz and Offenbach are the great industrial centres, and the manufactures comprise machinery, cottons, linens, hosiery, paper, papier-maché, oil, chemicals, snuff, leather, carriages, &c. H. has one university (at Giessen), six gymnasia, ten *real-schulen*, two teachers' seminaries, and 1760 *volks-schulen*. In 1875 the pop. comprised 584,391 Protestants, 239,088 Roman Catholics, and 25,373 Jews. H. is, by the constitution of 1820, a hereditary monarchy, and the legislature is vested in two chambers of representatives. But a council of state, and the four ministers of the administration, really transact the government business. The troops, forming the twenty-fifth division of the imperial army, are included in the eleventh army corps. The budget for 1876–78 gave the revenue at £1,127,206, and the expenditure at £1,014,728. In 1876 the public debt, chiefly for railways, amounted to £1,443,968. Besides the supreme court of appeal at Darmstadt, the capital, there are inferior tribunals at Mainz, Giessen, Offenbach, and throughout the country.

History.—Georg I., youngest son of Philipp the Magnanimous, founded H. in 1567, having received the upper grafship of Katzenellenbogen, including the town of Darmstadt, and later (1583) one-third of the dominion of his brother. His patrimony was divided among his three sons at his death (1596), the main line being continued in Ludwig V., while the youngest son, Friedrich, founded the junior line of Hessen-Homburg (q. v.). H. suffered severely during the Thirty Years' War, but prospered on the whole during the 17th and 18th centuries, gaining various additions of territory. Its debt was paid off by Ludwig IX., who left to his son, Ludwig X., a dominion with a pop. of 300,000 at his death in 1790. Ludwig X. joined the Confederation of the Rhine, and obtained from Napoleon large accessions of territory, and the title of grand duke (Ludwig I.) in 1806. He followed the fortunes of Napoleon consistently till after the battle of Leipsic, when he luckily changed to the side of the allies just in time. In 1814 he joined the German Confederation, and, by decision of the Congress of Vienna, made large cessions of his newly-acquired territory on the right bank of the Rhine (pop. 185,000) to Prussia, Hessen-Kassel, and Bavaria, but was granted as indemnity part of the old French department of Mont-Tonnère (with Bingen and Mainz), and most of the principality of Isenberg (total pop. 203,854). From the latter accession he assumed the title of Rhenish grand duke. The original constitution of 1820 was met by a storm of opposition, and as year by year the clamour went up for reforms, they were granted tardily. Ludwig I. died in 1830, and his grandson, Ludwig III., who ascended the throne in 1848, concluded a special military convention with Prussia in 1867, by which the army of H. became part of that of the N. German Confederation. As such it took part in the Franco-Prussian war of 1870. See Walther, *Handbuch für Geschichte und Landes-Kunde von H.* (Darms. 1841); Steiner, *Geschichte des Grossherzogthums H.* (5 vols. Darms. 1833–34); Buchner, *Das Grossherzogthum H. in seiner Polit. und Socialen Entwickelung* (Darms. 1850).

Hess'en-Hom'burg, a former langrafdom of Germany, was founded by Friedrich, grandson of Philipp the Magnanimous, in 1596. It lay in the basin of the Rhine, and was divided into the provinces of Homburg and Meisenheim, having an area of 105 sq. miles, and a pop. (1861) of 26,817. It received the addition of Meissenberg from the Congress of Vienna, and was admitted to the German Confederation in 1817. On the failure of the direct line, it reverted to Hessen-Darmstadt, March 24, 1866, and was ceded to Prussia, September 3, 1866.

Hess'en-Kass'el (*Kurhessen*, 'Electoral Hessen'), a German principality till 1866, with an area of 5943 sq. miles, and a pop. of 738,500, and since then part of the Prussian province of Hessen-Nassau. It belonged to the older line of the house of H., having been founded in 1567 by the landgraf Wilhelm IV., 'the Wise,' the eldest son of Philipp the Magnanimous. Moritz, son of Wilhelm, adopted the Reformed faith, and abdicated (1627) in favour of his son, Wilhelm V., who began the practice of hiring out Hessian troops, and was placed under the ban of the empire by siding with Sweden in the Thirty Years' War. Friedrich I. having succeeded to the Swedish throne as husband of Ulrike Eleonore, sister of Karl XII. (1720), he resigned H.-K. to his brother, Wilhelm VIII., who fought valiantly along with England and Hanover in the Seven Years' War. His son, Friedrich II., is chiefly remembered for joining the Romish Church, and for having hired to England, at a cost of £3,161,516 sterling, 22,000 of his mercenaries to fight in the American War of Independence (1776–84). He lived splendidly, and amassed an immense treasure. Wilhelm IX., his son and successor, frequently changed sides during the Napoleonic wars, and procured the elevation of H.-K. into an electorate in 1803. First acting as an ally of Great Britain and of Prussia, he then threw in his lot with Napoleon, but after the battle of Jena the French Emperor expelled him from H.-K., and merged his dominion in the new kingdom of Westphalia. In 1813, when the French power in Germany was overthrown, he returned with many fair promises of reforms, which were cancelled in the first moment of security. At the Congress of Vienna, to the great indignation of existing crowned heads, he strove hard to be made king, like the Electors of Saxony and Bavaria. He died in

1821, and in the reign of his son, the Elector Wilhelm II., the discontent of the Hessians increased, till it broke out in open revolt in 1830. The Elector abdicated (1831) in favour of Prince Friedrich Wilhelm, who only plunged H.-K. deeper into the quagmire of oppressive taxation and political intrigue. The French Revolution of 1848 frightened him into liberal concessions, part of which were carried out, but soon matters drifted back into the old channel; the hated Hassenpflug drew on himself the charge of treason; the Elector had to fly along with the Minister to Hanover and then to Frankfurt. The military intervention of the Frankfurt Diet procured the restoration of the Elector in 1850, but the conflict was resumed on the introduction of a new constitution in 1852. H.-K. was now little better than a despotism, and from 1834 to 1861 its population decreased nearly 7 per cent. In the Austro-Prussian war of 1866 it took the side of Austria, and was, according to the policy of Bismarck, incorporated with Prussia. Friedrich Wilhelm was carried as a prisoner to Stettin, but was set at liberty in 1867. See Röth, *Hess. Geschichte* (2 vols. Kass. 1855); Wippermann, *Kurhessen seit den Freiheitskriegen* (Kass. 1850).

Hess'en-Nass'au, a province of Prussia (since 1866), embracing old Hessen-Kassel, the duchy of Nassau, the landgrafdom of Hessen-Homburg, and the city of Frankfurt. Area, 5943 sq. miles; pop. (1875) 1,467,898. It lies between Bavaria and the province of Saxony, Hanover, Rhenish-Prussia, and Westphalia, and encircles the large northern portion of Hessen-Darmstadt. It is partly bounded in the W. by the Rhine, in the S. by the Main, and in the E. by the Weser, and has an extreme length from S.W. to N.E. of 175 miles. The surface is much diversified, is broken by the Westerwald, Taunus, Rhöngebirge, and other ranges, and is watered by the Lahn, Fulda, Kinzig, &c. The soil is fertile, and there is much agriculture, cattle-rearing, and vintaging. H. yields about 45,000 hogsheads of wine yearly; among the kinds specially famous are Rüdesheimer, Johannisberg, and Hochheimer. Its manufactures are cloths, yarn, iron, jewellery, pottery, leather, chemicals, brandy, &c.; and its minerals are iron, coal, silver, copper, and marble. H. is the richest part of Germany for mineral springs, having 125, of which the most celebrated are those of Wiesbaden, Kronthal, Ems, Schlangenbad, Schwalbach, and Nieder-Selters. The chief town is Kassel.

Hess'ian Fly (*Cecidomyia destructor*), a dipterous insect inhabiting the United States, the larvæ of which are exceedingly destructive to corn crops. Wheat in particular suffers from its attacks. The adult fly is black, with dusky wings. Two broods are produced each year.

Hes'ychasts (from Gr. *hēsychazō*, 'I am quiet'), a community of monks at Mount Athos in the 14th c., who sought the extinction of all the passions by means of contemplation. A charge was brought against them before the Patriarch of Constantinople by Barlaam, an abbot there, who applied to them the epithets of Messalians (Aram. 'those who pray,' Ezra vi. 10), or Euchites (Gr. from *euchē*, 'a prayer'), the name of a mystical sect in the 4th c., and designating generally those who laboured to elevate the soul to God by prayer and contemplation, and of *Omphalopsychoi* (Gr. 'navel-souls'), from their practice of sitting a long time every day with their eyes fixed on their belly. In this posture, they boasted, a divine light, the same as that seen by the disciples at the Transfiguration on Mount Tabor, beamed forth upon them. They found an advocate in Gregory Palamas, and when the cause was tried in a series of councils from 1337 to 1351, the H. were acquitted and the Barlaamites condemned. See Mosheim's *Eccl. Hist.* (Reid's ed.).

Hesy'chius, a Greek grammarian of Alexandria, who lived about the end of the 4th, or, according to others, in the 6th c., author of a Greek lexicon, chiefly compiled from earlier writers, but of great value for literary and archæological information. The best edition is Alberti's, by Ruhnken (Leyden, 1746-66). —**H. of Miletus** lived about the beginning of the 6th c., and wrote *Onomasticon*, an alphabetical synopsis of the greatest learned men of Greece (ed. of Orelli, Leips. 1820); and a *Chronicon*, or universal history, from the Assyrian Belus to the year 518, which is now lost.

Heterocer'cal Tail, the name given by Agassiz to the tails of such fishes as possess the upper lobe greatly developed over the lower. Such a conformation is seen in the sturgeon, shark, dogfish, skate, &c. In these the spine extends into the upper lobe of the tail, to a greater or less extent. In the opposite condition—*homocercal*—in which the lobes of the tail are equal, as in the salmon, herring, &c., the spine does not extend to the tail-fin, but terminates with the body.

Heterogangliа'ta, Professor Owen's term for the sub-kingdom *Mollusca* (q. v.), suggested by the fact that the nervous masses or *ganglia* are scattered or disposed through the body in an irregular manner. Thus typically in molluscous animals one ganglion (*cephalic*) exists in the head, a second in the foot (*pedal*), and a third (*branchial*) in the neighbourhood of the heart and gills; these being connected by nervous or *commissural* cords. The term is employed by Owen in contradistinction to *Homogangliata*, applied to the *Articulate* or *annulose* animals, in allusion to the regularly-disposed nature and form of the nervous system.

Heterogen'esis, a name used synonymously with *Abiogenesis* or *Archebiosis*, and therefore indicating a belief in the origin of living organisms from non-living or inorganic matter, without the pre-existence of parent germs or organisms. See GENERATION, SPONTANEOUS.

Heterop'oda, a division of *Gasteropoda* (q. v.) represented by the genera *Carinaria*, *Firola*, *Atalanta*, &c., in which the shell is rudimentary or absent, the 'foot' being converted into a flattened ventral fin-like organ, while the animals are free-swimming and oceanic in habits. The H. are also known by the name *Nucleobranchiata*, the two included families being the family *Atalantidæ* and *Firolidæ*.

Het'man, or **At'aman**, the general of the Cossacks (q. v.), was anciently elected by the whole people, and possessed an absolute power of life and death. After the submission of the Cossacks to the Russian Government (1654), the office was left untouched, until in 1708 the effort of Mazeppa (q. v.) to make himself independent led Peter the Great largely to curtail its privileges. From that date the post remained unfilled till the election, in 1750, of Count Rasumowski, who received, however, a yearly sum of 500,000 roubles in place of the lands and taxes of his predecessors. The Ukraine hetmanship was finally abolished by the Empress Catherine; the H. of the Don Cossacks still retaining vestiges of authority. In Poland, also, there was (from 1581) an officer called *great H.*, appointed by the king. His power over the army was ordinarily unbounded, but wholly ceased when the king took the field. To him the army swore allegiance, and all prisoners and ransoms fell to him; but he might take no part in the national assemblies or kingly elections. His subordinate was called *field-H.* Both offices were abolished in 1702.

Heve'lius, Johannes, or **Johann Höv'elke**, a German astronomer, born at Danzig, January 28, 1611, studied at Leyden, and travelled from 1630 to 1634 through Holland, England, and France. In 1641 he built an observatory at his own house, where he observed a transit of Mercury in 1661, the first observed after Gussendi. He died January 28, 1687. H.'s chief works are *Selenographia* (1647); *Cometographia* (1668); and *Machina Cœlestis* (2 vols. 1673-79). His life was written by Westphalen (Königsberg, 1820), and by Seidemann (Zittau, 1864).

Heves', a village in the comitat of the same name, Hungary, 60 miles E. of Pesth, with a trade in hemp and flax. Pop. (1869) 5703.

Hex'achord, a series of six musical tones, having some historical, but no practical importance in music.

Hex'agon, a geometrical figure of six sides and six angles. The *regular* H. has its sides and angles equal, and if it is inscribed in a circle, each side is equal in length to the radius of the circle. This gives a simple method for describing a H. See Euclid's *Elements*, book iv. Of all figures which, when placed contiguously, completely occupy space, the H. contains the greatest area with a given perimeter.

Hexahe'dron is a solid figure bounded by six faces, and therefore includes the cube. The term is very much restricted to crystallography.

Hexam'eter (Gr. *hex*, 'six,' and *mětron*, 'a measure'), the chief form of verse among the Greeks and Romans. It comprises six feet, which may be either dactyls or spondees, the last being always a spondee, or at least a trochee, which the *arsis* or stress of the voice at the end of the verse makes virtually a spondee. When the fifth foot is a spondee, the verse is called *spondaic*. The H. was the verse in which the great classical epics—the *Iliad*, *Odyssey*, and *Æneid*—were cast. It has been employed in modern times in German and English poetry. Goethe, Klopstock, Eberhard, and Voss have written German hexameters with considerable success, but it is totally incompatible with the structure of English diction. The so-called English hexameters are slovenly, cumbrous, and unmusical; a 'tumbling metre,' having a totally different rhythm from that of Greek and Latin verse. The least unsuccessful attempt in recent English poetry to use the measure is Kingsley's *Andromeda;* Longfellow's *Evangeline* being neither truly dactylic nor spondaic, while Clough's *Vacation Ramble* can hardly be regarded as a serious attempt to obey the laws of the H.

Hexap'la (Gr. 'the sixfold') was an edition of the Septuagint (q. v.) prepared by Origen (q. v.) for the use of Christians unacquainted with Hebrew, so that they might know how far that translation, as it then existed, differed from the Hebrew text. The six columns of the work were occupied as follows:—(1) The Hebrew text in Hebrew characters; (2) the same in Greek characters; (3) the translation of Aquila (q. v.); (4) that of Symmachus (q. v.); (5) the Septuagint; (6) the translation of Theodotion. Passages in the LXX. not in the Hebrew he marked with an *obelisk*, and passages in the Hebrew not in the LXX. he supplied from the other translations, and marked them with an *asterisk*. Fifty years after Origen's death (beginning of 4th c.) this work was discovered by Eusebius and placed in the library of Pamphilus at Cæsarea. As there is no further trace of it, it probably perished when Cæsarea was destroyed by the Arabs, 653.

Hex'ham, a town of England, in the county of Northumberland, on the Tyne, 20 miles W. of Newcastle by railway. It is surrounded with orchards, nursery grounds, and market-gardens, and has beautiful remains of St. Wilfrid's monastery (674); a cruciform abbey church of 1113, rich in stone and wood carving, with a tower 100 feet high; and a townhall and exchange in Italian style, built in 1866. Besides glovemaking there is some tanning, brewing, and iron and brass founding. The Tyne is here crossed by a bridge of nine arches. Pop. (1871) 5331. H. is the *Hagustald* or *Hestaldesham* ('the place of priests'?) of the Angles. It was made a bishopric by St. Wilfrid in 674, was joined to Lindisfarne in 883, and eventually became part of the see of Durham. The Scots frequently plundered it, and in the vicinity was fought the battle of H. between Yorkists and Lancastrians in 1463.

Hey'lin, Peter, D.D., was born in Burford, Oxfordshire, November 29, 1600, and educated at Oxford, became (1629) chaplain-in-ordinary to Charles I., and was appointed to a number of livings, which, with his personal property, he forfeited on the King's execution. At the Restoration he was made subdean of Westminster, and died May 8, 1662. His works include an *Ecclesia Vindicata, or a Defence of the Church of England, Life of Bishop Laud, History of the Sabbath, Examen Historicum, Microcosmos*, a once popular description of the globe, &c.

Hey'ne, Christian Gottlob, a great German scholar, was born of very poor parents at Chemnitz, Upper Saxony, September 25, 1729. With difficulty he obtained an elementary education, and poverty still hampered him at Leipsic University. Appointed (1753) under-clerk in Count Brühl's library at Dresden, he was again unsettled by the Seven Years' War (1756–63). During his Dresden residence, however, he managed to publish an edition of *Tibullus* and of the *Enchiridion* of Epictetus, which at once placed the humble official in the front rank of German scholars. In 1763 he was made Professor of Eloquence at Göttingen University, chiefly on the recommendation of Ruhnken, who had recognised the high merit of his *Tibullus* and *Epictetus*. Here he remained till his death, July 14, 1812. Among his editions of the classics, in addition to the two mentioned, the chief are those of *Virgil* (1767–1803), *Pindar* (1774–98), and *Apollodorus* (1787–1803). Besides this, he accomplished an enormous amount of work, literary and academic. H. is regarded as the founder of a new epoch in classical study, from his penetrating insight and lucid exposition. See Heeren, *H.'s Biographie* (Gött. 1813), and Carlyle's eloquent and appreciative essay on the work.

Hey'se, Johann Christian August, a German grammarian, born 21st April 1764 at Nordhausen, Prussian Saxony, studied at Göttingen, and after holding various scholastic offices, finally became director of the gymnasium and girls' school in Magdeburg, where he died, 27th June 1829. He was author of *Theoretisch-praktische Deutsche Grammatik* (5th ed. 1838–49), *Deutsche Schulgrammatik* (21st ed. 1868), &c.—**Karl Wilhelm Ludwig H.**, a philologist, son of the preceding, born 15th October 1797 at Oldenburg; from 1819–27 was tutor in the family of Mendelssohn-Bartholdy (q. v.); in 1829 was appointed Professor of Philosophy in Berlin University; and died there, 25th November 1855. He wrote *Handwörterbuch der Deutschen Sprache* (3 vols. Magd. 1838–49), *System der Sprachwissenschaft* (Berl. 1856), &c.—His son, **Paul Johann Ludwig H.**, a favourite poet and novelist, was born 15th March 1830, at Berlin, and educated there and at Bonn. After a lengthened tour in Switzerland and Italy, H. settled (1854) at Munich, where he married, and has since resided. Among his numerous works may be mentioned *Ulrica* (1852) and *Thekla* (1858), epics; *Ludwig der Bayer*, *Colberg*, and *Die Sabinerinnen* (1859), tragedies; and *La Rabbiata* (1858) and *Mexaner Novellen* (1864), romances. A beautiful novelette of Ligurian coast-life by H. appeared in the *Rundschau* (Berlin) of January 1877.

Hey'wood, an industrial town of England in Lancashire, on the Roach, 8½ miles N. of Manchester by railway. It has extensive manufactures of cotton goods, iron, boilers, machinery, &c., and in the vicinity are large coal-mines. The town has grown rapidly. Pop. (1871) 12,824.

Hey'wood, John, surnamed the 'Epigrammatist,' was born (it is supposed) at N. Mims in Hertfordshire, and was educated at Oxford. He obtained the friendship of Sir Thomas More and of Queen Mary, but left England on the accession of Elizabeth, and died at Mechlin in 1565. H. is remembered in English literature as a writer of interludes or dramatic pieces of a satirical nature, intermediate both in point of time and character between the *Moralities* and the Elizabethan Plays. The best-known are *A Mery Play between the Pardoner and the Frere, the Curate, and Neybour Pratt* (1532), and *The Foure P.'s, a very Mery Enterlude of a Palmer, a Pardoner, a Potecary, aud a Pedlar*, the date of which is unknown. Besides interludes, H. wrote some 600 epigrams, none of which exhibit a very deadly wit. H. was an ardent Catholic, and his two sons **Ellis** and **Jasper** both joined the Society of Jesus. Before entering on an ecclesiastical career they had given evidence of literary talent. Jasper became Provincial of the Jesuits of England, and died at Naples in 1598. He contributed to the *Paradise of Dainty Devices*.—**Thomas H.**, an Elizabethan dramatist, was a native of Lincolnshire, and was educated at Cambridge; becoming a Fellow of Peterhouse. We find him writing for the stage in 1596, and for upwards of forty years he was a most industrious and prolific author. He died about 1641. Twenty-three of his pieces are still extant. Among others may be mentioned *A Woman Killed with Kindness, The English Traveller, A Challenge for Beauty, Lancashire Witches, Rape of Lucrece, Love's Mistress, Joan as Good as my Lady*, &c. H. has a fine poetic fancy, enriched with classic memories that are sometimes too much for him; his humour is genuine, and his songs have a true lyric flow and dainty sweetness of sentiment.

Hezeki'ah (Heb. 'strength of Jehovah'), the son and successor of Ahaz, king of Judah, reigned twenty-nine years in Jerusalem (B.C. 726–697, 2 Kings xviii.–xx., 2 Chron. xxix.–xxxii.). Immediately on his accession he set himself to carry out a religious reformation, to abolish the idolatry which had been introduced by his father, to restore the true worship of Jehovah, and to restrict it to the temple at Jerusalem. As regards his foreign relations, the best critics are of opinion that the invasion in the fourteenth year of his reign (2 Kings xviii. 13, Isa. xxxvi. 1) was not made by Sennacherib, but by his father, Sargon, who in the tenth year of his reign (the fourteenth of H.) sent an expedition into Palestine and Egypt (Isa. xx. 1, Nah. iii. 8–10). Now, as H. was unmolested by this expedition, it is probable that he had not yet thrown off his allegiance to the king of Assyria. His famous illness (2 Kings xx., Isa. xxxviii.) must have taken place at this time also, as he was promised fifteen years to his life, and he only reigned twenty-nine years. On his recovery ambassadors were sent by Merodach-Baladan, king of Babylon, and vassal of the king of Assyria, ostensibly to congratulate the king on his recovery, but also probably to form an alliance with H. for throwing off the Assyrian yoke. After Sargon was succeeded by Sennacherib (B.C. 702), H. made a league with Egypt (Isa. xxx., xxxi., *cf.* xxxvi. 6–9), and refused to pay the tribute which his father had agreed to pay to the king of Assyria in the time of Tiglath-Pileser (2 Kings xvi. 7). Sennacherib thereupon led an army against him, and took 'all the fenced cities of Judah' (2 Kings xviii. 13–16, Isa. xxxvi. 1), Jerusalem being saved only by H. giving him 'all the silver that was found in the house of the Lord, and in the treasures of the king's house.' After a futile expedition into Egypt, Sennacherib a second time invaded the dominions of H. (2 Kings xviii. 17, xix. 37, 2 Chron. xxxii., Isa. xxxvi., xxxvii.), in the twenty-eighth year of his reign (B.C. 698). Jerusalem was saved on this occasion by the death of 185,000 of the Assyrians in a single night (explained by some as caused by an attack of Tirhakah, king of Ethiopia, who had shortly before obliged Sennacherib to raise the siege of Pelusium in Egypt; by others ascribed to the pestilence), in consequence of which Sennacherib fled to Nineveh. At what period of the reign of H. his defeat of the Philistines (2 Kings xviii. 8) ought to be placed, we have no means of determining.

Hi'bernation is the state of torpor in which many animals—such as bats, bears, dormice, &c.—pass the colder months or season of the year. In addition to the mammals or warm-blooded animals just mentioned, almost all reptiles and amphibia pass the colder months in a hibernating condition, whilst some fishes (*e.g.*, the Lepidosirens, q. v.) may exemplify this habit. Some molluscs (*e.g.*, snails), and many insects appear to hibernate; the beetles presenting not a few examples of hibernating forms. According to Dr. Marshall Hall, hibernating animals present us with 'an ultimate faculty of assuming an augmented degree of irritability of the muscular fibre, a power possessed by all animals within certain limits, but by the hibernating animals beyond the usual limits.' Dr. Hall regards sleep as the physiological counterpart of H. H. according to him is a state of profound sleep; and ordinary sleep presents us with the initiatory stage of H. The influence of cold in inducing H. has been in all probability greatly exaggerated; this condition simply exercising an effect in producing sleep. H., although generally occurring during the winter season, is not absolutely confined to that portion of the year. Cuvier remarks that the Tenrecs (q. v.) or Madagascar hedgehogs pass three months of the year in a lethargic condition, even although these animals inhabit the torrid zone. As regards the *physiological* or *functional* relations of the hibernating state, it may be noted that the respiratory movements, or those of breathing, are diminished from their general number and force. This result is just what physiology would lead us to expect. Frequency of respiration depends on, and at the same time contributes to, the maintenance of animal heat; and as the temperature sinks in H., the respirations must be less frequent in consequence. The *temperature* in hibernating animals usually sinks to within a few degrees above that of the surrounding media; and, with decreased respiration and temperature, we may reasonably believe that the blood becomes 'more and more venous,' and aids in inducing within the brain and nerve centres a state of torpor. In the hibernating animal the vital processes of the body sink to the minimum degree of activity, while some—such as digestion and sanguification in their ordinary aspects—may be entirely suspended. The *circulation*, as observed in the wing of the bat, is slow and inert; while the functions of the nervous system are limited to those *automatic* or *excito-motor* acts connected with respiration, &c. An interesting fact connected with the *nutrition* of the bodies of some hibernating animals is that these animals retire to their winter quarters provided with a due supply of fatty matters, while they appear in spring, after their sleep, in a meagre and lean condition. The body in such a case has been feeding on the nutritive stores laid up within its tissues.

Hiber'nia, Ibernia, Ivernia, Ierne, various forms of the ancient name of Ireland. *Hibernia* first occurs in Cæsar, the oldest form of the name being *Ierne*, which is found in Aristotle and in an old poem on the Argonautic expedition, which dates, probably, from about the 5th c. B.C. Pomponius Mela uses the form *Iverna*, Pliny *Hibernia*, Strabo *Ierne*, and Ptolemy *Ivernia*. All these are varieties of the native Celtic or Erse, *Erin* or *Eri*, the similarity of which to the Greek *hiera* led Avienus to describe it as the 'sacred isle.' Ptolemy alone of ancient authors gives an account of H., which he describes minutely and with tolerable accuracy. Many of the geographical names mentioned in Ptolemy, survive, *e.g.*, *Oboca*, Avoca, *Bargus*, Barrow, *Liboius*, Liffy, *Senus*, Shannon, *Eblana*, Dublin, *Nagnatae*, Connaught, &c. Although Agricola projected an invasion of H., the Romans never sought to conquer the island. Its inhabitants, the ancestors of the modern Irish, were Gaelic Celts, with probably an infusion of Iberians from Spain. The occurrence of the Teutonic name *Cauci* and the British *Brigantes* on the W. coast suggests the early presence of colonies from Britain and Germany. The *Scoti*, who migrated from H. to what is now called Scotland, are first mentioned by Claudian.

Hibis'cus, a very large genus of *Malvaceæ*, the majority of which are natives of the tropics, though a few are found in temperate regions, and one species occurs in the S. of Europe. On account of their showy flowers, they are favourites with the gardener, *e.g.*, the variable *H. Rosa Sinensis* is a well-known ornament of our hothouses, and *H. Syriacus*, with its profusion of flowers, has long been cultivated as a hardy shrub in many parts of Britain. All possess the mucilaginous properties common to the order, and several are eaten in their native countries as potherbs, while their inner bark yields more or less fibre. Ambaree hemp or bastard jute is obtained from *H. cannabinus*.

Hicc'up, or **Hicc'ough**, consists of a convulsive catch of the respiratory muscles, attended with a peculiar sonorous sound, produced in the larynx, and followed by expiration. It most commonly occurs in paroxysms of varying duration, repeated at short intervals; the movements concerned in its production being spasmodic contraction of the diaphragm and constriction in the glottis. H. may be caused by irritation of the glottis, as from peppers; by gastric derangement, as from the prolonged use of alcohol, excessive acidity, and the ingestion of cold water; by emptiness or over-distension of the stomach, as in the case of infants during suckling; and is a frequent accompaniment of hysteria, dyspepsia, and certain diseases attended with great debility. A paroxysm of H. may sometimes be cut short by a strong mental effort, or by having the attention withdrawn from it by some other object; or the irritation, if slight, may be removed by swallowing cold water or small pieces of ice. In some cases opiates, antimonials, or diffusible stimulants, as ammonia or camphor, may be necessary.

Hickes, George, D.D., an English scholar and divine, was born June 20, 1642, at Newsham in Yorkshire, entered St. John's College, Oxford, in 1659, and in 1664 became Fellow of Lincoln College. Two years later H. took holy orders, and after travelling for some time on the Continent, was appointed in 1676 chaplain to the Duke of Lauderdale. In the next year he accompanied the Duke to Edinburgh, and in 1678 received the degree of D.D. from the University of Glasgow, the same honour being conferred on him by Oxford University in 1679. H. subsequently obtained considerable preferment; but refusing to take the oath of allegiance to King William at the Revolution of 1688, he lost his Deanery of Worcester and other benefices. He died December 15, 1715. H. was the author of numerous pamphlets and polemical writings which are now forgotten; his reputation for scholarship rests on the *Thesaurus, or Treasury of the Northern Tongues* (3 vols. Oxford, 1705), a work displaying much antiquarian and philological knowledge.

Hick'ory, a N. American genus of large forest trees, of which the scientific name is *Carya*, belonging to *Juglandaceæ*, and closely related to the walnuts. Their timber is of great strength, weight, and toughness, and is much used for the manufacture of barrel-hoops, axe and whip handles, handspikes, &c., where toughness and elasticity are necessary. It will not stand exposure, and is liable to the attacks of insects, consequently is not suitable for building purposes. The nuts of some of the species are eaten, that of the peccan or Illinois H.-nut being the best, next to it that of the shag-bark H. (*Carya alba*).

Hidal'go, the name given to a Spanish nobleman of inferior rank. The word is derived either from *hijo del Goto*, 'son of the Goth,' that is, of noble descent, of Gothic, as opposed to Moorish blood, or from *hijo de alguno*, 'son of somebody.'

Hiera'cium, a large genus of plants of the natural order *Compositæ* (q. v.). See HAWKWEED.

Hi'erarchy (from Gr. *hierarchēs*, 'a steward or president of sacred rites, a bishop') means properly the order of bishops, and then the whole series of the orders of ministry in the Christian Church. The H. embraces the power of *jurisdiction* and of *order*, considered as a principality. The H. of order, which pertains to all clergy, according to the measure of their power, by ministration of the sacraments and preaching the gospel, aims at elevating and hallowing the spiritual life; the H. of jurisdiction, which pertains to prelates alone, is for the promotion of exterior discipline. In the one, the clerical characters or the ecclesiastical office only is regarded; in the other, the degree or rank in jurisdiction of a prelate is alone considered. The first form of a Christian H., in the modern sense, was bishop, presbyter, and deacon. This was gradually developed both upwards, by the creation of metropolitans, archbishops, and patriarchs, and downwards, by the creation of sub-deacons, acolytes, &c. The ultimate development of the H. in the Western Church was into a pure monarchy or papacy; in the Eastern Church it has always remained aristocratical and patriarchal. (See BISHOP.) See Blunt's *Dict. of Doct. and Hist. Theology* (1872).

Hierat'ic Writing. See HIEROGLYPHICS.

Hi'ero (Gr. *Hieron*), tyrant of Syracuse, succeeded his brother Gelon in 478, warred against Theron of Agrigentum, and afterwards against Theron's son Thrasydæus, whom he utterly defeated, gained a great victory over the Etruscan fleet off Cumae in 474, and was repeatedly successful in the Olympic and Pythian games. H. was a famous patron of literature and philosophy, and Æschylus, Pindar, Bacchylides, Xenophanes, Simonides, and Epicharmus resided at his court. His victories in the Greek games were sung by Pindar, and Xenophon's *Hieron* is an imaginary dialogue between H. and Simonides. H. died at Catana in 467.—**H.**, King of Syracuse, son of Hierocles, a descendant of Gelmond, a slave, distinguished himself in the Sicilian wars of Pyrrhus, was made general of the whole Syracusan forces, and after winning a signal victory over the Mamertines, became King of Syracuse in 270 B.C. He allied himself with the Carthaginians against the Romans, but after suffering defeat in 263 was the faithful supporter of Rome even amid the victories of Hannibal. He ruled with justice and clemency, gave great care to finance, and embellished Syracuse with many fine buildings. H. died in 216. Theocritus celebrates H. in his 16th Idyl.

Hier'ocles, a Neo-Platonist who flourished at Alexandria during the 5th c., of whose life nothing is known. He wrote *On Providence, Fate, and the Harmony between the Divine Government and Man's Freewill*, of which only a few fragments remain (Morelli, Par. 1593), *On Justice, Reverence of the Gods, and the Domestic and Social Virtues*, now lost, except several extracts in Stobæus, and a commentary on the golden verses of Pythagoras, which contains some valuable information as to the Pythagorean doctrine, and of which the best edition is by Mullach (Berl. 1853). *Asteia*, a collection of facetiæ, has been ascribed to H., but probably belongs to a later era. The best edition of the *Asteia* is by Schier (Leips. 1768).

Hieroglyph'ics. In 1799 a French artillery officer, Bouchart, discovered at the redoubt of St. Julian an oblong slab of black syenite with three inscriptions, one in H. proper, one in Greek, and one in what the Greek text calls the enchorial or popular character. This is the famous Rosetta stone. It contains an address by the Memphis priests to Ptolemy Epiphanes. Besides this, the French Government publication *Description de l'Egypte* (new ed. in 36 vols. 1828–31) contained several monuments and papyri. Though the Dane Zœga had already in his *De Symbolicis* (1798), proceeding mainly on Coptic materials, pointed out that H. were phonetic signs, *not merely symbolical and mythical representations*, and Barthélemy had also suggested that the rings on the monuments contained the names of kings, the study of the Rosetta stone was hampered by this error being repeated, also by the notion that the enchorial or demotic was purely alphabetical and not partly symbolical, and the same as the hieratic writing in the older papyri. The enchorial is really Coptic, differing from H. in individual words and also in declensions. De Sacy first observed the recurring groups of characters representing Ptolemy, Bernice, and Alexander. These were decomposed into letters by the Swede Akerblad, who also added the enchorial groups of Chemi (Egypt), Phuro (the king), Nierpheni (the temples), Urb (priests). Thomas Young's *Conjectural Translation* appeared in 1814. It gives 100 alphabetical characters, and thirty additional recurring groups, and brings out the symbolic element in the enchorial. He also made some progress in the derivation of the cursive or hieratic writing from the H. In his *Rudiments of an Egyptian Dictionary in the Ancient Enchorial Character* (1830), he added to the ascertained names of kings, but his H. alphabet never went beyond the proper names. The demotic papyri at Berlin were further investigated by Rosegarten and De Saulcy, but the great name in this subject is that of Champollion le Jeune, who, following up the lines of Akerblad and Young, and starting from a profound knowledge of Coptic, soon arrived at the conception of homophone signs (*i.e.*, different figures representing one and the same sound), the necessary foundation of a H. alphabet. Deciphering the phonetic signs on several of the royal rings, which he compared with equivalent Greek inscriptions, comparing also the funereal papyri, he produced in 1824 his famous *Précis du Système Hiéroglyphique*. It distinguishes 232 alphabetic signs. Champollion was followed by Ipollite Rosellini, whose dictionary gives the value of the phonetic and determinative, and also of the symbolic H.; Françesco Salvolini, whose name is connected with the Rosetta stone and the Sallier papyrus, and who suggested that the phonetic sign might indicate the initial sound not merely of the name of the object, but also of the object of which it was the symbol; Richard Lepsius, who pointed out that many of Champollion's 'letters' were not of universal application; Hincks, who discovered that every letter has a normal vowel not written (but written in the hieratic); Birch, who described certain signs as determinative not of sense but of sound. Other writers on the grammar are Chabas, Deveria, and De Rougé in France; Goodwin and Heath in England; and Brugsch in Germany. The chief ancient account of H. is that left by Clemens of Alexandria. He mentions (1) the demotic (popular), or epistolographic, or enchorial (so distinguished from the Ptolemaic Greek), the idiom of private, domestic, and commercial affairs, the basis of the modern Coptic; (2) the hieratic, used for religion and science by the sacred scribes, a running hand formed from the H., and with more symbolical elements than the enchorial; (3) the H. proper, which practically meant the linear H. in the sacred books derived from the pictorial signs on the monuments. But Clemens speaks more of the pictorial H., which are either *kyriological*, *i.e.*, simple images, as *sun*, *moon*, *ship*, *scales*, *bed*, *bull*, *loaf*, *fish*, *goose*, &c.; or very obvious symbols—as where a flat roof with stars represents the night; or remoter symbols (generally for more abstract ideas), visible metaphors, in fact, the part being taken for the whole, an effect for its cause, &c. Thus a 'milk-pail' may mean milk, and a 'man throwing arrows' may mean tumult. The gods are often represented by their sacred animals. Clemens also mentions the 'anaglyphs,' an enigmatical or cabalistic character (in which a serpent represents the star-courses, and a beetle represents the sun). This, however, seems to have been a comparatively recent contrivance of the priesthood, who dealt largely in esoteric meanings. But while the oldest writing is a representation of objects, not of sounds, it must not be supposed that it was, like the Mexican, pure picture-writing. Only the simplest ideas could be expressed that way. A system of abbreviation and composition gradually grew up. Milk and wine are represented by the vessels which usually hold them. Water is shown by three zigzag lines, which are now seen on pottery all over the world. These lines became straight in the linear H. Add the figure of a kid, and you have the H. for *thirst*. *White* is denoted by a bulb, probably an onion. A palm branch means the *year*; and because the words for good and lute were the same, a lute stands for the good and beautiful. This important principle of homophony appears again in the identification of *eye* and *child*. The principle of determination is also important. It distinguishes the individual from the genus, and qualifies the former by an image of the latter; *e.g.*, the sycamore becomes a sign for all trees. It includes the grammatical signs, such as a short vertical stroke for noun masculine; the addition of a segment for noun feminine; two extended arms with palms downwards negate the following sentence; dual and plural numbers are expressed by two and three vertical lines; and the personal pronoun by a human figure. Homophony led to the invention of syllabic writing, the pictorial hieroglyphic appearing as the first letter or syllable of the whole word, of which the phonetic elements follow. As many of the oldest Egyptian words were monosyllabic, so under this syllabic system there were some syllabic signs which were purely phonetic, *i.e.*, they are capable of indicating the sound of the word they represent without exclusive reference to the one object denoted by this word. These syllabic phonetics, as they are called by Bunsen, gradually become the later phonetic alphabet. As regards the number of H., there have been determined (1) of the signs of objects (whether descriptive or symbolic) at least 400, the most frequent objects being the human figure in various postures, and works of art; (2) of determinatives, as above defined, at least 120; (3) of phonetics, both syllabic and alphabetic, which do not lose their connection with particular things by acquiring a connection with particular sounds, about seventy; (4) of mixed sounds, *i.e.*, objective signs followed by one or two phonetic H. which represent the sound of the corresponding word, generally its last letter, at least fifty-seven. We may add some specimens of the H. numerals—

| ∩ c [illegible] 7

1 10 100 1000 10,000

The units are expressed by strokes, but always in groups; as 6 or 3 + 3 = ||| over |||. We may also mention among the grammatical signs the roll of papyrus, which indicates a full stop; the cross bar (×) which indicates a verb; the stretched legs which indicate an active verb. See Chabas, *Papyrus Magique d'Harris* (4to, Chal. 1861); De Rougé, *Étude d'une Stèle Égyptienne* (Par. 1858); Brugsch, *Hieroglyphisch-Demotisches Wörterbuch* (4 vols. Leips. 1867–68); and *Grammaire Hiéroglyphique* (4to, Leips. 1872).

Hier'ophant, or Mys'tagogue, the priest who initiated candidates into the Eleusinian mysteries, in which he was supposed to represent the demiurge or creator of the world. He was necessarily an Athenian citizen descended from the hero Eumolpus, and free from any moral or physical defect. He held the office for life, and was not permitted to marry.

High Bailiff. See BAILIFF, HIGH.

High Commission Court, an oppressive ecclesiastical court established by Queen Elizabeth, was abolished by 16 Car. I. An attempt to revive it by James II. promoted the revolution of 1688.

High Constable. See CONSTABLE.

High Court of Justice. See COURT OF JUDICATURE, SUPREME, ACT.

High Places were thought by most ancient nations to be the best on which to worship their deities, as men there were nearer to heaven and to the object of their worship; hence it was common to build altars and chapels on the tops of mountains and hills, for the offering of sacrifices and other worship. That the Hebrews followed this practice, as well as other nations, for the worship both of false gods and of Jehovah himself, is abundantly evident from the Bible. Thus Abraham built an altar on a mountain at Bethel (Gen. xii. 8); and Samuel, Solomon, and all the people offered sacrifices on H. P. (1 Sam. ix. 12; 1 Kings iii. 2–4). Even after the building of Solomon's temple the practice was generally continued (2 Kings xii. 3, xiv. 4), until Hezekiah and Josiah abolished the H. P. and restricted the worship of Jehovah to the temple at Jerusalem (2 Kings xviii. 4, xxiii. 13).

High Priest was the head of the priesthood among the Israelites, and had certain functions which the ordinary priests were not entitled to perform. (1) The H. P. alone could enter the holy of holies in the tabernacle and the temple, which even he did only once a year, on the great day of atonement (Lev. xvi.); and (2) he alone could consult the Lord by means of the oracle of the Ephod (q. v.) and the Urim and Thummim (q. v.), although some modern critics maintain that this latter privilege —of giving oracles, as well as wearing the ephod—belonged originally to all the priests alike (*cf.* Chron. xv. 27; 1 Sam. ii. 28, &c.), and was only restricted to the H. P. by the priestly legislature of the post-exilian period. *Dress.*—Besides those articles of dress which he had in common with the ordinary priests, namely, an embroidered linen tunic, linen girdle, drawers, and turban (four pieces), the H. P. had a distinctive dress consisting of a breastplate, on which were set twelve precious stones, the ephod, the robe of the ephod, and an upper turban or metre (four pieces; Exod. xxviii.).

High Seas. By international law every country has certain exclusive rights over what is called the *mare clausum*, that is, the sea within three miles of its coast. Of these rights the most important is that of fishing. Beyond three miles from the coast the seas are called the H. S., and no nation has any exclusive right over them. It has recently been decided in the case of the *Franconia* that English courts have no criminal jurisdiction over foreign vessels within three miles of the English coast.

High Steward, a legal peer appointed by the crown to superintend the trial of any peer indicted for treason or felony. A peer so indicted can only be tried by the court of the H.S.

High Treason. See TREASON.

High'gate, a suburb of London, 5 miles N. of the General Post-office, is pleasantly situated on hilly ground. It contains many fine villas, seven churches, and several chapels and schools, an infirmary with 550 beds, and a smallpox hospital. The North London Cemetery is at H. Pop. (1871) 5339.

High'land Regiments, the general name of eight British infantry regiments that were originally raised in the Highlands, and that still wear the Highland costume. These are the 42d (see BLACK WATCH), the 71st (raised in 1777), the 72d (in 1777), the 74th (in 1787), the 78th or Ross-shire Buffs (in 1793), the 79th or Cameronian Highlanders (in 1805), the 92d or Gordon Highlanders (in 1796), and the 93d or Sutherland Highlanders (in 1800). Though these regiments are recruited in the Highlands, some twenty per cent. of the men are English and Irish. They are distinguished by various tartans.

Highways, Law Regarding. Every parish is bound to keep the highway passing through it in repair unless there be legal provision to the contrary. Surveyors are by statute elected annually by the parishioners at their first meeting for the nomination of overseers of the poor. A highway is a road leading from one town to another, whether it be a footway, a horse and foot way, or a cartway. Every one has a right of thoroughfare. The general and amending Act of highways is the 25 and 26 Vict. c. 61. It provides that notice having been given by the clerk of the peace, at the instance of five or more justices, to churchwardens or overseers of parishes, justices in general or quarter sessions may issue a provisional order dividing their county or part of it into *highway districts*, or constituting the whole county a *highway district*, for the more convenient management of H., and directions are given for the legal execution of the scheme. Penalties are enacted against riding on footpaths, and various other public nuisances connected with it. No one is entitled to use any part of a highway except for passage or traffic, even though the use seem to be for the public benefit. Telegraph posts cannot be legally put up except under Act of Parliament. Ground under a highway belongs to the adjoining owners; hence an owner may work a mine under a road, so long as he leaves enough soil to support it. Any one but the owner breaking the surface is liable in damage for trespass. The laws of Scotland as regards H. are essentially the same as those of England. See BAR, TOLL.

Hig'gler is one who carries small articles from door to door and retails them. See HAWKER.

Hilary, St., of Poictiers, a father of the Church, born early in the 4th c., of heathen parents, on reaching maturity embraced Christianity, and about 350 was elected to the bishopric of his native city, Poictiers. He is chiefly distinguished by his zeal against the Arians, which won him the title of *Malleus Arianorum*, and led to his banishment to Phrygia by Constantius II. (356). In his exile, however, H. still so harassed his opponents —at the Council of Seleucia (359) denouncing the Emperor as antichrist—that, to be rid of him, he was soon permitted to return to his see. Under Julian he laboured hard to extirpate the Arian heresy, and when in 364 Auxentius was nominated Bishop of Milan by Valentinian I., H. protested against the appointment, and created such confusion that he was ordered forthwith to retire to his diocese. He died January 7, 367. Of his writings nine exist of certain, two of doubtful authenticity, while seven have perished. See the *Vita Hilarii ex ipsius potissimum Scriptis collecta*, prefixed to the best edition of his works by the Benedictine Constant (Par. 1693, 2d ed. Veron. 1730).—**H. of Arles**, born about 400 in Gallia Belgica, was educated at the Abbey of Lérins, and took the monastic vows, which he abandoned in 429 for the bishopric of Arles. In 441 H. became involved in a controversy with Pope Leo I., the Great, arising from the deposition of a Bishop of Besançon, Chelidonius. The latter carried an appeal to Rome, whither he was followed by H., who refused, however, to recognise in the Pope more than an arbitrator. Leo thereupon reinstated Chelidonius, and, supported by a rescript of the Emperor Valentinian III. (445), deposed H. himself, who, fearing for his own liberty, had stolen from Rome, and crossed the Alps on foot. The dispute is an important one, as showing the antiquity of Ultramontanism (q. v.). H. died at Arles, 449. The only two of his works extant were published in the *Bibliotheca Patrum Maxima*, vol. viii. (Lyon, 1677), and in Barralis's *Chronologia Lirinensis* (Lyon, 1613), the latter also containing a *Vita Hilarii*, ascribed to Honoratus, Bishop of Marseille (460).

Hilary Term. See TERM.

Hildburghaus'en, a town of Germany, in the duchy of Sachsen-Meiningen, on the river Werra, and the Eisenach-Koburg Railway. It was the residence of the Dukes of Sachsen-H. till 1826; and has some interesting buildings, and also manufactures of cloth, tobacco, machinery, &c. Pop. (1875) 5162.

Hildebrand. See GREGORY VII.

Hil'den, a thriving town of Prussia, in the Rheinland, and on the Itterbach, 9 miles E.S.E. of Düsseldorf by rail. It has extensive manufactures of cotton and linen goods, cassimeres, &c. Pop. (1875) 6799.

Hil'desheim, a town of Prussia, in the province of Hanover, on the Innerste, 30 miles S.E. of Hanover by rail. It is a quaint, placid, old town, the see of a bishop since 822, and has a cathedral of date 1015, with famous bronze gates and glass paintings; a beautiful church of St. Godehard, with triple-towers, built in 1133, and restored in 1852; and the basilica church of St. Michael founded in 1022. It is still the see of a Roman Catholic bishop, and has considerable trade in corn, linen, and yarn, but slight industries. Pop. (1875) 22,581. On the Galgenberg, in the vicinity, were found sixty silver vessels of finest Roman make in 1868.

Hill Mustard. See BUNIAS.

Hill, Rowland, Viscount, an English general, belonging to the Shropshire Hills, was a son of Sir John Hill of Hawkstone, and was born August 11, 1772. At the age of fifteen he entered the army, and obtained speedy promotion. He was lieutenant-colonel of the 90th Regiment in its Egyptian campaign, and was sent to Spain in 1808 in command of a brigade. For distinguished services at Corunna, Talavera, and Arroyo de Molinos, he was created a baron and G.C.B., and was voted a pension of £2000, with the thanks of Parliament. He was present at Waterloo, and was second in command of the army of occupation in France. In 1828 he became commander-in-chief, and on his resignation from ill health in 1842, was created a viscount. H. died December 10, 1842.

Hill, Sir Rowland, author of the penny postal system, born at Kidderminster, 3d December 1795. In his youth he assisted his father in a school near Birmingham, and in 1835 was appointed Secretary to the Commissioners for the Colonisation of S. Australia. A pamphlet, published by him in 1837, in favour of penny postage, engaged the attention of the House of Commons; 2000 petitions were presented in its favour, and his plan was carried out early in 1840, after an experimental charge of 4d. had been tried. H. received an appointment in the Treasury, but Sir Robert Peel's Government dispensed with his services in 1841, on the ground that they were no longer required, and the more grateful public thereupon subscribed a testimonial to him of £13,360. In 1845 he became Chairman of the London and Brighton Railway, in 1846 Secretary to the Postmaster-General, and in 1854 Chief Secretary to the Post-Office. He was made a K.C.B. in 1860, and retired from office in 1864 with full pay of £2000 and a parliamentary grant of £20,000. In the same year he received the honorary degree of D.C.L. His brothers, **Matthew Davenport H.** and **Frederick H.**, have also signalised themselves by philanthropic activity.

Hill States of the Punjaub, India. A collection of twenty petty states, which are all in relation with the Punjaub Government through the Superintendent of the Hill States. They lie between the Sutlej and Jumna rivers, and stretch from the plains of Umballa to the borders of the Chinese Empire; area, about 5441 sq. miles; estimated pop. 386,800. The chiefs are all Rajputs, and most of them owe their power to the direct grant of the British after the Gurkha war in 1815.

Hilla, or **El-Hilleh**, a garrisoned town in the vilayet of Bagdad, in Asiatic Turkey, 56 miles S. of Bagdad, on both banks of the Euphrates, here 450 feet broad and crossed by a pontoon bridge. It is partly walled, has fifteen Shiite mosques, various bazaars, and is famous for its sour milk, fish, and dates. Its manufactures are silks (*kds*), leather, and date-spirits. H. is built on the ruins of Babylon. Pop. variously estimated from 6000 to 30,000, mostly Shiite Arabs, Persians, and Jews.

Hill'el 'the Elder,' a Jewish Rabbi belonging to the sect of the Pharisees, was born at Babylon about B.C. 75, and died about A.D. 10. About B.C. 36 he settled in Jerusalem, where he supported himself and family by the labour of his hands, and at the same time attended the lectures of the Rabbis Shmemajah and Abtalion, paying the half of his earnings for admission. Such was his thirst for knowledge, and so well did he profit by his opportunities, that about B.C. 30 he was elected president of the Sanhedrim. In modern times H. has been called the teacher of Jesus (Renan), and the reformer of Judaism (Geiger). Be that as it may, 'by his self-denying and holy life, as well as by his great wisdom and learning,' he exercised such an influence both on the theology and literature of the Jews as to earn the title of 'the second Ezra,' or restorer of the law. He differed from his rival teacher, Shammai, by a more liberal interpretation of the law in some things, dictated by a more gentle and yielding spirit; and hence arose endless disputes between the disciples of the two. H. inculcated as the very kernel of the law, 'Whatsoever thou wouldst not that a man should do to thee, do not thou to him.'—**H. II.**, elected president of the Sanhedrim about 330 A.D., is chiefly remarkable for his introduction of the calendar still used by the Jews.

Hil'ted, in heraldry, signifies having a handle.

Hil'versum, a village of N. Holland, 15 miles S.E. of Amsterdam, has manufactures of cottons, carpets, spinning and dyeing wool, &c. Pop. 6300.

Himala'ya ('the abode of snow'), a range of mountains in the S. of Central Asia, the highest in the world, bounds the peninsula of India on the N., from Afghanistan to Burmah, separating it from Thibet; total length along the curve, nearly 15,000 miles; average elevation, from 16,000 to 18,000 feet. The limit of perpetual snow varies on the S. from 16,000 to 19,000 feet, on the N. from 17,000 to 18,000 feet; the lowest glacier extends as low as 10,500 feet. There are 45 peaks known to be higher than any in the rest of the world; the highest is Gouri Sunkur and Mount Everest, in Nepaul, 29,002 feet; the next, Dapsang, in the Karakorum range, 28,278 feet; the third, Kinchinjunga, above Darjeeling, 28,156 feet. The highest point ever reached by man is believed to have been in August 1855, when the brothers Schlagentweit ascended Ibi Gamin, in the Karakorum H., a height of 22,259 feet. The highest pass regularly used for commerce is believed to be the Parang Pass, in Spiti, 18,500 feet. Leh, the capital of Ladakh, is 11,257 feet above the sea, and there are Buddhist monasteries permanently inhabited 4000 feet higher. Trees grow up to a height of 11,800 feet; but there are pastures in Thibet 16,000 feet; monkeys and tigers are seen up to 11,000 feet, leopards up to 14,000 feet; fish have been found in rivulets 1000 feet higher. The most elevated British sanatarium is at Chini, 9096 feet; Simla is 7156 feet; Darjeeling, 6905.

The geological structure is gneiss and a schistose formation. There are no plains and few lakes. The most characteristic trees on the lower slopes are the deodara and the rhododendron, and yet lower down, the *sal*. Fringing the plains of India lies the Terni, a strip of malarious jungle-grown marsh. In the H. rise the Ganges, the Jumna, the Sutlej, the Indus, and the Brahmaputra. The three last flow between, and penetrate by steep gorges, the loftiest ridges of the chain; and the gorge of the Indus terminates the H. proper on the W., as the Brahmaputra does on the E. Very little of British territory extends up the mountains, which chiefly belong to Cashmere, Gurhwal, Nepaul, Sikkim, and Bhootan; the northern slopes terminate in the plateau of Thibet. See Dr. Royle's *Botany of the H. Mountains* (Lond. 1839); Dr. Hooker's *Himalayan Journals* (Lond. 1854); and Wilson's *Abode of Snow* (1875).

Hinck'ley, a town of England, in Leicestershire, 99 miles N.N.W. of London by rail. It has a church of the 14th c. with a richly-carved oak ceiling, is the centre of the brown cotton hose industry, and carries on brewing, malting, lime-burning, and the making of needles and weaving frames. H. extends into Warwickshire. Pop. (1871) 6902.

Hinc'mar, a noted Frankish Churchman, was born in the year 806. He was trained as a monk in the Abbey of St. Denis, and having acquired high favour at the court of Karl the Bald, was appointed Archbishop of Rheims in 845. H.'s tenure of this dignity was distinguished by the independent attitude which he took up towards the Papal See. His election to the Archbishopric had been opposed by Lothar, the brother of King Karl, and by the Pope; but on this occasion H. triumphed. His later contests with the Papacy, however, were not so successful. H. had treated with the utmost severity the heretical theologian Gottschalk, who had been handed over to him for discipline by the Council of Mainz; and to this conduct Rothad, Bishop of Soissons, objected. H. accordingly entertained hostile feelings towards his bishop, and took advantage of the deposition of a priest by Rothad in 862 to provoke a quarrel. The priest appealed to H., who ordered his restoration; Rothad refused, and was in consequence deposed and imprisoned by a Council convened by H. at Soissons. Rothad thereupon appealed to Pope Nicholas, who summoned H. to appear at Rome in person, and answer to the charges against him. H. sent a legate, but as he still refused to restore the Bishop, the Pope heard the cause over again, acquitted Rothad, and compelled H. to yield. Throughout the remainder of his life the Archbishop exerted almost supreme authority over Church and State in the Western Frankish state, always using his great power in the interests of ecclesiastical liberty. He died at Epernay in 882. The collected works of H. were published by Sirmond (Par. 1645).

Hind, the name given to the female Stag (q. v.), but also to the females of foreign deer, or to the females of various species of Antelopes (q. v.). The young female deer, in ancient forestry, assumed the rank of H. on attaining its third year.

Hind, John Russell, F.R.S., an English astronomer, was born May 12, 1823, at Nottingham, where his father was a lace manufacturer. He early began the study of astronomy, and in 1840, through the influence of Sir Charles Wheatstone, obtained a situation in the Magnetical and Meteorological Department of Greenwich Observatory. In 1843 he was sent to determine the longitude of Valencia, and on his return in 1844 was appointed observer in Mr. G. Bishop's private observatory at Regent's Park. Here he laboured with great assiduity, and discovered nine asteroids—four of them in the latter half of 1852. For this he received the Lalande medal from the Academy of Sciences, Paris, and a prize of 300 francs. H. is editor of the *Nautical Almanac*. He was also awarded the gold medal of the Royal Astronomical Society, and obtained a pension of £200 per annum. His chief works are the *Solar System* (1846), *Expected Return of the Great Comet of* 1264 *and* 1556 (1848), *Astronomical Dictionary* (1852), *Replies to Questions on Comet of* 1556 (1852), *Illustrated London Astronomy* (1853), *Elements of Algebra* (1855), and his *Descriptive Treatise on Comets* (1857).

Hind'ley, a rapidly increasing town of Lancashire, England, 3 miles S.E. of Wigan by railway, carries on cotton-spinning and cotton manufactures, and is surrounded by numerous coal-works. Pop. (1871), 10,627.

Hindu'ism. The religions of India are treated of generally under the heading INDIA; but it will be convenient in this place to give a brief notice of the system of religious faith, ceremonial observance, and social custom, which constitutes the life of the great bulk of the Indian people. According to the general census (1867–72) of British India, excluding the native states, the Hindus proper number 139½ millions, or 73 per cent. of the total population. This classification, being based upon religious as opposed to ethnological principles, excludes not only the Mohammedans and Buddhists, but also the Sikhs and the pure aboriginal tribes. The census also shows that it is in the S. of the peninsula that H. is most prevalent. In Mysore, Madras, and Coorg, the Hindus form more than 90 per cent., diminishing to 86 per cent. in the N.W. Province, 79 per cent. in Bombay, including Scinde, 64 per cent. in Bengal, and only 35 per cent. in the Punjaub. But even among the Hindus thus distinguished, all gradations may be found in the acceptance of the fundamental doctrines of H. These fundamental doctrines may be said to gather round the one central principle of the recognition of the sanctity of the Brahmin caste; and H. in this sense is a convertible term with Brahminism. It is important to observe that H., though now a crystallised system, draws absolutely none of its binding authority from the early Sanskrit books. The Vedas, everywhere recognised as the Hindu Scriptures, nowhere even imply the existence of castes or of a distinct sacerdotal order. Their religion is simply nature-worship of a peculiarly pure type, external phenomena being personified as conscious beings (*devas* = the shining ones). The subsequent growth of caste, the separation of the Brahmins, and the adoption of the modern pantheon, have been plausibly assigned to the circumstance that the original Aryan-speaking race conquered and civilised, but did not thoroughly amalgamate with, the various aboriginal tribes of the peninsula. This circumstance, combined with the necessities of the climate, caused ceremonial purity and social exclusiveness to be regarded as religious duties; while the subject people, as some sort of compensation for their degraded condition, were enabled to impose upon their conquerors the toleration, if not the adoption, of their own indigenous gods, and their barbarous forms of worship. At the present day, the most popular deity throughout India, especially in the S., is not Brahma the creator, nor Vishnu the preserver, but Siva the destroyer, adored in conjunction with his bloody wife Kali. Of the three sects into which modern Hindus are commonly divided, two, the Sivites and the Saktas, are devoted respectively to Siva and his wife, while Brahma has no special following. Similarly, the horrible practices of *Suttee* (q. v.) and of female infanticide, and the extraordinary veneration in which the cow is held, are none of them of ancient date, but comparatively recent excrescences on the primitive system.

With regard to the future of H., it must be recollected that it is not a body of theological dogmas, such as might reasonably be expected to undergo development, but a deeply-rooted system of customary observance, which, in the unchanging East, among a people sunk in the most abject poverty and the densest ignorance, forms the one tie which binds man to man, family to family, and generation to generation. See H. H. Wilson's *Essays on the Religion of the Hindus*, Muir's *Sanskrit Texts*, Lassen's *Indische Alterthumskunde*, and Sherring's *Castes of Benares*.

Hindu' Kush, or **Indian Caucasus** (anc. *Paropamisus*), a lofty range of mountains in the S.W. of Central Asia, separated from the Himalayas by the valley of the Indus. This region is supposed to have been the cradle of the Aryan race. The highest mountain, from which the range takes its name, is Hindu Koh, estimated to exceed 20,000 feet; the highest pass is the Khawak Pass, 13,200 feet. The main geological structure is granite; vegetation is scanty even on the lower slopes. The chief rivers that rise in the range are the Oxus, running N.W. into the Aral Sea, and the Helmund, which flows S.W., and loses itself in the deserts of Persia.

Hindustan' (Pers. 'the land of the Hindus'), a name not uncommonly applied to the whole of the Indian peninsula, but properly limited to that extensive plain which lies between the Himalayas on the N. and the Vindhya mountains on the S., and which is bounded by Bengal proper on the E. and the Punjaub on the W. This is the upper valley of the Ganges, comprising, according to British political divisions, the N.W. Province, Oude, and Behar. Here was the early home of the first Sanskrit-speaking immigrants, and here again was the centre of Mohammedan rule. The language spoken is Hindi, which is also used in the Central Provinces and part of the Punjaub. Concerning this language Professor Wilson states that it is spoken by more than 30,000,000 of people; its grammar is, in the main, that of Hindustani, while nine-tenths of the words are Sanskrit. The Hindustani language proper, which is also called Urdu ('belonging to the camp'), has been formed by an admixture of the original speech of the Mohammedan conquerors with that of the Hindus; about one-third is Arabic or Persian. It is the language of the native army, of domestic servants, and to some extent of the trading classes. As a vernacular, it is only in use in the Mussulman cities of Delhi and parts of Oude and Lucknow, and throughout the Punjaub. It has been called the *lingua franca* of India. See INDIA.

Hinge (from the verb 'to hang'), a joint such as is applied to a door or shutter to enable it to be opened or closed. In ancient times, doors, whether of wood, stone, or metal, were made to turn on projecting vertical pieces at the top and bottom, holes being made to receive them. The Greeks and Romans made hinges resembling a sort now in use. In the British Museum may be seen bronze hinges of Roman manufacture having two straps with projecting divisions of a hollow cylinder which are united by an axial pin. The doors of Solomon's temple were hung on hinges of gold. Modern hinges are chiefly made of iron or brass. They are contrived in a great variety of forms, some involving principles of applied engineering. 'Butts' are commonly used for doors and shutters, one kind of them, called the 'rising butt,' has the hollow cylinder divided helically, and so 'serves the double purpose of a spring to shut the door, and also of a rising hinge,' whereby the carpet or other obstruction may be cleared. 'Double-action spring' hinges allow of a door being opened both ways while it closes of itself. The common ⊢ shaped H. placed on gates and heavy doors is called a 'cross-garnet.'

Hingunghat', a town in the Central Provinces, British India, not far from the Wardha coal branch of the Indian Peninsula Railway; pop. (1872) 9415. It is the emporium of the local trade, especially for raw cotton, of which it exports £120,000 worth in the year. The H. cotton has earned a name in the Bombay market as one of the best indigenous staples, and the seed has been distributed in other parts of India. A model cotton farm was established here in 1868.

Hinn'om, Valley of. See GEHENNA.

Hinn'y, the name given to the hybrid progeny of the stallion and the female ass; the *mule* being the offspring of the male ass and the mare. The H. is an animal usually of smaller size than the mule, its body, as a rule, being also of clumsier form.

Hinojo'sa-del-Du'que, a city of Spain in the province of Cordova, 45 miles N.N.W. of the city of Cordova. It stands in a mountainous region, is an old Moorish town, and is cleanly and well built. H. has some linen and woollen manufactures. Pop. about 8000.

Hiou'en-Thsang, a famous Chinese traveller, born A.D. 603. He became a Buddhist priest, and in his twentieth year began to journey from convent to convent, comparing their respective versions of the Buddhist law. Struck by the discrepancies in these documents, he resolved to journey to India, and there collect the sacred books and consult the Buddhist sages. He set out in 628, and wandered through Dzungaria, Mongolia, and Transoxiana, finally passing by Balkh and Kabul into India. Thence he returned to China by Kashgar and Yarkand, laden with a valuable collection of 657 books relating to the Buddhist creed. He was received with great honour, and the Emperor offered to appoint him Minister, an offer which he declined. After spending his last years in a monastery in translating the works which he had gathered together during his travels, H. died in 664. He wrote a history of Western countries entitled *Ta-Thang Si-yu-ki Chi-oeull-kiouen*, which has been translated into French by M. Stanislas Julien (Par. 1857), and an account of his travels, which was continued by Hoeï-li, the whole work being also translated by M. Stanislas Julien (Par. 1853). These works contain much valuable information, especially as to Hindustan in the 7th c.

Hip, or **Hep**, the fleshy calyx-tube (fruit) of the rose, containing numerous coriaceous or bony achenes (seeds) beset with hairs, which excite itching if applied to the skin. When ripe, and the seeds removed, the scarlet remainder has a sweet, subacid, agreeable taste. Mixed as a pulp with twice its weight of sugar, a confection is formed which is used as a basis for pills and electuaries. Dr. Prior traces the derivation of H. to the middle-age Latin *jujuba*. See also *Ortus Sanitatis*, c. ccxx.

Hip Joint, a large ball-and-socket joint formed by the globular head of the femur being lodged in the cotyloid cavity or acetabulum of the innominate bone. The opposing surfaces are covered by cartilage, the bones are kept in apposition by various ligaments, and the whole of the joint is lined by a delicate membrane, termed a synovial membrane. Movement is allowed in every direction.

Disease of the Hip Joint.—Hip disease may be of an acute, subacute, or chronic inflammatory character, most commonly occurring in strumous subjects, before the age of puberty, the morbid action being generally excited by very slight causes, as over-exertion, a sprain, a fall, or exposure to cold. The hip joint being composed of the soft structures, the acetabulum, and the head of the femur, the diseases thereof may be described as *arthritic*, *acetabular*, and *femoral*; pain, suppuration, dislocation, and anchylosis being more or less common to each variety of the affection. The *arthritic* form may commence in any of the soft structures composing the joint, but most frequently in the cartilage covering the head of the femur, the symptoms being those attending acute inflammation—excruciating local pain *within* the joint, with spasms of the limb, marked by nocturnal exacerbations. The limb is everted, abducted, and motionless. There is usually some fulness about the anterior part or outer side of the joint, and sometimes elongation of the limb, from the capsule being distended with fluid, occasionally terminating in rupture of the capsule, and sudden dislocation of the bone on to the dorsum ilii. In the acute form, recovery may take place with stiffness, partial anchylosis, wasting, and shortening of the limb; but, in the majority of cases, abscesses are formed, resulting in shortening from absorption of the head of the bone, or dislocation out of the acetabulum. In the most favourable cases, a year or two will elapse before the limb can be used freely, and there is generally some stiffness. In the *acetabular* form there is pain *around* the hip, and often abscess in the iliac fossa, eventually passing down under Poupart's ligament, or by the side of the rectum, or through the sciatic notch into the gluteal region. The *femoral* form of hip disease is usually subacute, the prominent symptoms being a limping, shuffling gait with *eversion*, slight *abduction*, the knee being partially bent, and the limb apparently shorter than the other. There is usually pain in the hip, which is increased by pressure, standing, or walking, and also by abduction, rotation of the limb outwards, and particularly by striking the heel or knee. Abscesses, in this form of hip disease, occur under the glutei muscles, sometimes under the pectineus muscle, causing severe pain on the inner side of the thigh; and, at this stage, there is shortening with *adduction* and *inversion*, owing to the alteration in the muscular action. Advance of the disease is attended with fatty degeneration, absorption, or disintegration from the formation of abscesses. The treatment of hip diseases depends upon the form, the acuteness, and the severity of the local and constitutional symptoms. When inflammation has been subdued, absolute rest must be secured—as by the application of the starch bandage. When abscesses form they must be opened early, and when dislocation occurs it must be reduced, as a cure may occur with anchylosis. In certain severe cases there is no hope of cure except by excision of the diseased portions, and such operations have been recently performed with great success under Professor Lister's antiseptic mode of treatment.

Hippar'chus, the first and greatest of Greek astronomers, flourished in the 2d c. B.C. Suidas makes him a native of Bithynia, and gives 160–125 B.C. as the time during which he flourished. Ptolemy adds that he made observations upon the sun and moon at Rhodes. The titles of eleven works attributed to him alone remain, and from these and the statements of later writers, a list of his many and important discoveries is compiled. He drew up a catalogue of stars, discovered the precession of the equinoxes and the motion of the moon's nodes, corrected the length of the year, showed that the sun varied its distance from the earth, and that a longer time elapsed between the spring and autumn equinoxes than between the autumn and spring, and made a wonderfully accurate determination of the distance of the moon. See Delambre's *Historie de l'Astronomie Ancienne* (1817), and Marcoz's *Astronomie Solaire d'Hipparque* (1828).

Hippar'ion, an extinct genus of horses or *Equidæ* (q. v.), which is considered by the evolutionists to represent a progenitor of the existing horse. The remains of the H. are confined to the Upper Miocene and Pliocene periods. It possessed *three* distinctly developed toes, the outer two, however, not touching the ground; while in the existing horse only one toe, the third, is fully developed, and the other two are represented in quite a rudimentary condition by the *splint-bones*. It is curious to note that in another fossil horse, the *Anchitherium*, of older (Upper Eocene and Lower Miocene) age than the H., all three toes touched the ground. The Anchitheriun may therefore be viewed as the parent-stock from which the H. was derived.

Hippocam'pus, a curious genus of Teleostean fishes, including the little forms familiarly known as 'sea-horses,' from the shape of the head. They belong to the order *Lophobranchii* ('tuft-gilled'), in which the gills exist as a series of tufts on the branchial arches, while the bones of the head are consolidated, and the scales are of the *ganoid* variety, the skeleton being cartilaginous. The sea-horses have long flexible tails, which they coil round fixed objects; and both rest and swim in an upright position, chiefly by means of the little dorsal fins. They are common in the English Channel, and may be found in large aquaria. One of the most curious features in their life history is the possession by the *male* H. of a ventral 'pouch,' in which the young are hatched and protected.

Hipp'ocras, a spiced wine, used medicinally, so called from Hippocrates, the celebrated physician. It was highly prized in the 14th and 15th centuries, when the then rare spices grains of paradise, cinnamon, and ginger were employed as flavouring ingredients.

Hippoc'rates, the most famous physician of antiquity, born in the island of Cos, about 460 B.C., was the son of Heraclides, an Asclepiad, and Phaenarete, a Heraclid. After being instructed in medicine by his father and by Herodicus, and having practised in his native island, he travelled through various parts of Hellas, and died at Larissa, in Thessaly, about 357. These meagre facts are supplemented with a vast mass of fable. There are few ancient writers about whom so much has been written as H. Of the writings, more than sixty in number, which have come down to us under his name, only a few are held genuine—viz., *Prognōstikon; Aphorismoi; Epidēmiōn Biblia; Peri Diaitēs Oxeōn; Peri Aerōn, Hydatōn, Topōn; Peri tōn en Kephalē Trōmatōn*. Most of the others are believed to have been written by his followers. There were also many commentaries on his writings by ancient physicians, the most important being that of Galen. H. divided the causes of disease into two great classes, the one comprising the variations of climate and situation, and the other different kinds and quantities of food taken by individuals. He argued from natural analogy that heat and cold, moisture and dryness, succeeded one another in the body throughout the year. His 'Humoral Pathology' recognised four humours (blood, phlegm, black and yellow bile), in which diseases first settled, and the crasis or due blending of which was health. A patient recovering experienced certain changes in his humour called *coctions*, which were followed by a *crisis* or expulsion of the morbid matter occurring at definite periods, called 'critical days.' His treatment was cautious, attending chiefly to diet, and watching the operations of nature. The apophthegms interspersed through his writings are terse and telling; but his works themselves carry conciseness to obscurity. The best editions of his entire writings are those of C. G. Kühn (3 vols. Leips. 1825–27), and of Littré, with a French translation (10 vols. Par. 1839–61). See also Dr. Adams' English translation of *The Genuine Works of Hippocrates* (2 vols. 1849).

Hipp'ocrene (Gr. *hippos*, 'a horse,' and *krēnē*, 'a spring'), a fountain on Mount Helicon, in Bœotia, which the winged horse Pegasus (q. v.) was said to have struck forth with his hoof. Sacred to Apollo and the Muses, it bestowed the gift of song on all who drank of its waters. H. has been identified with a spring at Makariotissa.

Hippodami'a, in Greek mythology, a daughter of Œnomaus, king of Pisa in Elis, and the Pleiad Sterope. An oracle had foretold Œnomaus' death to be connected with his daughter's marriage, and he therefore proclaimed that none should wed her unless he had first vanquished himself in a chariot race, while all who lost should be put to death. Many tried and failed, till Pelops, by bribing Myrtilus, Œnomaus' charioteer, to take out the linchpins of the king's wheels, won the race. Œnomaus killed himself, and Pelops thus obtained both his kingdom and daughter. For the sequel of the myth see PELOPS.

Hipp'odrome (Gr. *hippos*, 'a horse,' and *dromos*, 'a course'), the Greek term for a racecourse, corresponding to the Latin Circus (q. v.). There seems to have been little difference between the two, except in point of width, the Romans allowing only four chariots to start at once, while with the Greeks the number was unlimited. In the centre of the course stood two pillars (*stēlai*), 400 yards apart, one forming the starting, and the other the turning post, the chariots having to make the circuit twelve times. In the *At Meidan* (Turk. 'horse place') at Constantinople we have a fine specimen of an ancient H. Constructed by Severus and adorned by Constantine, it was originally 800 yards long and 200 wide, but has been greatly encroached on by modern buildings. The Byzantine hippodromes long outlived the Roman circi, and under Justinian (A.D. 501) we find two factions—the Blues or Venetians, and the Greens—which, originating in the H., carried their feud into public and private affairs, and in 532 were the cause of party fights in which 30,000 persons perished. These parties ended only with the Byzantine Empire, though the H. itself does not appear to have been used after 1204. H. is now applied, like circus, to any exhibition of horsemanship.

Hipp'ogriff (Gr. *hippos*, 'a horse,' and *gryps*, 'a griffin'), a fabulous monster, half horse half griffin, frequently alluded to by the poets, *e.g.*, by Milton in *Paradise Regained*, books iv. v.

Hippol'ytus, a bishop of Portus in the 3d c., was a disciple of Irenæus. It is supposed that he was banished to Sardinia A.D. 235, and on returning the next year was martyred at Ostia. A book of great value as a source of information regarding the early Christian Church, professing as it does to refute thirty-two heresies, although it deals chiefly with Gnosticism, was brought from Mount Athos in 1842, and being regarded as the work of Origen, was published in 1851 under the title of *Originous Philosophoumena ē kata Pasōn Haireseōn Elegchos*. But on the back of a statue of H. which was dug up on the site of his chapel, in the year 1551, there was found a list of his works, including a book *Peri tou Pantos*, a book which is claimed by the author of the above work. The *Elegchos* is therefore, on this and other grounds, ascribed now to H. Most of his other works have either perished or only exist now in fragments. See Bunsen's *H. and his Age* (1852); Döllinger's *Hippolytus und Kallistus* (1853); Wordsworth's *St. Hippolytus* (1853); Volkmar's *Hippolytus und die Röm. Zeitgenossen* (1855).

Hippoph'agi (Gr. 'horse-eaters,' from *hippos*, 'a horse,' and *phagein*, 'to eat'), a title bestowed by the Greeks on two tribes—the H. Sarmatæ (Slavs) and the H. Scythæ (Ugrians)—who dwelt to the N.E. of the Caspian. The nomad Mongols of those parts still use horse-flesh and fermented mare's milk as articles of diet.

Hippopot'amus (Gr. *hippos*, 'a horse,' and *potamos*, 'a river'), a genus of *Ungulate* mammals represented by a single species, the *H. amphibius*, or 'river-horse' of S. African rivers. It forms the type of a special family, which has been constituted for its reception, and which is distinguished by having four hoofed toes on each foot—the animal thus belonging to the *Artiodactyle* or 'even-toed' group of Ungulata. The head is large, and the body massive and clumsy; the average length 11 or 12 feet. The muzzle is very broad; the eyes and ears are of small size, and the skin of very thick texture, and but sparsely covered with hairs. The teeth are represented by four incisors, two canines, and twelve or fourteen molars in each jaw, the crowns of the latter teeth being very broad, and adapted for grinding vegetable matters, such as roots and grasses, on which the animal feeds. The upper canines are of small size, but

Hippopotamus.

their lower neighbours attain a very great size, and project in the form of unshapely tusks from the jaw—these lower canines having chisel-shaped edges. The H. very nearly approaches the Elephant (q. v.) in its bulk and strength, and appears, on the whole, to be comparatively inoffensive, but attacks its enemies with great fury when roused or irritated. Various African explorers have remarked its habit of suddenly rising from the depths of some pool or river in which it had been taking its *siesta* during the heat of the day, and overturning canoes and other river-craft. A male H. and his mate have lived for some years in the gardens of the Zoological Society of London. These animals have bred in captivity; one specimen, appropriately named 'Guy Fawkes,' because born on November 5, died at an early period of its existence. The H., as seen in captivity, immerses itself in its water tank, leaving only the nostrils above water, and remains in its bath for extended periods. The prevailing colour is a dark-brown, which appears to assume a greyer tint with age. In habits, the H. is gregarious, and roams about in bands of from twenty to thirty. It is captured by pitfalls, and is also killed by means of an apparatus consisting of a poisoned spear driven into a heavy log of wood which falls down upon the neck of the animal, through the cord which attaches the log being broken by the animal's passage. The H. may also be harpooned in its native rivers, and is thereafter chased until it succumbs to the hunters. The Dutch name of the H. is the 'zee-koe,' 'lake' or 'sea cow.' The flesh is valued for its delicacy, and the fat is also utilised, while the hide makes a thick and valuable leather, and the teeth afford ivory. A second species (*Chœropsis Liberiensis*), said to differ from the common H. in possessing only two lower incisors, inhabits W. Africa.

Fossil species of H. occur in Tertiary deposits, the most familiar extinct form being the *H. major* of Pliocene and Pleistocene formations, found in Britain and over S. Europe. Fossil species of H., belonging to the genus *Hexaprotodon* (possessing six molars in each jaw), occur in the Miocene deposits of the Siwalik Hills of India.

Hippu'ric Acid occurs in considerable quantity in the urine of herbivorous animals, and was first obtained by Rowelli from the urine of the cow and camel. It is also present, though in minute quantity, in the human urine, its amount increasing in certain diseases, such as chorea, diabetes, &c. To prepare it, fresh cows' urine is evaporated to a sixth of its volume and mixed with excess of hydrochloric acid. A dense crystalline precipitate of impure H. A. results, which may be purified by boiling with milk of lime, filtering, precipitating the solution with carbonate of potash, again filtering, and finally precipitating with excess of hydrochloric acid. H. A. is a colourless substance, which crystallises in long needles. It is very slightly soluble in cold water, but more readily in boiling water and alcohol. It is insoluble in ether. Its solution reddens litmus, and it unites with bases to form salts. When its solution is boiled for some time with dilute acid, H. A. takes up the elements of water and is decomposed, yielding Benzoic Acid (q. v.) and Glycocoll.

$$\underbrace{C_9N_9NO_3}_{\text{Hippuric acid.}} + \underbrace{H_2O}_{\text{Water.}} = \underbrace{C_2H_5NO_2}_{\text{Glycocoll.}} + \underbrace{C_7H_6O_2}_{\text{Benzoic acid.}}$$

This change takes place in cows' urine when it putrifies, and is employed practically in the manufacture of benzoic acid. Conversely, if benzoic acid be swallowed, it is excreted as H. A. H. A. has been prepared artificially by heating the silver salt of glycocoll (prepared from acetic acid) with chloride of benzoyl (prepared from benzoic acid).

$$\underbrace{C_2H_4AgNO_2}_{\text{Glycocoll silver.}} + \underbrace{C_7H_5Cl}_{\text{Chloride of benzoyl.}} = \underbrace{C_9H_9NO_3}_{\text{Hippuric acid.}} + \underbrace{AgCl}_{\text{Chloride of silver.}}$$

Hippu'ris, a genus of aquatic plants, belonging to the natural order *Haloragaceæ*. *H. vulgaris* is the common mare's tail which is abundant in Britain, and also occurs in N. America. It is one of the plants that grow in the hot water proceeding from the geysers in Iceland. In France the plant is called *Pesse d'Cau*, and in Germany *Schafthalm*.

Hippuri'tes, a fossil genus of shells, the exact zoological position of which was for long a matter of doubt, but which appears to be rightly included in the class *Lamellibranchiata*, represented by the oysters, cockles, &c. The difficulty of deciding as to the nature of these shells arose from the peculiar shape of these structures. The shell is inversely conical, and may attain a length of 12 inches or more. It was attached, like the familiar oysters, to the sea-bed by the larger conical valve, and was closed by a smaller and free valve with a central *umbo* or 'beak.' Dr. S. P. Woodward says that these 'shells are the most problematical of all fossils; there are no recent shells which can be supposed to belong to the same family, and the condition in which they usually occur has involved them in greater obscurity.' The H. are confined to the Cretaceous or Chalk rocks, and occur in Britain, S. Europe, N. America, W. Indies, Egypt, and Algeria. *H. Toucasiana* is a familiar species.

Hi'ring is a contract by which one engages the service or property of another for recompense. The term is never applied to any contract for the use of money. You *borrow* five shillings, and you *borrow* a thousand pounds at such a rate of interest. (See BORROWING.) The chief legal questions which occur between parties under contracts of H. are connected with loss of the subject or damage done to it. The leading principle of the law is that the hire covers ordinary wear and accidental loss or damage, unless these are caused by the fault of the hirer. Very nice legal questions however arise. Suppose a man engaged to do a piece of work for a given sum, and does it very badly, is he entitled to be paid? This would clearly depend on circumstances. The fault might lie with whoever engaged him having selected an incompetent man, or it might lie in the man having misrepresented his qualifications. An important question is, should the hirer be called on to show that he used due care, or the owner to prove want of due care on the part of the hirer? According to English law the *Onus Probandi* (q. v.) lies on the owner; according to Scotch law it lies on the hirer.

Hirsch'berg, a town in the province of Silesia, Prussia, on the Bober, 65 miles W.S.W. of Breslau by rail. It is beautifully situated at the base of the Riesengebirge, has a large Gothic church (Protestant), and is encircled by double walls. H. is the centre of the Silesian linen trade. Pop. (1875) 12,970, of whom more than half are Protestants.

Hispan'ia, the Latin, as **Ibe'ria** was the Greek, title for the south-western peninsula, now divided into Spain and Portugal. The name H. was derived by Bochart from the Phœnician *sapan* or *span*, 'a rabbit;' but W. von Humboldt's derivation from the Basque *españa*, 'a border' is preferable. Iberia, on the other hand, is thought to contain the same root as Aryan (q. v.). Who the earliest inhabitants of H. were—whether Celts or Basques—is still a disputed question, the answer to which must be found in an investigation of the ancient names occurring in Ptolemy, Strabo, Pliny, and other writers. An analysis of these seems to indicate that the Celts were the conquering, the Basques the conquered race. Thus, as a rule, the Celtic names are those of towns or fortresses, the termination *briga* being especially prominent; while the Basque are characteristic of natural objects—*e.g.*, in *Asturia* we recognise the Euskarian *asta*, 'rock,' and *uria*, 'water.' Against this theory, however, must be set the names Durius (Celt. *duor*, 'water') and Vinnius (Celt. *pen*, 'head'). The Phœnicians were early acquainted with H., where they seem to have exercised a great civilising influence as founders of trading cities on or near the coast. The names Gadeira (Cadiz), Asido (Medina Sidonia), and Carthagena are identical with the Tyrian or Carthaginian Geder (*gadir*, 'an enclosure'), Sidon, and Carthage; and similarly Malaga, Seville, Lisbon, Tarragona, Cordova, &c., all point to a Phœnician origin. (See HAMILCAR, HASDRUBAL, and HANNIBAL.) The conquest of H. by Rome, commenced by Scipio Africanus Major (q. v.), was almost complete in B.C. 171. The constant presence of Roman armies necessarily exercised an important influence on the language and customs of the natives, and the fusion of the Iberian and Roman races was greatly accelerated by the foundation under Augustus of many important colonies, *e.g.*, *Cæsar Augusta* (Zaragoza), *Pax Augusta* (Badajoz), and others. The modern name Portugal is also Latin, being a corruption of *Pax Julia*. The history of the conquest of H. (409) by the barbarians is given under SPAIN. See W. von Humboldt's *Prüfung der Untersuchungen über die Urbewohner Hispaniens* (Berl. 1821).

Hispanio'la ('little Spain'), the name given by the Spaniards to the island of Hayti (q. v.).

Hissar' ('citadel'), the chief town of the district of the same name, province of the Punjaub, British India, on the western Jumna Canal, 102 miles W. of Delhi; pop. (1868) 14,133. It was founded in 1352 by the Emperor Feroz Shah, for a hunting residence, and was supplied with water from his canal. A large area is still covered with ruined tombs and broken bricks. In the neighbourhood is a large Government farm for breeding cattle.—The *district* of H., which is almost entirely shut in by the native states of Bikanîr and Puttealah, has an area of 3539 sq. miles; pop. (1868) 484,681. The soil is a sandy desert, except where watered by the canal; it suffered severely in the famine of 1868-69. The crops are millet, gram, wheat, cotton, and coriander. The trade centres in the town of Bhawani, and chiefly consists of cotton and cotton goods, sugar, brassware, and salt.

Histol'ogy. See ANATOMY.

Hit, a town in the vilayet of Bagdad, Asiatic Turkey, 90 miles W.N.W. of Bagdad, on the right bank of the Euphrates. It is noted for its bitumen and naphtha springs, which yielded material for building Babylon. H. is the *Is* of Herodotus. Pop. 2000.

Hitch'cock, Edward, D.D., LL.D., an American geologist, born at Deerfield, Massachusetts, May 24, 1793. He became Principal of Deerfield Academy in 1815, Congregational pastor at Conway in 1821, and President of Amherst College in 1845, with the chair of geology. Under his care this school made most satisfactory progress. As the state geologist, a position he was appointed to in 1830, he made an entire geological survey of Massachusetts, the first attempt of the kind in any country. He was also for a time geologist for a district of New York State and of Vermont. In 1850 he was commissioned by the Government of Massachusetts to examine the agricultural schools in Europe, and he afterwards published a valuable report. He was the first President of the American Geological Association. H. died 27th February 1864. Among his works, which extend to more than 20 volumes, are *Geology of the Connecticut Valley* (1823), *Reports on the Geology of the State of Massachusetts* (1831-42), *Ichnology of New England* (1840, supp. 1865), *Fossil Footmarks in the United States* (1848), *Elementary Geology* (1840, enlarged 1854), *Religion of Geology* (1851), the last two the most popular of his writings, and *Reminiscences of Amherst College* (1863).

Hitch'in, a town of Hertfordshire, England, 14 miles N.W. of Hertford, on the river Hiz, and a station on the Great Northern Railway. It has large breweries, and carries on a trade in corn, malt, and flour. Straw-plaiting gives employment to a considerable number of females. Pop. (1871) 7630.

Hit'eren, an island on the coast of Norway, 47 miles W. of Trondhjem, and 28 miles long. Area, 220 sq. miles. Pop. 2300, living on the shores and subsisting by fishing.

Hitopade'sa (from Sansk. *hita*, 'good,' and *upadesa*, 'advice'), is the name of a famous Sanskrit collection of fables which is highly valued by the Hindus for its ethical instruction. It forms part of a larger work—the *Pantschatantra* (q. v.). The stories in one shape or another have found their way into nearly every national literature in Asia and Europe. The H. has been edited by Johnson (2d ed. 1864) and by M. Müller (1865).

Hitt'ites, or descendants of Heth, the second son of Canaan (Gen. x. 15), inhabited the southern part of the land of Canaan, and seem to have been one of the most important of its tribes. In the time of Abraham they were settled in Hebron and its neighbourhood (Gen. xxiii.). They are mentioned in almost all the lists of the Canaanitish tribes; sometimes the Canaanites, H., and Amorites (or Hivites), or the H. and Amorites stand for the whole; and in one passage (Josh. i. 4; *cf.* Deut. xi. 23, 24) the H. alone. In later times they were found in the N. of Palestine, under a confederacy of petty kings, who were conquered by the Egyptian king Seti I. (about 1340 B.C.), and their town of Kadesh (Edessa, mod. *Hums*), situated on an island in the Orontes, taken. At a still later period they imported horses and chariots from Egypt (1 Kings x. 29), by which they became a terror to their neighbours (2 Kings vii. 6). Although there is no mention of their deity in connection with Solomon's wives (1 Kings xi. 1), it appears from the Egyptian monuments that the H., like the Hyk-shos, worshipped the god Seti or Seth, known to the Egyptians as Tiphon. The local goddess of Kadesh was Anata or Anaitis, the Bellona or Canaanitish goddess of war.

Hitz'ig, Ferdinand, a distinguished German exegete and critic of the Old Testament, was born 23d June 1807, at Hauingen in Baden, studied at Heidelberg, at Halle (under Gesenius), and at Göttingen, where he graduated and became a lecturer in the university. In 1833 he was called to Zürich, which he left in 1861 for Heidelberg; and there he laboured till his death, 22d January 1875. His lectures covered the whole ground of Old Testament study and the Semitic tongue, nor was he a stranger in New Testament criticism. Free from dogmatic prejudice, H. may be reckoned among the historico-critical rationalists. But he surpassed all his compeers in the acuteness, boldness, and ingenuity of his hypotheses. His *Begriff der Kritik am A. T.* and his *Übersetzung und Auslegung des Propheten Josaias* (Heid. 1833) founded H.'s fame. The latter work was followed by commentaries on the Psalms, the twelve minor prophets, Jeremiah, Ezekiel, and Daniel, the Song of Solomon, Proverbs, and (in 1874) Job. Among other works are the *Urgeschichte und Mythologie der Philistäer* (1846), *Johannes Marcus und Seine Schriften* (1843), and the *Geschichte der Volkes Israel* (1869).

Hivao'a, the island of the Marquesas, in the S. Pacific, about lat. 10° S. and long. 139° W. It is traversed by a mountain range that attains a height of 4200 feet. The inhabitants, 6500 in number, are amongst the wildest Polynesians, and have remained unaffected by various Catholic and Protestant missions.

Hiv'ites (Heb. 'midlanders' or 'villagers'), a tribe of Canaanites mentioned in the history of Jacob as occupying territory near the centre of Palestine (Gen. xxxiv. 2), where they were also in the time of Joshua (Josh. ix.). The main body, however, seems to have been in the N., at the foot of Hermon and Lebanon (Josh. xi. 3; Judges iii. 3; *cf.* 2 Sam. xxiv. 7). But as they were not one of the most important tribes, they seem sometimes to be included under the Amorites.

H'Lass'a, or simply **Lass'a**, the capital of Tibet, on the N. side of the Himalayas, in a mountainous region, 11,700 feet above the sea. It lies on the right bank of the Kichu Sangpo, an affluent of the Brahmaputra, 40 miles N.E. of Palti Lake. Here is the Buddha-la, or hill of Buddha, the residence of the Dalai-lama, hierarch of Buddhism throughout Mongolia. A fine road leads from the town to the hill, which is covered with splendid temples and palaces, burdened by a wealth of ornamental gold and jewels. H'.L. is visited by thousands of pilgrims, many of whom stay to complete theological and other studies, and all of whom bring presents for the Dalai-lama. There is a large trade in gold, velvet, silk, cashmere, and precious stones. Pop. estimated at 50,000. H'L., from which foreigners are excluded, was visited by Captain Montgomerie in 1866.

Hlodowig, or **Chlodowig** (Lat. *Clovis* and *Chlodovechus*, whence *Ludovicus*. H. is the same name as the German *Ludwig* and the modern French *Louis*), son of Childeric, king of the Salian Franks, who in the 5th c. occupied the region of the Lower Rhine, began to rule in 481, when he was about fifteen years of age. In 486 he fell upon Northern Gaul, overthrew Syagrius, the nominal representative of Rome, and shortly afterwards married Hlotehild (Fr. Clotilde), a Christian, daughter of a Burgundian chief. After his victory over the Allemans at Tolbiac in 496, H. was baptised in Rheims, and after forcing Gondebald, king of the Burgundians, to own himself his 'man,' in 507 he broke the Visigothic power in the S. of Gaul, where his barbarity stirred up the bitter enmity which the S. long bore for the N. of France. Shortly afterwards Anastasius, emperor of the East, sent him the title of *Consul Romanus*, and in 511 he died. H. was a bloodthirsty, treacherous savage, with a great deal of coarse energy and dogged ambition. He loaded the clergy with gifts, and had an important influence on the rise of the Church militant. See Kitchin's *History of France* (vol. i. 1873).

Hoad'ley, Benjamin, D.D., an English prelate, was born at Westerham, Kent, November 14, 1676, and educated at Norwich and Cambridge. In 1701 he became lecturer at St. Mildred's-in-the-Poultry, London, and in 1704 obtained the rectory of St. Peter-le-Poor. H. early displayed great controversial ability, and soon became the acknowledged champion of Whig or Low Church principles, his most famous disputes being with Calamy on the reasonableness of conformity, and with Atterbury on non-resistance. Though much opposed by the clergy, his views were popular, and applauded by Parliament, and Mrs. Howland, a sympathetic admirer, presented him to the living of Streatham. In 1715, on the accession of George I., he became Bishop of Bangor, but never visited his diocese. A sermon preached by him in 1717 on the text 'My kingdom is not of this world,' contending that the Church could claim no civil power, provoked the celebrated Bangorian controversy, in which he was opposed by Sherlock, Hare, Law, &c. From Bangor he was transferred to Hereford in 1721, to Salisbury in 1723, and to Winchester in 1734, where he died, April 17, 1761. His works were published in 3 vols. fol. in 1773.

Hoang-ho ('yellow river'), a great river of China, rises in Lake Ala-nor, in Tibet, flows first in a north-easterly direction through part of Mongolia, then S., passing the Great Wall, and forming the boundary between Shen-si and Shan-si, and finally W. and N.W. traversing Ho-nan and Shan-tung, and entering the Gulf of Pe-chi-li. It is rapid and tortuous, and in its lower course scarcely navigable. Its name is derived from the yellow clay it deposits along its banks and at its mouth. Its chief affluent is the Wei-ho, and the principal towns it passes are Lan-chu and Kai-fung. In its lower course the bed of the H. often lies above the level of the surrounding country, and one of the most fertile provinces in the empire is protected from inundation by embankments and canals maintained at a cost of 7,000,000 dollars yearly. The H., which has a length of about 2400 miles, entered the Yellow Sea some 300 miles further S. till 1853, when it broke into its new course.

Hoarfrost. See DEW.

Hoarse'ness. See THROAT, DISEASES OF.

Ho'bart Town, the capital of Tasmania, is beautifully situated at the foot of Mount Wellington (4166 feet), on the river Derwent, The harbour is of the first rank, capable of accommodating ships of any tonnage. The town is laid out in the form of a square, and the streets are wide, straight, and lighted with gas. The public buildings are numerous and handsome, the chief being the governor's residence, houses of parliament, and townhall. There are also Anglican and Roman Catholic cathedrals, and thirty-one other places of worship. The city likewise contains sixty-two private, seven public, and three ragged schools. Brewing, jam-making for export, and shipbuilding, are the chief industries of H. T., which carries on an extensive trade with the neighbouring colonies (principally with Victoria) and with the mother country. A line of railway connects it with Launceston on the N. side of the island. H. T. is a favourite health resort of the wealthy citizens of Melbourne, Sydney, and Adelaide during the summer months. Pop. 19,000.

Hobb'ema, Minderhout, a well-known Dutch landscape painter of the 17th c. Except that he was a contemporary of Berghem, Lingelbach, and J. van Loo, who executed the figures in H.'s landscapes, we know nothing of his life, though, from a similarity of styles, it has been conjectured that he was a pupil of Ruysdael. His pictures, mostly forests with ruins, are scattered over the galleries of Vienna, Berlin, &c.

Hobbes', Thomas, an influential English thinker, the son of a Protestant clergyman, was born at Malmesbury, 5th April 1588. After study at Oxford, and travel in Europe as a tutor, he became secretary to Bacon, and through his patron, Lord Devonshire, made the friendship of Ben Jonson and Herbert of Cherbury. In 1628 appeared his translation of *Thucydides*, meant to prevent the Civil War. After repeated visits to the Continent, in which he met Mersenne and Galileo, he in 1642 published *Elementa Philosophica de Cive*. On the breaking out of Civil War he withdrew to France, where he corresponded with Descartes and Gassendi, and composed his *Human Nature*, his *De Corpore Politico*, and the *Leviathan* (1651), which cost him his post of mathematical tutor to Charles II., who, while bending to the clamour of the Church against H.'s supposed atheism, treated H. with great kindness, and gave him a pension. Returning to England in 1652, he wrote his famous *Letter on Liberty and Necessity*, which called forth the eloquence of Bishop Bramhall. H. was also engaged in a mathematical controversy with Wallis. While the House of Commons passed a censure on his books, Cosmo de Medici and many other great foreigners came to visit H. and to do him honour. After his eighty-fifth year this wonderful old man wrote his life in Latin verse, and published translations of the *Iliad* and the *Odyssey*. His *Behemoth, or History of the Civil War from* 1640 *to* 1660, was not published till after his death, which took place 4th December 1679. H. was a man of singularly quiet and simple life. Dr. Kennet in his *Memoirs of the Cavendishes* relates how he took exercise in the morning, and retired after dinner to his study, 'where ten or twelve pipes of tobacco were laid out for him.' His converse with great persons never spoiled his native independence of character. He has no equal in English literature for boldness and originality of speculation, or for absolute lucidity of expression. He first discussed government on grounds of reason, and started the fiction of an original contract, creating the Leviathan or Commonwealth for mutual protection and defence. But in destroying the religious and patriarchal theories of society, he laid the basis for despotism, by transferring all rights from the subject to the monarch, except that of self-preservation. Power came from the people, and was given for the people's good, but H. did not recognise a right of resistance, the responsibility of princes, or the supremacy of representative assemblies. The first part of the *Leviathan*, 'On Man,' contains a powerful analysis of the simple and complex passions. The standard of public and private interest is enlightened self-interest; all feelings are self-regarding; the power of the state and the perception of public utility are the real sanctions of conscience. To this we add religion; for H. (himself a sceptic) declared faith in Christ and obedience to the state to be necessary to salvation. In morals H. was answered by Cumberland, Clarke, and Wollaston. A magnificent edition of his works in 11 vols. was published by Sir William Molesworth in 1842-45.

Hobb'y (*Falco subbuteo*), a species of *Falconidæ* or Falcons (q. v.), occurring throughout Europe, and also in Asia and Africa. It is of a slate-grey colour on the upper parts, the feathers exhibiting yellowish-white edges, and the under parts being of lighter tints than the upper. The average length is from 11 to 13 inches. The H. is by no means a common British bird. It was used by the falconer to bring down smaller game.

Hob'oken, a city of New Jersey, on the river Hudson, adjoining Jersey City, was founded by the Dutch in the 17th c. Lying opposite New York, it was formerly a favourite place of residence for the merchants of that city. H. is the terminus of four lines of European steamers, and of the Morris and Esser, the Delaware, Lackawanna, and Western Railways. It supplies New York with coal, has large foundries, and manufactures machinery and lead-pencils. H. contains several good schools, including the Stevens' Institute of Technology, which has eight professors, and the Martha Institute. Pop. (1870) 20,297.

Hoche, Lazare, a great French general, born at Montreuil, 25th June 1768, was at first a stable-boy, then joined the army, and when the Revolution came had risen to the rank of sergeant. He soon got a lieutenant's commission, and served at Thionville and Neerwinde under Dumouriez. Carnot saw his ability, and sent him as brigadier-general to Dunkirk, invested by the Duke of York, where his success gained for him the command of the army of the Moselle. Here, however, Brunswick kept the line of the Vosges, until H. effected a junction with Pichegru on the Rhine, when the Austrians evacuated Alsace. In 1794 he was called to the command of the army of the W. He showed great skill, patriotism, and humanity in dealing with the fanatical Chouans, who maintained a guerilla war in a difficult country. He crushed the Quiberon expedition of Charette, and disapproved of the *noyades* and other excesses by which the republican cause was disgraced. After taking part in the abortive descent on Bantry Bay, the brave soldier at the head of the army of the Sambre and Meuse made a brilliant dash across the Rhine to Giessen, where the articles of Leoben stopped him. After the *coup d'etat* of Fructidor, for which H. had offered Barras and the majority of the Directory the use of his army, in spite of the rage of the *Clichien* party, he succeeded Moreau in the command of the army of Germany. H.'s military talent and sincere republicanism might have altered the whole history of France, but he died suddenly, probably by poison, on 8th September 1797. He received a magnificent funeral. See the biographies of H. by Privat (1798), Rousselin (1798), and Dourille (1844).

Hoch'heim, a town in the province of Hessen-Nassau, Prussia, on the banks of the Main, 3 miles W. of Mainz by rail. It has given name to a superior class of Hock wines. Pop. 2494.

Hoch'kirch, a village in the kingdom of Saxony, 7 miles S.E. of Bautzen, notable as the scene of one of the battles in the Seven Years' War, in which Friedrich the Great was completely routed by the Austrians under Daun, October 14, 1758.

Hoch'städt, a town of Bavaria, on the Danube, where took place the 'battle of Blenheim' (q. v.), so called by the English from a neighbouring village, the scene of a decisive incident in the fight.

Hodg'kinson, Eaton, a distinguished engineer, was born at Anderton, near Norwich, Cheshire, February 26, 1789. When twenty-one years of age he settled in Manchester, and there begun the study of mechanics. He became Professor of Mechanical Engineering in the University College, London, in 1847. Six years earlier he had been elected a Fellow of the Royal Society, when he received the royal gold medal for his *Experimental Researches on the Strength of Pillars of Cast-iron and of other Materials.* These were carried on at the expense of Sir W. Fairbairn (q. v.) of Manchester, with whom he also co-operated in determining, experimentally and theoretically, the best form and proportions of the Britannia Tubular Bridge (q. v.). His valuable investigations on the strength of materials and the resistance of structures to stresses of all kinds were published in the *Transactions* of the British Association, in the *Philosophical Transactions*, and in the *Manchester Transactions.* H. died, June 1861, at Broughton, near Manchester.

Ho'dograph of a moving particle is the curve passing through the extremity of those lines which, drawn from a fixed point as origin, represent in direction and magnitude the velocities of the particle at the different points of its path. The H. of a projectile moving in a parabola is evidently a vertical straight line, since the horizontal component of the velocity at every point is constant. Again, the H. of a point moving uniformly in a circle is another circle whose centre is the origin from which the velocities were laid down. The H. of a planet is a circle which is, however, placed excentrically with respect to the origin. The method of construction of this curve shows that, just as the tangent at any point of an orbit gives the direction in which the particle is moving, so the tangent to the H. gives the direction of acceleration. This curve was invented by Sir W. R. Hamilton; and its application to planetary motion has resulted in most simple and elegant geometrical constructions. See Hamilton's *Quaternions*, Thomson and Tait's *Natural Philosophy*, Tait and Steele's *Dynamics of a Particle*, and Clerk Maxwell's *Matter and Motion.*

Hodom'eter is an instrument which, by an arrangement of toothed wheels connected with the axle of a vehicle, registers the number of revolutions which the wheel makes, and thus affords data for the calculation of the distance traversed.

Hod'son, Major William, one of the leading characters of the Indian Mutiny. In the early years of his service in India, he had been selected for civil employment under the Lawrences in the Punjaub. The outbreak of the Mutiny in May 1857 revealed his peculiar qualities. He was immediately appointed to the staff, and was intrusted with the raising of a new regiment of irregular cavalry—'Hodson's Horse.' Through the siege of Delhi he performed admirable service as chief of the intelligence department, which brought him into close communication with the rebel royal family. On the capture of the city, he received orders to bring in *alive* the last of the Mogul Emperors, who had taken refuge in the tomb of Humayun, outside the walls. This he safely effected, and then went to fetch the Shahzadas, or royal princes. They also surrendered to him; but on the way to the city he ordered his prisoners to strip themselves of their jewels, &c., and then he shot them dead with his own hand. The general wrote, 'H., as a partisan officer, has not his equal.' A few months afterwards H. was himself killed in the final storming of the Kaisar Bagh, the royal palace at Lucknow. See *Life of Major William H.* by his brother, and Sir J. W. Kaye's *History of the Sepoy War.*

Hoe, a simple tool used in gardening and agriculture for freeing the ground from weeds, stirring up earth, thinning drilled seedlings, and other like operations. In gardening two varieties of H. are used: (1) the Dutch H., which has a flat cutting blade attached to its long handle in the same plane, and is worked by pushing only, for under-cutting weeds and dressing walks; and (2) the common or draw H. which has its blade fastened at a right angle to the handle. The chief use of this kind of H. is in cleaning drilled crops, and thinning or hoeing drilled seedlings, as in the case of turnips; but it is also found to be a useful implement in many other agricultural operations. A horse-H. is a machine having a series of H. blades mounted upon it, which is used for cleaning and tilling between drills. Special forms of hoes for use on sugar and cotton plantations are extensively manufactured at Birmingham.

Hoe'ven, Jan van der, a Dutch naturalist, was born February 9, 1801, at Rotterdam. He studied medicine at Leyden, where he became Professor of Zoology in 1835. He is the author of several important works and numerous memoirs; but his greatest is *Handbock der Dierkunde* (2 vols. 1827–33, 2d ed. 1846).—His elder brother, **Cornelis Pruys van der H.,** is a medical professor at Leyden and the author of several historical medical works.

Hof, a town of Bavaria, in Upper Franconia, on the Saale, 40 miles N.E. of Bayreuth by rail. It has manufactures of woollens, cottons, hosiery, beer, and iron wares, and an active transit trade. It was partly destroyed by fire in 1823. Pop. (1875) 18,267.

Ho'fer, Andreas, the Tyrolese patriot, was born November 22, 1767, at St. Leonard's, in the valley of Passey, where his father was an innkeeper. H. succeeded to his father's business, combining with it wine-selling and horse-dealing, until the wars of the first Napoleon gave him the opportunity of obtaining distinction. The courage and boldness of H. made him leader among his compatriots, and under his command the Tyrolese took an honourable part in the wars of Austria against the French. Shortly before the battle of Wagram, a formidable insurrection against the French Emperor was raised in the Tyrol at the instance of the Archduke Johann of Austria, and of this H. became the ruling spirit. Such was his success, that in the three days, April 11 to April 13, 1809, the province was completely cleared of the enemy; but Napoleon having defeated the great armies of Austria, this local triumph was of comparatively little moment. The Tyrol was ceded by Austria to France, and H., though he struggled to the uttermost, was eventually driven into hiding. He was betrayed into the hands of the French by a priest named Douay, who had formerly been his friend; taken to Mantua, tried and condemned, and there shot, February 20, 1810. H.'s heroic defence of his country was subsequently acknowledged by the ennobling of his family, and a statue of him has been erected at Innsbrück, where he is buried. See the biographies of H. by Weber (Innsbr. 1852), Rapp (Innsbr. 1852), and Weidinger (3d ed. Leips. 1861).

Hoffmann, August Heinrich (H. von Fallersleben), a German poet and philologist, was born at Fallersleben, Lüneburg, 2d April 1798, educated at the Helmstedt and Brunswick gymnasia, and the universities of Göttingen and Bonn. A friendship contracted with the brothers Grimm (1818) led him to abandon the study of theology for that of the German language and literature. Appointed keeper of the University Library, Breslau (1823), H. became Extraordinary Professor of the German Language and Literature in that university 1830), and Ordinary Professor (1835); but lost his post through the publication of *Unpolitische Lieder* (1842), and for six years wandered, a political refugee, through Germany, Switzerland, and Italy. Re-established (1848) in his Prussian civic rights, and pensioned, H. married, and settled successively on the Rhine and at Bingerbrück, Neuwied, and Weimar, at the last place editing unsuccessfully the *Weimarisches Jahrbuch* (Hanov. 1854–

1857). In 1860 he was appointed librarian to the Duke of Ratibor. His chief works are *Horæ Belgicæ* (12 vols. Leips. and Berl. 1830–62), *Geschichte des Deutschen Kirchenliedes bis auf Luther* (Bresl. 1832; 3d ed. Hannov. 1861), *Die Deutsche Philologie im Grundriss* (Berl. 1836), philological studies; editions of *Reineke Vos* (Berl. 1834) and *Theophilus* (2 vols. Hannov. 1853–54); and *Gedichte* (6th ed. Hannov. 1864), *Rheinleben* (Neuwied, 1865), *Soldatenlieder* (Mainz, 1851), *Fünfzig Kinderlieder* (Leips. 1843), &c., original poems.

Hoffmann, Ernst Theod. Amadeus (properly **Wilhelm**), a German novelist, born January 24, 1776, at Königsberg in Prussia, studied law there, and entering the state service, was appointed Government Assessor for Posen (1800). Some of his caricatures offending his superiors, H. was transferred as councillor to Plock and (1803) to Warsaw. The entrance of the French (1806) into that city cut short H.'s diplomatic career, and for nine years he was forced to support himself by contributing to a Leipsic musical journal, and acting as director to a Dresden opera company. But 1816 saw him re-established as a councillor in Berlin, where he died, July 24, 1822. Among his works may be noticed *Phantasiestücke in Callot's Manier* (Bamb. 1814; 3d ed. Leips. 1825); *Lebensansichten des Kater Murr* (2 vols. Berl. 1821–22); and *Der Doppelgänger* (Brünn, 1824). H.'s *Ausgewählte Schriften* appeared at Berlin (10 vols. 1827–28), and a complete edition of his works (12 vols. 1857). In the genius of H. there is a strange compound of ghostly fantasy and mocking satire; and in spite of certain repellent qualities that disfigured both the man and his works, his novels have the supreme merit of riveting the attention of the reader. See J. E. Hitzig, *Aus H.'s Leben und Nachlass* (2 vols. Berl. 1823).

Hoffmann, Friedrich, a distinguished German physician, was born at Halle, February 19, 1660. He studied at Jena and Erfurt, returning to Jena in 1681 to take his doctor's degree. After several years spent in travelling through England and Holland, he began practice at Minden in Westphalia in 1685. Three years later he removed to Halberstadt; and in 1693 was appointed Professor of Medicine in the University of Halle, by Friedrich, Elector of Brandenburg, afterwards King of Prussia. In 1708, at the King's request, he removed to Berlin, but returned in 1712 to Halle, where he died, November 12, 1742. As a physician and professor of medicine he was second only to Boerhaave (q. v.), who at that time made the school of Leyden famous. He wrote numerous works, many of which were collected and published at Geneva in 1740. His great works, however, are his *Medicina Rationalis Systematica* (9 vols. 1718–40) and his *Medicina Consultatoria* (12 vols. 1721–39).

Hoffmann's Anodyne Liquor, the *compound spirit of sulphuric ether* of the London pharmacopœia, is a mixture of ether, etherial oil, and alcohol, being similar in properties to *Spiritus ætheris*, which is composed of ether, one, and rectified spirit, two parts. It is a powerful diffusive stimulant, expectorant and antispasmodic, in doses of from thirty to sixty minims.

Hofmann, August Wilhelm, a German chemist, was born April 8, 1818, at Giessen, where for a time he acted as assistant to Liebig. In 1845 he came to England to superintend the Royal College of Chemistry, which now forms part of the Royal School of Mines. He has contributed many valuable papers on organic chemistry to various chemical and scientific journals, and is especially known for his researches in connection with aniline dyes. H. has edited along with Dr. Bence Jones several of the editions of Fownes' *Manual of Chemistry*, and is himself the author of a work on the subject entitled *Einleitung in die Moderne Chemie* (3 vols. 1867). In 1868 he was appointed Professor of Chemistry in Berlin.

Hof'wyl, a Swiss village 6 miles N. of Bern, noted as the seat of an educational and agricultural establishment founded by Von Fellenberg (q. v.) in 1808, and carried on by his relatives till 1840.

Hog ('the grunting animal;' Welsh, *hwch*; Bret. *houc'ha*, 'to grunt'), the name given to various genera of mammals belonging to the order *Ungulata* (q. v.), and to the *Omnivorous* group of the order. The H. is *Artiodactylate ungulata*, as the feet are even-toed, and have each two functional or well-developed toes, with two rudimentary digits in addition; the latter not reaching the ground. The canine teeth are largely developed, especially in the males, in which they form tusk-like organs, and the lower incisors or front teeth are usually inclined forwards. The molar teeth may number from six to fourteen in each jaw. The stomach generally exhibits a semi-complex structure, but is by no means of compound nature, as in the ruminantia. The H. has a truncated snout of cylindrical shape, and provided with a cartilaginous tip; the conformation of the snout and its muscular development making it an efficient burrowing organ. The skin in many cases is sparsely covered with coarse hair or bristles, but in the wild H. or varieties, hair may be abundantly developed. The tail is never of great length, and in some cases is represented by a mere tubercle. Of the H. the most familiar is the wild H. or boar (*Sus scrofa*), still found in the European forests, where it is hunted by dogs, and where its pursuit constitutes a sport by no means unattended with danger. In olden times the wild H. was hunted on foot with the spear; in modern days the chase is kept up on horseback, the huntsmen being seconded by dogs and armed with the rifle. The domesticated varieties of our pigs have sprung from the wild boar, the nearest descendants of which in England are probably to be found in the Hampshire forest-pigs. In its natural state the H. feeds on acorns, nuts, and roots, and is a cleanly animal; the depraved habits and tastes of its domesticated descendants having been induced by artificial feeding. The flesh is palatable; and the wild boar is not unknown in Britain as a dainty morsel, the *gout* of which is supposed to be increased and improved by its high or semi-putrescent condition. The Jews and Mahometans esteem the H. an unclean animal, and the use of the flesh is forbidden by their religious tenets. The flesh of the domestic pig undoubtedly serves as a harbour for the embryo-form of the *Tænia solium* or common tapeworm of man. But when the flesh is thoroughly cooked, all danger from the parasites ceases, as continued exposure to a high temperature kills them. The H. produces from eight to twelve young twice annually. When duly trained, it exhibits a high degree of intelligence. The India wild H. or boar is closely allied to the European species, and is especially destructive to fields of sugar-cane. The pursuit of this animal—popularly named 'pig-sticking'—affords amusement to English residents in India. The bush H. of S. Africa (*Cheiropotamus Africanus*), also named the Bosch Vark by the Dutch, has large tusks and swollen cheeks, while the hair is long; the ears being well developed with prominent tufts. The average length is 5 feet, and the height 2½ feet. The colour is dark brown, sometimes varied with lighter tints. The Babyroussa H. (q. v.), another notable species, is found in the E. Archipelago. There is also in Papua a H. named the *Sus Papuensis*, attaining a length of 1½ or 2 feet. The wart hogs of Africa are so named from the possession of a warty process under each eye.

Ho'garth, William, a celebrated English painter and engraver, was born in Ship Court, Old Bailey, London, 10th December 1697, and bound apprentice to Ellis Gamble, a goldsmith of Cranbourn Street, in 1712. Starting in business on his own account (1720) as an heraldic engraver, H. presently applied himself to copper-engraving, his eighteen illustrations to Butler's *Hudibras* appearing in 1726–27. In 1729 he formed a secret marriage with a daughter of Sir James Thornhill (at whose academy he had studied in 1724), and during the years 1727–30 turned out dozens of portraits, with no great profit to himself. But the series of the 'Harlot's Progress' (1733, destroyed by fire, 1755) at once marked the true bent of H.'s genius, won him a name, and, by the sale of 2000 plates, laid the foundation of his later competence. Then came in quick succession (1734–38) the 'Rake's Progress,' 'Strolling Actresses in a Barn,' and the 'Distressed Poet,' all adding largely to the reputation of this 'Juvenal in oils.' After a few mistaken essays in the field of historical painting, H. came back to the more congenial line of modern satire, and issued his 'Distressed Poet' (1741); 'Marriage à la Mode' (1745), bought in 1797 by Mr. Angerstein for £1381, and now in the National Gallery; 'Industry and Idleness' (1747), 'March to Finchley' (1748), 'Calais Gate' (1749), &c. In 1750 H. bought a villa at Chiswick, in 1757 was elected a councillor and honorary member of the Imperial Academy of Augsburg, and the same year succeeded his father-in-law as sergeant-painter to George II. He died in Leicester Square, London, 25th October 1764, and was buried at Chiswick, his wife surviving him thirty-five years. Numerous editions of H.'s works have been published both at home and abroad, the best being those by T. Clerk (1812) and Nichols (3 vols. Lond.

1820–22). See *W. H., Painter, Engraver, and Philosopher*, by G. Sala, in the *Cornhill Magazine* (vol. i.–ii.), collected and republished in 1867, and G. F. Waagen's *Kunstwerke und Künstler in England und Paris* (3 vols. Berl. 1837–39).

Hogg, James, 'the Ettrick Shepherd,' a Scottish poet, was born in the Forest of Ettrick, Selkirkshire, January 25, 1772. From his boyhood he followed the occupation of a shepherd, and early won a local reputation as a song-writer. In 1801 he became acquainted with Scott, to whom he handed over a number of the old ballads collected in the *Border Minstrelsy*, and in 1803 he issued the *Mountain Bard*. After making an unlucky farming speculation, he became editor of the *Spy*, an Edinburgh journal, a contributor to *Blackwood's Magazine*, and an intimate associate with various literary celebrities, among others with Scott and Wilson, the latter of whom widely popularised, and in a coarse way idealised, him in the *Noctes Ambrosianæ*. H. published the *Queen's Wake* in 1813, married in 1814, and was again unsuccessful as a farmer, after which he devoted himself mainly to literature, and wrote both in prose and verse with considerable profit until his death at Altrive, November 21, 1835. Besides the *Queen's Wake*, his best work, he produced *Madoc of the Moor*, *The Pilgrims of the Sun*, *Queen Hynde*, *The Jacobite Relics of Scotland*, *The Border Garland*, several wild but interesting Scottish stories, *Lay Sermons*, and a *Life of Sir Walter Scott*. His larger poems, sometimes disfigured by affectation and ineptitudes, abound in rich description, thrilling weirdness, and subtle, delicate imagination. His lyrics, of which the finest are the *Skylark*, and *When the Kye comes Hame*, are characteristically Scottish in their stirring or plaintive melody, their sweet intensity of pathos, their fresh, natural colour, and their genuine Arcadian sentiment. A collected edition of H.'s poems, with a biography of the author, was published at London by J. Wilson, in 5 vols. 1850–52.

Hogmanay', a name in use in Scotland for the last day of the year. The word is very variously explained; some, for example, deriving it from a French phrase, *au qui menez*, 'to the misletoe lead,' others from *hoggu-nott*, or *hogenat*, a Scandinavian word for 'killing-night,' *i.e.*, the eve of the feast. *Hagmena*, doubtless the same as H., is a N. of England name for the last *period* of the year.

Hog Plum, the name current in Brazil and the W. Indies for the fruit of several species of spondias, a genus belonging to the natural order *Anacardiaceæ*, and so called from being extensively used to fatten swine. The genus has a wide distribution through the tropics of both hemispheres, furnishing in the Society Islands, Abyssinia, India, &c., an article of native food. Various species, as *S. mangifera*, *S. tuberosa*, and *S. Mombin*, are also valued for sundry medicinal qualifications.

Hog Rat, the name given to a species of Rodent (q. v.) quadrupeds, belonging to the genus *Capromys*, and found in S. America and Cuba. It is also named sand rat, is somewhat hoglike in shape, and inhabits trees. The tail is long and hairy, and the average size is that of a small rabbit.

Hogs'head, an ancient measure of capacity, still used in Britain and America as a standard measure for wine and beer. The wine H. contains 63 gallons, the beer H. 54. In the United States a H. of tobacco varies from 750 to 1200 pounds in the different States.

Hohenlin'den, anc. *Hollinden* ('the hollow place of the lime-trees'), a village in Upper Bavaria, Germany, 25 miles E. of Munich, is famous as the scene of the defeat, inflicted during a snowstorm, on the Austrians, under the Archduke Johann, by the French, led by Moreau, December 3, 1800. The Austrian losses amounted to 8000 killed and wounded, 11,000 prisoners, and 100 pieces of artillery. The victory, which led to the peace of Lunéville, is the subject of one of Campbell's fiery lyrics.

Hoh'enlohe, a former Countship and Principality of Franconia, S. Germany, with an area of 680 sq. miles, and a pop. in 1805 of 108,600, was mediatised by the Rhein-Bund in 1806, and is now partly included in Bavaria and partly in Würtemberg. The family, which was founded in the 12th c. by Count Gottfried, friend of the Emperor Heinrich VI., divided (1551) into two main branches, still existing—the Lutheran H.-Neuenstein, with the lines H.-Lagenburg, H.-Oehringen or Ingelfingen, and H.-Kirchberg (died out in 1861); and the Roman Catholic H.-Waldenburg, with the lines H.-Waldenburg-Bartenstein and H.-Waldenburg-Schillingsfürst. In 1744 the Counts of H. were made Princes of the Empire. **Friedrich Ludwig**, Prince of H.-Ingelfingen (born 1746, died 1818), received the command of the Prussian army when the Duke of Brunswick was wounded at Jena, and infamously capitulated at Prenzlau with 17,000 men, October 28, 1806. **Ludwig Aloysius**, prince of H.-Waldenburg-Bartenstein (born 1765, died 1829), fought with distinction against Napoleon under French, Dutch, and Austrian colours, and was made marshal and peer of France. **Alexander Leopold Franz Emmerich**, Prince of H.-Waldenburg-Schillingsfürst (born 1794), was educated by Jesuits, became a priest, wrote mystical books, caused some sensation as a miraculous healer, and died, 1849, as Bishop of Sardica *in partibus*. **Clodwig**, prince of the same line, was born 31st March 1819, and became Minister of Foreign Affairs for Bavaria, and did much to promote a good understanding with Prussia. As vice-president of the Zollverein (1868–69) he showed himself a friend of German unity, incurring the bitter hostility of the Bavarian anti-unionists. He was forced to resign office on the eve of the Franco-Prussian war, but was appointed French ambassador in 1874.

Hoh'enstaufen, a princely German family founded in the middle of the 11th c. by Friedrich von Büren, and which derived its name from Von Büren's Castle of Hohenstaufen ('high rock'), on the Danube, 30 miles below Stuttgart. Von Büren's son, Friedrich von Staufen or H., distinguished himself so much at the battle of Merseburg (1080), that Heinrich IV., whose daughter Agnes he married, made him Duke of Swabia. Friedrich came into conflict with the Welfs or Guelfs, and his family were called by the Italians Ghibellines from their castle of Weiblingen. The sons of Friedrich—Friedrich II. and Konrad, Dukes of Swabia and Franconia—on Heinrich V.'s death grasped unsuccessfully at the imperial title, and after a fierce war they were forced to yield in 1135; but in 1138 Konrad was elected emperor, and the imperial office remained in the family above a century, being held by Konrad III. (q. v.), Friedrich I. (q. v.), Heinrich VI. (q. v.), Philip (q. v.), Friedrich II. (q. v.), and Konrad IV. (q. v.). The last prince was poisoned in Southern Italy in 1254, and the male line of the Hohenstaufens died with his son Konradin, who fell in 1268 when striving to gain the kingdom of Naples. In 1280 a branch of the family, descended from Constance, daughter of Manfred (q. v.), half-brother of Konrad IV., became rulers of Sicily, Constance having married Peter III. of Aragon. See Raumer's *Geschichte der H.* (4th ed. 6 vols. 1871).

Hoh'enstein ('high rock'), a town in the kingdom of Saxony, 10 miles W.S.W. of Chemnitz by railway. It is a seat of the cotton manufacture, and possesses a mineral spring. Pop. (1875) 5726.

Hohenzoll'ern, or **Zoll'ern**, is the name of a castle on a conical peak in the northern slope of the Swabian Alps, near the town of Hechingen, the cradle of an illustrious line of German princes. The family of H. traces its descent back to a Graf Thassilo, said to have founded the castle about the year 800. The first to assume the name of H. or Zollern were two counts, Burchard and Wezel, who fell in battle about 1061. Graf Friedrich III. von Zolre, who died about 1200, was one of the most trusty councillors of the Emperors Friedrich I. and Heinrich VI., and was by the latter appointed Burggraf of Nürnberg. Through his Austrian wife he came into possession of extensive estates in Franconia and Austria. His grandson Konrad II. made over the original family title and estates to his nephew Friedrich; retaining for himself the newly-acquired lands and the title Burggraf of Nürnberg. Since that time the H. family has been maintained in the two lines, the elder or *Franconian* and the *Swabian*. Friedrich III., son of Konrad II., head of the former line, acquired in Baireuth and its mines a valuable addition to his domains. Before 1330 several townships and the city of Anspach (Ansbach) were added by purchase. And by the middle of the 14th c. the Burggrafs of Nürnberg were the most powerful lords in all Franconia. Friedrich V. was made a prince of the empire in 1363. In 1411 the Emperor conferred the domain of Brandenburg on the house of H., and in 1415 the title of Elector. Friedrich III., eleventh in succession from the first Elector of Brandenburg, became, as Friedrich I., the first king of Prussia; and in the person of William I. of Prussia, in descent from the first king, the house of H. has attained to the imperial crown of Germany. The Swabian line did not become prominent until the 16th c., but gradually added the territory of Sigmaringen, Vöhringen, and Hechingen to the patrimonial domain of H.; and about the beginning of the 17th c., this line separated into the branches of H.-Hechingen and H.-Sigmaringen. In virtue of family compacts made in 1695, 1707, and 1821, the representatives of both these branches retired into private life (7th December 1849), with the rank of princes, leaving the seigniory of H. to Friedrich-Wilhelm IV., King of Prussia, as being head of the whole house of H. The principality of H. is accordingly now a Prussian province. It consists of a long strip of land, extending from the Neckar southward across the Danube to near the lake of Constance. It is completely encircled by Baden and Würtemberg, has an area of 439 sq. miles and (in 1871) a pop. of 65,558. See Barth's *Hohenzoll. Chronik* (Sigmar. 1860).

Höh'scheid, an important industrial town of Rhenish Prussia, 17 miles S.E. of Düsseldorf. Its chief industries are in lead and iron. Pop. (1875) 9958.

Hokian'ga, a river and township in the N. Island of New Zealand, near its northern extremity. The river enters the sea by a spacious estuary, forming a safe and commodious harbour, its mouth being in 35° 30′ S. lat., 173° 26′ E. long. Large quantities of timber, chiefly that of the valuable Kauri Pine (q. v.), are exported from the district.

Hokitik'a, a town on the W. coast of the Middle Island of New Zealand. Shortly after the discovery of the Westland diggings in 1865, H. sprang into existence, rapidly growing into a town of 10,000 inhabitants, with a gold export of more than £750,000 in a single year. H. has since declined with the gold fields, on which it is dependent, and in 1876 its population was only 3600, or, inclusive of the neighbouring district, 7380. H. is situated at the mouth of a small river of the same name, with a bad bar harbour.

Hol'bach, Paul Heinrich Dietrich, Baron d', a philosopher of German origin, was born in 1723 at Heidelsheim, in the Palatinate. Coming to Paris with plenty of money, he gathered about him a social clique of Encyclopædists, such as Diderot, Galiani, D'Alembert, Ragnal, Helvetius, Marmontel, &c. His house was for years the centre of 'free' thought in France. H., a kindly, luxurious, rather dull man, was personally a great favourite. He wrote on physics, chemistry, and mineralogy for the *Encyclopédie*, translating many scientific works from the German. In his *Christianisme Dévoilé* (1767) he attacked both the dogmas and the moral teaching of Christianity, and denied that religion was essential to political security. In 1770 appeared his *Système de la Nature*, republished as *Le Bon Sens*, a very popular work among the lower classes, who were caught by the simplicity of its crude materialism, and which Voltaire indignantly criticised in his article 'God' in the *Encyclopédie*. *Le Système Social* is an attempt to construct a scheme of social order and duty without reference to religion. H. died 21st January 1789. See *Memoires* of the Abbé Morellet, Grimm's *Correspondance*, and *Les Diners de Baron D'H.*, by Mme. de Genlis.

Hol'bein, Hans (the Younger), a great German painter, was born about 1497, Grünstadt and Augsburg contending for the honour of being his birthplace. Taught painting by his father, H. the Elder, he attracted notice as early as 1512, and four years later settled at Basel, where he seems to have led a gay, roystering life, and whence, in 1526, he proceeded to England with a recommendation from his friend Erasmus to Sir Thomas More. H. spent three years in More's house upon the Thames, and in 1529 was appointed court-painter to Henry VIII. with a salary of £30 a year. The year following H. revisited Basel, where he had left a wife and family, but immediately returned with them to England, and in this land of his adoption passed the remainder of his days in the busy practice of his art. The date of his death has been a subject of much controversy. By Walpole and others he is stated to have fallen a victim to the plague of 1554. But we find no record of any such pestilence in that year, and the recent discovery of H.'s will, bearing date of administration November 29, 1543, may be regarded as decisive of the question. Consequently the many 'Holbeins' subsequent to the latter year have had to be reattributed. The whole subject, indeed, of this master's works is a perplexing one. Even of his masterpiece, 'The Family of the Burgomaster Meyer,' two copies exist—the one at Darmstadt, the other in the Dresden Gallery—concerning which connoisseurs differ as to which is the original, which the *replica*. Among H.'s other works may be noticed a 'Last Supper' and 'Passion' at Basel; an 'Adoration of the Shepherds and Kings' at Freiburg; the 'Barber-Surgeons receiving their Diploma from Henry VIII.,' in the Barbers' Hall, London; and portraits of Erasmus, Gyzen, Moretto, Melanchthon, and Jane Seymour, in the galleries respectively of Berlin, Dresden, Hanover, and Vienna. H. was further an admirable wood-engraver—his 'Dance of Death' (q. v.) being most familiar to us—whilst his skill as a designer for glass-painting is shown in the noble windows of King's College Chapel, Cambridge. The freedom and accuracy of his drawing, the truth and brilliancy of his colour, and his exquisite finish, entitle him to be reckoned among the great masters. See Hegner, *Hans Holbein der Jüngere* (Berl. 1827); Bartolozzi, *H.'s Portraits of the Court of Henry VIII.* (Lond. 1828); Wornum's *Life of H.* (Lond. 1867); and Woltmann, *Holbein und seine Zeit* (Leips. 1867, 2d ed. 1874). The *H. Society*, founded in 1868, has for its object the encouragement of a taste for old wood-engravings by the production of photo-lithographic copies.

Hol'berg, Ludvig, one of the greatest names in modern Danish literature, was born at Bergen in Norway, November 6, 1684, and studied at Copenhagen University. After visiting Germany, Holland, France, and England, he returned to Copenhagen, where in 1718 he was made Professor of Metaphysics, and two years later Professor of Oratory and member of the 'Consistorium.' From this period date his satires, the first-fruits of his literary activity. *Peder Paars*, a heroic satire in iambics (1719–20), *Hans Mikkelsens Fire Skjemtedigte* (1722), *Hans Mikkelsens Metamorphosis* (1726), were already written when, led by an accident to write for the stage, he found there a field peculiarly favourable to his genius. In quick succession he produced a long series of comedies, *Hans Mikkelsens Comedier* (7 vols. 1723–54), which form the groundwork of the Danish comic drama. They are full of lively, powerful humour, and present a great variety of original characters. *Nils Klims, Underjordiske Reise*, a satirical romance, was written in Latin (1741), but was soon translated into several languages. H. also turned his attention to history, producing *Danmarks Historie* (finished 1762–63), *Jödiske Historie* (1742), *Almindelig Kirkehistorie* (1739), as well as four volumes of parallel lives of heroes and heroines in Plutarch's manner (1753–57). His *Epistler* (5 vols. 1748–54) are full of thought and wit, but *Moralske Fabler* (1751) are comparatively uninteresting. He was ennobled in 1746, and died 28th January 1754. K. L. Rahbek published in 21 vols. *Udvalgte Skrifter*, but it is only in recent years that the Holberg Society have produced critical editions of his greatest writings by Liebenberg, Brunn, &c. See Prutz, *H., Leben und Schriften* (Stuttg. 1857); Smith, *H.'s Levnet og Populære Skrifter* (Copenh. 1858); Legrelle, *H. considéré comme Imitateur de Molière* (Paris, 1864).

Hol'cus, a genus of grass, two species of which are indigenous to Britain. See SOFT GRASS.

Hold, the interior part of a ship nearest the keel, which runs from stem to stern. In merchantmen the cargo is mainly stowed in the H., which, in men-of-war, contains the ship's stores. It is divided into compartments by bulk-heads.

Holding, a term of Scotch feudal law equivalent to *tenure* (see TENURES) in England. H. expresses the services due to the Superior (q. v.), and marks by the words—*Feu* (q. v.) or *Blench*—the nature of the connection between the superior and Vassal (q. v.). When any one holds *feu*, he holds his land for a yearly payment. *Blench* denotes a nominal duty, as a penny Scots. See also DOMINIUM, GROUND ANNUAL, BURGAGE TENURE.

Holding Over, an English law term, denoting the keeping possession of land or a tenement beyond the term of agreement. In this case the tenancy is held to be renewed on the same terms and for the same period. But if notice of quitting has been given on either side, and the tenant refuse to go at the proper time, he is liable in double rent. In Scotch law see RELOCATION, TACIT.

Hol'idays (in law). The national H. in England are Christmas Day, Good Friday, and the Queen's birthday. 34 and 35 Vict. c. 17 makes Easter Monday, the Monday in Whitsun Week, the first Monday in August, and the 26th December, bank H. in England and Ireland. Bank H. in Scotland, under the same Act, are New Year's Day, Christmas Day, Good Friday, and the first Mondays of May and August, If either of the two first falls on a Sunday, the following Monday is a holiday. If a bill of exchange falls due on a Sunday, it must be paid the day before; when it falls due on a bank holiday, it is payable the day after. The sole authority by which a legal holiday can be constituted in any part of the United Kingdom is an Act of Parliament.

Hol'inshed, Raphael, an English chronicler, born about the beginning of the 16th c., was educated, says Anthony à Wood, at one of the universities, and died about 1580. He wrote *The Chronicles of Englande, Scotlande, and Irelande* (2 vols. Lond. 1577; mod. ed. 6 vols. 1807–8), in which he was assisted by William Harrison, who composed the most valuable part—the prefatory account of England in the 15th c.—John Hooker, who translated the *Conquest of Ireland* from Giraldus Cambrensis, and Richard Stanihurst, who produced the portion describing Ireland. H. is now mainly known for having furnished Shakespeare with materials for his English historical plays.

Hol'kar, the hereditary appellative of the great Mahratta family that rules at Indore in Central India. The founder, Mulhar Rao H., a Sudra of the shepherd caste, and a cavalry soldier in the army of the Peishwa, died in 1766. He was succeeded by Ahalya Barji, the widow of his son, an extraordinary woman, who reigned for thirty years, and founded the city of Indore. She is now worshipped in Malwa as an incarnation of the deity. The descendants of her adopted son are still on the throne. The H. dynasty were the military rivals of Scindiah (q. v.) of Gwalior. See Grant Duff's *History of the Mahrattas* (Lond. 1826). See also INDORE and MAHRATTAS.

Holl'and ('hollow-land'), a name frequently given to the former republic of the Seven Provinces and to the present kingdom of the Netherlands, was originally that of an old countship almost co-extensive with the modern provinces of North and South H. See NETHERLANDS.

Holland, North, a province of the Netherlands, mainly consists of the peninsula that encloses the Zuider Zee on the W., and also comprises, of the series of islands stretching N. therefrom—Wieringen, Texel, Vlieland, and Ter Schelling. Area, 955 sq. miles; pop. (1875) 629,345. The peninsula is traversed from Amsterdam in the S. to Helder in the N. by the great N. Holland Canal, and is separated from the mainland by the Y (*Het Ij*), the Wijkermeer, and N. Sea Canal, carried across a narrow neck of land (*Holland op Zijn Smalst*). The fertile and well-cultured marsh land is drained by many steam-pumps, watermills, and canals, and protected from the sea by enormous dunes and dykes. There is much cattle-rearing, and the chief products are cheese, butter, and oats. In the S. lay the old Haarlem Lake (q. v.). The chief town is Amsterdam.—**South H.**, a province lying between the former and the mouths of the Rhine, is bounded E. by Utrecht and Gelderland, and W. by the North Sea. Area, 1162 sq. miles; pop. (1875) 748,162. It is flat and low-lying, and includes the islands Voorne, Putten, Over-Flakkee, Ijsselmonde, Rozenburg, Beijerland, Strijen, &c. There are many canals, sloughs (*sloten*), and ponds (*polder*), and the chief rivers are the Old Rhine, Ijssel, Lek, Merwede, Hollands-Diep, and Maas. The islands have a loamy soil, and yield corn and flax; the so-called Westland is famed for its fruit and vegetables. The principal industries are cattle-rearing, cheese-making and fishing. The capital is the Hague, and other towns are Rotterdam, Leyden, Gouda, Dordrecht, and Delft.

Holland, Henry Richard Fox Vassall-Holland, third baron, an English statesman, nephew of Charles James Fox, was born at Winterslow House, Wilts, 23d November 1773, and succeeded to the title in 1774. He was educated at Eton and Christchurch, and carefully trained by his uncle for a political career. In 1798 he made his maiden parliamentary speech, and was thereafter a frequent debater in the House of Lords. He protested against the imprisonment of Napoleon, opposed the slave-trade and the corn-laws, and was throughout life a staunch and consistent Whig. He was Lord Privy Seal under Lord Grenville for a few months, and was in opposition with his party till 1830, when he became Chancellor of the Duchy of Lancaster in Lord Grey's Ministry, and subsequently in that of Lord Melbourne. He died October 22, 1840. H. was a generous patron of literature and the fine arts, and his courtly grace of manner and amiability of character endeared him to many friends. His own contributions to literature are not unimportant. He wrote two fine biographies of Guillen de Castro and Lope de Vega (Lond. 1805, 2d. ed. 1817), and translated three Spanish comedies (Lond. 1807); drew up an admirable life of his great uncle, which he prefixed to an edition (1808) of Fox's *History of the Reign of James II.*, and edited the *Memoirs of Lord Waldegrave* (Lond. 1822). Two posthumous works from his pen, *Foreign Reminiscences*, and *Memoirs of the Whig Party*, edited by his son, **Henry Edward Fox**, fourth **Lord H.** (born 1802, died 1859), were published respectively in 1850 and 1854. The Princess Marie Lichtenstein, adopted daughter of the last Lord H., has published an interesting history of *Holland House* (2 vols. Lond. 1873).

Holland, Sir Henry, Bart., an English physician, born at Knutsford, Cheshire, October 27, 1788, studied at London, Glasgow, and Edinburgh, and took his degree of M.D. at the last of these universities in 1811. After travelling for two years in the E. of Europe, an account of which he published in 1815, he settled in London, and rose to great eminence in his profession, being elected a Fellow of the Royal College of Physicians in 1828. He was appointed Physician in Ordinary to the Prince Consort in 1840, to the Queen in 1852, and was made a baronet in 1853. His practice was one of the largest in London, and he attended in succession seven Prime Ministers. During many years he annually set apart two months for foreign travel, and it was after returning from a tour in Russia that he died suddenly on October 27, 1873, at the age of eighty-five. His intellect was vigorous and unimpaired to the last. His best-known works are *Medical Notes and Reflections* (1839), *Chapters on Mental Physiology* (1852), *Essays on Scientific and other Subjects* (1862), *Recollections of Past Life* (1872), and *Fragmentary Papers on Science* (1875). His son, Sir Henry Thurston H., born 1825, is M.P. for Midhurst, and was Assistant Secretary for the Colonies, 1870–74.

Hollow-Ware, a trade term for hollow articles of cast-iron or wrought-iron, as pots, saucepans, and kettles. The maufacture of 'tinned' H. W. is chiefly carried on in the midland district of England, while that of 'black' or untinned is concentrated in the W. of Scotland.

Holl'y, the genus *Ilex*, belonging to the natural order *Aquifoliaceæ*, consists of about 150 species, ranging through the tropical and temperate regions of the world (excepting N. W. America), and especially abundant in S. America. *I. Aquifolium*, or common H., so well known for its useful and decorative purposes, exists through Europe as an indigenous plant, penetrating also into Western Asia. In Britain it is a true native (ascending to 1000 feet in the Highlands), though very often planted in copses, &c., and its frequency is further increased from the fruit being eaten by birds and the seed thereby distributed. The varieties produced and perpetuated by cultivation for ornamental purposes are very numerous and diverse in aspect. The beautiful hard and fine-grained white wood is in considerable demand for such purposes as the handles of small tools, inlaying work, &c. In the neighbourhood of large towns H.-trees are frequently shamefully mutilated by unscrupulous persons stripping off the bark to make birdlime, or stealing the berried branches at Christmas time. Another prominent species, known as Paraguay tea, or by its native name of *Maté*, is the *I. Paraguayensis* of botanists. In S. America it occupies the same place in domestic economy that Chinese tea does with us. See MATÉ.

Holl'yhock. Of this old-established and favourite garden plant the origin is a species of *Malvaceæ* named *Althæa rosa*, a native of China and the S. of Europe. By attentive cultivation the flower has been greatly developed in size, and diversified in its colour-shades, so that the gardeners' kinds now form a long list. The leaves furnish a blue dye, and in Greece a demulcent drink is prepared from the roots.

Holmes, Oliver Wendell, M.D., an American writer of prose and verse, was born at Cambridge, Massachusetts, August 29, 1809. He graduated at Harvard in 1829, took a doctor's degree in 1836, was made Professor of Physiology and Anatomy at Dartmouth in 1838, and in 1847 became Professor of the same subject in the Massachusetts Medical School, Boston. He is the author of *Poetry* (1836), *Terpsichore* (1843), *Urania* (1846), *Astræa* (1850), *Elsie Venner, a Romance of Destiny* (1861), *Songs in many Keys* (1864), *The Guardian Angel* (1868); but his fame is chiefly due to his *Autocrat of the Breakfast-Table* (1857), and its companions *The Professor at the*

Breakfast-Table (1860), and *The Poet at the Breakfast-Table* (1872), delightful prose papers full of shrewd wisdom tinged with poetry, of wit and rich humour shaded and mellowed with pathos. His verses are generally turned with the happiest fluency and grace, and abound in piquant touches of sentiment and sparkling flashes of satire. H. has also written several medical pamphlets, in which his literary felicity adds a charm to his scientific knowledge.

Holocan'thus, a well-known genus of *Teleostean* fishes, belonging to the sub-order *Acanthopterygii* and to the family *Squamipennes* ('scaly-finned'). The body is very broad and compressed, and the fins more or less spinous. The species of H. are confined to tropical seas. A familiar form is the *H. semicirculatus*, or semi-lunar H., so named from the crescentic shape of the blue and white lines marking the sides of the tail and body. The ground colour is black. Other species are the ringed H. (*H. annularis*), the spotted H. (*H. maculosus*), the ciliated H. (*H. ciliaris*), the emperor H. (*H. imperator*), and the arched H. (*H. arcuatus*).

Hol'ocaust. See SACRIFICE.

Hol'ograph (Gr. *holos*, 'whole,' and *graphē*, 'a writing'), in Scotch law, is a deed written by the granter. Owing to the difficulty of forgery, it is held valid without attestation, or Testing Clause (q. v.). When stated in the deed that it is in the handwriting of the granter, it is presumed to be so though the contrary may be proved. When it does not bear to have been written by the granter, it may be proved to have been so by comparison of admittedly genuine handwriting, or by the evidence of those who saw it written. A H. deed not attested does not prove the date which may be given to it. In English law there is no distinction between H. deeds and other deeds.

Holopty'chius (Gr. *holos*, 'whole,' and *ptychē*, 'a wrinkle'), a well-known genus of fossil *Ganoid* (q. v.) fishes, possessing scales of *cycloidal* form, and included in the division *Glyptodipterini*, in which two dorsal fins are developed, the pectoral fins being lobate. This group in turn forms a division of the sub-order *Crossopterygidæ*, in which the fins are 'fringed.' The genus H. had the two dorsal fins set far back on the body, whilst the pectorals were very long and the ventrals placed near the tail. The scales, which are of the *ganoid* kind, are rounded, overlapping, and have wrinkled surfaces, while the tail is unequally lobed. The H. is confined to the Devonian or Old Red Sandstone rocks. The genus *Rhizodus*, of the Carboniferous formations, is closely allied to H. Some specimens of H. attain a length of 12 feet.

Holothu'ria, Trepang', or Bêche-de-Mer, names given to the members of an order (*Holothuroidea*) of *Echinodermata* (q. v.), allied to the sea-urchins, starfishes, &c., and which are known by the name of 'sea-cucumbers.' See BÊCHE-DE-MER.

Hol'stein (anc. *Holtsatia*, 'the settlement in the woods'), a former duchy of Denmark, and since 1866 part of the Prussian province of Slesvig-H. (q. v.). It lies between the Baltic and the N. Sea, and is separated in the N. from Slesvig by the Eider river and Slesvig-H. Canal, and in the S. from Hanover by the Elbe. Towards the centre it extends in low hills and sandy heaths, affording excellent grazing and is watered by the Stör, Eider, and Trave. In the E. the soil is rich and well cultivated, but in the W. the surface is low and marshy, protected from the sea by dykes. The chief industries are cattle-rearing, husbandry, and cheese and butter making. Among the natural products are peat, salt, amber (from the Baltic coast), and lime. The principal towns are Kiel and Altona. A considerable number of the inhabitants are Frisians, and the spoken languages are German and Danish. Most of the peasants speak Platt-Deutsch. The Duchy of H. was formed in the 14th c. out of a countship of the same name, and was increased by the addition of the countship of Stormarn, the Frisian district of Ditmarsh (q. v.), and the province of Wagrien. The King of Denmark, as Duke of H., was a member of the German Confederation.

Hol'ster (Dutch, *holster*, 'a case for a pistol,' akin to Old Eng. *heolster*, 'a hiding-place or recess'), a leather case for a horseman's pistol, placed at the fore part of a saddle.

Holte'nia, a peculiar genus of sponges, inhabiting the deep seas, and known as an 'anchoring sponge,' from the fact that the body has no stem or root, but fixes itself in the mud of the sea-bed by a long beard or bunch of delicate thread-like spicules. The *H. Carpenteri*, named after Dr. Carpenter, one of its discoverers, is the familiar species. H. is one of the *Siliceous* or flinty sponges.

Holy Alliance, the name given to an arrangement signed at Paris (26th September 1815) by the sovereigns of Russia, Prussia, and Austria. It was the conception of the Czar Alexander, inspired by Mdme. Krudener. The parties engage in the name of the Holy Trinity to treat one another as brothers, and to act as Christian fathers to their subjects and armies. At the Congress of Aix-la-Chapelle (1818) France joined the alliance, which was really a conspiracy for mutual intervention in the case of revolution against the legitimate despotic dynasties of the day—a league against the public good or political liberty. Its programme, in fact, resembled the declaration of war made in 1792 by Austria and Prussia against the new-born freedom of France. This was clearly seen in the Troppau circular (8th December 1820), which recommended intervention in Naples, where the liberal Constitution of Cadiz had been proclaimed, and which was answered by Castlereagh (then British Foreign Secretary), to the effect that (apart from the constitutional reasons preventing a British sovereign from becoming a party to such an alliance) it was only where British interests were seriously threatened that he could recognise a lawful ground for interfering in a political revolution. In the same way, at the Congress of Verona (October 1822), Wellington protested against the suggestion of Chateaubriand and others that the French army should assist the cause of despotism in Spain. Upon the revolt of the Spanish colonies in South America there was some talk of 'holy pressure' being applied by the Continental powers on behalf of the mother country. This gave rise to the Monroe Doctrine in the United States, which declared that any attempt to coerce the South American Republics would be regarded by the States as an unfriendly act; and also that European colonisation of America would be resisted. The H. A. does not seem to have long survived the Czar Alexander. The unctuous blasphemy of its terms makes it unique in the literature of diplomacy. To Canning belongs the chief credit of keeping Britain free from all complicity.

Holy Coat is our Saviour's seamless coat (*cf.* John xix. 23), which tradition says was discovered, along with the cross on which he was crucified, by Helena, the mother of the Emperor Constantine, on her visit to Palestine in 326. Part of the cross she gave to the city of Jerusalem, and sent the rest to her son; the coat she sent to Treves, where it has been preserved as a priceless relic ever since, having been exhibited to admiring multitudes so late as 1844. The miracles wrought by it are commemorated on the 1st October in the Gregorian Calendar.

Holy Family, an art term comprehending all representations of the Virgin and Child, alone or attended by SS. Anna, Joseph, John Baptist, or others of her kinsfolk. Christ is most frequently represented as lying on his mother's lap, or standing at her knee, whilst St. John—who is often depicted as the older of the two—stands by, attended by a lamb, or at least bearing his *Ecce Agnus* staff, and already dressed in camel's hair. Joseph, when present, often sits in the background reading. In Murillo's famous H. F. in the National Gallery, the first and third persons of the Trinity hover above the group, the Father as an aged man upborne by angels, the Spirit in the form of a dove. The term H. F. is also sometimes incorrectly applied to 'votive pictures,' where, besides the leading figures, others of the donors themselves, or of their patron saints, are introduced in attitudes of adoration. Such is Raphael's 'Madonna di San Sisto' at Dresden.

Holy Ghost, or **Holy Spirit**, in Christian theology, is the third person of the Trinity (q. v.). As the second person is called the Son or the Word, as the image or revealer of God, so the third is called Spirit, as his breath or power. He is called prominently *holy*, to indicate both his nature and operations, being absolutely holy in his nature, and the cause of holiness in all creatures. See PROCESSION OF THE HOLY GHOST.

Holy Grass, the common name for *Hierochloa borealis*, a sweet-scented grass found sparingly in Britain near Thurso, but abundant in Iceland, and also met with in Asia, America, and New Zealand. In Germany it is strewn at the doors of churches on special occasions; hence its name.

Hol'yhead, a seaport of Wales, in the county of Anglesey, on the N. side of the island of the same name, 25 miles W. of Bangor, and 275 N.W. of London by railway. It has been the chief mail-packet station for Ireland since the time of William III., and is a splendid harbour of refuge, protected by a colossal breakwater of hard H. limestone. The nearest English port to Dublin, it is connected with Kingston, 70 miles distant, by telegraphic cable. The passage from Dublin to H. takes four hours, and thence to London by mail-train, seven hours. Outside the harbour is H. Bay, with the Skerries light in the N. Together with Beaumaris, Amlwch, and Llangefni, H. returns one member to Parliament. Pop. (1871) 5916.—**H. Island** (Welsh, *Ynys Gybi*) lies to the W. of Anglesey, from which it is separated by a *traeth* that dries at low water, and is crossed by the bridges of the great Irish coast road and the Chester and H. Railway. Area, 6000 acres; pop. (1871) 7191. It is 7 miles long from N.W. to S.E., and 3 miles broad, and is for the most part barren and hilly, affording some good pasture. The coast, haunted by seafowl, is mostly precipitous, and is much caverned. On the South-Stack islet to the N.W. stands a lighthouse.

Holy Island, or **Lin'disfarne**, an islet, or island peninsula, 4 miles long and 2 broad, lies off the Northumberland coast, 13 miles S. of Berwick, and 3½ from Beal, on the Great Northern Railway. It is distant 2 miles from the mainland, with which, however, it is connected by sands at low tide. It has a village (pop. 876), and interesting remains of an old castle and of the once famous abbey. An episcopal see was planted here under Oswald, King of Northumbria, in the first half of the 7th c., by Aidan (q. v.), a Scotch monk from Iona, whom the king invited hither to revive the Christianity which had nearly perished in consequence of the victories of the heathen Mercians. The bishopric was removed for safety from Danish marauders to Chester-le-Street (893), and finally to Durham.

Holy Land. See PALESTINE.

Holy Phial, or **Sainte Ampoule**, an inexhaustible flask of oil said to have been brought from heaven by a dove to St. Remy at the coronation of Hlodowig I. (496) at Rheims, and thenceforward employed at the coronation of every French king down to Louis XVI. The H. P. was broken during the Revolution, but a fragment survived until the Bourbon restoration, and was found still to contain a portion of the sacred oil, which was used at the coronation of Charles X. (1825).

Order of the H. P.—An ancient French order of knighthood, composed of the four chief nobles of Champagne, who, at French coronations were delivered over to the clergy of Rheims Cathedral as pledges for the safe return of the H. P.

Holy Places for the first three or four centuries of the Christian era meant those places hallowed by the presence of our Lord, especially the scenes of his nativity, crucifixion, resurrection, and ascension. After a certain time these H. P. began to be visited for the purpose of stimulating devotion, or under the notion that prayer in them was more acceptable to God than when made elsewhere. The first great impulse to these pilgrimages was given by Helena, the mother of the Emperor Constantine, who, according to Eusebius, visited Jerusalem in 326, and 'left a fruit of her piety to posterity' in two churches built 'one at the cave of the Nativity, the other on the mount of the Ascension.' According to the same authority, Constantine caused first an oratory and then a magnificent church to be built over the holy sepulchre. A traveller from Gaul who visited Palestine in the 4th c. mentions a basilica which was built by Constantine on the place of the birth of Christ at Bethlehem. Before the middle of the 4th c. it was reported that the very cross on which Christ suffered had been discovered; the latest tradition on the subject being that it was found by the Empress Helena. From the 4th c. other places began to acquire a sacred odour, as the scene of a martyr's sufferings or the shrine of his relics, and received the name of H. P. By the close of the 5th c. a custom began to prevail of sending penitents to various shrines, partly as a penance, and partly to obtain the intercession of the saint of the place.

Holy Roman Empire. See ROMAN EMPIRE.

Hol'yrood ('holy cross'), a royal palace in Edinburgh, long the chief seat of the Scottish court, is a venerable pile standing at the foot of the ridge ending in the Castle Rock, and at the entrance to the Queen's Park, with a romantic background formed by Arthur's Seat and Salisbury Crags. The old palace of H., founded by King James IV., was the court residence of Queen Mary and James VI. The present building is a quadrangle with cloistered interior court and lordly turrets in the prevailing taste of Louis XIV.'s reign, designed by Sir William Bruce of Kinross, and built in the time of Charles II. It has been temporarily occupied by Charles Edward Stuart, the exiled Comte d'Artois, afterwards Charles X. of France, George IV., and the present Prince of Wales. It is occasionally visited by the reigning sovereign on her way to and from the Highlands. The picture gallery (150 feet by 27) contains some 100 portraits of Scottish kings, one or two authentic, the rest imaginary, from Fergus I. to James VII., by De Wit.

The Abbey of H.—An abbey of canons regular of the order of St. Augustine, founded by David I. about 1128, was removed hither from within the castle walls in 1174. A well-known legend of the 15th c. tells of the rescue of David from a stag at bay by the miraculous appearance of a cross, and of the king's commemorative dedication of an abbey to the Black Rood of Scotland (q. v.). The abbey received many gifts and privileges, and early became one of the wealthiest of Scottish ecclesiastical foundations. It was a royal residence from the 13th c. till the erection of an adjoining palace by James IV., whose marriage with Margaret Tudor was here celebrated in 1503. The abbey was burned by the English in 1385, in 1544, and in 1547, was always restored, and after the Reformation was used as Canongate parish church (1560–1670). In 1687, James II., who here for a time held a viceregal court, reserved it for Roman Catholic service. During the Revolution of 1688 it was partly destroyed by the mob, and lay in neglect for many years. In 1758 it was covered with a roof of heavy freestone, which gave way two years later, greatly injuring the ground work and column shafts. The roofless nave of the old abbey still exhibits, among many later additions, various traces of 12th c. work, and contains the tombs of David II., James II., James V., Rizzio, &c. The precincts and park afford a sanctuary for debtors. See ABBEY.

Holy Water, the use of, in the Christian Church, is a practice probably of pagan origin (*cf.* Virgil's *Æn.* vi. 230). The *Aquaminarium* or *Perirrantērion* was a vessel of water mixed with salt and blessed by a priest placed at the entrance of heathen temples, with which the worshippers might sprinkle themselves as they entered, or be sprinkled by the priest with an *aspersorium* or *aspergillum* (sprinkling brush). During the first centuries the Fathers spoke of the custom as purely heathenish, and condemned it as impious and detestable, but it seems, from the directions regarding it in the Forged Decretals (q. v.), to have taken considerable hold in the Church by the 8th c. or 9th c. H. W. was used in all benedictions of palm and olive branches, vestments, corporals, candles, houses, herds, fields, and in private houses. The chief use of it in modern times is for worshippers marking the sign of the cross on their forehead as they enter a church. The practice is not observed by Protestants.

Holy Week, the week preceding the festival of Easter, was observed in the Church from a very early period with peculiar solemnity, as it included the anniversaries of the principal events connected with our Lord's Passion—Palm Sunday (q. v.) and Good Friday (q. v.). By the end of the 4th c. the observance of H. W. was in full operation, various enactments having been made for that purpose. The whole week was observed as far as possible as a strict fast, from midnight on Palm Sunday till cock-crow on Easter day, when the fasting and mourning gave place to rejoicing. All business was suspended, the law courts were closed, all actions at law ceased, and all work was, as far as possible, laid aside for seven days before and after Easter. Those in prison for debt and all but the more heinous crimes were liberated, slaves were manumitted, and liberal almsgiving prevailed. The observance of the week properly began on the Saturday before Palm Sunday, when the raising of Lazarus from the dead was commemorated, with reference to John xii. 1-9.

Hol'ywell, a thriving town of Wales, in Flintshire, to the S.W. of the estuary of the Dee, 4½ miles N.W. of Flint by rail. It has large manufactures of cottons, flannels, Roman cement, and paper, and in the vicinity are extensive limestone quarries, and mines of coal and lead. H. sends one member to Parliament. The Well of St. Winifred, perhaps the most copious spring in the kingdom, was formerly believed to possess sovereign virtues, and attracted many pilgrims. Pop. (1871) 7961.

Hom'age (Med. Lat. *homagium*, from *homo*, 'a man,' a vassal being spoken of as his superior's 'man'), the service by which, in the middle ages, a vassal acknowledged his dependence on his feudal superior. (See FEUDALISM.) *Liege H.* implied absolute allegiance, which could not be broken; but *simple H.* bound him making it only while he held the fief for which it was rendered. The word H. is not used in Scotch law, and in English law only signifies the acknowledgment which the lord of the manor receives from a tenant.

Homalop'tera (Gr. 'level-winged'), a division of the insect order *Diptera* (q. v.), sometimes also named *Pupipara*. In this group the *Hippoboscidæ* or forest-flies and the bat-lice (*Nycteribiidæ*) are included. The larvæ of some species have the power of producing other larvæ within their bodies by a process of internal budding or gemmation.

Hom'burg (H. von der Höhe), formerly the capital of the landgrafdom of Hessen-Homburg, has been since 1866 a town in the Prussian province of Hessen-Nassau, 50 miles N. of Frankfurt. Formerly notorious for its public gaming-tables, H. is still famous for the beauty of its scenery and its mineral waters. The parks and public buildings are on a magnificent scale. Pop. (1875) 8294.

Home, Henry, Lord Kames, a Scottish philosopher, was born at Kames, in Berwickshire, in 1696, and came to the Scotch bar in 1724 without passing through a university. He was, however, an omnivorous student. In 1728 appeared his *Remarkable Decisions of the Court of Session from* 1716 *to* 1728. In 1752 H. was made a judge in the Court of Session. His marriage with Miss Drummond gave him an opportunity of introducing large agricultural improvements (summer fallow, &c.) at Blair Drummond. In reclaiming Kincardine Moss he set a useful example; and as a member of the Board for Scotch Fisheries, Arts, and Manufactures, and of the Commission for the Management of Forfeited Estates, he encouraged enclosures, drainage, the flax trade, and sheep-breeding. As a civil judge he was extremely learned, but too metaphysical and impulsive. His house in Edinburgh was the centre of a small intellectual coterie. H. died 27th December 1782. Among his professional writings may be mentioned his *Abridgment of Statute Law*, *Historical Law Tracts*, *Principles of Equity*, and *Elucidations Respecting the Common and Statute Law of Scotland*. But his chief literary activity was displayed in metaphysics. In his *Essays on the Principles of Morality and Religion*, published under the name of Sopho in 1757, he attacked his friend David Hume's analysis of conscience, justice, property, &c. H.'s later works, *Introduction to the Art of Thinking*, *Elements of Criticism*, and *Sketches of the History of Man* (1761-74), contain many amusing speculations based on insufficient data. His last production was *Loose Hints on Education* (1781), written in his eighty-fifth year. See Tytler's *Memoirs of the Life and Writings of H.* (2 vols. Edinb. 1807).

Home, John, a Scottish dramatist, born at Leith, 22d September 1722, studied for the Church, and became minister of Athelstaneford. There he wrote his tragedy of *Douglas*, which was first acted at Edinburgh in 1756. It was hailed with boundless enthusiasm, and had an equally flattering reception at Covent Garden, London, in 1757. But the Scottish clergy were so indignant at a clergyman's having written a play that H. was forced to resign his living. Lord Bute then appointed him to a sinecure office, and in 1760 he received a pension of £300 a year. After writing the now utterly forgotten dramas of *Agis*, *Aquileia*, *Alonzo*, and *The Fatal Discovery*, and long associating with Hume, Blair, Robertson, and the other Scottish literary men of the time, H. died 5th September 1808. The plot of *Douglas* is romantic and pathetic, but the dialogue is generally flat and conventional, with a few happy lines and touches of true feeling. See Henry Mackenzie's *Life of J. H. the Dramatist* (Edinb. 1822).

Hom'elyn, a species of *Raidæ* or Rays (q. v.), zoologically termed the *Raia maculata*, and found on the S. coasts of England, whence it is obtained for the London markets. The thornback and H. are nearly allied. The eyes are large, and the sides are marked with dark spots.

Ho'mer, the earliest and the greatest of epic poets, stands forth as a grand shadowy being to whom all nations have paid willing homage. The ancient biographies of H. which have come down to us cannot be regarded as authentic history; still from these, and from the universal belief of the ancients in his individuality, as well as from the internal evidence of the poems themselves, the almost unanimous verdict of English and of later Continental criticism has been in favour of a personal author of the *Iliad* and *Odyssey*. The honour of giving birth to him was disputed by seven cities—Smyrna, Chios, Colophon, Salamis, Rhodos, Argos, Athenæ. Of these, the first seems to have the best claim. Legendary evidence, dialect—the Ionic—the allusions and general colouring of the poems favour this view. The chronology of H. is very uncertain. His period, however, was unquestionably long before the recognised system of reckoning dates by Olympiads (776 B.C.). Herodotus places H. at least 400 years before his own time, *i.e.*, about 884 B.C. His date is generally set down as 962–927 B.C.; that of the composition of the *Iliad* and *Odyssey* as 940–927 B.C. In this view he would be born about a dozen years after the death of Solomon, when the revolt of the ten tribes broke up the Hebrew monarchy, and led to the establishment of the kingdoms of Judah and Israel. We have said that the idea of an authorship of the two great Greek epics other than that of H. never entered the minds of the ancients. For nearly eighteen centuries of the Christian era his claim remained all but undisputed. In 1795, however, F. H. Wolf, in his famous *Prolegomena*, endeavoured to overthrow the doctrine of the unity of the Homeric poems, and to show that these were really small, separate, and independent epic songs written down, interwoven, and fashioned into one great work by Pisistratus (q. v.). In this startling statement Wolf but reproduced the unheeded or forgotten conjectures of Casaubon (1559-1614), and Bentley (1662–1742), not to speak of other scholars, French and Italian. Wolf's theory, startling though it was, and albeit met with much opposition, and subjected to material modifications by subsequent discussions, has never been wholly overthrown. Moreover, it has done more towards a critical understanding of the *Iliad* than any work on the same subject. The question that lies at the bottom of all Wolf's inquiry is, whether the Homeric poems were *written* or not. Into this question, though in itself extremely interesting, we shall not here inquire. What chiefly concerns us is that H. was a minstrel—an *aoidos*—a character well known in this country, and famous in the medieval literature of Europe. H. was the prince of minstrels, but as much above all succeeding ballad-mongers as Sir Walter Scott excels the village minstrel. His poetry, viewed as the model and consummation of the epic minstrelsy, is characterised by intense national feeling, great pictorial ornamentation, and a freshness which gives to the events of the far-distant past the aroma of yesterday. It is pervaded throughout by a solemn grandeur and a serene divinity, which gave to it, to the *Iliad* especially, the character of a Bible or Psalter in the eyes of the ancient Greeks. The chief English versions either of both epics or of one are those of Chapman, Hobbes, Pope, Cowper, Sotheby, Derby, and Worseley. See the Histories of Greek Literature by Colonel Mure and K. O. Müller, the special works on H. by Gladstone, and *H. and the Iliad* by Professor Blackie.

Hom'icidal Ma'nia (the *Monomanie meurtrière* of the French) is a blind, irresistible tendency to destroy life, developed under certain morbid conditions of the brain. The disposition to injure others, or to destroy life, may be constant or paroxysmal in an insane person, and may be associated with general incoherence, delusions, illusions, or hallucinations. The motive for the act may be *destruction*, the insane person being under an impulse of blind rage; or it may be *preservation*, he being under the impression that his life is in danger from the person he assaults; or it may originate from a sense of *moral obligation*, being in obedience to a command supposed to be divine. There are certain congenital conditions of the brain truly morbid, and frequently associated with hereditary tendency, in virtue of which the individual, though sane, is on the borderland of insanity, and it not unfrequently happens that excitation of the brain from organic or functional disease, or from the stimulus of alcoholic drinks, results, in such cases, in an outburst of H. M. When such outbreaks are obviously associated with delusions, and where there is marked hereditary tendency, the person is deemed insane and irresponsible, unless it be the case that the excitation has been the result of stimulants voluntarily taken. But there are also cases of H. M. described as *emotional insanity*, in which a criminal act may be committed in consequence of cerebro-mental disease, without any apparent lesion of the perceptive and reasoning powers, and the mental disorder may be of a sudden and transitory nature. In such cases there is, probably, always some preceding morbid feelings, both mental and physical, and in some cases there may be suspicion of revenge. In emotional H. M., the result of disease, there is usually no premeditation, no motive, or only a trivial one; no accomplice, and no effort to escape. The attack may be excited by the sight of a weapon, or by hearing of a murder, and the deed is usually perpetrated with the utmost *sang froid*, and is not followed by any remorse. According to the law, every person is assumed to be responsible for his acts unless the contrary is proved; but a person may be sound *intellectually* and know what is right and what is wrong, and unsound *emotionally*, being powerless to refrain from doing what is wrong. Numerous cases of this kind have been brought to light in connection with medical jurisprudence. See Krafft-Ebing's *Die Lehre von der Mania Transitoria für Aerzte und Juristen dargestellt* (Erlangen, 1865); *American Journal of Insanity* (1872); *Edinburgh Medical Journal* (1862); *Journal of Mental Science* (1872); Tardieu, *Étude Médico-Legale sur la Folie* (1872); Brierre de Boismont, *De la Folie Raisonnante*, &c. (1867); Despine, *Psychologie Naturelle* (1868); the works of Esquirol and Marc, and *Psychological Medicine*, by Drs. Bucknill and Tuke (3d ed. 1874).

Hom'icide, in law, is the killing of a human being. It may be *justifiable* as done from necessity, or *excusable* as done unintentionally or in self-defence, or *felonious* as done from malice and forethought. It is then either *Murder, Manslaughter*, or *Suicide*. H. is justifiable in preventing an atrocious crime, the principle of the law being that when any one tries to commit a capital crime it is lawful to kill him to prevent it. It is not lawful to shoot a man for trespassing; but to shoot a burglar might probably be held justifiable, as done in self-defence.

Hom'ildon Hill, near Wooler in Northumberland, was the scene of a battle (14th September 1402) between the Scotch under the command of Murdach Steward, son of the Regent Albany, and Archibald Earl Douglas, and the English, led by the Earl of Northumberland and his son Hotspur. The former, who were returning home from a successful raid, were disastrously defeated, and their commanders taken prisoners.

Homilet'ics (Gr. *homiletikē*, sc. *technē*, 'art') is the science that treats of homilies, and the best way to compose and deliver them; a subject on which numerous treatises have been written since St. Augustine wrote the first one, namely, his *De Doctrina Christiana*.

Homilia'rium (Eccl. Lat. 'a collection of homilies'). At an early period the custom began to prevail in the Church of preaching, for one reason or other, the homilies or sermons of others. In course of time this led to the formation of collections of homilies written by eminent writers, intended especially for the use of those who were too ill-instructed to compose discourses of their own, but who were strictly enjoined to preach them in the vernacular of their congregation. A collection of discourses written by the Venerable Bede was much used in this way. In the end of the 8th c. Karl the Great ordered Paul Warnefrid to prepare an improved H., and recommended it to be used in the churches of Gaul. An English H. was compiled by Ælfric, perhaps the Archbishop of York (1023-51), which was probably founded on several earlier ones. A metrical English H. was composed about the middle of the 13th c., and has been partly edited by Mr. Small, librarian to the University of Edinburgh. The *Liber Festivalis*, printed by Caxton 1482, was a H., as were also the Homilies (q. v.) published under Edward VI. and Elizabeth.

Hom'ilies, of the Church of England, are a collection of discourses, appointed to be read in churches 'on any Sunday or holy day when there is no sermon,' but no longer in use. There are two books of them, of which the first was composed (probably by Cranmer, Ridley, and Latimer) and published in the reign of Edward VI. (1547). The second was perhaps prepared at this time also, but did not appear till they were both published together, along with the ARTICLES (q. v.), under Elizabeth (1562).

Hom'ily (Gr. *hōmilia*, 'intercourse'), in its classical sense meant the instruction given by a philosopher to his pupils, which was generally given in familiar conversation. It was thus applied in the Christian Church to a simple, popular address by a presbyter to a congregation. It passed into Latin in the same sense about the 5th c., and became the technical term for a religious address founded on a passage of Scripture. The earliest homilies so called are those of Origen (3d c.). The most famous that have been preserved, besides Origen's, are those of Clement of Alexandria, Chrysostom, Augustine, Athanasius, Gregory Nazianzen, Gregory the Great, Cyril of Jerusalem, and Cyril of Alexandria. At the present day the name is used loosely as a synonym for sermon; when any definiteness is attached to it, it means an exposition of a passage of Scripture.

Homœop'athy (Gr. *homoios*, 'like,' and *pathos*, 'affection') is a system of medicine introduced into practice in Germany by Samuel Hahnemann at the close of the last century, the fundamental therapeutical law being *similia similibus curentur*, 'let like things be cured by like,' the phrase being expressive of the relation between the effects of the medicine and the disease. In reasoning out his theory, Hahnemann ascribed to all preceding physicians the adoption of one or other, or of both combined, of two fundamental therapeutical principles, one of which he called *allœopathy*, and the other *antipathy*; in the former, remedies being administered from their presumed power over the hidden causes of disease; and in the latter, from their producing in the healthy body symptoms of a kind opposed to those of the disease, on the principle of *contraria contrariis curentur*. H. is, in theory, a universal as well as an exclusive method, and the only method by which disease ever has been or ever can be cured by art; and, in consequence, the practice of medicine, other than upon the principle of H., has always been a 'fatal art,' except by accident. The theory of H. was reasoned out, inductively, before a single experiment had been made. In order to reduce the theory to practice, it was necessary to ascertain the precise action of medicinal substances on the healthy organism; and to accomplish this, experiments were made, and a record of effects kept, out of which a 'proving' of the medicines was compiled, the design of the 'proving' being to ascertain, with the utmost possible accuracy, all the properties of the substance *proven*. The fundamental rules for the practice of H. may be stated thus:—(1) Ascertain the effects of medicinal substances upon persons in health; (2) select the remedies whose action corresponds with the symptoms of the patient under treatment; (3) give the remedy by itself alone; (4) the dose should be so small as not to cause any general disturbance of the system, its action being limited to that portion of the body which is in a morbid condition. To fulfil the latter condition it was necessary to ascertain, by experiment, the effect of medicinal agents upon diseased structures, the amount of effect depending upon the form in which they were administered, and the condition of the person to whom they were administered. This led to the adoption of the wholly novel system of infinitesimal doses; for Hahnemann maintained that the $\frac{1}{100000}$th of a grain of belladonna was sufficient for the purpose of homœopathic cure in the case of scarlatina. Medicinal doses in H. are all expressed by fractions. There is first the *mother tincture*, one drop of which being added to 99 drops of alcohol constitutes the *first dilution*, and is marked **1**. A drop of the first dilution is then added to 99 drops of alcohol, which constitutes the *second dilution*, and is marked **2**; and so on until number 30 is reached, which is the highest recommended. On the same principle one grain of an insoluble substance may be triturated with 99 grains of sugar of milk, and so on till the sixth trituration is reached, when it is *presumed* that all substances become soluble in alcohol, and, afterwards, alcoholic dilutions are made, in the same way as the vegetable tincture, until the thirtieth dilution is reached. The $\frac{1}{100}$th of a drop of a tincture, or of a grain of an insoluble substance, is the most powerful dose in H., and the decillionth of a drop is the weakest recommended, an almost inconceivably minute fraction of any complex substance. From the year 1818 to 1836, H. was forbidden to be practised in Austria, except under powerful patronage; but in the latter year Dr. Fleischmann undertook the charge of an hospital in Vienna for the treatment of cholera patients on the condition that he was to be allowed to employ H. in their treatment; and, shortly after the Emperor issued an ordinance legalising the practice of H. by any duly qualified medical practitioner. From Germany, H. spread over Europe and America, and was introduced into England, in the year 1827, by Dr. Quin, physician to the King of the Belgians.

H. being a system of medicine essentially revolutionary, both in theory and practice, has met with violent opposition, as might have been anticipated, more especially as Hahnemann and his disciples applied to those who differed from them in opinion the offensive sobriquet *allæopathist* and *antipathist*. H. begins with an assumption, *similia similibus curentur*, and ends with an assumption, *the curative property of a medicine is developed in a much higher degree by an inconceivably minute than by a palpable dose*. The system of H. breaks down if it fails in one point, the fundamental principle being comprehensive and exclusive. Since the days of Hahnemann, the science and practice of medicine has made rapid and sure advances, more especially in the great departments of physiology, chemistry, and pathology; and by the aid of the microscope disease-processes have been investigated with an accuracy undreamt of in his day, and with the effect of undermining the system so vauntingly propounded. The class of parasitic diseases embraces now, not simply the tapeworm and the acarus scabei, but many diseases formerly supposed to be due only to organic change; and if the germ theory of disease be accepted as a fact, more especially in its relation to the specific forms, the homœopathic system necessarily collapses, both in theory and practice; for if certain diseases depend upon the existence and multiplication of living organisms within the body, the only possible *cure* consists in the destruction of these organisms by *antidotes*.

Homoganglia'ta. See HETEROGANGLIATA.

Homologa'tion, a term of Scotch law, signifying an act approving of a deed; the effect being to make that deed, though defective, binding to the person who homologates. The paying of interest due under the deed, or discharging an obligation come under in it, is held to be H. There is no identical term in English law; but there are similar ones, as *Confirmation, Part performance, Estoppel* (q. v.), &c.

Homol'ogous, in geometry, is a term applied to two or more magnitudes which correspond exactly as regards their external circumstances. Thus, the sides which are opposite the corresponding angles of similar triangles are H. sides. In *biology*, organs are termed H. when they correspond in structure and development, though they may differ in their functions.

Homol'ogy is a term now employed by comparative anatomists to designate those organs found in the same body, or in the bodies of different animals, which are structurally composed of the same anatomical elements. Thus the arm of a man, the wing of a bat, the wing of a bird, the fore-leg of a horse, the pectoral fin of a fish, and the flapper of a seal or whale, are all modifications of the anterior extremity of a vertibrate animal, and they are homologous structures. H. is the correlative of *analogy*, a term employed to designate relations in function, but not in structure. Thus the wing of a bird is not homologous with the wing of a butterfly, because it is constructed in a different way, but it is analogous to it, inasmuch as both serve the purposes of flight.

Homoou'sios (Gr. from *homos*, 'the same,' and *ousia*, 'substance') was the term adopted by the Council of Nice (325) to express the relation existing between the Son of God and the Father, or that the divine nature of the former is exactly the same as that of the latter, in opposition to the doctrine of the Arians that the Son, having a beginning and being derived from the Father, was inferior to the latter. *Homoiousios* was the term adopted by the Semi-Arians, as a compromise between the Catholic doctrine and that of the Arians.

Homop'tera (Gr. *homos*, 'the same,' and *pteron*, 'a wing'), a division of *Hemipterous* insects, in which the front wings are entirely membranous; the sucker originating in the inferior part of the head near the thorax, and the wings folding over one another when at rest. The females are provided with an ovipositor, and the antennæ are of small size. To this division belong the *Aphides* or plant-lice; the *Coccidæ* or cochineal insects; the *Cicadas*, and lantern-flies (*Fulgora*).

Ho-nan' ('south of the river'), a province of China, partly bounded on the N. by the Hoang-ho (q. v.). It is singularly fertile lowland, except in the S.W. angle, which is traversed by the Pe-ling mountains. The Hoang-ho is in various parts higher than the surrounding country, which it frequently inundates. Kai-fong, the capital, lies on the right bank of the great river; it was the capital of the empire in the reign of Fubi, and is the residence of the remnant of the Jews of China.

Hondu'ras, a Central American republic, is bounded E. by the Caribbean Sea, W. by the Pacific and San Salvador, N. by Guatemala and the Gulf of H., and S. by Nicaragua. Area, 47,108 sq. miles; pop. about 400,000. It has a mountainous interior, diversified by plateaux, terraces, and fertile valleys, the great chain being the Sierra Madre, which separates at Mereidon into two branches, the Selaque Mountains (10,000 feet), and the easterly range that bears the name Espiritu Santo and Grita. The E. coast is low, and in part abounds with lagoons, as the Laguna de Cartago, and Laguna de Cartine; to the W. of long. 85°, however, it rises in rugged cliffs, and is fringed with islands, among which are the Bay Islands belonging to Jamaica. H. only touches the Pacific at Fonseca Bay, where it has several good harbours. The chief rivers are the Segovia, 300 miles, the boundary between H. and Nicaragua; the Patuca, with its affluent the Guayape, noted for its rich gold-washings; and the Ulua, navigable for 90 miles by steamers. The climate is hot, and the rainy season is heralded by violent hurricanes. The valleys and lowlands are clad with the rich vegetation of the tropics; the plateaux yield abundantly the fruits and plants of the temperate zone, and the mountains are covered with forests of mahogany and other cabinet-wood trees. Besides timber, the country produces gums, drugs, dye-stuffs, sugar-cane, tobacco, coffee, cotton, and cochineal. H. is rich in gold, silver, copper, coal, and marble, which are, however, little wrought. Most of the inhabitants are engaged in cattle-rearing. The exports amounted (1872) in value to £306,250. Cottons and silks are imported from England, cutlery and machinery from the United States. The capital is Comayagua, and the eastern ports are Omoa, Trujillo, and Puerto Cortes. Of the inhabitants, 180,000 are Indians, 200,000 mestizoes, 6000 negroes, and the remainder whites of Spanish descent. The religion is Roman Catholic, and there is little public education. The executive is vested in a President, elected for four years, the legislative in a Senate and Chamber of Deputies. In 1876 the foreign debt amounted to £5,990,108. A railway across H. is to extend from Puerto Cortez to Fonseca Bay, 225 miles, but only 53 miles were completed in 1875. H. was discovered by Columbus in 1502, and taken possession of by the Spaniards in 1523. Later it formed part of the Spanish Guatemala, but became a republic in 1824. After being torn for years by civil war, H. began in 1872 a wretched struggle with Guatemala and San Salvador, which only ended on the exhaustion of both sides, June 1876. See *H., Descriptive, Historical, and Statistical*, by E. G. Squier (Lond. 1870).

Honduras, Bay of, (H. in Spanish means 'deep water'), in the Caribbean Sea, between Honduras, Guatemala, and Balize, receives, among other streams, the Balize, Montagua, and Ulua, and contains many islands, of which the largest is Turneffe.

Honduras, British. See BALIZE.

Hones (Old. Eng. *hán*, Ice. *hein*, 'a whetstone') and **Whetstones** are employed for whetting or sharpening edge-tools and cutting instruments generally. They are composed largely of silica in a finely divided state, and to it their abrasive action is due. Some are used with sperm or neat's-foot oil, others with water, and a few dry. The finer varieties are prepared in different forms, called 'slab,' 'slip,' and 'pencil.' Oilstones for fine cutlery are procured in Leicestershire and North Wales. The hard kinds of the water-of-Ayr stone are also useful as whetstones. The *batts* or keen gritty sandstones obtained in Devonshire, Yorkshire, and Fifeshire are employed for whetting scythes, &c. The Turkey and German H. or oilstones, found respectively in Asia Minor and in slate-hills near Ratisbon, are most esteemed. The other varieties imported into Great Britain are commercially known as the Arkansas, Washita, Peruvian, and Persian oilstones, the Italian water-hone, the Canadian whetstone, and the Norwegian and Russian *ragstones*.

Hon'esty. The small genus *Lunaria* of the natural order *Cruciferæ* is a native of Central and Southern Europe; and in the first catalogue extant of an English garden, viz., that of Gerard (1596), we find the two species *L. biennis* and *L. rediviva* are included. The former he calls 'white satin or honestie,' and the name H. is no doubt taken from the *transparency* of the large silvery partition of the seed pouch.

Hon'ey (Old Eng. *hunig*, Ger. and Dut. *honig*, Dan. *honning*, Swed. *honing*, Icel. *hunáng*) is the sweet syrupy substance extracted by bees from the nectaries of flowers, and deposited by them in cells of wax, an assemblage of which forms a honeycomb. (See WAX.) H. consists essentially of grape-sugar or glucose, in the modified forms known chemically as dextrose and lævulose; and peculiarities of its flavour and colour are more due to the nature of the flowers whence it is obtained than to the kind of bees which collect it. In the Scotch Highlands H. is very largely obtained from heather flowers, and the product is brownish in colour, with a distinct flavour of its own. English H. is chiefly obtained from furze and broom flowers, and, of course, from the cultivated flowers of gardens. The celebrated Narbonne H. owes its peculiar flavour to rosemary and other allied labiate flowers, and it is imitated by artificially flavouring common H. with rosemary. H. in Russia and Eastern Europe is very largely derived from lime-tree flowers, which yield a much-esteemed variety, and from the flowers of the buckwheat plant. Many plants yield H. having noxious or poisonous properties, of which the Trebizond H., derived from *Azalea pontica*, is a famous example. A considerable quantity of H. is imported into England from the forests of S. America. H. is extracted from the comb by simply straining in a very gentle heat, and when so run it forms a thin, transparent syrup. Gradually semi-crystalline grains form in it, and ultimately the H. separates into a thin syrup and a solid sugary portion. H. is often of use medicinally from its laxative influence, and it enters into many minor pharmaceutical preparations, both on account of its pleasant taste as well as for a certain amount of pectoral and demulcent effect it possesses.

Honey Bear (*Cercoleptes candivolvulus*), a species of Carnivorous mammalia inhabiting S. America, and also known by the names Kinkajou and Potto. Its average size is that of a large cat, and its colour is a light brown, marked with darker bands. The tongue is very long and protrusible, and is used, as indicated by the name of the animal, for searching in the nests of wild bees for the honey there accumulated. The tail is prehensile, and assists the animal in climbing upon trees. The H. B. appears to be nocturnal in its habits, and is readily domesticated.

Honey Buzzard (*Pernis apivorus*), a species of Raptorial birds included in the sub-family of the *Milvinæ*, or Kites. It derives its name from its habit of feeding on insects, and especially on bees. Honey itself does not form part of the food, but the persistence with which the bird pursues insects is remarkable. The average length is 22 inches, the females being larger than the males. The colour is a dark or blackish-brown above, the under parts are of a lighter brown. The tail is variegated with light and dark bands of brown. The nest is constructed in high trees, and the eggs, two in number, are reddish coloured.

Honeycomb Moth, or **Bee Moth**, the names given to a species of moths belonging to the genus Galleria, included in the family *Pyralidæ*, or that of the vine moths. They have broad wings, indented on the outer edge. *G. cereana* is a familiar species. Its colour is a dusky grey. It constructs galleries amid the honeycombs of bees. The larvæ are yellow with brown dots, and live in the pupa state within thick white cocoons. Two broods are produced each year in April and August, and the larvæ become moths in three weeks.

Honeydew, a sugary secretion from the leaves of plants in hot weather.

Honey-Eaters, or **Honey-Suckers**, the name popularly given to the birds belonging to the family *Meliphagidæ*, of the order Insessores, sub-order Tenuirostres. They are for the most part found only in Australia, are sociable in their habits, and of handsome plumage. Their bills are long, slender, and curved, while their tongues are feathered, to enable them the better to extract the honey which forms their principal food, though they also feed upon fruits and small insects. Among the principal species the following may be noted:—The New Holland creeper (*Meliphaga Novæ Hollandiæ*), very common in New S. Wales; the bell-bird (*Myzantha melanophrys*), whose tinkling note is a welcome indication that water is to be found not far off; the rifleman or rifle-bird (*Ptilornis paradisea*); and the regent-bird (*Sericulus melinus*), the adult male of which is of a golden yellow, beautifully contrasted with a velvety black. The tui-tui or poe, of New Zealand (*Prosthemadera Novæ Zelandiæ*), is of the size and colour of a starling, with two bunches of white feathers on the throat, supposed to resemble a clergyman's bands, whence it is known to the colonists as the parson-bird. It possesses considerable powers of song and mimicry, and is also esteemed as an article of food.

Honey Guide ('Indicator'), the name applied to a genus of Scansorial or climbing birds, from the fondness they evince for wild bees and their honey. The beak is long and curved. The H. G. are included in the cuckoo family (*Cuculidæ*), and have the third to the fifth quills the longest in the wings. The great H. G. (*I. major*) occurs in S. Africa, whilst other species are found in India and Borneo. The lesser H. G. (*I. minor*) is also a S. African species. The colour of the former is dark-brown above, and greyish-white below. Both sexes assist in incubation, and the eggs, which number three or four, are of a brownish-white hue.

Honey Locust-Tree. See LOCUST-TREE.

Honeystone, or **Mell'ite**, a mineral found in some parts of Prussia and Austria, which crystallises in square octohedrons, and can be cut with a knife. In chemical composition it is essentially mellate of alumina.

Hon'eysuckle. In poetry and popular usage the woodbine (*Lonicera Periclymenum*) is meant by H., but, says Dr. Prior, 'it is very doubtful to what plant the word properly belongs.' Gerard in 1599 applies it as we do, whereas Parkinson makes it denote meadow clover. The large genus *Lonicera*, which takes its name from a German botanist, belongs to the natural order *Caprifoliaceæ*, and is distributed through the temperate and warm regions of the northern hemisphere. In addition to our common species, two others now appear in British floras, viz., perfoliate H. (*L. caprifolium*) and fly H. (*L. xylosteum*). The latter is perhaps native in two or three counties of S. England, the first is certainly only an introduction. Both are commonly planted in shrubberies, &c., as is also trumpet H. (*L. sempervirens*), a handsome climbing N. American species with evergreen leaves and scarlet flowers. *L. Japonica* is frequently figured in Chinese drawings.

Hon'fleur, a town of France, department of Calvados, on the left bank of the Seine, 7 miles S.E. of Havre. Its streets are narrow and winding, and it contains several interesting buildings of the 16th c. It has a well-sheltered port, large fisheries, imports of coal, wood, and iron; and exports of fruit, eggs, poultry, &c. There is some shipbuilding, and sugar, biscuits, and oil are manufactured. Pop. (1872) 15,475.

Hong-Kong properly **Hiang-Kiang** (the place of 'fragrant streams'), an English island off the S.E. coast of China, at the mouth of the Chu-kiang, 75 miles S.E. of Canton. Area, 29 sq. miles; pop. (1874) 121,985, of whom 115,564 are Chinese, 4931 Europeans and Americans, and 1490 natives of Manilla. The island is 9 miles long, of irregular shape, bare and mountainous, rising to a height of 1825 feet. The rocks are chiefly granite, serpentine, and syenite. H. has a fairly good climate. From May to October (83°–90° F.) there is much rain and great heat; but the four winter months (40°–75° F.) are dry, and even occasionally chilly. The change of temperature is, however, apt to engender disease of the kidneys. On the N. side of the island is the city of Victoria, with a deep commodious harbour. It extends for about 3 miles along the bay, from the foot of the hills to the water's edge, and has a cathedral, a governor's house, a bishop's palace, an exchange, an hospital, good free schools for the poorer Chinese, and fine public gardens. The chief imports (value, 1875, £3,599,811) are cotton goods, opium, and ships' supplies; the exports (value, 1875, £1,154,910) are tea (11,702,812 lbs.), silk, spices, opium, rice, and China ware. In spite of the increase of direct communication with the various ports, H. still remains the great financial centre of the China trade. Bombay, Calcutta, San Francisco, Canton, Macao, and Singapore steamers go and come almost daily, and the harbour is thronged by thousands of junks and other sailing vessels. In 1872 the total tonnage of vessels entering and clearing was 3,777,676. Other havens for large steamers are Aberdeen on the S. coast and Kow-lung on the peninsula of the same name, opposite Victoria. The colony, which includes a maritime strip of the mainland, is under a governor and legislative council, and yields a surplus (£14,290 in 1874) of revenue after defraying the expense of a strong police force of Indian Sepoys. The island was ceded in perpetuity to Great Britain in 1843.

Hon'iton, an old town of England, Devonshire, in the rich valley of the Otter, 17 miles N.E. of Exeter by rail. It gives name to the fine 'H. lace' still manufactured here, and in most of the towns and villages of Devonshire. The industry was introduced in the time of Elizabeth by the Lollards. H. returned two members to Parliament till it was disfranchised in 1868. Pop. (1871) 3464.

Honolu'lu, the capital of the Sandwich Islands, is situated on the S. shore of the island of Oahu, in lat. 21° 18′ N. and long. 157° 55′ W. It has a fine deep harbour, formed by a breach in the coral reef that girds the islands, and lined with spacious wharves. The city is embowered in tropical foliage, and has a healthy, equable climate, with a temperature ranging from 60° to 87° F. Its chief buildings are the royal palace, the parliament house, a Roman Catholic cathedral, an Anglican church, the hospital, a post-office, and a theatre. Steamers touch here regularly in the passage between Australia, New Zealand, China, Japan, and San Francisco. In 1872 there entered the port 138 merchant vessels (96,957 tons), of which 86 were American, and 47 whalers. The exports, chiefly sugar, paddy, tallow, coffee, wool, and whale oil and bone, amount in value (1872) to 1,402,685 dollars; the imports, building materials, cottons, woollens, silks, provisions, lumber, &c., to 1,583,583 dollars. Pop. (1872) 14,852.

Hon'or, in English law, is a superior manor or seigniory. An H. may be held by grant or prescription; but the crown cannot create one without an Act of Parliament. There are eighty in England.

Honora'rium, the name given to a counsel's or physician's fees, which were presumably a present given beforehand. Consequently a lawyer or physician could not legally recover unpaid fees; but this no longer applies to physicians.

Hono'rius, the name of several popes. The first was Bishop of Rome from 625 till 638, and was condemned as a heretic by the 6th Œcumenical Council at Constantinople, 680 A.D., for having adopted the doctrine of the Monothelites. This circumstance has been a serious obstacle in the way of the supporters of papal infallibility, and the questions suggested by H.'s heresy and condemnation have been keenly discussed. See Hefele's *Die Honorius-frage* (1870).—**H. II.** was appointed Pope under imperial influence in 1061, a few weeks after Alexander II. had been nominated by Hildebrand and the other cardinals. He was repudiated by two councils, never exercised papal authority, and died in obscurity in 1072.—Another H., sometimes called **H. III.**, but generally reckoned **H. II.**, Pope from 1124 to 1130, was compelled by Count Roger of Sicily to surrender the papal fiefs of Calabria and Apulia; his elder brother Arcadius (q. v.) obtaining the East. A fourth **H.**, from 1216–1227, crowned Friedrich II. emperor, was a friend of the new Mendicant order, and also of the Teutonic knights; and yet another from 1285–87, who chiefly busied himself with Sicilian politics.

Hono'rius, Fla'vius, second son of the Roman Emperor Theodosius I., was born in 384. On the death of his father in 395, the empire was divided, and H. succeeded quietly to the western portion. But as he was a minor, all affairs were at first entrusted to Stilicho (q. v.), whose prudence and force of character did much for H.'s reign, until he fell a victim to the intrigues of the eunuch Olympius at Ravenna in 408. This able general, whose daughter Maria H. had married, repulsed the Visigothic irruption in 402–3, as well as that of Rhadagaisus in 405–6; but after his death Alaric again entered Italy, and sacked Rome in 410, dying however in the same year. Constantius now appeared to deliver the empire, defeating the usurper Constantine in 411, and turning back the barbarians, for which services he was rewarded with the hand of H.'s sister Placidia, and declared Augustus by H., but survived only seven months. In this reign Britain, Gaul, Spain, and Pannonia fell away from the Roman Empire. H.'s residence, at first fixed at Milan, was in his later years at Ravenna, where he died, 27th August 423. His character was feeble, faithless, and cruel. See Gibbon's *Decline and Fall of the Roman Empire.*

Honourable Ordinaries. See ORDINARIES.

Honours, Military and Naval. See SALUTES.

Hon'theim, Johann Nikolaus von, a famous opponent of papal tyranny belonging to the ranks of the Catholic hierarchy, was born at Trier (Treves), 27th June 1701, and educated at Louvain, Leyden, and Rome. On his return to Trier, he was appointed to various offices of importance in State and Church by the Elector Georg, and was finally, in 1748, made a Suffragan of the Archbishop. His *Historia Trevirensis Diplomatica* was published in 1750, the *Prodromus* in 1757; but the work *De Statu Ecclesiæ Liber Singularis* (Frankf. 1763), put forth under the pseudonym Justinus Febronius, attracted a wider and keener interest than the others. It was designed to further union amongst the distending Christian sects and parties, and in defending the liberties of the Church it attacked overweening papal assumptions. The hostility of Rome did not directly assault H., powerfully supported as he was; but the perpetual harassment to which he was subjected led him in his old age to make a partial retractation. He died at Montquintin, 2d September 1790.

Honved' ('defenders of the land'), a name used in Hungary in 1848 for the volunteers raised to repel the incursions of the Serbs, then used for the whole national army during the revolutionary war. The force of honveds now existing was constituted in 1868. It is supplementary to the regular army and landwehr, and is composed of such able-bodied men as are not yet or no longer required to serve either in the army or in the Hungarian reserve. Most of the force are very young men.

Hood, Robin, a celebrated outlaw, who is traditionally assigned to the beginning of the 13th c. The first mention of him is in the *Vision of Piers the Plowman* (1362–78), 'But I can rymes of Robyn hood' (Pass. v. l. 402); and the next in Wyntown's *Orygynale Cronykil* (circa 1420), where 'Lytell John and Robyne Hude' are both spoken of rather kindly (B. vii. ll. 3523–24). Wynkin de Worde printed *The Lytel Geste of Robyn Hood* about 1495, and Major, early in the 16th c., described him as 'of all thieves the prince and the most gentle thief.' R. H. is the subject of many ballads and legends, for which see the *R. H. Collection*, 2 vols., published by Ritson in 1795, and enlarged by J. M. Gutch in 1847, and *Percy's Reliques*. Mr. Thomas Wright, in his *Essay on the Middle Ages*, doubts the existence of such a person; but the Rev. J. Hunter, in *Critical and Historical Tracts*, stoutly maintains his historic reality, and endeavours to identify him with a certain Robyn Hod, sometime a porteur to King Edward II. Thierry suggests that he was a Saxon patriot carrying on a guerilla warfare against Norman oppression, while others consider that he was a follower of Simon de Montfort; and Ritson submits that his name was Robert Fitzooth, and that he had a claim to the Earldom of Huntingdon, but in support of this there does not appear a shadow of evidence. The haunts of the R. H. of popular tradition were Barnsdale in Yorkshire, and notably Sherwood Forest in Nottingham, where Stow relates that he 'entertained 100 tall men and good archers with such spoils and thefts as he got, on whom 400 (were they ever so strong) durst not give the onset. He suffered no woman to be oppressed, violated, or otherwise molested. Poor men's goods he spared, abundantly relieving them with that which by theft he got from abbeys and the houses of rich old carles.' His prowess in combat, skill in archery, and, above all, his levelling of rich with poor by force of arms, have made him a preeminent favourite of the people, along with his companions, the most famous of whom are his henchman Little John, his mistress, Maid Marian, and his jovial chaplain, Friar Tuck.

Hood, Samuel, Viscount, an English admiral, was the son of the vicar of Thorn Cliffe, Devonshire, and was born 12th December 1724. He entered the navy in 1740. As commander of a fifty-gun ship he captured a French frigate of equal strength in 1757, and another in 1759, when he was made post-captain. He served in the Mediterranean till the close of the war in 1763. In 1780 he was sent as rear-admiral to the W. Indies, and brilliantly distinguished himself in the actions with the Comte de Grasse on 9th and 12th April 1782. In 1784 he was elected member for Westminster. As admiral in the Mediterranean he took Toulon in 1793, and before evacuating it destroyed the arsenal and many ships of war. He drove the French out of Corsica in 1794. In 1796 he was appointed

Governor of Greenwich Hospital. He was created a baronet in 1778, an Irish peer in 1782, and a viscount in the peerage of Great Britain in 1796. H. died June 27, 1816. His younger brother, Alexander, created Viscount Bridport in 1801, was also a celebrated admiral. He died 3d May 1814.

Hood, Thomas, an English poet and humorist, of Scotch extraction, was the son of a bookseller in London, where he was born, May 23, 1799. He was apprenticed to an engraver; but his health being delicate, was sent to Dundee to recruit, and his first literary effusion appeared in the *Dundee Advertiser* in 1814. Returning to London in 1820, he became sub-editor of the *London Magazine*, and the success of some poetical efforts made him choose authorship definitely as a profession. In 1825 he published *Odes and Addresses to Great People*, conjointly with his brother-in-law, J. W. Reynolds, and in 1826 *Whims and Oddities*. His *Comic Annual*, which amusingly caricatured passing events, appeared regularly from 1830 to 1838, an additional volume in 1842, and *H.'s Own* was started in 1838. *Up the Rhine* appeared in 1839, and he edited the *London Magazine* from 1841 to 1844, when he began *H.'s Magazine*. All his life he struggled against bad health, and a long and wasting illness, borne with much gentleness, terminated in his death on May 3, 1845. See *Memorials of T. H.*, edited by his son and daughters, published in 1860. H. was a master of the grotesque and the ridiculous, the prince of punsters, and a poet of clear shining lustre. His writings breathe a tender sympathy with suffering and poverty, and a large-hearted charity. *The Bridge of Sighs*, *Eugene Aram*, *The Song of the Shirt*, *The Lady's Dream*, *The Deathbed*, and many of his minor poems, are things of exquisite beauty, and will live with the language. His entire works with Life, in 10 vols., were printed in 1869-73, edited by his son, Thomas Hood, who was born in 1835, was for many years editor of *Fun*, and died November 20, 1874.

Hoofs (Old Eng. *hôf*, Dut. *hoef*, Ger. *huf*, Dan. *hov*, anything that *shields* or *covers*), the name given to the largely developed 'nails' which protect and invest the toes of many mammals. Their typical development is well seen in the horse, the care of whose hoof and the treatment of the diseases to which it is subject are matters of extreme importance. Brittle H. arise from inattention, from long periods of dryness, and sometimes from general debility. When H. 'crack,' they become liable to sores and ulcers which are very difficult to heal. Careful washing and frequent oiling are the best preventives of disease. Undue paring is a cause of lameness. Rest and attention to the general health are the chief things to be attended to in the treatment of ordinary affections of the H., but when the H. are cracked or worn, blistering and other measures may become necessary. See HORSE-SHOEING.

Hooft, Pieter, a Dutch historian, born at Amsterdam, 16th March 1581; after studying at Leyden University, he travelled for a time in Germany, France, and especially Italy. On returning to Holland he devoted himself to historical study and writing after the manner of Tacitus, whose works he translated into Dutch. *Het leven van Koning Hendrik IV.* (Amsterd. 1626-52); *Geschiedenis der Huis Medici* (Amsterd. 1649); *Nederlandsche Historien* (2 vols. Amsterd. 1642-54; newer ed. by Hecker, 5 vols. Grön. 1843-46), embracing the years 1556 to 1587, are his most important works. H. was also a distinguished lyrist and tragic poet. His *Gedichten* (Amsterd. 1656; edited by Bilderdijk, 3 vols. Leyd. 1823) and his letters (edited by Huydecooper, 1738) are regarded as models. H. died at the Hague, 21st May 1647. His influence on the development of Dutch has been very great.

Hoogh'ly (*Hugli*), the most southern mouth of the Ganges, on which Calcutta is situated, and the only one now used by large ships. This name is applied from the junction of the Bhagirutti and Jelinghi at Nuddea town to the sea at Saugor Island, 160 miles in all; at the latter point the estuary is 15 miles wide, opposite Calcutta only 1 mile, now spanned by a floating bridge which cost £220,000. The tributaries are the Damudah and the Rupnarain, both on the right bank. Sandbanks are continually forming in the channel, and destructive cyclones sometimes occur; the bore or tidal wave is well known. The H. retains the sanctity of the Ganges, and on its bank are many historic sites. It is navigable up to Chandernagore, and the port of Calcutta extends along 10 miles.

Hooghly, the chief town of the district of the same name, province of Bengal, British India, 27 miles N. of Calcutta. Pop. (1872), together with the former Dutch settlement of Chinsurah, 34.761. H. is said to have been founded in 1537 by the Portuguese, who were expelled by the Mohammedans in 1628. The first English factory in Bengal was planted here in 1642. The principal building is the Imambara, a religious college of Mussulman learning with a large endowment. The first printing-press in Bengal was set up here in 1778.—The *district* of H., which borders the H. river on the W., has an area, including Howrah, of 1424 sq. miles; and a pop. (1872) of 1,488,556, or 1045 to the sq. mile, the greatest density in all India, and probably throughout the whole world. The soil is very fertile, and supplies vegetables and fruit for the Calcutta market; the manufactures and through trade are also considerable.

Hook, Theodore Edward, novelist and dramatist, was born in London, September 22, 1788. He was educated at Harrow and Oxford. Almost fabulous stories are told of his powers as an improvisatore, but they were wonderful enough to astound Coleridge and mystify Sheridan. The hero of a hundred drawing-rooms, he was petted and fêted by the leaders of society. The Prince Regent, fascinated by his splendid versatility, procured for him the Treasurership of the Mauritius with £2000 a year. To that island H. was sent in 1813, where he spent five delightful years. But in 1818 there was a deficit of £20,000 in the treasury, and H. was found guilty of the grossest carelessness and recalled. His life, from 1818 to its close, is one of extraordinary vigour, both in the pursuit of literature and pleasure. In these twenty-three years he produced thirty-eight volumes, besides numberless squibs, papers, and sketches. In 1820 he started the *John Bull* newspaper, to attack Queen Caroline and champion high Toryism. He was in prison from 1823 to 1825 for his debt to the crown, which he never made any attempt to discharge, although he was making on an average £3000 a year by his writings. His *Sayings and Doings* appeared from 1824 to 1828; *Maxwell*, his best novel, in 1830; *Love and Pride* in 1833; *Gilbert Gurney*, almost an autobiography in fiction, in 1835; *Jack Brag* in 1837; *Gurney Married* in 1839, and *Peregrine Bunce* in 1842. H. died August 24, 1841. See *Life and Remains of T. E. H.*, by the Rev. R. H. D. Barham (2 vols. 1849).—**Rev. Walter Farquhar H., D.D.**, son of the Rev. Dr. J. Hook, and nephew of the preceding, was born March 13, 1798, and educated at Winchester and Oxford. Ordained in 1821, he became Chaplain-ordinary to George IV., and subsequently to William IV. and Queen Victoria. He was vicar of Leeds from 1837 till 1859, when he was appointed Dean of Chichester, during which time he did much in the way of church and school extension. Though a High Churchman, he was a liberal educationist. His *Ecclesiastical Biography* and *Church Dictionary* are standard works of reference. He also published the *Lives of the Archbishops of Canterbury*, and many sermons and pamphlets. He died October 20, 1875.

Hooke, Robert, a distinguished natural philosopher, was born at Freshwater in the Isle of Wight, July 18, 1635. In 1664 he became Professor of Geometry in Gresham College, London, and in 1677 was appointed secretary to the Royal Society, in the formation of which, seventeen years earlier, he had taken a most active part. In the *Transactions* of this Society are numerous and most valuable papers by him, bearing on almost every department of physical science, and foreshadowing many of the discoveries of his contemporaries and successors. His suggestion of the law of gravitation, and his researches into the cause of the colours of thin plates, roused a controversy between him and Newton. Among other valuable inventions he constructed the spirit level, the marine barometer, a reflecting quadrant, and a dividing engine; he suggested the freezing and boiling points of water as convenient and fixed standards for measuring temperature, and the pendulum as a standard measure; he enunciated the law of elasticity—*ut tensio sic vis*—and invented the well-known and most valuable *universal joint*. His chief works are *Micrographia* (1666) and *Lectiones Cutlerianæ* (1678-79). He died at London, March 3, 1702.

Hook'er, Richard, one of the greatest of English theologians and prose writers, was born of a poor family at Heavitree, in or near Exeter, about 1554. His schoolmaster, seeing his abilities, brought him under the notice of Jewel, Bishop of Salisbury, who gave him a pension and had him admitted as a clerk or sizar to Corpus Christi, Oxford. In 1577 he was made Fellow of his college, and in 1579 Hebrew lecturer, and in the same year was, for some unknown cause, expelled. He became preacher at St. Paul's, London, and after, in 1586, making a marriage which proved very unhappy, settled in the living of Drayton, Beauchamp, Buckinghamshire. In 1584–85 he was, through Archbishop Whitgift's influence, elected Master of the Temple, where Travers, the afternoon lecturer, maintained Presbyterianism, while H. upheld Episcopacy. 'The pulpit,' says Fuller, 'spake pure Canterbury in the morning, and Geneva in the afternoon.' In 1591 H. received the living of Boscombe, near Salisbury, where he wrote his *Ecclesiastical Polity*, of which the first four books were published in 1594, the fifth being issued in 1597. In 1595 he removed from Boscombe to the better living of Bishopsborne, near Canterbury, where he died, 2d November 1600. The sixth and eighth books of the *Polity* were published in 1651, the seventh in 1662. It has been argued by Walton and others that the three last books were distorted by the Presbyterian friends of H.'s wife; but this, though probable, has not been conclusively proved. Mr. Keble, however (the latest and best editor of H.), has shown that the sixth book is utterly lost, and that what now stands for it is matter quite irrelevant, though possibly obtained from H.'s papers. The *Ecclesiastical Polity* is an elaborate defence of the English Church, based on philosophical rather than on theological grounds, H. asserting, in opposition to the dogmatism of the Presbyterian Cartwright, that 'no form of church government had ever been of indispensable obligation;' that divine order exists in moral relations as well as in written revelation, and that the human reason can distinguish the laws of this order as well as the eternal from the temporal in Scripture. The reasoning, though sometimes hazy, is generally conducted with depth, cogency, and calm dignity; H.'s tranquil eloquence being nobly free from the angry partisanship of his age. Hallam, in his *Const. Hist.* (c. iv.), says that H. 'mingled in these vulgar controversies like a knight of romance among caitiff brawlers, with arms of finer temper, and worthy to be proved on a nobler field.' But for a certain arrogant scorn of the question at issue, this might be accepted as a just representation. H.'s style is unadorned in comparison with that of the other great Elizabethans. It is grave and elaborately rhythmical, its stately periods flowing on with a golden wealth of language and solemn music. Its faults are want of simplicity, occasional intricacy and awkwardness, and an unpleasant frequency of Latin idioms. See Isaac Walton's *Life of H.* (2d ed. 1670), and the biography in Keble's edition of H.'s Works (4 vols. Lond. 1836). The first book, with a prefatory memoir by R. W. Church, forms a volume (1868) in the *Clarendon Press Series*.

Hook'er, Sir William Jackson, F.R.S., a celebrated English botanist, was born at Norwich in 1785. He was Professor of Botany in Glasgow University from 1821 to 1841. In 1836 he was knighted, and in 1841 became director of the botanical gardens at Kew, where he died, August 12, 1865. His chief works are the *Monograph of the British Jungermanniæ* (1812–16), *Icones Filicum* (in conjunction with Dr. Greville, 2 vols. 1826–37), *The British Flora* (1830), the later editions of which have been published under the joint editorship of H. and Dr. Walker Arnott, *Icones Plantarum* (1837–60), *A Century of Orchidaceous Plants* (1846–53), *British Ferns* (1862).—**Joseph Dalton H., M.D., C.B., F.R.S.**, the only surviving son of the preceding, was born at Glasgow in 1817. In 1839 he accompanied the *Erebus* to the Antarctic Ocean as assistant-surgeon, and on his return published *Flora Antarctica*, a valuable contribution to the geographical distribution of plants. In 1847 he journeyed to the Himalayas, where he remained four years studying the flora. His *Himalayan Journals* (1852) are a most valuable addition to botanical literature. In 1855 he was appointed assistant-director of the Kew Gardens, and succeeded to the directorship on his father's death in 1865. In 1868 he was President of the British Association. In 1871 he brought home a valuable collection of plants from Morocco. He is at present (1877) the President of the Royal Society of London, a position to which he was elected in 1873. His latest works are *The Student's Flora of the British Islands* (1870), and *The Flora of British India* (1874).

Hooks and Eyes are well-known useful fastenings for wearing apparel and other articles. They are made from iron or brass wire or sheet-metal by the aid of machinery. There are numerous modifications of the ordinary hook, which has the body bent into a 'beak' that engages in a circular eye, both of the articles having lateral rings for attachment to the garment. The hook is sometimes provided with a 'spring' or 'tongue' for preventing the eye becoming accidentally disengaged.

Hook-Squid, a name given to certain genera of Cuttle-fishes (q. v.), from the hooked processes with which the suckers of the arms are furnished. These hooks not only increase the prehensile power of the arms, but serve to attach the one elongated tentacle to the other, so as to bring the muscular power of these two largest arms to bear upon any object. The H. S. are allied to our common squids, and belong to the family *Teuthidæ*. The genus *Onychoteuthis* includes the most familiar species.

Hoop Ash. See Nettle-Tree.

Hoop'er, John, an English Protestant martyr, born in Somersetshire about 1495, and educated at Oxford. He became a Cistercian monk, but embracing the Reformation, was obliged to leave England in 1540, and lived in France and Switzerland till Edward VI.'s accession. In 1550 he was nominated Bishop of Gloucester, and was imprisoned for some months for a refusal to wear vestments. The matter was compromised, and he received the Bishopric of Worcester *in commendam* in 1552. On Queen Mary's accession he was committed to the Fleet, tried by Gardiner on January 28, 1555, and, refusing to recant, was burned at Gloucester, February 9, 1555, meeting death with admirable courage. His works were published by the Parker Society in 2 vols. in 1843 and 1852.

Hoop'ing-Cough, or **Pertuss'is**, is an infectious and sometimes epidemic specific disease, preceded and accompanied by fever, attacking children mostly during the spring and autumn months. H.-C. has a period of incubation, usually of five or six days after exposure, followed by fever and catarrh, which may last from one to eight days or longer, being the first stage of the disease. The second stage is indicated by a remission of the fever, and the appearance of the characteristic *whoop*, the disease being then fully formed. The approach of the fit is indicated by a titillation of the glottis, a sharp pain in the chest, and a spasmodic contraction of the diaphragm, so rapid and convulsive that the air is almost instantly expelled from the lungs, nearly suffocating the patient. When the diaphragm relaxes, the violent inspiration which follows gives rise to the characteristic *whoop*. In ordinary cases the paroxysms recur every two hours, but in more severe cases, especially during the second and third week, every quarter of an hour or oftener, the patient being well during the intervals. The duration of the second stage is from two to eight weeks, but the whole duration is exceedingly variable, sometimes terminating in two or three days, or extending over several months. H.-C. is frequently complicated with inflammation of the mucous membrane of the bronchia, of the soft tissues of the lungs, of the stomach or intestines, or of the serous membranes of the brain. H.-C. is induced by a specific poison, probably of the nature of a vegetable parasite, the germs being communicable from one subject to another by *fomites*, and is, consequently, a preventible disease. It seldom affects the same person oftener than once, and but few children escape it. The mortality from H.-C. is considerable, and is greater in towns than in the country. *Treatment:*—Narcotics, such as belladonna, hemlock, hyoscyamus and opium, have no specific action, but are useful in allaying the paroxysms and shortening the spasmodic period. Cochineal is an anodyne which sometimes affords relief, but all treatment is merely palliative; for in H.-C., as in typhus, cholera, and many other affections of a similar class, the nature of the agent which modifies and gives a specific character to the disorder is unknown. The disease is most successfully treated by topical applications administered by inhalation.

Hoop'oe (*Upupa*), a genus of Insessorial birds, belonging to the group *Tenuirostres* (q. v.), and forming the type of a special family (*Upupidæ*). In the genus *Upupa*, the bill is slender and curved throughout, and the nostrils are covered by a scale. The tarsi are invested with broad scales or plates, and the tail is long and even. The outer toe is longer than the inner, and the claw of the hinder toe is long and straight. The name H. is derived from the cry of the bird, the common species of which (*U. epops*) is found in N. Africa, on the European continent, and in Asia, and occasionally, though rarely, in England. The H. attains a length of 13 inches. Its colours are white, buff, and black. It has a remarkable crest of feathers, of a reddish-buff hue, tipped with black. Its food consists of insects. The nest is built in hollow trees, and the eggs—of a light grey—vary in number from four to seven. The young are hatched in June. To the family *Upupidæ* also belong the genus *Epimachus*, or that of the plume-birds, and the genus *Neomorpha*, inhabiting New Zealand.

Hoops. See CRINOLINE.

Hoorn, a seaport in the province of N. Holland, in the Netherlands, on the Zuider Zee, 10 miles E. of Alkmaar. Its walls have given place to promenades, and there is considerable shipbuilding and fishing. It has a naval college, and a trade in butter and cheese. Pop. (1875) 9503.

Hop (the name was adopted from the Netherlands along with the culture of the plant about the year 1520) belongs to *Humulus Lupulus*, sole British representative of the natural order *Cannabinaceæ* or *Cannabineæ*. The plant is indigenous in Mid and South England, and is elsewhere native throughout temperate Europe, Asia, and N. America. It is a perennial, producing yearly long, weak, tough, roughish, twining stems, and opposite, lobed, coarsely-toothed leaves, which bear a general resemblance to those of the vine, but are harsh to the touch. The male and female flowers are produced on separate plants. The males grow in loose drooping panicles, whilst the females form yellowish-green catkins or stroboli, which are produced either singly or in clusters, and are composed of a number of membranous partly overwrapping concave scales, each having two inconspicuous flowers at its base. These catkins increase in size during the progress of ripening, and when full grown, constitute the brewer's 'hops.' Their active qualities reside principally in an adherent golden yellow powder (*lupuline*), and in brewing they serve the important purposes of checking acetous fermentation, and thus rendering the beer capable of being kept, of clarifying the beer, and of imparting to it an agreeable bitterness and flavour. Extract, tincture, and infusion of hops are used medicinally as soporifics, and the young shoots for use as asparagus are a common article of sale in some of the Continental vegetable markets.

Cultivation of Hops.—The cultivation of hops as a branch of agricultural industry is chiefly carried on in the S.E. counties of England, Kent being the great 'H.-garden' of England. The growth of hops gives to the country a peculiar aspect, as the plants, being climbers, have to be supported on multitudes of poles. The H. attains its full growth in the third year of its existence, and it requires considerable attention. The chief manures used to favour its growth are animal matters, such as hair, skin, blood, fish, &c. The H.-picking season begins in September. Thousands of persons of the poorer classes then migrate to the H.-fields from London and other large towns. The hops are conveyed to the *kilns* in which the process of drying is carried on; this process is conducted most carefully, in order to avoid inducing chemical changes, which would destroy the quality of the lupuline. Huge bags are made up of the dried hops and conveyed to market for sale. Hops exhibit many varieties in favour with growers, each variety being found to be adapted to certain soils. The *Golding hops*, numbering many sub-varieties, as the Jones' variety and the Farnham variety, are in the highest repute. In 1875, 254,444 cwts. of hops (value £1,188,054) were imported from the Continent and America. In Britain about 550,000,000 gallons of ale and porter are brewed annually, and to each bushel of malt used in brewing about 1 lb. of hops is added. The duty formerly levied on hops has been removed, and hence every encouragement is given to the cultivation of this product abroad. The addition of hops to malt liquors not only imparts to them an aroma and flavour, but also tends to keep them in a wholesome condition. See BEER.

Hop Clover is *Trifolium procumbens*, and so called from the resemblance of its heads of flowers to little catkins of hops.

Hope, Thomas, an English author and connoisseur, descended from the Hopes of Amsterdam, was born in London about 1770. At eighteen becoming master of a large fortune, he spent eight years of travel in the study of the architectures of the East, and on his return to England applied these studies practically to the enlargement and decoration of his mansion in Duchess Street, Portland Place, London. In 1805 H. published *Household Furniture*, a work which, though ridiculed in the *Edinburgh Review*, gave a great impulse to decorative art in England. To it succeeded *Costume of the Ancients* (1809), *Modern Costumes* (1812), and a novel, *Anastasius, or Memoirs of a Modern Greek at the Close of the 18th c.* (1819). The last, published anonymously, was at the time commonly ascribed to Byron, and called forth a eulogistic criticism from Sydney Smith, the *Edinburgh* assailant of 'the gentleman upholsterer.' H. married Louisa Beresford, daughter of the Archbishop of Tuam, and died February 3, 1831. Two posthumous works of H. are his *Historical Essays on Architecture* (3 vols. 1831), and the brilliant but extravagant treatise *On the Origin and Prospects of Man* (2 vols. 1837), which was subsequently suppressed.—**Alexander James Beresford H., M.P., LL.D.**, son of the preceding, was born in 1820, and educated at Harrow and Trinity College, Cambridge, where he took his B.A. in 1841. In 1842 he married Lady Mildred Cecil, a daughter of the Marquis of Salisbury, in 1844 founded a missionary college (St. Augustine's) at Canterbury, and in 1865–67 was President of the Royal Institute of British Architects. H. sat for Maidstone 1841–52, and again in 1857; was defeated for the University of Cambridge (1859) and for Stoke-upon-Trent (1862), but was elected for the latter borough in 1865, and for the University, which he still represents, in 1868. He is the author of *Letters on Church Matters by D.C.L.*; *Worship in the Church of England* (1874), &c., and is best known as a prominent member of the High Church party.

Hop Flea (*Haltica concinna*), a species of *Coleoptera* or beetles, belonging to the family *Chrysomelidæ*. It attains a length of $\frac{1}{10}$th of an inch. This small insect does great damage to the young shoots. The turnip flea beetle (*H. striolata*), and the grapeleaf flea beetle (*H. chalybea*), also belong to this genus.

Hop Fly (*Aphis humuli*), a species of plant-lice or *Aphides* (q. v.), *Hemipterous* insects, infesting many trees and shrubs, and causing great damage, especially to young plants. It has even been asserted that on its absence the prosperity of the hop crop chiefly depends. The H. F. is not a true fly. Like other aphides, it produces winged males and females at the end of autumn, and these in turn produce eggs, from which, in the succeeding spring, wingless females are developed. The curious fact has also been noticed that these wingless females produce generations of others without the presence of any male insects, the latter not appearing until the succeeding autumn. The H. F. is of green colour, banded with black.

Hôpital, Michel de l'. See L'HÔPITAL.

Hop'kins, Samuel, D.D., an American theologian, born at Waterbury, Connecticut, U.S., September 17, 1721, studied at Yale College, became pastor at Housatonic (now Great Barrington), Massachusetts, and at Newport, where he died, December 20, 1803. He wrote a number of sermons, a Life of President Edwards, a system of theology (new ed. Bost. 1852), &c., and has given rise to the *Hopkinsians*, a Calvinistic sect who hold that all sin is selfishness, and all virtue disinterested benevolence.

Hora'tius, Flacc'us Quin'tus, a great Latin lyrist, and the most popular in modern times of all Greek and Roman authors, was born December 8, 65 B.C., near Venusia (mod. Venosa), where his father, a Venusian freedman, who had been a collector (*coactor*) either of the public revenue, or, more probably, of the money at auctions, had bought a small farm. Here H. spent his earliest years, and here, according to a charming story told in one of his lyrics, he was found when a child sleeping in the summer woods amid laurel and myrtle strewn over him by the wild doves. When he came to boyhood, his father, though a poor man, had him carefully educated at Rome under one Orbilius, whose fondness for castigating his pupils H. has commemorated. Between the ages of seventeen and twenty he studied literature and philosophy at Athens, and in B.C. 43 he joined the army of Brutus, his brief military career ending at Philippi, where, he says, he cast away his shield and fled. When he returned to Italy, about 41 B.C., he found his small estate confiscated, but contrived, we do not know how, to obtain a kind of clerkship in the quæstor's department, on the salary of which he managed to live with great frugality. About this time he produced his *Epodes*, and won the reputation of being a brilliant, stinging satirist. In 39 B.C. he was introduced through Virgil and Varius to Mæcenas, who became his lifelong patron and friend, and about 33 B.C. gave him the 'Sabine farm,' immortalised in his verse, a small estate in the secluded valley of Ustica, 30 miles from Rome. In this retreat H. spent much of his later years, delighting to escape again and again from the dust and din of the capital to its shady hills and cool streams. About 27 B.C. he won the patronage of Augustus, who proposed to make him his secretary, an offer which the poet declined, and who gave him a fine villa at Tibur. His juvenile republican fervour had cooled, and he celebrated the praises of the Emperor in strains of glowing and partly sincere adulation. He became intimate with the leading Roman authors and statesmen, and his life glided tranquilly and happily away in refined epicurean pleasures, in polishing his verses, and in light, rural occupations. H. died, shortly after the death of Mæcenas, aged nearly fifty-seven, on November 17, 8 B.C. His works include the *Satires* (bk. i. about 35 B.C., bk. ii. about 33 B.C.); the *Epodes* (about 31 B.C.); the *Odes* (bk. i., ii., iii., about 24 B.C., bk. iv. about 14 B.C.); the *Epistles* (bk. i. about 20 B.C., bk. ii. uncertain); the *Carmen Seculare* (17 B.C.); the *Ars Poetica* (uncertain, but belonging to his last years). H.'s *Odes* have not the unstudied grace, spiritual rapture, and dewy freshness of such lyrics as those of Burns, but they are inimitable in artistic effect; they embalm in the most translucent and mellifluous Latin poetic flowers culled from the Greek song-writers, while there is a distinctively national character in their occasional stateliness, their solemn moral teachings, and the fragrance which they breathe of the old rural life of Italy. The *Satires* and *Epistles* are H.'s most natural and original works. They are written in a style at once terse, polished, and colloquial; they are full of shrewd wisdom melting into humour, of earnest precepts enlivened by personal gossip and racy anecdote; and they contain the most vivid pictures of ancient Roman life both in the luxurious capital and in the neighbouring country district. The *editio princeps* of H. was issued at Milan in 1470. Among the best modern editions are those of Orelli (3d ed. 1850–52), Haupt (1861), Macleane, and Wickham (1875). Of the very numerous translations of H. into English, the best are those of Conington, Martin, and Newman.

Hör'de, a town of Prussia, province of Westphalia, on the river Emscher, 33 miles S. of Munster, with which it is connected by railway. It lies in the centre of great coal-mines, and has quite recently set up immense ironworks. Pop. (1875) 12,852.

Horde'olum, or **Stye**, is a farunculus or small boil projecting from the edge of the eyelid, implicating merely the cellular tissue. If slow in bursting, the abscess may be opened with the point of a lancet.

Hordeum, a genus of Grasses (q. v.). See BARLEY.

Horeb. See SINAI.

Hore'hound, so called from its *whitish* appearance ('hoar,' Old Eng. *har*, in the sense of white or grey, is still seen in *hoar*-frost, and is common in the form *hoary*), and from its being formerly supposed to be a cure for the bite of a mad dog. With qualifying words, H. is applied to three plants belonging to different genera of the natural order *Labiatæ*. Common or white H. (*Marrubium vulgare*), occasionally met with as a wild or semi-wild plant in Britain, is widely distributed through Europe, part of Asia, and N. Africa, and has, moreover, become naturalised in N. America. It was once employed in many diseases, but has fallen into disuse except as a domestic remedy in chest complaints. *Ballota nigra* is presumably called 'black H.' from its general resemblance to the above combined with dark flowers. It is equally well known as 'stinking H.' from its nauseous odour, and is common in many parts of Britain. Abroad it has much the same distribution as common H. Again, in *Lycopus Europæus* the family likeness has doubtless originated the name of 'water H.' It is found in watery places throughout Britain excepting the N. of Scotland; and in addition to a range same as common and black H., is a native of Australia and N. America. It does not appear ever to have been brought into the rustic pharmacopœia. Its other name of gipsywort was given, says Lyte (1578), 'because the rogues and runagates which call themselves Egyptians do colour themselves black with [the juice of] this herb.'

Hori'zon (from Gr. *horizō*, 'I bound'), the apparent line of meeting of the earth and sky. The true astronomical H. for any point in the earth's surface is the great circle on the sphere of the heavens corresponding to the terrestrial circle whose pole is situated at that point.

Hor'mayr, Joseph Freiherr von, statesman and historiographer, was born at Innsbruck, January 20, 1781. In 1801 he became secretary to the court at Vienna, in 1809 planned the operations for the expulsion of the French from the Tyrol, and subsequently, in spite of the greatest difficulties, maintained the defence of the country. Called in 1815 to be imperial historiographer, he in 1828 passed into the diplomatic service of Bavaria, and died at Munich, 5th November 1848. Among his works are *Geschichte der Gefürsteten Grafschaft Tirol* (1806–08); *Œsterreichischer Plutarch* (1807–20, in 20 vols.); *Alleg. Geschichte der Neuesten Zeit* (1817–19, 2d ed. 1851); *Das Land Tirol und der Tirolerkrieg von* 1809 (1845).

Horn or **Hoorn, Cape**, is the most southerly point of America, the extremity of an island of the same name, in the archipelago of Tierra del Fuego, lat. 50° 59′ S., 67° 16′ W. The island is a bare precipitous rock, with a perennially antarctic climate. The cape was first doubled by Schouten, a native of Hoorn, in 1569, and since then this course has been preferred to the Strait of Magellan.

Horn (Fr. *horn*, Ital. *corno*), a wind instrument consisting of a coiled brass tube with mouthpiece and bell-shaped opening. The tones, produced simply by the agency of lips and breath, are the 'Harmonics' (q. v.) of the sound represented by the whole length of the tube, and are called 'open notes.' Let the hand partially close the 'bell,' and the intermediate or 'shut' notes are obtained. C is the normal key, but by the use of certain crooks the pitch may be changed; in other words, the H. may be played in any key. The H. 'part' is written in C and in the treble clef, but the *sounds* may belong to another key, and even the C horn plays an octave below, *e.g.*—

Horns with pistons and those with valves give the whole scale in 'open' notes. In the orchestra there are usually two, sometimes four horns. The 'English H.' is little used.

Horn'beam. Gerard says of the wood of the common H. that it grows 'so hard and tough with age as to be more like horn than wood.' Either this or its former use to yoke horned cattle may have originated the name. In scientific nomenclature it is known as *Carpinus Betulus*, a native of S. England as well as the bulk of European countries and W. Asia. It only occurs as a planted tree in Scotland and Ireland. Along with the oak, beech, and nut, it belongs to *Cupuliferæ*, by some merged into *Amentiferæ*, by others kept as a distinct natural order, and there are three other species of the genus also inhabitants of the N. temperate zone. The foliage of common H. resembles that of beech, but is opaque, not shining, and, like the beech, the leaves may remain attached to the twigs long after autumnal death. This qualification, combined with non-injury from renewed cutting and clipping, has led to an extensive employment of the plant for hedge-making, especially for those used as screens in nursery gardens. If in erecting a fence the plants are arranged so as to cross each other, and are bound together at the points of intersection after removal of the adjacent bark, they will unite at these places, and in process of time a living palisade can be formed of any length. Some very curious illustrations of this fact are detailed and figured by Mr. M'Nab in vol. x. of *Transactions of Edinburgh Botanical Society*. When well-grown, *C. Betulus* rises into a beautiful tree 50 to 70 feet high; its wood is white, heavy, close-grained and tough, burns well, and produces good charcoal.

Horn'bill (*Buceros*), the name given to various species of Conirostral birds, from the large size and texture of the bill. The wings have their third and fourth quills longest. The tail is long, and the tarsi broadly scaled. The face and throat are nearly bare, and the head commonly bears a horny protuberance of helmet-like shape and of varying size. The familiar species of H. are the common or rhinoceros H. (*B. rhinoceros*), the white-crested H. (*B. albocristatus*), the crested H. (*B. cristatus*), the two-horned H. (*B. bicornis*), and the woodpecker H. (*B. pica*). The beak of the H. is of small size when the bird is hatched, but increases disproportionately as growth proceeds. The bird inhabits Africa and India. The common H. is mainly of black colour, but dusky grey below. The tail is grey and the bill yellow. Its length is about 10 inches. The white-crested H. is of a deep black colour, but the crest is white.

Horn'blende, an important group of minerals, crystallising in oblique rhombic prisms, varying in colour from white to black through all shades of green, grey, and brown, and ranging between degrees 5 and 6 of the scale of hardness. Silicia is the principal ingredient, with variable quantities of oxides of aluminum, calcium, iron, magnesium, and fluorine. There are two distinct groups of varieties, the light coloured and the dark coloured. Among the former are placed *Actinolite*, which includes most of the light-green kinds, and *Asbestus*, which occurs in easily separable fibres, and includes the well-known *mountain leather* and *mountain cork*. These contain little alumina or iron. *Common H.* is typical of the dark-coloured varieties, and is an essential constituent of certain rock, such as syenite, trap, H.-slate, &c.

Horn'book was at first a tablet with the letters of the alphabet either printed or written in black-letter, and covered with a thin plate of transparent horn to preserve it from injury, whence the name. The Lord's Prayer was generally placed beneath the alphabet, and the Roman numerals were likewise frequently added. Before the invention of printing, a H. was of vellum, covered with written characters. Hornbooks were in common use as the first reading-primers for children down to the time of George II. They have now dropped wholly out of use, but the name survives as applied to a book which contains the earliest rudiments of any branch of knowledge. There are very few extant specimens of old hornbooks. Tablets of this kind seem to have been mostly English.

Horn'castle, a town of England, Lincolnshire, at the confluence of the Bain and Waring, 21 miles E. of Lincoln, and 130 N. of London by railway. It has a church of St. Mary, with a square tower, dating from the time of Henry VII., a free grammar school, founded in the reign of Elizabeth, a trade in corn, wool, and coals, and some malting and brewing. The great H. horse-fair (8th–21st August) is perhaps the most important in the kingdom, and attracts Continental dealers. Pop. (1871) 4865. H. has traces of a Roman station, and is the Old English *Hyrn-Ceastre* or 'castle at the horn or angle.'

Horne, Richard Hengist, an English poet whose merit is somewhat greater than his fame, was born in London in 1803. Besides certain dramatic pieces, *Cosmo de Medici*, *The Death of Marlowe*, *Gregory the Seventh*, &c., he has written two notable works, an epic poem, entitled *Orion* (1843), and *A New Spirit of the Age* (1844), a collection of critical essays, partly the work of Elizabeth B. Browning. The former, although sarcastically published at a *farthing* (new ed. 1876 at 9s.), is really a poem of some classic purity and eloquence. In 1846 appeared his *Ballad Romances*. From 1852 to 1869 H. lived in Australia, latterly holding the office of 'Gold Commissioner.' In 1877 he published *Letters of Mrs E. B. Browning addressed to R. H. Horne* (2 vols.), chiefly concerning 'A New Spirit of the Age.'

Horne, Thomas Hartwell, D.D., a biblical critic, was born October 20, 1780, and was educated at Christ's Hospital. The death of his parents prevented him from passing on to the University, and he was compelled to become a lawyer's clerk. All his leisure, however, was devoted to learned study, and in 1818 appeared his *Introduction to the Critical Study and Knowledge of the Holy Scriptures*, which procured him the degree of M.A. from Aberdeen. Next year he was ordained by the Bishop of London. He was afterwards made B.D. of Cambridge, and D.D. of the University of Pennsylvania. H. published no fewer than forty-five works, some of them against Roman Catholic dogmas. He died 27th June 1860. See *Reminiscences of T. H. Horne by his Daughter* (Lond. 1862).

Hor'net (*Vespa crabro*), a species of *Vesparia* or wasps, common in England, but rare in Scotland. It is the largest of the British wasps. The H. is coloured black on the chest or thorax, the head is reddish, and the abdomen is yellow, with three brown points or marks on each joint. It is a singularly vicious insect, and has become the symbol of any very troublesome assailant. The nest is frequently built in the neighbourhood of man, and is found in outhouses and like situations. H. communities do not contain a large number of individuals; but in the disposition of the colony the same division of members is found that is seen in bees and ants—namely, into males, females, and neuters or makers.

Horning, a term of Scotch law denoting the process by which a debtor is charged to pay his debts before he or his estate is seized. By special statute letters of H. are authorised to pass on bills of exchange, the protest on which has been recorded in any competent court; but it is now largely superseded by other statutory forms of enforcing decrees.

Horn'pipe, an old English instrument ('horne-pipes of Cornewaile'—*Chaucer*) still in use in Wales, consisting of a wooden pipe with horn at each end. Also the name of a lively dance accompanied by the H. formerly.

Horns (Lat. *cornua*) are the appendages developed from the *epidermis* or outer layer of the skin in many mammals. They vary greatly in texture, structure, and situation. The H. of sheep, goats, and antelopes are *hollow*, and hence the name *Cavicornia* (q. v.) given to this group of animals. These hollow H. are further persistent; in other words, they are never cast or shed. In the *Cervidæ* (q. v.) or Deer (q. v.), on the contrary, the H. are *solid*, and are named *antlers*. They are usually much branched, the complications of form increasing with age, and they are cast each year, to be reproduced of increased size at the breeding season. These antlers are borne on the frontal bone, and the process of annual growth may fitly be cómpared to that whereby new bone is produced to repair an injured portion. Another difference in form between the H. of antelopes and those of deer is that the former are not branched, although they may be ringed or annulated. In man, horny growths, consisting of modifications and abnormal developments of the epidermis, have been developed, and have required removal by a surgical operation. Several specimens of H. removed from various situations in the human body are contained, *e.g.*, in the Anatomical Museum of the University of Edinburgh; and an account of some of the more remarkable growths of this kind may be found in Syme's *Principles of Surgery*; and in Sir James Paget's *Surgical Pathology*, devoted to pathological anatomy. The number of H. developed in animals is usually two; but in certain species of antelopes (*e.g.*, the Chickara or four-horned Indian antelope) four H. occur.

Manufactures of Horn.—The H. of animals as used for manufacturing purposes are of two kinds, having altogether distinct properties and applications. The hard or bony deer horn is almost exclusively used for the handles of pocket and other knives, and for this purpose the antlers of the axis or spotted Indian deer (*Axis maculata*) are extensively imported into this country. The principal source of hollow horn for manufacturing purposes is the common ox, the horns of which are brought to England in vast quantities from S. America, Australia, and Russia. The hoofs of oxen, being exactly the same in structure as the horns, are also used for all purposes to which horn is applied. Buffalo horn is imported from India, China, and the Cape of Good Hope, and forms a very valuable article in H. M. The chief demand for horn is in combmaking (see COMB), and the solid tips which the comb manufacturers do not use are utilised by the button manufacturers of Birmingham, or in Sheffield for making knife-handles, razor-scales, umbrella-handles, and other articles. Formerly a large quantity of horn was used by itinerant tradesmen in making spoons, but these are now largely supplanted by cheap metal spoons. Cuttings, scraps, and waste of horn are of great value in the manufacture of prussiate of potash, and of artificial manure.

Horny Tissues, the name given in physiology to such tissues as enter into the composition of horns, hairs, nails, hoofs, whalebone, and other substances. In its simplest state horn appears to consist of an albuminous substance, which is distinguished from albumen and fibrin chiefly by containing a larger amount of sulphur. Hair, for example, contains 10 per cent. of sulphur; nails, 6 to 8 per cent. The horny tissues have a greater or less quantity of the substance to which Simon gave the name of *keratin*. These tissues are not soluble in water, ether, or alcohol; but are soluble in caustic potash, and in sulphuric, nitric, and hydrochloric acids. The H. T. in morphological and microscopic composition exhibit a close analogy with the skin structures. Horn proper is modified *epidermis*—the latter being the outer layer of the skin, while feathers and allied products are secreted by the *dermis* or under layer. In hair and feathers an appreciable proportion of *silica* or flint exists; and colouring matters—notably iron and copper—are obtained by analysis.

Horol'ogy (Gr. *hōra*, 'any defined portion of time,' and *logia*, 'a discourse') is the science which treats of the construction of machines for marking and measuring the flight of time. The motions of the heavenly bodies relatively to the earth give our first standard intervals of time, the year, the month, the day; and it is the subdivision of the last and smallest of these into intervals more convenient for practical purposes that is the great concern of H. The first apparatus in use was, no doubt, the sun-dial (see DIAL), which registered the progress of the sun through the sky by a shadow cast upon a graduated plate. It was, however, useless during night, or when the day-sky was overclouded. The next decided advance was the construction of the Clepsydra (q. v.), which measured the hours by the efflux of water from a graduated vessel. It was introduced into Rome by Scipio Nusica about 158 B.C. Subsequent improvements were made by the addition of a toothed wheel and index, which were driven by the outflowing water. By the substitution of a descending weight to drive the wheel, water was dispensed with, but now a regulator was necessary to render the downward motion of the weight uniform. With the invention of the first escapement, the construction of clocks proper may be said to begin. In 1288 a clock was set up in Old Palace Yard; and in the succeeding century clock-towers became a feature in Bologne, Strasburg, Courtray, and other Continental towns. The clock set up by Heinrich von Wick in Paris in the year 1379 is one of the most famous of these earlier mechanisms. No great improvement was made till the middle of the 17th c. In 1641 an English clockmaker, Harris by name, perceived the possibility of regulating the action of the escapement by means of a pendulum, which Galileo had shown to be practically, for small oscillations, isochronous in its beats. It was Huyghens, however, the Dutch physicist, who first constructed a pendulum clock. The escapement or crown wheel, which had hitherto been set vertical, was by him set horizontal, and the pallets were attached to the horizontal rod from which the pendulum hung. From this time all clocks which could lay claim to any accuracy were provided with a pendulum; and subsequent improvements were merely modifications in detail of the action of the escapement, or of the form or material of the different parts of the mechanism. England took the foremost place in the development of the science, as the names of Hook, Graham, Harrison, Earnshaw, Dent, Frodsham, Shepherd, Airy, and others sufficiently testify.

In considering the essentials of a timepiece, the first part to be noticed is the moving power. In large-sized clocks this is a raised weight; in chronometers, watches, and smaller clocks, it is a coiled, elastic, highly-tempered spring. The weight in descending, or the spring in uncoiling, sets a cylinder in rotation, and this rotatory motion is transmitted through wheels and pinions to the hands, which by their motion in front of the graduated dial-plate indicate the hours, minutes, and seconds. The descent of the weight must, however, be regulated, and this is effected by means of the escapement and pendulum. The escapement is simply the mechanism which transforms the rotatory motion of the wheels into the oscillatory motion of the pendulum; and the pendulum, in virtue of its isochronism, reacts upon the escapement, rendering its action, and therefore the motion of the whole clock-train, more uniform. The time of beat of the pendulum is, however, seriously effected by external circumstances; and this must tell upon the *rate* of the clock. If the beat becomes slower, the clock must lose; if faster, it must gain. The most serious error in this respect arises from the change of length of the pendulum due to variation of temperature. To remedy this, several methods have been suggested and employed, the most notable of which are Harrison's *gridiron* pendulum, and Graham's *mercurial* pendulum. (See PENDULUM.) Other minuter errors are no doubt occasioned by the fact that the pendulum in ordinary clocks is moving freely only during a small portion of its oscillation, on account of the pressure existing between the pallet and the escapement wheel, and also possibly by the further well-known fact that, except for arcs of vibration, small in comparison to its length, the pendulum is not sufficiently isochronous, but that, in our more accurate astronomical clocks, the variation in beat might be appreciable. The former defect is very evident in Graham's celebrated *dead-beat* escapement, which is so admirable in many other respects. To remedy these minor errors, Sir William Thomson has devised a new astronomical clock, whose special merits are the small oscillation which the second's pendulum makes (not more than half-a-centimetre on each side of its middle position), and the simple mechanism of the escapement, in which the pallet touches the tooth of the escapement-wheel during $\frac{1}{300}$th of the time of the pendulum's oscillation. For a detailed description of this escapement, see *Nature* for January 11, 1877 (page 228, vol. xv.). When the moving power is a mainspring, the motion is regulated in the first place by the escapement and balance-wheel. The same great cause of error, variation of temperature, exists here also, and compensation is necessary. (See BALANCE-WHEEL.) The most important improvement in this direction, especially for marine chronometers, since the time of Earnshaw, has been made by Mr. Hartnup. For each chronometer there is a certain particular temperature for which the compensation is perfect. Hartnup finds that the rate is fastest at this temperature; and that the rate at any other temperature is calculated with great accuracy by subtracting from the maximum rate the number obtained by multiplying the square of the difference of temperature by a certain constant co-efficient. His method has been experimentally tested, and proved far superior to any other in present use. Evidently a great desideratum in a good chronometer is that this critical temperature be as nearly as possible the mean temperature at which the chronometer is used. The escapement in spring-clocks and watches has undergone various modifications. Here we cannot do more than mention the various kinds by name, referring to some treatise on the subject for their description. Those in most general use are the *lever*, the *duplex*, the *vertical*, the *horizontal*, and the *detached* escapements. The last is that employed in the modern chronometer. The escapement and balance-wheel, however, are not sufficient to regulate the uncoiling of the spring; and that for this reason—the more the spring uncoils, the slower is its rate of uncoiling, the weaker therefore the motive force which it exerts upon the mechanism. To equalise this variable force, a very beautiful contrivance called the *fusee* has been introduced. The fusee is in reality a variable lever, conical in shape, and communicating with the works by means of the toothed fusee-wheel, which is fixed concentrically at its base. The mainspring is contained in a cylindrical box, which, by its uncoiling, it makes rotate. This rotation is communicated to the fusee through the medium of the chain; and as this chain uncoils from the fusee, the point at which it acts upon the fusee is pushed further and further from the centre of rotation, the *leverage* is therefore increased, and the force necessary to give the fusee a certain rotation diminished. As delicacy in the construction of timepieces increased, it soon became apparent that there should be an apparatus to keep the machine going while it was being wound up—that there should be, in technical words, a *maintaining power*. Huyghens kept his clock in motion by an arrangement of pulleys and an endless cord. Harrison's contrivance, known as the *going fusee*, is that now in general use. In the hollow of the fusee-wheel, a circular spring is fitted in such a manner that, by its reaction, it keeps up the motion of the fusee-wheel while the winding-up is taking place. It is impossible here to describe the mechanisms which are necessary for striking the hours, half-hours, and quarters, or to more than mention the complications which *repeating-watches* require.

The manufacture of watches gives an excellent example of the principle of division of labour. The maker who sends out the finished article to the public does not construct a single part of the mechanism himself—he merely combines what he gets from other sources. The motion-work comes from one, the escapement from another, the spring from a third, and the case, dial, glass, &c., from other quarters. The *movements* of watches are chiefly constructed in Lancashire, and especially in Prescot; and from Clerkenwell district, London, the great majority are turned out upon the market. Switzerland, long a great centre of watchmaking, has of recent years been in great part superseded by America. See Reed's *Treatise on Clock and Watch Making;* Derham's *Artificial Clockmaker;* Denison's *Rudimentary Treatise on Clocks;* Earnsham's *Explanations of Time-keepers;* and Berthoud's *Histoire de la Mesure du Tems.*

Horop'ter, a term used in physiological optics to denote that combination of all those points in space which, for any one position of the eyes, appears single. The H. is really a circular line, of which the chord is formed by the distance between the eyes, whilst the size of the circle is determined by three points, viz., by the two eyes and the point towards which their axes converge.

Hor'oscope (Gr. *hōra*, 'an hour,' and *skopeō*, 'I observe'), in astrology, was a representation of the relative positions of the heavenly bodies at the birth of an individual. It was supposed to indicate his future destiny.

Hors-de-Combat (a French phrase, meaning literally, 'out of the fighting'), is applied to a combatant or combatants quite disabled from continuing a struggle.

Horse (*Equus*), a genus of mammalia included in the order *Ungulata* (q. v.), or that of the 'hoofed' quadrupeds, and in the *Perissodactyle* (odd-toed) section of that order. In former systems of mammalian classification, the H. formed the type of a distinct sub-order named the *Solidungula* ('single-toed'). This name is still retained to designate the division in which the H. and its neighbours, the zebras and asses, are included. The characters of the Solidungula are—(1) that a single toe only is developed. This toe is enclosed in a largely developed nail—the hoof. In the extinct H. named *Hipparion* (q. v.) two rudimentary toes existed, while in the still older fossil H. *Anchitheriun* all three toes touched the ground. The existing H. has two very rudimentary toes, represented by the 'splint-bones,' but these, while demonstrating the probable descent of the H. from a three-toed form, are of no account in its existing structure. (2) A discontinuous or interrupted series of teeth exists in each jaw. Canine teeth of small size are developed in the males only, and fall out sooner or later. The skin is hairy, and the neck is provided with a mane. The teeth number six incisors, two canines (in the males only), eight premolars and six molars in each jaw, and the incisors are of similar form in each jaw. In the H. seven cervical or neck-vertebræ, twenty-four dorso-lumbar segments, five sacral, and seventeen caudal or tail vertebræ exist. The skeleton of the limbs exhibits a special development in connection with the running powers of the animal. In addition to the length of the *phalanges* or bones of the fingers, the wrist is specially adapted to the requirements of the horse's life, from its situation in the middle of the fore-limb; the wrist-joint of the H. being popularly but erroneously termed the 'knee.' The 'heel' is similarly situated in the hind-limb, and constitutes the 'hock.' The movements of the limbs are restricted to a fore and backward movement, the fore-arm being fixed in the position of *pronation*—a state exhibited by the fore-arm of man when the palm of the hand is turned downwards, the elbow resting on a fixed surface. The upper arm and thigh are enclosed within the skin and muscular tissues, and are not perceptible or distinct externally. Seven carpal or wrist bones exist. The bones of the pelvis are very long, and the crests of the *ilia* or haunch bones are wide. The thigh has a third trochanter, and the upper extremity of the fibula is abortive. There are six or seven tarsal or ankle bones. In connection with peculiarities in the skeleton, the *muscles* of the H. evince many striking and special features. The milk-teeth include six incisors, two canines, and four premolars in each jaw; the molars, as in other mammals, being wanting in the milk set. The milk-teeth are present at birth, with the exception of the outer incisors, which are developed during the first few months of life. A wide interval or *diastema* exists between the canines and molars. The groove or hollow existing in the incisor teeth becomes filled with foreign matter, and as the tooth wears, a very characteristic mark is thus produced. As age advances, this mark, owing to the wear of the tooth, disappears, and hence the value of the mark as a test of the age of the H. The *digestive system* of the H. is estimated to attain a length eight times that of the body. The stomach is single, and does not exhibit the complications characteristic of the *Ruminantia* (q. v.). There is a very large *cæcum* (or first portion of the large intestine). No gall-bladder is developed, but in the division or septum separating the ventricles of the heart a cartilage is found. The hemispheres of the brain (*cerebral hemispheres*) are long, and do not project beyond the cerebellum when the brain is regarded from the upper surface. The *testes* of the male pass into a *scrotum*, and the penis is large and provided with a prepuce. The *uterus* exhibits a division at its fundus or base, with two *cornua* or 'horns.' The mare goes with young eleven months, and during the development of the embryo the *Allantois* (q. v.) covers the whole of the internal surface of the chlorion, and ceases to invest the amnion.

The *Solidungula* is divided into two genera—the genus *Equus*, represented by the H., with horny patches on the inner sides of both fore and hind limbs, while the tail is bushy; and the asses (*Asinus*) with horny patches on the inner sides of the fore limbs only, while the tail is tufted. The *domestic history* of the H. resembles that of all animals which have been domesticated by man: a process of *variation* has been inaugurated, the results of which are seen in the remarkable differences perceptible between the breeds or races of these animals. The clumsy dray-H. and the fleet, supple, well-bred racer are apparently quite different animals, and save for the fact that both are horses, might be considered, as far as external characters are concerned, to represent distinct species. But one distinct species of H. is recognised as having formed the parent-stock from which the breeds or races have been derived. This species is the *Equus caballus*, the original habitat of which appears to have been Central Asia. In Tartary, at present, herds of wild horses are found, exemplifying the primitive state of the species, and in the N. American prairies, where the 'mustangs' or wild horses—propagated from domesticated forms allowed to run wild—are found in great numbers, the return to the natural and primitive state is also witnessed. These herds appear to be led by an old and wary male, who directs the movements of his companions. The young males are said to be excluded from the old herds, and are forced to exist in herds by themselves, until they are able to select or attract females, and thus to form a little community or family circle of their own. The wild H. of Tartary is usually of a reddish-brown hue, and has a very dark mark along the spine. In Tartary the flesh of the H. is eaten, and its milk is used for food, while the skin and hair supply the nomadic tribes with materials for making tents and clothing. The American mustang is a powerful animal, showing a nearer approach to the Tarpan or Tartary H. than to domesticated breeds. It roams through the prairies in vast herds, and is caught chiefly by means of the *lasso*. The *Arabian* H. has long been celebrated for its docility, intelligence, and powers of endurance. The *Kochlami* breed of Arabian horses is perhaps the most celebrated of all the varieties, and is esteemed an exceedingly valuable animal on account of its variety and purity of blood. The Arabian breed has a long body, an arched neck, and delicate or slender limbs. Of ordinary breeds of English horses, the racehorses form well-known examples. They prove the value of training and selection in producing an animal in which speed and endurance are most desirable qualities. One of the most celebrated of the kind was 'Eclipse,' whose feats are probably unequalled in the annals of racing. In the hunter, speed is less requisite than endurance and strength of limb. The frame of the hunter is more compact than that of the racer. The Flemish and Belgian horses are noted for their solid bulk and strength, and amongst British breeds the Clydesdale carthorses are second to none as models of strength.

The stables in which horses are kept should be well ventilated and periodically whitewashed with lime, more especially when any epidemic disorder is prevalent. A good supply of pure water is a necessity, and the quality of the food an item second in importance only to the regulation of the times and periods when food should be supplied. Corn and hay are the staple articles of dietary, 10 or 12 lbs. of oats *per diem* being a fair average quantity of corn for a H. Bruised oats are to be preferred, and horses in hard work are the better of having a bran-mash given them once or twice weekly, provided they can be allowed to rest the day afterwards. The care of the mare during gestation and parturition, and other details of like nature, belong to the province of veterinary medicine. It is here sufficient to say that interference with the normal process of parturition in the H. is seldom called for. *Castration* is performed by veterinary surgeons on foals when a year old; and after attaining the third year the H. may be gradually and gently inured to hard work. See the works of Youatt, Gamgee, Fitzwygram, and Sydney.

Horse Chestnut, or **Chesnut**, a tree that, from its highly ornamental appearance, is now extensively planted throughout Europe wherever the climate will permit its growth. It is the *Æsculus Hippocastanum* of Linnæus, belonging to the natural order *Sapindaceæ*, and was introduced from the East about the middle of the 16th c. Northern India is often named as its native home, but it is not now known there in a wild state (Boissier, *Fl. Orient*, i. 497). It thrives well in Britain, generally towards mid-May standing forth prominently in all the gorgeousness of leaf and blossom, in striking contrast to the unassuming but more useful trees. Both foliage and flower, even to a casual observer, proclaim a foreign origin. The pyramidal panicle of flowers when in perfection is very beautiful; they soon, however, become tarnished, and most of the blossoms speedily drop off, a small proportion only maturing seed. The capsular, three-celled fruit, beset with spines, fall when ripe, and splitting open, display the roundish polished seed. These 'nuts' are too bitter for human food, and to express this coarseness in contrast to the edible chestnut there is little doubt the prefix 'horse' was given. Deer, goats, and sheep will eat them, but they are refused by the horse. The timber, owing to rapid growth, is soft and of little value. An American species of H.-C. (*Œ. Ohioensis*) is inferior in beauty to the above. In the sub-genus *Pavia*, with a smooth fruit-capsule, are included some handsome trees and shrubs, of which the red-flowered H.-C. (*P. rubra*), the yellow-flowered H.-C. (*P. flava*), and *P. discolor* are in cultivation for ornament. The seeds of *P. Indica* are, according to Dr. Royle, eaten in the Himalayas in time of scarcity, and the fruit is applied externally for rheumatism.

Horse-Fly. See FOREST FLY.

Horse Guards, a large old-fashioned stone building in Whitehall, London, with an archway leading to St. James' Park, where the business of several departments of the War Office is carried on, including the Fortification and Barrack branches, and the Home District and Paymaster Control offices. In 1871 the military functions here exercised were placed under the control of the Secretary of State for War, whose authority had previously been limited to the civil administration of the War Office. See *The Horse Guards*, by Lieut.-Colonel Hort (Lond. 1850).

Horse Guards, Royal, the 3d heavy cavalry regiment, and one of the finest in the British army, formed in the year 1661. As part of the household brigade, the R. H. G. are usually stationed in or near London. Though seldom sent on foreign service, they fought in the Peninsula and at Waterloo. The uniform is blue, with helmet and cuirass, and the horses are black. Strength of the regiment in 1876—27 officers, 64 non-commissioned officers, and 343 rank and file, with 275 horses.

Horse-Leech. See LEECH.

Horsens, an old town of Denmark, in the E. of Jutland, at the mouth of the Bygholms-Aa, and on the H. Fjord, 15 miles N.E. of Veile by rail. It has considerable trade, and some manufacture of tobacco, &c. The river is crossed by four bridges. Pop. (1874) 10,501.

Horse'manship, the art of riding and managing the horse, has been highly esteemed from remote times, especially by nations much given to war and the chase. The Numidians and Mauritanians rode without saddle, and guided their horses by touching either side of the neck with a switch. The Persians, who early began to use a kind of saddle, could make their horses kneel at mounting. The Thessalians were noted horsemen, whence probably the fable that their country was originally inhabited by centaurs. The rider of the Roman circus, to whom some writers apply the title *equus desultorius*, practised various feats, *e.g.*, leaping from one horse to another when running at full speed. Perhaps the earliest regular treatise on H. is that by Xenophon, from which it appears that the horse was ridden either barebacked or with a cloth or skin secured by a band. Stirrups came into use about the 5th c., but regular saddles were not known till the 14th c., and were first made chiefly of wood. The tournaments encouraged the love of riding, and riding-schools arose at Naples and elsewhere. Louis XIII. received lessons from Pluvinel in the court of the Louvre. The folio volume of De la Guerinière on H., with plates by Parrocel, appeared in 1733. See Mayhew, *Illustrated Horse Management*, Daumas, *Horses of the Sahara*, and Waite, *Graceful Riding*.

Horse-Power is the unit employed in estimating the power of a steam-engine, and is a measure of the work which that machine can do. It is equivalent to 33,000 foot-pounds, where a foot-pound is the work which must be done to raise a pound weight through a distance of one foot at the surface of the earth.

Horse-Racing, a favourite sport of great antiquity. It was introduced into the Grecian games 648 B.C., and a race for mares alone, called Calpe, was instituted 150 years later. The Romans were very fond of the sport; but it is extremely improbable that they introduced it into England. It may, however, be reasonably traced to the tournaments of the middle ages. In the time of Henry VIII. it was a common amusement. James I. patronised and fostered it, and Charles I. instituted a royal plate and kept a stud at Newmarket. About this time barbs and other Eastern horses were imported, and the breed became greatly improved, the most famous sires of winners being Darley's Arabian and the Godolphin Arabian, the latter purchased from a cart in Paris. Since then there has been very little foreign importation, nor has it been needed; as severe yet careful training, combined with high feeding, have made the English racer for swiftness and endurance immeasurably superior to the steed of the desert. Queen Anne ran horses in her own name, the Prince Regent kept a magnificent stud, and the sport has latterly been stamped not only with royal but with parliamentary approval, the House of Commons having adjourned every Derby-day since 1847 till now.

Chester is the oldest meeting in England, but the metropolis of racing is Newmarket, which has the finest course and training-ground in the world, and where seven meetings are annually held. The Heath is the property of the Jockey Club, the supreme turf tribunal, composed (1877) of 102 members. There were in this year ninety-eight places of sport in England, fourteen in Scotland, and eleven in Ireland. In Great Britain 1907 races were run in 1876, in which 2054 separate horses competed, and the prizes offered were £300,000. Thirty-four royal plates were granted of 200 guineas each. The greatest sporting carnival is the summer meeting at Epsom; the most fashionable meetings are 'royal' Ascot, and 'glorious' Goodwood.

Formerly, horses of five and six years of age competed for the great prizes of the year, which are now limited to three-year olds. These are the Two Thousand Guineas (Newmarket, April), the Derby (Epsom, May), and the St. Leger (Doncaster, September). The One Thousand Guineas and the Oaks are for fillies alone. There are about 2500 thoroughbred brood-mares in Great Britain, and the price of a promising foal runs from a few hundreds to £2000. Nearly 300 foals are entered for the Derby, of which about one-tenth come to the post. The fastest recorded time for the Derby course of 1½ miles is 2 m. 43 s., accomplished by Blair-Athol in 1864. The weights of the jockeys (who are lavishly paid) for the three-year old races are 8 st. 7 lb. for colts, and 8 st. 3 lb. for fillies, but handicap races with the weights varied, according to the powers of the horses, are very common. Steeplechasing over rough ground is also popular.

Enormous sums change hands on every racecourse, as, besides private speculators, there are scores of professional betting-men. Betting-houses have been recently abolished, but Tattersall's, the great turf-exchange, still remains.

The sport has become acclimatised in many European countries and in the colonies. The French, by purchasing many of the finest English stallions and brood-mares, are becoming formidable rivals. In America, trotting-races are much in vogue. See *History of Horse-Racing*, published by Saunders, Otley, & Co., 1863; also the *Racing Calendar*, an annual publication.

Horse-Radish. The genus or sub-genus *Armoracia*, belonging to the natural order *Cruciferæ*, of which *A. rusticana* or common H.-R. is well known for its use as a condiment, &c., whilst its large coarse root-leaves and tall stem, bearing a profusion of white flowers, renders it prominent in the kitchen-garden. So tenacious of life is the root-stock, that pieces thrown from the garden to the manure-heap, or washed down by a stream to some suitable resting-place, are quite sufficient in course of time to found a bed of the plant in such out-of-the-way localities that it has the position and surroundings of a wild plant. It is not, however, a native of Britain; indeed, its exact origin is unknown. As mentioned under Aconite, the 'root' of that plant has several times been mistaken for H.-R., and with terrible results. In the former it is tapering, of a dark-brown colour externally, and the first taste is bitter. In H.-R. there is not the tapering form, the external colour is dirty white, and odour and taste are at first pungent and acrid.

Horse-Radish-Tree. The root of *Moringa pterygosperma*, like horse-radish, is pungent to the taste, hence the name the tree has acquired. The seeds, called ben-nuts, yield oil of ben, used by watchmakers. It is a native of India.

Horses, Sale and Exchange of. The property in horses is not easily changed without consent of the owner, for a purchaser does not become proprietor of a stolen horse unless it has been bought in *open* market, according to statutory directions. The owner of a stolen horse legally sold may redeem it on payment or tender of the price within six months after it is stolen. A warranty of *soundness* regarding a horse implies an assurance against constitutional defects. A temporary defect does not make a horse legally *unsound*. The law is the same regarding exchanges as in sales. Delivery on one side at least is required to prove a contract of exchange. An agreement for the sale of a horse is held to be an agreement 'relating to the sale of goods,' and so to come under the Statute of Frauds; therefore a written receipt for the price, containing the warranty or other condition of sale, is admissible, stamped as a receipt, as evidence of the contract. When a defect contrary to the warranty is discovered, the horse must be returned immediately, unless there be a stipulation to the contrary.

Horse-Shoeing. The art of fitting an iron protection to the hoof of the horse is one of great antiquity. It is unfortunate that the art, as commonly practised by modern farriers, shows but little improvement upon old methods. It proceeds upon the idea that every variety of hoof must be made, through paring and other treatment, to conform to the one type of shoe—an idea which is the root of much mischief in farriery. The hoof is subjected to a process of paring, which, in the hands of a careless smith, is simply tantamount to the destruction of the support which should suffice for the lodgment of the shoe; and an equally careless and empiric method of fastening shoes may be credited with causing a vast amount of lameness. Instead of the wholesale paring to which the hoof is usually subjected, the outer crust, impacted by the pressure of the old shoe, should be lightly and carefully removed with the knife. In particular, the 'frog,' or triangular prominent space between the 'bars' of the sole, requires careful treatment; this portion, one of the most necessary supports of the foot, being frequently destroyed by the shoer. The toe, or front of the hoof, should also be very slightly pared, so as to form a flat surface for the reception of the 'clip' of the shoe, which is often large and very clumsily made. Various modifications of fastening the shoe must be adopted and used in different cases, but the nails should, as a rule, be driven if anything obliquely into the hoof, and then carefully hammered down on the outer surface after the points are broken off. Filing and rasping the ends of the nails are unnecessary. A well-made shoe should last for three weeks at least. The light-running horse should be provided with a shoe of plain structure without heels or tips. The shoe of the heavy draught-horse, on the contrary, requires tips and heels to afford stout points of resistance, but the heels are often clumsily made and too large in size. The treatment of *corns*, to which the feet of horses are liable, consists in judicious paring and shoeing, with the avoidance of undue pressure. Corns usually appear in the angles of the hoof, between the heel and bars. Leather pads, with or without tow-stuffing, are to be regarded only as temporary methods of relieving tender soles.

Horses, Stealing. Any one stealing a horse, or any one counselling or helping the thief, is liable in a penalty ranging from two years' imprisonment, with or without hard labour, to fourteen years' penal servitude.

Horsh'am, a picturesque old town of England, in Sussexshire, on a branch of the Arun river, 37 miles S.S.W. of London by rail. It has a large church of St. Mary dating from the reign of King John, a Gothic courthouse, and a grammar-school founded by Richard Collier in 1532. There is an extensive trade in corn, timber, &c. H. sends one member to Parliament. Pop. (1871) 7831.

Hors'ley, Samuel, a learned prelate, born in London in 1733. He was educated at Westminster and Cambridge, and soon after taking orders succeeded his father as rector of Newington Butts. In addition to this living, which he held for many years, not a few of the good things of the Church were showered on him by influential patrons. His learned leisure was firstly given to science, and he was appointed Secretary to the Royal Society in 1773, having been elected a Fellow in 1767. In 1776 he projected a complete edition of Newton's works, in five quarto volumes, the last of which appeared in 1785. During their publication he fought his famous theological duel with Dr. Priestley. The latter's *History of the Corruptions of Christianity*, defending materialism and unitarianism, was the subject of a furious onslaught in a charge delivered by H. to his congregation, and a vigorous epistolary battle ensued, H. publishing his seventeen letters to Dr. Priestley in 1789. The orthodox party were delighted, and honours and emoluments crowded thickly on their champion. He received in succession the bishoprics of St. David's, Rochester (with the deanery of Westminster), and St. Asaph's. In the House of Lords he was a warm supporter of Pitt. He died 4th October 1806. H. was a variously gifted man, a weighty scholar, a learned theologian, an ardent politician, and a vigilant prelate; he awakens a certain respectful admiration, which would be considerably strengthened if we could only persuade ourselves that he really knew anything of the religion he so forcibly upheld. A complete list of his very numerous works on classical, mathematical, scientific, and biblical subjects will be found in Nichols' *Literary Anecdotes of the Eighteenth Century*, published in 1812. See the collected edition of his theological works (Longman, 6 vols. 1845).

Horticul'tural Soci'eties are now so wide spread through civilised countries, that their utility is fully proved by their general acceptance, and it may appear remarkable, in the history of such an ancient art as horticulture, that their growth lies within the compass of the present century. There is no doubt that not only the large societies holding international meetings, but also the associations belonging to provincial districts, and even to individual villages, have effected much good for horticulture. The Royal Horticultural Society of London, which obtained its charter in 1808, is looked upon as the parent English society. The Caledonian Horticultural Society at Edinburgh dates from 1809. The first society of the kind was formed at Altenburg in 1803, and now almost every town of Germany has one; the various societies form a union, and meet in a botanical congress yearly. The *Société d'Horticulture de Paris* was established in 1827, and has done much to encourage gardening, both by the annual distribution of prizes and by the publication of the *Annales d'Horticulture*.

Hor'ticulture, from Lat. *hortus*, or **Gar'dening**, from Ger. *garten*, is the name given to the cultivation of a piece of ground enclosed for the production of flowers, culinary vegetables, and fruits. It is thus broadly separated from Agriculture (q. v.) and from Arboriculture (q. v.). Still it touches upon these departments of industry by including what is necessary for the practical maintenance of market, nursery, and botanic gardens; and we further find that certain staples of the farm, as also various items of the arboriculturalist's care, are commonly intrusted in a smaller extent to the gardener's charge. The recognition of, and painstaking obedience to, the rules that observation and common sense show to be nature's ordinances in the vegetable kingdom, is alike necessary, whether the area of cultivation be the farm, the plantation, the nobleman's garden, or the cottager's plot.

In the selection of ground for a garden, the three most important points to be considered are the soil, the situation and surroundings, and the water supply. Loams on a moderate retentive subsoil are the best soils, and are characterised, according to the earths that prevail in them, as a sandy or clayey loam; or, according to their degree of friability, as a free loam, a stiff loam, &c. In general, much more depends on the texture of a soil, and its capacity for retaining or parting with water and heat, than on its chemical composition. The depth of soil of a garden should not be less than two to four feet. As to situation, a garden should be so placed that it may receive the full benefit of a free untainted atmosphere, and so obtain whatever is desirable from light, heat, moisture, and aerial circulation. The water arrangements must be negative and positive, that is to say, a complete system of underground drainage must be formed, and at the same time a water supply should never be wanting. Of course, the detailed practice of gardening varies considerably in different countries on account of the difference of climate, &c.

To become a proficient gardener in the present day, the individual must acquire his knowledge by a system of physical and mental work, commencing in early life. In particular, he must cultivate his powers of observation and reasoning, and he ought to educate himself to be a botanist as well as a gardener. The neglect of this in the past is apparent in the confusion and nonsense that even still exists in the gardener's nomenclature. The range of a gardener's duties is very wide. He should understand soils, their proper working, and the organic and inorganic manures with which it is necessary to improve them; the varieties of animal and vegetable life injurious to the plants under his charge, and the most effective preventives and antidotes; the diseases and accidents of plants; the implements used in horticulture; the structures and edifices, fixed, portable, and temporary, that are best approved in the various departments of a garden; the operations of propagation, whether by seeds, cuttings, layers, grafting, or budding; the art of selecting and improving plants in culture, and all the addenda of transplanting, potting, training, pruning, sheltering, retarding, and resting; the rotation of crops; the operations of horticultural design and taste; the forcing department; the exact culture of diverse kinds of ornamental trees, shrubs, and herbs, of the numerous kitchen-garden and orchard products, and of such specialties as the orchids amongst flowers, and the pine-apple among fruits. Finally, to bear himself in such a manner to those around him that all may work in happy unison with him.

The earliest accounts we have of gardens are those recorded in the Bible. The Egyptians, the Persians, and other remote nations, prided themselves on their magnificent gardens. Those of Epicurus, and of Pisistratus, Cimon, and Theophrastus, were the most famous in Greece. The gorgeous gardens of Lucullus, Sallust, Crassus, Pompey, Seneca, &c., show the delight which the Romans took in them. The Romans were, perhaps, the first who introduced the art of H. into Western Europe. But it was not until the reign of Henry VIII. that H. made any particular advance in England. We learn, indeed, from Dr. Bulleyn's *Bulwark of Defence* (1562), that excellent apples, pears, plums, cherries, and hops were of native growth, but these were supplemented by important additions from Holland and France, and the impetus thereby rendered developed H. very considerably during the remaining Tudor and succeeding reigns up to the Civil War. This is amply shown by the writings of Gerard and Parkinson (1597, 1629, and 1643). Since then, H. has made continuous scientific progress.

Ho'rus, the Latinised form of *hor*, *har*, or *her*, was the name of an Egyptian god, identified by Herodotus with the Greek Apollo. H. generally appears as the deity of the sun or of the light of day, and his name is probably connected with the Semitic root *hur*, 'light.' The Egyptian myth latterly recognised two gods of the name, the elder a son of Seb (Kronos) and Nut (Rhea), the younger a son of Osiris and Isis, but their functions were the same. H. was represented under the symbol of a falcon.

Horváth, Michael, a Hungarian historian, born at Szentes, in the comitat of Csongrad, 20th October 1809, was educated at Szegedin and Watizen, and took priest's orders in 1830. In 1844 he was made Professor of Hungarian at the Vienna Theresianum, and three years later Dean of Hatvan, in the neighbourhood of Pesth. Here H. formed that close connection with the Liberal movement which raised him in 1848 to the see of Csanád, and the year after obtained him the portfolio of Education. On the downfall of the insurrection H. effected his escape from Hungary, and passed eighteen years of exile at Paris, Genoa, Nice, &c., but in 1866 obtained permission to return, and has since been repeatedly elected by Szegedin to the Hungarian Diet. His most important works are *A Magyarok' Törtenete* ('History of Hungary,' 1842–46, new ed. 1861); *Huszonöt év Magyarország Történélból* ('Twenty-five Years of Hungarian History,' 2 vols. 1863); *Magyarország Függetlenségi Harczának Törtenete* 1848 *és* 1849-*ben* ('History of the War of Independence in Hungary in 1848–49,' 3 vols. 1865), and *Felelet Kossuth Leveleire* ('Answer to Kossuth's Letters,' 1867). H. is now (1877) President of the Historical Academy at Pesth.—There is also an **Istvan H.** (born 1784, died 1846) who has a place in the historical literature of Hungary.

Hose'a (Heb. 'help,' or 'helper'), one of the twelve 'minor' Hebrew prophets, 'prophesied in the days of Uzziah, Jotham, Ahaz, and Hezekiah, kings of Judah, and in the days of Jeroboam (II.) king of Israel' (about B.C. 790–725), and probably in the kingdom of Israel. The book of his prophecies, which appears to contain a general summary of the leading thoughts contained in his public addresses, may be divided into two parts, i.–iii. and iv.–xiv.; the first giving a symbolical representation of the past, present, and future history of the people of God; the second expanding and illustrating the revelation of the first, in describing their adoption, rebellion, chastisement, and rejection, the conversion of the Gentiles, and the future repentance and restoration of Israel.

Hoshungabad', the chief town of the district of the same name, in the Central Province, British India, on the left bank of the Nerbudda river, 338 miles S. of Agra, and 144 E. of Mhow. Pop. (1872) 8032. It is a centre of the trade in Manchester piece-goods, and exports raw cotton and grain.—The *district* of H., which occupies the S. valley of the Nerbudda, has an area of 4222 sq. miles; pop. (1872) 440,186. In the valley is the 'black cotton soil,' which produces gram, wheat, and oil seeds, and an increasing quantity of cotton. The export trade in these commodities is very large. Coal is found commonly, and the district is now traversed by railway.

Ho'siery, a term derived from the Old English *hos*, the name given to close-fitting breeches reaching down to the knee, which were worn in early times. It now includes specially the manufacture of stockings, but also that of all close-fitting under-clothing made principally of worsted yarn with the peculiar elastic structure resulting from the stocking-stitch. The plain stocking-stitch is made of a single continuous thread of yarn, and results from drawing one loop successively through a series of other loops. The ordinary way of accomplishing this, with two or more wires, is so universally familiar that it requires no description here, and it would be equally useless to attempt to describe the numerous fancy stitches and ornamental forms which result from various combinations of stitches. The H. trade is an extensive and valuable industry, centring chiefly in Nottingham and Belper in England, but there the work is done in factories with the stocking-frame, the original form of which was invented by Mr. Lee of Cambridge in 1589. On the stocking-frame a flat web is only produced, which in the case of stockings and all 'round' articles has to be seamed up by hand labour. A variety of ingenious machinery, chiefly of American invention, has of recent years been adapted for automatically knitting round hosiery, and some of these are now being much used in domestic work and small establishments. The most favourably known are the Lamb Knitting Machine and the 'Little Rapid.'

Hos'mer, Harriet, an American sculptor, and the daughter of a physician who became a professor in the Medical College of St. Louis, was born at Waterton, Massachusetts, 3d October 1831. In youth she strengthened a feeble constitution by active outdoor exercise and a raid into the Far West, ending in a visit to the Dakota Indians. After studying anatomy at St. Louis, where she produced a beautiful 'Hesper,' among other original pieces, she went to Rome in 1852, and was received into Gibson's studio. The statue of 'Puck,' sent to Boston in 1856, won her the favour of the American public. Among her more important works are busts of 'Daphne' and 'Medusa,' the full-lengths of 'Œnone' and 'Beatrice Cenci,' the colossal 'Zenobia in Chains,' and the 'Sleeping Fawn' exhibited at the Paris Exposition of 1867. A faithful disciple of Canova, through the influence of Gibson she works out the classic ideas of her school with a vigour and versatility that give a vital grace to its cruder conventionalities. She resides in Rome.

Hos'pice (Fr. from Lat. *hospitium*, 'a place where strangers are entertained,' from *hospes*, 'a guest'), a place for entertaining travellers in the Alps, and inhabited by monks. There are hospices on the Simplon, Little St. Bernard, Mount Cenis, and Great St. Bernard—the last being the oldest H. See HOSPITAL.

Hos'pital (probably derived through the Latin from Sanskrit *gosha*, 'a station for cows,' and *pâti*, 'master'), as the name indicates, meant originally any place where guests are received gratuitously. Such a place was also called *hôtel dieu*, *maison dieu*, and *hospice*. At first the Catholic bishop had the charge of the poor, whether sick or not, of widows, orphans, and strangers. Then for a period one-fourth of the fixed revenue of the Church was assigned to the poor. But as hospitals were founded by private benevolence, some were made ecclesiastical benefices, and put under the superintendence of the bishop as titular, while others became purely lay institutions. The civil and canon laws also mention a variety of similar *domus religiosæ* in the Eastern Empire, viz., the Xenodochium, where pilgrims and strangers were received; the Noscomium, managed by Parabolani for the benefit of the sick; the Procotrophium, for the poor and beggars; the Orphanotrophium, for orphans; the Brephotrophium, for abandoned children; the Gerontozomium, for the aged poor and for maimed persons; the Grotophonium, where a certain class of women were received. Separate provision was made at an early date for lepers. The *Hôtel Dieu* of Paris is one of the oldest of such institutions in the West. It is referred to in a decree of the Council of Paris (829) ordering the canons to give a tenth of their church lands to the H. of St. Christopher. There was from time to time great abuse of these endowments, the popes sometimes granting collations in perpetuity. The Council of Trent accordingly directed the will of the pious founders to be observed, and, anticipating the English doctrine of *Cy-près*, where the expressed purposes failed, that a kindred charity, in the discretion of the bishop, should be carried out. The greater number of the hospitals were in the hands of Augustinian monks, and the wish of the reforming party in the Church was to take the charities from secular priests, and put them under the management of respectable laymen, who should submit inventories and accounts to the bishop. Minor hospitals have been established for the administration of the sacraments, and in large towns for the entertainment of members of particular religious orders engaged in travel. The latter were called *hospices*, and were disfavoured by the Church as against convent discipline. Under the canon law all hospitals enjoyed the privileges of the Church, and an exemption from all taxes, even that for the building of schools. (For the modern representatives of these institutions, see De Liefde, *Six Months among the Charities of Europe*, 2 vols., 1865.)

In Scotland, one-half of the educational endowments, or about £79,000, is devoted to *hospitals*. This does not include places which, like Cowane's and Spittal's in Stirling, Hutcheson's in Glasgow, Gillespie's in Edinburgh, were really almshouses for the 'aged,' 'poor,' 'decayed guild brethren,' and the like. In many cases, also, either by custom and change of circumstances, or by Provisional Order under the 'Endowed Institutions (Scotland) Act, 1869,' the funds have been applied educationally in paying the school fees of poor children, or in supplementing the salaries of teachers. In a few cases the converse process has taken place. Some endowments are absolutely wasted on account of the restrictive conditions which cannot be fulfilled. The large funds held by the Guildry of Aberdeen and the Incorporated Trades of Stirling admittedly require a change in administration. The word *H.*, however, as applied to an institution for the maintenance, education, and clothing of orphan or destitute children, was introduced from England in 1624 by George Heriot. His scheme, founded on Christ's H., London, has been largely imitated, and there are now in Scotland twenty-six hospitals, educating 1510 foundationers (chiefly from the petty tradesmen and skilled artisan classes) between the ages of seven and fourteen, at a cost varying from £12 to £54 per head—a cost by no means proportional to the educational results. Opinion has of late run strongly against the monastic system, which is said to depress the intelligence and moral standard of the children; and under the Act of 1869 the Merchant Company of Edinburgh and the governors of the Bathgate Academy have converted their institutions into great day schools, and introduced the principle of competition among applicants for foundations. The two advantages of the monastic system, viz., regular attendance and wholesome diet, may always be secured by a judicious system of boarding out. Three-fifths of the foundationers in Scotland are orphans. There is always an entrance examination. In Fettes College the foundationers provide their own clothes. There has, no doubt, been a pauperising influence, as in Heriot's H., where many persons bought burgess tickets in order to entitle their children to admission. A royal commission, which reported in 1875, recommended universal boarding out, admission of day scholars, and the institution of scholastic foundations for secondary instruction. The great H. of Heriot, with its income of £20,000, spends considerable sums on apprentice fees, bursaries, and the system of free day schools for the Edinburgh poor. This last improvement was made under an Act of Parliament in 1836. The other large hospitals of Edinburgh are John Watson's (founded in 1759 'to prevent child murder by receiving pregnant women,' but altered by statute in 1822), which receives fatherless boys and girls, chiefly from the professional part of the middle class; Donaldson's, founded in 1833, which gives part of its accommodation to deaf mutes. The smaller Scotch hospitals, not before mentioned, are the Boys' and Girls', Gordon's, Orphan and Destitute Females, Orphan Asylum, and Shaw's at Aberdeen; Spier's in Ayrshire; Muirhead's at Dumfries; Morgan's and the Orphan Institution at Dundee; the Orphan and Trades Maiden at Edinburgh; Cauvin's at Duddingstone; Elgin Institution; the Scott Institution at Greenock; Brookland's at Kirkpatrick-Durham; Douglas Free School at Newton-Stewart; Schaw's at Prestonpans; Stiell's at Tranent; Speyside Charity, Grantown.

Of medical hospitals it is impossible to give any detailed account. They are partly endowed, partly supported by private subscriptions. The oldest of the London hospitals are St. Thomas, Bartholomew's, and Bethlehem, all founded in the middle of the 16th c. Many more belong to the reign of George II. when (in 1736) the Edinburgh Royal Infirmary was founded. This infirmary revised its constitution by Act of Parliament in 1870. It is now managed by the representatives of the Court of Contributors, and some *ex officiis* managers. New premises, on a very large scale, are being erected. There is, of course, a tendency to specialise the work of each H., and in those larger ones (as the Middlesex) which remain general, the organisation of the treatment of disease is more strictly carried out. Hence, the great value of hospitals as practical schools of medical study. The nine great hospitals of Dublin have for many years been under a Statutory Board of Superintendence, who have an income of £36,000. Here and there (as in Chalmers' H., Edinburgh) the *maison de santé* or *sanatorium* principle has been attempted, a higher class of patients paying moderate fees for board and advice. Gratuitous *dispensaries* of medicine are usually worked in connection with the larger hospitals.

In regard to civil hospitals, the 19th c. has been marked (1) by a great advance in the scientific construction of H. buildings; (2) by a recognition of the necessity of having *educated* nurses; (3) by the voluntary service (sometimes religious, sometimes secular) of many educated ladies in the capacity of nurses.

Hospital.—In English law a H. is a corporation founded for a charitable object. By 39 Eliz. c. 5 any one seized of an estate in Fee Simple (q. v.) may by deed enrolled in Chancery found a H. for relief of the poor, to continue for ever, and by two more statutes of the same reign the Lord Chancellor is empowered to issue a commission to inquire into abuses and breaches of trust in H. foundations.

Hospitals, Military, form part of the Army Medical Department, which is under the control of the Director General, assisted by the Administrative Officers of the Medical, Sanitary, and Statistical Branches. The latter (viz., the Surgeon-General and Deputy Surgeon-General) preside at Medical Boards and inspect hospitals, barracks, and camps. The Army Hospital Corps consist of two ranks: (1) captain of orderlies; (2) lieutenant of orderlies. The compounder of medicines acts as ward-master, and a corporal generally acts as pack storekeeper. There are *station hospitals* and hospitals at district *headquarters* for the reception of sick from all corps in garrison. The tendency under Lord Cardwell's unification system is to separate medical officers (who are appointed by the Director-General) entirely from regiments, and attach them to a general medical organisation for the army. In general, all non-commissioned officers and soldiers, and their wives and children, are entitled, subject to the regulation stoppages, to attendance, medicine, and diet. All the foreign invalids pass through Netley to their appropriate district hospitals. The staff of the *general hospitals* includes a governor or commandant, separate medical and sanitary officers, a registrar, and superintendent of nurses. The governor, who is nominated by the Commander-in-chief, has very large powers, including military authority over officers. It cannot be said that the Army Medical Department is as yet permanently organised. See *The Army Medical Regulations and Circulars of* 1873–76.

Hospital, Naval. The chief features of naval hospitals are that the medical officers (who often act gratuitously in civil hospitals) are always paid; that the patients being of different ranks, very different arrangements have to be made; that they are subject to the public rules of the service (*e.g.*, a post-captain as superintendent, and one nurse to every seven patients); that the officers survey invalids and pensioners, examine recruits, and issue stores to the service afloat. The chief naval hospitals are the Melville, Chatham; the Royal, Plymouth; the Haslar, Portsmouth. The last is on a magnificent scale, with a 'Zymotic Department,' for the treatment of exanthematous fevers, a large system of baths, and 50 acres of ground. Greenwich H., with an income of £138,000 (part of which used to come from the old tax known as 'Merchant Seamen's Sixpences'), has practically given up the in-pensioner principle, and now distributes ninepence a day to seamen and marines over seventy years of age, and who have been naval pensioners for ten years, and fivepence a day to those over fifty-five who have been pensioners for five years.

Hospitall'ers (Fr. from Lat. *hospitium*, 'a place for receiving strangers'), were at first religious fraternities which gave food and lodging to pilgrims. From one of these institutions at Jerusalem arose, about the beginning of the 12th c., the order of the Knights Hospitallers afterwards known as the Knights of St. John of Jerusalem (q. v.).

Hos'podar, formerly the usual title for the princes of Moldavia and Wallachia, is a Slavic word signifying lord or master, and appears in dialectically differing forms such as *Gospod* and *Gospodar*. The native Rumanian title is *domnu*, a corrupt form of the Latin *dominus*.

Host (Lat. *hostia*) means literally a sacrificial victim or offering. Thus in the Vulgate *hostia* is the word used for that which is rendered 'sacrifice' in English in Rom. xii. 1.; and it is applied to Christ in Eph. v. 2 and Heb. x. 12. It then came to be applied to the bread and wine of the Eucharist taken together as representing the body of Christ, but was afterwards restricted to the bread alone. The Roman Catholic practice of the adoration of the H., a wafer of unleavened bread, is connected with the doctrine of Transubstantiation (q. v.).

Höst, Jens Kragh, one of the most prolific of Danish writers at the close of the 18th and in the first half of the 19th c., in history, æsthetics, law, and language, was born of Danish parents, 15th September 1772, at St. Thomas in the West Indies. When H. was four years old his parents came to Copenhagen. He graduated at the university in 1792, and from that year held various legal appointments till 1808, when difficulties arising from a too free expression of his opinions led him to retire into private and literary life. He died 26th March 1844. H. was one of the Scandinavian 'Literaturselskab,' whose object was to use literature to promote the union and unity of the Scandinavian kingdoms. The best-known work of H. is *Grev Struensee og hans Ministerium* (3 vols. 1824; improved in Germ. trans. 2 vols. 1826–27), but several other of his historical writings are valuable, especially those treating of the time of Christian VII.

Hostil'ius, Tullus, according to the Roman legend, was the third King of Rome, succeeding Numa B.C. 670. In his reign a war with Alba was decided by the famed combat of the Horatii and Curiatii, and was followed by others with Veii and Fidenæ. In the last, H., hard pressed, vowed temples to Pallor and Pavor, and after the victory tore asunder with chariots the Alban dictator, razing his city, and transferring its inhabitants to the Mons Cælius of Rome. His defeat of the Sabines H. similarly owed to a vow to double the number of the Salii, or priests of Mamers; but in 638, a pestilence arising, he, like Numa, attempted conjurations, and with his whole house was consumed by fire from heaven. The destruction of Alba and fusion of the Roman and Alban tribes probably contain germs of historic truth; according to Niebuhr, 'this point of real history stands like an oasis in the midst of legends.'

Hot'bed, in gardening, a bed or heap of fresh horse-dung, spent tan, leaves, or other moist composts, fermenting and evolving heat, for raising plants. When the violence of the fermentation has passed, and the bed has acquired the desired temperature, mould is laid on the top, and potted seeds and plants placed therein; and the whole is covered with a glazed frame. Kitchen vegetables, as salad plants, cucumbers, and melons, are frequently raised in a H. The exposure should be southerly, and protection from high winds by high walls and trees should be afforded.

Hotchpot, in English law, means the bringing together of sums of money or of effects with a view to dividing them. When a child has received an advance from the personal estate of a deceased father, he must bring that advance into H. before he will be allowed to share with the other children; that is, the advance is placed to the debit of him who has received it, in dividing the personal estate of the deceased under the statute of distribution. In Scotch law see COLLATION.

Hotels', Law Regarding. Commissioners and officers of excise are prohibited from granting to the keepers of hotels or spirit shops a license to retail any *excisable* liquor to be consumed on the premises unless the magistrates' license for the sale of beer has been previously obtained. For Scotch law see FORBES MACKENZIE ACT, NAUTÆ, CAUPONES, STABULARI. English and Scotch law see INNKEEPER.

Ho'tham, a suburb of Melbourne, but under distinct municipal government. It is situated on the N.W. side of the city. Pop. 16,000.

Hot'house, in gardening, a term loosely applied to glazed structures provided with heating apparatus for the sustenance and growth of plants that cannot be grown out of doors. In this signification it embraces the Conservatory (q. v.) and Greenhouse (q. v.). A H., however, differs from these in having a high temperature requisite for rearing tropical plants constantly maintained. The damp stove and the dry stove, the bark stove, and the forcing-house for forcing the growth of fruits, are all used in hothouses. See HOT-WALLS.

Hott'entots, a native race of S. Africa, occupying a region that stretches N. from Cape Colony to Mossamedes, and is bounded on the W. by the Atlantic, and E. by the Kala-harri waste. Their country is divided by the two great tribes into Damara-land in the N., and Namaqua-land (q. v.) in the S.; part of the latter section, known as Little Namanqua-land, lying to the S. of the Orange River, is included in Cape Colony. The basin of the Orange River as far W. as the Orange Free State, and S. to the province of Victoria W. is thinly peopled by the degraded Bosjesmans (*Saab*), the Griquas (*i.e.*, bastards, see GRIQUALAND), are a tribe of mixed Dutch and Hottentot origin. The purer Namanquas, Damaras, and Ovampos are tall, warlike, intelligent people. They call themselves collectively Quai-quae or Koi-Koin, and the name H. (written by Dampier *Hodmadods*) is probably either a sobriquet (*Hot en Tot*) given to the race by the Dutch in mimicry of their clicking speech, or, as Pritchard suggests, a corruption of *H'outeniqua*, the name of a particular tribe. By Latham the H. are ranked among the Atlantidæ, while Blumenbach classes them with the Ethiopians. They curiously combine many features of the Mongolian and the Negro. Slim, well-built, with high cheek-bones, sallow complexion, and oblique, widely separated eyes, they have thick lips, flat noses, and woolly hair. When young, the Hottentot has generally a graceful figure, but in advanced life the females especially are extremely ugly, having loose, distended breasts and nates of unusual dimensions. The speech of the pure H. is the so-called 'click' language (see BUSHMAN LANGUAGE), abounding in horrid nasal clicks (expressed by *t'*) and gutturals, and attractive only as a storehouse of the native folk-lore. The H. are mostly nomad hunters or rearers of cattle, living in kraals or villages. They make their own weapons (poisoned arrows, javelins, and spears), some coarse earthenware, the sheep-skin cloaks that form their sole attire in winter, rude kinds of reed flutes, and three-stringed guitars. Though almost destitute of any religious ideas, they have eagerly received the instruction of various Moravian missionaries. They were made known to Europeans as a distinct race in 1509, when they were found to occupy the country as far S. as Table Bay. The Dutch settlers acquired the flocks and herds of many of the tribes in exchange for rum and brandy, and eventually held the natives in their employment as slaves. A considerable number of H. are now engaged as good, steady workmen throughout Cape Colony. See Fritsch, *Drei Jahre in Südafrika* (1869) and *Die Eingebornen Südafrika* (1872); Dr. Bleek, *Comparative Grammar of the S. African Languages* (Cape Town, 1862); *Reynard the Fox in S. Afria, or Hottentot Fables and Tales* (Lond. 1864); and *Brief Account of Bushman Folklore and other Texts* (1875). A *Bushman-English Grammar and Dictionary* by Dr. Bleek (1877) is in course of preparation for the press.

Hotto'nia, a small genus of aquatic plants belonging to the natural order *Primulaceæ*, and named after Hotton, an early Leyden professor of botany. *H. palustris*, called water-violet, is not an uncommon English plant, but does not extend into Scotland. It may readily be known by its submerged, imperfectly whorled, pectinate leaves, and its erect raceme of whorled lilac flowers with a yellow eye, rising from 5 to 9 inches above the surface of the water. It is a good plant for aquaria.

Hot-Walls, in gardening, are walls built hollow for the passage of steam or hot-water pipes, or with flues for the circulation of heated air from a furnace. They are employed in rearing fruit-trees, placed against them, and for the preservation of tender plants in localities higher than the 50° of latitude.

Houghton-le-Spring, a town of England, in Durhamshire, 6 miles N.E. of Durham, and 6½ S.W. of Sunderland by rail. It has a large trade in the fine coal, limestone, and freestone of the district, besides extensive iron foundries, breweries, brick-kilns, &c. H. was long the residence of Bernhard Gilpin, 'the Apostle of the North.' Pop. (1871) 5276.

Hought'on, Richard Monckton Milnes, first Baron, poet and politician, only son of R. P. Milnes, Esq., of Fryston Hall, Yorkshire, was born June 19, 1809. He graduated at Trinity College, Cambridge, in 1831, and entered Parliament as member for Pontefract in 1837, which seat he held till 1863, when he was created a peer. Originally a Conservative, he afterwards became a supporter of the Whigs, advocating free trade, popular education, religious equality, and concurrent endowment. He sympathised with oppressed nationalities, and interested himself in penal reform, introducing a bill for the establishment of reformatories in 1846. He has published various works of travel and on politics, and has always been a generous friend of struggling merit. Several of his biographical sketches were reissued as *Monographs, Personal and Social*, in 1873. H.'s *Poems of Many Years, Palm Leaves*, &c., were collected in 1876, and published with a preface by himself. They display fine fancy, are rhythmical, and written in a pure and simple style. Among the most popular are two dainty ballads, *The Brookside* and *Good Night and Good Morning*. H. edited the first complete collection of Keat's poems in 1877.

Hound (Old Eng. *hund*, akin to Lat. *can*-is, Gr. *kuōn*, and Sansk. *çvan*, perhaps onomatopœic, from the bark of the animal), a very general name given especially to dogs which are used in hunting. The H. is a dog possessed of great powers of scent. The Bloodhound (q. v.), Deerhound (q. v.), and Fox-hound (q. v.) are good examples; but these breeds have become mixed with other varieties, and in many cases have greatly deteriorated. In general, hounds are short-haired and powerfully-built, with broad muzzles, strong jaws, and pendant ears. The eyes are of moderate size, and the tail is slender.

Hound's-Tongue, an equivalent of Cynoglossum, a genus of *Boraginaceæ*, distributed through temperate and tropical regions. The name is derived from the texture of the leaf surface of some of the species. Common H. (*C. officinalis*) ranges through Europe, N. Africa, Siberia, and W. Asia: in Britain it is not uncommon in sandy ground near the coast, and to a less extent in fields and waste places inland. The genus contains about forty species.

Houns'low, a town of England, in the county of Middlesex, 3½ N.W. of Richmond, and 12 W. of London by rail. Before the opening of the railway to Southampton and Bath, H. had a most extensive posting business, nearly 500 coaches passing through it every day. The neighbouring heath was a favourite haunt of highwaymen down to the present century. It is now partly occupied by military barracks, partly enclosed, and the town is surrounded by many fine villas. The chief industries are carriage-building, market-gardening, and brickmaking. Pop. (1871) 9394. H. is the *Hondeslawe* of Domesday Book, and the Heath was a royal preserve till the time of Charles II.

Hour, an interval of time, twenty-four of which make up one day. The division of the common day, or time during which the sun is above the horizon, into twelve portions dates from a remote antiquity; but the similar division of the night was introduced first at Rome during the Punic wars. These intervals of time varied in length with the variations of day and night, which result from the sequence of the seasons. In modern reckoning, the twenty-four hours which make up one whole day are usually divided into two sets of twelve hours each, reckoning from midnight to midday, and from midday to midnight. The Italians, however, use twenty-four hours beginning with sunset, while astronomers are in the habit of making their day begin at midday, and reckoning twenty-four hours till the succeeding midday.

Hour-Glass, a kind of clepsydra, which measures the passing of time by the running of water or sand from one glass to another. Its indications must, of course, depend much upon the temperature and humidity of the atmosphere.

Housaton'ic, a river of N. America, rises in Berkshire county, Massachusetts, 1000 feet above sea-level, flows S. through Connecticut, and falls into Long Island Sound at Milford Point, after a course of about 120 miles, 14 of which are tidal. The H. is a picturesque stream, and supplies water-power to numerous manufactories.

House. In England it is not lawful to break into any one's house in execution of a civil warrant, but stratagem may be used to enter peaceably. Force may be used to execute a criminal warrant. The law holds the employment of any force requisite to defend a H. against trespassers or burglars justifiable. It is, of course, impossible to lay down a rule as to what force may be requisite to its end, each case depending on its own circumstances. (See HOMICIDE.) In Scotland a messenger may get leave from the court to break open the door in execution of a civil or criminal warrant. See BURGLARY, HOUSEBREAKING.

House'breaking is the most criminal form of theft. It is committed if the natural security of the house has been overcome. But it is not committed if the thief enters by an open door or window. When entry is effected by connivance with a resident of the house, the accomplice is also guilty of H., and should the crime amount to burglary in the actual thief, it will be burglary in the accomplice. See BURGLARY.

Housebuilder Moth (*Oiketicus Sandersii*), a peculiar genus of Moths (q. v.) occurring in the W. Indies, and so named from the habit of the larvæ in fastening bits of wood and leaves together, so as to form a habitation for itself. It (H. M.) appears to possess the power of closing the aperture at will. The females are wingless, and the body of the male is hairy. The antennæ are of comb-like form at the base, and the wings are covered with hairs.

House'burning; in Scotch law, see FIRE-RAISING; in English law, see ARSON.

House-Fly (*Musca domestica*), a species of *Diptera* or flies, belonging to the family *Muscidæ*, in which the antennæ are three-jointed, the proboscis having a fleshy lobe at its tip, while the maxillary palpi are single-jointed. The larvæ are footless grubs, and have hook-like mandibles or jaws. The H.-F. has a peculiar tongue, formed of the modified *labium* or lower lip. When a fly alights on a piece of sugar, this tongue may be seen unfolded, the broad extremity dividing into two flat, leaf-like bodies, furnished with suckers with which the insect laps up the sweet morsels. The inside of the broad tip of the tongue is rough and file-like, and it is by the action of this organ that the polish of books and furniture is damaged. The early stages of the H.-F. are passed amid manure, and it remains in the pupa or chrysalis state from eight to fourteen days. The H.-F. is infested by fungi; and the ichneumon-flies also prey upon it. The feet are terminated by minute discs furnished with a gummy secretion and provided with suckers, whereby the animal is enabled to walk on flat surfaces.

House'hold Troops, six of the best-appointed of British regiments, consist of the 1st and 2d Life, Royal Horse, Grenadier, Coldstream, and Scots Fusilier Guards. As their peculiar functions are to escort royalty and to defend the capital, their usual quarters are in the metropolitan and Windsor barracks. Their strength in 1876 was 1302 cavalry, with 825 horses, and 5950 infantry, and their pay and allowances, £283,607.

House'-Leek. The word leek here has no connection with the onion family, being simply the Old English *leac*, a 'plant,' so the H.-L. means a plant grown on a house. We confine it to *Sempervivum tectorum*, a European and W. Asian species of the natural order *Crassulaceæ*, which has for centuries been grown on the roofs of houses, outbuildings, &c., in Britain, as a handy relief for such casualties as burns, cuts, stings, and ulcers. In country places the bruised leaf is still used for these purposes. The sempervivums, as the name indicates, are remarkable for retention of vitality under adverse circumstances. The species number about forty, and with allied genera have recently come greatly into vogue for garden-beds and rock-gardens.

House'maid's Knee is an inflammation of the bursa or sac intervening between the patella or knee-cap and the skin, and is generally caused by pressure from kneeling. Treatment:—when inflamed, leeching, followed by tepid lead-lotions, or poultices; when chronic, painting with tincture of iodine, tapping, and injecting with iodine, or passing a seton through the sac. If suppuration has taken place, the sac must be freely opened, and the pus evacuated.

House of Commons and **House of Lords.** See PARLIAMENT.

House of Correction. The distinction between H. of C. and other prisons is abolished. See PRISONS, REFORMATORY.

House Rents. In England an action to recover H. R. can be brought till six years after the date of falling due. In Scotland H. R. prescribe in three years, under the Triennial Prescription Act of 1579. For English law, see LANDLORD AND TENANT; for Scotch law, see LEASE, CONTRACT OF.

Houss'a, or **Hauss'a**, a territory of the Sudan, Central Africa, in about 12°–13° N., and long. 5°–10° E. It is in part low land, inundated during the rainy season by the Niger and its affluents, and in part elevated tableland, enclosed by ranges of rocky hills. Some tribes of the Houssas are independent, others are subject to the Fellatahs.

Hous'ton, a city of Texas, U.S., on both sides of the navigable Buffalo Bayou, 50 miles N.W. of Galveston by rail. It is the railway centre of Texas, has manufactures of cotton, soap, Portland cement, ploughs, carriages, &c., and three daily and five weekly newspapers. The place is named after Samuel Houston (q. v.). Pop. (1870) 9382.

Houston, Samuel, an American general, born near Lexington, in Virginia, 2d March 1793. In his boyhood he ran from home, and for several years lived with the Cherokee Indians, after which he enlisted in the army, and fought with distinction against the English and the Creek Indians, being severely wounded at Tallapoosa, March 24, 1814. He next practised as a lawyer at Nashville, and successively became major-general, representative in Congress, and Governor of Tennessee. Three months after his marriage in 1829, he suddenly left his wife and civilisation, and was formally admitted a chief of the Cherokees. He emerged from his wigwam to take command of the Texan army in the war against Santa Anna, and on April 21, 1836, gained the brilliant victory of San Jacinto, which secured the independence of Texas. He was elected President of Texas in 1836, and again in 1841; and his administration, though beset with difficulties, was able and successful. On the absorption of Texas by the United States, H. was returned as senator for that State. In 1859 he was appointed Governor of Texas, but he retired on the outbreak of the Civil War. He died at Huntersville, Texas, July 25, 1863.

How'ard is the name of the family which popularly ranks as the noblest of English noble houses. The origin of the name is doubtful. By some it is derived from Hereward, 'the last of the English.' But a plausible derivation (see Isaac Taylor's *Names and Places*, p. 361) regards it as another form of Hogarth, said to have been originally Hog-ward; so that by the irony of history the boast of having 'all the blood of all the Howards' in one's veins vaunts descent from a race of swineherds. The famous *family* of H. cannot be traced further back than **Sir William H.**, Chief-Justice in the days of Edward I. His grandson became an admiral of the fleet and sheriff of Norfolk. The growing dignity of the Howards was greatly advanced by the marriage of the admiral's grandson to the co-heiress of the noble house of Mowbray, dukes of Norfolk. The son of this union, **Sir John H.**, was a distinguished supporter of the White Rose, fought gallantly in France, became sheriff of Norfolk and Suffolk, and was made treasurer of the royal household. His services against the Lancastrians at sea and by land was finally rewarded by being created first Lord H., and then in 1483 Duke of Norfolk; he was further named Earl Marshal of England, and Lord Admiral of England, Ireland, and Aquitaine. But he fell at Bosworth, and his family were deprived of his dignities. His son, who had been made Earl of Surrey, after three years' imprisonment had the family honours restored, and served the Tudors well at Flodden (q. v.). His son, third Duke of Norfolk, was father of the gallant but ill-fated Earl of Surrey (q. v.), who died on the scaffold by Henry VIII.'s procurement, and narrowly escaped a like fate himself. The head of the fourth Duke came to the block on Tower Hill, for treasonous intrigues on behalf of Mary of Scotland. James I. and Charles II. between them restored the H. family to its ancient honours, which are now enjoyed by the fifteenth Duke of Norfolk. The family is now chiefly conspicuous by its adherence to Roman Catholicism. The earldoms of Carlisle, of Suffolk, and of Effingham are held also by representatives of this family; and the Barons H. de Walden and H. of Glossop are members of the English peerage. Several titles now extinct were at various times conferred on Howards; and innumerable untitled county families can still count kinship with the head of this illustrious house.

Howard, John, the philanthropist, was born at Hackney, London, 2d September 1726. His father was a wealthy upholsterer, from whom he inherited a considerable fortune. In 1756, when on a voyage to Lisbon, he was taken prisoner by the French, and remained for some time in captivity. It was probably his own experience of a prison that first suggested to him the resolution he afterwards took, of devoting his life to bettering the condition of prisons and prisoners. For this purpose he began to visit jails in 1773, and spent the rest of his life in travelling repeatedly throughout the whole of England and over the whole of Europe, with the satisfaction of knowing that his labours were in most instances productive of good results. In 1777 he published his *State of Prisons in England and Wales, with Preliminary Observations, and an Account of some Foreign Prisons* (new ed. 1780). In 1785 he began to visit the principal lazarettos in Europe, of which he published an account in 1789. He died at Kherson, on the Black Sea, 20th January 1790, from a fever caught in the course of his benevolent labours. Besides the great work of his life, he did much good in his own district by building artisans' cottages and establishing schools. H. was fond of horticulture and of scientific study and experiments, some of which he communicated to the Royal Society. See Dixon's *H. and the Prison World of Europe* (5th ed. Lond. 1854), and Field's *Correspondence of H.* (Lond. 1855).

Howe, John, one of the greatest of the Puritan divines, was born at Loughborough in Leicestershire, May 17, 1630, educated partly at Cambridge and partly at Oxford, ordained in 1653, and settled as pastor at Great Torrington in Devon. The energy and duration of his religious exercises were something marvellous. He began with his flock 'at 9 A.M., prayed during a quarter of an hour for blessing upon the day's work, then read and explained a chapter for three quarters of an hour, then prayed for an hour, then preached for an hour, and prayed again for half an hour, then retired for a quarter of an hour's refreshment—the people singing all the while—returned to his pulpit, prayed for another hour, preached for another hour, and finished at 4 P.M. with one half-hour more of prayer, doing it all singly, and with his whole soul in it all' (Morley's *English Literature*, pp. 613–14). In 1657 he was made chaplain to Cromwell, securing the esteem and praise of the fiercest enemies of his party. At the Restoration he retired first to Devon and then to Ireland, but in 1676 became pastor of a Nonconformist congregation in London. In 1685 he settled at Utrecht as a schoolmaster, but returned to London after James's Declaration, and died 2d April 1706. His great work, *A Good Man the Living Temple of God*, was published partly in 1676; the second part not till 1702. Others once famous, and still worthy of fame, are *The Solemn Inquiry Concerning the Possibility of a Trinity* (1695), *The Redeemer's Tears over Lost Worlds* (1685), *On the Carnality of Religious Contention* (1693), and *The Redeemer's Dominion over the Invisible World* (1700). See Henry Rogers's *Life and Character of John H.* (Lond. 1836).

Howe, Richard, Earl, a British admiral, second son of the second Viscount Howe, was born in 1725. In 1739 he left Eton and entered the navy, obtaining the rank of post-captain when twenty years of age for important services in intercepting French stores for the Pretender. His seizure of two French frigates off Newfoundland in 1755 was the prelude to the Seven Years' War. He destroyed the fort of Aix in 1757, reduced Cherbourg in 1758, and in the disaster at St. Cas his presence of mind in covering the re-embarkation of the British saved many lives. Next year he showed conspicuous bravery in the great battle of Quiberon, and captured two French ships. After the war he became in succession a lord of the Admiralty, Treasurer of the Navy, and Commander-in-Chief in the Mediterranean. In 1776 he took New York and Philadelphia, in 1778 defeated D'Estaing off Rhode Island, and in 1782 relieved Gibraltar. In the latter year he was created a Viscount of the United Kingdom, and an Earl in 1788. On 1st Juue 1794 he completely routed the French fleet off Ushant, and was made a Knight of the Garter. He suppressed a mutiny at Portsmouth in 1797, and died August 5, 1799. He was a bold and skilful officer, and the ablest sea-captain of his time. See Barrow's *Life of Lord H.* (Lond. 1838).

Howe, Samuel Gridley, M.D., an American physician, was born at Boston, Mass., November 10, 1801. He served as surgeon in the Greek war of independence (1824–27), and organised a medical staff, of which he was made the head. After his return to America, he became interested in the education of the blind, visited Europe with the view of studying the various systems in use, and suffered imprisonment in Prussia for six weeks for attempting to carry help to the Poles. Since 1832 he has been superintendent of the Perkins Asylum for the Blind, Massachusetts; and in 1871 was one of the United States Commissioners to San Domingo. His chief works are *An Historical Sketch of the Greek Revolution* (1828), and *Reader for the Blind* (1839).

How'itt, William and Mary, two popular and meritorious English authors. William H. was born at Heanon in Derbyshire in 1795, and married in 1823 Mary H. (Miss Botham), born at Uttoxeter in 1800. In the year of their marriage they jointly published *The Forest Minstrel*, and in 1827 the *Desolation of Eyam* and other poems. Besides contributing largely to periodical literature, they have since published, jointly and separately, very many works. A residence in Heidelberg from 1840 to 1842 led them to study German and Scandinavian literature, an outcome of which was their *Literature and Romance of Northern Europe* (2 vols. 1851–52). W. H. has written the *History of Priestcraft*, *Student Life in Germany*, *The Homes and Haunts of the British Poets*, *The Ruined Castles of Great Britain and Ireland*, *Land Labour and Gold*, an account of two years' residence in Australia (1852–54), a *History of the Supernatural*, &c. For some time Mr. H. edited the *People's Journal*, which was started in 1846, but has long ceased to exist. M. H.'s best-known works are *The Seven Temptations*, dramatic sketches, *Wood-Leighton*, a novel, a series of *Tales for the People and their Children*, and translations of the tales of Fredrika Bremer and Hans Ch. Andersen.

How'itzers (Ger. *haubitze*, from *haufen*, 'to fill'), light field-guns for throwing shells at short ranges.

Howl'er, or **Howling Monkey,** a name given to certain genera of *Platyrhine* or New World monkeys, from the loud noises they are capable of making. The voice is rendered powerful and resonant by the presence of large sacs within the larynx or organ of voice. The tail is prehensile. The Ursine H. (*Mycetes ursinus*) is one of the best-known species. This animal is of a reddish-brown hue, and has a prominent beard. The howling monkeys herd in large troops in tropical forests, and make most discordant noises.

How'rah, the chief town of the district of the same name, in Bengal, British India, included within Hooghly (q. v.), on the right bank of the Hooghly river, which is here nearly one mile wide, exactly opposite to Calcutta; pop. (1872) 97,784. It is really a transpontine suburb of Calcutta, with which it was connected in 1875 by a massive pontoon bridge, at a cost of £220,000. H. is the terminus of the East Indian Railway. It has busy dockyards, flourishing mills and manufactures, the botanical gardens and Bishop's College; here also reside many of the business people of Calcutta. At the end of last century it was a mere village.

Howth, a seaport of Ireland, in the county of Dublin, on the N. side of H. Head, 10 miles E.N.E. of Dublin by rail. Its harbour, constructed by Government at a cost of half a million sterling, is obstructed by sandbanks. The chief industry is fishing. Pop. (1871) 1948.—**H. Head,** an almost insulated promontory, enclosing the N. side of Dublin Bay, is 3 miles long and 2 broad, and has bold picturesque shores. The hill of H. is visible for many miles. The name is a corruption of the Danish *hoved*, 'a head;' but the original designation is *Ben Edair*, 'the hill of Edair,' probably a legendary chief of the Tuatha de Danann.

Hoy'a, a genus of *Asclepiadaceæ* containing some of the most ornamental among the plants cultivated in our hothouses. *H. carnosa* receives the name of wax-flowers from the peculiar aspect of its blossoms.

Hoy, next to Pomona, the largest of the Orkney Islands, lies 15 miles S.W. of Kirkwall. It is a precipitous mass of sandstone, 15 miles long and 6 broad, rising from the sea in rugged cliffs 1000 feet high in the W., and opening here and there in deep gorges. Of its three peaks, the Ward Hill reaches a height of 1555 feet. Pop. (1871) 1385. To the S.W. is a grotesque insulated pillar 300 feet high, called the Old Man of H. The island is haunted by myriads of seafowl.

Hualla'ga, or **Ucaya'li,** a tributary of the Amazon, 500 miles long, rises in the Peruvian Andes, flows in a northerly direction to join the Maïnas, and form the Marañon. It is wholly within Peru.

Huaman'ga, the former name of the city of Ayacucho (q. v.).

Huancaveli'ca, or **Guancabeli'ca,** the capital of a province of Peru, on the E. side of the Andes, 11,000 feet high, has extensive mines of gold and quicksilver. Pop. 5000.

Huanu'co, an old town of Peru, in the beautiful valley of the H., a tributary of the Maïnas, in the Andes. It lacks means of transit for the sugar and corn crops of the valley. Pop. 5000.

Huaraz', the chief town of a province of the same name, Peru, beautifully situated on the Santa, 150 miles S.E. of Trusillo. The inhabitants are mostly mestizoes, engaged in agriculture and gardening. Pop. 8000.

Huas'co, a seaport of Chili, province of Atacama, at the mouth of a river of the same name, 90 miles S.W. of Copiapo. It owes its prosperity to the mining of copper, of which it exports £345,000 worth annually. Pop. 7000.

Hubb (Habb), the only river of Scinde, India, besides the Indus, which finds its way to the sea. It rises in Kelat, forms for some distance the boundary between Scinde and Beloochistan, and after a total course of 100 miles, falls into the Arabian Sea N.W. of Cape Monze. The water has been greatly utilised for irrigation by a Mohammedan proprietor.

Hu'ber, François, a Swiss naturalist, was born at Geneva, July 2, 1750. Though blind for the greater part of his life, he made valuable investigations into the habits of bees, receiving much assistance from his wife and a domestic servant named Burnens. His results were collected and published in his *Nouvelles Observationes sur les Abeilles* (1796). He was latterly aided by his son, **Pierre H.** (born 1777, died January 1841), who was the author of a valuable work entitled, *Histoire des Mœurs des Fournis Indigènes*. H. died at Lausaune, December 22, 1831.

Hu'ber, Ludwig Ferdinand, a German author of note, was born at Paris in 1764, became secretary to the Saxon legation at Mainz in 1787, was editor of the *Allgemeine Zeitung* from 1798 to 1803, and died 24th December 1804. His *Sammtliche Werke*, consisting chiefly of plays original and adapted from the French, were published by his wife in 4 vols. 1806–9.—**Therese H.,** wife of the preceding, was the daughter of the illustrious scholar Heyne (q. v.), and was born at Göttingen, 7th May 1764. She was married first to Johann Georg Forster (q. v.), and after his death to H. As a novelist she has a distinct place in German literature. She writes for her own sex chiefly. An edition of her works, in 6 vols., was published by her son (Leips. 1830–33).—**Victor Aimé H.**, an historico-literary and political writer, son of Ludwig F. and Therese H., was born at Stuttgart, 10th March 1800, became Professor of the History of Literature at Rostock in 1833, went to Marburg three years later as Professor of Modern Languages and Literature, and from 1843 to 1850 held the same appointment in the University of Berlin. He died at Wernigerode in the Harz, 19th July 1870. H. had a wide knowledge and a fine appreciation of the Romance literatures. Among his chief works are the *Geschichte des C.* (1829), *Chronica del lid* (1844), *Die Neu-Romantische Pœsie in Frankreich* (1833), *Die Skizzen aus Spanien* (1828–35), *Reisebriefe aus Belgien* (1855).

Hu'bert, Saint, Bishop of Liège, son of Bertrand of Guienne, was chief functionary at the court of the Frankish king Theodoric. At the suggestion of his friend and teacher Bishop Lamprecht of Maastricht, and through sorrow for the death of his wife Floribane, he sought a hermit's life, but after the martyrdom of Lamprecht returned to succeed him as Bishop of Maastricht and Liège in 708. He died in 727, and the legend tells that long afterwards his body was found still undecayed. In 827 he was canonised, and his corpse buried in a Benedictine monastery named Ardenne, whose name was changed to St. H. Another legend tells how, when H. was hunting one Good Friday in the Ardennes Hills, he came upon a stag with a gleaming crucifix between its horns, which admonished him for his passionate love of the chase, and persuaded him to a life of contemplation. Oddly enough, this story made him the patron saint of hunters. Many orders of knighthood were formed in his honour, courts held great hunting feasts on his name-day (3d November), and the common people believed that St. Peter had intrusted him with the *key* to the cure of possessed persons and those bitten by mad dogs.

Hu'bertsburg, a former royal hunting-castle in the circle of Leipsic, Saxony, near Mügeln, was built by Augustus III. in 1721. It is now an asylum and prison. The Peace of H., which ended the Seven Years' War, was signed here, 15th February 1763.

Hub'li, a flourishing town in the district of Dharwar, province of Bombay, British India, 290 miles S.E. of Bombay. Pop. (1872) 37,961. It stands on the main road from the S. Mahratta country to the Malabar coast, on the line of the proposed State Railway, and is a great emporium for cotton.

Hüb'ner, Rudolf Julius Benno, an historical painter of the 'Düsseldorf' school, born (1806) at Oels in Silesia, studied (1821) under W. Schadow (q. v.) at Berlin, where he exhibited his earliest work, 'Boaz and Ruth,' but in 1826 followed his master to Düsseldorf. H. travelled in Italy, and on his return settled (1839) at Dresden, where he has since resided, and where in 1841 he obtained the Professorship of Painting in the Academy. His works are marked by great purity of colour and design, but are somewhat deficient in depth and energy. Chief among them are the 'Fisherman' (1828), 'Samson Breaking the Pillars,' 'Christ and the Evangelists' (1835), and 'Happiness and Sleep' (1842).

Huc, Évariste Régis, a French missionary to China, was born at Toulouse, 1st August 1813, was educated there and in Paris, and ordained by the Lazarist fathers in 1839. He devoted himself to the Chinese Mission, and sailed immediately after his ordination. He studied eighteen months in Macao, and then, with dyed skin, pigtail, and Chinese costume, started for the interior. After directing a Chinese mission in the southern provinces, H. resided for a time in Pekin, whence he passed into Mongolia, translating several religious works into the Mongol tongue. In 1844 the Vicar Apostolic of Mongolia sent H. on the chief mission of his life, an expedition through Mongolia into Thibet. This was undertaken in company with M. Gabet, another Lazarist, and a Thibetan convert; and in spite of enormous difficulties, delays, and dangers, Lassa was reached by the missionaries. Their stay there was interrupted by Chinese influence; and in 1846 H. was again at Macao. He sailed homewards in ill health in 1849, and spent the remainder of his life in literary labour. H. died March 31, 1860. His *Souvenirs d'un Voyage dans la Tartarie, le Thibet et la Chine* (1852, Eng. trans. by Hazlitt, 1852) is one of the most interesting of books of travel; and his *L'Empire Chinois* (1854), and *Le Christianisme en Chine, en Tartarie et en Thibet* (1857–58), have also been translated into English.

Hudd'ersfield, a town of England in the W. Riding of Yorkshire, at the confluence of the Holme and the Colne, 16 miles S.W. of Leeds by railway. It ranks next to Leeds in the manufacture of woollens and mixed fabrics; among its products being doeskins, beavers, fancy trouserings, mohairs, rugs, Angolas, Bedford and worsted cords, quiltings, challies, &c. There are also extensive steam-engine and boiler factories, chemical-works, dye-houses, fulling-mills, &c. Among the public buildings are the church of St. Peter, rebuilt in 1837 at a cost of £10,000, St. Paul's Church, built by the Parliamentary Commissioners in 1830, St. Thomas's Church, with a richly carved pulpit of Caen stone, a circular cloth hall with circumference of 2640 feet, a chamber of commerce, and a proprietary college connected with the London University. The houses are almost entirely built of sandstone. H. has various charities, including the Dole Land of 25 acres, and a large hospital. Pop. (1871) 74,358. H. sends one member to Parliament. In the vicinity are numerous coal-mines and quarries. The united stream of the Holme and Colne is lined with mills in its course of 3 miles before reaching the Calder. At Lockwood, about half a mile from the town, are the Spa baths, the waters of which are strongly sulphurous. H. has more than quadrupled in wealth and population during the present century.

Hud'son, a town of New York, U.S., on the E. bank of H. River, at the head of navigation, 115 miles N. of New York, and 36 S. of Albany. It has fifteen churches, an old-established academy, orphan asylum, &c., and a thriving river-trade. Pop. (1870) 8615.

Hudson, a river of New York, U.S., and one of the most important streams of N. America, is formed by two branches, which rise in the Adirondacs, 4000 feet above sea-level, and unite some 40 miles from their respective sources. In its upper portion the H. is circuitous and much interrupted by cataracts, the Great, Jessups, Hadley, and Glen's Falls, but from the last-named point it strikes a southerly course, which it maintains to its mouth in New York Bay. It has a total length of 300 miles, and is navigable to Hudson (117 miles) for first-class shipping, and to Troy, the highest tidal point (166 miles), for smaller craft. The western tributaries are the Sacandaga, Mohawk (q. v.), Catskill, Rondout, and Wallkill; the eastern, the Schroon, Hoosick, Battenkill, Kinderhook, and Croton. The chief towns upon the banks of the H. are Troy, Albany, Hudson, Newburg, and New York. It is connected by canals with Lakes Erie and Champlain, and by the Delaware and Hudson Canal with the coal-fields of Pennsylvania; and a plan is now on foot to render the upper waters navigable as high as Fort Edward, 28 miles above Troy, by means of locks and dams. The H. abounds in fish, shad, sturgeon, and bass; and salmon have been lately introduced. It owes its name to Henry Hudson (q. v.), who discovered it in 1609.

Hudson, George, 'the railway king,' was born in York in 1800. On the birth of the railway system he was a bold and eager speculator, and erelong became the central figure of that astounding movement. His early schemes were enormously successful, and brought him a large fortune. He was thrice elected Mayor of York, and from 1845 to 1859 he was member for Sunderland. But his rocket-like ascent was followed by a no less sudden collapse. Some of his companies sank, the prosperity of others was found to be only upon paper, and thereupon his name ceased to conjure. Greatly impoverished, he spent the remainder of his life chiefly abroad. Some friends bought him an annuity; but he died, shortly after its purchase, December 14, 1871. See Carlyle's *Essay on G. H.*

Hudson, Henry, an English discoverer, whose name is commemorated by a bay, river, strait, and city in America. The only records of his life are from 1607 to 1610, when he made four voyages in search of a northern passage, the first in a small ship manned by eleven men. In his third voyage he sailed up the Hudson River. In 1610 he discovered Hudson's Bay, and hoping he had solved the north-west problem, determined to winter there. His crew thereupon mutinied, and sent him adrift with a few others in a boat, which was never again heard of. See Purchas' *Pilgrimes* and Parker's *Voyages*, also the *Voyages of H. H.*, edited by G. Asher (Lond. 1860).

Hudson, Sir James, diplomatist, grandson of the first Marquis Townshend, was born in London in 1810. He was educated at Rugby and Westminster, and was page and private secretary to King William IV. He acted as Secretary of Legation at Washington from 1838 to 1843, when he was transferred to a similar post at the Hague. In 1845 he was appointed Secretary of Legation at Rio Janeiro, where he ultimately became Minister, and after a brief official residence in Florence he was sent to Turin in 1852 as Minister-Plenipotentiary. Here he gave his hearty sympathy to the new-born movement towards Italian unity and liberty, and was instrumental in enlisting Sardinia as an ally against Russia. He was created a K.C.B. on 2d May 1855, and a G.C.B. in 1863, on his retirement from Turin.

Hudson's Bay, an extensive inlet in the heart of British N. America, lies between 51°–64° N. lat. and 78°–95° W. long., is about 800 miles long by 600 broad, and communicates with the Atlantic by Hudson's Strait, and with the Polar waters by Fox Channel. Area, 300,000 sq. miles. H. B. is indented by James Bay on the S., Button Bay on the W., and Chesterfield Bay on the N.W. The south-western shores are low and marshy, but elsewhere they are rocky and often precipitous. The surface is studded by numerous sandbanks and islands (of which Southampton Island in the N. is the largest), and is frozen over for eight months of the year. Innumerable rivers of no great size fall into H. B., the Churchill, Nelson, Severn, and Albany being the most important. H. B. was discovered in 1517 by Sebastian Cabot (q. v.), but received its name from Henry Hudson (q. v.).—**H. Strait** connects H. B. with Davis Strait, and so with the Atlantic. It is 450 miles long, and 60 to 100 wide, and is blocked with ice the greater part of the year.

Hudson's Bay Company, a corporation chartered 2d May 1670 by Charles II. with the perpetual exclusive right of trading in the territory watered by all the streams flowing into Hudson's Bay. The company in succession erected forts on the Rupert, the Moose, Albany, and Nelson rivers, and at first confined its operations within modest dimensions. The Indians were willing to barter the skins of the animals they trapped for trifles, and the trade was consequently, notwithstanding its limitation and the fierce hostility of the French, so lucrative that the capital of the company, which had been paying large dividends, was trebled in 1710. The forts were gradually increased and strengthened, and by 1781 the field of operations included the basins of the Saskatchewan and Coppermine rivers and had reached Athabasca. The charter had never been confirmed by Parliament, and was therefore on an unsatisfactory footing, but private traders were so opposed by the company that it maintained a monopoly of the fur trade until 1783. In that year a rival society on a large scale, the North-Western Company of Montreal, was projected, which established stations beyond the Rocky Mountains, and a violent and even bloody contest for supremacy ensued. The older company sold pieces of land on Lake Winnipeg and Red River to colonisers, and the younger company disputing this power, destroyed the settlement. At length in 1821 an amicable settlement took place, the surviving partners of the North-Western Company agreeing to coalesce with the H. B. C. The united company at once obtained an extension of its powers. An Act of Parliament (1st and 2d Geo. IV., cap. 66) gave it the sole right for twenty-one years of trading in the 'Indian territories,' or in the entire country west of its territory in Rupert's Land, which monopoly was renewed by the crown in 1838 for a further term of twenty-one years. Until 1859 the corporation had therefore the entire possession of all British North America, excepting the basin of the St. Lawrence and of territory since ceded to the United States. The 4,000,000 sq. miles governed by them were partitioned into four departments—the Montreal, Southern, Western, and Columbian—under the management of 25 chief factors, 28 chief traders, and a staff of about 1400 employés; the forts extending from Labrador to the Pacific and from the St. Lawrence to the Arctic Ocean. On the whole the administration was just and humane, the Indians being treated with kindness and consideration. In 1869, on the suggestion of Earl Granville, then Colonial Secretary, the territory of the company was transferred to the Dominion of Canada for £300,000, and was finally transformed into the province of Manitoba in 1870. The commerce of the company remains unaffected, notwithstanding the loss of its power and monopoly. The trade, which is almost entirely in furs, exported to and sold by auction in London was, till recently, carried on with the natives by a standard valuation based on the market price of a beaver. The proceeds of furs and other imports in 1876 were £291,566, the profits for the year £98,345, and the capital employed in carrying on trade £1,003,710.

Hué, Phu-thua-thien, or **Fu-chuan,** the chief town of Anam, on a river of the same name, and 10 miles from its entrance into the Gulf of Tonquin. It was fortified under the direction of French officers (1801–20), is well built, and has a large citadel, but is accessible only to small vessels on account of a bar in the river. The royal palace is a large building; most of the dwelling-houses are of bamboo. H. is a great weapon-depôt for the interior. Pop. 100,000.

Hue and Cry, a term of English law denoting the supposed pursuit of a felon. Upon every robbery committed the Statute of Winchester, 13 Geo. I., directs that pursuit shall be made from town to town and from county to county, and that H. and C. shall be raised till the felon be delivered to the sheriff. And that the H. and C. may be more effectual, the Hundred (q. v.) was bound to answer for any robbery committed within its bounds unless the felon was taken. This liability is now restricted to liability in damage for mischief done by riotous assemblies. No action can be maintained where the damage is less than £30. Maliciously to raise a H. and C. against any one is criminal, and renders the offender liable in damages.

Huel'va, the chief town of a province of the same name, Spain, on a peninsula at the confluence of the Odiel and Tinto, 63 miles W.S.W. of Seville by rail. It has an extensive tunny fishery, and has greatly increased in importance since the recent opening of the rich copper-mines in the vicinity. In 1872 the exports, chiefly copper, manganese, wine (£11,900 worth), oranges, raisins, oil, almonds, and figs, amounted in value to £651,559; and the imports, mainly British coal, iron, and machinery, to £240,197. There entered the port (1872) 1054 vessels of 188,745 tons, of which 237 were British. H. is the ancient *Onuba*, a place of Phœnician origin, and was fortified and called by the Arabs Velba or Vuelba. Pop. 8423.

Huer'ta, Vicente Garcia de la, a Spanish poet, was born at Zafra, Estremadura, in 1734, studied at Salamanca, and repairing to Madrid, obtained the post of keeper of the royal library, and was elected a member of various literary societies. H. was an ardent and successful upholder of the national drama, as against the French or classical school of Luzan and his followers, but he was often blinded by an exaggerated patriotism, and apt unduly to depreciate the works of his opponents. *La Raquel* (1778), a play turning on the amour of Alfonso VIII. with a Jewish maiden, led to H.'s temporary banishment to Oran, but won an immense popularity, which it still retains. H. died at Madrid, March 12, 1817. He published *Vocabulario Militar Español* (Mad. 1760), Lives of the great soldiers of Spain; *Obras Poeticas* (2 vols. Mad. 1778–79); and *Teatro Español* (17 vols. Mad. 1785–86), a collection of old Spanish plays.

Hues'ca, a town of Spain, capital of a province of the same name, stands a mile distant from the W. bank of the Tisuela, and 40 miles E.N.E. of Zaragoza by railway. It is a bishop's see, has a fine Gothic cathedral of the 15th c., a townhall, bull-arena, &c., and is girt by ruinous walls, of whose ninety-nine towers two only remain. The university, founded by Pedro IV. in 1354, is now suppressed; but Charles V.'s Colegio de Santiago, Jayme Callen's Colegio de San Vincente (1587), and the Seminario de Santa Cruz (1580) still exist. Pop. 9874. H. was the Roman *Osca*, and the *Weschka* of the Moors, who held it from 713 to 1096, when it was wrested from them by Pedro I., and long continued to be the residence of the kings of Aragon.

Hues'car, a town of Granada, Spain, on the Guardal, 75 miles N.E. of Granada, has manufactures of linen and woollen fabrics. Pop. 7332.

Hu'et, Pierre Daniel, a French scholar and prelate, was born at Caen, February 8, 1630. After being educated at the Jesuit College in his native town, he visited Queen Christina of Sweden with his friend Bochart, and there found the MS. of Origen that first suggested his special study of that father's works. In 1670 he was appointed tutor to the Dauphin, together with Bossuet, with whom also he superintended the publication of the classics 'in usum Delphini.' In 1674 he became a member of the Academy. In 1676 he took orders, and in 1678 received the abbacy of Aunay, in 1685 the bishopric of Soissons, and in 1693 the bishopric of Avranches. Resigning this in 1699 on account of failing health, he was made Abbot of Fontenai, near Caen. He died January 26, 1721. H. was a man of wide sympathies, and many scholars of opposite creeds were among his friends. He has importance partly as a worker in the history of literature, partly as an opponent of the Cartesians, to whom he at one time belonged. His chief works are *Origenis Commentaria in Sacras Scripturas* (2 vols. Rouen, 1668); *Demonstratio Evangelica* (1679); *Quæstiones Alnetanæ* (1690); *Traité de la Situation du Paradis Terrestre* (1691); *De Navigationibus Salomonis* (1698); *Histoire du Commerce et de la Navigation des Anciens* (1716). An interesting autobiography of H., *P. D. Huetii Commentarii de Rebus ad eum Pertinentibus* (The Hague, 1718) was translated into English by Dr. Aikin (2 vols. Lond. 1810), and into French (Par. 1853). See the Abbé Flottes's *Étude sur Daniel Huet, Évêque d'Avranches* (Montpel. 1857).

Hu'feland, Christopher Wilhelm, a physician famous in his own time, born 12th August 1762, at Langensalza in Thuringia, was first (1783–93) a physician at Weimar, then (till 1801) professor at Jena, and finally Clinical Professor at Berlin, where he died, 25th August 1836. He was a man of probity, but of weak character, who by seeking to please all parties involved himself in perverted views and inconsistencies, which he had afterwards to retract. Yet in practical matters he did lasting service in various ways, and his work *Ueber die Ursachen, Erkenntniss, und Heilung der Skrofelkrankheit* (Berl. 1795), was translated into several languages.

Hug, Johann Leonhard, a learned Catholic scholar and divine, was born at Constance, 1st June 1765, and educated at the University of Freiburg. He studied also in France and Italy. Consecrated a priest in 1789, he was called to be professor at Freiburg in 1791, and there he laboured till his death, 11th March 1846. His principal work, *Einleitung in die Schriften des Neuen Testaments* (Stutt. 1808, 4th ed. 1847), which was soon translated into French and English, was conservative in its views. He is also known by his work on *Die Erfindung der Buchstabenschrift* (1801), and by his *Gutachten über das Leben Jesu von D. F. Strauss* (Freib. 1840–44).

Hughes, Thomas, author and social economist, son of the late John Hughes, Esq., of Donnington Priory, was born October 20, 1823, and educated at Rugby and Oxford. He graduated in 1845, and was called to the bar in 1848. He published *Tom Brown's Schooldays* in 1856, the best story of schoolboy life in English literature. It has made Rugby known and loved throughout Britain and America. Among his other works are *The Scouring of the White Horse* (1858), *Tom Brown at Oxford* (1861), *Religio Laici* (1862), *Alfred the Great* (1869), and *Memoirs of a Brother* (1873). Mr. Hughes sat as a Liberal in Parliament for Lambeth 1865–68, and for Frome 1868–74. He is an authority upon social questions, and, as a warm friend to the working classes, has been a successful mediator in strikes and trade disputes. A disciple and friend of the late Frederick Maurice, his opinions are purified and impassioned by warm Christian feeling.

Hugo, Victor Marie, Vicomte, was born at Besançon, February 26, 1802. His father, General H., was a devoted supporter of Napoleon, and H.'s early years were spent partly in France, partly in Italy and Spain, where the General held various posts. On the fall of Napoleon his father and mother separated, and H. was placed in the École Polytechnique to prepare for a military career. During the years 1819–22 he gained three prizes at the Floral Games of Toulouse, and in 1822 he became famous by the publication of the first volume of his *Odes et Balades*. He now married Mlle. Foucher, who had previously refused him on the ground of his poverty. His next works, two prose pieces, *Hans d'Islande* (1823), and *Bug-Jargal* (1825), first showed the bold, antithetic, and at times spasmodic, manner characteristic of H. *Les Orientales* (1828), passionate odes, were eagerly welcomed; and in 1829 the production of his drama *Hernani* led to a fierce contest between the Classicists and H.'s friends the Romanticists, in which the latter were victorious. In 1845 Louis Philippe made H. a peer of France, and in 1848 the Parisians elected him both to the Legislative and Constituent Assemblies. About this time he became a Red Republican in politics, and in 1852 was banished from France by Napoleon III., whom he shortly afterwards assailed in a stinging brochure, *Napoleon le Petit*. He lived mainly at Jersey and Guernsey from 1852 until the fall of the Empire, when he was returned to the National Assembly at Bordeaux, but soon resigned, and after being driven from Brussels for his sympathy with the Commune, returned to Paris in 1871. Besides those already mentioned, H.'s works include *Notre Dame de Paris*, his first great novel (1831); *Les Chants des Crépuscule* (1835); *Les Voix Intérieures* (1837); *Les Rayons et les Ombres* (1840); *Châtiments* (1853); *Contemplations* (1856); *Le Légende des Siècles*, his grandest poem (1859 and 1877); *Les Miserables*, one of the best modern works of fiction (1862); *Les Travailleurs de la Mer* (1866); *L'Homme qui rit* (1869); and *Quatre-vingt-treize* (1874). H. is the greatest of French poets and novelists. He possesses a superb imaginative gift, and excels in vivid dramatic power, in analysis of character, in the presentation of intense emotion, and in descriptions of nature full of sombre, mysterious grandeur. He has wrought a wonderful reform in French poetry, banishing the old cramping rules, and imbuing it with new strength and sweetness. His poems contain lyrics of exquisite loveliness, though they are sometimes marred by over-audacious fancies and flaming colour. His marvellous fictions are also far too dithyrambic in style, and are weakened by undue aiming at effect.—**Charles Victor H.**, son of the preceding, born 2d November 1826, is an author and politician of some note; his brother, **François Victor H.**, born 22d October 1828, is favourably known to Englishmen by his translation of Shakespeare into French, in 13 vols (1860–64).

Hu'guenots, the name by which those who accepted the Reformed faith in France became generally known in the 16th c. There has been much doubtful speculation as to the origin of the name. Professor Mahn enumerates fifteen derivations, and himself inclines to that which associates the name with Hugues, an obscure heretic. With more probability the name has been derived from the German *Eidgenossen*, 'confederates' (by the French pronounced *Higuenos*), or from *Huc Nos*, the opening words of one of the earliest public documents of the H. See FRENCH PROTESTANT CHUCH.

Huile de Cade, obtained by the dry distillation of the wood of *Juniperus oxycedrus*, is almost entirely manufactured in France, and is chiefly employed, externally, in veterinary medicine, but occasionally on the human subject in obstinate skin diseases.

Hul'da, or Hol'da ('the friendly'), the old German goddess of marriage, the guardian of domestic life, and patroness of agriculture. She figures greatly in legend, and formerly the phrase, 'Hulda is making her bed,' was applied to the falling snow.

Hulk (Old Eng. *hulce*, 'a ship'), the body of a ship, especially if applied to an old unseaworthy vessel. The *hulks* are old ships formerly used as prisons. A *sheer-H.* is an old ship fitted up with machinery for fixing or removing a ship's masts.

Hull (Old Eng. *hule*, 'the shell or crust'), the body of a vessel, exclusive of the masts and rigging. *H. down* is said of a ship when her H. is beneath the horizon.

Hull, or Kingston-on-Hull, a thriving port of England, in the E. Riding of Yorkshire, is situated on a low plain at the entrance of the Hull into the Humber, 20 miles from the mouth of the latter, 53 E.S.E. of York, and 145 N. of London by rail. It has a rich Gothic church of the Holy Trinity, with a transept supposed to be the oldest brick building in England; a town-hall (1866) in the Italian style, faced with Streatly and Portland stone, and having a tower 135 feet high, and shafts of red Mansfield stone; a grammar-school, founded by Bishop Alcock in 1486; the Trinity House, an hospital for decayed sailors, to which is attached a nautical school; the Charter House, founded in 1384; Lister's Hospital, established by Sir J. Lister in 1642, a new theatre, &c. One of the chief ports for the trade with Germany and the Baltic, it receives in exchange for the cloths and yarns of York and Lancashire large quantities of grain, cattle, timber, wool, flax, hemp, rape, linseed, tallow, potatoes, &c. The docks, which are provided with railway lines, steam-cranes, &c., cover an area of over 100 acres. The Royal Albert Dock was opened by the Prince of Wales, July 21, 1869.

There entered the port (1875) 4631 vessels of 1,615,956 tons, and cleared 4355, of 1,454,642 tons. H. is a principal station for the Continental steam-packets, and sends two members to Parliament. Pop. (1871) 123,408. The town was purchased from the monastery of Melsa by Edward I., who changed its name from *Myton Wyk* to *Kyngestown-super-Hull*, gave it a charter, and constructed its harbour. Fortified by Edward II. in 1322, it was the first place to resist the authority of Charles I. on the outbreak of the Civil War. A great fire (damage, £100,000) occurred on the 15th August 1864.

Hull'ah, John P., musical composer and teacher, was born at Worcester in 1812. He studied theory under W. Horsley, and singing under Cruvelli (1829-35). H. has exerted himself in spreading the knowledge of music among the middle classes by the system which bears his name. From 1844 to 1874 he was Professor of Vocal Music at King's College, London, and in 1876 the degree of LL.D. was conferred upon him by the University of Edinburgh. Among his works are *History of Modern Music* (1862-75), and *Lectures on the Transition Period of Musical History* (1865-76).

Hul'sean Lectures, a course of from four to six sermons preached annually at Cambridge by a lecturer appointed in accordance with the will of the Rev. John Hulse of Elworth in Cheshire, who was born at Middlewich in 1708, and died 14th December 1790. On the same foundation are two scholarships in St. John's College, Cambridge, where Hulse was educated, the Hulsean Prize and the Hulsean Professorship of Divinity, the latter being substituted by an Order in Council in 1860 for the office of Christian advocate, instituted by the will of the founder, a portentous document extending to 400 pages folio.

Hu'manism and **Hu'manists.** Humanism was the form of culture that, after the restoration of Greek and Latin learning between the 14th and 16th centuries—especially after the taking of Constantinople in 1453, which sent Greek scholars to Italy—found its only models of thought and expression in ancient literature. At first a welcome release from the medieval suppression of human nature, it gradually produced a slavish imitation of classic forms of speech, especially those of Cicero. From the school at Deventer in the Netherlands 'humanistic studies' (*humaniora*) were diffused throughout Europe N. of the Alps. The Humanists paved the way for the Reformation, partly by struggling against the abuse of ecclesiastical authority, partly by their study of the Bible in the original tongues, although the humanistic attitude was often hostile to every kind of theological dogma. *Humanity* means everything that gives man a character in opposition to the brute, but especially the harmonious development of his moral and intellectual faculties.

Humanita'rians, a certain class of Christians in the first three centuries who asserted the mere and sole humanity of Christ, and denied his divinity in any and every sense of the term; some of them holding, however, to an extraordinary humanity in Christ, and others only to an ordinary. Under this general name of H., which again is a subdivision under the more general name of Anti-Trinitarians, are classed all those sects, such as the Ebionites (q. v.), &c., who denied both the deity and divinity of Christ.

Humayun', the second of the Mogul Emperors of India, son of Baber, and father of Akbar the Great. He reigned from 1530 to 1543, when he was defeated and driven out by his Afghan rival, Sher Khan. In 1555 he recovered his kingdom, but died in the following year. He lies buried under a white marble mausoleum at Delhi, erected by his widow, Hamida Banu, at a cost of £150,000.

Hum'ber, the estuary of the Ouse and Trent, 40 miles long, and from 1 to 8 broad, separates the counties of Lincoln and York, and has a direction first E. and then S.E. On its N. shore is Hull; on its S., Great Grimsby. It is somewhat obstructed by silting. At its mouth it is narrowed by the promontory of Holderness, the S.E. extremity of Yorkshire, which tapers out in Spurn Point to within 4 miles of the Lincoln shore.

Humble-Bee (*Bombus*), a genus of bees closely allied to the honey-bees, and living, like the latter, in social colonies. The common H.-B. (*B. terrestris*) is a familiar British insect, distinguished by the large size of its body, by the hairy covering of the body, and by the yellow and black bands which mark the upper surface. The tibiæ or shins of the hinder legs are two-spined. The nests of humble-bees are constructed underground, and vary in the number of their cells. The latter are loosely connected together, and are of oval shape. Three kinds of individuals—as in the honey-bees—males, females, and neuters or makers, constitute the H.-B. colony. The honey of these bees is fragrant, but appears to differ in its nature from that of the honey-bees. The *Bombus muscorum*, or foggie bee, constructs its nest of 'fog' or moss, and is also termed the 'carder bee,' from the manner in which it weaves the fibres of the moss together. *B. lapidarius*, or the red-tailed bee, constructs a nest amongst stone-heaps. A familiar species is the *B. Orientalis*, which attains a considerable size. The females of H.-B. colonies exist in each nest in considerable numbers, a feature in their economy in which they differ from the honey-bees. In the nests of the latter, a single female only, the 'queen-bee,' is permitted to exist.

Hum'boldt, Karl Wilhelm von, a German scholar and statesman, was born at Potsdam, 22d June 1767, of a noble Pomeranian family. After a home education, under the pedagogist Campe and the philosopher Engel, he studied at Göttingen under such men as Heyne the philologist, and was introduced to Jacobi and Müller, then leaders in German literature. A visit to Paris in 1789 suggested his essay on the *Limits of the Action of the State*, on which Mr. Mill has founded his essay on *Liberty*. The doctrine of individualism, the only desirable liberty, he thought, had been lost sight of in the French revolutions. The book is marked by a lofty sense of human dignity. H. now went to Wolf at Halle, and began an ardent study of Hellenic life through philological research. At Jena he formed an equally close friendship with Schiller, then lecturing on æsthetics; and there he also met Schlegel, the translator of Shakespeare; Goethe, who was writing *Hermann und Dorothea* (which H. afterwards made the text of his æsthetic essays), and Fichte. Inspired with the idea of writing a history of human culture, he began a four years' travel through S. Europe. Much of his experience is preserved in letters to his friends. In 1801 he became Prussian ambassador at the court of Pius VII., where his charming wife (herself a good Greek scholar) kept a brilliant salon, visited by Mme. de Stael, Courier, Thorwaldsen, Tieck, &c. In 1808 H. became Prussian Minister of Public Instruction and Religion, immediately after the audacious decree of Napoleon dismissing the patriot Stein and forfeiting his property. In 1810 he founded the University of Berlin, and became ambassador at Vienna, in which capacity he signed the Articles of Prag in 1813, which secured Austria to the coalition, and probably decided the fate of Napoleon. His clearness and steadfastness of purpose made him the match of Talleyrand and Metternich. At the Congress of Vienna he argued for the separation of Germany and Austria, which he saw to be inevitable, and was strongly opposed to the Holy Alliance. After this he gradually lost faith in the Prussian government, from which he was dismissed in 1819. The rest of his life was devoted to comparative philology, for which science he ransacked the dialects of three continents. One of his largest treatises traces the Sanskrit elements in the island of Java; another discusses the Basque idioms of Spain. He died at Tegel, near Berlin, 8th April 1835. H.'s *Sämmtliche Werke*, with a preface by his brother Alexander, were published in 7 vols. Berl. 1841-52. The best study of H. is by Haym, *Lebensbild und Charakteristik* (Berl. 1856). See also *W. von H.'s Briefen an eine Freundin* (7th ed. 1863).—**Friedrich Heinrich Alexander von H.**, brother of the preceding, was born at Berlin, 14th September 1769. The pupil of Heyne and Blumenbach, he early showed (in his memoir on the basaltic rocks of the Rhine) a passion for observation and travel. This was fostered by the acquaintance of Forster, a companion of Captain Cook, and by the teaching of Werner, under whom he studied botany at Freiberg. From 1792-97 he was director-general of mines in Anspach and Baireuth, but he found time for a literary partnership with Schiller in *Die Horen*, and for independent researches in the subjects of irrespirable gases and muscular irritability. Disappointed by war in his expectations of visiting Italy and Egypt, H., after making the acquaintance of Berthollet and Laplace at Paris, set out with Bonpland on his American tour in 1799. Exploring Venezuela from Cumana, they passed from the Orinoco to the Amazon. In 1801 he passed through Carthagena to Callao in Peru, and next year ascending to the plain of Bogota, he visited some of the volcanic Cordilleras and reached Quito. He climbed Chimborazo as he had climbed Teneriffe. Passing through Mexico, he visited Jefferson at Washington, and reached Bordeaux in the autumn of 1804. From 1805 to 1827 his life was spent at Paris, editing the enormous results of his expedition in seven great works on geography, ethnography, geology, and natural history—the whole forming a colossal treatise in 29 vols. (1807-27), with 1425 coloured engravings. The most interesting sections to the general reader are his *Voyages aux Régions équinoxiales du Nouveau Continent* (3 vols. Par. 1809-25; Ger. ed. 6 vols. Stutt. 1825-32); *Essai Politique sur le Royaume de la Nouvelle-Espagne* (2 vols. Par. 1811); and *Essai sur la Géographie des Plantes* (Par. 1805; Ger. ed. Tübing. 1807). In this period he also worked with Gay-Lussac on atmospheric and hypsometric observations, formed a friendship with Arago, and visited London with his brother Wilhelm. In 1829 the indefatigable explorer left his recently formed home at Berlin for a journey through Siberia to the borders of China, and back by Astrakhan and the Caspian to Moscow, the fruit of which was his *Asie Centrale* (3 vols. Par. 1843; Ger. ed. 2 vols. Berl. 1843-44), a work full of important new matter on minerals and the science of climate. All his works are marked by vivid description, as well as a free play of philosophic thought. Among his great geographical 'finds' in Asia were the Plain of Gobi, and the true height of Lake Baikal. H. was now at the height of his fame as a public man in Berlin, Paris, and London. In 1835-38 appeared his *Examen critique de la Géographie du Nouveau Continent* (Par. 1835-38; Ger. ed. 3 vols. Berl. 1836). He warmly asserted the possibility of a Panama Canal with fewer locks than the Caledonian. In the period 1845-62 he produced his most widely-read book, the *Kosmos* (5 vols.), a development of his earlier *Ansichten der Natur* (Fr. *Tableaux de la Nature*). In this he sums up in picturesque style his treasures of knowledge. The classification of rocks into eruptive, sedimentary, metamorphic, and conglomerate is given. His distribution of animals and plants is based on isothermal lines. He also generalises what was known of the interior and exterior planets, and the intermediate asteroids, of terrestrial magnetism, earthquakes, and volcanos. 'The modern Aristotle' died full of years and honours, 6th May 1859. See H.'s *Briefe an Varnhagen von Ense* (5th ed. 1861); *an Bunsen* (1869); also Life by Karl Bruhns (Eng. trans. 2 vols. Lond. 1874); Klencke's *A. V. Humboldt* (6th ed. 1870); and Goethe's *Briefwechsel mit den Gebrüdern von H.*, edited by F. T. Bratanek (Leips. 1876).

Humboldt River, a river of Nevada, U.S., rises in the H. mountains, and, after a course of 384 miles in a S.W. direction, loses itself in the H. Sink, a marsh surrounded by a desert. The H. is unnavigable even by boats; the largest tributary is the Little H.

Hume, David, philosopher and historian, born at Edinburgh, April 26, 1711, was the second son of Joseph Hume, of Ninewells, Chirnside, Berwickshire, and a daughter of President Falconer. His father died early. In 1723 he went to Edinburgh University, where he read chiefly 'books of reasoning and philosophy, poetry, and the polite authors,' and where he wrote *An Historical Essay on Chivalry and Modern Honour*. His early experiences are described by himself in his famous letters to Michael Ramsay and Dr. Cheyne. He came to the conclusion that 'moral philosophy was founded more on invention than experience.' In 1731 he passed through a strange bodily and mental crisis; and in 1734, after trying to settle in a merchant's business at Bristol, he went to France, where he spent three years in Paris, Rheims, and La Flèche. To 1737 belongs his *Treatise of Human Nature*, sold for £50 to John Noone, Cheapside. The volume on *Ethics* (revised by Hutcheson, and published by Longman), and the *Essays, Moral and Political*, followed in 1741-42, the former of which was very unsuccessful. One review, however, in *The Works of the Learned* compared these works to the juvenile efforts of Milton and Raphael. The *Treatise of Human Nature* was not, as commonly supposed, suppressed by H. For some years H. acted as companion to the Marquis of Annandale, and as judge-advocate to the forces on the Port L'Orient expedition, and as secretary to General St. Clair at Vienna and Turin, and from 1752 to 1756 he was librarian of the Advocates' Library. Refusing an invitation from Millar to edit a London paper, he republished a portion of his *Treatise* as *Inquiry Concerning the Human Understanding*, and the *Inquiry Concerning the Principles of Morals*. In his autobiography he laments the failure of these books, while Dr. Middleton's *Free Inquiry* was making a great sensation. To this period also belong the beginning of his *History of England* and his *Natural History of Religion*, which Warburton asked Millar the bookseller to suppress. From 1763 to 1766 he acted as Secretary of Embassy to Lord Hertford in Paris, where he received great attention from D'Alembert, Marmontel, Diderot, Helvetius, Tugot, Holbach, Buffon, &c. He says: 'I eat nothing but ambrosie, drink nothing but nectar, breathe nothing but incense, and tread on nothing but flowers.' His *Political Discourses* had already been translated into French by a Provençal named Macwillon, Secretary to the King of Poland. On his return Princess Amelia proposed to make him a bishop, and he was appointed a sort of Under Secretary of State for Scotland. The rest of his life was spent in 'St. David' Street, Edinburgh, where he enjoyed the friendship of Robertson, Cullen, Black, Blair, the two Homes, 'Jupiter' Carlyle, Ferguson, Smith. In April 1776 he wrote *My Own Life*, which was posthumously published by Adam Smith, H.'s literary executor, and which, along with Smith's affectionate and dignified letter to Strahan, drew down the wrath of John Wesley in his Halifax sermon. After an exhausting illness borne with cheerful fortitude, H. died August 26, 1776. It is impossible here to describe the philosophy of H., the greatest of modern metaphysicians. He pushed the doctrine of the relativity of human knowledge to its results; and in the then state of mental and social science he could perhaps do no more. He did not attempt to construct a positive system, and the German and Scottish philosophies which have since opposed his teaching perhaps show that, while right in principles of investigation, he had not sufficiently appreciated the facts of mind and society. Indications of his teaching on the fundamental questions of metaphysics will be found in other articles. In ethics he maintained, against Butler, Price, and Hutcheson, that both reason and sentiment enter into moral determinations; that the approbation of virtue varies with its social utility; that justice is really founded on the distinctions of private property; that natural generosity or sympathy co-operates with self-interest in forming moral feeling. There is a great deal of superficial partiality in the *History of England* (continued by Smollett), but it is still a delightful book, with remarkable information for the time in which it appeared. There is a *Life of H.* by Dr. Hill Burton, and a careful edition of his philosophical works by Messrs. Grosse & Green (Oxford, 1875).

Hume, Joseph, a politician whose influence for good is still felt in English finance, was born at Montrose, Scotland, in 1777, educated for the medical profession, and went out as assistant army surgeon in the Mahratta war in 1800. As interpreter and paymaster he rendered numerous services, and returned to England in 1808 with a considerable fortune. He had shown a taste for Oriental languages, but his desire was for political life. After representing Weymouth for a few months in 1812, and some years of travel, he was, in 1818, returned for the Montrose burghs, which he represented till 1830. This trust was renewed in 1842 till his death. In the interval he sat for Middlesex and Kilkenny. Through the teaching of Bentham and a natural capacity for figures he became a leader of the philosophical radicals below the gangway. The practical form of his principles was to insist on rigid economy and financial reform in all branches of the public accounts. The repeal of the combination laws, export and import duties, municipal and colonial administration, election expenses, Catholic emancipation, and electoral reforms also engaged his attention. In 1835 he warmly denounced the Orange lodges. H. died, 20th February 1855, at Burnley Hall, Norfolk. His function was one indispensable to the purity of the public accounts, for he not only objected to improper expenditure, but the fear of his objection was often sufficient to prevent its being stated. See Martineau's *History of England during the Thirty Years' Peace.*

Hu'mea, a genus of composite plants, of which *H. elegans*, a native of Australia, is the best-known species, and grown in gardens for its ornamental and graceful drooping habit. The plant when bruised emits a balsamic odour.

Hum'erus (Lat.) is the bone of the upper arm, extending from the scapula to the bones of the fore-arm, with which it is articulated. See ARM.

Humetté, in heraldry, is an ordinary—*e.g.*, a cross, *couped* or cut off so that it does not reach the shield's edge.

Hu'mic Acid (Lat. *humus*, 'the earth') occurs in certain circumstances in slowly decaying vegetable matter, and is met with in bog-earth, peat, turf, and other soils. Its colour is dark brown, and its composition is represented by the formula $C_{34}H_{15}O_9$. Sugar boiled with a dilute mineral acid gives a deposit which, when treated with ammonia and an acid, leaves H. A. behind.

Humirpore' (Hamirpur), the chief town of the district of the same name, in the N.W. Provinces, British India, at the confluence of the Betwa and Jumna rivers, 155 miles S.E. from Agra, and 110 N.W. from Allahabad. Pop. (1872) 7007.—The *district* of H. has an area of 2287 sq. miles; pop. (1872) 529,137. It is noted for artificial lakes encircling rock temples, now used for irrigation. The principal crops are gram, wheat, millet, and oilseeds, with a little cotton; the trade is insignificant. As in the rest of Bundlecund, the Mutiny of 1857 was made the occasion for murder and rapine.

Hummell'er, an agricultural machine for breaking off the awns of barley. It may either be attached to the thrashing-machine or be worked separately. There are various forms of it. The *cylindrical* H. consists of a vertical cylinder of wire-gauze having a revolving central shaft armed with thin flat iron blades, which remove the stumps of the awns as the barley, fed from a hopper, passes through the machine.

Humm'ing Bird, the name applied to many genera and species of Insessorial birds belonging to the section *Tenuirostres* ('slender-billed'), and especially to the family *Trochilidæ*. In this family the bill is very slender, and its tip is sharp. The nostrils are usually covered with a large scale. The wings are long and pointed, as also is the tail. In the typical genus *Trochilus* the edges of the upper mandible overlap the lower mandible at the base. The first quill of the wings is shorter than the second quill. The tail is forked, and has two feathers projecting beyond the others. The inner toe is shorter than the outer. The humming birds form a large group, extending over all parts of the New World, from the furthest N. to Tierra del Fuego. Many species are very limited and local in distribution, being found in many instances within a narrow area. These birds evince, perhaps, of the whole feathered creation, the brightest hues and most varied colours. Some of the species are of small size, looking hardly larger than bees, and appear like iridescent glittering gems as they flit among the flowers. Bailey's expression—

Humming Bird (ruff-necked).

> 'Bright humming bird of gem-like plumeletage,
> By western Indians "living sunbeam" named,'

is a most appropriate and happy description of many of these forms. When they fly they produce a buzzing sound with their wings, this sound having given origin to their name. The food consists of honey and flower-juices, but most of the species also feed on small insects. The tongue is of remarkable structure. It can be protruded to a great length from the mouth, and is specially adapted for sucking up the flower-juices, whilst the structure of the bill is also well fitted for probing flowers. Most of the humming birds lay only two eggs. One of the best-known species is the ruby and moated H. B. (*Trochilus colubris*), found in N. America, and ranging over a large extent of country. Its general colour is a light metallic green glossed with gold, the under parts being of whitish hue, and the throat of a ruby red colour. The wings, as is commonly seen in humming birds, are of purplish-brown hue. The long-tailed H. B. (*T. polytmus*) of Jamaica is another familiar species, coloured light green above, and emerald green below, the tail being black. Its average length is 9 inches, inclusive of the ring-tail feathers. Other species belong to the genera *Heliactin* (sun genus), *Topaza* (topaz humming birds), *Heliomaster* (star-throats), *Eutoxeres* (sickle-bills), *Microchœra* (snow-caps), *Lophornis* (coquettes), &c.

Hu'moralists, a term used in medical literature to designate a sect who based their pathology upon the influence of the humors. See PATHOLOGY.

Hu'mulus, the genus of plants to which the Hop (q. v.) belongs.

Hu-nan' ('S. of the lakes'), a province of China, lying between the Nan-ling Mountains on the S. and the river Yang-tse-kiang. Area, 83,229 sq. miles; pop. 20,048,969. It is singularly fertile, and within its northern frontier lies the largest of Chinese lakes, Tung-ling-hw, with an area of 300 sq. miles, into which flow the Jüan-kiang and Hing-kiang, after watering the province. The chief products are tea and rice; among the minerals are coal, iron, lead, and malachite. The capital is Chang-sha, on the Hing-kiang. The H. teas are mainly sent to Hankow (q. v.).

Hun'dred, or **Wa'pentake**, was perhaps the area in which 100 warriors of the invading Teutons had their primitive settlement. Wapentake points to an armed gathering of freemen. It is disputed whether the *lathes* (into which Kent is divided, probably from Jutish *lething*, 'a levy'), the *rapes* of Sussex, the *trithings* or Ridings of Yorkshire were originally the same. In some cases there was a subdivision into an H. Originally denoting personal relations, the H. in the laws of Eadgar (959–975) denotes the territorial subdivision of shire or kingdom. There was a H. *gemot*, convened by the H. *ealdor*, and attended by the local thegns and representatives from the towns. The court consisted in theory of all local freeholders, and had both civil and criminal jurisdictions. It was attended by the king's *gerêfa*, to collect the *wite* or fine for offences. It enrolled persons claiming frankpledge, each in his tithing. The H. seems to correspond to the Archaic Irish *tuath* or *cantsed*, the Scandinavian *fylk*, the Slavonic *pulk*, the Gothic *gavi* or *gau*. Perhaps, however, the *herath* or *haerred*, a division of the fylk, would be nearer to the H. In Gothland there was a precisely similar division called *hundari*. The 'thing' of the fylk answered to the 'môt' of the H. The Latin name for fylk, 'centena,' is preserved in canton. The *pagus* of Cæsar and Tacitus was probably a more compact organisation than the H., and resembles more the Irish *baile*, which by the usual duodenary subdivision gave twelve *seisreachs*, just as in E. Anglia the H. gave twelve *leets*.

Hun'gary (Magyar, *Magyar Orszâg*, 'land of the Magyars,' Slav. *Vengria*, Ger. *Ungarn*, Fr. *Hongrie*), the independent Transleithan kingdom that with Austria forms the dualistic Austro-Hungarian empire. It consists of the crown land of H. Proper, Transylvania, Croatia, Slavonia, and the military frontier, and has a total area of 125,041 sq. miles, and a pop. (1869) of 15,509,455. With the Cisleithan portion of the state it is connected by a common dynasty and by a common Parliament ('the Delegations') of 120 members, of whom 60 are returned by each of the two sections of the empire. The Delegations legislate in imperial affairs, war, finance, foreign relations, &c. Internal legislation is vested in a responsible Ministry and in a Reichstag (at Pesth), consisting of the Magnatentafel (*Förendek*) of 731 members (1876), and of the Ständentafel (*Rendek*) of 444 representatives. The Emperor of Austria is called King of H. in all public acts. In 1875 the revenue of H. was £21,213,850, and the expenditure £22,746,415. For several years there have been increasing deficits, which have led to the contraction of a special debt, amounting in 1876 to £35,400,000. H. contributes 319,632 men to the army of the empire, according to the law of 1868.

Physical Aspect and Products.—The *crown land* of H. Proper has an area of 87,043 sq. miles, and a pop. (1869) of 11,633,162. It has an extreme length from E. to W. of 550 miles, and a breadth of 340, is mainly a vast plain with rich pastures and fertile tilths, bounded on the N. and E. by the Carpathians and on the W. by the Noric Alps, and partly intersected by the Danube and the Theiss, with their numerous tributaries. Treeless grass-flats (*pussten*), dotted with sand-dunes and swamps (*hansag*), extend along the great rivers. The Danube enters H. by the *Porta Hungarica*, in the Leitha Mountains, 30 miles E. of Vienna, then flows in an easterly direction for 115 miles, after which it turns abruptly S. to the frontier (185 miles), where it receives the Drave from the W.; it finally flows E., receiving the Theiss (828 miles) from the N., and forming the southern boundary. Other tributaries from the left are the March, Waag,

Neutra, Gran, and Eipel; from the right, the Raab and Leitha. The largest lakes of H. are the Balaton (q. v.) and the Neusiedler See (q. v.); in the Carpathians are many *Meeraugen* ('sea-eyes') or lakelets. The climate is somewhat extreme both in winter and summer, the plains being often swept by the bora and the sirocco (called the *föhn*), and the crops destroyed by sudden and violent hailstorms. The surface is occupied to the extent of one-third by magnificent forests of oak (especially in Barânya, between the Danube and Drave), beech, elm, birch, and pine; one-third is cultivated, yielding oats, barley, rye, maize, wheat, hemp, flax, tobacco, woad, madder, saffron, &c. The vegetation embraces nearly all the indigenous and many of the imported plants of Europe. Among the principal fruits, growing chiefly in the comitats of Zala, Somogy, Barânya, Behar, Arad, Berégh, Szaithmar, and Gömör, are the grape, plum, peach, walnut, almond, and fig. The vine is cultivated over 1220 sq. miles, and the best wine is the golden-green Tokay of the Hegyallja Mountains; while the white wine (of Pesth, Magyáret, &c.) is equal to the finest Rhenish. The forests, swarming with game, still afford a refuge to the wild-boar and wolf; and one of the chief occupations is the rearing of horses, sheep, and cattle. In wealth of precious metals H. ranks only inferior to Russia, and has some 2000 mines and 60 smelting furnaces. The minerals found are gold (£60,000 worth yearly), silver (£137,400 worth), copper, quicksilver, pig-iron, coal, and rock-salt. There are many mineral springs. Besides the internal communication afforded by the Danube, its navigable affluents and by canals (Baczker-Bega and Sarviz), H. has in operation (1875) 3999 miles of railways.

Ethnology, &c.—In no other country of Europe is there an equal variety of races. The pop. consisted in 1871 of 5,604,200 Magyars, 1,596,633 Germans, 1,248,217 Rumanians, 1,517,099 Slovaks, 206,600 Croats, 267,654 Serbs, 469,203 Ruthenes, and 715,266 Jews, Gypsies, Bulgarians, &c. Of these again, 5,884,472 are Roman Catholics (with three archbishops at Gran, Kalócsa, and Erlau), 982,142 Greek Catholics (under the patriarch-archbishop of Lemberg), 2,589,758 Protestants (mostly Calvinists), 1,141,216 Byzantine Greek Catholics, and 517,338 Jews. Education is in a comparatively forward state; 47 per cent. of the men and 55 of the women can read and write. In 1871 there were 99 upper and 47 lower gymnasia, with 30,992 pupils and 1624 teachers; 11 upper and 17 lower *realschulen*, with 5472 pupils and 267 teachers, besides many religious seminaries. The University of Pesth in 1875 had 1912 students and 122 professors; and connected therewith is a seminary for the training of teachers. The Government grant to churches and schools was £392,420 in 1875.

Language and Literature.—Magyar, the name of the dominant people of H., is also that of their language. The Magyars are the most numerous section of the Ugrians (q. v.), and their language closely resembles that of the Finns, especially in its grammatical forms and in its vocables. It has a more strident sound than Finnish on account of its compound sibilants *cs* and *cz*. The four principal dialects are the Palócz of the Mátra mountains, in which are the greatest number of ancient words; the Györi, prevailing in the Raab valley; the Bihari, spoken in the basin of the Theiss; and the Székely of Transylvania, containing many Tartar words. Christianity was introduced into H. about the end of the 10th c., and with it came the Roman alphabet, and Latin as the language of the Church, the law courts, and of literature. The 13th c. saw the foundation of many schools and libraries; but the native language only found vent in translations of the Bible (as early as 1384), and in hymns and ballads. From Bohemia the Reformation found its way hither, and its chief literary results are the translations of the Bible by Komjáti (1533), Pesti (1536), Sylvester (1541), Heltai (1546), Székely (1548), and Melius (1565); and native Magyar chronicles by Székely (1559), Temesvári (1569), Heltai (1572), &c. But on the accession of the Hapsburg family Latin was confirmed as the official language, and the Jesuits (from 1561) threw discredit on Magyar as being a veil for heresy. In the 17th c. Latin enjoyed almost undisputed supremacy. It was the language of the first regular Hungarian newspaper, begun in 1721. As in Poland, Latin here made the nearest approach to 'a vernacular without becoming one' (Latham.) A bibliographical list of all Magyar works gives only twenty-nine trivial publications for the year 1784. But in that year Joseph II.'s attempt to substitute German for Latin awakened the national spirit, and, by resolution of the Diet at Presburg, Magyar became henceforth the language of law courts and schools. The first Magyar journal, by Matthias Ráth, appeared in 1781. It was followed in 1788 by Kazinczy's *Magyar Museum*, which gave impetus to the reviving literature. A national theatre was opened at Pesth (1793), where was produced the first Magyar comedy, by Karoly Kisfaludy, in 1817, and where the plays of Joseph Szigligeti subsequently (since 1834) laid the foundation of a rich native drama. In 1836 began to appear the Baron Josika's brilliant series of historical romances. Louis Kossuth, in editing the *Pesti Hirlap* (1841–44), did much to improve the language in flexibility and elegance. Sándor Kisfaludy (author of *Himfy's Love*, 1817) is perhaps the earliest, Sándor Petöfi is the greatest of the recent Magyar poets, who have given at least to the lyric in its weird pathos and its wild freedom the charm and character of national life. Eminent among song-writers are Victor Dalmady, who has been compared to Moore; Vajda, a fiery, voluptuous lyrist; and Endrödy, the genial author of *Tücsökdalok* ('Songs of Crickets'). The greatest living representative of fiction (1877) is Maurice Jókai. There is a Petöfi Society for the encouragement of *belles lettres*, and an historical academy, presided over by Horváth, and receiving from Government a yearly subsidy of 50,000 florins. The latter body publishes the valuable *Monumenta Hungariæ Historica*. In 1877, according to the *Vasarnap Ujság*, there are 268 Magyar periodicals, 128 of which are issued in Buda-Pesth, 139 in provincial towns, and 1 abroad. H. also has 146 foreign journals, 85 of which are in German, 42 in Slavonic, 13 in Rumanic, 4 in Italian, 1 in Hebrew, and 1 in French.

History.—The country now known as H. was formerly a Roman possession, forming part of Dacia and Pannonia. It was overrun by the Franks, Huns, and Avars, and towards the end of the 9th c. was divided into many petty kingdoms of Slavs, Bulgarians, Wallachians, and others. Under Almus and his son Arpad (q. v.), the hero of Hungarian romance, the Magyars advanced from the region of the Ural Mountains and took possession of the land far beyond the Theiss about 894. They conquered the country between the Danube and the Drave to the foot of the Styrian Alps in 899. The broad lands thus acquired were divided by covenant among 108 chiefs under fealty to the house of Arpad, and thus remained till Stephen I. (997–1038), broke the power of the nobles by establishing a monarchy. As a reward for his vigorous exertions on behalf of the Latin Church he received from Pope Sylvester II., in the year 1000, a crown that still forms the upper part of the *sacra regni Hungariæ corona*. Besides introducing Christianity among his people, he divided the country into ten bishoprics and founded classical and theological schools. He also greatly developed the military and civil administration, portioning the country into seventy-two comitats. In the subsequent reigns of Peter I. (1038–46), Andreas I. (1046–60), and of Bela I. (1060–63), there was much reactionary fighting against Christianity. In the dark, eventless period that follows, the valorous Vladislav I. (1077–95), and Coloman the 'learned' lawgiver (1095–1114), stand out in bold relief. In the time of Gejza II. (1141–61) Flemish settlers inaugurated mining in the Carpathians. Andreas II. (1205–35) was forced by the nobles to sign the *Bulla Aurea*, the great charter of Hungarian liberty; his son, Bela IV. (1235–70), though unable to stem the invasion of the Mongols (1241–43), sharply punished Friedrich II. of Austria for ungenerous conduct during the occupation of the barbarians. The Arpad dynasty expired with Andreas III. (13th January 1301), and the Duke Charles Robert of Anjou succeeded by marriage to the throne in 1307. Lewis I. (1342–81) extended the domination of H. far into Poland and Russia, and eventually united his crown with that of Poland in 1370. As son-in-law of Lewis, the Emperor Sigismund of Germany became King of H., and in his reign occurred the inroad of the Turks (1391) and the Hussite wars. During the reigns of Vladislav III. and Vladislav IV. the wars with the Turks excited the attention of all Christendom, and out of these arose the hero János Hunyady (q. v.), whose son, Matthias Corvinus (q. v.), was elected King of H. in 1458. Matthias more than justified his election by his indomitable valour in battle against Turks, Poles, and Austrians, and by the wisdom which generously encouraged a taste for art and literature. He was succeeded by the Bohemian King, Lewis II. (1490–1516), in whose reign broke out the Peasant War, which was subdued by the famous János Zápolya, after which the whole of the peasantry was reduced to serfdom. Lewis II. was killed in the battle of Mohacz (q. v.), the crowning disgrace of H. at the hands of the Turk. By marriage of his sister Anna with Ferdinand of Austria, H. fell to the house of Hapsburg in 1526. The subsequent history of H. is given in the article on the empire of Austria. See also Gebhardi, *Geschichte von Ungarn* (4 vols. Leips. 1778–82); Katona, *Historia Critica Ducum et Regum Hungariæ* (42 vols. Pesth, 1779–1808); Fessler, *Geschichte der Ungarn und ihrer Landsassen* (10 vols. Leips., new ed. 1867); Mailáth, *Geschichte der Magyaren* (5 vols. Vien. 1828–31); Alderstein, *Archiv des Ungar. Ministeriums* (3 vols. Altenburg, 1851); Görgei, *Mein Leben und Wirken in Ungarn* (2 vols. Leips. 1852); Falk, *Széchenyi István gróf es Kora* ('Széchenyi and his Time,' Pesth, 1868); Horváth, *Magyarország történelme* ('History of H.,' 6 vols. Pesth, 1860–63); Karl Keleti, *Länder der Ungarischen Krone* (Pesth, 1872); F. von Löher, *Die Magyaren und andere Ungarn* (Leips. 1874); A. J. Patterson, *The Magyars, their Country and its Institutions* (Lond. 1870); J. Hunfalvi, *A Magyar-Osztrák Monarchia rövid statisztikaja* (Pesth, 1874); and Paul Hunfalvi, *Ethnography of H.* (Pesth, 1876).

Hungary Water, an alcoholic perfume, obtained by distilling grape-spirit over Hungarian rosemary, the essential oil of which is thereby extracted. The recipe for its preparation is said to have been given by a hermit to a queen of Hungary in the 14th c. This legend Beckmann (*History of Inventions*) rejects as fiction.

Hun'gerford (formerly *Ingleford*, originally *Englaford*, 'the ford of the Angles'), an English market-town, partly in Wilts, partly in Berkshire, 61½ miles W. of London by railway, stands on the Kennet, a fine trout-stream, and is traversed by the old Roman road to Bath. Pop. (1871) 3064. Here William III. met James II.'s agents in 1688.

Hün'ingen (formerly Fr. *Huningue*), a town of Germany, in Ober-Elsass, on the left bank of the Rhine, 4 miles N. of Basel by railway. It had fortifications by Vauban till 1814. In the vicinity there is an establishment (founded 1852) for the breeding of fish, which has an area of over seventy acres. The Rhine is here crossed by a pontoon bridge. Pop. (1875) 1456.

Huns (Lat. *Hunni*, Gr. *Ounnoi* and *Chounoi*), a set of Scythian nomads, probably of Mongolian race, who first appeared in the Plains of Tartary threatening the Chinese frontier about 200 B.C. They then moved westward to the district between the Caspian and the Dniester, where they almost destroyed the Alani. Passing still westward to the Danube in the second half of the 4th c. (Christian), they drove the Visigoths and the Gruthungi or Ostrogoths into Roman territory. Partly helped by the Goths, they next attacked Rome itself, and at Adrianople defeated the imperial armies and killed the Emperor Valens. The period of their greatest power was under Attila, in the middle of the 5th c. His death seems to have dissolved the bond of union among the various tribes, who, pressed by the Goths, fell back across the Don, some of them settling in Pannonia. The name appears in Hungary. The Nepthalitæ or White H. invaded Persia in the time of Firoze. The H. are now undoubtedly lost; we have not enough to identify them by. See Gibbon's *Decline and Fall of the Roman Empire*, and De Guigne's *Histoire des H.*

Hunt, James Henry Leigh, an English poet, essayist, and journalist, was the son of a West Indian lawyer, and was born at Southgate, Middlesex, October 19, 1784. He was educated at Christ's Hospital, and in 1802 published *Juvenilia*, a volume of poems. After remaining a short time in a lawyer's office, and afterwards in the War Office, he became, at the age of twenty, dramatic critic to his brother's paper the *News*, and thenceforth led an exclusively literary life. In 1808 the two Hunts started the *Examiner*, and from 1813 to 1815 Leigh was imprisoned for having penned sarcasms on the Prince Regent. He produced in 1816 the *Story of Rimini*, a fine poem, which was heartily reviled by the critics, but the *Indicator*, a weekly modelled on the *Spectator*, which he started in 1819, had considerable success. H. went to Italy in 1821, and joined with Byron and Shelley in bringing out the *Liberal*, but the paper was a failure, and H. quarrelled with Byron, whom he assailed in his *Lord Byron and some of his Contemporaries*. He returned to England in 1825, and spent the rest of his life in London, starting the *Tatler* and *London Journal*, writing to periodicals, and producing various works in prose and verse, as *Captain Sword and Captain Pen*, a poem (1839), *The Legend of Florence*, a play (1841), *Imagination and Fancy* (1845), *Wit and Humour* (1846), *Stories from the Italian Poets* (1846), *Men, Women, and Books* (1847), *A Jar of Honey from Mount Hybla* (1847), *The Lovers* (1848), his *Autobiography* (1850, 2d ed. 1861), *The Religion of the Heart* (1853), *The Old Court Suburb* (1855), &c. H. died August 28, 1859. H. was a radical in politics, and held a vague optimistic deism. His poems have a pleasing lightness and airy fancy, abound in tender but not deep romantic sentiment, and are imbued with a peculiar blossomy freshness. His essays are exquisitely simple and graceful in style, containing much delicate criticism and Addisonian humour. See *H.'s Letters and Correspondence*, edited by his son, Thornton Hunt, in 1862.

Hunt, William Holman, an English painter, was born in London in 1827. As a young artist he was one of the founders of the pre-Raphaelite school, and all his works show the intense study of nature and minute accuracy in depicting it aimed at by that body. His earlier subjects were taken from scenes in romance and poetry, but he has latterly painted chiefly religious pictures, of which he has produced a splendid series, including the 'Hireling Shepherd' (1852), 'The Light of the World' (1854), 'The Scapegoat' (1856), 'Christ in the Temple' (1860), and 'The Shadow of Death' (1873). The two last-named works were the fruits of several years' study in Palestine, were separately exhibited, and sold for enormous sums. Among his secular pictures are 'Valentine receiving Sylvia from Proteus' (1851), 'Claudio and Isabella' (1853), 'Our English Coasts' (1853), and 'The Festival of St. Swithin' (1868). Mr. Hunt is at present (1877) engaged on an important painting at Jerusalem, where he has a studio.

Hunt, William, an English water-colour painter, born in London in 1790, became a member of the Society of Painters in Water-colours in 1824, and won high rank as an artist. He died in 1864. His works display scrupulous fidelity to nature, and combine delicate poetic feeling with breadth of effect and rich accuracy of detail. Mr. Ruskin places H. among the greatest English colourists, and especially praises his sympathetic representation of peasant boys. Among H.'s paintings are 'Peasant Girl,' 'Farmhouse Beauty,' 'Old Pilot,' 'Bunch of May,' 'Roses,' 'Fast Asleep,' 'Oak Trees,' &c.

Hun'ter, William, a distinguished Scottish surgeon, born at Long Calderwood, in the parish of Kilbride, Lanarkshire, 23d May 1718, was educated for the Church, but meeting with William Cullen (q. v.) about 1739, he agreed to enter with him into a medical partnership, each partner studying and practising in alternate years. This, however, did not last long, for H. went to London, and began to lecture on surgery at the Society of Naval Surgeons (1744). He afterwards took the subject of anatomy, and finally that of midwifery. In 1764 he became Physician Extraordinary to the Queen; in 1767 he entered the Royal Society, and in 1781 succeeded Fothergill as President of the College of Physicians. He died 30th March 1783, very wealthy. His successes as a teacher and practitioner had been great. His brother and others helped him in the lectures. He was the first great scientific accoucheur. The dispute with his brother about the determination of the structure of the placenta was probably not due to his fault. His chief work was the *Anatomia Humani Gravidi Uteri* (Birmingham 1774; English Lond. 1794), with plates from his own dissections. His occasional writings all refer to obstetric problems: they include the discovery of the varicose aneurism. His offer to found an anatomical school in London having been refused by Government, he left his museum in Windmill Street (with preparations, coins, books, and natural history specimens), with £8000 in trust to convey to Glasgow University at the expiry of thirty years. This was done. The coins were catalogued by Dr. Combe. See Simmens, *Account of W. H.* (Lond. 1783).—**John H.**, younger brother of the preceding, also born at Long Calderwood, 14th July 1728, received no university education. He worked three years in a carpenter's shop, and then went (1768) to London to help his brother William in the dissecting-room. After long surgical training in the hospitals, under Cheselden and others, in 1759 he was regularly associated with his brother in lecturing. After two years' voyage to recruit his exhausted strength (for he studied intensely), he began surgical practice in 1763. This grew slowly, and he found it necessary to teach. Jenner and Home were among his pupils. In 1768 he became Surgeon to St. George's Hospital, having previously entered the Royal Society. His great exertions left him subject to heart disease, which his rough fiery nature made more dangerous. He died of this disease, October 18, 1794. H. was one of the first to see clearly how much physiology depended on the comparative sciences of form and function. He accordingly ransacked menageries to fill a house which he kept at Brompton for purposes of experiment and dissection. He had many doubtful relations with body-snatchers, and one amusing story is told of the enthusiasm with which he watched a huge Irishman, O'Brien, whose skeleton he had resolved to get. One consequence of this was that he was always in want of money; his museum (afterwards bought by Government for £15,000) having cost him £70,000. Until Owen prepared the Hunterian catalogues, it was not known how vast was H.'s knowledge, his ten volumes of MS. notes and designs having been destroyed after his death. Filled with his own general views of the science of life, H. had a contempt for books. He probably owed one or two ideas to Harvey. Among his more famous writings we may mention, on the *Descent of the Testis* (1762), a development of Sharp's observation of congenital hernia; on *Absorption by Veins* (or rather *non-absorption*, a doctrine exploded by Majendie); on the *Natural History of the Human Teeth* (a development of Leuwenhoh's thesis); on the *Digestion of the Stomach after Death* (shown in the perforations of healthy stomachs); *Anatomical Observations on the Torpedo* (1773), proceeding on the idea thrown out by Bancroft (the friend of Priestley and Franklin), that the violence of the torpedo was due to electricity; *An Account of Air-Receptacles in Birds*, the honour of which discovery was disputed by Peter Cowper; on the *Heat of Animals*, or rather on the power of resisting cold possessed by cold-blooded animals, a continuation of the experiments of Duhamel on warm-blooded animals; *Observations on Inflammation of the Internal Coat of the Veins* (1784), a theory of phlebitis which was taken up afterwards by Abernethy; *Treatise on the Venereal Disease; Treatise on Blood, Inflammation, and Gunshot Wounds*, in which he tries to explain several pathological phenomena by the analogy of the coagulation of the blood. H. disputes with Desault the application of Anel's method of ligature *above* the sac to aneurisms on large arteries without opening the sac. H.'s views on fossil bones and monsters (or cases of arrested development) have been largely verified by later investigations. The best edition of H.'s works is Palmer's (4 vols. 1835), to which is prefixed a *Life of H.* by Ottey. There are other biographies by Home, Foote, and Adams.

Hunting Dog (*Lycaon venaticus*), a species of Canidæ or dogs found in S. Africa, and also known by the name 'hyæna dog.' These dogs live in packs, and in a natural state are wild and bold. The colour is a reddish brown marked with black and white. The ears are large and prominent, and the nose and muzzle are black. The tail is bushy, and is white at its base and black at the tip. The fore feet possess four toes only.

Hun'tingdon, the chief town in the county of H., England, on the left bank of the Ouse, 59 miles N. of London by rail. It extends for about a mile along the line of the ancient Ermine Street, and is near the site of the Roman station of *Durolapons*. Here are the county hospital and lunatic asylum, a grammar-school with two exhibitions to Cambridge, works for making perforated bricks, breweries, an iron foundry, &c. H. has a weekly cornmarket. An old stone bridge of six arches across the Ouse connects H. with the suburban village of Godmanchester. Pop. (1871) 4243. H. sends one member to Parliament. It is the birthplace of Oliver Cromwell.

Huntingdon, Seliña, Countess of, the daughter of the second Earl Ferrers, was born August 24, 1707. She married in 1728 Theophilus, Earl of H., whose death in 1746 was nearly accompanied by that of four of her seven children. On her bereavement she sought comfort in the revival movement of Wesley and Whitefield, attaching herself to the latter as the leader of Calvinistic Methodism, and spending her ample fortune in the endowment of numerous chapels and a college. On her death, June 17, 1791, there were 64 chapels (now over 100) belonging to the 'C. of H.'s connection.' The peculiarity of the sect is that it adapts the liturgy of the Church of England to the congregational system of government.

Huntingdonshire, the third smallest county of England, is bounded by the counties of Bedford, Northampton, and Cambridge. Area, 327 sq. miles; pop. (1871) 63,708. It is slightly hilly in the S., but in the N. forms part of the fen-country. The chief rivers are the Ouse and Nen, and the sub-soil is in great part Oxford clay. Portions of the 'meres' have been converted by draining and cultivation into the richest of English meadows. The principal crops are wheat, oats, beans, barley, hemp, hay, and clover. In 1876 there were 100,848 acres under corn crops, 21,597 under green crops, and 59,098 in permanent pasture, exclusive of hill and heath; also 24,725 head of cattle, 156,245 sheep, and 17,971 pigs. The manufactures are mainly bricks and tiles, paper, parchment, madder, beer, and leather. H. sends two members to Parliament. It is crossed by two Roman roads, and has yielded many antiquities, including urns, coins, and encaustic tiles.

Hunting Horn, a slightly curved horn, known as the H. H., is a common bearing in heraldry. When there is a band round the horn it is said to be *garnished*. The *bugle-horn* in heraldry is a semicircular horn.

Hunting Spider (*Salticus scenicus*), sometimes also named the zebra spider, from its brown colour being variegated with white bands, is a common British spider of active habits, found on walls and on trees, pursuing its prey with great persistence and agility. Three pairs of spinnerets exist in the H. S., which has also very long legs.

Hunt'ly, a town of Scotland, Aberdeenshire, in the hilly district of Strathbogie, at the confluence of the Deveron and Bogie, 24 miles N.W. of Aberdeen by rail. It has some linen industry, and a trade in grain, leather, bricks, &c. H. gives the title of Marquis to the Gordon family, of whose old castle (demolished after the battle of Glenlivet, 1594) there are ruins near Deveron bridge. Pop. (1871) 3570.

Hunts'ville, a town of Alabama, U.S., 10 miles N. of the Tennessee river, on a spur of the Cumberland mountains, has several fine public buildings, a brass and iron foundry, planing-mills, &c. Pop. (1870) 4907.

Hun'yady, János Corvin, a Hungarian hero, was born at Hunyad, in Transylvania, in 1387. A baseless legend made him the son of Emperor Sigismund and Elizabeth Palæologus. He first appears in 1439 supporting the usurper Vladislav of Poland on the throne of Hungary against the infant heir of Emperor Albrecht II. To reward his services at Belgrad and elsewhere against the Turks of Amurath (who called him Yanko), he was made Vaivod of Transylvania. Another great victory at Nissa led to the Peace of Szegedin (12th July 1444). After the disaster of Varna (10th November 1444), in which Vladislav was killed, H. acted as governor-general till 1453. He often co-operated with the Albanian Prince Scanderbeg against the Turks. H. was superseded in political power by Count Ulrich of Cilly, but gave a closing proof of his power as a popular military leader by raising the siege of Belgrad (14th July 1456), when Mahomet II. lost a large army and his whole cannon (300 pieces). H. died at Semlin, 10th September of the same year. His second son became King Matthias of Hungary.

Hu-pé ('north of the lakes'), a province in the heart of China, in the basin of the Yang-tse-kiang. Area, 69,480; pop. 28,584,564. It is named from the network of lakes in the S., along the course of the Yang-tse, which here receives its great affluent the Han-kiang. H. is perhaps the most highly cultivated and productive of all the provinces of China. It gives name to a famous tea, produces also hemp and tobacco, and exports raw silks. Wu-chang-fu, on the Yang-tse, is the capital, and its suburb of Hankow (q. v.) was opened to foreign commerce in 1858.

Hup'feld, Hermann, an eminent German linguist and theologian, was born at Marburg in 1796, studied Hebrew and exegesis under the guidance of Gesenius at Halle, he became Professor of Oriental Languages at Marburg in 1827, and was called to Halle as the successor of Gesenius in 1843. He died 24th April 1866. H. was a thoroughly scientific scholar in the circle of Oriental languages, and his work, though fragmentary, is of great value for the grammar and exegesis of the Old Testament. His masterpiece is the *Uebersetzung und Auslegung der Psalmen* (4 vols. Gotha, 1855-61). Other important productions are *Ueber Begriff und Methode der sog. Biblischen Einleitung* (Marb. 1844), *Die Quellen der Genesis aufs Neue untersucht* (Berl. 1853), and *Untersuchungen über die Feste der Hebräer* (Halle, 1851-64).

Hu'ra belongs to the Spurge family or *Euphorbiaceæ*, and is represented by a single species, a native of tropical America, called *H. crepitans*, the sandbox-tree. It grows 30 to 40 feet high, branches widely, and possessing a dense mass of foliage, is planted for the sake of its shade. The segments of the curious hard-shelled fruit, which is about the size of a small flattened orange, when ripe, burst from the common axis with a report like that of a pistol, hence sometimes called 'the monkey's dinner-bell.' The green seeds are emetic and violently purgative, and the milky juice characteristic of the order is abundant and venomous.

Hurd, Richard, D.D., an accomplished scholar and a bishop of the English Church, was born 13th January 1720, at Congreve, in Staffordshire, studied at Cambridge, and was ordained priest in 1744. His commentary on Horace's *Ars Poetica*, published in 1749, procured for him an introduction to Bishop Warburton. After holding several livings, he became in 1775 Bishop of Lichfield and Coventry, and in 1781 of Worcester. He declined the primacy in 1783, and died 28th May 1808. The best known of his works are his edition of the *Ars Poetica*, his *Dialogues, Moral and Political* (1765), his *Letters on Romance and Chivalry*, his *Twelve Discourses on the Prophecies*, his *Sermons*, his edition (1788) of the works of Warburton in 17 vols., his *Life of Warburton* (1795), &c. H. had an elegant, acute, and persuasive intellect, but did not sufficiently disdain the arts of a sophist. See the Life prefixed to the *Complete Works of H.* (8 vols. Lond. 1810).

Hurd'les, wicker frames of about 6 feet by 2 feet 9 inches used in warfare to form fences. *H.-batteries*, invented by Sir William Congreve, are made by arranging H. in the form of triangles and filling up the space between them with earth.

Hurdui, the chief town of the district of the same name, in the province of Oude, British India, and a station on the railway, 62 miles N.W. of Lucknow. Pop. (1869) 6415.—The *district* of H., which lies between the Ganges and the Gumti, has an area of 2292 sq. miles. Pop. (1869) 930,977.

Hurd'war (*Hari-dwar*, 'the gate of Hari or Vishnu'), a town in the district of Seharunpur, N.W. Province, British India, on the right bank of the Ganges, 924 miles N.W. of Calcutta. Pop. (1872) 4800. The Ganges here debouches on the plain, being still 1024 feet above the sea; and this spot is the most holy place of pilgrimage in its entire course. The bathing season is in April. It is said that 100,000 persons come annually, and thrice that number every twelfth year; the next of these great occasions will occur in 1883. H. was sacked by Timur in 1398, and has often been the scene of battles between rival sects of pilgrims. In 1819, 430 persons were trampled to death.

Hurdygurdy (the Continental *Leyer* or *Bauern-leyer*), a flat, oblong musical instrument with four strings. Two strings produce a drone-bass; the simplest melodies only can be played on the other two.

Hu'ron, the central and third largest of the five great N. American lakes of the St. Lawrence basin, divides the State of Michigan from Upper Canada, has an area of 23,800 sq. miles, a circuit of over 1000 miles, and a maximum depth of 1800 feet. The Manitoulin Islands (q. v.) and the peninsula of Cabot's Head separate it into two unequal portions, the easternmost of which is named Georgian Bay. H. is connected with Superior by St. Mary's, and with Michigan by Mackinac Strait, its outlet being by the St. Clair River. It lies 574 feet above sea-level, is subject to violent tempests, abounds in fish, and is remarkable for the purity and coldness of its water, being frozen over for five months in the year. The affluents of H. are numerous but unimportant, the chief being the French river and Severn, flowing into Georgian Bay, and, on the western side, the Saginaw.

Hurons. See INDIANS, AMERICAN.

Hurryhur' (*Harihara*), a British cantonment in the State of Mysore, Southern India, on the right bank of the Tungabudra river, a tributary of the Kistna, 132 miles N.W. of Seringapatam, and 320 N.W. of Madras. Pop. (1871) 6401.

Hurst, in heraldry, a clump of trees.

Hûs (commonly but incorrectly spelt **Huss**), **Johannes**, a martyr to his persistent and outspoken testimony against prevailing abuses in the Christian Church, was born in 1369 (or 1373) at Husinecz in Bohemia, studied philosophy and theology at the University of Prag, and graduated in 1396. Having in 1398 begun to teach in the university, he was, in 1401, made Dean of the Faculty of Philosophy and in the same year was appointed preacher in the Bethlehem Chapel, where the sermons were delivered in the vernacular Czech. He soon came thus to exert a powerful influence on the people; and, partly owing to his familiarity with the works of Wiclif, becoming deeply convinced of the corrupt condition of Christian morals and practice, he thundered not less energetically against the corruptions of higher and lower clergy than against the sins of the common folk. This and his defence of some of Wiclif's theses soon brought him into direct conflict with the ecclesiastical authorities. At first favoured by his Archbishop and supported by the King, H. in 1409 greatly furthered his cause in Bohemia by a reform of the university, the result of which was that upwards of 5000 foreign students and professors left Prag, leaving the management of the university in the hands of the native Bohemians. Yet, in 1411, H. was excommunicated and summoned to Rome, whither he declined to go. But as Prag was put under interdict so long as it gave shelter to the excommunicated theologian, he, in 1412, forsook the city and lived under the protection of the nobles who favoured his cause. When the universal council to which he had appealed was assembled at Constance, H. accepted the summons to defend himself there. Soon after his arrival, in November 1414, he was, in defiance of the safe-conduct granted by the Emperor Sigismund, thrown into prison. Not till June 1415 was he brought before the council; at three successive sittings the defence made by H., sick and solitary but steadfast, was unheeded, and on the 6th July, as he refused to withdraw errors which had not been proved against him from Scripture, he was condemned to be degraded and burnt, and his ashes to be thrown into the Rhine. The sentence was fulfilled that day. He died firm in the faith he had his life long preached. Practical in the turn of his mind, H. addressed himself to the special corruptions with which circumstances forced him into contact, and did not always draw the full consequences of his teaching, still less develop a well-defined system. How far he was from being a thoroughgoing follower of Wiclif is apparent from the fact that he nowhere says anything against the adoration of relics, against celibacy or monasticism. And though firm as a rock, he was not the man to found a new church or foresee the bearings of a great enterprise; he was of the stuff of which martyrs, not reformers, were made. In person he was tall and pale of countenance. His enemies admitted the irreproachableness of his life and the loveliness of his character. His chief works are *Actus pro defensione libr. Joannis Wiclif de Trinitate, Quæstio de Indulgentiis, contra Bullam Papæ Joannis XXIII.*, and *De Ecclesia*, together with sermons in the Czech language (the orthography of which he systematised), and a few poems. Ulrich von Hutten first began to edit H.'s works in his *Historia et Monumenta Jo. Huss atque Hieron. Pragensis* (Nürnmb. 1588, new ed. 1715). See Wendt's *Geschichte von H. und den Hussiten* (Magdeb. 1845); Helfert, *H. und Hieronymus* (Prag, 1853); Höfler, *Magister Johannes H.* (Prag, 1864); and Bezold, *König Sigismund und die Reichskriege gegen die Husiten* (Munich, 1877).

Hus'band and Wife. By the law of England the *personal* Estate (q. v.) (and articles there referred to) belonging to a woman before her marriage, on her marriage vests absolutely in her husband. But see under CONTRACT, *Contract of Marriage*. Of *real* property, the freehold and inheritance of the wife, the husband only receives the profit during her life. The law gives the same limited power to the husband over any real estate accruing to the wife during Coverture (q. v.). A married woman cannot make a legally binding contract without the expressed or implied consent of her husband. If a wife sell the goods of her husband, or dispose of them, the sale or disposal is void; or if she buys goods without his consent, he is not chargeable with them, but this consent will be held implied in matters usually under the management of a wife. A note or bill drawn by a married woman during coverture is void; so is her endorsation. A husband may restrain the person of his wife in case of gross misconduct, but if the restraint be unreasonable the law will relieve the wife by a writ of *Habeas Corpus*. If the wife be injured in person or property, she can bring no action for redress without the concurrence of her husband. Neither can she be sued without citing him as defendant, unless he is dead in a legal sense. (See CIVIL DEATH.) By 16 and 17 Vict. c. 83 husbands and wives are made admissible witnesses for or against each other in any civil judicial inquiry, but they are not so in criminal cases. In treason the wife may be evidence for the crown against her husband; so may she also be in an indictment for Abduction (q. v.) and marriage. In indictment for Bigamy (q. v.), though the lawful husband or wife cannot be a witness, the man or woman misled may be. When a husband has allowed his wife to act as his agent, her evidence respecting her agency is admissible. Thus when a wife made a bargain for board for herself and husband, an action against him for relative payment was decided in favour of the plaintiff. A husband is bound to maintain his wife according to his rank and means, and if she contract debt for goods requisite for this maintenance he is bound to pay it. But this obligation ceases if she leave her husband without his consent, on his giving public notice of his dissent to her absence. If a husband expels his wife from his house for legal misconduct, her subsequent contracts do not bind him. If the wife elopes the husband is no longer bound. But his liability continues if she justifiably leaves her husband, as when she leaves on reasonable suspicion of personal violence, though no violence has been committed. If a man marry a wife with children, he is not by the act of marriage bound to support them, but if they live with him he will incur the legal liability of a father. (See PARENT AND CHILD.) The legal relation of H. and W. was defined in the Court of Criminal Appeal, June 3, 1854. A woman had fled with her paramour from her husband's house, taking with her some money, a considerable portion of which was found in the man's possession when he was arrested. He was tried for stealing the money, and convicted. The conviction was appealed against on the ground that a wife cannot rob her husband, and consequently that the convict could not have received stolen property. The conviction was sustained, the court finding that while the general rule of law was that a wife could not steal from her husband, in this case the woman had by her misconduct lost the privileges of a wife, and consequently forfeited her implied authority over the goods of her husband. The law of Scotland does not materially differ from that of England as regards the legal relation of H. and W. In both countries these may be altered by anti-nuptial contract, or by post-nuptial contract if the husband be solvent at the date of executing the deed. The latter contract is in England binding on wife and children in all cases, while in Scotland it only is so if they get by it a better provision than they would otherwise have got. The mode by which the legal relation of H. and W. may be entered into is essentially different in Scotland from what it is in England. See MARRIAGE LAWS, DIVORCE, ADULTERY.

Hus'bandry, Servants in. Differences between masters and S. in H. may be determined summarily by a Justice of the Peace, on examination of parties on oath, if the sum in dispute does not exceed £10. Any S. in H. absenting himself during the term of his contract, written or verbal, is guilty of a misdemeanour, and is liable to be sent to prison with hard labour for three months, or to be mulcted in part of his wages. The law applies to women-servants also.

Husch, the chief town of the circle of Faltchi, Moldavia, near the border of Bessarabia, 8 miles W. of the Pruth, and 40 S.E. of Jassy. It was founded over 400 years ago by Hussites, is the seat of a Greek bishop, and has a trade in corn and wine. Here the Russians and Turks signed the treaty of 1701. Pop. 18,000.

Hushiarpur', the chief town of the district of the same name, in the Province of the Punjaub, British India, 90 miles E. of Lahore, and close by the old city of Hurrianah, has a special manufacture of white damask cotton cloth. Pop. (1868) 13,022. —The *district* of H., which lies in the Jullundhur Doab, between the Sutlej and Beas rivers, has an area of 2086 sq. miles; pop. (1868) 938,890. The crops are wheat, Indian-corn, barley, rice, cotton, and sugar-cane.

Hus'kisson, William, an English statesman and financier, was born at Birch Moreton, Worcestershire, March 11, 1770, and educated in Paris. He was a member of the 'Societé de 1789,' and took great interest in its commercial discussions. He became Secretary to the British Parisian ambassador, and on his return to England, Under Secretary of State in 1795. He was appointed Secretary of the Treasury (1804), Commissioner of Woods and Forests (1822), President of the Board of Trade (1822), Colonial and War Secretary (1827), and Foreign Secretary (1828), and represented Morpeth, Liskeard, Harwich, Chichester, and Liverpool in succession. He was killed by a locomotive engine on the opening of the Liverpool and Manchester line, September 15, 1830. H. had a profound financial knowledge, and his speeches (published with a biographical memoir in 1831 in 3 vols.) have never been surpassed for clearness of reasoning and mastery of detail. His statesmanlike measures for removing restrictions on commerce, particularly a bill carried in 1823, were without doubt the great precursors of the Free Trade movement.

Hussars' (Magyar, from *Husz*, 'twenty,' every twenty families being obliged to furnish one man), a species of light cavalry, of which in 1877 there were thirteen regiments in the British army. They originated in Hungary, and in the 17th and 18th centuries regiments of the kind were formed in France, Prussia, Russia, and England. They are armed with sabres, pistols, and carbines or rifles, and are adapted for close-fighting, scouring the country, and harassing the enemy.

Huss'ites (properly **Husites**) were the warlike adherents of Hus (q. v.). Hus was not merely a martyr to his faith, but was amongst all ranks and classes in Bohemia regarded as a national hero. In September 1415 a national assembly defied the Council of Constance, and resolved that every Bohemian proprietor might have the doctrines of Hus preached throughout his territories. The formation of a Catholic League intensified the excitement. Soon thousands were pledged not merely to take arms for the vindication of Hus's teaching, but to take revenge on the minions of a bloody church and a treacherous emperor. Amongst the H. two parties were formed. One, headed by the city of Prag and its university, were willing to be content with a few moderate concessions, including the use of the cup in communion to the laity, and from this circumstance are generally called *Calixtines*. The other party, known as *Taborites*, from their chief stronghold, the hill town of Tabor, went to an extreme in their opposition to all the existing arrangements in the Catholic Church, and soon ran into apocalyptical fanaticism. The latter party was headed by Nicolaus of Husinecz and John Ziska, and in 1419 fought a bloody battle at Prag. Under Ziska, the Taborites sacked monasteries and churches, and exercised great cruelties on priests and monks; and after the death of the king, Wenzel, obtained the support of the moderate H. in resisting the claim of the hated Emperor Sigismund to the Bohemian crown. For fifteen years Sigismund was unable to make head against the H., and as the various parties were united only against the common enemy, Bohemia was all that time in a state of anarchy. The result has been that in Franconia, Saxony, Silesia, and other Catholic districts of Austria, the name of the H. is still remembered with a shudder. Not only in great battles such as Deutschbrod (1422), but in smaller engagements, Ziska continually routed the imperial troops. After his death in 1424, the mass his energy and military success had held together broke into smaller parties. Those who held most closely to Ziska's aims called themselves the 'orphans,' and formed a middle party between Calixtines and Taborites, while the larger party of the Taborites took Procop as their commander. The new leader brilliantly displayed his capacities in the decisive victories at Miesz and Tachau in 1427 and 1431, gained over greatly superior numbers of imperial troops. Meanwhile the Calixtines had obtained the upper hand in the councils of the nation; the moderate H. saw their way to a compact with the Catholic party, and, united with the latter, entirely defeated the recalcitrant Taborites at Böhmischbrod, 30th May 1434, and for ever broke their strength, though as late as 1453 the Taborites maintained themselves as a party. After a final defeat in that year, the Taborites disappear in the *Bohemian Brethren* (q. v.). The victorious Calixtines, after certain concessions afterwards faithlessly withdrawn, agreed in 1436 to recognise Sigismund as King of Bohemia; and ultimately, in 1575, such as had not been crushed into conformity with the Catholic Church, united themselves with the Bohemian Brethren. See Palacky, *Geschichte von Böhmen;* and Bezold, *König Sigismund und die Reichskriege gegen die Husiten* (Munich, 1877).

Hus'tings (lit. a 'house court;' Old Eng. *hus*, 'house,' and Dan. *ting*, a 'court of justice'), is a court held before the Lord Mayor, Recorder, and Sheriffs of London. It is the Supreme Court of the city.

Hu'sum, a seaport in the province of Slesvig-Holstein, Prussia, on the North Sea coast, 22 miles W. of Slesvig. It has some industry in tobacco, leather, and spirits, and wool and cattle markets. Pop. (1875) 5765.

Hut, in military affairs, houses used instead of tents, formed either of wood, when they are called *log-huts* or *frame-huts*, the latter being more carefully constructed, or of clay, when they are called *pisé-huts*, the last being common in France. Huts vary greatly in size, being sometimes made to hold only one man, sometimes to hold 100 men.

Hutch'eson, Francis, a Scottish metaphysician, was born 8th August 1694, at Drumalig, near Saintfield, county Down. He was the son of a Presbyterian minister of Ballyrea, whose father had crossed from Scotland during the earlier persecution. After a private training in scholasticism, he studied at Glasgow under Gershom Carmichael (called by Sir W. Hamilton 'the founder of Scottish philosophy') and the heretical John Simson, one of the fountains of 'New Light.' The influence of Hoadley and Clarke was at this time considerable, and when in 1716 H. accepted a charge at Magherally, his preference for natural over Calvinistic theology was so distasteful to his flock that he left the pulpit and opened a school at Dublin. In 1725 he produced his *Inquiry into the Original of our Ideas of Beauty and Virtue*, which he defended against Philaretus, a son of Bishop Burnet, in the *London Journal* of 1728, in which year he also published *An Essay on the Nature and Conduct of the Passions and Affections, with Illustrations of the Moral Sense.* In 1729 he succeeded Carmichael at Glasgow, where he lectured on natural religion, morals, jurisprudence, and government, and read and expounded the great moral philosophers of Greece and Rome. His inaugural address was *De Hominum Socialitate.* At this time H., Simson (the mathematican), Dunlop (Greek), and Leechman (theology), attracted many students from Ireland and England to Glasgow, where the printers Foulis were also established. Among H.'s pupils was Adam Smith. With Leechman H. laboured 'to put a new face on Scotch theology.' In 1735 he wrote a pamphlet against patronage. He also published in Latin educational compendiums of logic and metaphysics, and helped Moore to translate and edit the *Meditations* of Antoninus. In 1745 he was nominated by the Edinburgh Town Council to the Chair of Moral Philosophy there, which he declined. He died 8th August 1746. In psychology H. was, on the whole, of Locke's school. He did not attempt the analysis of the primary qualities. But interest chiefly attaches to his theory of the moral sense, the sensations of which he keeps apart from (1) the pleasures and pains of imagination (arising from harmony, novelty, grandeur, &c.); (2) the pleasures and pains of sympathy; and (3) the sense of honour founded on the approbation and disapprobation of others. The pleasure of conscience caused by the contemplation of whatever tends to the happiness of others is a primitive feeling. He omits altogether the element of responsibility or obligation. He illustrates skilfully the growth of secondary desires, and defends the underived existence of disinterested feeling. H. was not a profound, but a clear and graceful writer. He did much to form a rational moderate party in both college and church. See the *Life of H.* by Dr. Leechman, prefixed to an edition of his *System of Moral Philosophy*, published by H.'s son in 1755.

Hutch'inson, Anne, founder of a sect of Antinomians in America, was born at Alford in Lincolnshire, England, in 1591, and emigrated to Boston in 1634. Her views were opposed by the clergy of Massachusetts, and she was banished from the State in 1637. She removed to Rhode Island, and in 1642 to the Dutch territory, where she was killed by Indians in 1643.

Hutchinson, John, founder of the school of cabalistical interpreters of Scripture known as *Hutchinsonians*, was born in 1674 at Spennithorne, in Yorkshire. He was employed as steward by the Duke of Somerset, and afterwards received a comfortable sinecure through the influence of the same noble patron. In a curious work entitled *Moses's Principia*, of which a fresh part appeared in 1724, H. assailed the Newtonian theory of gravitation on the authority of Scripture; and till the end of his life continued to publish occasional volumes, in which the attempt is made by fanciful treatment of the texts, words, and root syllables of the Hebrew Scriptures, to extract thence a complete system, not merely of theology and philosophy, but of astronomy and natural history. Amongst the followers of H., who was a mere ignorant dabbler, possessed neither of learning nor ability, were not a few men of high academical and ecclesiastical position. *The Philosophical and Theological Works of the Late Truly Learned John H., Esq.*, appeared in 1748 in 12 vols.

Hutchinson, Lucy, a Puritan lady, who has won a place in literature by an admirable memoir of her husband, Colonel John Hutchinson, was born 29th January 1620, and married in 1638. Colonel Hutchinson was a member of the high court of judiciary that sentenced Charles I. to death. At the Restoration he was arrested, and died a prisoner in Sandown Castle, 11th September 1664. His wife survived him many years. The work which has made both herself and her husband famous was not published till 1806. In a graceful and appreciative review, Lord Jeffrey compares her to 'the Valerias and Portias of antiquity.'

Hutt'en, Ulrich von, the fiery champion of *humanism*, indefatigable in his efforts for freeing the German nation from the yoke of Italian ecclesiasticism, was descended from an ancient knightly family in Franconia, and was born at Steckelberg, in Hessen, 22d April 1488. He escaped from the monastery of Fulda and the monastic life to which he was destined by his family, and at the universities of Erfurt, Frankfurt on the Oder, Greifswald, and later in Italy, he was won to the cause of the new classical learning—the *Renaissance* of pure literature. The aquaintance made with Aquinas (q. v.) at Cologne and with canon law at Pavia and Bologna only provided material for displaying his contempt for the old scholasticism. His sojourn in Italy provoked him to intense abhorrence of the influence exercised on German affairs by the 'Roman tyrants,' as he called the popes. A family feud with the Duke of Würtemberg raised his ire against the arbitrary power of the minor German princes. He took up with zeal the cause of Reuchlin against the Dominicans; in the biting satire of the *Epistolæ Obscurorum Virorum*, at least in the second part, a large share must unquestionably be ascribed to H. When Luther adopted a position of decided hostility to Rome, H. greeted him as a fellow-worker, though conscious that their aims were almost as different as the methods by which they sought to gain them. H.'s zeal was less for the purity of doctrine or for the promotion of piety than for the restoration of political and intellectual freedom and unity in Germany; but he was keenly persuaded that the papal system was contrary to the spread of Christianity and hostile to human freedom. After 1520 H. was deeply engaged in intrigue for securing the ends he sought by military combination of well-affected nobles, cities, and peasants; and found in Franz von Sickingen a captain after his own heart. H.'s inseparable companions through life, poverty, sickness (in great measure the result of dissipated habits), and bitter hostilities, followed him to Switzerland, where, in 1523, he was working for Sickingen's cause. Here he engaged in a bitter controversy with Erasmus, whom he regarded as an apostate from the cause he had once done so much to forward, when, hearing of Sickingen's defeat and death, he died broken-hearted on the island of Ufenau in the Lake of Zürich, 29th August 1523—a man not without many faults, but a brilliant example of self-devoting, consuming zeal for truth and right. A collected edition of H.'s works, in 5 vols., was published by Böcking in 1859-62. See Strauss's *Ulrich von H.* (Leips. 2 vols. 1857).

Hutt'on, Charles, an English mathematician, was born at Newcastle-on-Tyne, August 14, 1737. He was almost entirely self-taught, and conducted with success a school in his native town till 1773, when he was called to the Chair of Mathematics in the Royal Military Academy at Woolwich. In 1775 he was charged by the Royal Society with the duty of deducing the earth's mean density from the observations made by Maskelyne upon the attraction of Schiehallion. He enriched the *Philoso-*

phical Transactions with many valuable papers, and published his famous *Mathematical Tables* in 1785. His *Tracts on Mathematical and Philosophical Subjects* (3 vols.) appeared in the succeeding year, and the *Compendious Measurer* and the *Elements of Conic Sections* in 1787. His other chief works are *A Mathematical and Philosophical Dictionary* (1795–96), *A Course of Mathematics* (3 vols. 1798–1801), *Recreations in Mathematics and Natural Philosophy* (translated, with additions, from the French of Montucla, 4 vols. 1803), and, together with Shaw and Pearson, an *Abridgment of the Philosophical Transactions* (18 vols. 1804–9). While at Woolwich, his attention was naturally attracted to Gunnery (q. v.), and his experiments with Robin's ballistic pendulum form perhaps his most important contributions to practical science. In 1806 his health obliged him to resign his post, and retire on a government pension of £500 per annum. H. died in London, January 27, 1823.

Hutton, James, a Scottish geologist, was born at Edinburgh, June 3, 1726. He studied medicine at Edinburgh, Paris, and Leyden, where he took his doctor's degree in 1749. On his return in 1750, he worked as a practical farmer for some time; but the love for chemistry, which he had always shown, finally led him to the study of mineralogy. To better prosecute this science, he undertook journeys into England and through the North of Scotland, and ultimately became fully absorbed in the much wider science of Geology (q. v.), which was then in its infancy. His discovery of granite veins forms an important event in the progress of geology, and his *Theory of the Earth* (communicated to the Royal Society of Edinburgh in 1777, published 1795) entitles him to a foremost place among modern geologists. It roused a bitter controversy, and was vigorously attacked by the Wernerians. His *Theory of Rain*, which is now recognised as generally accurate, was criticised and combated by De Luc. H. died March 26, 1797.

Hux'ley, Thomas Henry, was born at Ealing, Middlesex, May 4, 1825. In 1842 he entered the Medical School of Charing Cross Hospital, and in 1845 passed the first M.B. examination at the University of London, especially distinguishing himself in anatomy and physiology. In the succeeding year he accompanied H.M.S. *Rattlesnake* to the Southern Seas as assistant-surgeon, investigated with great success the fauna of those regions, and communicated to the Royal Society several important papers, the first of which (1849) bears the title *On the Anatomy and Affinities of the Family of the Medusæ*. He returned home in 1850, was elected a Fellow of the Royal Society in 1851, and succeeded Edward Forbes in the Chair of Natural History in the Royal School of Mines in 1854, a post which he still holds. In 1870 he presided at the meeting of the British Association, was elected Lord Rector of Aberdeen University in 1872, and lectured on natural history at Edinburgh University during the summer sessions of 1875–76 in room of Sir Wyville Thomson, then absent on the *Challenger Expedition*. H. is universally recognised as one of the foremost biologists of the day. All his writings exhibit his wide grasp of the facts and principles of the science in which he labours, as well as his true philosophical acumen in detecting essential relationships between different animal groups as a basis for generalised conceptions; while as a teacher and expounder he stands pre-eminent in his department. His rare powers are well shown in his classification of the whole animal kingdom, but especially in the elucidation of the comparative anatomy of the vertebrata. His extension of Darwin's theory of natural selection, and the great impulse which he has given to the doctrine of evolution, merit particular attention. His chief works are *Man's Place in Nature* (1863), *Lectures on Comparative Anatomy* (1864), *Lessons in Elementary Physiology* (1866, 2d ed. 1868), *An Introduction to the Classification of Animals* (1869), *Lay Sermons, Addresses, and Reviews* (1870, 2d ed. 1871), *Manual of the Anatomy of Vertebrated Animals* (1871), *Critiques and Addresses* (1873); and, with W. T. T. Dyer, the article *Biology* in the *Encyclopædia Britannica* (9th ed. vol. iii. 1875).

Huy, a fortified town in the province of Liege, Belgium, at the confluence of the Hoyoux and the Maas, 17 miles S.W. of Liege by rail. It lies in a wild, hilly district, has a Gothic church of Notre Dame dating from 1311, and carries on a large trade in the coal and iron from the neighbouring mines. The former abbey of Neufmoustier (*Novum Monasterium*), was founded at H. by Peter the Hermit after the first Crusade. H. was taken by Marlborough and Coehoorn in 1703. Pop. (1874) 11,420.

Huy'ghens van Zuglichem, Christian, a celebrated natural philosopher, was born at the Hague, in Holland, April 14, 1629. In 1645 he entered the University of Leyden as a law student, devoting most of his energies, however, to the study of mathematics. He studied later at Breda, and in 1651 published his first work, *Theoremata de Quadratura Hyperbolis, Ellipsis, et Circuli, ex dato Portionum Gravitatis Centro*—a work which placed him among the first mathematicians of the age. In 1655 he discovered, by means of a telescope constructed by himself, the fourth satellite of Saturn, and later proved the existence of the ring. His results were published in his *Systema Saturninum* (1659), where also is described for the first time the *micrometer*, an invaluable instrument in astronomical research. About this time he applied the pendulum to the regulation of clocks—undoubtedly the greatest of his practical inventions, which forms the subject of his important treatise *Horologium Oscillatum* (1658). In 1660 he visited England, and in 1666 settled in Paris, where he remained till 1681, when he returned to his native town. In 1690 he published his famous treatise on light, in which he proved, upon the undulatory hypothesis, by most beautiful geometrical constructions, not merely the ordinary laws of reflection and refraction, but also the hitherto inexplicable phenomenon of double refraction. Another of his optical discoveries is the polarisation of light by reflection. H. died at the Hague, June 8, 1695. S' Gravesande published his *Opera Varia* (4 vols. 1724), and, as a supplement, *Opera Reliqua* (2 vols. 1728). His unpublished manuscripts were collected under the title *Opera Posthuma* (1700). See the *Vita Hugenii* prefixed to his *Opera Varia*.

Huy'sum, Jan van, an exquisite Dutch painter, was born at Amsterdam in 1682. His father, Justus H., also a painter, carefully educated him in his own branch of the art, viz., landscape painting, which Jan cultivated with great success. Latterly, however, he betook himself to flower and fruit pieces, and in this style he reached the highest degree of excellence. Nothing can surpass the delicacy, mellowness, and natural beauty of his work. In all he executed, it is said, between 1000 and 1400 pictures. The best specimens of his genius are in the galleries of Vienna, Munich, Dresden, and St. Petersburg. H. died at Amsterdam in 1749. His three brothers, Justus van H. (ob. ætat. 22), Nikolaus van H., and Jakob van H. (died in London 1740), were also painters of some note.

Hu'zara (*Hazara*), the most northerly district of British India, province of the Punjaub. Area, 3000 sq. miles; pop. (1868) 367,218. It is bounded on the W. by the Indus; and the country is mainly mountainous. Snow falls as low as 4000 feet. The crops are maize, wheat, and barley, and there are large flocks of sheep and goats. The chief town is H. or Abbotabad, 125 miles E. of Peshawur, where there are cantonments for 1500 men. In 1857 the sepoy regiment mutinied, and was pursued and cut to pieces among the mountains.

Hwang-Ho. See Hoang-Ho.

Hy'acinth, a mineral variety of the species *Zircon* (q. v.). occurring in grains in Ceylon and several European localities, such as Auvergne and Bohemia.

Hyacinth, a plant to which frequent allusion is made by the Greek poets, but which, from the vague way they use the names of flowers, it is impossible to identify. As now understood, H. is the genus *Hyacinthus*. This genus belongs to the section of the natural order *Liliaceæ*, with united perianth segments (*gamopetalous*), capsular fruit, and racemose inflorescence, and contains about thirty species, of which three-fourths are natives of Persia, Asia Minor, Syria, and countries bordering the Mediterranean. From one of these, viz., *H. orientalis*, the various coloured single or double hyacinths of the garden and the greenhouse have been produced. Grown indoors in H.-glasses they form an enlivening and favourite ornament in the early months of the year. Some six species of H. are peculiar to our Cape of Good Hope colonies. The grape-H. belongs to another genus named *Muscari*, and the popular name originates from the small roundish purple flowers being arranged in clusters on the top of the stalk (scape), something like grapes in a bunch. There are about twenty species, one of which is possibly a native of Britain; several of them are grown in gardens. The wild or wood H. or bluebell is a *Scilla*, in which genus the petals or segments of the perianth are *not* united, but free.

Hyacinthus orientalis.

Hy'acinthe, Père (Charles Loyson), a Catholic schismatic, was born at Orleans, 10th March 1827, studied at the Academy of Pau, of which his father was rector, entered the seminary of St. Sulpice (1845), migrated thence to Paris (1846), and received priest's orders, 17th June 1851. Successively Professor of Philosophy at Avignon, and of Theology at Nantes (1854), he exchanged the latter post for the cure of the church of St. Sulpice, and four years later entered first the Dominican, then the Carmelite order, accomplishing his noviciate at Branssay. After preaching at Lyon, Bordeaux, &c., in 1864 H. came to Paris, where, as superior of the Carmelite monastery at Passy, he delivered some eloquent courses of sermons at the Madeleine and Notre Dame (1865-69). His oratory, however, was better than his orthodoxy, and a speech addressed to the International League of Peace, in which he classed the Jewish, Catholic, and Protestant religions as 'the three great religions of civilised peoples,' caused his suspension, July 1869. This H. answered by a manifesto (September 20) appealing to the forthcoming Œcumenical Council; but at the same time renouncing his vows, he was excommunicated, and shortly after left Paris on a visit to the United States. In September 1871 he appeared at the 'Old Catholic' Congress at Munich, and on September 2, 1872, contracted a civil marriage with an American lady, the widow of Mr. E. Meriman, who has since borne him a son. Elected, April 1873, a curé of the 'Liberal Catholics' at Geneva, he resigned the post in 1874, on the ground that 'Liberal Catholicism was neither Liberal in politics nor Catholic in religion,' and has since officiated in a church of his own establishing. H. has lectured occasionally in England, where he numbers among his friends Mr. Gladstone, Dean Stanley, and Professor Jowett.

Hy'ades (Gr. 'rainers,' from *hyein*, 'to rain,' Lat. *Pluviæ*), five stars clustered in the face of the constellation Taurus, the rise of which simultaneously with the sun was thought by the ancients to portend rainy weather. The story connected with them is variously given.

Hya-Hya. See Cow-Tree.

Hyæ'na (*Hyæna*), a genus of Carnivorous mammals included in the family *Hyænidæ*, and possessing six incisors, two canines, and two molars in each jaw; eight premolars existing in the upper and six in the lower jaw. All the feet possess four toes, and the tail is short. The body exhibits a singular conformation in that it slopes in a very marked manner from the shoulders to the hind quarters. These animals are cowardly and timid, and appear chiefly to subsist on the carrion left by other animals. The H. will only attack smaller animals, or press larger animals when the latter are solitary, and when the H. is supported in the attack by numbers of its own kind. These animals exist in Asia and Africa, and several very distinct species are known to zoologists. The striped or crested H. (*H. striata*) attains a length of 4 or 5 feet. Its colour is greyish brown, but it may be readily recognised by the black stripes which mark the sides and limbs. The ears are long and pointed. The brown H. (*Crocuta rufa*) derives its name from the general brown line of its fur. The spotted H. (*C.* or *H. maculata*) is, perhaps, the most familiar of these animals. It is common in S. Africa, and is named the 'tiger wolf,' from its peculiar marked ferocity; whilst the name 'laughing H.' has been given to this animal from its strange cries. Its average length is 5½ feet, and its height at the shoulder 2½ feet. The head is short and the muzzle broad; the colour being brown, marked in an irregular manner with black spots. The tail measures about 16 inches; and there is a kind of rough mane on the back and withers. The power of the jaws and jaw-muscles in the H. is well exemplified by the ease with which these animals split up the largest bones into splinters.

Hunting Hyæna.

Hyalone'ma, a very peculiar genus of animals, known popularly as the 'glass-rope zoophyte,' and apparently composed of two distinct animal forms closely united together. The organism consists (1) of a cap-shaped sponge (*Carteria*), to which is attached (2) a long twisted coil of flinty or siliceous fibres; and encrusting these fibres is found (3) a colony of little polypes, resembling the sea-anemones in their essential nature. *H. Sieboldii* was first brought from Japanese seas, but allied species have been dredged elsewhere, especially off the coast of Portugal. The peculiar nature of the H. has formed a puzzle to zoologists. By some it has been placed among the *Zoantharia* in the *Cœlenterate* sub-kingdom of animals, from the consideration that the little polypes manufacture the flinty coil. But as no cœlenterate are known to secrete a *flinty* coral or hard parts, this view has been rejected by others, who maintain that the true artificer of the flinty coil is the sponge; the polypes in this latter view being regarded as parasitic. On the whole, this latter opinion—supported by Wyville Thomson, Loven, &c. —is the most probable.

Hyberna'tion. See Hibernation.

Hyb'la, three towns in Sicily, from one or other of which came the honey so often alluded to by ancient poets, namely, *H. Major*, on the S. slope of Ætna; *H. Minor*, or *Megara Hyblæa*, founded on the E. coast by Dorians of Megara in Greece in 728 B.C., under Syracuse from the earlier part of the 5th c. B.C., but insignificant after its sack by the Romans during the second Punic War; and *H. Heræa*, in the S., between Agrigentum and Syracuse.

Hyb'odus (Gr. 'hump-toothed'), a genus of extinct fishes belonging to the order *Elasmobranchii* (q. v.), and to the division *Cestraphori* of that order. H. remains occur plentifully in Triassic and Oolitic rocks, and less abundantly in the Chalk series. The teeth are shark-like in conformation, but are somewhat blunted in shape. Each tooth includes a central cone, having smaller or secondary cones on either side. The fossil fin species, or 'ichthyodorulites' of H., are grooved longitudinally, and are toothed on their hinder edges. The teeth and fin species form, in fact, the only portions of these fishes which have been preserved in a fossil state.

Hy'brid (from Gr. *hybris*, 'wanton excess,' 'licentiousness'), the name given to the progeny of animals assumed or believed to be distinct *species*. Thus the progeny of a male horse and female ass is a H. named the Hinny (q. v.), that of the mare and the he-ass, a H. named the Mule (q. v.). Here the distinctly *specific* nature of the horse and ass is assumed, and, in point of fact, is generally admitted. In determining the nature of any animal presumed to be a H., it is evident the chief test must rest with the determination of the truly and distinct specific nature of the parents. The definition of a species of animals or plants is by no means an easy matter, since the ideas of naturalists regarding species have greatly altered within the past few years. A species is not now regarded as the invariable and stable quantity which the older zoologists and botanists defined it to be; the modern tendency in biological speculation is to regard each species as capable of *varying* to a greater or less extent. A species thus produces *varieties*, and when distinct *varieties* interbreed, the progeny are not named hybrids but *mongrels*. To understand the difficulties which beset the determination of hybrids, it is necessary to bear in mind that each species may be regarded from two points of view—(1) in reference to structure, that is, *morphologically*, and (2) in reference to functions, that is, *physiologically*. It is clearly the physiological idea of species which is concerned in the production of hybrids, since the fertility of two forms is a matter to be decided from a functional or physiological point of view. A general survey of the animal and plant creations would show us that as a rule distinct species of animals and plants present little or no tendency to interbreed. When two individuals representing two distinct species do interbreed, the species will be found almost invariably to be near neighbours, and to posssess a very close structural and physiological relationship. The further we go from the type of the genus the less likelihood is there of hybrids being produced. Hybrids have been thus readily enough produced by 'crossing' the horse and ass as already remarked, and by interbreeding the sheep and goat. It is worthy of remark, however, that there appears to exist a preference, as it were, on the part of one or other *sex* for the successful production of hybrids. Thus in some cases (exemplified by the horse and ass) the male of one species when crossed with the female of the opposite species produce a more perfect H. than when the female of the first species is crossed with the male of the second. The male ass and mare produce a stronger H., and one more likely to be fertile or to produce young, than the offspring of the stallion and the female ass. The he-goat united with the ewe produces a physiologically more perfect H. than that resulting from the union of the ram with the she-goat, the greater physiological perfection of the former H. being evinced by its capability of producing young. Other cases of hybrids have been proved to occur indiscriminately between the horse, ass, and zebra. The dog breeds freely with the wolf, and the resulting hybrids are by no means sterile; the lion and tiger have also produced a H. progeny. The offspring of the swan and goose are fertile, and pheasants have been successfully bred with allied species. Rabbits and hares are perfectly prolific *inter se*, and among fishes hybrids have been artificially produced by fertilising the eggs of one species with male fluid from another. In plants the production of first hybrids takes place very frequently, but the degree of fertility which these hybrids may exhibit has not been definitely ascertained. The plant species is if anything more elastic in its nature than the animal species, in so far at least as the production of first crosses are concerned. Mr. Darwin remarks that the prevailing idea among naturalists is, 'that species, when intercrossed, have been specially endowed with sterility in order to prevent their confusion;' yet he adds, 'although I know of hardly any thoroughly well authenticated cases of perfectly fertile H. animals, I have reason to believe that the hybrids from *Cervulus vaginalis* and *Reevesii*, and from *Phasianus colchicus* with *P. torquatus* are perfectly fertile. M. Quatrefages states that the hybrids from certain moths (bombyx, cynthia, and arrindia) were proved in Paris to be fertile *inter se* for eight generations.' The result of Mr. Darwin's considerations tends to show that every degree of fertility probably exists in H. races, ranging indeed 'from zero to perfect fertility.' At the same time, the question regarded generally may be summed up by stating that sooner or later the fertility of hybrids becomes impaired. The conditions which produce these forms may be competent to continue their fertility for several generations, but no evidence is at hand to prove that this fertility is permanent, or that any one race of plants or animals represents the results of permanent hybridisation originally induced between two distinct species.

Hybrid Disease. The only instance of H. D. which has been described is Rötheln or Rubeola (q. v.), a disease developed from the combined poisons of two fevers, measles and scarlatina. Dr. Kütner, of Dresden, states that he has seen occasionally in the same individual portions of the skin presenting the scarlatina eruption, while in other parts the eruption of measles was to be seen, and cases have also been described in which the eruption was hybridous. It is possible that an individual may suffer from two diseases of the zymotic type at the same time; but the possibility must also be admitted of the existence of H. D., and the theory receives confirmation from recent investigations regarding the Germ Theory of Disease (q. v.). It is probable that Dengue (q. v.) belongs to the class of H. D.

Hyde', a town of England, in Cheshire, on the river Tame and the Peak and Forest Canal, 7 miles E. of Manchester by rail. It has extensive cotton-mills, printworks, iron foundries, and machine factories. In the vicinity are numerous collieries. H. is an old market-town, but its thriving industries are of recent date. Pop. (1871) 14,223.

Hyde, Edward. See CLARENDON, EDWARD HYDE, EARL OF.

Hy'der (*Haidar*) **Al'i**, the most formidable enemy that the British ever encountered in India, either in diplomacy or war, was born in 1728, and first served as a trooper under the Hindu Rajah of Mysore. He usurped the throne in 1759, and founded a Mohammedan empire over the entire S. of the Peninsula, except the Carnatic. H. headed a native league to expel the British from India, and also allied himself with the French. His first war with the British lasted from 1767 to 1769, and was terminated by a peace dictated by himself under the walls of Madras. He next became involved with the Mahrattas, but after a severe defeat maintained his power. The second war with the British broke out in 1779. It is memorable for the devastation of the Carnatic, and for the victory of Sir Eyre Coote at Porto Novo in 1781. H. A. himself died 7th December 1782, before the termination of the war, bequeathing his dominions and his policy of enmity against the British to his son, Tippoo Sahib.

Hy'dnum, a large genus of hymenomycetous fungi, distinguished by the hymenium consisting of prickles projecting from the pileus. *H. repandum*, a common species in woods, is good eating if properly cooked.

Hy'dra (Gr. 'water snake'), a monster fabled in ancient times to have infested the marsh of Lerna near Argos. It was the offspring of Typhon and Echidna, or of the Titan Pallas and Styx, and had nine heads, which, as Hercules (q. v.), who had been sent to attack it, struck them off with his club, were succeeded by twice as many more. At last the hero, aided by his servant Iolaus, burned off the heads, burying the middle one, which was immortal, under a huge rock, and poisoned his arrows by tinging them with the blood of the H. As 'killing the H.' was a Greek proverb for labour in vain, so the term H. is often applied to some irrepressible pest, *e.g.*, the 'H. of revolution.'

Hydra, an island of Greece, 11 miles long and 3 broad, off the eastern peninsula of the Morea, from which it is separated by a strait 5 miles wide. Area, 45 sq. miles; pop. (1871) 11,684, mostly Albanians. It is included in the nomarchy of Argolis and Corinth, and is barren and hilly (1800 feet high), destitute of wood and wells. A strongly-fortified town, also called H., on the N. shore, is one of the most beautiful in Greece, and has a good harbour, some cotton and silk industries, shipbuilding, &c. Pop. 7380. The island, uninhabited in ancient times, was settled by Albanians and Greeks who fled hither from Turkish oppression in the 15th and 16th centuries. Before the War of Liberation, H. was regarded as the richest island in this archipelago. The Hydriotes played a prominent part in the war, and are still admirable sailors. Much of their trade has found its way to more advantageous ports since 1825.

Hydra, or Common Fresh-Water Po'lype, a little animal attaining a length of a quarter of an inch, found in fresh-water ponds and ditches. The common species, *H. viridis*, receives its green colour from the development of *chlorophyll*. *H. fusca*—the 'long-armed H.'—of a brown colour, is so named from the possession of long arms or tentacles which surround the mouth. The body of a H. is simply a little tube, composed of two layers or tissues (*ectoderm* and *endoderm*), attached to weeds, &c., by one extremity, the *hydrorhiza*, whilst at the free extremity or mouth surrounded by tentacles, from four or five to ten or more are found. The tentacles capture the prey, consisting of water-fleas and other minute organisms, and along with the body-tissues are richly provided with stinging-cells named *cnidæ* or thread-cells. These thread-cells contain a fluid and a thread or filament which lies coiled up within the interior of the cell. On being irritated in any way, the thread-cell ruptures, the fluid escapes, and the thread is everted, and coming in contact with the tissues of the prey, serves to paralyse and to kill the latter. The bases of the threads of H.'s thread-cells are armed with three little recurved hooks. The simple interior of the body-cavity serves as a digestive system, and the *cilia* or vibratile filaments lining the endoderm serve to circulate through the body the products of digestion. *Reproduction* in H. may be performed in three ways. Trembley of Geneva, in 1744, published his researches on the H. and showed that these polypes might be artificially divided in various ways, with the result of producing new hydræ by the division of a single individual. This process may therefore be termed one of *artificial fission.* Reproduction by *gemmation* or *budding* also takes place in the warmer months of the year, young buds growing on the side of the parent body, and gradually growing into the likeness of the latter. These buds, however, drop off sooner or later to seek a lodgment and begin life on their own account. The H. also reproduces its like by means of *sexual* reproduction. Eggs are produced in an *ovarium* situated near the base of the body, *spermatozoa* or *male* elements being developed in *spermaria* at the base of the tentacles. After fertilisation the eggs undergo segmentation, and finally the *blastoderm*, or germinal membrane, gives origin to the two layers of the body of the H., and a mouth and tentacles being developed, the adult form is matured. The H. forms the type of the class *Hydrozoa* of the *Cœlenterate* sub-kingdom of animals, the class being represented by zoophytes, jellyfishes, and the like.

Hy'drabad (*Haidarabad*, 'the city of Haidar, or the lion'), the name of two important towns in India. 1. The capital of the Nizam's Dominions (q. v.), in the centre of the Deccan, on the Mussi river, a tributary of the Kistna, 962 miles or 91 hours by rail S.W. of Calcutta, and 449 miles or 27 hours E. of Bombay. It is a walled city, the third largest in India, containing, with its extensive suburbs, a population of 450,000 souls. H. was founded in 1589, to supersede the old capital, Golconda, 8 miles distant, and it contains many handsome buildings, palaces, mosques, and tanks. The British Residency is also a fine structure on the opposite side of the river, here crossed by a stone bridge of nine arches, erected by a British officer in 1831. The cantonments of Secunderabad lie about 4 miles N. H. is famous for a permanent horse-market, and for its fruit-gardens. The large Mohammedan population is disposed to be turbulent. 2. Sometimes spelled Hyderabad for distinction, the chief town of the district of the same name in Scinde, just below the bifurcation of the delta of the Indus, 88 miles N.E. of Kurachi, with which it is connected by railway. Pop. (1872) 35,272. It was the former capital of the province, and is strongly built on an elevated plateau, with a conspicuous citadel. The cantonments, lying to the N. and W., contain about 1300 men and officers. In the neighbourhood are several handsome tombs of the Kalhora and Talpur Mohammedan dynasties, and the British Residency, where Outram was besieged in 1843. There are famous manufactures of gold, silver, and silk-embroidered fabrics, and of carpets; the former manufacture of arms and armour is now decayed. The trade is very considerable, the municipal tolls on certain articles alone realising £6000 per annum.—H. *district*, which borders the left bank of the Indus, has an area of 9053 sq. miles; pop. (1872) 721,947. Like the rest of Scinde, it forms a sandy desert wherever it is not irrigated by a network of canals. See *Gazetteer of Scinde*, by Mr. A. W. Hughes (Lond. 1874).

Hy'dracids, or Hy'drogen Acids, a name sometimes given to those hydrogen compounds which contain no oxygen, and which exhibit all the characteristics of true acids. Such, for instance, are hydrochloric acid (HCl), hydrobromic acid (HBr), hydrocyanic acid (HCN), &c. Some chemists regard the presence of hydrogen as necessary to the formation of an acid, so that all acids are H., and anhydrous acids (such as sulphuric anhydride, SO_3) have no real existence. See ACIDS.

Hy'dragogues. See CATHARTICS.

Hydrang'ea, a genus of showy shrubs, giving name to a suborder of the *Saxifragaceæ.* The best-known species is *H. hortensis*, a Chinese plant introduced into Kew Garden towards the end of the last century by Sir Joseph Banks. In the S. and S.W. of England it thrives well in the open air, and in those parts claims the attention of the stranger by its luxuriance and handsome appearance in the gardens of both rich and poor. Its almost globular clusters of flowers nearly hide the branches and foliage, and are like an enlarged mass of blossom of the guelder-rose or snow-ball tree, but they vary in colour from white to pink and a peculiar blue shade. In the greenhouse it looks somewhat coarse.

Hy'drates are salts in which water plays the part either of the base or of the acid. For instance hydrated sulphuric acid is really a salt, with water as its base; for its formula (H_2SO_4) differs from sulphate of potash (K_2SO_4) in nothing except in the substitution of the base K_2O for H_2O. The name H. should be more properly restricted to those salts which result from the action of a base upon water, which here acts as an acid. The best known of these salts are hydrate of baryta (H_2BaO_2), and hydrate of lime or slaked lime (H_2CaO_2).

Hydrau'lics may be regarded as the practical aspect of hydrodynamics. It considers the construction of machines which depend for their action upon the motion or pressure of fluids, and is intimately concerned with the collection and transporting of fluids for useful ends. So wide and varied are its latter applications that it is impossible here to enter into these, which are better considered under such headings as Breakwaters, Canals, Docks, Harbours, Pumps, &c. As indicated above, machines which derive their motive power from fluid agency fall to be treated under two headings—according as they depend on fluid-motion or fluid-pressure. To the former class belong the waterwheel, turbine (see WATER-POWER), Barker's Mill, and the more modern inventions known as *hydraulic engines.* These do not differ in general construction from ordinary steam-engines—the really distinguishing feature being the use of water instead of steam to drive the piston-rod. There is little question that our greatest possible source of hydraulic power is to be found in the energy of the tides, but the difficulty of utilising this immense store of energy has yet to be overcome. Hydraulic machines of the other class, those which act through fluid pressure, have assumed within the last twenty or thirty years a great practical importance, especially in the working of apparatus for loading and unloading goods, and for closing and opening docks. The hydrostatic principle involved is that of the Hydrostatic Press (q. v.), by means of which it is practically possible to exert a pressure so enormous as to be beyond the strength of the strongest materials. A number of different cranes may thus be set in operation by being simply connected mechanically with a powerful press worked by means of an ordinary steam-engine.

Hy'drides are compounds of metals or salt radicals with hydrogen. Arseniureted hydrogen (AsH_3), and antimoniureted hydrogen (SbH_3) are both well-known gases. Marsh gas is sometimes spoken of as the hydride of methyl (CH_3H), and similarly with the higher series of saturated hydrocarbons.

Hydrocar'bons, formerly called carbo-hydrogens, are compounds of carbon and hydrogen, and are perhaps the most numerous and important of all the carbon compounds. The number of these bodies has gradually increased with the progress of chemical science, and at the present moment amounts to hundreds. Besides possessing considerable theoretical interest, the H. are of immense practical value. They are employed for illuminating purposes, as sources of a great many colouring matters, as solvents of fats, resins, &c., for lubricating machinery, and for a host of other purposes. The limits of this article prevent us from entering into a detailed description of these interesting bodies, and from showing how the existence of so many compounds of two elements can be accounted for. We must content ourselves with explaining the plan which has been adopted in their classification, at the same time pointing out a few of the most important properties of the leading groups.

The classification of the H. depends upon the relative proportion of carbon and hydrogen which they contain. In each series there is a definite relation between the number of carbon and hydrogen atoms contained in its different members, and this relation may be expressed by a formula. Thus in the series of paraffines, or saturated H., the number of hydrogen atoms which any member contains is equal to twice the number of carbon atoms, plus two. The formula expressive of this relation is $C_n H_{2n+2}$, in which n = the number of carbon atoms. Each member of this series differs from the preceding member by containing an atom more carbon and two atoms more hydrogen. Such a series is said to be *homologous*, and it will be observed that all the other series of H. are homologous. The different series of H. differ from one another in containing less and less hydrogen, the formulæ expressive of their composition showing that the quantity of hydrogen diminishes by two atoms in each case. If, instead of vertical columns, the lateral columns be examined, it will be seen that they consist of H. containing the same number of carbon atoms, but fewer and fewer hydrogen atoms. A series, each term of which differs from the preceding term by two atoms less hydrogen, is called an *isologous* series.

With regard to the nomenclature of the H., the system proposed by Hofmann is the simplest and most useful. In it a prefix indicates the number of carbon atoms, a vowel the number of hydrogen atoms.

Saturated Series. C_nH_{2n+2}. Paramnes.	Diatomic Series. C_nH_{2n}. Olefines.	Tetratomic Series C_nH_{2n-2}. Acetylenes.	C_nH_{2n-4}.	C_nH_{2n-6}. Benzol Series.
Methane, CH_4				
Ethane, C_2H_6	Ethene, C_2H_4	Ethine, C_2H_2		
Propane, C_3H_8	Propene, C_3H_6	Propine, C_3H_4		
Beutane, C_4H_{10}	Butene, C_4H_8	Butine, C_4H_6		
Pentane, C_5H_{12}	Pentene, C_5H_{10}	Pentine, C_5H_8	Pentone, C_5H_6	
Hexane, C_6H_{14}	Hexene, C_6H_{12}	Hexine, C_6H_{10}	Hexone, C_6H_8	Hexune, C_6H_6
Heptane, C_7H_{16}	Heptene, C_7H_{14}	Heptine, C_7H_{12}	Heptonel C_7H_{10}	Heptune, C_7H_8
Octane, C_8H_{18}	Octene, C_8H_{16}	Octine, C_8H_{14}	Octone, C_8H_{12}	Octune, C_8H_{10}
&c.	&c.	&c.	&c.	&c.

The above table contains the five most important groups of H. and a few of the more important members of each group, but besides the above there are a great many H. known, corresponding with groups containing very much less hydrogen. Thus styrol C_8H_8 belongs to a group the general formula of which is C^nH_{2n-8}. Napthalene $C_{10}H_8$ to one which is C_nH_{2n-12}. Whilst chrysene $C_{18}H_8$ is a hydrocarbon of a group containing so little hydrogen that its general formula is C_nH_{2n-24}. A little consideration will show that only H. containing many carbon atoms can belong to groups so poor in hydrogen. Thus it is obvious that no H. containing twelve atoms of carbon could belong to the series C_nH_{2n-24}. The nomenclature of the H. not contained in the above table has up to the present time been arbitrary.

Saturated Series of H. or Paraffines.—These are called saturated because they cannot combine with any element or group of elements directly; a fact which is owing to the complete saturation of all the atomicities of each carbon atom, partly by neighbouring carbon atoms, partly by hydrogen atoms, as will be seen from the graphic formula of methane (marsh gas), ethane, and propane. See 'Atomicity' in Art. CHEMISTRY.

```
     H             H  H            H  H  H
     |             |  |            |  |  |
  H—C—H        H—C—C—H        H—C—C—C—H
     |             |  |            |  |  |
     H             H  H            H  H  H
  Methane.        Ethane.         Propane.
```

They are, however, acted on by chlorine and bromine, giving rise to substances in which their hydrogen is gradually replaced by the haloid: thus—

$$\underbrace{CH_4}_{\text{Marsh gas.}} + \underbrace{Cl_2}_{\text{Chlorine.}} = \underbrace{CH_3Cl}_{\text{Chloride of methyl.}} + \underbrace{HCl}_{\text{Hydrochloric acid.}}$$

$$\underbrace{CH_3Cl}_{\text{Chloride of Methyl.}} + \underbrace{Cl_2}_{\text{Chlorine.}} = \underbrace{CH_2Cl_2}_{\text{Chloride of methylene.}} + \underbrace{HCl}_{\text{Hydrochloric acid.}}$$

$$\underbrace{CH_2Cl_2}_{\text{Chloride of methylene.}} + \underbrace{Cl_2}_{\text{Chlorine.}} = \underbrace{CHCl_3}_{\text{Chloroform.}} + \underbrace{HCl}_{\text{Hydrochloric acid.}}$$

$$\underbrace{CHCl_3}_{\text{Chloroform.}} + \underbrace{Cl_2}_{\text{Chlorine.}} = \underbrace{CCl_4}_{\text{Chloride of carbon.}} + \underbrace{HCl}_{\text{Hydrochloric acid.}}$$

Nearly all the members of this series have been obtained from American petroleum by fractional distillation. Solid paraffine consists of a mixture of the higher members. Marsh gas is formed by the gradual decomposition of vegetable matter in presence of water. The first four of the series are gaseous at ordinary temperatures, the next sixteen are liquids, and the remainder solids. A gradual increase is observed in their boiling points and specific gravity. They are employed practically for a great many purposes.

Diatomic Hydrocarbons or Olefines.—These have been obtained by the removal of water from alcohols of the series $C_nH_{2n+2}O$; thus—

$$CnH_{2n}O - H_2O = CnH_{2n}$$

$$\underbrace{C_2H_6O}_{\text{Ordinary alcohol.}} - \underbrace{H_2O}_{\text{Water.}} = \underbrace{C_2H_4}_{\text{Ethylene.}}$$

and by many other reactions. Some of them appear to occur in petroleum. Unlike the paraffines, they can combine directly with certain elements, especially with chlorine or bromine, forming products of addition; thus—

$$\underbrace{C_2H_4}_{\text{Ethylene.}} + \underbrace{Cl_2}_{\text{Chlorine.}} = \underbrace{C_2H_4Cl_2}_{\text{Chloride of ethylene or Dutch liquid.}}$$

The olefines do not possess any practical importance further than that one or two of them (Ethylene and Propylene) occur in coal-gas, and contribute in considerable measure to its illuminating properties.

Acetylene Series.—These H. have been chiefly obtained by the removal of hydrochloric or hydrobromic acid from the product of addition of chlorine or bromine with the olefines, by treating them with caustic potash dissolved in alcohol; thus—

$$\underbrace{C_2H_4Cl_2}_{\text{Chloride of ethylene.}} + \underbrace{2KHO}_{\text{Caustic potash.}} = \underbrace{2H_2O}_{\text{Water.}} + \underbrace{2KCl}_{\text{Chloride of potassium.}} + \underbrace{C_2H_2}_{\text{Acetylene.}}$$

They can combine with two or four atoms of chlorine and bromine; thus—

$$\underbrace{C_2H_2}_{\text{Acetylene (ethine).}} + \underbrace{Br_2}_{\text{Bromine.}} = \underbrace{C_2H_2Br_2}_{\text{Ditromide of acetylene.}}$$

$$\underbrace{C_2H_2}_{\text{Acetylene (ethine).}} + \underbrace{2Br_2}_{\text{Bromine.}} = \underbrace{CHBr}_{\text{Tetra-bromide of acetylene.}}$$

Acetylene occurs in small quantity in coal-gas, and is produced when various H. burn in a limited supply of air. The other members of the series are unimportant.

CnH_{2n-4} Series is unimportant, and but few of its members have been obtained. They are prepared by removal of hydrobromic acid (by alcoholic potash) from substances similar to dibromide of acetylene—

$$\underbrace{C_5H_8Br_2}_{\text{Dibromide of pentone.}} - \underbrace{2HBr}_{\text{Hydro-bromic acid.}} = \underbrace{C_5H_6}_{\text{Pentone.}}$$

Benzol Series.—This is perhaps the most important series of all the H., not only from the chemist's point of view, but to the world at large, as the compounds of benzol and its homologues are in many cases of the greatest practical importance. Most of the artificial colouring matters—the aniline and alizarine dyes—carbolic acid, and other valuable products, are derived from them.

Benzol and other H. of the series are produced when coal is distilled at a comparatively high temperature, as in the manufacture of coal-gas. They are separated from the tar which is produced by the process of fractional distillation. (See DISTILLATION.) It is remarkable that at a lower temperature than is employed in the distillation of coals for gas, little or none of the benzol series is produced, but principally the paraffines. Thus two distinct sets of products may be obtained at will from coal, each set possessing considerable practical importance. Benzol does not readily yield products of addition when treated with chlorine or bromine, nevertheless a compound $C_6H_6Cl_6$ has been obtained. The action of the haloid is usually to replace the hydrogen and yield products of substitution; thus—

$$\underbrace{C_6H_6}_{\text{Benzol.}} + \underbrace{Cl_2}_{\text{Chlorine.}} = \underbrace{C_6H_5Cl}_{\text{Chloride of phenyl.}} + \underbrace{HCl}_{\text{Hydro-chloric acid.}}$$

By continuing the chlorination, a body having the formula

C_6Cl_6 may be obtained. The H. of this series are remarkable for the readiness with which they yield nitro- and sulpho-derivatives when treated with nitric or sulphuric acids ; thus—

$$\underbrace{C_6H_6}_{\text{Benzol.}} + \underbrace{HNO_3}_{\text{Nitric acid.}} = \underbrace{C_6H_5(NO_2)}_{\text{Nitro-benzol.}} + \underbrace{H_2O}_{\text{Water.}}$$

$$\underbrace{C_6H_6}_{\text{Benzol.}} + \underbrace{H_2SO_4}_{\text{Sulphuric acid.}} = \underbrace{C_6H_5HSO_3}_{\text{Benzol-sulphonic acid.}} + \underbrace{H_2O}_{\text{Water.}}$$

The study of the benzol derivatives has added largely to the number of organic substances, and has opened up new fields of research and speculation. The properties of these substances are indeed of such a special character that they are usually considered as a separate group, to which the name of *aromatic bodies* has been given.

Hy'drocele (Gr. *hydōr*, 'water,' and *kēlē*, 'a swelling') is the medical term for dropsy of the tunica vaginalis, the serous membrane, or investing sac of the Testis (q. v.). H. may occur as the result of acute orchitis, but more commonly as a chronic disease. It begins with a swelling and sense of weight about the testis, the tumour becoming oval or pyriform in shape, smooth, and uniformly tense and hard, and often having a semi-elastic feeling. The most characteristic sign of H. is its translucency by transmitted light. The *palliative* treatment of H. consists in wearing a suspensory bandage, or in tapping with a fine trochar. The *curative* treatment has for its object the excitation of a sufficient degree of inflammation in the tunica vaginalis to restore the balance between secretion and absorption, and this is most effectually done by tapping, followed by the injection of the tincture of iodine through the canula into the tunica vaginalis.

Hydroceph'alus (Gr. *hydōr*, 'water,' and *kephalē*, 'the head'), or **Water in the Head**, is a disease of the brain resulting in an effusion of serous fluid between the membranes of the brain or within its ventricles. H. may be congenital, depending upon defective development or disease during fœtal life; or it may occur at some period in after-life, but most frequently during infancy, in an acute or chronic form. Effusion of serum into the ventricles or into the cavity of the arachnoid is generally accompanied by some lesion of the brain or of its membranes, so that H. is usually acute and inflammatory at its commencement. The fluid effused is sometimes very great, filling the whole cavity of the arachnoid as well as the ventricles, and the greater part is generally contained in the lateral ventricles, and in lesser quantity in the third and fourth ventricles, the effusion being frequently associated with tubercules in the brain or membranes. The form of the head (which is often enormously large) is sometimes very irregular, one side being much larger than the other, and the bones of the skull are very thin and transparent, the sutures being commonly separated from each other, at their superior portions, by a wide extent of membrane. The membranes are generally thickened, and the brain is sometimes so compressed, that but little of the organ remains. Acute H. is divided into three stages: (1) the stage of irritability; (2) that of diminished sensibility; and (3) that of convulsions or palsy. The *first stage* is generally preceded by giddiness and general constitutional disorder. Then the senses of sight and hearing become morbidly acute; the pupils are contracted or dilated, and the eyebrows are knit; there is great fretfulness of temper; the sleep is short and disturbed, and the patient wakens up with a scream, and complains of headache, the more prominent symptoms being those of *meningitis*. In the *second stage*, the child lies in a state of stupor, the eyes being half-closed, dull and heavy, sometimes staring or squinting, and the pupils are contracted or expanded. The patient utters shrill piercing screams, and the hands are tremulous, and engaged in picking the nose or mouth. In the *third stage*, the patient either sinks or recovers, and when the former is the case, the pulse becomes more frequent, the eye red and dim, and delirium, partial or general convulsions, or paralysis of one limb or one side, follow. The duration of the acute form of H. is about three weeks, each stage averaging about a week. In chronic H., when the disease is fully formed, whether it be congenital or not, the child is generally of feeble intellect, irascible, of extreme muscular debility, often epileptic, and either paralytic or scarcely able to walk. The remote causes of H. are often obscure, but they are principally referred to injuries of the head, inflammation of the ear, dentition, worms, the retrocession of cutaneous eruptions, the action of morbid poisons, as that of scarlet fever, pertussis, and measles; and of constitutional diseases, as tuberculosis and syphilis. The period of greatest liability to H. occurs between the second and fifth years. There is also a morbid state resembling H., called spurious H., or hydrocephaloid disease. Spurious H. occurs among children from a few months to two or three years of age, of a delicate constitution, or who have suffered from debilitating diseases, and is indicated by heaviness of the head, a remarkable expression of langour and drowsiness, the eyes being unattracted by any object put before them, and the pupils insensible to light. The disease is one of debility or atrophy. In *acute* and *chronic* H., where there is plethora, or inflammation, or an approach to inflammation, the surface of the fontanelle is convex and prominent; but in *spurious* H., where there is emptiness and want of support, the fontanelle is concave and depressed.

The chances of recovery are favourable during the first stage, if the treatment be judicious; but not so during the second stage. Blood-letting and active purgation have been said to yield the most satisfactory results; but the disease has been more successfully treated on the principles of hydrotherapia. Such cases, however, should be left to the care of a skilled physician only. The disease was first described by Dr. Whyte, *Observations on Dropsy in the Brain* (Edinb. 1768). See also *Diseases of Infancy and Childhood* by Dr. West (Lond. 1865).

Hydrocharid'eæ, an order of Monocotyledons, which takes its name from *Hydrocharis Morsus-ranæ*, the frog-bit, a rather pretty white-flowered floating aquatic, not uncommon in ponds and ditches in England, but not reaching N. into Scotland. Other genera of this order are anacharis, stratiotes and vallisneria.

Hydrochlo'rate of Ammo'nia, or **Sal Ammo'niac**, is employed in medicine as an expectorant in chronic bronchitis, and is useful in rheumatism, portal dropsy, hepatites, scrofulous, and syphilitic enlargements of the glands, and in facial neuralgia. A saturated solution applied to corns and warts removes them, and acts as a stimulant and resolvant in enlarged bursæ. Ten grains in a glassful of cold water, frequently repeated, allays fits of coughing.

Hydrochlo'ric Acid (HCl) is a compound of hydrogen and chlorine, which is gaseous under ordinary conditions. Its aqueous solution has long been known in the arts under the names of *muriatic acid* and *spirit of salt*. Chlorine and hydrogen, when mixed in equal volumes, unite with a violent explosion in direct sunlight to form two volumes of H. A. In diffuse daylight they combine gradually; and in darkness no combination takes place. Chlorine has so strong an affinity for hydrogen that it often abstracts that element from its compounds. Thus turpentine ($C_{10}H_{16}$) ignites in chlorine and burns with a sooty flame, depositing carbon and evolving H. A. Commercially H. A. is very cheap; and this is due to its being produced in immense quantities as a by-product in the manufacture of the carbonate of soda. (See SODA.) It is the direct result of the action of sulphuric acid upon common salt, the other product of the reaction being sulphate of soda, the preparation of which is a necessary preliminary in the manufacture of the carbonate.

Pure H. A. is a colourless gas. It may be liquefied under extreme pressure, but it has never yet been obtained in the solid condition. It has a strong affinity for water, one volume of which at 0° C. can absorb 400 volumes of the acid. When, as a gas, it is brought into contact with moist air, it absorbs the moisture and produces an evident cloud. A strong solution of H. A., if heated, evolves the gas until the solution contains 20·2 per cent. of the acid, when it distils over like a single liquid compound at a temperature of 110° C. On the other hand, a weak solution when heated loses water till the same strength is reached, and then distils over unchanged. The existence of this particular solution, which is known as 'H. A. of constant boiling-point,' suggests that it is a real chemical compound; but that it is not so is proved by the fact that the strength of H. A. of constant boiling-point varies with the pressure under which the solution is formed. H. A. is readily acted upon by certain metals, evolving hydrogen, and leaving behind the chloride of the metal. Zinc gives such a reaction. Again, when treated with certain metallic peroxides, H. A. produces the metallic chloride, water, and free chlorine. Thus Chlorine (q. v.) is ordinarily prepared by acting upon peroxide of manganese (MnO_2) with H. A.

Hydrochloric Acid is given medicinally in a very dilute form as a refrigerant, antiseptic, and tonic, and is applied, diluted with an equal quantity of water, to diphtheric patches in the throat. In cases of poisoning by H. A., the antidotes are chalk, magnesia, and emollient drinks.

Hydrocot'yle, a genus of *Umbellifera*, of which the best-known species is *H. vulgaris*, a very common British plant in marshes and boggy ground, and is popularly known as marsh pennywort, from its round leaves, or white rot, from its supposed injury to sheep. The genus numbers about seventy species, distributed through the temperate and tropical regions of the world.

Hydrocyan'ic or **Prussic Acid** (HCN) is a compound of carbon, hydrogen, and nitrogen, discovered by Scheele in 1782. It may be prepared pure by passing sulphuretted hydrogen (H_2S) over dry cyanide of mercury ($Hg(CN)_2$), maintained at a temperature of from 30° to 40° C. Sulphide of mercury (HgS) is left behind, and H. A. passes off in a state of vapour, and is condensed to a liquid in a U-shaped tube surrounded by a freezing mixture. Acetylene (C_2H_2) and nitrogen when mixed and fired by an electric spark also produce H. A. The pure substance is a colourless liquid at ordinary temperatures; it boils at 26°·5 C., and solidifies to a crystalline solid at 15° C. Its vapour burns with a violet flame. H. A. mixes with water in all proportions, but seems to form with it a compound having a definite chemical constitution represented by the formula $2HCN,3H_2O$. Whether pure or in solution, it tends of itself to decompose, especially under the action of light, depositing a brown substance. This action may be hindered by addition of a minute quantity of a mineral acid. The dilute aqueous solution employed in medicine is prepared by distilling a mixture of water, ferrocyanide of potassium, and sulphuric acid, when sulphate of potassium, ferrocyanide of potassium and iron, and H. A. result. Solution of H. A. is feebly acid, but acts upon oxide of mercury (HgO) to produce cyanide of mercury and water. By chemists, H. A. is regarded as a true hydracid (see HYDRACIDS), containing hydrogen united to a group of elements (CN) called Cyanogen (q. v.). The metallic cyanides resemble in constitution the haloid salts (chlorides, bromides, &c.), exactly as H. A. resembles the acids. Under its more popular name of prussic acid it is well known as a deadly and violent poison. Great caution is therefore necessary in experimenting with it even when it is in solution, since the inhalation of its vapour in very small quantity is sufficient to cause giddiness and headache. No real antidotes are known, but the usual remedies are ammonia and chlorine, which appear to act by exciting the nervous system.

Hydrocyanic Acid is employed medicinally as a sedative and antispasmodic in cases of vomiting, gastrodynia, and in dyspeptic palpitation. It is used externally as a lotion or ointment to allay itching of the skin; and, as a vapour, it is sometimes applied to the eye, or inhaled. In cases of poisoning, the antidotes are exposure to air currents, artificial respiration, and cold affusions. Freshly precipitated oxide of iron, with an alkaline carbonate, should also be given.

Hydrodynam'ics is the branch of dynamical science which treats of the motions and equilibrium of a material system, part or all of which is fluid. It may be thus said to investigate, on the one hand, the conditions of equilibrium of a fluid mass, and of a rigid system immersed in fluid; and, on the other hand, the motions of fluids in fluids or in confined channels, and the motions of solids through fluids. The subject naturally then divides into two parts, according as the system under consideration is or is not in equilibrium.

1. *Hydrostatics.*—In establishing the fundamental principles of hydrostatics, it is necessary to define what is strictly meant by a *fluid*. A *perfect* fluid is an unrealisable conception, and is defined as a body incapable of resisting a change of shape. It can therefore experience no tangential stress; and accordingly the pressure which the fluid exerts on any surface, whether of a solid or of a contiguous portion of the fluid, is at every point perpendicular to the surface. It is almost self-evident that, if a material system be in equilibrium, we may suppose any portion of that system to become rigid and fixed without destroying the equilibrium. Keeping this consideration in view, imagine the fluid to be contained in a closed vessel, and to be wholly uninfluenced by external force, such as gravity. The resultant pressure of the fluid upon any portion of a spherical surface must pass through the centre of the sphere, because each component pressure does so. Suppose, then, a portion of the fluid in the form of a plano-convex lens to be solidified. Since the resultant pressure on the convex side must equal the resultant in the plane side, the latter must pass through the centre of the sphere of which the convex surface is a part, and must therefore, being perpendicular to the plane, pass through the centre of the circular area. The resultant pressure accordingly on any circular area of a plane surface passes through the centre, and therefore the pressure is the same at all points of a plane. Hence the resultant pressure on any plane surface passes through its centre of inertia. Now, consider the pressures upon the bounding planes of a triangular prism. The three resultant pressures evidently act in a plane cutting the prism at right angles. If we draw the triangle of section, we may represent the pressures by lines perpendicular to the sides of the triangle at their middle points. They must accordingly meet in a point, and being in equilibrium, must be proportional to the lengths of their respective sides, *i.e.*, to the breadth, and therefore area, of the faces of the prism. Hence the resultant pressures on the faces are proportional to the areas of the faces, and therefore the pressure is the same in any two planes that meet. Summing up our results, it appears that the pressure is the same at every point of the fluid, when the pressure is dependent only on the pressure exerted by the enclosing vessel. If external forces act upon the fluid, the pressure will be the same in all directions at any one point, but will vary continuously from point to point. Thus, when gravity is the force to be considered, and the fluid incompressible of density ρ, the increase of pressure per unit of length as we descend is, in kinetic units $g\rho$, where g represents the force of gravity. The pressure is obviously the same along any horizontal plane; in other words, the surfaces of *equal pressure* are horizontal planes. If equilibrium exists under the action of any forces which constitute a conservative system (see ENERGY), the surfaces of equal pressure are coincident with the surfaces of equal density, and are everywhere perpendicular to the lines of resultant force; and indeed equilibrium cannot exist except this latter condition be fulfilled.

If a solid be immersed in a fluid, it will sink or float according as it is specifically heavier or lighter than the fluid. According to the principle of Archimedes, any body which is kept immersed loses in weight, and this loss is exactly equal to the weight of the fluid displaced, in other words, to the weight of the quantity of fluid equal in volume to the immersed body. Accordingly, a body will weigh less in a heavier fluid than in a lighter, a principle which affords an easy method of comparing the specific gravities of different fluids. If the immersed body be lighter specifically than the surrounding, it will have, so to speak, a *negative* weight, and will tend to rise. If the fluid be incompressible, the body will rise to the free surface and float there; and if the fluid be elastic, the body will rise till it becomes, bulk for bulk, of the same weight as the surrounding fluid. That point in a body at which the resultant hydrostatic pressure may be supposed to act is called the centre of pressure; and the discussion of its position is most important when we come to treat of the equilibrium of solids and fluids. Suppose a body to be floating at the surface of a liquid; it is buoyed up by the upward pressure of the liquid, which is equal and opposite to the downward weight of the body: the body is then in equilibrium under the action of two forces—the weight of the body acting downwards at its centre of gravity, and the pressure of the liquid acting upwards through the centre of pressure. For a position of equilibrium, then, these two centres must lie in the same vertical line. If they happen to coincide, the body may float in any position whatsoever. If they do not coincide, the only position of stable equilibrium is that position which brings the centre of gravity vertically *below* the centre of pressure. To make this clear, suppose the centre of gravity to be the higher; there will be, of course, equilibrium when the two are in the same vertical line, but the equilibrium will be essentially unstable. For consider the effect of a minute rotation of the body round a horizontal axis, perpendicular to the line joining the centres (this instantaneous centre of rotation is called the *metacentre*), and the motion, however slight, will call into action a couple, which will tend to turn the body *away* from its former position, which is, therefore, one of unstable equilibrium. If the centre of gravity be below the centre of pressure, a similar minute displacement will, it is true, call into action a couple; but this couple will tend to bring the body *back* to its old position, which is, therefore, one of stable equilibrium. Accordingly, it is of importance in the building of ships to put the centre of gravity as low as possible. See EQUILIBRIUM.

Under the statics of fluids must also be included the theorems relating to surfaces of equilibrium in rotating masses of fluid. For instance, if a mass of liquid contained in a rigid cylindrical box be set in rotation round its axis of figure, the surfaces of equal pressure under the action of gravity are no longer planes, but paraboloids of revolutions with their vertices pointing downwards; so that at the free surface, if there be one, the liquid will appear concave. The most important problem in this connection, and one whose general solution has not yet been attempted, is to find all the forms of equilibrium which a mass of homogeneous incompressible fluid, held together by the mutual gravitation of its parts, and rotating with uniform angular velocity, may assume. Newton and Maclaurin discovered that an oblate ellipsoid of revolution was such a form—the angular velocity for a given eccentricity being proportional to the square root of the density. Another form, as first discovered by Jacobi in 1834, is an ellipsoid with three unequal axes, of which the least is the axis of rotation. These problems derive their great interest from their evidently close connection with the figure of the earth, and they have engaged the attention of the most profound mathematicians of the last two centuries.

2. *Hydrokinetics.*—As long as we confined ourselves to problems of equilibrium, there was no danger in regarding all fluids as satisfying the definition of a perfect fluid. But in problems of fluid-motion it is otherwise. All fluids are *viscous*, and therefore resist more or less a change of shape. This viscosity is very different for different liquids, a fact which may be at once seen by comparing the properties of such liquids as tar or treacle with those of water or ether. The latter are what are known as mobile liquids, and in their motions they most nearly approach the ideal incompressible fluid. If a jet of water be projected into the air, each particle will travel as any other projectile would. If we neglect the resistance of the air, or project the jet *in vacuo*, the path which each particle describes will be a parabola, and therefore the continuous stream of water will assume a parabolic form. The dimensions of this parabola will depend upon the velocity of projection and the angle of elevation. (See PROJECTILES.) If the jet be projected horizontally, the vertex of the parabola will be at the origin of the jet; and if it be projected vertically, the parabola will become in theory a straight line. Practically, however, the mutual collisions of the particles and the physical impossibility for one material current to travel opposite to and in the same course as another, necessitate the spreading out of the water on all sides as it reaches its highest limit. The best method of producing a steady stream of water is to provide a vessel with an orifice near its base, through which the water is pushed by the pressure of the column in the vessel. If the orifice be small, we may consider the kinetic energy of the issuing stream to be equal to the loss of potential energy of the whole due to the depression of the free surface. Hence the velocity with which an incompressible fluid escapes from a small orifice is the same as would be acquired by falling from the free surface to the level of the orifice. If the stream be then projected vertically upwards, it will rise almost to the height of the free surface, and this is the principle upon which all our artificial fountains are constructed. If the orifice be simply a hole in the side of the vessel, it is evident that the issuing stream is made up of innumerable streams in the liquid inside the vessel converging towards the orifice. This produces as a first effect the continuous contraction of the stream for some little distance beyond the orifice—a contraction which is more rapid the nearer the section is to the orifice. The direct dynamical effect of this contraction is the increased velocity of the issuing jet; and thus is explained the greater velocity, which experiment shows the jet to have, than is indicated by the theory given above. It is a question of great practical moment as to how the efflux of water will be affected if the issuing stream, instead of being projected into the air, is carried along a pipe of given form and dimensions. If a stream of fluid travel along a tube, completely filling it at every section, at the surface of contact friction comes strongly into play, so that the fluid in the centre necessarily moves fastest. Consequently in every fluid which is moving in a prescribed path there is a kind of *shearing* motion (see STRAIN), so that particles originally in a straight line are no longer so, but lie on a hyperbolic-shaped curve which points with its vertex in the direction of motion of the fluid. Rivers, currents, winds, all show this peculiarity, but in none can it be so well remarked as in Glaciers (q. v.).

Passing to the consideration of the motion of solids in fluids, it is evident first of all that a solid moving in a perfect fluid would experience no resistance. The resistance which experiment shows us to exist in all such cases is due then to the imperfection of our fluids—in other words, to their *viscosity*. Resistance in itself has no existence. It is merely a convenient term for a transformation of some of the kinetic energy of the moving solid into a less evident form. The solid in moving through the fluid must do work in altering the relative positions of the fluid particles, since the fluid is not perfect; and this alteration may so take place as to result in the formation of currents, eddies, and waves, the energy of whose motions, together with the amount of heat evolved, will of course be the equivalent of the kinetic energy lost by the solid. This introduces us at once to the more abstruse questions of waves and eddies. The former are treated more fully under their special heading, and the latter under VORTEX. At the meeting of the British Association in 1876, Professor Osborne Reynolds gave most valuable information regarding the relation of vortex-motion to solids moving through liquids. Helmholtz showed that vortex-motion could neither be created nor destroyed in a perfect fluid—so that if it once existed, it must exist for ever, and if it did not exist at any instant, it never could exist. Inasmuch as our fluids are imperfect, vortex-motion can be easily produced, and indeed is always a result of a displacement such as that occasioned by the motion of a solid through a liquid. One of Reynolds's many beautiful results is that a body shaped like a watchglass, convex on the one side and concave on the other, will, if wholly immerged in water, move with less resistance when its concave side is directed forward than when its convex side is. This result is at first so antagonistic to all preconceived ideas of the relation existing between the form of a body and the resistance offered to it, that it merits a closer attention. When a vortex-ring is directed fairly against a disc-shaped solid, which is immerged in the fluid, and whose plane is perpendicular to the direction of motion of the vortex ring, it will carry the disc along with it. But the disc by its own motion may be made to generate a vortex ring which will follow in the wake of the disc. Now in the case of the watchglass-shaped body, a more perfect vortex ring is generated by the body when its concavity is first, and this ring travels exactly at the same rate as the body. When the convexity is first, the vortex ring is not so perfectly formed as above, and lags behind, so that the body is forced to throw off another vortex ring, which behaves precisely as the former, and necessitates the formation of a third. The kinetic energy of the body is thus gradually used up in generating a succession of vortex rings; and accordingly the body comes to rest sooner than in the other case, where one vortex ring was formed once for all. The true nature of the phenomena which occur in the motion of a solid through a fluid is still very imperfectly understood, but there can be little doubt that the theory of vortex motion as elaborated by Professors Helmholtz and Sir W. Thomson must henceforth have a most important bearing upon the further elucidation of the science. Many facts and experiments have necessarily been omitted in such an article as the present, but these may be obtained from any good ordinary text-book on physics. The principles of hydrostatics are established in a lucid and elementary manner in Thomson and Tait's *Natural Philosophy*, where also are given the usual mathematical formulæ which apply to a fluid system in equilibrium.

Hy'dro-Fluo'ric Acid. See FLUORINE.

Hy'drogen, one of the chemical constituents of water, was first recognised as an element by Cavendish in 1766. By acting upon metals with dilute acids he obtained a gas which was capable of burning in air, and which he accordingly named 'inflammable air' or gas. Later, when its properties had been more thoroughly investigated, it was discovered that its combustion resulted in the production of water—hence its present name *H.* (Gr. 'water-producing'). The gas is also obtained native, but in small quantity, as an emanation from the earth in Tuscany and Iceland. It exists, however, in vast quantities in the chromosphere of the sun and other stars—being the principal constituent of the coloured flames or prominences which have of late years been so fully studied. (See SUN.) In combination with other metals it occurs constantly on our globe, not only in water, but as an important element in all organic compounds. It may be obtained by analysis from water in three distinct ways —by *electrolytic action*, when H. is given off at the negative pole (see ELECTROLYSIS); by *dissociation* of the vapour of water into its components by passing it through a red hot iron tube, when the iron absorbs the oxygen and lets the H. go free; and by the *chemical action* of certain metals, such as sodium and potassium, which have a strong affinity for oxygen. Practically, H. is prepared by the action of a dilute solution of a strong acid (such as sulphuric or hydrochloric) upon a metal, usually iron or zinc—the metal and the H. changing places. Thus, sulphuric acid acting on zinc produces sulphate of zinc and free H.

H. is a colourless inodorous gas, which has never yet been obtained in the liquid state. It is the lightest known substance, 11·16 litres weighing only 1 gramme at ordinary temperature and pressure; while the same volume of air weighs 14·49 grammes. By chemists, accordingly, the H. atom has been taken as the unit with which to compare the atomic weights of the other elements. If two volumes of H. be mixed with one volume of oxygen, no combination takes place; but by the application of a flame or the passage of an electric spark, a sharp explosion ensues, and water is formed. This formation of water by synthesis may be represented by the equation

$$2H_2 + O_2 = 2H_2O$$

which indicates that for every three volumes of the mixture two volumes of steam at the temperature of combustion are formed. If a jet of H. be burned in oxygen, a very intense heat results, which has been utilised as a source of light in the oxyhydrogen or Drummond Light (q. v.), and as an agent for fusing and melting platinum. Further, the strong affinity of H. for oxygen renders it a powerful reducing agent, a property which is made use of in the reduction of metallic oxides. Under the influence of sunlight, H. combines directly with chlorine to form Hydrochloric Acid (q. v.). In combination with carbon, or with carbon and oxygen, it forms innumerable compounds and groups of compounds (see ALCOHOL, FATS, HYDROCARBONS, OILS, &c.), which are of great practical importance. In many of its actions H. strongly resembles a metal; and indeed its compounds, which are commonly called acids, may be regarded as *salts* in which H. plays the part of the metal. Thus, sulphuric acid (H_2SO_4) may be regarded as sulphate of H., corresponding to the sulphates of potassium, sodium, &c. H. forms with oxygen another compound, *Peroxide of H.*, which has the formula H_2O_2. It is prepared by passing a stream of carbonic anhydride through peroxide of barium (BaO_2) suspended in water, when carbonate of barium and peroxide of H. result. It is a peculiarly unstable compound, liquid at ordinary temperature, and decomposing into water and oxygen. The presence of gold, silver, or platinum hastens this decomposition without the metal itself experiencing any change; while, if the oxide of one of these metals is employed, the decomposition of the peroxide of H. is accompanied by the decomposition of the metallic oxide.

Hydrog'raphy (Gr. *hydōr*, 'water,' and *graphē*, 'description') is that branch of physical geography which describes the oceans, seas, and rivers, with their physical phenomena. It takes particular account of the configuration of the land and sea, of soundings, currents, islands, shoals, &c.; includes the construction of charts and maps; and is consequently of inestimable service to the navigator. In all important maritime nations, hydrographers are Government officials. In Britain the chief hydrographer is usually a retired captain in the navy.

Hy'dromancy (Gr. *hydōr*, 'water' and *manteia*, 'divination'), a kind of divination by means of radiations from water or from bright objects thrown into it. It was practised by the Romans, and, according to Varro, originated among the Persians.

Hydroma'nia. See PELLAGRA and SUICIDE.

Hydrom'eter, the name now universally given to instruments for measuring the specific gravities of liquids, the principles of the construction of which are described under AREOMETER.

Hy'dromys, a genus of Rodents, represented by the *H. chrysogaster* or beaver rat of Van Diemen's Land. This animal swims and dives with great facility. Its colour is a rich brown, tinted with golden lines on the under parts, sides, and shoulders. The tip of the tail is white. The body is long, and the total length of the animal is about 2 feet. The hind feet are webbed. The teeth include two incisors, two premolars, and two molars in each jaw.

Hydrop'athy, or **Hydrother'apy** (Gr. *hydōr*, 'water,' and *therapeia*, 'care,' or 'cure;' hence popularly termed the 'water-cure'), a system of practical medicine in which the applications of water, in combination with general hygienic measures, are chiefly relied upon in the treatment of disease. Water has been prescribed, externally and internally, by physicians from the remotest times as a therapeutic agent in the treatment of acute and chronic diseases, but it was not till the beginning of the present century that the various modes of application were reduced to a system by Vincent Priessnitz, a Silesian farmer, the father of the present system of H. Priessnitz was not an educated physician, and could not understand the philosophy of his own practice; so that both he and his immediate followers ran into numerous extravagancies by endeavouring to construct a new system of universal medicine, based upon an imperfect and incomplete system of physiology and pathology, instead of professing to institute only a system of hygienic medicine. In consequence of the absurd pretensions and mistaken zeal of the early advocates of H., the progress of the practice was much retarded; but hydrotherapy is now admitted to its proper place in therapeutics as a valuable aid to nature's strivings after health—the *vis medicatrix naturæ*.

A certain quantity of water or fluid aliment is necessary for digestion, and for the metamorphosis of tissues, whether it be physiological or pathological, and water, in larger quantity, promotes the functional activity of the kidneys, and the cutaneous transpiration, increasing the excretion of urea, chloride of sodium and phosphoric acid. The intense craving for cold water, in certain forms of disease, is an expression of nature regarding rapid tissue-changes taking place in the system, the extraction of the fluid constituents of the blood or tissues, or an abnormal increase in their solid constituents; and the barbarous system of forbidding water, in such cases, not only retarded the cure, but imperilled the patient's life. Water should be administered freely, but not in very large quantities at a time, in every case of illness in which great thirst is experienced.

The physiological effects of the external application of cold and hot water have been described in the article Bath (q. v.), but there are certain forms of baths frequently had recourse to in hydrotherapia which may be briefly described. Instead of the warm or hot bath, the vapour of water in the form of the Turkish Bath (q. v.), or the steam bath is frequently used, and similar objects may be attained by means of the warm or hot wet-packing. The *Turkish bath* consists in the exposure of the body in suitable apartments to the vapour of hot water at a temperature gradually increased from 96° to 140° Fahr. The bath should not exceed fifteen minutes in duration, and should be followed by the cold or shower bath conjoined with friction. When special arrangements are not available, the same end may be attained by causing the patient to sit on a low stool with a blanket pinned about his neck, and under this the vapour of water may be conducted, or generated by means of a spirit lamp. The *warm* or *hot wet-packing* is applied by enveloping the body, or some part of it, in cloths wrung out of hot water, and then covering with blankets, a mode of applying moist heat which may be advantageously used. The *cold wet-pack* consists in wrapping the body in a linen sheet wrung out in cold water, blankets being afterwards wrapped round the body of the patient. When reaction is fully established, the wet-pack should be removed, and the body well rubbed with dry towels. When active diaphoresis is desired, the patient must be well enveloped in blankets, and remain within them for an hour or more. The *wet-pack* may be applied with water at any degree of temperature. The *rubbing wet-pack* consists in enveloping the body with a sheet dipped in cold water, and rubbing vigorously with the sheet to induce reaction quickly, the skin being afterwards dried by means of coarse towels. The *douche* consists in the impact against the body of a column of water from a height which should not be greater than 10 feet, the column not being larger than 4 inches. It may be applied by means of a pitcher or water-bucket, or by a hose attached to a water-pipe, and, in the latter case, it may be applied in any direction, and the effect may be regulated by the size of the stream and the force with which it is thrown against the part. There are various local baths, such as the sitz-bath, the uses of which are indicated by their names.

The applications of water in the treatment of disease are numerous and important, but it should be always remembered that the advocates of H. profess to do nothing more than aid the *vis medicatrix naturæ.* To do so effectually, however, implies a complete knowledge of physiology and pathology, as well as a discriminating knowledge of the symptoms of disease, otherwise the reparative processes of nature may be ignorantly retarded, and with fatal results. Modes of treatment which might be of great benefit to one person might be fatal to another through carelessness or an error in diagnosis.

The following are some of the diseases which have been treated successfully on hydropathic principles. *Tonsillitis, diphtheria,* and *spasmodic croup,* may be greatly benefited by the topical application of ice to the fauces, by the wet-pack to the neck, or by cold affusions. Habitual constipation may be overcome, sometimes, by the use of cold water before breakfast, and bleeding hæmorrhoids by a daily rectal injection of cold water. Pure water is an effective diuretic in *acute desquamative nephritis,* and the internal use of water may be supplemented by hot water fomentations to the lumbar region. The Turkish bath is of great service in cases of *chronic muscular rheumatism,* and stiffness, the result of *acute rheumatism. Lead, mercurial,* and *paludal cachexia,* are relieved by the Turkish bath and the wet-pack, and, in such cases, free diaphoresis should be encouraged. The treatment of *fevers* by means of cold baths has been recently revived and extensively practised. The fever patient is put into a bath about the normal temperature of the body (98° Fahr.), and the water is cooled by the addition of ice to 80° Fahr. or even to 40° Fahr., according to the effect produced on the temperature of the body, which, for this purpose, should be taken in the rectum. When a positive reduction of the fever heat has occurred, the patient should be wiped dry, placed in bed, and covered with blankets. The bath may be used from two to six times each day, and for from five minutes to half-an-hour. The appliances for administering baths to fever patients are—a strong sheet for lifting the patient into the bath tub, a bath and clinical thermometer for noting the variations of the temperature of the water and body. In such cases the wet-packing, although not so efficacious as the bath, may be used as a powerful means of reducing fever heat. Some practitioners administer the baths regularly in cases of enteric fever, at six A.M., one to three P.M., and seven P.M. By this mode of treatment the mortality is said to be less, and the complications fewer, excepting hæmorrhage, than by other modes of treatment. H. thus applied is of great advantage in the *hyperpyrexia* of *acute rheumatism, delirium tremens, fevers,* &c., and also in *typho-malarial fever.* Scarlatina, measles, smallpox, cerebro-spinal meningitis, are advantageously treated in the same way, or by means of the cold or hot wet-pack. The wet-packing is efficacious in *acute rheumatism,* and the Turkish bath in chronic rheumatism and gout. In *acute cerebral congestion* the cold douche may be applied to the head, or a piece of ice to the nape of the neck, while the feet are immersed in warm water. The same line of treatment is of value in *inflammatory affections* of the meninges, *meningeal hæmorrhage, sunstroke* or *thermic fever,* where the range of temperature is very high, and also in *delirium tremens,* when there is no great depression of the bodily powers; but in cases where there are symptoms of atheroma of the cerebral arteries, or of cardiac disease, the treatment is of doubtful utility, and in some cases may cause mischief. Bucknill and Tuke recommend the shower bath in cases of *intercurrent mania* and *monomania,* and in *melancholia,* and the warm bath at 95° Fahr. to subdue the excitement and sleeplessness of various forms of insanity. *Lesions of the spinal meninges* and of the *cord* are remediable by similar means. In *inflammatory affections of the chest* the hot wet-pack diminishes the pain and relieves the inflammation, and hot or cold applications may be used by means of spongio-piline. Ice bags to the chest and back is of great utility in pulmonary hæmorrhage, in *inflammatory affections of the abdominal organs, strangulated hernia, hæmorrhoids, bubo,* and *swelled testicle;* and cold water, by means of injections, are of great utility in *uterine* hæmorrhage, and hot water, in cases of *chronic metritis.* See *Principles and Practice of the Water Cure,* by Dr. James Wilson; the works of Dr. Edward Johnson; and also Dr. Lane's treatise, *H. or Hygienic Medicine;* and for more recent information see *Beobachtungen und Versuche über die Andwendung des kalten Wassers bei fieberhaften Krankhaften,* by Professor Liebermeister (Leips. 1868); Ziemssen's *Cyclopædia,* vol. i.; *Handbuch der allgemeinen und speciellen Balneotherapie,* by Dr. Valentiner, 1873; *Observations on the Treatment of Hyperpyrexia,* by Dr. Wilson Fox; *Lancet,* vol. ii. 1871, p. 231 *et seq.*

Hydropho'bia (Gr. *hydōr,* 'water,' and *phobos,* 'fear'), a disease produced in the human species by the inoculation of a specific poison derived from animals of the canine or feline race while suffering from *rabies.* The saliva or secretion issuing from the mouth of the diseased animal is the medium of inoculation, either through a wound or a thin epidermis without abrasion, and there is no case on record in which the disease has ever originated *de novo* in man. H., the most distressing disease to which man is subject, is fortunately of rare occurrence in this country, so much so, indeed, that its very existence has been doubted by some, who have ascribed death, in such cases, to the influence of morbid imagination. Rabies is extremely rare, even among dogs, and there can be no manner of doubt that it is communicable to man; but it does not follow that every person bitten by a dog suffering from rabies is seized with H. The specific virus may not be excreted, or it may be so in small quantity, or it may not be present on that portion of the teeth by which the bite is inflicted; so that a dog suffering from rabies may not communicate the disease to those bitten by it, or it may communicate it to one or more, according to the circumstances under which the wound is inflicted. Hitherto rabies in the dog and its analogue H. in man, has been much more common in France, Germany, Italy, and Holland than in Great Britain, but within recent years cases of H. have been on the increase in this country. In 1866 there were thirty-six deaths from H. in England, and none in Scotland; but in the twelve years 1855–66 there were twelve cases in Scotland, and within a few months, in 1876–77, four cases of H. terminated fatally in the city of Glasgow alone, the disease being marked by the well-known characteristic symptoms. H. appears generally in an epidemic form, but its distribution is always in a direct ratio with the prevalence of *rabies* among the canine species. From 1800 till 1860 no case of H. had occurred in Dresden; but in 1863 ten cases were known to have occurred throughout Saxony, coincident with the appearance of *rabies.* In 1864 there were 33 cases, in 1865, 227, in 1866, 287, and in 1867, 250. Preventive measures were then adopted, and the epidemic subsided. In 1867, owing to the public alarm which had been excited in this country, a 'Metropolitan Street Act' was passed, which enabled the police to seize all vagrant dogs, and in July 1871 an 'Act to provide further protection against dogs' was passed, the Act being applicable to Great Britain and Ireland. The wound inflicted by the bite generally heals readily, there being nothing in its appearance, during the healing process, to distinguish it from an ordinary dog-bite, nor do any constitutional effects immediately supervene, the poison lying dormant or latent in the system. It is probable that during the period of latency, which may vary from a few weeks to several months, the *materies morbi* is gradually undergoing some development, and increasing in quantity, and that the result of this growth and development is the morbid symptoms manifested in the nervous centres. If this hypothesis be correct, the great variation in the period of latency may be accounted for, as such changes may be produced more rapidly in one subject than in another. As a general rule, the constitutional symptoms do not appear earlier than the fortieth day after inoculation, and rarely after two years; but cases are on record of their occurrence on the day following the injury, and extreme cases, after an interval of five and even nine years. The period of incubation of the specific poison of H. is therefore indefinite.

The earliest symptom of H. is pain, or some unusual sensation, such as aching, tingling, burning, coldness, numbness or stiffness in the cicatrix, which generally swells, becomes of a red or livid colour, and sometimes opens up afresh, discharging a thick ichorous fluid instead of pus. This local change is accompanied with general nervous disturbance, the patient becoming dejected, morose, irritable, restless, and sleepless; there is usually great intolerance of bright and sudden light, currents of cold air, the sudden appearance of strangers, and pains in various parts of the body are experienced. After the continuance of these symptoms for an indefinite period, stiffness or tightness is experienced in the throat, swallowing, especially of liquids, is accomplished with difficulty, and rigors supervene. As the disease advances, swallowing excites the most painful spasms in the back part of the throat, and the indescribably painful sensations which ensue cause the patient to dread the very sight or thought of liquids, although intense thirst may be experienced, and hence the designation of the disease, H., or 'water-fear.' These prominent symptoms are accompanied with nervous paroxysms, sensations of stricture or oppression about the throat and chest, painful and embarrassed breathing, a peculiar sighing and sobbing movement, a sense of impending suffocation, and most markedly, a horribly violent convulsion or spasm of the muscles of the larynx and pharynx, preventing swallowing, and retarding the entrance of air to the windpipe. Shuddering tremors, resembling general convulsions, agitate the body, and there is always, at intervals, a fearful expression of anxiety, terror, or despair, which once seen, can never be forgotten. There is seldom any disturbance of the intellectual faculties; but some or other of the special senses are frequently morbidly acute. Paroxysms are brought on by the slightest causes, such as the sound of water poured from one vessel to another, a current of cold air, or any cold substance applied to the body; the sight of liquids or the shining surface of a mirror; the suggestion of ideas connected with swallowing, or the recollection of sufferings experienced in former attempts. In H. there are frequently hallucinations of sight and of hearing, hyperæsthesia of the skin, exaltation of the senses, and satyriasis and nymphomania are occasionally present. A copious secretion of a viscid tenacious mucus in the fauces—'the hydrophobic slaver,'—is another characteristic symptom. The mouth is often full of mucus, which flows from its corners, or which the patient spits out upon everything around him, as if the dread of swallowing it induced an instant and eager expulsive effort. Although general incoherence is very unusual, there are frequently paroxysms of mental excitement approaching to insanity, but entirely distinct in their essential features from an attack of acute mania. Not unfrequently the patient is aware of the approach of these attacks, and, being fearful of the loss of self-control, begs to be restrained; but it is in comparatively rare instances that he gives way to wild fury, and the desire to bite is rare. Cases of general maniacal excitement do occur, characterised by outbursts of extreme violence and fury, followed by a state of listless gloom, dejection, and apathy. The disease generally terminates fatally between the second and fifth day, though it sometimes runs on to the seventh, eighth, or ninth day. Death most commonly takes place with well-marked symptoms of asphyxia, due to convulsions of the respiratory muscles, but, in some cases, it occurs as a consequence of complete exhaustion, or as a result of paralysis. Death has been the inevitable termination of H. in every well-authenticated case. Although H. is obviously connected with disorder of the nerve centres, no notable alteration in the minute structure of the brain and nerve tissues has, until very recently, been detected. In 1872 Dr. Clifford Allbut examined specimens taken from the central convolutions, the central ganglia, the medulla oblongata, and the spinal cord, and found the following morbid conditions, but in different degrees, present in all: (1) Great vascular congestion, with transudation into the surrounding tissues. In the grey centres the vessels were distended, their walls thickened, and here and there were seen patches of nuclear proliferation. There was diminished consistence, especially of the medulla. (2) Hæmorrhages, and in many places a refracting material outside the vessels, due apparently to exudations. (3) Little gaps caused by the disappearance of nerve strands, which had passed through granular disintegration. In 1877 Dr. Joseph Coats of Glasgow made microscopic examinations of the cicatrix, and of portions of the cord and medulla oblongata. In the former he found the skin and fat infiltrated with round cells, and transparent globular bodies, like drops of exuded fluid, on the internal walls of the vessels; and in the latter he found accumulations of round cells in the perivascular spaces of the medium-sized vessels, and similar cells around the ganglion cells, and in all parts of the system there were numerous amyloid bodies. These appearances are evidence of great irritation of the central nervous system, and also of parts near the cicatrix, the irritation being probably due to the specific virus introduced. Professor Maurice Benedikt describes somewhat similar appearances, certain of which he ascribes to the transformation of the red corpuscles of the blood. See *Rabies and H.*, by G. Fleming (Lond. 1872); *The Lancet* (Lond. February and March, 1877); *Virchow's Archiv.* (1876).

Hydrophylla'ceæ, an order of herbs, shrubs, and trees, chiefly natives of North America, of which about eighty species are described. None are of commercial or special economic importance, and only a few are cultivated for ornament. Of these, the best known are *Nemophila insignis*, introduced by Mr. Douglas from California, *N. maculata*, and two or three species of *Eutoca*. In India the beaten leaves of *Hydrolea Zeylanica* are used as a poultice.

Hydrostati'c Press, better known in its portable forms as *Bramah's Press*, is a machine which is capable of exerting enormous pressure. As its name implies, it depends for its action upon the properties of fluids. The hydrostatic principle which is involved is frequently termed the *hydrostatic paradox*, but it is simply the law already proved under hydrodynamics, that in a fluid at rest, under the action of gravity, the surfaces of equal pressure are horizontal planes. Consequently the shape of the containing vessel can have absolutely no effect upon the variation of pressure throughout the fluid mass. Imagine two cylindrical vessels of different diameters to be set vertically and connected below by a tube, so that water may pass freely from one to the other. If water be then poured in, it will rise to precisely the same height in both vessels, however much these vessels may differ in size. This apparent *balancing* of the larger column by the smaller constitutes the so-called paradox. Though the *total* pressure on any horizontal section of the larger column is greater than the total pressure on the corresponding section of the smaller, yet the pressure on unit area of these surfaces is the same, and this is the necessary and sufficient condition for equilibrium. The truth implied here is precisely the same as that which is stated in the popular saying, 'Water seeks its own level.' Suppose now that the cross-section of the smaller column is unit area, and that of the larger a. Then if p be the pressure exerted on the former, pa is that exerted on the latter. If an increased pressure be applied to the smaller surface so as to lower its level by a distance x, the larger surface will be raised through a distance $\frac{x}{a}$; and, therefore, the work done in both cases being the same, $Px = W\frac{x}{a}$, when W is the whole weight raised, and is evidently greater than P in the ratio of $a:1$. Accordingly if $a = 100$, the weight which a power P can raise is $100\,P$; so that by increasing the relative dimensions of the larger cylinder, a greater weight can be raised, though, of course, at a correspondingly smaller rate.

Hydrostat'ics. See HYDRODYNAMICS.

Hydrosulphu'ric Acid, or **Sulphuretted Hydrogen** (H_2S), a strongly odorous and colourless gas, evolved from decomposing albuminoid substances, such as rotten eggs. It emanates from the soil in many volcanic districts, and occurs dissolved in certain mineral springs—those, for example, of Harrowgate, Aix-la-Chapelle, Barèges, &c. Artificially it is readily prepared by the action of a strong acid upon certain metallic sulphides. The most convenient for this purpose is sulphide of iron (FeS), which, if treated with dilute sulphuric acid, results in the evolution of H. A.—leaving sulphate of iron behind in solution. It may be prepared by the action of hydrochloric acid upon sulphide of antimony (Sb_2S_3), H. A. and chloride of antimony ($SbCl_3$) resulting. This gas is condensable to a colourless liquid under seventeen atmospheres of pressure at 10° C. It burns readily in air, producing sulphurous anhydride (SO_2) and water. At 18° C. 1 volume of water dissolves 2½ volumes of H. A.; and this aqueous solution is of prime importance in the laboratory to the analytical chemist. When solutions of certain metallic salts are treated with solution of H. A., the corresponding metallic sulphide is precipitated. The salts of another set of metals, whose sulphides are soluble in, or are acted upon by, strong acids, require for the precipitation of the sulphide the addition of ammonia to neutralise the hydrochloric acid, which is a necessary resultant constituent in the reaction. A third group gives no precipitate either in an acid or a basic solution. Copper, lead, bismuth, silver, antimony, &c., exhibit the first action; iron, zinc, nickel, cobalt, manganese, &c., the second; and magnesium, barium, sodium, potassium, &c., the third. H. A. is poisonous when inhaled; but its solution, introduced into the stomach, is not injurious, and has, besides, valuable medicinal properties.

Hydrothor'ax (Gr. *hydŏr*, 'water,' and *thorax*, 'the chest'), or **Water in the Chest**, is the term applied to effusions of serum into the cavity of the chest, which may occur in either or both sides. It is generally the result of pre-existing disease of the pleura, lungs, heart, or great vessels; or of zymotic or constitutional diseases. The fluid, which varies in quantity, may be limpid and colourless; but it is generally citron-coloured, and contains fibrine, albumen, and sometimes urea, when complicated with Bright's disease of the kidneys. H. is occasionally the result of slight pleurisy, rarely of severe; and, when secondary, it may co-exist with almost every chronic affection of the liver, kidneys, or heart; and is then generally preceded by swelling of the legs and eyelids. The physical symptoms are dulness on percussion; bronchial and sometimes tracheal respiration; bronchophony, and occasionally ægophany; and the absence of expansion, on respiration, on the side of the seat of the effusion. H. is an extremely serious disease, and its treatment is difficult. Tapping by means of the trocar and canula may be performed under the following circumstances—(1) When there is severe permanent dyspnœa, the fluid filling, or nearly filling, the pleural cavity; (2) when there are occasional attacks of orthopnœa, threatening death, although the fluid may not more than half fill the cavity; (3) when means for absorption by other methods have failed; (4) in chronic idiopathic H. with extensive effusion. See *Clinical Medicine* by Professor Gairdner.

Hydrozo'a, one of the two classes into which *Cœlenterate* (q. v.) animals are divided. The H. differ from the remaining class, that of the corals and sea-anemones (*Actinozoa*) in the non-possession of a stomach sac, and in the fact that the reproductive organs are external in the H. The H. are represented by zoophytes, jellyfishes, and allied forms; many other forms being of compound nature. The following are the orders into which this class is divided:—

	ORDERS.	
Sub-class 1. HYDROIDA,	1. *Hydrida*, . . .	Ex. Hydra.
	2. *Corynida*, . . .	Ex. Cordylophora.
	3. *Sertularida*, . .	Ex. Sea-firs.
	4. *Campanularida*,	Ex. Campanularia.
Sub-class 2. SIPHONOPHORA,	5. *Calycophoridæ*, .	Ex. Diphyes.
	6. *Physophoridæ*, .	Ex. Physalia.
Sub-class 3. DISCOPHORA, .	7. *Medusida*, . .	Ex. Jellyfishes.
	8. *Lucernarida*, .	Ex. Lucernaria.
Sub-class 4. GRAPTOLITIDÆ,	,,, ...	Ex. Graptolites (extinct).

Hyères', an old town in the department of Var, France, 8 miles E. of Toulon, romantically situated on a steep rocky hill, commanding a splendid view of the Mediterranean (3 miles distant) and the Isles d'Hyères (Porquerolles, Point Gros, du Levant, &c.), called by the ancients Stœchades. Besides its quaint old ramparts, it has a church of St. Louis of the 13th c. and remains of a Roman villa. There is an active trade in oil, wine, and fruits. The summer is delicious, but the winter is cold and rainy. Pop. (1872) 5197.

Hygiei'a (Gr. 'health'), the ancient Greek goddess of health, was the daughter or wife of Æsculapius (q. v.), in whose temples, as at Athens, Argos, and Corinth, she usually shared. Conceived as the goddess of mental health, she was sometimes even identified with Athena. Works of art display her as a long-robed maiden feeding a serpent from a cup.

Hygiene (Gr. *hygieinos*, 'good for the health') is that department of medical therapeutics which treats of the preservation of health, and discovers proper means for the continuance of that state, and for the prevention and arrest of constitutional diseases. H. has respect to man in his social as well as in his individual condition. The laws of H. have reference to man in the different stages of his existence, viz., during the periods of development, maturity, and decay; to his congenital condition, as regards robustness or delicacy of organism, and liability to constitutional diseases; to his geographical position in the globe, as regards temperature and climatology generally, and also to the race to which he belongs. The chief subjects of H. are diet, air, water, beverages, and condiments; conditions of soil, habitations, clothing, cleanliness, exercise, individual hygienic management, the disposal of the dead, preventible diseases, disinfection, and statistics. Many valuable contributions have been recently made to H. both in this country and on the Continent, but the best is a *Manual of Practical H.*, by Dr. Parkes (4th ed. Lond. 1873). See also *The Management of Infancy*, by Dr. Combe, edited by Sir James Clarke (9th ed. Lond. 1860), and *Public Health*, by Dr. Parkes (Lond. 1876).

Hygrom'etry (Gr. *hygros*, 'moist,' and *metron*, 'a measure') is the branch of meteorological science which treats of the state of the air as regards the moisture it contains. At all times the atmosphere contains a greater or less quantity of water vapour; and the maximum quantity which a given volume of air can hold in given circumstances depends upon the temperature of the air. The higher the temperature the greater is the amount of water vapour which can be held in suspension; and when the atmosphere contains nearly this maximum quantity, it is said to be *saturated*. In these circumstances a slight fall of temperature will be almost certainly followed by a deposition of moisture, either in the form of dew or rain. The temperature at which this *first* deposition occurs is called the *dew-point*, and its determination is obviously a measure of the relative humidity of the air, the temperature and barometric pressure being of course known. The general humidity may be indicated in several ways—for example, as in Saussure's hygroscope, by a hair which elongates when moist and contracts when dry, or by a piece of catgut which untwists when moist and twists when dry. Such, however, can give no quantitive indications, and cannot therefore in strictness be called *hygrometers*. All true hygrometers measure the humidity as suggested above by determining the dew-point. Daniell's hygrometer consists of a U-shaped tube inverted, and terminated at each end by a bulb. The one bulb contains a quantity of ether and a delicate thermometer immersed in the liquid, while the other contains nothing but vapour of ether. The exterior of the latter is covered with some fine muslin-like fabric, and on it when the determination is to be made a few drops of ether are dropped. The evaporation of this ether produces intense cold, which condenses the ether-vapour in the bulb; and as a natural consequence the liquid ether in the other bulb evaporates, rapidly cooling during the operation till its temperature reaches just below the dew-point, when, of course, deposition takes place on the exterior surface of the bulb. Read on the enclosed thermometer the temperature of first deposition, and then take the reading when the dew disappears as the temperature rises. The mean of the two gives the dew-point. Regnault's hygrometer is constructed upon the same principle; but the ether, which is placed in a glass tube covered externally with a thin coating of silver, is evaporated by forcing air through it. Its indications are much more exact than those of Daniell's. The hygrometer in most general use is, however, that which is known as the *wet-and-dry-bulb* thermometer. Two similar thermometers are fixed side by side, the bulb of the one being covered with muslin which is kept moist by the capillary action of a few threads of darning-cotton which lead into a small vessel close at hand. This covered bulb is therefore always cooler than the other on account of the evaporation which is always going on, and which is greater the drier the surrounding air is. The nearer the readings of the two thermometers are, the more moist must the atmosphere be.

Hyk'shos (*hyk*, 'ruler,' and *shasu*, 'shepherds or nomads'), is the name given to the chiefs of some Arabian or Phœnician tribes who invaded Egypt probably in the 16th c. B.C., and maintained a dominion there by force for 100 years. Their first king was *Saites*, or *Salatis*, or *Set*, who fixed his court at Memphis, founded the city of Abaris, near Pelusium, and levied a corn tax in Lower Egypt, the Egyptian King Rasekenu still holding Thebes. The British Museum papyrus calls the H. 'lepers.' *Saites* was succeeded by Beon, Apechnas, Apophis, Janias, and Asselto. The insulting demand for workmen and materials to build a temple to the strange god *Sutech* or *Set* at last roused the Egyptians to combined resistance, and about 1450 B.C. *Chebros-Amosis* or *Aahmes*, the founder of the 18th native dynasty, drove the H., to the number of 240,000, out of the land, a number of the lower people remaining to work as slaves along with the Israelites. It is probable that the Potiphar who promoted Joseph was a shepherd king at Heliopolis. It has also been suggested that the H. are the people named by the Israelites *Philistines* or *foreigners* (a name which they apparently carried from *Pelusium* to *Palestine*). It is also said that the H. were Caphtorites from the island of Caphtor in the Eastern Delta (*cf.* Gen. x. 14; Deut. ii. 23; Jer. xlvii. 4).

Hylæosau'rus (Gr. 'tree lizard'), a genus of extinct reptiles, belonging to the order *Deinosauria*. Their remains occur in the Wealden formations of the S.E. of England. The familiar species is *H. Oweni*. H. appears to have had an exoskeleton of scales and bony tubercles; the teeth were of small size, and were closely set; and the tail was long. Probably the back was provided with a spiny crest, such as is possessed by many living lizards.

Hy'men, or **Hymenæ'us**, in Greek mythology, was the god of marriage, and, according to one legend, the son of Apollo and one of the Muses, according to another, of Dionysus and Aphrodite. He is represented as a fair, winged youth, bearing a bridal torch and veil, and taller than Eros. He was invoked in the *Hymenæus* or bridal-song, of which the *H. O Hymenæe* of Catullus is a beautiful example.

Hymenop'tera (Gr. 'membrane-winged'), an order of *Holometabolic* insects, undergoing a complete metamorphosis, and represented by the wasps, ants, bees, hornets, and allied forms. The wings are four in number, and are wholly membraneous; the *nervures* or supporting ribs of the wings small and slender. The head is large, and in addition to the compound eyes, has three *ocelli* in simple eyes. The mouth partakes of the character of the masticatory or biting variety, combined with the suctorial form of mouth. The abdomen bears at its extremity appendages modified to serve as ovipositors (as in saw-flies) or (as in bees, &c.) for a sting or *aculeus*. The larvæ are quite unlike the perfect insect, and are usually short, cylindrical, and footless. The chrysalis has the limbs free, and is usually contained within a slight silky cocoon, which, however, in the saw-flies is thick. The H., according to Dana, exhibit the *normal size* of the insect type. The antennæ or feelers are short; the thorax is rounded; and the abdomen numbers seven segments in the males and six in the females. The H. inhabit the warm and temperate regions of the earth, and in habits are more terrestrial than most other insects. In the exhibition of instincts of a very high order, they differ widely from other groups of insects, and are grouped in many cases into *social communities*. It is to be noted, however, that the acts of bees, wasps, and ants are to be accounted of *excito-motor* kind, that is, depending for stimulation and direction upon external circumstances, of which the insect has no intelligent appreciation. The young ant or bee, liberated from its chrysalis, at once enters upon its duties, and performs them as perfectly as at the close of its existence. No experience is afforded the insect. The H. first appear in a fossil state in the Jurassic rocks.

Hymett'us, a mountain in Attica, subdivided into the Greater H.—now *Telō-Vuni*, and the Lesser H.—now *Maurō-Vuni*. It was anciently covered with woods, and was and is famous for its honey—

> 'There flowery hill Hymettus, with the sound
> Of bees' industrious murmur.'

Hymn (Gr. *hymnos*), an ode in praise of a deity. The earliest examples of the H. in Greek literature were those known as the *Homeric hymns*, which are partly epic in character, while the later hymns of Pindar and Callimachus are lyrical. There are several hymns in the Vedas, but the crowning examples of this form of poetry are the Psalms of David. The early Christians produced many noble Latin hymns, *e.g.*, the *Te Deum* (q. v.), the *Gloria in Excelsis*, and the *Tersanctus*. Until the 10th c. many hymns were composed in Greek by Clemens Alexandrinus, Gregory Nazianzen, John Damascene, Andrew of Crete, Metrophanes, &c.; while down to the 15th c. a rich Latin hymnology, generally fervent, musical, and sonorous, was produced by Ambrose, who founded a school of hymnists, Prudentius, Fortunatus, Gregory, St. Bernard, Peter Damiani, Hilderbert, Hildegarde, Thomas Aquinas, Thomas a Celano, author of the *Dies Iræ* and *Veni Creator Spiritus*; Jacopol, author of *Stabat Mater*, &c. In England hymnology arose after the Reformation; among the chief English hymnists being Herbert, Ken, Baxter, Mant, Doddridge, Toplady, Watts, Wesley, Montgomery, Heber, Keble, Lyte, &c. See Neale's *Hymns of the Eastern Church*, Mrs. Browning's *Greek Christian Poets*, Koch's *Geschichte des Deutschen Kirchenlieds*, Mone's *Hymni Latini Medii Ævi* (Friburg, 1856), and *Hymns Ancient and Modern, with Accompanying Tunes* (revised and enlarged edition, 1875).

Hy'oid, a bone situated at the base of the tongue, between the chin and the thyroid cartilage of larynx. It is shaped somewhat like the letter U, hence the name, from U, the Greek letter *upsilon*, and *eidos*, 'shape.' Although comparatively small in man, it attains great size, complexity of structure, and functional importance in the lower vertebrates. See *Lessons in Elementary Anatomy*, by St. George Mivart (Lond. Macmillan & Co. 1873, page 123).

Hyoscy'amus, the genus of plants to which the Henbane (q. v.) belongs.

Hypa'tia, the daughter of Theon the Younger, a mathematician, was born at Alexandria, between A.D. 370 and 380. She was thoroughly trained in mathematics and metaphysics, and her brilliant accomplishments lent an additional charm to the loveliness of her person. After the death of Julian the Apostate, like many members of the Neo-Platonic school of Alexandria, she went to Athens, where she probably was admitted to the esoteric theurgy of the younger Plutarch. Returning to Alexandria, she taught philosophy with enthusiasm and success. Synesius, Bishop of Cyrene, was her pupil. The rumours that she married Isidorus, and that she wrote to Cyril about her conversion to Christianity, seem to be without foundation. This noble woman at last fell a victim to the quarrel between Bishop Cyril and her friend, the Prefect Orestes. Fanatical monks at the head of a Christian mob, and probably authorised by Cyril, killed her with great brutality and outrage at the Cæsarea church, March 415. Suidas says H. wrote commentaries on Diophantus and the Conics of Apollonius of Perga. There are several letters from Synesius to H. extant. Her story is the subject of a splendid historical romance by Charles Kingsley.

Hyperæsthe'sia (Gr. *hyper*, 'over,' and *aisthēsis*, 'sensation'), or excessive sensibility, is a disease of the nervous structure, the prominent symptom being exalted irritability. The term H. is more commonly applied to excessive sensibility of the skin, which is sometimes so great that the slightest touch by the finger, and the weight and pressure of dress, occasion severe pain.

Hyper'bola, a central curve of the second order. It is one of the conic sections, and may be obtained by cutting a right cone by a plane, which makes with the side of the cone any angle less than the semi-vertical angle of the cone. For every property of the Ellipse (q. v.), there is a similar property of the H., but the latter is at once distinguished from the former by its infinite branches, and by its asymptotic nature. That is to say, for every such curve there are two straight lines which pass through the centre, and which continually approach the infinite branches of the H., but never meet them—which are, in other words, tangents at infinity. It may be defined further as the locus of points, the *difference* of whose distances from two fixed points (called the *foci*) is a constant quantity. Its equation referred to its principal diameters (a and b) is $\frac{x^2}{a^2} - \frac{y^2}{b^2} = 1$; and if the asymptotes be taken as the axes of co-ordinates, the equation assumes the simple form $4\,xy = a^2 + b^2$. When $a = b$, the asymptotes are at right angles to each other, and the curve is called the *equilateral H.* *Hyperboloids* are surfaces of the second order, which are cut by certain planes in hyperbolas. There are two distinct kinds of these surfaces, distinguished as *hyperboloids of one sheet* and *hyperboloids of two sheets*. Their equations are respectively $\frac{x^2}{a^2} + \frac{y^2}{b^2} - \frac{z^2}{c^2} = 1$, and $\frac{x^2}{a^2} - \frac{y^2}{b^2} - \frac{z^2}{c^2} = 1$.

Hyper'bole (Gr. *hyper*, 'over,' and *ballō*, 'I cast'), a figure of rhetoric, especially common in Oriental style, which consists in magnifying an object beyond its natural bounds, not by the introduction of qualities which do not, but by the exaggeration of those which do belong to it. A familiar instance of a H. is that of Virgil where he describes Camilla (*Æn.* vii.) as so fleet that she could skim the waves without wetting the sole of her foot.

Hyperbo'reans (*i.e.*, 'dwellers at the back of the north wind'), the name bestowed by the ancients on a sacred nation said to live beyond the Rhipæan mountains, from a cavern in which issued the cutting blasts (Gr. *rhipai*) of Boreas to the southward. The H., thus sheltered from cold and storms, are represented by Pindar (*Pyth.* x. 56) as free from sin and suffering, abstaining from flesh, and living a thousand years; and Pliny adds that, wearying of their easy life, they leapt, crowned with flowers, into the sea. In Æschylus we find the phrase *tychē hyperboreos*, to signify 'more than mortal pleasure.'

Hypericin'eæ, or **Hyperica'ceæ**, is a natural order of some 220 described species, distributed through the temperate zones and the montane districts of warmer regions. The principal genus is *Hypericum*, consisting of 160 species of herbaceous and shrubbery plants, and it is the only one that represents the order in Europe. Eleven species of it are natives of Britain. In many hypericaceous plants a yellow resinous juice exists, as in the allied order *Guttiferæ* (q. v.); this is much developed in the American species of Vismia, and is collected under the name of American gamboge.

Hype'rion (by the ancients directly derived from Gr. *hyper*, 'above,' and *iōn*, 'going,' but from the length of the penultimate seemingly a shortened form of the patronymic Hyperionion), a Titan, son of Uranus ('heaven') and Gaia ('earth'), and husband of his sister Euryphaessa ('far-shining'), who bore him Helios, Selene, and Eos (the sun, moon, and dawn). Helios himself is styled H. by Homer. The myth is unmistakably of solar origin.

Hyper'trophy (Gr. *hyper*, 'over,' and *trophē*, 'nutrition'), a term in medicine signifying the enlargement of a part of the body from increased exercise, excessive nutrition, or disease processes. The following conditions give rise to H.:—(1) The increased exercise of a part in its healthy function; (2) an increased accumulation in the blood of the particular materials which a part appropriates in its nutrition or in secretion; (3) an increased afflux of healthy blood.

Hy'phen (Gr. *huphen*, 'into one'), a mark (-) implying that two words are connected, *e.g.*, self love.

Hypnot'ics (Gr. *hypnos*, 'sleep'), medicines which tend to produce sleep, called also *soporifics* and *sedatives*. The group consists of cannabis indica, chloral, chloroform, codeia, conium, croton-chloral, hyoscyamus, lupulus, morphia, opium, papaver, sumbul, &c.

Hyp'notism, a name given to a variety of somnambulism produced artificially by causing the person to gaze fixedly at a near object. See SOMNAMBULISM.

Hyp'num, the principal genus of the *Hypnæi*, a large natural order of lateral fruited mosses. The species occur in all parts of the world, and include many of the largest and most ornamental mosses. *H. tamariscinum*, a common British species, is used by the artificial flower makers in the construction of their moss-roses, and other species are used by birdstuffers, &c. H. by modern authorities is broken up into numerous genera or sub-genera.

Hyp'ocaust (Lat. *hypocaustum*, from Gr. *hypo*, 'under,' and *kaiō*, 'I burn'), in architecture, hollow cells communicating with each other and connected with an oven or furnace, for the dissemination of streams of heated air under the floor and through the flued walls of an apartment. In the baths of ancient Rome the H. served to heat the water, and to maintain a high temperature in the thermal chambers. A similar arrangement was also adopted in private houses.

Hypochœ'ris, popularly **Cat's Ear**, a small genus of the natural order *Compositæ* ranging under its *Chicoraceæ* or chicory tribe. *H. radicata* is one of the commonest British plants in pastures and other grass grounds. By its vigorous growth and its leaves spreading close to the surface it usurps the place of better fodder within its area, and is therefore a mischievous weed.

Hypochlor'ous Acid (Cl_2O), a powerfully explosive gas, produced by passing chlorine over dry oxide of mercury contained in a tube surrounded by ice. It is dark orange in colour, has a strong chlorine odour, and liquefies at 20° C. under ordinary pressure. It dissolves easily in water; and the solution is a powerful bleaching agent, a characteristic common to its salts, the hypochlorites.

Hypochondri'asis (Gr. *hypo*, 'under,' and *chondros*, 'cartilage'), a disease characterised by uneasiness about the region of the stomach and liver, dyspepsia, extreme sensitivity of the nervous system, depression, apprehension of impending evil, morbid suspicion, aversion to society, and loss of mental and bodily energy. These symptoms frequently increase to such an extent as to result in insanity. *Hypochondrical insanity* is developed when H. passes beyond the control of the will, the entire attention being directed to the state of the system, the sensations being exalted and misinterpreted, and consists essentially in the transference of phenomena, subjective or mental in origin, into what appears to be a real material change appreciable sometimes by others. The sensations, however, may proceed from organic or functional disease, or they may be ordinary sensations, excited and intensified by the act of attention, and ascribed to other causes than those which produce them. Hypochondriacal insanity is one of the principal forms which *melancholia* assumes, and those affected with it are liable to a class of singular delusions, chiefly as regards personal identity and metamorphosis. A patient may imagine that the abdomen or the head is the abode of animals of various kinds; that the body is made of butter or glass; that he has been transformed into some other person, or into an inferior animal; or, more remarkable still, into some inanimate object, as a teapot, a pump-handle, a beer-barrel, or a mutton chop. Such extraordinary delusions are not by any means uncommon among the insane. Such delusions and hallucinations are apt to originate homicidal and suicidal acts, and very frequently do so. See *De l'Hypochondrie et du Suicide*, by Dr. Falret; *Psychological Medicine*, by Drs. Bucknill and Tuke (Lond. 1874).

Hypos'tasis (Gr. 'real being'), in Greek philosophy, meant a real personal subsistence, which was the only meaning the word had before the time of Arius (q. v.). But as the idea of reality in the word also applies to substance and being (Gr. *ousia*), when Arius said there are three *hypostases*, he meant three natures or substances. There being at first no equivalent for *ousia*, H. was translated into Latin sometimes by *substantia*, and sometimes by *subsistentia*. This gave rise to great confusion and much misunderstanding, till the Council of Antioch (341) fixed the distinction between H. and *ousia*, and restricted *substantia* to the latter, leaving H. to be represented by *persona*, which was the proper equivalent of its meaning in the Catholic doctrine.

Hypostat'ic Union is the term used to denote the union of the divine and human natures in Christ. Regarding this union orthodox theology holds—(1) That in the person of Christ the two natures are inseparably united; yet (2) without being mixed or confounded; (3) that none of the attributes of either of the natures is transferred to the other; (4) that it is not a mere indwelling of the divine nature in the human, a moral or sympathetic union, nor a temporary and mutable relation; and (5) that it is of such a nature that Christ is but one person.

Hypoth'ec (Gr. *hypothēkē*, 'a pledge') is a security established by law in Scotland in favour of a creditor over a subject belonging to his debtor. A landlord has a H. over the furniture or crops of his tenant for the current rent. A law-agent has a H. over legal documents in his possession, the property of his client, for his Bill of Costs (q. v.) or Expenses (q. v.). The corresponding term of English law is *lien*. See LIENS.

Hypotheca'tion is a term of maritime law, denoting the security which can be created over a ship for repair in an emergency. The owner does not become personally liable under H.

Hypoth'enuse, or **Hypot'enuse** (Gr. *hypoteinousa scil. grammē*, 'the line that stretches under'), in geometry, is the side which subtends the right angle of a right-angled triangle. The square described upon it is equal to the sum of the squares described in the other two sides.

Hypoth'esis (Gr. 'what is placed under'). All hypotheses must be subjected to the test of experiment; but the mere absence of any phenomenon inconsistent with the H. must not be accepted as having much weight in establishing its truth. The grand test of the truth of an H. is not merely that it should explain in a simple manner a variety of phenomena, but that it should indicate existing but still unknown phenomena, and the direction in which to search for these. It is in this way especially that gravitation has been raised to form an H. to a law, as witness the discovery of Neptune; and it is on this ground chiefly that we rest assured of the truth of the conservation of energy. Thus, also, has the undulatory theory of light successfully coped with its rival the corpuscular theory, which had to be abandoned as soon as facts came to light which were demonstratively inconsistent with it. In biology, again, Darwin's theory of natural selection, which aims at accounting for the present distribution of life as a result of evolution, is a very good example of a fruitful H.

Hypsilan'tis. See YPSILANTI.

Hyracoi'dea, an important order of Mammalia founded to include the genus *Hyrax*, of which the *H. Syriacus* or 'coney' of Scripture (see DAMAN) is a typical species, a second species being the *H. Capensis* or 'klipdas' of South Africa, also known to the colonists as the 'badger.' The order H. has been specially constructed for these animals, inasmuch as they do not fall naturally within the boundary of any other order of existing mammals. By many zoologists they were and are placed among the rhinoceroses from the similarity of their molar teeth. But the characters derived from teeth are apt to be deceptive, and as the incisors of the upper jaw grow from permanent pulps like those of the *Rodentia* (q. v.), the H. by other naturalists are included in the latter group. The question of the affinities of H. seem, however, to be most satisfactorily settled by instituting a distinct order, distinguished by having no canine teeth, and four incisors, four premolars, and six molars in each jaw. The front feet have four and the hinder feet three toes, and the digits have hoof-like nails. The collar-bones or clavicles are undeveloped. The nose and ears are short, and the tail is rudimentary. The Placenta (q. v.) is *deciduate* and *zonary*, and thus comes to differ from that of ungulata in which the placenta is non-deciduate.

Hy'rax. See DAMAN and HYRACOIDEA.

Hyracothe'rium, an extinct genus of Mammalia, so named from its supposed affinities to the little *Hyrax* or 'coney.' (See HYRACOIDEA.) The H. remains occur in the Eocene rocks of the Tertiary period. Owen described another fossil which he named *Pliolophus* as forming with H. 'a well-marked section of the odd-hoofed (*Perissodactyle*) herbivores, which preceded the palæotherian family in time, and retained more of the general ungulate type. By some palæontologists the genus *Pliolophus* of Owen is merged into the genus H., a course apparently warranted from a consideration of the very close homologies of the remains. The London clay (Eocene) has afforded the remains of H. in most perfect preservation. The species included under the genus H. may be enumerated as H. (*Pliolophus*) *vulpiceps*, *H. leporinum*, and *H. cuniculus*.

Hyrca'nia, an ancient province of Persia, the modern Mazanderán, was bounded N. by the Caspian or Hyrcanian Sea, E. by the Oxus, S. by the Montes Sariphi (Hazari), which separated it from Parthia, and W. by Mons Koronus and the river Charindas, dividing it from Media. The part of H. near the sea is stated by Strabo to have been extremely fertile, yielding wine, fruits, but no corn; whilst the mountains were covered with dense forests, infested by tigers, and abounding in wild bees. The Hyrcani, according to Xenophon, were subdued by the Assyrians, and Curtius says there were 6000 of them in the army of Darius. The name H. is supposed to survive in the modern Gurkan, a town to the E. of Astrabad.

Hyrca'nus, John, a Jewish prince, and son of Simon Maccabæus, succeeded on the death of his father, B.C. 135, to the government of Judæa and the high priesthood. The country had been at war with Syria, and he was forced to conclude a peace on disadvantageous terms, but in B.C. 130 he threw off the Syrian yoke. He next seized various places in Syria, Phœnicia, and Arabia, conquered the Idumæans, took Shechem, destroyed Samaria and the temple on Mount Gerizim, and renewed the league with the Romans. After this he governed Judæa, Samaria, and Galilee for two years, till his death, B.C. 107.—**H. II.**, the son of Alexander Jannæus, succeeded on the death of his father, B.C. 79, to the government of Judæa and the high priesthood. Three months after the death of his mother, who had survived her husband nine years, he was ousted by his younger brother Aristobulus, who was at first assisted by the Romans. H., however, applied to Pompey, and was by him reinstated in his government, but as a tributary of Rome, B.C. 63. When Antipater was made Procurator of Judæa, B.C. 47, H. was continued in the high priesthood. His grand-daughter Mariamne married Herod the Great, by whom he himself was put to death, B.C. 31.

Hyrtl, Joseph, a celebrated modern anatomist, was born at Eisenstadt in Hungary, 7th December 1811, studied at Vienna, and in 1837 was appointed Professor of Anatomy in Prag. In 1845 he was elected to the Anatomy chair at Vienna, where he has formed a fine anatomical museum. His chief works are *Lehrbuch der Anatomie des Menschen* (1847, 11th ed. 1870); *Handbuch der Topographischen Anatomie* (1847, 5th ed. 1865); *Beiträge zur Morphologie der Urogenitalorgane der Fische* (1850); *Handbuch der Praktischen Zergliederungskunst* (1860). They have been translated into most European languages.

Hyss'op, the genus *Hyssopus*, belonging to the natural order *Labiatæ*. *H. officinalis*, or common H., a native of South Europe, is supposed to be the plant mentioned by Dioscorides, and it was much cultivated and used in the past as a carminative, &c., Garard recording six varieties in his garden in 1596. It has now fallen into disuse. The H. of our authorised version of the Bible is considered by the best authorities to mean a species of capparis. (See CAPERS.) The hedge H. of the old herbalists is a gratiola.

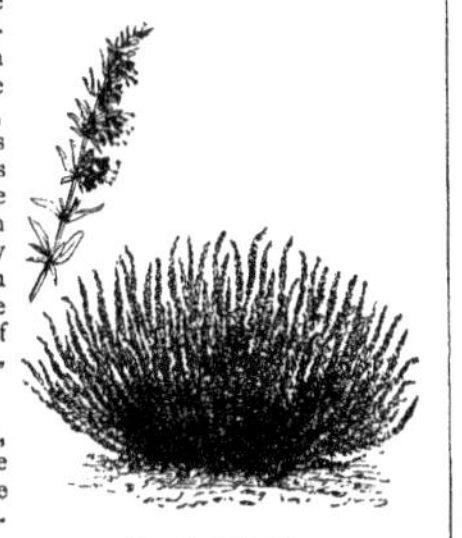

Hyssop officinalis.

Hyste'ria (Gr. *hystera*, 'the womb') is a disease characterised by convulsive struggling, with alternate remissions and exacerbations, generally accompanied by a sense of suffocation, and probably associated with some morbid state of the emotional or sensori-motor centres. H. has been referred (1) to a morbid condition of the uterus; (2) to a morbid state of the cerebral structures; (3) to a morbid excitability of the whole nervous system implying paralysis of some nervous centres. Post-mortem appearances afford negative results only. H. is divided into three forms—(1) That in which there is the sensation of suffocation, as of a ball rising in the throat—the *globus hystericus*—but without convulsions; (2) that in which the *globus hystericus* occurs with convulsions; and (3) those irregular phenomena which often appear during the intervals of severe attacks. The milder form begins with pains in the left side, or some part of the abdomen, and there is usually nervous excitement or depression, followed by the sensation of a ball, rising apparently from the lower portion of the abdomen, and proceeding upwards, with various convolutions, to the stomach; and thence to the throat, causing an intense sense of suffocation. The attack is followed by headache, stiffness of the neck, copious discharge of urine, and great flatulent distension of the abdomen. In the more severe cases, when the *globus hystericus* reaches the throat, the patient falls, apparently unconscious, and violently convulsed, the convulsions being sometimes so strong that several persons may be required to restrain the patient, who writhes to and fro, agitates the limbs, beats the breast, tears the hair, screams, shrieks, laughs, cries, and sobs alternately. The veins of the neck are distended, and the carotids beat with violence; the respiration is slow and laborious, owing to spasms about the pharynx and glottis causing the patient to grasp the neck and throat. The head is generally thrown back, so that the throat projects; the eyelids are closed, but tremulous; the nostrils distended; the jaws often firmly clenched; but there is no distortion of the countenance, and the cheeks are at rest. In severe cases there may be loss of consciousness, but this is not a common accompaniment of the convulsions of H. The fit may last from a few minutes to two or three hours. H. is frequently connected with menstrual disorder. Pains under or in the mammæ—the *hysterical breast* (*clavus hystericus*)—lumbar pains, and palpitation, are common; but the morbid sensibility is chiefly in the integuments. The pain of H. is increased when the attention is directed towards it, but lessens when the attention is withdrawn. The convulsive paroxysms of H. may be mistaken for epilepsy; but there is never complete loss of sensibility and perception. H. is not attended with ultimate danger either to body or mind. The first thing to be done during the fit is to loosen everything tight about the person; to admit a free current of air, and to drench the face and head with cold water; for the hysterical state is one from which the patient can be roused, and, in this respect, it is markedly dissimilar to that of epilepsy and apoplexy.

Hys'trix. See PORCUPINE.

Hythe, one of the Cinque Ports, Kent, England, 77 miles by rail S.E. of London. It lies in a hollow nearly a mile from the coast, and consists mainly of one long street. In the 16th c. it was one of the chief ports in the Channel, but since then has greatly declined. Its prosperity revived during the French war, large forces being stationed in the town, and considerable military works being undertaken, but it has again lost much of its importance. It contains a fine old church about to be restored, two hospitals, a gaol, the National School of Musketry, and a theatre. The neighbouring country is rich in fine ruins and antiquarian remains, Saltwood, Lympne (the *Portus Lemanus* of the Romans), Snowfall Castle, &c. Folkestone, Sandgate, and other places are comprised in the parliamentary borough of H., which returns one member to Parliament. Pop. (1871) of the municipal borough, 3383; of the parliamentary borough, 24,078.

I.

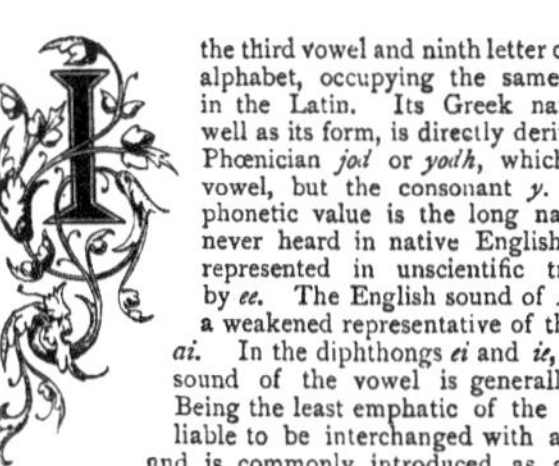

the third vowel and ninth letter of the English alphabet, occupying the same position as in the Latin. Its Greek name, *iota*, as well as its form, is directly derived from the Phœnician *jod* or *yodh*, which was not a vowel, but the consonant *y*. Its proper phonetic value is the long narrow sound, never heard in native English words, but represented in unscientific transliteration by *ee*. The English sound of *I* is properly a weakened representative of the diphthong *ai*. In the diphthongs *ei* and *ie*, the original sound of the vowel is generally preserved. Being the least emphatic of the vowels, *I* is liable to be interchanged with any of them, and is commonly introduced as a mere connecting sound, or as an enclitic particle, especially in Greek. For interchanges, Lat. *pingere* = Fr. *peindre*, Eng. 'paint;' Lat. *bibere*=Fr. *buvoir*, Ital. *bevere*. The form of this vowel is also insignificant. Comp. 'not one jot nor one tittle.'

As a numeral, I. stands for 'one' both in the Roman and Arabic notation. As an abbreviation, I.H.S. stands for *Jesus Hominum Salvator*, whereas IHS, without the stops, is said to represent the first three letters of the sacred name.

Iam'bics (from Gr. *iaptō*, 'I assail,' because first used by the satiric writers), a metre consisting of iambi (⏑ –) or equivalent feet, said to have been invented by Archilochus (q. v.). All I. agree in requiring a cæsura or pause in the middle of the verse, but they differ in the number of their feet, the commonest variety, the tragic trimeter, containing six. Drayton employed this metre in his *Polyolbion*, *e.g.*—

When Phœ | bus lifts | his head | out of | the win | ter's wave;

but the decasyllabic or pentameter blank verse and heroics of the English dramatists and epic poets are the forms of iambic metre most familiar to us.

Iam'blichus of Chalcis in Cœle-Syria, the scholar of Plotinus, was a Neo-Platonist philosopher who lived in the time of Constantine, and died about 330 A.D. The centre of his system is a theogony which shows how from the original One, attributeless and beyond the sphere of contradictions, the intelligible world sprang, whence again arose the intellectual world, and from it the psychical. To this latter world belonged all the deities of the Greek and Oriental mythologies, the whole system forming a speculative justification of polytheism in which the Pythagorean mystical numbers play a larger part than any truly Platonic thought. His chief work in ten books, some of which are lost, is the *Peri Aireseos Pythagorou* ('On the Choice of Pythagoras'). The best edition of I.'s remains is that of Kiessling (1813-15). There were other persons of this name in antiquity, but none were noteworthy.

Ianthi'na, a peculiar genus of *Gasteropodous* Mollusca, popularly known by the name of 'violet snails.' They inhabit the sea, and are included in the family *Haliotidæ* or 'ear shells,' but may also form the type of a special family, that of the *Ianthidæ*. The shell exactly resembles that of the common snail in shape. It is of delicate texture, and of a deep violet hue at the base, the spire being white. The foot is small, but secretes a remarkable 'raft' or 'float,' formed of air cells, to the under surface of which the eggs are attached, the animal and its eggs thus floating about at the surface of the water. The I. occur in great numbers on the Atlantic Ocean, and may be driven by storms on the S. coasts of Britain.

Ibarr'a, a town in the N. of Ecuador, at the E. base of the volcano of Cutacache, 60 miles N.E. of Quito. It has some trade in the cotton and sugar of the surrounding country. Pop. 13,200. I. was visited by a severe earthquake in 1868.

Ibe'ria. See HISPANIA.

Ibe'ris. See CANDYTUFT.

I'bex, or **Bouquetin**, a genus of *Capridæ* or goats, scientifically known as the *Capra I.*, and also under the name of Steinbock. The characteristics of this genus consist in the very large size of the horns of the males, which are wrinkled transversely, and have a series of knobs or tubercles on their outer faces. The 'muzzle' is hairy. The I. is found in the Alps and other mountainous parts of Europe; that of the Pyrenees differing only in a few unimportant points from the Alpine I.

Ibex.

I'bis (*Ibis*), a genus of *Grallatorial* or wading birds, belonging to the sub-family *Tantalinæ*, in which the bill is long, slender, and curved, the sides being gradually compressed towards the tip. The wings are long, and the tail even. The inner toe is shorter than the outer, and the hinder toe is long. In the genus I. itself, the nostrils exist in a narrow groove, and the wings have the first and second quills longest. The head is only partly covered with feathers. The allied genus *Geronticus* has been constructed for the reception of several species of I., which have the third and fourth quills longest, and the head almost destitute of feathers, while the tarsi are covered with hexagonal scales. The sacred I. (*I. religiosa*) is one of the most familiar species of these birds. Its colour is a silvery white, the plumage being of loose character. The secondary wing-feathers and the head and neck plumage are black. This bird derives its name from its intimate association with the religion of ancient Egypt. It arrives in Egypt when the Nile begins to rise, and its appearance was doubtless associated with the cause of the rising of the waters. Its food consists of snakes, molluscs, and insects. The scarlet I. (*I. ruber*) has a glossy scarlet plumage; and the glossy I. (*I. falcinellus*) is a third species, which inhabits N. Africa, and which occasionally appears in Britain. Its colour is a very deep brown, almost passing into black. The white I. (*I. alba*), a native of N. America, has a snow-white plumage. The straw-necked I., inhabiting Australia (*Geronticus spinicollis*), has a black head and neck, the lower part of the neck being white, while drooping feathers of a light hue depend from the neck. The back is a glossy black. The remains of these birds occur in the Egyptian tombs. They were embalmed, and received many marks of honour and esteem during life. The feathers were believed to frighten away the crocodile; and as it bred in other lands, the Egyptians believed it to be of miraculous origin. Its food and drink were believed to be of pure kind, and after

Ibis.

death its body was thought to be incapable of undergoing putrefaction. The shape of the body was even taken as symbolical of the human heart, and the hues of the body were held to represent the light of the moon. In the remains of a mummified I., Cuvier was enabled to detect the scales and bones of snakes, which proved the nature of the food of these birds.

Ib'rahim Pasha, a real or adopted son of Mehemet Ali, was born at Cavalla in Rumilia in 1789. After subduing the Wahabis in 1816, he received the command of the Egyptian army, which he organised on European models. He would have crushed the Greeks in 1828 but for the intervention of the Great Powers. In 1831, in the war in Syria against the Porte, he took Gaza, Acre, and Antioch, and with 30,000 troops routed 60,000 Turks at Konieh. He next acted as Governor of Syria. On the renewal of hostilities in 1839, he defeated the Turkish army at Nisib, but foreign interference and the English successes in Syria forced him to retreat to Egypt. He succeeded Mehemet Ali as Viceroy of Egypt, but died soon afterwards at Cairo, November 9, 1848. I. was a brave soldier, and an able if severe administrator.

Ibrail'. See BRAILA.

Ib'sen, Hen'rik, a Norwegian poet, born at Skien in 1828, and now (1877) residing at Dresden. His chief works are dramatic, and divide themselves into two classes—his early dramas, drawn from middle-age history, *Gyldet paa Solhaug* (1856); *Fru-Inger paa Österraad* (1857); *Hærmændene paa Helgeland* (1858); *Kongsemnerne* (1864); and his later ones, *Brand* (1866); *Peer Gynt* (1867); *De Unges Feorbund* (1869), in which subjects from the present time are treated with rare knowledge of human nature and the keenest irony. The last especially entitles him to high esteem, but his lyric poems, of which a collection came out at Copenhagen in 1871, are also very fine. Most think the drama *Kaiser og Galilœer* (1873, English translation by Catherine Ray, 1876) his greatest work. I. received a pension from the Storthing in 1866.

Ice (Old Eng. *is;* Dan. and Icel. *is;* Ger. *eis*), the form which water assumes when it solidifies on freezing. The temperature at which this occurs at ordinary atmospheric pressures is known as the *freezing-point*, and is one of the standard temperatures used in thermometry. (See THERMOMETER.) It is the zero of the centigrade scale, and as such will be regarded throughout this article. If we take a pound of water, say at 10° C., and cool it, we observe that it contracts in volume as its temperature is lowered, until its temperature is very approximately 4° C. This is called the point of *maximum density;* for if the temperature be further diminished, the water expands. This simultaneous increase in volume and lowering in temperature continues till the temperature falls to 0° C., after which no change in temperature is observable. Further cooling results in the transformation of the water into I., and not until it is wholly transformed into I. can a change of temperature be produced. When water becomes I. it undergoes considerable expansion, and therefore ice floats on water. Further, water at 0° C. can have no melting effect upon I. at the same temperature, because there cannot be a transference of heat between them; and conversely ice at 0° C. cannot convert water into I. The freezing-point of water, however, depends not merely upon temperature, but, as shown by Professor James Thomson, upon pressure. Increase of pressure lowers the freezing-point; so that if I. at 0° C. is subjected to an increased pressure, part of it melts. Remove the pressure and it freezes again. This is no doubt the property which makes the formation of a snowball possible, which explains the *fact* of relegation, discovered independently by Dollfuss-Ausset and Faraday, and which affords a *raison-d'être* of glacier-motion. (See GLACIER.) I. has a glassy, transparent appearance, but unlike glass, it is wonderfully regular in its internal constitution, crystallising in most beautiful and varied forms of hexagonal crystals. I. plays an important part in the economy of nature. It frequently exists in the higher regions of the atmosphere as minute crystals, giving rise by the combination of their several reflections to Halos (q. v.) and mock-suns. As snow, hail, and hoar-frost, it is often evident; but it is seen on its grandest scale in the Glaciers (q. v.) of snow-capped ranges, and in the ice-floes of the polar zones. In the Arctic and Antarctic regions the huge glaciers which line the coasts of the snow-clad lands are daily letting loose their pinnacled fragments, which slowly drift towards warmer climes. These icebergs, as they are called, are sometimes of immense dimensions, and are frequently met with as far S. as 37° N. lat., and as far N. as 44° S. lat. The expansive force with which water becomes I. is further a powerful geological agent in the disintegration of rocks and the loosening of soils.

Ice-Trade and Artificial Production.—I. is a substance of great and daily-increasing importance in many industrial operations, in the preservation of food, in the preparation of I.-creams and drinks, and in medical practice, &c. In temperate and warm countries a constant supply can only be maintained either by storing up in suitable I.-houses the natural product of winter, or by the use of some of the numerous forms of freezing machines which have been introduced. Both systems of securing a supply of I. are extensively practised in Great Britain; and in addition to a very uncertain and fluctuating supply obtained from native lakes and rivers during winter, a large and constantly increasing quantity is annually imported, chiefly from Norwegian lakes. The importation of I. into Great Britain began in 1840, when a company was formed for bringing it from Wenham Lake, near Boston, U.S., but that company's I. is now Norwegian. I. has long been artificially produced on a small scale by the use of freezing mixtures, such as a mixture of snow and common salt, a solution of nitrate of ammonia, or of nitrate of ammonia with carbonate of soda, and several other like substances. Most of the machines for manufacturing I. at present in use depend in principle on the abstraction of heat from any liquid operated on by the vaporisation of liquid ammonia or ether. In the first freezing machine used—invented by Shaw in 1839—sulphuric ether was employed. The same agent is used in Harrison's machine, invented in 1856 and improved by Messrs. Siebe in 1862. Carré of Paris in 1860 introduced a machine in which ammonia is employed, which also is the refrigerating medium in Reece's machine, patented in 1867. In Tellier's system pyroligneous ether is used, but he also employs anhydrous liquid ammonia for refrigerating on board ship. Mr. A. C. Kirk of Glasgow produces a freezing temperature by compressing atmospheric air, and extracting the heat developed by the pressure by means of a current of water. On permitting the compressed air so cooled to expand, it becomes sufficiently cold to freeze water. The imports of I. into Great Britain fluctuate enormously, according to the amount of home produce during winter, and partly also owing to the nature of the summer. The growth of the trade is, however, indicated by the fact that whereas the imports in 1854 were not more than 2000 tons, they now (1877) average more than 100,000 tons. The consumption in Continental and American cities is enormous, it being estimated that in Paris as much as 400 tons per week are used. In America the I. trade centres in Boston, whence the material is exported to every tropical country in the world. The American I. industry gives employment to more than 10,000 persons, and engages a capital of about 6,000,000 dollars.

Ice'berg. See ICE.

Ice'land is a large island belonging to Denmark in the N. Atlantic Ocean, about 190 miles from Greenland and 600 from Norway. Its greatest diameter (from E. to W.) is 330 miles, and its area, including the many surrounding islets, 39,690 sq. miles, of which 16,730 are coast-land, inhabited by 70,417 people (1871). All the rest is bare ice and snow-clad mountains (*jöklar*), or valleys of lava or sand, with scanty copse and greensward here and there. Except on the S., the coast is much indented. The chief inlets are Faxafjördr on the W.; Breidifjördr and Hunaflói, and between them Isafjardardjup, on the N.W.; Skagafjördr and many of less size on the N. and E. The Gulf Stream has great influence on I., as also a Polar current which sends huge icefields against the N. coast about every third year. The greater part of the island is a plateau averaging 2000 feet high, with mountain masses of tufa and trap, resulting from eruptions in the tertiary period. Great volcanic activity exists still, especially in the S., where are Hekla and Kötlugjá. In the interior there is a large lava field, Odadahraun, which has issued from several volcanoes, Trolladyngia, Herdubried (5447 feet), &c., and is continued by a chain of volcanoes up to Husavik in the N. The chief *jöklar* are Vatna or Klofa, with Skaptár, Skeidarar, and Orœfa (in all 3500 sq. miles; greatest height, 6426 feet, of which Mr. Watts reached 6150 in 1875); Hofs, Eyjafjalla (5590 feet), and Snœfells (5976 feet). Skaptár had a frightful eruption in 1783. Mud volcanoes and sulphur pools are very common. Mineral wells (*ölkeldur, i.e.,* 'beer springs') are frequent in the W. Of the many lakes of I., most are very deep, and some have neither affluent nor outlet. They are called *vötn*, and are probably old craters. The largest are Thíngvallavatn, Hvitárvatn, and Myvatn. The rivers, chiefly *jökull* streams of unpalatable water, are broad and short (70 to 90 miles at most). The largest in the S. half are Thorsá, Markarfljót, and two named Hvitá; in the N. Laxá and Lagarfljót, the last as wide in its lower course as the Rhine at Köln. The climate of I. is tolerably mild in the plains, but the atmosphere is generally damp and foggy. The average temperature at Reykjavik is 41·2°. June, July, and August are free from snow. The air is constantly in motion, and fearful storms occur frequently. On the plains of volcanic sand rage great whirlwinds of fog and dust (*mistur*). Auroras and parhelia are not uncommon sights. In the N. of the island the longest day in summer and the longest night in winter extend each to a week. In I. barley, oats, and rye can be cultivated, but their ripening is so uncertain, that it is cheaper to buy corn than to grow it. Many farms, however, have a *tun* or piece of land for grass enclosed with stone walls. From the middle of July to September many of the people leave the coast for the haymaking on the plains in the interior. Three species of birch prevail in I., but seldom reach more than 8 to 10 feet. Only one tree in the island is 25 feet high. In early times trees grew much higher, and some say were large enough for ship-building. The lowest plant-region extends from the coast to a height of 1600 feet; the middle one attains to 2660 feet, producing grass and dwarf-birch, great stretches of heather and bilberries, here a source of food, and various kinds of moss, especially the *Icelandic Moss* (q. v.), which, cooked with milk, serves instead of bread in the N. and E. of I.; and the highest, presenting dwarf-willows, *Azalea procumbens*, *Gentiana nivalis*, &c., is bounded by the snow-line 2880 to 3200 feet above the sea. The domestic animal most important to the Icelanders is the sheep. Their wool is not shorn, but torn off when loose, as on the Faröes, and the dung used not more for manure than for fuel. Rot is very prevalent. Horses of a small, sure-footed, mountain breed are much employed in I., and are exported to this country. Many of these live almost wild. In some places their flesh is used for food. Reindeer, introduced in 1770, roam wild in great herds on the plains of the interior. Gnats are produced in immense swarms, especially about the Myvatn. These supply food to birds and fishes, both of which abound in I. The salmon fisheries of Hvitá and Laxá are very important, and many kinds of fish are found in great numbers on the coast. From February to May, the fishing season, almost all the population live at the coast: 150 French and Dutch ships yearly take part in the codfishing, which is very rich. Sixteen species of seals and whales frequent the surrounding seas, and there are sixty-two species of birds on the island. Ptarmigan, of easy capture and pleasant flesh, swarm on the mountains, and various kinds of birds (eider duck, guillemots, &c.) abound along the coast.

The Icelanders are mainly of Scandinavian blood, and their speech deviates little from the Old Scandinavian. They are in general poor, but honest, patriotic, and well educated. Most of their houses are ill-ventilated and of the meanest description. Their food chiefly consists of fish, bread, and milk in various forms. Dropsy is a very common disease. The principal imports are rye, barley, spirits, coffee, chicory, sugar, and tobacco; the exports—fish, tallow, wool, knitted woollen articles, skins, eider-down, feathers, and Iceland-spar. Each amount to about £130,000. Trade has been free since 1855; and in summer communication is regular from the chief town (Reykjavik) to Leith and Copenhagen.

The Irish probably discovered I. about 800. Between 860 and 870 it was visited by two Norwegians, after one of whom it was called Gardarsholm, a name subsequently changed to I. (from the drift-ice). Many Norwegian district-kings, after the defeat of Hafrsfjord in 872 (see HARALD HAARFAGER), repaired to I. for freedom, the first settlers reaching the island under Ingólfr in 874. In about sixty years all the habitable parts of the island were occupied. Patriarchal government was first instituted; district affairs were discussed in meetings called *Things*, but from 929 a General Assembly or *Althing* met at Thíngvalla. Towards the end of the 10th c. the Icelanders discovered Greenland, and about the beginning of the 11th c. the mainland of America. Christianity was established in 1000, largely through the exertions of the Norwegian king Olaf Tryggvesön. Wasting feuds between the chiefs enabled Hakon IV. (Hakonsön) of Norway to reduce I. in 1262-64, after which it prosperity gradually declined. On the union of Norway with Denmark in 1380, I. was transferred to Danish rule. The Reformation struggle lasted from 1540 to 1551. The Althing was abolished in 1800, but re-established in 1843. On January 5, 1874, after a thirty years' conflict, I. received a freer constitution from Denmark. See Sartorius von Waltershausen, *Physisch-geographische Skizze von Island* (Gött. 1847); Thienemann, *Reisen im Norden Europas, vorzüglich in Island* (Leips. 1827); G. G. Winkler, *Island: Seine Bewohner, Landesbildung und Vulcanische Natur* (Brunsw. 1861); P. Schleiszner, *Island undersögt fra et lægevidenskabligt Synpunkt* (Copenh. 1849); Zirkel and Preyer, *Reise nach Island im Sommer* 1860 (Leips. 1862); Maurer, *Island von seiner ersten Entdeckung bis zum Untergange des Freistaats* (Munich, 1784); Gröndal, *Um natturu Islands* (Copenh. 1874); R. F. Burton, *Ultima Thule, or a Summer in Iceland* (Edinb. 1875); Watt, *Across the Vatna Jökull* (Lond. 1877).

Iceland Moss (*Cetraria Islandica*), a plant of three or four inches in height, and in colour olive brown, consisting of an erect foliaceous and tufted thallus, having the segments laciniated. I. M. grows very abundantly on the surface of the ground, more especially on mountains, in exposed situations in high northern latitudes, and receives its vernacular name through confusion with genuine mosses. I. M. contains 80 per cent of farinaceous matter, insoluble in alcohol, ether, and cold water, but soluble in boiling water; also a starch-like body called *inuline*, and a bitter principle, *cetraric* acid, soluble in water and alkaline solution. I. M., deprived of its bitter principle, is used as food by the Icelanders, and as a light farinaceous article of diet by invalids suffering from *dyspepsia*, *chronic dysentery*, *phthisis*, and *chronic catarrh*. It is frequently confounded with Irish moss; but neither of the two is a moss; the latter being a small seaweed. See CARRAGEEN.

Iceland Moss.

Ice Plant, the current designation of *Mesembryanthemum crystallinum*, the only species of that immense and truly beautiful genus that is European. In England it is commonly grown in gardens. Both scientific and popular names originate from the plant being covered with watery vesicles which glisten in the sun like fragments of ice.

Ichneu'mon, a genus of small carnivorous animals belonging to the *Viverridæ* or civet family. The genus *Herpestes* includes the best-known species of I. In this genus the legs are short; the feet have five toes; the ears are small and rounded, and the claws large and curved. The hair is long and bristly, and the teeth number forty. The common I. (*H. Ichneumon*) inhabits N. Africa. It is popularly known as 'Pharaoh's rat,' and, like the Ibis (q. v.), appears to have received special attention and honour from the ancient Egyptians. It is still plentiful in Egypt, being domesticated and kept in the house like a cat. The I. is an exterminator of all kinds of reptiles, snakes, lizards, and crocodiles' eggs being greedily devoured by it. The colour is brown variegated with grey tints; the average length about 3 feet. The Indian I. or mungoos (*H. griseus*) is of a grey colour, and is famous for its habit of attacking the Cobra (q. v.), the deadliest of Indian snakes, and for its apparent immunity from the venom of its enemy. The crab-eating I. or urva (*Urva cancrivorus*) is so named from its habit of feeding on crabs, like the crab-eating racoon. Other species of I. are the garangan or Javanese I. (*H. Javanicus*), of a rich chestnut brown; and the banded mungoos or I. (*H. fasciatus*), so named from the dark bands which cross the spine.

Ichneumon.

Ichneumon Fly, the name given to various species of *Hymenopterous* insects belonging to the family *Ichneumonidæ*. The body is long and slender, while the *ovipositor* or egg-depositor is well developed, and exists at the extremity of the abdomen. This organ is protected by a sheath. The larvæ are soft, footless grubs. The eggs of the I. flies are deposited on the larvæ of certain species of *Coleoptera* or beetles, on *Hymenopterous* larvæ, and on those of other insects. The genus I. itself is represented by such species as the *I. suturalis* and *I. paratus*, the larvæ of which are deposited on the larvæ of the *Leucania unipunctata*, a *Lepidopterous* insect. Other genera and species of I. flies are *Evania*, of which the *E. lævigata* is parasitic on the cockroach; *Fœnus*, of which *F. jaculator* infests the nests of sand-wasps (*Crabro*); *Ophion*, of which *O. macrurum* attacks the American silkworm (*Telea polyphemus*); *Anomalon*, of which *A. vesparum* infests wasps; *Pimpla*, of which *P. instigator* is a familiar species, infesting the larvæ of the cabbage-butterfly, and *Microgaster*, exemplified by *M. glomerulus*, also infesting the caterpillars of the cabbage-butterfly.

Ichnol'ogy (Gr. 'footprint lore'), the science that determines the nature of fossil footprints. Many extinct animals have left traces of their movements upon soft formations, such as sand or mud, these formations afterwards becoming consolidated into rocks, which thus bear evidence of the life of the period at which they were formed. It is perfectly clear that I., as a department of palæontological science, is founded upon comparative anatomy. Only the skilled anatomist, who is conversant with the structure of the limbs and feet of existing animals, is entitled to express an opinion as to the kind of foot which may have made an impression upon a once soft formation. The more perfectly the science of comparative anatomy can be applied to the examination of footprints, the greater hope is there of arriving at a just conception of the forms which have made the impressions, and the same opinion must necessarily be expressed with regard to the examination of fossil remains themselves. The department of I. may be said to include the investigation of all traces of animal life, whether consisting of actual footprints or of impressions of other surfaces than those of the feet, or of lower animals which possess no distinct limbs. Thus worm-burrows, the impressions of shells, &c., fall naturally under the consideration of this branch of geological science. The impression of an animal or its hard parts may persist after the animal itself has disappeared through the action of chemical change or of other influences. In other cases, soft-bodied animals, such as sea-anemones, and even the delicate jellyfishes, have left impressions which, in the absence of hard parts in the animals, have, nevertheless, served to perpetuate their existence, and have afforded means of speculating with tolerable certainty on the nature and relations of such organisms. Thus, in the fine-grained lithographic slates of Solenhofen in Bavaria, which in their soft and primitive condition must have been capable of receiving and retaining the slightest and most delicate impression, traces of medusidæ or jellyfishes have been found. Many soft seaweeds are known to us as fossils by their impressions only; and inorganic things, such as raindrops, ripple-waves on a sea-beach, footmarks, and sun-cracks, are similarly reproduced in a fossil and petrified state. Evidence of the existence of marine worms is obtained from the tracks and burrows these worms have left in the sand and mud of their primitive habitations. From the Lower Cambrian rocks up to the present day, annelid tracks are common, and names have been given to the *burrows* (*Scolithus*, *Histioderma*, and *Arenicolites*), although in some cases, and when first discovered, the petrified tracks were described as the fossilised worms themselves. *Scolithus* made long straight burrows; those of *Histioderma* were curved and terminated in a little heap; that of *Arenicolites* is a small burrow formed after a looped fashion; *Grossopodia* from the Silurian rocks exhibits windings and undulations; while one genus, *Palæochorda*, was formerly thought to represent traces of marine plants.

The *Vertebrate* animals, however, are unquestionably those which present examples of the science of I. in fullest detail, and amongst the vertebrates, the reptiles, birds, and quadrupeds are the classes demanding attention from the palæontologist. In 1828 the existence of tortoises in past times was inferred by Dr. Duncan from the impressions of footprints seen on sandstones in Dumfriesshire. Footprints of birds and reptiles are often well preserved, the footprint having first been made on the soft mud or clay of sea-beaches, which may become sun-dried, and adapted to resist the pressure of the matter which covers the impression at the next inflow of the tide; while dry sand may be blown by the wind into an impression and may fill it up. Among the best-known examples of *Ichnites* or fossil footprints are those named *Protichnites septem-notatus*, by Owen, from the Cambrian rocks. These impressions were produced most probably by some extinct crustacean or crablike animal. The famous *Cheirotherium* ('hand-beast') impressions were first described in 1834, and resemble the footprints of a salamander-like animal possessing five toes. The subsequent discovery of the huge extinct amphibians named *Labyrinthodons* (q. v.) afforded the clue to the source of the cheirotherium marks. In 1835 large footprints resembling those of birds were observed in sandstone slabs of Triassic age from the banks of the Connecticut River in the United States. The evidence afforded by these prints tend to show (1) that they are the footprints of a biped; (2) that the impressions are three-toed; and (3) that the numerical progression of the bones of the toes was the same as that seen in existing birds. The largest footprint is 22 inches long and 12 inches wide. The idea that these footprints represent those of birds has been rejected by some palæontologists in favour of the opinion that they are those of extinct reptiles which may have possessed the power of walking upon two limbs.

Ich'thus (Gr. 'a fish'), the name given to the earliest kind of Christian amulets, because the initials of the Greek for Jesus Christ, Son of God, Saviour, made up this word.

Ichthyodor'ulite (Gr. 'fish-spear stone'), the name given to the fossilised fin-spines of fishes, chiefly belonging to the orders *Elasmobranchii* (q. v.), sharks, &c., and *Ganoidei* (q. v.), sturgeons, &c. A few Teleostean fishes, such as the *Siluridæ* or sheat-fishes, also have fin-spines, but these are unknown in the older formations in which I. occur. The earliest remains of I. occur at the close of the Upper Silurian system of rocks. The genus *Onchus* is one of the earliest genera founded upon the characters of the I. occurring in Upper Silurian strata. In Old Red Sandstone or Devonian rocks these fossils also occur.

Ichthyol'ogy (Gr. 'the science of fishes') is a department of zoology not now prosecuted as a distinct branch of science. The day of special departments of natural history—such as conchology, malacology, and the like—has almost disappeared. Apart from its relations to modern science, I. has always held an important place in zoological science. Aristotle and Pliny in classic times, Willoughby and Ray during last century, and Agassiz and Owen at the present time, represent the chief workers in this department. In particular, the labours of the late Professor Agassiz are to be borne in mind as having advanced our knowledge of fossil fishes especially. Agassiz proposed many important modifications of the classification of fishes, the chief of which was a proposal to arrange fishes according to the structure of their scales.

Ichthyop'sida, one of the chief divisions or provinces into which Vertebrate animals are divided. The I. include the fishes and Amphibians (q. v.) (frogs, newts, &c.). The distinctive features of the I., or those, in other words, in which fishes and amphibians agree, consist in the fact that the *blood* is cold and the red blood corpuscles *nucleated*; gills or branchiæ may form, as in fishes, the only breathing organs, or may be conjoined with lungs, as in amphibia. Neither *Amnion* (q. v.) nor *Allantois* (q. v.), are represented in the development of the I. The skull may be altogether wanting, as in the lancelet and the spine may persist as a notochord without developing any distinct bony spine-elements. The occipital condyles of the skull may be double, or only one may be developed, whilst a condyle may be wanting. The *exoskeleton*, consisting of scales, &c., is never developed to any great extent. The digestive system may terminate in a cloaca; when a cloaca is wanting, the intestine terminates in front of the urinary organs. The *heart* may be tubular (lancelet), bilocular (two-chambered, as in fishes), or trilocular (three-chambered, as in amphibia). Two *aortic arches*, at least, exist in the adult, and no *diaphragm* is developed. The *kidneys* simply represent the wolffian bodies of the embryo. No mammary glands are developed. The remaining principal divisions of vertebrata are the *Sauropsida* reptiles and birds, and *Mammalia*.

Ichthyosau'rus (Gr. 'fish-reptile'), an extinct genus of large reptilia, belonging to the order *Ichthyosauria* or *Ichthyopterygia*

(Owen). This group was distinguished by the fishlike form of the body. No distinct neck was developed, and in all probability the body was covered with a smooth wrinkled skin; no traces of scales or any hard covering having been found. The vertebræ were numerous, bony, and markedly bi-concave in form (*amphicœlous*). No sacrum, sternum (breastbone), or sternal ribs were developed. Clavicles or collar-bones were present, and false or abdominal ribs were developed. The orbits or eye-cavities were very large, and the eye had a ring of bony plates in the sclerotic or outer coat. The teeth, which were numerous, were not developed in sockets, but were lodged in a common groove. Both pairs of limbs existed in the form of swimming-paddles, the number of the *phalanges* or finger-bones being very great. In all probability a vertical caudal-fin or tail-fin was present. The remains of I. are exclusively confined to the Mesozoic rocks, being found in the Lias, Oolite, and Chalk. These animals must have been both numerous and large. Specimens have been met with which exceed 20 feet in length. The structure of the vertebræ, the short whalelike neck, and the large development of the paddles, evidently adapted them for a marine life. Along with their neighbours the *Plesiosauri*, they must have roamed far out to sea; and that they occasionally rested on the land is proved by the examination of the shoulder-girdle, which supports the fore-limbs. That they were carnivorous in habits is proved by an examination of their fossil excrement or *coprolites*, which contain fragments of the scales and bones of Ganoid (q. v.) fishes which were contemporaries of the I. in the primitive oceans. Dr. Buckland says that the enormous eye (the orbit in some specimens measuring 4 inches in its largest diameter) of which the sclerotic plates formed the front, was an optical instrument of varied and prodigious power, enabling the I. to descry its prey at great or little distances, in the obscurity of night, and in the depths of the sea. About thirty species are known to geologists.

Ichythyo'sis. See Fish-Skin Disease.

Ic'ica, a tropical genus of *Amyridaceæ*, consisting principally of large trees, belonging to mid-America, and possessing the balsamic juice for which the order is noted. So highly saturated is *I. heptaphylla* with this odoriferous resin that the timber is used for torches, and is called in Guiana, incense-wood. Another species, *I. altissima*, from its fragrant smell, is termed cedar-wood. Like the cedar, it is distasteful to insect vermin, and is consequently in request for household furniture. On account of its large growth, its durability, and the facility with which it is wrought, it is also chosen by the Indians for the manufacture of their canoes. A third species of the same region yields Elemi (q. v.).

I'cicles, in heraldry, are charges similar to the drops in the bearing known as Gussé, but more elongated.

Icil'ius, the name of a plebeian gens which, in the 5th c. B.C., played a leading part in the struggle at Rome between the patricians and plebeians. Seven of the name figure in history, of whom the most important are—(1) **Spurius I.**, who, as tribune of the plebs, in 492, enacted the popular *Lex Icilia*, augmenting the tribunal powers, and in 491 was thrown from the Tarpeian Rock; and (2) **Lucius I.**, who enacted a law assigning the Aventine to the plebs in 496, and six years later headed the outbreak against the decemvirs. See Appius Claudius.

Icolm Kill'. See Iona.

I'cones (Gr. *eikones*, 'images'), pictorial representations of plants. The word is commonly quoted Ic.

Ico'nium. See Konieh.

Icon'oclasts (Gr. *eikôn*, 'image,' and *klazô*, 'I break') is the name given to those in the 8th c. who were opposed to image-worship in the church, and did their best to put it down. It might be said that the first of the I. was Izid or Jesid, an Arab prince, who in 715 commanded all pictures to be removed from the churches in his dominions. Leo the Isaurian, an Eastern Roman emperor (716), declared himself opposed to idolatry, and first (726) ordered images to be hung higher, that they might not be kissed, and then (730) all to be removed from the churches. His son and successor, Constantine V., published another edict against images (741), and all that had been left were effaced by scraping or whitewashing the walls. By a general council convened by him at Constantinople in 754, severe penalties were enacted for image-worship. But on the death of Leo IV. (780), the Iconolaters were triumphant under his widow, Irene, who convened a council at Nicæa (787), by which the worship of images and of the cross was re-established. Leo the Armenian (813) was a decided enemy to image-worship, but it was restored by Theodora, the widow of Theophilus (died 842), and the consent of the Church given by a council held at Constantinople (869), and confirmed by another in 879. In the West, it was decreed by a council held at Gentilly in 767, under Pippin, that images might be endured 'so that they were not had for worship, veneration, and adoration.' Again, under Karl the Great, a council held at Frankfurt (794) condemned the adoration which the synod of the Greeks had declared to be due to images, although it allowed the use of them.

Icy Cape, a promontory in the N. of Alaska, N. America, on the W. Georgian coast, 160 miles W.S.W. of Point Barrow. It was the furthest point reached by Cook in his voyage through Behring Strait in 1778.

I'da, an offshoot of the Taurus range, in Asia Minor, which, extending from Phrygia into Western Mysia, attained in Gargarus (the modern Kazdag) an elevation of 4650 feet. I. was anciently covered with woods, was the source of countless streams (the Simois, Scamander, &c.), and, according to Homer, abounded in wild beasts. At its western base stood Troy (q. v.), and the entire range is associated with numerous Greek myths. A second I., forming the central and loftiest point of the mountain system of Crete, has been identified with the modern Psiloriti (7674 feet), was sacred to Zeus, who, according to one myth, was brought up on its slopes, and was the home of the Idæan Dactyls, the legendary discoverers of metallurgy.

I'daho, a western territory of the United States, N. America, is bounded N. by British Columbia, E. by Montana and Wyoming, S. by Utah and Nevada, and W. by Oregon and Washington. Area, 86,294 sq. miles; pop. (1870) 20,583, of whom 8915 were Indians, and 4274 Chinese. The chief rivers are Clark's Fork and Lewis or Snake River, both affluents of the Columbia (q. v.), and the Bear River, which falls into the Great Salt Lake. The Bitter Root Mountains, offsets of the Rocky Mountains, attain in their loftiest points an altitude of over 13,000 feet, and the town of Florence (11,100 feet above the sea) is the highest city in the United States. There are numerous lakes throughout the territory. The rainfall is small, but the valleys are extremely fertile, and the mountains clothed with forests up to the snow-line. The discovery of gold in 1852 led to the settlement of I., which up till 1863 formed a portion of the territory of Oregon. It has no railroads, and no good roads of any length. In 1872 the yield of gold and silver amounted to $8,000,000. Lead, coal, iron, and building-stone are also found. The principal towns are Boisé City (the capital), I., Lewiston, and Silver City.

Ide (*Leuciscus Idus*), a Teleostean fish belonging to the carp family (*cyprinidæ*) and to the genus *Leuciscus*, which includes the dace, chub, &c. It is found in lakes and rivers in N. Europe, and appears to ascend the latter in April and May to spawn.

Ide'a is properly the general name for those secondary and less intense feelings which, though they are taken to imply objective excitants that acted at a past time, do not imply their present action. This, of course, applies to those feelings initiated from within, called emotions, as well as to those initiated outside, called sensations. These ideas afterwards form into various relations of likeness and unlikeness, coexistence and sequence, and also into various tracts of consciousness, differing greatly in the clearness with which the separate or successive elements are distinguished. Thus, subject to the control and suggestion of actual sensation, the undercurrent of mental life is made up. This revivability or recoverability of feeling, or rather of clusters of feelings, is the most fundamental fact of mind. The process is one for the most part generally independent of will. There is a scale of facility with which different feelings can be represented; from the intense feelings of sight down to the vague feeling of hunger. The recovery is more difficult in the case of emotions, for some time is occupied in imagining the circumstances calculated to produce it. The ease of recovery also depends very much on the vividness of *pre-*

sent feelings, but this condition is less powerful when the revived and the present feelings belong to different orders; a circumstance which points to localisation of function. Original strength and frequency of repetition are constant conditions of revivability; and the first of these often depends on the temporary state of repair of the nervous centre affected, on the activity of the general circulation, and on the vital character of the blood. An exalted state, produced by exercise, emotion, or even disease, is the most favourable for revival. These conditions must also be allowed for at the time of revival. Indeed, under the influence of opium and hashish, the revived impressions have sometimes more than their original strength. The revivability of relations, or of forms of thought, apart from their contents, stands in a very different position. Whether the compound relations be of coexistence, sequence, or difference, they are more distinctly representable and more enduring in memory. The succession of emotions is more easily recovered than the emotions themselves; and most easily where the emotions are such as to have many relations to other things, including other relations. The same antagonism exists between similar orders of represented relations as in the case of feelings. In the history of philosophy, the word I. has, of course, had many and various meanings. We have the Platonic ideas of the Divine mind, eternal models or archetypes of sensible things, about which alone science is conversant; the sensible species, *aporroai*, or phantasms, which by many of the Greek schools, and generally down to the time of Descartes, were supposed to have an undefined likeness to the external object which they represented; the image of Locke, at least as regards primary qualities; and the Berkleian I. which, far from being a mere species of mental modification, was supposed to have an independent objective existence in the Divine mind when not present to the human. The question whether the I. resembles the *ideatum*, is now generally abandoned as insoluble, man being unable to get outside his own mind, except to the effect of recognising, and to some extent predicting, an order of facts, the essential nature of which is unknown. I. is also frequently used to denote the fundamental conception from which a work of art or a scientific demonstration proceeds.

Id'eler, Christian Ludwig, a Prussian astronomer and chronologist, was born September 21, 1766, at Gross-Brese, near Perleberg. In 1821 he became a professor in Berlin University, and in 1839 was chosen an honorary member of the Institute of France. He died August 10, 1846. His great work is his *Handbuch der Mathematischen und Technischen Chronologie* (2 vols. Berl. 1825–26), which treats fully of the reckoning of time among the ancients.—His son, **Julius Ludwig I.** (born 1809, died 1842), was the author of *Meteorologia Veterum Græcorum et Romanorum* (Berl. 1832), and *Physici et Medici Græci Minores* (2 vols. Berl. 1841–42), &c.

Iden'tity has various meanings. There is the verbal I. satirised by Locke in his chapter on Trifling Propositions (Essay, iv. 8), and of which a specimen is the great ontological maxim 'whatever is, is.' There is logical I., which includes subjects possessing the same attribute or attributes, *i.e.*, belonging to the same species. Hence, the law of I. appears along with those of contradiction and excluded middle as a fundamental law of thought; and from these, formal logicians develop the abstract rules of syllogism, the 'dictum de omni et nullo,' &c. These so-called laws are simply different modes of expressing that we cannot at the same time *believe* both a proposition and its contradictory opposite, and that we cannot at the same time *disbelieve* both. They are conditions of thought, and without them language would have no meaning or title to belief. In an important chapter (ii. 27) Locke discusses the identity and diversity of various classes of substances. Plants and animals are supposed to maintain their I., though the particles of matter composing them are in a state of continual flux. Inorganic substances also are said to retain their I., though subjected to temporary changes of condition. Even the primary qualities may be interfered with without destroying I. These puzzles are avoided by the analysis of material substance into permanent possibility of sensation. But the more difficult question of personal I. remains. Locke (who has on this subject a long controversy with the Bishop of Worcester on the Resurrection) says this may mean (1) the same numerical soul, (2) the same physical animal, (3) the same soul and body together. It is defined by himself as the consciousness of continued existence, but, as he inclined to the belief in an immaterial substance or *ego*, he probably does not differ much from Butler, who said that consciousness presupposed I. In the belief in memory there is no doubt involved more than the mere consciousness of a succession of feelings in time. There is the recognition of the reality of the past feeling; and out of the past and also the expected future there is constantly growing the notion of self, which is not, as some have supposed, a simple and definite idea, but varies according to the particular character and the particular trains of memory, fancy, or expectation with which the character most strongly sympathises. Self accompanies all deliberate acts of consciousness, but not those ideas which, when reproduced, are not remembered. But whether a spiritual self can exist apart from a material self is a point on which neither physiology nor psychology is likely to throw any light. There is an anthropological doctrine of some importance called the psychical I. of the human race. It rests on the number of striking mental analogies observed between the most dissimilar and widely-separated races. Nearly all nations have reached a single or double decimal system. Circumcision was perhaps at one time universal wherever the sanitary reasons existed, and is still much more widely practised than is generally supposed. So with skin-painting, tattooing, flattening the heads of children, sexual connection with a brother's widow, the salute of rubbing noses, the custom of ratifying bonds of friendship by an exchange of names, that of travellers adding each a stone to hill-cairns, the *couvade* or inlying of the father; all these at one time thought to be idiosyncrasies of a particular tribe or nation are now found to exist or to have existed almost all over the world among people between whom there was no possibility of intercourse. In legal proceedings the proof of I. of a human body has often depended on the question whether cicatrices or tattoo-marks might have disappeared, or might have been produced at a certain time; these being among the most durable of bodily signs. A dispute as to I. of sex raises the difficult and fortunately rare question of Hermaphroditism.

Ides. See CALENDS.

Id'iocy is an abnormal condition of the intellect, depending upon defective development or disease during fœtal life; or upon arrested development during infancy or childhood up to puberty. A dement is deprived of powers which he once possessed, but an idiot is characterised by absence of powers which he never possessed. An imbecile is weak in all his mental faculties; but the intellect of an idiot is not only dwarfed, but deformed; while feebleness of will is often as remarkable as deficiency of power of apprehension. There are different degrees of I. depending upon the extent to which the cerebro-spinal system is involved. In the lowest form, the functions of *organic* or *vegetative* life are imperfectly performed; and the functions of *animal* life are likewise impaired, so that he may be scarcely alive to external impressions, and barely possess the power of executing spontaneous acts. In the most abject state of I. he is blind, deaf and dumb, and the excretions are passed involuntarily. There are, however, many grades of intellectual and moral capacity among idiots, and all, except the very lowest, are susceptible, in a corresponding degree, to management, training, and education. It may be stated, generally, that the greater the organic deformities, and the smaller the head, the imperfections of sensibility and intelligence will be the more marked; but the heads of many idiots are unusually large. The chief characteristics of I. are the vacant stare, thick everted lips, the slavering mouth, irregular teeth, squinting, and absence or defect of the senses of sight, hearing, speech, taste, or smell. The extent to which the cerebro-spinal system is involved is frequently manifested by bodily as well as mental deformity, and the idiot is frequently a dwarf, or he may be unable to walk, or to balance himself while sitting, or he may walk with a staggering gait. I. is very frequently associated with epilepsy; cerebral disease, as hydrocephalus; paralysis; disorder of the process of dentition, and general arrest of development during infancy. Some one faculty is frequently exempted from the dulling of the rest, as a perception of tune, an idea of numbers, a mechanical occupation, certain sympathies, and the capacity for imitation; and the measure of success attending educational efforts depends upon a correct appreciation of the dormant or latent capacity. The more celebrated establishments for the education of idiots in Great Britain are at Earlswood, Reigate, Baldovan, Forfarshire, and Larbert, Stirlingshire. See Seguin, *Traitment Morale, &c. des Idiots* (Par. 1846); *Report to the Legislature of Massachusetts upon Idiocy*, by S. G. Howe (Bost. 1848); Abbot's *Handbook of Idiocy*, Buckminster Brown; *Treatment and Cure of Cretins and Idiots;* and the works of Esquirol, Coke, Prichard, and *Psychological Medicine*, by Bucknill and Tuke (Lond. 1874).

Id'iots and Lun'atics, Law Regarding. They are not chargeable with their acts, however these may be of a criminal nature in the same. It is often exceedingly difficult to determine the line between legal sanity and legal insanity. He who causes a madman to commit a crime is held guilty of that crime.

Idol'atry (Gr. *eidōlolatreia*, from *eidōlon*, 'an image,' and *latreia*, 'worship'). An idol is a likeness or figure of any object worshipped as a divinity, or as representing a divinity. A classification of all the forms of I., which is thus regarded as synonymous with false religion, has been made under the heads of (1) Fetishism (q. v.), or low nature-worship, (2) Shamanism (q. v.), (3) Sabæism (q. v.), or high nature-worship, (4) worship of deceased ancestors, and (5) the worship of abstractions or mental qualities; all other systems being regarded as mixtures or combinations of these five. The religion of the ancient Assyrians and Babylonians was a system of high nature-worship. That of the ancient Egyptians was a phase of Fetishism, being chiefly a worship of animals, &c. The Hebrews were remarkable for their early conception of Monotheism, but there are distinct traces of I. among them down to a late period. The other gods referred to (Josh. xxiv. 2) as worshipped by their fathers must have been the gods of the ancient Assyrians (see Smith's *Chaldæan Acc. of Genesis*). The gods or teraphim of Laban, as well as those of Jacob's household (Gen. xxxi. 30, xxxv. 4), were probably connected with ancestor-worship. The I. into which they fell in the wilderness, the worship of Jehovah under the figure of a bull (Exod. xxxii.), and of Saturn (Amos v. 26. *cf.* Acts vii. 43), was a species of nature-worship, as was also the I. of which there are so many traces in their history long after they settled in Canaan. Indeed, they do not seem to have realised till the time of the Babylonish exile that the worship of Jehovah was incompatible with that of Baal, Ashtoreth, the sun, Chemosh, Molech, &c. (*cf.* 1 Kings xi. 1-8; 2 Kings xxiii. 11-13). But, as it has been said, they went to Babylon a nation of idolaters, and returned a nation of puritans. The Christian Church, again, had to contend with the I. of the Greek, Latin, and Celtic races; and it is remarkable how much I. there was lingering in Europe long after it was regarded as being Christianised. Regarding a certain amount of disguised I. which crept into the Church itself, see IMAGE-WORSHIP.

Id'ria, Ober, a town of Austria, in Carniola, and on the Idriza, 30 miles N. of Trieste. Its quicksilver mines are among the richest in Europe, employing 700 men, and yielding 3000 cwts. of metal annually. Pop. (1869) 3813.

Idumæ'a. See EDOM.

Idun', Ydun', or **Idun'a,** in the Northern mythology a goddess of the race of the dwarfs, wife of Bragi (q. v.), who kept in a box the apples by eating which the gods had perpetual youth. A story of the *Younger Edda* makes I. be seized by the giant Thiassi, aided by Loki, who was compelled by the gods to bring her back.

I'dyll, or **Idyl** (Gr. *eidullion*, from *eidos*, a 'form' or 'figure;' Lat. *idyllium*, 'a small image'), was at first strictly a short pastoral poem, a distinction being sometimes made between the *eclogue*, which was said to demand dramatic dialogue, and the I., which demanded mere narration. The I. did not long retain a solely pastoral character. The idylls of Theocritus give glimpses of town as well as country life, though the idea of rural descriptions is still vaguely associated with the spirit of poetry. Tennyson's *Idylls of the King* are only idyllic in so far as they are non-lyrical, and as each tells a complete story.

Ig'lau, one of the oldest and largest towns of Moravia, Austria, on the Iglawa, 130 miles N.W. of Vienna by rail. It has an old Gothic church of St. Jakob, and extensive manufactures of woollen cloths, paper, glass, tobacco, &c. The river is here crossed by a stone bridge. To the E. of the town are two granite pillars, one marking the Bohemian border, the other the spot where Ferdinand I. took the oath of allegiance to Bohemia on its passing to the House of Hapsburg in 1527. Pop. (1869) 17,427. By the Treaty of I. the Emperor Sigismund agreed to observe the Prag Compact, and became King of Bohemia, 5th July 1436.

Ignat'ieff, Nicolas Paulovitch, a Russian general and diplomatist, born about 1830. While still young he became a general, and was sent on a mission to Pekin, where he negotiated a favourable commercial treaty with China. He had for some time charge of the Asiatic department in the Russian Foreign Office, and became Minister at Constantinople, July 26, 1864. Here he exercised great influence over the Sultan Abdul Assiz. On the latter's dethronement and the outbreak of the war with Servia and Montenegro, he strongly championed the Slavonian cause, and an ultimatum presented by him in October 1876 forced the Porte to grant an armistice. He was the Russian plenipotentiary at the Conference at Constantinople, Christmas 1876, and on its failure withdrew with the other ambassadors temporarily from that capital. In March 1877 he visited the principal courts of Europe on the Eastern question, and in London was the guest of the Marquis of Salisbury, his colleague at the Conference, the result of which was the signature of the London Protocol. He is understood to have great conversational powers, to be a master of diplomacy, and to be marked out for even greater advancement in the Russian state.

Igna'tius, Bishop of Antioch, is one of the so-called Apostolic Fathers (q. v.), and is said to have been a disciple of St. John. Eusebius records the tradition that he suffered martyrdom by being torn to pieces by wild beasts at Rome in the reign of Trajan, but whether in 107 or 116 is not clear. There are extant a number of epistles bearing the name of I., regarding which there has been much controversy. From Smyrna, according to Eusebius, he wrote four epistles—to the Churches of Ephesus, Magnesia, Tralles, and Rome; and from Troas three—to the Churches of Philadelphia and Smyrna, and to Polycarp (q. v.). These seven, of which there are longer and shorter copies, have generally been considered authentic and genuine in the shorter form; other five in Greek, and as many more in Latin, have been universally rejected. The circumstance that has chiefly been the occasion of the controversy regarding the seven is that in them the dignity and authority of bishops are exalted higher than in any other writings of the same age. For this reason the epistles have been highly prized and strenuously defended by the advocates of the apostolic origin of Episcopacy, and as strenuously assailed by divines of the Reformed Churches. A Syriac version of three of them, those to Polycarp, the Ephesians, and the Romans, was recently discovered in the Egyptian desert of Nitria. These Syriac copies are shorter even than the short Greek copies, and the passages omitted in the Syriac are chiefly those that magnify the office of a bishop and enforce the doctrine of the deity of Christ. See Cureton's *Anc. Syr. Version of the Epistles of I.* (Lond. 1845).

Ignatius, St., Patriarch of Constantinople, son of the Emperor Michael I., was born about 800. His original name was Nicetas, which he changed to I., when, on the deposition of his father by Leo V. (813), he was forced to become a monk. As such I. was ordained priest by Basil of Paros, became abbot of the monastery of Satyrus at Constantinople, and in 846 succeeded Methodius in the patriarchate of that city. I. was a vigorous opponent of the Iconoclasts (q. v.), and in this opposition was supported by Theodora, the regent for her infant son, Michael III.; but the latter, on attaining majority, was led by the intrigues of his uncle, Bardas, whose vices I. had reproved, to depose I. (858) and secure the election in his place of the iconoclastic Photius (q. v.). Although Pope Nicholas I. refused to recognise the transaction, Photius retained the patriarchate till 867, when, under Basil I. (q. v.), he was in turn deposed and I. reinstated, an eighth general council assembling at Constantinople in 869 to ratify both events. I. died October 23, 878.

Ignatius', St., Beans, the name given by old writers to certain seeds introduced into the Dutch shops about 200 years ago, and extolled as a remedy against cholera. From the quantity of strychnia they contain, their origin is surmised to be a species of *Strychnos*. The genus *Ignatia*, in which they were placed by the younger Linnæus, does not exist in nature; he founded it on specimens belonging to two genera.

Ig'neous Rocks include all rocks which have consolidated from fusion. In their mode of formation they are distinguished from the other two great groups of rocks—the *aqueous* and the *metamorphic*. The former are produced by consolidation from solution, or by deposition from suspension; while the latter have been altered from their first condition by intense heat or crushing, without, however, being completely fused. If the earth be a cooling body, all rocks must originally have been igneous, so that the ultimate constituents of aqueous and therefore of metamorphic rocks are of igneous origin. I. R. are characterised by an absence of stratification, except such as might result from the flow of one lava stream over another, or from the deposition of successive showers of volcanic ashes and scoriæ. Chemically, all such rocks are composed essentially of silicates, which belong to one of two great classes—the *magnesia* and the *alumina* silicates. For purposes of classification, I. R. are divided into (*a*) *volcanic*, including those which have consolidated at the surface; and (*b*) *plutonic*, embracing those which have formed at some distance below it. Practically it is found more convenient to look upon the latter as consisting of two divisions, *trappean* and *granitic*, the former of which is intermediate to the volcanic and granitic, and is defined only vaguely. The truly volcanic include such rocks as trachyte, obsidian, pumice, dolerite, basalt, doleritic breccias, and tuffs, &c.; the trappean include felstone, pitchstone, porphyrite, diallage rock, greenstone, &c.; and the granitic include the various varieties of granite and syenite.

Ig'nis Fat'uus (Lat. foolish fire'), a luminous meteor which is sometimes seen in marshy places, flitting over the ground at a short distance above the surface. Cases are on record of its having been mistaken for a lamp, and the traveller thus decoyed has perished in the bog. It is usually pale blue in colour, but varies much in size and shape, and in the steadiness of its appearance. No satisfactory explanation has yet been given, and the probability is that there are several distinct kinds of I. F. due to different causes. Some may be caused by the escape of phosphureted hydrogen (PH_3), which ignites spontaneously when it comes into contact with the air; others by the combustion of light carbureted hydrogen or *marsh gas* (CH_4); while others may be a species of phosphorescence. It is not confined to true marshes, but is sometimes observed in churchyards and near stagnant pools. Its appearances are most frequent in the autumn or late summer, from a short time after sunset to early morning. It was long an object of superstitious dread amongst the common people, as its various names, of which *Will-o'-the-wisp*, *Jack-a-lantern*, and *Spunkie* are the most familiar, indicate.

Ignorance of the Law, or **Ignorantia Juris**, is no legal extenuation for any crime, offence, or breach of contract. Ignorance of fact may, however, have a material effect in civil questions. See BONA FIDES and CONDICTIO INDEBITI.

Ignoran'tines (*Frères Ignorantins*), called also the *Congregation of Christian Doctrine*, are a Jesuit association founded in 1724 by the Abbé de la Salle. They give instruction gratis in the primary schools, the main aim being to inculcate submission to the hierarchy. They continued to maintain Jesuit influence, even after the regular order had been expelled from France in 1764. When the I. were themselves compelled to leave France in 1790, they possessed twelve institutions there. Taking refuge in Italy, they were allowed to return by Napoleon, who encouraged their labours. Recently they had about 400 institutions, and nearly 700 schools under their management in France. They have also branches in Italy, Germany, Bohemia, England, and Ireland.

Iguala'da, a town in the province of Barcelona, Spain, on the Noya, 40 miles W.N.W. of Barcelona, at the S. base of the Montserrat. It is a gloomy town with a beautiful suburb, and has a trade in wine, oil, fruits, &c., besides manufactures of cottons, woollens, paper, and firearms. Pop. 14,000.

Igua'na, the typical genus of a large family (*Iguanidæ*) of *Lacertilia* or lizards, found in both Old and New Worlds, and distinguished by a very thick, fleshy tongue, divided at its extremity only, and incapable of being protruded from the mouth. The back usually bears a prominent spinous crest or ridge, and the throat has a large dewlap, or fold of skin. The body is covered with imbricated or overlapping scales. The head is broad and flat, and provided with spines or lobes. The eyes have well-developed lids. The genus is divided into two sections. In the one group, represented by American species, the teeth are attached to the inner sides of the jaw-bones. The Old World species, on the contrary, have the teeth attached to the outer aspect of the jaw-bones. The common I. (*I. tuberculata*) is abundant in tropical America. It attains a length of 4 or 5 feet. The colour is green, varied with lines of the same colour, the tail being banded with brown, and the back having a comb-like crest. The throat fold is also mottled on its front margin. The teeth have serrated and compressed crowns, the food consisting of fruits and seeds. The naked-necked I. (*I. delicatissima*) has no tubercles on the neck-skin, and the colour is a bluish-green. Other genera include the horned I. (*Metopoceros cornutus*), and the marbled I. (*Polychrus marmoratus*) of Brazil and Central America.

Iguan'odon, an extinct genus of *Reptilia*, including some of the largest and most remarkable reptilian forms. The I. remains occur exclusively in the Cretaceous or Chalk formations, being especially found in Wealden strata, these latter formations representing a great deposit of estuarine, or delta-like matter. The I. must have attained an average length of 60 feet. It derives its name from the resemblance the teeth bear to those of the living Iguana (q. v.). The thigh measures from 4 to 5 feet in length, and in its smallest circumference about 22 inches. The fore limbs were very small as compared with the hind limbs, and it has been suggested that the I. may have occasionally walked upon the hind limbs alone, thus giving origin to paired impressions of footprints similar to those described in the article ICHNOLOGY (q. v.). The teeth are obtuse, and somewhat triangular. The surfaces are crenated, and present closely set wavy ridges. In old teeth the crowns are found to be worn —a proof that they were used in masticating and triturating the substances upon which the animals fed. In very many points of its organisation the I. appears to exhibit close resemblance to birds. Huxley on this account includes the I. and its neighbours (*Megalosaurus*, &c.) along with a singular little bird-like reptile) named *Compsognathus* in one great order of extinct reptiles, to which the name *Ornithoscelida* is given. *I. Mantellii*—named after Dr. Mantell, the discoverer of the genus—is the most familiar form. The hinder feet had three toes only, a fact which may serve to correlate the footprints (usually believed to be those of birds) observed in certain rocks along with those of the I.

Ih're, Johan, a great Swedish philologist, born at Lund, where his father was a professor, March 3, 1707. On his father's death he went to live at Upsala with his maternal grandfather, Archbishop Steuch, and graduated there in 1731. After a scientific tour for three years in Germany, Holland, England, France, and Denmark, he was appointed Professor of Belles-lettres at Upsala University. He died December 1, 1780. His chief works are: *Utkast till föreläsninger öfver Svenska språket* (Upsala, 1745; Stockholm, 1751); *Vetustus Catalogus Regum Suiogothorum* (Upsala, 1752-1755); *Svenskt dialect-Lexicon* (1766); *Ulphilas Illustratus* (*ibid.*, 1759); *Upsalia Illustrata* (*ibid.*, 1762-72), and *Glossarium Suiogothicum* (*ibid.*, 1769), his greatest production, giving the meaning and etymology of all Swedish words.

Il'chester, or **Iv'elchester**, a market-town of England, in Somersetshire on the Yeo or Ivel, 5 miles N. of Yeovil, and 33 S.S.W. of Bath. It is regarded, on account of its position, and of the traces of a Roman wall and ditch, as the *Ichalis* of Ptolemy, and at the *Domesday* survey had six churches, and was the residence of 107 burgesses. King John gave it a charter, which was renewed in the reign of Mary. Formerly it had some industries in silk and thread lace. Pop. (1871) 743. Roger Bacon was born here in 1214.

Ile-de-France, a former province of France, bounded N. by Picardy, W. by Normandy, S. by Orléannais, and E. by Champagne, so called because originally enclosed by the Seine, Marne, Oise, Aisne, and Ourcq. It had an area of 9543 sq. miles, and was (1790) subdivided into the departments of Seine, Seine-et-Oise, and Oise, and parts of Aisne, Seine-et-Marne, and Eure-et-Loire. Paris (q. v.) was the capital of I.-de-F., and hence from the 6th c. onwards the history of the province is closely connected with that of the city and its rulers. See CAPET, HOUSE OF; FRANCE; and KAROLINGS.

Iletzkij-Gorodok, a town in the government of Orenburg, Russia, on the Ilek, 6 miles S. of its confluence with the river Ural, and 80 miles S. by W. of Orenburg. Near it are the great government salt-works, yielding from eighteen to seventy-two million lbs. yearly of the finest Russian salt. The salt-bed is of vast extent and unknown depth, and is only covered by some 4 feet of soil. Pop. 2886. I. was founded by Cossacks in 1737.

Il'eus, Misere'ri Mei, or **Il'iac Passion,** is the term applied to a severe variety of colic, accompanied by obstinate vomiting, inversion of the action of the bowels, and frequently terminating in fœcal vomiting and death. I. may be caused by inflammation, cancer, or structural disease of the intestines; or by some mechanical obstruction. The disease is of the most serious nature, and requires immediate and skilled treatment.

I'lex, the scientific name for Holly (q. v.). I. is also the name of a species of oak, a native of S. Europe, and often planted in this country, called evergreen or holm oak (Quercus I.). This tree is *the* oak of many classical writers. The wood is of good quality, and the bark is used by tanners.

Il'fracombe ('Ælfric's coombe or dingle'), a seaport and watering-place of England, in N. Devonshire, picturesquely nestled in a cove among hills on the Bristol Channel coast, 11 miles N. of Barnstaple. Its harbour, among the best on the S. side of the Channel, consists of a natural basin surrounded by rocks, and is protected by a pier. The fine sandy beach attracts many visitors in summer. There is some fishing, and a coasting trade. Pop. (1871) 4721. I. had formerly a continental trade, and in Edward III.'s time sent six ships to the siege of Calais, while Liverpool only sent one.

Iliss'us. See ATHENS and ATTICA.

Ilha'vo, a town of Portugal, province of Beira, 38 miles S. of Oporto, near the sea-coast, has large glassworks in its neighbourhood at Vista Alegre. Pop. 8200, mostly fishermen.

Ilium. See TROY.

Ilium. The I. is a part of the innominate or pelvic bone, which, with its fellow on the opposite side, along with the sacrum and coccyx, forms the pelvis. In early life the innominate bone is formed of three parts, the ilium, ischium, and os pubis, but these in advanced life become fused together to form one bone.

Il'keston, a town of England, in Derbyshire, in the valley of the Erewash, 8 miles N.W. of Nottingham by rail. Its manufactures are chiefly stone bottles, drain pipes, earthenware, and bricks. I. has held a high position among English spas since the discovery of a spring of mineral water, resembling Seltzer, in 1830. Pop. (1871) 9662. The name I. was anciently spelled *Elchestane.*

Ille-et-Vilaine', a maritime department in the N.W. of France, is bounded N. by Manche and the English Channel, W. by Côtes du Nord and Morbihan, S. by Loire Inférieure, and E. by Mayenne. Area, 2597 sq. miles; pop. (1872) 589,532. I.-et-V. is traversed in the N. by a granitic range, at no point exceeding 800 feet in height, and is watered mainly by the Vilaine and Ille, which unite at Rennes. The soil is poorly cultivated, half the entire surface being heath or forest, but in the N. the plain of Dol yields good crops of cereals, and cider-making is a general and important source of wealth. Cattle-rearing, iron-mining, and linen-spinning are the chief industries, and there are five sea-ports in the department, one canal, and one main railway—the Paris-à-Brest—with two branches. The principal towns are Rennes (the capital), St. Malo, Fougères, and Vitré.

Illegibil'ity, in a material part of a deed, may be fatal to it. See CANCELLING, ERASURE.

Illegit'imacy. See BASTARD.

Illi'cium, a genus of evergreen shrubs or low trees belonging to the natural order *Magnoliaceæ,* inhabitants of both hemispheres. When bruised, the leaves, &c., exhale a strong odour like that of aniseed. The stellate fruit of a Chinese species is commonly used to flavour food among E. Asian nations; it is also taken as a stomachic, and is known commercially as star or Chinese anise. A Japan species (*I. religiosum*) is held in high estimation, and employed in various religious ceremonies by the natives. The leaves of *I. floridanum,* a native of S. United States, are said to possess poisonous properties. See ANISE.

Illima'ni, a mountain in the Bolevian Andes, 24,550 feet high. See ANDES.

Illinoi's one of the United States of America, is bounded N. by Wisconsin, E. by Lake Michigan and Indiana, S. by Kentucky, and W. by Missouri and Iowa. Area, 55,410 sq. miles; pop. (1870) 2,539,891. The surface is extremely flat, consisting for the most part of fertile prairies, interrupted here and there by clumps of oak, black-walnut, sugar-maple, sycamore, &c. The river Mississippi forms the western, the Ohio the southern, and the Wabash, part of the eastern boundary. Other rivers are the I. (500 miles long), Kaskaskia, and Rock River, tributaries of the Mississippi. The geological formation is chiefly Carboniferous; the coal measures are extensive (45,000 sq. miles), but only to a small extent workable. There are 400 mines, yielding annually some three million tons. In the N.W. are rich mines of argentiferous galenga. The climate is generally healthy, but bilious and intermittent fevers are common in the low and swampy bottom-lands of the S. In the bottom-lands the loam, based on clay, is from 25 to 100 feet deep. The chief crops are corn, wheat, oats, hay, rye, barley, buckwheat, tobacco, hemp, and flax. Among the wild animals are the coyote, or prairie wolf, the wild-cat and red-fox; game is abundant, including the hare, wild turkey, prairie rye-hen, &c. The chief industries are flour-milling, the packing of pork and other meats, distilling and malting, and the making of machinery. Chicago, Quincy, Peoria, and Springfield are among the principal cities. I. has a greater extent of railway than any of the other States, there being 6116 miles in 1874. The important I. and Michigan Canal, opened in 1848, is carried from the Chicago River W. for 96 miles to the I. River, thus connecting the great lakes with the Gulf of Mexico. The first white settlements in this region (Kaskaskia, Kaliokia, &c.) were made by the French from Canada (1682), following in the path of the explorer Sieur de la Salle 1679), who here found a tribe of Indians, whom he named in his journal the Illini, and after whom he named the river I. The region fell to the English Government on the conquest of Canada in 1763, and to the United States after the War of Independence. It was converted into a State in 1818. Long struggles with the Indians culminated in what was called the Black Hawk War, which led to their final expulsion from the State in 1832. In 1840 the Mormons removed hither from Missouri, and built the city of Nauvoo, but in an outburst of popular feeling the brothers Joseph and Hyrum Smith were murdered in June 1844, and in the following autumn their followers, to the number of 20,000, left the State under the guidance of Brigham Young.

Illinois Industrial University, at Urbana, 85 miles E.N.E. of Springfield by rail, was opened in 1869, for the purpose of teaching agriculture and the mechanic arts, including military tactics, &c. It received from Congress a land grant of 480,000 acres, and 300,000 dollars from the State of I.; its assets amount to nearly one million dollars, and its annual revenue to 40,000 dollars. There are connected with it experimental farms, nursery grounds, &c. In 1873 it was attended by 338 men and 76 women, and had 13 professors, 9 assistants, &c. The University cannot confer degrees.

Illumina'ti, The, were founded by Adam Weishaupt, who was born at Ingolstadt in the year 1748. Weishaupt was a pupil of the Jesuits, and for some time a professor of canon law. In 1778, along with Nicolai, the Berlin bookseller, and some other Italians and Germans, he founded his society for teaching brotherly love and diffusing knowledge. The members took ancient names, such as Lucian and Spartacus; they called Munich Athens, and Vienna Rome. The organisation included Novice or Minerval, who must be a freemason, the illuminatus minor, 5 degrees of masonry, and 4 degrees of mysteries. The final doctrine taught to the initiated was the disappearance of ranks and inequalities of wealth in society, and the restoration of the patriarchal state by peaceful means, if possible. The leading members or Areopagites were Zwack, Hertel, Berger, Baader, Batz, and Constanza. Zwack projected a sisterhood of illuminatæ and wrote a satire on religion called *Horus,* which was sold at Leipsic fair. The general position of the society seems to have been one of coarse negative criticism of existing forms of religion. In 1782, in consequence of the evidence given by the Masonic Lodge Theodore, the I. were banished from Bavaria, Weishaupt becoming a Privy

Councillor in Saxe-Gotha. The 'German Union' was revived shortly afterwards by Dr. Bahrdt. Illuminism, introduced by Bode, Busche, Mirabeau, and others, to the French masonic societies of the *Chevaliers bienfaisans, Martinistes, Philalètes*, and *Amis Réunis*, had through the Jacobin clubs an important influence in preparing the Revolution of 1789. See Robison, *Proofs of a Conspiracy* (Edinb. 1797). Nearly a dozen descriptive works were printed at Munich in 1786–88.

Illu'sions are mental phenomena, depending upon a morbid condition of the organs of the special senses, but especially of the organ of sight. See HALLUCINATIONS.

Illyr'icum (Gr. *Illyris*, rarely *Illyria*), a name applied in ancient times to a wide tract of land occupied by barbarous tribes W. of Macedonia and Mœsia, and stretching from Epirus to the junction of the Savus and Dravus. The river Drilo (*Drin*) divided it into two portions—*Illyris Romana* or *Barbara* (the modern Dalmatia, Herzegovina, and Montenegro, with part of Croatia, Bosnia, and Albania), and *Illyris Graeca* (including the greater part of Albania), the former inhabited by three separate tribes—the Japydes, partly Illyrian and partly Celtic, in the interior of the N.; the Liburni, along the coast from the Arsia to the Titius, famous for their seamanship and swift vessels; and the Dalmatæ, who held the coast from the Titius to the Drilo. During the Empire, Illyrian, and especially Dalmatian, soldiers were much employed. *Illyris Graeca*, also called Epirus Nova, was a wild and rugged region, unproductive except on the southern coast, and inhabited by tribes dangerous to the Macedonian kings from an early period. In 229 the Romans, exasperated by their piracy, overran their territory and subjected them to a yearly tribute. The I. of Constantine was one of the great provinces of the Roman Empire, divided into *I. Occidentale*, comprising I. proper, Noricum, and Pannonia; and *I. Orientale*, including Thrace, Macedonia, Moesia, and Dacia.

Il'men, a lake of Russia, in the government of Novgorod, has an area of 340 sq. miles, is 30 miles long and 24 broad, and is connected by the Volchov with Lake Ladoga, which lies 100 miles further N. It receives the Shelon, Lovat, Msta, &c., abounds in fish (bream, saudres, and smelt), and is frequently visited by storms. Its banks were formerly inhabited by the Slavic tribes who called the Russian kingdom into existence by inviting Rurik the Varangian Russ from Sweden to become their ruler in 862. On its N. side lies Novgorod, on its S. Staraja Russa, the capital of a great military colony that surrounds the lake on three sides.

Il'minster, an old market-town of England, in Somersetshire, on the Isle, 13 miles S.E. of Taunton by rail. It has woollen, cloth, and flax mills, chemical works, and brickfields, besides some brewing, tanning, and glove-making. There is an old cruciform church and a grammar school (founded by H. Waldron in 1550), which has an endowment of some £1000, with four exhibitions at Oxford University. Pop. (1871) 2431.

Il Obeid. See EL OBEID.

Ils'ley (East), a market-town of England in Berkshire, on the Downs, 56 miles W. of London, and near the Great Western Railway. Its well-known sheep markets begin on the Wednesday fortnight before Easter, and are held every alternate Wednesday till July. At the great sheep fair (26th of August) as many as 50,000 sheep and lambs have been penned for sale. In the vicinity are several packs of hounds, and the Downs are noted for their coursing meetings. Pop. (1871) 608.—**West I.** (pop. 424) is distant about a mile.

Ilyan'thus, a familiar genus of *Actinozoa* or sea-anemones, differs from its common neighbours by its conical shape, and its slender and pointed base. Probably I. lives with its base attached in the mud of the sea. The family *Ilyanthidæ* includes the nearly-allied genus *Arachnactis*, an anemone which lives a free life, and fixes itself at will. The common sea-anemones, on the other hand, are usually firmly rooted and fixed to rocks and stones. *I. Scoticus*, or the 'Scottish Pearlet,' is a familiar species.

Im'age Wor'ship, in the Christian Church, to which alone the present article refers, began with the use of certain symbolical figures. The earliest of these was the sign of the cross made with the hand. Wooden crosses then began to be set up in various places, and figures to be embroidered on cloth, &c. Next the Good Shepherd or Christ under the figure of a lamb was painted or etched on various articles, especially the chalice used in the eucharist. By and by religious art advanced from symbolism to represent figures partly historical and partly symbolical or ideal—a favourite subject, *e.g.*, being the offering of Isaac, because it symbolised the death of Christ—and then pictorial images, purely historical. In the 4th c. the use of images—of the apostles and martyrs, and pictures of scenes from the Old and New Testaments—increased to such an extent that the walls of churches were covered with frescoes and paintings. (Wooden figures of saints were probably not introduced till the 9th c.) At first these images were intended merely to instruct the ignorant; they were 'the Bible of the poor,' 'the Scriptures of the laity,' but gradually they were credited with working miracles, and in short with a part of the supposed powers of the saints, or of Christ or his mother, according to the representation. Thus Pope Gregory I., in describing the true use of images, points to the very abuse into which ignorant people, not yet weaned from heathen ideas and practices, could not fail to fall. 'They who are ignorant of letters may at least read on the walls by seeing there what they cannot read in books. . . . It is one thing to adore a picture, another to learn by the story of the picture what ought to be adored. . . . If any one wishes to make images, by no means stop him, but by all means stop the worship of images.' In the Greek Church, however, I. W. was avowed, and defended thus: 'That in worshipping the image of God the material wood and colours were not worshipped, but laying hold of the lifeless representation of Christ the worshipper seemed to lay hold of, and to worship Christ through it.' This expresses the principle on which I. W. has generally been defended, a principle which was enunciated by the Council of Nicæa (787; see ICONOCLASTS), namely, that the worship paid the image terminates on the object which it represents. The same council declared that they were not to be worshipped with *latreia*, or the reverence due to God, but with salutations and reverent prostrations. The Council of Trent decreed that to the images of Christ and the saints 'due reverence' should be paid, without defining the nature of that reverence. Among Romish writers various opinions are found on the subject. Some hold that the image itself is not to be worshipped in any sense, but merely that the original is to be worshipped before it; others that images ought properly to be honoured in themselves, but with an inferior honour to that paid to their originals, and hence that no image is to be adored with the worship of *latreia*. Others, again, hold that the same honour is due to the image as to the original, and hence that the image of Christ is to be adored with the worship of *latreia*, that of the Virgin with *hyperdoulia*, and those of ordinary saints with the worship of *doulia*. Regarding the violent controversy which occurred in the Church in the 8th c., on the subject of I. W., see ICONOCLASTS.

Imag'inary Quan'tity, in algebra, is the name given to an *even* root of a negative quantity. For instance, $\sqrt{-a^2}$ has no meaning in ordinary algebra, because $-a^2$ is the square of no possible quantity, positive or negative, integral or fractional. $\sqrt{-a^2}$ may be written $a\sqrt{-1}$; and this symbol $\sqrt{-1}$, or $(-1)^{\frac{1}{2}}$, or (as some put it) $(-)^{\frac{1}{2}}$ is recognised as *the imaginary* or *impossible* quantity of algebra. Its constant occurrence in higher analysis is evidence that it must have some meaning; but not until Sir W. R. Hamilton developed his calculus of QUATERNIONS (q. v.) was this meaning clearly brought out.

Imagina'tion, in the strictest sense of the term, is that faculty of the mind which represents. The mind by means of perception admits new objects within the sphere of consciousness: knowledge thus acquired is retained by memory proper: the ideas stored by memory are reproduced either by suggestion or recollection, and kept continuously before the mental eye by I. Not only do these faculties of retention, reproduction, and representation vary relatively in individuals, but they are together strong or weak in regard to the same class of subjects. Any one, for example, acquainted with Celtic literature will recollect that a vivid sense of colour distinguishes the Cymric and Gaelic bards. Or, again, it is well known that there have been prodigies capable of playing on musical instruments long passages but once heard, who yet were notably deficient otherwise in mental capacity. From this it may be seen that I. is partial, but only as the subordinate faculties are partial, giving to their work its stamp of greater permanency. It is further to be noted, as a fact well established, that I. depends on no part of the cerebral arrangement exclusively, but makes use of all the organs of sense. Experiment has proved that any part of the brain may be injured or destroyed without impairing the representative faculty, while, on the other hand, injury done to the intracranial portion of any external organ of sense invariably affects that faculty.

In the more popular acceptation of the term, I. becomes not only representative but creative. Choosing among the facts given by memory, it combines and adds to these, and from them produces something which may be unlike anything ever actually experienced. It is not necessary that what it produces conform to truth. It may subtract from any actual combination of qualities—as in the conception of a ghost, which is supposed to have the appearance without the body of a man; or it may add to these—as in the representation of a winged bull. Nevertheless, analysis of such products will show them to be entirely composed of elements previously given in experience. Nor can I., free as it is, escape the laws of thought; there must be a certain congruity in its acts. To imagine a square circle, for example, would be impossible.

I. is commonly represented as courted by art, but shunned by science. No view could be more erroneous. To I. the great majority of scientific discoverers owe their successes, for without its aid no hypothesis could be formed. The Greek poets personified nature by no other act of the mind than that by which later philosophers sought its scientific explanation. In science I. not only leads to actual discovery, but hypothetically explains what can never be directly observed; as, for instance, the sensation of light or colour. It leads the artist from simple observation to conceptions of the beautiful. In morals it gives to each man his individual and ideal end of life, and in religion shapes for him the object that he worships.

Imaum', or **Imâm** (Arab. 'teacher'), the title of a Mohammedan functionary, whose duties answer somewhat to those of a parish priest—assisting at circumcisions, marriages, funerals, &c. He occupies a pulpit (*mimbar*) in the S.E. angle of the mosque, is distinguished from laymen by the superior height of his turban, is treated with great reverence, but, from the lowness of his stipend, is often obliged to combine some other employment with his religious duties. Two imaums are usually attached to each mosque, under the superintendence of a *khatib*, or higher minister, also called *I.'ul Djumâ* ('Friday I.'), from his performing the solemn noonday service on Friday. The sultan himself, as successor of Mohammed, is known as *the* I.

Imæ'us, a classic derivative from the Sanskrit *hima*, 'snow;' comp. Gr. *cheima* and Lat. *hiems* 'winter' or 'snow-time,' anciently given to part of the Hindu-Kush or the Himalayan range.

Imbatt'led. See Embattled.

Imbecil'ity, or **Fee'bleness of In'tellect**, may be congenital or infantile, depending upon arrested development of the mental powers during foetal life, or, more frequently, during infancy. I. denotes a lesser degree of mental deficiency than Idiocy (q. v.), and, when present from birth, the sensitive and intellectual faculties are somewhat developed, and are susceptible of the influences of education; so that many imbeciles are able to take care of themselves, and to perform many of the ordinary duties of life. The intellect of the *idiot* is dwarfed and distorted; that of the *dement* has been deprived of powers formerly possessed; but that of the *imbecile* is undeveloped or but partially so. Imbeciles are affectionate but passionate, and have frequently a strong tendency to theft; while some are prone to incendiary, and, still more frequently, to homicidal acts, there being in the same person, and at the same time, an absence or depression of the intellectual faculties, and an excess or exaltation of the affective faculties. There are various classes of mental weakness which have special reference to I. In the *first*, the imbecile is incapable of forming a judgment on a new subject, however simple it may be; although he may judge correctly regarding familiar subjects. In the *second*, he is less able to judge regarding his accustomed occupations, being confused especially in regard to time and identity. In the *third*, there is much less self-control, the imbecile being delusive, passionate, suspicious, and misanthropic. I. involves congenital defect in, or arrested development of, the centre of the nervous system essential to the operations of the mind, which is, therefore, capable only of limited improvement. See *Psychological Medicine* by Drs. Bucknill and Tuke (Lond. 1874).

Imbecility does not, by the law of England, prevent a man from managing his own affairs, nor does it protect him from the consequence of his acts. See Fraud, Idiots and Lunatics. Scotch law, Interdiction.

Im'bros (now *Embro*), an island of Turkey, included in the vilayet of Brusa, 10 miles W. of the entrance to the Dardanelles. Area, 130 sq. miles; pop. 6000. It is well wooded and hilly, rising to a height of 1845 feet above the sea. There is some export of oil, corn, wine, &c. The chief town and port is Kastro; the only other considerable place is Skinudi in the interior.

Imbrued', in heraldry, signifies bloody, dropping with blood.

Imereth'i, a former independent state of Georgia (q. v.), now included in the Russian government of Kutais, in the lieutenacy of the Caucasus.

Imita'tion, in music, is the succession of similar phrases in different 'parts.' The imitated phrase is called *subject* or *antecedent*; the imitating phrase, *answer* or *consequent*. The answer may vary from the subject in accent, pitch, length of notes, and direction of movement. I. 'serves to develop the ideas, to connect the parts, and to give unity of design to the whole' of a composition.

Im'itative Insan'ity. See Epidemic Mental Disease.

Immac'ulate Concep'tion is the name of a doctrine promulgated in a bull of Pope Pius IX. (1854), to the effect 'that the Blessed Virgin Mary was (by the grace and favour of Almighty God) preserved perfectly free from all taint of original sin from the very moment when she was conceived by her mother.' It is likewise the name of a festival of the Roman Catholic Church, on the 8th December, also observed in the Anglican Church under the name of the Conception of the Blessed Virgin Mary, and in the Eastern Church, on the 9th December, under the name of the Conception of Anne, the mother of the mother of God. The form in which the doctrine first appeared, was that since God says of Jeremiah, 'Before thou camest forth out of the womb, I sanctified thee' (Jer. i. 5), the same might be said of the Virgin Mary. The earliest authentic historical trace of it, as now understood, appears in an epistle of St. Bernard written (1140) to the canons of Lyons, in which he affirms that the festival, which was observed in the Cathedral at Lyons, and by the Franciscans at Rome, is a novelty in the Church, and condemns the doctrine, although he admits the sanctification of the Virgin in her mother's womb. Half a century later the doctrine formed one of the themes of controversy between the Thomists and Scotists. Thomas Aquinas followed St. Bernard in his moderate statement of the doctrine, and was followed by his order, the Dominicans; Duns Scotus supported the extreme view, and was followed by his order, the Franciscans. Sixtus IV. published two bulls (1477 and 1483) excommunicating all on either side who asserted or denied the belief in the doctrine to be heresy, on the ground that it had not yet been settled by the Holy See. The Council of Trent added to its decree regarding original sin that it did not include the blessed and immaculate Virgin Mary, the mother of God. The controversy still continued, however, till the doctrine was finally imposed as an article of faith on the Roman communion by the bull of Pius IX. mentioned above. See Blunt's *Dict. of Doct.* and *Hist. Theology* (Lond. 1872).

Immemo'rial U'sage. By the law of England, a custom uninterrupted since the beginning of the reign of Richard I. acquires legal validity. See Easement, Prescription.

Immoral'ity in Law. While the law protects the good and the bad alike, it will not take cognisance of any transaction, the nature of which it holds to be contrary to public morality. Thus, as it holds betting and gambling to be so, it will not enforce payment of a bet or gaming debt

Immort'ality. The belief in I. has been found almost without exception among the aborigines of America, as well as among the Polynesians, Papuans, and Australians, among the greater number of Asiatics, among the ancient inhabitants of Europe, and all the Hamites of N. Africa from the Nile to the Canaries. The belief may often be inferred from the mode of burial. Thus, Egyptians provided their mummies with wheat, that they might have seed-corn at the resurrection; the Caribs place maize-seeds, and the Babylonians placed date-stones on the tombs. The sacrifice of slaves, as in the 'Adah' or *great custom* of Dahomey, and the wholesale strangling of wives at the funeral of a Fiji prince, show the same thing. The Hottentots place the corpse in the cramped position of a fœtus, expecting a second birth. This rude belief is not confined to the I. of men. The Itelines of Kamchatka believe in the renewal 'of the smallest fly.' The Jesuit missionaries found that the Inca-Peruvians and many N. American tribes believed in the eternal existence of prototypes or essences. The Fijians add a very practical belief that cocoa-nut trees are also immortal. But many negroes have no belief in I. The Lataka chief said to Sir S. Baker, 'Can a dead man come out of his grave unless he is dug up?' Wherever, among negroes and Polynesians, a distinct worship of departed chiefs is observed, there is apparently belief in I. It has been suggested that the belief rests on dreaming; as negroes have been found who believe in the continued existence of one or two generations, but forget those further back. Buddhism is founded on the perpetual transmigration of souls. Confucianism denies I. The doctrine of the resurrection is distinctly taught in the dualistic Iranian religion of Zoroaster. It also appears in the Egyptian trial, and in the creed of the Badagas of India, which compels souls to pass through a column of fire in order to reach the land of the blessed. While the Jews were free from Shamanism (or magic religion), they did not for centuries embrace the Iranian notion of I.—at least the Pentateuch is silent on the subject. The 'grave' or 'hell' of the Old Testament is even less than the Greek Hades—a prison-house of feeble shades who can never revisit the realm of light. The retributions of the just and the wicked were all to be in this life. In the person of Christ the doctrine first became a *clear fact*—he 'brought life and immortality to light in the gospel.' In the Christian theology the doctrine of I. in the form of a heaven reserved for the faithful, and a hell reserved for those unreconciled to God, is of vital importance. Before Mohammed the Arabs did not believe in I. It was this doctrine which specially repelled the higher classes of his countrymen. His paradise was a sensual one in those points in which the Mohammedan character is sensual. The truth of the doctrine of I. is often inferred from the necessity (on the assumption of a just Providence) of redressing the inequalities of the present life. But it is the flood of conviction which Christianity has poured into the human mind that gives any reality to the ethical conception of a 'just Providence.'

Immortelles'. See EVERLASTING FLOWERS.

Imo'la, a town of Italy, in the province of Ravenna, on the Santerno, 10 miles N.W. of Faenza. It stands on the railway between Bologna and Ancona, has some fine palaces, manufactures of leather, oil, wax, glass, silks, bricks, majolica, &c. It was the ancient *Forum Cornelii*, so called because founded by L. Cornelius Sulla. Pop. (1872) 28,328.

Impale'ment, in heraldry, the marshalling two coats-of-arms side by side upon one shield, is effected by dividing it into two equal parts by a vertical line called the pale. Alliance by marriage has been denoted by I. since the close of the 14th c., the husband's arms forming the dexter, the wife's the sinister half; and similarly bishops, deans, and kings-of-arms impale their paternal arms with those of their sees or offices. The impaled arms of husband and wife are not hereditary, but may be borne by the survivor of either of them. While, however, a widower marrying again is entitled to bear the arms of both wives, a widow does not bear those of her former husband unless he was a peer. The earliest method of I. was by Dimidiation (q. v.).

Impana'tion (Lat. *in*, and *panis*, 'bread') is a term which was invented by Luther, from the analogy of 'incarnation,' to express the union between the outward and the inward parts in the Eucharist. It is practically synonymous with Consubstantiation (q. v.).

Impeach'ment is an indictment presented by the House of Commons to the House of Lords accusing a commoner of a high political misdemeanour, or accusing a peer of any crime. On the trial of Warren Hastings, a doubt was raised as to whether the House of Lords was bound by the same rules of evidence as bind inferior courts. It was decided that the House of Lords was so bound. The last I. was that of Lord Melville in 1805.

Impeachment of Waste. When an estate in England is given to any one *without I. of W.* he is entitled to cut timber, and has other reasonable privileges; any unreasonable exercise of these may be restrained by injunction from Chancery division. There is no corresponding term of Scotch law; but there are similar privileges and checks.

Impenetrabil'ity, in physics, is an essential property of matter, implying that no two portions of matter can occupy the same space at the same moment of time. See MATTER.

Imper'ative, The Categor'ical, is the central element of Kant's ethical philosophy, and is the name Kant gave to the fundamental law of the pure practical reason. It is called categorical, because it appeals to us directly, independently of all motives outside its own scope, wholly without any reference to the prospect of profit or pleasure to be derived from the course of action it demands, and was thus formulated by Kant: 'Act so that the maxim of thy will may ever stand as the principle of a universal system of law.'

Impe'rial Crown, properly that worn by the German King as Roman Emperor, a crown similar in shape to a Mitre (q. v.). The term I. C. is now applied to all kingly crowns. See CROWN.

Impeti'go, a disease of the skin attacking primarily the mouths of the hair follicles, and giving rise to an effusion of pus. The pustules are usually small, like the vesicles of eczema; but they are sometimes large and confluent, especially on the scalp. They are usually arranged in thickly-set clusters, occupying a small extent of surface, but they are sometimes distributed more or less generally over the surface of the body. When they burst, there remains a rough, yellowish, transparent crust of considerable thickness. The mode of distribution of the pustules, the locality and the severity of the disease, give rise to the nomenclature of varieties, as *I. figurata*, *I. sparsa*, *I. scabida*, *I. erythematica*, *I. capitis*. Treatment:—During the inflammatory stage, emollient and sedative fomentations, and water dressings; afterwards a coating of the benzoated oxide of zinc ointment, a weak solution of nitrate of silver, a liniment of olive oil and lime-water, or of glycerine and carbolic acid in the ratio of 1 to 20.

Impeyan' Pheasant, or **Mo'nal** (*Lophophorus Impeyanus*), a genus and species of Rasorial birds belonging to the family *Phasianidæ* or pheasants, and distinguished by having the bill broad at the base, the upper mandible projecting over the lower. The nostrils are partly covered with feathers, and the wings have their fourth and fifth quills longest. The tarsi are spurred in the males, and covered with large scales. The head and throat are green, with a metallic lustre, the former bearing a crest consisting of quills with broad extremities. The lower part of the neck and upper part of the back are purple, and the tail is reddish brown. A snow-white line marks the middle of the back. The rest of the plumage is of a bluish tint. The colour of the females is brown. The food consists chiefly of roots. The I. P. inhabits the upper regions of the Himalayas.

Impon'derables was the name given to light, heat, electricity, and magnetism, when these were supposed to be material. See ENERGY.

Importa'tion and Exporta'tion. Commodities brought from foreign countries and articles of home produce sent abroad are called imports and exports respectively. Under each country a statement is given of its imports and exports. Among articles the importation of which into Great Britain is forbidden, are copyright books, false money, extracts of coffee, tea, &c., snuff-work, immoral books and prints. See CUSTOMS DUTIES.

Im'ports and Ex'ports. See BALANCE OF TRADE.

Impos'ture. See BEGGARS, LAW OF ENGLAND RELATIVE TO.

Im'potency, in law, is valid ground for either a husband or a wife having the marriage dissolved by law.

Impound'ing a Doc'ument is the phrase used in law to denote that a judge has retained a document produced at a trial, instead of returning it to its owner. The object of this act is to enable a prosecution to be legally effected.

Impounding Cattle, in English law, denotes the right of an occupant of land to seize cattle found straying on such land, and to drive them to the nearest 'pound' (Ger. *pfand*) or 'pledge-place,' if it be within three miles; if not, he may keep them on his own premises, but must take proper care of them. The owner can only recover them by paying the expenses of their keep. In Scotland the phrase used is 'poinding.'

Impress'ment of Seamen was for long the means used to man the British navy. The lawfulness of the procedure appears to rest mainly on national necessity, no statute having declared the power to belong to the crown; though there are statutes which imply that it does. The implication chiefly arises from the statutory declaration of special exemptions. According to Lord Kenyon, the right of impressment is founded on common law, and extends over all seafaring persons. An endeavour has been made to lessen the necessity of naval impressments by a system of registration of merchant seamen, and by encouraging the voluntary enlistment of seamen into the royal navy.

Impris'onment. The Act 32 and 33 Vict. c. 62 abolishes I. for nonpayment of debt, unless for default of payment of certain penalties. The Act, however, gives power to a judge to arrest a debtor to the amount of £50, when it is proved that the debtor is about to quit England. Provision is also made for the punishment of fraudulent debtors. The frauds specified consist generally of false representations regarding property, collusive transfers of it, and other practices for the misleading and deception of creditors. Fraudulently obtaining credit renders the offender liable to a year's imprisonment with hard labour. In Scotland, I. for debt has not yet been abolished, and may be enforced by a creditor against a debtor to the amount of £8, 6s. 8d. See BANKRUPTCY, for Eng. and Scot. law; especially Scotch, see CESSIO BONORUM. For criminal I., see COMMITMENT FOR TRIAL, BAIL.

Improba'tion, a term of Scotch law denoting the disproving and setting aside of writs *ex facie* probative, on the ground of falsehood or forgery.

Impropria'tion and **Appropria'tion,** terms used to denote the transfer of ecclesiastical property or revenue from the benefice to the use of a layman or of a bishop or spiritual corporation. On the dissolution of religious houses in the reign of Henry VIII., a statute was passed giving the property which had belonged to them to the king. Grants by the crown from this source are called *impropriations*, because, according to Spelman, they are diverted from their proper use. A benefice held by a bishop or religious corporation is an *appropriation*; when held by a layman it is an *impropriation*.

Improvisato're and **Improvisatrice** are the names given in Italy to men and women who have the curious gift of composing offhand and reciting verses to almost any extent on almost any subject, but especially on political subjects. The art there is an old one, Brother Philip in the time of Sixtus V. having been a great I. In this century Gianni of Genoa and the Ricci of Florence are the most prominent figures. The siege of Rome in 1847 produced some fine improvisatori. There is generally an accompaniment on the guitar. The Italian language is very favourable to this composition, which is also in keeping with the melodious, impetuous character of the inhabitants. But improvisatori are quite an institution of savage life. Thus, among the Mandingo negroes there is a class of *singing men*, who extemporise in honour of the chief or any one else who will pay them, and who also recite historical events. The Zulu royal heralds are remarkable for their impromptu volubility and total disregard of pauses. In Abyssinia the improvisatori, who are generally through Africa recognised as a distinct profession, like the troubadours and minstrels, attend funerals and chant the praises of the dead.

Impul'sive Insan'ity is not a distinct form of mental disease, but has reference, principally, to the sudden accession of symptoms of a peculiar class. In general, there are well-marked premonitory symptoms prior to the full development of mental disease; but it occasionally happens that the symptoms are obscure, and, in some cases, quite imperceptible. Sudden outbreaks of acute mania, or the sudden lapsing into a state of dementia, are not illustrations of I. I., for such are associated with great disturbance of the nervous centres, indicated by general incoherence and delusions. I. I. is, strictly speaking, the sudden development of a Monomania (q. v.) in which a propensity is involved, the more marked illustrations being cases of homicidal and suicidal mania, pyromania, kleptomania, dipsomania, nymphomania, and satyriasis.

Imputa'tion, in theological language, means attributing anything to a person or persons as the meritorious reason of reward or punishment, that is, of the bestowal of good or the infliction of evil. So far as the meaning of the word is concerned, it makes no difference whether the thing imputed be sin or righteousness, and therefore the same thing is meant whether the I. of Adam's sin to us, of our sins to Christ, or of Christ's righteousness to believers, be referred to. 1. The I. of Adam's sin to his posterity seems to be implied in the Pauline theology, and has certainly been a doctrine of the Church since the time of Augustine, who laid down the proposition that 'as all men have sinned in Adam, they are justly exposed to the vengeance of God because of this hereditary sin and guilt of sin.' A subject of controversy at the time of the Reformation, as it had been all along, was the relation of this I. to hereditary corruption of nature. (See ORIGINAL SIN.) And in the 17th c. an attempt was made to distinguish between 'mediate' and 'immediate' I. La Place of Saumur advanced the theory that there is no direct or immediate I. of Adam's sin to his posterity, but an indirect or mediate I. of it, founded on the fact that we derive a corrupt nature from him. In opposition to this theory the Formula Consensus Helvetici stated the full and distinct Calvinistic doctrine on the subject, namely, that 'it does not appear how hereditary corruption, as spiritual death, could fall upon the entire human race by the just judgment of God, unless some fault, . . . bringing in the penalty of that death, had preceded. . . . Wherefore man, previous to the commission of any single or actual transgression, is exposed to the divine wrath and curse from his very birth, . . . first, on account of the transgression and disobedience which he committed in the loins of Adam; and, secondly,' &c. 2. Regarding the I. of our sins to Christ, Calvinistic divines explain that it is not thereby meant 'that he was morally criminal on account of them, or that the demerit of them rested upon him, but that he undertook to answer the demands of justice for the sins of men.' 3. So the I. of the righteousness of Christ to believers is explained to mean 'not that the merit of his righteousness is their personal merit, nor that it constitutes their moral character, but that the righteousness of Christ having been wrought out for the benefit of his people, in their name, by him as their representative, it is laid to their account, so that God can be just in justifying the ungodly.' See Hodge's *Systematic Theology* (Edinb. 1873).

Inaja' Palm. The I. P. of the Brazilians—the 'Cocurito' of Humboldt's writings—is the *Maximiliana regia* of botanists, a magnificent palm forming one of the most conspicuous ornaments of the primitive forests of the Amazon region. It frequently reaches 100 feet in height, bearing a crown of gigantic pinnate leaves 30 to 40 feet long. The woody boatlike spathes remain on the trunk for years after flower and fruit have fallen. They are used by the Indians for baskets, cradles, and cooking utensils.

Inarch'ing, or **Graft'ing by Approach,** differs from ordinary Grafting (q. v.) in the scion being attached to the parent tree during the process of union, and only separated from it when that union is accomplished. It is necessary, therefore, that the plants operated upon be placed near each other so that their branches may overwrap. The position of the intended junction being selected, a piece of bark is removed from both scion and stock, the parts are fitted together so that their cambium layers may coincide, and the process of tying and protecting follows as in common grafting. After union the scion is severed, and may subsequently be cut off close to its new stock. I. is well adapted for the young shoots of oranges, camellias, &c. It effects the same results as grafting.

In Artic'ulo Mor'tis, a phrase used in Scotch law to denote the execution of a deed on *Deathbed* (q. v.).

Incanta'tion (Lat. *incantatio*, 'an enchanting,' from *in* and *canto*, 'I sing or chant') is a form of passionate, generally rhythmical, speech, which is supposed to have a *controlling effect* over gods or demons, or even natural forces. It is therefore the opposite of prayer or supplication. Theoretically it can hardly be discussed apart from the other rituals by which Shamanism or religious magic deludes its followers. The Shaman is generally able to throw himself into a nervous excitement, his mouth foaming, his limbs convulsed. He selects as apprentices epileptic persons. The negroes prefer dwarfs and albinos. The Siberian priest, the N. American medicine-man, the S. American *playe*, with their drums, horns, or *maracca* (a rattle consisting of a hollow gourd filled with hard seeds), all profess by the production of certain sounds to remove illness or bad weather, or plagues of any kind. The shell-trumpet of Papua is a similar case. The same principle also appears in some forms of sacrifice and other symbolical acts, and even in the revolving prayer-wheels of the Buddhists. So also with the devil-dancers of the wild Veddahs. Clad in green leaves, they shuffle round an offering of eatables placed on a tripod, and gradually work themselves with moans and screams into a paroxysm, and thus extort the secret of curing disease. The Tasmanian doctors use a rattle of dead men's bones. Among the Dyaks, if conversation does not compel the spirit, gongs are used by the medical profession. The Bechuana prophets leap and shout in a peculiar manner, or strike the ground with a club; and many of the African fetish-men practise ventriloquism so as to obtain an audible answer to their I. The holy fetish jargon is unintelligible to the rest of the tribe. The Kaffir handling-doctors dance, drum, put mysterious questions, and receive answers. The Bushmen cry out a set form of furious words against the thunder. Among the Todas of N. India the priest pronounces an I. over every bell-cow added to the herd. The *ohja*, or exorcist of the Bodo tribe, sits before thirteen leaves sprinkled with rice, swinging a pendulum and muttering rapidly. This compels one god of the thirteen to confess what he has been doing. Among the Kamchatdales the old women avert disease by whispering on the fins of fishes and on blades of sweet grass. The Mishmi priest drives evil from the house by a monotonous chant, flourishing a fan in one hand and rattling a box of pebbles in the other. The *modus operandi* of I. is not clear. Among very savage people mere loudness, harshness, or shrillness is thought important; it terrifies the gods. But generally the force of alliteration and rhythm, rhyme and cadence, is resorted to in order to express the intensity of feeling; and much of the impressive effect depends not only on the accessories, but on the principle of repetition. Long after the decay of explicit belief in particular supernatural agencies, there survives a confused belief in I. as a mere form of words. So far as the cure or other benefit depended on faith, on the impression made on the mind of the patient, it may still be obtained.

Incarna'tion (from Lat. *in*, and *caro, carnis*, 'flesh') is the theological term for the doctrine that the second person of the Trinity, the divine Logos, was united with the person of Jesus (q. v.), the son of the Virgin Mary (John i. 14). The mere conception of an I. is not peculiar to Christianity. Krishna was an I. of the second person of the Indian trinity, born of a virgin of a royal line (Jones' *Asiatic Researches*); and the Buddhas (see BUDDHISM) were either men exalted to the Buddhaship, or an I. of Vishnu or of Brahma. Again, all the forms of Sun-worship (q. v.), in Egypt, Persia, Phœnicia, Greece, &c., had their I. in the person of Osiris, Mithra, Adonis or Thammuz, Atys, Dionysus or Bacchus, &c.

In'cas, or **Yncas** (a Peruvian word signifying 'chiefs'), the name given in Peru before the Spanish conquest to the sovereign and princes of the blood. See PERU.

In'cense (Lat. *incensum*, 'what is set on fire,' from *incendo*, 'I put fire to') is a compound of several sweet spices, the burning of which, so as to raise a smoke and fragrant smell, formed a part of the religious rites of most ancient nations. Among others, it was used by the Israelites, both in their idolatrous worship (Jer. xi. 12), and in connection with their sacrifices to Jehovah (Exod. xxx. 34-38). The proper compound was equal parts of stacte, onycha, galbanum, and Frankincense (q. v.), and so much salt (Exod. xxx. 35, 'tempered'), which, as the symbol of incorruptibility, was present in all offerings (Lev. ii. 13). In the Christian Church there is no trace of I. as a part of worship proper during the first four centuries. It was early used, however, in the caves and catacombs in which the first Christians often worshipped as a disinfectant and to counteract offensive smells, and in the 5th c. or 6th c. it began to be used as a part of the worship. The use of I. being regarded by Protestants as an idolatrous practice, was one of the things rejected by them at the Reformation.

Incensed', or **An'imé**, a heraldic epithet applied to wild animals having fire issuing from their ears and mouth.

In'cest (Lat. *in*, 'not,' and *castus*, 'chaste') is the simulated marriage or the sexual intercourse of persons legally forbidden to intermarry on account of relationship or of Affinity (q. v.). The offence was at one time capital in England. It is now cognisable only by the ecclesiastical courts. In Scotland I. still renders the offender liable to the punishment of death. It is not probable, however, that the extreme penalty would be inflicted.

Inch, Inis, Innis, Inish, Ennis, variants of the same Gaelic word, denoting primarily the islands formed by the branching or encircling of rivers, of which the 'Inches' of Perth are still examples. *Inch* is the prevalent form in Scotland, *Inis* in Ireland; but both occur in each of these countries. The words were afterwards applied to islets in the sea or in lakes, *e.g.*, Inchkeith, Inchcolm, in Scotland; Inisturk, Inishmore, Inishmann, in Ireland.

Inch, in British linear measure, is the twelfth part of a foot, or the thirty-sixth part of the imperial standard Yard (q. v.).

Inch'bald, Elizabeth, *née* **Simpson**, an English actress, dramatist, and novelist, born of Roman Catholic parents at Stanningfield, Suffolk, 15th October 1753, came to London at the age of sixteen to seek a theatrical engagement. From the dangers and temptations to which her youth and beauty exposed her she was only freed by her marriage in 1772 with Mr. I., an actor to whom she had applied for counsel and protection. The same year she made her début at Bristol, acted subsequently with her husband at Edinburgh, Glasgow, York, &c., and made a short tour in France. Mr. I. dying at Leeds in 1779, she contracted an engagement at Covent Garden, London (1780–89), and during this period produced a farce, *The Mogul Tale*, and other pieces, the success of which led her finally to quit the stage and apply herself wholly to literature. Mrs. I. died at Kensington, 1st August 1821. She published in all ten plays, three collections of plays, and two novels; but of these, the last—*A Simple Story* (1791) and *Nature and Art* (1796)—are the works by which she is now remembered, and have indeed taken their place among the standard novels of the language. Her Memoirs were published by J. Boaden (2 vols. 1833), but an autobiography, for which Phillips the publisher had offered £1000, she destroyed by the advice of her director.

Inchcolm' ('St. Colm's Inch'), an islet, about one mile long, in the Firth of Forth, 5 miles N.W. of Leith, and included in the parish of Aberdour, in Fifeshire. It is separated from the Fife shore by 'Mortimer's Deep,' which has a breadth of one mile. It was anciently called Acmona, is said to have been the residence of St. Colm or Columba while attempting the conversion of the Picts, and was the site of an abbey of Austin canons founded by King Alexander I. in 1123, and of which there are interesting remains, including a fine stone-roofed oratory and a beautiful chapter-house. Walter Bower, the continuator of Fordun's *Scoti-Chronicon*, was abbot from 1418 till 1449. A detailed history of I. appears in the *Proceedings of the Society of Antiquaries of Scotland* (vol. ii. pp. 489–528).

Inchkeith', an island in the Firth of Forth, included in the county of Fife, Scotland, 2½ miles N. of Leith. It is about half a mile long, and has a rocky surface that rises to a height of 180 feet at the N. end, where there is a lighthouse with a revolving light visible for 18 miles. It is supposed to be the *Caer Giudi* of Bede, and the site of a monastery founded by St. Adamnan, the biographer of St. Columba, between 679 and 704. It was seized and fortified by the English in 1547, recovered by the French auxiliaries in 1549, and dismantled in 1567. It was early the property of the Keith family, reverted to the crown, and subsequently became the property of the Buccleuchs.

In'cidence, Angle of, is the angle at which a ray of light or radiant heat falls upon a surface. See LIGHT, OPTICS.

In'cident Dil'igence, a term of Scotch law applied to a process to compel the attendance of witnesses and havers. In England, the same end is obtained by writ of *Duces Tecum* (q. v.). See also DILIGENCE.

Inclined' Plane, a simple form of machine, by means of which a man may raise to a given height a heavy body which he cannot lift. It is merely a plane inclined to the horizontal at an angle other than 90°. If a body of weight W, be drawn up an I. P. of length l to a height h, the whole amount of work done is evidently (neglecting friction) equal to the work which must be done to raise W to the height h, and is therefore represented by the product Wh. (See ENERGY.) The same work may, however, be estimated as the product of the force (F) which has to be exerted to draw up the weight into the distance through which it acts, *i.e.*, may be written $F \times l$. Hence $F = W\frac{h}{l}$; so that the ratio of the weight to the power which can support it is as the length of the plane to its height. In practical questions, Friction (q. v.) must be taken into account, and it always acts in a direction contrary to that in which the body tends to move.

In Cœ'na Dom'ini, or **Pastora'lis,** is the name of a Papal bull, which has been traced back to Gregory XI. (A.D. 1370), and which was regularly published at Rome every Holy Thursday down at least to 1773. It relates to discipline, and recognition has been denied to it by almost every country in Europe. Its rejection is made the subject of Article XVII. of the famous Declaration of the liberties of the Gallican Church. The bull anathematises heretics and their abettors, those who read or print their books, schismatics, all persons and universities who appeal to a future council, pirates and wreckers, those who impose or augment tolls without leave of the Pope, those who supply the Saracen or Turk, or other enemies of Christ, with arms or aid, those who prevent persons coming to Rome, or stop supplies, those who appeal to secular power against the execution of the letter apostolic, secular judges who bring ecclesiastical persons before their tribunals, and those who exact contributions from such persons. It was the attempt of Clement XIII., in 1768, to enforce the bull in Parma, that led to a strong expression of opinion against it by several European powers, and ultimately to the triumph of the *Regalisti* party at Rome, and the suppression of the Jesuits. The English Roman Catholics hold the bull to be obsolete. See *Lord Arundel's Letter to Mr. Plumptre,* (Lond. 1848), and various pamphlets published in the same year by Hatchard.

Incombus'tible Fab'rics are made of the fibrous mineral *asbestos* (Gr. 'unconsumable'), which remains uninjured in the intensest heat. The ancients wrapped the dead in tissues of that material to preserve their ashes after cremation. Ordinary textile fabrics are protected from the effects of fire by steeping them in saline solutions. See FIREPROOFING.

Income-Tax is a tax originally imposed by Sir Robert Peel in 1842 on all incomes in Great Britain above £150 a year. By 16 and 17 Vict. c. 34 the tax was extended to Ireland. Its range has been from 2d. to 1s. 4d. per pound.

Incommen'surable, in mathematics, is a term used with reference to two quantities which have not a common measure, or, in other words, which are not multiples of any one unit, however small that unit may be taken. Such a pair is the side of a square and its diagonal, the area of a circle and that of the circumscribed square, the quantities $\sqrt{2}$ and $\sqrt{3}$, and so on.

Incorpora'tion. See CORPORATION.

Incuba'tion, a name applied to the habit practised by many birds and by some reptiles of sitting on their eggs, and thus favouring the development of the young by the heat of the parent body. The period occupied in the process varies greatly. The humming-birds and many other smaller birds generally incubate for ten or twelve days, canaries from fifteen to eighteen days, whilst the duck and turkey sit for a month, and the common hen three weeks. The swan incubates for the long period of forty or forty-five days. The duration of the incubatory period varies according to the external temperature, being slightly extended if the weather be cold. Artificial I. has been practised with success in France and elsewhere, various machines having been invented with a view to surrounding the eggs by the proper degree of temperature during the sitting period. See *Ure's Dictionary of Arts and Sciences,* vol. ii. p. 496 (5th ed. 1860).

Incubation of Diseases, or the period of latency, designates the interval that elapses between the time when the infective matter is received into the system, until the first symptoms of the disease become manifest, or the interval before the infection received can be again communicated. The period of I. of D. of the zymotic type varies, it being much longer in some diseases than in others, as in cholera, which may be fully expressed in a day, and in hydrophobia, which may not be developed for several months. In each disease, also, the constant quantity of the period of incubation varies according to the constitution of the person affected, the amount and intensity of the contagium, and the mode by which it is conveyed into the system. In some constitutions the contagium germinates and multiplies more rapidly than in others, and there seems to be a considerable variety as regards virulence of type, by which the constitution is more or less rapidly and severely impressed. Specific contagium affects the system most rapidly when injected into a vein or a visceral serous-cavity, but less so by means of inoculation or contact with an open sore. As a general rule, contagium acts more rapidly and certainly when introduced by inhalation than by ingestion. The disease germs may be intercepted in the air-passages, or destroyed by the juices of the stomach, or the condition of the blood may be such as to neutralise their development. The period of I. of D. is most certainly ascertained by means of inoculation, and it has been demonstrated that some diseases cannot show themselves except after a certain interval, and that this interval is definite within certain limits. As a general rule, when the period of incubation is long, the period of infection is short, and *vice versa.* During the I. of D. the specific germs evidently undergo a process of development and increase, after the same fashion as the germs of plants and the ova of animals, each specific disease germ having its own definite period. In each particular case the period of I. of D. is marked by its own peculiar symptoms; but such are not so clearly defined as the symptoms characteristic of the period of invasion, nor of those marking the period of full development.

Incum'bent is the holder of an ecclesiastical benefice in England or Ireland. The term is not technical in Scotland in civil or ecclesiastical law.

Incumbered Estates Court. See LANDED ESTATES COURT.

Incum'brances, a general term for pecuniary burdens on land.

Incunab'ula (Lat. lit. 'swaddling clothes;' hence 'beginnings') is the name given to the early printed works which immediately succeeded the image or block books, and which are all dated prior to 1500. There are probably at least 18,000 I., chiefly from the presses of Mainz, Bamberg, Cologne, Strassburg, Rome, and Venice. In the very early specimens, no printer's name, date, or place of printing, title-page, or titles to chapters, appear. Catchwords and signatures for the direction of the binder took the place of the older *register.* (an alphabetical list of the first words of chapters), and preceded the numbering of pages. The primitive Gothic or black-letter types soon gave place to Roman, and in 1501 Aldus introduced *italics.* In Caxton's books commas and periods are represented by oblique strokes. Blanks were often left for illuminated capital letters. Coloured frontispieces were also frequent, a common subject being the author at his desk. Except by the great Parisian and Venetian printers of the time, devices, *vignettes,* or ciphers were not used to mark the particular press. Herbert, Ames, and Dibdin are the chief writers on English I., the best collections of which were in the Lambeth and Althorp libraries. The most important general authorities are Laire's *Index* (1791); Serna Santander's *Dictionary* (1805); Maittaire's *Annals* (1719), on which was founded Panzer's *Annals,* 10 vols. (1793–1803),

Hain's *Repertorium Bibliographicum*, 4 vols. (1826-38), which mentions 16,299 books.

In'cus, one of the small bones in the middle ear. Shaped somewhat like an anvil or bicuspid tooth, it unites on the one side with the *malleus*, or mallet (which is connected with the membrane of the drum), and on the other with the *stapes* or stirrup, which fits into the oval window of the internal ear. It is thus the middle link in the chain of bones, and it transmits the vibrations of the *membrana tympani*, or drum of the ear, to the internal ear. See EAR.

Inde'cent Exhibi'tions, or **Expo'sure**, or **Prac'tices**, are offences of various kinds punishable by statute in England, and in Scotland by common law.

Indefectibil'ity of the Church includes its Perpetuity, by which it is free from failure of its members, and its Inerrancy and Infallibility, by which it is free from failure in holding and declaring the truth. For the perpetuity of the Church such passages of Scripture are cited as Isa. lxi. 9; Dan. ii. 44; Matt. xvi. 18, xxviii. 20; John xiv. 16, 17, and the following arguments adduced: that 'the consummation of all things is delayed only till the servants of God are sealed' (1 Cor. xv. 28; Rev. vi. 9-11), so that when faith fails the end will be (Luke xviii. 8), and that as God will have all men to be saved, and come to the knowledge of the truth, the Church could not fail without a failure of God's mercy. See INFALLIBILITY.

Indem'nity Deed is in English law a deed in security of the fulfilment of an obligation. The similar deed in Scotland is called a *bond of relief*.

Inden'ted, one of the partition lines of a heraldic shield, serrated like *Dancetté* (q. v.), but with smaller notches.

Inden'ture. Formerly it was held in England that there ought to be as many copies of a deed as there were parties to it, and that each copy should be notched at the margin so as to correspond with the others—hence the name of I. See DEED.

Indepen'dents are a sect of Christians whose history properly dates from the Commonwealth, although, like every other Christian sect, they hold that theirs is the genuine primitive form of church government. The sect was founded by John Robinson, a Brownist minister at Leyden, about 1610, and in 1616 Mr. Jacob, who had adopted the sentiments of Robinson, established the first Independent congregation in England. Owing to the persecution of Nonconformists at the time, they did not dare to show themselves openly in the country till 1640. In the Westminster Assembly five of the divines belonged to the I., but they were completely overpowered by the Presbyterians. They were afterwards favoured by Cromwell, however, and in consequence increased greatly in numbers and influence. In 1658, being now a numerous and wealthy body, and having obtained the consent of the Protector, they convened a synod, and drew up a 'Declaration of the Faith and Order owned and practised in the Congregational Churches in England.' This Declaration was virtually a republication of the Westminster Confession, with the omission of those passages which maintained the Presbyterian discipline, and with the addition of a chapter in which the Independent scheme is asserted and explained. At the Restoration (1660) the I. lost all their political importance. They suffered much also from the Act of Uniformity (1662), the Conventicle Act (1664), and the Five-Mile Act (1665). Their sufferings had been increased also by a want of agreement with the Presbyterians, but in 1691 the two bodies came to a partial agreement, which was ratified (and made to include the Baptists) in 1696, and again about 1730. From the close of the reign of Queen Anne (1714), while Presbyterianism gradually declined in England, the I. rallied, until they now stand at the head of the Protestant Dissenters in England, if not in mere numbers, at least in political energy and intellectual culture.

The name of I. was assumed by the sect in their Apology published in 1644, but finding afterwards that it was also adopted by other sects and parties with whose tenets they had no sympathy, they discarded it, and adopted instead the name of Congregational Brethren. This name is derived from a point in their church government, the circumstance, namely, that whereas in the Presbyterian Church the government of each congregation is vested in a session composed of the pastor and ruling-elders, in the Congregational Church it is vested in all the members of the congregation. They also differ from the Presbyterians in holding that each congregation is entirely exempt from any extraneous jurisdiction, a tenet from which was derived their original name of I. The following are the principal items of statistical information regarding the Congregationalists in Great Britain and the Colonies (1877):—There are in England and Wales 2862 churches, with 2496 ministers; in Scotland, 109 churches, with 120 ministers; in Ireland, 28 churches, with 26 ministers; in the smaller British Islands, 18 churches, with 8 ministers; in the Colonies, 329 churches, with 301 ministers, besides 148 missionaries of the London Missionary Society, and 98 native ordained missionaries connected with the denomination. Of colleges and institutes for ministerial training there are in England and Wales 13, with 40 professors and 392 students; in Scotland, 1, with 3 professors and 9 students; in the Colonies, 3, with 9 professors and 29 students. See Vaughan's *Congregationalism* (Lond. 1842); Dexter's *Congregationalism* (Boston, U.S., 1868); *Congregational Year Book*.

Indeter'minate, in algebra, is a term applied to a class of problems which have an infinite number of solutions. An equation which involves two unknown quantities is in general indeterminate, for it requires *two* simultaneous equations to fully determine two independent variables. As a simple example of an I. problem the following may be given:—Find two numbers such that, if twice the one be subtracted from three times the other, the difference is unity. This is satisfied by the numbers 1 and 1, 3 and 4, 5 and 7, 7 and 10, and so on; and has therefore an infinite number of rational solutions.

In'dex (Expurgato'rius) is the catalogue or table of books the reading of which is forbidden by the Congregation of the Holy Office, according to instructions originally issued by Paul IV., under pain of excommunication and perpetual infamy. The first considerable edition was by a committee of the Council of Trent. The names of the books and of the authors, and a separate list of anonymous books, are given. To publish, print, or to have in one's possession, is as wicked as to read. 'Prava doctrina' is the form of objection. The authority of the I. does not depend on the dogma of Infallibility, but on the Catholic duty of obedience. Every bishop can forbid the use of a book in his diocese. The authority is not fully admitted in all Catholic countries, though in most great deference is paid to it as a warning or advice. Decrees are sometimes issued against booksellers, forbidding them to sell or contract for a certain book, and directing their shops to be closed. A book is sometimes damned '*donec corrigatur*,' and then it is the duty of those concerned to submit proposed corrections to the Congregation. In passing laws against heretics, the Church, or the Catholic state, has always made special provision for the destruction of their books. Thus Innocent II. dealt with the books of Abelard, and the Council of Constance with those of Wiclif and Huss. In fact, that a book is by a heretic is sufficient, though it contain no heretical matter. The old rule of the Council of Trent damning all anonymous books is now relaxed. Thus all Protestant literature on the one hand, and such heretical works as Fénélon's *Explanation of the Maxims* and Dupin's *Ecclesiastical Law*, are forbidden. A convenient reprint with preface by Mr. Gibbings was published at Dublin in 1837.

In'dia is the geographical term properly applied to the central peninsula of Southern Asia, which is bounded on its landward base by the Himalaya Mountains and the rivers Indus and Brahmaputra. The name was originally brought into use by the Greeks, having been formed from the Sanskrit 'Sindh,' 'the land of the Indus,' which in its Persian form became Hindustan (q. v.). In this article, however, the word India will be understood in its modern political signification, as comprehending the entire region over which Queen Victoria exercises supremacy as Empress of I. Since the proclamation of that title, dated 28th April 1876, it is no longer necessary to maintain the former distinction between British and Native I. The old geographical heading of Further I. for the peninsula to the E., comprising Burmah, Siam, &c., may also be suffered to become obsolete.

I., then, in the modern political sense, excludes Ceylon, as also the Straits Settlements of Singapore, &c., but includes the Punjaub and British Burmah, as well as the small islands in the Bay of Bengal and the Indian Ocean. The outlying station of Aden, at the

S.W. corner of Arabia, though administered from I., must be omitted owing to its geographical remoteness. I. forms an irregularly-shaped tract, with few natural boundaries except the sea. It extends from Cashmere in the N. to Cape Comorin in the S.; and from the mouths of the Indus in the W. to beyond the mouths of the Irawaddy in the E., about 19,000 miles each way. On the N. are Chinese Tartary or Yarkund, Thibet, Nepaul, and Bhootan, the two first of which lie beyond the Himalayas, the two latter within their southern ranges; on the N.E. are the unexplored hills which cut off British territory from Burmah and China; on the N.W., Afghanistan and Beluchistan are separated by the Suleiman and Hala Mountains; in all other directions there is open seaboard.

The following table, taken from the 'Statistical Abstract relating to British I.' (1874), shows in detail the area and population of each British province, according to actual census taken between 1867 and 1872, together with estimates for the aggregates of the feudatory states and foreign possessions, some of which enumerations are fairly accurate and others merely conjectural:—

AREA and POPULATION of BRITISH INDIA, with estimate for the Native States and Foreign Possessions.

Provinces.	Under British Administration.		Native States.		Total.	
	Area in sq. miles.	Population.	Area in sq. miles.	Population.	Area in sq. miles.	Population.
Government of India—						
Ajmere	2,754	316,590	...	...	2,754	316,590
Berar	17,624	2,231,565	...	..	17,624	2,231,565
Mysore	29,323	5,055,412	...	...	29,325	5,055,412
Coorg	2,000	168,312	...	...	2,000	168,312
Central India and Bundelcund	...	...	88,738	8,360,571	88,738	8,360,571
Rajputana	...	...	128,126	9,261,607	128,126	9,261,607
Nizam's Dominions or Hyderabad	...	...	80,000	9,000,000	80,000	9,000,000
Munnipoor	...	...	7,584	126,000	7,584	126,000
Bengal	158,595	60,595.524	38,936	2,271,943	197,531	62,867,467
Assam	53,856	4,132,019	...	...	53,856	4,132,019
North-West Provinces	81,403	30,781,204	6,311	1,091,810	87,714	31,873,014
Oude	23,992	11,220,232	...	...	23,992	11,220,232
Punjaub	104,975	17,611,498	115,287	5,567,478	220,262	23,178,976
Central Provinces	84,963	8,201,519	28,834	1,049,710	113,797	9,251,229
British Burmah	88,556	2,747,148	...	...	88,556	2,747,148
Madras	124,499	30,203,009	23,290	4,756,235	147,789	34,959,244
Bombay	124,462	16,349,206	72,209	8,840,103	196,671	25,189,309
Total for British India	897,004	189,613,238	589,315	50,325,457	1,486,319	239,938,695
French Possessions	...	...	...	...	196	259,981
Portuguese Possessions	...	...	...	...	1,610	527,517
Total of all India	...	...	...	...	1,488,125	240,726,193

The *Physical Aspect* is extremely varied, and represents the grandeur of tropical phenomena on a most impressive scale. The Himalaya Mountains exhibit both the loftiest peaks and the highest level of elevation in the world; their southern slopes drop abruptly on the wide plain of Hindustan Proper, where they are fringed by the *terai* jungle, fatal to Europeans during most seasons of the year. To the S. of this plain, again, lies the mountain plateau of the Deccan, which is bounded on the N. by the Vindhya Hills, and extends between the Eastern and Western Ghauts almost to the southern point of the peninsula. From these several ranges, which catch the entire rainfall brought up from the sea by the monsoons, issue innumerable torrents, which finally form a few great rivers, and annually inundate the low-lying lands for miles on each side. The total area that drains eastward into the Bay of Bengal is about 1,442,000 sq. miles; while the drainage of about 630,000 sq. miles flows westward into the Indian Ocean. The delta formed by the confluence of the Ganges and the Brahmaputra, which two rivers alone have a basin of over 750,000 sq. miles, is perhaps the most fertile spot in the world; while the embouchures of the Irawaddy, the Mahanuddy, the Godavery and the Kistna are hardly less so. The Indus, on the other hand, which is in length the first river of the country, winds through a desert and rainless tract, and neither brings down natural fertility nor gives birth to commerce. S. of the junction of the Sutlej with this river lies the Thur Desert, a sandy and almost uninhabited region, covering 68,000 sq. miles.

The *Geology* of I. has been the study of a special department for the last quarter of a century. On the whole, but few extraordinary features of scientific or commercial interest have been disclosed. The great mountains are mostly composed of metamorphic rocks, which protrude through later formations of sandstone and conglomerate. Limestone, in the form of laterite and *kankar*, is common in the neighbourhood of the alluvial river basins. The mineral wealth of India consists of coal, iron, and salt. Gold is washed by wild tribes in many hill torrents, but not remuneratively. Copper is mined in several places in the Himalayas. Very rich tin deposits are known to exist in the S. of British Burmah. Antimony abounds in the Himalayas; and cobalt and alum are found in Rajputana. Saltpetre effloresces from the soil in Behar, but the manufacture has fallen off. The chief coal-fields lie between the valleys of the Ganges and the Godavery, but isolated deposits are found in many parts of the country. The geological formation which yields nearly all the coal is known as the Damuda; it is the same as that of the Australian beds, and differs but slightly from the carboniferous strata of Europe. The total area of the coal measures is computed at 35,000 sq. miles. In Ranigunj there are forty-four coal-mines at work; and now (1877) the East Indian Railway is entirely supplied from its own colleries at Kurhurbari. Iron in various forms is scattered throughout India, and has always been wrought by native methods. Hitherto it has failed to attract English capital. The great Salt Range in the N. of the Punjaub is said to be the most valuable deposit of the substance known to exist, and the yield is increasing year by year. Much salt is also obtained in the dry season from the lakes in Rajputana, and by solar evaporation along the coasts of Madras and Bombay.

The *Climate* of India is thoroughly tropical, except in the more favoured hill stations. The year naturally divides into three seasons—the rains, from June to October; the cold weather, from November to February; and the hot weather, from February to June. There are, of course, local variations, but the periodicity of the Monsoons (q. v.) determines the regular sequence. The extreme hot weather, accompanied by sandy winds in some parts of India, and by a steamy dampness in Bengal, is most feared by Europeans, though it has been ascertained to be the least unhealthy season for the natives. The mean temperature of Calcutta is 79° F.; the highest recorded, 106°; the lowest, 53°, giving a mean range of 53°. The mean temperature of Madras and Bombay is somewhat higher, and that of Delhi considerably lower. The chief meteorological interest of I. centres upon the rainfall, upon which depends the success of the harvests. The amount of rain that falls in different tracts varies excessively. In the N.W. corner of I., composing half the Punjaub and all Scinde, less than 15 inches falls in the year, and irrigation is an absolute necessity; whereas at Cherra Pûnji in the Assam Hills as much as 805 inches have been registered (366 in the single month of January 1861). For the proper cultivation of rice, an annual fall of 72 inches is said to be necessary; but it is required, above all, that this amount should be distributed through the proper seasons. The Bay of Bengal is the home where originate the tremendous cyclones which occasionally devastate the E. coast of I., especially the neighbourhood of Calcutta. The calamity of October 1876 is said to have swept away in one night 250,000 souls at the estuary of the Brahmaputra.

Vegetable Productions.—The extraordinary fertility of many parts of I. has passed into a proverb. The bountiful rice and the useful cocoa-nut palm have found a place in the Hindu religion. But it is a mistake to suppose that rice is the universal food of the people. It is only in the swamps of Bengal Proper, Orissa, Burmah, and the coast of Madras that its cultivation largely predominates; and even there, health requires that pulses, &c., should be consumed with it. Throughout the rest of I., various sorts of millets, barley, wheat, gram, and maize, form the staple food-grains, though rice is always preferred by those who can obtain it. Opium, cotton, jute, and indigo, the four great crops for exportation, are all very local in their production. Opium is confined to the mid valley of the Ganges and to Malwa; the best cotton comes from the Central Provinces and the south of Bombay; jute is grown nowhere but in E. Bengal, and indigo chiefly in Behar. Sugar is widely manufactured both from the sugar-cane and the date-palm; but, as with tobacco, little is produced beyond what is required for local consumption. Oilseeds of many kinds are grown as cold-weather crops. Fruit-trees, vegetables, and spices of all sorts abound. In the river basins the productiveness of the soil is so great that three crops are sometimes raised from the same field, on which no manure is put, and which is never allowed to lie fallow. The modes of agriculture, though primitive, are exceedingly laborious, and the principles which underly the rotation of crops are not unknown. The products raised under European supervision, excluding indigo, are coffee and tea, both of which are grown in the hills, on virgin soil cleared of jungle. Coffee is grown in Mysore and Coorg; the exports in 1875 were valued at £1,308,000. Tea is chiefly grown in Assam, Darjeeling, and Chittagong; the exports in 1875 were £1,963,000, which shows a steady annual increase. Cinchona, for the preparation of quinine, has been successfully introduced into these same hills; and experiments are now being made with ipecacuanha. A special department for the care of the forests was first organised in Bombay in 1846; and now a carefully trained staff is annually sent out from England. The forest reserves cover more than 6,000,000 acres, the revenue from which considerably exceeds the expenditure. The most valuable forests are on the lower hill ranges; among the timber trees are teak, *sal*, deodara, sandalwood, blackwood, and ironwood. Caoutchouc is an important product of the N.E. frontier, being brought in from the forests by the wild tribes of Assam and Burmah.

Animals.—Among domestic animals the first place is due to the sacred ox or humped zebu, which is used for ploughing, for draught, and for milk. The finest breeds come from Gujerat and Hurrianah; the cattle of Bengal are miserably dwarfed. The buffalo is also largely used for ploughing, and thrives best where the oxen are worst. The horses are not good; even the breeds of the Deccan and Kattywar have degenerated, and it has become difficult to obtain remounts for the cavalry except by importation. Elephants are mainly kept for ostentation; the chief supply now comes from the N. and N.E. frontier. Throughout Bengal and Assam about 250 are captured annually. The finest goats are bred in the neighbourhood of Patna, sheep in the Punjaub and N.W. Provinces. Pigs are only eaten by low castes. The tiger is still common in many parts; like all other wild animals, he is only driven back by the advance of cultivation. His ravages are not so much dreaded by the villagers as are those of the wild hog and deer, whose numbers he keeps down. It is only the confirmed man-eater that they fear, who, on his part, generally avoids Europeans. Other common beasts of prey are leopards, wolves, hyenas, bears, jackals, and wild dogs. The largest game are the elephant, rhinoceros, and bison. The lion is said to be found in a few special tracts. Fixed rewards are given by Government for the heads of certain wild animals; but poisonous snakes annually destroy far more lives than do tigers, their victims being estimated at as many as 20,000 a year. In times of inundation, the snakes take refuge in the raised villages.

People.—The average density of the population in British I. is 211 persons to the square mile, varying from 468 in the province of Oude to 31 in British Burmah. In Great Britain and Ireland the average pop. per sq. mile is 265. There is a comparative absence of large towns, only 44 containing more than 50,000 inhabitants. Of the total pop. 73½ per cent. are called Hindus, and 21½ per cent. are Mohammedans, leaving 5 per cent. for Buddhists, Christians, Hill Tribes, &c. Nearly all the Buddhists are in British Burmah; those assigned to Bombay are probably Jains (q. v.). The Christians (mostly in Madras and Burmah) number nearly 900,000, of whom about 250,000 have European blood. French missions have been especially successful among the aboriginal tribe of Karens (q. v.). In Scinde the Mohammedans form 78 per cent. of the population; in the Punjaub, 53 per cent.; in Eastern Bengal, 49 per cent.; whereas throughout the entire S. of the peninsula their numbers are singularly insignificant. The term 'Hindu' has been used with great looseness in the several census reports, and has doubtless been applied to many semi-Hinduised aborigines. The total number of Brahmins is over 10,000,000, most numerous in the N.W. Provinces and Oude. The second caste in rank, the Kshattriyas or Rajputs, numbers 5½ millions. The remaining castes it is impossible to discriminate.

The ethnological history of I. yet remains to be written; it would yield very different results from those indicated above. Neither the Hindus nor the Mohammedans form an homogeneous section. Comparatively few of those who are called Hindus can justly lay claim to the august Aryan lineage; and still fewer of the Mohammedans are of Mongolian or even foreign descent. As tested by language, there can be no doubt that almost the entire population of Madras is Dravidian; and tested by colour and physiognomy, the large majority both of the Hindus and Mohammedans of Bengal must also be referred to an aboriginal origin. It is in Hindustan Proper, *i.e.*, in Behar and the N.W. Provinces, and in the Punjaub, that we can alone look for the pure-bred Aryan immigrant, whether under the name of Hindu or Mussulman. The aboriginal tribes, as might be expected, muster strongest in the hilly tracts of Central I., where they have remained almost unchanged since the first advent of a Sanskrit-speaking colony. The Bheels, the Gondhs, the Koles and Mundas, the Sonthals and the Oraons, are the best-known names. Some of them are certainly Dravidian, while others have been connected with the Indo-Chinese races on the N.E. frontier. A negroid origin, however, has been plausibly assigned to many of these tribes.

The Languages and Literature of I. are more specially alluded to in separate articles. The spoken tongues may be divided into four great classes:—(1) Those that are demonstrably derivatives from the Sanskrit of the original Aryan conquerors, such as Hindi, Bengali, Urya, and Gujeratti; (2) those introduced by the later Mohammedan invaders, of which Hindustani (q. v.) is the language of military life, civil administration, and commerce, Persian of diplomacy, and Arabic of religious instruction; to this class may be added Pushtu, used beyond the Indus; (3) the various Dravidian Tongues (q. v.) spoken throughout the S. of the peninsula, and also by some aboriginal tribes in Central I.; (4) a privative group, including the barbarous dialects of the hill races, of which little is yet known. Many of these have Indo-Chinese affinities, and a sub-group may be formed out of the Kolarian tribes of Chota Nagpore. The alphabets used in writing may all be referred to two sources: the Deva-nagari character of the Sanskrit, which has been adopted even by the Dravidians; and the Persian. Sanskrit literature refers itself back to the remotest antiquity. It opens with the Vedas (q. v.), or hymns of ritual and praise, the sacred book of the Brahmins. Then follow the epics, the mythical histories, the commentaries, the codes of law and the dramas, which together constitute a body of original literature second only to that of the Greeks. European influence has not only diffused some knowledge of English among the upper classes, especially in Bengal, but has also directly stimulated the culture of the native languages. Philology has given a new start to the study of Sanskrit, even among the pundits of Benares; while the industry of the missionaries and the needs of our administration have raised not a few of the vernacular dialects to the dignity of printed languages. The native press is gradually establishing itself as a potent instrument for disseminating knowledge.

Religion.—Figures have already been given to show the comparative distribution of the two great creeds of I. It cannot be said that either is at present actively proselytising. A few outcaste Hindus annually embrace the faith of Islam, and even of late years some of the hill tribes have displayed a tendency to submit themselves *en masse* to the Brahmins. But on the whole, the positions of Hinduism and Mohammedanism remain as firmly fixed as do the limits which separate the Protestants from the Roman Catholics of Europe; and the adherents of the rival faiths live on as good terms as the two Christian sects in Switzerland or Bavaria. Hinduism is described *sub voce*. The Mohammedans of I. have lately taken part in the religious revival that originated among the Wahhabis of Arabia. In Bengal especially, where they were once scarcely to be distinguished from their Hindu fellow-villagers, they have now reformed themselves in accordance with the traditions of primitive orthodoxy. Speaking generally, they are more litigious and turbulent than Hindus; they are proportionally less numerous among the landlord class, and are less enterprising in commerce. It is as ordinary cultivators and boatmen that they are best known. The vast majority belong to the Suni sect. The various forms of faith professed by the hill tribes are mainly based upon worship of the elements. The sun, mountains, and rivers supply the chief gods. Demon worship is not so common as is often supposed, and human sacrifice was only resorted to on exceptional occasions, even by the Gondhs. But the belief in witchcraft is universally prevalent. Altogether, it seems not improbable that the low opinion commonly entertained of these races is due, not so much to the character of their religion, as to reports spread by the Hindus, who abhor them for their dark colour and their unclean habits of feeding. It is among these primitive people that the Protestant missionaries have, of late years, been most successful. Statistics for 1872 show that there were in that year 318,363 Protestant converts in I. and Ceylon, of whom one half are in Madras. The great majority of Roman Catholic converts are also to be found in the same Presidency, but their number is not increasing. The Brahmo-Somajh (q. v.), or reformed theistic sect of Hindus, founded in 1830 by Rajah Rammohun Roy, counts many firmly established communities, especially in Bengal Proper; and its influence is greater than would be represented by the actual number of its professed adherents. The Parsees, the exiled fire-worshippers from Persia, number 69,000, chiefly in Bombay, where they are well known as the most speculative of merchants. The Jews number only 7600. In Calcutta there is an Armenian colony, of old date and high position. The Sikhs, who are a sect of military enthusiasts, repudiating caste and other Brahminical doctrines, are almost confined to the Punjaub; but even there they do not form more than 6 per cent. of the total population, being most numerous in the neighbourhood of Lahore.

Material Condition of the People.—The great majority of the people are directly dependent upon their own agriculture. The census returns according to occupation, which are not entirely trustworthy, show 56 per cent. of the total adult males as 'agricultural,' and an additional 12 per cent. as 'labourers.' The condition of the ordinary cultivator varies considerably. In Madras and Bombay, where the Land Settlement is made directly with him, and in the Punjaub also, where the settlement is made with the village community of which he is a member, his lot is distinctly a happy one. He is a peasant proprietor under favourable circumstances, with every stimulus to exertion and security for the fruits of his toil. In Bengal, however, in Oude, and in great part of the N.W. Provinces, where the land-tax is paid primarily by the landlord, his position is not so good. Under exceptionally favourable circumstances, as in the alluvial swamps of Eastern Bengal, where spare land is yet abundant, he can maintain himself in comfortable independence; but throughout the greater part of the Gangetic valley, the small farmers are little better off than were the cottiers of Ireland before the famine in that country, and the day-labourers are hardly removed above serfdom. Both rent and wages are commonly paid in kind, and the rates of each are directly determined by the minimum at which life can be supported. In addition, the village usurer or Mahajan (q. v.) is always at hand to appropriate the profits of a favourable season. It is in these same tracts, as might be expected, that the pressure of population upon the soil is most severe. The Hindu will not permanently leave his native village, even when there is abundance of uncultivated jungle not far off; and systematic emigration has as yet proved a failure. But despite great poverty and the hopelessness of improvement, the ordinary cultivator is by no means miserable. His patience and good temper have become a proverb; and the charitableness inculcated by his religion renders any poor-law superfluous. The total number of coolie emigrants in 1875 was only 25,325, of whom 20,230 embarked from Calcutta, 1886 from Madras, and 3209 from French ports. The destination was either Mauritius, Natal, or the W. Indies. These numbers indicate no increase during the previous ten years. The number of emigrants to the tea districts of Assam in the same year was 22,288, and from Bengal to Burmah 7397. About 70,000 coolies annually cross from S. India to work on the coffee plantations of Ceylon.

Health and Sanitation.—The sanitary commissioner accepts as approximately correct a calculation which estimates the average duration of life in I. at 30 years and 8 months, at which rate the average mortality would be 32·57 per thousand. In many parts of the country, especially in Bengal, cholera exists in an endemic form; but fevers and bowel complaints are ordinarily the most fatal forms of disease. It has been noticed that the cold season is the most unhealthy for the natives. Smallpox continues to cause many deaths annually, though inoculation is now prohibited over large areas, and voluntary vaccination is on the increase. At the capital cities there are excellent medical hospitals; charitable dispensaries, with Government subsidies, are scattered throughout the rural tracts; and quinine, the only real preventive and remedy in the case of fever, is now cheaply produced in the country, and widely distributed. Bad water and bad drainage are acknowledged as the main cause of much of the disease in I. The new water-supply and sewage-scheme has had some effect in improving the health of Calcutta, and a similar result may be expected from the works at Madras.

Education has been widely disseminated of late years. Though much yet remains to be done, I. will now bear comparison with the more backward countries of Europe. The present system dates from 1854. The plan laid down in that year by Sir C. Wood (Lord Halifax) established an education department for each province; founded universities for granting degrees (after the model of the University of London), with which the existing colleges were affiliated; reorganised the middle-class schools in which English is taught; and encouraged the indigenous village schools for giving primary instruction in the vernacular. This latter class of schools has always existed throughout I.; but up to the date already mentioned, efficient vernacular teaching had been the proud monopoly of the missionaries. Universities were founded at the three presidency towns in 1857, when the Mutiny was at its height. There are now forty affiliated colleges, besides special institutions for the study of Oriental languages, medicine and engineering, and schools of art. In the year ending March 1875, the total number of candidates at the three universities for the entrance examination was 5280, of whom 2012 passed; 175 persons passed for B.A., and twenty-one passed for M.A. with honours. During the same year there were, throughout all I. under British administration, 74,050 educational institutions of all kinds, attended by 1,660,202 pupils. The work of female education, closely connected with *zenana* visitation, still remains almost confined to missionaries and their wives.

The *Commerce and Trade* of I. is very large, and annually increasing. It may be divided into maritime commerce (foreign and coasting), internal trade, and the trans-Himalayan traffic. For the year 1875, the total number of sailing and steam vessels, with cargoes and in ballast, that entered British Indian ports was 19,875, with a tonnage of 4,903,827; of these, as many as 13,528 vessels (including 10,002 native craft), with a tonnage of 2,461,266, were engaged in the coasting trade. The foreign trade proper is, of course, mostly conducted direct with the United Kingdom; next in order come Ceylon, the Red Sea and Persian Gulf, the Straits Settlements, China, Mauritius, France, Australia, and the United States. The total value of the imports, including Government stores and treasure, was £44,363,134; of the exports, £57,984,539. The former of these figures is somewhat below, and the latter somewhat above, the average for the last ten years, which shows a general balance of trade in favour of I., amounting to about £11,000,000 sterling annually. This balance is supposed to be satisfied by the Indian Secretary's bills on I., which are sold periodically in London. Striking an average for the last ten years, the imports of treasure (almost solely silver) exceed the exports by an average of nearly £10,000,000 a year, so that the strict balance of trade, as shown by the excess of exports over imports in merchandise proper, may be placed at £20,000,000 sterling annually. Among the imports the following are the chief items for 1875:—Cotton manufactures, £16,263,560, the largest total yet reached, as compared with £11,849,214 in 1866; cotton twist and yarn, £3,157,780, as compared with £1,961,144 in 1866; metals, manufactured and unmanufactured, £2,607,096; machinery and millwork, £1,185,943, as compared with £586,182 in 1866; Government stores, £1,576,851. Among the exports, raw cotton, 627,209,661 lbs., valued at £15,257,342, against 803,150,424 lbs., valued at £35,587,389 in 1866; opium, £11,956,972, a very constant item; grains and pulse (including rice, but excluding wheat), £4,765,334; jute and manufactures of jute, £3,484,522, against £1,083,522 in 1866; seeds, £3,235,948, against £1,750,197 in 1866; hides and skins, £2,677,767, against £609,803 in 1866; indigo, £2,576,302; tea, £1,963,550, against £309,899 in 1866; cotton manufactures, £1,426,538; coffee, £1,307,919, against £785,102 in 1866. It will thus be seen that the apparent decline in exports is solely due to the decreased value of cotton, as compared with a period when the American ports were closed; and that the new staples of jute, seeds, hides, tea, and coffee, show a most satisfactory progress. It must always be recollected that these figures include British Burmah, but exclude Ceylon. The internal trade passes by road, water, and railway. Few statistics on this subject are available, but the traffic is known to be very great. In 1875, the railways throughout I. carried a total of 4,388,649 tons of goods and minerals, besides 505,621 head of live stock. The trade statistics of the Punjaub, which are not entirely trustworthy, show a total of about 1,520,000 tons, valued, but evidently overvalued, at 16 millions sterling. A most comprehensive system of boat registration, which has lately been established on all the great waterways of Bengal, reveals an annual traffic within that province, in heavy goods alone, of about 30 million tons. The entire trade of Patna, the emporium of Behar, is estimated at about 1½ million tons a year; the registered river-borne traffic for six months only was valued at over 3 millions sterling. The trans-Himalayan trade passes by recognised mountain passes either through Afghanistan, Cashmere, or Nepaul.

Manufactures throughout I. are undergoing a change. Many old industries, such as cotton and silk weaving, and salt-making, have been largely superseded by the competition of the cheaper imported articles. Specialties, however, such as the brocades and embroidery of the Punjaub, the saddlery of Cawnpore, the jewellers' work of Trichinopoly, Cuttack, &c., and the trade of potters and braziers generally throughout the country, still flourish; European capital, also, has introduced, and is continuing to introduce, new employments for the disengaged or surplus labour. Indigo, tea, and coffee each require a large number of hands; while the cotton-mills of Bombay, and the jute and paper mills of Bengal, are illustrating the capacity of the natives for new forms of skilled handicraft. In 1872 there were in Bombay 18 steam factories, employing 4500 looms, 405,000 spindles, and 10,000 hands, and turning out daily 100,000 lbs. of yarn. Apart from the local demand, the produce is finding its way into the markets of Russia, America, and China.

Means of Communication have been immensely improved under British rule, and it is by their efficiency in seasons of drought, more even than by irrigation, that local scarcity can be prevented from intensifying into famine. Railways, which now stretch over the length and breadth of the peninsula, were partly no doubt laid out for military purposes, following the lines of the Grand Trunk Roads. The main lines have been constructed by private companies, to whom the Government has guaranteed 5 per cent. interest on their outlay, retaining an option of purchase. Since the time of Lord Mayo, it has been determined that future lines, which must chiefly be feeders, shall be made and worked directly by the State. At the close of 1875, the total length of lines open (both guaranteed and State, and including some railways in native territory) was 6497 miles; the number of passengers, 26¾ millions; the number of tons of goods and minerals carried, 4,388,649; the gross receipts, £7,412,079; the gross expenses, £3,764,311; the total capital expended, £102,128,893, of which 92 millions was on guaranteed railways; the number of persons killed was 208, injured, 267. The telegraph statistics for the same date (including Ceylon) are as follow:—Miles of wire, 33,798; offices open, 225; messages (including State and free), 883,727; receipts, £203,881; expenditure, £338,731. The postal statistics show a very large increase, amounting almost to twofold, during the past ten years. In 1875 the number of post-offices open was 3408; the establishment numbered 25,942 persons; the revenue was £719,587; the expenditure, £729,191.

Administration.—Subject to the distant control exercised by the Secretary of State in England, who is aided by a salaried council of fifteen members, the supreme government of I. is vested in the Governor-General or Viceroy, the latter of which titles was assumed after the fall of the East India Company in 1858. The Governor-General in his turn is assisted by two councils, the Executive and the Legislative, and all his public acts run in the name of 'the Governor-General *in* Council.' Theoretically, he is supreme at the council board, and on him rests the sole responsibility; but in practice his position somewhat resembles that of the Prime Minister in a Cabinet. The Executive Council is composed of the Commander-in-Chief and five other 'members,' each of whom is intrusted with a special department; the Legislative Council contains in addition several non-official members, including a few distinguished natives. For ordinary civil administration the whole area of British India is divided into that portion which is directly under the Governor-General, and the Provinces, nine in number, which have each a separate government. The Native States also may be divided on the same principle. The four tracts of Ajmere, Berar, Mysore, and Coorg, under the Governor-General, represent recently-acquired territory, which it has not been thought convenient to attach to any of the old-established provinces. The separate administrations are the 'Presidencies' of Madras and Bombay (including Scinde), each under a governor appointed from England; the Lieutenant-Governorships of Bengal, the N.W. Provinces, and the Punjaub; and the Chief Commissionerships of Oude, the Central Provinces, British Burmah, and Assam. To nearly all these provinces are attached a larger or smaller number of Native States; but by far the more important of the feudatory chiefs, whose territory lies in the centre of the peninsula, are in immediate relation with the supreme government. The Governors of Madras and Bombay have each both Executive and Legislative Councils; Bengal has a Legislative Council; the remaining provinces are under the sole authority of their respective Lieutenant-Governors or Chief Commissioners. Each province is divided into districts or *zillahs*, and the districts are usually subdivided into subdivisions, called sometimes *talooks*. The districts, which vary much in size, constitute the field of work of one responsible official, known as a Collector-Magistrate or Deputy-Commissioner, who is required to perform an infinite variety of administrative duties. The judicial work proper rests in other hands. The entire civil staff may be arranged in three classes—the covenanted servants, who are selected by open competition in England; the uncovenanted servants, who are nominated in India; and the officers of the Indian staff corps who have received civil employment. The covenanted servants, the inheritors of Haileybury traditions, and 'the Indian Civil Service' *par excellence*, enjoy a monopoly of the higher appointments in what are known as the Regulation Districts, the old-established regions in which the codes are in full force. The other two classes are eligible for the non-Regulation Districts, including the whole of the Punjaub and Oude.

Army.—For military purposes the old threefold division into the Presidencies of Bengal, Madras, and Bombay, is maintained; everything that was not historically included under either of the two last mentioned being arbitrarily placed under Bengal. But this classification is only kept up as a staff distinction, for the troops of each Presidency are by no means confined within their proper geographical limits. The total strength of the army in 1875 amounted to 190,175 officers and men, of whom 104,174 belonged to the Bengal establishment. The European army numbered 66,313, of whom 6086 were officers, including 2357 belonging to the staff corps. The native army numbered 123,682, of whom only 180 were officers. Among the Europeans 12,305 were artillery, 4347 cavalry, 354 engineers, 45,962 infantry; while 151 are returned as general officers unemployed. Before the Mutiny of 1857 the army of the Company was composed of about 45,000 Europeans and 232,000 natives. The European troops are for the most part housed in new and healthy barracks, in connection with certain recognised hill sanitariums; and through communication by rail is now open to every important station except Peshawur and Hydrabad. The death-rate in 1874 was only 1·389 per cent. as opposed to an average of 2·299 per cent. for the previous ten years. The British forces are chiefly stationed in the Punjaub and along the valley of the Ganges. The military expenditure in 1875 was £15,375,159, of which £3,617,778 was spent in England. The total shows a considerable decrease during the past ten years. To the volunteer corps was allotted £13,248. The above figures, of course, exclude the various armies of the Native States, which are estimated to number 314,598 men, with 3488 serviceable pieces of artillery.

Revenue and Expenditure.—Owing to the constant changes in the system of keeping accounts, it is almost impossible to give a sketch of the finances of I. which shall not be misleading. Since 1872 both revenue and expenditure have been affected by the transfer of certain items to 'Provincial Services,' in accordance with a reform inaugurated by Lord Mayo; and the present finance minister, Sir J. Strachey, proposes to extend this principle. On the expenditure side there is a fundamental distinction drawn between ordinary expenditure, and that on 'public works extraordinary.' These latter are officially defined as 'public works that the Government have decided may be carried on by loans, if necessary.' As a matter of fact, they represent the capital account of a commercial undertaking; and as the Government have now resolved to construct railways themselves, this heading of extraordinary expenditure is evidently destined to maintain itself. In addition, the item of 'Famine Relief' has recently appeared on the expenditure side, amounting during the four years from 1874 to 1878 to an estimated total of £11,000,000, or an average of more than £2,000,000 a year. The balance-sheet for the financial year ending 31st March 1875 may be thus stated:—Gross revenue, £50,570,171; total expenditure, £54,500,545, of which £4,249,571 was for public works extraordinary, and £2,237,860 for famine relief; deficit, £3,930,374. The budget estimates for 1877–78 place the revenue at £52,192,700; the expenditure at £56,442,400, including £3,628,000 for public works extraordinary, and £2,150,000 for famine relief; deficit, £4,249,700. For 1875 the chief items of revenue were as follow:—Land revenue, £21,296,793; opium, £8,556,629; salt, £6,227,301; excise and forest, £2,929,424; stamps, £2,758,042; customs, £2,678,479; public works, £1,047,735. The income-tax, which had realised £2,000,000 in 1871, was finally abolished in 1873. The chief items of expenditure in 1875 were:—Army, £15,375,159; refunds, charges of collection, assignments under treaties, &c., £9,510,766; interest on debt, &c., £5,412,055; provincial services (police, education, &c.), £5,148,744; State railways (capital), £3,014,180; public works, £2,504,230; law and justice, £2,298,180; famine relief, £2,237,860; railways (guaranteed interest), £1,483,839; loss by exchange on home remittances, £897,878. The total debt of I., exclusive of the £12,000,000 sterling forming the capital stock of the East I. Company, amounted in 1875 to £118,333,794, of which £70,000,000 bore interest in I. and £48,000,000 in England. The total shows an increase of £28,000,000 during the past ten years. The most important financial reforms required in I. are admitted to be the abolition of inland customs lines, and the equalisation and reduction of the salt duties. The Government is also pledged to abolish the import duties on cotton goods with the least possible delay.

The *Land Revenue* in 1875 amounted to £21,296,793, or 42 per cent. of the total receipts; and its collection forms so large a portion of the duties of the administrative staff, that the district officer is still commonly styled 'Collector.' Including a few local rates and cesses, the average incidence of the land-tax throughout British I. is estimated to be 9½d. per acre of gross area, 2s. 8d. per acre of revenue-paying cultivated area, 13s. 1½d. per adult male agriculturist, and 2s. 4½d. per head of total population. But the incidence, no less than the mode of assessment, varies extremely in the different provinces, being 3s. 10½d. per head in Bombay, and only 1s. 2¾d. in Bengal. This tax, which may more properly be regarded as the rental reserved by the State as its proprietary right in the soil, is of extreme antiquity in I., being indeed indigenous to all settled Oriental countries. The tax is universally paid in cash; and numerous permanent interests in the soil have in many provinces been suffered to grow up between the State and the cultivator. In Bengal a permanent settlement of the land revenue was adopted by Lord Cornwallis in 1793, in accordance with which the *zamindars* or official rent-collectors were acknowledged as ordinary English landlords, and a rent-charge was fixed in perpetuity. In Madras the *ryotwary* system proper is in force, by which an annual settlement is made with each separate cultivator. In Bombay, the system is also *ryotwary*, except that the settlement lasts for thirty years. In the N.W. Provinces, a thirty years' settlement is made with the recognised proprietor of each village or township, whether such proprietor be the village community itself, a landlord proper, or a family group of landlords. In Oude, the settlement, made after the Mutiny of 1857, has conferred rights in perpetuity on the *talookdars* or large landlords. In the Punjaub the village communities, which have maintained their integrity more fully than elsewhere in I., pay the revenue assessed for periods of thirty years; and in the small province of Assam the village head-man is responsible for the annual assessment. There can be no doubt that the position of the cultivator is universally better where the settlement is made directly with himself. Whether the assessment should be fixed or variable is still a matter of discussion.

The monetary system of I. is based upon a silver standard alone. The unit is the rupee, weighing 180 grains (165 pure), a coin which is said to have been first introduced in 1542. Its nominal value is about 2s., but the exchange with England has been known to fall to 1s. 7d. It is subdivided into sixteen annas, each of which again contains twelve pies. The anna, therefore, is equal to three halfpence, and the pie to half a farthing. Several of the larger Native States still retain the prerogative of coinage, but the only two Government mints now open are at Calcutta and Bombay. The former gold coins—the Mohammedan mohur = 16 rupees, and the Madras pagoda = 3½ rupees—have practically ceased to be in circulation. Enumeration in account is effected by means of lacs and crores, the former meaning 100,000, the latter 10,000,000. In the year 1875 there was coined £14,034 in gold, £4,896,884 in silver, and £111,334 in copper, and the mint profit was £159,021. Chartered banks are established at the three Presidency towns; but the paper currency is for the most part a direct Government issue of promissory notes, which may be cashed at all the local treasuries within the circle of issue. The average amount of note circulation in 1875 was £10,670,407, and the profit on issue was £198,015. The unit of weight throughout the greater part of I. is the *seer*, which, as fixed by Government, exactly corresponds to the metrical kilogramme, being equal to 2·205 lbs; but this has nowhere come into use. For practical purposes the *seer* equals 2 lbs. The table is 16 *chuttucks* = 1 *seer*, 40 *seers* = 1 *maund* or 80 lbs. The unit of land measure is the *beegah*, which again is extremely variable. The Government standard *beegah* is equal to 14,400 square feet, or almost precisely one-third of an acre. The *seer* is used not only for weighing, but also for liquid measure. The price of grain is estimated by the number of *seers* that may be obtained for a rupee.

The *Native States* are more particularly described under their several names. The most important are the ancient Hindu states of Rajputana, which cover 128,126 sq. miles, and contain a pop. of 9,000,000; Hyderabad, or the Dominions of the Nizam, the first Mohammedan potentate in the peninsula, area, 80,000 sq. miles, pop. 9,000,000; the three great Mahratta states of Baroda, Gwalior, and Indore, ruled over respectively by the Guicowar, Scindiah, and Holkar, with a total area of 45,593 sq. miles, and a pop. of 5,000,000; the Himalayan valley of Cashmere, whose chief owes his power to a British grant, area, 79,784 sq. miles, pop. 1,537,000; the flourishing southern states of Travancore and Cochin, area, 8091 sq. miles, pop. 2,909,732. The total revenue of all the chiefs is estimated at £14,500,000 sterling; the tribute they pay to the British is only £741,465. It would be hazardous to attempt to define the exact relations between these feudatories and the paramount power. Of the 153 chieftains who are recognised, some are mere heads of wild hill tribes, others are really subject noblemen or squires, while those named above possess the majority of the attributes of independent sovereignty. None can exercise the right of adoption without an express grant or *sunnud;* and the greatest of them, when admitted to the presence of the viceroy, presents his *nuzzur* or present, which is throughout the East the acknowledged mark of inferiority. They may not levy war against one another, and a guarantee for internal order exists in the right of dethronement and the establishment of a temporary British administration, which has not seldom been exercised by the paramount power.

The French and the Portuguese still retain territory in I. The French capital is Pondicherry (q. v.), on the Coromandel coast; the colony sends a member both to the Versailles Senate and the House of Representatives. The Portuguese seat of government is the city of Goa (q. v.). Many Christians of mixed Portuguese descent are to be found scattered through British territory, especially in the neighbourhood of Dacca and Chittagong, where they are known as Feringhees (q. v.). The Dutch settlements, of which Chinsurah on the Hooghly was the chief, were ceded to Great Britain in exchange for the island of Java in 1825. The Danish settlements of Tranquebar and Serampore were transferred to the East India Company in 1845, in consideration of the sum of £125,000.

History.—The history of I. is the record of a succession of waves of conquest, which almost without exception have burst upon the country from the N.W. In early prehistoric times we may picture to ourselves I. as inhabited by three races, each of which might well claim to be regarded as aboriginal. In the S. were the Dravidian peoples (q. v.) who still hold their own in language and national characteristics, though they early accepted the faith of Brahminism from the Aryan invaders. Siva-worship and the adoration of the *linga* are thought to be the contribution of the Dravidians to modern Hinduism. In the centre of the peninsula were uncivilised tribes, dark in colour and negroid in physiognomy, with whom the Aryans first came into collision, and who are now represented by the hill tribes of Koles and Sonthals, and perhaps the Gondhs, but whose blood is largely to be found in all the Hindu low castes. Sorcery and the practice of human sacrifice are peculiar superstitions of these tribes. Finally, near the N.E. frontier and along the Himalayas was a race of Thibetan or Chinese origin, who may be now identified most distinctly in the numerous caste of Kochs with its many offshoots. It is in this country that the impure mysteries of the Tantras retain their firmest hold.

It is impossible to fix even an approximate date for the first Aryan immigration. It is only certain that the invaders came from the N.W., that they drove out or enslaved aboriginal inhabitants of a darker hue than themselves, and spread very gradually S.E. along the valley of the Ganges, in which tract alone (Hindustan Proper, q. v.) do they still form the bulk of the population. It was partly by their superior physique, but still more by their finer intellectual and moral organisation, that the Aryans exercised their dominant influence over the indigenous races of the entire peninsula. Theirs was not an invasion of conquest, such as leads to a warfare of extermination, but rather the imposition of a higher civilisation, justified by the permanence of its results. The invaders carried with them the germs of the two religions—Hinduism and Buddhism—which still constitute the faith of about one half of the human species. The history proper of I. does not commence until the Hindus, as we may call the amalgamated population, are firmly settled in the land. The prior events are only matter for conjecture. The war of the Mahabharata may preserve some relics of historical fact, but their discovery is now even more impossible than in the analogous cases of the Trojan War or the Niebelungen Lied. The earliest authentic facts we possess come from the Greek historians, who recognised the general unity of the races inhabiting the country, and also the exceeding density of the population. They further teach us that I. never formed one solid empire, but was always broken up into states of varying power and area.

The invasion of Alexander, also from the N.W., is the next fact in Indian history. His army refused to follow him beyond the region of the Punjaub; but the effect of this first penetration of Europeans into I. spread much wider. A new civilisation, and above all a new style of art, were disclosed to the Hindus, and a direct route for maritime commerce was opened by the naval expedition of Nearchus. Recent archæological discoveries have shown that Hellenic influence, exhibited in coins, sculpture, and architecture, remained for some time predominant in the N.W. It is by the light of these facts that two obscure events in Indian history may perhaps be rightly understood. These events are the immigration of a supposed Scythian race, whose descendants are to be traced in the Jats, the modern Sikhs, and the constant allusions to be found in the Hindu chronicles treating of this period to the Yavanas, a name that connects with Ionia and Javan, and is etymologically interpreted to mean 'goers.' This period also saw both the rise and downfall of Buddhism, a most curious and perplexing epoch in Indian history. The life of Gautama himself is now fixed by scholars as being almost co-extensive with the 5th c. B.C. Within 150 years after his death, *i.e.*, in 250 B.C., Asoka the King of Magadha held his great council at Pataliputra, the Palibothra of the Greeks and the modern Patna, in accordance with which the doctrines of the new religion were engraved on pillars which still exist, and thus published to the furthest corners of the peninsula. Soon after the commencement of the Christian era Buddhism began to decline. Hiouen Thsang (q. v.), a Chinese pilgrim who traversed great part of I. in the 7th c. A.D., found it everywhere weak and corrupt; and within two hundred years afterwards, the Buddhists had been entirely exterminated from their native country by the victorious Brahminists, who were themselves soon destined to fall before the Mohammedan invader.

The Mussulman invasion of I. is not one isolated event, but a constant succession of inroads and immigrations of hardy barbarians from the mountains of Afghanistan and the steppes of Central Asia, which continued for a period of almost 800 years, from Mahmoud of Ghuzni to Nadir Shah. The N.W. corner of I. was of course the most exposed to these attacks, and it took many centuries before the S. of the peninsula fell under Mohammedan rule. The first recorded conquest is that of Mahmoud (q. v.) of Ghuzni, the great Asiatic conqueror of his generation, who is said to have marched his armies across the Indus no less than nine times. In the year 1001 he led forth his famous expedition against the Hindu shrine of Somnauth in Gujerat, the sacking of which temple is regarded as marking the general downfall of Hindu supremacy. But his dynasty was not long-lived; and a series of petty Mussulman monarchies fixed themselves, for longer or shorter periods, at what were even then recognised as the capital cities of Lahore and Delhi. In 1211 the sanguinary Genghiz Khan (q. v.) swept over the upper plains of Hindustan; and in 1397 Timur (q. v.) the Tartar followed in his track, leaving a name behind him which is remembered by the Hindus at the present day. During this period the Mohammedans were gradually extending their power, not as one empire but as independent dynasties, in Bengal, Malwa, the Deccan, and Gujerat. But the real subjection of I. dates from the first battle of Paniput in 1525, by which Baber (q. v.), a descendant of Timur and the first of the Great Moghuls, established himself at Delhi, not as a temporary immigrant, but as a step towards his design of erecting a united Indian empire. His son Humayun suffered reverses; but his grandson, Akbar (q. v.) the Great, and his successors, firmly secured their power from Cabul and Cashmere to the S. of the peninsula. I. was thus, for the first time in history, formed into one political unity; but it would be an error to suppose that the Moghul dynasty at any time exercised the real attributes of sovereignty over this wide area. The early emperors were continually in arms, warring not only against their Mohammedan rivals, but also against confederacies of the dispossessed Hindu chieftains who had retired into the inaccessible tract now known as Rajputana. And as soon as these foes were severally defeated, the final causes of the downfall of the Delhi empire began to show themselves. On the one hand, the local Mohammedan officials—the Nazim of the Deccan, the Nawab Nazim of Bengal, the Nawab Vizier of Oude—gradually asserted a practical independence; while the power at court fell into the hands of palace intriguers, who deposed and set up emperors at their pleasure. On the other hand, the subject Hindus took advantage of these dissensions, and as represented by the Mahratta horsemen fought it out on equal terms with their former masters. By this time, also, European nations had come upon the scene.

In the year 1498 the Portuguese admiral, Vasco de Gama, landed at Calicut, on the Malabar coast of Southern I., and his countrymen retained their monopoly of trade for more than a century. The early history of the East India Company (q. v.) has already been given; it will be enough in this place to record the dates of the more important events which changed a corporation of traders into one of the most powerful governments in the world. It was in Bengal, by accident rather than by intention, that the weakness of Oriental power was first demonstrated. The battle of Plassey was won by Clive in 1757; but not till 1765, as the result of the equally decisive victory of Buxar, which brought the British into direct connection with the Moghul Emperor, Shah Alum, was their status of traders definitely exchanged for that of territorial rulers. On 12th August of that year the Dewani, or financial administration of Bengal, Behar, and Orissa, was formally made over to the Company by imperial grant. It fell to Warren Hastings and Lord Cornwallis (1773–93) to organise these new dominions, and show the possibility of governing I. under European supervision. In the S. of I. a different set of circumstances required to be encountered. The French were there settled as the rivals, and occasionally the successful rivals, of the English; and in addition, Hyder Ali and his son Tippoo illustrated the capacities for warfare, diplomacy, and administration which continually present themselves sporadically in the East. The fall of Seringapatam in 1799 marks the final establishment of British supremacy, which has never since been contested in that quarter. The Governor-Generalship of Lord Wellesley (1798–1805) is generally regarded as the epoch which practically inaugurated the principle that every native prince holds his power subject to the approval of England. The Nazim, the Peishwa, and the Guicowar were compelled to accept subsidiary treaties, the Mahratta confederation was broken by the victories of Assaye and Laswaree, and the Moghul Emperor was restored to his throne at Delhi by a British escort. The next great event in Indian history was the disastrous invasion of Afghanistan (1838–42), which was not justifiable in its origin, and which led to the greatest blow that British prestige has ever suffered in the East. There followed upon this expedition the conquest of Scinde and the Punjaub, the only two outlying corners of I. that yet remained entirely under native rule. Scinde was won by the signal victory of Meanee in 1843; but the Punjaub was not finally annexed till 1849, when the second Sikh campaign was closed by the battle of Gujerat. This annexation was one of the first acts of the administration of Lord Dalhousie, Governor-General from 1848–55, a period which was signalised by the introduction of railways and telegraphs into I., and by the opening of steam communication by the overland route. But Lord Dalhousie's rule was still more strongly impressed upon the native mind by the conquest of the Punjaub beyond the Sutlej, and of Burmah beyond the 'black water,' and by the deliberate enunciation of the doctrine of 'lapse,' in accordance with which the states of Oude, Nagpore, and Sattara successively passed under British administration, away from those who were popularly regarded as their rightful princes. All these changes, whether of civilisation or of policy, profoundly unsettled the minds of the people. The Mohammedans had never forgotten that their government had been overthrown by the British, and all the disinherited chiefs and landlords combined to take advantage of a temporary discontent among the Bengal sepoys. The result was the Mutiny of 1857, which fell most unexpectedly upon those who were actually on the spot, and of which it is now hopeless to attempt to discriminate all the immediate causes. The first outbreak was of a cavalry regiment stationed at Meerut in May 1857, which marched to the neighbouring city of Delhi, and forthwith all the N.W. Provinces, Oude, and Central I. were in a blaze. The Punjaub was firmly held by Lawrence and his able lieutenants, the civil population of Bengal were quiet throughout, the Madras and Bombay sepoys did not mutiny, and the great majority of the native chiefs remained loyal. It were useless to recount the sufferings of the Europeans—men, women, and children—who were thus miserably cut off, or the stern retribution which was afterwards meted out to the rebels. Delhi was recaptured by storm in September 1857; but it was not till the middle of 1859 that the whole of Central I. was finally pacified.

These events led to the last scene in the drama of Indian history. In August 1858 the Act of Parliament was passed by which all the powers of the East India Company were vested in the Queen, and a new system of government (described above) was organised for the country. Lord Canning was the Governor-General through all this troublous time (1856–62), and the first viceroy of the Queen. Since this date there have been various frontier expeditions; but historical interest has centred round questions of internal administration, among which the successful dealing with periodical famine occupies the foremost place. The auspicious tour of the Prince of Wales throughout the length and breadth of I. during the cold weather of 1875–76, and the proclamation of Queen Victoria as 'Kaiser-i-Hind' at Delhi on 1st January 1877, are the only remaining events worthy of notice.

Among books on I. the following are the most valuable:—*The Statement Exhibiting the Moral and Material Progress*, annually laid before Parliament as a Blue Book, of which the number for 1872–73 by Mr. Clements Markham, with maps, is especially useful; *The Statistical Abstract Relating to British I.*, also published annually, giving a comparison by decennial periods; the statistical accounts of each province, district by district, of which the greater part are already printed. These are edited and partly compiled by Dr. W. W. Hunter, who is now commencing an alphabetical Imperial Gazetteer of all I., to supersede Thornton's *Gazetteer*, of which the last edition was published in 1859; *The History of British I.*, by James Mill, continued by Prof. H. H. Wilson; the popular history by Dr. Marshman. For the early periods, Elphinstone's *History of I., the Hindu and Mohammedan Periods* (4th ed. 1864); Elliott's *History of I., as told by its own Historians* (1867), of which posthumous volumes are still appearing; Mr. Talboys Wheeler's three volumes. For special periods, General Briggs' *History of the Deccan*, Prof. Stewart's *History of Bengal*, Grant Duff's *History of the Mahrattas*, Cunningham's *History of the Sikhs*, Sir J. Kaye's Histories of the Afghan Campaign and of the Sepoy War, the same author's memoirs of many distinguished Anglo-Indians, and Dr. Hunter's *Annals of Rural Bengal*, *Orissa*, and a *Life of Lord Mayo* give a most interesting description of various aspects of Indian life. See also Fergusson's *History of Indian Architecture*, Col. Cunningham's *Ancient Geography of I.*, Col. Dalton's *Descriptive Ethnology of Bengal* (Calcutta, 1872), and the numerous works published by Messrs. Allen & Co., the publishers to the I. Office, which are most expensively illustrated.

India'na, one of the United States of America, bounded N. by Michigan and Lake Michigan, E. by Ohio, S.E. and S. by Kentucky, and W. by Illinois. Area, 33,809 sq. miles; pop. (1870) 1,680,637. The surface is generally level, with rolling prairies and deep river-valleys. The chief rivers are the Wabash, Great Miami, the Maumee, and the Ohio. The soil is very fertile, and the climate is variable, the summer heat and winter cold being both intense. There are large forests, especially in the E., of black walnut, red maple, oak, elm, hickory, &c. I. is one of the richest grain-growing States. Large crops of wheat, rye, Indian-corn, &c., are raised, and vines flourish along the Ohio. Hemp, flax, and sugar are produced, and cattle are reared in great numbers. I. has coalfields of about 7700 sq. miles in area; and much of the coal is of the best quality. The manufactures, which are rapidly increasing, comprise woollens, iron goods, machinery, agricultural instruments, &c., but the chief industries are flour-making and wood-cutting. I. is intersected by numerous railways, there being (1874) 3837 miles of railroad in the State. The chief towns are Indianapolis, the State capital, Fort Wayne, Evansville, Terre Haute, New Albany, Lafayette, and Madison. I. was at first part of the French possessions, and was ceded to the English in 1763. Together with the rest of the N.W. Territory it was transferred to the United States by the treaty of 1783. The early settlers suffered greatly from the attacks of the Indians, which were finally put an end to by successful conflicts in 1811 and 1815. I. was made a State of the Union 11th December 1816.

Indianap'olis, the capital of Indiana, U.S., stands near the middle of the State, on the White River, and is connected by rail with many of the great American cities. Its streets are wide and mostly lined with trees, and there is a large park in the centre. There are seventy churches, large state and county courthouses, an imposing chamber of commerce, a masonic hall, oddfellows' hall, academy of music, and many other fine edifices. I. has numerous benevolent institutions, a city hospital, dispensary, national surgical institute, homes for orphans, &c. The city lies in a rich corn-growing district, and has extensive grain and mineral trade, and very large manufactures of iron and brass work, furniture, carriages, cottons, woollens, &c. The first settlement at I. was made in 1819, and the town became the State capital in 1824. Pop. (1850) 8091, (1860) 18,000, (1870) 48,244. A belt railway to surround the city was in course of construction in 1875.

In'dian Ar'chitecture has been best treated in the elaborate publications of Mr. Fergusson, especially *History of I. A.* (Lond. 1876). The subject may be divided into two branches: (1) the indigenous style, and (2) the style introduced by the Mohammedan invaders. The first refers back to the earliest rise of

Buddhism, in the centuries immediately preceding the Christian era. The oldest buildings that remain take the form of rock-cut caverns, which were used either as temples proper, containing images of Buddha, or as monasteries for the habitation of the celibate Buddhist priests. The most primitive of the caves are situated in Behar and Orissa, but all the most ornamented are to be found in Western India. The form of architecture foreshadowed by these rock-temples has been traced in Burmah and Java, and indeed wherever the Buddhist faith is still prevalent. In India Proper a change, or rather a development, of architectural style was caused by the religious revival which restored Brahminism as the orthodox belief. In the temples of the Jains (q. v.), Buddhist features were to a considerable extent retained; but among the Hindus proper a new style of architecture arose, which reached its greatest splendour in the pagodas of the S. But however much a pagoda may differ in outward appearance from a cavern, yet modifications were only gradually effected, and the main plan of the two remains unchanged. The Mohammedan conquerors brought with them a style of architecture, common to the whole people of Islam, which is generally known as Moorish or Saracenic. Both the ground plan, and the general rules of building, are the same for a mosque at Delhi, Constantinople, or Cordova. The monuments of the early Afghan dynasties are of a comparatively rude type. But the wealth and taste of the united Moghul Empire were bestowed on the patronage of architecture above all the other arts. In grace of design, purity of ornamentation, and beauty of material, the tombs, mosques, and pillars of Agra and Delhi have never been surpassed, and it is suspected that the assistance both of Hindu and European artificers was invoked for their erection. Hitherto the British Government has done little for the advance of I. A. The native grandees and princes build themselves palaces according to a style of bastard classicism, for which they find but too much encouragement in some of the monuments which we have raised. But within the past few years, schools of art in the Presidency towns have given encouragement to native taste, and the designs for public buildings have been thrown open to local competition. See Fergusson's *History of Indian Architecture* (Lond. 1875).

Indian Clove Bark. See CLOVE BARK.

Indian-Corn, or **Maize,** was entirely unknown as an article of food in Great Britain and Ireland till the failure of the potato crop in 1846, when, for the first time, public attention in this country was directed to the very important position this grain held as the food corn of the population of a large part of Europe as well as America. In 1847 a large quantity was imported, of which a great part was destined for Ireland, partly on account of private enterprise and partly by contract with the Irish Relief Commissioners, in order to meet the general destitution caused by the want of potatoes, which had been the staff of life throughout the country. The use of the 'yellow meal,' as it was called, caused a great outcry in the workhouses and other places where the relief was administered, but the prejudice soon passed away, and I.-C. has since been an article of considerable consumption for food in Ireland. The imports, which had been practically *nil* up to 1847, are now very important, having been in 1875 1,021,924 tons (value £8,119,957), of which—

602,930 tons were from the	United States.
193,502 ,, ,, ,,	Turkey.
59,435 ,, ,, ,,	Austrian Territories.
43,689 ,, ,, ,,	British North America.

Of corn-meal in 1875 the quantity imported was 7376 cwts. The use of this grain in Great Britain is not to any extent for human food in its raw state; it is chiefly for feeding purposes, and it is found that no grain is more useful for fattening cattle and pigs, taking weight for weight, and that in judicious mixture it is most valuable for feeding horses which have hard and rapid work. A large quantity is, however, consumed in Great Britain in the form of 'prepared corn,' or, as it is usually styled, 'Corn Flour;' this being the starch of the I.-C. adapted for the food of infants and invalids, and for puddings. This article was patented by Messrs. T. Kingsford & Sons of Oswego, U.S., in 1848, and was immediately introduced into Great Britain, where it attracted considerable attention. The original makers still continue to occupy the first place in the trade, which is now of very considerable dimensions, their output being upwards of 26 tons per diem; but the manufacturers of 'Corn Flour' in Scotland, chiefly Messrs. Brown & Polson of Paisley, do a very large business, and the article is in everyday use among all classes of the community. The calyx of the seed-producing flower of the I.-C. is a tough lance-shaped leaf of 6 or 8 inches in length, and is well known as the covering of the oranges which are imported in enormous quantities from St. Michael's and the other Azore islands. It is also used in many countries as the stuffing of beds, for which it is particularly suitable. See MAIZE.

Indian Fig. See PRICKLY PEAR.

Indian-Ink, properly **China-Ink,** a preparation much used by artists and draughtsmen, is composed of very fine lamp-black, made into a paste with a proportion of gelatinous matter, perfumed with musk or other odorous matter, and cast into cakes or sticks. Much factitious I.-I. is manufactured in Europe, but it is immensely inferior in quality to that made in China or Japan.

Indian Matting is made from *Cyperus corymbosus*, a sedge-like plant common about Calcutta, &c. The flowering stems when green are split into three or four pieces, which, in drying, contract so that the edges overlap each other; in this state they are woven into mats for floors of rooms, &c.

Indian Ocean (the *Erythra* of Herodotus) separates Africa on the W. from Malaysia, Australia, and Tasmania on the E., and extends from India and Beloochistan on the N. as far southward as the Antarctic Circle. From the Cape of Good Hope to South Cape in Tasmania its breadth is upwards of 6000 miles, and its area has been variously computed at from 17 to 25 millions of sq. miles. The I. O. includes several minor seas, as the Red Sea, Arabian Sea, Persian Gulf, and Bay of Bengal. Ceylon and Madagascar are its chief islands, the others—if we exclude the Indian Archipelago as bounding rather than belonging to the I. O.—being neither large nor numerous; and the most important rivers that flow into it are the Zambezi of Africa, the Euphrates, Indus, Ganges, and Irawadi of Asia, and the Murray of Australia. The temperature of the I. O. is exceptionally high; periodical currents are numerous, the constant, few; chief of the latter being the Mozambique Current, the Agulhas or Cape Current, the Equatorial, and the Counter-Current. (See CURRENTS, OCEAN.) Pearl-fishing is the leading industry connected with its waters. The Monsoons (q. v.) of the I. O., by rendering navigation peculiarly easy, early led the Phœnicians to establish trading settlements both on the Red Sea and Persian Gulf; and Humboldt's identification of Ophir, whence Solomon procured apes (*kophim*), peacocks (*thukkiim*), and sandalwood (*algummin*), with India—these names being all of Sanskrit origin—shows at how remote a period a regular communication between East and West by way of the Arabian Sea must have existed.

Indian Red, or **Persian Earth,** is a marone-coloured ferruginous earth used as a painter's pigment, and obtained from the hills near Chingleput as well as from Persia. An imitation is manufactured in this country by mixing oxide of iron with colcothar.

Indian Territory, a country set apart by the United States Government as a permanent home for such Indian tribes as can be induced to settle. Area, 68,991 sq. miles; pop. (1870) 68,152, of whom 59,367 were Indians (24,967 on reservations and at agencies, more or less civilised, and 34,400 nomads), 2407 whites, and 6378 coloured persons of African descent. Among the tribes settled here are the Cherokees, Choctaws, Creeks, Chickasaws, Seminoles, &c. The country is bounded N. by Kansas, E. by Missouri and Arkansas, S. and W. by Texas; it slopes gently from the Rocky Mountains in the extreme N.W. to the basin of the Mississippi, and is watered by the Arkansas River, by its tributaries the N. and S. Canadians, Cimarron, Neosho, &c., and by the Red River, that forms the southern boundary. The Cross Timbers, a belt of forest, from 5 to 30 miles broad, separate the eastern region of rich upland prairies, luxuriant woodlands, and fertile river-bottoms from the sterile tableland of the N.W., where the vegetation is limited to the thorny cacti, yuccas, and grey sagebush. In the S.E. are the low ranges of the Washita, Poteau, and San Bois mountains. The climate is warm, and droughts are frequent, but farming is carried on to a considerable extent by the Indians. In 1872, 204,674 acres of improved land yielded 6,739,355 bushels of wheat, &c., and the total value of real and personal property, on which no taxes are levied, amounted to 16,987,818 dollars. Among the towns, none of which are of any size, are Tahlequah, capital of the Cherokee country; Caddo, capital of the Choctaws; and Vinita, the junction of the Missouri, Kansas, and Texas and S.W. branch of the Pacific Railways. One newspaper is printed in the Cherokee language, another in Creek or Choctaw. The government is in the hands of the various tribes. They are not represented in Congress, but as occasion requires, send their chiefs to Washington to state their complaints. The territory, originally set aside in 1832, had an area of 195,274 sq. miles, but was diminished by the withdrawal of Kansas and part of Nebraska. During the Civil War several of the tribes took the side of the S., and were temporarily held to have forfeited their lands.

Indians, American. The aboriginal inhabitants of N. and S. America received the name Indians from the belief of the discoverers and early conquerors of the New World that America was a part of Asia. Ethnologically the various tribes seem to have sprung from a common stock, but their relation to the races of the Old World has not yet been clearly determined. No links have been discovered connecting their speech with Old World tongues, and even the common features of their own numerous dialects cannot be precisely defined. Physically they are lithe and slender, of a reddish copper colour, with long, black hair, prominent cheek-bones, dark eyes, and low foreheads. They display greater uniformity in their mental and bodily characteristics than can be found in any other races spread over an equal extent of territory. They are remarkable for apathetic endurance of pain, sullen haughtiness, courage, dissimulation, and cruelty, and excel all other savage races in reflectiveness, perseverance, and passionate intensity of feeling. Their languages are distinguished by the endless wealth of conjugational forms, by the tendency to express a cluster of naturally connected ideas by a single word, their inflexional variety enabling them to indicate very subtle shades of meaning. Efforts have been made to trace an affinity between their speech and the Mongolian, Polynesian, Tungusian, &c., but most scholars of any weight regard such attempts as futile and fantastic. About four-fifths of N. America was formerly held by tribes speaking, at most, not more than four distinct tongues, viz., the *Eskimo*, spoken along the shores of the Arctic Ocean; the *Athabascan*, spoken in the lands S. of the Eskimo region, between Hudson's Bay and the Rocky Mountains; the *Algonkin*, the most rich and widespread of all N. American Indian tongues, spoken from about 50° N. latitude, as far S. as the confluence of the Ohio and Mississippi, W. to the Rocky Mountains, and E. to the Atlantic, the Algonkin tribes especially clustering along the Mississippi Valley, the *Dakota* or *Sioux*, spoken in the lands of the Dakotas, between the Mississippi and the Rocky Mountains, and from the Saskatchewan Sea to the Arkansas River. These linguistic divisions correspond to the four great families of North American tribes. For Eskimo see the separate article. Among the numerous tribes of the Athabascans were the Chepewyans, Dog-Ribs, Sussees, Apaches, Slave, and Beaver Indians; to the Algonkin family belonged the Satiskaas or Blackfeet, and the Chippeways; while the Dakota collection of tribes included the Santees, Brulees, Tetons, Urkpapas, Ogalallahs, Yanktons, &c. Within the vast territory of the Algonkins lay the *Iroquois*, who spoke a different language from the Algonkins and includes the Hurons, Eries, Tuscaroras, &c. Other great families, though inferior to the four principal tribal clusters, were the *Chahta-Muskoki*, lying along the lower Mississippi, and comprising the Seminoles, Muskokis or Creeks, Choctaws, Chicasas, Alabamas, &c., and the *Cherokees* who dwelt along the Tennessee River and held parts of what are now Georgia and Alabama. The Pawnees and Comanches, tribes lying along the Mexican frontier, differ in speech from the Dakotas, though their dialects have erroneously been included under the Dakotas. These great families held N. America from the Arctic Ocean S. to Mexico, from Mexico S. to Chili; and at the time of the Spanish conquest the region between the Pacific and the Gulf of Mexico and the lands on the western seaboard of S. America were held by peoples originally of the same stock as the nomads of N. America, but possessing a very high civilisation. For these, see MEXICO and PERU. See also INDIAN TERRITORY, and Schoolcraft's *Historical and Statistical Information Respecting the Indian Tribes* (6 vols. 4to, 1851–56); Ludewig's *Literature of American Aboriginal Languages*, Field's *Essay towards an Indian Bibliography* (New York, 1873); for the Algonkin, the works of Duponceau, Pickering, and Gallantin; for the languages of S. America, Von Martius' *Beiträge zur Ethnographieund Sprachenkunde Amerikas* (Leips. 1867); and A. d'Orbigny's *L'Homme Américain* (Par. 1839); and as an aid to the comparison of N. and S. American languages, J. J. von Tschudi's *Quichua Sprache* (Vien. 1853).

Indian Yellow, or **Puree**, is a yellow pigment, imported from India and China, and much used by artists, both as an oil and a water-colour. The substance is apparently of animal origin, but its source is not yet accurately known. Chemically it consists of an acid substance, pureic or euxanthic acid, combined with magnesia.

India-Rubber. See CAOUTCHOUC.

Indica'tor. See HONEY GUIDE.

Indic'tion, a word primarily signifying a tax, but afterwards a chronological period or cycle of fifteen years. It first began to be used by Church writers in the time of Athanasius (4th c.). The practice was formally adopted by the popes in the 12th c., and the number of indictions was reckoned from the birth of Christ, which, however, does not correspond with the first, but the fourth year of an I. The rule, therefore, for finding the I. of any year in the Christian era is to add 3, and divide by 15. The quotient will give the I., and the remainder the year of the I.

Indict'ment is the name in England and in Scotland of the written accusation of crime against any one who is to be tried before a jury. In England, in common cases of felony and misdemeanour, the clerk of indictments prepares the document from the depositions returned to the court by the committing magistrate. Sometimes the I. is framed by a barrister or crown draftsman, in which case the clerk only passes it, receiving his fee as if he had drawn it. The names of the witnesses for the prosecution are written on the back of the I. In Scotland, the I. runs in the name of the Lord Advocate, and is addressed to the prisoner.

Indiges'tion, or **Dyspep'sia**, is the term used to indicate that state of the stomach in which it is incapable of performing its natural and healthy functions. It is, therefore, an abnormal functional state, which is sometimes due to sympathetic relations with other organs which are themselves in a morbid condition, the irritation being due to reflex action; thus vomiting is frequently associated with disease of the lungs, brain, liver, and uterus, and is an early result of shock from injuries or surgical operations. The term is more frequently applied to disease processes in the stomach and alimentary canal, such as a scanty secretion of the gastric juice, resulting in long retention of food by the stomach owing to slowness of digestion. This gives rise to a sensation of weight and uneasiness at the pit of the stomach, and sometimes to severe pain both in the stomach and alimentary canal, owing to the irritation of the unaltered ingesta, which frequently appear as such in the stools. Food in this condition is peculiarly liable to decomposition with the evolution of fetid gases, causing flatulence and eructations, prominent symptoms in all cases of I. Loss of appetite is a common symptom of I., but the appetite is occasionally excessive, and even ravenous. Nausea and vomiting frequently occur immediately after a meal, or after the lapse of two or three hours, and the food may be ejected in the same condition as when taken, or in an acid condition, or bitter from the admixture of bile.

Treatment.—When I. depends upon congestion, catarrh, or ulceration, the remedies are chiefly dietetic; as a sparing and easily digested diet, and total abstinence from all alcoholic drinks. In severe cases counter-irritants may be applied over the stomach, and the patient may have small quantities of iced water to sip, or small pieces of ice to suck. When there is ulceration, the diet should consist of milk with bread, semolina, sago, tapioca, biscuit-powder, Indian-meal, or iced-milk combined with one-quarter to one-third of lime-water. Constipation should be counteracted by enemata, and astringent medicines should be given, such as oil of turpentine, acetate of lead and opium, alum and tannic acid. The chief rules of treatment are to use albumenoid food in as liquid a state as possible; to partake of it in small quantities at a time and at regular intervals; to aid the digestive process by the administration of pepsine or by alkalies, that the food may pass into the intestines and be digested there rather than by the stomach. When mineral acids are prescribed, it should be borne in mind that sulphuric acid is astringent, that hydrochloric acid promotes digestion, and nitric acid secretion. When loss of appetite is atonic, the appropriate medicines are bitters, such as quinine, gentian, calumba, chiretta, &c., combined with mineral acids. See *The Causes, Symptoms, and Treatment of Imperfect Digestion* by Dr. Leared.

Indigir'ka, a river in the E. of Siberia, government of Vakutsk, rises in the Aldansk Mountains, has a northerly direction, and enters the Arctic Ocean after a course of 800 miles.

In'digo, the name of various plants, the most important of which belong to the genus *Indigofera*. This genus numbers some 250 to 300 species, spread through all tropical regions, and also abundant at the Cape. The one that yields the chief supply of the beautiful and important blue dye is *I. tinctoria*, now universally grown in India, but whether it is a native of the country is doubtful. It is a shrub 4 to 5 feet high, with twiggy, woody, thin, silvery branches, leaves 1 to 2 inches long, leaflets opposite membranous turning blackish when dried, flowers reddish-yellow in lax racemes 2 to 4 inches long, pods nearly straight, about an inch long. *I. Anil*, a native of the W. Indies and America, is also commonly cultivated in India; it differs chiefly from the above in its short congested racemes and pod turned back like a sickle. An inferior kind of I. is prepared from the leaves of *Wrightia tinctoria* of the dog-bane family, and the leaves of a couple of species of *Marsdeniæ* (natural order *Asclepiadaceæ*) yield a blue dye resembling I. *Tephrosia apollinea*, a native of Egypt and Nubia, also furnishes a kind of I., also *Polygonum Chinense*, a native of China, and, before the E. Indies were opened to trade, the blue colouring matter of *Isatis tinctoria* was largely used throughout Europe. See WOAD.

Indigo.

The valuable blue-dyeing substance derives its name from India, the country of its original production, whence it was known to the ancient Romans as *Indicum*. It did not come prominently into use in Europe till the 16th c., and its employment met the most strenuous opposition in all Western countries, laws enacted against its use having continued unrepealed till comparatively recent times.

I. does not exist ready found in the plants from which it is obtained, but is the result of a fermentation to which they are subjected. Two methods of dealing with the plants are pursued in Bengal, in one of which fresh leaves and green stems are employed, and in the other dried leaves are treated. In dealing with fresh leaves, they are thrown in bundles into large stone tanks and covered with water, where, for from nine to fourteen hours, according to the temperature, they are left undergoing a brisk fermentation. When by its colour the supernatant liquor is deemed to have arrived at the proper point, it is carefully drawn off to a cistern at a lower level, into which a dozen of naked men enter, armed with long bamboo rods, and splash about the liquid for two or three hours. Steam machinery is now coming into use for this process of 'beating.' Gradually the liquor passes from its first yellow into a green colour which indicates the formation of I. It is allowed to precipitate, and the supernatant liquid is drained away by degrees. The precipitate is conveyed to a boiler and boiled for two or three hours, after which it is run into a decipping vat or cistern having a false bottom, in which it is allowed to drain. The solid mass is thereafter squeezed in a screw press, cut by wire into cubical pieces of about 3 inches, and placed on wicker shelves to dry. In manufacturing I. with dry leaves, the leaves after drying in the sun are stored for three or four weeks, during which they change from a bright green colour to a pale bluish-grey. In this state the leaves have only to be macerated a short time in the water to give up their tinctorial principle, and the subsequent processes of agitation, boiling, &c., are the same as with fresh leaves.

The theory of the formation of I. now generally adopted is that evolved by Schunk from his investigations of the conditions under which it is obtained from the woad plant. From that plant he isolated a peculiar principle to which he gave the name Indican. Indican is a kind of glucoside, very soluble in water and alcohol, which, under the influence of acids, of weak alkalies, and even spontaneously during the evaporation of its solutions, separates into a sugar indiglucine and indigotine, the essential principle of I. It is therefore supposed that indican is present in all the plants from which I. may be prepared, and that in the manufacturing process the indican is liberated by fermentation and dissolved in the first vat, and that the fermentation and the oxidation in the second vat determines the separation of the indigotine, along with which other products, brown, yellow, and red, are precipitated to form commercial I.

The I. of commerce varies much in quality, appearance, and tinctorial value, as might be expected from the diverse plants, countries, and methods of its preparation. It has been separated into three classes according to the continent of production as follows:—(1) Asiatic I., embracing Bengal, Oude, Coromandel, Madras, and Java varieties; (2) African I., including Egyptian, Reunion, and Senegal; and (3) American I., which comprehends Guatemala, Caracas, Mexican, Brazilian, Carolina, and Antilles. Of these varieties, the most highly valued are Bengal, Java, and Guatemala.

I. is a most valuable and extensively-employed dye-stuff in calico-printing and woollen-cloth dyeing. As indigotine the tinctorial principle of I. is perfectly insoluble in any of the ordinary solvents—water, alcohol, oils, acids, or alkalies; it cannot be fixed upon any fibre till it is brought into a soluble condition. When from any source it takes into its composition two additional atoms of hydrogen it changes to a white colour, and then as white or hydrogenised I. it is readily soluble in alkaline compounds, in which state it is applied to textile substances. By subsequent exposure it quickly again oxidises to its blue colour, and so becomes a very fast permanent dye. There are numerous methods by which blue I. is reduced and prepared for dyeing and painting.

The quantity of I. imported into Great Britain during the year 1875 was 59,608 cwt., of which the greater part came from British E. Indian possessions. The export from British India during 1874 (which was somewhat above the average) was 115,980 cwt., valued at 2½ millions sterling. In Bengal the manufacture is almost entirely in the hands of Europeans, who take land on lease from the landlords, and obtain the plant from the cultivators under an organised system of advances. Since 1860 this industry has rapidly decayed in the Gangetic delta; but throughout N. Behar, and especially in Tirhut, the area under I. is on the increase. The seed requires to be renewed annually from the N.W. Provinces. The crop is very uncertain, but a favourable year will return cent. per cent. upon capital.

In'dium, this metallic element was discovered by Reich and Richter in 1863 during the spectroscopic examination of the zinc-blende of Freiberg. It is a very scarce element. The Freiberg blende, containing 25 to 30 parts in 100,000, occurs in only a few localities, and is always associated with zinc, from the ores of which it is separated by a complex and difficult process. In the metallic state I. is lustrous, white, soft—marking paper like lead—and malleable. Its specific gravity is 7·42. It fuses at 176°, and when heated sufficiently high it volatilises and burns with a blue flame. Its combining weight is 113·4; in which case the formula of the chloride of I. is $InCl_3$.

Indivis'ible, or **Pro Indivi'so Prop'erty**. *Pro indiviso* is the legal term used to denote the right to a property which belongs to several persons in common. Each *pro indiviso* proprietor has the same equal but undivided right, and is entitled to the joint use of the subject and an equal share in its produce. Mutual consent is necessary in all acts of management or disposal. Each proprietor may, however, sell his *pro indiviso* share, the purchaser coming into his place. Any of the parties may enforce by legal action, when the subject in its nature is indivisible, a sale and division of the price, and where division is possible, a division of the property. A common way in which the right arises is when a person possessed of an estate dies intestate leaving only female issue, his daughters succeed as equal *pro indiviso* proprietors to the estate.

Indo-Germanic Languages. See ARYAN LANGUAGES.

Indore', the capital of the state of the same name in Central India, separated into the old and new town by the Kutka River, 402 miles S.W. from Agra and 377 N.E. from Bombay. Pop. 15,000. There are no buildings of importance. The British cantonments are at Mhow, 13 miles S.E. In 1857 I. was the scene of a massacre of Europeans; the prince, though suspected at the time, is now known to have stood loyal.

The *state* of I., which is crossed by the Vindhya range and the Nerbudda River, has an area of about 8000 sq. miles; pop. 635,000; revenue, £500,000. The soil is fertile, and produces the well-known Malwa opium, cotton, wheat, sugar-cane, and tobacco. By the close of 1875, three-quarters of a million had been spent on the Holkar State Railway, which connects with the Great India Peninsula system, and 57 miles were open. The effective military force is 24 guns and 28,000 horse and foot. The ruler is Holkar, the third of the great Mahratta families. The first of the name was a shepherd's son, and a distinguished military chief; his descendants have suffered many vicissitudes in alliance or rivalry with Scindia and in wars with the British. The territory has generally been well administered, and the present Maharajah has a high reputation as his own finance minister. The I. Agency is the seat of a British Resident, who controls several other minor chiefs. I. was visited by the Prince of Wales in the spring of 1876. See also HOLKAR and MAHRATTAS.

Indorsed', Endorsed', Addorsed', a heraldic term applied to two animals or two Inanimate Charges (q. v.) placed *back to back*.

Indorse'ment, the writing on the back of a negotiable instrument, transferring the property therein specified; usually, however, the signature of the holder of a bill of exchange or promissory note, called, if alone, a *blank* I., but if accompanied by the name of the transferee, a *special* I. or I. *in full*. The indorser may avoid liability to suretyship by employing such restricting words as *without recourse*. In English law, the term I. is applied to anything whatever written on the back of a writ or deed. See BILL and BILL OF EXCHANGE.

In'dra (akin to Sansk. *indu*, 'drop, sap'), the *Jupiter pluvius* of the Hindu pantheon, was, according to the Vedas, the son of the common Aryan divinity Dyu (Zeus, Jupiter, Tyr), whom, indeed, he almost wholly superseded, whilst inheriting many of his attributes. It is easy to understand how in a dry climate like that of India the rain-giving qualities of the heavens should predominate over the conception of brightness which we find in the root of *divus*, and which in the moister settlements of the Aryans of the western immigration might well retain its ancient significance. I., then, is the fertilising and all-seeing sky, who pours the milk of the cloud-cows upon the earth, and in the *Rámáyana* is represented, like Argus, as having a thousand eyes and four arms, in which we see, perhaps, the four quarters of the heavens. He vanquishes with his thunderbolt the demon Vritra (*vri*, 'to hide or wrap'), the cloud which obscures the sun, the robber who confines the fruitful cows in his dark cavern-house. From this achievement I. came to be regarded as the god of victory generally, and as the special champion of the Aryans in their contest with the aborigines of the peninsula. Hence the popularity of his worship. In Vedic times I., like Zeus, was supreme, or only shared his sovereignty with Agni (fire), Surya (the sun), Ushas (the dawn), and the Maruts (winds). In the Puranas, however, he ranks only as lord of the inferior divinities, and is the object of poetic rather than of national veneration. The nature-character of the myth had faded, and I. in the later legends becomes merely a vehicle for sensuous descriptions of the charms of his paradise (*Swarga*), his nymphs (*Apsarases*), his singers (*Gandharvas*), &c. Sculptures of I. occur in the caves of Ellora and Elephanta, and representations of him are given in Moor's *Hindu Pantheon*, in which he appears seated on a three-trunked elephant, a tree growing from his head, and peacocks perching on its branches.

Indre, a central department of France, formed out of the old provinces of Berri, Orléannais, and Marche. It is bounded N. by Loir-et-Cher, E. by Cher, S. by Creuse and Haute Vienne, and W. by Vienne and Indre-et-Loire. Area, 2624 sq. miles; pop. (1872) 277,693. I. is watered by the Indre, Creuse, and Claise, is everywhere flat, and in the western district of Brenne abounds in malarious pools of stagnant water. Sheep, geese, and turkeys are largely reared, and an inferior wine produced. Iron-mining is a growing industry, and there are manufactures of paper, cotton, &c. Châteauroux (see CHÂTEAU) is the capital, and other towns are Issoudun (q. v.), Argenton, and Levroux. The Paris-à-Agen Railway traverses I.

The *river* I. rises in Cher, flows N.W. through the department to which it gives name, enters Indre-et-Loire, and joins the Loire at a point between Langeais and La Chapelle after a course of 142 miles.

Indre-et-Loire, a central department of France, formed out of the old province of Touraine. It is bounded N. by Sarthe, E. by Loir-et-Cher and Indre, S. by Vienne, and W. by Maine-et-Loire. Area, 2360 sq. miles; pop. (1872) 317,027. The chief rivers are the Loire and its navigable affluents, the Cher, Indre, and Vienne. The district in the neighbourhood of the Loire is so fertile as to have won the title of the 'Garden of France,' but agriculture is in a backward state. The northern portion is mainly heath or forest. Hemp, truffles, and fruits are largely cultivated; and the vineyards yield on an average 17,000,000 gallons of wine annually. The cloth, silk, and leather manufactures date from a period previous to the revocation of the Edict of Nantes, while iron, gunpowder, and sugar are important modern industries. I. is traversed by two main railroads and one branch line, and is connected with the Canal-du-Berry by the Cher-à-la-Loire Canal. The chief towns are Tours (the capital), Amboise, Chinon, and Loches.

Indu'ciæ Lega'les, a term of Scotch law denoting the days between the citation of a defender and the day on which he is bound to appear in the action or process. 'So many days to answer to,' is the corresponding English phrase.

Induc'tion has deen defined as the process of discovering and proving general propositions. It passes from the known to the unknown, and from the particular to the general. It is therefore distinguished from deduction, which never reaches conclusions more general than the premises from which it starts. The tacit assumption on which all I. proceeds is, of course, the invariable sequence of cause and effect. Practically, therefore, I. does not consist in saying in any particular case, 'because B has followed A in the past, B will follow A in the future.' It rather consists in ascertaining A and B. This is easy enough in many familiar cases, where the true sequence forces itself constantly into notice: *e.g.*, light and heat as effects of the sun's rays. But it is often difficult, because A is constantly combining with C and D; or, without combination of causes, the effects of C and D coincide with and obscure B; or B may be produced by E, something totally different from A; or B is constantly growing or dwindling, and cannot be fixed, even after it has disappeared. The problem of I., therefore, is to eliminate from the effect whatever may be due to antecedents other than A. If other antecedents are known to be present, and their effects are also generally known, this may or may not be easily done, according to the subject-matter of I. In chemical, biological, and sociological inquiries this might not be easy, as the behaviour of the superfluous antecedents under the particular conditions might be a question of doubt. But if it be not known what are the effects generally of all the antecedents except A, or if it be not known whether antecedents other than A are present or not, or even if they be apparently absent, the real difficulties of I. then arise. The ordinary methods of reasoning are to infer a true sequence between A and B (1) because they are found together in a number of instances; (2) because B is present in one case and absent in another, between which the only difference is the presence of A in the first case, and the absence of A in the second; (3) because the same observation as in No. 2 has been made in a number of positive instances and a number of negative instances; (4) because there is nothing but A left to account for B; (5) because whenever A increases or diminishes, B does the same. If direct experiment were possible in all cases, if the reasoner had complete control over the antecedents, and could vary them at pleasure, the process would be simpler, and would be exposed only to the very serious risks of error in adjustment and in the observation of results. But in most cases experiment is impossible, and in many cases where fresh antecedents may be introduced, or some existing ones removed at will, there is a substantial *status quo* which makes the result very uncertain indeed. This is eminently the case with the human body. In other cases, *e.g.*, Kepler's law, and the law of refraction of light, the discovery of the true sequence is made only after an immense series of observations, and by the intervention of numerical and geometrical relations. Similarly, by the comparison of statistics extending over centuries, statists endeavour to trace the effect of a particular institution or particular physical cause. It must not be supposed that I. leads in every case to a certain result. It implies proof to a certain extent, and is therefore distinguished from unverified hypothesis or mere analogy. But it frequently affords only empirical laws, which, not themselves ultimate, probably depend on the collocation of original causes, or the derivative successions and co-existences among their separate effects. The success of I. really depends on the accuracy and range of several operations subsidiary to I., such as observation and description, abstraction, naming, and classification by natural groups or by series. This is illustrated in ethnology, where the definition of race is not yet settled. Formal logicians have endeavoured, by the use of symbols, to construct test-inductions of ideal validity. The utility of this is doubtful.

Induction of a clergyman in England, is the ceremony denoting the giving him possession of a benefice. The inductor places the hand of the clergyman on the church-door, then, opening the door, puts him into the church. A bell is then tolled, which is supposed to give the parishioners notice to whom the tithes and dues are to be paid. I. in Scotland is performed by the presbytery.

Induction. See ELECTRICITY and MAGNETISM.

Indul'gence (legal Lat. *indulgentia*, 'a remission of punishment or of taxes'), in ecclesiastical writers meant (1) remission of sins, such, for example, as was held to be effected in or by baptism. But (2) it meant 'such a lightening of ecclesiastical penalties, in consideration of the state of the offender, as St. Paul practised (2 Cor. ii. 6–11). Up to the end of the 3d c. no canons for regulating Penance (q. v.), had been passed. The time required for the ordinary course of penance, in which the penitents had to pass through four stages—mourners, hearers, kneelers, co-standers—occupied a considerable number of years. The Council of Ancyra (314), however, gave the bishops power to shorten or to lengthen the period of an offender's penance; and the Council of Nice (325) gave them power to deal more gently with penitents who showed true repentance. Thus matters stood till the end of the 7th c., when the first change was effected by the Penitential of Theodore of Canterbury (668), which introduced the practice of redeeming penance at a stated and graduated rate of fines. The next step was the granting of exemption from all penance to those going on a pilgrimage or joining a crusade. One step more led to the recognised office of pardoner, the scandalous abuses of which first roused the wrath of Luther. The following is the form of the diplomas sold by Tetzel: 'May our Lord Jesus Christ have pity upon thee, A. B., and absolve thee by the merits of his most holy passion. And I, in virtue of the apostolic commission which has been committed to me, absolve thee from all ecclesiastical censures, judgments, and penalties, which thou mayest have deserved; further, from all the excesses, sins, and crimes which thou mayest have committed, however great or enormous they may be, and extending to all cases whatever, even were they reserved to our most holy father the Pope and to the Apostolic See. I wipe out all the stains of inability, and all the marks of infamy, which thou mayest in that respect have drawn upon thee. I remit for thee the pains thou mightest have had to endure in purgatory. . . . So that at the moment of thy death, the gate by which souls pass into the place of pains and torments will be shut upon thee, while, on the contrary, that which leads to the paradise of joy will be open to thee.' The doctrine of I., as now held by the Church of Rome, rests on the following grounds:—(1) That satisfaction has to be made to God for the remission of the temporal penalties for sin which remain to be paid in this world or in purgatory, over and above the eternal punishment which may be remitted on confession and contrition. (2) That the Church has always considered herself possessed of the authority to mitigate the penance which she enjoins. (3) That the sufferings of the saints in union with, and by virtue of, Christ's merits are available towards this mitigation. (4) That such mitigations, when prudently and justly granted, are conducive to the spiritual welfare of Christians.

In'dus (*Sindhu*, 'water'), a river of India, the first in length, and that with which the European world was first acquainted. It rises in Thibet, not far from the sources of the Sutlej and the Brahmaputra, under the Kailas Mountain, at a height of about 18,000 feet. It first flows N.W. through Cashmere, and then turns S. to penetrate the gorge between the Himalaya and the Hindu Koosh. It enters the plain just above Attock, where it is joined by the Cabul River from the W., at the spot where it was crossed by Alexander the Great. Here also it first becomes navigable, and thence flows nearly due S. through the Punjaub and Scinde into the Indian Ocean, which it enters near Kurachi by several mouths. Its navigable portion is 942 miles long; its total length about 1800 miles; its drainage basin about 372,700 sq. miles. About 450 miles below Attock, the I. receives on its left bank the Punjnud, which conveys the five streams that constitute the Punjaub. From the sea up to this point it is navigated by the steamers of the Indian Flotilla, in connection with the half-completed railway. The plain through which it runs would be a sandy desert if it were not watered by a network of canals. The I. basin has, in fact, been from time immemorial the home of artificial irrigation. The chief town on its banks is Hyderabad, situated just below the bifurcation of the Delta; Kurachi is a little W. of its most western mouth. Its channels are very changeable, and its diluviating action most destructive; its silt, also, is less fertilising than that of most great rivers which annually rise in flood. As is the case with the Ganges, neither its volume nor normal width increase as it approaches the sea. At present, the largest and most useful mouth is the Hajamro. Its value for trade is less than might be anticipated. The registration at Sakhar shows about 3000 tons, worth £47,000, going up stream; and 18,000 tons, worth £448,000, down stream. Apart from native craft, steamers make about fifty passages each way in the year; about £6000 is annually expended on river conservancy, and nearly as much is received in tolls. The I. Valley State Railway, which will shortly be opened from Hyderabad to Mûltan, will bring Kurachi into direct connection with the rest of India. The I. nowhere now forms the political boundary of British territory.

Indu'sial Limestone, a fresh-water limestone found in Auvergne, so named from the great numbers of indusiæ or cases of the larvæ of *Phryganea* which abound in it.

Indu'sium, a thin membrane often covering the clusters of capsules or sporangia of ferns.

Indus'trial Access'ion, a term of Scoth law, borrowed from the Roman, denoting the addition made to the value of a subject by human art or labour.

Indus'trial Schools, as recognised by the law of Great Britain, are schools specially devoted to the education of 'vagrant, destitute, and disorderly' children, and to which juvenile offenders may be sent by a magistrate. These schools are synonymous in character and purpose with the so-called Ragged Schools (q. v.); the former, however, are certified by Government, while the latter are strictly voluntary. The certified I. S., indeed, hold an intermediate position between the Ragged Schools and the Reformatory Schools (q. v.), as institutions intended to prevent the spread of crime. The previous legislation in regard to such schools was consolidated by an Act of 1866, by which the magistrate was empowered to send to a certified industrial school (1) children under fourteen found begging; (2) children under twelve charged with offences; (3) refractory children under fourteen in charge of parent; and (4) refractory children under fourteen in pauper school or workhouse. This Act was extended to Ireland in 1868. In 1875 there were 86 I. S. in England, and 28 in Scotland, attended by 11,776 children (by 8230 in England, and 3546 in Scotland). Of the schools in England, 6251 were Protestant and 1979 Roman Catholic; of those in Scotland, 3104 were Protestant and 442 Roman Catholic. As many as eight I. S. were opened in 1875, and there can be little doubt of their future increase under the present Act, supplemented as it has been by the powers given to School Boards under the Education Act not only to use such schools, but to establish them at the expense of the rates. The receipts of I. S. in 1875 amounted to £268,525; the Treasury allowance was £136,698; subscriptions and legacies, £51,445; payment from rates—county, £14,193; borough, £14,193; profit from industrial department, £16,904; fees for voluntary inmates, £6868. The trades taught are tailoring, shoemaking, brush-making, firewood cutting, and box-making. Frequent attempts have been made to introduce the teaching of industrial arts into ordinary elementary schools. The chief obstacle is the desire of parents to see their children receive an intellectual in preference to a manual training. In elementary schools for girls industrial work has been successfully introduced to the extent of sewing, shaping, knitting, and netting. Training schools in special departments have also been fairly successful, as in the case of the Glasnevan Agricultural Training School and of the various Training Ships. See *Reports on Certified Industrial and Reformatory Schools* (19 vols. 1856–76).

Iner'tia (Lat.) is a general property of matter, in virtue of which all bodies tend to preserve their state of motion or rest. It expresses the fact that matter itself is *inert*, and changes its condition only when acted upon by external agencies.

Inescut'cheon, in heraldry, a small shield, in the fesse point. When there are more than one small shield, they are called escutcheons.

Infallibil'ity of the Church is divided into *passive* and *active*. By passive I. or Inerrancy, is meant that 'the Church must always have a tenure of truth sufficient for salvation,' and that any doctrine which can be said by its universal acceptance to be the deliberate ascertained voice of the Church, must be from God. In support of which doctrine are cited such promises as John xvi. 13; 1 John ii. 27, and the declaration that the spirit which dwells in the Church is a spirit of knowledge and understanding (Col. i. 9, ii. 3, iii. 10). This theory, which is held more or less by all Episcopal Churches, is very different from the doctrine of I. held by the Church of Rome: namely, that 'the Church is divinely appointed to be the infallible teacher of men in all things pertaining to faith and practice;' in other words, that she can never possibly teach anything erroneous. But there is a controversy in the Church of Rome itself—between the Gallican and the Ultramontane party—as to the organ of the Church in its I. According to the former, the bishops, as the official successors of the apostles, and in their collective capacity, are infallible as teachers; according to the latter, the Pope, who is the Vicar of Christ, and is not subject to a general council, is the organ through which the infallible teaching of the Church is given, his I. not being personal, however, so as to depend on his personal character, but official, so that he is the organ of the Holy Spirit when speaking *ex cathedra*. The theory of Papal I. was sanctioned in the Œcumenical Council of 1870, and is therefore now the faith of the Church.

Infamed', or **Defamed',** a term in heraldry used to denote that an animal has lost its tail, and is thus 'defamed' or disgraced.

In'famous. A person is legally I. who has been convicted of crime, or whose generally bad reputation can be proved by questions put to himself. Formerly in the United Kingdom infamy of a witness was valid ground on which to reject his testimony. It is now taken for what it may be worth.

Infant, in law. See AGE.

Infan'te (Lat. *infans*, 'an infant'), the title of the younger sons of the Kings of Spain and Portugal, the heir-apparent being styled in the former country Prince of the Asturias, or simply the Prince, and in the latter Prince of Beira, or (till 1825) of Brazil. The younger princesses of the royal house are similarly called *infantas*. I. is an ancient title, occurring in a document of the year 999, but was originally applied to all hidalgos. The *infantado*, or appanage of an I. or infanta, gave name to a district of four villages in the province of Guadalajara, which was erected into a dukedom in 1476.

Infan'ticide may be regarded as an archaic institution or as a modern crime. The systematic exposure of children which took place at Sparta, and still disgraces China, was dictated in the one case by political, in the other by economical, reasons. The advantages of weeding from a community its weaker or its superfluous members were clearly pointed out by Plato in his *Republic*. Not merely is a burden removed from the survivors, but the reproduction of feeble and diseased human beings is prevented. The disadvantage would consist in the starvation of the finer sympathies and educated conscience of society. It must, however, be kept in view, that in primitive times the conditions were often very different. Not only was there less realised wealth on which superfluous persons might exist, but there were fewer employments in which the weak or the deformed might gain a livelihood. There are various forms of I., extending to the children of concubines, of stranger fathers, and of mothers who die from sickness. The Beloochis use opium and drowning in milk: hence the proverb, 'The lady's daughter died drinking milk.' In general the practice is confined to female children, as being more dependent on others, especially in a warlike tribe. This is probably due also in some measure to the old practice of exogamy, which compelled the men of the tribe to seek a wife outside its ranks. Among some of the hill tribes of India female children are placed at the door of the cattle pen so as to be trampled to death by the buffaloes. According to the statement of an old member of a Toda tribe (who seem to be otherwise affectionate to their children) it was only on account of extreme poverty (each family having only one *putkuli* or mantle) that they smothered and buried all girls *after the first*. The I. of male children is very rare, and is generally based on religious considerations. Certain children of the Khond tribes, *e.g.*, are set apart by the priests for sacrifice. I., as a branch of human sacrifice, was of course extensively practised under the Phœnician and other extinct civilisations. But among certain African races children are selected as sacrifices for sacrilege, or where, as on the death of a chief, the killing of lower animals is not thought sufficient. I. is also caused by special superstitions, as in Bambarra, where if a male child of one of the king's wives is born on a Friday its throat is at once cut. In Mexico children of noble birth were regularly sacrificed to the god of rain. In Central America bastard children were occasionally killed in the temples, and their blood used in the making of a sort of sacred wafer; and another class of boys, named Mojas, were specially preserved for sacrifice to the sun.

In modern times I. is a well-known crime, following generally on illicit intercourse. The killing of lawful children is rare. The motive of shame also leads to the kindred crimes of criminal abortion and concealment of pregnancy. Compassion for these unhappy mothers led in 1809 to a statute which introduced to Scotland the last-named offence. Formerly, as in England, the charge was murder, and it was often difficult to prove complete birth. It was suggested in 1866 that the killing of a child during birth, or within seven days thereafter, should in England be made an offence punishable with penal servitude or imprisonment. This has not been done, and the common law is therefore forced to assume (in deference to public opinion) that every new-born child has been born dead, until the contrary appears from evidence in court. Such cases generally result in verdicts of culpable homicide. The crucial tests of life in a child seem to be the colour, volume, consistency, absolute weight, and buoyancy of the lungs; but a child may be born alive, and therefore murdered, before it has breathed. The hydrostatic test, or watching whether the lungs sink or swim in water, only goes to the fact of breathing. Respiration, however, may be simulated by artificial inflation, and may also occur *before* and not *after* birth. The common modes of I. are suffocation, drowning, and exposure. It must be recollected that the *natural* causes of death in new-born children are numerous.

Infants, Liabilities of. Under the age of seven an infant cannot be capitally punished, but at fourteen he may. Regarding the liabilities of an infant between seven and fourteen there is great uncertainty; for it depends on the capacity to distinguish between the good and evil tendency of actions. Sir M. Hale mentions the capital conviction of a girl of thirteen, who was burned for killing her mistress. A boy still younger, he tells us, was hanged for killing his companion, on the ground of his having hid himself, and that the hiding showed that he knew he had done wrong; the maxim of the law being—*malice is equivalent to age*. See AGE, and articles there referred to; also GUARDIAN.

Infant Life Protection Act, 1872. This important statute was passed for the better protection of infants intrusted to persons to be nursed or maintained for hire or reward; but it does not extend over the relatives or guardians of an infant, nor over persons receiving one under the Poor Law Acts. Houses are to be registered with the local authority, who is to make byelaws regulating the number of infants to be received in each registered house. In non-registered houses, only one infant is to be kept for hire, or two may be kept if twins. Notice of death must be given to the Crown within twenty-four hours after the event.

Infanticide, Law Regarding. See BIRTH, CONCEALMENT OF; PREGNANCY, CONCEALMENT OF.

In'fantry (Lat. *infans*, 'child,' or 'servant,' first applied to servants on foot, and then to foot-soldiers—*infanteria*), the foot-soldiers of an army, as distinguished from the cavalry and artillery. I. formed the chief strength of the Greek and Roman armies, and after falling into insignificance during the middle ages, when battles were mainly decided by heavy cavalry, began to rise in importance from the end of the 14th c., and now forms the chief body of an army.

Infec'tion denotes a specific virus generated in diseased persons, and capable of reproducing itself when implanted in the system of otherwise healthy persons; but in this acceptation it is more properly termed *infective matter*. I. also signifies the *communication* of such specific virus from a diseased to a healthy person. I. and Contagion (q. v.) are used as synonymous in a great majority of cases.

Infec'tious Diseas'es are those maladies which are capable of being communicated from one person to another, and the class comprehends nearly the entire miasmatic order of zymotic disease, such as smallpox, vaccinia, chicken-pox, measles, scarlet fever, rubeola, dengue, erysipelas, plague, enteric fever, typhus fever, yellow fever, hooping-cough, diphtheria, croup, cholera, syphilis, and gonorrhœa; and also certain diseases communicable from the lower animals to man; such as cowpox, hydrophobia, glanders, and farcy, and malignant pustule (q. v.). I. D. include also transmissible parasitic diseases—the entozoa, the epizoa, and the epiphytes, such as tapeworms, fluke-like parasites, round worms, lousiness, itch, ringworm, scald-head or favus, tinea decalvans, and fungus-foot of India (q. v.). Various attempts have been made by special enactments, such as quarantine regulations and Public Health Acts, to limit the ravages of I. D.; but as yet no such comprehensive measure has been adopted for the protection of healthy men as has been enforced for the protection of healthy cattle, and the more important clauses in the Public Health Acts are permissive in their character, and, consequently, generally ignored.

Infeft'ment, a term of Scotch law denoting the giving of symbolical possession of heritable (real) property; the legal evidence of which is an Instrument of Sasine (q. v.).

In'finite, in mathematics, is applied to a quantity which is greater or smaller than any assignable quantity, however great or however small that quantity may be. An infinitely small quantity is not strictly nothing, but it is so small that it makes no appreciable difference when added to or subtracted from an ordinary conceivable quantity, and that further its square may be neglected in comparison to itself. As an example of an infinitely great quantity the sum of the natural numbers to infinity may be given. By taking a sufficient number of terms, the sum can be made greater than any assignable quantity, and this is all that is mathematically meant when we say that $1 + 2 + 3 + 4 + \ldots$ to infinity is infinity.

In metaphysics the term I. has no universally accepted meaning. The best thinkers, however, maintain that it denotes nothing positive, but is only an expression of our inability to transcend in conception the limits of matter and space.

Infin'itive. See VERB.

Inflamma'tion is the reaction of a living tissue against an injury, and the term comprehends 'an assemblage of phenomena held in relation with each other by the circumstance that they are all effects of the same injurious agency, and that they all form parts of one process, of which the various stages follow each other in more or less orderly succession.' These phenomena, the result of mechanical or chemical injury, depend on changes in the structural elements of the tissues, and they may have their seat also in the blood-vessels themselves, as muscular tubes (the contractile elements of which are under the immediate control of the vaso-motor nervous system), or as mere conduits for the conveyance and distribution of the blood. I., therefore, consists of textural and vascular changes, but the former are subordinate and consequent to the latter; for although a living part cannot be injured without the elements of its tissues undergoing germinative changes, such changes, resulting in the production and multiplication of young cells, are never the first effects of which the reaction of a living tissue against an injury consists. The first local effect is vascular, and the state of contraction of the smallest arteries within and around the seat of the injury is altered or modified so as to determine an increased supply of blood to the injured part, and the walls of the capillaries undergo changes in consequence of which the liquor sanguinis and corpuscles ooze out into the lymphatic spaces containing the elements of the tissues. In consequence of this exudation the tissue elements begin to germinate, but the tissue may be acted on directly by the peculiar cause of the I., or indirectly by the exuded liquor sanguinis with which it is irrigated, and it is probable that in the majority of inflammations the excitation of the tissues is indirect or secondary, being due to the exuded liquor sanguinis. Textural germination may occur as the direct result of mechanical or chemical injury, without any antecedent inflammation; but such results, if they ever take place, are, at all events, exceptional. I., if of considerable extent, is invariably attended with more or less fever, limited in duration and degree by the limits of the injury which caused it, and is designated as *simple* or *normal* I.; but when the I. extends beyond the direct and primary operation of its cause, inducing similar inflammations in other parts, and disordering the vital functions of the whole body, inducing those states expressed by such terms as *irritative fever*, *pyæmia*, or *septicæmia*, the I. may be appropriately termed *infective*. Infective I. is characterised by peculiar appearances at the original seat of I., and by the appearance of new foci of I. along the course of the infected channels, and in the occurrence of changes in the physical and organoleptic characters of the blood itself, indicating that it is impregnated with the infective poison. It has been discovered that in all acute infective inflammations microzymes abound in the exudation-liquids, and that the same forms are also to be found in the blood of the infected animals, their presence being a constant accompaniment of all acute infective suppurations. These organisms, permeating the exudation liquids, are various, and have characteristic appearances to which distinctive terms are applied, but they may be divided into two groups, according to the circumstances under which they occur. Of these groups, the *rod form* is the type of one, and the *dumb-bell form* of another. Where the development of microzymes is going on with great rapidity, as in the exudation-liquid of intense infective-peritonitis, single *rod-forms*, not larger than $\frac{1}{1000}$ millimetre in length, are found, and the less acute the process of I. may be, the larger are the *rods*, and the more symmetrical is their arrangement of filaments, end to end. In the exudation liquids of a subcutaneous abscess, or of a chronic peritonitis, there are scarcely any *rod-forms*, the prevalent *forms* being *spheroids*, *dumb-bells*, and *chains*. On no single occasion has any form of mycelium been discovered in infective liquids charged with microzymes, and the microzymes of ordinary drinking water neither originate from fungi nor develop to them. In the various forms of secondary I. the exudation liquids of ordinary I. are always endowed with toxical properties not possessed by other animal fluids, and which produce local I. in the living tissues with which such liquids are brought into contact; or acute general disorder, consequent on their existence in the circulation or in the tissues. It has also been demonstrated that in the transmission of infective I. by inoculation, an *augmentation of infective activity* takes place of such a nature that, from an inconsiderable and transitory product at first, a product is eventually obtained possessing toxical powers of the most intense virulence. The presence of characteristic organic forms in infective exudations, affords *in itself* no conclusive proof that these bodies are the cause of the infectiveness; but as these infinitely minute organisms are present in every intensely infective inflammation, we may conclude that they have an important relation to the morbid process.

Nearly all the tissues and organs of the body may be the seat of I., so that the various diseases resulting from I. are numerous and complicated, and the more important are described under their specific names, which, as a general rule, terminate in the affix *itis*, denoting I. I. of the lungs, however, is usually designated pneumonia, instead of pneumonitis. See the experimental researches of Hunter, Thomson, Wilson, Philips, Hughes, Bennett, Wharton Jones, John Simon, Paget, Lister, and the recent investigations of Dr. Burdon Sanderson, *Reports of an Experimental Study of Inflammations*, contained in the *Reports of the Medical Officer of the Privy Council and Local Government Board* (new series, No. vi. 1875).

Inflec'tion is the general term employed by grammarians to denote the changes which words undergo when placed in relation to one another in a clause or sentence. Most of these changes take place in the terminations of words, and these have been proved by philologists to represent separate words joined to the stem or root. In course of time these suffixes became merged in the root-word itself, and gave rise to case, number, person, tense, mood, and voice. In the Indo-European tongues, there can be no doubt that the terminations of the persons in the different tenses of verbs are personal suffixes, or pronominal forms disguised by time, or by that constant change which is the universal law of language. The most common forms of the personal suffixes are—sing. *mi, si, ti*, representing respectively the pronouns *ma, twa* (*swa*), *ta*. The plural forms *mas, tas, nti*, are more obscure. The most ingenious explanation yet offered makes *mas* = *ma* + *twa*, *i.e.*, 'I and thou,' 'we;' *matwa* would become *matwi, masi, mas*. So *twatwa*, 'thou and thou,' 'ye,' would become *twatwi, twasi, tas*. The third form, which differs from the singular only by the insertion of *n* before *ti*, has not yet been satisfactorily accounted for. The Latin differs but little from the Sanskrit in these forms, *e.g.*, *su-m, es, es-t, su-mus, es-tis, su-nt*. The verb was further inflected so as to express different times of action, and this by a process quite distinct from the combination of a nominal or verbal base with a pronominal suffix. In the Latin verb, for example, the terminations in *bam, bo, avi*, &c., are made up of already inflected forms, from *i*, to go, and *as* and *fu*, to be; thus *amabo* = *amare-fuo*, 'I am to love.' Many philologists, however, consider *bo* and *bam* to be divergent forms of the root *bhu*, 'to be,' in which case *bo* and *bam* would be added to the root *ama*. That auxiliary verbs do in some languages do duty as inflections is shown by the French future *aimer-ai*, 'I have to love.' Other modes of I. are by prefixes known as *augment* and *reduplication*, *e.g.*, Gr. *tuptō*, imperfect, *e-tupton*, perfect, *te-tupha*; Lat. *tundo*, perfect, *tu-tudi*. Thus far we have spoken of I. only with regard to person, number, and tense. The various moods and voices of verbs were in like manner distinguished by suffixes, but whether these are pronominal or verbal is not clear. It remains to say a few words on the I. of nouns and adjectives. The nominative case (denoting the subject) ended in *s* in masculine, sometimes also in feminine, nouns, as—Gr. *hippo-s*, Lat. *equu-s, nube-s, Gaiu-s*. In all such cases *s* is most likely the pronoun of the third person 'he' or 'she,' for gender is no natural distinction in language. The accusative (denoting the object) was usually marked by the suffix *m*. The locative case, distinguished by the suffix *i*, originally denoted *in a place*; the dative, with suffix *ai*, probably a modification of the locative, expressed *bodily inclination towards an object*. The ablative, with a variety of suffixes, in its primary signification denoted *from a place*; while what is commonly called the instrumental case, with the two suffixes *ā* and *bhi*, possessed a meaning much less definite. In Sanskrit the *ā* form is very common; it is found in Greek in words like *hama, tacha*, &c. In Latin the *bhi* form is seen in *tibi, sibi, ibi, ubi*; in epic Greek in *biē-phi*, 'with strength.' In modern languages the work of I. is performed in great measure by articles, prepositions, pronouns, and auxiliary verbs. From those modern tongues in which it does exist, I. is rapidly disappearing. In French, for instance, though it remains in the verb in the written tongue, it has almost vanished from the spoken language. The loss of I. in modern tongues can hardly be looked upon as a misfortune, for if it has robbed them of the simplicity and elasticity of earlier forms of speech, it has invested them with a clearness, a directness, and a precision peculiarly their own. See Peile's *Philology* (Lond. 1877).

Inflores'cence (Lat. *in*, and *florescere*, 'to begin to blossom') is the manner in which flowers are arranged, and the form of I. not only determines the habit of a plant, but is also of value in its systematic classification. It is (1) *terminal* or *determinate* when at the summit of a stem or leafy branch; (2) *auxiliary* or *indeterminate* when arising in the axil of a Bract (q. v.), the stem or branch ending in leaf-buds. The former (1) is nearly always *centrifugal*, *i.e.*, the terminal or the central flower opens first, and the others downwards or outwards in regular progression; the latter (2) is always *centripetal*, *i.e.*, the lowest or outermost first open. To the main axis of the I. the term *rachis* is applied; the stalk supporting a cluster of flowers (sometimes a single flower) is a *peduncle*; and if single-flowered branches are given off by a peduncle, they are termed *pedicels*; a leafless peduncle arising as if from the root is a *scape*. Flowers that are not stalked are *sessile*. The principal forms of I. are—*Spike*, a simple (*i.e.*, undivided) axis with sessile flowers; *raceme*, a simple axis with stalked flowers; *panicle*, a raceme with branched peduncles; *corymb*, a raceme with the peduncles becoming gradually shorter as they approach the top, so that all the flowers are about on a level; *umbel*, when many stalked flowers spring from one point, and reach about the same level; *partial* umbels are umbels seated on the branches of an umbel, when the whole forms a *compound* umbel; *head* or *capitulum*, when several sessile or nearly sessile flowers are collected into a compact head-like cluster; *cyme*, formed of a terminal flower, beneath which are branches each having a terminal flower, together with lateral branches again similarly dividing, and so on; a *globose* cyme has flowers so placed as to form a globose mass; a *scorpioid* cyme produces only the external branch of each pair except the first. *Catkins* are deciduous unisexual *spikes* of crowded flowers, and the *spadices* of various monocotyledons and the *ears* and *spikelets* of grasses are forms of the spike. Different forms of I. may arise from varied combinations of some two of the above primary forms.

Influen'za is a specific febrile disease of the miasmatic order of zymotic disease, frequently-prevailing as an epidemic, and attended with an extreme degree of lassitude and prostration. The most prominent symptoms of I. are chills and great sensibility to cold over the surface of the body. The mucous membranes lining the air passages are chiefly affected, the nostrils discharging an acrid fluid, accompanied with coughing and a yellowish expectoration, which is most troublesome at night. The eyes are injected and watery, and there is intense frontal headache, especially over the eyes, sometimes attended with giddiness, delirium, or lethargy and excessive insomnia. The fever attending I. is sometimes very severe, and the type varies in different epidemics and localities. The sense of taste is generally disordered, and there is great oppression over the region of the heart. In 1311 and 1403 I. was very fatal in France, and in the year 1557 it prevailed as an epidemic over the whole of the northern hemisphere, beginning in Asia and terminating in America. I. was epidemic in the years 1729, 1743, 1775, 1782, and in 1831, 1833, 1837, 1847, and prevailed in both summer and winter, lasting nearly the same time, from four to six weeks, in the different towns and cities attacked. The specific poison of I. probably affects animals as well as man, for when I. has prevailed as an epidemic, a similar disease has been epizoötic among horses and dogs, as in the years 1728, 1732, 1775. I. is endemic in the tropics, at least in Eastern Africa, and is frequently confounded with ague, which, in some respects, it closely resembles. In this country the type of the fever is remittent, with exacerbations in the evening, generally terminating in abundant perspiration after a duration of from two to four days; but in Germany the fever is sometimes intermittent. The more severe cases are followed by serous inflammation and red hepatisation of the lungs, terminating fatally. The nature of the epidemic influence which gives rise to I. is unknown, but sudden changes of temperature assist in the development of the poison, and exposure to cold predisposes to the disease. The chief indications in the treatment of I. are to relieve the bowels by an active cathartic, to promote perspiration by warmth, and to counteract the febrile symptoms by the administration of quinine in full doses. Pulmonary complications are to be treated on the same principles as special diseases of the pulmonary tissues.

In For'ma Pau'peris, a term used to denote that a person is allowed to sue 'as a pauper'—that is, without payment of court fees and other costs.

Informa'tion by the Crown, is a term of English law denoting a mode of carrying on a criminal process without the intervention of a grand jury. Information in name of the Queen is filed *ex officio* by the Attorney-General, and is only directed against an offender, to delay punishing whom might be dangerous to the state or to the public peace.

Infor'mer. In English law various statutes enact penalties for offences, and award part, or the whole, to the person whose information has led to the conviction of the offender. In such cases, it is usually provided that any one may prosecute. He who does so is called the I. Any one informing and compromising with the accused is by statute disabled from again suing as an I. Public prosecutors in Scotland are bound to give the name of their I., who is liable in damage if the information be false, the falsehood being aggravated if malicious.

Infundibula'ta, the name given to one of the divisions of the class *Polyzoa* (q. v.), distinguished by having the tentacles arranged in a round or orbicular fashion, and by the absence of an *epistome* or valvular lid for closing the mouth of the cells. The sea-mats or *flustræ* exemplify this group.

Infu'sions, or **Infu'sa**, are aqueous solutions of vegetable substances, generally prepared with boiling water, but, in some cases, made at a lower temperature—as *infusum calumbæ*—to prevent the starch-matter from being dissolved. Concentrated I. are very largely used; but, though convenient and economical, they have not the aroma of the freshly-made infusion. To obviate putrefactive changes, small bottles, filled to the brim with recently-made infusion, are placed in a boiler with hay and water, and kept at the boiling-point for five minutes, and are then tied over with a bladder, and stoppered while hot. I. thus treated may be preserved good for several weeks. I. prepared by Percolation (q. v.) are less liable to decay than by the ordinary method of infusion.

Infuso'ria, the name given to the highest class of the *Protozoa* (q. v.). This group of animalcules is defined by having a *mouth*, by the general presence of *Cilia* (q. v.), and by the inability to protrude the body into *pseudopodia* or prehensile processes. The body, as in all protozoa, is composed of *Protoplasm* (q. v.), and the body-substance exhibits a division into three layers, the outer being named the *cuticle*, the middle the *cortical layer*, and the innermost layer the *chyme mass*. These animalcules are for the most part of microscopic size; the smallest existing as mere specks under the highest powers of the best microscopes. Under the general name of I., a great variety of very dissimilar beings were included by the older naturalists. Thus *Diatomaceæ* (now regarded as low vegetable organisms), the *Rotifera*, or 'wheel animalcules,' and many others, were formerly included under this name; the more perfect investigation of their structure, however, resulting in their being separated from the present class, and allocated to different groups of the animal or plant worlds. The great majority of infusorians are free-swimming animalcules, some, as the *Vorticellæ* or 'bell animalcules,' being borne on a contractile stalk; while others, as *Epistylis*, are branched but not contractile; *Carchesium* being both branched and contractile. *Stentor*, or the 'trumpet animalcule,' a common denizen of our pools, can attach itself at will to fixed objects, swimming freely at other times by means of the *cilia*, which constitute the locomotive organs of the class. The mouth exists as a small orifice surrounded by cilia, which sweep particles of nutriment into the orifice. These particles pass into the general substance of the body, and are digested by the surrounding protoplasm. Ehrenberg, who was one of the first to investigate the structure of these animalcules, supposed that each food particle was lodged in a distinct stomach. This observation was founded on an error, and hence Ehrenberg's name of *Polygastrica* ('many-stomached'), applied to the I., has passed from the vocabulary of the zoologist. Certain clear spaces, named *contractile vesicles*, are seen to expand and contract with a regular and rhythmical motion in the bodies of I. It has been supposed that these bodies represent rudimentary hearts. Reproduction in I. takes place by *fission* or simple division of the body substance into two or more new animalcules; by *gemmation* or budding; and by *encystation*, this latter being a process consisting of the division of the body-substance into small portions, each of which, when liberated, becomes a perfect animalcule. The *nucleus* and *nucleolus* seen within the bodies of many I. are believed to represent reproductive organs, and hence these bodies are supposed to possess intimate relations with the process last alluded to. The *classification* of the I. is still under the consideration of zoologists. The system most commoly received is that wherein the class is divided into three orders: (1) *Ciliata*, which includes the great majority of these animalcules, in which the body-surface is more or less completely provided with *cilia*; *e.g.*, *Vorticella*, *Epistylis*, *Paramœcium*, *Stentor*, &c.; (2) *Flagellata*, including those forms in which the *cilia* are reduced to one or two in number; *e.g.*, *Peranema* and *Anisonema*; (3) *Suctoria*, so called from the fact that the body has tubular filaments provided with suckers at their tips. Whether or not the suctorial I.—represented by *Acineta*—are distinct and separate I., or are merely stages in the development of other forms, are facts which have not exactly been determined.

The name I. is derived from the Latin *infusum*, an infusion, and is applied to these creatures from the fact that they are usually found wherever collections of animal or vegetable matter are exposed to the atmosphere. Hence the I. have become of special interest to biologists as beings which, according to one school of thought, may be produced by *spontaneous generation* or *abiogenesis*, *i.e.*, without the presence of parent-germs or organisms. The 'germ-theory,' on the other hand, which holds that the germs of these and allied organisms are carried by the atmosphere, and develop into mature forms when surrounded by proper conditions, is a thoroughly logical hypothesis, and accounts in a perfectly natural manner for their appearance in infusions. (See GENERATION, SPONTANEOUS.) The name *Fossil I.* has been erroneously applied to the fossilised flinty shells of minute animals known as *Polycystinæ*, which are allied to the *Foraminifera*.

In'gelow, Jean, an English poet and novelist, was born in Boston, Lincolnshire, about 1830. She published *Tales of Orris* in 1860. A collection of *Poems* which appeared in 1863, containing *Divided*, *Songs of Seven*, *The Letter L Divided*, *The High Tide*, &c., established her fame, and has passed through many editions. Her subsequent works include *A Story of Doom and other Poems* (1867), *Mopsa the Fairy* (1869), *Little Wonder Horn* (1872), and *Off the Skelligs* (a novel in 4 vols. 1873). Her poems are remarkable for depth of feeling and high artistic power, and her tales for children are charming.

Ing'emann, Bernhard Severin, a great Danish poet and novelist, was born May 28, 1789, at Torkildstrup, in the island of Falster, and educated at Copenhagen University. While yet a student, he published in 1811 a volume of poems, and after a tour (1818–19) in Germany, France, Switzerland, and Italy, became (in 1822) 'Lector' in Danish language and literature at Sorö Academy, of which institution he had the general direction from 1843 to its dissolution in 1849. He died 24th February 1862. I. was a writer of great fertility in various fields. He himself divided his literary life into three periods—the first (1811–14) romantic, subjective, sentimental, and devoted to poetry; the second objective, and given to the drama; and the third (from 1821) to poems and to historical novels illustrative of the middle ages in Denmark. These are excellent imitations of Scott, and in great favour with the people. His chief works are an epic poem, *Valdemar den Store og hans Mænd* (1824), his masterpiece; the novels *Valdemar Seier* (1826); *Erik Menveds Barndom* (1828); *Kong Erik og de Fredlöse* (1833); *Prinds Otto af Danmark* (1835); the dramatic poem *Renegaten* (1838), and tale, *Salomons Ring* (1839); and the poems *Dronning Margrete* (1836), and *Holger Danske* (1827). *Kunnuk og Naja* (1842), a tale of Greenland life; *Landsbybörnene* (1852), a romance; *Confirmationsgave* (1854), and the poems *Tankebreve fra en Afdöd* (1855), and *Guldæblet* (1856), may be also mentioned. His *Samlede Skrifter* are published in four sets. *Dramatiske Digte* (6 vols. Copenh. 1843); *Historiske Digte og Romaner* (12 vols. 1847–51); *Eventyr og Fortællinger* (12 vols. 1847–56); *Romaner, Sange, og Eventyrdigte* (9 vols. 1845–64). *Levnetsbog*, an autobiography of I., appeared at Copenhagen in 1862.

Inglis, The Right Hon. John, an eminent Scottish lawyer, son of the Rev. Dr. Inglis, a minister of the Established Church, was born in 1810, and studied at Glasgow and Oxford. He was called to the Scotch bar in 1835, was made Solicitor-General for Scotland in 1852, and shortly afterwards became Lord Advocate. He was appointed Lord Justice-Clerk of Scotland in 1858, and in the same year was returned for Stamford. In 1859 he was made D.C.L. and a member of the Privy Council.

He was appointed Lord Justice-General and President of the Court of Session in 1867, and Chancellor of Edinburgh University in 1869. I. is one of the keenest, strongest, and most legal intellects adorning the Scotch Bench.

In'golstadt, originally called **Ingoldestadt,** a Bavarian city defended by fortifications of imposing strength, is situated at the confluence of the Schutter with the Danube, 50 miles N. of Munich by rail. It possesses a castle, convent, nunnery, and three churches, one of which is for Protestants, and another is the colossal church of the Virgin (*Liebfrauenkirche*), built early in the 15th c., where lie the bones of Eck, Luther's antagonist. I. was fortified in 1250, and for more than 300 years was the seat of a university, founded in 1472, transferred to Landshut in 1800, and finally incorporated in 1826 with the University of Munich. By the Latin writers of the 16th c. I. was called *Auripolis* and *Chrysopolis* ('Golden City'). It has no manufactures of any importance, and depends chiefly on the agricultural industry of the neighbourhood. Pop. (1871) 13,157.

In'gres, Jean Dominique Auguste, a French painter, was born at Montauban, September 15, 1781. He studied in the *atélier* of David, and in 1801 gained the first prize of the École des Beaux Arts. In 1804 he painted a portrait of the First Consul, which so pleased Napoleon that he gave I. a sitting for a second, which appeared in 1806. He studied in Rome (1806–20) and in Florence (1820–24), during which time he produced many large classical, historical, and religious pictures, such as 'Œdipe expliquant l'Enigme,' 'L'Entrée de Charles V. à Paris,' &c. In 1825 he was elected a member of the Institute, and Professor in the École des Beaux Arts. 'L'Apothéose d'Homère,' one of his finest efforts, was painted for the Louvre in 1827. In 1829 he became Director of the French Academy at Rome, and while there he painted 'Le Martyre de St. Symphonea,' 'Stratonice,' and a portrait of 'Cherubini.' On his return to France some ten years later, every possible honour was showered upon him by the state. A special room was set apart in the Paris Exposition Universelle of 1855 for forty of his pictures. He exhibited 'La Source,' one of his best pictures, when eighty years of age. He was named a Senator in 1862, and died January 14, 1867. I. has been almost idolised by his countrymen, though no artist has been subjected to more searching criticism. His style is founded on that of David, tempered by a study of the great Italian masters, particularly of Raphael. His merits are originality in conception, wondrous grace of outline, and conscientiousness in labour; his defects, a certain hardness in drawing and unreality in colour. He has exercised enormous influence over modern art in France. Over a hundred engravings of his works were published by Mons. A. Reveil in 1851.

Ingross'ing or **Engross'ing** a deed, means the making a fair copy from the draft for signature. The corresponding term of Scotch law is 'extending a deed.' See TESTING CLAUSE. English law, ATTESTATION.

Ingulf, Abbot of Crowland, was, until Sir Francis Palgrave led important evidence in 1826 to prove the contrary, generally believed to be the author of the *History of Crowland* (*Historia Monasterii Croylandensis*). More recently (1870) Mr. Freeman has decided that 'it is quite certain he did not write the book which is called by his name;' the same historian concluding that 'it must have been written several hundred years later.' I., according to the *Historia*, was born in London (1030), educated at Westminster and Oxford, became secretary to William, Duke of Normandy, undertook a pilgrimage to the Holy Land along with Sigfrid, Duke of Mainz, passed through many vicissitudes in the East, returned to Normandy, became a monk in the Abbey of Fontenelle, from which he was advanced to the office of prior. In 1076, through William the Conqueror's influence, he was transferred to the Abbey of Crowland in Lincolnshire, whose history he was understood to have continued from 664 till 1091. I. died of gout (1109). Three editions of the works attributed to him have been published; by Savile (1596), Gale (1684), and Bohn in his *Antiquarian Library*.

Inher'itance. See HEIR AT LAW, HEIR PRESUMPTIVE.

Inhibi'tion is a process of Scotch law by which a debtor, having heritable (real) estate, is prohibited from alienating or burdening it, until the debt due to the inhibiting creditor is provided for.

Inhib'itory Action, this is a term applied by modern physiologists to designate a peculiar action of the nervous system by which one nervous centre or set of nerve-fibres can restrain or moderate the action of another. The most notable example is the influence of the pneumogastric or vagus nerve on the action of the heart. When this nerve is cut the heart beats faster, and when the end of the nerve next the heart is stimulated by electric currents, the heart beats more slowly, and if the stimulus be sufficiently powerful, the heart will stop beating in a condition of complete relaxation. It is well known that the heart has in its own substance ganglia or knots of nervous matter which regulate its rhythmic movements. These ganglia may apparently be restrained in their action by this nerve; but the exact way in which this is accomplished is quite unknown. I. A. plays an important part in all nervous mechanisms, and in all probability the influence of the will may be accounted for by supposing that certain higher centres in the brain have no power of governing or controlling lower centres.

In'ia, a peculiar genus of *Cetacea* (q. v.), or whale-like mammalia, found inhabiting the rivers of Bolivia, often at a distance of over 2000 miles from the sea. The average length of the males is about 12 or 14 feet; of the females, 7 feet. The only species is the *I. Boliviensis*. These mammals agree with the dolphins and their neighbours in essential structure, and are included in the family *Delphinidæ*. The head is somewhat pointed; and the colour is black above, and white on the under parts.

Injec'tions are fluid medicines thrown into the passages or cavities of the body by means of a syringe or elastic bag. Fluids injected into the rectum are termed Clysters (q. v.). Medicines are occasionally administered by injecting under the skin, called hypodermic medication, to produce local, and sometimes constitutional effects. Blood is also occasionally injected into the veins in cases of severe and sudden hæmorrhage. See TRANSFUSION OF BLOOD.

Injunc'tion is a writ in English law to prevent or stop the procedure of an illegal or inequitable act. Disregard of I. renders the offender liable to punishment for contempt of court. The similar process in Scotland is called *Interdict*.

Ink (Fr. *encre*; Ital. *enchiostro*; Lat. *encaustum*, the purple red ink used only in the signature of the Emperors) is the coloured fluid used for forming written characters, and the viscous material employed for printing impressions from types, plates, or lithographic stone, &c. The two classes of materials thus indicated are essentially different from each other, and will be separately noticed. *Writing-inks* are of many colours, and prepared from numerous tinctorial substances. The essential qualities of a good I. are, that it should flow freely from the pen, which it should not corrode or destroy; that it should not turn mouldy or thicken on exposure; that it should so bite into the paper as not be washed out; and, finally, that it should not fade or disappear with age or exposure. Ordinary *black I.* is a solution of a compound tanno-gallate of iron held in suspension by the addition of gum arabic or a similar compound. The following recipe yields an excellent black I:—Of the best blue Aleppo galls, well bruised, 4 oz. are macerated for a fortnight in a quart of distilled water. To this are added 1½ oz. of gum arabic dissolved in water, and ½ oz. of lump sugar. When well mixed, 1½ oz. of crushed green copperas (ferric sulphate) is added, and the whole is then occasionally shaken up for two or three days. After a week or two the I. is ready for use, and to prevent mouldiness, a drop or two of carbolic acid, or a little essential oil, may be added. *Copying-I.* may be made by adding sugar to ordinary black I.; but the best copying I. is made from roasted galls, by which a portion of pyro-gallic acid is formed, a substance much more soluble in water than ordinary gallic acid. *Red I.* of the finest quality is made from cochineal with liquor of ammonia, but Brazil-wood with acetic acid, garancine, and other red dyes are also employed. *Blue I.* is prepared by dissolving Prussian blue in oxalic acid, and by various other agents. *Purple I.* and *violet I.* are made from a strong decoction of logwood, to which a little alum and tin crystals are added, and I. of almost any colour can be obtained by similarly treating the various dye-stuffs. I. prepared from various aniline colours have been much used of recent years. *Marking I.* is generally a solution of nitrate of silver, which on exposure to heat and air darkens and communicates an indelible stain. *Gold and silver I.* are made by mixing finely-powdered leaf of either metal with gum arabic. *Sympathetic I.*, or I. which becomes visible only when acted on by heat or by some chemical preparation, may be prepared from many substances, but the best are certain salts of cobalt.

Printing-I. is of two principal kinds, first, for typography, and second, for lithographic or copper-plate printing. *Typographic I.* is prepared by boiling and burning linseed oil in an iron pot till it becomes thick and gluey, to which black resin and brown soap in certain proportions are added, and the whole well incorporated over a fire. To this, for black, fine lamp-black is added and a very small quantity of indigo and Prussian blue, and for coloured inks the various coloured pigments are substituted for the lamp-black, &c. *Lithographic I.* is a compound of resinous substances with wax, tallow, hard soap, and lamp-black. See LITHOGRAPHY.

Ink'ermann, properly **Ink'jermann**, a village in the W. of the Crimean peninsula, Russia, at the mouth of the Tchernajathales, 5 miles E. of Sevastopol, is famous as the scene of an English-French victory over the Russians, 5th November 1854. A force of 14,000, including part of the Household Guards, successfully resisted the advance, under cover of drizzling rain, of the Russian army, 60,000 strong, and finally drove it back. I. has been called a 'soldier's battle' on account of the extent to which the issue depended on personal intrepidity and physical force. An explosion of some 100,000 lbs. of gunpowder occurred at I. causing great loss of life, 15th November 1855.

In'land Bill of Exchange. See under BILL, BILL OF EXCHANGE.

Inlay'ing is the art of inserting into excisions in metal, wood, or stone, materials of a different colour or texture, or of a more costly description. One process of metal I. is described under DAMASCENING, and by operations similar to those there mentioned the celebrated Indian Bidri or Biddery ware is produced. It consists of a zinc alloy enriched with silver. It takes its name from Bider in the Deccan, where it is extensively manufactured. The decoration of furniture by inlays of light-coloured and valuable woods and ivory was widely practised in Italy during the Renaissance, and in France at even a later period. 'Intarsiatura,' or 'Tarsia,' is the Italian term denoting this style of art; in France and England it is called *marqueterie* or marquetry. Buhl or Boule work is a kind of marquetry. The Persians long excelled in I. articles of wood with ivory, white and stained, arranged in minute geometrical patterns. Most of this work is now executed at Bombay and Goa. The choir fittings of the Certosa di la Pavia are richly decorated with small pieces of ivory. The name *Certosina* has been applied to this combination of walnut or cypress-wood and ivory. The Chinese and Japanese enrich their lacquerwork with inlays of mother-of-pearl and coloured stones. Variegated marbles, agates, cornelians, and other precious stones were inlaid in furniture in Italy during the 15th and 16th centuries. The most magnificent display of stone inlay is that of the Taj-Mahal at Agra.

Inn (the *Œnus* of the Romans), the largest of the Alpine tributaries of the Danube (q. v.), rises from the Lungin Lake at the Septimer Pass in the Engadine (q. v.) valley, which is situated in the S.E. part of Graubünden, or Grisons (q. v.), a canton of Switzerland. From its source at Malojasattel, 5874 feet above the sea, to the town of Passau, where it joins the right bank of the Danube, at a height of 920 feet, it has a north-easterly course of 309 miles. Entering the Tyrol at the Finstermünz Pass, it traverses the Upper Inn Valley and the Lower Inn Valley, becoming navigable at Hall, near Innsbruck; then passing through the Kalkalpen at Kufstein, it enters Bavaria, and makes a semicircular sweep northwards till joined by the Salzach from the S., when, following its original direction, it becomes, as far as Passau, the boundary between Bavaria and Austria.

Innate' Ideas, the name first given by Descartes to certain ideas which it was assumed could not be the product of experience, but must have been, as it were, folded up in the original mould of the mind or thinking faculty, and developed with its growth—from *within*, not from *without*. Among the ideas supposed to be thus 'innate,' are those denoted by the terms God, Eternity, Infinitude, Duty, and, generally speaking, the transcendental conceptions of the 'Pure Reason.' Locke in his *Essay on the Human Understanding* combats the doctrine of I. I. See Tenneman's *Manual of the History of Philosophy.*

Inner House. Scotch law, see COURT OF SESSION.

Inner Temple. See INNS OF COURT.

Inn'es, Cosmo, was born September 9, 1798, at Durris, on Deeside, Aberdeenshire, admitted to the bar in 1822, became Sheriff of Morayshire in 1840, and occupied that position with much credit until 1852, when he was appointed Clerk to the Second Division of the Court of Session. I. was elected to the Chair of History in the University of Edinburgh in 1846. In the labours of the Bannatyne, Maitland, and Spalding Clubs he took a prominent part, the fruits of which were shown in the collating and editing of nearly all the Chartularies of the religious houses. His patient study of public records and contemporary documents is seen to greatest advantage in *Scotland in the Middle Ages*, and in *Sketches of Early Scottish History*, whilst his keen insight into the political and ecclesiastical constitution of antique Scotland may be judged from his introduction to the first volume of *Scots Acts*. From 1865 until his death at Killin, July 31, 1874, he was chiefly engaged in preparing for the press the *Rescinded Acts*, in indexing the folio edition of the *Acts of the Scots Parliament*, a task for which his incomparable skill in deciphering and extracting the meaning of old writings rendered him peculiarly fit, and in preparing for the press his *Lectures on Scottish Legal Antiquities* (1872). Shortly before his death he wrote a brief and appreciative memoir of Dean Ramsay. See *Memoir of C. I.* (Edinb. Paterson, 1874).

Innes, Thomas, was born at Drumgask, parish of Aboyne, Aberdeenshire (1662), sent for his education to the University of Paris (1677), returned to Scotland (1698), where he officiated as priest at Inveravon. In 1701 I. returned to Paris, where, at the Scots College, he devoted himself to writing a history of Scotland, and from the nature of his researches he may be regarded as the first critical inquirer in that field. *A Critical Essay on the Ancient Inhabitants of the Northern Parts of Britain or Scotland* was published at London, 1729. It has a permanent value owing to the conscientious spirit in which he consulted original manuscripts, and, according to his lights, rejected all material based upon irresponsible rumour. I. also wrote one volume of a *Civil and Ecclesiastical History of Scotland*, carried down by him to the year 597 A.D., which, with an unfinished account of two centuries more, has been published by the Spalding Club. I. died at Paris, January 28, 1744.

Innis. See INCH.

Inn'keeper, Law Affecting the. An innkeeper is bound to receive all guests or travellers, and to provide them with necessary food and lodging, unless he can show a reasonable excuse for his refusal. While he is not bound to allow a guest to choose his room, he cannot impose unreasonable terms. If the innkeeper refuse to entertain a guest on tender of a reasonable price, not only may his house be suppressed, but he may be indicted and fined at the suit of the crown, and damage may be awarded against him to the person rejected. If a guest be robbed, the innkeeper is bound to compensate the loss, unless the guest was robbed by his own servant or companion. This liability can only be limited by argument or due notice. But the innkeeper is only answerable for those things which are *within* his house. It has lately been decided that an innkeeper cannot detain the *person* of his guest, nor take off his clothes in order to secure payment of a bill. 26 & 27 Vict. c. 41 limits the liability of the inkeeper as above defined to the value of £30, unless the loss has occurred through his wilful neglect, or unless the property stolen or injured has been deposited *expressly* for safe custody with the innkeeper, who, if such tender be made, is bound to receive it. There does not appear to be any essential difference in the law of England and that of Scotland as affecting innkeepers. In neither country is the host answerable for loss or damage to his guest's property from Act of God (q. v.).

Inn'ocent, the name of thirteen Popes, of whom the following are the most notable :—**I. I.**, born at Albano, near Rome, Pope from 402 to his death, 12th March 417, claimed, as the successor of St. Peter, the settlement of all weighty matters (*causæ majores*), promoted celibacy amongst the clergy, bitterly opposed the Novatians, and approved the condemnation of Pelagianism passed by the Councils of Milevi and Carthage. His learning and prudence were such that his advice on Church matters was in constant request; and in his epistles, written in a tone of mingled instruction and command, Leo and his successors afterwards found much to justify their assertion of the universal authority of the Roman See. The best edition of these, his only extant writings, is in vol. i. of Coustant's *Epistolæ Pontificum Romanorum* (Par. 1721), and reprinted in the 8th vol. of Galland's *Bibliotheca Patrum* (Ven. 1765–81). I. was canonised by the Church, the 28th July (which Baronius gives as the date of his death) being his saint's-day.—**I. III.** (1198–1216), previously Lothario, Count of Segni, born 1161 at Anagni, and descended from a great Gothic family, was brought up at Rome, and studied theology and canon law at Paris and Bologna. He was chosen Pope when scarcely thirty-seven years old, and shortly after his accession compelled the imperial prefect in Rome to do him homage, thereby disowning feudal dependence on the Emperor. The Romans, however, forced him to submit. I. placed himself at the head of the league of cities in Lombardy and Tuscany, and on the death of the Empress-dowager Constantia was made guardian of her son (Friedrich II.), who had already been chosen Emperor. This duty he discharged in a liberal-minded way, also ruling as regent of the two Sicilies with energy and ability. When the Emperors Otto IV. and Philip of Swabia contended for the chief power in Germany, he confirmed the choice of the former, who in return recognised I.'s right to the March of Ancona, Ravenna, and Pentapolis; but afterwards, when Otto laid claim to Italy, the Pope excommunicated him and raised Friedrich II. to the throne. He excommunicated Philippe Auguste, King of France, for repudiating his Queen, the Danish Princess Ingeborg, and laid France under an interdict, until the king had to yield. He had a successful contest with John (q. v.) of England respecting the choice of bishops; assigned kings to Bulgaria and Wallachia; was absolute in Poland, Hungary, Servia, and Bosnia; imposed a yearly tax on Portugal and Aragon; but could not bow Sverre, King of Norway, who died excommunicated. I. was the instigator of the Fourth Crusade (q. v.). Confident of his power, he called in 1215 a general council in the Lateran (q. v.) of 500 bishops and 900 abbots, besides many temporal princes, and the Patriarchs of Constantinople and Jerusalem. Among these he took his seat 'as the head of a great family of nations, who with paternal authority orders his house,' and in the opening speech he compared himself to 'the sun, who lends the moon (*i.e.*, the state) her light.' This council sanctioned the doctrine of transubstantiation, forbade Bible-reading, and enjoined yearly absolution. The year after I. died of a violent fever. Closely resembling Gregory VII. in force of genius and will, he had yet more learning and depth of feeling. He hated all wrong, was a refuge to the distressed, but a bitter persecutor of all he thought heretics. His own life was spent in self-denial, his court was without magnificence, all his revenues were devoted to the Church. His life object was the elevation of the Papal chair by the firm establishment of its temporal power, and the deliverance of Italy from the Emperor, especially the separation of Naples and Sicily from Germany. In all this he saw the means of exercising an unrestricted power over all Christian nations. The authority of the Roman See is thought to have been never greater than during the pontificate of I. His letters (Baluze, Par. 1682) well illustrate his character and relations to his time. For I.'s life and writings, see Hurter, *Gesch. I. III. und seiner Zeitgenossen* (Hamb. 1834–42).—**I. XI.**, a Pope zealous above all for the restoration of a purer and more rigid morality in Church and State, held the See of Rome from 1676 till 1689; having been born in 1611, a scion of the noble house of the Odescalchi. He waged perpetual war with all irregularities in the personal or official conduct of the clergy, and sought to regulate the minds of the Roman citizens. The Jesuit morality he unsparingly condemned, especially and expressly in the bull of the year 1679. He came into conflict with Louis XIV. in the matter of the right hitherto claimed by ambassadors in Rome to make their palaces an asylum for criminals; put the French ambassador under excommunication, and ultimately carried his point. He also disputed persistently, though in vain, Louis's claim to draw and manage the revenues of vacant bishoprics; and this too, though he applauded the king for his persecution of the Jesuits, and celebrated the revocation of the Edict of Nantes by a solemn Te Deum. The privileges claimed by the Church of France, the *Gallican Propositions*, were solemnly and publicly condemned by I. in 1681. He died in 1689. See Ranke's *Die Röm. Päpste, ihre Kirche und ihr Staat im 16 und 17 Jahrh.*

Inn'ocents, Feast of Holy, observed in the Western Church on the 28th December, in the Eastern on the 29th, is in commemoration of the massacre by Herod of the boys in Bethlehem 'from two years old and under' (Matt. ii. 16), who were regarded as the first martyrs for Christ. Combined at first with Epiphany, a special day was afterwards set apart for the F. of H. I., perhaps as early as the 5th c.

Innom'inate Artery, the first large branch leading off from the arch of the aorta, is the channel through which the blood flows to the right side of the head and neck and to the right arm.

Inns'bruck, the capital of Tyrol, Austria, at the confluence of the Inn with the Sill, 95 miles S. of Munich by rail, in a magnificent valley, fenced in on the N. by rugged calcareous mountain masses, near 9000 feet high, and on the S. by the wooded flanks of the Brenner, with grand dolomite peaks behind. I., constituted a city in 1234, stands on the right side of the river, its suburb on the other side being called St. Nikolaus. The streets are wide and handsome, and contain many stately buildings, amongst which are eleven churches, five monasteries, a Jesuit college, the university, and the theatre. In the Franciscan Church (1563), adorned by the magnificent cenotaph of the Emperor Maximilian I., and monuments of Tyrolese worthies, Christina of Sweden, daughter of the Protestant champion Gustavus Adolphus, made public profession of the Catholic faith in 1651. The university, founded in 1672, and more than once suppressed and restored, has about fifty professors and 650 students. The manufactures are silk, gloves, cotton, and hardware. The position of I. on the railway into Italy renders its transit trade important. Pop. (1869) 16,324, of whom 5000 are soldiers.

Inns of Court are four societies in London for students-at-law, having the exclusive right of calling to the bar. They are the Inner Temple, Middle Temple, Lincoln's Inn, and Gray's Inn. Each inn is governed by its own Benchers (q. v.), who fill up the vacancies in their own body. The benchers of each inn exercise the power of calling to the bar the members of their own inn. (See BARRISTERS.) They have also authority to Disbar (q. v.). The inns of Chancery are subordinate to the I. of C. They are Clifford's Inn, Clement's Inn, Lyon's Inn, New Inn, Furnival's Inn, Thavie's Inn, Staple Inn, and Barnard's Inn. A committee appointed by the benchers of the four I. of C. have decided that ordained clergyman shall not in future be excluded from the bar. Any inn of court may refuse to call any one to the bar without giving a reason for refusal; but no one of fair character is ever excluded.

Innuen'do (Lat. *in*, 'toward,' and *nuo*, 'I nod'), in rhetoric a figure of speech in which the meaning is delicately hinted or insinuated, instead of being plainly expressed. It is effectively used for purposes of sarcasm. The bad oratory of a speaker was thus pitilessly described—'He did his party all the harm in his power; he spoke for it, and voted against it.'

Innuendo, a term of English law procedure, denoting an averment that the signification of an *initial* or of a doubtful word is that which the pleading attaches to it.

Inocar'pus, a small genus of trees belonging to *Leguminosæ*. The seeds of *I. ederlis*, called Ratti by the natives of Tahiti, &c., are used as an article of food both in the Pacific and the Indian Archipelago, being roasted in ashes or boiled, when they have somewhat the flavour of chestnut.

Inocula'tion (Lat. *inoculo*; *in* and *oculus*, 'the eye'), is the act or practice of communicating a disease to a person in health by inserting contagious matter in his skin or flesh, the process being analogous to that of grafting. Many diseases may be thus communicated; but the practice has been chiefly confined to the communication of smallpox and of cowpox which is intended as substitute for it. When the virus of smallpox, taken from a pustule after the commencement of the eighth day, is inserted in or beneath the skin of a person who has not previously suffered from smallpox, the following phenomena are observed:—Shortly after the insertion of the virus, systemic disturbance takes place. On the second day a shrivelled stain is seen at the point where the virus was introduced; on the third day there is a papular elevation; on the fourth day the papule becomes vesicular, and local irritation commences; on the sixth day there is stiffness in the axilla, and general constitutional disturbance; occasionally on the seventh day, but oftener on the eighth, rigors occur with faintishness, pain in the back, headache and vomiting, a disagreeable taste in the mouth, and offensive breath, after which the eruption appears. When I. is practised, the eruption appears on the eighth day; but when communicated by infection, on the fourteenth. The artificial disease produced by I. is much less dangerous than ordinary smallpox, and it is an almost certain means of preventing a subsequent attack of the disease. The importance of I. as regards personal safety has been long recognised both in India, China, and Europe; but it was not till about 1717 that the operation became generally known in this country, through the influence of Lady Mary Wortley Montagu, who had her own daughter publicly inoculated. Two of the children of Caroline, Princess of Wales, were inoculated, which gave a sanction to the practice. The safety conferred by I. was undoubted, and the mortality resulting from it was but trifling; but the effect upon the community at large was very pernicious, as foci for dissemination were established, which increased the spread of smallpox amongst those who were not protected by I., and the total number of deaths from smallpox increased in one hundred years in the ratio of about five to four. At the beginning of the 18th c. about one-fourteenth of the population died of smallpox, but at the latter end of the same century the number increased to one-tenth, probably in consequence of I. For such obvious reasons the operation of inoculating the poison of smallpox has been rendered illegal in this country by the passing of the Vaccination Act in 1841. See *Smallpox and Vaccination Historically and Medically Considered*, by Dr. Collinson, and *The History of Smallpox*, by Dr. Moore.

In'osite ($C_6H_{12}O_6$), a variety of Glucose (q. v.) found in certain animal organs and in the unripe fruit of certain plants. Its prismatic crystals dissolve in water; and though not fermenting in yeast, it undergoes lactic fermentation when in contact with cheese or flesh.

Inowrac'law, or **Jung'breslau** ('young Breslau'), a town of Prussia, in Posen, 26 miles S.S.E. of Bromberg by rail. A large rock-salt mine was opened here in 1871. Pop. (1875) 9139.

In Part'ibus Infide'lium (Lat. 'in the regions of the unbelievers') is a phrase applied in the Church of Rome since the 13th c. to those archbishops and bishops who have no diocese. The titles are, as a rule, taken from places in the East which were once episcopal sees. In 1877 the total number of these dignitaries was 164.

In'quest. See CORONER.

Inquisi'tion, in canon law, means either a judicial proceeding merely on public report, without accuser or informer, or else a particular tribunal established by the Popes to judge Spanish heretics. Before Constantine, the only authority was the bishops, and the only punishment was excommunication. After that, the emperors frequently passed laws inflicting heavy civil penalties on the various heretical sects. No doubt, persons were appointed to carry out these laws, but it is about A.D. 382 in a law of Theodosius against the Manichæan sects that the name *inquisitors* first occurs; they were to be named by the Prætorian Prefect. These laws gradually increase in severity; legal disabilities, banishment, forfeiture, death, are necessarily proclaimed. The principle is that '*whoever violates the religion established by God sins against public order.*' In 541 the decrees of the four general councils were made part of the imperial statute book, and all suspects who could not satisfy the Church of their innocence were declared *infamous*. The third Lateran Council distinguishes between spiritual penalties and those inflicted by the aid of the civil courts, but by this time the councils had undoubtedly assumed a power of defining penalties which Bossuet, Fleury, and others, refer to the implied consent of the secular power. Fleury says the I. began at the Council of Verona (1184), where the bishops and certain lay lords were directed to search out suspects, penitents, and 'relapsed' persons according to public rumour, and to appoint *commissioners* to help them in the business. *Rainier* and *Guy*, sent by Innocent III. to the Albigenses in 1198, were probably the first true inquisitors. But even the Dominicans sent to Languedoc in 1233 had no regular jurisdiction; it was merely their 'holy office' to stir up the crusade with the cross of cloth upon the breast, to urge the civil magistrates to punish. It was Gregory IX. who first clearly defined the functions and procedure of the inquisitorial missions sent to different countries. Their operations were much facilitated by the laws passed by the Emperor Friedrich II. (himself a sceptic), which sentenced obstinate heretics to the stake, and penitents to perpetual imprisonment. A bull of 1252 shows that in Italy the rectors and consuls of the municipalities were to cooperate with the Dominicans and the bishops, who are the lawful judges of heresy. There are traces of concordats between the Pope and certain States for the erection of an I., which was generally put into the hands of an order of monks. The excesses of the 'Fratres Prædicatores' frightened and enraged the people. Apparently, the name of the informer was kept secret, the evidence was taken down before a notary and two priests, the accused got no list of witnesses, was kept in prison till his trial, and was tortured into confession. If the evidence was insufficient, he was still compelled to 'abjure' with certain penalties. The 'relapsed' heretic was instantly *relaxatus*, or handed over to the magistrate, who gave him the choice of strangling in private and burning in public. But it was in Spain that the I. flourished most. By a bull of 1483 Thomas Torquemada (called in Latin *Turrecremata*) was appointed Inquisitor-General for that country. He sat in a 'Consejo de la suprema Inquisicion,' without appeal to Rome. His legal assessors, Gutierrez and Medina, drew up the famous articles, which are not so unfair or severe as the rules which had previously been put in force by the national Spanish inquisitors against the new 'Christians' or Jews. In particular, a list of witnesses was given, and property was not confiscated. The Spanish I. was introduced into Sicily, but was totally different from the constitutional inquisitions which were permitted in the Italian States. (See Sarpi's *History of Venetian I.*, 1638.) In Naples down to 1799 there was a 'Tribunale contro quello del Sant Uffizio,' expressly formed to protect the kingdom from the Roman I. In 1543 Paul III. founded the 'Congregation of the Holy Office,' which consisted of six cardinals, with power over all inquisitors, except the Spanish, and with power to proceed, punish, confiscate in the first instance, and also on appeal. This afterwards became the 'Holy Roman and Universal I.,' several officers called *consultors* and *qualificators* (who drew the cases) being added. This body still exists, watching specially over the conduct of the clergy and the publications of the press. Pius VII. abolished torture. 'It holds,' says Lacordaire (in his *Mémoire pour le Rétablissement des Frères Prêcheurs*), 'a middle place between the civil tribunals (which look only to external acts) and the purely voluntary confessional. It is the only court in the world which for three centuries has not shed a drop of blood.' The I. was made use of by the Guises against the Huguenots in France, but not since the Edict of Nantes. The Spanish I. (of which the history has been written by Llorente), after a short period of suspension under Napoleon, was finally suppressed in 1820. The last burning took place in 1781. The punishment of spiritual crimes has now been universally assumed by the secular courts, or by ecclesiastical courts which have received their constitution from the civil law. See the histories of Nigrinus (1582), Paramo (1598), Marsolier (1613), Limborch, the best of the old works (1692), Rule (1874); for I. in France, De la Mothe-Largon (1829); in Spain, Gonsalvi (1567), Arnold (1609), Bebel (1692), Puigblanch (Eng. trans. by Walton, 1816), De Maistre, *Lettres sur l'Inquisition Espagnole* (1822), Hefele, *Ximenes* (2d ed. 1851, trans. by Dalton 1860); in Portugal, Herculano (1858), and at Goa, Dellon (1663). See also Brandt's *Netherlands*, M'Crie's *Spain* and *Italy*, Ranke's *Popes*, the works of Prescott and Motley; and Hauréau, *Bernard Délicieux et l'Inquisition Albigeoise* (Par. 1877). Prescott's statements regarding the I. have been reviewed by Archb. Spalding, *Miscellanea* (1866).

Inrol'ment. For safe custody and evidence, deeds are sometimes inrolled upon the records of a division of the High Court of Justice, or of a Court of Quarter Sessions. I. of a deed does not make it a record. A record is the I. of judicial matter transacted in a court of record, and of which the court takes notice; but I. of a deed is a private act of those concerned.

Insan'ity is 'a condition of the mind in which a false action of conception or judgment, a defective power of the will, or an uncontrollable violence of the emotions and instincts, have, separately or conjointly, been produced by disease, the cerebro-mental disorder being of such a nature as to suspend or impair the action of the healthy will.' *Non compos mentis* is the general legal term used to include persons labouring under mental disabilities, and four classes were comprised under this term by Coke: 1. Idiot, or fool natural, who from his nativity by a perpetual infirmity is *non compos mentis.* 2. A person who was of good sound memory, and by sickness, grief, or other accident wholly loses his memory and understanding. 3. A lunatic, *lunaticus*, who has sometimes his understanding and sometimes not, *qui gaudet lucidis intervallis*, and therefore he is called *non compos mentis* so long as he has not understanding. 4. A person who, by his own vicious acts, for a time deprives himself of his memory and understanding, as he that is drunken; but such a person has no privilege by this voluntary contracted madness.

Various classifications of I. have been proposed by Alienists, and the International Congress of Alienists, at their meeting in Paris in 1867, drew up the following classification, which is a combination of the ætiological and the symptomatological methods:—1. Simple I. comprehends the different varieties of mania, melancholia and monomania, circular I. and mixed I., delusion of persecution, moral I., and the dementia following these different forms of I. 2. Epileptic I. means I. with epilepsy, whether the convulsive affection has preceded the I. and has seemed to have been the cause, or whether it has appeared during the course of the mental disease only as a symptom or complication. 3. Paralytic I. or dementia should be considered as a distinct morbid entity, and not at all as a complication, a termination of certain forms of I. There should be comprehended, then, under the name of paralytic insane, all the insane who show, in any degree whatever, the characteristic symptoms of this disease. 4. Senile dementia is the slow and progressive enfeeblement of the intellectual and moral faculties consequent upon old age. 5. Organic dementia embraces all the varieties of dementia other than the preceding, and which are caused by organic lesions of the brain, nearly always local, and presenting, as almost constant symptoms, hemiplegic occurrences more or less prolonged. 6. Idiocy is characterised by the absence or arrest of the development of the intellectual and moral faculties, imbecility and weakness of mind constituting two degrees or varieties. 7. Cretinism is characterised by a lesion of the intellectual faculties, more or less analogous to that observed in idiocy, but with which is uniformly associated a characteristic vicious conformation of the body, an arrest of the development of the entirety of the organism. Under the titles of 'ill-defined forms,' 'other forms,' are to be set down all the varieties of mental alienation which it shall seem impossible to associate with any of the preceding typical forms. Drs. Bucknill and Tuke, in their standard work on *Psychological Medicine*, group mental defects and disorders under five great divisions:—The *first*, comprising idiocy, imbecility, and cretinism, states of undeveloped intellectual power. The *second*, dementia, a state in which intellectual power has been destroyed. The *third*, delusional insanity, or those states in which marked delusion is present, whether assuming a melancholy character (*Melancholia* with delusion), an exalted character (*Monomania* with delusion; the intellectual monomania of Esquirol), or a distinctive character (*Homicidal* and *Suicidal I.*, &c., with delusion). The *fourth*, emotional I., or morbid states of the emotions without delusion, whether of a melancholy character (*Melancholia simplex*), or of an exalted character (partial exaltation; the affective monomania of Esquirol), or whether marked by a perverted moral sense, or by impulses chiefly of a destructive character (*Homicidal I.*, &c., without delusion or mental weakness; instinctive monomania of Esquirol), constituting moral or emotional I. *proper.* The *fifth*, mania, a state of general mental excitement or exaltation. All these forms or varieties of I. are liable to complication with epilepsy, or, if acquired, with general paralysis. According to the summing-up of the Master in Lunacy in the case of Windham in 1862, 'mere weakness of character, mere liability to impulse, or susceptibility of influence, good or bad, mere imprudence, extravagance, recklessness, eccentricity, or immorality—no, not all these put together would suffice, unless they (the jury) believed themselves justified, on a view of the whole evidence, in referring them to a morbid condition of intellect.' See Shelford's *Law of Lunatics;* Collinson *On Lunacy;* Bucknill and Tuke, *Psychological Medicine* (Lond. 1874); *The Journal of Mental Science* (Lond.).

Insanity, Law Regarding. See IDIOTS AND LUNATICS.

Inscrip'tions (Lat. '*in*, 'on,' and *scribo*, 'I write'), characters engraved on some durable material, as stone or metal, are often of extreme antiquity. How old and widespread the practice was of thus recording public events is shown by the fact that the radical notion of the Gypsy *chinava*, the Gr. *graphō*, the Lat. *scribo*, and the Eng. *write*, is always that of 'scratching' or 'engraving.' The earliest known I.—those of Egypt—are supposed to be at least 500 years older than the first writings on papyrus, being assigned to the reign of Sent, of the second dynasty (3000 B.C.). Next in point of date come the cuneiform I. of Assyria (2000 B.C.); the Chinese (1200 B.C.), the inscription of Yu (2205 B.C.) being of doubtful authenticity; the Phœnician (900 B.C.); the Greek (665 B.C.); the Lycian (530–335 B.C.); the Indian (400 B.C.); and the Roman (145 B.C.). The dates of the Etruscan I., of the Runes of Scandinavia, the Oghams of the Celts, as also of the picture-writings of the Mexican Aztecs, have not yet been determined. With the Renaissance sprang up a taste for the collection of I. as of other antiquities, the discovery of many important monuments—*e.g.*, of the Eugubine Tables—belonging to that period; and in 1663 the Académie des I. was founded by Louis XIV. (See INSTITUTE OF FRANCE.) But up to the present century scholars had confined themselves to the interpretation of Greek and Latin I.; and the hieroglyphics of the Pyramids, the cuneiform records of the rocks of Behistun, the Himyaritic tablets of Southern Arabia, remained a dead letter. The first impulse to their decipherment was given by the discovery of the Rosetta Stone in 1799; and since that date the ancient Egyptian, Zend, Accadian, and other extinct languages have been recovered, mainly through the labours of such men as De Sacy and Champollion, Grotefend and Rask. The gains to the historian and philologist from this branch of study have been immense, as in many instances the sole surviving remains of the history and language of a people were contained in its I. In one case only, that of the Etruscan monuments, have all attempts at interpretation resulted as yet in failure. But the art of decipherment is still young, and some day it will doubtless force from the I. of Etruria the full ethnic and linguistic history of their lost and forgotten founders. A striking instance of the application of that art was furnished in the case of some Norse Runes engraved on one of the stone lions that surmount the entrance to Venice Arsenal. These have been deciphered, from photographs, by Professor Rafn of Copenhagen, and found to record the capture by Harald Hardraga of the Piræus, from which these lions were originally brought to Venice. See CUNEIFORM, EUGUBINE TABLES, GRAFFITI, HIEROGLYPHICS, MOABITE STONE, OGHAMS, ROSETTA STONE, and RUNES.

Insec'ta ('insects'), a class of *Arthropodia* (that is, higher annulose animals, with jointed limbs), distinguished (1) by having the head, chest, and abdomen distinctly marked and separable; (2) by having not more than three pairs of legs in the adult state; (3) by having the legs borne by the thoracic segments only; (4) by usually having two pairs of wings; (5) by the possession of *tracheæ* or air-tubes as the breathing or respiratory organs; and (6) by being provided with a single pair of *antennæ* or 'feelers.' The insect class is one exhibiting a decided uniformity of type and structure. Extreme variations are no doubt seen within its limits, but these variations are themselves sharply marked off from neighbouring classes and groups. The examination of this group of animals may be pursued according to a defined order, beginning with the consideration of the *exoskeleton* or outer layer of the body. In the insect, as in the crustacean, the hard parts of the body form an outer and protecting casing, which also serves for the attachment of muscles. The outer covering of the body in insects is usually of *chitinous* or horny nature; and each somite or joint of the body appears to exhibit a structure composed of six pieces. Thus the upper or back (dorsal) half of each segment is named the *tergum*, the lower half is known as the *sternum*, the side pieces as *pleura*, the sternum being further subdivided into *epimeral* and *episternal* pieces. The *insect body* itself is composed of some twenty segments, of which five or six form the head; the thorax or chest is invariably composed of three joints; while those of the abdomen may number from nine to eleven. The *head segments* are united to form an apparently single mass; and the appendages of this region are modified for sensory purposes, and also to serve as masticatory organs, or those connected with the mouth apparatus. The appendages of the *head* may be examined in order, and consist of *eyes*, *antennæ* or feelers, and the *organs of the mouth*. The antennæ of insects never exceed two in number, and present great variations in form and size. In their simplest form they exist as straight, jointed filaments, but in many insects they are forked, in others club-shaped, while in some they may mimic forms of vegetation, and appear in the likeness of ferns and other objects. The function of these antennæ is undoubtedly that of acting as organs of touch; but it is highly probable that they may subserve other functions, *e.g.*, taste, or even hearing. The *eyes* of insects consist of simple eyes or *ocelli*, and of large *compound* eyes, the latter being formed of aggregations of simple eyes. Each simple eye consists of a little hexagonal *facet*, and includes a *lens*, nerve filament, and other structures entering into the essential composition of an eye. In many insects large numbers of facets exist in the compound eyes. The ants have 50 facets, some butterflies 4000. The eyes may be supported on short stalks or *peduncles*, but the latter are never movable, as in crustaceans. The organs of the *mouth* in insects present a striking *homology* or similarity in fundamental structure. Two chief types of mouth are found in insects. The biting or *masticatory* mouth is well shown in beetles. It includes (*a*) a *labrum* or upper lip, (*b*) a pair of *mandibles* or larger jaws, which in insects never bear *palpi* or organs of touch, (*c*) a pair of lesser jaws or *maxillæ*, which bear one or two pairs of *palpi* (*maxillary palpi*), and (*d*) a lower lip or *labium*, with *labial palpi*, this latter structure being in reality composed of a coalescent and second pair of maxillæ. This latter and primitive condition of the *labium* is seen in Orthopterous insects and certain *Neuroptera*. Other structures often mentioned in connection with the mouth of insects are the *ligula* or front portion of the labium; the ligula being sometimes divided (as in some beetles—*Carabidæ*—and in bees) into three lobes, of which the two outer are named the *paraglossæ*, the middle process being termed the *lingua* or tongue. The second form of mouth is termed *suctorial*. It is seen in butterflies, and is adapted for the prehension of flower juices. Here the same parts are to be viewed as in the mouth of the beetle, only having undergone considerable modifications, and exhibiting a functional adaptation to the work of suction. The (*a*) labrum is now rudimentary, as also are the (*b*) mandibles, but the (*c*) maxillæ are drawn out, and are greatly elongated to form a tubular organ, the *anthia* or *proboscis*, by means of which flower juices are sucked up. The maxillary palpi are small, and the (*d*) labium is small, but its palpi are greatly developed, and form two hairy pads or cushions, between which the proboscis is coiled up when at rest. Thus we find in the butterfly the same fundamental composition of mouth as in the beetle. In wasps and bees, a variety of mouth is found which presents us with a combination of the masticatory and suctorial types. The (*a*) labrum and (*b*) mandibles exist as in the beetle; the (*c*) maxillæ being developed to form long sheaths protecting the (*d*) labium, which exists as in the form of a tongue. In the bugs and their allies (*Hemiptera*), the (*b*) mandibles and (*c*) maxillæ exist as sharp lancets, while the (*d*) labium forms a protective sheath. In the flies (*Diptera*), the (*d*) labium undergoes a great development, and forms a prominent tongue, the other parts of the mouth being developed simply as sheaths to the labium. The *thorax* or chest of the insect consists of three segments, named respectively, as we proceed backwards, the *prothorax*, *mesothorax*, and *metathorax*. The prothorax bears the first pair of legs; the mesothorax, the second pair of legs and first pair of wings; and the metathorax, the third pair of legs and second pair of wings. The *legs* of insects may be more numerous in the larval than in the adult stage, and may be terminated in various ways. The last joints of the leg constitute the *tarsus*. The *wings* are delicate expansions of the integument, and consist each of two delicate membranes, between which the supporting ribs or *nervures* are stretched. The nervures are in reality hollow tubes, and are to be regarded as extensions of the *respiratory* or breathing system, the wings being adapted by their movements to assist in respiration. In most insects two wings are developed; in the flies the front pair only is present; and in the *stylops*, or bee-parasite, the hinder pair is alone represented; whilst in the lice, fleas, and in the females of some winged genera (*e.g.*, cockroaches), wings may be wanting. The *muscles* of insects lie beneath the integument, of which, indeed, they form a mere continuation. The fibres of the muscles are not gathered into distinct bundles as in higher animals, and exhibit in many cases a *striated* or striped structure. The muscular system of many insects, and especially in some larvæ, is exceedingly complicated. Lyonnet found in the larva of the goat-moth 228 muscles in the head alone; the entire body possessing 3993 muscles. The muscular power of insects is, relatively to the size of the body, very great. The flea leaps 200 times its own height, and some beetles will support and move about under weights out of all proportion to their size; a beetle weighing a few grains only will escape from a pressure of 20 to 30 ounces. The *digestive system* varies with the habits and food of the animal similarly to the mouth. In *stylops*, or the bee-parasite, and in young bees, the intestine ends in a blind sac; these insects living on fluids, and having no solid excreta to get rid of. There are three coats found on investigating the structure of the digestive system; an inner or *mucous*, a middle or *muscular* coat, and an outer or *peritoneal*. The *œsophagus* or gullet may have a *crop* (the sucking stomach of flies, bees, and butterflies); and a *gizzard* and true stomach or *preventriculus* also exist. There is, in fact, a singular likeness between the confirmation of the digestive system of birds and that of insects. The intestine is divided into a *small* and *large* portion. *Salivary glands* exist in the mouth in many cases. No true *liver* exists, the place of this gland being supplied by *biliary tubes*. The *kidneys* are represented by *urinary tubes*. The *heart* lies dorsally, or on the back-surface, and consists of a long pulsatile sac, divided into seven or eight compartments separated from each other by valves. The flow of blood through the heart takes place towards the head, each chamber sending blood onwards to the compartment before it. At the head the blood appears to escape from the vessels, and freely circulates slowly through the *sinuses* of the body, or the ill-defined spaces which exist between the various tissues and organs. The blood itself is usually colourless, and contains corpuscular elements. During this latter stage of its circulation, it is subjected to the action of the *respiratory system*, which in insects consists of *air-tubes* or *tracheæ*. Each *trachea* is an elastic tube, formed, like the wing, of two delicate membranes, between which a spiral filament is coiled up; this filament preventing the collapse of the tube and permitting of its adjustment to the movements of the body. The *tracheæ* extend everywhere throughout the body of the insect, being distributed in greatest quantity to the active tissues—such as the muscular tissue—of the body. The insect thus, like the bird, may be said to breathe in every part, and is rendered in this way light and buoyant for flight. The acts of respiration and inspiration are effected by the contraction and expansion of the abdominal segments, aided by the wing movements. The air is admitted to the tracheæ by apertures called *spiracles*, which can be closed at will, and which exist generally to the number of eleven on each side of the body. The *nervous system* lies ventrally, or on the floor of the body, and consists of a chain of *ganglia* or nerve-knots, typically double, but usually united to form a single cord. The *præ-œsophageal* and *infra-œsophageal* ganglia, or those situated above and below the gullet, are especially large. Insects are *diœcious*; that is, have the *sexes* situated in *distinct individuals*. *Reproduction* takes place through the production and development of *ova* or eggs, but in certain cases—exemplified by the case of the *Aphides* or plant-lice—peculiar phenomena may be observed in the generative process, since female insects are known to produce eggs and young without the presence or influence of a male insect. (See PARTHENOGENESIS.) The male organs include a *penis* or copulatory organ, *vesiculæ seminales*, *vasa deferentia*, and *testés*, the latter being glandular and tubular in form, and being situated in the abdominal cavity, on each side of the alimentary canal. The female organs include a simple tubular *ovary* and an *oviduct*; a *spermatheca*, or receptacle in which the male fluid may be stored up being sometimes found—as in queen bees. The *eggs* vary in form and size; and in some insects (*Melophagus* and *Braula*), the *larva*, or young insect, may be perfectly formed before it is expelled from the female organs.

The *development* of I. presents many interesting features connected with the occurrence of what is known as *transformation* or *metamorphosis*. This name is used to indicate the series of changes, of a greater or less extent, which the insect undergoes in passing from its miniature to the adult state. Considered in a cursory manner, *metamorphosis* may be said to correspond to the developmental stages passed by the young of most other animals while still *within* the egg. While within the egg, the body of the insect soon becomes segmented, and sooner or later—in such insects as flies, bees, beetles, and butterflies—escapes from the egg as the *larva* or *caterpillar*. This latter is a worm-like creature, which feeds voraciously, grows largely, and makes for itself an investing case or cocoon, in which it passes the second or *pupa* stage of its existence. Occasionally the *chrysalis* or *pupa case* may be formed by the larval skin. Within the pupa case a wonderful transformation takes place; the larval body being literally broken down by the process of *histolysis*, while its elements are rebuilt and transformed through the process of *histogenesis* into that of the *imago* or perfect insect, which, provided with wings and sexual organs, sooner or later escapes from the pupa case, and ascends into the air in pursuit of a free existence. Such a metamorphosis as that just described is termed *complete* or *holometabolic*. In this case, the larva is unlike the perfect insect or *imago*, and the pupa is quiescent. In the grasshoppers, crickets, dragonflies, bugs, &c., the metamorphosis is termed *incomplete* or *hemimetabolic*. The larval grasshopper, for example, closely resembles the perfect insect in form, and the chrysalis or pupa is active, and differs from the *imago* chiefly in the absence of wings and in the non-development of sexual organs. Some lower insects (lice, spring-tails, &c.) undergo no metamorphosis whatever, and do not differ from the *imago* on leaving the egg, save in respect of size. These latter are named *ametabolic* insects. Metamorphosis in some insects may extend over long periods of time. The cockchaffer passes three years in attaining its perfect form, and the gold beetles and other insects occupy a similar period in undergoing development. The process of development is retarded by cold. Reaumur kept a butterfly pupa for two years in an icehouse, and during that period the insect exhibited no tendency to further development, but became the *imago* on being removed to a warmer place.

Classification of I.—Insects have been classified according to very different methods. Probably the most simple and natural arrangement of the class is that detailed in the following table, in which the characters of the orders are also given:—

	ORDERS.
Section A.—AMETABOLA. Undergoing no metamorphosis and wanting wings; eyes simple, sometimes wanting.	1. ANOPLURA—Ex. Lice. Insects having suctorial mouth and simple eyes only. 2. MALLOPHAGA—Ex. Bird-lice. Mouth masticatory. 3. THYSANURA—Ex. Spring-tails, *Poduræ*, &c. Abdomen having long appendages.
Section B.—HEMIMETABOLA. Metamorphosis incomplete; larva differing from imago chiefly in absence of wings; pupa active.	4. HEMIPTERA—Ex. Bugs. Mouth suctorial, beak-shaped; wings four, with anterior halves horny in some. 5. ORTHOPTERA—Ex. Crickets, Locusts, Grasshoppers, Cockroaches, &c. Wings straight-veined, front pair usually of leathery consistence; mouth masticatory. 6. NEUROPTERA—Ex. Termites, Dragonflies, Mayflies, &c. Mouth masticatory; wings large and membranous; larvæ active and hexapod.
Section C.—HOLOMETABOLA. Metamorphosis complete; larva unlike imago, pupa quiescent.	7. APHANIPTERA—Ex. Fleas. Wings absent; mouth suctorial. 8. DIPTERA—Ex. Flies. Hinder wings absent; mouth suctorial. 9. LEPIDOPTERA—Ex. Butterflies and Moths. Wings four, covered with scales; mouth suctorial. 10. HYMENOPTERA—Ex. Bees, Wasps, Ants. Mouth partly masticatory and partly suctorial; wings four, membranous. 11. STREPSIPTERA—Ex. Stylops or Bee-parasite. Anterior wings wanting, and replaced by twisted filaments; hinder wings developed in males only; jaws rudimentary. 12. COLEOPTERA—Ex. Beetles. Front wings horny, forming elytra or sheaths for the posterior pair; mouth masticatory.

The *origin* of insects (or their *ætiology*), according to Darwin's theory, has been discussed by Sir J. Lubbock, amongst others. This author assumes that insects have 'descended from ancestors more or less resembling the genus *Campodea* (insects belonging to the order *Thysanura*), with a body divided into head, thorax, and abdomen; the head provided with mouth parts, eyes, and one pair of antennæ; the thorax with three pairs of legs; and the abdomen, in all probability, with caudal appendages. . . . From what lower group the Campodea type was itself derived is a question of great difficulty. Fritz Müller, indeed, says, "If all the classes of Arthropoda (Crustacea, Insecta, Myreopoda, and Arachnida) are indeed all branches of a common stem (and of this there can scarcely be a doubt), it is evident that the water-inhabiting and water-breathing Crustacea must be regarded as the original stem from which the other terrestrial classes, with their tracheal respiration, have branched off."' *Fossil* insects are first known to occur in the Devonian rocks of N. America. These earliest fossil forms belong to the *Neuropterous* order. In Carboniferous rocks the remains of *Neuroptera*, *Orthoptera*, and *Coleopterous* insects occur; while in Jurassic formations the orders *Hemiptera* and *Hymenoptera* are first represented. The *Diptera* and *Lepidoptera* first appear in rocks belonging to the Tertiary system.

Insectiv'ora, an order of Mammals, represented by the moles, shrews, hedgehogs, and their allies. In these animals the *Placenta* (q. v.) is discoidal and deciduate, the collar-bones are well developed, and the animals walk on the soles of their feet (*Plantigrade*). The feet have each five toes. Incisor, canine, and molar teeth are present in all cases, the molars being provided with little points or *cusps*, adapted for crushing the insects on which the I. feed. The animals are of small size. They hybernate during winter. As a rule they are subterranean in habits, and active chiefly during the night. They are distributed throughout the world, with the exception of S. America and Australia. The *Talpidæ* (moles), *Soricidæ* (shrew-mice), and *Erinaceidæ* (hedgehogs), are the three included families.

Insesso'res, Pass'eres, or **Perch'ing Birds**, an order of the class Birds (q. v.), distinguished chiefly by the negative characters of the forms included within its limits. They are represented by most of our common and smaller birds. The toes are four in number, and are directed three forwards and one backwards; some forms, however, exemplified by the swifts, having the under toe also turned forwards. The toes and tarsi are covered with scales, and the outer toe is commonly united to the middle toe at its base. The primary quill-feathers of the wings usually number ten, the first of these feathers being generally of small size. The tail is composed in most I. of twelve feathers. The form of the bill varies greatly, and is used as a basis for the classification and division of the order. The chief sections are the *Conirostres* (q. v.), the *Dentirostres* (q. v.), the *Fissirostres* (q. v.), and the *Tenuirostres* (q. v.).

Insol'vency. See BANKRUPTCY.

Inspec'tor (Lat. *inspicio*, 'I look into'), a military title somewhat loosely applied to any officer charged with regimental or half-yearly inspection, &c. There are inspectors-general of infantry, cavalry, and artillery, of musketry and volunteers, and also in the medical branch of the service of hospitals. In the police force an I. is the officer next in rank to a superintendent.

Inspec'torship, Deed of, is a deed by which inspectors of the dealings of an insolvent person are appointed for a limited period, or till he has paid his debts, or such composition *for them* as the creditors have agreed to accept. See BANKRUPTCY.

Inspectors of Schools. See PUBLIC SCHOOLS.

Inspira'tion (Lat. *inspiratio*, from *in*, and *spiro*, 'I breathe'), according to the orthodox doctrine of the Church, means the influence of the Holy Spirit on the minds of the writers of the Scriptures, which rendered them the organs of God for the infallible communication of his mind and will, and in virtue of which the Scriptures are regarded as the Word of God. The earliest theory of I. (1), held regarding the Old Testament Scriptures by the Jews, and afterwards applied by Christians both to the Old Testament and New Testament, regarded it as *verbal*, meaning that the very words and phrases as well as the subject-matter emanated from the Holy Spirit. In reference to the manner in which the human agents are affected, this has been called the Mechanical theory, according to which the sacred writers were mere automata in the hands of the Spirit, as pens which wrote what he dictated, or as harps from which he drew what sounds he pleased. It is unnecessary to enter into objections to this theory, because in its original extreme form it is now generally abandoned in favour of (2) *Plenary* I., which is defined as a divine influence which is 'full and sufficient to secure its end,' that end being 'the perfect infallibility of the Scriptures in every part as a record of faith and doctrine, both in thought and verbal expression.' According to this definition, *plenary* I. does not differ much from *verbal* I. in its results. The chief difference lies in the manner in which it is held to operate on the human agents. According to this theory, which has been called the Dynamical, the Holy Spirit is regarded as exerting an influence which guides and directs the human agents, not as exerting a power which supersedes all their energies. The sacred writers, who were employed as the organs of God, so that what they taught he taught, were used according to their different natures and their peculiar gifts and endowments, writing out of the fulness of their own thoughts and feelings, and employing the language and modes of expression which were the most natural and appropriate to them. The proofs adduced that this is the Scriptural view of I. are as follows:—1. From the signification and usage of the word, as in 2 Tim. iii. 16; 2 Pet. i. 21. 2. From the meaning of the word 'prophet,' who is represented in the Old Testament as the mouth of God:—Isa. li. 16; Jer. i. 9, *cf.* Jer. xxxvi. 17, 18; Exod. iv. 14–16, vii. 1. 3. From the declarations that what the prophets said the Spirit said:—Matt. xxii. 43; Ps. xcv. 8, *cf.* Heb. iii. 7; Jer. xxxi. 33–34, *cf.* Heb. x. 15–17; Ps. ii. 1, *cf.* Acts iv. 25; Acts xxviii. 25. II. The I. of the New Testament writers in the same way is held to be proved:—(1) By the promise of the Holy Spirit given by Christ; (2) a promise which was fulfilled on the day of Pentecost; (3) after which they claim to be the infallible organs of God in all their teaching (*cf.* 1 Cor. xiv. 37; 1 Thess. ii. 13; 1 John v. 10); (4) by the testimony of St. Paul (1 Cor. ii. 7–13); (5) claims which were all duly authenticated by (*a*) the nature of the truths which they communicated, (*b*) the power which these truths exerted, (*c*) the inward witness of the Spirit (1 John v. 10, ii. 20), and (*d*) miraculous gifts (2 Cor. xii. 12; Heb. ii. 4).

It is objected to this theory of *plenary* I. that the sacred writers (1) contradict (*a*) themselves and (*b*) each other, and (2) teach error—what is false in history, science, and morality. To which it is replied (1) in reference to the discrepancies and contradictions, that (*a*) they are for the most part trivial, (*b*) the great majority are only apparent, (*c*) many of them may fairly be ascribed to the errors of transcribers, and (*d*) the marvel and the miracle is that there are so few of any real importance. (2) In answer to the second class of objections it is remarked, (*a*) that we must distinguish between what the sacred writers themselves thought or believed, and what they teach; (*b*) that the language of the Bible being that of common life, is founded upon apparent and not upon scientific truth; (*c*) that there is a great distinction between theories, which are often contradicted by the Bible, and facts, which never are; and (*d*) that there is also a distinction to be made between the Bible and our interpretation of it, the latter of which must yield if proved to be wrong.

Other theories of I. may be noticed:—1. That which goes by the name of *gracious* I., according to which the sacred writers were merely holy men under (1) the ordinary guidance of the Spirit, or (2) a pre-eminent degree of spiritual illumination. 2. The theory of *partial* I. One form of which (1) is that only some parts of the Bible are infallible; *e.g.* (*a*) the Law and the Prophets, (*b*) the New Testament, or (*c*) the discourses of Christ, respectively. (2) Others limit the I. to the doctrinal teaching, as distinguished from mere matters of fact; (3) others, to the thoughts as distinguished from the words; and (4) others hold that there were different degrees of divine guidance. 3. Some have held that I. was simply an exaltation of intuitional consciousness, *i.e.*, that it took the place in the writers of great genius and great goodness, with the same results. See Hodge's *Syst. Theology* (Edinb. 1873); Gaussen's *Theopneustia* (Lond. 1841).

Installa'tion, in church law, means the ceremony by which a canon or prebendary is legally confirmed in a benefice. The similar ceremony for the confirmation of a bishop is 'enthronisation;' for that of a rector, 'induction.'

In'sterburg, a town of Prussia in the province of E. Preussen, on the Inster, 60 miles E. of Königsberg by rail, has manufactures of beet-sugar, woollens, cottons, hosiery, and machinery. A number of Scottish families settled in trade here in the 17th c. I. was once a seat of the Teutonic knights. Pop. (1875) 16,380.

In'stinct (Lat. *instinctus*, from *instinguere*, 'to urge on'), the general name under which the nervous acts of lower animals, as applied to the regulation of their lives, are included. The term, however, has been commonly restricted to denominate those acts more especially in which the lower animals appear to imitate the actions of man. Very frequently, however, this distinction is more apparent than real. Impulses of the same nature, as far as observation or hypothesis may determine, animate man and lower animals; for example, when danger threatens, and when the 'I.' of self-preservation becomes a leading idea in the mind. Many acts of man's life are regulated by experience, and are primarily gained through experience, in the same manner in which many lower animals gain a knowledge of their surroundings. At the same time, and while admitting the common origin and similar nature of many of the acts of man and lower animals, there exists in the operations of the human mind an evident appreciation of the nature and reasons of its own operations and working. We have, in fact, to account for the due explanation of the superiority of man's mental organisation, by admitting the development of *consciousness* or the knowledge of self, and of the why and wherefore of our acts. As Dr. Carpenter remarks, the study of comparative anatomy demonstrates that it is in man that the *cerebrum* or true brain attains its highest development, and it is in man that the degree of *intelligence*—'using the latter term as a comprehensive expression of that series of mental actions which consists in the *intentional* adaptation of means to ends, based on definite *ideas* as to the nature of both'—is found accordingly to attain its highest phase. Brain development and the possession of an *intelligence* which stands out in marked contrast to pure unreasoning *instinct*, stand in a direct ratio to each other. '*Instinctive* actions,' according to Dr. Carpenter, 'are performed automatically, in obedience to internal impulses, without even the perception of their adaptiveness on the part of the being who is the agent in them; these impulses being called into play by impressions on the nervous system, which are made either by external objects, or by changes in the individual organism.' The justness of this distinction becomes obvious when we analyse our own consciousness, and distinguish our own instinctive actions from those which involve intelligence; for we are thus led to perceive that, in regard to those operations which are most closely concerned in the maintenance of our own lives, and in the continuance of the race, provision has been made in the mechanism of the automatic portion of our nervous system, so as to render them independent of the exercise of Intelligence or the asertion of the Will on our part. 'Thus,' continues Dr. Carpenter, 'the infant seeks the nipple, and puts its muscles into suctorial action, without any knowledge that by so doing it will relieve the uneasy feeling of hunger; and if we could imagine a man coming into the world with the full possession of all his faculties, we may feel tolerably certain that he would not wait to eat until he had learned by experience his dependence upon food.'

Some recent utterances on the *automatic doctrine* of animals appear to have confused in a singular manner the faculties which man exhibits in virtue of his intelligent consciousness, and those which the lower animals exhibit in virtue of their lower instincts alone. That many acts in man are of automatic or instinctive and unreasoning character cannot be denied; but this admission is by no means tantamount to the assertion that *all* human acts are such. It may even be rationally supposed that the intelligence and consciousness of man has arisen gradually out of the original automatism of his nature; just as the infant, as it grows, gradually acquires through experience the knowledge and consciousness of its own existence and of its surroundings. But from the analysis of our own mental acts we conclude that we not only possess a conscious intelligent knowledge of ourselves, but that through this intelligence we possess the power of specially adapting the acts of our lives to whatever circumstances may from time to time arise and affect us. It is unquestionably in this latter phase of their character that human acts differ most typically from the mere *instincts* of lower animals. The chief characters of purely instinctive acts may be briefly summarised as consisting (1) in their marked *uniformity* and *unvarying repetition* in and by the individuals of the species which exhibit them; (2) in their being performed under such circumstances (as when a *newly-born* ant or bee enters at once on the performance of all its duties) that the idea of *experience* is completely negatived; (3) by their being performed under circumstances strongly suggestive of the *absence* of adaptive intelligence, as, for example, 'when a tame beaver attempts to build its dam across a room, or when bees attempt to make a new *queen* out of a drone (or male) larva.' The operations of intelligence and reason, on the contrary, are not only performed with a *purposive character*, but are susceptible of *gradual improvement* under the tuition of experience.

In'stitute a term of Scotch entail law denoting the person first in the destination. Those that follow are called *substitutes*.

In'stitute of France, a corporative body comprising the five great scientific and artistic societies of Paris, is a lineal descendant of the French Academy, founded with forty members by Richelieu, 25th January 1635, for the cultivation of the language generally, and the special work of preparing a (hitherto, 1877, unfinished) dictionary. The French Academy, with the affiliated Academies of Fine Arts (1648), Sciences (1666), and Inscriptions (1701), was suppressed at the Revolution by the Convention, 8th August 1793, and replaced under the Directory, 25th October 1795, by the National Institute, which, consisting of 144 members, was divided into the three classes, physics and mathematics, literature and fine arts, morals and politics. Of these classes, the last was abolished, and the two first broken up into four, by Napoleon, 23d January 1810; whilst with the Bourbon restoration came the re-establishment of the four ante-revolutionary academies, which, increased to five by the addition of an Academy of Morals and Politics, 26th October 1832, have ever since constituted the I. of F., its prefix only—Royal, National, or Imperial—varying with the corresponding changes in the form of government.

In its present form, then, the Institute consists of (1) the French Academy with 40 members, an annual State grant of 85,000 francs, prizes for eloquence and history of 4000 francs, the Montyon prize for virtue of 20,000 francs, and the Gobert history prize of 10,000 francs; (2) the Academy of Inscriptions and Belles Lettres, with 40 ordinary, 10 honorary, 8 foreign, and 50 corresponding members, and a second Gobert history prize; (3) the Academy of Sciences, having 65 ordinary, 10 honorary, 8 foreign, and 100 corresponding members, and eleven prizes, several of them of 10,000 francs apiece; (4) the Academy of Fine Arts, with 40 ordinary, 10 honorary, 10 foreign, and 40 corresponding members; and (5) the Academy of Morals and Politics, which has 40 ordinary, 6 honorary, 6 foreign, and 40 corresponding members. Thus, in all, there are 225 ordinary, 36 honorary, and 230 corresponding members, with 32 foreign associates. In the list of foreigners connected with the Institute occur the familiar names of Herschel, Faraday, Hamilton, Max Müller, and Grote, while of its French members may be mentioned Ampère, Arago, Gay Lussac, Thiers, Michelet, Gerôme—all, indeed, that are most distinguished in French literature, art, and science of the present century. The Institute holds two public sessions weekly, on Monday and Friday, at 3 P.M., in the Palais de l'Institut, opposite the Louvre.

In'stitutes, the name given to the treatise on the principles of Roman Law (q. v.) drawn up in the reign of Justinian (q. v.).

Institu'tion, in church law, is the ceremony by which a bishop commits to a clerk who is presented to a church living the spiritual welfare of its people.

In'strument is a semi-technical term in the law of England denoting a testamentary writing, and sometimes it is used in a wider sense. In Scotch law it is usually applied to notarial documents.

Instrumenta'tion, the art of using several musical instruments in combination, or of writing appropriately for the 'Orchestra' (q. v.). See Berlioz's *Modern I. and Orchestration* (Lond. 1858).

Instruments, Musical, are of three classes—(1) stringed I.; (2) wind I.; (3) I. of percussion. In the first class the strings may be touched by the fingers (*e.g.*, harp), by a bow (*e.g.*, violin), or by hammers (*e.g.*, pianoforte). The organ, trumpet, oboe, and flute are representative examples of the second class; the first has bellows and keyboard, the second is of brass, the third has reeds, the fourth has no reeds. The drum is an instrument of percussion.

Insurance, Life. Insurance, as a prosperous business, did not to any large extent exist before the 19th c. It has now become for the upper and middle classes almost as great an institution as the benefit societies of the lower classes. It is used not merely as a family provision, but as a security in loans. It is also the easiest and safest method of saving money. The business is carried on by—(1) Mutual societies, of which the members insure one another, a guarantee fund being formed, and the whole surplus profits going to increase the value of the policies; (2) Proprietary companies, of which the shareholders give to the public the security of their subscribed capital, and are therefore entitled in the first place to the profits. But competition has caused most proprietary companies to give a large share of the profits to the policy-holders, who therefore in many cases secure not merely an insurance against risk, but a very profitable investment. As an Act of 1870 requires a deposit of £20,000 from new companies, it is unlikely that more mutual societies will come into existence. There are many varieties of L. I. business. The Tontine principle was a scale of benefits varying with the age of the policy. Most companies offer a choice of rates for participation or non-participation in profits; and the premium, or consideration given by the assured, may be paid in many different ways. In all cases, however, the contract is only renewable annually, and the company does not undertake to continue its business beyond the year. The liability is to pay only on death, but a small surrender-value is usually given when A, who has paid a certain number of premiums, wishes to drop his policy. The huge failures of the Albert and the European, caused by reckless amalgamation, have called public attention to the financial principles of L. I.; and under an Act of 1870 the companies are obliged to return to the Board of Trade certain accounts which are supposed to test their solvency. In the premiums charged there are three elements: the pure risk, the rate of interest on investment, and the loading for expenses. Even as regards the first two, the practice is various. The chief tables, or tabulated results of mortality, on which the calculation of risk has been based, are the Carlisle, the Northampton, the seventeen offices' experience, and the recently published experience of the Institute. Each company adjusts its theoretical expectation of life to its own experience. The results are no doubt in some degree temporary and local, but, together with a careful selection of lives, they are enough to make L. I. the safest of all businesses. The reports of the Registrar-General are of great use in determining the special risks which are accepted at special rates. The interest allowed for in the premium may be 3, 3½, or 4. It is in the matter of expenses of management and excessive commission to agents that the most discreditable features and the greatest varieties of L. I. occur. Commissions to solicitors and other persons not insurance agents is simply a robbing of the public. Comparative freedom from this was one element of strength in the mutual companies. A fair test of the soundness of an office which has been in existence for some years is to observe the percentage which working expenses bear to premium income. It was excessive expenditure that led to foolish amalgamation, by which women and aged persons often found that their solvent debtor had disappeared without notice, leaving an insolvent substitute behind. By an Act of 1872, however, the public are so far protected that 'novation' will now be held not to have taken place where an agreement to that effect has not been signed. Little requires to be said of the legal aspects of the familiar contract of L. I. It is not a contract of indemnity, but it is one in which the most exuberant good faith is required from both parties. Obviously, it depends on a true disclosure of health, age, profession, and every other circumstance which materially affects the risk.

Accident Insurance has very recently become a large business. 'Millions of people cannot afford to be run over;' and the leading feature of this business is to insure against complete or partial disablement through accidental causes, against which the assured could not reasonably protect himself, and to which he has not contributed by acting illegally or negligently. Very various classifications of professions and trades, as more or less hazardous, are used. Special policies for railway accidents are issued, and the risk of death is often included. Injuries due to somnambulism, intoxication, or inflicted by other persons, are generally excluded.

Marine Insurance was in its primitive form merely a loan or advance, repayable on safe arrival, the *fœnus nauticum* (12 per cent.) of the Roman Empire escaping the rules of the Church against interest. This is seen in the *Bödemerey* of the *Recessus* of Lübeck; indeed, bottomry seems to be of Hanseatic, not Mediterranean, origin. The first regular Chamber of Assurance is mentioned as at Bruges in 1310 by the *Chronyk van Vlændern.* In England, probably a system of mutual guarantee prevailed among the Easterlings of the steelyard; the famous Act of 43 Eliz. c. 12, erecting a special court to try M. I. cases, speaks of the policy as an immemorial usage. Premiums of insurance, 'preus de seguretats,' are traced in 1435 at Barcelona, where over-insurance, 'valegnen mes o menys,' is prohibited, and also the insurance of foreign vessels. At Venice, in 1468, the Pregadi denounce deck-loading under severe penalties. At Florence *scritta* or underwriting was supervised by public *deputati*, and *sensali*, or brokers. It was undoubtedly the Lombards, the 'Pope's merchants' in London, who introduced to England the word *polizza*, or promise, and the phrase till lately used, 'In the name of God' (Dio la Salvi). Every policy issued at Lloyd's still refers to Lombard Street. From the *Guidon de la Mer* (Rouen, 1590), it appears that unwritten insurances, called 'confidence bargains,' were at one time the rule. The spread of M. I. in England was hindered by 'Cauder's patent,' a monopoly granted by Elizabeth, which threw 120 notaries-public out of work. Among the 'Kauphy' houses of London in the 17th c., which gave an impetus to the business, was that of Edward Lloyd in Tower Street, and afterwards in Lombard Street, described in the *Tatler* and the *Spectator.* In 1696 *Lloyd's News* was started for six months, to reappear in 1726 as *Lloyd's List*, both being summaries of commercial intelligence. The miscellaneous auction pulpit at Lloyd's was gradually restricted to the shipping trade, and it became a meeting-place for underwriters. In 1720 Speaker Onslow and Lord Chetwynd obtained by payments to Exchequer the charters of the 'London Assurance Corporation' and the 'Royal Exchange Assurance Corporation.' This monopoly against insurance partnerships was said to be required from the frequent failures of private insurers. The underwriters retained about nine-tenths of the business. The *List* was published twice a week; the early entries from Greenock are fifteen days after date. About 1770 gambling insurance on public events having become very common, the underwriters acquired the property of the *List*, and shortly after, under the leadership of J. Augerstein, removed to the Royal Exchange, where they founded New Lloyd's. In 1786 appeared the work of Park summing up the judicial decisions of Lord Mansfield, who had now elaborated the distinction between valued and open policies, the prime cost being expressed in the former, voyage and time policies, warranties of seaworthiness and representations, particular and general average, &c. There is no branch of law in which sound common sense and the usage of trade have had a larger share in determining. The policies were generally 'warranted free from average, except general or the ship be stranded,' but by an Act in 1746 open-water policies, 'interest or no interest,' were prohibited. In 1779 the present printed form of policy was adopted by New Lloyd's. The American and French wars made insurance much more general, and Lloyd's was recognised by the Government as superintending the despatch of convoys, and consulted for news and with regard to commercial treaties. In 1802 Lloyd's distinguished themselves by founding the Lifeboat Institution, and next year they started the Patriotic Fund by a subscription of £20,000. From the evidence given before a committee in 1810 it appeared that M. I. was very profitable, but that the underwriters dealt very liberally with respectable merchants. This committee considered the question of repealing the monopoly of 1820, but this was not done until in 1824, when Nathan Rothschild, Montefiore, and Gompertz got an Act incorporating the 'Alliance.' Attention was called in 1810 to the imperfect laws punishing insurance frauds, which, though Walpole in 1725 had extended them to barratry against the writers and by the owners, still permitted the owners to recover on the policies. The case of Captain Codling in 1802 had revealed an immense amount of systematic scuttling, and it was stated that one-third of insurance claims were fraudulent. The 'Alliance' was followed by the 'Indemnity' and the 'Marine,' the latter of which in 1867–69 paid dividends of 44 per cent. The Limited Liability Acts brought many more into existence, and the American War gave them artificial profits for several years. The recent history of the trade is contained in *The Underwriting of* 1872, by Mr. Danson, Liverpool. Lloyd's had a ship's list or registry as early as 1730. In 1780 the appointment of surveyors is traced. The classification was so strict that for thirty-four years the shipowners had a rival register called the *Long Shore Book*, a very worthless production. In 1834 both this and Lloyd's *Old Book* were merged in *Lloyd's Register of British and Foreign Shipping*, which is managed by a committee of merchants, shipowners, and writers (twenty-four of London and fifteen from the chief outposts), and employs fifty-two surveyors in the United Kingdom and fifty abroad, and is represented by 1200 agents. The income from survey fees and sale of registers is £40,000 per annum. There are five classes of wooden ships: viz., A (black), A (red), Æ, E, I. Iron vessels are certified as $\underset{A}{A}$, $\underset{B}{A}$, $\underset{C}{A}$. About one-half of British vessels are placed in the register, and one-half of that number (or 8000) are classed, the rest being expunged, expired, or without character assigned. There is a French Lloyd's, called Bureau Veritas, managed by M. Bal, which grants certificates much more easily. The English Lloyd's, consisting of 710 members, was incorporated by statute in 1871. The M. I. companies subscribe for information, on which more than £10,000 per annum is spent. The index showing the precise whereabouts and character of a ship, and the 'captain's register,' giving a sketch of each officer, are marvels of skilful arrangement constantly revised. The rates of premiums for the great ocean routes depend on the time of year, on an analysis of the wreck registers of the Board of Trade, and on the cargo and character of the ship.

Fire Insurance has been traced back to 1667, when the 'Fire Office' issued policies in London. Shortly after the great fire the corporation of London undertook the business. The sixpenny stamp was imposed in 1694. Before this there existed a practice of asking compensation for fire by fire briefs issued by the Chancellor to a particular locality. On the Continent, just as fire, water, and robbery were provided against by the ancient gilds, so in the customary laws which succeeded them (notably in the Cora or Customs of Furnes, A.D. 1240) special notice is taken of fires. Quite recently the experiments of compulsory state and municipal F. I., carried out in Zurich, Denmark, and Poland, have been very seriously discussed in the United States. During the 18th c. the rule seems to have been to insure three-fourths value only. In 1776 Adam Smith observed that only one house in 100 was insured against fire. In 1802 Sir F. M. Eden estimated the insurable property in the United Kingdom at 612 millions. Braidwood's *Fire Engine*, &c., published at Edinburgh in 1830, gives local statistics of some interest. Porter in his *Progress of the Nation* shows that in the first half of the 19th c. the sums *insured* increased 210 per cent.; the total in 1867 being 722 millions. About the same time Mr. Samuel Brown made the first serious effort in the statistics of the subject, and found that in 100 cases, buildings and contents were insured in 37, buildings only in 15, contents only in 14, and neither in 33. The London Fire Brigade Records, published in 1870, show the principal causes of fire very minutely, the chief being—candles, 11 per cent.; curtains, 9 per cent.; flues, 7 per cent.; gas, 7 per cent.; sparks of fire, 4 per cent.; unknown, 32 per cent. The fires from unknown causes are naturally the more destructive, and they visibly increase as trade becomes depressed. In 1869 the *percentage* duty was wholly abolished. In 1872, the fire premiums received by twenty-six British offices amounted to £5,297,762; their losses to £3,722,504; and in 1874 the business done in London alone reached the sum of £540,000,000. The contract of F. I. is one of indemnity, and the insurer may either restore the property or pay the fair value. As a general rule, rent and profits are not insured, but floating and blanket policies are common; they cover the excess beyond specific policies, wherever the goods may lie. Misstatement of value vitiates a policy. The difficult question of adjustment between these policies are treated in *The Average Clause*, by Mr. Atkins, published 1866. Generally, also, goods held in trust or commission are excluded, and special rates charged for valuables and dangerous localities. Other subjects of indemnity insurance are cattle, glass, steam-boiler, carriage, &c. In hail insurance the principle of consequential damages is admitted. Fire business is done by companies: there is only one private fire underwriter in the world, viz., Mr. Wheeden of Baltimore, U.S.

Intaglio (pron. *intalyo*, Ital. 'an incision') denotes engraved work sunk into a gem, as distinguished from work in relief. (See CAMEO.) The cylindrical seals of the Assyrians exhibit the earliest known work of this kind. The ancient Greeks and Romans produced *intagli* of great beauty in abundance, and set them in signet rings. The artists of the Renaissance, and more recent periods, executed their work on a larger field than the ancient gem-engravers.

In'tegral Cal'culus and **Integra'tion.** See CALCULUS.

In'tellect. See MIND.

Intem'perance means, in a general sense, want of moderation or due restraint, and hence, appropriately and emphatically, habitual indulgence in spirituous liquors, with or without intoxication. Spirituous liquors are obtained from a variety of sources in different parts of the world, and are in general use in most countries. The *arrack* of the Hindus and Malays is obtained from rice or areca-nut; the *raki* of the Greeks and Turks, from rice; the *toddy* of the Hindus, from the cocoa-nut; the *bojah* of the Mahrattas, and the *murwa* of the Sikkim, from eleusine corocana; the *samshoo* of the Chinese, and the *sâcie* of the Japanese, from rice; the *kawa* of the Pacific Islanders, from macropiper; the *pulque* of the Mexicans, from agave; the *chica* of the S. Americans, from maize; the *koumiss* of the Tartars, from mares' milk; the *vodki* of the Russians and Poles, from potato; the *tallah* of the Abyssinians, from millet; and the *alcoholic stimulants* in general use among European nations, from a well-known variety of sources. Probably the sole reason why alcoholic stimulants are in such general use consists in the hilarity produced as an immediate effect. The agreeable exhilaration which follows their use is, however, transient in its nature, and, in order to keep it up, repeated doses must be taken, eventually resulting in I., and the formation of a morbid appetite or craving for stimulants. Until recently, science sanctioned the belief that alcohol is a food, which, in the advancing stages of civilisation, becomes more requisite than ever; but investigation now shows that it is only entitled to a place among the *luxuries*, and not among the *necessaries* of life. The physiological and medicinal action of alcohol has been discussed under *Alcohol* (q. v.); but it is a matter of the highest importance to determine when the extreme limit of the useful effect of alcohol is reached. On the supposition that the appearance of alcohol in the urine is a sign that as much has been taken as can be disposed of by the body, and that this indicates the commencement of the poisonous stage, manifested by narcosis, loss of appetite, increased rapidity of the heart's action, and dilatation of the small vessels, Drs. Anstie and Parkes and Count Wollowiez ascertained, by a series of rigid experiments on powerful healthy men, accustomed to the use of alcohol, that the extreme limit of the useful effect is produced by some quantity between 1 and 1½ fluid ounces in twenty-four hours. The experiments were not intended to show that the daily use of alcohol to this amount was necessary or even beneficial, but to mark the limit beyond which the use of alcohol was positively injurious, or the extreme boundary line between temperance and intemperance. Dr. B. W. Richardson recently made a series of elaborate scientific researches on alcohol which he summarises as follows:—'I learned purely by experimental observation that, in its action on the living body, this chemical substance, alcohol, deranges the constitution of the blood; unduly excites the heart and the respiration; paralyses the minute blood-vessels; increases and decreases, according to the degree of its application, the functions of the digestive organs, of the liver, and of the kidneys; disturbs the regularity of nervous action; lowers the animal temperature; and lessens the muscular power.' The results of the purely scientific researches of Drs. Parker, Anstie, and Richardson are strikingly confirmed by experience. No one can entertain a moment's doubt that the effect of I. in any alcoholic beverage is to cause premature old age, to predispose to, and result in, organic diseases which greatly shorten life; but very remarkable evidence in support of the scientific deductions of Dr. Richardson is given by the statistics of the United Kingdom Temperance and General Provident Institution. One section consists of abstainers, and another of persons selected as not known to be intemperate. The claims for five years (1860–70) anticipated in the temperance section were £100,446; but there were actually only claims for £72,676. In the general section, the anticipated claims were £196,352 and the actual claims were no less than £230,297. The amount of bonuses paid to each £1000 whole-life policy in the two sections for the same five years shows the much greater longevity of the abstaining section, and demonstrates that at every age at entrance the abstainer has a very great advantage, even over those who, though not intemperate, use alcohol in what is called moderation. The section of non-abstainers showed a mortality of 7 per cent. below the calculated average of life, and from bonuses of premium paid received 34 per cent.; but the section of abstainers showed a mortality of 26 per cent. below the average, and received from bonuses 53 per cent. In regard to the administration of alcoholic stimulants in *sickness*, Dr. Parkes says, 'I believe they are often of great use, although, like many other strong medicines, they require to be given carefully. The fashionable plan of giving great quantities of strong spirits is happily dying out, and is being replaced by a more careful practice.' Sir Henry Thomson says, 'As with many other medicines, its employment is apt to be greatly abused, and thus wine or spirit is taken when not in the least degree necessary, often when it is absolutely injurious; for people who enjoy tolerable health, but nevertheless find *digestion slow* or *imperfect*, or *the circulation languid*—popular forms of excuse for taking wine—it seems to me more frequently a dangerous snare than a tolerable remedy.' See *Practical Hygiene*, by Dr. Parkes (Lond. 1873); *Medical History of the War in the Crimea*, by Sir John Hall (vol. i.); *Physiology of Temperance*, by Dr. Carpenter; *Degenerative Changes induced by Alcohol*, by Dr. Dickinson (*Lancet*, November 1872); *Diseases of Modern Life*, by Dr. Richardson (Lond. 1876); and a *Course of Six Cantor Lectures*, delivered before the Society of Arts, by Dr. Richardson. See also articles on ALCOHOL, DELIRIUM TREMENS, and DIPSOMANIA.

Inten'dant (Lat. *intendens*, 'attending to'), one who has the oversight of some special department, as I. of Marine, I. of Finance, &c. In France, before the revolution of 1789, the Intendants of the provinces answered to the modern Préfets (q. v.). They dated from the 16th c., but owed their definite organisation to Richelieu (1636). At present the name *Intendants Militaires* is applied to an administrative corps which superintends the commissariat, pay, quarters, &c., of the troops in the field. It was established July 29, 1819, and consists of an I.-in-chief, 28 intendants, 140 sub-intendants, and 80 adjutants.

Inter'calary Day, in the calendar, is a day inserted at certain periods to keep the civil year approximately coincident with the solar year. The 29th of February, which is inserted every fourth or *leap* year, is of this character.

Intercess'ion of Christ with God for sinners, in theological language, is the exercise of his priestly office, in which he is engaged for ever at the right hand of the Father. Man's need of an intercessor arose from his loss of the right of communion with God by the Fall, a privilege which was restored in Christ, who was constituted our high priest by the union of his divine and human natures, the latter furnishing both priest and victim (Heb. iv. 15, vii. 25, ix. 14). It is held by Roman Catholics, as well as certain other Christians, that saints in heaven are to some extent partakers with Christ in this work of I. See INVOCATION OF SAINTS.

Intercolumnia'tion (Lat. *intercolumnium*, from *inter*, 'between,' and *columna*, 'a column'), the space between two columns of a building, which, among the ancients, might be of various extent—either aræostyle, 4 diameters of the shaft of the column; diastyle, 3; eustyle, 2¼, the favourite width; systyle, 2; or pyknostyle, 1½.

In'terdict (Ecclesiastical). See EXCOMMUNICATION.

Interdict, in Scotch law, is an order of the Court of Session, or of an inferior court, to prevent an illegal act or to stop illegal procedure. The applicant for an I. must show a title and prove that he has an interest in the act or procedure complained of. The similar remedy of English law is Injunction (q. v.).

Interdic'tion is, in Scotch law, a system of judicial restraint, provided for those, legally speaking, of facile nature. (See

FACILITY.) The remedy may be had at the instance of the facile person himself, or it may be procured against his wish at the instance of a near kinsman. In the latter case, it is called *judicial I.* In both cases the effort is to appoint trustees, whose consent is necessary to the validity of any deed affecting the heritable estate of the imbecile.

In'terest is the sum of money paid for the loan or use of another sum, generally estimated at so much *per cent.*, or per £100. The sum for which the I. is paid is called the *principal,* and the I. upon a hundred is called the *rate.* The I. is further proportional to the time, so that whatever is paid for £100 for one year, double that amount is paid for two years. The principal and I. together make the *amouut,* and this is the whole sum which is paid back to the lender. I. is either simple or compound. The former is reckoned upon the principal only, however long the period over which the loan extends; the latter is reckoned not only on the principal but also upon the I. as it becomes due. Thus, suppose the I. per annum upon a £100 to be £5, then, reckoning at simple I., the whole amount after ten years will be £150. At compound I., however, the I. for the second year is not, as above, £5, but is £5, 5s., being the I. charged upon £105, which is the original principal together with the first year's interest. Representing [the principal by P, the annual rate per cent. by r, the time by n, and the I. by I, the relation between these at simple interest is evidently

$$P \times \frac{r}{100} \times n = I, \text{ or } Prn = 100\ I,$$

from which, if any three are given, the fourth may at once be found. If the reckoning be at compound I., the formula is more complicated. At the end of the first year, the interest $= P \times \frac{r}{100}$, and the principal then becomes $P + P \times \frac{r}{100} = P(1 + \frac{r}{100})$. At the end of the second year, the I. is accordingly $P\ (1 + \frac{r}{100}) \times \frac{r}{100}$, and the amount on which to reckon for the ensuing year is

$$P(1 + \frac{r}{100}) + P\ (1 + \frac{r}{100}) \times \frac{r}{100} = P\ (1 + \frac{r}{100})^2.$$

Similarly the amount at the end of the third year is $P\ (1 + \frac{r}{100})^3$; and that at the end of the ninth year is $P\ (1 + \frac{r}{100})^9$. As an example, any sum of money put out at five per cent. compound interest, would nearly double itself in fourteen years. This is equivalent to saying that $(1 + \frac{1}{20})^{14}$ is nearly equal to 2.

Law Regarding Interest of Money.—The statute of 12 Anne, c. 16, made five per cent. the legal interest in Great Britain, describes usury, then a crime, imposes penalties upon it, and declares the contract null. By 17 and 18 Vict. c. 90, all acts against usury were repealed. This Act, however, declares that the expressions *legal* or *current* rate of interest shall mean the same as formerly. It is also declared that the laws as to pawnbrokers are not affected by the new Act. (See PAWNBROKING.) Interest may be due *ex lege;* that is, by the act of the law, as is the case of bills of exchange, which bear interest from their date of falling due, or it may be due under agreement. In the latter case, the rate at which interest falls to be charged depends wholly on stipulation. Legal interest is five per cent. The law hardly ever awards compound interest—or interest with *annual rests,* as it is often called in the law of England—to any one.

Interfe'rence of Light is the name given to a class of remarkable optical phenomena, of which the most striking is the production, under certain circumstances, of darkness by the coming together of two rays of light. The explanation which the undulatory theory affords of this phenomenon is so simple and beautiful as to carry with it, to the appreciative mind, the irresistible conviction that light travels in waves through the ether or space-pervading medium. Imagine a lake of water stretching indefinitely in all directions, and let a stone be dropped in from above. A series of concentric circular waves will be propagated from that point as centre where the stone struck the surface. This is very analogous to the propagation of light through the ether, except that the light waves form concentric spheres and not circles, and the particles of ether vibrate in *all* directions tangential to the spherical surface, and not merely in *one* direction as the up-and-down vibrating water particles do. If two series of equal waves meet at a point such that crest coincides with crest and trough with trough, the result will be a series of waves, each of which has nearly twice the amplitude of either of the constituents, if the latter are small. But if they should meet so that trough coincides with crest and crest with trough, the result will be a dead level or no wave motion at all. Consider, then, two series of waves of equal length diverging from two centres. For all points whose distances from these centres are equal, or differ by any whole number of wave-lengths, crest will come with crest and trough with trough, and increased brightness will result; while for all points whose distances differ by half a wave-length or by any odd multiple of half a wave-length, crest and trough will coincide and darkness will ensue, since darkness is merely the *absence* of the vibrations which constitute light. In the former case, the waves are said to meet in the *same phase;* in the latter case, they meet in *opposite phases.* Consequently wherever circumstances are such that two series of waves meet in opposite phases, the phenomenon of darkness produced by two lights will take place. A very instructive experiment is that devised by Young, to whom we owe the first complete explanation of the phenomena of interference. Light is allowed to diverge from two minute apertures and fall directly upon a plane screen, which is perpendicular to the axes of the two luminous cones; all points in the screen which are equidistant from the two sources of light will be luminous, and similarly for all points at which the waves from the two sources meet in the same phase. These points will appear arranged along bright bands, which form hyperbolas with the exception of the rectilinear band formed in the centre, and which are separated by dark spaces. The points along the central line of these dark bands are those points at which the waves of light meet in opposite phases. The alternation of distinctly-marked bright and dark bands, or fringes, as they are called, is only possible when homogeneous light is used. When white light is employed, the fringes will be coloured bands, which, after a few successions, are effaced by the overlapping of the fringes of different colours. An application of the same principles of wave interference has accounted for many more complex phenomena, into which it is impossible here to enter. A special set of interference phenomena is considered under DIFFRACTION, and a fuller treatment of the first principles of the undulatory theory will be found under LIGHT. The best English elementary treatise on the subject is Lloyd's *Wave Theory of Light,* to which the reader is referred for a complete elucidation of this branch of physical science.

In'terim (Lat. 'in the meantime') was the name given to certain documents drawn up in connection with the scheme of the Emperor Karl V. to conciliate the Lutherans, and make it possible for them to remain in the Church till a general council should assemble to settle the matters in dispute. The first I. was discussed at a conference held at Ratisbon (1541) between Eck, Pflug, and Gropper on the one side, and Melanchthon, Bucer, and Pistorius on the other. The second I. was drawn up by order of the Emperor, and discussed at the Diet of Augsburg, 1548; but, giving satisfaction to neither party, it was repealed in 1552. The third I. was a document embodying the opinions of Melanchthon and the other divines convened at Leipsic (1548) by Moritz, Elector of Saxony, to consider the I. of Augsburg.

Interjection (Lat. *interjectio,* from *inter,* 'between,' and *jacio,* 'I throw'), a word expressing a sudden passion or emotion of the mind. It is not so much the expression of a thought as the interruption of the sequence of thought, and as being a mere exclamation, it does not stand in grammatical relation to any word in the sentence in which it occurs. The I. is thus the lowest form of speech, and is nearly allied to the sounds emitted by the lower animals, *e.g.*, the bark of the dog, the grunt of the pig, &c. Many of the interjections in English are abbreviated forms of phrases or sentences. Such are Good-bye ! = God be with you; Adieu ! = I commend you to God; Marry ! = by Mary (the Virgin). Many adverbs, prepositions, verbs, &c., are used as interjections. In written speech the I. or the clause in which it occurs is followed by the sign (!).

Interlak'en ('between the lakes'), a beautiful Swiss village in the canton of Bern, on the low land called *Bödeli*, between the lakes of Thun and Brienz, which are 2 miles apart. A double avenue of walnuts lines the Höheweg, which is flanked by hotels, and extends from the adjacent village of Aarmühle to the upper bridge over the Aar. Pop. 1896. I. is noted for its whey-cure. It is a great centre for excursions into the Bernese Oberland, of which there is a magnificent view to the S.

Interlinea'tions in a deed are, legally speaking, additions or corrections, whether literally so or written on the margin. The initials or signature of the granter of the deed should be written across the I., and in Scotland the fact should be mentioned in the testing clause. An I. not properly executed is not, if unimportant, fatal to a deed; but it is very desirable either to avoid correction, or to have it properly executed. See ERASURE, ILLEGIBILITY.

Interlocu'tor, in Scotch law, means the judgment of a law court. The word is not used in English law; but in both countries the term *Interlocutory decree* is used to denote a judgment which is not final, but is merely a step in the case.

In'terlude, Intermezz'a (mus.). A short movement played between the acts of a drama, or between certain portions of a church-service.

Intermitt'ent Fever. See AGUE.

Interna'tional, The, a cosmopolitan association of trades unions, which has spread its ramifications throughout Europe, and whose primary principle was not political but social revolution, was organised at London in 1862, the year of the International Exhibition, 'to establish common interests among the working classes in different countries of the world.' At a meeting attended by delegates of ten nationalities, held at St. Martin's Hall, London, September 28, 1864, under the presidency of G. Odger, a new character—that of political action—was imparted to the society by its voting the publication of the revolutionary statutes and manifestoes of Dr. Karl Marx, whose programme of administration was finally adopted, in preference to those of Mazzini and Bakunin, at meetings held in the four following years at Geneva, Lausanne, Brussels, and Basel. In 1868 the French branch of the I. was prosecuted by the Government, the names of Assi, Duval, and nine other leaders of the subsequent Paris Commune first emerging in the course of this trial. Among the avowed aims of the advanced members of the I. at this period should be noted the abolition of marriage, religion, and inheritance, and the constitution of land as collective property; while its workings were shown in the support of the Paris bronze-workers in their strike of 1867, and of the Geneva builders in 1868, by English trades unions, the latter in turn being upheld in their strikes by the prohibition on the part of the I. against the importation of cheap labour into England from the Continent. With the struggle of the Paris Commune in 1871, the I. may be said to have at present culminated. At a meeting held at the Hague, September 4, 1872, Marx, the president, denounced Favre as a wretch and Trochu as a traitor, and a resolution was passed expressing 'admiration for the heroism of the champions who have fallen for the rights of the people,' and sending 'a greeting to all those who are still in chains.' Still, these sentiments failed to find favour with a large body who desired simply an international trades union, while the leaders were bent on political revolution in their own communistic sense, and two days later the congress broke up in dissension, the English, Swiss, Spanish, and Italian delegates forming a European confederation apart from the extreme section, which, under Marx and the French Communists, has transferred its headquarters from London to New York. Except in Spain, where in 1873 Internationalist revolts broke out in Murcia, little has been heard during the last five years of the society. Its members are stated to be still on the increase in Europe; but in America, though possessing branches in most of the large cities, the I. cannot be said as yet to command a numerous or influential following, only 2000 persons taking part in the 'demonstration' held at New York, December 17, 1871. See Onslow Yorke, *The Secret History of the I.* (Lond. 1874).

International Law. The term I. L. is, strictly speaking, a contradiction, for the common analysis of law implies not only a command or prohibition, but a sovereign power capable of enforcing this on subjects. Did such an authority exist, the law if enforced would then not be international, in the sense of applying to the relations between completely independent sovereigns, for a part of sovereignty would have been surrendered. I. L. may, however, be most usefully defined as certain rules which have been generally adopted by Christian States in their intercourse with one another. The practice of a few States is not sufficient to support a rule, and the practice between less civilised races, or between superior and inferior (*e.g.*, England and China) is generally left out of account. In the Amphictyonic Council of Greece and the *Jus Fetiale* at Rome there is nothing answering to modern I. L. except in so far as the latter treats of the rights and ceremonial usages of heralds or ambassadors. In medieval times the Pope exercised a species of international jurisdiction, for which his power of dispensing with the performance of solemn obligations must have been very useful. Many points were discussed by Suarez, Ayala, and Albericus Gentilis, but the system of I. L. was first generally stated by Grotius in the beginning of the 17th c. Since then a great literature has appeared, in which two schools are most conspicuous—(1) Those who, like Puffendorf, and many German and French writers, endeavour to develop *à priori* the jural relations of States, their definitions of rights and obligations being for the most part borrowed from individual morality; (2) those who, like Grotius, the eminent American writers Wheaton and Keat, and the English writers Twiss and Phillimore, content themselves with tracing the limits and the principles which seem to be involved in historical precedents of comparatively modern date. Several plans have been suggested to supply an umpire or authority who should both ascertain and enforce the law, which is in a very uncertain state. Such were St. Pierre's *Projêt de Paix Perpetuelle* (1729), which consisted in a perpetual league of the European States, having in all, singly or in groups, twenty votes, the right of war being renounced, and a vote of three-fourths being conclusive; Bentham's plan of a general congress (1789), which included the renunciation of colonies, reduction of armaments, and the furnishing of a contingent to enforce the congress decrees; Kant's plan, expressed in his essay *Zum Ewigen Frieden* (1795), for the abolition of standing armies, universal republican institutions, and world citizenship. (See also Ladd's Prize Essay on a Congress of Nations, for the American Peace Society, Boston, 1840.) This idea is still cherished by the amiable *savans* of the 'International Law Congress,' established at Ghent in 1873. In the present condition of the world its realisation would obviously afford opportunities for oppression. Among recent instances of international arbitration, one of the most important was that between the United States and Great Britain for the settlement of the disputed claims arising out of the depredations of the *Alabama* (q. v.) and other Confederate cruisers built and sent from England during the civil war. The arbitration was preceded by a joint high commission of the two Governments, by which the treaty of Washington was negotiated, arranging for an arbitration at Geneva, to proceed according to certain fixed rules of neutrality. The arbitration was followed in 1873 by a vote in the House of Commons, by which it was resolved 'that an humble address be presented to her Majesty praying that she will be graciously pleased to instruct her principal Secretary of State for Foreign Affairs to enter into communication with foreign powers with a view to further improvement in I. L., and the establishment of a general and permanent system of international arbitration.' A conference on the subject of I. L., attended by representatives from America, England, France, Germany, Italy, Spain, Switzerland, Belgium, and Holland, was held at Brussels, 10th October 1873. From the literature of the whole subject we select:—Robert von Mohl, *Geschichte und Literatur der Staatswissenschaft* (3 vols. Erlangen, 1855–58); Laurent, *Histoire du Droit des Gens* (Ghent, 1850); Pardessus, *Collection des Lois Maritimes Antérieures au 18ème Siècle* (6 vols. Par. 1828–45), including the *Assises des Bourgeois du Royaume de Jérusalemme*, the *Jugements d'Oleron*, and the *Jugements de Damme*, the *Consolato del Mare* (composed at Barcelona), the Sea Code of Wisby, the *Guidon de la Mer*, the laws of the Hanseatic League, and the famous French *Ordonnance Maritime of* 1681; De Martens, *Recueil des Principaux Traités de Paix*, which has been continued in various supplements; Koch, *Abrége de l'Histoire des Traités de Paix* (recast by Schöll, 15 vols. Par. 1818); Emmerich de Vattel, *Droit des Gens* (published at Leyden, 1758; best edition by Pinheiro-Ferreira, Par. 1838); De

Martens, *Précis du Droit des Gens Moderne de l'Europe* (Gött. 1789; edition by Pinheiro-Ferreira, Par 1855); Heffter, *Das Europäische Völkerrecht der Gegenwart* (3d ed. Berl. 1855). The best work on the consular service is De Miltitz, *Manuel des Consuls*, 1843; on private I. L., Fœlix, *Traité du Droit International Privé* (3d ed. Par. 1856); and the eighth volume of Savigny's *System des Heutigen Romischen Rechts* (translated by Guthrie); Prof. Bluntschli, *Modernes Völkerrecht der Civilisirten Staaten, als Rechtsbuch Dargestellt* (Heidelb. 1868; French trans. under the title *Droit International Codifié*); and D. D. Field, *Draft Outline of an International Code* (Lond. 1872).

Interplead'er Suit is a suit in the Chancery division in England, or in the Court of Chancery in Ireland, to determine which of two or more claimants is entitled to the thing claimed. The corresponding process of Scotch law is called *Multiple-poinding* (q. v.).

Interpola'tion, in mathematics, is the operation of inserting between two terms of a series other terms which shall conform to the series. It also includes the much more general and difficult problem of finding the general *form* of a function, for which certain particular values are given. In physical science it is consequently a method of great importance, since by its means the law regulating a phenomenon can be deduced from particular observed cases of the phenomenon. Its complete theory requires the aid of the highest branches of algebra, and is intimately connected with the calculus of finite differences.

In'terval, in music, is the distance (or 'difference in acuteness and gravity') between two musical sounds. An I. is named according to the number of degrees (on the *stave*) of which it consists, the two extremes being counted. The octave and every I. less than that are called 'simple.' Larger intervals than the octave are called 'compound,' but in harmony the 9th, 11th, and 13th are often treated as independent intervals. Intervals are also classified as 'diatonic' and 'chromatic;' the former are such as occur in an unaltered diatonic scale, while the latter are 'augmentations' and 'diminutions' of the former by one semitone. Thus G to A♯ is an 'augmented 2d.' The diagram contains a specimen of each simple diatonic I., with the names most commonly used.

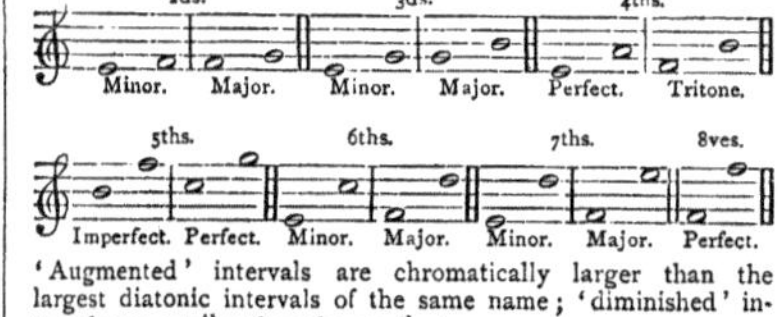

'Augmented' intervals are chromatically larger than the largest diatonic intervals of the same name; 'diminished' intervals are smaller than the smallest.

Intes'tacy is the legal term for the condition of one who died without a will. The eldest son inherits the real property of an intestate. In England he takes, in addition, his share of the personal estate; but not so in Scotland. (See COLLATION; Eng. law, HOTCHPOT.) Failing the eldest son and his issue, then the real estate descends to the second, third, and all other sons of the intestate, respectively in order of birth, and to their issue in like order. (See HEIR-AT-LAW; HEIR PRESUMPTIVE; BROTHERS, LAW OF SUCCESSION AMONG.) Regarding the division of the personal property of an intestate in England, see DISTRIBUTIONS, STATUTE OF; Scot. law, CONQUEST, SUCCESSION.

Intestine is the name given to that portion of the alimentary canal extending from the stomach to the anus. It is divided primarily into two parts, the *small* and the *large* I. The *small* I., about 20 feet in length in the adult, has been subdivided by anatomists into three portions—first, the *duodenum*, about 10 to 12 inches in length, next the stomach; second, the *jejunum*, consisting of many convolutions, and measuring about 8 feet in length; and, third, the *ileum*, forming the remainder, and terminating in the great I. The small I. is a tube formed of several coats having different functions. Externally it is covered almost entirely by a thin covering formed by the serous membrane which lines the abdominal cavity. This membrane is derived from the web called the *mesentery*, which connects the bowel with the trunk. The mesentery is double up to the inner margin of the bowel. There the two layers separate, so as to form a sheath for the bowel, covering its outer surface. Thus the bowel is connected with the body, and is covered by a smooth membrane which permits its various movements with a minimum of friction. The mesentery also conveys to and from the bowel blood-vessels, lymphatics, and nerves. Beneath the serous membrane there is a muscular coat formed of involuntary or non-striated muscular fibres, and consisting of two layers—an outer longitudinal, and an inner circular layer. These muscular coats by their contractility, under the influence of the nervous system, mechanically propel onwards the semi-digested matter in the bowel. Such movements are usually called *peristaltic*. Within the muscular coat a thin layer of connective tissue is found, in which vessels, nerves, and lymphatics ramify, and within this there is the internal coat or lining membrane of the I. When examined by the naked eye, this presents a shaggy or flocculent appearance like velvet, due to the presence of innumerable small processes projecting from its surface, called *villi*. It also shows a number of transverse folds or wrinkles, which are most marked when the bowel is not distended, called *valvulæ conniventes*. These folds increase the absorptive surface of the bowel. The mucous membrane of the small I. is probably the most important physiologically. By structures found in it at least three distinct functions are performed, namely, (1) absorption by blood-vessels, (2) absorption by special organs in the villi called *lacteals*, and (3) the secretion of various fluids by glands. (1) The mucous membrane is abundantly supplied by vessels which, by a process probably of a physical character similar to endosmotic action by dead membranes, absorb soluble matters directly into the blood. Such matters are water, salts, sugar (formed by the action of saliva on starch), and soluble forms of albumen known as *peptones*, produced by the influence of the gastric juice on albuminates. They pass into the blood, and are carried in the first instance to the liver. (2) The *fats* are absorbed chiefly by the lacteals in the villi. Each villus is a minute finger-shaped projection from the lining membrane of the bowel. In its interior and near its centre there is a delicate vessel, termed a lacteal, which during digestion is found, when examined microscopically, to be filled with fatty matter. The lacteal unites with others from adjacent villi to form a larger vessel, which carries the absorbed matter to glands in the mesentery, where it undergoes changes fitting it for the formation of blood. Covering the villus there are numerous epithelial cells of columnar form, which probably, in the first instance, absorb the fatty matter and transmit it to the lacteal. (3) The secretory structures in the small I. are of two kinds—first, numerous small tubular glands, which absorb throughout its whole course; and, second, of racemose glands, which are found only in the upper part of the duodenum, that is, next the stomach. The first are known as Lieberkühn's glands; while the second are named, also after their discoverer, Brunner's glands. These glands secrete the intestinal juice, a clear, limpid, alkaline or neutral fluid, which has been found to have the property (1) of converting starch into sugar; and (2) of acting slightly on albuminous compounds, changing these into peptones. As the food passes along the small I. it is termed *chyme*. It is mixed with the bile, pancreatic juice, and intestinal juices. Each of these have definite actions on it, the general result of which is to fit certain portions for being absorbed. Absorption takes place, as already mentioned, by two channels—first, by the vessels; and, second, by the lacteals of the villi. As it passes slowly along the bowel the nutritious portions of the food are gradually absorbed, and when it reaches the great I. it is nearly non-nutritious, and it assumes a fœcal odour. (In the small I. two other kinds of glands are found, named the solitary and agminated glands of Peyer; but these belong to the system of blood-glands, and have to do, not with the formation of any secretion for the I., but with the preparation of blood.)

The great I. consists also of three parts—first, the *cæcum*, which is next the ileum, and which is found in that part of the abdominal cavity above the right groin; second, the *colon*, which passes upwards on the right side to nearly the level of the liver, then transversely across the body, and then downwards on the left side, so as to terminate in the third portion or *rectum*, which passes through the pelvis and ends at the anus. The great I. is short, but much more capacious, considering its length, than the small I. It has the same coats as those already described, but two points require to be specially noticed. First, the longitudinal layer of involuntary muscular fibres, instead of being uniformly disposed around the bowel, as in the small I., is arranged in three distinct bundles, and as these are shorter than the length of the bowel, the latter presents a peculiar sacculated or puckered appearance, as if it had constrictions at certain intervals; second, the mucous membrane has no villi. The alimentary matter in the great I. has lost nearly all its nutritious properties, and is not fit for absorption It now gradually, as it passes along the bowel, acquires more and more of a fœcal character, probably because fermentations and decompositions go on, the result of which is the formation of compounds of fœcal odour, and because a true process of *excretion* also takes place in this portion of the alimentary canal. Here, doubtless, matters are separated from the blood, which, if retained, would prove injurious; and thus the great I. is not only an organ of excretion, so far as the refuse material of food is concerned, but also as regards matters separated directly from the blood, which are mixed with bile and intestinal secretions.

Intestinal Diseases are morbid conditions characterised by functional disorders, lesions of texture, or both combined, of the lesser intestinal canal, the organic lesions being, in many respects, identical with similar lesions affecting the stomach. The functional disorders are different, depending upon irritation or perverted action, and are expressed by a peculiar set of symptoms, such as spasms, colic, flatulence, constipation, various forms of diarrhœa, hæmorrhages, &c. I. D. are numerous and very frequently complicated, being the concomitants or sequelæ of a variety of systemic disorders which attack the intestinal canal as well as other tissues and organs of the body, directly or indirectly. Indeed there are but few disorders which do not implicate the intestinal track mediately or immediately. The several parts under which the intestinal canal is anatomically described are influenced by local inflammatory processes, resulting in lesions of texture, and by a variety of organic changes and consequent disordered functions. *Softening of tissues* may take place in the small intestines, but it is less common than in the stomach. *Glandular lesions* and *degenerations* are of much more frequent occurrence, resulting in atrophy or hypertrophy of the mucous membrane of the intestines, the glandular structure being altered or altogether replaced. These changes are usually associated with other complex morbid processes, as in constitutional diseases or organic lesions leading to impairment of health, and during the progress of some zymotic diseases as *cholera*, *dysentery*, and *enteric fever*. *Erythematous congestion* of the mucous surface, depending upon a variety of causes, such as changes of temperature, errors in diet, &c., produces intestinal catarrh, variously named *enteria*, *diarrhœa mucosa*, *summer* and *autumn diarrhœa*, and is usually associated with a congested state of the liver, the prominent symptoms being frequent fluid alvine discharges, gripping pains and tenesmus; but the belly is not painful when pressed, as in peritonitis, or acute inflammation of the bowels. (See DIARRHŒA.) *Inflammation of the intestines*, or *Enteritis* (q. v.), seldom affects the intestine throughout its whole extent, and the symptoms generally express themselves in the ileum. The intestinal mucous membrane is, like the spleen, liver, and kidney, subject to *waxy*, or *Amyloid Degeneration* (q. v.), the arterial capillaries of the villi and the surrounding mucous and submucous tissues being chiefly affected, and frequently to such an extent that the villi drop off, the mucous membrane being also destroyed; and ulcers are developed which penetrate deeply into the tissue, resulting in fatal hæmorrhage or perforation. *Colic*, *ileus*, *volvulus*, *intus-susception*, and *invagination* are the names for a variety of severe and dangerous I. D. which are described under their appropriate headings. See also RECTUM, DISEASES OF.

Intona'tion, when it does not mean *Intoning* (q. v.), refers to the sounds of the scale. The pitch of each of these sounds bears an arithmetical ratio to that of the keynote. The notes of a keyed instrument do not represent perfectly correct I. See TEMPERAMENT and HARMONICS, and consult Woolhouse's *Essay on Musical Intervals, &c.* (Lond. 1835).

Into'ning, the practice of singing a part of the church-service, including the delivery of the prayers, in a monotone. This is the custom in the Roman Catholic, the English, and the Lutheran Churches, though in the last two it is not universal. Prayers were commonly intoned by the Jews, and this practice is also widely diffused among barbarous tribes.

Intoxica'tion. See INTEMPERANCE.

Intra'dos (Fr., from Lat. *intra*, 'within,' and Fr. *dos*, from Lat. *dorsum*, 'back'), in architecture, the inner or lower line of an arch, or the flat surface of a vault turned towards the interior of a building, in opposition to the *Extrados*, or outer curve of the voussoirs or wedge-shaped stones forming an arch or vault.

Intrench'ment. See FORTIFICATION.

In'troit, music sung in the Roman Catholic service while the priest goes to the altar to celebrate the mass, and that sung in the corresponding part of the Anglican service.

Intromiss'ion, in Scotch law, is the assuming of the possession and management of property belonging to another. When this is done according to law, it is called *legal I.* When done contrary to law, it is called *vicious* I. The latter term is especially applied to an heir's unwarrantable dealing with the movable estate of his ancestor.

Intui'tion ('a looking upon,' from Lat. *in*, and *tueor*, 'I look') is a term used in philosophy to denote a power which a certain school supposes the mind to possess of instantaneously perceiving the truth of things without a process of reasoning. That the mind really possesses any such power is more than questionable. On the other hand, it may be admitted that mental operations sometimes transact themselves with a swiftness so incalculable, that their process fails to obtain the notice of consciousness. See MIND.

Intus-Suscep'tion is the accidental insertion of one portion of intestine into another, and is a most serious disorder, generally terminating fatally. I.-S. occurs more frequently in infancy and childhood than at any other period of life. The colic is extremely severe, and there are remissions and exacerbations of pain, increasing in violence with each repetition.

In'ula, a genus of the *Compositæ* family, numbering some fifty species, of which six are natives of Britain, notably the ploughman's spikenard, the golden samphire, and the flea-bane; whilst Elecampane (q. v.) is perhaps only naturalised with us from former cottage-garden cultivation.

In'ulin, a starchy material obtainable from various plants; differing from ordinary starch in being coloured yellowish-brown by iodine. See ELECAMPANE.

In'uus, a genus of *Catarhina* (q. v.) or Old World monkeys, of which that inhabiting the Rock of Gibraltar is an example. This species, representing the only wild European monkey, was bred from ancestors imported from the opposite coast of Africa.

In'valides, Hôtel des, the Chelsea Hospital of Paris, stands near the S.E. angle of the Champ de Mars, and occupies 28 acres. It was built (1671–75) by Louis XIV. from designs by Bruant, with accommodation for 5000 disabled veterans; but in 1872 contained less than half that number of privates, and 160 officers. Each of its inmates receives, besides board and lodging, a small monthly pension—from 30 francs for a colonel to 2 francs for a private. The Hôtel is a four-storied structure with a façade of 612 feet, is divided into five large and fifteen smaller courts, has a library of 30,000 volumes, and in its western wing contains the Artillery Museum. The chapel is rendered by its gilded dome (328 feet), designed by Mansard, one of the most conspicuous objects of Paris. Here are buried Vauban, Turenne, Duroc, and Bertrand, and hither the body of Napoleon I. was brought from St Helena, September 15, 1840.

Inven'tors and Pa'tentees. See PATENTEES AND INVENTORS.

In'ventory, in English law, is a list and description of goods and chattels. It is especially applied to the list of a deceased person's effects made up by his executor or administrator. In Scotland it has a wider application. See BENEFICIUM INVENTARII.

In Ventre Sa Mere, a term in English law denoting an unborn child. It is especially applied to the Fœtus (q. v.) whose father dies before its birth. A child so born has the same legal rights as if born during the lifetime of its father.

Inver'ary, the capital of Argyleshire, and long the chief town of the Western Highlands of Scotland, lies on a small bay on the W. side and near the head of Loch Fyne, at the mouth of the small river Aray, 60 miles N.W. by W. of Glasgow. It mainly consists of one street, running E. and W., near the centre of which stands an old square church, and an obelisk to the memory of seventeen Campbells who were executed without trial by Montrose in 1685. A stone bridge here crosses the Aray, and there is a ferry to St. Catherine's on the E. shore of Loch Fyne. Regular steamboat communication is maintained with Glasgow. The only industry is the herring fishery. Pop. (1871) 905. I. was made a burgh of barony in 1472, and a royal burgh in 1648. The old town lay a little to the N., and was deserted for the present one about 1742. With Oban, Irvine, Ayr, and Campbeltown, I. sends one member to Parliament. In the vicinity is I. Castle, the residence of the Duke of Argyle.

Invercar'gill, a town in the south or middle island of New Zealand, situated on a small estuary known as the New River, in 46° 27′ S. lat. and 168° 25′ E. long. Only small vessels can reach I., the larger ones loading and discharging at Bluff Harbour, 18 miles distant, with which I. is connected by rail. Pop. (1875) 6000.

Inverness', the chief town of the county of the same name, Scotland, on both banks of the Ness, about a mile from its mouth, 156 miles N.N.W. of Edinburgh by rail. It is picturesquely situated at the N. end of the great glen of Scotland, and is popularly regarded as the capital of the Highlands. The principal buildings are the castle, built on the site of an old royal fortress in 1835; the cathedral of St. Andrews, in Decorated Gothic style, erected at a cost of £20,000 in 1866; a townhall and exchange of date 1708. The I. Academy was founded by royal charter in 1792, and endowed by Captain W. Mackintosh with £20,000. The *Clach-na-cudden* ('stone of the tubs,' from having served as a resting-place for those carrying water from the river), a blue lozenge-shaped stone, long regarded as the palladium of the town, is preserved in the High Street, near the town-cross. There is a trade by the Moray Firth and the Caledonian Canal in grain, potatoes, spirits, &c., and manufactures of woollen cloth, leather, spirits, iron and brass wares, sailcloth, &c. In 1875 there entered the port 1862 vessels of 210,313 tons, and cleared 1524 of 175,941. The river is crossed by a wooden bridge, a modern suspension bridge, a foot-bridge, and a railway bridge. I. has three newspapers, and with Forres, Fortrose, and Nairn, sends one member to Parliament. Pop. (1871) 14,510. I. received a borough charter from William the Lion in the 12th c. In 1411 it was sacked by Donald, Lord of the Isles. As 'a solitary outpost of civilisation' (Macaulay), it suffered greatly from the wild descents of the Highlanders. The town strongly supported the Stuart cause, and after the '45 some thirty-six men were executed here. The old castle, of which there are no remains, was seized by the adherents of Edward I. in 1303, and recovered by Robert Bruce. James I. is said to have held a parliament here in 1427. It was taken by Cromwell in 1649, and destroyed by Prince Charles Edward in 1746.

Inverness'-shire, the largest county of Scotland, is bounded E. by Nairn, Elgin, Banff, and Aberdeen, W. by Ross-shire and the Atlantic, S. by Argyle and Perth, and N. by Ross-shire. It includes the western islands of Skye, N. and S. Uist, Barra, and Harris, the southern portion of Lewis. Area 4256 sq. miles; pop. (1871) 87,480. The insular portion alone has an area of 1150 sq. miles. The mainland is extremely mountainous. Glenmore (q. v.), or the Great Glen of Scotland, traverses it in the direction of its greatest length, and along the bottom of the glen stretch Lochs Lochy (10 miles long), Oich (4), and Ness (27) linked together and with the sea at both ends by the Caledonian Canal (q. v.). The Grampians form the S. boundary of I., rising in Ben Nevis, the highest peak in Great Britain, to a height of 4406 feet; other heights are Ben Aulder (3757 feet), Cairn Gorm (4090), and to the N. of Glenmore, Mam Suil (3862), Ben Scrian (3188), Ben Douran (3517), Mealfourvounie (2730), Scuir-na-Lapich (3740). Between the Grampians and the lateral range of the Monadhleadh mountains, a broad strath is watered by the Spey; other rivers flowing N.E. are the Findhorn, Nairn, and Beauly; the Foyers flows into Loch Ness, the Garry into Loch Oich, and the Spean into Loch Eil, a western arm of the sea. The 'Fall of Foyers' is one of the glories of the country. A large part of the surface is covered with heath (especially in the southern district of Badenoch), and with forests of fir and pine, but the glens and straths are fertile and well cultivated. The W. coast is indented by Lochs Hourn, Nevis, Nanuagh, Moidart, &c. In 1876 there were 40,221 acres under corn crops, 19,553 under green crops, 26,895 under clover, sanfoin, and grasses in rotation, and 35,228 in permanent pasture, exclusive of mountain or heath; the number of horses was 9008, of cattle 53,242, of sheep 724,518, and of pigs 4127. The chief crops are barley, oats, rye, wheat, potatoes, and turnips. In a varied geological formation, the prevailing rocks are gneiss, mica, slate, granite, and porphyry. Game is abundant, including the roe and red deer, Alpine hare, otter, hawk, and eagle. Gaelic is the prevailing language. The only burgh is Inverness; other places are Beauly, Fort William, Fort Augustus, and Fort George. The county is traversed by splendid military roads, constructed in the 18th c. The Highland Railway enters I. to the E. of Loch Errocht, and continues N.E. through Strathspey.

Inver'sion (1) of *intervals* (in music) takes place when the lower note is replaced by that an octave higher, or *vice versâ*. Thus—

3rd = Inv. 7th = Inv. 5th = Inv.

6th. 2d. 4th.

(2) I. of *chords*. (See HARMONY.) (3) I. of *parts*. (See DOUBLE COUNTERPOINT.) (4) I. of *phrases*, also called inverse movement; where a subject and its answer (see IMITATION) move in opposite directions but with the same intervals, *e.g.*, the opening of 'Egypt was Glad,' in *Israel in Egypt*, by Handel.

Invertebra'ta, a name applied collectively to include the groups of animals of lower rank than the *Vertebrata* (q. v.). The characters of I. are those which may be regarded as negative when applied to vertebrates. Thus I. have no spine or *Notochord* (q. v.). They have generally numerous limbs; jaws in the form of modified limbs, or consisting of hard parts developed in the lining membrane of the mouth; no *absorbent vessels*, and no *portal system* of veins; and their nervous system is not shut off or specialised from the general body-cavity. The invertebrate groups are the *Protozoa*, *Cœlenterata*, *Echinozoa*, *Annulosa*, and *Mollusca*, all of which are described in special articles.

Inves'titure (late Lat. *investitura*, from Lat. *in* and *vestire*, 'to put in possession') is 'the putting ecclesiastics in possession of their temporalities by a formal act of the civil power.' Previous to the 9th c. there were no forms for this peculiar to the clergy, further than the ordinary symbolical form according to which the sovereign delivered to his vassals a written instrument, green twig, &c., to signify the transfer of the dominion over the property which they held from him, the common name for which form was 'traditio.' The mode of investing bishops and abbots with the ring and crozier, which were the insignia of their office, the one being the symbol of the sacred mysteries, and the other the pastoral staff, was introduced at the time when sovereigns assumed to themselves the power of conferring sacerdotal offices. In order to secure the power of conferring the sacred offices on whom they pleased, as soon as any of the higher officers in the Church died, they required the staff and ring to be transferred to them. These were delivered to the man of the sovereign's choice, who thereafter repaired to the metropolitan, and, delivering them to him, was reinvested with them after they were consecrated. This custom led to scandalous practices in the sale of benefices, and Pope Gregory VII., in his attempt to put down simony and his battle for the aggrandisement of the Church, decreed in a council held at Rome 1075, that 'if any person in future accepts a bishopric or an abbacy from the hands of a layman, such person shall not be regarded as a bishop or an abbot, nor shall he enter a church, till he has given up the place thus illegally obtained. . . . And every individual, be he emperor or king, who bestows investiture in connection with such an office, shall be excluded from Church communion.' The conflict waged by Gregory and succeeding

Popes on this matter ended (at the Diet of Worms, 1122) in the clergy getting the right of election of bishops and abbots, while the sovereigns retained the right of I., not with the ring and staff, but with the touch of the sceptre.

Investiture, a term of Scotch law denoting the act of giving feudal possession of heritable property. This is now done by registration of the deed of conveyance.

Invocation of Angels and Saints is practised in the Romish and Eastern Churches, the following distinction being made, however, in the different kinds or degrees of worship:—*Douleia*, the worship due to angels and saints; *hyperdouleia*, due to the Virgin Mary; and *latreia*, due to God alone. In the first three centuries of the Church all worship of angels and saints was considered idolatrous. In the beginning of the 4th c., during the Arian controversy, an argument for the proper divinity of Christ was drawn from the worship offered to him, on the obvious ground that worship could not be offered to any creature, but to God alone. Indeed, the ground on which worship could be offered to saints was cut away by the opinion of the fathers that they did not enter into the enjoyment of the beatific vision till after the day of judgment. At first, too, it may be, the worship in the chapels built at the tombs of martyrs was offered to God, and the offerings laid on the altars made to him, the chapels and altars being simply memorials of the martyrs. But the pagan practice of building temples and making votive offerings to gods and demigods is well known, and it would have been wonderful if ignorant people, full of pagan notions, had not entertained similar sentiments towards the angels and saints of Christianity, and sought to express them in a similar way. Thus Hlothar, King of France, built a church to St. Vincent, who had helped him against the Goths. The modern Roman Catholic doctrine on the subject (*Council of Trent*) is, that 'the saints, who reign with Christ, and guardian angels, offer prayers to God for men; that it is good and useful to invoke them, and, on account of the benefits to be obtained from God through Jesus Christ, to flee to them for help.' The objections which Protestants generally urge against the practice are:—(1) That it is at least superstitious, being founded on the assumption—of which, it is asserted, there is no Scripture proof—that the spirits of the dead are accessible to the living, and capable of hearing and answering their prayers. (2) That in actual practice it involves all the elements of idolatry, even although it were granted that the doctrine as expounded by theologians does not. That blessings are actually sought by the people at the hands of creatures which God alone can bestow. And not only so, but that this implies the possession by creatures of attributes which belong to God alone, since it is assumed that the saints are omnipresent, or at least that they can hear prayers addressed to them from all parts of the earth at the same time. See Hodge's *Syst. Theology* (Edinb. 1873); Gieseler's *Lehrbuch der Kirchengeschichte* (Bonn, 1855, Eng. trans. by Davidson).

In'voice (from the Italian *avviso*), literally a letter of 'advice' or information respecting the despatch of goods, giving particulars of their quantity and price.

Involu'cre, the whorled bracts at the base of an umbel or head of flowers, or sometimes below a single flower. An *involucel* is the I. of a *partial umbel*. See INFLORESCENCE.

In'volute. See EVOLUTE.

Involu'tion. See EVOLUTION AND INVOLUTION.

I'odine. This element was discovered in 1811 by Bernard Courtois, a saltpetre manufacturer of Paris. He noticed that the iron vessels he used for crystallising the salts were corroded by keeping the mother liquors in them. On distilling these liquors with sulphuric acid, he got a substance which, when heated, was converted into a splendid purple vapour. This body was subsequently investigated by Gay-Lussac and Sir Humphry Davy, who pointed out its resemblance to chlorine. The name I. (*ion*, 'violet') was given to it from the colour of its vapour. I. is a very widely-distributed, but nowhere abundant element. It occurs in minute quantity in many mineral waters; combined with mercury, silver, and lead; combined with sodium, potassium, and magnesium; in salt mines and brine springs; in several land plants; in plants growing on the sea-shore, and in sea-water itself, but only in minute quantity. Sea-plants, however, such as *Fucus digitatus*, *F. saccharinus*, *Neva umbilicalis*, and many others, as well as sponges, and other sea-animals, assimilate I. from the sea-water, and retain it in small but such appreciable quantity that it is from these sources that I. is usually manufactured. The sea-weed, either drifted on shore from deep water or cut from the rocks at ebb-tide, is dried and incinerated at as low a temperature as possible. The semi-fused ash is black or grey, somewhat deliquescent, and is known technically as *kelp*. The kelp is dissolved in hot water, the liquor concentrated, and a quantity of salts removed by crystallisation. The liquor or I. ley is next mixed with sulphuric acid, which sets free several gases, and produces a fresh crop of crystals. The liquor is then run into an earthenware or leaden still connected with a series of receivers. It is heated gently in the still, and binoxide of manganese having been added, the I. is liberated, rises in vapour, and passes over into the receivers, in which it condenses. If necessary, it can be purified by sublimation. There is a different method of dealing with the sea-weed from that just described. Instead of being converted with kelp, the sea-weed is thoroughly dried, compressed, and heated in iron retorts at a regulated temperature. Gas is given off, tar and ammonia distil over, and a fixed residue remains in the retorts, consisting of charcoal and all the fixed salts, including iodides and bromides. The residue is lixiviated with water, the salts separated by crystallisation, and the mother liquors treated with sulphuric acid and binoxide of manganese to separate the I., as in the previous process. I. crystallises in rhombic octahedra, which by spontaneous sublimation are obtained of great beauty and with a brilliant lustre, but in general it is got in plates or crystalline masses, with an inferior lustre, like blacklead. Pure I. is black. Its specific gravity is 4·948: it is soft, and easily powdered. It is somewhat volatile at the ordinary temperature; when heated, it fuses about 113° C., and boils at 175° C., giving off a purple vapour. It does not conduct electricity. I. has a peculiar odour; its vapour attacks the eyes, nostrils, and windpipe: it has a harsh taste, and is very poisonous. It stains the skin yellow or brown, but the stain can be readily removed by an alkali; if kept in contact with the skin, it gradually corrodes it. I. is sparingly soluble in water; it dissolves more easily in alcohol and ether, especially if iodide of potassium be present. The solutions are brown. In bisulphide of carbon it dissolves with a rich purple colour. I. combines with all the metals, and with most of the non-metallic elements. It readily combines with and dissolves iron and zinc when digested with these metals in water; it forms compounds with antimony, arsenic, bismuth, cadmium, copper, iron, lead, mercury, potassium, silver, and zinc, most of which are of importance in the arts, in medicine, and in practical chemistry. With oxygen it forms iodic anhydride (I_2O_5), and there are also known iodic acid (HIO_3), and periodic acid (HIO_4). Hydriodic acid (HI) is best obtained by cautiously heating I., red phosphorus, and water together. It is a colourless, fuming gas, very soluble in water, with a strongly acid reaction, and decomposes on keeping, with liberation of I. When I. is digested with cold, strong ammonia, a black powder is obtained containing iodide of nitrogen. When dried, the powder explodes violently with the slightest touch, and sometimes spontaneously. I. in solution is recognised by the beautiful blue colour it gives to starch, paste, or starch solution. If the I. is free the blue colour is at once obtained; but if the I. is in combination, it must be liberated by the cautious addition of chlorine, bleaching-powder, or similar re-agent. The combining weight of I. is 127.

Io'doform (CHI_3) is a substance which is analogous in composition to chloroform, but differs from it in properties: it has been used in medicine in cases of neuralgia and sciatica, and in certain virulent diseases. It is prepared by acting on alcohol, and many other bodies, with iodine and potash. It is obtained in yellow crystalline scales, and has a peculiar smell. It is insoluble in water, but dissolves in chloroform and in ether, and sparingly in alcohol.

Io'na, a celebrated island, about 3½ miles long by 1 to 1½ broad, at the S.W. end of Mull, Argyleshire, from which it is separated by a narrow channel. Pop. about 300. Of old it was known as *I* (pronounced *ee*) = 'the island.' Adamnan, in his *Life of St. Columba*, following the fashion of the time in making the name into a Latin adjective, writes *Ioua insula*. Some transcriber mistaking the *u* for *n* wrote *Iona*, and thus it has continued. In Gaelic it is known as *I. Chalum Cille* = 'the island of Calum of the Church.' In 563 St. Columba (q. v.) and twelve companions founded the monastery of I., remarkable for this feature in its constitution, viz., that the abbot exercised jurisdiction over the bishop in his neighbourhood. Owing to the high character for learning and piety maintained by the successors of Columba in I., the churches which the saint founded, all regarded the mother church with greatest reverence, and for 200 years it continued to grow in fame and power. In the beginning of the 9th c. the island was ravaged by the Danes. The 'relics' of Columba were transferred to Kells, in Ireland, whence some of them were sent to Dunkeld, in Scotland. The cathedral of Durham also claimed the possession of some. During the next 300 years the sea-rovers frequently repeated their visits, plundering and slaying. In the 11th c. Magnus Barefoot, King of Norway, having conquered the Hebrides, placed I. under the jurisdiction of the Archbishop of Trondjheim; but when Somerled, Lord of the Isles, married the daughter of Magnus' successor, the Southern Hebrides were given up to him, and I. was restored to its original place. Its monastic authority, however, decreased as Diocesan Episcopacy spread throughout Scotland after the reign of Malcolm Canmore; and when its church was made the cathedral of the Bishopric of the Isles its peculiar character necessarily disappeared.

The antiquities of the place are interesting more for the profound associations connected with them than for the appearance which they present. The walls of the small cathedral and its square tower, belonging to the beginning of the 13th c., are still standing. The remains of St. Oran's Chapel (ascribed to Queen Margaret in the 12th c.) and of the 'Nunnery' are also to be seen, and several other chapels are spoken of as having at one time existed. The Cross of St. Martin, 14 feet high, is the finest specimen extant of the Celtic cross. Maclean's Cross, 10 feet high, is also beautiful. There are other smaller ones; but the story of Sacheverell, unsupported by any evidence, of the 360 crosses cast into the sea by order of the Presbyterian Synod of Argyle, is treated by Dr. Reeves, and all who have examined the subject, as an absolute fable. Of the cemeteries, the oldest is 'the Druids';' after it comes *Rélig Orain*, 'St. Oran's Burial Ground,' and *Iomaire nan Righrean* = 'the ridge of the kings,' said to contain the dust of several kings of Scotland, Ireland, France, Denmark, and the North of England. See Montalembert's *Monks of the West*, which gives a glowing but misleading account of I.; the Duke of Argyle's *Iona* (Lond. 1871): for pictorial representations of the existing monuments, Graham's *Sketches;* and for accurate knowledge of 'the monastery of I.,' Dr. Reeves' admirable work.

Io'nia, a country on the western coast of Asia Minor, which extended for 90 miles along the Ægean Sea from Phocæa in the N. to Miletus in the S., but penetrated only a few miles inland. Its inhabitants, the Ionians, derived their name from the eponymous hero Ion, and according to the myth immigrated from Greece in 1044 B.C.; but recent writers have questioned whether they did not rather arrive at the shores of the Ægean immediately from the East, and trace a connection between the names Ion and Javan (a son of Japheth), the Ionians and the Yavanas of Sanskrit literature. I. originally contained twelve states (increased to thirteen by the addition of Smyrna in the 7th c. B.C.), which, independent of each other, yet formed a confederacy—the Ionian League—for common purposes, and held regular meetings at Panonium, on the northern slope of Mount Mycale. (See CLAZOMENÆ, COLOPHON, EPHESUS, MILETUS, SAMOS, SCIO, and SMYRNA.) The Ionians were a maritime race, and early cultivators of the arts and sciences, giving rise to a philosophy, and to styles of architecture and painting, whilst their soft and vocal dialect, the Ionic, was that of Homer, Hesiod, and the epic poets generally. They passed successively under the sway of the Lydians (about 700 B.C) and the Persians (557), revolted unsuccessfully against the latter in 500, and again with better result in 479, became for a short time dependent upon Athens, but in 387 were again made over to Persia. On the overthrow of the Persian monarchy by Alexander, the Ionian cities were annexed to Macedonia, along with which they fell under the Romans, still retaining great commercial and artistic importance, which only perished with the irruption of the Turks in the middle ages.

Io'nian Islands, a chain of some forty islands, extending along the W. and S. coast of Greece, and having a total area of 1041 sq. miles, and a pop. (1870) of 18,879. The names of the seven largest are Corfu, Cephalonia, Santa Maura, Ithaki, Zante, Cerigo, and Paxo. They are for the most part mountainous, and have little wood and water, but enjoy a delicious climate. Among the abundant mineral products are marble, coal, pitch, sulphur, and salt, while the fertile valleys and coast plains yield grapes, olives, roses, cotton, flax, &c. In the earliest ages of Greece, the islands were under hereditary princes of their own, who subsequently made way for republican constitutions. They suffered in all the vicissitudes of Hellas, and on the division of the Roman power fell to the Byzantine Empire, but were seized by the Duke of Calabria (afterwards King of Naples) in 1081. In the beginning of the 15th c. they passed to the Venetians, who retained them till the overthrow of the republic by Napoleon in 1797, when they were ceded to France. They were taken possession of by Russia and Turkey in 1800, by France in 1807, and by England in 1809. In 1815 they were formed into the Septinsular Republic under the English protectorate. The government was at first stringent, but in 1848 the franchise was lowered, ballot was introduced, and freedom allowed to the press. Immediately followed a demand for annexation to Greece. Sir Henry Ward suppressed an insurrection in 1849, but Mr. Gladstone's intercessions as special commissioner in 1858 was fruitless. The islands were transferred to Greece by treaty concluded in London 28th May 1867. They had cost England £100,000 yearly. See Davy, *The I. I. under British Protection* (Lond. 1851); Ansted, *The I. I.* (Lond. 1863); Kirkwall, *Four Years in the I. I.* (2 vols. Lond. 1864).

Ionian Mode. See GREGORIAN CHANT.

Ionian School, a collective title for several of the earliest Greek philosophers, from Thales to Anaxagoras, whose speculations were of physical and pantheistic character, and who for the most part were natives of Ionia in Asia Minor. See HELLENIC PHILOSOPHY; and Ritter, *Geschichte der Ionischen Philosophie* (Berl. 1821).

Ion'ic Order. See COLUMN and GRECIAN ARCHITECTURE.

I'owa, one of the United States, lies between the Mississippi on the E. and the Missouri on the S. and W., and is bounded on the N. by Minnesota. Area, 55,045 sq. miles; pop. (1870) 1,182,933. The country is extremely flat, consisting for the most part of 'rolling' prairie considerably above the level of the sea, and is worn into deep rocky gullies by the numerous tributaries of the two great boundary rivers. There are many small lakes, chief of which are Spirit Lake (area, 14 sq. miles), Okoboji (15 miles long), and Clear Lake (4 miles), and extensive forests of oak, elm, cotton-wood, black walnut, hickory, linden, maple, &c. The climate is mild and equable, and the principal crops are corn, wheat, oats, barley, buckwheat, and rye. The surface is covered with diluvial deposits, and these again with alluvium in the river bottoms. The upper coal-measures occupy the whole S.W. portion of the State, while the N.E. is traversed by a tract of Lower Silurian. The I. coal-field has an area of some 7000 sq. miles. Besides coal, which is extensively mined, the minerals found include lead (argentiferous galenga ore), iron, gypsum, and limestone. Chief among the exports of I. are flour, timber, cut meats, and tobacco. Des Moines is the capital, but the only town of more than 25,000 of a pop. are Davenport and Dubuque. In 1874 there were 3800 miles of railroad, and over 300 newspapers in the State. As part of the Louisiana purchase, the county of I. came to the United States in 1803. I. territory was organised in 1839, and admitted to the Union as a State in 1846. In 1870 the number of Indians in I. had dwindled to 48.

Iowa City, the capital of Johnson county, in Iowa, U.S., at the head of navigation on the I. river, 115 miles W. of Rock Island by rail. It was the State capital till 1857, when it gave place to Des Moines, and is still the seat of the State college. It has fifteen churches, extensive manufactures of woollens, flax, oil, &c., and a large local trade. Pop. (1870) 5914.—**I. College** was founded in 1847 by an association of Congregationalists and Presbyterians, but is free from all church influence. The endowment is under 100,000 dollars, and the number of students is about 250; ladies were admitted in 1867. A fine new building, supplied with chemical laboratories, was erected in 1872.

Ipecacuanh'a is the dried rhizome of *Cephælis ipecacuanha*, a Brazilian plant belonging to the Peruvian bark family. It is largely employed in medicine as an emetic and as an expectorant, and was formerly highly esteemed in dysentery. The active principle is emetin, an alkaloid contained in the rind of the 'root.' These roots are about the thickness of a goose quill, of various shades of brown, are contorted, knotted, and annulated; consequently are very characteristic, so that spurious I. may readily be detected. The discovery that the plant can be propagated from the leaf as well as by divisions of the rhizome, has facilitated its present extensive cultivation in India, from whence it is hoped we shall in the future draw our chief supply.

The Medicinal Properties of I.—I. in large doses acts as an emetic, and in small doses as an expectorant and diaphoretic. When it is absorbed it acts upon the mucous surfaces of the respiratory organs and the alimentary canal, and is useful in certain bronchial affections, and also in the acute stage of dysentery. The dose of I. as an expectorant, &c., is from ½ to 2 grains, and as an emetic from 15 to 30 grains. In acute dysentery I. is given in emetic doses, and the first generally causes emesis; but a certain tolerance is established, and large doses can afterwards be given without causing nausea and vomiting. The preparations are *pilula I. cum scilla, pulvis I. comp.* (Dover's powder), *lozenges* of I., and in combination with *morphia; vinum I.* and *syrupus* I. Dose—of the *powder*, 5 to 10 grains; of the *wine*, 5 to 40 minims; and of the *syrup*, 15 to 60 minims.

Iphigeni'a, according to Greek legend, was the daughter of Agamemnon and Clytæmnestra, and was brought in her youth to Chalcis, that her sacrifice might propitiate Artemis, who would not, the seer Calchas declared, otherwise allow the Greek fleet to sail to Troy, Agamemnon having slain a stag sacred to the goddess, or having, according to another story, vowed to sacrifice to her the most beautiful production of the year in which I. was born. When I. was about to be sacrificed Artemis bore her away in a cloud to Tauris, where she became priestess of the goddess, and where she afterwards recognised and saved her fugitive brother Orestes (q. v.), with whom, and her sister Electra, she returned to Mycenæ. According to one tradition she died there, though others assert that Artemis changed her into Hecate, a third story being that she received immortal youth and became the wife of Achilles in the island of Leuce. Her story is the subject of Euripides' tragedies, *I. at Aulis* and *I. at Tauris*. The incident of her intended sacrifice is beautifully told by Ovid. Lucretius also refers to it in a fine passage, and Landor has an exquisite poem on I.

Ipomæ'a, a large genus of the *Convolvulus* family; in many cases being plants with long twining stems, arising from a largely-developed root-stock which contains an acrid juice of purgative properties. (See JALAP.) The handsome flowers have brought several species into cultivation as ornamental plants.

Ipomæa purpura.

Ipsambul'. See ABOUSAMBUL.

Ip'swich, the chief town of Suffolk, England, on a gentle acclivity rising from the N. bank of the Orwell (which above I. is called the Gipping), 12 miles from the sea, and 68 miles N.E. of London by the Great Eastern Railway. It has a few quaint old houses ornamented with plaster mouldings, and is enlivened by many fine villas. Its principal buildings are the church of St. Mary-le-Tower, in richly decorated Second Pointed style; the Roman Catholic church of St. Pancras, with a lofty flèche; a handsome townhall, the façade of which has an open arcade supporting four large statues. Its grammar-school, founded by Cardinal Wolsey, and endowed by Elizabeth, has seven scholarships, including one established as a memorial of the Prince Consort, who laid the foundation-stone of the present buildings in 1847. There are beautiful horticultural gardens, and among the manufactures are agricultural implements, artificial manure, leather and tackle. The harbour admits vessels of 500 tons, and there is an active trade in iron wares, coal, timber, and agricultural produce. Steamers ply regularly between I. and Harwich and London. In 1875 there entered the port 2543 vessels of 179,895 tons; and cleared, 2007, of 140,218 tons. I. was incorporated in the reign of John, and sends two members to Parliament. Pop. (1871) 42,947.

Ipswich, the third largest town in Queensland, is situated on the river Bremner, 25 miles W. of Brisbane (q. v.), with which it is connected both by railway and steamer. Cotton and maize are extensively grown in the neighbourhood, and the cultivation of the sugar-cane has also been commenced. Coal is plentiful and easily worked. The town is pleasantly situated and well built. Pop. (1875) 6000.

Irak'-Aj'ami, a central province of Persia, bounded N. by the Kizl-Ozan River and Elburz Mountains, E. by Khorasan and the Great Salt Desert, S. by Khuzistan and Fars, and W. by Turkish territory. It is 520 miles long and 450 broad, and is almost entirely mountainous, the treeless ranges extending from E. to W., and opening here and there in valleys seldom exceeding 15 miles in width. The mountains send down various rivers—the Karun, Kerkah, Diala, &c. Agriculture is only carried on near the villages, where cotton, rice, various grains, opium, fruits, manna, &c., are produced. The chief towns are Teheran, Ispahan, Natanz, Kashan, and Hamadan. The climate varies from the excessive heat along the verge of the deserts to the wintry severity of the uplands. Among the manufactures are silks, velvets, chintzes, gold and silver brocades, carpets, arms, cutlery, and sweetmeats. The I. militia is organised in eleven regiments of 1000 men each, and are under the command of the proprietors of estates.

Irak'-Ar'abi, a province of Turkey in Asia, lying between the Tigris and Euphrates, and including a strip of land between the Euphrates and the desert. It corresponds to the ancient Babylonia, and contains the ruins of Babylon, Seleucia, and Ctesiphon. See TURKEY IN ASIA, and BABYLONIA.

Iran', the native name of Persia, part of which was known to the Greeks and Romans as *Ariana*. In the Zendavesta the term is *Airya*. See ARYAN.

Irbit', a town of Eastern Russia, in the government of Perm, at the confluence of the I. and Nitsa, and 106 miles E.N.E. of Ekaterinburg. A yearly fair (founded in 1630) is held here in February, which is second only to that of Nijni-Novgorod (q. v.), and attracts upwards of 60,000 traders from all parts of Russia, from Greece, Armenia, Siberia, Persia, and even China. The chief articles of trade are home-manufactured goods, tea, furs, sugar, and wine; of secondary importance are foreign manufactured goods, leather, hardwares, and jewellery. In 1872 the estimated value of the goods offered for sale was £7,500,000; of sales effected, £7,000,000. Pop. 4212.

Ire'land is 'the land of *Eire*,' a word of uncertain derivation. Some think it connected with the Celtic *iar*, 'the West;' others suppose it to be the name of an ancient Irish queen; while others again see in it the root 'ar' ('to till'), which plays so important a part in Aryan philology. The island was known to the Greeks by the name *Ierne* (Erin), 'the island of Eire,' and to the Romans by the name *Hibernia*. It is the second largest of the British Isles, is washed on the N., S., and W. sides by the Atlantic Ocean, and is separated from Great Britain by the N. Channel, the Irish Sea, and St. George's Channel in lat. 51° 2′ 6″—55° 23′ N. and long. 5° 26′—10° 28′ W. It has a length from N.E. to S.W. of 306 miles, a breadth from E. to W. of 180 miles, and a coast-line of 2200 miles, or one mile of coast to every 15 sq. miles of surface. The coast along the E. is for the most part flat and little indented, but on the other sides is bold and rocky, running out in lofty headlands, and opening in many deep inlets to the Atlantic surge. In the E. the chief bays are Belfast Lough, Strangford Lough, Dundrum Bay, Carlingford Lough, Dundalk Bay, Dublin Bay, and Wexford Harbour; in the W., Donegal Bay, Sligo Bay, Clew Bay, Galway Bay, the estuaries of the rivers Shannon and Kenmare, Tralee Bay, Dingle Bay, Bantry Bay, and Dunmanus Bay; in the N., Lough Foyle, Mulroy

Bay, and Lough Swilly; in the S., Cork, Waterford, and Youghal harbours, and Dungarvan Bay. Among the promontories are Malin Head, Bangore Head, and Fair Head in the N.; Carnsore Point, Knockadoon Head, Old Kinsale Head, and Mizen Head in the S.; Bloody Foreland, Teelin Head, Benwee Head, Achill Head, Aghros Point, Slyne Head, Loop Head, Dunmore Head, Kerry Head, Boulus Head, Crow Head, and Sheep's Head in the W.; and Ballyquintin Point, St. John's Point, Ballagan Point, Dunany Point, Howth Head, Wicklow Head, Cahore Point, and Greenmore Point in the E. The most southernly point is at Cape Clear, the extremity of Clear Island, to the S.W. of county Cork. The islands are for the most part very small, and lie close to the mainland; they plentifully fringe the W. coast, where the principal ones, proceeding from N. to S., are the Tory, Arranmore, Mullet, Achill, Clare, Innis Turk, Innis Bofin, Gorumna, Inishmore, Inishmaan, Inisheer, the Blaskets, the Valentia, Skelligs, Bear and Clear islands. Other islands are Rathlin, N. of Antrim; Copeland, N.E. of Donaghadee; the Skerries, Lambay, and Ireland's Eye, E. of Dublin; Saltees, S. of Wexford, and Cove in Cork Harbour. Of the 5000 islands and rocks belonging to I. only 245 were inhabited in 1871. Valentia Island off Kerry is the terminus of the Atlantic cables. I. is divided into the four provinces of Ulster, Leinster, Munster, and Connaught, and these are again subdivided into thirty-two counties, the areas and population of which are as follows, according to the census of 1871:—

Counties.	Area in stat. acres.	Pop. 1871.	Chief towns.
LEINSTER—			
Carlow . . .	221,342	51,650	Carlow.
Dublin . . .	226,894	405,262	Dublin.
Kildare . . .	418,496	83,614	Athy.
Kilkenny . . .	509,732	109,479	Kilkenny.
King's County . .	493,984	75,900	Tullamore.
Longford . . .	269,409	64,501	Longford.
Louth. . . .	201,601	70,511	Dundalk.
Meath . . .	579,861	95,558	Trim.
Drogheda . . .	453	13,510	Drogheda.
Queen's County .	424,853	79,771	Maryborough.
Westmeath . .	453,468	78,432	Mullingar.
Wexford . . .	576,588	132,666	Wexford.
Wicklow . . .	500,178	78,699	Wicklow.
MUNSTER—			
Clare	827,993	147,864	Ennis.
Cork	1,849,684	517,076	Cork.
Kerry . . .	1,185,917	196,586	Tralee.
Limerick . . .	680,842	191,936	Limerick.
Tipperary . . .	1,061,730	216,713	Clonmel.
Waterford . . .	461,551	123,310	Waterford.
ULSTER—			
Antrim . . .	762,080	404,015	Belfast.
Armagh . . .	328,086	179,260	Armagh.
Cavan . . .	477,394	140,735	Cavan.
Donegal . . .	1,197,154	218,334	Lifford.
Down	612,409	293,449	Downpatrick.
Fermanagh . .	457,369	92,794	Enniskillen.
Londonderry . .	522,315	173,906	Londonderry.
Monaghan . . .	319,741	114,969	Monaghan.
Tyrone . . .	806,658	215,766	Omagh.
CONNAUGHT—			
Galway . . .	1,566,352	248,458	Galway.
Leitrim . . .	392,363	95,562	Carrick.
Mayo	1,363,883	246,030	Castlebar.
Roscommon . .	607,691	140,670	Roscommon.
Sligo	461,796	115,493	Sligo.
Total .	20,819,867	5,512,479	

In no country of Europe has there been of late years such vicissitudes in population. In 1801 the population amounted to 5,395,456; in 1811 it rose to 5,937,856; in 1821, to 6,801,827; in 1831, to 7,767,401; and in 1841, to 8,175,124; but sank to 6,552,385 in 1851, and to 5,798,564 in 1861. According to the Registrar-General, the number of emigrants from I. in 1852 was 190,322; in 1857, 95,081; in 1863, 117,229; in 1870, 74,855; and in 1875, 51,462.

Physical Aspect.—The great central portion of I., from Dublin to Galway, and from Tipperary to the shores of Lough Neagh, is extremely flat, and the mountains by which the interior plain is fringed are broken into isolated groups. Not less than 2,830,000 acres of the surface is bog or morass, which is quite uncultivatable, and gives a dreary aspect to the country. The largest single morass is the Bog of Allen (see ALLEN, BOG OF), covering great parts of Meath, King's County, and Kildare. The central plain is traversed by a few low ranges of hills, chief of which are the Slieve-Bloom mountains, rising in Mount Kieper to a height of 2278 feet, and separating the basin of the Shannon from that of the Barrow and Suir. The highest mountains of I. are Macgillicuddy's Reeks in the S.W. (county Kerry), which rise in Carran-Tual, the loftiest peak in the island, to 3414 feet, and in Mangerton, S.E. of Lake Killarney, to 2756 feet; Mount Brandon (3127 feet), the second highest peak in I., is also situated in Kerry to the N. of Dingle Bay. Other ranges are the Mourne Mountains in Down, the highest summit, Slieve Donard, being 2796 feet; Glenocum Mountains in Antrim, 1817 feet high in Mount Trostan, and extending from Belfast to Fair Head; Carntogher Mountains, in Londonderry, attaining in Mount Sawell 2090 feet; the Donegal Mountains, in which the principal peaks are Errigal, 2466 feet, and Blue Stack, 2219 feet; the Nephin-Beg Mountains (2646 feet) in Mayo; the mountains of Joyce's Country (the Twelve Pins, 2395 feet), and of Connemara (Muilrea, 2688 feet), between Clew Bay and Galway Bay; the Slieve Baughta Mountains in the S.E. of Galway; the Vermine Mountains in Tipperary; Galteemore (3007); Knockmeledown (2598) in Waterford; and the group with Lugnaquilla (3039), and Kippur (2473) in Wicklow. The great *rivers* of I. rise in the central plain, and generally string together numerous lakes or *loughs*, while several of them have been rendered navigable almost to their source by means of locks and lateral cuttings. The Shannon is the longest river in I., having a length (with windings) of 220 miles. The rivers that flow from the central plain and empty themselves into the Atlantic on the W. coast are the Shannon, Corrib, Moy, and Erne; on the N. coast, the Foyle and Bann; on the S. coast, the Suir, Barrow, Lee, and Blackwater; on the E. coast, the Slaney, Liffey, Boyne, and Lagan. Internal communication is greatly extended by an artificial water system embracing the Lagan, Newry, Ulster, Royal, Grand, and Athy Canals. The loughs are many and of great extent; Lough Neagh, in Ulster, with an area of 153 sq. miles, being the largest sheet of water in the British Isles. The total area of all the Irish lakes is 984 sq. miles, and the principal of them are Neagh, Corrib, Erne, Derg, Ree, and Mask. On the Shannon are Loughs Derg, Ree, Boffin, Corry, and Allen; on the Corrib are Mask and Corrib; on the Moy are Conn and Cullen; on the Erne are Oughter and Erne. The lakes of Killarney (q. v.), in Kerry, and under shadow of the loftiest mountains in the island, are widely famed for their romantic beauty. The coast inlets are in some cases called loughs, *e.g.*, Loughs Foyle and Swilly, and Belfast and Strangford Loughs.

Climate.—The climate of I. is milder and moister than that of Great Britain, owing to its lying further into the Atlantic, and coming more directly under the influence of the Gulf Stream. The mean temperature in winter is 41°, in spring 47°, in summer 60°, and in autumn 51° F. The difference in mean temperature between N. and S. is only 3° F. The annual rainfall throughout I. is estimated at 40 inches. It is much greater in the W. and S., especially in the mountainous region of Kerry; but at certain points on the E. coast the rainfall scarcely exceeds 25 inches. In winter I. is visited by prevailing S.W. winds, mild and full of moisture, while it is less exposed than Great Britain to the chill easterly winds of spring.

Geology.—The island is divided geologically into three great sections—the central plain of Carboniferous limestone, the Silurian district in the N., and that of the Cambrian rocks, resembling those of N. Wales, in the S. Greatest of these is the central plain, which is occupied by one of the largest aggregates of beds of Carboniferous limestone in the world. The plain is formed by wavy beds of the lower part of the Carboniferous limestone, from which the coal measures, to the thickness of from 2000 to 6000 feet, have been denuded, and which is covered here and there with limestone gravel. Its surface is overlaid with peat-moss and fresh-water marl, in which have been found remains of recently extinct animals. The structure is beautifully exhibited in the hills of Queen's County on the E., and on the W. in the hills of Burren, 1000 feet high, that sweep for some 20 miles along the S. side of Galway Bay. To the S. the limestone is succeeded by a series of black shales, and grey gritstones or flagstones, containing in their upper portion thin coal beds. Cambrian rocks, beds of grit, and slate of dull green, brown, and purple hues, occur in Wexford in the extreme S.E., in Wicklow, and in Howth Head, Dublin county. In Kerry and Cork the principal rocks are the sandstones and slates of the Devonian age. The northern portion of the country is allied in geological character to the W. of Scotland, the prevailing Silurian rocks being intruded by granite and basalt, *e.g.*, at the Giant's Causeway (q. v.). Here also occur Permian, Cretaceous, and Triassic formations; near Belfast there are beds of gypsum and rock-salt. One of the finest known examples of steady direction of cleavage planes is in the S. of I., over the whole of which, from Dublin to the Mizen Head and the Dingle Promontory, the direction of cleavage, according to Jukes, 'seldom varies 10° from E. 25° N., whatever rocks it traverses.'

Soil and Productions.—The soil of I. is for the most part fit for cultivation, while much of it is singularly fertile. Though there must at one time have been immense forests of oak, as evidenced by the great tracts of bog, the surface is now extremely bare. The moist climate clothes the plains and valleys with the richest pasture, procuring for I. the name of the Emerald Isle. In the S.W. many of the wild plants of the N. of Spain grow. In 1876 there were under all kinds of crops, bare fallow, grass, and permanent pasture, 15,724,954 acres; 1,848,487 of corn crops (incuding beans and peas); 1,363,224 of green crops; 11,652 bare fallow; 1,861,464 grasses, clover, &c., under rotation; 10,507,249 in permanent pasture. The chief crops are barley, wheat, rye, beans, potatoes, turnips, marigolds, and cabbage. Flax is also cultivated to the extent of 130,000 acres, especially in Ulster. The system of cultivation is very defective, though various agricultural schools have been established throughout the country since 1831. The recent Irish Land Act, from which much benefit is expected, provides fixity of tenure, compensation for improvements, and facilities for converting leaseholds into freeholds. In 1875 the number of separate holdings was 585,483, and of these 51,459 were of not more than one acre. The live-stock was as follows in 1876:—horses, 479,000; cattle, 4,113,000; sheep, 4,007,000; and pigs, 1,424,000.

Industries, Commerce, &c.—The most important manufacture of I. is that of linen, of which Belfast is the centre. In the towns on the N.E. and W. muslin-sewing and lace-making are considerable industries. Woollen manufactures are carried on to a limited extent in Dublin, Cork, Waterford, Kilkenny, &c., and there are also industries in woollen and worsted goods, in silk, jute, &c. According to official returns, in 1875 there were in I. 8 cotton factories, employing 3075 persons; 60 woollen factories, employing 1506 persons; 149 flax or linen factories, employing 60,316 persons; 4 hemp factories, employing 341 persons; 11 jute factories, employing 2094 persons; 2 silk factories, employing 400 persons; and 1 worsted factory, employing 12 persons. Of the whole employed inhabitants, 32¼ per cent. are men, and 68¾ per cent. are women. I. has a comparatively large number of coal-pits, but an annual output not exceeding 165,000 tons. There is a considerable amount of whisky-distilling and porter-brewing. The fisheries have of late years greatly declined; in 1846 they employed 20,000 vessels and 100,000 persons; and in 1872 not more than 8000 vessels and 31,000 persons. The seas around I. are singularly rich in cod, ling, hake, herrings, pilchards, &c. The trade of I. is almost entirely with Great Britain, and is mainly in grain, potatoes, cattle, and whisky. In 1871 there were 1776 vessels, of 218,162 tons, and 11,887 men, registered at the ports. The gross receipts of custom for I. amounted to £1,755,487 in 1875.

Railways, &c.—In 1876 there were in I. 2148 miles of railway open for traffic. The total capital contributed up to 1875 was £30,246,175, and the receipts of that year amounted to £2,633,103. The number of private telegraphic messages forwarded in 1875 was 1,434,996.

Education.—The educational returns for I. are less favourable than for any other portion of the United Kingdom. In 1872 36 per cent. of the men and 46 of the women in signing their marriage register were unable to write their names. A system of national education was established in 1845 under the management of a body of commissioners. The principle laid down was one which has not been extended to England and Scotland, viz., that there should be 'united secular, and (when wanted) separate religious instruction.' In 1871 there were 6914 national schools with 1,021,700 pupils, of whom 822,016 were Roman Catholics, 113,227 Presbyterians, and 78,789 Episcopalians. The parliamentary grant in 1871 amounted to £408,388. The 'secular' teaching of the national schools is somewhat coldly regarded by the various Churches, and the Church Education Society has (1870) some 350 schools attended by 52,166 pupils, of whom 44,662 are Episcopalians, 3747 other Protestants, and 3757 Roman Catholics. There are also 587 higher schools with 25,055 pupils. Among the chief educational institutions are Dublin University (q. v.) and the Queen's Colleges (q. v.) at Belfast, Cork, and Galway. Maynooth College (15 miles N.W. of Dublin) is an institution for the training of Roman Catholic priests, supported at public expense, and attended by 520 students. At Dublin there is a Royal Hibernian Military School.

Religion.—According to the census of 1871 there were in I. 4,141,933 Roman Catholics; 683,295 Episcopalians; 558,238 Presbyterians; 41,815 Methodists; 4485 Independents; 4643 Baptists; 3834 Quakers; and 258 Jews. The Roman Catholic Church is under the Archbishops of Armagh, Cashel, Dublin, and Tuam, and twenty-three bishops. The Protestant Episcopal Church of I., formerly in civil union with the Church of England, under two archbishops and ten bishops, ceased to be a state establishment on and after 1st January 1871, by Act of Parliament, 32 and 33 Vict., cap. 42. The endowments have been dispensed so liberally that only a trifling sum will remain after meeting all liabilities. A payment of £500,000 was made to the disestablished Church in lieu of its private endowment, of £372,332 to Maynooth College, and of £90,000 to Nonconformist bodies, leaving in 1875 property valued at £16,750,000. Annuities and other liabilities are estimated to dispose of £11,560,000 of this amount, and there will thus remain a sum of £5,190,000, which is to be devoted to national purposes.

Government.—I. is represented in the Imperial Parliament by thirty-two members of the House of Lords and 105 of the House of Commons. A Lord-Lieutenant is head of the executive government, and is assisted by a Privy Council and Chief Secretary. The judicial system resembles that of England, and has a Landed Estates Court. In I. there are no fewer than 12,000 police, of whom some 400 are mounted.

History.—The ancient traditional inhabitants of I., the Firbolgs and Danauns, are said to have been conquered in early times by the Milesians or Gaels. Almost everything, however, is legendary and uncertain in the history of I. till the 5th c. A.D., when the inhabitants are called Scots. About the time that English invaders were beginning to harry the south coast of Britain, the Scots were passing in fleets of coracles from the coast of Antrim to found the little kingdom of Scotland in the S. and W. of Argyle. Christianity had found its way to I. before the appearance of St. Patrick (q. v.), but it only attained its complete supremacy about a century after his death. The conversion of the Irish at a time when Christianity was struggling for existence in Italy, Gaul, and Spain, raised their country to a position of honour that it has never since known among the nations of Western Europe. Towards the end of the 6th c. extensive monasteries arose throughout the island, and these soon became the illustrious centres of letters and arts. 'The science and biblical knowledge which fled from the Continent took refuge in famous schools, which made Durrow and Armagh the universities of the West.' For the missionary zeal that flamed up a ready field was found among the Frisians of the northern seas and the Picts of the Highlands. Among the more famous of the Irish apostles are Columba (q. v.), Adamnan (q. v.), his biographer, Columbanus (q. v.), founder of monasteries in Burgundy and the Apennines, Gallus, who gave name to the Swiss canton of St. Gall (q. v.), and Ferghal or Virgilius, the evangeliser of Carinthia. The labours of Aidan (q. v.) and the monks of Lindisfarne led to a claim for the annexation of England to the Irish Church that was only reversed by the Council of Whitby in 664. But the Celtic Church, that had risen to power so rapidly, was devoid of regular organisation, and shared the fate of the clan system on which its government was based. By the 12th c. its learning had disappeared, its religion had dwindled into superstition and ascetic exercise, and its spiritual influence was lost in tribal quarrel and ecclesiastical controversy. Its head, the Coarb or Archbishop of Armagh, sank into the hereditary chieftain of a clan; its bishops were without diocese, and often mere dependants of the greater monasteries. But the Church only shared in a general anarchy that it was unable to check. From the earliest times I. seems to have been divided into the four principalities of Ulster, Leinster, Munster, and Connaught, long subject to the central authority of the Ard-righ or King of Leinster, whose territorial possession was Meath, and who usually resided at

Tara. The supremacy of the over-king and even of the minor kingships gradually became merely nominal, while the only recognised institution remaining was the primitive sept, tribe, or clan, whose chieftainship was hereditary, passing not from father to son, but to the eldest member of the ruling family at the time. (See BREHON LAWS.) The incursions of the Danes began about the end of the 8th c., and led to a series of destructive struggles that lasted for three hundred years, and gradually extinguished Irish civilisation. Brian Boroimhe inflicted such a blow on the invaders in his victory at Clontarf near Dublin (1014) as thenceforth restricted them to the coast towns they had founded, Dublin, Waterford, &c., where they remained distinct in blood and manners, at feud with the surrounding tribes, though occasionally forced to pay tribute to the Irish kings. The coast cities had meantime renewed the intercourse of England with I. by the slave-trade, which the Conqueror and Bishop Wulfstan temporarily suppressed at Bristol, and by receiving the ordination of their bishops from the See of Canterbury. The slave-trade had filled I. with kidnapped Englishmen, and defied alike the royal prohibition and the spiritual menaces of the English Church. Henry II. obtained (1155) the sanction of Pope Hadrian IV. to an invasion of I., his ostensible aim being to 'subject the people to laws, to extirpate vicious customs, to respect the native churches, and to enforce the payment of Peter's pence.' The project was abandoned, however, on account of the opposition it met with in a great council of the English baronage. Fourteen years later, Dermot MacMurragh, King of Leinster, appeared at the English court, and did homage to Henry for the dominions from which he had been driven by one of the endless tribal wars. He returned to I. in 1169 with promises of aid, and was soon followed by a band of a hundred and forty knights, sixty men-at-arms, and three or four hundred Welsh archers. The small force proved invincible among the Irish kernes, and Dermot was reinstated, and added to his former possessions Dublin and other eastern towns. Richard of Clare, Earl of Pembroke and Striguil, a ruined baron, surnamed 'Strongbow,' married Eva, Dermot's daughter, and succeeded (1171) to the kingship of Leinster, but to appease Henry was forced to surrender Dublin to the crown, and to do homage for his dominion as an English lordship. In 1172 Henry visited I. with a large force, received homage from all the native rulers save the King of Connaught and the chiefs of Ulster, and was recognised by the bishops as their lord in the Synod of Cashel. Before carrying out his scheme of complete conquest, he was recalled by the troubles in Normandy, but he granted charters to Fitz Gislebert, Le Gros, De Cogan, De Lacy, De Courcy, and other Anglo-Norman adventurers, to take possession of the independent parts of the island by force. De Courcy entered Ulster, and settled at Downpatrick. In 1184 Henry made his youngest son, John, Lord of I., but the levity of the young prince, who mocked the native chieftains and plucked them in derision by the beard, excited disturbances which led to his recall. The invaders, unable to make themselves masters of the island, were hemmed up in what was called the 'English Pale,' comprising the districts of Drogheda, Dublin, Wexford, Waterford, and Cork. All the lawless ferocity of feudalism broke out in the 13th c. under the barons, who observed a mere shadow of fealty to the English crown. The English settlers within the Pale were harried alike by the Irish septs and the baron protectors. John headed an expedition in 1212, and drove the leading barons into exile, but anarchy burst forth again on his departure. The Irish with an allied Scottish force under Edward Bruce, were defeated by the barons on the bloody field of Athenry (1316) with the loss of eleven thousand men, including almost the whole of the great clan of the O'Connors. But from this period the barons sank gradually into Irish chieftains. The statute of Kilkenny (1367) in vain forbade any man of English blood to adopt the Irish name, dress, or language. Richard II. landed with an army of overpowering strength, reduced the whole island to subjection, knighted at Dublin the four over-kings, received homage from seventy-five chiefs, strove to reform the government and enforce improved laws; but the withdrawal of his soldiers was the signal for a return to misrule. Henry VII. adopted the policy of increasing, since he could not restrain, the power of the barons; and when the great Earl of Desmond defied the authority of the Government, he made him Lord Deputy. The Earls of Desmond, the Fitzgeralds or Geraldines, who had acquired unbounded power in E. Munster and Kildare, continued to govern I. in the name of the crown till the accession of Henry VIII., when they were completely overthrown by Skeffington the new Lord Deputy. Their discomfiture was mainly due to the unexpected destruction by a train of artillery of Maynooth, the stronghold from which the Geraldines menaced Dublin. Henry had no sooner subjected the barons than he set himself to the task of 'making Ireland English.' This was to be done gradually, by the enforcement of justice and legal rule. The sole test of loyalty was the acceptance of an English title, and the education of a son at the English court. In 1541 Henry assumed the title of King of I., and the conciliatory scheme was like to win its end, when the island was again plunged into strife by a fatal attempt, continued during the reign of Edward VI., to thrust upon it the Reformation doctrines. The population on both sides of the Pale united in opposition 'as Catholics,' and the old faith was restored by Mary. The slow conciliation of the chiefs, however, gave way to the sterner and speedier policy of supplanting by force the Irish septs by English colonists, as in the case of the O'Connor's country, which was converted into shire-land under the names of King's and Queen's County, in honour of Philip and Mary. The result was a revolt in the N., and the appearance of the valorous Shane O'Neill, the successor to the Earldom of Tyrone, according to Irish law. Shane for a time ably resisted Sussex, and subsequently made a feint of submission at London to Elizabeth, but again revolted with the ambitious hope of adding Connaught to his dominion of Ulster. He was at last signally defeated (1567) by Sir Henry Sidney. In 1579 an attempted Papal rising was fiercely suppressed, a small Spanish force that had landed in Kerry was put to the sword, the Earl of Desmond was defeated, and his estates in Munster were given over to English settlers. But a more formidable revolt (1598) of the great northern tribes under Hugh O'Neill, Earl of Tyrone, who had been brought up at the English court, was only quelled after three years' hard fighting, directed by Lord Mountjoy. A Spanish force which landed at Kinsale had to surrender; a chain of forts was thrown across the conquered country; and the work of devastation was completed by a famine. A death-blow was dealt to the old tribal system by the settlement of the acquired province on the basis of a purely English polity. The chiefs were legally deprived of their tribal authority, and reduced simply to nobles or landowners; the clansmen rose from subjects into tenants, rendering to their lords only fixed dues and services; the English system of judges and trial by jury took the place of Brehon law. In the reign of James I. was effected the great revolutionary measure known as the 'Plantation of Ulster' (1610). Two-thirds of the N. of I., declared to have been confiscated to the crown, was cleared of Irishry and allotted to new Scotch and English settlers, and the foundation laid of the subsequent industrial prosperity of Ulster. Strafford by his system of 'Thorough' (1633) weakened and cowed I. for a time, but in playing off religious parties against each other he stirred the passions which found vent in the Irish massacre of some 40,000 Protestants in 1641. The revolt that followed was crushed out by Cromwell, in whose vengeful campaign the more memorable incidents are the taking of Drogheda, and the ineffectual siege of Waterford. The revolutionary wars raged in I. for four years (1688–72), the native Irish siding with James II. William's most brilliant success was the battle of the Boyne (1690); the determined but hopeless defence of Limerick was the last display of national bravery. For the next hundred years I. remained passive under a terrible legal tyranny. The more stringent penal statutes against the Catholics were repealed too late to hinder the rebellion of 1798, which was suppressed at Vinegar Hill. The Act of Union with Great Britain passed into law 1st January 1801, and from this date the history of I. merges in that of Great Britain (q. v.). Important circumstances and phases of later Irish history are also described in such articles as CATHOLIC EMANCIPATION, FENIANISM, O'CONNELL. See *The Annals of the Four Masters*, edited by Dr. O'Donovan (Dubl. 1856); Dr. Lanigan's *Ecclesiastical History of I.* (Dubl. 1829); Professor O'Curry's *Lectures on the Materials of Ancient Irish History* (Dubl. 1861); Froude's *English in I. in the Eighteenth Century* (3 vols. Lond. 1872–74); and other authorities given in Green's *Short History of the English People.*

Ireland, Law Regarding. Since the legislative incorporation with Great Britain, taking effect from 1st January 1801, other measures have been adopted for uniting the interests of the two countries. In 1819 an Act was passed for consolidating the exchequers of England and Ireland. By 6 Geo. IV. c. 79 the currency of Ireland is assimilated to that of Great Britain, and all mercantile and pecuniary transactions are to be done in the currency of the United Kingdom. By the Catholic Emancipation (q. v.) Act, the disabilities to which the great majority of the Irish population had been subjected were removed. The Acts for facilitating the sale of encumbered estates having proved beneficial; their provisions were amended in 1858, and a permanent court erected for the sale and transfer of land. 26 Vict. c. 11 introduced a complete system of registration of births and deaths. 36 and 37 Vict. c. 21 abolished tests in Trinity College and in the University of Dublin. 32 and 33 Vict. c. 42 dissolved the union between the Churches of England and Ireland from 1st January 1870, and abolished the right of Irish bishops to sit in the House of Lords.

Irenæ'us, St., Bishop of Lyon, one of the most famous of the 2d c. fathers, was an Asiatic Greek, born probably at Smyrna between the years 120 and 140. He was a disciple of Polycarp, who is supposed to have sent him to Gaul as presbyter to Pothinus, the founder of the churches of Lyon and Vienne. On the martyrdom of the latter (177), I. succeeded him in his bishopric, which he held until 202, when, according to tradition, he was himself beheaded in the persecution of Severus. He made many converts from heathenism, was an active opponent of the Gnostics, and in the controversy between the Eastern and Western Churches as to the time and manner of celebrating Easter (q. v.), addressed a moderate letter to Pope Victor, which aided the postponement of the question until the Council of Nicæa (325). We possess but one of I.'s writings in its entirety, *Adversus Hæreses*, and that in a barbarous Latin translation of the 4th c. It was published first by Erasmus (Basel, 1526), and again with the fragments by Gallasius (Par. 1570), but the best edition is that of Grabe (Oxf. 1702).

Ire'ne (Gr. *eirēnē*, 'peace'), a Byzantine empress born about 752 at Athens. At seventeen she became the wife of Leo, son of Constantine V., who was fascinated by her beauty, and in 780 she succeeded Leo as ruler, during her son Constantine VI.'s minority. One of her chief aims was to restore image-worship in the Eastern Empire, which she effected through a council at Nicæa in 789. Her son at length flung off her authority and became emperor in 790, but I. in 797 contrived to gain imperial power, and caused him to be blinded. 'For five years,' says Gibbon, 'her reign was crowned with external splendour; and if she could silence the voice of conscience, she neither heard nor regarded the reproaches of mankind.' She is said to have offered herself in marriage to Karl the Great, who rejected the proposal. I. ruled with considerable ability until 802, when she was deposed by her grand treasurer, Nicephorus, who banished her to Lesbos, where she was forced to maintain herself by spinning, and where she is said to have died of grief in 803. She has been canonised by the Greek Church. See Gibbon's *Decline and Fall of the Roman Empire* (ch. xlviii.).

Ire'ton, Henry, one of Cromwell's generals, belonged to a Nottinghamshire family, was born in 1610, educated at Cambridge, and became a lawyer. In the Civil War he took the side of the Parliament, and his legal skill was of much service to his party. He fought at Naseby, and became one of the most trusted lieutenants of the Protector, a daughter of whom he married. He signed the King's death-warrant, and succeeded Cromwell in the chief command in Ireland in 1649, governing with severity. He died of fever at Limerick, November 26, 1651, and was buried at Westminster. At the Restoration his corpse was disinterred, and burned at Tyburn. He was austere and fanatical, but of upright, incorruptible character.

Iriar'tia, a small genus of handsome and singular *Palmæ*, with stems supported on a cone of emersed prickly roots. *I. exorrhiza* is one of the commonest Amazon palms. Well-grown plants of *I. ventricosa* are from 60 to 100 feet high, with the cone of exserted roots 2 to 12 feet. Canoes are sometimes extemporised from the bellied trunk by splitting off lengthwise a little less than half of it, hollowing out the remainder and stopping up the ends with clay. From a slender little species of the Rio Negro region—*I. setigera*—the natives commonly make their blowing-canes.

Irid'eæ, or **Irida'ceæ,** an order of monocotyledonous herbaceous plants with tuberous roots or creeping root-stock, narrow leaves, and generally handsome flowers springing from spathe-like bracteæ; chiefly extra-tropical in their distribution, and numbering about fifty genera and five hundred species. The British representatives of the order are Crocus, Iris, Gladiolus, Trichonema. Along with these numerous foreign genera furnish some of the best-known florist's flowers, *e.g.*, Ixia, Tritonia. At the Cape the order is abundantly represented, not confined to any one district, soil, or elevation, but abounding from one end of the colony to the other, and covering the ground in the months of September and October with a sheet of blooms 'that resemble nothing so much as a shower of gaudy butterflies.'

Irid'ium, an element discovered by Smithson Tennant in 1804 along with osmium, in the residue of the action of aqua regia on crude platinum. On account of the variety of colours assumed by its compounds it was called I. (from Gr. *iris*, 'the rainbow'). It is a scarce metal, being found associated with platinum and osmium in certain rare minerals. I. is a hard, brittle, white metal; specific gravity, 21·15. It is not acted on by acids; but when heated with nitre it gradually oxidises and dissolves. It forms three chlorides, $IrCl_2$ (the protochloride), $IrCl_3$, and $IrCl_4$, with corresponding oxides and sulphides. On account of its hardness it has been used for pointing gold pens. The combining weight of I. is 198.

I'ris, a genus of beautiful, hardy perennials belonging to Irideæ (q. v.), of which many varieties are commonly cultivated in gardens, and one species, under the name of yellow flag, is a well-known ornament of our British river-banks, ditches, &c. A rarer English species is met with in chalk and limestone districts, on hedge-banks, and in copses, called *I. fœtidissima*, from the nauseous smell emitted by the plant when bruised. In contrast to this, *I. florentina*, a species of the Mediterranean region, yields the violet-scented Orris-root (q. v.). The old name of flower-de-luce, applied to this genus, is a corruption of fleur-de-Louis, a white-flowered I. (so supposed), being the shield-device adopted by Louis VII. of France.

Iris Pseud-acorus.

I'ris, in Greek mythology, is the daughter of Thaumas and Electra, the parents of the Harpies, a virgin goddess, who is given in the *Iliad* as the messenger of the gods, an office held in the *Odyssey* by Hermes. In the later poets she appears as the wife of Zephyrus and mother of Eros. No antique statues of I. exist, but in the bas-reliefs and on vases she is usually a young maiden with winged shoulders, dressed in a light upper garment with a long, loose robe beneath, and bearing a herald's staff and flower. The conception of I. as messenger of the gods doubtless arose from a personification of the rainbow, appearing suddenly and as suddenly 'evanishing amid the storm,' and regarded as a bridge uniting earth and heaven.

Iris, in physiology, is a muscular curtain in the eye, perforated by a hole known as the pupil. (See EYE.) The I. is formed of involuntary muscular fibres arranged in two sets—(1) A radiating set, under the control of the sympathetic nerve, which on contraction dilate the pupil; and (2) a circular set, found chiefly near the margin of the pupil, under the control of the third cranial nerve, which have the effect of contracting the pupil. These fibres, through their nervous supply, are stimulated to contract by the action of light on the retina of the eye. Thus the amount of the dilatation of the pupil is regulated by the strength of the stimulus of light. With a strong light the pupil contracts, and with a weak light the pupil dilates. Certain substances have a definite action on the I. Thus atropine, the active principle of Belladonna, dilates, while physostigmine, the active principle of Calabar bean, contracts it. The functions of the I. are—(1) to regulate and moderate the amount of light passing into the eye; (2) to correct the defect of spherical aberration by cutting off the outer rays of the pencil of light; (3) to assist in accommodation for near objects by contracting and thus cutting off the outer divergent rays. Without the intervention of the I., these outer rays would, by the sphericity of the cornea and lens, be brought to a focus in front of the retina, and thus there would be an uneven or blurred image. See EYE.

I'rish Language and Literature. The Celtic language is divided into two great branches, the Cymric and the Gaelic, the latter of which embraces the three varieties popularly known as Irish, Scotch, and Manx Gaelic. It is a matter of dispute whether these three should be treated as mere varieties or as distinct dialects. There are differences of such importance both in vocables and in grammatical structure between Irish and Scotch as to make the term 'dialect' applicable to each; but Manx, having adopted a phonetic system of writing, and renounced everything specifically characteristic of Gaelic except the mere words, is undeserving of such a distinction. Here we confine ourselves chiefly to the Irish. Several antiquaries maintain that pagan Ireland possessed an alphabet of its own, and speak much of an 'Ogham character,' as well as of a *Beth-Luis-Nion* alphabet; but the writing, though unquestionably old, belongs to Christian times, and is really in the Roman character of the 5th c., modified slightly in some instances. The Irish, however, adopted only eighteen of the Roman letters, rejecting j, k, q, v, w, x, y, z. The Scotch also reject these, while the Cymric and Manx use the modern English alphabet with its twenty-six letters. Both dialects agree in a peculiarity known to no other branch of the Aryan language, viz., that the harmony of vowels requires, if the vowel of the first syllable of a word be broad, that in the next syllable must also be broad, and *vice versâ*—a troublesome rule unknown of old, condemned by grammarians, but observed by all later writers. Both are now destitute of a neuter gender, though they formerly used it. In both, the terminal inflections of nouns and verbs are very few, while initial inflection, the special characteristic of the Celtic, prevails to a great extent, the first letter of a word being modified by the preceding word. In Irish this is known as *eclipsis* and aspiration. In writing Gaelic several combinations of consonants are used, which, according to the present mode of pronunciation, are entirely mute, and strangers consider these combinations as formidable obstacles to the mastering of the language. The truth is, however, that these groups of letters, necessary for preserving any trace of etymology, are to the ear simple and uniform, each combination invariably preserving its own distinctive sound, and such anomalies as occur in English, where we have one group, *e.g.*, *ough*, sounded as in *dough*, *plough*, *through*, *enough*, are never met with in Gaelic. Poetry was cultivated with very great care both in Ireland and Scotland, and while final rhymes, as in English, are not unknown, the prevailing rhythm of Gaelic poetry is 'assonance' as distinguished from 'consonance,' *i.e.*, a correspondence between the vowel sounds quite regardless of the consonants. This correspondence is often between the final syllable of one line and the middle syllable of the next; but whatever be the position of the assonants, the number of feet in the line is attended to with the utmost regularity.

Poets were generally treated in ancient Ireland with the highest respect, and enjoyed very valuable privileges. An *Ollamh*, the highest literary degree or title in philosophy, sat at the table next to the king, and the lower degrees possessed corresponding honours which are too numerous to specify here. An immense quantity of ancient Irish MSS., ranging from the 8th to the 17th c., is still preserved. The oldest MSS. speak of still older ones, which now are unfortunately lost, and thus it is probable that, at least from the introduction of Christianity into Ireland (5th c.), native literature was carefully cultivated. Professor E. O'Curry, the highest authority, says that in the libraries of Trinity College, Dublin, and of the Royal Irish Academy alone, there is to be found what, if printed, would fill 50,000 quarto pages. In Oxford, in Cambridge, in the British Museum, in the Vatican Library, Rome, in that of the Cathedral of Milan, in the monasteries of Bobio, Wurzburg, and St. Gall, as well as in many private collections at home and abroad, there are thousands more to be found. The contents of these MSS. are extremely varied, including martyrologies, festologies, treatises on scientific subjects, translations from the classics, genealogies of all the distinguished families in Ireland, and innumerable romantic tales in prose and in verse. The most valuable, however, are historical annals, civil and ecclesiastical, and the Brehon Laws (q. v.), several volumes of which are now published with an English translation and notes. The close of the 18th c. witnessed the death of the Irish tongue as a vehicle of literary composition; but Irish wit, humour, pathos, and melody are immortal, and even in the alien tones of the English tongue we can recognise the exquisite and fascinating qualities of the national genius. Goldsmith, Burke, Sheridan, Moore, Banim, Carleton, Lever, Mahony (Prout), &c., have adorned the muses of Albion with fresh grace and splendour. Though no longer a literary dialect, the I. L. is spoken by nearly three millions in Ireland, and by many hundreds of thousands in America and Australia.

Among the scholars who have recently distinguished themselves by their knowledge of Gaelic are Whitley Stokes, Drs. Everet, Petrie, O'Donovan, Reeves, O'Connor, Professor O'Curry, and notably the German Zeuss. His *Grammatica Celtica*, O'Donovan's *Irish Grammar*, and O'Reilly's *Dictionary* will be found useful to the learner; but O'Curry's *Lectures* are *the* authority on ancient Irish literature.

Irish Moss. See CARRAGEEN.

Irish Sea, separating in part Ireland from England, lies between the North Channel in the N. and St. George's Channel in the S., and extends to a breadth of 150 miles between Dundalk and Morecambe Bays. It forms a vast inlet on the English coast, contains the Isles of Man and Anglesey, and attains a depth of 80 fathoms.

Iri'tis is the term applied to inflammation of the iris, the muscular structure which divides the cavity of the Eye (q. v.) into an anterior and posterior chamber. The iris is composed of muscular fibres, nerves, and blood-vessels, cellular tissue, and a pigmentary and serous membrane; and the inflammation to which it is generally subject is of the adhesive kind, so that in the course of a neglected or misunderstood attack of I. the pupil may become obliterated by an effusion of coagulable lymph, causing permanent blindness unless relieved by an operation. The most prominent symptoms of I. are (1) pain in the eye and round the orbit, generally most intense at night; (2) contraction, irregularity, or a fixed state of the pupil; (3) discolouration of the iris, from increased vascularity and effusion of lymph; (4) effusion of lymph into the pupil and posterior or anterior chambers; (5) adhesion of the iris to the capsule of the lens, or to the cornea; (6) tubercules, pustules, or abscesses of the iris; (7) opacity of the lens or its capsules, causing (8) dimness of sight or blindness. The most frequent causes of I. are sudden changes from heat to cold, exposure to cold draughts, overuse of the eye on minute objects, especially by artificial light. I. frequently depends also on constitutional syphilis and scrofula, and on gonorrhœa, followed by synovitis, operating through the constitution. I. may depend also on actual injury, and is a concomitant of other diseases of the eyeball. In the *first stage* of I. there is increased vascularity of the cornea, discolouration of the iris, inactivity of the pupil, dimness of sight, and pain. In the *second*, there is dimness of vision, from effusion of lymph into the pupil, and contraction thereof, abscesses, adhesions, and increase of pain. In the *third*, there is obliteration of the pupil, opacity of the lens, insensibility of the retina, flattening of the eyeball, and protrusion of the choroid through the sclerotica. The treatment of I. has for its objects to subdue the congestion, to prevent the effusion of lymph or promote its absorption, to prevent the contraction of the pupil, or to dilate it if contracted, and to alleviate pain. To attain such ends, recourse is had to blood-letting and counter-irritants, the use of cathartics and diuretics, nauseants and opiates, mercury, and the iodide of potassium. Belladonna is necessary, in nearly all cases, for the purpose of dilating the pupil.

Irkutsk', a Russian government in Eastern Siberia, is bounded E. by Jakutsk, Trans-Baikal and Lake Baikal, S. by Chinese Mongolia, E. by Jeniseisk, and N. by Jakutsk. Area, 309,108 sq. miles; pop. (1870) 703,950. It is very mountainous, and is watered by the Lena, and the Angara, the upper stream of the Jenisei. The chief products are gold, silver, lead, precious stones (amethysts, emeralds, jasper, topaz), and furs, including those of the reindeer, sable, fox, seal, and ermine. The inhabitants are mainly Buriats, Tunguses, and Russians.—I., the capital, lies at the confluence of the Irut and the Angara, and has a pop. of 22,800. It is one of the chief trading towns in Siberia, a centre of Russian administration, and has an active commerce with China. Lying 1200 feet above the sea-level, it has a healthy climate, but the winter cold is intense.

Iron (Old Eng. *iren;* Ger. *eisen;* connected with Lat. *aes,* 'bronze') is the most important of all metals. It is rarely found native, but in combination with oxygen and other elements its presence is universal over the earth's surface. The metal is obtained from its ores by a lengthened series of processes afterwards described. When pure, iron is white and extremely soft and tough, with a specific gravity of 7·8. It is the most tenacious of all metals, and is difficult of fusion. In its normal state it is strongly magnetic, but loses its magnetism when heated to a dull red. Iron does not oxidise in air at ordinary temperatures, but when heated to redness becomes covered with a coat of black oxide. It, however, speedily tarnishes when in the presence of both air and water, the *rust* which is produced being a hydrate of the sesqui-oxide. Iron gives rise to two series of salts, known as the *ferrous* (Lat. *ferrum,* 'iron') and *ferric* salts. The ferrous chloride ($FeCl_2$) produced by acting upon iron with dilute hydrochloric acid may be taken as the type of the former, and ferric chloride (Fe_2Cl_6) prepared by dissolving ferric oxide in hydrochloric acid as the type of the latter. The corresponding oxides are FeO and Fe_2O_3; but besides these there is an intermediate oxide, commonly called *magnetic* or *black* oxide, having the composition Fe_3O_4. Ferrous oxide is a powerful base with a strong tendency to absorb oxygen and pass into the ferric or sesqui-oxide. The soluble ferrous salts have usually a pale green colour and a disagreeable metallic taste. The most important of these salts is the ferrous sulphate ($FeSO_4$, $7H_2O$), known also as *green vitriol* and *copperas,* which may be obtained by dissolving iron in dilute sulphuric acid. It is generally obtained on a large scale, however, from iron pyrites, the mineral ferric sulphide (FeS_2), which oxidises readily in the presence of moisture. It forms double salts with the sulphates of potassium and ammonium, which have the formulæ $FeK_2(SO_4)_2 6H_2O$ and $Fe(NH_4)_2(SO_4)_2 6H_2O$. The salts are isomorphous with the corresponding Magnesium (q. v.) salts. *Ferrous Nitrate* ($Fe(NO_3)_2$) is prepared by the action of dilute nitric acid upon ferrous sulphide (FeS). It forms pale green and very soluble crystals. *Ferrous Carbonate* ($FeCO_3$) occurs in nature as *spathose iron ore* or *iron spar.* It may be obtained as a whitish precipitate by mixing solutions of a ferrous salt and an alkaline carbonate. The *ferrous sulphide* (FeS) is a blackish brittle compound formed by heating iron and sulphur together. It evolves sulphuretted hydrogen (H_2S) when acted on by dilute acids, and for this purpose is constantly employed in the laboratory. *Ferric oxide* (Fe_2O_3) is a feeble base. It is the main constituent of red and brown Hæmatite (q. v.). As a fine powder this oxide is bright red, and is accordingly used as a pigment. It forms ferric salts, which are reddish in colour and have an acid reaction. They are not of great importance, the best known being the ferric sulphate ($Fe_2O_3 3SO_3$), which with sulphates of potassium and ammonium yields salts resembling in form and constitution the alums (see ALUM), the ferric nitrate, which is deep red in colour and used in dyeing, and the ferric sulphide (FeS_2), which occurs in nature as iron pyrites, the material chiefly employed in the manufacture of Sulphuric Acid (q. v.). (See PYRITES.) Iron is also a constituent in the important salts known as the ferro-cyanides and ferri-cyanides. (See FERRI-CYANOGEN and FERRO-CYANOGEN.)

Metallurgy of I.—The art of extracting iron from its ores has been known and practised from a period anterior to historical record, although it was not the first metal used by the human race. The production of metallic iron on a small scale is a very simple operation, and the primitive process by which it was extracted is yet prosecuted among the rude tribes of Central Africa, who thereby produce malleable iron of a very superior quality. The direct production of malleable iron from ores is still also among civilised communities an operation of some importance, being carried on in the N. of Spain and the S. of France, in India, and also in the United States and Canada. The type of the processes carried on in all these localities may be found in the Catalan forge of Spain, which consists of a hearth or furnace built of refractory sandstone into which the ore to be reduced is piled. The ore is covered over with charcoal, and when the furnace is in operation it is supplied with a blast by a nozzle passing through a wall built in the rear of the furnace. In this case the reduction of the metal from its ore—an oxide—is effected by the action of the carbonic oxide formed by the combustion of the fuel.

Iron is prepared and employed in the three different conditions of cast or pig iron, malleable iron, and steel, all of which possess properties so distinct as to give them the practical value of different metals. Pig-iron results from a combination of the metal with from 2 to 6 per cent. of carbon; malleable or wrought iron is almost free from carbon; and steel is intermediate in composition and properties between the other two, while it possesses the peculiar property of being hardened or softened at will by the process of *tempering.* In modern metallurgy, the ordinary method of manufacture is first to extract the metal in the form of pig or crude cast-iron. Pig-iron in its turn forms the basis from which both malleable iron and steel are formed. Till within very recent times steel was prepared only from malleable iron by recombining with the metal a portion of the carbon previously extracted from it in its conversion from pig into malleable iron. Now, by the Bessemer and other processes hereafter alluded to, steel is very extensively prepared direct from pig-iron without passing the metal through the processes necessary for the production of malleable iron.

Iron ores occur widespread over the globe in great abundance, although the varieties used by smelters are not numerous. Those of greater importance are carbonates of iron, generally associated in seams or nodular masses with coal deposits. The clayband or argillaceous ores and the blackband ores of Great Britain are carbonates of iron combined respectively with more or less of clayey or carbonaceous impurities, whence their names. From these alone the greater part of the iron smelted at the present day is produced. The Cleveland ore, worked in the N. of Yorkshire, and the spathose, or sparry ore, are also carbonates, and form extensive and important sources of iron. Of the oxides which are used to yield iron, the varieties of Hæmatite (q. v.) are the most important; magnetic iron ore—magnetite or loadstone—is a very valuable ore in Sweden and the N. of Europe generally, being the source of the greater part of the famous Swedish bar-iron, from which the finest quality of crucible cast-steel is prepared. Iron pyrites, the impure sulphide of iron, is also now to some extent a source of metallic iron after yielding its sulphur for sulphuric-acid-making, and in the case of Spanish ores being further treated by the wet process for the extraction of copper.

Production of Pig-Iron.—When, instead of smelting ore on a low or open hearth, a furnace of a lofty conical form is employed, the metal thereby obtained is in the condition of cast or pig iron. The blast-furnace, in which pig-metal is produced, is a comparatively modern invention, but except in the few cases of manufacturing malleable iron by the direct method already alluded to, it is now exclusively used for smelting from the ores. The most important and valuable invention of modern times in connection with the blast-furnace was the introduction of the hot blast by Neilson of Glasgow in 1828. The immediate result of the application of the hot blast was that whereas formerly 8 tons of fuel were required to produce 1 ton of pig-iron, by the year 1833 the same weight of iron was obtained with the expenditure of 2 tons 13 cwt. of coal. Now 1 ton of pig-iron can be produced by the use of from 17 to 20 cwt. of fuel. No improvement of subsequent introduction, although many of them have been of great importance and value, has affected the principles upon which the operations of the blast-furnaces are conducted. (See BLAST-FURNACE.) In smelting blackband or clayband, the ore is first broken into large pieces, and calcined generally in heaps in the open air. Alternate layers of fuel, calcined ore, and limestone flux are then introduced into the furnace, which is constantly kept filled to the 'throat.' The combustion of the fuel in the lower part of the furnace produces carbonic acid, liberating thereby an enormous heat. The ore at that point is reduced to the metallic condition, and sinks to the bottom of the furnace. In its progress upwards, the carbonic acid, meeting fresh fuel, is reduced to carbonic oxide, by which the temperature of the gas is much decreased; but meeting next the metallic oxide of the ore, it is again changed into carbonic acid, with a simultaneous production of metallic iron; and so changes go on throughout all the layers in the stack, carbonic acid being given off from the limestone in the upper part of the furnace. The working of a blast-furnace is continuous, and the periods at which the metal is withdrawn varies according to circumstances. The capacity of furnaces and the amount of iron they produce per week also vary very widely, some containing only about 1000 cubic feet of space, while the cubic contents of others measure 30,000 feet and upwards, a pair in the Cleveland district having a capacity of no less than 41,149 feet. The yield of pig-iron per day ranges from 20 to 80 or 90 tons; and three furnaces of the largest capacity now produce in a given time more iron than was manufactured in the whole country little more than a century ago. A furnace of 7500 cubic feet capacity consumes about 5400 feet of air per minute or 1700 tons per week, a weight considerably in excess of its total solid contents. Four principal varieties of pig-iron are generally recognised, numbered 1, 2, 3, and 4, respectively. The first is dark grey in colour, with large crystalline grains in its structure, soft and very fluid when melted, and it forms the best 'foundry pig.' No. 2 is also grey, with smaller crystals, soft, and from its liquidity when melted suitable also for foundry purposes. No. 3 is mottled in appearance, and intermediate between 2 and 4; and No. 4 is hard, brittle, and white in fracture, and melts only imperfectly. Nos. 3 and 4 are converted into malleable iron. The brands of different makers possess distinctive qualities, and in some districts the pigs are differently classed into six varieties.

Malleable Iron Manufacture.—Ordinary pig-iron, in addition to the carbon in its composition, contains a small percentage of silicon, sulphur, phosphorus, and other impurities, a large proportion of which along with the carbon is removed in the operations by which the pig is converted into malleable iron. These substances are got rid of by the action of oxygen on the molten metal. The pigs are usually first *refined* in a *finery* furnace, in which charges of a little more than a ton of the metal are melted under the influence of a cold blast. In the process, which occupies about two hours, almost the whole of the silicon and phosphorus and much of the carbon are removed. The refined metal is next introduced in small charges into the puddling-furnace, which is of the reverberatory kind, and in it the mass is again brought into a state of fusion. It is periodically stirred up to promote the oxidation of the carbon and remaining impurities, and gradually it swells up and becomes a stiff granular mass. In the later stage of puddling the heat is forced and all air carefully excluded, after which the puddler collects on the end of an iron rod a mass as heavy as he can manipulate, which is called a *bloom*. The bloom is hammered either under a steam-hammer or squeezed in a *shingling* press to remove the slag mixed with or adhering to the iron. The metal is then passed through the grooved rollers of a rolling-mill to draw it out into bars. The bars are cut into pieces, piled in a reverberatory furnace and heated to the welding-point, and again passed through the rolling-mill. This operation is repeated several times in the production of fine iron, and in the final stage it is passed between rollers having grooves of the section T, angle, bar, round, rail, or other, in which the metal is to be finished. The refining process in the manufacture of malleable iron is now frequently omitted, and the pigs are carried direct to the puddling furnace. The process when the finery operation is omitted is called *pig-boiling*. Much attention has been devoted of late years to the question of mechanical puddling of iron, and several processes for avoiding the severe manual labour of the old method have been devised, the most important being that of Mr. Danks, an American.

Malleable Cast-Iron, a preparation which has now come into extensive use, and in which certain advantages of both varieties are combined, is prepared by packing iron castings in powdered hæmatite and exposing them to a red heat for some time. Thereby the oxygen of the hæmatite removes a certain proportion of the carbon of the cast-iron, producing a skin of malleable iron, thick in proportion to the duration of the operation. The process of preparing malleable cast-iron is thus exactly the converse of the case-hardening of malleable iron, which operation consists of giving a skin of steel to malleable iron by exposing it to heat packed in charcoal. For the manufacture of steel see STEEL.

Statistics of the Iron Trade.—In 1874 the total quantity of iron ore smelted in Great Britain amounted to 15,854,077 tons, of which 14,844,936 tons were raised in the United Kingdom, the remainder having been imported. The quantities of pig-iron produced in the same year, and the number of furnaces in blast, were as follows:—

	Pig-iron in tons.	Furnaces in blast.
England	4,417,139	430
Wales	766,592	96
Scotland	807,677	123
Total, .	5,991,408	649

Owing to the depressed state of the iron trade in Great Britain, the above number of furnaces in blast falls short by one-third of the number of furnaces *built*.

The United Kingdom exported in 1875:—

	Tons.	Value.
Iron, pig and puddled . . .	947,827	£3,449,916
Bar, angle, &c.	276,068	2,725,907
Railroad	545,781	5,453,836
Tinned plates	138,363	3,686,607
Steel, unwrought	29,858	1,073,733
Iron, cast or wrought . . .	239,869	4,342,492
Hoops, sheets, and boiler-plates .	204,483	3,304,148
Old iron and wire	63,831	782,874
Combined steel and iron wares .	11,026	827,754
Total, .	2,457,306	25,647,267

And imported during the same period:—

	Tons.	Value.
Iron, unwrought bars . . .	89,822	£1,320,059
Wrought iron and steel . . .	1,159,762	1,422,799

The above statistics are exclusive of the export of machinery, the value of which in 1875 was £11,058,647. The steam-engines exported alone amounted to £2,631,333.

Iron Bark, the name popularly given in Australia to different species of Eucalyptus (q. v.), on account of the extreme hardness of their bark. The species number about a dozen, and are distinguished by the colonists according to the smoothness of their bark and the size of their leaves. *E. resinifera* may be taken as the typical species. The average height of the trees is from 80 to 100 feet, and their circumference sometimes reaches 25 feet. Their timber is very strong and durable, and is in high repute in Australia for shipbuilding, piles for wharves, &c.

Iron Cross, a Prussian order, founded March 10, 1813, by Friedrich Wilhelm III. as a mark of distinction for services in the War of Liberation. The knights of the I. C. consist of two classes besides the possessors of the grand cross, which is only obtained by the gainer of a great victory, or the successful besieger or heroic defender of a fortress. The decoration consists of a black cast-iron cross, mounted with silver, bearing the flourish F. W., the date 1813, the imperial crown, and a wreath of oak-leaves. The order was renewed on the occasion of the French war of 1870.

Iron Crown (of the Lombard kings). Few questions have been more warmly contested by the older writers than the significance of the crown assumed by the Holy Roman Emperors at Aachen, Monza, and Rome. 'They tell us,' says Dr. James Bryce, 'that the Roman was golden, the German silver, and the Italian iron, the metal corresponding to the dignity of each realm.' 'There seems to be no doubt,' adds the same writer, 'that the allegory created the fact, and that all these crowns were of gold or of gilded silver.' The distinctive feature of the crown of the Lombard kings is a strip of iron passing round the inner circumference, which tradition held to have been forged from a nail of the true cross. The outer circle of the crown, composed of a band of gold, is adorned with sapphires, rubies, and emeralds, set in blue enamel. When Henri, Count of Luxemburg, received (in 1310) the imperial title, he also won the I. C. In May 26, 1805, when Napoleon entered Milan, he placed it on his own head, pronouncing the formula used by the Lombard kings on these occasions, 'God hath given it me;

beware who touches it.' He also founded an order of knighthood named from the I. C., which, having disappeared, was revived (in 1816) by Emperor Franz I. The crown, removed by the Austrians (1859) to Mantua, is now in Vienna.

Iron Mask, Man with the (Fr. *L'homme au masque de fer*), the name given to a state prisoner confined in the Bastille by Louis XIV., concerning whose identity fifty-three writers have advanced no less than twenty-six different hypotheses. Of documents put forward as contemporaneous and serving to elucidate the mystery, some are certainly fictitious, others only questionably refer to this particular prisoner, and three alone are of indisputable authenticity. These are two passages from the journal of Dujonca, lieutenant of the king at the Bastille, and an entry in the burial registers of the church of St. Paul, all three preserved in the archives of the Arsenal, and first published by Père Griffet, confessor to the Bastille, in his *Traité des Différents Sortes de Preuves qui servent à établir la Verité dans l'Histoire* (Liége, 1769). From them we gather that on Thursday, 18th September 1698, St. Mars, the new governor of the Bastille, arrived from the Ile Ste. Marguerite, bringing with him a prisoner (name unknown) *whom he had formerly guarded at Pignerol* (of which fortress St. Mars was governor from 1664 to 1681), and whose face was always concealed by a black velvet mask; that this prisoner died 19th November 1703, and was buried on the 20th in the cemetery of St. Paul, his name being given in the register as 'Marchiali,' and his age as 'forty-five or thereabouts.' Who was this prisoner? He has been identified with such well-known historical characters as (1) Louis de Bourbon, Comte de Vermandois, a natural son of Louis XIV. and Mademoiselle de la Vaillière (born 2d October 1667, died at Courtrai, 18th November 1683)—in the anonymous *Mémoires Sécrets de Perse* (Amst. 1745), the earliest work upon the subject, followed by Père Griffet; (2) François de Vendôme, Duc de Beaufort (born January 1616, killed in Candia, 25th June 1669)—by Lagrange Chancel in *L'Année Littéraire* for 1759, followed by a writer in *All the Year Round* (1876); (3) James, Duke of Monmouth (q. v.) (beheaded at London, 15th July 1685)—by Saint-Foix, in *L'Année Littéraire* for 1768, a theory adopted by M. de Sévelinges in the article 'Monmouth' of Michaud's *Biographie Universelle;* (4) Fouquet, the celebrated Superintendent of Finances (born 1615, died a prisoner at Pignerol, March 22, 1680)—in *Loisirs d'un Patriote Français* (Par. 1789), followed by M. Paul Lecroix in his *Histoire de l'Homme au Masque de Fer* (Par. 1840); (5) Arwediks, an Armenian patriarch (kidnapped 1706, imprisoned at Marseille, Mont St. Michel, and the Bastille, and died a Catholic, at Paris, July 21, 1711)—by the Chevalier de Taulès in his *L'Homme au Masque de Fer* (Par. 1825), followed by Hammer, the German historian. Again, imaginary personages have been evoked to fit the character. In 1754 some Dutch savants tried to prove that the M. with the I. M. was (6) the true father of Louis XIV. (born 5th September 1638), while by Cubières in the *Voyage à la Bastille* (Par. 1789) he was affirmed to be (7) the twin-brother of that sovereign, from whose marriage with the daughter of a gaoler, Bonpart, Las Cases (q. v.) actually derived the Bonaparte family. Others have seen in him (8) an elder brother, the son of Anne of Austria by an unknown father, conjectured by Luchet in *Remarques sur le Masque de Fer* (1783) to have been no other than the Duke of Buckingham (q. v.), who last met the Queen in the June of 1625. This theory of an elder brother, started by the editor of the seventh edition of the *Dictionnaire Philosophique*—probably Voltaire himself, who had already discussed the question, without hazarding an opinion, in his *Siècle de Louis XIV.* (Berl. 1751) and *Essai sur les Mœurs*—is favoured by Michelet in his *Histoire de France*, vol. xii. p. 435, and has been popularised by Dumas in the *Vicomte de Bragelonne*.

All these theories were regarded as superseded by that which made the M. with the I. M. a minister of Duke Charles IV. of Mantua, one Ercole Antonio Matthioli, who, having deceived Louis XIV. in certain negotiations for the surrender of Casale (q. v.), was secretly arrested, May 2, 1679, and conveyed to Pignerol, an account of the transaction being given in a pamphlet, *La Prudenza Triomfante di Casale* (Köln, 1682). Suggested by the Baron d'Heiss in the *Journal Encyclopédique* for 1770, this theory was adopted in the *Correspondance Interceptée* (1789) of the Chevalier de B——, who confounds, however, Matthioli with another agent of the Duke, the Count Girolamo Magni; and during the present century it has been supported by Roux-Fazillac, *Recherches sur l'Homme au Masque de Fer* (1800), Delort, *Histoire de l'Homme*, &c. (1825), and M. Marius Topin, *L'Homme*, &c. (1869, Eng. trans. 1870). This latest advocate of the Matthioli system maintains that Matthioli did not die, as has been supposed, in the January of 1687, but remained at Pignerol till March 19, 1694, when he was transferred to the Ile Ste. Marguerite; and a comparison of dates and of the documents first published in M. Topin's work would seem at first sight to go far to establish a theory, the grand objection to which—very cursorily dismissed by M. Topin—is that at Pignerol, at least, Matthioli certainly did not wear a mask, nor was he isolated from the other prisoners. So far, however, from being definitely settled, the whole question is reopened in M. Jung's *La Verité sur le Masque de Fer* (Par. 1873), which assumes the prisoner to have been the head of a plot for the assassination of Louis XIV.—possibly a Chevalier de Kiffenbach—and advances a mass of fresh unpublished documents in confirmation of that theory. But though, as less is known of this Kiffenbach, so it is harder to prove that he could not have been the man, yet the question, Whose was the face behind the I. M.? cannot be pronounced conclusively determined, and indeed is one that to all appearance will never receive a wholly satisfactory solution.

Irons. See BILBOES.

Iron'wood, a name variously applied in many different countries to the hardest and heaviest wood of that country. In botanical nomenclature the Greek equivalent, *Lideroxylon,* is a widely-distributed genus of *Sapotaceæ.*

I'rony (Gr. *eirōneia,* 'dissimulation'), a figure of rhetoric in which words by some peculiar form or tone of expression are made to convey a meaning precisely the reverse of their literal sense. Ex. 'No doubt but ye are the people, and wisdom will die with you' (Job xii. 2). 'The story of the astronomical observations, extending over 31,000 years, sent from Babylon to Aristotle, would be a conclusive proof of the antiquity of the Chaldæan astronomy, if it were true' (Sir G. Cornwall Lewis).

Iro'quois See INDIANS, AMERICAN.

Irra'tional is a term applied to numerical quantities, which cannot be expressed by a finite number of figures. Thus $\sqrt{2}$, or the diagonal of the unit square, is an I. quantity. So also is the circumference of the circle of unit radius, a quantity usually symbolised by the Greek letter π.

Irrawadd'y (Irawad'i), the 'great river' of Burmah, which flows nearly due S. from the E. limit of the Himalayas into the Bay of Bengal: total length, about 1060 miles; drainage basin, about 150,800 sq. miles. It receives no important tributaries. On its banks are Bhamo, 640 miles from the sea, up to which point it is navigable even for steamers; Mandalay, the present capital of Independent Burmah, and Rangoon, the capital of British Burmah. Its delta lies between the Rangoon and Bassein rivers, which are both navigated by ships of the largest tonnage. Extensive embankments here protect the most productive rice-fields in the world. About 240 miles of the I. lie in British territory. In 1874-75 the I. flotilla had a fleet of nine steamers and nineteen flats; in addition to the steamers, 8203 laden boats passed up the river, and 8819 passed down. The king of Burmah has also steamers of his own. A State Railway is now in process of construction up the I. valley, on which, up to 1875, £82,000 had been expended. See RANGOON.

Irredu'cible Case, the name given to the case of a cubic equation, which cannot be solved by Cardan's Rule. See CUBIC EQUATION.

Irriga'tion (Lat. *irrigatio,* 'watering'), signifies the watering of the soil to increase its productiveness. Rain, springs, and the flooding of rivers are natural irrigating agencies. Egypt owes its fertility to the annual inundation of the Nile, a phenomenon which is supposed to have first suggested the art of artificial I. to the Egyptians. In dry, arid countries, artificial I., which may be defined as the conservation and regulated distribution of the natural water supply, is absolutely essential to agriculture. China is the most efficiently irrigated country in the world, and in

India many vast works of I. have been carried out. Artificial I. is conducted mainly from canals, which draw their supplies from a river or perennial stream, across which a dam is thrown to raise the surface level and divert the water into the new channels. Minor canals branch off from the main canal, and these feed the distributaries that convey the water over the fields. Wells and tanks or reservoirs are also employed to supply the watercourses. The water may either trickle over the fields by gravitation, or be pumped up from a lower level by means of levers or wheels.

In India two great systems of I. prevail, which may be distinguished as (1) the I. of deltas; (2) the I. of Doabs (q. v.). The one system, chiefly adopted on the E. coast of Madras, is applicable to the large tracts of rich alluvial soil at the mouths of great rivers, and these are efficiently irrigated by main and branch canals supplied from the rivers, dams or *anicuts* being constructed just above the delta head. An additional feature of this system is the existence of vast storage tanks, the works of former native rulers. The province of Madras is said to possess 43,000 of these tanks, mostly formed by throwing embankments across hill gorges, which are transformed by rainfall and local drainage into artificial lakes. The Veranam tank has an embankment 12 miles long and an area of 35 sq. miles. The other system is practised in Northern India, and deals with the elevated country far inland, running along each side of the river-banks. The most important examples are to be found at the foot of the Himalayas, where the rivers Ganges, Jumna, and Sutlej first debouch upon the plain of Hindustan. Inundation canals fed by rivers in flood are abundant in the Punjaub and other regions. These canals water the crops of autumn, but do not benefit the crops of spring, because the rivers are then low; the canals are then cleared of the silt deposited during inundation. Apart from the initial difficulty of expense, I. in India is not unaccompanied with drawbacks of its own. It has been discovered, especially in parts of the N.W. Provinces, that excessive I. tends on the one hand to engender a malarious diathesis in the population, and, on the other, to produce a saline efflorescence, known as *reh*, which is fatal to the crops. I. is a great good; but the one real safeguard against periodical famines lies in the improvement of the local means of communication.

Many extensive permanent works of I. have been constructed in Europe, more particularly in Spain, Italy, and France. The old Moors were skilful irrigators, and the fruitfulness of the *huertas* of Valencia, Murcia, and other Spanish provinces is due in great measure to the splendid machinery laid down by them 600 years ago. In England I. has not hitherto received attention commensurate with its importance, and it is chiefly confined to water-meadows or grass-lands, whereas on the Continent all kinds of agricultural produce are systematically watered. The water-meadows of the Duke of Portland at Clipstone Park, Nottinghamshire, are noteworthy. The I. of water-meadows is conducted by laying out the ground, nearly level, in a series of parallel ridges and valleys, and a narrow channel is made along the top of each ridge for the passage of water from the main conduit. The water, overflowing, trickles down the sides of the ridges, and falling into the intervening gutters is carried by them to the drain. When the ground has a uniform slope, the 'catch-water' system is pursued, in which the main drain charged with all the surplus water from the upper part of the slope becomes in turn a distributing channel to a lower tract, and so on successively. Perfectly level ground may also be irrigated from underground drains. All water is not alike adapted for purposes of I. Spring or river water may be impregnated with matter noxious to plants, therefore it is of prime importance to determine its suitableness beforehand. Good drainage should, of course, exist in water-meadows, and after the water has run for two or three weeks it should be withdrawn for some days to give the soil time to dry and air.

The question of I. in relation to the disposal of liquid sewage is assuming an important aspect; and the study now devoted to it is earnest that steps will soon be taken to extend a plan that is already in successful operation in many towns in England, likewise at Edinburgh—where rude sewage I. has been followed for upwards of a century—and Paris, and which is shortly to be tried at Brussels and Berlin. See Moncrieff, *I. in Southern Europe* (1868); Roberts, *I. in Spain* (1867); *Madras I. Reports*; Baird Smith, *Italian I.* (1855); *I. in Madras Provinces* (1856); Aymard, *Irrigations du Midi de l'Espagne* (1864); Nadault de Buffon, *Des Canaux d'I. de l'Italie Septentrionale*; and the chapter on I. in *The Progress Report of India for* 1872-73.

Irritabil'ity of Plants. In plants, from the lowest algæ to the highest development of vegetable life, certain sensible movements and actions not referable to mere elasticity or to the hygroscopic nature of the tissues have been noticed, which are classed together under the head of vegetable irritability. The motive cause is often obscure, but the use in many cases is obvious, and the writings of Darwin and of certain other observers have raised the subject to one of intense interest to the biologist. Reference must be made to these special writings, it being impossible to give even an outline in a short encyclopædia article.

Irr'itancy (Lat. *irritus*, 'of no effect'), a term of Scotch law. The I. of a right is its forfeiture in consequence of neglect or contravention. It may take place by force of the law alone (*ex lege*), or in consequence of stipulation. By the former, is the I. of a feu from non-payment of the feu during two years. Legal I. is incurred by a lessee allowing his rent to fall into arrear for two years, or by the lessee deserting or neglecting to cultivate the farm at the usual time. *Irritant Clause* is a clause in a Scotch deed of entail by which certain acts by the holder under the deed are declared void.

Irrita'tion is the term applied to morbid or artificially produced excitement of the vital actions. I. may be produced artificially by the application of irritants, such as *acetic acid*, *sinapisms*, *ammonia*, *camphor*, *turpentine*, *cantharides*, *iodine*, *mercury*, and *tartrate of antimony*. The action of many medicinal substances is due to I. alone, such as certain active cathartics. The term I. is frequently applied to what is strictly due to reflex action artificially produced, or to the result of healthy or morbid conditions; thus I. of the fauces may excite vomiting or coughing; the gravid uterus or abdominal tumours may cause sickness and vomiting; calculi, vomiting and tenesmus; while I. from intestinal worms affects the nostrils.

Ir'tish, an affluent of the Obi (q. v.), in W. Siberia, rises in the Altai Mountains, flows through the Zaisan Lake, has a winding north-easterly course through the governments of Semipalatinsk and Tobolsk, and joins the Obi, near Troitsk, 200 miles N. of Tobolsk. It receives the Ishim and Tobol, and has a length of 2080 miles.

Ir'vine, a town of Scotland, in Ayrshire, on a river of the same name, about a mile from its mouth on the Firth of Clyde, and 23 miles S.W. of Glasgow, with which it is connected by railway. It has two fine churches, and near the harbour there are three extensive chemical works, two of which cover 20 acres, and employ 300 men each. The manufactures are chiefly soda ash, bleaching powder, copper extracted by the wet process (the small quantities of gold and silver in the ores being recovered), and bichromate of potash. The wharf of the harbour was extended in 1873. Gravitation water is (1877) being brought into I., from a distance of 6 miles, at a cost of £30,000. The river is crossed by a handsome stone bridge of four arches. The academy of I. is a higher class school. Pop. (1870) 4299; including Fullarton on the opposite bank of the river, 6866. With Ayr, Campbeltown, Oban, and Inverary, I. sends one member to Parliament. I. is an old royal burgh, and was the site of a convent of White Friars, founded by the Fullartons in the 14th c. It is the birthplace of the poet Montgomery and of the novelist Galt.

Ir'ving, Edward, a great Scottish preacher, was born at Annan, Dumfriesshire, in 1792, studied at Edinburgh University, where he was a distinguished student, especially in mathematics; taught about a year in Haddington, and about seven in Kirkcaldy, latterly attending also the Divinity Hall in Edinburgh. In 1819 he was licensed a preacher of the Church of Scotland by the Presbytery of Annan. When on the point of setting out as a missionary to Persia he was appointed assistant to Dr. Chalmers in Glasgow, and for two years, says the biographer of the latter, 'Dr. Chalmers was refreshed and sustained by the congenial fellowship and efficient co-operation of a like-minded and noble associate.' In 1822 he was called to London to be pastor of the Caledonian Chapel there, and for two years enjoyed unprecedented popularity. An exalted, antique eloquence, full of an elaborate grace and pomp, that rivalled the best literature of the old English divines, marked his discourses, and compelled for a time the homage of the London 'world.' The tendency to mysticism, which he had always shown, grew upon him, however, and found scope in the exposition of unfulfilled prophecy. He then adopted the opinion that want of faith alone prevented the miraculous gifts possessed by the primitive Church from being enjoyed yet. Arraigned by the Presbytery of London in 1830 for heresy regarding the person of Christ, of whom he maintained that 'our Lord took upon him fallen and sinful flesh, with like appetites and desires as are found in us,' he was deposed by the Presbytery of Annan in 1833, and died in Glasgow next year, in the forty-third year of his age. His friend Carlyle says of I., 'his head, when the fog-Babylon had not obscured it, was of strong, far-reaching insight,' and 'his was the freest, bravest, brotherliest human soul mine ever came in contact with.' See Carlyle's *Miscellaneous Essays*, and Mrs. Oliphant's *Life of E. I.* (Lond. 1862).

Irving, John Henry Brodribb, a modern actor, was born February 6, 1838, and made his first appearance on the stage at Sunderland, September 29, 1856. He received a ten years' theatrical training in provincial theatres, playing successively in Edinburgh, Glasgow, Manchester, and Liverpool. His first London engagement was as Doricourt in the *Belle's Stratagem*, at the Lyceum Theatre. In the popular comedy of the *Two Roses* he played Digby Grand for three hundred nights at the Vaudeville. On November 20, 1871, he appeared at the Lyceum as Mathias in *The Bells*, a performance which caused a great sensation. At the last-named theatre he still (1877) remains, having appeared there as Charles I., Richelieu, Eugene Aram, Hamlet, Macbeth, Othello, and Richard III., with great approbation. His first provincial tour in 1876 was an almost unprecedented triumph. In his Shakespearian impersonations he has shown a tendency to break through stage tradition, and may be regarded as the leader of the Realistic school. Critics differ as to the merits of these performances, but all agree that he is an actor of striking force and singular originality. In melodrama he has no living rival.

Irving, Washington, an illustrious American author, the son of a Scotch merchant in New York, was born in that city, April 3, 1783. He left the study of law in 1803 to travel for his health in Europe, returning in 1806. His first work of any note was the burlesque *History of New York*, by Diedrich Knickerbocker (1809), which was widely read, its dainty satire and happy humour exciting the warm admiration of Walter Scott. He became a partner in the commercial house of Irving Brothers, and in 1815 went as its Liverpool representative to England, where he was cordially received in literary circles. Literature had till now been only a pastime to him, but in 1817 his house failed, and his pen became his only capital. Scott (whose hospitality he afterwards commemorated in *Recollections of Abbotsford*) generously interested himself on I.'s behalf, and induced Murray to publish the *Sketch-Book* in 1820. This was followed by *Bracebridge Hall* (1822) and *Tales of a Traveller* (1824). Their success was great and deserved. His polished style, bright fancy, and delicate wit, wrung from the English public an acknowledgment that a classic author had at length risen in America, who, not unworthily, wore the mantle of Addison. Taking up his residence in Spain, I. struck a new mine of literary wealth. *The Life and Voyages of Christopher Columbus* (1828), *The Conquest of Granada* (1829), and *The Alhambra* (1832), displayed his fine powers as a historian, and procured for him, along with Hallam, a medal from George IV. for historical eminence. He returned to America in 1832, and, with the exception of a residence as Minister at Madrid, 1842-45, remained there till his death. His chief works during this time were the *Tour on the Prairies* (1835), *Adventures of Captain Bonneville* (1837), *Life of Goldsmith* (1846), *Mahomet and his Successors* (1849), *Chronicles of Wolfcote Roost* (1855), and the *Life of Washington*, his crowning effort (1855-59). During his life 600,000 copies of his works were sold in America, and they had also a vast popularity in this country. His private character was high and pure. He died at his residence, Sunnyside, an old Dutch mansion on the Hudson, in the 'Sleepy Hollow' of his story, November 28, 1859. See Pierre Irving's *Life and Letters of W. I.* (4 vols. Lond. 1862-64).

Ir'vingites are a small sect of Christians founded by the Rev. E. Irving (q. v.). This name, however, they disclaim, as following no earthly leader, and assume that of the Apostolic Catholic Church. When Irving was deposed in 1833 his followers took another place of worship. On his death in 1834 a pastor was appointed in his place, and other six congregations were formed in London. Besides about thirty congregations in England, there are now congregations in Scotland, Ireland, the Continent, and America, but with small numbers. The only standards of faith which they recognise are the Apostles', Nicene, and Athanasian creeds. Their most peculiar tenet is that Apostles (of whom there ought to be twelve), Prophets, Evangelists, and Pastors are the ministers of the Church for all time, designed, along with the power and gift of the Holy Spirit, to prepare Christ's followers for his second coming. Another peculiarity of the Apostolic Catholic Church is the extraordinary use made in it of material symbols—*e.g.*, oil, light, incense, vestments, &c.—as exponents of spiritual realities. They hold that these belong to the gospel dispensation as much as the use of water in baptism, and of bread and wine in the Eucharist. The congregations are under the charge of angels or bishops, priests, and deacons; the ministry being supported by the tithes of the income of the members and freewill offerings. The hours of worship in fully-equipped churches are very frequent—at six, morning and evening, at nine, and at three. The Eucharist, which is regarded as a real sacrifice of the body of Christ, is celebrated every Sunday, and frequently in the course of the week. From holding the doctrine of the real presence of Christ, consecrated elements are kept on the altar at the time of ordinary worship. See Baxter's *Irvingism, its Rise*, &c. (1836).

I'saac (Heb. 'laughter'), the Hebrew patriarch, was son of Abraham (q. v.) and Sarah. When forty years old he married his cousin Rebecca (Gen. xxiv., *cf.* xxv. 20), by whom he had two sons, Esau (q. v.) and Jacob (q. v.). He died at Hebron at the age of 180, and was buried by his two sons in the cave of Machpelah (Gen. xxxv. 28, 29).

Isaac I., Eastern Roman Emperor, who succeeded the deposed Michael VI., founded the Comnenian dynasty (see BYZANTINE EMPIRE) in 1056. He had previously been employed in important civil and military services by Basil II. I.'s reign was marked by two principal events—the internal economical struggle which he carried on against the clergy in order to force contributions from them to the taxation of the country, and (1059) the warfare with the Hungarians, whom he was successful in keeping at bay. I. ceded his crown in the same year to Constantine Ducas, under the impression that he was a dying man. In 1061 he died in a convent to which he had retired, leaving behind him a reputation for moral strength, political capacity, and literary power. His erudition is embalmed in some Homeric Scholia, in a work upon the Greek and Trojan chiefs, and in a volume *On the Works of Homer*.

Isabell'a of Castile, daughter of Juan II., born at Madrigal, 22d April 1451, married Ferdinand of Aragon, 19th October 1469, and succeeded her half-brother Enrique IV. on the thrones of Castile and Leon, 13th December 1474. Her husband becoming King of Aragon ten years later under the title Ferdinand V., the royal consorts assumed the titles King and Queen of Spain. The great events of their united reigns have been already noticed under FERDINAND, but it is to the genius of Isabella, who jealously maintained her independent sovereignty, that many of them are rightly assignable. Thus she spurred her husband to the conquest of Granada from the Moors (1481), and herself shared in the trials and dangers of the campaign; hers is the glory of having fitted out at her own expense the first expedition of Columbus (1492); but on her must rest the blot of having in 1478 procured a bull from Sixtus IV. for the introduction of the Holy Office into Castile, and of having caused the expulsion of the Jews from that country. Isabella died at Medina del Campo, November 26, 1504. She had five children, of whom one, Juana, was mother of Karl V., and another the unfortunate Catharine of Aragon. See Prescott's *History of Ferdinand and Isabella* (1838).—**I. II.**, ex-Queen of Spain, born at Madrid, October 10, 1830, succeeded her father, Ferdinand VII., September 29, 1833, under the regency of her mother, Maria-Christina. The latter resigned in 1840 in favour of Espartero, and on October 15, 1843, I. was declared by the Cortes to have attained her majority, and three years later married her cousin, Don Francisco de Assisi. Five children were the fruit of this marriage, which, solely dictated by policy, proved an unhappy one. I.'s reign of thirty-five years witnessed the downfall of 40 ministries and 500 ministers, and was in fact but a series of alternate triumphs and defeats on the part of Narvaez, Espartero, and O'Donnell. Her court was the most profligate in Europe, and even the Golden Rose, sent her by Pio Nono in 1868, failed to rehabilitate her private character. Still, good-natured and liberal, I. was popular with the mass of the Spanish people, and this popularity was heightened by an attempt upon her life in 1852 by a priest, Martin Marino. Prim's first attempt at revolt, in 1866, was a failure; his second, in 1868, forced I. to quit her throne, and, with a favourite, Marfori, take refuge in France. On June 15, 1870, she abdicated in favour of her son, Alfonso XII. (q. v.), at Paris, where, with the exception of a visit to Geneva during the Franco-Prussian war, she resided till 1876, when she returned to Spain.

Isabella the Catholic, American Order of, a Spanish order of knighthood, founded by Ferdinand VII., March 24, 1815, was originally designed for the defenders of the Spanish possessions in America, but is now bestowed for merit generally. The king is its head, and there are three classes—Grand Crosses, Commanders, and Knights.

Isa'iah (Heb. 'Jehovah's salvation') the greatest prophet of the kingdom of Judah, was the son of Amos, who is otherwise unknown. The age to which he belonged was the reigns of Uzziah (who died B.C. 759), Jotham, Ahaz, and Hezekiah (B.C. 728–699). He was thus the contemporary of Micah and (probably) Joel in Judah, and of Hosea and Amos in Israel. The latest period for which we have certain information of the prophet's ministry is about the fourteenth year of the reign of Hezekiah (B.C. 714; 2 Kings xx.; Isa. xxxviii. 39), that is, forty-six years after the death of Uzziah, at which time he was probably ordained to the prophetic office (Isa. vi. 1–9). But there is some reason to believe that he continued his work till the reign of Manasseh. He wrote a history both of Uzziah and Hezekiah (2 Chron. xxvi. 22, xxxii. 32), both being presumably written after the king's death. There is also an ancient tradition, whatever value may be attached to it, according to which he suffered martyrdom under Manasseh by being sawn asunder. The book of the prophecies of I. naturally divides itself into three parts: chapters i.–xxxv., xxxvi.–xxxix., and xl.–lxvi. Till the end of last century the whole book was by universal consent (with one exception) attributed to one and the same author. That exception was Aben Esra, who as early as the 12th c. had maintained the opinion that the author of the last part was a prophet of the time of the Babylonish exile. This is the part which modern critics are most confident cannot be from the hand of I.; but there are passages even in the first part, *e.g.*, ii. 2–4, xiii. 1, xiv. 23, xxi. 1–10, xxxiv., xxxv., which some attribute to other prophets and times. On the other hand, there are not wanting able and learned critics who controvert all this, and vindicate the integrity of the book, and the unity of the authorship in all its divisions. The literature of I. is perhaps the very noblest in the whole range of the Old Testament. Never did sublime hopes clothe themselves in more brilliant imaginative forms. The spiritual exaltation is at times so intense, the future of the prophetic vision so full of thrilling joy and heavenly beauty, that one shrinks from seeking their origin in the mere patriotic yearnings of an impassioned exile. Nothing in history is worthy of them but the character and work of Christ, and hence the Church in all ages has been wont to speak of I. as, *par excellence*, the evangelical or Messianic prophet. See Ewald's *Propheten des Alten Bundes*.

I'sar, a tributary of the Danube, in Bavaria, rises in a lava ridge in Tyrol, rushes impetuously through the Porta Claudia in the Chalk Alps, flows N. and N.E. through the Dachauer and Erdinger morasses, passes Munich and Landshut, receives the Amper, and joins the Danube at Deggendorf, after a course of 216 miles. Much timber is floated down the I. from the mountains.

Is'atin ($C_{16}H_{10}N_2O_2$), the body produced by boiling indigo with nitric acid till the blue colour disappears through oxidation. Brilliant red prismatic crystals form when the hot solution cools. It is soluble both in alcohol and in water, and turns violet on addition of an alkali.

Is'chia (Gr. *Pithecusa;* Class. Lat. *Ænaria* or *Inarime;* Med. Lat. *Iscala*), a beautiful island at the entrance to the Gulf of Naples, and 5 miles from the mainland, with an area of 25 sq. miles, and a pop. (1874) of 24,000. It is rocky and of volcanic origin, rising in Monte Epomeo (anc. *Epopos*) to a height of 2574. It is widely celebrated for its charming climate, its delicious wines and fruits, its mineral springs, and valuable potter's clay. I., the capital, has a castle, and a pop. of 2930. The island is often visited by severe earthquakes, but the most recent irruption of Epomeo was in 1302. The celebrated general Marchese Pescara was born in 1489 at the castle of I., which later was defended gallantly by his sister Constance against the forces of Louis XII. of France. Her family was rewarded with the government of I., which they retained till 1734. The town of I. (pop. 6546) is the seat of a bishop, and has a lofty insulated fort connected with the land by a pier. Other towns are Casamicciola and Forio.

Is'chium is the name given to a portion of the innominate or pelvic bone. It forms the posterior and lower portion of this bone (in man), and in the sitting posture the body rests chiefly on the two ischia.

Isch'l, a very popular bathing-place, and the seat of an imperial residence, in the heart of the 'Salzkammergut' district in Upper Austria, beautifully situated 1520 feet above the sea and 50 miles S.S.W. of Linz, in a magnificent valley on the river Traun, a small affluent of the Danube. The climate is very mild and equal, and of great benefit to consumptive patients. Its saltworks produce about 200,000 tons of salt yearly, and the salt-baths are highly esteemed. Pop. 6215.

Ise'o, Lago d' (the *Sebinus Lacus* of Pliny), a lake of Northern Italy, dividing the provinces of Brescia and Bergamo, and inferior for magnitude and beauty only to the three great lakes. It is 620 feet above sea-level, about 18 miles long from N. to S. by 2–3 broad, and 1000 feet deep, and is fed by the Oglio (*Ollius*) and Borlazzo. Steamboats ply upon it from Sarnico at the S. extremity to Iseo, an ancient town at its head, with (1871) 1784 inhabitants. In the L. d'I. rises the rocky island of Monte d'Isola, 1½ miles long, and containing two fishing villages.

Isère', a S.E. department of France, bounded N. and W. by the Rhone, S. by Ardèche and Drome, and E. by Savoie. Area, 3200 sq. miles; pop. (1872) 575,784. To the N. of the river I., which bisects the department in a S.W. direction, stretch fertile plains, but S. of it is a romantic highland, abounding in pine-woods, glaciers, and mountains, the loftiest of which is L'Aiguille-de-Meije (12,308 feet). In spite of a variable climate, agriculture is highly developed in I., and its vineyards yield some 10,000,000 gallons of excellent white and red wines annually. Iron-mining, silkworm-rearing, and glove-making are also important industries. I. is traversed by the Paris-à-Lyon Railway, with six branch lines. The chief towns are Grenoble (the capital), Voiron, and Vienne.

The *river* I. rises at a height of about 7000 feet in the Col d'Iseran in Savoie, winds in a general south-westerly direction through that department, and those of I. and Drôme, and falls into the Rhone at Coufoulin, 8 miles N. of Valence. Its chief tributaries are the Arc, Bréda, and Drac.

Iserlohn', a town in the province of Westphalia, Prussia, on the Baar, 14 miles S.E. of Dortmund, stands picturesquely in a hilly district, and is an important trade centre, its manufactures, which date from the 18th c., being chiefly of ironware, needles, and wire. I. itself has seventeen large manufactories, and the whole neighbourhood abounds in foundries, paper-mills, &c. Pop. (1875) 16,868.

Iser'nia (the *Æsernia* of the Samnites), a town of Italy, in the province of Campobasso, stands on an isolated eminence 29 miles N.E. of Caianello. It is now a dirty and confined place, consisting of one long street, but in the ime of Trajan was a municipal town of some importance, as is attested by a Roman aqueduct and the remains of a fine bridge. The walls still present fragments of ancient polygonal work, believed to be of Samnite origin. Pop. (1871) 7715.

Ish'mael (Heb. 'God hears'), the eldest son of Abraham, by his Egyptian concubine Hagar, was born at Mamre, fourteen years before the birth of Isaac (Gen. xvi. 3–16, *cf.* xxi. 5). He married an Egyptian wife (xxi. 21), and was the progenitor of the tribes in the N. and W. of the Arabian peninsula (xxv. 12–18).

According to some modern critics, the object of the story is to give an account of the Ishmaelites, or wandering Arab tribes, in relation to the Hebrews. Thus the Ishmaelites were related to them, but not their equals. I. was older than Isaac, but his mother was an Egyptian; or, the Ishmaelites had been an independent people before the Israelites, but had not preserved the purity of their blood.

Is'idore of Seville, born at Carthagena about A.D. 570, became Bishop of Seville about 600. He presided at the second Council of Seville (619), and at that of Toledo (633), and died 636. From the variety and extent of his knowledge, as exhibited in his numerous writings, I. must be regarded not only as an influential ecclesiastic, but as one of the most learned men of his time. The complete works of I., which included doctrinal, exegetical, canonical, and historical writings, and the most important of which was *Originum sive Etymologiarum Libri* xx., an encyclopædia of arts and science, treating of all the subjects in literature, science, and religion studied at the time, were published in 7 vols. 4to by Arevali at Rome (1797–1803).

Isidor'ian Decre'tals professed to be a collection made by Isidore of Seville (q. v.) of Decretal Epistles of the bishops of Rome from Clement I. to Damasus I. (384). The collection contains genuine decretals and canons, but most of them are deliberate forgeries. The real author and the exact time and place of publication are unknown. Coming to light about 830–845, they were eagerly taken up by the Popes as favouring their pretensions to absolute supremacy over the Church, were appealed to in public transactions, and were circulated in various collections without suspicion till the Reformation. The 'Donatio Constantini M.' a fiction of an earlier time, conferring on the Bishop of Rome the sovereignty of the city of Rome, of Italy, and of the Western Provinces, was adopted into them, and formed the first stepping-stone on which the Pope tried to raise himself even above the state. The authenticity of the I. D. was first seriously attacked in the Magdeburg Centuriators (q. v.). Against this attack they were defended by the Jesuit Turrianus, but the forgery was incontrovertibly exposed by Blondell in his *Pseudo-Isidorus et Turrianus Vapulantes* (Geneva, 1628). Even Roman Catholic writers now admit the forgery, contending only that they were not the cause, but merely the expression, of the ecclesiastical development which was in progress at the time. See Gieseler's *Lehrbuch Kirchengeschichte* (Bonn, 1855; Eng. trans. by Davidson).

I'singlass. See GELATINE.

I'sis (the Græcised form of *Hes*), an Egyptian goddess, daughter of Seb and Nut, sister and wife of Osiris, and mother of Horus, is represented by a throne in the hieroglyphics, where she is styled 'queen of heaven' and 'mother-goddess.' Regarded by the Egyptians as both a celestial and terrestrial divinity, I. was identified by the Greeks with Demeter, by the Romans with Ceres, and by Tacitus (*Germ.* 9) with the German Hertha. The earliest seat of her cultus was at This, in Upper Egypt, and other shrines peculiarly sacred to her were at Philæ, Dendera, Memphis, and Busiris. Her worship became general in Egypt under the eighteenth dynasty, spread thence to Greece and Asia Minor early in the 3d c. B.C., and was introduced into Rome in the time of Sulla. There the licentiousness of her mysteries led to numerous enactments against their celebration from B.C. 58 down to the time of Vespasian, when along with Serapis she was formally admitted into the Roman pantheon, and a temple erected in her honour in the Campus Martius. In works of art I. is usually clad in a long tunic gathered on the breast in a knot; her head is sometimes horned, sometimes crowned with a lotus-blossom; and in her right hand she bears the sistrum. Her son Horus frequently stands by her side. See Bunsen, *Egyptens Stelle in der Weltgeschichte*; Sir G. Wilkinson, *Manners and Customs of the Ancient Egyptians*; and Birch, *Gall. Ant.*

Isis. See THAMES.

Iskanderun', or **Alexandrett'a**, a town of Asiatic Turkey, in the vilayet of Aleppo, on the E. side of the Gulf of I. (*Sinus Issicus*), and 78 miles N.W. of Aleppo, of which it is the port, is a decayed place, surrounded by malarious marshes. In 1874, 439 vessels of 175,138 tons entered and cleared the port, and the total value of imports and exports amounted to £2,207,976. Pop. about 1000. I. was the ancient *Alexandria ad Issum*, founded by Alexander the Great to commemorate the battle of Issus (q. v.), B.C. 333; and a place in the neighbourhood named Jacob's Well has been identified with the *Myriandrus* of Xenophon. Tancred took I. in 1097; and it was the scene of a defeat of the Turks by the Egyptians, April 13, 1832.

Is'la de Pi'nos, a West Indian island, lying 30 miles S. of Cuba, to which it belongs. Area, 800 sq. miles; estimated pop. 2000. The surface is mountainous, the Sierra de la Canada attaining a height of 1600 feet; the climate healthy and the soil extremely fertile. Iron, silver, and mahogany are the chief products of the island, the capital of which is Nueva Gerona. I. de P. was discovered by Columbus in 1494, and was long a rendezvous for pirates and bucaneers.

Islam', or **Eslam'**, the name by which the followers of Mohammed call their faith, means self-devotion to God. He who professes I. is a *Moslem*, a word common in the corrupt form *Mussulman*.

Isl'and, in Old Eng. *ealand* or *igland*, *i.e.*, 'land in water,' or 'waterland.' The word is properly spelled *iland* (*e.g.*, 'and come vnto an *iland* waste and voyd,' *Færie Queene*, book xi. c. 6), the *s* in the modern spelling being due to a fanciful connection with the Fr. *isle*, derived from Lat. *insula*. In geography an I. means a piece of land surrounded by water. A large group of islands is called an Archipelago (q. v.). Next to Australia, which is sometimes regarded as a continent, the largest I. in the world is Borneo. Most of the groups near continents, which themselves are merely islands on a much larger scale, have been connected with the mainland at one time. Oceanic or pelagic islands are usually either volcanic or coralline. See CORAL ISLANDS.

Islands of the Blessed (Gr. *hai tōn makarōn nēsoi*; Lat. *Fortunatæ Insulæ*), in Greek mythology, were placed far beyond the Pillars of Hercules on the western verge of Oceanus, and were identified by Hesiod and Pindar with Elysium (q. v.). In later times the name was transferred to the Canary, Madeira, and Azores groups, which first became known to the Romans at the close of the civil wars of Marius and Sulla; but the existence of the ancient myth suggests that these islands may have been accidently discovered by earlier Phœnician or even Etruscan navigators.

Isl'ay, one of the largest islands of the inner Hebrides, included in Argyleshire, Scotland, lies 1 mile S.W. of Jura, and 15 miles W. of the promontory of Kintyre. Area, 220 sq. miles; pop. (1870) 8143. It is perhaps the most populous and productive of the Hebrides, is 25 miles long and 22 broad, and the surface is hilly in the E. and N. The highest points are Ben Varn, 1500 feet; and Ben Ronastel, 1050 feet. The great bight of Loch-indaal converts the western portion into a large peninsula. About a third of the surface is under corn and green crops, and lead, copper, manganese, and marble are obtained in considerable quantity. There is abundance of deer and wildfowl, and a productive salmon-fishery. The chief villages are Port Ellen, with a pop. of about 1000, and the fishing station of Ascaig. Eight distilleries in the island yield annually 400,000 gallons of whisky. The exports include large numbers of black cattle and sheep. I. was a favourite residence of the Lords of the Isles, and passed to their rivals the Campbells about 1616.

Isle of Man. See MAN, ISLE OF.

Isles, Lord of the, a title borne by the descendants of Somerled (or Samuel, Gael. Somhairle), thane of Argyle, who in 1135, on the expulsion of the Norwegians from Arran and Bute by David I., seems to have received a grant of these and other islands from that monarch. On Somerled's assassination in 1164, his dominions were divided between his three sons, Dugal, Angus, and Reginald—Mull, Coll, Tiree, and Jura falling to the eldest; Islay, Kintyre, and half Arran to the second; Bute and the remaining half of Arran to the third. The last subsequently added Dugal's inheritance to his own, and in his line was vested the Lordship of the Isles. Angus Oig, great-grandson to Reginald, fought under Bruce at Bannockburn (1314), and is the hero of Scott's *L. of the I.*, and Angus's grandson Donald was defeated at Harlaw (q. v.) in 1411 by the Earl of Mar, and forced to surrender the Earldom of Ross, which he had seized in his wife's right. With the death of John, son of Donald, in 1498, the direct line terminated, and though various bastard members of the house assumed the title, their claims were never recognised. The Lordship of the Isles was annexed to the Scottish crown December 3, 1540, and from it the Prince of Wales now derives one of his titles.

Is'lington, a suburb of London, in the parliamentary borough of Finsbury, forming the greater part of the Northern postal district, and embracing Highbury, Holloway, Barnsbury, Kingsland, &c. A country village in the beginning of the century, it had in 1871 a pop. of 213,778. Being only 2 miles from the bank, it is greatly inhabited by City men. It abounds in churches and charitable institutions. The Agricultural Hall is the largest building of the kind in London.

Is'maelites (*Ismaili*), a branch of the Mohammedan sect of the Shiites, or upholders of the claims of Ali (q. v.) to the califate, derived their name from Ismail (*circa* 722 A.D.), the seventh Imaum in descent from Ali. They seem to have existed under the early Abbasides, but were first organised in the 10th c. by Abdallah Ibn Maimun, a Persian, to whose influence may be ascribed the singular compound of Islamism and Zoroastrianism observable in the tenets of the I. This Abdallah preached the advent of a Messiah who should be greater than Mohammed, and by his esoteric interpretation of the Koran laid himself and his followers open to charges of atheism and immorality. The I. in their turn gave birth in the 11th c. to the Assassins (q. v.); and by the remnants of that sect, after its suppression in 1272, Ismaelite doctrines have been handed down to our own time. At present there are the Syrian I. of Massyad, and the Persian I. of Rudbar in Khorassan.

Ismail', formerly **Tutch'ikov**, a fortified river-port of Moldavia, on the Kilia, an arm of the Danube, 40 miles from its entrance into the Black Sea. It was destroyed by Suwaroff in 1789, but was rebuilt, and is now a thriving city. In 1872 it exported 167,478 quarters of wheat, 37,867 of maize, 14,363 of barley, 11,267 of rye, and 5068 cwts. of wool. Steamers ply regularly between I. and Braïla. Pop. 26,000. I. was ceded to Russia at the peace of Bucharest in 1812, and became the station of the Russian fleet of the Danube. It reverted to Turkey by the treaty of Paris in 1856, and is now part of Rumania.

Ismail Pasha, Khedive of Egypt, second son of Ibrahim Pasha, was born in 1830, and educated at Paris. He became general-in-chief of the Egyptian army in 1862, and succeeded his uncle, Said Pasha, as fifth viceroy in 1863, securing in 1866, by enormous presents to the Porte, a direct line of succession for his house. In the same year he sent 30,000 troops to subdue the insurrection in Crete. In 1867 he received the title of Khedive. His assumption of sovereignty, and the regal style in which he entertained several crowned heads and 10,000 guests at the opening of the Suez Canal in 1869, excited the jealousy of the Sultan, and he was ordered to reduce his naval and military establishments. By a firman in 1873, however, he obtained complete control over his army, and several important concessions. Meanwhile, ostensibly to suppress the slave trade, he had sent various expeditions far southwards along the basin of the Nile, which greatly extended his sway. He employed many foreigners in the embellishment of his capital, and spent excessive sums for civil and warlike purposes. Notwithstanding the huge capital raised by him by loans in 1868 and 1873, his finances were in 1876 in so unsatisfactory a condition that he was compelled to sell his Suez Canal shares to the British Government, who sent Mr. Cave, as special commissioner, to investigate his accounts. Neither this mission nor that of Mr. Goschen and Monsieur Joubert later, in the interests of the British and French bondholders, have as yet (1877) restored his credit in any great degree. In the war of the Turks with Servia in 1876, and with Russia in 1877, he rendered the Porte active military assistance.

Ismail'ia, a town of Lower Egypt, situated on the Suez Canal, and on the N. shore of Lake Timsah, 147 miles. E.S.E. of Alexandria by railway. It was founded in 1863, as the headquarters for the general direction of the canal works, and is named after the Khedive, Ismail Pasha (q. v.). It lies at the E. end of the Suez Company's freshwater canal, which was opened April 9, 1877, and is intended, since the choking of the Canopus branch of the Nile, as a more direct channel to the ocean highway for the grain, cotton-seed, and sugar of Upper Egypt. Lake Timsah is spacious enough to receive a fleet of merchantmen, but as yet the warehouses and cotton-presses are at Alexandria. Passengers from Cairo and Alexandria to Suez can only be conveyed *via* Zagazig and I. since the abandonment of the old desert line in 1874. Pop. 4000.

I'sobaric or **Isobaromet'ric Lines** are lines drawn through those localities for which the mean annual barometric pressure is the same. They are constructed upon the same principle and have the same properties as Isotherms (q. v.) and contour lines. See GRAPHICAL REPRESENTATION.

Isocar'dia, a genus of *Lamellibranchiate* Molluscs, belonging to the family *Cyprinidæ*, and familarly known as 'heart-cockles' from the form of the shells, the beaks of which are widely separate, and of sub-spiral arrangement. *I. cor* is a familiar species. These shells are first found as fossils in the Triassic rocks, and are very abundant in the Oolitic formations and in the Chalk system.

Isoc'hronism. See CYCLOID and PENDULUM.

Isoclin'ic and **Isogon'ic Lines** are lines of equal magnetic inclination and declination respectively. See MAGNETISM.

Isoc'rates, a famous Athenian orator, who from bodily weakness and timidity did not appear as a political speaker, but devoted himself to teaching eloquence, and preparing written orations. He became rich by his instructions, being said to have had about 100 disciples, who paid him 1000 drachmæ each. After the rule of the thirty tyrants, he busied himself with preparing legal harangues for others. Going to Chios in 392 B.C., he entered a new path, publishing so-called epideictic orations, and continued this practice, together with his teaching, after his return to Athens in 388. Born in 436, eight years after Xenophon and Aristophanes, and eight years before Plato, he died in 338, two years before the accession of Alexander the Great. The tradition, given by Pausanias and Lucian, that grief for the defeat at Chæronea was the cause of his death, though accepted in Milton's allusion to the 'Dishonest victory, fatal to liberty, which killed with report that old man eloquent,' has been proved by Blass to be untrue. Twenty-one of his speeches are preserved, the *Codex Urbinas*, probably the most perfect of all Greek MSS., containing nineteen. In the purest Attic dialect, and in a clear but highly artificial style, they treat subjects of social and political importance, and are written to be read, not spoken. The best known is the *Panegyrikos*, a sort of festival-speech, recounting the services of Athens to Hellas, and justifying her hegemony. The *Editio Princeps* of I. is by Demetrius Chalcondylas (Milan, 1493), and the first Aldine edition is dated 1513. The edition of Jerome Wolf (1548, 1551, 1570), containing the first modern *Commentary* on I., and that of Koraes (Paris, 1807–8), are the best for exegesis, those of Baiter and Sauppe (Zürich, 1839) and Benseler (Leips. 1851, 1856) being the best for textual criticism.

Isom'erism. This term is applied to a phenomenon especially observable in the chemistry of carbon compounds. It frequently occurs that bodies differing in properties and functions are found on ultimate analysis to contain their elements, carbon and hydrogen, with oxygen and nitrogen, as the case may be, in the same proportion; in other words, have the same percentage composition. Such bodies are called *isomeric*, or of equal parts (*isomeres*). On closer investigation, however, differences appear which have led to the subdivision of isomeric bodies into various classes. In certain cases, while the percentage composition is the same, the molecular magnitude as determined by the vapour density is different. Thus ethylene and butylene contain the same proportions of carbon and hydrogen, but the vapour density of butylene being double that of ethylene, the formula assigned to it is C_4H_8, while that of ethylene is C_2H_4. The same is the case with propylene, C_3H_6, and hexylene, C_6H_{12}. Similarly the formula of acetic acid is $C_2H_4O_2$, of lactic acid $C_3H_6O_3$, of grape-sugar $C_6H_{12}O_6$, each being a whole multiple of the formula CH_2O, which expresses in the simplest form the ratio in which the elements exist in these compounds. Other examples are afforded by acetylene, C_2H_2, and benzol, C_6H_6; cyanic acid, CHNO, fulminic acid, $C_2H_2N_2O_2$ (which, however, is only known in the form of fulminates), and cyanuric acid, $C_3H_3N_3O_3$. Compounds which, like those just quoted, are multiples of some simple formula, are said to be polymeric; and when a body in the course of a chemical action appears to be changed into another with a multiple of the original formula, as when pyridine (C_5H_5N) is converted into dipyridine ($C_{10}H_{10}N_2$), it is said to be polymerised. Other bodies again exhibit not only identity in percentage composition, but identity of molecular weight. For instance, the formula $C_3H_6O_2$ expresses the molecular weight of propionic acid, methyl acetic ether, and ethyl formic ether. But these bodies are obtained from different sources in different ways, and they yield quite different substances when acted on by the same chemical reagent. It is assumed, therefore, that in such cases the proximate composition of the bodies is different, and attempts are made by modifying the general formula to express the difference of composition. Substances the I. of which is explainable by the assumption of the existence in them of radicles of different magnitudes are called *metameric*. There are other classes of substances the I. of which cannot thus be accounted for. These have the same molecular weight, they exhibit differences, however, in specific gravity, boiling point, and other properties; and while they behave in a similar manner with some chemical reagents, they may behave very differently with others. Such a set of bodies are found in the butylic alcohols, the lactic acids, and other compounds. These might be called isomeric in the strict sense of the term. The difference in such cases is supposed to be explained by assuming that the so-called atoms of carbon, hydrogen, and other elements are united in different ways, and to express these different arrangements *structural* formulæ are employed. Such formulæ are useful for remembering the experimental differences between the bodies.

Isomor'phism. This word, signifying equality of form, was first employed by Mitscherlich to denote a connection which he pointed out between chemical composition and crystalline form, in papers communicated to the Berlin Academy in 1819 and following year. It was well known that quite different bodies, such as galena, common salt, iron pyrites, fluor spar, &c., could crystallise in the same form, but Mitscherlich showed that bodies of quite different composition had the same crystalline form, and that equality of form indicated not exactly the same composition, but similar composition from different elements, and that analogy of composition was often accompanied by similarity of form, and was probably the cause of it. I. is on the whole more strikingly exhibited by classes of compounds than by the elements themselves. In some cases elements are isomorphous, such as arsenic and antimony, and these give rise to isomorphous compounds; but there are isomorphous compounds the analogous elements of which are not isomorphous, as in the case of zinc and iron, and there are also similarly constituted compounds which are not isomorphous. Among the more important and commonly occurring isomorphous groups of salts may be mentioned the alums, the sulphates of which, sulphate of magnesium (Epsom salt), is the type, including sulphate of zinc, nickel, cobalt, iron, and other metals, with the corresponding double sulphates, the chromates and the manganates, the perchlorates and permanganates, the chloride, bromide, and iodide of potassium, the carbonates analogous to Iceland spar, and the compounds of ammonium and potassium, such as the nitrate.

Isop'oda, an order of *Crustacea* (q. v.), in which the head is separable from the first segment, which have feet. The eyes are unstalked, and of compound nature. Generally there are seven pairs of limbs borne on the thorax or chest; the body is more or less flexible, and can be rolled into a ball-shaped form for purposes of defence. The joints of the abdomen are united, and form a broad shield, beneath which the gills are protected. The I. are represented by such genus as the familiar slaters or woodlice (*Oniscus*), and by the water-slaters. Some I. (*Bopyridæ*) live as parasites on other crustacea, and one (*Limnoria terebrans*) bores into wood, and effects great destruction on wooden piers and like erections. The I. first occur as fossils in Devonian rocks.

Is'otherms (Gr. *isos*, 'equal,' and *thermos*, 'warm') are lines drawn through places which have the same mean temperature. The mean temperature may be taken for the summer months, the winter months, or for the whole year; and on account of the irregularity of the configuration of the surface of the earth, these three systems present very different appearances. They give very valuable information as regards the probable nature of the climate of any locality, and are therefore of great importance in meteorology. See CLIMATE.

Ispahan', the largest city of Persia, capital of Irak-Ajami, on the left bank of the Zainderud, and in a rich plain, 220 miles S. of Teheran. It is beautifully embowered in groves and orchards, but its streets are narrow, dirty, and crooked, and part of the city is in ruins, haunted by the jackal and fox. The houses are mostly of earth or brick, and only one storey high, while the bazaars are very extensive, it being possible to walk under cover continuously for some three miles. The principal buildings are the college called Madrasse Shah Sultan Huseyn, the magnificently ornamented gates of which are carved and embossed with verses from the Koran; the college mosque, supporting a fine cupola, and faced by two minarets; the palace of the Chehl Situn (*i.e.*, 'forty columns'), a wonder of marble, glass, and gilding, situated in an immense square, laid out with chenar-trees and artificial lakes, and the modern palace of Fattehabad, a noble pile in good repair. The manufactures include the most expensive velvets and satins, gold and silver trinkets, coarse nankeen and calico, firearms and sword blades, glass, earthenware, sweetmeats, &c. I. has a good water supply, and is the emporium of a large trade with India, Afghanistan, and Turkey. Pop. variously estimated, but is not less than 200,000. I., the capital of Irak under the Califs of Bagdad, was taken in 1387 by Timur, who is said to have put to death 70,000 of the inhabitants. It became the capital of Persia, and one of the greatest cities of Asia under Shah Abbas in the 17th c., but was sacked by the Afghans in 1722. The Kajars made Teheran the capital in 1795.

Israel. See JEWS.

Issoire (anc. *Issiodurum*), a town in the department of Puy-de-Dôme, France, stands on the river Crouze, 20 miles S.S.E. of Clermont by rail, in a plain circled by mountains. It has an interesting old church, St. Paul's, some trade in cattle, hemp, walnut-oil, and wine, and manufactures of woollens and agricultural instruments. Pop. (1872) 5876.

Issoudun, a town in the department of Indre, France, on the Théols, 18 miles N.E. of Chateauroux, connected by rail with Orleans. It has an old church of the 15th c., considerable trade in wine and cattle, and manufactures of wool, linen, ironmongery, and cutlery. Pop. (1872) 14,230.

Iss'ue, in law, means the question of fact submitted to a jury See FEIGNED I.

Iss'us (Gr. *Issos* or *Issoi*), a seaport of Cilicia, Asia Minor, on a bay of the same name, famous as the scene of Alexander the Great's victory over Darius Codomannus in 333 B.C. I. is probably the modern Ajazzo.

Istalif', a beautiful town of Afghanistan, on a small tributary of the Cabul river, 20 miles N.N.W. of Cabul. It is terraced on the mountain side, crowned by the magnificent shenars of the Hazrat Eshan's shrine, and girt with the richest orchards and vineyards. The inhabitants, about 15,000 in number, are handsome, agile Tajaks, reputed to be the best of Afghan foot-soldiers. They weave coarse cloth, in which there is a trade with Turkistan. I. was in great part destroyed by the British in 1842.

Isth'mian Games, forming one of the four Pan-Hellenic festivals, derived their name from the Corinthian isthmus on which they were celebrated in honour of Poseidon (Neptune). The temple of Poseidon was situated at the narrowest part of the isthmus, and near it were the theatre and stadium of white marble. This festival was said to have been instituted by Sisyphus and restored by Theseus, and was originally held every eighth year, but after Olymp. 49 every third year. The games were the same as those held at Olympia, including, besides athletic exercises and horse and chariot racing, contests in music and poetry. Victors were crowned with a simple pine-garland, and their statues were placed in the famous temple, while their envied success reflected high honour alike on their family and birthplace. The management of the games was conducted by the Corinthians, but certain honourable distinctions were reserved for the Athenians. In 228 B.C. the Romans were privileged to take part in the games, and it is conjectured that soon after the time of Cæsar there began to be introduced fights with wild beasts. At a late period of the Roman Empire the games had been sunk into coarse gladiatorial shows, but they continued to be celebrated till the 4th c. A.D.

Isth'mus (Gr.) is the name of a narrow neck of land connecting two continents, *e.g.*, the isthmuses of Darien and Suez, or a peninsula with the mainland, *e.g.*, the I. of Corinth, to which the name was perhaps first applied. It was often used alone by the Hellenes to designate this particular I.

Is'tria (anc. *Histria*), an Austrian markgrafdom, of which the greater part is a peninsula running into the Adriatic near its northern end. It now forms part of the Austrian Küstenland. The surface is mountainous, the highest peak being Monte Maggiore, 4400 feet high. The climate is warm and dry, but exposed to biting winds. The soil produces oil, figs, and excellent wine in abundance. The inhabitants, Italian in the town, and Slavic in the country districts, live by shipbuilding, sea-going, salt-boiling, cattle-breeding, and oil and wine manufacture. The coast is full of good harbours. I. formed a part of the old kingdom of Illyria. Rovigno, Capo d'Istria, and Pirano are among the towns. Area, 1908 sq. miles; pop. (1869) 254,076.

Italian Art. (1) *Painting.*—The founder of Italian painting was Cimabue (q. v.), born about 1240, and his pupil Giotto (q. v.) freed art from stiffness and Byzantine mannerism, and is the first great representative of the Florentine school. Orcagna, who died about 1370, produced gloomy and grotesque works, illustrating the faith of medieval Christianity; and a school of religious painters, characterised by sweetness, delicate imagination, and mystic piety of spirit, arose at Siena during the 14th c. Among the Italian painters belonging to the 14th c. are Gaddi, Giottino, Giovanni da Melano, Spinello, Aretino, Pietro, &c. From 1400 to 1470 is a second great period. Art became more varied and fanciful in subject, and gained rapidly a mastery of technicalities. Perspective and anatomy were studied, religious allegories yielded to scenes and figures from everyday life. Among the leading painters of this period were Masaccio (q. v.), Uccello, Castagno, and Gozzoli. As the 15th c. advances Italian painting becomes gradually imbued with the Renaissance spirit—with naturalism, vivacity, and love of classic themes—Leonardo da Vinci being the link between the 15th c. artists and the great 16th c. masters Michael Angelo and Raphael. In the works of Lippo Lippi, Filippino Lippi, Mantegna, Botticelli, and Ghirlandajo we trace the dawn of a new artistic spirit, while Fra Angelico stands apart, his works reflecting the visionary medieval spirit. From 1470 to 1550 may be roughly regarded as the period in which the influence of the Renaissance on painting is strongest—in which Italian art culminates. To the latter part of the 15th c. belong Mantegna, Perugino, Francia, the Bellini, Signorelli, and Fra Bartolommeo. This period abounds in work splendid in conception and exquisite in execution, but not attained to the unrivalled grandeur and beauty of the period embraced in the first half of the 16th c.—the age of Michael Angelo (q. v.), Raphael (q. v.), Giorgione (q. v.), Correggio (q. v.), Andrea del Sarto (q. v.), and Titian (q. v.). Leonardo da Vinci (q. v.) might chronologically be ranked among the earlier cluster of the Renaissance painters, as he died in 1519, but ranks with the greatest masters of the 16th c. Leonardo's work is exquisitely subtle and original, with a grotesque, bizarre element absent from Raphael's creations, which are the perfection of harmony, accurate design, and luminous beauty. Correggio's paintings show almost no passion or deep thought, they are unsurpassed for blooming, delicate colour, for wanton, sensuous loveliness. The Venetian school was a later outcome than the Florentine, and achieved for colour what the Florentine did for form. The great Venetian paintings are far less thoughtful and subtle than the Florentine; they display the utmost glory of sensuous beauty, the sublimity of noble colour. The greatest Venetian masters are Veronese (q. v.), whose works are a splendid reflection of material gorgeousness; Tintoretto (q. v.), a stormy, fiery genius, who loved the most daring and tragic themes; and Titian (q. v.), who carried the mastery of glowing yet unsating colour to the height of achievable perfection. Among the secondary Venetians were Palma, Bonifazio, Bordone, the Robusti, the Caliari, the Bassani. In the great 16th c. painters, Italian art gained its zenith, and decadence rapidly ensued. Among the later painters are the Carracci (q. v.), Guido (q. v.), Domenichino (q. v.), and Caravaggio (q. v.). But pictorial art became steadily more sensual and strained, and in the Bolognese and Neapolitan schools degenerated into coarse animalism, depicting repulsive scenes of bloodshed and sensuality. Of this last stage of artistic degradation the leading representative is Salvator Rosa (q. v.). Besides the works of Vasari and Lanzi, see Rosini, *Storia della Pittura Italiana* (Pisa, 2d ed. 7 vols. 1848–52); and Crowe and Cavalcaselle, *History of Painting in Italy* (Lond. 1864–66).

(2) *Music.*—In Italy the old Græco-Roman melodies were partly adapted to Christian hymns, and in the 4th c. Bishop Ambrosius introduced religious chaunts adapted to the four modes of the Greeks. Gregory the Great in the 6th c. gave a new development to religious music, founded many singing schools, and elaborated the choral song, the foundation of church music. (See GREGORY THE GREAT and GREGORIAN CHAUNT.) Guido of Arezzo, a Benedictine of the 13th c., improved the manner of writing musical notes, and divided the scale into hecachords. Music, favoured by the Popes, was gradually viewed as a science. Many instruments were invented in the 15th c., and in the 16th notable composers appeared in Palestrina, Felice Anerio, and Nanini da Vallerano. Venice and Rome were the great musical centres, but the nation as a whole was renowned throughout Europe for prominence in music. In the 17th c. operas began to be performed, and the severe state church music of the 15th and 16th centuries gave place to a florid, somewhat effeminate, and more popular style. Unfortunately the zealous culture of vocal music led to the comparative neglect of instrumentation, and consequently, the Italian music is lacking in depth and richness of harmony. Among the 17th c. composers are Sully, Corelli, and Frescobaldi. To the 18th c. belong the famous violinist Paganini, and the composers Caldara, Brescianello, Galuppi, Jomelli, Porpora, Pergolese, Piccini, Cherubini, &c. The leading composers of the 19th c. are Spontini, Bellini, Donizetti, Verdi, and Rossini.

(3) *Architecture.*—'Italian architecture' is the name given to the style which arose in Italy in the 15th c., and which was formed by an adaptation of the old Roman style. Its founder was Filippo Brunelleschi. Inspired with enthusiasm for classical antiquity by the newly-discovered work of Vitruvius, he studied with zealous assiduity the architectural relics of the Eternal City, and his cupola of the cathedral at Florence is a masterpiece of artistic beauty and boldness. The new style was not a slavish reproduction of old buildings, but a free imitation of the massive edifices of ancient Rome. Its great fault was a want of unity, the general form of the structures being modern, while the parts were copied from various ancient models. Brunelleschi's most distinguished successors in the 15th c. were Leone Battista Alberti, Michelozzo, Michelozzi, and Benedetto da Majano, the authors of the fine Florentine palace style. Three schools of Italian architecture are reckoned—the Venetian, Florentine, and Roman—the last bearing a closer resemblance than the others to the ancient classical style. The Renaissance gave a great impetus to the imitation of antique structures, and a large number of churches, built on semi-classic designs, were raised in Italy, being distinguished especially by the introduction of the Dome (q. v.). Of these, by far the noblest is St. Peter's in Rome. From the 16th c. the greatest names in Italian architecture are Bramante, whose Romanesque work is frequent in Rome; Peruzzi, architect of the Farnesina and the Palazzo Massimi; San Gallo, who planned the Palazzo Farnese; Vignolo, Fontana, Giocondo, Falconetto, San Michelé, of whose works some beautiful specimens may be seen at Canossa, Verona, and Venice, Sansovino, Palladio (q. v.), whose fame is over all Western Europe, Ammanati, Maderno, Bernini, Borromini, Simonetti, Morelli, and Poletti.

Italian Language and Literature. (1) *Language.*—Like the French, the I. L. is a branch of the *Romana Rustica*, or provincial Latin of the Empire, mingled with barbaric words. The Italian speech early abounded in dialectic varieties, due partly to provincial differences in the *Romana Rustica*, and partly to the divergences of race among the Teutonic barbarians. (See ROMANCE LANGUAGES.) The classic literary speech seems to have arisen from the language spoken in the Italian cities, which was mainly cultivated by Tuscan writers. Consequently the literary language is mainly Tuscan, though the other provinces contributed largely to enrich it. The speech received new strength and majesty from Dante, new polish from Boccaccio, while Petrarch imbued it with a peculiar softness and pliancy from his study of the Provençal. At the end of the 14th c. it was in a condition of the ripest culture. During the 16th c. Italian was temporarily injured by the Renaissance enthusiasm for Latin, but was speedily re-established as the medium of literature. The chief dialects of modern Italian are:—The Sicilian, which shows traces of Greek, Arabic, Norman, Provençal, and French; the Neapolitan; the Calabrian; the Roman, at first the rudest of all the dialects, and now the most intelligible, though not the most polished; Norcian; the Tuscan, which contains several distinct branches; the Bolognese, inelegant and truncated; the Venetian, the softest and most musical; the Friulian, which has a large French and Slavonic element; the Paduan; the Lombardian, at one extremity shading into the Venetian, and at the other resembling the Bolognese, and including (1) the Bergamese, harsh and contracted; (2) the Milanese, showing Northern influence in its consonant endings; and (3) the Piedmontese, a blending of Italian and French; the Genoese has also much in common with the French, while the Corsican is said to show strong affinity with the Tuscan, and the Sardinian is a many-coloured dialect, in which Carthaginian, Greek, Arabic, Gothic, Frankish, and Aragonese words are, as it were, crumbled down and imbedded.

The Italians cannot hitherto be said to have treated the grammar of their language with scientific thoroughness. The first who collected observations on the language was Cardinal Bembo, whose work, begun in 1500, first appeared in 1525 under the title *Prose*. Only a few small unimportant works, by Fortunio, Liburnio, Marcantonio Flaminio, appeared earlier. The *Prose*, in the form of a dialogue, are neither thorough nor complete, and treat only of Boccaccio and Petrarch. The exertions of Count Trissino to regulate and establish orthography, after a long struggle, only resulted in the letters *v* and *j* being recognised as proper consonants. Other grammatical works, which formed at this time epochs, and exercised a lasting influence, are the *Ercolano* of Barchi (Flor. 1570), the object of which was to establish the claims of the Florentines to the right of self-government in language; the *Avvertimenti della Lingua* by Salviati (2 vols. Ven. and Flor. 1584–86), which treated diffusely of letters, and some of the parts of speech, especially the noun and article; *Della lingua Toscana* by Buommattei (Flor. 1648), the first tolerably complete grammar, adopted and published by the *Accademia della Crusca* as their own. A rich mine of observations and examples is to be found in the *Osservazioni della Lingua* by Cinonio (Ant. Mambelli, part 1, Forli, 1685; part 2, Ferrara, 1644; 4 vols. Milan, 1809), where the verbs and particles are treated in alphabetical order. A most erudite and bold work is that of Bartoli, *Il Torto e'l Diritto del non si può* (Rome, 1655). The first systematic, complete grammar, furnished with good examples, and from which almost all later ones have sprung, is *Regole et Osservazioni*, by Corticelli (Bolog. 1785). Mastrofini (1814), Nannucci (from 1813), Gherardini, Antolini have published works on individual parts of the language. The most of the later Italian grammars, such as those by Ambrosoli, Ponza, Biagioli, Valentini, Robello, Troya, Semeria, Puoti, &c., are of no importance. There are some admirable German works on the Italian tongue—*e.g.*, the *Ital. Sprachlehre* by Fernow (2 parts, Tüb. 1804); and Blanc's *Ital. Grammatik* (Halle, 1840), which is the first attempt at a historico-etymological work on the language.

Italian lexicography begins in the 16th c. with a collection of words by Minerbi (1535), Fabricio de Luna (1536), and Accaritio (1543). *Le Ricchezze della lingua Volgare* (1543), and *Della Fabbrica del Mondo* (1546), by Alunno, are somewhat richer. A more complete lexicon is the *Memoriale della Lingua* by Pergamini (1658). At length there was published, first in Venice (1612), the *Vocabolario degli Accademici della Crusca*, which was limited with pedantic strictness almost exclusively to the writers of the *Trecento* and to the Florentines, who had collected with great diligence all mutilations, all improper expressions and phrases of the people, but had paid no attention to the language of science and art. A second slightly changed edition was published at Venice (1623); the third, considerably enlarged (3 vols. 1691); and the fourth (6 vols. 1729–38) at Florence. The publication of a fifth edition, much richer in words and examples, but entirely in the spirit of the earlier editions, was begun in 1843 at Florence. This work has been made the basis of many others, amongst which are the lexicons of Ant. Cesari (6 vols. Verona, 1806) and Guiseppi Manuzzi (4 vols. Flor. 1836–44; 2d ed. 1862, *et seq.*). The first not Florentine but really Italian dictionary is the *Dizionario Enciclopedico*, by Francesco Alberti (6 vols. Lucca, 1797–1805). Of the later large dictionaries, the best are *Dizionario della Lingua Italiana* (7 vols. Bolog. 1819–26), *Dizionario Universale della Lingua Italiana*, by Mortara, Bellini, Codagni, and Mainardi (8 vols. Mant. 1845–56), the dictionaries by Tommaseo and Bellini (Turin, 1864, *et seq.*), Carena (2 vols. Turin, 1851–53), Bolza (Vien. 1851–53), Fanfani (2 vols. Flor. 1855; *Vocabulario dell' uso Toscano*, Flor. 1863), Trinchera (2 vols. Milan, 1864). Tommaseo (6th ed. 2 vols. Milan, 1855), and Zechini (new ed. Turin, 1864) are the authors of dictionaries of Italian synonyms.

(2) *Literature.*—The history of I. L. begins in the 12th c., the earliest poet of note being a Sicilian, Ciullo d'Alcamo, who died in 1194. Between D'Alcamo and Dante the chief writers were Bruno, Anselmo, Brunetto Latini, Guinicelli, Ruggieri, and Fra Guittone d'Arezzo. Contemporary with Dante, the principal poet was Guido Cavalcanti. After Dante (q. v.), the greatest medieval poet, the chief writers were Boccaccio (q. v.) and Petrarch (q. v.). The age from 1400 to 1500—the time when the Italian Renaissance was in full bloom—produced a throng of elegant scholars. (See RENAISSANCE.) The leading poets of the epoch were Poliziano (q. v.), Pulci (q. v.), and Boiardo (q. v.). During this period, authors enamoured of the loveliness of the revived classical literature strove to ignore medieval writings, to replace the Italian speech by Latin as the language of culture. Poliziano, however, introduced a new epoch, by blending classic and Italian influences, by instilling classic purity of style into the Italian tongue. Among other writers of this age are Ugolino, and Michel Verini, Naldio, Pontano, Landino, and Sannazzaro (q. v.). From 1500 to 1600 is the second great period in I. L.—the age of the poets Ariosto (q. v.), Trissino, Ruccellai, Bembo, (q. v.), Pietro Aretino (q. v.), Castiglione, Fracastoro, Berni (q. v.), Guarini (q. v.), and Tasso (q. v.). The poetry of the age is full of a sensual gorgeousness, and breathes a peculiar ironical, indifferent spirit, while it is occasionally servile and emasculate in its tone. Among the chief writers of fiction, which was generally lively and indecent, are Bandello, Firenzuola, Grazzini, Straparola, Parabosco, and Giraldi. The greatest prose writers are Guicciardini (q. v.) and Macchiavelli (q. v.). Other historians of this period are Bembo (q. v.), Giovio, Nardi, Sarpi (q. v.), Bartoli, Bentivoglio, &c. The interest of much of the history is marred by an unfortunate tendency to ape the manner of Livy and other Latin historians, leading to dreary diffuseness and stilted rhetoric. The 17th c. is a time of poetic decline, but is rich in prose. Among the poets are Filicaja, Chiabrera, Marini, Tassoni, and Redi, while the prose writers include Speroni, Castiglione, Massuccio, Davila (q. v.), &c. The verse of the time was marred by the affectations of the *Seicentisti*, a school of writers of whom the foremost was Marini, who indulged in strange euphemistic freaks. To the 18th c. belong the poets Fortiguerra, Frugoni, Maffei, Riccoboni, Metastasio (q. v.), Goldoni (q. v.), Gozzi (q. v.), Alfieri (q. v.), Monti (q. v.). The greatest Italian historian of the century is Muratori (q. v.). Other historians of the 18th c. are Tiraboschi and Giannone.

To the 19th c. belong the poets Manzoni (q. v.), Maffei, Leopardi (q. v.), Silvio Pellico (q. v.), Foscolo (q. v.), Tommaseo, Borghi, Arici, Taddei, Grossi, Prati, Niccolini, Giusti (q. v.), Baldachini, Torti, Barbieri, Sestini, &c.; the prose-writers Coletta, Botta, Litta, Cantu, Amari, La Farina, Farini, Balbo, Villari, Corniani, Selvatico; the philosophers, Galluppi, Gioberti (q. v.), Mamiani, and Rosmini. Manzoni has founded a school of writers of historical novels, among whom are Rosmini, Grossi, Cantu, D'Azeglio (q. v.), and Guerrazzi (q. v.). The patriot and political theorist Mazzini (q. v.) also deserves honourable mention. The long struggle against Austria imbued Italian literature with a rebellious, patriotic spirit, which found vent occasionally in bitter mockery and sorrowful retrospect, and at last in jubilant enthusiasm. None of the most recent Italian writers have produced a masterpiece, but much of their poetry is fervid, sweet, and graceful, and the new school of fiction is marked by delicacy of sentiment and considerable psychological insight and skill in the representation of manners. Many of the best-known Italian writers of this century have owed their popularity to the political tenor of their works rather than to their intrinsic literary merits, and, as a whole, the recent I. L. will not bear comparison with the recent literature of Germany or of France. The Italian prose writings of the present age rank higher than the contemporary Italian poetry, and periodical literature is now being widely cultivated. The great variety of dialects prevailing in the country has all along partly crippled Italian authors, many of whom could only acquire command of the classic Tuscan by dint of studious effort. This drawback will, in all likelihood, gradually vanish now that Italy has been formed into a united nation.

Of the works on the history of I. L., besides the numerous writings on the history of the literature and of the scholars of individual provinces and towns, the following are conspicuous:—Crescimbeni, *Storia della volgar Poesia* (6 vols. Rome, 1698; Venice, 1731); Quadrio, *Storia e Regione d'ogni Poesia* (7 vols. Bologna, 1739; Milan, 1741–52); Mazzucchelli, *Gli Scrittori d'Italia* (vols. i.–vi., Brescia, 1753–63), in alphabetical order, but only embracing the two first letters; Tiraboschi, *Storia della Letteratura Italiana* (14 vols. Modena, 1772–83; 16 vols. 1787–94; 12 vols. Rome, 1785; 16 vols. Milan, 1822–26, and since often reprinted), on which all later works are based, and which found a continuator in Lombardi in the *Storia della Letteratura Italiana nel Secolo* 18 (4 vols. Modena, 1827–30), and in Levati in the *Saggio sulla Storia della Letteratura Italiana ne' primi* 25 *Anni del Secolo* 19 (Milan, 1831); Corniani, *Secoli della Letteratura Italiana* (9 vols. Brescia, 1818–19; continued by Ticozzi, 2 vols. Milan, 1832–33); Ugoni, *Della Letteratura Italiana* (3 vols. Brescia, 1820–22); Maffei, *Storia della Letteratura Italiana* (2d ed. 4 vols. Milan, 1834); Emiliani-Giudici, *Storia della Letteratura Italiana* (2d ed. 2 vols. Flor. 1855); Rovani, *Storia delle Lettere e belle Arti in Italia* (3 vols. Milan, 1856–58); Ambrosoli, *Manuale della Letteratura Italiana* (2d ed. 4 vols. Flor. 1864); Ruth, *Geschichte der Ital. Poesie* (2 vols. Leips. 1844–47; new ed. 1867); Ebert, *Handbuch der Ital. Nationalliteratur* (Marburg, 1863).

Ital'ic Ver'sion (Lat. *Vetus Itala*) was a Latin version of the Scriptures, the Old Testament being from the LXX. It differed slightly from the Vetus Latina of the North African Church, and was that which was in common use in the N. of Italy till Jerome (died 420) produced his Vulgate (q. v.).

It'aly (*Regno d'Italia*), the midmost of the three great peninsulas in the S. of Europe, is only connected in the N. with the mainland where it is bounded W. by France, N. by the Swiss cantons of Valais, Uri, and the Grisons, and by Austrian Tyrol and Carinthia, E. by Austrian Carniola, extending in lat. 36° 42'–46° 40' N. and long 6° 35'–18° 30' E. In outline it is strikingly like a long, high-heeled boot, which stretches in a direction S.E., and parallel to the coast-line of Austria and Turkey, and the toe of which, the Calabrian promontory, approaches, at the Strait of Messina, the island of Sicily. It is washed on the E. by the Adriatic, S. by the Ionian Sea, and W. by the Tyrrhene and Ligurian Seas, and has a coast-line of 3237 miles, broken by few deep indentations. Proceeding along the coast from N.W., the chief promontories are Portofino in the Gulf of Genoa; Piombino and Ortobello in the Maremma; Cape Linaro S. of Civita Vecchia; Cape of Anzo S. of the Tiber; the rocky headlands of Circello, Algalone, and Posilipo, Cape Campanella, separating the Bay of Naples from the Gulf of Salerno; Capes Licosa, Palinoro, Falconara, and Vaticano; Spartivento, in the extreme S. of Calabria; Capes delle' Colonne and Santa Maria di Luca on either side of the Gulf of Taranto; and on the Adriatic side, the peninsula of Gargano (the spur of the Italian boot), the Point of Ancona, and the delta of the Po. The chief inlets besides those already mentioned are the sheltered Gulf of Spezia (the great naval arsenal of I.), the Bay of Grosseto, the Gulfs of Gaeta, Policastro, Santa Eufemia, and Squillace; and in the Adriatic, the Gulfs of Manfredonia, and Venice. Among the principal islands, which are treated of in separate articles, are Sicily, Sardinia, the Lipari Isles, Ischia, and Capria without the Bay of Naples; Ponza Isles further N., and Elba opposite Piombino. The mainland has an extreme length of 830 miles, and a mean breadth of 138 miles. I. is divided into 69 provinces, grouped in 16 compartments, and subdivided into 197 circles (*circondari*), in which are 8382 communes or townships. The country is generally regarded as comprising the three sections of Northern, Central, and Southern I., and the areas and the populations of its provinces was as follows, according to the census of 1861 and of 31st December 1871:—

Provinces.	Area in sq. miles.	Pop. 1861.	Pop. 1871.
NORTHERN ITALY.			
Piedmont—			
Alessandria	1951	645,607	683 473
Cuneo	2755	597,279	615,930
Novaro	2526	579,385	567,212
Turin	4067	941,992	967,540
Liguria—			
Genoa	1588	650,143	716,284
Port Maurizio	467	121,330	126,953
Lombardy—			
Bergamo	1087	347,235	368,141
Brescia	1643	434,219	450,750
Como	1050	457,434	480,339
Cremona	631	285,148	300,595
Mantua	950	262,819	288,769
Milan	1125	948,320	1,009,774
Pavia	1292	419,785	448,357
Sondria	1261	106,040	120,722
Venetia—			
Belluno	1270	167,229	175,350
Padua	754	304,762	364,355
Rovigo	650	180,647	200,929
Treviso	941	308,483	352,538
Udine	2515	440,542	481,786
Venice	848	294,450	335,379
Verona	1060	316,493	367,701
Vicenza	1016	327,674	363,022
Emilia—			
Bologna	1390	407,452	439,166
Ferrara	1010	199,158	215,369
Forli	719	224,463	233,969
Modena	965	260,591	272,845
Parma	1250	256,029	264,509
Piacenza	965	218,569	225,750
Ravenna	742	209,518	219,625
Reggio-Emilia	876	230,054	240,635
CENTRAL ITALY.			
Umbria and Marches—			
Perugia	3719	513,019	549,833
Ancona	736	254,849	262,359
Ascoli-Picino	810	196,030	203,009
Macerata	1056	229,626	236,719
Pesaro and Urbino	1114	202,568	213,060
Tuscany—			
Arezzo	1277	219,559	239,901
Florence	2367	696,214	766,326
Grosseto	1686	100,626	107,449
Leghorn	108	116,811	118,851
Lucca	576	236,161	280,070
Massa-Carrara	687	140,733	161,944
Pisa	1179	243,028	265,295
Siena	1465	193,935	205,918
Rome—			
Latium	4601	750,415	835,324
SOUTHERN ITALY.			
Abruzzi and Molise—			
Aquila	2509	309,451	333,791
Campobasso	1777	346,007	363,943
Chieti	1114	327,316	339,961
Teramo	1283	230,061	245,617
Campania—			
Avelino	1408	255,621	375,103
Benevento	692	220,506	231,914
Caserta	2206	653,464	696,328
Naples	401	867,983	907,714
Salerno	2130	528,256	541,738
Apulia—			
Bari	2292	554,042	604,365
Foggia	2953	312,885	319,164
Lecce	3293	447,982	493,263
Basilicata—			
Potenza	4121	492,959	501,880
Calabria—			
Catanzaro	2306	384,159	412,226
Cosenza	2840	431,922	443,483
Reggio	1514	324,546	353,606
Sicily—			
Caltanisetta	1455	223,178	230 066
Catania	1969	450,460	479,850
Girgenti	1491	263,880	289.018
Messina	1767	394,761	419,286
Palermo	1964	584,929	615,905
Syracuse, or Noto	1427	259,613	294,874
Trapani	1214	214,981	236,324
Sardinia—			
Cagliari	5256	372,097	392,958
Sassari	4141	215,967	243,607
Total	114,268	24,903,450	26,709,809

Physical Aspect.—The surface of I. is rich in the beauty of its rivers and flora, extends in broad, fertile plains, and rises in snow-capped mountain masses, enclosing fair, sequestered valleys. The backbone of the peninsula is the chain of the Apennines (q. v.), which forms near Genoa a continuation of the Maritime Alps, traverses the entire length of I., and attains in Monte Corno (the Gran Sasso d'Italia), among the wild highlands of Abruzzo, its greatest height of 9590 feet. Other peaks to the S. of Monte Corno, as Mont Amaro or Majella (9131 feet), Monte Vellino (8180), Monte Meta (7835), and Monte Pollino (7070), are capped with snow for some nine months in the year. Steep and rocky around the Gulf of Genoa and towards the Adriatic, the Apennines for the most part decline gently to the plains on the N. and W., here and there throwing out minor spurs. In the N. of I. the Alps (q. v.) form a magnificent circling frontier, in which the principal heights are Mont Blanc (15,798 feet), Monte Rosa (15,210), the Matterhorn (14,833), Monte Viso (12,567), and Mont Cenis (11,457); the two chief summits lying wholly in I. are the Grand Paradis (13,300), and the beautiful Grivola or Corne de Cogne (13,028), offshoots of the Graian Alps. Although sloping gradually to the N., the Alps are scarped and precipitous towards I., so that while the Rhone has a fall of 5250 feet in 92 miles, the Po makes an equal descent in 22 miles. The height of the snow-line is 9500 feet, and the whole Alpine chain abounds in glaciers, there being over 400 between Mont Blanc and Tyrol, some of which are about 15 miles long and 2½ wide, with a depth of 1640 feet. The chief passes are the Col di Tenda (5890 feet), Mont Cenis (6772), Great St. Bernard (8169), Simplon (6575), St. Gothard (6804), Splügen (6942), Brenner (4659), Stelvio (9095), and Semmering (4287). *Plains.*—The great northern plain of I., including Piedmont, Lombardy, and Emilia, and forming the basin of the Po, is unrivalled in the richness of its soil, the wealth of its productions, the density of its population, and the number of its towns. The other plains of I. are those of Venetia, Tuscany, Romagna, Campagna (Terra di Lavoro), and the Tavoliere of Apulia, from which the fine plain of Basilicata stretches round the Gulf of Taranto. The Roman plain is barren and desolate, but the coast-plains of Southern I. are singularly beautiful and luxuriantly fertile. *Valleys.*—Of the Alpine valleys, the only two that have a longitudinal direction are those of Aosta and the Valtelline. The other large valleys, some thirty-six in number, are normal to the chain, and most of them contain beautiful lakes, and send down copious streams. The valleys in the wild highlands of Abruzzo and Calabria are famed alike for their wealth of brilliant vegetation and charms of scenery. Vallombrosa, through which the Arno flows, and 'where the Etrurian shades high over-archt imbowr,' is hallowed by Milton's well-known lines.

Hydrography.—Owing to the peninsular character of I. and the direction of the mountains there are few important rivers, but innumerable mountain torrents. By far the largest river is the Po (q. v.), which rises in Monte Viso, on the French border, flows through Piedmont, separates Lombardy from Parma, Modena, and Ferrara, and enters the Adriatic by several channels about 30 miles S. of Venice, after a course of 330 miles. The chief of its many tributaries are, from the N., the Dora Baltea, Sesia, Ticino, Adda, Oglia, and Mincio; and from the S., the Tanaro, Trebbia, Nure, Taro, Parma, and Secchia. The Po annually deposits at its mouth forty million cubic feet of alluvium, thus extending its delta yearly at a mean of 230 feet. Among the other rivers of I. are the Adige, Brenta, Piave, Tagliamento, Aterno, Sangro, Metaura, and Ofanto, flowing into the Adriatic; the Arno, Tiber, Ombrone, Garigliano, and Volturno, entering the Tyrrhenian Sea; and the Bradano and Basente, draining into the Gulf of Taranto. Most of the rivers are only navigable to barges or coasting boats. *Lakes.*—I. is studded with many fine lakes, the chief of which are cradled in the Alpine valleys, as Maggiore, Como, Garda, &c., and are each celebrated for unique, enchanting beauties. Garda (45 miles long) is the largest, and Maggiore (perhaps the most beautiful), contains the famous Borromean Islands (q. v.). Other lakes are the Castiglione and Orbitella in the Tuscan Maremma, Chiusa, also in Tuscany; Perugia, in Umbria; Bolsena and Bracciano in Latium; Fondi in Caserta; Fucino in Abruzzo; and Salpi on the coast of Apulia. The coast valleys of Comacchio, S. of the Po, now form an immense pool or lagoon, 164 miles in circuit, and from 3 to 6 feet deep, in which there are valuable fisheries. *Canals.*—There are numerous canals, for irrigation as well as traffic, in the N. of I., the finest being the Canal Cavour in Piedmont, with a length of 52 miles, and the Naviglio Grande or Ticinello, 28 miles long, connecting Milan with the Ticino. The latter was begun in 1179, and many of the other canals are also of early date. Extensive canals have been constructed for the drainage of the Pontine marshes. The total length of canals in I. is 435 miles. I. has a vast number of mineral and thermal springs.

Geology and Mineralogy.—The great basin of the Po, the coast-region from Genoa to Civita Vecchia, and the entire belt between the Apennines and the Adriatic, are covered with Tertiary and post-Tertiary strata. The higher ridges of the Alps consist of gneiss and other primary rocks, flanked with limestone, sandstone, slate, &c. The Apennines as far as Calabria are formed of calcareous and serpentine rocks, and of graywacke, on which lie thick deposits of gypsum and beds of sulphur. But the most notable feature in the geology of I. is its volcanic system, comprising the Euganean hills of Lombardy, the group of Santa Fiora in Tuscany, Viterbo and the formations around Rome, Sant' Agata, Rocca Morfina, and Vesuvius (the only active volcano on the European continent), with its Campi Flegrei (Phlegræan Fields), Etna, in Sicily, and Stromboli, &c., in the Lipari Isles. Extinct craters abound throughout the whole length of the Apennines, and the territories of Arezzo, Perugia, Spoleto, &c., present the best-known examples in the world of volcanic action in their broken surfaces. The minerals of I. are numerous, but are not mined extensively. In the Alps are found iron, copper, lead, quicksilver, rock-salt, and some gold and silver; in the Apennines, copper, quicksilver, cobalt, manganese, &c. Coal is plentiful in Venetia and Tuscany, and in various parts occur salt, alum, and borax. Of great value are the volcanic products, nitre, sulphur, and lava; nearly all the sulphur employed in Europe is obtained from Sicily. Other minerals are the sea-green marble of Bocchetta, the gold-veined of Porto Venere, the statuary marble of Carrara, the jasper of Berga, the black marble of Pistoja, the giallo and lapis-lazuli of Siena, the alabaster of Volterra, the porphyries and rock-crystals of Aosta, and the chalcedonies and agates of Tuscany.

Climate.—The climate of I. is singularly fine, in spite of the winter severity in the N. and the almost tropical heat in the S. In the great northern plains the lakes freeze in winter, and the orange and lemon will not ripen in the open air; the central and southern plains are favoured with an almost perpetual spring. Snow falls, on an average, only two days annually at Rome, Florence, Naples, and Palermo, and five days at Venice. The annual mean temperature at Genoa is 61° F., at Florence 59°, at Bologna 58°, at Milan and Venice 56°, at Rome 60°, at Naples 61°, and at Syracuse 65°; the highest temperature at Rome is 95°, and in Sicily 104°. In the N. and in the interior it rains more during summer than winter, while the reverse is the case along the coast and in the S. The annual rainfall at Perugia is 39 inches, at Genoa 52, at Florence 49, and at Naples 34. During summer a deadly malaria is generated in the Tuscan Maremma, in the Pontine marshes and Venetian lagoons. Unfavourable winds are the tramontana or piercing wind of the mountains, and the blighting sirocco, which frequently sweeps the southern coasts.

Botany and Agriculture.—In I. are drawn together the characteristic floras of Western Asia, of N. Africa, and of all the countries of Europe. According to Cesati, the flowering plants of Lombardy alone number 2568 species. Among the tropical plants which grow in the S. are the cotton-plant, sugar-cane, date-palm, pistachio and papyrus; the Indian fig, a species of cactus, grows wild in Sicily. The oak and chestnut clothe the mountain sides to a height of 4000 feet; wheat thrives at 4500 feet, and the beech at 6000. The Apennines in Central I. are covered with a rich vegetation up to 3200 feet, while the lower zone is occupied by the palm, orange, citron, and olive. Above the dense forests and fine pasture of the Alps the *Alpine flora* rises to a height of 9500 feet, comprising the juniper, alder, rhododendron, willow, saxifrages, mosses, &c. The total extent of the forests in I. is about 12,350,000 acres. Except in the N., agriculture is in an extremely backward state. In abundant years the supply of grain exceeds the consumption, and in years of scarcity it falls short by about one-tenth. Two-fifths of the surface is arable, and the chief crops are wheat, maize, rye, barley, oats, and rice. Other important products are silk, wine

(780,000,000 gallons, of which 208,000,000 are yielded by Sicily), oil (30,560,000 gallons), hemp (50,000 tons), and tobacco (325,000 metric quintals). The mulberry is extensively cultivated, and the fruits exported are oranges, citrons, lemons, dates, melons, &c. The vine flourishes everywhere, but the wines are inferior to those of Spain and France, and they are mainly exported from Naples and Sicily. The finest Sicilian wines are those of Marsala; the choicest of Naples are the red *Lacryma Christi* and *Vino d'Asti*. There is considerable dairy-farming in Lombardy, and the produce of cheese and butter is valued at not less than £3,000,000.

Zoology.—Among the wild animals of I. are the wolf, lynx, boar, deer, marmot, fox, and wild-cat, and characteristic birds are the vulture, ibis, pelican, and flamingo. Various species of African water-fowl are found on the southern coast; the small birds *ortolans* and *beccafico* are esteemed as dainties. The tunny, anchovy, sardine, pilchard and mackerel fisheries of the Mediterranean are of great value. The rivers yield large quantities of salmon, trout, sturgeon, lampreys, tench, barbel, &c., while the lagoons abound with eels. Locusts occasionally appear in devastating swarms; butterflies are remarkable for their variety and beauty; and the seas are rich in molluscs, crustaceans, sponges, corals, &c. The bee and silkworm are of great economic importance, and a feature of insect life is the nocturnal firefly. Of the domestic animals the estimated number of black cattle or oxen is 3,700,000, of sheep and goats 12,000,000, of horses and mules 1,400,000, and of swine 4,000,000. I. has a comparatively small number of cattle.

Manufactures.—The principal manufacture is silk, the yearly value of spun silk alone being £5,200,000, independent of the tissues, among which the most valuable is velvet, produced of especially fine quality at Genoa. Woollens are manufactured, particularly at Biella and other places in Piedmont, to the value of £2,640,000. The cotton industry flourishes in Liguria, Piedmont, Lombardy, and Friuli, the production of spun cotton amounting to £1,400,000, and of cotton cloths to £3,200,000. There is an extensive straw-plait industry, chiefly at Leghorn and throughout Tuscany. So defective is the manufacture of wines, that they deteriorate with keeping, and are unfit to bear transport. Celebrated manufactures are the filigree work of Genoa, the coral ornaments of Naples and Leghorn, the wrought marbles of Carrara and Lucca, the perfumery and essences of Tuscany, and the mirrors, mosaics, and enamels of Venice. The traditionary skill of the Ligurian shipbuilders is now aided by good technical schools, especially by the Nautical Institute of Genoa. In 1875 there were in construction at fifteen shipyards of Liguria 103 vessels of 107,900 tons, or 1057 tons each.

Commerce.—The exports, silks, olive-oil, sulphur, fruits, anchovies, &c., amounted in 1875 to £42,286,040; the imports, the hardware and textiles of Great Britain, wool from the Levant, corn from Odessa, &c., to £48,602,040. Most of the raw and thrown silk imported into England from France is not produced in that country but in I. In 1874 there entered the ports of I. 118,446 vessels of 12,053,330 tons, and cleared 117,010 of 11,976,143 tons. The mercantile marine consisted in 1876 of 17,562 sailing vessels and 103 steamers, with a total of 949,813 tons.

Railways, &c.—In 1876 there were 4817 miles of railway open for traffic, of which 1016 belonged to the state. Since the opening of the Mont Cenis (see CENIS, MONT) tunnel in 1870 the E. Indian mails from England have been conveyed *via* Brindisi. The line across the Semmering Pass, completed in 1853, connects the railway system of I. with that of Austria. In 1876 there were 12,622 miles of telegraph lines, about two-thirds of which belong to the state.

Finance.—The budget for 1876 estimated the total receipts at £53,766,564, and the expenditure at £58,917,672. Since the establishment of the kingdom in 1866 till 1876 there have been deficits varying in amount from £1,743,000 to £24,668,000 in 1866. In 1875 the public debt amounted to 400 millions sterling. The deficits have been produced chiefly by the vicissitudes of the revolution, by military expenses, and by the construction of railways. The money, weights, and measures of I. are the same in all but name as those of France; the lira of 100 centisimi = the franc, or 25s. sterling.

Army and Navy.—By law of 7th June 1875, all men capable of carrying arms are held liable for service till the end of their thirty-ninth year, and must serve eight or nine years in the standing army, three or four in the milice mobile (*Landwehr*), and seven in the milice territoriale (*Landsturm*). In 1876 the standing army comprised a total of 409,426 (20,171 on peace furlough), besides 13,694 officers; the additional reserves bringing it up to a total of 867,886, with 18,836 officers. The artillery has a total of 1640 pieces. In 1876 the navy consisted of 81 war-vessels, carrying 671 guns, having a force of 13,316 sailors and marines. It includes two of the most powerful ironclads yet constructed, viz., the *Duilio* and *Dandolo*, double turret-ships, with armour 22 inches thick throughout, armed each with four 100-ton Armstrong guns. Two enormous vessels are designed, to be called the *Italia* and *Vittoria Emmanuele*, each to be of 14,000 tons, covered with armour of 36 inches. Under the superintendence of the able Minister, Saint Bon, the navy is being gradually transformed.

Education.—The percentage of the population that could not read was 78·29 in 1861, and 73·29 in 1871. Elementary instruction is now compulsory and gratuitous. There are 43,380 elementary schools, with (1872) 1,745,467 pupils, and several normal schools, giving a three years' course, attended by some 6000 intending masters and mistresses. Classical instruction is given in 104 national gymnasia to 8268 pupils, and in 79 royal lyceums to 3773 pupils. The Government technical schools, with physico-mathematical, commercial, agronomical, and industrial sections, are 135 in number, and have 10,659 pupils. At Milan and Portici are two large agricultural schools. Besides the 17 universities, Bologna, Padua, Florence, Rome, Naples, &c., with their 10,524 students, there are 3 free universities, 3 institutions for engineers, and 2 for literary and scientific culture. Of the 33 public libraries of I., the most important is the Magliabecchiana at Florence, with 280,000 printed vols. and 14,000 MSS. The state grant for education is £600,000.

Religion.—The *Statuto fondamentale del Regno* enacts in its first article that 'the Catholic Apostolic and Roman religion is the sole religion of the state.' A royal decree of 9th October 1870 declared that 'Rome and the Roman provinces shall constitute an integral part of the kingdom of I.,' and recognised the Pope as supreme head of the Church, retaining his dignities as a reigning prince, and all other prerogatives of absolute and independent sovereignty. The hierarchy in I. consists of 45 archbishops and 198 bishops. But the royal consent to the installation of a bishop or archbishop is now necessary. According to the census of 1871 the population comprised 26,658,679 Roman Catholics, 58,651 Protestants, 35,356 Jews, and 48,468 of other or of no professed faith. Freedom of worship, formerly denied except to the Waldensians in Piedmont, is now allowed throughout the country. The suppression by Government of several of the orders, and the enforced sale of their land, has greatly curtailed the Church revenues. In 1869 there were seven priests to every thousand inhabitants.

Government and Administration.—The Government of I. is a limited monarchy, established by constitution of 17th March 1861. The legislative power is vested in the King and in a Parliament consisting of a Senato, the members of which (270 in 1876) are nominated by the King for life, and in a Camera de' Deputati of 508 deputies, elected by a free suffrage. Neither senators nor deputies receive any salary or other indemnity. Entire freedom of the press and right of association are among the constitutional liberties. The Government appoints prefects of provinces and syndics of towns, and most of the governmental offices are elective. The judicial system of I. comprises conciliatory judges, who conciliate litigants and settle minor cases; prætors, who have jurisdiction of offences punishable with three months' imprisonment or a fine not exceeding £12, and decide civil cases not involving more than £60; tribunals with which lie appeals from the prætors, and above which are higher courts of appeal and courts of cassation. Little satisfaction has resulted as yet from the system of juries before the courts of assize.

History.—For the history of Italy to the fall of the Roman Empire see ROME. On the dethronement of Romulus Augustulus in 476, Zeno the Byzantine Emperor was nominally made ruler of Italy, the real power in that country being wielded by Odoacer, King of the Heruli, who bore the title of Imperial Regent. In 489 Theodoric, King of the Ostrogoths, overthrew Odoacer, founded a Gothic monarchy in Italy, and restored the country to a prosperity unknown since the days of the Antonines. But on Theodoric's death in 526 the shortlived Teutonic kingdom began to crumble away, and the hopes of a united Italy were lost. In the reign of Justinian the Byzantine troops drove the Ostrogoths from Italy, which was then governed for the Eastern emperors by an exarch, who dwelt at Ravenna (see EXARCHATE). In 568 the Lombards (q. v.) poured into Northern Italy, founded a kingdom there, and threatened the imperial power. Meanwhile, as the exarch's influence weakened, the papal power increased, aided largely by Gregory the Great's conversion of the Lombard Arians to the Catholic faith, and by the rupture between the Eastern and Western Churches, which loosened the bonds holding Italy to the Byzantine Empire. About the middle of the 8th c. the Pope, unable to withstand the Lombards, and deserted by the emperors, appealed to the Franks, and after the Papacy received aid from Pippin, the Frankish ruler, and from Karl the Great, the latter was proclaimed Emperor at Rome in 800, and the Western Empire was restored. Under Karl's feeble successors the Italian nobles became practically independent sovereigns, and the country was invaded by the Saracens, who seized on Southern Italy. At the close of the 9th c. the Byzantine power revived in the S., the Greeks wrested part of the land from the Saracens, and constituted it a province of the Eastern Empire under a ruler entitled the *Patrician*. On the breaking up of the Karoling Empire in 887, Italy became a separate kingdom and the scene of strife between various Teutonic invaders; the land was ravaged by Norsemen and Magyars, and the power of the Papacy dwindled. At length, in 962, Otto the Great, King of the Germans, put an end to the feeble line of Italian kings, and was crowned Emperor at Rome. Henceforth the sovereign of Italy was a German prince, whose authority repeatedly waxed and waned, and was speedily assailed by the growing power of the Papacy and the great Italian cities, which were now becoming independent republics. In the first half of the 10th c. the Normans conquered Calabria, Apulia, and Sicily, and destroyed the commerce of the southern cities, whose maritime greatness devolved upon Venice, Genoa, and Pisa. The Lombard cities, of which the chief was Milan, became practically independent, though owning a shadowy allegiance to the Holy Roman Empire. But during the great struggle between Heinrich IV. and Hildebrand (see HEINRICH IV. and GREGORY VII.) in the latter part of the 11th c., they mostly supported the Pope. Free civic life flourished far more vigorously in Italy than in any other country during the middle ages. This was due to the absence of any strong central power, and to the fact that Italy was never permanently occupied by any of the Teutonic tribes who destroyed the empire, and was more deeply impressed with Roman municipal institutions than any other part of Europe. Unfortunately the great Italian republics were bitterly jealous of each other, and instead of uniting in a compact federation, by playing into the hands of foreign rulers led to the prolonged enslavement of Italy. The failure of the Teutons to found a compact kingdom in Italy, and the evil effects of the Holy Roman Empire, kept the country broken up into small mutually jealous states until the recent establishment of the Italian kingdom. Medieval Italian history is much more complicated than the history of any other European state, the influences at work being far more varied. The republics never held all the land, never flung off formal allegiance to the Emperor of the Romans; their constitutions were partly inherited from Roman times, but were greatly modified by Teutonic influences, excepting in the case of Venice, which was isolated from the rest of Italy, and was never under a Teutonic ruler. Feudalism never took deep root in Italy—the nobles being early forced into the ranks of citizens in the great republics—except in the S., where the weakness of the nominal Greek rule favoured the growth of independent sovereignties. During the struggle between the papal and imperial power, most of the leading cities embraced the Guelphic cause, though many—and notably Pisa—aided the Emperor. (See GUELPHS AND GHIBELLINES, GREGORY VII., HEINRICH IV.) On Friedrich I.'s (q. v.) invasion of Italy, in the latter part of the 12th c., the northern cities banded against him in the Lombard League, and finally, after their victory at Legnano (1176), reduced the imperial power in Italy to a nominal suzerainty. During the 12th and 13th centuries the Italian republics were in their zenith of power. (See FLORENCE, MILAN, GENOA, VENICE, PISA.) The 14th and 15th centuries are the 'age of the despots'—the period when free civic government was supplanted by tyrannies, in which Italy remained destitute of central government and almost devoid of republican rule, while she was still only slightly influenced by feudalism. The banishment of the popes to Avignon removed the papal influence, which, though not strong enough to submit Italy to the rule of the pontiffs, kept the various powers of the peninsula in a kind of vague coherence, and was able to check the growth of an independent state in the N. The rise of the tyrants was favoured by the overlordship wielded by the Pope and Emperor, who gave a show of legitimate rule to adventurers willing to become their partisans. In the 15th c. the military spirit of the Italians dwindled away owing to the custom of employing mercenaries, the force of the various states and cities was sapped by endless virulent feuds, and at the end of the century the discovery of America diverted commerce from I. to Western Europe. When France, England, Austria, and Spain had become compact nations, I. was a cluster of contending princedoms. Her rulers, instead of confederating, in which lay their only hope of safety, endeavoured to use France, Spain, and Austria for the furtherance of their ends in Italian politics. The result was that I. was reduced to become the arena on which European quarrels were fought out. In 1494 Charles VIII. of France invaded the peninsula; his successor, Louis XII., made a similar expedition; and I. was the scene of the long contest between François I. and Karl V. During the 16th c., I., though ruled by Italians, was mainly in the power of Karl V.'s successors on the Spanish throne; and by the treaty of Lyons, in 1601, the French were excluded from the peninsula, and the change of Savoy into an Italian state was greatly advanced. In 1631 Mantua and Montferrat were bestowed on Charles of Nevers, who supported the French interests; and in the latter half of the century Louis XIV. made attempts on Savoy. But during the 17th c. I. enjoyed comparative peace until 1696, when the war of the Spanish Succession (q. v.), broke out. Austria seized Milan, Mantua, and Montferrat in 1706, and Naples and Sardinia in 1714. Savoy won Sicily, and handed over that island to Austria, receiving Sardinia in its stead, from which the house of Savoy took their royal title. Before 1750 all I., saving a few isolated republics and the Papal States, was divided among the houses of Lorraine, Bourbon, and Savoy. Forty years of slavery and apathy followed, till in 1792 the French Republic invaded Savoy. Napoleon (q. v.) formed the Cisalpine Republic in 1796, and the Roman Republic in 1798, and in 1804 added the crown of Italy to his imperial crown, making his brother Joseph king of Naples in 1805. In 1815 the affairs of Italy were reconstituted by the Congress of Vienna. Austria annexed the Lombardo-Venetian provinces; the Archduke Ferdinand of Austria became again Grand Duke of Tuscany; the King of Sardinia was restored to his dominions; the papal territories were almost wholly restored; and Ferdinand IV. was made King of the Two Sicilies. The Italians, galled by the detested Austrian rule, formed secret societies, of which the chief was that of the Carbonari (q. v.), to create a free united Italy, but in 1821 the Austrians quelled the revolutionary forces, and restored the former tyranny in Piedmont, Sicily, and Naples. Austria then established a system of terrorism and inquisitorial oppression throughout the country. Abortive revolutions flared out in Modena and the papal territory in 1831, and the Italians vainly looked for French succour. About this time the party known as Young Italy was founded by Giuseppe Mazzini (q. v.), whose aim was to expel the Austrians by a volunteer army, and until 1844 repeated but futile efforts were made to shake off the Austrian yoke. Another party, that of the *Moderates*, now arose, who looked forward to a united Italian kingdom. In 1848 the struggle with Austria was renewed in the north, but the King of Sardinia was beaten at Custozo, and the Austrians placed the country under martial law. About this time Garibaldi (q. v.) emerged as a guerilla leader in the N.; the Moderate party declined, and the Republicans strengthened; war was renewed; the Piedmontese were defeated at Novara (1849); but a republic was established at Rome, with Mazzini at its head. The French now assailed the Italians, and Garibaldi, after beating King Ferdinand's army at Palestrina, held Rome for about a month, when the French captured the city. Insurrection was again foiled. The Italians now began to look to Victor Emmanuel, King of Sardinia, as their champion. In 1859 he formed an alliance with France. The French entered Italy, beat the Austrians at Magenta and Solferino, and in 1860 Tuscany, Modena, Parma, and Romagna were united to Sardinia. In the same year Garibaldi with a volunteer force overthrew the atrocious despotism of Sicily and Naples, and Victor Emmanuel, who had forbidden Garibaldi's expedition, reaped the benefits, being proclaimed King of all Italy, and receiving Sicily and Naples. Venetia and the Papal States were still to be freed. In 1866 Italy took advantage of the Austro-Prussian war to wrest Venetia from Austria. In the following year Garibaldi marched on Rome. He routed the papal troops at Monte Rotondo, but the French Emperor's army defeated the Italians at Mentana. In 1870, after Napoleon III. surrendered at Sedan, Victor Emmanuel seized Rome, which became the capital of Italy, and the temporal power of the Pope came to an end. Since then Italy has made great progress in political reform and in mercantile and agricultural prosperity.

Itch, or **Scab'ies**, is an affection of the skin, characterised by scaliness, vesicles, and in some cases by pustules and excoriations. It is accompanied with excessive itching, which is augmented by warmth and stimulating food and drinks, giving rise to accidental abrasions and scratches. I. is caused by the *acarus scabiei*, which burrows within the epidermis and excites the papillary surface of the derma. The scaliness is caused by the burrowing of the *acarus*. On the surface of the vesicle there is a minute spot or streak, the point of entrance within the epidermis, and from it a whitish line may be traced into the neighbouring epidermis—the *burrow* of the acarus—and at its termination, under a slight elevation of the epidermis, the acarus lies concealed. The eruption of I. is most common between the fingers, at first, and from thence it extends to the wrists, flexures of the elbow, axillæ, abdomen, and the whole body. The most prominent symptom is intense itching, which is increased by scratching. When the patient is young and robust, I. spreads rapidly, and causes insupportable pruritis; but when weak and infirm, its progress is slow, the eruption partial, and the itching moderate. I. may be confounded with eczema, prurigo, lichen, impetigo, and ecthyma; but in I. there is the peculiar scaliness and undermining of the epidermis, the conical vesicles with acuminated and transparent points, and the *actual presence* of the acarus, which may be placed under the microscope. I. is always communicated by contact either immediately or through the contact of clothing. In strong and healthy children, the period of incubation is from two to four days; but in adults the usual period is a week or ten days, and during winter it may be extended to a fortnight or three weeks, and among the aged the period may be more extended still. The treatment of I. is purely local, the object being the extermination of the acarus and its ova. The first step to be taken is the preparation of the skin for the reception of medicaments by a thorough ablution with a warm solution of subcarbonate of potash, containing about half a pound to a gallon of water. After drying the skin, simple sulphur ointment should be rubbed into the entire skin, particularly into the affected parts, morning and evening, for two days. Flannel should be worn next the skin during treatment, and on the morning of the third day the body should be washed with warm water and soap. The process should be repeated to secure the destruction of ova which may not have been developed at the time of treatment. All articles of clothing should be boiled or exposed to a high temperature, or destroyed, to ensure the destruction of the acari and ova. Instead of the sulphur ointment, *stavesacre ointment* may be similarly used for four days, four times a day. Sponging with vinegar may be adopted in the case of young children. See *Diseases of the Skin*, by Erasmus Wilson.

Itch-Mite (*Sarcoptes scabiei*), a genus of *Arachnida* (q. v.) belonging to the *Acarina* or mite order, and infesting the human skin, in which it develops pustules, noted for the intense itching and irritation they produce. The I.-M. was first recognised in the 12 c. by an Arabian author as the cause of the itch disease, but the existence of the animal was long regarded as hypothetical. The body is rounded and oval shaped; the mandibles or jaws are of needle-like conformation; and the legs very short, and composed each of three joints. The female itch insect differs from the male in having the two hinder pairs of legs only partially developed, each leg ending in a long bristle. The average length of the female I.-M. is about one-fifth or one-sixth of a line in length, and one-seventh in breadth. The surface of the body is covered with bristles. Allied species infest the horse (*S. equi*), cat (*S. felix*), dog (*S. canis*), and pig.

Ith'aca, now **Ithaki** or **Thiaki**, one of the Ionian Islands (q. v.), the smallest next to Paxo, situated a little to the N.E. of Cephalonia (q. v.). Its area of 35½ sq. miles presents a constant succession of rugged limestone crags, with some pleasant valleys interspersed. The soil is light but well tilled, and the climate very healthy. The pop. is 11,910, and that of Vathi, the chief town, 3372. I. was the island of Ulysses (q. v.). There still exist cyclopean ruins of great antiquity, and many places seem to bear identification with scenes in Homer's poems.

Ith'aca, the capital of Tompkin's County, in the State of New York, U.S., on the Cayuga Lake, 180 miles N.W. of New York city, with which it is connected by railway. It is a busy centre of the Pennsylvania anthracite coal-trade, and the seat of Cornell University (q. v.), which in 1872 had 33 resident professors and 494 students. The manufactures are glass, leather, paper, calendar clocks, machinery, &c. Pop. (1870) 8462.

Itin'erary (the Lat. *itinerarium*, from *iter*, 'a journey'), a list of the stations between two main points of a route, together with the distances between them. The chief writings of this kind preserved from antiquity are *Itineraria Antonini*, comprising *I. provinciarum*, which gives the routes between the different Roman provinces of Europe, Asia, and Africa, and *I. maritimum*, a catalogue of the sea-passages most used; *I. Hierosolymitanum*, written by a Christian in 333 A.D. for the use of travellers from Burdigala (Bordeaux) to Jerusalem (best edition of both, Pinder and Parthey, Berl. 1848); and *I. Alexandri* (published by Angelo Mai at Milan, 1817), an account of Alexander the Great's expedition to Persia, drawn up about 338 A.D.

It'ri, a town of S. Italy, in the province of Caserta, half-way between Fondi and Gaeta, is a poor but picturesque place, with a ruined castle, and is best known in connection with Fra Diavolo (q. v.), who was born here in 1760. Pop. (1871) 6542.

I'tu, or **Y'tu**, a town of Brazil, in the province of São Paulo, 3 miles from the S. bank of the Tiete, and 48 N.W. of São Paulo, is a thriving centre of agricultural produce, and has some fine churches, two convents, a lazaretto, &c. Large quantities of sugar are produced in the neighbourhood, and I. has celebrated breeds of horses and mules. Pop. about 10,000.

Iturbide, Don Augustin de, a Mexican usurper, the son of a Biscayan nobleman and a creole, was born at Valladolid, Mexico, September 27, 1783. He joined the army in 1805, and received command of the 'army of the north' in 1820. On the Mexican revolution in 1822 he was proclaimed Emperor (18th May), but soon quarrelled with Congress, and was forced to abdicate. He removed to Europe, but landing in Mexico in 1824 with revolutionary designs, was seized by the authorities at Padilla, and shot, 19th July 1824. In the year of his death he published an autobiography (Eng. trans. by Quin, same year).

Itz'ehoe, a town of Prussia, in the province of Slesvig-Holstein, on the navigable Stör, 15 miles from its entrance into the Elbe, and 60 N.W. of Hamburg by rail. It has manufactures of tobacco, cement, chicory, &c., also distilleries and sugar-refineries. Pop. (1875) 9786. I. arose about a castle built here by Karl the Great in 809, and bore the names successively of Esseveldoburg and Eselsfleth, or Ezeho. It was joined to Holstein by Adolf IV. in 1238, and became the residence of the Holstein Dukes. In the Thirty Years' War it was twice taken by Tilly, and was partly destroyed by the Swedes in 1657.

Iu'lus, the genus of *Myriapoda* (q. v.), including the forms familiarly known as *Millepedes*, or 'thousand-feet,' and as 'hairy worms'—the supposed 'hairs' seen on the sides of the body being in reality numerous and minute legs. The I. is nearly related to the Centipede (q. v.). The body is cylindrical, and the head large and distinct. The antennæ are long and many-jointed; the eyes simple, and situated at the base of the feelers. The average length is about 2½ or 3 inches. The I. is found beneath the bark of trees, under stones, moss, and in damp places generally. It has the power of rolling the body for defence into a spiral form, the feet being contained within the inner whorl of the spire. The I. form the type of the order *Chilognatha*, in which the mandibles or larger jaws are without *palpi* or feelers, and are covered by a lower lip or labium formed of the united *maxillæ* or lesser jaws. *I. terrestris* is a familiar species; others are *I. Canadensis* found in N. America, and *I. multistriatus* in the Western States of America.

Ivan', or **Iwan** (Russian form of the Gr. *Ioannes*, Eng. John), is the name of six Russian Grand-Dukes and Czars. During the Mongol dominion, **I. I. Danilovitch Kalita** (*i.e.*, 'money-bag,' from his constantly carrying such to relieve the poor), Grand-Duke of Moscow, 1328–1340, sought to make his city the capital of Russia, and succeeded in removing thither from Vladimir the seat of the Metropolitan. His younger son, **I. II. Ivanovitch** (1353–59), lost in battle with the Lithuanians a wide extent of land on the Dnieper, and died a monk.—**I. III.** (as Czar, **I. I.**) **Vasiljevitch the Great** (1462–1505), founder of the Russian Empire, was born 22d January 1440. Gradually uniting the other Russian duchies with that of Moscow, he freed Russia from the Mongol power, and subdued Novgorod in 1478. In 1472 he married Sophia, niece of the last Byzantine Emperor, which gave him a claim on the Greek Empire, and led to the double-headed Byzantine eagle being placed on the Russian arms. He died October 1503 at Moscow.—**I. II. Vasiljevitch Grosnji** (*i.e.*, 'terrible'), Czar 1533–84, grandson of the preceding, was born 25th August 1530. He did more than all his predecessors to further the civilisation of his half-savage people, but his cruelty was excessive. In his reign foreign, especially German, artisans and scholars were introduced into Russia. Trade, which at that time could only be carried on through Archangel, he promoted by striking a treaty with Elizabeth of England. He established a standing army, the Strelitzes. Though unfortunate in his wars with Poland and Sweden for Livonia, I. extended his dominions with the conquest of Kasan (1552) and of Astrakhan (1554), the remains of the Mongol realm, and acquired Siberia by accepting Jermak Timofejev's offer of submission. He died 18th March 1584.—**I. III. Alexievitch**, of the house of Romanov, elder half-brother of Peter the Great, and father of Anna Ivanovna (q. v.), was born in 1666, and in 1682 became Czar together with Peter. Weakness of mind and body unfitted him for power. He resigned in 1688, and died 29th January 1696.—**I. IV. Antonovitch**, grandson of the preceding, son of Prince Anton Ulrich of Brunswick-Wolfenbüttel and the Russian Grand-Duchess Anna Carlovna (q. v.), born 23d August 1740, was by his great-aunt the Empress Anna appointed her successor, and at her death, when only two months old, was proclaimed Czar under the regency of Biron. In a few days Biron was displaced by I.'s mother, but I. had already (6th December 1741) been dethroned by Elizabeth, daughter of Peter the Great. She placed him in several prisons in succession, and finally at Schlüsselburg. Here, during the reign of Catherine II., in consequence of an attempt of a Lieutenant Mirovitch to deliver him, he was put to death (16th July 1764), which the garrison were ordered to do in the last extremity.

Ivan'ova, a village of Russia, on the river Uvod, in the government of Vladimir, 215 miles N.E. of Moscow, in a territory possessed by the Counts Sheremetieff since 1714. From the extent of its manufacturing industry, I. has been called the Russian Manchester. It has itself 130 calico factories, annually preparing one million pieces, and as the centre of the cotton manufacture of Russia, gives employment to 50,000 operatives here and in the surrounding district, producing goods yearly to the value of 2½ million pounds sterling. Pop. (1870) 6000.

Ives, St., a seaport and market-town, N. coast of Cornwall, 15 miles N.W. of Land's End, lies at the N.E. extremity of a deep bay of the same name, and has a commodious harbour. The chief industry is the pilchard-fishery, but boat-building is also carried on (in 1875 23 vessels of 390 tons), and there are valuable tin and copper mines in the neighbourhood. A line connecting St. I. with the W. Cornwall Railway was opened in May 1877. St. I. returns one member to Parliament. Pop. (1871) 6965.

Ives, St., a town of England, in Huntingdonshire, 72 miles N. of London by rail, on the left bank of the Ouse, which is here crossed by an ancient bridge of six arches. Brewing and malting are the leading industries. Pop. (1871) 3248. Its earlier name, Slepe, survived in Slepe Hall, the residence of Oliver Cromwell (1631–35).

Ivi'za (Lat. *Ebŭsus* or *Ebūsus*), the larger of two islands in the Mediterranean, forming part of the Balearic group, and anciently known as the Pityusæ Insulæ, now belonging to the Spanish province of Mallorca. *Ophiussa* (now Formentara), the other island, was uninhabited. Area of I., 221 sq. miles; pop. 22,170. The chief town, I., is fortified, has a harbour, and exports salt. Pop. 5100.

I'vory (Fr. *ivoire*, from the Lat. *ebur*, Sansk. *ibha*, 'an elephant'), a dense substance of bony nature used in the arts, and obtained from various animals. I. represents the largely developed tooth substance (or *dentine*) of such animals as the elephant, mammoth, narwhal, hippopotamus, &c. The microscopic investigation of I. shows that its substance is perforated by numerous fine tubes, which open internally into the central portion or *pulp cavity* of the tooth, and which by their outer extremities come in contact with the under surface of the enamel or cement which coats the tooth. The tubes of I. exhibit gentle curvatures, and divide and subdivide in a regular and dichotomous manner. The average diameter of these tubules is the $\frac{1}{1500}$th of an inch, and in a living tooth they contain infinitesimal prolongations of the pulp-substance. Chemically examined, I. contains less *animal* matter than bone; 28 parts of animal matter existing to 72 of earthy or mineral matter in 100 parts of I. The large development of I. in the Elephant (q. v.), is due to the continuous growth of the teeth, which spring from permanent pulps, the upper incisors or front teeth forming the tusks. In the narwhal the great development of a single tooth, the exact nature of which is undetermined, produces a long spirally-twisted horn, which may attain a length of 8 or 9 feet.

Elephant I. is very valuable as an article of commerce, and is obtained from three sources—1st, from the tusks of the Asiatic elephant, 2d, from the African elephant, and 3d, from the fossil remains of the mammoth or great prehistoric elephant. Asiatic I. is very white, but tends to become yellow on exposure to the air, and on this account is less valuable than the African variety. The latter in its green or fresh state has a warm tint, and no appearance of grain, but as the oil it contains dissipates the I. whitens; it has usually a closer texture, works harder, and takes a better polish than the Asiatic. It is the most valuable article of commerce in Central Africa, and by all the trade routes from the interior vast quantities are sent out annually. The mammoth I., found in great abundance in the N. of Siberia, supplies the Russian market, and a portion of it finds its way to Great Britain. It is of a rather marbly white appearance, and is comparatively brittle. I. has been a favourite substance on which to execute artistic carvings from the most remote period, and the existence of plaques of very large size favours the opinion that the ancients possessed a means of artificially flattening it which is now lost. At the present day the demand for I. far exceeds the supply, and it constantly tends to increase in value. It is used for knife handles, billiard balls, pianoforte keys, for inlaying, and innumerable other useful and ornamental purposes. Dieppe is now, perhaps, the most extensive I.-factory in Europe.

Ivory, Vegetable. This article, now in extensive use as a substitute for ivory, is obtained from one or two species of *Palms* constituting the genus *Phytelephas*, abounding in the lower eastern slopes of the Andes, and descending along the course of the rivers a few hundred miles. In *P. macrocarpa* the fruit is 9 to 12 inches in diameter, containing numerous carpels, of which only four are fertilised. The albumen of the unripe seeds is drunk while watery, or rather when it becomes fleshy, the taste being something like that of cocoa-nut in the same immature state; but when ripe it is so hard and ivory-like as to defy the teeth of any animal, and becomes the I.-nut of commerce, chiefly employed in the manufacture of buttons, umbrella handles, knobs for doors, inlaying, and toys.

Ivre'a, the *Eporedia* of the Romans, colonised by them as a bulwark against the Alpine tribes, a town of North Italy, on the Dora Baltea, and 33 miles N.E. of Turin. It has a bishop's residence, a citadel, and an old cathedral. Pop. (1874) 9125. The Markgrafdom of I., created by Karl the Great after the conquest of the kingdom of Lombardy, took its name from this town. After Karl III. was driven out of Italy in 887, the Markgrafs of I. were among the aspirants to the crown of Italy, of which Berengar possessed himself in 950. When the Markgraf Harduin set himself up as king in opposition to the Emperor Heinrich II., and was overcome, Heinrich incorporated I. (1018) in the German Empire. Friedrich II. granted it to the House of Savoy, to which it still belongs.

Ivry, a town to the S.E. of the walls of Paris, and near the left bank of the Seine, in the department of that name. The chief industries are ropemaking and the manufacture of animal charcoal and chemicals. Pop. (1872) 1989; of commune, 11,176.

I'vy (Old Eng. *ifig;* Ger. *epheu;* med. Lat. *iva;* yew is from the same word, written *iua*). Common I. is the *Hedera Helix* of botanists, the only British representative of the natural order *Araliaceæ*, and certainly one of the best-known constituents of British flora. There are many varieties, though Dr. Hooker limits the genus to two species. I. thrives poorly in the United States, owing to greater extremes of climate. The medicinal properties are of no importance.

Ixi'on, according to early Hellenic tradition, was a Thessalian prince, and king of the Lapithæ or Phlegyes. After his marriage with Dia he treacherously murdered her father, Deïoneus, who had demanded certain bridal gifts. All the gods were indignant, but Zeus purified him of the crime, after which the ingrate strove to win the love of Hera. Zeus created a phantom resembling her, and by it I. became the father of the Centaurs. For his lust and treachery he was chained by Hermes to a winged or fiery wheel, which whirled perpetually in the lower world or in the air.

Ixmiquil'pan, a town of Mexico, in the state of Hidalgo, on the river Montezuma, 80 miles N. of the city of Mexico. In its vicinity are several silver-mines, owned by English companies. For several months in 1861 it was the headquarters of General Zuloaga, who claimed to be President of the Republic. Pop. 10,000, mostly Otomi Indians.

Izucar', a thriving town of Mexico, in the state of Puebla, near the base of Popocatepetl, and in the rich valley of the Mescala. It is the S. terminus of a railway from Puebla (constructed in 1875), and has a trade in the sugar and other products of the country. Pop. 12,000. General Matamoros gained a great victory at I. over the Spainards, 24th February 1812.

J.

J the tenth letter in the English alphabet, occupying the same position as in the Latin and Phœnician. In Greek it was unknown, and the Phœnician *jod* or *yodh* was sounded something between a *y* and a soft *g*. In Latin it was not distinguished in form from *i*; and indeed it is only within the last three centuries that it has been differentiated in writing from that vowel, by being merely continued below the line. In German it is pronounced as *y*; in Spanish as a guttural aspirate; in French as *zh*; and in English as *dzh*, precisely the sound of the soft *g*. J occurs in many of the Oriental alphabets; and English is the only language into which it can be translated without the awkwardness of a double consonant. Examples of its interchanges are: Lat. *jugum*, Ger. *joch*, Gr. *zygon*, Eng. yoke; Eng. 'journey' and 'journal,' from Lat. *diurnus*; Ital. *Giovanni*, from Lat. and Gr. *Ioannes*.

As an abbreviation, J.P. stands for justice of the peace.

Ja'biru (*Myctŏria*), a genus of *Grallatorial* or wading birds, represented by the Australian J. (*M. Australis*), and by other species. These birds belong to the *Ciconinæ* or sub-family of the storks. The bill is very large, and has its tip turned upwards. The second and third quills are the longest. The species occur in S. America, Africa, and Australia. The head and upper part of the neck are destitute of feathers. The birds may measure from 4 to 5 feet in height. The Australian J. is green on the head and neck, the same colour, but darker, prevailing on the back. The food consists of fishes, and especially of eels; nearly two pounds of the latter fishes have been taken from the stomach of one specimen.

Jaboran'di, a plant of the natural order *Rutaceæ*, said to be the *Pilocarpus pennatifolius* of Lemaire. An alkaloid named *pilocarpine* has been extracted from the leaves and bark, and in lesser quantity from the wood, by Mr. Gerrard; and experiments on the lower animals showed the following results:—A $\frac{1}{16}$th of a grain injected into the jugular vein produced profuse salivation almost instantly, caused a retardation of the heart's action, and had a marked influence on the blood pressure. In frogs, the smallest doses produced an extremely viscid condition of the skin; larger doses, well-marked neurotic symptoms, and larger still, powerful tetanic spasms. J. applied to the eye contracts the pupil. More recent experiments show that J. has powerful chologue properties, and hence its denomination *vegetable mercury*. In the human subject J. is the most powerful sialogogue and sudorific known. See *Year-Book of Pharmacy* (Lond. 1875), *Edinburgh Medical Journal*, article J., by Dr. W. Craig (1876).

Jab'ua, the capital of the State of the same name, in connection with the Bheel Agency in Central India, 92 miles W. from Mhow. Area of the *state*, 1500 sq. miles; pop. 55,000, mostly Bheels; revenue, £25,000; tribute, £147. The chief is a Rajput, who was loyal during the Mutiny; he is tributary to Holkar.

Jacamar' (*Galbula*), a well-known genus of birds, a species of which inhabits the New World. They are included in the order *Insessores* (q. v.), and in the section *Fissirostres* (q. v.). The sub-family *Galbulinæ*, constructed for their reception, is characterised by a long bill and a tapering tail. In the genus *Galbula* the bill is square and straight, and the nostrils are in a small groove. The tarsi are feathered, and the hinder toe is very small. The food consists of insects. The green J. (*G. viridis*) and Paradise J. (*G. Paradisea*) are familiar species. The latter occurs in Surinam. It is brown, marked with bright hues; the neck and wing-coverts are white; the back has a golden-green lustre; the two central feathers of the tail are very long. In the plumage of the green J. green tints predominate. Its size is about that of the English kingfisher. The allied genus *Jacamerops* includes the great J. (*J. grandis*), also green, with a very broad bill. The genus *Jacamaralcyon* includes the three-toed J. (*J. tridactyla*).

Ja'cana (*Parra*), a genus of *Grallatorial* birds, remarkable for the long toes, which enable them to walk over water-plants. The common J. (*Parra J.*) inhabits S. America; other species are found in Africa, Asia, and Australia. These birds are nearly allied to the Screamers, and are distinguished, as a genus, by a bill which has the sides compressed, by the third quill being the longest, and by the tail being short and partly hidden by its coverts. The head and part of the neck may be naked. The common J. is black. The Chinese J. or Meewa (*Hydrophasianus Sinensis*) is equally at home on land or water. It resembles the pheasant—hence the generic name *hydrophasianus* ('water-pheasant'). The body is a deep chocolate-brown; the head, neck, and throat are white; the back of the neck is orange, and the legs and beak are green.

Jacaran'da, the Brazilian name of the trees that furnish the true Rosewood (q. v.), as well as of several species of Machærium (Leguminosæ), which yield an inferior wood. It is often confounded with the genus J. belonging to Bignoniaceæ.

Jacita'ra Palm (*Desmoncus macracanthos*), one of a genus peculiar to tropical America. The flexible stems climb or trail 50 or 60 feet, and the hooked spines of the leaves are a great annoyance to the traveller. The Indians plait strips of the stems into strainers to extract the poisonous juice from the mandioc.

Jack (*Artocarpus integrifolia*), a species of trees allied to the bread-fruit, is a native of the E. Indies. It produces a much larger fruit than the bread-fruit tree, and the timber, which is at first of pale colour, but subsequently becomes as dark as mahogany, is extensively used for making furniture.

Jack-a-Lantern. See Ignis Fatuus.

Jack'al (a corruption of Sp. and Fr. *chacal*, Pers. *shacal*), a species of *Carnivorous* mammalia, closely allied to the dog, and included in the family *Canidæ*. These animals inhabit Africa and Asia, and are sometimes met with in immense packs. The common J. (*C. aureus*), or Kholah, is found in India, Ceylon, and other parts of Asia. The pupil of the eye is circular, the tail bushy, and the ears prominent and pointed. The dental formula resembles that of the dog. The fur is yellow, which has given origin to the specific name of *aureus*.

Jackal.

The average size is that of a large fox. The J. has frequently been named the 'lion's provider,' from the belief that it guided the king of beasts to prey. But there appears to be no truth in this idea; the J. usually accompanies the larger carnivora in the hope, no doubt, of participating in their prey. The animal is nocturnal in habits and cowardly in nature. The black-backed J. (*C. mesomelas*) inhabits S. Africa, from which fact it also receives the name of 'Cape J.' It has white and black markings on the back, this peculiarity distinguishing it from the Asiatic species.

Jack'ass, Laughing, the name given by the Australian colonists to the great brown kingfisher, *Dacelo gigantea*, a bird of the family *Halcyonidæ*, tribe *Fissirostres*, and order *Insessores*. It derives its popular name from its peculiar note, resembling a boisterous gurgling laugh, in imitation of which the L. J. is called by the aboriginals the 'gogobera.' Unlike other kingfishers, it does not take its prey from the water. It is invaluable as a destroyer of snakes, and also lives on lizards, insects, and mice. It is easily domesticated, and is then frequently allowed to wander freely about house or garden.

Jack'daw (*Corvus monedula*), a species of *Corvidæ* or crows, distinguished by a grey patch on the crown of the head and at the root of the neck, and by being smaller than the rook or crow. It is a familiar British bird, and is easily tamed and trained to talk. The nest is built in ruined places, crevices of rocks, hollow trees, and like situations; instinct leading the J. to protect its young from stoats and polecats by selecting inaccessible places. The average length of the J. is 14 inches. The eggs number five or six, and are bluish white.

Jack'son, (1) a city of Michigan, U.S., and a great railway junction on the Grand River, 76 miles W. of Detroit. It has extensive foundries, engine-works, sal-soda factories, flour and planing mills, fireclay works, &c., and in the vicinity are productive coal-mines. The city was incorporated in 1857, and is the seat of Michigan State prison. A feature is its fine trotting park. Pop. (1870) 11,447.—(2) The capital of Mississippi, U.S., on the W. side of the Pearl River, 45 miles E. of Vicksburg by rail. It carries on an active trade in cotton and other products, comprises among its public buildings the State-house and penitentiary, institutions for the blind and for the deaf and dumb, and a lunatic asylum, and is the seat of the United States courts. Pop. (1870) 4234, of whom about half are coloured.—(3) A city of Tennessee, U.S., at the junction of the Mississippi Central and the Mobile and Ohio railways, 72 miles N.E. of Memphis. Its cotton trade is important (125 business houses), and it is the seat of the West Tennessee College. Pop. (1870) 4119, rapidly increasing.

Jackson, Andrew, the seventh President of the United States, was born of Scotch-Irish parentage at Waxhaw settlement, in Tennessee, March 15, 1767. After serving through the American Revolution, J. turned lawyer, became senator, judge of the Supreme Court, and major-general of the Tennessee army. In 1813 the Creek Indians made war on the South-western States, and J. defeated them at Talladega, Emuckfaw, and Tallapoosa. He was made major-general of the United States army in 1814, and in that year conducted a vigorous campaign against the British in Florida. From the Spanish he captured Pensacola (September), and (January 8, 1815) successfully defended New Orleans against the attack of General Pakenham. J. was appointed governor of the new territory of Florida in 1821, and was elected to the United States Senate, and nominated by the Tennessee Legislature to the Presidency in 1823. A strong Democrat, he was elected in 1828, and re-elected in 1832. Two struggles marked his period of office the first conducted against the extreme members of his own party in South Carolina, who refused to accept the tariff of lowered import duties; the second against the Federals, who, backed by the National Bank, opposed his re-election. J. deprived the bank of its charter and withdrew from it the public money. He died near Nashville, June 8, 1845. J. was a man of excitable temperament, but was endowed with a natural power for command and an indomitable energy and force of character. See Lives of J. by Eaton (1824), Cobbett (1834), Amos Kendall (1844), and by James Parton (3 vols. New York, 1859).

Jackson, Thomas Jonathan, an American general, was born at Clarksburg, in Virginia, January 21, 1824, was educated at the military academy of West Point, 1842–46, served in the Mexican war, and rose to the rank of lieutenant in 1847, was elected Professor of Mathematics and Military Science in the Virginia State Military Institute in 1852, and was appointed Brigadier-General in the Confederate army in 1861. His resolute conduct at the first battle of Bull Run earned for him the name of 'Stonewall J.' At the junction of the Shenandoah with the Potomac (June 27, 1862), J. defeated a Federal force 70,000 strong under M'Clellan. In August he defeated the Federals at Cedar Mountain and Gainsville; during their first invasion of Maryland, he took Harper's Ferry, with 11,000 prisoners; and at the battle of Chancellorville he successfully attacked the Federal right. When riding back from reconnoitring, he was mistaken by his own men and shot, May 10, 1863. J. was conspicuous for the swift dexterity of his movements, whilst his personal daring and tactical skill earned him the affection and esteem of his soldiers. He moulded the raw Valley Virginians into the famous 'Stonewall brigade.' See *Life of Stonewall J.* by J. Esten Cooke (New York, 1876).

Jackson, William, an English composer of great originality and grace, was born at Exeter, May 1730, studied under Travers of the Chapel Royal in London, and returning to his native city, was appointed organist of the cathedral in 1777. He published four collections of vocal and one of instrumental music, besides three operas, and was the author of *Thirty Letters on Various Subjects, On the Present State of Music*, &c. J. was also a landscape painter, closely following his friend Gainsborough. He died at Exeter, 12th July 1803.

Jack'sonville, a city of Illinois, U.S. situated in a fertile prairie, near the Mauvaiseterre Creek, a branch of Illinois River, 30 miles W. of Springfield by rail. It is known as the 'Athens of the West,' and among its public buildings are various State asylums and the Illinois College (Congregational), Illinois Female College (Methodist), Illinois Conservatory of Music, &c. Its industries in woollens, ironwares, and flour are rapidly developing. Pop. (1870) 9203.

Ja'cob. Of the name J. (Heb.) as in the case of Esau, two different derivations are given, as some say, by different writers: the one from the literal meaning of *akab*, 'to take hold of the heel' (Gen. xxv. 26), the other from the figurative meaning, 'to circumvent' (Gen. xxvii. 36). According to some critics, the chief object of the story of J.'s life after he fled from his home (Gen. xxviii. 1) was to show that the Israelites had no Canaanitish blood in their veins, to assign its proper rank to each of the tribes [the sons of the beloved Rachel, *i.e.*, the tribes of Ephraim, Manasseh, and Benjamin, being the chief, and the sons of Leah (Reuben, Simeon, Levi, Judah, Issachar, and Zebulon) of nobler blood than the sons of the slaves (Dan, Naphtali, Gad, and Asher)], to teach that there ought to be friendly relations between Israel and Syria, and to explain the origin of the worship of teraphim in Israel. The Scripture narrative is familiar to every one. See ESAU.

Jacobabad, or **Khangurh**, the chief town of the Upper Frontier district, Scinde, British India, near the border of Beluchistan, about 200 miles N. of Hydrabad. Pop. (1872) 10,714. It contains the cantonments of the Scinde Horse and Jacob's Rifle Regiment. The town was founded in 1847 by General Sir J. Jacob, to whom it owes its excellent roads, canals, and public buildings. It contains the stone mausoleum of its founder, who died here in 1858. See *Gazetteer of Scinde*, by A. W. Hughes (Lond. 1874).

Jaco'bi, Johann Georg, a German poet, born 2d September 1740, at Düsseldorf, studied at Göttingen, and became Professor of Philosophy and Eloquence at Halle. In 1794, Joseph II. made him Professor of the Fine Arts at Freiburg, in the Breisgau. J. died January 4, 1814. His collected works, chiefly pleasant lyric poems, including also cantatas, operas, and the comedy *Die Wallfahrt nach Compostella*, appeared at Zürich (7 vols. 1807–13). See *Life of J.* by Ittner (Zür. 1825).—**Friedrich Heinrich J.**, brother of the preceding, was born at Düsseldorf, 25th January 1743. After studying at Geneva, and managing his father's business from 1763 to 1772, he was appointed councillor in the Exchequer, and in 1779 privy councillor and 'referent' of taxes in Munich. Returning to Düsseldorf in 1780, he spent his leisure on his estate of Pempelfort in philosophical study and social intercourse. In 1794 he went to Holstein, where he lived until 1804, when he was made a member of the newly-founded Academy of Sciences at Munich, of which he was president from 1807 to 1813. He died 10th March 1819. As the founder of the 'Philosophy of Faith' he makes war alike upon Kant and the rationalism of the Illuminati, maintaining that not only our knowledge of the supernatural, but also our certainty of the existence of an external world, depend not on reasoning, but on an immediate acceptance or faith, which he later calls *reason*. The feelings are related to reason as the senses to the understanding, but unlike the senses, are incapable of error. Nature conceals God; the supernatural in man himself reveals him. His whole philosophy is of a subjective nature. Though a mystic, his mysticism did not take the form of dogma. J.'s works, *Allwill's Briefsammlung* (1792), and *Woldemar* (1799), are philosophical romances; *Etwas, was Lessing gesagt hat* (1782), *Briefe über die Lehre des Spinoza* (1785), *David Hume über den Glauben* (1787), *Sendschreiben an Fichte* (1799), *Ueber das Unternehmen des Kriticismus, die Vernunft zu Verstand zu bringen* (1801), *Von den Göttlichen Dingen und ihrer Offenbarung* (1811), are philosophical treatises. His collected writings appeared in 6 vols. (1812-24), his correspondence in 2 vols. (1825-27), followed by the *Briefwechsel zwischen Goethe und J.* (Leips. 1846). See Schlichtegroll, Weiller, and Thiersch, *Friedr. Heinr. J. nach seinem Leben, Lehren und Wirken* (Mün. 1819), and J.'s *Biographie* by Zirngiebl (1867).

Jacobi, Karl Gustav Jakob, a German mathematician, was born at Potsdam, December 10, 1804, studied at the University of Berlin, and in 1827 obtained the Chair of Mathematics at Königsberg. His great work, *Fundamenta Nova Theoriæ Functionum Ellipticarum* (1829), contains only a part of his valuable researches on this abstruse branch of mathematics. He successively visited England, Scotland, France, and Italy, and on his return to Germany removed from Königsberg to Berlin, where he died, February 18, 1851. J. is the author of another work entitled *Canon Arithmeticus* (1839); but it is in Crelle's *Journal für die reine und angewandte Mathematik* that his most powerful and original memoirs appear.—His brother, **Moritz Hermann J.**, born at Potsdam, 21st September 1801, has also won celebrity in applied science. See his discovery, *Die Galvanoplastik* (St. Petersb. 1840), and *Mémoire sur l'Application de l'Électro-Magnetisme au Mouvement des Machines* (St. Petersb. 1836).

Jac'obins, originally the name of the French Dominicans, who were so called from the circumstance that a church dedicated to St. James had been given to them on their settlement in Paris in the 13th c. During the French Revolution of 1789 the chief club of *La Montagne* took the name on account of its meeting in a Dominican monastery in the Rue St. Honoré. At first members of the club were selected from those who sat in the National Assembly, but its privileges were soon enlarged under the government of Robespierre. By its influence and that of the Cordeliers, the revolutionary scene of June 20, 1792, took place, and (July 11) the raising of the insurrectionary army under the walls of Paris, whilst on the 10th of August they dictated their own terms for a National Convention, which met on the 21st of September. 'They are Lords of the Articles,' writes Carlyle, 'they originate debates for the legislative; discuss peace and war; settle beforehand what the legislative is to do.' The death of the king (January 21, 1793), the establishment of the *Comité du Salut Public*, the decree for the arrest of the Girondist members, and the subsequent establishment of a sanguinary despotism, whose acts are known as the Reign of Terror, may all be traced in part to the action of the J. The revolution of the 9th Thermidor (1794) put an end to the club, their hall being closed by an order of the Convention, after which retribution was dealt out to the members. The J. gave rise to an extensive literature of plays, poems, and pamphlets, as *Les Secrets des J.*, *La Jacobiniade*, *Les Crimes des J.*, published in Paris between 1790 and 1795.

Jac'obites, sometimes used as a name synonymous with the Monophysites (q. v.) of the Eastern Church, are properly confined to Syria and Mesopotamia; their Patriarch, called of Antioch, and always taking the name Ignatius, residing at Diarbekir, according to some authorities at Zaaferan, near Mardin. The name is derived either from the Apostle James (Jacobus), or much more probably from a famous Bishop (Jacobus) of Nisibis in the 6th c., who did much to preserve the sect in a time of persecution.

Jac'obites, the name given to the partisans of James II. after the revolution of 1688. They were most numerous in Scotland, where they stirred up the rebellions of 1715 and 1745. They were not wholly extinguished as a party till the death of Charles Edward Stuart in 1788.

Jacobite Songs, a distinct class of Scotch melodies, in which are celebrated the gallantry of the later princes of the Stuart dynasty, their successes, their misfortunes, their kindliness and gift of personal fascination. These songs are pathetic, humorous, and satirical, and the fine Scottish airs to which they are set, or which have been composed for them, are admirably expressive of the varying shades of sentiment, and afford in themselves high testimony to the racy and genuine musical genius of the Scottish people. Many of the most beautiful and popular of the songs were written either in the present, or towards the close of the last century, in many cases long after all direct personal feeling towards the Stuarts had of necessity died out. Burns was too fully occupied with painting the simple rustic habits of the peasantry to feel much real interest in Jacobite matters, and consequently those of his songs inspired by Jacobite feeling are very few in number. Allan Cunningham, however, and James Hogg have given us many excellent J. S.; the famous 'Wae's me for Prince Charlie,' written by W. Glen of Glasgow, is of modern date, while the less celebrated modern songs by writers in all parts of Scotland are numberless. All the finer airs have been *reset* by one or other of the great musical composers of modern times; but it is questionable whether the sets of the J. S. occurring in Thomson's collection of Scottish songs are surpassed by those in any similar work. See Hogg's *Jacobite Relics* (reissue, Gardner, Paisley, 1874).

Jacob's Ladder (*Polemonium cæruleum*), a plant belonging to the natural order *Polemoniaceæ*. It is a perennial herbaceous plant, with clusters of pretty blue or white flowers, and is frequently cultivated. The plant is astringent.

Jaco'by, Johann, a notable Prussian politician, was born May 1, 1805, in Königsberg, studied medicine there and at Heidelberg, and settled in his native town as a physician. By his professional skill and disinterested kindness of disposition he soon won the love and confidence of his fellow-citizens. It was, however, by his political activity that his reputation spread to wider circles, and when in 1841 his pamphlet *Vier Fragen beantwortet von einem Ostpreussen* (Mannh. 1841), ('Four Questions answered by an East Prussian'), appeared, his name became famous throughout all Germany. This publication upon the constitutional rights of the Prussian people was under the then existing circumstances a great political act, and although the Prussian Government subjected J. to many press prosecutions, he was invariably acquitted. In 1848 he was elected to the Prussian National Assembly, having previously taken part in the Frankfurt preliminary parliament. After the dissolution of the second Prussian Chamber in 1849, J. went back to Frankfurt, and accompanied the 'rump Parliament' to Stuttgart. On his return to Königsberg he was thrown into prison and accused of high treason, but was again acquitted by a Prussian jury, and from that time his whole political life was devoted to the furtherance of the principles of advanced Liberalism. In 1870 he had to expiate a public declaration against the annexation of Alsace and Lorraine by a lengthened imprisonment. He also lost his seat in Parliament. Retiring from public life, he now devoted himself entirely to scientific study. His death took place March 6, 1877. Singularly forbearing towards his opponents, rigid towards himself, inflexible in his opposition to tyranny, of undaunted courage in his advocacy of right and truth, J. will live in the memory of every Prussian patriot. His proud answer to King Wilhelm: 'It is the misfortune of kings that they will not listen to truth,' will long be remembered by his countrymen.

Jacquard', an ingenious apparatus, invented by J. M. Jacquard (born at Lyon, 1752), to facilitate the production of figured silk fabrics. It dispenses with the services of a drawboy, who formerly co-operated with the weaver in manipulating the harness-cords. Jacquard exhibited his valuable machine at Paris in 1801, and five years later the municipality of Lyons purchased the right of applying it to the city looms. For a time manufacturers and operatives bitterly opposed its introduction; but long before the death of the inventor, near Lyon, 7th August 1834, it was fully established in public favour. The J. may be adapted to any figure-weaving loom, enabling the most intricate designs to be as easily produced as plain fabrics. It is fitted to the top of the loom. The diagram shows the principal features of the mechanism in cross-section. Vertical wires *aa*, arranged in several rows of eight, are at their lower extremities attached to the harness-cords of the loom, while their upper ends

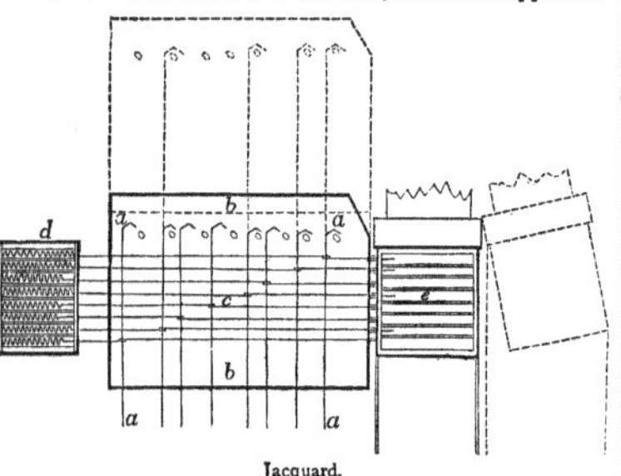

Jacquard.

are bent, and hook on to small bars fixed to a plate *b*, which can be raised at pleasure by means of a long lever in connection with a treadle. Each wire has a companion horizontal needle, through the eye of which it passes. These needles, *c*, are free to move laterally, and with pressure from the right hand they are driven into the box *d*, containing spiral springs, one for each needle. A four-sided barrel, movable on its axis, and pierced on each face with holes coinciding in number and position with the end of the needles, is represented by *e*. It is carried at the lower end of a vibrating frame called the *press*, and when in its lowest position the protruding ends of the needles enter the perforations in the face turned inwards. But if some of the holes be covered, it is obvious that the corresponding needles will be driven into the spring case, thereby carrying their companion wires off their bars, and that the remaining undisturbed wires may then be lifted. This manœuvre is performed by a 'card' of mill-board or stout paper of the same size as a face of the barrel. Each weft thread in the design to be woven has a representative 'card,' perforated in a manner consistent with the needles intended to enter the barrel, or in other words, in accordance with the warp threads to be simultaneously raised for the shot of the weft. The 'cards' requisite to form the whole design are joined in an endless band which travels round the barrel with its rotation. When a 'card' has performed its function of unhooking certain wires, the remainder are drawn up (as indicated by the dotted lines on the diagram), and the warp threads pertaining to them are thereby elevated; the shots of weft and colour as required are then thrown. Simultaneously with the elevation of the wires the *press* is thrown outwards, releasing the compressed springs, which thereon restore the disturbed needles and accompanying wires to their original places. On the descent of the plate the hooks of the replaced wires grasp their respective bars, and the barrel, which meanwhile has made a quarter rotation, presents the next 'card' to the needles. Another series of wires is thus selected for elevation; the same process is repeated through the entire number of perforated 'cards.'

The perforation of the cards is effected by an ingenious machine designed on a principle analogous to the J. The cardmaker is provided with an enlarged pattern, drawn and coloured, of the figure to be woven, and guided by it he *reads in* the design by interlacing threads of weft with vertical cords, which represent the warp. He then draws forward the cords that lie over the weft thread forming the first line of the figure; this tension gives forward motion to certain horizontal needles. A plate, perforated, and holding a punch in each hole, rests in front of the needles, and in front of this *punch-holder* is placed a similar plate called the *punch-receiver*. The needles, which are set in motion by the drawn cords, drive the companion punches from the holder into the receiver; the latter is then removed, and covered with a blank card through which the punches are thrust at one pressing. The receiver and the punches are next restored to their original position, and by manipulating the upper cords of the second line of the figure, another lot of punches is selected, and properly disposed for piercing a second 'card,' and so on through each line of the figure. Each card as produced is numbered, and the whole are afterwards laced together in proper order.

Jacq'uerie, derived from Jacques Bonhomme, the familiar name applied to French rustics, is the name given to the rising of the French peasantry which began (May 1358) in the neighbourhood of Clermont and Beauvais. Though it was simultaneous with a revolt in Paris which had as its aim the imposition of a constitutional check upon the monarchical power, it was not dignified by the same political purpose. After the battle of Poitiers, when Jean II., the Good, was imprisoned in England, and the Dauphin was fighting for existence against Marcel and the King of Navarre, the enslaved peasants found an opportunity for avenging their condition. The rebellion was simply one of hunger and vengeance, and found vent to itself in razing the feudal châteaux to the ground, in outraging and murdering the wives and children of the nobility. An effort was made by Marcel to direct the J. towards a definite revolutionary purpose, but in besieging Meaux, the serfs were routed by Gaston Phœbus and Captal de Buch. In revenge the peasantry were subjected to a prolonged and sanguinary massacre at the hands of the nobility. See *Sismondi* (vol. x. pp. 530–533), and Kitchin's *History of France* (vol. ii. Lond. 1877).

Jactitat'ion of Marriage is a suit which may be brought in the English Divorce Court. Its object is to compel any one averring that he or she is married to another, not admitting that it is so, to produce proof of the averment. If this is not done, decree passes ordering the claimant to keep perpetual silence on the subject, and making future averment of no legal effect.

Jade. (Fr *jade*, Ital. *gidda*), a term under which several mineral species allied in physical appearances and properties are included. They are silicates of lime, magnesia, soda, and alumina, one or other base being absent in some and predominating in others. The variety of J. known as nephrite is very highly esteemed in China for ornamental purposes, being carved in a most elaborate fashion by the Chinese. It varies in colour from a leek-green to a pale milky-white. It was also formerly much used in New Zealand for axe-heads and grotesque charms, the latter being greatly treasured by the Maoris.

Jaën (Arab. *Jejan*, later *Jayenu-l-harir*, 'J. of the Silk,' referring to its former silk industries), the picturesque capital of a province of the same name, Spain, on the Rio de J., a branch of the Guadalquivir, 50 miles N. of Granada and 65 W. of Cordova. It is the seat of a bishop, is girt with Moorish walls, and guarded by an old castle, has two cathedrals, fourteen convents, various hospitals, libraries, and art galleries, an institute and theatre, and beautiful promenades. Under the Moors in the 12th c. J. reached its greatest point of prosperity, and was encircled by no fewer than 500 silk-weaving villages. Pop. 22,938. To the E., in the valley of the Rio-Tercero, are the much-frequented mineral springs of Ivalacuz, with a temperature of 24° F.—The *province* is part of Andalusia (q. v.), and was formerly an independent kingdom of the Moors till its conquest by Ferdinand III. in 1234, when it was added to the kingdom of Castile. It lies in the basin of the Guadalquivir, and is fertile and rich in metals. Area, 5184 sq. miles; pop. (1870) 392,100.

Jafferabad', the chief town of the native state of the same name, in Kattywar, India, on the estuary of the small river Ranuy.—The *state* of J., or Jingira, lies partly in the Kattywar peninsula and partly on the coast S. of Bombay; the latter portion is commonly known as the Hubshi, from the Abyssinian origin of the ruling dynasty. Area, 324 sq. miles; pop. (1872) 71,996; revenue, £32,700. The administration has of late been much improved by direct British management. The Nawab of J., or Hubshi Sidi, is the descendant of the admiral of the Mohammedan fleet who resisted the Mahrattas in his island of Jingia. The first treaty with the British dates from 1733.

Jaffnapatam', a town in the N.E. corner of Ceylon, and on a small island of the same name, sometimes described as a peninsula. It was originally a Dutch settlement, of which it still bears traces. It has some trade in tobacco and the various products of the cocoa-nut palm. Estimated pop. 8000.

Jagell'o, or **Jagjell'o**, born in 1354, succeeded his father, Olgerd in 1381 as Grand-Duke of Lithuania. In 1386 he received the crown of Poland as Vladislav II., being chosen by the Polish nation husband to Hedwig, daughter of Lewis the Great of Hungary, on condition of renouncing and abolishing paganism. He founded the bishopric of Wilna and the University of Cracow (hence called the 'Academy of J.'), gained a decisive victory at Tannenberg (1410) over the Teutonic knights, and died May 31, 1434. His two sons, Vladislav III. and Casimir IV., followed him in succession, and J. was thus the founder of the *Jagellon Dynasty*, which ruled Poland till the death of Sigismund in August 1572, and gave Hungary three kings, of which the two last were also kings of Bohemia. By the marriage of Sigismund II.'s sister, Catharina Jagellonika, with the Swedish king Johan III., was formed a female line of Jagellons in the House of Vasa, which gave Poland three kings.

Jä'gerndorf (Krnov), a frontier town of Austrian Silesia, on the Oppa, 39 miles N.E. of Olmütz. It is capital of the Duchy of J. belonging (since 1623) to the Lichtenstein princes, whose castle, Lobenstein, is here. It manufactures linens, woollens, paper, and machinery. Pop. (1869) 8121.

Jagg'ernaut. See JUGG'ERNAUT.

Jagg'ery, a variety of crude sugar obtained from the palm in India. The flowering shoot of the palm is bruised on three successive mornings, a thin slice is cut off on the four following mornings, and the juice which flows out is collected in an earthen dish tied to the stump. The juice, if boiled down at once, yields the brown sugar called J. From the juice the fermented liquor called *toddy* is prepared; and if toddy be distilled, a good spirit is obtained, which constitutes one variety of *arrack*. Twelve trees yield about six gallons of J. daily, on an average.

Jagheer' (*jagir*), a Persian word, signifying 'that which occupies a position,' is in common use throughout India for a grant of land by the Government, revenue free, either terminable or not with the life of the grantee, and sometimes subject to conditions. It closely corresponds to the fief of medieval Europe. The most celebrated of these grants in history are the J. granted to the East India Company by the Nabob of the Carnatic, which now forms the Madras district of Chingleput; and the J. given to Lord Clive for life by the Nabob of Bengal in 1759.

Jaguar' (*Leopardus*, or *Felis Onca*), a species of Felidæ, or Carnivorous Mammalia, closely allied to the leopard of the Old World, and inhabiting S. America. The name 'Ounce' is sometimes applied to this animal. The fur of the J. is spotted as in the leopard, the spots being rosette-shaped, and of larger size than those of the leopard, whilst each spot has a very prominent central black mark. The spinal region is marked with a very prominent row of black spots. The breast bears three black bars not found in the leopard, and the tail of the J. is shorter in proportion to the size of body than the leopard's. The J. may equal the tiger in size and in strength. It seldom seeks to encounter man, unless pressed by hunger, or when set at bay. Its food consists of monkeys and other quadrupeds, and being an expert climber, it is the terror of arboreal animals. The J. is taken in traps, and the skin is of considerable commercial value.

Jaguar.

Jahn, Johann, a Roman Catholic divine and biblical critic, was born 18th June 1750, at Taswitz in Moravia, and studied at Xnaim, Olmütz, and Bruck. After taking orders (1775) he for a time filled the pastoral office, but was called to be Professor of Oriental Languages and Biblical Hermeneutics in the Lyceum of Olmütz in 1784. In 1789 he became professor of the same subjects at the University of Vienna. Though his views were conservative compared with those of Protestant biblical scholars, the novelty of his opinions among Catholic teachers led to a vehement outcry. He was compelled to desist from teaching in 1806, and accepted a canonry. He died 16th August 1816. J.'s most valuable works, the *Einleitung in die Göttlichen Schriften des Alten Bundes* (1793, 2d ed. 1803), and the *Biblische Archæologie*, his best work (1797–1805), were ultimately put by the Church in the index of prohibited books. Save the *Enchiridion Hermeneuticæ* (1812) and the *Vaticinia Prophetarum de Jesu Messia* (1815), his other works were mainly grammatical, and illustrated the Hebrew, Chaldee, Syriac, and Arabic languages.

Jail Fever has had many other popular appellations, as *hospital fever*, *ship fever*, *camp fever*, but is known now to have been but a severe form of *Typhus Fever* (q. v.). J. F. is described as having spread in our courts of justice, giving rise to what was termed 'The Black Assize' (q. v.), the last of which happened at the sessions of the Old Bailey in 1756, when the lord mayor, two of the judges, and several eminent persons died, having been infected by the prisoners. By attention to sanitary arrangements, J. F. has been reduced to a minimum in our prisons.

Jains, or **Jain'as**, a religious sect in India, intermediate between the Hindus and the Buddhists. Their origin and history are among the unsettled questions of Oriental scholarship; but it seems probable that they arose during the decline of Buddhism about the 8th c. A.D. Both tradition and architectural remains show that they were once predominant over a great part of the peninsula. Their present headquarters are Rajputana and Gujerat; but individual members are scattered throughout India, and they take the lead everywhere in commerce and banking. They are especially numerous in Lower Bengal, and have settled permanently in the neighbourhood of Murshedabad. Their most celebrated place of worship and of pilgrimage is Parasnath Hill in Chota Nagpore.

The philosophy of the J. is a manifest adaptation of the Buddhist doctrine of *nirvana*, and their religious beliefs and ceremonies are largely borrowed from the same source. The characteristic objects of worship are the twenty-four Tirthankaras or Jinas, deified saints, from whom the name of the sect is derived. The J. deny the divine authority of the Vedas, and are most strict in their respect for animal life. They are divided into two great divisions—the Digambara, 'skyclad' or naked; and Svetambara or 'white robed.' See Lassen's *Indische Alterthumskunde*, vol. iv., Essays by Colebrooke and Wilson, and Translations by the Rev. J. Stevenson.

Jájpore' ('town of the shrine'), a town in the district of Cuttack, Bengal, British India, on the right bank of the Byturn river, 180 miles S.S.W. of Calcutta. Pop. (1872) 10,753. It was the capital of Orissa before the rise of Cuttack in the 11th c.; and it contains numerous temples and sculptures of the Sivite sect of Hindus, which have been defaced by the Mohammedans. A great religious fair is still held here. See Dr. W. Hunter's *Orissa* (Lond. 1872).

Jakutsk', chief town of a Russian district of the same name in E. Siberia, on the left bank of the Lena. It is the centre of the N. Siberian fur trade, and the headquarters of the Russo-American Fur Trade Company. A great fair is held here annually from 1st July to 1st August. Although not the most northerly, J. is reckoned the coldest town in the world; it suffers greatly from the scarcity of drinking-water, which is supplied by melting ice. Among the articles of traffic, which are mostly despatched to Okhotsk, are the skins of sables, foxes, bears, &c., mammoth, buffalo, and other tusks and bones brought from the Lena's mouth and from Liakovski island in New Siberia Archipelago. Pop. 6100.—The *district* of J. is the vast region not included in the Siberian governments, and to the N. of the Amur territory has an area of 1,517,061 sq. miles, and a pop. (1870) of 231,977, mostly Jakut, Tungus, and Jukagir nomads. It is traversed by several mountain ranges, and watered by the Lena, Kolyma, Indigirka, &c. The chief occupations are hunting, fishing, and the herding of sheep, horses, and reindeer.

Jal'ap, the dried tubers of the *Exogonium Purga* (Convolvulaceæ), imported from Mexico, constitutes officinal J. Commercial J. consists of irregular egg-like roots, dark brown in colour, furrowed and contorted. J. is heavy, tough, and horny; the fracture is resinous, of a pale brown or dingy-white colour. It has a faint odour, and is mawkish, with acrid aftertaste. The virtue of J. depends on a resin, which can be extracted by rectified spirit. The crude substance, *Resina Jalapæ* (*B.P.*), is black, brittle, and lustrous. From it, by the action of ether, a residue is got having the composition $C_{31}H_{50}O_{16}$, called *Convolvulin*. This body is a strong purgative.

Another body called *Jalapin* ($C_{34}H_{56}O_{16}$) is obtained from the *Ipomœa orizabensis*, a Mexican plant, which is frequently used to adulterate true J., and known as *fusiform* or *woody* J. Jalapin differs from convolvulin by being soluble in ether. *Tampico J.* is the product of the Mexican plant *Ipomœa simulans.* This variety closely resembles true J., but is usually smaller, and more elongated. It is said also to be less powerful in its action. J. is named from the town of Jalapa, whence it was first brought to Europe in 1610.

Medicinal Properties of J.—J. is a brisk cathartic, producing copious watery discharges, and from its hydragogic powers it is specially useful in cases of dropsy. When administered by itself, it sometimes operates painfully, and is, therefore, usually combined with *bitartrate of potash* and *ginger*, in the form of *compound powder of J.* The pharmaceutical preparations are the *extract*, the *resin*, and the *tincture.* Jalapin is simply the resin decolorised by animal charcoal, and is less liable to irritate the bowels. Dose of the *powder*, 10 to 30 grains; of the *compound powder*, 20 to 60 grains; of the *resin* and of *jalapine*, 2 to 5 grains; of the *extract*, 5 to 15 grains, and of the *tincture*, ½ drm. to 2 drms.

Jala'pa, one of the two capitals of the State of Vera Cruz, Mexico, on the slopes of the Cordilleras, 6 miles N.W. of the port of Vera Cruz. It is 4500 feet above the sea, and enjoys one of the finest climates in the world, is the residence of the wealthy merchants of Vera Cruz, to which city a railway was all but completed in 1875. J. is the seat of a bishop, and has Government buildings, high-class schools, three newspapers, cotton and cigar factories, tanneries, potteries, &c. Pop. 15,000. J. was founded in the time of Cortes, and has played a prominent part in Mexican politics. It was occupied by American troops in 1847–48. See Rivera's *Historie de J.* (5 vols. 1870–71).

Jalun', a town in a district of the same name, N.W. Provinces, British India, 110 miles S.E. of Agra. Pop. (1872) 10,197. It is always liable to inundation, and is unhealthy.—The *district* of J., lies between the native state of Gwalior, the Jumna and the Betwo rivers. Area, 1553 sq. miles; pop. (1872) 404,447. The crops are millets, gram, wheat, cotton, and the *al* dye. The chief town is Urai, but Kalpi and Kuch are the centres of trade. In the Mutiny most of the European residents were murdered, and it was not till the month of September 1857 that Sir Hugh Rose was able to restore order, after many engagements.

Jamai'ca (the Carib *Xaymaca*, 'land of wood and water'), the most important British island in the W. Indies, is in the group of the Greater Antilles, and lies 90 miles S. of Cuba, in lat. 17° 40′–18° 30′ N., and in long. 76° 15′–78° 25′. Area, 4193 sq. miles; pop. (1871) 506,154, of whom 13,101 were whites, 101,346 mulattoes, 391,707 blacks. The island has an extreme length from Morant Point in the E. to S. Negril Point in the W. of 150 miles, and a breadth from Portland Point in the S. to Point Galina in the N. of 50 miles. Its chief inlets are Kingston Harbour, Old Harbour, and Morant Bay in the S., but there are innumerable creeks and coves. It is traversed by the picturesque Blue Mountains (q. v.), which attain a height in one peak of 7150 feet, and are luxuriantly clad with forests of cedar, mahogany, bread-fruit, cotton, fustic, satin-wood, and palm trees, and with pimento groves. The range slopes gently to the N., but is rugged and precipitous to the S., and on both sides sends down innumerable torrents. Of the more considerable streams, the longest is the Black River, with a course of 30 miles, navigable by flat-bottomed boats and canoes. The lower and more level part of J. is in the S.E., and here are the principal sugar-plantations, and chief centres of population, as Kingston, Port Royal, and Spanish Town. The Pedro Plains and Savannah la Mer in the extreme W. are in great part covered with swamps. The climate of J. is hot and unhealthy along the shores and in the valleys, but at an elevation of 1500 feet it is delightful. In summer the thermometer occasionally rises to 100°, and in winter it sinks to 60°. Near Kingston Harbour the mean is 81° F.; at an altitude of 4000 feet it is 68°. Snow has never been observed even on the highest peaks, but heavy hail sometimes falls. The sea-breeze that prevails on the low coast is popularly known as the 'Doctor.' The rainy seasons, in April and May, and in September, October, and November, are preceded by an oppressive stagnation of atmosphere, and ushered in by thunderstorms and hurricanes. Earthquakes are not unfrequent; those of 1692 and 1780 were especially destructive. Besides yellow and bilious fever, the common diseases include typhus and cholera; an epidemic outbreak of cholera in 1850–52 carried off some 30,000 inhabitants. The soil is extremely fertile; coffee can be cultivated at a height of 5000 feet, while sugar, indigo, and tobacco flourish in the plains and valleys. Other productions are arrowroot, ginger, turmeric, cacao, maize, yams, casava and sweet potatoes; the fruits are singularly abundant, including the pine-apple, pomegranate, orange, shaddock, fig, sweet-lemon, citron, mango, banana, &c. Of the animals, the more notable are the agoutis, iguanas, and various species of monkeys; alligators are numerous, and also parrots, humming-birds, mosquitos, &c. Fish abound in the sea and rivers, and swarms of rats destroy about a twentieth of the sugar-canes. Domestic animals have long been successfully introduced from Europe. The emancipation of the slaves in 1834 was followed by a falling off in the staple products of the island—sugar, rum, and coffee; but it is only fair to mention that this falling off had begun as early as 1820, or even earlier. Since 1865 trade has been gradually reviving, but the rich resources of the island are as yet far from being fully developed. The total value of the exports in 1874 amounted to £1,442,081, that of the imports to £1,762,817 (the largest sum since 1859). Of the exports, the chief articles were sugar, 28,398 hogsheads (value £482,779); coffee, 10,351,570 lbs. (£338,165); rum, 29,378 gallons (£293,878); logwood, 62,803 tons (£147,564); pimento, 5,761,273 lbs. (£36,008); and ginger, 1,181,789 lbs. (£21,103). The imports are mainly provisions, coal, and manufactured goods. The total tonnage of vessels entering and clearing in 1874 (exclusive of coasting trade) was 806,526. J., to which are annexed for administrative purposes the Turks and Caicos Islands, by Act of Parliament of 1873, is under a Governor-General appointed by the Crown, and an elective assembly. The Governor is the chief civil and military authority. In 1874 the public revenue was £536,799, and the expenditure £537,263, while the debt amounted to £665,537.

History.—Discovered by Columbus during his second voyage in 1494, J. received its first Spanish settlement in 1509. In fifty years the cruelty of the conquerors exterminated the native inhabitants. An English force, commissioned by Oliver Cromwell, and commanded by Penn and Venables, captured the island, which was ceded to England by the treaty of Madrid in 1670. The Maroons, the forsaken negro slaves of the Spaniards, defied the English for 140 years, but were subdued in 1795. The slaves were emancipated 1st August 1834. The immediate results of this noble act were unfavourable; hundreds of sugar and coffee estates were abandoned by the liberated slaves; planters associated to reduce wages and advance the rent of huts; negroes settled idly in the mountains, and an unsuccessful effort was made to introduce Chinese coolies. At last in 1865 the discontent of the negroes broke forth in a revolt, which was rigorously suppressed by Governor Eyre (q. v.). The negroes began with the massacre of twenty-three whites, but the island was promptly placed under martial law, about 1000 houses were burned, many rebels were hanged, and some flogged. The Governor was thanked by the Jamaica Assembly for suppressing the rebellion, but was recalled to England to answer charges of over-severity. Exonerated by a commission of inquiry, a vigorous but vain effort was made to bring him to trial by those who disapproved of his policy. The catastrophe of 1865 marks the beginning of a new life in the colony. Education is spreading among the blacks (grant to schools in 1866, £4622; in 1872, £19,403), poverty among them is disappearing, crime is diminishing, several of the long-forsaken sugar-estates have been taken up, and among other signs of improvement is the construction of new roads, harbours, and canals. See Michael Scott's *Tom Cringle*, Edward's *History of J.*, Stewart's *Past and Present State of J.*, Kingsley's *At Last*, and Trollope's *West Indies.*

Jamaica Bark. See CARIBEE BARK.

Jamb, in architecture, is the side of a window, door, &c.

James, the Elder, the son of Zebedee, was called with his brother John to be a disciple of Christ (Matt. iv. 21), and, along with his brother and Peter, of all the disciples, seems to have enjoyed the closest familiarity with his Lord (*cf.* Mark v. 37, ix. 2, xiv. 33). There is no further mention of him till he was beheaded by Herod Agrippa I. in the year 44 (Acts xii. 2). 2. J., the son of Alpheus, was one of the twelve apostles (Matt. x. 3). If Alpheus and Cleopas be, as some maintain, merely two forms of the Aramaic name Chalpha, J. the Less (Mark xv. 40; John xix. 25) would be the same person; and if his mother Mary was the sister of the mother of Jesus, *i.e.*, unless there be four and not three women mentioned, John xix. 25, this J. was the first-cousin of Jesus. 3. J., the brother of Jesus (Matt. xiii. 55; Gal. i. 19), is doubtless the same as the J. of Acts xii. 17, &c. It is contended by some that he is the same as J. the Less (?), the son of Alpheus, on the ground that J., Joses, Simon, and Jude were not brothers, but first cousins of Jesus (see above). 4. J., the brother of Jude (Luke vi. 16; Acts i. 13; Jude i.), is probably the same as J. (3), whether the same as (2) or not. **The Epistle of J.** is variously supposed to have been written by or in the name either of J. (2) or (3), if these be different persons, and the time it was written variously fixed at from A.D. 45 to 68. According to chap. i., it was addressed to Jewish Christians out of Palestine. The main object of the epistle was to censure the errors connected with their Christian life, and to console them in adverse circumstances. The style is marked by great literary beauty; and the mode of thought is distinctly different from that of Paul or John. The critical literature on the epistle is very extensive, and has been reviewed by Professor Berschlag in *Studien und Kritiken* (1874). See also *The Catholic Epistle of St. James, a revised text with translation, introduction, and notes*, by F. T. Bassett, M.A. (Lond. 1877).

James I., son of Robert III., King of Scotland, was born at Dunfermline, 1391. It was resolved to send him to the court of France, Scotland's ancient ally, for protection and education, and he sailed in March 1409. The vessel was captured by an English ship of war, and the prince was carried a prisoner to London. On the death of his father in 1406, J. was acknowledged king by the Scottish Parliament; but no serious effort was made to effect his release and recall, and the government of the country remained in the hands of his uncle, the Duke of Albany. A romantic attachment, which forms the subject of the *Kingis Quhair* (King's Quire or Book), led to his marriage with Joan Beaufort, niece of Henry IV. of England, and having arranged a seven years' truce with England, he set out for Scotland, and was crowned at Scone, 21st May 1424. The young king devoted himself to the revision of old and the enactment of new laws, to the general survey and valuation of all landed property, the repression of mendicancy, the regulation of weights and measures, and the assimilation of the Scots Parliament to that of England. Eight months after his restoration he suddenly arrested twenty-nine of the leading nobles who were supposed to have been instrumental in keeping him so long from his rightful inheritance. Of these, the Duke of Albany and his two sons were executed on the 'heading hill,' Stirling, and a younger son was hunted, taken, and executed. J. broke the almost independent power of Donald of the Isles. In 1434 his daughter was sent to France, where eventually she was married to the Dauphin, afterwards Louis XI. The reforms introduced by J. promoted the wealth and the civil liberty of the humbler classes, and in proportion checked the hitherto unbridled powers of the feudal aristocracy; while the forfeiture of the estates of the Earl of March and of the Earl of Strathearn spread the greatest discontent and alarm among a number of the smaller barons. Sir Robert Graham, a kinsman of the Earl of Strathearn, having accused the king in Parliament of encroachments on the territorial aristocracy, was subsequently driven to seek refuge among the Highlanders north of the Tay. In the winter of 1436–37, J. was passing his Christmas at the monastery of the Black Friars in Perth, when, on the night of the 20th February, Graham with three hundred Highland outlaws burst in upon him and despatched him in a vault in which he had sought to conceal himself. Besides his *Kingis Quhair* (printed in 1783 and edited by William Tytler, Lord Woodhouselee), which is in the allegorical style of the age, but is illumined by a pure, airy fancy, J. is accredited with the authorship of *Christis Kirk of the Grene* and *Peblis to the Play*. If this popular belief could be established, J. would rank in the history of Scottish literature as the first of those graphic humourists who have sought the sources of their inspiration in the pastimes and pleasures of humble life, and as the originator not only of the ornate and courtly poesy of Scotland, but of that vivid and joyous realism which attained its perfection in the verse of Burns.—**James II.**, born in 1430, was crowned at Holyrood in 1437. Sir Robert Graham and his confederates in the assassination of James I., were captured, and tortured to death at Stirling and Edinburgh. The two most ambitious and crafty men of the time were Sir William Crichton, governor of Edinburgh Castle, and Sir Alexander Livingstone, governor of Stirling Castle. The former endeavouring to obtain the undivided control of the infant king, the queen-mother fled with the boy to Livingstone, who, repeating Crichton's tactics, began as guardian of the king to exercise the prerogatives of royalty. Crichton seized the king as he was taking exercise in the park, hurried him off to Edinburgh, and once more found himself able to dictate to almost all the Scottish nobility. At this period (1439) the great house of Douglas was represented by a proud and extravagant youth of seventeen, who affected the state and grandeur of royalty. Crichton invited Douglas to visit the king in Edinburgh Castle; the Earl came accompanied by his brother, and both were beheaded (see DOUGLAS, FAMILY OF). Their cousin William married the sister of the murdered youths, and thus reunited the whole of the Douglas dominions. He sought still further to increase his influence by entering into a bond or agreement with two great noblemen, the Earls of Crauford and Ross, to support each other against all enemies. A paction of this description threatened the very existence of the Stuart dynasty, and in 1452 the king invited Douglas to Stirling with the object of persuading him to break the bond. This the Earl refused to do, and the discussion becoming impassioned, the king stabbed Douglas, who was afterwards despatched by the royal attendants. Civil war now burst forth between the royal forces and those of the Douglas family, but the contest was eventually closed by the forfeiture (1454) of the Douglas estates, the greater part of which passed to the Earl of Angus. England was now being desolated by the Wars of the Roses, and J. made an effort to recover Berwick and the castle of Roxburgh. The royal army, supported by a force under the Lord of the Isles, laid siege to Roxburgh Castle. Here for the first time the Scots troops employed artillery. By the accidental bursting of a cannon, the king was killed on the spot, 3d August 1460.—**James III.**, King of Scotland, son of James II., was born June 1452. From 1460 to 1465 the government of the country and the care of the king were vested in Kennedy, Bishop of St. Andrews, but on the 9th July 1466 the young king was kidnapped at Linlithgow and the prerogatives of viceroyalty assumed by the Boyd family, one of whom, Thomas, the eldest son, married the king's sister, the Princess Mary, and was created Earl of Arran. In 1467 J. was betrothed to Margaret, daughter of Christian, King of Norway and Denmark, who offered the Orkney and Shetland Islands as security for his daughter's dowry. The marriage was celebrated in July 1469, and the pledged islands being forfeited, were acquired by the Scottish crown. The fall of the Boyd family, after a parliamentary trial for high treason, occurred during the same year. Lord Boyd was obliged to flee to England, Alexander his brother was executed for treason, and Arran was divorced from the king's sister. The Lord of the Isles submitted to the king and yielded up the earldom of Ross and other lands. As a compensation he was created a Scottish peer, and was presented with considerable lands in central Scotland. In 1471 the bishopric of St. Andrews was created an archiepiscopal or metropolitan see. The king, himself an amateur in the arts and a recluse, chose to heap his favours upon artificers. His two brothers, the Duke of Albany and the Earl of Mar, he regarded with jealousy and treated as his enemies. Mar died suspiciously at Craigmillar Castle. Albany, forced to flee to France, was invited to England by King Edward, and signed a treaty with that monarch by which he was enfeoffed—on parchment—with the Scottish sovereignty. Meantime (1482), believing that England threatened war, J. assembled a great army on the Boroughmuir and marched toward the Border. On this expedition the king's chief favourite, Cochrane, a 'mason,' or architect, was intrusted with an important command. Enraged at this fresh instance of the king's infatuation, the leaders of the Scottish army, which had now advanced as far S. as Lauder, seized several of the favourites, Cochrane, Rogers a musician, Torphichen a fencing-master, Hommel a tailor, and Leonard a shoemaker, and hanged them over Lauder Bridge. In 1488 a widespread confederacy organised for the purpose of dethroning the king drew to a head. The royal army and that of the confederates, with the king's eldest son at their head, met at Sauchie Burn, between Bannockburn and Stirling, where a skirmish took place, 18th June

1488. The unwarlike king was seized with panic, and in his headlong retreat was thrown from his horse, and afterwards killed 'of mischance.'—**James IV.**, son of the preceding, born 17th March 1471, ascended the throne on the death of James III., in 1488. In 1495 he received Perkin Warbeck, the pretended rightful heir to the throne of England, with splendid hospitality, gave him Lady Catherine Gordon, granddaughter of James I., in marriage, and fitted out expeditions in 1496 and 1497 to accompany the Pretender into England. On the 8th August 1502, he married Margaret, Princess of England. After the death of Henry VII. of England, in 1509, difficulties, arising originally from quarrels and reprisals at sea, occurred between the two countries. Other causes of quarrel were the withholding, on the part of Henry VIII., of the jewels and treasure which James's queen should have inherited on the death of her father, Henry VII., and the existing alliance between Scotland and France. James assembled an army, and, marching south, fought and lost the disastrous battle of Flodden (q. v.), in which he and the flower of the Scottish nobility of that day perished, 9th September 1513.—**James V.**, son of the preceding, was born 10th April 1512. In 1514, the queen, his mother, married the Earl of Angus, but the Parliament, alarmed at the increased power of the Douglasses, intrusted the government of the country to the Duke of Albany, who was summoned from France to assume the office of Regent. In 1524, disgusted with the severe unyielding temper of the contending parties in Scotland, Albany finally returned to France. In August of the same year J. assumed the royal functions under the advice of the queen and the Lords of Council. The Earl of Angus, who had been living for some time at the English court, and had been won over to the interests of Henry VIII., returned to Scotland in 1525. In 1526 the king ceased to be a minor, and chose as his guardians the Earl of Angus and the Lords Argyle and Errol. Angus kept the boy-king a close prisoner, and allying himself with the Earl of Arran, commenced to rule with despotic authority. In May 1528, the king, then residing at Falkland, succeeded in making his escape, and riding to Stirling, found refuge in the castle. The estates of Angus were forfeited, and the Earl fled to England in 1528. But the house of Douglas, of which he was the head, had still many adherents. In 1531 James marched to the borders, and put to death many of the chiefs, including John Armstrong and his brother Thomas, who, after being invited to a conference, were seized, convicted of theft, and hanged. The king then marched with an army to suppress disturbances in the Highlands and Islands, the result of the expedition being that Argyle, Lieutenant of the W., and Craufurd, Lieutenant of the N., were deprived of their office and local influence. This was only one of a persistent series of measures for curbing the power of the great aristocratic houses. Disaffection spread among a number of the barons, and in 1532 Scotland was invaded by an English force under Northumberland, in which the Earl of Angus and several of his apostate kinsmen fought. A border war raged between the two countries till the peace of 1534. J. married Magdalen, daughter of the king of France, in 1537; but she dying a few months afterwards, he espoused Marie, widow of the Duc de Longueville, and daughter of the Duc de Guise, in 1538. Provoked by J.'s refusal to be a party to a conference on ecclesiastical matters, Henry VIII. sent an invading force across the border in 1542. A Scottish army opposed the invaders, but refused to pursue them over the border. Unseemly discussion and disorder prevailed in J.'s camp, and a body of 300 English cavalry taking advantage of the confusion, charged the Scots, and completely routed them. J., broken in body by an intemperate mode of life, sank under the dishonour of this defeat, and died at Falkland Palace, December 13, 1542. For the fuller history of the first five Jameses see the Histories of Tytler and Hill Burton.—**James VI.** of Scotland and **I.** of England, the son of Mary Queen of Scots, by her second husband, Henry Stewart, Lord Darnley, was born at Edinburgh, 19th June 1566. In the following year Mary was forced by the insurgent nobles to resign the crown to the infant J. who was proclaimed king on 29th July. In 1570 J. was placed under the tutorship of the famous George Buchanan (q. v.). During the stormy years of his childhood, passed at Stirling Castle, the regency was successively in the hands of the Earls Murray, Lennox, Mar, and Morton, until on the overthrow of the last J. placed himself at the head of the Government in 1578. For some years, however, he remained under the influence and control of the Duke of Lennox (Esmè Stewart) and the Earl of Arran. At the 'Raid of Ruthven,' 22d August 1581, the king was kidnapped by the confederate lords, who held him in custody for ten months. On the 23d November 1589 he married the Princess Anne of Denmark. Ignoble disturbances organised by the 'Popish lords,' chiefly Bothwell and Huntly, and fierce debates between the king's 'Commission of Finance,' and the zealots of the kirk, occupied the rival parties of the country from 1592 to 1597. The singular 'Gowrie Conspiracy' (q. v.) took place in 1600. In 1603 James succeeded to the English throne, and was crowned at Westminster, July 25. The Gunpowder Plot (q. v.), a Catholic conspiracy to destroy the king and Parliament, was discovered in 1605. The king's ungainly appearance, his undignified bearing, and the recklessness with which he lavished wealth and honour on unworthy favourites, rendered him unpopular with an influential section of the English nobility. Such was his coarse extravagance that after a few years of peace he had doubled the amount of the debt that had been contracted by Elizabeth after fifteen years of war. His first expedient for raising supplies was the arbitrary imposition of taxes on the imports and exports of the country; and as the commerce of the country was now rapidly extending, the experiment was found, for a time, to answer. The Commons (in 1610, and again in 1614) remonstrated against these imposts as illegal, and supplies were refused until illegal taxation and other grievances were redressed. James dissolved both Parliaments. Misled by his theory of the divine right and absolute authority of kings, he now resolved to govern without any Parliament. He continued to levy customs, to issue letters to the landholders demanding 'benevolences' or loans, to sell peerages, and to openly interfere with the natural course of justice. James's foreign policy was as disastrous as his home measures were illegal, profligate, and mean. He proclaimed an alliance with Spain, on the eve of a great struggle on the Continent between Protestantism and Catholicism, and to this suicidal alliance the life of Sir Walter Raleigh (q. v.) was among the first of the many sacrifices paid. J. died 27th March 1625. In Henri IV.'s phrase, he was 'the wisest fool in Christendom.' Despicable as were his personal qualities, he was 'a ripe scholar, with a considerable fund of shrewdness, of mother wit, and ready repartee.' He was widely read, especially in theological matters, and among his voluminous writings are *Essays of a Prentice in the Divine Art of Poesy* (Edinb. 1584); *Dæmonologie* (1597); *True Law of Free Monarchies* (1598); *Basilikon Doron* (1599); *Triplici Nodo Triplex Cuneus* (1605); *Remonstrance for the Right of Kings* (1615); and *Counterblast to Tobacco* (1616). These works are full of 'canny humour,' and abound with 'quaint, incisive phrases, with puns and epigrams, and touches of irony which still retain their flavour,' but have now mainly an historical interest. See Nichol's *Progresses, Processions, and Festivities of J. I.* (3 vols. Lond. 1829); D'Israeli, *Inquiry into the Literary and Political Character of J. I.* (Lond. 1816); Gardner, *History of England from the Accession of J. I.* (Lond. 1875); and various authorities given in Green's *Short History of the English People* (1875).—**James II.** of England and **VII.** of Scotland, brother of Charles II., was born in London, 15th October 1633. He became Duke of York, escaped from the Parliamentarians, and sought refuge in the Low Countries in 1648; served with distinction under Turenne and Condé, and was made Captain-General in Italy by Mazarin in 1656. In 1660 he was appointed Lord High Admiral of England and Lord Warden of the Cinque Ports, and married Anne, daughter of Lord Chancellor Hyde; after whose death he married Maria Beatrice, daughter of the Duke of Modena, in 1673. He avowed himself a Catholic in 1671; and though a bill excluding him on account of his religion from succession to the crown had passed in the Lower House in 1680, he ascended the throne without opposition on the death of his brother, February 6, 1685. His first public act was to pledge himself to preserve the laws inviolate and to protect the Church; and Parliament enthusiastically voted him a revenue of nearly two millions for life. Two risings took place in 1685—one in the W. under the Duke of Monmouth, who by many was believed to be the legitimate son of Charles II., and therefore the true heir to the throne, and the other a Protestant movement in the N., under the Earl of Argyle. The latter rising was soon suppressed and its leader beheaded; the former collapsed on Sedgemoor (q. v.), where Monmouth (q. v.) was put to flight, to be captured a few days afterwards, and remorselessly sent to the block. The rebels were hunted down, burned, hanged, whipped, and sold into slavery with a ferocity that filled the land with horror, and earned for Judge Jeffreys (q. v.), who presided over the 'Bloody Assize,' a reputation for cruelty unsurpassed in the annals of any age or country. In 1686, James abolished the Test Act, revoked the laws forbidding Catholic priests to conduct worship publicly according to the Catholic form, refilled the streets of London with monks and friars in their religious garb, endeavoured to convert Oxford and Cambridge into Catholic seminaries, and appointed Catholics to many of the chief offices in Church, state, and army. In 1687 he issued the famous 'Declaration of Indulgence,' which formally abrogated all tests as qualifications for religious or civil appointments, and re-issued it on the 27th April 1688 with the command that it should be read in all the churches. Archbishop Sancroft and his six suffragan bishops protested against publishing what they deemed an illegal document. The seven churchmen were committed to the Tower and brought to trial on the 29th June. Their acquittal was the result of the overwhelming force of public sympathy and indignation. The country was now in revolution; William of Orange arrived in England, on the invitation of a number of the leading nobles and statesmen, on the 5th November 1688, and J. flying from the country to France, was received and pensioned by Louis XIV. The defeat of the battle of the Boyne (q. v.) ruined all J.'s hopes of conquering England from Ireland, and retiring to St. Germains, he died there, 6th September 1701. See Clarke's *Life of J. II.* (2 vols. Lond. 1816); the *Life* in Macpherson's *Original Papers*; and M. Mignet's *Négociations Relatives à la Succession d'Espagne* (Par. 1835), which is indispensable for a real knowledge of this and the preceding period; also Macaulay's *History of England.*

James, George Payne Rainsford, a voluminous writer of historical romances, was born in London in 1801. He published his first novel, *Richelieu*, in 1828, his second, *Darnley*, in 1830, and subsequently about a hundred works of the same kind. His romances bear a strong family resemblance, and are somewhat puerile in conception, but are agreeable, and even skilful narratives. *De Lorme, Mary of Burgundy*, and others are still widely read. He also wrote histories of various French and English princes, and was made historiographer-royal by William IV. In 1850 he was appointed consul at Massachusetts, and in 1858 at Venice, where he died, June 9, 1860.

James, John Angell, a popular Evangelical writer, was born June 6, 1785. From the age of twenty till his death (October 1, 1859) he was pastor of Carr's Lane Congregational Chapel, Birmingham. He was an eloquent and imaginative preacher. Many of his writings have attained extraordinary popularity, *The Anxious Inquirer, Christian Father's Present to his Children*, &c., having sold by hundreds of thousands. See his *Life and Letters* by R. W. Dale (1861).

James River, a river of the United States, rises about the centre of, and is entirely within, the State of Virginia. It cuts through the Blue Ridge, and has a course generally E.S.E., passing Lynchburgh and Richmond, widening into a splendid estuary 66 miles long, and entering Chesapeake Bay by Hampton Roads, the best harbour on the Atlantic coast. The J. R. is 450 miles long, and is navigable as far as Richmond for steamers and schooners of 130 tons. By an extension of the J. R. and Kanawha Canal it is proposed to connect the Ohio River and the above at a cost of sixty million dollars. See *Annual Report of the U. S. Chief of Engineers* (1874).

Jameson, George, a Scottish portrait-painter, was born (1586) at Aberdeen, and settled about 1620 in his native town. Walpole has called him 'the Vandyck of Scotland,' and it is said that he studied with Vandyck under Rubens. Charles I. sat to J. in 1633, and he was largely employed by the Scotch nobility. At Taymouth Castle, in the colleges of the University of Aberdeen and in the Advocates' Library, are specimens of his work. J.'s portraits want the sense of movement and the gradations of light and shade visible in the Dutch masters; his heads are painted on a dark ground, and upon them the most of his work is concentrated. He died at Edinburgh in 1644. 'It must be admitted,' says Mr. J. H. Burton, 'that the claims to immortality of this one Scots painter are founded somewhat on the poverty of neighbours.'

Jameson, Mrs. Anna, authoress and art critic, was born in Dublin, 19th May 1797. Her first works were notes of travel and lives of celebrated females. *Characteristics of Women* (1832) is a fine analysis of Shakespeare's heroines. She commenced art criticism in 1842 with a *Handbook to Public Galleries of Art in London*, and was an industrious expounder of art till the close of her life, publishing many valuable volumes, illustrated by beautiful etchings. The most important of these are *Sacred and Legendary Art* (2 vols. 1848), and the *History of Our Lord as exemplified in Works of Art* (1860), continued by Lady Eastlake, and completed in 1864. Mrs. J., who laboured much for the social elevation of women, died March 17, 1860.

James's Bay, a large inlet in the S. of Hudson's Bay, in lat. 51°-55° N. and long. 79°-82° 30′ W. It receives the rivers Albany, Moose, Rupert, and E. Maine, abounds in shoals and islands, and along its S. shores are extensive marshes. It was named from Captain James, who wintered here in 1631-32.

James's Palace, St., an irregular brick building south of Pall Mall, originally a hospital, enlarged and partly rebuilt by Henry VIII. It was the royal residence from the burning of Whitehall till the opening of Buckingham Palace. Till 1861 drawing rooms were held here, and it is still used for levees. *St. James' Park*, 91 acres in extent, lies S. to the rear of the palace. The fine avenues, broad walks, and ponds were planned under Charles I. The picturesqueness of the gardens is enhanced by the surrounding palaces, Government offices, and other fine buildings.

James's Powder is a patent medicine introduced by Dr. Robert James, who died in 1776. From the analysis of the medicine it appears to consist mainly of *antimonious acid, phosphate of lime*, and *oxide of antimony*, the two former making up the bulk of the medicine. The pharmacopœial preparation, *pulvis antimonialis* contains one part of *oxide of antimony* and two of precipitated *phosphate of lime.* J. P. is prescribed as a sudorific in fevers and rheumatic affections, in doses of from 2 to 6 grains.

Jamestown (1) a post-village of New York, U.S., on the outlet of Chautauqua Lake, 50 miles W. of Buffalo, and 2½ miles from the Pittsburg Railway. It has ten churches, two newspapers, extensive manufactures of alpaca and woollens, &c. Pop. (1870) 5336. (2) A township of Virginia, the first permanent English settlement in America. It lies on a peninsula 32 miles from the mouth of the James River, and has a pop. of 1088. Settled originally by a band of 107 colonists under Wingfield, Christopher Newport, and Bartholomew Gosnold, April 26, 1607, and named after James I., it soon became the capital of a thriving colony; and in 1619 a House of Burgesses, the first legislative assembly in British America, met here. J. began to decline after the seat of government was removed to Williamsburg, was in part burned during the rebellion of 1676, and was the scene of an engagement between Wayne and Lord Cornwallis in 1781.

Jamieson, Rev. John, was born in Glasgow, March 3, 1759, attended lectures at the University of his native place in his tenth year, and afterwards at Edinburgh; was licensed to preach, 1779; ordained pastor at Forfar, 1781; and transferred to Edinburgh, 1797. After publishing some poems, sermons, and theological works, he issued an *Etymological Dictionary of the Scottish Language* (1808-9), an *Abridgment* (in 1818), and a *Supplement* (in 1825). This work is chiefly important as a record of pure Scotch before it had ceased to be spoken among the educated classes. His philological theory of the origin of Lowland Scotch is utterly worthless, but the value of the work as a treasury of the peculiar forms of Northern English used in Scotland is not impaired by its perverse etymologies. J. published *An Historical Account of the Ancient Culdees of Iona, and of their Settlement in Scotland, England, and Ireland* (1811), *Hermes Scythicus* (1814), besides editing Barbour and Blind Harry with due credulity. He died at Edinburgh, July 12, 1838.

Jamieson, Robert, a Scottish naturalist, was born at Leith, July 11, 1774. He studied medicine at Edinburgh University, but ultimately directed his whole attention to natural history. In 1800 he went to Freyberg and worked under Werner, and in 1804 was elected Professor of Natural History at Edinburgh. In 1819, along with Brewster, he started the *Edinburgh Philosophical Journal*, and in 1826 founded the *New Philo-*

sophical Journal, which he edited till his death on April 10, 1857. J.'s chief works are *A System of Mineralogy* (1804, 3d ed. 1823), the *Elements of Geognosy* (1809), *Manual of Minerals*, &c. (1821), and the *Elements of Mineralogy* (1837).

Janes'ville, a city of Wisconsin, U.S., on both sides of Rock River, 70 miles W.S.W. of Milwaukee by rail. Among its industrial establishments are a large reaper-factory and machine-shops, and there are extensive manufactures of boots and shoes, carriages, &c. The State institute for the blind is at J., also excellent musical schools. Pop. (1870) 8789.

Jan'in, Jules Gabriel, a French novelist and critic, was born at St. Etienne, 24th December 1804, educated at the college of Louis-le-Grand in Paris, and began a literary career by writing political satires in *Figaro* and *Messager des Chambres*. In 1829 appeared his first novel, *L'Ane Mort et la jeune Femme Guillotinée*, a sensational satire on Victor Hugo as a pioneer of Romanticism. At intervals there followed *Barnave*, *Contes Fantastiques*, *Contes Nouveaux*, *Voyage de Victor Ogier*, *Les Catacombes*, *Les Symphonies de l'Hiver*, sketches to the *Revue de Paris*, &c. But his most characteristic works were the *feuilletons* of the *Journal des Debats*, begun in 1833 and continued till his death. Steeped in classical literature, with a style full of brightness and charm in its aerial movement from one impalpable idea to another, light, free, and sparkling, J. discoursed to the Parisians with immense acceptance, earning for himself the title of *le Prince de la Critique*. In 1870 he was elected a member of the Academy, and died 20th June 1874. See M. Piedagnel's *Jules Janin* (Par. 1876).

Ján'ina (Slav. 'St. John's town;' in Turk. *Jânya*), the capital of a vilayet of the same name, in the S.W. of Turkey, on the W. side of Lake J. (anc. *Pambotis*). It has sixteen mosques, eight Greek churches, two Greek colleges, and two synagogues. The Pasha resides in a fort surrounded by a ditch. J. still manufactures a considerable amount of gold-stuffs, silks, morocco-leather, coloured linen, &c. The artisans are mostly Greeks. Pop. 30,000. Ali Pasha (q. v.) usurped the pashalic of J. in 1807 and held it till 1820, during which time order was firmly restored and the pop. of the capital rose to 50,000. The Lake of J. is 12 miles long and 3 broad, and at its S. end stood the ancient Dodona with its famous temple.

Jan'issaries ('new soldiers'), were a well-disciplined body of Turkish infantry, originally composed of a tribute of children taken from Christian subjects by Orkhan (1330) and Amurath I. (1362). After special privileges were granted to them, Turks joined their ranks, and they were divided into regular and irregular troops. They acted both as police and members of the Sultan's bodyguard, but their power became in time so dangerous and their initiative in insurrection so frequent, that they were dissolved with great slaughter by Sultan Mahmoud II. in 1826.

Jan Mayen's Land, an island in the Arctic Ocean between Iceland and Spitzbergen, in lat. 70° 29′ N., and long. 7° 31′ W. It is volcanic, and its highest points, Beerenberberg (6640 feet) and Esk (1500), are still occasionally active. It is named after a Dutchman who discovered it in 1611.

Jan of Leyden (properly **Jan Bockelson** or **Bockold**), born at Leyden about 1510, was a tailor in his native town, where he also kept an inn, amusing his guests with his poetry and acting. Making the acquaintance of Jan Mathison of Haarlem, a baker, in 1553, he accompanied him to Münster, where he soon became the chief of the Anabaptists. After his friend's death in 1534, B. was proclaimed king of 'the new Zion,' and gave himself out as a prophet. In order to marry Mathison's widow he introduced polygamy, and had at last seventeen wives. He lived with great magnificence, and practised the utmost cruelty. Considering himself the founder of the millennium, this madman sent out twenty-eight apostles, and appointed twelve 'dukes' to rule the world under him. The town was long besieged in vain by the Bishop of Münster, but was taken (24th June 1535) after a valiant defence; B. was seized with his ministers Knipperdolling and Krechting, and put to death, 23d January 1536.

Jan'sen, Cornelius, a famous Catholic divine, was born, 28th October 1585, at the village of Akoi in N. Holland, studied at Utrecht and Louvain, and after a residence in Paris and Bayonne returned to Louvain, where he passed as doctor in 1617, and became professor in 1630. In 1635 he became Bishop of Ypres. A zealous student of the great Latin fathers, he taught Augustine's theology on the fall, original sin, grace, and predestination, and at his death, 6th May 1638, left as his testament to posterity his *Augustinus seu Doctrina Augustini de Humanæ Naturæ Sanitate, Ægritudine, Medicina, adversus Pelagianos et Massilienses*, published at Louvain in 1640, at Paris in 1641, and at Rouen in 1643.

Jansenism was the name by which the doctrinal system of J. became famous after his death. As early as 1641 the Jesuits disputed publicly against his views, but defenders were found amongst Benedictines, Augustinians, priests of the Oratory, and part of the Dominicans, the hereditary enemies of the Jesuits. Soon the controversy spread over all ranks; even court circles took sides. J.'s views were most brilliantly supported by such scholars as Arnauld, Nicole, and Pascal; the monastery of Port Royal was the recognised hearth of Jansenism. In 1642 the *Augustinus* was condemned as heretical by the bull *In eminenti*. But steady opposition to this was offered by many bishops and universities. In 1653 four selected propositions from J.'s work were formally pronounced heretical by Innocent X. The controversy grew hotter on both sides till in 1668 a temporary truce was obtained, the bishops admitting that the propositions condemned were heretical, but declining to admit that they were Jansenists. The bigoted Louis XIV. would hear of no concession to Jansenism, and by persecution forced many Jansenists to flee into the Netherlands. The next important step of the controversy was the publication of a French New Testament by Quesnel, with a commentary, in a Jansenistic spirit. This it was which in 1713 drew from Rome the famous constitution *Unigenitus*, in which 101 propositions from Quesnel's Testament, including not a few doctrines taught by the most approved fathers of the Church, and even some distinctly Tridentine assertions were summarily declared heretical and dangerous. The community of Port Royal were expelled and their buildings destroyed. The constitution provoked fierce hostility in France. A large party of the French clergy protested against the bull, declining to accept it save with modifications. And when the Pope threatened excommunication, they appealed to a general council of the Church. The *appellants* were headed by four bishops, and joined by many who were not themselves Jansenists, including Cardinal Noailles. Even when in 1719 excommunication was finally fulminated against the appellants, the Parliament of Paris, the Sorbonne, and other theological faculties remained steadfast. But the papal policy triumphed at last; Noailles and the most distinguished of the appellants were found amongst the *Acceptants*. Appellants and Jansenists were now no longer tolerated in France; again there was an exodus to Holland; and though the spirit of Jansenism still lived in the French clergy, what was latterly associated with the name of Jansenism was a wild superstition cherished chiefly amongst the uneducated. François of Paris, a noted appellant, died steadfast to his testimony. His grave was visited by multitudes, and miracles of healing were reported thence. The alleged miracles were seriously investigated even by such Protestant theologians as Mosheim, and were made use of by Hume in his famous *Essay on Miracles* The community of refugee Jansenists, calling themselves officially 'disciples of St. Augustine,' have since 1723 had an Archbishop of Utrecht and the Bishops of Haarlem and Deventer to preside over them. They profess still to belong to the Catholic Church, and recognise the Pope as visible head of the Church. They have about twenty congregations, over 5000 members, and from them the Old Catholics of Germany have had a measure of sympathy and help.

Jan'ssens, Abraham, a Flemish painter, born at Antwerp about 1569, died 1631, was a pupil of Jan Snellinck and a contemporary of Rubens. Many historical pictures by J. may be found in the Flemish churches, and there are some in Dresden, Munich, Vienna, and Berlin. His torchlight scenes are specially famous.—**Cornelis J.**, a Flemish portrait-painter, whose historical pictures are also admired, died at Amsterdam in 1665.—**Victor Honorius J.**, a Flemish historical painter, born at Brussels in 1664, died in 1739. He formed his style by the study of Albani in Italy.

Janua'rius, Order of St., an order of knighthood founded 6th July 1738 by Charles III. of Spain (then King of Sicily), abolished in 1806, but renewed in 1814. An octagonal gold cross in white and red, adorned with lilies of gold, with an image of St. Januarius bearing an open book on the obverse, and an open book and the two phials of the legend; on the reverse is the badge of the order, which comprehends *Cavalieri di Grazia*, and a higher class called *Cavalieri di Giustizia*, who must be of a house ennobled at least four generations.

Januarius, St. (San Gennaro), Bishop of Beneventum in Campania, was beheaded under the Emperor Diocletian about the beginning of the 4th c. His body was brought to Naples by Bishop St. Severus, in the time of Constantine, and deposited in the cathedral, which is dedicated to St. J., the patron saint of Naples. His head, with two phials (*ampullæ*) said to contain his blood, is preserved in a separate chapel, and it is affirmed that the blood usually becomes liquid when brought near the head. The relics are exhibited thrice yearly, on the 19th September (anniversary of his death), the first Sunday in May, and 16th December, and these are the greatest festivals of Naples. The Romish Church recognises fourteen other martyrs named J.

Jan'uary, the first month of the year According to Roman legend, *Januarius* was the name given by Numa to the first of the two months added by him to the ten of Romulus to make a pure solar year, and was called after Janus, the beginner of all things, as being the month next after the winter solstice, when the sun resumes his journey (Ovid., *Fast.* i. 163). The consuls received office (from B.C. 153 at least) on the 1st of this month, which thereby became the 1st of the civil year. See YEAR.

Ja'nus, an Italian divinity of great antiquity. J. and Jana (the feminine form) were identical with Dianus and Diana, worshipped as the sun and moon. J. was represented as bearing a sceptre and key, and as having two faces, the one young and the other old, looking opposite ways, and seems to have been worshipped by the Italian tribes in the remotest times, but has no place in the Greek mythology. He was the god of beginning and entering; his name was mentioned first in prayers, and his festival fell on the first day of the month Januarius, on which occasion friends gave one another *strenæ* or gifts of sweetmeats and copper coins with the double head of J. on the obverse, and on the reverse a ship's prow, and offered to him incense, wine, barley, and cakes called *janual*. As opener of the day he was called *Matutinus Pater*. Close to the N.E. corner of the Roman Forum was the temple of J. built by Numa. But as there were in Rome other shrines of J., and all open archways were called *Jani*, this temple is not to be confounded with the *J. quadrifrons*, still extant, a massive double archway of Greek marble covered with bas-reliefs descriptive of a sacrifice. The Romans connected the word J. with *janua* (door). Max Müller (*Science of Language*, vol. ii. 452), comparing *Jan* (the older form of J.) with Greek *Zēn* and Sanskrit *dyav-an*, adds, 'He was likewise called *Janonius* and *Quirinus*, and was, as far as we can judge, another personification of *Dyu*, the "sky," with special reference, however, to the year.'

Japan' (the native *Nipon* or *Dāi Nipon*, *i.e.*, 'land of the rising sun'), an insular empire in the E. of Asia, comprising the four large islands of Nipon (the Japanese mainland), Sikok, Kiusiu, and Yesso, and as many as 3500 smaller ones, including the Kurile Islands. The large islands form a crescent extending in a direction N.N.E. from Corea to the Russian island of Saghalien, and thence the Kurile Islands stretch still further N.E. between the N. Pacific and the Sea of Okhotsk to the southern point of Kamtchatka. The large islands are washed on the E. by the N. Pacific, and on the W. by the Sea of J., and are separated in the S. from the Corea by a channel 500 miles wide. According to the official reports the total area is 156,604 sq. miles, and the pop. (1875) 32,794,897. By far the largest of the four principal islands is Nipon, which has an area of some 95,000 sq. miles, and gives name to the empire. Yesso, with an area of 30,000 sq. miles, lies N. of Nipon, and Sikok (10,000 sq. miles), and Kiusiu (16,000) lies to the S.W. The coast is in great part bold and rocky, and is indented with many deep bays, forming excellent harbours. The empire is divided into five *kies* or departments, which surround the imperial capital, and eight *dōs* or large districts, which are subdivided into seventy-two *kens* or provinces. The two principal cities are Miako, the ancient seat of government, and Yedo, the present capital.

Physical Aspect.—The principal islands are traversed by mountain ranges, which here and there attain a great elevation, and in which there are many volcanoes. The most extensive range is Hakoni in Nipon, and the highest summit in all J. is Fusiyama ('sacred mountain'), an extinct volcano, 80 miles S.W. of Yedo, with a height of 14,170 feet, and a perpetual cap of dazzling snow. The volcanic mountain of Wunsentake, on a western promontory of Kiusiu, also rises above the perpetual snow line. In Yesso the mountains near the coast are 8000 feet high, but a large part of the island is still unexplored. The islands of J. are strongly affected by volcanic actions, and are frequently visited by earthquakes, especially in the N.E. Though impetuous, the rivers are short and shallow; they are subject to numerous freshets during the rainy season, and the mouths of most of them are obstructed by sand-bars. The three chief rivers are the Torregawa, Sinanogawa, and Kisogawa. The only considerable freshwater lake is Biwako or Lake Umi in Nipon, near the city of Miako, and it is 40 miles long and 12 wide. Throughout the mainland there are many lakelets and hot springs. The village of Mionoska, with its sulphur springs, 65 miles S.W. of Yedo, and within the sacred precincts of Hakoni, is the Baden-Baden of the Japanese aristocracy.

Climate, Botany, and Agriculture.—The climate of J. varies greatly, but in the central part, which is the most densely populated, it is generally mild and agreeable. In the extreme S. the heat is often oppressive, while in Yesso the mercury sometimes sinks far below zero, the snow falling to a great depth in the valleys. The greatest heat of J. (96° F. in the shade) is less debilitating than that of the Indian or Chinese coast. The W. coast of Nipon is said to be much colder than the E., and this is attributed to a constant current setting S.W. from the Sea of Okhotsk. October and November are the finest months in the whole year; June, July, and August are those of the annual rains, which fall in long-continued, deluging showers. The sun is occasionally hidden by fogs for several days together. September brings the fearful typhoons, which cause such havoc along the E. coast of the empire. The flora of J. strikingly resembles that of N. America. The grandest forest trees are the evergreen oak, the maple, and sycamore. In Nipon and Yesso there are large forests of pine, chestnut, beech, elm, dwarf-oak, elder, cypress, &c. Peculiarities of Japanese flora are the camphor tree (*Laurus camphora*), the lacquer tree (*Rhus vernicifera*), the wax tree (*Rhus succedanea*), and the paper mulberry (*Brousonetia papyrifera*), the bark of which is converted into paper. In the S. grow bamboos, bananas, tree-ferns, the sago and other palms, and not less than 150 species of evergreen trees. Among the many flowering plants are the azalea, camellia, marigold, and water-lily. Fruits are abundant, comprising figs, lemons, oranges, apricots, peaches, plums, a species of citron, &c. The Japanese are good agriculturists, and pay great attention to irrigation, manures, and the rotation of crops. Their soil, a fertile, friable loam, is chiefly under tea and rice, but other products are cotton, tobacco, wheat, maize, millet, potatoes, turnips, beans and peas, carrots, melons, gourds, and cucumbers. European machinery is fast coming into common use.

Mineralogy.—The great mineral wealth of J. has been long known, an extensive export of copper, silver, and gold having been begun by the Dutch as early as 1545. Gold and silver are said to be richly distributed in the N. of Nipon, and in the N.E. of Nambu are the famous gold mines of Natsumai. Copper is the principal metal of J., and of the many kinds bar-copper is the most valuable. There are large iron-mines in Yesso, and the purest sulphur is found here and in the neighbouring islands in almost inexhaustible quantities. Lead as well as copper is wrought near Hakodadi, and rich beds of superior coal occur throughout the four large islands. Ambergris and pearls of fine quality are found along the shores. Among the other mineral products of J. are a reddish naphtha, agates, cornelians, jaspers, alum, talc, felspar, basalt, and red and grey granites.

Zoology.—Almost the only wild animals in J. are wolves, foxes, wild boars, and hares, and even these are only found in the remote parts. The law, however, protects wild deer. The sheep, goat, ass, and mule are alike unknown. Oxen and cows are only used as beasts of burden, as flesh meat is never eaten, and even milk and butter are not common articles of food. Dogs are regarded as sacred, and cats are plentiful, yet the islands are plagued with rats and mice. The waters abound in fish, which, in addition to rice, forms the staple food of the people. The birds are very numerous, including the falcon, pheasant, heron, crane, lark, teal, mandarin-duck, &c. Among the few reptiles are varieties of snakes, lizards, and the tortoise. The most peculiar insects are the winged grasshopper, the white ant, and many brilliant coloured moths.

Inhabitants, Manners, and Customs.—The Japanese are regarded by Latham as Turanians, and by Prichard as Malays. Their language is, more than that of any other island, purely and exclusively insular, *i.e.*, it has no congener on the continent with which it can be immediately connected or from which it can be definitely derived. In Yesso the Japanese is intrusive, the original language being the Aino or Kurilian. Physically, the people are generally olive-complexioned, and have oval heads and faces, high foreheads, rounded frontal bones, small dark eyes, and heavy arched eyebrows. They are singularly well-made, are easy and active in their motions, agreeable and sprightly in their manners, and on the testimony of the Marquis de Beauvoir, 'certainly the most polished people on the earth.' Proud and suspicious, the upper classes despise industrial pursuits, and glory in military life, carrying the sentiment of personal honour far beyond any other race. They are, however, imbued by a love of knowledge, are ingenious, clean, and frugal; are 'great tea-drinkers, great tobacco-smokers, and great talkers,' and, it may be added, great letter-writers. They dress in loose robes of white or brightly coloured silk or cotton, and wear neat little sandals of plaited straw. On the back of the dress is usually embroidered the armorial device of the wearer or of his master—in red, blue, green, and yellow—or a designation of the wearer's trade. Many of the men are only clad in a loin-cloth and sandals, and are tattooed from head to foot in the most brilliant colours, with figures of dragons, women, warriors, &c. The ladies fasten their long black hair in three stages by ornamented pins; they frequently powder and paint their cheeks and gild their lips. After marriage they have a strange custom of blackening the teeth and shaving off the eyebrows. Priests and doctors shave the whole head, but the usual custom is to train the hair into a pigtail about 4 inches long. The wooden houses, of which the greater part of the towns consist, are marvels of joinery, built without a single nail, and entirely destitute of painting. A light roof is supported by a frame of pine-wood, and the walls of a transparent cotton-paper, slipped into double grooves, can be removed by one turn of the hand. During the day the little kiosks are open to the four winds, and at night, when the wall-curtains are drawn, they glow like lanterns. Fires, of course, are common, and as checks there are numerous watch-towers and regular native fire brigades. Perhaps the two most distinctive customs of J. are the Harri-kari (q. v.), a legalised honourable mode of suicide, and the promiscuous bathing which is general throughout the country. The people observe many holidays, and delight in theatre-going, dancing, juggling, and wrestling. The use of opium is rigidly prohibited, but there is considerable indulgence in saki, a spirit distilled from rice. Great honour is paid to the dead, and the cemeteries are adorned with beautiful carved granite monuments.

Industries and Commerce.—The Japanese are singularly skilful in the manufacture of silks and cottons, and are unsurpassed by any nation in the world for the exquisite beauty of their porcelain, lacquer-work, and bronzes. They early received the art of lithochrome-printing from the Chinese, and are now admirable engravers of maps and book-illustrations. The native artists are familiar with, and practise, the rules of perspective, contrary to the common opinion, which is based on pictures that are sold in Yedo for the tenth part of a penny. See Audsley and Bowes, *Keramic Art of J.* (Parts 1 and 2, Liverp. 1876). The chief exports are tea, raw silk, silkworm's eggs, copper, dried fish, rice, coal, and tobacco; and the staple imports are cotton and woollen fabrics, arms, and ammunition. In 1875 the total value of the former amounted to £3,602,978, and of the latter to £5,893,413. British exports to J. amounted to £2,460,227, and the imports thence to £377,791. Most of the ports are linked together by telegraph, and in 1876 railways were completed from Hiogo to Osaka and Kioto (50 miles) and from Yedo to Yokohama (20 miles).

Government, Finance, &c.—The system of government, established in 1869, is one of absolute monarchy. The Mikado ('the venerable') is supreme in temporal and spiritual affairs, and acts through an executive ministry, divided (in imitation of that of France under Napoleon III.) into the eight departments of the Imperial House of Foreign Affairs, of War, the Navy, Finances, the Interior, Justice, Education, and Ecclesiastical Affairs. A *sain*, or senate of thirty members, and a *shoïn*, or Council of State, of an undetermined number of members, are both nominated by the Mikado. Affairs of unusual importance are decided by a Great Council, presided over by the Mikado, and consisting of the shoïn, the prime minister, vice-prime minister, with five advisers, and the ministers and vice-ministers of the eight departments. Ordinary matters are decided by ministers individually or in cabinet. Since 1871 the administration in the provinces has been in the hands of prefects, who cannot carry into execution sentences of death or banishment until they are confirmed by the Minister of Justice. In 1874, according to official returns, the revenue amounted to £9,750,000, and the expenditure to £9,320,000. The chief source of revenue is the land-tax (levied in rice); other sources are the maritime and customs' duties, stamps, taxes on alcoholic liquors, &c. In a published budget, approved by the Great Council, the estimated revenue for the financial year 1875–76 was £13,717,653, and the expenditure, £13,699,701. In 1875 the public debt consisted of £5,143,000 internal, and £1,102,000 foreign liabilities. The national coins are the silver ichibu = 1s. 4½d., and the yen or dollar = 4s. An imperial mint, with machinery made in England, was opened at Osaka in 1870, and the new coins are 10, 5, and 2½ dollar pieces; and 50, 20, and 5 cents, besides several small copper coins. In 1874 the number of letters transmitted was 17,095,842, and there were in J. 3244 post-offices. The army of J., under the command of the Mikado, does not probably exceed 80,000 men. A decree of 1872 made liability to arms universal, but had not been given effect to by 1876. Japanese officers have in recent years been instructed by the French at Yokohama. In 1876 the navy comprised two ironclad corvettes, two wooden corvettes, three schooners, one gunboat, one transport, and one yacht; and was manned by 1200 sailors, including 67 artillery-men and 260 marines. Three ironclads—a frigate of 2500 tons and two corvettes of 1700 tons each—were being constructed in England in 1876. Naval instruction is given by thirty-one English officers, who arrived in the country in 1872.

Religion and Education.—The two great religions are Sintuism (*sin*, 'the gods,' and *syu*, 'faith') and Buddhism, while the higher classes are partial to the teaching of Confucius. Sintuism is the ancient faith of the country, and there are only ninety-seven Sintu temples, while the number of Buddhist temples is not less than 296,900. Education has recently made great strides, the annual grant being now about £60,000. At the expense of the Government many young men have been sent to study in America (till 1875 about 500), England, France, and Germany. In 1871 America was visited by five young lady students. A law of 1872 decreed the establishment of 53,760 schools, the expense of which is to fall eventually on the people. Native education is widely diffused, the common people can generally read and write Japanese, and the cultured are more or less advanced in the study of Chinese, which has been to them a classical language. Yedo has a university (attended in 1875 by 345 students), comprising colleges of medicine, jurisprudence, philosophy, mining, &c. There are also a school of foreign languages, and a normal school for teachers. Books and newspapers in Japanese and English are daily multiplying.

Language and Literature.—In J. there are three alphabets—(1) the *Kata-Kana* ('side letters'), anciently derived from Chinese hieroglyphics, and used chiefly by scholars; (2) the *Karina*, now called simply *Kana*, with forty-eight letters, which is syllabary; and (3) another form of the *Kana*, invented by a Buddhist priest about 1000 years ago for the purpose of assimilating its letters to those of the sacred books. The simplified Kana or *Hira-Kana* ('plain letters') is most in use. The Japanese, with its seventy-two syllables, is one of the most flexible and melodious of spoken languages. See E. M. Satow, *English-Japanese Dictionary* (1876), and Alcock's *Japanese Grammar* (1861). The literature, which is voluminous, is divided into three general classes—(1) *Kangaku*, or Chinese classical literature and works regarding it, including the Buddhist literature; (2) *Wagaku*, or a strictly native literature of history, geography, art, and old metrical legends; and (3) *Kasaku*, or the literature of fiction, which is singularly varied and extensive.

History.—The authentic chronology of J. goes back to 667 before the Christian era, and the first great historical character is the Mikado Sinmu, who after a career of conquest founded a dynasty which has endured for upwards of twenty-five centuries. Much of the early history is of a purely local interest and character. In 1192 the reins of government were plucked from the hands of a feeble sovereign by Yoritomo, the Shiogun or generalissimo (called in recent times the *Tycoon*, from the Chinese *Tai Koon* 'great lord'). A permanent system was thus established by which the latter residing at Yedo remained his actual ruler, though doing homage to the Mikado at Miako. The Europeans later took the Shiogun for emperor and the Mikado for a spiritual dignitary. In 1543 the Portuguese traders first found their way hither, and St. Francis Xavier followed in 1549. In 1603 Tokugawa Jyeyas ('the illustrious'), whose descendants held the Shiogunate till 1868, inaugurated a policy of isolation, which closed the ports against an increasing foreign traffic, and stamped out the Roman Catholic religion by the massacre of some 50,000 converts. A single Dutch factory was allowed to remain on the island of Hirado, but the system of rigid exclusion triumphed till 1853, when Commodore Perry led a squadron of U. S. war-ships into the harbour of Yokohama, and wrested from the Shiogun the first of the series of modern treaties. Since 1854, the ports of Kanagawa, Yokohama, Nagasaki, Hiogo, Osaka, Hakodate, Yedo, Niigata, and Kagoshima have been opened to foreign commerce. The *Daimios* or territorial princes, alienated by the unauthorised acts of the Shiogun, were bitterly opposed to the invasion of foreigners. Many assassinations occurred during the subsequent ten years, but the bombardment of Kagosuhima Chioshiu by the English and allied fleets (1863) tended to produce a complete revolution of opinion in favour of foreign relations. The Shiogun was deposed and the Mikado was placed at the head of the reformed government in 1868. In 1870 a great embassy visited the United States and Europe, and subsequently the calendar of the western nations was substituted for that of old J., and English was adopted as the official language. The Daimios, who in 1862 numbered 216, with revenues ranging from £15,000 to £915,500, and who had long played the part of independent sovereigns, submitted to the Mikado after more or less resistance. The *Samurai*, the former military class, nearly 2 millions in number, have been deprived of their pensions and incomes, which kept the country in poverty for centuries, and the disaffection thus caused has shown itself in a series of insurrections. The defiant isolation of the powerful and warlike Satsuma clan still frustrates the efforts of government to effect complete imperial unity. After the suppression of the revolt at Kumamoto in February 1877 great apprehension was felt of a general rising of the Satsuma, which would be a severer trial than the government has had to face since the Restoration. See Sir R. Alcock's *Capital of the Tycoon* (2 vols. Lond. 1863); Lawrence Oliphant's *Narrative of Lord Elgin's Mission* (Lond. 1859); and the works of Lindau (Par. 1864); Dickson (Lond. 1869); Du Pin (Par. 1868); Jephson and Elmhirst (Lond. 1869); Humbert (Par. 1870); Taylor (New York, 1871); Mitford (*Tales of Old J.*, 2 vols. Lond. 1871); F. O. Adams (2 vols. Lond. 1875); Mossman (Lond. 1875); Bousquet (Par. 1876); and Griffis (New York, 1876).

Japann'ing, the term for the process of applying varnish or Lacquer (q. v.) to articles of wood, metal, and papier-mâché, and hardening it by heat. The art is carried to great perfection in Japan, whence the name. In J. metal, a japan ground, prepared with a pigment and shellac or animé varnish is first applied, and then the varnish alone in successive coats; each coat is dried and hardened in an oven before another is laid on. Decoration in colour and gold is placed on the japan ground with peculiar gold-size made with boiled linseed oil, animé, and vermilion. The article is finished by being polished with felt and fine powdered pumice, and with oil to give final lustre. Wood and papier-mâché are similarly treated.

Japh'eth (Heb., apparently derived in Gen. ix. 27, from *pathach*, 'to extend,' but more probably from *yaphach*, 'to be fair'; *cf.* Ham, 'sun-burnt') was one of the three sons of Noah (Gen. v. 32). His seven sons were the progenitors of the non-Semitic and non-Hamitic races, who at first occupied 'the isles of the Gentiles' (Gen. x.). There is a noteworthy resemblance in the names between J. and *Japetos*, the ancestor of the human race according to the Greeks.

Japu'ra, a tributary of the Amazon, 1000 miles long, rises in the Eranadian Andes, Columbia, flows E. and joins the larger river about 10 miles above Ega.

Jargoni'sing, the utterance of uncouth and unintelligible sounds, is, when combined with great excitement, one of the symptoms of acute or paroxysmal mania, and is more properly designated *general incoherence*. The utterance of such sounds is common to idiots, dements, and the lower grades of imbeciles.

Jarnac, Battle of, was fought near the town of that name (13th March 1569) on the banks of the Charente, between the Catholic army of the Duc d'Anjou, afterwards Henri III., and the Huguenot troops of Coligny. Owing to the self-will of the Protestant gentlemen and their want of obedience, Coligny, while leading off the vanguard of his army from the Charente, was surprised by the Duc d'Anjou. Condé, who galloped back from the front with some cavalry, was slain, and the Protestants were defeated. See Kitchin's *History of France* (vol. ii. Lond. 1877). The town of J. has a pop. (1872) of 3864, a trade in wine and brandy, and has given the title of Comte to several persons, *e.g.*, to the French minister to England, who died in 1875.

Jar'oslav, a central government of European Russia, formerly a principality. Area 122,988 sq. miles; pop. (1870) 1,000,748. It is watered by the Volga, Mologa, Scheksna, and Kostroma, and of the surface five-twelfths is arable land, and one-third is covered with forest. The chief industries are the growing, spinning, and weaving of flax, kitchen-gardening, and the manufacture of hardware (springs, nails, &c.). The inhabitants are skilful and industrious, and the women are famed for their beauty throughout Russia. The chief towns are J., Uglitch, Rybinsk, Rostov, and Mologa.

Jaroslav, the capital of the government, on the right bank of the Volga, where it is joined by the Kotorost, 165 miles N.N.E. of Moscow by rail. It is a handsome city, with countless towers and cupolas. The river banks are lined with palaces, and there are sixty-six churches and three convents. The market-place (*Gostinoike Dvor*) is of extreme size, and among the manufactures are linens, cottons, large bells, white-lead, and silks. Pop. (1870) 27,268. J., said to have been founded by Jaroslav the Great in the 10th c., is one of the oldest towns of Russia. It was long the residence of the feudal princes of J., and suffered frequently at the hands of the Mongols.

Jarr'ah (*Eucalyptus marginata*), a valuable tree found only in Western Australia, where it forms extensive forests. It is large, but is liable to early decay at the heart. When sound, and felled at the proper season, the J. timber is of great value for use as wharf piles, railway sleepers, and telegraph posts, as it then contains a pungent acid which repels even the *teredo navalis* and white ant. Large quantities of it are exported to the other Australian colonies and to India. J. is also used for parts of ships under water, and vessels planked with it do not require copper sheathing. The wood, however, cracks in the sun, and will not bear a heavy transverse strain. See Laslett's *Timber and Timber Trees* (1875).

Ja'shar, Book of, is mentioned in two passages of the Old Testament (Josh. x. 13, and 2 Sam. i. 18), from which it appears to have been a collection of heroic poems. The origin of the name is obscure. As to its contents various opinions have prevailed. It has been identified with the Pentateuch, Genesis, Numbers, Deuteronomy, and Judges respectively. Two rabbinical books of Jashar have been published: one by Jacob Meir or R. Tam, at Cracow, 1586; the other at Venice, 1625. A forgery called *The B. of J. translated into English from the Hebrew by Alcuin of Britain*, was published at Bristol, in 1751, by Jacob Ilive. But the most famous of all is *J.: Fragmenta Archetypa Carminum Hebraicorum Collegit, &c.*, by J. W. Donaldson (Berl. 1854). In this work the author undertakes to collect the scattered parts of the book referred to in the Old Testament, on the foundation of the two passages in which it is mentioned, and 'a true perception of the meaning of the term *J.*,' which he makes to be *just* and *righteous*, and which contains 'the substantial expression of the religious and theocratic ideas of the chosen people—their idea of the nature of God (the just One: *cf.* Deut. xxxii. 4), and of his dealings with men, of the connection between man's duty and man's happiness, and of all that was and ought to be distinctive of their own nature, in contrast to the condition of the nation before it was specially selected by God (making Israel, from *J.* and *El*, to be those whom God has made just and happy), and to the other nations from whom they were separated.' See Donaldson's *Christian Orthodoxy* (1857), and an essay on J. in E. Deutsch's *Remains* (1874).

Jas'min, Jacques, or **Jaquon Jansemin,** a famous Languedoc poet, was born at Agen, 6th March 1798, became a barber, and attracted customers to his shop not only by the skilful use of his razor, but by his singular spontaneity in the composition of verse in the patois of the S. of France. In 1835 he published a collection of romances, burlesques, poems, and odes (*Las Papillotos*), and the same year *L'Abuglo de Castel-Cuillé*, (in 1840) *Françonnette*, (1844) *Marthe-la-Folle*, (1845) *Les Deux Frères Jumeaux*, (1849) *La Semaine d'un Fils*, all of them written in patois, and dealing with the common theme of local tradition. His rapid power of improvisation J. corrected by devoting himself to poetry as an art, and added to the qualities of wit, liveliness, and dash a truthfulness, simplicity, sobriety, and power of appropriate condensation which induced Sainte Beuve to classify him with Theocritus, Horace, and Gray. In using the patois of his native district, J. elevated it to the dignity of classical perfection which it had attained during the 13th c. 'If,' it was said concerning him, 'France had ten poets of J.'s influence, she would have no revolution to fear.' J. was elected member of the Academies of Bordeaux and Agen, Chevalier of the Legion of Honour (1846), and died 4th October 1864, in his native town.

Jas'mine, or **Jess'amine,** a name given to several plants of the natural order *Jasminaceæ*. They are shrubs or climbing plants, with clusters of white or yellow flowers, and are highly prized both for their beauty and the fragrance of their flowers. Some of the plants have medicinal properties; the leaves of one species being used against tapeworm, the root of another against ringworm. The fragrant essential oil of J. is obtained from *J. officinale* and *grandiflorum*.

Ja'son. See ARGONAUTS.

Jas'per, an opaque variety of massive quartz, of which there are several varieties differing in colour and external appearance. Common or red J. is of a bright blood colour, owing to the presence of peroxide of iron; Egyptian J. is streaked, banded, or mottled with yellow and brown, approaching the agate in appearance; porcelain J. is formed of clay rock by the action of heat, and is a kind of natural porcelain. The varieties of J. take a fine polish, and are much used for engraving cheap seals and the commoner kinds of ornamental lapidary work.

Jass'y (Slav. 'the marshy place'), the capital of Moldavia, Roumania, on the swampy Bachlui, an affluent of the Pruth, 9 miles W. of the main stream, which forms the Russian frontier, and on the malarious slopes of the Kopoberg Mountains. It is for the most part regularly built, but is intersected by crooked alleys; and the palatial mansions, the Chika Vogorides and Sturdza, of the Bojars are enclosed in walled courts, surrounded by filthy huts. There are seventy Greek churches, ten convents, one Protestant, one Roman Catholic, and one Armenian church, many small synagogues, a large new metropolitan church, a church of the Three Saints, built in the 13th c., the Ministerial and Assembly buildings, around which are the barracks, a handsome theatre, fine shops and warehouses, and innumerable khans or Eastern restaurants. The Kopo is a beautiful public garden. Owing to the dust and mud of the streets there is an unusual demand for conveyances, the estimated number of private equipages being 1300, of droskies 5000, and of horses 13,000. Skuleni, the port of J., is 8 miles down the river. J. has a wretched Tartar suburb, and a suburb called Pokurar, occupied by German artificers. Pop. 90,000, of whom one-third are Galician and Russian Jews, and 5500 Bojars, with 3000 gypsies and 3300 servants. According to Vaillant, the Jews of J. are the descendants of the Avars who embraced Judaism. They have Tartar physiognomies, and their rabbis call themselves Khagans.

Jász-Berény, a town of Hungary, in the free district of Jazygia, on the Zagyva, 45 miles E. of Pesth. It includes two woody river islands, and has a Greek church, a Franciscan convent, a townhouse, gymnasium, &c. There is a trade in corn, cattle, and wine. A monument in the heart of the town is said to mark the grave of Attila. Pop. (1869) 20,233.

Jat, Jut, or **Jaut,** the name of the dominant tribe throughout the Punjaub, also found in Scinde, Rajputana, and the N.W. Provinces. In religion the Jats are indiscriminately Mohammedans, Hindus, or Sikhs, but the first of these three form the majority. In physiognomy they are decidedly Aryan, and they make excellent soldiers. Their methods of cultivation are good, and they are also breeders of cattle and camels. The democratic village community exists among the Jats in its full perfection. Their language is a derivative of Sanskrit, not widely differing from the Hindi. A plausible theory assigns to the Jats a Scythic origin. See Campbell's *Ethnology of India*, in the *Journal of the Asiatic Society* for 1866.

Játi'va, San Felipe de, an old town of Spain, in Valencia, on the Guadamar, 20 miles from the coast, and 40 S. by E. of Valencia by rail. Its alamada is ornamented with a palm-alley. The great castle has been several times used as a state prison. Pop. 13,200. J. is the Roman *Setabis*, and was anciently famed for its flax and linen manufactures. The Borjas (Ital. *Borgias*) are an old J. family.

Jat'ropha, a genus of plants (*Euphorbiaceæ*), some of which yield an oil, and others very poisonous juices, the active principle of which appears to be prussic acid. The *J. manihot* yields a poisonous juice and much starch. The root is disintegrated and the starch extracted from it, which, after having been washed and dried, constitutes Brazilian arrowroot or tapioca. The seed-kernels of *J. curcas* yield about 37 per cent. of an oil which is colourless, and is devoid of smell and marked taste; but it is powerfully purgative, 10–15 drops producing an effect. On account of its being so much more powerful than castor-oil—which is also derived from a Euphorbiaceous plant—it used to be called *Oleum infernale*. It is surpassed, however, in activity by Croton oil (*C. tiglium*, Euphorb.).

Jau'er (Slav. 'the place of the maple-tree'), a town in the province of Silesia, Prussia, on the Neisse, 37 miles W. of Breslau, is noted for its corn trade and sausage-making, and was formerly capital of the principality of J., which extended to 1218 sq. miles. J. was once the centre of the Silesian linen trade, but suffered severely from the Thirty Years' War. Pop. (1875) 10,404.

Jaun'dice, Ic'terus, or the **Yellows,** are terms which comprehend a group of diseases of the liver, the prominent symptom of which is the yellow colour of many of the different tissues and fluids of the body, but more especially of the conjunctiva and the connective tissue. The first symptom of J. is a yellowness of the white of the eyes, then of the roots of the nails, next of the face and the neck, and ultimately of the whole body. At the earliest stage, the urine becomes of a deep-red colour, stains the linen yellow, and is changed to a deep green by the addition of nitric acid; and, at the same time, the evacuations are of a white, clayish colour, generally relaxed, but sometimes constipated. J. is always associated with a white tongue, a bitter taste in the mouth, distaste for food, inaptitude for all exertion, great depression of spirits; and there is, occasionally, some slight pain over the liver, headache, nausea, and vomiting. J. may arise in two ways:—(1) By the mechanical obstruction to the passage of the bile into the intestines, and the consequent *reabsorption* of the detained fluid into the blood. This condition may be caused by the obstruction of a calculus in the common hepatic duct; by obstruction of the gall-ducts from tumours in the liver, disease of the head of the pancreas, or of the duodenum. (2) By *suppression* of the biliary secretion, arising from some morbid condition of the liver itself, in consequence of which biliary ingredients may accumulate in the circulation. *Treatment:*—When J. is due to *congestion* of the liver, mercurial purgatives in combination with aloes and nux vomica with rhubarb; but acids and alkalies are contra-indicated. Benzoic acid is useful in cases of innervation; but injurious when there is obstruction. Podophilin, combined with hyoscyamus, is useful in cases of suppressed secretion, and with vegetable tonics in feeble liver; but is also contra-indicated in obstruction. Sulphate of magnesia, in drachm doses, with fifteen grains of carbonate of magnesia, and half a drachm of aromatic spirits of ammonia, given three times daily before meals, is also highly recommended. See Dr. Harley *On Jaundice*, Dr. Budd *On Diseases of the Liver.*

Ja'va, or **Yava-Dwipa** ('barley island'), the finest of the larger Sunda Islands, in the Indian Archipelago, and one of the richest countries in the world, lies in lat. 5° 2'–8° 0' 50" S., and in long. 105° 12'–114° 0' 39" E. It is separated on the W. from Sumatra by the Sunda Strait, 25 miles wide; on the E. from Bali by the Bali Strait, which narrows to 6 miles; and on the N. from Borneo by the wide expanse of the shallow Sunda or J. Sea; while in the S. it is washed by the open Indian Ocean. Area, 51,336 sq. miles. Its extreme length from E. to W. is 660 miles, and its greatest breadth 140 miles. From E. to W. it is traversed by an irregular mountain range, richly clad with magnificent forests, and attaining its greatest heights of 12,250 feet in Semiru, and of 11,320 in Slamat. Active volcanoes are numerous, especially in the S.E., and are remarkable for their great discharges of sulphur and sulphurous gases. Fish cannot live in the sea near the mouth of a stream that issues from the lake in the vicinity of Jaschem (a volcano in the E. of J.) owing to the waters being so impregnated with sulphuric acid; and the Vale of Poison, near Batar, is strewn with the bones of animals that have been killed by the exhalations of carbonic acid gas. The eruptions of Papandayang in 1772 and of Galunggong in 1822 were very destructive. The mountains in the S. are steep and rugged, but in the N. they decline more gradually to the low coast plains and mangrove swamps. The navigation of the coast is difficult, but in the N. there are a few good harbours, as those of Batavia and Surabaya, and several fine roadsteads. Of the many short and rapid streams, only a few are navigable, as the Solo, Kediri, and Tjimanock. J. is in great part covered by luxuriant and valuable forests of teak, drammar-pine, fig-trees, &c. Coffee, the staple product, is cultivated to a height of 2000 feet, and other abundant crops are sugar, cotton, rice, indigo, tobacco, and spices. Buffaloes are generally used in agriculture, and among the wild animals are the king-tiger, the one-horned rhinoceros, the wild ox, two varieties of the wild hog, large bats five feet across the wings, and many kinds of apes, while the waters are abundantly stocked with fish. Gold-dust is found in several rivers; mineral springs are numerous; coal and rock-salt occur in the mountains, but there is no mining. The climate is unhealthy only in the marshy regions of the N. coast; the temperature in the lowland is very equal, seldom rising above 90° F., or falling below 70° F. During the equinoxes there are generally violent winds and thunderstorms; the wet season, with its W. winds, lasts intermittingly from October to March. Earthquakes are not unfrequent; that of 1867 is said to have killed 300 persons. In 1873 the pop., which has nearly quadrupled since 1816, amounted to 17,855,840, of whom 27,009 were Europeans, 190,603 Chinese, 22,958 Arabs and others, and the rest natives. The Javanese are the most civilised people of the Malay race. Small in stature, yellow in colour, patient and cheerful in temperament, they are perhaps the best agriculturists in Asia, and show much industrial skill and ingenuity. They are chiefly employed as agricultural labourers, and are professed Mohammedans. The language of the greater part of J. differs considerably from Malay proper, and from Sundese, which is spoken in the W. of the island. It has twenty consonants and six vowel sounds. It is rich in fine objective distinctions, but is utterly lacking in abstract expressions. The literary fragments—dubious chronicles, religious writings, and resetting of Hindu poems—are of very early date.

The most important colonial possession of the Netherlands, J. is under a governor-general and a deliberative council of five members. Including the island of Madura (q. v.) it is divided into twenty-three residencies, each governed by a resident, who is in constant intercourse with the native chiefs. The scheme of administration is known as the 'culture system,' and was established by Van den Bosch in 1832. It provides for official control and superintendence of native labour, so as to develop most extensively the cultivation of articles for the European market. Formerly the labour of the natives was enforced in almost all agricultural operations; it is now required only on sugar and coffee plantations, and by an Act of 1870 the forced cultivation of the sugar-cane is to be totally abolished in the next twenty years. All the land belongs to the Government except the private estates in the N.W. residencies. The revenue is chiefly derived from the sale of articles at a price far above the cost of production under the 'culture system.' In 1875 the revenue was £10,433,690, and the expenditure was £9,588,458. The trade is for the most part with the Netherlands and (exclusive of specie) the imports in 1874 amounted to £7,529,000, and the exports to £11,971,000. In 1875 the value of the exports to Great Britain was £1,442,607 and of the imports therefrom £1,577,980. About one-half of the rice is shipped to Borneo and China. The *Nederlandsche Handel Maatschappij*, established in Amsterdam in 1824, is sole agent in buying and importing into J. all Government supplies, and of exporting the produce of the colony and selling it in Europe. In 1876 there were in the island 160 miles of railway, comprising lines from Samarang to Djokdjokarta and from Batavia to Buitenzorg. An Act for the construction of a network of railways at the cost of the Government was passed in 1875. J. is connected by telegraph with China, Australia, Europe, and America, and has an army of about 30,000 men and 1200 commissioned officers; more than one-half of the former are natives, and all the latter are Europeans except (1876) seven natives of high rank. In 1876 the navy consisted of 1 screw-frigate, 2 corvettes, and 26 smaller steamers.

The early faith of the Javanese was Buddhism, and throughout the island are scattered many Buddhist temples. (See BORO BUDDOR.) Mohammedanism found its way hither in the 14th c. In 1511 the Portuguese first visited J., and in 1595 the Dutch erected the first factory. After much fighting the island was nominally made a Dutch colony in 1677. On the incorporation of Holland by France in 1811, the English took J., but restored it to the Dutch five years later. In 1830 the whole island was subjugated, after a fierce protracted struggle with the natives. See Sir Stamford Raffles, *History of Java* (2 vols. Lond. 1817); Müller *Beschreibung der Insel Java* (Berl. 1860); Wallace, *The Malay Archipelago* (Lond. 1869); Goeverneur, *Nederlandsch Indië* (Leyden, 1870); and Wenzelburger, *Nederländisch-Ostindien* in *Unsere Zeit*, vol. ix. (Leips. 1873).

Jav'elin (Fr. *javeline*, from Armor. *gavlin*, connected with Ger. *gabel*, 'a fork'), a light dart, used in hunting, and hence the word is often erroneously derived from the Span. *javal*, 'a wild boar.' The J. corresponds to the *cidôn* of the Old Testament, the *hyssos* of Polybius, and the *pilum* of Roman writers. The last was about 6 feet 9 inches long; had a barbed iron head and a shaft of tough wood, and was used either to throw or thrust with. Two *pila* formed with a sword the equipment of the *hastati*.

Jaw, the name applied in anatomy to two bones, viz., the *upper* and *lower*. *Upper Jaw or Maxilla Superior* is one of the principal bones of the face. It enters also into the floor of the orbit, the floor and lateral portions of the nasal cavity, and forms the greater part of the hard palate. It consists of an *ascending* or *nasal* process, which is situated superiorly; an *alveolar* process situated inferiorly, which contains the sockets for the upper teeth; a *nasal surface* situated internally, in which surface there is an opening leading into a large cavity situated within the bone and called the Antrum of Highmore, and an *external surface*, convex in shape, which forms the anterior and lateral parts of the face. To the upper J. are attached various muscles which act principally upon the lips and angles of the mouth.

Lower Jaw or Mandible.—A bone which is present in vertebrate animals, and which has its representative in some of the classes of invertebrate animals. In the vertebrate kingdom, the condition of the lower J. forms, along with other conditions, a means of subdividing this kingdom into three sections. In birds and reptiles each half of the J. is made up of several pieces, and the bone articulates with the temporal bone of the skull, not directly, but by the intervention of a bone, the *quadrate bone*. In most reptiles the halves are only loosely connected, and the teeth are not usually placed in distinct sockets. In mammals, each half of the lower J. is composed of only a single piece, and articulates directly with the temporal bone of the skull. There is no *quadrate bone*. The teeth in all the members of this class are planted in distinct sockets.

Lower Jaw in man is the strongest bone of the face. It consists of a middle portion placed horizontally, the *body*, and two ascending processes, the *rami*. The *body* is marked in the middle line by a rough ridge, placed vertically, and marking the original division of the bone into two parts. This ridge is called the *symphysis*. The inferior border of the bone is thicker nearer the middle line than in the rest of its extent. This thicker portion, by being everted slightly, gives rise to the prominence called the chin. The superior or alveolar border is hollowed out for the lower teeth. On the internal surface of the bone, near the symphysis, there are four tubercles or prominences, situated in pairs, and below these tubercles two depressions. These tubercles and depressions give attachment to muscles which depress the lower J., and therefore open the mouth; or, if the lower J. be held immovable by the action of other muscles, they will, by their action, elevate the larynx. The external and internal surfaces of the *rami* are rough for the attachment of muscles. The muscles attached to this bone are to *the body* muscles which act upon the lower lip and angles of the mouth, and to the *ramus* muscles concerned in mastication. The form of the *angle* varies at different periods of life. The lower J. is united to the rest of the skull by means of the condyle, which articulates with a depression on the temporal bone. This depression, the *glenoid fossa*, is deepened by the presence of an inter-articular fibro-cartilage, biconcave in shape. The bones are held in position by an external and an internal lateral ligament, and by a capsular ligament which closely envelops the joint. These ligaments allow of the movements of elevation, depression, a gliding movement backwards and forwards, and a certain amount of lateral movement. To facilitate such movements there are two synovial membranes in the joint; one between the glenoid fossa and the upper surface of the inter-articular fibro-cartilage, and one between the condyle and the lower surface of the same cartilage. One of the muscles, the *external pterygoid*, is attached not only to the neck of the J., but also into the inter-articular fibro-cartilage, the object of this arrangement being to pull forward the cartilage along with the condyle, and thus lessen the risk of dislocation of the J., which would be liable to occur in the absence of such a provision.

Jaxar'tes (Arab. *Saihún*, Pers. *Sír Daria*, 'Yellow River'), the Greek name of a large river rising in the Thian Shan Mountains in Central Asia, and flowing W. and N.W. through the valley of Khokan and the sandy desert of Kizil-Kum into the Sea of Aral, separating Sogdiana from Scythia. The J. was supposed to fall into the N. part of the Caspian (which is first distinguished from the Sea of Aral by Ammianus Marcellinus in the 4th c. A.D.), but the accounts of it in ancient writers are very conflicting. The Jaxartæ, a Scythian tribe, lived on its banks. The sources of the J. were first discovered by Baron Kaulbars in 1869. In its lower course its banks are low, and consist of sand or clayey soil impregnated with salt. Before reaching the Kizil-Kum steppes it flows through a land that is only equalled in luxuriant vegetation by the richest valleys of India. Its length is estimated at 1800 miles, of which 900 are navigable. The J. below Khojend is now in the Russian territory of Turkestan, and on its banks the forts of Aralsk, Kásaly, Karmákchi, and Perovsky, form the famous so-called 'line of the Sír Daria.'

Jay (*Garrulus*) a genus of Insessorial birds or perchers, belonging to the *Conirostres*, and to the *Corvidæ* or crow family. It is distinguished by a bill of moderate size, the nostrils being hidden by plumes. The fourth, fifth, and sixth quills are the longest. The hinder toe is straight and long. The genus is represented by a well-known English bird. The harsh screams of the common J. (*G. glandarius*), and its imitative powers, have won for the name 'J.' a somewhat unenviable reputation. The J. is the size of a pigeon, and is brownish above, glossed with purple. The head has a crest of grey feathers spotted with black. The wings and tail are black, and the wing-coverts banded with black. Two broods are produced each year. The eggs number four or five, and are of a yellowish white. The food consists of caterpillars, insects, fruits, and berries, and even the young of other birds. In 1744 the J. was condemned by a statute, and a reward of 3d. for the head of each J. was offered, on account of the supposed injuries which it inflicted on young trees. The blue J. (*Cyanocorax cristatus*) of N. America is well known. The colour is a light bluish purple. The head has a blue erectile crest. The bird is active and predatory in habits, attacking even the hawk.

Jay.

Jay, John, an American statesman, first Chief Justice of the United States, was born in New York, December 12, 1745, called to the bar in 1768, and elected to Congress in 1774. He took a leading part in the War of Independence. In 1779 he was appointed Minister at Madrid, and he signed the treaty of peace at Paris in 1783. In that year he became Foreign Secretary, in 1789 Chief Justice, and in 1794 Ambassador at London. He was Governor of New York State 1795–1801, after which he retired to private life. He died May 17, 1829. He was a leading Federalist, and his services to the American cause were only surpassed by those of Washington. See his Life by his son, William J. (1833).

Jaya-Deva, the most popular poet of the Hindus, was born near Burdwan, in Lower Bengal, some time between the 11th and 16th c. A.D. His great work is the *Gita Govinda*, which has been admirably translated by Mr. Edwin Arnold (*The Indian Song of Songs*, Lond. 1875). It represents the amours of Krishna, an incarnation of Vishnu, with the milkmaids of Brindaban, and his final reconciliation with his true lover, Radha. A mystical interpretation has sometimes been placed upon the erotic language of the poem.

Jeanne Darc ('the Maid of Orleans'), daughter of a peasant, was born 6th January 1412, at Domremy, a village in Champagne on the Meuse, and showed an early tendency towards a fervent form of religious belief. The cause of Henri VI. (q. v.) was being pushed in France during J.'s girlhood, and in the midst of war she heard, as she believed, a clear angel's voice calling her 'to have pity on the fair realm of France,' St. Catherine, St. Marguerite, and St. Michael all appearing and offering her aid. Convinced of her divine mission, she sought the Dauphin (Charles VII.) at Chinon. After submitting to the interrogatories of learned churchmen, 'who wearied her with their words,' she was put in command of a body of soldiers, and set out to Orleans to raise the English siege, in which she was successful, 29th April 1429. J. then sought the Dauphin at Loches, overcoming the jealousy of his advisers, and triumphing over the enemy at Patay, June 18, led him to Rheims, where he was crowned, July 17, 1429. J. was captured, May 23, 1430, whilst engaged in a sortie at Compiègne against the Burgundians, was placed under guard by John of Luxembourg, and sold by him for 16,000 francs to the English. 'No man had pity on her. The king and his crew of favourites made no sign; the Archbishop of Rheims denounced her; the clergy of the English party followed his leading; the University of Paris, utterly incapable of discerning her heroism, clamoured that she should be handed over to the Holy Office; the Inquisition claimed her as its victim.' In despair she flung herself from her cell window at Beaurevoir, but survived the fall, was conveyed to Rouen, subjected to a long trial on the charges of sorcery and witchcraft, and burnt 31st May 1431. The doubts regarding the story of her death expressed by Viguier, Delapierre, and others, though supported by some curious evidence, have not found much acceptance among critics. See Delapierre's *Doute Historique* (1855). 'The noble figure of the heroine of France stands out in amazing beauty against the background of treachery, meanness, cruelty, and smoke of devouring fire. In all she is lifted far above her countrymen and her age; in all she is perfect in her simplicity, piety, self-devotion. She stands alone on the page of history' (Kitchin, *History of France*, vol. i. p. 537). See also *Procès de Condamnation*, by Jules Quicherat, and *Histoire de J. D.*, by De Beauregard.

Jed'burgh, a picturesque old border town of Scotland, and capital of Roxburghshire, on the left bank of the Jed, 10 miles S.S.W. of Kelso, and 56 S.E. of Edinburgh by rail. It was founded by Ecgred, Bishop of Lindisfarne, between 829 and 854, was made a royal burgh by David I., and became the chief town on the Middle Marches. In the fastness of its forest, and guarded by a castle, it was frequently the residence of the Scottish kings, and the rendezvous of their armies. Its chief architectural feature is its magnificent ruined abbey, an exquisite example of the transition from Norman to Early English style. It was founded by David I. in 1118 or 1147 for Augustine friars from Beauvais, and has a tower 120 feet high, arches of a singularly mixed character, a beautifully-interlaced arcade, and a

St. Catherine's rose-window (Flamboyant). The abbey was burned by the Earl of Hertford in 1544. The present jail of the town occupies the site of the old castle. J. holds a fair industrial position; its principal manufactures are blankets, shawls, plaids, boots and shoes, and hosiery. The town is girt with gardens and orchards. Pop. (1871) 3322. Together with Haddington, Dunbar, North Berwick, and Lauder, J. sends one member to Parliament. J. was often sacked in the border wars, and its existing records only extend back to 1619.

Jedd'ah, or **Jiddah,** a walled town of Arabia, in Hedjaz, on the Red Sea, 60 miles W. of Mecca. It is surrounded by barren deserts, and the rain-water is carefully gathered in cisterns. As port of Mecca it carries on an important trade, exporting coffee, and importing provisions from Egypt, manufactured goods from India, &c. Thousands of pilgrims pass through J. yearly. A massacre of the Christians took place here June 15, 1858, and the town was bombarded by the English in the August following. Pop. estimated variously at from 10,000 to 20,000.

Jeejeeb'hoy, Sir Jamset'jee, the title indissolubly annexed by an Act of the Indian Legislature to the holder of the baronetcy conferred (1857) on the great Parsee merchant of the same name. He was born at Bombay, 15th July 1783 and died 15th April 1859, after a life equally famous for the accumulation of wealth and its charitable disposition. The commercial development of Bombay, especially as regards the export of raw cotton, is historically associated with his name; and both at Bombay and Poonah are to be seen monuments of his munificence. He was succeeded by his son, whose original name was Cursetjee Jamsetjee.

Jeff'erson City, the capital of Missouri, U.S., on the S. bank of the Missouri River, opposite Cedar City, and on the Pacific Railway. It is the seat of J. C. College (Episcopal), and has a state-house, the armoury and penitentiary of the State, eight churches, a Lincoln institute, a normal school for coloured children, large flourmills, foundries, and a factory for farm implements. Pop. (1870) 4420. There is much coal and iron in the vicinity.

Jefferson, Joseph, an American comedian, was born at Philadelphia, February 20, 1829, and became an actor when very young. His *Rip Van Winkle,* which he has played almost continuously since its first production at the Adelphi Theatre, London, 1865, is admired as much in this country as America as one of the finest of modern dramatic creations.

Jefferson, Thomas, an American statesman, was born April 13, 1743, at Albemarle County, Virginia, U.S., studied at Williamsburg, was elected (1769) to the Virginia House of Burgesses, and became a member of Assembly (1773). The form of words of the Declaration of Independence was supplied by J., though many expressions were toned down by his colleagues. After serving as Governor of Virginia and Minister to France, J. became (1789) Secretary of State under Washington, and led the Democratic party, showing a leaning at the same time to France. After the outbreak of the Revolution, he took office (1797) as Vice-president, and (1801) was elevated to the Presidency. During his tenure of office (until 1807) Louisiana was purchased from the French Government for £3,300,000, and active preparations were made for engaging in war with Great Britain. J.'s chief literary work is entitled *Notes on Virginia.* His views were at all times extreme, and his temper hot, but his career was marked by consistent honesty of conduct. He died 4th July 1826. His collected Works comprise 9 vols. 8vo. See *Memoirs and Correspondence* by his grandson, T. J. Randolph (4 vols. 1829), and Lives by George Tucker (2 vols. 1837), by G. H. Randall (3 vols. 1858), by Sarah N. Randolph (1 vol. 1871), and by James Parton (1 vol. 1874).

Jeffrey, Francis, Lord, was born in Edinburgh October 23, 1773, went in his eighth year to the High School of Edinburgh, in his fifteenth to the University of Glasgow, in 1791 to Queen's College, Oxford, and in 1792 to the law classes of the Edinburgh University. Here he joined the Speculative Society, and formed a friendship with Scott, Brougham, Horner, and others. In 1794 he was called to the bar, and began writing for the *Monthly Review,* married (1801), and (1802) became editor of the *Edinburgh Review* (q. v.), which was started at the suggestion of Sydney Smith, and which J. conducted for twenty-six years. His practice at the bar flourished apace, and after being chosen Lord Rector of the University of Glasgow (1821), Dean of the Faculty of Advocates (1829), Lord Advocate (1830), he was returned to Parliament for the Perth, Forfar, and Dundee Burghs (1830), for Walton (1831), for Edinburgh (1832), and took his seat as a Judge of the Court of Session in 1834. J.'s numerous and varied contributions to the *Review* have been published in a selection of volumes (1843), but have scarcely stood the test of time like those of Macaulay and Carlyle. It is safe to say, however, that the most trenchant and characteristic of his essays remain uncollected. J.'s most marked qualities as a critic were rapid discernment and penetration, to which he added a certain brightness of fancy, a fine if not strong scholarship, and a copious diction. In sympathetic insight he was too often deficient, notoriously so in his estimate of Wordsworth, a trait which discovers itself also in his *Treatise on Beauty.* He died at Craigcrook Castle, 26th January 1850. See Lord Cockburn's *Life of J.* (2 vols. Edinb. 1852).

Jeff'reys, George, Baron, was born at Acton, Denbighshire, in 1640, educated at Shrewsbury and Westminster, entered the Inner Temple, and commenced pleading without being regularly called to the bar at Kingston Assizes in 1666. A drunkard and bully, but of quick and vigorous parts, he won an extensive Old Bailey practice as a Roundhead and persecutor of the Catholics. In 1677, however, he turned renegade, found a patron in James Duke of York, was knighted, and the year after appointed Recorder of London. Created successively King's Serjeant, Chief Justice of Chester, and baronet (1681); J. acted as crown's counsel or judge against Russell and Sydney, Baxter and Oates, was made Chief Justice of the King's Bench in 1683, and on the accession of James II. was raised to the peerage with the title of Baron J. of Wem. In the 'Bloody Assize' that followed Monmouth's revolt, J. found work after his own heart, hanging 350 prisoners and transporting 841 as slaves to the plantations. For these services he was rewarded by the Lord Chancellorship. He showed himself a ready tool to all the king's misdeeds, notably as head of the new High Court of Commission (1686), and in the trial of the Seven Bishops (1688). He sought to follow James's example of flight, but was caught disguised as a sailor in Wapping, and committed to the Tower, where he died, April 18, 1689.

Jehan'abad, (1) a town of India, in the district of Burdwan, with a pop. (1872) of 13,409, is a centre of the weaving trade; (2) a town in Gya District, India, with a pop. (1872) of 21,022, is also the home of cotton-weavers and of general commerce.

Jehangir' (*Jahangir*), a Moghul emperor who reigned at Delhi from 1605 to 1628. He was the son and successor of the great Akbar, and it was in his reign that the Rajputs first submitted to the Mohammedan power. J. himself married a Rajput princess; but his better-known wife was the beautiful Nur Jehan, whose name was placed on the imperial currency, and who lies buried with him in a marble mausoleum near Lahore.

Jeho'vah is the name of the Supreme Being, which, according to the third commandment of the Jewish decalogue (Exod. xx. 7), was not to be uttered—a law which the Jews have always faithfully observed, substituting for it either the name Adonai, 'Lord,' or Elohim, 'God.' According to Exod. iii. 14, and vi. 2, the name is connected with the verb *hayah, havah,* 'to be,' and would thus mean 'He is,' indicating the self-existence, the unchangeableness and faithfulness of God. Again, according to Exod. vi. 2–8, the name was not known to the Patriarchs, but was revealed to Moses as the name by which the God of Israel was to be distinguished from all other deities. The time here indicated actually corresponds with the chronological use of the name in Hebrew literature, but, on the other hand, the statement appears to be contradicted by the fact that the name occurs frequently throughout the Book of Genesis, being known not only to Abraham (xiv. 22), Isaac (xxvi. 22), and Jacob (xxviii. 16), but to Noah (ix. 26), Lamech (v. 29), and even Eve (iv. 1), and it is asserted generally that in the time of Enos 'men began to call on the name of J.' (iv. 26). One hypothesis to account for this discrepancy is that the passages in Genesis in which the name occurs are interpolations by a later writer; another is that Exod. vi. 2–8 does not mean that the name had been unknown before the time of Moses, but that the nature of J., to which the name particularly belonged, had not been fully revealed.

Jeisk, a town in the country of the Kuban Cossacks, in Cis-Caucasia, Russia, on a tongue of land between the Sea of Azov and the river Jeja, 50 miles S.W. of Taganrog, was founded in 1849, and is in a very flourishing state, being an agricultural centre, with a pop. of 16,747.

Jelat'ma, or **Jelati'na**, a town of Russia, on the Oka, in the government of Tambov, 170 miles E.S.E. of Moscow, with manufactures of woollens, sulphur, and vitriol. Pop. 7107.

Jeléz', a town of Russia, in the government of Orel, on the Sosna, 218 miles S. of Moscow. It has many gardens, fifteen churches, several manufactories, and its wheaten flour is famed throughout Russia. Pop. 30,540.

Jellachich de Buzim, Joseph, Baron, was born at Peterwardein, Austrian Slavonia, October 16, 1801, entered the Austrian army as sub-lieutenant of dragoons, 1819, went to Italy as captain of a regiment, 1830, and passed through the grades of major, lieutenant-colonel, and colonel. In 1848, when the court of Vienna had privately stirred up the Croatians, Dalmatians, and Serbs, to attack the Magyars, J. became the ban or commander-in-chief of the combined nationalities, led them across the Drave (September), and suffered a defeat. Afterwards at the battle of Swechat he defeated the Magyars. In the campaign of 1848–49 he was under the command of Prince Windischgrätz. The defeat at Hegyes, 14th July 1849, paralysed him for the rest of the war. At its close he was made civil and military governor of Croatia and Slavonia. J. died at Agram, May 20, 1859. In 1851 a volume of verse by J. was published at Vienna.

Jellalabadd' (*Jalalabaa*), the chief town of a district of the same name, in Afghanistan, at the head of the Khyber Pass, on the right bank of the Cabul River, 100 miles E. of Cabul, and 91 W. of Peshawar. Its trade chiefly consists of the export of fruit and timber. Pop. variously estimated at from 3000 to 10,000. J. is celebrated for the gallant defence made by Sir Robert Sale and 'the illustrious garrison' against the Afghans, from November 1841 to April 1842.—The *district* of J. has an estimated pop. of 100,000. The revenue is about £40,000, and the staple crops are Indian corn and barley.

Jellinghi (*Jalangi*), a river of Bengal, the second offshoot of the Ganges, which branches off from the main stream at the village of J., and joins the Bhagirutti at Nuddea to form the Hooghly. It is the least obstructed of the direct river routes to Calcutta; the annual boat-traffic is about 30,000 tons a year.

Jell'yfish, the name given popularly to *Cœlenterate* animals belonging to the class *Hydrozoa*, and to the section *Discophora*. They are very common in the summer season around the British coasts. Each J. is a clear glassy bell, the clapper being represented by the *manubrium* or mouth of the animal. The smallest J. are the floating reproductive bodies of Zoophytes (q. v.), the true J. or *Medusidæ* corresponding to the 'Naked-eyed' Medusæ of the earlier zoologists.

Jemappes', a town of Belgium, in the province of Hainault, 2½ miles W. of Mons by rail, with extensive brewing and tanning industries, and large coal-mines in the neighbourhood. Pop. (1874) 11,274. It is famous as the scene of the victory of the French under Dumouriez and the Duc de Chartres (afterwards Louis-Philippe) over the Austrians, November 6, 1792. By this battle the whole of the Netherlands fell into the hands of the Republicans.

Je'na, a town of Germany, in the Grand-Duchy of Sachsen-Weimar-Eisenach, stands surrounded by hills at the confluence of the Saale and Leutra, on the eastern skirts of the Thüringer Wald, 9 miles S.E. of Apolda, and 23 N.W. of Rudolstadt by rail. Pop. (1872) 8197. Here Goethe composed his *Hermann und Dorothea* (1797), Schiller his *Wallenstein* (1799), and the houses of these and many other illustrious residents, are marked by tablets, erected in 1858, on occasion of the tercentenary of the university. Founded by Duke Johann Friedrich the Generous, February 2, 1558, as a home of the 'new learning,' the University of J. attained its zenith during the years 1787–1806, when it included among its professors men so distinguished as Hegel, Fichte, Voss, and the brothers Schlegel. It possesses a library, observatory, and botanical gardens, and in June 1876 had seventy-three professors and teachers, 440 students, half of whom were in philosophy, and a yearly revenue of £6000.—The *battle of J.* is a collective name often given to two separate engagements which took place on the same day, 14th October 1806—one at Auerstadt, 4½ miles N. of J., between 60,000 Saxons and Prussians under Duke Karl of Brunswick, who was mortally wounded, and 30,000 French under Davout; the other on the heights round J., between 70,000 Prussians under the Prince of Hohenlohe and the Graf von Tauenzien, and 90,000 French commanded by Napoleon in person. In both the Germans were totally defeated; and their defeat led to that utter subjugation and humiliation of the 'fatherland,' typified in the hare-hunt held two years later upon the battlefield of J. by the French and Russian emperors.

Jenn'er, Edward, M.D., the discoverer of vaccination, was born at Berkeley, Gloucester, 17th May 1749. After serving his apprenticeship to Mr. Ludlow, a surgeon at Cirencester, near Bristol, he removed to London, where he became a pupil of the celebrated anatomist John Hunter. Returning to Berkeley, he soon acquired an extensive practice, and in 1788 published his first scientific memoir *On the Natural History of the Cuckoo*, which appeared in the *Philosophical Transactions*. Meanwhile he had been studying the nature of cow-pox, and after a long series of careful experiments established the truth of the local tradition that one who had suffered from cow-pox was insusceptible to small-pox. He discovered what variety of cow-pox afforded the best protection, and in 1796 made the experiment which has resulted in such benefit to mankind. His two memoirs, *An Inquiry into the Causes and Effects of the Cow-Pox* (1798), and *Further Observations on the Variolæ Vaccinæ or Cow-Pox* (1799), roused general interest, and resulted in the wide-spread acceptance by medical men both at home and abroad of his theory and methods. Honours and rewards followed. He was elected an honorary member of nearly all the scientific societies, and received a grant of £20,000 from Parliament. He died at Berkeley, January 25, 1823. See Baron's *Life and Correspondence of J.* (Lond. 1827, 2 vols. 1838).

Jenner, Sir William, Bart., was born at Chatham in 1815, and was educated at University College, London. In 1844 he graduated as M.D., and four years later was appointed Professor of Pathological Anatomy in the University College. In 1852 he was elected Fellow of the Royal College of Physicians, and in 1862 was gazetted Physician in Ordinary to the Queen, and in the same year became Professor of the Principles and Practice of Medicine at the University College. In 1863 he was appointed Physician to the Prince of Wales, whom he attended during his severe illness in 1871–72. In recognition of his services then rendered he was made a K.C.B., having previously been created a baronet in 1868. He has written several papers of medical interest, and is widely known as the first who established that typhus fever and typhoid fever differed in kind.

Jer'boa (*Dipus*), a genus of Rodent mammalia, distinguished by very short fore-limbs, the hind-limbs on the other hand being very long, and the animal progressing by a series of leaps. The tail is long and heavy. The J. has two incisors, two pre-molars, and four molars in each jaw. The ears are short; the fore-feet have five toes, the hinder feet three. The common J. (*D. Ægyptus*) is found in N. Africa and Egypt. It attains the size of a large rat, and is of a light-brown hue above, the under parts being white. The long tail preserves the balance of the animal in leaping. The J. lives in burrows. Its flesh is esteemed palatable. The Gerbilles of Africa and India, and the Alactaga of Siberia, are nearly allied forms.

Jerboa.

Jeremi'ah (Heb. 'Jehovah casts') prophesied from the thirteenth year of Josiah, King of Judah (about B.C. 628; Jer. i. 2, *cf.* xxv. 3), down to the destruction of Jerusalem, and after, a period of about forty years. When Jerusalem was besieged by the Chaldean army, J. was imprisoned for predicting that the city would be captured and burned by the besiegers, and remained in confinement till the end of the siege (xxxiv.–xxxviii.). After the capture, he remained at first in Jerusalem, and afterwards at Mizpah with Gedaliah (xxxix.–xl. 6). After the murder of Gedaliah and his adherents he was carried off by the Jewish princes to Egypt, where he probably remained till his death. There is a tradition, however, that he was stoned to death by his countrymen, and another that he escaped with Baruch to Babylon, where he died in peace. On the return from Babylon, the prophecies of J. were collected as those of the second greatest of the prophets of Israel. In the Babylonian Talmud he is even reckoned the first. The fulfilment of his predictions of the restoration of the Jews caused him to be regarded as the guardian and patron-saint of the nation; and, as in the case of Moses and Elijah, a vague expectation prevailed that he would re-appear among them to prepare the way for the Messiah (*cf.* Matt. xvi. 14). The greatest difficulty connected with the writings of J. is the variation between the Hebrew text and the lxx., the latter of which differs considerably from the former in parts of the translation, as well as in the arrangement. The genuineness of the following passages has been called in question by some modern critics: x. 1–16, xxx., xxxi., xxxiii., and lii., and l. and li, are thought to contain many interpolations. The literary beauty of the prophecies is great. In soft tenderness of sentiment J. has no equal among his countrymen. Several of the most pathetic of the psalms have also been ascribed to him.

Jer'icho, anciently an important city of Canaan, in a plain cut through by the Jordan, from which it is distant westward about 6 miles. It was the first place stormed and destroyed by the Israelites after crossing the Jordan, was rebuilt by Hiel the Bethelite, in the reign of Ahab, about 918 B.C., and became famous for its prophetical 'school' (2 Kings ii. 4, *et seq.*). J. was a favourite residence of Herod the Great. It figures in the life of our Lord, who here restored sight to the blind (Matt. xx. 30; Mark x. 46; Luke xviii. 35) and accepted the hospitality of Zaccheus. The city was again destroyed by Vespasian, rebuilt under Hadrian, captured and recaptured during the Crusades, and has now dwindled to a wretched village (*Richa* or *Ericha*) of some 200 inhabitants.

Jerked Beef is a kind of dried beef largely prepared in S. America, Mexico, and Texas. In the River Plate countries J. B. is called *charqui* (whence probably comes the English name), and in N. America it is called *tasajo*. Some years ago Uruguay exported enormous quantities to Great Britain, but it did not gain favour. *Tasajo* is largely consumed by the negroes in the W. Indies.

Jerome, Saint, is the Anglicised name by which we know **Sophronius Eusebius Hieronymus,** one of the most copious authors of the ancient Latin Church, and the most learned father of his time. Born in 341 or 342, at Stridon, in Dalmatia, he was carefully educated by his wealthy parents, and at Rome he nurtured that love for the classics of Greece and Italy which he afterwards regarded as a dangerous temptation. He soon felt a leaning to Christianity, and after travels in the Rhineland and in Gaul, was baptized at Rome in 360. In 373 he settled at Antioch in Syria, and next year began a four years' course of ascetic self-mortification and exegetical study as a hermit in a wilderness. Ordained presbyter in Antioch, he passed, after a sojourn in Constantinople and Alexandria, to Rome, where he was received with great favour by his friend the Bishop Damasus, but created many enemies by the success with which he converted sons and daughters of noble Roman houses to asceticism and celibacy. In 386 he founded, by help of one of his wealthy converts, a monastery at Bethlehem, where he lived and laboured, with one brief interruption, till his death in 418 or 419. J. opened to the Westerns the treasures of Oriental learning; his zeal and labour were indefatigable, but his character is tarnished by vanity, jealousy, and passionate intolerance. Unworthy anxiety to preserve the good fame of orthodoxy led him to assail Origen, whose enthusiastic and deeply indebted pupil he once had been, and repeatedly to suppress his own real opinions. But he laid a deep debt of gratitude on the Church, especially by his exegetical labours, and by that new Latin version of the Bible still used by the Western Church, the Vulgate. The best edition of J.'s works, comprising letters, commentaries, and treatises in theology, is by Vallarsi (Verona, 1734, 11 vols.); see Zöckler's *Hieronymus* (Gotha, 1865).

Jerome of Prag was born at Prag in Bohemia in the second half of the 14th c., studied at Paris, Köln, Oxford, and Heidelberg, took the degree of Bachelor of Theology in 1399, and soon became famous by his eloquence and learning. He threw himself passionately into the reform movement begun by his friend Hus (q. v.). When the latter was on his trial at Constance, J. hastened to defend him, but was himself arrested at Hirschau, in April 1415, and after a long imprisonment, during which he recanted his heresies and then recanted his recantation, he was burnt, 30th May 1416. See the Biographies of Heller (Tüb. 1835) and Becker (Nordling. 1858).

Jerr'old, Douglas, an English dramatist and man of letters, the son of a theatrical manager, was born in London, January 3, 1803. He was sent to sea in 1813, but left after two years to enter a printer's office. The compositor soon blossomed into an author. *Black Eyed Susan*, his first great success (1829), ran for 300 nights at the Surrey. *The Rent Day*, *Time works Wonders*, and *Bubbles of a Day*, are among the best of his plays. After 1840 he was chiefly a journalist, contributing to *Punch*, *Blackwood*, the *Athenæum*, &c. In *Punch* appeared *The Caudle Lectures*, *The Story of a Feather*, *Punch's Letters to his Son*, *Punch's Complete Letter Writer*, &c. *Lloyd's Newspaper* was started under his editorship in 1852. He died June 8, 1857. His writings sparkle with epigram and bristle with caustic wit and pungent satire. But his fierceness against abuses was the outburst of a feeling heart. As Leigh Hunt said, 'If he had the sting of a bee he had also its honey.' His *Life and Remains* were published in 1858 by his son, **William Blanchard J.,** who was born in 1826, succeeded his father as editor of *Lloyd's*, and has published many works—*Imperial Paris* (1855), *London*, illustrated by Doré (1872), *Life of Napoleon III.* (1874–75), &c.

Jer'sey, the largest and most productive of the Channel Islands (q. v.), lies about 15 miles W. of the coast of Cotentin in France, and the same distance S.E. of the Island of Guernsey. Area 28,717 statute acres; pop. (1871) 56,627. It is 10 miles long from E. to W., and 6 broad from N. to S., is high and rocky in the N., and slopes to the S. and E., where the coast is low, shelving, and broken by many bays and coves. The interior is well-wooded, and is watered by several small streams. On the S. coast is the bay of St. Aubin, on which lie the principal town of St. Helier (q. v.), and the quaint little town of St. Aubin, with its miniature castle. The only other considerable town is St. Martin, on the E. coast. J. has a singularly mild climate, the mean temperature being 52° F. Snow seldom falls, and continued frosts are rare. The myrtle, vine, peach, apricot, and plum grow in the open air. Although the holdings seldom exceed 15 acres, agriculture is in a forward state. The crops are wheat, barley, hay, turnips, potatoes, mangel-wurzel, parsnips, and carrots. Much fruit is also exported, including the famous Chaumontel pears, and the fisheries are very valuable. There is total exemption from import duties, and the exports to England are only subject to the same duties as are paid on the produce within Great Britain. J., like other Channel Islands, is governed by its own laws. The States of J. consist of the lieutenant-governor and the bailiff of the royal court, appointed by the crown; twelve jurats, elected for life by the ratepayers; twelve constables, rectors of the twelve parishes; and fourteen deputies. The bailiff and twelve jurats constitute the Court of Judicature; from their decisions an appeal lies to the Queen in council. The inhabitants speak a corrupt French dialect, but English is understood generally. French is the language of the law courts, and of the church service. The chief educational institution is the Victoria College, which has exhibitions to Oxford and Cambridge. J. is the *Cæsarea* ('Cæsar's isle') of the Romans. It has belonged to the English crown since the Norman conquest, and was unsuccessfully attacked by the French in the reign of Edward III., and during the Wars of the Roses. J. was the temporary refuge of Henry VII. while Earl of Richmond, and at a later period of Charles II. The French captured the town of St. Helier in 1781, but were forced to surrender by Major Pierson. The grand old castle of Mont Orgueil, at Gorey Harbour, was the prison of Prynne and the Parliamentarians. See the Rev. P. Falle, *History of J.*, and the interesting historical publications of the *Société Jerviaise*, founded in 1873.

Jersey City, the capital of Hudson county, New Jersey, U.S., on the W. bank of the Hudson river, opposite the S. part of New York city, of which it is really a suburb, and with which it is connected by five ferries. It is the terminus of six railways of the Morris Canal from Eastern Pennsylvania, and of the Cunard steamship line; it has considerable foreign commerce, but as it is included in the customs district of New York, no separate returns are obtainable. J. has over sixty churches, forty-four schools, five newspapers (two German), and large manufactories of glass, iron, steel, zinc, tin, copper, boilers, machinery, locomotives, soap, candles, watches, &c. An extensive abattoir, for the daily supply of the New York market, was opened in 1874. J. C. has arisen very rapidly. There was no settlement on Paulus Hook, as the locality was called, at the beginning of the present century. The city had only a pop. of 6856 in 1820, but was increased by the annexation of Van Vorst township in 1851, of Hudson and Bergen cities in 1870, and of Grenville village in 1872. Pop. in 1860, 29,227; in 1870, 82,546.

Jeru'salem (Heb. 'inheritance, or foundation of peace') appears first in the Bible under the name of *Jebus* or *Jebusi* (Josh. xv. 8; xviii. 16, 28; Jude xix. 10, 11), which is described as situated on the boundary between the territories of the tribes of Judah and Benjamin. As has been remarked, the most striking peculiarity in the annals of J. is the number and severity of the sieges it has undergone. The men of Judah took it about B.C. 1400 (Judges i. 8), but the citadel was not taken from the Jebusites till the time of David, who captured it, and made J. his capital, surrounding the whole city with a wall. In the reign of Rehoboam, J. was taken without resistance (about B.C. 970) by Shishak, King of Egypt, who plundered the Temple and palace built by Solomon (1 Kings xiv. 25; 2 Chron. xii. 2–9), in that of Jehoram, by the Philistines and Arabians (2 Chron. xxi. 16, 17), and in that of Amaziah, by Joash, King of Israel, who broke down 400 cubits of the N. wall. It was besieged in the reign of Ahaz by the united armies of Israel and Syria, but seems to have escaped being plundered at this time (2 Kings xvi. 5). In the fourteenth year of the reign of Hezekiah (about B.C. 711), a Chaldean army advanced against J., from which it would seem to have been twice in danger, but escaped the first time by Hezekiah paying a large tribute, and the second time by the death in one night of 185,000 of the Chaldeans (2 Kings xviii., xix.; 2 Chron. xxxii.; Isa. xxxvi.). According to the Chronicler J. must have been taken by Nebuchadnezzar in the reign of Jehoiakin, when the king and the vessels of the house of the Lord were carried away to Babylon (2 Chron. xxxvi. 5–7). It was so at any rate under Jehoiakin when the Temple and palace were plundered, and 10,000 of the Jews carried off to Babylon. It was finally taken in the reign of Zedekiah by Nebuchadnezzar (B.C. 588), when the walls were levelled with the ground, the temple, palace, and other more important buildings burnt, and the bulk of the remaining inhabitants carried off to Babylon (2 Kings xxv.; 2 Chron. xxxvi.; Jer. lii.). In the second year after the return from Babylon (B.C. 534) the foundation of the Temple was laid; it was finished in the sixth year of Darius (B.C. 516: Ezra iii. 8; Esdras vii. 5). The rebuilding of the walls was not attempted till the arrival of Nehemiah (B.C. 445), by whose exertions it was accomplished in fifty-two days (Neh. ii.–vi.). There is a story, whether authentic or not, that J. was visited by Alexander the Great, after the capture of Tyre (B.C. 331). It was taken (about B.C. 320) by Ptolemy Soter, and remained in the hands of the Ptolemies till finally taken by Antiochus the Great (B.C. 198). Besieged and pillaged by Antiochus Epiphanes (B.C. 170), besieged for a short time by Aretas (B.C. 65), it was taken by Pompey (B.C. 63), when 12,000 of the inhabitants were slain, and the walls razed to the ground, and besieged and taken by Herod (B.C. 37). The greatest siege of all was by the Romans under Vespasian and Titus (A.D. 70); when taken, the city was totally destroyed, and the nation dispersed. After the capture of the city by Severus (A.D. 135), Hadrian literally razed to the ground the ruins left by Titus, and built a heathen city, which he called Ælia Capitolina. The old name was not revived till Constantine built the *Martyrion* (335) on the spot where the Crucifixion of Christ took place. The city was now undisturbed by war till it was besieged by the forces of Chosroes, King of Persia (614). Falling into the hands of the Romans again on the defeat of Chosroes by Heraclius (628), it was taken by the Mohammedans in 637, who held it with various vicissitudes till it was finally taken by the Turks in 1076. Taken by the first Crusaders (see CRUSADES) in 1099, it was retaken by Saladin in 1187. Falling into the hands of the Turks, along with Syria and Egypt, in 1517, it has belonged to the Ottoman Empire ever since, the only change being that from 1832 to 1841 it was subject to the Pasha of Egypt. Pop. of the modern J. from 15,000 to 30,000.

Topography.—J. stands on the southern extremity of a plateau bounded by the two ravines of Kedron on the E. and Hinnom on the S. and W. A third ravine, the Tyropœon, beginning at the junction of the Kedron and Hinnom, and rising up to the level of the plateau on the N.W., divides the city into two unequal halves. On the eastern spur, Mount Moriah, stood the temples of Solomon, Zerubbabel, and Herod; on the western, which is 120 feet higher, was 'the upper city' of Josephus. This western 'hill' is that which has always been known as Mount Zion, at least since the time of Constantine; but it has been maintained that in Old Testament times Zion was the eastern 'hill.' In course of time three different walls were built for the defence of J. The first was built by David to enclose the original city around the citadel he had taken from the Jebusites (2 Sam. v., *cf.* Josephus), and strengthened and extended by Solomon, doubtless so as to connect the buildings on Moriah with the rest of the city. The second was built round a part of the N. side by Hezekiah, in preparation for the attack of the Chaldeans (2 Chr. xxxii. 5). The third was built beyond the last, round the whole of the N. side, by Herod Agrippa, A.D. 45. The two most difficult points to determine in the topography of the city are, the site of the Temple, and that of the Sepulchre of Christ. (1). The Temple.—On Mount Moriah there is a large open space called *Haram es-sherif* ('Noble Sanctuary'), measuring about 1500 feet (from N. to S.) by 900 feet. In the centre is a raised platform on which stands the Mosque *Kubbet es-sakhra* ('Dome of the Rock'). Somewhere within this sanctuary the temple of the Jews must have stood; but the exact position of its site has been long a subject of the keenest controversy among travellers, two theories having been chiefly favoured: the one, that the temple area occupied the whole of the sanctuary; the other, that it was confined to a space of about 600 feet square in the S.W. corner. New light has been thrown on the subject by the excavations of Captain Warren, who has discovered that the N.E., S.E., and S.W. corners of the sanctuary are made up, from a great depth, of *debris*, and that the ridge of Moriah descends very steeply on these three sides, so that under the N.E. corner the rock is 162 feet below the present level, under the S.W. corner 150 feet, and under the S.E. corner 163 feet. As this *debris* is plainly an accumulation from the sundry demolitions of the buildings on Moriah, there can have been little or none of it in the time of Solomon, hence in all probability his temple was built on the ridge of Moriah. As the result of his labours Captain Warren concludes that its site would be a rectangle about 900 feet from E. to W. by 600 feet, at a distance of 300 feet from the S. wall of the sanctuary; and that Solomon's palace had occupied a position under the S.E. corner. The same authority considers that, to meet all the requirements of the descriptions, Herod's temple must have occupied the whole southern side of the sanctuary, covering an area of about 900 feet square. (2). The Holy Sepulchre.—There is a church in modern J. called the Church of the Holy Sepulchre, situated in the N.W. quarter of the city. The question whether this church actually marks the site of the sepulchre of Christ, or is in the same place as the one built by Constantine (335), supposing that he was correct with his site, depends so far on whether or not the spot was outside the walls of the city at the time of the crucifixion, as is required by the gospel narrative. It is certainly well within the modern wall, but those who contend for the authenticity of the site maintain that the city spread out and surrounded it after the time of Constantine. See Robinson's *Biblical Researches* (3d ed. Lond. 1871); Stanley's *Sinai and Palestine* (new ed. Lond. 1867); Warren's *Recovery of Jerusalem* (1871).

Jeru'salem Ar'tichoke, a plant of the same natural order as the common sunflower, grows 6 or 8 feet high, has large rough leaves and yellow flowers. The roots are creeping, and produce in autumn, like the potato, several round yellowish or reddish tubers which are used as food. The leaves are given to cattle. The name Jerusalem is a corruption of the Italian *Girasole*, 'sunflower,' and artichoke implies a resemblance in flavour to the common Artichoke (q. v.).

Jer'vis, John, Earl of St. Vincent, an English admiral, was born at Meaford Hall, Staffordshire, January 9, 1734. He entered the navy in his tenth year, and was made lieutenant in 1755, and captain in 1759. In 1782 he captured a French frigate, and received the order of the Bath. He was appointed Rear-Admiral of the Blue in 1787, and of the White in 1790. In 1793 he was naval commander of the expedition which took Martinique and reduced Guadaloupe. His greatest achievement was the defeat of the Spanish fleet of twenty-seven great ships, off Cape St. Vincent, on February 14, 1797, his fleet numbering only fifteen. It procured him an earldom and a pension of £3000. J. was First Lord of the Admiralty, 1801–1804. In 1821 he was appointed Admiral of the Fleet. He died March 13, 1823, and was buried at St. Paul's, where a monument is erected to his memory.

Je'si (the ancient *Æsis*), a town in the province of Ancona, Italy, 17 miles S.W. of the town of Ancona, with important manufactures of paper, silk, linen, and woollen hosiery, and trade in wine and olives. J. was the birthplace of the Romano-German Emperor, Friedrich II., and of Spontini, the composer. Pop. (1871) 13,472.

Jess'amine. See JASMINE.

Jess'ant, issuing from the middle of a Fesse (q. v.). A leopard's head *jessant de lis* has a *fleur-de-lis* passing through it.

Jess'o. See YESSO.

Jessore' (*Yashohara* = depriving others of fame), the chief town of the district of the same name, in Bengal, British India, on the Bhyrab river, 77 miles N.E. of Calcutta; pop. (1872) 8152. It has little trade, but a good school and a church. In the neighbourhood is the residence of the Rajah of J., an old Hindu family.—The *district* of J., which occupies the centre of the Gangetic delta, and is bounded and permeated by numerous offshoots of the great river, has an area of 3658 sq. miles; pop. (1872) 2,075,021. This tract has only recently been formed by alluvion, and merges imperceptibly into the Sunderbunds proper. The crops are rice, pulses, indigo, and the date and cocoanut palm. The exports are considerable, and also the manufacture of date sugar. In one town 5000 tons of this sugar are made annually, some of which is sent to England. From the Sunderbunds are despatched large quantities of firewood, and round by the same route comes the surplus produce of E. Bengal. The centres of trade are Keshubpur, Kotchandpur, and Khulna (Mr. Westland's *Report on J.*, Calcutta, 2d ed. 1875).

Jes'ter. See COURT FOOL.

Jes'uits. The Society of Jesus, founded in 1540, was one of the chief instrumentalities by which the Church of Rome recovered so rapidly from the shock of the Reformation, and regained so much of her influence in the world. As has been remarked, Ignatius Loyola (q. v.), the founder of the order, bore the same part in the Catholic reaction which Luther bore in the great Protestant movement. The nucleus of the society was formed at Paris by Loyola himself and two young men—Faber, a Savoyard, and Xavier, of Pampeluna—who shared his rooms in the College of St. Barbara. These three, three other Spaniards—Salmeron, Lainez, and Bobadilla—and a Portuguese, Rodriguez, took the vow of chastity, and 'to proceed to Jerusalem, after finishing their studies, there to live in poverty, and dedicate their days to the conversion of the Saracens, or if that were found to be impracticable, next to offer their services to the Pope, agreeing to go whithersoever he might assign them their labours, without condition and without reward.' In 1537 they were in Venice, with three other companions, prepared to set out on their pilgrimage; but this was delayed owing to the war between the Venetians and the Turks, and the project was never carried out. Meantime Loyola became acquainted in Venice with the constitution of the Theatines (q. v.), by which he was deeply impressed, and the conviction was formed in his mind that to turn their labours to the best advantage he and his companions must become regular priests. Accordingly they all entered priests' orders, and devoted themselves to preaching, assuming now the name of the 'Company of Jesus,' from the idea that they were a company of soldiers under the command of Christ, and fighting against his enemies, according to the old military associations of Loyola, who besides did not wish that the company should be called by his own name. After preaching for a time at Vicenza, they repaired to Rome, where, although they were regarded at first with suspicion, and met with considerable opposition, their mode of life and zeal in preaching, teaching the young and tending the sick, soon gained them so many adherents and friends, that they were in a position to formally organise the society, and apply to the Pope for his sanction to its institution. This sanction was readily granted, first with certain restrictions in 1540, and then absolutely and unconditionally in 1543. They deserved the special attention and patronage of the pontiff, for at a time of defection and opposition, they had sprung up a body of enthusiastic and zealous men entirely devoted to his service. To the vows of chastity and poverty they had taken at Paris, and the general vow of obedience to the order, they added a fourth and special vow 'to perform whatsoever the reigning pontiff should command them; to go forth into all lands, amongst Turks, heathens, or heretics, wherever he might please to send them, without hesitation or delay, as without question, condition, or reward.' The arrangements of the society were complete when Loyola was unanimously elected by the six oldest members the president or general, who 'should dispense offices and grades at his own pleasure, should form the rules of their constitution, with the advice and aid of the members, but should alone have the power of commanding in every instance, and should be honoured by all as though Christ himself were present in his person.'

The great aim of the constitution of the order was to release its members from all external obligations, so as to absorb their whole being in the society, and to inspire each individual with a new principle of life and action, with this peculiarity, however, that the full development of all the faculties of each was desired. The new principle of life and motive to action was obedience: obedience absolute and unconditional, without a thought or question as to its object or consequences. Every member of the society had to resign himself, in total and blind submission to the will of his superiors, to be led 'like a thing without life, as the staff, for example, that the superior holds in his hand, to be turned to any purpose seeming good to him.' The love of kindred was denounced as a carnal inclination; all property had to be given up unreservedly for the benefit of the poor, and the members were not permitted to aspire to any higher rank, or to accept ecclesiastical dignities, for these 'might have involved the fulfilment of duties, or the forming of relations, over which the society could no longer exercise control.' As at first constituted, when it was complete, the society was composed of four grades of members: novices, scholars, coadjutors, and professed members. (1) In the general was vested for life the power of wielding the unquestioning obedience of the whole order. Being responsible to no one for the use made of it, he exercised a kind of Papal authority on a small scale. (2) The *professed* were those who have passed through all the preparatory stages, and have taken the four vows of the order. From them alone the general and higher officials could be chosen, such as superiors of provinces, colleges, and houses, who were all named by the general, and held office for three years. (3) But as the professed were all bound by their fourth and special vow to perpetual travels in the service of the Pope, the *coadjutors* were instituted; the *spiritual* to fill certain posts which required constant residence, such as the superintendence of colleges and provinces; the *secular*, or lay brothers, to take care of the alms which constituted the living of the professed in their houses, and of the revenues which the colleges were permitted to have. Both were bound only by the three vows of poverty, chastity, and obedience to the order, and that only as simple vows which in certain cases could be cancelled. (4) The *scholars*, or *scholastics*, were those engaged in the prescribed course of study or in teaching in the schools of the order. (5) The *novices* were those engaged in a two-years' course of religious exercises and ascetic practices preparatory to becoming scholastics.

The rapidity with which the order increased in numbers, and the extraordinary influence which it acquired among all classes of society, were due to several peculiarities. First, by the arrangements of the system for cutting off the members from all external obligations and relations, and for merging all individuality in a life of mutual supervision and subordination, a compact and perfect unity was formed. Secondly, by casting off the more ascetic and cumbrous forms of monastic devotion, excess in religious exercises was avoided, with the consequent deterioration of physical and mental energy, and the highest culture of the faculties of each was as far as possible attained. Thus also they were left with more leisure and energy for performing what was regarded as their real work, namely, tending the sick, preaching, acting as confessors, and teaching. In education they followed a carefully-considered system, dividing the schools into classes, and pursuing in these a method strictly uniform. From paying great attention to the moral training they were favoured by the civil power, and, what helped greatly to fill their schools, all their instruction was gratuitous. Whenever one of their colleges was founded in a place no private person needed to incur any further expense in the education of his children. Then the best talent among the pupils was, if possible, appropriated for the order, and in this way an incalculable amount of influence was acquired wherever they had schools established. But, perhaps, the most direct and immediate source of their influence was the confessional. As confessors they have been described as the the most rigid and as the most indulgent of spiritual directors. Doubtless they were both the one and the other. In this, as in their whole system, the secret of their success lay in the knowledge of human nature they displayed, and the confessors could be strict or lax as best suited the temper of the penitent. Such is a sketch of the constitution of the society as first completely developed; a history of the J. would virtually be a history of the Roman Catholic Church (q. v.) since the Reformation. In the 17th c. great changes were introduced. The most important was that the 'professed' members had become advanced to the possession of power. (1) They took part, *e.g.*, in the management of the revenues of the colleges, and became rectors and provincials, offices which used to belong to the coadjutors alone. (2) By introducing the practice of associating a *vicar* with their general, they were able to depose their chief without any alleged offence on his part; thus subverting the fundamental principle of their system, obedience. (3) By siding with the house of Bourbon in their conflicts with Rome, they went against their supreme principle of obedience to the Pope. (4) Another principle really essential to the original constitution—that all worldly connections should be set aside—was also overturned, for now each wealthy member, when making a transfer of his property to the society, did so with the clear understanding that this was in favour of the particular college to which he had attached himself, and even frequently in such a way that he retained the management of it in his own hands. (5) They even devoted themselves to the acquisition of wealth by commerce. In short, the purpose of the society was not now what it had been, to subjugate the world and imbue it with the spirit of religion. On the contrary, their own spirit had been corrupted by the world, and all their aim and labour now was to aggrandise themselves. To maintain the influence which was now gradually slipping from their grasp, they not only modified and perverted the rules of the society, as described above, but even the doctrines of religion and the precepts of morality. In the 18th c. they were still powerful, being still the confessors of princes and nobles, and holding in their hands the education of the young; but they were in ever-increasing conflict with the new tendencies of the age. Their presence at the courts of Europe was becoming intolerable. Under various pretexts they were banished from Portugal in 1759, suppressed in France 1764, in Spain 1767, and afterwards in Naples, Parma, and Modena, and such was the pressure brought to bear by these courts upon Rome that in 1773 Pope Clement XIV. issued a bull, 'Impelled by the duty of restoring concord to the Church, convinced that the Society of Jesus can no longer effect those purposes for which it was founded, and moved by other reasons, we do extirpate and abolish the Society of Jesus.' The order, however, was not completely crushed by this suppression, but began to raise its head again at the beginning of the century, was re-established by Pope Pius VII. in 1814, and has been a powerful agent in all the subsequent policy of the Papacy. See Wolf's *Allgem. Gesch. der Jesuiten* (2d August 1803); Poynder's *Hist. of the J.* (Lond. 1816); Ranke's *Hist. of the Popes* (Eng. trans. Lond. 1850); Cartwright's *The Jesuits* (Lond. 1876).

Jesuits' Bark. See CINCHONA.

Je'sus, the Greek form of the Hebrew Joshua or Jeshua, a contraction of Jehoshua, 'help of Jehovah,' or 'Saviour,' was the name given to the founder of Christianity before his birth (Matt. i. 21). J., the son of a virgin, was born at Bethlehem (Luke ii. 4-6), according to the received chronology, in the year A.U.C. 754, but as he was born in the lifetime of Herod the Great (Matt. ii. 1), who is known to have died in the year A.U.C. 750, his birth was probably in the year B.C. 4. His crucifixion is generally placed in the year A.D. 33; if then the date of his birth given above be correct, he would have been in the thirty-seventh year of his age at the time. Almost the only source of information regarding the life of Christ is the New Testament, and especially the four Gospels. But there has been much discussion in modern times as to how far the Gospels are to be regarded as records of actual history, the fourth especially meeting with much hostile criticism. Various explanations of their existence in their present form have been given by modern biblical critics, and various pictures of J. have been drawn, according to the idea of the writers of what he must have been. Thus Strauss, in his *Leben Jesu*, undertook to show that not merely in the accounts of the infancy, but in most of the important supernatural events of the life of J., the only really plausible explanation is the mythical, that is, that mere opinions, or 'the wholly gratuitous fabrications of the imagination' had gradually come to be believed, and were put down as facts. Renan, in his *Vie de J.*, although accepting much more of the historical materials at his command as genuine, still produced a picture greatly modified from that ordinarily received, laying great stress on two points especially, namely, the gradual alteration which time and circumstances produced in the conceptions and language of J., and 'the manner in which miracles grew up, as it were, around the steps of every great prophet and reformer in the East.' We have two striking English pictures of Christ, one by the author of *Ecce Homo*, and another by Mr. Arnold in his *Literature and Dogma*; and the number will be increased indefinitely so long as each writer makes his own modification of the gospel history. The controversy regarding the authenticity and genuineness of the evangelical narrative is necessarily one of the profoundest interest and importance. Everything hangs upon it, and it is certain that all thoughtful believers—not merely erudite or eloquent theologians—will sooner or later have to weigh the evidence as it has never been weighed before. If the Gospels stand the test of impartial criticism, then the historical J. is not the myth of Strauss, but that Divine Redeemer in whom Christendom has trusted for 1800 years.

Jesus College, Cambridge, founded in 1496 by John Alcock, Bishop of Ely, and endowed with the possessions of the nunnery of St. Rhadegund, consists of a master (appointed by the Bishop of Ely) and of sixteen fellows, six of whom must be in orders. It has fifteen foundation scholarships of from £20 to £50; seventeen of from £40 to £50, founded by Tobias Rustat, for the sons of deceased, or in default of such, of living clergymen; seven close, and two open, scholarships. The college holds the presentation to sixteen livings. In the chapel, a cruciform structure, recently restored, is some fine painted glass. Cranmer, Flamstead, Hartley, Sterne, and Coleridge were students of J. C. In 1875 the number of undergraduates was 144.

Jesus College, Oxford, founded by Dr. Hugh Ap-Rhys in 1571, consists of a principal, thirteen fellows (seven of whom must be natives of Wales or Monmouthshire), and twenty-two scholars. It has also thirty exhibitions of £40 a year, and the presentation to twenty livings. In 1876 the college had thirty-six commoners and eleven members of Congregation. By 17 and 18 Vict. c. 81, one fellowship, founded by Charles I., was to be applied, on its next avoidance, to the maintenance of scholars from the Channel Islands, another to the purposes of the professoriate of the university, and four others to augment the number and value of the open scholarships. A Celtic chair was founded in 1876 by the principal and fellows of J. C., and by them endowed with £500 a year, the stipend being made up by £600 out of the university chest.

Jesus, Son of Sirach. See ECCLESIASTICUS.

Jet (Fr. *jais*, Old Fr. *jayet*, badly formed from the Lat. *gagātes*, see below), a lustrous mineral of a velvety-black colour, resembling glance-coal, found in thin scattered beds in the upper lias shale in Yorkshire, and in marly strata in Spain, France, and Saxony. Authorities are not agreed upon its origin. Some believe that it is bituminised wood or a variety of lignite; others that it is an indurated petroleum. It takes a good polish, and is easily carved. The production of personal ornaments in J. is the staple industry of Whitby, one-third of the population of that town being directly supported by it. In 1863 the industry realised £55,000, and in 1873 upwards of £90,000. J., the *gagates* of the ancients, derived its name from the river Gagas, in Lycia, Asia Minor, where it was first discovered. It was formed into bracelets by the ancient Britons, and J. remains are common in Europe wherever the Romans have dwelt.

Jet'sam (Fr. *jeter*, 'to throw'), a legal term used to denote goods thrown into the sea. Till claimed by the owner such goods are the property of the Crown. See FLOTSAM and JETTISON.

Jett'ison is the legal term denoting the justifiable throwing overboard of a ship's cargo or of part of it. Occasion for J. occurs chiefly during a storm, or to prevent capture. The necessity for the measure must be determined by the master and a majority of the mariners. The owners of the ship and of the cargo saved are liable to the owners of the goods thrown out. See AVERAGE.

Jev'ons, William Stanley, an English political economist, was born at Liverpool in 1835, and educated at University College, London, where he graduated in 1862. In 1866 he was appointed Professor of Logic, Mental and Moral Philosophy, and Cobden Lecturer in Political Economy, in Owen's College, Manchester, and in 1875 received the honorary degree of LL.D. from Edinburgh University. He has written several pamphlets bearing upon questions of political economy, but is best known by his *Elementary Lessons in Logic* (1870), and *Principles of Science* (1874).

Jew, Wandering, is the subject of a legend which represents a Jew called Ahasuerus as compelled to undertake an eternal and unresting journey through the world, because he drove Christ from his door when he wished to rest from the toil of carrying his cross. The fiction has appeared in different shapes throughout various literatures. *Le Juif Errant* (1844-45), of Eugene Sue, a tale levelled at the Jesuits, is the most important outcome of the tradition in modern times. For the literature of the subject see Grässe, *Die Sage vom Ewigen Juden*.

Jewel (Fr. *joyau;* Old Fr. *jouel*, from the Lat. *gaudium*, 'a joy or delight'), is an article of personal ornament made of precious metals, as gold or silver, of any of the precious stones, or of these in combination.

Jew'el, John, an English Protestant divine, born 24th May 1522, at Berrynarbor, Devonshire, entered Merton College, Oxford, at the early age of thirteen, but migrated to Corpus, whence he took his B.A. degree in 1540, and became a tutor of that college. On the accession of Edward VI. J. openly professed the Reformed faith, which he had previously practised in secret, and he acted as secretary to Peter Martyr on occasion of a public discussion at Oxford between the latter and certain Catholic divines. In 1551 he took his B.D., and at the same time obtained the living of Sunningwell, Berks, only to lose it in 1553 on the restoration of Catholicism by Mary. A temporary recantation was followed by flight, and for four years J. lived in exile at Frankfurt and Strassburg, at the latter place acting as vice-master of a college founded by his old friend Peter Martyr. Returning home at Mary's death, he was made Bishop of Salisbury by Elizabeth in 1559, and in that position signalised himself by his animosity to the old religion, and specially by a challenge, issued in a sermon preached at Paul's Cross, to produce a single writer of the first six Christian centuries who held the tenets of the Roman Church. This led to a controversy between the Jesuit Harding and himself, in the course of which he published his *Apologia Ecclesiæ Anglicanæ* (Lond. 1562), which has been translated into six different languages. J. died at Monkton Farleigh, Wilts, 21st September 1571. His *Works* have been edited by Dr. R. Jelf (8 vols. Oxf. Clar. Press. 1847).

Jew'ellery consists of manufactured articles in precious metals, stones, and other valuable materials used for purposes of personal decoration. The material in which the jeweller works and the subdivisions of his trade are very numerous. Gold and silver, diamonds, emeralds, rubies, garnets, amethysts, pearls, coral, topazes, cairngorms, and agates, are among the principal materials used for J., and these mostly are dealt with in different ways by special artizans. The ornamental effect of the various stones is developed or heightened by cutting and setting in a particular manner, and the metals are enriched by chasing, engraving, inlaying, and enamelling. The J. of special countries and periods is very distinct in its character, and is found to be dependent for its peculiarities on the artistic development of the races fabricating it, and also on the nature of the materials at the disposal of the makers. Birmingham is at the present day the great emporium of the cheap J. trade. The manufacture of imitation J. in electro-gilt metal with imitation precious stones of 'straw' or 'paste' is known as the gilt toy trade (see GILT TOYS). A higher class of Birmingham manufacture consists of plated J. in which a thin plate of gold covers the copper or other base metal of which the body of the work is composed. J. is also made in Birmingham from a compound called 'common gold,' and which consists of only 7 parts of gold to 17 of alloy, while '9 carat gold' having 15 parts of alloy is a compound having the sanction of a hall mark, and which is more extensively employed than any other quality of gold. Scotch J., in which silver, agates, and cairngorms are the leading materials, is also an important feature in the Birmingham trade. The manufacturers of Clerkenwell in London compete with the Birmingham traders in the better class of trade J. Details regarding the J. manufacture will be found in Gee's *Practical Gold Worker* (Lond. Crosby, Lockwood & Co. 1877.)

Jewish Sects. Several lists of J. S. are given by Christian fathers. Epiphanius (*Hæreses*) enumerates seven: the Pharisees, Sadducees, Ossenes (Essenes), Hemerobaptists, Scribes, Nazaræans, Herodians. Hegesippus (Eusebius, *H. E.*) gives the same list, except the last three, for which he substitutes the Galilæans, Masbothæans, and Samaritans. Justin Martyr mentions (*Dial. c. Triph.*) six: the Sadducees, Genistæ, Meristæ, Galilæans, Hellenians, and Pharisee-Baptists. Of these some were not properly sects in the ordinary sense at all; they could only be described as parties in the nation following certain religious or political tendencies. The last period of the existence of the Jewish nation was materially affected by the rise of a most bitter party spirit, which actually contributed greatly to the dissolution of the nation. The peculiar phase of Israelitish patriotism had always been that they were 'a people dwelling alone' (Num. xxiii. 9). The ultra-development of this idea had been exhibited in the time of Judas Maccabæus by the *Chasidim* (q. v.). This party becoming dissolved, there remained a puritan party known as the *Essenes* (q. v.), and a moderate party represented by the *Pharisees* (q. v.). The Pharisees, so far from having been a sect, were simply the people, in contradistinction to 'the leaven of Herod,' the aristocratic, free-thinking *Sadducees* (q. v.). Regarding the *Herodian* party mentioned by the Evangelists (Matt. xxii. 16; Mark iii. 6, xii. 13) there is little information to be had. They seem at least to have belonged to the Sadducees, if indeed the two names be not synonymous (Matt. xvi. 6; *cf.* Mark viii. 15). It has been supposed that they were the Galilean party who were eager to get the honour of royalty for Herod Antipas. The *Galilæans* were the followers of Judas of Gamala, who, when Archelaus was banished (A.D. 6), Judæa incorporated into Syria, and the Roman census introduced (*cf.* Acts v. 37), called the Jews to arms in defence of their liberties. The *Zealots*, who were so prominent during the years 66 to 70, were the same party. Holding it to be unlawful to submit to or pray for a foreign prince, they desired to be zealous for the honour and service of the God of Israel, like Phinehas the grandson of Aaron (Num. xxv.), and Mattathias at Modin (1 Macc. ii. 23). The *Hemero-Baptists* in the above list of Epiphanius, probably the same as the Pharisee-Baptists of Justin's list, were so called from their daily ablutions, and were evidently akin to the Essenes. The *Nazaræans* (Heb. *nezer*, 'a branch') of Epiphanius' list, perhaps the same as the *Genistæ* (properly *genitæ*, from Gr. *genos*, 'stock') and *Meristæ* of Justin's list, professed to be primitive Jews of the true stock. Justin's *Hellenians* were probably the Herodians. The *Masbothæans* were an obscure sect of free-thinkers who denied the providence of God and the immortality of the soul! not Sabbatarians as they are erroneously represented by some writers to be. The *Gorthæans* are described by Eusebius as a sect founded by Gorthæus, a follower of Simon Magus. See KARAITES, SABBATHAIS ZEDI.

Jews (Heb. *Jehudim* 'Judæans') was the name originally applied to the inhabitants of the kingdom of Judah, after the revolt of the ten tribes under Jeroboam (*cf.* 2 Kings xvi. 6). After the Captivity, as the majority of those who returned to Palestine belonged to the old kingdom of Judah, the name was applied to the whole nation, and even extended to those scattered abroad (*cf.* Dan. iii. 8; Esth. iii. 4). The history of the J. might conveniently be divided into several periods:—(1) The first, down to the settlement in Canaan; (2) from the settlement in Canaan to the beginning of the monarchy; (3) from the reign of Saul to the Babylonish Captivity; (4) from the Captivity to the destruction of Jerusalem by Titus; and (5) the modern period, from the destruction of Jerusalem to the present time.

First Period.—According to Gen. x. 22 (*cf.* xi. 10–32) the five sons of Shem were Elam (Elymais, on the Persian Gulf beyond the Tigris), Asshur (the Assyrians), Arphaxad (Arrapachitis, the most northerly country of Assyria: Ptolemy), Lud (the Lydians of Asia Minor), and Aram (the Aramæans). From Arphaxad, the centre of the whole region occupied by those Semitic tribes, at some pre-historic period, some families emigrated westwards to the higher Mesopotamia [Gen. xi. 31: Arphaxad = *Arph-casd* = *Ur Casdim*, Heb. for Ur of the Chaldees]. A part of this colony settled there (in Haran), another part passed on to the S.W. towards the coast of the Mediterranean. Branches of them called the Moabites and Ammonites, settled to the E. of Canaan; another, Edom, took possession of the mountains of Seir, S. of the Dead Sea; other two, Midian and Ishmael, pushed farther to the S. into the Arabian peninsula (Gen. xxv.); and the branch of the Hebrews crossed the Jordan into Canaan under the conduct of Abraham (q. v.: Gen. xii.). The Hebrews having been greatly strengthened by the arrival of another company from Haran under the conduct of Jacob (q. v.: Gen. xxxv.), continued their wanderings still farther to the S.-W., and settled in the Land of Goshen in the N.-E. of Egypt, where they found rich pasture for their cattle, and whither, in fact, a family of the tribe (Joseph) had already found its way (Gen. xlvi., xlvii.). It is a difficult matter to determine the exact date of the arrival of the Israelites in Egypt, or the length of their stay, but there are distinct traces in Egyptian history of a Shemitic invasion. About the year B.C. 2100 Shemitic hordes from Central Asia invaded the eastern Delta, and seized the kingdom of Memphis, driving the native kings to the S. For more than 400 years these foreign conquerors, called on the monuments *Amu* ('shepherds of oxen'), *Aadu* ('detested, wicked ones'), and their kings *Hykshos* (*hyk-shasu*, 'ruler of shepherds'), held the country in subjection. But about B.C. 1660 Upper Egypt, which had been tributary, rose against them, and regained its independence; and about B.C. 1580 king Thutmosis, taking their fortified camp at Tanis (Avaris) on the E. of the Nile, drove them from the country. Josephus tries to identify the Hykshos with his countrymen, but it seems incredible that, if the Israelites had ever actually held possession of Egypt, there should have been no tradition of it among them. It is much more probable that they are intended by 'the lepers' (all foreigners being unclean to the Egyptians) described in the other fragment of Manetho preserved by Josephus. The Exodus (q. v.) probably took place about the year B.C. 1320, or, according to the ordinary chronology, about 170 years earlier. All danger from the Egyptians being removed, as soon as the Red Sea was passed, the Israelites set out along the shore of that sea towards Mount Sinai, their wants being supplied on the way thither by Manna (q. v.), quails, and water—first the bitter water of Marah (q. v.), sweetened by a certain tree (Exod. xv. 25), and then from the rock in Horeb (q. v.: Exod. xvii. 1–7). At Rephidim they defeated the Amalekites, who attacked them (Exod. xvii. 8–16), and there they were visited by Jethro the priest of Midian, and father-in-law of Moses, by whose advice the administration of justice was improved (Exod. xviii.). But the most glorious manifestation of the presence of Jehovah was on Sinai (q. v.), where the law was delivered to Moses, and a covenant made with Israel (Exod. xix., xx.), the people being nevertheless engaged at the very time making and worshipping the image of a bull, probably an idolatrous representation of Jehovah himself (Exod. xxxii.). At the end of two years from the time when they left Egypt they arrived at the southern frontier of Canaan, but finding that this fertile country was held at the time by fierce and gigantic tribes, they were afraid to attempt the invasion of the country, and turned back to continue their nomadic life in the desert (Num. xiii., xiv.). Little is recorded of their life during the next thirty-eight years; almost the only particular being the rebellion of Korah, Dathan, and Abiram against Moses and Aaron (Num. xvi., xvii.). In the fortieth year from their leaving Egypt the Israelites again approach the land of Canaan, this time on the eastern frontier, and a great number of most important events follow in rapid succession, in fact seem to be crowded into an incredibly short space of time—the last seven months of this year. On the first day of the fifth month Aaron dies on Mount Hor (Num. xx. 22–29, xxxiii. 38). That month being spent in mourning for Aaron, the Israelites march round Edom, defeat Sihon, king of the Amorites, and Og, king of Bashan, and fraternise with the Moabites long enough to take part in the unchaste worship of Baal-peor (Num. xxi.–xxv.). Moses having died in the land of Moab (Deut. xxxiv.), they are led into Canaan by Joshua (q. v.) about B.C. 1280, and in two battles that able general completely crushed the resistance of the inhabitants (*cf.* Josh. ii. 9–13, ix. 24), after which he took their towns one after another with little difficulty (Josh. i.–xxiv.).

Second Period.—The account of the rapid and comparatively easy conquest of the country by Joshua is considerably modified by the picture of the state of the country given in the Book of Judges, from which it appears that the Canaanitish tribes were very far from being completely subdued centuries after the death of Joshua. The period of the Judges was the period of the first formation of the nation. The tribes had now exchanged their nomadic life for that of agriculturists, and they were brought into contact with two nations in particular—the Phœnicians and Philistines—both in a more advanced state of civilisation than themselves. The Phœnicians, entirely engrossed with trade and commerce, were peaceful neighbours. The Philistines, on the other hand, with their five chief cities, Gaza, Askelon, Ashdod, Gath, and Ekron, were a warlike nation, and proved themselves very troublesome neighbours. But even in the interior of the country, besides the Gibeonites, who made a treaty with Joshua for the peaceful possession of their towns (Josh. ix.; *cf.* 2 Sam. xxi. 1–4), many of the inhabitants remained unsubdued and independent. Jebus was not taken till the reign of David (2 Sam. v. 6–9; *cf.* Jud. xix. 10–12), and Gezer not till the time of Solomon (1 Kings ix. 16). Others, again, of the Canaanites proper, as well as from among the neighbouring nations, allied themselves with the Israelites, or even became amalgamated with them: *cf.* Jud. i. 16, Caleb the Kenezite (Josh. xiv. 6–15), Heber the Kenite (Jud. v. 24), Doeg the Edomite (1 Sam. xxi. 7), Amasa the Ishmaelite (2 Sam. xvii. 25), Ittai the Gittite, *i.e.*, a Philistine of Gath (2 Sam. xv. 19–22), Ahimelech and Uriah the Hittites (1 Sam. xxvi. 6, 2 Sam. xxiii. 39), Zelek the Ammonite (2 Sam. xxiii. 37), Ithmah the Moabite (1 Chron. xi. 46). That there was yet no proper unity in the nation is clear from the fact there was a jealousy and rivalry among the tribes so strong as sometimes to produce war between them (*cf.* Jud. viii. 1–7, xvii.–xxi.), and that the wars which almost always brought calamity only on single tribes, were regarded with indifference by the rest of the tribes, the deliverance being generally effected by an alliance of one or two. The following is a summary, according to the book of Judges, of the nations by which parts of the country were conquered and held in subjection for a time, and the judges by whom the foreigners were defeated: I. King of Mesopotamia, 8 years servitude: Othniel, 40 years of peace. II. Moabites, 18; Ehud, 80. III. Philistines: Shamgar. IV. Canaanites, 20; Deborah and Barak, 40. V. Midianites, 7; Gideon, 40; Abimelech, 3; Tola, 23; Jair, 22. VI. Ammonites and Philistines, 18; Jephthah, 6; Ibzan, 7; Elon, 10; Abdon, 8; Philistines, 40; Samson, 20 (probably meant to be included within the 40 of servitude); Eli, 40 (perhaps partly or altogether synchronous with the 40 years' oppression by the Philistines; interregnum, 20; Samuel). The so-called 'Judges' might for the most part more properly be called warriors or heroes. The first who deserved the name was Eli, in whose person was united the offices of judge and priest, which was the first step towards the establishment of a monarchy. It began to be apparent to all the tribes that unless the state of disunion and rivalry which had prevailed so long was put an end to, they would never be able to hold their own against the surrounding tribes, and that their only hope of maintaining their existence as a nation was to have a king like the neighbouring nations. More than one attempt had been made to introduce the regal form of government during the period of the Judges (*cf.* viii., ix.), but unsuccessfully, because prematurely. Gideon doubtless expressed the sentiments of the majority at the time when he declared that the evils of a monarchy were greater than its advantages; and the parable of Jotham expresses unbounded contempt for that form of government. But the national mind was clearly advancing in that direction, and at last it was resolved that they would have a king, notwithstanding the protestations of Samuel (q. v.). That prophet represented the old conservative spirit of the nation, according to which Jehovah was their king; from which idea this period at the close of which Samuel stands has been called the Theocracy. The choice of a king was hurried on by the successes of the Philistines. The Ark of the Covenant (q. v.), which had been carried into battle as the symbol of the Divine presence, was captured by them, and the sanctuary at Shiloh, in which the ark had been kept since the conquest, seems to have been destroyed.

3. *Period of the Monarchy.* At this crisis of the national life, the nation possessed in Samuel a notable leader and adviser. The last of the Judges and the first of the Prophets (q. v.), he was the inaugurator of the first of the kings, Saul the son of Kish, of the tribe of Benjamin, who began to reign about B.C. 1100. Having inaugurated his reign by defeating the Ammonites, who were threatening the people of Jabesh-Gilead, kindred of the Benjamites, he next attacked the Philistines, and carried on the war against them so vigorously and successfully that they were driven out of the country for a time. After the defeat of the Philistines, instead of disbanding his army, he assumed an offensive attitude towards the tribes who had formerly proved themselves hostile and troublesome, and making war on the Moabites, Ammonites, Edomites, the kings of Zobah, and the Amalekites, he 'vexed' them all. It is thus clear that under his rule Israel became a united and formidable nation. The nucleus of a standing army was formed (1 Sam. xiii. 2, xiv. 50, 'host'), and a bodyguard established (xvi. 15, 17). A new sanctuary also was established at Nob (xxi. 1). But Saul fell short of the zeal which was thought to be necessary by Samuel and the prophets and Nazarites (q. v.), produced by the religious revival which he had awakened. According to them religious reformation, zeal in the worship of Jehovah, was the one road to national prosperity, and therefore everything Canaanitish and heathenish must be rooted out, cost what it might. For a time Saul ruled entirely in this spirit (*cf.* 1 Sam. x. 9–12); he persecuted the necromancers and wizards (1 Sam. xxviii. 9), raised altars to Jehovah, and would not have hesitated to sacrifice his own son in fulfilment of a vow. Whether it was that latterly his heart revolted against the wholesale bloodshed involved in carrying out this spirit, he began to display a milder policy, and from this time, although the great mass of the people remained faithful to him, he was opposed by Samuel and his party. Saul having failed in this way, Samuel anointed as his successor one who was to be 'a man after God's own heart,' David (q. v.), the son of Jesse, of the tribe of Judah. On the death of Saul, who fell in battle against the Philistines at Mount Gilboa, the greater part of the tribes of Israel remained faithful to his son Ishbosheth, who, a feeble man himself, was supported by his courageous cousin Abner, and established himself at Mahanaim beyond Jordan. David was proclaimed king by his own tribe, and made Hebron his capital. On the death of Ishbosheth, two years after, David was acknowledged as king by all the tribes. Some time after he took the stronghold of Jebus, and after reigning seven years and a half at Hebron removed to Jerusalem (q. v.), and by bringing thither the Ark of God made it the religious capital of the country. The reign of David (1058–1018) was upon the whole marked by great prosperity. He was almost invariably successful in his wars—against the Philistines, Moabites, Ammonites, Edomites, and Syrians (2 Sam. viii., x.; 1 Chron. xviii., xix.)—and extended the boundary of his kingdom towards the N. and the E. At home he was surrounded by a royal state quite unknown in the time of Saul. The military organisation of Saul was greatly developed by David. (1) All males capable of bearing arms had to be in training for a month yearly in time of peace, being divided for that purpose into twelve divisions (1 Chron. xxvii. 1–15). (2) There was also a small standing army, the nucleus of which was the band of 600 men who had gathered round him before the death of Saul (2 Sam. xxiii. 8–39, 1 Chron. xi. 10–47); and (3) a body-guard, nominally at least composed of foreigners—'the Cherethites and the Pelethites (Cretans and refugees: Stanley; 2 Sam. viii. 18). New arrangements were also made in connection with pastoral, agricultural, financial, and judicial matters (1 Chron. xxvi., xxvii). But the most notable of David's institutions were the religious. Two prophets —Gad and Nathan—acted as his advisers (2 Sam. vii., xxiv. 11). There were also two high-priests, Abiathar and Zadok, subordinate prophets especially trained in music (1 Chron. xxv.), and Levites (1 Chron. xxvi.). At the head of the whole was David himself as Prophet, Priest (2 Sam. vi. 14, 17), and Psalmist. As the conqueror of his country's enemies, the administrator of justice, and the religious guide of his people, David might well seem in their eyes the 'light' of Israel (2 Sam. xxi. 17); and in after times David's reign was looked back to as the golden age of the nation's history. Even Solomon's reign (B.C. 1018–978), with all its glory, was regarded with far less admiration than David's. He could perform miracles of wisdom, had immense wealth, built a magnificent Temple (q. v.) for Jehovah, besides a splendid palace, and altogether his magnificence was something unparalleled even in the East; but all this was too much at the expense of the people to be gratefully or very admiringly remembered. His subjects were heavily taxed and obliged to serve for little at his great works. Besides, the national glory abroad was tarnished (*cf.* 1 Kings ix. 10–14, xi. 14, 23). The discontent which had been openly expressed even in the lifetime of Solomon (1 Kings xi. 26–40) exploded altogether owing to the obstinacy of his successor Rehoboam; and eleven of the tribes, headed by Ephraim, formed an independent kingdom under Jeroboam, which received the name of the kingdom of Israel, while the tribe of Judah, and it alone, remained faithful to the house of David under the name of the kingdom of Judah. Although the nation of the J. was really perpetuated through the kingdom of Judah, with which also the prestige of the house of David remained, so that the ordinary impression, which indeed is conveyed in the history, is that that kingdom represented the nation, yet in reality the kingdom of Israel was to a great extent the kingdom of the whole nation. At the death of Saul Ishbosheth was made king over *all* Israel, and David only over the tribe of Judah (2 Sam. ii. 4, 8, 9); and so it was at the death of Solomon with Jeroboam and Rehoboam (1 Kings xii. 20). The kingdom of Israel still extended from the Mediterranean to the Euphrates, and from the extreme N. to the frontier of Judah. Even the tribes of Simeon and Benjamin, which were almost enclosed within Judah, did not give their undivided allegiance to that tribe. In the historical books the disruption under Jeroboam was as much a thing from the Lord as the establishment of the monarchy had been (1 Kings xi. 31–39); Jeroboam was supported by the prophets Shemaiah and Ahijah, as David had been by Samuel. However, nearly the entire history of the kingdom is made up of bloodshed and confusion. In the 254 years of the monarchy nine different families occupied the throne, and according to the historian not one of the nineteen kings was free from the general charge of depravity. Of one after another, it is said, 'he did that which was evil in the sight of the Lord.' Pekah made an alliance with Rezin, King of Syria, against Ahaz, King of Judah. Ahaz thereupon applied for help to Tiglath-Pileser, King of Assyria, who conquered Israel, carrying away the two and a half trans-Jordanic tribes, and making the rest tributary (B.C. 738). Ten years later Hoshea revolted from Assyria, which brought Shalmaneser, the son of Tiglath-Pileser, upon him; Samaria was taken, and the ten tribes were carried off to Assyria (B.C. 721), and never more heard of. During the 388 years that the kingdom of Judah lasted, twenty kings, all of the house of David, occupied the throne, six of whom—Asa, Jehoshaphat, Uzziah, Jotham, Hezekiah, and Josiah—are mentioned with special praise, while several, *e.g.*, Jehoram, Ahaz, Manasseh, and Amon, are described as excessively wicked. Ahaz, as we have seen, sought the aid of Tiglath-Pileser, the bitter fruits of which alliance he and his successors reaped. It cost himself a heavy tribute, Hezekiah most of his treasury, Manasseh his liberty, and Josiah his life. Jehoahaz was carried captive to Egypt, Jehoiakim was deposed by Nebuchadnezzar, as was his son Jehoiakim, who was carried off to Babylon. Zedekiah his successor having revolted, Nebuchadnezzar came a third time against Jerusalem and took it. The city was burned, the temple destroyed, and the greater part of the nation carried off to Babylon (B.C. 587).

Fourth Period, from the Captivity to the destruction of Jerusalem.—When the decree of Cyrus was issued (B.C. 536, Ezra i.) permitting the J. to return, an expedition numbering 42,360 returned to Palestine, and although they settled at first in the towns they belonged to they soon afterwards assembled at Jerusalem and commenced the rebuilding of the temple (Ez. iii.), which was finished in the year B.C. 516. The wall of the city was rebuilt (B.C. 445), in spite of the opposition of Sanballat and Tobias (Neh.ii.-vi.), who were leading men among the Samaritans (q. v.). After the time of Nehemiah (B.C. 420) Judea continued for nearly a century subject to Persia, as part of the satrapy of Syria, the government being entrusted to the High Priest, subject to the control of the Syrian governor. When the Persians were conquered by Alexander the Great (B.C. 331) it fell into the power of that monarch. Whatever truth there may be in the story of Alexander's visit to Jerusalem (Jos. *Ant.* xi. 8, 4), when he built his city of Alexandria he placed in it a great number of J. and gave them the same privileges as his Greek subjects. After Alexander's death (B.C. 323) Judea ultimately fell to Ptolemy Lagus as part of the monarchy of Egypt (B.C. 301), and by the encouragement given to the people to settle there, Egypt became an important seat of the Jewish population. At Jerusalem the prosperity of the J. was much promoted by the administration of the excellent High Priest, Simon the Just (died B.C. 291), who repaired and fortified the city and temple. After being tributary to Egypt for about a century, Judea next became subject to Antiochus the Great, King of Syria (B.C. 198), although the government still remained in the hands of the High Priest and a national council. The country was now divided into the five provinces of Galilee, Samaria, and Judea in the W., and Trachonitis and Peræa on the E. of the Jordan. Being situated between Syria and Egypt it was greatly harassed by the frequent wars between these two countries. But to the conservative, patriotic part of the nation, what appeared to be the greatest danger of the time was that Judaism would give way before the Hellenic influences introduced by their Syrian rulers, that the nation would cease to be 'a people dwelling alone' (Num. xxiii. 9), and become simply a part of the Syrian empire. There was a party with Hellenic tendencies in the nation itself. Thus in the time of Antiochus Epiphanes (B.C. 175) the High Priest Joshua did everything in his power to introduce Greek manners among the people, *e.g.*, by establishing a gymnasium at Jerusalem, sending a contribution to the games held at Tyre in honour of Melkarth, &c. Antiochus, seeing danger to his own authority during his wars with Egypt in the commotions which were produced by struggles for the possession of the high priesthood, came with an army to Jerusalem and plundered it (B.C. 169). Two years after an army of 22,000 men under Apollonius entered the country, and the obvious aim of all his proceedings was to obliterate the individuality of the nation by destroying the national religion. Taking Jerusalem, with a terrible massacre of its inhabitants, he prohibited all sacrifices, festivals, and rites in honour of Jehovah. And not only so, but an altar to Jupiter Capitolinus was erected upon the altar of burnt-offering in the temple, the worst of all being that a number of the people joined in the heathen rites (1 Macc. i.). But the national spirit was not to be so easily crushed. The opposition, at first passive, many allowing themselves to be tortured and put to death rather than take part in the heathen worship (1 Macc. vi.-vii), broke into open rebellion at Modin. At that place the people, roused by an old priest Mattathias, attacked and slew the officers of Antiochus, who were offering sacrifices. The little band who fled to the wilderness gradually increased, and on the death of Mattathias (B.C. 166) was commanded by his son Judas, surnamed Maccabæus ('the hammer'). After a series of brilliant victories, Judas was able to take possession of Jerusalem and the temple (B.C. 164), although a Syrian garrison continued to hold the stronghold (Acra) built by Apollonius. The temple was consecrated anew to the service of God, and the daily sacrifices resumed on the same day (25th December) on which, three years before, the first sacrifice to Jupiter Capitolinus had been offered; and this restoration was afterwards celebrated by the Feast of the Dedication (*cf.* John x. 22). After various vicissitudes, Judas being killed in the disastrous battle of Eleasa (B.C. 160), the independence of the J. was finally acknowledged by the Syrian king (B.C. 138). Under the Asmonæan princes, as the family of Mattathias were called, Judea became a free state, supported by regular troops, and forming alliances with other powers, even with Rome herself. But in B.C. 63 Pompey seized the pretext of the war between John Hyrcanus and his brother to make himself master of Jerusalem, although the independence of the J. was ostensibly respected. In the year 37 B.C. Herod the Great (q. v.) took Jerusalem from Antigonus, the last of the Asmonæan princes, and established himself King of the Jews, tributary to Rome. Under Herod the Jewish state again rose into importance and respect. He at least perpetuated his fame, although he could not conciliate the people, who hated him as a foreigner and a sycophant at Rome, by replacing Zerubbabel's temple by a much more magnificent structure. Just before his death (B.C. 4) there occurred the greatest event in Jewish history, although they themselves do not recognise it as such, namely, the birth of Jesus (q. v.). The Roman yoke was no less hateful to the J. than every other foreign dominion had been, and, aggravated by the misgovernment of various rulers, became every year more intolerable. In A.D. 6, when Judea, with Samaria, was incorporated with the Roman empire as a subdivision of the province of Syria, a rising had taken place under Judas of Gamala (See JEWISH SECTS; Galileans, *cf.* Acts v. 37), and at last under Gessius Florus the whole nation rose in revolt (A.D. 66). They at first met with some success, but were hopelessly weakened by being divided into parties which fought against each other. In fact, the real clew to the history of the J., from before the time of Antiochus Epiphanes till the fall of Jerusalem, is the existence of a bitter party-spirit. The body of the people, the true leaven of the J., under the influence of the Scribes or expounders of the law, were utterly opposed to all foreign relations whatsoever. Hence they continually resisted the policy of the more tolerant priestly aristocracy, with their foreign leanings, such as those of the High Priest Joshua, who Græcised his name to Jason. Under the Asmonæan princes the two classes came to be known as the parties of the Pharisees (q. v.) and Sadducees (q. v.), whose general political tendencies were those just described. Thus, when the war broke out, there was a peace party and a war party, the latter composed of zealots, who scouted the idea of all compromise, and were resolved to gain their freedom or perish. As there belonged to the latter party a band of assassins ready to put out of the way all opposed to them, and the party itself was divided into two factions, when Jerusalem was invested by the Roman army, the streets ran with the blood of J. slain by their own countrymen. By the fall of Jerusalem (A.D. 70), and the burning of the temple, not only the war, but the existence of the J. as a nation was virtually at an end; the most of those who had not been killed were scattered among the nations.

5. *Modern Period.*—Some convulsive struggles of the dying nation appeared in risings under Trajan (98–117) in Africa, Cyprus, and Mesopotamia, and under Hadrian in Palestine (130: see BAR-COCHBA). After the suppression of this last insurrection the final dispersion of the J. from Palestine was made. Hadrian, desiring completely to obliterate Jerusalem, built on its ruins a Roman city, with a temple to Jupiter Capitolinus, to which he gave the name of Ælia Capitolina, and which the J. were forbidden to enter on pain of death. (See JERUSALEM.) Under Antoninus Pius the scattered remains of the nation were restored to their privileges and permitted to form establishments in the different Roman provinces, to acquire the freedom of Rome, and enjoy municipal honours. The patriarch, who had fixed his residence at Tiberias, was empowered to appoint subordinates, and to receive an annual contribution from his dispersed brethren. These were allowed to erect synagogues in many cities, and openly to celebrate their festivals; and as a rule they settled down into peaceable and industrious subjects. Their enthusiasm was roused by the permission given by the Emperor Julian to rebuild the temple. Assembling from all the provinces of the empire they commenced the work (362), but the attempt was defeated by an earthquake, a whirlwind, and a fiery eruption from the ground (see Gibbon's *Decline and Fall*), regarded as a judgment of God on the impious attempt of Julian to falsify the predictions of Christ (Matt. xxiv. 2). Church historians mention the conversion of many J. to Christianity from the 4th c. onward; but the fact does the Christians little credit, for in almost every case they merely submitted to the rite of baptism to save themselves from fierce persecution or from death. Thus in the 5th c. 540 were baptized in Minorca, after their synagogue had been burned and themselves driven to starve among the rocks. The kings of Gaul and Spain by similar means compelled great numbers to submit to baptism, sometimes incited

thereto by the bishops, although sometimes against the wish of the Roman pontiffs. The same policy was followed by the Byzantine Emperor Heraclius (610–641). Many of the J. had settled in Arabia, where they were allowed to remain in peace till the time of Mohammed. That prophet did all in his power to gain them over to his opinions; the new religion, in fact, having much in common with the Jewish. But although he gained a few converts the majority repelled his advances. He thereupon attacked them, and those who were not killed were driven from the country and sought refuge in Syria. To return to Europe, in the 11th c. great sufferings were inflicted on the J. by the first armies of the Crusaders, who in their wanderings through Europe everywhere put to death with horrid cruelty those who would not submit to baptism. And from this time they were constantly exposed to explosions of popular fury. It gradually came to be understood that the J. had no *rights;* and only by special permission from the sovereign, for which they had to pay heavily, and under severe restrictions, were they allowed to reside anywhere. Often too the measure was adopted of banishing them completely from the country unless they embraced Christianity by a certain time. In this manner they were driven from England (1290), and more than once from Italy, Germany, France, Spain, and Portugal; an honourable exception to this intolerance being shown by Holland, where many of them found an asylum. When the Black Death visited Europe (1348–49) the cruelties to which the J. were subjected in the outbreak of fanaticism at the time (see FLAGELLANTS) are described as having been quite unparalleled. In Spain, 200,000 were compelled to undergo baptism in 1391, and as many lost their lives. Relief came in the 18th c. The oppressive laws against the J. began to be repealed, Friedrich the Great having had the honour of beginning the reform. In 1750 he enacted certain measures for their relief in his dominions; in 1791 they were acknowledged as citizens on taking the oath of allegiance; and in Germany they are now almost, if not altogether, on an equality with Christians. In other countries the reform has been so slow, that even yet there are some remains of the former oppression. In Great Britain, by statutes passed in the present reign (Victoria), the J. are on the same footing as British subjects, with the exception that a Jew *may* be excluded from the Houses of Parliament by the wording of the oath of allegiance, which contains the clause, 'I make this declaration upon the faith of a Christian,' and is especially excluded from several of the highest offices of State. These are specified at the close of this article in the paragraph entitled *Law Regarding Jews.*

Religion.—Having sketched the outward facts of their history, it will now be necessary to take a brief review of the religion of the J., with which their history is so intimately connected. The religion of the J. is generally regarded as having been a pure Monotheism from the time of Abraham, but it is now contended by many Biblical scholars that this conception of the Deity was not held by the people generally till a comparatively late period of their national existence, that at an earlier period they were Polytheists, and that the worship of their national god, Jehovah, was a higher kind of nature-worship, similar to that of the kindred Semitic tribes, Ammon, Moab, &c., and included even human sacrifices. The following are some of the considerations on which this position is maintained. First of all, in order to understand what was the primitive form of the religion of the J., it is most essential to remember that they were not an isolated nation in the midst of aliens, but simply one of the branches of the Semitic migration which flowed down towards the Levant from Central Asia, so that they were akin, as in language and manners, so also, it cannot be doubted, in religion to the Ammonites, Moabites, Edomites, and other branches which settled on the E. and S. of Canaan, and more remotely with the coast-tribes, the Phœnicians and Philistines. It is contended, then, that the Shemites generally were Polytheists, and that the Hebrews were no exception. The religion of the kindred tribes around Canaan was a higher kind of nature-worship. Their gods were the rulers of nature. Molech (Heb. *melech*, 'king,' *i.e.*, 'of heaven') or Milcom of the Ammonites (1 Kings xi. 5, 7), and Chemosh of the Moabites were sun-gods, representing the terrible and destructive aspect of nature, and propitiated with human sacrifices (2 Kings iii. 27). But the fertilising, productive power of nature was also worshipped as Baal ('Lord,' *i.e.*, 'of heaven'), in connection with which there was a duality of deities, the male and the female. Along with Molech, represented with the head of a bull, was Astarte, the moon-goddess, represented by the horns; along with Baal was Ashera (q. v.: *cf.* 1 Kings xviii. 19); and the nature of the rites of Baal-peor is well known (Num. xxv.). Now, in the first place, there is abundant evidence that these gods of the surrounding nations were at least occasionally worshipped by the J. down to the Babylonish captivity. Although this worship was denounced by the prophets, and attempts made to root it out by several of the kings, these denunciations and more or less successful attempts only prove how extensive was the evil they sought to counteract. In the reign of Solomon, Ashtoreth, Milcom, Chemosh, and Molech were worshipped at Jerusalem (1 Kings xi.). The worship of Baal was the established religion in the kingdom of Israel in the time of Ahab, and kept its hold, notwithstanding the work of Elijah, till the fall of the kingdom (2 Kings xvii. 16, 17). In the kingdom of Judah the worship of Molech was practised to a great extent, especially in the reigns of Ahaz, who established a place for sacrificing children to him in the Valley of Hinnom, setting the example by offering up his own son (2 Kings xvi. 3; 2 Chron. xxviii. 1–4), and of Manasseh (2 Kings xxi. 1–6). The work which Josiah had to do in his reform shows to what an extent the people had given themselves up to this worship; but, at anyrate, it is maintained, there is enough of evidence to show that Molech, Baal, and the rest were, during considerable periods of history, regarded as deities as well as Jehovah. That the primitive stock in Ur of the Chaldees were Polytheists, as well as the Hebrews at least till they left Egypt, is expressly mentioned (Josh. xxiv. 2, 14; Ezek. xx. 5, 8; *cf.* Gen. xxxi. 30; xxxv. 2). The next question is, was there any resemblance between Jehovah, the national God of the J., and these other gods; and it is maintained that the very fact of his being regarded as one of the Semitic deities, three or four of whom could be worshipped at the same time along with himself, implies a certain similarity between Jehovah and them. It is also pointed out that the golden image of a young bull, which Aaron called the god who had brought them out of Egypt (*cf.* Ps. cvi. 20, which says they changed 'their glory,' that is, their god, 'into the similitude of an ox'), and before which Aaron built an altar, proclaiming to the people 'To-morrow is a feast to Jehovah' (Exod. xxxii. 1–6), has a remarkable resemblance to the bull-headed Molech. Still more remarkable than this image were those set up by Jeroboam at Dan and Bethel, regarding which he used the very language which Aaron had used of his one. Now the kingdom of Israel was the national kingdom, and there cannot be a doubt that Jeroboam intended to establish in his kingdom the national religion, although it was in such a sensuous form as to be condemned by the prophets who had supported him. His act was intended as a piece of deep policy (1 Kings xii. 28: he 'took counsel'), and setting up the two sanctuaries would have had the effect he intended if they were for the same worship as obtained at Jerusalem, but not otherwise. There might have been some meaning in his establishing the worship of Baal, Molech, or some of the other Semitic gods, for worshipping whom the ten tribes had been rent from the house of David (1 Kings xi. 31–34); that would have afforded them a rival attraction to Jerusalem. But as that is evidently not what is meant, the explanation generally given is that the bulls were images of the god Apis, with whom Jeroboam had been familiar while in Egypt, and to whose worship it is presumed the Israelites would also take quite readily. But, not to mention that the god Apis was always in the form of a living bull, and the improbability of Aaron and Jeroboam declaring that the people owed their deliverance from Egypt to an Egyptian god, it seems incredible that nine-tenths of the nation should all at once have adopted the worship of a god utterly unknown to them, in preference to any Semitic deity. At anyrate we must conclude that the worship at Dan and Bethel was either totally strange to the people, or else was closely akin to that of Solomon's temple, in which there was a four-*horned* altar and a brazen sea supported by twelve brazen oxen. It has been mentioned that the other Semitic deities were worshipped even with human sacrifices, and it is maintained that there are several tolerably clear hints and allusions which show that the practice was not unknown in the worship of Jehovah. The narrative of Abraham's offering (Gen. xxii.) is unintelligible unless the idea of such sacrifices had been a familiar one to him. Jephthah actually sacrificed his child to Jehovah (Judg. xi. 30, 31, 39); Samuel hewed Agag in pieces before Jehovah (1 Sam. xv. 33); David and the Gibeonites sacrificed seven of the sons of Saul to Jehovah (2 Sam. xxi. 1-6); and it seems to have been part of the worship at Bethel under Jeroboam (Hosea xiii. 2, 'sacrificers of men'). The rite of circumcision is also supposed to be a relic of the practice of human sacrifices. A trace of the same thing is found in the law which gave to Jehovah the first-born of man as well as of beast, the former being redeemed by paying a sum of money to the priest (Exod. xiii. 1-16). It is pointed out that other traces of nature-worship appear in the close connection between their festivals and the seasons: the three chief were the Easter Feast (see PASSOVER) and the Feast of Harvest, at which the first-fruits were offered to Jehovah, and the Feast of Ingathering (Exod. xxiii. 14-17); in the great importance attached to the *moon* or month: the Feast of the New Moon came next to the Sabbath (Num. xxviii. 9-15); and in the sacred number *seven*, which is supposed to be a relic of star-worship, and connected with the seven planets. The whole cycle of the earlier Festivals (q. v.) was regulated by the number seven, in days, weeks, months, and years; and according to the prophet Amos the planet Saturn was worshipped in the wilderness (Amos v. 26; *cf.* Acts vii. 43).

Although the polytheistic notions described above lingered in the minds of the people down to a late period of the national existence, a new era began under Moses. It has been pointed out that several of the details of the Mosaic worship were borrowed from the Egyptians, *e.g.*, the Ark (q. v.), the Urim and Thummim (q. v.), and the priestly vestments, but be this as it may, the national deity of the J. as conceived by Moses was raised far above the nature-gods of the Egyptians, whom he had vanquished in the Plagues, and in the deliverance of his people. With Moses he was the creator and the Lord of nature, which perhaps is the meaning of the new name Jehovah (q. v.) now given to him. But the greatest feature of the Mosaic reformation was the connection established between religion and the moral life. However unable to grasp the idea that there were no gods but Jehovah at all, it was an extraordinary advance for the people, to learn, as they did through Moses, that Jehovah differed from all the other gods in this respect that he desired to be worshipped not only with sacrifices and festivals, but by the observance of moral precepts. It was alongside of and through this differentiation of Jehovah from all other gods that the idea of Monotheism was gradually developed. This was the principle which was contended for so strongly by Samuel, the first of the prophets, in connection with the choice of a king; as it was by the succeeding prophets, who declared that Jehovah had no pleasure in their sacrifices and festivals, for the worship he desired was 'to do justly, and to love mercy, and to walk humbly with their God' (*cf.* Isa. i.; Micah vi. 6-8). The J. were finally weaned from polytheism during their Captivity in Babylonia. There they came in contact with the religion of the Persians, which was a dualism (see PARSEES); and the influence of this contact is thought to be traceable in the development of their ideas regarding the immortality of the soul, Angels (q. v.), Demons (q. v.), Satan (q. v.), &c. After the Captivity the worship in the temple became more severely spiritual than formerly. The institution of the Synagogue (q. v.) was also established; brought thither from Babylonia, where the exiles used to assemble periodically to listen to the exhortations of the prophets or the reading of the Scriptures.

Language and Literature.—The Semitic Languages (q. v.) have been divided into three divisions—the Northern or Aramaic, to which the Chaldee and Syrian belong, the Middle or Hebrew, and the Southern or Arabic. The almost unquestioned opinion used to be that the Hebrew was spoken by Abraham from the first, that in fact it was the one Holy Language that was spoken before the confusion of tongues. The principal argument for this opinion is drawn from 'the fact that the proper names of persons and places which occur in the oldest portions of Genesis clearly show a Hebrew derivation,' *e.g.*, Adam, Eve, Eden, Abel, Nod, Enoch, &c. But it has been pointed out that these are not pure names, but appellatives applied to the objects in allusion to their history, which implies that this was done at a later time; while for others of the names the Hebrew does not afford an etymology at all, *e.g.*, most of the names in Gen. iv. 17, 18 (as well as Tubal-Cain) and v. 12-25. As to Abraham and the tribe he led from Haran, there can be no doubt that till they arrived in Canaan the language they spoke was the Aramaic, which remained the language of Abraham's nephew Laban, as we see from Gen. xxxi. 47. The heap of stones erected by Jacob and Laban received from the former a Hebrew name (Galeed), and from the latter a Chaldee one (Jegar-sahadutha), *cf.* Deut. xxvi. 5. From this it would appear that Abraham's tribe must have adopted the Hebrew language, which was originally very closely akin to the Phœnician, after they settled in Canaan. This view is supposed to be confirmed by several circumstances—(1.) In all the intercourse which there was between the Hebrews and the Canaanites, there is no intimation of any diversity of language. (2.) The names of Canaanitish persons and places are Hebrew, *e.g.*, Kirjath-sepher (Heb. 'city of book'), Shechem (Heb. 'shoulder'), Abimelech (Heb. 'father of the king'), Melchizedek (Heb. 'king of righteousness'). (3.) Importance is attached by some to the fact that Isaiah (xix. 18) calls the Hebrew the language of Canaan. The earliest knowledge we have of Hebrew is derived from the Old Testament, which is composed in that language, with the exception of Ezra iv. 8-vii. 18; vii. 12-26; Jer. x. 11; Dan. ii. 4-vii. And the language of the earlier writings is in such an advanced stage of perfection that the difference between them and the later is very slight. Indeed the purest Hebrew is the oldest, and what change there is in the later is rather a degeneracy. The separation implied in Gen. xxxi. 47 between it and the Aramaic must have taken place before the composition of the earliest writings. It is a matter of controversy how long the Hebrew remained the spoken language of the people. The most prevalent opinion, both among J. and Christians, has been that it was so only down to the Captivity. The principal argument for this opinion is found in Neh. viii. 8, which is understood to mean that when the law was read to the people it had to be interpreted to them in Chaldee, the word *m'phorash* ('distinctly') being held as equivalent to 'interpreted.' It is contended, on the other hand, that the meaning of the word here, as in other passages, is just that given in the authorized version, 'distinctly, audibly,' and that it is not implied that the explanation given after the reading was in another language. Further, it is maintained that the Hebrew must have remained the vernacular of the J. in Palestine, even after the Captivity, because several of the canonical books which were intended to have an immediate influence on the people were written in it. Still, the Aramaic became the vernacular of the J. who remained in Babylonia, and in course of time of those in Palestine also; a change which was chiefly effected in the latter country during the Syrian dominion (B.C. 198-138). Aramaic was next adopted as the written language, as appears from the fragments in the books of Ezra and Daniel. The Hellenistic J., however, living in countries where Greek was spoken, adopted that language as their vernacular, and translated their Scriptures into it. (See SEPTUAGINT.) It is generally assumed, from the fact that the four Gospels were written in Greek, with the exception perhaps of Matthew (the original of which may have been written in Aramaic), that that language was the vernacular in Palestine in the time of Christ. (See Roberts's *Discussions on the Gospels.*) But if Greek had been well understood at Jerusalem in the time of Christ it must have been much more so in the time of Josephus, who belonged to the next generation; whereas he, a well-educated Jew, remarkable for his love of learning, tells us that he had only acquired it with great labour, after he was forty years of age, for the special purpose of writing his history, and that although he had acquired a grammatical knowledge of it, the habitual use of his native tongue prevented his accurate utterance of it (*Ant.* xx. 11, 2; *Con. Ap.* i. 9). In a number of other passages of his writings he expressly refers to the fact that his countrymen were completely ignorant of Greek. The study of the Scriptures, at anyrate, which was carried on in regular schools in Babylonia and Palestine, was not from the Septuagint but the original text. After the destruction of Jerusalem the chief school was at Tiberias, but after the death of Rabbi Jehuda II. (275) the great seat of Biblical learning was in Babylonia. The language used by Jewish writers of this period was the Aramaic, and partly the Hebrew. After the 10th c. they began to make some use of the Arabic, which, by the spread of Mohammedanism, had driven out the Aramaic. After this, however, scholarship among the J. was found farther to the west; first in Spain and the north of Africa, where, from intercourse with the Moors, Arabic was the language used, and later in France and Germany, where the use of Hebrew was resumed. For further particulars regarding the literature, see APOCRYPHA, BIBLE, CABALA, MASORA, MIDRASH, TALMUD, TARGUM.—Authorities: Basnage, *Histoire des Juifs* (Rotterd. 1706); Ewald's *Gesch. d. Volkes Israel* (3d ed. 1864-69; Eng. transl. 1869); Milman's *History of the J.* (new ed. 1863); Stanley's *Jewish Church* (6th ed. 1875); Kuenen's *Religion of Israel* (1874); Picciotti's *Anglo-Jewish History* (Lond. 1876); and Ignaz Goldziher's *Mythology among the J.* (Eng. transl. Lond. 1877).

Law Regarding Jews.—Previous Acts which prescribed certain forms of declaration to be made by J. on taking office were repealed in 1868, and a uniform oath prescribed for all. (See AFFIRMATION OATH.) By 21 and 22 Vict. c. 49, Parliament was opened to the J., either House being empowered to admit them by a resolution dispensing with the phrase '*upon the true faith of a Christian*,' and in 1866 J. were empowered to sit in Parliament on taking an oath similar to that taken by members of other religious sects. But J. are still disqualified for the offices of Regent of the kingdom, Lord Chancellor, or Lord-Lieutenant of Ireland, or Her Majesty's High Commissioner to the General Assembly of the Church of Scotland. J. born in the United Kingdom are subjects of the Queen.

Jew's Harp, or **Trump**, a small metal instrument, capable of producing very beautiful sounds. It is held in the mouth, while a vibrating tongue is touched by the forefinger. The J. H. has long been known in many parts of the world. The name is a corruption either of Fr. *jeu* (a 'game'), or of the Eng. *jaw*.

Jew's Mallow. See CORCHORUS.

Jew's Thorn. See JUJUBE and PALIURUS.

Jeypore' (Jaipur), the capital of the native state of the same name, in Rajputana, India, 140 miles W. of Agra, and a station on the new Rajputana Railway. It was founded in the early part of the 18th c. by the great astronomer and statesman Jai Singh, who removed here the seat of government from Amber. It stands in a plain, surrounded by stony hills, and is regarded as the most handsome and regularly built town in India, with numerous gardens and palaces.

(1) The *state* of J., formerly known as Amher, from the original capital, lies W. of Gwalior, and has an area of about 15,250 sq. miles; pop. about 2,000,000; revenue, £475,000, and about twice as much more is absorbed by feudal and religious grants; tribute, £40,000; army, 72 guns, 4450 horse, and 15,858 foot. The soil is sandy and rocky, but great part is irrigated from wells, and cattle are numerous. There are mines of copper, alum, iron, and cobalt; 40,000 tons of salt are raised from the Sambhur Lake, half of which is within J., now leased to the British Government. In 1874-75 about £400,000 worth of European piece goods was ascertained to be imported into this state. The ruling dynasty, which dates from 967 A.D., has produced many distinguished men, and was in favour with the Delhi emperors. The ravages of the Mahrattas rendered necessary an appeal to British protection in 1817. The present (1877) Maharajah is an enlightened ruler, and spends large sums on public works. His loyalty during the Mutiny, and charitableness during the Rajputana famine of 1868, were conspicuous. Since 1869 he has been a member of the Legislative Council of India. J. was visited by the Prince of Wales in 1876. See *India and its Native Princes*, by Louis Rousselet (Lond. 1875).

Jeypore Agency. A collection of semi-independent hill states in the district of Vizagapatam, Madras Presidency, British India, lying between the E. Ghauts and the state of Bustar in the Central Provinces; area 13,041 sq. miles; pop. (1871) 766,128. The Rajah of J. has an income of £3000, and pays a tribute of £1600. This tract is inhabited by the aboriginal tribe of Khonds, and was notorious for the regular practice of human sacrifice, which is known to have continued as late as 1855. The victims, called *meriahs*, were bought as children in the plains, and carefully bred up for the purpose. Four sub-magistrates are now stationed in this tract.

Jeysulmere' (Jasalmir = the rocky oasis of Jasal), the capital of the native state of the same name, in Rajputana, India, 1290 miles N.W. of Calcutta, said to have been founded in 1156 A.D. It stands on a rocky ridge, and the houses are built of yellow sandstone, elaborately carved. The citadel contains the palace, which is surmounted by a metal umbrella on a stone shaft. The *state* of J., which lies in the Great Indian Desert, between Bikanir and Scinde, has an area of about 12,250 sq. miles; pop. about 75,000; net revenue, about £10,000. It is a waste of sand hills and rocky ridges, and no running streams. Millet forms the only food-crop, and camels are used for ploughing. There is considerable through trade.

Jhallawur', a native state in Rajputana, India, in connection with the Haraoti Agency; area, about 2500 sq. miles; pop. about 226,000; revenue estimated at £160,000; tribute, £8000. It was formed by the British only in 1838 out of the state of Kotah, to provide for a descendant of the minister of the latter state. The soil is rich, and produces opium; the hills are well-known hunting ground for tigers.

Jhan'si, the chief town of the district of the same name, N.W. Provinces, British India, 245 miles W. of Allahabad; pop. (1872) 536, besides European and native troops. This only refers to the new town; the old town, which was handed over to the native state of Gwalior in 1861, is estimated to contain 30,000 persons. In the latter is the fort, built by the Mahrattas, which entirely commands the British station; the houses are of brick and the streets regular. The new town is known as Jehanabad. In June 1857 the sepoys mutinied; and with the express approval of the disinherited Ranee of J., massacred all the Europeans to the number of 66. The fort was retaken by Sir Hugh Rose in April 1858. The *district* of J. has an area of 1567 sq. miles; pop. (1872) 317,826. The largest town is Mow.

Jheend (Jhind), the capital of the native state of the same name, Punjaub, India, on the Feroz Canal, 979 miles N.W. of Calcutta. It is a considerable place. The state of J. has an area of 985 square miles; pop. 190,475; revenue, £60,000; army, 2000 men. The ruling dynasty, which was founded by a Sikh in 1763, has always been loyal to the British, and received considerable accession of territory after the Mutiny. The Rajah with his troops served through the siege of Delhi. See Leppel Griffin's *Rajahs of the Punjaub* (Lahore, 1870).

Jhe'lum (Jhilam), the ancient Hydaspes, one of the five rivers of the Punjaub, India. It rises in the N.E. of Cashmere, flows W. through that state, and turns S. through a narrow pass into the plain of the Punjaub. It is navigable up to the town of J., and again in the valley of Cashmere. It finally joins the Chenaub after a total course of about 490 miles. It was on the bank of this river that Alexander defeated Porus, and founded the city of Bucephala; the spot is identified with Jelalpore.

Jhelum, the chief town of the district of the same name, Punjaub, British India, on the right bank of the J. river, 100 miles N.E. of Lahore; pop. (1868) 5158. It is a modern town, with one native regiment in the cantonments; the only business is boat-building. The river is here crossed by the new Northern State Railway, on a bridge of fifty spans which cost £147,000. The *district* of J., which lies E. of the river, has an area of 3909 sq. miles; pop. (1868) 500,988. It is celebrated for containing the Salt Range, of which the hills are about 3000 feet high, and the beds of salt from 150 to 200 feet thick. 'Nowhere else in the world are deposits of such extent and purity known to exist.' The chief mine is called after Lord Mayo; it yields a revenue to Government of £300,000 per annum. Coal and other minerals are also found. There are many monuments of antiquity in the district.

Jhung (Jhang), the chief town of the district of the same name, Punjaub, British India, 96 miles N.E. of Multan; pop. (1868) 9124. It is a considerable centre of local trade. The imports are valued at £80,000; the exports at £65,000. The *district* of J., which lies mostly in the arid tract between the rivers Jhelum, Chenaub, and Ravee, has an area of 5702 sq. miles; pop. (1868) 348,027. The most populous town is Mughianah.

Jib, a large sail of triangular form running from the bowsprit to the masthead in small vessels, and from the jib-boom (a spar running out from the extremity of the bowsprit) to the fore-top-masthead in large ones. The J. has effect in bringing the ship's head to leeward when the wind is a-beam.

Jidd'ah. See JEDDAH.

Jig (*gigue*, *giga*), a lively dance for one or more performers. J. tunes have been written in Britain from the 16th c. onwards. The rhythms are various, but 'triplets' are an almost constant element in them. The J. is found as a movement in a *Suite* (q. v.) from the end of the 17th c. to the time of Haydn, and was gradually transformed into the 'last movement' of a sonata.

Jigg'er, a ship's tackle with a block at one end and a sheave at the other, used to 'hold on' to the cable, *i.e.*, keep it tight as it leaves the windlass.

Jihun'. See OXUS.

Jikad'ze, or **Shikat'ze**, the capital of the district of Zang, in Tibet, on the right bank of the Zangbo, 190 miles W. of H'Lassa. It contains a number of palaces, temples, and tombs, richly ornamented. The chief building is an immense palace or temple, the residence of one of the principal lamas, who has a suite of over 4000 persons. Pop. supposed to be about 100,000.

Jo'achim, Joseph, a celebrated violinist, born near Presburg, in Hungary, of Jewish parents, July 15, 1831. His teachers were Böhm, David, Moritz, and Hauptmann. From the Vienna Conservatoire he went to Leipzig, and was at the Gewandhaus for seven years. In 1850 he was made Director of Concerts at Weimar, in 1853 Master of the Hanover Chapel Royal, and in 1869 a Director in the Berlin Conservatoire. He appears annually in England, and was made Doctor of Music by the University of Cambridge in March 1877. J. is perhaps the most brilliant and powerful violinist of this century.

Jo'achimstahl (Joachimov), a Bohemian town 35 miles S. of Chemnitz, situated in the Erzgebirge, 2400 feet above the sea, and on the Weseritz, a branch of the Eger. Pop. 5641. J. was once twice as large, owing to its mines of silver, which, discovered in 1516, yielded, at the close of the 16th c., 20,000 marks, but now produce only 8500. There are also mines of iron, lead, and tin, and paper and coarse lace are manufactured. Large silver coins, first struck here in 1519, were called *Joachimsthaler*, from which shortened has arisen the German *thaler* and American *dollar*.

Joan of Arc. See JEANNE DARC.

Joan, Pope, was believed during the 13th c. to have been an Englishwoman of great learning, lewdness, and ability, who rose to the highest rank in the Catholic Church on the death of Leo IV., whom she succeeded (855), the supposition being that she was a man. It was also believed concerning her that between the Colosseum and the Church of St. Clement, Rome, she was seized with the pangs of childbirth, and died after holding the papal office for two years and five months. The prevalence of this belief gave rise to one of the most noteworthy controversies in history, the result of which is that both Catholic and Protestant writers have agreed in rejecting the tale as a groundless fiction. The authorities on which the story is based are Marianus Scotus, Martinus Polonus, and Stephen de Bourbon, the most recent believer in its authenticity being Professor Kist of Leyden. Panvinius, Blondel, Leibnitz, and Wensing are the most weighty authorities against its credibility.

Job, Book of, is one of the finest of the Old Testament Scriptures. The traditional view regarding it has been that Job was a real person, and the book a record of facts. The tendency among modern scholars is to regard it as a dramatic poem, as it is called even in the Talmud, with a historical prologue and epilogue, intended to teach certain ideas. But even by those who regard it in this light, the writer's aim is differently understood. Some have conceived it to be simply to set forth Job as an example of patience under suffering, or to set forth the conflict and victory of the pious in the heaviest troubles; but if this be the nature of the book, its aim undoubtedly is to throw light on the Divine procedure in the connection between evil and the moral conduct of men. The idea prevalent among the Israelites was that the lot of men in this world, both generally and in detail, was determined entirely by their moral character and conduct, so that every outward calamity was a punishment for some known or unknown sin, as prosperity was the reward of piety. This idea is expressed in the book in the speeches of Job's friends; and is shown to be a false one by the whole scope of the book, not merely by Job's replies to his friends, but by the prologue, according to which unparalleled calamities befell a pre-eminently pious man, and by the epilogue, in which God is made to admonish the friends, and impose an atoning sacrifice upon them because they had not spoken rightly of him as Job had done. The author and date of the book can only be conjectured. The Talmud ascribes it to Moses, and some assign to it even an earlier date. But from xiii. 26 and xxxi. 35 it appears that at the time of the composition it was customary to make a charge against any one before a tribunal in writing; and this alone would fix it down at least to the time of Moses, before which there is no trace of the art of writing (see Ewald, *History of Israel*). It is supposed also, from xii. 17–19, that the author had witnessed some such circumstances as he describes. On the other hand, since Ezekiel, Jeremiah, and the author of Proverbs i.–ix. seem to have been acquainted with it (*cf.* Jer. xx. 14–18 with Job iii., and Ezekiel xiv. 14–20), it must have been composed before the Babylonian exile. It was therefore most probably written between the Assyrian and Babylonian exiles. There is some reason to suppose that the discourses of Elihu (xxxii.–xxxvii.) are a later interpolation. See Bleek's *Einl. in das A. T.* (Eng. trans. 1869).

Job's Tears (*Coix lachryma*), a native grass of the E. Indies and Japan. The large round shining seeds have, when unripe, some resemblance to heavy tear-drops—hence the name. It is said to have strengthening and diuretic qualities.

Joc'elin of Brakelond, a Norman Englishman, native of St. Edmundsbury, who lived in the reign of King John, was monk and chaplain of the monastery of his native place. He wrote *Chronica Jocelini de Brakelonda* when in that position, recording the deeds of Abbot Samson, his superior, in a 'kind of monk or dog-Latin.' Carlyle in *Past and Present* gives a vivid, if occasionally strained, account of his book and contents, comparing him to Boswell, and describing him as a man 'of patient, peaceable, loving, clear-smiling nature.' 'Then also he has a pleasant wit.' See *Chronica*, edited by J. G. Rokewood (Camden Society, London, 1840).

Jodhpore', the capital of the native state of the same name in Rajputana, India, 358 miles S.W. of Delhi, and 1128 miles W. of Calcutta. It was founded by the Rajah Jodha in 1459, who removed hither the seat of government from Mandor, 5 miles N., where there are still fine tanks and marble ruins. J. is built on a rocky ridge, 300 feet above the plain, and contains many large tanks, wells, and freestone edifices, with a strong citadel, and a wall five miles in circumference.

The *state* of J., which is also known as Marwar, lies between Jeypore and Scinde, and is the largest of the Rajputana states. Area, about 35,672 sq. miles; pop. 1,783,600; revenue, £250,000; but twice as much is absorbed in feudal and religious grants; tribute, £21,300. The greater part consists of sandy or gravelly plains and grass jungle, on which are bred horses, camels, and cattle. Salt is manufactured in immense quantities at the Sambhur Lake, half of which adjoins the State, and is leased to the British; the other minerals are tin, lead, iron, alum, limestone, sandstone, and marble. The climate is healthy, but J. is liable to severe droughts. The other towns, besides J., are Nagore in the N.E., and Pali in the S. The only river is the Luni, or Salt River, which ultimately loses itself in the Runn of Kutch. The ravages of the Pindarees rendered necessary an appeal to British protection in 1818. Six years afterwards Marwar was made over to the British, and is still administered by us. The present (1877) chief, Jeswunt Singh, is a vigorous administrator. See *India and its Native Princes*, by L. Rousselet (Lond. 1875).

Jo'el (Heb. 'Jehovah is God') was one of the prophets of Judah, the date of whose prophesying has been fixed by different scholars at very various times, varying from the 10th c. to the 6th c. B.C. The most probable opinion is that he was a contemporary of Amos in the reign of Uzziah (B.C. 810–758; *cf.* i. 4, i. 25 with Amos iv. 6–9, and iii. 4–8 with Amos i. 6–10). It is also debated among critics (1) whether the description of locusts and their devastation is to be understood literally, or figuratively of hostile armies and their ravages, as *e.g.* those of Tiglath-Pileser, Shalmaneser, Sennacherib, Nebuchadnezzar, &c.; and (2) whether it is a description of a present plague or a prophecy of a future one.

Joe Miller, a term applied to stale threadbare jokes, from the name of a comic actor who died in 1738. He was a noted coiner or retailer of good things, a collection of which was published anonymously by John Mottley in 1739, with the title of *J. M.'s Jests, or the Wit's Vade Mecum.* In ten years the work, which is greatly marred by coarseness, passed through fifteen editions. *The Family J. M., a Drawing-Room Jest Book* (1848) is a more palatable publication. A facsimile of the original edition of 1739 was issued by Chatto & Windus in 1870.

Joggle, a term in masonry variously applied to any sort of jointing in which one stone is let or fitted into another with a notch or curve, so as to keep them both from slipping.

Johann' von Schwaben, also called **Johann the Parricide**, born about 1288, was the son of Rudolf, Duke of Swabia, and grandson of Rudolf, Duke of Habsburg. His uncle, the Emperor Albrecht I. (q. v.), having refused to make over to him, on his coming of age, the Duchy of Kyburg, which he had inherited from his mother Agnes, a Bohemian princess, J. conspired with some other Upper Swabian knights and killed him near Windisch, while he was crossing the river Reuss on an expedition to punish the mountaineers of the three rebel cantons of Switzerland. The conspirators fled, and all, save one Von Wart, died in wretchedness and obscurity, J., it is said by some, as a monk at Pisa in 1360.

Johann'a, the most prosperous and picturesque of the Comoro Isles (q. v.), between Madagascar and the E. coast of Africa.

John was the name borne by twenty-three of the Popes.—**John I.**, afterwards canonised, was Pope from 523 to 526. Sent on a successful mission to the emperor at Constantinople by the Arian king Theodoric, he was nevertheless thrown into prison at Ravenna on his return, and died there.—**John VIII.**, a Roman, Pope from 872 to 882, unpopular in Italy on account of his partiality for the Western Franks, crowned Karl the Bald Emperor, in spite of the protest by Ludwig the German, and at the next vacancy he supported the claims of Karl the Fat to the imperial crown. In the hope of securing jurisdiction in Bulgaria, he intrigued with the Greek emperor Basil, and recognised the banished Photius as Patriarch of Constantinople. Foiled in his expectations, he subsequently condemned Photius.—**John XII.** (956–964) was the first Pope who changed his name on assuming the papal dignity, and was formerly named Octavianus. He was but eighteen years of age when he became Pope, and he speedily covered himself with infamy by his licentiousness. He invited the German king Otho I. to assist him against Berengar II., crowned him Emperor, but proving disloyal, was deposed by Otho.—**John XXII.** (1316–34), born at Cahors in 1244, was a learned and distinguished canonist ere he took service as chancellor of the King of Naples. He became in succession bishop of Fréjus, archbishop of Avignon, and cardinal and bishop of Porto, and being in 1316 elected Pope at Lyon, he continued to maintain his residence in Avignon. He took lofty ground with the Emperor; and when the contest arose between Ludwig of Bavaria and Friedrich of Austria, he did his best to make the papacy supreme over the Empire. When fortune declared for Ludwig, he cited him before him, and when he refused to appear, excommunicated him. In Italy the Pope had the Guelph party to support him. He freely excommunicated the Ghibelline leaders, as well as the numerous scholars and divines, who denied the Pope's right to decide in civil cases. Meanwhile Ludwig entered Italy; had himself crowned emperor by bishops; and citing J. to appear before him to answer charges of heresy and high treason, he proceeded to depose him, and made Nicholas V. Pope. But when Ludwig left Italy, the Ghibelline cause decayed, and J., though he never visited Rome, soon secured his power again. He did much to defend Christendom from Mohammedan aggression; and when he died at Avignon left a treasury well filled by means of unexampled extortion.—**John XXIII.** (1410–1415), a Neapolitan, was made Pope in spite of his moral character, but was a man of great ability. When a council had become absolutely inevitable, by reason of the controversy with John Huss, J. summoned it to Constance. The same council finally found him guilty of seventy shameful deeds, and deposed him. J. spent some years in prison, but was pardoned by Pope Martin V., and died at Florence in 1419. For most of the above see Artaud de Montor's *Histoire des Souveraines Pontifes* (8 vols. Par. 1847–49).

John, youngest son of Henry II. and Eleanor of Guienne, was born at Oxford 24th December 1166. In 1185 Ireland was placed under his control, and, after having intrigued against his father (1189) and his brother Richard (until 1199), he was elected King of England. Arthur of Brittany, his nephew, was supported in France by King Philippe, but at Mirabel he came into J.'s power, and was despatched in prison. In 1200 J. divorced Hawisia of Gloucester and married Isabelle of Angoulême, and during the next few years lost Normandy, Anjou, and Guienne. 'The separation,' says Professor Stubbs, 'did much for England. Henceforth the king is mainly if not solely king of England, and the welfare of England the main if not the sole object of English counsels.' A dispute about the right of electing the Archbishop of Canterbury (1205) drew forth an interdict from Pope Innocent III., which (1212) was increased to a declaration that J.'s vassals were absolved from their allegiance. On May 15, 1213, J. made an abject submission, accepting Stephen Langton as Archbishop of Canterbury. Immediately a baronial quarrel arose owing to the increase of taxation, the hosts of mercenaries, and the plundering of the Church, which culminated (June 15, 1215) at Runnymede, near Windsor, where J. was compelled to sign the Magna Charta (q. v.). 'Although it is not the foundation of English liberty, it is the first, the clearest, the most united, and historically the most important of all the great enunciations of it, and it was a revelation of the possibility of freedom to the medieval world.' Though Archbishop Langton had sided with the barons, the Pope annulled the charter, and a war arose between the king and his subjects, who at last offered the crown to Louis, son of Philippe of France. On the 18th October 1216 J. died at Newark, in the midst of the war. 'Of all the kings he was,' writes Professor Stubbs, 'the most vicious, the most profane, the most tyrannical, the most false, the most short-sighted, the most unscrupulous;' and yet it is certain that he had the hereditary cleverness and vivacity of his race, with all the inborn resources of the warrior. See Pearson's *History of England* (vol. ii.), Stubbs' *Early Plantagenets*, and *Documents Illustrated, &c.*, Green's *Short History of the English People.*

John, Don, of Austria. See JUAN, DON, OF AUSTRIA.

John, Eve of St. According to Luke i. 26, 36, John the Baptist was older than Christ by six months, so that the birthday of the latter having been fixed at the Winter solstice, that of the former falls at the Summer solstice—the 24th of June. Owing to this circumstance several heathen practices passed into the observance of the Christian festival. The most prominent of these is the custom which used to prevail all over Europe, as well as in the E., and in some places has not yet altogether died out, of kindling great fires on midsummer eve, which was simply a relic of sun-worship, of the same nature as the rites observed at the Winter solstice (see YULE) and on May-day (see BELTEIN). These heathen practices, at first opposed, gradually came to be tolerated, and were finally adopted by the Church as her own. The fires of midsummer eve got the name of St. John's fire, being explained by the Church as an allusion to the words of Christ (John v. 35) regarding John: 'He was a burning and a shining light.' A curious mystical connection was also early observed between the Baptist's words regarding Christ (John iii. 30): 'He must increase, but I must decrease,' and the fact that after Christmas the days lengthen, and after midsummer shorten.

John, Knights of St., the oldest of the religious orders of knights in the middle ages, originated (1048) in a society of merchants at Amalfi for the defence of pilgrims to Jerusalem. These merchants founded at the sepulchre of Jesus in Jerusalem a church and cloister, whose inmates lived after the rules of the Benedictines; and soon afterwards a hospital for poor and sick pilgrims was added, dedicated to St. John the Baptist, wherefore the monks were named the Hospital-brothers of St. John of Jerusalem. Released at the conquest of Jerusalem in 1099 from severe persecution by the Seljuk Turks, the order increased in importance, and under its first superior, Gérard Tonque, received a constitution from Pope Pascal II. Gérard's successor, Raimond of Puy, changed the institution to a religious order of knights in 1118, adding to the monastic vows a solemn engagement to join in battle against the infidel, and himself taking the title of master of the order, which was now to consist of three classes—knights, of noble birth, to bear arms; priests or chaplains, to officiate in religious worship; and serving brothers, to tend the sick and relieve pilgrims. Under the favour of the Popes it rapidly increased, but gradually deviated more and more from its original objects. Monasteries called *commanderies* were planted in lands far from Palestine, the proper theatre for the K. of St. J., in order to raise money for their holy wars. After the taking of Jerusalem by Saladin in 1187, they removed to Ptolemais, and afterwards (in 1291) to Limisso in Cyprus. In 1309 they conquered Rhodes, and called themselves *Knights of Rhodes*; but after a hard struggle with the Turks had to surrender the island to Soliman II. in 1522. They then wandered about for a time without forming a permanent settlement, till Karl V., in 1530, gave them Malta, Gozo, and Comino, as a fief, after which they were called *Knights of Malta*. The Reformation cost them their possessions in England, the Netherlands, and Scandinavia. The Revolution in France had the same result, and when Napoleon I. took Malta in 1798, they were driven thence. The last grand-master, Hompesch, laid down his authority at Trieste, and in his stead was chosen the Emperor Paul of Russia, but the election was set aside on the protestation of the Pope, and to avoid a conflict with Russia the Elector of Bavaria abolished the order in his dominions. In 1810–11 the order was abolished in Prussia, and all its property confiscated; while the name was retained in *Der Preussische Johanniterorden*, which, founded in 1812 as a decoration reserved for nobility, was in 1852 developed to an evangelical order of knights, for the care of the sick, under King Friedrich Wilhelm IV.'s brother, Prince Karl, with branches in several Prussian and other German provinces. This order was very active in the wars of 1864, 1866, and 1870–71. After the fall of Napoleon I. the K. of St. J. sought in vain to be restored to Malta, but the Pope permitted the removal of the chapter to Ferrara (in 1826), and afterwards to Rome (1834). The arms of the order consisted of an octagonal silver cross on a red ground, with a crown surrounded with a garland of roses. In peace the knights wore a long white mantle with a white octagonal cross on the breast; in war they had a red coat with a cross of the common shape on the breast and back. The K. of St. J. still preserve at Rome, Venice, Naples, and Prag, the shadow of the *Grand Priories* that once were widely established among European nations, and one of which (at Clerkenwell) gave its holder the title of First Baron of England.

John, Prester. See PRESTER JOHN.

John, St., the Apostle, was the son of Zebedee, a fisherman of Galilee, and followed that occupation himself till his call to be a disciple of Christ (Matt. iv. 21, 22; Mark i. 19, 20), from whom he received special marks of affection, above even Peter and his own elder brother James. The traditional history of the latter part of John's life is that he remained at Jerusalem till about 48, when he went to Asia Minor, and there founded several churches, residing chiefly at Ephesus; that under Nero (54–68), or Domitian (81–96), he was banished to Patmos, where he received the vision of the Apocalypse; that on his liberation he returned to Ephesus, where he wrote his Gospel and Epistles about (90–100), and remained till his death, about 100, in the hundredth year of his age. The writings ascribed to him are the Fourth Gospel, the three Epistles which bear his name, and the Apocalypse (q. v.). It is round the Fourth Gospel that the hottest war of controversy has raged in connection with the Life of Christ, because it is contended by those who question its authenticity and fix its date, some of them, so late as 150, that it gives a more fully developed and altogether different conception of Christ from that of the Synoptists. (See GOSPELS.) The authenticity of the First Epistle must stand or fall with that of the Gospel, for almost all agree that it is by the same author. The tradition that the second and third Epistles were written by St. J. is ancient, but they were classed by Eusebius among those writings which in his time were not received by all the ecclesiastical authorities. They may have been written by John *the elder* (*cf.* II. 1, III. 1), who lived at Ephesus, and was sometimes confounded with St. J.

John, St., the fourth largest city in the Dominion of Canada, and the emporium of New Brunswick, lies at the mouth on the left bank of the river of the same name. Its harbour is free from ice owing to the tide-falls of the Bay of Fundy, and this gives it an advantage over all the Dominion ports. The town is now connected by railway with all parts of the Dominion, and has a fine cathedral of the Immaculate Conception, handsome state buildings, a penitentiary, lunatic asylum, hospital, skating-rink, three daily, one tri-weekly, and eight weekly newspapers, &c. It exports large quantities of pine timber to America, of deals to England, and of shooks to the W. Indies, and carries on an active shipbuilding trade. The river is spanned by a fine suspension bridge 640 feet long. Pop., including the suburb of Portland, 45,000.

The *river* St. J. rises in Maine, U.S., forms the international boundary for about 60 miles, flows mainly in a S.E. direction through New Brunswick, and enters the Bay of Fundy after a course of 450 miles. It is navigable for vessels of 150 tons to Fredericton, a distance of 80 miles.

John of Leyden. See JAN OF LEYDEN.

John o' Groat's House, on a rocky promontory 1½ miles W. of Duncansbay Head in Caithness, was long and widely known as marking the limit of Scotland on the N.; *e.g.*, 'frae Maidenkirk to Johnny Groat's' (Burns). The legend of John o' Groat or Groot is told by Robert Chambers in his *Picture of Scotland*. The descendants of a Hollander of the above name who had settled in this remote spot in the reign of James IV., having quarrelled about precedence, one of the eight members of the family restored peace by erecting an octagonal building entered by a door on every side, and containing a table of the same shape. Whatever may be the value of the legend, there is documentary evidence to prove the existence of a family of this name near Duncansby Head as far back as the close of the 15th c., and various representatives of the family are said to exist in the present day (1877), among others, a Mrs. Cruickshanks in Pulteneytown, Wick. The site of J. o' G.'s H. is still outlined on the turf. Most probably the legend was suggested by the odd shape of what was formerly a ferry-house for the Orkneys. See *Statistical Account of Scotland*.

John (III.) Sobies'ki, King of Poland, son of the Castellan of Cracow (a great warrior and statesman), was born at Olesko, in Galicia, June 2, 1624, and, along with his brother Mark, received an excellent education. Both brothers were abroad at their father's death, when they entered the Polish army, which had just been defeated by the Russians at Pilawiecz. Mark fell in an action at the river Bug, but his brother distinguished himself so that he became the terror of the Turks and Tartars. In 1665 he became a marshal, in 1667 commander-in-chief and woiwode of Cracow, and (11th November 1673) inflicted a great defeat on the Turkish army at Choczim. He was chosen King of Poland 21st May 1674, and with his wife, the daughter of a French marquis, was crowned at Cracow in 1676. The war against the Turks was continued with the utmost vigour; and on the 12th September 1683 J. S. performed his greatest exploit, the relief of Vienna when besieged by the Grand Vizier with 200,000 men, and defeat of the Turks outside the walls of the town. But neither from the delivered Austrians nor from his own subjects did the hero receive support to fitly follow up this success, which therefore had not the fruits that might have been expected. He died of apoplexy 17th June 1696.

John's, St., the capital, commercial emporium, and seat of government of Newfoundland, British N. America, lies picturesquely about 3 miles from Cape Spear, the most easterly point of land on the American side of the Atlantic. It has a fine harbour entered by the 'narrows,' and enclosed by hills rising abruptly to a height of 600 feet on each side. Its chief buildings are the Anglican cathedral designed by Sir G. G. Scott, and the Roman Catholic cathedral erected at a cost of $800,000. The industries are biscuit-baking, founding, oil-refining, tanning, distilling, &c. The town is connected with continental America by telegraph, and by regular steam lines with Halifax, Montreal, and New York. Pop. in 1802, 3420; in 1869, 22,553. Sir Humphrey Gilbert landed here when taking possession of the island in 1583.—**J., St.**, a beautiful town in the province of Quebec, Dominion of Canada, on the W. bank of the river Richelieu, at the head of Chambly Canal and of the navigable waters of Lake Champlain, and on the Grand Trunk Railway. It has saw, planing, and grist mills, several foundries and brick-fields, and a considerable trade in grain, timber, firewood, &c. Pop. 4000. St. J.'s is connected by a bridge with Iberville, or St. Athanase, on the opposite side of the river.

John's, St., the capital of Antigua, and residence of the governor of the Leeward Islands, is situated in the N.E. of the island, at the head of a wide but shallow bay. It has a cathedral, a courthouse, a large market, &c., and exports considerable sugar, rum, and molasses. The temperature ranges from 96° to 62° F., and the average rainfall is 45 inches. Rain-water is gathered in cisterns. Pop. 8515.

John's, St., College, Cambridge, was founded in 1511 under the will of Lady Margaret, Countess of Richmond and Derby, and mother of Henry VII. Owing to the death of the foundress (1509) before the full completion of her designs, great difficulty was experienced in establishing the college on as large a scale as was originally intended; and it was mainly through the exertions of Fisher (q. v.), Bishop of Rochester, that sufficient funds were obtained to endow thirty-two fellowships. The college at present consists of a master, fifty-six fellows, sixty foundation and eight minor scholars, and forty-nine sizars. The fellowships and scholarships are open to all British subjects without restriction, except that the fellows must be in priest's orders within seven years of their M.A. The college sets £6700 apart from its annual revenues for the maintenance of scholarships, exhibitions, &c., and £180 for prizes. It has fifty-one livings in its presentation. St. J., which ranks second only to Trinity, is the great mathematical and North Country college. The buildings consist of four courts, the first of which is entered by a fine gateway, and contains the magnificent chapel, erected in 1867, from designs by Sir G. G. Scott, and moulded on the Sainte Chapelle of Paris. Its tower is the most conspicuous object in Cambridge. In 1875 the number of undergraduates was 381.

John'son, Andrew, seventeenth President of the United States, was born at Raleigh, N. Carolina, December 29, 1808. He never was at school, and was almost entirely self-taught. Apprenticed to a tailor, he went in 1826 to Tennessee, and settled in Greenville, becoming mayor in 1830. He was elected to the State legislature in 1835, and again in 1839. Next year he canvassed Tennessee in the Democratic interest for Van Buren. He sat in Congress from 1843 to 1853, when he became Governor of Tennessee, and he was elected to the United States Senate in 1857. He there supported the slave-holding and Democratic party generally, but when secession was mooted vigorously opposed it, and took the side of the North. As military governor at Nashville in 1862 he showed courage and ability in maintaining order. He was elected Vice-President in 1864, and on the assassination of Lincoln was sworn President, April 15, 1865. Though he had spoken violently against the South, he acted moderately, and granted general amnesties, to the chagrin of his Republican supporters. His Congress was hostile, and the contempt he showed for it in vetoing its decisions, and in dismissing Mr. Stanton, his war secretary, led to his impeachment in February 1688. J. was, however, acquitted. His term expired in March 1869. He was elected to the Senate in 1875, but died 31st July of the same year. See *Lives* by Savage (1865), Moore (1865), Foster (1866), and *Trial of A. J.* (3 vols. 1868).

Johnson, Reverdy, an American lawyer and statesman, was born at Annapolis, Maryland, May 21, 1796. He was admitted to the bar in 1815, elected a Maryland senator in 1821, was a United States senator 1845–49 and 1863–68, and Attorney-General of the United States 1849–53. In June 1868 he was sent as ambassador to London, where he negotiated a treaty on the Alabama Claims. This was, however, rejected by the Senate, and he was recalled in 1869, and has since resided at Baltimore.

John'son, Samuel, was born 18th September 1709, at Lichfield, in Staffordshire, England, where his father was a bookseller. After five years' schooling in his native city, one at Stourbridge, and two years' loitering at home, he entered Pembroke College, Oxford, in 1728, and whilst there produced a Latin version of the *Messiah* (1731), which won the applause of the whole university, as also of its author, Pope. Forced by poverty to leave college without a degree, he was for a time usher in the school of Market Bosworth, next lived at Birmingham, where he translated Lobo's *Voyage to Abyssinia* (1735), and having in 1736 married a Mrs. Porter, a widow of forty-eight, who brought him £800, started a boarding-school on his own account near Lichfield. The venture failed, and in 1737 J. came to London, with David Garrick, one of his three pupils, and an unfinished tragedy, *Irene* (acted in 1749). Private patronage was dead, the patronage of the public was only arising, and during the twenty-five years that J. led the life of a Grub Street hack, he was always in straitened circumstances, like his friend Savage (q. v.), whose life he published (1744). For *London*, an imitation of Juvenal's third satire, he got but £10, though it ran through an edition in a week, whilst his connection with Cave's *Gentleman's Magazine*, in which he wrote the parliamentary debates, besides prefaces, lives, and miscellaneous papers, was equally unremunerative. But he had made himself a name, and in 1747 Dodsley with four other firms engaged him for £1575 to compile his *Dictionary* (completed in 1755). Other works that greatly added to his reputation were the *Rambler* (1750–52, the last number appearing three days before his wife's death), *Idler* (1758–60), and *Rasselas* (1759), which last was written in the evenings of one week, and brought its author £125. In 1762 he received a pension of £300, and thenceforth wrote comparatively little, the *Lives of the Poets* (1779–81) being his only considerable work. In 1763 he met Boswell (q. v.), and in 1765 made the acquaintance of the Thrales, of whose family he came to be almost regarded as a member. The founding of the Literary Club (see CLUB), the receipt of an LL.D. diploma from Trinity College, Dublin (1765), visits to the Hebrides (1773), Wales (1774), and France (1775)—these are the most marked events of J.'s closing years. He died 13th December 1784 in Bolt Court, and was buried in Westminster Abbey. J.'s writings during his lifetime were popular beyond belief, his *Rambler* being ranked above the *Spectator*, his criticisms regarded as infallible. To us they seem commonplace, disfigured by mannerism, cramped, and warped by prejudice. A High Churchman, he was lenient to Catholics, but would credit no good of a Dissenter; a Tory, to him a Whig was 'vile,' whilst as a critic he preferred Pope's *Iliad* to Homer's, sneered at Bishop Percy's ballads, and could see no merit in *Gulliver*, *Tom Jones*, or *Tristram Shandy*. His style is a caricature of Sir Thomas Browne's. The dignity of the older writer becomes in J. pomposity; his quaintness, affectation; and a natural if overstrained niceness of diction, leads him to a studied avoidance of all that is native and home-grown in the English speech. Yet his name has become immortal through Boswell's *Life*. There we see the man as he lived, and looked, and thought. We mark the 'Sage's' uncouth person and tender heart, his weaknesses and kindnesses, his contradictions and solid learning, and above all we have such a vivid picture of the life and thought of his century as meets us in no autobiography or set history of the times. It may be added that a certain deep, rugged, honesty of soul exalts him above all his contemporaries, and gives to his character, though not to his writings, a permanent interest and vitality. The best editions of J.'s works are those by Hawkins (15 vols. Lond. 1787–89) and Murphy (12 vols. Lond. 1792; new ed. 1824). See Boswell's *Life*, and the Essays of Macaulay and Carlyle.

Johnson, Thomas, an English botanist, was born at Selby in Yorkshire, brought up as an apothecary in London, the University of Oxford conferring on him the degree of doctor of physic, and died in September 1644 from a wound received whilst fighting in the royal cause at Basing. He was the first who published an account of a botanical exploration in England (*Iter Cantianum*, 1629), the first who gave a catalogue of a defined botanising ground (*Ericetum Hampstediense*, 1632), the first who separated British plants from foreign ones (*Mercurius Botanicus*, 1634), and from his greatly improved edition of Gerard's *Herbal*, describing 2850 plants (1633).

John'ston, Alexander Keith, LL.D., F.R.S., a celebrated cartographer, was born at Kirkhill, in Edinburghshire, Scotland, 28th December 1804, served his apprenticeship as an engraver, travelled extensively, and studied the principal modern languages. Among the best of his many works are a *National Atlas* (folio, 1843), a *Physical Atlas of Natural Phenomena* (1847–49, 2d ed. 1854–56), for which he received the assistance of Brewster, Murchison, and others, and a *Royal Atlas of Geography* (1861). He may be regarded as the first of the great modern cartographers, and his maps surprised the world into delighted admiration by their fullness, accuracy, and beautiful engraving. Honours were showered upon him, and the Geographical Society of Paris proclaimed his *Physical Atlas* to be 'one of the most magnificent monuments that had yet been raised to the scientific genius of the age.' J. died at Ben Rhydding, 9th July 1871. His son, bearing the same name, is honourably known as a S. American traveller and a geographical writer.

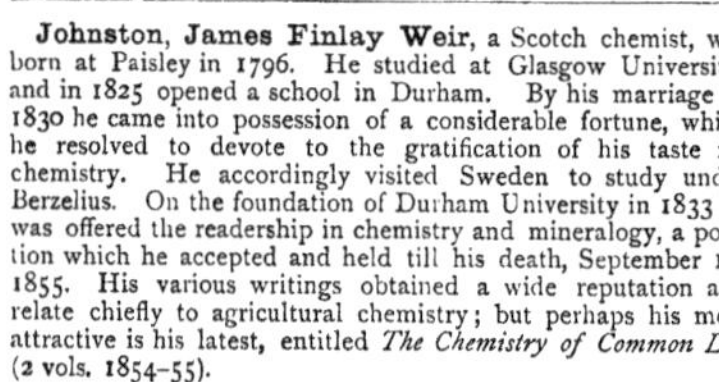

Johnston, James Finlay Weir, a Scotch chemist, was born at Paisley in 1796. He studied at Glasgow University, and in 1825 opened a school in Durham. By his marriage in 1830 he came into possession of a considerable fortune, which he resolved to devote to the gratification of his taste for chemistry. He accordingly visited Sweden to study under Berzelius. On the foundation of Durham University in 1833 he was offered the readership in chemistry and mineralogy, a position which he accepted and held till his death, September 18, 1855. His various writings obtained a wide reputation and relate chiefly to agricultural chemistry; but perhaps his most attractive is his latest, entitled *The Chemistry of Common Life* (2 vols. 1854-55).

Johnston, Joseph Eccleston, an able Confederate general, was born in Virginia, February 1807. In 1829 he entered the U.S. army. He served as captain of engineers in the Mexican war and became a colonel. In 1860 he was made quartermaster-general, resigning April 22, 1861, to enter the Confederate service. He led the Southern soldiery at Bull's Run, and in the spring of 1862 held the command at Richmond. Wounded at Fair Oaks, May 31, 1862, on his recovery he was made general of the army in Tennessee. Here and in Georgia he sustained a series of reverses, and finally was superseded by Hood, July 17, 1864. Later he was called to lead the scattered forces in Georgia, S. Carolina, and Florida, but was unable to stem Sherman's victorious march. On hearing of Lee's surrender of the main army he capitulated to Sherman, April 26, 1865. Since the war he has resided in Georgia actively labouring for the resuscitation of the shattered South. See his *Narrative of Military Operations* (New York, 1874).

John'stone, a town of Scotland, in the county of Renfrew, on the Black Cart river, 2 miles W. of Paisley by rail. It has sprung into existence since 1781, and is now a thriving industrial centre, with large cotton factories, flax-mills, machine-shops, brass and iron foundries, &c. In the vicinity are extensive collieries. The 'Brig of J.' here spans the river. Pop. (1871) 6882. Cattle and horse fairs are held at J. in January and July.

Johnstown, a town in Pennsylvania, U.S., between the Conemangh River in the N. and Stoney Creek on the S., 79 miles E. of Pittsburg by rail. It is on the Pennsylvania Canal, and has a rolling-mill and Bessemer steel work (in 1875 employing 6000 men), a woollen-mill, tannery, cement works, &c. The surrounding hills are rich in iron, bituminous coal, limestone, cement, and fireclay. Pop. (1871) 6028, but greatly increased since the census.

John the Baptist (Heb. 'God-granted'), a native of Judæa, and the son of Zacharias, a priest (Luke i., *cf.* Jos.), was beheaded by Herod Antipas. Closely allied to the Essenes in disregard of bodily comforts and dislike to the busy haunts of men, J. in spirit more closely resembled the old prophets. From the time of Zerubbabel there was a change in the form of the Jewish Messianic hopes. The Messiah (q. v.) is now, at least with the prophets, the Angel or Messenger of the Covenant (Mal. iii. 1), and in preparation for the glorious day of the Sun of Righteousness Elijah the prophet is to reappear to *convert* both old and young (Mal. iv. 2, 5, 6); or this harbinger is to be like the herald who proclaimed the return of the exiles from Babylonia (Isa. xl. 1-5). This mission J. fulfilled by preaching in connection with the simple rite of baptism, which was substituted for the dead service of sacrifice, a higher righteousness of heart and life, 'that the regeneration of the human spirit was to be accomplished, not by ceremonies or opinions, but by moral uprightness.' See Stanley's *Jewish Church* (2d ed. Lond. 1875).

John the Baptist, St., College of, Oxford, was founded in 1555 by Sir Thomas White, Knt., alderman of London, on the site of a Cistercian monastery. The original foundation consisted of a president, fifty fellows and scholars, a chaplain, an organist, six clerks, eight choristers, and two sextons. At present there are eighteen open life fellowships; four Fereday fellowships tenable for fourteen years, founded in 1854; five open and twenty-eight close scholarships, twenty-one of which are tenable for seven years by persons elected from Merchant Taylors' School; and four Casperol scholarships, tenable for four years. The college presents to thirty-one livings. In 1876 the number of members of Congregation was 17, and of commoners 89.

Johore', a Mohammedan state on the most southern point of the Malayan peninsula, 15 miles S. of Singapore, founded in 1511 by the inhabitants of Malacca, who had been driven out by the Portuguese. Area 20,000 sq. miles; pop. 40,000 Malays, and 60,000 Chinese. Exports, gambier, pepper, and tea. British relations with the Sultan of J. date from 1818; six years later he ceded the island of Singapore. The present ruler is a most enlightened prince, and has greatly developed the resources of the country. In 1866 he visited England, and was created a Maharajah. He has also received the orders of the Star of India, and of St. Michael and St. George.

Joint. By *J.*, or *articulation*, is meant the connection which exists between the different bones and cartilages of which a living body is composed. The form of the J. and the kind of connection between the bones entering into the J. vary, the variations depending upon the amount of movement allowed in the articulation. In some, the movement allowed is little or none, and to these the term *synarthrosis*, or *immovable* joint, has been applied; in others, a considerable amount of movement is allowed, these are called *diarthrosis* or *movable* joints. An intermediate class is formed between the two extremes, the *amphiarthrosis* or *mixed* joints. In the *immovable* joints, the bones are separated from each other only by the periosteum or lining membrane of the bone. They are not separated from each other by a synovial cavity. This kind of J. is found between the various bones which form the skull and face, with the exception of the lower jaw. In the *movable* joints the portion of the bones which enter into the articulation is enlarged and coated over with cartilage. The surfaces of the cartilages are lubricated by synovial fluid, which is secreted by the synovial membrane which envelops the articulation. The object of the cartilage and fluid is to make the surfaces smooth and diminish friction during movement. The joints which are included in this division are subdivided according to the kind of movement permitted. (1) *Arthrodia.*—Here the bones have flat surfaces, and are closely connected by ligaments. The only motion permitted is a gliding movement. The joints between the carpal bones are examples. (2) *Ginglymus* or hinge-J.—Here the surfaces of the bones are of such a shape that movements of flexion and extension only are permitted. The bones are connected by ligaments which also resist any other movement. The elbow and ankle joints, and the joints of the fingers may be taken as typical examples. (3) *Enarthrosis* or ball and socket-joint, where movement in all directions is permitted. Here one of the bones has a rounded portion or head upon it, and it is in contact with, and moves in a depression or socket in the other bone. The ligaments are also arranged so as only to limit movement, when that movement is becoming excessive in any direction. The bones are held together by atmospheric pressure, and by the action of the muscles surrounding the J. The hip and shoulder joints are examples of this class. (4) *Mixed Joints.*—The bones entering into this form of J. are separated by fibro-cartilage, and have either no synovial membrane, or the membrane is present only in a portion of the articulation. This form of J. is found in those parts of the body where stability is required, but where some amount of motion is necessary. Thus we have examples in the articulations between the bodies of the vertebræ. Here the amount of motion between two contiguous bodies is not great, but in the column, as a whole, there is a considerable amount. This can be noted when we bend the body in order to pick up something from the ground.

Diseases of the Joints.—The various joints of the body may become the seat of disease of an inflammatory or strumous character, or of malignant degeneration; and such diseases may give rise to various morbid conditions, such as rigidity, Anchylosis (q. v.), and the formation of foreign bodies within their cavities. Until the time of the late Sir B. Brodie, D. of the J. were called by surgeons *Arthritis* (q. v.), and by the public *white swellings*. Inflammation of the synovial membrane or *Synovitis* is the most common of all the articular affections, and usually results from cold in rheumatic or syphilitic constitutions, and, in such cases, more joints than one are generally affected; but it may also be occasioned by injury, and, in such cases, the other textures that enter into the formation of the joint are usually implicated. This form may terminate in *hydrarthrosis*, or dropsy of the joint, which, in strumous constitutions, frequently runs on to suppurative destruction; or the serous membrane may become lined with pendulous growths which occasionally become detached as loose substances of a fibrous structure. Adhesions are also frequently formed which result in stiffness of the joints. The symptoms of D. of the J. vary according to the joints affected and the nature of the affection; the most marked symptoms, in all cases, being pain, heat, and swelling. In the larger joints, such as the ankle, knee, and hip joints, the pain is usually very severe, and is much aggravated by motion and pressure. The mode of treatment varies in like manner, but the general indications are perfect rest; the usual means for subduing inflammation and alleviating pain in the acute stage, and in the subacute and chronic stage, rest and counter-irritants.

Joint and Several, an English law phrase meaning that an obligation is come under, or a contract entered into, by each of several parties in connection with each other, and also independently. The general rule of law in England is that unless otherwise stipulated, a contract is only *joint*, hence if an action is brought to compel fulfilment, it must be brought against all the parties bound. But where the words J. and S. are used—as, 'we A. B. and C. jointly and severally bind and oblige ourselves, or promise,' &c.—then the holder of the obligation may sue A. B. or C. alone, the party sued having a claim of relief against the others. In Scotland, the general rule of law in *joint* obligations is that each debtor is bound *pro rata* only; but where each is bound *conjunctly and severally*—the Scotch equivalent to J. and S.—then each is liable *Singuli in Solidum*, and the creditor may exact full performance from one, or from any number he chooses proportionally, leaving them to account with one another.

Joint Fir. See SEA GRAPE.

Joint-Stock Companies, Law Regarding. The principle of limited liability among the members of J.-S. C. was first introduced by the Act 18 and 19 Vict. c. 133. At that time there were various statutes affecting the incorporation, regulation, and winding-up of trading companies. These were consolidated and amended by the Companies Act of 1862, which was again amended by the Act of 1867. By these statutes, seven or more persons associated for any lawful purpose may, by subscribing their names to a memorandum of association, form an incorporated company with or without limited liability. An annual list of the members of a company is to be forwarded to the registrar of J.-S. C., and the list is to be open to public inspection. Provision is made to protect the public from adventurers getting up companies, to punish delinquent directors, and to prevent their flight. And though the offence of a delinquent director or other official of a joint-stock company is one for which the offender is criminally liable, he may be compelled to pay a sum to the company as compensation for his misconduct. It not unfrequently happens that in launching joint-stock adventures delusive prospects of gain are held out to induce the public to join in them. When any one has thus been misled by a statement distinctly untrue, the Chancery division will annul the contract; but some latitude of statement is allowed, according to the decision in the case of Kisch *v.* The Central Railway Company of Venezuela. Lord-Justice Turner said that it was unfortunately universally known that the prospectus of a company never contained an accurate account, so that the validity of a bargain founded on such a document could not be tried by so strict a test as another kind of bargain could be tried by. A mere exaggerated view or casual inaccuracy in a prospectus would not justify the setting aside of a bargain founded on it. On the other hand, the Court required that where a contract was founded on the statement of one of the parties to it, that statement should be *bonâ fide.* By sec. 4 no partnership of more than ten persons is to be formed for banking purposes unless it is registered under the Act, or is formed under some other statute or letters-patent. Nor is any partnership of more than twenty persons to be formed for the purpose of gain, unless it is registered or is formed under an Act of Parliament or letters-patent, or constituted for the working of mines within the jurisdiction of the Stannaries (q. v.). A partnership of fewer than twenty persons is not bound to register, but it may do so with or without limited liability. Petitions to wind up companies must be presented in England to the Chancery division, who may refer the question to the Court of Bankruptcy. The Act applies to the United Kingdom, being in Scotland adapted to the legal institutions of that kingdom. See PARTNERSHIP, LAW REGARDING.

Joint-Tenancy. See under COMMON—COMMON, TENANCY IN.

Joint Trade, or **Adventure**, is a partnership for a special object, as for the working of a mine. The rights and liabilities of such a partnership depend mainly on the terms of the contract. But the personal creditors of one partner cannot appropriate the joint-stock to his own payment until the debts of the concern are paid and the other partners have received their shares. See PARTNERSHIP, LAW REGARDING.

Join'ture, in English law, is a provision made for a wife in the event of her surviving her husband. If the J. be provided after marriage the wife may either accept it or claim her *Dower* (q. v.), (see also BAR OF DOWER). A J. is not forfeited by the adultery of the wife as dower is. In Scotch law the word is used in a similar sense.

Joinville, Jean, Sieur or **Sire de**, descended from one of the most illustrious families of Champagne, was born (1224) in the district of Châlons-sur-Marne, was early attached to the court of the King of Navarre, joined a crusade with St. Louis (1248), engaged in many battles, and returned (1254), married Alix de Resnel (1261). J. declined to follow the king on the crusade of 1270 on the plea that when he was beyond sea his people were compelled to suffer too many hardships at the hands of the King of Navarre. Even in his ninety-second year J. obeyed the summons to appear in the battle-field, and he lived through the reigns of six kings. M. Francisque Michel thinks it probable that he died in 1317. In 1853 a bronze statue was erected to his memory in the town which bears his name. Medieval literature furnishes no history exactly comparable to J.'s *Histoire de St. Louis* for simplicity of narrative, naïveté of detail, and sober truthfulness of method. See Max Müller's *Chips from a German Workshop*, vol. iii. p. 159.

Joists. See FLOORS.

Jol'iet, a city of Illinois, U.S., on the Aux des Plaines River and the Illinois and Michigan Canal, 36 miles S.W. of Chicago by rail. It is the seat of the state penitentiary, perhaps the largest institution of the kind in the country, usually containing 1300 convicts, who are employed industrially. J. has an immense iron and steel work (employing some 2500 men), large building-stone quarries, cement works and brickfields. It is near the Wilmington coalfields, and draws an abundant water supply from sixteen artesian wells. Pop. (1870) 7263.

Jolly-Boat (a corruption of *yawl*-boat, comp. Dutch *Jol*, Ger. and Dan. *Jolle*), a small broad boat used by ships' stewards for communicating with the shore.

Jomini, Henri, Baron, a distinguished soldier and military author, was born at Payerne, Switzerland, March 6, 1779. He joined the French army and served under Ney in Germany in 1805, in which year he published his *Traité des Grandes Opérations Militaires*. He was made a baron for gallantry at Jena, after which he served in Spain and Russia. Badly treated by Napoleon, he went over to the allies, became a Russian general, and fought in the Turkish war of 1828. He retired to Brussels in 1855, and died at Passy, March 24, 1869. J. wrote many military works of great excellence, and the *Vie de Napoleon* (4 vols. 1827).

Jo'nah (Heb. 'dove'), a Hebrew prophet, who lived not later than the reign of Jeroboam II. (B.C. 824–783; 2 Kings xiv. 25). If therefore the opinion that the Book of J. was composed by the prophet himself were correct, it would be one of the oldest prophetical writings which have been preserved. Some maintain the historical nature of the book without reference to the writer or date of composition. The language used by Christ (Matt. xii. 39–41; xvi. 4; Luke xi. 29) is felt by many to compel the adoption of this view. Others, however, find difficulties in the way of regarding it as pure history: (1) in the improbability that the whole of the inhabitants of Nineveh should immediately have felt such remorse at the call to repentance of an unknown foreigner, there being besides no trace of the event in the history of the city; (2) in the fact that the name of the king in whose time it happened is not mentioned; (3) that J. should not only live seventy-two hours in the belly of a fish, but in that position compose a psalm, which it is distinctly stated he did (ii. 2–9); and maintain that the aim of the book was to teach, in opposition to the narrow-minded idea of the Jews, that Jehovah was the God of their nation alone, that he embraces all nations within his fatherly love.

Jones, Ernest, Chartist and poet, was born 25th January 1819 at Berlin, his father, Major J., residing in Holstein as aide-de-camp to the Duke of Cumberland. Educated at the Lüneburg Gymnasium and the University of Göttingen, he was called to the bar by the Society of the Middle Temple, April 19, 1844, but devoting himself to Chartism (q. v.), became editor of three of its organs, stood unsuccessfully for Halifax (1847), and in 1848 was sentenced to two years' imprisonment for a seditious speech delivered at a monster Chartist meeting held on Kensington Common. In prison he wrote with his own blood on the flyleaves of a prayer-book—so he tells us in the dedication—*The Revolt of Hindustan* (1857). He published several other poems, besides three volumes of tales, travelled the northern circuit, contested Nottingham in 1853 and again in 1857, and Manchester (where he resided) in 1868, but always without success, and died at the latter place, January 26, 1869.

Jones, In'igo, the father of modern English architecture, was born in London in 1572. He studied in Italy, and in 1605 returned to England, where he designed the scenery of the court masques of James I. While thus engaged he excited the antagonism of Ben Jonson, but had the royal favour. After some years of further study in Italy, he finally took up his residence in London. Among his finest efforts are the noble Banqueting House at Whitehall, and the front of Wilton House. He designed the Corinthian Portico of St. Paul's, the Covent Garden Piazza, Heriot's Hospital, Edinburgh, and many fine buildings. His unfulfilled plans for a gigantic palace for James I. were published in 1727. He died June 1653. J. was a follower of Palladio. See Memoirs of his Life, by Peter Cunningham.

Jones, Owen, the Mæcenas of Welsh literature, was born in the Vale of Myvyr, Denbighshire, in 1741, and came early to London, where he made a considerable fortune as a furrier in Thames Street, and where he died September 26, 1814. He founded the Gwyneddigion Society (1771), published an edition of the poems of Davydd ab Gwilym (1789), the *Myvyrian Archæology of Wales* (3 vols. 1801–7), &c., and formed a collection of transcripts of ancient Welsh MSS. (50 vols. 4to.), which is now in the British Museum.

Jones, John Paul, a famous buccaneer, son of a gardener named Paul, was born at Arbigland, Kirkcudbright, North Britain, July 6, 1747. He went to sea at twelve, and in 1773 settled in Virginia under the name of Jones. Shortly after the outbreak of the war with Great Britain, he obtained the command of an American ship, and made great havoc of British commerce. In April 1778, he landed by night at Whitehaven, plundered the house of the Earl of Selkirk, and seized 200 prisoners. Next year he threatened Leith, but was driven back by a gale, when he captured the *Serapis*, a British frigate, off Flamboro'. After the war, he was for some time an Admiral in the Russian navy. He died in Paris, July 18, 1792. J. was fiery, impetuous, and boastful. The *Mémoires* which appeared at Paris in 1789 (Edinb. 1830) are of doubtful authenticity. See the Biographies by Sherburne (Wash. 1826), Simms (New York, 1845), J. S. C. Abbott (New York, 1875).

Jones, Sir William, next to Colebrooke the greatest English Orientalist, was born in London, 28th September 1746, was educated at Harrow and Oxford, and was tutor to Lord Althorp, son of Earl Spencer, from 1765 to 1770. He devoted himself early and eagerly to the study of Oriental languages, and published a French translation of a Persian *Life of Nadir Shah* (1770); a *Persian Grammar* (1771); *Commentaries on Asiatic Poetry* (1774), and translations of seven Arabic poems under the collective title *Modllakat* (1780). Called to the bar in 1774, he issued several legal essays, and was appointed a judge in the Supreme Court of Judicature in Bengal in 1783. In 1784 he founded the Asiatic Society at Calcutta, of which he was the first president, and to the transactions of which he was a voluminous contributor. His later works were a translation from Sanskrit of Kâlidâsa's play of *Sakuntala*, one of the finest gems of Eastern Literature, and a masterly translation of the *Laws of Manu* (1794), extracts from the Vedas, and tales, poems, and legal works from the Indian languages. While busy with a digest of Hindu and Mohammedan laws, he died at Calcutta, 27th April 1794. His writings are marked by a highly cultivated taste, and a singular power of assimilating the exotic beauty of Eastern poetry. But his studies rather bespeak the æsthetic devotion of the litterateur than the severe critical labour of the scholar. 'The really difficult works, the grammatical treatises and commentaries, the philosophical systems, and, before all, the immense literature of the Vedic period, were never seriously approached by him' (Max Müller). Colebrooke, however, was in greatest measure indebted to him, and he certainly gave an incalculable impulse to Oriental scholarship. An edition of his works in 6 vols. was issued by Lady J. in 1799, and another in 13 vols. with a *Life* by Lord Teignmouth, in 1807.

Jone'sia, a genus of trees found in the Malay Peninsula, Japan, &c., belonging to the same family as the laburnum. They have large glossy leaves, a foot or more long, and clusters of bright scarlet flowers, and are named after the great Oriental scholar.

Jongleurs. See TROUVERES and TROUBADOURS.

Jönköping, a town in the district of Smaaland, Sweden, has manufactures of lucifer matches, paper-hangings, and hardware. Pop. (1871) 11,254. J. was a trading town as early as the 13th c., and was fortified till the middle of the 17th c. It has been several times burnt.

Jon'quil, a common garden plant, is a species of Narcissus (q. v.) or daffodil, with *rush*-like leaves (Lat. *juncus*, 'a rush'). A fine perfume is extracted from its flowers.

Jon'son, Ben, playwright and lyrist, was born at Westminster in 1573, a month after the death of his father, a clergyman of Scottish descent. Through the kindness of Camden he received a free education at Westminster School, but being removed thence at an early age, he was for a while apprentice to a bricklayer, then saw a few months' service in the Netherlands, and finally obtained an engagement at the Curtain Theatre in Shoreditch as player and dramatist. His works of this period are lost, and we know little of his life, beyond that he married a shrewish wife, probably in 1592. Next, from an entry in Henslowe's diary (July 28, 1597), he seems to have made one of the Rose company, and then we follow him to the Globe, where his *Every Man in his Humour* was brought out in 1598 on the recommendation of Shakespeare, and was followed by its inferior antitype, *Every Man out of his Humour*. For slaying an actor of the Rose, one Gabriel Spencer, in a duel (1598), he was imprisoned, in prison turning Catholic, and on his release engaged in a string of squabbles with the playwrights of that theatre. J.'s *Cynthia's Revels* (1600) and *Poetaster* (1601) evoked Dekker's *Satiromastix*, in which our poet's origin and history are handled with Aristophanic licence. His first tragedy, *Richard Crook-back*, was acted in 1602, and the year after appeared *Sejanus*, which he is supposed to have written in conjunction with Shakespeare. For the first two years of James's reign he confined himself to the production of masques, but a comedy, *Eastward Ho* (1604), the joint work of J., Chapman, and Marston, caused the arrest of its authors for reflections on the Scotch, and they narrowly escaped the slitting of ears and noses. The next few years of J.'s life yielded nine plays and masques, witnessed his return to Protestantism, and marked the zenith of the Mermaid Club, composed of Shakespeare, J., Beaumont, Fletcher, and others. In 1613 J. went to France as tutor to Sir Walter Raleigh's son, and on his return published *Bartholomew Fair* (1614), and *The Devil's an Ass* (1616). He had already issued a book of *Epigrams* and *The Forest*, and now for nine years withdrew from dramatic labours, in 1618 paying his memorable visit to Drummond of Hawthornden; but in 1619 he received the degree of M.A. from the University of Oxford, and from the king the poet-laureateship, with a pension of 100 marks. His wife was dead, a precious library destroyed by fire, and J., quitting his old Bankside residence, established himself outside Temple Bar, near the Devil Tavern, where he founded the new Apollo Club, with Herrick, Suckling, Carew, and all the list of poets 'sealed of the tribe of Ben.' Up to James's death J. wrote but one yearly masque for the Court Twelfth Night revels, but then he had once more to turn to the theatres for support. But, enfeebled by palsy, his hand had lost its cunning. His last plays, *The Magnetic Lady* (1632) and *Tale of a Tub* (1633) are 'poor dotages,' and their author, pursued by ancient feuds, died August 6, 1637. He was buried in Westminster Abbey, in an upright position, on his grave the words, 'O rare Ben

Jonson.' J.'s plays, as we have them, are sixteen in number, his masques thirty-five. To the comedies already cited must be added *The Silent Woman* (1603), *Volpone* (1605), and *The Alchemist* (1610). These all are like himself, with his 'mountain belly' and his 'rocky face'—great but gross, full of shrewd insight and vigorous common sense, but wanting in fineness of thought and human sympathy. In the realm of pure fancy, as in *Cynthia* and the unfinished fragment, *The Sad Shepherd*, J. rises to higher things; but his tragedies, based closely on the classic models, are imitative rather than assimilating. His truest fame rests on his lyrics, which, always beautiful, are often unsurpassed. *Drink to Me Only with Thine Eyes*, *See the Chariot*, with the epitaphs on Lord Herbert and the Countess of Pembroke, can never die. The best edition of J.'s works is that by Gifford, republished with introduction and appendices by Lieut.-Col. Cunningham (9 vols. Lond. 1875).

Joonaghur' (Junaghar). The chief town of the native state of the same name in Kattywar, India, 235 miles N.W. of Bombay, and 150 W. of Surat. Pop. (1872) 20,025. It is a meanly-built town, with a wall 5 miles in circumference; it contains a strong citadel, and a handsome mosque with pillars of granite and a pulpit of marble.—The *state* of J., which ranks first in Kattywar, has 890 villages; pop. (1872) 380,921; revenue, £150,000; tribute, £7000. Within its boundaries lie the sacred mountain of Girnar (q. v.), the old temple of Somnauth, and the port of Verawal. The ruling Mohammedan dynasty established itself over the Rajputs in 1735. The treaty with the English dates from 1808; and a second treaty regarding shipping was agreed to in 1846. The present (1877) Nawaub, an enlightened prince, is a K.C.S.I.; he receives tribute from several minor chiefs in the Kattywar peninsula.

Jopp'a (Heb. *Yapho*, 'beauty'), a sea-port about 34 miles N.W. of Jerusalem, according to Josephus originally belonged to the Phœnicians (*Ant.* xiii. 15, 4). It is first mentioned in the Bible as being in the portion of Dan (Josh. xix. 46). Here the timber for Solomon's temple, as well as for Zerubbabel's, was landed when brought from Lebanon (2 Chron. ii. 16; Ezra iii. 7). Here Jonah took ship 'to flee unto Tarshish' (Jonah i. 3); as, according to Strabo (*Geogr.*), Andromeda was exposed to the whale at the same place. And here St. Peter had his famous vision (Acts x. 9–16). The modern Jaffa, which between crusaders and infidels underwent as many vicissitudes as Jerusalem itself, is a town of 15,000 inhabitants. In 1875 its exports (wheat, barley, sesame, olive oil, soap, and oranges) amounted in value to £258,156; and the imports (rice, coffee, sugar, cottons, and timber) to £110,667.

Jor'daens, or **Jordaans, Jakob**, a Flemish painter and engraver, born at Antwerp 19th May 1594, died in 1678. He was a pupil of Adam van Oort, for whose daughter's sake, it is said, he refrained from going to Italy, contenting himself with copying the works of the Italian masters that he found in the Netherlands. He was a friend of Rubens. As a colourist J. has even been compared with that painter; but is without taste in design. His greatest pictures are at Paris and Dresden.

Jor'dan (Heb. *Yarden*, 'the descender'), which forms the eastern boundary of Palestine, and for its size is perhaps the most famous river in the world, takes its rise from a number of streams which burst from the slopes of Lebanon and Hermon. The united stream flows through the Lake Merom (mod. *el Huleh*), and southwards to the Lake of Tiberias (q. v.), the distance between the lakes being 9 miles, and the fall about 600 feet. Still flowing nearly due S., in 60 miles of latitude, but in an actual course of 200 miles, it falls into the Dead Sea (q. v.), which is about 650 feet below the level of the Lake of Tiberias, and 1317 below that of the Mediterranean.

Jornan'des, or **Jordanes**, a Goth, who was state secretary to the king of the Alani in the time of the Emperor Justinian. Adopting Christianity, he took orders and became a bishop, some say of Ravenna in Italy. J. is the author of two Latin works, *De Getarum* (*Gothorum*) *Origine et Rebus Gestis*, giving the history of the Goths down to the submission to Belisarius in 541 A.D., a work of immense value in spite of its blunders (best edition, that of Closs; Stuttg. 1861); and *De Regnorum ac Temporum Successione*, an abstract of general history down to 552, with some valuable information about northern nations.

Jor'tin, John, D.D., an English divine and author of Huguenot descent, was born at London, October 23, 1698. Passing from the Charterhouse to Jesus College, Cambridge, he gained a fellowship in 1719, and was ordained priest in 1723, having already published a volume of Latin poems, *Lusus Poetici* (Camb. 1722). In 1727 he accepted the college living of Swavesey, Cambridgeshire, but resigned it the year following, and repairing to London soon attracted notice by his eloquent sermons. After holding the rectories of St. Dunstan-in-the-East (1751) and Eastwell in Kent, he was appointed in 1762 domestic chaplain to Dr. Osbaldeston, Bishop of London, who also gave him a prebend of St. Paul's, the living of Kensington, and in 1764 the archdeaconry of London. He died September 5, 1770. Besides sermons, J. published eleven works, which have been issued in a uniform edition, and of which may be noticed *Remarks on Ecclesiastical History* (3 vols. 1751–54), *Life of Erasmus* (2 vols. 1758–60), and *Remarks upon the Works of Erasmus* (1760).

Jorull'o, a volcano of Mexico, in the state of Michoacan, 150 miles W.S.W. of Mexico city. From a plain 2880 feet above the sea, J. was suddenly thrown up to a height of 4265 feet on 8th September 1759. But several of its many cones soon sank, and of those still remaining only a few discharge even vapour. The sides of J. are clad with forests.

Jo'seph I., son of Leopold I., German Emperor, born at Vienna, July 26, 1678, was crowned hereditary prince of Hungary, 1687, King of the Romans in 1690, and Emperor in 1705. J. carried on the paternal wars against Bavaria owing to the Elector's sympathy with France, but his antipathy to the latter country came to an end (1707), after which he presented his brother, Charles II. of Spain, with Milan. J. was an ambitious but prudent emperor, who worked a useful reform in fiscal law, and established the Chamber of Justice. He died April 17, 1711. —**Joseph II.**, eldest son of Franz I. and Maria-Theresa, was born at Vienna, March 13, 1741. He was early placed under the tuition of Count Batthyany, a Hungarian, and, though naturally timid, showed a leaning towards arms which his mother repressed. In 1760 he married Isabella, eldest daughter of Philip of Parma; in May 27, 1764, was elected King of the Romans at Frankfurt; became Emperor 18th August 1765; and married Marie Joseph, daughter of Karl VII., 28th May 1767. He tried in vain to wrest the complete power out of his mother's hands, being first of all entrusted only with the armies. Then he inculcated economy in all branches, setting the example by the simplicity of his own surroundings. Having begun a course of travels (1764) through Hungary, he returned thither (1768), went to Rome incognito (1769), travelled through Bohemia, Moravia, and his own dominions (1772), and arrived in France (1777), where he was but coldly received by his brother-in-law, Louis XVI. After the death of Maximilian-Joseph of Bavaria, J. attempted a war of aggrandisement in his territory, known as 'the Potato War,' that brought small results, owing to the opposition of Friedrich the Great and the lukewarmness of Maria-Theresa. In other efforts of the same kind he was not more successful, but his domestic policy was most beneficial. He introduced various ecclesiastical reforms, mitigated the condition of the Jews, equalised the administration of justice, and introduced comparative freedom of worship. He died 20th February 1790. See Pezzl, *Characteristik J.'s II.* (Vien. 1790); Gross-Hoffinger, *Lebens- und Regierungs-geschichte J.'s II.* (4 vols. Stuttg. 1835–37); Paganel, *Histoire de J. II.* (Par. 1843); Burckhardt, *Kaiser J. II.* (Meissen, 1835); Heyne, *Geschichte Kaiser J.'s II.* (Leips. 1848); Arneth (1867–69).

Jos'éphine, Marie Joseph Rose, was born at Trois-Ilets in the island of Martinique, June 23d, 1763, educated in the convent of Port Royal, landed in France (1779), and married Alexandre, Marquis of Beauharnais. He proved faithless to her after the first year, and in 1788 she returned to Martinique with her daughter Hortense, rejoined him in 1790, and lived with him until he was executed by order of the Convention, May 5, 1794. Two years later she married General Bonaparte, and in 1800 went to live at the Tuileries, and organised state receptions with great success, her personal qualities of refinement, taste, and amiability showing to perfect advantage. J. became empress 28th November 1804, her son Eugene (by her first marriage) being appointed Viceroy of Italy, her daughter Hortense becoming

Queen of Holland. For political reasons, J., having no issue by her second marriage, was divorced by Napoleon 16th December 1809. Towards the end of 1811 she took up her residence at Malmaison, giving full scope to her taste for art, botany, and natural history, and died May 29, 1814. J. was kind, timid, luxurious, and a little deceitful, but merited better things at the hand of the Emperor. See Aubenas, *Histoire de l'Impératrice Joséphine* (1857-59).

Jose'phus, Flavius, the Jewish historian, was born at Jerusalem A.D. 37. If his own account, the only authority we have, is to be believed, at the age of fourteen he was a prodigy of learning. At the age of sixteen he set out for Rome to plead the cause of some imprisoned Jewish priests. He suffered shipwreck on his voyage, and had a narrow escape from drowning, but reached his destination in safety, and through the patronage of Poppæa gained his cause. The Jewish war against the Romans broke out (66) soon after his return, and although he was opposed to the insurrection, he accepted the command in Galilee. Having fallen into the hands of the Romans on the capture of the town of Jotapata, which he was defending, his life was spared, but he was kept in captivity till Vespasian's elevation to the throne, which he had predicted, took place (70). J. was with Titus at the siege of Jerusalem, and afterwards accompanied him to Rome, where he spent the rest of his life (died about 100) kindly treated by Vespasian, Titus, and Domitian, and occupied in writing his various works. These are:—*A History of the Jewish War* (from the capture of Jerusalem by Antiochus Ep. B.C. 170), first written in Hebrew and then translated into Greek; *The Jewish Antiquities*, a history of the Jews from the Creation to A.D. 66; an *Autobiography*; and a *Treatise against Apion*, on the antiquity of the Jewish nation. The best editions of J.'s works are by Havercamp (2 vols. Amst. 1726), Oberthür (3 vols. Leips. 1782-85), and Richter (6 vols. Leips. 1825-27).

Josh'ua (Heb. *Yehoshua*, 'whose help is Jehovah'), formerly called Hoshea ('deliverance,' Num. xiii. 8, 16), the son of Nun, of the tribe of Ephraim, was appointed by Moses general of the army of Israel when they were attacked by the Amalekites at Sinai (Exodus xvii. 9), one of the spies for exploring Canaan (Num. xiii.), and finally to lead the people into Canaan after his own death (Num. xxvii. 18-23, Deut. xxxi. 14, 23). After fulfilling the task entrusted to him with valour and discretion (see JEWS), he died at the age of 110 (about B.C. 1427), and was buried at Timnath-serah (Josh. xxiv.). The book of J., which contains an account of the conquest of Canaan by the Israelites, and its division among the twelve tribes, was supposed by most Jewish and early Christian writers to have been composed by J. himself, some maintaining the same thing yet. But its composition has been ascribed by others to one of the elders who survived J., to Eleazar, to Phinehas, to Samuel, and to Jeremiah; to some one in the time of Saul, of Josiah, or even after the Babylonish Captivity.

Josi'ah (Heb. 'Jehovah heals'), the son of Amon, King of Judah, succeeded his father on the throne at the age of eight (about B.C. 640), and reigned thirty-one years, when he met his death in a battle with Pharaoh-necho, whose march against the Chaldeans he attempted to check. Brought up under the influence of a circle of remarkable persons—Shaphan the scribe, Hilkiah the high priest, and Huldah the prophetess—he zealously seconded their desire for a religious reformation. Hilkiah had found a copy of the Book of the Law, which had a great effect both on the king and the people, being as completely strange to them as if it had never existed before, which indeed some affirm to have been the original form of the Book of Deuteronomy and composed at that time. At any rate, J. repaired the temple of Jehovah, established his worship as the national religion, and caused all High Places (q. v.), Asheras (q. v.), and every trace of worship paid to any of the other Semitic deities, to be destroyed.

Jósika, Miklos (*Nicholas*), a Hungarian novelist, born of a noble family at Torda in Transylvania, 28th September 1796. In 1834 he appeared in the Transylvanian diet in the ranks of the opposition, and took part in the political movements in Hungary from 1835 to 1840. In 1836 he produced the tale *Abafi*, and continued till 1848 to publish as many as sixty novels on subjects drawn from Hungarian history. Of these, the most famous are *Az Utolsó Bátory* (1838), *A Csehek Magyarországban* (1840), *Josika Istvan* (1847). J. acted in 1847 as Transylvanian deputy for the political union of Transylvania and Hungary, took part in the Revolution of 1848, but was forced to fly, and took up his abode in Brussels in 1850. Of his later romances the chief are *Esther* (1853) and *A Négvâriak* (1865). He died at Dresden, February 27, 1865. J. resembles his model, Scott, but has quite an original freshness and colour.

Jost, Isaak Mark, a German Jew, born at Bernburg 22d February 1793, was a second Josephus. Though born of poor parents, by extraordinary diligence he acquired an excellent education, and great proficiency in the Semitic as well as in the classical and modern languages. He taught a school at Berlin for seventeen years (1816-33), and the Jewish High School at Frankfort from 1835 till his death 25th November 1860. His chief works were *Geschichte d. Israeliten* (9 vols. Berl. 1820-28); an abridgment of the above, *Gesch. d. Isr. Volkes* (2 vols. 1831-32); a continuation, *Neuere Gesch. d. Isr.* (1866-67); and *Gesch. d. Judenthums* (3 vols. 1857-59), embodying all the results of his life's work.

Joudpore. See JODHPORE.

Jouff'roy, Théodore Simon, a French philosopher, was born in the hamlet of Pomtets, on the heights of the Jura, 7th July 1796, went to Paris in 1813 to the Normal School, accepted with M. Cousin the Royalist restoration 'as more favourable to thought than the empire,' became attached (1822) to the Bourbon College, having previously composed two theses, *Le Beau et le Sublime* and *La Causalité*. In 1824 he joined the staff of *Le Globe*, and took his place on it as 'le philosophe generalisateur,' besides contributing articles upon history and geography. His collected writings consist of translations from the Scotch philosophers Stewart and Reid, a volume of *Mélanges Philosophiques* (1833), and *Nouveaux Mélanges* published after his death. He died 4th February 1842. Like Coleridge, J. projected several works which he never completed, and to a power of profuse meditative conversation he added the affliction of great literary indolence.

Jougs, Juggs, or **Joggs** (Fr. *joug*, Lat. *jugum*, allied to the Eng. *yoke* and Ger. *joch*), the name of an instrument of punishment used in Scotland at least as early as the 16th c., consisting of an iron collar suspended by a few links of chain in some public place, and fitted with a padlock for fastening it upon an offender's neck. They were sometimes accompanied with the Branks (q. v.). J., which have also been used in Holland, and probably in other countries, have not been employed in Scotland for a century, but are still occasionally seen hanging at country churches—*e.g.*, at Duddingstone, near Edinburgh.

Joule, James Prescott, F.R.S., D.C.L., &c., a celebrated living physicist, was born at Salford, near Manchester, December 24, 1818. Though associated in business with his father till 1854, he early turned his attention to science, and finally became as enthusiastic and careful an experimenter as his teacher Joseph Dalton (q. v.). At the age of nineteen, he constructed an electro-magnetic machine; and in 1840 he was led into a series of experiments to determine the law regulating the evolution of heat by an electric current. This resulted in obtaining in 1843 a first approximation to the dynamical equivalent of heat, and suggested that brilliant series of experiments which established the true theory of heat and the doctrine of the conservation of Energy (q. v.), and obtained for the investigator a world-wide reputation. He has since made valuable experimental researches into the thermal conditions of fluids under various circumstances. He received the royal medal from the Royal Society in 1852, and the Copley Medal in 1860, in recognition of his valuable services to science. He is a member of all the principal scientific societies both at home and abroad. He was president of the British Association in 1873, and in 1875 was made doctor of mathematics and physics by the University of Leyden. His numerous memoirs are published in the *Philosophical Transactions*.

Jounpore' (*Jaunpur*), the chief town of the district of the same name, N.W. Provinces, British India, on both banks of the Gumtee River, 55 miles N.E. of Allahabad. Pop. (1872) 23,327. The town contains a stone fort, a handsome mosque, and many ruins; the river, which is navigable, is crossed by an ancient bridge.—The *district* of J. has an area of 1556 sq. miles; pop. (1872) 1,025,961. The soil is fertile, and irrigated from wells.

Jour'dan, Jean Baptiste, Comte, son of a surgeon, was born at Limoges, 29th April 1762, entered the army (1778), made five campaigns in America, and rose to be General of Division (July 1793). He commanded the French army of the N., and won the battle of Wattignies. In 1794 he commanded with success the army of the Moselle and the army of the Sambre and Meuse, gaining (26th June) the battle of Fleurus. J. was checked by the Archduke Karl in Germany (1796), and owing to his reverses was compelled to resign his post. He became a member of the Council of Five Hundred (1797), carried the law of conscription (September 5, 1798), and was excluded from the Chamber, having opposed the dictatorship of Napoleon. He accompanied Joseph Bonaparte into Spain, and fought against Wellington. Louis XVIII. made him a Comte, and he took his place as a constitutional politician. He died November 23, 1833.

Joust, or **Juste** (Old Fr. *jouste*, Ital. *giostra*), is defined by Ducange as a single combat or duel, while a tournament was an encounter of two troops of combatants; but the distinction seems to be an arbitrary one, and the terms are used synonymously by old writers.

Jowar' (*Jawar*), the chief town of the native state of the same name, in India, 68 miles N. of Bombay. It is an insignificant place, lying within the British district of Tanna. The *state* of J. has an area of about 534 sq. miles; pop. (1872) 37,406; revenue about £6000; no tribute is demanded, but a nuzzurana or relief of £2000 is paid to the British on the accession of the Rajah. Timber is the most valuable of the productions. The dynasty is said to have been very powerful when founded 500 years ago. The present Rajah, a minor, is now (1877) being educated at Poonah.

Jow'ett, Rev. Benjamin, D.D., an English scholar and theological critic, born at Camberwell in 1817, was educated at St. Paul's School, London, and became a student of Balliol College, Oxford, in 1835, a fellow in 1838, and tutor in 1842, in which year he was also ordained. In 1853 he served on and compiled the report of a commission to consider the application of the competitive system to the Indian civil service, of which Macaulay and Lord Ashburton were also members, and in 1855 was appointed, through Lord Palmerston, Regius Professor of Greek. An article by J., *On the Interpretation of Scripture*, in the famous *Essays and Reviews* (1860), led to his trial and acquittal in the Vice-Chancellor's court on a charge of heresy. In 1870 he succeeded Dr. Scott as Master of Balliol, and in 1875 received from the University of Leyden the honorary degree of D.D. J. has published a commentary on three of the Pauline epistles (1855), a translation of the *Dialogues of Plato* (4 vols. Oxf. 1871; 2d ed. 5 vols. 1876), and an edition of the *Republic*. He is a refined, subtle, suggestive, but inconclusive thinker.

Jow'rah (*Jaura*), the chief town of the native state of the same name in Central India, on the Piria river, 260 miles S.W. of Gwalior, and 94 N.W. from Mhow. The river is here crossed by a handsome bridge of porphyritic stone. The *state* of J., which is the second Mohammedan power in Central India, has an area of 872 sq. miles; pop. about 85,000; revenue, £65,524; tribute, £15,902. The best Malwa opium is grown here to the amount of 100 chests a year. The Nawab is descended from a leader of Pindari marauders.

Ju'an, the Spanish form of John. **Don Juan of Austria** was the illegitimate son of the Emperor Karl V. and Barbara Blomberg, born 24th February 1546. After his father's death he was recognised by his half brother Philip II., and thereafter educated along with the Prince of Parma and the infante Don Carlos. The loyalty with which he tracked out Don Carlos' political intrigues procured him the command of a fleet of galleys for the defence of the coast against the African pirates, and of an army with which he crushed the Moorish rising in Granada (1569–70). His greatest exploit was the victory of Lepanto (7th October 1571), in which he defeated and partly destroyed the Turkish fleet. In 1573 he besieged Tunis, and two years afterwards was sent to the Netherlands as Stadtholder, where (31st January 1578) he gained the victory of Gemblours, but died during the siege of Namur on the 1st October of the same year.

Juan, Don. See DON JUAN.

Juan Fernan'dez, an island in the S. Pacific, situated in 33° 37′ S. lat., 78° 53′ W. long., about 360 miles from the coast of Chili, to which it belongs. It is 18 miles long and 6 broad, and very mountainous, the highest peak reaching an elevation of 3000 feet. The island is leased by a Chilian merchant, who employs the inhabitants (about forty in number) in cutting wood, herding cattle, and seal-hunting. J. F. produces excellent timber, and abounds in fruit and vegetables, on which account it is a favourite place of call for ships requiring fresh provisions. It is chiefly known as having been from 1704 to 1709 the solitary residence of Alexander Selkirk, a Scotch sailor, who was the original of Defoe's *Robinson Crusoe*. An iron tablet to his memory was erected on the island in 1868 by the officers of H.M.S. *Topaze*. See Spry's *Cruise of H.M.S. Challenger* (1876).

Juar'ez, Benito, President of Mexico, was of Indian extraction, and was born at Ixtlan, 21st March 1806. After filling various legal offices he became Governor of Oxacaca in 1848. He was banished by Santa Anna in 1853. On the latter's downfall he was made President of the Supreme Court, and succeeded Comonfort as President of Mexico in 1858. The clerical party, first under Zuloaga, and afterwards under Miramon, opposed him and drove him to Vera Cruz, but J. defeated them at Silva, August 14, 1860, and re-entered Mexico, January 12, 1861, where he declared the confiscation of the Church property. The suspension of payment of the State's debts brought about the armed intervention of France, Spain, and Great Britain. Negotiations at Soledad, January 19, 1862, resulted in the withdrawal of the two latter powers, but the French army remained, captured Mexico on May 31, 1863, and placed the Archduke Maximilian on the throne. J. still held out, carrying on a guerilla warfare with the moral support of the United States, and that country induced Napoleon to withdraw his troops in 1866. Maximilian was thereupon defeated and executed June 19, 1867. J. was re-elected President in October 1867, and died July 18, 1872. J. was an unusually able and enlightened governor, and his death was a national calamity.

Jubae'a. *J. spectabilis* is the coquito palm of Chili. It has a tall straight trunk 30 to 40 feet high, surmounted by a crown of large pinnate leaves. A sweet syrup called palm honey is got by boiling the sap of the tree.

Jubbulpore' (*Jabalpur* = the town on the hill), the chief town of the district of the same name, Central Provinces, British India, on the right bank of the Nerbudda, 615 miles N.E. of Bombay and 224 S.W. of Allahabad. Pop. (1872) 55,188. It has always been a centre of trade, and latterly has risen to great importance as the railway junction by which Bombay is directly connected with Calcutta and Delhi. In 1868, before the opening of the railway, the exports were estimated at £80,000, the imports at £464,000. The town itself is modern, the streets are wide and regular, and the houses well built. There is a large cantonment for all arms, and a school of industry, where tents and carpets are largely manufactured by Thug and Dacoit 'approvers.' The *district* of J., which consists of hill ranges and fertile river valleys, has an area of 3918 sq. miles; pop. (1872) 528,859. Coal and iron are both worked by European capital, and there are other valuable minerals. The forests, which are preserved by Government, furnish lac and the tussur silk-worm. The manufactures are iron, cotton-cloth, and brass utensils, in which a considerable trade is carried on, as also in raw cotton. In 1875 the imports at the railway station were 8000 tons, of which one-fourth were sugar; the exports were 9000 tons, of which one-half were cotton.

Ju'bilee, or **Year of Jubilee** (Heb. *yobel*, 'a ram,' then (meton.) 'a ram's horn,' and finally, *the sound* produced by the horn), literally the year of blowing the horn (*cf.* the day of blowing the horn, *i.e.*, the New Year, Num. xxix. 1), among the Israelites was the next year after seven Sabbatical Years (q. v.), that is every fiftieth year, in which (1) the soil had rest from tillage and harvest; (2) all the land which had been alienated reverted to the families to whom it was originally allotted; and (3) all bondmen of Hebrew blood, who had not spontaneously submitted to perpetual slavery (Ex. xxi. 6) were liberated (Lev. xxv. 8–16, 23–55). (4) Josephus (*Ants.* iii. 2, 3) declares that all debts were also remitted, and although the Bible only speaks of this in connection with the Sabbatical year (Deut. xv. 1, 2), it seems to be implied in the J. as well, since all in bondage for debt were liberated.

Jubilee in the Romish Church is a time of indulgence in which confessors may absolve in all reserved cases from all censures, greater excommunications, suspensions from offices, benefices, and interdicts, and can commute vows, except those of religion, perpetual chastity, or pilgrimages to Rome, Jerusalem, or Compostella. Pope Boniface VIII. in the year 1300 sent an epistle throughout Christendom to the effect that in every centennial year all who should confess and lament their sins, and devoutly visit the Church of St. Peter and St. Paul at Rome, should receive plenary absolution of their sins. Plenary indulgences had hitherto been confined to the Crusaders, but the belief had long prevailed that Romish indulgences were more efficient than any others, the pilgrims who travelled to Rome for them being under the immediate protection of the Pope. Accordingly the number of pilgrims who visited Rome in 1300 was about 2,000,000. And as these had brought many gifts to the Pope and much wealth to the city, Clement VI. repeated the J. in 1350. Urban VI. in 1389 reduced the interval to thirty-three years, the length of our Saviour's life; and Nicholas V. (1447-55) appointed it to be held every twenty-five years.

Ju'dah (Heb. *yehudah*, 'praised, celebrated') was the fourth son of Jacob (q. v.) and Leah (Gen. xxix. 35). The tribe of J. was the most powerful of the Israelitish confederation, and the great rival of Ephraim (q. v.). On the death of Saul it elected David king, and eventually succeeded in establishing him as king of the whole nation. On the revolt of the other tribes under Jeroboam, it remained faithful to the house of David (1 Kings xii. 20), and constituted the kingdom of J., which outlasted that of Israel. See JEWS.

Judai'zers. See EBIONITES.

Jud'as Tree belongs to the same family as the laburnum. The purple flowers appear before the leaves, and are followed by large brown pods which remain on the tree all the year. The flowers are often pickled in vinegar. Popular legend says that Judas hanged himself on this tree, hence its name.

Jude (Gr. *Ioudas*, Heb. *Judah*), 'the brother of James' (1), who is generally understood to have been J. Lebbæus or Thaddæus (Matt. x. 3; Luke vi. 16), and 'the Lord's brother' of Matt. xiii. 55. The *Epistle of J.*, the least important in the canon of the New Testament, was one of the last to be received, and was like to have been thrown out at the Reformation. On the other hand, its very insignificance, and the absence from it of everything that could serve as a motive for forgery, are arguments for its authenticity.

Judge-Advocate-General, a civil official appointed in the reign of Charles II. to serve as public prosecutor in courts-martial, but whose functions since 1829 have been confined to acting as military adviser of the crown. Sir R. Phillimore, Judge of the Admiralty Court, was appointed, May 17, 1871, 'to hold that office until a new arrangement of its duties can be effected.' In the U.S. army the J.-A.-G. is an officer holding supreme legal authority in all military matters, who resides at Washington, bears the rank of brigadier-general, and by an Act of Congress, June 23, 1874, is assisted in his duties by four judge-advocates with the rank of major.

Judges. The judges of the superior courts in England are appointed by the Crown, and since 1688 various Acts have been passed to secure their independence in their discharge of their duties. 13 Will. III. c. 2, enacts that their commission shall not as formerly continue *during pleasure*, but during good behaviour, unless an address requesting their dismissal be presented from both Houses of Parliament. In 1825 Acts were passed to abolish the sale of offices in the Courts of Queen's Bench and Common Pleas, and substituting fixed salaries and retiring pensions. See COURT OF JUDICATURE, SUPREME ACTS. For Scotch law, see COURT OF SESSION.

Judges, Book of, records the history of the Israelites from the death of Joshua till the time of Samuel the prophet. The so-called 'judges' (Heb. *Shophetim*, 'rulers of the people'), of whom there were fifteen, including Eli and Samuel, were mostly warriors or heroes, who appeared at times of great danger and distress, and delivered the nation, or rather particular tribes, from their foreign oppressors, and 'ruled' over them for a number of years (see JEWS). The only analogy to this office to be found in any other nation is that of the Phœnician Suffetes (perhaps the same name) of Tyre and Carthage. The period covered by the book, from the sum of the dates given, is 410 years; and the 450 of Acts xiii. 20 is got by adding forty years for Eli (1 Sam. iv. 18). This, however, does not correspond with 1 Kings vi. i, where the whole period from the Exodus to the building of Solomon's temple is given as 480, and various arbitrary methods of getting over the difficulty have been resorted to.

Judgment is a term used in Christian theology; 'For we must all appear before the judgment seat of Christ; that every one may receive the things done in his body, according to that he hath done, whether it be good or bad' (2 Cor. v. 10).

Judgment.—In English law, after the verdict follows the J. of the Court. It may be suspended or arrested when there has been any defect in the trial. Cause for suspension may arise from want of due notice of trial, improper behaviour of the jury among themselves, or of the plaintiff towards them, misdirection of the judge, or exorbitant damage. On these and similar grounds a new trial may be awarded. But if two juries return the same or a similar verdict, a third trial is seldom allowed. If the J. be not appealed against, suspended, or reversed, the sentence of the law may then be put in force by *execution.* See EXECUTION, CIVIL. For Scotch law, see DECREE.

Judgment, Final. It is a doctrine of natural and revealed religion that God is the moral ruler of men, and that there is a future state of reward and punishment, in which the inequalities and anomalies here permitted shall be adjusted. The doctrine of the Christian Church regarding the F. J., which is to settle all this, is that it is a definite future event, when the eternal destiny of all shall be finally determined, that Christ is to be the judge, that it is to take place at the second coming of Christ and the general resurrection, and that the persons to be judged are men and angels.

Judi'cial Committ'ee, of the Privy Council, consists of the Lord Chancellor, Lord Justices, Lord Chief-Justices, Judges, Vice-Chancellors, Master of the Rolls, Judges of the Admiralty, Bankruptcy, and Prerogative Courts, with the bishops for ecclesiastical purposes; and two more members may be summoned by the Queen. Appeal may be taken to this Court from the Admiralty and Ecclesiastical Courts, and from the Courts of the British colonies and dominions abroad.

Judi'cial Fac'tor, in Scotch law, is an administrator appointed by the Court of Session, on petition, to take charge of the estates of minors, lunatics, or absent persons. The J. F. must in his management conform to the provisions of the Act of Sederunt, 13th February 1730, and of the Pupils Protection Act (q. v.).

Judi'cial Ratifica'tion. See RATIFICATION BY A WIFE.

Judi'cial Remit', in Scotch law, is a reference by a Court to some one specially skilled to report on a case, or on some portion of it. Matters are thus frequently submitted to accountants and engineers. *Reference to an expert to report* is the corresponding term of English law.

Judi'cial Separa'tion, in English law, is the term for the separation of a husband and wife by decree of the Court of Divorce (see DIVORCE). It may be obtained by a husband or by a wife on the ground of adultery, cruelty, or desertion without cause for two years and upwards. The legal effect of J. S. depends on the terms of the order; the judge having considerable discretion, so as to deal with a petition according to its merits. A certain income may be awarded to the wife, and her future earnings may be protected from her husband and his creditors; in which case the husband is no longer responsible for his wife's debts. J. S. does not divorce husband and wife, so that under it neither can marry again. A husband and wife are not legally entitled to live separately, except by common consent; and a voluntary separation does not affect the legal position of married persons. For Scotch law, see SEPARATION OF MARRIED PERSONS.

Ju'dith, Book of, is one of the Old Testament apocryphal writings, and narrates the exploit of a Jewish widow of Bethulia, who by slaying Holofernes, an Assyrian general invading Judæa, was the means of freeing her country from the impending danger. The historical difficulties of the book have led commentators to treat it either as pure fiction or allegory—making the widow to be the Jewish nation (Heb. *Jehudith*), or at most to be only founded on fact.

Jugg'ernauth (Jagannath, 'the Lord of the World'), the title by which the Hindu god Vishnu is worshipped at the town of Puri in Orissa, which town is often called, though erroneously, by the same name. The shrine here is among the most popular places of pilgrimage in all India; the annual attendance having been estimated at 300,000; the annual revenue of the priests, &c., at £67,000. The great pagoda, which is thought to be nearly 700 years old, is 200 feet high, and is conspicuous from the sea. The idol consists of a log of wood, painted blue, without hands or feet. It is waited upon as if it were a living being, and is supplied daily with food, &c., of the richest kind. The car festival, which takes place annually in March, attracts 100,000 devotees. The ceremony consists in drawing the god to his country seat. The vulgar stories of deliberate self-immolation committed on this occasion are gross exaggerations; but it would be difficult to over-estimate the sum of deaths caused by the diseases engendered among the vast assemblage. It has been stated that 10,000 pilgrims die yearly, despite all the efforts of the British administration; and that cholera may be dispersed from this centre over the rest of the globe. See Dr. W. Hunter's *Orissa*, vol. i. (Lond. 1872).

Jugg'ler (akin to Ger. *gaukeln*, 'to move hastily,' and in no way connected with the Lat. *joculator* from *jocus*), an artist in legerdemain or sleight of hand, is the modern representative of the Gr. *thaumatopoios*, the Lat. *præstigiator*, and the *jogelour* of Chaucer and Piers Plowman. Whilst these, however, were all mere acrobats, modern jugglery undoubtedly owes much to the older Magic (q. v.). How close is the connection between the two has been shown in ancient times in the case of Moses and the Egyptian magicians, in our own day by the competition between Robert Houdin and the *marabouts* or priests of Algeria, and still more recently by the rival performances of Messrs Cooke and Maskelyne on the one hand, the Davenport Brothers, Slade, and their like on the other. At any rate, the art of juggling, like magic, certainly originated in the East. From India, too, Western jugglery probably received a fresh impulse by the arrival of the Gypsies (q. v.), who may have introduced many of our modern feats of legerdemain. See Reginald Scot's black-letter *Discoverie of Witchcraft* (Lond. 1584), and the works of W. H. Cremer, published by Chatto & Windus.

Ju'glans and Juglanda'ceæ. See WALNUT.

Jug'ular Vein, one of the large veins on either side of the neck, so named from Lat. '*jugulum*, the collar-bone, which 'joins' (*jungere*) the neck and shoulders.

Jugur'tha, king of Numidia, son of Mastanabal, was appointed by his uncle, Micipsa, to a share in the succession with his sons Adherbal and Hiempsal. In 116 B.C. J. caused Hiempsal to be killed; and though Adherbal sought help from the Romans, J. bought them off by bribery, and finally caused his cousin to be put to death in the town of Cirta (112 B.C.). The Romans now made war on J., who with great skill baffled their efforts for a time. At last Q. Cæcilius Metellus, gained a decisive victory at the river Muthul. J. then fled to Bocchus, King of Mauretania, who gave him up to the Romans (106 B.C.). He graced the triumph of Marius as a prisoner in 104 B.C., and thereafter suffered death by starvation. The history of the war against J. is related by Sallust.

Ju'jube, a genus of stiff thorny shrubs or sometimes small trees belonging to the same family as the Buckthorn (q. v.). Their fleshy, berry-like fruit has an agreeable flavour, and when dried forms the jujubes of commerce. Syrup of jujubes is used as a medicine in coughs, fevers, &c. One species is called Jew's thorn because it is said to have supplied the crown of thorns put on our Saviour's head.

Ju'lia, the only child of the Roman Emperor Augustus, born 39 B.C., was the daughter of his second wife Scribonia. She was distinguished for beauty and cultivation of mind, and was first married (25 B.C.) to M. C. Marcellus, her cousin; then (23 B.C.) to M. Agrippa; and finally (12 B.C.)—through the intrigues of Livia, who wished to secure the succession to her son—to Tiberius Nero, afterwards emperor. This marriage lasted till Augustus banished her (A.D. 2) for her licentiousness to the island Pandataria, near Naples. Five years afterwards she was removed to Rhegium, where she died in A.D. 14. Only her daughters Julia and Agrippina (q. v.) survived her; two of her sons, Caius and Lucius Cæsar, died before her, and one, Agrippa, Tiberius put to death.—An elder J. was the daughter of C. Julius Cæsar, and wife of Pompeius, and died 54 B.C.

Ju'lian the Apos'tate (Flavius Claudius Julianus), born at Constantinople, November 17, 332, was a nephew of Constantine the Great (q. v.), whose son and successor, Constantius II., murdered all the male descendants of Constantine Chlorus by his second wife (337), J. and his elder half-brother, Gallus, alone escaping from the butchery. The two brothers received a monkish education in various parts of Asia Minor, till in 351 Gallus was created Cæsar and governor of the East, and on his execution at Milan (354) J. was removed to Italy, and kept for some months in strict captivity. Through the mediation of the Empress Eusebia he was allowed to proceed to Athens (355), there to perfect his study of Greek literature and philosophy, but in the November of the same year was recalled to Milan, and himself proclaimed Cæsar, receiving the Transalpine provinces and the hand of his cousin Helena. His administration in Gaul was vigorous and popular. He defeated 35,000 Alemanni near Strasburg (357), forced the Franks to come to terms of peace, and thrice crossed the Rhine to carry the war into the enemy's country. But these successes revived the smouldering jealousy of his uncle, who in 360 ordered off four of the finest Gallic legions to Persia. Thereupon the troops saluted J. as Augustus, and he, after vain attempts to treat with the Emperor, marched upon Constantinople. Constantius set out from Syria to meet him, but died at Mopsocrene in Cilicia, November 3, 361. For ten years J. had been a Christian in name only; he now openly professed paganism, sacrificed to Jupiter, and strove by his pen and authority to suppress the new religion. Though he published an edict of toleration, he closed the Christian schools, compelled Christians to contribute to the erection of heathen shrines, and sought to falsify the words of Christ by rebuilding the Jewish temple. But this last flash of heathendom was destined to be short-lived. In 363 J. set out from Antioch at the head of 65,000 men on an expedition against the Persians. He crossed the Euphrates and Tigris, but failing to take Ctesiphon, was forced by want of provisions to retreat. In a skirmish he was mortally wounded by a javelin, and died the next night, June 26, 363. Few characters have been more hotly contested than that of J.—exalted by heathen, and debased by Christian writers. Religion apart, he was certainly a sagacious ruler, and even as a pagan he displayed virtues and self-restraint which put to shame many of his so-called Christian successors. The teachings of early instructors (men who had often professed Christianity from purely interested motives), the hypocrisy of Constantius, the mutual persecutions of the orthodox and Arians—all had tended to revolt him from the faith of the Galilean, whilst his vanity was fed by the hopes of reviving the antique glories of his race in its religion, and of winning for himself the proud title of 'philosopher.' Of his writings there are extant eighty-three letters, nine orations, and three epigrams, besides the *Kaisares* and *Antiochikos*, the last a satire on the effeminate inhabitants of Antioch. His most important work, *Kata Christianōn*, is only known to us in fragments. J.'s style is pure, but marred by a servile imitation of classic models, and all his writings are mere echoes of the Neo-Platonists, whose doctrines he so laboured to resuscitate. The best edition of his complete works is Spanheim's (Leips. 1696); of the letters, Heyler's (Mainz, 1828). See the splendid but partial sketch of J.'s career in Gibbon's *Decline and Fall* (ch. xix., xxii., xxiii., xxiv.).

Julian Epoch, in chronology, is the epoch or commencement of the Julian Calendar. See CALENDAR.

Jü'lich (Fr. *Juliers*), formerly a duchy (1600 sq. miles), on the W. bank of the Rhine, is now a part of Rhenish Prussia. It was a countship before its union with Berg (q. v.) in 1348.—J. (Lat. *Juliacum*), once capital of the duchy, on the river Roer, 26 miles W. of Köln, is said to have been founded by Julius Cæsar, has lively trade, and a pop. of 4802.

Julien, Stanislas-Aignan, the foremost Chinese scholar of this century, was born at Orleans, September 20, 1799. In

1821 he became Professor of Greek at the College de France, shortly thereafter he turned his attention to the Chinese language, and displayed so surprising a facility in the mastery of that tongue that in twelve months he could venture to publish a translation of the philosopher Mencius (1824), which immediately made his fame as a sinologue. Besides writing several valuable works on Chinese grammar, J. continued from time to time to give Europe translations from the treasures of Chinese lore, including tales, such as *Yu-Kiao-ei, ou les Deux Cousines* (1863), plays, *Hoei-lan-Ki, ou l'Histoire du Cercle de Craie* (1832), and Chinese technical treatises. The *Vie de Hiouen-Thsang* (1853), the travels of a Buddhist pilgrim, illustrated also J.'s knowledge of Sanskrit. In 1852 he was appointed Professor of Chinese on the death of Rémusat, and in 1855 became president of the college. J. died 14th February 1873.

Ju'lius, the name of three Popes, two of whom are historically conspicuous.—**J. II.** (1503-13), previously Julianus della Novere, a nephew of Sixtus IV., was a warrior, a statesman, and a friend of art and science, and throughout his pontificate strenuously laboured to increase the power of the papal chair. With the Emperor Maximilian I. and the French King Louis XII. he formed (1508) the League of Cambray against Venice, but soon after took part with Venice in the 'Holy League' against France, and drove the French from Italy. Louis caused a Council to be held at Pisa (1511) independent of J.'s authority, but it proved a signal failure, and at the fifth Lateran Council in 1512 the King was excommunicated. He then advanced against J., but was defeated and forced to leave Italy. J. founded the new Church of St. Peter, and died 21st February 1513.—**J. III.** (1550-55), previously Gianmaria de' Medici, was one of the four papal legates who opened the Council of Trent. In 1551 he had again to open the Council, but it was dissolved in 1552 through the interference of the Elector Moritz. J. had a contest with Venice on account of the Inquisition, and endeavoured to unite the Nestorians to the Romish Church. His dissolute life ended 23d March 1555.

Jullundhur' (*Jallandar*), the chief town of the district of the same name, Punjaub, British India, near the right bank of the Sutlej, and a station on the Delhi Railway. Pop. (1868) 45,607. It was once the capital of the Punjaub, and contains many mausoleums of the Lodi-Afghan dynasty. It is now the seat of flourishing silk manufactures, and of trade with the Trans-Himalayan countries. The J. Doab, or tract between the Beas and Sutlej rivers, which was ceded to the British in 1846, is extremely fertile, and is famous for its fruit trees.—The *district* has an area of 1326 sq. miles; pop. (1868) 794,764.

Julus. See IULUS.

July' (Lat. *Julius*), the seventh month of our year, with the Romans was the fifth, the name being changed (45 B.C.) from Quintilis, in honour of Julius Cæsar.

Jumalpore' (*Jamalpur*), a town in the district of Monghyr, Bengal, British India, 721 miles N.W. of Calcutta; pop. (1872) 10,453. It contains the largest iron workshops in India, the property of the East India Railway.

Jumbusir' (Jambusar), a town in the district of Broach, Bombay, British India, near the estuary of the Nerbudda, 212 miles N.W. of Bombay; pop. (1872) 14,924. Exports: cotton, grain, and coarse cloth.

Jumill'ah, a town in the province of Murcia, Spain, on the Jua River, 35 miles N. of Murcia. It has manufactures of ovens and earthenware. Pop. 9613.

Jummu' (Jamu), a town in the native state of Cashmere, India, on the Chenaub, in the lower Himalayas; pop. about 8000. It contains the palace of the Rajah of Cashmere, and is the capital of a tract which formed the earliest possession of the present ruling family. It has manufactures of shawls, &c. The cultivation of the vine and the hop plant have lately been introduced in the neighbourhood. J. was visited by the Prince of Wales in the spring of 1876.

Jum'na (Jamna, named after the goddess *Yamuna*), the chief tributary of the Ganges, rises in Gurhwal, under the Jumnotri peaks, at an elevation of 10,849 feet, not far from the source of the Ganges. It flows first S.W., and, after receiving many mountain torrents, debouches on the plain of Hindustan at Badshahmahal, where the canal system commences. It then turns S.E., and flowing past the towns of Delhi, Muttra, Agra, Calpee, Etawah, &c., joins the Ganges beneath the rocky citadel of Allahabad, after a total course of about 860 miles. At its source are the hot springs of Jumnotri, which have a temperature nearly equal to that of boiling water. At its confluence is the sacred ghaut of Tribeni; its water is here perfectly clear, while that of the Ganges is turbid. Its chief tributaries are the Chumbul, Sind, Betwa, and Cane, on the right bank; and the Hindon and Seengur on the left. It is navigable up to Delhi, where there is a bridge of boats; and it is crossed by the railway near Saharunpore.

The Jumna Canal System is divided into the Western, the Eastern, and the Agra Canals. The Western J. Canal was the first canal undertaken by the British in India, having been commenced in 1823 and completed in 1843. To a great extent it follows the old cuttings of Firoz Shah and Akbar, but great engineering difficulties were overcome. It irrigates 400,000 acres in the Punjaub districts of Kurnal, Delhi, Hissar, and Rohtuck, and supplies Delhi with water; total cost, £311,693; net receipts in 1872-73, £92,500, or 31 per cent. on capital; aggregate length of watercourses, 728 miles. The Eastern J. Canal was commenced shortly afterwards, to water the tract between the J. and the Hindon, and the two now take off from a common head. This also partly follows old works of the Mahomedans. Area irrigated, 200,000 acres; net returns in 1872-73, £30,774, or 16 per cent. on outlay; length of canals and distributaries, 755 miles. The Agra Canal, which has just been completed, will water 350,000 acres in Gurgaon, Muttra, and Agra. The water is diverted just below Delhi by a masonry weir 2428 feet long.

Jump'ing Hare (*Helamys capensis*), or 'Spring haas,' a genus of *Rodentia*, so named from the leaps they are enabled to make by the help of their long hinder limbs. The J. H. inhabits S. Africa. Its colour is a dark or reddish brown, and the tail is very long and provided with stiff hairs.

Junca'ceæ, or **Rush Family**, consists of about 200 species of plants growing chiefly in cold and temperate climates. Their hollow or flat leaves are used for mats and chair-bottoms, and the pith for wicks of candles.

June, the sixth month of our year, was with the Romans the fourth, and was so called either from Juno (comp. Ovid's *Mensis Junonius*), or from the first consul, Junius Brutus.

Jung (*Jang*), a common native name in India, of Persian derivation, signifying 'battle.' Sir J. Behaudur, the late prime minister and 'Mayor of the Palace' to the titular Rajah of Nepal, was born in 1815; he was hereditary ruler of two large estates, and became practical ruler of Nepal in 1845 by means of the unscrupulous removal of all his rivals. In 1850 he visited England, and his favourable reception by the queen, and in London society, determined his policy towards the British, and also towards his own subjects. He assisted Britain during the Mutiny at the head of 16,000 men, who all received the Mutiny medal, while Sir J. himself was created G.C.B., and subsequently K.C.S.I. In 1876 he magnificently entertained the Prince of Wales in the Nepal terai, which affords the best tiger preserves in India. He died suddenly in February 1877, and was peaceably succeeded in authority by his brother.

Jung, Johann Heinrich, called **Stilling**, a German writer, born September 12, 1740, at Im-grund in Nassau, was first a tailor, then studied medicine at Strasburg, where he became a friend of Goethe. He practised medicine at Elberfeld from 1772, and became famous for curing cataract, was made Professor of General Science at Marburg in 1787, returned to Heidelberg in 1804, and died at Karlsruhe, April 2, 1817. J. was a man of simple character and fine feeling. His works are marked by religious mysticism and lively fancy. The chief are *Theobald oder die Schwärmer* (1797), *Theorie der Geisterkunde* (1808), *Scenen aus dem Geisterreiche* (1803). J.'s representations of different periods of his life are collected in 1859 in *Lebensgeschichte J. Stillings.*

Jungermann'ia, a genus to which formerly nearly all the Liverworts with distinct stems and leaves were placed. It is now much restricted, the numerous species having been separated into many genera. See HEPATICÆ.

Jung'frau (Ger. 'maiden'), a conspicuous peak of the Bernese Alps, and one of the most beautiful mountains of Switzerland, rises to a height of 13,700 feet, on the N. boundary of Valais. It was first ascended by six peasants in 1828; and then by Agassiz, Forbes, and others in 1841.

Jungipore' (Jangipur), a town in Murshedabad district, Bengal, British India, on the left bank of the Bhagirutti, 130 miles N. of Calcutta. Pop. (1872) 11,361. It is a great mart of river traffic, and also of the silk trade.

Jun'gle-Fowl, a name applied to various kinds of Rasorial or Gallinaceous birds. Of these, the most typical, perhaps, is the Australian J.-F. (*Megapodius tumulus*), an example of the *Megapodinæ*, or 'large-footed' birds, noted for gathering together large quantities of earth to contain its eggs. These mounds act as artificial incubators, and in size may measure 60 feet as to circumference, and 15 feet in height. The J.-F. is brown, and blackish-grey above, the latter tint prevailing on the under parts. The eggs are deposited from the end of August till March. The jungle-fowls of Asia are allied to the ordinary English fowls.

Jun'iper, a name given to several trees or shrubs belonging to the natural order *Coniferæ*. They are evergreens, having their flowers in catkins, narrow awl-shaped leaves, and a berry-like fruit of a bluish colour. The berries (which are really succulent *cones*) take two years to ripen—the name J. (Lat. *juniperus*, 'junior') implying that it *brings forth younger* berries while the others are ripening—and are used to flavour gin. The wood of several species is hard and fragrant, that of *J. Bermudiana*, or Bermudas cedar, being used for pencil-making, cabinets, &c.

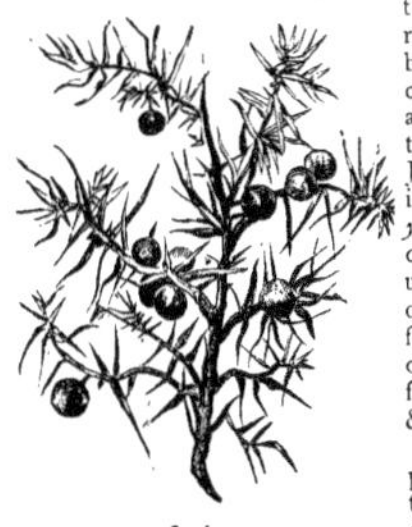
Juniper.

The berries yield about one per cent of a mixture of volatile oils, one of which has the composition of oil-of-turpentine ($C_{10}H_{16}$), boils at 160°, and is lævorotatory; the other has the formula ($C_{20}H_{32}$), boils at 205°, and is also lævorotatory. The berries contain nearly one-third of their weight of sugar and wax, resin, acetic, malic, and firmic acids, pectin, albuminous matters, fibre, inorganic matter, and a small quantity of a substance called juniperin is also contained in them. The essential oil is the constituent of chief value.

Medicinal Properties of J.—The oil of J. is stimulant and carminative, but is chiefly used in medicine as a diuretic in debilitated dropsical cases. It is administered in doses of from 1 to 3 minims, and the *spirit*, composed of 1 part of oil and 49 of rectified spirit, in doses of from 30 to 60 minims. J. tar, the French *Huile de Cade*, is used in obstinate skin diseases.

Ju'nius, Letters of, a celebrated series of political tracts which appeared in Woodfall's *Public Advertiser* from January 21, 1769, to January 21, 1772, were fifty-nine in number (including the fifteen by 'Philo-Junius'), and were reissued in a revised and collected form in 1772. To their author have also been ascribed the pre-Junian letters signed 'Poplicola,' the first of which appeared April 28, 1767, as well as some of the minor letters which, under various signatures, supplemented or reinforced the views of 'Junius.' The time of their appearance—the close of the Grafton and rise of the North ministry—was a critical one, with a king bent on asserting his prerogative, a parliament torn by political and private enmities, troubles in America and on the Continent, and at home a rancorous struggle for the liberties of the press. All these topics the *Letters* handled with an energy and sarcasm, a grace of style and happiness of expression, worthy of the most brilliant writers of the period. But their great and lasting interest lay in their personality (Delolme alone, of all the persons mentioned, wholly escaping the writer's lash), in the minute knowledge they displayed of affairs of State and of matters of private history, and above all, in the fact that their authorship remained and still remains a mystery. 'My secret,' said the Unknown, 'shall die with me.' Burke, Wilkes, Tooke, Lyttelton—all these and a dozen other writers were in turn identified with 'Junius,' but none on other than the merest guesswork. The claims of Sir Philip Francis (q. v.), however, first advanced in 1812, were supported by Taylor in his *Junius Identified with a Celebrated Living Character* (1816) by arguments accepted as conclusive by Brougham, De Quincey, and Macaulay. The theory is based on a comparison of handwriting, character, and style, as shown in Francis's acknowledged writings, on his supposed facilities for acquiring the special knowledge displayed throughout the *Letters*, and on his conduct and language respecting them *after* they had been attributed to him. On the other hand, it is on precisely these points that his claims are contested by the 'Anti-Franciscans,' who have the advantage of shifting the *onus probandi* on the upholders of the theory. See Parkes' and Merivale's *Memoirs of Sir Philip Francis* (2 vols. Lond. 1867); Professor F. Brockhaus' *Die Briefe des Junius* (Leips. 1876); and Hayward's *More about Junius* in vol. lxxvi. of *Fraser's Magazine*.

Junk (Dutch *jong*, possibly from Chinese *yong*, 'the sea'), a three-masted, flat-bottomed vessel of from 100 to 300 tons' burden, used by the Chinese, Japanese, and Malays. It has a lofty poop and forecastle, a wooden anchor, lateen sails of matting, and on each side of the bows an eye is painted, as in the ancient Greek trireme. Though extremely clumsy, junks have made voyages to England and America, but they are now being gradually superseded by vessels built on European lines.

Ju'no (originally *Jovino*) the wife of Jupiter, identified with the Greek Hera (q. v.) and Etruscan Cupra, as the patroness of marriage was called *Matrona*, *Pronuba*, and *Jugalis*, and as the goddess of childbirth *Lucina*, identified with the Greek Ilithyia. In early times J. was worshipped at Lanuvium as *Sospita* or 'Saviour.' Her cult was formally introduced at Rome from Veii, but even before this the Romans worshipped her as J. *Regina* or 'Queen of Heaven.' The mint stood close to the temple of J. *Moneta* on the Capitoline. The first of every month was sacred to J., who had a special festival (the *Matronalia*) on the 1st of March. J. is usually represented after the type of Hera.

Ju'not, Andoche, Duc d'Abrantès, a French general, was born October 23, 1771, at Bussy-le-Grand, studied at the College of Châtillon, became aide-de-camp to Napoleon, with whom he went to Egypt (1798) where he was created General of Brigade. In 1805 Napoleon sent him to Portugal as ambassador, but he returned to Paris in 1806, of which he was nominated governor in 1807. Soon after he received the command of an army invading Portugal, and entered Lisbon in triumph. For this last service he was created Duc d'Abrantès. Having failed in the battle of Vimeiro he fell a little in Napoleon's estimation, and in 1812 lost his confidence still further when in command of an army destined to act against Russia. J. was then sent to govern Venice and Illyria, but during a fever cast himself from a window, and died at his father's house at Montbard near Dijon, 22d July 1813. See Mme. d'Abrantès' *Memoires* (Par. 1831–35).

Jun'ta (Span. an 'union'), a term applied in Spain to an assembly called together or meeting voluntarily for a political object. Juntas have from 1808 up to recent times played an important part in Spanish history, having several times placed themselves at the head of political movements, and undertaken the direction of affairs.

Jupati' Palm, found in the coast region of the Amazon valley, has a stem 6 or 8 feet high, but its gigantic spiny leaves, 40 to 50 feet long, and erect, being supported on leaf-stalks 12 feet long, give the plant the appearance of being from 60 to 70 feet high. The leaf-stalks are used for walls of houses, &c., and their pith is used as cork. It is the only scaly-fruited palm of America that has pinnate leaves, all the others having fan-shaped leaves.

Ju'piter (contracted from *Diovis pater*, or *Diespiter*, the 'heavenly father'), identified with the Etruscan Tina or Tinia and the Greek Zeus, was the supreme deity of the Romans, and received worship on the Capitoline as *Optimus*, *Maximus*, *Capi-*

tolinus, and *Tarpeius*. As lord of the heavens, he was called *Pluvius*, *Tonans*, *Fulgurator*, *Lucetius*, &c. J. was the tutelar deity of Rome, and had many surnames from attributes of power and success in war. A great festival of J., called the *Feriæ Latinæ*, held yearly on the Alban Mount, was said to have been instituted in honour of the union of Rome and the states of Latium, and a sacred feast named the *Epulum Jovis* fell on the 13th November. The care of his worship belonged to the *Flamen Dialis*, who held the highest rank among priests. Representations of J. follow the type of the Greek Zeus (q. v.).

Jupiter is the largest planet of our solar system. Its mean distance from the sun is 478,000,000 of miles; its period of revolution or year 4,332·585 mean solar days; the excentricity of orbit ·04816; the inclination of the plane of its motion to the ecliptic 1° 18′ 30″; its diameter about 85,000 miles; and the period of its rotation round its axis only 9 hours, 55 minutes, 26 seconds. A direct effect of this rapid rotation is the evident oblateness of the planet's disk, the compression at the poles being as much as $\frac{1}{17}$ of the equatorial diameter. Its density is about one-fourth that of the earth, while its *mass* has been estimated by Airy, Bessel, Von Asten and others, from observations of the elongation of a satellite, or from the measured perturbations upon comets and asteroids, to be between $\frac{1}{1047}$ and $\frac{1}{1048}$ of the sun's mass. When viewed through a telescope, the surface of J. presents a streaked appearance, which Sir John Herschel has explained as probably due to trade-winds acting upon the cloud masses in the planet's atmosphere. Subsequent study of the surface, however, has led some authorities to take up the view that J. in its physical condition bears little resemblance to our earth, but is in reality a molten mass in a state of great activity, throwing out on all sides masses of semi-transparent vapour. It is this vapour we see, and not the planet's true body, which is hid from us just as the true nucleus of the sun is hid behind the glowing chromosphere. J. has four satellites, which were first discovered by Galileo (q. v.). They suffer eclipse exactly as our moon does. The eclipses are announced in the *Nautical Almanac*, and may be used for determining longitude. They are also of historic interest, since it was by observations of them that Römer was led to the determination of the velocity of Light (q. v.). See SOLAR SYSTEM.

Ju'ra, a mountain range extending in a north-easterly direction for a distance of 450 miles from the river Rhone to the Fichtelgebirge in Central Germany, where the Main has its source. It is divided by the Rhine into two portions, known as the Swiss and German J. respectively. The former lies chiefly in France, and gives name to a French department. It consists of a number of parallel ridges separated by narrow and deep valleys, through which small streams flow S. to the Rhone. The principal heights are Col de la Neige (5342 feet), Reculet (5330), Mont Credoz (5250), Grand Colombier (5230), Mont Tendre (5212), and La Montagne de Dôle (5210). The German J. presents a wholly different aspect, being rather a succession of plateaux of moderate height with few intersecting streams. It looks S.E. over the basin of the Danube. The heights are insignificant, the highest being Oberhohenberg (3300 feet). Geologically, the J. consists of a characteristic limestone, which is contemporaneous with our oolites.

Ju'ra, a department of France, on the Swiss frontier, traversed from N. to S. Area, 1924 sq. miles; pop. (1872) 287,634. It is watered by the Ain, Bienne, Doubs, Loue, and Seille. The mountains are clad with pine forests and fine pasture, and the valleys and plains yield abundance of grain and wine, to the extent yearly of 505,000 hectolitres, and to the value of 5,000,000 francs. A notable product is the yellow wine of Château-Chalons, known as the *Madère Français*. The mining and working of iron is a leading industry. J. is traversed by several lines of railway. Lons-le-Saubnier is the capital, and other towns are Dôle, Sainte Claude, Arbois, and Poligny.

Jura (Scand. *deor-oe*, 'deer island'), the fourth largest island of the Inner Hebrides, is separated from the mainland of Argyleshire by the Sound of J., 10 miles broad, and from Islay (q. v.) in the S.E. by a long channel that narrows to half a mile. It is 27 miles long and from 5 to 7 broad, and is bleak and mountainous, rising to a height of 2560 feet in the Paps of J., three round-topped summits. The W. coast, which is wild and rocky, is indented by the narrow Loch Tarbet to a depth of 4 miles. A belt of plain stretching along the E. coast yields some oats, barley, flax, and potatoes, and is dotted with a few fishing villages. Red deer and other game abound, and there is a considerable export of black cattle. Pop. (1871) 761. Between J. and the island of Scarba in the N. is the whirlpool of Corryvrechan (q. v.).

Jurass'ic Series. See OOLITIC SERIES.

Jurisdic'tion in law means the legal authority of Court or judge. Objection to J. is in England called a plea to the J. The same in Scotland is included in what are called *preliminary* pleas. See CONFLICT OF LAWS, INTERNATIONAL LAW.

Jurispru'dence is the term used to denote the science or philosophy of Law (q. v.), or an exposition of the principles on which positive law is based. See Austin's *Province of J. Determined*.

Jury, Grand. See GRAND JURY.

Jury, Trial by. This mode of legal trial has existed in England from immemorial time. By 6 Geo. IV. c. 50 several abuses which had crept into the system were removed. According to the Jury Act the church wardens and overseers of the poor are required to make out an alphabetical list before the 1st September each year of all men in their respective parishes qualified to serve on juries. The summons of every common juror must be at least ten days, and of every special juror at least three days before he has to attend; but in the City of London, and in the county of Middlesex six days are allowed between summons and appearance. Judges may direct the sheriff to summon 144 jurors, but not more, to attend the assizes on their respective circuits, to serve indiscriminately on civil and criminal trials. These are to be divided into two sets, one of which is to attend at the beginning, the other, at the end, of the assizes. On the jurors' names being called they may be objected to, or *challenged*, as it is called, as improper persons to form a jury. Challenge to the *array* is an objection to the whole list, or *panel*, of jurors. Challenge to the *poll* is an objection to an individual. A *special* jury is one in which jurors are selected from the better educated classes, to try a cause involving a question of more than ordinary difficulty. If after a jury have retired to consider their verdict they have meat, drink, fire, or candle without consent of the Court, and before finding their verdict, they are liable to be fined. If any juryman speaks to either party to a suit, or to his agent after retiring, or if the jury cast lots for whom they shall find, the verdict will be set aside. No new evidence can be adduced after the jury have retired. They may have a witness recalled to repeat his evidence in *open* court, but not privately. When a criminal trial cannot be finished in one day, the Court may adjourn till next morning, but the jury must be kept so as to have no communication except with each other. In trials for misdemeanour the jurors may be allowed to go home on engaging not to allow themselves to be spoken to on the subject of the trial. In civil cases the jury may separate until the judge has summed up, after which they cannot do so. In England a jury must be unanimous in its finding. If they cannot agree after having been in deliberation for a reasonable length of time they are discharged. A new jury may then be summoned and the process repeated. In civil cases if there has been any mistake on the part of the judge, or any misconduct on the part of the jury, the losing party will be allowed a new trial. But in a criminal case under the same circumstances no new trial will be allowed, either in England or in Scotland. In the latter country T. by J. in civil cases was introduced according to the English practice in 1815; but unanimity is not required in returning the Verdict (q. v.). See also GUILTY, GRAND JURY, JUDGMENT, CIVIL.

Jury-mast (probably contracted from *injury-mast*), a temporary mast in a ship.

Jus Devolu'tum, a phrase used in Scotch ecclesiastical law to denote the right which devolves upon a presbytery to appoint a minister to a vacant charge, if the congregation fail to do so within six months.

Jus Gen'tium. See INTERNATIONAL LAW.

Jushpore' (*Jashpur*), a native state in Chota Nagpur, India, in political connection with the Bengal Government. Area, 1947 sq. miles; pop. (1872) 66,926; revenue about £2000; tribute £77, 10s., paid through the neighbouring chief of Sargujah. The chief place is Jushporenuggur, or Jugdispore. The staple crop is rice; gold is found by washing in the river Id.

Jus Mari'ti, a term of Roman law and of Scotch law, denoting the right which a husband acquires by marriage over his wife's property. See under CONTRACT—*Contract of Marriage*.

Jus Relic'tæ, a term of Scotch law, denoting the share of the *Goods in Communion* (q. v.) to which a wife is entitled on the death of her husband.

Jus Representatio'nis, a term adopted by the Scotch law from the Roman, to denote the rule of law by which the descendant of an elder brother takes the place of his father in succeeding to heritage before the younger brothers of his father. Formerly there was no J. R. regarding movable property; but this was changed by 18 Vict. c. 23, so that the issue of a predeceasing next of kin take the place of their parent in intestate succession. See SUCCESSION, EXECUTORS, INTESTACY.

Jussieu, Antoine de, the earliest of the famous botanists of this name, was born at Lyon, 22d April 1686, became Professor of Botany at the Jardin du Roi in 1708, and died at Paris, April 12, 1758. He was a most indefatigable working botanist, travelled through various foreign countries collecting plants, and wrote several works on his favourite science. He was ably assisted by his brother, **Bernard de J.**, who was born at Lyon in 1699, accompanied Antoine in his various travels, became demonstrator at the Jardin du Roi in 1722, and died at Paris, November 6, 1777. As superintendent of the botanical garden at Trianon, he arranged the plants according to a system which was afterwards elaborated by his nephew.—**Antoine Laurent de J.**, son of Antoine, was born at Lyon, April 12, 1748. He was carefully trained in botanical science by his uncle Bernard, whose method of classification he adopted and developed. As Professor of Botany in the Jardin du Roi, he had peculiar opportunities for establishing the new system, which, on the completion of his *Genera Plantarum* (1778–89), at once superseded the convenient, but evidently artificial, classification of Linnæus. (See BOTANY.) In 1790 he organised, with the aid of Daubenton, Lemonnier, and others, the Museum of Natural History, became in 1804 Professor of Botany in the University of Paris, and died September 17, 1836.—**Adrien de J.**, son of the preceding, was born at Paris, December 23, 1797, and passed his whole life at the Museum of Natural History, where he succeeded his father as Professor of Botany in 1826. He died June 29, 1853. He was the author of numerous and important memoirs on various natural orders, and wrote besides a work entitled *Cours Élémentaire de Botanique* (Par. 1848), which was translated into nearly every European language, and was for long the standard treatise on the subject.

Jus'tice may be considered as a moral habit of the mind, or objectively as a course of conduct in certain circumstances. In the first sense it is described by psychologists as the cardinal social virtue; in the second it is treated of by moralists and lawyers as criminal J., civil J., abstract J. But the meaning of the word is extremely vague. It is said to be just that crimes should be punished: that contracts should be enforced: that the infirm poor should be supported: that society should frown on certain vices: that the laws should treat all classes in the same manner: that persons who have received benefits should feel grateful. Even the operations of nature have been described as just, but this generally with reference to some human duty of prevision or precaution. There is almost always some reference to the interests of others than the actor, but it is sometimes said that a man is unjust to himself (as through intemperance, overwork, &c.), and, in fact, J. has been applied to the conditions of well-being, to the right balance and harmony of forces, to the adaptation of organism to environment in the individual and in society. On the other hand, teachers of natural law distinguish between J. and charity: between duties of perfect obligation which imply co-relative rights to demand performance, and duties of imperfect obligation which are binding only on conscience. This distinction cannot be maintained on grounds of natural law; for either a man is entitled to nothing but what positive law gives him, or every member of society is entitled to demand that all the other members shall live a perfectly virtuous life. The word J. comes from the Latin *jussum*, 'what has been ordered;' and the Greek δίκαιον from δίκη, 'a suit-at-law,' δίκη first meaning the manner of doing things, then the prescribed manner. The root idea is therefore conformity to law, either existing or which ought to exist. Penal sanction is common to J. and to moral obligation. But J. seems to be distinguished by the presence of a desire to punish or to reward a definite object. This springs from personal resentment for injury and the instinct of self-defence, which feelings are extended to the case of others being injured (at first only within the family, caste, tribe, or clan), or to ideal cases. Such is the origin of the peculiar force of the sentiment of J., but the sentiment does not become strictly moral until it is subordinated to the social sympathies. J. is violated equally by wrongful aggression and by the wrongful withholding of rights; hence the sacred shibboleth of liberty, equality, fraternity. Expediency may demand what is inconsistent with abstract J., but the history of human freedom is the gradual recognition of social inequalities as inexpedient and therefore unjust. There are many classical discussions of J.: as in Plato's *Republic* (where it is put for the health of the state); Aristotle's Eudemian Books, where the Pythagorean idea of J. as retaliation is discarded for the famous distinction of distributive J. according to merit fixed by the state constitution, and corrective or reparative J.; among the Stoics, who, in order to make the individual independent, minimised his responsibility for others; among the Epicureans, who based J. on the feeling of reciprocity or joint interest; the school of Hobbes and Hume, which, on the assumption that for the sake of peace primitive society has surrendered a portion of its unlimited rights of enjoyment, resolves J. into the respect of property and the performance of covenants; the intellectual intuition school of Clarke and Wollaston, who identify injustice with falsehood or contradiction. We may also mention the maxim of Kant, 'Act as if the maxim of your action ought by your will to become the universal law of nature;' and the definition of Herbert Spencer as 'the mutual limitations of man's actions necessitated by their co-existence as units of society; limitations the perfect observance of which constitutes that state of equilibrium forming the goal of political progress.' This is merely a biological way of putting the golden rule of Christianity, which merges the distinction of social and personal duty in the higher conception of 'living to God.'

Jus'tice, College of. See COLLEGE OF JUSTICE.

Justice, Lord Chief. The principal judge of the Queen's Bench division is entitled L. C.-J. of England. There is also a L. C.-J. of the Common Pleas division.

Justice Courts. See JUSTICE, LORD-CHIEF.

Justices of the Peace. The Lord Chancellor, the Lord Treasurer, and all the Justices of the Queen's Bench are *ex officio* conservators of the peace. J. of the P. for the county are usually appointed on the recommendation of the Lord-Lieutenant. Their powers and duties depend on their commission. These powers are generally to suppress riots, and otherwise to preserve the peace, and to commit for trial those accused of crime. Their duties have been greatly increased by late Acts of Parliament, as regards the regulation of gaols and houses of correction, in taking cognisance of various offences against the vagrant, game, and revenue laws, and in the licensing of public houses. By statute, every Justice of the Peace must have an estate of £100 per annum, clear of incumbrance, or the immediate reversion of reserved rents to the amount of £300, and if he acts without qualification he forfeits £100. 34 and 35 Vict. c. 18 repeals the law disqualifying attorneys and other lawyers in practice from being J. of the P. for counties; retaining the disqualification, however, as regards the counties in which they carry on their profession. A Justice of the Peace acts *ministerially* or *judicially*—*ministerially* in preserving the peace, hearing charges against offenders, issuing summonses or warrants, bailing the supposed offender or committing him for trial—*judicially* when he convicts for an offence. His conviction drawn in due form is conclusive. If a Justice of the Peace act illegally, maliciously, or corruptly, he is punishable by information or indictment. When a criminal information is applied for against a magistrate, the question for the Court is not whether the Act founded on was right, but whether or not it proceeded from an unjust, oppressive, or corrupt motive.

In Scotland an endeavour was made to introduce the office of Justice of the Peace by the Act 1587 c. 82, but it required repeated enactments to lay the foundation of the system, which was not fully done till the passing of the Act 1661 c. 38. By the Articles of Union the laws for regulating the trade, customs, and excise in Scotland are assimilated to those of England; and accordingly J. of the P., in Scotland, are vested with the same powers as they have in England, in matters which affect the customs and excise; and by the statute 6 Anne c. 6, the same powers were given to J. of the P. in Scotland, which had formerly been held by J. of the P. in England in relation to the preservation of the peace; leaving the trials and judgments to be regulated by Scotch forms and customs. In England some of the more eminent of the Justices form what is called a *quorum*, without whose presence certain business cannot be transacted. This arrangement has never been introduced into Scotland, where no particular qualification of rank or property is essential.

Justice-Clerk, Lord, a judicial officer in Scotland second in rank to the Lord Justice-General, in whose absence he presides in the Court of Justiciary. Usually the L. J.-C. presides over the Second Division of the Court of Session.

Justice-General, Lord, is the highest judge of the Court of Session in Scotland. He is also called the Lord President of the Court of Session.

Justices, Lords, were officials appointed by the sovereign, on leaving the kingdom, to carry on certain of the regal functions; for example, the summoning or prorogation of Parliament, and the disposal of church preferment in the gift of the crown. The last appointment of L. J. was by George IV. on visiting Hanover. Queen Victoria has never delegated her authority on leaving the kingdom; the highest legal authorities being of opinion that it is unnecessary to do so.

Justices' Clerk is in England an officer appointed by the Justices of the Peace to advise them in their legal administration. The appointment, which is paid by fees, is usually given to a solicitor of good local position.

Justi'ciary Court. The supreme criminal court of Scotland is so called. Its jurisdiction extends over the country, and over all crimes. It is an appellate court as regards inferior criminal tribunals, its decisions being final. It usually sits in Edinburgh, but it holds circuit courts, for which purpose the kingdom is divided into three divisions, the South, the West, and the North. A circuit court is held thrice a year in Glasgow.

Jus'tifiable Hom'icide. See HOMICIDE.

Justifica'tion, in Pauline theology, is the declaration of God by which remission of his sins is granted to the sinner in view of his faith. Properly the only possible way in which this could have been accomplished was by the sinner suffering death. But it became possible for him to be justified without actually suffering death through the conjunction of three things equally indispensable—the grace of God, the blood of Christ, and the faith of man. (1) First of all Christ died; (2) the sinner by faith may be so joined to Christ, become so essentially one with him, that in his death the old man dies, so as to rise in Christ's resurrection as a new man; and (3) God in his grace is willing to substitute this mystical death (*of the sinner*) in Christ for real death, and so he who dies thus is justified (Rom. vi. 2–11; Gal. ii. 20; 2 Cor. v. 14, 'then all died').

After the Reformation, the Roman Catholic doctrine, which of course did not originate then, was that J. and Sanctification constituted the one act of *making just*. The Protestant doctrine was that J. is a forensic act performed by God, antecedent to the work of Sanctification. Roman Catholics also differed from Protestants in holding that good works are a necessary condition of salvation *in addition* to faith.

Jus'tin, a Roman historian, not later than the 4th or 5th c. A.D., author of *Historiarum Philippicarum Libri XLIV.*, still extant, taken from the lost *Historiæ Philippicæ* of Trogus Pompeius, a contemporary of Augustus. The *editio princeps* of J. was printed at Venice by Jenson in 1470. Frotscher's edition (in 3 vols. Leips. 1827) is the most useful.

Justin I. *the Elder*, Eastern Roman Emperor, was born in the hamlet of Tauresium (450 A.D.) in Dardania. Originally a Slav or Gothic shepherd, he went to Constantinople to seek his fortune. Being enrolled in the guards he made himself famous for courage in the wars with Persia, and rose from tribune to senator and commander-in-chief. On the death of Anastasius I. in 518 he was proclaimed emperor, though he could neither read nor write. J. left the administration of affairs to Proclus, allied himself with the adherents of the Orthodox Church, and (520) adopted his nephew Justinian (q. v.). A war with the King of Persia, the occurrence at Antioch of a disastrous earthquake, and the measures he adopted for making good its ravages, are the chief events of his later career. He died August 1, 527.—**J. II.** *the Younger*, nephew of Justinian, ruled from 565 to 574, when he became insane. He died 26th September 578. In his reign the Lombards wrested Italy from the empire.

Justin'ian I. (Flavius Anicius Justinianus; Slav. *upravda*, 'upright,' of which Justin and Justinian are supposed to be Latin translations), was born at Tauresium, the modern Kustendje (q. v.), 11th May 483. He was educated at Constantinople, and following the fortunes of his uncle, Justin I. (q. v.), was by him appointed commander-in-chief of the Asiatic armies (520), consul (521), and co-emperor (527). Justin dying in the August of the same year, J. was crowned head of the Eastern Roman empire, with Theodora for his colleague, the actress and courtesan whom he had wedded in 525, and who exercised so baneful an influence upon his reign. She it was who urged J. to his vain attempt to coerce the Monophysites into orthodoxy, and her partiality towards the 'Blues' led to the terrible faction fight of the Hippodrome (532), in which 30,000 persons lost their lives. The external history of J.'s reign is that of the conquests of his generals, Belisarius (q. v.) and Narses (q. v.), which for a time partially reunited Italy to the empire, but diverted men's minds from the growing assaults of Persia and the other nations of the East, from whence the final ruin was to come. These wars, too, so drained the imperial treasuries that taxes heavy and unequal fell on J.'s own immediate subjects like a hailstorm. At home the Emperor abolished the consulship, and closed the Neo-Platonic schools of Athens and Alexandria. He built twenty-six churches in Constantinople, that of St. Sophia among the number, and lavished £200,000 on the embellishment of Antioch, while the enormous expenditure entailed by his fortifications in Thrace and Asia was barely compensated by the introduction into Europe of the silkworm by Nestorian missionaries returned from China. J. died November 14, 565, leaving to his nephew, Justin II. (q. v.), an empire vast but unwieldy, outwardly imposing but rotten at the core. His character presents a strange medley of virtues and vices, for, whilst frugal, kindly, and of exemplary private life, he was vain, jealous, and rapacious, and his ingratitude to Belisarius is an eternal infamy. He has left at least one lasting monument to his genius in the *Corpus Juris Civilis*, comprising the code, digests or pandects, institutes, and novells. These, executed under his directions by Tribonian (q. v.), first shaped the Roman law into a definite code, and have formed the groundwork of the civil law of most civilised nations. See Gibbon's *Decline and Fall*.

Justin Martyr, a Christian apologist, was born at Neapolis (anc. Shechem, mod. Nablus), in Samaria, somewhere between the years 89 and 118 A.D. His father was a heathen, and he himself was by turns a Stoic, Peripatetic, and Platonist, till meeting one day with a meek and venerable old man on a lonely spot by the sea-shore, he was led by his discourse, first to a study of the Hebrew prophets, and thence to a profession of the Christian faith (119–40). J. did not, however, discard his old pursuits. He rather saw in Christianity the highest of all philosophies, gathering in its focus the rays of truth that had been scattered throughout the various heathen systems. As such he commended it to Antoninus 'the Philosopher,' and as such he defended it from the assaults of learned Jews. He is said to have suffered martyrdom, on occasion of a second visit to Rome, about the year 165. Of the writings assigned to J. three are undoubtedly his work, the first and second *Apologia pro Christianis*, and the *Cum Tryphone Judæo Dialogus*; four are of questionable authenticity, and five are certainly spurious. Eight others are either wholly lost, or exist only in fragments. The *editio princeps* was published by Stephanus (Par. 1551), and the best and most recent edition is that of Otto (3 vols. Jena, 1842–46). There is an English translation of J.'s works in the *Ante-Nicene Library*

(Edinb. 1867). See Semisch, *Justinus der Märtyrer* (2 vols. Bresl. 1840–42).

Just Intona'tion, in music, is tuning related notes to their true relative pitch. See TEMPERAMENT.

Jute is the textile fibre obtained from the stalks of *Corchorus capsularis* and *C. olitorius*, two closely-allied plants belonging to the natural order *Tiliaceæ*, natives of and cultivated throughout the greater part of Bengal. The two plants are precisely similar in external appearance, leaves, and flowers, the only points of difference being the greater height to which *C. capsularis* attains—5 to 10 feet as against 5 to 6—and the form of the seed capsule, which in *C. capsularis* is wrinkled and globose, while in the other it forms a long slender cylinder. There are various other species of *Corchorus* growing in *Bengal*, but these alone are the sources of J. The term J. is the Anglicised form of the Orissa name *jhat*, derived from the ancient Sanskrit *jhat;* the Bengalee name is *pat* or *kosha*.

The plant has been cultivated and its fibre used in Bengal from time immemorial, where also its fresh green leaves have been, and still are, employed as a pot-herb; but it is only in very recent times that its fibre has attained the position of an important article of export. In the year 1793, 100 tons of the fibre was sent to England by the officers of the East Indian Company, under its native name of *pat*. It was very favourably reported on as being 'not hemp, but a species of flax superior in quality to any known in the trade, 1000 tons of which,' says the report, 'would readily go off annually at from £40 to £60 per ton.' Two years later Dr. Roxburgh prepared and sent to England a bale of the fibre under the name of J., which he learned from the Orissa gardeners; and this constitutes the first time the English term was applied to the fibre. From that date a small fluctuating export trade sprang up, but it was not reckoned sufficiently important to merit a special heading in the Calcutta Custom House records till the year 1828-29. In that year 364 cwts. were exported, and thereafter the exports grew with extraordinary rapidity till in 1872–73, not less than 7,250,000 cwt. were shipped from Calcutta, valued at nearly £4,000,000 sterling; and into Great Britain alone in 1874 the quantity imported was 4,270,164 cwts. At the same time the local manufacture has also developed with great rapidity. About fifteen mills with English machinery and controlled by English capitalists are now working in the neighbourhood of Calcutta. Fifty million Gunny Bags (q. v.) are annually exported, to the value of more than £1,000,000. The native Indian manufacture is chiefly confined to gunny bags, gunny cloth, twine, and coarse paper.

For the cultivation of the J. plant, a rich alluvial soil, a hot, moist climate, and an abundant rainfall appear to be most favourable. The seed is sown broadcast from the latter half of March till June, and reaped from August to October in different localities. The cultivation is chiefly confined to the lower valley of the Brahmaputra, where the Mahommedan population is in the majority. Its rapid extension is due to the enterprise of the petty farmers, stimulated by the commercial demand; and it has greatly added to the prosperity of this class, who rely upon it for paying their rent. The fibre is separated from the woody stalk by a process of steeping, similar to that practised with flax and hemp. When separated it is washed in water, dried in the sun, and made up into hanks, which are collected by retail dealers for despatch to the markets of Serajgunge, Naraingunge, &c. It is pressed into bales, for exportation, at Calcutta in screw presses, the bales weighing 300, 350, or 400 lbs. About seven million cwts. are annually received in that city by native boat, steamer, and rail, of which two million cwts. are consumed locally.

The fibre of J. is long, smooth, and glossy; and it possesses a brownish yellow tint, which can only be discharged with great difficulty by bleaching. On this account it has not yet been successfully employed as a white paper-making material, although on several occasions the *Dundee Advertiser* has been printed on a very fair paper made from pure J. The fibre takes brilliant dye colours readily, but they are all comparatively fugitive. One of the most remarkable properties of J. is the facility with which it can be prepared to imitate other and more valuable articles, as wool, silk, and even human hair. On this account it is much used for inferior classes of carpeting, for adulterating or imitating silk textures, and for making stage wigs, tresses, and ladies' hair pads. The staple manufacture, however, consists of 'hessians,' a coarse fabric for packing, sackings, Osnaburgs, mattings, ducks, and other heavy cloths. The process employed in preparing, spinning, and weaving J. are essentially the same as those used for flax, but the machinery is heavier.

The great seat of the J. manufacture is Dundee in Scotland. There the fibre became an important staple during the Crimean war (1853–55); and the outbreak of the American civil war, with the consequent cotton famine, gave the trade an enormous impetus. In 1838 only 1136 tons were consumed by Dundee manufacturers, in 1847 the consumption had risen to 6966 tons; in 1854 it was 16,590, and in 1872, the year of its greatest prosperity, the trade demand was 96,000 tons. To a limited extent the manufacture is prosecuted in Glasgow and at Barrow-in-Furness, besides various Continental and American localities. See *Report of the J. Commission* (1 vol. fol. Calc. 1874).

Jü'terbogk (named after the Slavic god of spring), a town in the province of Brandenburg, Prussia, 28 miles S. of Potsdam, on the Nuthe, an affluent of the Havel, with woollen manufactures and a pop. (1875) of 6852. Near J. is the battlefield of Dennewitz (q. v.).

Jut'land. See DENMARK.

Juvena'lis, Decimus Junius, the most earnest and trenchant of Roman satirists, was born at Aquinum, an inconsiderable town of the Volsci. The year of his birth is unknown. Dodwell, an inexact authority, sets it down as 38 A.D. Teuffel, with greater caution and with some regard to historical fitness, gives the period of J. as 47–130 A.D. Mr. Walford (see *Juvenal* in Blackwood's *Ancient Classics for English Readers*) dismisses this interesting question with the words, 'The dates of his birth and of his death are alike disputed.' 'That the only facts with regard to Juvenal on which we can implicitly rely are that he flourished towards the close of the 1st. c., that Aquinum was, if not the place of his nativity, at least his chosen residence, and that he is in all probability the friend whom Martial addresses in three epigrams.' From his boyhood till he attained the age of thirty-five nothing is known of him save that he devoted himself to the study of eloquence, according to the practice of the time, more for his own amusement than for gain or professional advancement. Satire—the sphere in which the genius of Juvenal worked—was a purely Roman growth. It began with Lucilius, and was continued by the witty, delicate, graceful Horace. To him succeeded J., in every respect distinct, earnest, strong, intensely human, with a depth of sentiment, a real sorrow, and a despairing earnestness, new in the literature of the world, if we except a few passages in the Hebrew Scriptures. His satires, sixteen in number, cover a wide field. Their onslaughts on tyranny, corruption in morals and policy, silly vices, and vagrant fancies have a perennial vitality. J. was the Hogarth of his time. Though much better known to the English public than many of the *dii majores* of Latin literature, he is still very imperfectly appreciated. Dryden's version of five of his satires are at best but fair. Dr. Johnson's *London* and *Vanity of Human Wishes* are vigorous imitations of two of the most notable. Gifford's version is on the whole terse, pungent, and scholarly; but a really good translation of J. has still to be executed. The *editio princeps* of J. was published at Venice, 1470, folio. The editions of Ruperti (2 vols. Leips. 1801); Lemain (2 vols. Par. 1823); Jahn (Berl. 1851); and J. E. B. Mayor (with commentary, Lond. 1869), may be noted as works deserving the attention of scholars. Continental translations are numerous. That of Hertzberg and W. W. Teuffel (Stuttg. 1864–67) is distinguished by singular felicity of diction, force, and character. With all their epigrammatic turn and satiric power the French have failed in giving us a good translation of J.

Ju'venile Offen'ders. To avoid the evils of the long imprisonment of the J. O. before trial, 10 and 11 Vict. c. 82, enacts that persons not exceeding fourteen years of age, accused of simple larceny or of aiding in its commission, may be summarily convicted by two justices, and sentenced to imprisonment for a period not exceeding three calendar months, with or without hard labour, or to forfeit a sum not exceeding £3; and if the offender be a male he may be once whipped in addition to the other punishment, or instead of it. If either the accused or their parents object to a summary conviction, justices are to proceed as before the passing of the Act, which is extended by 13 and 14 Vict. c. 37, and by 25 Vict. c. 18. The Acts apply to Scotland.

K.

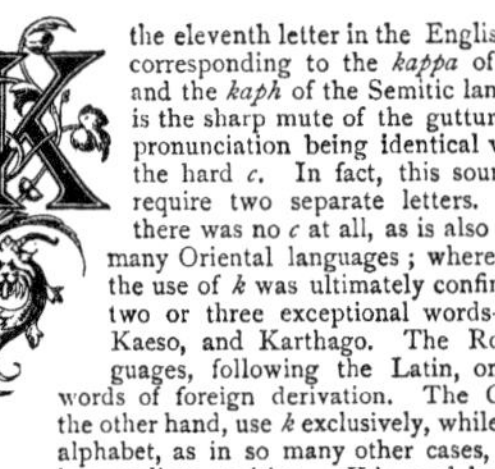

the eleventh letter in the English alphabet, corresponding to the *kappa* of the Greeks and the *kaph* of the Semitic languages. It is the sharp mute of the guttural series, its pronunciation being identical with that of the hard *c*. In fact, this sound does not require two separate letters. In Greek there was no *c* at all, as is also the case in many Oriental languages; whereas in Latin the use of *k* was ultimately confined to some two or three exceptional words—Kalendae, Kaeso, and Karthago. The Romance languages, following the Latin, only use *k* in words of foreign derivation. The Germans, on the other hand, use *k* exclusively, while the English alphabet, as in so many other cases, occupies an intermediate position. *K* is used by us in native words as an initial chiefly before *e*, *i*, and *n*, and as in German, to strengthen *c* when terminating a monosyllable, as *luck*. Modern usage drops the final *k* in such Greek derivatives as *music*. The Semitic *kaph* is to be distinguished carefully from *koph*, which latter has been borrowed in the form of *q*. For the interchanges of *k* compare Carolus, Charles, Karl; and 'knee,' Lat. *genu*. See also *C* and *G*. As an abbreviation, *K*. stands for knight, as in K.C.B. = Knight Commander of the Bath.

Ka'aba (Arab. 'square house'), a rectangular building, 38 feet high and 28 feet broad, in the mosque at Mecca, said to have been built by Abraham for the worship of the One God, into the S. corner of which is fixed the large stone called *Hadschar-el-Aswad*, given to Abraham by the angel Gabriel, once pure white, but now black with the kisses of penitents, or, as others say, with its own tears for men's sins. Frequent repairs, especially those of the Sultan Mustapha in 1630, have left only a small portion of the original building. Instead of Jerusalem, Mohammed made the K. the *Kiblah*, *i.e.*, the object in the direction of which worshippers must turn in praying, and ordered pilgrimages to be made to it. It was an Arab place of worship even before Mohammed, who destroyed the 365 idols that surrounded it. The K. receives annually a new outer covering of black silk, embroidered in gold with verses of the Koran, and round it are many porches and other places of devotion, as well as the well of Zem-Zem, where pilgrims wash. The whole is enclosed by a great covered passage, and is called *Medschid-el-Haram* ('holy mosque').

Kaama. See HARTEBEEST.

Kab'yles (properly *K'baïl*, 'confederates,' the plural of the Arabic *K'bila*, 'a league'), the name of the Berbers of Algeria and Tunis. The K. are one of the chief indigenous peoples of N.W. Africa, distinct from the Æthiopic or black population, and unquestionably of the same stock as the nations of antiquity known as Mauretanians, Numidians, Getulians, &c. They are brave but vindictive, of ordinary stature, well-built and handsome, with complexions ranging from dark-brown to a dirty yellow, with straight hair, scant beards, and black eyes. The pop. of Algeria was 2,448,691 in 1875, and of this number it was estimated that one-third were K. See ALGERIA and BERBERS.

Kadur', a town, but since 1865 not the chief town, of the district of the same name in the state of Mysore, India, 145 miles N.W. of Bangalore. Pop. (1871) 2733.—The *district* of K. has an area of 2294 sq. miles; pop. (1871) 333,925. Coffee cultivation in S. India originated here. Berries were brought from Mecca two centuries ago, and Europeans commenced planting about 1835. There are now 13,000 gardens, covering 60,000 acres.

Kaff'a (so called by the Genoese, from the Tartar *Kefê*), or **Feodo'sia**, a fortified port of Russia, in the Crimea, on a bay of the same name, an inlet of the Black Sea, 55 miles W.S.W. of Kertch. It was the chief seat of the Genoese trade in the 13th c., and when it fell to the Turks it was called 'Little Stambul,' and had 100,000 inhabitants, 51 mosques, and 171 springs. It was the residence of the Tartar Khans from 1774 till its conquest by the Russians in 1783. The higher part of the town contains the Tartar citadel and barracks. K. is the entrepôt of a large caravan trade, and has great magazines. Its exports, chiefly wheat, hides, and goat's hair, amounted to 817,474 roubles in 1873. Pop. 8482.

Kaffaristan' (Arab. *Kafir*, 'unbeliever,' and the Pers. word *istân*, 'place or abode'), a region of Afghanistan, on the southern slopes of the Hindu Kush, which has never been visited by Europeans. It is inhabited by a race called Kaffar Siahposh, who are not of the same religion or origin as the neighbouring Afghans and Tartars. In language, religion, and even physiognomy they are akin to the Hindus. They cherish an hereditary feud with all Mohammedans, and are disposed to claim relationship with the English.

Kaffir Corn. See SORGHO GRASS.

Kaff'irs, or **Kafirs**, the name of a race inhabiting S.E. Africa, from Sofala to the Great Fish River, and inland as far as Lake Ngami and the southern basin of the Zambesi. The word *Kafir* is of Arabic origin, signifying infidel, and was vaguely applied by the old Arab invaders of Eastern Africa to all the non-Mohammedan peoples with which they came in contact. The K. are of a modified negro type, the divergence from the pure negro increasing with the distance from the tropic. They are tall, slimmer than the negro, sinewy, and exceedingly active. Their colour is a dark-brown, which deepens into black in some of the northern tribes. The hair is black and curly, and the skin emits the same peculiar odour as that of the negro, but the lips are less prominent, and the nose is higher and frequently even hooked.

The K. are divided into many independent tribes, each owning allegiance to its own chieftain. In Zululand the principal tribes are the Amazulu and Amatabele; in Bechuanaland the Makololo and Batoka; and in Natal, Kaffraria Proper, and the Transkeian districts of Cape Colony, the Amapondo, Amaxosa, Amagcaleka, Tambookies, Basutos, and Amafengu, or Fingoes. The two last are of Zulu origin, and are more peaceful and inclined to a settled mode of life than the K. The Fingoes (*i.e.*, 'dogs') were reduced to slavery by the Amaxosa, but were set free by Sir B. D'Urban in 1835, and were settled along the frontier as a barrier between their former masters and the colonists, a policy which has proved very successful.

Five great wars have taken place between the K. and the British power in S. Africa. The first, in 1811–12, resulted in the K. being driven out of the Zuurveld into the region E. of the Great Fish River. The second, in 1818–19, was caused by a pseudo prophet, named Makanna, under whose leadership the K. suddenly overran the district from which they had been expelled, and attacked Grahamstown. After a desperate struggle they were completely defeated, and the district between the Great Fish River and Koonap Kat was added to the colony. The third war, in 1834–35, was marked, like the others, by the temporary success of the K. and their ultimate defeat with great slaughter. The fourth war took place in 1846-48, originating in a wanton outrage perpetrated by the K., who sustained a crushing reverse at the Gwanga. The war resulted in the extension of the British frontier to the Keiskamma, while the territory between that river and the Great Kei was reserved for occupation by the K. under the name of British Kaffraria (see CAPE COLONY). In 1850 the last great war broke out, being instigated by another self-styled prophet named Umlangene. The crisis was heightened by the unexpected rebellion of the Hottentots, and peace was not restored till March 1853. This war alone cost more than £2,000,000. Since then no serious conflict has taken place between the British power and the K., though a sanguinary contest between the Zulus and the Boers of the Transvaal took place in 1876-7. See TRANSVAAL.

The K. are a brave though treacherous race, and are a curious compound of shrewdness and superstition. They have but vague ideas of God, and like most other savages they seek rather to propitiate an evil spirit than to adore a good one. A belief in witchcraft is universal. Nevertheless their reasoning powers are remarkably good. Many of the K., especially in Basutoland and Fingoland, have been converted to Christianity by the missionaries of various denominations. The K. is by nature a herdsman, and does not care much for agriculture. His great care is for his cattle, which form his wealth. Cases exist of K. purchasing and successfully working farms, and (in Natal) sugar-mills, but these are very exceptional, save among the Fingoes. Few also of the K. take to mechanical pursuits or trade. The women build the huts and cultivate the crops of millet and maize. Their position is less degraded than among the Hottentots, though polygamy is general. Before the general introduction of firearms, the national weapons of the K. were assegais or lances and clubs, a large shield of ox hide being carried as a defence. The bow and arrow were not used by the K., though in general use among the Bushmen. A blanket is now the Kaffir's usual garment, having superseded the ox-hide formerly worn. In war time, however, the warriors entirely dispense with clothing, substituting for it a coating of red clay. The Kaffir language is sonorous and pleasing when pure, but on the Cape frontier it has become corrupted by an infusion of the peculiar Hottentot 'clicks' and Dutch words. There is no written character.

It is impossible to arrive at a reliable estimate of the numbers of the K. According to the colonial Blue Book the number of K. in Cape Colony in 1875 was 335,000. To these must be added 220,000 in Kaffraria, 300,000 in Natal, 25,000 in Orange Free State, 1,000,000 in the Transvaal, and probably 1,000,000 more in the regions beyond European settlement, making a grand total of about 2,880,000. See Shooter, *The Kaffirs of Natal* (1857); *Proceedings of the Commission relative to the Kaffirs* (Maritzb. 1852); Maclean, *Kaffir Lands and Customs* (1858); Holden, *Past and Future of Kaffir Tribes* (1855); Thomson, *Travels in S. Africa* (1872).

Kaffra'ria is the name once given to the whole of the coast region of S. Africa between Sofala and the Great Fish River, but now restricted to the independent territory between the Great Kei River and Natal, the inland boundary being the Transkeian districts of Cape Colony. The area thus included forms a rectangle of about 7500 sq. miles. It consists in great measure of a grassy plateau about 2500 feet above the sea level, but near the coast the surface is broken and rugged. The rivers flow in deep *kloofs* or gorges, and are mere torrents unsuited for navigation. The coast is rocky and shelterless. The country is well watered and fertile, and even under the very imperfect cultivation of the Kaffirs yields good crops of maize, millet, and Kaffir corn. The Kaffirs also rear large herds of cattle and goats, whose hides and skins they dispose of to the settlers of Cape Colony. The total absence of roads and bridges, however, and the still uncivilised condition of the Kaffirs, confine the trade to small limits. The principal tribes are the Amapondos and the Amagcalekas. Pop. estimated at 220,000.

Kaffraria, British, now part of Cape Colony (q. v.), but formerly an indepenent settlement, is bounded E. by free Kaffraria, W. by the province of Victoria, N. by that of Queenstown, and S. by the Indian Ocean. Area, 4500 sq. miles; pop. 86,201, of whom 2376 are European grantees, 2327 German settlers, 3380 'other Europeans,' and the remainder are natives, chiefly Amaxosa and Amafengu Kaffirs. The natural boundaries of the country are the Great Kei River in the E., the Keis Kamma in the W., and the bold range of the Amatola Mountains, which attain a height of 5000 feet, in the N. Chief of the many streams of K. are the Chumie, Buffalo, and Gonubi, but none of these are navigable. From the high grassy plateaus of the interior numerous fertile valleys open to the sea. The headquarters of the military and seat of the government are at King William's Town, of which the port is East London, at the mouth of Buffalo River. The territory of K. was occupied after the Kafir war of 1846-47, was made an independent colony in 1861, but was annexed to Cape Colony in 1866.

Kain, a term in Scotch law denoting rent paid in kind.

Kai'ra, the chief town of the district of the same name, Bombay, British India, 265 miles N. of Bombay; pop. (1872) 12,681. It is a well-built walled town, with a Jain temple and other handsome public buildings. The *district* of K., which is much interlaced with the native state of Baroda, has an area of 1561 sq. miles; pop. (1872) 782,733. Cotton, sugar-cane, and tobacco are grown.

Kairwan', a town of Tunis, N. Africa, 75 miles S. of the city of Tunis, with a pop. of 12,000, and manufactures of fur and leather. K. was founded in 672 by the Arabs, was long the capital of Moslem Africa, and is still considered a sacred town. It has 20 mosques and numerous chapels, and to the magnificent Okbah Mosque, resting on 500 pillars, numerous pilgrimages are made.

Kaisariyeh, a town of Asia Minor, in the vilayet of Angora, on the Kara-su (*Melas*), 161 miles S.E. of Angora. It stands in a fertile but highly volcanic district, and has suffered much from earthquakes. Grain, dye-stuffs, and saltpetre are the chief articles of trade. K. is the ancient *Cæsarea* (q. v.), and there are numerous ruins about the town. Estimated pop. 40,000.

Kaiser-i-Hind (Emperor of India), the Persian, or rather Hindostani, title by which Queen Victoria was proclaimed Empress at the great Durbar at Delhi on 1st January 1877. This title, which was settled after much consideration, commends itself to Persian scholars. The term 'Kaiser' has been erroneously conjectured from its spelling to be borrowed from the German, but it is, in truth, a well-known Persian word, derived through the Arabic from the Greek, and is to be found in a hackneyed quotation from the epic poet Firdousi. Persian is the court and diplomatic language of India; and under the disguise of Hindostani, was until lately the regular language of British administration.

Kaiserslau'tern, or **Lau'tern** (*Lutrea*), a town in the Rhenish Palatinate on the river Lauter, 32 miles W. of Mannheim, with breweries, tanneries, iron works, cotton manufactories, and an important fruit market. Pop. 17,867. K. was the scene of a fierce and bloody battle (28th, 29th, 30th November 1793) between the Duke of Brunswick and Hoche, in which the latter was repulsed.

Kákapo, the Maori name of the ground or night parrot of New Zealand, *Strigops habroptilus*, belonging to the family Psittacidæ (q. v.). It is remarkable as possessing a considerable development of wing, and yet never attempting to fly. On this account it is being rapidly exterminated, chiefly by dogs and rats, and is already very rare, except in the wild and uninhabited region at the S.W. extremity of the colony.

Kalafat', or **Calafatu**, a fortified town in the S.W. of Wallachia, on the left bank of the Danube, opposite the Turkish Widdin. It commands a winding stretch of the Danube, and was the scene of severe conflicts between the Russians and Turks in 1829 and again in 1854. Pop. 2500. There was continuous cannonading between K. and Widdin at the beginning of the Russo-Turkish war in May 1877.

Kalamazoo', capital of a county of the same name, in Michigan, U.S., on the river K., 143 miles W. of Detroit by rail. It is the seat of K. College, incorporated in 1855, and attended by ninety-eight male and seventy-one female students in 1872. There is splendid water-power, and the manufactures are extensive, comprising machinery, steel springs, carriages, pianos, &c. There is a fine public park and a driving park, with a superior track. Pop. (1870) 9181.

Kal'be, or **Cal'be**, a town in the province of Saxony, Prussia, on the left bank of the Saale, 10 miles S.S.E. of Schönebeck by rail, carries on spinning, weaving, and manufactures of cloth, frieze, paper, sugar, and tobacco. Pop. (1875) 7940.

Kale, Sea. See SEA KALE.

Kale is an open-leaved variety of the polymorphous cabbage plant, technically called *Brassica oleracea, acephala*. It is cultivated as a winter and spring vegetable. There are many sub-varieties, some of which are handsomely variegated; hence their use for garnishing desserts, for filling flower beds, or forming the ribbon borders of gardens in winter.

Kalei'doscope (Gr. *kalos*, 'beautiful,' *eidos*, 'form,' and *skopeō*, 'I see'), a philosophical toy invented by Sir David Brewster. Two plane reflecting surfaces are fitted longitudinally in a cylindrical tube, making an angle of 60° with one another. At the one end of the tube is a small hole for looking through, and at the other is a flat glass cell containing fragments of coloured glass. On looking through the tube towards the light, the particular figure in which the fragments may happen to congregate will be observed five times reflected, and these, together with the direct image, form a symmetrical pattern, which may be varied continuously by turning round the tube, and permitting the fragments to take up other relative positions.

Kaleva'la. See FINNISH LITERATURE.

Kali', the goddess who figures most prominently in the Hindu religion. As Parvati, she appears as the wife of the destroyer, Siva; as Durga, she has given her name to the Durga Pujah festival, the great annual holiday of Bengal; her other names are Bhawani and Devi. She has been identified with the Isis of Egypt and the Greek Hecate. K. was not known in the earliest period of the Mahabharata; and there is much plausibility in the theory that her bloody worship, with that of her husband, was borrowed from the aboriginal tribes. It is abundantly established that human sacrifices were, even to a recent period, offered in her honour, though such a practice is most abhorrent to the primitive spirit of Hinduism. K. is represented of a dark blue colour, with distorted countenance, and a necklace of human heads. It is said that the name of Calcutta is derived from K.-ghat.

Kâlidâ'sa, the greatest of all Indian dramatists, according to tradition, flourished in the reign of King Vikramaditya (57 B.C.), of whose court at Ujjayini (Oujein) he was one of the 'nine jewels' or illustrious men. More probably, however, he lived about the commencement of the 3d c. A.D., Lassen assigning him the date 250 A.D., whilst Dr. Bhau Daji places him as late as the reign of a Vikramaditya of the 6th c. He wrote but three plays, the *Sakuntala, Vikramorvasi*, and *Malavikagnimitra*, of which the first and by far the most celebrated exists in three recensions, the Bengali, Devanagari, and one in the S. of India. It has been translated into English by Sir W. Jones (1789) and Monier Williams (1853; verse trans. 1856), into French by Chezy (1830), and into German by Forster (1790), Meyer (1851), and four others. The best editions are by Böhtlingk (1842) and Pandit Tarkabagish (1860). This drama elicited the unqualified praise of Goethe, and is styled by Max Müller 'the finest of Eastern gems.' K. was also author of three of the six *Maha-kavyas* ('great poems') and of the *Ritu-samhara*, a short but well-known poem on the six seasons of the year. These last are often truly poetical and display a fertile imagination, but are too studied and artificial, being marred by a puerile love of alliteration and play upon words. See Monier Williams, *Indian Wisdom* (Lond. 1876).

Kaliha'ri, or **Kalaha'ri Desert**, a waste region in S. Africa, between 21°–29° S. lat., and 19°–25° E. long., covering an area of 200,000 sq. miles. It is a plateau of light-coloured soft sand, about 3700 feet above the sea-level, and during most of the year is rainless. The surface is nevertheless clothed with a dense vegetation of bushes and creeping tuberous plants, which support large herds of antelopes, while lions, leopards, and other carnivora are to be found near the few places where water exists. The K. D. is inhabited by wandering tribes of Bushmen, and by the Bakalahari, a pastoral race of Bechuana origin. They manage to extract water from the ground at a few 'sucking-places,' and trade chiefly in karosses, or skin-mantles.

Kal'isz, or **Kal'ish** (probably the *Calisia* of Ptolemy), a walled town in the government of the same name, Russia, on the Prosna, 62 miles N.E. of Breslau, with great trade and manufactures of cloth, was the scene of August II.'s victory over the Swedes 27th October 1706, and of the Russo-Prussian treaty of 28th February 1813. K. was founded in the 7th c. Pop. about 20,000 (7500 Jews).

Kal'mar, a seaport town in the Swedish län of the same name, on the W. shore of the Kalmarsund, opposite Oland, and 48 miles N.E. of Karlskrona, with important ship-building, manufactures of sugar and tobacco, and large trade, especially in wood and fish. There is a fine cathedral, and in the old castle, Kalmarslot, was concluded the Union of Kalmar (1397). Pop. (1868) 9421; of län 236,503.

Kal'mia, a genus of N. American evergreen shrubs belonging to the heath family (*Ericaceæ*), and so named by Linnæus after his fellow countryman, Peter Kalm. Various species are frequent in gardens, from the large growing *K. latifolia* to the small *K. glauca*. The leaves and shoots are deleterious to cattle, whilst honey from the flowers, and the flesh of game fed on the berries are poisonous to man.

Kal'muks (called by themselves *Derben-Eret* or *Dörbön-Oirat*, and by the Tartars *Khalimik*), **Oelöt**, or **Eleutes**, the most numerous of the Mongol races, are partly Chinese, partly Russian subjects, and extend from the steppes of the Don and Volga to the deserts and mountain ranges of Upper Asia. Four distinct types are recognised, the Khoshots, the Dsongars, the Derbets, and the Torgots. It is from the K. that the unfavourable descriptions of the Mongols as flat-faced and of a dirty yellow complexion have been drawn. Yet they are now considerably intermingled with their neighbours the Russians, Persians, and Turks. The history of the K. is closely connected with the great Asian conquests from Attila to Timur. They are mostly Buddhists, and are nomadic and warlike, living in felt-covered tents, their possessions being horses and sheep. Their priests have a sort of theological learning drawn from Chinese and Tibetan sources. See Latham, *Native Races of the Russian Empire* (Lond. 1854), von Hellwald, *The Russians in Central Asia* (trans. by Wirgman, Lond. 1874).

Kaloc'sa, a town in the comitat of Pesth, Hungary, near the Danube, 170 miles S.E. of Vienna, has a cathedral, an archbishop's palace, and a library of 30,000 vols. Pop. (1869) 16,302.

Kalong' (*Pteropus*), the name given to a genus of *Cheiroptera* (q. v.), or bats, forming the type of the *Frugivorous*, or fruit-eating group of the order. The K. proper is the *Pteropus Edulis* of Java, but the Roussette (*P. rubricollis*) is another familiar species. The name 'flying fox' is often applied to the K., from the shape of the head. The fur is usually reddish. The K. flits about at night, feeding on fruits and vegetable matters. It inhabits the Eastern Archipelago. The first-named species may attain an expanse of wings measuring 4 or 5 feet, and includes some of the largest of the Cheiroptera.

Kalu'ga, a central government of Russia, lies immediately S.W. of Moscow. Area, 11,934 sq. miles; pop. (1870) 984,255. It is a fertile plain, watered by the Oka, Shisdra, and Ugra, and of which one-half is cultivated and one-fourth covered with forest. Hemp is one of the chief crops, and there is an active industry in coal-mining and in making sailcloth and other coarse wares.

Kaluga, the capital of the government, lies at the confluence of the Oka and Jatschenka, 115 miles S.W. of Moscow. It is a beautiful town, the seat of a bishop, and has thirty-five churches, a great artillery park, large powder magazines, manufactures of leather, sailcloth, oil, sugar, &c., and an important trade in corn, oil, and honey. Pop. 38,608.

Ka'ma, or 'little Volga,' the largest affluent of the Volga in Russia, rises in the woods that clothe the W. slopes of the Urals, in Viatka. It flows in a S.W. direction through Perm, Orenburg, and Volga, and has a length of 1100 miles, of which all but 40 miles are available for an important traffic. The K. abounds in salmon and other fish.

Kam'ala, or **Wurr'us**, is a fine, granular, orange-red powder, which consists of the minute glands that cover the capsules of

Rottlera tinctoria, imported from India, where it is used as a dye for silk. K. is a purgative, and has been extensively used in India in the treatment of tape-worm. The worm is generally passed entire, and almost always *dead*, the head being generally detected. Dose, 60 to 120 grains of the powder, suspended in gruel, mucilage, or syrup, followed, if necessary, by half a fluid ounce of castor oil. A second dose is seldom required.

Kamieniec' Podolsk', the capital of the government of Podolia, Russia, near the border of Austrian Galicia, on a steep chalk rock overlooking the Smotrycza, 9 miles above its entrance into the Dniester. It consists of a lower and upper town, is the seat of a Greek archbishop, and of a Roman and an Armenian bishop, and has an old castle, a beautiful Gothic cathedral, and a considerable trade, mostly in the hands of the Jews. Pop. 22,611. K. was long one of the strongest bulwarks of Poland against the Turks, and fell to Russia in 1793.

Kam'pen, a port in the province of Over-Yssel, Netherlands, at the mouth of the river Yssel, 43 miles N.E. of Amsterdam, is a neat town, with important trade. Pop. (1875) 12,163.

Kampti', a flourishing town in the District of Nagpore, Central Provinces, British India, on the right bank of the river Kanhan, 9 miles N.E. of Nagpore, and 520 miles E. of Bombay by rail. Pop. (1872) 48,831. There is a cantonment here for all arms, established in 1821, from which time dates the prosperity of the town. The trade is very large, consisting chiefly of agricultural produce, timber, cotton-goods, and salt; in 1868-69 the imports were valued at £595,083, the exports at £187,607.

Kamptu'licon, the name given to a kind of floorcloth invented about 1843 and prepared by incorporating ground cork with masticated caoutchouc, rolling the mass into sheets and drying. It may be readily stained with mosaic or other patterns. It wears well, is waterproof, and much warmer than the ordinary oilcloth. The manufacture of K. received a great impetus through Sir Charles Barry employing it to cover the corridors of the Houses of Parliament. In inferior varieties of K., oxidised linseed oil, sawdust, peat, chalk, pitch, and other matters are often combined.

Kamrup', a district of Assam, British India, on both banks of the Brahmaputra; area, 3631 sq. miles; pop. (1872) 561,681. The chief town is Gowhatee (q. v.). K. is famous as the centre of a great Hindu kingdom of this name, which extended over all N. Bengal and Assam before the Mahommedan conquest.

Kamtchat'ka, a peninsula in the E. of Siberia, and in the Russian coast province, extends in a southerly direction, enclosing the Sea of Okhotsk on the E. It is 850 miles long, and has an extreme breadth of 250 miles, is traversed from N. to S. by two parallel ranges of volcanic mountains. Of the twelve active volcanoes, Kliutschevskaia (16,152 feet) is the highest in Asia, and was in full irruption in 1829. The only considerable river is the K., which is 150 miles long, and waters one of the few valleys of the peninsula, extending between the two mountain ranges. Even in the valleys the climate does not admit of cultivation, and the soil is for the most part stony. Winter lasts for nine months, and severe frosts frequently extend into summer. There are forests of birch and pine. Among the wild animals are the bear, sable, fox, otter, wolf, seal, and beaver. The only domestic animal is the dog, a peculiar species, that lives on fish, does not bark, and is used in drawing sledges. The inhabitants, about 20,000 in number, are mostly Kamtchadales, Korjäkes, and Lamuts. The chief town, Petropaulovski (q. v.), on the E. coast, is the centre of the Russian fur trade. K. was annexed to Russia in 1697.

Kam'yshin, a town in the government of Saratov, Russia, on the W. bank of the Volga, 120 miles below Saratov. It has many large workshops and gardens, and in the vicinity is a German colony. Pop. 15,698.

Kanaga'wa, a seaport of Japan, on the W. side of the Bay of Yedo, and 2 miles N. of Yokohamo, on a railway between the latter town and Yedo. It was opened to foreign commerce in 1859, and rapidly became the seat of an extensive trade, which of late years has in great part been transferred to Yokohamo. K. is still the seat of the foreign consuls. Its trade is not represented in separate returns. It is 18 miles by rail S. of Yedo, and the total receipts for goods and passengers between K. and Yedo was 431,576 dollars in 1875. Pop. estimated at about 60,000. The exports are raw silk, tea, silkworm-egg cards, cocoons, lacquer ware, copper, and tobacco.

Kana'ris, Konstantin, born about 1790 in the Greek island Ipsara, originally an obscure shipmaster, distinguished himself during the Greek War of Independence by destroying Turkish war ships. On the 19th June 1822 he burned the admiral's ship at Chios, and on the 22d November another admiral's ship at Tenedos. On the 17th August 1824 he revenged the devastation of Ipsara by burning some Turkish ships at Samos, and delivered that island from a similar fate; but failed in an attempt to destroy the fleet at Alexandria in August 1825. From 1827, when he was set over a squadron, he frequently held the office of Minister of Marine under King Otho, who, in 1861, offered him the admiralship, which he declined. K. was with a brief interruption Premier of Greece from March 1864 to March 1865.

Kanda'vu, one of the principal islands of the Fiji group (q. v.), situated in 19° S. lat., 178° 15' E. long. It is 26 miles long, and of very irregular form, being only half a mile wide in the centre. At the W. extremity is Mount Washington (3800 feet), the highest peak in the Fiji Islands. K. is the calling-place of the mail steamers running between San Francisco, Sydney, and New Zealand.

Kane, Elisha, Kent, M.D., a celebrated American traveller, was born at Philadelphia, February 3, 1820. After graduating at Pennsylvania University in 1843, he entered the navy, and visited China as physician to the embassy. Subsequently he travelled in Egypt and Western Africa; and on his return to America in 1846 served in the Mexican War. In 1850 he accompanied the first Grinnell expedition in search of Sir John Franklin as surgeon. In the second expedition (1853-55) he acted as commander and reached what he regarded as an open polar sea in N. lat 80° 20'. His health was so injured by the hardships which all Arctic explorers have experienced that he died within eighteen months after his return, at Havana, February 16, 1857. He wrote narratives of the two expeditions, entitled *United States Grinnell Expedition in search of Sir John Franklin* (1853, 2d edit. 1857), and *Arctic Explorations in the years* 1853, 1854, *and* 1855 (2 vols. 1856).

Kane, Sir Robert, M.D., F.R.S., an eminent chemist, was born at Dublin in 1810. He commenced his studies at Meath Hospital, and obtained his diploma in 1832. The same year he projected the *Dublin Journal of Medical Science*, which he edited till 1834. Shortly after he was elected professor of chemistry to the Apothecaries' Hall, a post which he resigned in 1845. From 1844 to 1847 he was professor of natural philosophy to the Royal Dublin Society, and in the latter year he obtained the Cunningham gold medal from the Royal Academy for his discoveries in chemistry. He took an active part in the formation of the Museum of Industry at St. Stephen's Green, of which he was created director in 1846. The same year he was knighted and was appointed one of the Irish Relief Commissioners. In 1864 he resigned the presidency of Queen's College, Cork, which he held for several years previously. As an author he is best known by his *Elements of Chemistry* (1842) and his *Industrial Resources of Ireland* (1844); but besides these he has written valuable memoirs on chemical subjects, notably one *On the Colouring Matter of Lichens* in the *Philosophical Transactions* (1840).

Kangaroo', a genus of quadrupeds belonging to the order Marsupialia (q. v.), and found only in Australia and a few of the neighbouring islands. Fty-six species have been described. The true K. (*Macropus*) measures about 5 feet in length from the tip of the nose to the root of the tail, and to the extremity of the latter organ fully 3 feet more. The fore-legs are very much shorter and weaker than the hind-legs, and serve rather as arms, the K. not using them in progression, though it rests upon them when feeding. The toes on each of the fore-paws are five in number, and are furnished with claws. The hind-feet are unusually long, the tarsus without the claws measuring 12 inches in length. The toes are only four in number, and the fourth is armed with a very large solid claw. The tail is very muscular, and sometimes measures a foot in circumference at the root. It materially aids the K. in its mode of locomotion, which consists of a series of bounds on the hind-feet alone, the distance covered by every such leap sometimes exceeding 15 feet. The head is small and elegantly shaped, the ears and eyes large. The teeth consist of eight incisors, four premolars, and sixteen molars. The K. feeds upon grass and the leaves of bushes, and has been observed to chew the cud.

Kangaroo.

The K. as a rule is a mild and timid animal, but the larger species, such as *M. major* (called 'old man' or 'boomer' by the colonists), and *Ophranter rufus*, the great red K., fights desperately when driven to bay. The great K. (*M. major*) is not found in the north of Australia, but some of the species are found all over the continent. They are in most cases smaller than *Macropus*, and possess other points of difference. Two species of terrestrial K., belonging to the genus *Dorcopsis*, inhabit New Guinea and the Aru and Mysol Islands. The tree K. (*Dendrolagus*), also indigenous to New Guinea, by an elongation of the fore-paws is enabled to climb trees, upon whose foliage it feeds. Kangaroos have so increased in numbers in Australia in consequence of the extermination of the Dingo (q. v.), that the squatters or large sheep-owners find it necessary to have *battues* occasionally to keep them in check, and a law designed to have the same effect was passed by the Queensland Legislature in 1876. The K. breeds freely in captivity, and has been successfully acclimatised in the open ground in the parks of noblemen in the S. of England, as well as in France.

The flesh of some kinds of K. is excellent eating, and K.-tail soup is now largely manufactured for use on shipboard, &c. The furs of the smaller kinds are beginning to be sought after, and first-rate leather is made from the hides of the larger species.

Interesting discoveries of fossil remains of the K. have been made in cave deposits and other post-Tertiary strata of Australia. Among the extinct genera of which remains have been found is the diprotodon, which appears to have occupied a place between the K. and the Wombat (q. v.), and is believed by Professor Owen to have been as large as a rhinoceros.

Kangaroo Apple, the popular name of the plant *Solanum laciniatum*, found in Australia, Tasmania, and Peru. When ripe the fruit is wholesome, but when unripe it is acrid and dangerous.

Kangaroo Grass is the colonial name of *Anthistiria Australis*, the most generally distributed plant in Australia. It is tall, with long twisted awns, and is much prized as fodder for cattle.

Kangaroo-Rat, Potoroo, or **Bettong**, are names given in Australia to marsupial animals belonging to the genus *Hypsiprymnus*, of the family *Macropodidæ*. They differ from the true kangaroos in having a distinct canine tooth in the upper jaw, in the œsophagus being removed from the commencement to the termination of the middle division of the sacculated compartment, and in the fore-feet and claws being adapted for burrowing. The tail, also, is not used to assist locomotion, but in the sub-genus *Bettongia* it is in some degree prehensile. The K.-R. is about the size of a hare or rabbit, and subsists upon roots and grasses. About a dozen species are known, the chief of which are *H. rufescens, H. murinus*, and *H. cuniculus*. The last, which is also the largest, is confined to Tasmania.

Kangaroo Thorn, is *Acacia armata*, much grown in Australia for hedges, forming an impenetrable fence.

Kang'ra, the chief town of the district of the same name, Punjaub, British India, is the site of an extensive hill-fort or *kot*, of historical importance.—The *district* of K., which lies among the Himalayas N.W. of Simla, has an area of 8988 sq. miles; pop. (1868) 743,882. Wheat, barley, and rice are the food crops. Tea cultivation was introduced here at an early date. In 1872, there were twenty-eight plantations, with a yield of 428,655 lbs.; the yield per acre was 130 lbs. Potatoes, also, are now extensively grown. A fair established in 1867 at Palampore, for the trans-Himalayan trade, is annually attended by 30,000 persons.

Ka'no, a town of Houssa, Central Africa, is the great entrepôt of English and American wares, the former coming from the N. across the desert of Sahara, the latter from the Bight of Benin. Cloth-dyeing is an important native industry, which has rendered K. famous throughout the whole of Central Africa. Estimated pop. 30,000 to 40,000.

Kan'sas, a State of the American Union, bounded E. by Missouri, W. by Colorado, N. by Nebraska, and S. by the Indian territory. Area, 81,318 sq. miles; pop. in 1860, 107,206; in 1870, 373,299; in 1874, nearly 600,000. The country slopes gently from the base of the Rocky Mountains to the river Missouri, which forms part of the eastern boundary, and receives from K. the river of the same name. The K. River is of no commercial value; it receives the Republican, Solomon's Fork, Big Blue, Grasshopper, and innumerable smaller tributaries. The only other important river is the Arkansas, a tributary of the Mississippi. According to the State Agricultural Report, 95 per cent. of K. is prairie, and only 5 per cent. forest. The river-bottoms of the centre and E., in which the loam is often 50 feet deep, are grown with forests of cotton-wood, red and white elm, oak, black walnut, sycamore, cedar, maple, &c.; in the W. the grama and buffalo grasses afford excellent pasture. Agriculture is being profitably carried far W. of the margin of what was known as the 'Great American Desert.' In 1874 there were 3,669,769 acres under cultivation, and the total value of the crops was nearly 30 million dollars; the amount of winter wheat was 6,870,606 bushels; of spring wheat, 3,010,777; of corn, 12,283,142; of oats, 4,064,424; of potatoes, 1,497,328; of sorghum, 540,338 gallons; of cotton, 11,657 lbs.; of flax, 265,704 lbs., and of tobacco, 29,384 lbs. In the same year K. had 202,962 horses, 749,959 cattle, 22,034 mules and asses, 84,838 sheep, and 356,916 swine. The cheese made amounted to 430,849 lbs., and the butter to 7,457,110 lbs. Among the wrought minerals are bituminous coal, lime, marble, salt, gypsum, and kaolin; there are considerable deposits of brown hæmatite and other iron ores, which have been worked but slightly. The aggregate coal-measures have an area of 22,256 sq. miles. The climate is temperate and healthy. Leavenworth (q. v.) is the largest city; Topeka is the capital, and other towns are Lawrence, Fort Scott, and Wyandotte. In 1874 the 1839 miles of railway were completed; two lines, the K. Pacific and Atchison, Topeka, and Santa Fé, traverse the State from E. to W. K. was organised as a territory in 1854, and, after a long and fierce struggle between northern and southern settlers, slavery was prohibited, and the territory was admitted to the Union as a State in 1861. The growth of its population is unparalleled even in the United States for rapidity. A disastrous visitation of grasshoppers or locusts destroyed one-third of Indian corn crops in 1874.

Kansas, a city of Missouri, U.S., one mile E. of the K. frontier, on the right bank of the Missouri, just below the mouth of the K. river, is the centre of an immense land and river traffic, and the converging point (1875) of nine completed railways, and of four or five others in course of construction. Its chief trade is in live-stock, the completion (1873) of a railway line having connected it with the great stock-raising regions of Texas. The receipts of cattle in 1875 were 227,669, valued at $3,415,035; of hogs 220,956, valued at $2,131,178. The pork-packing business has increased from 13,000 hogs in 1868 to 200,000 in 1873. The amount of grain received in 1873 was 1,718,280 bushels. The whole Missouri valley as far N. as Omaha is supplied with coal from the vicinity of K. The Missouri is crossed by a bridge 1400 feet long, erected at a cost of one million dollars. Pop. in 1860, 4418; in 1870, 32,260.

Kan-su, a province of China, lies between Tibet in the S. and Mongolia in the N., and has an estimated area of 260,599 sq. miles; and a pop. of 19,512,716. It is in great part mountainous, and is traversed from E. to W. by the winding upper course of the Hoang-ho. The capital is Lan-chow.

Kant, Immanuel, the founder of the German philosophy, was born at Königsberg, 22d April 1724. In 1740 he became a student of theology in the university of his native town, but applied himself principally to philosophy, mathematics, and physics. After fifteen years spent as *privat docent*, he was made at the age of forty-six Professor of Philosophy, and in 1781 published the first edition of his great work the *Kritik der reinen Vernunft* ('Critique of the Pure Reason'). In 1788 appeared the *Kritik der Praktischen Vernunft* ('Critique of the Practical Reason') and in 1790 the *Kritik der Urtheilskraft* ('Critique of the Faculty of Judgment'). K. led a very quiet life, and always refused to quit his native town. Besides being eminent in philosophy, he was also one of the greatest authorities of his time upon physical geography. He died February 12, 1804. K.'s philosophy is mainly a theory of perception, and comes in logical and historical order after that of Hume. The latter, following out the consequences of the extreme nominalism of Berkeley, had reached the conclusion that in ultimate analysis all existence was reducible to a train of atomic sensations, standing in no real relation to one another except that of succession. All other relations, and notably that of cause and effect, were therefore fictions superinduced by the associative power of the mind. K. saw that if this were admitted all knowledge or experience which is made up of these relations, and depends particularly upon the invariability of the law of cause and effect, must be a delusion, for if the sensations which are at present the objects of consciousness stand in no real relation to those which may in future be so, the belief in uniformity of nature must be without any true foundation. He saw, moreover, that this uniformity is presupposed by all human intelligence, and therefore he set himself to investigate the nature and limits of human knowledge in the *Kritik der reinen Vernunft*, the results of which may be briefly summarised as follows:—The antithesis between subject and object is partially at least transcended in the conclusion that the mind, far from being merely passive in experience, is really the main factor in its constitution. Into perception, according to K., there enter the following elements: (*a*) the action of an unknowable thing in itself upon mind, supplying to it a chaotic manifold of sensation, which (*b*) is received into the pure forms of sensibility, in one or both of which thought apprehends all its objects, time and space, and (*c*) arranged in certain definite intelligible relations termed categories (relations of quantity, quality, causality, substantiality, &c.) by the constitutive action of that pure impersonal thought called by K. the synthetic unity of transcendental apperception, which is identical in all individual thinking, being without the sphere of time. Experience as thus constituted is the only legitimate object of reason, which whenever it seeks to transcend it and speculate about metempirical entities such as God or the soul, falls into certain inevitable self-contradictions called antinomies. The only reality, so far as science is concerned, is the region of time and space, all else is unknowable.

With this result K. commences the investigation in the *Kritik der Praktischen Vernunft* of the question, Can reason determine the will independently of experience? The will being a thing in itself is obviously free from that law of causality which rules in the region of experience only, and it is therefore capable of determination by itself, that is by reason, for K. practically identifies the two. But the only law of action which can be laid down *a priori* apart from experience is this, to act at all times from a maxim fit for being made a universal principle of conduct. For the fulfilment of the moral postulate of a harmony between duty and wellbeing, there is necessary a future state and a moral orderer of the universe, two results which in the *Kritik der reinen Vernunft* were found to be theoretically unprovable.

Midway between simple apprehension and reasoning lies judgment, which, as its function is to subsume the particular under the universal, naturally refers the empirical plurality of nature to a supersensual transcendental principle as ground of unity to this plurality. The *Kritik der Urtheilskraft*, therefore, deals with the conception of design in nature, and seeks to show that there is no contradiction between the mechanical and teleological explanations, since the co-operation of percipient thought with things in themselves in the constitution of nature affords two distinct points of view from which to regard it. This *Kritik*, though the least known, was perhaps the most important of the three in its results, for out of its principles grew the majority of the salient features in the post-Kantian metaphysics.

Besides the three Critiques, K. published *Religion innerhalb der Grenzen der blossen Vernunft*, in which he applies the critical method to theology, the *Metaphysische Anfangsgründe der Naturwissenschaft*, the *Grundlegung der Metaphysik der Sitten*, *Prolegomena zu einer jeden künftigen Metaphysik*, with a number of other less important works. His successors submitted his system to a thorough criticism, the outcome of which was the rejection of the doctrine of things in themselves, and the declaration that the world of experience, which to K. was only phenomenal, was the only reality, in other words, a thoroughgoing identification of knowing and being. This was effected chiefly by Fichte, Schelling, and Hegel (q. v.). Modern German philosophy is tending strongly to seek in K. a foundation for its metaphysico-empirical speculations.

The leading English works upon K. are Professor Caird's *Philosophy of K.* (1877), and Professor Mahaffy's *Critical Philosophy for English Readers*. An excellent *Introduction to the Critical Philosophy* has been written by W. H. S. Monck. There are translations of the *Kritik der Reinen Vernunft* and the *Prolegomena* by Meiklejohn and Mahaffy respectively, of the *Metaphysik der Sitten* by Semple and Abbott, the former of whom has also translated the *Religion innerhalb der Grenzen der blossen Vernunft*. See Borowski, *Darstellung des Leb. und Charact. Kants*, 1804, and Schubert's *K.'s Biographie* in *K.'s Werke* edited by Rosenkranz and Schubert (Leips. Voss, 1838–42, 12 vols., also in 8 vols. 1867–69). There is also a good edition of K.'s works by Hartenstein, Modes, and Baumann (10 vols. Leips. 1838–39).

Kaolin, or **Porcelain Clay**, is the clay which results from the decomposition of Felspar (q. v.), water replacing the potash and part of the silica. It occurs in Cornwall, near Limoges in France, and in Saxony; also in China and Japan. The word K. is of Chinese origin, being a corruption of *Kauling* or *high-ridge*, the name of a hill near Jauchan Fu, where the material is obtained in quantity. All our finer porcelain ware is made of this clay, the constitution of which may be represented by the formula $Al_2O_3, 2SiO_2 + m H_2O$.

Kap'ila. See SANKHYA.

Kar'aites (Heb. *karaim*, 'scripturists'), were a sect which sprang up about the middle of the 8th c. among the Jews in the E. The founder of the sect was Anan ben David. He and his followers rejected the Talmud, and set themselves to the study of the Old Testament; although their literature was not confined to this subject alone, but embraced almost the whole domain of theology. The sect, which soon spread among the Jews in the W., now drags out a feeble existence in a few communities. The ten articles of their creed are—(1) All things were created (2) by an uncreated being, (3) who is without form, and is in every respect one alone; (4) who sent Moses, and (5) by Moses his perfect law, which (6) the faithful are bound to know; (7) who guided the prophets by his spirit, who (8) will raise the dead, and (9) judge them according to their works; who (10) has not rejected his people, but has sent them salvation by Messiah the son of David. See Blunt's *Dict. of Sects, &c.* (1874).

Karaka is the name given by the New Zealand natives to the tree *Corynocarpus lævigata*. See CORYNOCARPUS.

Karaman', a decayed town of Asia Minor, in the vilayet of Konieh, 64 miles S.E. of the town of that name, contains from two to three thousand houses, mostly like the mosques in ruins, and has some manufactures of coarse cotton and woollen stuffs. Estimated pop. 12,000. The former eyalet of K. corresponded to the modern vilayet of Konieh (q. v.).

Karam'sin, Nicolas Michailovitch, the best of Russian historians, born at Michailovka in the government of Orenburg, December 12th, 1765, was educated at Moscow, and served while young in the army. On returning from a lengthened tour through Germany, France, and England, he published with success his *Letters of a Russian Traveller*. Making literature his profession, he founded the *Aglaia*, a review, and the *Moscow Journal*, many numbers of which were said to be entirely written by himself. His labours soon obtained for him the post of imperial historiographer, a sinecure giving him both leisure and means, which he devoted to his life's work, the *History of*

Russia. Thirteen years of incessant toil were bestowed upon the first eight volumes of this history; but its success rewarded the author abundantly. In 1824 other three volumes appeared, bringing the account down to the reign of Ivan V., but the twelfth and last volume had to be written by the author's friend Bludov, minister of interior. K. died, 3d June 1826. An edition of his works in 18 vols. was published at St. Petersburg in 1835, to which additions with his correspondence were made in 1862.

Karasu'-Bazar', a town of Russia, in the Crimea, on the Karasu, 26 miles E.N.E. of Simferopol. The manufactures, which are in the hands of the Jews and Armenians, are of morocco, candles, soap, &c. Pop. (1870). 11,669.

Karatchef', a town of Russia, in the government of Orel, 24 miles W. of Briansk, on the Snesheta, existed in the 12th c. In its neighbourhood are hundreds of oil-mills and tar-furnaces. Pop. (1870) 11,267.

Kare'lia, the old name of the S.E. part of the grand duchy of Finland and the adjoining tracts of Russia.

Karens', a hill tribe in British Burmah, numbering about 330,000 souls. Some wander about the hills, while others have settled as cultivators on the plains. Their traditions have a singular Jewish tinge, and they have afforded to the American Baptist and French Roman Catholic Missions a most successful field of labour. Out of 330,000 in all British Burmah, about 30,000 have been converted. They have also signalised themselves by their readiness to accept British rule. See *The K. of the Golden Chersonese*, by Colonel Macmahon (Lond. 1876).

Karikel'. See CARRICAL.

Karl the Great, the greatest of the Frankish kings, in whose person the dignity of Roman Emperor was first conferred on a Teuton, was the elder son of Pippin the Short, and succeeded, on the death of his father in 768, to the western half of the Frankish state, which extended from Frisia to the Pyrenees; Elsass, Burgundy, and Provence, however, forming part of the inheritance of Karlmann. K. had previously received the titles of king and Roman patrician from the Pope. After reducing the rebellious Duke of Aquitaine, K., in spite of the threatened anathema of Pope Stephen III., married the daughter of Desiderius, King of the Lombards, whom he shortly afterwards repudiated for Hildegarda, the daughter of the Suabian King. The first of K.'s Capitularies, passed at the *Mallum*, or National Assembly of 769, prohibited priests from having several wives and from following the army. After the death of Karlmann had given K. an opportunity of seizing the inheritance of his nephews, who fled with their mother Gilberga to Lombardy, the great war against the Saxons, between the Rhine, the Weser, and the Elbe (which lasted thirty-three years), was begun, and in 773–74 was followed by the successful expedition against Pavia and other Lombard strongholds, which was undertaken at the suggestion of Pope Adrian I., and which procured for K. the title of the King of the Lombards. Friuli, Switzerland, and the turbulent Tassilo of Bavaria now acknowledged the Frankish supremacy; many of the Westphalian Saxons were compelled to submit, attended the National Assembly of Paderborn in 777, and received Christian baptism. Soon after, K. was recalled from Aragon and Catalonia (where he had assisted the Abbasside faction against the Ommiad Calif of Cordova) by the insurrection of Wittikind (Widukind) on the Rhine. On the way, the ambuscade of Roncesvaux took place. In 781 several matters took K. again to Rome; the proposed marriage between his eldest daughter and Constantine V., the son of Irene; the slave-traffic with the East; and the quarrels between the Pope (who claimed Lombardy as a gift from K.) and the Italian dukes. The severity with which, at the close of the war in Brunswick, K. punished the second revolt of Wittikind, protracted the Saxon struggle for independence till 785, when Wittikind became a Christian. Soon after, the allegiance of the Thuringians, the Bretons, and the S. Lombards was secured. The successful campaigns against the Slav population between the Elbe and the Oder, and against the Huns, were followed in 793 by the apostasy and revolt of the Saxons, and the Saracen invasion of Aquitaine (the district between the Loire, the Rhone, and the Ebro.) In 796 the celebrated Council of Frankfurt was held, in which image worship and the Felician heresy were condemned, K. publishing the *Karoline Books* on the former question. The revolt against Pope Leo III. gave K. an opportunity in 800 of revisiting Rome. The dignitaries of the Church declined to inquire into the charges brought against the Pope, who declared his innocence, and his enemies were found guilty of calumny. In return for this the Pope crowned K. Emperor of the Romans, and endeavoured to unite the two empires by arranging a marriage between K. and Irene. In the year 801, among the embassies who sought K.'s favour from Spain, Constantinople, &c., came one from Harun-al-Raschid, bearing the keys of the Holy Sepulchre. At this time begins the more continuous series of *Capitularies* which throw so much light on the ecclesiastical, military, and social affairs of the time. They deal with such matters as benefit of clergy; the feudal and personal obligations of military service; the imperial deputies or assize judges, called *Missi Dominici*, who also looked after the revenues of the royal cities, and minutely regulated agriculture and trade; the system of personal laws under which K.'s Saxon, Lombard, and Frankish subjects lived. In 804, in order to make room for Slav tribes who had acknowledged his supremacy, the 'Consul' repeated his favourite policy of transporting to Gaul and Lombardy great bodies of Saxons from beyond the Elbe. He also seconded the efforts of Ingo, the evangelist of the Avars. At the Assembly of 806 the empire was divided between K.'s three sons—Karl, Hludwig, and Pippin: the first obtaining the northern part of Gaul and Germany; the second Italy and Bavaria; the third Aquitania, Burgundy, Provence, and the March of Spain. About this time the successes of the Moors, the Greeks, the Danes or Normans, at various points of the vast frontier, showed the real insecurity of the empire; they resulted in treaties of peace in 810, K. apparently feeling that he should now act on the defensive. In that year and the following his sons Pippin and Karl died, and Hludwig was accordingly solemnly crowned emperor by his father in the church at Aachen, the consent of the Assembly having been obtained. K. now gave himself up to devotional exercises, almsgiving, and the revisal of sacred books. He died after a short fever January 28, 814, at Aachen, where also he was buried. Boulainvilliers praises K. as the founder of perpetual succession in fiefs, De Mably as the protector of the common people against the nobles, Montesquieu as a model legislator, others have described him as a perfect hero. His secretary, Eginhard, has left a pleasing picture of the simplicity of his manners, of his eloquence in Latin, which he knew as well as his native German, though he never learned to write, of his anxiety to promote learning, which induced him to invite the teachers of grammar and arithmetic from Rome to fill his public schools, and to assist Alcuin in founding the academy and school of the palace. K. was undoubtedly a religious, patriotic man, affectionate to his family, and having a high conception of his public duty. See Sismondi, *Histoire des Français*; Dippold, *Leben Kaiser K.'s des Grossen* (Tüb. 1810); Gaillard, *Histoire de Charlemagne* (4 vols. Par., 2d ed. 1819); Abel, *Jahrbücher des Fränk. Reichs unter K. dem Grossen* (Berl. 1866 *et seq.*); Lorenz, *K's. des Grossen Privat- und Hofleben* in Raumer's *Histor. Taschenbuch* (1832); Gagern, *K. der Grosse* (Darmst. 1845); Kitchen, *History of France* (Lond. 1873), and Freeman, *Historical Essays* (Lond. 1872).—**Karl IV.**, *Emperor of the Romans*, born May 14, 1316, was the son of Johann of Luxemburg, King of Bohemia, and succeeded to the empire on the death of Ludwig of Bavaria in 1347, but not without many disputes among the electors, who were alarmed by the deference paid by K. to the Pope. After being consecrated in Rome in 1354, he published his celebrated Golden Bull, which names the seven electors, the Archbishops of Mainz, Köln, and Tryer, the King of Bohemia, the Kur-graf, the Duke of Saxony, and the Markgraf of Brandenburg. He then irritated the Pope, by asking for Church reform when the empire was overrun by brigands. He almost destroyed imperial influence in Italy (where the *Visconti* were now powerful) by selling towns and territories. The 'Alliance of Suabia' was formed during his reign. He died at Prag, November 29, 1378. See Pelzel, *Geschichte Kaiser K. IV.*, and Dönniges, *Geschichte des Deutschen Kaiserthums im 14 Jahrh.* (Berl. 1841).—**Karl V.**, born at Ghent, February 24, 1500, son of Philipp the Handsome, Archduke of Austria, and of Juana, a daughter of Ferdinand and Isabella of Aragon and Castile. Carefully educated by Guillaume of Croy, and Adrian of Utrecht, he became, on the death of Ferdinand in 1516, the first king of Spain. He had previously been called the Prince of Asturias. His mother was associated with him on the throne, and Ximenes acted as Regent. In 1519, on Maximilian's death, he was elected to the imperial throne in preference to François I. Almost his first act was to call the Diet of Worms for the suppression of Luther's heresy. War soon broke out with France, and after the unsuccessful attack on Mézières, K. concluded with Wolsey a treaty against France, promising to marry the Princess Mary of England. The French being driven from Milan with the help of Leo X., K. put down the *Santa Junta* formed by the Spanish towns. The struggle in Piedmont ended in the defeat of François at Pavia (1525), and the forfeiture of Sforza's possessions. Next year K. married Isabella, daughter of Emmanuel of Portugal. Clement VII. having formed a league against K., the Constable of Bourbon, who had held the French in check in Piedmont, sacked Rome, and took the Pope prisoner. The Peace of the Ladies at Cambrai (1529) brought a lull in hostilities, and K. was crowned at Bologna King of Lombardy and Emperor of the Romans. He at the same time restored the Sforza and the Medicis. In the meantime the Diet of Augsburg had led to the league of Schmalkalden, and the unity of the German empire was lost. The expedition against Suleiman II., who was assisting Zapolya against K.'s brother Ferdinand, and in support of Muley Hassem in Tunis, was followed by several campaigns on French territory without result; and the truce of Nices gave K. time to assert despotic authority in Spain, and to alter the constitution of the ancient Cortes. After the collapse of the Algiers expedition, the Emperor caused his son Philip to be recognised as King in Castile and Aragon. The Diet of Speyer (1544) furnished the means for another invasion of France, but when K. proceeded to put into execution the early decrees of the Council of Trent, the Protestant princes took the alarm and formed the Confederation, which was dissolved by the defection of Moritz of Hessen and Sachsen, and the victory of Mühlberg. François I. being now dead, the Emperor was able to devote himself to the forcible propagation of Catholic doctrine and the *Interim* of Augsburg, until the revolt of Moritz brought about a measure of toleration in the treaty of Passau (1552). The attempt to recover Metz, Toul, and Verdun having failed, and Philip being married to Mary Tudor, K., whose health was now broken, resigned the empire to Ferdinand on 25th October 1555, and the crown of Spain to Philip, 15th January 1556. On 24th February 1557 he entered the monastery of St. Just, near Placentia, where he remained till his death on 21st September 1558. Though he had fallen into a religious melancholy, he still retained his interest in politics, and was constantly 'advising' his son and others. In spite of the heavy taxes with which K. oppressed Spain, the Netherlands, Milan, Naples, Sicily, and the Spanish colonies in the New World, he left a large debt behind him, with instructions to his son to preserve the Catholic faith and to show no quarter to heretics. He showed great skill in dealing with the political equilibrium of Europe and with the religious passions of the Church and the Reform party, his main object being the aggrandisement of himself and his family. Robertson's *History* is still a leading English authority on his life and times. Sir William Stirling Maxwell's *Cloister Life* is also authoritative. Other works are Lanz, *Correspondenz des Kaisers K. V.*, Gachard, *Correspondence de Charles Quint;* Guntram, *Kaiser K. V.*, and Motley's *Rise of the Dutch Republic.*—**Karl VI.**, born 1st October 1685, the son of Leopold I., claimed the throne of Spain on the death of Karl II. (1st November 1700), who had, however, bequeathed it to his sister's grandson, Philippe of Anjou. K. prosecuted his claim most vigorously, carrying on the 'War of the Spanish Succession' from 1704 to 1711 in the heart of Spain itself. On his succeeding his brother Joseph I. as Emperor, his allies were unwilling to prolong the war, and made with France the Peace of Utrecht (1713), and by the Peace of Rastadt (1714) K. accepted the secure possession of Milan and Mantua, Naples, Sardinia, and the Netherlands. The next few years were occupied by the brilliant campaign of Prince Eugène of Savoy against the Turks, ending in the Peace of Passarowitz. K. next assured the succession of his daughter Maria-Theresa (he had no sons) by the Pragmatic Sanction. In 1733 Austria and Russia combined to support the claims of August III. to the Polish crown. This 'Polish Succession' war cost K. the Two Sicilies and a part of Milan: it was, however, successful in its immediate object, though ultimately disastrous to Poland. His war with the Turks, ending with the Peace of Belgrade (1739), further diminished his possessions on the E. frontier. K. executed a great number of public works, and, had his reign been peaceful, might have greatly advanced his country, though his attachment to the ecclesiastical orders and a feudal aristocracy was somewhat blind. He died 20th October 1740. See Förster, *Die Höfe und Cabinete Europas im 18 Jahrh.*—**Karl VII.**, born 6th August 1697 at Brussels, son of Maximilian-Emmanuel, Elector of Bavaria, was first governor of the Netherlands, then served in the Turkish war, and succeeded his father in 1726. He married Maria Emilia, a daughter of Joseph I., and on the death of Karl VI. he claimed the imperial crown as descended from Anna, the daughter of Ferdinand I., and in terms of the will of Ferdinand. Allying himself with France and Spain, he marched on Linz and Prag, and was unanimously elected Emperor in 1742. The troops of Maria-Theresa then occupied Bavaria and Bohemia, and drove K. to Frankfurt. After the victories of Friedrich the Great and Seckendorf he returned to Munich, where he died 20th January 1745.

Kings of Sweden.—**K. IX.**, the youngest son of Gustaf Vasa, after acting for several years as regent for his nephew, Sigismund of Poland, succeeded to the throne in 1599 after the defeat of the Polish forces at Stängelro. K. had already, as leader of the Protestants in the reign of his brother Johann and in supporting the resolutions of Upsala (1593), helped to make Sweden a Protestant country, and he now treated the Catholic nobility who desired an elective monarchy with severity. His admission of burghers and peasants to definite political rights and his care for trade brought him the title of the Peasant King (Bondarkonungen). He conducted against Denmark the Kalmar war, which arose out of conflicting claims to the Riga trade, intervened in Russian politics during the rebellion of Demetrius, and actively urged the formation of a Protestant union in Europe. He died, aged sixty, at Nyköping in 1611, leaving as his successor the heroic Gustaf Adolf, a son by his second wife, Christina of Holstein-Gottorp.—**K. X. Gustaf**, a nephew of Gustaf Adolf, succeeded to the throne of Sweden on the abdication of his cousin Christina in 1654. His short reign was full of wars. He defeated the Poles at Warsaw in 1656, obtained from Denmark by the Peace of Roeskilde (1658) the provinces of Skaania, Halland and Bleking, and was only driven from the Kattegat by the intervention of the English and Dutch. He died in 1660, aged thirty-eight. His father being the Count Palatine Johan Kasimir, K. and his descendants have been called the Palatinate dynasty. —**K. XI.**, the infant son of the preceding, succeeded, but from 1660 to 1675 the country was misgoverned by a council of regency appointed by the will of the late king. Peace was negotiated with Russia and the Polish King John Kasimir, but when in 1674 an expedition in aid of the French was undertaken against the Elector of Brandenburg, and when in the following year Denmark and Holland declared war against Sweden, K. found in the defeats of Fehrbellin and Oland that the council had entirely neglected both army and navy. The war continued till the Peace of St. Germains (1679), when K. recovered the territory of Pommern and married the Danish Princess Ulrika Eleanore. With the help of Gillenstjerna K. now addressed himself to internal finance. By claiming a large sum of wrongful appropriations from former ministers, and by the right of 'reduction' or retaking of crown lands granted out within the preceding thirty years, he saved the state from bankruptcy. In doing so he came into conflict with the noble grantees and with the national estates, which body he forced in 1693 to acknowledge his sovereignty as absolute. K. was ignorant, but energetic, and popular with the poor. He died, aged forty-two, in 1697, and was succeeded by his eldest son **K. XII.**, who, at the age of fifteen, being declared major by the estates, crowned himself without taking any oath of fidelity. His youth gave little promise of his subsequent distinction, and accordingly in 1700 Frederik IV. of Denmark and Augustus of Poland (who had entered into a treaty with the Czar Peter) took this opportunity of attacking Holstein-Gottorp and Livonia. Procuring some vessels from the English king, K. showed his military genius by an immediate bombardment of Copenhagen, and, imposing his terms on Frederik, next marched to the relief of Riga and to Narva in Ingermannland, where on 30th November 1700 he defeated 60,000 Russians under De Croy with a force of 8000 Swedes. K. then advanced into Poland, stormed Warsaw, compelled Augustus after the battles of Klissov and Pultusk to resign, and secured the election in 1704 of Stanislas Lesczinski, the young Voivod of Posen. For six years K. remained in

Poland and Sachsen, his influence being so great that at his request Joseph I. granted liberty of conscience to the Silesian Protestants. The designs of the Czar on Ingermannland and Livonia recalled K. to Russia in 1707. Dissuaded by the Cossack Ivan Mazeppa from a projected attack on Moscow, he turned S. to the Ukraine, and after a severe winter in camp was completely defeated at Pultava on 27th June 1709, the Cossacks having deserted, and a wound preventing him from commanding in person. This was the signal for attack on Sweden, and, while General Stenbock and his army of 'wooden shoes' was engaged with the Danes, whom they drove out of Skaania, the Russians took possession of parts of Esthonia and Livonia. K., who had escaped to Turkey, persuaded Achmed III. to make war on the Czar, but soon found himself a prisoner of the Porte at Dimotika. From this he escaped in 1714, rode across Europe in fourteen days under the assumed name of Peter Frisch, and threw himself into Stralsund, which he defended against the united Russians, Saxons, and Danes. With the help of his minister Görtz K. now energetically recruited his army, Lund being the headquarters; but just as an alliance with Russia and Spain was being completed, the 'Demürbasch' (Ironhead), as the Turks called K., was shot in the trenches before Frederikshald on 11th December 1718. His life has been written in almost every European tongue. His simple life and manner, his bravery, his brilliant success and tragic reverses, endeared him to his people, who recall with pride the 'Karolinska tiden' (Karl's time). K.'s chaplain, Norberg, wrote the Biography of his master; Adlerberg published memorials of his military career; Voltaire's *Histoire de Charles XII.* has (or had) a European fame, but the most authoritative work is Lundblad's *Konung Carls XII. Historia* (Stockh. 2 vols. 1830; Ger. transl. Hamb. 2 vols. 1835–40).—**K. XIII.**, born at Stockholm 7th October 1748, the son of Adolf Fredrik, King of Sweden, and Louise Ulrike, the sister of Friedrich the Great, had distinguished himself in the naval war of his brother Gustaf III. against Russia, and had, as Duke of Södermanland, been chosen as regent in 1792, when his French proclivities and the arrogance of his minister Reuterholm gave dissatisfaction. In 1809, when the eccentric Gustaf IV. was declared to have forfeited the crown, K. was elected king, the Diet being at the same reorganised on a constitutional basis. Owing to the generalship of Bernadotte, who on the death of Prince Christian August of Augustenborg in 1809, had been chosen Crown Prince, K. became in 1814, King of Sweden and Norway, the two Diets, the Riksdag and the Storthing, remaining distinct. K. died on 5th February 1818.—**K. XIV.**, originally Jean Baptiste Jules Bernadotte, made by Napoleon Prince of Porte-Corvo, but called by the Swedes K. Johan, was born at Pau, 26th January 1764. Although a brilliant general, he had, through his firmness in resisting Napoleon's ambition in 1799, never enjoyed his master's confidence. Suspicion followed him to Sweden, where Napoleon, relying on the Treaty of Paris, treated him with great indignity and forced him into the Continental Alliance. K., however, kept up trade with England, and took advantage of the seizure of Pomerania to declare war against France in 1812, and at Grossbeeren and Dennewitz contributed decisive victories to the cause of the allies. Sweden had lost Finland and Aaland to Russia in 1809, and at the Congress of Vienna Pomerania was ceded to Prussia for a sum in money, but under the vigorous rule of the 'burgher-king,' she rapidly developed her trade, threw off a large public debt, and supplied herself with a good system of education and of internal communication. Although K. had adopted the national religion, he could not learn the language; and towards the close of his reign his persecution of liberal writers and his decided preference for aristocratic interests destroyed his popularity. The names of Berzelius (chemist), Geyer (historian), Tegnér (poet), Fogelberg (sculptor), show the advance of Sweden during this reign. K. died 8th March 1844 and was succeeded by his son Oscar.—**K. XV.**, the eldest son of Oscar I. and Josephine of Leuchtenberg, granddaughter of the French empress Josephine, succeeded to the united crown on his father's death in 1859. From 1857 he had carried on the administration as regent. K. extended the railway system and conciliated the Norwegians, who were jealous of the predominance of Swedish interests. In 1866 he introduced the present constitution of the Diet, viz., a chamber of members chosen for nine years by the provincial Landsthings, and a chamber of members chosen by universal suffrage to decide special questions. K. died in 1872, and was succeeded by his brother Oscar II. His daughter Lovisa (Louisa) is wife of the present Crown Prince of Denmark.

Karl, Ludwig, Archduke of Austria, born 5th September 1771, a son of Leopold II., and younger brother of Franz II., first showed his military genius in 1793. He became Governor of the Low Countries, and in 1796–97, as Commander-in-Chief of the Austrian and Imperial armies, he drove back Moreau and Jourdan beyond the Rhine and captured Kehl. After the Congress of Rastadt, he took the field against Jourdan in Suabia, and was opposed to Massena in Switzerland. He subsequently became Governor-General of Bohemia, and Minister of War, the Treaty of Luneville being adjusted by him. In 1805 he again confronted Massena in Italy, while Napoleon pushed on by Ulm to Austerlitz. After the Peace of Presburg, K. was appointed Chief of the Aulic Council of War and Generalissimo of the Austrian forces. In the great battles of 1809—Eckmühl, Aspern, and Wagram—although constantly worsted by the genius of Napoleon and his brilliant staff of generals, K. showed great coolness and determination. This was his last campaign. K. lived till 30th April 1847. He wrote *Strategics*, and a *History of the Campaign of* 1799.

Karl Martel, a natural son of Pippin of Herstall, was born about 690 A.D., and was in prison at Metz when his father died, 16th December 714, leaving to an infant grandson Theodebald, the office of Mayor of the Palace. The wars which ensued between Neustria (Chilperich [Hilperik] II., the King, and Raganfried, the mayor, had formed a league with the Frisians) and Austrasia soon brought K., whose bravery was known, to the head of the Austrasian armies, which he led to conquest at Vincy near Cambrai in 717. He was then made Duke of the Austrasian Franks at Köln, and Hlothar IV. was declared king. The mission of Boniface tended to strengthen K. on his Saxon frontiers, while in spite of the help given by Odo (Eudes) of Aquitania the Neustrian mayor was again defeated at Soissons. Hlothar then died, and K. arranged that Chilperich should be nominal king of both divisions of France, and himself mayor in both. On the death of Chilperich, K. chose as king Theoderich, a boy six years old. Like the other 'Do-nothing kings' Theoderich lived without influence (720–37). During that period K. led six expeditions to the N. and E.; the Germans, Bavarians, and Frisians submitted, but as K. built no fortresses, and could not therefore leave garrisons, the Saxons maintained their independence. In the meantime the generals of the Ommiad Calif Hashem had established themselves at Narbonne, and by repeated expeditions driven back the Aquitanians on the Loire. In 732 K. met the Saracen army near Poitiers, and decisively checked its farther advance; the name *Martel* ('hammer'), however, was given him by chroniclers long subsequently. After campaigns in Frisia and against the independent nobility of Burgundy and Provence, K. in 737 retook Avignon from the Saracens, and besieged for some time Narbonne itself, then commanded by Abd-el-rahman, and in retreating set fire to Nismes. In this year Theoderich died. It is remarkable that K., while he retained in his person the military command, the administration of justice, the arrangement of provincial affairs, &c., did not think it necessary to confine Theoderich to the palace, but permitted him to move about freely with his court. The help of the Lombards, and the dissensions of Abd-el-Melek and Offa in Spain, which resulted in the separation of the Cordovan Emirate from the Califate of Bagdad, at last brought about comparative quiet on the S. frontier. K. rewarded his victorious army with Church lands, for which in 858 the French clergy, in asking Hludwig the German to restore the property, decided that their saviour from the Moslem power was condemned to eternal torture not merely for his own sins, but for the sins of those who had endowed the Church. In 741 Pope Gregory III., who had quarrelled with the Emperor Leo on the image-worship question, and had interfered between the Lombards and the Duke of Spoleto, sought K.'s protection against the former. The matter was amicably arranged, and on the 21st October of the same year K. died at Quiercy near Compiegne, leaving to his son Karlmann, Austrasia with Suabia and Thuringia, and to Pippin, Neustria, Burgundy, and Provence. See Breysig's *Karl Martell* (1869), and Kitchen's *History of France* (Lond. 1873).

Karls'bad ('Karls' bath'), a celebrated watering-place of Bohemia, in the pine-clad valley of the Tepel, a tributary of the

Eger, 76 miles W.N.W. of Prag by rail. The springs, according to a tradition, were discovered by Karl IV. in 1347. They have a maximum temperature of 167° F., and gush forth with violence from apertures in the hard rock (*Sprundelschale*) on which the most of the town is built. The oldest, hottest, and most copious spring is the Sprundel, which rises in a volume 1½ feet in diameter to a height of 3 feet (formerly 6 feet). Especially efficacious in liver complaints, the waters chiefly contain sulphur, salt, and carbonate of soda. About two million gallons are discharged daily. There were 18,000 visitors in 1872. K. has a theatre and many fine hotels, reading-rooms, and cafés. Goethe frequently resided here. Pop. (1869) 7291.

Karls'burg or **Belgrad** (formerly *Weissenburg*, Magyar *Károly-fejérvár* or *Gyula*), a fortified town of Transylvania, Hungary, on the river Maros, 58 miles by rail N.W. of Hermannstadt, named after Karl VI., and built on the site of the ancient *Apulum*, is a bishop's see, has a cathedral with the tombs of the Hunyads, an observatory, and a mint. There is a large wine-trade. Pop. (1869) 7955.

Karlskro'na, or **Ble'king**, a län of Göthaland in Sweden, surrounded by Christianstad, Kronoberg, Kalmar, and the Baltic Sea, has a rocky surface with extensive woods and many lakes. Except from 1332 to 1360, K. belonged to Denmark till 1658. Area, 1164 sq. miles; pop. (1876) 131,812.—K., the chief town, is the main station and arsenal of the Swedish fleet, was founded by Karl XI. in 1680, and lies 240 miles S.W. of Stockholm on several rocky islets connected by bridges. Its excellent harbour is strongly defended by the forts Kungsholm and Drottningsskär, and has docks cut out of granite, covering 20,580 sq. yards. K. has a sailors' hospital, schools of navigation and shipbuilding, and many naval workshops and stores. Tobacco and sugar are manufactured. Pop. (1876) 16,877.

Karls'ruhe, capital of the Grand-Duchy of Baden, S. Germany, 45 miles N.E. of Strassburg, and 3 miles from the right bank of the Rhine, is a regularly-built town, with streets stretching out from the Schloss (founded about 1750) like the ribs of a fan, and divided by the 'Lange Strasse' into a northern and southern part. K. was founded in 1715 by the Markgraf Karl III., and has a polytechnic school, an observatory, a botanic garden, a library of 100,000 volumes, and rich art-collections. There are extensive manufactures of machinery, carriages, furniture, and jewellery. Pop. (1875) 42,768.

Karl'stad, a town of Sweden, in the län of Wermland, is situated on the island of Tingvalla, on the N. side of the Wener Lake, 160 miles W. of Stockholm by rail. It is connected with the mainland by two bridges, one of which is the longest and finest stone bridge in Sweden. K. is the seat of a bishop, and has an important haven, a beautiful cathedral, a gymnasium, an observatory, a theatre, &c. It exports copper, iron, and timber through the Gotha Canal. Pop. (1874) 5433. K. was founded by Karl IX. in 1548.

Karl'stadt, a fortified town of Austria, in Croatia, on the Kulpa, and 33 miles S.W. of Agram by rail. It has an old castle with a large armoury, and is a busy commercial place. Pop. (1869) 5175.

Karma'thians, a Mohammedan sect founded in Persia about 900 A.D. by Abu Said Al-Karmata, an Ismaelite missionary who mastered Irak, Syria, and a great part of Arabia, but was assassinated in 914. Under his son and successor, Abu Tahir, the K. attacked Mecca (930), butchered the pilgrims, profaned the Kaaba (q. v.), and carried off the Black Stone to Lahsa, their capital, where it remained for twenty years. Abu Tahir died in 943, and thenceforth the power of the K. declined. They were defeated at Kufa in 986, and again in 989, but retained Lahsa until 1041, and remnants of them, according to Palgrave, still linger on at Hasa. Their tenets seem to have been identical with those of Ismaelitism, without the foreign elements of the latter; to have been, in short, a free-thinking form of Islam. Wine was allowed, and prayer, fasting, and other observances of the older law were treated esoterically. See Palgrave, *Central and Eastern Arabia* (2 vols. 1865.)

Kar'olings (sons, *i.e.*, descendants of Karl) were members of the second dynasty of Frankish kings. Their lineage may be traced to Pippin of Herstall, who after the battle of Testri (687), as Mayor of the Palace and Duke of the Franks, practically superseded the Merwings, though he did not dethrone them. It was not until 753, however, that Pippin, the son of Karl Martel, was actually elected and crowned king at Soissons. In 768 his kingdom passed to Karl and Karlmann, the former upon his brother's death extending his dominions from the Atlantic to the Lower Vistula, and accepting at the hands of Pope Leo III. the title of Emperor of the Romans. At Aachen (in 813) Hludwig the Pious was crowned as his father's successor, but (in 817) he voluntarily divided the empire among his sons Lothar, Pippin, and Hludwig, afterwards (829) making a new kingdom for his son Karl by a second marriage. After much fighting a final division of the empire was made, Lotharingia falling to Lothar and Karolingia to Karl, whilst Hludwig received the Teutonic kingdom which became Germany. Under Karl the Fat, the son of Hludwig the German, the empire was again united until 887, when, owing to his incompetence, he was dethroned at Tribur. Arnulf, his illegitimate nephew, was next successor, and Hludwig the Child came after. With him (910) ended the Karolingian dynasty in Germany. Odo (Eudes), Count of Paris, was elected king of Karolingia, and 'there followed about a hundred years of shifting to and fro between his new family and the old family of the K.' Hludwig V., the last Karolingian king, died at Laon (987), and 'this was the real beginning of the modern kingdom of France.' See Bryce's *Holy Roman Empire* (1875); Freeman's *General Sketch*; Maine's *Ancient Law* (1861).

Kar'oly, or **Nagy-Ka'roly** (*Hirsch*), a town in the comitat of Czathmár, Hungary, 200 miles E. by N. of Pesth, with which it is connected by rail. K. has linen and woollen weaving, and the fertile neighbourhood produces much wine, maize, and tobacco. Pop. (1875) 12,754.

Karr, Jean-Baptiste-Alphonse, a French writer, born at Paris, November 24, 1808, studied at and became a teacher in the Collège Bourbon, and published his first novel, *Sous les Tilleuls*, in 1832. Others followed in quick succession, and in 1839 he became editor-in-chief of *Figaro*, the same year starting the monthly *Les Guêpes*, which had a great success. He was made Chevalier of the Légion d'Honneur in 1845, but after the revolution of 1848, being defeated in the Seine Inférieure elections, withdrew to Nice, where he has continued to write for the *Revue des Deux Mondes* and other journals. Of his thirty or forty works the best known are *Voyage autour de mon Jardin* (1845), and *Promenades hors de mon Jardin* (1857). They abound in terse, incisive observations, and witty criticisms of society. The *Esprit d'A. Karr: Pensées extraites de ses Œuvres Complètes* appeared in 1877.

Karroo' (a Hottentot word signifying 'dry or barren') is a term applied in Cape Colony primarily to the barren plateaux lying between the Nieuwveld, Roggeveld, Langeberg, and Zwarteberg ranges, and thence to barren plains generally. The soil of the K. consists of shallow but fertile deposits of red clay on a substratum of blue schistose slate. It is in many parts impregnated with saline matter, but when irrigated produces good crops. The Great K. is about 3000 feet above the sea-level, and the Little K., or Kannaland, 1000 feet lower. Both are subject to great extremes of temperature. They have evidently at one time formed the beds of lakes, and abound in fossil saurian remains peculiar to this region. Large flocks of sheep are now pastured on the K., and the value of land there has quintupled within the last few years.

Kars, a fortified town in the vilayet of Erzerum, in Asiatic Turkey, lies 22 miles W. of the Russian frontier, on a tributary of the Aras (anc. *Araxes*), 6000 feet above the sea, and 110 miles E.N.E. of Erzerum. There are two isolated and walled suburbs, containing over a third of the inhabitants. The town is defended by a massive old castle, perched on a precipitous rock. It is the eastern key to Asia Minor, and has an extensive transit trade, but the climate is severe. In 1828 it was taken by the Russians, under Mouravieff, but during the Crimean War it was gallantly defended by a Turkish garrison, 17,000 strong, under the command of General Williams, against a greatly superior Russian force. The siege began on the 16th June, and after a vain effort on the part of the Russians to take the place by storm (September 29), lingered on till famine compelled its surrender on the 30th November 1855. Pop. 12,000. K. forms part of the famous Turkish quadrilateral in Asia Minor (composed of K.,

Erzerum, Batoum, and Ardahan), and at this moment (June 1877) is in imminent danger of being stormed by the Russians.

Kar'shi (anc. *Nakhsheb*), the second most important town in the khanat of Bokhára, Central Asia, 90 miles S.E. of the town of that name, has an extensive transit trade with India, and Kábul, and Bokhára. Its pop., 25,000, chiefly Usbeks, supply the best of the Bokharian soldiers, and its knives and swords are in great request through all Asia. There are Russian cantonments here.

Karwar', a seaport in the district of N. Canara, Bombay, British India, at the mouth of a stream called Konai, 300 miles S. from Bombay. Pop. (1873) 13,263. Here is shipped the cotton of Dharwar and the S. Mahratta country. A state railway has been sanctioned to Hubli, and it is proposed to protect the harbour by throwing out a granite breakwater for a mile and a half. There is at present safe anchorage during the S.W. monsoon.

Kasan', or **Kazan'** (Tartar, 'kettle') a government of E. Russia, surrounded by the governments Viatka, Ufá, Simbirsk, and Nishegorod. The area, 24,600 sq. miles, mainly consists of a well cultivated, undulating plain (two-fifths covered with wood) drained by the Volga, with its affluents the Kama, Kasanka, &c., broken, however, in the E. by offshoots from the Ural Mountains. K. is subject to great extremes of temperature. Tillage and cattle-rearing are the chief industries. Pop. (1870) 1,670,337, chiefly Russians, with 400,000 Tartars and other Asiatics. The Khanat of K., which arose about the end of the 14th c., on Timur's conquest of the Kiptshak kingdom, covered the present governments of K., Simbirsk, Pensa, Viatka and Perm; its rulers constantly warred with the Russian grand-dukes, till vanquished by Ivan I. in 1487, and finally subdued by Ivan II. in 1552.—K., the chief town, near the junction of the Volga and Kasanka, 205 miles E. of Nishnij-Novgorod, is the seat of a metropolitan bishop, has a cathedral, a university, and thirty-eight churches, manufactures leather, hardware, soap, cloth, and cotton, and has a large trade with Siberia. Pop. (1870) 78,602 (one-fourth Mahommedans). See E. T. Turnerelli's *Kazan, the Ancient Capital of the Tartar Khans* (2 vols. Lond. 1854); Latham's *Native Races of Russia* (Lond. 1854).

Kasanlik', a town of Turkey, in the vilayet of Adrianople, at the entrance to the Balkan Pass, 85 miles N.W. of Adrianople. It lies in a fertile and well-irrigated plain, and produces fine attar of roses (5000 lbs. of blossoming rose-leaves yielding 1 lb. of perfume, valued at about £18), walnuts (£19,995 worth yearly), and beautiful walnut timber. Pop. 10,000.

Kaschan' (*Kassa*), the principal town in the N.E. of Hungary, in Abujvar, on the right bank of the Hernád, 130 miles N.E. of Pesth by rail. It is the seat of a bishop, and has forty-one Roman Catholic churches, one Protestant, and one Greek church, a Government academy, with a library, an important seminary, and a theatre. The cathedral of St. Elizabeth is a beautiful Gothic building, with a tower of the 13th c., and twenty-seven altars. K. has fayence, paper, and tobacco industries, and a considerable trade in wine, grain, and tobacco. Pop. (1869) 21,742.

Kashan', a town of Persia, in Irak Ajami, on a stony plain fringing the great salt desert, 128 miles S. of Teheran. It is girt by feeble walls, and embowered in mulberry groves; its finest building is the *medresh* or college built by the Shah. K. is a great industrial centre. It supplies all Persia with copper wares (perforated lanterns, ingenious portable cooking utensils, &c.), which are generally tinned and whitened so as to resemble silver. Its flowered silks (*shal kashai*) are exquisite imitations of the richest Cashmere shawls. Other noted manufactures are cotton-stuffs and velvets. Pop. 30,000.

Kashgar'. See CASHGAR.

Kashin', a town in the government of Tver, Russia, on the Kashinka, an affluent of the Volga, 74 miles N.E. of Tver, with trade in provisions and linen, large annual fairs, and manufactures of paper, leather, sacks, and hosiery. K. has twenty-eight churches. Pop. (1870) 7516.

Kass'el, formerly capital of the electorate of Hessen, and now seat of the government of the Prussian province of Hessen-Nassau on the Fulda, 85 miles S. of Hanover by rail. The Fulda separates the Altstadt and Ober-Neustadt from the Unter-Neustadt, and is crossed by two bridges. The Great Friedrichs-Platz is enclosed on the E. by the Old Palace of the Electors, the New Palace and the Museum (erected by the Landgraf Friedrich II. in 1779), and on the W. by stately dwelling-houses. Other notable buildings are the Protestant church of St. Martin, in Gothic style, with nave of the 14th c., restored in 1842; the Bellevue-Schloss, containing a celebrated picture-gallery, founded by Prince Wilhelm of Hessen at the beginning of the 18th c., and which is specially rich in Dutch and Flemish works; an observatory, two hospitals, an opera-house, two theatres, &c. The collection in the Museum Fridericianum was begun by the Hessen princes at the close of the 16th c., and comprises ancient sculptures, Roman and Florentine mosaics, curious clocks, art objects in ivory, gold, silver, and agate, a natural history section, armoury, a library of 200,000 vols., &c. The Auegarten, or Karlsaue, by the river side, beautifully laid out by Le Nôtre in 1709, is the favourite resort of the inhabitants. K. has some manufacture of cottons, woollens, silks, lace, carpets, scientific instruments, &c. Pop. (1875) 53,043. The town appears as *Chassala* in the rolls of Konrad I., as early as 913. It received freedom and privileges in 1239. After the Peace of Tilsit, 1807, K. was made the capital of Westphalia. Distant nearly 4 miles is Wilhelmshöhe, formerly the residence of the Elector of Hessen, and celebrated for its beautiful grounds and fountains. Napoleon III. was a prisoner here during the latter part of the Franco-Prussian war in 1870–71. See Lynker's *K. und die schönsten Punkte der Umgegend* (4th ed. Kass. 1856).

Kassimof' (formerly *Gorodez*), a town of Russia, in the government of Riazan, 69 miles N.E. of the town of that name, on the Oka. It has a large yearly fair, extensive tow and leather manufactures, and there are numerous glass-furnaces in the neighbourhood. Pop. (1870) 14,102.

Kastamu'ni, a town of Asia Minor, the capital of a vilayet of the same name, on the Gök Irmak ('blue river'), 113 miles N.E. of Angora. It is a decayed place, with trifling manufactures of copper, leather, and cotton. Estimated pop. 40,000.—The *vilayet* of K. has an area of 20,400 sq. miles, and a pop. (according to the *Almanach de Gotha*, 1877) of 772,010.

Ka'ter, Captain Henry, F.R.S., was born at Bristol, April 16, 1777. In 1794 he obtained a commission in the 12th regiment of foot, then stationed in India, where in the succeeding year he aided in the trigonometrical survey of that country. After seven years' stay he was obliged through ill health to return to England. In 1814 he retired upon half pay, and devoted the remainder of his life to science. He died at London, April 26, 1835. K. is best known for his invaluable experiments to determine the length of the seconds' pendulum, and for his labours in constructing standards of weights and measures. He was a member of most of the scientific societies at home and abroad, and was presented by the Czar of Russia with the order of St. Anne and a diamond snuffbox for his services in relation to the Russian standards of weights and measures.

Kat'rine, Loch, a beautiful lake of the Scottish Highlands, near the S.W. border of Perthshire. It is 8 miles long and about three-quarters of a mile broad, is approached from the E. by the romantic defile of the Trossachs, and is overshadowed on the S. by the riven mass of Ben Venue. The splendid scenery of the region is minutely described in Scott's *Lady of the Lake*. L. K. supplies Glasgow with water, which is conveyed through the mountain side by a tunnel 6975 feet long, and subsequently by aqueducts and pipes for a distance of 25 miles.

Kat River,, a tributary of the Great Fish River, Cape Colony. An interesting Hottentot settlement was formed in its upper valleys in 1829, but was broken up after the Hottentot rebellion of 1851–52.—The *district* is now included in that of Stockenström. It is mountainous, well wooded, and fertile. Pop. 5700 of all races, including many Europeans.

Kattamándu, or **Cattemundoo**, the East Indian name for the inspissated juice of one or more species of *Euphorbia*. It is a substance analogous to gutta-percha, and is used in India for cementing metal surfaces.

Kattywar' (Kathiawar), the name of a district in India, derived from the dominant tribe of Katties, said to be of Scythian origin, which has been politically extended to the whole peninsula of Gujerat, lying N.E. of Bombay between the Runn of Kutch and the Gulf of Cambay. Area, 22,339 sq. miles; pop. (1872) 2,312,629. It is well watered by rivers rising in the central plateau, and carries on a brisk trade in cotton, wool, grain, hides, &c. The export of cotton in 1874–75 was valued at £2,500,000. The breed of horses is famous; and lions, said to be black and maneless, here alone in India take the place of tigers. K. is divided into four *pranths* or counties, each under a European official, and there are more than 200 petty chiefs subordinate to the K. Political Agency. Many of these are tributary to the Gaekwar of Baroda. The administration has been greatly improved of late years; and the ancient state of internal anarchy has now ceased. A railway was opened in 1872 in the N. of this tract. The English headquarters is Rajkote, where there is a public school for the young chiefs. Among historical sites are the hill of Girnar (q. v.) and the temple of Somnauth (q. v.). The chiefs are mostly Rajputs, and in former days they were infamous for the practice of female infanticide. The leading principalities are Jhownuggur, Nowanuggur, and Bhownuggur. See Wyllie's *Essays*, ed. by W. W. Hunter (Lond. 1875).

Katun'ga, or **Ejeo**, a town in the Fellata territory, W. Africa, 220 miles N.E. of Abomey, has a lively trade in grain, sheep, cloth, &c. Estimated pop. 16,000.

Katz'bach, a river of Prussian Silesia, on whose banks at Wahlstatt (the scene of a Tartar defeat in 1241) was fought the battle of K., August 26, 1813, between 100,000 French under Macdonald and 90,000 Germans under Blücher. The latter had drawn Macdonald across the K. and Neisse, only to drive him back into their waters, swollen by rain, which had also damped the powder, so that the battle was one of bayonet and butt-end. When the floods went down, thousands of French corpses were seen sticking in the mud. The total loss on the side of the French was 18,000 prisoners, 12,000 dead and wounded, 2 eagles, and 103 guns; on that of the Germans, only 1000 men. Blücher received the title Prince of Wahlstatt, and Macdonald, returning almost alone to Dresden, announced to Napoleon, 'Your army of the Bober no longer exists.'

Kauff'mann, Angelica, a well-known painter, born October 30, 1741, at Chur in the Grisons, received her first instruction from her father, and after twelve years' study in Italy came to London (1765), where she achieved a brilliant success, painting the portraits of the royal family, and being elected one of the thirty-six original members of the Royal Academy. A marriage with a Swedish adventurer, the *soi-disant* Comte de Horn, was followed by a separation (1768), and in 1781 Angelica married a landscape-painter, Antonio Zucchi, who had followed her from Venice. Returning to Italy the year after, she there lost both husband and fortune (1795), and died at Rome, November 5, 1807. Her pictures—graceful but feeble allegories, often introducing her own beautiful portrait—abound in all the galleries of Europe; and a fresh interest has lately been lent to her history by its forming the basis of a charming fiction by Miss Thackeray—*Miss Angel* (Lond. 1875).

Kauf'mann, K., Von, a distinguished Russian general of German descent, was educated at the Military School for Engineers, served with brilliant success in the Caucasus, acquiring the rank of general and the post of chief of the field officers under Mouravieff. During the Crimean War he was chosen to settle with General Williams the conditions for the capitulation of Kars. He was successively appointed chief of the staff of the Grand Duke Nicholas, Minister of War, and Governor of Lithuania *vice* General Mouravieff, in 1865. To K. and Millutin is due the credit of entirely re-organising the army. In 1867 K. was nominated Governor-General of the vast Asiatic territories of the Sír Daría and Semivetshkaia. After long negotiations with the refractory Emir of Bokhára, K. defeated the forces sent against him, and concluded a treaty (1868) by which Samarcand and a large territory was ceded to Russia. In 1873 followed the taking of Khiva, K.'s masterpiece of generalship. Surrounded on all sides by immense deserts, Khiva was approached by three columns, comprising 12,000 men, from the Caspian, from Orenburg, and from Tashkend, the last of these being under his own command. The troops were skilfully extricated from the hardships of their terrible march, and Khiva was taken on the 10th June 1873. In consequence of a treaty between Russia and England the army was withdrawn from Khiva, but the campaign greatly extended Russian dominion, and established the unconditional authority of Russia in Central Asia. Tashkend is K.'s residence. His last act was the invasion and conquest of Khokan in 1875.

Kaul'bach, Wilhelm Von, was born in 1804, at Arolsen, capital of the principality of Waldeck. Without exhibiting any particular leanings towards art in his youth, K. was entered at the Academy of Dusseldorf, and set to work at some frescoes of Cornelius. In 1825 he followed Cornelius to Munich, where he executed 'Apollo and the Muses' for the ceiling of a concert-hall, and worked at the story of Psyche upon the walls of the Prince of Birckenfeld's palace. His 'Victory of Herman over the Romans,' and 'The House of Fools,' gave him a European reputation which was more than sustained by the 'Combat of Souls,' the 'Destruction of Jerusalem by Titus,' and the historical tableaux composed (1847–66) for the decoration of the staircase of the Berlin Museum. K. has been blamed for an absence of warmth in colouring, and a certain frigidity in execution, but universal admiration has been bestowed upon his imaginative power, his mastery over various expressions, and the depth of his general conceptions. K. died April 7, 1874.

Kau'nitz, Wenzel Anton, Prince Von, the youngest son of Maximilian Ulric, Graf von Rietberg, was born at Vienna, February 2, 1711. At first destined for the Church, on the death of his brother he embraced a diplomatic career, attended the universities of Vienna, Leipsic, and Leyden, and from 1732 to 1735 travelled in Germany, Italy, France, and England. Under Karl VI. he acted as second imperial commissioner at the Diet of Ratisbon. Under Maria Theresa, in 1741, he executed a great mission at Florence, in 1742 acted as Minister at Turin, in 1744 Plenipotentiary to the Netherlands, in 1747 Ambassador to the Congress of Aix-la-Chapelle, and in 1750 Ambassador to the Court of France. Franz I. created him a feudatory Prince of the Empire, but his influence declined under Joseph II. until (1790–92) he was replaced at the head of the state by Leopold II. K. died June 24, 1794. *Le cocher de l'Europe* was a familiar phrase used regarding K. by his contemporaries, to indicate the fact that he wielded the reins of universal statesmanship. His devotion to the House of Austria rather than the empire to which he belonged narrowed his views, though these were always applied with energy and skill. To profound political knowledge, K. added the graces of an extensive literary culture.

Kau'ri, sometimes erroneously written **Cow'rie** and **Cow'die**, the native name of the pine *Dammara Australis*, found only in New Zealand, N. of the parallel of 37° S. lat. The K. is a noble tree, sometimes reaching a height of 140 feet, with an average girth of 10 to 15 feet, though Laslett (*Timber and Timber Trees*) mentions having seen two specimens whose circumference was 48 and 72 feet respectively. The timber of the K. is straw-coloured, close grained, and readily worked, and it combines the qualities of strength, elasticity, lightness, and durability to a degree entitling it to a place in the first rank among timbers. For masts and spars especially the K. is unrivalled. With regard to the resin which exudes from the K. see DAMMAR.

Kaye, Sir John William, the distinguished chronicler of various epochs in the history of the British rule in India, was born in London in 1814. In 1822 he passed from Addiscombe into the Bengal Artillery, but resigned military service for literary pursuits in 1841. He founded the *Calcutta Review*; and eventually entered the Home Service, and filled the appointment of Secretary in the Secret and Political Department of the India Office from 1859 to 1874. K. died 24th July 1876. Among his works may be mentioned *The History of the War in Afghanistan*; *The History of the Sepoy War in India*, of which he lived to publish only the third volume, out of a promised four; and *The Life and Correspondence of Sir John Malcolm*. His peculiar merit is to have used his official and private sources of information so as to popularise among Englishmen the great events and leading heroes of Indian history.

Kazaly, a Russian town and fort in Turkestan, and on the Sír-Daría (anc. *Jaxartes*) 40 miles from its mouth. It is the first of the forts on the so-called 'line of the Sír-Daría,' and was founded in 1847. The earthworks of the fort, which is garrisoned by 1000 men, are 200 yards square, surrounded by a ditch. Between the fort and river is the navy yard, and on the land side is the thriving town of K. with a pop. of over 5000. There is here a Cossack colony, and the chief products are cotton and a wine of excellent quality.

Kazan'. See KASAN.

Kean, Edmund, tragedian, born in London, November 4, 1787. The son of an actress, he figured as Cupid in a ballet as soon as he could stand, and became when very young a strolling player. His *debut* as Shylock at Drury Lane on January 26, 1814, was, according to Hazlitt, the 'first gleam of genius breaking athwart the gloom of the stage.' Densely packed houses for many seasons were inspired and terrified by his Richard, Othello, and Macbeth. The awful realism of his Sir Giles Overreach on one occasion sent an entire house into hysterics, Lord Byron into a convulsive fit. His fame spread with his travels, and for twenty years he was the dramatic meteor both of England and America. Dissipation at length ruined his powers and health. He died 15th May 1833. K. had marvellous powers of expression, and was the most intense depicter of the passions that ever trod the English stage. See Memoirs by Proctor (1835) and by Hawkins (1869).—**Charles K.**, tragedian, son of the preceding, was born in 1811 and educated at Eton. As a young man he acted along with his father. With scarce a tithe of the latter's genius, care and study made him a respectable actor. In 1842 he married Miss Ellen Tree, an accomplished Shakesperian actress. In 1850 he took the Princess' Theatre, where for several years he produced gorgeous and tasteful Shakesperian revivals. He died January 22, 1868.

Keats, John, was born in London, October 29, 1795. Little promise of a poet could be found in him when a schoolboy; but the reading of the *Faerie Queene* burst the floodgates of his imagination, and the *Lines in Imitation of Spenser* are supposed to be his earliest attempt in verse. Removed from school, K. became for five years apprentice to a surgeon at Edmonton, and thence proceeded to London to follow his profession. But friendships formed with such men as Leigh Hunt, Hazlitt, Haydon, Godwin, Dilke, and Basil Montague soon drew him into the paths of literature. His first venture, a series of juvenile poems, passed unheeded by press or public. In 1818 he again produced a volume, containing *Endymion*, and a few smaller pieces. Although little general attention was at first called forth by these poems, their author was detected and attacked as a member of the Cockney school by the *Quarterly Review* and *Blackwood's Magazine*. The effect of this attack upon K. himself has been greatly exaggerated. While treating the critics with apparent contempt, he yet made use of the lesson so roughly taught, and in his last volume, *Tales and Poems*, containing, with shorter pieces, *Hyperion*, and the *Eve of Saint Agnes*, won for himself a foremost place in English poetry. Nothing richer in colour, daintier in phrase, or more delicious in melody exists in our literature than the *Ode to a Nightingale*, *On a Grecian Urn*, *To Autumn*, and the *Eve of Saint Agnes*. Byron thought the fragment of *Hyperion* as sublime as Æschylus. There is a sober gorgeousness in the diction that strikingly contrasts with the flowery and fantastic juvenilities of *Endymion*, and shows that the genius of K. was rapidly ripening to a splendid harvest. But the ravages of hereditary disease, hastened by an unfortunate passion, carried him off in the brightness of his youth. He died at Rome, 27th February 1820, and lies there in the Protestant cemetery, close by the grave of Shelley, whose *Elegy of Adonais* is the noblest tribute to a brother poet in English literature. The only complete edition of K.'s poems is that edited by Lord Houghton (Lond. Bell & Sons, 1877).

Keble, John, an English poet, son of the Rev. John K., was born at Fairford, Gloucestershire, April 25, 1792. He studied at Corpus Christi, Oxford, and after becoming a university tutor and examiner, devoted himself to the life of a parish priest. In 1827, he published *The Christian Year, or Thoughts in verse for the Sundays and Holydays throughout the Year*, which had a very great success. He became Professor of Poetry at Oxford in 1831, and was one of the chief movers in the 'Puseyite' movement, contributing to the famous *Tracts for the Times*. He received the living of Hursley in 1835, published *Lyra Innocentium* in 1846, *Sermons Academical and Occasional* in 1848, and wrote *A Life of Wilson, Bishop of Sodor and Man*, and several High Church pamphlets. He retained great influence in his party until his death at Bournemouth, March 29, 1865. K. holds a high place among English devotional poets, his verses breathing deep religious sentiment and genuine love of nature. See Shairp's *Studies in Poetry and Philosophy* (1868).

Keble College, Oxford, founded by subscription as a memorial to the late Rev. John Keble (q. v.), was incorporated by royal charter bearing date June 6, 1870, by which it is declared to be 'founded and constituted with the especial object and intent of providing persons desirous of academical education, and willing to live economically, with a college wherein sober living and high culture of the mind may be combined with Christian training, based upon the principles of the Church of England.' The college is governed by a warden and a council of not less than nine, nor more than twelve members. In 1876 it had five tutors, four lecturers, a precentor and a bursar, eleven scholars, five exhibitioners, three students of music, and 122 commoners. It presents to three livings. The buildings, of red brick, are from the design of Mr. W. Butterfield. The foundation-stone was laid April 25, 1860, and the dedication took place June 23, 1870. A splendid chapel has since been erected.

Kecskemét' (*Egopolis*), a town of Hungary, in the county of Pesth, and in a sandy plain 54 miles S.E. of Pesth by rail. It has four large churches, important manufactures of soap, leather, and wheaten bread, and famous cattle, sheep, and horse markets. Pop. (1869) 41,195, of whom one-third are Protestants.

Kedge, a small anchor, employed to steady a vessel when riding in a tidal river, and to prevent her fouling the bower anchor, particularly at the turn of the tide. Among other purposes it is used to move a ship along in a harbour, the K. being carried out and let go from a boat. This operation is called *kedging* or *warping*.

Ke'dron (Heb. 'turbid') is a 'mountain ravine (not a 'brook,' as in the A. V.), in most places narrow, with precipitous banks of naked limestone,' although in places the easy slopes and bottom are capable of cultivation. It begins in a slight depression on the summit of the plateau 1½ mile N.W. of Jerusalem. Running for about ½ mile towards the city it turns to the E., and holds that direction for about ¾ mile, at a distance of about ½ mile to the N. of the city. It then turns to the S. and widens; but is soon contracted again by the Mount of Olives on the E. and Bezetha on the W. Farther down, Moriah on the W. and Olives on the E. rise precipitously from a torrent bed. Below the point where it is joined by the Tyropœon (see JERUSALEM), K. again expands into a level fruitful tract, which extends to the mouth of Hinnom, where K. ends, at a distance from its head of about 2¾ miles.

Keel (Old Eng. *Ceol*, Dutch and Ger. *Kiel*), that part of a ship which extends along the bottom from stem to stern, and on which the whole superstructure is built. In wooden vessels the K. consists of several lengths of wood scarfed together end ways. Occasionally it is protected from injury by a strong piece of timber called a *false K.* *Bilge-keels* are fastened to the bottom of a ship parallel to the main K. to prevent heavy rolling or drifting to leeward, and with the same object *sliding keels*, pieces of wood or iron that may be lowered through the main K., are used. In iron ships the K. is usually formed of lengths of bar iron welded together.

Keel'age, dues levied on a ship entering a port or harbour.

Keel'hauling (Dutch *Kielhaalen*), a punishment, now obsolete, practised in the Dutch navy, and introduced into the English navy during the reign of William III. It consisted of dropping the delinquent, having weights to his feet, from a yard-arm and dragging him through the water under the keel to the other side of the vessel. Colloquially K. signifies a vexatious examination, or galling conduct of an official towards a subordinate.

Keel'son, or **Kel'son,** in shipbuilding, an internal keel placed directly over and securely fastened to the external keel. It serves to bind together the floor-timbers and gives increased strength to the ship. Pieces of timber or angle iron placed on each side of the K. are termed *sister keelsons*.

Keep (from Old Eng. *cēpan*, 'to hold'), a stronghold constructed in the centre of a castle or fortress as a place of retreat for last defence, also called *Donjon* (q. v.).

Keeper of the Great Seal. See GREAT SEAL.

Keigh'ly, a town of England, in the W. Riding of Yorkshire, on the Aire, 9½ miles N.W. of Bradford by rail. It is a busy centre of the worsted trade, producing yarns and fancy goods, and also manufacturing much paper, machinery, &c. Besides several good churches it has a free grammar school and a handsome mechanics institute, opened in 1870. Pop. (1870) 19,775.

Kei River, Great, forms the boundary between Cape Colony and Kaffraria. The country on its upper waters is level and fertile, but on the lower part of its course the land is wild and rugged, and unfit for cultivation. The mouth of the K. is blocked against vessels by an impassable bar.

Keiskamm'a, a river of Cape Colony, draining the S. and E. slopes of the Amatola mountains. It falls into the Indian Ocean in 33° 14′ S. lat., 27° 20′ E. long. Though a fine stream, it is useless for purposes of navigation.

Keith, the Family of, is no doubt a very ancient one, but the legends of its origin given in Buchan's *Ballads of the N.E. Coast* do not deserve attention. The hereditary office of Grand Marischal is said to have been given to a K. by Malcolm II. after a battle with the Danes. Sir Robert K. stood high in the confidence of Edward I., but afterwards joined Robert Bruce and received from him the lands of Buchan in Aberdeenshire, to which by a marriage with the Frasers the family added the Kincardineshire estates on which their castle of Dunottar was built. In 1458 Sir William was created *Earl* Marischal and Lord K. The fourth Earl, 'William of the Tower,' who took a leading part in the Reformation, was one of the wealthiest nobles of that time, having a rental of 270,000 merks and lands in Haddington, Linlithgow, Kincardine, Aberdeen, Banff, Elgin, and Caithness. The fifth Earl negotiated the marriage of James VI. and Anne of Denmark; founded and endowed Marischal College, Aberdeen (1593); granted its original charter to Peterhead; acted as lieutenant of the north in the time of the Spanish Plot; and was royal commissioner in the Scottish Parliament of 1607. At the Union (1707) another earl protested that it should not prejudice the rights of Great Marischal, which the family had held for 700 years. His sons **George, Earl Marischal** and **James K.** are both famous in history. The former was captain of the guard under Queen Anne, and on her death, although a Protestant, he was strongly urged to proclaim James Stuart at Charing Cross. He waited for the rising of 1715, when he defeated one portion of Argyle's army at Sheriffmuir and received the Pretender at Newburgh and Fetteresso. Both brothers had to leave Scotland. After some years of intrigue with Carl XII. and Alberoni, they reappeared in the Hebrides in concert with the Ormond Expedition, but were defeated at Glenshiel by Wightman (1719). For several years the Earl acted as confidential political agent for the Pretender and the Chevalier at the courts of Spain and France, but he took no part in the '45. He seems to have quarrelled with the Stuarts and then entered the diplomatic service of Friedrich the Great, just as Tyrconnel entered the diplomatic service of France. As Governor of Neuchâtel, he became extremely intimate with Rousseau, who, in his *Confessions*, describes 'this illustrious and virtuous Scotchman.' In 1759 Lord Chatham got the sentence of attainder reversed, and the earl returned to Scotland, taking the oath of allegiance in the Court of King's Bench, and inheriting the Earldom of Kintore. He was said to have furnished to the English Government some valuable information regarding the Bourbon Family compact. Finding his old house of Inverugie destroyed, he returned to Berlin, where Friedrich gave him a house near the Sans Souci Gardens, and where he died 28th May 1778. He adopted a Turkish girl, whom, when a baby, his brother had rescued at Oczakow. Carlyle calls him 'a cheery old soul, honest as the sunlight, with a fine small vein of gaiety.' **James K.**, the younger brother, after serving in the Irish Brigade and in the Spanish expedition to Gibraltar, entered the military service of Russia and distinguished himself under Münnich against the Turks at Oczakow (1737), and under Lacy against the Swedish Wrangel at Wilmanstrand (1741). He set his face against the habitual cruelty of the Russian army. He was at London in 1740, and assisted in carrying out the Peace of Abo against the rebellious Dalecarlians in 1743. A young Prince Repnin having been unjustly preferred to a command in 1747, K. left the service of Elizabeth for that of Friedrich the Great, who at once made him field marshal with an income of £1200. 'The sagacious gentleman with the broad accent' became a great favourite, not only in military but in literary matters. After brilliant exploits in the Seven Years' War, at Prag, Rossbach, and Olmutz, K. was shot dead in the battle of Hochkirk (1758). He was buried in the Garnison Kirche there, the inscription over his grave being written by Metastasio, and statues by Tassaert to him and to his companions Schwerin, Winterfield, and Seidlitz were erected on the Wilhelm Platz at Berlin. Quite lately, the German Emperor sent a bronze statue of K. to Peterhead. Like his brother, K., who was educated by Bishop Keith, wrote well. He has left part of an autobiography, an account of the Prussian Court, and some letters about Russia. The best life was published at Berlin in 1844. See also *Correspondence of Sir Robert Murray Keith* (Lond. 1749). The latter was a diplomatist of some note, who in 1771 brought Matilda, the divorced Queen of Denmark and sister of George III., to Hanover.

Kelat', the capital of the state of Beluchistan on the N.W. frontier of India, 392 miles N. of Kurrachee and 225 E. of Jacobabad; with these two towns, which are both in Scinde, it is connected by tolerable roads. K. occupies an important position, at the upper end of the Bolan pass, both for military and commercial purposes. It was occupied by the British during the Afghan War; and the most important diplomatic event in recent Indian history is the K. treaty of 1877, by which the Khan receives an annual subsidy of £10,000, and a British Agent resides at his court with a strong military escort of all arms. A line of telegraph has been already laid down, and it is proposed to construct a railway. In fact, the mediatization of K. has been carried into execution so as to outflank a possible enemy in Afghanistan.

Kell'ermann, François Christophe, Duc de Valmy, a Marshal of France, was born near Strassburg, May 30, 1735. He entered the army when seventeen, served in the Seven Years' War, and later in Russia. Embracing the Revolution, as commander on the Moselle in 1792 he gained the decisive victory of Valmy, which drove the Prussians out of France. In 1793 he was general of the army of the Alps. Under Napoleon he was a commander of reserves. After Elba he supported the Bourbons. K. died September 12, 1820. From the *Mémoires* he left, his son wrote a *Histoire de la Campagne de* 1800 (Par. 1854).

Kells, an ancient town of Ireland, in the county of Meath, Leinster, on the Blackwater, 39 miles N.W. of Dublin by rail. It has an old church and round tower, a handsome Roman Catholic church, a fever hospital, some lace industry, six great yearly fairs, and a considerable retail trade. Pop. (1870) 2953. K., in Irish Gael. *Ceanannus* ('head abode'), was a royal residence down to the 6th c., 'when King Dermot MacKerval granted it to St. Columkille, after which time it lost its pagan associations, and soon became a great ecclesiastical centre.' See Joyce's *Irish Names of Places*, 2d series (Dub. 1875). Ceanannus was shortened into *Kenlis*, and that into K. The town gave title to a bishop, was plundered by the Danes in the 12th c., became a stronghold of the English Pale, and sent two members to the Irish Parliament previous to the Act of Union.

THE END OF VOL. III.

www.ingramcontent.com/pod-product-compliance
Lightning Source LLC
LaVergne TN
LVHW021107110826
845150LV00001B/192

* 9 7 8 1 4 2 5 5 6 4 7 7 3 *